ISBN 978-0-260-11764-9
PIBN 10928991

THE

AMERICAN AND ENGLISH

ENCYCLOPÆDIA

OF

LAW.

COMPILED UNDER THE EDITORIAL SUPERVISION OF

JOHN HOUSTON MERRILL,

Editor of the American and English Railroad Cases and the American and English Corporation Cases.

VOLUME IV.

NORTHPORT, LONG ISLAND, N. Y.:

EDWARD THOMPSON, LAW PUBLISHER.

1888.

PARTIAL LIST OF CONTRIBUTORS, VOLUME IV.

Contribution, ...	HENRY B. BARTOW, of the Philadelphia Bar.
Contributory Negligence, .	WILLIAM H. RUSSELL, of the Chattanooga (Tenn.) Bar.
Conversion, ...	D. H. PINGREY, of the Bloomington (Ill.) Bar.
Coroner, ...	EDW. P. ALLINSON and BOIES PENROSE, of the Philadelphia Bar.
Corporations:	
Organization, ...	CHAS. CHAUNCEY BINNEY, of the Philadelphia Bar.
Name, ... *Domicile,*	ALBERT B. WEIMER and H. S. P. NICHOLS, of the Philadelphia Bar.
Powers and Liabilities,	JNO. HOUSTON MERRILL and LUTHER E. HEWITT, of the Philadelphia Bar.
Consolidation, ...	J. PERCY KEATING, of the Philadelphia Bar.
Actions By and Against,	CHAS. CHAUNCEY BINNEY, of the Philadelphia Bar.
Dissolution, ...	ALBERT B WEIMER and H. S. P. NICHOLS, of the Philadelphia Bar.
Costs, ...	CHAS. A. ROBBINS, of the Lincoln (Neb.) Bar.
County, ... *County Commissioners,* .	EDW. P. ALLINSON and BOIES PENROSE, of the Philadelphia Bar.
County Seat, ... *Coupons,*	W. M. MCKINNEY, Associate Editor of the Am. & Eng. R. R. Cases.
Courts, ...	ALBERT B. WEIMER, of the Philadelphia Bar.
Covenants, ...	JAMES M. KERR, of the Rochester (N. Y.) Bar.
Creditor's Bill, ...	HENRY T. DECHERT, of the Philadelphia Bar.
Criminal Conspiracy, . . *Criminal Law,*	ROBERT DESTY, Author of Am. Crim. Law, etc , etc.
Criminal Procedure, . .	JAMES M. KERR, of the Rochester (N. Y.) Bar.
Crossings, ...	WILLIAM H. RUSSELL, of the Chattanooga (Tenn.) Bar.
Dam, ...	W. HOWARD FALKNER, of the Philadelphia Bar.

PARTIAL LIST OF CONTRIBUTORS, VOLUME IV.

TABLE OF TITLES AND DEFINITIONS.

See Index for numerous sub-titles and definitions contained in the notes.

THE

AMERICAN AND ENGLISH

ENCYCLOPÆDIA OF LAW.

CONTRARY. — See notes 1 and 2.

CONTRIBUTION. See also CO-TENANCY; CORPORATIONS; GENERAL AVERAGE; INSURANCE; JETTISON; PARTNERSHIP; SHIPPING; SURETYSHIP.

1. **Definition.** — The payment by each or any one of several parties who are liable in company with others of his proportionate part of the whole liability or loss, to one or more of the parties so liable upon whom the whole loss has fallen, or who has been compelled to discharge the whole liability.[3]

2. **In General.** — Whenever one of several parties who are bound by a common charge discharges the same for the benefit of all, he has a right to call upon his co-debtors for contribution.[4]

The doctrine of contribution is not so much founded on contract as on the principle of equity and justice, that, where the interest is common, the burden also shall be common.[5]

1. **Contrary to Law.** — On motion for new trial means, "contrary to the general principles of the law as applicable to the facts." Buskirk's Practice, p. 239; Bosseker *v.* Cramer, 18 Ind. 44; Candy *v.* Hanmore, 76 Ind. 125.

2. **Contrary Intent in Trust Deed.** — A trust deed which omits to provide for filling a vacancy in the number of trustees upon the happening of an event not contemplated by the parties to that instrument, does not, by that mere omission, show an intention "contrary" to an appointment of a new trustee in the mode provided by the English Conveyancing Act of 1881 (44 and 45 Vict. c. 41), s. 31, sub-secs. 1, 3, 6, 7. *In re* Coates to Parsons, 34 Ch. D. 370.

3. Bouvier's Law Dict.

4. See Bispham's Eq. § 328; Adams's Eq *267. Stirling *v.* Forrester, 3 Bligh, 590; Aspinwall *v.* Sacchi, 57 N Y. 331; Wood *v.* Leland, 1 Met. (Mass.) 389.

The voluntary act of one party in expending money for the benefit of all, will not create a right to contribution. See Webster's App. 86 Pa. St. 409; Watson *v.* Wilcox, 39 Wis. 643.

An agreement by several parties to equally aid, comfort, and take care of a third party, when sick, may warrant a decree in equity for contribution. Odiorne *v.* Moulton (S C. of N. H. 1887), 9 Atlantic Rep. 625

5. Campbell *v.* Mesier, 4 Johns. Ch (N. Y) 334; s. c., 6 Johns Ch. (N. Y.) 21;

3. Between Sureties. — The right of contribution arises between sureties where one has been called on to make good the principal's default, and has paid more than his share of the entire liability.[1]

Allen *v.* Wood, 3 Ired. Eq. (N. C.) 386; Mills *v.* Hyde, 19 Vt. 59; White *v.* Banks, 21 Ala. 705; Russell *v.* Failer, 1 Ohio St. 327; Oldham *v.* Broom, 28 Ohio St. 41; Van Petten *v.* Richardson, 68 Mo. 380; Wells *v.* Miller, 66 N. Y. 255.

"The principle," observes Lord Redesdale in Stirling *v.* Forrester, 3 Bligh, 59, "established in the case of Dering *v.* Lord Winchelsea (1 Cox, 318), is universal, that the right and duty of contribution is founded in doctrines of equity: it does not depend upon contract. If several persons are indebted, and one makes the payment, the creditor is bound in conscience, if not by contract, to give to the party paying the debt all his remedies against the other debtors."

While contribution was originally only enforceable by courts of equity, subsequently jurisdiction was assumed by courts of law and relief administered on the ground of an implied assumpsit.

See notes to Dering *v.* Earl of Winchelsea, 1 Lead. Cas. Eq. *106; Fletcher *v.* Grover, 11 N. H. 368; Bachelder *v.* Fisk, 17 Mass. 464; Mason *v.* Lord, 20 Pick. (Mass.) 447; Mills *v.* Hyde, 19 Vt. 59; Norton *v.* Coons, 3 Denio (N. Y.), 130; Wilder *v.* Butterfield, 50 How. (N. Y.) 399; Rindge *v.* Baker, 57 N. Y. 209, 215; s. c., 15 Am. Rep. 475; Powers *v.* Nash, 37 Me. 322; Jeffries *v.* Ferguson, 87 Mo. 244.

Field, C. J., in Chipman *v.* Morrill, 20 Cal. 131, 135, discussing the principle upon which the doctrines of contribution depends, says, "The principle is, that, where there is a common liability, equality of burthen is equity. Courts of equity, therefore, naturally took jurisdiction of cases of contribution, where one surety had paid more than his just proportion. But the equitable doctrine, in progress of time, became so well established that parties were presumed to enter into contracts of suretyship upon its knowledge; and consequently, upon a mutual understanding that if the principal failed, each would be bound to share with the others a proportionate loss. Courts of common law thereupon assumed jurisdiction to enforce contribution between the sureties, proceeding on the principle that from their joint undertaking there was an implied promise on the part of each surety to contribute his share, if necessary, to make up the common loss. Craythorne *v.* Swinburne, 14 Vesey, 164; Lansdale's Adm'rs & Heirs *v.* Cox, 7 T. B. Mon. (Ky.) 403; Campbell *v.* Mesier, 4 Johns. Ch. (N. Y.) 339; 1 Maddock's Ch. 236; Fletcher *v.* Grover, 11 N. H. 369."

The jurisdiction of equity, however, to enforce contribution, remains unimpaired. Wayland *v.* Tucker, 4 Gratt. (Va.) 268; Couch *v.* Terry's Adm'rs, 12 Ala. 225, 228; Mitchell's, etc., Adm'rs *v.* Sproul, 5 J. J. Marsh. (Ky.) 264, 270; Wright *v.* Hunter, 5 Ves. 792. And the remedy in equity is in many respects superior. Campbell *v.* Mesier, 4 Johns. Ch. (N. Y.) 334; Black *v.* Shreeve, 3 Halst. Ch. (N. J.) 440; Cowell *v.* Edwards, 2 Bos. & P. 268.

"In many cases, especially where the sureties were numerous, and some of them were insolvent, or where some of the sureties had died, courts of equity were alone adequate to afford complete remedy." Per *Field, C. J.*, in Chipman *v.* Merrill, 20 Cal. 135. In equity the rights of all the parties can be fully adjusted and protected. Bank of Poughkeepsie *v.* Ibbotson, 24 Wend. (N. Y.) 479; Pfohl *v.* Simpson, 74 N. Y. 137; Thebris *v.* Smiley, 110 Ill. 316. See also Waters *v.* Riley, 2 Har. & G. (Md.) 305; York *v.* Peck, 14 Barb. (N. Y.) 644; Chaffee *v.* Jones, 19 Pick. (Mass.) 260.

1. Adams's Equity, *269; Norton *v.* Soule, 2 Me. 341; Crowdus *v.* Shelby, 6 J. J. Marsh. (Ky.) 62; Pinkston *v.* Taliaferro, 9 Ala. 547; Yates *v.* Donaldson, 5 Md. 389; Newcomb *v.* Gibson, 127 Mass. 396; Harvey *v.* Drew, 82 Ill. 606.

A judgment, execution and payment of the amount thereof, are quite enough to sustain a co-surety who asks for contribution. Wyckoff *v.* Gardner (N. J. Ch. 1886), 5 Atlantic Rep. 801.

In an action by a surety against a co-surety for contribution, the latter cannot defend by setting up, by way of set-off, a cause of action existing in favor of the principal against the plaintiff. O'Blenis *v.* Karing, 57 N. Y. 649.

Sureties may join in an action to recover from a co-surety the amount paid for his benefit, when, each being liable for the full amount, they joined in making the payment by a contribution agreed on among themselves for that purpose. Clapp *v.* Rice, 15 Gray (Mass.), 557; s. c., 77 Am. Dec. 387; Fletcher *v.* Jackson, 23 Vermont, 581; s. c., 56 Am. Dec. 98.

The right of contribution does not arise until the surety has paid more than his share of the debt. Rutherford *v.* Branch Bank, 14 Ala. 92; Lytle *v.* Pope, 11 B. Mon. (Ky.) 309; Van Petten *v.* Richardson, 68 Mo 379; Wood *v.* Leland, 1 Met. (Mass.) 387; City of Keokuk *v.* Love. 31 Iowa, 119.

In Davies *v.* Humphreys, 6 M. & W. 168, *Parke, B.*, says, "What, then, is the nature of the equity upon which the right of action

But the payment, upon which the claim for contribution is founded, must have been compulsory; that is, one which the surety could

depends? Is it that when one surety has paid any part of the debt, he shall have a right to call on his co-surety or co-sureties to bear a proportion of the burthen? or that, when he has paid more than his share, he shall have a right to be reimbursed whatever he has paid beyond it? or, must the whole of the debt be paid by him, or some one liable, before he has a right to sue for contribution at all? We are not without authority on this subject, and it is in favor of the second of these propositions. Lord Eldon, in the case of *Ex parte* Gifford (2 B. & P. 269), states, that sureties stand with regard to each other in a relation which gives rise to this right amongst others, *that if one pays more than his proportion*, there shall be a contribution for a proportion of the excess beyond the proportion which, in all events, he is to pay; and he expressly says, 'that, unless one surety should pay more than his moiety, he would not pay enough to bring an assumpsit against the other.' And this appears to us to be very reasonable; for, if a surety pays a part of the debt only, and less than his moiety, he cannot be entitled to call on his co-surety, who might himself subsequently pay an equal or greater portion of the debt. In the former of which cases, such co-surety would have no contribution to pay; and in the latter, he would have one to receive."

The action for contribution may be sustained without proof of a previous demand upon the co-surety. Chaffee *v.* Jones, 19 Pick. (Mass.) 260; Collins *v.* Boyd, 14 Ala. 505; Morrison *v.* Poyntz, 7 Dana (Ky.), 307; s. c., 32 Am. Dec. 92. See, however, Carpenter *v.* Kelly, 9 Ohio, 106, where it is *held* that no liability on the part of the co-surety arises until he has had notice that the surety has paid the debt. See also Sherrod *v.* Woodard, 4 Dev. (N. C.) 360.

Costs and Expenses of Suit. — The right of co-sureties to compel contribution for costs and expenses incurred in defending a suit, depends upon whether the defence was made under such circumstances as to be regarded hopeful and prudent. If so, the expenses of defence may always be recovered. Per *Redfield, J.*, in Fletcher *v.* Jackson, 23 Vt. 581; s. c., 56 Am. Dec. 98, 102; Marsh *v.* Harrington, 18 Vt. 150; Davis *v.* Emerson, 17 Me. 64; Kemp *v.* Finden, 12 M. & W. 421.

In Davis *v.* Emerson, 17 Me. 64, judgment had been recovered against an insolvent principal and his two sureties, and had been paid by one of them. *Held*, that the surety so paying, might recover of his co-surety one-half of the costs, as well as of the debt. *Weston, C. J.*, said, "The plaintiff paid the execution, including the costs. The failure to pay, which occasioned the costs, was imputable to the defendant, as much as to the plaintiff. As the defendant was liable for half the execution, to that extent, the plaintiff paid money for his use and benefit. The costs cannot be distinguished from the debt. Every equitable principle which entitles the plaintiff to contribution for the one, applies equally to the other." *Compare* Boardman *v.* Paige, 4 N. H. 431; Knight *v.* Hughes, Moo. & M. 247; s. c., 3 Car. & P. 467; Comegys *v.* The State Bank, 6 Ind. 357.

Compromise by Surety. — If the surety compromises the claim, his co-sureties are entitled to the benefit of the compromise. Hickman *v.* McCurdy, 7 J. J. Marsh. (Ky.) 555; Swan's Estate, 4 Ired. Eq. (N. C.) 209; Tarr *v.* Ravenscroft, 12 Gratt (W. Va.) 642.

Surety is discharged by a Release of the Principal. — The liability of a surety for contribution is discharged by a general release given by his co-sureties to the principal of all liability for any sums they should pay, and it makes no difference that the release was only given to enable the principal to testify in a suit against the surety for contribution. Fletcher *v.* Jackson, 23 Vt. 581; s. c., 56 Am. Dec. 98; Hobart *v.* Stone, 10 Pick. (Mass.) 215. See, however, Hall *v.* Hutchens, 3 M. & K. 426.

Estate of Deceased Co-surety liable for Contribution. — The executor or administrator of a deceased co-surety may be called upon for contribution. Bachelder *v.* Fisk, 17 Mass. 264; Johnson *v.* Harvey, 84 N. Y. 363; s. c., 38 Am. Rep. 515; Sibley *v.* McAllister, 8 N. H. 389; Malin *v.* Bull, 13 S. & R. (Pa.) 441. In Bradley *v.* Burwell, 3 Denio (N. Y.), 62, B. and G. became sureties for S., as guardian of a minor, in a joint bond executed by the three, conditioned for the due execution of the trust by the guardian. *After the death of G.*, the guardian committed a breach of his duty, on account of which the obligee recovered a judgment against S. and B., which B., the surviving surety, paid. *Held*, that B. could maintain an action against the executors of G. to recover a moiety of the amount so paid by him.

When Statute of Limitations begins to run. — The right of action attaches as soon as a surety has paid more than his share of the debt, and the statute of limitations begins to run from the time of the payment of the money. Sherrod *v.* Woodward, 4 Dev. (N. C.) 360; Ponder *v.* Carter, 12 Ired. L. (N. C.) 242; Wood *v.* Leland, 1 not legally resist.[1] Sureties for the same principal and for the same engagement are entitled to contribution, although bound by

Met. (Mass.) 387; Singleton *v.* Townsend, 45 Mo. 379; Preslar *v.* Stallworth, 37 Ala. 402; Broughton *v.* Robinson, 11 Ala. 922; Davies *v.* Humphreys, 6 M. & W. 153.

Whether Surety must show Insolvency of Principal. — In equity the rule is, that it must appear that the principal is insolvent, or unable to pay, before the surety is entitled to contribution from his co-surety. Atkinson *v.* Stewart, 2 B. Mon. (Ky.) 348; Morrison *v.* Poyntz, 7 Dana (Ky.), 307; Bolling *v.* Doneghy, 1 Duv. (Ky.) 220; Daniel *v.* Ballard, 2 Dana (Ky.), 296; Pearson *v.* Duckham, 3 Litt. (Ky.) 385; Allen *v.* Wood, 3 Ired. Eq. (N. C.) 386; Burrows *v.* McWhann, 1 Desaus. (S. C.) 409.

The surety must show that he has used due diligence, without effect, to obtain reimbursement. McCormack *v.* Obannon, 3 Munf. (Va.) 484; Morrison *v.* Poyntz, 7 Dana (Ky.), 307; s. c., 32 Am. Dec. 92. In the case last cited, *Robertson, C. J.*, said, "It is well settled, that, in equity, a surety who has paid the debt is not entitled to contribution from a co-surety, as long as he may be able, by ordinary diligence, to obtain restitution or indemnity from the principal debtor; and that, before any payment of the debt, any one of several sureties may maintain a bill against his co-sureties and their principal to compel the latter to pay it, if he be able, or the former to contribute to the payment of it, if he should be unable to pay it."

But in an action at law, a surety who has paid the debt may recover contribution from a co-surety, without showing the insolvency of the principal. Judah *v.* Mieme, 5 Blackf. (Ind.) 171; Rankin *v.* Collins, 50 Ind. 158; Goodall *v.* Wentworth, 20 Me. 322; Brisendine *v.* Martin, 1 Ired (N. C) 296; Roberts *v.* Adams, 6 Port. (Ala) 361; Odlin *v.* Greenleaf, 3 N. H 270; Buckner's Adm'r *v.* Stuart, 34 Ala. 529. *Compare* Morrison *v.* Poyntz, 7 Dana (Ky), 307.

Insolvency of a Co-Surety. — In equity, where one of the sureties is insolvent, his share is apportioned among the rest, in favor of the surety asking contribution. Dodd *v.* Winn, 27 Mo. 501; Young *v.* Lyons, 8 Gill (Md.), 166; North *v.* Brace, 30 Conn. 72; Security Ins. Co. *v.* St. Paul Ins. Co., 50 Conn. 233; Stothoff *v.* Dunham, 19 N. J. (Law) 181; Mayor of Burwich *v.* Murray, 7 De G. Mac. & G. 497; Cowell *v.* Edwards, 2 Bos. & P. 268. And courts of law, in some of the States, follow the rule in equity. Mills *v.* Hyde, 19 Vt. 59; Henderson *v.* McDuffee, 5 N. H. 38; Preston *v.* Preston, 4 Gratt. (Va) 88; Harris *v.* Ferguson, 2 Bailey (S C), 397, 401; Boardman *v.* Paige, 11 N. H. 432, 440; Magruder *v.* Admire, 4 Mo. App. 133.

Removal of Co-Surety from the State Equivalent to Insolvency. — In an action by a co-surety for contribution, the share to be recovered is determined by the number of solvent co-sureties in the State. Liddell *v.* Wiswell, 59 Vt. 365; s. c., 8 Atlantic Rep. 680. Removal from the State has the same effect upon the rights and liabilities of the remaining sureties as insolvency. McKenna *v.* George, 2 Rich. Eq. (S. C.) 15; Boardman *v.* Paige, 11 N. H. 431; Liddell *v.* Wiswell, 59 Vt. 365.

1. Aldrich *v.* Aldrich, 56 Vt. 324; Russell *v.* Failor, 1 Ohio St. 327; s. c., 59 Am. Dec. 631; Bradley *v.* Burwell, 3 Denio (N. Y.), 61; Skillin *v.* Merrill, 16 Mass. 40; Pitt *v.* Purssord, 8 M & W. 538; Cowell *v.* Edwards, 2 Bos. & Pull. 268. Thus, a surety, by voluntarily paying money on a void note, cannot impose an obligation upon a co-surety for contribution. Russell *v.* Failor, 1 Ohio St. 327.

In Skillin *v.* Merrill, 16 Mass. 40, the plaintiff and defendant were sureties in a bail bond conditioned for the appearance of the principal, and for his abiding the judgment in a certain suit, and with the privilege of surrendering him at any time before final judgment against them upon *scire facias*, they paying the costs of that suit. The plaintiff, in good faith, paid the judgment recovered against the principal, but before the *scire facias* was served, and the action entered in court. *Held*, that he could not recover contribution of his co-surety. *Parker, C. J.*, said, "This action being for contribution by one surety against another, cannot be maintained, except by showing a just and equitable ground for contribution. In the case of a voluntary payment of money actually due, to avoid a suit, there is no doubt that he who pays the money may compel his co-surety to contribute. But the contract in this case is of a different nature. . . . He (the defendant) was not absolutely indebted in consequence of becoming bail, or because *non est inventus* was returned upon the execution. The law gave him the means of avoiding the debt, by surrendering the principal before judgment upon the *scire facias*, upon the penalty of the costs of that suit only. Of this privilege he was deprived by the voluntary interference of the plaintiff; and for that cause he is not equitably bound to contribute a moiety of the debt and costs."

Payment where the Cause of Action is barred. — A surety who has neglected to interpose a legal defence, as of the statute different instruments and at different times.[1] They are also entitled to the benefit of all securities which have been taken by any one of them to indemnify himself against the joint liability.[2]

of limitations, cannot claim contribution from his co-sureties. Fordham *v.* Wallis, 17 Jurist, 228. In Shelton *v.* Farmer, 9 Bush (Ky.), 314, the plaintiff, who had paid a judgment recovered against him as surety, brought suit against the heirs of his co-surety for contribution. At the time judgment was entered against plaintiff, the cause of action against the co-surety was barred by the statute of limitations. *Held*, that plaintiff could not recover, as payment of the judgment relieved the co-surety of no burden. See, however, Camp *v.* Bostwick, 20 Ohio St. 337, where it is held that the estate of a surety which has been released from its direct liability by the statute of limitations, is liable to contribute to a co-surety who has paid more than his moiety of the debt.

A surety who has paid money for a guardian, which the latter owed upon his bond, and which the surety is bound to make good, is not obliged to wait for judgment or execution, but, by paying without them, undertakes the burden of showing that he was actually bound to pay. Fishback *v.* Weaver, 34 Ark. 569. See also Mauri *v.* Heffernan, 13 Johns. (N. Y.); Minneapolis Mill Co. *v.* Wheeler, 31 Minn. 121; Harvey *v.* Drew, 82 Ill. 606. It is no objection to an action for contribution, that the plaintiff, after judgment against him as surety, paid voluntarily without waiting for an execution to be issued. Bradley *v.* Burwell, 3 Denio (N. Y.), 61.

When Payment is deemed Compulsory. —A payment is deemed to be compulsory when the party making it cannot legally resist it. Aldrich *v.* Aldrich, 56 Vt. 324; s. c., 48 Am. Rep. 791. In this case, the parties to the action were co-sureties on a note, all the parties to which lived in Vermont. After the statute of limitations had run against the note, the plaintiff, in good faith, went to New Hampshire, where the statute was no defence; and a judgment was recovered against him on the note, and he was compelled to pay it. *Held*, that the payment was compulsory, and defendant must contribute. *Royce, C. J.*, said, "Did the plaintiff, by voluntarily going into New Hampshire, and thus giving the payee of the note an opportunity to institute the proceedings which terminated in a judgment against him, release his co-surety from his liability for contribution? It will be noticed that it is not alleged that the plaintiff went into New Hampshire with any fraudulent intent, or for the purpose of giving an opportunity to have the process served upon him. A voluntary payment of an obligation by a surety, which he is not under a legal obligation to make, does not give a right of action against a co-surety for contribution. But where the payment is compulsory, the rule is different; in such case the payment by one surety gives a right of action against co-sureties for contribution. And a payment is deemed in law to be compulsory when the party making it cannot legally resist it. The payment of a judgment while it is collectible comes within the definition of a compulsory payment."

1. Dering *v.* Earl of Winchelsea, 1 Cox, 318, Chaffee *v.* Jones, 19 Pick. (Mass.) 260, 264; Armitage *v.* Pulver, 37 N. Y. 494; Aspinwall *v.* Sacchi, 57 N. Y. 331; Breckenridge *v.* Taylor, 5 Dana (Ky.), 110; Harris *v.* Ferguson, 2 Bailey (S. C.), 397; Butler *v.* Birkey, 13 Ohio, N. S. 514. Thus, if there be several sureties in an official bond, and subsequently another bond be given in the same form as the previous one, for the general conduct of the person, all the sureties in both bonds are liable to contribution among one another Bell *v.* Jasper, 2 Ired. Eq. (N. C.) 597; McKenna *v* George, 2 Rich. Eq. (S. C.) 15; Bosley *v.* Taylor, 5 Dana (Ky.), 157; American note to Dering *v.* Earl of Winchelsea, 1 Lead. Cas. Eq. 154. But no right of contribution exists where some are sureties in a replevin bond, and others in a *supersedeas* bond, as the liabilities imposed by the respective bonds are of different natures. Kellar *v.* Williams, 10 Bush (Ky.), 216.

Where it distinctly appears that the suretyship of each is a separate and distinct transaction, there is no right of contribution of one surety against the other. See Kellar *v.* Williams, 10 Bush (Ky.), 216; Armitage *v.* Pulver, 37 N. Y. 494; Hartwell *v.* Smith, 15 Ohio St. 200; Moore *v.* Isley, 2 Dev. & Bat. (N. C.) 372; Langford *v* Perrin, 5 Leigh (Va), 552.

2. Guild *v.* Butler, 127 Mass. 386; McCune *v.* Belt, 45 Mo 174; Fishback *v.* Weaver, 34 Ark. 569, 580; Gilbert *v.* Neeley, 35 Ark. 24; Miller *v.* Sawyer, 30 Vt 412; Aldrich *v.* Hapgood, 39 Vt. 617; Hall *v.* Robinson, 8 Ired (N. C.) 56; Silvey *v.* Dowell, 53 Ill. 260; Parham *v.* Green, 46 N. C. 436; Seebert *v.* Thompson, 8 Kan. 65; Steele *v.* Mealing, 24 Ala. 285; Brown *v.* Ray, 18 N. H. 102. In Agnew *v.* Bell, 4 Watts (Pa.), 33, *Kennedy, J.*, says, "Sureties are bound to observe good faith toward each other; and when funds are placed by the principal in the hands of one surety, to be applied either to the payment of the debt, or for the purpose of indemnifying him against any loss that may arise from

4. Between Partners. — Contribution lies by one partner against the other partners for any excess which he has paid beyond his share, if, upon a winding-up of the partnership affairs, such a balance appears in his favor; or if, upon a dissolution, he has been compelled to pay any sum for which he ought to be indemnified.[1]

the suretyship, he must be considered as holding them for the common benefit of all concerned." So, in Moore *v.* Moore, 4 Hawk. (N. C.), 360; s. c., 15 Am. Dec. 523, *Henderson, J.*, says, where "one surety stipulates for a separate indemnity, such indemnity is reached by his co-surety, upon the ground, either that it was intended for the benefit of all, or that the taking it was a fraud upon the others. In such cases, courts of equity convert him into a trustee, not permitting him to allege his own turpitude or selfishness as a protection; for they enter into the agreement under a belief of perfect equality."

One surety who has obtained security from his principal debtor by a mortgage must be regarded as a trustee for the other, as the mortgage inures to the benefit of all the sureties, and he is bound to the exercise of the duties which attach to that relation. If such surety gives up such security without the consent of his co-surety, he cannot obtain contribution from him. Taylor *v.* Morrison, 26 Ala. 728; s. c., 62 Am. Dec. 747.

Where a creditor, who is also a surety, takes security both for the debt due to him and for his liability as surety, he will be entitled to have his own debt paid first in full, before applying any part of the security for the benefit of his co-sureties. Brown *v.* Ray, 18 N. H. 102; Hess's Estate, 69 Pa. St. 272; Field *v.* Hamilton, 45 Vt. 35; Magee *v.* Leggett, 48 Miss. 139; McCune *v.* Belt, 45 Mo. 174.

1. Story's Eq. Juris. § 504; Taylor *v.* Coffury, 18 Ill. 422; Payne *v.* Matthews, 6 Paige (N. Y.), 19; Noel *v.* Bowman, 2 Litt. (Ky.) 46; Kelly *v.* Kaffmann, 18 Pa. St. 351; Fletcher *v.* Brown, 7 Humph. (Tenn.) 385; *Ex parte* Letts *v.* Steer, 26 L. J. Ch. 455.

The usual and most effectual remedy is in equity, where an account of all the partnership transactions can be taken. See Collyer on Partnership, 324 and note. McGunn *v.* Hanlin, 29 Mich. 477; McFadden *v.* Sallada, 6 Pa. St. 283; White *v.* Harlow, 5 Gray (Mass.), 463; Sells *v.* Hubbell's Adm'rs, 2 Johns. Ch. (N. Y.) 394; Wright *v.* Hunter, 5 Ves. 792.

Where, after the assets of a firm have been divided, one partner is compelled to pay outstanding debts, he may sue for contribution. Eskins *v.* Knox, 6 Rich. (S. C.) 14. See also Forbes *v.* Webster, 2 Vt. 58; Olleman *v.* Reagan, 28 Ind. 109; Evans *v.* Clapp, 123 Mass. 165.

In Kelly *v.* Kaffmann, 18 Pa. St. 351, two partners had been engaged in purchasing and selling cattle. Most of the cattle had been sold, and one of the partners agreed to take the residue of the cattle at a stipulated price per head. They settled their partnership accounts, and divided the assets. For some of the cattle sold, a note was given to the firm, which was received by the plaintiff, who indorsed it, and had it discounted, and applied the proceeds to the credit of the firm. The debtor failing to pay the note, plaintiff paid it, and brought an action against the other partner for contribution. *Held*, that defendant was liable to contribution in the absence of an agreement to the contrary.

A partner who has been compelled to pay the whole of a firm debt cannot sue his co-partner-at-law for a contribution while the accounts of the partnership remain unsettled Laurence *v.* Clark, 9 Dana (Ky.), 257; s. c., 35 Am. Dec. 133.

Where one partner advances money to another to relieve him from liability upon an execution issued for debts due the firm, and takes his note therefor, an action may be brought by him thereon without reference to the partnership. Chamberlain *v.* Walker, 10 Allen (Mass.), 429.

Accommodation Indorsers. — As between accommodation indorsers, the doctrine of contribution does not apply. McDonald *v.* Magruder, 3 Pet. (U. S.) 478; McNeilly *v.* Patchin, 23 Mo. 41; McCune *v.* Belt, 45 Mo. 174; Stiles *v.* Eastman, 1 Kelly (Ga.), 205. *Compare* Douglas *v.* Waddle, 1 Ham. (O.) 413; s c., 13 Am. Dec. 630; Daniel *v.* McRae, 2 Hawk. (N. C.) 590; s. c., 11 Am. Dec. 787. In the absence of an express or implied agreement, changing the liability of indorsers *inter se*, they are bound to pay in the order in which their names appear on the paper. Spence *v.* Barclay, 8 Ala. 581; Aiken *v.* Barkley, 2 Speers' Law (S. C.), 747; s. c., 42 Am. Dec. 397.

In Bank of U. S. *v.* Beirne, 1 Gratt. (Va.) 234, *Scott, J.*, says, "The legal effect of several successive indorsements is, that each indorser has a right to look for indemnity to all the indorsers who precede him, whether they indorse for the accommodation of the drawer, or for value received, unless there be an agreement *aliunde* different from that evidenced by the indorsements." See also Ross *v.* Espy, 66 Pa. St. 481; Shaw *v.* Knox, 98 Mass.

5. Joint Owners of Property. — Contribution is also enforced between joint owners of property, for expenses incurred for the common benefit.[1]

(*a*) *Tenants in Common.* — The right of contribution also arises, in certain cases, between tenants in common.[2]

214; Givens *v.* Merchants' Nat. Bank, 85 Ill. 443; Easterly *v.* Barber, 66 N. Y. 433.

As between the indorsers themselves, it may be shown by parol that they were all accommodation indorsers, and were by agreement between themselves co-sureties. Smith *v.* Morrill, 54 Me. 48; Clapp *v.* Rice, 13 Gray (Mass.), 403; Nurre *v.* Chittenden, 56 Ind. 463; Davis *v.* Morgan, 64 N. C. 570. But the burden of proof to show that such an agreement exists, is upon him who seeks the benefit of it. Hogue *v.* Davis, 8 Gratt. (Va.) 4; Sweet *v.* McAllister, 4 Allen (Mass.), 353.

Between Insurers. — In cases of double insurance, that is, when two or more policies are taken out upon the same interest, the insurer paying the loss will have a claim for contribution against the other insurers for their respective proportions. Gordon *v.* London Assurance Co., 1 Burr. 492; Lucas *v.* Jefferson Ins. Co, 6 Cow. (N. Y.) 635; Stacy *v.* Franklin Fire Ins. Co., 2 W. & S. (Pa) 506, Merrick *v.* Germania Fire Ins. Co., 54 Pa. St. 277; Peoria, etc., Ins. Co. *v.* Lewis, 18 Ill. 553; Hough *v.* People's Ins. Co., 36 Md. 398.

The several insurers of the same subject-matter against the same risk are regarded as if they were one, each standing as co-surety with the others, according to the amount insured. May on Insurance, § 434; Liverpool, etc., Ins. Co. *v.* Verdier, 33 Mich. 138; Tuck *v.* Hartford Fire Ins. Co., 5 N. H. 326.

Policies usually contain a clause, that, in case of double insurance, each company shall only be liable for its respective proportion of the loss. See May on Insurance, § 13; Home Ins. Co. *v.* Baltimore Warehouse Co., 93 U. S. 527. If, therefore, a company whose policy contains this provision pay more than its share, it can have no remedy for contribution against the other insurers, for the principle of contribution only applies where the party paying was under a legal obligation to pay. Lucas *v.* Jefferson Ins. Co., 6 Cowen (N. Y.), 635; Haley *v.* Ins. Co., 12 Gray (Mass.), 545.

Between Stockholders of Corporations. — A stockholder who has been compelled to pay more than his share of the corporate debts may have an action for contribution against the other stockholders. Aspinwall *v.* Torrance, 1 Lans. (N. Y.) 381; Gray *v.* Coffin, 9 Cush. (Mass.) 192; Stewart *v.* Lay, 45 Iowa, 604; Farrow *v.* Bivings, 13 Rich. Eq. (S. C.) 25; Umsted *v.* Buskirk, 17 Ohio St. 113; Matthews *v.* Albert, 24 Md. 527; Hadley *v.* Russell, 40 N. H. 109; Brinham *v.* Wellersburg Coal Co., 47 Pa. St. 49.

Between Directors. — If a director who has been compelled to pay a corporate debt through an omission of duty, which the law imposed equally upon all the directors, such as the filing of an annual certificate or report, he is entitled to contribution from the others. Nickerson *v.* Wheeler, 118 Mass. 295. See, however, a contrary decision in Andrews *v.* Murray, 33 Barb. (N. Y.) 354.

In Ashhurst *v.* Mason, L. R. 20 Eq. 225, 236, the directors of a company, acting *ultra vires*, passed a resolution under which certain shares of the company were purchased with its funds, and transferred to one of the directors in trust for the company. The transaction was free from bad faith or moral turpitude. The company having been wound up, this director was compelled to pay calls in respect of shares. *Held*, that he could maintain a bill in equity for contribution from his co-directors. *Bacon, V. C.*, said, "It would be against every principle of justice and reason that the persons who were parties to the transaction should say to the one of them who, by their resolution and direction, is by name only the person under a legal liability, that he should bear that exclusively, as between him and themselves."

Where by statute the officers of a corporation are made primarily liable, and the stockholders only secondarily liable, for its debts, the former, who have been compelled to pay corporate debts, cannot maintain a bill in equity against the latter for contribution. Stone *v.* Fenno, 6 Allen (Mass.), 579. *Bigelow, C. J.*, said, "The rule of law, as well as of equity, is, that all who are bound by a common obligation shall stand relatively to one another in that state of equality in regard to a loss or payment, which corresponds with the equality of risk or responsibility which rests upon them under their original contract or liability. . . . But where there is no such equality, the right of contribution does not exist."

1. See Gardner *v.* Diederichs, 41 Ill. 158; Young *v.* Williams, 17 Conn. 393; Dech's App. 57 Pa. St. 467; Mumford *v.* Brown, 6 Cowen (N. Y.), 475; Leigh *v.* Dickeson, 12 Q. B. D. 194; Rogers *v.* MacKenzie, 4 Ves. 752.

2. **Repairs.** — One tenant in common can compel another to contribute to such

(*b*) *Part Owners of Ships.* — Whenever the ship is reasonably repaired by the consent of all the owners, for the common benefit,

repairs to a house or mill belonging to them, as are necessary to its preservation or use. Alexander *v.* Ellison, 79 Ky. 148; Gardner *v.* Diederichs, 41 Ill. 158; Anderson *v.* Greble, 1 Ashm. (Pa.) 136; Beaty *v.* Bordwell, 91 Pa. St. 438; Denman *v.* Prince, 40 Barb. (N. Y.) 217.

See also Co. Litt. 200, b, where Lord Coke says, that owners are "bound *pro bono publico*, to maintain houses and mills, which are for the habitation and use of men."

But the rule does not extend to the case of fences enclosing wood or arable lands. See Lewis Bowles' Case, 11 Co. 79 b., 82 b.; Story on Partnership, § 422; Alexander *v.* Ellison, 79 Ky. 148.

A tenant in common is liable to his co-tenant for repairs that are absolutely necessary to houses and mills already erected and in being, which fall into decay; but the rule does not apply to woodland or arable land. Beaty *v.* Bordwell, 91 Pa. St. 438.

In this case, the parties had purchased, and held as tenants in common, a farm containing eighty acres. Bordwell had the possession thereof, and had expended money in pulling and removing stumps, and claimed to be allowed for one-half of the sum so expended. *Held*, that his co-tenant was not liable.

Request and Refusal to join in Repairs. — It has been held, however, that one tenant in common cannot recover against another for repairs, though necessary and proper, unless he has requested his co-tenant to join in the repairs, and the latter has refused. Mumford *v.* Brown, 6 Cowen (N. Y.), 475; Taylor *v.* Baldwin, 10 Barb. (N. Y.) 582; Doane *v.* Badger, 12 Mass. 65; Stevens *v.* Thompson, 17 N. H. 103; Kidder *v.* Rixford, 16 Vt. 172.

The assent of a co-tenant to necessary repairs may be presumed from the peculiar relation of the parties, some of whom were non-residents, and the beneficial character of the acts done. Haven *v.* Mehlgarten, 19 Ill. 95.

In Louisiana, joint owners must contribute ratably to useful expenses incurred on the property by a joint owner managing it, when they have made no opposition to such expenses. Percy *v.* Millandon, 18 Martin (La.), 616.

In Loring *v.* Bacon, 4 Mass. 575, A. owned a room on the lower floor of a dwelling-house, and the cellar under it; and B. owned the chamber over the room, and the remainder of the house. The roof becoming ruinous, B. made the necessary repairs, after a demand upon A., and a refusal to join therein. *Held*, that A. was not liable to contribute to such repairs, as the parties had distinct dwelling-houses.

Rule in Massachusetts. — In Massachusetts, a tenant in common who makes necessary repairs upon the common property without the consent of his co-tenant cannot maintain an action at law against him to recover contribution for the cost thereof. Calvert *v.* Aldrich, 99 Mass. 74. See also Converse *v.* Ferre, 11 Mass. 325.

In Calvert *v.* Aldrich, 99 Mass. 74, *Foster, J.*, says, "The difficulty in the way of awarding damages in favor of one tenant in common against his co-tenant for neglecting to repair, is that both parties are equally bound to make the repairs, and neither is more in default than the other for a failure to do so. Upon a review of all the authorities, we can find no instance in England or this country in which, between co-tenants, an action at law of any kind has been sustained, either for contribution or damages, after one has made needful repairs in which the other refused to join."

In New Hampshire, Maine, and Massachusetts, the repair of mills is regulated by statute. See Bellows *v.* Dewey, 9 N. H. 278; Buck *v.* Spofford, 31 Me. 34; Carver *v.* Miller, 4 Mass. 559.

Improvements — A tenant in common who puts improvements, as buildings, etc., on the land, is not entitled to charge either the land or his co-tenant with the value thereof or the expense incurred in making them. Thurston *v.* Dickinson, 2 Rich. Eq. (S C.) 317; Taylor *v.* Baldwin, 10 Barb. (N.Y.) 582; Walter *v.* Greenwood, 29 Minn. 87; Stevens *v.* Thompson, 17 N. H. 103; Crest *v.* Jack, 3 Watts (Pa.), 238; Dech's App. 57 Pa. St. 572; Elrod *v.* Keller, 89 Ind. 382; Bazemore *v.* Davis, 55 Ga. 504; Drennen *v.* Walker, 21 Ark. 557.

In Thurston *v.* Dickinson, 2 Rich. Eq. (S. C.) 317, Chancellor Johnson said, "The general rule clearly is, that if one of several tenants in common make improvements on the common property, neither the property nor his co-tenants are chargeable with their value or the expenses incurred in making them. . . . He can, at any moment, obtain a severance, and use his own portion as he may think fit; and, if he will expend money in the improvement of the common property, he is no more to be favored than one who wilfully spends money in improving his neighbor's lands without his consent."

In Thompson *v.* Bostick, 1 McM. Eq. (S. C.) 75, a tenant in possession erected a cotton-gin on the premises *Held*, that his and one part owner has paid for the expense incurred, he can call upon the others for contribution.[1]

(*c*) *Owners of Party-Walls.* — For the cases in which contribution is enforced between the owners of party-walls, see note 2.

co-tenant was not chargeable with any portion of its value. One tenant in common cannot be made liable to the others for expensive and valuable improvements, which are not repairs in the strict sense of that term, and not necessary to preserve the premises from dilapidation and ruin, and to save the property, in the absence of an express or implied contract to pay for them. Taylor *v.* Baldwin, 10 Barb. (N. Y.) 582.

In Walter *v.* Greenwood, 29 Minn. 87, one tenant in common built upon the common property a frame-barn of the value of six hundred dollars, and sought contribution therefor from his co-tenant, who had full knowledge of its construction, and made no objection thereto. *Held*, that the co-tenant was not liable for any portion of the cost of the improvements. See also Stevens *v.* Thompson, 17 N H. 103; Thurston *v.* Dickinson, 2 Rich. Eq. (S. C.) 317; Taylor *v.* Baldwin, 10 Barb. (N. Y.) 582.

In Crest *v.* Jack, 3 Watts (Pa.), 238, by permission of some of the tenants in common, a house was erected upon the common property. Jack, one of the co-tenants, did not consent to the erection of the building, but knew of its being built, and made no objection thereto *Held*, that he was not liable for his proportion of the moneys expended in building the house. *Sergeant, J.*, said, "One joint tenant, or tenant in common, cannot erect buildings or make improvements on the common property without the consent of the rest, and then claim to hold until reimbursed a proportion of the moneys expended; nor can he authorize this to be done by a third person. If he desires to improve without asking the assent of a co-proprietor, his course is to have his share set off by partition, and to deal with that as he may see proper."

Where a co-tenant has assented to the improvements, or authorized them to be made, he is liable to account for his *pro rata* share of the cost thereof. Baird *v.* Jackson, 98 Ill. 78; Prentice *v.* Janssen, 79 N. Y. 478; Houston *v.* McCluney, 8 W. Va 135.

Partition where Improvements have been made. — A tenant in common of land, who has erected thereon a house without the knowledge or consent of his co-tenant, is not entitled to have partition made of the land without the house, and to have that part of the land on which the house stands set off to him Husband *v.* Aldrich, 135 Mass. 317. See, however, Dean *v.* O'Meara, 47 Ill. 120, where it is held that in a suit for partition of lands, where improvements had been made by one tenant in common, the court should direct in making partition, that the portion improved be assigned to the one making such improvements, without taking into consideration the value of the improvements. And in case such division cannot be made, the court will so apportion the purchase-money as to give to such tenant in common the increased value of the property derived from the improvements, besides his *pro rata* interest in the land. See also Louvalle *v.* Menard, 1 Gilman (Ill.), 39; Kurtz *v.* Hilner, 55 Ill. 514; Borah *v.* Archer, 7 Dana (Ky.), 176.

Taxes and Encumbrances. — A co-tenant who pays taxes, or removes encumbrances, is entitled to be reimbursed. Weare *v.* Van Meter, 42 Iowa, 128; Wilton *v.* Tazwell, 86 Ill. 29; Allen *v.* Poole, 54 Miss. 323; Davidson *v.* Wallace, 53 Miss. 475.

In Wilton *v.* Tazwell, 86 Ill. 29, one tenant in common of lands subject to a widow's dower and homestead rights, procured their release at a reasonable price. *Held*, that he was entitled to contribution from his co-tenant, who had received the benefit of the release.

1. Story on Partnership, § 419; Starbuck *v.* Shaw, 10 Gray (Mass.), 492; Sheehan *v.* Dalrymple, 19 Mich. 239.

But in the absence of any agreement between the owners, express or implied, sanctioning such repairs, no right of contribution exists in favor of the owner, who has paid for the same. Story on Partnership, § 421; Curling *v.* Robertson, 7 Man. & G. 336; Brodie *v.* Howard, 17 C. B. (84 E. C. L.) 109; Hardy *v.* Sproule, 31 Me. 71; Pentz *v.* Clarke, 41 Md. 327; Stedman *v.* Feidler, 20 N. Y. 437.

Story, however, in his work on Partnership, § 423, considers this doctrine of doubtful propriety. And see Sheehan *v.* Dalrymple, 19 Mich. 239, where it was held, that joint owners of a vessel are bound to pay each his own share of the expense of repairs; and, without clear evidence of a special agreement to the contrary, the law will imply a promise by one owner to repay to the other any sum paid by the latter beyond his half of such repairs.

2. **Party-Walls.** — Where a party-wall becomes ruinous and unsafe, and incapable of being repaired, and is rebuilt by one of the owners, the other may be compelled to contribute ratably to the expense of the new

(*d*) *General Average.* — In case of a general average loss, a claim for contribution arises.[1]

wall. Campbell *v.* Mesier, 4 Johns. Ch. 334.

In this case, Chancellor Kent said, "The parties had equality of right and interest in the party-wall, and it became absolutely necessary to have it rebuilt. It was for the equal benefit of the owners of both houses, and the plaintiff ought not to be left to bear the whole burthen. The inconvenience of the repair was inevitable, and as small and as temporary as the nature of the case admitted. . . . I am very forcibly struck with the equity of the demand. The houses on each side of the lot were old and almost untenable; and it would be the height of injustice to deny to the plaintiff the right of pulling down such a common wall, and of erecting a new one suitable to the value of the lot, in the most crowded part of a commercial city. It would be equally unjust to oblige him to do it at his exclusive expense, when the lot of the defendant was equally benefited by the erection, and much enhanced in value." The chancellor was of the opinion, however, that the defendant was not bound to contribute to building the new wall higher than the old; nor, if materials of a different and unusual kind were used, was he bound to pay any part of the extra expense.

In Sherred *v.* Cisco, 4 Sandf. (N. Y.) 480, a party-wall, built at the joint expense, was destroyed by fire. The owner of one of the two lots upon which it stood, proceeded, without the agreement or concurrence of the owner of the other lot, to build a new wall on the site of the old. The owner of the other lot subsequently built on his lot, and rested his beams on the new wall *Held*, that he was not liable to contribute to the owner of the adjoining lot any portion of the expense of erecting such wall. See also Partridge *v.* Gilbert, 15 N. Y. 601.

Where the party-wall is expressly built for the use of two buildings erected at the same time, without any express agreement as to who should pay for the wall, the owner who builds and pays for it is entitled to contribution from the other for his proportion of the cost thereof. Huck *v.* Flentye, 80 Ill. 258.

In Day *v.* Caton, 119 Mass. 513; s. c., 20 Am. Rep. 347, plaintiff sued to recover the value of one-half of a brick party-wall built by him, partly on his estate, and partly on that of the defendant. The court instructed the jury as follows: "If the jury find that the plaintiff undertook and completed the building of the wall with the expectation that the defendant would pay him for it, and the defendant had reason to know that the plaintiff was so acting with that expectation, and allowed him so to act without objection, then the jury might infer a promise on the part of the defendant to pay the plaintiff." *Held*, that this instruction was not erroneous.

Where, under a parol agreement between two adjoining owners to jointly build a party-wall, the parties have gone on and built a portion of the wall, one party, who has prepared his materials and planned his building, relying upon the performance of the contract, may, after notice to the other, complete the wall, and recover of him one-half of the expense. Rindge *v.* Baker, 57 N. Y. 209.

Additions to Party-Wall used by Co-Owner. — In Sanders *v.* Martin, 2 Lea (Tenn.), 213; s. c., 31 Am. Rep. 598, the plaintiff extended the party-wall above and below for his own convenience, with the consent of the defendant, the owner of the adjoining lot, who used the extension by improvements on his lot. *Held*, that the plaintiff was entitled to contribution from the co-owner, who was liable for one-half of the value of the additions at the time they were actually used by him. *Cooper, J.*, said, "If one owner can rebuild a party-wall which has become dangerous, and compel contribution, it is clearly upon the equitable and moral principle that the expenditure is for the benefit of both, and that the right of easement is a sufficient basis upon which to justify interference and raise an implied contract. The same basis exists where a wall is added to and actually used."

Destruction by Fire. — In case a party-wall is destroyed by fire, there is no implied obligation to contribute towards rebuilding it. Automarchi's Executor *v.* Russell, 63 Ala. 356; s. c., 35 Am. Rep. 40; Sherred *v.* Cisco, 4 Sandf. (N. Y.) 489; List *v.* Hornbrook, 2 W. Va. 340; Orman *v.* Day, 5 Fla. 385.

Where houses having a party-wall are accidentally destroyed by fire, leaving the wall standing, the easement in the wall ceases, and either owner may dispose as he pleases of the part on his ground. Hoffman *v.* Kuhn, 57 Miss. 746; s. c., 34 Am. Rep. 491.

If one adjacent proprietor rebuilds on the same foundation, he cannot compel a purchaser from the other proprietor to contribute to the cost of the wall, or make compensation for using it in the subsequent erection of a building on the adjacent lot. Automarchi's Executor *v.* Russell, 63 Ala. 356.

1. The Toledo, etc., Co. *v.* Speares, 16 Ind. 52; Munck *v.* Holmes, 25 Pa. St.

366; Bevan *v.* Bank of U. S., 4 Whart. (Pa.) 301.

General average in maritime law is a contribution made by the owners of a vessel and cargo, and all concerned in the success of her voyage, towards a loss sustained by some of the parties interested, for the benefit of all. Wilson *v.* Cross, 33 Cal. 60.

When it becomes necessary for the general safety to make a jettison, or other sacrifice of a part of the interest at risk, the loss must be made good by contribution, to be assessed upon what is saved of ship, cargo, and freight. Phillips on Ins. § 1279.

"General average contribution," says *Mr. Justice Clifford* in "Star of Hope," 9 Wall. (U. S.) 203, 228, "is defined to be a contribution by all the parties in a sea adventure to make good the loss sustained by one of their number on account of sacrifices voluntarily made of part of the ship or cargo, to save the residue and the lives of those on board from an impending peril, or for extraordinary expenses necessarily incurred by one or more of the parties for the general benefit of all the interests embarked in the enterprise."

There are three essentials, without all of which there can be no claim for general average. There must be a common danger, a voluntary loss, and a saving thereby of the imperilled property, — in other words, the sacrifice must be voluntary, necessary, and successful. See 1 Parsons on Maritime Law, 288; Barnard *v.* Adams, 10 Howard (U. S.), 270, 303; The "Congress," 1 Biss. (C. C.) 42; "Star of Hope," 9 Wall. (U. S.) 203.

Terre Tenants. — Where there are several purchasers in succession at different times of parts of a tract of land bound by a judgment, there is no equality, and no case for contribution between the purchasers. Clowes *v.* Dickenson, 5 Johns. Ch. (N. Y.) 235, 241; Lock *v.* Fulford, 52 Ill. 166; Cary *v.* Folsom, 14 Ohio, 365; Holden *v.* Pike, 24 Me. 427; Brown *v.* Simons, 44 N. H. 475.

If the debtor sells a portion of land bound by a judgment, the remaining land in the hands of the debtor, or his heir or vendee, must first be proceeded against by the judgment creditor, before the land of the prior purchaser can be levied on. Per *Sergeant, J.*, in Taylor's Executors *v.* Maris, 5 Rawle (Pa.), 55. See also Nailer *v.* Stanley, 10 S. & R. (Pa.) 450; Clowes *v.* Dickenson, 5 Johns. Ch. (N. Y.) 235; Sir Wm. Harbert's Case, 3 Co. 11.

If one owning several tracts of land, bound by a judgment against him, sells one tract to A., the remaining tract being more than sufficient to pay the judgment, and afterwards sells one of the remaining tracts to B., who has notice of the circumstances, if B.'s tract is taken in execution, and the judgment satisfied by the sale of it, B. cannot maintain assumpsit on an implied promise against A. for contribution. Nailer *v.* Stanley, 10 S. & R. (Pa.) 450. See also Cowden's Est. 1 Pa. St. 267; Jones *v.* Myrick, 8 Gratt. (Va.) 180; Hunt *v.* Mansfield, 31 Conn. 488; Cooper *v.* Bigby, 13 Mich. 463.

Heirs, Devisees, and Legatees. — An heir who has paid the debts of his ancestor, after a deficiency in the personal assets, is entitled to contribution from his co-heirs out of the estate descended to them. Taylor *v.* Taylor, 8 B. Mon. (Ky.) 419; s. c., 48 Am. Dec. 400; Schermerhorn *v.* Barhydt, 9 Paige (N. Y.), 28.

If the portion of one heir has been taken to pay the debt of the ancestor, he is entitled to contribution from his co-heirs. Clowes *v.* Dickenson, 5 Johns. Ch. (N. Y.) 235.

Where one specific legacy, upon a deficiency of assets, is applied to the payment of debts, other specific legatees will be compelled to contribute. Snow *v.* Callum. 1 Desaus (S. C.) 543.

If specific legacies have been applied to the payment of specialty debts, the specific legatees are entitled to contribution against the devisees of the real estate; but when applied to the payment of simple contract debts, no right of contribution exists against the devisees of the real estate. Chase *v.* Lockerman, 11 Gill & John. (Md.) 185; s. c., 35 Am. Dec. 277.

Where the personal estate and proceeds of real estate, out of which the debts and pecuniary legacies are to be paid, prove insufficient, the general pecuniary legatees cannot compel contribution from specific devisees to equalize the loss arising from the deficiency. Glass *v.* Dunn, 17 Ohio St. 413.

Specific devisees can compel contribution from each other where the land devised to either is taken for payment of debts which are not charged, or secured by mortgage or other lien, upon the same. Glass *v.* Dunn, 17 Ohio St. 413.

Where the executor has in his hands funds sufficient to pay all the legacies, and, after paying some of them, squanders or misapplies the residue of the fund, the unpaid legatees cannot resort to the others for contribution. Sims *v.* Sims, 2 Stock. (N. J.) 158. See also Peeples *v.* Horton, 39 Miss. 406.

See generally, Thomas *v.* Thomas, 2 C. E. Green. (N. J.) 356; *In re* Moulton, 48 Cal 191; Livingston *v.* Livingston, 3 Johns. Ch. (N. Y.) 148; Graham *v.* Dickinson, 3 Barb. Ch. (N. Y.) 169.

6. Between Wrong-Doers. — The general rule is, that no right of contribution exists between wrong-doers.[1] But the rule is con-

1. Merryweather *v.* Nixan, 8 T. R. 186; Colburn *v.* Patmore, 4 Cr. M. & R. 73; Pearson *v.* Skelton, 1 M. & W. 504; Minnis *v.* Johnson, 1 Duv. (Ky.) 171; Nichols *v.* Nowling, 82 Ind. 488; Cumpston *v.* Lambert, 18 Ohio, 81; s. c., 51 Am. Dec. 442; Herr *v.* Barber, 2 Mackey (D. C.), 545; Percy *v.* Clary, 32 Md. 245; Coventry *v.* Barton, 17 Johns. (N. Y.) 142; s. c., 8 Am. Dec 376; Miller *v.* Fenton, 11 Paige (N. Y.), 18; Wehle *v.* Haviland, 42 How. Pr. (N. Y.) 399; Selz *v.* Unna, 6 Wall. (U. S.) 327. One wrong-doer cannot maintain an action for contribution against another, although he may have been compelled to pay all of the damages arising from the tort committed by both. Hunt *v.* Lane, 9 Ind. 248; Churchill *v.* Holt, 131 Mass 67.

A statute imposed upon each trustee of a manufacturing company the duty of making a report of its capital, etc., and made the trustees jointly and severally liable for its debts for neglecting to file the report mentioned. The plaintiff, one of the trustees, alleging that he had discharged certain debts of the company for which the statute had made all the trustees personally liable, in consequence of their neglect brought an action for contribution against the other trustees. *Held*, that plaintiff was a wrong-doer, and could not recover. Andrews *v.* Murray, 33 Barb. (N. Y.) 354. See, however, Nickerson *v.* Wheeler, 118 Mass. 295, where it was held that if the property of the president of a manufacturing corporation is taken in satisfaction of an execution issued on a decree in equity against himself and the other officers by which they are decreed to be personally liable to a creditor of the corporation for neglect to file the certificate required by statute, he may maintain a bill in equity against the other officers for contribution. See also Aspinwall *v.* Sacchi, 57 N. Y.

In Rend *v.* Chicago, etc., Railway Co., 8 Bradwell (Ill.), 517, plaintiff having been obliged to pay a judgment recovered against it for an injury to one of its passengers caused by a collision between a loaded wagon of defendant's and one of plaintiff's horse-cars, brought suit against defendants for contribution for the damages so paid. *Held*, that if the injury was the result of the joint negligence of both parties, plaintiff could not recover.

In Cumpston *v.* Lambert, 18 Ohio, 81, defendant was a justice of the peace, and as such, had called upon the plaintiff to assist him in arresting one William Razor, and promised to indemnify him for so doing. The arrest was afterwards held to be unlawful, and judgment was recovered against the plaintiff therefor, which he paid, and brought suit on the contract of indemnity. *Held*, that plaintiff could not recover. *Compare* Jacobs *v.* Pollard, 10 Cush (Mass.) 287.

In Spalding *v.* Oakes, 42 Vt. 343, the plaintiff and the defendant were the joint owners of a vicious ram, whose propensity to butt was known to both parties. The animal was kept for the separate use of both: each having the immediate charge of him, from time to time, as occasion required. While being kept by the defendant, on his farm, with plaintiff's assent, the ram, in consequence of not being properly restrained, committed an act of violence, for which an action was brought, and a judgment recovered against both owners for the damages. The plaintiff, having paid the judgment, brought suit for contribution against the defendant. Held, that both parties had neglected their duty to restrain the animal, and were wrong-doers between whom there could be no contribution.

If a person leaves a hatchway in the sidewalk connected with his premises in an unsafe condition, so that an injury to a traveller on the street is liable to happen in consequence of it, and another person so interferes with the hatchway as to cause it to be more dangerous, and a traveller is injured by the hatchway, the occupant of the premises is *in pari delicto* with the other person and cannot recover contribution of him, it compelled to pay damages recovered in an action by the injured person. Churchill *v.* Holt, 131 Mass. 67.

In Atkins *v.* Johnson, 43 Vt. 78, plaintiff was the publisher of a newspaper, and brought suit upon an agreement in writing made by defendant, that, if plaintiff would publish in his newspaper an article entitled "A Jack at All Trades exposed," the defendant would save him harmless from the consequence thereof. The article proved to be a libel; and a judgment was recovered against plaintiff for the publication thereof, which he was obliged to pay. *Held*, that the parties were joint wrong-doers, and that the agreement could not be enforced. *Pierpont, C. J.*, said, "In this case, both these parties knew that they were arranging for, and consummating, an illegal act, one that subjects them to legal liability, hoping, to be sure, that they might defend it; but the plaintiff, fearing they might not be able to do so, sought to protect himself from the consequences, by taking a contract of indemnity from the defendant. To say, under such circumstances, that these parties were not joint wrong-doers, within the full spirit fined to cases where the person seeking redress knew, or must be presumed to have known, that the act was unlawful.[1]

and meaning of the general rule, would be an entire perversion of the plainest and simplest proposition. This being so, the law will not interfere in aid of either. It will not inquire which of the two are most in the wrong, with a view of adjusting the equities between them; but, regarding both as having been understandingly engaged in a violation of the law, it will leave them as it finds them, to adjust their differences between themselves as they best may."

In Shackell *v.* Rosier, 29 Com. L. 438; s. c., 2 Bing. (N. C.) 234, the plaintiff, at the request of defendant, published in his newspaper an article libellous on its face, but which the defendant assured him was true. The party aggrieved having brought an action against plaintiff for the libel, the defendant thereupon promised him that, if he would defend the suit, he, the defendant, would indemnify him for all costs and damages. A recovery was had in that suit, and plaintiff sued for the indemnity. There was a verdict for the plaintiff, which the court set aside, *Bosanquet, J.*, observing that "the act done by the plaintiff here was unlawful within his own knowledge."

1. Adamson *v.* Jervis, 4 Bing. 72; Wooley *v.* Batte, 2 Car. & P. 417, Pearson *v.* Skelton, 1 M. & W. 504; Jacobs *v.* Pollard, 10 Cush. (Mass.) 287; s. c., 57 Am. Dec. 105; Bailey *v.* Bussing, 28 Conn. 455; Moore *v.* Appleton, 26 Ala. 633; Acheson *v.* Miller, 2 Ohio St. 203; s. c., 59 Am. Dec. 663; Goldsborough *v.* Darst, 9 Brad. (Ill). 205; Sherner *v.* Spear, 92 N. C. 148; Horbach *v.* Elder, 18 Pa. St. 33; Armstrong Co *v.* Clarion Co., 66 Pa. St. 218.

It has been said that the test for determining whether there shall be contribution between wrong-doers is the common-sense rule, "namely, that when parties think they are doing a legal and proper act, contribution will be had; but when the parties are conscious of doing a wrong, courts will not interfere" Per *Caldwell, J*, in Acheson *v.* Miller, 2 Ohio St. 203; s. c, 59 Am. Dec. 663. See also Grund *v.* Van Vleck, 69 Ill. 479; Ives *v.* Jones, 3 Ired. L. (N. C.) 538. The true rule, however, seems to be, that where there has been an intentional violation of law, or where the wrong-doer is presumed to have known that the act was unlawful, no right of contribution exists. Barley *v.* Bussing, 28 Conn. 455; Moore *v.* Appleton, 26 Ala 633; Jacobs *v.* Pollard, 10 Cush (Mass.) 287; s. c, 57 Am. Dec. 105; Armstrong Co., *v.* Clarion Co, 66 Pa. St. 218; Adamson *v.* Jervis, 4 Bing. 66, 73; Betts *v.* Gibbons, 2 Ad. & Ell. 57, 74.

In Jacobs *v.* Pollard, 10 Cush (Mass) 287, the plaintiff seized certain cattle while alleged to be damage-feasant, and delivered them to the defendant as field-driver, who, at plaintiff's request, sold them at auction, and received the proceeds. The proceedings were irregular, and the owner of the cattle recovered judgment against both parties as joint trespassers, and plaintiff was obliged to pay the judgment. *Held*, that the parties having acted in good faith in making the seizure, the plaintiff was entitled to recover of defendant the money received for the sale of the cattle.

Bigelow, J., said, "No one can be permitted to relieve himself from the consequences of having intentionally committed an unlawful act, by seeking an indemnity or contribution from those with whom, or by whose authority, such unlawful act was committed. But justice and sound policy, upon which this salutary rule is founded, alike require that it should not be extended to cases where parties have acted in good faith, without any unlawful design, or for the purpose of asserting a right in themselves or others, although they may have thereby infringed upon the legal rights of third persons. It is only when a person knows, or must be presumed to know, that his act was unlawful, that the law will refuse to aid him in seeking an indemnity or contribution. It is the unlawful intention to violate another's rights, or a wilful ignorance and disregard of those rights, which deprives a party of his legal remedy in such cases."

Wrong-Doers by Inference of Law. — In Pearson *v.* Skelton, 1 M. & W. 504, one stage-proprietor, who had been sued for the negligence of a driver, and damages had been recovered against him, which he had paid, sought contribution from another of the proprietors. *Held*, that the rule that no contribution exists between tort-feasors, does not apply to a case where the party seeking contribution was a tort-feasor only by inference of law, but is confined to cases where it must be presumed that the party knew he was committing an unlawful act.

A traveller, passing over a bridge which was maintainable by two counties, was injured by its breaking down. He recovered damages in an action for negligence against one of the counties. *Held*, that county might recover contribution from the other Armstrong Co. *v.* Clarion Co., 66 Pa. St 218.

Rule where the Parties are not In Pari Delicto. — Where the parties are not *in pari delicto*, and one is compelled to pay the damages, he may sue the other for contribution. Thus, in Lowell *v.* Boston & L. R. R., 23 Pick. (Mass.) 24; s. c., 34 Am. Dec. 33, the defendants, in constructing a railroad from Boston to Lowell, had occasion to make excavations in one of the highways in Lowell, which plaintiffs were bound to keep in repair, whereby it became necessary to place barriers across the highway for the protection of travellers. The defendants afterwards removed the barriers, and neglected to replace them, so that two persons, driving along the highway in the night-time, were precipitated into the deep cut made by defendants, and greatly injured, and on account thereof recovered double damages against the plaintiffs, which they were compelled to pay. *Held*, that the plaintiffs were entitled to contribution from defendants to the extent of single damages, for the loss suffered by the fault of defendants' servants.

Wilde, J., said, "Our law does not, in every case, disallow an action, by one wrongdoer against another, to recover damages incurred in consequence of their joint offence. The rule is, *in pari delicto potior est conditio defendentis.* If the parties are not equally criminal, the principal delinquent may be held responsible to his codelinquent for damages incurred by their joint offence. In respect to offences in which is involved any moral delinquency or turpitude, all parties are deemed equally guilty, and courts will not inquire into their relative guilt. But where the offence is merely *malum prohibitum*, and is in no respect immoral, it is not against the policy of the law to inquire into the relative delinquency of the parties, and to administer justice between them, although both parties are wrong-doers." See also Campbell *v.* Somerville, 114 Mass. 334; City of Chicago *v.* Robbins, 2 Black (U. S.), 418; Gridley *v.* City of Bloomington, 68 Ill. 47. Contribution lies where, through the negligence of the defendants, the plaintiff has been obliged to pay damages Minneapolis Mill Co *v.* Wheeler, 31 Minn. 121.

Where a traveller falls into an excavation in the street of a city, made by the negligence of an abutting owner, and recovers damages of the city, the city is entitled to contribution from the owner. Westfield *v.* Mayo, 122 Mass. 100; Centreville *v.* Woods, 57 Ind. 192; Portland *v.* Richardson, 54 Me. 46; Brooklyn *v.* Brooklyn City R. Co, 47 N. Y. 475; Robbins *v* Chicago, 4 Wall. (U. S.) 657.

The rule that one of two joint tort-feasors cannot maintain an action against the other for contribution, does not apply where one does the act, or creates the nuisance, and the other does not join therein, but is thereby exposed to liability, and suffers damage Churchill *v.* Holt, 127 Mass. 165; Gray *v.* Boston Gas Light Co., 114 Mass. 149; Horbach *v.* Elder, 18 Pa. St. 33; Bailey *v.* Bussing, 28 Conn. 455.

In Wooley *v.* Batte, 2 Car. & P. 417, one stage proprietor having been sued for an injury to a passenger through the negligence of the driver, and having paid the damages, was allowed to recover contribution from his co-proprietor, upon proving that he was not personally present when the accident happened. So, in Bailey *v.* Bussing, 28 Conn. 455, a judgment was recovered against three defendants, jointly interested in the running of a stage, for an injury caused to a traveller upon the road by the negligence of one of the defendants, who was driving One of the other defendants was compelled to pay the whole amount of the judgment, and brought an action against the defendant whose negligence had caused the injury for contribution. *Held*, that plaintiff was entitled to recover. *Ellsworth, J.*, observed, "We must look for personal participation, personal culpability, personal knowledge. If we do not find these circumstances, but perceive only a liability in the eye of the law, growing out of a mere relation to the perpetrator of the wrong, the maxim of law that there is no contribution among wrong-doers is not to be applied."

Where the defendant, without the permission of the plaintiff, attached to the plaintiff's chimney a telegraph-wire, which rendered it unsafe, and ultimately caused it to fall and injure a horse and wagon then passing, and the injury caused thereby plaintiff was obliged to pay for, *held*, that defendant was liable to plaintiff for the amount so paid. Gray *v.* Boston Gas Light Co, 114 Mass. 149. *Endicott, J.*, said, "When two parties, acting together, commit an illegal or wrongful act, the party who is held responsible in damages for the act cannot have indemnity or contribution from the other, because both are equally culpable, *or participes criminis*, and the damage results from their joint offence. This rule does not apply when one does the act, or creates the nuisance, and the other does not join therein, but is thereby exposed to liability, and suffers damage. He may recover from the party whose wrongful act has thus exposed him. In such case the parties are not *in pari delicto* as to each other, though as to third persons either may be held liable."

A joint trespasser is entitled to contribution for fees paid by him to the counsel who defended the suit. Percy *v.* Clary, 32 Md. 245

Authorities for Contribution. — Adams's Equity; Bispham's Equity; Chitty on Contracts; Story's Eq. Juris.; Article in 8 Am. L. Reg. (U. S.) 449; Article in 6 Albany, L. J. 23, on "Contribution between Wrong-Doers."

CONTRIBUTORY NEGLIGENCE.

1. The General Rule.—It has long been a settled rule of the common law, that, for injuries negligently inflicted upon one person by another, there can be no recovery of damages if the injured person by his own negligence, or by the negligence of another legally imputable to him, proximately contributed to the injury.[1]

1. **The Rule stated.**—There is no doubt that the principles which govern in the law of contributory negligence were known in the Roman Law (Wharton on Neg. 2d ed. § 300; Pollock on Torts, 484), and probably from this source the rule was derived by the Common Law (Beach on Con. Neg. § 1). But as applicable in cases of tortious injury by negligence, the doctrine of contributory negligence, substantially as it now prevails, was first enunciated in Butterfield v. Forrester, 11 East, 60; s. c., 2 Thompson on Neg. 1104. The case was as follows: "This was an action on the case for obstructing a highway, by means of which obstruction the plaintiff, who was riding along the road, was thrown down, with his horse, and injured, etc. At the trial before *Bayley, J.*, at Derby, it appeared that the defendant, for the purpose of making some repairs to his house, which was close by the roadside, at one end of the town, had put up a pole across this part of the road, a free passage being left by another branch or street in the same direction; that the plaintiff left a public house not far distant from the place in question at eight o'clock in the evening in August, when they were just beginning to light candles, but while there was light enough left to discern the obstruction at one hundred yards' distance, and the witness, who proved this, said that, if the plaintiff had not been riding very hard, he might have observed and avoided it. The plaintiff, however, who was riding violently, did not observe it, but rode against it, and fell with his horse, and was much hurt in consequence of the accident, and there was no evidence of his being intoxicated at the time. On this evidence, *Bayley, J.*, directed the jury, that if a person riding with reasonable and ordinary care could have seen and avoided the obstruction, and if they were satisfied that the plaintiff was riding along the street extremely hard, and without ordinary care, they should find a verdict for the defendant, which they did accordingly." In the Court of King's Bench it was contended that this direction was wrong, and that, on the above facts, plaintiff was entitled to re-

2. Difficulties in its Application. — While this general rule is recognized in all jurisdictions where the common law prevails, yet may difficulties have arisen in its practical application, and it is only in recent years that the doctrines of contributory negligence have become reasonably well settled.[1]

cover. But the case was thus disposed of by *Lord Ellenborough, C. J.*: "A party is not to cast himself upon an obstruction which has been made by the fault of another, and avail himself of it, if he do not himself use common and ordinary caution to be in the right. In cases of persons riding upon what is considered to be the wrong side of the road, that would not authorize another purposely to ride up against them. One person being in fault will not dispense with another's using ordinary care for himself. Two things must concur to support this action, — an obstruction in the road by the fault of the defendant, and no want of ordinary care to avoid it on the part of the plaintiff."

The doctrine thus laid down in 1809 by the English Court of King's Bench has never since been doubted or denied, and this case has been cited with approval and followed in every jurisdiction where the common law prevails. Freer *v.* Cameron, 4 Rich. (S. Car.) 228; 55 Am. Dec. 663, and list of authorities collected in note at pp. 666 and 667; Wharton on Neg. (2d ed.) § 300, note 3; Beach on Con. Neg § 7, p. 15, note 2; Deering on Neg. § 12, note 2; Patterson's Ry. Ac. Law, § 45, p. 47, note 1; Cooley on Torts, 675, notes 1 and 2. *American* statements of the general doctrine are forcible and frequent. "It has been a rule of law from time immemorial, and it is not likely to be changed in all time to come, that there can be no recovery for an injury caused by the mutual default of both parties. When it can be shown that it would not have happened except for the culpable negligence of the party injured, concurring with that of the other party, no action can be maintained." Pennsylvania R. Co. *v.* Aspell, 23 Pa. St. 147; s. c., 62 Am. Dec. 323.

"When there has been mutual negligence, and the negligence of each party was the proximate cause of the injury, no action whatever can be sustained." Traw *v.* Vermont Cent. R. Co., 24 Vt. 487; s. c., 58 Am. Dec. 191, 196; Timmons *v.* Cent. Ohio R. Co., 6 Ohio St. 109; Haley *v.* Chicago, etc., R., 21 Iowa, 25; Button *v.* Hudson River R. Co., 18 N. Y. 257; Needham *v.* San Francisco, etc., R. Co, 37 Cal. 409; Reynolds *v.* Hindman, 32 Iowa, 149; Stucke *v.* Milwaukee, etc., R. Co., 9 Wis. 214.

"If the injury was the result of the carelessness of the plaintiff, and could have been avoided by the exercise of ordinary vigilance, he should not recover." President, etc., *v.* Gullett, 15 Ind. 487.

"The general rule is, that one who receives an injury from the negligence of another may maintain an action for his damages. Upon this rule, a natural and reasonable exception has been ingrafted, that if the injured party, by his own negligence, has contributed to the injury, he cannot maintain an action." Chapman *v.* New Haven R. Co., 19 N. Y. 341; s. c., 75 Am. Dec. 344.

"The law is well settled that there can be no recovery if the plaintiff's negligence or want of care contributed in any way to the injury complained of." Indianapolis *v.* Cook, 99 Ind. 11.

"Whenever there is negligence on the part of the plaintiff, contributing directly, or as a proximate cause, to the occurrence from which the injury arises, such negligence will prevent the plaintiff from recovery." Murphy *v.* Deane, 101 Mass. 455; s. c., 3 Am. Rep. 390, 396.

Reason for the Rule. — "The reason why, in cases of mutual concurring negligence, neither party can maintain an action against the other, is not that the wrong of one is set off against the wrong of the other: it is that the law cannot measure how much of the damage suffered is attributable to the plaintiff's own fault. If he were allowed to recover, it might be that he would obtain from the other party compensation for his own misconduct." Heil *v.* Glanding, 42 Pa. St. 493, 498.

"The law has no scales to determine in such cases whose wrong-doing weighed most in the compound that occasioned the mischief." L. S. N. R. Co. *v.* Norton, 24 Pa. St. 469. And see Beach on Cont. Neg § 6.

1. Indefiniteness of Rule. — "Scarcely any theme, in the whole range of legal science, has been more fruitful in adjudications, than the subject of contributory negligence; but the multiplicity of decisions on this point has not by any means cleared it of difficulties. On the contrary, it has in some respects seemed rather to 'darken counsel,' by the introduction of a great variety of metaphysical refinements and subtile distinctions" Note to Freer *v.* Cameron, 55 Am Dec. 666.

"These doctrines remain little more than metaphysical abstractions, tending to confuse courts and juries, and to defeat the ends of justice, unless there can be extracted from them a definite practical rule

3. Scope of this Discussion. — In the articles in this work upon the various topics and relations wherein the principles of law relating to contributory negligence have application, the special modifications and concrete applications of those principles will be treated.[1] Whence it follows, that the general doctrines of the law of contributory negligence will form the principal subject of this article, and contributory negligence in its special phases and particular applications will only be treated of incidentally and by way of illustration.[2]

4. Contributory Negligence defined. — Contributory negligence is a want of ordinary care upon the part of a person injured by the actionable negligence of another, combining and concurring with that negligence, and contributing to the injury as a proximate cause thereof, without which the injury would not have occurred.[3]

or rules. We are convinced, after a study of the adjudications of both the English and American courts, that the whole subject of contributory negligence remains in a state of great confusion and uncertainty. The doctrinal formulas, already laid down in the preceding sections, are reiterated in many judicial opinions without their import being understood by the judges who make use of them; and even those judges, who, by study, seem to have acquired definite theoretical views of the import of these expressions, are unable to agree upon any definite rules with respect to their application." With these statements, Mr. Thompson closes a review of the general principles of the law of contributory negligence (2 Thompson on Neg. 1155, § 7); and hence the difficulties of laying down "definite" and "practical" rules, for the application of those principles, may be apprehended. Notwithstanding the difficulty of the task, we shall endeavor without discussion or argument to formulate in this article "definite" and "practical" rules, which can be supported both upon principle and authority; and it is believed, that if the principles of the subject are developed in logical order, as they have been evolved by the cases, many of the difficulties in their application will disappear.

1. **Contributory Negligence in Special Relations.** — See, for example, such topics as HIGHWAYS, MASTER AND SERVANT, CARRIERS OF PASSENGERS, GOODS AND LIVE-STOCK, BAILMENTS, RAILROADS, ANIMALS, FENCE LAWS, BANKS AND BANKING, BRIDGES, ATTORNEYS, OFFICERS, MUNICIPAL CORPORATIONS, TELEGRAPH COMPANIES, TURNPIKE COMPANIES, INSURANCE, and many other titles. In these articles, instances of the application of the general rules laid down here will be found multiplied.

2. **General Principles only stated.** — Illustrations herein are necessarily chosen from almost every branch of the law in which the doctrines of contributory negligence are enforced. But while the principles which govern in all relations are stated, with their application, more complete collections of authorities must be looked for under other appropriate titles.

3. **Various Definitions.** — "Contributory negligence may, therefore, be defined to be that want of reasonable care upon the part of the person injured which concurred with the negligence of the railway [defendant] in causing the injury." Patterson's Ry. Ac. Law, p. 48, § 47.

"If the plaintiff or party injured, by the exercise of ordinary care under the circumstances, might have avoided the consequences of the defendant's negligence, but did not, the case is one of mutual fault, and the law will neither cast all the consequences upon the defendant, nor will it attempt any apportionment thereof." Cooley on Torts, 674.

"The obligation to use ordinary care, so as to avoid receiving injury as well as to avoid inflicting it, governs the relation of all who are exercising independent rights. One who, by the breach of this duty, has shared in bringing an injury upon himself, cannot complain of another, who, by a breach of the corresponding duty, has also shared in producing it. In an action for negligence, two conditions must concur, — a performance of duty by the plaintiff, and a breach of duty by the defendant. The more approved statement of the doctrine of contributory negligence is, that a person cannot recover for an injury to which he contributed by his own want of ordinary care." Pierce on Railroads, 323.

"One who is injured by the mere negligence of another, cannot recover at law or in equity any compensation for his injury, if he, by his own or his agent's ordinary negligence or wilful wrong, proximately contributed to produce the injury of which

5. Negligence of the Defendant. — There can be no contributory negligence on the part of a plaintiff, except in cases where there has been negligence upon the part of the defendant. Contributory negligence exists only when the negligence of both parties has combined and concurred in producing the injury.[1]

6. Elements of Contributory Negligence. — Assuming as a postulate, the negligence of a defendant as a proximate cause of an injury, then the essential elements of contributory negligence on the part of a person injured are: 1. A failure on his part, or on the part of some person with whose negligence he is chargeable, to exercise ordinary care to avoid injury; and, 2. A proximate connection between such failure to exercise ordinary care, and the injury, so direct and immediate, that, but for such want of ordinary care, the injury would not have occurred.[2] That is, the

he complains, so that, but for his concurring and co-operating fault, the injury would not have happened to him, except where the more proximate cause of the injury is the omission of the other party, after becoming aware of the danger to which the former party is exposed, to use a proper degree of care to avoid injuring him." Shearman & Redfield on Neg. § 25.

"Contributory negligence, in its legal signification, is such an act or omission, on the part of a plaintiff, amounting to a want of ordinary care, as, concurring or co-operating with the negligent act of the defendant, is a proximate cause of the injury complained of." Beach on Con. Neg. §§ 3, 7.

"Contributory negligence in law is that sort of negligence on the part of a plaintiff which is the proximate, and not the remote, cause of the injury." Whittaker's Smith on Neg. 373.

And see the philosophical description of contributory negligence in Pollock on Torts, 374-379.

The definition of Smith, quoted above, is misleading, because he would make plaintiff's negligence, which is the sole proximate cause of an injury, contributory negligence. This error, which is common, has been well corrected in a West Virginia case, where the true meaning of contributory negligence is accurately stated. "Properly speaking, contributory negligence, as the very words import, arises when the plaintiff as well as the defendant has done some act negligently, or has omitted through negligence to do some act which it was their respective duty to do, and the combined negligence of the two parties has directly produced the injury." Washington *v.* B. & O. R. Co., 17 W. Va. 190; s. c., 10 Am. & Eng. R. R. Cas. 749, 755.

1. Defendant must be Negligent.—"There can be no contributory negligence, except where the defendant has been guilty of negligence to which the plaintiff's negligence could contribute. An assault and battery is not negligence. The former is intentional: the latter is unintentional." Ruter *v.* Foy, 46 Iowa, 132; Steinmetz *v.* Kelly, 72 Ind. 442; s. c., 37 Am. Rep. 170; Patterson's Ry. Acc. Law, § 50, p. 49; Beach on Con. Neg. § 22, p. 69.

Thus, no matter how negligent the plaintiff may be, he is not guilty of contributory negligence if purposely injured by the defendant. Carter *v.* Louisville, etc., R. Co., 98 Ind. 552; s. c., 22 Am. & Eng. R. R. Cas. 360.

The negligence of defendant must be shown before any question of contributory negligence can arise.

Simms *v.* So. Car. R. Co. (So. Car. 1887), 2 S. E. Rep. 486.

Thus, in Harris *v.* Minneapolis, etc., R. Co., 33 Minn. 459, the case was reversed because there was no evidence of defendant's negligence, and the question of decedent's negligence was not considered; but on another trial it was held, that defendant's negligence having been sufficiently shown, the question of decedent's contributory negligence arose. Harris *v.* Minneapolis, etc., R. Co. (Minn. 1887), 33 N. W. Rep. 12.

2. Negligence of Plaintiff must be Proximate. — "In order to constitute such negligence as will bar a recovery of damages, these two elements must in every case concur: 1. A want of ordinary care on the part of the plaintiff. . . . 2. A proximate connection between this want of ordinary care and the injury complained of." 2 Thompson on Neg. 1148, § 3; Beach on Con. Neg. 19. This is an accurate statement of the abstract legal doctrine, but it affords no test by which to determine when the causal connection between the failure of ordinary care and the injury exists. In the rules laid down in the text, and well supported by authorities, we have endeavored to formulate such a test. Thus, negligence of the defendant and the negligence of the plaintiff must have been so inextricably mingled together, jointly and in combination causing the injury, that it cannot be said that the injury would have happened had the plaintiff, or person injured, been free from fault at the time of the injury.[1] But plaintiff's act or omission when only a remote cause,[2] or a mere antecedent occasion,[3] or condition,[4] of the injury is not contributory negligence.[5]

7. The Want of Ordinary Care. — Considering these elements in their order, we find it established, by an overwhelming weight of authority, that there must have been a want of ordinary care, under the circumstances of the case, contributing to the injury, as an efficient and proper cause thereof, before *contributory* negligence can exist.[6] But when such want of ordinary care exists,

it has been said, "Mere negligence, or want of ordinary care or caution, will not disentitle the plaintiff to recover, unless it be such, that, but for that negligence, or want of ordinary care and caution, the misfortune could not have happened." Tuff *v.* Warman, 5 C. B. N. S. 573, 585.

"To defeat the right of action, it must appear that, but for the negligence of the party injured operating as an efficient cause of the injury, in connection with the negligence or misconduct of the defendant, the injury would not have happened." Note to Freer *v.* Cameron, 55 Am. Dec. 668.

And it seems that the rule, as stated in the text, is fully warranted by many cases. Kentucky Cent. R. Co. *v.* Thomas, 79 Ky. 160; s. c., 1 Am. & Eng. R. R. Cas. 79, 80; 42 Am. Rep. 208; Railroad Co. *v.* Jones, 95 U. S. 439; Paducah, etc., R. Co *v.* Hoehl, 12 Bush (Ky.), 41; Pennsylvania R. Co. *v.* Righter, 42 N. J. L. 180; Colorado, etc., R. Co. *v.* Holmes, 5 Colo. 197; s. c., 8 Am. & Eng. R. R. Cas. 410; Woods *v.* Jones, 34 La. Ann. 1086; s. c., 15 Am. Rep. 555; Richmond, etc., R. Co. *v.* Morris, 31 Gratt. (Va.) 200; Richmond, etc., R. R. Co. *v.* Anderson, 31 Gratt. (Va.) 812; Murphy *v.* Deane, 101 Mass. 455; s. c., 3 Am. Rep. 390; Sullivan *v.* Louisville Bridge Co., 9 Bush (Ky.), 81; 2 Thomp. on Neg. 1151; Wharton on Neg. § 324; Pierce on R. R. 326; Patterson's Ry. Acc. Law, § 45; 2 Wood's Ry. Law, 1255-1257; Radley *v.* London, etc., R. Co., L. R. 1 App. Cas. 754.

1. "**Contributory negligence is a defence which confesses and avoids the plaintiff's case, and must be made out by showing affirmatively, not only that the plaintiff was guilty of negligence, but that such negligence co-operated with the negligence of the defendant to produce the injury." Kentucky R. Co. *v.* Thomas, 79 Ky. 160; s. c., 1 Am. & Eng. R. R. Cas. 81.**

"**When,** however, the two circumstances occur at the same time, the defendant is not charged with the duty of taking care of the plaintiff, inasmuch as the sudden occurrence of the plaintiff's act gives him no opportunity to do so. The two acts of negligence being concurrent, each is held to contribute to the result." Spencer *v.* B. & O. R. Co., 4 Mackey (D. C.), 138; s. c., 54 Am. Rep. 269, 272.

2. Plaintiff's Remote Negligence. — 2 Thompson on Neg. 1151; Shearman & Redf. on Neg. § 25; Pierce on R. R. 326, 327; Beach on Con. Neg. §§ 10, 18; Kerwhacker *v.* Cleveland, etc., R. Co., 3 Ohio St. 172; s. c., 62 Am. Dec. 246; Trow *v.* Vt. Cent. R. Co., 24 Vt. 487; s. c., 58 Am. Dec. 191; Davies *v.* Mann, 10 Mee. & W. 545; s. c., 2 Thompson on Neg. 1105; Doggett *v.* Richmond, etc., R. Co., 78 N. Car. 305; Walsh *v.* Mississippi, etc., Trans. Co., 52 Mo. 434; Pacific R. Co. *v.* Hauts, 12 Kan. 328; Whalen *v.* St. Louis, etc., R. Co., 60 Mo. 323; State *v.* Manchester, etc., R. Co., 52 N. H. 528; Nare *v.* Flock, 90 Ind. 206; Kennard *v.* Burton, 25 Me. 39; s. c., 43 Am. Dec. 249.

3. Scheffer *v.* R. R. Co., 105 U. S. 249; s. c., 8 Am. & Eng. R. R. Cas. 59; Shearman *v.* Western Stage Co, 24 Iowa, 515, 563; Hussey *v.* Ryan, 64 Md. 426; s. c., 54 Am. Rep. 772; Murray *v.* McShane, 52 Md. 217; s. c., 36 Am. Rep. 367; Varney *v.* Manchester, 58 N. H. 430; s. c., 42 Am. Rep. 592.

4. Bigelow on Torts, 307; Wharton on Neg. §§ 324-327; Pierce on Railroads, 327; White *v.* Long, 128 Mass. 598; Thirteenth & F. Sts. R. Co. *v.* Boudrou, 92 Pa. St. 475; s. c., 2 Am. & Eng. R. R. Cas. 30; Northern Cent. R. Co. *v.* State, 29 Md. 420; Weymire *v.* Wolfe, 52 Iowa, 533; Harriman *v.* Pittsburgh, etc, R. Co., 12 N. E. Rep. (Ohio) 451, 462.

5. Wharton on Negligence, §§ 85, 86.

6. Proximate Want of Ordinary Care must exist. — Butterfield *v.* Forrester, 11 East, it will bar a recovery, no matter whether, in point of time, it pre-

60; s. c., 2 Thompson on Neg. 1104; Smith *v.* Smith, 2 Pick. (Mass.) 621; s. c., 13 Am. Dec. 464; Kennard *v.* Burton, 25 Me. 39; s. c., 43 Am. Dec. 249, 253; Steele *v.* Cent. R. Co., 43 Iowa, 109; Hughes *v.* Muscatine, 44 Iowa, 672; Priest *v.* Nicholls, 116 Mass. 401; Railroad Co. *v.* Jones, 95 U. S. 439; Bridge *v.* Grand Junction R. Co., 3 Mees. & W. 244; Hill *v.* New Orleans, etc., R. Co., 11 La. Ann. 292; Mercer *v.* New Orleans, etc., R. Co., 23 La. Ann. 214; Runyon *v.* Cent. R. Co., 25 N. J. L. 556; Gothard *v.* Alabama, etc., R. Co., 67 Ala. 114; s. c., 12 Rep. 69; Chicago, etc., R. Co. *v.* Johnson, 103 Ill. 512; s. c., 8 Am. & Eng. R. R. Cas. 225; Richmond, etc., R. Co. *v.* Morris, 31 Gratt. (Va.) 200; Jalie *v.* Cardinal, 35 Wis. 118; Strong *v.* Sacramento, etc., R. Co., 61 Cal. 326; s. c., 8 Am. & Eng. R. R. Cas. 273; President, etc., *v.* Gullett, 15 Ind. 487; Beatty *v.* Gilmore, 16 Pa. St. 463; s. c., 55 Am. Dec. 514; Griffin *v.* Willow, 43 Wis. 509; Hammond *v.* Mukwa, 40 Wis. 35; Lilley *v.* Fletcher, 1 So. Rep. (Ala.) 273; Smith *v.* N. Y. Cent. R. Co., 38 Hun (N. Y.), 33; Marble *v.* Ross, 124 Mass. 44; Indianapolis, etc., R. Co. *v.* Stout, 53 Ind. 143, 148; Terre Haute, etc., R. Co. *v.* Graham, 95 Ind. 286, 291; s. c., 12 Am. & Eng R. R. Cas. 77; Daley *v.* Norwich, etc., R. Co., 26 Conn. 591; Williams *v.* Clinton, 28 Conn. 266; Fox *v.* Glastenbury, 29 Conn. 204; Creamer *v.* Portland, 36 Wis. 92, 99; Greany *v.* Long Island, etc., R. R. Co., 101 N. Y. 419, 425-427; s. c., 24 Am. & Eng. R. R Cas. 473.

The general rule of ordinary care on the part of the plaintiff has thus been stated in a recent case:—

"The defendant's negligence upon this branch of the case, upon this disputed testimony, became a question which was proper to be submitted to the jury. But this alone, resolved in plaintiff's favor, would not entitle him to a verdict. He must also show that he himself was in the exercise of ordinary care, and free from any negligence which contributed to the injury." Thompson *v.* Flint, etc., R. Co., 57 Mich. 300; s. c., 23 Am. & Eng R. R. Cas. 289, 295.

And in a *Wisconsin* case the rule was thus admirably expressed:—

"If the plaintiff was guilty of any want of ordinary care and prudence, however slight, which neglect contributed directly to produce the injury, he cannot recover. It is not the law that slight negligence on the part of the plaintiff will defeat the action. Slight negligence is the want of extraordinary care and prudence; and the law does not require of a person injured by the carelessness of others, the exercise of that high degree of caution as a condition precedent to his right to recover damages for the injuries thus sustained." Creamer *v.* Portland, 36 Wis. 92.

So it is said, "An examination of the cases leads to the conclusion, that the correct rule is, that if the party by the want of ordinary care contributed to produce the injury, he will not be entitled to recover." Kennard *v.* Burton, 25 Me. 39; s. c., 43 Am. Dec. 253.

And again: "In the legal sense, he [plaintiff] was innocent of negligence, unless there was a want of ordinary care and prudence on his part. The rule is not that any degree of negligence, however slight, which directly concurs in producing the injury, will prevent a recovery; but if the negligence of the plaintiff, amounting to the absence of ordinary care, shall contribute proximately, in any degree, to the injury, the plaintiff shall not recover." Strong *v.* Sacramento, etc., R. Co., 61 Cal. 326; s. c., 8 Am. & Eng R. R. Cas. 275; Robinson *v.* R. Co., 48 Cal. 423.

There are cases that apparently conflict with this doctrine, by holding that "the plaintiff must be entirely free from any negligence whatever, contributing to the injury." New Jersey Ex. Co. *v.* Nichols, 33 N. J. L. 434; Wilds *v.* Hudson River R. Co., 24 N. Y. 430; Philadelphia, etc., R. Co. *v.* Boyer, 97 Pa. St. 91; s. c., 2 Am. & Eng. R. R. Cas. 172; Griffen *v.* New York, etc., R. Co., 40 N. Y. 34; Vanderplank *v.* Miller, Moody, & M. 169; Toledo, etc., R. Co. *v.* Goddard, 25 Ind. 185; Terre Haute, etc., R. Co. *v.* Graham, 95 Ind. 286; s. c., 12 Am. & Eng. R. R. Cas. 77. But it is doubtful if these cases really conflict with the great mass of authority. In all of them, the degrees of negligence are repudiated, and it follows that they use the term negligence as meaning a want of ordinary care under the circumstances. Hence, when they say that, in order to charge defendant, it must be a case of unmixed negligence, or that plaintiff's negligence must not have contributed to his injury in any degree, they only declare the general rule, that, if plaintiff's want of ordinary care contributed to his injury, he cannot recover.

Creamer *v.* Portland, quoted *supra*. Thus it is said in Terre Haute, etc., R. R. Co. *v.* Graham, 95 Ind. 291; s. c., 12 Am. & Eng. R. R. Cas. 77. "It is the general doctrine, and the settled law of this State, that, where negligence is the issue, it must be a case of unmixed negligence; that, in such case, a party cannot recover if it appear that, by the want of ordinary care and prudence on his part, he contributed to the injury, or if, by the exercise of ordinary care, he might have prevented the injury."

ceded,[1] succeeded,[2] or came into existence contemporaneously[3] with, the negligence of the defendant, provided it proximately combined with such negligence in causing the injury.[4]

8. No Degrees of Negligence. — In determining whether there has been a want of ordinary care, the so-called degrees of negligence; namely, "slight," "ordinary," and "gross" negligence, are not to be considered.[5]

The division of negligence into degrees is not recognized in jurisdictions where the doctrine of contributory negligence prevails.[6] Indeed, it is declared by high authority to be misleading in practice, and unscientific in principle.[7]

1. **When it does, Recovery barred.** — Chicago, etc., R. Co. v. Clark, 2 Bradw. (Ill.) 116; Illinois, etc., R. v. Hall, 72 Ill. 222; Illinois, etc., R. v. Hetherington, 83 Ill. 510; Pennsylvania R. Co. v. Morgan, 82 Pa. St. 134; Carroll v. Minnesota Valley R. Co., 13 Minn. 930; Pierce on Railroads, 327; Shearman & Redf. on Neg. § 33; Beach on Cont. Neg. 21; Deering on Neg. § 14.

2. Martensen v. Chicago, etc., R. Co., 60 Iowa, 705; s. c., 11 Am. & Eng. R. R. Cas. 233; Butterfield v. Forrester, 11 East, 60; Brown v. Milwaukee, etc., R. Co., 22 Minn. 165; Jackson v. County Com'rs, 76 N. Car. 282; Illinois, etc., R. Co. v McClelland, 42 Ill. 355; Beach on Cont. Neg. 21.

3. O'Brien v. McGlinchy, 68 Me. 552; Doggett v. Richmond, etc., R. Co., 78 N. Car. 305. Chicago, etc., R. Co. v. Becker, 76 Ill. 26; s. c., 84 Ill. 483; Moak's Underhill on Torts, 285; Beach on Cont. Neg. 21.

4. The causal connection in such cases must not be overlooked. Indeed, the doctrines already laid down in the text must be viewed in connection with the discussion farther on of the rule that the law looks at the proximate, and not the remote, cause of an injury in fixing the liability for its existence. See, in this connection, Isbell v. New York, etc., R. R. Co, 27 Conn. 393, 406; s. c., 71 Am. Dec. 78, and note; Murphy v. Deane, 101 Mass. 455; s. c., 3 Am. Rep. 390; Pierce on R. 327, and note 2.

5. **There are no Degrees of Negligence.** — Steamboat "New World" v. King, 16 How. (U. S.) 469, 474; Terre Haute, etc., R. Co. v. Graham, 95 Ind. 286, 293; s. c., 12 Am. & Eng. R. R. Cas. 77; Milwaukee, etc., R. Co. v. Arms, 91 U. S. 489, 494; Cooley on Torts, 630; Smith v. N. Y. Cent. R. Co., 24 N. Y. 222, 241; Deering on Neg. § 11; Patterson's Ry. Acc. Law, 8

6. The statement of the text is not too broad when limited to cases where the principles of contributory negligence are applicable. Pennsylvania Co. v. Roney, 89 Ind. 453; s. c., 46 Am. Rep. 173; s. c, 12 Am. & Eng. R. R. Cas. 223; Wilds v. Hudson River R. Co., 24 N. Y. 432; O'Keefe v. Chicago, etc., R. Co., 32 Iowa, 467; Wharton on Neg. § 64; Deering on Neg. § 11; Patterson's Ry. Acc. Law, 8; Cooley on Torts, 630; Beach on Cont. Neg. 19, 80. In other words, where the doctrine of contributory negligence is applied, if it appears that the plaintiff, by a want of ordinary care, has proximately contributed to his own injury, he cannot recover by saying that the negligence of the defendant was greater in degree than his own. "The parties being mutually in fault, there can be no apportionment of damages. The law has no scales to determine in such cases whose wrong-doing weighed most in the compound that occasioned the mischief." Railroad Co. v. Norton, 24 Pa. St. 465; s. c., 64 Am. Dec. 674. And, often as it is denied, this is the rule, even where the doctrine of comparative negligence prevails. Abend v. Terre Haute R. Co., 111 Ill. 203; s. c., 53 Am. Rep. 616; s. c., 17 Am. & Eng. R. R. Cas. 614. The truth is, that the rule of comparative negligence is not applicable to cases where the rule of contributory negligence should be applied. The distinction between degrees of negligence is preserved in *Illinois*, but it is never invoked when there has been a want of ordinary care on the part of plaintiff. See title "COMPARATIVE NEGLIGENCE," 3 Am. & Eng. Encyc. of Law.

7. Thus, Chief Justice Cockburn, in his dissenting opinion in the Geneva Award cases, says, —

"The older authorities, indeed, speak of three degrees of negligence, and of gross negligence, as being necessary in some cases to found liability; but the tendency of modern decisions has been to apply in all cases the sound practical rule, that, in determining the question of negligence, the true test is, whether there has been, with reference to the particular subject-matter, that reasonable degree of diligence and care which a man of ordinary prudence and capacity might be expected to exercise in the same circumstances." Quoted, 6 Alb. Law J 313, where many other similar

9. The Test of Ordinary Care. — It follows that the only test by which it can be determined whether ordinary care has been used or omitted in any particular case, is the test of negligence in general, which may be formulated thus: —

There has been no want of ordinary care when, under all the circumstances and surroundings of the case, the person injured, or those whose negligence is imputable to him, did or omitted nothing which an ordinarily careful and prudent person, similarly situated, would not have done or omitted; and, conversely, there has been a want of ordinary care when, under all the circumstances and surroundings of the case, something has been done or omitted that an ordinarily careful and prudent person, so situated, would not have done or omitted to do.[1]

criticisms are collected. See also N. Y. Cent. R. Co. *v.* Lockwood, 17 Wall. (U. S.) 357; Deering on Neg. § 11, and cases cited and the authorities cited in the two preceding notes. But, as holding a contrary view in a limited sense, see Shearman & Redf. on Neg. §§ 16, 17; Wharton on Neg. (2d ed.) §§ 44-65.

1. **The Meaning of "Ordinary Care."** — Freer *v.* Cameron, 55 Am. Dec. 663 and note; s. c., 4 Rich. (S. Car.) Law, 228; Mayor *v.* Bailey, 2 Denio (N. Y.), 433; State *v.* Manchester, etc., R. Co., 52 N. H. 528, 552; Beisigel *v.* N. Y. Cent. R. Co., 34 N. Y. 622, 628, 632; Davis *v.* N. Y. Cent., etc., R. Co., 47 N. Y. 400; Ditberner *v.* Chicago, etc., R. Co., 47 Wis. 138; Cleveland, etc., R. Co. *v.* Crawford, 24 Ohio St. 631, 638; Creed *v.* Penn. R. Co., 86 Pa. St. 139, 145; Beers *v.* Housatonic R. Co., 19 Conn. 566, 571, 572; Ernst *v.* Hudson River R. Co., 35 N. Y. 9; Manly *v.* Wilmington, etc., R. Co., 74 N. Car. 655, 660; Mackay *v* N. Y. Cent. R. Co., 35 N. Y. 75, 80; Tucker *v.* Henniker, 41 N. H. 317; Madison *v.* Ross, 3 Ind. 236; s. c., 54 Am. Dec. 481; Nitro-Glycerine Case, 15 Wall. (U. S.) 524; Morgan *v.* Cox, 22 Mo. 373; Northern Cent. R. Co. *v.* State, 29 Md. 420; Brown *v.* Milwaukee, etc., R. Co., 22 Minn. 165; Moore *v.* Cent. R. Co., 24 N. J. L. 268; Wyandotte *v.* White, 13 Kan. 191; Wheeler *v.* Westport, 30 Wis. 392; Ward *v.* Milwaukee, etc., R. Co., 29 Wis. 144, Stokes *v.* Saltonstall, 13 Pet. (U. S.) 181; Railroad Co. *v.* Pollard, 22 Wall. (U. S.) 341; Reynolds *v.* Burlington, 52 Vt. 300; Strong *v.* Sacramento, etc., R. Co., 61 Cal. 321; s. c., 8 Am. & Eng. R. R. Cas. 273; Aurora, etc., R. Co. *v.* Grimes, 13 Ill. 585; Wilson *v.* Cunningham, 3 Cal. 241; s. c., 58 Am. Dec. 407; Blyth *v.* Birmingham Water-Works Co., 11 Exch. 784; Hays *v.* Millar, 77 Pa. St. 238; Beach on Cont. Neg. § 9; Deering on Neg. § 15; Shearman & Redf. on Neg. §§ 29, 30; Pierce on R. R. 318, 324, 325; Patterson's Ry. Acc. Law, 45-50; 2 Thomp. on Neg. 1149, 1150.

The test of ordinary care formulated in the text, and supported in a general way by the foregoing authorities, has beenstated by the courts as follows: —

"There is no absolute rule as to what constitutes negligence. When a higher degree of care is demanded under some circumstances than under others, when the standard shifts with the circumstances of the case, when both the duty and the extent of its performance are to be ascertained as facts, a jury alone can determine what is negligence, and whether it has been proved." West Philadelphia R. Co. *v.* Gallagher, 108 Pa St. 524; s. c., 27 Am. & Eng. R. R. Cas. 204.

"The rights and duties of parties grow out of the circumstances in which they are placed." Pennsylvania R. Co. *v.* Kilgore, 32 Pa. St. 292; s. c., 72 Am. Dec. 787.

"What is reasonable skill, proper care and diligence, etc., can only be determined, as matter of fact, by the jury. It is impossible to establish any general rule upon so indefinite a subject; and it is impossible to make juries, or merely practical men anywhere, determine these matters except upon the circumstances of each particular case." Robinson *v.* Cone, 22 Vt. 213; s. c., 54 Am. Dec. 67, 74.

"The degree of care and foresight which it is necessary to use, in cases of this description, must always be in proportion to the nature and magnitude of the injury that will be likely to result from the occurrence which is to be anticipated and guarded against; and it should be that care and prudence which a discreet and cautious individual would or ought to use if the whole risk and loss were to be his own exclusively." Walworth, Chancellor, Mayor *v.* Bailey, 2 Denio (N. Y.), 433, 440.

And in a recent case, involving the question of care in crossing a railway, it is said,

10. Slight Want of Ordinary Care. — And, while the degrees of negligence are not recognized in determining whether there has been contributory negligence, yet the slightest want of ordinary care, as above defined and tested, will constitute contributory negligence, if, in combination with the negligence of the defendant, it causes the injury.[1]

"The plaintiff is not bound to see: he is bound to make all reasonable effort to see, that a careful, prudent man would make in like circumstances. He is not to provide against any certain result. He is to make an effort for a result that will give safety, — such effort as caution, care, and prudence will dictate." Greany R. Co. *v.* Long Island, etc., R. Co., 101 N. Y. 419; s. c., 24 Am. & Eng. R. R. Cas. 476.

So, in a similar case, it is said, "What constitutes negligence in a given exigency is generally a question for the jury, and not for the court. Negligence is want of ordinary care under the circumstances; the standard is therefore necessarily variable; no fixed rule of duty can be formed which can apply to all cases. A course of conduct justly regarded as resulting from the exercise of ordinary care, under some circumstances, would exhibit the grossest degree of negligence under other circumstances: the opportunity for deliberation and action, the degree of danger, and many other considerations of a like nature, affect the standard of care which may be reasonably required in a particular case." Schum *v.* Pennsylvania R. Co, 107 Pa. St. 8; s. c., 52 Am. Rep. 469.

And, more exactly in line with the text, it has been said, "The general doctrine is perfectly familiar to us, that, when the negligence of the injured party contributes directly to the injury complained of, the law will afford no redress. . . . But negligence is a relative term, and is defined to be 'the omission to do something which a reasonable man, guided by those considerations which ordinarily regulate the conduct of human affairs, would do, or doing something which a prudent and reasonable man would not do.' Moreover, it is not absolute or intrinsic, but always relates to some circumstance of time, place, or persons." Jamison *v.* San Jose, etc., R. Co, 55 Cal. 593; s. c., 3 Am. & Eng. R. R. Cas. 351, 352; Broom's Leg. Max. 329; Richardson *v.* Kier, 34 Cal. 63.

And although a plaintiff may, by his acts or omissions, have proximately contributed to his own injury, yet, if he was not in fault in so doing, he may recover. "It is possible for the plaintiff not only to contribute to, but even to be himself, the immediate cause of his own injury, and yet to recover compensation therefor. If his share in the transaction was innocent, and not incautious, it furnishes no excuse for the defendant." Shearman & Redf. on Neg. § 28.

Thus, where "the plaintiff carried on a varnish-factory adjoining defendant's railway, and in the manufacture exposed benzine out of doors on his premises, which was ignited by sparks from defendant's engine, and caused the destruction of the factory," it was held that plaintiff was not guilty of contributory negligence. Kalbfleisch *v.* Long Island R. Co., 102 N. Y. 520; s. c., 29 Am. & Eng. R. R. Cas. 179; 55 Am. Rep. 832; S. P. Fero *v.* Buffalo, etc., R. Co., 22 N. Y. 215.

And there are numerous recent cases which recognize this doctrine, and assert the principle, that plaintiff's act or omission contributing to the injury must be such as a person of ordinary care and prudence would not have been guilty of under the circumstances, or it does not constitute contributory negligence. Patten *v.* St. Louis, etc., R. Co., 87 Mo. 117; s. c., 23 Am. & Eng. R. R. Cas. 364; 56 Am. Rep. 446; Louisville, etc, R. Co. *v.* Richardson, 66 Ind. 43; s. c., 32 Am. Rep. 94; Pittsburgh, etc., R. Co. *v.* Jones, 86 Ind. 496; s. c., 11 Am. & Eng. R. R. Cas. 76; 44 Am. Rep. 334; Richmond, etc., R. Co. *v.* Medley, 75 Va. 499; s. c., 7 Am. & Eng. R. R. Cas. 493; 40 Am. Rep. 734; Kellogg *v.* Chicago, etc., R. Co., 26 Wis. 223; s. c., 7 Am. Rep 69; Iron R. Co. *v.* Mowery, 36 Ohio St. 418; s. c., 3 Am. & Eng. R. R. Cas. 361; South Cov., etc., R. Co. *v.* Ware (Ky. 1886), 27 Am. & Eng. R. R. Cas. 206; Jeffrey *v.* Keokuk & D. R. Co., 56 Iowa. 546; s. c., 5 Am. & Eng. R. R. Cas. 568.

1. **Slight Want of, constitutes Negligence.** — "If the plaintiff was guilty of any want of ordinary care and prudence, however slight, which neglect contributed directly to produce the injury, he cannot recover." Creamer *v.* Portland, 36 Wis. 92; Hammond *v.* Mukwa, 40 Wis. 35; Otis *v.* Janesville, 47 Wis. 422; Strong *v.* Sacramento & Placerville R. Co., 61 Cal. 321; s. c., 8 Am. & Eng. R. R. Cas. 273, 275; Baltimore, etc., R. Co. *v.* Fitzpatrick, 35 Md. 32; Manly *v.* Wilmington, etc., R. Co., 74 N. Car. 655; Kerwhacker *v.* Cleveland, etc, R. Co, 3 Ohio St. 172; s. c., 62 Am. Dec. 246; Dush *v.* Fitzhugh, 2 Lea (Tenn.), 307; Houston, etc., R. Co. *v.* Gorbett, 49 Tex. 573; Bridge *v.* Grand Junction Ry. Co., 3 Mee & W. 244; Terre Haute, etc., R. Co. *v.* Graham, 95 Ind. 286, 291;

11. How the Elements must combine. — But a want of ordinary care on the part of the plaintiff, or the person injured, will not prevent a recovery if such want of ordinary care was not a proximate cause of the injury.[1] Nor will the fact that the person injured proximately contributed to his own injury by his conduct, constitute contributory negligence, if he was not guilty of a want of ordinary care.[2] Hence, there must be a want of ordinary care contributing to the injury as a proximate cause before contributory negligence can exist.[3]

s. c., 12 Am. & Eng. R. R. Cas. 77; Dowling *v.* Allen (Mo.), 5 West. Rep. 371, 372; Monongahela City *v.* Fischer, 111 Pa. St. 9; s. c., 13 Am. & Eng. Corp. Cas. 431; 56 Am. Rep. 241. It must be borne in mind that the term "slight negligence," as used in some of these cases, means always slight want of ordinary care, and never a want of extraordinary care, or of the slightest degree of care, a distinction which seems to have escaped Mr. Beach. Beach on Cont Neg. 20 and 21, and note 1, p. 21.

There is a difference of opinion as to the utility of the doctrine laid down in the text. Mr. Beach pronounces it "ingenious and philosophical, and capable of useful application" (Beach, Con. Neg. 20); while Mr. Freeman says, "This distinction between slight negligence and slight want of ordinary care is exceedingly minute, and in practice it would be very difficult to make an average jury comprehend it." Note to Freer *v.* Cameron, 55 Am Dec. 670, 671. But it seems that Mr. Freeman overlooks the marked difference between a slight want of ordinary care, which is negligence by reason of the very fact that it is a failure of ordinary care (Pierce on R. R. 324), and that omi sion of extraordinary care which is usually denominated slight negligence (Story on Bailments, § 17), but which, where the only standard is that of ordinary care, is not negligence at all. "In cases like the one now before us, each party is required to exercise ordinary care, and neither party is required to exercise great or extraordinary care. The want of ordinary care is ordinary negligence; but the want of great or extraordinary care is only slight negligence; and while either party will be held to be guilty of culpable negligence if found to be guilty of ordinary negligence, yet neither party will be held to be guilty of culpable negligence if found to be guilty of only slight negligence." *Valentine, J.*, in Kansas Pac. R. Co *v.* Peary, 29 Kan. 169; s. c., 11 Am. & Eng. R. R. Cas. 260, 271, citing the Wisconsin cases.

1. Causal Connection of Elements. — In the discussion of causal connection which follows, the application of this rule will be shown. It is sufficient here to cite the general authorities for it. Pierce on Railroads, 326, 327; Wharton on Neg. § 323 *et seq.*; Shearman & Redf. on Neg. § 33; 2 Thomp. on Neg. 1151 *et seq.*; Cooley on Torts, 674, 675; 2 Wood's Ry. Law, 1255–1257; Beach on Cont. Neg. 25; note to Freer *v.* Cameron, 55 Am. Dec. 668; Davies *v.* Mann, 10 Mee. & W. 545; s. c., 2 Thomp. on Neg. 1105; Radley *v.* London, etc., Ry. Co., L. R. 1 App. Cas. 754; s. c., 2 Thomp. on Neg. 1108; Puff *v.* Warman, 2 C. B. (N. S.) 740; s. c., 5 C. B. (N. S.) 573; Murphy *v.* Deane, 101 Mass. 455; s. c., 3 Am. Rep. 390; Scheffer *v.* R. R. Co., 105 U. S. 249; s c., 8 Am. & Eng. R. R. Cas. 61.

2. Proximate Contribution not Enough. — This principle has been illustrated in note 22, *ante*, and other illustrations are plentiful. Thus, a person exercising ordinary care may suddenly, without fault on his own part, be put into a position of danger that requires him to adopt a perilous alternative in attempting to escape the immediate danger. If, in doing this, he is injured by the negligence of another, he is not guilty of contributory negligence, even though, had he remained passive in the first instance, he would have escaped injury Jones *v.* Boyce, 1 Stark. (N. J.) 493; Stevenson *v.* Chicago, etc., R. Co., 18 Fed. Rep. 493; Buel *v.* N. Y. Cent. R. Co., 31 N. Y. 314; Chicago, etc., R. Co. *v.* Becker, 76 Ill. 25; Linnehan *v.* Sampson, 126 Mass. 506; s. c., 30 Am. Rep. 692; Galena, etc., R. Co. *v.* Yarwood, 17 Ill. 500; Indianapolis, etc., R. Co. *v.* Stout, 53 Ind. 143; Mobile, etc., R. Co. *v.* Ashcroft, 48 Ala. 15; Georgia, etc., Banking Co. *v.* Rhodes, 56 Ga. 645; Turner *v.* Buchanan, 82 Ind. 147; s. c., 42 Am. Rep. 485; Wilson *v.* Northern Pac. R. Co., 26 Minn. 278; s. c., 37 Am. Rep. 410; Pittsburgh, etc., R. Co *v.* Rohrman (Pa.), 12 Am. & Eng. R. R. Cas. 176, and note; Lowery *v.* R. Co., 99 N. Y. 158; s. c., 23 Am. & Eng. R. R. Cas. 276; Wharton on Neg. §§ 304, 305, 377; Beach on Cont. Neg. §§ 14, 15; Patterson's Ry. Acc. Law, 62 *et seq.*; Pierce on R. R. 328, 329; South Covington, etc., R. *v.* Ware (Ky.), 27 Am. & Eng. R. R. Cas. 206; Nare *v.* Flock, 90 Ind. 211; Louisville, etc., R. Co. *v.* Richardson, 66 Ind. 43, 48; s. c., 32 Am. Rep. 94; Iron R. Co. *v.* Mowery, 36 Ohio St. 418; s. c., 3 Am. & Eng. R. R. Cas. 361.

3. There must also be a Want of Ordinary Care. — This results as a logical con-

12. Proximate and Remote Causes. — In the application of the principle that the law looks at the proximate, and not at the remote, cause of an injury, lies the great difficulty in the law of contributory negligence.[1] No general rule for determining when causes are proximate, and when remote, has yet been formulated.[2] But the principles that govern the determination of the question are well settled.[3] When it is once established that a person, injured by the negligence of another, has been guilty of a want of ordinary care, it becomes necessary to determine whether such want of ordinary care proximately contributed to the injury, as an efficient cause, or only remotely, as a condition or remote cause, thereof.[4] If it proximately contributed, there can be no recovery; but if it was only a remote cause or condition of the injury, a recovery can be had.[5] A want of ordinary care may be said to

sequence, and is, of course, well settled. Beach on Cont. Neg. §§ 3, 7, 10, 11; 2 Thomp. on Neg. 1148-1155; Shearman & Redf. on Neg. § 33; Pollock on Torts, 378, and the authorities cited to the two preceding notes.

1. **Causa Proxima et non Remota Spectatur.** — 2 Thomp. on Neg. 1155; Wharton on Neg. § 85. The maxim of the law is, "*In jure non remota causa sed proxima spectatur.*" Broom's Max. 165, of which Lord Bacon says, —

"It were infinite for the law to consider the causes of causes, and their impulsions one of another, therefore it contenteth itself with the immediate cause, and judgeth of acts by that without looking to any further degree." Maxims, Reg. 1. But this does not help us to tell when a cause is proximate, and when remote.

2. "To a sound judgment must be left each particular case." Harrison *v.* Berkley, 1 Strobh. L. (S. Car.) 525; s. c., 47 Am. Dec. 578. "Many cases illustrate, but none define, what is an immediate, or what is a remote, cause. Indeed, such a cause seems incapable of any strict definition which will suit every case." Fairbanks *v.* Kerr, 70 Pa. St. 86; s. c., 10 Am. Rep. 664. "There can be no fixed and immediate rule upon the subject that can be applied to all cases. Much must, therefore, as is often said, depend upon the circumstances of each particular case." Page *v.* Bucksport, 64 Me 51.

3. With the law of causal connection in the field of negligence in general, we do not here deal. Perhaps the principles that must be invoked to determine when a cause is proximate and when remote, have never been better stated than by Judge Cooley. Cooley on Torts, 68-80. See also Scheffer *v.* R. Co., 105 U. S. 251; s. c., 8 Am. & Eng. R. R. Cas. 59; Ins. Co. *v.* Tweed, 7 Wall (U. S.) 44; Terre Haute, etc., R. Co. *v.* Buck, 96 Ind. 350; s. c., 18 Am. & Eng. R. R. Cas. 234; Henry *v.* St. Louis, etc., R. Co., 76 Mo. 288; s. c., 12 Am. & Eng. R. R. Cas. 136; Lewis *v.* Flint, etc., R Co., 54 Mich. 55; s c., 18 Am. & Eng. R. R. Cas. 263; opinion by *Cooley, C. J.*

4. Pierce on Railroads, 326, 327; 2 Thomp. on Neg. 1151; Beach on Cont. Neg. § 3; 55 Am. 668, note to Freer *v.* Cameron; Pollock on Torts, 378.

5. **The Doctrine of Davies v. Mann.** — Here we encounter two distinct lines of authority, of which Butterfield *v.* Forrester, 11 East, 60, heads one; and Davies *v.* Mann, 10 Mee. & W. 545; s. c., 2 Thompson on Neg. 1105, the other. In the first case the general rule was laid down, which has never since been denied, that a want of ordinary care on his own part, proximately contributing to his injury, will prevent a person injured by the negligence of another from recovering. In the second case, decided in 1842, the correctness of the doctrine in Butterfield *v.* Forrester was conceded; but it was *held* that it had no application to the case before the court, on the ground that plaintiff's want of ordinary care did not constitute contributory negligence, because it was a remote cause or mere condition of the injury, resulting from defendant's negligence, and did not proximately contribute to it. In other words, defendant's negligence was held the sole proximate cause of the injury sustained by plaintiff, the principle being that the negligence of defendant arising subsequently to that of plaintiff, and plaintiff's negligence being so obvious that defendant could, by the exercise of ordinary care, have discovered it in time to have avoided inflicting the injury, defendant's failure to discover such want of care on plaintiff's part was itself the negligence proximately and directly causing the injury, with no intervening negligence on plaintiff's part to break the causal connection between defendant's negligence and the injury. As sustaining this statement

contribute proximately to an injury when it is an active and efficient cause of the injury in any degree, however slight, and not the mere condition or occasion of it.[1] But it is not a proximate

of the rule, and of the effect of the decision in Davies *v.* Mann, see Wharton on Neg. §§ 323 to 327; Pollock on Torts, 378, 379; Shearman & Redf. on Neg. § 25; Pierce on Railroads, 326, 327; Patterson's Ry. Acc. Law, pp. 51–56, and especially § 58, p. 55. And so have the courts applied the case of Davies *v.* Mann, both in this country and in England. Trow *v.* Vermont Cent. R. Co., 24 Vt. 487; s. c., 58 Am. Dec. 191, 196, 197; Isbell *v.* New York, etc., R. Co., 27 Conn. 393; s. c., 71 Am. Dec. 78, 83; Spencer *v.* Baltimore & Ohio R. Co., 4 Mackey (D. C.), 138; s. c., 54 Am. Rep. 272; *The Bernina*, 12 Prob. Div. 58; s. c., 57 Am. Rep. 494, 509, note.

So also a *dictum* in the case of Davies *v.* Mann may be cited as sustaining the doctrine that contributory negligence is not a defence where an injury is wilfully inflicted. Terre Haute, etc., R. Co. *v.* Graham, 46 Ind. 243.

Recent text-writers have criticised the rule in Davies *v.* Mann, and have declared the case "a mischief-making authority." Beach on Con. Neg. § 5; 2 Thomp. on Neg. 1155. But Mr. Thompson has shown how the rule can be usefully and practically applied, — 2 Thomp. on Neg. 1157, — and there is little prospect of its abandonment by the courts as a safe and proper rule in its practical effects.

1. Slight Want of Ordinary Care not Slight Negligence. — Bigelow on Torts, 311; Beach on Con. Neg. 36; Wharton on Neg. § 303; Shearman & Redf. on Neg. § 33; McAunich *v.* Mississippi, etc, R. Co., 20 Iowa, 338; Muldowney *v.* Illinois, etc., R. Co., 39 Iowa, 615; Haley *v.* Chicago, etc., R. Co., 21 Iowa, 15; Sullivan *v.* Louisville Bridge Co., 9 Bush (Ky.), 81, 90; Tuff *v.* Warman, 5 C. B. (N. S.), 573; 2 Thomp. on Neg. 1152; Murphy *v.* Deane, 101 Mass. 455; s. c., 3 Am. Rep. 390; Greenland *v.* Chaplin, 5 Exch. 248; Norris *v.* Litchfield, 35 N. H. 271; s. c., 69 Am. Dec. 546; Pennsylvania R. Co. *v.* Righter, 42 N. J. L. 180; s. c., 2 Am. & Eng. R. R. Cas. 220; Creamer *v.* Portland, 36 Wis. 92; Marble *v.* Worcester, 4 Gray (Mass.), 395; Chicago, etc., R. Co. *v.* Becker, 76 Ill. 25, 30; Monongahela City *v.* Fisher (Pa. 1886), 13 Am. & Eng. Corp. Cas. 431; *Valentine, J.*, in Kansas Pac. R. Co. *v.* Peary, 29 Kan. 169; s. c., 11 Am. & Eng. R. R. Cas. 260. *Compare* Chicago, etc., R. Co. *v.* Johnson, 103 Ill. 512; s. c., 8 Am. & Eng. R. R. Cas. 225.

But it must be Proximate to bar Recovery. — "The act or omission on the part of a plaintiff claimed to have contributed to the injury must have direct relation to the act or omission charged to be negligence on the part of the defendant." McQuitken *v.* Cent. Pac. R. Co., 64 Cal. 463; s. c., 16 Am. & Eng. R. R. Cas. 353.

"The negligence of the plaintiff which defeats a recovery must be a proximate cause of the injury." Fowler *v.* B. & O. R. Co., 18 W. Va. 579; s. c., 8 Am. & Eng. R. R. Cas. 480, 482.

"When the negligence of the party injured did not in any degree contribute to the immediate cause of the accident, such negligence ought not to be set up in answer to the action." Greenland *v.* Chaplin, 5 Exch. 248.

"When there has been mutual negligence on the part of the plaintiff and defendant, and the negligence of each was the proximate cause of the injury, no action can be sustained." Trow *v.* Vt. Cent. R. Co., 24 Vt. 487; s. c., 58 Am. Dec. 191.

"Properly speaking, contributory negligence, as the very words import, arises when the plaintiff as well as the defendant has done some act negligently, or has omitted through negligence to do some act which it was their respective duty to do, and the combined negligence of the two parties has directly produced the injury. . . . On the contrary, if the act of the defendant is the immediate cause of the injury, no preceding negligence or improper conduct of the plaintiff would prevent him from recovering; for in such a case his preceding negligence or improper conduct would not be in law regarded as any part of the cause of the injury, and would not therefore be held to be contributory negligence. The plaintiff's preceding negligence or improper conduct is in such case a mere condition, and not a cause of the injury. Though it may be in such a case, that the injury could not possibly have happened without this preceding negligence or improper conduct of the plaintiff, — that is, without circumstances being in the actual condition in which the plaintiff had improperly placed them, — he may in such case nevertheless recover; for in the view of the law, which never looks to the remote cause, which we have called a condition, but only the proximate cause, the injury in such a case would be held to be caused by the defendant only." Washington *v.* B. & O. R. R. Co., 17 W. Va. 190; s. c., 10 Am. & Eng. R. R. Cas. 749, 755, 756.

"Although the plaintiff was wrongfully upon the cars, the conductor was bound to exercise reasonable care and prudence in removing him. The rule that the plaintiff cause of the injury when the negligence of the person inflicting it is a more immediate efficient cause.[1] That is, when the negligence of the person inflicting the injury is subsequent to, and independent of, the carelessness of the person injured, and ordinary care, on the part of the person inflicting the injury, would have discovered the carelessness of the person injured in time to have avoided its effects, and prevented injuring him, there is no contributory negligence, because the fault of the injured party becomes remote in the chain of causation.[2] In such a case, the

cannot recover of his own wrong as well as that of the defendant, has conduced to the injury which he has sustained, is confined to cases where his wrong or negligence has immediately or proximately contributed to the result." Meeks v. Southern Pac. R. R. Co., 56 Cal. 513; s. c., 8 Am. & Eng. R. R. Cas. 314, 319, 320.

"Negligence, which does not contribute to results, need not be regarded." Marcott v. Railroad Co., 4 Am. & Eng. R. R. Cas. 548, 551; s. c., 47 Mich. 1, 49 Mich. 99.

"It is clear that a plaintiff may recover, though he did not use due care, if his negligence in no wise *caused* the accident resulting in his injury." Thirteenth & F Sts. Pass. R. v. Boudrou, 92 Pa. St. 475; s. c., 2 Am. & Eng. R. R. Cas. 30, 34.

1. **Not Proximate when Defendant's Negligence More Immediate Efficient Cause.** — Pac. R. Co. v. Hauts, 12 Kan. 328; Walsh v. Mississippi, etc., Trans. Co., 52 Mo. 434; Whalen v. St. L., etc., R. Co., 60 Mo. 323; State v. Manchester, etc., R. Co., 52 N. H. 528; Manly v. Wilmington, etc., R. Co., 74 N. Car. 655; Kerwhacker v. Railroad Co., 3 Ohio St. 172; s. c., 62 Am. Dec. 246; Radley v. London, etc., R. Co., L. R. 1 App. Cas. 759; s. c., 2 Thomp. on Neg. 1108; Mark v. Hudson, etc., B. Co., 56 How. Pr. 108; Gunter v. Wicker, 85 N. Car. 310; Weymire v. Wolfe, 52 Iowa, 533; Needham v. R. R. Co., 37 Cal. 409; Brown v. Hannibal, etc., R. Co., 50 Mo. 461; s. c., 11 Am. Rep. 420; Richmond, etc., R. Co. v. Anderson, 31 Gratt. (Va.) 812; s. c., 31 Am. Rep. 750; Button v. Hudson River R. Co., 18 N. Y. 248, 258.

"Another qualification to the general rule, that there is no liability upon the defendant when the plaintiff has contributed to the injury, exists when, though both parties be in fault, the defendant has been the immediate and proximate cause of the injury." Vicksburg, etc., R. Co. v. Pa., 31 Miss. 156; s. c., 66 Am. Dec. 552, 554, 569.

"That plaintiff's conduct exhibited an utter disregard of caution, there can scarcely be a doubt. Still, if this want of caution did not proximately contribute to the accident, and the carelessness of the railroad company alone was the immediate cause of it, plaintiff might recover." Pittsburgh, etc., R. Co. v. Karns, 13 Ind. 87, 89.

"When the negligence of the defendant is proximate, and that of the plaintiff remote, the action can be sustained, although the plaintiff is not entirely without fault." Richmond, etc., R. Co. v. Anderson, 31 Gratt. (Va.) 812; s. c., 31 Am. Rep. 754.

"When the negligence of the defendant is the proximate cause of the injury, but that of the plaintiff only remote, consisting of some act or omission not occurring at the time of the injury, the action for reparation is maintainable." Kerwhacker v. R. R. Co., 3 Ohio St. 172; s. c., 62 Am. Dec. 246, 266.

"When the negligence of the defendant is the proximate cause of the injury, but that of the plaintiff only remote, consisting of some act or omission not occurring at the time of the injury, the action for reparation is maintainable." Zemp v. Wilmington, etc., R. Co, 9 Rich. L. (S. Car.) 84; s. c., 64 Am. Dec. 763, 768.

"The true ground of contributory negligence being a bar to recovery, is that it is the proximate cause of the mischief; and negligence on the plaintiff's part, which is only part of the inducing causes, will not disable him." Pollock on Torts, 378.

In a leading *Missouri* case, the following statement of the rule in an instruction was approved: "Although the deceased may have been guilty of misconduct, or failed to exercise ordinary care or prudence while a passenger on defendant's boat, which may have contributed remotely to the death of deceased, yet if the employees, or either of them, of the defendant, were guilty of negligence which was the immediate cause of the death, and with the exercise of prudence by said employees, or either of them, said injury and death might have been prevented, the defendant is liable." Morrissey v. Wiggins Ferry Co., 47 Mo. 521; s. c., Thomp on Carriers of Pass. 243.

2. **The Rule in Tuff v. Warman.** — Tuff v. Warman, 2 C. B. N. S. 740; 5 C. B. N. S. 573; 27 L. J. C. P. 322; Radley v. London, etc., R. Co., L. R. 1 App. Cas. 754; s. c., 2 Thomp. on Neg. 1108; Isbell v. New York, etc., R. Co., 27 Conn. 393. s. c., 71 Am. Dec. 78; Baltimore, etc., R.

want of ordinary care on the part of the injured person is held not a juridical cause of his injury, but only a condition of its

Co. *v.* Kan. (Md.), 28 Am. & Eng. R. R. Cas. 580, 584; Beach on Cont. Neg. 58, § 18; Pollock on Torts, 375, 376; Note to Freer *v.* Cameron, 55 Am. Dec. 669; Cooley on Torts, 675; Smith on Neg. (Am. ed.) 374-376; Patterson's Ry. Acc. L. 51; 2 Am. & Eng. Ency. of L. 748, § 17, note 4, where many cases bearing generally upon the question are collected.

"The leading case which settled the doctrine in its modern form, is Tuff *v.* Warman, 2 C. B. N. S. 740. The action was against the pilot of a steamer in the Thames for running down the plaintiff's barge. The plaintiff's own evidence showed that there was no lookout on the barge. As to the conduct of the steamer, the evidence was conflicting; but, according to the plaintiff's witnesses, she might easily have cleared the barge. *Willes, J.*, left it to the jury to say whether the want of a lookout was negligence on the part of the plaintiff, and, if so, whether it 'directly contributed to the accident.' This was objected to as too favorable to the plaintiff, but was upheld both in the full court of Common Pleas, and in the Exchequer Chamber. In the considered judgment on appeal, it is said that the proper question for the jury is, 'whether the damage was occasioned entirely by the negligence or improper conduct of the defendant, or whether the plaintiff himself so far contributed to the misfortune by his own negligence, or want of ordinary and common care and caution, that but for such negligence, or want of ordinary care and caution on his part, the misfortune would not have happened.' But negligence will not disentitle the plaintiff to recover, unless it be such that without it the harm complained of could not have happened; 'nor if the defendant might, by the exercise of care on his part, have avoided the consequences of the neglect or carelessness of the plaintiff.'" Pollock on Torts, 375, 376.

The doctrine thus enunciated in Tuff *v.* Warman, 2 C. B. N. S. 740, when correctly applied, is unobjectionable, but the language used by the court has been the subject of some criticism: "We think it is manifest that the rule thus laid down in Tuff *v.* Warman is not the correct rule of law which governs ordinary cases of injury by negligence; but whenever there is negligence on the part of the plaintiff, contributing directly, or as a proximate cause, to the occurrence from which the injury arises, such negligence will prevent the plaintiff from recovery." Murphy *v.* Deane, 101 Mass. 455; s. c., 3 Am. Rep. 390.

In general, however, Tuff *v.* Warman is recognized as authority; and it has been followed in many cases, both in England and the United States.

Perhaps the best illustration of the true application of the principle occurs in the case of Radley *v.* London, etc., R. Co., L. R. 1 App. Cas. 754; s. c., 2 Thomp. on Neg. 1108, where the facts were that, "A railway was in the habit of taking full trucks from the siding of a colliery owner, and returning the empty trucks there. On this siding was a bridge eight feet high from the ground. On a Saturday afternoon, when all the colliery men had left work, the servants of the railway ran some trucks on the siding. All but one were empty, and that one contained another truck, and their joint height amounted to eleven feet. On the Sunday evening the railway servants brought on the siding many other empty trucks, and pushed forward all those previously left on the siding. Some resistance was felt: the power of the engine pushing the trucks was increased, and the two trucks, the joint height of which amounted to eleven feet, struck the bridge, and broke it down. In action to recover damages for the injury, the defence of contributory negligence was set up. The judge, at the trial, told the jury that the plaintiffs must satisfy them that the accident happened solely through the negligence of the defendant's servants, for if both sides were negligent, so as to contribute to the accident, the plaintiffs could not recover." The jury found, under this direction, that there was contributory negligence, and the verdict was for the defendant. On a final appeal to the House of Lords, it was *held* that there was a question of fact for the jury as to plaintiff's negligence, but that the law had not been sufficiently stated to them. "They had not been clearly informed, as they should have been, that not every negligence on the part of the plaintiff, which in any degree contributes to the mischief, will bar him of his remedy, but only such negligence that the defendant could not, by the exercise of ordinary care, have avoided the result." Pollock on Torts, 377.

It is said in the opinion, "It is true that in part of his summing up the learned judge pointed attention to the conduct of the engine-driver, in determining to force his way through the obstruction, as fit to be considered by the jury on the question of negligence; *but he failed to add that if they thought the engine-driver might at this stage of the matter, by ordinary care, have avoided all accident, any previous negligence of the plaintiff's would not prevent them from recovering.* In point of fact, the evidence occurrence.[1] Conversely, when the carelessness of the person inflicting the injury is antecedent to the negligence of the person injured, and the latter might, by ordinary care, have discovered the failure of the former to use such care in time to have avoided the injury, there can be no recovery, because the intervening negligence of the injured person is the direct and proximate cause of his injury.[2] And upon the principle that one will be charged

was strong to show that this was the immediate cause of the accident, and the jury might well think that ordinary care and diligence on the part of the engine-driver would, notwithstanding any previous negligence of the plaintiffs in leaving the loaded-up truck on the line, have made the accident impossible. The substantial defect of the learned judge's charge is, that the question was never put to the jury." 1 App. Cas. 760.

Perhaps the principle of these cases has never been better stated than in a late Missouri case, where it is said, —

"If the negligence of a defendant, which contributed directly to cause the injury, occurred after the danger in which the injured party had placed himself by his own negligence, was, or, by the exercise of reasonable care, might have been, discovered by the defendant in time to have averted the injury, however gross the negligence of the injured party may have been in placing himself in such position of danger.' Donohue *v.* St. Louis, etc., R. Co., 91 Mo. 357; s. c, 28 Am. & Eng. R. R. Cas. 673, 677. See also to same doctrine, Keim *v.* Union R., etc., Co., 90 Mo. 314; Kelley *v.* Hannibal, etc, R Co, 75 Mo. 138; s. c., 13 Am. & Eng R. R. Cas. 638; Frick *v.* St. L., etc., R. Co., 75 Mo. 595; s. c., 8 Am. & Eng. R. R. Cas. 280, 10 Id. 780; Werner *v.* Cit. R Co, 81 Mo. 374; Maher *v.* R. R. Co., 64 Mo. 267; Harlan *v.* Hannibal, etc., R. Co, 65 Mo. 22; Adams *v.* R R. Co., 74 Mo. 553; s. c., 7 Am. & Eng. R. R. Cas. 414.

And the supreme court of *Maryland* thus states the same doctrine: "The governing principle established by the courts may now be stated in a very few words. If both parties have been negligent, but want of due care and caution on the part of the plaintiff was the direct cause of the injury, or, in other words, if the injury could not have been sustained, if the plaintiff had not been careless and neglectful in providing for his safety, there can be no recovery in the action. But if, on the other hand, it is apparent from the evidence that the plaintiff, although negligent, would have suffered no injury had proper care and caution been observed by the defendant, the right of action is maintainable." Baltimore, etc., R. Co. *v.* Kean (Md.), 28 Am. & Eng. R. R. Cas. 580, 584.

How applied to Trespassers. — But it seems that the doctrine of the *Missouri* cases above cited will not be invoked to hold a defendant liable for an injury to a trespasser, unless his danger was *actually* discovered. Rine *v.* Chicago, etc., R. Co., 88 Mo. 392; s. c, 25 Am. & Eng. R. R. Cas. 545; Keim *v.* Union R, etc., Co., 90 Mo. 314; Donohue *v.* St. Louis, etc., R Co., 91 Mo. 357; s. c., 28 Am. & Eng. R. R. Cas 677; Bell *v.* H. & St. Joe. R. R Co., 86 Mo. 599 And so it has been held in other jurisdictions. Little Rock, etc., R Co. *v.* Carenesse (Ark.), 2 S. W. Rep. 505, St. Louis, etc., R. Co. *v.* Monday (Ark. 1887), 4 S. W. Rep. 782; Hughes *v.* Galveston, etc., R. Co. (Tex.), 4 S. W. Rep. 219; McAllister *v.* Burlington, etc., R Co, 64 Iowa, 395; s. c, 19 Am. & Eng. R. R. Cas. 108; Burtnett *v.* Burlington, etc., R. Co., 16 Neb. 332; s. c., 19 Am. & Eng R. R. Cas. 25; International, etc., R Co *v.* Smith, 62 Tex. 252; s. c., 19 Am & Eng. R. R. Cas. 21; Cent. R. Co *v.* Brinson, 70 Ga. 207; s. c., 19 Am. & Eng. R. R. Cas. 42; Patterson's Ry. Acc Law, 192; Beach on Cont. Neg. §§ 67, 68. But these cases may rest on the principle that it is no want of ordinary care not to look out for persons where they have no right to be. And the train men in such cases, even when a trespasser is seen, may usually depend on him to leave the track in time to avoid injury, if he appears to be a person of average capacity. See Hughes *v.* Galveston, etc., R, *above;* Mobile, etc., R. Co. *v.* Stroud (Miss. 1887), 2 So Rep 171. But see Frazer *v.* South & N. Ala R. Co. (Ala. 1887), 28 Am. & Eng. R. R. Cas. 565.

1. Wharton on Neg. § 323; Pollock on Torts, 378; Pierce on Railroads, 327.

2. **Plaintiff's Subsequent Negligence a Bar** — Gothard *v.* Alabama, etc., R. Co., 67 Ala. 114; Macon, etc, R. Co *v* Winn, 19 Ga 440; Hoehl *v.* Muscatine, 57 Iowa, 444; Walsh *v.* Miss., etc, Trans Co., 52 Mo 434; Dudley *v.* Camden, etc., Ferry Co, 45 N. J. L 368; s. c, 29 Alb. L. J. 42; Irwin *v.* Sprigg, 6 Gill (Md), 200; s c., 46 Am. Dec. 667; Flower *v.* Adam, 2 Taunt 314; Wetherley *v.* Regent's Canal Co, 12 C B. N. S. 1; Alston *v* Herring, 11 Ex. 822; Illinois, etc., R. *v.* McClelland, 42 Ill. 355; Toledo, etc., R. *v.* Pindar, 53 Ill. 447;

with notice of that which by ordinary care he might have known, it is held that if either party to an action involving the questions of negligence and contributory negligence, should, by the exercise of ordinary care, have discovered the negligence of the other, after its occurrence, in time to have foreseen and avoided its consequences, then such party is held to have notice; and his negligence in not discovering the negligence of the other, under such circumstances, is held the sole proximate cause of a following injury.[1] But if, in the exercise of ordinary care, the one party would not have discovered the negligence of the other in time to have avoided the injury, the rule just stated has no application;[2] and it is only when the negligence of one party is subsequent to that of the other, that the rule can be invoked.[3] When the negligence of the two parties is concurrent at the time of the injury, it makes no difference that one discovered the negligence of the other before the catastrophe, but too late to prevent it.[4] In such

s. c., 5 Am. Rep. 57; Beach on Cont. Neg. § 19.

"The established doctrine now is, that, although the defendant's misconduct may have been the primary cause of the injury complained of, yet the plaintiff cannot recover in an action of this kind, if the proximate and immediate cause of the damage can be traced to a want of ordinary care and caution on his part." Irwin *v.* Sprigg, 6 Gill (Md.), 200; s. c., 46 Am. Dec. 667, 669; Richmond, etc, R. Co. *v.* Anderson's Adm'r, 31 Gratt. (Va.) 812; s. c., 31 Am. Rep. 750, 754; Lilly *v.* Fletcher (Ala.), 1 So. Rep. 273. And note as of special value the language of *Green, P. J.*, in Washington *v.* B. & O. R. Co., 17 W. Va. 190; s. c., 10 Am. & Eng. R. Cas. 749, 755.

1. Rule when Negligence might have been discovered by Ordinary Care.— Patterson's Ry. Acc. Law, 51; Smith on Neg. (Am. ed.) 374-376; 2 Thomp. on Neg. 1157; Barker *v.* Savage, 45 N. Y. 191, 194; Brown *v.* Lynn, 31 Pa. St. 510; Northern, etc., R. *v.* State, 29 Md. 420; Locke *v.* R. Co., 15 Minn. 350; Nelson *v.* Atlantic, etc., R. Co., 68 Mo. 593; O'Keefe *v.* Chicago, etc., R. Co., 32 Iowa, 467; Morris *v.* Chicago, etc., R. Co., 45 Iowa, 29; Donohue *v.* St. Louis, etc., R. Co., 91 Mo. 673; s. c., 28 Am. & Eng. R. R. Cas. 673; Purinton *v.* Me. Cent. R. Co., 78 Me. 569; and see generally the cases cited, note 33, *supra*.

2. When the Rule does not apply.— Maryland Cent. R. Co. *v.* Newbern, 62 Md. 391; s. c., 19 Am. & Eng. R. R. Cas. 261; Kean *v.* B. & O. R. Co., 61 Md. 154; s. c., 19 Am. & Eng. R. R. Cas. 321; Kelley *v.* Hannibal, etc., R. Co., 75 Mo. 138; s. c, 13 Am. & Eng. R. R. Cas. 638; Colorado Cent. R. Co *v.* Holmes, 5 Colo. 197; s. c, 8 Am. & Eng. R. R. Cas. 410; Chicago, etc., R. Co. *v.* Johnson, 103 Ill. 512; s. c, 8 Am. & Eng. R. R. Cas. 225, 231; Price *v.* St. L., etc., R. Co., 72 Mo. 414; s. c., 3 Am. & Eng. R. R. Cas. 365, 377; Texas, etc., R. Co. *v.* Barfield (Tex.), 3 S. W. Rep. 665.

"But where the manifestation of the peril and the catastrophe are so close, in point of time, as to leave no room for preventive effort, the rule (as above stated) will not apply." Frazer *v.* S. & N. Ala. R. Co. (Ala.), 28 Am. & Eng. R. R. Cas. 565. And see Hughes *v.* Galveston, etc., R. Co. (Tex. 1887), 4 S. W. Rep 219; Mobile, etc., R. Co. *v.* Stroud (Miss. 1887), 2 So. Rep. 171.

3. When it can be invoked.— Beach on Cont. Neg. 59 and 60; Murphy *v.* Deane, 101 Mass. 455; s. c., 3 Am. Rep. 390; Bigelow on Torts, 311.

4. Has No Application when Negligence Concurrent.— Frazer *v.* S. & N. Ala. R. Co. (Ala.), 28 Am. & Eng. R. R. Cas. 565; Murphy *v.* Deane, 101 Mass. 455; s. c., 3 Am. Rep 390.

"On the other hand, it is sometimes said that the plaintiff may be entitled to recover, if the defendant might, by the exercise of care on his part, have avoided the consequences of the negligence of the plaintiff. But this doctrine appears to be applicable only to cases in which the plaintiff's negligence precedes that of the defendant. Where the negligence of the two persons is contemporaneous, and the fault of each operates directly to cause the injury, the rule is declared to be, that the plaintiff cannot recover, if by due care on his part he might have avoided the consequences of the negligence of the defendant." Bigelow on Torts, 311; Zimmerman *v.* Hannibal, etc., R. Co., 71 Mo. 476; s. c., 2 Am. & Eng. R. R. Cas. 191, 196.

case the negligence of each is proximate, and contributory negligence bars a recovery.[1]

13. Aggravation of Injury by Plaintiff's Negligence. — But, while the negligence of the injured person contributing proximately to his injury will bar his recovery of damages, it is held that when he was guilty of no negligence contributing to the injury, negligence upon his part after the injury, by which it is aggravated, will not prevent him from recovering damages for so much of the injury as the original wrong-doer caused by his negligence.[2] In such cases it seems that the damages may be apportioned o allowance made by the jury for that portion of the injury due t plaintiff's fault.[3]

14. Injury enhanced by Disease. — And in cases where defendant's negligence caused a disease,[4] developed a latent tendency to disease,[5] aggravated a prior disease,[6] or led in immediate sequence to disease,[7] defendant must respond in damages for such part of the diseased condition as his negligence caused;[8] and if there can be no apportionment, or if it cannot be said that the disease would have existed apart from the injury inflicted by the defendant, then

1. Bigelow on Torts, 311, 312; Beach on Cont. Neg. 71; Lucas *v.* New Bedford, etc., R. Co., 6 Gray (Mass.), 64; Waite *v.* N. E. R. Co., 9 El. & Bl. 719; Robinson *v.* Cone, 22 Vt. 213; s. c., 54 Am. Dec. 67; Murphy *v.* Deane, 101 Mass. 455; s. c., 3 Am. Rep. 390. In considering the case of Murphy *v.* Deane, it should be borne in mind that many of its statements are fully applicable only where the rule prevails that the burden of disproving contributory negligence is on the plaintiff. Such is not the *English* rule.

2. **Plaintiff's Negligence after Injury.** — Shearman & Redf. on Neg. § 32 and note; Beach on Cont. Neg. 64; Stebbins *v.* Cent. Vt. R. Co., 54 Vt. 464; s. c., 11 Am. & Eng. R. R. Cas. 79; 41 Am. Rep. 855; Greenland *v.* Chaplin, 5 Exch. 243; Thomas *v.* Kenyon, 1 Daly (N. Y.), 132; Sills *v.* Brown, 9 Car & P. 601; Secord *v.* St. Paul, etc., R. Co., 5 McCrary (U. S.), 515; s. c., 18 Fed. Rep. 221; Louisville, etc., R. Co. *v.* Falvey, 104 Ind. 409, 424, 425; s. c., 23 Am. &. Eng. R. R. Cas. 522.

3. **May lead to Apportionment of Damages.** — Beach on Cont. Neg. p. 73, § 24; L. N. A. & C. R. Co. *v.* Falvey, 104 Ind. 409; s. c., 23 Am. & Eng. R. R. Cas. 522; Gould *v.* McKenna, 86 Pa. St. 297; s. c., 27 Am. Rep. 705, 706; Nitro-Phosphate Co. *v.* Docks Co., 9 L. R. Ch. Div. 503; Hunt *v.* Lowell Gas Co., 1 Allen (Mass.), 343; Chase *v.* N. Y., etc., R. Co., 24 Barb. (N. Y.) 273; Sherman *v.* Fall River Iron Co, 2 Allen (Mass.), 524; Matthews *v.* Warner, 29 Gratt. (Va.) 570; s. c., 26 Am. Rep. 396; Hibbard *v.* Thompson, 109 Mass. 286; Fay *v.* Parker, 53 N. H. 342; s. c., 16 Am. Rep. 270, 287, 288.

4. **Defendant's Negligence, causing a Disease** — Baltimore, etc., R. Co. *v.* Kemp, 61 Md. 74; s. c., 18 Am. & Eng. R. R. Cas. 220; s. c., 47 Am. Rep. 381, 48 Am. Rep. 134; Ginna *v.* Railroad Co., 8 Hun (N. Y.), 494, 67 N. Y. 596; Houston, etc., R. *v.* Leslie, 57 Tex. 83; s. c., 9 Am. & Eng. R. R. Cas. 407.

5. **Developing a Latent Tendency to Disease.** — Stewart *v.* Ripon, 38 Wis. 584; Jeffersonville, etc., R. Co. *v.* Riley, 39 Ind. 568.

6. **Aggravating a Prior Disease.** — Louisville, etc., R. Co. *v.* Falvey, 104 Ind. 409; s. c., 23 Am. & Eng. R. R. Cas. 522; Allison *v.* Chicago, etc., R Co., 42 Iowa, 274; N. C. R. Co. *v.* State, 29 Md. 420; McNamara *v.* Clintonville, 62 Wis. 207; s. c., 51 Am. Rep. 722.

7. **Leading directly to Disease.** — Terre Haute, etc., R. Co. *v.* Buck, 96 Ind. 346; s. c., 18 Am. & Eng. R. R. Cas. 234; 49 Am. Rep. 168; Williams *v.* Vanderbilt, 28 N. Y. 217; Beauchamp *v.* Saginaw Mining Co., 50 Mich. 163; s. c., 45 Am. Rep. 30; Jucker *v.* Chicago, etc., R. Co., 52 Wis. 150; s. c, 2 Am. & Eng. R. R. Cas. 41; Delie *v.* Chicago, etc., R. Co., 51 Wis. 400; s. c., 5 Am. & Eng. R. R. Cas. 464; Heim *v.* McCaughan, 32 Miss. 17.

8. **Measure of Damages: How apportioned.** — Louisville, etc., R. Co. *v.* Jones, 108 Ind. 551; s. c., 28 Am. & Eng. R. R. Cas. 170; Louisville, etc., R. Co. *v.* Falvey, 104 Ind. 409; s. c., 23 Am. & Eng. R. R. Cas. 522; Com. *v.* Warner, 4 McLean (U. S.), 464; State *v.* Morea, 2 Ala. 275; Com. *v.* Fox, 7 Gray (Mass.), 585; McAllister *v.* State, 17 Ala. 434; Com. *v.* Green, 1 Ashm.

defendant is responsible for the diseased condition.[1] But when the diseased condition exists independently of the injury, and does not flow from it as a natural consequence following in direct sequence, the defendant's liability is only for such consequences as, independently of the diseased condition, were directly and immediately caused by his negligence;[2] yet if he knew of the diseased condition, and could have foreseen that it would aggravate an injury inflicted by his negligence, he is liable for the entire consequences that flow from the combination of his negligence with the existing diseased condition.[3] And so defendant is liable for negligently causing a natural function or condition to become disordered, and must respond in damages for all the direct and natural consequences, however unusual or unexpected;[4] and this doctrine is particularly applicable when the person guilty of the negligence owes a special duty to the person injured,—for example, to carry safely.[5] In such cases it is generally held that the action, although it may arise out of contract, sounds in tort, and the negligent person must answer for all the natural consequences of his wrongful act.[6] The principle, as applied to carriers of passengers,

(Pa.) 289; Mobile, etc., R. Co. *v.* McArthur, 43 Miss. 180.

1. When no Apportionment. — Patterson's Ry. Acc. Law, 28, 29; Beach on Cont. Neg. § 24; McNamara *v.* Clintonville, 62 Wis. 207; s. c., 51 Am. Rep. 722; Ehrgott *v.* Mayor, 96 N Y. 264; s. c., 48 Am. Rep. 622; King *v.* Cohoes, 77 N. Y. 83; s. c., 33 Am Rep. 574

"Here, as I understand the findings of the jury, the plaintiff's injuries would not have been suffered but for the strain and shock of the accident. While both causes were proximate, that was the nearest and most direct. Still further. It was certainly impossible for the plaintiff to prove, or for the jury to find, how much of the injury was due to either cause alone. It was wholly impossible to apportion the damages between the two causes. Shall this difficulty deprive the plaintiff of all remedy? We answer, No. The wrong of the defendant placed the plaintiff in this dilemma, and it cannot complain if it is held for the entire damage." *Earl, J.*, in Ehrgott *v.* Mayor, 96 N. Y 264; s. c., 48 Am. Rep. 622.

2. Defendant not liable for Consequences of Disease alone. — Kitteringham *v.* Sioux City, etc., R. Co., 62 Iowa, 285, s. c., 18 Am. & Eng. R. R. Cas. 14; Indianapolis, etc., R. Co *v.* Birney, 71 Ill. 391; Louisville, etc, R. Co. *v.* Jones, 108 Ind. 551; s c., 28 Am. & Eng R. R. Cas. 170; Louisville, etc, R. Co. *v.* Falvey, 104 Ind. 409, s c., 23 Am. & Eng. R. R. Cas. 522, Scheffer *v* Railroad Co., 105 U S. 249: s. c., 8 Am & Eng. R. R. Cas. 59; Pullman Palace Car Co *v* Barker, 4 Colo 344; s c, 34 Am. Rep. 89: Gould *v.* McKenna, 86 Pa. St. 297, s. c, 27 Am. Rep. 705; Beach on Cont. Neg. § 24; Barry *v.* U. S. Mut. Acc. Ass'n, 23 Fed. Rep. 712, 716; McCarthy *v.* Trav. Ins. Co, 8 Ins. L. J. 208.

3. But liable for Aggravation: When? — Stewart *v.* Ripon, 38 Wis. 584; Bigelow on Torts, 313; Pullman Palace Car Co. *v.* Barker, 4 Colo. 344; s. c., 34 Am. Rep. 89; New Orleans, etc., R. Co. *v.* Statham, 42 Miss. 607; 1 Sutherland on Dam. 79.

4. And for All Natural Consequences of Injury. — Brown *v.* Chicago, etc., R. Co., 54 Wis. 342; s. c., 3 Am. & Eng. R. R. Cas. 444; 41 Am. Rep. 41 and note; Oliver *v.* La Valle, 36 Wis. 592; Heinl *v.* McCaughan, 32 Miss. 17; Barbee *v.* Reese, 60 Miss. 906; Fitzpatrick *v.* Great Western R., 12 Up. Can. (Q. B.) 645; 2 Wood's Ry. Law, 1233-1237.

5. Especially when owing Special Duty. — Baltimore, etc., R. Co. *v.* Kemp, 61 Md. 619; s. c., 18 Am & Eng R. R. Cas. 229, 232; 2 Wood's Ry. Law, 1232.

6 The Action may arise in Contract, but sounds in Tort — Lake Erie, etc., R. Co. *v.* Acres, 108 Ind. 548; s. c., 28 Am. & Eng. R. R. Cas. 112; Cincinnati, etc., R. Co. *v.* Eaton, 94 Ind. 474; s. c., 18 Am. & Eng R. R. Cas. 254; Lake Erie, etc., R. Co. *v.* Fixe, 88 Ind. 381; s. c., 11 Am. & Eng. R. R. Cas. 109; Ehrgott *v.* Mayor. 96 N. Y. 264; s. c., 48 Am. Rep. 622; Creign *v.* Brooklyn, etc, R. Co., 75 N. Y. 192; School Dist. *v.* Boston, etc., Ry. Co., 102 Mass. 552; Nevin *v.* Pullman Palace Car Co., 106 Ill. 222; s. c., 11 Am & Eng. R. R. Cas. 92 and note, 46 Am. Rep. 688; Baltimore, etc., R. *v.* Kemp, 61 Md. 619; s. c., 18 Am. & Eng. R. R. Cas. 229, 233;

is, that they should be liable for any consequences of their negligence which are proximately and in natural sequence caused by such negligence, even though such consequences would not ordinarily have been expected to follow.[1] But it would seem that a carrier should not be held liable for a diseased condition when it cannot be told whether the condition is in any manner attributable to the negligence of the carrier, or wholly arises from other causes.[2] In other words, the plaintiff must show, by a preponderance of the evidence, that his diseased condition is due, in whole or in part, to the negligence of the defendant; and this he does not do if the evidence shows another probable efficient cause of the condition, without showing that such other probable cause was not really the efficient, immediate cause thereof.[3] But where no other proximate cause of a diseased condition or injury except defendant's negligence can be found, then such negligence will be held the sole proximate cause thereof.[4] And, subsequently, developed diseases, apparently flowing from defendant's negligence, must be shown to be due to some other cause, or defendant's negligence will be held the proximate cause of such condition.[5] And in all such cases it should be left to the jury, under proper instructions, to determine whether the diseased condition is in

Brown *v.* Chicago, etc., R. Co., 54 Wis. 342; s. c., 41 Am. Rep. 41 and note; Patterson's Ry. Acc. Law, 386 *et seq.*

But where the action is in form purely *ex contractu*, only such damages can be recovered as could reasonably have been foreseen, when the contract was made, as likely to follow its breach, or which flow naturally from such breach. Hobbs *v.* Railroad Co., L. R. 10 Q. B. 111; Hadley *v.* Boxendale, 9 Exch. 341; Walsh *v.* Chicago, etc., R. Co., 42 Wis. 23; s. c., 24 Am. Rep. 376; Murdock *v.* Boston, etc., R. Co., 133 Mass. 15; s. c., 6 Am. & Eng. R. R. Cas 406; Pullman Palace Car Co. *v.* Barker, 4 Colo. 344; s. c., 34 Am. Rep. 89; Indianapolis, etc., R. Co. *v.* Binney, 71 Ill. 391; Francis *v.* St. Louis Transfer Co., 5 Mo App. 7.

1. **Not Necessary that Particular Consequences could have been foreseen.** — Cooley on Torts, 68, 69; Shearman & Redf. on Neg. § 594; Wharton on Neg. § 97 *et seq.*, Terre Haute, etc., R. Co. *v.* Buck, 96 Ind. 346; s. c., 18 Am. & Eng. R. R. Cas. 234; Milwaukee, etc., R. Co. *v* Kellogg, 94 U. S. 469, 475; Smith *v.* London & S. W. R. Co., 6 C. P. 14; Patterson's Ry. Acc. Law, 9, 28; 1 Sutherland on Dam. 21 *et seq.*; Id. 47 *et seq.*; Beauchamp *v.* Saginaw Mining Co., 50 Mich. 163; Baltimore, etc., R. *v.* Kemp, 61 Md. 74; s. c., 18 Am. & Eng. R. R. Cas. 220; McNamara *v.* Clintonville, 62 Wis. 207; s. c., 51 Am. Rep. 722.

2. **No Liability, if Negligence not shown to be Cause of Disease.** — Kitteringham *v.* Railroad Co., 62 Iowa, 285; s. c., 18 Am. & Eng. R. R. Cas. 14; Scheffer *v.* Railroad Co., 105 U. S. 249, s. c., 8 Am. & Eng. R. R. Cas. 59; Barry *v.* U. S. Mut. Acc. Ass'n, 23 Fed. Rep. 712, 716, Jackson *v.* St. Louis, etc., R. Co., 87 Mo. 422; s. c., 25 Am. & Eng. R. R. Cas. 327.

3. **And Diseased Condition must be traced to Injury.** — Patterson's Ry. Acc. Law, 435; Searles *v.* Manhattan R. Co., 101 N. Y. 661, 662; s. c., 25 Am. & Eng. R. R. Cas. 358; Reading, etc., R. Co. *v.* Eckert, 2 Central Rep. 790, 793; Marble *v.* Worcester, 4 Gray (Mass.), 402; Dubuque, etc., Ass'n *v.* City, 30 Iowa, 176.

4. **But this is done if no other Efficient Cause Appears** — Scheffer *v.* Railroad Co, 105 U. S. 249; s. c., 8 Am. & Eng. R. R. Cas. 61; Terre Haute, etc., R. Co. *v.* Buck 96 Ind. 346; s. c., 18 Am. & Eng. R. R. Cas. 234.

5. **And if Another Cause exists, Defendant must show it.** — Patterson's Ry. Acc. Law, 28; Beauchamp *v.* Saginaw Mining Co., 50 Mich. 163; s. c., 45 Am. Rep. 30; Houston, etc., R. Co. *v.* Fredericka (Texas Sup Ct. 1882); Baltimore, etc., R. Co. *v.* Kemp, 61 Md. 74, 619; s. c., 18 Am. & Eng. R. R. Cas. 220; Jucker *v.* Chicago, etc., R. Co, 52 Wis. 150; s. c., 2 Am. & Eng. R. R. Cas. 41; Delie *v.* Chicago, etc, R. Co, 51 Wis. 400; s. c., 5 Am & Eng. R. R. Cas. 464; Louisville, etc., R. Co. *v.* Jones, 108 Ind., s. c., 28 Am. & Eng. R. R. Cas. 170.

whole or in part attributable to defendant's negligence,[1] and whether the plaintiff's conduct — he having notice of a prior disease, or predisposition to disease — was such as to constitute contributory negligence, and become a proximate cause of an aggravation or development of the disease.[2] But where an injury or disease is caused by the negligence of a defendant, it will be no defence for him that such injury or disease was enhanced by surgical treatment, provided the person injured used reasonable care in the selection of a surgeon.[3]

15. **Special Application of the Doctrine.** — In the foregoing sections of this article the general principles of the law of contributory negligence have been stated; and we may now consider some special applications of those principles, thus: —

16. **Plaintiff's Previous Knowledge of the Danger.** — If the injured person had no actual knowledge of the danger that threatened him, and if in the exercise of ordinary care under the circumstances he would not have apprehended such danger in time to have avoided the consequences of defendant's negligence, he cannot be charged with contributory negligence.[4] It follows that there must

1. **But it is for the Jury to determine the Question.** — Louisville R. Co. *v.* Falvey, 104 Ind. 409; s. c., 23 Am. & Eng. R. R. Cas. 522; Louisville R. Co. *v.* Jones, 108 Ind.; s. c., 28 Am. & Eng. R. R. Cas. 170; Terre Haute R. Co. *v.* Buck, 96 Ind. 346; s. c., 18 Am. & Eng. R. R. Cas. 234; Brown *v.* Chicago, etc., R. Co., 54 Wis. 342; s. c., 3 Am. & Eng. R. R. Cas. 444; 41 Am. Rep. 41; Baltimore, etc., R. Co. *v.* Kemp, 61 Md. 74, 619; s. c., 18 Am. & Eng. R. R. Cas. 220; 48 Am. Rep. 134.

2. **Diseased Condition as Evidence of Contributory Negligence.** — The principle stated in the text legitimately results from the preceding doctrines, although, perhaps, it cannot be supported by any direct authority. If a man in the last stages of heart disease should become a passenger on a railway train, knowing his own condition, but giving no notice of it to the carrier, and while being carried by the railway his death should be occasioned and hastened by a slight shock, insufficient to injure even a delicate woman, it might very properly be left to the jury to say whether the passenger had not assumed the risk, or been guilty of contributory negligence, in so taking passage; and perhaps in such case it might be said, as matter of law, the facts being undisputed, that the heart disease was the proximate cause, and the railway shock only the immediate occasion, of the death of the passenger. The case of Jackson *v.* Railroad Co., 87 Mo. 422; s. c., 25 Am. & Eng. R. R. Cas. 327, supports the doctrine of this illustration as to proximate cause; and Reading, etc., R. Co. *v.* Eckert (Pa.), 2 Cent. Rep. 790, 793, may be regarded as in line with the text, as well as with the doctrine, of this note. See also Renneker *v.* So. Car. R. Co., 20 So. Car. 218; s. c., 18 Am. & Eng. R. R. Cas. 149, 152, 153; Willetts *v.* Buffalo, etc., R. Co., 14 Barb. (N. Y.) 585.

3. **Surgical Treatment enhancing Effects of Injury.** — Sauter *v.* Railroad Co., 66 N. Y. 50; s. c., 23 Am. Rep. 18; Lyons *v.* Erie R., 57 N. Y. 489; Collins *v.* Council Bluffs, etc., R. Co., 32 Iowa, 324; s. c., 7 Am. Rep. 200; Ginna *v.* Railroad Co., 8 Hun (N. Y.), 494; 67 N. Y. 596; Page *v.* Sumpter, 53 Wis. 652; Pullman Palace Car Co. *v.* Bluhm, 109 Ill. 20; s. c., 18 Am. & Eng R. R. Cas. 87.

4. **Plaintiff Ignorant of Danger.** — Freer *v.* Cameron, 4 Rich. (S. Car.) 228; s. c., 55 Am. Dec. 663 and note 672; 2 Thomp. on Neg. 1172, § 18; Beach on Cont. Neg. 38; Deering on Neg. § 16; Jeffrey *v.* Keokuk, etc., R. Co., 56 Iowa, 546; s. c., 5 Am. & Eng. R. R. Cas. 568; Langan *v.* St. Louis, etc., R. Co., 72 Mo. 392; s. c., 3 Am. & Eng. R. R. Cas. 355; Dush *v.* Fitzhugh, 2 Lea (Tenn.), 307; McGuire *v.* Spence, 91 N. Y. 303; Gray *v.* Scott, 66 Pa. St. 345; Fowler *v.* Baltimore, etc., R. Co., 18 W. Va. 579; s. c., 8 Am. & Eng. R. R. Cas. 480; Washington *v.* B. & O. R. Co., 17 W. Va. 190; s. c., 10 Am. & Eng. R. R. Cas. 749; Thirteenth St., etc., R. Co. *v.* Boudrou, 92 Pa. St. 475; s. c., 2 Am. & Eng. R. R. Cas. 30, 37 Am. Rep. 707; McGarry *v.* Loomis, 63 N. Y. 104; s. c., 20 Am. Rep. 510; Varney *v.* Manchester, 58 N. H. 430; s. c., 42 Am. Rep. 592; Murray *v.* McShane, 52 Md. 217; s. c., 36 Am. Rep. 367; Bennett *v.* Railroad Co., 102 U. S. 577; s. c., 1 Am.

be knowledge of the danger, or sufficient reason to apprehend it, to put a reasonable and careful man on his guard, or there can be no contributory negligence.[1] But even though the person injured knew of the danger, or had reason to apprehend it, yet it does not necessarily follow that he has been guilty of contributory negligence. Notwithstanding his knowledge of or reason to apprehend danger, he may have been in the exercise of ordinary care to avoid injury; and in such event his injury may be solely due to the negligence of another.[2] Thus one may voluntarily and unnecessarily expose himself or his property to a known danger, without being guilty of contributory negligence, as a matter of

& Eng. R. R. Cas. 71; Hayward *v.* Merrill, 94 Ill. 349; s. c., 34 Am. Rep. 229 and note.

"Contributory negligence is not imputable to a person for failing to look out for a danger, when, under the surrounding circumstances, the person sought to be charged with it had no reason to suspect that danger was to be apprehended." Langan *v.* St. Louis, etc., R. Co., 72 Mo. 392; s. c., 3 Am. & Eng. R. R. Cas. 355.

It is also somewhat loosely said that a person is not chargeable with contributory negligence in failing to anticipate the fault or negligence of another, — 2 Thomp. on Neg. 1172, § 18; Shearman & Redf. on Neg. § 31; Deering on Neg. § 16, — and that one person has a right to rely upon the presumption that another will act with due care, Shearman & Redf. on Neg. § 31; Deering on Neg. § 16; and many cases are cited in support of these statements of the rule. Kellogg *v.* Chicago, etc., R. Co., 26 Wis. 223; Fox *v.* Sackett, 10 Allen (Mass.), 535; Baker *v.* Pendergast (Ohio), 8 Cent. L. J. 334; Damour *v.* Lyons, 44 Iowa, 276; Shea *v.* Potrero, etc., R. Co., 44 Cal. 414; Cleveland, etc., R. Co. *v.* Gerry, 8 Ohio St. 570; Robinson *v.* Railroad Co., 48 Cal. 409; Harpell *v.* Curtis, 1 E. D. Smith (N. Y.), 78; Brown *v.* Lynn, 31 Pa. St. 510; Fraler *v.* Water Co., 12 Cal. 555; Newson *v.* N. Y. Cent. R. Co., 29 N. Y. 383; Snyder *v.* Railroad Co., 11 W. Va. 14; Kansas Pac. R. *v.* Ward, 4 Colo. 30; Morrisey *v.* Wiggins Ferry Co., 47 Mo. 521; s. c., Thomp. Car. of Pass. 243; The Mongerton, 1 Swabey, 120; Vennall *v.* Garner, 1 Cr. & M. 21; Ernst *v.* Hudson River R. Co., 35 N. Y. 9, 35; Barton *v.* Syracuse, 37 Barb. (N. Y.) 292, 299; Gee *v.* Metropolitan R. Co., L. R. 8 Q. B. 161, 171; Carroll *v.* New Haven R. Co., 1 Duer (N. Y.), 571; Reeves *v.* Delaware, etc., R. Co., Pa. St. 454; Fisk *v.* Wait, 104 Mass. 71; Moulton *v.* Aldrich, 28 Kan. 300; Foy *v.* Brighton, etc., R. Co., 18 C. B. (N. S.) 225; Clayards *v.* Dettrick, 12 Q. B. 439; Beisiegel *v.* N. Y. Cent. R. Co., 34 N. Y. 622; Philadelphia & Trenton R. Co. *v.* Hogan, 47 Pa. St. 244. But these cases do not have the meaning that is imputed to them by the rule as stated. They hold either, 1st, the doctrine of the text, that it is not contributory negligence not to look out for danger when there is no reason to apprehend any, or 2d, that a mere failure to anticipate the negligence or wrong-doing of another is not contributory negligence when it does not amount to a want of ordinary care, or is only a remote cause or the mere condition of the injury; and so the rule is understood and stated by Mr. Beach. Beach on Cont. Neg. § 13.

1. **Reason to apprehend Danger must exist.** — Deering on Neg. § 16; Beach on Cont. Neg. p. 39; Cases cited in note 4, page 34.

2. **But Knowledge of Danger not Negligence, per se.** — Beach on Cont. Neg. pp. 39, 40; Shearman & Redf. on Neg. § 31; Deering on Neg. §§ 23, 24; Weed *v.* Balston Spa, 76 N. Y. 329; Turner *v.* Buchanan, 82 Ind. 147; s. c., 42 Am. Rep. 485; Henry Co. T. Co. *v.* Jackson, 86 Ind. 111; s. c., 44 Am. Rep. 274; Osage City *v.* Brown, 27 Kan. 74; Mahoney *v.* Metropolitan R. Co., 104 Mass. 13; Dewire *v.* Bailey, 131 Mass. 169; s. c., 41 Am. Rep. 219; Thomas *v.* Mayor, etc., 28 Hun (N. Y.), 110; Estelle *v.* Lake Crystal, 27 Minn. 243; Wheeler *v.* Westport, 30 Wis. 392; Albion *v.* Hetrick, 90 Ind. 545; Jeffrey *v.* Keokuk, etc., R. Co., 56 Iowa, 546; s. c., 5 Am. & Eng. R. R. Cas. 568; Dublin, etc., R. Co. *v.* Slattery, 3 L. R. App. Cas. 1155; s. c., 19 Alb. L. J. 70; Reed *v.* Northfield, 13 Pick. (Mass.) 94; s. c., 23 Am. Dec. 662; Frost *v.* Waltham, 12 Allen (Mass.), 86; Snow *v.* Housatonic R. Co., 8 Allen (Mass.), 450; Coombs *v.* New Bedford Cordage Co., 102 Mass. 572, 585; s. c., 3 Am. Rep. 506; Marble *v.* Ross, 124 Mass. 44; Evans *v.* Utica, 69 N. Y. 166; s. c., 25 Am. Rep. 165; Bassett *v.* Fish, 75 N. Y. 303; Ochsenbein *v.* Shapley, 85 N. Y. 214; Schaefler *v.* Sandusky, 33 Ohio St. 246; Pittsburgh, etc., R. Co. *v.* Taylor, 104 Pa. St. 306; s. c., 49 Am. Rep. 580; Iron R. Co. *v.* Mowery, 36 Ohio St. 418; s. c., 3 Am. & Eng. R. R. Cas. 361.

law;[1] and while in so doing he is held to assume all risks of injury which a careful and prudent person would apprehend as likely to flow from his conduct,[2] yet if injured by the negligence of another, without any negligence upon his own part proximately contributing to the injury, he may recover;[3] and it is usually held a question for the jury whether he was in exercise of due care to avoid the known danger.[4] But there seems to be a presumption of fact, which may be rebutted, that there has been contributory negligence.[5]

1. **And Exposure to a Known Danger not always Negligence.** — Beach on Cont. Neg. p. 39; Clayards *v.* Dettrick, 12 Q. B. 439; Filer *v.* N. Y. Cent. R. Co., 49 N. Y. 47; s. c., 10 Am. Rep. 327; Albion *v.* Hetrick, 90 Ind. 545; s. c., 46 Am. Rep. 230; Kalbfleisch *v.* Long Island R. Co., 102 N. Y. 520; s. c., 29 Am. & Eng. R. R. Cas. 179, 55 Am. Rep. 833; Baldwin *v.* St. Louis, etc., R. Co., 63 Iowa, 210; s. c., 15 Am. & Eng. R. R. Cas. 166; Greenleaf *v.* Dubuque, etc., R. Co., 33 Iowa, 52, 59; Holmes *v.* Clark, 6 Hurl. & N. 349, 7 Hurl. & N. 937; s. c., 2 Thomp. on Neg. 953, 966; Dublin, etc., R. Co. *v.* Slattery, 3 L. R. App. Cas. 1155; s. c., 19 Alb. L. J. 70; Rexter *v.* Storin, 73 N. Y. 601; Wassner *v.* Delaware, etc., R. Co., 80 N. Y. 212; s. c., 1 Am. & Eng. R. R. Cas. 122, 36 Am. Rep. 608.

"It is not a universal rule that the defendant is excused from liability merely because the plaintiff, knowing of the danger caused by defendant's negligence, voluntarily incurs that danger." Harris *v.* Township of Clinton (Mich. 1887), 7 West. Rep. 666.

So where a tenant, while using a stairway left in an unsafe condition by the landlord, was injured, it was said, "The fact, if proved, that the plaintiff had previous knowledge that the stairs were in a dangerous condition, would not be conclusive evidence that the plaintiff was not in the exercise of due care." Looney *v.* McLean, 129 Mass. 33; s. c., 37 Am. Rep. 295; Dewire *v.* Bailey, 131 Mass. 169; s. c., 45 Am. Rep. 219.

"The fact that a person voluntarily takes some risk, is not conclusive evidence, under all the circumstances, that he is not using due care." Lawless *v.* Conn. River R. Co., 136 Mass. 1; s. c., 18 Am. & Eng. R. R. Cas. 96.

2. **But Person so exposing Himself assumes Ordinary Risks.** — Goldstein *v.* Chicago, etc., R. Co., 46 Wis. 404; Pittsburgh, etc., R. Co. *v.* Collins, 87 Pa. St. 405; s. c., 30 Am. Rep. 371.

Plaintiff "voluntarily and needlessly put himself in a highly dangerous place, — a place, however, where he might go without incurring any liability as a wrong-doer, but where his own safety required his attention to his surroundings without one moment's interruption. If he risked himself in such a place, he must take whatever injury came from his own want of attention to danger." Baltimore, etc., R. Co. *v.* Depew, 40 Ohio St. 121, 127; s. c., 12 Am. & Eng. R. R. Cas. 64. See also Erie *v.* Magill, 101 Pa. St. 616; s. c., 47 Am. Rep. 739; Corlett *v.* Leavenworth, 27 Kan. 673; Mehan *v.* Syracuse, etc., R. Co., 73 N. Y. 585, Mansfield, etc., Coal Co. *v.* McEnery, 91 Pa. St. 185; s. c., 33 Am. Rep. 662.

3. **When he may recover for Negligent Injury.** — "Some risks are taken by the most prudent men; and the plaintiff is not debarred from recovery for his injury if he has adopted the course which most prudent men would take under similar circumstances" (Shearman & Redf. on Neg. § 31). "This doctrine has often been applied, and is peculiarly applicable to cases like this. The obstruction is seen in the street. There is room to pass it. It is not known that it will cause fright; and the traveller, with due care, knowing the temper of his horses, and having control of them, believing there is no danger, attempts to pass. In doing this, he is not guilty of negligence. He takes the risk which a prudent man would take, and nothing more. Such an assumption of risk affords no excuse for the wrongdoer, — the party who wrongfully placed the obstruction in the street." Turner *v.* Buchanan, 82 Ind. 147; s. c., 42 Am. Rep. 485; Mahoney *v.* Metropolitan R. Co., 104 Mass. 73; Dewire *v.* Bailey, 131 Mass. 169; s. c., 41 Am. Rep. 219.

4. **In such Cases Jury to decide** — Hanlon *v.* Keokuk, 7 Iowa, 488; s. c., 74 Am. Dec. 276; Harris *v.* Township of Clinton (Mich. 1887), 7 West. Rep. 666; Dewire *v.* Bailey, 131 Mass. 169; s. c., 41 Am. Rep. 219. And this is the rule, even though it may be clear that the plaintiff's conduct in an endeavor to avoid danger actually contributed to his injury. Iron R. Co. *v.* Mowery, 36 Ohio St. 418; s. c., 3 Am. & Eng. R. R. Cas. 361.

5. **But there is a Rebuttable Presumption of Contributory Negligence.** — Wyatt *v.* Citizens' R. Co., 55 Mo. 585; Marble *v.* Ross, 124 Mass. 44; Smith *v.* St. Joseph,

17. Danger incurred to save Life. — It is said that one who is injured by the negligence of another while attempting to save the life of a person imperilled by that negligence, is not himself guilty of contributory negligence.[1] But the true rule in such cases is, that contributory negligence is a question of fact for the jury.[2] And if it appears that the attempt was not so rash as to entail certain injury, a recovery will be sustained.[3] "The fact that the injured person did some act by which he incurred or increased danger does not necessarily involve negligence which will prevent a recovery when the danger was created by some unlawful act" of the person inflicting the injury.[4] But it would seem that the contributory negligence of the person sought to be saved will be imputed to the savior;[5] yet if the act of the latter could have been discovered by the exercise of ordinary care by the defendant in time to have avoided the infliction of the injury, although the danger of the person saved would not have been, the defendant is liable.[6] And so the defendant is liable when the person saved

45 Mo. 449; Forks Township *v.* King, 84 Pa. St. 230; Estelle *v.* Lake Crystal, 27 Minn. 243; Frost *v.* Waltham, 12 Allen (Mass.), 85; Osage City *v.* Brown, 27 Kan. 74; Wheeler *v.* Westport, 30 Wis. 392; Evans *v.* Utica, 69 N. Y. 166; s. c., 25 Am. Rep. 165; Reed *v.* Northfield, 13 Pick. (Mass.) 94; s. c., 23 Am. Dec. 662; Beach on Cont. Neg. p. 40.

1. **Not Contributory Negligence to try to save Life.** — Beach on Cont. Neg. p. 45. In the opening part of § 15 of his excellent work Mr. Beach thus broadly states the rule; but this statement may be considered as qualified by the doctrines that immediately follow. Whether it is negligent under the circumstances cannot usually be determined by the court as a matter of law.

2. **But the Question is for the Jury.** — Linnehan *v.* Sampson, 126 Mass. 506; s. c., 30 Am. Rep. 692.

3. **When a Recovery may be had.** — Eckert *v.* L. I. R. Co., 57 Barb. (N. Y.) 555; 43 N. Y. 503; s. c., 3 Am. Rep. 721.

4. **Danger created by Wrongful Act.** — Pierce on Railroads, 328, Twomley *v.* Cent. Park, etc., R. Co., 69 N. Y. 158; s. c., 25 Am. Rep. 162 and note.

5. **Is Negligence of Saved imputable to Savior?** — "Why was Hiatt injured? Because his father was carelessly remaining upon the railroad track, in front of an approaching train, which it was his duty to avoid, . . but which he carelessly failed to do. If it be said that the father was old and feeble, and unable to get out of the way of the train, then we say, the carelessness, the rashness, of going upon the track in front of an approaching train was still greater, and involves those who were with the old man, to some extent, in the carelessness, in not preventing him from going upon the track; or, at all events, keeping close to him with watchfulness while he was on it." Evansville, etc., R. Co. *v.* Hiatt, 17 Ind. 102, 104.

The doctrine of the text is certainly reasonable. The person inflicting the injury should not be held liable unless he would have been liable to the person originally in danger, except in cases where he could, by the exercise of ordinary care, have discovered the danger of the rescuer in time to have avoided injuring him. See Donahoe *v.* Wabash, etc., R. Co., 83 Mo 560; s. c., 53 Am. Rep 594.

6. **When not Imputable: Related Questions.** — "It is to be observed that it is only when the railroad company, by its own negligence, created the danger, or through its negligence is about to strike a person in danger, that a third person can voluntarily expose himself to peril in an effort to rescue such person, and recover for an injury he may sustain in that attempt. For instance, if a man is lying on the track of a railroad intoxicated or asleep, but in such a position that he could not be seen by the men managing an approaching train, and they had no warning of his situation, and another seeing his danger should go upon the track to save his life, and be injured by the train, he could not recover *unless the train men were guilty of negligence with respect to the rescuer, occurring after the beginning of his attempt.*" Donahoe *v.* Wabash, etc., R. Co., 83 Mo. 560; s. c., 53 Am. Rep 594; Evansville, etc., R. Co. *v.* Hiatt, 17 Ind. 102, 104.

was incapable of contributory negligence,[1] or was free from such negligence,[2] provided there was negligence on the part of the defendant toward such person or toward the plaintiff.[3]

18. Danger incurred in Discharge of Duty. — A person whose duty it is to care for the safety of others intrusted to his care, is not guilty of contributory negligence in remaining at his post of duty and sacrificing his life in endeavoring to avert a danger to those in his care, but from which he might have escaped himself.[4] He whose duty it is to care for the safety of others, may do so, even though his duty leads him into great and visible dangers, and not be chargeable with contributory negligence.[5] But the injured person must not have created the danger or been guilty of the negligence from whose consequences he tried to save others, or his recovery will be barred.[6] And it must appear that he was in

1. **Person saved non sui Juris.** — "No negligence is imputable to a child as young as the one killed by this train." Donahoe *v.* Wabash, etc., R. Co., 83 Mo. 560; s. c., 53 Am. Rep. 594, 597; Eckert *v.* Long Island R. Co., 43 N. Y. 502; s. c., 3 Am. Rep. 721

2. **If Person saved not Negligent, Defendant liable.** — Perhaps no direct authority can be found for this position, but it follows of necessity from the doctrines of the cases heretofore cited. If the person saved was in danger without fault on his own part, then the person who rescued him could stand in no worse posi'on; but the doctrine might be qualified if the attempt at rescue should be made under such circumstances that it would be manifest that there was little hope of success, and if injury, in fact, followed to the person first in danger and the intended rescuer.

3. **Provided Defendant was Negligent.** — In the case of Donahoe *v.* Wabash R. Co., 83 Mo. 560; s. c., 53 Am. Rep. 594, already quoted from extensively, the facts were, that the plaintiff, Mrs. Donahoe, was struck and injured by a train while trying to save the life of her infant child, which had wandered upon a railroad track in front of an approaching train. In the course of a very admirable opinion, *Henry, J.*, said, "If the railroad company is not chargeable with negligence with respect to the person in danger, the case of the person who attempted to rescue him, and was injured must be determined with reference to the negligence of the company in its conduct toward him, and his in making the attempt. In other words, the negligence of the company as to the person in danger is imputed to the company with respect to him who attempts the rescue; and if not guilty of negligence as to such person, then it is only liable for negligence occurring with regard to the rescuer, after his efforts to rescue the person in danger commenced." And this was all that was decided in the much misunderstood case of Evansville, etc., R. Co *v.* Hiatt, 17 Ind. 102. It is there said, "As the injured party, then, was in fault in continuing so long upon the track, if not, indeed, in going upon it at all under the circumstances, and the railroad operatives, after they discovered the condition of the persons, were guilty of no neglect in trying to avoid the collision, the plaintiff cannot recover." In another part of the opinion it is said that the railroad employees "were guilty of no manner of negligence whatever," and this was the basis of the decision.

4. **Not Contributory Negligence to discharge Duty.** — "A locomotive engineer, killed by remaining upon his engine when a collision was imminent, and taking measures to stop his train, is not chargeable with contributory negligence as matter of law, although he might have escaped injury by leaving his post." Head note Cottrill *v* Chicago, Milwaukee, & St. Paul R. Co., 32 Am. Rep 796· s. c., 47 Wis. 634; Patterson's Ry. Acc. Law, page 378, § 331.

5. **Even though Dangers are Apparent.** — "An engineer who remains at his post and faces danger is not to be deemed negligent. An engineer in charge of a train laden with men, women, and children, is not bound to leap from his engine to escape impending danger. If he believes his duty requires him to do what he can to save those under his charge, and he braves death in the discharge of that duty, the law has for him no censure, but has, on the contrary, high commendation and respect." Pennsylvania Co *v.* Roney, 89 Ind. 453; s c., 12 Am. & Eng. R. R. Cas. 223; 46 Am. Rep. 173; Central R. Co. *v.* Crosby, 74 Ga. 737; s. c., 58 Am. Rep. 463.

6. **But Persons so injured must have been Free from Fault.** — Central R. Co. *v.* Sears, 61 Ga. 279.

the discharge of duty,[1] and could not, by the exercise of ordinary care, have performed his whole duty, and yet escaped the danger.[2] So a person who goes into a place of danger in the discharge of a public or official duty which rendered such exposure to danger necessary, and is there injured by the negligence of another, is not guilty of contributory negligence in incurring the danger, if he used due care under the circumstances to avoid injury therefrom.[3]

And the same principle applies where danger is knowingly incurred in the discharge of a private duty of imperative obligation, as where one goes into danger in the performance of necessary work;[4] but in many such cases as this, the person going into the place of danger is held to have assumed the risk of injury from the known danger;[5] although he may recover for an injury resulting from the negligence of another, and which he could not

1. **And in the Discharge of Duty.** — Atlanta, etc., R. Co. *v.* Ray, 70 Ga. 674; s. c., 22 Am. & Eng. R. R. Cas. 281; Cent. R. *v.* Sears, 61 Ga. 279.

2. **Where Ordinary Care would not have avoided Injury.** — Cottrill *v.* Chicago, Milwaukee, & St. Paul R. Co., 47 Wis. 634; s. c., 32 Am. Rep. 796; Central R. Co. *v.* Crosby, 74 Ga. 737; s. c., 58 Am. Rep. 463.

3. **Injury when in Danger because of Public Duty.** — Thus, a customs officer searching for smugglers along a wharf, and injured by falling into an opening left unguarded and unlighted, can recover, although, had he carried a light, he might have avoided the injury.

"It is noticeable that in arguing this point [contributory negligence] on the motion, the learned counsel for defendants fall back in part upon their original contention that the customs officer 'was obliged to move about at his own peril.' Not so. His duty carried him there in consequence of, and in connection with, the business which defendants had established there. The jury probably thought that, if he went as a section of a torchlight procession, he might as well have staid at home; that he was not in search of an honest man, and had no need of a lantern." Law *v.* Grand Trunk R. Co., 72 Me. 313; s. c., 39 Am. Rep. 331.

4. **Or Private Duty of Imperative Obligation.** — Thus, when a common seaman, over his protests, was forced to go into a dangerous place by the commands of his superior, and was there injured, it was *held* that he was entitled to recover; and the case was distinguished from those cases which hold that an employee cannot recover for an injury resulting from his work in a dangerous place, the hazards of which he knew and assumed in taking employment.

"The master has an absolute authority on board his ship, and his orders, if not unlawful, are and must be imperative: submission is amongst the first duties of the seaman. The seaman on the voyage has no alternative but to obey, or suffer punishment." Thompson *v.* Herman, 47 Wis. 602; s. c., 32 Am. Rep. 784.

And when a railway freight brakeman was killed by a collision between two freight-cars, caused by the negligence of the company, it was held that he was not guilty of contributory negligence in climbing upon one of the cars, and setting the brakes, in the endeavor to save the company's property; and that, on the facts, he was not injured by a danger of the employment whose risk he had assumed. Kelley *v.* Chicago, etc., R. Co., 50 Wis. 381; s. c., 2 Am. & Eng. R. R. Cas. 65.

So it was held that a railroad engineer was not guilty of contributory negligence in reversing his engine after it had left the track by the negligence of the company, although his arm was broken by so doing, and his only purpose was to save the property of the company from further injury, as he might himself have escaped by leaping to the ground. Knapp *v.* Sioux City, etc., R. Co., 61 Iowa, 91; s. c., 18 Am. & Eng. R. R. Cas. 60; 50 Am. Rep. 56(?). And see Snow *v.* Housatonic R. Co., 8 Allen (Mass.), 441.

5. **But the Risks of Injury are often assumed.** — Contributory negligence and assumption of the risk of injury from a known danger, or the ordinary hazards of an employment, are often confounded, but are in reality essentially different. 2 Thompson on Neg. 1147, § 2. Later on we shall note the distinction more fully. It has its principal application in cases where an employee is held, by the contract of employment, to assume the usual dangers and risks of the business he undertakes.

reasonably have foreseen as one of the hazards of the place.[1] In such an instance the injury results, not from a known danger, the risks of which were assumed, but from some extraneous cause.[2]

19. Defendant's Knowledge of the Danger. — The converse of some of the foregoing rules may be found in the doctrine, that, if defendant knew, or had reason to apprehend, special dangers from his acts or omissions, or had greater capacity for understanding the harmful results likely to flow from his conduct than the injured person had, he will be liable, notwithstanding acts or omissions on the part of the injured person, that with equal knowledge of the danger, or capacity to apprehend it, would have been contributory negligence.[3] This, however, is but a special application of the general rule, that, in determining whether plaintiff was guilty of a want of ordinary care, contributing to his injury, his conduct and that of the defendant must be considered in the light of the attending circumstances; and, when so considered, a want of extraordinary care on the part of the plaintiff is not sufficient to bar his action, if the defendant, knowing of dangers which the plaintiff had no reason to apprehend, was guilty of a want of ordinary care to avoid injuring the plaintiff.[4]

Wood's Master and Servant (2d ed.), § 326, *et seq.*; Simmons *v.* Chicago, etc., R. Co., 110 Ill. 340; s. c., 18 Am. & Eng. R. R. Cas. 50; Farwell *v.* Boston, etc., R. Co., 4 Met. (Mass.) 49; s. c., 38 Am. Dec. 339; Murray *v.* So. Car. R. Co., 1 McMullan's (S. Car.), 385; s. c., 36 Am. Dec. 268 and note.

As applications of the doctrine when no contractual relation exists, see Goldstein *v.* Chicago, etc., Co., 46 Wis. 404; Wohlfohrt *v.* Beckert, 92 N. Y. 490; s. c., 44 Am. Rep. 406.

1. **In so far as reasonably to be foreseen.** — Wood's Law of M. & S. 2d ed. §§ 349, 353, 357, 359, 385, 386, 387.

2. Gray *v.* Scott, 66 Pa. St. 345.

3. **Defendant liable if he knew of Danger when Plaintiff Ignorant of.** — Thus, where a common laborer in an iron foundry was directed by the foreman to assist another employee in carrying a ladleful of molten iron over an icy passage-way, and in so doing was killed by an explosion resulting from the spilling of the molten metal on the ice, it was *held* that, although he had assumed the ordinary risks of the employment, and perhaps been careless in carrying the metal, yet he was not guilty of contributory negligence, and could not be held to have assumed the risk of the danger which caused his injury, because he was ignorant of the effects that would follow the contact of the molten metal with the ice, of which danger the foreman had full knowledge, and failed to warn him. He took the risk of slipping, and may even have been careless in allowing the iron to spill, but he was not in a position to know the real danger, or apprehend the injury that would result: hence the negligence of the foreman in sending him over the ice with the ladle of iron was the only negligent cause of the injury. In other words, the injured man, in view of his knowledge, exercised ordinary care, while the foreman, in view of his knowledge, did not. Smith *v.* Car Works (Mich.), 12 Am. & Eng. Corp. Cas. 269; Lynch *v.* Nurdin, 1 Q. B. 29; Clark *v.* Chambers, L. R. 3 Q. B. Div. 327; Stout *v* Sioux City, etc., R. Co., 2 Dill. (U. S.) 294; Railroad Co. *v.* Stout, 17 Wall. 657; Keffe *v.* Milwaukee, etc., R. Co., 21 Minn. 207; s. c., 18 Am. Rep. 393; Harriman *v.* Pittsburgh, etc., R. Co. (Ohio), 12 N. E. Rep. 451; Philadelphia, etc., R. Co. *v.* Spearen, 47 Pa. St. 300; Baltimore, etc., R. Co. *v.* Rowan, 104 Ind. 88; s. c., 23 Am. & Eng R. R. Cas. 390; Louisville, etc., R. Co. *v.* Frowley, 110 Ind. 18, 22; s. c., 28 Am. & Eng R. R. Cas. 308; Ford *v.* Fitchburg R. Co., 110 Mass. 240; s. c., 14 Am. Rep. 598; Holden *v.* Fitchburg R. Co., 129 Mass. 268; s. c., 2 Am. & Eng. R. R. Cas. 94, 37 Am. Rep. 343; Davis *v.* Cent. Vt. R. Co., 55 Vt. 84; s. c., 11 Am. & Eng. R. R. Cas. 173, 45 Am. Rep. 590; Vosburgh *v.* Lake Shore, etc., R. Co., 94 N. Y. 374; s. c., 15 Am. & Eng. R. R. Cas. 249, 46 Am. Rep. 148; Pennsylvania R. Co. *v.* Ogier, 35 Pa. St. 60; s. c., 78 Am. Dec. 322; Bransom *v.* Labrot, 81 Ky. 638; s. c., 50 Am. Rep. 193, 196; Jones *v.* Florence Mining Co., 66 Wis. 268; s. c., 57 Am. Rep. 269; St. Louis, etc., R. Co. *v.* Valirius, 56 Ind 511.

4. **This a General Principle.** — Beach on Cont. Neg pp. 20, 21, Strong *v.* Sacra-

20. Inevitable Accident. — There is no liability for an injury inflicted by one person on another, even though the injured person be free from fault, if the cause of the injury was unusual, and one which reasonable and careful human foresight could not have foreseen as such, and which under the circumstances such care and foresight should not have guarded against.[1] Such an injury, without any want of ordinary care on the part of the person inflicting it, is held an inevitable accident. But where an accident and want of ordinary care concur in producing an injury, the negligent person is liable for the consequences if without his negligence the injury would not have been caused by the accident alone.[2]

mento & Placerville R. Co., 61 Cal. 321; s. c., 8 Am. & Eng. R. R. Cas. 273; Whirley v. Whiteman, 1 Head (Tenn.), 611; Kerwhacker v. Cleveland, etc., R. Co., 3 Ohio St. 172; s. c., 62 Am. Dec. 246.

1. **Inevitable Accident causing Injury.** — Beach on Cont. Neg. pp. 38, 39; Cooley on Torts, 80; 1 Am. & Eng. Ency. of L. 82, tit. "Accident;" id. 173, tit. "Act of God."

"No case or principle can be found, or if found can be maintained, subjecting an individual to liability for an act done without fault on his part. . . . All the cases concede that an injury arising from inevitable accident, or, which in law or reason is the same thing, from an act that ordinary human care and foresight are unable to guard against, is but the misfortune of the sufferer, and lays no foundation for legal responsibility." Harvey v. Dunlop (Lalois Sup.), Hill & Denio (N. Y.), 193; Holmes v. Mather, L. R. 10 Exch. 261; s. c., 16 Am. Rep. 384; Brown v. Collins, 53 N. H. 442; s. c., 16 Am. Rep. 372; 1 Thomp. on Neg. 61; the Nitro-Glycerine Case, 15 Wall. (U. S.) 524; s. c., 1 Thomp. on Neg. 42; Lasee v. Buchanan, 51 N. Y. 476; s. c., 10 Am. Rep. 623; 1 Thomp. on Neg. 47; Sheldon v. Sherman, 42 N. Y. 484; s. c., 1 Am. Rep. 569; Bizzell v. Booker, 16 Ark. 308.

2. **Accident and Negligence in Combination.** — "An accident may be defined as an event happening unexpectedly and without fault; if there is any fault, there is liability." Cooley on Torts, 80, note 2; Leame v. Bray, 3 East, 593.

The distinction between an accident and an act of God seems to be, that in one case there is not, and in the other case there is, the presence and operation of *vis major.* Patterson's Ry. Acc. Law, 35, 1 Am. & Eng. Ency. of L. 144, § 2.

But, as stated in the text, if negligence combines and concurs with either an inevitable accident or the act of God as a proximate cause of an injury, without which it would not have occurred, the negligent person is liable. 1 Am. & Eng. Ency. of L. 176, § 5, tit. "Act of God," 2 Thomp. on Neg. 1085, § 3, 1087, § 4; Patterson's Ry. Acc. Law, 34; Lord's Bailiff-Jurats, etc., v. Corp. of Trinity House, L. R. 5 Exch. 204, L. R. 7 Exch. 247; s. c., 2 Thomp. on Neg. 1063, Salisbury v. Herchenroder, 106 Mass. 458; s. c., 2 Thomp. on Neg. 1067, 8 Am. Rep. 354.

In the case last cited it is said, "The fact that a natural cause contributes to produce an injury which could not have happened without the unlawful act of the defendant, does not make the act so remote as to excuse him."

And the same principle has been stated thus: "We apprehend that the concurring negligence which, when concurring with the act of God, produces the injury, must be such as in itself is a real producing cause of the injury, and not merely a fanciful or speculative or microscopic negligence, which may not have been in the least degree the cause of the injury. In other words, if the act of God in this particular case was of such an overwhelming and destructive character as, by its own force, and independent of the particular negligence alleged or shown, produced the injury, there would be no liability, though there was some negligence in the maintenance of the particular structure. To create liability, it must have required the combined effect of the act of God and the concurring negligence to produce the injury." Balt., etc., R. Co. v. School Dist., 96 Pa. St. 65; s. c., 2 Am. & Eng. R. R. Cas. 166; Ellett v. St. Louis, etc., R. Co., 76 Mo. 518; s. c., 12 Am. & Eng. R. R. Cas. 183; Phila., etc., R. Co. v. Anderson, 94 Pa. St. 356; s. c., 6 Am. & Eng. R. R. Cas. 407; Davis v. Cent. Vt. R. Co., 54 Vt. 84; s. c., 11 Am. & Eng. R. R. Cas. 173; Lambkin v. Railroad Co., 5 App. Cas. (Eng.) 352; Dixon v. M. Board of Works, 7 Q. B. D. 418; Truitt v. Hannibal, etc., R. Co., 62 Mo. 527.

21. Natural Consequences always Proximate. — But a want of ordinary care substantially contributing to cause an injury is not excused because the particular consequences are unusual and unexpected, and such as would not ordinarily have been foreseen, provided the want of ordinary care was such that it might have been foreseen that some injury was likely to result from it. Natural consequences are always proximate, in the absence of any intervening efficient cause, even though such consequences had never followed before, and could not have been anticipated.[1] And a want of ordinary care on the part of the injured person contributing in natural and unbroken, though unusual and extraordinary, sequence to cause the injury, breaks the chain of causation, and becomes an intervening cause of the injury that relieves the person inflicting the injury from liability.[2]

22. Contributory Negligence of Children. — While the test of ordinary care is applied throughout the entire law of negligence, yet, as we have seen, it is ordinary care under the circumstances and conditions.[3] Thus, what would be ordinary care for one person, might be culpable negligence in another; and conduct which on the part of a person of full age and average capacity would be held contributory negligence, as a matter of law, might be ordi-

1. **Unusual Consequences may be Proximate.** — Cooley on Torts, 70, 75; Pollock on Torts, 32–45; Wharton on Neg. §§ 74–78; Terre Haute, etc., R. Co. *v.* Buck, 96 Ind. 346; s. c., 18 Am. & Eng. R. R. Cas. 234, 49 Am. Rep. 168; Baltimore, etc., R. Co. *v.* Kemp, 61 Md. 74 and 619; s. c., 18 Am. & Eng. R. R. Cas. 220; Jeffersonville, etc., R. Co. *v.* Riley, 39 Ind. 568; Binford *v.* Johnson, 82 Ind. 426; s. c., 42 Am. Rep. 508; Bellman *v.* Indianapolis, etc., R. Co., 76 Ind. 166; s. c, 6 Am. & Eng. R. R. Cas. 41; 40 Am. Rep. 230; Milwaukee, etc., R. Co. *v.* Kellogg, 94 U. S. 469; Smith *v.* London & S. W. Ry., 6 C. P. 14; Beauchamp *v.* Saginaw Mining Co., 50 Mich. 163; s. c., 45 Am. Rep. 30; Thomas *v.* Winchester, 6 N. Y. 397; Scott *v.* Shepherd, 2 W. Black. 892; Ricker *v.* Freeman, 50 N. H. 420; s. c., 9 Am. Rep. 267; Ins. Co. *v.* Tweed, 7 Wall. (U. S.) 44; Griggs *v.* Fleckenstein, 14 Minn. 81.

"It is not simply because the relation of cause and effect may be somewhat involved in obscurity, and therefore difficult to trace, that the principle obtains that only the natural and proximate results of a wrongful act are to be regarded. It is only where there may be a more direct and immediate sufficient cause of the effect complained of, that the more remote cause will not be charged with the effect. If a given result can be directly traced to a particular cause as the natural and proximate effect, why should not such effect be regarded by the law, even though such cause may not always, and under all conditions of things, produce like results? . . . Hence the general rule is, that, in actions of tort like the present, the wrong-doer is liable for all the direct injury resulting from his wrongful act, and that, too, although the extent or special nature of the resulting injury could not with certainty have been foreseen or contemplated as the probable result of the act done." *Alvey, C. J.*, in Baltimore, etc., R. Co. *v.* Kemp, 61 Md. 74; s. c., 18 Am. & Eng. R. R. Cas. 220. See also 1 Sutherland on Dam. 62; 2 Suth. Dam. 714, 715; 1 Addison on Torts, 5.

2. Wharton on Neg. §§ 133, 300.

3. **Ordinary Care under the Circumstances.** — *Ante* §§ 7, 9, 10: "'Ordinary care' is a term that has relation to the situation of parties, and the business in which they are engaged. It is used here as synonymous with the term 'reasonable care,' as used by the courts in England. Care and diligence should vary according to the exigencies which require vigilance and attention, conforming in amount and degree to the particular circumstances under which they are to be exerted." Fletcher *v.* Boston, etc., R. Co., 1 Allen (Mass.), 9; s. c., 79 Am. Dec. 695; Holly *v.* Gas Light Co., 8 Gray (Mass.), 23; s. c, 69 Am. Dec. 233; Beach on Cont. Neg. 23; Shearman & Redf. on Neg. § 30; Robinson *v.* Cone, 22 Vt. 213; s. c., 54 Am. Dec. 73; Lynch *v.* Nurdin, 1 Ad. & El. N. S. 28; s. c., 41 Eng. Com. L. 422; 2 Thomp. on Neg. 1140.

nary care in a child of tender years.[1] Hence it follows, that children so young as to be *non sui juris* cannot be guilty of contributory negligence.[2] And children who have attained an age where they are not wholly irresponsible are not required to exercise the same care and prudence that would be demanded of an adult similarly situated, but only the care of a child of equal age and ordinary childish care and prudence.[3] And even when a

1. **The Standard of Care varies with Age and Capacity.** — "The age and inexperience of the party may be taken into consideration, in passing upon the question of negligence alleged against him. For instance, no negligence is imputable to a child, although its own carelessness may produce its injury; and less care and foresight are exacted of an inexperienced youth than of a man of mature years." Dowling *v* Allen, 88 Mo 293.

2. **Infants of Tender Years Incapable of Negligence.** — 2 Thomps. on Neg. 1180, 1181, § 31; Beach on Cont. Neg. 120, 121; Deering on Neg. § 21

"The child was only three years and two months old, and clearly within the adjudged cases in which infants have been held not *sui juris*, or responsible for their own conduct." Ihl *v.* Forty-second St., etc., R. Co., 47 N. Y. 317; s. c., 7 Am. Rep. 450.

"No negligence is imputable to a child as young as the one killed by this train." Donohoe *v.* Wabash, etc., R. Co, 83 Mo 560; s. c., 53 Am. Rep. 594, 597.

"The rule above stated [of contributory negligence] does not apply when the party plaintiff is an idiot, insane person, or an infant of such tender years as to be incapable of taking care of himself or herself, or incapable of apprehending danger, or of the exercise of prudence or foresight in avoiding danger. In this case the child, Lulu Frick [aged two years], was incapable of contributory negligence." Frick *v.* St Louis, etc., R. Co., 75 Mo. 595; s. c., 8 Am. & Eng. R. R. Cas. 280; 10 Id 780, S. P. Smith *v.* Atchison, etc., R. Co., 25 Kan. 738; s. c., 4 Am. & Eng. R. R. Cas. 554.

And there are many other cases to the same effect, holding children all the way from one to seven years old *non sui juris*, as a matter of law Schmidt *v.* Milwaukee, etc., R. Co., 23 Wis. 186; Kreig *v.* Wells, 1 E. D. Smith (N Y.), 76; Mangam *v.* Brooklyn, etc., R. Co., 38 N. Y. 455; s. c., 36 Barb. (N. Y.) 230; Hartfield *v.* Roper, 21 Wend. (N. Y.) 615; s. c., 34 Am. Dec. 273; Wright *v.* Malden, etc., R. Co., 4 Allen (Mass.), 283; Toledo, etc., R. Co. *v.* Grable, 88 Ill. 441; Callahan *v.* Bean, 9 Allen (Mass.), 401; Evansville, etc., R. Co. *v.* Wolf, 59 Ind. 89; O'Flaherty *v.* Union R. Co, 45 Mo. 70; Mascheck *v.* St Louis, etc., R. Co., 3 Mo. App. 600; s. c., 71 Mo. 276; s c., 2 Am. & Eng. R. R Cas. 38; La Fayette, etc., R. Co *v.* Huffman, 28 Ind. 287; Pittsburgh, etc., R. Co. *v.* Caldwell, 74 Pa. St. 421; Jeffersonville, etc., R. Co. *v.* Bowen, 40 Ind. 545; McGarry *v.* Loomis, 63 N. Y. 104; s. c., 20 Am. Rep. 510; North Penn. R. Co. *v.* Mahoney, 57 Pa. St. 187; Lehman *v.* Brooklyn, 29 Barb. (N. Y.) 234; Gavin *v.* Chicago, 97 Ill. 66; Bay Shore R. Co. *v.* Harris, 67 Ala. 6; Morgan *v.* Ill. & St. Louis Bridge Co., 5 Dill. (U S.) 96; McGeary *v.* Eastern R. Co.. 135 Mass. 363, s. c., 15 Am. & Eng. R. R. Cas. 407; Texas, etc., R. Co. *v.* O'Donnell, 58 Tex. 27; s. c., 10 Am. & Eng. R. R. Cas. 712; Chicago *v.* Starr's Adm'r, 42 Ill 174; Meeks *v.* So. Pac. R. Co., 52 Cal. 604; Pittsburgh, etc., R. Co *v.* Vining, 27 Ind. 513; Norfolk, etc., R. Co. *v.* Ormsby, 27 Gratt. (Va.) 455; Chicago *v.* Hesing, 83 Ill. 204; Chicago, etc., R. Co. *v.* Gregory, 58 Ill. 226; Cent. Trust Co. *v.* Wabash, etc., R. Co., 31 Fed. Rep. 246.

When Care of Child for the Jury. — But where there is a question whether the child is of sufficient age and discretion to be capable of some care for his own safety, the question of his capacity and its degree is for the jury. 2 Thomp. on Neg. 1182; Honeysberger *v.* Second Avenue R. Co, 1 Keyes (N. Y.), 570; s. c., 33 How. Pr. (N. Y.) 195; Lovett *v.* Railroad Co., 9 Allen (Mass.), 557; Karr *v.* Parks, 48 Cal. 188; Drew *v.* Sixth Avenue R. Co., 26 N Y. 49; Oldfield *v.* N. Y., etc., R. Co., 14 N. Y. 310; Casgrove *v.* Ogden, 49 N. Y. 255; Barksdull *v.* N. O., etc., R. Co., 23 La. An. 180, St. Paul *v.* Kirby, 8 Minn. 154; Mulligan *v.* Curtis, 100 Mass. 512; Chicago, etc., R. Co *v.* Becker, 76 Ill. 25; s. c., 84 Ill. 483; Railroad Co. *v.* Gladman, 15 Wall. (U. S.) 401. And in such cases it seems that the child's capacity for exercising care is to be determined by the same standard that would be applied in ascertaining its capacity to commit crime. Rockford, etc., R. Co. *v.* Delaney, 82 Ill. 198; s. c., 25 Am. Rep. 308; Chicago, etc., R. Co. *v* Becker, 76 Ill. 32; West Phil., etc., R. Co. *v.* Gallagher, 108 Pa. St. 504; 27 Am. & Eng. R. R. Cas. 204. A "child" is a boy not above fourteen, or a girl not above twelve, years of age. Bell *v.* State, 18 Tex. Ct. App. 53; s. c., 51 Am. Rep 293.

3. **The "Ordinary Care" of a Child.** — "If the jury find that the plaintiff was of

child has reached years of discretion, and become, as a matter of law, responsible for his conduct, no higher degree of care will be exacted of him than is usually exercised by persons of similar age, judgment, and experience.[1] Thus, a minor employee injured by the negligence of a fellow-servant, or by defects in machinery, or by obviously dangerous appliances, will not necessarily be barred from maintaining an action against his employer for the injuries, although guilty of conduct which in an adult would have amounted to contributory negligence, or an assumption of the risk of injury.[2] In such cases while a minor employee is held to have assumed the risks of the employment, yet it is only such risks as one of his age, discretion, and experience can be said to have comprehended that he will be charged with having assumed.[3] And he

such capacity that he was in the street without negligence, either on the part of himself or his parents, then the question arises, what degree of care he was bound to exercise. . . . Certainly the jury could not find that a boy nine years old must exercise the capacity of an adult; but it was implied that, if it was proper for him to be there, it was only necessary for him to exercise such capacity as he had. School-children who are properly sent to school unattended must use such reasonable care as school-children can. It must be reasonable care adapted to the circumstances, or, in other words, the ordinary care of school-children." Lynch *v.* Smith, 104 Mass. 52; s. c., 44 Am. Rep. 188.

"It is well settled that the conduct of an infant of tender years is not to be judged by the same rules which govern that of an adult. While it is the general rule in regard to an adult, that to entitle him to recover damages for an injury resulting from the fault or negligence of another, he must himself have been free from fault, such is not the rule in regard to an infant of tender years. The care and caution required of a child is according to its maturity and capacity only, and this is to be determined in each case by the circumstances of that case." Railroad Co. *v.* Stout, 17 Wall. (U. S.) 657. And to same effect see Evansich *v.* R. Co, 57 Tex. 126; s. c., 6 Am. & Eng. R. R. Cas. 182; 44 Am. Rep. 586.

1. **"Due Care" of a Child not that of an Adult.** — "It was necessary that the plaintiff, though a boy, should prove that he was in the exercise of due care; but due care on his part did not require the judgment and thoughtfulness which would be expected of an adult under the same circumstances. It is that degree of care which could reasonably be expected from a boy of his age and capacity." Plumley *v.* Birge, 124 Mass. 57; s. c., 26 Am. Rep 645.

"The caution required is according to the maturity and capacity of the child; and this is to be determined in each case by the circumstances of that case." Railroad Co. *v.* Gladman, 15 Wall. (U. S.) 401, 406. See also Duffy *v.* Mo. Pac. R. (Mo.) 2 West. Rep. 198, 201; Philadelphia, etc., R. Co. *v.* Spearen, 47 Pa. St. 300; Cooper *v.* L. S., etc., R. Co. (Mich. 1887), 33 N. W. Rep. 306; Kunz *v.* Troy (N. Y.), 10 N. E. Rep. 442.

2. **Care required of a Child Employee.** — In stepping over a revolving shaft at a point where there was a set-screw, a boy of seventeen years, in the employ of defendant, sustained severe injuries by the set-screw catching the leg of his trousers. He knew of the presence of the shaft, but had never taken particular notice of the set-screw, and had received no warning of its dangers. In the course of an opinion holding that he could recover, it was said, "It is not a conclusion of law, from the fact that plaintiff was aware of the existence of the set-screw, and was seventeen years old, and sprightly for one of his years, that he was aware of the risk and danger of passing over the shaft while it was in motion." Dowling *v.* Allen, 74 Mo. 13; s. c., 41 Am. Rep. 298.

"A servant knowing the facts may be utterly ignorant of the risks." *Cockburn, C. J.*, in Clarke *v.* Holmes, 7 H. & N. 937; Railroad Co. *v.* Fort, 17 Wall. (U. S.) 553.

3. **Only assumes Risks within his Comprehension.** — "If in this case the plaintiff was too young and inexperienced to appreciate the danger to which he was exposed, then conduct on his part which would be negligence in one aware of the danger might not be imputed as negligence to him. But if the jury should find that he was aware of the danger to which he was exposed, any negligence on his part which contributed directly to his injury will defeat his action." Dowling *v.* Allen, 88 Mo. 293.

may recover for injuries resulting from dangers that, by reason of youth, immaturity, and inexperience, he was unable to fully apprehend, and the perils of which had not been explained to him.[1] Nor will a child negligently injured upon a railroad, or by defects in a public highway, or by dangerous machinery, or explosives, or in any other way, be charged with contributory negligence, if, at the time of such injury, he was doing what might have been expected of an ordinarily careful and prudent child of the same age, making due allowance for the natural instincts of childhood.[2]

1. May recover when injured by Uncomprehended Dangers.—"The rule contended for by the appellant, that the employee impliedly assumes the risks of the service, and of such dangers as are obvious and open to ordinary observation, does not embrace such risks as the employer knows, or which by the exercise of reasonable care he might have known, beforehand, that the employee, by reason of his immaturity and inexperience, is ignorant of, or such as the employer knows, the employee, without experience, cannot appreciate or avoid without instruction or warning. . . . The *gravamen* of such a case is the omission of duty on the part of the employer, in failing to instruct an inexperienced servant, who, although he may see the danger, may nevertheless be utterly ignorant of the risk, or of the manner of performing the service, so as to avoid injury therefrom." Louisville, etc., R. Co. *v.* Frowley, 110 Ind. 18, 24; s. c., 28 Am. & Eng. R. R. Cas. 308.

"If the owners of dangerous machinery, by their foreman, employ a young person about it quite inexperienced in its use, either without proper directions as to its use or with directions which are improper, and which are likely to lead to danger, of which *the* young person is not aware, and of which they *are* aware; as it is their duty to take reasonable care to avert such danger, they are responsible for any injury which may ensue from the use of such machinery." *Cockburn, C. J.*, in Grizzle *v.* Frost, 3 Fost. & Fin. 622.

2. Allowance made for Childish Instincts.—"Children, wherever they go, must be expected to act upon childish instincts and impulses; and others who are chargeable with a duty of care and caution toward them must calculate upon this, and take precautions accordingly. If they leave exposed to the observation of children any thing which would be tempting to them, and which they, in their immature judgment, might naturally suppose they were at liberty to handle or play with, they should expect that liberty to be taken." *Cooley, J. J.*, in Powers *v.* Harlow, 53 Mich. 507; s. c., 51 Am. Rep. 154.

And see a recent interesting case in Ohio, where a dangerous torpedo was placed upon a railroad track by employees of the railway company, and left unwatched. A boy, going to the track, had his curiosity excited by the torpedo, and, picking it up, tried to open the box, during which operation it exploded, injuring the plaintiff, a boy of ten years, who with childish curiosity had drawn near to see what his comrade had found. In this case a recovery was sustained, and all the leading cases reviewed in the course of the elaborate opinion. Harriman *v.* Pittsburgh, etc., R. Co. (Ohio, 1887), 12 N. E. Rep. 451.

It is upon the principle stated in the text that what are known as the "Turn-Table Cases" rest. In them, children attracted by railway turn-tables left unguarded and unlocked, and injured while playing on the tables, have been permitted to recover,—first, because it might have been apprehended that children would be attracted by such appliances; and, second, because the turn-tables served as implied invitations to children with childish instincts, and the railway companies were bound not to leave such temptations in their way. Railroad Co. *v.* Stout, 17 Wall. (U. S.) 657; Evansich *v.* Gulf, etc., R. Co., 57 Tex. 126; s. c., 6 Am. & Eng. R. R. Cas. 182; 44 Am Rep. 586; Kansas Cent. R. Co. *v.* Fitzsimmons, 22 Kan. 686; s. c., 18 Am. & Eng. R. R. Cas. 34; 31 Am. Rep. 203; Keffe *v.* Railroad Co., 21 Minn. 207; s. c., 18 Am. Rep. 393; and in this last case it is said, "Now, what an express invitation would be to an adult, the temptation of an attractive plaything is to a child of tender years." Atchison etc., R. Co. *v.* Bailey, 12 Neb. 333; s. c., 10 Am. & Eng. R. R. Cas. 742; Koans *v.* St. Louis, etc., R. Co., 65 Mo. 592; Nagle *v.* Mo Pac. R. Co., 75 Mo. 653; s. c., 10 Am. & Eng. R. R. Cas. 702, 42 Am. Rep. 418.

But in such cases the negligence, both of the railway company and the child, seems to be for the jury. Kolsti *v.* Minneapolis, etc., R. Co., 32 Minn. 133; s. c., 19 Am. & Eng. R. R. Cas. 140; Atchison, etc., R. Co. *v.* Bailey, 12 Neb. 333; s. c., 10 Am. & Eng. R. R. Cas. 742. But there is one unsatisfactory case where it was held as matter of law that the defendant had not been guilty of negligence, the turn-table being in an

Hence a person negligently injuring a child may be held liable under circumstances where contributory negligence would have barred an adult.[1] And conversely, a much higher grade of care and watchfulness must be exercised to avoid injuring children than would constitute ordinary care towards an adult; that is, what is ordinary care towards an adult of full capacity, may be culpable negligence towards a child.[2] As the standard of care thus varies with the age, capacity, and experience of the child, it is usually, if not always, where the child is not wholly irresponsible, a question of fact for the jury whether a child exercised the ordinary care and prudence of a child similarly situated; and if such care was exercised, a recovery can be had for an injury negligently inflicted, no matter how far the care used by the child falls short of the standard which the law erects for determining what is ordinary care in a person of full age and capacity.[3] But this will not warrant a recovery when the child suddenly put himself in a dangerous place where there was no reason to expect him, and too late for the danger to be averted by the person inflicting the injury.[4] And, of course, there can be no recovery if the injury did not result from negligence,[5] or if it came from a

isolated place, and latched in the ordinary manner. St. Louis, etc., R. Co. *v.* Bell, 81 Ill. 76; s. c., 25 Am. Rep. 269.

1. **Infancy and Helplessness often excuse.**—"A child's age and helplessness may, however, often excuse where one of mature age would be adjudged in fault, and may also often make an act negligent as to him that would not be so as to one of riper years." Indianapolis, etc., R. Co. *v.* Pitzer, 109 Ind. 179; s. c., 25 Am. & Eng. R. R. Cas. 313.

2. **But Great Care must be exercised toward a Child.**—"It is a reasonable and necessary rule that a higher degree of care should be exercised toward a child incapable of using discretion commensurate with the perils of his situation than one of mature age and capacity; hence conduct which toward the general public might be up to the standard of due care, may be gross or wilful negligence when considered in reference to children of tender age and immature experience." Bransom *v.* Labrot, 81 Ky. 638; s. c., 50 Am. Rep. 193; Robinson *v.* Cone, 22 Vt. 213; s. c., 54 Am. Dec. 67.

3. **Ordinary Care of Child for the Jury, When.**—"The question of discretion in the child, and of consequent responsibility for negligence, was not one for the court, and to be determined upon demurrer, but was for the jury. In no class of cases can this practical experience of juries be more wisely applied than in that we are considering. We find accordingly, although not uniform or harmonious, that the authorities justify us in holding in the case before us, that although the facts are undisputed, it is for the jury and not for the judge to determine whether proper care was given, or whether they establish negligence. A court cannot declare, as a matter of law, that a child of seven years is *sui juris*; and when from the age of the child there may be doubt upon that question, it should be submitted to the jury." Evansich *v.* Railroad Co., 57 Tex. 126; s. c., 6 Am. & Eng. R. R. Cas. 182, 44 Am. Rep. 586. See to same effect Lynch *v.* Smith, 104 Mass. 52; s. c., Am. Rep. 188.

4. **No Liability for Sudden Act of Child.**—"It is hence manifest that this accident occurred, not because of any defect in the vehicle, nor from the neglect of the person in charge of it, but from the sudden and unanticipated act of the child itself, which could neither be foreseen nor guarded against; and it is a fact that the thoughtless impulse of a child may bring about an accident for which even a railroad company will not be held liable." Hestonville Pass. R. Co. *v.* Connell, 88 Pa. St. 520; s. c., 32 Am. Rep. 472; citing Philadelphia, etc., R. Co. *v.* Spearen, 11 Wright (Pa.), 300.

And upon this same ground the case of Nagle *v.* Allegheny, etc., R. Co., 88 Pa. St. 35; s. c., 32 Am. Rep. 413, might well have been placed. But it was there *held*, as matter of law, that a boy of fourteen years had been guilty of negligence.

5. **If Defendant not Negligent, not Liable.**—The youth of the plaintiff, as was said

danger fully apprehended by the infant, and of which he had assumed the risks, having the capacity to comprehend and avoid the danger.[1] So if a minor has reached years of discretion, and is fully capable of comprehending danger and using sufficient care to avoid it, he may be guilty of contributory negligence as a matter of law.[2] Many of the general rules here stated are not fully applicable where a child is a trespasser without inducement, license, or invitation, express or implied; but in such cases a recovery is generally denied on the ground that no duty of special

by *Agnew, J.*, in Flower *v.* R. Co., 69 Pa. 210; s. c., 8 Am. Rep. 251, "may excuse him from concurring negligence, but it cannot supply the place of negligence on the part of the company." *Hough, J.*, in Sherman *v.* Hannibal, etc., R. Co., 72 Mo. 62; s. c., 4 Am. & Eng. R. R. Cas. 589.

"Where the injury is caused by the actual negligence of the company, the incapacity of a child of this age [nineteen months] to know the danger, and to avoid it, shields it from responsibility for its acts. If there be no negligence on the part of the company, then the incapacity of the child creates no liability." Kay *v.* Pa. R. Co., 65 Pa. St. 269; s. c., 3 Am. Rep. 628, 634. And to S. P., see Cauley *v.* Pittsburgh, etc., R. Co., 95 Pa. St. 398; s. c., 4 Am. & Eng. R. R. Cas. 533, 40 Am. Rep. 664; Central Branch, etc., R. Co. *v.* Henigh, 23 Kan. 347; s. c., 31 Am. Rep. 210, note: Patterson's Ry. Acc. L. 72, § 75; Bishop *v.* Union R. Co., 14 R. I. 314; s. c., 51 Am. Rep. 386.

1. **Injury from Risks assumed by Child.** — Thus, in McGinnis *v.* C. S. Bridge Co., 49 Mich. 466; s. c., 8 Am. & Eng. R. R. Cas. 135, where plaintiff claimed a right to recover, on the ground that, being immature and inexperienced, he had been sent by defendant into danger the full extent of which he did not comprehend, it was said by the court, "The first ground was shown to be untenable by the plaintiff's own evidence. He was past twenty years of age; was not shown to be wanting in average intelligence of those of his age, and his duties were explained to him when he entered upon the employment. He besides understood the very danger into which he fell, and had in mind the purpose to avoid it. It was thus made to appear, by his own examination, that he was not sent into unknown dangers, and that he was not exposed to risks which he, through immaturity or for any other reason, failed to comprehend."

"It is said by the learned counsel for the respondent that infancy and inexperience do not modify the rule of fellow-servants. But that statement only holds good when it appears that such employee has been properly instructed by his employer as to the dangers of his employment, or has acquired knowledge of such dangers from other sources. When he has been properly instructed, and knows the danger of his employment, then he stands on the same footing as any other employee, and cannot recover for any injury caused by the negligence of a fellow-servant." Jones *v.* Florence Mining Co., 66 Wis. 268; s. c., 57 Am. Rep. 269, 276; Atlas Engine Works *v.* Randall, 100 Ind. 293; s. c., 50 Am. Rep. 798; Williams *v.* Churchill, 137 Mass. 243; s. c., 50 Am. Rep. 304; Fones *v.* Phillips, 39 Ark. 17; s. c., 43 Am. Rep. 264; Dowling *v.* Allen, 74 Mo. 13; s. c., 41 Am. Rep. 298; Coombs *v.* New Bedford Cordage Co., 102 Mass. 572; s. c., 3 Am. Rep. 506.

"Here again it should be observed that the master will not be thus liable, if the circumstances are such as to show that the servant is competent to apprehend the danger, and expressly or impliedly assumes the risk." Pittsburgh, etc., R. Co. *v.* Adams, 105 Ind. 151, 167; s. c., 23 Am. & Eng. R. R. Cas. 418. And so where the minor employee, although not warned of the danger by his master, had obtained knowledge from other sources, and fully realized the risks he was taking. Sullivan *v.* India M. Co., 113 Mass. 396. And see to same effect as foregoing, Atlas Engine Works *v.* Randall, 100 Ind. 293; s. c., 50 Am. Rep. 798; Williams *v.* Churchill, 137 Mass. 243; s. c., 50 Am. Rep. 304; Curran *v.* Merchants' M. Co., 130 Mass. 374; s. c., 39 Am. Rep. 457; Coombs *v.* New Bedford Cordage Co., 102 Mass. 572; s. c., 3 Am. Rep. 506, Fones *v.* Phillips, 39 Ark. 17; s. c., 43 Am. Rep. 264; Dowling *v.* Allen, 74 Mo. 13; s. c., 41 Am. Rep. 298.

2. **A Minor may be Guilty of Negligence as Matter of Law.** — Thus, when an intelligent boy of fourteen years, knowing of the dangers of machinery generally, and familiar with a railroad adjacent to his place of work, heedlessly ran onto the track in front of a locomotive, and was killed, it was held as a matter of law that he was guilty of contributory negligence. Nagle *v.* Allegheny Valley R. Co., 88 Pa. St. 35; s. c., 32 Am. Rep. 413. And see Dietrich *v.* Baltimore, etc., R. Co., 58 Md. 347; s. c.,

care was owing to the child while a naked trespasser.[1] The foregoing principles apply with equal force to cases where injuries to idiots, lunatics, or weak-minded persons are in question, except that in such cases the very appearance of the person is not necessarily, as it is in the case of children of tender years, a warning to every one that he is not to be held to the adult standard of ordinary care.[2]

23. Erroneous Conduct of Plaintiff caused by Defendant. — When the plaintiff acts erroneously through fright or excitement induced by defendant's negligence, or adopts a perilous alternative in the endeavor to avoid an injury threatened by such negligence, or is lulled into fancied security by defendant's conduct, and then acts mistakenly in endeavoring to avoid an unexpected danger negligently caused by defendant, or is induced to incur danger, not obviously certain to result in injury, by defendant's directions or assurances of safety, upon which he relies, he is not guilty of contributory negligence as a matter of law.[3] And even though the

11 Am. & Eng. R. R. Cas. 115, where, the facts being undisputed, a boy of fourteen was held guilty of negligence as a matter of law. *Contra*, Haycroft *v.* Lake Shore, etc., R. Co., 64 N. Y. 636, where it was held a question for the jury to say whether a girl of seventeen, injured because of her own heedlessness, had been guilty of contributory negligence. Patterson's Ry. Acc. L. 70.

1. Rules modified when Child a Trespasser. — Central Branch R. Co. *v.* Henigh, 23 Kan. 347; s. c., 31 Am. Rep. 210, note; Cauley *v.* Pittsburgh, etc., R. Co., 95 Pa. St. 398; s. c., 4 Am. & Eng. R. R. Cas. 533, 40 Am. Rep. 664.

In Hydraulic Works Co. *v.* Orr, 83 Pa. St. 32; s. c., 31 Am. Rep. 208, note, the distinctions between cases in which there is and is not a liability to an infant trespasser are admirably stated. In that case a recovery was sustained because the trespassing child was allured upon the premises by the fascinations of the very death-trap in which he was caught. In the course of the opinion it was said, "But it has often been said, duties arise out of circumstances. Hence, where the owner has reason to apprehend danger, owing to the peculiar situation of his property and its openness to accident, the rule will vary." See also Schilling *v.* Abernethy, 112 Pa. St. 437; s. c., 56 Am. Rep. 320; Powers *v.* Harlow, 53 Mich. 507; s. c., 51 Am. Rep. 153.

This question will be more fully considered when we come to treat of "Children as Trespassers," *post*, § 26.

2. Same Rules apply to a Person non Compos Mentis. — Shearman & Redf. on Neg. § 51; Deering on Neg. § 20; Wharton on Neg § 306.

3. Defendant putting Plaintiff in Danger. — "But though in fact it may be hazardous 'to alight from a moving train,' a passenger who does so at the instance or direction of the conductor, or other employee in the management of the train, on whose opinion or judgment in the matter he has the right to rely, *and where the risk or danger was not apparent*, cannot be chargeable with negligence." St. Louis, etc., R. Co. *v.* Cantrell, 37 Ark. 519; s. c., 8 Am & Eng. R. R. Cas. 198; 40 Am. Rep. 105; Georgia R. Co. *v.* McCurdy, 45 Ga. 288; s. c., 12 Am. Rep. 577. In this latter case the conductor had agreed to stop at an unusual stopping-place, and let the plaintiff off. The train slacked its speed, so that it was not obviously very dangerous to alight, and, in obedience to the directions of the conductor, plaintiff sprang off, and was injured. The court thus states the scene: "Who that has seen much railroad travel can fail to see in his mind the picture of this scene? — the conductor in a pet; his train bound to slack up its speed at an unusual point; the passenger conscious that he was giving unusual trouble; the train slacks its speed; he stands ready, the conductor ready also, to give the word — now jump! None but a timid and yet resolute man would fail, and jump he did. And the court held that it was not contributory negligence, under the circumstances, to get off in the only manner that the conduct of the railway company permitted.

In Patton *v.* Western, etc., R. Co. (N. Car.), 1 S. E. Rep. 863, a railroad section-master, with power to hire, direct, and discharge men, suddenly ordered a new and inexperienced section-hand, in the injured person might have escaped the injury so brought upon him but for his hasty and mistaken conduct in the face of danger, yet defendant's negligence is the sole juridical cause of the injury, and plaintiff's error of judgment only its condition, when plaintiff was placed in the position of danger without previous negligence on his own part.[1] But plaintiff cannot recover when his own

course of his employment, to jump from a swiftly moving train, which order was obeyed; and it was *held* that, as plaintiff acted in the course of duty on a sudden command to do an extra-hazardous thing, that he was entitled to recover for injuries resulting therefrom, and that the section-master, in giving the command, was not a fellow-servant, but a vice-principal.

In Fowler *v.* B. & O. R. Co., 18 W. Va. 579; s. c., 8 Am. & Eng. R. R. Cas. 480, the plaintiff, in the night-time, went upon a railway track, by directions of the conductor of a freight-train on which he was a passenger, to assist in caring for some cattle which he had in one of the cars in the train. He was assured by the conductor that it was safe to do this, and had nothing to fear from any other train, as the freight was entitled to the track upon which he would have to stand, or along which he would pass. While standing in such track, caring for his cattle, plaintiff was struck and injured by an express-train, which came upon him without warning. It was held that he had a right to rely upon the assurances of the conductor, and that he was not guilty of contributory negligence in not keeping a lookout for the train that injured him.

"If I place a man in such a situation that he must adopt a perilous alternative, I am responsible for the consequences." Lord Ellenborough in Jones *v.* Boyce, 1 Stark. 493; s. c., Thomp. Car. of Pass. 246.

"If, therefore, a person should leap from the car under the influence of a well-grounded fear that a fatal collision is about to take place, his claim against the company for the injury he may suffer will be as good as if the same mischief had been done by the apprehended collision itself." *Black, J.*: Pa. Railroad Co. *v.* Aspell, 23 Pa. St. 147; s. c., Thomp. Car. of Pass. 252, 62 Am. Dec. 323; Chicago, etc., R. Co. *v.* Randolph, 53 Ill. 510; s. c., 5 Am. Rep. 60; Wesley City Coal Co. *v.* Healer, 84 Ill. 126; Chicago *v.* Hesing, 83 Ill. 204; Lambeth *v.* Railroad Co., 66 N. Car. 494; s. c., 8 Am. Rep. 508; Files *v.* N. Y. Cent. R. Co., 49 N. Y. 47; s. c., 10 Am. Rep. 327; Kelley *v.* Hannibal, etc., R. Co., 70 Mo. 604; Doss *v.* Railroad Co., 59 Mo. 27; s. c., 21 Am. Rep. 371; Loyd *v.* Hannibal, etc., R. Co., 53 Mo. 509; Penna. R. Co. *v.* Kilgore, 32 Pa. St. 292; Delaware, etc., Co. *v.* Webster (Pa.), 27 Am. & Eng. R. R. Cas. 160; B & O. R. Co. *v.* Leapley (Md.), 27 Am. &. Eng. R. R. Cas. 167; Western, etc., R. Co. *v.* Wilson, 71 Ga. 22; L. & N. R. Co. *v.* Kelley, 92 Ind. 371; s. c., 13 Am. & Eng. R. R. Cas. 1; Pool *v.* Chicago, etc., R. Co., 53 Wis. 659; s. c., 3 Am. & Eng. R. R. Cas. 332; Johnson *v.* West Chester, etc., R. Co., 70 Pa. St. 357; Indianapolis, etc., R. Co. *v.* Stout, 53 Ind. 143; Indianapolis, etc., R. Co. *v.* Carr, 35 Ind. 510; Karr *v.* Parks, 48 Cal. 188; Cook *v.* Cent. R. R. Co., 67 Ala. 533; Delamatyr *v.* Milwaukee, etc., R. Co., 24 Wis. 578; Ingalls *v.* Bills, 9 Metc. (Mass.) 1; s. c., 43 Am. Dec. 346; Carr *v.* Parham, 24 Ala. 21; Penna. R. Co. *v.* McCloskey, 23 Pa. St. 526; Penna. R. Co. *v.* Henderson, 51 Pa. St. 315; Cleveland, etc., R. Co. *v.* Manson, 30 Ohio St. 451; McIntyre *v.* N. Y. Cent. R. Co., 37 N. Y. 287; Penna. R. Co. *v.* Ogier, 35 Pa. St. 60; South Covington, etc., R. Co. *v.* Ware (Ky.), 27 Am & Eng. R. R. Cas. 206; Harris *v.* Township of Clinton (Mich.), 7 West. Rep. 666.

And see, generally, upon the subjects of this section, 2 Thomp. on Neg. 1092, § 8; 1173, § 19; 1174, § 20; Patterson's Ry. Acc. Law, pp. 14–23, 62; Beach on Cont. Neg. 42–44, 71, 72.

1. Plaintiff's Erroneous Act not a Proximate Cause, When.—"When the negligence of the agents puts a passenger in such a situation that the danger of remaining on the car is apparently as great as would be encountered in jumping off, the right to compensation is not lost by doing the latter; and this rule holds good even where the event has shown that he might have remained inside with more safety." *Black, J.*, in Pa. Railroad Co. *v.* Aspell, 23 Pa. St. 147; s. c., 62 Am. Dec.; s. c., Thomp. Car. of Pass. 252; Stokes *v.* Saltonstall, 13 Pet. (U. S.) 181.

"If the jury had found, as they might from the evidence, that, through defendant's negligence, the unexpected, sudden, and rapid approach of the car placed Hemberg, without his fault, in a position of apparent peril, requiring instant action to escape, and that the peril, and shouting by the brakeman and others, frightened and bewildered him, so that for the moment he was incapable of deliberating, and choosing the safest course to pursue, the defendant cannot allege it as negligence in law on his part, so as to prevent his recovery, that he adopted an unsafe course, if it was a natural negligence combined and concurred with that of the defendant in putting him in the position of peril.[1]

24. Illegal Conduct of Plaintiff as Contributory Negligence. — It is not contributory negligence, *per se*, for the injured person, at the time of his injury, to be engaged in a violation of law, either positive or negative in its character. Before an illegal act or omission can be held contributory negligence, it must appear that such act or omission was a proximate cause of the injury.[2] It is usually

result of the fright and bewilderment so caused by defendant's negligence, such as might occur to one acting with ordinary prudence. . . . If the jury had been satisfied from the evidence, as they might have been, that the car was run in negligently; that it was not negligence in Hemberg not to see the car till it was close upon him, and if he then ran upon the track his doing so was through terror and loss of self-possession caused by defendant's negligence, his doing so was not negligence." Mark *v.* St. Paul, etc., R. Co., 30 Minn. 493; s. c., 12 Am. & Eng. R. R. Cas. 86; Wilson *v.* N. Pac. R. Co., 26 Minn. 278; s. c., 37 Am. Rep. 410; Buel *v.* N. Y. Cent. R. Co., 31 N. Y. 314; Twomley *v.* Cent. Park, etc., R. Co., 69 N. Y. 158; s. c., 25 Am. Rep. 162; Coulter *v.* Am. Exp. Co., 56 N. Y. 585; Frink *v.* Potter, 17 Ill. 406; Schultz *v.* Chicago, etc., R. Co., 44 Wis. 638; Hoff *v.* Minneapolis, etc., R. Co., 14 Fed. Rep. 558; Moore *v.* Central R. Co., 47 Iowa, 688; Mark *v.* St. Paul, etc., R. Co., 30 Minn. 493; s. c., 12 Am. & Eng. R. R. Cas. 86; Stevenson *v.* Chicago, etc., R. Co., 18 Fed. Rep. 493; Siegrist *v.* Arnot, 10 Mo. App. 197; Chicago, etc., R. Co. *v.* Becker, 76 Ill. 25, 29; Penna. R. Co. *v.* Werner, 89 Pa. St. 59; Galena, etc., R. Co. *v.* Yarwood, 17 Ill. 509; s. c., 65 Am. Dec. 682; Turner *v.* Buchanan, 82 Ind. 147; s. c., 42 Am. Rep. 484; Pittsburgh, etc., R. R. Co. *v.* Rohrman (Penn.), 12 Am. & Eng. R. R. Cas. 176 and note, p. 180; Iron R. Co. *v.* Mowery, 36 Ohio St. 418; s. c., 3 Am. & Eng. R. R. Cas. 361, 38 Am. Rep. 597; Collins *v.* Davidson, 19 Fed. Rep. 83; Richmond, etc., R. Co. *v.* Morris, 31 Gratt. (Va.) 200.

1. But Plaintiff's Contributory Negligence bars him. — "A railroad company is not liable to a passenger for an accident which the passenger might have prevented by ordinary attention to his own safety, even though the agents in charge of the train are also remiss in their duty. From these principles it follows very clearly that, if a passenger is negligently carried beyond the station where he intended to stop, and where he had a right to be let off, he can recover compensation for the inconvenience, the loss of time, and the labor of travelling back, because these are the direct consequences of the wrong done to him. But if he is foolhardy enough to jump off without waiting for the train to stop, he does it at his own risk, because this is gross imprudence, for which he can blame nobody but himself. If there be any man who does not know that such leaps are extremely dangerous, especially when taken in the dark, his friends should see that he does not travel by railroad." *Jere. Black, J.*, in Pa. Railroad Co. *v.* Aspell, 23 Pa. St. 147; s. c., Thomp. Car. of Pass. 252; Chicago, etc., R. Co. *v.* Hazzard, 26 Ill. 373; Frost *v.* Grand Trunk R. Co., 10 Allen (Mass.), 387; Woolery *v.* Louisville, etc., R. Co., 107 Ind. 381; s. c., 27 Am. & Eng. R. R. Cas. 210.

2. Illegal Conduct not Negligence Per Se. — "The defendant's counsel contends that the simple fact that the plaintiff is in the act of violating the law at the time of the injury, is a bar to the right of recovery. Undoubtedly there are many cases where the contemporaneous violation of the law by the plaintiff is so connected with his claim for damages as to preclude his recovery; but to lay down such a rule as the counsel claims, and to disregard the distinction implied in the ruling of which he complains, would be productive oftentimes of palpable injustice. The fact that a party plaintiff, in an action of this description, was at the time of the injury passing another wayfarer on the wrong side of the street, or without giving him half the road, or that he was travelling on runners without bells, in contravention of the statute, or that he was smoking a cigar in the streets in violation of a municipal ordinance, while it might subject the offender to a penalty, will not excuse the town for a neglect to make its ways safe and convenient for travellers, if the commission of the plaintiff's offence did not in any degree contribute to produce the injury of which he complains." Baker *v.* Portland, 58 Me. 199; s. c., 4 Am. Rep. 274.

"And it is true generally, that while no person can maintain an action to which he must trace his title through his own breach of the law, yet the fact that he is breaking the law does not leave him remediless for injuries wilfully or carelessly done to him, and to which his own conduct has not contributed." Steele *v.* Burkhardt, 104 Mass.

held that the mere collateral wrong-doing of the plaintiff cannot, of itself, bar him of his action when it did not proximately contribute to the injury.[1]

25. Plaintiff a Trespasser. — Upon analogous principles, a mere trespass is not contributory negligence *per se*, and, before it can be held contributory negligence, it must appear that it was an efficient and direct cause of an injury complained of, producing the injury in combination with the negligence of the defendant; and if plaintiff was at the place of injury by the invitation, license, or consent of the defendant, express or implied, the question is simply one of ordinary care apart from the trespass. But if the plaintiff was a naked trespasser, to whom the defendant owed no duty, he cannot recover merely because he used ordinary care after becoming a trespasser. By becoming a trespasser, a person assumes the risks attendant on the trespass; and he must show

59; s. c., 6 Am. Rep. 191; Cook *v.* Johnson, 58 Mich. 437; s. c., 55 Am. Rep. 703; Pittsburgh, etc., Co. *v.* Staley, 41 Ohio St. 118; s. c., 19 Am. & Eng. R. R. Cas. 118, 52 Am. Rep. 74; Billings *v.* Breinig, 45 Mich. 65; Haas *v.* Railroad Co., 47 Mich. 401; s. c., 8 Am. & Eng. R. R. Cas. 268; Knupfle *v.* Knickerbocker Ice Co., 84 N. Y. 488; Western & Atl. R. Co. *v.* Jones, 65 Ga. 631; s. c., 8 Am. & Eng. R. R. Cas. 267; Pakalinsky *v.* Railroad Co., 82 N. Y. 424; s. c., 2 Am. & Eng. R. R. Cas. 251; Neanow *v.* Uttech, 46 Wis. 581; Davidson *v.* Portland, 69 Me. 116; s. c., 31 Am. Rep. 253; Spofford *v.* Harlow, 3 Allen (Mass.), 176; Welch *v.* Wesson, 6 Gray (Mass.), 505; Steele *v.* Burkhardt, 104 Mass. 59; s. c., 6 Am. Rep. 191; Hall *v.* Ripley, 119 Mass. 135; Bigelow *v.* Reed, 51 Me. 325; Hamilton *v.* Goding, 55 Me. 419; Griggs *v.* Fleckenstein, 14 Minn. 81; Baker *v.* Portland, 58 Me. 199; s. c., 4 Am. Rep. 274; Patterson's Ry. Acc. Law, pp. 64, 65; Beach on Cont. Neg. § 16.

1. **It must proximately contribute to be a Bar.** — "The fact that one who sustains an injury by the negligent or wrongful act of another, may have been, at the time of such injury, acting in disobedience of his collateral obligation to the State, which required of him the observance of the Sunday laws, will not prevent a recovery from one whose wrongful or negligent act or omission was the proximate cause of such injury." Louisville, etc., R. Co. *v.* Frawley, 110 Ind. 18, 30; s. c., 28 Am. & Eng. R. R. Cas. 308, citing Patterson's Ry. Acc. Law, pp. 64, 65; Beach on Cont. Neg. 186, 187, 270, 278; Cooley on Torts, p. 155; 21 Cent. L. J. 525; Mahoney *v.* Cook, 26 Pa. St. 342; Philadelphia, etc., R. Co. *v.* Philadelphia, etc., Co., 23 How. (U. S.) 209; Schmid *v.* Humphrey, 48 Iowa, 652; s. c., 30 Am. Rep. 414; Knowlton *v.* Milwaukee, etc., R. Co., 59 Wis. 278; Wood's Ry. Law, § 318; Wentworth *v.* Jefferson, 60 N. H. 158; Opsahl *v.* Judd, 30 Minn. 126; Carroll *v.* R. Co., 58 N. Y. 126; s. c., 17 Am. Rep. 221; Platz *v.* Cohoes, 89 N. Y. 219; s. c., 42 Am. Rep. 286; Stewart *v.* Davis, 31 Ark. 518; s. c., 25 Am. Rep. 576; Baldwin *v.* Barney, 12 R. I. 392; s. c., 34 Am. Rep. 670.

But it must not be overlooked, as it seems to have been in a measure in the above case, that, when plaintiff is compelled to found his action in his own violation of law, he cannot recover. Cooley on Torts, p. 156, note 1; Holt *v.* Green, 73 Pa. St. 198–200; s. c., 13 Am. Rep. 737; Gregg *v.* Wyman, 4 Cush. (Mass.) 322; Way *v.* Foster, 1 Allen (Mass.), 408; Smith *v.* Boston, etc., R. Co., 120 Mass. 490; s. c., 21 Am. Rep. 538; Crossman *v.* Lynn, 121 Mass. 301; Bosworth *v.* Swansey, 10 Met. (Mass.) 363; s. c., 43 Am. Dec. 441; Johnson *v.* Mo. Pac. R. Co., 18 Neb. 690; s. c., 23 Am. & Eng. R. R. Cas. 429; Woodman *v.* Hubbard, 25 N. H. 67; Phalen *v.* Clark, 19 Conn. 421; s. c., 50 Am. Dec. 253; Bank *v.* Highland St. R. Co., 133 Mass. 485; Parker *v.* Nashua, 59 N. H. 402; Read *v.* B. & A. R. R. Co. (Mass.), 140 Mass. 199; De Groot *v.* Van Duzer, 20 Wend. (N. Y.) 390. These cases and the rule just stated, however, turn usually upon the proposition that plaintiff cannot recover except through an illegal contract which is the foundation of his right of action; and when he can make out a case of injury independent of the illegal contract, a recovery may be had. Frost *v.* Plumb (Conn.), 13 Am. L. Reg. (N. S.) 537; Williams *v.* Hastings, 59 N. H. 373; Bernhard *v.* Lupping, 36 Mo. 341; Read *v.* B. & A. R. Co. (Mass.), 140 Mass. 199, 227; McGrath *v.* Merwin, 112 Mass. 467; Tamplin *v.* Still, 77 Ala 374.

that defendant, by some negligence subsequent to the trespass, inflicted an injury upon him that could have been avoided by the exercise of ordinary care toward a trespasser, before he can recover.[1]

1. **A Trespass as an Element of Negligence.** — 2 Thomp. on Neg. 1162, § 12; 1 Thomp. on Neg. 300 *et seq.*; Beach on Cont. Neg. §§ 17, 67, 71, 72, 80; Patterson's Ry. Acc. Law, 182; Deering on Neg. § 25; Wharton on Neg. § 346; Shearman & Redf. on Neg. § 38; Marble *v.* Ross, 124 Mass. 44; Nullaney *v.* Spence, 15 Abb. Pr. N. S. (N. Y.) 319; Daly *v.* Norwich, etc., R. Co., 26 Conn. 591; Norris *v.* Litchfield, 35 N. H. 271; s. c., 69 Am. Dec. 546; Brown *v.* Lynn, 31 Pa. St. 510; Loomis *v.* Terry, 17 Wend. (N. Y.) 496; Isbell *v.* N. Y., etc., R. Co., 27 Conn. 393; Whirley *v.* Whiteman, 1 Head (Tenn.), 611; Kerwhacker *v.* Cleveland, etc., R. Co., 3 Ohio St. 172; s. c., 62 Am. Dec. 246; Johnson *v.* Patterson, 14 Conn. 1; s. c., 35 Am. Dec. 96; Freer *v.* Cameron, 4 Rich. (S. C.) Law, 228; s. c., 55 Am. Dec. 663; Woolf *v.* Chalker, 31 Conn. 121, 131; Birge *v.* Gardner, 19 Conn. 512; s. c., 50 Am. Dec. 261; Little Rock, etc., R. Co. *v.* Pankhurst, 36 Ark. 371; s. c., 5 Am. & Eng. R. R. Cas. 535; Herring *v.* Wilmington, etc., R. Co., 10 Ired. (N. Car.) 402; s. c, 51 Am. Dec. 395; Meeks *v.* R. Co., 56 Cal. 13; s. c., 8 Am. & Eng. Corp. Cas. 314, 38 Am Rep. 67; Southwestern, etc., R. Co. *v.* Hankerson, 61 Ga. 114; Houston & Texas Central R. Co. *v.* Sympkins, 54 Tex. 615; s. c., 38 Am. Rep. 632; Mayor of Colchester *v.* Brooke, 7 Q. B. 339; Sanders *v.* Reister, 1 Dak. 151; Terre Haute, etc., R. Co. *v.* Graham, 95 Ind. 286; s. c., 12 Am. & Eng. R. R. Cas. 77, 48 Am. Rep. 719; Mason *v.* Mo. Pac. R. Co., 27 Kan. 83; s. c., 6 Am. & Eng. R. R. Cas. 1, 41 Am. Rep. 405; Chicago, etc., R. Co. *v.* Kellam, 92 Ill. 245; s. c., 34 Am. Rep. 128; Isabel *v.* Hannibal, etc., R. Co., 60 Mo. 475; Mulherrin *v.* Delaware, etc., R. Co., 81 Pa. St. 366; Baltimore, etc., R. Co. *v.* State, 33 Md. 542; Weymire *v.* Wolfe, 52 Iowa, 533; Lake Shore, etc, R. Co. *v.* Miller, 25 Mich. 279; Hargreaves *v.* Deacon, 25 Mich. 1; Zoebisch *v.* Tarbell, 10 Allen (Mass.), 385; Lary *v.* Cleveland, etc., R. Co., 78 Ind. 323; s. c., 3 Am. & Eng. R. R. Cas. 471, 41 Am. Rep. 572; Parker *v.* Portland Pub. Co., 69 Me 173; s. c., 31 Am. Rep. 262; Gramlich *v.* Wurst, 86 Penn. St. 74; s. c., 27 Am. Rep. 684; Severy *v.* Nickerson, 120 Mass. 306; s. c, 21 Am. Rep. 514; Pierce *v.* Whitcomb, 48 Vt. 127; s. c., 21 Am. Rep. 120; Ills., etc., R. Co. *v.* Godfrey, 71 Ill. 500; s. c., 22 Am. Rep. 112; Hardcastle *v.* Railroad Co., 4 Hurl. & N. 67; s. c., 28 L. J. (Exch.) 139; Stone *v.* Jackson, 16 C. B. 199; s. c., 32 Eng. Law & Eq. 349; Sweeny *v.* Old Colony, etc., R. Co., 10 Allen (Mass.), 368; Graves *v.* Thomas, 95 Ind. 361; s. c., 48 Am. Rep. 727; Campbell *v.* Boyd, 88 N. Car. 129; s. c., 43 Am. Rep. 740; Buesching *v.* Gas Co., 73 Mo. 219; s. c., 39 Am. Rep. 503; Hayward *v.* Merrill, 94 Ill. 349; s. c., 34 Am. Rep. 229; McAlpin *v.* Powell, 70 N. Y. 126; s. c., 26 Am. Rep. 555; Campbell *v.* Portland Sugar Co., 62 Me. 552; s. c., 16 Am. Rep. 503; McKone *v.* Michigan, etc., R. Co., 51 Mich. 601; s. c., 47 Am. Rep. 596; Davis *v.* Chicago, etc., R. Co., 58 Wis. 646; s. c., 15 Am. & Eng. R. R. Cas. 424, 46 Am. Rep. 667; Bennett *v.* Railroad Co., 102 U. S. 577; s. c., 1 Am. & Eng. R. R. Cas. 71; Barry *v.* N. Y., etc., R. Co., 92 N. Y. 289; s. c., 13 Am. & Eng. R. R. Cas. 615; Indermaur *v.* Dames, L. R. 1 C. P. 274; s. c., L. R. 2 C. P. 311; s. c., 1 Thomp. on Neg. 283; Smith *v.* Dock Co., L. R. 3 C. P. 326; Davis *v.* Cent. Cong. Soc., 129 Mass. 367; Carleton *v.* Franconia Iron Co., 99 Mass. 216; Gilbert *v.* Nagle, 118 Mass. 278; Larue *v* Hotel Co., 116 Mass. 67; Ackert *v.* Lansing, 59 N. Y. 646; Camp *v.* Wood, 76 N. Y. 92; s. c., 32 Am. Rep. 282; Pastene *v.* Adams, 49 Cal. 87; Hayward *v.* Merrill, 94 Ill. 349; s. c., 34 Am. Rep. 229; Pierce *v.* Whitcomb, 48 Vt. 127; s. c., 21 Am. Rep. 120; Totten *v.* Phipps, 52 N. Y. 354; Nare *v.* Flock, 90 Ind. 205; Bush *v.* Brainard, 1 Cow. (N. Y.) 78; s. c., 13 Am. Dec. 513; Munger *v.* Tonawanda R. R. Co., 4 N. Y. 349; s. c., 53 Am. Dec. 384; Carter *v.* Columbia, etc., R. Co., 19 S. Car. 20; s. c., 15 Am. & Eng. R. R. Cas. 414, 45 Am. Rep. 754; Everhart *v.* Terre Haute, etc., R. Co., 78 Ind. 292; s. c., 4 Am. & Eng. R. R. Cas. 599, 41 Am. Rep. 567; Haughey *v.* Hart, 62 Iowa, 96; s. c., 49 Am. Rep. 138; Baltimore, etc., R. Co. *v.* Depew, 40 Ohio St. 121; s. c., 12 Am. & Eng. R. R. Cas. 64; Houston, etc., R. Co. *v.* Richards, 59 Tex. 373; s. c., 12 Am. & Eng. R. R. Cas. 70; Davis *v.* Chicago, etc., R. Co., 58 Wis. 646; s. c., 15 Am. & Eng. R. R Cas. 424, 46 Am. Rep. 667; Hogan *v.* Chicago, etc., R. Co., 59 Wis 139; s. c., 15 Am. & Eng. R. R. Cas. 439; East. Tenn., etc, R. Co. *v.* Fain, 12 Lea (Tenn.), 35; s. c., 19 Am. & Eng. R. R. Cas. 102; Central R. Co. *v.* Brinson, 70 Ga. 207; s. c., 19 Am. & Eng. R. R. Cas. 42; McClelland *v.* Louisville, etc., R. Co., 94 Ind. 276; s. c, 18 Am. & Eng. R. R. Cas. 260; Learoyd *v.* Godfrey, 138 Mass. 315; Evansville, etc., R. Co. *v.* Griffin, 100 Ind. 221; s. c., 50 Am.

26. Children as Trespassers. — A child injured while trespassing has no right of action, unless injured by the negligence of defendant when the injury might have been avoided by ordinary care on defendant's part. But when a child of tender years commits a mere technical trespass, and is injured by agencies that to an adult would be open and obvious warnings of danger, but not so to a child, he is not debarred from recovering, if the things instrumental in his injury were left exposed and unguarded, and were of such a character as to be likely to attract children, excite their curiosity, and lead to their injury, while they were pursuing their childish instincts. Such dangerous and attractive instrumentalities become an invitation by implication.[1]

Rep. 783; Powers v. Harlow, 53 Mich. 507; s. c., 51 Am. Rep. 154; Crogan v. Schiele, 53 Conn. 186; s. c., 55 Am. Rep. 88; Larmore v. Iron Co., 101 N. Y. 391; s. c., 54 Am. Rep. 718; Schilling v. Abernethy, 112 Pa. St. 437; s. c., 56 Am. Rep. 320; Hamilton v. Texas, etc., R. Co., 64 Tex. 251; s. c., 21 Am. & Eng. R. R. Cas. 336, 53 Am. Rep. 756; Jones v. Nichols, 46 Ark. 207; s. c, 55 Am. Rep. 575.

1. **Infant Trespassers: the Turn-table Cases.** — Harriman v. Pittsburg, etc., R. Co. (Ohio), 12 N. E. Rep. 451; Phila., etc., R. Co. v. Spearen, 47 Pa. St. 300; Duffy v. Mo. Pac. R. Co. (Mo. Ct. of App.), 2 Western Rep. 198; Taylor v. Delaware, etc., Co., 113 Pa. St. 162; s. c., 57 Am. Rep. 446; Barry v. N. Y., etc., R. Co., 92 N. Y. 289; s. c., 13 Am. & Eng. R. R. Cas. 615, 44 Am. Rep. 377; Schilling v. Abernethey, 112 Pa. St. 437; s. c., 56 Am. Rep. 320; Biddle v. Hestonville, etc., R. Co., 112 Pa. St. 551; s. c., 26 Am. & Eng. R. R. Cas. 208; Keyser v. Chicago, etc., R. Co., 56 Mich. 559; Branson v. Labrat, 81 Ky. 638; s. c., 50 Am. Rep. 193; Scoville v. Hannibal, etc., R. Co., 81 Mo. 434; Western, etc., R. Co. v. Wilson, 71 Ga. 22; Baltimore, etc., R. Co. v. Schwindling, 101 Pa. St. 258; s. c., 8 Am. & Eng. R. R. Cas. 544; 47 Am. Rep. 706; Central R. Co. v. Brinson, 70 Ga. 207; s. c., 19 Am. & Eng. R. R. Cas. 42; 11 Galveston, etc., R. Co. v. Moore, 59 Tex. 64; s. c., 10 Am. & Eng. R. R. Cas. 746; 46 Am. Rep. 265; Lynch v. Nurdin, 1 Q. B. 29; s. c., 2 Thomp. on Neg. 1140; Clark v. Chambers, 3 Q. B. Div. 327, 329; s. c., 7 Cent. L. J. 11; 17 Alb. L. J. 505; Railroad Co. v. Stout, 17 Wall. (U. S.) 657; s. c., 2 Dill. (U. S.) 294; Keffe v. Milwaukee, etc., R. Co. 21 Minn. 207; s. c., 18 Am. Rep. 393; Kerr v. Forgue, 54 Ill. 482; s. c., 5 Am. Rep. 146; Chicago v. Starr, 42 Ill. 174; Nagel v. Mo., etc, R. Co., 75 Mo. 653; s. c., 10 Am. & Eng. R. R. Cas. 702; 42 Am. Rep. 418; Evansich v. Gulf, etc., R. Co., 57 Tex. 126; s. c., 6 Am. & Eng. R. R. Cas. 182, 44 Am. Rep. 586; Kansas, etc., R. Co. v. Fitzsimmons, 22 Kan. 686; s. c., 31 Am. Rep. 203; Koons v. St. Louis, etc., R. Co., 65 Mo. 592; St. Louis, etc., R. Co. v. Bell, 81 Ill. 76; s. c., 25 Am. Rep. 269; Birge v. Gardner, 19 Conn. 507; s. c., 50 Am. Dec. 261; Casgrove v. Ogden, 49 N. Y. 255; Whirley v. Whiteman, 1 Head (Tenn.), 611; Meitens v. Dodge, 38 Wis. 300; s. c., 20 Am. Rep. 6; Hydraulic Works v. Orr, 83 Pa. St. 332; Vanderbeck v. Hendry, 34 N. J. L. 467; Hughes v. Macfie, 2 Hurl. & Colt. 744; Mangan v. Atterton, L. R. 1 Exch. 239; Lane v. Atlantic Works, 107 Mass. 104; s. c. again, 111 Mass. 136; Lyons v. Brookline, 119 Mass. 491. (See Criticisms Mass. Rule 4 Am. Law Rev. 405, 1870.) Wood v. Independent School Dist., 44 Iowa, 27; Boland v. Railroad Co., 36 Mo. 484; Gillespie v. McGowen, 100 Pa. St. 144; Rockford, etc., R. Co. v. Delaney, 82 Ill. 198; s. c., 25 Am. Rep. 308; Isabel v. Hannibal, etc., R. Co., 60 Mo. 475; Kay v. Pa. R. Co., 65 Pa. St. 269; s. c., 3 Am. Rep. 628; Penna. R. Co. v. Lewis, 79 Pa. St. 33; Penna. R. Co. v. Morgan, 82 Pa. St. 134; Byrne v. R. Co., 83 N. Y. 620; Meyer v. Midland Pac. R. Co., 2 Neb. 319; Johnson v. Chicago, etc., R. Co., 56 Wis. 274; s. c., 8 Am. & Eng. R. R. Cas. 471; Fitzpatrick v. Railroad Co., 128 Mass. 13; Plumley v. Birge, 124 Mass. 57; s. c., 26 Am. Rep. 645; Munn v. Reed, 4 Allen (Mass.), 431; Dowd v. Chicopee, 116 Mass. 193; Morrissey v. Railroad Co., 126 Mass. 377; s. c., 30 Am. Rep. 686; Cent. Branch R. Co. v. Henigh, 23 Kan. 347; s. c., 33 Am. Rep. 167; Smith v. Atchison, etc., R. Co., 25 Kan. 738; 28 Kan. 541; s. c., 4 Am. & Eng. R. R. Cas. 554; Conley v. Railroad Co., 95 Pa. St. 398; s. c., 40 Am. Rep. 664; Moore v. Railroad Co., 99 Pa. St. 301; s. c., 44 Am. Rep. 106; Sweeny v. Old Colony R. Co., 10 Allen (Mass.), 368; Daley v. Norwich, etc., R. Co., 26 Conn. 591; Hicks v. Pacific R Co., 64 Mo. 430; Chicago, etc., R. Co. v. Murray, 71 Ill. 601; Railroad Co. v. Gladman, 15 Wall (U. S) 401; Chicago, etc., R. Co.

27. Plaintiff and Defendant in Privity. — In some relations, where one party owes the other a special duty, contractual or otherwise, a higher degree of care and foresight is required of the one owing the duty, than of the one to whom it is owing. The test is still that of ordinary care; but what would be ordinary care for one party to the relation, might be negligence in the other because of the higher duty resting upon him.[1]

28. Carriers of Passengers. — The principle stated is well illustrated by the co-relative duties of carrier and passenger. The carrier, being under special obligations to care for the safety of the passenger, must exercise the greatest practical degree of care, skill, and foresight to avoid injuring him. For the slightest failure to use ordinary care, he is liable, if injury follows; and the ordinary care required is that high degree of care that careful and prudent persons, with similar duties resting upon them, would exercise. It is a much higher grade of care than one owes to a stranger or trespasser.[2]

v. Dewey, 26 Ill. 255, 259; Pittsburgh, etc., R. Co. *v.* Bumstead, 48 Ill. 221; Penna. R. Co. *v.* Morgan, 82 Pa. St. 134; North Pa. R. Co. *v.* Mahoney, 57 Pa. St. 187; Norfolk, etc., R. Co. *v.* Ormsby, 27 Gratt. (Va.) 455; Rauch *v.* Loyd, 31 Pa. St. 358; Penna. R. Co. *v.* Kelley, 31 Pa. St. 372; Manly *v.* Wilmington, etc., R. Co., 74 N. Car. 655; Phila. & Reading R. Co. *v.* Hummell, 44 Pa. St. 375; Ostertog *v.* Pac. R. Co., 64 Mo. 421; Snyder *v.* Hannibal, etc., R. Co., 60 Mo. 413; Bulger *v.* Albany, etc., R. Co., 42 N. Y. 459; Citizens' St. R. Co. *v.* Carey, 56 Ind. 396; Nolan *v.* N. Y., etc., R. Co., 53 Conn. 461; s. c., 25 Am. & Eng R. R. Cas. 342; Durkee *v.* Cent. Pac. R. Co (Cal. 1885), 25 Am. & Eng. R. R. Cas. and note reviewing many cases; Union Pac. R. Co. *v.* Dunden (Kan. 1887), 14 Pac. Rep. 501; Schmidt *v.* Kansas City Dist. Co. (Mo.), 7 West. Rep. 124; Ecliff *v.* Wabash, etc., R. Co. (Mich.), 7 West. Rep 462; s. c., 31 N. W. Rep. 180; Indianapolis, etc., R. Co. *v.* Pitzer, 109 Ind. 179; s. c., 25 Am. & Eng. R. R. Cas. 313.

1. **"Ordinary Care" in Relations of Privity.** — This is only another way of stating the doctrine that ordinary care varies with the circumstances and conditions of the parties, and hence each party to a relation of privity must exercise that care which an ordinarily careful and prudent person so situated would exercise. Reeves *v.* Delaware, etc., R. Co., 30 Pa. St. 454; s. c., 72 Am. Dec. 713; Sullivan *v.* Scripture, 3 Allen (Mass.), 566; Fallon *v.* Boston, 3 Allen (Mass.), 39; Cunningham *v.* Hall, 4 Allen (Mass.), 276; 2 Wood's Ry. Law, 1074 *et seq.*; Thomp. on Carriers, 257; Jeffersonville, etc., R. Co. *v.* Hendricks, 26 Ind. 228; Price *v.* St. Louis, etc., R. Co., 72 Mo. 414; s. c., 3 Am. & Eng. R. R. Cas. 365.

2. **Ordinary Care of Carriers of Passengers.** — Ingalls *v.* Bills, 9 Metc. (Mass.) 1; s. c., 43 Am. Dec. 346 and note; Pennsylvania Co. *v.* Roy, 102 U. S. 451; s. c., 1 Am. & Eng. R. R. Cas. 225; Bedford, etc., R. Co. *v.* Rainbolt, 99 Ind. 551; s. c., 21 Am. & Eng. R. R. Cas. 466; Cleveland, etc., R. Co. *v.* Newell, 104 Ind. 264; s. c., 23 Am. & Eng. R. R. Cas. 492; Louisville, etc., R. Co. *v.* Thompson, 107 Ind. 442; s. c., 27 Am. & Eng. R. R. Cas. 88, 329; Louisville, etc., R. Co. *v.* Pedigo, 108 Ind. 481; s. c., 27 Am. & Eng. R. R. Cas. 310; 2 Am. & Eng. Ency. of L. 745, § 11, *et seq.*; Ford *v.* London, etc., R. Co., 2 Fost. & Fin. 730; Redhead *v.* Midland R. Co., L. R. 2 Q. B. 412; s. c., L. R. 4 Q. B. 379; Stokes *v.* Saltonstall, 13 Pet. (U. S.) 181; Phila., etc., R. Co. *v.* Derby, 14 How. (U. S.) 468; Penna. R. Co. *v.* Roy, 102 U. S. 451; s. c., 1 Am. & Eng. R. R. Cas. 225; Baltimore, etc., R. Co. *v.* Wightman, 29 Gratt. (Va.) 431; s. c., 26 Am. Rep. 384; Taylor *v.* Grand Trunk R. Co., 48 N. H. 304; s. c., 2 Am. Rep. 229; Laing *v.* Calder, 8 Pa. St. 479; s. c., 49 Am. Dec. 533; Farish *v.* Reigle, 11 Gratt. (Va.) 697; s. c., 62 Am. Dec. 666; McElroy *v.* Nashua, etc., R. Co., 4 Cush. (Mass.) 400; Union Pac. R. Co. *v.* Hand, 7 Kan. 380; Simmons *v.* New Bedford, etc., R. Co., 97 Mass. 36; Keokuk, etc., Packet Co. *v.* True, 88 Ill. 608; Philadelphia, etc., R. Co. *v.* Boyer, 97 Pa. St 91; s c., 2 Am. & Eng. R. R. Cas. 172; Lemon *v.* Chanslor, 68 Mo. 340; s. c., 30 Am. Rep. 799; Peters *v.* Rylands, 20 Pa. St. 497; s. c., 59 Am Dec. 746; Galena, etc., R. Co. *v.* Fay, 16 Ill. 558; s. c., 63 Am. Dec 323; Carroll *v.* Railroad Co., 58 N. Y.

On the other hand, the passenger has a right to depend upon the carrier owing him the duty of safe carriage, to perform it; and, while ordinary care to avoid injury devolves upon the passenger, yet such ordinary care is usually only to resign himself passively to the care of the carrier, conform to the carrier's reasonable rules and regulations, obey his directions, and avoid voluntary conduct causing an unnecessary exposure to danger.[1] The passenger can depend upon the means and appliances furnished for carrying him, and for his care and comfort, without making any special examination of them; and, while using and depending upon them in an ordinary manner, he is not guilty of contributory negligence, if negligently injured by defects therein, of which he had no notice.[2] But if the passenger unnecessarily exposes him-

126, 138; s. c., 17 Am. Rep. 228; Thomp. on Car. of Pass. 200; Wheaton v. Railroad Co., 36 Cal. 590; Kansas, etc., R. Co. v. Miller, 2 Col. 442; Hall v. Steamboat Co., 13 Conn. 319; Fuller v. Naugatuck R. Co., 21 Conn. 557, Crawford v. Railroad Co., 62 Ga. 566: Brunswick, etc, R. Co. v. Gale, 56 Ga. 322; Louisville, etc, R. Co. v. Wearns, 80 Ky. 420; s. c., 8 Am. & Eng. R. R. Cas. 399; Black v. N. O. & Carrollton Co, 10 La Ann. 33; Knight v. Portland, etc, R. Co, 56 Me. 234; Johnson v. Winona, etc., R. Co., 11 Minn. 296; McLean v. Burbank, 11 Minn. 227; Gilson v. Jackson Co., etc., R. Co., 76 Mo. 282; s. c., 12 Am. & Eng. R. R. Cas. 132; Nashville, etc, R Co. v. Messino, 1 Sneed (Tenn), 220; McKinney v. Neil, 1 McLean (U. S.), 540; Bowen v. N. Y. Cent. R. Co, 18 N. Y. 408; Tuller v. Talbot, 23 Ill. 357; Central, etc., R. Co. v. Perry, 58 Ga. 461; Mad River, etc., R. Co. v. Barber, 5 Ohio St. 541; s. c, 67 Am. Dec. 312; Hegeman v. Railroad Co., 13 N. Y. 9; s. c., 64 Am. Dec. 517; Hadley v. Cross, 34 Vt. 586; s c., 80 Am. Dec. 699; Hyman v. Nye, L. R. 6 Q. B. 685; s. c., 29 Moak's Eng. Rep. 769; Feital v. Middlesex, etc., R. Co., 109 Mass. 398; s. c., 12 Am. Rep. 725; Nashville, etc., R. Co. v Elliott, 1 Caldw. (Tenn.) 611; s. c, 78 Am. Dec 506; Frink v. Coe, 4 G. Greene (Iowa), 555; s. c, 61 Am. Dec. 141 Sales v. West. Stage Co., 4 Iowa, 547; Raymond v. Burlington, etc., R. Co., 62 Iowa, 152; s. c., 18 Am. & Eng R. R. Cas. 217, 13 Am. & Eng. R. R. Cas. 6; Smith v. St Paul City R. Co., 32 Minn. 1; s. c., 16 Am & Eng R. R. Cas. 310; N.Y., etc., R. Co. v. Daugherty (1882, Pa.), 6 Am. & Eng. R. R. Cas. 139; International, etc., R. Co v. Halloren, 53 Tex. Rep. 46; s. c., 3 Am. & Eng. R. R Cas. 343; George v. St. Louis, etc., R. Co., 34 Ark. 613; s. c., 1 Am. & Eng. R. R. Cas 294; Louisville, etc., R. Co. v. Ritter (Ky), 28 Am. & Eng. R. R. Cas 167; Louisville, etc., R. Co. v. Thompson, 107 Ind. 442; s. c., 27 Am. & Eng. R. R. Cas. 88; Louisville, etc., R. Co. v. Pedigo, 108 Ind. 481; s. c., 27 Am. & Eng. R. R. Cas. 310; Leslie v. Wabash, etc., R. Co., 88 Mo. 50; s. c., 26 Am. & Eng R. R. Cas. 229.

1. "**Ordinary Care" of a Passenger.** — Beach on Cont. Neg. §§ 51–57; 2 Wood's Ry. Law, 1083–1087; 2 Thomp. on Neg. 1172, § 18; Sheridan v. Brooklyn, etc., R. Co., 36 N. Y. 39; Houston, etc., R. Co. v. Gorbett, 49 Tex. 473; Lawrenceburg, etc., R. Co. v. Montgomery, 7 Ind 474; Lafayette R. Co. v. Sims, 27 Ind. 59; Galena, etc., R. Co. v. Fay, 16 Ill. 558; s. c., 63 Am. Dec. 323; Louisville & N. R. Co. v. Kelley, 92 Ind. 371; s.c., 13 Am. & Eng. R. R. Cas. 1; 47 Am. Rep. 149; Kentucky Cent. R. Co. v. Thomas, 79 Ky. 160; s. c., 1 Am. & Eng. R. R. Cas. 79, 42 Am. Rep 208; Houston, etc., R. Co. v. Clemmans, 55 Tex. 88; s. c., 8 Am. & Eng R. R. Cas. 396, 40 Am. Rep. 799; Railroad Co. v. Jones, 95 U. S., 439; Germantown Pass. R. Co. v. Walling, 97 Pa. St. 55; s.c., 2 Am. & Eng. R. R. Cas. 20, and note; 37 Am. Rep. 711, note.

2. **He has a Right to depend on Carrier's Appliances.** — Hegeman v. West. R. Co., 13 N Y. 9; s. c., 64 Am. Dec. 517; Steinweg v. Erie R Co., 43 N. Y. 123; s. c., 3 Am Rep. 673; Thomp. Car. of Pass. 220, § 13; Grand Rapids, etc., R. Co. v. Huntley, 38 Mich. 537; s. c., 31 Am. Rep. 321; Meier v. Penna R. Co., 64 Pa. St. 225; s. c., 3 Am. Rep. 581; Ladd v. Railroad Co., 119 Mass. 412; Grand Rapids & Ind. R. Co v. Boyd, 65 Ind. 526; Redhead v. Midland R. Co., L. R. 4 Q. B. 379; Taylor v. Grand Trunk R. Co., 48 N. H. 304; s. c., 2 Am. Rep. 229; McPadden v. Railroad Co., 44 N. Y. 478; s. c., 4 Am. Rep. 705; Burgess v. Great West'n R., 6 C. B. N. S. 923; Hulbert v. N. Y. Cent. R. Co., 40 N. Y. 145, C. & I. C. R. Co. v. Farrell, 31 Ind. 408; Bennett v. Railroad Co., 102 U. S. 577; s. c., 1 Am. & Eng. R. R. Cas 71; Hartwig v. Railroad Co., 49 Wis 358, s. c., 1

self to danger, goes into an unauthorized place or position of danger, or violates the reasonable rules and regulations made to secure his safety, he cannot recover if such conduct contributed to an injury which he would otherwise have escaped.[1] And the

Am. & Eng. R. R. Cas. 65; and see cases cited to note 121 *supra*.

1. **But he must not voluntarily go into Danger.**—Todd *v.* Old Colony R. Co., 7 Allen (Mass.), 207; s. c., 80 Am. Dec. 49; Louisville, etc., R. Co. *v.* Lickings, 5 Bush (Ky.), 1; Indianapolis, etc., R. Co. *v.* Rutherford, 29 Ind. 82; Pittsburgh, etc., R. Co. *v.* Andrews, 39 Md. 329; s. c., 18 Am. Rep. 568; Holbrook *v.* Railroad Co., 12 N. Y. 236; Pittsburgh, etc., R. Co. *v.* McClurg, 56 Pa. St. 294; Spencer *v.* Milwaukee, etc., Railroad Co., 17 Wis. 503; Chicago, etc., R. Co. *v.* Pandram, 51 Ill. 333; Penna. Co. *v.* Langdon, 92 Pa. St. 21; s. c., 1 Am. & Eng R. R. Cas. 87; Jacobus *v.* St. Paul, etc., R. Co., 20 Minn. 125; Watson *v.* Railway Co., 24 U. C. Q. B. 98; Hickey *v.* Boston, etc., R. Co., 14 Allen (Mass.), 429; Quinn *v.* Railroad Co., 51 Ill. 495; Buel *v.* Railroad Co., 31 N. Y. 314; Willis *v.* Long Island R. Co., 34 N. Y. 670; Zemp *v.* Railroad Co., 9 Rich. L. (So. Car.) 84; Meesel *v.* Lynn, etc., R. Co., 8 Allen (Mass.), 234; Augusta, etc., R. Co. *v.* Renz, 55 Ga. 126; Spooner *v.* Brooklyn City R. Co., 54 N. Y. 230; s. c., 13 Am. Rep. 570; Robertson *v.* Railroad Co., 22 Barb. (N. Y.) 91; Keith *v.* Pinkham, 43 Me. 501; Phillips *v.* Rensselaer, etc., R. Co., 49 N. Y., 177; Knight *v.* Pontchartrain R. Co., 15 La. An. 105; Harper *v.* Erie R. Co., 32 N. J. L. 88; Chicago, etc., R. Co. *v.* Scates, 90 Ill. 586; Lambeth *v.* N. Car. R. Co., 66 N. Car. 494; Filer *v.* N. Y. Cent. R. Co., 68 N. Y. 124; s. c., 10 Am. Rep. 327; Wyatt *v.* Citizens' R. Co., 55 Mo. 485; Price *v.* St. Louis, etc., R. Co., 72 Mo. 414; s. c., 3 Am. & Eng. R. R. Cas. 365; Johnson *v.* West Chester, etc., R. Co., 70 Pa. St. 357; Ill. Cent. R. Co. *v.* Able, 59 Ill. 131; Georgia, etc., R. Co. *v.* McCurdy, 45 Ga. 288; s. c., 12 Am. Rep. 577; Jamison *v.* San José, etc., R. Co., 55 Cal. 593; s. c., 3 Am. & Eng. R. R. Cas. 350; Gee *v.* Metropolitan R. Co., L. R. 8 Q. B. 161; Vicksburg, etc., R. Co. *v.* Hart, 61 Miss. 468, s. c., 19 Am. & Eng. R. R. Cas. 521; Texas, etc., R. Co. *v.* Murphy, 46 Tex. 356; s. c., 26 Am. Rep. 272; Harvey *v.* Railroad Co., 116 Mass. 269; Galveston, Harrisburg, etc., R. Co. *v.* Smith, 59 Tex. 406; Loyd *v.* Hannibal, etc., R. Co., 53 Mo. 509; Penna. R. Co. *v.* Kilgore, 32 Pa. St. 292; Brooks *v.* Boston, etc., R. Co., 135 Mass. 21; s. c., 16 Am. & Eng. R. R. Cas. 345; Doss *v.* Railroad Co., 59 Mo. 27; s. c., 21 Am. Rep. 371; Kelley *v.* H. & St. Joseph R. Co., 70 Mo. 604; Penna. R. Co. *v.* Aspell, 23 Pa. St. 147; s. c. 62 Am. Dec. 323; Jewell *v.* Chicago, etc., R. Co., 54 Wis. 610; s. c., 6 Am. & Eng. R. R. Cas. 379, 41 Am. Rep. 63; Richmond, etc., R. Co. *v.* Morris, 31 Gratt. (Va.) 200; Cumberland, etc., R. Co. *v.* Maugans, 61 Md. 53; s. c., 18 Am. & Eng. R. R. Cas. 182; Central, etc., R. Co. *v.* Letcher, 69 Ala. 106; s. c., 12 Am. & Eng. R. R. Cas. 115; 44 Am. Rep. 505; South, etc., R. Co. *v.* Singleton, 66 Ga. 252; s. c., 67 Ga. 306; Lucas *v.* Railroad Co., 6 Gray (Mass.), 64; Morrison *v.* Erie R. Co., 56 N. Y. 302; Dougherty *v.* Chicago, etc., R. Co., 86 Ill. 467; Lake Shore, etc., R. Co. *v.* Bangs, 47 Mich. 470; Mitchell *v.* Railroad Co., 51 Mich. 236; s. c., 47 Am. Rep. 566: Houston, etc., R. Co. *v.* Leslie, 57 Tex. 83; s. c., 9 Am. & Eng. R. R. Cas. 407; see Ill., etc., R. Co. *v.* Green, 81 Ill. 19; s. c., 25 Am. Rep. 255; Com. *v.* Boston, etc., R. Co., 129 Mass. 500; s. c., 1 Am. & Eng. R. Cas. 457; 37 Am. Rep. 382; Chicago, etc., R. Co. *v.* Randolph, 53 Ill. 510; s. c., 5 Am. Rep. 60; Cincinnati, etc., R. Co. *v.* Peters, 80 Ind. 168; s. c., 6 Am. & Eng. R. R. Cas. 126; Penna. R. Co. *v.* Dean, 92 Ind. 459; s. c., 18 Am. & Eng. R. R. Cas. 188; Higley *v.* Gilmer, 3 Mont. 90; s. c., 35 Am. Rep. 450; Alabama, etc., R. Co. *v.* Hawk, 72 Ala. 112; s. c., 18 Am. & Eng. R. R. Cas. 192; Camden, etc., R. Co. *v.* Hoosey, 99 Pa. St. 492; s. c., 44 Am. Rep. 120; Quinn *v.* Illinois, etc., R. Co., 51 Ill. 495; McIntyre *v.* N. Y. Cent. R. Co., 43 Barb. (N. Y.) 532; s. c., 37 N. Y. 287; Louisville, etc., R. Co. *v.* Kelley, 92 Ind. 371; s.c., 13 Am. & Eng. R. R. Cas. 1; 47 Am. Rep. 149; Penna. R. Co. *v.* Langdon, 92 Pa. St. 21; s. c., 1 Am. & Eng. R. R. Cas. 87; 37 Am. Rep. 651; Kentucky, etc., R. Co. *v.* Thomas, 79 Ky. 160; s. c., 1 Am. & Eng. R. R. Cas. 79, 42 Am. Rep. 208; Houston, etc., R. Co. *v.* Clemmans, 55 Tex. 88; s. c., 8 Am. & Eng. R. R. Cas. 396, 40 Am. Rep. 799; Dunn *v.* Grand Trunk R. Co., 58 Me. 187; s. c., 4 Am. Rep. 267; Jacobus *v.* St. Paul, etc., R. Co., 20 Minn. 125; s. c., 18 Am. Rep. 360; Waterbury *v.* N. Y., etc., R. Co., 21 Blatchf. (U. S.) 314; Austin *v.* Great West., etc., R. Co., L. R. 2 Q. B. 442; Carter *v.* Louisville, etc., R. Co., 98 Ind. 552; s. c., 49 Am. Rep. 780; Houston, etc., R. Co. *v.* Moore, 49 Tex. 31; s. c., 30 Am. Rep. 98; Sherman *v.* Hannibal, etc., R. Co., 72 Mo. 62; s. c., 4 Am. & Eng. R. R. Cas. 589; 37 Am. Rep. 423; Eaton *v.* Delaware, etc., R. Co., 57 N. Y. 382; s. c., 15 Am. Rep. 513; Hoar *v.* Maine Cent. R. Co., 70 Me. 65; s. c., 35 Am. Rep. 299; McQueen *v.* Cent. Branch U. P. R. Co., 30 Kan. 689; s. c., 15

passenger may put himself in so dangerous a place, in violation of the rules and directions of the carrier, that it will be held that the carrier owed him no duty while voluntarily in such place, and that he cannot recover for injuries received while so exposed, unless the carrier inflicts them wilfully.[1]

29. Travellers on Streets and Highways. — A non-contractual relation wherein greater care is required of the one party than of the other, is that which exists between a municipal corporation and a traveller on a public street or highway, when the law imposes upon the municipality the duty of keeping streets and highways reasonably safe for public travel, and renders them liable for injuries resulting from failures in this respect. It is the duty of such a municipality to keep its streets and highways reasonably safe for travel, and when they are in process of repair, defective, or unsafe, to see that proper signals and warnings of danger are given to travellers. A traveller upon a street or highway has a right to depend upon the performance of this duty without special investigation; and if injured by defects therein of which he had no notice, while travelling along the street in an ordinary manner, and relying upon the performance of duty by the municipality, he is not guilty of contributory negligence.[2] And it is not contributory negligence *per se* to use a highway, street, or bridge that is known to be defective; but if the traveller uses ordinary care to avoid injury from such defects, and is injured notwithstanding such care, it is a question for the jury whether he was guilty of contributory negligence in using the highway with knowledge of the defects.[3] But any want of ordinary care on the part of the

Am. & Eng. R. R. Cas. 226; Pool *v.* Chicago, etc., R. Co., 53 Wis. 657; s. c., 3 Am. & Eng. R. R. Cas. 332; Little Rock, etc., R. Co. *v.* Miles, 40 Ark. 298; s. c., 13 Am. & Eng. R. R. Cas. 10; 48 Am. Rep. 10; McCorkle *v.* Chicago, etc., R. Co., 61 Iowa, 555; s. c., 18 Am. & Eng. R. R. Cas. 156; but see Indianapolis, etc., R. Co. *v.* Horst, 93 U. S. 291; Creed *v.* Railroad Co., 86 Pa. St. 139; s. c., 27 Am. Rep. 693; Arnold *v.* Ill. Cent. R. Co., 83 Ill. 273; s. c., 25 Am. Rep. 383; Lucas *v.* Milwaukee & St. Paul R. Co., 33 Wis. 41; s. c., 14 Am. Rep. 735; Dun *v.* Seabord, etc., R. Co, 78 Va. 645; s. c., 18 Am. & Eng. R. R. Cas. 363, 49 Am. Rep. 388; Pittsburgh, etc., R. Co. *v.* McClurg, 56 Pa. St. 295; Pittsburgh, etc., R. Co. *v.* Andrews, 39 Md. 329; s. c., 17 Am. Rep. 568; Barton *v.* St. Louis, etc., R. Co., 52 Mo. 253; s. c., 14 Am. Rep. 418; Chicago, etc., R. Co. *v.* Pandram, 51 Ill. 333; s. c., 2 Am. Rep. 306; Farlow *v.* Kelley, 108 U. S. 288; s. c., 11 Am. & Eng R. R. Cas. 104; Spencer *v.* Milwaukee, etc, R. Co., 17 Wis. 503; Western, etc., R. Co. *v.* Stanley, 61 Md. 266; s. c., 18 Am. & Eng. R. R. Cas. 206; 48 Am. Rep. 96; Gee *v.* Metropolitan R. Co., L. R. 8 Q. B. 161; 5 Moak's Eng. Rep. 169; Railroad Co. *v.* Hanning, 15 Wall. (U. S.) 649; Sweeny *v.* Old Colony R. R. Co., 10 Allen, 373.

1. **And if he does, may release Carrier from Duty.** — Penn. R. Co. *v.* Langdon, 92 Pa. St. 21; s. c., 1 Am. & Eng. R. R. Cas. 87; 37 Am. Rep. 651; Kentucky Cent. R. Co. *v.* Thomas, 79 Ky. 160; s. c., 1 Am. & Eng. R. R. Cas. 79; 42 Am. Rep. 208; Houston, etc., R. Co. *v.* Clemmans, 55 Tex. 88; s. c., 8 Am. & Eng. R. R. Cas. 396, 40 Am. Rep. 799; Higler *v.* Gilmer, 3 Mont. 90; s. c., 35 Am. Rep. 450; Railroad Co. *v.* Jones, 95 U. S. 439; Beach on Cont. Neg. 159, § 55.

2. **A Non-Contractual Special Duty.** — Kenyon *v.* Indianapolis, 1 Ind. 129; Indianapolis *v.* Gaston, 58 Ind. 224; Elkhart *v.* Ritter, 66 Ind. 136; Board of Com'rs *v.* Legg, 110 Ind. 479; Thompson *v.* Bridgewater, 7 Pick. (Mass.) 188; Jordon *v.* City of Hannibal, 87 Mo. 673; s. c., 15 Am. & Eng. Corp. Cas. 246; Plattsmouth *v.* Mitchell (Neb. 1886), 15 Am. & Eng. Corp. Cas. 233; Dooley *v.* Meriden, 44 Conn. 117; s. c., 26 Am. Rep. 433.

3. **Using Defective Highway with Knowledge of Defects.** — Reed *v.* Northfield, 13

traveller, which contributes proximately to his injury, will bar his recovery; and where his want of care is undeniable, he will be held guilty of contributory negligence as a matter of law.[1]

30. Master and Servant. — When the relation of master and servant exists, a special duty devolves upon the master to provide for the safety of his servant in many important respects.[2] In such relationship the servant assumes the risk of injury from all the ordinary dangers that necessarily accompany the employment, and from any unusual dangers incident to the employment of which he has notice before voluntarily exposing himself to them.[3]

Pick. (Mass.) 94; s. c., 23 Am. Dec. 662; Marble *v.* Worcester, 4 Gray (Mass.), 404; Frost *v.* Waltham, 12 Allen (Mass.), 86; Snow *v.* Housatonic R. Co., 8 Allen (Mass.), 450; Henry Co. Turnpike Co. *v.* Jackson, 86 Ind. 111; s. c., 44 Am. Rep. 274; Toledo, etc., R. Co. *v.* Bronnagan, 75 Ind. 490; s. c., 5 Am. & Eng. R. R. Cas. 630; Indianapolis *v.* Cook, 99 Ind. 10, 13; Estelle *v.* Lake Crystal, 27 Minn. 243; Evans *v.* Utica, 69 N. Y. 166; s. c., 25 Am. Rep. 165; Weed *v.* Ballston Spa, 76 N. Y. 329; Kenworthy *v.* Ironton, 41 Wis. 647; Griffin *v.* Auburn, 58 N. H. 121; Co. Com'rs *v.* Burgess, 61 Md. 29; Bullock *v.* New York, 99 N. Y. 654; Loewer *v.* Sedalia, 77 Mo. 431; Nare *v.* Flock, 90 Ind. 205; s. c., 46 Am. Rep. 205; Smith *v.* Lowell, 6 Allen (Mass.), 39; Hanlon *v.* Keokuk, 7 Iowa, 488; s. c., 74 Am. Dec. 276; Montgomery *v.* Wright, 72 Ala. 411; s. c., 47 Am. Rep. 422.

1. **Any Want of Ordinary Care will bar Traveller.** — Butterfield *v.* Forrester, 11 East, 60; Smith *v.* Smith, 2 Pick. (Mass.) 621; s. c., 13 Am. Dec. 464; Reed *v.* Northfield, 13 Pick. (Mass.) 94; s. c., 23 Am. Dec. 662; Hibbard *v.* Thompson, 109 Mass. 288; Johnson *v.* Whitefield, 18 Me. 286; s. c., 36 Am. Dec. 721; French *v.* Brunswick, 21 Me. 29; s. c., 38 Am. Dec. 250; Raymond *v.* Lowell, 6 Cush. (Mass.) 524; s. c., 53 Am. Dec. 57; Gerald *v.* Boston, 108 Mass. 584; Baker *v.* Portland, 58 Me. 199; s. c., 4 Am. Rep. 274; Steele *v.* Burkhardt, 104 Mass. 59; s. c., 6 Am. Rep. 191; Vicksburg *v.* Hennessy, 54 Miss. 363; s. c., 28 Am. Rep. 354; Evans *v.* Utica, 69 N. Y. 166; s. c., 25 Am. Rep. 165; King *v.* Thompson, 87 Pa. St. 365; s. c., 30 Am. Rep. 364; Bruker *v.* Covington, 69 Ind. 33; s. c., 35 Am. Rep. 202; Albion *v.* Hetrick, 90 Ind. 545; s. c., 46 Am. Rep. 230; Montgomery *v.* Wright, 72 Ala. 411; s. c., 47 Am. Rep. 739; Bloomington *v.* Perdue, 99 Ill. 329; Huntington *v.* Breen, 77 Ind. 29; Henry Co. Turnpike Co. *v.* Jackson, 86 Ind. 111; s. c., 44 Am. Rep. 274; Wilson *v.* Trafalgar, 93 Ind. 287; McLaury *v.* McGregor, 54 Iowa, 717; Munger *v.* Marshalltown, 56 Iowa, 215; s. c., 59 Iowa, 763; Parkhill *v.* Brighton, 61 Iowa, 103; Osage City *v.* Brown, 27 Kan. 74; Salina *v.* Trasper, 27 Kan. 545; Maultby *v.* Leavenworth, 28 Kan. 745; Loewer *v.* Sedalia, 77 Mo. 431; Drew *v.* Sutton, 55 Vt. 586; s. c., 45 Am. Rep. 644; Durant *v.* Palmer, 29 N. J. L. 544; Dewire *v.* Bailey, 131 Mass. 169; s. c., 41 Am. Rep. 219; Weston *v.* Railroad Co., 73 N. Y. 595; Hutchinson *v.* Collins, 90 Ill. 410; Aurora *v.* Hillman, 90 Ill. 61; Erie *v.* Magill, 101 Pa. St. 616; s. c., 47 Am. Rep. 739; Schaefler *v.* Sandusky, 33 Ohio St. 246; s. c., 31 Am. Rep. 533; Centralia *v.* Krouse, 64 Ill. 19; Parkhill *v.* Brighton, 61 Iowa, 103; Corbett *v.* Leavenworth, 27 Kan. 673; Wilson *v.* Charlestown, 8 Allen (Mass.), 137; President, etc., of Mt. Vernon *v.* Desouchett, 2 Ind. 586; s. c., 54 Am. Dec. 467; Bruker *v.* Covington, 69 Ind. 33; s. c., 35 Am. Rep. 202; King *v.* Thompson, 87 Pa. St. 365; s. c., 30 Am. Rep. 364; Indianapolis *v.* Cook, 99 Ind. 10.

2. **Master and Servant · Special Duty of Master.** — Cooley on Torts, 549–564; Wood's Law of Master and Servant (2d ed.), §§ 326–456; 3 Wood's Ry. Law, §§ 370–398; Beach on Cont. Neg. §§ 94–145; Farwell *v.* Boston, etc., R. Co., 4 Met. 49; s. c., 38 Am. Dec. 339. See also "The Criterion of Fellow-Service," an admirable article by Geo. W. Easley, Esq., 25 Am. & Eng. R. R. Cas., 513, where the duties of the master are clearly and forcibly stated.

3. **Risks assumed by Servant.** — Wood's Law of Master and Servant (2d ed.), §§ 326, 327, 352, 385; 3 Wood's Ry. Law, §§ 386, 387; Beach on Cont. Neg. §§ 139, 140; Murray *v.* So. Car. R. Co., 1 McMullan's (S. Car.), 385; s. c., 36 Am. Dec. 268 and note; Farwell *v.* Boston, etc., R. Co., 4 Met. (Mass.) 49; s. c., 38 Am. Dec. 339; Priestley *v.* Fowler, 3 M. & W. 1; Lovell *v.* Howell, 1 L. R. C. P. Div. 167; Warner *v.* Erie R. Co., 39 N. Y. 468; McDermott *v.* Pac. R. Co., 30 Mo. 115; Indianapolis, etc., R. Co. *v.* Love, 10 Ind. 556; Thayer *v.* St. Louis, etc., R. Co., 22 Ind. 26; Hayden *v.* Smithville Manuf. Co., 29 Conn. 548, 558; Skipp *v.* Eastern Counties R. Co., 9 Exch. 223; Griffiths *v.* Gidlow, 3 Hurl. &

But there is a marked distinction between assumption of the risk of injury and contributory negligence.[1] And where the servant is injured by the failure of his master to exercise ordinary care for his safety, his assumption of the risks of the employment will not prevent a recovery if he was in the use of ordinary care at the time of his injury, and was discharging his duties in a usual and ordinary manner.[2] Thus, the master is liable for an injury to a servant resulting from the master's failure to use ordinary care in any of the following respects; viz., To warn the servant of extraneous risks and unusual dangers known to the master, but unknown to the servant;[3] to instruct an immature or inexperi-

Norm. 654; Davis *v.* Detroit, etc., R. Co., 20 Mich. 105; s. c., 4 Am. Rep. 364; McGlynn *v.* Brodie, 31 Cal. 376; Huddleston *v.* Lowell Mch. Shops, 106 Mass. 282; Coombs *v.* N. B. Cordage Co., 102 Mass. 585; s. c., 3 Am. Rep. 506; Sullivan *v.* India Manuf. Co., 113 Mass. 398; Kray *v.* Chicago, etc., R. Co., 32 Iowa, 357; Buzzell *v.* Laconia, etc., Co., 48 Me. 113; Atlas Engine Works *v.* Randall, 100 Ind. 293; s. c., 50 Am. Rep. 798; Leary *v.* Boston, etc., R. Co., 139 Mass. 580; s. c., 23 Am. & Eng. R. R. Cas. 393, 52 Am. Rep. 733 and note; Rasmussan *v.* Chicago, etc., R. Co., 65 Iowa, 236; s. c., 18 Am. & Eng. R. R. Cas. 54; Rodman *v.* Mich. Cent. R. R. Co. (Mich. 1884), 17 Am. & Eng. R. R. Cas. 321; Campbell *v.* Penna. R. Co. (Penn. 1886), 24 Am. & Eng. R. R. Cas. 427 and note; Cook *v.* St. Paul, etc., R. Co., 34 Minn. 45; Columbus, etc., R. Co. *v.* Webb, 12 Ohio St. 475; Sweeny *v.* Berlin Jones, etc., Co., 101 N. Y. 520; Foley *v.* Chicago, etc., R. Co., 48 Mich. 622; s. c., 6 Am. & Eng. R. R. Cas. 161; and see cases collected in note, 25 Am. & Eng. R. R. Cas. 521; Flyn *v.* Kansas, etc., R. Co., 78 Mo. 195; s. c., 18 Am. & Eng. R. R. Cas. 18, 47 Am. Rep. 99; Bunt *v.* Sierra, etc., Co., 24 Fed. Rep. 847 and note.

1. **Assumption of the Risks not Contributory Negligence.** — Beach on Cont. Neg. 370; Louisville, etc., R. Co. *v.* Orr, 84 Ind. 50, 53; s. c, 8 Am. & Eng. R. R. Cas. 94; Flyn *v.* Kansas City, etc., R. Co., 78 Mo. 195; s. c., 18 Am. & Eng. R. R. Cas. 23, 47 Am. Rep. 99; Aldridge *v.* Mid. Blast Furn. Co., 78 Mo. 564; Callahan *v.* Warne, 40 Mo. 136; Waldhier *v.* Hannibal, etc., R. Co., 71 Mo. 519; s. c., 2 Am. & Eng. R. R. Cas. 146; Coombs *v.* New B. Cordage Co., 102 Mass. 596; Baird *v.* Railroad Co., 61 Iowa, 359; s. c., 12 Am. & Eng. R. R. Co. 75; Smith on Neg. 149, 159; Shearman & Redf. on Neg. 126, § 96; 2 Thomp. on Neg. 1147, 1148; Corey *v.* Hannibal, etc., R. Co, 86 Mo. 635; s. c., 28 Am. & Eng. R. R. Cas. 382.

2. **When Assumption of Risks does not bar Servant.** — "The rule of law which exempts the master from responsibility to the servant for injuries received from the ordinary risks of his employment, including the negligence of his fellow-servants, does not excuse the exercise of ordinary care in supplying and maintaining proper instrumentalities for the performance of the work required. One who enters the employment of another has a right to count on this duty, and is not required to assume the risks of the master's negligence in this respect" Ford *v.* Fitchburg R. Co., 110 Mass. 241; s. c., 14 Am. Rep. 598; S. P. Hough *v.* Railway Co., 100 U. S. 213; Holden *v.* Fitchburg R. Co., 129 Mass. 268; s. c., 2 Am. & Eng. R. R. Cas. 94; Booth *v.* Boston, etc., R. Co., 73 N. Y. 38; s. c., 29 Am. Rep. 79 and note; Davis *v.* Cent. Vt. R. Co., 55 Vt. 84; s. c., 11 Am. & Eng. R. R. Co., 173, 45 Am. Rep. 590; Vosburgh *v.* Lake Shore, etc., R. Co., 94 N. Y. 374; s. c., 15 Am. & Eng. R. R. Cas. 249, 46 Am. Rep. 148; Pantzar *v.* T. F. I. Mining Co., 99 N. Y. 368.

"A servant has a right, himself exercising ordinary care, to rely upon his master's care and diligence. He is not bound to watch his master as he is his fellow-servant. The rights are reciprocal: the master has his duty, as the servant has his. When the master's duty is negligently done, he it is who is guilty of a breach of duty, although he acted through the medium of an agent. . . . It is clear, upon principle, that, where the duty rests directly on the master, and he authorizes an agent or servant to perform that duty, he is bound to answer to a servant injured by the negligent performance of the duty." Indiana Car Co. *v.* Parker, 100 Ind. 182, 188 *et seq.*; Beach on Cont. Neg. 351, note 1.

3. **Extraneous Risks: Failure to warn Servant of.** — It is upon this principle that the case of Chicago, etc., R. Co. *v.* Ross, 112 U. S. 377; s. c., 17 Am. & Eng. R. R. Cas. 501, rests, and nothing more than this is decided by that case, which Mr. Beach (Cont. Neg. § 114) and others seem disposed to regard as having overturned the doctrines of Farwell *v.* Boston, etc., R.

enced servant, and warn him of dangers accompanying the work,

Co., 4 Metc. (Mass.) 49, and Bartonshill Coal Co. *v.* Reid, 3 Macq. 295, but which is not, in reality, in conflict therewith. It is one of the legal duties of the master to give his servant warning of any extraneous and unusual danger to which he may be subjected; and if he fails to use ordinary care to do so, and the servant is injured, the master is liable, because the injury did not flow from any risk assumed by the servant, but from the personal negligence of the master. Nor can the master avoid liability by making it the duty of an agent to give such warning, and then, if it is not given, say that the negligence was that of a fellow-servant. In such cases the maxim *qui facit per alium facit per se* applies as between the master and the servant entitled to the warning; and the servant or agent appointed to give the warning, no matter what his grade or rank in the general service of the master, becomes, ***for such purpose***, the *alter ego* of the master. His act is the master's act, his failure the master's failure. Indiana Car Co. *v.* Parker.

In a recent Indiana case, *Elliott, J.*, accurately and forcibly states these distinctions, saying, "The complaint of the appellee alleges that he was employed by the appellant; that while engaged in the discharge of the duties of his employment, he received an injury, and that this injury was caused by the fault and negligence of the appellant in providing unsafe and defective machinery. . . . The facts which it is necessary to consider in connection with the rules of law stated are these: The appellant is a foreign corporation, with its chief officers and agents in another State; it owned and operated a car-manufactory at Cambridge City in this State; this factory was under the general control and management of John McCrie; the wood-shop in which the appellee was injured, and where he was employed, was under the immediate control of John Higginson, as foreman.

"It is obvious that the rules of law will preclude the appellee from recovering upon the ground that the foreman, in the discharge of his duties as foreman, was guilty of negligence. While Higginson was acting merely as foreman, and not discharging a duty owing by the master to its servants, he was the fellow-servant of the appellee. The duties of his position as foreman did not make him any thing more than a co-employee with a higher rank and greater authority than the appellee; and so long as he kept within the line of his duties as foreman, he was a fellow-servant serving a common master. If the negligence which caused the injury occurred while Higginson was engaged in the performance of the duties imposed upon him as an employee in the same general line of service with the appellee, the employer is not liable, because the liability to injury from the negligence of a fellow-servant is one of the risks of the service which the servant assumes in entering upon it. The servant does not assume any risk arising from a breach of duty by the master, but does assume the risk of a breach of duty by his co-servants. It is clear that counsel's theory that the appellee is entitled to recover on the ground that the foreman was guilty of negligence in the performance of his duty as foreman, cannot be maintained; and if there is no other ground upon which the appellee can plant his right to a recovery, this appeal must be sustained.

"It is the duty of the master to provide suitable and safe machinery, reasonably well adapted to perform the work to which it is devoted, without endangering the lives or limbs of those employed to operate it. The master is not bound to use the highest care, nor to secure the latest and most improved machinery, but he is bound to use care, skill, and prudence in selecting and maintaining machinery and appliances, and for a negligent omission of this duty he is answerable to a servant injured by the omission. Umback *v.* Lake Shore, etc., R. Co., 83 Ind. 191, 193; s. c., 8 Am. & Eng. R. R. Cas. 98; Boyce *v.* Fitzpatrick, ***supra***; Lake Shore, etc., R. Co. *v.* McCormick, 74 Ind. 440; s. c., 5 Am. & Eng. R. R. Cas. 474; Lawless *v.* Connecticut River R. Co., 136 Mass. 1; 18 Am. & Eng. R. R. Cas. 96; Trask *v.* California, etc., R. Co., 63 Cal. 96; s. c., 11 Am. & Eng. R. R. Cas. 192; Payne *v.* Reese, 100 Pa. St. 301, Hough *v.* Railroad Co., 100 U. S. 213; Railroad Co. *v.* Fort, 17 Wall. (U. S.) 553; Ford *v.* Fitchburg R. R. Co., 110 Mass. 241; s. c., 14 Am. Rep. 598; Paterson *v.* Wallace, 1 Macq. 798; Corcoran *v.* Holbrook, 59 N. Y. 517; s. c., 17 Am. Rep. 369; Ellis *v.* N. Y., etc., R. Co., 95 N. Y. 546; s. c., 17 Am. & Eng. R. R. Cas. 641; Wilson *v.* Willimantic, etc., Co., 50 Conn. 433; s. c., 47 Am. Rep. 653, 655; Vosburgh *v.* Lake Shore, etc., R. Co., 94 N. Y. 374; s. c., 15 Am. & Eng. R. R. Cas. 249; 46 Am. Rep. 148; Wood's Master and Servant (2d ed.), 686; 2 Thomp. on Neg. 972; Whart. Neg. § 211.

"The duty which the master owes to the servant, is one which he cannot rid himself of by casting it upon an agent, officer, or servant employed by him. The distinction between a negligent performance of duty by an agent or servant, and the negligent omission of duty by the master himself, is but not obvious as such to one of his capacity and experience;[1]

an important one. Where the duty is one owing by the master, and he intrusts its performance to an agent, the agent's negligence is that of the master. As the master is charged with the imperative duty of providing safe and suitable appliances, this duty he must perform; and if he intrusts it to an agent, and the agent performs it in his place, the agent's act is that of the master. In authorizing an agent to perform such an act, the principal is, in legal contemplation, himself acting when the agent acts, for he who acts by an agent acts by himself. This principle does not conflict with any of the general rules we have stated, for the agent assumes, by authority, the master's place, and does what the law commands the master to do. He is for the occasion, and in the eyes of the law, the master. If it be true that the agent's act is the master's act, then it must be true that the negligence involved in the act is that of the master himself. The rule which absolves the master from liability for the negligence of the fellow-servant has no application whatever, where the agent stands in the master's place. The reason of the rule fails; and where the reason fails, so does the rule itself. The reasons which support the rule are that servants take the risks of the employments upon which they enter, and that public policy requires that fellow-servants should 'each be an observer of the conduct of the other.' Farwell *v.* Boston, etc., R. Co., 4 Met. (Mass.) 49.

"The first of these reasons completely fails when it is brought to mind that the servant does not assume the risk arising from unsafe and unsuitable machinery and appliances. The second as surely and completely fails when we affirm, as under all the authorities affirm we must, that the duty to provide safe appliances rests upon the master, and not on any servant; for, surely, servants are not bound to be observers of the master's conduct. It is, therefore, not at all difficult to clearly discriminate and broadly mark the difference between a case where it is the master's duty, as master, that is neglected, and a case where it is the fellow-servant's duty, as servant, that is negligently performed. A servant has a right, himself exercising ordinary care, to rely upon his master's care and diligence. He is not bound to watch his master as he is his fellow-servant. The rights are reciprocal — the master has his duty as the servant has his. When the master's duty is negligently done, he it is who is guilty of a breach of duty, although he acted through the medium of an agent. If the master were permitted to escape his duty by shifting it to an agent, the practical result would be his entire absolution from the duty which the law imposes. The law will not permit this result, for it will not permit a duty to be evaded, but will require performance by the person upon whom it has fixed it. A different rule from that stated would, in such a case as this, wholly relieve the master from obligation to his servants, for here the foreign corporation acted by its agents, and none of its chief officers were ever at the factory in Cambridge City. If it cannot be held responsible for the negligence of these agents in selecting, arranging, and maintaining his machinery, the result will be that it is wholly absolved from its duty to its agents and servants." Indiana Car Co. *v.* Parker, 100 Ind. 181.

The Ross Case. — And this was the doctrine of the Ross case (112 U. S. 377). In that case the plaintiff was injured while acting as engineer of a freight train on defendant's road, by a collision between such train and a gravel train. It appeared that plaintiff was not negligent, that his train was on time, and, in the absence of telegraphic orders to him, was entitled to the track. The company sent the gravel train out on the schedule time of the freight train, and then sent telegraphic orders to the engineer and conductor, but *delivered the messages to the conductor, making it his duty to convey the orders to the engineer.* This he negligently failed to do, and the collision followed. It was correctly *held*, that the conductor's negligence was that of the master, and not that of a fellow-servant. Nothing more than this was necessary to the decision of the case; and further than this, it cannot be considered authoritative, four of the nine judges having dissented There are many other cases supporting the doctrine of the text. Strohlendorf *v.* Rosenthal, 30 Wis. 674; McGowan *v.* La Platte M. & S. Co., 3 McCrary (U. S.), 393; Smith *v.* Car Works (Mich. 1886), 12 Am. & Eng. Corp. Cas. 269; Parkhurst *v.* Johnson, 50 Mich. 70; s. c., 45 Am. Rep. 28; Perry *v.* Marsh, 25 Ala. 659; Smith *v.* Oxford Iron Co., 42 N. J. L. 467; s. c., 36 Am. Rep. 535; Baltimore, etc., R. Co. *v.* Whittington, 30 Gratt. (Va) 805; Wheeler *v.* Wason Manf. Co., 135 Mass. 294; Walsh *v.* Peet Valve Co., 110 Mass. 23; Baxter *v.* Roberts, 44 Cal. 187; Spelman *v.* Fisher Iron Co, 56 Barb. (N. Y.) 151; Mo Pac. R. Co. *v.* Callbreath, cited, note, 28 Am. & Eng R. R. Cas. 556, 557; s. c., 6 Tex. Law Rev 584.

1. Master's Duty to Immature and Inexperienced Servants. — "We think it is now to provide suitable machinery, tools, and appliances to carry on the business about which the servant is engaged;[1] to inspect and

clearly settled that if a master employs a servant to do work in a dangerous place, or where the mode of doing the work is dangerous and apparent to a person of capacity and knowledge of the subject, yet if the servant employed to do work of such a dangerous character, or in a dangerous place, from youth, inexperience, ignorance, or want of general capacity, may fail to appreciate the dangers, it is a breach of duty on the part of the master to expose a servant of such character, even with his own consent, to such dangers unless he first gives him such instructions or cautions as will enable him to comprehend them, and do his work safely, with proper care on his part. . . . There are many reasons given by the courts for holding to the rule above stated, the most satisfactory of which are, (1) that the master owes a duty toward an employee who is directed to perform a dangerous and hazardous work, or to perform his work in a dangerous place, when the employee, from want of age, experience, or general capacity, does not comprehend the dangers, to point out to him the dangers incident to the employment, and thus enable him to comprehend and avoid them, and that neglect to discharge such duty is gross negligence on the part of the employer; (2) that such an employee does not assume the risk of the dangers incident to such hazardous employment, because he does not comprehend them, and the law will not, therefore, presume that he contracted to assume them." Jones *v.* Florence Mining Co., 66 Wis. 268; s. c., 57 Am. Rep. 269.

"We think the doctrine equally well settled by the authorities, that although the machinery, or that part of it complained of as especially dangerous, is visible, yet if, by reason of the youth and inexperience of the servant, he is not aware of the danger to which he is exposed in operating it, or approaching near to it, it is the duty of the master to apprise him of the danger if known to him. . . . It is not a conclusion of law, from the fact that plaintiff was aware of the existence of the set-screw, and was seventeen years old, and sprightly for one of his years, that he was aware of the risk and danger of passing over the shaft while it was in motion." Dowling *v.* Allen, 74 Mo. 13; s. c., 41 Am. Rep. 298; s. c. (second hearing), 5 West. Rep. 370.

In a leading case in Michigan, *Cooley, J.*, said, "He took an inexperienced man into a place of danger without apprising him of the risks, and without any warning that danger was to be anticipated. It is true the workmen in the business testify that they do not consider it dangerous, and probably it is not to one who fully understands it; but this man did not fully understand it, and the danger and loss of life came to him in consequence. The negligence consisted mainly in not informing him." Parkhurst *v.* Johnson, 50 Mich. 70; s. c., 45 Am. Rep. 28. And to the same effect are many other cases. Grizzle *v.* Frost, 3 Fost. & Fin. 622; Bartonshill Coal Co. *v.* Reid, 3 Macq. 266, 295; Bartonshill Coal Co. *v.* McGuire, 3 Macq. 311; Clark *v.* Holmes, 7 H. & N. 937; Railroad Co. *v.* Fort, 17 Wall. (U. S.) 553; Coombs *v.* N. B. Cordage Co., 102 Mass. 572; s. c., 3 Am. Rep. 506; s. c., 102 Mass. 595; Smith *v.* Oxford Iron Co., 13 Vroom (N. J.), 467; s. c., 36 Am. Rep. 535; Louisville, etc., R. Co. *v.* Frawley, 110 Ind. 18; s. c, 28 Am. & Eng. R. R. Cas. 308; Hill *v.* Gust, 55 Ind. 45; Sullivan *v.* India Manf. Co., 113 Mass. 396; Smith *v.* Car Works (Mich. 1886), 12 Am. & Eng. Corp. Cas. 269; Pittsburgh, etc., R. Co. *v.* Adams, 105 Ind. 151, 165; s. c., 23 Am. & Eng. R. R. Cas. 408; O'Connor *v.* Adams, 120 Mass. 427; Ryan *v.* Tarbox, 135 Mass. 207; Wheeler *v.* Wason Manf. Co., 135 Mass. 294; Allen *v.* Burlington, etc., R. Co, 57 Iowa, 623.

When Certain Doctrines do not apply. — But the doctrines of the foregoing cases cannot be properly invoked in any case where the dangers were open and obvious, and the servant, although immature or inexperienced, had sufficient capacity to fully comprehend them; nor are they applicable when the servant, although not warned by the master, has from some other source obtained full information of the danger, and is of sufficient capacity to have avoided it after it became known to him. Williams *v.* Churchill, 137 Mass. 243; s. c., 50 Am. Rep. 304; Sullivan *v.* India Manf. Co., 113 Mass. 396; Coombs *v.* N. B. Cordage Co., 102 Mass. 572 and 595; s. c., 3 Am. Rep. 506; Rock *v.* Indian Orchard Mills (Mass. 1886), 16 Am. & Eng. Corp. Cas. 114; Fones *v.* Phillips, 39 Ark. 17; s. c., 43 Am. Rep. 264; Hathaway *v.* Mich. Cent. R. Co, 51 Mich. 253; s. c., 12 Am. & Eng. R. R. Cas. 249; 47 Am. Rep. 569; Atlas Engine Works *v.* Randall, 100 Ind. 293; s. c., 50 Am. Rep. 798; McGinnis *v.* C. S. B. Co., 49 Mich. 466; s. c., 8 Am. & Eng. R. R. Cas. 135; Viets *v.* Toledo, etc., R. Co., 55 Mich. 120; s. c., 18 Am. & Eng. R. Cas. 11.

1. **Master's Duty to provide Suitable Appliances.** — In Hough *v.* Railroad Co., 100 U. S. 213, Mr. Justice Harlan, after stating the general rule that the servant assumes the natural and ordinary risks of

repair machinery, tools, and appliances;[1] to provide a safe place for the servant to do his work, the ordinary hazards of the business excepted;[2] to guard against a danger to the servant of which

his employment, but that the rule does not apply in all cases, says, "One, and perhaps the most important, of those exceptions, arises from the obligation of the master—whether a natural person or a corporate body—not to expose the servant, when conducting the master's business, to perils or hazards against which he may be guarded by proper diligence upon the part of the master. To that end the master is bound to observe all the care which prudence and the exigencies of the situation require, in providing the servant with machinery or other instrumentalities adequately safe for use by the latter. It is implied in the contract between the parties that the servant risks the dangers which ordinarily attend, or are incident to, the business in which he voluntarily engages for compensation, among which is the carelessness of those, at least in the same work or employment, with whose habits, conduct, and capacity he has, in the course of his duties, an opportunity to become acquainted, and against whose neglect or incompetency he may himself take such precautions as his inclination or judgment may suggest. But it is equally implied in the same contract that the master shall supply the physical means and agencies for the conduct of his business. It is also implied, and public policy requires, that, in selecting such means, he shall not be wanting in proper care. His negligence in that regard is not a hazard usually or necessarily attendant upon the business. Nor is it one which the servant, in legal contemplation, is presumed to risk, for the obvious reason that the servant who is to use the instrumentalities provided by the master has ordinarily no connection with their purchase, in the first instance, or with their preservation or maintenance in suitable condition after they have been supplied by the master." Hence it was held that the master must, in all cases, use ordinary care, either in person, or by his agents, to provide his servant with safe and suitable machinery and appliances, and see that he was not injured by any failure in this respect. And such is the general rule. Sioux City, etc, R. Co. v. Finlayson, 16 Neb. 578; s. c, 18 Am. & Eng. R. R. Cas. 68 and note; Booth v. Boston, etc., R. Co., 67 N. Y. 593; Probst v. Delamater, 100 N. Y. 266; Indiana Car Co. v. Parker, 100 Ind. 181; Bean v. Steam Nav. Co., 24 Fed. Rep. 124; Phila., etc, R. Co. v Keenan, 103 Pa. St. 124; Holden v. Fitchburg R. Co., 129 Mass. 268; s. c., 2 Am. & Eng. R. R. Cas 94. 37 Am. Rep. 343; Cowles v. Richmond, etc., R. Co., 84 N. Car. 309; s. c., 2 Am. & Eng. R. R. Cas. 90, 37 Am. Rep. 620; Gibson v. Pacific R. Co., 46 Mo. 163; s. c., 2 Am. Rep. 497, 2 Thomp. on Neg. 944; Penna. Co. v. Lynch, 90 Ill. 333; Chicago, etc., R. Co. v. Platt, 89 Ill. 141; Columbus, etc., R. Co. v. Troesch, 68 Ill. 545; s. c., 18 Am. Rep. 578; Chicago & N. W. R. Co. v. Taylor, 69 Ill. 461; Ft. Wayne, etc., R. Co. v. Gildersleeve, 33 Mich. 134; and see generally Wood's Master and Servant (2d ed.), § 326 *et seq.;* Patterson's Ry. Acc. Law, §§ 284, 285; Beach on Cont. Neg. § 123 and cases cited; 25 Am. & Eng. R. R. Cas. note p. 518; 5 Am. & Eng. R. R. Cas. note pp. 504-507.

1. Master's Duty to inspect and repair.—"It will not do to say that, having furnished suitable and proper machinery and appliances, the corporation can thereafter remain passive. The duty of inspection is affirmative, and must be continuously fulfilled, and positively performed. In ascertaining whether this has been done or not, the character of the business should be considered, and any thing short of this would not be ordinary care." Brown v. Chicago, etc., R. Co., 53 Iowa, 595; s. c., 36 Am. Rep. 243; Baker v. Allegheny R. Co, 95 Pa. St. 211; s. c., 8 Am. & Eng. R. R. Cas. 141, 40 Am. Rep. 634; Frazier v. Penna. Co., 38 Pa. St. 104; Warner v. Erie R. Co., 39 N. Y. 468; Fuller v. Jewett, 80 N. Y. 46; s. c., 1 Am. & Eng. R. R. Cas. 109, 36 Am. Rep. 575; Long v. Pac. R. Co., 65 Mo. 225; Spicer v. South Boston Iron Co., 138 Mass. 426; Ford v. Fitchburg R. Co., 110 Mass. 240; s. c., 14 Am. Rep. 598; Solomon R. Co. v. Jones, 30 Kan. 601; s. c., 15 Am. & Eng. R. R. Cas. 201; Johnson v. Richmond, etc., R. Co., 81 N. Car. 446; Shanny v. Androscoggin Mills, 66 Me. 420; Smoot v. Mobile, etc., R. Co., 67 Ala. 13; Toledo, etc., R. Co. v. Conroy, 68 Ill. 560; Davis v. Cent. Vt. R. Co., 55 Vt. 84; s. c., 8 Am. & Eng. R. R. Cas. 173, 45 Am. Rep. 590; Houston, etc., R. Co. v. Dunham, 49 Tex. 181; Indiana Car Co. v. Parker, 100 Ind. 181; Covey v. Hannibal, etc., R. Co, 86 Mo. 635; s. c., 28 Am. Rep. 382; Beach on Cont. Neg. § 124; Patterson's Ry. Acc. Law, §§ 286-289.

2. Master's Duty to provide Safe Place to work.—"In all cases at common law a master assumes the duty toward his servant of exercising reasonable care and diligence to provide the servant with a reasonably safe place in which to work." Atchison, etc., R. Co. v. Moore, 29 Kan. 632; s. c, 11 Am. & Eng. R. R. Cas 243;

he has been notified, and which he has promised to obviate, or assured the servant did not exist; [1] to make and promulgate proper rules and regulations for the conduct of the business about which the servant is engaged; [2] to employ and retain competent

Hannibal, etc., R. Co. v. Fox, 31 Kan. 587; s. c., 15 Am. & Eng. R. R. Cas. 325; Lake Shore, etc., R. Co. v. Lavalley, 36 Ohio St. 221; s. c., 5 Am. & Eng. R. R. Cas. 549; Moore v. Wabash, etc., R. Co., 85 Mo. 588; s. c., 21 Am. & Eng. R. R. Cas. 509; Boyd v. Graham, 5 Mo. App. 403; Ferren v. Old Colony R. Co., 9 N. E. Rep. 608; Coombs v. N. B. Cordage Co., 102 Mass. 572; s. c., 3 Am. Rep. 506; Cayzer v. Taylor, 10 Gray (Mass.), 274; s. c., 69 Am. Dec. 274; Arkarson v. Dennison, 117 Mass. 407; Benzin v. Steinway, 101 N. Y. 547; s. c., 2 Cent. Rep. 491; Stringham v. Stewart, 100 N. Y. 516; Ryan v. Fowler, 24 N. Y. 410; Beach on Cont. Neg. § 123.

1. **Master's Duty to obviate Danger of which he has Notice.** — "If the engineer, after discovering or recognizing the defective condition of the cow-catcher or pilot, had continued to use the engine without giving notice thereof to the proper officers of the company, he would, undoubtedly, have been guilty of such contributory negligence as to bar a recovery, so far as such defect was found to have been the efficient cause of the death. He would be held in that case to have himself risked the dangers which might result from the use of the engine in such defective condition. But 'there can be no doubt that where a master has expressly promised to repair a defect, the servant can recover for an injury caused thereby, within such a period of time after the promise as it would be reasonable to allow for its performance, and, as we think, for an injury suffered within any period which would not preclude all reasonable expectation that the promise might be kept.' Shearman & Redf on Neg. § 96; Conroy v. Vulcan Iron Wks., 62 Mo. 35; Patterson v. Pittsburgh, etc., R. Co., 76 Pa. St. 389; Le Clair v. the First Div. St. P., etc., R. Co., 20 Minn. 9; Brabbits v. Chicago, etc., R. Co., 38 Wis. 289. 'If the servant,' says Mr. Cooley, in his work on Torts, 559, 'having a right to abandon the service because it is dangerous, refrains from doing so in consequence of assurances that the danger shall be removed, the duty to remove the danger is manifest and imperative, and the master is not in the exercise of ordinary care unless or until he makes his assurances good. Moreover, the assurances remove all ground for the argument that the servant, by continuing the employment, engages to assume the risks.' And such seems to be the rule recognized in the English courts. Holmes v. Worthington, 2 Fos. & Fin. 533; Holmes v. Clarke, 6 H. & N. 937; Clarke v. Holmes, 7 H. & N. 937. We may add, that it was for the jury to say whether the defect in the cow-catcher or pilot was such that none but a reckless engineer, utterly careless of his safety, would have used the engine without its being removed. If, under all the circumstances, and in view of the promises to remedy the defect, the engineer was not wanting in due care in continuing to use the engine, then the company will not be excused for the omission to supply proper machinery, upon the ground of contributory negligence. That the engineer knew of the alleged defect was not, under the circumstances, and as matter of law, absolutely conclusive of want of due care on his part." Hough v. Railroad Co., 100 U. S. 213, 224, 225. See also Daley v. Schoaf, 28 Hun (N. Y.), 314 Parody v. Railroad Co., 15 Fed. Rep. 205; Clarke v. Holmes, 7 Hurl. & Norm. 937; Porter v. Hannibal, etc., R. Co., 71 Mo. 66; s. c., 2 Am. & Eng. R. R. Cas. 44; Howd v. Miss. Cent. R. Co., 50 Miss. 178; Kroy v. Chicago, etc., R. Co., 32 Iowa, 357; Galveston R. Co. v. Drew, 59 Tex. 10; s. c., 46 Am. Rep. 261; East Tenn., etc., R. Co. v. Duffield, 12 Lea (Tenn.), 63; s. c., 18 Am. & Eng. R. R. Cas. 35; 47 Am. Rep. 319; Snow v. Housatonic R. Co., 8 Allen (Mass.), 441; Huddleston v. Machine Shop, 106 Mass. 282; Mo. Furnace Co. v. Abend, 107 Ill. 44; s. c., 47 Am. Rep. 425; Greene v. Minneapolis, etc., R. Co., 31 Minn. 248; s. c., 15 Am. & Eng. R. R. Cas. 214; 47 Am. Rep. 785; Manf'g Co v. Morrissey, 40 Ohio St. 148; s. c., 48 Am. Rep 669.

2. **Master's Duty to make and promulgate Rules.** — Wood's Master and Servant (2d ed.), § 403; Vose v. Lancashire, etc., R. Co., 2 H & N. 728; Haynes v. East Tenn., etc., R. Co., 3 Coldw. (Tenn.) 222; Chicago, etc., R. Co. v. Taylor, 69 Ill. 461; s. c., 18 Am. Rep. 626; and in Lake Shore, etc., R. Co. v. Lavalley, 36 Ohio St. 221, 226; s. c., 5 Am. & Eng. R. R. Cas. 549, it is said, "It was the duty of the company to make such provision or regulations for the safety of its employees as would afford them reasonable protection from the dangers incident to the performance of their respective duties. . . . The services, therefore, required of these hands were peculiarly dangerous; and it was the duty of the company to make reasonable regulations or provision to protect them from the dan-

and trustworthy servants, and to see that he has enough such servants to safely and properly carry on the business in which the servant is engaged.[1] The obligation resting upon the master to

gers to which they were exposed from moving trains and cars, while engaged in the discharge of their duties."

1. Master's Duty to employ and retain Competent Servants. — Wood's Law of Master and Servant (2d ed.), §§ 394-396; Beach on Cont. Neg. §§ 127-129; Patterson's Ry. Acc. Law, §§ 293-297.

In a recent case the Supreme Court of the United States has considered this question very fully, and *Mr. Justice Harlan*, delivering the opinion of the court, quotes from the case of Hough *v.* Railway Co. (100 U. S. 213) these parts relating to the duty resting upon the master to provide and maintain safe machinery and appliances, and applying the principles there enunciated to the questions before the court, says, "These observations as to the degree of care to be exercised by a railroad corporation in providing and maintaining machinery for use by employees apply with equal force to the employment and retention of the employees themselves. . . . The decisions, with few exceptions not important to be mentioned, are to the effect that the corporation must exercise ordinary care. But, according to the best-considered adjudications, and upon the clearest grounds of necessity and good faith, ordinary care in the selection and retention of servants and agents implies that degree of diligence and precaution which the exigencies of the particular service reasonably require. It is such care as, in view of the consequences that may result from negligence on the part of employees, is fairly commensurate with the perils or dangers likely to be encountered. . . . That the court did not use the word "ordinary" in its charge is of no consequence, since the jury were rightly instructed as to the degree of diligence which the company was bound to exercise in the employment of telegraphic night operators. The court correctly said that that was a position of great responsibility, and, in view of the consequences which might result to employees from the carelessness of telegraphic operators, upon whose reports depended the movement of trains, the defendant was under a duty to exercise "proper and great care" to select competent persons for that branch of its service. But that there might be no misapprehension as to what was in law such care, as applicable to this case, the court proceeded, in the same connection, to say that the law presumed the exercise by the company of proper diligence, and, unless it was affirmatively shown that the incapacity of McHenry when employed, or after his employment and before the collision, *was known to it or by reasonable diligence could have been ascertained*, the plaintiff was not entitled to recover. Ordinary care, then, and the jury were, in effect, so informed, implies the exercise of reasonable diligence; and reasonable diligence implies, as between the employer and employee, such watchfulness, caution, and foresight as, under all the circumstances of the particular service, a corporation controlled by careful, prudent officers ought to exercise." Wabash R. Co. *v.* McDaniel, 107 U. S. 454; s. c., 11 Am. & Eng. R. R. Cas 158. See also A. & F. R. Co. *v.* Waller, 48 Ala. 459; Laning *v.* N. Y. Cent. R. R. Co., 49 N. Y. 521; s. c., 10 Am. Rep. 417, is one of the leading cases upon this subject, and the opinion of *Folger, J.*, is a model of judicial reasoning. Kray *v.* Chicago, etc., R Co., 32 Iowa, 357; Strahlendorf *v.* Rosenthal, 30 Wis. 674; Rohback *v.* Union Pac. R. Co., 43 Mo 187; Maxwell *v.* Hannibal, etc., R. Co., 85 Mo. 95; Brothers *v.* Cartter, 52 Mo. 373; s. c., 14 Am. Rep. 424; McDermott *v.* Railroad Co., 30 Mo. 115; Wiggett *v.* Fox, 36 Eng. L. & Eq. 486; King *v.* Boston, etc., R. Co., 9 Cush. (Mass.) 112; Caldwell *v.* Brown, 53 Pa. St. 453; Manville *v.* Cleveland, etc., R. Co., 11 Ohio St. 417; Haskin *v.* Railroad Co., 65 Barb. (N. Y.) 129; Faulkner *v.* Erie R. Co., 49 Barb. (N. Y.) 324; Thayer *v.* Railroad Co., 22 Ind. 26; Chicago, etc., R. Co. *v.* Harvey, 28 Ind. 28, Gilman *v.* East. R. Co., 10 Allen (Mass.); 233; Ill. Cent. R. Co. *v.* Jewell, 46 Ill. 99; Davis *v* Detroit, etc., R. Co., 20 Mich. 105; Harper *v.* Indianapolis, etc., R. Co., 47 Mo. 567; s. c., 4 Am. Rep 353; s. c., 44 Mo. 480; Gibson *v.* Pac. R. Co, 46 Mo. 163; Mann *v.* Delaware, etc., C. Co., 91 N. Y. 495; s. c., 12 Am. & Eng. R. R. Cas. 199; Columbus, etc., R. Co. *v.* Troesch, 68 Ill. 545; s. c., 18 Am. Rep. 578; Beaulieu *v.* Portland Co., 48 Me. 291; Brickner *v.* N. Y. Cent. R. Co., 49 N. Y. 672; Chicago, etc., R. Co. *v.* Doyle, 18 Kan. 58; Brown *v.* Maxwell, 6 Hill (N. Y.), 592, s. c., 41 Am. Dec 771; Toledo, etc., R. Co. *v.* Durkin, 76 Ill. 397; Cowles *v.* Richmond, etc, R. Co., 84 N. Car. 309; s. c, 2 Am. & Eng. R. R. Cas. 90, 37 Am. Rep. 620; Houston, etc., R. Co. *v.* Oram, 49 Tex. 341; Tyson *v.* North & South Alabama R. Co., 61 Ala. 554; s. c., 32 Am. Rep. 8; McMahon *v.* Davidson, 12 Minn. 357; Hogan *v.* Cent. Pac. R. Co., 49 Cal. 128; McDonald *v.* Hazeltine, 53 Cal. 35; Summerhays *v.* Kansas Pac. R. Co., 2 Colo. 484; Chapman *v.* Erie R. Co 55 N. Y. 579; Mentzer *v.* Armour, 18 Fed. Rep. 571; s. c., 5 McCrary use ordinary care in these respects, is personal in character, and cannot be delegated to another so as to relieve the master from liability. Hence the servant does not assume the risks of injury by reason of a negligent failure on the part of the master to perform such duties, and when injured by such failure is not guilty of contributory negligence, if he was at the time exercising ordinary care to avoid injury, and discharging his own duties in a careful and prudent manner.[1] And it is not contributory negligence for the servant to obey the orders of the master, whereby he is exposed to an unusual and unexpected danger out of the line of his employment, unless the danger was fully realized by him, and was so imminent and obvious that it was apparent to a person of ordinary prudence that an injury would follow obedience.[2]

(C. C.), 617; Delaware, etc., Canal Co. v. Carroll, 89 Pa. St. 374; Huffman v. Railroad Co., 78 Mo. 50; s. c., 17 Am. & Eng. R. R. Cas. 625; Keasey v. Kansas City, etc., R. Co., 79 Mo. 362; s. c., 17 Am. & Eng. R. R. Cas. 638; Mass. v. Railroad Co., 49 Mo. 167; Indiana Manuf. Co. v. Milican, 87 Ind. 87; Booth v. Boston, etc., R. Co., 73 N. Y. 38; s. c., 29 Am. Rep. 97; East Tenn., etc., R. Co. v. Gurley, 12 Lea (Tenn.), 46; s. c., 17 Am. & Eng. R. R. Cas. 568; Luebke v. Chicago, etc., R. Co., 59 Wis. 127; s. c., 15 Am. & Eng. R. R. Cas. 183, 48 Am. Rep. 483; Corson v. Maine, etc., R. Co., 76 Me. 244; s. c., 17 Am. & Eng. R. R. Cas. 634; Michigan, etc., R. Co. v. Dolan, 32 Mich. 510; Blake v. Maine, etc., R. Co., 70 Me. 60; s. c., 35 Am. Rep. 297; Crispin v. Babbitt, 81 N. Y. 516; s. c., 37 Am. Rep. 521; Mitchell v. Robinson, 80 Ind. 281; s. c., 41 Am. Rep. 812; Ryan v. Bagaley, 50 Mich. 179; s. c., 45 Am. Rep. 35; Wilson v. Willimantic, etc., Co., 50 Conn. 433; s. c., 47 Am. Rep. 653; Gunter v. Manuf. Co., 18 S. Car. 362; s. c., 44 Am. Rep. 573; Patterson v. Wallace, 1 Macq. H. of L. 748; Tarrant v. Webb, 18 C. B. 797; Railroad Co. v. Decker, 82 Pa. St. 119; Michigan, etc., R. Co. v. Gilbert, 46 Mich. 176; s. c., 2 Am. & Eng. R. R. Cas. 230; Ohio, etc., R. Co. v. Collarn, 73 Ind. 261; s. c., 5 Am. & Eng. R. R. Cas. 554; Pittsburgh, etc., R. Co. v. Ruby, 38 Ind. 294.

1. **Master cannot delegate these Duties, and avoid Liability.** — Hough v. Railroad Co., 100 U. S. 213; Benzing v. Steinway, 101 N. Y. 547; Stringham v. Stewart, 100 N. Y. 516; s. c., 1 Cent. Rep. 779; Flike v. Boston, etc., R. Co., 53 N. Y. 549; s. c., 13 Am. Rep. 545; Crispin v. Babbitt, 81 N. Y. 516; s. c., 37 Am. Rep. 521; Laning v. N. Y. Cent. R. Co., 49 N. Y. 521; s. c., 10 Am. Rep. 417; Brothers v. Cartter, 52 Mo. 378; s. c., 14 Am. Rep. 424; Gunter v. Manuf. Co., 18 So. Car. 262; s. c., 44 Am. Rep. 573; Indiana Car Co. v. Parker, 100 Ind. 181, and cases therein cited; Wabash R. Co. v. McDaniel, 107 U. S. 454; s. c., 11 Am. & Eng. R. R. Cas. 158; Mulvey v. R. I. Locomotive Works, 14 R. I. 204.

2. **Master exposing Servant to Unusual Dangers.** — While the servant assumes the ordinary risks of his employment, and, as a general rule, such extraordinary risks as he may knowingly and voluntarily see fit to encounter, he does not stand upon the same footing as the master as respects the matter of care in inspecting and investigating the risks to which he may be exposed. He has a right to presume that the master will do his duty in that respect; so that, when directed by proper authority to perform certain services, or to perform them in a certain place, he will ordinarily be justified in obeying orders without being chargeable with contributory negligence or with the assumption of the risks of so doing. This proposition is, however, subject to the qualification that he must not rashly and deliberately expose himself to unnecessary and unreasonable risks which he knows and appreciates. Cook v. St. Paul, etc., R. Co., 34 Minn. 45.

"It may be, as stated in Wood on Master and Servant, p. 900, that 'an order given by a foreman to do an act within the line of a servant's duty, in the execution of which an injury arises, is not such an act of authority, on the part of the foreman, as renders the master liable for the consequences;' but if the order is given to do an act at a time or under circumstances which renders the doing of the act extra-hazardous, the rule, as stated, can have no application. The principal is liable, unless to obey the order was plainly to imperil life or limb. Obedience is the primary duty of the servant, and he may, within reasonable bounds, trust to the superior judgment of the master." Stephens v. H. & St. Jos. R. Co., 86 Mo. 221; s. c., 28 Am. & Eng. R. R. Cas. 538; Chicago, etc., R. Co. v. Bayfield, 37 Mich. 205; Patterson

31. Other Relations. — There are many other relations to which the principles illustrated in the last three sections are applicable, and among them may be named innkeeper and guest, bailor and bailee, attorney and client, physician and patient, guardian and ward; and in all of them the rule is, that each party must exercise that care which a careful and prudent person so situated would exercise, and any failure to do so is a failure to use ordinary care.

32. Contributory Negligence where there is no Privity. — Where a relation of privity exists, the degree of care necessary to constitute ordinary care is higher upon the person owing affirmative duties than upon the one of whom only negative duties can be exacted; on the other hand, where no special duty is owing, either party doing a thing wrong in itself or in violation of a positive law will have to exercise greater care to avoid inflicting or receiving an injury, while a wrong-doer, than would otherwise be necessary, and the degree of carefulness necessary to constitute ordinary care is, in such cases, less for the non-wrong-doer than for the one engaged in a violation of law. These principles have already been fully illustrated.[1] But where no relation of privity exists, and neither party is guilty of any collateral wrong-doing at the time an injury occurs, the rights and duties of the parties are equal, mutual, and reciprocal, and the care which should be exercised by ordinarily careful and prudent persons so situated is all that is required of either.[2] In such cases the parties are strangers in law, having equal obligations imposed upon them to care for their own and each other's safety; and such obligations, and the

v. Pittsburgh, etc., R. Co., 76 Pa. St. 389; Flike *v.* Boston, etc., R. Co., 53 N. Y. 549; s. c., 13 Am. Rep. 545; Clayards *v.* Dettrick, 12 Q. B. 439; Keegan *v.* Kavanagh, 62 Mo. 230; Roberts *v.* Smith, 2 Hurl. & N. 213; Connolly *v.* Paillon, 41 Barb. (N. Y.) 366; Lalor *v.* Chicago, etc., R. Co., 52 Ill. 401; Mann *v.* Oriental Print Works, 11 R. I. 152; Railroad Co. *v.* Fort, 17 Wall. (U. S.) 553; East Tenn., etc., R. Co. *v.* Duffield, 12 Lea (Tenn.), 63; s. c., 18 Am. & Eng. R. R. Cas. 35, 47 Am. Rep. 319; Guthrie *v.* Louisville, etc., R. Co., 11 Lea (Tenn.), 372; s. c., 15 Am. & Eng. R. R. Cas. 209, 47 Am. Rep. 286; Broderick *v.* Detroit Union R. Station and Depot Co., 56 Mich. 261; s. c., 56 Am. Rep. 382; Hawkins *v.* Johnson, 105 Ind. 29; s. c., 55 Am. Rep. 169 and note; Haley *v.* Case, 142 Mass. 316; Beach on Cont. Neg. § 132; Wood on M. & S. (2d ed.) § 387; 2 Thomp. on Neg. 974-976. But see McDermott *v.* Hannibal, etc., R. Co., 87 Mo. 285; s. c., 28 Am. & Eng. R. R. Cas. 528; Cummings *v.* Collis, 61 Mo. 520; Williams *v.* Churchill, 137 Mass. 243; s. c., 50 Am. Rep. 304; Russell *v.* Tillotson, 140 Mass. 201; Taylor *v.* Manuf. Co., 140 Mass. 150; Leary *v.* Boston, etc., R. Co., 139 Mass. 580; s. c., 23 Am. & Eng. R. R. Cas. 383; Campbell *v.* Penna. R. Co. (Penn. 1886), 24 Am. & Eng. R. R. Cas. 427 and note.

1. **Violation of Positive Law as affecting Negligence.** — *Ante*, §§ 24 and 25; Beach on Cont. Neg. p. 189, § 62; Toledo, etc., R. Co. *v.* Grush, 67 Ill. 262; s. c., 16 Am. Rep. 618; Campbell *v.* Portland Sugar Co., 62 Me. 552; s. c., 16 Am. Rep. 503; Tobin *v.* R. Co., 59 Me. 183; s. c., 8 Am. Rep. 415; McDonald *v.* Chicago, etc., R. Co., 26 Iowa, 124; Wendell *v.* Baxter, 12 Gray (Mass.), 494; Pittsburgh *v.* Grier, 22 Pa. St. 54; s. c., 60 Am. Dec. 65; McKone *v.* Mich. Cent. R. Co., 51 Mich. 601; s. c., 47 Am. Rep. 596; Bennett *v.* Louisville, etc., R. Co., 102 U. S. 577; s. c., 1 Am. & Eng. R. R. Cas. 71; Pittsburgh, etc., R. Co. *v.* Bingham, 29 Ohio St. 364; s. c., 23 Am. Rep. 751; Sweeny *v.* Old Colony, etc., R. Co., 10 Allen (Mass.), 368; Gillis *v.* Penna. R. Co., 59 Pa. St. 129; Severy *v.* Nickerson, 120 Mass. 306; s. c., 21 Am. Rep. 514; Illinois, etc., R. Co. *v.* Godfrey, 71 Ill. 500; s. c., 22 Am. Rep. 112. See also Beach on Cont. Neg. § 17.

2. **When Rights and Duties are equal.** — Pierce on Railroads, 340; Indiana Cent. R. Co. *v.* Hudelson, 13 Ind. 325, 328.

care and duties flowing from them, vary widely according to the character of the parties, and the circumstances and conditions which surround them and control their conduct. The test of "ordinary care under the circumstances" is applied to determine when they have been negligent and when not, and it is quite unnecessary to enumerate all the special applications of the rules already laid down.[1] But their application in the concrete may be well illustrated by the doctrines relating to —

33. Contributory Negligence at Railway Crossings. — At highway crossings, a railway company is bound to exercise ordinary care to avoid injuring persons upon the crossing;[2] and the duty of persons using the crossing is to exercise the same kind of care.[3] Those who attempt to cross a railroad track at a public highway crossing, must exercise ordinary care, in view of all the surrounding circumstances, to avoid receiving an injury by collision with trains.[4] But, in the very nature of things, the standard of such

1. **The Standard of Ordinary Care varies with Circumstances.** — See 69 Am. Dec. note, p. 628; Mad River, etc., R. Co. *v.* Barber, 5 Ohio St. 541, s. c., 67 Am. Dec. 312; N. Y., etc., R. Co. *v.* Schuyler, 34 N. Y. 30, 52; Wells *v.* N. Y. Cent. R. Co., 24 N. Y. 188; Boniface *v.* Relyea, 5 Abb. Pr. N. S. (N. Y.) 268; s. c., 36 How. Pr. (N. Y.) 465.

2. **Railroad's Duty at Highway Crossings.** — Pierce on Railroads, 340–342, 346, 347, where the duty of the company is accurately and tersely stated; Patterson's Ry. Acc. Law, pp. 157–167; Beach on Cont. Neg. §§ 64, 65; Brand *v.* Schenectady, etc., R. Co., 8 Barb. (N. Y.) 368; Beers *v.* Housatonic R. Co., 19 Conn. 566; Bellefontaine R. Co. *v.* Snyder, 24 Ohio St. 670, 676; Huvett *v.* Phila., etc., R. Co., 23 Pa. St. 373; Runyon *v.* Cent. R. Co., 1 Dutch. (N. J.) 556, 558; Kennedy *v.* N. Mo. R. Co., 36 Mo. 351, Continental Improvement Co. *v.* Stead, 95 U. S. 161; Chicago, etc., R. Co. *v.* Lee, 87 Ill. 454; Harlan *v.* St. Louis, etc., R. Co., 65 Mo. 22; Stillson *v.* Hannibal, etc., R. Co., 67 Mo. 671; Wilds *v.* Hudson River, etc., R. Co., 24 N. Y. 430; 29 N. Y. 315; Warner *v.* New York Cent. R. Co., 44 N. Y. 465; Robinson *v.* West. Pac. R. Co., 48 Cal. 409; Louisville, etc., R. Co. *v.* Head, 80 Ind. 117; s. c., 4 Am. & Eng. R. R. Cas. 619; Smedis *v.* Brooklyn, etc., R. Co., 88 N. Y. 13; s. c., 8 Am. & Eng. R. R. Cas. 445; Penna. R. Co. *v.* Goodman, 62 Pa. St. 329; Black *v.* Railroad Co., 38 Iowa, 515; State *v.* Baltimore & Ohio R. Co., 24 Md. 84; Powell *v.* Mo. Pac. R. Co., 76 Mo. 80; s. c., 8 Am. & Eng. R. R. Cas. 467; Railroad Co. *v.* Ritchie, 102 Pa. St. 425; s. c., 19 Am. & Eng. R. R. Cas. 267; Louisville, etc., R. Co. *v.* Milan, 9 Lea (Tenn.), 223; s. c., 13 Am. & Eng. R. R. Cas. 507; Shaber *v.* St. Paul, etc., R. Co., 28 Minn. 103; s. c., 2 Am. & Eng. R. R. Cas. 185; Richardson *v.* N. Y., etc., R. Co., 46 N. Y. 846; Eaton *v.* Fitchburg R. Co., 129 Mass 364; s. c., 2 Am. & Eng. R. R. Cas. 183; James *v.* Great West'n R. L. R. 2 C. P. 634, note; Bilbee *v.* Railroad Co., 18 C. B. N. S. 584; s. c., 114 E. C. L.; Funston *v.* Chicago, etc., R. Co., 61 Iowa, 452; s. c., 14 Am. & Eng. R. R. Cas. 640; Nehrbas *v.* Cent. Pac. R. Co., 62 Cal. 320; s. c., 14 Am. & Eng. R. R. Cas. 670; Dimick *v.* Chicago, etc., R. Co., 80 Ill. 338; West *v.* New Jersey, etc., R. Co., 3 Vroom (N. J.), 91; Hutchinson *v.* St. Paul, etc., R. Co., 32 Minn. 398; s. c., 19 Am & Eng. R. R. Cas 280; Kissenger *v.* N. Y., etc., R. Co., 56 N. Y. 538; Savannah, etc., R. Co. *v.* Shearer, 58 Ala. 672; Kay *v.* Penna. R. Co., 65 Pa. St. 269; Ferguson *v.* Wisconsin Cent. R. Co., 63 Wis. 145; s. c., 19 Am. & Eng. R. R. Cas. 285; Howard *v.* St. Paul, etc., R. Co., 32 Minn. 214; s. c., 19 Am. & Eng. R. R. Cas. 283; Penna. R. Co. *v.* State, 61 Md. 108; s. c., 19 Am. & Eng. R. R. Cas. 326; Bohan *v.* Milwaukee, etc., R. Co., 58 Wis. 30; s. c., 15 Am. & Eng. R. R. Cas. 374; s. c., 61 Wis. 391; 19 Am. & Eng. R R. Cas. 276; Marcott *v.* Marquette, etc., R. Co., 47 Mich. 1; s. c., 4 Am. & Eng. R. R. Cas. 548; St. Louis, etc., R. Co. *v.* Matthias, 50 Ind. 65; Frick *v.* St. Louis, etc., R. Co., 75 Mo. 595; s. c., 8 Am & Eng. R. R. Cas. 280.

3. **Traveller's Duty at Railroad Crossings.** — Pierce on Railroad, 342; Reeves *v.* Delaware, etc., R. Co, 30 Pa. St. 454; s. c., 72 Am. Dec. 713; Chicago, etc., R. Co. *v.* Still, 19 Ill. 499; s. c., 71 Am. Dec. 236, and cases cited to last note.

4. **It is Ordinary Care under the Circumstances.** — "But while the road is held to this degree of care, it is equally the duty of a person crossing the track of a railroad to

care cannot be absolutely fixed.[1] Yet in some jurisdictions it is held that a failure to stop, look, and listen, before entering upon a railway track, is not merely evidence of negligence, but is negligence *per se*,[2] and, as such, will bar a recovery, unless it affirmatively appears that it did not proximately contribute to the injury.[3] And so stringent is the rule in Pennsylvania, that, when a traveller cannot otherwise determine whether a train is coming, it seems he must get out and go forward to the track before attempting to cross with his vehicle, or take the risk of being held guilty of contributory negligence.[4] But in other jurisdictions such a precaution

be on his guard, and to see that he is not incurring danger to himself and to his property. He has no right to shut his eyes and close his ears to the danger he is liable to incur at such a place; and if he does, then he must be responsible for the consequences of his carelessness." Chicago, etc., R. Co. *v.* Still, 19 Ill. 499; s. c., 71 Am. Dec. 236; Railroad Co. *v.* Houston, 95 U. S. 697, 702; Haas *v.* Grand Rapids Railroad Co., 47 Mich. 401; s. c., 8 Am. & Eng. R. R. Cas. 268; Parker *v.* Railroad Co., 86 N. C. 224; s. c., 8 Am. & Eng. R. R. Cas. 420; Continental Imp. Co. *v.* Stead, 95 U. S. 161; Baltimore, etc., R. Co. *v* Owings (Md. 1886), 28 Am. & Eng. R. R. Cas. 639.

1. The Standard cannot be absolutely fixed.—"'Ordinary care' is a term that has relation to the situation of parties and the business in which they are engaged. It is used here as synonymous with the term 'reasonable care,' as used by the courts of England. 'Care and diligence should vary according to the exigencies which require vigilance and attention, conforming in amount and degree to the particular circumstances under which they are to be exerted.'" Fletcher *v.* Boston, etc., R. Co., 1 Allen (Mass.), 9; s. c., 79 Am. Dec. 695; Holly *v.* Boston Gas Light Co. 8 Gray (Mass.), 131; s. c., 69 Am. Dec. 233; Marietta, etc., R. Co. *v.* Picksley, 24 Ohio St. 654; Cleveland, etc., R. Co. *v.* Terry, 8 Ohio St. 570; Penna. R. Co. *v.* Ogier, 35 Pa. St. 60; s. c., 78 Am. Dec. 322.

2. The "Stop, Look, and Listen" Rule.—"There never was a more important principle settled than that the fact of the failure to stop immediately before crossing a railroad track is not merely evidence of negligence for the jury, but negligence *per se*, and a question for the court." Sharswood, J., in Penna. R. Co. *v.* Beale, 73 Pa. St. 504; s. c., 13 Am. Rep. 753; North Penn. R. Co. *v.* Heileman, 49 Pa. St. 60; s. c., 1 Thomp. on Neg. 401. "It was unquestionably the decedent's duty to stop, look, and listen for approaching trains, before attempting to cross the track of defendant's road; and if he failed to observe this precaution, his failure was not merely evidence of negligence, it was negligence in itself." Penna. R. Co. *v.* Weber, 76 Pa. St. 157; s. c., 18 Am. Rep. 407; Reading, etc., R. Co. *v.* Ritchie, 102 Pa. St. 425; s. c., 19 Am. & Eng. R. R. Cas. 267; Penna. Canal Co. *v.* Bentley, 66 Pa. St. 30; Phila., etc., R. Co. *v.* Hogeland (Md. 1886), 5 Cent. Rep. 587, 589.

3. Where the Rule does not govern.—It should not be overlooked that the Pennsylvania rule that a failure to stop, look, and listen is negligence *per se*, has no application to a case where the failure to stop, look, and listen was not a proximate cause of a subsequent injury. Thus, when plaintiff drove on a crossing without stopping to look or listen, but would have crossed in safety if his horse's foot had not become fast, by reason of a defect in the crossing, and his horse and vehicle were injured several minutes later by the negligent management of a train, while he was trying to extricate the horse's foot from the crossing, it was *held*, that the failure to stop, look, and listen did not contribute to the injury, and would not bar a recovery. Baughman *v.* Shenango, etc., R. Co., 92 Pa. St. 335; s. c., 6 Am. & Eng. R. R. Cas. 51, 37 Am. Rep. 690.

But where it does not thus affirmatively appear that the failure to stop, look, and listen was not a proximate cause of the injury, it seems that in Pennsylvania and other States holding such failure negligence *per se*, it will be presumed to have contributed to the injury. Phila., etc., R. Co. *v.* Hogeland, 66 Md. 149; Reading, etc., R. Co. *v.* Ritchie, 102 Pa. St. 425; s. c., 19 Am. & Eng. R. R. Cas. 267.

4. When Traveller must lead his Horse in Pennsylvania.—"If the traveller cannot see the track by looking out, whether from fog, or other cause, he should get out, and, if necessary, lead his horse and wagon." Penna. R. Co. *v.* Beale, 73 Pa. St. 504; s. c., 13 Am. Rep. 753; Lehigh Valley, etc., R. Co. *v.* Brandtmaier, 113 Pa. St. 610; Cent. R. R. Co. *v.* Fuller, 84 Penn. St. 226; but see Penna., etc., R. Co. *v.* Ackerman, 74 Pa. St. 265.

is not necessary to constitute "ordinary care;"[1] and the general rule is, that a person about to cross a track must bear in mind the dangers attendant upon crossing, and vigilantly use his senses of sight and hearing in the endeavor to avoid injury.[2] And if the

1. **Such Precaution not required Elsewhere.** — Pittsburgh, etc., R. Co. *v.* Wright, 80 Ind. 182; s. c., 5 Am. & Eng. R. R. Cas. 628; Davis *v.* N. Y., etc., R. Co., 47 N. Y. 400; Weber *v.* N. Y., etc., R. Co., 58 N. Y. 451; s. c., 67 N. Y. 587; Duffey *v.* Chicago, etc., R. Co., 32 Wis. 269; Continental Imp. Co. *v.* Stead, 95 U. S. 161. In a late Missouri case it was expressly held that the law did not require a traveller to take such precautions as the dictum of Judge Sharswood, in the Beale case, would seem to require. Huckshold *v.* St. Louis, etc., R. Co. (Mo. 1887), 28 Am. & Eng. R. R. Cas. 659.

2. **General Rule as to Care required of Traveller.** — The best general statement of the rule is that of Mr. Pierce, who says, "A traveller upon a highway, when approaching a railroad-crossing, ought to make a vigilant use of his senses of sight and hearing, in order to avoid a collision. This precaution is dictated by common prudence. He should listen for signals, and look in the different directions from which a train may come. If by neglect of this duty he suffers injury from a passing train, he cannot recover of the company, although it may itself be chargeable with negligence, or have failed to give the signals required by statute, or be running at the time at a speed exceeding the legal rate." — Pierce on Railroads, p. 343; Steves *v.* Oswego, etc., R. Co., 18 N. Y. 422; Wilds *v.* Hudson River R. Co., 29 N. Y. 315, 24 N. Y. 430, 440; Gonzales *v.* N. Y., etc., R. Co., 38 N. Y. 440; Ernst *v.* Hudson River R. Co., 39 N. Y. 61, 35 N. Y. 9, 32 Barb. (N. Y.) 159; Wilcox *v.* Rome, etc., R. Co., 39 N. Y. 358; Beisiegel *v.* N. Y. Cent. R. Co., 40 N. Y. 9; Grippen *v.* N. Y. Cent. R. Co., 40 N. Y. 34; Baxter *v.* Troy, etc., R. Co., 41 N. Y. 502; Harty *v.* Central R. Co., 42 N. Y. 468; Warner *v.* N. Y. Cent. R. Co., 44 N. Y. 465, 469; Gorton *v.* Erie R. Co., 45 N. Y. 660; Davis *v.* N. Y. Cent., etc., R. Co., 47 N. Y. 400; Reynolds *v.* N. Y. Cent., etc., R. Co., 58 N. Y., 248, 2 Thomp. & C. (N. Y.) 644; Weber *v.* N. Y. Cent., etc., R. Co., 58 N. Y. 451, 67 N. Y. 587; McGrath *v.* N. Y. Cent., etc., R. Co., 59 N. Y. 468, 1 Hun (N. Y.), 437, 3 Thomp. & C. (N. Y.) 776; Mitchell *v.* N. Y. Cent., etc., R. Co., 64 N. Y. 655; Salter *v.* Utica, etc., R. Co., 75 N. Y. 273, 13 Hun (N. Y.), 187; Cordell *v.* N. Y. Cent., etc., R. Co., 75 N. Y. 330, 70 N. Y. 119, 64 N. Y. 535; Adolph *v.* Central Park, etc., R. Co., 76 N. Y. 530, 65 N. Y. 554; Sheffield *v.* Rochester, etc., R. Co., 21 Barb. (N. Y.) 339; Brooks *v.* Buffalo, etc., R. Co., 25 Barb. (N. Y.) 600; Dascomb *v.* Buffalo, etc., R. Co., 27 Barb. (N. Y.) 221; Havens *v.* Erie R. Co., 53 Barb. (N. Y.) 328; Haight *v.* N. Y. Cent. R. Co., 7 Lans. (N. Y.) 11. Elwood *v.* N. Y. Cent., etc., R. Co., 4 Hun (N. Y.), 808; Bunn *v.* Delaware, etc., R. Co., 6 Hun (N. Y.), 303; Sutherland *v.* N. Y. Cent. etc., R. Co., 41 N. Y. Superior, 17; Chicago, etc., R. Co. *v.* Houston, 95 U. S. 697; Graws *v.* Maine Cent. R. Co., 67 Me. 100; Butterfield *v.* Western R. Co., 10 Allen (Mass.), 532; Allyn *v.* Boston, etc., R. Co., 105 Mass. 77; Brooks *v.* Somerville, 106 Mass. 271; Blaker *v.* New Jersey Midland R. Co., 3 Stewart (N. J.), 240; Lyman *v.* Phila., etc., R. Co., 4 Houst. (Del.) 583; Morris, etc., R. Co. *v.* Haslan, 4 Vroom (N. J.), 147; Reeves *v.* Delaware, etc., R. Co., 30 Pa. St. 454, 464; North Penna. R. Co. *v.* Heileman, 49 Pa. St. 60; Penna. R. Co. *v.* Goodman, 62 Pa. St. 329; Nagle *v.* Allegheny Valley R. Co., 88 Pa. St. 35; Baltimore, etc., R. Co. *v.* Sherman, 30 Gratt. (Va.) 602, 629; Bellefontaine, etc., R. Co. *v.* Snyder, 24 Ohio St. 670, 18 Ohio St. 399; Pa. Co., etc., *v.* Rathgeb, 32 Ohio St. 66; Baltimore, etc., R. Co. *v.* Whitacre, 35 Ohio St. 627, 24 Ohio St. 642; Chicago, etc., R. Co. *v.* Still, 19 Ill. 499; Chicago, etc., R. Co. *v.* Gretzner, 46 Ill. 74, 82; Chicago, etc., R. Co. *v.* Sweeney, 52 Ill. 325; Chicago, etc., R. Co. *v.* Jacobs, 63 Ill. 178; Chicago, etc., R. Co. *v.* Bell, 70 Ill. 102; Illinois Cent. R. Co. *v.* Goddard, 72 Ill. 567; Chicago, etc., R. Co. *v.* Van Patten, 64 Ill. 510, 64 Ill. 512; Chicago, etc., R. Co. *v.* Hatch, 79 Ill. 137; Chicago, etc., R. Co. *v.* Harwood, 80 Ill. 88; Rockford, etc., R. Co. *v.* Byam, 80 Ill. 528; Chicago, etc., R. Co. *v.* Damerell, 81 Ill. 450; Illinois Cent. R. Co. *v.* Hetherington, 83 Ill. 510; Chicago, etc., R. Co. *v.* Becker, 84 Ill. 483; Lake Shore, etc., R. Co. *v.* Sunderland, 2 Bradw. (Ill.) 307; Lake Shore, etc., R. Co. *v.* Clemens, 5 Bradw. (Ill.) 77; Bellefontaine R. Co. *v.* Hunter, 33 Ind. 335; Toledo, etc., R. Co. *v.* Shuckman, 50 Ind. 42; St. Louis, etc., R. Co. *v.* Mathias, 50 Ind. 65; Pa. R. Co. *v.* Sinclair, 62 Ind. 301; Artz *v.* Chicago, etc., R. Co., 34 Iowa, 153; 38 Iowa, 293; 44 Iowa, 284; Carlin *v.* Chicago, etc., R. Co., 37 Iowa, 316; 31 Iowa, 370; Benton *v.* Central R. Co., 42 Iowa, 192; Lang *v.* Holiday Creek R. & C. M. Co., 49 Iowa, 469; Starry *v.* Dubuque, etc., R. Co., 51 Iowa, 419; Lake Shore, etc., R. Co. *v.* Miller, 25 Mich. 274, 290,

traveller looked and listened, or did all that a prudent man would have done under the circumstances, it will not be said, as matter of law, that he should have stopped;[1] nor will a failure to stop,

291; Haas v. Chicago, etc., R. Co., 41 Wis. 44; Brown v. Milwaukee, etc., R. Co., 22 Minn. 165; Salen v. Virginia, etc., R. Co., 13 Nev. 106; Bunting v. Central Pac. R. Co., 14 Nev. 351; Fletcher v. Atlantic, etc., R. Co., 64 Mo. 484; Leduke v. St. Louis, etc., R. Co., 4 Mo. App. 485; New Orleans, etc., R. Co. v. Mitchell, 52 Miss. 808; Zeigler v. North Eastern R. Co., 5 S. Car. 221, 7 S. Car. 402; South, etc., R. Co. v. Thompson, 62 Ala. 494; Flemming v. Western Pac. R. Co., 49 Cal. 253; Northern Cent. R. Co. v. State, 20 Am. & Eng. R. R. Cas. 219; Dublin, etc., R. Co. v. Slattery, L. R. 3 App. Cas. 1155; Ir. R. 8 C. L. 531; Ir. R. 10 C. L. 256; Nicholls v. Great Western R. Co., 27 Upper Canada, Q. B. 382; Daniel v. Metropolitan R. Co., 5 H. L. 45; s. c., L. R. 3 C. B. 591; State v. Maine Cent. R. Co., 76 Me. 357; s. c., 19 Am. & Eng. R. R. Cas. 312, 49 Am. Rep. 622; Phila., etc., R. Co. v. Stebbing, 62 Md. 504; s. c., 19 Am. & Eng. R. R. Cas. 36; Cleveland, etc., R. Co. v. Crawford, 24 Ohio St. 631; s. c., 15 Am. Rep. 633; Louisville, etc., R. Co. v. Goetz, 79 Ky. 442; s. c., 14 Am. & Eng. R. R. Cas. 627, 42 Am. Rep. 227; Penna. R. Co. v. Beale, 73 Penn. St. 504; s. c., 13 Am. Rep. 753; Karle v. Kansas, etc., R. Co., 55 Mo. 476; Kennedy v. North Mo. R. Co., 36 Id. 351; Whalen v. St. Louis, etc., R. Co., 60 Id. 323; Bernhardt v. Rensselaer, etc., R. Co., 1 Abb. App. Dec. (N. Y.) 131; s. c., 32 Barb. (N. Y.) 165, 18 How. Pr. (N. Y.) 427, 19 How. Pr. (N. Y.) 199; Beisegel v. N. Y., etc., R. Co., 14 Abb. Pr. (N. S.) (N. Y.) 29; s. c., 40 N. Y. 9; Eaton v. Erie R. Co., 51 N. Y. 544; Maginnis v. N. Y., etc., R. Co., 52 N. Y. 215; Central, etc., R. Co. v. Moore, 24 N. J. L. 824; Indianapolis R. Co. v. Stout, 53 Ind. 143; Mercer v. New Orleans, etc., R. Co., 23 La. Ann. 214; Continental Improvement Co. v. Stead, 95 U. S. 161; Cooley on Torts, 673; Reading, etc., R. Co. v. Ritchie, 102 Pa. St. 425; s. c., 19 Am. & Eng. R. R. Cas. 267; Gothard v. Ala. Great Southern, etc., R. Co., 67 Ala. 114; Chicago, etc., R. Co. v. Demick, 96 Ill. 42; s. c., 2 Am. & Eng. R. R. Cas. 201; Penna. R. Co. v. Rudel, 100 Ill. 603; s. c., 6 Am. & Eng. R. R. Cas. 30; Peoria, etc., R. Co. v. Clayberg, 107 Ill. 644; s. c., 15 Am. & Eng. R. R. Cas. 356; Terre Haute, etc., R. Co. v. Clark, 73 Ind. 168; s. c., 6 Am. & Eng. R. R. Cas. 84; Pittsburgh, etc., R. Co. v. Martin, 82 Ind. 476; s. c., 8 Am. & Eng. R. R. Cas. 253; Laverenz v. C. R. I., etc., R. Co., 56 Iowa, 689; s. c., 6 Am. & Eng. R. R. Cas. 274; Funston v. Chicago, etc., R. R. Co., 61 Iowa, 452; s. c., 14 Am. & Eng. R. R. Cas. 640; Wheelwright v. Boston, etc., R. Co., 135 Mass. 225; s. c., 16 Am. & Eng. R. R. Cas. 315; Johnson v. Chicago, etc., R. Co., 77 Mo. 546; I. & Galveston, etc., R. Co. v. Bracken, 59 Tex. 71; s. c., 14 Am. & Eng. R. R. Cas. 691; Galveston, etc., R. Co. v. Graves, 59 Tex. 330; Feild v. Chicago, etc., R. Co., 4 McCrary (C. C.), 593; Tully v. Fitchburg R. Co., 134 Mass. 499; s. c., 14 Am. & Eng. R. R. Cas. 682; Kelly v. Hannibal, etc., R. Co., 75 Mo. 138; s. c., 13 Am. & Eng. R. R. Cas. 638; Powell v. Mo. Pac. R. Co., 76 Mo. 80; s. c., 8 Am. & Eng. R. R. Cas. 467; Randall v. Conn., etc., R. Co., 132 Mass. 469; Schofield v. Chicago R. Co., 2 McCrary (C. C.), 268; Plummer v. Eastern R. Co., 73 Me. 591; s. c., 6 Am. & Eng. R. R. Cas. 165; Stubley v. London R. Co., L. R. 1 Exch. 13; Cliff v. Midland R. Co., 5 Q. B. 258; Telfer v. North, etc., R. Co., 30 N. J. Law, 188; State v. Manchester, etc., R. Co., 52 N. H. 528; Webb v. Portland, etc., R. Co., 57 Me. 117; McCall v. N. Y. Cent. R. Co., 54 N. Y. 642; Gillespie v. Newburgh, 54 N. Y. 468; Belton v. Baxter, 54 N. Y. 245; Wilson v. Charlestown, 8 Allen (Mass.), 138; De Armand v. New Orleans, etc., R. Co., 23 La. Ann. 264; Hanover, etc., R. Co. v. Coyle, 55 Pa. St. 396; St. Louis, etc., R. Co. v. Manly, 58 Ill. 300; Illinois, etc., R. Co. v. Baches, 55 Ill. 379; Penna. Canal Co. v. Bently, 66 Pa. St. 30; Lehigh Valley R. Co. v. Hall, 61 Pa. St. 361; Baltimore, etc., R. Co. v. Breinig, 25 Md. 378; Kelly v. Hendrie, 26 Md. 255; Brown v. Milwaukee, etc., R. Co., 22 Minn. 165; Stackus v. N. Y. & R. R. Co., 79 N. Y. 464; Chicago, etc., R. R. Co. v. McKean, 40 Ill. 218; Chicago, etc., R. Co. v. Still, 19 Ill. 499; Linfield v. Old Colony R. Co, 10 Cush. (Mass.) 562; Baughman v. Shenango, etc., R. Co., 92 Pa. St. 335; s. c., 6 Am. & Eng. R. R. Cas. 51, 37 Am. Rep. 690; Schofield v. Chicago, etc., R. Co., 114 U. S. 615; s. c., 19 Am. & Eng. R. R. Cas. 353.

1. **Not Negligence, per se, not to stop.**— "With respect to the degree of care with which a person travelling on a highway should approach a railroad crossing, the court below was right in its instruction to the jury that it is not in all cases his duty to stop and listen to ascertain if a train may be coming that his duty in that regard must depend on the circumstances of the case, of which the jury are to judge." Shaber v. St. Paul, etc., R. Co, 28 Minn. 103; s. c., 2 & Am. & Eng. R. R. Cas. 185; Garland v. Chicago, etc., R. Co., 8 Ill App. 571; Spencer v. Ill. Cent. R. Co., 29 Iowa,

look, and listen be held negligent when the circumstances were such that an observance of these precautions would have been unavailing as a guard against injury.[1] Hence a failure to stop, look, and listen is not contributory negligence *per se.*[2] Yet when

55; Dolan *v.* Canal Co., 71 N. Y. 285; Kellogg *v.* N. Y. Cent. R. Co., 79 N. Y. 72; Zimmerman *v.* Hannibal, etc., R. Co., 71 Mo. 476; s. c., 2 Am. & Eng. R. R. Cas. 191; Donohue *v.* St. Louis R. Co. (Mo. 1886), 28 Am. & Eng. R. R. Cas. 673; Petty *v.* Hannibal, etc., R. Co. (Mo. 1886), 28 Am. Eng. R. R. Cas. 618; Peart *v.* Grand Trunk R. Co., 10 Ont. App. 191; s. c., 24 Am. & Eng. R. R. Cas. 239; Maryland Cent. R. Co. *v.* Newbern, 62 Md. 391; s. c., 19 Am. & Eng. R. R. Cas. 261; Eilert *v.* Green Bay & Minn. Railroad Co., 48 Wis. 606. "The plaintiff was riding in a wagon, and did not stop his horse to listen for the cars. The defendant contends that this fact should, as matter of law, preclude the plaintiff from recovering in this action. The fact is not conclusive evidence of negligence: it was for the judgment of the jury in connection with its circumstances." Tyler *v.* N. Y., etc., R. Co., 137 Mass. 238; s. c., 19 Am. & Eng. R. R. Cas. 296. See also Patterson's Ry. Acc. Law, § 176; Terre Haute, etc., R. Co. *v.* Clark, 73 Ind. 168; s. c., 6 Am. & Eng. R. R. Cas. 84.

1. **Failure to stop, look, or listen: When not Negligent.** — "A person thus about to cross a railroad, to be free from negligence, must take such precaution as could reasonably be expected of an ordinarily prudent person under like circumstances. It is upon this reason that the requirement to look and listen is based. So far as the precaution would be useless, it is not required. Whether reasonable caution was exercised by the intestate in approaching, depended upon the nature and extent of his knowledge of facts, and his opportunity for knowledge. He was required to act like an ordinarily prudent man. A prudent man's attention may be diverted so that he will fail to look and listen, and the evidence may be such as to make it proper to leave to the jury the question whether it was negligence for him to so fail. There may be circumstances which excuse the taking of the usually necessary precaution of looking and listening. Chicago, etc., R. Co. *v.* Hedges, 105 Ind. 398, 406; s. c., 25 Am. & Eng. R. R. Cas. 550; Pittsburgh, etc., R. Co. *v.* Martin, 82 Ind. 476; s. c., 8 Am. & Eng. R. R. Cas. 253; Penna. Co. *v.* Rudel, 100 Ill. 603; s. c., 6 Am. & Eng. R. R. Cas. 30; Laverenz *v.* Chicago, etc., R. Co., 56 Iowa, 689; s. c., 6 Am. & Eng. R. R. Cas. 274; Carlin *v.* Railroad Co., 37 Iowa, 316; Benton *v.* Railroad Co., 42 Iowa, 192; Artz *v.* Railroad Co., 34 Iowa, 153; Smedis *v.* Brooklyn, etc., R. Co., 88 N. Y. 13; s. c., 8 Am. & Eng. R. R. Cas. 445; Com. *v.* Fitchburg R. Co., 10 Allen (Mass.), 189; Craig *v.* New York, etc., R. Co., 118 Mass. 431; Webb *v.* Portland, etc., R. Co., 57 Me. 117; Johnson *v.* Hudson River R. Co., 20 N. Y. 66; Continental Imp. Co. *v.* Stead, 95 U. S. 161; Penna. R. Co. *v.* Ogier, 35 Pa. St. 60; Fordham *v.* London, etc., R. Co., L. R. 3 C. P. 368; Stubley *v.* London, etc., R. Co., L. R. 1 Exch. 13; French *v.* Taunton Branch R. Co., 116 Mass. 537; Hinckley *v.* Cape Cod, etc., R. Co., 120 Mass. 257; Chicago, etc., R. Co. *v.* Garvey, 58 Ill. 83; Butler *v.* Milwaukee, etc., R. Co., 28 Wis. 487; Terry *v.* Jewett, 78 N. Y. 338.

2. **Failure to stop, look, or listen not Negligence per se.** This follows of necessity if the doctrines of the cases cited in two preceding notes are good law; and the principles laid down in them seem to be incontrovertible. Nor is this doctrine at all in conflict with the rule "That ordinary prudence requires one who enters upon so dangerous a place as a railroad-crossing to use his senses, to listen, to look, or to take some precaution for the purpose of ascertaining whether he may cross in safety." Ormsbee *v.* Boston, etc., R. Co., 14 R. I. 102; s. c, 51 Am. Rep. 354, 355, and cases cited. There is no doubt that where it appears beyond controversy that a failure to stop, look, or listen was a proximate cause of an injury, the courts will hold such failure contributory negligence, as a matter of law. Schofield *v.* Railroad Co., 114 U. S. 615; s. c., 19 Am. & Eng. R. R. Cas. 353; Hixson *v.* St. Louis, etc., R. Co., 80 Mo. 335. But this is a very different matter from holding a failure to stop, look, or listen negligence *per se* sufficient to bar a recovery. In the one line of cases it is properly held that a failure to stop, look, or listen was negligence, *as a matter of law*, upon the undisputed facts, because ordinary care required the precaution, and the failure to take it was a proximate cause of the injury that followed. In other words, there is a difference between *negligence per se*, without regard to the surrounding circumstances, and *negligence as a matter of law*, in view of all the circumstances. And it will be noticed that in most, if not all, the cases, including those in Pennsylvania, where the doctrine that it is negligence *per se* not to stop, look, and listen, is enunciated, the facts were such that the court would have been justified in holding that

the facts are undisputed, and it appears that a failure to stop, look, or listen proximately contributed to an injury which would otherwise have been avoided, such failure should be held contributory negligence as a matter of law.[1] But if the facts are disputed, or it is doubtful whether, under the circumstances, the failure to stop, look, or listen was negligence proximately contributing to the injury, the question of a failure to use ordinary care, and of the effect of a failure to stop, look, or listen, should be left to the jury.[2]

there had been contributory negligence as matter of law, because the failure to stop, look, or listen had been a proximate cause of the injury, which would have been avoided by ordinary care. See Patterson's Ry. Acc. Law, § 175.

1. **But such Failure may be Negligent as a Matter of Law.** — "Negligence of the company's employés in these particulars was no excuse for negligence on her part. She was bound to listen and look before attempting to cross the railroad track, in order to avoid an approaching train, and not to walk carelessly into the place of possible danger. Had she used her senses, she could not have failed both to hear and to see the train which was coming. If she omitted to use them, and walked thoughtlessly upon the track, she was guilty of culpable negligence, and so far contributed to her injuries as to deprive her of any right to complain of others. If, using them, she saw the train coming, and yet undertook to cross the track, instead of waiting for the train to pass, and was injured, the consequences of her mistake and temerity cannot be cast upon the defendant. No railroad company can be held for a failure of experiments of that kind. If one chooses, in such a position, to take risks, he must bear the possible consequences of failure." Chicago & Rock Island, etc., R. Co. *v.* Houston, 95 U. S. 697; Schofield *v.* Chicago, etc., R. Co., 114 U. S. 615; s. c., 19 Am. & Eng. R. R. Cas. 353; Baltimore, etc., R. Co. *v.* Hobbs (Md 1884), 19 Am. & Eng. R. R. Cas., 337; Mynning *v.* Detroit, etc., R. Co. (Mich. 1887), 28 Am. & Eng. R. R. Cas. 667; Harris *v.* Minneapolis, etc., R. Co. (Minn. 1887), 33 N. W. Rep. 12; Brown *v.* Milwaukee, etc., R. Co., 22 Minn. 165; Baltimore, etc., R. Co. *v.* Mali (Md. 1886), 28 Am. & Eng. R. R. Cas. 628; State *v.* B. & O. R. Co., 58 Md. 482; s. c., 15 Am. & Eng. R. R. Cas. 409; Hixson *v.* St. Louis, etc., R. Co., 80 Mo. 335; Zimmerman *v.* Hannibal, etc., R. Co., 71 Mo. 476; s. c., 2 Am. & Eng R. R. Cas. 191; Turner *v.* Hannibal, etc., R. Co., 74 Mo. 603; s. c., 6 Am. & Eng. R. R. Cas. 58; Henze *v.* St. Louis, etc., R. Co., 71 Mo. 636; s. c., 2 Am. & Eng. R. R. Cas. 212; Taylor *v.* Mo. Pac. R. Co., 86 Mo. 467; Terre Haute, etc., R. Co. *v.* Clark, 73 Ind. 168; s. c., 6 Am. & Eng. R. R. Cas. 84; Tolman *v.* Syracuse, etc., R. Co., 98 N. Y. 198; s. c., 23 Am. & Eng. R. R. Cas. 313; 50 Am. Rep. 649; Union Pac. R. Co. *v.* Adams, 33 Kan. 427; s. c., 19 Am. & Eng. R. R. Cas. 376; Schaefert *v.* Chicago, etc., R. Co., 62 Iowa, 624; s. c., 14 Am. & Eng. R. R. Cas. 696; Pence *v.* Chicago, etc., R. Co., 63 Iowa, 746; s. c., 19 Am. & Eng. R. R. Cas. 366; Tully *v.* Fitchburg R. Co., 134 Mass. 499; s. c., 14 Am. & Eng. R. R. Cas. 682; Kelley *v.* Hannibal, etc., R. Co., 75 Mo. 138; s. c., 13 Am. & Eng. R. R. Cas. 638; Powell *v.* Mo. Pac. R. Co, 76 Mo. 80; s. c., 8 Am. & Eng. R. R. Cas. 467; Abbett *v.* Chicago, etc., R. Co., 30 Minn. 482; Haus *v.* Grand Rapids, etc., R. Co., 47 Mich. 401; s. c., 8 Am. & Eng. R. R. Cas. 268; Kelly *v.* Penn., etc., R. Co. (Pa.), 8 Atl. Rep. 856; Merkle *v.* N. Y., etc, R. Co., 49 N. J. 473; Fox *v.* Mo. Pac. R. Co., 85 Mo. 679; Houston, etc., R. Co. *v.* Richards, 59 Tex. 373; s. c., 12 Am. & Eng. R. R. Cas. 70; Penna. Co. *v.* Movel, 40 Ohio St. 338; Rogstad *v.* St. Paul, etc., R. Co., 31 Minn. 208; s. c., 14 Am. & Eng. R. R. Cas. 648; Flemming *v.* Western Pacific R. Co, 49 Cal. 253; Cleveland, etc., R. Co. *v.* Elliott, 28 Ohio St. 340.

2. **The Question generally for the Jury.** — Thus the supreme court of Ohio say, "Again, failure to look or listen for an approaching train, though such failure may contribute to the injury, cannot, under all circumstances, be regarded as negligence. . . . When, therefore, a person about to cross a railroad track under a given state of circumstances, exercises that degree and amount of care which prudent persons usually exercise under like circumstances, he is without fault. In other words, when the circumstances are such that prudent persons would not ordinarily look or listen for an approaching train, there is no negligence in omitting to look or listen. If this be correct, it is plain, as a general rule, that whether contributory negligence existed or not, is a mixed question of law and fact; that is to say, a fact for the jury to find from such testimony as the law regards competent to prove it, and to be found in accordance with such rules as the court may give to the jury for their guidance. Cleveland, etc., R. Co. *v.* Crawford, 24

The traveller, however, is rigidly required to do all that care and prudence would dictate to avoid injury; and the greater the danger, the greater the care that must be exercised to avoid it.[1] And where, because of physical infirmities, darkness, snow, fog, the inclemency of the weather, buildings, or other obstructions and hindrances, it is more than usually difficult to see or hear, greater precautions must be taken to avoid injury than would otherwise be necessary; and, under such circumstances, there can be no excuse for a failure to adopt such reasonable precautions as would probably have prevented the injury.[2] Nor will a failure upon the part of the railway company to give warnings or take precautions required by statute, excuse a want of ordinary care, upon the part of a traveller at a highway crossing, which directly contributes to his injury.[3] But if the company be guilty of conduct that would render the statutory warnings unavailing, and a traveller be injured in consequence, when he would otherwise have escaped injury, the misconduct of the company is the sole proximate cause of the injury.[4] So a person injured upon a highway railway crossing

Ohio St. 631; s. c., 15 Am. Rep 633; Petty v Hannibal, etc., R. Co. (Mo. 1886), 28 Am. & Eng. R. R. Cas. 618; Hathaway v. East Tenn., etc., R. Co., 29 Fed. Rep. 489; Greauy v. Long Island R. Co., 101 N. Y. 419; s. c., 24 Am. & Eng. R. R. Cas. 473; Penna. R. Co v. Garvey, 108 Pa. St. 369; Drain v. St. Louis, etc., R. Co., 86 Mo. 574; Lincoln v. Gillilan, 18 Neb. 114; Johnson v. Mo. Pac. R. Co., 18 Neb. 690; Palmer v. Detroit, etc., R. Co., 56 Mich. 1; Ferguson v. Wisconsin, etc., R. Co., 63 Wis. 145; s. c., 19 Am. & Eng. R. R. Cas. 285; Orange, etc., H. R. Co. v. Ward, 47 N. J. L. 560; Leavitt v. Chicago, etc., R. Co., 64 Wis. 228; Tyler v. N. Y., etc, R. Co., 137 Mass. 238; s. c., 19 Am. & Eng. R. R. Cas. 276; Hutchinson v. St. Paul, etc., R. Co. 32 Minn. 398; s. c., 19 Am. & Eng. R. R Cas. 280; Copley v. New Haven, etc, R. Co., 136 Mass. 6; s. c., 19 Am. & Eng. R. R. Cas. 372; Scott v. Wilmington, etc., R. Co. (N. Car. 1887), 2 S. E. Rep. 151; Loucks v. Chicago, etc., R. Co., 31 Minn. 526; s. c, 19 Am. & Eng. R. R. Cas. 305; Nehrbas v. Central Pacific R. Co., 62 Cal. 320; s. c., 14 Am. & Eng R. R. Cas. 670; Funston v. Chicago, etc., R. Co., 61 Iowa, 452; s. c., 14 Am. & Eng. R. R. Cas. 640; Stackus v. N. Y. Central, etc., R. Co., 79 N. Y. 464; Detroit, etc., R. Co. v. Van Steinburg, 17 Mich. 99; Beisiegel v. N. Y., etc, R. Co., 34 N. Y. 622.

1 **The greater the Danger, the greater the Care.** — Baltimore, etc., R. Co., v. Whitacre, 35 Ohio St. 627.

2. **Unusual Difficulties require Unusual Precautions.** — Nicholson v. Erie R. Co, 41 N. Y. 525; Hanover R. Co. v. Coyle, 55 Pa. St. 396; Rothe v. Milwaukee, etc., R. Co, 21 Wis. 256; Butterfield v. Western R. Co., 10 Allen (Mass.), 532; Elkins v. Boston, etc., R. Co., 115 Mass. 190; Chicago, etc., R. Co. v. Still, 19 Ill. 499; Steves v. Oswego, etc., R. Co., 18 N. Y. 422; Ill. etc., R. Co. v. Ebert, 74 Ill. 399; Penna. R. Co. v. Werner, 89 Pa. St. 59; Roithe v. Milwaukee, etc., R. Co., 21 Wis. 258; Sheffield v. Rochester, etc., R. Co., 21 Barb. (N. Y.) 339; Penna. R. Co. v. Maryland, 61 Md. 108; s. c., 19 Am. & Eng. R. R. Cas. 326.

3. **Failure of Company to give Statutory Signals.** — Stepp v. Chicago, etc., R. Co., 85 Mo. 225; Williams v. Chicago, etc., R. Co., 64 Wis. 1; s. c., 23 Am. & Eng. R. R. Cas. 274, where it is held that although "the whistle is not blown, nor the bell rung, on the locomotive before crossing the highway, as required by statute, the railroad company is not liable for an injury resulting from a collision at such a crossing if the negligence of the person injured contributed thereto." Wabash, etc., R. Co. v. Wallace, 110 Ill. 114; s. c., 19 Am. & Eng. R. R. Cas. 359; Houston, etc., R. Co. v. Nixon, 52 Tex. 19; Cleveland & Columbus, etc., R. Co. v. Elliott, 28 Ohio St. 340; Shaw v. Jewett, 86 N. Y. 616; s. c., 6 Am. & Eng. R. R. Cas. 111; Hinckley v. Cape Cod R. Co., 120 Mass. 257.

4. **Statutory Warnings rendered Unavailing.** — "It is negligence in a railroad company to run trains so near together at a highway crossing as to make the statutory signals unavailing to warn travellers on the highway;" and where an injury follows, that would probably have been avoided had not the train been so run, — that is, when it appears that the plaintiff exercised such care

can recover, in spite of his own negligence, if the injury was inflicted upon him wilfully.[1] And notwithstanding negligence upon the part of the person injured, he may recover if the railway company, after such negligence occurred, could, by the exercise of ordinary care, have discovered it in time to have avoided inflicting the injury.[2] So if a railway company, by its servants, invites or directs a traveller to cross, he has a right to presume that the company's agent knows what the company's conduct will be, and is not guilty of contributory negligence in obeying, even though a train be approaching.[3] Yet this presumption will not avail him when it would have been apparent to an ordinarily prudent man that an injury would certainly follow an attempt to cross;[4] and if, with full knowledge of the near approach of a train, a traveller attempts to cross in advance of it, and merely miscalculates his ability to do so in safety, there can be no recovery for a resulting injury.[5] But there are cases where it is not negligence, as a matter of law, to attempt to cross in front of an advancing train.[6]

as could have avoided the injury, had the signals availed to warn him of danger, — a recovery may be sustained. Chicago, etc., R. Co. *v.* Boggs, 101 Ind. 522; s. c., 23 Am. & Eng. R. R. Cas. 282, 51 Am. Rep. 761. See also N. Y., etc., R. Co. *v.* Randel, 47 N. J. L. 144; s. c., 23 Am. & Eng. R. R. Cas. 308; Shaber *v.* St. Paul, etc., R. Co., 28 Minn. 103; s. c., 2 Am. & Eng. R. R. Cas. 185; Leonard *v.* N. Y., etc., R. Co., 42 N. Y. Super. Ct. 225; Powell *v.* N. Y., etc., R. Co., 22 Hun (N. Y.), 56; Beisiegel *v.* N. Y. Cent. R. Co., 34 N. Y. 622; Casey *v.* N. Y., etc., R. Co., 78 N. Y. 518; N. J., etc., R. Co. *v.* West, 32 N. J. L. 91. See Penna. R. Co. *v.* Fortney, 90 Pa. St. 323; s. c., 1 Am. & Eng. R. R. Cas. 128.

1. **Injury wilful.** — Terre Haute, etc., R. Co. *v.* Graham, 95 Ind. 286; s. c., 12 Am. & Eng. R. R. Cas. 77; Carter *v.* Louisville, etc, R. Co., 98 Ind. 552; s. c., 22 Am. & Eng. R. R. Cas. 360; Louisville, etc., R. Co. *v.* Schmidt, 106 Ind. 73; Penna. R. Co. *v.* Sinclair, 62 Ind. 301.

2. **Plaintiff's Negligence remote.** — "Counsel indulge in a criticism of the cases in which this court has held that, if negligence of the defendant which contributed directly to cause the injury occurred after the danger in which the injured party had placed himself by his own negligence, was or by the exercise of reasonable care might have been discovered by the defendant in time to have averted the injury, then the defendant is liable, however gross the negligence of the injured party may have been in placing himself in such a position of danger. Such is the well-established doctrine of this court." Donohue *v.* St. Louis, etc, R. Co. (Mo. 1886), 28 Am. & Eng. R. R. Cas. 673; Werner *v.* Citizen's R. Co., 81 Mo. 374; Kelly *v.* Hannibal, etc., R. Co., 75 Mo. 138; s. c., 13 Am. & Eng. R. R. Cas. 638; Frick *v.* St. Louis, etc., R. Co., 75 Mo. 595; s. c., 8 Am. & Eng. R. R. Cas. 280; Keim *v.* Union R. (Mo. 1887), 2 S. W. Rep. 427; Little Rock, etc., R. Co. *v.* Cavanesty (Ark. 1886), 2 S. W. Rep. 505; St. Louis, etc., R. Co. *v.* Monday (Ark. 1887), 4 S. W. Rep. 782; Maher *v.* Atlantic, etc., R. Co, 64 Mo. 267; Harlan *v.* St. Louis, etc., R. Co., 65 Mo. 22; Adams *v.* Hannibal, etc., R. Co., 74 Mo. 553; s. c., 7 Am. & Eng. R. R. Cas. 414; Morris *v.* Chicago, etc., R. Co., 45 Iowa, 29; Chicago, etc., R. Co. *v.* Hogarth, 38 Ill. 370.

3. **Invitation to Cross.** — Sweeney *v.* Old Colony R. Co., 10 Allen (Mass.), 368; Peck *v.* Michigan, etc., R. Co. (Mich. 1885), 19 Am. & Eng. R. R. Cas. 257; Phila., etc., R. Co. *v.* Killips, 88 Pa. St. 405; Wheelock *v.* Boston, etc., R. Co., 195 Mass. 203; Ernst *v.* Hudson River R. Co., 35 N. Y. 9; s. c., 39 N. Y. 61; Dolan *v.* Delaware, etc., Co., 71 N. Y. 285; Sharpe *v.* Glushing, 96 N. Y. 676; s. c., 19 Am. & Eng. R. R. Cas. 372; Bayley *v.* Eastern R. Co., 125 Mass. 62; Borst *v.* Lake Shore, etc., R. Co, 4 Hun (N. Y.), 346.

4. Chicago, etc., R. Co. *v.* Spring, 13 Ill. (app.) 174.

5. **Crossing in Front of Approaching Train.** — Bellefontaine R. Co. *v.* Hunter, 33 Ind. 335; s. c., 5 Am. Rep. 201; Chicago, etc., R. Co. *v.* Fears, 53 Ill. 115; Schwartz *v.* Hudson River, etc., R. Co., 4 Robt. (N. Y.) 347.

6. **It is not always Negligent to do so.** — Detroit & Milwaukee, etc., R. Co. *v.* Van Steinburg, 17 Mich. 99; Langhoff *v.* Milwaukee, etc., R. Co., 19 Wis. 489; Aaron *v.* Second Ave. R. Co., 2 Daley (N. Y.), 127; Baxter *v.* Second Ave. R. Co., 30 Howard's Pr. (N. Y.) 219; s. c., 3 Robt. (N. Y.) 510.

It has been held that negligence upon the part of the person injured will be presumed from the mere fact of injury at a railway crossing;[1] and it has been held, that, in the absence of evidence of his negligence, the presumption that the injured person exercised care will prevail.[2] This conflict seems to arise from the different rules prevailing as to the burden of proof being upon plaintiff or defendant in cases where contributory negligence is an issue.[3] But the true rule is, that there is no presumption either

1. **Presumption of Negligence.** — In a recent case in Indiana this doctrine was carried to the extent of holding that where a person was killed upon a railway crossing, and it was not affirmatively shown that he had been free from negligence, the presumption would be, that he had been guilty of contributory negligence, and consequently that no recovery could be had, even though there was evidence of negligence upon the part of the railroad company, and no evidence of negligence on the part of the deceased. In the course of the opinion *Mitchell, J.*, said, "It will not do to say, however, as the instruction in effect does, that if the plaintiff can show the defendant's negligence and his injury, he may leave his own conduct to conjecture, and recover. He must show the facts, — as well those which relate to his share in the transaction as those which relate to the defendant's; and if, upon the whole case, an inference of negligence arises against the defendant, and of due care on his part, he may recover. The fact that a person travelling on a highway comes in collision with a train on a railway crossing, is of itself sufficient to suggest a presumption of contributory negligence against him in a suit for compensation." And in accordance with this doctrine an instruction was held erroneous that stated the law to be, that if negligence of the defendant was proved, and no contributory negligence, or ground for inferring it, shown by the evidence, that plaintiff had sufficiently shown the deceased free from fault, and that "in the absence of circumstances to show or suggest it, there is no presumption of contributory negligence." Ind., etc., R. Co. *v.* Greene, 106 Ind. 279; s. c., 25 Am. & Eng. R. R. Cas. 322, 55 Am. Rep. 736.

So it has been held in Maine: "In an action for the death of a traveller on a highway at a railway crossing, there is no presumption that he used due care, and evidence as to his character and habits of carefulness is incompetent." Chase *v.* Maine, etc., R. Co., 77 Me. 62; s. c., 19 Am. & Eng. R. R. Cas. 356, 52 Am. Rep. 744; State *v.* Maine, etc., R. Co., 76 Me. 357; s. c., 19 Am. & Eng. R. R. Cas. 312, 49 Am. Rep. 622.

2. **Presumption of Due Care.** — Thus, in Pennsylvania, where the "Stop, look, and listen," doctrine is applied most rigidly, it is held that it is not incumbent on the plaintiff to show affirmatively that the decedent, killed upon a railway crossing, stopped, looked, and listened, before attempting to cross the track. In a recent case of this character, the Supreme Court of Pennsylvania says, "The common-law presumption is that every one does his duty, until the contrary is proved; and in the absence of all evidence on the subject, the presumption is, that the decedent observed the precautions which the law prescribed. In the case at bar no witness was called who saw the occurrence; there is no evidence whatever, whether, in fact, the decedent did stop and look and listen; the presumption is that he did; proof of that fact was no part of plaintiff's case. The presumption is of fact merely, and may be rebutted; but we are without evidence on the subject. All that we have is, that, as he came upon the railroad, he was struck down by the locomotive." And it was held that a recovery could be sustained. Schum *v.* Penna., etc., R. Co., 107 Pa. St 8; s. c., 52 Am. Rep. 468; Penna., etc., R. Co. *v.* Weber, 76 Pa. St. 157; s. c., 18 Am. Rep. 407. See also Buesching *v.* Gas Co., 73 Mo. 219; s. c., 39 Am. Rep. 503; Petty *v.* Hannibal, etc., R. Co. (Mo. 1886), 28 Am. & Eng. R. R. Cas. 618, 626.

And it has been held that a jury may infer due care, and the absence of contributory negligence, on the part of a deceased person, from the general and well-known disposition of mankind to take care of themselves, and keep out of danger. Northern Cent. R. Co. *v.* State, 31 Md. 357; Johnson *v.* Hudson River R. Co., 20 N. Y. 65; Gay *v.* Winter, 34 Cal. 153; Lehigh Valley R. Co. *v.* Hall, 61 Pa. St. 361.

3. **Whence this Conflict.** — Buesching *v.* Gas Co., 73 Mo. 219; s. c., 39 Am. Rep. 503; Petty *v.* Hannibal, etc., R. Co. (Mo. 1886), 28 Am. & Eng. R. R. Cas. 618, 626; Indiana, etc., R. Co. *v.* Greene, 106 Ind. 279; s. c., 23 Am. & Eng. R. R. Cas. 322, 55 Am. Rep. 736; Little Rock, etc., R. Co. *v.* Ubanks (Ark.), 3 S. W. Rep. 808; Cincinnati, etc., R. Co. *v.* Butler, 103 Ind. 31; s. c., 23 Am. & Eng. R. R. Cas. 262. And

way; and when negligence on the part of the railway company sufficient to account for the injury has been shown, and there is no evidence of contributory fault, the burden of the issue should shift, and plaintiff be entitled to recover, unless contributory negligence be affirmatively proved, the principle being that a sufficient cause having been shown, and no intervening efficient cause appearing, the negligence of the company should be held the sole proximate cause of the injury.[1] As the mere fact of the injury

see Glasscock *v.* Central Pacific R. Co. (Cal. 1887), 14 Pacific Rep. 518, and note on the various branches of this subject.

1. **The True Rule: No Presumption Either Way.**—"In cases where such issues are made, the question of contributory negligence on the part of plaintiff or his intestate, and of negligence on the part of defendant, causing the injury complained of, should be considered and determined upon the same principles and by the same rules exactly. *There is no presumption of negligence as against either party, except such as arises upon the facts proved. Indeed, the presumption of law is, that neither party was guilty of negligence; and such presumption must prevail until overcome by proof.*" Cleveland, etc., R. Co. *v.* Crawford, 24 Ohio St. 631; s. c., 15 Am. Rep. 633.

"But it is urged that, inasmuch as no witness testifies that the intestate looked to see, or listened to hear, if defendant's train was approaching, it must be assumed that he did not, and that such omission was negligence on his part. We know of no such rule. While it is true that a traveller, on approaching a railroad crossing, is bound to look and listen for an approaching train before undertaking to cross, it is only where it appears from the evidence that he might have seen had he looked, or might have heard had he listened, that the jury is authorized to find that he did not look, or did not listen.' Smedis *v.* Brooklyn, etc., R. Co., 88 N. Y.; s. c., 8 Am. & Eng. R. R. Cas. 445.

"When the plaintiff shows negligence on the part of defendant, and there is nothing to imply that the plaintiff brought on the injury by his own negligence, then the burden of proof is on the defendant to show that plaintiff was guilty of negligence." Cassidy *v.* Angell, 12 R. I. 447; s. c., 34 Am. Rep. 690.

"While those on the highway when about crossing a railroad track, must exercise proper diligence and care with reference to their own safety, where there is an absence of evidence as to the care exercised by the party injured, as in this case, it is not to be presumed that the deceased recklessly and carelessly imperilled his own life, or entered upon the track of the railroad knowing of the train's approach." Louisville, etc., R. Co. *v.* Goetz, 79 Ky. 442; s. c., 14 Am. & Eng. R. R. Cas. 627, 42 Am. Rep. 227.

So the doctrine of the text, that when an efficient, adequate cause appears, it must be held the sole proximate cause in the absence of evidence or any other, is easily supported. Thus, "An efficient, adequate cause being found must be deemed the true cause, unless some other cause, not incidental to it, but independent of it, is shown to have intervened between it and the result." Adams *v.* Young, 44 Ohio St. 80; s. c., 58 Am. Rep. 789; Kellogg *v.* Chicago, etc., R. Co., 26 Wis. 223; s. c., 7 Am. Rep. 69.

In Milwaukee, etc., R. Co. *v.* Kellogg, 94 U. S. 469, it was said, "Where there is no intermediate, efficient cause, the original wrong must be considered as reaching to effect and proximate to it. In such cases it is necessary to determine the proximate cause of the injury or death; and defendant's negligence once established, and no other proximate cause being shown, such negligence should be held the sole proximate cause." Ins. Co. *v.* Tweed, 7 Wall. (U. S.) 44; Scheffer *v.* Washington, etc., R. Co., 105 U. S. 251; s. c., 8 Am. & Eng. R. R. Cas. 61. See also Cooley on Torts, 664; Penna. Co. *v.* Marshall, 119 Ill. 399; Gulf, etc., R. Co. *v.* Rediker (Tex. 1886), 2 S. W. Rep. 513; Gugenheim *v.* Lake Shore, etc., R. Co. (Mich. 1887), 9 Western Rep. 906; s. c., 33 N. W. Rep. 161; s. c. (first trial), 57 Mich. 488.

In a recent Illinois case the doctrine stated in the text seems to have been directly declared. It was there held that at the conclusion of plaintiff's evidence it would have been proper to have non-suited the plaintiff, *because no evidence had been given of negligence upon the part of the defendant, but that when it appeared from the evidence given for defendant that it had been guilty of negligence, a recovery could be sustained without direct proof that the deceased was free from fault.* Chicago, etc., R. Co. *v.* Carey, 115 Ill. 115; s. c., 2 West Rep. 73; Raymond *v.* Burlington, etc., R. Co., 65 Iowa, 152; s. c., 18 Am. & Eng. R. R. Cas. 217; Phila., etc., R. Co. *v.* Boyer, 97 Pa. St. 91; s. c., 2 Am. & Eng. R. R. Cas. 172; Savannah, etc., R. Co. *v.* Barber, 71 Ga.

raises no presumption that the railway company was negligent, it certainly should not raise one that the injured person was.[1] The rules here laid down, like most other doctrines of the law of negligence, are founded upon the care to be expected of a careful and prudent man under such circumstances, and, in accord with principles already stated, they are somewhat modified in their application to children of tender years; or, rather, the railway company is charged with notice of the fact that children, as well as adults, may be upon the highway, and must exercise greater care to avoid injuring them than an adult is entitled to demand.[2]

34. Intoxication as an Element of Contributory Negligence. — The fact that a person when injured was intoxicated, does not constitute contributory negligence *per se*,[3] but it is a circumstance that

644; Phila., etc., R. Co. *v.* Stebbing, 62 Md. 504; s. c., 19 Am. & Eng. R. R. Cas. 36; Jones *v.* N. Y. Cent., etc., R. Co., 28 Hun (N. Y.), 364; Smedis *v.* Brooklyn, etc., R. Co., 23 Hun (N. Y.), 279.

"If the plaintiff's evidence shows an injury by defendant's negligence, and does not raise the implication that his own contributed, the burden of proof of such contributory negligence as will defeat the recovery, rests upon the defendant." Baltimore, etc., R. Co. *v.* Whitacre, 35 Ohio St. 627, 630; Ill., etc., R. Co. *v.* Cragin, 71 Ill. 177; Penna. R. Co. *v.* Goodman, 62 Pa. St. 239.

It may be thought that these principles are only applicable in jurisdictions where the burden of proof of contributory negligence is upon the defendant, but a little reflection will show that this is not true. Even where the burden of proving freedom from contributory negligence is on the plaintiff, it is quite sufficient, on principle, to show that the defendant's negligence was adequate to have caused the injury, and that there is no evidence of any other sufficient cause — that is, no evidence of fault on the plaintiff's part, or that of the deceased. In such case the law must ascribe the injury to the only cause found.

1. **Why No Presumption should arise.** — "Indeed, the presumption of law is that neither party was guilty of negligence, and such presumption must prevail until overcome by proof. As a general rule, the existence of negligence, on either side, is a fact to be ascertained by the jury under proper instructions from the court." Cleveland, etc., R. Co. *v.* Crawford, 24 Ohio St. 631; s. c., 15 Am. Rep. 633; Savannah, etc., R. Co. *v.* Geiger, 21 Fla. 669; s. c., 29 Am. & Eng. R. R. Cas. 274, 58 Am. Rep. 697.

"In actions for injury by negligence, where there is nothing in plaintiff's evidence tending to show contributory negligence, the presumption will be that there is no contributory negligence, and this presumption remains until the contrary is shown." Pittsburgh, Cincinnati, etc., R. Co. *v.* Fleming, 30 Ohio St. 480, 485.

2. **Modification of Doctrine when Persons non sui juris.** — "Contributory Negligence of Children," *ante*, § 22. It is held that more care is required towards children of tender years at crossings than toward adults. Thurber *v.* Harlem, etc., R. Co., 60 N. Y. 326; O'Mara *v.* Hudson River R. Co., 38 N. Y. 445; McGovern *v.* N. Y., etc., R. Co., 67 N. Y. 421; Elkins *v.* Boston, etc., R. Co., 115 Mass. 190; Chicago, etc., R. Co. *v.* Becker, 84 Ill. 483; Costello *v.* Syracuse, etc., R. Co., 6 Barb. (N. Y.) 92; Haas *v.* Chicago, etc., R. Co., 41 Wis. 44; Paducah, etc., R. Co. *v.* Hoche, 12 Bush (Ky.), 41; Boland *v.* Missouri, etc., R. Co., 36 Mo. 484; Isabel *v.* Hannibal, etc., R. Co., 60 Mo. 475; Chicago, etc, R. Co. *v.* Murray, 71 Ill. 601; Johnson *v.* Chicago, etc., R. Co., 49 Wis. 529; s. c., 1 Am. & Eng. R. R. Cas., and note collecting many cases on this and related topics; Mobile, etc., R. Co. *v.* Crenshaw, 65 Ala. 567; s. c., 8 Am. & Eng. R. R. Cas. 340; Schwier *v.* N. Y. Cent. R. Co., 90 N. Y. 558; s. c., 14 Am. & Eng. R. R. Cas. 656; Wendall *v.* N. Y. Cent. R. Co., 91 N. Y. 420; s. c., 14 Am. & Eng. R. R. Cas. 663; Nehrbras *v.* Cent. Pac. R. Co., 62 Cal. 320; s. c., 14 Am. & Eng. R. R. Cas. 670.

3. **Intoxication not Negligence per se.** — Lower *v.* Sedalia, 77 Mo. 431; s. c., 2 Am. & Eng. Corp. Cas. 658; 2 Thomp. on Neg. 1174, § 22; 2 Thomp. on Neg. 1203, § 50; Stuart *v.* Machias Port, 48 Me. 477; Weymire *v.* Wolf, 52 Iowa, 533; Salina *v.* Trosper, 27 Kan. 545; Alger *v.* Lowell, 3 Allen (Mass.), 403; Robinson *v.* Pioche, 5 Cal. 460; Ditchett *v.* Spuytendyval, etc., R. Co., 5 Hun (N. Y.), 165; Thorpe *v.* Brookfield, 36 Conn. 320; Shearman & Redf. on Neg. § 487; Beach on Cont. Neg. § 66 and 146; Houston, etc., R. Co. *v.* Reason, 61 Tex. 613; Fitzgerald *v.* Weston, 52 Wis. 354; Baker *v.* Portland, 58 Me. 199; s. c., 4 Am. Rep. 274.

may be considered as bearing upon the question of due care,[1] and if the intoxication actually contributed to the injury, the plaintiff cannot recover.[2] The principle is, that a person cannot voluntarily incapacitate himself from the ability to exercise ordinary care, and then recover for an injury to which a want of ordinary care upon his part while so intoxicated proximately contributes.[3] Therefore the ordinary care required of an intoxicated person is the same care which would be required from a sober person;[4] but if defendant knew of plaintiff's intoxication before the injury, then defendant would be required to exercise greater care to avoid inflicting an injury upon him than if he were sober.[5]

35. Blindness and Deafness.—That a person blind or deaf is injured in a public and dangerous place, where sight and hearing

1. **But it may be Evidence of Negligence.**—Yarnall *v.* St. Louis, etc., R. Co., 75 Mo. 575; s. c., 10 Am. & Eng. R. R. Cas. 726; Baltimore, etc., R. Co. *v.* Boteler, 38 Md. 568; Healey *v.* N. Y., 3 Hun (N. Y.), 708; Cramer *v.* Burlington, 42 Iowa, 315; Burns *v.* Elba, 32 Wis. 605; Aurora *v.* Hillman, 90 Ill. 61; S. W. R. Co. *v.* Handherson, 61 Ga. 114; Marquette, etc., R. Co. *v.* Hanford's Adm'r, 39 Mich. 537; O'Keefe *v.* Chicago, etc., R. Co., 32 Iowa, 467; Wallace *v.* St. Louis, etc., R. Co., 74 Mo. 549; Button *v.* Hudson River R. Co., 18 N. Y. 248.

2. **If a Proximate Cause of Injury is a Bar.**—McClelland *v.* Louisville, etc., R. Co., 94 Ind. 276; s. c., 18 Am. & Eng. R. R. Cas. 260; Houston, etc., R. Co. *v.* Reason, 61 Tex. 613; Lower *v.* Sedalia, 77 Mo. 431; s. c., 2 Am. & Eng. Cor. Cas. 658; Ill. Cent. R. Co. *v.* Cragan, 71 Ill. 177; Little Rock, etc., R. Co. *v.* Parkhurst, 36 Ark. 371; s. c., 5 Am. & Eng. R. R. Cas. 535; Cassiday *v.* Stockbridge, 21 Vt. 391; Bradley *v.* Second Ave. R. Co., 8 Daly (N. Y.), 289; Davis *v.* Oregon, etc., R. Co., 8 Oregon, 172; Wood *v.* Andes, 18 N. Y. 543; McGuire *v.* Middlesex R. Co., 115 Mass. 239; Meyer *v.* Pacific R. Co, 40 Mo. 151.

3. **Voluntary Incapacity no Excuse.**—This doctrine is plainly deducible from the cases cited: and see Railroad Co. *v.* Valleley, 32 Ohio St. 345; s. c., 30 Am. Rep. 601; Thorp *v.* Brookfield, 36 Conn. 320; Toledo, etc., R. Co. *v.* Riley, 47 Ill. 514.

4. **Standard of "Ordinary Care" governs.**—"It was the duty of the plaintiff to use every care and precaution to avoid falling from said bridge that a sober man of ordinary prudence would have used under the circumstance; and if he failed to use such care and precaution, and such failure contributed directly to causing his injuries, he cannot recover." Lower *v.* Sedalia, 77 Mo. 431; s. c., 2 Am. & Eng. Cor. Cas. 658; Kean *v.* Baltimore, etc., R. Co., 61 Md. 154; s. c., 19 Am. & Eng. R. R. Cas. 321; Toledo, etc., R. Co. *v.* Riley, 74 Ill. 70; Chicago, etc., R. Co. *v.* Bell, 70 Ill. 102; Chicago City R. Co. *v.* Lewis, 5 Bradw. app. (Ill.) 242.

5. **But not if Defendant had Notice.**—"Preventive remedies must therefore always be proportioned to the case in its peculiar circumstances, imminency of the danger, the evil to be avoided, and the means at hand to avoid it. And herein is no novel or strange doctrine of the law. It is as old as the moral law itself, and is laid down in the earliest books on jurisprudence. . . . An intoxicated man is lying on the travelled part of a highway helpless, if not unconscious: must I not use care to avoid him? May I say he has no right to encumber the highway, and therefore carelessly continue my progress regardless of the consequences; or if such a man has taken refuge in a field of grass or a hedge of bushes, may the owner of the field, knowing the fact, continue to mow on or fell trees as if it were not so? Or if the intoxicated man has entered a private lane or byway, and will be run over if the owner does not stop his team which is passing through it, must he not stop them? It must be so that an unnecessary injury negligently inflicted in these and kindred cases is wrong, and therefore unlawful." Isbell *v.* N. Y., etc., R. Co., 27 Conn. 393; s. c., 71 Am. Dec. 78; Louisville, etc., R. Co. *v.* Sullivan, 81 Ky. 624; s. c., 16 Am. & Eng. R. R. cas. 390, 50 Am. Rep. 186; Weymire *v.* Wolfe, 52 Iowa, 533; St. Louis, etc., R. Co. *v.* Wilkinson, 46 Ark. 513; Kean *v.* Baltimore, etc, R. Co., 61 Md. 154; s. c., 19 Am. & Eng. R. R. Cas. 321; Houston, etc., R. Co. *v.* Simkins, 54 Tex. 615; s. c., 6 Am. & Eng. R. R. Cas. 11; Dinwiddie, adm'r, *v.* Louisville, etc., R. Co., 9 Lea (Tenn.), 309; s. c., 15 Am. & Eng. R. R. Cas. 483; Gill *v.* Rochester, etc., R. Co., 37 Hun (N. Y.), 107; Telfer *v.* Northern R. Co., 30 N. J. L. 188; Schieshold *v.* Railroad Co., 40 Cal. 447.

are ordinarily required, does not establish contributory negligence as a matter of law, but the blindness or deafness may be considered upon the question of due care, and as an evidence of contributory negligence; and if it appears that the defect of sight or hearing, coupled with the exposure to danger, was the cause of an injury which otherwise would not have occurred, it may be held that contributory negligence exists as a matter of law.[1] It is clear that the misfortune of being blind or deaf does not relieve the afflicted person from the duty to exercise ordinary care, but rather imposes upon him the duty of greater precautions to avoid injury.[2]

36. Wilful Injuries. — The doctrines of contributory negligence have no application in cases where the injury is inflicted by the wilful act or omission of the defendant; and in such cases contributory negligence is not a defence, and in its legal sense cannot exist.[3] Wilfulness and negligence are the opposites of each other, the one signifying the presence of intention or purpose, the other its absence.[4] This distinction has not always been observed,

1. **Effect of Blindness or Deafness on Doctrines of Negligence.** — Harris *v.* Uebelhoer, 75 N. Y. 169; Salem *v.* Goller, 76 Ind. 291; Sluper *v.* Sandown, 52 Vt. 251. It is contributory negligence for one of defective eyesight or hearing to walk upon a railroad track at a time when a train is known to be due. Maloy *v.* Wabash, etc., R. Co., 84 Mo. 270; Davenport *v.* Ruckman, 10 Bosworth (N. Y.), 20, 37 N. Y. 568; Shapley *v.* Wyman, 134 Mass. 118; Stewart *v.* Rippon, 38 Wis. 584; Phillips *v.* Dickerson, 85 Ill. 11; O'Mara *v.* Hudson, etc., R. Co., 38 N. Y. 445; Holmes's Common Law, 109.

2. **Does not relieve from Duty of "Ordinary Care."** — Cleveland, Columbus, etc., R. Co. *v.* Terry, 8 Ohio St. 570; Purl *v.* St. Louis, etc., R. Co, 72 Mo. 168; Winn *v.* Lowell, 1 Allen (Mass.), 177; Simmerman *v.* H. & St. J. R. Co., 71 Mo. 476; s. c., 2 Am. & Eng. R. R. Cas. 191; Ill. Central R. Co. *v.* Buckner, 28 Ill. 299; Gonzales *v.* N. Y., etc., R. Co., 1 Jones & S. (N. Y.) 57; Peach *v.* Utica, 10 Hun (N. Y.), 477; City of Centralia *v.* Krouze, 64 Ill. 19; Central, etc., R. Co. *v.* Feller, 84 Pa. St. 226; Morris, etc., R. Co. *v.* Haslan, 33 N. J. L. 147; West *v.* N. J., etc., Trans. Co., 32 N. J. L. 91; Elkins *v.* Boston, etc., R. Co., 115 Mass. 190.

3. **Wilful Injuries and Contributory Negligence.** — Beach on Cont. Neg. §§ 17, 21, and 22; Patterson's Ry. Acc. L. § 54, *ante* § 5.

"When wilfulness is an element in the conduct of the party charged, the case ceases to be one of negligence, and contributory negligence ceases to be a defence." Terre Haute, etc., R. Co. *v.* Graham, 95 Ind. 286, 293; s. c., 12 Am. & Eng. R. R. Cas. 77; Brownell *v.* Flagler, 5 Hill (N. Y.), 282; Sanford *v.* 8th Ave. R. Co., 23 N. Y. 343; Louisville, etc., R. Co. *v.* Collins, 2 Duvall (Ky.), 114; Mathews *v.* Warner, 29 Gratt. (Va.) 570; Ruter *v.* Foy, 46 Iowa, 132.

4. **Wilfulness negatives Negligence.** — "Where an intention to commit an injury exists, whether the intention be actual or constructive only, the wrongful act ceases to be a mere negligent injury, but becomes one of violence or aggression." Penna. Co. *v.* Sinclair, 62 Ind. 301; s. c., 30 Am. Rep. 185.

"The words 'wilful negligence' used in conjunction have not always been employed with strict regard for accuracy of expression. To say that an injury resulted from the negligence or wilful conduct of another is to affirm that the same act is the result of two exactly opposite mental conditions. It is to affirm in one breath that the act was done through inattention, thoughtlessly, heedlessly, and at the same time purposely and by design. It seems to be supposed that, by coupling the words together, the middle ground between negligence and wilfulness, between cases of nonfeasance and misfeasance, may be arrived at. It is only necessary to say that the distinction between cases falling within one class or the other is clear and well defined, and cases in any other class are aided by importing attributes pertaining to the other." Louisville, etc., R. Co. *v.* Bryan, 107 Ind. 51, 54; Terre Haute, etc., R. Co. *v.* Graham, 95 Ind. 286; s. c., 12 Am. & Eng. R. R. Cas. 77.

In Tonawanda R. Co. *v.* Munger, 5 Denio (N. Y.), 255; s. c., 49 Am. Dec. 239, consequently there are cases that use the terms "gross" or "wilful" negligence to designate wilful injuries.[1] Late cases have made the distinction clear.[2] And the principle of the responsibility of the wilful wrong-doer for all the consequences of his misconduct is really an old one.[3] The negligence of one person in carelessly exposing himself to danger, is no excuse for another who wilfully inflicts an injury upon him.[4]

37. Lord Campbell's Act: Contributory Negligence of Decedent. — In all the States of the United States, there are statutes modelled upon, and preserving the main features of, the English statute known as Lord Campbell's Act.[5] These statutes permit a recovery by the personal representatives or relatives of a person killed by the negligence of another; but all of them provide that no action can be maintained for an injury causing death, unless decedent, in his lifetime, could have maintained an action for injuries inflicted in the same manner and under the same circumstances.[6] Under this provision of these statutes no action can

it is said, "Negligence, even when gross, is but the omission of duty: it is not designed and intentional mischief."

1. **"Gross" or "Wilful" Negligence a Misnomer.** — Louisville, etc., R. Co. *v.* Collins, 2 Duvall (Ky.), 114; Louisville, etc., R. Co. *v.* Robinson, 4 Bush (Ky.), 507; Louisville, etc., Canal Co. *v.* Murphy's Admr., 9 Bush (Ky.), 521; St. Louis, etc., R. Co. *v.* Todd, 36 Ill. 409; Kerwhacker *v.* Cleveland, Columbus, etc., R. Co, 3 Ohio St. 172; s. c., 62 Am. Dec. 246; Hartfeld *v.* Roper, 21 Wend. (N.Y.) 615; s. c., 34 Am. Dec. 273; Evansville, etc., R. Co. *v.* Loudermilk, 15 Ind. 120; Claxton *v.* Lexington, etc., R. Co., 13 Bush (Ky.), 636; Louisville, etc., R. Co. *v.* Yandell, 17 B. Mon. (Ky.) 586; Jeffersonville, etc., R. Co. *v.* Riley, 39 Ind. 568; Drake *v.* Kieley, 93 Pa. St. 492; Clark *v.* Chambers, L. R. 3 Q. B. Div. 327; s. c., 7 Cent. L. J. 11.

2. **The Difference made clear.** — Penna. Co. *v.* Sinclair, 62 Ind. 301; Louisville, etc., R. Co. *v.* Bryan, 107 Ind. 51; Chicago, etc., R. Co. *v.* Hedges, 105 Ind. 398; s. c., 25 Am. & Eng. R. R. Cas. 550; Terre Haute, etc., R. Co. *v.* Graham, 95 Ind. 286; s. c., 12 Am. & Eng. R. R. Cas. 77; Louisville, etc., R. Co. *v.* Schmidt, 106 Ind. 73; Louisville, etc., R. Co. *v.* Ader, 110 Ind. 376; Ivans *v.* Cincinnati, etc., R. Co., 103 Ind. 27; s. c., 23 Am. & Eng. R. R. Cas. 258; Carter *v.* Louisville, etc., R. Co., 98 Ind. 552; s. c., 22 Am. & Eng. R. R. Cas. 360; Indianapolis, etc., R. Co. *v.* McClaren, 62 Ind. 566.

3. **Liability for Remote Consequences.** — Bigelow on Torts, p. 313, and note 4; Loop *v.* Litchfield, 42 N. Y. 358, 360; Conklin *v.* Thompson, 29 Barb. (N. Y.) 220; Binford *v.* Johnson, 82 Ind. 429; Weick *v.* Lander, 75 Ill. 93; Forney *v.* Geldmacher, 75 Mo. 113; Bloom *v.* Franklin Ins. Co., 97 Ind. 478; Bellinan *v.* Railroad Co., 76 Ind. 178; s. c., 6 Am. & Eng. R. R. Cas. 401; Reynolds *v.* Clarke, Lord Raym., 1401; Strange, 635; Scott *v.* Shepherd (the Squib case), opinion of *DeGray, J.*; 2 Wm. Black. 892; Ricker *v.* Freeman, 50 N. H. 420; s. c, 9 Am. Rep. 267; Holmes's Com. L. p. 92; Walls *v.* State, 7 Blackf. (Ind.) 573; Regina *v.* Hicklin, L. R. 3 Q. B. D. 360; 1 Bishop, Cr. L. (7 ed) § 327-333; Marble *v.* Worcester, 4 Gray (Mass.), 405; Thomas *v.* Winchester, 6 N. Y. 397; s. c., 57 Am. Dec. 455, and note.

4. **Negligence No Excuse for Wilfulness.** — In Carter *v.* L. N. A. & C. R. Co., 98 Ind. 552; s. c., 22 Am. & Eng. R. R. Cas. 360, it is said, "There was, according to the averments, that something more than mere negligence, which evinces a purpose to injure. Here the injury was the direct result of the aggressive act of the appellee's servant. The act of pushing appellant off the engine was the proximate cause of the injury, but the wrong of appellant was not proximate to the injury so as to preclude his right to recover."

5. **Liability for Injuries causing Death.** — Beach on Cont. Neg. § 20; Carey *v.* Berkshire R. Co, 1 Cush. (Mass.) 475; s. c., 48 Am. Dec. 616, and note; 9 and 10 Victoria, chap. 93; Shearman & Redf. on Neg. (3d ed) § 290-296; Patterson's Ry. Acc. L. 397-414.

6. **Statutes Effective only if Decedent would have had an Action.** — Shearman & Redf. on Neg. (3d ed) § 297-301; 3 Wood's Ry. Law, 1530-1542; Patterson's Ry. Acc. L. § 351.

be sustained if it appears that decedent was guilty of contributory negligence,[1] but whether he was guilty of contributory negligence is determined by the rules that govern in ordinary cases.[2]

38. Imputable Contributory Negligence. — Imputable contributory negligence, which will bar the plaintiff from recovery, exists when the plaintiff, although not chargeable with personal negligence, has been by the negligence of a person in privity with him, and with whose fault he is chargeable, exposed to the injury which he received through the negligence of the defendant.[3] In cases of this character, if the negligence of the person exposing the plaintiff to injury is a proximate cause of the injury, plaintiff cannot recover because the contributory negligence of such person will be imputed to him;[4] but before the contributory negligence of a person other than the plaintiff himself can serve as a defence to an action for a negligent injury of the plaintiff, it must appear, — 1. That such person was guilty of negligence. 2. That such negligence was a proximate cause of the injury. 3. That the plaintiff ought to be charged with such negligence as though it had been his own.[5] These rules are clear as mere legal doctrines, but in their application much difficulty arises.[6] The application of the doctrine to cases of two classes is particularly in dispute; viz., 1, To cases where a passenger is injured by the contributory negligence of his carrier, and the negligence of a third person;

1. **Decedent's Contributory Negligence a Bar.** — Shearman & Redf. on. Neg. (3d ed.) § 302; Lofton *v.* Vogles, 17 Ind. 105; Rowland *v.* Cannon, 35 Ga. 105, *Denman, C. J.*; Tucker *v.* Chaplin, 2 Carr. and K. 730, *Park, B.*; Armsworth *v.* Southeastern R Co., 11 Jurist, 758; Wilds *v.* Hudson River R. Co., 24 N. Y. 430; Johnson *v.* Hudson River R. Co., 20 N. Y. 65; Button *v.* Hudson River R. Co., 18 N. Y. 248; Witherley *v.* Regent's Canal Co., 12 C. B. (N. S.) 2; Louisville, etc., R. Co. *v.* Collins, 2 Duvall (Ky.), 114; Martin *v.* Wallace, 40 Ga. 52.

2. **The Question determined by the Usual Rules.** — Cooley on Torts, 264; Pierce on Railroads, 391; Evansville, etc., R. Co. *v.* Lowdermilk, 15 Ind. 120; Richmond, etc., R. Co. *v.* Anderson, 31 Gratt. (Va.) 812; s. c., 31 Am. Rep. 750; Beach on Cont. Neg. § 20; Pierce on Railroads, 385-400.

3. **Imputable Contributory Negligence.** — Shearman & Redf. on Neg. § 46; Whittaker's Smith on Neg. 405; Wharton on Neg. § 344*a*; Beach on Cont. Neg. §§ 32, 33; Thomp. on Car. of Pass. 284, § 1; Cooley on Torts, 684; Toledo, etc., R. Co. *v.* Goddard, 25 Ind. 185; Schular *v.* Hudson River R. Co., 38 Barb. (N. Y.) 653; Puterbaugh *v.* Reasor, 9 Ohio St. 484; Beck *v.* East River F. Co., 6 Robt. (N. Y.) 82.

4. **Bars when a Proximate Cause of Injury.** — Shearman & Redf. on Neg. § 46, Thomp. on Car. of Pass. 291, § 7; Deering on Neg. § 27; Callahan *v.* Sharp, 27 Hun (N. Y.), 85; Forks Tp. *v.* King, 84 Pa. St. 230; Puterbaugh *v.* Reasor, 9 Ohio St. 484; Toledo, etc., R. Co. *v.* Goddard, 25 Ind. 185; Peck *v.* N. Y., etc., R. Co., 50 Conn. 379; s. c., 14 Am. & Eng. R. R. Cas. 633; Carlisle *v.* Shealdon, 38 Vt. 440; Joliet *v.* Seward, 86 Ill. 402; Lake Shore, etc., R. Co *v.* Miller, 25 Mich. 274; Otis *v.* Jonesville, 47 Wis. 422; Waite *v.* N. E. R. Co., El. Bl. & El. 719, 728, 735; Ohio, etc., R. Co. *v.* Stratton, 78 Ill. 88, Gulf, etc., R. Co. *v.* Greenlee, 62 Tex. 344; s. c., 23 Am. & Eng. R. R. Cas. 322.

5. **What must appear to make imputable.** — Beach on Cont. Neg. §§ 32, 33; Robinson *v.* N. Y. Cent. R. Co., 66 N. Y. 11; s. c., 23 Am. Rep. 1; Gray *v.* Philadelphia, etc., R. Co., 22 Am. & Eng. R. R. Cas. 351; s. c., 23 Blatchf. (U. S.) 262; Beck *v.* East. R. F. Co., 6 Robt. (N. Y.) 82; St. Clair St. R. Co. *v.* Eadie, 43 Ohio St. 91; s. c., 23 Am. & Eng. R. R. Cas. 269; Follman *v.* Mankato (Minn. 1866), 15 Am. & Eng. Corp. Cas. 238.

6. **Difficulties in Application of Rule.** — Pollock on Torts, 382-385; Follman *v.* City of Mankato (Minn. 1886), 15 Am. & Eng. Corp. Cas. 238; Prideaux *v.* City of Mineral Point, 43 Wis. 513; Gray *v.* Philadelphia, etc., R. Co., 23 Blatchf. (U. S.) 262; 22 Am. & Eng. R. R. Cas. 351, and note.

2. To cases where a child, so young as to be *non sui juris*, and incapable of personal negligence, is exposed to danger by the neglect of its parents, guardian, or custodian, and injured, while so exposed, by the negligence of a third person.[1] Considering these cases in their order, it may be said, that, in the first class of cases, it is now the rule in the United States courts, in England, and in most of the States of the United States, that the contributory negligence of a carrier is not attributable to a passenger;[2] but in some of the United States the doctrine that it is imputable, and will bar a recovery, has been established.[3] Yet it would seem

1. **Where the Main Conflict arises.** — The conflict among text writers and courts upon the question whether the doctrines of imputable negligence are applicable in either one of the cases stated, may readily be seen by a comparison of the text-books and cases. See Pollock on Torts, 382–385; Thomp. on Car. of Pass. 284–294; Wharton on Neg. §§ 309–322; Id. § 395; Patterson's Ry. Acc. L. 78–87; Id. 90–94; Shearman & Redf. on Neg. §§ 46–52; 2 Thomp. on Neg. 1180–1190; Beach on Cont. Neg. §§ 32–48; Deering on Neg. §§ 27, 28; Whittaker's Smith on Neg. 405–418; note to Freer *v.* Cameron, 55 Am. Dec. 677; Borough of Carlisle *v.* Brisbane, 57 Am. Rep. 483, and note; s. c., 113 Pa. St. 544; Gray *v.* Railroad Co., 22 Am. & Eng. R. R. Cas. 351, and note. For particular points of difference, see the notes that follow.

2. **Carrier and Passenger.** — UNITED STATES COURTS. — Little *v.* Hackett, 116 U. S. 366; Gray *v.* Philadelphia, etc., R. Co., 23 Blatchf. (U. S. C. C.) 262. ENGLAND. — *The Bernina*, 12 Prob. Div. 58; s. c., 57 Am. Rep. 494, note; Tuff *v.* Warman, 5 C. B. (N. S.) 573; *The Milan*, Lush. Adm. 388. STATE COURTS. — Bennett *v.* New Jersey Railroad, etc., Co., 36 N. J. L. 225; s. c., Thomp. on Car. 281; 13 Am. Rep. 435; Chapman *v.* N. H. R. Co., 19 N. Y. 341; s. c., 75 Am. Dec. 344; New York, etc., R. Co. *v.* Steinbrenner, 47 N. J. L. 161; s. c., 23 Am. & Eng. R. R. Cas. 330, 54 Am. Rep. 126; Colegrove *v.* Railroad Co., 20 N. Y. 492; Webster *v.* Hudson River R. Co., 38 N. Y. 262; Perry *v.* Lansing, 17 Hun (N. Y.), 37; Robinson *v.* Railroad Co., 66 N. Y. 11; s. c., 23 Am. Rep. 1; Dyer *v.* Erie R. Co., 71 N. Y. 228; Masterson *v.* N. Y. Cent., etc., R. Co., 84 N. Y. 247; s. c., 38 Am. Rep. 510, 3 Am. & Eng. R. R. Cas. 408; McCallum *v.* Railroad Co., 38 Hun (N. Y.), 569; Cuddy *v.* Horn, 46 Mich. 596; s. c., 41 Am. Rep. 178; Malmsten *v.* Marquette H. & O. R. Co., 49 Mich. 94; s. c., 8 Am. & Eng. R. R. Cas. 291; Tompkins *v.* Clay St. R. Co., 66 Cal. 163; s. c., 18 Am. & Eng. R. R. Cas. 144; Danville Tp. Co. *v.* Stewart, 2 Metc. (Ky.) 119; Louisville, etc., R. Co. *v.* Case, 9 Bush (Ky.), 728; Eaton *v.* Boston, etc., R. Co., 11 Allen (Mass.), 500; Pittsburgh, etc., R. Co. *v.* Spencer, 98 Ind. 186; s. c., 21 Am. & Eng. R. R. Cas. 478; Wabash, etc., R. Co. *v.* Shacklett, 105 Ill. 364; s. c., 12 Am. & Eng. R. R. Cas. 166; 44 Am. Rep. 791; Transfer Co. *v.* Kelly, 36 Ohio St. 86; s. c., 3 Am. & Eng. R. R. Cas. 335, 38 Am. Rep. 558; St. Clear Str. R. Co. *v.* Eadie, 43 Ohio St. 91; s. c., 23 Am. & Eng. R. R. Cas. 269, 54 Am. Rep. 802; Follman *v.* Mankato (Minn. 1886), 15 Am. & Eng. Corp. Cas. 238; Philadelphia, etc., R. Co. *v.* Hogeland (Md. 1886), 66 Md. 149; s. c., 57 Am. Rep. 492; Holzab *v.* Railroad Co., 38 La. An. 185; s. c., 58 Am. Rep. 177.

3. **The Pennsylvania Rule.** — Lockhart *v.* Lichtenthaler, 46 Pa. St. 151; Philadelphia, etc., R. Co. *v.* Boyer, 97 Pa. St. 91; s. c., 2 Am. & Eng. R. R. Cas. 172. But the Pennsylvania court refuses to apply the rule except to public carriers, and holds that a person injured by the negligence of a third person, and the contributory negligence of the driver of a private vehicle in which the injured person is riding, is not barred in an action against such third person by the driver's contributory negligence. Carlisle *v.* Brisbane, 113 Pa. St. 544; s. c., 57 Am. Rep. 483.

On the other hand, in Iowa and Wisconsin the rule of Thorogood *v.* Bryan has been applied in the cases of persons injured by the contributory negligence of the driver while riding in private vehicles. Artz *v.* Chicago, etc., R. Co., 34 Iowa, 153; Payne *v.* Chicago, etc., R. Co., 39 Iowa, 523; Slater *v.* B. C. R. & N. R. Co. (Iowa, 1887), 32 N. W. Rep. 264; Prideaux *v.* Mineral Point, 43 Wis. 513; s. c., 28 Am. Rep. 558; Haufe *v.* Fulton, 29 Wis. 296; s. c., 9 Am. Rep. 568; s. c., 34 Wis. 608; 17 Am. Rep. 463; Otis *v.* Jonesville, 47 Wis. 422.

So there are cases which hold the contributory negligence of a husband, driving a private vehicle, a bar to an action brought by a wife to recover for injuries resulting from the negligence of a third person while she was in such vehicle so driven by that the recent repudiation of the doctrine of Thorogood *v.* Bryan [1] by the Supreme Court of the United States,[2] and the distinct

her husband. Carlisle *v.* Sheldon, 38 Vt. 440; Huntoon *v.* Trumbull, 2 McCrary (U. S.), 314; Gulf, etc., R. Co. *v.* Green'ee (Tex.), 23 Am. & Eng. R. R. Cas. 322. But see Platz *v.* Cohoes, 24 Hun (N. Y.), 101. And it has been *held*, that the contributory negligence of a master bars a servant. Lake Shore, etc., R. Co. *v.* Miller, 25 Mich. 274.

1. **Thorogood v. Bryan.**—Thorogood *v.* Bryan, 8 C. B. 115; s. c., Thompson on Carriers, 273. In this case it was *held*, that a passenger in an omnibus injured by the negligence of the driver of another omnibus had no action against the latter, because the driver of the omnibus carrying the passenger, by his negligence, contributed to the injury. It was said that the plaintiff, being a passenger voluntarily, was so far identified with the carriage in which he was travelling, that want of care on the part of the driver of such carriage would bar the plaintiff's action. The passenger was said to stand in the position of a master responsible for the acts of the driver as though those of a servant. See opinions of Coltman, Maule, Cresswell, and Williams, judges.

2. **Little v. Hackett.**—Little *v.* Hackett, 116 U. S. 366, where it is said, "The doctrine resting upon the principle that no one is to be denied a remedy for injuries sustained, without fault by him or by a party under his control and direction, is qualified by cases in the English courts, wherein it is held that a party who trusts himself to a public conveyance is in some way identified with those who have it in charge, and that he can only recover against a wrong-doer when they who are in charge can recover; in other words, that their contributory negligence is imputable to him so as to preclude his recovery for an injury when they, by reason of such negligence, could not recover. The leading case to this effect is Thorogood *v.* Bryan, decided by the court of common pleas in 1849, 8 C. B. 114. It there appeared that the husband of the plaintiff, whose administratrix she was, was a passenger in an omnibus. The defendant, Mrs. Bryan, was the proprietress of another omnibus running on the same line of road. Both vehicles had started together, and frequently passed each other, as either stopped to take up or set down a passenger. The deceased, wishing to alight, did not wait for the omnibus to draw up to the curb, but got out whilst it was in motion, and far enough from the path to allow another carriage to pass on the near side. The defendant's omnibus coming up at the moment, he was run over, and in a few days afterwards died of the injuries sustained. The court, among other things, instructed the jury that if they were of the opinion that want of care on the part of the driver of the omnibus in which the deceased was a passenger, in not drawing up to the curb to put him down, had been conducive to the injury, the jury must be for the defendant, although her driver was also guilty of negligence. The jury found for the defendant, and the court discharged a rule for a new trial for misdirection, thus sustaining the instruction. The grounds of its decision were, as stated by *Mr. Justice Coltman*, that the deceased, having trusted the party by selecting the particular conveyance in which he was carried, had so far identified himself with the owner and her servants, that if any injury resulted from their negligence, he must be considered a party to it. 'In other words,' to quote his language, 'the passenger is so far identified with the carriage in which he is travelling, that want of care on the part of the driver will be a defence of the driver of the carriage which directly caused the injury.' *Mr. Justice Maule*, in the same case, said that the passenger 'chose his own conveyance, and must take the consequences of any default of the driver he thought fit to trust.' *Mr. Justice Cresswell* said, 'If the driver of the omnibus deceased was in had, by his negligence or want of due care or skill, contributed to any injury from a collision, his master clearly could maintain no action, and I must confess I see no reason why a passenger who employs the driver to carry him stands in any different position. *Mr. Justice Williams* added that he was of the same opinion. He said, 'I think the passenger must, for this purpose, be considered as identified with the person having the management of the omnibus he was conveyed by.'

"What is meant by the passenger being 'identified with the carriage' or 'with the person having its management,' is not very clear. In a recent case, in which the court of exchequer applied the same test to a passenger in a railway train which collided with a number of loaded wagons that were being shunted from a siding by the defendant, another railway company, Baron Pollock said that he understood it to mean 'that the plaintiff, for the purpose of the action, must be taken to be in the same position as the owner of the omnibus or his driver.' Armstrong *v.* Lancashire, etc., R. Co., L. R. 10 Exch. 47, 52. Assuming this to be the correct explanation, it is difficult to see upon what principle the passenger can be considered to be in the same position, with reference to the negligent act, as the driver who committed it, or as his master, the owner. Cases cited from the English courts, as we have seen, and numerous others decided in the courts of this country, show that the relation of master and servant does not exist between the passenger and the driver, or between the passenger and the owner. In the absence of this relation, the imputation of their negligence to the passenger, where no fault of omission or commission is chargeable to him, is against all legal rules. If their negligence could be imputed to him, it would render him equally with them responsible to third parties thereby injured, and would also preclude him from maintaining an action against the owner for injuries received by reason of it. But neither of these conclusions can be maintained; neither has the support of any adjudged cases entitled to consideration.

"The truth is, the decision in Thorogood v. Bryan rests upon indefensible ground. The identification of the passenger with the negligent driver or the owner, without his personal co-operation or encouragement, is a gratuitous assumption. There is no such identity. The parties are not in the same position. The owner of a public conveyance is a carrier, and the driver or the person managing it is his servant. Neither of them is the servant of the passenger, and his asserted identity with them is contradicted by the daily experience of the world.

"Thorogood v. Bryan has not escaped criticism in the English courts. In the court of the admiralty it has been openly disregarded. In *The Milan*, Dr. Lushington, the judge of the high court of admiralty, in speaking of that case, said, 'With due respect to the judges who decided that case, I do not consider that it is necessary for me to dissect the judgment; but I decline to be bound by it, because it is a single case; because I know, upon inquiry, that it has been doubted by high authority; because it appears to me not reconcilable with other principles laid down at common law; and lastly, because it is directly against Hay v. La Neve and the ordinary practice of the court of admiralty.' Lush. 388, 403.

"In this country the doctrine of Thorogood v. Bryan has not been generally followed. In Bennett v. New Jersey R. Co., 36 N. J. L. (7 Vroom) 225, and New York, etc., R. Co. v. Steinbrenner, 47 N. J. L. (18 Vroom) 161; s. c., 23 Am. and Eng. R. R. Cas. 330, it was elaborately examined by the supreme court and the court of errors of New Jersey in opinions of marked ability and learning, and was disapproved and rejected. In the first it was held that the driver of a horse-car was not the agent of the passenger so as to render the passenger chargeable for the driver's negligence. The car, in crossing the track of the railroad company, was struck by its train, and the passenger was injured; and he brought an action against the company. On the trial the defendant contended that there was evidence tending to show negligence by the driver of the horse-car, which was in part productive of the accident; and the presiding judge was requested to charge the jury, that, if this was so, the plaintiff was not entitled to recover; but the court instructed them that the carelessness of the driver would not affect the action, nor debar the plaintiff's right to recover for the negligence of the defendant. And this instruction was sustained by the court. In speaking of the 'identification' of the passenger in the omnibus with the driver, mentioned in Thorogood v. Bryan, the court, by the chief justice, said, 'Such identification could result only in one way; that is, by considering such driver the servant of the passenger. I can see no ground upon which such a relationship is to be founded. In a practical point of view, it certainly does not exist. The passenger has no control over the driver or agent in charge of the vehicle. And it is this right to control the conduct of the agent which is the foundation of the doctrine that the master is to be affected by the acts of his servant. To hold that the conductor of a street-car or a railroad train is the agent of the numerous passengers who may chance to be in it, would be a pure fiction. In reality there is no such agency; and if we impute it, and correctly apply legal principles, the passenger, on the occurrence of an accident from the carelessness of the person in charge of the vehicle in which he is being conveyed, would be without remedy. It is obvious, in a suit against the proprietor of the car in which he was a passenger, there would be no recovery if the driver or conductor of such car is to be regarded as the servant of the passenger. And so, on the same ground, each passenger would be liable to every person injured by the carelessness of such driver or conductor; because, if the negligence of such agent is to be attributed to the passenger for one purpose, it would be entirely arbitrary to say that he is not to be affected by it for other purposes' (7 Vroom, 227, 228).

"In the latter case, it appeared that the plaintiff had hired a coach and horses, with a driver, to take his family on a particular journey. In the course of the journey, while crossing the track of the railroad, the coach was struck by a passing train, and the plaintiff was injured. In an action brought by him against the railroad company, it was held that the relation of master and servant did not exist between him and the driver, and that the negligence of the latter, co-operating with that of persons in charge of the train, which caused the accident, was not imputable to the plaintiff, as contributory negligence, to bar his action.

"In New York a similar conclusion has been reached. In Chapman *v.* New Haven R. Co., 19 N. Y. 341, it appeared that there was a collision between the trains of two railroad companies, by which the plaintiff, a passenger of one of them, was injured. The court of appeals of that State held that a passenger by railroad was not so identified with the proprietors of the train conveying him, or with their servants, as to be responsible for their negligence; and that he might recover against the proprietors of another train for injuries sustained from a collision through their negligence, although there was such negligence in the management of the train conveying him as would have defeated an action by its owners. In giving the decision, the court referred to Thorogood *v.* Bryan, and said that it could see no justice in the doctrine in connection with that case; and that, to attribute to the passenger the negligence of the agents of the company, and thus bar his right to recover, was not applying any existing exception to the general rule of law, but was framing a new exception based on fiction, and inconsistent with justice. The case differed from Thorogood *v.* Bryan in that the vehicle carrying the plaintiff was a railway-train instead of an omnibus; but the doctrine of the English case, if sound, is as applicable to passengers on railway trains as to passengers in an omnibus; and it was so applied, as already stated, by the court of exchequer, in the recent case of Armstrong *v.* Lancashire & Yorkshire R. Co. In Dyer *v.* Erie Railway Co, 71 N. Y. 228, the plaintiff was injured while crossing the defendant's railroad track, on a public thoroughfare. He was riding in a wagon, by the permission and invitation of the owner of the horses and wagon. At that time, a train standing south of certain buildings, which prevented its being seen, had started to back over the crossing, without giving the driver of the wagon any warning of its approach. The horses, becoming frightened by the blowing-off of steam from engines in the vicinity, became unmanageable, and the plaintiff was thrown, or jumped from the wagon, and was injured by the train which was backing. It was held that no relation of principal and agent arose between the driver of the wagon and the plaintiff; and, although he travelled voluntarily, he was not responsible for the negligence of the driver, where he himself was not chargeable with negligence, and there was no claim that the driver was not competent to control and manage the horses.

"A similar doctrine is maintained by the courts of Ohio. In Transfer Co. *v.* Kelly, 36 Ohio State, 86, 91; s. c., 3 Am. & Eng. R. R. Cas. 335, the plaintiff, a passenger on a car owned by a street railroad company, was injured by its collision with a car of the Transfer Co. There was evidence tending to show that both companies were negligent, but the court held that the plaintiff, he not being in fault, could recover against the Transfer Co., and that the concurrent negligence of the company, on whose cars he was a passenger, could not be imputed to him, so as to charge him with contributory negligence. The Chief Justice, in delivering the opinion of the court, said, 'It seems to us, therefore, that the negligence of the company, or of its servants, should not be imputed to the passenger, where such negligence contributes to his injury jointly with the negligence of a third party, any more than it should be so imputed, where the negligence of the company, or its servants, was the sole cause of the injury.' 'Indeed,' the Chief Justice added, 'it seems as incredible to my mind that the right of a passenger to redress against a stranger for an injury caused directly and proximately by the latter's negligence, should be denied, on the ground that the negligence of his carrier contributed to his injury, he being without fault himself, as it would be to hold such passenger responsible for the negligence of his carrier, whereby an injury was inflicted upon a stranger. And of the last proposition it is enough to say that it is simply absurd.'

"In the Supreme Court of Illinois the same doctrine is maintained. In the recent cases of the Wabash, etc., R. Co. *v.* Schacklett, 105 Ill. 364; s. c., 12 Am. & Eng. R. R. Cas. 166, the doctrine of Thorogood's case was examined and rejected, the court holding that, where a passenger on a railway train is injured by the concurring negligence of servants of the company on whose train he is travelling, and of the servants of another company with whom he has not contracted, there being no fault or negligence on his part, he or his personal representatives may maintain an action against either company in default, and will not be restricted to an action against the company on whose train he was travelling.

"Similar decisions have been made in the courts of Kentucky, Michigan, and California. Danville, etc., Turnpike Co. *v.* Stewart, 2 Met. (Ky.) 119; Louisville, etc., R. Co. *v.* Case, 9 Bush (Ky.), 728; Cuddy *v.* Horn, 46 Mich. 596; Tompkins *v.* Clay St. R. Co., 66 Cal. 163; s. c., 18 Am. & Eng. R. R. Cas. 144.

"There is no distinction in principle whether the passenger be on a public con-

manner in which that case has now been overruled in England,[1] indicate an entire abandonment of the doctrine that the contributory negligence of a carrier should be imputed to a passenger.[2]

In the second class of cases, the doctrine of Hartfield *v.* Roper[3] is followed in some jurisdictions; and it is held that the negligent conduct of a parent, guardian, or custodian in allowing a child *non sui juris* to be negligently injured is contributory negligence, which must be imputed to the child.[4] But in other jurisdictions

veyance like a railroad train or an omnibus, or be on a hack hired from a public stand in the street for a drive. Those on a hack do not become responsible for the negligence of the driver if they exercise no control over him further than to indicate the route they wish to travel or the places to which they wish to go. If he is their agent, so that his negligence can be imputed to them to prevent their recovery against a third party, he must be their agent in all other respects, so far as the management of the carriage is concerned, and responsibilities to third parties would attach to them for injuries caused by his negligence in the course of his employment. But, as we have already stated, responsibility cannot, within any recognized rules of law, be fastened upon one who has in no way interfered with and controlled in the matter causing the injury. From the simple fact of hiring the carriage, or riding in it, no such liability can arise. The party hiring or riding must in some way have co-operated in producing the injury complained of before he incurs any liability for it. 'If the law were otherwise,' as said by Mr. Justice Dupue in the elaborate opinion in the latest case in New Jersey, 'not only the hirer of the coach, but also all the passengers in it, would be under a constraint to mount the box and superintend the conduct of the driver in the management and control of his team, or be put for remedy exclusively to an action against the irresponsible driver, or the equally irresponsible owner of a coach taken, it may be, from a coach-stand, for the consequences of an injury which was the product of the co-operating wrongful acts of the driver and of a third person, and that, too, though the passengers were ignorant of the character of the driver, and of the responsibility of the owner of the team, and strangers to the route over which they were to be carried.' New York, Lake Erie, etc., R. Co. *v.* Steinbrenner, 47 N. J. L. (18 Vroom) 161, 171; s. c., 23 Am. & Eng. R. R. Cas. 330.

"In this case, it was left to the jury to say whether the plaintiff had exercised any control over the conduct of the driver further than to indicate the places to which he wished him to drive. The instruction of the court below, that unless he did exercise such control, and require the driver to cross the track at the time the collision occurred, the negligence of the driver was not imputable to him so as to bar his right of action against the defendant, was therefore correct, and the judgment must be affirmed."

1. **Case of the Bernina.** — *The Bernina*, 12 Prob. Div. 58, s. c., 57 Am. Rep. 494, *et seq.*, note.

2. **When the Rule properly applicable.** — An examination of the cases cited will show a marked tendency to the entire abandonment of the doctrine of imputable negligence in cases of the class now under discussion. It may be questioned whether the rule has any proper application, except in cases where the maxim, *qui facit per alium facit per se*, can be invoked. Reedie *v.* London, etc., R. Co., 4 Exch. 244; Quarman *v.* Burnett, 6 M. & W. 499; *The Bernina*, 12 Prob. Div. 58; N. Y., etc., R. Co. *v.* Steinbrenner, 47 N. J. L. 161; s. c., 23 Am. & Eng. R. R. Cas. 330, 54 Am. Rep. 126 and note; St. Clair St. R. Co. *v.* Eadie, 43 Ohio St. 91; s. c., 23 Am. & Eng. R. R. Cas. 269; Cuddy *v.* Horn, 46 Mich. 596; s. c., 41 Am. Rep. 178; Little *v.* Hackett, 116 U. S. 366; Follman *v.* Mankato (Minn. 1886), 15 Am. & Eng. Corp. Cas. 238.

3. **Imputable Negligence of Parents: Hartfield v. Roper.** — Hartfield *v.* Roper, 21 Wend. (N. Y.) 615; s. c., 34 Am. Dec. 273; 2 Thomp. on Neg. 1121. In this case, it was *held*, that parents permitting a child two years old to be in a public highway unattended, are guilty of such contributory negligence as will defeat an action *in the child's name* for an injury done to it by the negligence of a traveller in the highway.

4. **Where held Imputable to Child.** — Gibbons *v.* Williams, 135 Mass. 333; McGeary *v.* Eastern R. Co., 135 Mass. 363; s. c., 15 Am. & Eng. R. R. Cas. 407; O'Connor *v.* Boston, etc., R. Co., 135 Mass. 352; s. c., 15 Am. & Eng. R. R. Cas. 362; Wright *v.* Malden, etc., R. Co., 4 Allen (Mass.), 283; Lynch *v.* Smith, 104 Mass. 52; s. c., 6 Am. Rep. 188; Schierhold *v.* North, etc., R. Co., 40 Cal. 447; Meeks *v.* Southern, etc., R. Co., 52 Cal. 604; s. c., 56 Cal. 513; 38 Am. Rep. 67; Gavin *v.* Chicago, 97 Ill. 66; s. c., 37

it is held that the negligence of the parent, guardian, or custodian is not imputable to the child, because it is in no way responsible for the danger, had no volition in establishing the relation of privity with the person whose negligence it is sought to impute to it, and should not be charged with the fault of such person in allowing it to be exposed to danger which it had neither the capacity to know nor avoid.[1] In England it has been held that the negligence of a person in the actual custody of a child, at the time of its injury, which contributes to the injury, may be imputed to the child.[2] And in some of the United States, similar decisions have

Am. Rep. 89; Toledo, etc., R. Co. *v.* Grable, 88 Ill. 441; Chicago *v.* Hesing, 83 Ill. 204; Evansville, etc., R. Co. *v.* Wolf, 59 Ind. 89; Jeffersonville, etc., R. Co. *v.* Bowen, 40 Ind. 545; Atchison, etc., R. Co. *v.* Smith, 28 Kan. 541; s. c., 8 Am. & Eng. R. R. Cas. 327; Leslie *v.* Lewiston, 62 Me. 468; Brown *v.* European, etc., R. Co., 58 Me. 384. *Compare* O'Brien *v.* McGlinchy, 68 Me. 552; McMahon *v.* Northern, etc., R. Co., 39 Md. 438; Baltimore, etc., R. Co. *v.* McDonnell, 43 Md. 534; Fitzgerald *v.* St. Paul, etc., R. Co., 29 Minn. 336; s. c., 8 Am. & Eng. R. R. Cas. 310; 43 Am. Rep. 212; Ihl *v.* Railroad Co., 47 N. Y. 323; s. c., 7 Am. Rep. 450; Casgrove *v.* Ogden, 49 N. Y. 255; s. c., 10 Am. Rep. 361; Mangam *v.* Brooklyn R. Co., 38 N. Y. 455.

Parent barred when Child not.—In considering these and similar cases, it should not be overlooked that there is a marked distinction between cases brought in the name of the child itself, and cases brought by the parents to recover for the injuries sustained by them by reason of the homicide or injury of the child. Thus, when the parents sue, their negligence in exposing the child to injury will bar their recovery. Smith *v.* Hestonville, etc., R. Co., 92 Pa. St. 450; s. c., 2 Am. & Eng. R. R. Cas. 12, 37 Am. Rep. 705; Battishill *v.* Humphrey (Mich. 1887), 23 Am. & Eng. R. R. Cas. 597; Williams *v.* Texas, etc., R. Co., 60 Tex. 205; s. c., 15 Am. & Eng. R. R. Cas. 403. And this is a correct rule in all jurisdictions. But, as the cases just cited show, the contributory negligence of the parent will not keep the child from recovering, except in jurisdictions that have fully adopted the rule in Hartfield *v.* Roper. Erie City Pass. R. Co. *v.* Schuster, 113 Pa. St. 412; s. c., 57 Am. Rep. 471; Glassy *v.* Hestonville, etc., R. Co., 57 Pa. St. 172; North Pa. Railroad Co. *v.* Mahoney, 57 Pa. St. 187.

And the Question of Imputability for the Jury.—It will also be noted that in Massachusetts, and several other jurisdictions, the rule of Hartfield *v.* Roper is held in the modified form. In Massachusetts the question of the contributory negligence of the parents which will bar the child is *always* held a question of fact for the jury, not of law for the court. McGeary *v.* Eastern R. Co., 135 Mass. 363; s. c., 15 Am. & Eng. R. R. Cas. 407; O'Connor *v.* Boston, etc., R. Co., 135 Mass. 352; s. c., 15 Am. & Eng. R. R. Cas. 362. See Beach on Cont. Neg. § 41; Patterson's Ry. Acc. L. § 93; Texas, etc., R. Co *v.* Herbeck, 60 Tex. 612; Galveston, etc., R. Co. *v.* Moore, 59 Tex. 64; s. c., 10 Am. & Eng. R. R. Cas. 746, 46 Am. Rep. 265; Robinson *v.* Cone, 22 Vt. 213; s. c., 2 Thomp. on Neg. 1129; s. c., 54 Am. Dec. 67; Norfolk, etc., R. Co. *v.* Ormsby, 27 Gratt. (Va.) 455.

1. **Where held Not Imputable.**—Government St. R. Co. *v.* Hanlon, 53 Ala. 70; Bay Shore, etc., R. Co. *v.* Harris, 67 Ala. 6; Birge *v.* Gardiner, 19 Conn. 507; s. c., 50 Am. Dec. 261; Bronson *v.* Southbury, 37 Conn. 199; Daley *v.* Norwich, etc., R. Co., 26 Conn. 591; s. c., 68 Am. Dec. 413; Frick *v.* St. Louis, etc., R. Co., 75 Mo. 542; s. c., 75 Mo. 595; 8 Am. & Eng. R. R. Cas. 280; Boland *v.* Missouri R. Co., 36 Mo. 490; Battishill *v.* Humphrey (Mich. 1887), 28 Am. & Eng. R. R. Cas. 597; s. c., 57 Am. Rep. 474, note; Huff *v.* Ames, 16 Neb. 139; s. c., 49 Am. Rep. 716; Bellefontaine R. Co. *v.* Snyder, 18 Ohio St. 400; Cleveland, etc., R. Co. *v.* Manson, 30 Ohio St. 451; St. Clair St. R. Co. *v.* Eadie, 43 Ohio St. 91; s. c., 23 Am. & Eng. R. R. Cas. 269; Erie City Pass. R. Co. *v.* Schuster, 113 Pa. St. 412; s. c., 57 Am. Rep. 471; Phila., etc., R. Co. *v.* Long, 75 Pa. St. 257; North Pa. R. Co. *v.* Mahoney, 57 Pa. St. 187; Smith *v.* O'Connor, 48 Pa. St. 218; Kay *v.* Penna R. Co., 65 Pa. St. 269; s. c., 3 Am. Rep. 628; Whirley *v.* Whiteman, 1 Head (Tenn.), 610.

2. **Negligence of Actual Custodian Imputable.**—Waite *v.* North-Eastern R. Co., El. Bl. & El. 719, 727; Beach on Cont. Neg. pp. 130–132; 2 Thomp. on Neg. 1182, § 32; Thomp. on Car. 291, § 7.

But Mr. Pollock regards this case as resting upon the principle that the foundation of defendant's liability was not shown, because it did not appear that the negligence of the defendant, rather than that of been made.[1] But it seems that these cases may be rested upon the doctrine of the identification of the child and its custodian at the moment of the injury; and in some of the English cases it is implied that the contractual obligations of the defendant to the custodian formed the only ground of action against the defendant, and therefore it would only be liable to the child when it would have been liable to the custodian.[2] The doctrine of Hartfield *v.* Roper is not applicable when the injured child, although *non sui juris*, has exercised ordinary care to avoid the injury,[3] or when the defendant, by the exercise of ordinary care, could have discovered the danger of the child in time to have avoided inflicting the injury;[4] and neither should it be applied in cases where the child is old enough to exercise a reasonable degree of care for its own safety, and is, because of this fact, released from the immediate custody of its parents or guardians.[5] The question then becomes the usual one of ordinary care, and the child may recover if it has exercised the ordinary care of a child.[6]

the custodian, was the proximate cause of the child's injury. Pollock on Torts, 382.

1. Ohio, etc., R. Co. *v.* Stratton, 78 Ill. 88; Stillson *v.* Hannibal, etc., R. Co., 67 Mo. 671; Lannen *v.* Albany Gas Co., 46 Barb. (N.Y.) 264; s. c., 44 N. Y. 459; Morrison *v.* Erie R. Co, 56 N. Y. 302; Kay *v.* Penna. R. Co., 65 Pa. St. 269, 276, 277; s. c., 3 Am. Rep. 628; Holly *v.* Boston Gas Lt. Co., 8 Gray (Mass.), 123; Carter *v.* Towne, 98 Mass. 567; s. c., 103 Mass. 507; Guthen *v.* Chicago, etc., R. Co., 22 Fed. Rep. 609; s. c., 19 Am. & Eng. R. R. Cas. 342; The Burgundia, 29 Fed. Rep. 404; 2 Thomp. on Neg. 1188, § 36; Patterson's Ry. Acc. L. § 94; Beach on Cont. Neg. pp. 130–132. But where the person in actual custody of the child is not in privity with it, and has no right to control it, his negligence is not attributable to the child. Thus, where a stranger rescued a child from one danger, and, while holding it in his arms, immediately exposed it to another danger, it was held that the child's right of action was not barred by the negligence of the stranger who held it. North Penna. R. Co. *v.* Mahoney, 57 Pa. St. 187. And see Pittsburgh, etc., R. Co. *v.* Caldwell, 74 Pa. St. 421; East Saginaw, etc., R. Co. *v.* Bohn, 27 Mich. 503; Bellefontaine, etc., R. Co. *v.* Snyder, 18 Ohio St. 400; Pat. Ry. Acc. L. § 95.

2. **This rests on Contract and Doctrine of Identification.** — Patterson's Ry. Acc. Law, §§ 89, 93, 94; Thomp. Car. of Pass. 291, § 7; Beach on Cont. Neg. pp. 131, 132; Waite *v.* North-East. R. Co., El. Bl. & El. 719, 728; 2 Thomp. on Neg. 1182, 1188, §§ 32, 36.

3. **When Child used Due Care, no Imputability.** — Lannen *v.* Gas Co., 46 Barb. (N. Y.) 264; s. c., 44 N. Y. 459; Ihl *v.* Railroad Co., 47 N. Y. 317; s. c., 7 Am. Rep. 450; McGarry *v.* Loomis, 63 N. Y. 104; s. c., 20 Am. Rep. 510; Lynch *v.* Smith, 104 Mass. 52; s. c., 6 Am. Rep. 188; Collins *v.* South Boston, etc., R. Co., 142 Mass. 301; s. c., 26 Am. & Eng R. R. Cas. 371; 56 Am Rep. 676; Munn *v.* Reed, 4 Allen (Mass.), 431; Mulligan *v.* Curtis, 100 Mass. 512; O'Brien *v.* McGlinchy, 68 Me. 552; Pittsburgh, etc, R. Co. *v.* Bumstead, 48 Ill. 221; McMahon *v.* Northern, etc., R. Co., 39 Md. 438.

4. **When Defendant could have avoided inflicting Injury.** — Davies *v.* Mann, 10 M. & W. 546; s. c., 2 Thomp on Neg. 1105; Meeks *v.* Railroad Co., 56 Cal. 513; s. c., 38 Am. Rep. 67; Baltimore, etc., R. Co. *v.* McDonnell, 43 Md. 534, 551; Patterson's Ry. Acc. L. § 93; 2 Thomp. on Neg. 1185, § 35; Wharton on Neg. § 314; Galveston, etc., R. Co. *v.* Moore, 59 Tex. 64; s. c., 10 Am. & Eng. R. R. Cas. 746; 46 Am. Rep. 265, 268.

5. **If Child sui juris, no Imputability.** — Lynch *v.* Smith, 104 Mass. 52; s. c., 6 Am. Rep. 188; McMahon *v.* New York, 33 N. Y. 642; Oakland R. Co. *v.* Fielding, 48 Pa. St. 320; Shearman & Redf. on Neg. (3d ed.) § 50; 2 Thomp. on Neg. 1180, § 31; Lynch *v.* Nurdin, 1 Q. B. 29; s. c., 2 Thomp. on Neg. 1140; Railroad Co. *v.* Gladman, 15 Wall. (U. S.) 401.

6. **Then a Question of "Ordinary Care of a Child."** — Beach on Cont. Neg. § 46; Meibus *v.* Dodge, 38 Wis. 300; s. c., 20 Am. Rep. 6; Plumley *v.* Birge, 124 Mass. 57; s. c., 26 Am. Rep. 645; Robinson *v.* Cone, 22 Vt. 213; s. c., 54 Am. Dec. 67; Thurber *v.* Harlem Bridge Co., 60 N. Y. 326.

39. Apportionment of Damages. — In cases of contributory negligence at common law, there can be no apportionment of damages, as there is in courts of admiralty.[1] But where the negligence of a defendant has been the sole cause of an injury to the plaintiff, and the plaintiff's subsequent negligence has enhanced the injury unnecessarily, the damages should be limited to the injury which would have resulted from defendant's negligence, had plaintiff exercised ordinary care after the injury.[2] Yet, when the plaintiff has exercised ordinary care, he can recover for an enhancement or aggravation of the injuries caused by defendant when such enhancement or aggravation results from an existing disease, or the development of a latent disease, or the perversion of a natural function or condition.[3] The existence of such disease or condition in the plaintiff is not negligence; but it would seem that there may be cases in which a person, sick or diseased, is barred from recovering for an aggravation or enhancement of such sickness or disease by the negligence of another, when, without notice to that other, he has exposed himself to injury while in such a condition as to make the results of a very slight injury serious.[4] Under such circumstances, if the negligence of the defendant would not ordinarily have resulted in injury to a person situated as plaintiff was, it is doubtful whether defendant is liable, and he should not

1. **No Apportionment at Common Law.** — Railroad Co. *v.* Norton, 24 Pa. St. 465; Greenland *v.* Chaplin, 5 Exch. 243; Beach, Cont. Neg. § 24. "The law does not apportion damages between parties whose joint negligence caused to one of them an injury." Cleveland, etc., R. Co. *v.* Elliott, 28 Ohio St. 340, 353.

2. **But Damages should be limited to Actual Effects.** — 1 Sutherland on Dam. 237; 2 Id. 729; Lyons *v.* Erie R. Co., 57 N. Y. 489; Gould *v.* McKenna, 86 Pa. St. 297; s. c., 27 Am. Rep. 705; Geiselman *v.* Scott, 25 Ohio St. 86; Nashville, etc., R. Co. *v.* Smith, 6 Heisk (Tenn.), 174; Louisville, etc., R. Co. *v.* Falvey, 104 Ind. 409; s. c, 23 Am. & Eng. R. R. Cas. 502; Nitro-Phosphate Co. *v.* Docks Co., 9 L. R. Ch. Div. 503; Sills *v.* Brown, 9 Car. & P. 601; Hunt *v.* Lowell Gas Co., 1 Allen (Mass.), 343; Shearman *v.* Fall River Co., 2 Allen (Mass.), 524; Hibbard *v.* Thompson, 109 Mass. 286; Stebbins *v.* Cent. Vt. R. Co., 54 Vt. 464; s. c., 11 Am. & Eng. R. R Cas. 79; 41 Am. Rep. 855; Matthews *v.* Warner, 29 Gratt. (Va.) 570; s. c., 26 Am. Rep. 396; Secord *v.* St. Paul, etc., R. Co., 5 McCrary (U. S.), 515; s. c, 18 Fed. Rep. 221; Patterson's Ry. Acc. L. 480.

3. **Yet Plaintiff may recover for Enhancement by Disease.** — Patterson's Ry. Acc. L. 28; Louisville, etc., R. Co. *v.* Jones, 108 Ind. 551; s. c, 28 Am. & Eng. R. R. Cas. 170; Louisville, etc., R. Co. *v.* Falvey, 104 Ind. 409; s. c., 23 Am. & Eng. R R Cas 522; Ehrgott *v.* Mayor, 96 N. Y. 264; s. c., 48 Am. Rep. 622; Brown *v.* Chicago, etc., R. Co., 54 Wis. 342; s. c., 3 Am. & Eng. R. R. Cas. 444; Houston, etc., R. Co. *v.* Leslie, 57 Tex. 83; s. c., 9 Am. & Eng. R. Cas. 407; Allison *v.* Chicago, etc., R. Co., 42 Iowa, 274, and see *ante*, §§ 13 and 14.

4. **But Disease may be Evidence of Contributory Negligence, when.** — Reading, etc., R. Co. *v.* Eckert, 2 Cent. Rep. 793 (Pa. 1886); Pullman Palace Car Co. *v.* Barker, 4 Colo. 344; s. c., 34 Am. Rep. 89; New Orleans, etc., R. Co. *v.* Statham, 42 Miss. 607; Hobbs *v.* London, etc., R. Co., L. R. 10 Q. B. 111. To the extent stated in the text, the case of Pullman Car Co. *v.* Barker, although often denied and criticised, may be sustained. The real trouble in that case was, that a correct principle was wrongly applied to a natural function or condition of common occurrence, and the existence of which in its female passengers the railroad company might reasonably have foreseen. Indeed, in its ultimate analysis, the question under consideration is always one of proximate cause. With notice of the existence of an unusual condition liable to enhance the results of a slight injury, liability for an enhancement by negligence arises when, without such negligence, there would be no liability, because the defendant would only be liable for such consequences as might reasonably have been foreseen. Kitteringham *v.* Sioux City, etc., R. Co., 62 Iowa, 285; s. c., 18 Am. & Eng. R. R. Cas. 14.

be held for any consequences except those directly caused by his negligence, and which might have been foreseen as its consequences.[1]

40. The Burden of Proof. — It is a moot question whether the burden of proving contributory negligence, or its absence, rests on plaintiff or defendant.[2] In some jurisdictions it is held, that, as the plaintiff cannot recover unless he was in the exercise of ordinary care at the time of the injury, he must both allege and prove that the injury occurred without negligence on his part;[3] and it is even said that there is a presumption that he was not using ordinary care.[4] On the other hand, it is held by a majority of the courts and most text-writers that there is a presumption of ordinary care in favor of plaintiff and defendant both, and that it devolves on plaintiff to prove a want of ordinary care on defendant's part, and on defendant to prove a want of such care on the part of plaintiff, contributing to his injury.[5] But in all jurisdic-

1. **When Diseased Condition should go in Mitigation of Damages.** — This rests upon the principle that for consequences which could not have been foreseen, and which would not have resulted in ordinary cases, there can be no liability unless the negligent person had notice, or by the exercise of ordinary care might have known, of the diseased condition or the tendency to disease that would enhance the effects of a slight injury; and in such cases it would seem that the proximate cause of such enhancement would be the negligence of the person injured in exposing himself to serious injury from a cause that ordinarily would not be productive of such injuries, without giving notice of the danger to the person guilty of the negligence that ordinarily would only have resulted in a slight injury, perhaps none at all. See, upon this question of proximate and remote causes, Hoag *v.* Lake Shore, etc., R. Co., 85 Pa. St. 293, 298; Shearman & Redf. on Neg. § 10; Sharp *v.* Powell, L. R. 7, C. P. 253; s. c., 2 Eng. Rep. (Moak's) 567; Brown *v.* Wabash R. Co., 20 Mo. App. 222; Francis *v.* St. Louis T. Co., 5 Mo. App. 7; Oil City Gas Co. *v.* Robinson, 99 Pa. St. 1; Shepherd *v.* Midland R. Co., 25 L. T. R. (N. S.) 879.

2. **The Burden of Proof Question.** — Cooley on Torts, 673; 2 Thomp. on Neg. 1175, § 24; Id. 1235, § 8; Shearman & Redf. on Neg. §§ 43, 44; Wharton on Neg. §§ 423-427; Patterson's Ry. Acc. L. 435, § 374; Pierce on Railroads, 298-300, 320; 2 Wood's Ry. Law, 1258-1261; Beach on Cont. Neg. 421-450; Whittaker's Smith on Neg. 381-384, notes.

3. **Where the Burden held on the Plaintiff.** — Cincinnati, etc., R. Co. *v.* Butler, 103 Ind. 31; s. c., 23 Am. & Eng. R. R. Cas. 262; Indiana, etc., R. Co. *v.* Greene, 106 Ind. 279; s. c., 25 Am. & Eng. R. R. Cas. 322, 55 Am. Rep. 736; Louisville, etc., R. Co. *v.* Orr, 84 Ind. 50; Mount Vernon *v.* Dusonchett, 2 Ind. 586; s. c., 54 Am. Dec. 467, 470; Hinckley *v.* Cape Cod, etc., R. Co., 120 Mass. 257; Stock *v.* Wood, 136 Mass. 353; State *v.* Maine Cent. R. Co., 76 Me. 357; s. c., 19 Am. & Eng. R. R. Cas. 312, 49 Am. Rep. 622; Kennard *v.* Burton, 25 Me. 39; s. c., 43 Am. Dec. 249; Vicksburg *v.* Hennessy, 54 Miss. 363; Moore *v.* Shreveport, 3 La. Ann. 645; Button *v.* Frink, 51 Conn. 342; Missouri Furnace Co. *v.* Abend, 107 Ill. 44; s. c., 47 Am. Rep. 425; Galena, etc., R. Co. *v.* Fay, 16 Ill. 558; s. c., 63 Am. Dec. 323; Greenleaf *v.* Ill., etc., R. Co., 29 Iowa, 14; s. c., 4 Am. Rep. 181; Slossen v. Burlington, etc., R. Co., 55 Ia. 294; s. c., 7 Am. & Eng. R. R. Cas. 509. But see Burns *v.* Chicago, etc., R. Co., 69 Iowa, 450; s. c., 28 Am. & Eng. R. R. Cas. 409; 58 Am. Rep. 227; Detroit & Milwaukee R. Co. *v.* Van Steinburg, 17 Mich. 99; Teifel *v.* Hilsendegin, 44 Mich. 461; Mitchell *v.* Chicago, etc., R. Co., 51 Mich. 236; s. c., 12 Am. & Eng. R. R. Cas. 163; 47 Am. Rep. 566; Doggett *v.* Richmond, etc., R. Co., 78 N. Car. 305; Walsh *v.* Oregon, etc., R. Co., 10 Oregon, 250.

4. **The Presumption of Negligence again.** — Indiana, etc., R. Co. *v.* Greene, 106 Ind. 279; s. c., 25 Am. & Eng. R. R. Cas. 322; 55 Am. Rep. 736; State *v.* Maine, etc., R. Co., 76 Me. 357; s. c., 19 Am. & Eng. R. R. Cas. 312; 49 Am. Rep. 622; Chase *v.* Maine. etc., R. Co., 77 Me. 62; s. c., 19 Am. & Eng. R. Cas. 356; Patterson's Ry. Acc. Law, § 378. But see Schum *v.* Penna. R. Co., 107 Pa. St.; s. c., 52 Am. Rep. 468; Penna R. Co. *v.* Weber, 76 Pa. St. 157; s. c., 18 Am. Rep. 407; Cassidy *v.* Angell, 12 R. I. 447; s. c., 34 Am. Rep. 690.

5. **Where the Burden held on Defendant.** — Hough *v.* Railroad Co, 100 U. S. 213;

tions, if plaintiff's declaration or evidence establishes his own contributory negligence, it bars his recovery, no matter where the burden rests.[1] And in jurisdictions where the burden of proving contributory negligence is on the defendant, plaintiff is only required to prove that the negligence of defendant was a cause of his injury in order to entitle him to recover, it being held sufficient for him to show a proximate cause adequate to account for the injury.[2] Perhaps the true doctrine is, that there is no pre-

Railroad Co. v. Gladman, 15 Wall. (U. S.) 401; Railroad Co. v. Horst, 93 U. S. 291; Smoot v. Wetumpka, 24 Ala. 112; Mobile, etc., R. Co. v. Crewnshaw, 65 Ala. 569; s. c., 8 Am. & Eng. R. R. Cas. 541; Thompson v. Duncan, 76 Ala. 334; McDougall v. Cent. R. Co., 63 Cal. 431; s. c., 12 Am. & Eng. R. R. Cas. 143; May v. Hanson, 5 Cal. 360; s. c, 63 Am. Dec. 135; Gay v. Winter, 34 Cal. 153; St. Louis, etc., R. Co. v. Weaver, 35 Kan. 412; s. c., 28 Am. & Eng. R. R. Cas. 341; Paducah, etc., R. Co. v. Hoehl, 12 Bush (Ky), 41; Kentucky, etc., R. Co. v. Thomas, 79 Ky. 160; s. c., 1 Am. & Eng. R. R. Cas. 79; Louisville, etc., R. Co. v. Goetz, 79 Ky. 442; s. c., 14 Am. & Eng. R. R. Cas. 627, 42 Am. Rep. 227; Thompson v. Cent., etc., R. Co., 54 Ga. 509; Prince George's Co. Com'rs v. Burgess, 61 Md. 29; Bacon v. Baltimore, etc., R. Co., 58 Md. 482; s. c., 15 Am. & Eng. R. R. Cas. 409; Hocum v. Weitherick, 22 Minn. 152; Texas, etc., R. Co. v. Orr, 46 Ark. 182; Little Rock, etc., R. Co. v. Atkins, 46 Ark. 423; Little Rock, etc., R. Co. v. Enbanks (Ark.), 3 S. W. Rep. 808; Lopez v. Cent. Arizona Min. Co., 1 Ariz. 464; Sanderson v. Frazier, 8 Colo. 79; s. c., 54 Am. Rep. 544, 547; Stepp v. Chicago R. Co., 85 Mo. 225; Buesching v. St. Louis Gas Co., 73 Mo. 219; s. c, 39 Am. Rep. 503; Lincoln v. Walker (Neb. 1884), 5 Am. & Eng. Corp. Cas. 610; Smith v. Eastern, etc., R. Co., 35 N. H. 356; New Jersey Ex. Co. v. Nichols, 33 N. J. L. 434; s. c., 33 N. J. L. 434; Cleveland, etc., R. Co. v. Crawford, 24 Ohio St. 631; s. c., 15 Am. Rep. 633; Baltimore, etc., R. Co. v. Whitacre, 35 Ohio St. 627; Cassidy v. Angell, 12 R. I. 447; s. c, 34 Am. Rep. 690; Carter v. Columbia, etc., R. Co., 19 So. Car. 20; s. c, 15 Am. & Eng. R. R. Cas. 414, 45 Am. Rep. 754; Roof v. Charlotte, etc., R. Co., 4 So. Car 61; Mares v. N. P. R. Co. (Dak. 1884), 17 Am. & Eng. R. R. Cas. 620; Houston, etc., R. Co. v. Cowser, 57 Tex. 293; Dallas, etc., R. Co. v. Spicker, 61 Tex. 427; s. c., 21 Am. & Eng. R. R. Cas. 160, 48 Am. Rep. 297; Texas P. R. Co. v. Davidson (1887), 4 S. W. Rep. 636; Prideaux v. Mineral Point, 43 Wis. 513; s. c., 28 Am. Rep. 558; Hoth v. Peters, 55 Wis. 405; Sheff v. Huntington, 16 W. Va. 307; Fowler v. Baltimore, etc., R. Co., 18 W. Va. 579; s. c., 8 Am. & Eng. R. R. Cas. 480; Barber v. Essex, 27 Vt. 62; Hill v. New Haven, 37 Vt. 501. But see Boree v. Danville, 53 Vt. 183; Holden v. Gas. Co., 3 C. B. 1; Muller v. Dist. of Col. (D. C. 1886), 5 Cent. Rep. 428; Bridge v. Grand Junction R. Co., 3 Mee. & W. 244; Martin v. Gt. N., etc., R. Co., 16 C. B. 179. The doctrines of the New York and Pennsylvania courts will be stated farther on. Perhaps they establish the true rule upon the question of the burden of proof.

1. **How when Plaintiff's Evidence shows Contributory Negligence.**—Pierce on Railroads, 320; Cooley on Torts, 673; Railroad Co. v. Gladman, 15 Wall. (U. S.) 401; Freck v. Philadelphia, etc., R. Co., 39 Md. 574; McQuillen v. Cent. Pac. R. Co., 50 Cal. 7; Lincoln v. Walker (Neb. 1884), 5 Am. & Eng. Corp Cas. 610; Prideaux v. Mineral Point, 43 Wis. 513; s. c., 28 Am. Rep. 558; Cassidy v. Angell, 12 R. I. 447; s. c., 34 Am. Rep. 690; Boss v. Providence, etc., R. Co. (R. I.), 21 Am. & Eng. R. R. Cas. 364; N. J. Ex. Co. v. Nichols, 33 N. J. L. 434; Berry v. Penna. R. Co., 48 N. J. L. 141; s. c., 26 Am. & Eng. R. R. Cas. 396; Baltimore, etc., R. Co. v. Whitacre, 35 Ohio St. 627; Winship v. Enfield, 42 N. H. 197.

2. **Proof required of Plaintiff when Burden on Defendant.**—"In view of the conflict in the authorities, we are compelled to adopt such rule as may seem most consonant with justice. This being so, there certainly is no presumption that the plaintiff was negligent. We therefore hold the rule to be, that, if the plaintiff can prove his case without showing contributory negligence, it is a matter of defence to be proved by the defendant." Lincoln v. Walker (Neb. 1884), 5 Am. & Eng. Corp. Cas. 610, 611; Prideaux v. Mineral Point, 43 Wis. 513; s. c., 28 Am. Rep. 558; Hoyt v. Hudson, 41 Wis. 105; s. c., 22 Am. Rep. 714; Daniel v. Met. R. Co., L. R. 3 C. B. 591; Id. 5 H. L. 45; Milwaukee, etc., R. Co. v. Hunter, 11 Wis. 160; s. c., 78 Am. Dec. 699; Johnson v. Hudson River R. Co., 20 N. Y. 65; s. c., 75 Am. Dec. 375 and note.

"It would seem that a plaintiff would be entitled in every case of this character to recover upon evidence which clearly makes a *prima facie* case, unless such case be resumption of either negligence or care which is applicable as a general rule in all cases, but that the question of the burden of proof should be determined on the facts of each case according to whether they show a duty of care on plaintiff or defendant.[1] On principle, it would seem sufficient to entitle plaintiff to recover for him to show a negligent injury by defendant, with nothing in the circumstances establishing contributory negligence on his part; and this done, it would devolve upon defendant to show plaintiff's contributory negligence affirmatively.[2]

butted by testimony offered by himself or by defendant." Dallas, etc., R. Co. *v.* Spicker, 61 Tex. 427; s. c., 48 Am. Rep. 297; Buesching *v.* Gas. Co., 73 Mo. 219; s. c., 39 Am. Rep. 503, and note; Kingston *v.* Gibbons (Pa. 1886), 5 Cent. Rep. 222.

1. **The True Rule as to the Burden of Proof.** — *Ante*, § 33, notes 173, 174; Burns *v.* Chicago, etc., R. Co., 69 Iowa, 450; s. c., 28 Am. & Eng. R. R. Cas. 409; 58 Am. Rep. 227, and note; Terpet *v.* Hilsendegan, 44 Mich. 461; Hart *v.* Hudson River Bridge Co., 80 N. Y. 622; Mayo *v.* Boston, etc., R. Co., 104 Mass. 137; Smith *v.* Boston Gas Co., 129 Mass. 318; Com. *v.* Boston & Lowell R. Co., 126 Mass. 61; Street R. Co. *v.* Nolthenius, 40 Ohio St. 376; s. c., 19 Am. & Eng. R. R. Cas. 191; Baltimore, etc., R. Co. *v.* Whitacre, 35 Ohio St. 627; Cleveland, etc., R. Co. *v.* Crawford, 24 Ohio St. 631, 636; s. c., 15 Am. Rep. 633. "I am of the opinion that it is not a rule of law of universal application, that the plaintiff must prove affirmatively that his own conduct on the occasion of the injury was cautious and prudent. The *onus probandi* in this, as in most other cases, depends upon the position of the affair as it stands upon the undisputed facts." *Denio, J.*, in Johnson *v.* Hudson R. R Co, 20 N. Y. 65; s. c., 75 Am. Dec. 375, and note. And such seems to be still the rule in New York, although Tolman *v.* Syracuse, etc., R. Co, 98 N. Y. 198; s. c., 23 Am. & Eng. R. R. Cas. 313; 50 Am. Rep. 649, has been cited as establishing the rule that plaintiff must affirmatively prove due care. Beach, Cont. Neg. 446. The real effect of the decision in the Johnson case is to hold that plaintiff may recover by showing negligence on the part of the defendant adequate to account for the injury inflicted when the circumstances establishing so much are also consistent with the exercise of ordinary care on plaintiff's part. This rests upon the principle, that a sufficient direct cause of an injury appearing, it will be held the sole proximate cause in the absence of evidence of any other cause. Adams *v.* Young, 44 Ohio St. 80; s. c, 58 Am. Rep. 789; Milwaukee, etc., R. Co. *v.* Kellogg, 94 U. S. 469. And that the Tolman case does not depart from the general New York rule, may be seen when it is considered that in that case the contributory negligence of the deceased affirmatively appeared, and it was impossible to infer from the facts and circumstances that he was in the exercise of due care. In another case reported in the same volume, it was *held* that plaintiff need not negative contributory negligence in his complaint. Lee *v.* Troy Cit. Gas Co., 98 N. Y. 115. And the effect of this decision is, that when plaintiff has shown the negligence of the defendant as a proximate cause sufficient to account for the injury, without showing fault on his own part, he is entitled to recover. And such is the doctrine in New York, as the learned editor of the Am. Reports understands it. Note to Buesching *v.* Gas Co., 39 Am. Rep. 512, 513; note to Burns *v.* Chicago, etc., R. Co., 58 Am. Rep. 229, 230; s. c., 28 Am. & Eng. R. R. Cas. 409. Where it is possible to infer due care, the question is for the jury. Byrne *v.* N. Y. Cent. R. Co., 104 N. Y. 362; s. c, 58 Am. Rep. 512; 83 N. Y. 620; Long Island R. Co. *v.* Greany, 101 N. Y. 419; s. c., 24 Am. & Eng. R. R. Cas. 473. And see Schum *v.* Railroad Co., 107 Pa. St. 8; s. c, 52 Am. Rep. 468; Penna. R. Co *v.* Weber, 76 Pa. St. 157; s. c., 18 Am. Rep. 407 · Railroad Co. *v.* Rowan, 66 Pa. St. 393; McKimble *v.* Boston, etc, R. Co., 139 Mass. 542; s. c., 21 Am. & Eng. R. R. Cas. 213.

2. **The Underlying Principle.** — Wharton on Neg. §§ 423, 426; Shearman & Redf. on Neg. § 44; Stephen's Dig. of Ev. Art. 95; Patterson's Ry. Acc. L. § 374, and cases cited; Burns *v.* Chicago, etc., R. Co., 69 Iowa, 450; s. c., 28 Am. & Eng. R. R. Cas. 409, 58 Am. Rep. 227; Cassidy *v.* Angell, 12 R. I. 447; s. c., 34 Am. Rep. 790; Dallas, etc., R. Co. *v.* Spicker, 61 Tex. 427; s. c., 21 Am. & Eng. R. R. Cas. 160, 48 Am. Rep. 297; Louisville, etc., R. Co. *v.* Goetz, 79 Ky. 442; s. c., 14 Am. & Eng. R. R. Cas. 627, 42 Am. Rep. 227; Lincoln *v.* Walker (Neb. 1884), 5 Am. & Eng. Corp. Cas. 610; Missouri Furnace Co. *v.* Abend. 107 Ill. 44; s. c, 47 Am. Rep. 425; Chicago, etc., R. Co. *v* Carey, 115 Ill. 115; Ill, etc., R. Co. *v.* Cragin, 71 Ill. 177; Penna. R. Co. *v.* Goodman, 62 Pa. St. 329; Hays *v.* Gal-

41. Law and Fact. — When the facts are disputed, or more than one inference can be fairly drawn from them as to the care, or want of care, of the plaintiff, the question of contributory negligence is for the jury;[1] but when the facts are undisputed, and but one inference regarding the care of the plaintiff can be drawn from them, the question is one of law for the court.[2] It is often said that negligence and contributory negligence are usually mixed questions of law and fact;[3] and, in a certain sense, this is true when the court does not determine the question as one of law alone; for, when the case goes to the jury, it is the duty of the court to tell the jury what facts, if proved, will constitute negligence or contributory negligence, and to explain and state the rule

lagher, 72 Pa. St. 136; Penna. R. Co. v. Weber, 76 Pa. St. 157; s. c., 18 Am. Rep. 407; Schum v. Penna. R. Co., 107 Pa. St. 8; s. c., 52 Am. Rep. 468; Stepp v. Chicago, etc., R. Co., 85 Mo. 225; Kingston v. Gibbons (Pa. 1886), 5 Cent. Rep. 222; Bueschimg v. St. Louis Gas Co., 73 Mo. 219; s. c., 39 Am. Rep. 503, and note; Prideaux v. Mineral Point, 43 Wis. 513; s. c., 28 Am. Rep. 558; Phila., etc., R. Co. v. Stebbing, 62 Md. 504; s. c., 19 Am. & Eng. R. R. Cas. 36.

"There is no presumption of negligence as against either party, except such as arises from the facts proved. Indeed, the presumption of law is, that neither party was guilty of negligence, and such presumption must prevail until overcome by proof. In actions for injury by negligence, where there is nothing in plaintiff's evidence tending to show contributory negligence, the presumption will be that there is no contributory negligence, and this presumption remains until the contrary is shown." Pittsburgh, etc., R. Co. v. Fleming, 30 Ohio St. 480, 485; Ruffner v. Cincinnati, etc., R. Co., 34 Ohio St. 96. But see Hinckley v. Cape Cod R. Co., 120 Mass. 257, where it is said that "mere proof that the negligence of defendant was a cause adequate to have produced the injury, will not enable plaintiff to recover, as it does not necessarily give rise to the inference of due care on his part, proof of which is essential to his case."

1. **Contributory Negligence: When for the Jury.** — Cooley on Torts, 666–671; Pierce on Railroads, 311 *et seq.*; Wharton on Neg. § 420; Patterson's Ry. Acc. L. §§ 382–384; 2 Thomp. on Neg. 1178, § 25; Id. 1239, § 13; Beach on Cont. Neg. § 163; Hathaway v. East Tenn., etc., R. Co., 29 Fed. Rep. 489; North Penn. R. Co. v. Heileman, 49 Pa. St. 60; s. c., 1 Thomp. on Neg. 401. "When the question arises upon a state of facts on which reasonable men may fairly arrive at different conclusions, the fact of negligence cannot be determined until one or other of these conclusions has been drawn by the jury. The inferences to be drawn from the evidence must either be certain and incontrovertible, or they cannot be decided by the court. Negligence cannot be conclusively established by a state of facts upon which fair-minded men may well differ." *Cooley, J.*, in Detroit, etc., R. Co. v. Van Steinburg, 17 Mich. 99; Hart v. Hudson R. B. Co., 80 N. Y. 622; Boss v. Providence, etc., R. Co. (R. I. 1885), 21 Am. & Eng. R. R. Cas. 364; Petty v. Hannibal, etc., R. Co. (Mo. 1886), 28 Am. & Eng. R. R. Cas. 618; Lehigh Valley R. Co. v. Greiner (Pa. 1886), 28 Am. & Eng. R. R. Cas. 397; Strand v. Chicago, etc., R. Co. (Mich. 1887), 28 Am. & Eng. R. R. Cas. 213; Fernandes v. Sacramento City R. Co., 52 Cal. 45; Jochem v. Robinson, 66 Wis. 638; s. c., 57 Am. Rep. 298.

2. **When for the Court.** — Beach on Cont. Neg. § 162; Todd v. Old Colony, etc., R. Co., 3 Allen (Mass.), 18; s. c., 80 Am. Dec. 49, and note; Merrill v. North Yarmouth, 78 Me. 200; s. c., 57 Am. Rep. 794; Larmore v. Crown Point Iron Co., 101 N. Y. 391; s. c., 54 Am. Rep. 718; Pierce v. Whitcomb, 48 Vt. 127; s. c., 21 Am. Rep. 120; Tolman v. Syracuse, etc., R. Co., 98 N. Y. 198; s. c., 23 Am. & Eng. R. R. Cas. 313, 50 Am. Rep. 649; Schofield v. Chicago, etc., R. Co., 114 U. S. 615; s. c., 19 Am. & Eng. R. R. Cas. 353; Baker v. Fehr, 97 Pa. St. 70; Indianapolis v. Cook, 99 Ind. 10; Lehigh Valley, etc., R. Co. v. Greiner (Pa. 1886), 28 Am. & Eng. R. R. Cas. 397; Filer v. N. Y. Cent. R. Co., 49 N. Y. 47; Reading, etc., R. Co. v. Ritchie, 102 Pa. St. 425; s. c., 19 Am. & Eng. R. R. Cas. 267.

3. **A Mixed Question of Law and Fact.** — Beach on Cont. Neg. § 161; Fernandes v. Sacramento, etc., R. Co., 52 Cal. 45, 50; Wharton on Neg. § 420; Cleveland, etc., R. Co. v. Terry, 8 Ohio St. 570–585; Trow v. Vt. Cent. R. Co., 24 Vt. 487; s. c., 58 Am. Dec. 191. And see, on submitting question of proximate cause to jury, opinion

of proximate cause.[1] This done, the jury must determine the facts, and apply to the facts proved the law as laid down by the court.[2]

42. Peculiar Modifications of Doctrine. — In some jurisdictions, peculiar modifications of the general doctrines of contributory negligence have been made, either by the courts or the legislatures; and the more important of these modifications are here noted.

The Rule in Illinois. — In Illinois the doctrine of comparative negligence prevails, and the Illinois rule has been fully treated already.[3] The results reached under that rule are not different from those following the application of the doctrine that a want of ordinary care on plaintiff's part contributing to his injury as a proximate cause thereof, bars his right of recovery.[4]

The Rule in Georgia. — In Georgia it is provided by statute, that, "If the plaintiff by ordinary care could have avoided the consequences to himself caused by the defendant's negligence, he is not entitled to recover. But in other cases the defendant is not relieved, although the plaintiff may in some way have contributed to the injury sustained."[5] It is also provided by statute, that "no person shall recover damages from a railroad company for injury to himself or to his property, where the same is done by his consent, or is caused by his own negligence. If the complainant and the agents of the company are both at fault, the former may recover; but the damages shall be diminished by the jury in proportion to the amount of default attributable to him."[6] These statutes are said to be declaratory of the common law as established by the decisions in Georgia prior to the code,[7] and those decisions should be considered in connection with the statutory provisions.[8] They do not establish the doctrine of comparative

of *Seymour D. Thompson, J.*, in Dunn *v.* Cass Ave., etc., R. Co., 21 Mo. App. Rep. 188.

1. **What this means.** — Baltimore, etc., R. Co. *v.* State, 36 Md. 366; Detroit, etc., R. Co. *v.* Van Steinburg, 17 Mich. 118; Met. R. Co. *v.* Jackson, L. R. 2 C. P. D. 125; Memphis, etc., R. Co. *v.* Whitfield, 44 Miss. 466; Montgomery *v.* Wright, 72 Ala. 411; s. c., 47 Am. Rep. 422; Pierce on Railroads, 322; Pennsylvania Co. *v.* Conlan, 101 Ill. 93; s. c., 6 Am. & Eng. R. R. Cas. 243; Pleasants *v.* Fant, 22 Wall. (U. S.) 121; Cumberland, etc., R. Co. *v.* State, 37 Md. 157; Bigelow's Lea. Cas. on Torts, 580, *et seq.*; Toledo, etc., R. Co. *v.* Goddard, 25 Ind. 185.

2. Pierce on Railroads, 311; 2 Thomp. on Neg. 1235, § 10.

3. **Comparative Negligence.** — See "Comparative Negligence," 3 Am. & Eng. Ency. of Law.

4. **It does not change Results.** — See title "Comparative Negligence," 3 Am. & Eng. Ency. of Law.

5. **The Georgia Statute.** — Code of Georgia, 1882, § 2972.

6. **Other Provisions.** — Code of Georgia, 1882, § 3034. See also Id. § 3033, which establishes the rule that, when persons property, or stock are injured by the running of the locomotives, cars, or other machinery of the railroad company, it will be presumed that such injury was negligent, and the burden of disproving negligence is upon the railroad company. See, as to rebuttal of this presumption, Central, etc., R. Co. *v.* Sanders, 73 Ga. 513; s. c., 27 Am. & Eng. R. R. Cas. 300.

7. **Said to declare Common Law Rule.** — "Both branches of the rule of liability, as laid down in these sections of the Code, are traceable to, and derived from, decisions of this court, made prior to the adoption of that body of laws." Cent. R. Co. of Ga. *v.* Brinson, 70 Ga. 207; s. c., 19 Am. & Eng. R. R. Cas. 50.

8. **Decisions before the Statute.** — It is out of these earlier decisions that the idea

negligence as it exists in Illinois.[1] From the latest cases it seems that the Georgia rule may be thus stated: The plaintiff cannot recover, —

(1) When he could, by ordinary care, have avoided the consequences of defendant's negligence;

(2) When the injury is done by his consent;

(3) When the injury is caused by his own negligence;

(4) When the defendant has been guilty of no negligence; but,

(5) The plaintiff may recover when his own negligence contributed to the injury caused by the negligence of the defendant, *provided*, the defendant might, by the exercise of ordinary care, have prevented the injury, but in such case the plaintiff's contributory negligence may be considered in mitigation of his damages.[2] If this latter rule be applied only in cases where the negligence of the plaintiff is antecedent to that of the defendant, and when defendant might, by the exercise of ordinary care, have discovered plaintiff's negligence in time to have avoided injuring him, it only differs from the rule elsewhere in allowing plaintiff's *remote* negligence to be considered in mitigation of damages.[3] But if it is

that the rule of comparative negligence prevails in Georgia has arisen. Brannon *v.* May, 17 Ga. 136; Macon, etc., R. Co. *v.* Davis, 13 Ga. 68; s. c., 18 Ga. 679; s. c., 27 Ga. 113; Macon, etc., R. Co. *v.* Winn, 19 Ga. 440; s. c., 26 Ga. 250. In the Winn case (19 Ga.), *Lumpkin, J.*, reviews the Davis and May cases, and says they do not conflict, and in the Winn case the doctrine of contributory negligence is correctly and fully stated as the law. Later cases use the terms "gross" and "slight" negligence in an improper manner, but never, we think, in a technical sense, for the purpose of comparison. Augusta, etc., R. Co. *v.* McElmurry, 24 Ga. 75; Rome *v.* Dodd, 58 Ga. 238; Cent., etc., R. Co. *v.* Gleason, 69 Ga. 200; Atlanta, etc., R. Co. *v.* Wyly, 65 Ga. 120; s. c., 8 Am. & Eng. R. R. Cas. 262; Thompson *v.* Cent. R. Co., 54 Ga. 509, Campbell *v.* Atlanta, etc., R. Co., 53 Ga. 488; s. c., 56 Ga. 586; Hendricks *v.* West. R. Co., 52 Ga. 467; Macon, etc., R. Co. *v.* Johnson, 38 Ga. 408; Yonge *v.* Kinney, 28 Ga. 111; Vickers *v.* Atlanta, etc., R. Co., 64 Ga. 308; s. c., 8 Am. & Eng. R. R. Cas. 337; Georgia, etc., R. Co. *v.* Neely, 56 Ga. 540; Southwestern, etc., R. Co. *v.* Johnson, 60 Ga. 667; Southwestern R. Co. *v.* Hankerson, 61 Ga. 114.

1. Not Comparative Negligence. — The effect of the decisions was really to declare the doctrine of Davies *v.* Mann, 1 Mee. & W. 564. And so Judge Redfield understood the McElmurry case (24 Ga. 75), note, 2 Am. Law Reg. (N. S.) 90; and to the same doctrine the Winn case in 19 Ga. 445 has been recently cited in Georgia. Higgins *v.* Cherokee R. Co., 73 Ga. 149; s. c., 27 Am. & Eng. R. R. Cas. 218, 228. The test is always that of ordinary care. M. & W. R. Co. *v.* Johnson, 38 Ga. 431; Macon, etc., R. Co. *v.* Davis, 18 Ga. 679. "*The term 'gross negligence,'* used in connection with such circumstances, has a relative rather than an absolute and strict signification, and, as thus used, *is the equivalent of acts which result* from a failure to observe that 'ordinary and reasonable care and diligence' prescribed by our Code." Cent. R. Co. *v.* Brinson, 70 Ga. 207; s. c., 19 Am. & Eng. R. R. Cas. 42, 67.

2. The Present Georgia Rule. — Central, etc., R. Co. *v.* Brinson, 70 Ga. 207; s. c., 19 Am. & Eng. R. R. Cas. 42; Georgia R. Co. *v.* Pittman, 73 Ga. 325; s. c., 26 Am. & Eng. R. R. Cas. 474; Higgins *v.* Cherokee, etc., R. Co., 73 Ga. 149; s. c., 27 Am. & Eng. R. R. Cas. 218. It should be noted that subdivision 5 of the rule has no application between master and servant. In cases of injuries to employees by the negligence of the master, the contributory negligence of the servant is an absolute bar to recovery, and the rule that it may be considered in mitigation of damages does not apply. Georgia R. Co. *v.* Ivey, 73 Ga. 499; s. c., 28 Am. & Eng. R. R. Cas. 392.

3. To What Cases applicable. — Thus, in Davies *v.* Mann (1 Mee. & W. 564), the plaintiff, having been guilty of negligence which the defendant, by the exercise of ordinary care, could have discovered in time to have avoided injuring plaintiff's donkey, it was held that plaintiff could recover, his negligence being remote, and that of defendant proximate. In such cases the remote negligence of plaintiff is not construed to permit a partial recovery where plaintiff's negligence is concurrent with the negligence of the defendant, and a proximate cause of the injury, then it establishes a rule for the apportionment of damages according to the respective fault of the parties.[1]

The Rule in Tennessee. — The doctrine of comparative negligence, although often said to do so, does not prevail in Tennessee.[2] And the terms "gross" and "slight" negligence as used in that State do not refer to the degrees of negligence, but are used in the sense of proximate and remote causes.[3] The only difference between the Tennessee rule and the general rule is, that in certain cases plaintiff's remote negligence may be considered in mitigation of damages.[4] His contributory negligence proximately

held a juridical cause of the injury, and cannot be considered in bar of the action, or in mitigation of damages. Wharton on Neg. (1st ed.) §§ 323-343. But it seems that in Georgia such remote negligence is treated as contributing to the injury; and hence it would have been held in Davies *v.* Mann, and has been held in similar cases, in that State, that such *antecedent* negligence on plaintiff's part, while it will not bar his action, may be considered in mitigation of his damages. 2 Thomp. on Neg. 1165, § 153. This is well illustrated by a late case, where the plaintiff's husband stood upon a railroad track, engaged in taking the numbers of ears on an adjacent track. While so standing, a locomotive came along the track towards him, and those in charge of the locomotive saw him, and discovered that he was making no effort to escape danger, and was apparently unconscious of it. They shouted at him, and without having tried to stop the locomotive, which they might have done, they struck and killed him. It was evident that the killing was not wilful, and that the men on the locomotive thought, until the last instant, that deceased would get off the track. It was held that plaintiff could recover, but that the conduct of her husband might be considered in mitigation of damages. Georgia, etc., R. Co. *v.* Pittman, 73 Ga. 325; s. c., 26 Am. & Eng. R. R. Cas. 474. And in this same case the jury were told that if the negligence of the deceased was the proximate cause of his death, no recovery could be had, and this question was submitted to the jury. And such, we think, is the clear meaning of the Brinson case, *supra.*

1. **Not applied if Plaintiff's Negligence Proximate.** — And this *Mr. Thompson* (Neg. 1165, § 15) and *Mr. Beach* (Cont. Neg. 92) seem to regard as the effect of the rule; but we think an examination of the Georgia cases cited will show that plaintiff's negligence is only considered in mitigation of damages when it is a remote cause of his injury, and that his proximate negligence always bars his action. Perhaps these distinctions have not always been clearly made or consistently adhered to, but they underlie the Georgia rule. Wharton on Neg. §§ 334, 335.

2. **In Tennessee Comparative Negligence not the Rule.** — "The doctrine of 'comparative negligence'" is "a doctrine correctly said not to be the law of this State." East Tenn., etc., R. *v.* Gurley, 12 Lea (Tenn.), 46, 55; s. c., 17 Am. & Eng. R. R. Cas. 568. The test is that of "ordinary care under the circumstances." Louisville, etc., R. Co. *v.* Gower, 85 Tenn. (1 Pickle) 465. And the proximateness or remoteness of such want of ordinary care determines the question of liability. Railroad Co. *v.* Fain, 12 Lea (Tenn.), 35; s. c., 19 Am. & Eng. R. R. Cas. 102.

3. **"Gross" and "Slight" mean "Proximate" and "Remote."** — "He is considered the author of the injury, by whose first or more gross negligence, *in the sense of proximate negligence,* it has been effected." Railroad Co. *v.* Fain, 12 Lea (Tenn.), 35, 40; s. c, 19 Am. & Eng. R. R. Cas. 102. And such was the meaning of the term, "*More gross* negligence," in the case of Whirley *v.* Whiteman, 1 Head (Tenn.), 610, 623, which case, in 1858, first laid down the Tennessee doctrine. East Tenn., etc., R. Co. *v* Gurley, 12 Lea (Tenn.), 46, 55-56; s. c., 17 Am. & Eng. R. R. Cas. 568.

4. **Plaintiff's Remote Negligence in Mitigation.** — The court "also charged them in relation to mutual or contributory negligence, that if both parties were guilty of some negligence, if the negligence of the plaintiff was the proximate and efficient cause of the injury, she could not recover; but if the defendant's negligence was the proximate and efficient cause of the injury, it would be liable; but in such case the negligence of the plaintiff should be taken into consideration by them in mitigation of

causing his injury in combination with the negligence of the defendant, wholly bars his action.[1] And where his negligence is the proximate, and that of the defendant the remote, cause of the injury, he cannot recover.[2] But he may recover, as in other States, when the defendant, by the use of ordinary care, could have discovered his danger in time to avoid injuring him;[3] yet in such cases his prior negligence, that exposes him to defendant's subsequent negligence, is looked to in mitigation of damages.[4] And it seems that cases of the character of Davies *v.* Mann are the only ones to which the rule in mitigation is applicable,[5] unless the action arises under the statute of Tennessee, which provides that if a railroad fails to adopt certain precautions, it shall be absolutely liable for injuries which follow the failure.[6] This statute has been construed to render a railroad company liable for a failure to take the precautions required, whether such failure caused the injury or not;[7] and consequently contributory

damages. This has been the established law in Tennessee since the case of Whirley *v.* Whiteman, 1 Head (Tenn.), 611." East Tenn., etc., R. Co. *v.* Conner, 15 Lea (Tenn.), 254, 258; Louisville, etc., R. Co. *v.* Fleming, 14 Lea, 130; s. c., 18 Am. & Eng. R. R. Cas. 347; Whirley *v.* Whiteman, 1 Head (Tenn.), 610; East Tenn., etc., Co. *v.* Gurley, 12 Lea (Tenn.), 46, 55; s. c., 17 Am. & Eng. R. R. Cas. 568.

1. **Proximate Contributory Negligence a Bar.** — "If a party by his own gross negligence brings an injury upon himself, or proximately contributes to such injury, he cannot recover. Neither can he recover in cases of mutual negligence, where both parties are equally blamable." East Tenn., etc., R. Co. *v.* Fain, 12 Lea (Tenn.), 35, 39, 40; s. c., 19 Am. & Eng. R. R. Cas. 102.

2. **Plaintiff's Negligence Proximate Cause.** — "If the injury was caused by the conduct, or was the immediate result of the conduct, of the plaintiff, to which the wrong of the defendant did not contribute as an immediate cause, then plaintiff should not recover, but should bear the results of his own conduct or neglect." East Tenn., etc., R. Co. *v.* Fain, 12 Lea (Tenn.), 35, 40; s. c., 19 Am. & Eng. R. R. Cas. 102; Nashville & C. R. R. Co. *v.* Carroll, 6 Heisk. (Tenn.) 347, 367; Louisville, etc., R. Co. *v.* Fleming, 14 Lea (Tenn.), 128; s. c., 18 Am. & Eng. R. R. Cas. 347.

3. **Plaintiff's Remote Negligence.** — "It never was the law that any citizen would not be responsible if he saw another on his track, even a trespasser, and rode over him, when he could have avoided it." Railroad Co. *v.* Humphreys, 12 Lea (Tenn.), 200, 204; s. c., 15 Am. & Eng. R. R. Cas. 472; Dush *v.* Fitzhugh, 2 Lea (Tenn.), 307; Louisville, etc., R. Co. *v.* Fleming, 14 Lea (Tenn.), 128; s. c., 18 Am. & Eng. R. R. Cas. 347.

4. **Is looked to in Mitigation of Damages.** — "In this State we hold that, although the injured party may contribute to the injury by his own carelessness or wrongful conduct, yet, if the act or negligence of the party inflicting the injury was the proximate cause of the injury, the latter will be liable in damages, the negligence or wrongful conduct of the party injured being taken into consideration by way of mitigation in estimating the damages." Louisville, etc., R. Co. *v.* Fleming, 14 Lea, 128; s. c., 18 Am. & Eng. R. R. Cas. 347; East Tenn., etc., R. Co. *v.* Fain, 12 Lea (Tenn.), 35; s. c., 19 Am. & Eng. R. R. Cas. 102; Nashville, etc., R Co. *v.* Carroll, 6 Heisk. (Tenn.) 347, 366, 367.

5. Davies *v.* Mann, 1 Mee. & W. 564; s. c., 2 Thomp. on Neg. 1105; Beach on Cont. Neg. § 30; and the cases heretofore cited in this section, particularly those in the preceding note.

6. **Except when Action is Statutory.** — Code of Tenn. 1884, §§ 1298–1300.

7. **When a Railroad's Liability is Absolute.** — "It will be observed that the statute does not make the liability of the company depend upon whether or not the accident or collision was the consequence of the failure of the employees to observe these precautions; but, on the contrary, the company shall be liable to all damages resulting from any accident or collision in all cases where the company fail to prove that the precautions were observed. Therefore, if the precautions have not been observed, the company is liable, although it may appear that the observance of the precautions would not have prevented the accident." Railroad Co. *v.* Walker, 11 Heisk. (Tenn.) 383, 385; Nashville, etc., R. Co. *v.* Thomas,

negligence will not bar a recovery, but it is held that it may be considered in mitigation of damages;[1] yet the statute requiring the precaution is said to be only declaratory of the common law.[2]

The Rule in Kentucky. — The rule of comparative negligence does not prevail in Kentucky[3] or Kansas.[4]

The general doctrine of contributory negligence is correctly applied in each State, but some confusion has arisen from the fact that the courts of each State have sometimes used the terms "gross" and "slight" negligence in place of the terms "proximate" and "remote" negligence, and that they have also used the term "gross negligence" as signifying wilfulness.[5] Indeed, there is a Kentucky statute which provides for the recovery of punitive damages in certain cases when death results from "wilful negligence," and some of the decisions under this statute have been mistaken for indorsements of the doctrine of compara-

5 Heisk. (Tenn.) 262; Collins *v.* East Tenn., etc., R. Co., 9 Heisk. (Tenn.) 841; Hill *v.* Louisville, etc., R. Co., 9 Heisk. (Tenn.) 823; Louisville, etc., R. Co. *v.* Connor, 9 Heisk. (Tenn.) 20.

Except when no Time to comply with Statute. — But if, after a person, animal, or obstruction appears on the track, there is not time to comply with the statutory requirements, the failure to do so will not render the company liable. East Tenn., etc., R. Co. *v.* Swaney, 5 Lea (Tenn.), 119; East Tenn., etc., R. Co. *v.* Scales, 2 Lea (Tenn.), 688.

1. **And Contributory Negligence is not considered.** — East Tenn., etc., R. Co. *v.* White, 5 Lea (Tenn.), 540; s. c., 8 Am. & Eng. R. R. Cas. 65; Railroad Co. *v.* Walker, 11 Heisk. (Tenn.) 383. This statute is applicable only to the injury of persons or property, by actual collision, on the roadway proper. It does not apply to passengers on a train, nor to persons, whether employees or strangers, in the yards of a railroad company. And it is *held*, that the provisions of the statute are for the benefit of the general public, and have no application to employees of the railway company. East Tenn., etc., R. Co. *v.* Rush, 15 Lea (Tenn.), 145; s. c., 25 Am. & Eng. R. R. Cas. 502, and cases cited therein.

2. **The Statute said to be Declaratory only.** — East Tenn., etc., R. Co. *v.* Pratt, 85 Tenn. (1 Pickle) 9, 13; Louisville & N. R. Co. *v.* Fleming, 14 Lea (Tenn.), 128, 139; s. c., 18 Am. & Eng. R. R. Cas. 347; East Tenn., etc., R. Co. *v.* Humphreys, 12 Lea (Tenn.), 200; s. c., 15 Am. & Eng. R. R. Cas. 472 and note.

3. **General Rule prevails in Kentucky.** — Beach on Cont. Neg. § 31. "When the defence is contributory negligence, the proper question for the jury is, whether the damage was occasioned entirely by the negligence or improper conduct of the defendant, or whether the plaintiff himself so far contributed to the misfortune by his own negligence, or want of ordinary or common care and caution, that, but for such negligence, or want of ordinary care and caution on his part, the misfortune would not have occurred." Kentucky Cent. R. Co. *v.* Thomas, 79 Ky. 160; s. c., 1 Am. & Eng. R. R. Cas. 79, 42 Am. Rep. 208.

4. **And also in Kansas.** — "This court has not adopted what is generally called the rule of comparative negligence. Under the law as settled in this State, ordinary negligence on the part of a plaintiff will defeat a recovery except in the case of wanton or wilful injury. Where two parties, of each of whom the exercise of ordinary care is required, are guilty of negligence, contributing to the injury of one of them, the injured party cannot recover damages therefor from the other on the sole ground that his negligence was less than that of the other; and generally the mere fact that the plaintiff has been guilty of less negligence than the defendant, will not authorize a recovery on his part." Kansas Pac. R. Co. *v.* Peavy, 29 Kan. 169; s. c., 11 Am. & Eng. R. R. Cas. 260; Atchison, etc., R. Co. *v.* Morgan, 31 Kan. 77; s. c., 13 Am. & Eng. R. R. Cas. 499.

5. Louisville, etc., R. Co. *v.* Collins, 2 Duvall (Ky.), 114; Louisville, etc., R. Co. *v.* Robinson, 4 Bush (Ky.), 507; Pac. R. Co. *v.* Houts, 12 Kan. 328; Kansas Pac. R. Co. *v.* Peavy, 29 Kan. 169; s. c., 11 Am. & Eng. R. R. Cas. 260; Sawyer *v.* Sauer, 10 Kan. 466; Atchison, etc., R. Co. *v.* Morgan, 31 Kan. 77; s. c., 13 Am. & Eng. R. R. Cas. 499. And see, for the real meaning of the Kansas cases, the concurring opinion of *Valentine, J.*, in the Peavy case, *supra*.

tive negligence.[1] The rule applied by courts of admiralty has already been sufficiently stated.[2]

Conclusion. — It would be useless to review all the merely cumulative cases on the subject of contributory negligence; but it is believed that no enunciation of principle has been overlooked, and it is hoped that all the doctrines of the subject have been clearly formulated and amply illustrated; and while the conclusions of others have not always been adopted, and have sometimes been dissented from, yet, in the main, this article is based upon the labor of others who have developed and illumined the subject.[3]

CONTROVERSY. — A dispute between two or more persons.[4]

1. 2 Stanton's Ky. Stat. 510, § 3; Gen'l Stat. Ky. ch. 57, § 3; Louisville, etc., R. Co. *v.* Sickings, 5 Bush (Ky.), 1; Louisville, etc., R. Co. *v.* Mahoney, 7 Bush (Ky.), 235, 255; Jacobs *v.* Louisville, etc., R. Co., 10 Bush (Ky.), 263.

2. Tit. "Comparative Negligence," 3 Am. & Eng. Ency. of Law.

3. **Authorities: Aim of this Article.** — See generally on the subject of contributory negligence, 3 Am. & Eng. Ency. of Law; Beach on Cont. Neg.; Thomp. on Neg.; Shearman & Redf. on Neg.; Wharton on Neg.; Whittaker's Smith on Neg.; Deering on Neg.; Cooley, Addison, and Pollock on Torts; Pierce on Railroads; Wood's Ry. Law; Patterson's Ry. Acc. Law. To all of these works, and especially to that of Mr. Beach, this article is greatly indebted. But while acknowledging such indebtedness, it is hoped that in the statement of principles nothing will be found at second hand. It has been the aim to state concisely the fundamental doctrines of the law of contributory negligence based upon a careful personal study of the cases in the light of legal reason. Hence in a number of instances the conclusions reached are not those of the text writers, but it is believed they are fully supported by the authorities and those fundamental principles which are the life of the law. It has been sought to state principles, not mere decided points. When the principles are understood, as Mr. Bishop says, the points will take care of themselves.

4. Bouvier's Law Dict.; Barber *v.* Kennedy, 18 Minn. 226.

Amount in Controversy. — See this work, vol. i. p. 563. See also Barber *v.* Kennedy, 18 Minn. 226, in which it was held that Minn. Gen. Stat. ch. 65, sec. 5, giving a justice jurisdiction in actions on contract for recovery of money only, if the sum claimed does not exceed $100, relates to the *sum claimed by the plaintiff*, and that the jurisdiction cannot be eluded by defendant's putting in a counter-claim, which, together with plaintiff's claim, or by itself, exceeds $100; nor does that statute, or construction of it, contravene Minn. constitution providing that no justice shall have jurisdiction in any civil action in which the amount in controversy exceeds $100. In this case, *Ripley, C. J.*, said, —

"The question raised by the defendant has, therefore, been passed upon and settled by the Supreme Court of the United States. The judiciary act provides that the circuit courts of the United States shall have original cognizance of all suits of a civil nature at law, or in equity, when the matter in dispute exceeds, exclusive of costs, the sum or value of $500. Under this section the amount "laid in the declaration is the sum in controversy. Green *v.* Liter, 8 Cranch (U. S.), 229; Gordon *v.* Linguist, 16 Pet. (U. S.) 97. . . . 'It has often been decided that if the plaintiff shall recover less than $500, it cannot affect the jurisdiction of the court, a greater sum being claimed in his writ.' Per McLean in Gordon *v.* Linguist, *supra.*"

"What the plaintiff thus claims is the matter in dispute, though that claim may be incapable of proof, or only in part well founded." Kanouse *v.* Martin, 15 Howard, 198, and cases cited. See, too, Castner *v.* Chandler, 2 Minn. 86–88.

On Appeal. — 1. On appeal by *defendant*, under New-York code, the sum in controversy is the amount of the *judgment* as rendered, and from which the appeal is taken. Graville *v.* New York Cent., etc., R. Co., 104 N. Y. Rep. 674; Brown *v.* Sigourney, 72 N. Y. 122. And if that, excluding costs, is not less than $500, it may be reviewed by the N. Y. court of appeals.

2. On appeal by *plaintiff*, the sum for which the *complaint* demands judgment is material. N. Y. Code, § 191, subd. 3; Graville *v.* N. Y. Cent., etc., R. Co., 104 U. S. 674.

Costs constitute no part of the amount in controversy, and are not included for the purpose of making a sum sufficient to give the Supreme Court jurisdiction. Maxfield *v.* Johnson, 30 Cal. 545; Moore *v.* Boner, 7 Bush (Ky.), 26.

CONVENIENCE. — Any thing which is a cause or source of comfort, help, or accommodation.[1] Fitness of time or place.[2]

CONVENIENT. — Suitable, appropriate, proper, reasonable;[3]

Interest: Judgment is not necessarily void because rendered for amount greater than the sum in controversy; for interest (so provided by Cal. constitution), though entering into the judgment, is yet not a part of the sum in controversy. Nor is the *cost of protest* of note. Bradley *v.* Kent, 22 Cal. 169.

Counter-claim. — The fact that defendant sets up a counter-claim in excess of the amount necessary in order to give the Supreme Court jurisdiction on appeal, does not confer jurisdiction on that court to hear the appeal; the *ad damnum* clause in the complaint is the "amount in controversy." Maxfield *v.* Johnson, 30 Cal. 545.

Defendant in a justice's court cannot set up counter-claim for amount greater than what he could sue on. Ibid.

Right to Office. — On *mandamus* to compel delivery by former sheriff of room, records, documents, keys, etc., inquiry cannot be made into the right to the office of sheriff, and appeal to Supreme Court will not lie, even though the office may exceed in value the "amount in controversy" necessary to bring a case into the court issuing the writ; for the right to office cannot be inquired. State *v.* Lagarde, 21 La. Ann. 18.

Mandamus to cancel Appeal. — However, where *quo warranto* is employed, then appeal will lie to Supreme Court if the records of the court appealed from show that the value of the office exceeds the "amount in controversy" necessary in cases on appeal. State *v.* Judge, 22 La. Ann. 49; explaining State *v.* Judge, 20 La. Ann. 574. But the Supreme Court will not permit affidavit as to salary to be made for the first time in that court. The proof must be made to the lower court, and appear on its records. 20 La. Ann. 49. Then, if appeal be refused, mandamus issues to compel its allowance. 20 La. Ann. 49.

1. Conveniences. — Where a turnpike act authorized any five or more trustees to make turnpikes, with such suitable out-buildings and "conveniences" as they thought necessary, on the intended line of the road, and the owner of the soil next adjoining a toll-house (erected in pursuance of the act) contracted with one of the trustees on behalf of the rest to sink a well for the convenience of the toll-house, the expense to be borne by each party equally, on the execution of the work suit was brought on behalf of the trustees to recover a moiety of the cost. It was objected that the sinking of the well in question was not within the scope or authority of the trustees, and, consequently, that the action was not maintainable; but the court sustained the verdict, saying, "The trustees are to make so many turnpikes as they shall think necessary on the line of the road, together with such suitable out-buildings and 'conveniences' as are necessary for the occupation of the turnpike and the collection of the tolls payable. Can it be doubted that a well is a suitable 'convenience' within the scope of the clause empowering the trustees to make turnpikes? Is the toll-gate keeper to live in the toll-house without water?" Newman *v.* Fletcher, 1 Dowl. & Ry. 202.

2. Where a father made a promise to A, that, if he should marry his daughter, "he (the father) would endeavor to do her equal justice with the rest of his daughters, as fast as it is in his power with *convenience*," and the marriage was afterwards had with his consent, it was *held* that such a promise was sufficiently certain and obligatory, and that in such a case the father had not his *lifetime* to perform it in, but in a *reasonable* time after the marriage (taking into consideration his property and other circumstances) he was bound to make an advancement to A, and to his daughter, A's wife, equal to the largest made to his other daughters. Chichester's Executrix *v.* Vass, Admr., 1 Munf. (Va.) 98.

3. With All Convenient Speed. — When such and kindred expressions are used in wills as to the payment of legacies, it has been *held* that the court will examine into the principles of convenience, and not leave the matter to the discretion of the executors. The legacies will be payable within a reasonable time, which has been generally considered to be one year. Sitwell *v.* Bernard, 6 Vesey, 520; Elwin *v.* Elwin, 8 Vesey, 547; Gillon *v.* Turnbull, 1 McCord, ch. (S. C.) 148.

So where the maker of a note made a payment thereon before it was legally demandable, in consideration of which the holder agreed to extend the time for payment of the balance of the note, after it should, by its terms, become due, until it was "convenient" for the maker to pay it, it was *held* that this extended the time of the note for such period as, under all the circumstances of the case, should be reasonable. Newsam *v.* Finch, 25 Barb. (N. Y.) 175.

On an agreement to make a certain payment when it should be "convenient" to make a final settlement, the court, *Bronson, J.*, said, "But suppose there was a promise to settle, it was not an undertaking to useful, advantageous, handy; affording convenience or accommodation.[1]

do so *when required by the plaintiff*. The language is, 'whenever it is *convenient* to make a final settlement.' The legal effect of such a stipulation is, I think, that the act shall be done *within a reasonable time*. It cannot mean that the thing shall be done on the *demand of the party*, for then he might demand immediately, and before a proper time had elapsed. 'Convenient,' as here used, must mean such a time for doing the act as, under all the circumstances of the case, should be reasonable." Howe's Executor *v.* Woodruff, 21 Wend. (N. Y.) 640.

Payable as Convenient.—This expression in a written contract providing for the payment of a certain sum is an extension of credit only: it cannot be construed to mean not payable at all. Black *v.* Bachelder, 120 Mass. 171.

1. As may be Most Convenient.—Under an authority given by charter to a railroad company to cross a river by bridge or ferry, "as may be most convenient," the railroad company are the judges as to which will be most "convenient." That a bridge would be less "convenient" to navigation than a ferry, does not deprive the company of the right to build a bridge. Attorney-General *ex rel*, etc., *v.* The N. Y. & Long Branch R. R. Co., 24 N. J. Eq. 49.

Where the trustees of an almshouse were empowered by letters-patent of incorporation to appoint and remove twenty-four inmates *toties quoties sibi conveniens fore videbetur*, on motion to expunge the names of the inmates from the registered list of freeholders, it was argued by counsel for the inmates as follows: "The appointment of the inmates of the hospital must be presumed to be an appointment for life, defeasible on certain conditions: they are, therefore, tenants for life. It is true that by the charter of Elizabeth the governors have the power of removing the inmates 'as often as it shall seem to be convenient to them;' but the term 'convenient' had not the same meaning then as now. It now means commodious. In Ainsworth's dictionary the word *conveniens* is rendered 'meet, suitable.' The meaning of the charter, therefore, is, that the inmates may be discharged only upon suitable or proper occasions, such as their misconduct would give rise to. This, consequently is not like an appointment *durante bene placito*." But it was *held* that the inmates appointed under this charter did not take an estate for life in the property enjoyed by them as such inmates, and were, therefore, not entitled to be registered as freeholders; the court, *Tindal, C. J.*, saying, "The patent of incorporation contains a power conferred upon the governors to nominate whom they may think proper as inmates of the hospital, and also a power to remove such inmates, which is given in the most general terms,—'So often as it shall seem to be "convenient" to them or the greater number of them.' I can scarcely conceive words of more general import than these, or conferring a wider exercise of discretion." Davis *v.* Waddington, 7 Man. & Gr. 37.

The County Board of Supervisors being empowered in Mississippi to erect and keep in repair in each county a "good and *convenient* court-house," it was *held* that they had the right to make an appropriation for setting shade-trees in the grounds connected with the court-house; the court, *Campbell, J.*, saying, "Shade-trees may be necessary to make a court-house 'good and convenient.' There is no express grant of power to have fences made around the court-house yard, or to dig wells or cisterns, or to protect the ground against washing; but as the law empowers the boards of supervisors to acquire so much ground as may be necessary and 'convenient' for the building and use of the court-house, and requires the erection and keeping in repair in each county of a 'good and *convenient* court-house,' it is incident to this to make *convenient* and protect this property by the means usually employed in such cases." Allgood *v.* Hill, 54 Miss. 666.

As is Most Convenient.—Where dower in certain lands was set out, "with privilege to pass and repass," etc., "as is most convenient," it was held that that expression meant the convenience of the tenant in dower; the court, *Park, J.*, saying, "The court further instructed the jury that the phrase, 'as is most convenient,' had reference solely to the convenience of the plaintiff. We see no error in this construction. The distribution says that the plaintiff shall have the right to pass and repass to the rooms particularly described 'as is most convenient.' *Convenient* to whom? Manifestly to the person to whom the right of passage is given. No other person is mentioned or referred to. The minds of the distributers are occupied in defining her rights. The first part of the clause gives her the right of passage; and the latter part, 'as is most convenient,' merely defines the way set out to her." Miles *v.* Douglas, 34 Conn. 393.

With All Convenient Speed.—The stipulations in a charter party that the vessel shall sail *with all convenient speed*, are not conditions precedent to the charterer's ob-

CONVENIENTLY. — With ease; without trouble; with reasonable diligence.[1]

CONVENTIONAL. — Depending on, or arising from, the mutual agreement of parties.[2]

CONVERSANT. — Living or residing; having one's abode; resident.[3]

ligation to load, unless, by the breach of such stipulations, the object of the voyage is wholly frustrated. In this case the court, *Pollock, C. B.*, said, "An intention to make any particular stipulation a condition precedent should be clearly and unambiguously expressed. There can be no doubt about a particular day; but what is a 'convenient speed,' or a 'reasonable time,' must always be a subject of contention. We may therefore fairly say, that, where a particular day is named, the time is unambiguously expressed; but, where the terms are so lax and ambiguous as to lead to a difference of opinion, then the stipulation is not a condition precedent." Jarrabochia *v.* Hickie, 1 H. & N. 183.

1. Where the California statute of 1862 (p. 398, sec. 11), relating to streets, required the contractor, in order to preserve his lien for street assessments, "to call upon the persons so assessed, or their agents, if they can be *conveniently* found, and demand payment of the amount assessed to each," it was *held* that a return by the contractor upon the warrants of the superintendent of streets, "that he could not *conveniently* find the defendant," without any thing to show what steps he had taken to find him, was insufficient; the court, *Rhodes, J.*, saying, "Impossibilities are not required of the contractor. He is not required to call on the owner, if he cannot be found; nor upon the agent (if he has an agent), if he cannot be found; nor to go upon the premises, if they are inaccessible. The warrant is a process which he is required to serve; and he is held to the same measure of diligence in its service as an officer holding legal process for service. He must make diligent search and inquiry for the person assessed. The word 'conveniently,' in the section requiring the contractor to call on the person assessed, if he can 'conveniently' be found, and demand payment, is very unusual in such a connection, though the proper interpretation may not be doubtful. It certainly does not mean that he should call on the owner of the lot, if it suits his *convenience*. It may, in one sense, be inconvenient for him to leave his residence, or to pass along a single block, or to enter the lot-owner's place of business, to demand payment; but that interpretation would make the requirement a useless and absurd one. Whatever it is the duty of an officer to do while engaged in the performance of services enjoined upon him by law, and may be accomplished by the exercise of reasonable diligence, that, it may be said, can 'conveniently' be done by him. The effort must be made to find the person assessed, before going in search of his agent; and the return must show that fact. If he is a non-resident of the city or State, or if he is temporarily absent, or if he has absconded, or if, after an attempt in good faith to find him, he cannot be found, there is no difficulty in stating the fact. The statute requires the return to state 'the nature and character of the demand;' and, as the continuance of the lien for two years depends on the return, there is a marked propriety in requiring the return to show a demand upon the person assessed, or a reason why it was not done before resorting to the other modes of making the demand. Suppose the fact was, as suggested by the defendant's counsel, that the defendant was as universally known, and as easily found, as any man in San Francisco, it is obvious that the return of the contractor, that he could not 'conveniently' find the defendant, would be the merest evasion. Had the return been, that the defendant 'cannot be found,' or that 'he could not find' the defendant, it would have been sufficient, so far as the personal demand is concerned, to show a compliance with the requirements of the statute; but, as it now stands, it is insufficient." Guerin *v.* Reese, 33 Cal. 292.

As soon as conveniently may be. — This phrase in wills has been held not to confer a large discretion, and a court of equity will take care that powers confided to trustee shall be honestly exercised for the benefit of the *cestui que trust*. See Walker *v.* Shore, 19 Vesey, 387, and the cases there cited.

2. **Conventional Estates.** — Those freeholds, not of inheritance, or estates for life, which are created by the express acts of the parties, in contradistinction to those which are legal, and arise from the operation and construction of law. 2 Blackstone, 120.

Conventional Services. — Those reserved by tenures upon grants made out of the Crown or Knight's Service. Hale's Analysis of the Common Law, p. 46.

3. A term of ancient law, as is seen by the following case: Declaration for goods

CONVERSATION. — See EVIDENCE.

CONVERSE. — To hold intercourse with; to commune.[1]

CONVERSION. — See EQUITY; HUSBAND AND WIFE; TROVER.

1. Definition. — Trover was originally an action of trespass on the case for damages against the finder of goods who refused to deliver them to the owner, but *converted* them to his own use. The gist of the action was the conversion. The word trover is from the French, *trouver*, to find. By legal fiction actions of trover were permitted against one who had in his possession, by whatever means, the personal property of another, who sold or used the same without the owner's consent, or refused to deliver them upon demand. In form trover is a fiction.[2] The form supposes that the defendant might have come lawfully by the possession of the goods; and if he did not, yet, by bringing this action, the plaintiff waives the trespass. No damages are recovered for the act of taking, but for the conversion.[3] Trover is a common-law action to recover the value of personal property converted by another to his own use. The plaintiff avers that on a certain day he was lawfully possessed of a certain chattel, and casually lost the same; that the defendant found it, and refuses to deliver it to the plaintiff, and has converted it to his own use. It is a form of trespass on the case. In the distant age, when it was first used, the plaintiff narrated accurately the facts in the case. Now the losing and finding have been regarded as merely

sold and delivered; defendant pleads in abatement, and traverses the "inhabitancy;" plaintiff demurs, that the Statute of Additions expresses the word "conversant;" that Rastall, and all the old entries, are so; and, indeed, some modern entries are "commorant," but none "inhabitant." This objection was *held* good; for a man may lodge in one parish, and work in another; he is "conversant" where he works. Judgment for plaintiff that defendant answer over. Shields *et al. v.* Cuthbertson, Barnes, 162.

1. An oath administered to an officer not to allow the jury to "converse," etc., is substantially the same as not allow them to "communicate." In this case the court, *Deaderick, C. J.*, said, "The officers were sworn to keep the jury together separate and apart from other citizens, and not to permit them to 'converse' with any other person, or to 'converse' with them themselves, about the case. It is insisted the oath should have been that they should not *communicate*, etc., and that the officers should not 'converse' with each other in their presence, etc. The oath as administered is substantially that insisted on. Webster defines 'converse' to mean 'to hold intercourse, to talk familiarly.' If kept separate and apart, and prevented from holding intercourse with others, the jury would certainly be free from the danger of corruption." Scott *v.* State, 7 Lea (Tenn.), 232.

2. 1 Chitty's Plead. 164; 2 Bl. Com. b. 3. 152.

3. Bouvier's Institutes, No. 3512.

legal fiction, which the defendant is not permitted to deny.[1] The action of tortiously converting chattels is commonly called "trover," meaning "to find," which was used in the old precedents of declarations; the plaintiff, by means of fiction, alleging that he had lost, and the defendant had found, and converted to his own use, the chattel in question. Trover is an action to recover damages for the conversion of chattels personal, or movable goods, to the value of the interest converted.[2] In the action of conversion, the declaration owns the real or supposed fact that the plaintiff casually lost his goods, and the defendant found and appropriated them.[3] Where a person finds the goods of another, or has them in his possession, and converts them to his own use without the consent of the owner, he is liable to the owner in an action of conversion. Refusal to restore the goods is *prima facie* sufficient evidence of the conversion, though it may not amount to a conversion.[4]

2. Trover, Trespass, Detinue, Replevin, distinguished. — The two principal differences between trespass and trover for personal property appropriated by the defendant are these: —

(1) In trespass the original taking is wrongful, or a taking made wrongful *ab initio* by subsequent conduct; while in trover the original taking is supposed to be lawful, and often the only wrong consists in a refusal to surrender a possession which was originally lawful, but the right to which has terminated.

(2) Trespass lies for a wrongful force; but the wrongful force is not conversion, when the owner's right is recognized. In trespass, there is a wrongful taking; in trover, a wrongful conversion.[5] The action of detinue is to recover chattels *in specie*, and not for damages for conversion. The action of replevin seeks to recover chattels personal *in specie* wrongfully withheld.[6] It may be added that detinue is an action of *ex contractu*; replevin, of *ex delicto*.

1. Puterbaugh's Com. L. Plead. 497.
2. Bigelow's Torts, 184.
3. Cooley's Torts, 441.
4. Wharton's L. Dict.; Miller *v.* Allen, 10 R. I. 49; Burroughs *v.* Bayne, 5 Hurl. & N. 296; Eslow *v.* Mitchell, 26 Mich. 500; Pillott *v.* Wilkinson, 2 Hurl. & C. 72; Dudley *v.* Abner, 52 Ala. 572; Hass *v.* Damon, 9 Iowa, 589: Laverty *v.* Snethen, 68 N. Y. 522; s. c., 23 Am. Rep. 184; Ireland *v.* Horseman, 65 Mo. 511; Adams *v.* McGlinchy, 62 Me. 533; Thompson *v.* Currier, 24 N. H. 237.
5. Cooley's Torts, 442; Wilson *v.* McLaughlin, 107 Mass. 587.
6. Bigelow's Torts, 185.

The action of detinue is the only remedy by suit at law for the recovery of personal chattels *in specie*, except in cases where replevin can be instituted. 1 Chitty, Plead. 111; 3 Bl. Com. 146, 152; Co. Lit. 296*b*.

In modern practice detinue is seldom used. Puterbaugh's Pract. 405.

Lord Mansfield defines conversion or trover to be a fiction in form, and in substance a remedy to recover the value of personal chattels wrongfully converted by another to his own use. No damages are recoverable for the act of taking: all must be for the act of converting. This is the tort or *maleficium*. 1 Chit. Pl. 146; Cooper *v.* Chitty, 1 Burr. (Eng.) 31. In replevin the plaintiff obtains possession of the goods at the beginning of the action, on giving security to prosecute his action, and to return the property if so decided. In detinue the property is to be returned by the final judgment and process thereon. Under the code the remedy by *claim and delivery* combines substantially the advantages of both of these actions. McLaughlin *v.* Piatti, 27 Cal. 451; Morgan *v.* Reynolds, 1 Montana, 163. Conversion, in trover, is the gist of the action. This consists in any tortious act by which the defendant deprives the plaintiff of his goods, either wholly or for a time. 2 Starkie, Ev. 842.

If a party has the personal property of

3. What Property may be converted. — Any property of a personal nature is subject to conversion, even though it has no value except to the owner.[1] Not only tangible property, but all property of a personal nature which may be converted. Trover lies for paper representatives of value, choses in action, and corporate stock.[2]

another in possession, and the owner makes a demand for it, and the person in possession refuses to deliver it, that will constitute a conversion of the property by the latter to his own use. Transportation Co. v. Sellick, 52 Ill. 249.

Cutting grass in ignorance of the true boundary, without attempting to remove it, or to prevent the plaintiff from so doing, but with the intent that it should be appropriated to another's use, is conversion. It is not necessary to a conversion that there should be a manual taking of the chattels in question, nor that it be shown that a party has applied it to his own use; a dominion exercised over it in exclusion, or in defiance of plaintiff's rights, is a conversion. Donahue v. Shippel (R. I.), 3 N. Eng. Rep. 866; Bristol v. Burt, 7 John. (N. Y.) 254; Liptrot v. Holmes, 1 Ga. 381; Reid v. Colcock, 1 Nott. & McC. (S. Car.) 592; R. R. Co. v. Car Works, 32 N. J. 517.

If the carrier of goods allows an officer to take goods he is transporting, it is no defence in an action of trover to plead that an officer took them, unless the officer had a legal right, which the defendant must show: if he does not show this, he is liable to the action of trover. Gibbons v. Farwell (Mich.), 26 N. W. Rep. 855.

A mortgagor cannot sustain trover against a mortgagee, or his assignee, in possession, after condition broken, for cutting and carrying away wood from the mortgaged premises. Place v. Sawtell, 142 Mass. 277. One who obtains goods from an insolvent debtor for the purpose of defrauding creditors, and sells them to a *bona fide* purchaser, is liable to the creditors for conversion. Smith v. Sands, 17 Neb. 498.

If a vendor is induced, by fraudulent representations, to sell property to an irresponsible party, and such party transfers it to a third party, who acts in good faith, without notice of fraud, the last vendee will hold the title as against the first owner. Curme v. Rauh, 100 Ind. 247; Parrish v. Thurston, 87 Ind. 437.

A party personated a member of a firm, and thereby obtained chattels. By this fraud no title passed, but remained in the vendor. The wrong-doer then sold the property through this firm, who received the consideration for the tort-feasor. When they sold the property, they sold chattels to which the original owner had a perfect title; and when they received the proceeds, they received money belonging to the original owner. This was a conversion, and they were liable in trover. Hamet v. Letcher, 37 Ohio St. 356; Baker v. Dinsmore, 72 Pa. St. 427; Moody v. Blake, 117 Mass. 23

1. Cooley's Torts, 447.

2. Ayres v. French, 41 Conn. 151; Payne v. Elliot, 54 Cal. 341; McAllister v. Kuhn, 96 U. S. 87. *Compare* Sewall v. Lancaster Bank, 17 S. & R. (Pa.) 285; Neiler v. Kelley, 69 Pa. St. 403; Romig v. Romig, 2 Rawle (Pa.), 241.

A note payable twelve months after date, given to an insurance company for premiums, was pledged by the company as collateral security for a loan less than its face. The note was paid and taken up by the maker before maturity. The company, becoming insolvent, made an assignment. The assignee brought trover for the note. This action was held maintainable, as the note was liable for the company's losses up to its maturity, and the measure of recovery was the balance of the note over the amount of the loan. Fell v. McHenry, 42 Pa. St 41. See Craig v. McHenry, 35 Pa. St. 120.

The maker of a note who has paid it, may maintain trover against the payee who has wrongfully disposed of it, whereby the maker had to pay it the second time. Buck v. Kent, 3 Vt. 99; Pierce v. Gilson, 9 Vt. 216; Murray v. Burling, 10 Johns. (N. Y.) 172; Otisfield v. Mayberry, 63 Me. 197. *Compare* Platt v. Potts, 11 Ired. (N. Car.) 266; Besherer v. Swisher, 3 N. J. 748.

Even a refusal to give up a paid note is a conversion, but the damages would only be nominal. Stone v. Clough, 41 N. H. 290; Spencer v. Dearth, 43 Vt. 98; Pierce v. Gilson, 9 Vt. 216. *Compare* Todd v. Crookshanks, 3 Johns. (N.Y.) 432; Lowremore v. Berry, 19 Ala. 130.

So when a payee gets wrongful possession of a note before it is delivered, the maker can maintain trover to regain it. Neal v. Hanson, 60 Me. 84; Evens v. Kymer, 1 B. & Adol. 528; Groggerley v. Cuthbert, 5 B. & P. 170.

Trover will lie for parish records. Baker v. Fales, 16 Mass. 487; Stebbins v. Jennings, 10 Pick. (Mass.) 172; Sawyer v. Baldwin, 11 Pick. (Mass.) 492.

When papers are used in evidence before a magistrate, and placed on file, trover will not lie for their recovery. Greene v. Mead, 18 N. H. 505.

Trover will lie to recover fixtures or buildings not belonging to the owner of the land where located, but to another. Russell v. Richards, 11 Me. 371; Hilborn v. Brown, 12 Me. 162; Smith v. Benson, 1 Hill (N. Y.), 176; Dame v. Dame, 38 N. H. 429; Crippin v. Morrison, 13 Mich. 23. *Compare* Oberton v. Williston, 31 Pa. St. 155; Prescott v. Wells, 3 Nev. 82.

Where a house, as between the parties, is personal property, trover will lie for its wrongful conversion. As, where it was so erected as to be personal property, or where the defendant is estopped by his own acts from denying that it is such. Davis v. Taylor, 41 Ill. 405, Jewett v. Partridge, 3 Fair. (Me.) 243; Pullen v. Bell, 40 Me. 314; Brown v. Wallis, 115 Mass. 156; Osgood v. Howard, 6 Greenlf. (Me.) 452; Chatterton v. Saul, 16 Ill. 149. *Compare* 2 Greenl. Ev. 522, § 635; 1 Cowan's Treaties, 291; Bacon's Abridg. tit. trover (B); Buffey v. Henderson, 8 Eng. L. & E. 305.

Trover lies for salt-pans, though fixed in the floor of a building; and whenever the fixed instrument, engine, or utensil is an accessory to a matter of a personal nature, it is considered as personalty. Elmes v. Mawe, 3 East, 53; Fitzherbert v. Shaw, 1 H. Black. 259.

Generally, however, the right of the tenant to remove fixtures remains only during his term, and, if removed afterwards, the landlord may maintain trover. Weeton v. Woodcock, 7 Mees. & W. 14. Cutting growing corn, and taking it away, will be sufficient conversion to maintain trover. Nelson v. Burt, 15 Mass. 203. Cutting trees without carrying them away has been held conversion. Sanderson v. Haverstick, 8 Barr (Pa. St.), 294. So, when a party cuts wood on another's land, and converts it into coal, trover will lie against him. Riddle v. Driver, 12 Ala. 590. A *bona fide* purchaser bought loads of earth from a party not the owner, and carried them away. The owner brought trover against the purchaser, and it was sustained. Riley v. Power Co., 11 Cush. (Mass.) 11. The plaintiff can waive its wrongful taking, and sue for the conversion. To this the defendant cannot complain. Wadleigh v. Janvrin, 41 N. H. 503.

A tenant, when he leaves the farm, has no right to sell the manure accumulated in the ordinary course of farming, unless there be expressed stipulations permitting it. If a party buys this manure with notice, the landlord can bring trespass or trover against him for the conversion. Middlebrook v. Corwin, 15 Wend. (N. Y.) 169; Fay v. Muzzey, 13 Gray (Mass.), 53; Daniels v. Pond, 21 Pick. (Mass.) 367; Perry v. Carr, 44 N. H. 118; Corey v. Bishop, 48 N. H. 146; Strong v. Doyle, 110 Mass. 92; Wetherbee v. Ellison, 19 Vt. 379; 1 Pars. Con. 430.

A debitor who has made a bill of his creditor's account, if the creditor gets wrongful possession of it, may maintain trover for its conversion. Fullman v. Cummings, 16 Vt. 697. If a contract for the sale of goods be complete, and binding under the law, yet the vendee acquires no property in them sufficient to authorize him to bring trover, provided any material act remains to be done before the delivery, in order to ascertain the quantity, or to distinguish the amount to be paid by the vendee, the purchaser cannot maintain trover until his portion has been ascertained and set apart. Dennis v. Alexander, 3 Barb. (N. Y.) 50; Baily v. Smith, 43 N. H. 141; Straus v. Ross, 25 Ind. 300; Barret v. Goddard, 3 Mason, C. C. 107; Mining Co. v. Senter, 26 Mich. 73; Groat v. Gile, 51 N. Y. 431; Scudder v. Bradbury, 106 Mass. 422; Frost v. Woodruff, 54 Ill. 155; Ormsbee v. Machir, 20 Ohio St. 295; Kaufman v. Stone, 25 Ark. 336; Gilman v. Hill, 36 N. H. 311; Prescott v. Locke, 51 N. H. 94; Gibbs v. Benjamin, 45 Vt. 124; Chase v. Willard, 57 Me. 157; Dyer v. Libby, 61 Me. 45; Foster v. Ropes, 111 Mass. 10; Mason v. Thompson, 18 Pick. (Mass.) 305; Riddle v. Varnum, 20 Pick. (Mass.) 280; McClung v. Kelly, 21 Iowa, 508; Freight Co. v. Stanard, 44 Mo. 70.

Delivery to the vendee is very strong evidence of a complete sale against any presumption arising from the fact that the goods sold have not been weighed, counted, and the like. Kelsea v. Haines, 41 N. H. 246. When the contract is for sale of a thing not specified, as of a certain quantity of goods in general, without a specific identification of them, the contract is an executory agreement, and the property does not pass. Browning v. Hamilton, 42 Ala. 484; Hutchinson v. Hunter, 7 Barr (Pa. St.), 140; Bell v. Farrar, 41 Ill. 400; Rodee v. Wade, 47 Barb. (N. Y.) 63; Haldeman v. Duncan, 51 Pa. St. 66; Warren v. Buckminster, 24 N. H. 336.

However, the law on this subject is not entirely settled. Olyphant v. Baker, 5 Denio (N. Y.), 379; Chapman v. Shepard, 39 Conn. 413; Waldron v. Chase, 37 Me. 414; Russell v. Carrington, 42 N. Y. 118; Pleasants v. Pendleton, 6 Rand. (Va.) 473.

Under a contract for supplying labor and materials, and making a chattel, no property passes to the vendee until the work is completed and delivered, or ready to be delivered. This is the law generally, unless a contrary intent is expressed or implied from the terms of the contract. Iron Co. v. Buffington, 103 Mass. 62; Williams v. Jackman, 16 Gray (Mass.), 511; McConihe v. R. R. Co., 20 N. Y. 495; Sandford v. Wiggin's Co., 27 Ind. 522; Elliot v.

4. What constitutes Conversion. — Conversion consists as a tort, either in the appropriation of the personal property of another to the party's own use and benefit, or in its destruction, or in exercising dominion over it, in exclusion and defiance of the rights of the owner or lawful possessor, or in withholding it from his possession, under a claim and title inconsistent with the owner's.[1] The action of trover is founded on the right of property and possession; and any act of a party, other than the owner, which militates against this conjoint right, in law, is a conversion. It is not necessary for a manual taking to make conversion, nor that the party has applied it to his own use. The question is, Does he exercise dominion over it in exclusion or in defiance of the owner's right? If he does, that is conversion, be it for his own or another's use.[2] It is conversion if one takes the property of another, and sells, or otherwise disposes of it, without the owner's authority;[3] or if he takes it for a temporary purpose only, in disregard of the owner's right, it is conversion.[4] The word conversion, by a long course of practice, has acquired a technical meaning, and means detaining goods, so as to deprive the owner, or person entitled to possession of them, of his dominion over them.[5] Any carrying away of a chattel for the use of one, without the owner's consent, or for a third party, amounts to a conversion, because it is inconsistent with the general right of dominion which the owner has in it, who is entitled to the use of it at all times and in all places. Such an asportation is conversion.[6] The wrongful act

Edwards, 6 Vroom (N. J.), 265; Andrews *v.* Durant, 11 N. Y. 35; Wright *v.* Tetlow, 99 Mass. 297.

There must be a tender and acceptance of the chattel before title passes. Moody *v.* Brown, 34 Me. 107; Mixer *v.* Howarth, 21 Pick. (Mass.) 205; McIntire *v.* Kline, 30 Miss. 361; Gamage *v.* Allander, 14 Tex. 414; Veazie *v.* Holmes, 40 Me. 60; Elliot *v.* Edwards, 6 Vroom (N. J.), 265

Trover lies for title-deeds. Wieser *v.* Zeisinger, 2 Yeates (Pa.), 537; Towle *v.* Louet, 6 Mass. 394. It lies for the conversion of negotiable instruments, certificate of stocks. Comparet *v.* Burr, 5 Blackf. (Ind.) 419; Todd *v.* Crookshanks, 3 John. (N. Y.) 432; Kingman *v.* Pierce, 17 Mass. 247; Dav *v.* Whitney, 1 Pick. (Mass.) 503; Jarvis *v.* Rogers, 15 Mass 105; Sewall *v.* Bank, 17 S. & R. (Pa.) 285. Trover lies for the conversion of bank-notes enclosed in a letter. Moody *v.* Keener, 7 Port (Ala.) 218. It lies for a copy of a record, which is private property. Jones *v.* Winckworth, Hard 111. Trover will not lie in general for a public record. 1 Chitty's Plead. 150. Trover lies for wild animals reclaimed. Amory *v.* Flyn, 10 Johns. (N. Y.) 102. It lies for coin described as such, because the thing itself is not to be recovered, but damages for the conversion. Viner's abr. action of Trover, E; Pettit *v.* Bouju, 1 Mo. 64. Trover is not the proper action, when the title to property is to be settled by a peculiar jurisdiction, as, for example, property taken on the high seas, and claimed as lawful prize, because in such case the courts of admiralty have exclusive jurisdiction. Sounaire *v.* Keating, 2 Gall. C. C., 325; Cam. & N. (N. C.) 115. *Compare* Miller *v.* The Resolution, 2 Dall. (Pa.) 1.

1. Shipwick *v.* Blanchard, 6 T. R. 299; Fouldes *v.* Willoughby, 8 Mees. & W. 540 Hutchinson *v.* Bobo, 1 Bailey (S. Car.), 546; Reid *v.* Colcock, 1 Nott. & McC. (S. Car.), 592; Reynolds *v.* Shuler, 5 Cowen (N. Y.), 323.

2. Liptrot *v.* Holmes, 1 Kelly (Ga.), 381.

3. Thompson *v.* Currier, 24 N. H. 237; Shaw *v.* Peckett, 25 Vt. 423; Blood *v.* Sayre, 17 Vt. 609.

4. Homer *v.* Thwing, 3 Pick. (Mass.) 492; Rotch *v.* Hawes, 12 Pick. (Mass.) 136; Horsely *v.* Branch, 1 Humph. (Tenn.) 199; Crocker *v.* Gallifer, 44 Me. 491; Fisher *v.* Kyle, 27 Mich. 454; Hull *v.* Corcoran, 107 Mass. 251.

5. Burroughs *v.* Bayne, 5 H. & N. 296.

6. Fouldes *v.* Willoughby, 8 Mees. & W. 540.

must be intended, and not merely accidental or negligent, though it is not necessary that the result which follows should have been contemplated.[1]

1. Bowlin *v.* Nye, 10 Cush. (Mass.) 416; Simmons *v.* Lillystone, 8 Exch. 431.

The wrongful taking of chattels of another who has the right to immediate possession, with intent to appropriate them to one's own use, or to some other person's than the owner; or destroying or altering their nature, is a conversion. Thurston *v.* Blanchard, 22 Pick. (Mass.) 18; Durell *v.* Mosher, 8 John. (N. Y.) 445; Harrington *v.* Payne, 15 John. (N. Y.) 431; Davis *v.* Duncan, 1 McCord (S. Car.), 413; Woodbury *v.* Long, 8 Pick. (Mass.) 543.

It is conversion for one to take goods from an officer seizing them on a defective writ of replevin. Adams *v.* McGlinchy, 62 Me. 533. Drawing a portion of liquor out of a barrel, and then filling it with water, is a conversion of the whole, because it changes the nature of the chattel. Dench *v.* Walker, 14 Mass. 500. If the taking be constructive, it is conversion, as when a person exercises dominion over property in opposition to the plaintiff's right. Murray *v.* Borling, 10 John. (N. Y.) 172; Bristol *v.* Burt, 7 John. (N. Y.) 254; Reynolds *v.* Shuler, 5 Cowen (N. Y.), 323. Unlawfully levying upon and selling chattels by a constable, without taking actual possession, is conversion on the part of the constable. Burke *v.* Baxter, 3 Mo. 207. Unlawfully seizing coals of plaintiff, in coal-house of another man, and selling them without removal, is a conversion by the party selling. Reynolds *v.* Shuler, 5 Cowen (N. Y.), 323.

If a party finds a timber-raft, lodged in a navigable river, and takes possession of it, and then sells a portion of the timber, and hires a person to assist in removing the part sold, and then sells the remainder to some person, but reserving to himself that part removed, it is conversion of the whole. Gentry *v.* Madden, 3 Pike (Ark.), 127. But if, after the conversion, with a full knowledge of the circumstances, the owner ratifies the wrongful act, or in any way becomes a party to the tort, the right to bring trover is lost. Hames *v.* Parkman, 20 Pick. (Mass.) 90.

The absolute and general owner of chattels may maintain trover, although he had sold or bailed them under a void contract, because he retains the present right. Smith *v.* Plomer, 15 East, 607. A verbal gift, without actual delivery, does not pass the property to the donee so as to enable him to bring suit. Irons *v.* Smallpiece, 2 B. & Ald. 551; Whiting *v.* Barrett, 7 Lansing (N. Y.), 106; Mahan *v.* United States, 16 Wall. (U. S.) 143; Wing *v.* Merchant, 57 Me. 383; Reeves *v.* Capper, 5 Bing. N. C. 136.

If goods are obtained by false pretences, under color of purchase, the vendee or his assignee acquires no property, and after demand may be sued in trover. Noble *v.* Adams, 7 Taunt. 59; Ferguson *v.* Carrington, 9 B. & C. 60; Anonymous, 6 Mod. 114. *Compare* Sheppard *v.* Shoolbred, 1 Car. & Marsh, 61. Trover may be brought against a fraudulent purchaser, or his vendee, with notice, without a previous demand, and before a tender of a note given in payment before the time of trial. Thurston *v.* Blanchard, 22 Pick. (Mass.) 18; Green *v.* Russell, 5 Hill (N. Y.), 183; Stevens *v.* Austin, 1 Met. (Mass.) 557; Ryan *v.* Brant, 42 Ill. 78; Bruner *v.* Dyhall, 42 Ill. 34. If a creditor by fraud receives goods from his debtor, and intends to apply them in satisfaction of his debt, the property not being changed, the debtor may maintain trover for the recovery of the goods. Woodworth *v.* Kissam, 15 John. (N. Y.) 186. When goods are sold to be paid for on delivery, and are delivered by the agent of the vendor, without receiving payment, the seller can maintain trover for their recovery. Kingman *v.* Hotaling, 25 Wend (N. Y.) 423; Centre Co. *v.* Smith, 12 Vt. 212. A finder of goods has a special property in them, and may sustain trover against any one who shall convert them but the true owner. McLaughlin *v.* Waite, 9 Cowen (N. Y.), 670; Clark *v.* Malony, 3 Harr. (N. J.) 68. A sheriff may maintain trover against any one taking property out of his hands, as he has a special property in it. Dillenback *v.* Jerome, 7 Cowen (N. Y.), 297; Barker *v.* Miller, 6 John. (N. Y.) 195; Pettes *v.* Marsh, 15 Vt. 454; Caldwell *v.* Eaton, 5 Mass. 399. But courts hold that the sheriff cannot sustain trover for goods taken on a *fieri facias* and a levy thereon, unless he has made a practical inventory of the goods, or has taken actual possession of them. Lloyd *v.* Wikoff, 6 Halst. (N. J.) 218; Brain *v.* Strait, Dudley (S. Car.), 19. A sheriff may support trover against his receiptor who refuses to re-deliver the goods intrusted to him. Sibly *v.* Story, 8 Vt. 15; Holt *v.* Burbank, 47 N. H. 164.

An agent is liable in trover, who, being given a note to have it discounted, and expressly cautioned not to give it unless he received the money, allowed another to do the business, and who appropriated the proceeds of the note. Lawrty *v.* Snethen, 68 N. Y. 522. If an agent disobeys instructions, and does what he is not authorized to do, and thereby his principal is damnified, trover can be sustained against the agent. Cairnes *v.* Bleecker, 12 Johns. (N. Y.)

300; Sarjeant v. Blunt, 16 Johns. (N. Y.) 74; Dean v. Turner, 31 Md. 52. If one takes property to sell, he is liable in trover if he exchanges it for other property, because he has no such authority. Haas v. Damon, 9 Iowa, 589.

A purchaser is liable in trover in a conditional sale, if he disposes of the goods bought, before he acquires property by payment. Sargent v. Gile, 8 N. H. 325; Grace v. McKissack, 49 Ala. 163. So is the vendee with notice from the first purchaser. Eaton v. Munroe, 52 Me. 63. If an officer levies upon property exempt from execution, and sells it, the owner can sue him in trover. Sanborn v. Hamilton, 18 Vt. 590. A more negligent injury is no conversion. Nelson v. Whetmore, 1 Rich. (S. Car.) 318. Trover cannot be maintained against an officer for the larceny of goods from him. Dorman v. Kane, 5 Allen (Mass.), 38.

If a mortgagor of personal property, or his agent, sell the entire property as owner, in exclusion of the rights of the mortgagee, such a sale is conversion. White v. Phelps, 12 N. H. 382. Driving a hired horse a greater distance than is agreed, or in a different direction, is conversion. Wheelock v. Wheelwright, 5 Mass. 104; Homer v. Thwing, 3 Pick. (Mass.) 492; Hart v. Skinner, 16 Vt. 138; Lucas v. Trumbull, 15 Gray (Mass.), 306. If an infant hires property, and puts it to a different use than that agreed to, he is liable in trover. Green v. Sperry, 16 Vt. 390; Homer v. Thwing, 3 Pick. (Mass.) 492; Eaton v. Hill, 50 N. H. 235.

A commission merchant who makes sales after his authority has ceased, but without notice to him of the fact, is not guilty of conversion, but is liable only for accounting. Jones v. Hodgkins, 61 Me. 480; Fifield v. R. R. Co., 62 Me. 77. Every tortious taking with intent to appropriate goods to the use of the taker, or to some other person than the owner, is a conversion. McPortland v. Read, 11 Allen (Mass.), 231; Coughlin v. Ball, 4 Allen (Mass.), 334.

If a party takes goods with the intent to use them, or the goods are destroyed or consumed, to the prejudice of the lawful owner, he is liable in trover. Spooner v. Holmes, 102 Mass. 506; Dearborn v. W. Nat. Bank, 58 Me. 273.

Trover lies for chattels taken by a wrongful distress. Drew v. Spaulding, 45 N. H. 472. Trover will lie against an officer when he has taken property upon an execution, issued upon a void judgment for want of jurisdiction of the court, or against any one receiving the property from the officer. Martin v. England, 5 Yerger (Tenn.), 313. When a party receives logs to be sawed into lumber on shares, and promised to give the owner security for his share, payable at a future day, but disposed of the property before the stipulated day of payment, the owner can sustain trover for his share, there being no change of property until the giving of the security. Rightmyer v. Raymond, 12 Wend. (N. Y.) 51; Whipple v. Gilpatrick, 19 Me. 427; Turner v. Waldo, 40 Vt. 51. Forbidding the owner of personal property from removing it from the land of the defendant, and claiming it to be his, makes the defendant liable in trover. Woodis v. Jordan, 62 Me. 490. Discounting a lost bill after notice, is a conversion. Lovell v. Martin, 4 Taunt. 799. It seems that the mere taking an assignment of goods from a person who has no right or authority to dispose of them, is a conversion: for this is an assumption by the assignee of the property in the chattels. Everett v. Coffin, 6 Wend. (N. Y.) 603; Rice v. Clark, 8 Vt. 109. One who merely receives goods into his possession and control, knowing that they were not lawfully in the possession of the assignor, but allows them to be taken away before demand by the same person, is not thereby guilty of conversion. Loring v. Mulcahy, 3 Allen (Mass.), 575; Fouldes v. Willoughby, 8 Mees. & W. 540; Simmons v. Lillystone, 8 Exch. 442; Hill v. Hayes, 38 Conn. 532.

Misdelivery by a carrier of goods, which he took upon himself to carry, is a conversion. Claflin v. R. R. Co., 7 Allen (Mass.), 341; Hawkins v. Hoffman, 6 Hill (N. Y.), 586; Bowlin v. Nye, 10 Cush. (Mass.) 417. Trover may be supported against a carrier or wharfinger who improperly breaks open a box. Tucker v. R. R. Co., 39 Conn. 447. A bare non-delivery of goods by a carrier is not a conversion. Robinson v. Austin, 2 Gray (Mass.), 564. But if he has the goods in his possession, and refuses to deliver them on demand, then he is liable in trover. Lockwood v. Bull, 1 Cowen (N. Y.), 322, Packard v. Getman, 4 Wend. (N. Y.) 613. Trover will lie against mortgagee of personal property who sells it before condition is broken. Eslow v. Mitchell, 26 Mich. 500. A town officer who removes a portion of a fence from the land of the owner, supposing it to be the town's, is liable for its value in trover. Smith v. Colby, 67 Me. 169. When chattels are left in the possession of the mortgagor, he has a special property in them, and can sustain trover against a wrong-doer. He also has a right of redemption, and may lawfully sell in recognition of the mortgagee. Such a sale is no conversion of the mortgagee's interest. White v. Phelps, 12 N. H. 382. But a sale in denial of the mortgagee's right would be a conversion in him, and perhaps in the vendee also. Millar v. Allen, 10 R. I. 49; Ashmead v. Kellogg,

23 Conn. 70; Coles v. Clark, 3 Cush. (Mass.) 399. If a mortgage is part due, and the mortgagor sells, this may be regarded as a foreclosure, and satisfaction to the extent of the sales. Eslow v. Mitchell, 26 Mich. 500. One who buys property must ascertain the ownership; for if he buys of one who has no authority to sell, and takes possession, he then denies the owner's right, and trover will lie against him. Miller v. Thompson, 60 Me. 322. If one contributes to the purchase-price, and gets the property insured in his own name, the seller having no title, the contributor will be jointly liable with the other. Abbott v. May, 50 Ala. 97; Williams v. Merle, 11 Wend. (N. Y.) 80; Hyde v. Noble, 13 N. H. 494; Clark v. Rideout, 39 N. H. 238.

If one buys property of a party who is not the owner, and disposes of it in the usual course of trade and in good faith, he is not protected, provided the vendor's possession was tortious. Hardman v. Booth, 1 H. & C. 803; Hallins v. Fowler, L R. 7 H. L. Cas. 757.

If an assignee of goods has a lien on them, and sells in his own favor, he is liable in trover: he can only retain them until his lien is satisfied. The authority to sell is a personal trust, and cannot be assigned. Terry v. Bamberger, 44 Conn. 558. If a person assists in taking goods wrongfully, though as an agent only, he is liable in trover. Agency is no protection in committing such a tort. Edgerly v. Whalan, 106 Mass. 307; McPortland v. Read, 11 Allen (Mass.), 231. It is a conversion for a party to purchase fruit from persons who have stolen it from the plaintiff's ground. Freeman v. Underwood, 66 Me. 229. If one hires a horse for another who drives it to death, while the hirer drives another beside it, the two persons are jointly liable to the owner for conversion. Banfield v. Whipple, 10 Allen (Mass.), 27.

To maintain trover, the plaintiff must prove that the goods were his, and, while they were his, they came into the defendant's possession, who converted them to his own use. A married woman bought goods, and died before paying for them. The husband took possession, and carried on the business. The creditor called on him for payment. The husband offered to sell the goods back; but the creditor refused the proposition, but found a purchaser who bought the goods from the husband, who delivered the proceeds to the creditor. Suit was brought by the administrator of the wife against the creditor for the selling-price. *Held*, no conversion by the creditor. Presley v. Powers, 81 Ill. 125. The government appropriated the horses of one man as the property of another who received payment therefor. The first man sustained trover against the latter for the amount received. Thomas v. Sternheimer, 29 Md. 268. An agister rode a horse fifteen miles, that had been placed in his keeping. The horse died soon after, but not in consequence of the riding. *Held*, no conversion. Murray v. Borling, 10 John. (N. Y.) 172. An agister was intrusted with fifty head of cattle to feed. He sold twenty of the best, and was held liable in trover for their full value. Atter v. Williams, 21 Ill. 119.

A planter employed an agent to take cotton to market, and to deliver it to a certain merchant. But the agent wilfully delivered it to another merchant, who sold it on the account of the agent, without notice of the fraud, and gave him the proceeds. The agent absconded with the money. *Held*, that the merchant thus selling was liable in trover to the true owner. Taylor v. Pope, 5 Cold. (Tenn.) 507. An innocent party purchased a stolen horse, and sent it to a repository for the sale of horses. The true owner demanded the horse of both the purchaser and the agister, who refused to deliver it. *Held*, conversion by both of them. Morrill v. Moulton, 40 Vt. 242. An owner of a horse placed him with a commission merchant for sale. This agent exchanged him for twenty-five dollars and another horse. *Held*, his authority ceased as commission merchant at the time of the exchange; that the owner was not liable for losses of subsequent exchanges, nor for board of the horses exchanged. Wing v. Neal (Me.), 2 Atl. Repr. 881.

If an agent, acting solely for his principal, without knowing of any wrong, sells property for his principal who has no right to dispose of it, the agent will not be liable in trover for conversion. Lenthold v. Fairchild (Minn.), 28 N. W. Rep. 218.

To constitute conversion, there must be some exercise of dominion over the property militating against the owner's rights. If a party hires a horse to go to a place without stopping, his mere delay in returning is not sufficient evidence of conversion. Evans v. Mason (N. H.), 5 Atl. Rep. 766. One having the lawful possession of another's chattel does not necessarily have a lien on it for the expense incurred in getting such possession; and his unlawful retention of it, claiming such a lien, in opposition to the owner's rights, makes him liable for conversion. Nutter v. Varney (N. H.), 5 Atl. Rep. 457.

Defendant was authorized to and did buy a horse on plaintiff's credit: the defendant held possession, and the plaintiff claimed a lien. The defendant exchanged the horse for another. Plaintiff claimed this was done with his consent, and that he had a lien on the second horse. The bill of sale

5. Conversion by Bailee. — When a bailee receives goods, without notice, from one who has a tortious possession, and delivers them in pursuance of the bailment, and before the rights of the true owner are known, the bailee will be protected.[1] After such notice the bailee acts at his peril. If he delivers to a party who is entitled to the possession, this will be his protection; and he may defend in the interest of the rightful owner before delivery.[2] If goods are taken from a bailee, on legal process, he will be protected.[3]

of the first vendor was admitted to show that the defendant was the sole owner. Aiken *v.* Kennison (Vt.), 7 East, Rep. 90.

A plaintiff can only recover *secundum allegata et probata*. Under a complaint of conversion of chattels, there can be no recovery for a misapplication of the proceeds of the sale of such property, when it appears that the possession of the property was obtained and sold by the defendant by the consent of plaintiff. Bixel *v.* Bixel, 107 Ind. 534.

For conversion of chattels, where it appeared that the plaintiff took a bill of sale from the supposed owner, and went with him to defendant's stable, where the property then was, and, in the defendant's absence, took a receipt from his foreman that he had received the goods of the plaintiff, but that the property was to remain where it was until defendant's return, this receipt was *held* admissible on the trial. Fennessy *v.* Spofford, 144 Mass. 22.

Trover may be maintained jointly against a party who cuts timber on the land of another, and the party who purchases such timber with notice. Smith *v.* Briggs, 64 Wis. 497.

An owner does not lose the right to sell or mortgage his chattels when they are in the wrongful possession of another. Dahill *v.* Booker, 140 Mass. 308.

In order to hold a party for alleged conversion and spoliation, it is necessary to prove that he or his agent took part in the conversion, or received a benefit therefrom in whole or in part. The Quantico Cotton, 24 Fed. Rep. 325.

If a landlord takes possession before the term expires, and without the tenant's consent, and then refuses the tenant permission to remove his personal property, he is liable in trover. Watts *v.* Lehman (Pa.), Leg. Int. May 22, 1885.

Shares of stock in a corporation are chattels personal; and if a party appropriates them wrongfully, he is liable for conversion. Budd *v.* Multnomah St R. R. Co., 12 Oregon, 271; s. c., 22 Am. & Eng. R. R. Cas. 27. If a party obtains an animal *feræ naturæ*, and in so doing commits a trespass, he gains no title. A hived a swarm of bees upon B's land without B's permission, and left the hive on B's premises. Two years thereafter, C took the hive, removed the bees and the honey, and replaced the box. After a demand upon C by A, he brought the action of trover. Held, he could not recover. Roxroth *v.* Coon (R. I.), Alb. L. J. Nov. 7, 1885. A party holds property on which he has a lien. Before he will surrender it, he demands a larger amount than is his due. This is conversion, and the amount actually due need not be tendered him. Hamilton *v.* McLaughlin (Mass.), 12 N. E. Rep. 424.

When a party is authorized by contract to take chattels and dispose of them, he cannot be held liable in trover, so long as he conforms to his instructions. Stockler *v.* Wooten (Ala.), 2 South. Rep. 703.

A party who has a valid lien under a verbal mortgage, on a crop which was not planted when the mortgage was given, may maintain trover against any one, who, with notice of such lien, converts the crop, when gathered, to his own use. Rees *v.* Coats, 65 Ala. 256. See Iron Works *v.* Renfro, 71 Ala. 577.

1. Nelson *v.* Iverson, 17 Ala. 216; Burdett *v.* Hunt, 25 Me. 419.

2. Bliven *v.* R. R. Co., 36 N. Y. 403; Bates *v.* Stanton, 1 Duer (N. Y.), 79; King *v.* Richards, 6 Whart. (Pa. St.) 418; Hardman *v.* Wilcock, 9 Bing. 382.

3. Bliven *v.* R. R. Co, 36 N. Y. 403; Wells *v.* Thornton, 45 Barb (N. Y.) 390, Van Winkle *v.* U. S. Mail S. S. Co., 37 Barb. (N. Y.) 122; Burton *v.* Wilkinson, 18 Vt. 186. *Compare* Kiff *v.* Old Colony Co., 117 Mass. 591. When a party is intrusted with goods of another, and transfers them to another without orders, it is a conversion. Syeds *v.* Hay, 4 T. R. 260. If a carrier by mistake delivers goods to the wrong person, he is liable in trover. Stevenson *v.* Hart, 4 Bing. 476. So with a wharfinger. Deveraux *v.* Barclay, 2 B & Old. 702; Price *v.* Oswego R. R. Co., 50 N. Y. 213; Adams *v.* Blankinsten, 2 Cal. 413; Winslow *v.* R. R. Co., 42 Vt. 700. If a party hire a horse or other chattel, and negligently kills or destroys it while driving or using, he is guilty of conversion. Woodman *v.* Hubbard, 25 N. H. 67; Wartworth *v.* McDuffe, 48 N. H. 402; Morton *v.*

Glouster, 46 Me. 520; Nodine v. Doherty, 46 Barb. (N. Y.) 59; R. R. Co. v. Towboat Co., 23 How. (U. S.) 209; Sutton v. Manwatosa, 29 Wis. 21; Hall v. Corcoran, 107 Mass. 251. *Compare* Gregg v. Wyman, 4 Cush. (Mass.) 322; Way v. Foster, 1 Allen (Mass.), 408.

A depositor of grain in grain-elevators, it would seem, retains his title. Warren v. Milliken, 57 Me. 97; Broadwell v. Howard, 77 Ill. 305; Cushing v. Breed, 14 Allen (Mass.), 376; Young v. Miles, 20 Wis. 615; Dole v. Olmstead, 36 Ill. 150. In this view the bailee would seem to have authority to change the bailor's tenancy in severalty, into a tenancy in common, and back again at will, or to substitute other grain of the same quality for that received. This differs from an ordinary bailee's powers. Burton v. Curyea, 40 Ill. 320.

If a bailee converts a chattel, an action of detinue will not be barred until the statutory time after a demand and refusal to deliver, although the bailor might have brought trover immediately on the conversion. Wilkinson v. Verity, L. C. 6 C. P. 206.

Trover lies against a person who illegally makes use of things found or delivered to him. Johnson v. Weedman, 4 Scan. (Ill.) 495; Liptrot v. Holmes, 1 Kelly (Ga.), 381. If a party be employed merely to keep or carry goods, and, having no beneficial interest in them, misuses the property thus intrusted to his care, he is liable in trover. Ripley v. Dolbier, 18 Me. 382; Lockwood v. Bull, 1 Cowen (N. Y.), 322; Rice v. Clark, 8 Vt. 109; Swift v. Mosely, 10 Vt. 208; Norton v. Kidder, 54 Me. 189. Trover is sustainable against a carrier who draws out part of the contents of a barrel, and fills it with water. Dench v. Walker, 14 Mass. 500. If carriers improperly break open a box, they are liable in trover. Tucker v. Housatonic R. R. Co., 39 Conn. 447. Trover will not lie for goods seized by legal process, and in the custody of the law. Jenner v. Joliffe, 9 John. (N. Y.) 381. Trover will not lie for goods taken from the plaintiff by virtue of a search-warrant. Pettigru v. Sanders, 2 Bailey (S. Car.), 549.

Trover lies against an officer who seizes property by legal process, but sells without notice. Wright v. Spencer, 1 Stewart (Ala.), 576; Perkins v. Thompson, 3 N. H. 144; Hall v. Moore, Add. (Pa.), 376. If a party is legally authorized to kill a dog, but converts him to his own use, he is liable in trover. Cummings v. Perham, 1 Met. (Mass.) 555. If a bailee of goods loses them by negligence merely, the remedy is not in trover, but in assumpsit. Moses v Norris, 4 N. H. 304; Johnson v. Strader, 3 Mo. 359; Hawkins v. Hoffman, 6 Hill (N. Y.), 586; Bowlin v. Nye, 10 Cush. (Mass.) 417; Packard v. Getman, 4 Wend. (N. Y.) 613. *Compare* Bank v. Leavitt, 17 Pick. (Mass.) 1. If a person receives a parcel to be forwarded by carrier, but loses it, trover will not lie against him. Williams v. Gesse, 3 Bing. N. C. 849. A bare non-delivery of chattels by a carrier is not a conversion, unless he refuses to deliver them after a demand on him. Robinson v. Austin, 2 Gray (Mass.), 564; Packard v. Getman, 4 Wend. (N. Y.) 613; Lockwood v. Bull, 1 Cowen (N. Y.), 322 The false assertion of a carrier that he has delivered the goods is no conversion. Attersol v. Briant, 1 Campb. 409.

The retention of property under a decree of court of competent jurisdiction, is no conversion. Hassack v. Masson, 4 Moore, 361.

In many cases of bailment, the bailee has no assignable interest. 1. Where the bailment is made upon trust in the personal skill, knowledge, or efficiency of the bailee. 2. Where the bailee has a mere lien upon the chattels intrusted to him. 3. Where the bailment is at will

In any of these cases the bailee has no assignable interest; and if he delivers them to other parties, the bailment ends, and the assignee acquires no title to the goods, and becomes liable in trover on refusing to surrender the goods to the owner. Bigelow's Torts, 194; Bailey v. Colby, 34 N. H. 29.

To pledge goods of another without his authority is a conversion. Carpenter v. Hale, 8 Gray (Mass.), 157. If an owner of goods stands by and permits them to be sold, interposing no objection, the vendee acquires a good title, and is not liable in trover to the owner. Pickard v. Sears, 6 Ad. & El. 469; Stephens v. Baird, 9 Cowen (N. Y.), 274; Dezell v. Adell, 3 Hill (N. Y.), 215; s. c., 38 Am. Dec. 628. A person having authority to sell goods of another must conform with the instructions: any material deviation will make him liable in trover. Haas v. Damon, 9 Iowa, 589. Appropriating property held in bailment to a use not contemplated in the contract of bailment, is a conversion. Isaac v. Clark, 3 Hulst. 306; Perham v. Coney, 117 Mass. 102.

It has been *held* that no right of action of trover arises, unless the bailee, in appropriating the chattel, injures it, provided he restores it to the owner. Johnson v. Weedman, 5 Scam. (Ill.) 495; Harvey v. Epes, 12 Gratt. (Va.) 153.

But this doctrine is doubted. The gist of the conversion is the usurpation of the owner's right of property, and not the actual damage inflicted. Perham v. Coney, 117 Mass. 102.

As to the passing of title and possession of grain in elevators by sale, see Cushing v. Breed, 14 Allen (Mass.), 376; Waldron v.

6. Conversion by Tenants in Common. — As a general rule, one tenant in common cannot sue his co-tenant, if the goods remain in the possession of the latter, although he refuses to permit the former to participate in the use of the chattels; because the possession of one is the possession of the other.[1] But if a tenant in common destroys the goods, or commits an act equivalent thereto, his co-tenant can recover the value of his share in trover.[2]

Chase, 37 Me. 414; Warren *v.* Milliken, 57 Me. 97; Dole *v.* Olmstead, 36 Ill. 150; Young *v.* Miles, 20 Wis. 615; Burton *v.* Curyea, 40 Ill. 320; Clark *v.* Griffith, 24 N. Y. 595; Russell *v.* Carrington, 42 N. Y. 118; Hall *v.* R. R. Co. 14 Allen (Mass.), 439. Where a bailee makes an actual conversion of grain, by mixing with other grain, he is liable in trover. Hadix *v.* Einstman, 14 Brad. (Ill.) 443.

Stock of a mining corporation was pledged as collateral security for a loan. The company, by legislative authority, afterwards reduced its capital, and proportionately reduced the nominal value of the shares of the capital stock. *Held*, the surrender by the pledgees of the original certificate of stock, and the acceptance of a new certificate for the same number of shares, was not a wrongful conversion. Dannel *v.* Wikoff (N. J.), 5 Cent. Rep. 820.

1. Cowan *v.* Buvers, 1 Cooke (Tenn.), 53; St. John 6 *v.* Standring, 2 Johns. (N. Y.) 468; Cole *v.* Terry, 2 Dev. & B. (N. C.) 252; Conover *v.* Earl, 26 Iowa, 167.

2. Delaney *v.* Root, 99 Mass. 546; Lowthorp *v.* Smith, 1 Hayw. (N. Car.) 255; Tubbs *v.* Richardson, 6 Vt. 442; Hurd *v.* Darling, 14 Vt. 214; Lucas *v.* Wasson, 3 Dev. (N. Car.) 398; Campbell *v.* Campbell, 2 Murph. (N. Car.) 65.

One tenant in common of a raft of logs, endeavoring to save it from loss, exercised entire ownership of it, against the consent of his co-tenant; yet such acts were not a conversion so that trover would lie against him. Kilgore *v.* Wood, 56 Me. 150. If property owned in common is capable of being measured, weighed, and thereby separated into portions, such as grain, then the owner has a right to separate his share from the whole, take and sell it. If one of such owners is in possession of the whole, and refuses the other co-owner to sever and take his part, he is then liable to an action in trover. Channon *v.* Lusk, 2 Lansing (N. Y.), 211. One tenant in common of a ship forcibly took it into his possession exclusively, and then secreted it from his co-tenant. Then sold it to a third person, who lost it at sea. This was conversion. Bernardiston *v.* Chapman, C. B Hil. T. 1 Geo. 1.

If one tenant in common takes control, and assumes to own the chattels held in common, and sells them, or rather attempts to sell them, his associate can maintain trover against him, so *held* by many of the American courts. Wilson *v* Reed, 3 John. (N. Y.) 175; Thompson *v.* Cook, 2 South. (N. J.) 580; Hyde *v.* Stone, 7 Wend. (N. Y.) 354; Weld *v.* Oliver, 21 Pick. (Mass.) 559; White *v.* Osburn, 21 Wend. (N. Y.) 72; Dyckman *v.* Valiente, 42 N. Y 347; Nowlen *v.* Colt, 6 Hill (N. Y.), 461; Williams *v.* Chadbourne, 6 Cal. 559; Burbank *v.* Crooker, 7 Gray (Mass.), 159; Wheeler *v.* Wheeler, 33 Me. 347; Dain *v.* Cowin, 22 Me. 347; White *v.* Brooks, 43 N. H. 402; Smith *v.* Tankersly, 20 Ala 212; Arthur *v.* Gayle, 38 Ala. 259. *Compare* Tubbs *v.* Richardson, 6 Vt. 442; Sanborn *v.* Morrill, 15 Vt. 700; Barton *v* Burton, 27 Vt. 93; Oviatt *v.* Sage, 7 Conn. 95; Pitt *v.* Petway, 12 Ired. (N. Car.) 69. Heath *v.* Hubbard, 4 East, 121. In Massachusetts it is *held* that one tenant may maintain trover against his co-tenant who has converted the chattels to his own use, such as the destruction of the chattel, or by its sale, or by such an appropriation that will exclude the other party from its enjoyment. Delaney *v.* Root, 99 Mass 547; 2 Greenl. Ev. sect. 646, note 4. If a creditor attach the whole property held in common for a debt owed him by one of the owners, and then sells the entire property, trover will lie against him for the interest of the co-tenants not in his debt. Ladd *v.* Hill, 4 Vt. 164; Bradly *v.* Arnold, 16 Vt 382. Under the common law if a woman converts goods before her marriage, or during it, without her husband, trover may be sustained against her and her husband. Kowing *v.* Manley, 49 N. Y. 192; Draper *v.* Fulkes, Yelv. 165. For a conversion of husband and wife jointly, the action of trover should be against him alone. But if the action is brought against both of them, it is good after verdict. Carleton *v.* Haywood, 49 N. H. 319.

As to what constitutes conversion by one tenant in common, is a question. Decisions conflict in the United States. In Vermont the claim, by one tenant in common, of exclusive ownership to the exclusion of the other, or the sale of the whole, cannot be

7. Demand of Possession, and Refusal to deliver. — When the conversion is direct, as by an illegal taking of the chattels, or a wrongful assumption of property, or a misuse of it, the conversion is complete without a demand. But when the conversion is indirect, a demand is necessary, because the defendant is in lawful possession of the goods, and there is no conversion, until he assumes a property in them.[1] A refusal to deliver the goods on the demand of the rightful owner shows an assumption of ownership of them, and is evidence of the prior conversion. The refusal of itself is not a conversion: it is only evidence of a conversion, and is open to explanation.[2]

The demand should be so made that the defendant can have no uncertainty as to what is meant, and by the owner, or his authorized agent, who must be entitled to receive the property.[3]

The demand should be made upon the person who has possession at the time, or upon his agent, or upon the party having the control over the chattel.[4]

The demand must be made before the action is brought.[5]

If the party upon whom the demand is made, having it in his power to make such delivery, refuses, it is only evidence of a prior conversion, not of itself conclusive, liable to be explained and rebutted.[6]

treated in law as the equivalent of loss or destruction, or as a conversion. Tubbs *v.* Richardson, 6 Vt. 442; Sanborn *v.* Morrill, 15 Vt. 700; Barton *v.* Burton, 27 Vt. 93. In Maine the mere claim by one tenant of exclusive ownership of a horse, was *held* not to be conversion. Dain *v.* Cowing, 22 Me. 347; Symonds *v.* Harris, 51 Me. 14; and see Gilbert *v.* Dickerson, 7 Wend. (N. Y.) 449. North Carolina holds a similar doctrine to Vermont, with this qualification, — the sale of the property out of the State by one tenant in common, may be considered as a loss or destruction. Pitt *v.* Petwey, 12 Ired. (N. Car.) 69. But generally a sale of the whole property by one tenant in common, without the authority of the other, is a conversion. Wheeler *v.* Wheeler, 33 Me. 347; Wilson *v.* Reed, 3 John. (N. Y.) 175; Hyde *v.* Stone, 9 Cowen (N. Y.), 230; s. c., 18 Am. Dec. 501; Neilson *v.* Slade, 49 Ala. 253.

It is conversion if one tenant takes a joint note for collection, and then surrenders it to the maker without getting payment. Winner *v.* Penniman, 35 Md. 163. If one tenant in common takes the joint property, and disposes of it to a third person for uses not justified by the joint holding, the other co-tenant may maintain trover against the vendee. Agnew *v.* Johnson, 17 Pa. St. 373; Collins *v.* Ayer, 57 Ind. 239.

A joint owner of a chattel is bound to bestow upon its preservation that care which a prudent person ordinarily uses with his own property. Guillot *v.* Dorsat, 4 Martin (La.), 203.

1. Wilton *v.* Girdestone, 5 B. & A. 587.

2. Thompson *v.* Rose, 16 Conn. 71; Sturges *v.* Keith, 57 Ill. 451; Coffin *v.* Anderson, 4 Blackf. (Ind.) 395; Beckman *v.* McKay, 14 Cal. 250; Dietus *v.* Fuss, 8 Md. 148; Lockwood *v.* Clayes, 8 Vt. 33; Jacoby *v.* Laussat, 6 S. & R. (Pa.) 300; Delano *v.* Curtis, 7 Allen (Mass.), 470.

3. 3 Bouvier's Inst. No. 3530; Phillips *v.* Robinson, 4 Bing. 106.

4. Knapp *v.* Winchester, 11 Vt. 351; Traylor *v.* Horrall, 4 Blackf. (Ind.) 317; Yale *v.* Saunders, 16 Vt. 243; Morris *v.* Thompson, 1 Rich. (S. Car.) 65.

5. Storm *v.* Livingston, 6 John. (N. Y.) 44.

6. 2 Greenl. Ev. sect. 644; Gilmore *v.* Newton, 9 Allen (Mass.), 171; Robinson *v.* Hartridge, 13 Fla. 501; Hagar *v.* Randall, 62 Me. 439.

A demand is not necessary if the taking is tortious, or if the actual conversion is otherwise proved. Davis *v.* Webb, 1 McCord (S. Car.), 213; Hewes *v.* McKinney, 3 Mo. 382; Farrington *v.* Payne, 15 John. (N. Y.) 431, 432; Riford *v.* Montgomery, 7 Vt. 411; Earle *v.* Van Buren, 2 Halst. (N. J.) 244; Newsum *v.* Newsum, 1 Leigh (Va.), 86. Or if the chattels wrongfully taken are delivered to a bailee, he is liable to the owner after demand and refusal to deliver. Doty *v.* Hawkins, 6 N. H. 247;

Houston *v.* Dyche, 1 Meigs (Tenn.), 76. The bailee may show that the property has perished, or has been lost without his fault, in which case he is not liable. Dearborn *v.* Nat. Bank, 58 Me. 273; Jefferson *v.* Hale, 31 Ark. 286. If it was taken from him by an armed force, he is not guilty. Abraham *v.* Nunn, 42 Ala. 51; Griffith *v.* Zipperwick, 28 Ohio St. 388.

If two hold goods, a demand on one is not sufficient to hold the other liable in trover. Mitchell *v.* Williams, 4 Hill (N. Y.). 13; White *v.* Demary, 2 N. H. 546; Griswold *v.* Plumb, 13 Mass. 298. A premature demand is invalid, and does not make the defendant liable. Hagar *v.* Randall, 62 Me. 439.

When an agent makes the demand, evidence of his authority ought to be shown in order to make the defendant liable for conversion. Watt *v.* Potter, 2 Mason, C. C. 77. *Compare* Ingalls *v.* Bulkley, 15 Ill. 224; Robinson *v.* Burleigh, 5 N. H. 225. If the demand is made on the agent, his refusal does not make him liable for conversion. Carey *v.* Bright, 58 Pa. St. 70. If, at the time of the demand, the property is present, and the defendant makes no objections to its being taken by the owner, though the duty devolved upon him to carry it to the owner's home, yet it is no conversion if he refuses to carry it. Farrar *v.* Rollins, 37 Vt. 295.

If the defendant on demand deliver the chattel, he is not guilty of trover. Quay *v.* McNinch, 2 Con. Ct. R 78; Chandler *v.* Partin, 2 Con Ct. R 72.

An unconditional refusal to deliver property to the rightful owner, though the property is away a great distance from the place of demand, is evidence of a conversion. Clark *v.* Hale, 34 Conn. 398; Fifield *v.* R. R. Co., 62 Me. 77. Setting up the rights of a third party by refusal to deliver, is a conversion. Atkinson *v.* Marshall, 12 L. J. R. N. S Exch. 117 If the party of whom the goods are demanded, *bona fide* and reasonably refuses, because he is not satisfied that the party demanding is the real owner, he is not liable in trover Sargent *v.* Gile, 8 N. H. 325; O'Connell *v.* Jacobs, 115 Mass. 21; Carroll *v.* Mix, 51 Barb. (N. Y.) 212; Leighton *v.* Shapley, 8 N. H. 359; Dowd *v* Wadsworth, 2 Day (Conn.), 130; Blaksenship *v.* Berry, 28 Tex. 448; Isaac *v.* Clark, 2 Bulst. 312; Green *v.* Dunn, 3 Campb. 215. The refusal to deliver goods on the ground that they are in the custody of the law, under a process against a third party, is no evidence of conversion. Verral *v.* Robinson, 2 Cromp. M. & R. 495. It is not a conversion for a servant to refuse to deliver the goods of his master until he had consulted him in order to obtain his instructions to deliver them. Carey *v.* Bright, 58 Pa. St. 70; Shotwell *v.* Few, 7 John. (N. Y.) 302; Hagar *v.* Randall, 62 Me. 439. If the demand be left at the house of the defendant, without personal service, a reasonable time must elapse for the defendant's reply, before he will be liable in trover. White *v.* Demary, 2 N. H. 546. The non-compliance with the demand after a reasonable time is presumptive evidence of conversion. Thompson *v.* Rose, 16 Conn. 71.

Generally the demand ought to be made of the person who holds the chattels in his own right personally. If that cannot be done, then a notice of the ownership of the goods, and a demand in writing to deliver them, should be left at the house of the tort-feasor. Logan *v.* Houlditch, 1 Esp. 22. When one ground of refusal is given, the defendant can take no other. If he has a lien on the chattel, but refuses to deliver it on other grounds, he waives his lien, and cannot resort to it thereafter. Clark *v.* Chamberlain, 2 M. & W. 78; Wilson *v.* Anderton, 1 B. & Ad. 450; West *v.* Tupper, 1 Bailey (S. Car.), 193. An absolute, unconditional, and unqualified refusal is equivalent to a conversion. Dent *v.* Chiles, 5 Stew. & Port. (Ala.) 383. The demand should be absolute and unconditional. Rushworth *v.* Taylor, 12 L. J. R. N. S. Q. B. 80. The demand should not be too large, nor of more things than could be rightfully claimed. Abington *v.* Lipscombe, 1 G & D 233. The nature of the refusal and the actions of the tort-feasor should be taken into consideration, in considering the demand. The person making the demand need not exhibit his title to the property as a part of the demand. Ratcliffe *v.* Vance, 2 Con. Ct. R. 239. To maintain trover against one who came lawfully into possession of chattels, a proper demand and refusal must be shown, unless there is proof of appropriation, or change in the condition of the chattels. Kime *v.* Dale, 14 Brad. (Ill.) 308. The decisions as to whether a purchaser from a bailee without authority to sell, can be held liable in trover without a demand for the goods, are conflicting The following decisions hold that the purchaser will be liable in trover without a demand: Mining Co. *v.* Tritte, 4 Nev 494; Frudo *v.* Anderson, 10 Mich. 357; Galvin *v.* Bacon, 2 Fairf. (Me.) 28, Stanley *v.* Gaylord, 1 Cush. (Mass.) 536, Parsons *v.* Webb, 8 Greenl. (Me.) 38. The following hold, with some modifications, that a demand must first be made before the defendant will become liable in trover: Sherry *v.* Picken, 10 Ind. 375; Marshall *v.* Davis, 1 Wend. (N. Y.) 109; Barrett *v.* Warren, 3 Hill (N. Y.) 348; Nash *v.* Mosher, 19 Wend. (N. Y.) 431; Justice *v.* Mendell, 14 B. Mon. (Ky.) 10; Talmadge *v.* Scudder, 38 Pa. St. 517.

8. Who may bring Trover. — A party, to support his action of trover, must, at the time of the conversion, have had complete property, either special or general, in the chattel, and the actual possession, or the right to the immediate possession, of it.[1] Absolute ownership of, or a special interest in, the chattel is sufficient to support trover.[2] Without this right of absolute or special property, the plaintiff cannot maintain his action of trover.[3]

The right of possession of chattels is sufficient to enable the general owner to bring trover, though he has not the actual possession at the time of the tortious act; because the ownership of goods draws to the owner the possession in contemplation of law. The plaintiff is deemed in possession at the time of the conversion.[4] A person having a special property of goods in his rightful possession can maintain trover against all persons who may wrongfully take the goods from him, even by the command of the general owner.[5]

The party having the special property of goods may maintain an action of trover against the owner himself for any unpermitted disturbance or refusal of his possession; because the owner cannot take goods himself, that he cannot authorize others to take.[6]

A person who has acquired possession of chattels unwarrantably, without title or right, cannot bring trover for the detention of goods against one who may wrongfully or otherwise take them from him.[7] To pledge the goods of another without authority is a conversion. The pledgee derives no right to the chattel, the act of the pledgor having re-invested the owner with his right of possession, who may bring trover for its recovery.[8]

When a party demands goods, which have come into possession of the landlord by death of his tenant to whom they were loaned, and the landlord replies, "Let some one who knows the goods come and get them," there is no conversion. Butler *v.* Jones (Ala.), 2 South. Rep. 300.

1. Drury *v.* Mutual Ins. Co., 38 Md. 242; Stephenson *v.* Little, 10 Mich. 433; Owens *v.* Weedman, 82 Ill. 409; Phillips *v.* Robinson, 4 Bing. 106; Sevier *v.* Holiday, 1 Hemp. C. C. 160; Glaze *v.* McMillion, 7 Porter (Ala.), 279; Hotchkiss *v.* McVickar, 12 John. (N. Y.) 403; Debow *v.* Colfax, 5 Halst. (N. J.) 128; Traylor *v.* Horrall, 4 Blackf. (Ind.) 317; Redman *v.* Gould, 7 Blackf. (Ind.) 361; Danley *v.* Rector, 5 Eng. (Ark.) 211; Kemp *v.* Thompson, 17 Ala. 9; Purdy *v.* McCullough, 3 Barr (Pa.), 466; Fulton *v.* Fulton, 48 Barb. (N. Y.) 581; Fairbanks *v.* Phelps, 22 Pick. (Mass.) 535; Cook *v.* Howard, 13 John. (N. Y.) 276.

2. Webb *v.* Fox, 7 T. R. 398.

3. Barton *v.* Dunning, 6 Blackf. (Ind.) 209; Glaze *v.* McMillion, 7 Porter (Ala.), 279.

4. Hyde *v.* Noble, 13 N. H. 494; Clark *v.* Rideout, 39 N. H. 238; Carter *v.* Kingman, 103 Mass. 517.

5. Autcolt *v.* Durling, 1 Dutch. (N. J.) 443.

6. Roberts *v.* Wyatt, 2 Taunt. 268.

7. Buckley *v.* Grass, 3 Best & S. 566; Kemp *v.* Thompson, 17 Ala. 9.

8. Carpenter *v.* Hale, 8 Gray (Mass.), 157.

A husband cannot bring trover for the conversion of the wife's chattels. Taylor *v.* Jones, 52 Ala. 78. In one case in New York the defendant was allowed to show property in a third person, without connecting himself with the right of such person. Rotan *v.* Fletcher, 15 Johns. (N. Y.) 206. In New York it has been also *held* that trover will lie against a stranger "on a bare possession." Daniels *v.* Ball, 11 Wend. (N. Y.) 57 note. In the same State it is *held* that a defendant cannot set up property in a third person without showing some claim, title, or interest in himself, derived from such third person. Duncan *v.* Spear, 11 Wend. (N. Y.) 54. See Harker *v.* Dement, 9 Gill (Md.), 7.

In Vermont the same doctrine is maintained. Knapp *v.* Winchester, 11 Vt. 351. Possession generally is sufficient to bring trover against a tort-feasor, until he shows a better title. Bartlett v. Hoyt, 29 N. H. 317; Carter v. Bennett, 4 Fla. 283; Coffin v. Anderson, 4 Blackf. (Ind.) 395; Burke v. Savage, 13 Allen (Mass.), 408; Cook v. Patterson, 35 Ala. 102; Vining v. Baker, 53 Me. 544; Swift v. Mosely, 10 Vt. 208; Duncan v. Spear, 11 Wend. (N. Y.) 54; Mount v. Cubberly, 4 Harr. (N. J.) 124; Barwick v. Barwick, 11 Ired. (N. Car.) 80; Fairbanks v. Phelps, 22 Pick. (Mass.) 535. Possession is not sufficient to hold property from the owner, when the title is void, made so by a defective instrument of conveyance. Sherman v. Matthews, 15 Gray (Mass.), 508.

The action of trover may be brought by the special or general owner, and judgment obtained by one is a bar to an action by the other. Smith v. James, 7 Cowen (N. Y.), 328. A mortgagee in possession of the chattels may bring trover for their conversion. Wolf v. O'Farrel, 1 Const. Ct. (S. Car.) 141.

A mortgagee may maintain trover against the mortgagor after the title of the mortgagee has become absolute, upon refusal of the mortgagor to deliver the property. Gifford v. Ford, 5 Vt. 532. And when the mortgagor has not the possession, he can bring trover for the goods after the conditions are broken. Ripley v. Dolbier, 18 Me. 382. If a mortgagor mixes the mortgaged goods with his own, and then sends them to a third person, who sells them, the goods being so mixed that they could not be separated, the mortgagee can bring trover against the consignee, and recover the whole value. Willard v. Rice, 11 Met. (Mass.) 493.

In the case of a simple bailment without reward, the bailor or the bailee can bring trover to recover goods wrongfully taken out of the bailee's possession. Faulkner v. Brown, 13 Wend. (N. Y.) 63.

A right of immediate possession at the time or before the conversion is essential to have the right to bring trover, but it is not necessary that the plaintiff's right in the chattel should have continued until the beginning of the suit. Barton v. Dunning, 6 Blackf. (Ind.) 209; Grady v. Newby, 6 Blackf. (Ind.) 442.

A vendor, in a void sale to a married woman, may bring trover against an officer who levies on the goods as property of the husband. Smith v. Plomer, 15 East, 607. A servant cannot bring trover for the conversion of his master's goods, since his possession is the possession of his master. Badger v. Manuf. Co., 70 Ill. 302; McConeghy v. McCaw, 31 Ala. 447; Jones v. Webster, 48 Ala. 109; Broughton v. Atchison, 52 Ala. 62; Robinson v. Kruse, 29 Ark. 576; Coles v. Clark, 3 Cush. (Mass.) 399; Chamberlain v. Clemence, 8 Gray (Mass.), 389; Spriggs v. Camp, 2 Speers (S. Car.), 181; Melody v. Chandler, 12 Me. 282.

A factor or bailee, or any other person with a right of his own, however small, can bring trover against a tort-feasor for taking property wrongfully from his possession, and may recover the whole value of the property, being accountable over to the general owner. Beger v. Bush, 50 Ala. 19.

If a party purchases goods of a person who has no title in them, and sells them in good faith, he will be liable to the owner for converting the goods. R. R. Co. v. Trenton, 3 Vroom (N. J.), 517; Beasely v. Mitchell, 9 Ala. 780; Hoffman v. Carew, 20 Wend. (N. Y.) 21; s. c., 22 Wend (N. Y.) 285; Heckle v. Lurney, 101 Mass. 344; Chapman v. Cole, 12 Gray (Mass.), 141; Browning v. Magill, 2 Harr. & J. (Md.) 308; Morrill v. Moulton, 40 Vt. 242. An auctioneer who, innocently, receives stolen goods, and sells them, or a person *bona fide* buys a stolen horse, and exercises dominion of it, he is liable in trover to the owners for conversion. Grunson v. State, 89 Ind. 533; Hoffman v. Carew, 20 Wend. (N. Y.) 21; Curme v. Rauh, 100 Ind. 247; Coles v. Clark, 3 Cush. (Mass.) 399; Hills v. Snell, 104 Mass. 173; Curtis v. Cane, 32 Vt 232. Where goods have been obtained under an invalid contract, and an action is pending on the contract, trover will not lie. Kimball v. Cunningham, 4 Mass. 502; Peters v. Ballistier, 3 Pick. (Mass.) 495. Where there is a fraudulent exchange of property, trover will not lie until all of the property is returned. Kimball v. Cunningham, 4 Mass. 502. The owner of cattle leased them with a farm for four years, with an agreement, that, at the end of four years, the lessee might return the cattle, or the price for them. The lessee sold the cattle before the expiration of the four years. *Held*, that this sale determined the lessee's right of possession; and the owner was permitted to maintain trover against both the seller and the vendee, for the cattle. Grant v. King, 14 Vt. 367; Turner v. Waldo, 40 Vt. 51. If an agent has authority to take a note, payable to his principal, but takes it payable to himself, the principal may waive the wrongful act, and maintain trover for its recovery. McNear v. Atwood, 17 Me. 434. An executor has a right to bring trover for the possession of chattels belonging to the estate. Kerby v. Quinn, 1 Rice (S. Car.), 254. The seller of goods may maintain trover against the vendee who gave in payment a check which was dishonored. Bank v. McCrea, 106 Ill. 281. Trover will lie for grain stored in a public warehouse, and mingled with other grain. Nat. Bank v. Meadowcroft, 95 Ill. 124. A real-estate broker has no lien on the title-deed and other papers put into his hands in order to sell a piece of realty, for his

9. Declaration, Requisites of. — 1. The declaration must state that the plaintiff was lawfully possessed of certain goods or chattels, with full description of them, avoiding repetition, as his own property, of a certain value, which should be mentioned; and that, being so possessed, he, on a certain day, which should be specified, casually lost said goods and chattels out of his possession. And that afterwards, on the day and year aforesaid, they came to the possession of the defendant by finding.[1] 2. The finding is generally used, but it would probably be sufficient to allege generally that the chattels came to the hands of the defendant.[2] 3. The averment should be that the defendant, well knowing that the said goods and chattels were the property of the plaintiff, and of right to belong and appertain to him, but contriving, and fraudulently intending, craftily and subtilely, to deceive and defraud the plaintiff in this behalf, has not yet delivered the said goods and chattels to the said plaintiff, although often requested so to do, but has hitherto refused, and still refuses, so to do; and afterwards, at a certain time mentioned, in said county, converted and disposed of the said goods and chattels to his (the defendant's) own use.[3] 4. To aver that the defendant took in his possession certain goods and chattels, the property of the plaintiff, that he refused, and still refuses, to deliver them to the plaintiff, though requested, and has converted them to his own use, is a sufficient averment.[4] 5. The plaintiff must also aver that he is entitled to possession.[5] 6. The declaration should lay the damages in a sum sufficient to cover the value of the article, and such other injury as the plaintiff may have sustained.[6]

All formal defects in a declaration are cured by a verdict when in favor of the plaintiff.[7] Where a declaration misstated the name of the defendant for that of the plaintiff, it was held that the mistake could be taken advantage of only by special demurrer; and, if there was a judgment by default, a special demurrer would not be allowed, except on the condition of pleading issuably.[8] Concisely stated, the declaration should show that the plaintiff was possessed of the goods as his own property, and that they came to the defendant's possession by finding, and that there is a conversion.[9]

charges and expenses. The refusal of him to return the papers until the payment of his charges, is a conversion; and, in trover for the same, these charges cannot be brought in as a set-off by the agent. Arthur *v.* Sylvester (Pa.), Leg. Int. Mar. 21, 1884; Weekly N. Cas. June 5, 1884.

1. 3 Bouvier's Inst. § 3538; Swier *v.* Holliday, 1 Hemp. C. C. 160; Good *v.* Harnish, 13 Serg. & R. (Pa.) 99; Carlisle *v.* Weston, 1 Met. (Mass.) 26; Heath *v.* Conway, 1 Bibb (Ky.), 398; Smith *v.* Hancock, 4 Bibb (Ky.), 222; Donaghe *v.* Rondebush, 4 Munf. (Va.) 251.

2. Puterbaugh's Pract. 507.

3. Steph. Pl. 48; Puterbaugh's Pract. 508.

4. Glenn *v.* Garrison, 2 Harr. (N. J.) 1.

5. Deorman *v.* Deorman, 5 Ala. 202.

6. 3 Bouvier's Inst. § 3540.

7. Good *v.* Harnish, 13 Serg. & R. (Pa.) 99; Chitty's Pl. 181.

8. McLure *v.* Vernon, 2 Hill (S. Car.), 420.

9. Chitty's Pl. 181.

The plaintiff, in order to succeed, must show general and absolute, or special, property in himself. Roberts *v.* Wyatt, 2

10. Defendant's Pleas. — In trover the general plea is ***not guilty***, under which many matters in discharge may be given in evidence. Release and statute of limitations must be pleaded if relied upon for a defence. The defendant may plead any thing specially which admits the property in the owner, and the conversion, but which justifies the latter.[1] Not guilty operates as a denial of the conversion only, and not the plaintiff's title to the goods.[2] A denial of the conversion is only equivalent to a plea of the general issue.[3] The defendant may plead a former recovery of damages, given in an action of trespass for the same trespass or conversion.[4]

A plea amounting to a general issue in trover is generally bad; as that the goods were sold pursuant to the plaintiff's orders,[5] or alleging property in the plaintiff, and that the goods were taken for rent.[6]

11. Verdict. — 1. *For Plaintiff.* — That he recover his damages and costs.

2. *For Defendant.* — That he recover his costs.[7]

Taunt. 268; Spoor *v.* Holland, 8 Wend. (N. Y.) 445.

When an article is manufactured upon special contract, and the price is paid in instalments as the work progresses, the payment of instalments, as they fall due, vests the property in the buyer. Johnson *v.* Hunt, 11 Wend. (N. Y.) 135. But if the contract is generally, without any express stipulations for advances, payment on account, will not vest the property. Bishop *v.* Crawshay, 3 B. & C. 416.

Possession, acquired in good faith and for a consideration, of bank-notes, bill of exchange or promissory note, when indorsed in blank, or payable to bearer; or a government bond, payable to the holder; or other negotiable security so payable or indorsed, — is sufficient evidence of title, without showing any title in the person from whom he received it. Story on Bills, sect. 415; 2 Greenl. Ev. § 639; 2 Phil. Ev. 222. An obligee can call the obligor to prove the contents of a bond. Smith *v.* Robertson, 4 Harr. & John. (Md.) 30. The plaintiff must show his right to present possession, and that he had such a right at the time of the conversion. If he has only special property, he must prove actual possession. Dennie *v.* Harris, 9 Pick. (Mass.) 364; Sheldon *v.* Soper, 14 John. (N. Y.) 352.

When the defendant has color of title, the plaintiff must show title and possession both in himself. Fightmaster *v.* Beasley, 7 Marsh., J. J. (Ky.) 410. The plaintiff must show that he has been injured by the conversion; for, if the goods have no value, he cannot recover damages. Miller *v.* Reigne, 2 Hill (S. Car.), 592.

In an action of trover to recover stock deposited as collateral security, the declaration must allege the conversion of the stock by defendant. Cumnock *v.* Institution, 142 Mass. 342.

In an action of trover, where possession is not sought, it need not be averred that the plaintiff is entitled to possession. Baals *v.* Stewart, 109 Ind. 371.

1. Hurst *v.* Clark, 19 Wend. (N. Y.) 463; Coffin *v.* Anderson, 4 Blackf. (Ind.) 395.

2. Chit. Pl. 530.

3. Fenlason *v.* Rackliff, 50 Me. 362.

4. Sanders *v.* Egerton, 2 Brev. (S. Car.) 45.

5. Kennedy *v.* Strong, 10 John. (N. Y.) 289.

6. Briggs *v.* Brown, 3 Hill (N. Y.), 87.

The defendant may show, in general, under *not guilty*, that the title of the goods was in himself absolutely, or as a joint owner with the plaintiff, or specially, as bailee, or that he had a right to retain on account of his lien. Skinner *v.* Upshaw, 2 Ld. Raym. 752. He can plead that he took the goods for a just cause, as for rent in arrears. Kline *v.* Husted, 3 Caines (N. Y.), 275. He may disprove the plaintiff's title by showing title in a stranger. Schermerhorn *v.* Van Volkenburgh, 11 John. (N. Y.) 529; Rotan *v.* Fletcher, 15 Johns. (N. Y.) 207. But, in showing the interest of such third party, he must connect in some way with himself, showing that he had some title in himself. Duncan *v.* Spear, 11 Wend. (N. Y.) 54. The defendant may plead accord and satisfaction, arbitrament and award. 1 Tidd's Pr. 598.

7. 3 Bouvier's Inst. §§ 3548 and 3550.

12. Damages. — (*a*) *Measure of Damages.* — In this country the measure of damages in trover, in general, is the value of the property converted at the time of the conversion, with interest from that period.[1]

The value of the property is beneficially equivalent to the property itself, and the interest for the delay is compensation for deprivation of property.[2]

1. Matthews *v.* Mevedger, 2 McLean, C. C. 145; Ewart *v.* Kerr, 2 McMullan (S. Car.), 141; Buford *v.* Fannen, 1 Bay (S. Car.), 273; McConnell *v.* Linton, 4 Watts (Pa.), 357; Harger *v.* McMaines, 4 Watts (Pa.), 418; Pierce *v.* Benjamin, 14 Pick. (Mass.) 356; Weld *v.* Oliver, 21 Pick. (Mass.) 559; Watt *v.* Porter, 2 Mason, C. C. 77; Lillard *v.* Whittaker, 3 Bibb (Ky.), 92; Washington Co. *v.* Webster, 62 Me. 362; Hepburn *v.* Sewell, 5 Harr. & J. (Md.) 211; Burney *v.* Pledger, 3 Rich. (S. Car.) 191; Kingsbury *v.* Smith, 13 N. H. 109; Robinson *v.* Hartridge, 13 Fla. 501; Stallenwerck *v.* Thatcher, 115 Mass. 224; Greeley *v.* Stilson, 27 Mich. 153; Winchester *v.* Craig, 33 Mich. 205; Yater *v.* Mullen, 24 Ind. 277; Turner *v.* Ritter, 58 Ill. 264; Jefferson *v.* Hale, 31 Ark. 286; Sledge *v.* Reid, 73 N. Car. 440; Thomas *v.* Sternheimer, 29 Md. 268; Herzberger *v.* Adams, 39 Md. 309; Polk *v.* Allen, 19 Mo. 467; Hurd *v.* Hubbell, 26 Conn. 389; Thrall *v.* Lathrop, 30 Vt. 307; Hayden *v.* Bartlett, 35 Me. 203; Tenney *v.* Bank, 20 Wis. 152; Carlyon *v.* Lannan, 4 Nev. 156; Neiler *v.* Kelley, 69 Pa. St. 403; Whitfield *v.* Whitfield, 40 Miss. 352; Newton *v.* White, 53 Ga. 395; Spencer *v.* Vance, 57 Mo. 427; Cole *v.* Ross, 9 B. Mon. (Ky.) 393; Spicer *v.* Waters, 65 Barb. (N. Y.) 227; Brisco *v.* McElween, 43 Miss. 556; Dixon *v.* Cadwell, 15 Ohio St. 412; Fowler *v.* Merrill, 11 How. (U. S.) 375; Bourne *v.* Ashley, 1 Low. (U. S. Dis. C.) 27; Jones *v.* Allen, 1 Head (Tenn.), 626; Lee *v.* Matthews, 10 Ala. 682; Moore *v.* Aldrich, 25 Tex. 276; Douglass *v.* Kraft, 9 Cal. 562; Boylan *v.* Huguet, 8 Nev. 345; Hamer *v.* Hathaway, 33 Cal. 117; Page *v.* Fowler, 39 Cal. 412; Riley *v.* Martin, 35 Ga. 136; Ryburn *v.* Pryor, 14 Ark. 505; Hatcher *v.* Pelham, 31 Tex. 201; Jenkins *v.* McConico. 26 Ala. 213; Robinson *v.* Barrows, 48 Me. 186; Davis *v.* Fairclough, 63 Mo. 61; Scull *v.* Briddle, 2 Wash. C. C. 150; Williams *v.* Crum, 27 Ala. 468; Linville *v.* Black, 5 Dana (Ky.), 177.

2. Ewing *v.* Blount, 20 Ala. 694.

No change by the tort-feasor should enhance the value so as to give the owner a new cause of action, or a new date for the valuation of the chattels. Dows *v.* Bank, 91 U. S. 618; Tome *v.* Dubois, 6 Wall. (U. S.) 548; Ins. Co. *v.* Dalrymple, 25 Md. 269; Newman *v.* Kane, 9 Nev. 234; Robinson *v.* Barrows, 48 Me. 186; Foote *v.* Merrill, 54 N. H. 490. *Compare* Ellis *v.* Wire, 33 Ind. 127; Final *v.* Backus, 18 Mich. 218; Baker *v.* Drake, 53 N. Y. 211. The plaintiff can recover the market value at the time of conversion, even though the goods have fallen in price. Devlin *v.* Pike, 5 Daly (N. Y.), 85; Barrante *v.* Garratt, 50 Cal. 112.

Where the defendant dug coal out of the plaintiff's mine, the damage was the value of the coal at the mouth of the shaft, less the expense of getting it there. Coal Co. *v.* Long, 81 Ill. 359.

Where the defendant cut timber on the plaintiff's land, the value was estimated after it was cut, the defendant's labor not counting. Bly *v.* United States, 4 Dillon, C. C. 464. *Compare* Nesbit *v.* St. Paul, 21 Minn. 491. If the property has little or no market value, the actual value to the owner is the just rule. Stickney *v.* Allen, 10 Gray (Mass.), 352; Starkey *v.* Kelly, 50 N. Y. 676; Bourne *v.* Ashley, 1 Lowell (U. S.), 27. Foreign goods' value should be that of the custom-house valuation of them in this country, if made at the time of the conversion. Caffe *v.* Bertrand, 1 How. App. Cas. (N. Y.) 224.

Goods wrongfully sold on execution should be valued at the price of the auction sale. Heinmuller *v.* Abbott, 34 N. Y. Super. Ct. 229. *Compare* Peters *v.* Mayor, 8 Hun (N. Y.), 405. A creditor took an absolute deed from his debtor as security. He sold the land. Held, liable for the proceeds of the sale less the debt. Meehan *v.* Forrester, 52 N. Y. 277. When land sold in fraud of the bankrupt law, the assignee can recover its value, irrespective of what it sold for. Clarion Bank *v.* Jones, 21 Wall. (U. S.) 325; Norman *v.* Cunningham, 5 Gratt. (Va.) 63. If the market is at a distance where the goods are to be sent, the value there may be taken with proper deductions for expenses. Saunders *v.* Clark, 106 Mass. 331; Cockburn *v.* Lumber Co. 54 Wis. 619. The market value will govern, rather than any special value to the owner, arising from his having contracted it or otherwise, the defendant not knowing of such special value. Brown *v.* Allen, 35 Iowa, 306; Gardner *v.* Field, 1 Gray (Mass.), 151; Watt *v.* Potter, 2 Mason,

C. C. 77. *Compare* France *v.* Gaudet, L. R. 6 Q. B. 199. If there is a market price for the property where taken, it will control rather than the place where it was to be shipped. Spicer *v.* Waters, 65 Barb. (N. Y.) 227. Stocks of goods cannot be valued at the retail price. Wehle *v.* Haviland, 69 N. Y. 448; State *v.* Smith, 31 Mo. 566; Nightingale *v.* Scannell, 18 Cal. 315; Haskell *v.* Hunter, 23 Mich. 305. If fixtures are severed from the freehold, their value is what they are worth as chattels. Clark *v.* Halford, 2 C. & K. 540; Ayer *v.* Bartlett, 9 Pick. (Mass.) 156.

Where the property fluctuates in value, the rule is not the same. The value may vary considerably between the time of conversion and the trial. Some of the courts hold the highest market value between the time of conversion and the beginning of the trial, and some add the qualification that the suit shall be commenced in a reasonable time. Markham *v.* Jaudon, 41 N. Y. 493; Morgan *v.* Gregg, 46 Barb. (N. Y.) 183; Stapleton *v.* King, 40 Iowa, 278; Kent *v.* Ginter, 23 Ind. 1; Stephenson *v.* Price, 30 Tex. 715; Johnson *v.* Marshall, 34 Ala. 522. The jury might award the highest market price in their discretion. Ewing *v.* Blount, 20 Ala. 694; Jenkins *v.* McConico, 26 Ala. 213. And this doctrine obtains especially where the property is subject to considerable fluctuation. Douglass *v.* Kraft, 9 Cal. 562; Hamer *v.* Hathaway, 33 Cal. 117. This last rule is qualified in Barrante *v.* Garratt, 58 Cal. 112. New York decisions would have the suit brought in a reasonable time; that is to say, if the property converted was always in market, the advance thereon from the conversion to the time of the trial may be allowed, provided the suit is brought in a reasonable time. Baker *v.* Drake, 53 N. Y. 211; Devlin *v.* Pike, 5 Daly (N. Y.), 85; Ormsby *v.* Vermont Copper Co., 56 N. Y. 623; Tyng *v.* Commercial Co, 58 N. Y. 308; Bank *v.* Bank, 60 N. Y. 40; Thayer *v.* Manly, 73 N. Y. 305; Harris *v.* Tumbridge, 83 N. Y. 92; s. c., 38 Am. Rep. 398. Under the code in California (1872, § 3336), the measure of damage is the value of the property at the time of conversion, with interest from that time; or, when the action has been commenced in a reasonable time the highest market value without interest at the option of the injured party; or a fair compensation for the time and money properly expended in the pursuit of the chattels. Fairbanks *v.* Williams, 58 Cal. 241. Georgia has a similar rule. See Georgia Code (1873), § 3077. See further the code practice as interpreted by the courts Clark *v.* Bates, 1 Dak. 43; Rhoda *v.* Alameda Co., 58 Cal. 357.

In Florida, in case stock is held for investment, the highest market value is the measure of damages. Moody *v.* Cault, 14 Fla. 50. In Pennsylvania the general rule is followed as to conversion of chattels. Neiler *v.* Kelly, 69 Pa. St. 403; Monk *v.* Bennett, 70 Pa. St. 484. But in the conversion of stocks, a qualification or modification is introduced. Where the consideration of the stock has been paid, the highest market value, with the dividends received between the conversion and the trial, is allowed as damage. Where the consideration is not paid, the damage is the difference between the consideration and the value of the stock, and the interest on the consideration and the dividends on the stock. Bank *v.* Montgomery, 26 Pa. St. 143. In an action to replace borrowed stock, the stock was the highest at the time of the trial, which value was allowed as damages. Musgrove, Beckendorff, 53 Pa. St. 310. But this rule is said to apply only in the case of a refusal to perform the contract, whereby the owner sustains the loss in the rise of the price of the stock. Phillips' Appeal, 68 Pa. St. 130. A party paid for stock, and then tendered it back under a condition of its sale; but the seller refused to accept it. The damages were the amount paid, and not the highest market price at the time of the refusal. Wagner *v.* Peterson, 83 Pa. St. 238. It is finally decided that this rule has no application to trover, and does not apply to ordinary stock contracts. It applies between trustees and beneficiary, or to cases where justice cannot be done by the ordinary and general rule in assessing damages. Coal Co. *v.* English, 86 Pa. St. 247; North *v.* Phillips, 89 Pa. St. 250.

The general rule is now departed from only in cases where this rule would not furnish adequate damages for the injury; for instance, the defendant has received an increase of the value which the plaintiff would have received but for the conversion. De Clerq, 46 Ill. 112; Symes *v.* Oliver, 13 Mich. 9; Ewant *v.* Kerr, 2 McMull (S. Car.), 141.

In Mississippi the court rejects the fluctuating rule, but admits qualifications (1) when the original act was wrongful; (2) when it was *bona fide*, but the defendant wrongfully converted it; (3) when the plaintiff seeks only to gain the price over the market value; (4) when the property has a special value to the plaintiff, and is withheld wilfully by the defendant. In these cases the damages are left largely with the jury. Whitfield *v.* Whitfield, 4 Miss. 352; Bickell *v.* Colton, 41 Miss. 368.

In Wisconsin the fluctuating rule or the highest price is adopted. Webster *v.* Mae, 35 Wis. 75; Weymouth *v.* R. R. Co., 17 Wis. 550. In North Carolina the value at the time of trial is taken; and, though the property has suffered injury, the defendant may surrender it, and damages be estimated for the withholding, including compensation for the decrease in value. Ins. Co. v. Davis, 70 N. Car. 485.

If the property has been largely increased in value by the tort-feasor, the improved value is generally the measure of damages. Bly v. U. S., 4 Dill, C. C. 464; Curtis v. Groat, 6 John. (N. Y.) 168; Riddle v. Driver, 12 Ala. 590; Nesbit v. Lumber Co., 21 Minn. 491; Ellis v. Wire, 33 Ind. 127; Snyder v. Vaux, 2 Rawle (Pa.), 423; Millar v. Humphries, 2 A. K. Marsh. (Ky.) 446; Smith v. Gowder, 22 Ga. 353; Eastman v. Harris, 4 La. Ann. 193; Davis v. Easley, 13 Ill. 192; Stuart v. Phelps, 39 Iowa, 14; Benjamin v. Benjamin, 15 Conn. 347.

Where chattels have become such by severance from realty by the tort-feasor, such as coal, timber, fixtures, minerals, grass, and the like, the measure of damages is the value at the instant when the chattel first becomes a chattel at its separation from the real estate, without further manipulation. Wetherbee v. Green, 22 Mich. 311; Moody v. Whitney, 38 Me. 174; Maye v. Tappan, 23 Cal. 306; Single v. Schneider, 24 Wis. 299; Potter v. Marder, 76 N. Car. 36; Foote v. Merrill, 54 N. H. 490; Tilden v. Johnson, 52 Vt. 628; Iron Co. v. Iron Works, 102 Mass. 80; Winchester v. Craig, 33 Mich. 205; Tome v. Dubois, 6 Wall. (U. S.) 548; Firmin v. Firmin, 9 Hun (N. Y), 571; Coal Co. v. Long, 81 Ill. 359; Kier v. Peterson, 41 Pa. St. 357; Young v. Lloyd, 65 Pa. St. 199; Heard v. James, 49 Miss. 236; U. S. v. Magoon, 3 McLean, C. C. 171; Cushing v. Longfellow, 26 Me. 306; Bennett v. Thompson, 13 Ired. (N. Car.) 146; Smith v. Gowder, 22 Ga. 353. The property carried to market is often increased in value, but this increase is no just cause for increase of damages to the owner. In this case the general rule is, that he recover the value at the place and at the time of conversion. Sanders v. Clark, 106 Mass. 331; Weymouth v. R. R. Co., 17 Wis. 550; Herdic v. Young, 55 Pa. St. 176; Tilden v. Johnson, 52 Vt. 628; Winchester v. Craig, 33 Mich. 205; Coal Co. v. Cox, 39 Md. 1. In regard to the confusion of goods, the measure of damages is the value at the time of conversion as if it occurred any other way. Ryder v. Hathaway, 21 Pick. (Mass.) 298; Hesseltine v. Stockwell, 30 Me. 237; Moody v. Whitney, 38 Me. 174; Wetherbee v. Green, 22 Mich. 311; Potter v. Marder, 76 N. Car. 36. Where the improved value is considered and taken when the chattel has been enhanced in value by the tort-feasor, and the rule of strict compensation cannot apply, the owner may take the entire property in which his goods have been converted Silsbury v. McCoon, 6 Hill (N. Y.), 425; Rice v. Hallenbeck, 19 Barb. (N. Y.) 664; Walther v. Wetmore, 1 E. D. Smith (N. Y.), 7.

If the confusion has been caused by mistake, the enhanced price is not generally adjudged the value of damages. Heard v. Jones, 49 Miss. 236; Forsyth v. Wells, 41 Pa. St. 291.

But there seems to be a doctrine of the decisions that the value of the whole property, when converted by admixture, or enhanced by the tort-feasor, should be the measure of damages. Single v. Schneider, 30 Wis. 570.

Where a broker disposes of, without authority, a stock which he holds for his principal, the measure of damages is the cost of replacing the stock within a reasonable time after such sale, and not the amount of money advanced by him for the purchase of the stock. Brewster v. Van Liew, 119 Ill. 554.

Where one to whom a conditional sale of personalty has been made, sells it to a third party, without the knowledge or consent of the first vendor, the third person acquires no better title as against the original vendor than the first buyer had, and may be held for conversion. Baals v. Stewart, 109 Ind. 371. A party buys lumber at a mill, and hauls it away, and sells it at fifteen dollars per thousand. The miller had wilfully cut the timber from the United States land, from which the lumber was made. The purchaser was an innocent party. *Held*, that the measure of damages for conversion of said timber was the value of the lumber at the mill before carriage. U. S. v. Heilmer, 26 Fed. Rep. 80.

An assignee can maintain trover against a wrong-doer for taking assigned property, even before filing his bond. The measure of damages is the true market value at the time of the conversion, with interest up to the rendition of the judgment. Schoolherr v. Hutchins (Tex.), 1 S. W. Rep. 266. The measure of damages for the conversion of a mere certificate of stock is not the value of the share which it represents, provided the ownership of the shares themselves is not affected. Daggett v. Davis, 53 Mich. 35.

In an action of trover, it appeared that the plaintiff had sued the defendant, who had stored the goods in his warehouse, for a mortgagee. The mortgagee, a year and a half after the beginning of the suit, took possession of the goods for conditions broken, and transferred them to the defendant to pay for storage. *Held*, taking the property for condition broken was an application of the property for the benefit of the plaintiff, and would go in mitigation of damages. Dahill v. Booker, 140 Mass. 308.

Stock of a corporation, wrongfully con-

(*b*) *Special Damages.* — Special damages are generally allowed, if set forth in the declaration; as where the plaintiff, being the true owner, has been compelled to expend money and time in searching for the chattels unlawfully taken. These damages are said to be immediately proximate to the defendant's wrong acts, and are proper. A reasonable compensation for this expenditure of time and money, beyond the interest and value, should be paid to the plaintiff.[1]

(*c*) *Exemplary Damages.* — Where the tort is wilful and malicious, and is attended with aggravating circumstances, exemplary damages may be allowed.[2]

(*d*) *Damages for Conversion of Money Securities.* — When trover is brought for the recovery of ***choses in action***, such as bills, notes, bonds, or other money securities, the measure of damages is the amount due on the security; the defendant having the right to reduce the valuation by showing payment, the insolvency of the maker, or any fact tending to invalidate the security.[3]

verted, may be valued by the jury; and this valuation will not be disturbed by the appellate court, provided there is testimony to sustain the jury's verdict. Hitchcock *v.* McElrath (Cal.), 14 Pac. Rep. 305.

1. McDonald *v.* North, 47 Barb. (N. Y.) 530; Saunders *v.* Brosius, 52 Mo. 49; Boylan *v.* Huguet, 8 Nev. 343; Forsyth *v.* Wells, 41 Pa. St. 291.

The plaintiff, to recover special damages, must at least allege them in his declaration. Barrelett *v.* Bellyard, 71 Ill. 280. The same rule applies in England. Moon *v.* Raphael, 2 Bing. (N. C.) 310; Hughes *v.* Quentin, 8 C. & P. 703; Barron *v.* Arnaud, 8 Q. B. 595.

If a party is entitled to recover special damages, they must be alleged and proved. Nunan *v.* San Francisco, 38 Cal. 689. If an owner is deprived of his chattels, it does not necessarily follow that he is obliged to incur expenses and loss of time in recovering them. Gray *v.* Bullard, 22 Minn. 278.

An action of trover was commenced against an officer for damages for the conversion of chattels, part of which the plaintiff held title to by bill of sale, and by chattel mortgage to the remainder. It was held that, the plaintiff having established his claim, his damages were the value of the property at the time of the conversion, with interest and a fair compensation for the time and money properly expended in the pursuit of the chattels, and, if the plaintiff had a chattel mortgage on the property, the amount of the mortgage debt with interest. Sherman *v.* Finch (Cal.), 11 Pac Rep. 847.

2. Prebble *v.* Kent, 10 Ind. 325; Mowry *v.* Wood, 12 Wis. 413; Forsyth *v.* Wells, 41 Pa. St. 291; Neiler *v.* Kelley, 69 Pa. St. 403; Day *v.* Woodworth, 13 How. (U. S.) 363; Dibble *v.* Morris, 26 Conn. 416; Berry *v.* Vantries, 12 S. & R. (Pa.) 89. But it is held in Pennsylvania that the alleged malice and wilfulness of the taking may be inquired into, and, when found, additional damages may be allowed in trover. Forsyth *v.* Wells, 41 Pa. St. 291; Neiler *v.* Kelley, 69 Pa. St. 403; Backenstoss *v.* Stahler, 33 Pa. St. 251.

3. Decker *v.* Mathews, 12 N. Y. 313; St. John *v.* O'Connel, 7 Porter (Ala.), 466; Menkens *v.* Menkens, 23 Mo. 252; Latham *v.* Brown, 16 Iowa, 118; Craig *v.* McHenry, 35 Pa. St. 120; Bredow *v.* Mutual, etc., 28 Mo. 181; Robert *v.* Berdell, 61 Barb. (N. Y.) 37; Turner *v.* Ritter, 58 Ill. 264; McPeters *v.* Phillips, 46 Ala. 496; Fisher *v.* Brown, 104 Mass. 259; Canton *v.* Smith, 65 Me. 203; Holt *v.* Van Eps, 1 Dak. 206; Seals *v.* Cummings, 8 Humph. (Tenn.) 442, Express Co. *v.* Parsons, 44 Ill. 312.

The presumption that the face value is the true measure of damages, has been denied, and proof required of the actual value. Brightman *v.* Reeves, 21 Tex. 70.

Stated accounts are within the general rule. O'Donoghue *v.* Corby, 22 Mo. 394. The defendant can show what the actual value is. Potter *v.* Merchants' Bank, 28 N. Y. 641. Latham *v.* Brown, 16 Iowa, 118; Zeigler *v.* Wells, Fargo, & Co., 23 Cal. 179.

The face value of a check which has been paid on a forged indorsement is the measure of damages, after demand and refusal to surrender it. Survey *v.* Wells, Fargo, & Co., 5 Colo. 124.

If the maker be insolvent, yet if the owner of the note could use the note for its full amount, this is his damages. Rose (*e*) *Mitigation of Damages.* — The gist of the action of trover is the conversion. The recovery of the property by the owner goes only in the mitigation of damages. So, if the tort-feasor re-delivers the property to the rightful owner, nominal damages only can be obtained. The owner will receive as compensation an amount in damages commensurate with his actual damages.[1] When an actual conversion has taken place, and the chattels still exist, and the wrong-doer offers to return them, the owner is not under any obligations to receive them.[2] But, in case the owner does receive the converted property from the tort-feasor, he does not thereby bar his action, but the return of the goods goes in mitigation of damages.[3]

v. Lewis, 10 Mich. 483. The defendant has the right to show, in reduction of damages, payment in part; the inability of the maker to pay; a release of the maker from his undertaking, or any legal matter which will decrease the value. Fell *v.* McHenry, 42 Pa. St. 41; Robinson *v.* Hurley, 11 Iowa, 410; Terry *v.* Allis, 20 Wis. 32; Booth *v.* Powers, 56 N. Y. 22; Ingalls *v.* Lord, 1 Cowen (N. Y.), 240; King *v.* Ham, 6 Allen (Mass.), 298; Brown *v.* Montgomery, 20 N. Y. 287.

In Pennsylvania it is held that trover cannot be maintained for *choses in action*, as a share of stock, but may be for the paper as evidence of debt. Sewall *v.* Bank, 17 S. & R. (Pa.) 285. And in such case the measure of damages is the debt of which the paper is the evidence. Romig *v.* Romig, 2 Rawle (Pa.), 241. In action for the conversion of a life insurance policy by the pledgee, the measure of damages was the value of the policy less the amount of the notes for which it was pledged. Wheeler *v.* Pereless, 43 Wis. 332; Fisher *v.* Brown, 104 Mass. 259. The rule of damages on an insurance policy is the same, it would seem, as if the action was brought by the insured upon the policy, subject to mitigation by evidence of the insolvency of the insurer. Kohne *v.* Ins. Co, 1 Wash. C. C. 93. For conversion of deeds and other instruments, damages will be allowed according to the loss in each case litigated. Mowry *v.* Wood, 12 Wis. 413; Coombe *v.* Samson, 1 D. & R. 201; Llyd *v.* Sadlier, 7 Ir. Jur. N. S. 15

An acceptor may bring trover for the conversion of a paid bill, and is entitled to recover in respect to the risk of liability. Stone *v.* Clough, 41 N. H. 290.

An owner of a bond mav recover for its conversion the sum he would be entitled to recover on it from the obligee. Romig *v.* Romig, 2 Rawle (Pa.), 241; Delany *v.* Hill, 1 Pittsb. (Pa.) 28.

Generally the insolvency of the parties liable on the converted papers may be shown in mitigation of damages. McPeters *v.* Phillip, 46 Ala. 496; Latham *v.* Brown, 16 Iowa, 118; Potter *v.* Bank, 28 N. Y. 641.

In trover to recover collaterals, the measure of damages is their market value. Loomis *v.* Stave, 72 Ill. 623.

1. Cook *v.* Loomis, 26 Conn. 483; Chamberlain *v.* Shaw, 18 Pick. (Mass.) 278.

2. Brewster *v.* Silliman, 38 N. Y. 423; Hanmer *v.* Wilsey, 17 Wend. (N. Y.) 91; Higgins *v.* Whitney, 24 Wend. (N. Y.) 379.

3. Gibbs *v.* Chase, 10 Mass. 125; Brewster *v.* Silliman, 38 N. Y. 423; Reynolds *v.* Shuler, 5 Cowen (N. Y.), 323; Murray *v.* Burling, Johns. (N. Y.) 172; Dailey *v.* Crowley, 5 Lans. (N. Y.) 301.

When the property has been returned and accepted, the measure of damages is the amount paid in getting back the chattels. Ford *v.* Williams, 24 N. Y. 359; Hurlburt *v.* Green, 41 Vt. 490; Sprague *v.* Brown, 40 Wis. 612. *Compare* Fitzgerald *v.* Blocher, 32 Ark. 742. In trover, courts of law are allowed to investigate the justice and equity of each particular case in manner and upon principle similar to that by which the defence of partial failure of consideration is maintained. McGowen *v.* Young, 2 Stew. & Port. (Ala.) 160. After the conversion, if the property comes back into the plaintiff's possession, and is accepted by him, this will go in mitigation of damages, though no agreement can be shown that the plaintiff consented to its return. Sparks *v.* Purdy, 11 Mo. 219; Yale *v.* Saunders, 16 Vt. 243; Brady *v.* Whitney, 24 Mich. 154; Hepburn *v.* Sewell, 5 Har. & J. (Md.) 211; Wheelock *v.* Wheelwright, 5 Mass. 104; Cook *v.* Loomis, 26 Conn. 483. If the owner sells the property after the conversion, he can recover only nominal damages. Brady v. Whitney, 24 Mich. 154. A mere offer to return the chattels will not reduce the damages. Norman *v.* Rogers, 29 Ark. 365; Stickney *v.* Allen, 10 Gray (Mass.), 352. An agent pawned his principal's watch, and the pledgee wrongfully sold it. The measure of damages was the value of the watch, irrespective of the money received by the agent. Van Arsdale *v.* Joiner, 44 Ga. 173. A pledgee who has converted stock can recoup the amount he has lawfully paid in assessments. McCalla *v.* Clark, 55 Ga. 53.

After the property is returned and accepted, the measure of damages is the market value at the time of the conversion, less the market-value at the time of its return. Irish *v.* Cloyes, 8 Vt. 30; Ewing *v.* Blount, 20 Ala. 694; Lucas *v.* Trumbull, 15 Gray (Mass.), 306. And this is not special damages, which must be set out in the declaration. Rank *v.* Rank, 5 Pa. St. 211. Where the property has been sold on legal process, and the proceeds applied to the payment of the owner's debts, or otherwise to his use, the facts may be shown in mitigation of damages. Pierce *v.* Benjamin, 14 Pick. (Mass.) 356; Dolittle *v.* McCullough, 7 Ohio St. 299; Howard *v.* Cooper, 45 N. H. 339; Stewart *v.* Martin, 16 Vt. 397. In Connecticut the sale of the converted property can be shown in mitigation of damages, if the process was in favor of the wrongdoer himself. Curtis *v.* Ward, 20 Conn. 204. But in New York the process must come through the agency of a third person, and not by the wrong-doer. Ball *v.* Liney, 48 N. Y. 6.

If the property is injured after conversion, and the conversion was wilful, the wrong-doer must stand the loss. Jamison *v.* Hendricks, 2 Blackf. (Ind.) 94. In this case the owner cannot be compelled to accept the property in mitigation of damages. Green *v.* Sperry, 16 Vt. 390; Hart *v.* Skinner, 16 Vt. 138; Shotwell *v.* Wendover, 1 John. (N. Y.) 65. But if the property came lawfully into the defendant's possession, and the conversion was only technical, and the property is in the same condition, the plaintiff will be compelled to take it back in mitigation of damages. Earle *v.* Holderness, 4 Bing. 462; Churchill *v.* Welsh, 47 Wis. 39; Bucklin *v.* Beals, 38 Vt. 653; R. R. Co. *v.* Bank, 32 Vt. 639; Cook *v.* Loomis, 26 Conn. 483; Thayer *v.* Manly, 8 Hun (N. Y.), 550; Rogers *v.* Crombie, 4 Greenlf. (Me.) 274; Tracey *v.* Good, 1 Clark (Pa.), 472; Stevens *v.* Low, 2 Hill (N. Y.), 132. But this compulsion, it would seem, is in the discretion of the court. Hart *v.* Skinner, 16 Vt. 138; Churchill *v.* Welsh, 47 Wis. 39.

The wrong-doer cannot apply the proceeds of the property to the plaintiff's use without his consent, and have it go in mitigation of damages. Wanamaker *v.* Bower, 36 Md. 42; Northrup *v.* McGill, 27 Mich. 234; Bringard *v* Stellwagen, 41 Mich. 54. If the defendant took the property to satisfy a debt owing to him by the plaintiff, under a void process, or by a void service of a legal process, it will not mitigate the damages in some of the States. Kelly *v.* Archer, 48 Barb. (N. Y.) 68; Butts *v.* Edwards, 2 Denio (N. Y.), 164; East *v.* Pace, 57 Ala. 521; Northrup *v.* McGill, 27 Mich. 234. But if the defendant has honestly endeavored to enforce a right, and ignorantly converts property because his power was wholly or partially defective, the courts generally consider the whole transaction, and award damages in their discretion. Tripp *v.* Grouner, 60 Ill. 474. If an officer sells without notice, and hence has converted, but applies the proceeds to the debt, the measure of damages is the proceeds plus the amount the property is supposed to have depreciated by a sale without notice. Pierce *v.* Benjamin, 14 Pick. (Mass.) 356. The motive by which a defendant was controlled in converting property is only admitted when introduced to repel any attempt by the plaintiff to recover exemplary damages, but not in mitigation. Harker *v.* Dement, 9 Gill (Md.), 7. A plaintiff, in searching for his property, may recover for money paid to satisfy an amount demanded by one in whose possession he found the property, — Keene *v.* Dilke, 4 Exch. 388, — or the amount he had to pay to obtain it at a wrongful public sale. Hurlburt *v.* Green, 41 Vt. 490; Baldwin *v.* Porter, 12 Conn. 473. An offer to return the property, which was rightfully declined by the plaintiff, is no mitigation of damages. Stickney *v.* Allen, 10 Gray (Mass.), 352. A part owner of a chattel may sue in trover for his interest in it; but the defendant may show the joint interest of the others in evidence, in mitigation of damages. If the plaintiff is a tenant in common, then the defendant can plead in abatement. But if he neglects such a plea, he can then avail himself of the plaintiff's want of title to the whole property. Wright *v.* Pratt, 31 Wis. 99; Sherman *v.* Iron Works Co., 5 Allen (Mass.), 213; Chandler *v.* Spear, 22 Vt. 388. Where a party sues two for a joint conversion, compromises with one, and takes judgment by default against the other, the measure of damages was the converted goods less the amount received from the one with whom a compromise was had. Heyer *v.* Carr, 6 R. I. 45.

An action will lie for the conversion of machinery in a shop, where the defendant had used it, but had not converted it, or had actual possession of it, but refused to have it removed by the rightful owner; subsequently the defendant told the plaintiff that he relinquished all claims to it. This was held in mitigation of damages. Delano *v.* Curtis, 7 Allen (Mass.), 470.

13. Judgment. — Judgment in trover for the value of the chattels vests the title in the defendant, according to some decisions.[1] But the present rule undoubtedly is that judgment and the satisfaction thereof passes the title to the defendant. This obtaining of the value by the plaintiff operates as a transfer of the title from the time of the conversion.[2]

14. Equitable Conversion. — The nature of conversion in equity is entirely dissimilar to conversion in trover. It has no point in common. By equitable conversion is meant the change of real property into personal, and personal into real, not actually taking place, but presumed to exist by construction or intendment of equity. Money directed to be used in the purchase of land, and land ordered sold and turned into money, are considered as that kind of property into which they were ordered to be converted, and this in whatever manner the direction is given, whether by will, contract, marriage articles, settlement, or otherwise.

For certain purposes of devolution and transfer, and in order that the rights of parties may be protected, it is often necessary to regard property as subject to rules applicable to it in its changed, and not in its original, state, although there is no actual change.[3]

15. Conversion of Wife's Choses in Action by Husband. — Under the common law, the wife's *choses*, or personals in possession, become the husband's absolutely on marriage. He may dispose of them during his life without the wife's consent. He may bequeath them by will; and after his death such *choses* are regarded as assets of

1. Carlisle *v.* Burley, 3 Me. 250; Rogers *v.* Moore, Rice (S. Car.), 60; Bogan *v.* Wilburn, 1 Spears (S. Car.), 179; Floyd *v.* Brown, 1 Rawle (Pa.), 121; Marsh *v.* Pier, 4 Rawle (Pa.), 273; Fox *v.* N. Liberties, 3 W. & S. (Pa.) 103; Merrick's Estate, 5 W. & S. (Pa.) 9; Curtis *v.* Groat, 6 Johns. (N. Y.), 168; Fox *v.* Prichett, 34 N. J. 13; Murrell *v* Johnson, 1 Hen. & Munf. (Va.) 450; White *v.* Philbrick, 5 Greenlf. (Me.) 147.

2. Hepburn *v.* Sewell, 5 Har. & J. (Md.) 211; Stirling *v.* Garritee, 18 Md. 468; Bacon *v.* Kimmell, 14 Mich. 201; Lovejoy *v.* Murray, 3 Wall. (U. S.) 1; Elliot *v.* Hayden, 104 Mass. 180; United Society *v.* Underwood, 11 Bush (Ky.), 265; Smith *v.* Smith, 51 N. H. 571; Bell *v.* Perry, 43 Iowa, 368; Brady *v.* Whitney, 24 Mich. 154.

The present English rule is, that the judgment and satisfaction transfer the title to the defendant. Brinsmead *v.* Harrison, L. R. 6 C. P. 584.

Where the judgment is for nominal damages, no property vests in the defendant. Barb. *v.* Fish, 8 Blackf. (Ind.) 481; Brady *v.* Whitney, 24 Mich. 154.

Where an executrix brings trover against a party for conversion of chattels belonging to the estate, and the property came to the defendant's possession, by direction of plaintiff to be sold, it is not conversion, provided the defendant paid the proceeds on debts of the deceased: he did not use the property for himself, but for the benefit of the estate. Rutherford *v.* Thompson, 14 Oregon, 236.

3. Craig *v.* Leslie, 3 Wheat. (U. S.) 563; Peter *v.* Beverly, 10 Pet. (U. S.) 532; Taylor *v.* Benham, 5 How. (U. S.) 233; Lorillard *v.* Caster, 5 Paige (N. Y.), 172; Rhinehard *v.* Harrison, Baldw. C. C. 177; Green *v.* Johnson, 4 Bush (Ky.), 164. Collins *v.* Champ, 15 B. Mon. (Ky.) 118; Kane *v.* Gott, 24 Wend. (N. Y.) 641; Lynn *v.* Gephant, 27 Md. 547; Allison *v.* Wilson, 13 S. & R. (Pa.) 330; Morrow *v.* Brenizer, 2 Rawle (Pa.), 185; Burr *v.* Sim, 1 Whart. (Pa.) 252; Parkinson's Appeal, 8 Casey (Pa.), 455; Scudder *v.* Vanarsdale, 2 Beas. (N. J.) 109; *Ex parte* McBee, 63 N. Car. 332; Smith *v.* McCrary, 3 Ind. Eq. (N. Car.) 204; Pratt *v.* Taliaferro, 3 Leigh (Va.), 419; Tazewell *v.* Smith, 1 Rand. (Va.) 313; Brolasky *v.* Gally, 1 P. F. Smith (Pa.), 509. The rule upon equitable conversions considers that which was agreed to be done as done, provided such would be lawful and just. Baden *v.* Countess, 2 Vern. 212; Lawes *v.* Bennett, 1 Cox, 167.

his estate, the title passing to the executor or administrator, to the exclusion of his wife, though she survives him.[1]

CONVEY. — To pass or hand on to another. To transfer,[2] especially to transfer property. To pass a title to any thing from

1. Co. Litt. 351b; Legg *v.* Legg, 8 Mass. 98; Winslow *v.* Crocker, 17 Me. 29; Morgan *v.* Bank, 14 Conn. 99; Hopkins *v.* Corey, 23 Miss. 54; Cropsey *v.* McKinsey, 30 Barb. (N. Y.) 47; Carleton *v.* Lovejoy, 54 Me. 445.

After the death of the wife her *choses in action* do not strictly go to the husband, but he may recover them, as her administrator; and after paying her debts, *dum sola*, for which her assets will be responsible, though, as husband, he will then be no longer liable for them, they will belong to him.

This right is given by the English Statute of Distribution, the provisions of which statutes have been re-enacted in most of the United States. Whitaker *v.* Whitaker, 6 Johns. (N. Y.) 112; Biggert *v.* Biggert, 7 Watts (Pa.), 563. By collecting money on her *choses in action*, and appropriating it, it becomes his own by this conversion; though in Pennsylvania this taking is only *prima facie* evidence of his conversion. Estate *v.* Hinds, 5 Whart. (Pa.) 138. The same doctrine is held in other decisions. *In re* Gray's Est. 1 Pa. St. 327; Timbens *v.* Katz, 6 W. & S. (Pa.) 290; Stanwood *v.* Stanwood, 17 Mass. 57; Phelps *v.* Phelps, 20 Pick. (Mass.) 556; Marston *v.* Carter, 12 N. H. 159. An assignment in bankruptcy, or under insolvent laws, of her husband, will not pass her property or right of survivorship. If the husband dies before the assignee reduces the wife's *choses in action* to possession, they survive to her; though in Pennsylvania, by statute, they pass to the assignee at once. Richwine *v.* Heim, 1 Pa. St. 373. Her right of survivorship holds in case the husband has placed the wife's *choses* as collateral security. Hartman *v.* Dowdel, 1 Rawle (Pa.), 279. A husband in a representative capacity cannot convert his wife's chattels, so that her right of survivorship will not be sustained. Estate *v.* Kintzinger, 2 Ashm. (Pa.) 455; Mayfield *v.* Clifton, 3 Stew. (Ala.) 375. Where a husband is compelled to apply to the chancery courts to recover his wife's *choses in action*, he will be required to make a reasonable provision for the support of his wife and children. These provisions are to be commensurate with her personal fortune, including what the husband has received heretofore. Howard *v.* Moffat, 2 John Ch. (N. Y.) 206; Dearing *v.* Fitzpatrick, 1 Meigs (Tenn.), 551; Kenny *v.* Udall, 5 John. Ch. (N. Y.) 464; Duval *v.* Bank, 1 Gill & John. (Md.) 282; Burr *v.* Browyer, 2 McCord (S. Car.), 368; Dumond *v.* Magee, 4 John. Ch. (N. Y.) 318. Personal property bequeathed to the wife without restrictions passes at once to the husband, like other things in possession. Shirley *v.* Shirley, 6 Paige (N. Y.), 363. Where real estate of wife is sold, and notes given payable to her, the property then becomes personalty in the shape of a *chose in action*. Taggart *v.* Boldin, 10 Md. 104; McCrary *v.* Foster, 1 Iowa, 271. The proceeds of a widow's dower vest in the second husband. Ellsworth *v.* Hinds, 5 Wis. 613; Bartlett *v.* Janeway, 4 Sand. (N. Y.) 396. *Compare* Barber *v.* Slade, 30 Vt. 191. If the husband refuses or neglects to reduce his wife's *choses in action* to possession, the property still vests in the wife. Mellinger *v.* Bausman, 45 Pa. St. 522.

At the present time the wife's right to her separate property is regulated by statute. The common law rule has been abrogated, or greatly modified, in all the States.

See HUSBAND AND WIFE, MARRIAGE, etc.

2. Thus, in construing the following instrument, "I have this day *conveyed* a note to J. E. S. against D. G. for $117.39, dated, etc., which note I hold myself accountable for the payment thereof, on condition the said J. E. S. uses proper exertion to collect the same;" and *holding* that the word "conveyed" did not import a consideration, the court, *Parker, J.*, said, "It was argued before us that the word 'conveyed' in this guaranty imported a consideration, and it was claimed to be equivalent to the word 'sold.' But I do not so understand its meaning. Webster defines it as signifying 'to carry, to bear, to pass, to transfer; to pass a title to any thing from one person to another, as by deed, assignment, or otherwise.' I may convey a farm without any consideration. The word is used in this instrument as synonymous with transfer, and certainly a promissory note may be conveyed or transferred without consideration. It passes by delivery, and may be by gift. In Newcomb *v.* Clark, 1 Denio (N. Y.), 226, it was *held* that the word 'agree' in a contract did not import a consideration. In that case, as in this, the question was whether there was a consideration expressed so as to take a promise to pay the debt of a third person out of the statute of frauds. I think the word 'convey' neither expresses, nor even implies, that any thing was paid, or promised to be paid, for the conveyance." Spicer *v.* Norton, 13 Barb. (N. Y.) 542.

one person to another as by deed, assignment or otherwise.[1]

1. Where a party has agreed to "convey" certain real estate, it is not enough for him to show that he has tendered a deed of it, but he must show that he had a title to it at the time, so that his deed would have "conveyed" the property. In this case the plaintiff sued the town of Greenwich for $600, which it had voted should be paid him when he should "convey" a certain bridge to the town, which bridge had been erected by the voluntary subscriptions of the plaintiff and others. The town refused to accept the deed when tendered, or to pay the $600 to the plaintiff. The court, *Sanford, J.*, said, "The plaintiff neither averred in his declaration, nor proved upon the trial, that he ever made or offered, or had the power to make, the proposed conveyance. He did indeed tender to the selectmen a deed purporting to 'convey' to the town that part (that is, one-half) of said bridge that lies in this State, and the selectmen refused to receive it. But the proposal was to convey 'the bridge,'—that is, the whole bridge,—and certain roads leading to it, so that the deed tendered was not such an one as the plaintiff proposed to make; and for that reason, if for no other, the selectmen were justified in refusing to accept it. Besides, the plaintiff offered no evidence of any title to the bridge. And no inference can be drawn from any thing appearing in the motion, that he had any title in himself, or any power from any one who had, to make such conveyance. On the contrary, we think the natural inference from the facts found by the superior courts is, that he had no such title or authority. To 'convey' real estate is, by an appropriate instrument, to transfer the legal title to it from the present owner to another. But, however appropriate for the purpose the deed may be upon its face, such deed is of no avail to prove the conveyance of a title, or the tender of such conveyance, unaccompanied by proof of its execution by the real owner of the property, or some one duly authorized to execute it in his behalf. The failure of the plaintiff, therefore, to prove that he was the owner of the bridge which his deed purported to 'convey,' was a failure to show the performance of a condition precedent on which his right of action against the town depended." Abendroth *v.* Town of Greenwich, 29 Conn. 356.

So where a contract read, "to *convey* the land by a deed of conveyance," it was *held* that this was not fulfilled by executing a deed of conveyance merely, for the party must be able to "convey" such a title as the other party had a right to expect, which is to be determined from the fair import of the terms used, with reference to the subject-matter; for said the court, *Redfield, J.*, "It has been argued in the present case, that the extent of plaintiff's obligation was fulfilled by the execution of a deed, and that it was at the risk of defendant whether it conveyed title. The agreement now in suit specifies the land sold, but is silent in regard to the title. The price was $650, and the covenant to 'convey' was in these words: 'to convey to said Samuel, by a deed of conveyance, a certain tract of land,' etc. Can it be with propriety said that this covenant is satisfied by the 'execution of a deed of conveyance'? Nothing could be more absurd. The contract is not to execute a deed merely, but to 'convey' by a deed, etc., *a certain tract of land.* Could language be more explicit? What is implied in *conveying* land? Surely, that the *title* shall be *conveyed.* I admit that when the contract is in terms, for the execution of a deed of conveyance, merely, the obligee must take the risk of the title, provided the party do not divest himself of the title which he had at the time of the contract. (Stow *v.* Stevens, 7 Vt. 27.) When, too, the contract in terms requires the execution of a deed with covenants, there may be reason to suppose the parties intended to look to the covenants as the muniments of the title. It was upon this ground that the case of Aikes *v.* Sandford, 5 Mass. 494, was decided. So also the cases of Parker *v.* Parmelee, 20 Johns. (N. Y.) 130, and Gazley *v.* Price, 16 Johns. (N. Y.) 266. These cases were very fully considered, and very ably illustrated in the opinions delivered by the late Ch. J. Spencer. It was correctly *held*, undoubtedly, that, when the contract *in terms* has reference to the deed only, it is a sufficient performance to execute such a deed as is specified. But when the contract expressly refers to the title to be conveyed, then the plaintiff, in order to recover, when the covenants are dependent upon each other, as in the present case, must not only aver readiness to 'convey,' but must prove his *ability* to 'convey' such title as is contemplated by the parties. (Jones *v.* Gardiner, 10 Johns. (N. Y.) 266.) The case of Judson *v.* Wass, 11 Johns. (N. Y.) 525, although an action of assumpsit, I consider involves the same principle with the present. There the purchaser refused to complete the sale, because the seller had no title to all the land sold, and the court *held* that he was not obliged to go forward with the contract. The contract there was to 'convey' the land: so was it here. How, then, is it material whether the contract was by deed, or in writing without seal, or without writing? It is a question of construction merely. And the *terms* must have the same force in all *forms* of contract. In contracts of this kind, as well as all others, we must frequently resort to the proof of the circumstances attending the transaction, although not specified in the writing, in order to determine the force of the terms used. Hence, when it is shown in the present case, that both the parties, at the time of the contract being made, understood that the plaintiff had only a leasehold title to the premises, and that no other could be obtained, we should not consider the contract as extending beyond the conveyance of such a title. To that extent, from the terms used, it is very obvious the plaintiff did intend to bind himself to convey an unincumbered title. This he had it not in his power to do. The defendant, therefore, was not obliged to part with his money. (Gazley *v.* Price, 16 Johns. (N. Y.) 266; Parker *v.* Parmelee, 20 Johns. (N. Y.) 130; Ferry *v.* Williams, 8 Taunton 62.) Where the contract refers to the instrument only, I think an obligation to 'convey' land by a *good* and *sufficient* deed, and to deliver possession of the same, does require that the defendant should either be in possession of the land, or at least that there should not be, at the time of the execution of his deed, an adverse possession, so as to render the deed inoperative." Lawrence *v.* Dole, 11 Vt. 549.

Give, grant, and convey. — These words are as comprehensive as any that can be used to "convey" the legal title. Young *v.* Ringo, 1 T. B. Mon. (Ky.) 30.

So where a deed was in the following words, — "For, and in consideration, etc., I do hereby assign and convey to James Coleman my right and title in said decree, and to the mortgage and mortgaged property therein specified, etc. Wm. May." Seal, — the court, *Mills, J.*, said, "The expressions used in this instrument, however informal and summary, certainly include the mortgaged estate; and the words used, especially the term 'convey,' we conceive are in meaning and effect sufficient to answer the requisites of a grant at common law, and under our statute concerning conveyances, and to carry with it the legal estate, and vest it in the grantee." Patterson *v.* Carneal, 3 A. K. Marsh. (Ky.) 618; s. c., 4 Wheel. Am. Com. Law, 249.

The true meaning of "convey" must be decided in each case by its special circumstances; for an agreement to "convey" by a quitclaim deed has reference to the title only as it was at the time of agreement, and not to one subsequently acquired. Woodcock *v.* Bennet, 1 Cow. (N. Y.) 711.

And a deed purporting to "convey" a fee-simple absolute, in order to pass a subsequently acquired title, must undertake to "convey" an indefeasible title; and must undertake to "convey," not the grantor's interest in the land, but the land itself, in such a manner that the grantee is not to be disturbed by any one. Gibson *v.* Chauteau, 39 Miss. 536.

Grant, bargain, sell, and convey. — These words, except where it is especially provided by statute, do not imply any covenants in a deed of conveyance of land in fee-simple. Bethell *v.* Bethell, 54 Ind. 428; Frost *v.* Raymond, 2 Caines (N. Y.), 188.

Therefore, where there is an agreement to "convey" land in fee-simple, it is satisfied by a conveyance without covenants Fuller *v.* Hubbard, 6 Cow. (N. Y.) 13. See Nixon *v.* Hyserott, 5 Johns. (N. Y.) 58.

Power to convey. — Where a testator, by his will, gave his executors "full power and authority to *convey* in fee-simple absolute, or otherwise in their discretion, all or any portion of my real estate, and to execute and deliver all proper deeds and instruments in writing therefor," it was *held* that the power to convey by all proper deeds, etc., implied a power to sell. Hamilton *v.* Hamilton, 98 Ill. 254.

While the word "convey" is a technical term relating to the disposition of interests in real property, see opinion of *Wright, J.*, in Dickerman *v.* Abrahams, 21 Barb. (N. Y.) 551, 561; yet where, by an antenuptial deed of settlement, it was stipulated that the wife should be permitted to make what disposition of the trust property she might choose, and that she should have the absolute and entire control over it, and dispose of the same by deed, will, or otherwise at her pleasure, and the trustee covenanted to "convey" the said estates and property as she should direct, it was *held*, that the term "convey" must have been used as well in reference to the personal as to the real estate, the court saying, "The term 'convey,' although usually applied to real estate, is very comprehensive in its meaning, and implies a transfer and assignment of personal property also. By reference to the recital in the deed and the covenant of the husband, we are enabled more fully to see in what sense the parties thereto understood it. In the recital it appears that the parties had mutually agreed that the intended husband should not interfere or meddle with her present or future acquired property, whether real or personal, and that the defendant should be permitted to make what disposition of the said property she might choose. And her intended husband covenanted that she might have the entire and absolute control over it, and dispose of the same by deed, will, or otherwise, at her pleasure. The intention of the defendant, and of the person next most interested,

To cause to pass by any channel, as to convey water by pipes.[1]

was, that she should have the absolute control of the property, and dispose of it at her pleasure. To carry out this intention, the trustee covenanted to 'convey' the said estates and property as she should direct. The term 'convey' must have been used as well in reference to the personal as to 'the real estate." Laycroft *v.* Hedden, 3 Green Ch. (N. J.) 512, 552.

Sold and conveyed. — Where a plaintiff in replevin, in order to prove property in himself, offered in evidence a deposition in which it was stated that the plaintiff's wife's father "sold and conveyed" to her the articles replevied, before her *marriage*, it was objected that the testimony was incompetent, because the language used by the witness proved that the contract of sale and conveyance was in writing. But the court *held* otherwise; *Gilchrist, J.*, saying, "If, from the testimony of the witness, it must be inferred that a bill of sale of the goods, or some written contract, was made by the father of Mrs. Brown, at the time to which the witness refers, the instrument should be produced, or its absence accounted for; and, unless that be done, there will be no evidence of property in the plaintiff. The first inquiry, then, is, whether the words 'sold and conveyed' be susceptible of the construction put upon them by the counsel for the defendant. According to the most approved modern lexicographer, the word 'sell' is used 'where something is given or delivered in exchange for money, or security for money.' The word 'convey' means 'to carry,' 'to transport,' 'to take to or from,' 'to import.' — *Richardson's New English Dictionary, in Verb.* According to Jacobs, a sale is the transferring the property of goods from one to another, upon a valuable consideration; and such is substantially the meaning given it by Chitty and Comyn on contracts. A 'conveyance' is a deed which passes or conveys land from one to another. — *Jac. Law Dict. in Verb.* But whether the definitions given by Jacobs be technically correct or not, the meaning of the words is to be ascertained by the context. The witness was speaking of property, a sale of which need not be proved by an instrument in writing. The defendant's argument is, substantially, that by using the words 'sold and conveyed' the same idea is communicated as if she had said 'sold and conveyed by an instrument in writing.' Now, the word 'sale' does not imply a written contract. The word 'convey,' if it imply a written instrument, refers to a deed of land. Had she been speaking of land, as it can be conveyed only by deed, the word would have implied a deed; but she was speaking only of personal chattels, and as we are called upon to criticise the language she used, and ascertain the ideas it might properly convey, our opinion is, that, considering the subject to which the words referred, they do not mean that any thing more was done than was necessary to transfer the property in the articles from the owner to Mrs. Brown, and that from them it cannot be inferred that there was an instrument in writing, that being unnecessary." Brown *v.* Fitz, 13 N. H. 283.

1. Where an agreement reserved the privilege of using all the water of a spring as formerly "conveyed," it was *held*, that the word "conveyed" meant the manner of conducting the water, and did not refer to the conveyance of the right; the court, *Black, J.*, saying, "The judge of the common pleas thought that the agreement of 1836 established a privilege to use the water, as it had been used previously. The plaintiff contends that it created a right limited and defined by the terms of the old grant. We are of opinion that the court below was right. The main argument of the plaintiff in error is, that the word 'convey' must be taken in its technical sense. It is true that a term of art in the law, when used in a written contract, is always understood by the courts according to the meaning which they have agreed to impress upon it, unless very strong reasons can be adduced to show that the parties meant something else by it; for instance, *heirs* and *heirs of his body* have a certain legal meaning, which will adhere to them until the contrary intent be clearly established, though it is well known that many, perhaps most, unprofessional persons, use them as synonymous with *children*. But it often happens that we have one and the same word for two ideas totally different. Of such a word we can never know the meaning, except by reference to the context. There is no better example of this than the word 'convey,' which may mean to *conduct* water from place to place, or to *transfer* title from one person to another. Assuming that in the latter sense it is a term of art (which it is not), we are still bound to receive it in its other meaning, if water was the subject-matter spoken of, since it would be absurd to speak of 'conveying water,' in a technical sense, from a spring to a paper-mill. Now, it was water that the agreement said should be *conveyed*, 'as it has formerly been conveyed.' The grammatical structure of the sentence leaves this in no doubt. The right or title is not referred to. The pronoun *it* can have no antecedent except *water*." Edelman *v.* Yeakel, 27 Pa. St 26.

CONVEYANCE. (See ABSTRACT OF TITLE; ACKNOWLEDGMENT; AGENCY; AMBIGUITY; ADVERSE POSSESSION; DEEDS.) —The act or instrument by which property in real estate is transferred.[1] A general word, comprehending the several modes of passing title to real estate.[2] The following instruments

1. This definition was given by *Sedgwick, J.*, in a case which decided that an indenture to lead to the uses of a common recovery was a "conveyance" within the meaning of the recording acts, and that where that part of such an indenture which was executed by the recoveror was acknowledged and recorded, it was not necessary that the part signed and sealed by the recoveree should be acknowledged and recorded; the judge saying, "As *grantor* is the most comprehensive word to signify one who conveys lands, so 'conveyance' is the common statute word to intend the deed, the act or instrument, by which property in real estate is transferred." Dudley *v.* Sumner, 5 Mass. 438, 472.

In *holding* that a freehold estate can only be conveyed by a deed or writing under seal, the court, *Scott, J.*, said, "It has been argued that there is nothing in our statute concerning 'conveyances' which requires an instrument conveying lands to be sealed. The statute uses the word 'conveyance' to designate all instruments conveying lands from one to another. Blackstone says, deeds, which serve to convey the property of lands and tenements from man to man, are commonly denominated conveyances. 2 Blackstone, 309. We have seen that, in England, the word 'conveyance' carries with it the idea of a sealed instrument. This word is used by our legislature in the sense in which it is understood in England. This seems apparent from the twenty-sixth section of the act relative to 'conveyances,' which declares that no covenant expressed or implied, in any 'conveyance,' shall bind a married woman, etc. A covenant cannot be created but by deed. The legislature, then, must have had in mind the idea of a sealed instrument, when the word 'conveyance' is used." McCabe *v.* Hunter, 7 Mo. 355.

In *holding* that a further charge in favor of the first mortgagee of land requires registration, the court, *Lord Cairns, L. C.*, said, "The question, then, is, whether the further charge of Potter & Brown was a 'deed or *conveyance*' within the meaning of the *West Riding Registry Act*. The wording of the act is not very clear, but we cannot read the first section without seeing that the documents intended to be registered were all deeds and 'conveyances' of or affecting lands within the *West Riding*. Is, then, an instrument not under seal, giving a charge on the equity of redemption in an estate, a 'conveyance' within the meaning of the act? There is no magical meaning in the word 'conveyance;' it denotes an instrument which carries from one person to another an interest in land. Now, an instrument giving to a person a charge upon land, gives him an interest in the land —if he has a mortgage already, it gives him a further interest; and so, whether made in favor of a person who has already a charge, or of another person, it is a 'conveyance' of an interest in the land." Credland *v.* Potter, 10 L. R. Ch. App. 8.

2. In construing the Mississippi code, which provides that "no *conveyance* or incumbrance for the separate debts of the husband shall be binding on the wife beyond the amount of her income," the court, *Simball, C. J.*, said, "The plain policy of the statute is, that she may sell her property, transfer or mortgage it. But if she pledges it as a security for the separate debt of her husband, whether that pledge is by a 'conveyance' absolute, by mortgage, or by deed of trust, it shall only have a limited effect. The legislative intention is that she shall not, beyond the income, make her property a security for her husband's debt, either by 'conveyance or incumbrance,' that is, by any form of instrument by which, under the law, a lien or hypothecation can be created. It will be observed that the word 'conveyance' is separated by the disjunction 'or' from 'incumbrance.' Those words are not used to convey the same idea. 'Conveyance,' being a general word, comprehends the several modes of passing title to real estate. It is defined to be 'the transfer of the title of land from one person, or class of persons, to another.' 1 Bouv. Law Dic. (12th ed.) 361. . . . We think that it is used in this statute in its general sense." Klein *v.* McNamara, 54 Miss. 90.

So in *holding* that a colorable sale and transfer of personal property, although void as against the creditors of the vendor, do not amount to an act of bankruptcy within the bankrupt law of the United States, unless executed by a fraudulent *deed or conveyance*, the court, *Sewall, J.*, said, "The transfer in this case was by a bill of parcels, a writing without seal, with a receipt for the amount, and a delivery of the articles sold by this memorandum. This 'conveyance' was not, in the opinion of the court, a 'conveyance' of chattels in the have been held to be conveyances:[1] The instrument or means

technical sense, or according to the legal construction of the clause cited from the statute. Whatever may be the loose and popular sense, or possible applications, of the term 'conveyance,' the legislature are not understood to speak in an indeterminate manner, especially if that construction would violate any general principle of jurisprudence. For in making a statute the legislature are understood to refer themselves to existing customs and rules, or, in other words, when using technical terms, to employ them in a precise and technical sense. The same term 'conveyance' is used in speaking of the transfer of lands and chattels, and different meanings must be given to the same word to apply it to the transaction in question." Livermore *v.* Bagley, 3 Mass. 487, 510.

1. **Wills.** A *will* is, in contemplation of law, a "conveyance;" therefore, under the act 3 Vict. c. 74, sec. 16 (Canadian Statute), which renders valid any deed or *conveyance* that may be made for the benefit of the Church of England, provided that such *deeds and conveyances* shall be made and executed six months, at least, before the death of the person conveying the same, and shall be registered not later than six months after his decease, it was *held* that a person may devise, as well as grant, by deed, lands to the Church of England, for the purposes of that act; *Robinson, C. J.*, saying, "It is a general principle in construing statutes, that we are to assume that the legislature did not use words idly, and without intending that any meaning should be attached to them. On the contrary, where they enumerate several things, as in this act, we are to give a several and distinct meaning to each word used, as if to express something distinct, whenever we can do so without departing from the natural and proper use of language. This rule holds in the construction of all statutes. We are, therefore, in the first instance, to suppose that when the legislature, throughout this clause, with one exception, used the words *deed or conveyance*, they did not mean deed alone; for, if they did, there was then no use for the words 'or conveyance,' as they would signify nothing. We must ask ourselves then, in the first place, is there any thing besides a deed by which lands may be made to pass, and which may by law be registered? A 'will' is an instrument by which lands may be passed, and which may be registered as this statute requires; and it is something different from a deed, and not included in that term. Then the next question is, can a will be properly said to be a 'conveyance'? If it can be, then by taking wills to be included in the word 'conveyance,' as used in this statute, a meaning is given to the word which makes it import something different from the other word, *deed*, and so shows that the legislature did not use the word idly and in vain. If, on the other hand, we cannot hold the will to be a 'conveyance' without perverting the proper legal import of the word, and using it in a sense unknown to the law, then we should hold 'wills' not to be comprehended in the word 'conveyance,' even though we should be driven in consequence to admit that the legislature must have used the word idly, and without intending that it should convey any distinct meaning; for, in fact, we know that this is nothing more than they do in an abundance of instances, which it would be easy to quote. It does not occur to me that, besides a deed, there is any other instrument for conveying land which can be registered, unless it be a will. Does a will, then, according to proper legal construction, come within the meaning of the word 'conveyance'? or, in plain words, is a will a 'conveyance'?

"In Sheppard's Touchstone, pages 1, 2, we are told that the common or general 'assurances or conveyances' of the kingdom that are made between subject and subject, and are of ordinary and daily use for the transferring of lands, tenements, and hereditaments from one to another, are of ten kinds, two of which are by matter of record, namely, fine and recovery; and the rest are by matter *of deed*." *Mr. Preston* corrects this passage by inserting in a parenthesis "(or in *pais* or by *will*, and commonly termed matters in *fait*)." And he enumerates the eight kinds of "conveyance," intended by Sheppard; namely, (1) by feoffment, (2) grant, (3) bargain and sale, (4) lease, (5) exchange, (6) surrender, (7) release or conveyance, (8) by devise, or by last will and testament. We see, then, that both by the author of the "Touchstone," and by his learned editor, *Mr. Preston*, wills are classed among the common "conveyances" of the kingdom, though the "Touchstone" does not draw the distinction which *Mr. Preston* does, and would even reckon them among "conveyances" by deed. *Mr. Preston* adds afterwards, "A feoffment, gift in tail, or lease, as an exchange in one county for other lands in the same county, or a surrender, may be without *deed*, as distinguished from a mere writing, and a writing is necessary only on account of the Statute of Frauds, 29 Car. II. c. 3, and a devise is an assurance by mere writing, with or without seal, and not by deed." *Mr. Justice Blackstone*, in his Commentaries, vol. ii. p. 378, says, "The last method of 'conveying' real property is by devise;" and in page 378 he adds, "A will of lands is considered by the courts of law, not so much in the nature of a testament as of a 'conveyance,' declaring the uses to which lands shall be subject, with this difference, that in *other conveyances* the actual subscription of the witnesses is not required by law, but in devises of lands subscription is now absolutely necessary by statute, in order to identify a 'conveyance' which, in its nature, can never be set up till after the death of the devisor; and upon this notion, that a devise affecting lands is merely a species of 'conveyance,' is founded this distinction betwixt devises and testaments of personal chattels, that the latter will operate upon whatever the testator dies possessed of, — the former only upon such real estates as were his at the time of executing and publishing his will." In Harwood *v.* Goodright, Cowper, 90, *Lord Mansfield* observed, "But a devise in England is an appointment of particular lands to a particular devisee, and is considered in the nature of a 'conveyance' by way of appointment, and upon that principle it is that no man can devise lands which he has not at the *date of such* 'conveyance.' Thus it appears that a devise is treated in law not merely as a 'conveyance,' but as being emphatically a 'conveyance,' so that on the principles of the common law nothing can pass under it but what the devisor, at the time of making his will, was in a condition to convey. We cannot therefore hold, in the face of these authorities, that the word 'conveyance' cannot include a devise." Baker *v.* Clark, 7 U. C. Q. B. 44.

But a gift of personalty is not a "conveyance;" and therefore, where an act (April 26, 1855, sect. 11) declared, "No estate, real or personal, shall hereafter be bequeathed, devised, or conveyed to any body politic, or to any person in trust for religious and charitable uses, except the same be done by deed or will, etc., at least one calendar month before the decease of the testator or alienor," and A, having made a will whereby she bequeathed legacies to charities, on finding her death imminent, executed a power of attorney to B, with instructions to sell her loans, and pay the amounts of her charitable legacies from the proceeds, all of which was done in her lifetime, but A died within a calendar month of the date of her will, and while the proceeds of the sale of the loans was still in B's hands, it was *held* that such a gift of personalty, not being a "conveyance" of property, was valid. McGlade's Appeal, 11 Weekly Notes of Cases (Pa.), 257.

Mortgages. — In some States, mortgages have been held to be "conveyances." Thus in Mississippi, in deciding that a mortgage in fee, made by the husband during coverture, bars his widow of dower, the court, *Simball, J.*, said, "A mortgage in fee serves a complex purpose: it is a security for a debt, and at the same time a 'conveyance' of the estate. In strictness it creates a conditional estate, or an estate upon defeasance. . . . We are unable to discover the reason why the husband may, for a valuable consideration, convey absolutely, so as to deprive the widow of dower, and yet a less 'conveyance' by way of mortgage not be within the act. Both are within its letter. If the husband should convey absolutely to his creditor, in satisfaction of his debt, it would hardly be pretended that the claim to dower would not be terminated. If he conveys conditionally, as security for the debt, the husband may redeem in his lifetime; if he fails, she may redeem, and call upon the heir for contribution; or, upon foreclosure, she may be endowed out of the surplus. In employing the term in the dower act (art. 162, code 467), 'conveyance,' 'conveyed,' we suppose that the legislature meant the sense in which the word is ordinarily used in our jurisprudence. It is a technical or *quasi*-technical word of precise and definite import. As defined by Bouvier (1 Law Dic. 346), '*Conveyance* is the transfer of the title to land by one person to another.' 'The instrument itself is called *a conveyance*.' It is a general term indicating the several modes of passing title. Such was the import given it in Sessions *v.* Bacon, 23 Miss. 273. The wife had power, with the concurrence of her husband, to 'convey' her separate property. The objection was, that this did not authorize her to mortgage it. But, argued the court, as the major includes the minor, if she may 'convey' absolutely, it is clear that she could exercise the less power of making a 'conditional conveyance.' . . . We are conducted to these conclusions, that a mortgage in fee, executed by the husband during the coverture, in good faith to secure a debt, is a '*conveyance* for a valuable consideration within the statute,' and imposes an incumbrance upon the estate, to which the dower of the widow is subordinate." Pickett *v.* Buckner, 45 Miss. 226.

So in California, the words "*conveyance* of real property," as used in sections 1213 and 1214 of the civil code, section 1215 of which defines the term "conveyance" used in the two preceding sections as embracing every instrument in writing by which any estate or interest in real property is created, aliened, mortgaged, or incumbered, or by which the title to any property may be affected, except wills, was *held* to include mortgages. Odd Fellows' Sav. Bank *v.* Banton, 46 Cal. 603. See Call *v.* Hastings, 3 Cal. 179.

In Iowa also, where the homestead statute provides that the homestead of every head of a family shall be exempt from judicial sale when there is no special declaration of the statute to the contrary, among which exceptions is, debts created by written contract by persons having the power to convey, and expressly stipulating that the homestead should be liable therefor, the court *held*, under a further provision of the same statute to the effect that a "conveyance" by the owner is of no validity unless the husband and wife (if the owner is married) concur in and sign such conveyance; that it was not essential to the validity of a mortgage of property occupied as a homestead, in the execution of which both the husband and wife concur, to expressly describe the property as a homestead, and to state that it is with reference to that fact that the "conveyance" is made; *Baldwin, J.*, saying, "It is not claimed by the complainant that the homestead of the defendants is liable under either of the exceptions as above stated; but it is submitted that the mortgage sought to be foreclosed is a 'conveyance' within the meaning of said section 1247, and that, when the defendants concurred in and signed the same, they thereby waived their right of exemption, and, when thus waived, their equity of redemption is liable to be foreclosed in the same manner as though the mortgaged property did not constitute the homestead. Did the legislature, in the adoption of this section, intend to embrace mortgages within the meaning of the term 'conveyance'? Giving to the word 'conveyance' a construction according to the approved usage of language, or the peculiar and appropriate meaning it has received in law, would it not apply to or include mortgages, as well as absolute transfers of titles? 'A mortgage is the *conveyance* of an estate by way of pledge for the security of a debt, and to become void upon the payment of it.' 4 Kent Com. 138. 'A mortgage may be described to be a *conveyance* of lands by a debtor to his creditor,' etc. Bouv. L. D. '*Mortuum vadium*, dead pledge, or mortgage, is where a debtor actually *conveys* lands to his creditor,' etc. Walker's Am. Law, 293. 'A mortgage is a *conveyance* of property, and passes it conditionally to the mortgagee.' United States *v.* Foster, 2 Cranch (U. S.), 358. 'A mortgage is not only a lien for a debt, but it is something more: it is a transfer of the property itself as a security for the debt.' Conrad *v.* Atlantic Insurance Co., 1 Pet. (U. S.) 441. 'A mortgage is the *conveyance* of an estate.' 1 Hilliard on Mortgages, 2. 'A mortgage not only creates a lien, but operates to transfer to the mortgagee a qualified or conditional estate,' etc.; 'and a mortgagee is a purchaser within the meaning of our registry law.' Porter *v.* Green, 4 Ia. 571. The authorities, without exception, speak of a mortgage as a 'conveyance.' We are inclined to think that our legislature regarded a 'conveyance' within the meaning of this section, not only from the general signification of the word as applicable to mortgages, but by the use of the word in other sections of the code, adopted at the same time this section was. In section 1232 the legislature provided that the form of a mortgage might be the same as a deed of 'conveyance,' adding that it should be void on condition, etc. So also in section 1256 it is provided that the owner of a homestead may change the metes and bounds thereof, but such change should not prejudice 'conveyances' or liens made or created previous thereto. What kind of 'conveyances' are here referred to? Not absolute *conveyances*, because no change of boundaries by the owner of the homestead could prejudice the rights of the vendee, where he had a title in fee-simple. To say that it referred to any other than 'conditional conveyances,' would render this section meaningless." Babcock *v.* Hoey, 11 Ia. 375.

So in the territory of Montana, it was *held* in January, 1887, that a "mortgage" is included within the words "grant or *conveyance*" as used in Rev. Stat. U. S. § 2262, providing that any grant or conveyance made by a settler of lands pre-empted before "final receipt shall be null and void, except in the hands of a *bona fide* purchaser for value." In this case the court, *Bach, J.*, said, "It is claimed by the appellants that the words 'grant or *conveyance*' do not include a mortgage; that a mortgage by our laws does not pass the title to the land, but is a mere security or lien for the note. The authorities are at variance upon this question. The Supreme Court of California has held that such a mortgage was absolutely void, as against the mortgagor and his assigns, excepting a *bona fide* purchaser. See Bull *v.* Shaw, 48 Cal. 455. The Supreme Court of Minnesota held mortgages to be within the terms 'grant and conveyance,' and that they were therefore void, except as provided in the statute in several cases, among others in McCue *v.* Smith, 9 Minn. 259; Woodbury *v.* Dorman, 15 Minn. 338. But the same court, in a later case, reversed that doctrine, and held that a mortgage was not included within the terms of the statute; and the court bases its decision upon the ground that a mortgage is a mere security, and does not act as a *conveyance*. See Jones *v.* Tainter, 15 Minn. 512. The Supreme Court of Kansas holds, with the California Supreme Court, that a mortgage does come within the terms of the statute. Brewster *v.* Madden, 15

Kan. 249. In the case of Owings *v.* Lichtenberger, 9 Copp, Land Owner, 197, in a letter dated Nov. 17, 1882, the Hon. Henry M. Teller, then Secretary of the Interior, writes upon this question as follows: 'It is claimed by plaintiff's counsel, that the mortgage given by plaintiff before his removal was a disposition of his homestead. . . . I do not think this view of the case can be maintained. At common law, the title passed to the mortgagee; but the rule of the common law has been changed by statute in most of the States, and in such States the legal title remains in the mortgagor. In Nebraska, a mortgage of real estate is a mere pledge or collateral security.' We think the honorable Secretary of the Interior and the Supreme Court of Minnesota apply the wrong rule of interpretation to the section 2262, by not first ascertaining what the nature of a mortgage is in Nebraska and Minnesota. They, in effect, declare that a United States statute is to be interpreted through the medium of a statute of a State. Whatever may be the meaning of the words 'grant or conveyance' in section 2262, it is certain that there cannot be two proper interpretations of the same statute. It is equally certain that the section contains one rule of law, and no more, on this subject, and that that rule applies to mortgages upon pre-emption lands, wherever situated, with the same force and effect. If the true interpretation of that section is to be governed by the character of a mortgage in the different States and Territories, there would be at least two distinct and contrary rules applying to mortgages and pre-emption claims; for some of the States hold that a mortgage passes the title, while others — by force of some statute, in most cases — hold that a mortgage is a mere security. We would then reach the conclusion that the validity of such a mortgage would depend upon the situation of the land. That, certainly, cannot be the law. A mortgage upon pre-emption lands, made before final entry, is either valid or void under that section. If valid in any State, it is valid everywhere; if void in one State, it is void in all States. The true rule of interpretation is, 'What did Congress mean?' The purpose of Congress undoubtedly was to furnish all and every encouragement to settlers upon the public lands, and to legislate so that, neither directly nor indirectly, by virtue of the law should those lands become the property of a few. And this section provides every possible safeguard against any alienation by the settler up to the time of the final 'conveyance' by the government. One portion of the section provides that the claimant shall make oath that 'he has not directly or indirectly made any agreement or contract, in any manner, with any person or persons whatsoever, by which the title which he might acquire from the Government of the United States should inure, in whole or in part, to the benefit of any person except himself.' These words show the evident purpose of the government; and, in the light of those words, the expression 'grant or conveyance' is clearly meant to include a mortgage. But there is a still further reason for such an interpretation. Section 2262 became a law in 1841. At that time, the courts of the State of New York were the only courts that held that a mortgage was a security only. Even at this late date, the following States, Alabama, Arkansas, Connecticut, Illinois, Kentucky, Maine, Maryland, Massachusetts, New Hampshire, New Jersey, North Carolina, Ohio, Pennsylvania, Rhode Island, Tennessee, Virginia, and West Virginia, hold the old common-law doctrine that the mortgagee has the legal title. In New York alone the courts, without the aid of a statute, hold a contrary doctrine. In the other States which hold a mortgage not to be a conveyance, the rule depends upon express statutes, passed long after 1841, when section 2262 was made law by act of Congress. Then we must consider what a mortgage was considered to be in the year 1841. And, so considering, we are forced to the conclusion that a mortgage is included within the words 'grant and conveyance,' in section 2262, and that the mortgage sought to be foreclosed in this action was absolutely void. The Supreme Court of the United States, as far as we can ascertain, has never ruled upon this question; but in the case of Warren *v.* Van Brunt, 19 Wall. (U. S.) 646, that court, speaking of the Minnesota cases, which held such mortgages void, said (page 655), "All contracts in violation of this important provision of the act are void, and are never enforced. It has been so decided many times by the Supreme Court of Minnesota. We are satisfied with these decisions." Bass *v.* Baker, 6 Montana, 442; s. c., 12 Pacific Rep. 922.

Again, in Wisconsin it has been *held* that the term "conveyance" in the recording act includes a mortgage. Rowell *v.* Williams, 54 Wis. 636.

Assignment of a Mortgage. — This also has been *held* to be a "conveyance" within the meaning of the recording acts; and in order to protect himself against a subsequent *bona fide* purchaser of the mortgage, whose assignment may be first recorded, the first assignee must record his assignment. Bank for Savings in N. Y. *v.* Frank, 45 N. Y. Super. Ct. 404.

Release. — So where a statute provided that every "conveyance" of real estate, not recorded in the office of the proper register of deeds, should be void against of carrying or transferring any thing from place to place; a

any purchaser in good faith, and for a valuable consideration, of the same real estate whose conveyance is first duly recorded, it was *held* that a *release*, as an instrument by which the title to real estate might be affected in law or equity, was a "conveyance" within the meaning of the statute; and a mortgagee having executed a sealed instrument releasing a portion of the mortgaged land, which release was not recorded, and subsequently assigned the mortgage, on foreclosure and sale of the whole land, all of which, including the released portion was purchased by defendant, it was *held* that as to the defendant the release was void. Palmer *v.* Bates, 22 Minn. 532.

Quitclaim Deed. — Under the statutes in Wisconsin, this has been held to amount to a deed of bargain and sale, and therefore to be a "conveyance." Cutler *v.* James, 64 Wis. 173.

Agreement creating an Easement. — As an easement is an interest in real estate, under the Minnesota statutes, such an instrument is *held* to be a "conveyance." Warner *v.* Rogers, 23 Minn. 34.

Leases. — A lease is not a "conveyance," and therefore it was *held* that a statute providing that a wife may not, without the joinder of her husband, *convey* certain real estate, does not prohibit her leasing the premises in her name alone for a term of years; the court, *Peters, C. J.*, saying, "A lease may be in a sense a 'conveyance,' but such is not the common accepted nor the accurate meaning of the term. When we say premises are leased, we generally mean that the use of them is transferred; and by the term conveyed, that the title is deeded. . . . An appeal to the authorities sustains the view advocated by the complainant. Jacob's Law Dictionary gives this as the old common-law definition of the word which is the key to the dispute: '"conveyance" is a deed which passes land from one man to another.' In Abenroth *v.* Greenwich, 29 Conn. 356, a party was to *convey* a bridge to a town. The court said, 'To *convey* real estate is by an appropriate instrument to transfer the legal title to it from the present owner to another.' In Mayor *v.* Mabie, 13 N. Y. 151, a question arose as to the meaning of the word 'conveyance' in a statute which provides that 'no covenants shall be implied in any "conveyance" of real estate; and it was *held* that a grant of wharfage for one year was not a "conveyance" of real estate. In Tone *v.* Brace, 11 Paige (N. Y.), 566, it was decided that a lease for a term of years was not, in the ordinary sense of the term, a "conveyance" of land. In the case of *In re* Hunter, 1 Edw. Ch. (N. Y.) 1, it was decided that where a person was to *convey* an estate he must transfer "the whole title." Mott *v.* Ruckman, 3 Blatch. (U. S.) 71, decides that a charter party is not a *conveyance* of a vessel, that it goes to the use, and not the title.'" Perkins *v.* Morse, 78 Me. 17; s. c., 57 Am. Rep. 780.

But in California a lease for a term exceeding one year was held a "conveyance" within the definition of that word as used in the recording act of 1850. Jones *v.* Marks, 47 Cal. 242.

Declaration of Trust. — In Wisconsin a written instrument in the form of a memorandum equivalent to a *declaration of trust* as to certain land, though not under seal, and without witnesses or acknowledgment, was *held* to be a "conveyance" under the Wisconsin statutes. White *v.* Fitzgerald, 19 Wis. 480.

Charter Party. — The act of Congress entitled, "An act to provide for recording the 'conveyances' of vessels, and for other purposes," does not extend to charter parties. Hill & Conn. *v.* the steamer 'Golden Gate," 1 Newb. Adm. (U. S.) 308; Mott *v.* Ruckman, 3 Blatchf. (U. S.) 71.

Conveyance implies no Covenants. — Where A. gave to B. a power of attorney to grant, bargain, sell, release, etc., in fee, certain lands, and on such sale "to execute, seal, and deliver in the name of A. such 'conveyances' and assurances in the law of the premises to the purchaser, in fee, as should be needful or necessary, according to the judgment of B. his attorney, it was *held* that B. had no power to execute a deed with the usual covenants of *seisin*, etc., so as to bind his principal, the court saying, 'The attorney was authorized to sell and to execute *conveyances and assurances* in the law, of the lands sold, but no authority was given to bind his principal by covenants. A 'conveyance' or assurance is good and perfect without either warranty or personal covenants; and therefore they are not necessarily implied in an authority to convey. All authority is to be strictly pursued, and an act varying in substance from it is void." Nixon *v.* Hyserott, 5 Johns. (N. Y.) 58.

Lawful Deed of Conveyance. — Where one covenanted to give a "lawful deed of *conveyance*," he may be fairly understood to mean a deed *conveying* a lawful or good title; and he is bound to produce his title to the defendant, and offer himself ready to execute a deed before he can recover the consideration money. Dearth *v.* Williamson, Adm. of Welsh, 2 S. & R. 498.

vessel or vehicle employed in the general conveyance of passengers.[1]

CONVEYANCING. (See ABSTRACT OF TITLE; CONVEY; CONVEYANCE; DEEDS; TRUSTS.) — Conveyancing is that part of the lawyer's business which relates to the alienation and transmission of property and other rights from one person to another, and to the framing of legal documents intended to create, define, transfer, and extinguish rights. It, therefore, includes the investigation of the title to lands, and the preparation of agreements,

1. **Public or Private Conveyance.**—Where an insurance company issued insurance tickets against death "caused by accident while travelling by *public or private conveyance* provided for the transportation of passengers," in two forms or classes, one known as the "travellers' risk," the other as the "general accident," the latter being sold for the highest price, and an engineer holding the ticket "general accident" was killed while on a railroad locomotive, it was *held* that the deceased was insured against all accidents, without regard to the capacity in which he was acting; that the ticket was intended to cover the accident by which he met his death, and that the insurance company was liable. Brown *v.* Railway Passenger Assurance Co., 45 Mo. 221.

Under a similar policy, a passenger injured while walking a short distance between a connecting steamboat and railway line, even though cabs were standing for hire, which might have been used, was *held* entitled to recover on the policy. Northrup *v.* Railway Passenger Assurance Co., 43 N. Y. 516.

On the other hand, where one took out an accident policy of insurance on his life, while "travelling by *public or private conveyance*," and having performed a part of his journey by steamer, which brought him to a certain village, he *walked* thence home about eight miles, it was *held* that while thus walking, he was not travelling by either *public* or *private conveyance*. It was argued by counsel that, "In Northrup *v.* Railway Passenger Assurance Co., 43 N. Y. 516, the contract was against accident while travelling by public or private *conveyance* provided for the transportation of its passengers. Yet the company was held liable though the death was caused while the party was *walking* from a steamboat landing to a railway station, a distance of seventy rods. This case regards the walking as part of the original journey in the public or private conveyance, and wisely; for few persons on a long journey are all the time in the rail carriages. The case does but carry out the injunction given by *Cockburn, C. J.*, in Trew *v.* Railway Passengers' Assurance Co., 30 L. J. Exchcq. 317: 'We ought not to give to these policies a construction which will defeat the protection of the assured in a large class of cases.' But independently of this. The words 'private conveyance' reasonably, and *ex vi termini*, include the case of a person pursuing a journey, or travelling by means of his own personal powers of locomotion; his limbs with their muscles and tendons, bones and joints — the primitive universal 'private conveyance' of man. 'Conveyance' is the instrument or means of carrying or transferring any thing from place to place. It is derived from *con* (with, by, along) and *via* (the way). It is used in this sense in the Scriptures, where it is said that the Saviour had *conveyed himself* away . . . And so in ordinary language, and in every-day life. Should a court direct its officer to '*convey* the prisoner to jail,' no one will doubt that the prisoner's walking to the place designated would be a literal and exact compliance with the order. If one were to say to an intruder '*convey* yourself away,' the speaker would have no idea but that the party should walk off; nor would the party himself expect that any thing else was meant." But the court, *Chase, C. J.*, said, "That the deceased was *travelling* is clear enough, but was travelling on foot, travelling by *public or private conveyance*. The contract must receive the construction which the language used fairly warrants. What was the understanding of the parties, or, rather, what understanding must naturally have been derived from the language used? It seems to us that walking would not naturally be presented to the mind as a means of *public* or *private conveyance*. *Public conveyance* naturally suggests a vessel or vehicle employed in the general *conveyance* of passengers. *Private conveyance* suggests a vehicle belonging to a private individual. If this was the sense in which the language was understood by the parties, the deceased was not, when injured, travelling, within the terms of the policy. There is nothing to show that it was not." Ripley *v.* Insurance Co., 16 Wall. (U. S.) 336.

wills, articles of association, private statutes, operating as conveyances, and many other instruments in addition to conveyances, properly so called.[1]

CONVICTED. — The past participle of the verb to CONVICT, which means, to find guilty of any crime, and to place under sentence, according to law.[2] It implies a trial, and verdict thereon.[3] It is sometimes used of civil sentences.[4]

1. Rap. & Law, Law Dic. *sub Verb.* See generally Sugden on Vendors, Preston on Conveyancing, Washburn on Real Property.

2. It has generally been held that the word "convicted" includes the final judgment, and that one who has been found guilty by the jury, but has not yet been sentenced, is not a "convicted" person.

Thus, where one was charged with voting, not being a qualified voter, for that he had been "*convicted* of the crime of burglary," on a motion to quash, because the indictment failed to show and allege defendant's disqualification in this, that it failed to allege any final judgment of a court of competent jurisdiction, the court overruled the motion, *White, P. J.*, saying, "The word 'convicted' used by the pleader has a definite signification in law. It means that a judgment of final condemnation has been pronounced against the accused. Penal Code, art. 27; 1 Bouv. L. Dic., word 'conviction.' To say that a party had been 'convicted,' and then add that he stood his final trial, and that judgment final was rendered against him, would be tautology. Moreover, the word 'convicted' is the proper statutory word to convey the idea that a party is disqualified from voting because he has been tried and condemned for a felony." Gallagher *v.* State, 10 Tex. App. 469.

So in Illinois it was *held* that it cannot be said that a person has been "convicted" of a crime, so as to render him incapable of giving testimony, until there has been a judgment rendered on the verdict of guilty. Faunce *v.* State, 51 Ill. 311.

So in England it has been *held* that the statute, 5 W. & M. C. 11, directing that no certiorari shall be granted on the part of a defendant to remove an indictment for a misdemeanor from the sessions before he shall enter into a recognizance, etc., to try at the next assizes; and that, "if the defendant prosecuting such certiorari be 'convicted,' the Court of King's Bench shall give reasonable costs to the prosecutor," and that the recognizance shall not be discharged till the costs taxed shall be paid, attaches only upon a defendant "convicted" by *judgment;* and therefore, if, after a verdict of guilty, the judgment is arrested, no costs can be taxed for the prosecutor. King *v.* Turner, 15 East, 570.

See 1 Hale, P. C., 686, where Lord *Hale*, commenting upon the stat. 5 Eliz. c. 14, against the forging or making of false deeds, etc., by which a person committing a second offence after his "*conviction* or condemnation of a former one, shall be deemed guilty of felony without benefit of clergy," has these words: "By 'conviction' I conceive is intended, not barely a 'conviction' by verdict where no judgment is given, but it must be a 'conviction' by judgment." For further examples see CONVICTION.

Every Person convicted of Felony. — An act (33 & 34 Vict. c. 29, s. 14) providing that "every person *convicted* of felony shall forever be disqualified from selling spirits by retail," was *held* to be retrospective, and to apply to a person "*convicted* of felony," either before or after the act passed; *Cockburn, C. J.*, saying, "On looking at the act, the words used seem to impert the intention to protect the public against persons 'convicted' in the past as well as in the future: the words are in effect equivalent to 'every *convicted* felon.'" Queen *v.* Vine, L. R. 10 Q. B. Div. 195.

3. A statute (11 & 12 Vict. c. 78) created a court of criminal appeal, and provided that, when any person should have been *convicted*, etc., the judge, etc., before whom the case was tried, might, in his discretion, reserve a case stated, with any questions of law for the consideration of said court. On an indictment to which the defendants demurred, upon judgment for the crown on the demurrer, the judge reserved the question as to the validity of the indictment; but it was *held* that the court had no jurisdiction, *Lord Campbell, C. J.*, saying, "I find no such power conferred upon us: the statute refers to questions which shall arise *upon the trial*, and which, *after the prisoner shall have been* 'convicted,' may be reserved for this court. Looking at the language employed, the word 'convicted' must be taken to mean 'convicted upon verdict,' and that really is the trial that takes place before the jury. There is no power here given us to investigate what is done upon demurrer before the trial begins." Reg. *v.* Faderman, 1 Temp. & M. 286; s. c., 1 Den. C. C. 565.

4. On the question as to whether a town court, constituted to try all civil actions,

CONVICTION. — The act of finding guilty of any crime, before a legal tribunal. This word is used sometimes as meaning the *verdict* of a jury, and at other times, in its more strictly legal sense, for the *sentence* of the court. For examples, see the notes: where held to imply a judgment;[1] where held an adjudication

and given all the powers in *civil* matters conferred upon justices, had jurisdiction over violation of the license laws, the court, *Young, C. J.*, said, "The difficulty, as it appears to me, has arisen out of a misapprehension of the scope and meaning of the words 'convicted' and 'conviction,' in the License Law, chapter 75. It was argued that a 'conviction' necessarily and exclusively applies to a criminal offence, punishable as a misdemeanor, and the proper subject of an indictment to be enforced by a warrant. Now, it may be conceded that this is the sense in which it is often understood, but not always so. *Bouvier*, in his Law Dictionary (2d ed.), says, 'This word means a condemnation. In its most extensive sense it signifies the giving judgment against a defendant, whether criminal or civil. In a more limited sense it means a judgment given against a criminal.' It is obvious that the legislature meant a conviction for penalties under chapter 75, in its extensive sense, otherwise they would never have perpetrated the absurdity of making them recoverable in the same manner and with the like costs as if they were private debts, and giving the form, not of a warrant, but of an execution." *In re* Fraser, 1 Russ. & G. (Nova Scotia) 354.

1. **Conviction denotes the Final Judgment of the Court.** — Thus, where an action was brought upon the Stat. 25 Geo. 2 C. 36, S. 5, against the defendants as overseers of the parish of Paddington for the sum of ten pounds, under the provisions of that statute, to wit, in case a person keeping a disorderly house in any parish, and being prosecuted on the information of two inhabitants of such parish, be *convicted*, the overseers are forthwith to pay ten pounds to each of such inhabitants; and it appeared that E. was prosecuted, and pleaded guilty to keeping a disorderly house, while F. and G. were overseers of the parish; and that after C. and D. succeeded them in that office, E. was called up for judgment and sentence, it was *held* that E. was not to be considered as *convicted* until the judgment of the court upon the indictment against him was pronounced, and therefore that the action was rightly brought against C. and D., and that their predecessors F. and G. were not liable, the court, *Tindal, C. J.*, saying, "The first question, then, is, Who were the overseers of the said parish at the time the 'conviction' took place? The information was laid in the year 1842, when the parties prosecuted pleaded guilty. The defendants contend that the 'conviction' took place at that time. The plaintiff, on the other hand, says that there was no 'conviction' then, nor till the parties were subsequently brought up and received the sentence of the court. The word 'conviction' is undoubtedly *verbum æquivocum*. It is sometimes used as meaning the *verdict* of a jury, and at other times in its more strictly legal sense, for the *sentence* of the court. In the passages cited from *Blackstone's Commentaries*, the term seems to be used in both senses. The question is, in which sense is it used in the statute now under consideration. And I cannot but think that the case of Sutton *v.* Bishop (4 Burr. 2283). The court there said, 'Though there is a distinction in criminal cases between the "conviction" and attainder, yet there is no such distinction in civil cases between verdict and judgment so that any effect can follow from a naked verdict. In a civil action no penalty takes place till judgment be given on the verdict. The penalty is demanded as a debt, and is not due till judgment is given. Any other construction would open the door to frauds. An offender would prosecute another to verdict, and therefore secure his own indemnity, and then proceed no farther.' Why does not the same reasoning apply to this case? If a verdict of a jury or a confession by the party were sufficient to satisfy the statute, a door would be equally open to fraud. So, again, the word 'acquittal' is *verbum æquivocum*. It is generally said that a party is acquitted by the jury, but, in fact, the acquittal is by the judgment of the court. A plea of *autrefois convict* or *autrefois acquit* can only be supported by proof of a judgment. Then, as these defendants were the overseers at the time that the judgment of the court was pronounced, I think they are properly made defendants in this action." Burgess *v.* Boetefeur, 7 Man. & G. 481, 504.

The case of Sutton *v.* Bishop, cited by the court above, is a singular one. Bishop, the defendant, had received a bribe of five guineas from one Earle. In order to indemnify himself, he determined to discover Earle, so as to avail himself of the eighth section of the Bribery Act (2 Geo. 2 C. 24), which enacts "that if any person offending against this act shall, within the space of twelve months next after such election, etc., discover any other person or persons offending against this act, so that such person or persons so discovered be thereupon *convicted*, such person so discovering, etc., shall be indemnified," etc. Accordingly, upon Bishop's statement, an action was brought under that act, by one Bingley against Earle. Two months afterwards an action by Sutton *v.* Bishop was brought, under the same section, for taking the bribe. Both these causes were set down for trial on the same day, and were actually tried within half an hour of each other; but the cause of Sutton *v.* Bishop standing first, the judge would not invert the order in which they stood upon his paper by trying the other cause of Bingley *v.* Earle first, though that action was first commenced: the consequence was, that Sutton got a verdict against Bishop, for Bishop could not show that he had made a discovery of another person so as to be thereupon *convicted*. Bingley, on the other hand, got a verdict against Earle upon the evidence of Bishop. But this verdict came too late to avail Bishop in his own cause at the suit of Sutton; for a verdict had already been given against him, which, as his counsel insisted, could not have happened if his cause had been tried first. On a motion by Bishop, the defendant, to set this verdict aside, it was made a question "what shall *amount* to a 'conviction' within the sense of this clause?" And the court said "that a *verdict alone* was *not* a 'conviction.' That in *civil* actions, a verdict is nothing without a judgment This is a civil action, an action of debt for a penalty: *nil debet* is pleaded. The defendant is not *convicted* of the debt till judgment." They were, therefore, of opinion that it ought to be completed by a judgment. But they were also of opinion, that after it should be so completed, it would relate back to the time of the original discovery. And they thought that Bingley ought to be at liberty to enter up his judgment, in order to entitle Bishop to his indemnity, or, at least, not to strip him of it. They thought also that Sutton should complete his judgment, but that his proceeding upon it should be stayed. Sutton *v.* Bishop, 4 Burr. 2282.

Under the provisions of the Revised Statutes of New York (2 R. S. 146, § 48), declaring that a wife convicted of adultery, in an action brought against her by her husband for divorce, shall not be entitled to dower in his real estate, it is only where, upon proof and a finding or verdict of adultery, the court has, in such action, given judgment of divorce against the wife that her right of dower is lost: the forfeiture is not in consequence of the offence, but of the judgment founded thereon. In this case the court said, "We cannot agree that the word 'conviction' means only the establishing her adultery as a fact by proof. We think that it is charged with the fuller meaning, that, upon proof and finding or verdict of her adultery, the court has given judgment of divorce against her, and dissolved the marriage between her and her husband." Schiffer *v.* Pruden, 64 N. Y. 47.

So under statutes disqualifying any person thereafter as a witness who "shall, upon *conviction*, be adjudged guilty of perjury," it was *held* that a person is not rendered incompetent until, by judgment, sentence has been pronounced upon him, — a verdict of guilty alone is not sufficient; the court, *Folger, J.*, saying, "We have lately, in civil cases, been called upon to construe statutes of similar import. We have *held* in them that there was no 'conviction' merely upon the finding of the question of fact, and that there must also be a judgment of the court. (Pitts *v.* Pitts, 52 N. Y. 593; Schiffer *v.* Pruden, 64 N. Y. 47.) Those cases arose under the acts relating to dower, and the forfeiture of it by adultery. We do not think that it is different under the criminal statutes involved in this case. In ordinary phrase, the meaning of the word 'conviction' is the finding, by the jury, of a verdict that the accused is guilty. But in legal parlance, it often denotes the final judgment of the court." Blaufus *v.* People, 69 N. Y. 107. See Keithler *v.* State, 10 Sm. & M. (Miss.) 192, 236; Sacia *v.* Decker, 1 N. Y. Civ. Pro. 47.

In a similar Massachusetts case it was *held* that the word "conviction" as used in the statutory provision that the "conviction" of any crime may be shown to affect the credibility of a witness in any proceeding, civil or criminal, in court or before a person having authority to receive evidence, implies a judgment of the court. Com. *v.* Gorham, 99 Mass. 420.

In Pennsylvania, where one was indicted for burglary, and the indictment set forth a former "conviction," and that the court gave judgment, but did not set forth what the judgment was, the prisoner pleaded guilty, and was sentenced to undergo an imprisonment at hard labor during his natural life, in accordance with the provisions of a statute (22d April, 1794, 3 Sm. Laws, 190) "that if a man shall commit burglary a second time, and be thereof legally 'convicted,' he shall be sentenced to undergo an imprisonment at hard labor during life," etc. On a writ of error this judgment was reversed, the court, *Tilghman, C. J.*, saying, "It was contended, on behalf of the commonwealth, that the judgment was good, because the defendant had been 'convicted' once before. If this appeared on the face of the indictment, the judgment would have been good. . . . But it does not appear in this indictment what judgment was given on the former indictment.

that the accused is guilty merely;[1] distinguished from attain-

It is, indeed, set forth, that the defendant was 'convicted' on a former indictment, and the court *gave judgment.* But what that judgment was, is not said. When the law speaks of 'conviction,' it means a *judgment,* and not merely a verdict, which in common parlance is called a 'conviction.'" Smith *v.* Com. 14 S. & R. (Pa.) 69.

See also Smith *v.* State, 6 Lea (Tenn.), 637, in which it was *held,* that, as the governor can only pardon *after* "*conviction,*" — and a conviction implies not simply a *verdict,* but also a *judgment,* — the governor's pardon cannot release the defendant from the costs in favor of third persons imposed on him by the *conviction.* See further on this point Com. *v.* Halloway, 2 Am. Law Reg. (N. S.) 474, note, and the cases there cited; State *v.* Mooney, 74 N. C. 98.

1. Conviction is merely an Adjudication that the Accused is guilty. — Thus, where a person accused of crime was ordered by a court of preliminary jurisdiction to enter recognizance for his appearance, and he neglected to do so, a *mittimus* was issued for him to be committed to await his trial, stating that he had been "convicted," and ordered to recognize. Upon a writ of personal replevin (*de homine replegiando*) the *mittimus* was held sufficient; the court, *Davis, J.,* saying, "It is alleged that the accused, upon his hearing, had been 'convicted' of the offence. Though the magistrate had no authority to sentence, he had authority to try the case. He required the accused to plead to the charge, and upon that plea, after the hearing, he 'convicted' him. 'Conviction' is an adjudication that the accused is guilty. It imports all that the statute requires before holding one to bail *and more.* It involves not only the *corpus delicti* and the *probable* guilt of the accused, but his *actual* guilt. I think the *mittimus* sufficient." Nason *v.* Staples, 48 Me 123.

In Massachusetts, where the constitution placed in the hands of the governor the power of pardoning offences, but provided that no pardon before "conviction" should avail the party pleading the same, it was *held* that a pardon granted after verdict of guilty, and before sentence, was valid. In this case, the question is so fully examined, in the opinion of *Judge Gray,* that it will bear quoting at some length. The judge says, "The ordinary legal meaning of 'conviction,' when used to designate a particular stage of a criminal prosecution triable by a jury, is the confession of the accused in open court, or the verdict returned against him by the jury, which ascertains and publishes the fact of his guilt; while 'judgment' or 'sentence' is the appropriate word to denote the action of the court before which the trial is had, declaring the consequences to the convict of the facts thus ascertained. The authorities upon this point are so numerous, that it will be sufficient to cite a few of those which show that such was the legal understanding and use of these words at the time of the adoption of our constitution. Upon a question of the meaning of legal language as used at that time, there is no higher authority than Blackstone's Commentaries, which were published in 1765, and of which Edmund Burke, in his speech on conciliation with the colonies, in 1775, said that he had heard that nearly as many copies had been sold in America as in England. Blackstone uniformly speaks of the verdict of a jury upon a plea of not guilty as constituting the 'conviction,' even while the case is still open to a motion for a new trial or in arrest of judgment. After discussing the granting of a new trial when the accused has been found guilty by the jury, and the conclusive effect of an acquittal, he adds, 'But if the jury find him guilty, he is then said to be "convicted" of the crime whereof he stands indicted — which "conviction" may accrue in two ways: either by his confessing the offence and pleading guilty, or by his being found so by the verdict of his country.' 4 Bl. Com. 362. . . . After describing the effect of 'sentence of death, the most terrible and highest judgment in the laws of England,' as attainting the criminal, and incapacitating him to be a witness, or to perform the functions of another man, he observes, 'This is after *judgment;* for there is a great difference between a man *convicted* and *attainted;* though they are frequently, through inaccuracy, confounded together. After "conviction" only, a man is liable to none of these disabilities, for there is still in contemplation of law a possibility of his innocence. Something may be offered in arrest of judgment; the indictment may be erroneous, which will render his guilt uncertain, and thereupon the present "conviction" may be quashed; he may obtain a pardon, or be allowed the benefit of clergy.' 4 Bl. Com. 380, 381. . . . The terms of our constitution clearly indicate that its framers had in mind these rules of the common law. The word 'conviction' was used in the same sense in many public acts of the government of this State, after it had thrown off the authority of the crown, and before the adoption of the Constitution of the Commonwealth. By statute 1776, ch. 32, § 18, it was provided that 'no miswriting, misspelling, false or improper English after 'conviction,' upon an indictment for treason should 'be any cause to stay or arrest judgment thereupon.' . . . The death-warrants of the same period, issued by the council exercising the executive power, preserve the same distinction between 'conviction' by the jury, and judgment of the court. For example, the warrant for the execution of Bathsheba Spooner, and others, for the murder of her husband in Worcester, in 1778, recites that the defendants 'were by verdict of our said county of Worcester *convict*, and thereupon' 'were by our justices of our said court adjudged to suffer the pains of death.' 2 Chandler's Criminal Trials, 378. . . . Mr. Dane, who was admitted to the bar before the adoption of the constitution, and was peculiarly learned in the law of his time, says, 'A man is *convict* by verdict, but not attainted before judgment.' 'Pardon is another special plea in bar.' 'By pleading a pardon in arrest of judgment, there is an advantage, as it stops the corruption of blood by preventing the attainder.' '*Conviction* is on confession or verdict.' 6 Dane Ab. 534, 536. See also 7 Dane Ab. 339, 340. In Commonwealth v. Richards, 17 Pick. 295, it was held that an appeal allowed by statute from the court of common pleas in a criminal case, to be claimed at 'the court before which such conviction shall be had,' must be claimed before the end of the term at which the verdict was returned; and *Chief Justice Shaw*, in delivering the opinion of the court, said, 'It has generally been considered, we believe, that, as the sentence is the final act in a criminal proceeding, it constitutes the judgment; and it is only from final judgments that appeals are to be taken. But, though such is the general rule of law, we think it has been changed by this statute, and that the statute itself has made a distinction between a "conviction" and a judgment. In general, the legal meaning of "conviction" is, that legal proceeding of record which ascertains the guilt of the party, and upon which the sentence or judgment is founded, as a verdict, a plea of guilty, an outlawry, and the like.' See also Commonwealth v. Andrews, 2 Mass. 409, and 3 Mass. 126. The use of words in our modern statutes is not the highest evidence of their meaning at the time of the adoption of the Constitution. But it may be observed that the Rev. Sts. c. 123, § 3, and the Gen. Sts. c. 158, § 5, provide that 'no person indicted for an offence shall be convicted thereof, unless by confession of his guilt in open court, or by admitting the truth of the charge against him by his plea or demurrer, or by the verdict of a jury accepted and recorded by the court.' It is by the defendant's own confession, plea, or demurrer, or by the verdict, that he is here declared to be 'convicted' without any action of the court in either alternative, except, in the latter, the mere formal acceptance and recording of the verdict, which implies no adjudication of the court upon the defendant's guilt. See also Rev. Sts. c. 137, § 11, and Gen. Sts. c. 172, § 16; Rev. Sts. c. 139, and Gen. Sts. c. 174, *passim*. 'When, indeed, the word 'conviction' is used to describe the effect of the guilt of the accused as judicially proved in one case, when pleaded or given in evidence in another, it is sometimes used in a more comprehensive sense, including the judgment of the court upon the verdict, or confession of guilt; as, for instance, in speaking of the plea of *autrefois convict*, or of the effect of guilt, judicially ascertained, as a disqualification of the convict. And it might be held to have the same meaning in the somewhat analogous case in which the constitution provides that 'no person shall ever be admitted to hold a seat in the legislature, or any office of trust or importance under the government of this Commonwealth, who shall in the due course of law have been "convicted" of bribery or corruption in obtaining an election or appointment.' Const. Mass. c. 6, art. 2. See Case of Falmouth, Mass. Election Cases (ed. 1853), 203. But Blackstone says, 'The plea of *autrefois convict*, or a former "conviction" for the same identical crime, though no judgment was ever given, or perhaps will be (being suspended by the benefit of clergy or other causes), is a good plea in bar to an indictment.' 4 Bl. Com. 336. And it is still an open question in this Commonwealth whether a verdict of guilty rendered upon a good indictment, and which has not been set aside, will, or will not, before judgment, support a plea of *autrefois convict*. 6 Dane Ab. 533; Commonwealth v. Roby, 12 Pick. 496, 510; Commonwealth v. Lahy, 8 Gray, 459, 461; Commonwealth v. Harris, 8 Gray, 470, 473. At the time of the adoption of the constitution, the word 'conviction' was ordinarily used to express the verdict only, even in treating of the disqualification of the convict as a witness. Lord Mansfield, for example, in 1774, where a witness was objected to as incompetent because he stood convicted of perjury, the record of which conviction was produced, said, 'A "conviction" upon a charge of perjury is not sufficient, unless followed by a judgment; I know of no instance in which a conviction alone has been an objection.' Lee v. Gansel, Cowp. 1, 3. In the earlier cases in this Commonwealth, the word 'conviction' was used in the same sense as applied to such a question, even before it had been settled whether a judgment was necessary to complete the disqualification of the witness. Upon the trial in this court in 1788 of an indictment against two for perjury, to which one pleaded guilty, and was offered as a witness for the

Commonwealth against the other, Mr. Justice (afterwards Chief Justice) Dana states, in his manuscript note of the case, 'To whom it is objected that, standing convict of the *crimen falsi*, he is disqualified to be a witness. It is answered that "conviction," though of the *crimen falsi*, is no disqualification, without it be followed by an infamous punishment, or, at least, until after judgment.' The witness was excluded by a divided court. Commonwealth *v.* Manley & Willis, Bristol, October Term, 1788. So in Cushman *v.* Soker, 2 Mass. 106, the court said, 'It is now settled that nothing short of a conviction on an indictment for *crimen falsi*, and a judgment on the conviction,' 'is a sufficient objection to the competency of a witness.' And in the latest case on that subject, in which it was held that a verdict without judgment was not such a 'conviction' as could be proved under Gen. Sts. c. 31, §13, in order to affect the credit of a witness, it was said, 'In its most common use, it signifies the finding of the jury that the prisoner is guilty.' Commonwealth *v.* Gorham, 99 Mass. 420." Com. *v.* Lockwood, 109 Mass. 323; s. c., 12 Am. Rep. 699.

Under the governor's power to grant a pardon conferred by the constitution of Virginia, art. 4, sec. 5, which declares that "he shall have power to remit fines and penalties in such cases, and under such rules and regulations as may be prescribed by law; and, except when the prosecution has been carried on by the house of delegates, to grant reprieves and pardons *after conviction*," — it was *held* that the governor has authority to pardon a person "convicted" of a felony by a verdict of the jury, before sentence is passed upon him by the court; *Judge Moncure* saying, after citing most of examples given in the last case, "It thus appears that the word 'conviction,' as used in our laws, ordinarily signifies the finding of the jury by verdict that the prisoner is guilty, or something equivalent thereto; but the word sometimes denotes the final judgment." Blair *v.* Com. 25 Gratt. 850.

Such a pardon may be granted pending an appeal; and when the case is called for argument upon the merits, the pardon may be pleaded in bar, since the words *after* "*conviction*" denotes a verdict of guilty rendered by a jury. State *v.* Alexander, 76 N. C. 231; s. c., 22 Am. Rep. 675.

In a United States case, arising in the district court of Oregon, for illegal voting, the defendant having forfeited his right to vote under the constitution of the State of Oregon, which declares (art. 2, § 3) that "the privilege of an elector shall be forfeited by a 'conviction' of any crime which is punishable by imprisonment in the penitentiary," it appeared that the defendant had been convicted of such a crime, punishable either by fine or imprisonment, and he was sentenced to pay a fine: it was *held*, that a crime is "punishable by imprisonment" in the penitentiary when by any law it may be so punished, and the fact that it also may be or is otherwise punished, does not change its grade or character in this respect, and that the term "conviction" as here used, is used in its primary and ordinary sense, and signifies a proving or finding that the defendant is guilty, either by the verdict of a jury or his plea to that effect, and does not include the sentence which follows thereon; the court, *Deady, J.*, saying, "In the argument for the defendant it has been assumed that 'conviction' of a crime includes and is the result of the judgment or sentence of the court imposing the punishment prescribed therefor. But this is altogether a mistake. The term 'conviction,' as its composition (*convinco, convictio*) sufficiently indicates, signifies the act of convicting or overcoming one, and, in criminal procedure, the overthrow of the defendant by the establishment of his guilt according to some known legal mode. These modes are, (1) by the plea of guilty, and (2) by the verdict of the jury. Speaking of the difference between 'conviction' and *attaint*, Lord Coke says, 'The difference between a man attainted and "convicted" is that a man is said "convict" before he hath judgment; as if a man be convict by confession, verdict, or recreancy.' To the same effect is the definition in Blount's Law Dic. *anno* 1670, *verbum*, 'convict.' . . . Bishop Stat. Crimes, § 348, says, 'The word "conviction" ordinarily signifies the finding of the jury, by verdict, that the prisoner is guilty. When it is said there has been a "conviction," or one is "convict," the meaning usually is not that sentence has been pronounced, but only that the verdict has been returned. So a plea of guilty by the defendant constitutes a conviction of him.' Mr. Justice Story in U. S. *v.* Gilbert, 2 Sumn. (U. S.) 40, while considering the maxim, 'No man is to be brought into jeopardy of his life more than once for the same offence,' said, '"*conviction*" does not mean the judgment passed upon the verdict;' and in the same case *held* that a plea of *autrefois convict* — a former 'conviction' — will be sustained by a confession or verdict, even when there has been no judgment. Citing 2 Hawk. Pleas of the Crown, c. 36, §§ 1, 10. In People *v.* Goldstein, 32 Cal. 432, it was *held* that a plea of guilty upon which no judgment was given was nevertheless a 'conviction,' and would therefore sustain a plea of former conviction to an indictment for the same offence. . . . But while this is the primary and usual meaning of the term 'conviction,' it is possible that it may be der;[1] a strong belief or persuasion, resting on what appears to be indisputable grounds.[2]

used in such a connection and under such circumstances as to have a secondary or unusual meaning, which would include the final judgment of the court. Bish. Stat. Crimes, § 348; Whart. Cr. P. & Pl. § 935. Yet in Stevens v. People, 1 Hill (N. Y.), 261, it was held sufficient, in an indictment for a second larceny, to allege a prior 'conviction' of the defendant, without averring that there was any judgment or sentence pronounced against him; but the contrary appears to have been held in Smith v. Com., 14 S. & R. (Pa.) 69. But there is nothing in the subject or the language of the clause of the constitution under consideration, to indicate that the term 'conviction' is used therein in any other than the ordinary sense. Of course, it is used there and elsewhere with the understanding that the 'conviction' was not afterwards set aside or annulled by the court. And this is probably the point of the ruling cited from 14 S. & R. (Pa.) *supra*, that the indictment, in alleging a prior 'conviction' of the defendant, should allege a judgment on the verdict, not as constituting the 'conviction,' but as conclusive evidence that it had not been set aside, and was still in force." United States v. Watkinds, 6 Fed. Rep. 152.

This view has been confirmed in a recent California case (1885) *holding* that a defendant convicted of a felony, not punishable with death, and not yet sentenced, who has appealed, is not entitled to be admitted to bail as a matter of right, it being a matter of discretion, not of right, after "conviction." *Ex parte* Brown, 68 Cal. 176; s. c., 8 Pac. Rep. 829. See, on the same point, People v. McGarigle & McDonald, 19 Chicago Leg. News, 347.

See also a Pennsylvania case in which under a statute providing that in all cases of "conviction" the costs shall be paid by the party *convicted*, but where the party shall have been discharged according to law, they shall be paid by the county, it was *held*, that a "conviction" by the jury was sufficient to give the prosecutor his costs, and that the defendant having pleaded a pardon in bar of sentence, and having discharged, the county was liable for the costs. York County v. Dalhousen, 45 Pa. St. 372.

In a United States case, in which certain claims were made for a reward offered for information which should lead to the forfeiture of any distillery, and to the conviction of the person engaged in operating it, it appeared that the persons said to have been "convicted" were found guilty by the jury, but that judgment on the verdict was suspended at the instance of the district attorney. It was *held*, that the conditions of the offer were complied with; the court, *Nott, J.*, saying, "The counsel for the defendants has also argued that the term 'conviction' in the offer of reward is to be construed . . . as meaning . . . 'trial and punishment.' We are of the same opinion, but draw from it a different inference, which is, that the statute enlarges rather than restricts the intent of the word 'conviction.' The informer's information led to an indictment, to a trial, and to a verdict of guilty. It also led to punishment, — not to a punishment by fine and imprisonment on the judgment of the court, but to a lesser, modified punishment, inflicted at the instance of the prosecuting officer, who deemed it best to hold the judgment in suspense over the heads of offenders as security for their future good behavior." Williams v. United States, 12 Ct. of Claims (U. S.), 192.

1. Conviction and Attainder distinguished. — In *holding* that the plea of *autrefois convict* is supported by proof of a lawful trial and verdict or confession on a sufficient indictment, though no judgment be given upon it, the court, *Sutherland, J.*, said, "In 1 Inst. 391, A, it is said, 'The difference between a man attainted and *convicted* is that a man is said *convict* before *he hath judgment*, as if a man be a convict by confession, *verdict*, or recreancy. And when he hath his *judgment* upon the *verdict*, confession, etc., then he is said to be *attaint*.' It is further said, 'By a *conviction* of a felon his goods and chattels are forfeited; but by *attainder*, that is, by judgment given, his lands and tenements are forfeited and his blood corrupted, and not before.' So in Jacob's Law Dict. (Attainted) it is said, 'Attainder of a criminal is larger than *conviction*: a man is *convicted* when he is found guilty, or confesses the crime *before judgment* had, but not attainted till judgment is passed upon him.' This shows the technical, common law definition of the word *convict or convicted*: a felon was 'convicted' by the verdict of the jury: he was *attainted* by the judgment rendered on the verdict." Shepherd v. People, 25 N. Y. 406. See Cozens v. Long, Penn. (N. J.) 764; Green v. Shumway, 39 N. Y. 430.

2. Abiding Conviction. — In *holding* that a charge to the jury on the subject of "reasonable doubt" as follows, "If you can truthfully say that you have an 'abiding conviction' of the defendant's guilt such as you would be willing to act upon in the more weighty and important matters relating to your own affairs, you have no

CONVOY.—In a warranty in a policy of insurance that a ship will sail with convoy, by the term "convoy" is to be understood "a naval force under the command of a person appointed by the government of the country to which the vessel insured belongs."[1]

COOLING TIME, in law, means time for the mind to become so calm and sedate as that it is supposed to contemplate, comprehend, and coolly act with reference to the consequences likely to ensue.[2] But no precise time in *hours* or *minutes* can be laid down by the court as a rule of law within which the passions *must be held* to have subsided, and reason to have resumed its control.[3]

CO-PARTIES.[4]

COPARCENARY.—A tenancy which arises when an inheritable estate descends from the ancestor to several persons possessing an equal title to it. It arises by act of law only; i.e., by descent, which, in relation to this subject, is of two kinds: (1) Descent by the common law, which takes place where an ancestor dies intestate, leaving two or more females as his co-heiresses; these all take together as coparceners or parceners, the law of primogeniture not obtaining among women in equal relationship to their ancestor; they are, however, deemed to be one heir; and (2) Descent by particular custom, as in the case of gavelkind lands, which descend to all the males in equal degree.[5]

COPY.—A copy is a true transcript of an original writing.[6] A *copy* of a book must be a transcript of the *language* in which the conceptions of the author are clothed; of something printed and embodied in a tangible shape. The same conceptions, clothed in another language, cannot constitute the same composition, nor can it be called a *transcript* or *copy* of the same book.[7] The words "a copy of a book" naturally import a transcript or copy of the entire book.[8]

reasonable doubt," was not erroneous, the court, *Field, J.*, said, "The word 'abiding' here has the signification of settled and fixed, a 'conviction' which may follow a careful examination and comparison of the whole evidence. It is difficult to conceive what amount of 'conviction' would leave the mind of a juror free from a reasonable doubt, if it be not one which is so settled and fixed as to control his action in the more weighty and important matters relating to his own affairs." Hopt *v.* People, 24 Rep. 129.

1. Peake Add. Cas. 143. note; D'Eguino *v.* Bewicke, 2 H. Black, 551.

2. Eanes *v.* The State, 10 Tex. App. 447.

3. Maher *v.* The People, 10 Mich. 223. See 2 Bish. Cr. L. §§ 711–13.

4. "The word 'co-parties,' as used in section 551 of the code, means parties to the judgment appealed from, not co-plaintiffs or co-defendants to the action. The appellant's co-defendants to the action were adverse to him, and not co-parties with him, or to the judgment rendered against him, within the meaning of the law." Hadley *v.* Hill, 73 Ind. 448, 449.

5. Whart. Law Lex.

6. Dickinson *v.* R. R. Co., 7 W. Va. 412.

7. Stowe *v.* Thomas, 2 Wall. Jr. (U. S.) 565; 2 Am. L. Reg. 229.

8. Rogers *v.* Jewett, 12 Month. L. Rep. (N. S.) 340. A statute permitting a party to file a "copy" of his account, is satisfied only by "'*a copy*,' not the *substance, amount*, or *balance* of the account claimed." M'Cormick *v.* Brookfield, South. (N. J.) 71.

Where a writ of capias described the defendant by the addition of "gentleman," which word was omitted in the copy served, *held*, that this was not a *copy* of the writ, in compliance with the statute regulating the mode of service. Cooke *v.* Vaughan, 4 M. & W. 69. But *held*, that if the defendant cannot be misled or prejudiced by a

"Copy" was also used in the sense of "copyright," signifying "an incorporeal right to the sole printing and publishing of somewhat intellectual, communicated by letters." [1]

See also EVIDENCE.

COPYHOLD. — A base tenure founded upon immemorial custom and usage. A copyhold estate is a parcel of the demesnes of a manor, held at the lord's will, and according to the customs of such manor, as evidenced by the rolls of the courts-baron in which they were entered. Such estates do not exist in the United States.

COPYRIGHT.

1. Definition. — Copyright is the exclusive right of printing or otherwise multiplying copies of a published literary work, and

mistake in the copy, the service is good. Furnace Co. *v.* Shepherd, 2 Hill (N. Y.), 414.

A "copy of the indictment," directed under act of Congress to be furnished to persons accused of treason, must contain "a copy of the caption." U. S. *v.* Insurgents of Pa., 2 Dall. (U. S.) 342.

Whether it is necessary that a "copy of articles of association" should contain the names of members as subscribed to the original articles, *quære*. Savings Bk. *v.* Ford, 27 Conn. 282.

A "copy of the record" means an entire copy, and not a mere extract. Edmiston *v.* Schwartz, 13 S. & R. (Pa.) 135. An act prohibiting the copying in any manner, of a picture, includes the reproduction thereof by the art of photography. Gambart *v.* Ball, 14 C. B. (N. S.) 306. *Willes, J.*, said, "Notwithstanding the ordinary rule of construction, that general words in a statute following particular are to be restricted in their meaning to the particular words preceding, I think the word 'copy' here may very well apply to a copying by any process by which copies may be indefinitely multiplied. To comprehend these, the act need not, as it appears to me, be construed to extend to a copying by hand."

So a "copy of a print" may vary in some trifling respects from the main design. "The question is, what is the meaning of the word 'copy' of a print. Now, in common parlance, there may be a copy of a print where there exist small variations from the original; and the question is, whether the words are used in that popular sense in this act of Parliament. . . . Every person, therefore, who sells a copy which comes so near the original as this, is thereby made liable to an action. There can be no reason why a person should not be liable where he sells a copy with a mere collusive variation; and I think we should put a narrow construction on the statute, if we held such a collusive variation from the original not to be a copy. A copy is that which comes so near the original as to give to every person seeing it the idea created by the original." West *v.* Francis, 5 B. & Ald. 737.

1. Lord Mansfield in Millar *v.* Taylor, 4 Burr. 2396, which he declares to have been its technical sense for ages. And see Jefferys *v.* Boosey, 4 H. L. C. 884, 888.

publishing and vending the same; the right of preventing all others from doing so.[1]

2. Property in Manuscript. — An author has, at common law, a property in his manuscript, and may obtain redress against any one who deprives him of it, or, by improperly obtaining a copy, endeavors to realize a profit by its publication; and there can be no doubt that the rights of an assignee of such manuscript would be protected by a court of chancery.[2]

(a) Dedication to the Public. — A manuscript is dedicated to the public by publication, and the exclusive property of the author in it ceases as soon as by publication it has become the property of the public, unless he has complied with the requirements of the statute, and secured a copyright.[3]

1. Stephens *v.* Cady, 14 How. (U. S.) 530; Stowe *v.* Thomas, 2 Wall. Jr. (U. S.) 547; Baker *v.* Selden, 11 Otto (U. S.), 99; Clemens *v.* Belford, 14 Fed. Rep. 728; Lawrence *v.* Dana, 4 Cliff. (U. S.) 1; Chappell *v.* Purday, 14 M. & W. 316; Millar *v.* Taylor, 4 Burr. 2311.

It is only conferred by statute. Although it was formerly held in England that at common law an author had a perpetual right in the products of his intellect, and although it has sometimes been doubted whether this part of the common law was not introduced in this country, it is now well settled in the United States and in England, that, by common law, an author has no exclusive right to a published literary work, the common law having been superseded by the statutes. Wheaton *v.* Peters, 8 Pet. (U. S.) 591; Clemens *v.* Belford, 14 Fed. Rep. 728; Crowe *v.* Aiken, 2 Biss. (U. S.) 208; Parton *v.* Prang, 3 Cliff. (U. S.) 537; Stevens *v.* Gladding, 17 How. (U. S.) 447; Clayton *v.* Stone, 2 Paine (U. S.), 382; Pulte *v.* Derby, 5 McLean (U. S.), 328; Stowe *v.* Thomas, 2 Wall. Jr. (U. S.) 547; Donaldson *v.* Beckett, 4 Burr. 2408; Millar *v.* Taylor, 4 Burr. 2303; Cambridge *v.* Bryer, 16 East, 319; Rees *v.* Peltzer, 75 Ill. 475.

When a person enters the field of authorship he can secure to himself the exclusive right to his writings by a copyright under the laws of the United States. If he publishes any thing of which he is the author or compiler, either under his own proper name or an assumed name, without protecting it by copyright, it becomes public property, and any person who chooses to do so has the right to republish it and to state the name of the author in such form in the book, either upon the titlepage or otherwise, as to show who was the writer or author thereof. Clemens *v.* Belford, 14 Fed. Rep. 728.

2. Wheaton *v.* Peters, 8 Pet. (U. S.) 591; Bartlett *v.* Crittenden, 5 McLean (U. S.), 32; Clemens *v.* Belford, 14 Fed. Rep. 728; Palmer *v.* De Witt, 47 N. Y. 552; s. c., 7 Am. Rep. 480; Parton *v.* Prang, 3 Cliff. (U. S.) 537; Crowe *v.* Aiken, 2 Biss. (U. S.) 208; Goldmark *v.* Kreling, 25 Fed. Rep. 349; Boucicault *v.* Fox, 5 Blatchf. (U. S.) 87; Jones *v.* Thorne, 1 N. Y. Leg. Obs. 408; Boucicault *v.* Wood, 2 Biss. (U. S.) 84; French *v.* Maguire, 55 How. Pr. (N. Y.) 471; Little *v.* Hall, 18 How. (U. S.) 165; Keene *v.* Wheatley, 9 Am. L. Reg. 33; Webb *v.* Rose, 4 Burr. 2330; Pope *v.* Curl, 2 Atk. 342; Manley *v.* Owens, Burr. 2320; Southey *v.* Sherwood, 2 Meriv. 434; Macklin *v.* Richardson, Amb. R. 694; Eyre *v.* Higbee, 22 How. Pr. (N. Y.) 207; French *v.* Maguire, 55 How. Pr. (N. Y.) 471.

An original operetta, consisting of libretto, score, and name, is property at common law, which, so far as unpublished, will be protected from fraudulent imitation by injunction, even though the operetta be an adaptation of an old play. Aronson *v.* Fleckenstein, 28 Fed. Rep. 75.

This principle holds good for the whole manuscript, or any part of it. Bartlett *v.* Crittenden, 5 McLean (U. S), 32.

An author may restrain the publication of literary matter purporting to have been written by him, but which in fact he never did write; and this rule applies in favor of persons known to the public under an assumed name. Clemens *v.* Belford, 14 Fed. Rep. 728.

Where written alterations are made to the manuscript of a play, by an actor in the employ of the manager who owns the manuscript, such alterations are the property of the owner of the manuscript. But unwritten additions are not the property of the owner of the manuscript: their use by the owner of another theatre to whom such actor has communicated them will, however, be enjoined. Keene *v.* Wheatley, 4 Phil. (Pa.) 157; s. c., 9 Am. Law Reg. 33.

3. Bartlett *v.* Crittenden, 5 McLean (U. S.), 32; Keene *v.* Wheatley, 4 Phil.

(Pa.) 157; s. c., 9 Am. Law Reg. 33; Parton v. Prang, 3 Cliff. (U. S.) 537; Carte v. Duff, 25 Fed. Rep. 183; Boucicault v. Wood, 2 Biss. (U. S.) 34; Tompkins v. Halleck, 133 Mass. 32.

An author cannot acquire a right to the protection of his writings under an assumed name as a trade-name or trade-mark, and no pseudonym, however ingenuous, novel, or quaint, can give one any more rights than he would have under his own name, or defeat the policy of the law that the publication of literary matter, without protection by copyright, has dedicated such matter to the public. Clemens v. Belford, 14 Fed. Rep. 728.

Unless a picture is covered by copyright, an unconditional sale of the picture also confers the right of making copies, and the publication of such copies. Parton v. Prang, 3 Cliff. (U. S.) 537.

A sale of a book naturally implies a publication. Baker v. Taylor, 2 Blatchf. (U. S.) 82.

Conditional consignments of printed books to a bookseller, with order not to sell before a specified day, is not a publication; but a sale after that period operates as a complete dedication of the work to the public. Wall v. Gordon, 12 Abb. Pr. N. S. (N. Y.) 349.

Delivery of copies of a report to the State, without proof of distribution, is not a publication. Myers v. Callaghan, 5 Fed. Rep. 726.

Permission to make a copy of the manuscript is not a publication. Bartlett v. Crittenden, 5 McLean (U. S.), 32; Forrester v. Waller, 2 Eden. 328; Queensbury v. Shebbeare, 2 Eden, 329.

Neither is the representation of a play. Boucicault v. Hart, 13 Blatchf. (U. S.) 47; Palmer v. De Witt, 47 N. Y. 532; s. c., 7 Am. Rep. 480; Roberts v. Myers, 23 Monthly L. Rep. 396; Keene v. Kimball, 23 Monthly L. Rep. 660; Crowe v. Aiken, 2 Biss. (U. S.) 208; Boucicault v. Fox, 5 Blatchf. (U. S.) 87; Tompkins v. Halleck, 133 Mass. 32; Shook v. Rankin, 6 Biss. (U. S.) 477.

The publication of a play, or representation acquired by phonographic reports or surreptitious means, is an infringement on the rights of the owner of the manuscript. Crowe v. Aiken, 2 Biss. (U. S.) 208; Keene v. Wheatley, 4 Phil. (Pa.) 157; s. c., 9 Am. Law Reg. 33; Shook v. Daly, 49 How. Pr. (N. Y.) 366; French v. Maguire, 55 How. Pr. (N. Y.) 471; Macklin v. Richardson, Ambl. 694.

Not so if such unauthorized representation is possible by means of the retention of the words in the memory of persons in the audience. Keene v. Wheatley, 4 Phil. (Pa.) 157; s. c., 9 Am. Law. Reg. 33; Keene v. Kimball, 16 Gray (Mass.), 545; French v. Maguire, 55 How. Pr. (N. Y.) 714; Keene v. Clarke, 5 Rob. (N. Y.) 38; Wallack v. Barney, 14 Am. L. Reg. N. S. 213.

A memorization of a play by actors while in the employ of the owner of a play, and with a view of producing the play for the benefit of such owner, is not such a memorization which will allow them to reproduce the play in another theatre, for the benefit of one not the owner of the play. Shook v. Rankin, 3 Cent. L. J. 210.

Compare, however, Tompkins v. Halleck, 133 Mass. 32, where it was held that the representation of a dramatic work, which the proprietor has never caused to be printed, and has not obtained a copyright of, if made without license of the proprietor, is a violation of his right, and may be restrained by injunction, although such representation is from a copy obtained by a spectator attending a public representation by the proprietor for money, and afterwards writing it from memory. French v. Conolly, 1 N. Y. Weekl. Dig. 197; Carte v. Ford, 15 Fed. Rep. 439.

A dedication to the public of a musical composition for the piano does not dedicate what it does not contain and what cannot be reproduced from it, and defendant does not, therefore, possess, and has no right to perform, such composition as set for an orchestra, although he should have the opportunity to copy it. Thomas v. Lennon, 14 Fed. Rep. 849.

An opera is more like a patented invention than a common book, as to the rule that he who obtains similar results, better or worse, by similar means, though the opportunity is furnished by an unprotected book, should be held to infringe the rights of the composer. Thomas v. Lennon, 14 Fed. Rep. 849.

This principle of Thomas v. Lennon, 14 Fed. Rep. 849, was, however, overruled in Carte v. Ford, 15 Fed. Rep. 439, where the non-resident alien authors of the comic opera of "Iolanthe," having sanctioned the publication in the United States of the libretto and vocal score, with a piano accompaniment, and having kept the orchestration in manuscript, it was *held*, that a person who had independently arranged a new orchestration, using for that purpose only the published vocal and piano-forte scores, could not be enjoined from publicly performing the opera with the new orchestration. It appearing that the orchestration was a subordinate accessory of the opera, *held*, that the use of the composer's name and the title of the opera would not be enjoined, provided the announcements of the performance were not so worded as to mislead the public into believing that the original orchestration, of which complainant had exclusive use, was to be performed. See also Goldmark v. Collmer, decided Nov. 1882, Circ. Ct. Cook Co. Illinois, cited in Carte *v.* Ford.

The representation of a dramatic work upon the stage is not a publication which will prevent the author or his assignee from obtaining a copyright. Keene *v.* Kimball, 16 Gray (Mass.), 545, 549; Roberts *v.* Myers, 13 Monthly L. Rep. 396; Boucicault *v.* Fox, 5 Blatchf. (U. S.) 87; Boucicault *v.* Wood, 2 Biss. (U. S.) 34; Boucicault *v.* Hart, 13 Blatchf. (U. S.) 47.

The publication in a foreign country of a play never published in the United States, is not a dedication to the public, unless such publication was made with the consent of the author. Boucicault *v.* Wood, 2 Biss. (U. S.) 34.

C., an alien, purchased from G. & S., British subjects, their right of the public representation in the United States of the comic opera, "The Mikado," of which G. was the author of the literary parts, and S. the author of the musical parts. They employed T., a citizen of the United States, to come to London, and prepare a piano-forte arrangement from the original orchestral score, with a view to copyrighting the same in the United States. After T. made the piano arrangement, proceedings were taken to copyright it as a new and original composition in the United States, and C. purchased the title of G., S., and T., to such copyright. After the recording in the office of the librarian of Congress of the title of this arrangement, the libretto and vocal score of the opera and piano-forte arrangement of T. were published and sold in England, with the consent of G and S. The orchestral score was never published, but kept by G. and S. for their own use and that of licensees to perform the opera. D. purchased in England a copy of the libretto, vocal score, and piano-forte arrangement, and procured a skilful musician to make an independent orchestration from the vocal score and piano score, and was about to produce the opera in New York City with words and voice parts substantially the same as those of the original, and with scenery, costumes, and stage business in imitation of the original, and with the orchestration, which he had procured to be made, and without claiming that he employed the orchestration of the original opera, when C. sought to enjoin the public representations. *Held*, that the publication of the libretto and vocal score of the opera in London, with the consent of the authors, was a dedication of their playright, or entire dramatic property in the opera to the public, notwithstanding their retention of the orchestral score in manuscript and the public representation would not be enjoined. Carte *v.* Duff, 25 Fed. Rep 183. See also Carte *v.* Ford, 15 Fed. Rep. 439.

Where the owner of the manuscript of a drama authorizes the publication of a novel based and founded upon the drama, such publication is not such a dedication to the public as will authorize the novel to be dramatized and put upon the stage without the authority of the persons owning the manuscript. Shook *v.* Rankin, 3 Centr. L. J. 210.

Publication of the songs and vocal score of an operetta, with the name of the operetta, does not make such name public property, so as to give to the public the right to use the name as applied to any other libretto, dialogue, and orchestra parts. The publication of the songs only gave to the public that which was published, and does not authorize the use of the name as applied to the operetta as a whole. Aronson *v.* Fleckenstein, 28 Fed. Rep. 75.

It has been held that voluntarily publishing pictures of a painting, is such a publishing of the painting as to furnish other parties the means of reproducing the pictures, without any invasion of the plaintiff's proprietary rights in the painting. Vertel *v.* Jacoby, 44 How. Pr. (N. Y.) 179. *Compare* Vertel *v.* Wood, 40 How. Pr. (N. Y.) 10.

Although the law recognizes a distinction between a painting and a print, a copyright for the former will protect its owner in the sale of copies thereof, even though they may appropriately be called prints, and a party who copies such copies will be guilty of infringement. The owner of a copyrighted painting by publishing lithographic copies thereof does not lose the right to restrain others from copying these copies Schumacher *v.* Schwencke, 30 Fed. Rep. 690.

Where a person compiled maps of the city of Chicago of a particular design from the public records into an atlas, and without taking out any copyright made several copies of the original in a form suitable for comprising atlases, sold several, and placed one copy in the hands of the city for public use, where any part of or the whole of it could be copied and used by any citizen, placing no restrictions on their use, *held*, that the author thereby dedicated the maps to public use, and consequently lost his common law proprietorship in them, and they became public property Rees *v.* Peltzer, 75 Ill. 475.

But where one made a map of the Nantucket Shoals, and deposited a copy in the navy department, it was held that it did not become thereby a public document which any one had a right to copy. Blunt *v.* Patten, 2 Paine (U. S.), 393.

It is the unquestioned law that in the case of letters the general property and the general rights incident to property belong to the writer, and the person to whom letters are addressed has but a limited

3. **What may be copyrighted.** — (*a*) *Statute.* — The Revised Statutes of the United States provide that any citizen of the United States, or resident therein, who shall be the author, inventor, designer, or proprietor of any book, map, chart, dramatic or musical composition, engraving, cut, print or photograph or negative thereof, or of a painting, drawing, chromo, statue, statuary, and of models or designs intended to be perfected as works of fine arts, and the executors, administrators or assigns of any such person shall, upon complying with the provisions of the statute, have the sole liberty of printing, reprinting, publishing, completing, copying, executing, finishing, and vending the same; and in the case of a dramatic composition, of publicly performing or representing it, or causing it to be performed or represented by others. And authors may reserve the right to dramatize or to translate their own works.[1]

(*b*) *Books.* — A book within the statute need not be a book in the common and ordinary acceptation of the word, viz., a volume made up of several sheets bound together: it may be printed only on one sheet, as the words of a song, or the music accompanying it.[2]

right or special property in such letters as a trustee or bailee for particular purposes, either of information or of protection or of support of his rights and character, and the publication of letters, even by the receiver, has been restrained where such publication was not made for purposes of protection or of support of his rights or character. Kiernan *v.* Manhattan Quotation Tel. Co., 50 How. Pr. (N. Y.) 194, 201; Folsom *v.* Marsh, 2 Story (U. S.), 100; United States *v.* Tanner, 6 McLean (U. S.), 128; Woolsey *v.* Judd, 4 Duer (N. Y.), 379.

Suit for protection of property at common law in a dramatic composition, e. g., an operetta, can be brought only by the licensee of a general owner, where such licensee has an exclusive license for a definite period, and, by the terms of his license, is to bring all the suits for the protection of his rights. Aronson *v.* Fleckenstein, 28 Fed. Rep. 75.

A part owner of a dramatic composition may protect his property by suit against a wrong-doer. Aronson *v.* Fleckenstein, 28 Fed. Rep. 75.

1. Rev. Stat. U. S. § 4952.

2. Clayton *v.* Stone, 2 Paine (U. S.), 383; Clementi *v.* Golding, 2 Camp. 25.

In deciding that a musical composition published on a single sheet of paper is privileged as a *book* within the statute of 8 Anne, c. 19, § 1, the court, *Ellenborough*, C. J., accepted the argument of Erskine in Hime *v.* Dale, sitting after May term, 1803, as follows: "There is nothing in the word 'book' to require that it shall consist of several sheets bound in leather or stitched in a marble cover. 'Book' is evidently the Saxon *boc*, and the latter term is from the *beech-tree*, the rind of which supplied the place of paper to our German ancestors. The Latin word *liber* is of a similar etymology, meaning originally only the bark of a tree. 'Book' may therefore be applied to any writing, and it has often been so used in the English language. The *horn book* consists of one small page, protected by an animal preparation, and in this State it has universally received the appellation of a 'book.' So in legal proceedings the copy of the pleadings after issue joined, whether it be long or short, is called the paper *book* or the demurrer *book*. In the Court of Exchequer a roll was anciently denominated a 'book,' and so continues in some instances to this day. An oath as old as the time of Edward I. runs in this form: 'And you shall deliver into the Court of Exchequer a *book* fairly written,' etc. But the 'book' delivered into court in fulfilment of this oath has always been a roll of parchment." Clementi *v.* Golding, 2 Campbell, 25, and notes; s. c., 11 East, 244; White *v.* Geroch, 2 B. & Al. 298; Clayton *v.* Stone, 2 Paine (U. S.), 382. See also Drury *v.* Ewing, 1 Bond (U. S.), 540; Scoville *v.* Toland, 6 West L. J. 84.

The act of 5th and 6th Vict. c. 45, § 2, declares that a *book* "shall be construed to mean and include every volume, part or division of a volume, pamphlet, sheet of letterpress, sheet of music or dramatic piece," under which it was held that a newspaper was not a "book" within the said act. Cox *v.* Land and Water Journal Co., L. R. 9 Eq. Cas. 324.

(*c*) *Compilations.* — A book, to be entitled to the protection of the copyright acts, need not be entirely original: it may be composed of old material, taken from sources common to all writers, as long as they are arranged and combined in a new and original form,

A diagram, with directions for cutting ladies' garments, printed on a single sheet of paper, was held to be a book. Drury *v.* Ewing, 1 Bond (U. S.), 540.

A label describing the virtues of certain medicine, and used to paste on the bottle, is not a book, under the statute, and cannot be copyrighted. Scoville *v.* Toland, 6 West. L. J. 84; Coffeen *v.* Brunton, 4 McLean (U. S.), 516.

A daily price current is not the subject of copyright. Clayton *v.* Stone, 2 Paine (U. S.), 382. *Compare* Kiernan *v.* Manhattan Quotation Tel. Co., 50 How. Pr. (N. Y.) 194.

Private letters may be copyrighted by the author of the letters. Folsom *v.* Marsh, 2 Story (U. S.), 100.

Abstracts of title are subjects of copyright. Banker *v.* Caldwell, 3 Minn. 94.

An illustrated newspaper has been held to be a book. Harper *v.* Shoppell, 26 Fed. Rep. 519.

A book explaining and illustrating a system of book-keeping may be copyrighted, but this gives no exclusive right to the system so explained. Baker *v.* Selden, 11 Otto (U. S.), 99.

The copyright of a book protects the whole book, and every part of it, including text, notes, illustrations, etc. White *v.* Geroch, 2 B. & A. 298; D'Almaine *v.* Boosey, 1 Y. & C. Exch. 288; Roworth *v.* Wilkes, 1 Camp. 94; Wilkins *v.* Aikin, 17 Ves. 422; Bradbury *v.* Hotten, L. R. 8 Exch. 1; Cobbett *v.* Woodward, L. R. 14 Eq. 407; Bogue *v.* Houlston, 5 De G. & Sm. 275.

And where it partly consists of literary matter, which cannot be legally protected, it will not affect the protection of the other part. Barfield *v.* Nicholson, 2 Sim. & St. 1; Lawrence *v.* Dana, 2 Am. L. T. R. (N. S.) 402; Low *v.* Ward, L. R. 6 Eq. 418; Cary *v.* Longman, 1 East, 360.

A book which has not been printed, but exists only in manuscript, may be the subject of copyright. Roberts *v.* Myers, 23 Law Rep. 396; 13 Law Rep. (N. S.) 396.

Foreign Books. — There can be no copyright on books published in a foreign country, nor on reproductions of such books published in this country. Where such reproduction contains notes, illustrations, or other new matter, not to be found in the original publication, such new matter may be protected by copyright. Sheldon *v.* Houghton, 5 Blatchf. (U. S.) 285.

Translations. — The translation of a foreign work may, however, be copyrighted, but is not protected by it to the extent of preventing others from publishing another independent translation of the same work. Shook *v.* Rankin, 6 Biss. (U. S.) 477; 3 Centr. L. J. 210; Emerson *v.* Davies, 3 Story (U. S.), 768; Rooney *v.* Kelly, 14 Ir. L. R. N. S. 158; Wyatt *v.* Barnard, 3 Ves. & B. 77.

Title of Book. — The simple title of a book, magazine, or other periodical, is not subject to be copyrighted. If it is to be protected as such, it must be protected under the statutes regulating the protection of trademarks. See TRADEMARKS. Osgood *v.* Allen, 1 Holmes (U. S.), 185; Benn *v.* Le Clercq, 18 Int. Rev. Rec. 94; Jollie *v.* Jaques, 1 Blatchf. (U. S.) 618.

The publisher of "Chatterbox," in England, having assigned the exclusive right to use and protect that name in this country, the assignee may maintain his action against any other person who undertakes to publish books under that name in the United States. Estes *v.* Williams, 21 Fed. Rep. 189. See TRADEMARKS. McLean *v.* Fleming, 96 U. S. 245.

New Editions. — A new edition of a copyrighted work is protected by the original copyright; but where new matter is inserted, such new matter will not be covered by the copyright, on the principle that nothing can be protected by it what was not in existence at the time it was granted. Lawrence *v.* Dana, 4 Cliff. (U. S.) 1; Farmer *v.* Calvert, Lith. Engr. and Map Publ. Co. 1 Flipp. (U. S.) 228.

This principle extends not only to books, but also to maps. Farmer *v.* Calvert, Lith Engr. & Map Publ. Co. 1 Flipp. (U. S.) 228.

A new edition of a copyrighted work may be published in a less number of volumes, and be protected by the original copyright, if notice thereof is properly published. Dwight *v.* Appleton, 1 N. Y. Leg. Obs. 195.

Where a new edition is substantially different from the original one, a new copyright may be acquired. The extent of the changes and alterations is immaterial, as long as they materially affect the work. Gray *v.* Russell, 1 Story (U. S.), 11; Lawrence *v.* Dana, 4 Cliff. (U. S.) 1; Banks *v.* McDivitt, 13 Blatchf. (U. S) 163; Black *v.* Murray, 9 Sc. Sess. Cas. (2d series) 341; Hedderwick *v.* Griffin, 3 Sc. Sess. Cas. (2d ser.) 383; Cary *v.* Longman, 1 East, 358; Cary *v.* Faden, 5 Ves. 24; Tonson *v.* Walker, 3 Swans, 672; Sweet *v.* Cater, 11 Sim. 572.

which gives it an application unknown before. Books "made and composed" in that manner are the proper subjects of copyright; and the author of such book has as much right in his plan, arrangement, and combination of the materials collected and presented as he has in his thoughts, sentiments, reflections, and opinions, or in the modes in which they are therein expressed and illustrated; but he cannot prevent others from using the old materials for a different purpose.[1]

1. Lawrence *v.* Dana, 4 Cliff. (U. S.) 1; Bullinger *v.* Mackey, 15 Blatchf. (U. S.) 550; Webb *v.* Powers, 2 Woodb. & M. (U. S.) 497; Greene *v.* Bishop, 1 Cliff. (U. S.) 199; Story *v.* Holcombe, 4 McLean (U. S.), 309; Lewis *v.* Fullerton, 2 Beav. 6; Curtis on Copyright, 180; Emerson *v.* Davies, 3 Story (U. S.), 768; Gray *v.* Russell, 1 Story (U. S.), 11.

Drone in his work on Copyrights, page 153, says, "These principles have been judicially recognized in the case of the following productions:—

"*General Miscellaneous Compilations.*—Jarrold *v.* Houlston, 3 Kay & J. 708; Pike *v.* Nicholas, 20 L. T. N. S. 906; L. R. 5 Ch. 251; Mack *v.* Petter, L. R. 14 Eq. 431; Hogg *v.* Scott, L. R. 18 Eq. 444; Gray *v.* Russell, 1 Story (U. S.), 11; Emerson *v.* Davies, 3 Story (U. S.), 768; Webb *v.* Powers, 2 Woodb. & M. (U. S.) 497; Greene *v.* Bishop, 1 Cliff. (U. S.) 186; Lawrence *v.* Cupples, 9 U. S. Pat. Off. Gaz. 254.

"*Annotations consisting of Common Materials.*—Story *v.* Holcombe, 4 McLean (U. S.), 306; Lawrence *v.* Dana, 2 Am. L. T. R. N. S. 402; Banks *v.* McDivitt, 13 Blatchf. (U. S.) 163; Black *v.* Murray, 9 Sc. Sess. Cas. 3d ser. 341.

"*Dictionaries.*—Barfield *v.* Nicholson, 2 Sim. & St. 1; Spiers *v.* Brown, 6 W. R. 352.

"*Books of Chronology.*—Trusler *v.* Murray, 1 East, 362.

"*Gazetteers.*—Lewis *v.* Fullerton, 2 Beav. 6.

"*Itineraries, Road and Guide Books.*—Cary *v.* Faden, 5 Ves. 24; Cary *v.* Longman, 1 East, 358; Murray *v.* Bogue, 1 Drew. 353.

"*Directories.*—Kelly *v.* Hooper, 4 Jur. 21; Kelly *v.* Morris, L. R. 1 Eq. 697; Morris *v.* Ashbee, L. R. 7 Eq. 34; Mathieson *v.* Harrod, L. R. 7 Eq. 270; Morris *v.* Wright, L. R. 5 Ch. 279; Kelly *v.* Hodge, 29 L. T. N. S. 387.

"*Maps and Charts.*—Blunt *v.* Patten, 2 Paine (U. S.), 393, 397; Stephens *v.* Cady, 14 How. (U. S.) 528; Stevens *v.* Gladding, 17 How. (U. S.) 447; Farmer *v.* Calvert, Lith. Engr. & Map Publ. Co. 5 Am. L. T. R. 168; Rees *v.* Peltzer, 75 Ill. 475; Stannard *v.* Lee, L. R. 6 Ch. 346.

"*Calendars.*—Matthewson *v.* Stockdale, 12 Ves. 270; Longman *v.* Winchester, 16 Ves. 269.

"*Catalogues.*—Wilkins *v.* Aikin, 17 Ves. 422; Hotten *v.* Arthur, 1 Hem. & M. 603; Hogg *v.* Scott, L. R. 18 Eq. 444.

"*Mathematical Tables.*—McNeill *v.* Williams, 11 Jur. 344; King *v.* Reed, 8 Ves. 223, note; Baily *v.* Taylor, L. J. 3 Ch. 66.

"*A List of Bounds.*—Cox *v.* Land & Water Journal Co., L. R. 9 Eq. 324.

"*Abstracts of Titles to Lands.*—Banker *v.* Caldwell, 3 Minn. 94.

"*Collections of Statistics.*—Scott *v.* Stanford, L. R. 3 Eq. 718; Maclean *v.* Moody, 20 Sc. Sess. Cas. 2d ser. 1154; Walford *v.* Johnston, 20 Sc. Sess. Cas. 2d ser. 1160, note.

"*Statutory Forms.*—Alexander *v.* Mackenzie, 9 Sess. Cas. 2d ser. 748.

"*Recipes.*—Rundell *v.* Murray, Jac. 311.

"*Designs.*—Grace *v.* Newman, L. R. 19 Eq. 623."

Public Documents.—A compilation from voluminous public documents, so arranged as to show readily the date and order of battles fought during the civil war, together with a list of casualties, may be copyrighted. Hanson *v.* Jaccard Jewelry Co., 32 Fed. Rep. 202.

An express and railroad guide consisting of a compilation of information regarding railroads, etc., may be copyrighted. Bullinger *v.* Mackey, 15 Blatchf. (U. S.) 550.

The copyright on a compilation of old matter does not protect the component parts independent from the mode of arrangement and combination: neither does it protect the mode of arrangement and combination independent of the component parts, but it protects only the two as combined. Gray *v.* Russell, 1 Story (U. S.), 11; Banks *v.* McDivitt, 13 Blatchf. (U. S.) 163; Lawrence *v.* Cupples, 9 U. S. Pat. Off. Gaz. 254; Lawrence *v.* Dana, 2 Am. L. T. R. N. S. 402; Farmer *v.* Calvert Lith. Engr. & Map. Pub. Co., 5 Am. L. T. R. 168; Webb *v.* Powers, 2 Woodb. & M. (U. S.) 497; Emerson *v.* Davies, 3 Story (U. S.), 768; Greene *v.* Bishop, 1 Cliff. (U. S.) 186; Jarrold *v.* Houlston, 3 K. & J. 708; Pike *v.* Nicholas L. R. 5 Ch. 251; Murray *v.* Bogue, 1 Drew, 353; Spiers *v.* Brown, 6 W. R. 352; Mack *v.* Petter, (*d*) *Abridgments.* — An abridgment of a literary work may be copyrighted when the abridgment does not consist merely in the omission of some of its parts, and the copying of the others.[1]

(*e*) *Law Reports.* — The reporter has a lawful right to a copyright on all original matter prepared by him, as head-notes, foot-notes, statements of facts, abstracts of the briefs of counsel, etc. But he is not entitled to copyright on matter of which he is not the author, as the opinion of the court, head-notes prepared by the court, etc.[2]

L. R. 14 Eq. 431; Barfield *v.* Nicholson, 2 Sim. & S. 1.

A mere copy of old matter without any new arrangement is not a compilation which may be copyrighted. Hedderwick *v.* Griffin, 3 Sc. Sess. Cas. 2d ser. 383; Rundell *v.* Murray, Jac. 314; Jollie *v.* Jaques, 1 Blatchf. (U. S.) 618; Boucicault *v.* Fox, 5 Blatchf. (U. S.) 87, 101.

No copyright can be had in the old matter independent from the arrangement; but where such matter has been abridged, digested, revised, or translated, an independent copyright will vest in it. Lawrence *v.* Dana, 2 Am. L. T. R. (N. S.) 402.

Valuable selections of poems or prose compositions are sometimes made and arranged with reference to their subject-matter; proverbs, quotations, etc., may be compiled so as to form useful collections; hymns may be selected and classified with a view to their use on appropriate occasions. Compilations of this kind may have a material value, due to the choice and arrangements of the selections, and in such case there seems to be no reason why they may not be proper subjects of copyright. Drone on Copyright, pp. 157, 158; citing Rundell *v.* Murray, Jac. 314; Marzials *v.* Gibbons, L. R. 9 Ch. 518.

1. Folsom *v.* Marsh, 2 Story (U. S.), 100; Gray *v.* Russell, 1 Story (U. S.), 11; Story *v.* Holcombe, 4 McLean (U. S.), 306; Lawrence *v.* Dana, 4 Cliff. (U. S.) 1; Greene *v.* Bishop, 1 Cliff. (U. S.) 186; Dodsley *v.* Kinnersley, Ambler, 403; Whittingham *v.* Wooler, 2 Swanst. 428; Tonson *v.* Walker, 3 Swanst. 672; Gyles *v.* Wilcox, 2 Atk. 141; Newberry's Case, Lofft. 775; Campbell *v.* Scott, 11 Sim. 38.

A digest of a work may be copyrighted. Sweet *v.* Benning, 16 C. B. 459.

2. Wheaton *v.* Peters, 8 Pet. (U. S.) 591; Myers *v.* Callaghan, 5 Fed. Rep. 726; 20 Fed. Rep. 441; Backus *v.* Gould, 7 How. (U. S.) 798; Banks *v.* Manchester, 23 Fed. Rep. 143; Little *v.* Gould, 2 Blatchf. (U. S.) 165; Banks *v.* McDivitt, 13 Blatchf. (U. S.) 163; Chase *v.* Sanborn, 6 U. S. Pat. Off. Gaz. 932; Little *v.* Hall, 18 How. (U. S.) 165; Butterworth *v.* Robinson, 5 Ves. 709; Saunders *v.* Smith, 3 My. & Cr. 711; Sweet *v.* Shaw, 3 Jur. 217; Sweet *v.* Benning, 16 C. B. 459.

A reporter employed with the understanding that the exclusive property, in the result of his labors, shall be in the State, is not entitled to a copyright even on his own production. Little *v.* Gould, 2 Blatchf. (U. S.) 165.

Neither a reporter nor a judge can have any copyright in the judicial decisions. The copyright to these decisions belongs to the State, who, however, usually waives this right, either by publishing without complying with the statute or by constitutional provision. See Drone on Copyright, pp. 161, 162; Wheaton *v.* Peters, 8 Pet. (U. S.) 591; Little *v.* Gould, 2 Blatchf. (U. S.) 165; Chase *v.* Sanborn, 6 U. S. Pat. Off. Gaz. 932. *Compare* Banks *v.* West Publ. Co., 27 Fed. Rep. 50.

The same principle holds good for public documents and statutes. Drone on Copyright, 164; Davidson *v.* Wheelock, 27 Fed. Rep. 61.

The statutes of Ohio authorize the publication of the reports of the Supreme Court, and of the Supreme Court commission, of the State, (1) under the direction of the supervisor of public printing; or (2) under a contract made by the Secretary of State. The official reporter, who receives from the State a fixed salary for his services, is required to secure a copyright for "each volume of the reports" published under the first method. The statute provides, that when the reports are published under the second method, the contractor "shall have the sole and exclusive right to publish such reports, so far as the State can confer the same," but imposes no requirement upon the reporter to secure copyright. No authority is given anywhere in the statutes to copyright the opinions of the judges. Advance sheets of volumes, included in the complainants' contract with the Secretary of State, were copyrighted by the reporter for the benefit of the State and of the complainants. The respondents published the opinions, *syllabi*, and statements of cases prepared by the judges, and contained in said advance sheets. *Held*, that the copyrights secured do not cover the matter pub-

(*f*) *Advertisements.* — There can be no copyright in advertisements as such. Publications which could otherwise not be copyrighted, as not possessing the essential qualities required for a copyright, cannot be copyrighted because they are used as advertisements. But such matter in an advertisement which is duly entitled to be copyrighted may be protected.[1]

(*g*) *Newspapers.* — There is no valid reason why newspapers, magazines, and other periodicals should not be copyrighted, although in the case of newspapers it is almost impracticable, and in practice not done.[2]

(*h*) *Musical and Dramatic Compositions* are covered by the statute, and this includes dramatizations, translations, and adaptations.[3]

lished by the respondent. The reporter might, in this case, copyright the volumes for the benefit of the complainants and of the State, but such copyright would protect only the portion of the volumes prepared by the reporter. Banks *v.* Manchester, 23 Fed. Rep. 143; Banks *v.* West Publ. Co., 27 Fed. Rep. 50.

1. Drone on Copyright, pp. 164 *et seq.*

An advertising card devised for the purpose of displaying paints of various colors, consisting of a sheet of paper having attached thereto square bits of paper painted in various colors, each square having a different color, with some lithographic work surrounding the squares advertising the sale of the colors, is neither a chart, map, print, cut, engraving, nor book within the meaning of the statute, and not the subject of a copyright. The exclusive right to employ a particular method of advertising wares cannot be acquired under the copyright laws. Ehret *v.* Pierce, 10 Fed. Rep. 553. See Collender *v.* Griffiths, 11 Blatchf. (U. S.) 212.

A chromo, if a meritorious work of art, may be copyrighted, though designed and used for gratuitous distribution as an advertisement for the purpose of attracting business. Yuengling *v.* Schile, 12 Fed. Rep. 97.

A painting only seven by four and a half inches in size, owned by a corporation, painted by an artist employed by the corporation from a design made by its president from a woodcut, may be copyrighted by the corporation. That such a painting could be readily lithographed, and used as an advertising label, will not affect the copyright. Schumacher *v.* Schwencke, 25 Fed. Rep. 466.

2. Drone on Copyright, 168, 170.

In England no one can have a copyright in newspapers. Cox *v.* Land & Water Journal Co., L. R. 9 Eq. 324; Platt *v.* Walter, 17 L. T. (N. S.) 159; Exp. Foss 2 De G., & J. 239.

3. Drone on Copyright, 175.

The copyright in musical compositions is more extensively protected than the copyright in dramatic pieces. Russell *v.* Smith, 15 Sim. 181.

The piano-forte score of an already existing opera, whether arranged by the composer himself or by another person, is the subject of copyright. Wood *v.* Boosey, 3 L. R. Q. B. 223; Atwill *v.* Ferrett, 2 Blatchf. (U. S.) 39; Carte *v.* Evans, 27 Fed. Rep. 861.

A person who writes words to an old air, and procures an accompaniment and publishes them together, is entitled to the copyright in the whole work. Leader *v.* Purday, 7 C. B. 4.

A party will be enjoined from using the title of a copyrighted dramatic composition, even for a composition entirely different from the one which was copyrighted. Shook *v.* Wood, 10 Phila. (Pa.) 373.

Charts, Photographs, etc. — The statute granting copyright protection to photographs and negatives thereof is not so clearly unconstitutional as to authorize the court at *nisi prius* to declare it invalid. Sarony *v.* Burrow-Giles Lith. Co., 17 Fed. Rep. 591; Schreiber *v.* Thornton, 17 Fed. Rep. 693.

Under the act of 1831 respecting copyrights, a photograph was not a subject of copyright. Wood *v.* Abbott, 5 Blatchf. (U. S.) 325.

The word "chart," as used in the copyright law, does not include sheets of paper exhibiting tabulated or methodically arranged information. Taylor *v.* Gilman, 24 Fed. Rep. 632. See CHART (vol. 3).

Plays. — The exclusive right to perform a play may also be secured by copyright. Rev. Stat. U. S. § 4966. Boucicault *v.* Hart, 13 Blatchf. (U. S.) 47; Daly *v.* Palmer, 6 Blatchf. (U. S.) 256; Boucicault *v.* Fox, 5 Blatchf. (U. S.) 87; Roberts *v.* Myers, 13 Month. L. Rep. 396.

4. Quality of Publications. — (*a*) *Indecent Publications.* — Publications which are of an indecent character, or otherwise have a tendency to disturb the public peace, corrupt morals, or libel individuals, are not protected by copyright.[1]

(*b*) *Originality.* — A work need not be strictly original to have a claim to copyright. But although composed entirely or in part of old and common matter, original and independent work must have been bestowed upon it by the author. Where two authors write on the same subject, and use the same common materials, both will be entitled to a copyright. And even where the products of their efforts would be substantially alike, this would not be absolute proof that one was a mere copy from the other.[2]

(*c*) *Literary Merit.* — There is no standard of literary merit required by the statutes to which a publication should come up, to be entitled to a copyright. Even works of very little literary merit have been held to be entitled to copyright where they served to propagate useful knowledge, or gave general information.[3]

1. Drone on Copyright, 181; Martinetti *v.* Maguire, 1 Deady (U. S.), 223.

If a play or any literary production is of an immoral character, it is no part of the office of a court to protect it by injunction or otherwise. The rights of the author are secondary to the right of the public to be protected from what is subversive of good morals. Shook *v.* Daly, 49 How. Pr. (N. Y.) 366, 368.

2. See compilations (*post*). Blunt *v.* Patten, 2 Paine (U. S.), 393; Banks *v.* McDivitt, 13 Blatchf. (U. S.) 163; Lawrence *v.* Cupples, 9 U. S. Pat Off. Gaz. 254; Farmer *v.* Calvert Lith. Engr. & Map Publ. Co., 1 Flipp. (U. S.) 228; Reed *v.* Carnsi, Tan., Dec. 72; Benn *v.* Le Clercq, 18 Int. Rev. Rec. 94; Gray *v.* Russell, 1 Story (U. S.), 11; Webb *v.* Powers, 2 Woodb. & M. (U. S.) 497; Lawrence *v.* Dana, 2 Am. L. T. R. N. S. 402, Greene *v.* Bishop, 1 Cliff. (U. S.) 186; Emerson *v.* Davies, 3 Story (U. S.), 768; Story *v.* Holcombe, 4 McLean (U. S.), 309; Barfield *v.* Nicholson, 2 Sim. & S. 1; Murray *v.* Bogue, 1 Drew 353; Spiers *v.* Brown, 6 W. R. 352; Pike *v.* Nicholas, L. R. 5 Ch. 251; Jeffrys *v.* Boosey, 4 H. L. Cas. 869.

A party, to be entitled to a copyright, must show that he is the author of the work, or that his title is derived from one sustaining that relation to the publication. Greene *v.* Bishop, 1 Cliff. (U. S.) 186.

One who deposits for copyright the title of a dramatic composition, which title is not original with him, cannot secure by such deposition the exclusive right to the title where it has already been applied to another dramatic composition founded on the same story. Benn *v.* Le Clerq, 18 Int. Rev. Rec. 94.

In music, not only new compositions, but any substantially new adaptation of an old piece, as an arrangement for the piano of a quadrille, waltz, etc., constitutes a valid claim. Schuberth *v.* Shaw, 19 Am. L. Reg. (N. S.) 248; Atwill *v.* Ferrett, 2 Blatchf. (U. S.) 39; Jollie *v.* Jaques, 1 Blatchf. (U. S.) 618.

But where an imported piece is simply transposed or differently arranged and adapted, no copyright will attach to it. Jollie *v.* Jaques, 1 Blatchf. (U. S.) 618.

In an action to recover the penalties provided by statute, the defendant may show in defence that the music was not original, that it was an abbreviation or alteration. Millett *v.* Snowden, 1 West. L. J. 240.

3. Drone on Copyright, 208 *et seq.* Scoville *v.* Toland, 6 West. L. J. 84; Coffeen *v.* Brunton, 4 McLean (U. S.), 516; Collender *v.* Griffiths, 11 Blatchf. (U. S.) 211; Maclean *v.* Moody, 20 Sc. Sess. 2d ser. 1163; Page *v.* Wisden, 20 L. T. (N. S.) 435.

A mere daily or weekly price-current has been held not to be subject to copyright. Clayton *v.* Stone, 2 Paine (U. S.), 382. *Compare* Kiernan *v.* Manhattan Quotation Tel. Co., 50 How. Pr. (N. Y.) 194.

A diagram, with directions for cutting ladies' garments, was held to be a subject for copyright. Drury *v.* Ewing, 1 Bond (U. S.), 540.

But prints of balloons and hanging baskets, with printing on them for embroidery, and cutting lines showing how the paper may be cut and joined to make the different parts fit together, and not intended as a mere pictorial representation of something, are not copyrightable. Rosenbach *v.* Dreyfuss, 2 Fed. Rep. 217.

5. Duration of Copyright. — A work protected by copyright is protected for twenty-eight years after the filing of the titlepage in the librarian's office; but such copyright may be extended for an additional term of fourteen years upon compliance with the requirements of the statute.[1]

6. Who entitled to Copyright. — (*a*) *Authors and Proprietors who are Citizens or Residents.* — The Statutes of the United States entitle to copyrights only authors or proprietors who are "citizens of the United States or residents therein." And with the exception of paintings, drawings, chromos, statues, statuary, models or designs, the statutes require not only that the party securing the copyright should be a citizen or resident of the United States, but also that the work should be a production of a party a citizen or resident. In case of death of the author, his executors or administrators succeed to his rights.[2]

(*b*) *Assignees.* — Not only the author has a right to protect his works by copyright, but this protection extends to his assignees;

The representation of a dramatic composition can only be enjoined by the one who has a literary property in it. A mere spectacle or arrangement of scenic effects, having no literary character, cannot be so enjoined. Martinetti *v.* Maguire, 1 Abb. (U. S.) 356.

1. Rev. Stat. U. S. §§ 4953, 4954.

The statute specifically provides that the renewal shall be for the benefit of the author if living, or for his widow and children if dead. Rev. Stat. U. S § 4954; Pierpont *v.* Fowle, 2 Woodb. & M. (U. S.) 41.

2. Rev. Stat. U. S. §§ 4952, 4971.

Although in section 4971 of the Revised Statutes of the United States, which provides that "nothing in this chapter shall be construed to prohibit the printing, publishing, importation, or sale of any book, map, chart, dramatic or musical composition, print, cut, engraving, or photograph, written, composed, or made by any person not a citizen of the United States nor resident therein," "paintings, drawings, chromos, statues, statuary, and models" have been omitted, the court held in Yuengling *v.* Schile, 12 Fed. Rep. 97, that such omission was probably accidental; that, holding that the owner of such "paintings, drawings, chromos, statues, statuary, and models," may be entitled to a copyright, although the artist or author was a non-resident alien, would be against the policy of the copyright law to protect American artists and authors only; and that the owners referred to are the purchasers of "such" map, chart, book, or books; i. e., of the works of resident authors only.

Congress refused repeatedly to grant protection to works of foreign authors, and in every copyright statute passed since the formation of the government has emphatically declared that such works are legitimate subjects of piracy. Drone on Copyright, 95. For an oversight of the efforts made in the United States to secure an international copyright, see the same work, pp. 92–96.

In the case of a work of which a citizen and a foreigner are joint authors, there is nothing to prevent a valid copyright from vesting in that part of which the former is the author, provided this can be separated from that written by the foreign author. If the parts cannot be separated, it would seem that copyright will not vest in any of it. Drone on Copyright, 232.

The question of residence is a mixed question of law and fact. It is not to be determined by the length of time a party remains in the country, nor by the fact whether he occupies his own house, or is merely a boarder or a lodger in the house of another, but by the intention existing in the mind of the person coupled with acts, which acts and intent are to indicate whether or not he is a resident of the place. Boucicault *v.* Wood, 2 Biss. (U. S.) 34.

Filing a declaration of intentions to become a citizen of the United States, does not make a party a resident. Carey *v.* Collier, 56 Nile's Reg. 262.

A chromo-lithograph, as in this case a highly and artistically colored picture of Gambrinus, used for the advertisement of lager beer, is nothing but a lithographic "print," and therefore is not excepted from the requirement of the statute that the author of such picture must be a citizen or resident of the United States, to entitle its owner to a copyright. Yuengling *v.* Schile, 12 Fed. Rep. 97, 107.

and it is not necessary that the copyright should be secured before assignment. The assignee of an unpublished work can secure a copyright in his own name as proprietor.[1]

1. U. S. Rev. Stat. § 4982; Paige *v.* Banks, 13 Wall. (U. S.) 608; Cowen *v.* Banks, 24 How. Pr. (N. Y.) 72; Lawrence Dana, 2 Am. L. T. R. N. S. 402; Folsom *v.* Marsh, 2 Story (U. S.), 100; Little *v.* Gould, 2 Blatchf. (U. S.) 165, 362; Pulte *v.* Derby, 5 McLean (U. S.), 328.

The form of assignment of a copyright is regulated by statute; but the form of assignment of a manuscript before copyright was obtained, and before publication, is regulated by the common law. So a manuscript otherwise subject to copyright may be copyrighted by an assignee under a common law assignment. U. S. Rev. Stat. § 4955; Little *v.* Gould, 2 Blatchf. (U. S.) 165; Lawrence *v.* Dana, 2 Am. L. T. R. N. S. 402; Carte *v.* Evans, 27 Fed. Rep. 861, 863.

A non-resident alien is not within our copyright law, but he may take and hold by assignment a copyright granted to one of our own citizens. Carte *v.* Evans, 27 Fed. Rep. 861, 863.

Employers and Employees. — It will depend on the terms of the agreement between a publisher and an author employed by him, whether the latter has a copyright in his works, or whether such copyright belongs to the former. The mere fact of employment does not vest the title to it in the publisher. Where there is an express agreement, the terms of the agreement determine the fact; and where there is no express agreement, the intention of the parties may be determined by the attending circumstances. Little *v.* Gould, 2 Blatchf. (U. S.) 165; Lawrence *v.* Dana, 2 Am. L. T. R. N. S. 402; Heine *v.* Appleton, 4 Blatchf. (U. S.) 125; Keene *v.* Wheatley, 4 Phila. (Pa.) 157; also 9 Am. Law Reg. 33; Boucicault *v.* Fox, 5 Blatchf. (U. S.) 87; Sweet *v.* Benning, 16 C. B. 459; Bishop of Hereford *v.* Griffin, 16 Sim. 190; Shepherd *v.* Conquest, 17 C. B. 427; Levi *v.* Rutley, L. R. 6 C. P. 523. *Compare* Pierpont *v.* Fowle, 2 Woodb. & M. (U. S.) 23, 46; Atwill *v.* Ferrett, 2 Blatchf. (U. S.) 39; Binns *v.* Woodruff, 2 Wash. (U. S.) 48.

N., under the employment of the Illinois Cent. R. Co., compiled a work entitled "Battles for the Union," etc. It was copyrighted in the name of H., the general passenger agent of the company. In an action by H. to restrain the publication by J., *held*, that an action for the infringement of a copyright may be maintained by the holder of the legal title thereof, though the beneficial ownership be in another. Hanson *v.* Jaccard Jewelry Co., 32 Fed. Rep. 202.

Whether paid writers for a periodical, magazine, or cyclopædia can have a copyright in their articles so as to prevent the publishers from publishing them in any other form but in the periodical for which they are written, depends also on their implied or express contract. Sweet *v.* Benning, 16 C. B. 459; Bishop of Hereford *v.* Griffin, 16 Sim. 190.

Although the copyright vests in the name of the party who takes it out, he may hold it in trust for the legal owner; and, where it does belong to another, a court of equity may compel an assignment. Lawrence *v.* Dana, 2 Am. L. T. N. S. 402; Little *v.* Gould, 2 Blatchf. (U. S.) 165; Pulte *v.* Derby, 5 McLean (U. S.), 328; Hazlitt *v.* Templeman, 13 L. T. N. S. 595.

An agreement between an author and an employer, the owner of a theatre, to write a play for him, which was to be represented at the theatre as long as it should draw, does not prevent the author from taking out a copyright in his own name. Such a contract is but a license to represent the play, and not an assignment. Roberts *v.* Myers, 13 Law Rep. N. S. 396.

An engraver in the employ of the government can have no copyright in a chart prepared for the government. Copyright 7 Op. Att'y Gen. 656.

One who merely employs another to design and execute a work of art for him, is not entitled to a copyright. Binns *v.* Woodruff, 4 Wash. (U. S.) 48; and see Atwill *v.* Ferrett, 2 Blatchf. (U. S.) 39.

Plaintiff engaged his services to defendant for a period of ten years as an author and inventor, and stipulated that the property in his productions should belong exclusively to defendant, including his time and services, in consideration of $5,000, to be paid to him annually, and certain other contingent provisions as to compensation. *Held*, that such a contract, and the transfer to defendant made in pursuance thereof, invested defendant with the exclusive property in the play copyrighted, and in the patented invention of the plaintiff contemplated in the terms of the engagement or contract. In such a contract there is no condition precedent or subsequent which can be invoked to defeat defendant's title, or re-invest plaintiff with any interest in the property, nor can he interfere with defendant's use of the property by injunction, or against defendant's wishes to use them himself. Mackaye *v.* Mallory, 12 Fed. Rep. 328.

An artist who accompanied a government expedition to Japan, in the capacity of

7. How is a Copyright acquired. — (*a*) *Statutory Requirements.* — Before a copyright can be granted, the Revised Statutes of the United States require, 1st, That a printed copy of the title of the book or other article, or a description of the painting, drawing, chromo, statue, statuary, or a model or design for a work of the fine arts, for which any person desires a copyright, shall be delivered at the Office of the Librarian of Congress, or be deposited in the mail addressed to said librarian; 2d, That within ten days from the publication thereof he shall deliver at the same office, or deposit in the mail addressed to said librarian, two copies of such copyright book or other article, or in case of a painting, drawing, statue, statuary, model or design for a work of the fine arts, a photograph of the same; 3d, That such person shall give notice of the copyright, by inserting in the several copies of every edition published, on the titlepage, or the page immediately following, if it be a book, or if a map, chart, musical composition, print, cut, engraving, photograph, painting, drawing, chromo, statue, statuary, or model or design intended to be perfected and completed as a work of the fine arts, by inscribing upon some portion of the face or front thereof, or on the face of the substance on which the same shall be mounted, the following words: "Entered according to Act of Congress, in the year , by A. B., in the Office of the Librarian of Congress at Washington."[1]

master's mate, and with the understanding that all sketches and drawings he should make should belong to the government, has no right to a copyright on his sketches, drawings, and engravings. They had become the property of the government. Heine *v.* Appleton, 4 Blatchf. (U. S.) 125; Com. *v.* Desilver, 3 Phila. (Pa.) 31.

An author who gratuitously furnishes to a widow annotations for a new edition of a work written by her husband, under an agreement that the copyright in the notes should afterward belong to him, may compel the widow in a court of equity to assign to him her interest in the copyright of the notes which she had taken out. Lawrence *v.* Dana, 4 Cliff. (U. S.) 1.

1. Rev. Stat. of U. S. §§ 4956, 4962.

It is optional with the owner of the copyright to insert the copyright notice, using the form as prescribed in § 4962 of the Rev. Stat., or to use the word "copyright," together with the year the copyright was entered, and the name of the party by whom it was taken out. 18 U. S. Stat. at Large, 78.

§ 4959 of the same statutes requires that the copies to be delivered to the Librarian of Congress shall be two complete printed copies of the best edition issued. Merrell *v.* Tice, 14 Otto (U. S.), 557.

No valid copyright attaches unless all the requirements of the statute have been complied with. Parkinson *v.* Laselle, 3 Sawyer (U. S.), 333; Chicago Music Co. *v.* Butler Paper Co., 19 Fed. Rep. 758; Benn *v.* Le Clercq, 18 Int. Rev. Rec. 94; Carillo *v.* Shook, 22 Int. Rev. Rec. 152; Centennial Catalogue Co. *v.* Porter, 2 Weekly Notes of Cases, 601; King *v.* Force, 2 Cr. C. C. 208; Boucicault *v.* Hart, 13 Blatchf. (U. S.) 47; Struve *v.* Schmedler, 4 Blatchf. (U. S.) 23; Marsh *v.* Warren, 4 Am. L. T. N. S. 126; Baker *v.* Taylor, 2 Blatchf. (U. S.) 82; Wheaton *v.* Peters, 8 Pet. (U. S.) 591; Chase *v.* Sanborn, 6 U. S. Pat. Off. Gaz. 932; Boucicault *v.* Wood, 2 Biss. (U. S.) 34; Lawrence *v.* Dana, 4 Cliff. (U. S.) 1. *Compare* Dwight *v.* Appleton, 1 N. Y. Leg. Obs. 195.

Although a copyright is not perfect until all the requirements are complied with, by taking the incipient step a right is acquired which chancery will protect until the other acts may be done. Pulte *v.* Derby, 5 McLean (U. S.), 328.

The publication must, however, follow the filing of the titlepage within a reasonable time. Boucicault *v.* Hart, 13 Blatchf. (U. S.) 47. *Compare* Farmer *v.* Calvert Lith. Engr. & Map Publ. Co, 1 Flipp. (U. S.) 228.

The copies of a copyright work required by section 4959 of the Revised Statutes to be deposited with the Librarian of Congress within ten days after publication, may be so deposited after the printing of the work, and before its formal publication. Chapman v. Ferry, 18 Fed. Rep. 539.

A firm deposited in the office of the Librarian of Congress the title of a book, in the following words: "Over One Thousand Recipes. The Lake-Side Cook-Book; A Complete Manual of Practical, Economical, Palatable, and Healthful Cookery. Chicago: Donnelley, Loyd & Co." The title with which the book was published was, "The Lake-Side Cook-Book, No. 1, a Complete Manual of Practical, Economical and Palatable and Healthful Cookery. By N. A. D.,"—followed by the imprint of the place of publication and the name of the proprietor, and the notice of the copyright on the titlepage. *Held*, that the variance was not material, and the title published was deposited in compliance with Rev. St. § 4956; Donnelley v. Ivers, 18 Fed. Rep. 592. See Carte v. Evans, 27 Fed. Rep. 861, 864.

The "printed" copy of the title of a book or other article, required by section 4956 of the Revised Statutes to be delivered or mailed to the Librarian of Congress, may be "printed" with a pen as well as type, with or without the aid of tracing-paper. Chapman v. Ferry, 18 Fed. Rep. 539.

When the required notice is plainly engraved on the plate from which a print is taken, within the line of a reasonable margin, and where it would not be covered when properly framed, it is impressed on the face within the meaning of the statute. Rossiter v. Hall, 5 Blatchf. (U. S.) 362.

The various provisions of law in relation to copyright should have a liberal construction, in order to give effect to what may be considered the inherent right of the author to his own work. Where a titlepage was deposited in January, 1867, and the notice stated, "entered, etc., in 1866," the court held that this was probably a mistake committed unintentionally, and did not invalidate the copyright. Myers v. Callaghan, 5 Fed. Rep. 726, 730. *Compare* Baker v. Taylor, 2 Blatchf. (U. S.) 82.

The object of inscribing upon copyright articles the word "copyright," with the year when the copyright was taken out, and the name of the party taking it out, is to give notice of the copyright to the public, to prevent a person from being punished who ignorantly and innocently reproduces the photograph without knowledge of the protecting copyright. Inserting in such a notice the initial of the Christian name and the full surname is a sufficient compliance with the law; it does not violate the letter of the law, and accomplishes its object. Sarony v. Burrow-Giles Lith. Co., 17 Fed. Rep. 591; 111 U. S. 53.

The only notice of copyright given in a printed book was the following, printed upon the page immediately following the titlepage: "Entered according to Act of Congress, in the Year 1878, by H. A. Jackson." *Held*, that the notice was not such a notice as required by the statute, and did not entitle the proprietor to maintain an action for infringement of copyright. Jackson v. Walkie, 29 Fed. Rep. 15.

An edition of a song was issued having a front cover, with an engraving thereon, and a list of seven songs, including the song in question, by a part of its title, over the name of the publisher, who claimed the copyright, and on the page where the music commenced the full title was printed, with the words, "Copyright, 1878," etc. *Held*, that this was a sufficient notice to the public of a claim of copyright, as required by act of Congress of 1874, § 1, and that there was no abandonment of the copyright. Blume v. Spear, 30 Fed. Rep. 629.

A. registered a copyright label in the Patent Office by the title of "Water-proof Drawing Ink," consisting of these words in one line, in an oblong formed of double lines, no notice of copyright or name of the owner being printed thereon, except by the words, "Registered, 3,693, 1883." *Held*, that, under the act of Congress of 1874, the label should at least have contained the word "copyright," with the year in which, and the person by whom, the copyright was taken out, instead of the statement of an entry in the office of the Librarian of Congress, as required by Rev. St. U. S. § 4962, in order to maintain a suit for infringement, and that a publication of such a defective notice was an abandonment of the copyright. Higgins v. Keuffel, 30 Fed. Rep. 627.

New editions of a copyrighted work are protected by the copyright on the first edition, when they contain no alterations or additions; but where they contain such improvements, alterations or additions, a new copyright must be taken out, and all the requirements of the statute again followed. Lawrence v. Dana, 2 Am. L. T. R. N. S. 402; Banks v. McDivitt, 13 Blatchf. (U. S.) 163; Farmer v. Calvert Lith. Engr. & Map Publ. Co., 5 Am. L. T. R. 168.

The original publication of the copyright need, in such a case, not be repeated in a succeeding edition, unless no new copyright is taken out. Lawrence v. Dana, 4 Cliff. (U. S.) 1. See Banks v. McDivitt, 13 Blatchf. (U. S.) 163.

Where a literary work consists of more than one volume, it has been held that the publication of the copyright need not occur in each volume. Dwight v. Appleton, 1 N. Y. Leg. Obs. 195.

Every person who shall insert or impress a copyright notice, or words of the same purport, in or upon any book, map, chart, (*b*) *By Assignment.* — A copyright may be acquired by assignment from the party who first took out the copyright. The statute provides that "copyrights shall be assignable in law by any instrument in writing, and such assignment shall be recorded in the office of the librarian within sixty days after its execution," in default of which it shall be void as to any subsequent purchaser or mortgagee for a valuable consideration without notice.[1]

musical composition, print, cut, engraving, or photograph, or other article for which he has not obtained a copyright, shall be liable to a penalty of one hundred dollars, for which, however, but one person can sue. Rev. Stat. U. S. § 4963; Ferrett *v.* Atwill, 1 Blatchf. (U. S.) 151.

To incur liability to the penalty, the notice must be printed on an article which may be copyrighted. Rosenbach *v.* Dreyfuss, 2 Fed. Rep. 217.

To secure a renewal of a copyright after the first term of twenty-eight years has expired, besides complying with the requirements of the statute, as in the case of an original copyright, within six months before the expiration of the term, a party trying to secure such renewal shall, within two months from the date of said renewal, cause a copy of the record thereof to be published in one or more newspapers printed in the United States for four weeks. Rev. Stat. U. S. § 4954; Wheaton *v.* Peters, 8 Pet. (U. S.) 591; Pierpont *v.* Fowle, 2 Wood. & M. 42.

1. Rev. Stat. U. S. § 4955; Webb *v.* Powers, 2 Wood. & M. (U. S.) 497; Pierpont *v.* Fowle, 2 Wood. & M. (U. S.) 42; Little *v.* Hall, 18 How. (U. S.) 165; Wheaton *v.* Peters, 8 Pet. (U. S.) 591.

In § 4964 it is required that the consent of the owner of a copyrighted work to make a reprint should be in writing, signed in the presence of two or more witnesses.

The word "manuscript," as used in the statute requiring the consent of the author or proprietor in writing, signed in the presence of two credible witnesses, to give the assignee the right to multiply and publish copies of the same, does not apply to pictures. A purchaser of a picture may acquire title to it by an oral contract with the lawful owner. Parton *v.* Prang, 3 Cliff. (U.S.) 537.

An agreement to assign an existing copyright may be by parol, and confers an equitable title. Gould *v.* Banks, 8 Wend. (N. Y.) 562; Lawrence *v.* Dana, 2 Am. L. T. R. N. S. 402; Carte *v.* Evans, 27 Fed. Rep. 861, 863.

Where one renders gratuitous services in editing a book for another, no written assignment is necessary to enable the one for whom the services are rendered to take out a copyright in his own name. Lawrence *v.* Dana, 4 Cliff. (U. S.) 1.

In case of bankruptcy, no written assignment between the bankrupt and his assignees seems to be necessary to effect a transfer of a copyright. *In re* Curry, 12 Ir. Eq. 391; Stevens *v.* Benning, 1 Kay & J. 168.

A sale of stereotype plates does not include a sale of the copyright attached to the work which may be printed with the plates, unless the intention of the parties also to sell the copyright is shown from the agreement or attending circumstances. Under a sale of such plates on execution, such copyright does not pass. Stevens *v.* Gladding, 17 How. (U. S.) 452; Stephens *v.* Cady, 14 How. (U. S.) 528, 531.

It seems that a copyright cannot be sold under execution, but the court may compel a transfer for the benefit of creditors. Stephens *v.* Cady, 14 How. (U. S.) 531; Cooper *v.* Gunn, 4 B. Monr. (Ky.) 594.

But where a copyright has been sold, the proceeds in the hands of the debtor may be attached. Cooper *v.* Gunn, 4 B. Monr. (Ky.) 594, 596.

An assignment of an existing copyright for twenty-eight years does not include an assignment of the renewal of the copyright for the additional term of fourteen years, unless specially expressed. Pierpont *v.* Fowle, 2 Woodb. & M. 41; Cowen *v.* Banks, 24 How. Pr. (N. Y.) 72.

It will be different where the assignment of the manuscript has been made before any copyright was taken out. In such a case an absolute right to the renewal will vest in the assignee. Pulte *v.* Derby, 5 McLean (U. S.), 328; Paige *v.* Banks, 7 Blatchf. (U. S.) 152; 13 Wall. (U. S.) 608.

To effect a valid assignment, the contract must be complete. Where plates, illustrations, and stamps were delivered to A., under an incomplete contract between him and B. for the sale of the same, together with a copyright on a book in the manufacture of which they were used, and $4,000 was paid as part consideration, and it was understood that a more definite contract was to be thereafter entered into, and reduced to writing, but B. refused to enter into a more definite contract, or comply with terms of the incomplete agreement, and proceeded to publish the book, *held*, 1st, that there was no assignment of the copyright; 2d, that B. was entitled to a

8. Infringement of Copyright. — (*a*) *Penalties.* — The statutes provide for the punishment of those who infringe upon the copyrights of others, by declaring that any person who shall unlawfully print, publish, or import, or sell, or expose for sale, any copy of a book, shall forfeit every copy thereof, and be liable in damages to the owner of the copyright; and in the case of maps, charts, musical compositions, prints, cuts, engravings, photographs, chromos, paintings, drawings, statues, statuary, and models or designs of articles of fine arts, the statutes provide a forfeiture of all the plates on which the same shall be copied, of every sheet thereof, either copied or printed, and one dollar for every sheet found in his possession; and in case of a painting, statue, or statuary, ten dollars for every copy of the same in his possession, or sold, or exposed for sale.[1]

return of the plates, etc., upon paying back to A. the $4,000 received with interest; and 3d, that under the peculiar circumstances of this case, B. was not entitled to damages or an accounting. Hubbard *v.* Thompson, 25 Fed. Rep. 188.

Part of the rights conferred by the statute may be assigned. Roberts *v.* Myers, 13 Monthly L. R. 396.

But the statutes of the United States do not expressly sanction transfers of limited local proprietorships of exclusive privileges. Such a transfer would operate as a mere license, and would be ineffectual as an assignment. Keene *v.* Wheatley, 4 Phila. (Pa.) 157; also 9 Am. Law Reg. 33.

Where A., the author of a work, before publication, conferred to a publisher the right to take out a copyright in his own name, and to print a thousand copies, paying A. a certain sum, and in case a new edition was needed, A. agreed to revise the edition, and that the publisher should sell as many copies as was called for, paying A. a certain amount per copy, *held*, that although the publishers were the lawful owners of the copyright, they could not transfer it, but that they could sell the plates, and transfer all their rights under the contract. Pulte *v.* Derby, 5 McLean (U. S.), 328.

Where a piano-forte arrangement of the orchestral score of an opera was made by a United States citizen with the consent of the non-resident foreign composers of the opera, and then transferred by him to a fellow-citizen, who procured a copyright which he assigned to a non-resident foreigner, acting as agent of the original composers of the opera, *held*, that there was nothing of evasion or violation of law, and that the assignee was entitled to the protection of the court against infringers. Carte *v.* Evans, 27 Fed. Rep. 861.

1. Rev. Stat. U. S. §§ 4965, 4966.

Similar punishment has been provided for the violation of the copyright of dramatic compositions, and for publishing any manuscript without consent of the author. Rev. Stat. U. S. §§ 4966, 4967.

Actions for forfeitures under the copyright laws must be brought within two years after the cause of action has arisen. Rev. Stat. U. S. § 4968.

Although in the case of "books," the statute uses the word "copy," it is settled that, when one book contains a substantial part of another, the former is, within the meaning of the law, "a copy" of the latter; and, although the courts may hold that the appropriation of an entire work is not necessary to subject the wrong-doer to the penalty of forfeiture, they may, on the other hand, hold that such penalty is not necessarily incurred by taking a part, though such part may be enough to amount to piracy, for which an action of damages will lie. In case of maps, charts, etc., the statute provides for damages and forfeitures in case of piracy of "the whole or in part." Drone on Copyright, pp. 488, 490.

In an action by several persons, being the proprietors of a duly copyrighted photograph, to recover, as well for the United States as for themselves, the penalty for infringement under the statute, it appeared that the defendant had caused lithographic copies of the photograph to be made, of which 14,800 were found in his possession or control. *Held*, that the defendant was liable to a penalty of one dollar for each copy so found in his possession or control. Schreiber *v.* Thornton, 17 Fed. Rep. 603.

The statute providing penalties and forfeiture for the infringement of a copyright is penal in its character, and must therefore be construed strictly. Where the agent of a firm published copies of a copyrighted photograph without the knowledge and consent of the members of the firm, although for the use of the firm, the firm was held not to be liable. Schreiber *v.* Sharpless, 6 (*b*) *What is an Infringement?*—It is not necessary that the whole, or even the larger portion, of a work should be taken in order to constitute an invasion of a copyright: if so much is taken that the value of the original is sensibly and materially diminished, or the labors of the original author are substantially, to an injurious extent, appropriated by another, such taking or appropriation is sufficient in point of law to maintain the suit.[1]

Fed. Rep. 175; Taylor *v.* Gilman, 24 Fed. Rep. 632.

An action for the penalty provided by the statute abates by the death of the defendant. Schreiber *v.* Sharpless, 17 Fed. Rep. 589; Exp. Schreiber, 3 Supr. C. Rep. 423.

The United States courts have exclusive jurisdiction of action, for an infringement of a copyright. Potter *v.* McPherson, 21 Hun (N. Y.), 559.

But a State court has jurisdiction of an action to determine the rights of the respective parties under an agreement by defendant with plaintiff for the exclusive right to have and perform a certain play. Widmer *v.* Greene, 56 How. Pr. (N. Y.) 91.

The penalty attached to an infringement of the copyright on maps, charts, etc., of one dollar for every sheet found in the possession of the offender, does not apply to sheets which have been in his possession. Backus *v.* Gould, 7 How. (U. S.) 798; Millett *v.* Snowden, 1 West. L. J. 230. *Compare* Dwight *v.* Appleton, 1 N. Y. Leg. Obs. 195.

The actual infringing prints can alone be recovered; and when the prints are out of the possession and beyond the control of the infringer, the proprietor of the copyright cannot recover of him their value in an action at law. Sarony *v.* Ehrich, 28 Fed. Rep. 79.

Vendors are liable for the sale of a book which invades the copyright of another, on the same principle, and for the same reasons, that the vendor of a machine or other mechanical structure in the case of patent rights is held liable for selling the manufactured article without the license or consent of the patentee. Greene *v.* Bishop, 1 Cliff. (U. S.) 186.

And in case of a copyrighted play, the vendor of a piratical copy is liable for a representation of the pirated play by the vendee. Daly *v.* Palmer, 6 Blatchf. (U. S.) 256.

Where the author of a book jointly with a firm of publishers took out a copyright on the book, and agreed to a division of territory in which each would have the exclusive right of sale, the publishers agreeing to supply the author with as many copies as he should need, at cost, and a difficulty afterward arose as to such cost, the author published himself an edition of the book, with some additions, and commenced to sell such edition in the territory allotted to the publishers. *Held*, that the contracts about the division of territory and the supply of copies were entirely distinct, and that, even if the publisher had violated his contract in regard to the supply, the author had no right to sell in the publisher's territory, either the original work or his own edition. Baldwin *v.* Baird, 25 Fed. Rep. 293.

In an action for penalties and forfeiture, for the breach of a copyright of certain chromos, the defendant cannot be compelled to produce in evidence his books of account, photographic plates, and copies of printed chromos. Johnson *v.* Donaldson, 3 Fed. Rep. 22; Atwill *v.* Ferrett, 2 Blatchf. (U. S.) 39; Chapman *v.* Ferry, 12 Fed. Rep. 693.

The penalties and forfeitures given by section 4965 of the Rev. St., for an infringement of a copyright, cannot be enforced in a suit in equity; and a prayer in a bill that the plate and unsold copies of a pirated map be delivered up to an officer of the court for cancellation and destruction, is demurrable, as asking for the enforcement of such forfeiture. Damages as well as profits may now be recovered in equity for an infringement of a patent, but not a copyright. Chapman *v.* Ferry, 12 Fed. Rep. 693; Stephens *v.* Cady, 2 Curt. (U. S.) 200; Stevens *v.* Gladding, 17 How. (U. S.) 453.

1. Greene *v.* Bishop, 1 Cliff. (U. S.) 186; Folsom *v.* Marsh, 2 Story (U. S.), 100; List Publ. Co. *v.* Keller, 30 Fed Rep. 772; Webb *v.* Powers, 2 Wood. & M. (U. S.) 514; Harper *v.* Shoppell, 26 Fed. Rep. 519.

A key, purporting to be for the use of teachers, to copyrighted text-books which contain an original method by which instruction in the English language is made interesting and effective by the use of sentences formed into diagrams under certain rules and principles of analysis, in which key are transcribed from the original works, diagrams, and also all the lesson-sentences arranged in diagrams according to said rules, is an infringement of the copyright. Reed *v.* Holliday, 19 Fed. Rep. 325.

Copying is not confined to literal repetition, but includes also the various modes in which the matter of any publications may be adopted, imitated, or transferred, with more or less colorable alterations, to disguise the piracy. Greene *v.* Bishop, 1 Cliff. (U. S.) 186; Lawrence *v.* Dana, 4 Cliff. (U. S.) 1; Emerson *v.* Davies, 3 Story (U. S.), 768.

It is of no consequence in what form the works of another are used; whether it be by a simple reprint, or by incorporating the whole, or a large portion thereof, in some larger work. Thus, if in one of the large encyclopædias of the present day, the whole or a large portion of a scientific treatise of another author should be incorporated, it would be just as much a piracy upon the copyright as if it were published in a single volume. Gray *v.* Russell, 1 Story (U. S.), 11.

The true test of piracy is to ascertain whether the defendant has in fact used the plan, arrangements, and illustrations of the plaintiff, as the model of his own book, with colorable alterations and variations only to disguise the use thereof; or whether his work is the result of his own labor, skill, and use of common materials and common sources of knowledge open to all men, and the resemblances are either accidental or arising from the nature of the subject. Emerson *v.* Davies, 3 Story (U. S.), 768.

Even if a work otherwise piratical be in some respects an improvement on the original work, it is still an infringement. Drury *v.* Ewing, 1 Bond (U. S.), 540.

If the parts which have been copied cannot be separated from those which are original, without destroying the use and value of the original matter, he who has made an improper use of that which did not belong to him must suffer the consequences of so doing. Emerson *v.* Davies, 3 Story (U. S.), 768; Lawrence *v.* Dana, 4 Cliff. (U. S.) 1.

But where, in such a case, the infringement is slight, and an injunction prohibiting the further sale of the book should be disproportionate and unjust, a suit at law for damages will be the more equitable remedy. Webb *v.* Powers, 2 Woodb. & M. (U. S.) 497; Greene *v.* Bishop, 1 Cliff. (U. S.) 186, 203.

The same principle which holds good in regard to books is applied to maps, charts, pictures, musical compositions, etc. The test is not whether the piratical production is an exact copy of the original, but whether it is substantially copied. A copy is that which comes so near to the original as to give to every person seeing it the idea created by the original. Farmer *v.* Calvert Lith. Engr. & Map. Publ. Co., 1 Flipp. (U. S.) 228; Blunt *v.* Patten, 2 Paine (U. S.), 393; Drury *v.* Ewing, 1 Bond (U. S.), 540; Emerson *v.* Davies, 3 Story (U. S.), 768; West *v.* Francis, 5 Barn. & Ald. 743.

Copying by means of photography is covered by the provision of the statutes. Rossiter *v.* Hall, 5 Blatchf. (U. S.) 362.

It is difficult to say, in some cases, what constitutes an infringement of the copyright of a map; but where the subsequent map appears to have been substantially copied from the prior one, without alteration or revision, except in scale and color, there is clearly an infringement, which authorizes a court of equity to enjoin the sale of such infringing map, and to require the publisher to account for the profits arising from the sale thereof. Chapman *v.* Ferry, 18 Fed. Rep. 539.

In the case of music, it is said that piracy substantially exists where the appropriated music, though adapted to a different purpose from that of the original, may still be recognized by the ear. The adding of variations makes no difference in the principle. D'Almaine *v.* Boosey, 1 Y. & C. Exch. 302; Daly *v.* Palmer, 6 Blatchf. (U. S.) 269. See also Reed *v.* Carnsi, Taney (U. S.), 72.

Republishing a copyrighted piece of music with slight omissions or alterations, does not prevent such publishing from being piratical. Neither will the fact that the words of a ballad are not original with the composer of the music authorize a piratical publication of such music. Millett *v.* Snowden, 1 West. L. J. 240.

A written work, consisting wholly of directions set in order for conveying the ideas of the author on a stage or public place, by means of characters who represent the narrative wholly by action, is a dramatic composition which may be protected by copyright. Such copyright is infringed by the representation of a substantially identical scene, if the appropriated series of events, when represented on the stage, although performed by new and different characters, using different language, is recognized by the spectator through any of the senses to which the representation is addressed, as conveying substantially the same impressions to, and exciting the same emotions in, the mind in the same sequence or order. Daly *v.* Palmer, 6 Blatchf. (U. S.) 256.

One who secures a copyright on a dramatic composition secures only the result of his own intellectual efforts. He cannot prevent others from composing a dramatic composition on the same subject, as long as they also only use their own intellectual powers. Benn *v.* Le Clercq, 18 Int. Rev. Rec. 94.

A copyright for a design for playing-cards may be infringed by the manufacture of cards strikingly similar to the copyrighted design in its main and distinctive features, although the cards manufactured differ from the copyrighted design in other particulars. Richardson *v.* Miller, 12 Pat. Off. Gaz. 3.

(c) *Proof of Infringement.* — Where infringement of a copyright is charged, the burden of proof is on the party making the charge; but where there is no direct proof on either side, it is upon the defendant to negative and explain any circumstantial evidence tending to show that an unlawful use has been made of the copyrighted book.[1]

Copying a copyrighted engraving by means of photography is an infringement of the copyright. Rossiter *v.* Hall, 5 Blatchf. (U. S.) 362.

The publication and sale of chromos designed from a picture found in a foreign publication do not constitute a breach of copyright of similar chromos, where such copyright was obtained after the circulation of such foreign publication, where the defendant did not avail himself either directly or indirectly of the plaintiff's production. Johnson *v.* Donaldson, 3 Fed. Rep. 22.

A book may in one part infringe the copyright of another book, and in other parts be no infringement; and in such a case the damages will not be extended beyond the injury. Story *v.* Holcombe, 4 McLean (U. S.), 306; Greene *v.* Bishop, 1 Cliff. (U. S.) 186; Emerson *v.* Davies, 3 Story (U. S.), 768.

1. Lawrence *v.* Dana, 4 Cliff. (U. S.) 1.

Clerical and typographical errors and peculiarities, including special translations from the original work, reproduced in the work complained of; coincidence of citation, as where authorities are cited in the same way by volume and page, or by chapter and section, and from the same edition of the work, and from the same place; identity in the plan and arrangement of the notes, and in the mode of combining and connecting the same with the text, — are strong circumstantial evidence which should be negatived or explained by the defendant. Lawrence *v.* Dana, 4 Cliff. (U. S.) 1. See also Blunt *v.* Patten, 2 Paine (U. S.), 393; List Publ. Co. *v.* Keller, 30 Fed. Rep. 772.

Where two authors, each preparing a work of the same character, as the map of the same State or county, and both make use of the same common source of information, the two works will be alike if correct, still there will be no infringement. Neither one of them will have the right, however, to avail himself of the enterprise, labor, and expense of the other in the ascertainment of those materials, and the combining and arrangement of them, and the representing them on paper, without being guilty of piracy. Farmer *v.* Calvert Lith. Engr. & Map Publ. Co., 1 Flipp. (U. S.) 228. See Bullinger *v.* Mackey, 15 Blatchf. (U. S.) 550.

In an action under the copyright laws, it is for the plaintiff to show his title to the copyright; but where the validity of the copyright is disputed, the burden of proof that the copyright is invalid is on the defendant. Chase *v.* Sanborn, 6 U. S. Pat. Off. Gaz. 933; Yuengling *v.* Schile, 12 Fed. Rep. 97; Parkinson *v.* Laselle, 3 Sawyer (U. S.), 330; Chicago Music Co. *v.* Butler Paper Co., 19 Fed. Rep. 758; Shook *v.* Rankin, 6 Biss. (U. S.) 477; Little *v.* Gould, 2 Blatchf. (U. S.) 165; Reed *v.* Carusi, Taney, 74; Rosenbach *v.* Dreyfuss, 2 Fed. Rep. 217; 2 Story Eq. Jur. (13th ed.) § 936, n. 5.

Where it is proved that the party claiming a copyright for a song, deposited two copies in the mail, and got a receipt from the Librarian of Congress acknowledging the receipt of two copies of the publication by its title in full, with the date over the official signature of the librarian, this will be considered evidence that two copies were delivered to the librarian as required by the act of Congress. Blume *v.* Spear, 30 Fed. Rep. 629.

In a court of equity it is, however, not necessary that a valid legal title to the copyright be established by the plaintiff. An equitable title to the copyright is sufficient to give him a cause of action in equity. Little *v.* Gould, 2 Blatchf. (U. S.) 165; Lawrence *v.* Dana, 4 Cliff. (U. S.) 1; Pulte *v.* Derby, 5 McLean (U. S.), 328.

Where the owner of a copyright either expressly or impliedly consents to an infringement of his copyright, as where in the employ of the defendant he assists in the publication without objecting to it, he will not be entitled to the copyright afterward. Heine *v.* Appleton, 4 Blatchf. (U. S.) 125. *Compare* Boucicault *v.* Fox, 5 Blatchf. (U. S.) 87.

Although no action for forfeiture under the statute can be maintained unless within two years after the cause of action has accrued, such restriction is not laid upon the right to bring an action in equity. Where the complainant is not guilty of laches, his suit will not be barred. Greene *v.* Bishop, 1 Cliff. (U. S.) 186; Boucicault *v.* Wood, 2 Biss. (U. S.) 34.

Judgment entered in a former action against a lithograph company, by whom prints were printed for an infringer of a copyright, is a bar to further recovery by the proprietor of the copyright in an action against the infringer for the value of the prints. Sarony *v.* Ehrich, 28 Fed. Rep. 79.

(*d*) *Fair Use.*—Although a copyrighted book cannot be copied, either as a whole or substantially, still a "*fair use*" of the book, as by quotations for criticism and review, etc., is not prohibited. What is such a "*fair use*" is not defined by the statutes, but must be decided by principles of law and equity as expressed in the decisions of the courts.[1]

1. A reviewer may fairly cite largely from the original work, if his design be really and truly to use the passages for the purpose of fair and reasonable criticism. Folsom *v.* Marsh, 2 Story (U. S.), 100; Harper *v.* Shoppell, 26 Fed. Rep. 519.

Extracts made for a review, or for a compilation, cannot be so extended in either case as to convey the same knowledge as the original work, nor can the privilege be so exercised as to supersede the original book. Story *v* Holcombe, 4 McLean (U. S.), 306; Greene *v.* Bishop, 1 Cliff. (U. S.) 186; Brammell *v.* Halcomb, 3 My. & Cr. 738; Folsom *v.* Marsh, 2 Story (U. S.), 100.

The privilege of fair use accorded to a subsequent writer must be such, and such only, as will not cause substantial injury to the proprietor of the first publication. Lawrence *v.* Dana, 4 Cliff. (U. S.) 1. See Webb *v.* Powers, 2 Woodb. & M. (U. S.) 497.

To ascertain whether the copying from a copyrighted work amounts to piracy or to "fair use," the court looks at the value more than at the quantity taken. Farmer *v.* Calvert Lith. Engr. & Map Publ. Co., 1 Flipp. (U. S.) 228; Gray *v.* Russell, 1 Story (U. S.), 11.

No man is entitled to avail himself of the previous labors of another, for the purpose of conveying to the public the same information, even though he may append additional information to that already published. Lawrence *v.* Dana, 4 Cliff. (U. S.) 1; Wheaton *v.* Peters, 8 Pet. (U. S.) 591; Scott *v.* Stanford, L. R 3 Eq. 724; Gray *v.* Russell, 1 Story (U. S.), 11.

Mere honest intention on the part of the one who infringes on a copyright will be no excuse, as the courts can look only at the result, and he must be presumed to intend all that the publication of his work effects. But evidence of innocent intention may have a bearing upon the question of "fair use;" and where it appeared that the amount taken was small, it would doubtless have some probative force in a court of equity in determining whether an application for an injunction should be granted or refused. It can, however, not be admitted that it is a legal defence where it appears that the party setting it up has invaded a copyright. Lawrence *v.* Dana, 4 Cliff. (U. S.) 1; Reed *v.* Holliday, 19 Fed. Rep. 325; Webb *v.* Powers, 2 Woodb. & M. (U. S.) 524; Story *v.* Holcombe, 4 McLean (U. S.), 306; Millett *v.* Snowden, 1 West. L. J. 240; Scott *v.* Stanford, L. R. 3 Eq. 723; Reade *v.* Lacy, 1 Johns. & H. 526; Cary *v.* Faden, 5 Ves. 23.

One who makes a plate from which a copy of a picture in an illustrated paper, that is copyrighted, can be produced, and sells the plate to another without intending or even expecting that it was to be used in competition with owner of the picture, is not guilty of infringement of the copyright. Harper *v.* Shoppell, 26 Fed. Rep. 519; and see Harper *v.* Shoppell, 28 Fed. Rep 613.

The rule appears now to be settled that the compiler of a work in which absolute originality is of necessity excluded, is entitled, without exposing himself to a charge of piracy, to make use of preceding works upon the subject, where he bestows such mental labor upon what he has taken, and subjects it to such revision and correction, as to produce an original result; provided, that he does not deny the use made of such preceding works, and the alterations are not merely colorable. Copinger's Law of Copyright, 91; Farmer *v.* Calvert Lith. Engr. & Map Publ. Co, 1 Flipp. (U. S.) 228. See also Banks *v.* McDivitt, 13 Blatchf. (U. S.) 163.

The law of copyright only requires a subsequent compiler of a directory to do for himself that which the first compiler has done. Where the commercial value of two society directories depends upon the judgment of the authors in the selection of names of persons of a certain social standing, each directory is original to the extent that the selection is original. Where the compiler of such directory uses a previous directory of the same character, to save himself the trouble of making an independent selection of the persons listed, though only to a very limited extent, he infringes the first compiler's copyright; but he may use the first compiler's book for the purpose of verifying the orthography of the names, or the correctness of the addresses, of the persons selected. List Publ. Co. *v.* Keller, 30 Fed. Rep. 772.

A publisher of a copyrighted series of maps of the city of New York has no exclusive right to the arbitrary signs used on his maps so as to prevent others to use the same signs on a series of maps for Philadelphia. Perris *v.* Hexamer, 9 Otto (U. S.), 674.

9. Injunctions. — (*a*) *Temporary.* — Whenever, in the opinion of the court, the circumstances of the case require it, they will grant an injunction, either temporary while awaiting a final decision, or permanent when the infringement on the copyright has been proved.[1]

There is nothing improper in an abridgment. If the leading design is truly to abridge and cheapen the price, and that by mental labor is faithfully done, it is no ground for prosecution by the owner of a copyright of the principal work. But it is otherwise if the abridgment or similar work be colorable and a mere substitute. Webb *v.* Powers, 2 Woodb. & M. (U. S.) 497; Folsom *v.* Marsh, 2 Story (U. S.), 100; Lawrence *v.* Dana, 4 Cliff. (U. S.) 1; Story *v.* Holcombe, 4 McLean (U. S.), 309; Greene *v.* Bishop, 1 Cliff. (U. S.) 186.

Drone, in his work on Copyright, holds a different view. See his reasoning, pp. 434 *et seq.*

A translation of a copyrighted work is no infringement of the copyright unless the right of translation and dramatization has been reserved by the author. Stowe *v.* Thomas, 2 Wall. Jr. (U. S.) 547; Reade *v.* Conquest, 9 C. B. N. S. 775; 11 C. B. N. S. 479; Toole *v.* Young, L. R. 9 Q. B. 523. *Contra*, Drone on Copyright, 445 *et seq.*

1. Where the plaintiff has made out a *prima facie* case in regard to his right of property to the copyright and the infringement, the court will grant a temporary injunction. Shook *v.* Rankin, 6 Biss. (U. S.) 477; Banks *v.* McDivitt, 13 Blatchf. (U. S.) 170; Little *v.* Gould, 2 Blatchf. (U. S.) 165, 185; Reed *v.* Holliday, 19 Fed. Rep. 325; Scribner *v.* Stoddart, 19 Am. L. Reg. N. S. 433; Lodge *v.* Stoddart, 9 Rep. 137; Pierpont *v.* Fowle, 2 Woodb. & M. (U. S.) 23; Atwill *v.* Ferrett, 2 Blatchf. (U. S.) 39.

If there appears a reasonable doubt as to the plaintiff's right, the court will refuse the injunction, and require him to try his title at law. Miller *v.* McElroy, 1 Am. L. Reg. O. S. 198; Ogle *v.* Edge, 4 Wash. (U. S. C. C.) 584; Ewer *v.* Coxe, 4 Wash. (U. S.) 487; Parkinson *v.* Laselle, 3 Sawyer (U. S.), 330. Or where there is a doubt as to the infringement. Blunt *v.* Patten, 2 Paine (U. S.), 397.

On a motion for a preliminary injunction to restrain an infringement of a copyright, when plaintiff has shown a copyright of a book, and a copy of a book having the same title, and has shown that defendant is publishing a book containing extracts from it, but has failed to show that the copy shown is a copy of the book copyrighted, and defendant denies that it is, *held*, that there is no ground for a preliminary injunction. Humphrey's Homœopathic Medicine Co. *v.* Armstrong, 30 Fed. Rep. 66.

Upon an application for an injunction to restrain infringement, it is not necessary to show that the piratical work is a substitute for the original. Reed *v.* Holliday, 19 Fed. Rep. 325.

Where the author of certain copyrighted articles had allowed them to be published in an encyclopædia published in a foreign country, the court refused to grant a temporary injunction interfering with a reprint in the United States of a volume of this encyclopædia containing the copyrighted articles. Scribner *v.* Stoddart, 19 Am. L. Reg. N. S. 433.

It is not necessary that a case should be decided in a court of law before an injunction can be issued. *Longyear, J.*, in Farmer *v.* Calvert Lith. Engr. & Map. Publ. Co., 1 Flipp. (U. S.) 228, said, "It is now well settled that both the right and the infringement may be set up and adjudicated in a court of equity without having first been determined at law," citing Phillips on Pat. Ch. 20-24; Hill. on Inj. 391, 392; 2 Story, Eq. Jur. 246-248; Stevens *v.* Gladding, 17 How. (U. S.) 447; Motte *v.* Bennett, 3 Fish. Pat. Cas. 642; Ogle *v.* Edge, 4 Wash. (U. S.) 584.

If infringement of a copyright is shown, the court will grant a temporary injunction without proof of actual damage. Reed *v.* Holliday, 19 Fed. Rep. 325.

A prayer for an injunction does not preclude plaintiff also to ask for the statutory penalties and forfeitures. Farmer *v.* Calvert Lith. Engr. & Map Publ. Co., 1 Flipp. (U. S.) 228.

An injunction to prevent infringement of a copyright may be granted, although a *qui tam* action for the penalty allowed by law is pending. Schumacher *v.* Schwencke, 25 Fed. Rep. 466.

A court of equity will not grant a preliminary injunction where it appears that the injury to plaintiff will be much less if refused than the injury to defendant if granted. Lodge *v.* Stoddart, 9 Rep. 137; 19 Am. L. Reg. 433; Spottiswoode *v.* Clarke, 2 Phillips, 157.

Where a temporary injunction is refused, the court may compel defendant to keep an account of all sales and profits while awaiting a final hearing. Blank *v.* Manufacturing Co., 3 Wall. Jr. (U. S.) 196.

Where a bill for the infringement of a copyright stated that the copyright claimed to have been infringed had been assigned to the complainant by the defendant, and (*b*) *Permanent Injunction.* — After the final hearing, when the court is satisfied that the copyright was infringed upon, a permanent injunction will be granted preventing further infringement. But in cases of doubt such injunction will be refused.[1]

(*c*) *Account of Profits.* — Incident to an injunction is generally an order of the court, requiring defendant to give an account of his profits on the pirated work, and to turn such profits over to the court for the benefit of the plaintiff.[2]

charged the defendant with having infringed said copyright by the publication of a book therein described, and in the prayer asked for a preliminary injunction, an accounting, etc., and where affidavits were filed against the injunction, which tended to prove that the contract which complainant claimed had operated as an assignment of said copyright had not been intended to so operate; that the agreements therein, to be performed by complainant, had not been performed by him; that said contract had been abrogated before the book complained of had been published; and that the publication of said book had not infringed said copyright, — *held*, that an injunction *simpliciter* should be refused, but that defendant should be required to give a bond to answer to any damages that might be adjudged against him in the case, and that he should be required to preserve an account of all the copies of said book which he had disposed of, and keep an account of all of said books which he might thereafter dispose of. Hubbard *v.* Thompson, 14 Fed. Rep. 689.

The owner of an opera that has not been copyrighted may obtain an injunction, on giving proper security, to prevent its presentation by an unauthorized party. When the owner of an uncopyrighted opera files a bill to restrain the unauthorized presentation thereof, and an order to show cause why the injunction should not issue is made, and no cause to the contrary having been shown, an injunction is granted on condition that a bond for $10,000 be given, and the bond offered is not accepted by the court, and the injunction dissolved, on defendant's executing an indemnity bond, a motion to set aside the order dissolving the injunction may be granted, when complainant offers to deposit in court as security a certified check for the amount of the required bond, or that amount in coin. Goldmark *v.* Kreling, 25 Fed. Rep. 349.

Situation of Parties to be considered. — Application was made by the plaintiff for an order *pendente lite*, restraining the defendant from circulating a guide-book containing matter infringing upon the copyright of plaintiff. *Held*, that the question of the damage that might be sustained by the defendant upon granting the order, as compared with that to the plaintiff by denying it, and the financial ability of the defendant to respond to any damages assessed against him, and the fact that there was no intent on the part of the defendant to appropriate the property of the plaintiff, and that it was done without the knowledge of the defendant by one employed to compile the work, — are all considerations which it is proper for the court to weigh in determining the question of granting or denying the application. Hanson *v.* Jaccard Jewelry Co., 32 Fed. Rep. 202.

1. Jollie *v.* Jaques, 1 Blatchf. (U. S.) 618; Folsom *v.* Marsh, 2 Story (U. S.), 100; Story *v.* Holcombe, 4 McLean (U. S.), 306; Greene *v.* Bishop, 1 Cliff. (U. S.) 186; Daly *v.* Palmer, 6 Blatchf. (U. S.) 256; Lawrence *v.* Dana, 4 Cliff. (U. S.) 1; Murray *v.* Bogue, 1 Drew, 353.

An injunction may be granted even when the merits of the case should not justify an action for penalties and forfeitures. Colburn *v.* Simms, 2 Hare, 558.

Where the injury is slight, or the granting of an injunction would do injustice to defendant, the injunction may be refused, and the complainant left to his remedies at common law. Webb *v.* Powers, 2 Woodb. & M. 497; Greene *v.* Bishop, 1 Cliff. (U. S.) 186.

The injunction need not cover the whole publication. It may prevent a further publication of only the pirated part. Greene *v.* Bishop, 1 Cliff. (U. S.) 203.

Where the pirated parts cannot be separated from the original, the whole publication will be prohibited. Lawrence *v.* Dana, 4 Cliff. (U. S.) 1.

2. No accounting as incident to an injunction can be granted unless asked for, either in a prayer for an accounting, or in a prayer for general relief. Stephens *v.* Cady, 2 Curt. (U. S.) 200; Stevens *v.* Gladdings, 17 How. (U. S.) 447.

Commissions received by a bookseller for the sale of a pirated book are profits, and must be accounted for to the owner of the copyright. Stevens *v.* Gladding, 2 Curt. (U. S.) 608.

A publisher who, having published and sold books in violation of the rights of the owner of the copyright, purchases such books, and re-sells them, may be charged

CORAL. — See CAMEO.

CORD. — A measure of wood or bark, containing one hundred and twenty-eight cubic feet, being the quantity contained in a pile

with the profit realized from the second sales, in addition to that realized from the first sales. Myers *v.* Callaghan, 24 Fed. Rep. 636.

M. owned the copyright of vols. 39 to 46 of the Illinois Reports, and the State reporter the copyright for the later volumes. C., who owned the copyright of vols. 1 to 31 inclusive, re-published and sold vols. 39 to 46, in violation of the rights of M., in full sets made up of the volumes owned by him, the infringing volumes, and volumes purchased from the reporter. *Held*, that the selling-price of the infringing volumes might be determined with sufficient accuracy by deducting from the amount received for a full set of reports the amount paid for the volumes purchased from the State reporter, and then dividing the balance by 46. Myers *v.* Callaghan, 24 Fed. Rep. 636.

Where the infringer has not been required by the decree of the court to surrender the unsold infringing volumes, but has been restrained from selling them, and has retained them in his possession, he cannot be credited for the cost of these volumes in order to determine the profits of those already sold.

Neither the amount paid by an infringer for editing the infringing volumes, nor the cost of stereotyping, will be allowed as an item of expense in producing them. Myers *v.* Callaghan, 24 Fed. Rep. 636.

When the infringers are partners, and under the partnership agreement each member is entitled to draw out of the business, for his personal expenses and support, a specific sum per annum, the amounts so drawn out by the respective partners cannot be included as part of the general expenses of the firm in conducting its business, in order to arrive at the percentage of such expenses. Myers *v.* Callaghan, 24 Fed. Rep. 636.

While a court will not presume that all the money received by a piratical publisher on the sale of his books is profit, still, as the proof as to the cost of producing the work is wholly in the control of the defendant, the complainant makes a *prima facie* case of right to recover by showing the selling-price and the usual manufacturers' cost. Myers *v.* Callaghan, 24 Fed. Rep. 636.

Where two parties own a copyright in common, and one of them, on his own expense, prints, publishes, and sells the book, he need not account to his co-owner for profits, unless required by an express agreement. Carter *v.* Bailey, 64 Me. 458.

If the owner of the copyright wishes to sell the published work directly, and only to individual subscribers, the statute protects him from interference by other dealers who offer surreptitiously-obtained copies of the genuine work without his consent, unless there be something in the circumstances of the particular case to estop him from relying on the privileges of his monopoly. The defendant procured genuinely-printed copies of Blaine's "Twenty Years of Congress," the copyright of which belonged to the plaintiff, who sold the work only by subscription to single buyers, from a dealer who had obtained them by purchase of an agent of the plaintiff, to whom they had been sent for delivery to such subscribers, but without the knowledge or consent of plaintiff, and against its instructions to the agent, and in violation of his agreement with the plaintiff not to disobey its instructions in that respect and of his bond to that effect, of which fraudulent conduct the defendant had no notice; but he abstained from making any inquiry into the circumstances of the dealer's possession and right to sell, well knowing that the plaintiff owned the copyright, and refused to sell otherwise than by subscription. *Held*, that he would be enjoined from selling these copies, and to account for the profits; that the above-stated circumstances required that he should have made inquiry, and that the failure to make such inquiry was equivalent to notice of the facts; but that the court had no power to enjoin the defendant from future dealing in the work without the consent of the plaintiff, or from any future interference with the trade of plaintiff's agent in the city where defendant resided. If the owner of the copyright undertake, by contract, to attach conditions of restriction to his sale of copies of the work, as, if he sells to canvassers upon agreement that they shall sell only by subscription, he must rely solely on the ordinary remedies for a breach of that agreement, and it is not within the protection of the copyright act. But it is otherwise if he sells the copies directly to subscribers through agents having no ownership of the copies sold, as in this case. The incidental protection of the statute belongs only to the owner of the copyright or some part of it, and cannot be transferred by him to mere owners of the copies having no interest in the ownership of the copyright. Henry Bill Publ. Co. *v.* Smythe, 27 Fed. Rep. 914. See Clemens *v.* Estes, 22 Fed. Rep. 899.

eight feet long, four feet broad, and four feet high. Such a pile is called a cord.[1]

CORN.—In England, corn is a comprehensive or general term including all kinds of grain.[2] In America its meaning is limited to maize or Indian corn.[3]

CORNER.—An angle made by two boundary lines at the point of intersection.[4]

A combination of capitalists for the purpose of holding or controlling the great bulk of any article in the market, or which may

1. Bouv. L. D.; Kennedy *v.* O. & S. R. R. Co., 67 Barb. (N. Y.) 169. A cord is defined by statute in several of the States to consist of a quantity equal to a pile eight feet in length, four feet in width, and four feet in height. Mass. Gen. Sts. (1882) c. 60, § 73; N. Car. Rev. Sts. (1883) § 3049; R. I. Pub. Sts. (1882) c. 128, § 1; Vt. Rev. Laws (1880), § 3711; Va. Code (1873), c. lxxxviii. § 8. Or of one hundred and twenty-eight cubic feet. Ohio Rev. Sts. (1883) § 4434; Va. Code (1873), c. lxxxviii. § 8. Provision is made in these statutes that the wood shall be well stowed and packed; and the measurement in Massachusetts, Rhode Island, and Vermont includes one-half of the kerf.

A declaration for the sale and delivery of a certain number of cords of wood must be interpreted as meaning cords such as the statute defines, and is not supported by proof of a special agreement that a less quantity should be delivered and accepted as a cord under the contract. Colton *v.* King, 2 Allen (Mass.), 317. And in Kennedy *v.* O. & S. R. R. Co., 67 Barb. (N. Y.) 169, it was said, "When a contract is made for the purchase and sale of a given number of cords of wood, the vendor is bound to deliver, and the vendee is entitled to receive, one hundred and twenty-eight cubic feet for each cord of wood so contracted for." It was accordingly *held*, that the purchaser, though informed that the wood was but three feet long, was not bound to accept a pile of such eight feet long by four feet high as a cord, in the absence of a special contract to do so, or a well-known custom or usage which recognizes such a pile as a cord.

Under the section of the Virginia Code, cited above, the statutory standard is to prevail, "any usage, by-law, or ordinance of any corporation, railroad, or other company to the contrary notwithstanding."

The sale of a part of a cord of wood is not a sale "by the cord" within an act providing a penalty for such, unless the wood is measured by the appointed measurer. Pray *v.* Burbank, 12 N. H. 267.

"Twenty-five cords of wood" is a sufficient description of the subject of a larceny in an indictment. It sufficiently indicates that the property was personal, and not real. State *v.* Parker, 34 Ark. 158.

2. R. & L. L. D.; Bouv. L. D.; Park on Ins. 112; 1 Parsons on Mar Ins. 627, n. 2. In the memorandum clause of a policy of insurance, corn was held to include pease and beans. Mason *v.* Skurray, Park on Ins. 112. Malt also comes within the designation as being corn in a manufactured state. Moody *v.* Surridge, 2 Esp. 633. But rice does not. Scott *v.* Bourdillion, 2 B. & P. (N. R.) 213.

3. 1 Parsons on Mar. Ins. 627, n. 2; Comm *v.* Pine, 2 Pa L J. Rep. 154. The word "corn," referring to grain, as used in this country, ordinarily means Indian corn, and not the cereal grains generally, unless the meaning is enlarged by the circumstances of its employment. Thus, a representation that a mill was capable of grinding forty bushels of corn per hour, is not shown to be untrue by proof that it would grind only fifteen bushels of mixed corn and oats per hour. Kerrick *v.* Van Dusen, 32 Minn. 317. In a larceny act "corn" does not mean a cereal, or wheat, or barley, or oats, but Indian maize, that having been the principal breadstuff here. Sullivan *v.* State, 53 Ala. 474.

In the same act, "outstanding crop of corn" means the crop in the field, not gathered thence and housed, without reference to its state: it is not confined to that which remains beyond the proper time for housing, or to matured corn in a condition to be housed. Sullivan *v.* State, 53 Ala. 474.

A bequest of "corn, fodder, meat, and other provisions on hand," includes wine and brandy, which the testator had laid in and provided for his own use. Mooney *v.* Evans, 6 Ired. (N. Car.) Eq. 363.

4. R. & L. L. D. A conveyance of a certain amount of land lying in the southwest corner of a certain section, describes the general position of the land with sufficient certainty. The "corner is a base point from which two sides of the land conveyed shall extend an equal distance, so as to include by parallel lines the quantity conveyed." Lessee of Walsh *v.* Ringer, 2 Ohio, 333.

be brought into the market, in order to prevent competition, and advance the price.[1] (See CONSPIRACY.)

CORONER. — See OFFICERS OF MUNICIPALITIES.

1. Definition. — Coroner or coronator, a very ancient officer at the common law, so called because he had principally to do with the pleas of the crown, or such wherein the king was immediately concerned.[2]

2. Different Kinds of Coroners at Common Law. — (a) *Virtute Officii.* — Under this head come the lord chief justice and puisne justices of the King's Bench, who are supreme and sovereign coroners respectively.[3]

(b) *Virtute Cartæ sive Commissionis.* — Coroners within particular liberties and franchises, over which the lords or heads of corporations are empowered to act themselves, or to create their own coroners, are so called because they exist by charter commission or privilege.[4]

1. Rapalje & Lawrence's Law Dict. And see also Sampson *v.* Shaw, 101 Mass. 145; Morris Run Coal Co. *v.* Barclay Coal Co. 68 Pa. St. 187; Carson on Crim. Conspiracies, 180; 4 Bla. Com. 158.

2. 1 Black Com. 346; 2 Inst. 31; 4 Inst. 271; Wharton's Law Dictionary, Jervis on Coroners, 1.

History. — At different periods in English history the coroner has borne different names. He was first called *serviens regis* (see Umfrev. Lex. Cor. XX.); and in the reign of Henry II. *coronarius* (see Wilkins' Leg. Ang. Sax. 337). By the time of Richard I. he was known as *custos placitorum coronæ* (see Wilkins, 346); in Magna Carta, and subsequent statutes, he is styled coronator. In Scotland he is called crowner, which is also a vulgar English appellation (see Jervis on Coroners, p. 2). So ancient is his office, that the origin is lost in antiquity. Some writers have ranked it coeval with the sheriff (see Mirror, c. 1, s. 3), but eminent authority have doubted this (see Bac. on Gov. 66, and 6 Vin. Abr. 242). Coke declares the sheriff to antedate the division of England into counties by Alfred, and to have existed in the time of the Romans as an officer of the consul (see Coke on Littleton, 168, a.). The coroner, however, certainly existed in the time of Alfred, for that king put to death a judge who had sentenced a party upon the coroner's record, without allowing the prisoner to traverse (see Bac. on Government, 6). The charter of King Athelstan to the monastery of St. John de Beverley, granted in 952, also mentions the coroner (see Dugd. Monast. 171).

The office, as at present constituted, was not clearly established until after the Norman Conquest. In the Capitula of Henry II., and in those of the reign of Richard I., the justices were enjoined to select "three knights and one clerk in each county," who were styled *custodes placitorum coronæ*. Crabb's Hist. of Eng. Law, c. xi. 1831.

3. 4 Rep. 57, b, 4 Inst. 73.

4. Mad. Excheq. 287. "The crown," says Sir John Jervis, p. 5, Jervis on Coroners, "may claim this privilege by prescription, but no subject may claim it otherwise than by grant from the crown." Co. Lit. 114 a; 2 Hawk. P. C. c. 9, s. 11; 9 Rep. 29 b. The stat. of Edw. I., 3 c. 6, confirming to the county the power of electing coroners, and all subsequent statutes relating to the election of county coroners, expressly exempts this privilege from their operation. Examples of this class of coroner are found

(*c*) *Virtute Electionis.* — Declaratory of the common law. The statute of Edward I. (West 1) c. 10, enacts, "That through all shires sufficient men shall be chosen to be coroners" The number was not defined, but varied by usage, there being in some shires six, in some four, in some two, and in some only one.[1] The number not being limited, the lord chancellor may at discretion, upon a petition of freeholders with the approbation of the justices, issue a writ for the election of one or more additional coroners.[2] Besides the coroners for the counties, every *borough* having a separate quarter sessions in England and Wales, is required under the provisions of the Municipal Corporation Act[3] to appoint a fit person, etc., to be coroner.[4] Coroners in England were chosen by all the freeholders of the county court[5] for life or good behavior, and were liable to be removed for cause by the writ *de coronatore exonerando.* There are several causes cited as good grounds for removal, such as being of unfit character, not having sufficient estate, lying in prison for a year, use of corrupt influence over a jury, also for being a common merchant. The writ issues on petition of freeholders, and must state the grounds of the objection to the coroner.[6]

3. Qualification and Remuneration in England. — (*a*) *Qualification.* — In the earlier days the coroner must needs be a knight, and have means enough to be able to maintain the office with dignity, and to answer for any fines imposed for misbehavior; for if he had not enough estate to meet the fine, it fell upon the county as a punishment for electing an insufficient officer.[7] Blackstone complains bitterly, that in his times "the office of coroner had

in Mayor of London, the Coroner of the Cinque Ports, of the Dean and Chapter of Westminster, the Bishop of Ely, and Stonaries of Cornwall, and many other exclusive jurisdictions. Jervis on Cor. p. 4.

On the more curious points of the common law, as applicable to coroners, the reader will do well to consult the excellent work by Sir John Jervis, on coroners, where the duties of coroners of *The Verge* and *The Admiralty* are well set forth. The subject of coroners is also treated of in the following volumes: Gwynne on Sheriffs and Coroners; Crocker on Sheriffs; Smith on Sheriffs.

1. 2 Inst. 175; F. N. B. 163; Jervis on Cor. 6; 2 Hale's Pleas of C. 55.

2. *In re* Coroner of Salop, 3 Swanst. 181.

3. 5 & 6 Will. IV. c. 76.

4. Reg. *v.* Grimshaw, 10 Q. B. 747.

5. 1 Blk. Com. 347.

6. Jervis on Cor. p. 94; S. P. C. 48; 2 Inst. 132; *Ex parte* Parnell, 1 J. & W. 451.

7. "At sessions ther was he lord and sire.
Ful often time he was knight of the shire.
. . . .
A shereve hadde he ben, and a countour
Was no wher swiche a worthy vavasour."
Description of the Frankelein. — CHAUCER.

3 Edw. I. c. 10 and Statute of Merton 20, Hen. III. c. 3, which assumes that all coroners were knights. Later, knighthood ceased to be a qualification; but statute 14 Edw. III. st. 1, c. 8, ordains "that no coroner be chosen unless he have land in fee sufficient in the same county whereof he may answer to all manner of people." Sir Edward Coke (2 Inst. 174) states that a coroner should have five qualities. "He should be *probus homo, legales homo;* of sufficient knowledge and understanding; of good ability and power to execute his office according to his knowledge; and, lastly, of diligence and attendance for the due execution of his office. And this for three purposes, — 1. The law presumes that he will do his duty, and not offend the law, at least for fear of punishment, whereunto his lands and goods are subject; 2. That he be able to answer the king all such fines and duties as belong to him, and to discharge the county thereof; 3. And lastly, that he may execute his office without bribery." For the office of coroner of a borough no qualification by estate, residence, or otherwise is required, all that is necessary is, that he is a fit person, not being an alderman or councillor. 5 & 6 Will. IV. c. 76.

been permitted to fall into low and indigent hands who desired to be chosen for the sake of the perquisites."[1]

(*b*) *Remuneration in England.* — In ancient times so great was the dignity of this office, that it was never presumed that coroners would condescend to be paid for their services.[2] Later on, beginning with 3 Hen. VII. c. 1, § 4, from time to time acts were passed entitling coroners to certain fees.[3] The growing evils and inconvenience of the fee system constantly felt, were finally recognized, and put an end to by a very recent statute, which provides for making the coroner a salaried officer.[4]

4. The Office in America. — The office of coroner was brought to America by the colonists along with the institutions of the common law, and may be said to exist in the several States with all common-law incidents, except so far as they may have been modified by statute.[5] Generally speaking, the coronor is a county officer, although in some States they are elected or appointed for districts and cities. *Coroners virtute officii* and *virtute cartæ sive commissionis* are not known to our law. Coroners in the United States may be classed under the head of coroners *virtute electionis.* Vacancies are filled by appointment of the appointing power for city or county, as the case might be; and, as county officers, vacancies would generally be filled by the governor.[6] Before he enters upon the duties of his office, the coroner must take the customary oath prescribed by law.[7]

The qualifications for the office must be found in those pre-

1. Blk. Com. vol. i. 347.

2. 1 Bl. Com. 347; 2 Inst. 173, 176; Stat. Wesm. 1, c. 10.

3. See Jervis on Coroners, 3d ed. 75, for a sketch of this legislation.

4. 23 & 24 Vict. c. 116.

Provision is also made by statute for expenses of inquest and fees of medical witnesses. Jervis on Coroners, 3d ed. 78–88.

5. The present defined powers of the coroner, both in Great Britain and America, except so far as they may be modified by statute, are derived from the English statute, *de officio coronatoris*, 4 Edw. I. § 2, which provides, "that where a death takes place suddenly under suspicious circumstances, the coroner shall, by his warrant, summon a jury to make due inquiry, upon view of body, into the manner of killing, who were present, and to examine the body; and that he may likewise commit any person to prison who may be adjudged as the author of the crime, and bind over the witnesses by recognizances to appear at the next term of court."

Previous to *Magna Carta*, coroners not only received accusations against offenders, but they also proceeded to try them.

6. See Statute Law for each State, title "Coroners." People *v.* Parker, 6 Hill (N. Y.), 49.

7. So far, however, as the rights of third persons and the public are concerned, his acts as such officer are valid, although he has not obeyed the statutory requirement and taken the oath. People *v.* Hopson, 1 Denio (N. Y.), 574.

Although it may be a misdemeanor for a coroner to enter upon or perform the duties of his office without having taken the oath of office, notwithstanding such neglect to take the oath of office, he will, so far as the rights of third persons and the public are concerned, be considered an officer *de facto.* People *ex rel.* Whiting *v.* Carrique, 2 Hill (N. Y.), 93; Paddock *v.* Cameron, 8 Cow. (N. Y.) 212.

Where a coroner has acted, the legal presumption is, that the facts existed which rendered his action proper in the particular instance. Kirk *v.* Murphy, 16 Tex. 654.

Where the objection to a return by a coroner was, that he had not received his official bond, or had not given a new one, *held*, that the want of a bond did not invalidate his official acts, as he was *de facto* a coroner. Mabry *v.* Turrentine, 8 Ired. (N. C.) L. 201. See also McHee *v.* Hoke, 2 Spears (S. C.), 138; and State *v.* Hill, 2 Spears (S. C.), 150.

scribed for the ordinary elective offices of a county in the respective States.[1] The office has not been abolished by the new constitution of Illinois.[2] In some States a justice of the peace may be called on to perform the duties of coroner when the coroner cannot be had in time.[3]

5. Powers and Duties generally. — The duties of coroner fall under two heads, — 1st, judicial; 2d, ministerial. What may be called the original jurisdiction of a coroner is judicial; when he acts in the place or stead of the sheriff, his duties are mainly ministerial.[4]

The duties imposed on the coroner by the common law and the laws of the different States may be summarized as follows: —

1 Coroners are conservators of the peace, and become magistrates by virtue of their election and appointment.[5]

2. To hold inquest[6] upon the bodies of persons slain, or who

1. In *New York* no person is capable of holding the office of coroner who at the time of his election or appointment shall not have attained the age of twenty-one, and who shall not then be a citizen of the State. Green *v.* Burke, 23 Wend. (N. Y.) 490.

In *New York*, coroners, when elected, hold their office for three years, whether they are elected at the close of a full term or to fill a vacancy. People *ex rel.* Gallup *v.* Green, 2 Wend. (N. Y.) 266, People *ex rel.* Bunn *v.* Coutont, 11 Wend. (N. Y.) 511.

By the constitution of *Maine* no person can exercise the several office of coroner and justice of the peace at the same time. Bamford *v.* Melvin, 7 Me. 14; Maddox *v.* Ewell, 2 Va. Cas. 59.

2. The office of coroner is not abolished by the new constitution of *Illinois*, and still exists within it. Wool *v.* Blanchard, 19 Ill. 38.

3. The provision of the *New Jersey* revised statutes authorizing a justice of the peace to act, but only when the coroner cannot be had in time to take the inquest, does not empower a justice to act without the exigency, although the justice may receive the first notice. The coroner on arriving may, at his option, assume control of the body, have the costs taxed, receive them from the treasurer, and pay the justice only reasonable compensation for the services rendered before arrival. State *v.* Erickson, 40 N. J. L. 159.

When a coroner is absent from the county, or unable to attend, a justice of the peace may hold an inquest, and in doing so has all the powers and can perform all the duties pertaining to a coroner. Stevens *v.* Coms., 46 Ind. 541.

Whether or not a coroner has authority to commit to jail a party charged with felony, it is too late to object to the authority of the coroner after a regular examination and indictment found for felony in the circuit court.

And if a justice of the peace acts as coroner, and commits a person to jail for felony, he may certify the fact of such committal as justice of the peace. Wormley *v.* Com., 10 Gratt. (Va.) 658.

4. By the common law the powers and duties of a coroner are both judicial and ministerial. His judicial authority relates to inquiries into cases of sudden death, by a jury of inquest, *super visum corporis*, at the place where the death happened, and also to inquiries concerning shipwreck and treasure-trove. In his ministerial capacity a coroner is merely a substitute for the sheriff, as where the sheriff is a party. Giles *v.* Brown, 1 Mill (S. C.), Const. 230.

A coroner holding an inquest is in the performance of functions judicial in their character. People *v.* Devine, 44 Cal. 452.

The coroner is a judicial officer, and has power to compel the attendance of witnesses by attachment. Coroner's Case, 11 Phila. (Pa.) 387; s. c., 7 Leg. Gaz. (Pa.) 125.

In re application of coroner, 1 Weekly Notes Cases (Pa.), 372, *Thayer, P. J.*, says, "The statute, 4 Edw. I., regulating the powers and duties of coroners is in force in Pennsylvania. His office is judicial as well as ministerial, — judicial in summoning witnesses, in the name of the Commonwealth, to appear before him for examination, and at the inquest he sits armed with the ordinary power of a judicial officer. He has a common-law power to compel obedience to his subpœnas."

5. Jervis on Coroners (3d ed.), 30.

This, says *Lord Hale*, appears evidently by stat. 3 Edw. I. c. 9, and 4 Edw. I.; *Officium Coronatoris*, 2 Hale, P. C. 107.

6. It is the duty of the coroner to inquire into the cause of all violent or extraordinary deaths. Lancaster *v.* Dern, 2 Grant (Pa.), 262.

have suddenly died, or who have been dangerously wounded, or found dead under such circumstances as to require an inquisition, within their jurisdiction.[1] This duty of taking inquests is the most important of the duties of coroner, and is regulated and defined in England by statute. 4 Edw. I. st. 2.[2]

3. To inquire of other felonies.[3]

4. To inquire of treasure-trove.[4]

5. To inquire of wrecks.[5]

6. Besides his judicial duties, the coroner has also a ministerial authority analogous to that of a sheriff, and executes process when just exception is taken to that officer.[6]

6. Rights and Liabilities. — (*a*) *Duration of Office.* — In *England* the coroner was chosen for life, subject to removal for cause by the writ *de coronatore exonerando.*[7] In this country he is elected for a term of years.

(*b*) *Rights.* — He could not by common law appoint a deputy for the performance of his judicial duties, and it may be safely laid down that a coroner has no power to appoint a deputy-coroner, except when special provision is made therefor by statute.[8] Coroners are exempt from serving offices which are inconsistent with duties of coroner, and are privileged from serving on juries.[9] They are also privileged from arrest when engaged in discharge of official duties.[10]

(*c*) *Liabilities.* — Coroners are liable to punishment as well for neglect of duty as for wilful misconduct in the execution of their office. They are liable to a criminal information, or may be indicted if they misconduct themselves in taking an inquisition.[11]

1. The sudden, violent deaths which are within the coroner's duty to inquire, are, from visitation of God; by chance or accident; by his own hand, as *felo de se;* by the hand of another where the offender is not known; and by the hand of another where the offender is known. 2 Hale's Cr. L. 62.

Before the statute of Magna Charta, coroners held pleas of the crown; but by cap. 17 of that statute (2 Inst. 30) their power in proceeding to trial and judgment is taken away. 2 Hale, P. C. 56.

Whenever a convict shall die in prison, it shall be the duty of the officials in charge, if any suspicious circumstances attach to the death, to summon the coroner; and it has been said, that, even if the prisoner die a natural death, the jailer ought to send for the coroner, as it may be presumed that the prisoner died by the ill-usage of the jailer. 2 Hale's Cr. L. 57.

2. Jervis on Coroners, p. 31.

The duties of coroners upon inquests, etc., cannot at common law be delegated. 2 Hale's Cr. L. 58.

3. 1 Britt. c. 2, s. 2; Mirr. of Just. ch. 1, § 13. See, however, Staund. P. C. 51; Hale. Sum. 171; 4 Inst. 271; 2 Inst. 32; 2 Hale, P. C. 65; and 2 Hawk. P. C. c. 9, s. 35.

4. Bract. b. 3, c. 6; 1 Britt. c. 2, s. 2; 2 Hawk. P. C. c. 9, s. 36.

5. Staund. P. C. 51; Bract. 120.

6. 4 Inst. 271; Hob. 85; Jervis on Coroners, p. 53; 2 Hawkins, P. C. 70.

7. 1 Bl. Com. 348; F. N. B. 163.

8. Crompton's Just. 227 a; 2 Hale, P. C. 57; 2 Fitz. Inst. 166. In *England* provision was made for the appointment of a deputy by 6 and 7 Victoria, c. 83; and similar provisions have been made in several States.

9. 2 Roll. Abr. 632, s. 4; F. N. B. 167.

10. Callaghan *v.* Twiss, 9 Ir. Law Rep. 422; *Ex parte* Deputy Coroner, 6 H. & N. 501.

11. Hale, P. C. 58; 1 Hen. 8, c. 7; 3 Hen. 7, c. 1; 3 Ed. I. c. 9; Rex *v.* Scory, 1 Leach, C. L. 43; Jervis on Coroners, p. 90.

Where a coroner inserted in an inquisition that three persons had been found guilty of murder by the jury, when in fact only one had been so found, he was adjudged to have committed forgery, and was found guilty. 3 Salk. 172. If a coroner

7. Coroner's Court. — The coroner's court is a court of record, of which the coroner is judge.[1] No action will be against the coroner for any matter done by him in the exercise of his judicial functions;[2] but he will be criminally responsible for corruption, misconduct, or neglect of duty.[3] The coroner has the power of excluding not only individuals, but the general public.[4] It is the duty of the coroner to instruct the jury on the law, but he is bound to accept the presentment which they may make.[5] He need not hold the inquest in the presence of the accused.[6] As the accused himself has no right to be present, so it follows that he has no right to be represented by counsel, nor to insist upon examination or cross-examination of witnesses.[7]

(*a*) *Jury.* — Every one summoned on a coroner's jury are bound to appear. They should be *probi et legales homines.* Jurors are not challengeable,[8] but they should be carefully selected.[9] It is the province of the jury to investigate and determine the facts of the case; they should not expect, nor need they obey, binding

has been guilty of corrupt practices in taking an inquisition, a *melius inquirendum* may be awarded to take a new inquest by special commissioners, who shall proceed without viewing the body, by the testimony only. 2 Hawk. P. C. c. 9, s. 56.

Coroners are liable in their ministerial character for an escape, 6 Mod. 37; for a false return, Freem. 191; and the court will exercise a summary jurisdiction over them, 8 Mod. 192. In fact, if coroners be guilty of any misconduct, either in a judicial or ministerial capacity, they are, according to the circumstances of the case, liable to removal, prosecution, or censure. Jervis on Cor. 94.

Where any act may be done by one coroner, as in the taking of an inquisition, his acts will not bind his co-coroners; but when the coroner's act is ministerial, all will be responsible for the acts of each civilly. 1 Mod. 198; 2 Mod. 23; Staund. P. C. 153 a.

A coroner holding an inquest on a dead body is not liable to an action for words falsely and maliciously spoken by him in his address to the jury. Thomas *v.* Charton, 2 B. & S. 475.

Liability for Misconduct. — The penalties to which coroners are subjected, by the Alabama act of 1833, for defaults in the execution of process, may be recovered in the summary mode pointed out by the act of 1807. The latter act, so far as it prescribes the remedy and mode of proceedings, is not repealed by the former. Patterson *v.* Gaston, 17 Ala. 223.

In a suit on a coroner's bond, proof that he had served and returned a writ directed to him as coroner, was held to be sufficient evidence that a commission had issued to him. Young *v.* Com., 6 Binn. (Pa.) 93.

A coroner is not liable for neglect to serve a writ against the sheriff of G., directed to the said sheriff of G. The writ not being directed to the coroner, he had no power to execute it, and was not liable for failure to return it. Brown *v.* Baker, 10 Humph. (Tenn.) 346. On this point see also Governor *v.* Lindsay, 14 Ala. 658.

1. 6 B. & C. 611.

2. 12 Rep. 24; Lutw. 935, 1560; 1 Ld. Raym. 454; Thomas *v.* Charton, 2 B. & S. 475.

3. Per Ld. Tenterden, 6 B. & C. 626.

4. 6 B. & C. 611. Cresfield *v.* Perine, 15 Hun (N. Y.), 200.

5. Comb. 386.

6. It is not necessary that a coroner, on holding an inquest on the body of a person dead or wounded, should take the testimony of the witnesses in the presence of the accused. Matter of Collins, 20 How Pr. 111.

The accused before a coroner, after an inquisition, has no right to require the examination of witnesses to establish his guilt or innocence. The process and the mittimus are based solely upon the inquisition. The coroner has no power to take testimony to establish the innocence of the prisoner, and then discharge him contrary to the finding of the jury. Matter of Collins, 11 Abb. (N. Y.) Pr. 406.

7. The weight of authority and reason sustains this proposition, although a contrary view is taken by Sir T. Smith in his history of the Commonwealth, p. 96. For a discussion of the question, see Jervis on Coroners, p. 245. See also 6 B. & C. 611.

8. Mir. c. 1, s 13.

9. Britt c. 2, s. 11 (ed. by Nichols).

instruction from the coroner. Respectful consideration should be shown by the jury to the coroner on all questions of law.[1]

8. The Inquisition. — The principal duty of the coroner is to hold an inquisition on the body of any person who may have come to a violent death, who has died in prison, who has been dangerously wounded, or whose death is accompanied by suspicious circumstances. The fearless and able execution of this duty is of the most paramount importance to the public, both as regards the punishment of the guilty and the protection of the innocent; and this high prerogative alone is sufficient to account for the ancient dignity of the office. The object of the inquest is to ascertain the cause of the death.[2]

An inquisition, properly speaking, is the written statement of the verdict of the jury, returned for the purpose of a particular inquiry, as distinguished from an indictment.[3] Where it contains the subject-matter of accusation, it is equivalent to the finding of a grand jury, and the parties may be tried and convicted upon it.[4] The caption is a necessary and essential part, and should be drawn up with precision, and contain the name of the county.[5]

The time and place when and where holden must appear with certainty;[6] also, that it was taken before a court of competent jurisdiction.[7] The name of deceased must be set out if known;[8] also, where the body lies;[9] also, that it was taken by the oaths of the within-named jurors,[10] and, it must expressly appear that the jurors are from the county or jurisdiction,[11] and that they present the inquisition upon oaths.[12] The verdict must be stated with legal precision and certainty, and the charge must be direct and positive.[13] The attestation is an essential part of the inquisition.[14]

Whenever the coroner shall receive notice of a sudden, suspicious, or violent death, of which it is his duty to inquire, it shall

1. Vaughn, Rep. 160.

2. It is the duty of the coroner to hold an inquest *super visum corporis* where he has cause to suspect the deceased was feloniously destroyed, or where his death was caused by violence. County of Northampton *v.* Imes, 2 Casey (Pa.), 156; Com. *v.* Harmon, 4 Barr (Pa.), 269; County of Lancaster *v.* Meshler, 4 Out. (Pa.) 624; Fayette Co. *v.* Batton, 108 Pa. St. 591; Lancaster *v.* Dern, 2 Grant (Pa.), 262.

It has been held in *England* that the coroner of X. has no jurisdiction to inquire into the case of a death occasioned by an accident happening outside of X. The mere fact of a body lying dead does not give the coroner jurisdiction, nor even the circumstance that the death was sudden. There ought to be a reasonable suspicion that the party came to his death by violent and unnatural means. Reg. *v.* Railroad Co., 2 A. & E. 759. See also 1 East's Pl. Cr. 382; Rex *v.* Kent, 1 East, 229; Rex *v.* Co., Nol. Ca. Just. P. 141.

3. Reg. *v.* Ingham, 5 B. & S. 257.

4. Jervis on Cor. 273.

5. 2 Hale, P. C. 163, 166.

6. Hale, P. C. 166; 2 Saund. 291; Rex *v.* Fernley, 1 T. R. 316; 2 Hawk. P. C. c. 25.

7. 22 Edw. IV. 13; Hale, Sum. 207; 2 Hawk. P. C. c. 25, § 119; 4 Rep. 41.

8. 2 Hawk. P. C. c. 25, §§ 71, 72.

9. 6 B. & C. 247.

10. Hale, P. C. 167.

11. Lambert *v.* Taylor, 4 B. & C. 138.

12. 2 Hawk. P. C. c. 25, § 126; 2 Hale, P. C. 167.

13. 2 Hale, P. C. c. 25, § 57.

14. It must be signed by the coroner and all jurors. Rex *v.* Justices of Norfolk, Nolan, 141. See also 6 B. & C. 247. The coroner's inquest being signed by the coroner, and duly certified by him, the jurors having signed by making their cross-marks, and the whole being certified by the coroner, who is a sworn officer, his certificate of the signature of the jury is sufficient. State *v.* Evans, 27 La. Ann. 297.

be his duty to go to the place where such person shall be, and forthwith summon his jury to the number required by the statute law of his State, being such as are qualified and not exempt from such service, to appear before him forthwith, at such place as he shall appoint to make inquisition concerning the death or wounding.

The place of holding the inquest must be in the county, and should be at a convenient place for such purpose nearest the body.[1]

After the jury are charged and sworn, they and the coroner go together and view and examine the body of the deceased. It will not be sufficient that they view the body separately and at different times;[2] and they cannot proceed upon the inquest until they shall have so viewed the body; and if it is buried, it must be dug up.[3] It is not necessary, however, that the inquest should be held where the jury is found; but, after the body has been viewed, the jury may return to some convenient place to hear the testimony of witnesses, and deliberate upon their verdict.[4]

The coroner exercising jurisdiction in the particular case, is the sole judge of the necessity of holding the inquest.[5] One inquisition may be held on several dead bodies killed by the same cause, or the coroner may hold a separate inquisition on each body.[6] In *England* the rule is, that there can be but one inquest upon a body, unless that taken be first set aside; and this rule has been followed in this country.[7] The jurors must be summoned by the coroner in person, unless the common-law rule is modified

1. The coroner can in no case hold an inquest except upon view of the body; and when it has been buried, he must dig it up again, and, after he and the jury have viewed it together, he shall cause it to be reburied. 2 Hawk. P. C. 77.

The provisions of the penal code (§ 311) of *New York*, describing the offence of body-stealing, does not apply to an exhuming of a body by a coroner, under whose direction an examination was made, there having been application and affidavits sufficient to give jurisdiction, although the person alleged to have been poisoned, was poisoned, if at all, in another State, and brought to New York for burial, and although there was no jury summoned. People *v.* Fitzgerald, 105 N. Y. 146.

2. King *v.* Ferrond, 3 Barn. & A. (Eng.) 260.

3. 2 Hale's Cr. L. 58.

4. Hawkins, P. C. 78.

Whenever six or more of the jurors shall appear, they shall be sworn by the coroner, and charged by him to inquire how and in what manner, and when and where, such person came to his death or hurt, and who such person was, and into all the circumstances attending such death or wounding, and to make a true inquisition according to the evidence offered to them, or arising from an inspection of the body. 2 Hale's Cr. L. 60.

5. Jameson *v.* County Coms., 64 Ind. 524.

An inquest ought not to be held, where defendant came to his death by being caught in machinery, which he himself was working, and no other person is suspected of contributing thereto. Crosby's Case, 3 Pitts. (Pa.) 425. See also Howorth's Case, 2 Leg. L. Reg. (Pa.) 119.

It is not necessary that an inquest should be held in the case of one dying with fever, apoplexy, or other disease. 2 Hale's Cr La. 57.

The presumption is, that the coroner acted in good faith and on sufficient cause Lancaster Co. *v.* Mishler, 100 Pa. St. 624

6. One inquisition may be held on several dead bodies of persons killed by the same cause, and who died at the same time. Croker on Coroners, § 950, p. 412, 2 ed. But see Fayette Co. *v.* Batton, 108 Pa. St. 591; Rombo *v.* Coms., 1 Chester Co. (Pa.) Rep 416.

7. In New York the English rule was followed. People *v.* Budge, 4 Parker, Cr. R. (N. Y.) 519.

by statute.[1] Care should be taken to secure an impartial jury and trial; but the jurors, when they appear, are not challengeable by either party.[2] The coroner may compel the attendance of jurors summoned.[3] Unless provision is made therefor by statute, a person summoned to attend on a coroner's jury is entitled to no compensation.[4] Where a person dies in one county, and is buried in another, and an inquest afterward becomes necessary, the coroner of the latter county is the proper officer to hold the inquest.[5]

The authority of the coroner in this branch of his office is necessarily judicial in its character.[6]

9. Proceedings on Inquest. — The coroner may issue subpœnas for witnesses, returnable forthwith, and may compel their attendance by attachment; and he should summon as such witnesses every person who in his opinion, or that of the jury, has any knowledge of the facts.[7]

He should also, as a general rule, summon a surgeon or physician, who should, in the presence of the jury, inspect the body, and give a professional opinion as to cause of death. He may under certain conditions employ experts to examine the body.[8]

1. The juror must be summoned in person. The coroner should, being vested with discretion, exercise great care in the selection of jurors: care should be taken not to summon any one related to the deceased, or to the suspect, nor any one prejudiced for or against him. The same care should be exercised in such a case to obtain a fair and impartial verdict, as upon the trial of the party accused of the offence. But the jurors who are selected and appear are not challengeable by either party. Hale's Cr. L. 59.

In *South Carolina*, by statute of 1797, the coroner must issue his warrant to a constable, to summon a jury of inquest; and, if a juror is summoned by the coroner in person, the summons is illegal. Cunningham *v.* Coroner, 2 Nott & M. (S. C.) 454.

2. T. W. Charlton (Ga.), R. 310.

3. The coroner's power to summon on inquests includes the incidental means of rendering that power efficient; and he may, therefore, rightfully impose a fine on a juror who refuses to attend. Exp. *v.* McAnnully, T. U. P. Charlton (Ga.), 310.

4. A person summoned to serve on a coroner's inquest is not entitled to any compensation. Green *v.* Wynne, 66 N. Car. 530.

There is no provision in the laws of Georgia for remunerating coroner's jurors. Kennedy *v.* Comans, 60 Ga. 612.

5. Jameson *v.* County Coms., 64 Ind. 524; County Coms. *v.* Jameson, 86 Ind. 154.

6. People *v.* Devine, 44 Cal. 452; Boislemere *v.* Co. Coms., 32 Mo. 375.

7. Smith on Shf. & Cor. p. 625; *In re* Coroner, 11 Phila. (Pa.) 387.

8. Smith on Shf. & Cor. 626.

Incident to the coroner's duty to hold inquests is the power to select physicians to make *post-mortem* examinations; and the county board has no right to control his choice, but must pay the physician whom he employs. Board *v.* Bond, 105 Ind. 102. And the authority of a coroner to employ a chemist to discover whether poison caused the death of one on whose body he holds an inquest, does not restrict him to the employment of a resident of the county. County Coms. *v.* Jameson, 86 Ind. 154.

Appointment of Surgeon. — The coroner has the right to select a surgeon to make a *post-mortem* examination at the expense of the county; the county commissioners cannot make a general appointment of a surgeon for such purposes. Allegheny Co. *v.* Shaw, 34 Pa. St. 301.

A coroner has authority to employ a physician for a *post-mortem*, but the county may not be liable to a fixed price agreed upon between the coroner and physician. Jameson *v.* Co. Coms., 64 Ind 524. See also Dearborn Co. *v.* Bond, 88 Ind. 102.

In taking an inquisition of death *super visum corporis*, the coroner, as a public agent, has authority to order a *post-mortem* examination at the public charge; and the physician or surgeon employed by him is employed by the county, and is entitled to a reasonable compensation from the county for his services. Allegheny Co. *v.* Watt, 3 Pa. St. 462; Com. *v.* Harmon, 4 Pa. St. 269.

The testimony should be reduced to writing;[1] and when thus taken officially, on an inquest, it is, under the circumstances, evidence against the party there or thereafter accused;[2] and the inquisition and testimony should be properly transmitted to the district attorney or proper authorities.[3]

The jury, having inspected the body, and heard the testimony, should retire for consideration of the case; from which consideration even the coroner is excluded, after having charged them, although they may take his opinion in questions of law which may arise in their deliberations.[4] Having agreed upon a verdict, they shall reduce the same to writing, which shall show before what coroner it was taken, and that it was taken by good and lawful men of the county who were duly sworn;[5] also when and where the same was taken; also how, when, and where the person came to his death or injury, who he was, and who was guilty, and in what manner.[6] If the person deceased, or the person causing the death, be unknown, the jury should so find.[7] The inquisition should be signed by the coroner and jury.[8]

If a crime has been committed, he shall bind over the material witnesses.[9] If there are no friends of deceased, he shall bury the body; and it is generally made the duty of the coroner to hand over the effects of deceased which are unclaimed to county treasurer or other designated authority.[10]

When the coroner's jury find that the deceased was killed or wounded by criminal means, it is his duty to issue a warrant for his arrest; and the accused is entitled to a hearing before a magistrate.[11]

And the testimony of a witness before the coroner, such person not being at the time under arrest, or charged with the crime, may be used against him on a subsequent trial for the alleged murder of the deceased.[12]

Where professional services are rendered by physician at inquests, at the request of the coroner, with no special agreement that he shall look to any other source than the coroner for payment, the latter is liable. Von Hoevenbergh *v.* Hasbrouck, 45 Barb. (N. Y.) 196. Paper on Medico-Legal Duties of Coroners, by Dr. Semmes, Amer. Law Reg. O. S. vol vi. 385.

1. People *v.* White, 22 Wend. 167.
2. Phil. Ev. 371 (7th Lon. ed.).
3. State *v.* Evans, 27 La. Ann. 297.
4. Crocker on Shf. *v.* Cor. 414.
5. 2 Hawkins, P. C. 77.
6. R. S. 1036, § 5.
7. 2 Hale, Cr. L. 63.
8. Rex *v.* Bowen, 6 Car. & P. 602; Rex *v.* Bennett, 6 Car. & P. 179; 2 Lewins, C. C. 125; Rex *v.* Nicholas, 7 Car. & P. 538.
9. Regina *v.* Taylor, 9 Car. & P. 672.
10. Crocker on Coroners, p. 416, § 964.

In Massachusetts coroners are required to deliver property found on or near the person of the deceased forthwith, to those entitled to its care or possession; and the refusal of coroners to deliver such property, on due demand, to the owner, amounts to conversion, for which they are liable Smiley *v.* Allen, 13 Allen (Mass.), 435.

11. One against whom a coroner's jury has found an inquisition is entitled to a hearing before a magistrate as if arrested, etc., under New York Code, § 145. *Re* Ramscor, 63 How. (N. Y.) Pr. 255.
12. Hendrickson *v.* The People, 2 Am. L. R. (O. S.) 531.

The testimony of a person examined as a witness before a coroner's jury, such person not being at the time under arrest or charged with crime, may be given in evidence against him on his subsequent trial for the alleged murder of the deceased. Hendrickson *v.* The People, 2 Am. L. R. (O. S.) 531.

10. Coroner's Duties as Sheriff.—When the office of sheriff has become vacant, the coroner becomes *ex-officio* sheriff; and all duties, rights, and powers of the sheriff, including power to appoint a deputy for the performance of the sheriff's duties, will devolve upon him, and the service of process by a deputy will be legal.[1]

A process or mandate in a civil action which must or may be served or executed by the coroners or coroner of the county, should be directed to the coroner or coroners.[2]

Where a coroner has acted in service of process, the legal presumption is, that the facts existed which rendered it proper for him to act.[3]

Process directed to and executed by a *de facto* coroner is good.[4]

And whether a coroner has power to commit to jail a party charged with felony, it is too late to object after a regular examination and an indictment found for felony.[5] Where a sheriff is interested in a matter, the coroner must serve the process, be it civil or criminal.[6]

1. Reed *v.* Reber, 62 Ill. 240; Yeargin *v.* Siler, 83 N. C. 348; Jervis on Cor. 75.

Under the revised statutes of Missouri the coroner is the proper officer to serve and execute all writs and precepts, and perform all other duties of the sheriff, when the latter is for any reason disqualified from discharging the duties of his office. 90 Mo. 37.

A coroner is authorized to serve process in the absence or in case of any disqualification of the sheriff; and where the record shows that process was so served, it will be presumed that the disabilities existed, unless the contrary be shown. Rodolph *v.* Myer, 1 Wash. T. 154.

And where the office of sheriff was vacant, and its duties were being performed by the coroner, and the coroner was party defendant to a bill in chancery, the facts justified the appointment of an elisor to serve the summons. Reed *v.* Moffatt, 62 Ill. 300.

A writ of replevin, directed to coroners, may be executed by a deputy specially authorized by one of the coroners. Jewell *v.* Hutchinson, 31 N. J. L. 71.

In South Carolina the coroner, being in his ministerial capacity merely the substitute of the sheriff, cannot act in that capacity when there is no sheriff in office; and a sheriff is not in office until he has given a bond according to law. Richardson *v.* Croft., 1 Bailey (S. C.), 264. But compare Paddock *v.* Cameron, 8 Cow. (N. Y.) 212.

The city coroner, and not the district coroner, is the proper officer to serve process on the city sheriff of Charleston. Miller *v.* Yeadon, 3 McCord (S. C.), 11.

2. Unless a mandate be directed to a particular county, or generally to the coroners of that county, the coroner to whom it is delivered has no authority to execute it, and is not liable for failure to return it. Brown *v.* Baker, 10 Humph. (Tenn.) 346; Governor *v.* Lindsay, 14 Ala. 658; Greshom *v.* Leverett, 10 Ala. 384.

3. Kittridge *v.* Bancroft, 1 Met. (Mass.) 508; Kirk *v.* Murphy, 16 Tex. 654; Rodolph *v.* Myer, 1 Wash. T. 154. *Contra*, see Com. *v.* Moore, 19 Pick. (Mass.) 339; Carlisle *v.* Weston, 21 Pick. (Mass.) 535, where it was held that service of process by a coroner, being, by virtue of special authority, the facts necessary to give him the power, should appear in the writ. And in Mays *v.* Forbes, 11 Tex. 284, it was *held* that, in order to entitle a coroner to serve a writ of error, the petition for the writ must state that there is no sheriff, or that there is some objection to him.

4. Gunby *v.* Welcher, 20 Ga. 336; Mabry *v.* Turrentine, 8 Ired. (N. C.) 201.

5. Wormley *v* Com., 10 Gratt. (Va.) 658.

6. A coroner who is deputy sheriff may as coroner serve a writ on another deputy of the sheriff. Colby *v.* Dillingham, 7 Mass. 475.

By the common law, when a coroner arrests a sheriff he is bound to make his own house or some other place a prison for the sheriff's detention; and he is liable for an escape if he commit him to the jail of which the sheriff by law has the charge. Day *v.* Brett, 6 Johns. (N. Y.) 22.

A coroner is authorized to serve criminal process upon the sheriff. Adams *v.* Vose, 1 Gray (Mass.), 51.

Under the New York Code, §§ 158, 419, the coroner may call to his aid the power of the county in a proper case in executing an order of arrest in an action in which

11. Expenses; Fees; Salary.—The proper expenses of a coroner's inquest are a charge against the county or town, and not against the State.[1] By the common law the coroner was entitled to neither fees nor salary, but compensation is now universally accorded. Generally speaking, the office is supported by fees, but in some places he has been made a salaried officer.[2] Where several persons are killed at the same time, and even owe their death to the same cause, the coroner may hold separate inquests on each body, and is entitled to fees in each case.[3] He may be entitled to his fees notwithstanding the jury finds that the deceased dies a natural death.[4]

the sheriff is a party. Slater *v.* Wood, 9 Bosw. (N. Y.) 15.

Where a coroner arrests a deputy jailer on execution, and carries him to jail, and neither the sheriff nor any keeper appointed by the sheriff is there to receive and confine him, the coroner has done his duty; and if the prisoner afterwards go at large, it is the escape of the sheriff. Colby *v.* Sampson, 5 Mass. 310.

When process is in the hands of a coroner, commanding him to seize property in the hands of the sheriff, which is regular on its face, the latter need not look behind it to inquire whether the prerequisite steps have been taken, nor whether the coroner was duly authorized to act. Governor *v.* Gibson, 14 Ala. 326.

In Kentucky, if a coroner serve a process on which a judgment is entered, the execution of the judgment must, by statute, be directed to and served by him, though the cause for directing the original process to him has ceased. Tuggle *v.* Smith, 6 T. B. Monroe (Ky.), 76.

The statutory provisions for service of process and protection thereunder apply to a coroner to whom a requisition has issued in a proceeding against the sheriff for the claim and delivery of personal property. Manning *v.* Keenan, 73 N. Y. 45.

Sales of Property by Coroner.—A coroner may convey land sold by him under execution. Winslow *v.* Austin, 5 J. J. Marsh. (Ky.) 411.

Though a coroner in his sales should pursue strictly the directions of the act which regulates sheriff's sales, yet a sale being advertised for a different day, to which the plaintiff, the defendant in execution, and the officer have all assented, cannot work the dissolution of a contract made at such sale by a third person who has been in no wise affected by the irregularity. O'Bannon *v.* Kirkland, 2 Strobh. (S. C.) 29.

1. The costs of a coroner's inquest are chargeable against the county, not against the State. Galloway *v.* Shelby Co., 7 Lea (Tenn.), 121.

Under Rhode Island Rev. Stat. ch. 333, the coroner can bring an action in his own name for all expenses attending an inquest which have been allowed by the town council. Hill *v* Mowry, 7 R. I. 167.

Where the coroner holds an inquest in land ceded to the United States, he is entitled to recover his fees from the county; no act of Congress has forbidden the holding of the inquest, under such circumstances. Allegheny Co. *v.* McClurg, 53 Pa. St. 482.

The fee of a coroner for summoning a jury not being fixed by statute, the county court may fix the amount at discretion, and the order is not reviewable. Cook *v.* Co., 8 Or. 170.

2. As to compensation of fees earned by a coroner which are made by law the basis of his salary, Phila. *v.* Gilbert, 37 Leg. Int. 376.

3. Where a coroner held inquest at the same time on seven bodies, of persons killed in one accident, *held*, that he is entitled to fees, in each case, for qualification, drawing and returning inquisition. Rombo *v.* Commissioners, 1 Chester Co. R. (Pa.) 416.

Nineteen persons came to their death suddenly and almost simultaneously by a mine explosion. The coroner held a separate inquest over each body, at the respective homes of the deceased, qualifying the same jury separately over each body, and the inquest returned a separate finding in each case. *Held*, that this was the necessary and proper course to pursue, under the circumstances, and that he was entitled to the legal fees in each case. Fayette Co. *v.* Batton, 108 Pa. St. 591.

4. The object of a coroner's inquest is to ascertain the cause of death. The authority of the coroner in this branch of his office is necessarily judicial in its character. Being the sole judge as to the propriety of holding the inquest, his action in that respect is not subject to revision by the county commissioners; and he is entitled to fees under the statute, notwithstanding the verdict of the coroner's jury discloses that the

A coroner cannot sustain an action to recover fees because of removal of a body from the county.[1]

CORPORAL. — Belonging or relating to the body.[2]

deceased died a natural death, and not by casualty or violence. Boislemere *v.* County Commissioners, 32 Mo. 375.

In an action by a coroner against a county to recover his fees for the making of an inquest, his inquisition upon the body of the deceased, signed by his physician, and signed and sealed by himself and his jury of six, is admissible in evidence, even though the paper has never been returned to any court, and is not marked filed, or recorded in any book kept by the coroner for that purpose.

Where a coroner makes an inquest, the presumption is that he has acted in good faith and on sufficient cause. In a suit by him against the county, however, to recover his fees, this presumption is not conclusive. Evidence is admissible to show that he acted in bad faith, and knowingly without sufficient cause or reason. County of Lancaster *v.* Mishler, 100 Pa. St. 624.

1. A coroner cannot sustain an action against one who has removed a dead body from the county, to recover fees which he might have charged upon holding an inquest. Fryer *v.* R. R. Co., 50 Ga. 581.

2. Webster.

Corporal Imbecility. — Sexual impotency, not necessarily permanent. Where it was alleged, as ground for a divorce, that the respondent was, at the time of marriage, "ever since has been, and now is, laboring under a corporal imbecility," the latter term was held not to import *ex vi termini*, a confirmed and incurable impotency. It has no precise technical meaning, and may be a merely temporary imbecility. Ferris *v.* Ferris, 8 Conn. 166.

Corporal Oath. — An oath taken by laying the hand on some part of the Holy Scriptures while the oath is administered. 3 Inst. 165; Just. Nov. 8, *ad fin.*; Id. 124, c. 1; Adams' Glos.; Burr. L. D.; Abb. L. D. Originally the book was taken in the hand, but subsequently mere touching was considered sufficient. The oath of proctors and advocates in the English consistory courts was, "Ego, A. B., ad ista sancta, Dei Evangelia, per me *corporaliter tacta*, juro, quod," etc. Burr. L. D.

In this country the term "corporal oath," as used in indictments for perjury, is considered to mean an oath taken according to the custom and usages of the country. Accordingly, such an indictment, alleging that the accused was sworn and took his corporal oath, is sustained by evidence that the oath was taken in the usual manner, as by holding up the hand. "The term, corporal oath," said the court, "must be considered as applying to any bodily assent to the oath of the witness." State *v.* Norris, 9 N. H. 96. The same point was decided in the same way in another State, where it was said, "However it may have been in somewhat olden time in Europe, we think that now, at least in our State, 'corporal oath' and 'solemn oath' are used synonymously, and an oath taken with uplifted hand may be properly described by either term." Jackson *v.* State, 1 Ind. 184. In this case was quoted, with approval, Webster's definition of corporal oath: "A solemn oath, so called from the ancient usage of touching the *corporale*, or cloth that covered the consecrated elements" in the Eucharist.

Where it was objected to an indictment for perjury, which alleged that the defendant did, "in due form of law, take his corporal oath," that it did not state that he took his oath on the Gospels, or in the presence of Almighty God by uplifted hand, the form used was held sufficient. The words "corporal oath" may stand for lifting an arm or other bodily member. Respub. *v.* Newell, 3 Yeates (Pa.), 412.

Corporal Punishment. — Any kind of corporal privation or suffering, inflicted directly by way of penalty for an offence. It includes imprisonment, and is set in contradistinction to fine. 7 Cowen (N. Y.), 525 n.; 1 Chit. Cr. L. 799; Whar. Cr. L. (7th ed.) § 3403.

CORPORATIONS (PRIVATE).—(See also AMOTION; BY-LAWS, DISFRANCHISEMENT; DIVIDENDS; FOREIGN CORPORATIONS; FRANCHISES; OFFICERS (PRIVATE CORPORATIONS); STOCK; STOCKHOLDERS; ULTRA VIRES.

For Particular Corporations, etc., see BANKS; BENEFICIAL ASSOCIATIONS; BOOM COMPANIES; BUILDING ASSOCIATIONS; CARRIERS OF GOODS; CARRIERS OF LIVE STOCK; CARRIERS OF PASSENGERS; EXPRESS COMPANIES; MUNICIPAL CORPORATIONS; RAILROADS; RELIGIOUS CORPORATIONS; and similar titles.)

A. Organization of Corporations.—1. Definition.—A corporation is a body consisting of one or more persons[1] established by law[2] for certain specific purposes, with the capacity of succession (either perpetual or for a limited period) and other special privi-

1. "A body-politic is a body to take in succession, framed (as to that capacity) by policy, and therefore it is called by Littleton a body-politic; and it is called a corporation or a body incorporate, because the persons are made into a body, and of a capacity to take and grant, etc." Co. Litt. 250 a.

A State is not a corporation, as the term is used in the United States revenue acts. Georgia *v.* Atkins, 35 Ga. 315.

2. By the common law of *England* and the *United States*, a corporation cannot, like a partnership, be constituted by the agreement of parties, but only under authority from the government. 1 Black. Com *472; Ang. & Am. §§ 66–75; Stowe *v.* Flagg, 72 Ill. 397; Atkins *v.* Mar. & Cin. R. Co., 15 Ohio St. 21; People *v* Assessors, 1 Hill (N. Y.), 616; State *v.* Bradford, 32 Vt. 50.

Acting as a corporation, without being legally constituted one, is an offence at common law, being a contempt of the king by usurping his prerogative. Knider *v.* Taylor, 3 Law Jour. 68; Duvergier *v.* Fellows, 5 Bing. 248; s. c., 5 M. & P. 403. See Quo Warranto

It follows that a corporation can have no legal existence out of the State creating it. The exercise of any power in another State depends on the will of that State. Gill *v.* Ky. Min. Co., 7 Bush (Ky.), 635; Thompson *v.* Waters, 25 Mich. 214; N. O., J. & G. N. R. Co. *v.* Wallace, 50 Miss. 244; Bank of Augusta *v.* Earle, 13 Pet. (U. S.) 512; O. & M. R. Co. *v.* Wheeler, 1 Black (U. S.), 286; Liverpool Ins. Co. *v.* Mass., 10 Wall. (U. S.) 566.

Hence all votes and proceedings of persons professing to act in the capacity of corporations, when assembled beyond the bounds of the State granting the charter of the corporation, are wholly void. Ang. & Am. § 498; Taylor, § 382; Aspinwall *v.* Ohio, etc., R. Co., 20 Ind. 492; Miller *v.* Ewer, 27 Me. 509; Freeman *v.* Machias, etc., Co., 38 Me. 433; Camp *v.* Byrne, 41 Mo. 525; Ormsby *v.* W. Cop. Mfg. Co, 56 N. Y. 623.

Being the creature of local law only,

leges not possessed by individuals, yet acting in many respects as an individual.[1]

2. Classification.—Corporations may be variously classified, depending on the point of view from which they are regarded. They may be—

(1) *Sole*, consisting of but one member at a time;[2] or *aggregate*. consisting of more than one member.[3]

(2) *Public*, for the purposes of government and the management of public affairs; or *private*, formed by voluntary agreement for private purposes.[4]

with privileges and immunities that cannot exist, without legislative permission, outside the State of its incorporation, it follows that though for the purposes of Federal jurisdiction a corporation is in some sense regarded as a citizen of that State (see FOREIGN CORPORATIONS), it cannot be so regarded in the sense of being "entitled to all the privileges and immunities of citizens in the several States," under the U. S. constitution. Paul *v.* Virginia. 8 Wall. (U. S.) 168; Tatem *v.* Wright. 3 Zab. (N. J.) 429, 445; Bard *v.* Poole, 12 N. Y. 495. 504.

A State can, of course, incorporate a corporation of another State. Grangers' L. & H. Ins Co. *v* Kamper, 73 Ala. 325; s. c. 6 Am. & Eng. Corp. Cas. 497; Bishop *v.* Brainerd, 28 Conn. 289. And see O. & M. R. Co. *v.* Wheeler, 1 Black (U. S.). 286. And it may recognize as a corporation a foreign body having the essential attributes of a corporation, even though the laws under which it was formed may expressly declare it not to be such. Oliver *v.* Liverpool, etc., Ins. Co., 100 Mass. 531; Liverpool, etc., Ins. Co. *v.* Mass., 10 Wall. (U. S) 566

A corporation chartered by the United States is not a foreign corporation in any State where it is established. Eby *v* N. P. R. Co., 6 W. N. C. (Pa.) 385. See FOREIGN CORPORATIONS.

1. Morawetz (2d Ed.), §§ 1, 227. For corporations as persons, see PERSONS.

2. The king of England has always been regarded as a sole corporation. Co. Litt. 43; 1 Black. Comm. *469; 1 Kyd on Corporations. 20.

A man may compose a corporation sole as trustee for the benefit of others, of which the most familiar instance is the chamberlain of the city of London, who may take a recognizance to himself and his successors in trust for the orphans. Fulwood's Case, 4 Co. 64; Cro. El. 464; 1 Kyd, 20.

Corporations sole are usually ecclesiastical, as a bishop or a vicar, and are therefore very rare in the United States Where the minister of a parish was, however, before the Revolution seized of a freehold as a *persona ecclesiæ* in the same manner as in England, he and his successors did not cease to be a corporation sole for that purpose after the States became independent. Town of Pawlet *v.* Clark, 9 Cro. (U. S.) 292: Weston *v.* Hunt, 2 Mass. 501; Brunswick *v.* Dunning, 7 Mass. 447.

There are some instances in which certain public officers are expressly empowered by statute to sue as corporations sole. Overseers *v.* Sears, 22 Pick (Mass) 125.

A corporation may be created, capable of being either sole or aggregate, e g., a grant of corporate powers may be made to one person, his associates and successors, and confers on him the right to exercise all the powers granted without taking associates. Penobscot Boom Co. *v.* Lamson, 16 Me. 224.

As the general laws under which private corporations are now usually formed always establish a minimum (usually five) for the number of subscribers to the certificate, no private corporation sole can be formed under these laws. See note 1, p. 187.

3. People *v.* Assessors, 1 Hill (N. Y), 616, 620

4. "Public corporations are generally esteemed such as exist for public political purposes only, such as towns, cities, parishes, and counties; and in many respects they are so, although they involve some private interests; but, strictly speaking, public corporations are such only as are founded by the government for public purposes, where the whole interests belong also to the government. If therefore, the foundation be private, though under the charter of the government, the corporation is private, however extensive the uses may be to which it is devoted, either by the bounty of the founder or the nature and objects

(3) *Ecclesiastical* (or *religious*),[1] for religious objects; or *lay*, for secular objects.[2]

of the institution. For instance, a bank created by the government for its own uses, whose stock is exclusively owned by the government, is, in the strictest sense, a public corporation. So a hospital created and endowed by the government for general charity. But a bank, whose stock is owned by private persons, is a private corporation, although it is erected by the government, and its objects and operations partake of a public nature. The same doctrine may be affirmed of insurance, canal, bridge, and turnpike companies. In all these cases the uses may, in a certain sense, be called public, but the corporations are private; as much so, indeed, as if the franchises were vested in a single person." Washington, J., in Dartmouth College *v.* Woodward, 4 Wheat. (U. S.) 518, 668. See also Osborn *v.* U. S. Bank, 7 Wheat. (U. S.) 738.

"The difference between these two classes of corporations is radical, and hence they are in many instances governed by widely different principles of law. Private corporations are associations formed by the voluntary agreement of their members, such as banking, railroad, and manufacturing companies. Public corporations are not voluntary associations at all, and there is no contractual relation between the corporators who compose them; they are merely government institutions, created by law, for the administration of the affairs of the community." Morawetz (2d Ed.), § 3. See Dillon on Mun. Corp. §§ 19-24; Ang. Am. §§ 30-34; Dean *v.* Davis, 51 Cal. & 406; People *v.* Morris, 13 Wend. (N. Y.) 325, 337; Bushell *v.* Com. Ins. Co., 15 S. & R. (Pa.) 186; Foster *v.* Fowler, 60 Pa. St. 27; Bennett's App., 65 Pa. St. 242.

In Miners' Ditch Co. *v.* Tellerbach, 37 Cal. 543, three classes were recognized: public municipal corporations, the object of which is to promote the public interest; corporations technically private, but of a *quasi* public character, having in view some public enterprise in which the public interests are involved, such as railroad, turnpike, and canal companies; and corporations strictly private.

In the popular meaning of the term, nearly every corporation is public, inasmuch as they are all created for the public benefit. Yet if the whole interest does not belong to the government, or if the corporation is not created for the administration of political or municipal power, it is a private corporation. Rundle *v.* D. & R. Canal Co., 1 Wall. Jr. (C. C. U. S.) 273, 290. To the same effect. Bk. of U. S. *v.* Planters' Bk., 9 Wheat. (U. S.) 907; Directors *v.* Houston, 71 Ill. 318; Miners' Bk. *v.* U. S., 1 Greene (Iowa), 553; Ten Eyck *v.* D. & R. Canal Co., 18 N. J. L. 200; Tinsman *v.* Bel. Del. R., 26 N. J. L. 148; Bonaparte *v.* C. & A. R. Co., 1 Bald. (C. C. U. S.) 205; Ala R. Co. *v.* Kidd, 29 Ala. 221; McCune *v.* Norwich Gas. Co., 30 Conn. 521; Commonwealth *v.* Lowell Gas. Co., 12 Allen (Mass.), 77; Roanoke R. Co. *v.* Davis, 2 Dev. & Bat. (N. Car.) 45; Bailey *v.* Mayor, etc., 3 Hill (N. Y.), 331; N. Y. C. R. Co. *v.* Met. Gas. Co., 63 N. Y. 326; Vincennes Univ. *v.* Indiana, 14 How. (U. S.) 268.

The fact that the State has an interest as one of the corporators does not make a corporation public. Bk. of U. S. *v.* Planters' Bk., 4 Wheat. (U. S.) 205; Turnpike Co. *v.* Wallace, 8 Watts (Pa.), 316. Nor that the corporation derives a part of its support from the government. Cleveland *v.* Stewart, 3 Ga 283. Nor that the corporation is employed in the service of the government. Thomson *v.* Pacific R., 9 Wall. (U. S.) 579. The same has been held where the entire interest was in the State. State Bk of So. Car. *v.* Gibbs, 3 McC. (S. Car.) 377.

"By becoming owner or stockholder the State descends from its sovereign dignity to individuality so far as to place it on an even footing of legal liability with other corporations of like character and purposes." Hutchinson *v.* W. & A. R. Co., 6 Tenn. 634. But the contrary has also been held. Trustees *v.* Winston, 5 St. & P. (Ala.) 17.

In the constitution of *Pennsylvania* (art. 16, sec. 13) the term "private corporation" is declared to include "all joint-stock companies or associations having any of the powers or privileges of corporations not possessed by individuals or partnerships." Similar provisions are found in the constitutions of *Alabama, California, Kansas, Louisiana, Michigan, Minnesota, North Carolina,* and *New York.*

1 Ang. & Ames, § 36.

The former name is usual in *England;* the latter, in the *United States.* Ang. & Ames, § 37.

2. Blackstone (i. 470) states that ecclesiastical corporations are where the members that compose it are entirely spiritual persons. This is not the case in the *United States,* where the vestry of a church, or other laymen holding an

(4) *Eleemosynary*, for charitable purposes;[1] or *civil*, for the transaction of public or private business.[2]

Besides corporations proper, there are *quasi* corporations, or corporations *sub modo*, i.e., associations and government institutions possessing only a portion of the attributes which distinguish ordinary public or private corporations.[3]

3. Ordinary Corporate Powers.—At the common law the ordinary powers, considered essential to every corporation, are these: [4]

(1) To have succession, by its corporate name,[5] either perpetually or for a limited period.

analogous office, are almost always members of the corporation.

Religious corporations in the *United States* "are not to be regarded as ecclesiastical corporations in the sense of the English law, which were composed entirely of ecclesiastical persons, and subject to the ecclesiastical judicatories, but as belonging to the class of civil corporations, to be controlled and managed according to the principles of the common law as administered by the ordinary tribunals of justice." Robertson *v.* Bidlious 11 N. Y. 243. See Terrett *v.* Taylor, 9 Cr. (U. S.) 43.

1 1 Kyd, 26; Asylum *v.* Phœnix Bk., 4 Conn. 272; State *v.* Adams, 44 Mo. 570; McKim *v.* Odom, 4 Bland Ch. (N. Y.) 407; Dartmouth College *v.* Woodward, 4 Wheat. (U. S.) 518, 681; Vincennes Univ. *v.* Indiana, 14 How. (U. S.) 268.

An academy receiving fees for tuition is not necessarily a corporation "for pecuniary profit." Sta. Clara Fem. Acad. *v.* Sullivan, 117 Ill. 375; s. c., 13 Am. & Eng. Corp. Cas. 11.

2 The universities of Oxford and Cambridge are civil, and not ecclesiastical nor eleemosynary. 1 Black. Com. 471.

3. Morawetz (2d Ed.), § 6; 2 Kent, *274.

The usual public *quasi*-corporations are counties, hundreds, townships, overseers of the poor, town supervisors, etc. See Adams *v.* Bank, 1 Me 363; Riddle *v.* Proprietors, 7 Mass. 169; Mower *v.* Leicester, 9 Mass. 352; School District *v.* Wood, 13 Mass. 193; Damon *v.* Granby, 2 Pick. (Mass.) 352; Rouse *v.* Moore, 18 Johns. (N. Y.) 407; N. Hempstead *v.* Hempstead, 2 Wend. (N. Y.) 109.

Joint-stock companies may be cited as *quasi* corporations of a private character. They are associations having some of the features of an ordinary common law copartnership, and some of those of a private corporation. Morawetz (2d Ed.), § 6.

4. For these powers in general, see 1 Blacks. Com. 475; 2 Kent Com. 277; 1 Kyd, 13, 69.

In the general laws of each State for the formation of corporations, it is provided that every corporation so formed shall have these powers.

5. Corporate Name.—Every corporation should have a name, by which it may be known as grantor and grantee, may sue and be sued, and do all other legal acts. Ang. & Ames, § 99. See case of Sutton's Hospital, 10 Co., 1 a, 28 b.

If a name be not expressly given in the charter, it may be assumed by implication from the nature of the powers granted. Anon., 1 Salk. 191.

A corporate name may be acquired by usage. Smith *v.* Plank Rd. Co., 30 Ala. 650.

The name should be distinct from that of any other body incorporated in the same State. Hence in Newby *v.* Or. Cent. R. Co., Deady (U. S. C. C.), 609, the court said: "The corporate name is a necessary element of a corporation's existence. Any suit which produces confusion or uncertainty concerning this name is well calculated to injuriously affect the identity and business of a corporation. And as a matter of fact, in some degree at least, the natural and necessary consequence of the wrongful appropriation of a corporate name is to injure the business and rights of the corporation by destroying or confusing its identity." An attempt to incorporate by the name of another corporation already existent in the same State was therefore enjoined.

The charter of a church will not be approved unless the corporate name adopted be entirely distinctive from that of any other association incorporated in the same locality. Pres. Ch. of Harrisburg, 2 Grant's Cas. (Pa.) 240.

There is no restriction, however, on the legal right of a corporation to take the name of a corporation of another State, though from a moral point of view

(2) To take and grant property, to contract obligations,[1] and to sue and be sued[2] by its corporate name in the same manner as an individual.

(3) To purchase lands and other property, and to receive grants of privileges and immunities, and to hold the same for the benefit of its members and their successors in common.[3]

(4) To have a common seal.[4]

such an act must be condemned. Lehigh Valley Coal Co. *v.* Hampden (U. S. Dist. Ct. Ill., 1885). 8 Am. & Eng. Corp. Cas. 201.

A corporation may have one name by which it may take and grant and another by which it may sue and be sued. A corporation by prescription may have several names to the same purpose, and *scire facias* will lie in one of the names on a judgment obtained in the other. It is said that a corporation by charter may be empowered to act and purchase by one name and sue and be sued by another, and may even be specially empowered to use more than one name to the same purpose. Ang. & Am. § 100; 1 Kyd. 229, 230; Anon., 3 Salk. 102; Minot *v.* Curtis, 7 Mass. 441.

Where one certain name, however, has been given by charter and adopted, the corporation can, in general, act by no other name; and where a corporation is required by the State to act for its own benefit, it must do this by its proper name. Glass *v.* Tipton, etc., Co., 32 Ind. 376.

If a corporation conveys by a wrong name, it cannot take advantage of this after receiving the consideration. African Soc. *v.* Varick, 13 John. (N. Y.) 38.

In grants to corporations, the name must be the same in substance as that given by the charter, but need not be the same in words and syllables. Rex *v.* Haughley, 1 Barn. & Ad. 655.

To sustain a devise to a corporation, it is sufficient to show that a particular corporation was meant, though the name be mistaken. Vansant *v.* Roberts, 3 Md. 119; First Parish *v.* Cole, 3 Pick. (Mass.) 232.

Place.—A corporation should be constituted as of some place. Ang. & Am. § 103; Potter *v.* Bank of Ithaca, 7 Hill (N. Y.) 530; Land Grant Ry. *v.* Coffey Co., 6 Kan. 245.

1. "It is well-settled, sound, and rational law, that contracts which the corporation has power to make may be made in the same manner that a natural person would make them, in the absence of any special restriction." Blunt *v.* Walker, 11 Wis. 334.

In Barry *v.* Merchants' Exch. Co., 1 Sand. Ch. (N. Y.) 280, the following propositions were laid down:

Every corporation has as such at common law the capacity to take and grant property and to contract obligations in the same manner as an individual.

Corporations, except when restrained by law, have the absolute *jus disponendi* of their property, whether of lands or chattels, and in its exercise are unlimited as to objects and quantity.

Corporations created for limited and special purposes, by the nature of which their common-law powers are restricted, may make all contracts necessary and usual in the case of the business they transact as a means to effect their objects, and within these limits, unless expressly prohibited by law or the provisions of their charters, may deal precisely as an individual might who sought to accomplish the same ends.

So in Reynolds *v.* Commissioners, 5 Ohio, 205, it was said, "a corporation, by the terms of its creation, has the same capacity to buy and sell that an individual has who is competent to make contracts."

2. **Right to Sue and be Sued**—It is even provided in the constitutions of some States that all corporations can sue and be sued like natural persons. See Constitutions of *Alabama* (art. 14, sec. 12), *California* (art. 12, sec. 4), *Kansas* (art. 12, sec. 6), *Michigan* (art. 15, sec. 11), *Minnesota* (art. 12, sec. 1), *Nebraska* (art. 13, sec. 3), *Nevada* (art. 8, sec. 5), *New York* (art. 8, sec. 3), *North Carolina* (art. 8, sec. 3).

In general, a corporation can be sued in transitory actions in any State where legal service of process can be had. Gill *v.* Ky. Min. Co., 7 Bush (Ky.), 635; N. O., J. & G. N. R. Co. *v.* Wallace, 50 Miss. 244.

By the constitutions of *Alabama* (art. 14, sec. 4) and *California* (art. 12, sec. 16) suits may be brought against a corporation in any county where it does business; and such is the general rule.

3. For restrictions of the right of corporations to hold real estate, see *infra* this title, POWERS OF CORPORATIONS.

4. See *infra* this title, POWERS OF CORPORATIONS.

(5) To make by-laws, which are considered as private statutes for the government of the corporate body.[1]

(6) To appoint and remove its officers, and expel members.[2]

A corporation has, however, no powers whatever, except those given by its charter or the law under which it is incorporated, either directly or as incidental to its existence.[3] The exercise of all corporate powers should be subject to the legal rights of individuals.[4]

4. Power of Creating Corporations.—The power of creating corporations is one appertaining to sovereignty, exercised by that branch of the government in which it is constitutionally vested.[5] Being a means by which other powers are exercised, and not an end of government in itself, it will, even if not expressly granted by a constitution, follow from the grant of other powers which are carried into execution by its means.[6] In the *United States*, the power belongs

1. See BY-LAWS.

2. See AMOTION.

3. See *infra* this title, POWERS OF CORPORATIONS. Dartmouth Coll. *v.* Woodward, 4 Wheat. (U. S.) 636; City Council *v.* Plank-Road Co., 31 Ala. 76; Holland *v.* City of San Francisco, 7 Cal. 361; Occum Co. *v.* Sprague Mfg. Co., 34 Conn. 541; Ohio Ins. Co. *v.* Munnemacher, 15 Ind. 294; Thompson *v.* Waters, 25 Mich. 214; Rochester Ins. Co. *v.* Martin, 13 Minn. 59; Ruggles *v.* Collier, 43 Mo. 353; Downing *v.* Mt. Washington, etc., Co., 40 N. H. 230; People *v.* Utica Ins. Co., 15 John. (N. Y.) 358; Farmers' L. & T. Co. *v.* Carroll, 5 Barb. (N. Y.) 613, 649; White's Bank *v.* Toledo Ins. Co., 12 Ohio St. 601.

The exercise of a corporate franchise, being restrictive of individual rights, cannot be extended beyond the letter and spirit of the act of incorporation. Beaty *v.* Knowler, 4 Pet. (U. S.) 152, 168.

The specific grant of certain powers in a charter is an implied prohibition of other and distinct powers. N. Y., etc., Ins. Co. *v.* Ely, 5 Conn. 560, 572; People *v.* Utica Ins Co., 15 John. (N. Y.) 358, 383; N. Y., etc., Ins. Co. *v.* Ely, 2 Cow. (N. Y.) 678, 699.

A corporation can make no contracts that are not necessary either directly or indirectly to effect the objects of its creation, and it can itself deny, in an action brought against it on a contract, its power to enter into it. Abbott *v.* B. & R. Stm. Pkt. Co., 1 Md. Ch 542.

A corporation created according to the rules of the common-law must be governed by it in its mode of organization, in the manner of exercising its powers, and in the use of the capacities conferred. When created in disregard of these rules, its existence, powers, capacities, and the mode of exercising them must depend on the law of its creation. Pen. Boom Co. *v.* Lamson, 16 Me. 224.

4. The constitutions of *California* (art. 12, sec. 8), *Colorado* (art. 15, sec. 8), *Georgia* (art. 4, sec. 2, 2), *Louisiana* (art. 235), *Missouri* (art. 12, sec. 5), and *Pennsylvania* (art. 16, sec. 3) provide that the exercise of the police power of the State shall never be so construed nor abridged as to permit corporations to conduct their business in such manner as to infringe the equal rights of individuals or the general wellbeing of the State.

5. Both before and for some time after the Norman conquest, the nobles had the power of conferring corporate privileges within their respective demesnes. 1 Kyd, 42. Eventually, however, this privilege was recognized as belonging to the king alone, who could exercise it either by his sole charter or by an act of parliament, both means being almost equally expressions of the royal will. With the growth of parliamentary power, certain bounds to the king's right to create a corporation by his sole charter became established, and it was held that the most important corporate franchises could be granted only by act of parliament, the royal assent to which, though a necessary ingredient as a matter of constitutional form, could not practically be withheld. The crown cannot, for instance, grant a charter conferring a monopoly or the power of imprisonment. 2 Kent, *276; 1 Kyd, 61; Ang. & Am. §§ 66–68.

6. McCulloch *v.* St. of Maryland, 4 Wheat. (U. S) 316, 409. On p. 441 Marshall, C. J, said: "The power of creating a corporation, though appertaining to sovereignty, is not like the power of

to Congress and the State legislatures [1] (being limited in the former

making war or levying taxes or regulating commerce, a great substantive and independent power, which cannot be implied as incidental to other powers or used as a means of executing them. It is never the end for which other powers are exercised, but a means by which other objects are accomplished. . . . No sufficient reason is therefore perceived why it may not pass as incidental to those powers which are expressly given if it be a direct mode of executing them."

1 Ang. & Am. § 71; Morawetz (2d Ed.), § 9.

Power of Congress.—Congress has power to create a corporation whenever such a measure is appropriate for carrying out any of the authorized purposes of the Federal government. Such a corporation, being designed to aid the government in the administration of the public service, cannot be controlled or affected by the States, except so far as Congress may permit. McCulloch *v.* Maryland, 4 Wheat. (U. S.) 316; Osborn *v.* Bk. of U. S., 9 Wheat. (U. S.) 708; Brown *v.* Maryland, 12 Wheat. (U. S.) 419; Weston *v.* Charleston, 2 Pet. (U. S.) 466; Farmers' Bank *v.* Dearing, 91 U. S. 29.

Power of the State Legislatures.—The authority of the legislature in this respect is absolute and unlimited, except by express restrictions of the fundamental law. Paschall *v.* Whitsett, 11 Ala. 472; Franklin Br. Co. *v.* Wood, 14 Ga. 80; Stowe *v.* Flagg, 72 Ill. 397; Aurora *v.* West, 9 Ind. 74; McKim *v.* Odom, 3 Bland (Md.), 407; Bk. of Chenango *v.* Brown, 26 N. Y. 467; Atkinson *v.* Mar. & Cin. R. Co., 15 Ohio St. 21; Murphy *v.* [illegible], 20 Pa. St. 415, 419; Hell *v.* Bk. of [illegible], Peck (Tenn.), 269; State *v.* [illegible], 22 Vt. 50; Briscoe *v.* Bk. of Comm. of Ky., 11 Pet. (U. S.) 257.

Trading companies or societies not expressly sanctioned by the legislature, pursuant to some general or special law, are nothing more than ordinary partnerships, and the laws respecting them are the same. Wells *v.* Gates, 18 Barb. (N. Y.) 554.

Where the constitution gives the legislative power in its discretion to create corporations by special charter, the courts cannot review the exercise of this discretion. U. S. Trust Co. *v.* Brady, 20 Barb. (N. Y.) 119.

A Territorial Legislature can also create corporations, subject to the right of Congress to disapprove and revoke its action. Ang. & Am. § 75; Vance *v.* F. & M. Bk. of Ind., 1 Blackf. (Ind.) 80; Riddick *v.* Amelin, 1 Mo. 5.

Restrictions on this Power.—The usual restriction is that which forbids the legislature, either wholly or with but few exceptions, to create corporations by special act. See Morawetz (2d Ed.), § 10; Stimson's Am. Stat. Law, § 441.

Where such restriction exists, a special act authorizing purchasers of a railroad's property at a foreclosure sale to organize and form a corporation with the same rights and franchises as belonged to the corporation whose property was taken, is unconstitutional and void. Atkinson *v.* M. & C. R. Co., 15 Ohio St. 21.

Where a legislature granted to specified individuals and their assigns certain powers and privileges, to take effect if they should within a certain time organize themselves into a corporation under existing laws, the act was held special, and therefore unconstitutional. The fact that the legislature in another act declared that the first act should be considered general, did not affect the matter. San Francisco *v.* Spring Valley W. W. Co., 48 Cal. 493.

The constitutions of several States forbid all special acts to extend, change, alter, or amend any charter or franchise already in force. Stimson Am. Stat. Law. § 440 (D).

An act authorizing any university or college to change its name before a certain date does not conflict with such a restriction. Hazelett *v.* Butler Univ., 84 Ind. 230.

Where there are no such restrictions, the fact that creation by special statute is forbidden is held not to affect alterations of charters or extension of their period of existence. Colton *v.* Miss., etc., Boom Co., 22 Minn. 372; St. Paul F. Ins. Co. *v.* Allis, 24 Minn. 75; Wallace *v.* Loomis, 97 U. S. 146.

By the constitution of *Delaware* (art. 2, sec. 17), every charter must be passed by a two-thirds majority in each house.

By the constitution of *Georgia* (art. 3, secs. 17, 18), the legislature has no power to create private corporations, except banking, insurance, railroad, canal, navigation, express, and telegraph companies, but shall prescribe by law the manner in which such powers shall be exercised by the courts.

By the constitution of *Rhode Island* (art. 4, sec. 17), bills to create corporations, other than religious, charitable, and the like, must be continued to the case to public purposes, and in the latter by the restrictions of the State constitutions), and it cannot be delegated.[1]

A corporation may also exist by prescription, which presupposes authorized and legitimate creation.[2]

5. How Corporations are Created.—The right to corporate existence was formerly granted only in exceptional cases, and by a special charter or act of incorporation in each instance ;[3] but the power of special legislation of this sort is now restricted or abolished by the constitutions of nearly all the States,[4] and corporations can now usually be formed by any persons who comply with certain general, in some States extremely simple, statutory requirements.[5]

next legislature, and public notice given of their pendency.

By the constitution of *South Carolina* (art. 12, sec. 5), all laws creating corporations shall have provisions to prevent and punish fraudulent misrepresentations as to the capital, property, and resources.

1. In *England*, Parliament can confer on any person the power to grant charters of incorporation. The same is true of the king; the grant in such a case being considered the king's act on the principle of *qui facit per alium facit per se*. 1 Bl. Com. 474; 1 Kyd, 50; Ang. & Am. 74.

In the *United States*, the principle *delegata potestas non potest delegari* is applied to the legislative power, and it is held that the legislature cannot delegate this to any other body or authority. Cooley's Const. Lims. 116; Morawetz (2d Ed.), § 15.

Where, however, the legislature has enacted that corporations may be formed upon compliance with certain conditions, it is no objection that ministerial duties, such as the issuing of a certificate or charter, must be performed by some judge or other officer before the incorporation takes effect; nor even that he must exercise his judgment in determining whether the law has been complied with, and the proposed corporation can properly be chartered under it. General corporation laws, even if not provided for by the constitution of a State, are constitutional. Franklin Bridge Co. *v.* Wood, 14 Ga. 80; Ames *v.* Port Huron Co., 6 Mich. 266; Keyser *v.* Trustees of Bremen, 16 Mo. 88; Thomas *v.* Dakin, 22 Wend. (N. Y.) 210; Greeneville, etc., R. Co. *v.* Johnson, 8 Baxt. (Tenn.) 332; Falconer *v.* Campbell, 2 McLean (C. C.), 195.

2. 1 Black. Com. *473; 2 Kent, *276; Ang. & Am. § 70; Greene *v.* Dennis, 6 Conn. 302; Hagerstown Tupke. Co. *v.* Creeger, 5 H. & J. (Md.) 122; Dillingham *v.* Snow, 7 Mass. 547; Stockbridge *v.* West Stockbridge, 12 Mass. 400; Bow *v.* Allenstown, 34 N. H. 351.

Where, however, it is clear that no charter has been granted, the exercise of corporate rights through a series of years will avail nothing. Douthitt *v.* Stimson, 63 Mo. 269.

3. The charter, and not the organization under it, creates the subscribers a corporation, at least so as to render contracts in favor of the corporation valid. Vermont Cent. R. Co. *v.* Clayes, 21 Vt. 30.

But it has been held in *Illinois* that there is no corporation until it is organized as authorized by the charter, nor does it possess franchises or faculties for it or others to exercise, until by such organization it acquires a complete existence. Gent *v.* M. & Mut. Ins. Co, 107 Ill. 652; s. c., 8 Am. & Eng. Corp. Cas. 306.

4. See *supra*, 4. POWER OF CREATING CORPORATIONS, notes.

5. In former times (the right to incorporate) was granted only in exceptional cases, by a special charter in each instance. It was therefore looked upon as something valuable, and was called a "franchise." At the present day, however, the prohibition of the common law has been in a great measure repealed by the general incorporation laws. What was formerly the exception has now become the general rule. All persons have now the right of forming corporate associations, upon complying with the simple formalities prescribed by statute. The right of forming a corporation, and of acting in a corporate capacity, under the general incorporation laws, can be called a "franchise" only in the sense in which the right of forming a limited partnership or of executing a conveyance of land by deed is a franchise. Morawetz (2d Ed.), § 923.

6. Incorporation by Special Charter.—To create a corporation by special act, no express words are requisite.[1] Where a corporation is necessary to accomplish the evident purpose of the act, the right to corporate existence may be gathered from the general language.[2] A grant of corporate power is sufficient.[3] Legislative recognition of a corporation as existing also dispenses with further proof of incorporation,[4] except in States where corporations are formed under general laws only.[5]

After a special charter has been obtained, its acceptance is the next, and an indispensable, preliminary to actual organization.[6] Acceptance should be signified by a formal vote at a meeting of the corporators called as provided in the charter;[7] and, on acceptance, the corporation begins to exist as such, and can proceed to organize by the election of permanent officers.[8] The records of such a meeting are the best evidence of the acceptance, but it may be presumed from organization under the charter and exercise of the corporate powers.[9]

1. Any words descriptive of the purpose of the legislature are sufficient. Rex *v.* Amery, 1 Term. 575; Conservators *v.* Ash, 10 B. & C. 349; Grangers' Ins. Co. *v.* Kamper, 73 Ala. 325; s. c., 6 Am. & Eng. Corp. Cas. 407; Mahoney *v.* State Bank, 4 Ark. 620; Denton *v.* Jackson, 2 John. Ch. (N. Y.) 325.

If the words "found," "erect," "establish," or "incorporate" are wanting, it is immaterial. The assent of the government may be given constructively or presumptively, without such words. Sutton's Hosp. Case, 10 Co. 23*a*, 306.

2. Walsh *v.* Trustees, 96 N. Y. 427; s. c., 6 Am. & Eng. Corp. Cas. 45.

In an act incorporating a bank, no persons were named as corporators, but the fund was placed under the management of a given number of directors, who were required to be elected by the legislature, and upon whom the usual banking powers were conferred. This was held sufficient. Murphy *v.* State Bank, 7 Ark. 57.

A resolve of the executive council of *Massachusetts*, establishing a military company "agreeably to military law," was held not to confer incorporation. Shelton *v.* Banks, 10 Gray (Mass.), 401.

3. Com'th *v.* W. C. R. Co., 3 Grant (Pa.), 200.

A grant of lands to individuals by the sovereign authority, to be possessed and enjoyed by them in a corporate character, in itself confers a capacity to take and hold in a corporate character. North Hempstead *v.* Hempstead, 2 Wend. (N. Y.) 109.

4. Peop. *v.* Farnham, 35 Ill. 562; McIntyre *v.* Zanesville Canal Co., 9 Ohio, 203; Williams *v.* Union Bank, 2 Humph. (Tenn.) 339.

A royal charter granting lands to a society recognizes or confers a corporate capacity to take and hold lands, and this with a statute of the State reciting that the society are a corporation holding lands, is sufficient *prima facie* proof of corporate existence and powers. Soc. Prop. Gos. *v.* Town of Pawlet, 4 Pet. (U. S.) 480.

5. If corporations cannot be created except under general laws, the mere recognition of a corporate body in acts of the legislature, as an existing corporation, cannot operate to give the organization validity. Oroville, etc., R. Co. *v.* Supervisors of Plumas, 37 Cal. 354.

6. A charter is inoperative until accepted, and so is the extension of a charter beyond the original term. Morawetz, § 21 *et seq.* 623; Ang. & Am. § 81; L. & K. Bk. *v.* Richardson, 1 Greenl. (Me.) 79; Hudson *v.* Carman, 41 Me. 84.

7. Hudson *v.* Carman, 41 Me. 84; Shortz *v.* Unangst, 3 W. & S. (Pa.) 45; Com'th *v.* Cullen, 13 Pa. 133. 143.

But there need be no formal vote if the charter does not require it. Coffin *v.* Collins, 17 Me. 440; B. O. & M. R. Co. *v.* Smith, 47 Me. 34.

8. Goshen Turnpike Co. *v.* Sears, 7 Conn. 86; Hudson *v.* Carman, 41 Me. 84; Riddle *v.* Proprs., 7 Mass. 184; Com'th *v.* Worcester Turnpike Co., 3 Pick. (Mass.) 327.

As all acts of a corporation as a body, outside the State of its incorporation, are invalid (*supra*, 2. CLASSIFICATION, notes), it follows that the organization, to be legal, must take place within the State. Freeman *v.* Machias, etc., Co., 38 Me. 343.

9. The acceptance of the charter must

7. Incorporation under General Laws.—Within this century the practice of granting charters by special act has been largely superseded by general laws,[1] providing that corporations may be formed by the voluntary association of at least a specified number of persons,[2] for the purposes and in the manner stated in the acts, and that, when formed, such corporations, by virtue of their existence as such, should have certain corporate powers (the usual powers mentioned *supra*, 3. ORDINARY CORPORATE POWERS), unless otherwise specially provided.[3] The provisions of these general laws may be outlined as follows: If a stock company is contemplated, a part of the stock must first be subscribed to, and in any case an organization must usually be effected by the election of directors or trustees.[4] A certificate, or articles of association,[5] is then pre-

be proved by the best evidence. The corporation's books are the best evidence of its doings. If they have not been kept, or are lost, or destroyed, or not accessible to the party who must prove acceptance, this may be proved by implication from the proved acts of the corporation. Hudson *v.* Carman, 41 Me. 84; Trott *v.* Warren, 2 Fair. (Me.) 227; Penobscot Boom Co. *v.* Lamson, 16 Me. 224; Sampson *v.* Bowdoinham Steam-mill Co., 36 Me. 78; Dedham Bk. *v.* Pickering, 3 Pick. (Mass.) 335; Charles Riv. Br. *v.* Warren Br., 7 Pick. (Mass.) 344; Russell *v.* McLellan, 14 Pick. (Mass.) 63; Middlesex Husbandmen *v.* Davis, 3 Met. (Mass.) 133; Narragansett Bk. *v.* Atlantic Silk Co., 3 Met. (Mass.) 282; F. & M. Bk. *v.* Jenks, 7 Met. (Mass.) 592; Cahill *v.* Kalamazoo M. I. Co., 7 Doug. (Mich.) 124; W. & M. R. Co. *v.* Saunders, 3 N. Car. 126; Bk. of U. S. *v.* Dandridge, 12 Wheat. (U. S.) 71.

Where a corporation had been formed and was doing business under a general law, and afterwards obtained a special charter with new and extended franchises, and the fact of acceptance was denied and the proof thereof claimed to be insufficient, it was held that the question of acceptance should have been submitted to the jury. "To prove the fact of acceptance," said the court, "it was only necessary to show, in connection with the act of incorporation itself, that the parties incorporated had actually used and exercised the powers and privileges conferred by the act, and if such user of powers and privileges could only be referred to the act of incorporation, such user would fully justify the presumption that the act of incorporation had been accepted." Hammond *v.* Straus, 53 Md. 1.

Election of officers is, however, only presumptive evidence of acceptance. Com'th *v.* Cullen, 13 Pa. St. 133.

The presumption of acceptance is rebutted by evidence that no proceedings were ever had under the charter, although some years have elapsed. Newton *v.* Carberry, 5 Cranch (C. C.), 632.

1. In *England* these laws are those known as the Companies Acts. For the constitutionality of such laws see *supra*, 4. POWER OF CREATING CORPORATIONS.

Incorporation under a general law is not destroyed, but only modified by the acceptance of a new special charter. Johnston *v.* Crawley, 25 Ga. 316.

2. In *Louisiana* it has been held that corporations are not persons within the meaning of such a provision, and therefore cannot participate in the formation of other corporations. F. & T. Ins. Co. *v.* New Harbor Co., 37 La. Ann. 233; s. c., 14 Am. & Eng. Corp. Cas. 1.

3. The powers obtained by such incorporations are necessarily restricted to those mentioned in the act. Medical Coll. Case, 3 Whart. (Pa.) 445.

The charter is void as to all powers and privileges granted beyond the provisions of the statute. Heck *v.* McEven, 12 Lea (Tenn.), 97; s. c., 6 Am. & Eng. Corp. Cas. 577.

If unauthorized provisions are added to the articles of incorporation, all acts done pursuant to such provisions will be void; but until the company is proceeded against for an abuse of its franchises, its rights as a corporation will not be affected by such unauthorized provisions. Eastern Plank R. Co. *v.* Vaughan, 14 N. Y. 516

4. See the last four items of the certificate as stated in the text.

In some States, e.g. *Illinois*, organization does not take place till after a license to organize is obtained. Rev. Sts Ill. 327; Stowe *v.* Flagg, 72 Ill. 397.

5. The latter term is usual in the Western States. In *California* the term

pared, which must be signed and acknowledged[1] by a certain number of the corporators,[2] usually setting forth—1. The name of the corporation;[3] 2. The purpose for which it is formed;[4] 3. The place or places where its business is to be transacted;[5] 4. The term for which it is to exist;[6] 5. The names and residences of the subscribers, if there be capital stock, and the number of shares taken by each; 6. The number of directors, and the names and residences of those chosen for the first year;[7] 7. The amount

"articles of incorporation" is used. 1 Hibb. Stats. § 5289.

1. Apart from statutory requirement, the certificate need not be either executed or acknowledged within the State. Humphreys *v.* Mooney, 5 Col. 282.

In *Pennsylvania* it must be acknowledged by at least three of the subscribers before the recorder of deeds of the county in which the chief business of the corporation is to be carried on, or in which the principal office is situated. Act of 29th Apr. 1874, § 3; 1 Purd. Dig. 337, 338.

Acknowledgment by all the subscribers is not necessary. In *Maryland* acknowledgment by five is sufficient. Hughes *v.* Antietam Mfg. Co., 34 Md. 316.

2. Citizenship of the Corporators.—Where the statute does not require any of the corporators to be citizens or residents of the State, such citizenship or residence is unnecessary. Humphreys *v.* Mooney, 5 Col. 282; Maine N. F. Co. *v.* Baumbach, 32 Fed. Rep. 205.

In *Pennsylvania* the certificate must be signed by five or more persons, three of whom at least must be citizens of the State. Act of 29th Apr. 1874, § 3; 1 Purd. Dig. 337, pl. 6.

Where the statute does not require the corporators to be subscribers to the stock, they need have no interest in the company. Densmore Oil Co. *v.* Densmore, 64 Pa. St. 43.

3. See *supra*, 3. ORDINARY CORPORATE POWERS, n., as to requisites of the name.

4. By the constitutions of *Alabama* (art. 14, sec. 5), *California* (art. 12, sec. 9), *Louisiana* (art. 237), *Missouri* (art. 12, sec. 7), and *Pennsylvania* (art. 16, sec. 6), no corporation can engage in any business other than that expressly authorized by its charter or the law under which it is formed.

The law authorizing incorporation for "hunting, fishing, or lawful sporting purposes" does not allow incorporation for the purpose of suing for violations of the game laws. Anc. City Sportsmen Club *v.* Miller, 7 Lans. (N. Y.) 412.

A medical college cannot be incorporated under a law for the incorporation of literary or scientific colleges and universities People *v.* Gunn, 96 N. Y. 317; s. c., 6 Am. & Eng. Corp. Cas. 584.

It has been held that telephone companies could incorporate under the law for the incorporation of telegraph companies. Wis. Telephone Co. *v.* Oshkosh, 62 Wis. 32; s. c., 8 Am. & Eng. Corp. Cas. 538.

It has been held that if, in preparing a certificate, the corporators employ only the words used in the statute to describe the general purposes of such incorporation, it is presumed that they intended to create a corporation of the same general nature and with the same general powers granted by the statute, rather than that by such words they sought to apply special limitations on the powers of the corporation. Whetstone *v.* Ottawa Univ., 13 Kan. 320.

A statement in the certificate that "the manner of carrying on the business shall be such as the association may from time to time prescribe" is insufficient. State *v.* Cent. Ohio, etc., Assn., 29 Ohio St. 399.

It must be the principal place or places of business for the purposes of taxation and service of process. Transportation Co. *v.* Scheu, 19 N. Y. 408; *In re* Enterprise M. B. Assn., 10 Phila. (Pa.) 380.

5. The *California* statute requiring the certificate to state the names of the city or town and county in which the principal place of business is to be located, is not complied with by a statement of the county merely. Harris *v.* McGregor, 29 Cal. 124.

But a failure to describe the place of business as the "principal place of business" is a mere technical error, which does not avoid the charter. *Ex parte* Spring Val. Water Works, 17 Cal. 132.

6. In many States the incorporation law fixes a limit to the existence of the companies formed under it. "Not to exceed forty years" is sufficiently definite where the act puts that limit to the existence of corporations. Hughes *v.* Antietam Mfg. Co., 34 Md. 316.

7. In *Pennsylvania* this provision has been held as plainly indicating "that the of the capital stock, if any, and the number of shares into which it is divided at its par value;[1] 8. That the required proportion of the capital stock has been paid in cash to the treasurer, stating his name and residence.[2]

In some States the parties to the certificate become a corporation on filing one copy with the clerk of the county court, or other specified officer, and a duplicate with the secretary of State,[3] and making known its material facts by publication in the newspapers within a certain time.[4] In other States public notice of the intention to apply for a charter must first be given,[5] after which the certificate is presented to the court or officer stated in the act,[6] who, if he find upon examination that the corporation is for a lawful purpose, and in accordance with public policy, and that all the legal forms have been complied with, shall approve the certificate[7]

application for incorporation is to be made by an existing association, presenting its constitution for legal approval." *In re* Red Men's Rel. Assn., 10 Phila. (Pa.) 546; *In re* Gibbs, 3 Pitts. (Pa.) 499.

In *California* it has been held that the certificate need not show that the signers previously constituted an existing society with rules and regulations, nor that the trustees named in the certificate were chosen in accordance therewith. R. C. Orph. Assn *v.* Abrams. 49 Cal. 455.

Directors need not be subscribers to the stock. *In re* Brit. Prov. Life Assn., L. R. 5 Ch. D. 306.

1. Where the certificate stated the capital stock as $500.000, and added, "said capital stock shall consist of five hundred shares at $100 per share," the discrepancy was not held fatal, as the subscription of the whole capital stock at a fixed value per share would necessarily determine the aggregate number of shares. Hughes *v.* Antietam Mfg. Co., 34 Md 316.

2. Giving a note is not such payment. Jersey City Gas Co. *v.* Dwight. 29 N. J. Eq 246; Leighty *v.* Turnpike Co., 14 S. & R. (Pa.) 434; Boyd *v.* Peach Bottom R. Co., 90 Pa. St. 169.

In *Nebraska*, corporations cannot begin business till the whole capital stock has been subscribed. Livesey *v.* Omaha Hotel Co., 5 Neb. 50.

3. Mokelumne Hill Min Co. *v.* Woodbury, 14 Cal 424; Cross *v* Pinckneyville Mill Co., 17 Ill. 54; Baker *v.* Backus, 32 Ill. 79; Indianapolis Min. Co *v.* Herkimer, 46 Ind 142; First Nat. Bank *v.* Davies, 43 Iowa, 434; Hunt *v.* Kansas Bridge Co., 11 Kan. 412; Hurt *v.* Salisbury, 55 Mo 310; Harrod *v.* Hamer. 32 Wis. 162

In *Illinois*, for corporations for profit, a license to obtain stock subscriptions is first granted by the secretary of State. and after complete organization a certificate to that effect is obtained from him. Rev. Stats. Ill. 327; Stowe *v.* Flagg, 72 Ill. 397

4. Heinig *v.* Adams & Westlake Mfg. Co., 81 Ky. 300; s. c., 1 Am. & Eng. Corp. Cas. 493.

5. The advertisement must state the object of the corporation, and the time and place when and where the application will be made. *In re* Parrish M. E. Ch., 3 Luz. Leg. Reg. (Pa.) 123; *In re* Enterprise M. B. Assn., 10 Phila. (Pa.) 380.

In *Pennsylvania*, pending the advertisement, the certificates of corporations not for profit must be lodged in the office of the court of common pleas for public inspection. *In re* Ch. of the Holy Communion. 8 Weekly Notes (Pa.). 357.

6. In *Pennsylvania* the certificate of a corporation not for profit is approved by a law judge of the county; that of a corporation for profit, by the governor. Act of 29th Apr. 1874, § 3 (1 Purd. Dig. 338, pll. 8. 9).

In *Georgia* the statutory requirement differs from both of the modes stated in the text. A petition is presented to the superior court for an act of incorporation. See Franklin Br. Co. *v.* Wood, 14 Ga. 80. *In re* Deveaux, 54 Ga. 673.

7. A provision that the members shall not enlist in the army or navy will not be approved. *In re* Mulholland Ben. Soc., 10 Phila. (Pa.) 19.

Nor will a certificate be approved if it contains an indefinite statement of the offences that may result in expulsion. Butchers' Ben. Assn., 38 Pa. St. 298; Ben. Assn. of Brotherly Unity, 38 Pa. St 299.

In *New York* approval by a justice of the supreme court is not conclusive as to whether the objects are within the pur-

(and, in some States, direct letters-patent to issue[1]). The certificate, and the order or decree approving it, must be recorded in a specified office, after which the corporation exists as such.[2] Whatever be the mode prescribed by the act, substantial compliance with all the provisions of it is required before the corporation can be said to be *in esse*.[3]

8. Defective or Illegal Incorporation and Organization.—A corporation must have a full and complete organization and existence as an entity, and in accordance with the law to which it owes its origin, before it can assume its franchises or enter into any kind of contract, or transact any business.[4] If business has been begun

view of the statute and the certificate in accordance with its requirements. People *v.* Nelson, 3 Lans. (N. Y.) 394; s. c., 10 Abb. Pr. N. S. (N. Y.) 200.

In *Georgia* an act of incorporation will be refused if the petition do not specify what the law requires. *In re* Deveaux, 54 Ga. 673. But the court has no discretion as to receiving the petition, and may be compelled thereto by *mandamus*. Franklin Bridge Co. *v.* Wood, 14 Ga. 80.

1. In *Pennsylvania* this is done in the case of corporations for profit. Act of 29th Apr. 1874, § 3; 1 Pur. Dig. 338, pl. 9.

2. Under a general incorporation law, when the instrument specifying the objects, articles, conditions, and name of the association, and whatever else the law may require, has been approved by the proper officer, and enrolled according to law, the persons associating become a corporation according to the objects, articles, and conditions contained in the instrument. These become their charter, and have the same force and effect in law as if they were specifically granted by special act. Society, etc., *v.* Com., 52 Pa. St. 125.

3. Harris *v.* McGregor, 29 Cal. 124; People *v.* Selfridge, 52 Cal. 331; McIntire *v.* McLain Ditching Co., 40 Ind. 104; Indianapolis, etc., Min. Co. *v.* Herkimer, 46 Ind. 142; Reed *v.* Richmond Street R. Co., 50 Ind. 342; Richmond Factory Co. *v.* Alexander, 61 Me. 351; Utley *v.* Union Tool Co., 11 Gray (Mass.) 139; Doyle *v.* Migner, 42 Mich. 332; Abbott *v.* Omaha Smelting Co., 4 Neb. 114; Unity Ins. Co. *v.* Crane, 43 N. H. 641; Childs *v.* Smith, 55 Barb. (N. Y.) 45, 53.

Where, however, the statute required the certificate to be filed with the county clerk and a duplicate with the secretary of State, and provided that when a certificate was filed the parties should be a corporation, it was held that, as to third parties, filing in the clerk's office alone was necessary. Mokelumne Hill Min. Co. *v.* Woodbury, 14 Cal. 424.

And in similar cases the filing with the secretary of State was held a condition precedent to the doing of business only, so that the stockholders were not jointly and severally liable as if no incorporation had been effected. First Nat. Bank *v.* Davies, 43 Iowa, 424; Harrod *v.* Hamer, 32 Wis. 162.

But the officers alone have been held liable on a note of the company issued by them under such circumstances. Hart *v.* Salisbury, 55 Mo. 310.

The *Kentucky* Gen. Stats. c. 56, §§ 5, 6, require, within three months from the filing of the articles, notice to be published, stating the name and general nature of the corporation, the amount of the stock, whether the stockholders' liability is limited, etc. This has been held a condition precedent; hence, where it had not been done, there was no corporation, and the property claimed to be corporate could be levied on as belonging to those claiming to be stockholders. Heinig *v.* Adams & Westlake Mfg. Co., 81 Ky. 300; s. c., 1 Am. & Eng. Corp. Cas. 493. So in *Iowa*. Clegg *v.* Hamilton, etc., Co., 61 Iowa, 121; s. c., 1 Am. & Eng. Corp. Cas. 496.

In *New York* a similar provision of the Connecticut statute has been held not so essential. Holmes *v.* Gilliland, 41 Barb. (N. Y.) 568.

As to unimportant omissions, see Humphreys *v.* Mooney, 5 Col. 282; Cross *v.* Pinckneyville Mill Co., 17 Ill. 54.

The rule stated in the text applies of course to all methods of becoming members. Wood *v.* Coosa, etc., R. Co., 32 Ga. 273; Carlisle *v.* S. V., etc., R. Co., 27 Mich. 315; Fiser *v.* Miss., etc., R. Co., 32 Miss. 359; Boyd *v.* P. B. R. Co., 90 Pa. St. 169.

4. Morawetz (2d Ed.), § 746; Gent *v* M. & M. Mut. Ins. Co., 107 Ill. 652; 6 Am. & Eng. Corp. Cas. 588. And see

under a defective organization, however, the defects may be remedied,[1] or the State may cure the irregularity by an enabling act,[2] or waive it by recognizing the corporation as in existence.[3]

If a corporation has acquired an existence *de facto* under color of law, the validity of its formation cannot be attacked collaterally, but only by proper *quo warranto* proceedings at the suggestion of the attorney-general.[4] Whether a company has actually acquired

cases cited in last note to paragraph 7, *supra*.

The reason is, that the corporation must exist *de facto* at the time it makes a contract. It cannot do this if its incorporation either has not taken place or is at an end. White *v.* Campbell, 5 Humph. (Tenn.) 38. See *infra* POWERS AND LIABILITIES OF CORPORATIONS.

"There is a manifest difference where a corporation is created by a special charter and there have been acts of user, and where individuals seek to form themselves into a corporation under the provisions of a general law. In the latter case it is only in pursuance of the provisions of the statute for such purpose that corporate existence can be acquired." Bigelow *v.* Gregory, 73 Ill 197.

Where a contract for the sale of land provided for payment when a certain corporation was formed, the contemplated organization was held to mean such acts of the associates as should form and set on foot, in practical existence, a body in which they should have rights and to which they would owe obligations, and through which they should possess rights against and incur obligations to each other, rather than an organization so exactly in accordance with the statute that it would successfully meet any scrutiny into its right which the sovereign power could institute. Childs *v.* Smith, 46 N. Y. 34.

1. But of course the members cannot ratify a defective incorporation without complying with the statutory prerequisites. Morawetz (2d Ed.). § 736.

A defectively organized corporation can sue if all the conditions precedent be complied with before the writ issues. Augur Axle Co. *v.* Whitney, 117 Mass. 461.

2. Workingmen's B. & L. Assn. *v.* Coleman, 89 Pa. St. 428.

A remedial statute, approving and ratifying an organization made without compliance with all statutory requisites, is constitutional. Central A. & M. Assoc. *v.* Ala. Gold L. I. Co., 70 Ala. 120; 3 Am. & Eng. Corp. Cas. 78.

3. People *v.* Perrin, 56 Cal. 345; Ill., etc., R. Co. *v.* Cook, 29 Ill. 237; Goodrich *v.* Reynolds, 31 Ill 490; Mitchell *v.* Deeds, 49 Ill. 416; Basshor *v.* Dressel, 34 Md. 503; St. Louis R. Co. *v.* Northwestern St. L. R. Co., 2 Mo. Ap. 69; Black Riv. R. Co. *v.* Barnard, 31 Barb. (N. Y.) 258; Cayuga, etc., R. Co. *v.* Kentucky Co., 64 N. Y. 186; Kanawha Coal Co. *v.* Kanawha, etc., Coal Co., 7 Blatchf. (C. C.) 391.

4. "When a body of men are acting as a corporation under color of apparent organization in pursuance of some charter or enabling act, their authority to act as a corporation cannot be questioned collaterally, but only in a direct proceeding in the nature of a *quo warranto*. Under such circumstances, if their organization is irregular they constitute a corporation *de facto*." Taylor Corp. § 145.

In an action by a mutual insurance company for assessments upon premium notes, the validity of the charter was conceded, but it was said to authorize insurance of cattle only, and that the contract for insurance of buildings, on account of which these assessments were made, was *ultra vires*. It was held that this was tantamount to calling in question the validity of the charter, which could not be done in a collateral proceeding. Freeland *v.* Pa. Cent. Ins. Co., 94 Pa. 504.

"The courts are bound to regard [a chartered company] as a corporation, so far as third persons are concerned, until it is dissolved by a judicial proceeding on behalf of the government that created it." Frost *v.* Frostburg Coal Co., 24 How (U. S.) 278, 284.

The State, which alone can incorporate, may waive the breach or acquiesce in the usurpation, and the wrong being to the State, and not to the individuals, so long as the State remains inactive the individuals must also acquiesce. Lehman Durr & Co. *v.* Warner, 61 Ala. 455; Central A. & M. Assoc. *v.* Ala. Gold L. I. Co., 70 Ala. 120; s. c., 3 Am. & Eng. Corp. Cas. 78; M. & P. Line *v.* Waganer, 71 Ala. 581; Bakersfield T. H. Assoc. *v.* Chester, 55 Cal 99; Humphreys *v.* Mooney, 5 Col. 282; Snelser *v.* W. & U. Turnpike Co., 82 Ind. 417; North *v.* State, 107 Ind. 356; s. c., 14 Am. & Eng. Corp. Cas. 7; Quinn *v.* Shields, 62 Iowa, 129; s. c., 1 Am. & Eng Corp. Cas. 498; B. & D. Bank *v.* Macdonald, 130 Mass. 264; French *v.*

such *de facto* existence or not, it is clear that its alleged incorporation cannot be denied, nor its members held liable as partners by those who have reaped the benefit of contracts made with it as a corporation.[1] But it is held, at least in some States, that parties cannot make use of a fictitious and clearly invalid incorporation to

Donohue, 29 Minn. 11; Studebaker Mfg. Co. *v.* Montgomery, 74 Mo. 101; Kishacoquillas, etc., Co. *v.* McConaby, 16 S. & R. (Pa.) 140; Bell *v.* Pennsylvania, etc., R. Co., 9 Cent. Rep. 138

Hence *quo warranto* cannot be brought for such a purpose at the suggestion of a private relator. Murphy *v.* Bank, 20 Pa. 415; Commonwealth *v.* P. & C. R. Co., 10 Weekly Notes (Pa.), 400.

If a corporation obtain an extension of its charter by false and colorable representations to the legislature, it may be made the ground of a *quo warranto*, but a stranger cannot take advantage of the fraud to deny the validity of the organization. Charles Riv. Br. *v.* Warren Br., 7 Pick. (Mass.) 344.

The *Michigan* statutes (How. Sts., § 8635) authorize the filing of an information, without leave of court, whenever it is claimed that a number of persons assume to act as a corporation within the State without being legally incorporated. Atty.-Genl. *v.* Lorman, 59 Mich 158.

If, on *quo warranto*, the decision be against the legality of the corporation, appropriate proceedings should be had by which the affairs of the *de facto* corporation should be wound up, the assets converted, and debts paid, and the surplus, if any, divided among the stockholders. People *v.* Flint, 64 Cal. 49; 1 Am. & Eng. Corp. Cas. 494.

1. In general, one who contracts with a corporation in the use of its corporate powers and franchises, and within the scope of such powers, is estopped from denying its corporate existence or inquiring into the regularity of its organization when an enforcement of the contract, or of a right arising under it, is sought. Cassall *v.* Cit. Mut. B. Assoc., 61 Ala. 232; Fresno C. & I Co. *v.* Warner (Cal.), 17 Am. & Eng. Corp. Cas. 37; Mitchell *v.* Deeds. 49 Ill 416; Jones *v.* Cin., etc., R. Co., 14 Ind. 89; Hubbard *v.* Chappell, 14 Ind. 601; Evansville, etc., R. Co. *v.* Evansville, 15 Ind. 395; State *v.* Bailey, 16 Ind. 46; Meikel *v.* Sav. Soc., 16 Ind. 181; Brownlee *v.* Ohio, etc., R. Co., 18 Ind. 68; Baker *v.* Neff, 73 Ind. 68; Johnson *v.* Gibson, 78 Ind. 282; Wash. Coll. *v.* Duke, 14 Iowa, 14; Agric. Bank *v.* Burr, 24 Me. 256; Hagerstown Turnpike Co. *v.* Creeger, 5 H. & J. (Md.) 122; Case *v.* Benedict, 9 Cush. (Mass.) 540; Worcester Med. Inst. *v.* Harding, 11 Cush. (Mass.) 285; Chester Glass Co. *v.* Dewey, 16 Mass. 94; Hamtranck *v.* Bank of Edwardsv., 2 Mo. 169; Cong. Soc. *v.* Perry, 6 N H. 164; Bank of Circlev. *v.* Remick, 15 Ohio, 222; Cochran *v.* Arnold, 58 Pa. St. 399; Spahr *v.* Farmers' Bank, 94 Pa. St. 429; Bank of U. S. *v.* Lyman, 20 Wall. (U. S.) 666; Connors *v.* Bolles, 94 U. S. 104; Smith *v.* Sheeley, 12 Wall. (U. S) 358; Chubb *v.* Upton, 95 U. S. 666; Or. R. Co. *v.* Or. R. & Nav. Co., 23 Fed. R. 232.

Especially where it is clear that credit was given to the alleged corporation and not to individuals. Stafford Bank *v.* Palmer, 47 Conn. 443; Cent. Cy. Sav. Bk *v.* Walker, 66 N. Y. 424.

Or where the contracting party was himself a member. McClinch *v.* Sturgis, 72 Me. 288.

One who is sued on his contract with a corporation cannot show in defence that the charter was obtained by fraud. Pattison *v.* Albany B. Assoc., 63 Ga. 373

Nor that it has been forfeited for non-user or mis-user. Trustees *v.* Hills, 6 Cow. (N. Y.) 23; Crump *v.* U. S. Min Co., 7 Gratt. (Va.) 352.

Nor that the officers who made the contract were not legally elected. Mech. Bk. *v.* Burnet Mfg. Co., 32 N. J. Eq. 236.

The view taken by the courts is that the contract supplies the necessary evidence of incorporation. Lehman *v.* Warner, 61 Ala. 455.

But it is otherwise if there are facts making it legally unjust to forbid a denial of corporate existence. Doyle *v.* Mizner, 42 Mich. 332; Esty Mfg. Co. *v.* Runnells, 55 Mich. 130; 8 Am. & Eng. Corp. Cas 225.

In an action by a corporation against subscribers to the articles of association, they are not estopped from denying the corporate existence, for their contract was not with the existing corporation. Rikhoff *v.* Brown's, etc., S. M. Co, 68 Ind. 388.

The rule stated in the text appears to hold even when the contracting party is himself the plaintiff. Gartside Coal Co. *v.* Maxwell, 22 Fed. R. 197; Blanchard *v.* Kaull, 44 Cal. 440; Humphreys *v.* Mooney, 5 Col. 282; P. & M. Bank *v.* Padgett, 69 Ga. 159; M. & M. Bank *v.* Storm, 38 Mich. 779.

escape the liabilities of partners as to contracts made by them.[1] A corporation cannot defend on the ground of defects in its organization.[2]

1. Mr. Morawetz, § 748, thinks the decisions on this point in conflict with those cited in the preceding note, and especially, it would seem, with those holding the contracting party estopped even when plaintiff. It is, however, perhaps possible to reconcile them. The rule is, that a corporation that has not a perfect existence cannot contract, but it may be fair to sustain the contract if the other party is not injured by it, and hence the exception of the cases of estoppel. If, however, the estoppel was applied in all cases, a pretended corporation might take advantage of its own wrong to the injury of an innocent party. Such, at least, seems to be the doctrine of Garnett *v.* Richardson, 35 Ark. 444; Bigelow *v.* Gregory, 73 Ill. 197; Kaiser *v.* Lawrence Sav. Bank, 56 Iowa, 104; Abbott *v.* Omaha Smelting Co., 4 Neb. 416; Hill *v.* Beach, 1 Beas. (N. J.) 31; Hess *v.* Werts, 4 S. & R. (Pa.) 356.

In Bank of Watertown *v.* Loudon, 45 N. Y. 410, the charter had expired, but the members agreed to carry on the business under the old name. They were of course liable as partners, even though the plaintiff had believed the corporation to be in existence.

In Richardson *v.* Pitts, 71 Mo. 128, the suit was between the associates and the directors, and it was held peculiarly inequitable for the former to attempt to escape liability for the acts that they had authorized.

In Martin *v.* Fewell, 79 Mo. 128, the plaintiffs had dealt with an agent, and were apparently ignorant that the principals even claimed to be a corporation, and they were held liable as partners. Pending their dealings with the plaintiffs the corporate organization was perfected, but this was held immaterial, as the plaintiffs had not been informed.

In Fuller *v.* Rowe, 57 N. Y. 23, and Cent. Cy. Sav. Bank *v.* Walker, 66 N. Y. 424 the members who had not known of any defects in the incorporation were held not liable as partners.

In State *v.* How, 1 Mich. 512, it was held that the defendants could not be liable as partners, for they had attempted to carry on a banking business, in which only corporations could engage. The notes issued by them being void, there was no right of action upon them.

Medill *v.* Collier, 16 Ohio St. 599, and Bank *v.* Hall, 35 Ohio St. 158, were also cases of illegal banking, but it was held those who had engaged in or authorized the transactions could not escape personal liability.

In Ash *v.* Guil, 97 Pa. St. 493, some members of an unincorporated association were similarly held liable on its certificates of indebtedness.

In *Massachusetts* the rule is that members of a defectively organized corporation cannot be held as partners. Fay *v.* Noble, 7 Cush. (Mass.) 188; Trowbridge *v.* Scudder, 11 Cush. (Mass.) 83; Bank of Salem *v.* Almy, 117 Mass. 476; Ward *v.* Brigham, 127 Mass. 24. The cases in this line are thought to be in conflict with the doctrine considered in this note. See Martin *v.* Fewell, 79 Mo. 401.

2. By the doctrine of estoppel, a corporation cannot avail itself, in defence to a suit, of any defect in its creation or failure on its part to comply with statutory requirements that are a condition precedent to its corporate existence. Bakersfield, etc., Assoc. *v.* Chester, 55 Cal. 98; Ewing *v.* Robeson, 15 Ind. 26; Hammond *v.* Straus, 53 Md. 1; Dooly *v.* Cheshire Glass Co., 15 Gray (Mass.), 494; Merrick *v.* Reynolds Eng. Co., 101 Mass. 381; Priest *v.* Essex Hat Co., 115 Mass. 380; Salem Nat. Bank *v.* Almy, 117 Mass. 476; Chamberlin *v.* Huguenot Mfg. Co., 118 Mass. 532; Rush *v.* Steamboat Co., 84 N. Car. 702; Whitney *v.* Wyman, 101 U. S. 392; Upton *v.* Hausborough, 3 Biss. (C. C.) 417.

A corporation which has enjoyed the benefits of a contract cannot plead that it was *ultra vires*. O. C. & A. R. Co. *v.* Pa. Transp. Co., 24 Pitts. L. J. (Pa.) 111.

The validity of the corporate organization, and of the acts of *de facto* officers, will be presumed in favor of creditors, and of third persons dealing with it in good faith, and the contrary cannot be set up as a defence by the company. Hackensack Water Co *v.* DeKay, 36 N. J. E. 548; s. c., 1 Am. & Eng. Corp. Cas. 670; City of Denver *v.* Mullen, 7 Col. 345; s. c., 4 Am. & Eng. Corp. Cas. 304; Tarbell *v.* Page, 24 Ill. 46; Thompson *v.* Candor, 60 Ill. 244; Aurora, etc., R. Co. *v.* Miller, 56 Ind. 88; Williamson *v.* Kokomo B. & L. Assoc., 89 Ind 339; s. c., 4 Am. & Eng. Corp. Cas. 172; Narragansett Bank *v.* Atlantic Silk Co., 3 Met. (Mass.) 282; Barrett *v.* Mead, 10 Allen (Mass.), 337; Walworth *v.* Brackett, 98 Mass. 98; Commonwealth *v.* Bakeman, 105 Mass. 53; Merchants' Bank *v.* Glen-

9. Liability for the Acts of the Promoters.—A corporation is not responsible for the acts nor bound by the contracts of its promoters done or entered into before incorporation,[1] unless it is made so either by its charter[2] or by its own express promise or ratification after incorporation,[3] or where it has accepted and re-

don Co., 120 Mass. 97; Swartout *v.* Mich., etc., R. Co., 24 Mich. 389; Society Perun *v.* Cleveland, 43 Ohio St. 481; s. c., 12 Am. & Eng. Corp. Cas. 40.

In particular, one who has taken part in the organization of a corporation, and represented it as such, is estopped from denying its existence. Close *v.* Glenwood Cem. Co., 107 U. S. 466; s. c., 1 Am. & Eng. Corp. Cas. 512; Abbott *v.* Aspinwall, 26 Barb. (N. Y.) 202; Eaton *v.* Aspinwall, 19 N. Y. 119.

It is no defence to a suit on a note of the corporation that the charter fails to define the period of its existence. E. Tenn. Ir. Mfg. Co. *v.* Gaskell, 2 Lea (Tenn.), 742.

If, however, the acts of a body sued as a corporation were not necessarily those of a corporation, it is not estopped from denying its corporate existence. Kirkpatrick *v.* Kiota U. P. Ch., 63 Iowa, 372.

1. The general principle is, that a corporation can be liable only for its own acts done after it had a legal existence. Promoters do not represent the corporation in any relation of agency, and have no authority to make preliminary contracts, binding the corporation when it shall be formed. Mere acceptance of the benefit of a contract does not imply a promise on the part of the corporation to adopt and perform it. Caledonian, etc., R. Co. *v.* Helensburgh, 2 Macq. 391; Payne *v.* N. S. W. Coal Co., 10 Ex. 283; N. Y. & N. H. R. Co. *v.* Ketchum, 27 Conn. 170; Safety Dep. L. I. Co. *v.* Smith, 65 Ill. 309; R. R., I. & St. L. R. Co. *v.* Sage, 65 Ill. 328; Western Screw & Mfg. Co. *v.* Cousley, 72 Ill. 531; Marchand *v.* Loan Assn., 26 La. Ann. 389; Franklin F. I. Co. *v.* Hart, 31 Md. 59; Penn Match Co. *v.* Hapgood, 141 Mass. 145; s. c., 7 N. E. Rep. 22; Carmody *v.* Powers (Mich.), 26 N. W. Rep. 801; Munson *v.* S. G., etc., R. Co., 103 N. Y. 58.

Hence, making application for insurance to a mutual insurance company before the proper certificate of the auditor of public accounts had been filed as required by law to perfect organization, and giving a premium note, constitute only a proposal to insure when the company shall be capable of transacting business. Gent *v.* M. & M. Mut. Ins. Co., 107 Ill. 652; s. c., 8 Am. & Eng. Corp. Cas. 306.

In *England*, under the act of 8 & 9 Vict. c. 110, which provided for provisional registration of joint-stock companies, and that the promoters might make certain contracts "conditional on the completion of the company," and to take effect after complete registration, it was held that a completely registered company was not liable on contracts made by the promoters before provisional registration, nor on those not made conditional on complete registration. Hutchinson *v.* Surrey Consumers' Assn., 13 C. B. 689; Gunn *v.* Lond. & Lan. Fire Ins. Co., 12 C. B. N. S. 694.

2. Tilson *v.* Warwick Gaslight Co., 4 B. & C. 962; *In re* B. & L. R. Co., L. R. 10 Ch. App. 177; Gent *v.* M. & M. Mut. Ins. Co., 107 Ill. 652; s. c., 8 Am. & Eng. Corp. Cas. 306.

3. Touche *v.* Met. Warehousing Co., L. R. 6 Ch. App. 671; Spiller *v.* Paris Rink Co., L. R. 7 Ch. D. 368; Whitney *v.* Wyman, 101 U. S. 392; Western Screw & Mfg. Co. *v.* Cousley, 72 Ill. 531; Franklin F. I. Co. *v.* Hart, 31 Md. 59; Macdonough *v.* Bk. of Houston, 34 Tex. 309.

Bonds issued by promoters before incorporation may be ratified by the directors after incorporation, so as to become valid obligations of the corporation. Wood *v.* Whellen, 93 Ill. 153.

A contract made by the promoters should be adopted by a corporation in the same way that its own contracts are made. Formal action by the board of directors is necessary in the former case only if it would be so in the latter. Battelle *v.* N. W. Cement Co. (Minn.), 33 N. W. Rep. 327.

In *England*, it is settled that a contract made on behalf of a corporation before it came into existence is a nullity, and cannot be ratified. Kelner *v.* Baxter, L. R. 2 C. P. 174; Scott *v.* Lord Ebury, 36 L. J. C. P. 161; Melhado *v.* Porto Alegre R. Co., L. R. 9 C. P. 503. It was at one time considered that this doctrine obtained in courts of law only, and in Spiller *v.* Paris Rink Co., L. R. 7 Ch. D. 368, Malins, V. C., held that such ratification was valid in equity. The later cases in the court of appeals, however, reassert the doctrine of Kelner *v.* Baxter, and maintain that the only result of the com-ceived the benefit of a contract made in its behalf with the understanding that it would be adopted by it.[1]

pany's availing itself of such a contract is the creation of an equitable liability (not on the contract, but for the benefits received thereby) on equitable grounds. *In re* Empress Eng. Co. L. R. 16 Ch. D. 125; *In re* North'd Ave. Hotel Co., L. R. 33 Ch. D. 16; s. c., 16 Am. & Eng. Corp. Cas. 89. See also *In re* Hereford Waggon Co., L. R. 2 Ch. D. 621; Taylor on Corp. § 87.

1. Where the contract was made in order to obtain the charter and bring the corporation into existence, the corporation would seem bound in equity to perform it. Thus in Edwards *v.* Grand Junc. R., 1 M. & Cr. 650, the promoters of the railway company had agreed with trustees of a turnpike that if the latter would not oppose the passage of the charter, the bridge to be built across the turnpike should be wider than provided in the charter, but after the charter was obtained the company began to build a bridge of the width authorized therein, and an injunction was granted because the company was bound not to use its power under the charter, which had been obtained by means of the agreement with the plaintiffs, in violation of that agreement.

So in Stanley *v.* Birkenhead R., 9 Sim. 264, there was a decree for the specific performance of a contract to pay a certain price for land required by the railway, in consideration of withdrawal of opposition to the charter. In both these cases there was an existing organization for the purpose of promoting the company, and the contract was made in the course of preliminary proceedings necessary to obtain the charter.

In Gooday *v.* C. & S. W. R., 15 Eng. L. & Eq. 596; s. c., 17 Beav. 132; Preston *v.* L. M., etc., R., 7 Eng. L. & Eq. 124; Webb *v.* D. L. & P. R., 9 Hare, 129, and other cases, this equity was carried still further, on the ground that the contracts, though made with the projectors, were properly on behalf of the intended companies, and with the view entertained by both parties at the time, of having them adopted by the companies when perfected and empowered to do so.

The doctrine of these cases is thus summed up in Redfield on Railways (5th Ed.), 18: "Whenever a third party enters into a contract with the promoters of a railway, which is intended to inure to the benefit of the company, and they take the benefit of the contract they will be bound to perform it upon the familiar principle that one who accepts the benefit of a contract, which another volunteers to perform in his name and on his behalf, is bound to take the burden with the benefit."

This doctrine was, however, disapproved, as extending the liabilities of the companies too far, in Caledonian R. Co. *v.* Helensburgh, 2 Macq. 391. In Bell's Gap R. Co. *v.* Christy, 79 Pa. St. 54, it is spoken of as "established in *England*, and to some extent recognized in this country." The authorities were reviewed in L. R. & Ft. S. R. Co. *v.* Perry, 37 Ark. 164, where the bondholders of an insolvent railroad having taken possession in order to complete it and save the land-grant, their agent contracted with the plaintiff for work and materials necessary to such completion. Afterwards they foreclosed, bought in all the property, privileges, and franchises of the corporation, and organized a new company for the same purpose as the old, and with an almost identical name. After such organization the president of the new company accepted the results and benefits of the contract and paid a part of the consideration. The judgment below was for the plaintiff, but the supreme court held that no valid contract with the new company had been proven, and said: "From all the authorities it seems clear, that, in order to recover in an action at law, the plaintiff must show either an express promise of the new company, or that the contract was made with persons then engaged in its formation, and taking preliminary steps thereto, and that the contract was made on behalf of the new company, in the expectation on the part of the plaintiff and with the assurance on the part of the projectors that it would become a corporate debt, and that the company afterward entered upon and enjoyed the benefit of the contract, and by no other title than that derived through it. From these circumstances an affirmance would be implied. . . . No authorities have gone the length of holding that any contract made with individuals, exclusively upon individual credit, will become the contract of any future corporation they may form for the more convenient management and use of the benefits of it."

The ruling in this case was expressly stated to be that of a court of law, but when the plaintiff subsequently filed an

B. Name of Corporation.—1. Importance of a Corporate Name.—It is essential that a corporation should have a name by which it may sue or be sued, and perform all legal acts. A corporation is recognized by law as having an existence as an artificial person distinct from the members which compose it. It is important that this separate existence should be identified by a name. The identity of the corporate name is also the principal means of effecting that perpetuity of succession which is one of the most important purposes of incorporation.

2. How Acquired.—The corporate name is usually stated in the charter. If no name is given in the charter a right to adopt a

amended complaint in equity, which came before the supreme court in Perry *v.* L. R. & F. S. R. Co., 44 Ark. 383, the equity side of the court held the same view, and said: "We do not think this is a case of a contract made with the promoters of a future corporation, upon the credit of the corporation to be formed, and with the intention mutually entertained that the corporation would be bound when organized. It rather appears a case of credit extended to the individual bondholders in person, and their liability will depend upon the authority vested in [the bondholders' agent]," and the decree in favor of the defendants was affirmed.

The cases of Low *v.* C. & P. Riv. R. Co., 46 N. H. 284, where it was held that acceptance of the contract was a ratification equivalent to an antecedent request, and that the company, taking the benefit of the services rendered with notice of the promise of compensation, was bound to perform the contract; and Hall *v.* Vt. & Mass. R. Co., 28 Vt. 401, where the necessity of the acts done (after incorporation, but before the organization was perfected) was held to imply a promise to pay for them, have been thought to go beyond the rule as recognized in America (see R., R. I. & St. L. R. Co. *v.* Sage, 65 Ill. 328), but the decisions seem warranted by the facts.

Where a contract to assign a patent when issued, and for royalty therefor, was made before the certificate was filed, but with the same parties that conducted the business afterward, and acting in the corporate name, and the patent was issued to the defendant company after organization, and they paid the royalty for a time, it was held that the corporation had, by availing itself of and acting under the agreement after organization, adopted and ratified it, and was bound by its provisions. Bommer *v.* Am. Spiral, etc., Co., 81 N. Y. 468. To the same effect, Chater *v.* S. F. Sugar Ref. Co., 19 Cal. 220.

Where a partnership was seeking to organize a corporation and it was necessary to borrow money in order to carry on the business until the company should be completely organized, and a mortgage was given to secure the debt, the concealment of the existence of this mortgage was held immaterial as regards the subscribers to the stock, as the company would have been equally liable for the amount secured thereby even if the mortgage had not been executed. Petrie *v.* Guelph Lumber Co., 11 Can. Sup. Ct. 451; s. c., 15 Am. & Eng. Corp. Cas. 487.

In Bergen *v.* Porpoise Fishing Co., 13 Am. & Eng. Corp. Cas. 1, it was held in *New Jersey* that where a company carried on business and held itself out to the world as a corporation, and afterwards completed its organization according to law, the assets should be made liable for the debts, though contracted before the organization was completed.

In a recent *Nebraska* case, after the articles were drawn up and signed by the promoters, but before they were recorded or filed, and before the time fixed therein for beginning the business, the president, with the approval of all the promoters executed and delivered a note in payment for property which came into his hands after the organization was perfected, and was used and enjoyed by the company. On these facts it was held that the assignee of the payee could recover from the company. Paxton Cattle Co. *v.* First Nat. Bk. of Arapahoe, 17 Am. & Eng. Corp. Cas. 1.

Where an express promise of the corporators is relied upon, it must have been made by a majority of them. Bell's Gap R. Co. *v.* Christy, 79 Pa. St. 54.

In such a case, the performance of the contract by the other party being necessary to enable the company to carry on its business, and being accepted, the jury may presume from this that the act of the president was authorized or subsequently ratified. Grape Sugar, etc., Mfg. Co. *v.* Small, 40 Md. 395.

name may be implied.[1] A name may be acquired by usage; and an old corporation may acquire a new name by reputation and usage.[2]

3. Misnomer.—Although the name of a corporation may be changed, the identity of the corporation itself is not affected. A contract entered into by a corporation under an assumed name may be enforced by either of the parties. In such a case the misnomer of the corporation has the same effect as a misnomer of an individual. The identity of the company may be established by the ordinary methods of proof.[3] In pleading, the corporate name

1. "A corporation must have a name, but that must be understood to be expressed either in the patent or implied in the nature of the thing; as, if the king should incorporate the inhabitants of Dale with powers to choose a mayor annually, though no name be given, yet it is a good corporation by the name of mayor and commonalty." Anon., 1 Salk. 191; College of Physicians *v.* Salmon, 3 Salk. 102; Pits *v.* James *et al.*, Hob. 122; Sharswood's Bl. Com. Bk. 1, 475.

When a general law for the incorporation of cities does not prescribe by what name existing corporations adopting its provisions shall be known, they might, and the court may presume they did, retain their former names. Johnson *v.* Common Council of the City of Indianapolis, 16 Ind. 227.

2. Names are necessary to the existence of corporations, but the authorities clearly show that although the name is usually given by charter, it is not indispensable that it should be so given, it may be derived from usage. Smith *v.* Plank Road Co., 30 Ala. 650; School District *v.* Blakeslee, 13 Conn. 227; Melledge *v.* Boston Iron Co., 59 Mass. 158; Dutch East India Co. *v.* Moses, 1 Stra. 612; Minot *v.* Curtis *et al.*, 7 Mass. 441; Alexander *v.* Berney, 28 N. J. Eq. 90.

A corporation may exist by prescription, and the persons acting in such corporate capacity are entitled to take, not in their natural names, but by a name which, if they were incorporated, would be a proper name of incorporation. Conservators of the River Tone *v.* Ash *et al.*, 10 B. & Cr. 349; Robie *et al.* *v.* Sedgwick *et al.*, 35 Barb. (N. Y.) 319; Stockbridge *v.* West Stockbridge, 12 Mass. 400; New Boston *v.* Dunbarton, 15 N. H. 201; Bow *v.* Allenstown, 34 N. H. 351.

A corporation might have two names, the one by prescription and the other by grant, or both by prescription, but not two by grant. Knight *et ux.* *v.* Mayor, etc., of Wells, 1 Ld. Raym. 80.

The power which created the corporation alone has power to change its name, but the identity of the corporation is not destroyed by its change of name. Shackleford *v.* Dangerfield, Law Rep. 3 C. P. 407; Girard *v.* Philadelphia, 7 Wall. (U. S.) 1; Episcopal Soc. *v.* Episcopal Church, 1 Pick. (Mass.) 372; Wardens, etc., *v.* Hall, 22 Conn. 125; Cahill *v.* Bigger, 8 B. Monr. (Ky.) 211; Rosenthal *v.* Madison, etc., R. Co., 10 Ind. 358.

3. A corporation, like a natural person, may be known and designated by several names, although it can have but one corporate designation. It has long been settled that it is not necessary, in order that a corporation be bound by its contracts, that they shall be made in its exact corporate name. If it appears from the allegations and proof that the obligation sued upon was intended to be the obligation of the corporation sued, a recovery will not be defeated by reason of the misnomer alone. Such a misnomer of the corporation will not prevent a recovery "either by or against the corporation in its true name, provided its identity with that intended by the parties to the instrument be assured in the pleadings and apparent in the proof." Clement *v.* City of Lathrop, 5 Am. & Eng. Corp. Cas. 563; Dutchess Cotton Mfg. Co. *v.* Davis, 14 Johns. (N. Y.) 238; All Saints' Church *v.* Lovett, 1 Hall (N. Y.). 191; Hammond *v.* Shepard, 29 How. Pr. (N. Y.) 188; Melford, etc., Turnpike Co. *v.* Brush, 10 Ohio, 111; People *v.* Runkel, 9 Johns. (N. Y.) 147; Hoboken Bldg. Assoc. *v.* Martin, 2 Beasl. (N. J.) 427; Boisgerard *v.* N.Y. Banking Co., 2 Sandf. Ch (N. Y.) 23; Brick District *v.* Bowen, 7 Upp. Can. Q. B. 471; Provisional, etc., Council of Bruce *v.* Cromar, 22 Upp. Can. Q. B. 321; Bridgeford *v.* Hall, 18 La. Ann. 211; Northwestern Distilling Co. *v.* Brant, 69 Ill. 658; Buckaway *v.* Allen, 17 Wend. (N. Y.) 40; Thatcher *v.* West River Nat. Bk., 19 Mich. 196; Asheville Div. No. 15 *v.* Aston, 92 N. Car. 578; Kentucky Seminary *v.* Wallace, 15 B.

must be strictly used;[1] but in the case of a devise or bequest to a corporation great latitude is allowed in the case of a misnomer.[2]

Monr. (Ky.) 35; Hagerstown Turnpike Co. v. Creeger, 5 Harris & J. (Md.) 122; Alloways Creek v. String, 5 Halst. (N. J.) 323; Woolwich v. Forrest, 1 Penning. (N. J.) 115; Middletown v. McCormick, 2 Penning (N. J.) 500; Douglass v. Branch Bank, 19 Ala. 659; Glass v. Tipton, etc., Co., 32 Ind. 376; Melledge v. Boston Iron Co., 59 Mass. 158.

If the name of a corporation has been changed, it must sue by its new name on its old contracts; the identity of the corporation may be shown by proof. Mayor, etc., of Colchester v. Seales, 3 Burr. 1866; Del. & Atl. R. Co. v. Quick, 3 Zab. (N. J.) 321; Episcopal Charitable Society v. Episcopal Church, 1 Pick. (Mass.) 372; Trustees of Northwestern College v. Schwagler, 37 Iowa, 577; Cahill v. Bigger, 8 B. Monr. (Ky.) 211; Rosenthal v. Madison & Ind. Plank Rd. Co., 10 Ind. 358; Scarborough v. Butler, 3 Lev. 237. But see Alexander v. Berney, 28 N. J. Eq. 90; Sunapee v. Eastman, 32 N. H. 470; Beene v. Cahawba R., 3 Ala. 660.

Taxes were assessed and a warrant for their collection issued against "The Souhegan Nail, Cotton and Woollen Corporation." The corporate name of the company was "The Souhegan Nail, Cotton and Woollen Factory." There being no other corporation of that character in the town, it was held that the corporation was substantially described by its corporate name and the tax legally assessed. The Souhegan, etc., Factory v. McConihe, 7 N. H. 309.

1. "In pleading, the style or corporate name must be strictly used; and while the law was that a corporation could speak only by its seal, the same strictness in the use of the style was also necessary in contracting. But when the courts began to allow these artificial beings the attributes of natural existence, and to permit them to contract pretty much in the ordinary manner of natural persons, a correspondent relaxation in the use of the exact corporate name for purposes of designation necessarily followed. A departure from the strict style of the corporation will not avoid its contract, if it substantially appear that the particular corporation was intended; and a latent ambiguity may, under proper averments, be explained by parol evidence, in this as in other cases, to show the intention." Turnpike Road v. Myers, 6 S. & R. (Pa.) 12; Medway Cotton Manufactory v. Adams *et al.*, 10 Mass. 360; Newport Mechanics' Mfg. Co. v. Starbird, 10 N. H. 123; Melledge v. Boston Iron Co., 5 Cush. (Mass.) 158; State v. Bell Telephone Co., 36 Ohio St. 296; Wilson & Co. v. Baker, 52 Iowa, 423; Mott v. Hicks, 1 Cowen (N. Y.), 513; Ryan v. Martin, 91 N. Car. 464; Franklin Ave. Savings Inst. v. Board of Education, 75 Mo. 408; Mayor of Stafford v. Bolton, 1 B. & P. 40; Lynn-Regis., 10 Rep. 120; N. Y. African Soc. v. Varick, 14 Johns. (N. Y.) 38; Gray v. Monongahela, etc., Co., 2 W. & S. (Pa.) 156; Northumberland Co. Bk. v. Eyer, 60 Pa. St. 436; Burnham v. Sav. Bk., 5 N. H. 446; Holreth v. Franklin Mill Co., 30 Ill. 151.

In a suit for infringement of a patent, the defendant was sued under an erroneous corporate name, but appeared and answered under that name without exception, and participated in further proceedings in the case until final hearing, and after four years sought to open the decree because of the erroneous name and character under which it was sued. *Held*, that under the circumstances the defendant was estopped from denying the name and character in which it was sued. Bate Refrigerating Co. v. Gillett, 31 Fed Rep. 809; Virginia, etc., Nav. Co. v. Steamboat jewess, Taney, 418.

2. "The general rule is, that where either a corporation or a natural person is so identified by the name and description in the will, as applied to the facts and circumstances, as to distinguish such person or corporation from all others, such person or corporation shall take the bequest, in the same manner as if no such discrepancy had appeared." Minot v. Boston Asylum, 7 Metc. (Mass.) 416; *In re* Killert's Trusts, 7 L. R. Ch. App. 170; Hospital v. Knight, 21 L. J. Rep. N. S. Eq. 537; Parish in Sutton v. Cole, 3 Pick. (Mass.) 232; Hornbeck's Extr. v. American Bible Soc. *et al.*, 2 Sandf. Ch. 133; New York Institution, etc., v. How, 10 N. Y. 84; Butten v. Am. Tract Soc., 23 Vt. 336; Newell's App., 24 Pa. 197; Domestic, etc., Missionary Society's App., 30 Pa. 425; Cresson's App., 30 Pa. 437; App. of Washington & Lee University, 111 Pa. 572; Vansant v. Roberts, 3 Md. 119; Chapin v. School District, 35 N. H. 445; Preachers' Aid Society v. Rich, 45 Me. 552; Atty.-Genl. v. Mayor, 7 Taunt. 546; Burdine v. Grand Lodge, 37 Ala. 478; St. Louis Hospital v. Williams, 19 Mo. 609; Appeal of Pennsylvania Industrial Home for Blind Women, 40 Leg. Intel. (Pa.) 242.

4. Right to the Exclusive Use of a Name.—Apart from any statute a corporation has a right to the exclusive use of its name, and this right will be protected upon the same principle that persons are protected in the use of trade-marks.[1]

C. Domicile of Corporations.—A corporation has implied authority under its charter to carry on business in the customary manner, wherever it is most profitable and convenient. It is, however, considered a citizen of the State which created it. It can exercise its functions in other States only so far as it may be permitted by the comity of the local sovereign. It has been said that a corporation has no faculty to emigrate. This means that a corporation has no power in itself to extend its franchises from the jurisdiction of the sovereignty which created it to another sovereignty by which permission has not been given it to carry on its business and exercise its franchises. This permission, however, is universally accorded as a matter of comity.[2] As a general rule, a

1. Goodyear Rubber Co. *v.* Goodyear Rubber Manufacturing Co., 8 Am. & Eng. Corp. Cas. 317; State *v.* McGrath (Sup. Ct. of Mo.), 5 S. W. Rep. 29; *Ex parte* Walker, 1 Tenn. Ch. 97; Howard *v.* Henriques *et al.*, 3 Sandf. Ch. (N. Y.) 725; Newby *v.* Oregon Central R. Co., Deady, 609; Holmes *v.* Holmes, etc., Manufacturing Co., 37 Conn. 278.

In *Illinois*, the "Drummond Tobacco Company," a corporation, sought to enjoin the incorporation of another company under the name of the "Drummond-Randle Tobacco Company." The court held that in the absence of a showing that injury to the plaintiff would result, equity would not interfere. 114 Illinois, 412.

2. "In the jurisprudence of the United States a corporation is regarded as in effect a citizen of the State which created it. It has no faculty to emigrate. It can exercise its franchises extra-territorially only so far as may be permitted by the policy or comity of other sovereignties. By the consent, express or implied, of the local government, it may transact there any business not *ultra vires*, and 'like a natural person, may have a special or constructive residence, so as to be charged with taxes and duties or be subjected to a special jurisdiction.' It is for the local sovereign to prescribe the terms and conditions upon which its presence by its agents and the conducting of its affairs shall be permitted." City of St. Louis *v.* Wiggins' Ferry Co., 78 U. S. 423; Chicago & Northwestern R. Co. *v.* Whitton, 80 U. S. 270; Muller *v.* Dows, 94 U. S. 444; Beaston *v.* Farmers' Bank of Delaware, 12 Pet. 102; Bank of Augusta *v.* Earle, 13 Pet. 519; Lafayette Ins. Co. *v.* French *et al.*, 59 U. S. 404; Paul *v.* Virginia, 75 U. S. 181; Germania Fire Ins. Co. *v.* Francis, 78 U. S. 210; Baltimore & Ohio R. Co. *v.* Koontz, 104 U. S. 5; Ohio & Miss. R. Co. *v.* Wheeler, 66 U. S 286; St. Clair *v.* Cox, 106 U. S. 350; Farnum *v.* Blackstone Canal Co., 1 Sumn. 46.

"The residence of a corporation, if it can be said to have a residence, is necessarily where it exercises corporate functions. It dwells in the place where its business is done. It is located where its franchises are exercised. It is present where it is engaged in the prosecution of the corporate enterprise. Bristol *v.* Chicago, etc., R. Co., 15 Ill. 436; Baldwin *v.* Miss., etc., R. Co., 5 Clarke (Iowa), 518; Louisville R. Co. *v* Letson, 2 How. (U. S.) 497; Conover *v.* Ins. Co., 10 How. Pr. 403; Hubbard *v.* Ins. Co., 11 How. Pr. 149; Glaize *v.* S. Car. R. Co., 1 Strob 79; Cromwell *v.* Ins. Co., 2 Rich. 512; Bank *v.* McKenzie, 2 Brock. C. C. 392; Adams *v.* Great Central R. Co., 6 Hurl. & N. 404; Smith *v.* Silver Valley Mining Co., 10 Am. & Eng. R. R Cas. 1; Balt. & Ohio R. Co. *v.* Glenn, 28 Md. 287; Gill *v.* Kentucky & Col. Co., 7 Bush (Ky.), 635; Cowardin *v.* Universal Life Ins. Co., 32 Gratt. (Va.) 445; Day *v.* Newark India Rubber Co., 1 Blatch. C. C. 628; Land Grant Co. *v.* Board of Commissioners, 6 Kan. 245; N. O., J. & G. N. R. Co. *v.* Wallace, 50 Miss. 244; Ormsby *v.* Mining Co., 56 N. Y. 623.

"In the case of a railroad, canal, or turnpike company, exercising its franchises in more than one county, and transacting business in each of them, with a local establishment for business purposes, it would seem to be reasonable on must have its central office in the State under whose organized. It must also hold its corporate meetings by which it was chartered.[1] Directors' meetings, may be held out of the State, the directors being merely the company.[2] A corporation created by concurrent of two States, receiving from each a charter, has a legal in each State, and may lawfully hold its meetings and its business in either.[3]

ERS AND LIABILITIES OF CORPORATIONS.—Construction of —(a) *General Principles.*—The charter of a corporation is ure of its powers. But no charter, certainly in modern ecifies all that a corporation may or may not do. The hich corporations may exercise are therefore expressed in charters, are raised by judicial construction out of those are read into the charter as powers which the law implies mere grant to a corporation of the right to exist. While powers are all traced to the same source, it will simplify sideration to thus classify them.

principles of construction have grown up about the charporations which are axiomatic; the most important of been already mentioned, viz., that the charter of a coris the measure of its powers.[4] In *England*, this rule be reversed, and there the powers of a corporation are d to be such as the charter does not expressly or impliedly [5] It results from this rule that a corporation can make

that the corporation might and where its operations were ally carried on." Rhodes v. Co., 98 Mass. 95; Baldwin R. Co., 5 Clarke (Iowa), oseggio, etc., R. Co. v. Me. 434; Richardson v. Bur- R. Co., 8 Clarke (Iowa), etc., R. Co. v. Board of 48 N. Y. 93; Harding v. R. Co., 80 Mo. 659; Edon Bank of Fla., 1 Fla. 136; rooklyn Ferry Co., 36 Barb. Thero v. Central R. Co., 2 Connecticut, etc., R. Co. v. Vt. 436.

the duty of a corporation to ncipal place of business, its records, and its principal offi the State which incorporated ment necessary to the fullest and visitorial power of the courts, and the efficient exeof in all proper cases which id corporation." State *ex rel.* ee, etc., R. Co., 45 Wis. 579. ce to this decision, Morawetz Corporations, § 361) says: tion is correct only provided re has expressed the policy of some special enactment or al system of legislation regarding incorporated companies. There is no such rule at common law. It is always implied in the grant of a charter of incorporation, where there is no indication to the contrary, that the company shall have its central office or place of management in the State under whose laws it was organized. This, however, is merely a rule applicable to the construction of charters, in determining the intention of the corporators and of the State, and is not an arbitrary rule of law."

2. McCall v. Byram Mfg. Co., 6 Conn. 458; Arms v. Conant, 36 Vt. 744; Wood Mining Co. v. Ring, 45 Ga. 34; Galveston R. Co. v. Cowdrey, 11 Wall. (U. S.) 459.

An authority given in a charter in general terms to certain persons to call the first meeting of the corporators does not authorize them to call such meeting at any place without the limits of the State. Miller v. Ewer, 27 Me. 509.

3. Covington Bridge Co. v. Mayer, 31 Ohio, 317; Blackburn v. Selma, etc., R. Co., 2 Flip. C. Ct. 525; Ohio Bridge Co. v. Wheeler, 66 U. S. 286; State v. Northern Central R. Co., 18 Md. 193; Sprague v. Hartford, etc., R. Co., 5 R. I. 233.

4. See cases cited in succeeding notes.

5. Morawetz Corp. (2d Ed.), citing Shrewsbury, etc., R. Co. v. Northwestern

no contracts beyond the purposes and scope of its charter. Where these powers are exceeded, the government may take away its charter; a court of equity will restrain the carrying out of the contract, and a court of law will sustain no action upon it.[1] The implied powers of corporations must result from the charter by necessary implication, regard being had to the objects of the grant. If ambiguity or doubt arises out of the terms of a charter, they must be resolved in favor of the public.[2] The enumeration of powers implies the exclusion of all others.[3]

R Co., 6 H L C. 113; Eastern Counties R. Co. *v.* Hawkes, 5 H. L. C. 348; National Marine Co. *v.* Donald, 28 L. J. Ex. 188; Shrewsbury, etc, R. Co. *v.* London, etc., R. Co., 22 L. J. Ch. 682; Atty-Gen. *v.* Great Northern R. Co., 1 Dr. & Sm. 154

1. In Memphis Grain & Elevator Co. *v.* Memphis etc., R. Co., 30 Am. & Eng. R. R. Cas. 522, the court observes: "In Davis *v.* Railroad Co., 131 Mass. 259, Chief Justice Gray, after saying the reported cases on the subject are so numerous that he will refer to comparatively few of them, adds: 'A corporation has power to do such business only as it is authorized by its act of incorporation to do, and no other. It is not held out by the government, nor by the stockholders, as authorized to make contracts which are beyond the purposes and scope of its charter. It is not vested with all the capacities of a natural person, or of an ordinary partnership, but with such only as its charter confers. If it exceeds its chartered powers, not only may the government take away its charter, but those who have subscribed to its stock may avoid any contract made by the corporation in clear excess of its powers. If it make a contract manifestly beyond the powers conferred by its charter, and therefore unlawful, a court of chancery, on application of a stockholder, will restrain the corporation from carrying out the contract; and a court of common law will sustain no action on the contract against the corporation. Every person who enters into a contract with a corporation is bound at his peril to take notice of the legal limits of its capacity. This is sound in reason and principle, and is the rule in this State."

Corporations possess only such powers and capacities as are specifically granted by an act of incorporation, or are necessary to carry into effect the powers thus granted; hence it can only make such contracts as are connected with the purpose for which it was created, and which are necessary either directly or incidentally to answer that end. Mobile, etc., R. Co. *v.* Franks, 41 Miss. 511; Abby *v.* Billups, 35 Miss. 68; s. c., 72 Am. Dec. 143.

In Diligent Fire Co. *v.* Commonwealth, 75 Pa. St. 291, the court observed: "A corporation being a mere creature of the law, possesses those powers only which are given to it by its charter, either expressly or impliedly, as necessary in strict furtherance of the objects of its creation. It can exercise no powers or authorities except such as are conferred or authorized by its charter, or those necessarily incident to the powers and authorities thus granted, and, in estimation of law, part of the same." Wolf *v.* Goddard, 9 Watts (Pa.), 550; Pennsylvania R. Co. *v* Canal Commissioners, 21 Pa. St. 9; Commonwealth *v.* Erie, etc., R. Co., 27 Pa. St. 339.

2. In Minturn *v.* La Rue, 64 U. S. 435, the court observed: "It is a well-settled rule of construction of grants by the legislature to corporations, whether public or private, that only such powers and rights can be exercised under them as are clearly comprehended within the words of the act or derived therefrom by necessary implication, regard being had to the objects of the grant. If any ambiguity or doubt arises out of the terms used by the legislature, it must be resolved in favor of the public. This principle has been so often applied in the construction of corporate powers that we need not stop to refer to authorities." See also Charles River Bridge *v.* Warren Bridge, 11 Pet. (U. S.) 422; Mills *v.* St. Clair Co., 8 How. (U. S.) 569; Fanning *v.* Gregoire, 16 How. (U. S.) 524.

The general power of a corporate body must be restricted by the nature and object of its institution. Korn *v.* Mut. Assur. Society, 6 Cranch (U. S.), 192.

3. In Thomas *v.* Railroad Co, 101 U.S. 71, the court observed: "We take the general doctrine to be in this country, though there may be exceptional cases and some authorities to the contrary, that the powers of corporations organized under legislative statutes are such and such only as those statutes confer. Conceding the

The rights of a corporation are determined by the law in force when it came into being.[1] And it is not the province of a court to enlarge the powers of a corporation beyond its charter limitations because circumstances have changed.[2] But the gift of new powers to a corporation does not destroy its identity nor change it into a new being.[3]

(f) *Charters as Contracts.*[4]—It is a well-known and thoroughly settled rule, that the charters of private corporations are contracts protected from invasion by that provision of the constitution of the United States which prohibits any State from passing a law impairing the obligation of contracts.[5] A charter incorporating a bank is a contract.[6] It has been held that the grant to a private corporation of an exclusive right to manufacture and distribute gas is a contract;[7] so of an exclusive privilege of supplying a

rule applicable to all statutes, that what is fairly implied is as much granted as what is expressed, it remains that the charter of a corporation is the measure of its powers, and that the enumeration of these powers implies the exclusion of all others." See also Green Bay, etc., Canal Co. v. Union Steamboat Co., 107 U. S. 98; Building Co. v. Hyde Park, 97 U. S. 659; Turnpike Co. v. Illinois, 96 U. S. 63; Dartmouth College v. Woodward, 4 Wheat. (U. S.) 636; Perrine v. Chesapeake, etc., Canal Co., 9 How. (U. S.) 184; Bank of Augusta v. Earle, 13 Pet. (U. S.) 587.

Corporations possess only the powers conferred by the statute creating them, and those necessarily implied. Huntingdon v. Nat. Sav. Bk. of D. C., 96 U. S. U. S. 388; Beaty v. Knowler, 4 Pet. (U. S.) 152; Runyan v. Coster, 14 Pet. (U. S.) 122; Russell v. Topping, 5 McLean (C. C.) 194; Weckler v. First National Bank, 42 Md. 581; Penn. & Nav. Co. v. Dandridge, 8 Gill & J. (Md.) 248; Le Couteulx v. Buffalo, 33 N. Y. 333; Auburn Plank-road v. Douglass, 5 Seld. (N. Y.) 444; Brady v. Mayor, 20 N. Y. 312; People v. Utica Ins. Co., 15 Johns. (N. Y.) 357; 8 Am. Dec. 243; White's Bank v. Toledo Ins. Co., 12 Ohio St. 601; Obermyer v. Williams, 15 Ohio, 31; Straus v. Eagle Ins. Co., 5 Ohio St. 59; Dowling v. Mt. Washington Road Co., 40 N. H. 230; Trustees v. Peaslee, 15 N. H. 330; New London v. Brainard, 22 Conn. 552; Fuller v. Plainfield Academy School, 6 Conn. 532; Occum Co. v. Sprague Mfg. Co., 34 Conn. 541; Shawmut Bank v. P. & M. R. Co., 31 Vt. 491; City Council v. Plank-road Co., 31 Ala. 76; Winter v. Muscogee, etc., R. Co., 11 Ga. 438; Bowling Green, etc., R. Co. v. Warren Co. Court, 10 Bush (Ky.), 712; Railroad v. Payne, 8 Rich. (S. Car.) 177; Matthews v. Skinker, 62 Mo. 329; Ruggles v. Collier, 43 Mo. 353; Vandall v. South, etc., Dock Co., 40 Cal. 83; Rochester Ins. Co. v. Martin, 13 Minn. 59.

1. Chesapeake & O. R. Co. v. Miller, 114 U. S. 176.

2. Perrine v. Chesapeake & Del. Canal Co., 9 How. (U. S.) 172.

3. Central R., etc., Co. v. Georgia, 92 U. S. 665.

4. For further treatment of the relations of corporations to the State creating them, see FRANCHISES.

5. Dartmouth College v. Woodward, 4 Wheat. (U. S.) 518; Chenango Bridge Co. v. Binghamton Bridge Co.,—"Binghamton Bride."—3 Wall. (U. S.) 51; Davis v. Gray, 16 Wall. (U. S.) 203; and cases cited in succeeding notes.

6. Providence Bank v. Billings, 4 Pet. (U. S.) 514.

Every valuable privilege given by the charter of a private corporation, and which conduced to its acceptance and an organization under it, is a contract which cannot be changed by the legislature, where the power so to do is not reserved in the charter. Piqua Branch Bank of Ohio v. Knoop, 16 How. (U. S.) 369.

7. The manufacture of gas, and its distribution by means of pipes laid under legislative authority in the streets and ways of a city, is not an ordinary business in which every one may engage as of common right, upon terms of equality; but is a franchise relating to matters of which the public may assume control, and, when not forbidden by the organic law of the State, may be granted by the legislature as a means of accomplishing public objects, to whomsoever and upon what terms it pleases.

The grant of the exclusive privilege in question is none the less a contract be-city with water.[1] Decisions upon this point are numerous, and, so far as this single doctrine is concerned, practically unanimous.[2]

A charter given without the reserved right to alter or repeal is not affected by subsequent changes in the statutes or constitutions of the States.[3] In addition to the implied condition that the privileges and franchises of a corporation shall not be abused, the condition is also implied that the corporation shall be subject to such reasonable regulations as the legislature may from time to time prescribe, which do not materially interfere with or obstruct the privileges the State has granted, and which serve only to secure the ends for which the corporation was created.[4] This doctrine was applied to the regulation of rates of freight by a railroad.[5] So a statute prescribing a mode of service of process upon a railroad company different from that provided for in its charter, is not void as impairing the obligation of contracts; the legislative power of change as to remedies may be exercised when it does not affect injuriously the rights which have been secured.[6] Other instances

cause the manufacture and distribution of gas, when not subjected to proper supervision, may work injury to the public; for such a grant does not restrict the power of the State to establish and enforce regulations not inconsistent with the essential right given to the company by its charter.

Before the adoption of the present constitution of Louisiana, the legislature had authority to grant to a private corporation an exclusive privilege of that character; and such grant constitutes a contract, the obligation of which cannot be impaired by a State law. New Orleans Gaslight Co. *v.* Louisiana Light, etc., Co., 115 U. S. 650.

The legislative grant to the Louisville Gas Company for the term of twenty years, of "the exclusive privilege of erecting and establishing gas works in the city of Louisville, and of vending coal-gas lights, and supplying the city and citizens with gas by means of public works," constitute a contract within the meaning of the National Constitution, and was not forbidden by the Bill of Rights of Kentucky, the services which the company undertook to perform being public services, affecting the interests and rights of the public generally. Louisville Gas Co. *v.* Citizens' Gaslight Co., 115 U. S. 683.

1 The charter of the New Orleans Water-works Company, granting to that corporation the exclusive privilege of supplying New Orleans and its inhabitants with water from the Mississippi River, constitutes a contract within the meaning of the contract clause of the United States Constitution. New Orleans Water-works Co. *v.* Rivers, 115 U. S 674; Atlantic City Water-works Co. *v.* Atlantic City, 39 N. J. Eq. 367.

2. Hartford Bridge Co. *v.* Union Ferry Co., 29 Conn. 210; Central Bridge Co. *v.* Lowell, 15 Gray (Mass.), 106; State *v.* Noyes, 47 Me. 189; State *v.* Accommodation Bank, 26 La. Ann. 288; Bank of Dominion *v.* McVeigh, 26 Gratt. (Va.) 457

3 Dodge *v.* Woolsey, 18 How. (U. S) 331; Mechanics and Traders' Bk. *v.* Thomas, 18 How. (U. S.) 384; Jefferson Branch Bank of Ohio *v.* Skelly, 1 Black. (U. S.) 436; Franklin Branch Bank of Ohio *v.* Ohio, 1 Black. (U. S.) 474; Henry County *v.* Nicolay, 95 U. S. 619; New Orleans Gas Light Co. *v.* Louisiana Light & H., etc., Co., 115 U. S. 650; New Orleans Water-works Co. *v.* Rivers, 115 U. S. 674.

4. Chicago Life Ins. Co. *v.* Needles, 113 U. S. 574.

5. When a charter of a railroad company declares that no by-law shall be made that is in conflict with the laws of the State, and that the rates of charge for conveyance of persons and property are to be regulated by by-law, only such charges can be collected as are allowed by the laws of the State. In such case, in the absence of direct legislation, the rates are subject only to the common-law limitation of reasonableness; but if the State establishes a maximum of rates, the rates fixed must conform to its requirements. Ruggles *v.* Illinois, 108 U. S. 536; Stone *v.* Farmers', etc., Co., 116 U. S 307; Chicago, etc., R. Co. *v.* Iowa, 94 U. S. 161; Peik *v.* Chicago, etc., R. Co., 94 U. S. 164.

6. Cairo, etc, R. Co. *v.* Hecht, 95 U. S. 168.

cation of similar principles will be found cited in the

ation of Power to Amend and Repeal.—Charters may nodified, or amended in all cases where the power to erved in the charter or in some antecedent general law.[2] on to repeal a charter must be express, or such as to cessary implication of an intention to repeal.[3] Such a e reserved to the State by a general law applicable to icorporation,[4] and is equally valid and effectual in such is a State, under a general law in existence when the corporation was granted, authorizing it to alter, amend, arters, may subject the corporation to taxation from

in the charter of a New ssociation, which re-enacts he law, cannot be regarded and is not within the pro- provision of the United ion. Sherman v. Smith,) 587.

ending a charter of a cor- ed with its assent, and corporate vote as an the charter, does not im- ion of the contract of the r. Pennsylvania College . (U. S.) 190.

scholarships between one s and individuals, before ere united, would not in- ture from altering, modi- nding the charter of the virtue of a right reserved or with the assent of the Pennsylvania College . (U. S.) 190.

in the charter of a bank, and notes of said institu- ceived in all payments of State," is a contract with he notes which the State but it does not extend to er the repeal of such pro- uff v. Trapnall, 10 How. up v. Drew, 10 How. (U.

ion in a charter, that it ered in any other manner ct of the legislature, is n express reservation to ke alterations in it. Penn- ge Cases, 13 Wall. (U. S.)

tc., Association v. Brown, 1; Bangor, etc., R. Co. v. 34; Webb v. Ridgely, 38

New York ("Miller v. l. (U. S.) 478.

4. Miller v. N. Y. State, 15 Wall. (U. S.) 478; Pennsylvania College Cases, 13 Wall. (U. S.) 190; Holyoke Water Power v. Lyman, 15 Wall. (U. S.) 500; Greenwood v. Union Freight R. Co., 105 U. S. 13, Shields v. Ohio, 95 U. S. 319.

While a general law is in force subjecting all charters to alteration, a charter is not exempt from such alteration although it expressly confers the same rights, privileges, and immunities possessed by a certain other corporation whose charter is not subject to such alteration. Hoge v. Richmond & Dan. R. Co., 99 U. S. 348.

Where the charter of a railroad company was subject to alteration or repeal, an amendment giving to a municipal corporation owning stock in the company the right to elect seven directors instead of four, as originally provided, in consequence of the failure of a large class of subscribers to the stock to make good their subscriptions, and of a necessary reduction of the stock and the shortening of the route, was not a violation of the contract. Miller v. State of New York, 15 Wall. (U. S.) 478.

Where an act incorporating a cemetery company provided for its alteration or repeal, an act passed twenty years after the cemetery had been laid out, improved, and used, and where two thousand burial lots had been sold, authorizing the owners of the burial-lots to elect a majority of the trustees, who were thereby created a board to control and manage the cemetery, with due regard to the equitable rights of all persons having any vested interest therein, and providing that a portion only of the receipts should be paid to the original proprietors, and the rest to the improvement and maintenance of the cemetery, was valid. Close v. Glenwood Cemetery, 107 U. S. 466.

which it was previously exempt.[1] In such case it may authorize the taking of the property of a corporation by right of eminent domain exercised by a subsequently created company.[2] The exercise of this reserved right, if deemed expedient, may result in absolute extinguishment as a corporate body.[3]

(*d*) *Effect of Police Power of States.*—The legislature cannot by any contract divest itself of the power to provide for the protection of the lives, health, and property of citizens, and the preservation of good order and public morals. All rights, including those under charters, are held subject to the police power of the State.[4] This doctrine has been applied, among others, to businesses which may become nuisances,[5] and to lotteries.[6]

(*e*) *Construction of Powers in Derogation of Common Right.*—It is a well-established principle, that if the powers or privileges which

1. Charleston *v.* Branch, 15 Wall. (U. S.) 470; Tomlinson *v.* Jessup, 15 Wall. (U. S.) 54.

2. If the legislature had the power to repeal the statute under which a company was organized, it can charter a new company, and confer the same powers on it as the former one possessed; and, so far as the property or franchises of the old company are necessary to the public use, it can authorize the new one to take them, on making due compensation therefor. Greenwood *v.* Union Freight R. Co., 105 U. S. 13.

3. Spring Valley Water-Works *v.* Schottler, 110 U. S. 347; Greenwood *v.* Union Freight R. Co., 105 U. S. 13.

A statute of a State, that all charters of corporations granted after its passage may be altered, amended, or repealed by the legislature, does not necessarily apply to supplements to an existing charter. A provision in a supplement to a charter, that such supplement and charter may be altered or amended by the legislature, does not apply to a contract with the corporation made in a supplement thereafter passed. New Jersey *v.* Yard, 95 U. S. 104.

Where a charter to erect a dam does not contain any stipulation or contract exempting them from such implied condition, such charter is subject to the power reserved to the legislature by a general law, in operation when the charters were granted, that all acts of incorporation may be amended, altered, or repealed at the pleasure of the legislature. The legislature, under such reserved power, may pass laws to enforce the duty to keep open fishways. Holyoke Water-Power Co. *v.* Lyman, 15 Wall. (U. S.) 500.

4. Boston Beer Co. *v.* Massachusetts, 97 U. S. 25; Northwestern Fertilizing Co. *v.* Hyde Park, 97 U. S. 659; Stone *v.* Mississippi, 101 U. S. 814; Butchers' Union, etc., Co. *v.* Crescent City, etc., Co., 111 U. S. 746.

5. A charter authorizing the manufacture of animal matter into a fertilizer is not a contract guaranteeing exemption from the exercise of the police power of the State, when the business becomes a nuisance by reason of the growth of population around the locality originally selected. Northwestern Fertilizing Co. *v.* Hyde Park, 97 U. S. 659.

A charter granted to a beer company for the manufacture of malt liquors gave the incidental right to dispose of the liquors manufactured; but where there was a general statute subjecting charters to alteration or repeal, there was no contract which was impaired by a subsequent statute prohibiting the manufacture and sale of intoxicating liquors in the State. Boston Beer Co. *v.* Massachusetts, 97 U. S. 25.

Although a State may give an exclusive right, for the time being, to particular persons or to a corporation to provide a stock landing and establish a slaughterhouse in a city, it has no power to continue such right so that no future legislature, nor even the same body, can repeal or modify it or grant similar privileges to others. Butchers' Union, etc., Co. *v.* Crescent City, etc., Co., 111 U.S. 746.

6. The legislature of the State cannot, by the charter of a lottery company, make a contract against future regulation or suppression of lotteries. No legislature can bargain away the public health or the public morals. Stone *v.* Mississippi, 101 U. S. 814.

corporation is authorized to exercise are in derogation of common right, the construction of the terms of the grant will be most strongly against the corporation.[1] Such powers come within this rule as the following: the grant of a right to build a bridge;[2] a ferry;[3] a railroad between certain termini;[4] the grant of a right

1. In Northwestern Fertilizing Co. v. Hyde Park, 97 U. S. 659, the court observed: "The rule of construction in this class of cases is that it shall be most strongly against the corporation. Every reasonable doubt is to be resolved adversely. Nothing is to be taken as conceded but what is given in unmistakable terms, or by an implication equally clear. The affirmative must be shown. Silence is negation, and doubt is fatal to the claim. This doctrine is vital to the public welfare. It is axiomatic in the jurisprudence of this court. It may be well to cite a few cases by way of illustration. In Protestant Christ Church v. Philadelphia Co., 24 How. (U. S.) 302; in Tucker v. Ferguson, 22 Wall. (U. S.) 595, property had been expressly exempted for the time from taxation. Taxes were imposed contrary to the terms of exemption in each case. The corporation objected. This court held that the forbearance was only a bounty or gratuity, and that there was no contract. In Bank v. Billings, 4 Pet. (U. S.) 515, the bank had been incorporated with the powers usually given to such institutions. The charter was silent as to taxation. The legislature imposed taxes. 'The power to tax involves the power to destroy.' McCulloch v. Maryland, 4 Wheat. (U. S.) 316. The bank resisted, and brought the case here for final determination. The court held that there was no immunity, and that the bank was liable for the taxes as an individual would have been." Minturn v. Larue, 23 How. (U. S.) 435; Rice v. Minnesota & N. W. R. Co., 1 Black (U. S.) 358; Chenango Bridge Co. v. Binghamton Bridge Co., 3 Wall. (U. S.) 51; Minot v. Philadelphia, W. & B. R. Co., 18 Wall. (U. S.) 206.

Exclusive rights to public franchises are not favored. If granted, they will be protected, but they will never be presumed. Wright v. Nagle, 101 U. S. 791; Ruggles v. Illinois, 108 U. S. 536. See also Chicago Life Ins. Co. v. Needles, 113 U. S. [illegible]; [illegible] v. Canton, 51 Miss. 335.

2. An Act incorporating a bridge company in the usual form, not explicitly granting any exclusive privileges, and containing no agreement by the State not to permit other bridges in competition, cannot be construed, by implication, to prevent the State from subsequently granting a charter to another company for a competing bridge. Charles River Bridge v. Warren Bridge, 11 Pet. (U. S.) 420.

The New Jersey Act (1790), and agreement under it between the commissioners and bridge-builders, constituted a contract that no bridge should be built within the designated limits except the two which the statute authorized. The prohibition of other bridges is so far a part of the contract, and only so far, as is necessary to enable the builders to reap the benefit of their right to collect toll for the use of their bridges. Bridge Proprs. v. Hoboken L. & I. Co., 1 Wall. 116.

Where the legislature gave to a company all the rights and privileges of a previous corporation, a restriction in the former charter that no other bridge should be built within two miles is a part of the latter charter. A company chartered to construct a bridge within the prohibited distance is a plain violation of the contract which the legislature made with the former company, and such a contract is within the protection of the U. S. constitution. Chenango Bridge Co. v. Binghamton Bridge Co., 3 Wall. (U. S.) 51.

3. A ferry merely licensed may be discontinued, and a statute providing that such a ferry should be discontinued after a certain bridge company had made repairs, was valid. The bridge company having repaired its bridge, a subsequent act re-establishing the ferry was void. East Hartford v. Hartford Bridge Co., 10 How. (U. S.) 511, 541.

4. The contract in a charter authorizing the company to construct a railroad between two points, in which the legislature pledged itself not to allow, for a certain time, any other railroad to be constructed between the same points, or for any portion of the distance, the probable effect of which would be to diminish the number of passengers travelling between those points upon the road authorized, is not impaired by the authorizing of a company whose road struck the first at nearly right angles, some distance from its termini, to extend its road to that terminus; and an injunction will not be granted to prohibit the building of such extension. Richmond, F. & P. R. Co. v. Louisa R. Co., 13 How. (U. S.) 71.

to create a monopoly;[1] to hold a lottery;[2] to commit indictable acts;[3] to take property by right of eminent domain;[4] to create a nuisance;[5] to levy charges upon the public, such as exercising the privileges of a turnpike company;[6] the grant of powers in-

1. **Monopolies.**—Ruggles *v.* Illinois, 108 U. S. 526; Bridge Proprs. *v.* Hoboken, etc., Co., 1 Wall. (U. S.) 116; Hartford *v.* Hartford Bridge Co., 10 How. (U. S.) 511; Richmond, etc., R. Co. *v.* Louisa R. Co., 13 How (U. S.) 71; Pratt *v.* Atlantic, etc., R. Co., 42 Me. 579; De Lancey *v.* Insurance Co., 52 N. H. 581; Isham *v.* Bennington Iron Co., 19 Vt. 248; Gaines *v.* Coates, 51 Miss 335.

The charter of the Charles River Bridge Co. is a written instrument, which must speak for itself and be interpreted by its own terms. The fact that any rights or privileges were formerly granted to Harvard College with reference to a ferry which has been superseded by the bridge, as payment of a large sum by the company to the college, cannot be used to extend the privileges of the bridge company beyond what the words of the charter naturally and legally import. Charles River Bridge *v.* Warren Bridge, 11 Pet. (U. S.) 420.

2. **Lotteries.**—In Stone *v.* Mississippi, 101 U. S 814, it was held that the legislature of a State could not, by the charter of a lottery company, make a contract against future regulation or suppression of lotteries. No legislature can bargain away the public health or the public morals

3. **Indictable Acts.**—In State *v.* Krebs, 64 N. Car. 604, it was held that general words in a charter are not to be construed to authorize a corporation to do indictable acts.

4. **Eminent Domain.**—Currier *v.* Marietta, etc., R. Co., 11 Ohio St. 228; Moorhead *v.* Little Miami, etc., R. Co., 17 Ohio. 340; New York, etc., R. Co. *v.* Kip, 46 N. Y. 546; Edward *v.* Lawrenceburgh, etc., R. Co., 7 Ind. 711; Hannibal Bridge Co *v* Schaubacker, 49 Mo. 555.

5. **Nuisances.**—The grant of powers and privileges by the legislature to do certain things, as to a railroad company to bring its trade into a city, does not carry with it immunity from damages for private nuisances resulting directly from the exercise of those powers and privileges. Baltimore & Potomac R. Co. *v.* Fifth Baptist Church, 108 U. S. 317; Babcock *v.* New Jersey Stock Yard Co., 20 N. J. Eq. 296; Hooker *v.* New Haven, etc., Co., 15 Conn. 312; Fertilizing Co. *v.* Hyde Park, 97 U. S. 659; Allegheny *v.* Ohio, etc., R. Co., 26 Pa. St. 355; Coates *v.* Mayor, etc., of N.Y., 7 Cow. (N. Y.) 585; Boston Beer Co *v.* Commonwealth, 97 U. S. 25; Butchers' Union, etc., Co. *v.* Crescent City, etc., Co., 111 U. S. 746.

6. **Turnpike Companies.**—In St. Clair County Turnpike Co. *v.* Illinois, 96 U. S. 63, the charter of a company gave it the right to erect certain toll gates and to exact certain tolls for twenty-five years and as much longer as the State failed to redeem the franchises therein granted by paying the cost of the work. This was a contract; but it related only to the turnpike then to be constructed. And where, when the terms of the charter had more than half expired, the State gave a company a new and additional privilege of using the bridge and dike, and of erecting toll-gates thereon, it cannot be presumed that it was intended to be a perpetual grant. The court observed: "At common law, a grant to a natural person, without words of inheritance, creates only an estate for the life of the grantee; for he can hold the property no longer than he himself exists. By analogy to this, a grant to a corporation aggregate, limited as to the duration of its existence, without words of perpetuity annexed to the grant, only creates an estate for the life of the corporation. In the present case the turnpike company was created to continue a corporate body only for the term of twenty-five years from the date of its charter, and although by necessary implication a further continuance, with the special faculty of holding and using the turnpike authorized by the calling until redeemed by the State, is given to it for that purpose, yet it is only by implication, arising from the necessity of the case, and therefore cannot be extended to every purpose and object. Grants of franchises are special privileges, and always to be construed most strongly against the donee and in favor of the public." See also Stockton, etc., R. Co. *v.* Barrett, 11 Cl. & F. 590.

Where there is no contract in the charter of a turnpike company that prohibits the legislature from authorizing the construction of a rival railroad, the construction and operation of the rival road are not the subject of legal redress. But if the charter contains such a contract, the breach of it on the part of the State furnishes no excuse for the neglect of the company to repair its road, while at the same time it insists upon collecting the istent with the individual responsibility of members under charter;[1] exemptions from taxation[2] and from the operation of ... laws;[3] the grant to one corporation of the rights and ... of another.[4]

Charters to be Fairly and Reasonably Construed.—The application of these rules, however, is not permitted to prevent a fair construction of the powers of corporations. Such construction ... to them certain implied or incidental powers, few of which ... expressed in terms in charters. The common law powers of corporations have already been referred to;[5] these, without any express provision, are deemed inseparable from every corpora-

Washington, etc., Turnpike Co. v. ...and, 3 Wall. (U. S.) 210.

...owers Inconsistent with the Responsibility of Members under the Charter.—In ... v. Pennsylvania State Co., 71 Pa. ..., the court observed: "Corporations are just what the law of their organization makes them,—no more, no ...; when there is anything in the ... for interpretation on account ... or indefinite language, we ... explain the meaning in view of the ... of the enactment,—its purpose,— ... consider the appropriateness of the ... used to the supposed purpose in ... the legislature." And it was held ... case, that a provision of the ... incorporation inconsistent with the ... responsibility of the members ... exemption of the common law, and ... strictly construed.

...Exemption from Taxation.—In Penn... R. Co. v. Canal Commissioners, ... St. 9, the court observed: "It may ... the privilege that the relators ... arise by implication out of ... charter, or some other of the acts ... by their counsel, if we saw an op... to give to them the broad in... which we sometimes apply to ... of a different character. The ... powers can never be created by ... enlarged by construction: ... is granted unless it be ex... in plain and unequivocal words, ... the intention of the legislature ... too plain to be misunder... When the State means to clothe ... body with a portion of her ... sovereignty and to disarm herself to ... of the powers which belong to ... so easy to say so that we will ... believe it to be meant when it is ..., and words of equivocal import ... inserted by mistake or fraud. ... consideration of justice and ... requires that they shall be treated ... when they do find their way ... of the legislature. In the construction of a charter, to be in doubt is to be resolved; and every resolution which springs from doubt is against the corporation. This is the rule sustained by all the courts in this country and in England." Morgan v. Louisiana, 93 U. S. 217; Railroad Co. v. Gaines, 97 U. S. 697; Railroad Co. v. Commissioners, 103 U. S. 1.

Exemptions from taxation are never presumed; on the contrary, the presumptions are always the other way. Memphis Gas Light Co. v. Shelby County, 109 U. S. 398; St. Louis, etc., R. Co. v. Loftin, 98 U. S. 559; Philadelphia, etc., R. Co. v. Maryland, 10 How. (U. S.) 376; Southwestern, etc., R. Co v. Wright, 116 U. S. 231; Academy v. Exeter, 58 N. H. 306; Roosevelt Hospital v. New York, 84 N. Y. 108; Fox's Appeal, 112 Pa. St. 339.

3. **Usury.**—Johnson v. Griffin Banking, etc., Co., 55 Ga. 691; Reiser v. William Tell, etc., Assoc., 39 Pa. St 137; Houser v. Hermann Bldg. Assoc., 41 Pa. St. 478; Tyng v. Commercial Warehouse Co., 58 N. Y. 308.

4. **Grant to Company of Rights and Privileges of Another.**—Packer v. Sunbury, etc., R. Co., 19 Pa. St. 211; Pennsylvania R. Co.'s App., 93 Pa. St. 150. See also Bowling Green, etc., R Co. v. Warren County Court, 10 Bush (Ky.), 711.

A grant to one company of the powers, rights, and privileges of another, for the purpose of making and using a railroad, carried with it only such rights and privileges as were essential to the operations of the company, and did not include exemption from taxation, which was one of the privileges of the company. Memphis & C. R. Co. v. Gaines, 97 U. S. 697; Annapolis, etc., R. Co. v. Anne Arundel County, 103 U. S. 1. *Compare* Humphrey v. Pegues, 16 Wall. (U. S.) 244; Tennessee v. Whitworth, 117 U. S. 139.

5. *Supra*, ORGANIZATION OF CORPORATIONS, p. 188.

tion.[1] General statutes authorizing the formation of corporations and special charters have not only left these implied powers untouched, but many others have been inferred as incidental[2] or auxiliary to expressly granted powers. It is a general rule, that a corporation, in order to attain its legitimate objects, may deal precisely as an individual may who seeks to accomplish the same ends;[3] it may exercise all the powers conferred by statute, and probably such powers as are usually exercised by similar corporations, and which are necessary to accomplish the purpose of such corporation, not in conflict with the laws of the State.[4] The same presumptions are made as to the character of their contracts,[5] the

1. Downing *v.* Mount Washington, etc., Co., 40 N. H. 230; White s Bank *v.* Toledo Ins. Co., 12 Ohio St. 601.

2. An incidental power is one that is directly and immediately appropriate to the execution of the specific grant, and not one that has a slight or remote relation to it. Hood *v.* New York, etc., R. Co., 22 Conn. 1; Buffett *v.* Troy, etc., R. Co., 40 N. Y. 176; Curtis *v.* Leavitt, 15 N. Y. 157.

3. Barry *v.* Merchants' Exch. Co., 1 Sandf. Ch. (N. Y.) 289, and cases cited in succeeding notes.

4. In Wendell *v.* State, 62 Wis. 304, the court observed: "It is not necessary that the articles of association shall designate with particularity all the powers which it may exercise when duly incorporated. It is sufficient that they designate in general terms the purposes for which the corporation is organized; and when organized, such corporation may exercise all the powers which are conferred upon such corporations by statute, and probably all such powers as are usually exercised by similar corporations and which are necessary to accomplish the purposes of such corporation, not in conflict with the laws of the State"

In Wellersburg, etc, Plank-road Co. *v.* Young, 12 Md. 476, it was held that the creation of a corporation for a specified purpose implies a power to use the necessary and usual means to effect that purpose. Bridgeport *v.* Railroad Co, 15 Conn. 475.

In Clark *v.* Farrington, 11 Wis. 306, it was held that the rule restricting the powers of corporations to those delegated ought not to be extended so far as to unwisely and unnecessarily cripple and restrain them as to the means of executing the powers that are delegated.

In Green Bay & M. R. Co. *v.* Union Steamboat Co., 107 U. S. 98, it was held that whatever under its charter and other general laws, reasonably construed, may fairly be regarded as incidental to the objects for which a corporation is created, is not to be taken as prohibited As in this case, a railroad corporation's charter empowered it to make such agreements "as the construction of their railroad, or its management, and the convenience and interest of the company and the conduct of its affairs may, in their judgment, require; also, to build and run steamboats, etc.,"—a contract with a steamboat company, by which the railroad company guaranteed a certain amount of receipts from a line of boats to be run in connection with the road, is not *ultra vires*. The court said: "The charter of a corporation read in connection with the general laws applicable to it, is the measure of its powers, and a contract manifestly beyond those powers will not sustain an action against the corporation. But whatever, under the charter or other general laws, reasonably construed, may fairly be regarded as incidental to the objects for which the corporation is created, is not to be taken as prohibited." Thomas *v.* Railroad Co., 101 U. S. 71; Davis *v.* Railroad Co., 135 Mass. 258; Atty.-Genl. *v.* Railroad Co., 5 App. Cas. 473.

5. In Ohio, etc., R Co. *v.* McCarthy, 96 U. S. 259, the court observed: "When a contract is not on its face necessarily beyond the scope of the power of the corporation by which it was made, it will, in the absence of proof to the contrary, be presumed to be valid. Corporations are presumed to contract within their powers. The doctrine of *ultra vires*, when invoked for or against a corporation, should not be allowed to prevail where it would defeat the ends of justice or work a legal wrong." Union W. Co. *v.* Murphy's Flat Fluming Co., 22 Cal. 620; Morris, etc., R. Co. *v.* Railroad Co., 29 N. J. Eq 542; Whitney Arms Co. *v.* Barlow, 63 N. Y. 62. See Young *v.* Tredegar Iron Co. (Tenn.), 2 S. W. Rep. 202.

their intentions, as would apply to individuals.[1] The c charter of a corporation can be questioned only by d not by those claiming adverse rights.[2]

Powers as to Property.—1. Power to Acquire Prop- poration has power to acquire unlimited personal less especially restricted by its charter,[3] and, subject to triction, it may do so by all the usual methods of le.[4]

nd, every corporation not expressly restricted there- charters or acts of Parliament creating them, may l, and deal with every species of personal property as ely as an ordinary individual.[5]

Take Property by Bequest.—Corporations have power aw to take property by bequest.[6] The following are bequests which have been sustained as bequests in ects within the scope of corporate duties: of money for the purchase of bread, and for the education of the ministry;[7] of money to purchase ground for a f money for the relief of indigent residents of a town.[9] a corporation of its own stock has been held valid.[10]

s, etc., Bank v. Risley, 19 Groff v. American, etc., N. Y. 124.

· Gas Light Co. v. Con- ., 40 N. J. Eq. 427; Rus- Pacific R. Co. (Tex.), 5

475; 2 Kent's Com. 227; ants' Exch. Co., 1 Sandf.

Spear v. Crawford, 14 13; Moss v. Averell, 10 v. Heineberg, 40 Vt. 81; 'aters, 25 Mich. 225. dgwick, 35 Barb. (N. Y.)

p. 104.

v. Orphans' Asylum Soc., 437; New York Institu- ow, 10 N. Y. 43; Dutch low, 52 Barb. (N.Y.) 228; v. King, 12 Mass. 546.

v. Lex, 17 S. & R. (Pa.) money to a church to be , annually, for ten years, the congregation; also a er sum for the education e ministry of the sect to egation legatee belonged,

etc., v. Elliott, 3 Rawle uest to the city of Phila- it to purchase a lot of ct thereon a hospital for nd and lame, was upheld, ng: "One of the very corporation is . . . the maintenance and care of its indigent blind and lame. The only thing peculiar to the fund is the direction to apply it, not to the general purposes of the corporation, but to particular objects within the scope of its corporate duties; and for the accomplishment of those objects it is clear that it has capacity to take and to act as a trustee."

9. Shotwell v. Mott, 2 Sandf. Ch. (N. Y.) 46. In this case a bequest for the relief of such indigent residents as the town trustees should select was upheld, and it was observed that had the bequest been to the trustees of the town directly, it would still have been good; for which Coggeshell, etc., v. Pelton, 7 Johns Ch. (N.Y.) 292, was cited. In the latter case the bequest was to a town to buy land and erect a town hall; the bequest was held valid.

In Viner (Charitable Uses, A. B.) a devise to poor people maintained in the hospitals in St. Thomas' parish, in Reading, is' mentioned; and because those poor could not take, and because the mayor and burgesses of the corporation of Reading had in fact the government of the hospital, it was decreed that the corporation should take for the benefit of the poor.

10. In Rivanna Navigation Co. v Dawson, 3 Gratt. (Va.) 19, it was held that a bequest to a corporation of its own stock was valid. *Compare* Morawetz on Corp. (2d Ed.) § 114.

A private corporation may take a bequest in trust for religious usage.[1] It has been held that a bequest is a contract within the meaning of a statute providing that no person sued on a contract made with a corporation shall in defence set up want of legal organization.[2] As to the right of foreign corporations to take by bequest or gift, see FOREIGN CORPORATIONS.[3]

3. Power to Hold Property in Trust.—A corporation with legal capacity to hold property may take and hold it in trust in the same manner and to the same extent as a private individual may do.[4] But a corporation cannot be a trustee for purposes foreign to its institution,[5] nor in a matter in which it has no interest.[6]

4. Power to Pledge.—A corporation may pledge wherever it may lawfully contract a debt.[7]

1. Protestant Episcopal Education Society *v.* Churchmen, 80 Va. 718.

2. Under *Iowa* Code, § 1089, that no person sued on a contract made with a corporation shall in defence set up want of legal organization, *held*, that heirs petitioning to set aside a bequest cannot allege illegal organization against a corporation seeking to maintain the validity of the bequest. A bequest is a "contract" within the meaning of the statute; and "defence" embraces resistance by plaintiff to rights asserted by defendant. Hence the statute applies. Quinn *v.* Shields, 62 Iowa, 129; s. c., 1 Am. & Eng. Corp. Cas. 498.

3. As to right of foreign corporations to take by bequest or gift, see FOREIGN CORPORATIONS. See also Thompson *v.* Swoope, 24 Pa. St. 480; Am. Bible Soc. *v.* Marshall, 15 Ohio St. 537; White *v.* Howard, 38 Conn. 342.

4. In Vidal *v.* Girard, 2 How. (U. S.) 187, the court observed: "Although it was in early times held that a corporation could not take and hold real and personal estate in trust, upon the ground that there was a defect of one of the requisites to create a good trustee, namely, the want of confidence in the person, yet that doctrine has long since been exploded as too artificial; and it is now held that where a corporation has a legal capacity to take real and personal estate, there it may take and hold it upon trust in the same manner and to the same extent as a private individual may do." First Congregational Soc. *v.* Atwater, 23 Conn. 34; Phillips' Academy *v.* King, 12 Mass. 246; First Parish, etc., *v.* Cole, 3 Pick. (Mass.) 232; Wade *v.* American, etc., Soc., 7 Sm. & M. (Miss.) 697; Mason *v.* Methodist Episcopal Ch., 27 N. J. Eq. 47; *In re* Howe, 1 Paige (N. Y.) 214; Robertson *v.* Bullions, 11 N.Y. 243, Farmers' Loan, etc., Co. *v.* Harmony, etc., Ins. Co., 51 Barb. (N.Y.) 33; Lincoln Savings Bank *v.* Ewing, 12 Lea (Tenn.), 598; Montpelier *v.* East Montpelier, 29 Vt. 12.

5. Trustees *v.* Peaslee, 15 N. H. 317.

6. A corporation cannot be a trustee in a matter in which it has no interest, but where property is devised to a corporation partly for its own use and partly in trust for others, the power to take the property for its own use carries with it the power to execute the trust in favor of others. *In re* Howe, 1 Paige (N. Y.), 214; Wetmore *v* Parker, 52 N. Y. 450.

In Bethlehem Borough *v* Perseverance Fire Co., 81 Pa. St. 445, it was held that a fire company whose object, as declared by its charter, was "the protection of the property of our fellow-citizens from fire," was not organized for the private gain of its members, nor could they divide its property among themselves or for their private purposes. For the declared object is a charitable one; the St. of 43 Eliz. c. 4 (Charitable Uses) though not in force in the State of the fire company (Pa.), yet marks out principles which, "as applied by chancery in England, have long been recognized as in force here by common usage. Witman *v.* Lex, 17 S. & R. 90; Babb *v.* Reed, 5 Rawle, 151," etc. See also Coggeshell *v.* Pelton, 7 Johns. Ch. (N.Y.) 294.

7. In Leo *v.* Union Pacific R. Co., 17 Fed. Rep. 273, the court observed: "The purpose to raise money to meet debts, or for other corporate uses, by pledge of these securities, seems to be clearly within the scope of the corporate powers, and lawful and proper. The corporation has these securities not yet due . . . It owes debts, and was created with the expectation that it would owe them, and has implied power to raise money to pay

It may pledge bonds[1] and stock issued by itself as security for its own debts.[2]

5. Power to Lease.—Corporations, unless expressly restrained by statute, have an unlimited power of alienation like that of an individual, and since the greater power includes the less they may lease property, which is but a partial or temporary alienation.[3]

tion. It is not disputed that it could sell these securities to raise money to pay its debts, and the power to pledge them is included fairly in the power to sell for the same purpose. Platt *v.* Union Pac. R. Co., 99 U. S. 48. The orator does not appear to be entitled to have the corporation restrained from raising the money by the pledge of the securities, for that seems to be entirely lawful; nor to have it restrained from using the money for outside purposes, for there is no sufficient allegation or admission of any intention of doing so if not restrained."

1. Combination Trust Co. *v.* Weed, 2 Fed. Rep. 24.

2. Morawetz on Corp. (2d Ed.) § 349, citing Lehman *v.* Tallassee Mfg. Co., 64 Ala. 567; Androscoggin R. Co. *v.* Auburn Bank, 48 Me. 335. See also Seymour *v.* New York, etc., R. Co., 84 N. Y. 502; Chouteau *v.* Allen, 70 Mo. 338. *Compare* Kean *v.* Johnson, 9 N. J. Eq. 401.

A transaction of this kind would in reality be a pledge of the power to issue the securities on non-payment of the debt, rather than a pledge of the securities themselves. *Compare* Burgess *v.* Seligman, 107 U. S. 20; Morawetz on Corp. (2d Ed.) § 830.

3. In Ardesco Oil Co. *v.* North Am. Oil, etc., Co., 66 Pa. St. 375, the court observed: "But corporations, unless expressly restrained by the act which establishes them or some other act of assembly, have and always have had an unlimited power over their respective properties, and may alienate and dispose of the same as fully as any individual may do in respect to his own property. Hence an insolvent corporation may make a general assignment for the benefit of its creditors, and this power may be exercised by the directors, unless special provision to the contrary is made by the charter. Dana *v.* Bank of the United States, 5 W. & S. (Pa.) 223. If they can alienate absolutely, they may lease, which is but a partial or temporary alienation. *Omne majus continet in se minus*." Featherstonhaugh *v.* Lee Moor Porcelain Clay Co., L. R., 1 Eq. 318; Simpson *v.* Westminster Palace Hotel Co., 8 H. L. Cas. 712; Forest *v.* Manchester, etc., R., 30 Beav. 40; Brown *v.* Winnisimmet Co., 11 Allen (Mass.), 326; Temple Grove Seminary *v.* Cramer, 98 N. Y. 121.

In Commissioners *v.* Atlantic, etc., R. Co., 77 N. Car. 289, it was held, instead of making distribution of surplus funds, a corporation might temporarily lend them on safe security.

Where the charter of a corporation only empowers it to sell the real estate necessary for the transaction of its business when not required for the uses of the corporation, it cannot lease such real estate nor maintain an action for rent under its lease, such leasing not being necessary to the exercise of the purposes for which the charter was given. Metropolitan Concert Co. *v.* Abbey, 52 N. Y. Super. Ct. 97.

In Crawford *v.* Longstreet, 43 N. J. L. 325, it was held that premises necessary for storing property and sheltering servants might be leased by a turnpike company.

In Northern Liberty Market Co. *v.* Kelly, 113 U. S. 199, the court refused to pass upon the question as to whether a corporation, empowered to hold and convey real estate for the objects of its incorporation, may convey an estate in fee, or any less estate in lands which it has purchased, and may therefore make a valid lease of them for any term of years, though extending beyond the limit of its corporate existence.

See views upon this subject in Morawetz on Corp. (2d Ed.) § 330.

A lease of the land of a corporation, made without authority by the president and treasurer of the corporation, to the president, may be ratified and affirmed by the stockholders. Mt. Washington Hotel Co. *v.* Marsh, 63 N. H. 230.

A corporation, like a natural person, may ratify any act which it can perform; and the entry into possession of a leased road in pursuance of a lease executed by its officers without due authority, and operating the same and paying the rent therefor, as reserved in said lease, is ample evidence of the ratification. Ore

6. Assignments by Corporations.—A corporation may make an assignment for the benefit of creditors unless prohibited by statute, and may do so with or without preferences, even though it be insolvent.[1] Assignments by corporations for the benefit of creditors with preference, are prohibited by statute in *New York*.[2] Shares of its stock, owned by a corporation, may be assigned to a creditor in satisfaction of the debt, and it makes no difference that the creditor was a trustee and took part in the proceedings authorizing the assignment, if the proceedings were afterwards ratified by the corporation.[3]

7. Power to Alienate Property.—Ordinarily the power of a corporation to alienate its property, unless restrained by statute, is unlimited;[4] but the legal right of stockholders to sell their stock does not authorize a sale in combination, by which the president

gonian R. Co. *v.* Oregon R. & Nav. Co., 28 Fed. Rep. 505.

1. White Water Valley Canal Co. *v.* Vallette, 62 U. S. 414; *Ex parte* Conway, 4 Ark. 348; Ringoe *v.* Biscoe, 13 Ark. 563; Savings Bank *v.* Bates 8 Conn 505; Catlin *v.* Eagle Bank, 6 Conn. 23; De Camp *v.* Alward, 52 Ind. 468; Reichwald *v.* Commercial Hotel Co., 106 Ill. 439; s. c., 5 Am. & Eng. Corp Cas 248; Sargent *v.* Webster, 13 Metc. (Mass.) 497; State *v* Bank of Md. 6 Gill & J (Md) 205; Union Bank *v.* Ellicott, 6 Gill & J. (Md.) 363; Merrick *v.* Bank of Metropolis 8 Gill (Md.) 59; Covert *v* Rogers, 38 Mich 363; Shockley *v* Fisher, 75 Mo. 498; Lionberger *v.* Broadway, etc , Bank, 10 Mo. App. 499; Pierce *v.* Emery, 32 N. H. 486; Arthur *v.* Commercial, etc., Bank, 17 Miss 394; Coats *v.* Donnell, 94 N. Y. 168; Ardesco Oil Co. *v.* North Am. Oil, etc., Co., 66 Pa St. 375; Dabney *v.* Bank, 3 S. Car. 124; Warner *v.* Mower, 11 Vt. 390; Whitwell *v* Warner, 20 Vt. 425; Planters' Bank *v* Whittle, 78 Va. 737; Lamb *v.* Cecil, 25 W. Va. 288.

An insolvent corporation may sell and transfer its property, and may prefer its creditors, unless prohibited by law. Bergen *v.* Porpoise Fishing Co. (N. J.), 8 Atl. Rep. 523. Following Wilkinson *v.* Bauerle, 41 N. J. Eq 635, 1 Smith's L. C. (7th Am. Ed.) 45.

In the absence of statutory prohibition, a corporation may sell and transfer its property, and may prefer one creditor to another, although it is insolvent. Since the repeal of the New Jersey "act to prevent frauds by incorporated companies," and the failure (June Term, 1886) to reenact the provisions of its second section, in the present revision, there exists no statutory prohibition against the sale of property or the preference of creditors by an insolvent corporation, except probably a preference by way of a confessed judgment, under the provisions of section 80 of the act concerning corporations. But corporations and their officers may not divert the corporate property from the payment of debts; and where such diversion deprives creditors of the opportunity to enforce their debts, relief may be had by the injured creditors. When the diversion charged is by a sale of corporate property to one of the directors taking part in the transaction as buyer and seller, it devolves on the directors to establish the good faith of the transaction, and that the sale produced the full value of the property. If not made in good faith, or if it did not produce the full value of the property, the directors taking part in the sale will be answerable to creditors for what was thus lost. Wilkinson *v.* Bauerle, 41 N. J. Eq. 635.

2. 1 R. S. (New York), ch. 18, tit. 2, art. i. § 9; re-enacted in Laws of 1882, ch. 409, § 187. See also National Shoe, etc., Bank *v.* Mechanics' Natl Bank, 89 N. Y. 467; Kingsley *v* First Natl. Bank, 31 Hun (N Y.), 329; Coats *v.* Donnell, 94 N. Y. 168; Morawetz Corp. (2d Ed.) § 804.

3. Reed *v.* Hayt, 51 N. Y. Super. Ct. 121.

An assignment which purports on its face to be the contract of a company, and is signed by the president for the company, is the company's contract. Gottfried *v.* Miller, 104 U. S. 521.

4 Wilson *v.* Miers, 10 C. B. N. S. 348; Ardesco Oil Co. *v.* North Am. Oil, etc., Co., 66 Pa St. 375; Dana *v.* Bank of United States, 5 W. & S. (Pa.) 223.

assigns all the stock and securities to the president of
pany, contrary to a provision of the constitution of
a forbidding one railroad corporation to control any
ad corporation owning or having under its control a
ompeting line.[1]

to Guaranty.—In a late case it was held that there was
ressed nor implied in a charter of a railroad company
iaranty a dividend on the stock of an elevator com-
t it has been held that a railroad might guaranty to a
ompany that its earnings would amount to a certain
a guaranty of the bonds of a properly leased railroad,[4]
cipal aid bonds lawfully issued,[5] have been sustained.

right of stockholders to
does not authorize a sale
by which the president of
ns all the stock and securi-.
ident of a rival company,
declared public policy of
nce such an assignment,
sident of the South Penn-
. to the president of the
. Co., the latter company
or competing line, is void
t. art. 17, § 4, forbidding
rporation to control any
corporation owning, or
ts control, a parallel or
In determining whether
parallel or competing line
another, traffic contracts
ads owned by the former
into consideration. The
"parallel or competing"
provisions, although in-
not yet in operation.
R. Co. v. Commonwealth,
p. 368. Compare Moss v.
. 449; Ernest v. Nicholls,

and stockholders of a
ld to A the entire stock,
to him all of the property
ion. A remained in pos-
property for three years,
nd managing it, and then
ers. The trustees closed
its after the sale, and did
s trustees until three years
he majority of them met
on account, and drew a
avor. *Held*, the trustees
such either *de jure* or *de*
corporation could not be
reason of the check, es-
was not misled. Orr
o. v. Reno Water Co., 17

his Grain & Elevator Co. v. Memphis, etc., R. Co., 30 Am. & Eng. R. R. Cas. 522, a railroad corporation empowered by its charter "to do all lawful acts properly incident to a corporation, and necessary and proper to the transaction of the business for which it is incorporated." Its charter also declared that it should "possess such additional powers as may be convenient for the due and successful execution of the powers granted in this charter." As an inducement for a subscription to its stock by an elevator company, the railroad attempted to guarantee an 8 per cent dividend on the elevator stock. But the court *held*, in a bill to enforce the contract, that the railroad was only concerned in its own success, and authorized to do such things as are necessary to the transaction of its business—the business for which it was incorporated. In no part of the grant of power is that of guaranteeing the success of another institution, person, or corporation to be found in either expression or implication. See also Davis v. Old Colony, etc., R. Co., 131 Mass. 258.

3. Green Bay, etc., R. Co. v. Union Steamboat Co., 107 U. S. 101; s. c., 13 Am. & Eng. R. R. Cas. 658, where it was held that a railroad may guarantee to a steamboat company that its earnings will amount to a certain sum. See also Flagg v. Metropolitan, etc., R. Co. (C. C. S. Dist. N. Y., 1882), 4 Am. & Eng. R. R. Cas. 140; State Board of Agriculture v. Citizens', etc. R. R., 47 Ind. 407.

4. In Low v. California, etc., R. Co., 52 Cal. 53, it was held that where one railroad had executed a lease of another railroad, which it had authority to do, it might properly guarantee the bonds of such railroad.

5. In Railroad Co. v. Howard, 7 Wall. (U. S.) 392, it was held that under the laws of *Iowa* a railroad company having

as well as negotiable municipal bonds indorsed by a railroad company.[1]

(F) **Power to Borrow Money.**—Private corporations have implied power to borrow money in the transaction of their legitimate business, unless expressly prohibited, and the legal presumption is that such acts were done in the regular course of their authorized business.[2] Banks have implied power to borrow money, when neces-

power to issue its own bonds in order to make its road may guarantee the bonds of cities and counties which have been lawfully issued, and are used as the means of accomplishing the same end.

1. In Bonner *v.* City of New Orleans, 2 Woods (C. C.), 135, a railroad company was held bound as indorser of a negotiable bond issued by a municipal corporation, payable to the railroad company or assigns in twenty years, which the company had transferred by indorsement; the municipality having failed to pay on demand at maturity, and the proper steps having been taken to charge the indorser.

2. Memphis, etc., R. Co. *v.* Dow, 120 U. S. 287; Mahoney Mining Co *v.* Anglo-Californian Bank, 104 U. S. 192.

In Chicago, etc., R. Co. *v.* Howard, 7 Wall. (U. S.) 392, the court observed: "Private corporations may borrow money or become parties to negotiable paper in the transaction of their legitimate business, unless expressly prohibited; and until the contrary is shown, the legal presumption is that their acts in that behalf were done in the regular course of their authorized business. Canal Co. *v.* Vallette, 21 How. (U. S.) 424; Partridge *v.* Badger, 25 Barb. (N.Y.) 146; Barry *v.* Merchants' Exch. Co., 1 Sandf Ch. (N. Y.) 280; Farnum *v.* Blackstone Canal Co., 1 Sumn. (C. C.) 46; Ang. & A. Corp. sec. 257; Story Bills, sec. 79."

In Rockwell *v.* Elkhorn Bank, 13 Wis. 653, the court observed: "It is a universally accepted principle, that corporations authorized generally to engage in a particular business have as an incident to such authority the power to contract debts in the legitimate transaction of such business, unless they are restrained by their charters or by statute from doing so. It is likewise an equally well-acknowledged rule, that the right to contract debt carries with it the power to give negotiable notes or bills in payment or security for such debts, unless the corporations are in like manner prohibited."

In Lucas *v.* Pitney, 27 N. J. Law, 221, the court observed: "If it may contract debts, it would seem clear that it may enter into obligations to pay those debts, or borrow money for that purpose."

Taylor *v.* Agricultural Association, 68 Ala. 229; Mobile, etc., R. Co. *v.* Talman, 15 Ala. 472; Alabama, etc., Ins. Co. *v.* Central, etc., Assoc., 54 Ala. 73; Oxford Iron Co. *v.* Spradley, 46 Ala. 98; Savannah, etc., R Co. *v.* Lancaster, 62 Ala. 555; Magee *v.* Mokelumne Hill Canal, etc., Co., 5 Cal. 258; Smith *v.* Eureka Flour Mills, 6 Cal. 1; Union Mining Co. *v.* Rocky Mountain, etc., Bank, 2 Col. 248; Bradley *v.* Ballard, 55 Ill. 413; Ward *v.* Johnson, 95 Ill. 215; Hamilton *v.* Newcastle, etc., R. Co., 9 Ind. 359; Smead *v.* Indianapolis, etc., R. Co., 11 Ind. 104; Thompson *v.* Lambert, 44 Iowa, 239; Commercial Bank *v.* Newport Manuf. Co., 1 B. Mon. (Ky.) 14; Booth *v.* Robinson, 55 Md. 419; Fay *v.* Noble, 12 Cush. (Mass.) 1; England *v.* Dearborn, 141 Mass. 590; Donnell *v.* Lewis County, etc., Bank, 80 Mo. 165; Connecticut River Savings Bank *v.* Fiske, 60 N. H. 363; Lucas *v.* Pitney, 27 N. J. Law, 221; Fifth Ward Savings Bank *v.* First Nat. Bank, 7 Atl. Rep. (N. J.) 318; Kent *v.* Quicksilver Mining Co., 78 N. Y. 159; Curtis *v.* Leavitt, 15 N. Y. 9; Barnes *v.* Ontario Bank, 19 N. Y. 152; Smith *v.* Law, 21 N. Y. 296; Nelson *v.* Eaton, 26 N. Y. 410; Beers *v.* Phœnix Glass Co., 14 Barb. (N. Y.) 358; Mead *v.* Keeler, 24 Barb. 20; Partridge *v.* Badger, 25 Barb. (N. Y.) 146; Clark *v.* Titcomb, 42 Barb. (N. Y.) 122; Barry *v.* Merchants' Exch. Co., 1 Sandf. Ch. (N. Y.) 280; Commissioners *v.* Atlantic, etc., R. Co., 77 N. Car. 289; Tucker *v.* City of Raleigh, 75 N. Car. 267; Larwell *v.* Hanover Savings Fund Soc., 40 Ohio St. 274; Bank of Chillicothe *v.* Chillicothe, 7 Ohio (Part II.), 31; Ridgway *v.* Farmers' Bank, 12 S. & R. (Pa.) 256; Philadelphia, etc., R. Co. *v.* Stichter, 21 Am. L. Reg. N. S. 713; Moss *v.* Harpeth Academy, 7 Heisk. (Tenn.) 285; Union Bank *v.* Jacobs, 6 Humph. (Tenn.) 515; Burr *v.* McDonald, 3 Gratt. (Va.) 215; Rockwell *v.* Elkhorn Bank, 13 Wis. 653; Australian, etc., Co. *v.* Mounsey, 4 prosecution of their business, and they may issue the ices of debt therefor.[1] The loan must be for a proper urpose.[2] Unless limited by express statutory provi- nount of money which a corporation may borrow is

This amount is sometimes limited by statute, either ter or by general laws.[4] It has been held that there tation to time upon the implied power of a corporation ioney which would prevent it from issuing irredeemable

AND LIABILITIES AS TO NEGOTIABLE INSTRUMENTS.—1. rer to Issue Negotiable Instruments.—It is well settled oration, unless prohibited, has implied power to issue notes when given for any of the legitimate purposes he company was incorporated.[6] Its power in this re- en either held or tacitly recognized to be coextensive ver to contract debts.[7] In the *United States* the right otiable instruments has been held to belong as an im-

hbs, etc., Case, L R. 10 Eq. Australasia *v.* Breillat, 6 152.

eavitt, 15 N. Y. 9; Barnes ik. 19 N. Y. 152; Bank of Breillat, 6 Moore's P. C. *v.* Mokelumne Hill Canal, L 258.

., Case. L. R. 12 Eq. 516. ferchants' Exch., etc., Co., V. Y.) 280.

ite, Co. *v* Canney, 54 N. in *v.* Sea F. L. A. Soc., 1 Fountaine *v.* Carmathen 316.

tion as to whether there is on upon the implied power n to borrow money, which its issue of irredeemable iscussed in the following ilelphia, etc., R. Co. *v.* up. Ct. 1883), 21 Am. Law 713, note; Barry *v.* Mer- o., 2 Sandf. Ch. (N. Y.) Philadelphia, etc., R. Co.,

harter allows the corpora- money on such terms as lay determine, and issue evidences of indebtedness, by it for less than their re not void for usury. Bank *v.* Lawrence Mfg. 3 S. E. Rep. 363. Western Tel. Co., 5 Biss. ford Iron Co. *v.* Spradley, lagee *v.* Mokelumne Hill o., 5 Cal. 258; Smith *v.* Mills Co., 6 Cal. 1; Ward 5 Ill. 215; Millard *v.* St. Academy, 8 Bradw. (Ill.) 341; Monument National Bank *v.* Globe Works, 101 Mass. 97; Fay *v.* Noble, 12 Cush. (Mass.) 1; Narragansett Bank *v.* Atlantic Silk Co., 3 Metc. (Mass.) 282; Cann *v.* Brigham, 39 Me. 35; Lucas *v.* Pitney, 27 N. J. Law. 221; Connecticut, etc., Ins. Co. *v.* Cleveland, etc., R. Co., 41 Barb. (N. Y.) 9; Mead *v.* Keeler, 24 Barb. (N. Y.) 20; Partridge *v.* Badger, 25 Barb. (N. Y.) 146; Curtis *v.* Leavitt, 15 N. Y. 9; Moss *v.* Averell, 10 N. Y. 449; Barry *v.* Merch. Exch. Co., 1 Sandf. Ch. (N. Y.) 280; Mechanics', etc., Banking Assoc. *v.* New York, etc., Co., 35 N. Y. 505; Straus *v.* Eagle Ins. Co., 5 Ohio St. 59; McMasters *v.* Reed, 1 Grant's Cas. (Pa.) 36; Union Bank *v.* Jacobs, 6 Humph. (Tenn.) 515; Rockwell *v.* Elkhorn Bank, 13 Wis. 653; Richmond, etc., R. Co. *v.* Snead, 19 Gratt. (Va.) 354.

7. Catron *v.* First Univ. Soc., 46 Iowa, 108; Pitman *v.* Kintner, 5 Blackf. (Ind.) 253; Moss *v.* Oakley, 2 Hill (N. Y.), 265; Kelly *v.* Mayor, etc., 4 Hill (N. Y.), 263; Hamilton *v.* New Castle, etc., R. Co., 9 Ind. 359; Auerbach *v.* Le Sueur Mill Co., 28 Minn. 291. See also Safford *v.* Wyckoff, 4 Hill (N. Y.), 442.

In Sullivan *v.* Murphy, 23 Minn. 7, Gilfillan, C. J., said: "Since the old rule that a corporation can only contract under its corporate seal has been relaxed so as not to apply to contracts in the daily and ordinary transaction of its business, there is no reason why such debts may not be evidenced by promissory notes."

Where promoters of a cattle corporation before its complete organization selected a president, who with their approval gave a note in the prospective plied power to the following corporations: Railroad companies,[1] canal companies,[2] turnpike companies,[3] mining companies,[4] insurance companies,[5] manufacturing companies,[6] and mill companies.[7] It has been recognized as to a church corporation for building purposes,[8] and permitted to a society for erecting a monument.[9] The right of building associations to give notes to members instead of money, the members giving mortgages to the building associations for the proceeds of the notes, the same as if they had received money, has been recognized in *Maryland*,[10] and apparently denied in *Pennsylvania* and *Ohio*.[11] In *England* this right seems to be permitted only to companies where the nature and character of their business requires it; it has been denied to building associations as an implied power,[12] to companies formed for the erection of public works,[13] for carrying on works abroad,[14] and to railroad companies,[15] mining companies,[16] gas companies,[17] water-

corporation's business. *Held*, that the president's indorser could recover thereon against the corporation. Paxton Cattle Co. *v.* First Natl. Bank of Arapahoe, 59 Am. Rep. 852 (21 Neb. 621).

1. **Railroad Companies.**—Frye *v.* Tucker, 24 Ill. 180; Lucas *v.* Pitney, 27 N. J. Law, 221; Olcott *v.* Tioga, etc., R. Co., 27 N. Y. 546; Hamilton *v.* New Castle, etc., R. Co., 9 Ind. 359; Railroad Co. *v.* Howard 7 Wall. (U. S.) 412.

But it has been held that the note must pertain to the company's business. Pearce *v.* Madison R. Co., 21 How 441, where a note given by a railroad company, on consolidation with another company, was held void because not given in a transaction within the ordinary power of a railroad corporation.

And it has been held, analogously to the English rule, that the burden is on the holder to show that the note was given in the transaction of the corporate business. McCullough *v.* Moss, 5 Denio (N. Y.), 58.

But the contrary has also been held. Hamilton *v.* Newcastle, etc. R. Co., 9 Ind. 361; Sparks *v.* State Bank. 7 Blackf. (Ind.) 469. Such also was the view, in passing, in Safford *v.* Wyckoff, 4 Hill (N. Y.), 442. See Hackensack Water Co. *v.* De Kay, 1 Am. & Eng. Corp Cas. 670 (36 N. J. L. 548).

2. **Canal Companies.**—McMasters *v.* Reed 1 Grant's Cas (Pa.) 56.

3. **Turnpike Companies.**—Lebanon, etc., Co. *v.* Adair, 85 Ind. 244.

4. **Mining Companies.**—Mahoney Mining Co. *v.* Anglo-Californian Bank, 104 U. S. 192; Moss *v.* Averell, 10 N. Y. 457. *Compare* Blood *v.* Marcuse, 38 Cal. 590.

5. **Insurance Companies.**—Hascall *v.* Life Association, etc., 5 Hun (N. Y.), 151. *Compare* Bacon *v.* Mississippi Ins. Co., 31 Miss. 116.

6. **Manufacturing Companies.**—Mechanics' Banking, etc., Assoc. *v.* New York, etc., Co. 35 N. Y. 505; Oxford Iron Co. *v.* Spradley, 46 Ala. 98; Monument National Bank *v.* Globe Works, 101 Mass. 57; National Bank of Republic *v.* Young (N. J.) 7 Atl. Rep. 488.

7. **Mill Companies.**—Smith *v.* Eureka Mills Co., 6 Cal. 1.

8. Catron *v.* First Univ. Society, 46 Iowa, 106.

9. Hayward *v.* Pilgrim Society, 21 Pick. (Mass.) 270.

10. Davis *v.* West Saratoga Building Union, 32 Md. 285; art. BUILDING ASSOCIATIONS, 2 Am. & Eng. Encyc of Law, 615.

11. Art. BUILDING ASSOCIATIONS, 2 Am. & Eng. Encyc. of Law. 615.

12. 2 Am & Eng. Encyc. of Law. 615.

13. **Erection of Public Works.**—Broughton *v.* Manchester Water Works Co., 3 B. & Ald. 1.

14. **Carrying on Works Abroad.**—Peruvian R. Co., 2 Ch. App. 617.

Right to issue negotiable paper has been denied in England to—

15. **Railroad Companies.**—Bateman *v.* Mid. Wales R. Co., L. R. 1 C. P. 499. *Compare* Peruvian R. Co. *v.* Thames, etc., Ins Co., L. R 2 Ch 617.

16. **Mining Companies.**—Dickinson *v.* Valpy, 10 B. & C. 128.

17. **Gas Company.**—Bramah *v.* Roberts, 3 Bing. N. C. 963.

s,[1] salt and gravel companies,[2] cemetery compa-
c companies.[3]

have also power to draw and accept drafts ange when not foreign or repugnant to the pur- arter;[5] they may issue bonds;[6] they have also o indorse negotiable paper,[7] but have no power

—Neale v. Turton,

Co.—Bult v. Mor-

teele v. Harmer, 14
t.
ompson v. Univer-
ch. 694. And see
22, prohibiting all
n Bank of England
notes at dates less

l. Walne R. Co., L.
ourt observed: "It
rated for the forma-
h a limited capital
borrowing money.
d power to accept
consequence would
ght bind themselves
unlimited extent, or
rase be an inquiry
given for the pay-
r for a purpose not
corporation."
Henry Iron Co., 12
51). In this case,
ney on drafts drawn
d by G. T. as agent
, the iron company
le although its true
ot used, but instead
e corporation.
nion Co., 19 Johns.
cepted by the com-
ture consignments
r them.
has power to give
payment of a debt,
perty for legitimate
R. Co., 40 Barb.
Olcott v. Tioga
tcall v. Life Assn.
N. Y.), 151; Barnes
N. Y. 152.
orporation to draw,
s upon bills of ex-
ign or repugnant to
arter, is well recog-
are few direct de-
See Story on Bills.
Commercial Paper,
and statute 3 and 4
although it prohibits
nking in short-time

notes, so as to avoid competition with Bank of England, yet as to other notes gives corporations and individuals the same remedies upon them as upon *inland bills of exchange*.

6. Miller v. Superior Machine Co., 79 Ill. 450, where an appeal bond was held valid. Commissioners, etc., v. Atlantic, etc., R. Co., 77 N. Car. 289. In this case Rodman, J., said: "A railroad corporation must have power to contract debts, and every corporation which has that power must also have power to acknowledge its indebtedness under its corporate seal, that is, to make its bonds." Williamsport v. Commonwealth, 84 Pa. St. 487; Commonwealth v. Pittsburg, 41 Pa. St. 278.

In Vicksburg v. Lombard, 51 Miss. 111, it was held that a municipality authorized to issue bonds had the implied power to make them negotiable. For the *Pennsylvania* law, which is peculiar in this connection, see Kerr v. Corry, 105 Pa. St. 282.

In Miller v. Superior Machine Co., 79 Ill. 450, the appeal bond was in the name of the company by its agent, with a scrawl seal. *Held*, that it will be presumed, in the absence of proof, that the seal used was the proper and only seal of the company.

Bonds of corporations shown to be intended as negotiable instruments by the forms in which they are issued and the mode of giving them circulation have come by usage and judicial recognition to be so regarded. White v. Vermont, etc., R. Co., 21 How. (U. S.) 575; New Albany, etc., Co. v. Smith, 23 Ind. 353; Virginia v. Maryland, 32 Md. 547; Haven v. Grand Junction R. Co., 109 Mass. 88; Philadelphia, etc., R. Co. v. Smith, 105 Pa. St. 195; Beaver County v. Armstrong, 44 Pa. St. 63; Carr v. Lefevre, 27 Pa. St. 418; National Exch. Bank v. Hartford, etc., R. Co., 8 R. I. 375.

7. As Breese, J., said, in Frye v. Tucker, 24 Ill. 180, respecting railroad companies: "That a railroad company can take a promissory note and negotiate it in the ordinary course of their business, cannot be questioned. It is a power inherent in all such corporations."

Nor will the fact that the charter proto become parties to bills or notes for the accommodation of others.[1]

2. Liabilities of Corporations upon Negotiable Instruments.—Liabilities of corporations upon negotiable instruments which differ from those of ordinary holders are explained by such considerations as the fact that corporations exercise powers limited by law, with notice of which persons dealing with them are charged, and that their dealings must be by means of agents whose authority is also

hibited dealings in commercial paper extend so as to prevent a land company from receiving and selling notes given for the sale of its lands. Buckley *v.* Briggs, 30 Mo. 452.

To use the language of Breese, J., again: "They [ordinary railroads] cannot, as a branch of their business, deal in notes and bills of exchange, but can make such paper subservient to the great design." Goodrich *v.* Reynolds, 31 Ill. 490.

A corporation cannot, as against a *bona fide* holder for value before maturity, set up in defence that its indorsement was for accommodation. Mechanics' Bkg. Assn. *v.* N. Y., etc., Co., 35 N. Y. 505. And where a corporation indorsed on an interest-warrant or coupon issued by another company a guaranty "for value received," it was held that the words "value received" imported sufficient consideration, and that the company could not be deemed an accommodation indorser or guarantor. Connect. Mut., etc., Co. *v.* Cleveland, etc., R. Co., 41 Barb. (N. Y.) 9. But unless the indorsement is in a form authorized by the corporation itself, or in a form as to which the conduct of the company has justified the belief that it was authorized by the corporation, the company will not be liable on the indorsement. Repeated instances of indorsement by a president in a certain manner may estop the company. See also Park Bank *v.* American, etc., Co., 53 N. Y. Super. Ct. 367.

1. A corporation created for the purpose of carrying on a manufacturing business has implied power to make negotiable paper for use in its business, but no power to become a party to bills or notes for the accommodation of others. When a corporation has power under any circumstances to issue negotiable paper, a *bona fide* holder may assume that it was issued under the proper circumstances, and such paper cannot, more than any other commercial paper, be impeached for infirmity. Notice which would put a prudent man on inquiry and lead to discovery of fraud will not vitiate the corporation's negotiable paper. National Bank of Republic *v.* Young (N. J.), 7 Atl. Rep. 488.

A private manufacturing company has no power to accepts drafts for the accommodation of its stockholders or others. The consent of the stockholders or directors cannot confer such power; and a previous course of dealing of the corporation will not enable the holder of such a draft to recover on it against the corporation, if he is not a holder for value, as well as in good faith, without notice that the acceptance was an accommodation acceptance. If an accommodation acceptance is given in behalf of a corporation by its treasurer, a holder who has received it upon a pre-existing debt, without an express agreement to release the debt, is not, under the *New York* law, a holder for value, so as to enable him to recover against the corporation. Webster *v.* Howe Machine Co. (Conn.), 8 Atl. Rep. 482.

An insurance company has no power to indorse accommodation paper. In *assumpsit* by a bank against a life-insurance company, on its indorsement of a note, it appeared that the company had but the usual powers; that the note, indorsed in its name by W., its president, was that of a railroad company, of which also he was president, and to the credit of which the proceeds were put on his procuring the note discounted at the bank; that W. had, with the assent of the insurance company directors, been the manager of that company's finances, and had signed and indorsed its paper to a large amount as its president; but it did not appear that he had made any use of the company's name, with the knowledge of the directors, which they considered as binding thereon, except where it was understood that the company received the proceeds or the direct benefit. *Held*, that the insurance company had no power to indorse an accommodation note for a third party; and even if it had, the facts gave W., as its president, no implied authority to sign its name for such purpose. Ætna Bank *v.* Charter Oak Life Ins. Co., 50 Conn. 167

questions arising are complicated by the doctrine of certain principles have become well settled.[1] ling in the negotiable securities of a corporation are h notice of the power of the corporation to make as conferred by its charter. If a power granted by ubject to a condition relating either to the form in urity shall be made in order to be valid, or relating iinary proceeding extraneous to the acts of the corofficers, securities issued not in a prescribed form, preliminary proceeding had, are subject to defences thereof, even in the hands of *bona fide* holders.[2] trine does not refer to those instances in which the uch securities is by the charter conditioned upon the f acts by the corporation or its officers, relating to nt of the affairs of the corporation. In such cases, ling with the corporation finds the acts to be within s powers under its charter, he has a right to assume ditions have been complied with.[3] The doctrine

uis Savings Bank v. Bank, 95 U. S. 557; Bank v. Globe Works, fayette Savings Bank Co., 2 Mo. App. 299; Bank v. Empire, etc., (N. Y.) 51; Culver v. Co., 91 Pa. St. 367. Water Co. v. De Kay, p. Cas. 670; Farmers', chers', etc., Bank, 16 o Davis v. Old Colony 288; Hoyt v. Thomp- ; Alexander v. Cauld-

tc., Bank v. Butchers', Y. 129, the court ob- n who deals directly n, or who takes its is presumed to know rporate powers. But s upon its face in all the corporation has , and its only defect extrinsic fact, such as ject for which it was t the person taking the as to such extraneous ce of which he is in no uld obviously conflict icy of the law in regard r." Bank of Genesee . Y. 309; Safford v. N. Y.), 442; Lafayette etc., Co., 2 Mo. App.

annot defend success- n innocent holder for value of a note of the corporation regular on its face on the ground that it was issued for an illegal purpose, as to buy stock of another corporation contrary to its charter, the stock having been delivered. Wright v. Pipe Line Co., 101 Pa. St. 204; s. c., 47 Am. Rep. 701; Ridgway v. Farmers' Bank, 12 S. & R. (Pa.) 256; Philadelphia, etc., R. Co. v. Lewis, 33 Pa. St. 33. See also Stoney v. American Life Ins. Co., 11 Paige (N. Y.), 635; Mechanics' Banking Assoc. v. New York, etc., Co., 35 N. Y. 505.

Where a mining company had power to borrow money for the purpose of the corporation, and to invest its president and secretary with authority to negotiate loans, to execute notes, and to sign checks drawn against its bank account, the existence of authority in such officers, where they have drawn checks making an overdraft, should be presumed. Mahoney Mining Co. v. Anglo-Californian Bank, 104 U. S. 192.

An officer of a corporation may, by the conduct of its directors or managers, be invested with capacity to bind the company by acts beyond those powers inherent in his office. Thus, when in the usual course of the business an officer has been allowed to manage its affairs, his authority may be implied from the manner in which he has been permitted to transact such business. In such cases the officer's authority does not depend so much on his title, or on the theoretical nature of his office as on the duties he is in the habit of performing. B. was presi-

which invalidates securities of a corporation within its apparent powers, but improperly, and therefore illegally, issued, for want of acts to be done by the corporation or its officers in the management of its internal affairs, applies only in favor of *bona fide* holders for value. A person who takes such a security with knowledge that the conditions on which alone the security was authorized were not fulfilled, is not protected, and in his hands the security is invalid, though the imperfection is in some matter relating to the internal affairs of the corporation which would be unavailable against a *bona fide* holder of the same security.[1]

3. Ratification, Acquiescence, Laches, etc.—There are also many instances of the liability of corporations upon negotiable instruments arising from an application of the doctrines of ratification, acquiescence, laches, etc., examples of which may be found in the notes.[2]

dent of the City Bank, and treasurer of a savings-bank. As treasurer of the savings-bank he was the custodian of certain coupon bonds payable to bearer, and negotiable securities, the property of the savings-bank. The City Bank was a debtor to the First National Bank, and transmitted to it three notes—one purporting to be made by J., another by P., and the third by the savings-bank. Accompanying these notes, and mentioned in them as collateral security, were a number of the bonds belonging to the savings-bank. The J. note was discounted to the credit of the City Bank; the other notes were credited to the City Bank on its indebtedness. These notes had apparently been held by the City Bank as business paper received under discount, and as such the First National Bank accepted them in good faith. The J. and P. notes were forgeries; the savings-bank note was made without authority, by the treasurer, B., who, also without authority, used the bonds, the savings-bank deriving no benefit from the transactions. In trover brought by the savings-bank against the First National Bank to recover the bonds, *held*, that, the bonds being negotiable securities, title to them passed to the First National Bank by the delivery of them by the City Bank, in whose possession and apparent ownership they were; and that their negotiable quality was not impaired by the fact that the J. note and P. note were forgeries, and that the savings-bank note was made without authority.

In addition to the above transaction, B., as treasurer of the savings-bank, obtained the discount by the First National Bank of two notes of the savings bank signed by him as treasurer. Accompanying these notes, and as collateral security, were certain other negotiable coupon bonds payable to bearer, belonging to the savings-bank. In trover for the last-mentioned bonds, *held*, (1) that the First National Bank, having dealt in this matter with an officer of the savings bank, whose duties, as defined by the charter and by common usage, were the duties of a special agent, assumed the risk of the authority of the officer to contract the loan and pledge the securities in payment, and (2) that an instruction to the jury that B., as treasurer, had no power, *virtute officii*, to borrow money for the savings-bank, and give its notes or pledge its securities in payment, but that if B. was held out by the managers, in the general course of the business, as being its agent, with such authority, his acts as such agent would be binding upon the company, was correct. Fifth Ward Savings Bank *v* First National Bank (N J.), 7 Atlantic Rep. 318.

1. Hackensack, etc., Water Co. *v* De Kay, 1 Am. & Eng. Corp. Cas. 670

The releasing, without consideration, a maker of a note from his indebtedness thereon to a corporation, is not an implied power of the secretary and treasurer Nor can the maker defend on the ground that he gave the note by agreement with the secretary and treasurer that he would not be called upon to pay it, without proof of power in the secretary and treasurer to make such agreement, the note having been given in renewal of a former note on which he was liable. The company in retaining the benefits of the officer's act obtains nothing to which it was not entitled. Moshannon Land and Lumber Co. *v.* Sloan 7 Atl. Rep. (Pa.) 102.

2. When directors authorize and direct sale of corporate property for payment of notes executed without authority in the

ransfer of Negotiable Securities.—Under a rule itle to property by or to a corporation will not nerely because the transaction involved an un- of corporate power on the part of the company, alidity of a transfer of negotiable paper by or nnot be successfully assailed upon this ground. estrain any attempt to use the funds or pledge oration by the use of negotiable securities not e scope of the charter.[1]

president and notes. Reich- otel Co., 106 Ill.

owed money, and t by its actuary, estly applied in iabilities of the tees individually action, and made of the note car. by the company, 101 U. S. 347.

of a company ground that the were also the any, where the re sanctioned by na Hotel Co. v.

le securities had the community, olution and vote, ce, and had cir- t on the part of train them, and r money on the , the corporation kie v. Cleveland, . (U. S.) 381.

officers of a cor- nissory note may uiescence of the ognition by it of, d officers in the horized business. h Missouri Coal,

tion was author- n property stored ssumed to bind it or one per cent, oration received. based on tobacco discounted a note ose order it was ted it indorsed as ration had recog- ons as valid, and en given by the corporation general power to manage its business. *Held*, that the corporation could not dispute its liability on the indorsement. Park Bank v. German-American Mut. Warehousing, etc., Co., 53 N. Y. Super. Ct. 367.

The general manager of a corporation, who was authorized to collect its checks, etc., presented a check belonging to it to a bank for payment. By mistake the bank overpaid him. *Held*, that the corporation was liable for the amount of the over-payment, without regard to whether the manager accounted to the corporation for the amount. Kansas Lumber Co. v. Central Bank, 34 Kan. 635.

A secretary of a corporation cannot, in the absence of special authority, bind the corporation by a "due bill" given a stockholder in consideration of his surrender of his stock. Gregory v. Lamb, 16 Neb. 205.

An acceptance of a bill by a corporation binds it, although the bill was drawn on an officer of the corporation. Louisville, Evansville, etc., R. Co. v. Caldwell, 98 Ind. 245.

A railroad corporation should be deemed to have ratified a settlement made by its directors by giving notes, where for ten years its liability on the notes was not questioned, where it paid interest on them, and accepted reports in which they were referred to as outstanding obligations. Kelley v. Newburyport & Amesbury Horse R. Co., 141 Mass. 496.

1. Morawetz Corp. (2d Ed.) § 275; Central, etc., R. Co. v. Collins, 40 Ga. 582; Hoole v. Great West. R. Co., L. R. 3 Ch. App. 262; White v. Carmarthen, etc., R. Co., 1 H. & M. 786.

In Hoole v. Railroad Co., L. R. 3 Ch. App. 262, a company having power to raise additional capital by the issue of shares, and to allot to them a preferential dividend, a general meeting sanctioned such issue, although the revenue which warranted a dividend had been diverted to pay pressing charges against the capital of the corporation; and it was

H. Powers as to Real Estate.—1. Power to Acquire Real Estate. —The power of corporations to hold real estate is regulated by general statutes, and in the grant of special charters in many of the States. A corporation has no rights of property except such as are derived from its charter. It holds such property only for the purpose for which it was created. Its rights are measured by its charter, and not by the common law.[1] Unless restrained by law, and except as so restrained, the implied power of corporations to acquire, hold, and dispose of real estate is undoubted.[2] A railroad corporation authorized to buy land for the purpose of procuring stone and other material necessary for the construction of the road has power to buy land for the purpose of getting cross-ties and fire-wood.[3] A corporation chartered to accumulate a fund to be loaned on real-estate security or divided among its members, can loan money to its members and take deeds of trust on realty as security, and sell or assign such contracts of loan.[4] Although the existence of a corporation may be limited by its charter, yet it is capable of holding real estate in fee.[5] Words of

voted that the shareholders should each receive additional shares equal in par value to the amount of the dividend he would have been entitled to but for said diversion of income to capital. The shares thus to be issued would be salable only at a large discount. *Held*, that a shareholder might maintain a bill to restrain the corporation from this course.

The language of McCay, J., in Central R. Co. *v.* Collins, 40 Ga. 582, in which case the subject of the transaction was stock in a rival road, is appropriate: "By becoming a stockholder he has contracted that a majority of the stockholders shall manage the affairs of the company within its proper sphere as a corporation, but no further; and any attempt to use the funds or pledge the credit of the company not within the legitimate scope of the charter, is a violation of the contract which the stockholders have made with each other, and of the rights—the contract rights—of any stockholder who chooses to say, 'I am not willing.' It may be that it will be to his advantage, but he may not think so, and he has a legal right to insist upon it that the company shall keep within the powers granted to it by its charter."

It is not a sufficient reply to the bill, that the plaintiff is not in good faith seeking the interests of the company, but is acting in the interests of a rival road. Each stockholder has a right to stand upon his contract, as provided by the charter. Central R. *v.* Collins, 40 Ga. 582.

In White *v.* Carmarthen, etc., R. Co., 1 Hem. &. M. (Eng. Chancery), 786, in 1863, Vice-Chancellor Wood was of opinion that the suit by the shareholder must be in form on behalf of all the shareholders, though it may be sustained notwithstanding their opposition. But in Hoole *v.* Gt. Western R. Co. (1867). L. R. 3 Ch. App. 252, Lord Cairns, in the court of appeals, was strongly of opinion that the member may maintain a bill in his own name, without suing on behalf of other persons as well as himself, to restrain the corporation from an act *ultra vires;* and Sir John Rolt, L. J., concurred with him in this; but they did not find it necessary to decide the point.

1. Perrine *v.* Ches. & Del. Canal Co., 9 How. (U. S.) 172.

The power of a corporation to agree with the owner for the purchase of lands includes the power to determine the price by a reference. Alexandria Canal Co. *v.* Swann, 5 How. (U. S.) 83.

2. 2 Kent's Comm; Morawetz Corp. (2d Ed) § 327; Callaway. etc., Co. *v.* Clark, 32 Mo. 305; Auerbach *v.* Le Sheur Mill Co., 28 Minn. 291; Ossipee, etc., Co. *v.* Canney, 54 N. H. 295; Moss *v.* Averell, 10 N. Y. 449; Asheville Division, etc., *v.* Aston, 92 N. Car. 578; Page *v.* Heineberg, 40 Vt. 81; State *v.* Madison, 7 Wis. 688. See also Hayward *v.* Davidson, 41 Ind. 212, where the court makes a classification of corporations with reference to their power to take and hold real estate.

3. Mallett *v.* Simpson, 94 N. Car. 37.

4. Detweiler *v.* Breckenkamp, 83 Mo. 45.

5 In Asheville Division, etc., *v.* Aston,

necessary to convey a fee-simple to corpora-. The same evidence available to prove owner- person in property may be used to establish the poration.[2] A corporation may become liable to a occupation of land.[3] It may also hold as tenant h a natural person.[4] But cannot take an estate in survivorship be an incident thereto.[5]

of a corporation to hold real estate is carefully re- terms of its charter. It has frequently been held d company cannot acquire land by exercising the nt domain for speculation or sale or to prevent com- r can a corporation take a lease of property not re- chartered purposes, and of no substantial use thereto, ntion of harassing another party by its use.[7] A

was held that although corporation be limited r of years, yet it is estates in fee. "The cease to exist, as such, of its prescribed limit y sooner by a forfeiture nforced by the State, as ividual must terminate nce, but each is capa- beyond this dura- operative words of the fficient to pass it." nberg, 40 Vt. 81, the "At common law cor- ly have the legal ca- fee to real property, holding that it is inci- ecation. This has been ttled, unless in a case tion purchases and un- real property for pur- side and foreign to the ation. In such a con- be that a stockholder, ceedings instituted for the control the acts of respect, and as the gal rights as a stock- ment. But however that city to take a grant in n England is only re- statutes of mortmain." New York, etc., R. ; People v. Mauran, 5 ; Rives v. Dudley, 3 126. Wheeler, 47 N. H. 488; r v. Sears, 22 Pick. on Canal Co. v. Young, 5. County Turnpike Co. v. 69, it was held that a tion aggregate, limited as to the duration of its existence, without words of perpetuity being annexed to the grant, only creates an estate for the life of the corporation. See the remarks upon this decision in Morawetz on Corp. (2d Ed.) § 330.

2. Lowe v. State, 46 Ind. 305.

3. If a railroad corporation occupies land after its agent has been notified by the owner that rent will be charged, it is liable to *assumpsit* for use and occupation. Illinois Central R. Co. v. Thompson, 116 Ill. 159.

4. Estell v. University of the South, 12 Lea (Tenn.), 476.

5. Telfair v. Howe, 3 Rich. Eq. (S. Car.) 235.

6. In Rensselaer, etc., R. Co. v. Davis, 43 N. Y. 137, a railroad company's acquisition of land by eminent domain was held unauthorized where it was attempted to be exercised for speculation or sale, or to prevent interference by competing lines or methods of transportation, or in aid of collateral enterprises remotely connected with the mining or operating of the road, although they may increase its revenue and business. See also Eldridge v. Smith, 34 Vt. 484; Nashville, etc., R. Co. v. Cowardin, 11 Humph. (Tenn.) 348; Hamilton v. Annapolis, etc., R. Co., 1 Md. 553; State v. Mansfield, 23 N. J. Law, 510; Pacific, etc., R. Co. v. Seely, 45 Mo. 212.

In Morgan v. Donovan, 53 Ala. 241, it was held that property bought of an opposition steamship line by a railroad, not with a view of employing it in connection with the business of the road, but to withdraw it from business, thereby promoting competition, was not authorized by the charter.

7. In Occum Co. v. Sprague Mfg. Co., 34 Conn. 529, it was held that a

corporation cannot purchase an equitable estate any more than a legal estate in land for an unauthorized purpose.[1] A national bank is not authorized under United States statutes to take real-estate security for money loaned.[2] The right of corporations or associations for religious or charitable purposes to hold real-estate in any territory of the United States is limited by United States statute.[3]

2. Statutes Regulating Power to Hold Real Estate.—In *England*, the statutes of mortmain rendered corporations incapable of purchasing lands. The earlier statutes were levelled at the religious houses, but it was later provided that civil or lay corporations were equally within the mischief and the prohibition, and lands conveyed to any third person for the use of the corporation were made liable to forfeiture in like manner as if conveyed directly in mortmain.[4] These statutes have not been re-enacted in the United States or generally assumed to be in force.[5] Statutes of

corporation chartered for a specific purpose has no power to take a lease of property not needed for that purpose, or of no substantial use for it, with the intention and for the purpose of harassing another party by the use, under the forms of law, of the supposed rights thus obtained.

1. In Coleman *v.* San Rafael Turnpike R. Co., 49 Cal. 517, it was held that a corporation could not hold by means of another name land which it could not hold in its own name, nor could it take a beneficial interest in such land. It would have no more right to purchase an equitable estate in land for an unauthorized purpose, than to purchase a legal estate under similar circumstances.

2. In Matthews *v.* Skinker, 62 Mo. 329, it was held under the provisions of the National Banking Act that a national bank was not authorized to take real-estate security for money loaned. Crocker *v.* Whitney, 71 N. Y. 161. *Compare* Spafford *v.* Bank, 37 Iowa, 181.

In Fowle *v.* Scully, 72 Pa. St. 486, it was held that such a bank might take real-estate security for a prior loan, if done in good faith. See also Woods *v.* People's Bank, 83 Pa. St. 57.

Other banks than national banks, unless restrained by their charters, have power to secure themselves against anticipated liabilities, as well as those existing at the time, by taking a mortgage. Bank of United States *v.* Dandridge, 12 Wheat. (U. S.) 64; Crocker *v.* Whitney, 71 N. Y. 161.

3. United States Rev. Stats., § 1890, provides: No corporation or association for religious or charitable purposes can acquire or hold real estate in any Territory of the United States of greater value than fifty thousand dollars, under penalty of forfeiture, and escheat to the United States.

A corporation, after accepting a deed of land purchased by one of its officers, cannot dispute the officer's authority to agree to pay a price additional to that recited as the consideration in the deed. Kickland *v.* Menasha Wooden-Ware Co. (Wis.) 31 No. West R. 471.

A and B, as officers of a corporation, bought a tract of land for the corporation without authority from the directors. The title was made to B, who executed several mortgages on it to A, to secure him in advances of money he had already made to the corporation, and afterwards made for it. A transferred the mortgages to a third person for value. B subsequently conveyed the land to the corporation. *Held*, the transferee, having paid full value, acquired good title to the mortgages; and the corporation having passed into the hands of a receiver, who sold the land, the transferee of the mortgages was entitled to be first paid, before other creditors, out of the fund realized from the sale of the land. Milroy *v.* Eager, 30 Fed. 544.

A deed of land by a corporation, to be valid, must, under Wis. R. S. § 2216, be signed by its president or other authorized officer, sealed with its seal, and countersigned by its secretary or clerk. Galloway *v.* Hamilton, 68 Wis. 651 (1887).

4. 2 Kent's Comm.

5. 1 Kyd on Corp. 78–104; 2 Kent's Comm. 282; Odell *v.* Odell, 10 Allen (Mass.), 1; Perin *v.* Carey, 24 How.

[illegible] incompetent to take title to real estate, a [illegible] void, but only voidable: the sovereign alone [illegible] valid until assailed in a direct proceeding insti[illegible].[9] This principle has been applied to heirs

[illegible], 7 R. I. [illegible] Vt. 81. [illegible] Lessee, 14 [illegible] observed: [illegible] supreme court of [illegible] of Leazure v. [illegible] is directly appli[illegible]. The question then [illegible] to the right of [illegible] to purchase, [illegible] lands in question: [illegible] distinction between [illegible] the right to [illegible] them to be very [illegible]; and that [illegible] in this respect [illegible] power to take [illegible] and that although [illegible] may be [illegible] office found, [illegible] by the govern[illegible] own laws, to vest [illegible] remains in the [illegible] to a purchaser, [illegible] which is not [illegible]wealth. Such [illegible] Pennsylvania, it must

[illegible] case expressly [illegible] decide how far [illegible] in force in [illegible] decision upon [illegible] v. Hillegas, 7 [illegible] the act April 6, [illegible] obvious policy of [illegible] to be, that al[illegible] either in that or [illegible] distinction being [illegible] purchase lands [illegible] Pennsylvania, yet [illegible] to be divested [illegible]wealth, which [illegible] the commonwealth

[illegible] v. Remington, 1 [illegible] Gibson observed: [illegible] have been [illegible] only so far as they [illegible] of property to super[illegible]rants to a corpora-tion without statutory license." This statement of the law is repeated by Woodward, C. J., in Miller v. Porter, 53 Pa. St. 292.

To the same effect are Grant v. Henry Clay Coal Co., 80 Pa. St. 218; Leazure v. Union Mutual Life Ins. Co., 91 Pa. St. 491, which hold that the validity of such conveyances and the power to hold land in excess of awful limits can only be questioned by the State in direct proceedings for that purpose.

In Goundie v. Northampton Water Co., 7 Pa. St. 233, it was held that the commonwealth alone can object to a want of capacity in a corporation to hold land which it was not authorised by its charter to purchase.

" But provisions of a similar character have been enacted by many of the States, and are not infrequently contained in special charters of incorporation." Morawetz Corp. (2d Ed.) § 328.

9. Cornell v. Colorado Springs Co., 100 U. S. 55; Jones v. Habersham, 107 U. S. 174.

Although a corporation is forbidden by its charter to hold real estate, yet a deed of land to it is valid until vacated by a direct proceeding by the State for that purpose. Mallett v. Simpson, 94 N. Car. 37; s. c., 55 Am. Rep. 594.

Under *Pennsylvania* statute, 1855, April 26 (1 Purd. 361), which forbids a foreign corporation to "acquire and hold" real estate, a deed of conveyance of land to such a corporation is not void. It passes the title, and the corporation may hold the land subject to the commonwealth's right of escheat.

The commonwealth alone can object to the legal capacity of a corporation to hold real estate. Hickory Farm Oil Co. v. Buffalo, N. Y. & Pac. R. Co., 32 Fed. 22.

No party except the State can object that a corporation is holding real estate in excess of its rights. Alexander v. Tolleston Club, 110 Ill. 65.

Plaintiff railroad company bought cer-

attempting to set aside a devise by their ancestor to a corporation;[1] to a grantor who has received full value for the property;[2] to a private person denying the capacity of a corporation *de facto* to hold land;[3] and to one damaging real estate.[4] A foreign corporation cannot avoid the effect of such a statute by purchasing the charter of a mining company, vesting the title to lands in the corporate name thereof, and issuing to itself the stock of such mining company.[5]

tain lands from the receiver of an insolvent railroad company, and then filed a bill to quiet its title to the lands. *Held*, that right to question its right to hold other lands than those necessary to the maintenance and operation of its road rests with the State alone. Russell *v.* Texas & P. R Co. (Tex.), 5 S. W. 686.

1. A corporation of one State not forbidden by the law of its being, may exercise within any other State the general powers conferred by its own charter, including the acquisition of real estate, unless it is prohibited from so doing either in the direct enactments of the latter State or by its public policy, to be deduced from the general course of legislation or from the settled adjudications of its highest court. Children and heirs at law of a citizen of Illinois who has conveyed to a New York corporation real estate in Illinois, cannot, in an action to set aside the conveyance upon the ground that it was against the public policy of Illinois, raise the question that the grantee corporation has acquired a larger quantity of real estate than its charter allowed. That question does not concern them if the title has passed by a valid conveyance from their ancestor. American & For. Ch. Union *v.* Yount, 101 U. S. 352.

In Jones *v.* Habersham, 107 U. S. 174, it was held that restrictions imposed by the charter of a corporation upon the amount of property that it may hold cannot be taken advantage of collaterally by private persons, but only in a direct proceeding by the State which created it. Held and applied in a case where heirs of a decedent filed a bill to have declared void certain devises to a charitable corporation, which, it was averred, would swell the amount owned by the corporation to a value greater than the charter authorized. See also Runyan *v.* Coster, 14 Pet. (U S.) 122, 131; Smith *v.* Sheeley, 12 Wall. (U. S.) 358, 361; Bogardus *v.* Trinity Church, 4 Sandf. Ch. (N. Y.) 633, 758; De Camp *v* Dobbins, 29 N. J. Eq. 36; Davis *v.* Old Colony R. Co., 131 Mass. 258, 273.

2. Myers *v.* Croft, 13 Wall. (U. S.) 291.

3. A corporation *de facto*, at least where there is a law under which a corporation may be formed for such purposes, is capable of taking and holding property as grantee, and conveyances to it will be valid as to all the world, except the State, in direct proceedings to inquire into its right to exercise corporate franchises. In an action brought by it to recover such property, no private person will be allowed to attack collaterally the regularity of the organization. East Norway Lake N. E. Lutheran Church *v.* Froislie (Minn.), 35 N. W. 260.

4. One damaging real estate held by a corporation cannot avoid responsibility by showing that the corporation was not permitted by its charter to acquire title to the property, or that it acquired it for purposes unauthorized by law. Farmers' Loan & Trust Co. *v.* Green Bay & Minn. R. Co., 11 Biss. (C. C.) 334.

Under the *New York* statute, insurance companies acquiring real estate by foreclosure must sell the same within five years, unless the superintendent of the insurance department shall certify that the interests of the company will suffer by a forced sale. *Held*, as the statute did not assume to divest title because of a failure to comply with the law, a company after five years could convey an estate thus acquired, although the certificate had not been obtained. Home Ins. Co. *v.* Head, 30 Hun (N. Y.), 405.

5. It is not possible for a foreign corporation, by any "device whatsoever," to acquire or hold real estate in *Pennsylvania* without especial authority so to do.

Under *Pennsylvania* act, April 2, 1855, prohibiting any corporation, not incorporated under the laws of the State, from holding real estate within the commonwealth, "directly in the corporate name, or by or through any trustee *or other* device whatsoever," unless specially authorized by law, a foreign corporation cannot, by purchasing the charter of a mining company, vesting the title to lands in the corporate name thereof, and procuring the issue to itself of the stock

orporations.—In *England*, corporations were ex-
the Statutes of Wills, and could not take real
ise; but there, by the Statute of Charitable Uses,
evised to a corporation for a charitable use, and a
ould support it. The Statute of Uses is in force
ited States, and the power of corporations to take
ise is regulated by statute.[1] It has been well
ever, that a distinction should be observed be-
s whose object is to regulate corporations in re-
wer of acquiring and holding property, and laws
to restrict the power of testators to dispose of
Where a corporation of another State is generally
e land, the prohibition, in the Statute of Wills of
ich it was created, against all devises of lands to
s not prevent it from taking and holding land in
of one of its citizens. The statute was intended
estamentary power of citizens of that State, not
d to define the capacity of testators, and not of
It has been held that a corporation incapable un-
its domicile of taking real estate by devise could
ier State, and that where such devise was made a
had no power to convert such real estate into
t payment thereof to such devisee.[4]
atute of Wills does not except bodies politic and
s privileges, corporations are competent to take
the words "person or persons," and the like;[5] but
e excepts bodies-corporate as competent devisees,
charter conferring a right to take by "purchase"
a right to take by devise;[6] and so of a provision

npany, become the
he State which it is
red to hold. If by
n corporation does
in the State, such
heat by proceedings
r above recited act.
is one thing for a
invest its surplus
of another corpora-
poration, authorized
the coal, iron, or
sts of the common-
er specified in the
; but it is another
t thing to purchase
ontrary to law," etc.
New York, L. E. &
tl. R. 756.

Swoope, 24 Pa. St
p. (2d Ed.) § 332.
v. Roberts, 3 Md.
kins, 49 Md. 423.

3. Thompson *v.* Swoope, 24 Pa. St. 474; White *v.* Howard, 38 Conn. 342; American Bible Society *v.* Marshall, 15 Ohio St. 537.

4. In Starkweather *v.* American Bible Soc., 72 Ill. 50, it was held that the American Bible Society, a corporation of the State of New York, because incapable under the laws of its domicile of taking real estate by devise, could not acquire real estate in Illinois by devise; and that when real estate is devised to a corporation incapable of acquiring title in that way, a court of chancery has no power to convert such real estate into money and direct payment thereof to such devisee.

5. Boone Corp. § 53; McDonough Will Case, 15 How. (U. S.) 367; Perin *v.* Carey, 24 How. (U. S.) 465; Inhabitants, etc., *v.* Cole, 3 Pick. (Mass.) 232; Chambers *v.* St. Louis, 29 Mo. 543; Girard *v.* Philadelphia, 7 Wall. (U. S.) 114.

6. Boone Corp. § 53; McCartee *v.*

of the charter declaring the corporation to be capable of "taking, purchasing, holding, and conveying real estate."[1]

4. Power to Mortgage Property.—The power of a corporation to mortgage its property is dependent upon the general right of disposal which it may possess. Where the latter right exists, the power to mortgage necessarily follows.[2] It may be

Orphans' Asylum Soc., 9 Cow. (N. Y.) 437; Canal Co. *v.* Railroad Co., 4 Gill (Md.), 1.

1. Boone on Corp. § 53; Theological Sem. *v.* Childs, 4 Paige (N. Y.), 419. *Compare* Downing *v.* Marshall, 23 N. Y. 366.

2. Reynolds *v.* Stark County, 5 Ohio, 205; Burt *v.* Rattle, 31 Ohio St. 116; Jackson *v.* Brown, 5 Wend. (N. Y.) 590; Gordon *v.* Preston, 1 Watts (Pa.), 385; Allen *v.* Montgomery R., 11 Ala. 437; Mobile R. *v.* Talman, 15 Ala. 472; State *v.* Rice, 65 Ala. 83; Phillips *v.* Winslow, 18 B. Mon. (Ky.) 431; West *v.* Madison Ag. Board, 82 Ill. 205; Pierce *v.* Emery, 32 N. H. 484; Millink *v.* Morris Canal, 3 Green Ch. (N. J.) 377; Curtis *v.* Leavitt, 15 N. Y. 9; Seymour *v.* Canandaigua R., 25 Barb. (N. Y.) 284; Farmers' Loan Co *v.* Hendrickson, 25 Barb. (N. Y.) 484; Parish *v.* Wheeler, 22 N. Y. 494; Pennock *v.* Coe, 23 How (N. Y.) 117; Shaw *v.* Bill, 95 U. S. 10; Jones *v.* Guaranty, etc., Co., 101 U. S. 622; Thompson *v.* Lambert, 44 Iowa, 239; Watts' Appeal, 78 Pa. St. 370; Howe *v.* Freeman, 14 Gray (Mass.) 566; Ellis *v.* Boston, H. & E. R., 107 Mass. 1.

In Pierce *v.* Emery, 32 N. H. 484, a mortgage made to trustees by a railroad corporation, in pursuance of an act of the legislature, to secure a loan, was held, on a proper construction of the act and of the deed, to convey to such trustees the whole road as an entirety, with all its rights and interests; and thereby to include as well subsequently acquired property as that belonging to the road at the date of the mortgage.

In Jones *v.* Guaranty and Indemnity Co., 101 U. S. 622, it was held that a corporation having authority to mortgage its property for the purpose of carrying on its business may make a mortgage to secure future advances.

The power of a corporation to mortgage its property is not restricted by a provision in its charter limiting the stock, and prescribing that no greater assessment should be laid than a certain amount, and that if a greater amount of money should be necessary, it should be raised by creating new shares. Richards *v.* Merrimac R., 44 N. H. 127.

Power to mortgage the property of a corporation for a particular purpose will not authorize the corporation to mortgage for different purposes, or to apply the funds so raised to other purposes. Boone on Corp. § 40; Trevilian *v.* Mayor of Exeter, 27 Eng. L. & Eq. 578; and see Leavitt *v.* Yates, 4 Edw. Ch. (N. Y.) 134.

A corporation has power to mortgage its property in order to raise money to carry on its business. England *v.* Dearborn, 141 Mass. 590.

Though a life-insurance company's charter provided that its "capital stock and funds shall be invested either in loans upon bonds and mortgages upon real estate or in loans upon United States stocks and bonds," *held*, that a properly executed and recorded mortgage to the company securing a promissory note given in consideration of a loan of the company's funds was valid. Washington Bank *v.* Continental Life Ins. Co., 41 Ohio St. 1.

The subsequent ratification, by the legislatures of different States, of the illegal act of a corporation which is domiciled in each of the States, in executing a mortgage, is equivalent to previous authority granted. Graham *v.* Boston, H. & E. R. Co., 118 U. S. 161.

A mortgage naming a corporation as the party of the first part, and reciting authority to execute it given to its president, although containing the personal covenant of the president of the corporation, and signed by him, and accompanied by his personal bond, was held to be the mortgage of the corporation, where it was shown that the money borrowed, for which it was given, was used for the corporation. Jones *v.* N. Y. Guaranty & Ind. Co., 101 U. S. 622.

In action for conversion of personalty to which plaintiffs claim title under a mortgage from a corporation, the introduction of the mortgage upon which the signature and seal appear to be regular and proper is sufficient to allow the jury to find that the mortgage is valid, the corporation duly established, and that

Jersey to give one creditor a preference over

to Mortgages upon Certain Corporations.—It is principle, that the right to mortgage is neces- s the legislature has restricted the power. This express provision in the charter, by a general ng the corporation under such a duty to the osure of the mortgage would prevent its fulfill- Hence it is said that a railroad company cannot or lease of any portion of its road, or of any to the operation of its road, without the con-

ıanufacturing corporations are restricted by ıging their property unless written assent of at he capital stock is recorded in the county where ated.[3]

ıame of the cor- ty to do so; and *rima facie* to es- e plaintiff as to lamilton v. Mc- East. Rep. 424. ly organized un- ed business and judgments were ring these debts l its legal organi- ertain mortgages , that the judg- reference in pay- ge. Bergen v. 1 N. J. Eq. 238; rp Cas. 1. preference of one tion over other a mortgage on not now (June by law, nor is it Vail v. Jameson

m, when not re- nay acquire lands executes a mort- be used to raise purposes, may the bonds to be em in the mort- urity for all the na, Marion, etc., 5. ersey R., 101 U. Winans, 17 How. Del., etc., Canal readwell v. Salis- ıy (Mass.), 409; n & Chelsea R., anoe Co. v. La-

fayette, etc., R., 50 Ind. 85; Pierce v. Emery, 32 N. H. 484; State v. Consolidation Coal Co., 46 Md. 115; Atl. & Pac. Tel. Co. v. Union Pac. R. Co., 1 McCrary (C. C.), 541. Nor can property necessary to enable a corporation to perform its duties to the public be taken on execution. Gue v. Tide Water Canal Co., 24 How. (U. S.) 257; City of Palestine v. Barnes, 50 Tex. 538. The same principles apply, of course, to mortgages. Hall v. Sullivan (U. S. Dist. N. H.), 2 Redf. R. Cas. 621; 21 Law Rep. 138; Comm. v. Smith, 10 Allen (Mass.), 448; Richardson v. Sibley, 11 Allen (Mass.), 65.

3. While under *New York* acts 1864, ch. 517, am. 1871, ch. 481, written assent of stockholders owning two thirds of the stock of a manufacturing corporation is indispensable to a valid mortgage, such assent, if given afterwards, will validate the mortgage if there are no intervening rights, even though the assent is not filed in the office of the clerk of the county where the mortgaged property is situated. Rochester Savings Bank v. Averell, 96 N. Y. 467.

Under the *New York* statute, a manufacturing corporation cannot give a mortgage for a debt not contracted in carrying on its business. A mortgage given for another purpose by a gas-light company is therefore invalid. Astor v. Westchester Gas Light Co., 33 Hun (N. Y.), 333. See also, for cases construing this statute, Lord v. Yonkers Fuel Gas Co., 99 N. Y. 547; Carpenter v. Black Hawk, etc., Co., 65 N. Y. 43; Vail v. Hamilton, 85 N. Y. 453; Jones v. Guaranty, etc. Co., 101 U. S. 622; Morawetz Corp. (2d Ed.) § 348.

A provision in articles of incorporation that "no instrument affecting the title to real estate shall be binding, unless ordered at a meeting of the official board," does not apply to a release of a mortgage.[1]

6. Mortgages of Corporate Franchises.—The weight of authority is to the effect that a corporation has no power to mortgage or sell its franchises unless expressly authorized.[2]

7. Conveyances by Corporations.—The right of alienation is an incident of ownership, and belongs to a corporation as well as to an individual, when no restraint is imposed in the charter.[3] It is a general principle, that a conveyance of property by a corporation may be executed, like a conveyance by an individual, through any agent having authority to represent the company for that purpose.[4]

1. Stevenson *v.* Polk (Iowa), 32 N. W. R. 340.

2. See also title FRANCHISES.

Thomas *v.* Railroad, 101 U. S. 73; Commonwealth *v.* Smith, 10 Allen (Mass.), 448; Richardson *v.* Sibley, 11 Allen (Mass.), 67; Susquehanna Bridge, etc., Co *v.* General Ins. Co., 3 Md. 305; Carpenter *v.* Black Hawk Mining Co., 65 N. Y. 43; Atkinson *v.* Marietta, etc., R. Co., 15 Ohio St. 21; Toledo Bank *v.* Bond, 1 Ohio St. 622; Hall *v.* Sullivan R. Co., 21 Law Reporter, 138; s. c., 2 Redf. Am. R. Cas. 621; Comm. *v.* Smith, 10 Allen (Mass.), 448; Coe *v.* Columbus, etc., R., 10 Ohio St. 372; Pierce *v.* Emery, 32 N. H. 486; Howe *v.* Freeman, 14 Gray (Mass.), 566; Shaer *v.* Norfolk Co. R., 5 Gray (Mass.), 162; State *v.* Morgan, 28 La. Ann. 482; Pullan *v.* Cincinnati, etc., R. Co., 4 Biss. (C. C.) 35. But see Shepley *v.* Railroad, 55 Me. 407; Kennebec & Portland R. *v.* Portland & Kennebec R., 59 Me. 23; Bardstown R. *v.* Metcalfe, 4 Metc. (Ky.) 199; Bank of Middleburg *v.* Egerton, 30 Vt. 182; Phila. *v.* W. U. Tel. Co., 11 Phila. (Pa.) 327. *Compare* Detroit *v.* Mutual Gas Co., 43 Mich. 594; Booth *v.* Robinson, 55 Md. 419; Meyer *v.* Johnson, 53 Ala. 324.

A consequence of this principle, where accepted, is, that the franchises of a corporation cannot be levied upon by execution, although the property of the corporation may be taken, unless the corporation would thereby be rendered incapable of performing its public duties. Gue *v.* Tide Water Canal Co., 24 How. (U. S.) 257; Randolph *v.* Larned, 27 N. J. Eq. 557; Stewart *v.* Jones, 40 Mo. 140; Louisville Water Co. *v.* Hamilton, 81 Ky. 517; Gooch *v.* McGee, 83 N. Car. 59; Richardson *v.* Sibley, 11 Allen (Mass.), 71; Susquehanna Canal Co. *v.* Bonham, 9 W. & S. (Pa.) 27; Foster *v.* Fowler, 60 Pa. St. 27. *Compare* Ovington Drawbridge Co. *v.* Sheperd, 21 How. (U. S.) 112; City of Palestine *v.* Barnes, 50 Tex. 538; Youngman *v.* Elmira, etc., R. Co., 65 Pa. St. 278; Girard Point, etc., Co. *v.* Southwark, etc., Co., 105 Pa. St. 251.

"Such an artificial being," says Curtis, J., "only the law can create, and when created it cannot transfer its own existence into another body, nor can it enable natural persons to act in its name, save as its agents or as members of the corporation, acting in conformity with the modes required or allowed by its charter. The franchise to be a corporation is therefore not a subject of sale and transfer unless the law by some positive provision has made it so, and pointed out the modes in which such sale and transfer may be effected." 21 Abraham, 71.

3. In Burton's App., 57 Pa. St. 213, the court observed: "The right of alienation is an incident of ownership, and belongs to a corporation as well as to an individual, when no restraint is imposed in the charter. Dana *v.* Bank of United States, 5 W. & S. (Pa.) 243; Walker *v.* Vincent, 19 Pa. St. 369; Sutton's Hospital, 10 Coke R. 30; Ang. & A. Corp. § 188."

4. Morawetz Corp. (2d Ed.) § 335; Musser *v.* Johnson, 42 Mo. 74. See also, generally, *infra*, USE OF CORPORATE SEAL.

In Morris *v.* Keil, 20 Minn. 531, the clause read: In testimony whereof, the said Oxford Female College has caused these presents to be signed by the president of its board of directors and countersigned by the secretary thereof, and its corporate seal to be hereto affixed, this 3d day of November, 1868. O. H. Stoddard *Pres.*; J. H. Hughes, *Secy.* A statute in that State declared "that

A corporation has no general authority as such to convey; specific authority is indispensable.[1] A corporation cannot appoint an agent to convey lands, except by vote of its directors or other managing board, in whom the power to sell is vested by charter or by the general law; and without legal proof of the corporate act, a deed purporting to be executed in its name by an agent is not evidence of title, though it may operate as an estoppel.[2] But the authority of the agent need not be by

authorized to hold real by the same by an agent for that purpose." claimed that thereby every corporate conveyance was observed: "We think of this provision was to in which a corporation conveyance of real estate. reason for supposing that to exclude the other practice of a convey-oration through one or icers,—for instance, its ary, or treasurer,—in-h an agent appointed by similar purpose."

Eagle Mountain Mining 427, it was held that a oration, the concluding In witness whereof, the has caused this indenture its president and attested and its common seal to the signatures and seal, uted as a common-law that a statute requiring ent and two other mem-ation shall sign its deed state is an enabling act, xclude the common-law

. Bynum, 9 Gray (Mass.), as held to be sufficiently here the clause was: "In the said Bristow County by George Atwood, their authorized for this pur-into set their name and he signature of the treas-porate seal.

r. Iowa Homestead Co., he court say that where al and the signatures of ting the deed are proved, esume the possession of e seal itself is *prima facie* t was affixed by proper ame effect see Hamilton (Mass.), 12 N. E. Rep. 8, the words were: "In testimony whereof, the said party of the first part (the corporation) have caused these presents to be signed by their president and their common seal to be affixed,"—followed by the signature of the president and the corporate seal.

In Blackshire *v.* Iowa Homestead Co., 39 Iowa, 624, in his dissenting opinion, Miller, C. J., observed: "The mere production in court of a deed purporting to be executed by a private corporation, under its corporate seal, is not sufficient evidence to establish the fact that it is the act and deed of the corporation. The seal will not prove itself. The court cannot presume, without some proof, that the seal is genuine, and was affixed by proper authority. Moises *v.* Thornton, 8 Tenn. R. 303; Jackson *v.* Pratt, 10 Johns. (N. Y.) 381; Mann, etc., *v.* Pentz, 2 Sandf. Ch. (N. Y.) 257; Foster *v.* Shaw, 7 S. & R. 156; Leasure *v.* Hilligas, 7 S. & R. 313. When, however, proof is made of the signatures of the officers or agents executing the instrument in its behalf, the seal will be presumed to be that of the corporation; and when the seal affixed to the deed is proved to be the corporate seal, it is *prima facie* evidence that it was affixed by proper authority. President, etc., *v.* Myers, 6 S. & R. 12; Adams *v.* His Creditors, 14 La. 455; Darnell *v.* Dickens, 4 Yerg. (Tenn.) 7; Burrill *v.* Nahant Bank, 2 Met. (Mass.) 163; Lovett *v.* Steam Saw Mill, etc., 6 Paige Ch. (N. Y.) 54; Flint *v.* Clinton Co., 12 N. H. 434."

1. In Stow *v.* Wyse, 7 Conn. 214, Daggett, J., said: "It may be incidental to his power as agent to borrow money, give promissory notes, and do many other acts in the ordinary course of the business of the company; but the idea is quite novel, that, merely as agent, he might sell or convey the real estate. To effect such an object a specific authority seems indispensable; nor is there any principle or precedent in support of the power. . . . The deed, therefore, cannot be upheld."

Adams, 4 Allen (Mass.),

2. Standifer *v.* Swann, 78 Ala. 88;

a power under seal.[1] A committee empowered by vote of a corporation to authorize the treasurer to convey real estate may communicate such authority orally.[2]

The corporate name should be used and the corporate seal must be affixed, though a seal adopted for the occasion has been permitted.[3] A deed of trust executed by officers of a corporation in

Tenney *v.* Lumber Co., 43 N. H. 355; Burr *v.* McDonald, 3 Gratt. (Va.) 215. Hopkins *v.* Gallatin Turnpike Co., 4 Humph. (Tenn.) 403.

If the corporation be held to have ratified the acts of one assuming to act as its agent in selling and conveying lands, by its knowledge of the fact that he was so acting, such ratification would only operate as an equitable estoppel, of which courts of law cannot take cognizance in an action involving the legal title. Standifer *v.* Swann, 78 Ala. 88.

1. In Hopkins *v.* Gallatin Turnpike Co., 4 Humph. (Tenn.) 403. the court observed: "The common-law rule, with regard to natural persons, that an agent, to bind his principal by deed must be empowered by deed himself, cannot, in the nature of things, be applied to corporations aggregate. These beings [are] of mere legal existence, and their board, *as such*, are, literally speaking, incapable of a personal act. They direct or assent by vote; but their most *immediate* mode of action must be by agents. If the corporation or its representative, the board, can assent primarily by *vote* alone, to say that it could constitute an agent to make a deed *only by deed* would be to say that it could constitute no such agent whatever: for, after all, who could seal the power of attorney but one empowered by vote?" See, to same effect, Beckwith *v.* Windsor Mfg. Co., 14 Conn. 603.

In Hopkins *v.* Gallatin Turnpike Co., 4 Humph. (Tenn.) 403, it was held that where the president of a corporation makes a deed on behalf of the corporation and affixes the seal of the corporation thereto, it will be presumed, in the absence of proof, that he was duly authorized by the vote of the board to make the deed. The contrary must be shown by the objecting party. See also Ang. & A. Corp (11th Ed.) § 224, and authorities there cited

2 Hutchins *v.* Byrnes, 9 Gray (Mass.), 367.

The mere fact that a deed has a corporate seal attached does not make it the act of the corporation, unless the seal was placed to it by some one duly authorized. Koehler *v.* Black River Falls Iron Co., 2 Black (U. S.), 715.

In Gashwiler *v.* Willis, 33 Cal. 12, it was held that an attempted conveyance of land was invalid when authorized by a shareholder's meeting, where the charter provided that "the powers of the corporation shall be exercised by a board of trustees." See Conro *v.* Port Henry Iron Co., 12 Barb. (N. Y.) 27.

3. Miners' Ditch Co. *v.* Zellerbach, 37 Cal. 543; Hutchins *v.* Byrnes, 9 Gray (Mass.), 367; Flint *v.* Clinton Co., 12 N. H. 430; Tenney *v.* East Warren Lumber Co, 43 N. H. 343; Hatch *v.* Barr, 1 Hamm. (1 Ohio) 390.

But the corporation will be bound by a deed sealed with another than their regular seal, a seal of any device, or a paper or wafer without mark, adopted by them for the occasion; as where, as in this case, the agents for the corporation, signing in its name by them as agents, with common seals opposite each officer's name. Tenney *v.* Lumber Co., 43 N H. 350, 354. See also McDaniels *v.* Flower, etc., Co., 22 Vt. 274.

The rule as to the *name* is traceable to Combes' Case, 9 Co. 76, and is there given: "2. It was resolved, that when any has authority to do any act, that he ought to do it in his own name, who gives the authority. The attorney cannot do it in his own name, nor as his proper act, but in the name and as the act of him who gave the authority. And where it was objected in the case at bar [that] the attorneys have made the surrender in their own names, for the entry is *Quod iidem Willielmus et Stephanus*, etc., *sursum reddiderunt*, etc., it was answered and resolved, *per totam curiam*, that they have well pursued their authority, for first they showed their letter of attorney, and then they *authoritate eis per præd' literam attornatus dat' sursum reddiderunt*, etc., which is as much as if they had said, We, as attorneys of T. Combes, surrender, etc. And both these ways are sufficient: I, as attorney of J. S., deliver you seizin; or, I, by force of this letter of attorney, deliver you seizin. And all that is well done, and a good pursuance of his authority."

The rule thus appears very plain; yet many decisions based upon it are really contrary to it It has been held that a

s by mistake, but intended as the deed of the cor-
eld capable of being reformed in equity.[1] A deed
ie corporators but not in the statutory mode has
Where the president or other officer of a corpora-
deed in his own name and under his own seal, it is
not the deed of the company.[3] The deed of a
be proved only by proving that the seal affixed is
corporation, or that it was affixed as the corporate

me of a corporation,
executed by a duly
nd purporting to con-
the principal, yet if
e of the deed is, "In
ave set my hand and
d is signed by the
be regarded as exe-
of the corporation or
it is entirely inopera-
g the agent adds to
attorney, for the prin-

Lessee v. Barr, 1
), a conveyance exe-
as agent in his own
s own seal as presi-.
to be a valid deed of
he court said: "The
the deed do not exe-
es are collected in 1
et seq.

nard Co. Agr. Board,
, said: "Equity pos-
reform the deed of
onform to the agree-
The deed was exe-
officers, for and on
ration. In equity, it
e corporation itself.
its these facts. The
upon is clearly the
ener," etc.

Moulton, 15 Vt. 519.
lington Iron Co., 19

arr, 1 Hamm. (Ohio)
ase, Spencer executed
his own name under
sident, and the court
antors named in the
it."

1 Net. 439, the deed
Benton, Jr., President
ngs Land Company,
etc., and was signed
way. *Held*, that it
See also Metropolis
, 14 Pet. (U. S.) 19.
ann, 2 Cush. (Mass.)
purporting to be the
England Silk Co., by

C. C., their treasurer, reciting that it was executed by him in behalf of the company, and as their treasurer, duly authorized for that purpose, and signed and sealed by him with his own name and seal, followed by the words "treasurer of the New England Silk Company," was held not a deed of the corporation. And Warner v. Mower, 11 Vt. 390 (1839), was distinguished from the prevailing decisions by the *Vermont* statute of 1815, providing that private business corporations might convey "by deed of such president reciting the vote of the corporation," the Vermont court conceding that the common-law rule was probably different.

In Isham v. Bennington Iron Co., 19 Vt. 230, this statute of 1815 was said not actually to require conveyance by an officer called a president. "It does not seem very important what the name of the officer or agent is; or whether he have any name; but the essence of the requisition is, that the deed must be executed in pursuance of some vote of the corporation, and that this vote must be recited in the deed."

Also in this last case a *Vermont* statute of 1797, requiring the deed to be "signed and sealed," was held not complied with by a deed signed by one as "chairman," and the fact that the corporate seal was set against the agent's name gave no virtue to the deed. The signing must be of the corporation's name. P. 251 *et seq.*

Bearing some resemblance to the above-mentioned *Vermont* act of 1815 is the *Georgia* statute chartering the Hawkinsville Bank, and providing that "the bills obligatory and credit notes, and all other contracts whatever, on behalf of said corporation, shall be binding upon the company, provided the same be signed by the president and countersigned or attested by the cashier of the said corporation." Under this charter it was held that a deed of land, made by the president and countersigned by the cashier, was a good conveyance. Veasey v. Graham, 17 Ga. 99.

seal by an officer of the corporation or other person, thereunto duly authorized.[1] Where the Statute of Frauds would render void a conveyance made by an individual, the same principles would apply to a corporation.[2]

8. Acknowledgment of Corporate Deeds.—The certificate should state the position of the officer affixing the corporate seal, his authority, that he knows the corporate seal, and that the same is affixed to the conveyance by order of the board of directors or other trustees of the corporation, and that he subscribed his name thereto as a witness of the execution thereof.[3] Where no statute regulates the execution and acknowledgment of corporate deeds, the officer affixing the seal is the party executing the deed within the meaning of statutes requiring deeds to be acknowledged by the grantor.[4]

I. USE OF CORPORATE SEAL.[5]—At common law, when a corporation is duly created, it is tacitly annexed as an incident that it may have a seal and may make or use what seal it will;[6] and this statement expresses the law as it is to-day.[7] It was also a doctrine of the common law, that a corporation spoke alone by its common seal, and its contracts and acts were only valid when its seal was affixed by a duly authorized agent;[8] but this rule has been wholly discarded.[9] For it has been substituted the universal rule, that a corporation is like an individual in its capacity to contract, appoint agents, and incur ordinary liabilities, and that the use of a seal is only necessary where its use would be required from an individual.[10]

1. Osborne *v.* Tunis. 25 N. J. Law, 633.

2. Smith *v.* Morse, 2 Cal. 524.

3. Lovett *v.* Steam Saw Mill Assoc., 6 Paige Ch. (N. Y.) 60.

In Frostburg Mut. Building Assoc. *v.* Bruce. 51 Md. 508, the certificate of the justice stated that the attorney of the corporation appeared and acknowledged the mortgage to be his act and deed, instead of the act and deed of the corporation. *Held*, that the acknowledgment was aided by intendment, and that it should be read and understood as the acknowledgment of the corporation by its attorney, according to what was the manifest intention. See also Muller *v.* Boom, 63 Tex. 91; Monroe *v.* Arledge, 23 Tex. 480; Eppricht *v.* Nickerson, 78 Mo. 483; more fully cited under ACKNOWLEDGMENTS, 1 Am. & Eng. Encyc. of Law, 159, 160.

4. Kelly *v.* Calhoun, 95 U. S. 710.

5. See generally, *supra*, POWERS AS TO REAL ESTATE; CONVEYANCES BY CORPORATIONS.

6. Co. Litt. 250 *a*; Com. Dig. Franchise, F. 13; Case of Sutton's Hospital, 10 Co. R. 30 *b*; 1 Kyd Corp. 259.

Character of Seal.—In Hendee *v.* Pinkerton, 14 Allen (Mass.), 381, the court observed: "The line must be drawn somewhere, and we are satisfied to draw it so as to exclude written or printed scrawls, scrolls, or devices; but so as to include an actual and permanent impression upon the substance of the paper of the common seal of a corporation." See also Bates *v.* Boston, etc., R. Co., 10 Allen (Mass.), 251; Haven *v.* Grand Junction R. Co., 12 Allen (Mass.), 337, Allen *v.* Sullivan R. Co., 32 N. H. 446.

7. Ransom *v.* Stonington, etc., Bank, 13 N. J. Eq. 212; South Baptist Soc. *v.* Clapp, 18 Barb. (N. Y.) 36; Bank *v.* Rutland, etc., R. Co., 30 Vt. 159; Tenney *v.* East Warren, etc., Co., 43 N. H. 343; Kansas City *v.* Hannibal, etc., R. Co., 77 Mo. 180; Johnston *v.* Crawley, 25 Ga. 316; Charleston *v.* Morehead, 2 Rich (S. Car.) 450.

8. Arnold *v.* Mayor of Poole, 4 Man. & G. 860; Mayor of Ludlow *v.* Charlton, 6 M. & W. 815.

9. 2 Kent's Com. 288; Bank of United States *v.* Dandridge, 12 Wheat (U. S.) 64.

10. Gottfried *v.* Miller, 104 U. S. 521; Fleckner *v.* Bank of United States, 8 Wheat. (U. S.) 338; Chesapeake, etc.,

ly the same rule prevails in *England.*[1]
nce of real property must purport to be made and the corporation acting by its duly authorized agent. s of simple contract the rule is not so strict, and an an instrument will be inferred from the general prinaw of agency.[2]
acting for the corporation in affixing a seal to an no longer, as at common law, required to have a seal.[3] This has been applied to an attorney or prosecutes a suit for a corporation,[4] or who consents to arbitration.[5] The corporate seal may be affixed properly authorized.[6]
bond of a municipal corporation was sufficiently the private seal of the president of the board of ere there was no common seal, and the corporation t without one.[7] An agreement made by the agent ion is a contract of the corporation, although made resolution of the board of directors, and though the s the private seal of the agent, if the agent was execute it, or the company ratified his act.[8] The s of a corporation in signing their names separately d affixing the corporate seal separately to each name xecution of a lease, their action being considered but not as vitiating the lease.[9]
ce of a seal gives rise to a *prima facie* presumption

app. 9 Pet. (U. S.) 541; polis v. Gottschlick, 14 rustees, etc., v. Moody," wley v. Genesee Mining Savings Bank v. Davis, ancroft v. Wilmington lemy, 5 Del. 577; Maher Ill. 266; Town of New as, 82 Ill. 259; Trustees, 53 Ind. 273; Maine Stage Me. 444; Badger v. Bank, 8; Santa Clara Mining ith, 49 Md. 389; Petrie Hen. 647; Buckley v. ; Goodwin v. Union N. H. 378; Crawford v. J. Law, 395; Whitford N. Y. 245; Sheldon v. 109. See also, *supra*, Land; Conveyances by Bellamy Mfg. Co., 12 N. H. 205; Santa Clara, etc., Assoc. v. Meredith, 49 Md. 389; Trundy v. Farrar, 32 Me. 225. See also, *supra*, Powers as to Real Estate; Conveyances by Corporations.

Guardians of Bethnal C. P. 91; Reuter v. ph Co., 6 El. & Bl. 341. Bennett, 27 L. J. C. P. ndon, etc., R., 5 Exch. 442. Johnson, 48 Mo 74. ited States v. Dandridge, 64; Despatch Line v.

4. Osborn v. Bank of U. S., 9 Wheat. (U. S.) 738.

5. Paret v. Bayonne, 39 N. J. Law, 559. *Compare* Cape Sable Company's Case, 3 Bland, 606.

6. Bason v. Mining Co., 90 N. Car. 417; Morris v. Keil, 20 Minn. 531. See also, *supra*, Powers as to Real Estate, Conveyances by Corporations.

7. In Deberry v. Holly Springs, 35 Miss. 385, it was held, where the charter of a municipal corporation authorized it "to have a common seal and to contract under the same or without it," an appeal bond of the corporation was sufficiently sealed with the private seal of the president of the board of selectmen, if there be no common seal.

8. Eureka Clothes Wringing Mach. Co. v. Bailey Washing & Wringing Mach. Co., 11 Wall. (U. S.) 488.

9. Jackson v. Walsh, 3 Johns. (N. Y.) 226; Clark v. Farmers' Wool Mfg. Co., 15 Wend. (N. Y.) 256.

that it was affixed by proper authority.[1] But this statement of the rule is criticised by an able writer.[2] The mere fact, however, that an instrument has the corporate seal attached does not make it the act of the corporation, unless the seal was placed to it by some one duly authorized.[3] A ratification by the corporation of an officer's use of the corporate seal may be presumed under certain circumstances.[4] The burden of proof is on the party impeaching, and the seal is *prima facie* evidence that officers did not exceed their authority.[5]

The effect of affixing the seal of a corporation to a contract is the same as when a seal is affixed to the contract of an individual: it renders the instrument a specialty.[6] It has also been held,

1. Indianapolis, etc., R. Co. *v.* Morganstern, 103 Ill. 149; Wood *v.* Whelen, 93 Ill. 153; Southern, etc., Assoc. *v.* Bustamente, 52 Cal 192; Solomon's Lodge *v.* Montmollin 58 Ga. 547; St. Louis Public Schools *v.* Risley. 28 Mo. 415; Chouquette *v.* Baruda, 28 Mo. 491; Trustees, etc., *v.* McKechnie, 90 N. Y. 618; St. John's Church *v.* Steinmetz, 18 Pa. St. 273.

2. "The meaning of these statements is not perfectly clear. The seal of a corporation certainly possesses no mysterious virtue not possessed by other seals; and a contract under seal executed by the agents of a corporation is subject to the same rules of evidence and of law as a similar contract executed by the agents of an individual. In order to prove the execution of a contract purporting to have been executed under the corporate seal, two facts must be shown: first, it must be shown that the agents by whom the contract purports to have been executed were in fact agents of the corporation, having authority to execute the contract in question, or contracts of that general description; and. secondly, it must be shown that the signatures are genuine, or, in other words, that these agents did actually execute that particular contract. The mere circumstance that a seal was affixed to the contract would evidently not tend to establish either one of these facts." Morawetz Corp. (2d Ed.) § 340.

3. Koehler *v.* Black River, etc., Co., 2 Black (U. S.), 715; Bank of United States *v.* Dandridge, 12 Wheat. (U. S.) 64.

4. A ratification of the use by the treasurer of the corporate seal on notes may be presumed where a committee of the directors pronounced the notes genuine; where interest was paid on them, and reports stating this fact were accepted. St. James' Parish *v.* Newburyport, etc., Horse R. Co., 141 Mass. 500.

5. Morris *v.* Keil, 20 Minn. 531; Flint *v.* Clinton Co., 12 N. H. 434; Tenney *v.* Lumber Co., 43 N. H. 534; Lovett *v.* Steam Saw Mill Assoc., 6 Paige (N. Y.), 60; Koehler *v.* Black River Falls Iron Co., 2 Black (U. S.), 717; Leggett *v.* New Jersey M. & B. Co., Saxt. Ch. (N. J.) 550; St. Louis, etc., Co. *v.* Risley, 28 Mo. 419; Choquette *v.* Baruda, 28 Mo. 497; Musser *v.* Johnson, 42 Mo. 74; Reed *v.* Bradley, 17 Ill. 325; Union Gold Mine Co. *v.* Bank, 2 Col. 226.

Denman, C. J., in Hill *v.* Manchester & Salford Water Works Co., 5 B. & Ad. 874. observed: "The plaintiff proved that the common seal of the company was affixed to the bond by the officer who had the legal custody of it, and so threw upon the defendants the burden of clearly proving that it was not set by their authority." To same effect: McCracken *v.* San Francisco, 16 Cal. 638; Levering *v.* Mayor, etc., of Memphis, 7 Humph. (Tenn.) 553; Turnpike Road *v.* Myers, 6 S & R. (Pa.) 12; Leggett *v.* N. J. Mfg., etc., Co., 1 Saxt. Ch. R. (N. J.) 541; Lovett *v* Steam Saw Mill Assoc., 6 Paige (N. Y.), 54; Burrill *v.* Nahant Bank, 2 Met. (Mass.) 163. Perhaps *contra:* Miller *v.* Ewer, 27 Me. 509; Johnson *v.* Bush, 3 Barb. Ch. (N. Y.) 207: "but the latter is not so considered," says Cope, J., in McCracken *v.* San Francisco, 16 Cal. 638.

6. In Clark *v.* Farmers' Mfg. Co., 15 Wend. (N. Y.), it was held that the effect of affixing the seal of a corporation to a contract is the same as when a seal is affixed to the contract of an individual: it renders the instrument a specialty. Further, that the agents of a corporation may enter into contracts under the corporate seal for the payment of money, in furtherance of the business of the corporation; it is not necessary they should subscribe their individual names to the contracts, but their doing so will not vitiate the

vithout objection,[1] that the common-law rule that an der seal imports a consideration, applies as strongly by a corporation acting within its powers, as to a

ND LIABILITIES AS TO CONTRACTS.—It is a well-settled corporations have implied power unless restrained by t as so restrained, to make all such contracts as will jects of their creation,[3] and that their dealings in this like those of an individual seeking to accomplish the This principle is directly or impliedly recognized in s which are referred to under other branches of this ave no powers as to contracts except such as are ex- d or necessarily implied,[5] and their contracts must he manner authorized by their charter.[6] While a n have no legal existence out of the boundaries of

ee also Boone on Corp. noist v. Carondelet, 8 r Androscoggin, etc., 349; Merritt v. Cole, 9 Clark v. Wool Mfg. N. Y.) 256; Steele v. . Co., 15 Wend. (N. Y.) ses do not state the law they hold that prom- not negotiable because rate seal." Morawetz 41. note.

a corporation is equally neans of evidencing its d by a simple contract see Cent. Nat. Bank v. . Co., 5 S. Car. 156; s. 2.

orp. (2d Ed.) § 341. . City of Alton, 3 Mc- ; Royal Bank, etc., v. etc., R. Co., 100 Mass.

orp. (2d Ed.) § 336, cit- etc., Canal Co. v. (U. S.) 424; Barry v. Co., 1 Sand. Ch. (N. n v. Lambert. 44 Iowa, R. Co. v. Evans, 6 Gray ottish, etc., R. Co. v. 415.

orations, par. 43, citing a, 48 Ill. 423; Strauss v. Ohio St. 59; Seibrecht 22 La. 496; Brooklyn . v. Slaughter, 33 Ind. First National Bank, 4 ch v. Detroit, 12 Mich. . Virginia City, 5 Nev. v. Manchester Water rn. & Ald. 1; Bateman Hurl & N. 328.

4. Boone on Corporations, § 43, *citing* Union Water Co. v. Murphy's Flat Fluming Co., 22 Cal. 620; Feeny v. People's Fire Ins. Co., 2 Robt. 599; State Bank v. Cape Fear Bank, 13 Ired. (N. Car.) 75.

A corporation without special authority may dispose of land, goods, and chattels, and in its legitimate business may make a bond, mortgage, note or draft, and compositions with creditors, or an assignment for their benefit, except when restrained by law. Whitewater Valley Canal Co. v. Vallette, 21 How (U S.) 414.

5. In Weckler v. First National Bank, 42 Md. 581, the court said: "In deciding whether a corporation can make a particular contract, it must be considered, in the first place, whether its charter or some statute binding upon it forbids or permits it to make such a contract; and if the charter and valid statutory law are silent upon the subject, in the second place, whether the power to make such a contract may not be implied on the part of the corporation as directly or incidentally necessary to enable it to fulfil the purpose of its existence; or whether the contract is entirely foreign to that purpose; a corporation has no other powers than such as are specifically granted, or such as are necessary for the purpose of carrying into effect the powers expressly granted."

6. **Power to Contract.**—A corporation can make no contracts and do no acts, either within or without the State which creates it, except such as are authorized by its charter, and in such a manner as the charter authorizes. Bank of Augusta v. Earle, 13 Pet. (U. S) 519.

the sovereignty by which it is created, its residence in one State creates no insuperable objection to its power to contract in another State.[1] Whenever a corporation makes a contract, it is a contract of the legal entity and not a contract of the individual members, and the only rights it can claim are those which are given to it as a legal entity.[2] Nearly every question which arises in litigation as to corporate liability upon contracts involves such considerations as whether or not the contract is *ultra vires*,[3] and, since all corporate acts and contracts are performed or made by its officers or agents,[4] whether or not the corporation is bound by an express

1. Bank of Augusta *v.* Earle, 13 Pet. (U. S.) 519; Runyan *v.* Coster, 14 Pet. (U. S.) 122; American & For. Ch Union *v.* Yount, 101 U. S. 352. See, generally, FOREIGN CORPORATIONS.

2. Bank of Augusta *v.* Earle, 13 Pet. (U. S) 519.

3. A corporation cannot enforce an executory contract made in excess of its powers. Nassau Bank *v.* Jones, 95 N. Y. 115.

Provisions in the charter of an insurance company merely enabling in their character are not restrictive of the general power to effect contracts in any lawful and convenient mode. Relief Fire Ins. Co. of N. Y. *v.* Shaw, 94 U. S. 574.

A court of equity will not, at the suit of a corporation, set aside a lease made by it to one of its directors after it has been executed over seven years before any objection is made to it, and has, during this time, been repeatedly ratified, and after a release of all claims executed by the corporation to the lessee on a full and final settlement between the parties, there being no evidence that the settlement was obtained by fraud or any improper conduct of either party, although the lease was executed in excess of the powers of the corporation. Pneumatic Gas Co. *v.* Berry, 113 U. S. 322.

Although a corporation has exceeded its corporate powers in making a contract of lease for a period beyond the term of its existence, where the lessee remains in possession of the property, a note given by him as a compromise for the notes originally given as the price of the lease will be valid. Northern Liberty Market Co. *v.* Kelly, 113 U. S. 199.

Certain residents of a county bound themselves for enough to pay for a right of way, and the company constructed the road. *Held*, that the promisors could not plead *ultra vires*. Chicago & Atlantic R. Co. *v.* Derkes, 103 Ind. 520.

A steamship corporation agreed to pay money to another steamship corporation for ceasing to exercise its franchises. *Held*, an illegal transaction, which equity would enjoin at the instance of a stockholder of the corporation which was to pay the money. Leslie *v.* Lorillard, 40 Hun (N. Y.), 392.

Although there may be a defect of power in a corporation to make a contract, yet if it is not in violation of its charter or of any statute, and the corporation has by its promise induced a party in execution of the contract to expend money and perform his part thereof, the corporation is liable on the contract. Hitchcock *v.* Galveston, 96 U. S 341.

In the absence of proof showing a want of authority on the part of a corporation in making a contract, or of a violation of its charter, a claim that the contract is *ultra vires* will not be upheld; every presumption is to the contrary. Rider Life-Raft Co. *v.* Roach, 97 N. Y. 378.

In a suit for money loaned a corporation, and used by it, the corporation cannot plead that it exceeded its statutory power to contract debts, or that the officers negotiating the loan were not properly authorized. Connecticut River Savings Bank *v.* Fiske, 60 N. H. 363.

4. A corporation can act only by its agents or servants. Barnes *v* Dist of Columbia, 91 U. S. 540; Maxwell *v.* Same, 91 U. S. 557.

Persons dealing with the managers of a corporation must take notice of the limitations imposed upon their authority by the act of incorporation. Pearce *v.* Madison & I. R. Co., 21 How. (U. S.) 441.

One who makes a special contract with the manager of a corporation is bound to notice limitations on the manager's authority. Smith *v.* Co operative Dress Assoc., 12 Daly (N. Y.), 304.

Rules and regulations of a corporation that no contracts shall be binding upon the corporation which are not in writing, signed by its president, cannot affect [illegible] ratification of its agents' acts.[1] The principles to be

[illegible] made by third parties with [illegible] corporation, without notice [illegible]. A verbal contract with the [illegible] of a railroad company to [illegible], etc., on the line of the [illegible] once a month, [illegible] to be paid for at current prices, such contract to last until the [illegible] is notified to stop, is not within the Statute of Frauds, requiring contracts not to be performed within a year to be in writing. Walker v. Wilmington, C. & N. R. Co. (S. Car.), 1 So. [illegible]

An innocent party is not affected by any defect of authority or other irregularity on the part of those acting for a corporation, if the contract could be valid under any circumstances. Merchants' National Bank v. State National Bank of Boston, 10 Wall. (U. S.) 604.

Whenever a corporation aggregate is acting within the scope of the legitimate purposes of its institution, all parol contracts made by its authorized agents are [illegible] promises of the corporation; and all duties imposed on them by law, and all benefits conferred at their request, raise implied promises, for the enforcement of which an action lies. Bank of Columbia v. Patterson, 7 Cranch (U. S.), 299. Chesapeake, etc., Canal Co. v. Knapp, 9 Pet. (U. S.) 541.

Where a contract was made with a [illegible] of a corporation who signed their own names, adding their description as [illegible], etc., and the other party in the negotiation addressed them in the name of the corporation, it was held to create a corporate, not an individual, liability. The intent alone was material; and it was held clear that both parties understood and meant that the contract was to be, and in fact was, with the corporation. Whitney v. Wyman, 101 U. S. [illegible]

Where a director of a corporation assumes a power never delegated, such, for instance, as to tell a merchant that the corporation will be responsible for goods furnished to an employee of the corporation, the merchant cannot charge the corporation for goods furnished in [illegible] that the corporation would pay for them. Rice v. Peninsular Club, 52 [illegible]. See also Woman's Christian Temperance Union v. Taylor, 8 Col. 75; [illegible] v. Virginia Lead Mining Co., 78 [illegible] v. Donaldson Lumber Co. [illegible] S. W. Rep. 703; Peterborough [illegible] v. Nashua, etc., R. Co., 59 N. H. [illegible]

A contract between two corporations is not void because all of the directors of one of the corporations are members of the board of directors of the other corporation. Alexander v. Williams, 14 Mo. App. 13.

1. A corporation, like an individual, may ratify the acts of its agents done in excess of authority. Marshall County v. Schenck, 5 Wall. (U. S.) 772.

A contract may be ratified by the stockholders of a corporation if it is made with full knowledge of all the material facts, although in ignorance of the legal effect of such facts. Kelley v. Newburyport & Amesbury Horse R. Co., 141 Mass. 496.

A corporation may ratify an act of its agent which it could have authorized. Greenleaf v. Norfolk Southern R. Co., 91 N. Car. 33. See also Poole v. West Point Butter & Cheese Assoc., 30 Fed. Rep. 813; Indianapolis Rolling Mill Co. v. St Louis, etc., R Co., 7 Sup. Ct. Rep. 542; Bancroft v. Wilmington Conference Academy, 5 Del. 577.

Where a corporation sues to set aside a contract claimed to have been agreed to by its directors in fraud of its rights, the other party to the contract cannot contend that the acquiescence of the corporation precludes its action. Metropolitan Elev. R. Co. v. Manhattan Elev. R Co., 11 Daly (N. Y.), 373; s. c., 14 Abb. N. Cas. (N Y.) 103.

In an action on a contract executed by the president of the defendant corporation, without authority from the directors, where the plaintiff has performed all the acts required of him by the contract, and relies on the acquiescence of the directors as a ratification, a charge that "all directors are presumed to know what it is their duty to know, what they are able to know, and what they undertook to know when they accepted the position," and "that, in the absence of direct and positive evidence of the knowledge of the directors, jurors have the right to assume that they are doing what they were appointed to do, and that they know what they were appointed to know," is erroneous The party relying on a ratification must show that the directors, or a majority of them, actually knew of the contract and its terms, and with such knowledge acquiesced in it. Murray v. C. N. Nelson Lumber Co. (Mass), 9 N. E. Rep 634.

Where a corporation has sold its property without legal authority to make the sale, an objection cannot be raised after applied to the contracts of corporations which relate to its property,[1] such as land,[2] the power to borrow money,[3] powers and liabilities as to negotiable instruments,[4] the use of the corporate seal,[5] etc., are treated elsewhere in this article, and to state them here would be needless repetition.

Liabilities of a corporation arising out of the acts and contracts of its officers will be treated under the title OFFICERS OF PRIVATE CORPORATIONS.

The principles to be applied in determining when and how far a contract of a corporation is *ultra vires* will be treated under the title ULTRA VIRES.

K. MISCELLANEOUS POWERS.—A corporation created for insuring property has no power to engage in banking.[6] A life or fire insurance company cannot issue marine-insurance policies.[7] A life and accident insurance company cannot issue fire-insurance policies.[8] Corporations cannot form a partnership unless expressly authorized,[9] but they may become estopped from interposing such a defence when sued upon a joint contract.[10] A corporation, as well as a natural person, may become a joint owner of a ferry if its charter

the contract has been subsequently carried into effect by the consent or ratification of all parties interested in the subject-matter of the sale. Chicago, R. I. & Pac. R. Co. *v.* Howard, 7 Wall. (U. S.) 392.

One who has contracted with a *de facto* corporation, either by making a subscription or otherwise, is estopped to deny its regular organization. Chubb *v.* Upton, 95 U. S. 665; Frost *v.* Frostburg Coal Co., 24 How. (U. S.) 278; Douglass County *v.* Bolles, 94 U. S. 104; Leavenworth County *v.* Barnes, 94 U. S. 70; Casey *v.* Galli, 94 U. S. 673; Close *v.* Glenwood Cemetery, 107 U. S. 466.

1. See *supra* this title, GENERAL POWERS AS TO PROPERTY.

2. See *supra* this title, POWERS AS TO LAND.

3. See *supra* this title, POWER TO BORROW MONEY.

4. See *supra* this title, POWERS AND LIABILITIES AS TO NEGOTIABLE INSTRUMENTS.

5. See *supra* this title, USE OF CORPORATE SEAL.

6. Blair *v.* Perpetual Ins. Co., 10 Mo. 559; Grand Lodge *v.* Waddill, 36 Ala. 313; Chambers *v.* Falkner, 65 Ala. 448. *Compare* Waddill *v.* Alabama, etc., R. Co., 35 Ala. 323.

In Mechanics', etc., Savings Bank *v.* Meriden Agency Co., 24 Conn. 159, where a charter authorized the corporation "to do a general insurance agency, commission and brokerage business, and such other things as are incidental to, and necessary in, the management of that business," this did not authorize the company to subscribe to the stock of a savings-bank and building association.

7. *Re* Phœnix Life Assur. Soc., 2 J. & H. 441.

8. Ashton *v.* Burbank, 2 Dill. (C. C.) 435.

9. Burke *v.* Concord, etc., R. Co., 8 Am. & Eng. R. R. Cas. 552; State *v.* Concord, etc., R. Co., 13 Am. & Eng. R. R. Cas. 94; Morris Run Coal Co. *v.* Barclay Coal Co., 68 Pa. St. 173; Smith *v.* Smith, 3 Desau. Ch. (S. Car.) 557. But see Allen *v.* Woonsocket Co., 11 R. I. 288; French *v.* Donohue, 29 Minn. 111.

10. Catskill Bank *v.* Gray, 14 Barb. (N. Y.) 471; Marine Bank *v.* Ogden, 29 Ill. 248; Racine, etc., R. Co. *v.* Farmers', etc., Co., 49 Ill. 331.

Defendant corporation, chartered to construct and operate a railroad between Savannah and Macon, and to organize and carry on a banking business, *held* to have no authority to enter into a partnership with a private individual to purchase and run a steamboat on the Chattahoochee river, forming no part of its route, and that it could not defeat liability for an injury caused by the negligence of an officer on a steamboat with the plea that the running of the steamboat was *ultra vires*, it being chartered only as a railroad and banking company. Central, etc., R. & Banking Co. *v.* Smith, 76 Ala. 572; s. c., 52 Am. Rep. 353.

n do not preclude it, and, like a natural person, may
ount for its share of the earnings.[1] There is no
iat a corporation is capable of purchasing and hold-
ock of another corporation, it not appearing under
nces they were acquired or held;[2] but the purchase
n of stock in another corporation is not necessarily
been held that a corporation aggregate has not the
o take an oath.[4] A manufacturing company may

ultnomah R. Co., 12 Am. Rep. 307.
ey, 46 Cal. 112.
is no implied right to another company for ntrolling its manage- Corp. (2d Ed.) § 431. Iarcy, 3 Woodb. & M. v. Collins, 40 Ga. 582; nnah, etc., R. Co., 43 hern R. Co. v. Eastern t L. J. Ch. 837. See. Leavenworth, etc., R. Booth v. Robinson, 55 iy a corporation hold ompany as an invest- e the usual method of wn proper business. poration to invest in ompany cannot be im- se both companies are lar kind of business. t carry on its business and not through the orporation. Mechan- Meriden Agency Co., umner v. Marcy, 3 Franklin Co. v. Lew- , 68 Me. 43; Berry v. N. Y.) 199. *Compare* k Co., 47 Conn. 141; Hill, etc., Mining Co., anklin Bank v. Com- Ohio St. 350. In Mill- etc., R. Co., 64 How. as held that a railroad cquired shares in an- ild not vote upon the ould collect the divi-

Bank v. National Ex- S. 679, it was held cks by national banks ibited by the Nation- ut such a prohibition e failure to grant the onest exercise of the nise a doubtful debt one owing by a bank, ten by a bank with a quent change or con- , so as to make good and reduce the anticipated loss. Such transaction does not amount to a dealing in stocks. See also First National Bank v. Hoch, 89 Pa. St. 324.

In Morawetz on Corp. (2d Ed.) § 432, the following is laid down: "No rule can be stated for determining, in all cases, whether or not a corporation may purchase shares in another company. Shares are, in reality, the interests belonging to the associates or part owners of the corporate concern; but in many instances they have a fixed value, and are dealt with as tangible property. The right to purchase and hold shares, therefore, depends upon the precise character of the shares and the circumstances of the case. Thus, a corporation whose charter authorizes it to invest its funds in an enterprise not requiring the direct supervision of its agents would be entitled to do this indirectly by purchasing shares in another company, but would have no right to buy shares for speculation. A corporation having authority to lend money on security would be entitled to receive shares of approved value as security, but would have no right to hold them to obtain the dividends, or in the hope of a speculative increase of their value. On the other hand, a corporation engaged in the business of buying and selling shares as a speculation would have no right to acquire them for any other purpose."

3. Hill v. Nisbet, 100 Ind. 341.

4. Alabama, etc., R. Co. v. Oaks, 37 Ala. 694.

A corporation, although unable, being a corporation, to take the oath required of trustees by *Tennessee* Code, § 1974, before entering on their duties, may yet take and hold estates as a trustee or mortgagee, and execute trusts in which it has an interest within the scope of its business. Perry on Trusts, secs. 42, 43. And a failure or inability to comply with this provision of the statute will not affect the validity of the deed, or divert the title vested by it. Vance v. Smith, 2 Heisk. (Tenn.) 343; Young v. Cardwell, 6 Lea (Tenn.), 171; Lincoln Savings Bk. v. Ewing, 12 Lea (Tenn.), 598.

buy patent rights to compete in business.[1] A corporation formed for the manufacture of spermaceti candles may purchase State bonds and engage to pay for them at a future day.[2] A boom company authorized to maintain a boom in a river wherever it should think best cannot obstruct navigation, alleging that it could not otherwise enjoy its privileges.[3] Corporations, as the owners of vessels, whether sail vessels or steamers, may maintain a salvage suit.[4] The power to have a board of directors is inherent in all private corporations. No special power need be conferred by statute.[5]

L. **Liability for Torts.**—It was formerly held that a corporation, having no soul, could not do a moral act, and therefore could not be liable in tort; but that doctrine is entirely obsolete,[6] and is regarded as more quaint than substantial.[7] It is now well settled that corporations will be held to respond in a civil action at the suit of an injured party, for every grade and description of forcible, malicious, and negligent tort or wrong which they commit, however foreign to their nature or beyond their granted powers the wrongful transaction or act may be.[8] It has often been held that in

1. Re British, etc., Cork Co., L. R. 1 Eq 231.

Railroad companies may adopt improvements. Mayor of Norwich v. Norfolk R Co. 4 El. & B. 397.

A corporation incorporated to turn gunstocks has implied authority to purchase a previously existing patent for turning gun-stocks and all other irregular forms. Blanchard's Gun Stock Factory v. Warner, 1 Blatchf. (C. C.) 277.

2. Indiana v. Woram, 6 Hill (N. Y.), 33.

3. Plummer v. Penobscot Lumbering Assoc., 67 Me. 363.

In Boom Corporation v. Whiting, 29 Me. 123, it was held that driving lumber was not within the scope of a company authorized to boom lumber. See also Boom Companies.

4. The Blackwall v. Saucelito, W. & S. T. Co., 10 Wall. (U. S.) 1; The Camanche v. Coast Wrecking Co., 8 Wall. (U S.) 448.

5. Hurlbut v. Marshall, 62 Wis. 590.

6. Johnson v. St. Louis Dispatch Co., 2 Mo. App. 570; Green v. London General Omnibus Co., 7 C. B. N. S. 290.

The opinion of Manwood, C. B., in 12 James I., was this, as touching corporations: "that they were invisible, immortall, and that they had no soule; and therefore no Subpœna lieth against them, because they have no Conscience nor soule; a Corporation, is a Body aggregate, none can create soules but God, but the King creates them, and therefore they have no soules; they cannot speak, nor appear in Person, but by Attorney, and this was the opinion of Manwood, Chief Baron, touching Corporations."

7. Barry, J., in Coulter's Case, 9 W. L. T. Rep. 209.

8. New York, etc., R. Co. v. Schuyler, 34 N. Y. 49; National Bank v. Graham, 100 U. S. 699; Peebles v. Patapsco Guano Co., 77 N. Car. 233. See also authorities cited in succeeding notes.

In Brokaw v. N. J. R., etc., Co., 32 N. J. L. 329, Depue, J., said: "In the earlier cases it was held that an action of trespass could not be maintained against a corporation aggregate, for the technical reason that a *capias* and *exigent*, the proper process in actions of trespass, would not lie against a corporation; but this technical objection was not uniformly yielded to, as instances of actions of trespass against corporations are to be met with as early as the year-books. A. & A. Corp. § 385; Notes to Maund v. Monmouthshire Canal Co., 4 M. & G. 454. As corporations became more numerous and were multiplied, until aggregated capital, seeking investment for the purposes of business, is generally invested under acts of incorporation to protect individuals from personal liability, technical objections which stood in the way of subjecting corporations to actions founded on torts have been entirely swept away, and corporations have been held liable for all torts, the same as individuals. That they may be sued in

octrine of *ultra vires* has no application.[1] Cor-
ole for the acts of their servants, while such serv-
d in the business of their principal, in the same
he same extent that individuals are liable under
es.[2] Upon a well-settled doctrine in the law of
nt, that the principal is liable for his agent's acts
n or incident to the agent's employment, and is
ise, it is important to consider, since corporations
ough agents, how far the agent's acts were within
authority.[3] The tendency of some decisions is to
d the doctrine of *ultra vires* in its application to
orations;[4] but it is said by a learned authority
no decision holding a corporation liable for a tort

ss *quare clausum* rmis, and ejectment, ished by the cases State v. Morris & 367."
he agents of a cor- *ntractu* or *in delicto*, ir employment, the nsible, as an indi- ilar circumstances. . R. Co. v. Quigley, 2; Merchants' Nat. Bank of Boston, 10 lean v. Platt, 99 U.
individuals, are lia- e and unskilful acts gents. Weightman ck (U. S.), 39. esponsible for acts r corporate powers, orate name and by ho were competent corporate powers. ot founded on con- y exercises of power , or are *quasi* crim- may be held to a ity for them to the ake City v. Hollis-
liable for all torts ants and agents, by oration, express or R. G. R. Co. v. ep. 1286.
k v. State Bank, 10 Goodspeed v. East onn. 530; Nat. Bk. . S. 699; Green's 64.
ng (N. Car., Nov. 923, the court em- hat the plea of *ultra* and that since au- was unnecessary to support recovery, an allegation of authority was unnecessary.

A corporation, when sued for a tort, cannot defend on the ground that the act from which the tort resulted was *ultra vires*. Gruber v. Washington & Jamesville R. Co., 92 N. Car. 1.

Corporations are liable for every wrong they commit; and in such cases the doctrine of *ultra vires* has no application. First Nat. Bank of Carlisle v. Graham, 100 U. S. 699.

A corporation cannot defeat liability for an injury caused by the negligence of an officer on a steamboat with the plea that the running of the steamboat was *ultra vires*, it being chartered only as a railroad and banking company. Central R. & Banking Co. v. Smith, 76 Ala. 572; s. c., 52 Am. Rep. 353.

2. National Bank v. Graham, 100 U. S. 699; and authorities cited in preceding notes.

3. See title AGENCY, 1 Am. & Eng. Encyc. of Law, 417 *et seq.*

In Craker v. Chicago & N. W. R. Co., 36 Wis. 657, a corporation was held liable in damages for its conductor's wrong in kissing a lady passenger, as it was within the conductor's duty to protect passengers from insult. See also Stewart v. Brooklyn, etc., R. Co., 90 N. Y. 588; s. c., 12 Am. & Eng. R. R. Cas. 183; Louisville, etc., R. Co. v. Kelley, 13 Am. & Eng. R. R. Cas. 1; Gilliam v. South, etc., R. Co., 15 Am. & Eng. R. R. Cas. 138; Bryan v. Chicago, etc., R. Co., 16 Am. & Eng. R. R. Cas. 335; International, etc., R. Co. v. Kentle, 16 Am. & Eng. R. R. Cas. 337; Louisville, etc., R. Co. v. Fleming, 18 Am. & Eng. R. R. Cas. 347; Heenrich v. Pullman Palace Car Co., 18 Am. & Eng. R. R. Cas. 379; Miller v. Burlington, etc., R. Co., 8 Neb. 219.

4. National Bank v. Graham, 100 U.

committed in the course of an *ultra vires* transaction on its face foreign to the corporate business, where the persons who could have objected to the transaction had not acquiesced in it.[1] Where there has been acquiescence and ratification by the corporation, such as its accepting the benefits of an *ultra vires* tort or retaining trust property of the person wronged, this will support an action against the corporation and estop it from pleading *ultra vires*.[2] Liability sometimes exists even where a servant of the corporation

S. 699; Merchants' Bank v. State Bank, 10 Wall. (U. S.) 604.

1. Taylor Corp. § 338. See Green's Brice's Ultra Vires, 364.

In Brokaw v. N. J. R., etc., Co., 32 N. J L. 332, Depue, J., said: "In considering the question, whether the agent has the authority of the corporation, so as to make it answerable for his act, the purposes for which the company was incorporated must not be overlooked. An authority given even by the board of directors, in express terms, will not, in all cases, be the authority of the corporation. The directors are only agents themselves, and their powers are necessarily limited within the scope of the purposes for which the corporation was created, beyond which they are not authorized to bind the corporation. To fix the liability of a corporation for the tortious act of one of its employees, done in obedience to the commands of its officers, the act must be connected with the transaction of the business for which the company was incorporated. If the directors should order an agent to take a person out of his house and beat him, the corporation could not be held for the assault and battery; or if the directors of a banking company should purchase a steamboat, and engage in transporting passengers, the corporation would not be liable for the misfeasance or nonfeasance of agents employed in that business. But if the directors of a corporation, having power to hold lands, order an agent to enter on lands and take possession of them for the legitimate uses of the company, his entry, if unlawful, will be the trespass of the corporation. So if the directors, acting in their official capacity, adopt rules and regulations for the transaction of the corporate business of the company, and provide for the enforcement of such rules and regulations, and authorize its agents or servants to carry them into effect, the corporation will be liable for the acts of such agents or servants in the course of such employment. In Railway Co. v Brown, 6 Exch. 325, Patterson, J., says: 'An action of trespass for assault and battery will lie against a corporation, whenever the corporation can authorize the act done, and it is done by their authority,'" etc.

In Weckler v. First Nat. Bk, 42 Md. 581, it was held that a national bank is not authorized to engage in selling railroad bonds on commission; and that, therefore, it cannot be held liable for false representations by its teller made in selling such bonds.

In Hood v. N. Y. & N. Haven R. Co., 22 Conn. 502, it was held that a railroad corporation was not estopped from setting up the defence of *ultra vires* in a suit for personal injury received beyond their terminus, by a practice of the railroad agents to sell tickets to a point beyond their terminus, contracting in such tickets to carry safely to the point mentioned. These last two cases may be compared with Alexander v. Relfe, 74 Mo. 495, and with Hutchinson v. Western & Atlantic R. Co., 6 Heisk. (Tenn.) 634, where the receipt of property in the first and of profits in the second case, and acquiescence in both, were held to make the defendant companies responsible in tort, the first for the property taken, the second for the death of a passenger. But they were actions not for breach of contract, but on the tort itself.

Agricultural society not liable for negligence of teamster whom it engaged to convey, in his own team, visitors to the society's fair, as the business of conveyance is beyond their scope. Bathe v. Decatur County Agricultural Soc. (Iowa), 34 N. W. Rep. 484.

2. In Alexander v. Relfe, 74 Mo. 495 (1881), an insurance corporation by giving its draft bought the stock, notes, and collaterals of an insolvent company, and afterwards a portion was paid on the draft, which meantime had been subdivided. With the notes and collaterals thus obtained and some cash the first company, actively assisted by the officers and directors of the insolvent company, bought 9763 of the 10,000 shares of the latter's capital stock, and the same were transferred to it. The offices of the old directors of the insolvent company be-

y.[1] The material inquiry is, was the assault or trespass
with the servant's employment.[2]

nt by the assignment, the
caused its own directors to
They then obtained amend-
isolvent company's charter.
etirement of a portion of
Thereupon they presented
on 9000 of the 9763 shares
tem, and by order of the
directors the treasurer of
mpany redeemed the shares
of the unpaid draft. *Held*,
least the affair was fraudu-
the first corporation could
to deny or evade its liability
that those wrongs resulted
cise of powers not granted
its organization.
Hutchinson v. Western &
Co., 6 Heisk. (Tenn.) 634, it
it is no defence to a cor-
how that a negligent act
injury resulted was not
the charter. If the corpora-
clear and explicit manner
e act as done in its business.
ving agents to superintend
g the profits arising from it.
the railroad company de-
g. albeit beyond its charter
considered), run a line of
he Tennessee in connection
, it was held liable to the
a person killed through
one of the steamers.
ast case may be compared
. & N. H. R. Co., 22 Conn.
a railroad company sold
e conveyance along its line.
stage to a point beyond its
purchaser of such a ticket
on the stage. *Held*, that
ntract was *ultra vires*, the
not liable.
rant's unauthorised tort is
e company, that will make
responsible. Railway Co.
tterson, J., 6 Excheq. 325,
aid in Hussey v. King (N.
Rep. 923, that a corporation
made liable for a malicious
by the mere ratification of it
completely terminated; that
must antedate that.
v. Consumers' Ice Co.,
7, Allen, J., said: "There
ions in several cases of
it for the wilful acts of the
master is not responsible.
Crickett, 1 East, 106; Hib-
& E. R. Co., 15 N. Y. 455;
ilcox, 19 Wend. [N. Y.] 343.)

But these intimations are subject to the material qualification, that the acts designated 'wilful' are not done in the course of the service, and were not such as the servant intended and believed to be to the interest of the master. In such case the master would not be excused from liability by reason of the quality of the act. (Limpus v. London Genl. Omnibus Co., 1 H. & C. 526; Seymour v. Greenwood, 6 H. & N. 359; *affirmed*, 7 H. & N. 355; Shea v. Sixth Ave. R. Co., 62 N. Y. 180; Jackson v. Second Ave. R. Co., 47 N. Y. 274.)"

In Terre Haute, etc., R. Co. v. Graham, 46 Ind. 239 (1874), it was held, after verdict and judgment for plaintiff, that a complaint was good which averred that defendant wilfully and purposely, and with great force, ran its locomotive against plaintiff, it having also averred (in another paragraph) that the servants were running defendant's train in the line of their duty. See Hussey v. King (N. Car. 1887), 3 So. East. Rep. 923.

On the other hand, it was said in Illinois Central R. Co. v. Downey, 18 Ill. 260 (1857): "If the injury was caused by the mere wilful act of the company's servants, and not in execution and furtherance of the business in which they were engaged, the company is not liable in this form of action [case]."

In Miller v. Burlington & Mo., etc., R., 8 Neb. 219, plaintiff's petition having alleged that defendants by their agent had wrongly and maliciously caused the arrest and holding over of plaintiff on the charge of burglary, the supreme court said: "But when an injury is committed by an employee of a corporation wilfully, and of his own malice, and not in the course of his employment, the corporation is not bound by his acts. And the same rule applies to the officers of a corporation in that regard as to its other agents. Goodspeed v. East Haddam Bank, 22 Conn. 541; Brokaw v. N. J. R. & Co., 3 Vroom, 331; Gillett v. Mo. Valley R. Co., 55 Mo. 315. The petition entirely fails to state that the parties charged were acting within the scope of their employment, or that the offence charged was committed in connection with the transaction of the business of the corporation. The demurrer was therefore properly sustained." This simply rests on the ordinary rule of liability of principal for servants' acts. See Helfrich v. Williams, 84 Ind. 553.

2. Thus in Porter v. C., R. I. & P.

An individual and a corporation may be joined in an action of trespass for assault and battery, or for malicious prosecution.[1] The fact that the State is the sole owner and stockholder does not exempt a corporation from liability and suit.[2]

1. Liability for Particular Torts.—(*a*) *Assault and Battery and False Imprisonment.*—A corporation may be liable for assault and battery, and false imprisonment.[3]

R Co., 41 Iowa, 358, employees running a train saw obstructions on the track, and plaintiff running from the place. They stopped the train, pursued and caught plaintiff, and took him to Des Moines, which was the nearest place where the employees could stop, and where resided a United States commissioner who might inquire into the violation of the United States law. No evidence sufficient appearing, plaintiff was discharged. He brought suit against the company. *Held*, that in the absence of any other authority from the company in this regard than that of the mere relation of employer and employee, the company was not liable. Judgment for plaintiff was accordingly reversed on appeal.

In Marion *v.* C., R. I. & P. R. Co., 59 Iowa, 428, Adams, J., said: "Where the question is as to whether the employer is liable for a wilful injury done by an employee, it is sometimes important to inquire whether the employee's purpose was to serve his employer by the wilful act. Ill. Cent. R. Co. *v.* Downey, 18 Ill. 259; Wright *v.* Wilcox, 19 Wend. (N.Y.) 343; Moore *v.* Sanborn, 2 Mich. 519; Croft *v.* Alison, 4 B. & Ald. 590; Johnson *v.* Barber, 5 Gilman (Ill.), 425; Foster *v.* Essex Bank, 17 Mass 479 The rule is that an employer is not liable for a wilful injury done by an employee, though done while in the course of his employment, unless the employee's purpose was to serve his employer by the wilful act. Where the employee is not acting within the course of his employment, the employer is not liable, even for the employee's negligence, and the mere purpose of the employee to serve his employer has no tendency to bring the act within the course of his employment.

"Where a female servant having authority to light fires in a house, but not to clean the chimneys, lit a fire for the sole purpose of cleaning a chimney, it was held that her employer was not liable for an injury caused by her negligence in lighting the fire. Mackenzie *v.* McLeod, 10 Bing. 385. See also Towanda Coal Co. *v.* Heenan, 86 Pa. St. 418." The court applied these principles to a case of injury to a ride-stealer who was violently pushed from the roof of a freight car by a brakeman, the authority to eject or remove trespassers being vested in the conductor, whom the brakeman did not consult.

In Hopkins *v.* Western Pac. R. Co., 50 Cal. 190, a railroad corporation was held not to be liable for a nuisance created by the use by its employees of a culvert which ran beneath the road as a privy, as the men in such use were not about the company's business.

In Edwards *v* London & Northwestern R. Co., L. R. 5 C. P. 445, it was held that a foreman porter who in the absence of a station master is in charge of a railway station has no implied authority to give in charge a person whom he suspects to be stealing the company s property; and if he gives in charge on such suspicion an innocent person, the company are not liable. Allen *v.* London & Southwestern R. Co., L. R. 6 Q. B. 65. *Compare* Goff *v.* Great Northern R. Co., 3 Ellis & Ellis (Q. B.), 672.

The president of an omnibus company directed its drivers to exclude all colored persons. *Held*, that he was individually liable for the ejection and personal injury of such persons, although an action might have been maintained against the company. (Scholfield, C.J., dissenting.) Peck *v.* Cooper, 112 Ill. 192; s. c., 54 Am. Rep. 231.

1. Brokaw *v.* N. J. R. & Transp. Co. *et al.*, 32 N. J. L. 328; 1 Vin. Ab. Abatement, Z, p. 32; Bro. Corporations, Pl. 24; Hewell *v.* Swift *et al.*, 3 Allen (Mass.), 420; Moore *v.* Fitchburg R. Co. *et al.*, 4 Gray, 465; Hussey *v.* King (N. Car., November, 1887), 3 So East. Rep. 923

2. Hutchinson *v.* Western & Atl. R. Co, 6 Heisk. (Tenn.) 634.

3. Denver & Rio Grande R. *v.* Harris, 122 U. S. 597.

In Lynch *v.* Metropolitan Elevated R. Co., 90 N. Y. 77. a rule of the company was that passengers should not be permitted by the gatekeepers to pass out from trains until they had produced their tickets or paid their fares. A passenger

corporation may be held liable for damages
eceit or false representations of its agents.[1]

'as prevented by the ing out, was arrested ight, although he engatekeeper appeared norning. Held, that ble for the arrest and irt said: "But it had could legally have er, before leaving its , should produce a , and if he did not, and there be detained l he did so. At most lebtor to the defendof his fare," etc. In see also American terson, 73 Ind. 430; Alb. R. Co., 104 Domestic Sewing s. 469; Goff v. Great Bilz & Ellis Q. B. ilroad Co. et al., 32

cided in 1822 that a be sued for assault rities in the time of Coke, Viner, are cited. reported in 1 Ohio, it was laid down in orations cannot be prosecution, slander, as that would make olders suffer with the ids v. State of Mis-13. But in Gillett v. 5 Mo. 319, Vories, J., v. State, said: "I is too general and arrent of the modern o to that extent. It the best-considered dern authorities, that es in which corporaiable for assaults and by their agents, for lieir agents, and even utions instituted by also Alexander v. 178, where distinction tions and contractual v. Life Assoc., 75

fuge, founded for the reformation of conorrigible youths, beanization, is not liaan assault by one of late. Perry v. House o; s. c., 52 Am. Rep.

1. Barwick v. Eng. Joint-stock Bank, L. R. 2 Exch. 259; Mackay v. Commercial Bank, L. R. 5 Privy Counc. Apps. 394; Ranger v. Gt. Western R. Co., 5 H. L. Cas. 72; Erie City Iron Works v. Barber, 106 Pa. St. 125; Peebles v. Patapsco Guano Co., 77 N. Car. 233; Cragie v. Hadley, 99 N. Y. 131; Candy v. Globe Rubber Co., 37 N. J. Eq. 175. But *compare* Western Bank of Scotland v. Addie, L. R. 1 H. L. Sc. 145, 157.

In Peebles v. Patapsco Guano Co., 77 N. Car. 233, defendant's agent falsely represented to plaintiff that a spurious article was the genuine Patapsco guano, of which defendant corporation was manufacturer. *Held*, such representation, necessarily fraudulent in law, must be taken as the corporation's act, and that plaintiff could recover from the company the damages caused by the deceit.

In Cragie v. Hadley, 99 N. Y. 131, the deceit was the acceptance by a bank cashier of a deposit at a time when the bank was hopelessly insolvent, and on the last day it continued its business. It was held that this was such a fraud as entitled plaintiffs to reclaim the drafts deposited or the proceeds. Citing Anonymous Case, 67 N. Y. 598. "And the fraudulent representations of the corporate agent may also give the other party the right to annul the contract." Taylor Priv. Corp. § 342, citing McClellan v. Scott, 24 Wis. 81; Derrick v. Lamar Ins. Co., 74 Ill 404; Henderson v. Railroad Co., 17 Tex. 560.

Corporations, as well as individuals, are held to a careful adherence to truth in their dealings with mankind, and cannot, by their representations or silence, involve others in onerous engagements, and then defeat the calculations and claims which their own conduct had superinduced. Zabriskie v. Cleveland, C. & C. R. Co., 23 How. (U. S.) 381; Moran v. Miami County, 2 Black (U. S.), 722.

In an action against a corporation for deceit by false representations made by its agent, on the sale of goods manufactured and sold by it for a particular purpose, there can be no recovery without proof of bad faith or absence of reasonable grounds of belief. Erie City Iron Works v. Barber, 106 Pa. St. 125; s. c., 51 Am. Rep. 508.

Where the superintendent of a rice mill endeavors to borrow money on the representation of his having rice in store with (*c*) *Trover and Conversion.*—A corporation may be liable in trover for conversion.[1]

(*d*) *Libel and Slander.*—A corporation is responsible for a libel published by its authority,[2] and it may be compelled to pay punitive damages therefor.[3]

the mill corporation, and offers as security a rice receipt in favor of the lender, by which the company, through said superintendent, acknowledges that the lender has so much rice on deposit, the proposed lender is put on notice of fraud, and if the representation is untrue he cannot recover from the corporation on the receipt. One cannot deal with third parties for his own individual benefit in the double capacity of individual and officer of a corporation; if he does, such third parties are charged with legal notice of fraud aginst the company. But the lender having also loaned money to a stranger upon the faith of another receipt signed by the superintendent, and acknowledging that the stranger had rice on deposit, *held*, that the company was liable on this receipt. Planters' Rice-mill Co *v.* Olmstead (Ga.). 3 S. E. 647. See also, *infra*, LIABILITY FOR FRAUD.

1. Beach *v.* Fulton Bank, 7 Cowen (N. Y.), 485; Yarborough *v.* Bank of England, 16 East, 6.

In Fishkill Savings Institute *v.* Bostwick, Receiver, 19 Hun (N. Y.). 354, plaintiff and the National Bank of Fishkill occupied for their business purposes the same offices, and the business of plaintiff with its depositors was conducted through the latter. One B. was cashier of the bank and treasurer of plaintiff, and active manager of both. He, without actual knowledge of the other officers of the bank, took from a depository in New York certain bonds of plaintiff's, and pledged them to secure a loan of money borrowed for and applied to the use of the bank. In action by the Savings Institute against the bank and its receiver, judgment was entered for plaintiff, which judgment was affirmed on appeal. See 80 N. Y. 162, where the court of appeals said that it was doubtful whether action for money had and received would lie, but that in either event it would not mete out full justice to confine plaintiff's recovery to the sum received by defendant bank but that the value taken from plaintiff should be allowed, in action for the tortious conversion.

2. Maynard *v.* Ins Co., 34 Cal. 48; s. c., 47 Cal. 207; Johnson *v.* St Louis Dispatch Co, 2 Mo. App 565; Evening Journal Assoc. *v.* McDermott, 44 N. J. Law, 430; Samuels *v.* Evening Mail Assoc. 9 Hun (N. Y.), 288; on appeal, 75 N. Y. 604 (reversing lower court as to exemplary damages, which the lower court refused to allow on the ground that the libel had been published but once, and had been promptly retracted). Howe Machine Co. *v.* Souder, 58 Ga. 64; Phila., W. & B. R. Co. *v.* Quigley, 21 How (U. S.) 202; Tench *v.* Gt. Western R. Co., 32 Up. Can. Q. B. 452.

In Phila., W. & B. R. Co. *v.* Quigley, 21 How. (U. S.) 202, it was held that the report of the directors respecting the conduct of the officers and agents of the company is a privileged communication, but that this privilege does not extend to the preservation of the report and evidence in a book for distribution among the stockholders or the community.

In Tench *v.* Great Western R. Co., 32 Up. Can. Q. B. 452, the libel was the publication by the general manager of a statement that plaintiff, a conductor, had been dismissed for dishonestly sending away uncancelled tickets. *Held*, that the publication would have been privileged if distributed only to employees, or if put up only in the company's private offices; but that placing it in offices and stations open to the public, was not within the privilege.

But if the libel were beyond the scope of the duties of the agent who wrote it, the corporation is not liable unless it ratify or adopt the misconduct. Southern Express Co. *v.* Fitzner, 59 Miss 581. And see Eastern Counties R. Co. *v.* Broom, 2 Eng. L & Eq. 406, where a railroad company was held not liable for malicious arrest caused by an officer outside of his employment.

"Whether a corporation can be guilty of express malice, so as to destroy a *prima facie* privilege arising from the occasion of publication, has not yet been decided; but *semble*, it can." Odgers on Lib & Sland. § 368, citing Lord Campbell, C. J., in E. B. & E. 121; 27 L. J. Q. B. 231.

3. Samuels *v.* Evening Mail Assoc., 75 N. Y. 604, sustaining the opinion of Davis, P. J. (in his opinion dissenting from the judgment of his court, reported in 9 Hun, 294), and reversing the order

iffer as to whether a corporation is liable for

.—An action may be maintained against a corpo-
damages caused by conspiracy.[2]

Prosecution.—An action lies against a corporation
›secution.[3]

ılow. Davis, P. J.,
ad accident cases
c no bearing upon
ase. They hold that
n is not chargeable
ages in cases of ac-
cause their agents
negligence, but that
n which charge the
th gross negligence
of the incompetency
›ad habits, or other
ring him unfit for
leghorn v. N. Y.
. Y. 44; s. c., 47 N.
cases, the falsity of
of malice sufficient
damages, the right
the discretion of a
ıry act done in the
lse libel," etc. See
, etc., Co., to Conn.
s. Co., 34 Cal. 54.
ournal Assoc. v. Mc-
Law, 430, where it
nce was rightly re-
llous publications of
"for the purpose of
of the defendant's
ion complained of."
orp. (2d Ed) § 727.
broadly that a cor-
eld responsible for
blished by its au-
cases cited are libel
nshend on Slander

" A corporation will
. be liable for any
officer, even though
ly for the benefit of
hin the scope of his
e proved that the cor-
red and directed that
y words, for a slan-
ıd tortious act of the
Libel and Slander

ting Oil Co. v. Stan-
& Eng. Corp. Cases,
on v. Metropolitan
Hun. (N. Y.), 366;
45; Reed v. Home
Mass. 443; Krulevitz v. Eastern R. Co., 140 Mass. 575; s. c., 26 Am. & Eng. R. R. Cas. 118; Western News Co. v. Wilmarth, 33 Kans. 510, Jordon v. Alabama, etc., R. Co., 74 Ala. 85.

In the *United States* malice may be imputed to a corporation, as will appear in the citations subsequently made. And see opinion by Walton, J., in Goddard v. Grand Trunk R., 57 Maine, 223.

In *England*, the decided weight of authority is the same way, though some hesitation has been evinced in that country to follow the new views of corporations, as in Abrath v. Northeastern R. Co., 26 Am. & Eng. R. R. Cas. 128, decided by the House of Lords. In that case, Lord Bramwell, speaking for himself and not for the lords, said that the malice of the servants ought not to be imputed to the corporation. The English decisions are reviewed in note 26 Am. & Eng. R. R. Cas. 134.

3 Boogher v. Life Assoc. of America, 75 Mo. 319, overruling Gillett v. Mo. Valley R. Co., 55 Mo. 315.

In Hussey v. King, 3 So. East. Rep. 923 (N. Car., November, 1887), it was held that allegation of authority, where the act complained of is *ultra vires*, is unnecessary. Morton v. Met. Ins Co., 34 Hun, 366; *affirmed* 103 N. Y. 645; Wheeless v. Second Nat. Bk., 1 Baxt. (Tenn.) 469; s. c, 25 Am. Rep. 783; Fenton v. Wilson Sewing Mach Co , 9 Phila. 189; Goodspeed v. East Haddam Bank, 22 Conn. 535. Vance v. Erie R. Co., 3 Vroom, 334; Carter v. Howe Machine Co., 51 Md. 290; Krulevitz v. Eastern R. Co., 140 Mass. 573. See Williams v. Ins. Co , 57 Miss. 759, where the subject is discussed at length; s. c., § 34 Am. Rep. 494, and note collating the cases.

Semble, that the corporation would not be liable by reason of ratification of a prosecution already completed and terminated by its agent. Morton v. Met. Ins. Co., 34 Hun (N. Y.), 366.

An action for malicious prosecution may lie against a corporation. (Overruling Owsley v. Montgomery & West Point R. Co., 37 Ala. 560.) Jordan v. Alabama Great Southern R. Co.. 74 Ala. 85; s. c., 49 Am. Rep 800; Pennsylvania Co. v. Weddle, 100 Ind. 138; s. c., (*g*) *Miscellaneous Torts.*—A corporation is answerable in an action for the vexatious and malicious interference with the business of another.[1] A corporation may be liable for damages for knowingly keeping a mischievous animal.[2] Under a *Connecticut* statute, giving an action for a vexatious civil suit, an action on the case may be maintained against a corporation.[3] A corporation may be liable in damages for a nuisance.[4] A bank may be liable for injuries through the gross neglect of its officers in the care of a special deposit.[5] An action lies against a corporation for its infringement of a patent.[6] An action may lie against a corporation for the neglect of a corporate duty by which the plaintiff suffers.[7]

(*h*) *Contempt of Court.*—Corporations, as well as individuals, are punishable for contempt of court.[8]

2. Exemplary Damages.—The great weight of authority establishes that corporations may be subjected to the payment of exemplary or punitive damages.[9] But where exemplary damages are to be

26 Am. & Eng. R. R. Cas. 120; Morton *v.* Metropolitan Life Ins. Co., 34 Hun (N. Y.), 366.

1. Green *v* London Omnibus Co., 7 C. B. N. S. 301.

2. Stiles *v.* Cardiff, etc., Co., 33 L. J. Q. B. 310.

3. Goodspeed *v.* East Haddam Bank, 22 Conn. 530.

4. See these principles illustrated by Balto. & Potomac R. Co. *v* Fifth Bapt. Church, 108 U. S. 317, where the railroad company constructed its works close to the church and Sunday school building of plaintiffs, and by their operations drowned the voice of the preacher, filled the church with soot and smoke, etc. *Held*, that a religious corporation could, as well as a private person, recover; that where its members suffer personal discomfort and apprehension of danger in the use of the corporate property, the corporation may recover for such injuries. Field, J.: "It admits indeed of grave doubt whether Congress could authorize the company to occupy and use any premises within the city limits, in a way which would subject others to physical discomfort and annoyance in the quiet use and enjoyment of their property, and at the same time exempt the company from the liability to suit for damages or compensation, to which individuals acting without such authority would be subject under like circumstances."

5. See the authorities reviewed in Vol. II. of this work, article BANKS AND BANKING, at p. 95, etc.

6. Poppenhusen *v.* N. Y., etc., Co., 2 Fish. Pat. Cas. 62. Action on the case will lie. Kneass *v.* Schuylkill Bk., 4 Wash. C. C. 9. See Goodyear *v.* Phelps, 3 Blatchf. (C. C.) 91.

7. In Riddle *v* Proprietors, 7 Mass 169, the neglect was to construct a canal of sufficient width and depth to allow the passage of certain rafts. The owner of such a raft, who paid the toll, but whose raft could not pass, brought trespass. *Held*, that he could recover.

8. People *v.* Albany, etc., R. Co., 12 Abb. Pr. (N. Y.) 171; First Cong. Ch. *v.* Muscatine, 2 Clarke (Iowa), 69; Golden Gate, etc., Co. *v.* Superior Court of Yuba Co., 2 West Coast Rep. (Cal.) 736; U. S. *v.* Memphis, etc., R., 6 Fed. Rep. 237; Mayor, etc., *v.* Ferry Co., 64 N. Y. 624.

Its effects may be sequestrated.—Judson *v.* Rossie Galena Co., 9 Paige's Ch (N. Y) 598; McKim *v.* Odom, 3 Bland's Ch. (Md.) 420,—or *distringas* may issue against it. McKim *v.* Odom, 3 Bland's Ch. (Md.) 420. It may be fined for violating injunction. Mayor, etc., *v.* Ferry Co., 64 N. Y. 622.

9. Samuels *v.* Evg. Mail Assoc., 9 Hun (N. Y.), 288; Atlantic & Gt. Western R. Co. *v.* Dunn, 19 Ohio St. 162; Pittsb., Ft. W. & C. R. Co. *v.* Slusser, 19 Ohio St. 157; Goddard *v.* Grand Trunk R., 57 Me. 202, 223; Singer Mfg. Co. *v.* Holdfodt, 86 Ill. 455; Phila., Wil & B. R Co. *v.* Larkin, 47 Md. 155; Heale *v.* Railroad Co., 1 Dillon (U. S. C. C., Iowa District), 568; Milwaukee & St Paul R. Co. *v.* Arms, 91 U. S. 489; Mendelsohn *v.* Anaheim Lighter Co., 40 Cal. 657; New Orleans, etc., R. Co. *v.* Statham, 42 Miss. 607. Denver, etc., R. Co. *v.* Harris, 122 U. S. 1146.

In the course of an interesting opinion by Walton, J., in Goddard *v.* Grand ondition and circumstances of the defendant may be A mere omission of duty, although grossly negligent, rded as sufficient to subject the corporation or indi- ndictive damages; but some intention to inflict the in- ckless, wanton disregard for the safety of others, should arrant punitive damages.[2]

TY FOR FRAUD.—Strictly speaking, a corporation can- e guilty of fraud; but where it is organized for the carrying on a trade or other speculation for profit, rming a railway, these objects can only be accom- ough the agency of individuals; and there can be no if the agents employed conduct themselves fraudu- hat if they had been acting for private employers per- om they were acting would have been affected by their ame principles must prevail where the principal under agent acts is a corporation.[3] A corporation has been

Me. 223, he says: "A cor- imaginative being. It has he mind of its servants; it ut the voice of its servants; hands with which to act of its servants. All its chief, as well as its schemes erprise, are conceived by and executed by human ese minds and hands are ninds and hands. All at- ore, to distinguish between e servant and the guilt of n, or the malice of the ser- aking of exemplary dama- malice of the corporation, tent of the servant and the the corporation, is sheer only tends to confuse the onfound the judgment. malice, nor suffering is his ideal existence called a And yet, under cover of its hority, there is in fact as ness, and as much that is unishment, as can be found . And since these ideal neither be hung, impris- l, nor put in the stocks,— no corrective influence can bear upon them except that loss,—it does seem to us ne of exemplary damages ficial in its application to its application to natural

ntly the doctrine is applied s of passengers, but it ap- orporations also. Mfg. Co. v. Holdfodt, 86 injury was by a sewing- machine company's agent. In Mendelsohn v. Anaheim Lighter Co., 40 Cal. 657, the court were ready to apply the doctrine to a carrier of lumber, had the evidence warranted. The court observed: "If a family picture, having no apprecia- ble market value, be delivered to a common carrier to be transported for hire, and if he wantonly destroy it, it is plain the damages would not be confined to the mere money value of the picture. In such cases the carrier would not only be guilty of a violation of the contract, but of a gross, wilful, and tortious breach of a duty enjoined upon him by law, for which he would be liable to punitive damages."

1. In Belknap v. Railroad Co., Sargent, J., said: "What would be sufficient as damages, by way of example and of pun- ishment, for a day laborer would be nothing by way either of example or as a punishment" to a wealthy corporation. But in the same case it was said that where actual damages only were to be awarded, the character, standing, condi- tion, or circumstances of the defendant are entirely immaterial; and so it was held in Hays v. Houston & Great North- ern R. Co., 46 Tex. 272.

2. N. O., etc., R. Co. v. Statham, 42 Miss. 620; Ill. Cent. R. Co. v. Hammer, 72 Ill. 347; Milwaukee, etc., R. Co. v. Arms, 91 U. S. 489; West. Un. Tel. Co. v. Eyser, 91 U. S. 495.

3. Ranger v. Great Western R. Co., 5 H. L. Cas. 86; Barwick v. English Joint Stock Bank, L. R. 2 Exch. 259; Phila- delphia, etc., R. Co. v. Derby, 14 How. (U. S.) 468; Henderson v. Railroad Co., 17 Tex. 560; Hale v. Union Mut., etc.,

onditior and circumstances of the defendant may be A mere omission of duty, although grossly negligent, rded as sufficient to subject the corporation or indi- punitive damages; but some intention to inflict the in- eckless, wanton disregard for the safety of others, should rant punitive damages.[9]

the Wants.—Strictly speaking a corporation can- c guilty of fault; but where it is organized for the carrying on a trade or other speculation for profit, ilding a railway, these objects can only be accom- ough the agency of individuals; and there can be no if the agents employed conduct themselves fraudu- if they had been acting for private employers, the they were acting would have been affected by their principle must prevail where the principal under- corporation. A corporation has been representation as to matters contained in the company's charter.[1] Ordinarily, liability does not exist if the agent was acting beyond the scope of his authority;[2] but the corporation may be charged with liability where the agent's acts were such as may fairly have been supposed to be within the power of an agent occupying his

1. A corporation is a body of limited powers derived wholly from its charter or general corporation law. Hence it has been held in the case of stock subscriptions that subscribers seeking to avoid their subscription cannot aver misrepresentation touching matters covered by the charter. Selma R. Co. *v.* Anderson, 51 Miss. 829; Irvin *v.* Turnpike Co., 2 Pa. 466.

2. In Washington Bank *v.* Lewis, 22 Pick. (Mass.) 24, it was held that the bank could recover from Lewis, upon a note which the latter had given to one of the bank's directors for discount, and which the director had pledged to the bank for a loan to said director. It appeared that the director had been authorized to procure notes for discount at times when money was abundant; but defendant, Lewis, knew that the director's power to procure notes on behalf of the bank only existed in such times, and knew that money was scarce when he parted with his note to the director. Udell *v.* Atherton, 7 H. & N. 172.

But if the corporation ratify the contract and avail itself of the benefits, it is liable. Henderson *v.* Railroad Co., 17 Tex. 560; Story on Agency, § 250, and notes; Wood's Field on Corp. § 295. If it ratify at all, it ratifies *in toto.* Wood's Field, § 295.

In case of the employment of several to do a particular business jointly, the corporation is equally responsible for each and all; for notice to either is notice to the principal. Bank of United States *v.* Davis, 2 Hill (N. Y.), 451. In this case a bill of exchange was sent to one of the directors of a bank for discount. The director was at the time a member of the board which ordered the discount to be made. He received the avails, alleging the discount to be for his own benefit. *Held,* that the bank was chargeable with notice of the fraud.

False Bills of Lading.—The authority of the carriers' agent to give bills of lading is generally limited to goods put on board the train or vessel. One who receives a bill of lading for goods never put aboard cannot recover thereon against the carrier without showing particular authority in the master or agent to sign the bill. Even one who is an innocent and *bona fide* holder cannot set up such a false bill against the carrier unless such special authority is shown. But this rule is not without opposition. In Grant *v.* Norway, 10 C. B. 687, it was held that, broad as is the authority of the master of a vessel, it does not extend to signing bills of lading for goods not put on board, and that all persons are bound to take notice that such is the rule. Grant *v.* Norway was followed in the Schooner Freeman *v.* Buckingham, 18 How. (U. S.) 191. The principle applies for a stronger reason to the shipping clerk of a railway, whose powers are obviously not so large as those of the captain of a ship. Coleman *v.* Riches, 16 C. B. 104. In Habbersty *v.* Ward, 8 Excheq. 330, the court went still further by a decision that when the master has once signed a bill of lading for goods that have actually been shipped his power is exhausted, and he cannot charge the owner by signing a second bill for the same goods.

But in Armour *v.* Michigan Central R. Co., 65 N. Y. 111, Grant *v.* Norway was disapproved, and railroad companies said to be estopped from questioning receipts signed by their agents, as against innocent *bona fide* holders for value. In Freeman *v.* Buckingham the goods were by the bill of lading deliverable to the consignor's order, while they were deliverable to the consignee's order in Armour *v.* Railroad Co., and the court attempted to draw a distinction based on this difference. In a Pennsylvania case, it was held that owing to the shipment having been made in New York, the decision must be based on Armour *v.* Railroad Co., but the court said that they were not prepared to admit that there was any material difference between the laws of the two States. Brooks *v.* N. Y., L. E. & W. R Co., 108 Pa. St. 529. See BILL OF LADING, 2 Am. & Eng. Encyc. of Law, 224.

If a corporation furnishes its secretary with money to pay its employees, and an employee monthly delivers to the secretary receipts for the month's salary, but leaves the money with the secretary, to be drawn against when desired, the corporation is not liable for the default position.[1] The weight of authority renders a corporation liable for the fraud of its agents, whether it has or has not derived benefit from the fraud;[2] but there is not wanting authority holding a

of the secretary in failing afterward, to pay over the amounts. Gardner *v.* Omnibus R. Co., 63 Cal. 326.

1. Davendorf *v.* Beardsley, 23 Barb. (N. Y.) 656. It was accordingly held that the company had constituted such person its agent to answer inquiries respecting the character, capital, and means of the corporation.

The manager of a bank is general agent. It was held in Barwick *v.* English Joint Stock Bank, L. R. 2 Ex. 259. that a bank was liable for misrepresentation by its manager, in giving plaintiff a written guarantee that the check of J. D., a customer of the bank, should be paid, on receipt of the government money due J. D., in priority to any other payment, "except to this bank." As a matter of fact, J. D.'s indebtedness to the bank was for a sum far beyond that payable to him by the government, and when the government paid him, his payment of the amount into the bank was credited on account, leaving nothing for plaintiff on the guarantee. *Held*, that there was evidence to go to the jury that the manager knew and intended that the guarantee should be unavailing, and fraudulently concealed from the plaintiff the fact which would make it so; and that the defendants would be liable for the agent's fraud.

So where a cashier of a bank falsely states to a surety that a note held by the bank has been paid, and the surety is thereby caused to yield up security held by himself, the bank is estopped to deny that the note was paid. For though the cashier ordinarily has no authority to discharge its debtors without payment, yet he is the proper one to whom to apply to ascertain whether the debt has been paid. Cocheco Nat. Bank *v.* Haskell, 51 N. H. 116; Derrick *v.* Lamar Ins. Co., 74 Ill. 404; Fire Ins. Co. *v.* Whitehill 50 Ill. 112. See also Sturges *v.* Circleville Bank, 11 Ohio St 153; BANKS AND BANKING, 2 Am. & Eng. Encyc. of Law, 118 *et seq.*

In Sharp *v.* Mayor, etc., of New York, 40 Barb. (N. Y.) 256, it was said: "It is urged that a corporation will not be affected by any representation made by an agent, unless the agent was directly authorized to make the particular statement. The principal is liable for the false representations of the agent made in and about the matter for which he was appointed agent, not on the ground of express authority given to the agent to make the statement, but on the ground that as to the particular matter for which the agent is appointed he stands in the place of the principal; and whatever he does or says in or about that matter is the act or declaration of the principal, for which the principal is just as liable as if he had personally done the act or made the declaration."

Power of Receivers to Collect Subscriptions to Stock Procured by Fraud – Litchfield Bank *v.* Peck, 29 Conn. 384; Upton *v.* Tribilcock, 91 U. S. 45. *Compare* Miller *v.* Wild Cat, etc., Co., 52 Ind. 1; Western Bank of Scotland *v.* Addie, 1 Sc & Div. App. 146.

2. British Mut. Bkg. Co. *v.* Charnwood Forest R. Co., 34 W. R. 718; 55 L. J. Q. B. 399. In that case the former secretary of a railway company induced plaintiffs to advance money on the security of certain stock of the company which he falsely represented belonged to the transferror. Plaintiffs had had former dealings with the said former secretary as secretary for the company, and had never been informed that he was not still such secretary. *Held*, that the corporation was liable. In Mackay *v.* Commercial Bk., L. R 5 Privy Counc. App. 394. the court did not decide this point; but the opinion evidently leans in favor of the liability In Swift *v.* Winterbotham, L. R. 8 Q. B. 244, a banking company was held liable for false representation in regard to the solvency of a certain person; and though the decision was reversed on another point, the liability for agent's fraud was not shaken. Nothing was said to show any benefit to the company. And see N. Y. & N. H. R. Co. *v.* Schuyler, 34 N. Y 30, where a corporation was held liable for stock over-issued by its president. *Compare* Wright's App., 99 Pa St. 425.

See authorities cited in succeeding note.

It is no ground for denying to a corporation the right to rescind a contract entered into through the fraud of its directors, that a new board exists. Metropolitan Elevated R Co. *v.* Manhattan Elevated R. Co., 11 Daly (N. Y.), 373; s. c., 14 Abb. N. Cas. (N. Y.) 103.

liable only to the extent of the benefits received.[1] The

h Authorities.—The leading
wick v. English Joint Stock
led in 1867, L. R. 2 Exch. 259.
er of a bank gave a written
hat he would honor the check
customer of the bank for oats
after supplied him, not exceed-
ain amount, on receipt of
t funds coming to said cus-
ng said check priority to any
ent except to the bank where-
were supplied by plaintiff.
nt of check was refused by the
because the indebtedness due
ar exceeded the government
eived; and this the manager
he gave the guarantee. *Held*,
vidence warranting a verdict
anager fraudulently intended
ee to be unavailing, and that
ants were liable for their
ud. See Bigelow on Fraud,
Swift v. Winterbotham, de-
3, L. R. 8 Q. B. 244. Here the
a bank in answer to inquiry
er one R. was responsible for
rote a reply favorable to R.'s
wing that his reply was false.
nce of the reply, plaintiff sold
for which he could not reason of R.'s insolvency. It
at the bank was liable for the
h was one in the course of
business. On another point,
he signature of the guarantor,
was reversed. L. R. 9 Q. B.
Justice Coleridge, rendering
in reversal, said: "This de-
not at all conflict with the
rwick v. London Joint-stock
. 2 Ex 259."
y v. Commercial Bank of New
L. R. 5 Priv. Counc. App.
Barwick v. English Joint
was approved, it being stated
ter is answerable for every
is servant or agent committed
se of the service and for the
nefit, though no express com-
ivity of the master be proved;
stinction could be drawn be-
ds and other wrongs; and that
s were liable for such deceit.
in this case was the sending,
er whose duty it was to obtain
of bills of exchange in which
as interested, of a telegram in
f the drawer of the bill, there-
ng that the drawer was con-
siness as theretofore, whereas
had absconded. In the judg-
ment of the House of Lords, Sir Montague Smith said: "It may be generally assumed that in mercantile transactions principals do not authorize their agents to act wrongfully, and consequently that frauds are beyond 'the scope of the agent's authority' in the narrowest sense of which the expression admits. But so narrow a sense would have the effect of enabling principals largely to avail themselves of the frauds of their agents, without suffering losses or incurring liabilities."

In British Mut. Bkg. Co. v. Charnwood Forest R. Co., L. R. 18 Q. B. D. 714; March, 1887, in the court of appeal, the rule stated by Willes, J., in Barwick v. English Joint Stock Bank, L. R. 2 Exch. 259, was again approved. "The general rule is, that the master is answerable for every such wrong of his servant or agent as is committed in the course of his service and for the master's benefit, though no express command or privity of the master be proved." However, it was held that the agent's fraud, if for his own benefit, was not "for the master's benefit," and hence could not render the corporation liable, even though the act was done in the course of the servant's employment.

In 1867, in Western Bank of Scotland v. Addie, L. R. 1 Scotch & Div. App. 145, Lord Cranworth expressed the opinion that a corporation can only be made responsible to the extent to which they have profited by such wrong; and the Lord Chancellor said that if, instead of seeking to set aside the contract, the person defrauded prefers an action of damages for the deceit such action cannot be maintained against the company, but only against the directors; and Lord Cranworth said a corporation cannot be called upon in its corporate character in action of deceit.

In Weir v. Bell, in 1878, 3 Exch D. 244, it was said by one of the judges,—Bramwell, L. J.,—that private masters are not responsible for acts done by the servant wilfully; and therefore he condemned the reasoning in Barwick v. English Joint Stock Bank, L. R. 2 Ex. 259, although he thought the decision itself was sustainable, because every person who authorizes another to act for him undertakes for the absence of fraud by that person in the execution of the authority.

In Blake v. Albion Life Assurance Socy., in 1878, L. R. 4 C. P. D. 94, Grove, extent of the liability is a general question, and not one relating peculiarly to corporations.[1]

1. Instances of Liability.—Instances of the liability of a corporation for fraud are as follows: Misrepresentations in notice of judicial sale of a railroad calculated to destroy competition among bidders;[2] procuring donations of property to a railroad by threatening to change its terminus;[3] fraud of agent in discharging and releasing mortgages;[4] in filling up certificates to holders of coupons;[5] in the issuance of stock certificates;[6] in other instances;[7]

J., said that it was fairly questionable whether the corporation could be made to pay damages for deceit by agent; but as the only claim was for return of money paid to the corporation, judgment was entered against the company.

American Authorities.—Corporations may be liable in action of deceit for the damage suffered, and not simply to the extent of benefit received Peebles *v.* Patapsco Guano Co., 77 N. Car. 233, where a spurious article was represented as the genuine. Taylor on Corporations, § 342; White *v.* Sawyer, 16 Gray (Mass), 586. Here it was held that two owners of a vessel are jointly liable in action of deceit for fraudulent representations made by one of them acting for both, in the sale of the vessel; and the damages are not limited to the profit derived by them, or either of them, from the fraud. Jeffrey *v* Bigelow, 13 Wend. (N. Y.) 518. Here an agent for the sale of sheep fraudulently sold some which were diseased, and the purchaser mixed the diseased sheep with others before owned by him, whereby the contagion was communicated through the entire flock. *Held*, that the principal was liable, not only as to the sheep sold, but for all the sheep to which the distemper was communicated. And see Bennett *v.* Judson, 21 N. Y. 238. On the other hand, it was held in *New Jersey* in 1881 that an innocent principal is not suable in tort for the agent's fraud. See *dictum* to same effect in Craig *v.* Ward, 3 Keyes (N. Y.), 393

1. Some authorities hold that the liability extends only to the benefit received; but the current of authority is that the liability equals the extent of the damage. Bigelow on Fraud (1888), 226 *et seq*; Pollock on Torts, 259; Barwick *v.* English Joint Stock Bank, L. R. 2 Exch. 259; White *v.* Sawyer, 16 Gray (Mass), 586; Kennedy *v.* McKay, 43 N J. L. 288.

2. Where the notice of the sale of a railroad under mortgage to secure railroad bonds, set forth that the sum due under the mortgage for the principal of bonds was two million dollars, with seventy thousand dollars interest, when in fact less than two hundred thousand dollars was held by *bona fide* holders for value, the remainder of the two millions being either in the hands of the directors or directly under their control, such notice was fraudulent, and of itself sufficient to vitiate the sale. James *v.* Railroad Co., 6 Wall. (U. S.) 752. "Deceptive notice was calculated to destroy all competition among the bidders, and, indeed, to exclude from the purchase every one except those engaged in the perpetration of the fraud."

3. Union Pac. R. Co. *v.* Durant, 3 Dillon (C. C.), 343. The oppression in this case was the causing of hope that Omaha would be the terminus of the road, and threatening to make Bellevue or Florence the terminus if citizens refused to donate lands. A bill filed by the company for conveyance was dismissed by the court, which held that the donors were entitled to have back again their lands.

4 The treasurer of a savings-bank, who had been authorized by a vote of the trustees to discharge and release mortgages, fraudulently interpolated in the record of the vote the word "assign" between the words "discharge" and "release." *Held*, that as between the bank and one who, misled by the record, took an assignment of a mortgage for value in good faith, the bank must bear the loss. Holden *v.* Phelps, 141 Mass. 456.

5. The president and treasurer of a railroad corporation confided to a clerk the duty of filling up and supplying certificates to the holders of coupons. The certificates were delivered, signed, to the clerk, who fraudulently filled them up and put them on the market, whence they came into the hands of innocent holders for value without notice of the fraud *Held*, the railroad corporation was responsible, and must bear the loss. Western Maryland R. Co. *v.* Franklin Bank, 60 Md. 36.

6. New York etc., R. Co. *v* Schuyler, 34 N. Y. 50. *Compare* Wright's App., 99 Pa. St. 425

7. See Derrick *v.* Lamar Ins. Co., 74

nt representations as to the financial condition of a com- ducing subscriptions to stock;[1] reports by directors and circulated by the corporation, unless they are mere statements as to possible profits, and accompanied by ts which afford the means of testing their accuracy;[2] tude is permitted in the issuance of a prospectus;[3] but representations cannot be tried by as strict a test as is n other cases, they are required to be fair, honest, and [4]

nd cases cited in preceding

ional Exch. Co., etc., v. Drew Jacq. (House of Lords) 103. ttering joint-stock company, to raise its shares in the mar- ented the concern as most and offered money to two of olders to buy further shares, ares accordingly were bought npany for such shareholders, ards became valueless; upon he company for repayment of advanced, it was held that de- the company had been guilty s a good defence. The gen- sts of society required that ions by directors should bind orporation, although the indi- posing it might be ignorant of ntation and of its falsehood. ld not be that the company efit by these misrepresenta- out being liable to be told, our fraud. See, generally,

al Exch. Co., etc., v. Drew Jacq (House of Lords) 103; wick, etc., R. & Land Co. v. 9 H. L. Cas. 711; In re Na- nt Steam Fuel Co., 4 Drewry,

sidering such a document as ctus of a company, allowance de for some latitude of state- s unfortunately so universally understood that the prospec- mpany never in fact contains curate account of its prospects ages, that the validity of bar- ed upon such instruments can- y be tried by as strict a test as lied in other cases. It is not prospectus contains exagger- of the advantages of the com- ch it relates, or contains some rifling errors or inaccuracies, urt would be justified in set- a bargain founded upon it. entral R. Co. of Venezuela, 3 S. 132.

4. Kisch v. Central R. Co. of Venezuela, 3 De G., J. & S. 132; Re Life Assoc. of England (Limited), 34 Beav. 639; Ross v. Estates Investment Co., L. R. 3 Eq. Ca. 122; Chester v. Spargo, 16 Weekly Reporter, 576.

In Kisch v. Central R. Co., 3 De G., J. & S. 132, plaintiff took shares in a railway company on the faith of a prospectus which referred to a concession for making the railway as having been made by the Venezuelan Government to the company, and stated that the contractor had guaranteed a dividend of £2½ per cent on the paid-up capital during the construction of the works, and that the Venezuelan Government had guaranteed a dividend of £9 per cent on the paid-up capital for twenty years. The concession had, in fact, been made to another company, and referred to the agreement for purchase; and the memorandum of association stated one of the objects of the company to be, acquiring, by purchase or otherwise, concessions from the Venezuelan Government. The guarantee of the contractor for interest during the construction was, in fact, limited to £20,000 in all (the whole capital being £500,000). The guarantee of the Venezuelan Government was for a dividend of 9 per cent while the line, without any default on the part of the company, failed to produce it. The documents giving the above guarantees were referred to in the articles without stating their contents. *Held*, that the plaintiff having, when he applied for the shares, agreed to be bound by the memorandum and articles of association, could not allege ignorance of their contents, and therefore, although the prospectus ought to have stated the fact of the concession having been acquired by purchase at a heavy price, *semble*, the plaintiff could not have established any title to relief on this ground. But *held*, that although the plaintiff must be treated as having notice of the memorandum and articles, he was not thereby affected by such knowledge of the contents of all the documents referred to but

Corporations have been held liable for issuing stock as full paid at less than its par value,[1] and for misrepresentations in railroad time tables.[2]

A corporation which conspires with an individual to obtain money under false representations can be made to yield the amount paid to it in an action of deceit.[3]

2. Matters of Pleading and Practice.—An agent's fraud, in an action of deceit, may be described in pleading as the wrong of the corporation.[4] The corporation and the agent guilty of the fraud may be sued jointly, since all are principals.[5]

not set forth in them, as to be debarred from complaining of any deceptive statement made to him respecting them; that he was entitled to rely on the representations in the prospectus as to the guarantees by the contractor and by the Venezuelan government, and that these representations were so far from being fair, honest, and *bona fide* statements, that he was entitled to be relieved from his shares. See also Smith's Case, L. R. 2 Ch. App. 611; Kennedy *v.* Panama, etc., Mail Co., L. R. 2 Q B. 580

1 As a general rule, it may be stated that the capital stock of a corporation is a trust fund for payment of its creditors; that persons trusting it have a right to assume that the amount of its stock issued indicates the amount of actual assets in its hands or subject to its call, to transact its business and meet the demands of its creditors. Therefore, on a sale of its stock as fully paid up, for less than its par value, creditors of the corporation may call upon the purchasers to make up the difference between the par value of the stock and the value at which it was sold. Chouteau Ins. Co. *v.* Floyd. 74 Mo 291; Ross *v.* Kelly, 36 Minn. 38 (1887); Upton *v.* Tribilcock, 91 U. S. 45; Bouton *v.* Dement, 11 West R 437 (Illinois, Nov. 1887). But this principle does not apply to mining corporations in *Minnesota* or *California*. Ross *v.* Kelly, 36 Minn. 38; *Re* South Mountain, etc., Min Co., 7 Sawy 30 (5 Fed. Rep. 403); s. c., 8 Sawy. 360 (14 Fed. Rep. 347). In *Minnesota*, on account of the provision of Gen. St. of 1878, § 149, providing that the stock of mining and smelting companies when sold, "purporting to be full paid," shall not be subject to further assessment; in *California*, on account of the custom in the organization of mining companies to fix the capital stock at a fictitious figure bearing no relation to the real value of the property.

2. Publication of railroad time-tables amounts to representation that trains will start as stated. A company which knowingly published false reports was held liable to a passenger who travelled with the expectation of making connections, but failed to do so owing to the false time-tables. Denton *v.* Great Northern R. Co., 5 El. & B. (85 E. C. L. R.) 860.

3 Blake *v.* Albion Life Assurance Soc., L. R. 4 C. P. Div. 94

4. Mackay *v.* Commercial Bank, L. R. 5 P. C. App. 391; Barwick *v.* English Joint Stock Bank, L. R. 2 Ex. 266.

In Raphael *v.* Goodman, 8 Ad & El. 565, the sheriff sued on a bond; plea, that the bond was obtained by the sheriff and others by fraud; proof, that it was obtained by the fraud of the officer. *Held*, the plea was sufficiently proved.

5. Swift *v.* Winterbotham, L. R. 8 Q. B 254.

In Cullen *v.* Thompson's Trustees, Lord Westbury says: "All persons directly concerned in the commission of a fraud are to be treated as principals."

Costs.—A bill by a purchaser of shares to have the purchase declared void, and to be relieved therefrom, contained many charges of fraud which plaintiff failed to prove. Other charges were sustained and the purchaser relieved; but because of the unsustained charges no costs were allowed Kisch *v.* Central R. Co. of Venezuela, 3 De G., J. & S. 122. When new stockholders have come in, or new debts created then the complainant cannot be relieved. Bigelow on Fraud, pp. 229 246.

Evidence—In action against a company to recover money obtained through fraud of defendants' agent, evidence of similar frauds on other persons by the same agent in the same manner, with the knowledge and for the benefit of defendants, is admissible on behalf of plaintiff. Blake *v.* Albion Life Assur. Soc., L. R. 4 C. P. D. 94.

2. Liability to Indictment.—1. Generally.—Malice and wilful intent cannot be predicated of a corporation, though they may well be of its members. A corporation cannot be indicted for treason or felony, or for crimes punishable by imprisonment.[1] Indictment lies against a corporation for a nuisance, and the liability may arise from a non-feasance, or an omission to perform a legal duty or obligation, as well as from a misfeasance, or the doing of any act unlawful in itself and injurious to the rights of others.[2] It may be

1. In State v. Morris & Essex R. Co., 23 N. J. Law, 360, Green, C. J., said: "The law is well settled, that a corporation aggregate is liable to indictment. It is said, indeed, by Blackstone, that a corporation cannot commit treason, felony, or other crime in its corporate capacity, citing the case of Sutton's Hospital, 10 Coke, 32. The original authority is simply that a corporation cannot commit treason. While it is conceded that a corporation cannot, from its nature, be guilty of treason, felony, or other crime involving *malus animus* in its commission, it is believed that there is no authority, ancient or modern, which denies the liability of a corporation aggregate to indictment, except an anonymous case, said to have been decided by Chief Justice Holt, in the court of king's bench, in the 13 Will. III. (1701). The case is reported in 12 Mod. 559, briefly as follows: 'Note per Holt, Chief Justice. A corporation is not indictable, but the particular members of it are.' It may well be doubted whether this is not one of those cases which extorted from Lord Holt the bitter complaint of his reporters, 'that the stuff which they published would make posterity think ill of his understanding, and that of his brethren on the bench.' Aside from the apocryphal character of the report, it is hardly credible that so learned and accurate a judge as Lord Holt should have laid down the broad proposition imputed to him by the reporter. It is certain that while he was chief justice of the king's bench there were cases before that court of indictments against *quasi* corporations for neglect to repair roads and bridges. Regina v. County of Wilts, 1 Salk. 359; The Queen v. Inhabitants of Cluworth, 6 Mod. 163; s. c., 1 Salk. 359. And in Anonymous v. Saintiff, 6 Mod. 255, Lord Holt himself held that if a common bridge be in decay, an indictment must of necessity lie for it, because an action will not lie without a special damage. It seems to be true, moreover, as was stated by Talfourd, Sergeant Arguendo, in The Queen v. Railway Co., 3 Queen's Bench, 227, that although there was at that time no direct authority in England for the position that a corporation aggregate is indictable in the corporate name, yet the course of precedents has been uniform for centuries, and the doctrine has frequently been taken for granted both in arguments and by the judges. The case of Langforth Bridge, Cro. Car. 365 (1635); Regina v. Inhabitants of the County of Wilts, 1 Salk. 359 (1705); The King v. Inhabitants of the West Riding of Yorkshire, 2 Blac. Rep. 685 (1770); Rex v. Inhabitants of Great Boughton, 5 Burr 2700 (1771); The King v. Inhabitants of Clifton, 5 D. & E. 499 (1794); Rex v. Corporation of Liverpool, 3 East, 86 (1802); Rex v. Mayor of Stratford upon-Avon, 14 East, 348 (1811); Rex v. City of Gloucester, Dougherty's Crown Cir. Ass. 249.

"Notwithstanding the frequent instances to be found in the books of indictments against aggregate corporations for neglect of duty imposed by law, the liability of a corporation to indictment was not expressly adjudicated in Westminster Hall until the very recent case of The Queen v. Birmingham & Gloucester R. Co., 9 Car. & Payne, 469, 3 Queen's Bench, 223. In that case it was directly adjudged that a corporation aggregate may be indicted by their corporate name for disobedience to an order of justices requiring such corporation to execute works pursuant to a statute.

"The same principle has been repeatedly recognized in the American courts, both before and since the decision in The Queen v. Birmingham & Gloucester R. Co. Mower v. Leicester, 9 Mass. 250; Howard v. North Bridgewater, 16 Pick. (Mass.) 190; Susquehanna & Bath Turnpike Co. v. People, 15 Wend. (N. Y.) 267; Freeholders v. Strader, 3 Harr. (N. J.) 108." *Compare* State v. Baltimore, etc. R. Co., 15 W. Va. 362.

2. Louisville & Nashville & Co. v. State, 3 Head (Tenn.), 523.

Where nuisance is complained of,

indicted for erecting and continuing a building, and placing and leaving railroad cars in the public highway;[1] for habitual failure to give signals or warnings of approaching trains where safety of travellers on intersecting roads demands it;[2] for cutting through and obstructing a public highway;[3] or for neglecting to repair a highway;[4] and notice of the defect is unnecessary,[5] nor does the imposition by the charter of a penalty for non-repair *ipso facto* take away liability to indictment;[6] for neglect to repair sea-banks, ditches, etc., protecting land from the sea, when the charter imposes such a public duty, the violation of which is a public offence.[7] For failure of a railroad company to obey a judicial order directing it to make certain arches to connect dissevered lands;[8] for permitting a pool of water to form on its land and

In *Virginia*, in Commonwealth *v.* Swift Run Gap Turnpike Co., 2 Va. Cas. 362, it was held that a corporation could not be indicted for a nuisance in obstructing a common highway.

In *Georgia*, in McDaniel *v.* Gate City Gas Light Co., 3 So. East. Rep. 693, the court observes: "We do not understand that in this State a corporation can be indicted for an offence."

In *Indiana*, the common law of England as to crimes was not a part of the State law; but Indiana Rev. St. 1881, § 1697, provides that corporations may be indicted for maintaining a public nuisance. It is held that this statute contemplates nuisances created before its passage as well as those created since. State *v.* Louisville, etc., R. Co. (Indiana, 1882) 10 Am. & Eng. R. R Cas. 286. "Every continuance of a nuisance is a fresh nuisance; no vested right can grow out of the commission of an indictable offence." *Compare* State *v.* Ohio, etc., R. Co., 23 Ind. 362; Indianapolis, etc., R. Co. *v.* State, 37 Ind. 493, which were cases arising under a prior statute.

1. State *v.* Morris, etc., R. Co., 23 N. J. Law, 360.

2. L. & N. R. Co. *v.* Commonwealth, 13 Bush (Ky.), 388. See also Louis., Cin & Lex. R. Co. *v.* Comm., 80 Ky. 143.

3. In addition to the authorities in previous notes may be mentioned that of Reg. *v.* Longton Gas Co., 2 El & E. 651, where it was held that the right of every householder to make such temporary obstruction of the highway or footway as may be necessarily incident to the enjoyment of his property, does not authorise his employing others to open trenches, deposit earth and bricks, etc., in order to construct a service pipe from a public gas main to the householder's dwelling, unless such others have parliamentary powers for such works. And it was held that a corporation not so authorized, and guilty of obstructing or cutting in this way, might be indicted for a nuisance. So in this country, the franchise of laying gas-pipes in the public streets must be granted by the legislature, or some local authority empowered to give it. State *v.* Cincinnati Gas Co., 18 Ohio St. 262, 291; 2 Dillon on Munic. Corp. § 691.

4. In State *v.* Morris, etc., R. Co., 23 N. J. Law, 364, the authorities on this point are collected; and see Mower *v.* Leicester, 9 Mass. 280; Commonwealth *v.* Worcester Turnpike Co., 3 Mass. 327; Syracuse, etc., Co. *v.* People, 66 Barb. (N. Y.) 25; Red River Turnpike Co. *v.* State, 1 Sneed (Tenn.), 474.

5. Syracuse, etc., Co. *v.* People, 66 Barb. (N. Y.) 25; Bragg *v.* Bangor City, 51 Me. 533; Angell on Highways, § 275 *et seq.*

6. Susquehanna, etc., Turnpike Co. *v.* People, 15 Wend. (N. Y.) 267; President, etc., *v.* People, 9 Barb. (N. Y.) 161.

7. Mayor, etc., of Lyme Regis *v.* Henley, 2 Cl. & Fin. 331.

8. Queen *v.* Birmingham, etc., R. Co., 3 Ad. & El. (N. S.) 223.

Where a corporation was created with authority to make a tramway, and to maintain the same for the passage of wagons and conveyance of goods on payment of toll, the corporation became charged with the obligation towards the public of continuing the road; and where they took up a part of the track in order to prevent competition with some collieries which the leading members of the company had acquired after the incorporation, the judges agreed that indictment was sustainable against the corporation; but as that was an inadequate remedy, they held that *mandamus* would become stagnant;[1] or to percolate upon land adjoining a canal.[2]

A corporation is not liable to indictment for maintaining a nuisance when in the hands of a receiver.[3]

A corporation may be indicted and fined for libel.[4] Where a statute prohibits a misdemeanor, and officers and employees of the corporation habitually commit the offence prohibited in such a way and at such times as to justify the inference that they had authority from the corporation, the offence may be imputed to the corporation.[5] A corporation would probably be liable to indictment for the act of its officer or employee, in issuing without the proper stamps papers which the law requires to be stamped, with intent to evade the act of Congress.[6] A corporation has been held liable to indictment for "Sabbath-breaking" in the shipment of goods on Sunday contrary to the provisions of a statute.[7]

It has been held that a corporation cannot be compelled to produce its books, or to allow their inspection, when so doing will expose it to indictment.[8]

issue commanding the reinstating of the road. King *v.* Severn & Wye R. Co., 2 B. & Ald 646.

1 Salem *v.* Eastern R. Co., 93 Mass. 431

2 Del. Div. Can. Co *v.* Commonwealth, 60 Pa. St. 367.

3. In State *v.* Vermont Central R. Co., 30 Vt 110, the defendant was indicted for blocking up a highway by stopping its cars upon the railroad. Bennett, J., said: "But if the railroad and all its concerns are in the hands of a receiver, and the company are under an injunction not to intermeddle with its concerns, it would seem difficult to maintain the proposition that still the company should be liable to an indictment for the acts of the receiver or of his agents. To hold the company liable in such a case would be indeed monstrous, as they had no power to control or prevent the acts complained of as a nuisance. No man or corporation should be made criminally responsible for acts which they have no power to prevent. It has been assumed by the attorney for the government that unless the prosecution is sustained the government are without the means of redress. But will that conclusion follow? Why may not the receiver be subjected to an indictment? If he has been guilty of a nuisance, it would seem difficult for him to defend under his commission from chancery. He was not placed above the law. But this is not a point before the court calling for a decision." New trial was granted, but the State's attorney elected to enter a *nolle prosequi*.

4. Odgers on Lib. *369; *per* Ld. Blackburn, in Pharmaceutical Soc. *v.* London, etc., Assoc., 5 App. Cas. 869. 870; dissenting from remarks of Bramwell, L. J., in the court below, 5 Q. B. D. 313.

It can be the subject of a criminal libel Brennan *v.* Tracey, 2 Mo. App. 540.

5. Where the agents of a corporation had been notoriously in the custom of giving to passengers notes for less than five dollars, contrary to the Pennsylvania Banking Act, it was held, in a civil action for the penalty, that this was sufficient proof that the corporation had authorized their conduct, and such action would lie against the corporation. Comm. *v.* Ohio & Pa. R. Co., 1 Grant's Cas. (Pa.) 329 The act termed the penalty a "civil" one.

6. United States *v.* Balt. & Ohio R. Co., U. S. Circuit Court, West Virginia District, August, 1868, reported in 7 Am. Law Reg. N. S. 757. The papers issued were receipts given by the platform-clerk of a common carrier, some for goods, some for money paid for carriage. The cases went off on another point, viz., that the act of Congress of 1864 did not subject such receipts to stamp duty, and the cases were settled by counsel.

7. State *v.* Baltimore, etc., R. Co, 15 W. Va. 362.

8. King *v.* Buckingham Justices, 8 B. & C. 375. In this case a county had been indicted for non repair of a bridge, and question arose whether the county or a certain parish was liable. The county obtained a rule *nisi* for liberty to

Liability to indictment is sometimes extended by statute.[1]

Where a charter confers upon a corporation privileges which in time become detrimental to the community, it cannot then be indicted for a nuisance, as this would be a breach of contract; the remedy is to take away the privilege.[2] Where by statute a cor-

inspect the parish books, but it was after argument discharged. See also King of the Two Sicilies *v.* Wilcox, 14 Jur. N. S. 751.

1. Reg. *v.* Great North of England R., 9 Q. B. 315.

Thus the ancient *Massachusetts* charter, 55, ch. 16, sec. 2, provided that where legal warning had been given any town of defect in any bridge or county highway and any person should lose his life through such defect, the county, or town, which should have remedied the defect should upon presentment in the shire court pay to the relatives, as there indicated, £100 This charter, which appears to be still in force, was many generations in advance of the statutes giving civil action in case of death.

Thus also railroads in *New Hampshire* were by the act of 1850 subjected to indictment and fine for loss of life through negligence of the company or their servants. Boston, Conc. & Mont. R. Co. *v.* State, 32 N. H. 215.

Such too is the *Maine* law.

In *Maryland*, the State is *pro forma* the plaintiff, but in that State the proceeding is a civil one.

Also, under the *Massachusetts* statute, indictment may be made either for injury or death; and the indictment for killing must aver particularly whether the killing was through the company's negligence, or through the negligence of the company's servants. Averment of one does not support proof of the other. Comm. *v.* Boston & M. R. Co., 8 Am. & Eng. R. R. Cas. 298.

2. Thus by their charter the proprietors of New Bedford Bridge were authorized to build a bridge "with two suitable draws, which shall be at least thirty feet wide." It was held that although Congress could interfere, the State legislature could not, so as to require the proprietors to maintain greater draws, nor could the State prosecute for a nuisance for want of the enlarged draws; but, on the other hand, the bridge was to have "two suitable" draws, and the court—not the legislature—had power to judge whether, in view of the increase of commerce, etc., the proprietors were maintaining draws suitable, and if not, indictment lay, although the draws might be "thirty feet wide." Comm. *v.* New Bedford Bridge, 2 Gray (Mass.), 339. And see Hookse *v.* Amoskeag Mfg. Co., 44 N. H. 105; Easton *v.* Same, 44 N. H. 143 *Compare, supra,* this title; CHARTER AS A CONTRACT.

It was said in a *Tennessee* case (Louisville & Nashv. R. Co. *v.* State, 3 Head. 524), that "undoubtedly, so long as the company keeps within its charter, it is not liable for a nuisance permissible under the charter. The work must be constructed without inconvenience to the public; but if it cannot be done without some inconvenience, it must be done with the least possible inconvenience." See also Queen *v.* Scott, 3 Ad. & El. (N. S.) 543; Northern Central R. Co. *v.* Commonwealth, 90 Pa. St. 306; Wood on Nuisances, ch. "Legalized Nuisances."

Legislative authority to build dams protects from indictment for the obstruction thereby caused. Gray *v.* City of Brooklyn, 50 Barb. (N. Y.), 365; Eastman *v.* Company, 44 N. H. 143.

In Hookset *v.* Amoskeag, etc., Company, 44 N. H. 105, a corporation, authorized by its charter to erect and maintain such dams across the Merrimack at A. as it it should deem necessary and proper for carrying on its works, erected a dam across the river at A., and thereby caused the water to be thrown back upon a bridge across the river in a public highway in the town of H., and thereby causing the destruction of the bridge. *Held*, that though this charter protected from indictment for nuisance, it furnished no defence to such corporation in an action on the case brought against it by the town of H.

In Delaware Division Canal Co. *v.* Commonwealth of Pennsylvania, 60 Pa. St. 367, Thompson, C. J., said: "It has not yet been decided that a nuisance created by the commonwealth resulting from, but not necessarily a part or parcel of, its works, may not be a nuisance when continued by a company. The analogy between the position of the commonwealth as proprietor, and that of a corporation, is not exact on the question of liability and relative duty, because the one is sovereign and the other subordinate. The maxim relating to the one is poration is given a certain privilege, and afterwards changes occur which would cause the exercise of the privilege to create a nuisance, the corporation must take proper measures to have the cause of the nuisance removed by those bound to remove it; and if the corporation continue the exercise of the privilege while it results in nuisance, it is indictable.[1] So where the corporation is authorized to exercise certain powers, but the statute does not authorize interference with vested rights, nor necessarily require anything to be done which would cause the nuisance, they cannot exercise those powers so as to create a nuisance.[2] The unreasonable use of a privilege will subject a corporation to indictment when it offends the whole public, but an actual injury need not be suffered by any person in order to constitute the offence.[3]

2. Pleading and Practice.—The period of limitation of indictments against corporations is that of indictments in general, in the absence of any contrary provision.[4] Where the name of a corporation is given, the corporate title must be strictly pursued, unless specification is made unnecessary by local statute.[5] Where a statute provides that a railroad corporation may be indicted for the death of a passenger through the negligence of servants of

that it can do no wrong, while the other may; and for this reason acts resulting from sovereignty are not indictable when done by the sovereign power. The commonwealth can neither be sued nor be indicted; but because this is so, I do not think it follows that such an immunity passes to the vendees of her property or rights. Railroad Company *v.* Duquesne Borough, 10 Wright (Pa.), 223, strongly sustains this view. It is in fact, however, not material to decide the point in this case." The indictment was for pools formed by percolating water. The defence was that the canal company used the canal in manner similar to that of the commonwealth when the State owned the canal; the jury found otherwise.

1 Queen *v.* Bradford Navigation Co., 6 Best & Smith, 629. Thus in the case just cited a canal company was authorized to collect its waters from certain streams which at that time—1771—were pure, but afterwards the growth of a neighboring town brought about so great a number of drains and sewers emptying into the chief stream that it became foul. It was held that the canal company's lessee was indictable for continuing to receive the water after the pollution, and thereby causing a nuisance through the country traversed by the canal. Blackburn, J.: "It throws on them the necessity of taking legal steps to compel the local board of health to do their duty in cleansing, etc; or, if that be found an inefficient remedy, to obtain a private act of parliament for the purpose." And query was raised as to whether the company was not also indictable.

2. Franklin Wharf Co. *v.* Portland, 67 Me. 46. Thus in Managers of Metropolitan Asylums District *v.* Hill, 44 L. T. R. (N. S.) 653, an incorporated body was authorized to build a hospital for infectious cases. Owners of adjacent land brought action against the corporation averring that the hospital was so constructed as to be a nuisance to them. The jury found that this was so. *Held*, that the action lay; that the order of authority was no defence. See Wood on Nuisance. See also Rex *v.* Pease, 4 B. & Ad. 30 (24 E. C. L. R.), where legislative authority which clearly contemplates the nuisance was held to constitute defence.

3. Cin. R. Co. *v.* Com., 80 Ky. 137. The offence here was obstructing a public road by leaving on it at a public crossing a hand-car, with buckets and clothes pendent, whereby horses were put to fright and flight, endangering lives. *Held*, an indictable offence.

4 Commonwealth *v* Boston etc., R. Co., 11 Cush. (Mass.) 512; Commonwealth *v.* East Boston Ferry Co., 13 Allen (Mass.), 589.

5. Wharton's Cr. Pl. & Pr. § 110; Archbold's Cr. Pr. 79; State *v.* New Jersey Turnpike Co., 1 Harr. (N. J.) 225; McGary *v.* People, 45 N. Y. 153.

the indictment need not set out the servant's re' an offence consists in an omission to do some ment must show how the defendant's obligation to ct arises.[2] It has been held that judgment may be st a corporation upon an indictment upon default after due notice to appear.[3] A corporation may nviction and ordered to abate the nuisance.[4] Cor- iot plead to an indictment the want of funds.[5]

TO TAXATION.—1. General Principles.—A complete the liability of a corporation to taxation would in- isideration of all the legal principles applicable to he taxation of the various kinds of corporations is statute in the different States. The power of the corporations as well as individuals and associations In the construction of tax laws applicable to cor-

lth v. Boston, etc., R. ss.) 518.

Jersey Turnpike Co., 5; State v. Hageman, .) 314; Rex v. Brough- oo. Failing in this, it State v. Turnpike Co., 25. But an indictment ndant's act of incorpo- uilding and use of a ng that defendant was nd maintain the same condition as to render convenient for travel- sufficiently the origin s liability to light the so as to support the nce in failing so to do. Bridge Corp., 12 Cush.

R. Co. v. State, 32

Southeastern R. Co., King v Severn & Wye Id. 650. And ordered nce, even though it be Del. Div. Canal Co. v. t. 367. In this case aid: "The owner of the isance is must not be ol the public right to nd what the law com- e for the benefit of the dual may not resist;" liott, 9 Pa. St. 375.

c., of W. & W. Turn- e. 9 Barb. (N. Y.) 174.

Corporate Duty Cannot forced by Indictment.— tc., R. Co., 2 B. & Ald. n Commrs., 2 Maule & th. etc., R. Co. v. Commonwealth (Pa.), 10 Am. & Eng. R. R. Cas. 321, and note.

Proceedings to Enforce Remedy by Indictment.—See Regina v. Birmingham, etc., R. Co., 3 Ad. & El. (N. S.) 223; Boston, etc., R. Co. v. State, 32 N. H. 215.

Liability of Corporations for Lessee's Nuisance.—See Queen v. Bradford Nav. Co., 6 B. & S. 629; King v. Pedley, 1 Ad. & El. 822; Gandy v. Zubber, 5 B. & S. 485; Rich v. Basterfield, 56 Eng. Com. Law Rep. 783.

Construction of Statutes.—See Commonwealth v. Demuth, 12 S. & R. (Pa.) 389; Benson v. Monson. etc., Co., 9 Metc. (Mass.) 562; Commonwealth v. Boston, etc., R. Co., 11 Cush. (Mass.) 516; Androscoggin Water Power Co. v. Bethel Steam Mill Co., 64 Me. 441; King of the Two Sicilies v. Willcox. 14 Jur. (N. S.) 751, Br. Stat. 7 & 8 Geo. IV. c. 28, s. 14. See also State v. Baltimore, etc., R. Co., 15 W. Va. 362; South Carolina R. Co. v. McDonald, 5 Ga. 531; Wales v. Muscatine City, 4 Iowa, 302; Stewart v. Waterloo Turnverein, 71 Iowa, 329.

6. See TAXATION.

7. In Bank of Pennsylvania v. Commonwealth, 19 Pa. St. 144, the court observed: "The taxing power is an incident of the highest sovereignty. It is an essential part of every independent government. By the constitution, and by the principles which lie at the foundation of every organized society, the State may tax all persons, natural or artificial, within her borders, and compel them to contribute such part of their property and income as the legislature may think right, to defray the expenses and meet

A tax cannot be unlawfully assessed upon a corporation which has the effect of imposing double taxation.[1] The capital stock of a corporation is personal property, and a tax levied on it is a personal tax.[2] Capital stock and shares of capital stock are two distinct things, separately assessable.[3]

2. Local Limitations upon Power to Tax.—Corporations, like natural persons, are liable to be taxed for their personal property in the places where they reside.[4] Foreign corporations conduct business in a State only by its express or implied permission founded upon comity, and are clearly liable to taxation.[5] The real property

exercise of the power. This limitation is restrained only by the will of the people, expressed in State constitutions or through elections, and by the condition that it must be so used as not to burden or embarrass the operations of the National government." It was accordingly held in that case that the property of the Union Pacific R., although the corporation was created by Congress, and the company is an agent of the general government, designed to be employed and actually employed in the legitimate service of the government, both military and postal, is not exempt from State taxation.

1. A tax cannot be lawfully assessed against the property of a corporation when the stock of the corporation is at the same time taxed to its owners. Cheshire County Telephone Co. v. State, 63 N. H. 167.

A statute imposing a tax upon the gross receipts of some railroads and upon the capital stock of others is unconstitutional for inequality. Worth v. Wilmington & Weldon R. Co., 89 N. Car. 291, s. c., 45 Am. Rep. 679.

The corporation being presumed to be taxed as "owner," in absence of any showing to the contrary, an assessment of stock to a shareholder will be considered void, as contravening the *California* constitutional inhibition of double taxation. San Francisco v. Mackey, 21 Fed. Rep. 539.

In State v. Cumberland, etc., R. Co., 40 Md. 22, it was held that a State cannot tax both the capital stock and the real and personal property of a corporation.

Deposits in savings-banks are not taxable to the bank and also to the depositors. Berry v. Windham, 59 N. H. 288, s. c., 47 Am. Rep. 202; Robinson v. Dover, 59 N. H. 521. See also Pullman Palace Car Co. v. State, 64 Tex. 274, s. c., 53 Am. Rep. 758; State v. United States, etc., Exp. Co., 60 N. H. 219; Mobile, etc., R. Co. v. Kennedy, 74 Ala. 566; Atchison, etc., R. Co. v. Howe, 32 Kans. 737; Veazie Bank v. Fenno, 8 Wall. (U. S.) 533.

A State tax law which provides different modes of assessment for different classes of property,—the law, however, to operate equally and impartially,—is not open to the objection of denying the "equal protection of the laws." Cincinnati, N. O., etc., R. Co. v. Kentucky, 115 U. S. 321.

In Railroad Tax Cases, 92 U. S. 663, it was held that while the *Illinois* constitution requires taxation in general to be uniform and equal, it declares in express terms that a large class of persons engaged in special pursuits, among whom are persons or corporations owning franchises and privileges, may be taxed as the legislature shall determine, by a general law, uniform as to the class upon which it operates; and under this provision a statute is not unconstitutional which prescribes a different rule of taxation for railroad companies from that for individuals.

2. Saup v. Morgan, 108 Ill. 326.

3. State Bank v. Richmond, 79 Va. 113.

4. Boone on Corporations, § 88, *citing* Union Bank v. State, 8 Yerg. (Tenn.) 490; Mohawk, etc., R. Co. v. Clute, 4 Paige (N. Y.), 384; McKeen v. Northampton County, 49 Pa. St. 519; Orange, etc., R. Co. v. City Council, etc., 17 Gratt. (Va.) 176; State v. Ill. Cent. R. Co., 27 Ill. 64; Jones v. Bridgeport, 36 Conn. 283; Middletown Ferry Co. v. Middletown, 40 Ill. 65. And see McHarg v. Eastman, 4 Robt. 635; Metcalf v. Messenger, 46 Barb. (N. Y.) 325; People v. Bay State, etc., Co., 17 Hun (N. Y.), 204; People v. Commrs., etc., 46 How. Pr. (N. Y.) 315.

See also Peter Cooper's Glue Factory v. McMahon, 15 Abb. Cas. (N. Y.) 314. *Compare* Manistique Lumber Co. v. Wetter, 58 Mich. 625.

5. Western Union Tel. Co. v. Mayer,

prohibition extends to renewals[1] thereof, as well as to the original creation.[2] Where the right to alter and amend charters is reserved, privileges granted may be abridged or destroyed,[3] and where the exemption forms no part of the contract it is subject to repeal.[4]

(m) *What Exemption Includes and Excludes.*—A valid exemption of corporate property from taxation has been held to include: Gross receipts and capital stock,[5] and the latter is exempted in the hands of shareholders;[6] capital stock of a cemetery company,[7] as well as its real estate held for burial purposes;[8] and the exemp-

Wilmington & W. R. Co. *v.* Reid, 13 Wall. (U. S.) 264; Raleigh & G. R. Co. *v.* Reid, 13 Wall. (U. S.) 269; Dodge *v.* Woolsey, 18 How. (U. S.) 331; Jefferson Branch Bank *v.* Skelly, 1 Black (N. S.), 436, Northwestern University *v.* People, 99 U. S. 309; St. Anna's Asylum *v.* New Orleans, 105 U. S. 362; Worth *v.* Petersburg R. Co., 89 N. Car. 301; Worth *v.* Seaboard, etc., R. Co., 89 N. Car. 310; Oliver *v.* Memphis, etc., R. Co., 30 Ark. 128, Neustadt *v.* Illinois Central, etc., R. Co., 31 Ill. 484; State *v.* Commissioners, 37 N. J. Law, 240.

The following terms in a charter, constituting the contract, that "this tax shall be in lieu and satisfaction of all other taxation or imposition whatsoever, by or under the authority of this State, or any law thereof," exclude the right of the State to revoke it at pleasure. New Jersey *v.* Yard, 95 U. S. 104.

1. Trask *v.* Maguire, 18 Wall. (U. S.) 391; Boody *v.* Watson, 63 N. H. 320.

2. Louisville & N. R. Co. *v.* Palmes, 109 U. S. 244.

Under *Louisiana* Constitution of 1868, property cannot be exempted from taxation unless actually used for church, school, or charitable purposes. In the charter of 1877 of the N. O. Water Works Co. the exemption from taxation is unconstitutional; it was only part of the consideration of the obligation to supply free water. In such case the city should be decreed to pay for its water to the value of the taxes recovered. New Orleans *v.* New Orleans Water Works Co., 36 La. Ann. 432.

3. A clause in the charter of a city railroad company that the company shall pay such license for each car run as is paid by other passenger railway companies in the city, which was thirty dollars, is not a contract that the license charged for such cars should never exceed the annual sum of thirty dollars, and is not protected from impairment by the United States constitution. A subsequent act of the legislature which requires such companies to pay the annual license of fifty dollars for each car is not unconstitutional as violating a contract. Where power to alter, revoke, or annul any charter of incorporation was vested in the legislature by the constitution of the State, before the defendant company was incorporated, the legislature may increase such license fee. Union Pass. R. Co. *v.* Philadelphia, 101 U S. 528. See also Ohio Life, etc., Co. *v.* De Bolt, 16 How. (U. S.) 416.

A provision in the amendment of a charter for ascertaining a tax by a certain mode is not a contract that no statute shall thereafter provide a different mode. Bailey *v.* Maguire, 22 Wall. (U. S.) 215.

4. St. Louis, etc., R. Co. *v.* Loftin, 30 Ark. 693; Louisville, etc., R. Co. *v.* Commonwealth, 10 Bush (Ky.), 43.

5. Worth *v.* Wilmington & Weldon R. Co., 89 N. Car. 291; s. c., 45 Am. Rep. 679; Worth *v.* Petersburg R. Co., 89 N. Car. 301; New Orleans *v.* Carondelet Canal, etc., Co., 36 La. Ann. 396.

6. Tennessee *v.* Whitworth, 117 U. S. 129.

A law pledging the faith of the State not to impose any further tax or burden upon banks if they would perform certain conditions, was an exemption of more than the franchise, and protected the stockholders from any tax upon them as individuals by reason of their tax. Gordon *v.* Appeal Tax Court, 3 How. (U. S.) 133.

7. Both the real estate used or dedicated to purposes of burial and the stock of a cemetery corporation are exempt from taxation. [Bermudez, C. J., and Manning, J., dissenting.] Metairie Cemetery Assoc. *v.* Assessors, 37 La. Ann. 32.

8. Metairie Cemetery Assoc. *v.* Assessors, 37 La. Ann. 32; Swan Point Cemetery Assoc. *v.* Tripp, 14 R. I. 199.

A statute of *Illinois*, passed in 1855, declares that all the property of the Northwestern University shall be forever tion extends to lands subsequently acquired,[1] church property,[2] road-bed, station buildings, workshops, etc., of a railroad company[3] taxes assessed but not collected,[4] State but not municipal taxes,[5] railroad franchises.[6]

A valid exemption of corporate property from taxation has been held to exclude: All property except such as is necessary for the company's business;[7] land not occupied by a railroad company, but likely to become necessary in future;[8] property of a railroad to be exempted when road was completed, before such completion;[9] house and lot of canal company used as superintendent's residence;[10] gasometers, gas-mains, and pipes of gas company;[11] land of religious corporation intended to be leased;[12] shares of stock in a foreign corporation under certain circumstances;[13] piles of staves;[14] assessments for street improvements;[15] lands of a corporation held as a mere convenience,[16] or for sale;[17] portion of

free from taxation. A statute of 1872 limited this exemption to land and other property in immediate use by the institution. *Held*, that the latter statute impaired the obligation of the contract of exemption found in the statute of 1855. Northwestern University *v.* People, 99 U. S. 309.

1. The charter of a cemetery corporation exempted all its real estate held for cemetery purposes from taxes and assessments. *Held*, that land subsequently acquired was exempt from a sewer assessment, although sewer assessments were not in vogue when the charter was granted. Swan Point Cemetery *v.* Tripp, 14 R. I. 199.

2. Property—e.g., church property—exempt "from all and every county and city tax," is exempt from sewer assessments. Erie *v.* Universalist Church, 105 Pa. St. 278.

3. Northern Pacific R. Co. *v.* Carland, 5 Mont. 146.

4. State *v.* Academy of Science, 13 Mo. App. 213.

5. *In re* Mayor, etc., 11 Johns. (N. Y.) 77; Baptist Church *v.* McAtee, 8 Bush (Ky.), 508; Insurance Co. *v.* New Orleans, 1 Woods (C. C.), 85.

6. Wilmington, etc., R. Co. *v.* Reid, 13 Wall. (U. S.) 264.

7. Where the charter of a corporation provides that it shall pay an annual tax on its corporate stock in lieu of all other taxes, the exemption extends only to the property necessary for the business of the company. Where the purposes for which a corporation may hold property are specified in connection with its exemption from taxation, only property acquired for such purposes is thus exempt. Bank of Commerce *v.* Tennessee, 104 U. S. 493.

8. Ramsey County *v.* Chicago, Milwaukee, etc., R. Co., 33 Minn. 537.

9. Vicksburg, Shreveport, etc., R. Co. *v.* Dennis, 116 U. S. 665.

10. State *v.* Cleaver, 46 N. J. L. 467.

11. Consolidated Gas Co. *v.* Baltimore, 62 Md. 588; s. c., 50 Am. Rep. 237.

12. Gibbons *v.* District of Columbia, 116 U. S. 404.

13. Under a statute which, like the Ohio Corporation, exempts from taxation shares of stock in corporations "the capital stock of which is taxed in the name of the company," shares of stock in a foreign corporation which pays taxes in the State only on that portion of its property therein situated, are not exempt. Sturges *v.* Carter, 114 U. S. 511.

14. Staves collected at various points and waiting to be cut to a uniform length and thickness, it being agreed that they might stand in piles for three months before being shipped, *held*, not exempt from taxation as being *in transitu*. Brown County Comrs. *v.* Standard Oil Co., 103 Ind. 302.

15. Sheehan *v.* Good Samaritan Hospital, 50 Mo. 155. See also Emery *v.* Gas Company, 28 Cal. 345; Bridgeport *v.* New York, etc., R. Co., 36 Conn. 255; Harlem, etc., Church *v.* Mayor, 5 Hun (N. Y.), 442; Brightman *v.* Kerner, 22 Wis. 54.

16. Railroad Co. *v.* Berks Co., 6 Pa. St. 70; Lackawanna Iron Co. *v.* Luzerne Co., 42 Pa. St. 424; People *v.* Cemetery Co., 86 Ill. 336.

17. Illinois, etc., R. Co. *v.* Irwin, 72 Ill. 452; Ordinary, etc., *v.* Central, etc., R. Co., 40 Ga. 646; State *v.* Hancock, 35

·tery company rented to sexton for residence and
ses;[1] railroad lands within the limits of an Indian

·f Exemptions.—Immunity from taxation is a per-
nd cannot be claimed by an assignee, purchaser,
mpany, etc., unless the statute creating the ex-
ly so provides.[2]
ms.—The right to claim exemption from taxation
ong acquiescence in a claim of the right to tax.[4]
supplying water to cities and villages in *Kentucky*
re not exempt from taxation because of benefits
governmental agencies.[5] Other miscellaneous au-
d in the notes.[6]

·bile, etc., R. Co. v.
·27; Richmond, etc.,
ners, 76 N. Car. 212.
, 16 Mo. App. 468.
Co. v. Fisher, 116

h v. Owensboro &
·1 Ky. 572; State v.
no.) 104; Memphis,
Kansas R. Commis-
609; St. Louis, etc.,
3 U. S. 465; Chesa-
v. Miller, 114 U. S.
Whitworth, 117 U. S.
R. Co. v. Berry, 41
Midland R. Co. v.

, an immunity from
ss to a purchaser of
pted as an incident
ay so pass if the law
rchase so provides.
ginia, etc., R. Co. v.
p. 614.
ht, 117 U. S. 648; s.
orp. Cas. 606. In this
is laid down, and the
an exemption from
n any case by long ac-
imposition of taxes,
an acquiescence of
eed a much shorter
nply sufficient for this
a conclusive pre-
der of the privilege.
e lost by non-user in
ven in a less time, if
tive acts of invasion.
e lost in the same
one of the common
a cause of forfeiture.
xemption from taxa-
privilege granted by
an individual, either
rtenant to his free-
hold, is a franchise. Non-user for sixty, or even thirty, years may well be regarded as presumptive proof of its abandonment or surrender."

5. A corporation, organized for supplying a city with water, and most of the stock of which is owned by the city, is not exempt from taxation in *Kentucky*, either expressly or by implication, because of the public benefits that it confers. Louisville Water Co. v. Hamilton, 81 Ky. 517; People v. Forrest, 97 N. Y. 97.

6. A State corporation cannot hold its property exempt from State taxation merely because it is entitled to certain benefits and subject to certain duties under the legislation of Congress, which legislation does not provide for such exemption, or indicate that it is essential to the full performance of its obligations to the government. Thomson v. Union Pac. R. (Thomson v. Pac. R.), 9 Wall. (U. S.) 579.

Where an exemption of the property of a corporation from taxes, by an act of a State legislature, was spontaneous, and no service or duty or other remunerative condition was imposed on the corporation, it belongs to the class of laws denominated *privilegia favorabilia*. It is not a necessary implication that the concession is perpetual, or what was designed to continue during the corporate existence. Such an interpretation is not to be favored, as the power of taxation is necessary to the existence of the State, and must be exerted according to the varying conditions of the commonwealth. It is the nature of such a privilege as the act confers, that it exists *bene placitum*, and may be revoked at the pleasure of the sovereign. An act of the same legislature partially repealing such exemption is not repugnant to the Constitution of

F. Consolidation of Corporations.—1. Definition.—Where the rights, franchises, and effects of two or more corporations are by legal authority and agreement of the parties combined and united into one whole, and committed to a single corporation, the stockholders of which are composed of those (so far as they choose to become such) of the companies thus agreeing, this is in law a consolidation, whether the consolidated company be a new one then created, or one of the original companies continuing in existence with only larger rights, capacities, and property.[1]

2. Reorganization is a term generally used to indicate the formation of an entirely new corporation for the purpose of purchasing the property of another corporation, and superseding it in business without incurring any liability to its creditors.[2] Whether the consolidating companies are extinguished or not depends upon the legislative intent as manifested in the statute under which consolidation is effected.[3]

3. Legislative Authority to Consolidate.—Corporations cannot be consolidated without the express sanction of the State.[4]

1. Meyer *v.* Johnston & Stewart, 64 Ala. 653. The term is analogous to *amalgamation* known to the English law, which has been declared to apply "where two or more companies agree to abandon their respective articles of association and register under new articles as one body." *In re* Bank of Hindustan, Higg's Case, 2 H. & M. 666; Dr. Dougan's Case, 28 L. T N. S. 60. "Two companies," says the vice-chancellor, "may be united either by fusion into a third or by one absorbing the other. The former process seems to correspond most nearly with the popular sense of the word 'amalgamation,' and I believe nobody really knows what amalgamation means."

Where the terms of the union were held not to amount to either amalgamation or consolidation. Powell *v.* N. Mo. R. 42 Mo. 63.

2. Morawetz on Private Corporations (2d Ed.), § 811; Houston & Tex. Cen. R. *v.* Shirley, 54 Tex. 125; Bruffett *et al. v.* Great Western R., 25 Ill. 353; Atkinson *et al. v.* Marietta, etc., R., 15 Ohio St. 21.

Conveyance of the Franchises.—The transfer or conveyance of the franchises of a corporation in pursuance of an act of the legislature amounts to a surrender or abandonment of the charter, and the grant by the legislature of a new charter to the transferees, subject to laws existing at the time of the grant. State of Ohio *v.* Sherman *et al.*, 22 Ohio St. 413.

3. Central R. & Banking Co. *v.* Georgia, 92 U. S. 665; Booe *v.* Junction R. Co., 10 Ind. 93.

Whether consolidation effects a dissolution of the old companies or not, *compare* McMahan *v.* Morrison, 16 Ind. 172; Clearwater *v.* Meredith, 1 Wall. (U.S.) 25; State *v.* Bailey, 16 Ind. 46; Chicago, etc., R. *v.* Moffitt, 75 Ill. 524; Zimmer *v.* State, 30 Ark. 677; Fee *v.* New Orleans, etc., Co., 35 La. Ann. 413; Thompson *v.* Abbott, 61 Mo. 176; Bishop *v.* Brainerd, 28 Conn. 289; Platt *v.* N. Y. & B. R., 26 Conn. 544; Commonwealth *v.* Atlantic, etc., R., 3 Pa. St. 9; Atlanta, etc., R. *v.* State of Georgia, 1 Am. & Eng. R. R. Cas. 399; L. & N. R. *v.* Palmes, 109 U. S. 244; B. & O. R. *v.* Gallahue's Admrs., 12 Gratt. (Va.) 655; Goshorn *et al. v.* Supervisors, 1 W. Va. 308; Ridgway Tp. *v.* Griswold, 1 McCrary (C. C.), 151; Maine Cen. R. *v.* Maine, 96 U. S. 509; s. c., State *v.* Maine Cen. R., 66 Me. 488; Shields *v.* Ohio, 95 U. S. 319. The statutes under which consolidation is effected sometimes expressly provide for the continuance of the constituent companies for certain purposes. Lightner *v.* Railroad, 1 Lowell (C. C.), 338; Whipple *v.* Railroad, 28 Kans. 474.

4. Clearwater *v.* Meredith, 1 Wall. (U. S.) 25; Pearce *v.* Madison, etc., R., 21 How. (U. S.) 442; Aspinwall *v.* Ohio & Miss. R., 20 Ind. 492; Black *v.* Canal Co., 24 N. J Eq. 455; N. Y., etc., Canal Co. *v.* Fulton Bank, 7 Wend. (N. Y.) 412; Charlton *v.* Newcastle, etc., R., 5 Jur. N. S. 1096; Blatchford *v.* Ross, 5 Abb Pr. N. S. (N Y) 434; s. c., 54 Barb. (N. Y.) 42; Church *v.* Financial Corp., Law Rep. 5 Eq. 450.

This sanction may be granted by a general law,[1] by the original charter of the consolidating companies,[2] by a statute passed before consolidation,[3] or by a subsequent ratification of an unauthorized consolidation.[4] The franchises of the consolidated company are measured by the act authorizing the consolidation, whether it describes the enterprise in terms and thus provides a complete constitution, or refers to the charters of the old companies expressly incorporating their provisions, or extends them by implication.[5]

4. Mode of Consolidation.—Where the statute provides for the mode of consolidation, every requirement must be strictly complied with;[6] but such compliance will be presumed in the ab-

Extent of Power.—Power to consolidate does not include power to lease, or enlarge the power to convey lands conferred by the charter. Mills *v.* Central R. Co., 41 N. J. Eq. 5; Archer *et al.* *v.* Terre Haute, etc., R., 102 Ill. 493.

1. The following States provide by their constitutions or by general act for consolidation:

Alabama: Civil Code, vol. 1, chap. 6—Railroads, §§ 1583-85; Insurance Cos., §§ 1541-46; Mining and Mfg. Cos., §§ 1565-69. *Arkansas:* Revised Stat. 1874, Railroads, sec. 4969, p. 866. *California:* Civil Code, § 361; 1 Hittell's Codes and Statutes—Mining Companies, 5361; Land and Building Companies, 5647, sec. 647; Railroads, 5473, sec. 473. *Colorado:* General Statutes (1883), Railroads, 353, p. 211; Corporations in general, 349, p 209. *Connecticut:* General Stat. Revis. of 1875: Insurance Cos., §§ 3-6, p. 307. *Indiana:* Revised Statutes (1881), art. 4, §§ 3965-3979. *Idaho:* Revised Statutes, sec. 2673. *Iowa:* Revised Code (1884), Railroads, sec. 1275, p. 332. *Illinois:* Revised Statutes (1887), § 50, p. 340. *Kansas:* Compiled Laws (1885), Railroads, 5221, § 47, p. 778. *Louisiana:* Const. 1879, art. 246; jurisdiction over interstate consolidating railroads, acts 1875, p. 18; Act Dec. 12, 1874, Business and Manufacturing Companies. *Michigan:* Howell's Statutes (1882), Railroads, §§ 3343-44; Mechanic Arts, §§ 3932-33; Mining Cos., §§ 4043-47, 4056-60, 4100-03, Religious Societies, §§ 4643-44; Churches of Christ, §§ 4692-95; School Districts, § 5041. *Minnesota:* Revised Statutes (1878), §§ 66-68, p. 381; as to railroads, Act March 3, 1881, P. L. 109. *Missouri.* Rev. Stat. (1879), sec. 789; Const. 1875, § 18, art. 411. *Nebraska:* Compiled Statutes (1885), Railroads, §§ 89-91, p. 198. *New Jersey:* Supplement to Revision of N. J. (1877-86), Railroads, § 20, p. 828; Storehouse, Pier, Dock, and Livestock Cos., §§ 71-75, p. 164. *New York:* L 1869, chap. 917; Rev. Stat. N. Y., 7th Ed., vol. 2, p. 1590. *Nevada:* Compiled Laws, 1873, Railroads, vol. 2, p. 301, § 3465. *Ohio:* Rev. Stat. (1884), Title II., ch. 2, secs. 3379-92. *Pennsylvania:* Act 29th April, 1874, § 42, P. L. 106; Act 16th May, 1861; Purd. 1429, State railroads; Act 24th March, 1865; Purd. 11th Ed., 1431. Interstate railroads; Constitution, art. xvii., § 4. *South Carolina:* General Statutes (1882), §§ 1425-32. *Texas:* Revised Stat. (1879), Telegraph Cos., art. 627, p. 104. *West Virginia:* Code (1887), 2d Ed., ch 54, sec. 53, p. 521. *Wisconsin:* Revised Statutes (1878), Improvement of Streams, § 1777, p. 518; Railroads, § 1833, p. 536.

The States of *Maine, Vermont, Massachusetts, Rhode Island, Connecticut, Delaware, Maryland, North Carolina, Virginia, Mississippi, Kentucky, Tennessee,* and *Oregon* have no general statutes authorizing consolidation.

2. Nugent *v.* Supervisors, 19 Wall. (U. S.) 241; Sparrow *v.* Evansville & Crawfordsville R., 7 Ind. 369.

3. Black *v.* Del. & Rar. Canal Co., 24 N. J. Eq. 455; Fisher *v.* Evansville & Crawfordsville R., 7 Ind. 412.

4. Bishop *v.* Brainerd, 28 Conn. 289; McAuley *v.* C. C. & I. C. R. Co., 83 Ill. 352; Mead *v.* N. Y., H. & N. R., 45 Conn. 219. Power given by statute to one railroad to consolidate with another has been held to authorize any other to join with it. In the Matter of Prospect Park, etc., Co., 67 N. Y. 371; Hill *v.* Nisbet, 100 Ind. 341; Mitchell *et al.* *v.* Deeds, 49 Ill. 418. But *compare* State *v.* Consolidation Coal Co., 46 Md. 11.

5. See Morawetz Private Corporations (2d Ed.), § 547.

6. Railroad *v.* Tharp, 28 Mich. 506; Mansfield, etc., R. *v.* Drinker, 30 Mich. 124; Tuttle *v.* Mich. Air Line, 25 Mich. 247; Rodgers *v.* Wells, 44 Mich. 411.

sence of evidence to the contrary, and cannot be inquired into collaterally.[1] If the statute only confers the naked power, the companies may by agreement fix the terms.[2] But no consolidation can take place without some action fully authorizing the same.[3]

5. Assent of Stockholders.—The consent of all the stockholders is necessary to a consolidation,[4] even when sanctioned by statute,[5] unless the same is contemplated in the original contract of subscription.[6] But the reservation by the State of the right to

1. Swartwout v. Railroad, 24 Mich. 389; Pittsburgh, etc., R. v. Rothschild, 18 Am. & Eng. R. R. Cas. 52; Lewis v. City of Clarendon, 6 Rep. 609.

2. Dimpfel v. Ohio, etc., R., 8 Rep. 641 (U. S. C. C. Illinois).

3. Mason v. Finch *et al.*, 28 Mich. 282.

4. Mowry v. Ind. & Cin. R., 4 Biss. 85; Pearce v. Madison, etc., R., 21 How. 441; Tuttle v. Mich. Air Line, 25 Mich. 247. In Zabriskie v. Hackensack & N. Y. R. Co., 3 C. E. Greene (N. J.), 183, Chancellor Zabriskie says: "It is also settled upon the principles of the common law in this State, and most of the States of the Union, that when a number of persons associate themselves as partners for a business and time specified in the agreement between them, or become members of a corporation for definite purposes and objects specified in their charter, which in such case is their contract and for a time settled by it, the objects and business of the partnership or corporation cannot be changed or abandoned or sold out within the time specified without the consent of all the partners or corporators: one partner or corporator, however small his interest, can prevent it. This rule is founded on principle—the great principle of protecting every man in his property by contracts entered into."

The act being *ultra vires* requires unanimous consent. Dr. Dougan's Case, 28 L. T. N. S. 60; Troy & Rutland R. v. Kerr, 17 Barb. (N. Y.) 581; New Orleans R. v. Harris, 27 Miss. 517. *Compare* Sprague v. Illinois Riv. R., 19 Ill. 177.

The majority have no power to make a single dissenting stockholder a member of the new company. Lanman v. Lebanon Valley R., 30 Pa. St. 42. But *compare* Treadwell v. Salisbury Mfg. Co., 7 Gray (Mass.), 393; Hodges v. New England Screw Co., 1 R. I. 347.

Implied Assent.—As to what amounts to such consent as will bind the stockholder by estoppel, see United Ports Co., etc., 41 L. J. Ch. 157; Boston, etc., R. v. N. Y., etc., R., 13 R. I. 264.

But assent cannot be implied to any change outside the scope of the contract. Hamilton Mutual Ins. Co. v. Hobart, 2 Gray (Mass.), 543; Mason v. Finch, 28 Mich. 286. See also Plank Road v. Arndt, 31 Pa. St. 317; Bank v. Charlotte, 85 N. Car. 453; Gardner v. Ins. Co., 33 N. Y. 421.

5. The legislature cannot, as a rule, by subsequent amendment of the charter authorize a consolidation by a majority vote. Kean v. Johnston, 9 N. J. Eq. 401; Boston, etc., R. v. N. Y., etc., R., 13 R. I. 268; Stevens v. Rutland, etc., R., 29 Vt. 545; Sparrow v. Evansville, etc., R., 7 Ind. 369. *Compare* Fee v. Gas Co., 35 La. Ann. 413.

Immaterial Changes.—It has been held, however, that where the legislative changes in the charter consist only of an increase of the corporate powers, or of a different organization of the corporate body, leaving it with power to execute substantially the original object of its creation, the dissenting stockholder is without remedy. Pacific R. v. Hughes, 22 Mo. 300; Marsh v. R. Co., 43 N. H. 526.

Eminent Domain.—Where the corporation has duties to perform to the public, the hindrance of a dissenting stockholder may be removed by the exercise of the right of eminent domain. See Green's Brice's Ultra Vires, 2d Am. Ed. p. 634, note; Field on Corporations, § 430; Black v. Del., etc., Canal Co., 9 C. E. Greene (N. J.), 455.

6. A clause in the charter providing that the company may be consolidated enters into the fundamental contract between the stockholders, and in such case consolidation can be effected by the majority. Sparrow v. Evansville, etc., R., 7 Ind. 369. See also Hanna v. Cincinnati, etc., R., 20 Ind. 30; Nugent v. Supervisors, 19 Wall. (U. S.) 25; Cork & Youghal R. v. Patterson, 37 Eng. L. & Eq. 398; Bish v. Johnson, 21 Ind. 299; Atchison, etc., R. v. Phillips Co., 25 Kans. 261; Sprague v. Railroad, 19 Ill. 174.

7. Status of Consolidated Company.—(*a*) *Rights, Privileges, Franchises and Property.*—Where two or more corporations are consolidated into one by agreement under legislative sanction, the new corporation becomes entitled to the rights, privileges, property, and franchises of the consolidating companies unless expressly restricted,[1] and the property of each is held subject to the same privileges and burdens as originally attached thereto.[2] When the effect of such consolidation is to dissolve the consolidating companies, thereby incapacitating them from the performance of the duties accompanying any exemption provided by their charters, they will be presumed to have abandoned such exemption.[3] Where the old companies are dissolved, the law in force at the time of consolidation governs and controls in determining the corporate rights and franchises of the new company,[4] and the liability of its stockholders.[5]

(*b*) *Liabilities and Duties.*—The consolidated company assumes

Ohio Canal Co. *v.* Webb, 9 Ohio St. 136; Barret *v.* Alton, etc., R., 13 Ill. 504; Sprague *v.* Ill Riv. R., 19 Ill. 174; Pac. R. *v.* Hughes, 22 Mo. 300; Railroad *v.* Dudley, 14 N. Y. 336.

Subscribers to Bonds.—A subscriber to the bonds of a company is released from liability on his subscription by a consolidation outside the scope of the original undertaking. New Jersey R *v.* Strait, 35 N. J. L. 322; Illinois, etc., R. *v.* Cook, 29 Ill. 237.

1. P., W. & B. R. *v.* Maryland, 10 How. (U. S.) 376; Nugent *v.* Supervisors, 19 Wall. (U. S.) 249; Green Co. *v.* Conness, 109 U. S. 104; Tomlinson *v.* Branch, 15 Wall. (U. S.) 460; Railroad *v.* Maine, 96 U. S. 499; Robertson *et al. v.* City of Rockford, 21 Ill. 451; Paine *et al v.* Lake Erie, etc., R., 31 Ind. 349, affirming the right of the consolidated company to compromise and settle a claim against one of the original companies and sustain an action to enforce a settlement. Branch *v.* City of Charleston, 92 U. S. 677; Lightner *v.* B. & A. R., 1 Lowell (C. C.), 338; Rome, etc., R. *v.* Ontario, etc., R., 16 Hun (N. Y.), 445; Hubbard *v.* Chappel, 14 Ind. 601; Miller *et al. v.* Lancaster, 5 Coldw. (Tenn.) 515. In Zanoier *v.* State, 30 Ark. 679, the original company was empowered by its charter "to make joint stock with any other railroad." A new constitution was afterwards adopted by the State, prohibiting the general assembly from granting special privileges or immunities. The company subsequently consolidated with another. *Held*, that the new company succeeded to the right of immunity granted the officers and servants of the old company by its charter from working on public roads.

Rights, Privileges, and Property.—The act authorizing consolidation usually provides that the new company shall possess the rights, privileges, and property of the consolidating companies. See Houston & Tex. Cen. R. *v.* Shirley, 54 Tex. 125. Under such grant passes the franchise to take land to build the road,—Railroad *v.* Blake, 9 Rich. 233,—and to mortgage the road,—Mead *v.* Railroad, 45 Conn. 199,—and to charge a fixed rate for transportation,—Fisher *v.* Railroad, 46 N. Y. 644. See *infra*, par. 12, TAXATION.

Right to *municipal subscriptions* to the capital stock is a privilege which passes to the consolidated company. County of Scotland *v.* Thomas, 94 U. S. 682, distinguishing Harshman *v.* Bates Co., 93 U. S. 569; County of Henry *v.* Nicolay, 95 U. S. 619; Thompson *v.* Abbott *et al.*, 61 Mo. 177. But see State *v.* Garonette, 67 Mo. 445; State *v.* Dallas, 72 Mo. 329. When the county subscribes to the stock of the consolidated company and issues bonds in payment therefor, it is estopped in an action on the bond from showing that the corporation so formed is not a corporation *de jure*. Lewis *v.* City of Clarendon, 6 Rep. 609. *Compare* Bank *v.* Charlotte, 85 N. Car. 433.

2. Delaware Tax Cases, 22 Wall. 206, P., W. & B. R. *v.* Maryland, 10 How. (U. S.) 376; Central R. *v.* Georgia, 92 U. S. 665; State *v.* Commrs. of R. R. Taxation, 3 N. J. L. 240; Chesapeake & Ohio R. *v.* Virginia, 94 U. S. 718.

3. Railroad *v.* Maine, 96 U. S. 499.

4. Shields *v.* Ohio, 95 U. S. 319.

5. Tibbals *v.* Libby, 87 Ill. 142.

the liabilities of the former companies on their contracts,[1] as well as for torts;[2] but creditors cannot be compelled to accept in the first instance the general liability of the new company in substitution of the old,[3] though not entitled to have the assets distributed as in case of a simple dissolution.[4] The duties of the old companies attach to the new company in respect to each as before consolidation.[5]

1. Columbus R. *v.* Powell, 40 Ind. 40; Chicago, etc., R. *v.* Moffitt, 75 Ill. 524; Miss. R. *v.* Chicago, etc., R., 58 Miss. 846; Sappington *et al.* *v.* Little Rock R., 37 Ark. 23; Boardman *et al.* *v.* Lake Shore R., 84 N. Y. 157; Montgomery, etc., R *v.* Boring, 51 Ga. 582; Railroad *v.* Fryer, 56 Tex. 600; Eaton, etc., R. *v.* Hunt, 20 Ind. 463; Mt. Pleasant *v.* Beckwith, 100 U. S. 514. In Railroad *v.* Jones, 29 Ind. 465, the court says: "By the consolidation both the old companies ceased to exist separately. The two corporations became merged in one. We cannot imagine how the Indianapolis & Cincinnati R. could afterwards be sued. Upon whom would process be served? It ceased to have any officers or agents. It ceased to be a separate legal entity. Instead of two, there was now but one corporation, made up of the mingled elements of the two pre-existing companies, so combined and merged that neither could be separately identified or brought into court. But what are the rights of creditors and persons upon whom torts have been committed by the vanished corporation? Must lawful claims be lost? That result cannot follow. Giving it the best consideration of which we are capable under the circumstances, we have reached the conclusion that for the purpose of assuming the liabilities of the constituent corporations the consolidated company should be deemed to be merely the same as each of its constituents, their existence continued in it under the new form and name, their liabilities still existing as before and capable of enforcement against the new company in the same way as if no change had occurred in its organization or name."

Limitation of Liability.—It has been held in many cases that the liability is limited to the assets of the debtor company joining in the consolidation, unless expressly assumed by the consolidating company or imposed by the consolidating statute. Shaw *v.* Railroad, 16 Gray (Mass.), 407; Prouty *v.* Railroad, 52 N. Y. 363; Railroad *v.* Skidmore, 69 Ill. 566; Railroad *v.* Harkin, 40 Ga. 709; Tyson *v.* Railroad, 13 Am. & Eng. R. R. Cas. 134. See Morawetz Private Corporations (2d Ed.), § 942.

Bona Fide Purchasers.—The liability does not attach to a *bona fide* purchaser of the franchises of a corporation by another for a valuable consideration. Powell *v.* Nor. Miss R., 42 Mo. 163.

Reorganization.—Nor does it attach to a reorganization by the purchaser on a foreclosure. Houston & Tex. Cen. R. *v.* Shirley, 54 Tex. 125; Smith *v.* Chicago, etc., R., 18 Wis. 1.

Survival of Old Companies.—The consolidating companies are sometimes continued in existence for the purpose of adjusting their liabilities, and provisions as to the method of enforcing it are usually inserted in the consolidating statutes. See Bruffett *v.* Railroad, 25 Ill. 353; Selma, etc., R. *v.* Harbin, 40 Ga. 706; Whipple *v.* Railroad, 28 Kan. 474. But the new company may be sued notwithstanding. Warren *v.* Railroad, 49 Ala. 582.

2. Coggin *v.* Central R., etc., 62 Ga. 685.

3. Railroad *v.* Moffitt, 75 Ill. 624. "The question," says the court, "is not whether the statute compels the creditor to accept the defendant corporation as a new debtor against his will, but whether it empowers the creditor or person injured to resort if he chooses in the first instance to the corporation which by the terms of the statute is made liable to him." See also New Bedford R *v.* Old Colony R., 120 Mass. 397; Warren *v.* Railroad, 49 Ala. 582; Bruffett *v.* Railroad, 25 Ill. 383; Smith *v.* Chesapeake & Ohio Canal Co., 14 Peters (U. S.), 45.

4. Wabash R. *v.* Ham, 114 U. S. 587. Nor have they any lien in any specific property of the consolidated company while it continues its business.

5. Gould *v* Langdon *et al.*, 43 Pa. St. 365; Peoria, etc., R. *v.* Mining Co., 68 Ill. 489; Railroad *v.* Smith, 75 Ill. 497; Pullman, etc., Co. *v.* Mo. Pac. R., 115 U. S. 587.

Restriction as to Rates.—Where a railroad of one company is purchased by another in pursuance of statutory authority, in the absence of statutory provision

8. Liens.—The lien of a mortgage on the property of a railroad company remains unaffected by consolidation,[1] and covers all acquisitions of the consolidated company which issue from and become part of the estate to which the mortgage applied.[2] Mortgages of the consolidated company have priority over unsecured creditors of the original companies.[3]

9. Interstate Consolidation.—Several States may co-operate in authorizing the consolidation of corporations chartered by each respectively.[4] The consolidated company in such case is viewed in each State as a distinct corporation,[5] with all the privileges and limitations by the laws of that State conferred on the old company.[6] One State may make a corporation of another State as there organized and conducted a corporation of its own as to any property within its territorial jurisdiction;[7] or it may authorize a

to the contrary the road passes to the purchaser subject to the same restrictions and limitations as to rates chargeable for transportation as attached to it in the hands of the vendor. Campbell *v.* Railroad, 23 Ohio St. 168.

Agreements for Sale.—The consolidated company is affected with notice of any agreements for sale effected by the old companies. McAlpine *v.* Union Pac. R., 23 Fed. Rep. 168.

As to *consequential damages*, see Northern Cen. R. *v.* Holland, 20 Weekly Notes of Cases (Pa.), 428.

1. Eaton, etc., R. *v.* Hunt *et al.*, 20 Ind. 457; Miss. Val. R. Co. *v.* Chicago, etc., R., 58 Miss. 846; Railroad *v.* Trust Co., 49 Ill. 331; The Key City, 14 Wall. 654.

2. Hamlin *et al.* *v.* Jerrard, 72 Mo. 62; Railroad *v.* Georgia, 92 U. S. 665.

3. Wabash R. *v.* Ham, 114 U. S. 587. See Blair *v.* St. Louis, etc., R., 24 Fed. Rep. 148.

4. Wilmer *v.* Atlanta, etc., R., 2 Woods (C.C.), 417; Railroad *v.* Maryland, 10 How. 393; Bishop *v.* Brainerd, 28 Conn. 289, Peck *v.* Chicago, etc., R., 94 U. S. 164; *In re* Sage, 70 N. Y. 220; Miller *v.* Dows, 94 U. S. 444; Richardson *v.* Railroad, 44 Vt. 613; Tomlinson *v.* Branch, 15 Wall. (U. S.) 460; State *v.* Railroad, 96 U. S. 499; Railroad *v.* Weber, 96 Ill. 443; Mead *et al.* *v.* Railroad, 45 Conn. 199. Such legislation is not repugnant to the provisions of the Federal Constitution, art. 1, § 8, sub. 3, conferring on Congress power to regulate commerce, in the absence of legislation by Congress. Boardman *v.* Railroad, 84 N. Y. 157.

5. Railroad *v.* Trust Co., 49 Ill. 331; Railroad *v.* Wheeler, 1 Black (U. S.) 297; Bridge Co. *v.* Adams County, 88 Ill. 615; Farnum *v.* Canal Co., 1 Sumn. (Mass.) 47; Burgher *v.* Co., 20 Am. & Eng. R. R. Cas. 608; Allegheny Co. *v.* Railroad, 51 Pa. St. 228; Delaware Tax Case, 18 Wall. (U. S.) 206; State *et al.* *v.* Metz, 32 N. J. L. 199. Graham *v.* Railroad, 14 Fed. Rep. 757. Maryland *v.* Railroad, 18 Md. 193; Railroad *v.* Railroad, 6 Biss. (C. C.) 219; Sprague *v.* Railroad, 5 R. I. 233. And is a citizen within the purview of its legislative enactments. Sage *v.* Railroad, 70 N. Y. 220.

6. Cooper *et al.* *v.* Corbin *et al.*, 105 Ill. 224.

7. B. & O. R. *v.* Gallahue's Admrs., 12 Gratt. (Va.) 655; Goshorn *v.* Supervisors, 1 W. Va. 308; McGregor *v.* Erie Co., 35 N. J. L. 118; Railroad *v.* Vance, 96 U. S. 450; Commonwealth, etc., *v.* Railroad, 58 Pa. St. 26.

Domicile.—In such case it has a legal domicile in both States, and may transact its corporate business and hold its meetings in either. Graham *et al.* *v.* Railroad, 118 U. S. 161; Bridge Co. *v.* Mager, 31 Ohio St. 318. "The only possible status," says the court in the latter case, "of a company acting under a charter from two States, is that it is an association incorporated in and by each of the States, and when acting as a corporation in either, it acts under the authority of the charter of the State in which it is then acting, and that only, the legislature of the other State having no operation beyond the territorial limit." See also Peik *v.* Railroad, 94 U. S. 164; Railroad *v.* Rothschild, 26 Am. & Eng. R. R. Cas. 50.

Control.—Its charter may be amended in one State so as to control its action and property there, though the amendment may be contrary to some statutory or constitutional provision of the other State.

The constitutional right of a citizen of one State to sue a corporation of another State in the Federal court of that other State, is not destroyed by a consolidation or joint incorporation by virtue of which the corporation is a citizen of the plaintiff's State as well.[1] But the Federal court of the plaintiff's State cannot assume jurisdiction by reason of the fact that the defendant corporation is likewise a citizen of another State.[2] Where a corporation of one State is merged by a transfer of its franchise and property into a corporation of another State, the latter becomes the consolidated company, and its citizenship is to be considered in determining the jurisdiction of the Federal court.[3] The jurisdiction of the Federal court may be exercised over the entire line of the consolidated company, whether within or without the State.[4]

(*b*) *State Courts.*—Two railroad corporations chartered under the laws of different States, and afterward consolidated under the laws of both, are separate in so far that each State is left the control over the charter it grants, and identical in so far that the corporations may represent each other in suits by or against either of them.[5] A mortgage made by a corporation created by different States on property situated in both is treated as one mortgage.[6] A decree of foreclosure is valid though part of the premises covered by it is in a sister State; and though the judgment cannot be enforced as to such property, yet where the trustee under the mortgage resides in the jurisdiction, the court may require him to execute a conveyance of the same to the purchaser in order that the whole security may be made effective.[7]

appears to be this: that the fact that there are railroad corporations created by different States which have been consolidated under the laws of those States, and the railroad operated by virtue of that consolidation as one entire line of road, will not prevent the corporation from being sued in one of these States as a corporation created by the laws of that State, provided the plaintiff is a citizen of a State other than that of the State which creates the corporation. The only law that operates upon it is the law of its own State. If the corporation is a defendant, that is expressly decided by the court in the two cases last cited. Now if that is so as to the defendant, why is there any difference where the plaintiff as a corporation brings the suit?"

1. Marshall *v.* B. & O. R., 16 How. (U. S.) 314; City of Wheeling *v.* Mayor, etc., 1 Hughes (C. C.), 90; Railroad *v.* Whitten, 13 Wall. (U. S.) 270.

The question whether the act of the legislature creates a new corporation or only enlarges the sphere of operations of a company already existing under the laws of another State, is of importance in this connection. Railroad *v.* Harris, 12 Wall. (U. S.) 82; Railroad *v.* Railroad, 10 Fed. Rep. 497; Callahan *v.* Railroad, 11 Fed. Rep. 536; Dennistoun *v.* Railroad, 1 Hilt. (N. Y.) 62.

2. Burgher *v.* Grand Rapids, etc., R., 20 Am. & Eng. R. R. Cas. 607; Uphoff *v.* Chicago, etc., R., 5 Fed. Rep. 545; Henen *v.* B. & O. R., 17 W. Va. 881; B. & O. R. *v.* P., W. & B. R., 17 W. Va. 812.

3. Antelope, etc., Co. *v.* Railroad, 4 McCrary (C. C.), 46; Railroad *v.* Railroad, 10 Fed. Rep. 497.

4. Wilmer *v.* Atlanta & Rich. Air Line, 2 Woods (C. C.), 418; Ellis *v.* Boston, etc., R., 107 Mass. 1; Blackburn *v.* Railroad, 2 Flipp. (C. C.) 525. As to method of sale, see Gibert *v.* Washington City, etc., Co., 1 Am. & Eng. R. R. Cas. 473.

5. Nashua, etc., R. *v.* Boston, etc., R., 16 Am. & Eng. R. R. Cas. 488; Horn *v.* Boston & M. R., 12 Am. & Eng. R. R. Cas. 287. See Maryland *v.* Railroad Co., 18 Md. 193.

6. Wood *v.* Goodwin, 49 Me. 260.

7. Union Trust Co. *v.* Rochester, etc., R., 24 Am. & Eng. R. R. Cas. 61; Muller *v.* Dows, 94 U. S. 450. *Compare* Pittsburg

ircumstances.[1] This right includes those of com-
,[2] refe[rring] them to arbitrators,[3] confessing judging ap[peal] bonds, and performing all other acts

ght to Sue.—*Libel.*—
nuoubled law that a
aintain an action for
authorities are com-
In Trenton Mut. F.
Perrine, 23 N. J. L.
s stated to be a mat-
sion. Green, C. J.,
revailing sentiment of
against it, but found
on for the objection.
of a corporation's
bility, soundness, and
way of its trade or
ding: "If, then, the
poration and that of
tial to its prosperity;
uniary loss, and even
on of its pecuniary
and malicious repre-
ould it not be entitled
ss?" Following the
unquet, J., in Hope
Beaumont, 10 Bing.
that unincorporated
: for a libel), it was
n may be maintained
aggregate for words
usly spoken or written
the way of its trade
the property and con-
ny, or of the officers,
ers of the company,
h special damage is
orporation;" and fur-
was on the company,
ers as individuals, so
ne could have a right
59 a similar decision
land in Met. Saloon
ns, 4 H. & N, 87, and
en followed in Hahne-
v. Beebe, 48 Ill. 87;
Bk. v. Thompson, 23
153; Knickerbocker L.
. 42 How. Pr. (N. Y.)
r, 34 N. Y. Super. Ct.

...als against corpora-
v. Tracy, 2 Mo. App.

...inst a nuisance. Cent.
4 Gray (Mass.), 474.
rporate name. Holmes
o., 37 Conn. 278; New-
R. Co., Deady (U. S.

Real and possessory

actions. 1 Kyd. 185; S. P. G. v. Wheeler, 2 Gall. (U. S. C. C.) 105.

For use and occupation. Stafford v. Till, 4 Bing. 54.

For purchase-money of land sold, even though the corporation may have had no authority to buy the land sold by it. Rutland R. Co. v. Proctor, 29 Vt. 93.

For malicious prosecution of a civil suit. South Royalton Bk. v. Suffolk Bk., 27 Vt. 505.

For salvage. The Comanche, 8 Wall, (U. S.) 448; The Blackwall, 10 Wall, (U. S.) 1.

For injuries to property in its possession; in which case the legal capacity of such corporation to hold the property cannot be inquired into. Cole Min. Co. v. V. & G. H. Water Co., 1 Saw. (U. S. C. C.) 470.

As petitioning creditor, for a commission in bankruptcy. *Ex parte* Bk. of Eng., 1 Swanst. 10; *Ex parte* Bk. of Ireland, 1 Mol. Ch. 261.

By attachment. Trenton Bkg. Co. v. Haverstick, 6 Hals. (N. J.) 171. And in such case the officers may give an attachment bond without any special statutory authority. Bk. of Augusta v. Conrey, 28 Miss. 667.

On a contract to pay money to the directors of the corporation. Thompson v. M. & M. G. R. Co, 98 Ind. 449.

Where a lease of corporate property provided that the dividends should be paid directly to the stockholders by the lessee, the corporation, representing their interests, is the proper party to enforce their claim. Pac. R. Co. v. Atl. & Pac. R. Co., 20 Fed. Rep. 277.

But a corporation cannot sue on a contract of the promoters, unless it became a party thereto after incorporation. Penn Match Co. v. Hapgood, 141 Mass. 145; and see *supra*, ORGANIZATION OF CORPORATIONS, *Liability for Acts of the Promoters.*

For remedies against its officers, see OFFICERS PRIVATE CORPORATIONS.

A corporation may prosecute criminally in certain cases, e.g. for embezzlement and libel. Whart. Crim. Law, §§ 1035, 1602.

2. Morawetz Corp. (2d Ed.) § 430.

3. Ang. & A. Corp. § 370; Alex. Canal Co. v. Swann, 5 How. (U. S.) 83; Sawyer v. Winn. Mill Co., 26 Me. 122; Day v. Essex Co. Bk., 13 Vt. 97.

4. Morawetz Corp. (2d Ed.) § 430. A

required of litigants.[1] A corporation may also properly support a suit out of the corporate funds, though not itself a party to the record, if it has an interest in the result; but such litigation must be for its benefit, and for an authorized purpose.[2] The dissolution of a corporation causes the abatement of all suits then pending by or against it.[3]

(*a*) *Jurisdiction of Federal Courts.*—The United States courts regard a corporation, for the purposes of their jurisdiction, as a citizen of the State by which it is chartered, irrespective of the citizenship of its members.[4] They also have jurisdiction over all

corporation may execute a power of attorney to confess judgment, waiving service, even though its charter provide a particular form of service. Millard *v.* St. F. X. Fem. Acad., 8 Ill. App. 341.

But a judgment, confessed by the promoters as such, does not affect the corporate property. Davidson *v.* Alexander, 84 N. Car. 621.

1. Morawetz Corp. (2d Ed.) § 430; Collins *v.* Hammock, 59 Ala. 448.

2. Morawetz Corp. (2d Ed.) § 430; Harbison *v.* First Pres. Soc., 46 Conn. 529; Baker *v.* Windham, 13 Me. 74; Babbitt *v.* Savoy, 3 Cush. (Mass.) 530; Butler *v.* Milwaukee, 15 Wis. 493.

3. Morawetz Corp. (2d Ed.) § 1031; Taylor Corp. § 435; Terry *v.* Merchants' Bk., 66 Ga. 177; Merrill *v.* Suffolk Bk., 31 Me. 57; Thornton *v.* M. F. R. Co., 123 Mass. 32; Bk. of Miss. *v.* Wrenn, 3 S. & M. (Miss.) 791; May *v.* State Bk., 2 Rob. (Va.) 56; Nat. Bk. *v.* Colby, 21 Wall. (U. S.) 609.

Where no issue had been raised as to the fact of corporate existence, but the corporation plaintiff introduced evidence of the articles of incorporation, and it appeared from them that the corporation had expired pending the suit, judgment on a verdict for the plaintiff was withheld. Eagle Chair Co. *v.* Kelsey, 23 Kan. 632.

An attachment against corporate property is dissolved by dissolution of the corporation. Paschall *v.* Whitsett, 11 Ala. 472; Bowker *v.* Hill, 60 Me. 172; F. & M. Bk. *v.* Little, 8 W. & S. (Pa.) 207. The contrary was held in Lindell *v.* Benton, 6 Mo 361. See, *infra*, DISSOLUTION OF CORPORATIONS.

4. **Corporate Citizenship.**—This is important as regards the right to sue and be sued in the Federal courts. In Strawbridge *v.* Curtiss, 3 Cr. (U. S.) 267 it was decided that where there were joint plaintiffs and joint defendants, each of the plaintiffs must be capable of suing each of the defendants in the Federal courts in order to support the jurisdiction. In U. S. Bk. *v.* Deveaux, 5 Cr. (U. S.) 61, the petition averred that the petitioners, "the president, directors, and company" of the bank, were citizens of Pennsylvania, and the defendants citizens of Georgia. The plea in abatement, that the petitioners "aver themselves to be a body politic and corporate, and that in that capacity these defendants say they cannot sue or be sued . . . in this . . . court," was sustained in the circuit court but overruled in the supreme court. Marshall, C. J., stated that while "no right is conferred on the bank by the act of incorporation to sue in the Federal courts," and a corporation "cannot be an alien or a citizen," yet that "where the members of a corporation are aliens, or citizens of a different State from the opposite party," the parties "come within the spirit and terms of the jurisdiction conferred by the constitution on the national tribunals." These two cases being applied to the facts before the court in Com. Bk. of Vicksburg *v.* Slocomb, 14 Pet. (U. S.) 60, it was held that *all* the members of a corporation must be citizens of different States from *any* of the opposite party. With the immense growth of corporations, the hardship of this rule became apparent; and in Louisville R. Co. *v.* Letson, 2 How. (U. S.) 497, 555, it was held that "a corporation created by a State to perform its functions under the authority of that State, and only suable there, though it may have members out of the State, seems to us to be a person, though an artificial one, inhabiting and belonging to that State and therefore entitled, for the purpose of suing and being sued, to be deemed a citizen of that State," and also that (p. 554) "a suit brought by a citizen of one State against a corporation by its corporate name in the State of its locality, by which it was created, and where its business is done, . . . is a suit, so far as jurisdiction is concerned,

against corporations chartered by Congress[1] (except regarding them as citizens of the States in which formed.

Liability to Suit.—This correlative liability was stated [illegible]. It includes all suits based on contract,[3] as

[illegible] the State where the
a citizen of another
was again con-
decision affirmed in
R. R. Co., 16 How.
Bronbridge Co.
(U. S.) 232; Rail-
13 Wall. (U. S.)
v. Brown, 94 U. S. 444.
it was expressly held
could not itself be a
in the sense in which
is used in the Federal
the purport of the
for jurisdictional
were conclus-
o be citizens of the State
This case' would
the main course of
of Daniel, J., in P.
14 How. (U. S.)
R. Co. v. Quigley,
based on a strict
"citizen" in the

ly, supposed that U. S.
x, 5 Cranch (U. S.). 61,
in Louisville R. Co. v.
(U. S.) 497, and so it
hat Wayne, J., in the
ghts, but, as a MS. note
n. Horace Binney, the
in U. S. Bank v. De-
hows; this is a mistake.
of U. S. Bank v. De-
ly that if the plaintiffs
the record as citizens of
nd the fact was so or was
murrer, the circuit court
of a suit in Georgia
st a citizen of Georgia.
no doubt of this. What
urt have decided since is
so, described or not, a
Pennsylvania may sue a
gia in the circuit court.
ch hold such description
be necessary have cer-
ruled, not U. S. Bank v.
also Pomeroy v. N. Y.,
Blatch. (C. C.) 702; Atkins
Blatch. (C. C.) 555; Minot
R. Co., 2 Abb. (C. C.)
Co. v. Detroit, etc., Co.,
U. S. 563.

Where a corporation gave a note to a citizen of the same State, and afterwards, in consideration of forbearance, by indorsement made it payable with higher interest to bearer, a *bona fide* holder, being a citizen of another State, was allowed to sue on it in the U. S. courts. Mfg. Co. v. Bradley, 105 U. S. 175.

If, however, the same parties are incorporated under the same name and for the same purposes in more than one State, they form so many distinct corporations, and cannot be joined as one and the same plaintiff incorporated in several States, and in that character sue in the Federal courts a citizen of any of the States in which they are incorporated. O. & M. R. Co. v. Wheeler, 1 Black (U. S.), 286.

By filing an answer, a corporation waives its right to object that it is not sued in the district of the State of its creation, even though the answer reserves the question of jurisdiction, and there is a demurrer to the jurisdiction and for want of equity. The facts showing want of jurisdiction should be set up in a plea in abatement. Blackburn v. S. M., etc., R. Co., 2 Flip. (C. C.) 525.

1. Morawetz, § 985; Osborn v. Bk. of U. S., 9 Wheat. (U. S.) 825; Pac. R. Removal Cases, 115 U. S. 1.

2. **National Banks.**—Under the National Banking Act of 1864, the circuit courts had jurisdiction of all suits brought by or against any national bank established in the district for which the court was held. Kennedy v. Gibson, 8 Wall. (U. S.) 498, 506; Wilson Co. v. Nat. Bk., 103 U. S. 770; Third Nat. Bk. v. Harrison, 8 Fed. R. 721. But this provision was held to apply only to transitory actions, not local actions or proceedings *in rem*. Casey v. Adams, 102 U. S. 66.

This exclusive jurisdiction was taken away by the act of July 12, 1882, c. 290, § 4, under which such banks are now subject to the jurisdiction of the State courts. Union Nat. Bk. v. Miller, 15 Fed. R. 703.

3. See *supra*, POWERS AND LIABILITIES AS TO CONTRACTS.

Assumpsit.—The question of whether a corporation can be sued in *assumpsit* is now one of historical interest only, even

in certain cases,[1] and is irrespective of the fact that the

v. Thiel Mfg. Co., 10 Conn. 384; Lowell v. B & L. R. Co., 23 Pick. (Mass.) 24.

Instances.—*Abuse and menace.* Goddard v. G. T. R. Co., 57 Me. 202. *Assault and battery.* E. C. R. Co. v. Broum, 6 Exch. 314; Jeffersonville R. Co. v. Rogers, 38 Ind 116; Moore v. Fitchb. R. Co., 4 Gray (Mass.), 465; Hewett v. Swift, 3 Allen (Mass.), 420; Holmes v. Wakefield, 12 Allen (Mass.), 580; Ramsden v. B. & A. R. Co., 104 Mass. 117; Brokaw v. N. J., etc., R. Co., 32 N. J. L. 328. *Fraudulent representations.* Nat. Exch. Co. v. Drew, 2 Macq. 103; Etting v. U. S. Bk., 11 Wheat. (U. S.) 59. *Illegal distress.* Smith v. Birm. Gas. Co., 1 A. & E. 526. *Libel.* Whitfield v. S. E. R. Co., E. B. & E. 115; P., W. & B. R. Co. v. Quigley, 21 How. (U. S.) 202. *Malicious prosecution and false imprisonment.* Goff v. G. N. R. Co., 3 E. & E. 672; Boogher v. Life Assn., 75 Mo. 319; Woodward v. St. L. & S. F. R. Co., 85 Mo. 142; Fulton v. Wilson S. M. Co., 9 Phila. (Pa.) 189. *Malicious prosecution of a civil suit.* Godspeed v. East Haddam Bk., 22 Conn. 530. *Trespass.* Maund v. Monmouthshire Can. Co., 4 M. & G. 452; Thayer v. Boston, 19 Pick. (Mass.) 511; Sheldon v. Kalamazoo, 24 Mich. 383. *Trespass for mesne profits and lower.* Yarborough v. Bk. of Eng., 16 East, 6; McCready v. Guardians of the Poor, 9 S. & R. (Pa.) 94. *Trespass on the case* for stopping a water-course. Chestnut Hill, etc., Tpke. Co. v. Rutter, 4 S. & R. (Pa.) 6.

The fact that the injury resulted from an act which was *ultra vires* is no defence. N. Y., L. E. & W. R. Co. v. Haring, 47 N. J. L. 137; s. c., 52 Am. R. 296. Hence where a railroad company undertook to run steamboats, though not authorized by its charter to do so, it was held liable for injuries received on the occasion of a collision of these boats. Hutchinson v. W. & A. R. Co., 6 Tenn. 634.

Where the charter made the stockholders personally liable for damages to private property by "the exercise of the privileges hereby conferred, or by the acts or omissions or neglect of the said company, its officers or agents," this did not prevent an action on the case against the corporation for injuries due to causes not strictly included in the provision. White Deer Cr. Imp. Co. v. Sassaman, 67 Pa. St. 415.

1. Indictment of a Corporation.—It was originally considered that a "corporation cannot do a personal tort to another, as a battery or wounding." Argument in Abbot of S. Bennet's v. Mayor of Norwich, Y. B. 21 Ed. IV. 7, 13; Sutton's Hosp. Ca., 5 Co 253; and in Anon., 12 Mod. 559, Lord Holt is reported as saying: "A corporation is not indictable, but the particular members of it are." This was probably not intended as a general proposition even then, and it is at present certainly limited to cases of felonies, assaults, riots, and malicious wrongs. Kyd, 225; Ang.& A.Corp. § 394; Morawetz, § 94; Wharton's Crim. Law, § 91. It has long been held that a corporation can be indicted for nonfeasance of a duty owing to the public. Sussex Co. v. Strader, 3 Harrison, 108; Reg. v. B. & G. R. Co., 9 Car. & P. 469; Same v. Same, 3 A. & E. N. S. 223. Though it was at one time held in *New York* that in such case the only criminal liability was in the officers personally. Kane v. People, 8 Wend. (N. Y.) 203. The same liability in cases of misfeasance was established in *England* in Reg. v. G. H. R. Co., 9 A. & E. N. S. 314.

In Reg. v. Scott, 3 A. & E. N. S. 543, a corporation obstructing a public road without making an equally convenient new one was indicted for a nuisance. In *America*, such an indictment was originally held not maintainable. State v. Great Works Co., 20 Me. 41; State v. O. & M. R. Co., 23 Ind. 362; Commonwealth v. S. W. R. G. Tpke. Co., 2 Va. Ca. 362. But the law is now abundantly settled the other way, and a corporation can be indicted for a nuisance of any kind. State v. L., N. A., etc., R. Co., 86 Ind. 114 (under statute); State v. Freeport, 43 Me. 198; State v. Portland, 74 Me. 268; Commonwealth v. V. & M. R. Co., 4 Gray (Mass.), 22; State v. M. & E. R. Co., 3 Zab. (N. J.) 360; State v. Useful Mfg. Soc., 42 N. J. L. 504; 44 N. J. L. 502; People v. Albany, 11 Wend. (N. Y.) 537; s. c., 27 Am. Dec. 95; N. C. R. Co. v. Commonwealth, 90 Pa. St. 300.

A corporation may be indicted for Sabbath breaking. State v. B. & O. R. Co., 15 W. Va. 362. And for libel. Rex v. Watson, 2 Term, 199; State v. Atchison, 3 Lea (Tenn.), 729. In the latter case certain individuals were joined as defendants, and the court said, in answer to the objection that a corporation could not be imprisoned: "It is true the corporation may not be imprisoned, but the fact that the same measure of punishment cannot be inflicted in this way cannot vitiate the

both at law and in equity, in their own names, in behalf of the company's interests, where it cannot or will not do so in its corporate capacity.[1] The pleadings must show either the refusal of the corporation to sue on proper request,[2] or that it is in the con-

1. Morawetz, § 239; Taylor Corp. §§ 138, 141; Allen *v.* Curtis, 26 Conn. 456; Gifford, 30 Iowa, 148; Peabody *v.* Flint, 6 All. (Mass.) 52; Marsh *v.* E. R., 40 N. H. 548.

The directors of a corporation are liable in equity as trustees for a fraudulent breach of trust. The principal party to sue is the corporation, but if it refuses on request, or is under control of the guilty parties, stockholders may sue in their individual names. Hodges *v.* N. E. Screw Co., 1 R. I. 321; Hazard *v.* Durant, 11 R. I. 195; Robinson *v.* Smith, 3 Pai (N. Y.) 222.

The owner of corporation bonds, secured by a lien on land of the corporation, has, as to such land, the same right of suit as a stockholder. Newby *v.* O. Cent. R. Co., 1 Saw (U. S. C. C.) 63.

It has been held that stockholders cannot, by a suit in their own names, assert corporate rights, but only protect them by means of preventive remedies. Samuels *v.* Cent. Overld. Exp. Co., McCa. (Kan.) 214.

2. The practical impossibility of a suit by the corporation must be alleged and proved. The leading case on this point is Foss *v.* Harbottle, 2 Hare, 461, where a bill was filed by two stockholders in behalf of themselves and all the others, except the defendants, against the directors and certain other persons, charging frauds on the company. The Vice-chancellor held that under the incorporation act the directors were the governing body, but subject to the superior control of the proprietors assembled in general meetings, the majority of whom have "power to bind the whole body, and every individual corporator must be taken to have come into the corporation upon the terms of being liable to be so bound." He objected that, for all that appeared in the bill, "whilst the court may be declaring the acts complained of to be void, at the suit of the present plaintiffs, who in fact may be the only proprietors who disapprove of them, the governing body of proprietors may defeat the decree by lawfully resolving upon the confirmation of the very acts which are the subject of the suit. In order that this suit may be sustained, it must be shown either that there is no such power as I have supposed remaining in the proprietors, or at least that all means have been resorted to and found ineffectual to set that body in motion." As there was no suggestion of any attempt to do this, the demurrers were sustained. Foss *v.* Harbottle has been repeatedly followed and its doctrine approved. Mozley *v* Alston, 1 Phil. 790; Lord *v.* Cop. Miners' Co., 2 Phil. 740; Gray *v.* Lewis, L. R. 8 Ch. App. 1035; MacDougall *v.* Gardiner, L. R. 1 Ch. D. 13.

The doctrine established both in *England* and *America* as to *equitable* jurisdiction in such cases is thus stated (on the authority of the above cases and others) by Miller, J., in Hawes *v.* Oakland, 104 U. S. 450:

"To enable a stockholder in a corporation to sustain in a court of equity in his own name a suit founded on a right of action existing in the corporation itself, and in which the corporation itself is the appropriate plaintiff, there must exist as the foundation of the suit—

"Some action or threatened action of the managing board of directors or trustees of the corporation which is beyond the authority conferred on them by their charter or other source of organization;

"Or such a fraudulent transaction, completed or contemplated by the acting managers, in connection with some other party or among themselves, or with other shareholders, as will result in a serious injury to the corporation, or to the interests of the other shareholders;

"Or where the board of directors or a majority of them are acting for their own interest, in a manner destructive of the corporation itself, or of the rights of the other shareholders;

"Or where the majority of shareholders themselves are oppressively and illegally pursuing a course in the name of the corporation, which is in violation of the rights of the other shareholders, and which can only be restrained by the aid of a court of equity.

"Before the shareholder is permitted in his own name to institute and conduct a litigation which usually belongs to the corporation, he should show to the satisfaction of the court that he has exhausted all the means within his reach to obtain within the corporation itself the redress of his grievances, or action in

der like circumstances, one or more stockholders may defend, in their own names, a suit brought against the corporation.[1]

A corporation should be made defendant in any suit affecting its property or franchises.[2] In certain cases, one or more stockholders may be joined as defendants.[3]

4. Service of Process.—A corporation may be sued wherever process[4]

for against it, but rather in its favor, it is eminently proper that it should be made a party, complainant or defendant. It could not be made complainant against its will, and, besides, its own agents joined in the fraudulent representations that were made. As a separate and independent personality, therefore, distinct from the stockholder interest, there was propriety in making it a party defendant. To the same effect: Dodge *v.* Woolsey, 18 How. (U. S.) 331; Davenport *v.* Dows, 18 Wall. (U. S.) 626; Samuel *v.* Holladay, 1 Wool. (U. S.) 400; French *v.* Gifford, 30 Iowa, 148; Smith *v.* Hurd, 12 Met. (Mass.) 371; Robinson *v.* Smith, 3 Paige (N. Y.), 222; Cunningham *v.* Pell, 5 Paige (N. Y.), 607; Gardiner *v.* Pollard, 10 Bos. (N. Y.) 674; Greaves *v.* George, 69 N. Y. 154; McAleer *v.* McMurray, 58 Pa. 126; Black *v.* Huggins, 2 Tenn. Ch. 780.

The rule is the same where a member seeks redress for a personal wrong which is also a wrong to the corporation, as where the directors of a mutual insurance company were sued for misappropriating money collected to pay the plaintiff. Brown *v.* Orr, 112 Pa. 233.

1. Similarly a stockholder may defend in his own name, where the directors refuse for the fraudulent purpose of sacrificing the interests of the stockholders. "In such a case it would be a reproach to the law, and especially in a court of equity, if the stockholders were remediless. . . . The court in its discretion will permit a stockholder to become a party defendant for the purpose of protecting his own interest against unfounded or illegal claims against the company; and he will also be permitted to appear on behalf of other stockholders who may desire to join him in the defence. . . . It is true the remedy is an extreme one, and should be admitted by the court with hesitation and caution; but it grows out of the necessity of the case and for the sake of justice, and may be the only remedy to prevent a flagrant wrong." Bronson *v.* La Crosse R. Co., 2 Wall. (U. S.) 283, 302.

And in such a case an answer filed by a stockholder, without showing that the corporation has refused to defend, should be struck out. Park *v.* N. Y. & K. Oil Co., 26 W. Va. 486.

An individual stockholder cannot appeal from a judgment against the corporation unless he conform his case to the rule above stated. State *v.* Fla. Cent. R. Co., 15 Fla. 690.

Where a fraud has been perpetrated by the directors, by which the property or interests of stockholders are effected, they can come in as parties to a suit against the corporation, and ask that their property be relieved from the effect of such fraud. Bayliss *v.* L. M., etc., R. Co., 8 Biss. (U. S. C. C.) 193.

2. See Dodge *v.* Woolsey, 18 How. (U. S.) 331, and other cases cited in next to last note.

The corporation is a necessary party to proceedings to restrain the usurpation of corporate franchises. People *v.* Flint, 64 Cal. 49.

In an action against partners, to enforce a lien, the answer was filed by a corporation alleging its incorporation and its title to the property. Judgment for the plaintiff was reversed on error, the corporation not having been made a party to the suit. Rousseau *v.* Hall, 55 Cal. 164.

3. Where stockholders are jointly and severally liable on bonds of a corporation, they are properly made defendants in a suit against the corporation on such bonds, to avoid a multiplicity of suits. M. & R. Phos. Co. *v.* Bradley, 105 U. S. 175.

The *Michigan* statute allows suits for labor done to be brought against a corporation either alone, or jointly with one or more stockholders. Where a claimant elected to sue a corporation alone, and recovered judgment, it was held that he could not afterwards bring another action on the same debt, or on a claim including it, against the corporation and the stockholders jointly. Milroy *v.* S. M. Iron Min. Co., 43 Mich. 231.

Such an action cannot be brought against stockholders only. Thompson *v.* Jewell, 43 Mich. 240.

4. The process against a corporation in actions at law must be by summons. 1 Kyd. 271; Ang. & A. Corp. § 637; Anon., 6 Mod. 183; Lynch *v.* Mechs. Bk., 13 Johns. (N. Y.) 137.

This is now usually provided by statute.

For commencement of suit by attachment, see FOREIGN CORPORATIONS.

For the old equity process, see SEQUESTRATION; SUBPŒNA.

denying it. At common law, and under some codes, a corporation can sue or be sued by the corporate name without further averment of incorporation or of authority to act and contract as a corporation,[1] but in some States the rule is otherwise.[2] The fact

A body sued as a corporation can, however, plead that it never was organized, nor had organization ever been attempted. Folsom *v.* Star Un. Lines, 54 Iowa, 490.

A *de facto* corporation may also prove a subsequent cessation of corporate functions. Dobson *v.* Simonton, 86 N. Car. 492. And the representative of a corporation, served with process, may plead in his own name that the corporation is extinct, and move to dismiss the suit. Kelly *v.* M. C. R. Co., 2 Flip. (U. S. C. C.) 581.

1. Ang. & A. Corp. § 632.

In Henriques *v.* D. W. I. Co., 2 Ld. Ray. 1532, it was said, *arguendo*, that "if the name is proper for a corporation they need not show how they were incorporated, because the name argues a corporation;" and the House of Lords so held.

In Zion Ch. *v.* St. Peter's Ch., 5 W. & S. (Pa.) 215, the defendants had requested the court to charge that the plaintiffs must "aver in the declaration that they are a corporation, setting out the title of the act creating the corporation and the date of its passage." This was refused, and, on the writ of error, the supreme said: ' No precedent of an averment of incorporation, or of a profert of the charter, has been produced in any declaration by a corporation; nor is there any reason why there should be one. Unlike a bond or grant of administration, it is no part of the title to sue any more than an act of baptism is part of such a title. Nothing but a deed or grant of administration is pleaded with a profert, and oyer cannot be demanded of a private statute even when a profert has been made of it. The name in this instance imports that the plaintiff is a body-politic, and had the fact been otherwise the plaintiff might have pleaded the want of an act of incorporation."

To the same effect. Woolf *v.* City S. B. Co., 7 M. G. & S. 103; Cent. Mfg. Co. *v.* Hartshorne, 3 Conn. 199; Frye *v.* Bk. of Ill., 10 Ill. 332; Spingle *v.* Ind., etc., R. Co., 21 Ill. 276; O'Donald *v.* Evansville, etc., R. Co., 14 Ind. 259; Heaston *v.* Cinn., etc., R. Co., 16 Ind. 275; Ryan *v.* Farmers' Bk., 5 Kan. 658; Lighte *v.* Everett Ins. Co., 5 Bos. (N. Y.) 716; Waterville Bk. *v.* Beltser, 13 How. Pr. (N. Y.) 270; Lithgow *v.* Commonwealth, 2 Va. Cas. 297; Rees *v.* Con. Bk., 5 Rand. (Va.) 326.

Where the name of a party to an action is such as to import that it is a corporation, and the cause proceeds to judgment without any allegation as to its incorporation, the judgment is not void. Whether in such a case the name imports a corporation, should, as a general rule, be left to judicial knowledge. S. Cecilia Acad. *v.* Hardin (Ga.), 3 S. E. Rep. 305.

In Stanly *v.* R. & D. R. Co., 89 N. C. 331, under the local code, the court said: "It is difficult to assign any sufficient reason why a corporation suing or sued should be designated by any further description than its corporate name, which does not apply with equal force to a natural person, the only purpose in either case being to point out the party to the action. The appearance and plea to the merits or answer is a concession of the sufficiency of the designation of the person, natural or artificial, and, if intended to be disputed, it should be under the present practice by answer." So under the section of the *Iowa* Code in regard to actions on written instruments, when "suit may be brought by or against any of the parties thereto, by the same name and description as those by which they are designated in such instrument." Harris Mfg. Co. *v.* Marsh, 49 Iowa, 11.

In La Grange Mill Co. *v.* Bennewitz, 28 Minn. 62, it was held that where the complaint alleged that the corporation plaintiff "entered into an agreement to and with each other," this included and implied the plaintiff's corporate capacity and power to make the agreement.

Where a company has authority, under a general statute, though not by its charter, to enter into the contract in suit, such authority need not be alleged in the declaration. Toppan *v.* C., C. & C. R. Co., 1 Flip. (U. S. C. C.) 74.

2. In Bliss on Code Pleading, § 246, it is stated that while domestic municipal corporations and domestic private corporations created by or under a public act need not aver their incorporation in the complaint, on the ground that the court will take judicial notice of the acts incorporating them, yet that "when a foreign corporation comes into court, or a domestic one created by a private act, or where private proceedings are necessary to its creation, the court cannot know of its legal existence; it is a question of fact

the face of the record, should be taken advantage of by demurrer.[1]

Corporate existence *de facto* is proved by the existence of a law authorizing it, and by user.[2] The presumption is usually in its favor.[3] If its admission be necessarily involved by statement of facts agreed upon, the parties cannot deny it.[4]

The pleadings should be in the name of the corporation, made[5]

In regard to code pleading, it has been said: "It is but reasonable that the statute should require the defendant, if he objects to the plaintiff's demand because he does not show a right to appear in court, to base his objection specifically upon that ground." Bliss on Code Pleading, § 408 a.

In *Missouri*, however, a general denial under the code puts the plaintiff's incorporation at issue, unless it took place by public act or the defendant is estopped. Girls' Ind. Home *v.* Fritchey, 10 Mo. App. 344.

1. Phœnix Bk. *v.* O'Donnell, 40 N. Y. 410; Maryville Coll. *v.* Bartlett, 8 Bax. (Tenn.) 231; Crane *v.* Reed, 3 Ut. 506.

Where corporate existence is properly alleged in the complaint, legal capacity to sue is presumed, and if no facts or circumstances to the contrary appear on the face of the complaint, it is not demurrable on the ground of want of such capacity. C. & C. R. Co. *v.* White, 14 S. Car. 51; C. & C. R. Co. *v.* Garland, 14 S. Car. 63.

2. "Two things are necessary to be shown in order to establish the existence of a corporation *de facto*, viz., the existence of a charter, or some law under which a corporation, with the powers assumed, might lawfully be created, and, second, a user by the party to the suit of the rights claimed to be conferred by such charter or law." M. E. U. Ch. *v.* Pickett, 19 N. Y. 482. See also Morawetz Corp. § 139; Taylor Corp. § 145; Miami Powr. Co. *v.* Hotchkiss, 17 Ill. App 622; Abbot *v.* Om. Smelt. Co., 4 Brown (Neb.) 419.

An answer showing the use of the corporate name and the exercise of corporate franchises, that the plaintiff was an officer, and had obtained a judgment against it, sufficiently shows the existence of the corporation. Johnson *v.* Gibson, 78 Ind. 282.

In a suit against a corporation and its officers, proof that for many years they acted as a corporation, and claimed to be such, has been held sufficient evidence of corporate existence. Tipton F. I. Co. *v.* Barnheisel, 92 Ind. 88; s. c., 5 Am. & Eng. Corp. Cas. 94.

A copy of the organization certificate of a national bank, certified and sealed by the comptroller of the currency, is sufficient evidence of corporate existence. Mix *v.* Bloomington Bk., 91 Ill. 20; Rock I. Bk. *v.* Loyhed, 28 Minn. 396.

In *California*, a copy of the articles of incorporation is sufficient. Fresno C. & I. Co. *v.* Warner, 17 Am. & Eng. Corp. Cas. 37.

Execution of a note and deed to a corporation have been held sufficient *prima facie* evidence of its existence. Brown *v.* S. A. Mtge. Co., 110 Ill. 235.

In case of a variance between the corporate name in the contract and that on which the suit is brought, evidence of mistake should be submitted to the jury. Hendel *v.* B. & D. Tpke. Co., 16 S. & R. (Pa.) 92. See EVIDENCE.

3. P. & M. Bk. *v.* Padgett, 69 Ga. 159; Sword *v.* Wickersham, 29 Kan. 746.

Where a corporation has gone into operation, and rights have been acquired under it, every presumption should be made in favor of its legal existence. White *v.* State, 69 Ind. 273; Hagerstown Tpke. Co. *v.* Creeger, 5 H. & J. (Md.) 122; All Sts. Ch. *v.* Lovett, 1 Hall (N. Y.), 191. And see *supra*, DEFECTIVE INCORPORATION, p. 197.

4. Rikhoff *v.* Brown's Rob., etc., Co., 68 Ind. 388.

5. In a suit against a corporation, the answer should be made by its principal officer, who should be able to admit or deny the facts charged and interrogated about, or to state his want of knowledge clearly and truly as a reason for doing neither." Hale *v.* Contin. L. I. Co., 16 Fed R. 718.

The answer must be filed by the officers at the time of filing. Mechs. Bk. *v.* Burnet Mfg. Co., 32 N. J. Eq 236.

As a corporation can only contract by its agents, it is sufficient to aver that the corporation made the contract in suit. Rochester *v.* Shaw, 100 Ind. 268. And the agent's authority may be proved by parol. Morrill *v.* C. T. Seg. Mfg. Co., 32 Hun (N. Y.), 843.

Under the *New York* Code, a corporation sued on a note must serve with its answer an order of court directing a trial,

7. Mandamus against Private Corporations.—Where a specific[1] duty is imposed on a corporation by its charter or the general law under which it is formed,[2] either in terms or by reasonable construction and implication, performance thereof may be compelled by *mandamus*, if no other specific or adequate remedy at law be available.[3] The writ may issue at the instance of a private citi-

may be so levied on. Plym. R. Co. *v.* Colwell, 39 Pa. 337; F. & C. Tpke. Co. *v.* Young, 8 Humph (Tenn.) 103.

Where a corporation exchanged land for its stock, which it retired, a creditor was held entitled to enforce his judgment against the land, though no fraud had been intended. Clapp *v.* Peterson, 104 Ill. 26.

1. The duty must be specific. "Where the case presents a single question, and calls for an act which is presently determinate, it is entirely practicable to direct the act by *mandamus*. But where the case contemplates something continuous yet variable in its conditions and aptitudes, the remedy by that process seems an unfit one. It is the office of a *mandamus* to direct the will, and obedience is to be enforced by process for contempt. It is therefore necessary to point out the very thing to be done, and a command to act according to circumstances would be futile." Diamond Match Co. *v.* Powers, 51 Mich. 145; s. c., 8 Am. & Eng. Corp. Cas. 144.

If the duty be discretionary, the rule does not apply. *Ex parte* Harris, 52 Ala. 87; People *v.* Loucks, 28 Cal. 68; People *v.* Sexton, 37 Cal. 532; Fulton *v.* Hanna, 40 Cal. 278; State *v.* Van Ness, 15 Fla. 317; State *v.* C. & C. Str. R. Co., 23 La. Ann. 333; E. Bost. Ferry Co. *v.* Boston, 101 Mass. 488; Swan *v.* Gray, 44 Miss. 393; People *v.* Leonard, 74 N. Y. 443; Turnpike Rd. *v.* Sandusky Co., 1 Ohio St. 149; Press Assoc. *v.* Nichols, 45 Vt. 7.

2. It must be a duty required by its charter, not merely created by contract. Parrott *v.* Bridgeport, 44 Conn. 180; State *v.* Rep. Riv. Br. Co., 20 Kan. 404; State *v.* Pat., etc., R. Co., 43 N. J. L. 505; State *v.* Zanesville, etc., Co., 16 Ohio St. 308; Ham *v.* T. W. & W. R. Co., 29 Ohio St. 174.

3. Rex *v.* Nottingham W. W., 6 A. & E. 355; Norris *v.* Irish Land Co., 8 E. & B. 512, U. P. R. Co. *v.* Hall, 91 U. S. 343, s. c., 3 Dill. (C. C.) 515; 4 Dill. (C. C.) 479; Chic., etc., R. Co. *v.* Crane, 113 U. S. 424; Fitch *v.* McDiarmid, 26 Ark. 482; Price *v.* Riverside L. & I. Co., 56 Cal. 431, State *v.* Hartf., etc., R. Co., 29 Conn. 538; State *v.* Van Ness, 15 Fla. 317; Habersham *v.* Can. Co., 26 Ga. 665; Chic., etc., R. Co. *v.* People, 56 Ill. 365; Fireman's Ins. Co. *v.* Mayor, 23 Md. 297; People *v.* State Ins. Co., 19 Mich. 292; State *v.* S. M. R. Co., 18 Minn. 40; State *v.* Board of Trustees, 4 Nev. 400; State *v.* Guerrero, 12 Nev. 105; People *v.* Pac. Mail, etc., Co., 50 Barb. (N. Y.) 280; s. c., 3 Abb. Pr. N. S. (N. Y.) 364; People *v.* Cummings, 72 N. Y. 433; Freon *v.* Carriage Co., 42 Ohio, 30; s. c., 10 Am. & Eng. Corp. Cas. 101; Can. Comrs. *v.* Willamette Trans. Co., 6 Ore. 219; M. M. Cem. Assoc. *v.* Commonwealth, 81 Pa. 235; Easton *v.* Leh. Water Co., 97 Pa. 554; State *v.* McIver, 2 S. Car. 25; Mob., etc., R. Co. *v.* Wisdom, 5 Heisk. (Tenn.) 125.

The jurisdiction is ancient and well established. High's Extr. Leg. Rem. § 276.

Mandamus lies to compel a corporation to recognize a person as a member, or to restore him to his corporate rights if improperly disfranchised or wrongly removed. Ang. & A. Corp. § 695; High's Ext. Leg. Rem. § 294; Wood's Field on Corp. § 462; Rex *v.* March, 2 Bur. 999; Da Costa *v.* Russia Co., 2 Str. 783; Med. & Sur Soc. *v.* Weatherly, 75 Ala. 248; s. c., 10 Am. & Eng. Corp. Cas. 26; State *v.* Geo. Med. Soc., 38 Ga. 608; State *v.* Cres. Cy. G. L. Co., 24 La. Ann. 318; Roehlen *v.* Aid Soc., 22 Mich. 86; People *v.* Med. Soc., 25 How Pr. 333; s. c., 32 N. Y. 187; Evans *v.* Phila. Club, 50 Pa. 107. But not when he has committed the offence charged. State *v.* Milw. Ch. of Com., 47 Wis. 671. See AMOTION.

To compel the directors to call a meeting for the election of officers. Rex *v.* Aldham Ins. Soc., 6 Eng. L. & E 365; s. c., 15 Jar. N. S. 1035; Orr *v.* Bracken Tpke. Co., 81 Ky. 593; s. c., 4 Am. & Eng. Corp. Cas. 231; State *v.* Wright, 10 Nev. 167; McNeely *v.* Woodruff, 13 N. J. L. 352; People *v.* Govs. of Alb. Hosp., 61 Barb. (N. Y.) 397; People *v.* Cummings, 72 N. Y. 433.

The writ implies that the election will be held in the manner provided by law. State *v.* Board of Trustees, 4 Nev. 400.

It lies to reinstate or admit to office

ten.[1] Unless the corporation has no power to do the act of its own motion, a previous demand for its performance must be shown.[2] If the duty be incumbent on the corporation as a whole, the writ should be addressed to it by its corporate name; if on one or more particular officers, they alone should be proceeded against.[3]

8. Quo Warranto Against Private Corporations.[4]—An information in the nature of the ancient writ of *quo warranto*[5] lies in cases of

there is a plain remedy at law or in equity. The most familiar instance is where it is sought to compel the issuance or transfer of certificates for specific shares of stock. In *England* and most of the States this cannot be done by *mandamus*. Rex *v.* Bk. of Eng., 2 Doug. 524; Rex *v.* Lond. Ass. Soc., 5 B. & Ald. 899; Am. Asy. *v.* Phœnix Bk., 4 Conn. 172; Tobey *v.* Hakes, 54 Conn. 274; s. c., 16 Am. & Eng. Corp. Cas 400; Bank *v.* Harrison, 66 Ga. 696 (except where stock has been sold at judicial sale); Townes *v.* Nichols, 73 Me. 515; Murray *v.* Stevens, 110 Mass. 95; Stackpole *v.* Seymour, 127 Mass. 104; Lamphere *v.* Un. Workmen, 47 Mich. 429; Baker *v.* Marshall, 15 Minn. 177; State *v.* Rombauer, 46 Mo. 155 (unless the corporation be under a legal liability to do so, and its refusal cannot be compensated for in damages. State *v.* St. L. Paint Mfg. Co., 21 Mo. App. 526); State *v.* Guerrero, 12 Nev. 105; Morgan *v.* Monmouth P. R. Co., 2 Dutch. (N. J.) 99; State *v.* Holliday, 3 Halst. (N. J.) 205; State *v.* Peop. Assoc., 43 N. J. L. 389; State *v.* Timken, 48 N. J. L. 87; s. c., 12 Am. & Eng. Corp. Cas. 34; Shipley *v.* Mechanics' Bk., 10 Johns. (N. Y.) 484; Cortwright *v.* Com. Bk., 20 Wend. 91; s. c., 22 Wend. 347; *Ex parte* Firemen's Ins. Co., 6 Hill (N. Y.), 243; People *v.* P. V. Coal Co., 10 How. Pr. 543; Cushman *v.* Thayer Mfg. Co., 76 N. Y. 365; Freon *v.* Carriage Co., 42 Ohio, 30; s. c., 10 Am. & Eng. Corp. Cas. 101; Durham *v.* Mon. S. M. Co., 9 Ore. 41.

In a few States the contrary is held. People *v.* Crockett, 9 Cal. 112; Campbell *v.* Morgan, 4 Ill. App. 105; G. M. Tpke. Co. *v.* Bailey, 45 Ind. 1; State *v.* Jeffersonville Bk., 89 Ind. 302 (a case of judicial sale); Cooper *v.* D. S. Can. Co., 2 Murph. (N. Car.) 195; State *v.* McIver, 2 S. Car. 25; State *v.* C. & C. R. Co., 16 S. Car. 524.

It will not lie to enforce the payment of a dividend which has been declared. Van Norman *v.* Cent. Car Co., 41 Mich. 166.

Nor to compel an act forbidden by an injunction. *Ex parte* Fleming, 4 Hill (N. Y.), 581; O. & I. R. Co. *v.* Commrs., 7 Ohio St. 278. Or an unlawful act. Ross *v.* Lane, 11 Miss. 695; People *v.* Fowler, 55 N. Y. 252. Or an impossible one. Silverthorn *v.* Warren R. Co., 33 N. J. L. 173

A *mandamus* will not be granted where not sought *bona fide*, nor for a proper purpose. Queen *v.* L. M. & N. R. Co., 21 L. J. Q. B. 284; People *v.* M. P. R. Co., 50 N. Y. Sup. Ct. 456.

1. "There is, we think, a decided preponderance of American authority in favor of the doctrine that a private person may move for a *mandamus* to enforce a public duty, not due to the government as such, without the intervention of the government law officer." Un. Pac. R. Co. *v.* Hall, 91 U. S. 343, 355.

2. Rex *v.* Wilts Can. Co., 3 A. & E. 477; Reg. *v.* B. & E. R. Co., 4 A. & E. N. S. 162 The demand must be definite and specific. Price *v.* Riverside S. & I. Co., 56 Cal. 431.

It has been held unnecessary where the duty was plain and unmistakable. Motta *v.* Primrose, 23 Md. 482.

3. Rex *v.* Abingdon, 1 Ld. Ray. 559; People *v.* Throop, 12 Wend. 183; People *v.* L. S. & M. S. R. Co., 11 Hun, 1.

If a majority of the directors can act, a *mandamus* will not be issued against a single dissenting director. *In re* White Riv. Bk., 23 Vt. 478.

4. See INFORMATION; QUO WARRANTO.

5. When *quo warranto* is referred to in this section, the information is, of course, always meant.

In some States special code proceedings have been substituted, but they are to the same effect and are governed by the same rules. People *v.* Thatcher, 55 N. Y. 528; People *v.* Hall, 80 N. Y. 117; State *v.* Doug. Co. R. Co., 10 Oregon, 198.

In *Tennessee*, equity proceedings have been substituted. State *v.* Turk, M. & Y. (Tenn.) 286; Atty.-Gen. *v.* Leaf, 9 Humph (Tenn.) 753; State *v.* W. Cr. Tpke. Co., 3 Tenn. Ch. 163. And in *Vermont*, proceedings by *scire facias*. Green *v.* St. Alban's Tr. Co., 57 Vt. 340; s. c., 10 Am. & Eng. Corp. Cas. 215.

gal occupation of corporate offices.[1] It is brought at the instance of the attorney-general,[2] and sometimes of other public officers,[3] except where only private or individual rights are concerned, when the relator may be a private citizen.[4] The court should use great

If for any of these causes the judgment is for the State, it works a forfeiture of the franchises and a dissolution of the corporation. See DISSOLUTION OF CORPORATIONS; FRANCHISES; ULTRA VIRES.

1. In *England*, intrusion into an office of a private corporation is not the subject of *quo warranto*, unless the corporation has public duties. King *v.* Ogden, 10 B. & C. 230; Queen *v.* Mousley, 8 A. & E. N. S. 946.

In *America* it has been held otherwise, on the ground that although in such a case no prerogative of the State has been usurped, a privilege granted by it has been abused. Davidson *v.* State, 20 Fla. 784; People *v.* Tibbetts, 4 Cow. (N. Y.) 358; Hallman *v.* Hovcomp, 5 Ohio St. 237; Commonwealth *v.* Arrison, 15 S. & R. (Pa.) 127; Commonwealth *v.* Graham, 64 Pa. 339.

Quo warranto has been held the only proper remedy where the acting treasurer of a company refuses to recognize the election of his successor or to turn over the corporate funds to him. Hunt *v.* Pleas. Hill Cem. Assn., 27 Kan. 734.

The remedy does not apply to a servant of the corporation. King *v.* Bedford Level, 6 East, 356. Not even to a professor in a college. Philips *v.* Commonwealth, 98 Pa. 394.

Subsequent resignation of the office is no defence to a *quo warranto* brought for such a purpose. State *v.* McDaniel, 22 Ohio St. 354. But the title of one assuming to act as a corporate officer cannot be tried in proceedings against his successor. Commonwealth *v.* Smith, 45 Pa. 59.

The application, being to the discretion of the court, must show the corporate office in question. The questions of the relators' acquiescence and of the effect on the corporation have to be considered. Rex *v.* Davis, 4 Bur. 2120; Rex *v.* Stacey, 1 Term, 1; Rex *v.* Bond, 2 Term, 677; Gunton *v.* Ingle, 4 Cr. (C. C.) 438.

In these proceedings the court can only oust the respondent from the office if he have not been legally elected thereto, and afford the party whose votes have been improperly rejected an opportunity of voting at another election. State *v.* McDaniel, 22 Ohio St. 354.

Where the real object of *quo warranto* against an officer is to test the validity of the charter, it will not be granted. Queen *v.* Taylor, 11 A. & E. 949. See OFFICERS OF CORPORATIONS.

2. Where the object of the proceedings is to forfeit the franchises or dissolve the corporation, they cannot be brought at the instance of a private citizen, even if a creditor. People *v.* N. Ch. R. Co., 83 Ill. 537; State *v.* P. & H. Tpke. Co., 1 Zab. (N. J.) 9; Commonwealth *v.* Farmers' Bank, 2 Gr. (Pa.) 392; Commonwealth *v.* Alleg. Br. Co., 20 Pa. 185; Murphy *v.* Farmers' Bank, 20 Pa. 415; Commonwealth *v.* P. G. & N. R. Co., 20 Pa. 518.

The contrary is held in *Oregon*, but as such private relator has no control over the case, the divergence is small. State *v.* Doug. Co. R. Co., 10 Oregon, 198.

It is within the discretion of the State, as represented by the attorney general, to begin the proceedings, as also to discontinue them. Commonwealth *v.* Un. Ins. Co., 5 Mass. 230; People *v.* Tobacco Co., 42 How. Pr. (N. Y.) 162.

Where the attorney-general proceeds, for the protection of the public, against illegal usurpation of corporate franchises, the information need not show title in the people to have the particular franchise exercised. The burden is on the defendant to show its title. People *v.* Utica Ins. Co., 15 John. (N. Y.) 358. But where the respondent's original title is admitted, but is claimed to have become forfeited, the burden is on the State. High's Ext. Leg. Rem. § 667 a; State *v.* Haskell, 14 Nev. 209.

3. Where a public officer, as the auditor of public accounts, is the relator, acting for the public interest, the prosecution is a public one. People *v.* Golden Rule Co., 114 Ill. 34; Murphy *v.* Farmers' Bank, 20 Pa. 415.

4. In such a case the relator must show title in himself. King *v.* Cudlipp, 6 Term. 503; King *v.* Cowell, 6 Dow. & R. 336; Miller *v.* English, 1 Zab. (N. J.) 317.

A corporator may be the relator in case of a usurpation of corporate offices, but he may be estopped by his acquiescence, as by participating in the meeting and acquiescing in the election though he knew that some votes were illegal. Rex *v.* Stacey, 1 Term, 1; State *v.* Lehre,

in the charter; (2) Upon the happening of a contingency prescribed by the charter; (3) By the surrender of the franchises to the State; (4) By act of the legislature; (5) By failure of an integral part of the corporation; (6) By forfeiture of the franchise in a proper judicial proceeding.

3. Dissolution by the Expiration of the Time Limited in the Charter.—Where a corporation is chartered to exist during a certain period of time or until a certain day, upon the expiration of the time or the happening of the day the corporate existence will cease.[1] In such a case the corporation cannot be continued even by the unanimous consent of the shareholders, nor can the legislature by renewing the charter revive the debts and liabilities owing to the original corporation.[2] On the other hand, if it is the intention of the charter that the corporation shall exist during a definite period of time, and that its business shall be carried on at all events during this period, a majority of the shareholders have no right to shorten the period even with the consent of the State.[3] But where the intention of the charter is merely to provide a limitation upon the duration of the franchises, the majority may wind up the business of the corporation whenever they deem this to be expedient.[4]

4. Dissolution upon the Happening of a Contingency prescribed by the Charter.—The franchises of a corporation may be so limited that they may expire upon a prescribed contingency, without the intervention of the courts to declare a forfeiture. Thus where the charter requires that the continued existence of the corporation shall depend upon its compliance with some requirement of the charter, and in case of noncompliance the corporate franchises are

second case mentioned by Blackstone does not apply to a corporation having shares of stock, which may be transferred by gift, sale, or inheritance. It applies, however, to clubs whose membership can only be maintained by the vote of the existing members.

In *England* a corporation may now by statute be wound up—1. Whenever the company has passed a special resolution requiring the company to be wound up by the court; 2. Whenever the company does not commence its business within a year from its incorporation, or suspends its business for the space of a whole year; 3. Whenever the members are reduced in number to less than seven; 4. Whenever the company is unable to pay its debts; 5. Whenever the court is of opinion that it is just and equitable that the company should be wound up. Companies Act, 1862, § 79. The cases under this act are collected in Ang. & A. Corp. p. 833.

1. Where a charter provided that a corporation should continue in existence "until the first day of January" the word "until" was construed to be exclusive in its meaning, and it was held that the charter expired on December 31. People *v.* Walker, 17 N. Y. 502; La Grange, etc., R. Co. *v.* Rainey, 7 Coldw. (Tenn.) 432; Bank of Miss. *v.* Wrenn, 3 Sm. & M. (Miss.) 791; Bank of Gallipolis *v.* Trimble, 6 B. Mon. (Ky.) 601; Asheville Division No. 15 *v.* Aston, 92 N. Car. 578.

2. Commercial Bank *v.* Lockwood, 2 Harring. (Del.) 8; Mason *v.* Pewabic Mining Co., 25 Fed. Rep. 882.

If a corporation previous to the expiration of the period of its corporate existence assigns to a trustee for the use of the shareholders, its unpaid paper, the trustee may sue on such paper in his own name after the expiration of the charter. Cooper *v.* Curtis, 30 Me 488.

3. Black *v.* Delaware, etc., Canal Co., 22 N. J. 403; Von Schmidt *v.* Huntington, 1 Cal 55.

4. 2 Morawetz on Corporations (2d Ed.), 396.

charter granted by himself.[1] In many of the United States a method of voluntary dissolution is provided by statute. Nonuser of its franchises by a corporation for a long period of time raises a presumption that the franchises have been surrendered to the State.[2] But the fact that a corporation has neglected to elect officers and to perform corporate acts does not of itself put an end to its corporate existence.[3] Nor will the disposal of all the prop-

Norris v. Mayor of Smithville, 1 Swan (Tenn.), 164; Curien v. Santini, 16 La. Ann. 27; Campbell v. Mississippi Union Bank, 6 How. (Miss.) 681; Enfield Toll Bridge Co. v. Connecticut River Co., 7 Conn. 45; Riddle v. Locks and Canals, 7 Mass. 185; McLaren v. Pennington, 1 Paige (N. Y.), 107; Canal v. Railroad, 4 Gill & J. (Md.) 1; 2 Kent's Com. 310; Mumma v. Potomac Co., 8 Pet. (U. S.) 281.

In Town v. Bank of River Raisin, 2 Doug. (Mich.) 538, it was said that "the modes in which a surrender is to be made, and as to what facts constitute a surrender, have been a fruitful subject of discussion in the courts of this country. In *England* the surrender is by deed to the king, by whom corporations are usually created by charter. In this country corporations are created by an act of the legislature, and it would seem to follow, in the absence of any statute prescribing the mode in which a surrender is to be made, that to become available, it must be accepted by the authority which created the corporation." In Taylor on Corporations, p. 313, it is suggested that the principle laid down in the older cases is at present of doubtful applicability. At the present time stock corporations are "almost universally organized under general enabling acts. A mode of dissolution is ordinarily provided; and if no such provision exists, the most experienced legal adviser might be puzzled to advise how an acceptance of the surrender of franchises could be brought about, unless by lobbying a special bill through the legislature. Besides, the idea of the necessity of the acceptance of a surrender of franchises on the part of the authority granting them seems intimately connected with the old doctrine—now certainly a thing of the past—that on the dissolution of a corporation all its debts were extinguished. There seems to be no valid reason why an ordinary stock corporation, charged with the performance of no public duty, should not be allowed to close up its business at any time, and dissolve."

In *Pennsylvania*, the act of April 9, 1856, provides for the dissolution of a corporation by petition of the corporation to the court of common pleas, "with the consent of the majority of the corporators duly convened." If the court is satisfied that the corporation may be dissolved without prejudice to the public interests or those of the corporators, it may enter a decree of dissolution. In Riddell v. Harmony Fire Co., 28 Legal Intelligencer (*Pa.*), 356, it was held that a proposed division of the property of the corporation among its members without a proceeding under the above act was illegal. See also Commonwealth v. Slifer, 53 Pa. St. 71. In the application of the Niagara Insurance Co., 1 Paige (N. Y.), 258, under a similar act in *New York* it was held that the court was not bound to decree a dissolution of a corporation simply because a majority of the directors and stockholders requested it to be done, but that where the owners of such a large proportion of the stock as three fourths found it for their interest to withdraw their capital, it would be deemed presumptive evidence that the interest of the stockholders generally would be promoted by a dissolution of the corporation. As to the power of the majority, see Wallamet Falls, etc., Canal Co. v. Kittridge, 5 Sawy. (C. C.) 44; Merchants', etc., Line v. Waganer, 71 Ala. 581; *In re* Woven Tape Skirt Co., 8 Hun (N. Y.), 508; Wilson v. Proprietors, 9 R. I. 590; Pratt v. Jewett, 9 Gray (Mass.), 34; *In re* Franklin Telegraph Co., 119 Mass. 447; Smith v. Smith, 3 Des. Ch. (S. Car.) 557; Ward v. Society of Attorneys, 1 Collyer, 370; Kean v. Johnson, 1 Stock. (N. J.) 401; New Orleans R. v. Harris, 27 Miss. 517; Abbott v. American Hard Rubber Co., 33 Barb. (N. Y.) 578.

1. 2 Kyd on Corporations, 447.

2. Brandon Iron Co. v. Gleason, 24 Vt. 238; Strickland v. Prichard, 37 Vt. 324; State v. Vincennes University, 5 Ind. 77. It cannot be set up collaterally that a corporation has forfeited its franchises by misuser or nonuser. Atlanta v. Gate-City Gaslight Co., 71 Ga. 106; Barren Creek Ditching Co. v. Beck, 99 Ind. 247.

3. 2 Morawetz on Corporations (2d Ed.),

consequence of this interpretation, it is now customary in the United States to provide in special charters of incorporation and in general corporation laws that the State shall have the right to repeal, alter, or amend the charter at its discretion.[1] The power

McLaren v. Pennington, 1 Paige (N. Y.), 107; Brown v. Hummel, 6 Pa. St. 86; Green v. Biddle, 8 Wheat. (U. S.) 1; State v. Heyward, 3 Rich. (S. Car.) 389; Society, etc., v. Morris Canal, Saxt. (N. J.) 157; People v. Manhattan Co., 9 Wend. (N. Y.) 351; Maryland University v. Williams, 9 G. & J. (Md.) 402; Commonwealth v. Cullen, 13 Pa. St. 132; Commercial Bank of Natchez v. State, 14 Miss. 599; Payne v. Baldwin, 3 S. & M. (Miss.) 661; Aberdeen Academy v. Aberdeen, 13 S. & M. (Miss.) 645; Barkus v. Lebanon, 11 N. H. 19; Young v. Harrison, 6 Ga. 130; Michigan State Bank v. Hastings, 1 Doug. (Mich.) 225; Coles v. Madison, Breese, 120; Bush v. Shipman, 4 Scam. (Ill.) 190; People v. Marshal, 1 Gilman (Ill.), 672; Bailey v. Railroad, 4 Harring. (Del.) 389; Bridge Co. v. Hoboken Co., 13 N. J. Eq. 81; Miners' Bank v. United States, 1 Greene (Iowa). 553; Edwards v. Jagers, 19 Ind. 407; State v. Noyes, 47 Me. 189; Le Clercq v. Gallipolis, 7 Ohio, 217; State v. Commercial Bank, 7 Ohio, 125; State v. Wash. Soc. Lib., 9 Ohio, 96; Boston R. Co v. Salem R. Co., 2 Gray (Mass.), 1; Commonwealth v. New Bedford Bridge, 2 Gray (Mass.), 339; Aurora Turnpike v. Holthouse, 7 Ind. 59; Louisville v. University of Louisville, 15 B. Mon. (Ky.) 642; Yarmouth v. North Yarmouth, 34 Me. 411; Bruffet v. G. W. R. Co., 25 Ill. 353; People v. Plank R. Co., 9 Miss. 285; Bank of the State v. Bank of Cape Fear, 13 Ired. (N. Car.) 75; Mills v. Williams, 11 Ired (N. Car.) 558; Hawthorne v. Calef, 2 Wall (U. S) 10; Wales v. Stetson, 2 Mass. 143; Nichols v. Bertram, 3 Pick. (Mass.) 342; King v. Dedham Bank, 15 Mass. 447; State v. Tombeckbee Bank, 2 Stew. (Ala.) 30; Central Bridge v. Lowell, 15 Gray (Mass.) 106; Bank of the Dominion v. McVeigh, 20 Gratt. (Va.) 457; Sloan v. Pacific R. Co., 61 Mo. 24; State v. Richmond & R. Co., 73 N. C. 527; Detroit v. Plank Road Co., 43 Mich. 140; 2 Kent Com 305; Ang. & A. Corp. 835; Cooley's Cons. Lim (5th Ed.) 337.

1. In Greenwood v. Freight Co., 105 U. S. 13, Mr. Justice Miller states the origin of this custom as follows: "It was, no doubt, with a view to suggest a method by which the State legislatures could retain, in a large measure, this important power, without violating the provision of the Federal constitution, that Mr. Justice Story, in his concurring opinion in the Dartmouth College Case, suggested that when the legislature was enacting a charter for a corporation, a provision in the statute reserving to the legislature the right to amend or repeal it must be held to be a part of the contract itself, and the subsequent exercise of the right would be in accordance with the contract, and could not, therefore, impair its obligation. . . . Wales v. Stetson, 2 Mass. 143 It would seem that the States were not slow to avail themselves of this suggestion, for while we have not time to examine their legislation for the result, we have in one of the cases cited to us as to the effect of a repeal (McLaren v. Pennington, 1 Paige (N. Y.) 102), in which the legislature of New Jersey, when chartering a bank with a capital of $400,000 in 1824, declared by its seventieth section that it should be lawful for the legislature at any time to alter, amend, and repeal the same. And Kent (2 Com. 307), speaking of what is proper in such a clause, cites as an example a charter by the New York legislature, of the date of Feb. 25. 1822. How long the legislature of Massachusetts continued to rely on a special reservation of this power in each charter as it was granted, it is unnecessary to inquire; for in 1831 it enacted as a law of general application, that all charters of corporations thereafter granted should be subject to amendment, alteration, and repeal, at the pleasure of the legislature: and such has been the law ever since. This history of the reservation clause in acts of incorporation supports our proposition, that whatever right, franchise, or power in the corporation depends for its existence upon the granting clauses of the charter, is lost by its repeal. This view is sustained by the decisions of this court and of other courts on the same question." Pennsylvania College Cases, 13 Wall. (U. S.) 190; Tomlinson v. Jessup, 15 Wall. (U. S.) 454; Railroad Co. v. Maine, 96 U. S. 499; Sinking Fund Cases, 99 U. S. 700; Railroad Co. v. Georgia, 98 U. S. 359; Erie & N. E. R. Co. v. Casey, 26 Pa. St. 287; Miners' Bank v. United States Bank, 1 Greene (Iowa), 553.

7. Dissolution by Failure of an Integral Part of the Corporation. —A corporation may be dissolved when it has lost an integral part of its organization, which part the corporation has no means of supplying, and without which the functions of the corporation cannot be exercised.[1] This method of dissolution occurs in the case of municipal and ecclesiastical corporations, and in the case of clubs and other societies, all of whose members are dead. It can seldom or never occur in the case of private corporations with transferable shares, whose officers may be elected by the stockholders.[2] In a corporation of this kind the membership is always

peal of a special charter by a general law. Nor is there any principle of law forbidding such repeal, without the use of words descriptive of the legislative intent to repeal the earlier statute. Repeals by implication are not favored. But the question is always one of legislative intent, and the intent to abrogate the particular enactment in an earlier statute by a general provision in a later statute is sufficiently manifested where the provisions of the two enactments are so inconsistent that they cannot stand together." See also Union Improvement Co. *v.* Commonwealth, 69 Pa. St. 140; Mechanics', etc., Bank *v.* Bridges, 30 N. J. Law 112.

In City of Grand Rapids *v.* Grand Rapids Hydraulic Co., 33 N. W. Rep. 749, it was stated that a corporation's charter cannot be repealed or amended by any statute which does not directly refer to it.

1. In Philips *v.* Wickham, 1 Paige (N. Y.), 596, the court said: "If a corporation consists of several integral parts, and some of those are gone, and the remaining parts have no power to supply the deficiency, the corporation is dissolved. As in the case in Rolle (1 Roll. Abr. 514, I.) where the corporation was to be composed of a certain number of brothers and sisters, and all the sisters were dead, and it was admitted that all grants and acts done by the brothers afterwards were void; for after the sisters were dead it was not a perfect corporation. But the case which is immediately afterwards stated by Rolle shows that if the brothers had possessed the power of appointing other sisters in the place of those who were dead the corporation might have been revived. So, Baron Comyn says, if a corporation refuses to continue the election of officers till all die who could make an election, the corporation is dissolved." So in Rex *v.* Pasmore (3 T. R. 245), Buller, J., said: "I am of opinion that whenever a corporation is reduced to such a state as to be incapable of acting or continuing itself, it is dissolved."

2. In Philips *v.* Wickham, 1 Paige (N. Y.), 596, it was decided that a *quasi* corporation, consisting of the owners of certain submerged lands, and having the power under a statute to conduct operations for the drainage of the lands, was not extinguished by the failure of the members to elect commissioners at the time and place fixed by the statute. The court held that the commissioners, who were annual officers, might be elected by the members at the period of the ensuing annual election. "No act," said the court, "is required to be done by the commissioners, except to report their proceedings for the last year to the meeting; and if there were no commissioners there could be no proceedings to report. The commissioners are not even required to preside at the meeting. There is nothing in the nature of the duties to be performed which necessarily requires a continued succession of commissioners." In Rose *v.* Turnpike Co., 3 Watts (Pa.), 48, Sergeant, J., said: "Our corporations bear little resemblance to the English municipal corporations either in design or constitution. The present, like many of our incorporations for civil purposes, either by special act of assembly or under the act of 1791, is not a corporation composed of several integral parts. The stockholders constitute the company, and the managers and officers are their agents, necessary for the conduct and management of the affairs of the company, but not essential to its existence as such, nor forming an integral part. The corporation exists *per se*, so far as is requisite to the maintenance of perpetual succession, and holding and preserving its franchises. The non existence of the managers does not imply the non-existence of the corporation. The latter is dormant during that time; its franchises are suspended for want of the means of

States.[1] The mode of proceeding at common law against a corporation to enforce a forfeiture is by *scire facias*, or by a writ of *quo warranto*, or by an information in the nature of *quo warranto*. A *scire facias* is proper where there is a legal body capable of acting, but who have been guilty of an abuse of the power intrusted to them. A *quo warranto* is necessary where there is a corporate body *de facto*, who take upon themselves to act as a body corporate without legal power so to do. In the *United States* it is customary to employ an information in the nature of a *quo warranto* both against corporations having a legal existence and against associations assuming corporate powers without authority.[2] Unless

1. In Commonwealth *v.* Union Fire & Marine Ins. Co., 5 Mass. 230, Parsons, C. J., said: "An information for the purpose of dissolving the corporation or of seizing its franchises cannot be prosecuted but by the authority of the commonwealth, to be exercised by the legislature, or by the attorney- or solicitor-general, acting under its direction, or *ex officio* in its behalf. For the commonwealth may waive any breaches of any condition expressed or implied on which the corporation was created; and we cannot give judgment for the seizure by the commonwealth of the franchises of any corporation unless the commonwealth be a party in interest to the suit."

In Matter of N. Y. Elevated R. Co., 70 N. Y. 337, Earl, J., said: "A cause of forfeiture cannot be taken advantage of or enforced against a corporation collaterally or incidentally, or in any other mode than by a direct proceeding for that purpose against the corporation; and the government creating the corporation can alone institute the proceeding; and it can waive a forfeiture, and this it can do expressly or by legislative acts recognizing the continued existence of the corporation." See also State *v.* Moore, 19 Ala. 514; New Jersey Southern R. Co. *v.* Long Branch Commissioners, 39 N.J. Law, 35; Chester Glass Co. *v.* Dewey, 15 Mass. 94; Commonwealth *v.* Lexington Turnpike Co., 6 B. Mon. (Ky.) 397; Society, etc., *v.* Morris Canal, Saxt. (N. J.) 157; Central Cross-town R. Co. *v.* Twenty-third Street R. Co., 54 How. Pr. (N. Y.) 185; Commonwealth *v.* Allegheny Bridge Co., 20 Pa. St. 185; Bank of U. S. *v.* Commonwealth, 17 Pa. St. 407; Dyer *v.* Walker, 40 Pa. St. 157; Murphy *v.* Farmers' Bank, 20 Pa. St. 415; Wight *v.* People, 15 Ill. 417; Baker *v.* Backus, 32 Ill. 79; State *v.* Real Est. Bank, 5 Ark. 596; Importing, etc., Co. *v.* Locke, 50 Ala. 334; Commonwealth *v.* Burrell, 7 Pa. St. 34; Banks *v.* Poitiaux, 3 Rand. (Va.) 142; West *v.* Carolina Life Ins. Co., 31 Ark. 476; Moore *v.* Schoppert, 22 W. Va. 282; Kishacoquillas Turnpike Co. *v.* McConaby, 16 S. & R. (Pa.) 144; Vernon Society *v.* Hills, 6 Cowen (N. Y.), 23; State *v.* Paterson Turnpike Co., 1 Zab. (N. J.) 9; Mosely *v.* Burrow, 52 Texas, 396; Toledo, etc., R. Co. *v.* Johnson, 49 Mich. 148; Enfield Toll Bridge Co. *v.* Connecticut River Co., 7 Conn. 45; Kellogg *v.* Union Co., 12 Conn. 7; Gaylord *v.* Fort Wayne, etc., R. Co., 6 Biss. (C. C.) 286; Penobscot Boom Co. *v.* Lamson, 16 Me. 231; State *v.* Vincennes University, 5 Ind. 89; Curien *v.* Santini, 16 La. Ann. 27; Proprietors of Baptist Meeting-house *v.* Webb, 66 Me. 398; Stoops *v.* Greensburgh, etc., Plank-road Co., 10 Ind. 47; Hartsville University *v.* Hamilton, 34 Ind. 506; Heard *v.* Talbot, 7 Gray (Mass.), 119; Bache *v.* Nashville, etc., Society, 10 Lea (Tenn.), 436; State *v.* White's Creek Turnpike Co., 3 Tenn. Ch. 163; Greenbrier Lumber Co. *v.* Ward (W. Va.), 3 S. E. Rep. 227; Asheville Division *v.* Aston, 92 N. Car. 578; State *v.* Butler, 15 Lea (Tenn.), 104; State *v.* Crawfordsville, etc., Turnpike Co., 102 Ind. 283.

2. Rex *v.* Pasmore, 3 T. R. 244; Ang. & A. Corp. §§ 731–765, and Morawetz on Corporations (2d Ed.), § 1030.

To authorize the institution of a suit in the name of the State to forfeit the charter of the corporation, it is not necessary that the legislature should by some general or special statute have authorized and directed the suit to be brought. If the legislature declares that a particular act of malfeasance or nonfeasance by a corporation or its officers shall work a forfeiture, it is the duty of the prosecuting officers of the State in case of such nonfeasance or malfeasance to institute a suit, and no further authority is necessary. State *v.* Southern Pacific R. Co., 24

form duties which it has assumed for the benefit of the public or which have been imposed upon it for reasons of public policy, it renders itself liable to forfeiture.[1] It is also liable to forfeiture where it fails to perform some act, the performance of which was a condition subsequent to the granting of the charter.[2] And where a private corporation has become wholly insolvent, and is thereby prevented from carrying on its business with safety to its creditors or to the public, it is its duty to wind up its affairs, and a failure to perform this duty may be punished by a compulsory

govern conditions annexed to them. The analogous cases of individual conditional grants will give the rule." See also State v. Pawtuxet Tpke. Co., 8 R. I. 182.

Where a bank was prohibited by its charter from making loans at a greater rate of discount than one half of one per cent for thirty days, and from dealing in promissory notes, and it wilfully violated these restrictions by discounting at higher rates than that allowed, and by dealing in promissory notes otherwise than by discounting them at the rate prescribed, it was held that such acts constituted a good ground of forfeiture. Commonwealth v. Commercial Bank of Pennsylvania, 28 Pa. St. 383. See also State v. Bradford, 32 Vt. 50; State v. Central Ohio, etc., Relief Assoc., 29 Ohio, 399; Charles River Bridge Co. v. Warren Bridge Co., 7 Pick. (Mass.) 371; State v. Bailey, 16 Ind. 46; Centre, etc., Turnpike Co. v. McConaby, 16 S. & R. (Pa.) 145; State v. Beck, 81 Ind. 501; State v. Kenyon, 51 Ind. 142. In People v. Utica Insurance Co., 15 Johns. (N. Y.) 358, a judgment of *ouster* was rendered against an insurance company which had undertaken to carry on banking operations without authority, and in violation of a general law restraining unauthorized banking. See also State Bank v. State, 1 Blackf. (Ind.) 267; People v. Phœnix Bank, 24 Wend. (N. Y.) 431; Commonwealth v. Union Fire, etc., Ins. Co., 5 Mass. 230. The withdrawing of stock under the form of loans on private security by a bank with intent to reduce the effective capital below the amount required by the charter, is a good cause of forfeiture. State v. Essex Bank, 8 Vt. 489. The contracting of debts or issuing of bills to a larger amount than the charter allows, or issuing with a fraudulent intention more paper than the bank can redeem, are causes of forfeiture. State Bank v. State, 1 Blackf. (Ind.) 270; Bank Commissioners v. Rhode Island Bank, 5 R. I. 12; Bank Commissioners v. Banks of Buffalo, 6 Paige (N. Y.) 497.

1. Long-continued neglect to repair their road by a turnpike company is a cause of forfeiture. People v. Fishkill, etc., Plank Road Co., 27 Barb. (N. Y.) 452; People v. Hillsdale Turnpike Co., 23 Wend. (N. Y.) 254; People v. Plymouth Plank Road Co., 32 Mich. 248; People v. Jackson, etc., Plank Road Co., 9 Mich. 285; State v. Royalton, etc., Turnpike Co., 11 Vt. 431; Turnpike Co. v. State, 3 Wall. (U. S.) 210.

Where a railroad company suffers its railroad to be sold on execution, and broken up in whole or in part, it renders itself liable to forfeiture. State v. Rives, 5 Ired. (N. C.) 309. See also State v. Minnesota Cent. R. Co. (Minn.), 30 Northwestern Rep. 816.

If a bridge necessary to render a road passable be carried away by a flood, the bridge company must rebuild it within a reasonable time or they will forfeit their charter. People v. Hillsdale Turnpike Co., 23 Wend. (N. Y.) 254; Enfield Toll Bridge v. Connecticut River, 7 Conn. 28.

The failure of a railroad company to comply with a provision in its charter requiring the president and directors of the company make an annual statement of its income and return the same to the general assembly, in order to enable the latter to regulate the tolls charged by the company, was held to be a cause for declaring the charter forfeited. Attorney-General v. Petersburg, etc., R. Co., 6 Ired. L. (N. Car.) 456.

In State v. Milwaukee, etc., R. Co., 45 Wis. 590, it was held that it was the duty of a railroad company "to keep its principal place of business, its books and records, and its principal officers within the State, to an extent necessary for the full-est jurisdiction and visitatorial power of the State and its courts, and the efficient exercise thereof in all proper cases which concern said corporation;" and that a total neglect of this duty would justify and demand a judgment of forfeiture of the franchises of the company. Darnell v. State (Ark.), 3 Southwestern Rep. 365.

2. People v. City Bank, 7 Col. 226.

upon the legal dissolution of a corporation all its real estate reverted to the grantor and its personal property to the king.[1] In equity, however, it is the rule that the capital or property and debts due to an ordinary trading or manufacturing corporation constitute a trust fund for the payment of the dues of creditors and stockholders; and a court of equity, which never allows a trust to fail for want of a trustee, will lay hold of this fund wherever it may be found, and apply it to the purposes of the trust.[2] In many of the States statutes have been passed provid-

Congress provides for such forfeiture whenever the directors themselves violate, or knowingly permit any officers, servants, or agents of the association to violate, any of the provisions of the act. The information filed against the bank by the comptroller of the currency disclosed several gross violations of the act by the directors; and the justice and validity of the decree were not questioned in the State court. With the forfeiture of its rights, privileges, and franchises the corporation was necessarily dissolved, as the decree adjudged. Its existence as a legal entity was thereupon ended; it was then a defunct institution, and judgment could no more be rendered against it in a suit previously commenced than judgment could be rendered against a dead man dying *pendente lite*. This is the rule with respect to all corporations whose chartered existence has come to an end, either by lapse of time or decree of forfeiture, unless by statute pending suits be allowed to proceed to judgment notwithstanding such dissolution. The prolongation of the corporate life for this specific purpose as much requires special legislative enactment as does the original creation of the corporation." See also Ingraham *v.* Terry, 11 Humph. (Tenn.) 572; Saltmarsh *v.* Planters' Bank, 17 Ala. 761; Pashall *v.* Whitsett, 11 Ala. 472; Greeley *v.* Smith, 3 Story (C. C.), 658; Mumma *v.* Potomac Co., 8 Pet. (U. S.) 281; Dobson *v.* Simonton, 86 N. Car. 492; City Ins. Co. *v.* Commercial Bank, 68 Ill. 350; Farmers', etc., Bank *v.* Little, 8 W. & S. (Pa.) 207; Bank of Miss. *v.* Wrenn, 3 Sm. & M. (Miss.) 791; Bank of Louisiana *v.* Williams, 19 La. Ann. 1; May *v.* State Bank, 2 Rob. (Va.) 56; Thornton *v.* Marginal Freight R. Co., 123 Mass. 32; Muscatine Turn Verein *v.* Funck, 18 Iowa, 473; Miami Exporting Co. *v.* Gano, 13 Ohio, 269. *Contra*, Lindell *v.* Benton, 6 Mo. 361. In Platt *v.* Archer it was held that a dissolution of a corporation by a decree of a State court would not abate proceedings in bankruptcy against the corporation, pending at the time the judgment was rendered. See also Hart *v.* Boston, etc., R. Co., 40 Conn. 524. A corporation may be enjoined by a Federal court from taking steps to procure its own dissolution in order to defeat legal proceedings instituted against it. Fisk *v.* Union Pacific R. Co., 10 Blatchf. (C. C.) 518.

1. 1 Blackstone Com. 484; Rex *v.* Pasmore, 3 T. R. 199; 2 Kyd on Corporations, 516; Erie R. Co. *v.* Casey, 26 Pa. St. 287.

2. In Mumma *v.* Potomac Co., 8 Pet. (U. S.) 281, the court said: "We are of opinion that the dissolution of the corporation under the acts of Virginia and Maryland cannot in any just sense be considered, within the clause of the Constitution of the United States on this subject, an impairing of the obligation of the contracts of the company by those States, any more than the death of a private person can be said to impair the obligation of his contracts. The obligation of those contracts survives; and the creditors may enforce their claims against any property belonging to the corporation, which has not passed into the hands of *bona fide* purchasers, but is still held in trust for the company, or for the stockholders thereof, at the time of its dissolution, in any mode permitted by the local laws." And in Curran *v.* Arkansas, 15 How. (U. S) 311, it is said: "If it be once admitted that the property of an insolvent trading corporation, while under the management of its officers, is a trust fund in their hands for the benefit of creditors, it follows that a court of equity, which never allows a trust to fail for want of a trustee, would see to the execution of that trust, although by the dissolution of the corporation the legal title to its property had been changed." See also Wright *v.* Petrie, 1 S. & M. (Miss.) 319; Nevitt *v.* Bank of Port Gibson, 6 S. & M. (Miss.) 513; Read *v.* Frankfort Bank, 23 Me. 318; Commercial Bank of Natchez *v.* Chambers, 8 Sm.

CORPOREAL. — Consisting of a material body, tangible, permanent.[1]

CORPSE. — See Dead Body.

CORPUS DELICTI.

1. **Definition.** — The term means literally the body of the offence or crime; that is, it means the substantial fact that a crime has been committed by some one.[2]

Corpus delicti is always made up of two elements, — first, of the fact that a certain result has been produced; second, of the fact that some one is criminally responsible for the result.[3]

2. **Burden of Proof.** — The onus of proving every thing essential to the establishment of the charge against the accused, lies on the prosecutor.[4]

3. **Confessions.** — An extra judicial confession, uncorroborated, is insufficient to authorize conviction. It is sufficient that there be such extrinsic corroborative circumstances as will, taken in connection with the confession, produce conviction of defendant's guilt in the minds of the jury.[5]

1. **Corporeal Hereditaments.** — Such as are of a material and tangible nature, such as may be perceived by the senses, consisting wholly of substantial and permanent objects, and may be comprehended under the general denomination of land. 2 Bla. Com. 17; Steph. Com. 159; Canfield *v.* Ford, 28 Barb. 339.

Corporeal Possession of land is a residence on, or occupation or cultivation of, the same. Dickson *v.* Marks, 10 La. Ann. 557.

2. Brown's L. Dict. 137.

3. Pitts *v.* State, 43 Miss. 472; State *v.* Dickson, 78 Mo. 438; Ruloff *v.* People, 18 N. Y. 179; People *v.* Bennett, 49 N. Y. 137; U. S. *v.* Williams, 1 Cliff. (U. S.) 25; 3 Greenl. Ev. § 30 (14th ed.); Malone's Cr. Briefs 304; Whart. Cr. Ev. § 325 (9th ed.).

Arson. — In arson, the *corpus delicti* consists, not alone of a building burned, but also of its having been wilfully fired by some responsible person. Burning by accidental and natural causes must be satisfactorily excluded, to constitute sufficient proof of a crime committed. Winslow *v.* State, 76 Ala. 42; Sam *v.* State, 33 Miss. 347; Phillips *v.* State, 29 Ga. 108. See Arson.

Burglary. — The *corpus delicti* consists of the breaking and entering by some person, of the dwelling-house of another, with intent to commit a felony therein. Johnson *v.* Commonwealth, 29 Gratt. (Va.) 796.

Homicide. — The *corpus delicti* in murder has two components, — death as the result, and the criminal agency of another as the means. Ruloff *v.* People, 18 N. Y. 179; People *v.* Bennett, 49 N. Y. 137; People *v.* Schryver, 42 N. Y. 1; s. c., 1 Am. Rep. 480; Smith *v.* Com., 21 Gratt. (Va.) 820.

4. In every case of homicide, the people must prove the *corpus delicti* beyond a reasonable doubt; and if the prisoner claims a justification, he must take upon himself the burden of satisfying the jury by a preponderance of evidence. On the trial of an indictment for manslaughter, the court charged the jury that it was for the prisoner to satisfy the jury, beyond a reasonable doubt, that the homicide was justifiable. *Held*, to be error. People *v.* Schryver, 42 N. Y. 1; s. c., 1 Am. Rep. 480. See also Com. *v.* York, 9 Met. (Mass.) 93; s. c., 43 Am. Dec. 373; U. S. *v.* Searcey, 26 Fed. Rep'r. 435; Ter. *v.* Monroe, 6 Pac. Rep'r. (Ariz.) 478.

5. See Confessions, vol. 3, p. 439.

A mere confession of the party charged with crime, uncorroborated by circumstances tending to inspire belief of its truth, is insufficient to justify conviction. Bergen *v.* People, 17 Ill. 426; s. c., 65 Am. Dec. 672; also, Rex *v.* White, Russ. & R. 508; Rex *v.* Eldridge, Russ. & R. 440; Rex *v.* Faulkner, Russ. & R. 481; Matthews *v.* State, 55 Ala. 187; Johnson *v.* State, 59 Ala. 34; Winslow *v.* State, 76 Ala. 42; People *v.* Jones, 31 Cal. 565; People *v.* Thrall, 50 Cal. 415; Nesbit *v.* State, 43 Ga. 239; Iowa *v.* Dubois, 6 N. W. Rep'r. 578; Williams *v.* People, 101 Ill. 382; People *v.*

CORRECT. — (*Adjective*) Right; conformable to truth; free from error.[1] (*Verb*) To chastise; to punish.[2]

CORRECTION. — See ASSAULT; MASTER AND SERVANT; PARENT AND CHILD.

CORRESPOND. — (1) To be adapted; to agree; (2) to have intercourse or communion.[3]

CORROBORATE (and see EVIDENCE) is used in a sense not materially different from its vernacular meaning, to denote the fortifying of evidence by some matter likely to inspire increased confidence. It is generally applied where the evidence already adduced is, if believed, sufficient for the purpose, but is liable to some suspicion, to remove which the party must produce auxiliary evidence.[4]

Com., 20 Gratt. (Va.) 796; State v. Davidson, 30 Vt. 377.

1. Webster.

In a contract in which it was agreed to "adjust and settle all the mutual accounts pertaining to the aforesaid business, . . . taking the annexed statement of disbursements and collections as correct to date," "correct" was held not to mean "complete." "The meaning and intent of the phrase is not, that the schedules should be peremptorily deemed to include all that was to be the subject of adjustment, . . . but that the schedules should be taken to be correct so far as they went, and as to the items therein specified." Accordingly, evidence in relation to items not included therein was properly considered by an arbitrator. Adams v. Macfarlane, 65 Me. 143.

Under an act requiring, in order to charge a person on the ratification of a contract made during infancy, that the subsequent promise or ratification should "be made by some writing signed by the party to be charged therewith," the words, "I certify the account to be correct and satisfactory," written at the end of a statement of the account, and duly signed, is not sufficient to charge the party. The expression means merely that the items are properly set out, and the sums charged are satisfactory. Rowe v. Hopwood, L. R. 4 Q. B. 1.

An application for life insurance contained the declaration, "I do hereby declare that the above written particulars are correct; . . . and if it shall hereafter appear that any fraudulent concealment or designedly untrue statement be contained therein, then . . . the policy shall be absolutely null and void." *Held*, the policy could only be avoided by a designedly untrue statement. Fowkes v. M. & L. L. A. & L. Assn., 3 B. & S. 529.

A mechanic's lien law requiring that the notice of the lien must contain a description of the property on which the lien is intended to be enforced, is to be construed no differently from a subsequent statute requiring a "correct" description to be contained in the notice. Gordon v. S. F. Canal Co., 1 McAllister (C. C.), 517.

2. Under a statute empowering a justice to commit servants, for any misdemeanor, miscarriage, or ill behavior in his or her service, to the house of correction, "there to remain and be corrected," the correction is a necessary part of the sentence, and must be corporal punishment by whipping. The King v. Hoseason, 14 East, 605.

3. Web. Dict.

Proviso that an annuity should cease if a woman should associate, continue to keep company, or cohabit, or criminally *correspond*, with J. F. *Held*, . . ." the words of the deed were as general as could be, and went much farther than the mere exclusion of criminal cohabitation; the intention was, to put a stop to all intercourse whatever between these two persons. The receiving a man's visits whenever he chooses to call, is associating with him. The parties had chosen to express themselves in those terms, and the words must receive their common meaning and acceptation. Lord Domer v. Knight, 1 Taunton, 417.

Correspondence. — The letters by one person to another, and the answers thereto. Bouvier's Law Dict.

4. Thus, it is said that no conviction may be had for seduction on the uncorroborated testimony of the woman; that testimony of an accomplice or of an impeached witness needs corroboration. Abbott's Law Dict.; Russell v. Commonwealth, 3 Bush (Ky.), 469.

. . . "'The defendant cannot be convicted upon the testimony of said Terrell alone, unless *corroborated* by other testimony tending to connect him with the offence committed; and the *corroboration* is not sufficient if it merely shows the commission of the

COSTS.

1. Definition. — Costs are the necessary expenses incurred by the parties in the prosecution or defence of an action or process at law or in equity.[1]

1. Bouvier's Law Dict.; Burrill's Law Dict.; Henry v. U. S., 15 Ct. of Cl. Rep. 162.

"A pecuniary allowance made by positive law to the successful party in a suit, or distinct proceeding within a suit, in consideration of and to reimburse his probable expenses." Abbott's Law Dict.

"The word 'costs' is a word of known legal signification. It signifies, when used in relation to the expenses of legal proceedings, the sums prescribed by law as charges for the services enumerated in the fee bill." Apperson *v.* Mut. Ben. L. Ins. Co., 38 N. J. L. 272.

A distinction has been made between *fees and costs*. "Costs are an allowance to *a party* for expenses incurred in conducting his suit; fees are a compensation to an *officer* for services rendered in the progress of a cause. . . . As between a party and the officer, charges for services rendered are costs [fees?]; as between the parties to the cause, being in contemplation of law charges actually paid by the successful party, or at least such as have created a responsibility to the officer, they are costs. . . . To avoid the vexation of an original suit for a trifling demand, it became a practice to include them in the execution as if they were a part of the successful party's costs; but they were in truth not so, as they might be recovered by the officer in a suit in his own name. In the identity of the usual mode of collection alone is there the least resemblance between costs and fees." Musser *v.* Good, 11 S. & R. (Pa.) 247.

Costs of the Day are costs incurred in preparing for trial on a certain day. Bouv. Law Dict.; Brown's Law Dict.

Costs de Incremento, or costs of increase, are those extra expenses which do not appear on the face of the proceedings, such as counsel's fees, expenses of witnesses, attendance on court, etc. Abbott's Law Dict.

Costs adjudged by the court in addition to those assessed by the jury. Bouv. Law Dict.

Costs are also *Interlocutory*, arising in the course of the suit; or *Final*, depending on the event of the suit. Bac. Abr. title "Costs;" 2 Tidd, Pr. 945.

Nature of Costs. — Costs are incident to the recovery, and are no part of the relief sought. Gray *v.* Dougherty, 25 Cal. 266; Knight *v.* Whitman, 6 Bush (Ky.), 51; Clark *v.* Rowling, 3 N. Y. 216. Hence they are no such part of the matter in dispute as to give a court jurisdiction by increasing the amount involved. Votan *v.* Reese, 20 Cal. 89.

Costs do not become a debt till judgment is rendered; and therefore a discharge in bankruptcy pending the determination of a suit does not relieve the bankrupt from paying them, nor will a conveyance of property before judgment in the suit be declared fraudulent as respects the costs. Pelham *v.* Aldrich, 8 Gray (Mass.), 515; s. c., 69 Am. Dec. 266; Dows *v.* Griswold, 122

unless expressly authorized by statute.[1] It is said that the court has no more jurisdiction to award costs than to grant relief. The rule is not universal, however; and where the court has jurisdiction of the parties, though not of the subject-matter, costs are frequently given,[2] especially where the want of jurisdiction does not clearly appear on the face of the writ, and is a fair subject of discussion.[3]

(*d*) *Who may grant.* — Neither court, jury, nor referees can award costs, unless authorized by law;[4] and where the rule is fixed by statute, it must be followed strictly.[5]

4. To Whom and against Whom granted. — (*a*) *In General.* — Ordinarily costs are paid by the defeated to the prevailing party.[6]

complete bar to all further proceedings in the suit thereby interposed by the legislature, then all voluntary control or agency of the parties in the disposition of the cause is ended *vi majori*, and neither can be regarded as the prevailing party," nor receive costs. Saco *v.* Gurney, 34 Me. 14.

1. [illegible] *v.* Slocum, 23 Ala. 668; [illegible] *v.* Boyd, 21 Ark. 264; Heflin *v.* Owens, [illegible] Ark. 265; Dever *v.* Mortragon, 4 Colo. [illegible]; [illegible] *v.* Hoev, 3 Colo. 279; Banks *v.* [illegible], 3 Litt. (Ky.) 332; Clark *v.* Rockwell, [illegible] Mass. 221; Williams *v.* Blunt, 2 Mass. [illegible]; Green *v.* Whiting, 1 Smed. & M. (Miss.) 579; Wingate *v.* Wallis, 5 Smed. & M. (Miss.) 249; Eames *v.* Carlisle, 3 N. H. 130; Norton *v.* McLeary, 8 Ohio St. 205; [illegible] *v.* Patterson, 4 Ohio, 200; Hopkins *v.* Brown, 5 R. I. 357; Walker *v.* Snowden, 2 Swan (Tenn.), 193; Taul's Admr. *v.* Collingsworth, 2 Yerg. (Tenn.) 579; Barlow *v.* Burr, 1 Vt. 488; Inglee *v.* Coolidge, 2 Wheat. (U. S.) 363; Maxfield *v.* Levy, 4 Dall. (U. S.) 330; Strader *v.* Graham, 18 How. (U. S.) 602; Pentlarge *v.* Kirby, 20 Fed. Rep. 898.

2. It is said that the defendant should not suffer by being forced to come into a court having no jurisdiction of the controversy, and also that the plaintiff should be estopped to deny jurisdiction so far as the question of costs is concerned. Moran *v.* [illegible], 11 B. Mon. (Ky.) 17; Brown *v.* Allen, 34 Me. 436; Harris *v.* Hutchins, 28 Me. 102; Elder *v.* Dwight Co., 4 Gray (Mass.), 201; Jordan *v.* Dennis, 7 Met. (Mass.) 590; Hunt *v.* Hanover, 8 Met. (Mass.) 343; State *v.* Thompson, 81 Mo. [illegible]; [illegible] *v.* Curd, 68 Mo. 282; State *v.* [illegible], 41 N. H. 238; Cumberland, etc., Co. *v.* Hoffman, 39 Barb. (N. Y.) 16; Paine *v.* Chase, 14 Wis. 653. See also Winchester *v.* Jackson, 3 Cranch (U. S.), 514.

And where a cause is remanded from a Federal to a State court, because the former has no jurisdiction, attorney's fees may be allowed as on final disposition of the cause. [illegible] Co. *v.* Higgins, 114 U. S. [illegible]; [illegible] *v.* Phillips, 27 Fed. Rep. [illegible].

3. Thomas *v.* White, 12 Mass. 367; Cary *v.* Daniels, 5 Met. (Mass.) 239; Osgood *v.* Thurston, 23 Pick. (Mass.) 110; Dixon *v.* Hill, 8 Ind. 147; Call *v.* Mitchell, 39 Me. 465; Balfour *v.* Mitchell, 12 Miss. 629.

4. *In re* Olmsted, 3 Dem. (N. Y.) 581; Guier *v.* Macfadon, 1 Ashm. (Pa.) 1; Bills *v.* Harris, 2 Va. Cas. 26; First National Bank *v.* Prescott, 27 Wis. 616.

That part of the jury's verdict giving unauthorized costs may be treated as surplusage. Connor *v.* Winton, 8 Ind. 315; s. c., 65 Am. Dec. 761; Corwin *v.* Thomas, 83 Ind. 111.

In an action *ex contractu* the jury should not consider costs. Bartholomew *v.* Bushnell, 20 Conn. 271; s. c., 52 Am. Dec. 338.

In an action *ex delicto* the jury may properly ask instructions as to the effect of the amount of the verdict on the costs. Elliott *v.* Brown, 2 Wend. (N. Y.) 497; s. c., 20 Am. Dec. 634; Waffle *v.* Dillenbeck, 39 Barb. (N. Y.) 123; Hicks *v.* Foster, 13 Barb. (N. Y.) 663. And they have been allowed to include costs in the amount of damages where punitive damages were proper, — Ives *v.* Carter, 24 Conn. 392; Dibble *v.* Morris, 26 Conn. 416; Campbell *v.* Short, 35 La. Ann. 465; Eatman *v.* New Orleans Pac. Ry., 35 La. Ann. 1018; Whipple *v.* Cumberland Mfg. Co., 2 Story (U. S.), 661, — as also the costs of a former action. Noyes *v.* Ward, 19 Conn. 250. *Compare* Jaudt *v.* South, 2 Dakota, 46; Barnard *v.* Poor, 21 Pick. (Mass.) 378; Lincoln *v.* S. & S. R. Co., 23 Wend. (N. Y.) 425; Stimpson *v.* Railroads, 1 Wall. Jr. (U. S.) 164; Day *v.* Woodworth, 13 How. (U. S.) 372. In action on covenants of warranty and seisin in the sale of real estate, and on breach of warranty of title to personal property, costs of a former action have been allowed. 3 Pars. Cont. (7 ed.) 165, 166, and cases cited.

5. McDonald *v.* Evans, 3 Oregon, 474; Wall *v.* Covington, 76 N. Car. 150.

6. It is said that there must be an express provision of law to permit the awarding of costs to or against one not a party to the record — Patterson *v.* Officers, 11 Ala. 740;

costs when acting in good faith for the benefit of the estate, the amount will be allowed him in his accounts.[1]

When he fails in an action based on a transaction to which he is himself a party, he is personally liable for the costs, whether he prosecutes or defends.[2]

(d) Trustees, Garnishees, and Plaintiffs in Cases of Interpleader.—Courts of equity having almost exclusive jurisdiction over suits between trustees and *cestuis que trust*, costs are governed by the special rules obtaining in equity.[3] Trustees prosecuting or defending without improper motives, and in doubtful cases, are generally entitled to costs out of the trust fund.[4] In suits between trustees and strangers respecting the trust fund, costs are usually awarded as in other cases where no trust is involved,[5] with the exception before made in favor of executors and administrators; but if the prosecution is just and proper, the unsuccessful trustee may be allowed his costs out of the fund.[6]

Where trustees, or other persons who are brought before a court as necessary parties, disclaim all interest and yield, costs should not be granted against them.[7]

1. Hardy v. Call, 16 Mass. 530; Morton v. Barrett, 22 Me. 257; Miles v. Bacon, 4 J. J. Marsh. (Ky.) 463. An executor who in good faith propounds a will, or resists a contest to vacate it, or seeks to have its construction settled, is entitled to have any costs incurred made a charge against the estate, and is also sometimes allowed reasonable attorney's fees. Henderson v. Simmons, 33 Ala. 291; s. c., 70 Am. Dec. 590; Phillips v. Phillips, 81 Ky. 328; Buchanan v. Lloyd, 64 Md. 306; Compton v. Barnes, 4 Gill (Md.), 55; s. c., 45 Am. Dec. 115; Craft v. Snook's Exrs., 2 Beasley Ch. (N. J.) 121; s. c., 78 Am. Dec. 94; Fidelity, etc., Co.'s Appeal, 99 Pa. St. 443. Where the construction sought was only as to a certain gift, it was held error to charge the costs against the whole estate. Cook v. Munn, 33 Hun (N. Y.), 25. And so one not an executor propounding or opposing a will in good faith may have his costs charged against the estate, though unsuccessful. Chaffee v. Baptist Convention, 10 Paige (N. Y.), 85; s. c., 40 Am. Dec. 225; Meurer's Will, 44 Wis. 392. And a provision in a will, that a child opposing it should pay costs, is nugatory. Hunt v. Holt, 40 N. J. Eq. 478.

2. "Whenever he [an executor or administrator] brings an action *in autre droit*, that is founded upon a transaction which arose in the lifetime of the testator or intestate, and fails, he shall not pay costs; but if for a cause to which he himself was a party, although the fruits of the suit, if successful, would be assets when received, yet if he fails, he shall pay the costs out of his own pocket. . . . The reason assigned for it, which is, that not being privy to the original transaction, he cannot be presumed to know exactly what the case may turn out to be upon investigation, and therefore shall not pay costs; but, on the other hand, where he is a party to it, and therefore must be presumed to know all about it, he will be held to act upon his own responsibility, and not to saddle the estate with the costs of the suit in case of failure." Potts v. Smith, 3 Rawle (Pa.), 361; s. c., 24 Am. Dec. 359. See also Buckland v. Gallup, 40 Hun (N. Y.), 61; Gebhart v. Shindle, 15 S. & R. (Pa.) 235; Jenkins v. Plume, 1 Salk. 207; Nicolas v. Killigrew, 1 Ld. Raym. 436; Hollis v. Smith, 10 East, 293; Boland v. Spencer, 8 T. R. 358; Pauler v. Delander, Ander. 357; Atkey v. Heard, Cro. Car. 219. *Compare* Carr's Exr. v. Anderson, 2 Hen. & M. (Va.) 361; Bull v. Palmer, 2 Lev. 165.

It should be borne in mind that the above rules are principally applicable under general statutes giving costs, while some States have special statutes regarding the liability for costs of executors and administrators; and also that in equity the subject rests largely in the discretion of the court.

3. See COSTS IN EQUITY, *post.*

4. 2 Perry on Trusts (2d ed.), 593, and cases cited. See COSTS OF EXECUTORS AND ADMINISTRATORS, *ante.*

5. 2 Perry on Trusts (2d ed.), 519.

6. 2 Perry on Trusts (2d ed.), 520, and cases cited. So of assignees for the benefit of creditors. Pettibone v. Stevens, 15 Conn. 19; s. c., 38 Am. Dec. 57; *In re* Edwards, 10 Daly (N. Y.), 68.

7. Adams v. Myers, 61 Wis. 385; 2 Perry on Trusts (2d ed.), 521.

(*f*) *Husband and Wife.* — Since at common law the husband was always joined with the wife in suits against third parties, and had the management of the cause (except in the few instances where she was treated as sole), he alone was liable for costs;[1] but where she can sue or be sued alone, and a binding judgment against her property be rendered, costs may be granted against her.[2]

In suits between husband and wife, when she sues out or defends against a peace warrant, or sues for a separate maintenance or alimony, or sues or defends in divorce proceedings, and is successful, she is entitled to her costs on the final disposition of the cause;[3] and, when *unsuccessful*, the prevailing opinion is, that she is not liable for his costs.[4] Costs have been awarded to her even where he prevailed.[5]

(*g*) *Assignors and Assignees.* — The assignor of a chose in action is liable for the costs of a suit brought by the assignee in his name, and is entitled in a proper case to be indemnified against them.[6] The real party in interest has also been held liable, even when not made so by statute.[7]

(*h*) *Stockholders.* — An action against stockholders is not based on any previous judgment against the corporation, but upon an original demand, and they are not liable for the costs of the suit against the corporation.[8]

(*i*) *Paupers.* — Permission to prosecute an action *in forma pauperis* does not relieve a party from costs already accrued.[9] In one case it was said, that the object of the statute was to afford him an opportunity to assert his rights, but not to relieve him

1. Stew. Husb. & Wf. sec. 437 and cases cited; Davis *v.* Lumpkin, 58 Miss. 377.

2. Musgrave *v.* Musgrave, 54 Ill. 186; Stew. Husb. & Wf. secs. 437 and 463.

3. Richardson *v.* Richardson, 4 Port. (Ala.) 467; s. c., 30 Am. Dec. 538; Thorndike *v.* Thorndike, 1 Wash. 189; 2 Bish. Mar. & Div. secs. 365 and 394.

4. Richardson *v.* Richardson, 4 Port. (Ala.) 467; Word *v.* Word, 29 Ga. 281; Finley *v.* Finley, 9 Dana (Ky.), 52; s. c., 33 Am. Dec. 528; Reavis *v.* Reavis, 1 Scam. (Ill.) 242; Thatcher *v.* Thatcher, 17 Ill. 66; De Rose *v.* De Rose, Hopk. Ch. (N. Y.) 100; Wood *v.* Wood, 2 Paige (N. Y.), 454; Garlick *v.* Strong, 3 Paige (N. Y.), 440; Martinez *v.* Lacero, 1 N. Mex. 208. See also Lockridge *v.* Lockridge, 3 Dana (Ky.), 28; s. c., 28 Am. Dec. 52; Erissman *v.* Erissman, 25 Ill. 136; Decamp *v.* Decamp, 1 Green Ch. (N. J.) 294. *Compare* Musgrave *v.* Musgrave, 54 Ill. 186.

5. Richardson *v.* Richardson, 4 Porter (Ala.), 467; McKay *v.* McKay, 6 Grant Ch. (Upp. Can.) 380. *Compare* Nikirk *v.* Nikirk, 3 Met. (Ky.) 432; Shoop's Appeal, 34 Pa. St. 233.

Suit Money. — The costs here referred to are costs in the American sense, the limited expenses of the party for witnesses, writs, etc., and not that broader allowance often granted the wife while the suit is pending, and more properly known as suit money and temporary alimony, with respect to which see chap. 25 Bish. Mar. & Div.; Stew. Husb. & Wf. sec. 463. See title "Alimony," 1 Am. & Eng. Encyc. of Law, 472. Suit money fully takes the place of costs in New Hampshire, in divorce cases. Whipp *v.* Whipp, 54 N. H. 461. Costs in divorce proceeding have been decreed against a third party interfering. Black *v.* Black, 5 Mont. 15.

6. Farmer's Bank *v.* Humphrey, 36 Vt. 554; s. c., 86 Am. Dec. 671.

7. Davenport *v.* Elizabeth, 43 N. J. L. 149; Schoolcraft *v.* Lathrop, 5 Cow. (N. Y.) 17; Norton *v.* Rich, 20 Johns. (N. Y.) 475.

8. Bailey *v.* Bancker, 3 Hill (N. Y.), 188; s. c., 38 Am. Dec. 625; Kingsland *v.* Braisted, 2 Lans. (N. Y.) 17. See further, Thompson on Liability of Stockholders, sec. 375.

9. Lyons *v.* Murat, 54 How. Pr. (N. Y.) 368; Brown *v.* Story, 1 Paige (N. Y.), 588.

(*d*) *Tender.*—A tender of the full amount due when kept good, or an offer to perform the duty required, will throw the costs of a subsequent action upon the plaintiff.[1] And after suit brought, a like full tender, including costs already incurred, made by leave of court, will shift upon the plaintiff all liability for future costs.[2] An offer to confess judgment or suffer default will sometimes have the same effect when the plaintiff fails to recover more than the amount of the offer.[3]

6. Costs on Pleas puis darrein Continuance, Voluntary Non-suit, Arrest of Judgment, etc.—A good plea *puis darrein continuance* admits that the plaintiff had a good cause of action, and defendant must pay costs till the time it is filed.[4] Where the plaintiff accepts a voluntary non-suit,[5] or his action is dismissed on account of a

115; Dunckel v. Farley, 1 How. Pr. (N. Y.) 166. But where the title is conceded, and a license only claimed, the title not being in question, costs will depend on the verdict or judgment. Meller v. Bayard, 15 Abb. Pr. (N. Y.) 449; Utter v. Gifford, 25 How. Pr. (N. Y.) 289. The record must show the title to be involved to carry full costs. Fowler v. Fowler, 52 Conn. 254; Hanly v. Borgmann, 52 Wis. 256.

1. Saunders v. Frost, 5 Pick. (Mass.) 259; s. c., 16 Am. Dec. 394; Seibert v. Gillette, 4 Mo. App. 565; Stowell v. Read, 16 N. H. 20; Holden v. Kynaston, 2 Beav. 204. A tender of the difference between the amount claimed and a valid set-off is sufficient. Smith v. Curtiss, 38 Mich. 393. A tender of the proper deed and a *pro rata* sum of money where the land falls short of the amount contracted for, will relieve from costs in a suit for specific performance. Walling v. Kennard, 10 Tex. 508; s. c., 60 Am. Dec. 216; Rucker v. Howard, 2 Bibb (Ky.), 166.

2. Shaw v. Southern, 10 Iowa, 415; Rucker v. Howard, 2 Bibb (Ky.), 166; Allen v. Wills, 4 La. Ann. 97; Columbian Ass'n v. Crump, 42 Md. 192; Murray v. Windley, 7 Ired. (N. Car.) 201; s. c., 47 Am. Dec. 325; Hay v. Ousterout, 3 Ohio, 384; State Bank v. Holcomb, 2 Halst. (N. J.) 193; s. c., 11 Am. Dec. 549. Where a mortgagee or his assignee avoids the mortgagor and his tender of interest due before action is commenced, the mortgagor may make tender pending such action, and the former will be liable for all costs. Noyes v. Clark, 7 Paige (N. Y.), 179; s. c., 32 Am. Dec. 620. A tender of the sum due for work on specific property made and accepted after suit brought for the recovery of the property, will not relieve the owner of costs, for the action was ill-founded when commenced. McIntyre v. Carver, 2 W. & S. (Pa.) 392; s. c., 37 Am. Dec. 519. After the acceptance of a tender, the recovery of a balance less than the specified statutory amount will not carry costs. Brooks v. Phœnix, etc., Co., 16 Blatchf. (U. S.) 182. A tender of the full amount claimed without costs before service of summons, has been held sufficient. Randall v. Bacon, 49 Vt. 20; 24 Am. Rep. 100. And where a full tender without costs is accepted, the case will not be further continued to award costs. Geiser v. Smith, 36 Wis. 295; s. c., 17 Am. Rep. 494. See further, Hand v. Philips, 18 Neb. 593; s. c., 53 Am. Rep. 824.

3. Rose v. Grinstead, 53 Ind. 202; Higgins v. Rines, 72 Me. 440; Bathgate v. Haskin, 63 N. Y. 261; Burnett v. Westfall, 15 How. Pr. (N. Y.) 420. But in King v. Harrison, 32 Kan. 215, *held*, that the offer must be accompanied with a tender of the amount. And defendant's costs, after tender or offer of judgment, may be set off against the judgment. Stone v. Wiatt, 31 Me. 409; s. c., 52 Am. Dec. 621.

4. Hitt v. Lacey, 3 Ala. 104; s. c., 36 Am. Dec. 440; Nettles v. Sweazea, 2 Mo. 100. So where defendant in ejectment acquires plaintiff's title pending the trial. Reid v. Hart, 45 Ark. 41. And on discharge in bankruptcy while the suit is pending. Shawe v. Wilmerdon, 2 Caines (N. Y.), 380. But the court may direct costs already incurred to be paid out of the bankrupt's estate. *Ex parte* Foster, 2 Story (U. S.), 131.

Release.—But on a compromise of the cause of action and a general release, silent on the question of costs, no costs will be given. Thompson v. Union Elevator Co., 77 Mo. 520; Kimball v. Wilson, 3 N. H. 96; s. c., 14 Am. Dec. 342; Watson v. Depeyster, 1 Caines (N. Y.), 66; Johnson v. Brannan, 5 Johns. (N. Y.) 268. An agreement that either party is to pay costs should be filed in court in order to be enforced by it. Murphy v. Smith, 86 Mo. 333.

5. Burlington, etc., R. Co. v. Sater, 1 Iowa, 421; Reynolds v. Plummer, 19 Me. 22; Dixon v. Parks, 1 Ves. Jr. 402. But

parties are partly wrong, the court may refuse to allow costs to either.[1]

On appeal from equity, an allowance of costs is generally treated as final, unless a palpable abuse of judicial discretion is shown.[2]

8. Costs in Criminal Cases. — By statute it is quite generally provided that a person convicted of crime shall bear the costs of the prosecution.[3] If a pardon is granted after conviction, but before sentence, *all* costs are remitted;[4] but if after sentence, the costs due an attorney or prosecutor are not remitted.[5] Some courts seem to hold, that, after sentence, costs due the State are a vested right, and cannot be remitted by a pardon;[6] but other courts reject this doctrine.[7]

A State, county, or municipal corporation is not liable for costs upon the acquittal of a person charged with crime, unless the

by petition in a pending action, costs are not granted to complainant. White v. Meday, 2 Edw. Ch. (N. Y.) 486; Langdon v. Roane's Ex., 6 Ala. 518; s. c., 41 Am. Dec. 60.

Express Decree. — There must be an express decree for costs, or they will be lost; and a cause will not be brought forward a term that they may be decreed. Lucas v. Moore, 139 Mass. 59; Stone v. Locke, 48 Me. 425; Eldridge v. Strenz, 39 N. Y. Super. Ct. 295.

Bill of Discovery. — It is a general rule that the plaintiff to a bill of discovery must pay costs, — Burnett v. Sanders, 4 Johns. Ch. (N. Y.) 503; King v. Clark, 3 Paige (N. Y.), 76; McCelvy v. Noble, 13 Rich. (S. Car.) 330, — but not the cost of exception to an improper answer. Price v. Tyson, 3 Bland Ch. (Md.) 392; s. c., 22 Am. Dec. 279. And, if defendant refuses to make voluntary disclosure of facts that plaintiff is entitled to know, he may be liable for costs. Weymouth v. Bower, 1 Ves. Jr. 416.

Where the officer's term expired while *quo warranto* proceedings were pending, they were continued and judgment entered, that the party in the right might have costs. People v. Loomis, 8 Wend. (N. Y.) 396; People v. Seaman, 5 Denio (N. Y.), 409. But in *mandamus* proceedings, under similar circumstances, the court refused to proceed with the case. Lacoste v. Duffy, 49 Tex. 767. For costs in *mandamus*, see High Extra. Leg. Rem. sec. 518.

Costs in Admiralty are discretionary as in equity. The "Florence P. Hall," 14 Fed. Rep. 408.

1. Bank of Utica v. Mersereau, 3 Barb. Ch. (N. Y.) 528; s. c., 49 Am. Dec. 189; Jones v. Wadsworth, 11 Phila. (Pa.) 239; Manning v. Ames, 38 Wis. 285; Reed v. Jones, 15 Wis. 40; Green v. Westcott, 13 Wis. 606. If the question is *novel*, costs are not given. Myer v. Hart, 40 Mich. 517; Hesse v. Briggs, 45 N. Y. Super. Ct. 417; Jones v. Mason, 5 Rand. (Va.) 577. So sometimes in a *friendly suit*. Smith v. Bank, 17 Mich. 479; State v. Adams, 58 Vt. 694. Equity will not inquire into the merits of a controversy settled by arbitration merely to award costs. Eastburn v. Kirk, 2 Johns. Ch. (N. Y.) 317.

2. Temple v. Lawson, 19 Ark. 148; Cowles v. Whitman, 10 Conn. 121; Howe v. Hutchinson, 105 Ill. 501; Shields v. Bogliolo, 7 Mo. 136; Smith v. Shaffer, 50 Md. 132; Belmont v. Pouvert, 38 N. Y. Super. Ct. 425; Lake v. Shumate, 20 S. Car. 23; Bratton v. Massey, 18 S. Car. 555; Sanborn v. Kittredge, 20 Vt. 632.

3. State v. Granville, 26 Kan. 158; Schlicht v. State, 56 Ind. 173; State v. Munds, 7 Oregon, 80. Though the statute uses general terms, the better practice seems to be not to impose costs upon conviction of a capital offence. Lanham v. State, 7 Tex. App. 126.

Where the charge is for a felony, and the conviction is for a misdemeanor, only costs pertaining to the latter grade of crime are imposed. State v. Granville, 26 Kan. 158.

Upon a joint conviction for an offence punishable by additional imprisonment to satisfy costs, the sentence of each should be for his proportion of costs. Desty's Am. Crim. L. sec. 54 c, and cases cited.

4. White v. State, 42 Miss. 635; Duncan v. Commonwealth, 4 S. & R. (Pa.) 449; State v. Underwood, 64 N. Car. 599; Watts' Case, Cro. Jac. 336.

5. State v. Mooney, 74 N. Car. 98; s. c., 21 Am. Rep. 487; State v. M. O'Blenis, 21 Mo. 272; Edwards v. State, 12 Ark. 122; 1 Bish. Cr. L. (7th ed.) p. 551, n. 1 and 2, and cases cited.

6. Estep v. Lacy, 35 Iowa, 419; s. c., 24 Am. Rep. 498; Schuylkill v. Reifsnyder, 46 Pa. St. 446.

7. Libby v. Nicola, 21 Ohio St. 414. And see 1 Bish. Cr. L. (7th ed.) sec. 910.

statute.[1] The right of the defendant to demand security for costs is sometimes waived by proceeding in the cause without such demand, after he has knowledge that he is entitled to such security.[2] Where an order to furnish security has been entered, the action will be stayed until the order is complied with, or, on call of the case for trial, it may be dismissed.[3]

(*b*) *Non-residents.*[4] — A rule requiring non-residents to furnish security for costs applies to plaintiffs who become non-resident after the commencement of the action,[5] but not to those who are abroad but temporarily.[6] It does not apply to non-resident plaintiffs who join in an action with residents.[7]

(*c*) *Suits in Forma Pauperis.* — The right to sue in the manner of a pauper seems to be limited to cases falling clearly within the statute; and the right to sue or prosecute an appeal in such manner, where security for costs is required, has been denied.[8]

A general statute does not include the State. State *v.* Taylor, 33 La. Ann. 1270.

The nominal party in a suit may sometimes require the party in interest to secure him against costs. Buckmaster *v.* Beames, 8 Ill. 97; Pierce *v.* Rubie, 39 Me. 205. And frequently the *prochein ami*, or guardian of an infant or *feme covert*, when irresponsible, may be required to furnish security for costs. Fulton *v.* Rosevelt, 1 Paige (N. Y.), 178; s. c., 19 Am. Dec. 409; Lawrence *v.* Lawrence, 3 Paige (N. Y.), 267; Wood *v.* Wood, 8 Wend. (N. Y.) 357; Towner *v.* Towner, 7 How. Pr. (N. Y.) 387; Green *v.* Harrison, 3 Sneed (Tenn.), 131; Hawkins *v.* Hawkins, 4 Sneed (Tenn.), 105; Pennington *v.* Alvin, 1 Sim. & Stu. 265; Walter *v.* Salter, Mosely, 47. *Compare* Anon. 1 Ves. Jr. 409; St. John *v.* Besborough, 1 Hogan (Ir.), 41. For instances of other parties required to furnish security, and additional security, see Bridges *v.* Canfield, 2 Edw. Ch. (N. Y.) 217; Conly *v.* Woonsocket, etc., Inst. 11 R. I. 147; Furman *v.* Campbell, 2 Ben. (U. S.) 472.

1. Newman *v.* Landrine, 1 McCarter (N. J.), 691; s. c., 82 Am. Dec. 249; 1 Daul. Pr. 35.

2. Heflin *v.* Rock Mills, 58 Ala. 613; Weber *v.* Moog, 12 Abb. N. C. (N. Y.) 106; Shuttleworth *v.* Dunlop, 34 N. J. Eq. 488; Goodrich *v.* Pendleton, 3 Johns. Ch. (N. Y.) 520; Long *v.* Tardy, 1 Johns. Ch. (N. Y.) 202; Craig *v.* Bolton, 2 Brown Ch. 609; Mellorucchy *v.* Mellorucchy, 2 Ves. Sr. 24; Prior *v.* White, 2 Molloy (Ir.), 361. *Held*, too late after defendant had answered. Sprague *v.* Haight, 54 Iowa, 446; Trustees *v.* Walters, 12 Ill. 154. And again after jury called. Wallace *v.* Collins, 5 Ark. 43; s. c., 39 Am. Dec. 359.

Filing security for costs is in some States an absolute pre-requisite to commencing an action by a non-resident, and the action may be dismissed where security has been filed since it was commenced. Stillman *v.* Dunklin, 43 Ala. 175; Morse *v.* Rankin, 51 Conn. 326; Sutro *v.* Simpson, 14 Fed. Rep. 370.

But in the absence of any provision as to the time of filing security for costs, it has been held that the defendant may ask, and the plaintiff give, security at any stage of the litigation, *if in good faith.* Lee *v.* Waller, 13 Ill. App. 403; Kimbark *v.* Blundin, 6 Ill. App. 539; Cox *v.* Hunt, 1 Blackf. (Ind.) 146; Cabell *v.* Payne, 2 J. J. Marsh. (Ky.) 134; Hugunin *v.* Thatcher, 18 Fed. Rep. 105; s. c., 21 Blatchf. (U. S.) 497.

3. Anderson *v.* Smith, 2 Mackey (D. C.), 1; Burns *v.* Mount, 28 N. J. Eq. 24; Newman *v.* Landrine, 1 McCarter (N. J.), 291; s. c., 82 Am. Dec. 249.

4. Foreign governments and princes are within the meaning of a rule requiring non-residents to give security for costs. Mexico *v.* Arrangois, 3 Abb. Pr. (N. Y.) 470; s. c., 11 How. Pr. 1, 576.

5. Malaby *v.* Hinkston, 4 Blackf. (Ind.) 127; Haney *v.* Marshall, 9 Md. 194; Newman *v.* Landrine, 1 McCarter, 291; s. c., 82 Am. Dec. 249; Anon. 2 Dick. 776; Weeks *v.* Cole, 14 Ves. 517. *Compare* Berry *v.* Griffith, 1 Har. & G. (Md.) 440. *Held*, not to apply where plaintiff became non-resident pending an appeal by defendant, the judgment standing unreversed. Flint *v.* Van Deusen, 24 Hun (N. Y.), 440.

6. Green *v.* Charnock, 1 Ves. St. 396.

7. *Ex parte* Jennison, 31 Ala. 392; Wood *v.* Goss, 24 Ill. 626; Jones *v.* Knauss, 33 N. J. Eq. 188. An order for security refused where the nominal party was non-resident, the party in interest being resident. Lewis *v.* Lewis, 25 Ala. 315.

8. Bolton *v.* Gardner, 3 Paige (N. Y.), 273; Campbell *v.* Chicago, etc., R., 23 Wis. 490.

Stuart v. Sanborn, 28 Fed. Rep. 299. But as to the latter part of the proposition, compare Clark v. Linneer, 1 Bailey (S. Car.), 189; Dowdell v. Parrish, 5 McLean (C. C.), 291; Spaulding v. Tucker, 2 Saw. (C. C.) 50; Woodruff v. Barney, 1 Bond (U. S.), 528; s. c., 2 Fisher's Pat. Cas. 245.

The fees of witnesses called in good faith, though neither subpœnaed nor examined, have been allowed. Farmer v. Storer, 11 Pick. (Mass.) 241; Wheeler v. Lozee, 12 How. Pr. (N. Y.) 446; Vence v. Speir, 18 How. Pr. (N. Y.) 168. *Compare* Meagher v. Van Zandt, 18 Nev. 230; Goodwin v. Smith, 68 Ind. 301. A party testifying in his own behalf is not entitled to fees. Christy v. Christy, 6 Paige (N. Y.), 170; Logan v. Thomas, 11 How. Pr. (N. Y.) 160; Stearn v. Miller, 30 How. Pr. (N. Y.) 71; Parker v. Martin, 3 Pittsb. (Pa.) 166; Grinnell v. Denison, 12 Wis. 402. *Compare* Rogers v. Chamberlain, 7 Abb. Pr. (N. Y.) 425. When he attends *solely* as a witness, however, he may recover fees. Barry v. McGrade, 14 Minn. 286; Van Duesen v. Bissell, 29 How. Pr. (N. Y.) 481; Hanna v. Dexter, 15 Abb. Pr. (N. Y.) 135; Howes v. Barber, 10 Eng. L. & Eq. 465. As also when called as a witness by his adversary. Goodwin v. Smith, 68 Ind. 301; Hewlett v. Brown, 1 Bosw. (N. Y.) 655; s. c., 7 Abb. Pr. 74.

An attorney has been disallowed fees as a witness in the court where he practises. McWilliams v. Hopkins, 1 Whart. (Pa.) 275. *Compare* Abbott v. Johnson, 41 Wis. 250; and see Tasker v. Schmidt, 25 How. Pr. (N. Y.) 340; Reynolds v. Warner, 7 Hill (N. Y.), 144; Butler v. Hobson, 7 Dowl. 157; s. c., 5 Bing. N. C. 128.

A party's expenses in attaching his own witness are not taxable costs. Rosekrans v. M'Intyre, 9 Wend. (N. Y.) 471. By a provision that the "costs of proving a document" whose execution is not admitted may be taxed against the party refusing to admit the execution, only taxable costs are meant, and not the extra expenses of getting witnesses to attend. Apperson v. [illegible], etc., Co., 38 N. J. L. 272.

Interpreters' Fees may be allowed. Meyer v. Foster, 16 Wis. 294.

Expenses of a Commission to take testimony are often allowed, — Finch v. Calvert, 13 How. Pr. (N. Y.) 13; Cox v. Charleston Ins. Co., 3 Rich. L. (S. Car.) 331; s. c., 45 Am. Dec. 771; Lamb v. Stone, 11 Pick. (Mass.) 527; Washington Bank v. Boston, etc., Co., 6 Pick. (Mass.) 375, — including the fees of witnesses under the commission. Hudson v. Sherman, 19 How. Pr. (N. Y.) 392; s. c., 11 Abb. Pr. 152. *Compare* Rousseau v. Ins. Co., 12 N. J. L. 95. And the costs of a deposition will not be disallowed because the witness was in attendance on the trial for the other side. Hunter v. International R. Co., 28 Fed. Rep. 842. In the absence of a customary regulation the reasonable worth of taking the testimony will be allowed. The "Frisia," 27 Fed. Rep. 480; Peters v. Rand, 108 Pa. St. 255.

Stenographers' Fees are sometimes allowed. Wright v. Wilson, 98 Ind. 112; Reynolds v. Mayor, 14 Abb. Pr. (N. Y.), 176, note 1; Gilman v. Oliver, 14 Abb. Pr. (N. Y.) 174; Sebley v. Nichols, 32 How. Pr. (N. Y.) 182; The E. Luckland, 19 Fed. Rep. 847. *Compare* Bridges v. Sheldon, 18 Blatchf. (U. S.) 507. The cost of a copy of minutes of evidence on motion for new trial allowed. Flood v. Moore, 2 Abb. N. C. (N. Y.) 91. But the cost of a transcript of the evidence for use in another trial disallowed. Hamilton v. Butler, 30 How. Pr. (N. Y.) 36; s. c., 19 Abb. Pr. 446. And a like transcript used in settling a bill of exceptions disallowed. James v. Emmett, etc., Co., 55 Mich. 347. A party must pay his own costs for reporting testimony for his own convenience. Pfandler, etc., Co. v. Pfandler, 39 Hun (N. Y.), 191. Stenographers' fees were ordered to be equally borne by the parties in Arnoux v. Phelan, 21 How. Pr. (N. Y.) 88.

Printing. — Costs of printing papers in a case, and briefs on appeal, are sometimes taxed against the failing party. Smith v. Smith, 30 Ala. 642; Hart v. Marshall, 4 Minn. 552; Salter v. N. & B. R. R., 86 N. Y. 401; Clayton v. Johnston, 82 N. Car. 423; Northampton Ins. Co. v. Stewart, 40 N. J. L. 103; Chambers v. Fisk, 22 Tex. 504; Southmayd v. Watertown, etc., Co., 47 Wis. 517; Dennis v. Eddy, 12 Blatchf. (U. S.) 195. But the costs of printing useless and prolix matter have been disallowed. Wilson v. Railroad, 57 Mich. 155; Personette v. Johnson, 40 N. J. Eq. 532; Crippen v. Brown, 11 Paige (N. Y.), 628; Rogers v. Rogers, 2 Paige (N. Y.), 458; Spang v. Robinson, 24 W. Va. 327. Also abstract of testimony. Hussey v. Bradley, 5 Blatchf. (U. S.) 210. Also testimony for convenience of court. Spaulding v. Tucker, 2 Sawy. (U. S.) 50. Also brief for argument below. Bowditch, etc., Co. v. Winslow, 3 Gray (Mass.), 415; *Ex parte* Hughes, 114 U. S. 548. *Compare* Neff v. Pennoyer, 3 Sawy. (U. S.) 335. Fees for advertising a sheriff's sale are costs, — Gardner v. Brown, 22 Ind. 447; Murphy v. Jones, 7 Mo. App. 569, — if the notice is not defective. Abbott v. Banfield, 43 N. H. 152.

Costs of Necessary Copies of deeds used in evidence are taxable. Inhabitants v. Mill, etc., Corps, 5 Pick. (Mass.) 540; Ela v. Knox, 46 N. H. 16; s. c., 88 Am. Dec. 179; G. & C. R. R. v. Evansich, 61 Tex. 3. Also of a copy of the record for the printer. Botsford v. Murphy, 48 Mich. 642. And of exceptions. Gardner v. Gardner, 2 Gray (Mass.), 434. Costs of copies of indorse-

(*r*) *Appeal from Taxation.* — An appeal from the taxation of costs must be promptly taken,[1] and in equity is strongly disfavored at all times.[2] Costs can be corrected only by direct appeal from the order or judgment granting them,[3] and not by collateral attack, as on appeal from an order refusing a new trial.[4]

13. **Payment and Collection of Costs.** — In the absence of a statute on the collection of costs, an action on the judgment is maintainable;[5] but they are commonly collected by issuing an execution on the judgment.[6] Mandamus will lie to compel the clerk to issue an execution.[7] Costs are sometimes collected by means of a personal attachment.[8] Where there is a second action or trial for the same cause, it may be stayed till the costs of the first action are paid.[9] A judgment for costs may also be availed of as a set-off in another action.[10]

CO-TENANCY. — See TENANTS IN COMMON.

COTTAGE. — A little house without land to it.[11]

unless actually paid. Jermain *v.* Lake Shore, etc., R., 31 Hun (N. Y.), 558; American, etc., Co. *v.* Sheldon, 28 Fed. Rep. 217. See also COLLECTION OF COSTS.

1. Shepherd *v.* Rand, 48 Me. 244; s. c., 77 Am. Dec. 225.

2. See COSTS IN EQUITY, *supra*, this title, 7.

3. Empire, etc., Co. *v.* Bonanza, etc., Co., 67 Cal. 406; Lasky *v.* Davis, 33 Cal. 677; Dowdy *v.* Norton, 41 Cal. 439; Rosa *v.* Jenkins, 31 Hun (N. Y.), 384; Burt *v.* Ambrose, 11 Oregon, 26. A judgment for costs alone, making no disposition of the matter in controversy, is not a "final" judgment from which an appeal lies. Scott *v.* Burton, 6 Tex. 322; s. c., 55 Am. Dec. 782; Warren *v.* Shuman, 5 Tex. 441.

4. Stevenson *v.* Smith, 28 Cal. 102; s. c., 87 Am. Dec. 107; Crosby *v.* Stephan, 97 N. Y. 606. Costs are commonly taxed by the clerk, but the court below may amend the record to include proper items. Lewis *v.* Ross, 37 Me. 230; s. c., 59 Am. Dec. 49. A justice must tax the costs within the time allowed him to enter judgment. Sibley *v.* Howard, 3 Denio (N. Y.), 72; s. c., 45 Am. Dec. 448.

5. Higgins *v.* Callahan, 10 Daly (N. Y.), 420; Hutchinson *v.* Gillespie, 11 Exch. 798; Cole *v.* Langer, 42 N. J. L. 381.

6. Beedle *v.* Mead, 81 Mo. 297; State *v.* Wallin, 89 N. Car. 578. And so in criminal cases. State *v.* Mends, 7 Oregon, 80.

7. Reg. *v.* Fletcher, 2 El. & Bl. 279.

8. State *v.* Kunkle, 39 N. J. L. 618; Schoen *v.* Schlessinger, 7 Abb. N. C. (N. Y.) 399; Colvard *v.* Oliver, 7 Wend. (N. Y.) 497; Norton *v.* Rich, 20 Johns. (N. Y.) 475; Reg. *v.* Johnson, 5 Q. B. 335. But see Cochran *v.* Gowen, 9 Phila. (Pa.) 339.

9. State *v.* Howe, 64 Ind. 18; Somers *v.* Sloan, 3 Harrison (N. J.), 46; s. c., 35 Am. Dec. 526; Peltier *v.* Receivers, 2 Green (N. J.), 391; Jackson *v.* Eddy, 2 Cow. (N. Y.) 598; Sands *v.* McClelan, 6 Cow. (N. Y.) 582; Miller *v.* Grice, 2 Rich. L. (S. Car.) 27; s. c., 44 Am. Dec. 271; Hoare *v.* Dickson, 7 C. B. 164. But see Warren *v.* Homested, 32 Me. 36; Daniels *v.* Moses, 12 S. Car. 130. And *habeas corpus* proceedings will not be stayed. People *v.* Mercein, 3 Hill (N. Y.), 399; s. c., 38 Am. Dec. 644. On *change of venue*, a justice cannot demand payment of costs already accrued, unless authorized by statute. O'Connell *v.* Gavett, 7 Colo. 40.

10. Porter *v.* Liscom, 22 Cal. 430; s. c., 83 Am. Dec. 76.

Authorities. — Beames (Eng.); Brightly (Pa.); Gray (Eng.); Hullock (Eng.); Mansel (Eng.); Marshall (Eng.); Parsons (N. Y. & O.); Pocock (Eng.); Sayer (Irish); Scott (Eng.); Bac. Abr. title "Costs;" 2 Tidd's Pr. 945–993; Perry on Trusts, chap. xxx.; 2 Bishop's Mar. & Div. chap. xxv.; 3 Williams's Executors, 1895–1899; Tyler on Infancy and Coverture (2d ed.), 211–213; 3 Wait's Pr. 453–461; 3 Wait's Law & Pr. (5th ed.) 850–860.

11. Hubbard *v.* Hubbard, 15 Ad. & El. (N. S.) 244; Young *v.* Sotheron, 2 B. & Ad. 628, n. 6.

Properly, however, a cottage seems to have always had a small portion of land attached to it (*fundi ascriptam portiunculam*), as appears also from the terms cot *land*, cot *sethland* (Spelman). And now, according to good authority, by grant of a cottage, a curtilage or garden will pass as included. 2 Ld. Raym. 1015; 6 Mod. 114; 4 Vin. Abr. 582; Shep. Touch. (by Preston) 94.

one professionally engaged in the trial or management of a cause in court; also, collectively, the legal advocates united in the management of a case. As distinguished from *attorney*, the latter is employed for the management of the mechanical parts of a case, while a *counsel* attends to the actual advocating of the cause. In this country the two functions are usually, if not always, united.[1]

COUNT. — A count is sometimes considered as synonymous with a declaration, and this was its original signification in the law-French; but it is now most generally considered as a part of a declaration, wherein the plaintiff set forth a distinct cause of action.[2] It was originally confined to the declaration in a *real* action.[3]

In criminal law the word "count" is used when, in one finding by the grand jury, the essential parts of two or more separate indictments, for crimes *apparently* distinct, are combined; the allegations for each being termed a "count," and the whole an "indictment." And an indictment in several counts, therefore, is a collection of several bills against the same defendant for offences which on their face appear distinct, under one caption, and found and indorsed collectively as true by the grand jury.[4]

"Counting upon" a statute consists in making *express reference* to it, as by the words "against the form of the statute," or "by force of the statute," in such case made and provided.[5]

COUNTER-CLAIM. — A counter-claim is substantially a cross-action by the defendant against the plaintiff, growing out of, or connected with, the subject-matter of the action.[6] A counter-

1. "Counsel or procure." — A person cannot be indicted under the 24 & 25 Vict. c. 94, s. 2, for "counselling, procuring, or commanding" another to commit a felony, unless such felony be actually committed by the other person. *Quære*, whether the words "solicit and incite" in an indictment are equivalent to "counsel, procure, or command." Reg. v. Gregory, L. R. 1, C.C. 77; 10 Cox, C.C. 459. One who has authority to prevent an illegal act being done, who chooses to stand by and see it done without exercising his authority, is properly convicted of "aiding, abetting, counselling, or procuring" the offence. Howells v. Wynne, 15 C. B. N. S. 3.

2. Cheetham v. Tillotson, 5 Johns. (N.Y.) [illegible].

3. Steph. Plead. 5th ed. 30.

4. Brown v. State, 4 S. W. Rep. 464 (Tex.), quoting 1 Bish. Crim. Proc. §§ 421, 422.

5. Hart v. B. & O. R. R. Co., 6 W. Va. 336, quoting Gould Plead. ch. 3, n. 3; likewise "pleading a statute is merely stating *the facts* which bring a case within it, without making mention or taking notice of the statute itself;" and "*reciting* a statute is quoting or stating its *contents*. A statute may therefore be *pleaded* without *reciting* or *counting upon* it, and may be *counted upon* without being *recited*."

6. Slone v. Slone, 2 Metc. (Ky.) 340.

"A counter-claim is a cause of action in favor of the defendant, upon which he might have sued the plaintiff, and obtained affirmative relief in a separate action." Belleau v. Thompson, 33 Cal. 497.

"The term *counter-claim*, of itself, imports a claim opposed to, or which qualifies, or at least in some degree affects, the plaintiff's cause of action." Dietrich v. Koch, 35 Wis. 626.

"A counter-claim is where the demand is against the plaintiff, and for which a judgment might be recovered against him." Tyler v. Willis, 33 Barb. (N. Y.) 333.

"The term 'counter-claim' being new to the law, as well as the dictionary, judges have sometimes exercised themselves with the duty of framing a definition. The term itself has always seemed to me simple and significant, and its meaning obvious. I understand that when the defendant has against the plaintiff a cause of action upon which he might have maintained a suit, such cause of action is a *counter-claim*. The parties then have *cross-demands*. When such a cross-demand is interposed by the

from *set-off*, under the English judicature acts, the latter appears to consist of a defence to the original claim of the plaintiff; a counter-claim being the assertion of a separate and independent demand, which does not answer or destroy the original claim of the plaintiff.[1] (See RECOUPMENT; SET-OFF.)

COUNTERFEITER. — In legal parlance, a counterfeiter is one who unlawfully makes base coin in imitation of the true metal, or forges false currency, or any instrument of writing bearing a likeness and similitude to that which is lawful and genuine, with an intention of deceiving and imposing upon mankind.[2]

COUNTERFEITING

1. **Definition.** — Counterfeiting coin is the making of false or spurious coin in the similitude of a genuine coin.[3]

1. Stooke v. Taylor, 5 Q. B. D. 577; Beddall v. Maitland, 17 Ch. D. 182.

Cross-Complaint. — "The difference between a counter-claim and a cross-complaint is this: in the former the defendant's cause of action is against the plaintiff, and in the latter against a co-defendant, or one not a party to the action." White v. Reagan, 32 Ark. 290.

2. Thirman v. Matthews, 1 Stew. (Ala.) [illegible].

"It has been said that the word counterfeiter has various significations. The dictionary has been referred to, and the treasures of Shakspeare have been called into requisition, to prove that the word has an innocent as well as a criminal meaning. Falstaff said to die was to counterfeit, for he was but a counterfeit who had not the life of a man; and when Sir Walter Blunt had assumed the dress and costume of the king, Douglas is made to say to him, 'Who are those that counterfeit the person of a king?' In Walker's Dictionary, a 'counterfeit or counterfeiter' is said to be 'one who personates another, an impostor, a forger.' In common parlance, a counterfeit is a likeness or resemblance, intended to deceive, and to be taken for that which is original and genuine, and, when applied to persons, is seldom used in an innocent sense."

3. 2 Bishop Cr. L. 7th ed. § 289; 1 Wharton Cr. L. 9th ed. § 749; U. S. v. Marigold, 9 How. (U. S.) 560.

Not only the making but also the importation into the United States of spurious coin, with intent to pass them; the passing or uttering of such coin; and the possession of any counterfeit current gold, silver, or minor coin, with intent to utter it, — have been made an offence by the statutes. In these cases a knowledge of the spurious character of the coin must exist to constitute the offence. Rev. Stat. U. S. §§ 5457, 5458; U. S. v. Marigold, 9 How. (U. S.) 560; U. S. v. Gardiner, 10 Pet. (U. S.) 618; U. S. v. King, 5 McLean (U. S.), 208; U. S. v. Burns, 5 McLean (U. S.), 23; U. S. v. Morrow, 4 Wash. (U. S.) 733.

The offence of counterfeiting includes also the mutilating of coin, the making or uttering of coin in resemblance of money, and the making or issuing of devices of minor coin. In all cases, however, the intent must exist to defraud, by passing them as current coin. Rev. Stat. U. S. §§ 5459, 5461, 5462.

So it includes the debasement of coin by officers of the mint. Rev. Stat. U. S. § 5460.

And the counterfeiting of postal money-orders, postal stamps, postal cards, and stamped envelopes. Rev. Stat. U. S. [illegible] 5463, 5464.

Foreign coins which are by law made current, or are in actual use and circulation in the United States, are also included. Rev. Stat. U. S. §§ 5457, 5459; Fight v. State, 7 Ohio, pt. 1, 180; s. c., 28 Am. Dec. 626.

But counterfeiting a coin not so current, is not punishable under the statute. U. S. v. Gardner, 10 Pet. (U. S.) 618; Com. v. Bond, 1 Gray (Mass.), 564; R. v. Humphrey, 1 Root (Conn.), 52.

Under a statute prohibiting the circulation of bank bills of a less denomination

ing pieces of metal which are not in the likeness or similitude of genuine coin.[1]

4. Counterfeiting Bills. — Falsely making, forging, or counterfeiting any note in imitation of, or purporting to be in imitation of, the circulating notes issued by any banking association, now or hereafter authorized, and acting under the laws of the United States; and also the counterfeiting of United States notes, treasury notes, national bank currency, and other obligations and securities of the United States, is an indictable offence under the statutes.[2]

1. U. S. v. Bogart, 9 Ben. (U. S.) 314; U. S. v. Hopkins, 26 Fed. Rep. 443; U. S. v. Morrow, 4 Wash. (U. S.) 733; U. S. v. Burns, 5 McLean (U. S.), 24; U. S. v. Marigold, 9 How. (U. S.) 560; U. S. v. Abrams, 21 Blatchf. (U. S.) 553; U. S. v. Bricker, 3 Phila. (Pa.) 426.

Where a coin was similar to a genuine United States coin in size, color, milling, and the devices on both sides, but differed from the genuine in weight and inscriptions, it was held to come under the statute. U. S. v. Hargrave, 17 Int. Rev. Rec. (N. Y.) 39.

The court will take judicial notice of the existence of the legal coins of the United States, including those made current by act of Congress: therefore the existence of these coins need not be proved under an indictment for counterfeiting them. U. S. v. Burns, 5 McLean (U. S.), 23; U. S. v. King, 5 McLean (U. S.), 208.

The passing of pieces of metal, apparently gold, octagon in shape, having on one side the device of an Indian, and on the other the inscription "¼ dollar Cal.," is not indictable under § 5461 Rev. Stat. U. S. A counterfeit coin must be in imitation of and resemble the genuine coin. It will be different where the spurious piece purports to be coin of the United States, although the devices with which it is impressed are so far from a similitude to the genuine as to be of original design. U. S. v. Bogart, 9 Ben. (U. S.) 314.

Where a counterfeit coin is in such a shape that it cannot pass in the condition in which it is, unless some labor be bestowed upon it to make it similar to the genuine coin, the statutory offence is not complete. U. S. v. Burns, 5 McLean (U. S.), 24; R. v. Varley, 1 East, P. C. 164.

But a party who has made false coins with intent to circulate them, and has carried the manufacture so far as to produce coins capable of being uttered as genuine coins, may be convicted of the offence described in Rev. Stat. § 5457, notwithstanding he intended to coat such coins with silver before putting them in circulation. U. S. v. Abrams, 18 Fed. Rep. 823.

To change, by any kind of manipulation, silver, copper, or any other metal, into the resemblance of some coin of the United States, or foreign coin, made current by law, or current as money in the United States, by gilding, electro-plating, or any other process, or coloring it so that it resembles gold, is an indictable offence, under chapter 24, act of Congress, Jan. 16, 1877; and a party so doing cannot excuse himself by showing what was his intention, or that he did not intend to use the coins he so made for fraudulent purposes, or that they should be so used by others, or that he was ignorant of the law. U. S. v. Russell, 22 Fed. Rep. 390; U. S. v. Peters, 2 Abb. (U. S.) 494; U. S. v. Moses, 4 Wash. (U. S.) 726. *Compare* U. S. v. King, 5 McLean (U. S.), 208.

Where a coin which had been regularly coined at the mint was afterwards punched and mutilated, and an appreciable amount of silver removed from it, and the hole plugged up with base metal, or with any substance other than silver, it is an act of counterfeiting; but it is otherwise where the hole was punched with a sharp instrument, leaving all the silver in the coin, though crowding it into a different shape. U. S. v. Lissner, 12 Fed. Rep. 840.

A genuine sovereign had been fraudulently filed at the edges to such an extent as to reduce the weight by one twenty-fourth part, and to remove the milling entirely, or almost entirely, and a new milling had been added in order to restore the appearance of the coin. *Held*, that the coin was false and counterfeit. R. v. Hermann, 4 L. R. Q. B. D. 284.

A sheriff may seize counterfeit coin, finished or unfinished, in the possession of a person arrested by him for counterfeiting, without the aid of any statute, as a measure of preventive justice. Such counterfeit coin may be detained as evidence to be used upon the trial of the person in whose possession it is found, though another person may claim to be the owner thereof, and such alleged owner cannot maintain trover for its recovery unless he can show that it was put in its questionable shape without his knowledge or consent. Spalding v. Preston, 21 Vt. 9; s. c., 50 Am. Dec. 68.

2. Rev. Stat. U. S. §§ 5413, 5414, 5415.

An indictment charging that defendant, on a day named, "caused to be printed

them fit for circulation, as by brightening them, he is guilty of the offence.[1]

6. Possession of Implements. — In many States, the possession of instruments and appliances adapted and designed for coining or making counterfeit coin, with intent to use the same, or cause or permit the same to be used in coining or making such coin, is made indictable by statute.[2]

7. Possession of Spurious Coin or Bills. — The possession of counterfeit coins or bank bills, with knowledge of their spurious character, and with intent to pass them, is a punishable offence under the statute.[3]

1. Bennick v. Com., 2 Va. Cas. 356. See also State v. Cheek, 13 Ired. (N. Car.) 114; U. S. v. Morrow, 4 Wash. (U. S.) 733.

Under the Connecticut statute, aiding in the act of counterfeiting is within both the letter and reason of the statute, as much as aiding in making the implements. State v. [illegible], Kirby (Conn.), 52.

Two persons may be joined in an indictment for having counterfeit notes in their possession. Hess v. State, 5 Ohio, 5.

If one pass counterfeit money, and another in any way aids and abets its passage with knowledge of the spurious character of the money, a criminal intent will be supposed, and both are guilty. State v. Hix, 15 Mo. 153. See U. S. v. Mitchell, Baldw. (U. S.) 366.

So is one who assists in preparing a plate from which counterfeit national bank notes are to be printed, indictable under the statute. U. S. v. Russvally, 3 Ben. (U. S.) 157.

The lessee or occupant of a house who knowingly permits his house to be used for counterfeiting, is guilty of assisting in making the coin. U. S. v. Tarr, 4 Phil. (Pa.) 405.

Where two persons are engaged in common criminal enterprise of uttering and publishing counterfeit bills, one of them may be questioned touching the part taken by the other in the passing or redemption of the bills. May v. State, 14 Ohio, 461; s. c. 45 Am. Dec. 548.

Where several persons are indicted for counterfeiting, and a foundation has been laid by proof of connection between them, evidence may be given on the separate trial of each, that parts of the machinery used by them for counterfeiting were found in the possession of others. U. S. v. Craig, 4 Wash. (U. S.) 729.

2. Com. v. Kent, 6 Metc. (Mass.) 221; State v. Griffin, 18 Vt. 198; People v. White, 34 Cal. 183; State v. Brown, 2 Oreg. 221; Bell v. State, 10 Ark. 536; Harlan v. People, 1 Doug. (Mich.) 207; People v. State, 6 Blackf. (Ind.) 95; Chamberlain v. State, 5 Blackf. (Ind.) 513; People v. Page, 1 Idaho T. 114; Miller v. People, 3 Ill. 233; State v. Collins, 3 Hawks. (N. Car.) 191; Bradford v. State, 3 Humph. (Tenn.) 370; Scott's Case, 1 Rob. (Va.) 695. See State v. Bowman, 6 Vt. 594.

The fact that various instruments and appliances for coining money were found in defendant's possession, may be evidence of criminal participation in the counterfeiting, unless the possession of such instruments and appliances is satisfactorily explained. U. S. v. Burns, 5 McLean (U. S.), 23; U. S. v. King, 5 McLean (U. S.), 208; Sutton v. State, 9 Ohio, 133; U. S. v. Craig, 4 Wash. (U. S.) 729.

The possession of an implement adapted and designed to make only one side of the coin, is an offence under the statute. Com. v. Kent, 6 Metc. (Mass.) 221; State v. Griffin, 18 Vt. 198.

Under these statutes the criminal intent must be proved. People v. White, 34 Cal. 183.

An averment that a defendant secretly kept instruments for counterfeiting, sufficiently shows a scienter. Sutton v. State, 9 Ohio, 133.

3. Com. v. Price, 10 Gray (Mass.), 472; Com. v. Cone, 2 Mass. 132; Sasser v. Ohio, 13 Ohio, 453; State v. Benham, 7 Conn. 416; U. S. v. Bicksler, 1 Mack. (U. S.) 341; State v. Washburn, 11 Iowa, 245; State v. Myers, 10 Iowa, 448; State v. Pierce, 8 Iowa, 231; State v. Shelton, 7 Humph. (Tenn.) 31; Gabe v. State, 6 Ark. 519.

The possession of a large quantity of spurious coin may be evidence before the jury of criminal participation in the counterfeiting. U. S. v. Burns, 5 McLean (U. S.), 23; U. S. v. King, 5 McLean (U. S.), 208.

But the possession of such bills purported to be on a bank which does not exist, is not indictable. Com. v. Morse, 2 Mass. 136.

Possession only for the benefit of another is within the statute. Sasser v. Ohio, 13 Ohio, 453.

The possession in one State of counterfeit bank bills, with the intent to pass them

3. Uttering. — To offer, whether accepted or not, a counterfeit coin or bank bill, with a representation by words or actions that the same is genuine, is an uttering under the statute.[1]

[illegible] of making alterations similar to those for which defendant is indicted, is not competent evidence against him. People v. [illegible], 3 Abb. App. Dec. (N. Y.) [illegible].

An indictment for having counterfeit money in possession need not describe the bills with the same minuteness as is required in an indictment for passing counterfeit bills. Jones v. State, 11 Ind. 357.

In an indictment for having counterfeit bank bills in possession, the fact that such bills are destroyed, or are in the prisoner's possession, is a good excuse for the want of a particular description of the notes. Armitage v. State, 13 Ind. 441.

Under an indictment for having counterfeit money in his possession, the court may permit experts to testify to the false character of bank bills without requiring proof that there is a bank in existence issuing genuine bills, of which those in question purport to be counterfeits. Jones v. State, 11 Ind. 357.

1. State v. Horner, 48 Mo. 520; Com. v. [illegible], 2 Binn. (Pa.) 332; U. S. v. Mitchell, 1 Baldw. (U. S.) 366; R. v. [illegible], 2 Leach, 644; R. v. Welch, 2 Den. C. C. [illegible].

And it does not matter whether it is given in charity or in payment for illegal transactions. [illegible] v. [illegible], 1 Brev. (S. Car.) 482; R. v. Ion, 2 Den. C. C. 484; R. v. ——, 1 Cox, C. C. 250.

Pledging a counterfeit bill with the intention to redeem it, is not passing it under the statute. Gentry v. State, 3 Yerg. (Tenn.) 451.

But a counterfeit coin or bank bill is not passed until it is received by the person to whom it is offered. Com. v. Searle, 2 Binn. (Pa.) 332; People v. Tomlinson, 35 Cal. 503; U. S. v. Mitchell, Bald. (U. S.) 366; Perdue v. State, 2 Humph. (Tenn.) 494. See McGregor v. State, 16 Ind. 9; Com. v. Hall, 4 Allen (Mass.), 305.

Selling. — Under a statute which makes it an offence to "utter, pass, and publish" counterfeit notes, without requiring in terms that they should be passed as "true," a conviction may be had upon evidence that they were sold as spurious notes with intent that they should be passed to the public as good notes; and it makes no difference that there is another statute which specially provides a punishment for "selling" spurious notes. U. S. v. Nelson, 1 Abb (U. S.) 135; State v. Wilkins, 17 Vt. 151; Hopkins v. Com., 3 Metc. (Mass.) 460, 464; Bevington v. State, 2 Ohio St. 160; Wilkinson v. State, 10 Ind. 372; King v. Franks, 2 Leach Cr. L. 644. *Compare* People v. Stewart, 4 Mich. 656.

An indictment charging a person with having counterfeit bank notes in his possession, and with making a sale of them, need not aver that the sale was for a consideration, or to the injury of any one. Hess v. State, 5 Ohio, 5; s. c., 22 Am. Dec. 767.

Having in possession counterfeit bank notes for the purpose of selling, bartering, or disposing of the same, and having such bank notes in possession with intent to pass the same to an innocent person as true and genuine, are different and distinct offences, and proof of the one will not support an indictment for either of the others. Hutchins v. State, 13 Ohio, 198; Vanvalkenburg v. State, 11 Ohio, 404.

Under a statute making the sale or barter of counterfeit coin a misdemeanor, a person who sells knowingly spurious coin is indictable, even though the buyer is not aware of the spurious character of the coin. Leonard v. State, 29 Ohio St. 408.

Imitation or resemblance must deceive persons of ordinary observation in order to sustain a conviction for passing a counterfeit bank note. Dement v. State, 2 Head (Tenn.), 505; s. c., 75 Am. Dec. 747; People v. Osmer, 4 Park. Cr. (N. Y.) 242; U. S. v. Turner, 7 Pet. (U. S.) 132; U. S. v. Burns, 5 McLean (U. S.), 23; U. S. v. King, 5 McLean (U. S.), 208; Clarke v. State, 8 Ohio St. 630; State v. McKenzie, 42 Me. 392.

Passing counterfeit money by an agent employed for that purpose is the same as if the money had been passed by defendant himself. U. S. v. Morrow, 4 Wash. (U. S.) 733; Com. v. Hill, 11 Mass. 136.

One receiving counterfeit money is bound to use due diligence in ascertaining its character, and in notifying the giver, provided the latter was ignorant of its character, and paid it in good faith. Atwood v. Cornwall, 28 Mich. 336; s. c., 15 Am. Rep. 219; Raymond v. Baar, 13 S. & R. (Pa.) 318; s. c., 15 Am. Dec. 603; Cucier v. Pennock, 14 S. & R. (Pa.) 56.

A party paying a debt with a counterfeit bill is liable immediately upon an implied promise or warranty that it was genuine, whether he knew it to be counterfeit or not, and a return of the bill before bringing the action is unnecessary, the bill being worthless. Watson v. Cresap, 1 B. Monr. (Ky.) 195; s. c., 36 Am. Dec. 572.

COUNTERPART. — One of two corresponding copies of a written instrument. When the several parts of an indenture are inter-

able to support an indictment for passing a counterfeit note. U. S. *v.* Roudenbush, 1 Baldw. (U. S.) 514.

Evidence. — If the jury are satisfied that the defendant uttered in payment and put away the note described in the indictment, that it was forged and false, and that the defendant knew it to be so, and put it upon the person named in the indictment, with the intent to defraud him, no other proof is necessary of the existence of the bank upon which it purported to be. McCartney *v.* State, 3 Ind. 353; s. c., 56 Am. Dec. 510; Jones *v.* State, 11 Ind. 360; State *v.* Hayden, 15 N. H. 355; People *v.* Chadwick, 2 Park. Cr. (N. Y.) 163; People *v.* Peabody, 25 Wend. (N. Y.) 472; People *v.* Davis, 21 Wend. (N. Y.) 310; Kennedy *v.* Com., 3 Metc. (Ky.) 36; U. S. *v.* Mitchell, 1 Baldw. (U. S.) 366; State *v.* Cole, 19 Wis. 141; Com. *v.* Smith, 6 S. & R. (Pa.) 568; Hobbs *v.* State, 9 Mo. 855. *Compare* State *v.* Brown, 4 R. I. 528; s. c., 70 Am. Dec. 168; State *v.* Twitty, 2 Hawks (N. Car.), 248; State *v.* Morton, 8 Wis. 352; State *v.* Newland, 7 Iowa, 242; s. c., 71 Am. Dec. 444; Com. *v.* Simonds, 11 Gray (Mass.), 306. And see Sasser *v.* Ohio, 13 Ohio, 453; Com. *v.* Carey, 2 Pick. (Mass.) 47; Benson *v.* State, 5 Minn. 19; White *v.* Com., 4 Binn. (Pa.) 418; Com. *v.* Whitmarsh, 4 Pick. (Mass.) 233; State *v.* Van Hart, 17 N. J. L. 327; Com. *v.* Houghton, 8 Mass. 107; State *v.* Ward, 2 Hawks (N. Car.), 443; Murray's Case, 5 Leigh (Va.), 720.

Where, under an indictment for uttering a counterfeit bank bill, a design to defraud an individual is set forth, it is not necessary to allege the existence of the bank of which it purports to be a bill. Com. *v.* Carey, 2 Pick. (Mass.) 47; State *v.* Hayden, 15 N. H. 355. But see De Bow *v.* People, 1 Den. (N. Y.) 9.

An indictment for passing counterfeit bank bills must profess to set out, not the effect, purport, or substance of the bill, but an exact copy of it. State *v.* Atkins, 5 Blackf. (Ind.) 458; Griffin *v.* State, 14 Ohio St. 55; Com. *v.* Clancy, 7 Allen (Mass.), 537. *Compare* State *v.* Smith, 31 Me. 120.

But the number of a bank bill, and the figures in the margin marking its amount, or ornamental devices found on the bill, are not parts of the bill, and need not be set out. Com. *v.* Bailey, 1 Mass. 62; U. S. *v.* Bennett, 17 Blatchf. (U. S.) 357; Com. *v.* Stevens, 1 Mass. 203; Com. *v.* Taylor, 5 Cush. (Mass.) 605; Hampton *v.* State, 8 Ind. 336; Griffin *v.* State, 14 Ohio St. 55.

The name of the State in the upper margin of the bill must, however, be set out, if not repeated in the body thereof. Com. *v.* Wilson, 2 Gray (Mass.), 70.

But it is not improper in such indictment to set out the names and residence of the engravers as the same appear upon the margin of the bill. Thompson *v.* State, 9 Ohio St. 354. And see Buckland's Case, 8 Leigh (Va.), 732.

A slight and unimportant variance, however, as where the same sound is preserved, and the sense not changed, will not make the indictment invalid. May *v.* State, 14 Ohio, 461; Houghton *v.* State, 2 Ohio St. 562; Mathena *v.* State, 20 Ark. 70. *Compare* Porter *v.* State, 15 Ind. 433.

In an indictment for passing counterfeit money, the name of the party to whom it was passed should be stated if known; and if unknown, this fact should be stated. Buckley *v.* State, 2 Greene (Iowa), 162; Gabe *v.* State, 6 Ark. 519.

An indictment which names the person whom the accused intended to defraud by the passing of the counterfeit coin, need not also name the person to whom the coin was passed. U. S. *v.* Benjandie, 1 Woods (U. S.), 294. See also U. S. *v.* Bicksler, 1 Mack. (U. S.) 341.

Under an indictment charging uttering and publishing coin current by law, usage, or custom, time is an ingredient of the offence; and an indictment for counterfeiting such coin, in which the time is not stated, is defective. Nicholson *v.* State, 18 Ala. 529; s. c., 54 Am. Dec. 168. *Compare* State *v.* Shoemaker, 7 Mo. 177.

For the purpose of showing that the defendant, in an indictment for uttering and passing as true a counterfeit bank bill, has made contradictory statements as to the person from whom he received it, an affidavit is admissible, made by him at a previous term, setting forth that an absent witness would testify, if present, that he lent the bill to defendant, and that, so far as he knew, the defendant was ignorant of the fact that it was counterfeit. Com. *v.* Starr, 4 Allen (Mass.), 301.

An indictment for the possession of counterfeit coin charged that the defendant "wilfully, feloniously, and knowingly did have in their possession," etc. *Held*, that their knowledge of its spurious character was as directly affirmed as their knowledge that it was in their possession, and that the knowledge of both facts was sufficiently affirmed. The circumstance that the affirmation was made in respect to the two facts in connection, did not vitiate or weaken the force of the allegation as to each separately. People *v.* Stanton, 39 Cal. 698.

the legislature uses the expression "the country," it is natural to suppose that they mean the country for which they are legislating.[1]

The word is used also to signify a *jury*, as in the expressions, "trial by the country," "conclusion to the country," "puts himself upon the country," etc.

COUNTIES. — See CORONER, COUNTY COMMISSIONERS, COUNTY SEAT, MUNICIPAL CORPORATIONS, OFFICERS OF MUNICIPALITIES, SHERIFF.

1. County defined and described. — (*a*) *Definitions.* — One of the civil divisions of a country for judicial and political purposes.[2] A local subdivision of a State created by the sovereign power of that State, of its own will, without the particular solicitation, consent, or concurrent action of the people who inhabit it. A local organization, which, for the purpose of civil administration, is invested with a few functions of corporate existence.[3]

(*b*) *The Derivation* of the term comitatus, or county, according to Blackstone, is from *Comes*, the count of the Franks, the name of the officer to whom its government was intrusted. The Saxon

1. Mansell v. Israel, 3 Bibb (Ky.), 514. "But the second ground assumed we apprehend clearly brings the plaintiff within the exception which prevents the statute from running against a person without the country. We cannot suppose, as was contended in the argument, that the expression 'the country' should be construed to mean the United States, and not this State."

See also ACROSS, BEYOND, INDIAN.

2. 1 Black. Com. 113.

3. Hamilton County v. Mighels, 7 Ohio St. 109.

The term county, and people of the county, may be used interchangeably. St. Louis Co. v. Griswold, 58 Mo. 175.

Counties are political divisions of the State, and are organized as a part of the machinery of the government, for the performance of functions of a public nature. Barton County v. Walser, 47 Mo. 189; Maury County v. Lewis Co., 1 Swan (Tenn.), 236; Laramie County v. Albany County, 92 U. S. 307; Granger v. Pulaski Co., 26 Ark. 37.

was and is the unit of government, while the two systems have met and modified each other in the Western States.

2. Corporate or Political Existence and its Incidents. — (*a*) *Organisation or Creation of Counties.* — The creation of counties is an act of the sovereign power of the State, and is not based on the particular solicitation, consent, or concurrent action of the people who inhabit them.[1] As a general rule, the power of the legislature, in the division of the State into counties, is absolute, and it may alter, modify, or destroy them as the public good may require.[2]

(*b*) *Powers of a County as a Corporation.* — 1. *Generally.* — A county is a political subdivision of the State, and may be said to act as a corporation with specific powers, through its officers as agents, whose duties are not only pointed out by law, but the mode of performing them laid down with accuracy and precision.[3] It is a public corporation, created by the mere will of the legislature, at whose pleasure, without constitutional prescriptions, its boundaries may be changed, or the county divided.[4]

In some States they are definitely recognized by the legislature and the courts as public corporations.[5]

Local Government in Illinois. By Albert Shaw. J. H. U. Studies. 1st series. No. 3.

Institutional Beginnings in a Western State. By Prof. Jesse Macy. J. H. U. Studies. 2d series. No. 7.

1. Coles *v.* Mad. Co., 1 Breese (Ill.), 115; Hamilton Co. *v.* Mighels, 7 Ohio St. 109. The county organization as distinguished from the State and the town is discussed in the case of People *v.* Stout, 23 Barb. (N. Y.) 338.

2. Public corporations, such as counties, are not within the principle that renders laws impairing the obligation of contracts unconstitutional. People *v.* Power, 25 Ill. 187.

Counties are the creatures of the legislative will. They are vested with certain corporate powers, in order to enable them to perform the duties required of them as part of the machinery of the State; and inasmuch as all their powers are derived from the legislature, the latter may enlarge, modify, or diminish them at any time. They cannot sustain their privilege or their existence upon any thing like a contract between them and the State, because there is not, and cannot be, any thing like reciprocity of stipulation, and their objects and duties are utterly incompatible with every thing in the nature of a compact. Hence the legislature may, unless prohibited by the constitution of a State or the organic law of a Territory, enlarge and diminish the area of a county whenever the public convenience or necessity requires, and make provision for the division of property belonging to it, and for the apportionment of its liabilities. But where it does not make any such provision, the general rule is, that the old county owns all the public property within the new limits, and is responsible for the debts contracted by it before the act organizing the new county, without any claim for contribution. Laramie Co. *v.* Albany Co., 92 U. S. 307; Chambers Co. *v.* Lee Co., 55 Ala. 534; Marengo Co. *v.* Coleman, 55 Ala. 605; Askew *v.* Hale Co., 54 Ala. 639; State *v.* Williams, 29 La. Ann. 779; Carrituck Co. *v.* Dare Co., 79 N. C. 565.

3. Shawnee Co. *v.* Carter, 2 Kan. 115.

4. Mills *v.* Williams, 11 Ired. (N. Car.) L. 558.

5. In *Illinois*, counties are public corporations, and can be changed, modified, enlarged, restrained, by the legislature, to suit the ever varying exigencies of the State. Coles *v.* Madison Co., 1 Breese (Ill.), 115.

In *Pennsylvania* a county is a corporation, and must be sued in its corporate name. Wilson *v.* Commissioners, 7 W. & S. (Pa.) 197. They can be sued only in the courts of the county itself. Lehigh Co. *v.* Kleckner, 5 W. & S. (Pa.) 181; Brown *v.* Somerset Co., 11 Mass. 221; Hecksher *v.* Phila., 20 W. N. C. (Pa.) 52.

In *Tennessee* they are held to have enough of the attributes of corporations to enable them to contract. Railroad Co. *v.* Davidson, 1 Sneed (Tenn.), 637.

So in *Minnesota* it is held that a *county* or other municipal corporation capable of holding real estate is capable of becoming a beneficiary under the act of Congress known as the Town Site Act. Blue Earth Co. *v.* Railroad Co., 28 Minn. 503; Bell

provisions will be found laid down in the constitutions, codes, and acts of the various States; that either as acknowledged public corporations, or as *quasi* corporations, they generally will be found invested with the following corporate powers:—

1. To sue and be sued by a corporate name.

2. To have a county seal.

3. To take and hold real estate within their respective limits, and also personal property, for such objects and purposes as county rates are, or may be, authorized by law, and for such other objects as may be expressly authorized by law.

4. To make such contracts as may be necessary and proper for the execution of the same objects and purposes.

5. These corporate powers to be exercised by commissioners, supervisors, or such officers as may be created and designated for that purpose by the several State legislatures.[1]

The following cases will illustrate certain miscellaneous general powers of counties as expounded by the courts of the several States.[2]

1. See title "Counties" in the Annual Acts of Assembly, Digests and Revisions of the Laws and Constitutions of the several States.

2. Counties created by a territorial legislature have power to bring suit, although the statute does not expressly give the authority to do so. Salt Lake Co. *v.* Golding, 2 Utah, 319.

A county may maintain an action to enjoin a railroad company from laying a track without any lawful authority along and in a county road. Stearns Co. *v.* Railroad Company, 32 N. W. Rep. 91.

A county has the legal capacity to sue for injuries to its highways. Lawrence Co. *v.* Chattaroi R. Co., 81 Ky. 225.

It may sue in ejectment or foreclosure. Lincoln Co. *v.* McClellan, 3 Mo. App. 312.

And a county has the right to employ counsel. Jordan *v.* Osceola Co., 59 Iowa, 388.

Under the laws of *Minnesota* a county can take and hold land in satisfaction of a lawful claim against a debtor. Shepard *v.* Murray Co., 33 Minn. 519.

Power of counties to sell their swamp lands is considered in Linville *v.* Bohanan, 60 Mo. 554; Audubon Co. *v.* County, 40 Iowa, 460; and Page Co. *v.* County, 41 Iowa, 115.

The fee of all streets in any city in *Kansas* is in the county for the use and benefit of the public. Smith *v.* City of Leavenworth, 15 Kan. 81.

The county property is for public use. Stone *v.* Charlestown, 114 Mass. 214.

The property of a county can be purchased only through the Board of Supervisors, except in cases where some other officer is specially authorized to make sale. McCrossin *v.* Lincoln Co., 57 Wis. 184.

As to powers of a county in the construction of bridges, validity and enforcement of contracts therefor, and proper application of county funds in payment, Clark *v.* Dayton, 6 Neb. 192; Follmer *v.* Nichols, 6 Neb. 204.

Building a public bridge may be a work of public improvement, in aid of which an issue of county bonds may be made, notwithstanding that the constructors of the bridge are to be authorized to collect tolls. Building Ass. *v.* Sherwin, 6 Neb. 48.

Under power to appropriate money to build a bridge, a county may do part when a foreign corporation does the rest. Kansas City Bridge Co. *v.* Commissioners, 34 Kan. 670.

In the absence of a statute or contract, one county cannot compel another to join in the erection or repair of a bridge across a stream separating them. Brown *v.* Merrick Co., 18 Neb. 355. See also BRIDGES, 2 Am. & Eng. Encyc. of Law, 540.

A county cannot sue out a writ of error to review a judgment in a proceeding to compel the commissioners to perform duties devolving upon them as individuals. Kitsap Co. *v.* Carson, 1 Wash. Ter. 419.

County authorities may not make a bargain with an agent to refund certain bonds on a commission, although an agent may be allowed reasonable compensation for services performed.

The court will not allow any one to speculate on the funds of a county by proffering advice on matters of law. Webster *v.* County of Lancaster, 30 N. W. Rep. 538.

The taxing power, being almost the highest prerogative of sovereignty, is conferred on the counties only by express grant of the legislature, or by necessary implication of its laws. The power to levy all needful taxes to pay all claims or demands on the county, and to cover all county purposes, is usually conferred.[1] The collection of certain State taxes are imposed on the counties, and the amount assessed against a county becomes a debt due.[2] After organization of a county, and qualification of its officers, taxes are payable to them, and not to the officers of the county to which it was formerly attached.[3]

But the rule is otherwise as to taxes levied and due prior to the complete organization of the new county.[4] The powers of counties in the matter of levying taxes, and the responsibility for the exercise of that power, must of necessity be greatly dependent upon the constitutions of the individual States and their fiscal legislation.[5]

1. Comrs. v. Alleghany, 20 Md. 449; McGuire v. Owsley Co., 7 B. Mo. (Ky.) 340.

As to limit of power of a county in *Arkansas* to levy a tax, see Worthen v. Badgett, 32 Ark. 496.

2. Multnomah v. State, 1 Deg. 358; Schuylkill v. Com., 36 Pa. St. 524.

But in *Kansas* it has been held that the duties imposed upon county officers in the collection of county taxes are imposed upon the officers, not upon the county. Atty.-Genl. v. Leavenworth Co., 2 Kan. 61.

And where taxes have been regularly assessed and returned, the responsibility of the county to the State on account thereof is fulfilled. People v. Monroe, 36 Mich. 70.

3. Railroad Company v. Brown Co., 18 Neb. 516; Morse v. Hitchcock, 19 Neb. 566.

4. See sec. 3 (*d*), and cases cited.

5. As to the powers of divers counties in the matter of local taxes, People v. Macoupin Co., 54 Ill. 217; State v. Spencer, 49 Mo. 342; Simmons v. Wilson, 66 N. Car. 336; Johnston v. Cleveland Co., 67 N. Car. 101.

As to whether a mining tax was properly assessed, White Pine Co. v. Ash, 5 Nev. 279.

The power of counties to tax is limited under the *Texas* act of 1848, organizing county courts, to subjects upon which a tax has been levied by the State. Baker v. Panola Co., 30 Texas, 86.

The *Illinois* constitution of 1848, requiring that taxes levied by counties, cities, etc., shall be uniform in respect to persons and property, is not contravened by a statute requiring a division and apportionment of county taxes, when collected, between the county and a city, and this although the apportionment should unjustly discriminate against the county. Sangamon Co. v. Springfield, 63 Ill. 66.

The *North Carolina* constitution, art. 5, § 7, restraining county commissioners from levying a tax more than double the State tax, does not apply to taxes levied to pay debts against the county existing at or before the adoption of the constitution. Houghton v. Commissioners, 70 N. Car. 466; Uzzle v. The Commissioners, 70 N. Car. 564; Edwards v. Commissioners, 70 N. Car. 571; Street v. Commissioners, 70 N. Car. 644.

A county has no lawful authority to make appropriations for any object for which authority, either express or implied, has not been given by the State legislature. Hirney v. Railroad Co., 32 Ind. 244; Hunter v. Campbell Co., 7 Cald. (Tenn.) 49.

Counties are authorized to levy assessments for local improvements without regard to cash valuation of the property assessed. *In re* Dowlan, 31 N. W. Rep. 517.

As to how the rights and duties of a county in levying taxes differ from those of the State, Wells v. Coles, 27 Ark. 603.

As to the power of counties to levy bridge and road taxes, Kinsey v. Pulaski Co., 2 Dill. 253. As to licenses, see State v. Knox, 52 Mo. 418.

A tax to pay bounties to volunteers has been held not to be for municipal purposes, and therefore unconstitutional. State v. Tappan, 29 Wis 664.

As to the extent of liability of a county for an illegal tax, Kellog v. Winnebago, 22 Wis. 97; Eaton v. Manitowoc, 40 Wis. 668.

A county is not liable to a tax-payer for taxes wrongly collected by the county treasurer and paid over to the State or municipalities other than the county. Price v. Lancaster Co., 18 Neb. 199.

As to how far the exercise of the power to levy a tax may be compelled by *mandamus*, Graham v. Parham, 32 Ark. 676.

The limitation of the State debt in the constitution does not affect the power of the legislature to allow the counties to contract debt.[1] An act authorizing county commissioners to organize turnpike companies, the cost to be assessed upon neighboring real estate, is constitutional.[2]

The legislature may not, by a mere legislative act, create an indebtedness from one county to another.[3]

The organic law of the State, as expressed in the State constitution, may, however, impose limitations on the legislature as to the division of existing counties, or the creation of new counties.[4]

in what order to pay county debts. McDonal v. Madux, 11 Cal. 187; State v. St. Louis Co., 34 Mo. 546.

But it will not be presumed to have appropriated county funds to the injury of third parties without express words. People v. Williams, 8 Cal. 97.

It may provide for funding of the debt of a county. Sharp v. Contra Costa Co., 34 Cal. 284; Chapman v. Morris, 28 Cal. 393.

The direction of a donation to a county, before it has been appropriated, or any right acquired under it, Cage v. Hogg, 1 Humph. (Tenn.) 48.

But it may not, by a retro-active act, confirm the illegal action of certain county commissioners in issuing certain bonds. Shawnee v. Carter, 2 Kansas, 115.

1. Pattison v. Yuba, 13 Cal. 175.

2. Goodrich v. Winchester Co., 26 Ind. 119.

3. But if, by hasty legislation, money is paid to one county which rightfully belongs to another, it is competent to provide for the correction of the error. Jackson v. La Crosse, 13 Wis. 490.

It may order reimbursement to one county by others, for the cost of trials removed there. Lycoming v. Union, 15 Pa. St. 166.

And if a county contract a debt, and before the same is due a new county is created out of it, the legislature may appoint commissioners to award the amount that the new county shall pay as its share. People v. Alameda Co., 26 Cal. 641.

4. The constitution of *Tennessee* declares that in the formation of a new county, no line of such county shall approach the court-house of any old county from which it shall be taken, nearer than twelve miles; therefore, if in the formation of a new county these restrictions are not adhered to, a court of chancery will, on the complaint of the older county, restore it to its original boundaries, and restrain the officers of the new county from the exercise of any jurisdiction within those boundaries. Maury County v. Lewis Co., 1 Swan. (Tenn.) 236.

Although chancery will, upon a proper application, restrain the commissioners from organizing a county, created by an act that is unconstitutional and void; yet, after the county has been organized, the court of chancery has no power to abolish it, or restrain existing officers from executing their several functions. Ford v. Farmer, 9 Humph. (Tenn.) 152.

The act to erect the county of Noble *held* not inconsistent with the constitution of Ohio. Evans v. Dudley, 1 Ohio St. 437.

Under the constitution of *New York*, there is no objection to the erection and organization of a county for municipal and judicial purposes only, until the next political apportionment of representation can be constitutionally made, with provision to secure to electors in the mean time the full enjoyment of the right of suffrage. The legislature are nowhere restrained, directed, or limited in regard to the nature, grade, or character of evidence which they must have as the basis of their action. In some specified cases their power is limited, and in others conditional, depending upon the existing of certain facts; but they must necessarily decide whether such facts exist, and the courts are bound to presume that the legislature acted upon good and sufficient evidence. De Comp. v. Eveland, 19 Barb. (N. Y.) 81.

Where the constitution requires that the legislature shall establish but one system of town and county government, which shall be as nearly uniform as possible, a special act making special provisions for one county, varying from those made by the general law, is unconstitutional. State v. Reardon, 24 Wis. 484; State v. Milwaukee Co., 25 Wis. 339.

The legislature of *Illinois* cannot abolish counties, remove county-seats, add the territory of one county to another, without submitting the act to the vote of the inhabitants affected by the change. People v. Marshall, 12 Ill. 391.

And where a State has full power to create counties, the exercise of this power is conclusive as to the existence of facts made by the constitution of the State prerequisite to such enactment. Lusher v. Scites, 4 W. Va. 11.

The multitude of cases to be found in the books are simply declaratory of the above proposition, or, as is more generally the case, have to do with the adjudication of cases involving the construction or interpretation of the various State constitutions, or the general or special laws which may have been passed from time to time. It is quite common for the constitution or laws of a State to provide that the lines of a new county, carved out of one or several old ones, shall not run within a certain limited distance of the county-seat;[1] also that the territory and population shall not be diminished below a certain limit;[2] and it is not infrequently provided that the question of the division of a county must be submitted to the decision of the qualified voters of the county in a manner provided by law, and that, before such division can be made, the approval of a certain proportion of the voters must be obtained.[3]

(b) *Legal Results of Change of County Boundaries, or Erection of a New County out of the Old, with Respect to whether Legal Proceedings are to be conducted in Courts of Old or of New County.* — Upon general principles of law, if part of the county is separated from it by annexation to another, or by the creation of a new county, the remaining part of the county retains all its property, powers, rights, duties, and privileges, and remains subject to all its obligations and duties, unless some express provision to the contrary be made by the acts authorizing the separation.[4]

turned over to Pamlico a fair proportion of certain county property within a year, — *held*, not operative to make the precise time of one year, of the essence of the obligation. Commissioners of Craven *v.* Commissioners of Pamlico, 73 N. Car. 298.

North Carolina Const. art. 7, § 3, provides that the first division of counties into townships shall be by the county commissioners; but it does not authorize them to make any subsequent division or alteration. The subsequent creation or alteration of counties is left with the legislature. Grady *v.* Commissioners of Lenoir, 74 N. Car. 101.

Although the creation of a county is a legislative function, a court of chancery may so far fix the boundaries of a new county as to secure to the old one so much of the territory as is declared inviolable, and may protect such other rights in the premises as are guaranteed by the organic law. Humphreys County *v.* Houston County, 4 Baxter (Tenn.), 593.

1. Gotcher *v.* Burrows, 9 Humph. (Tenn.) 585.

2. Bridgenor *v.* Rogers, 1 Caldw. (Tenn.) 259; State *v.* Larrabee, 1 Wis. 200; State *v.* Merriman, 6 Wis. 14.

3. Thus, a constitutional provision requiring the consent of two-thirds of the voters of a fraction of an old county before it can be taken to form part of a new county, does not mean two-thirds of the votes to be cast, but two-thirds of the qualified voters. Cocke *v.* Gooch, 5 Heisk. (Tenn.) 294; Stuart *v.* Bair, 8 Baxt. (Tenn.) 141.

The consent of a majority of the voters in the part taken off is only required in the case of new counties to be formed out of parts of old ones. Reynolds *v.* Holland, 35 Ark. 56.

In order to change the county lines of counties already organized, or to remove a county-seat, the legislature must pass a special law, which is perfect as a law when it leaves that body, but to take effect and become operative only after it has been approved by the electors of the county in question. Roos *v.* Swenson, 6 Minn. 428.

As to submission to the voters, see Taylor *v.* Taylor, 10 Minn. 107; People *v.* Reynolds, 10 Ill. 1; People *v.* Morrell, 21 Wend. (N. Y.) 563; State *v.* Elwood, 11 Wis. 17. *Compare* Hoswell *v.* Cram, 16 Wis. 343.

4. See note, 85 Am. Dec. 101.

School Commissioners *v.* School Commissioners, 35 Md. 206; Inhabitants of Hampshire *v.* Inhabitants of Franklin, 16 Mass. 86; Laramie Co. *v.* Albany Co., 92 U. S. 307, which case contains a comprehensive review of the law affecting the

Jurisdiction in Civil Cases where a New County is formed.— The division of a county or counties not being completed until the court of the new county is so far organized as to enable suits to be commenced in the new county, it may be laid down as a general rule of law, followed in most of the States, that, where the jurisdiction of the old court has once attached prior to the complete organization of the new county, it will not be divested by the subsequent organization. This is true, although the *res*, or the parties, may belong to the county, and the proceedings are initiated between the times of the formation and organization of the new county.[1]

1. Thus, a suit begun to foreclose a mortgage will not be defeated by a subsequent division. Buckinghouse *v.* Gregg, 19 Ind. 401.

And where chancery has once acquired and exercised jurisdiction, neither a change of boundaries, nor a change of residence of parties litigant, can arrest the prosecution of the suit. Arnold *v.* Styles, 2 Blackf. (Ind.) 391.

So, after formation of a new county, and before organization, a suit having been begun affecting title to real estate, upon which judgment was not entered until after such organization, the court of the old county has jurisdiction. Milk *v.* Kent, 60 Ind. 226.

In *Pennsylvania* the lien of a judgment having once attached, and the act dividing the county making no provision for keeping said lien alive as to lands within the new counties, the lien will either continue as at common law, or it may be preserved by revivals in the old county, without service of the process in the new. West's Ap. 5 Watts (Pa.), 87.

The same general principle has been applied to the administration of estates. Lindsay's Heirs *v.* McCormick, 2 A. K. Marsh. (Ky.) 229; Drake's Admrs. *v.* Vaughn, 6 J. J. Marsh. (Ky.) 147; State *v.* Jones, 4 Halst. (N. J.) 357.

And in *California*, where, after the death of the intestate, that portion of the county in which he resided at the time of death is erected into a new county, or attached to another county, the probate court of the old county still retains its jurisdiction over the administration. Harlan's Estate, 24 Cal. 182.

But in *Georgia* a contrary view has been taken. An act of the legislature had changed the territorial limits of a county pending a suit instituted respecting the title to certain lands. Judgment was obtained in the old county, and was about to be enforced by the eviction of the parties in the new county, when the court of the new county granted an injunction, on the ground that the jurisdiction of the court of the old county was ousted by the land falling within the new county after division. Kelly *v.* Tate, 43 Ga. 535.

And in *Alabama* it was *held* that, where a county was created out of several old ones, the right of defendants resident in the new county to have suits removed, must be exercised in a reasonable time. *Ex parte* Rhodes, 43 Ala. 373.

Tax Cases.— The rulings in tax cases are in conformity with the general rule as laid down above. Moss *v.* Shear, 25 Cal. 38; s. c., 85 Am. Dec. 94, and note, p. 103.

In Devor *v.* McClintock, 9 W. & S. (Pa.) 80, it was *held* where the boundary between two counties is changed after the assessors of the townships, embraced in the territory transferred, have made their assessments for the current year, and after the time for making and returning the assessments has passed, the old county, and not the new one, is entitled to assess, collect, and retain the taxes for that year in the transferred territory. Board of Morgan Co. *v.* Hendricks Co., 32 Ind. 234.

All rights of tax officers of an old county over territory transferred to another county remain for taxes levied before the transfer. Eckridge *v.* McGruden, 45 Miss. 294.

But for circumstances under which it was *held* that the old county could not recover the amount of taxes levied and collected in a new county, partly erected out of the old one, upon the subjects of taxation in such new county, Trinity Co. *v.* Polk Co., 58 Texas, 321.

In some States a justice of the peace, commissioned within a certain district and county, cannot act under his former appointment upon a division of the county, if his district falls entirely within the new county; but the rule is otherwise in other States. Respublica *v.* McClean, 4 Yeates (Pa.), 399. *Compare* Garey *v.* People, 9 Cowen (N. Y.), 640; People *v.* Morrell, 21 Wend. (N. Y.) 563; State *v.* Walker, 17 Ohio, 135; Exp. McCollum, 1 Cow. (N. Y.) 550; State *v.* Jacobs, 17 Ohio, 143.

is one of the extraordinary powers conferred on counties. That it is competent for the legislature, in the absence of specially restrictive constitutional limitations, to authorize a county to aid in the construction of railroads or such like corporations, is no longer an open question. The principle has been sustained by a long and almost unbroken line of decisions in the State and federal courts.[1] *Judge Dillon*, however, states, that, despite this line of decisions, "the soundness of this principle is open to grave question, viewed simply as one of constitutional law, and that, regarded in the light of its effects, this invention to aid the enterprise of private corporations has proved itself baneful in the last degree."[2] In the leading case of Sharpless *v.* Mayor of Philadelphia, *Black, C. J.*, while admitting the binding force of the prevailing interpretation of the law, vigorously challenges the wisdom of its exercise as a sound question of public policy, and foretells the evils which were bound to result therefrom.[3]

In *Iowa* this power in the legislature was first affirmed,[4] then denied,[5] the denial adhered to for seven years, to be virtually overthrown once more by a case which straddled both principle and precedent.[6] The legislature may even compel a county to subscribe to the capital stock of a railroad already built, to issue bonds in payment of the subscription, and to raise money to meet the same by taxation.[7] It may limit subscriptions by conditions precedent;[8]

1. See Dillon on Municipal Corporations, § 104, and cases cited in note. The history of the whole question dates back no farther than 1837; and Goddin *v.* Crump, 8 Leigh (Va.), 120, is the earliest case on the subject; s. c., 59 Am. Dec. 759, and note, 782. Sharpless *v.* Mayor, 21 Pa. St. 147, may be said to be the leading case. In Leavenworth Co. *v.* Miller, 7 Kansas, 479, the opinion of the court covers the ground exhaustively. The cases might be multiplied in different States, but they uniformly sustain the proposition, except in *Iowa*. The federal courts have followed the decisions of the State courts. Mitchell *v.* Burlington, 4 Wall. (U. S.) 270; Rogers *v.* Burlington, 3 Wall. (U. S.) 654; United States *v.* Clark Co., 96 U. S. 211.

2. Dillon on Mun. Corp. § 104.

3. In Sharpless *v.* Mayor, 21 Pa. St. 158, *C. J. Black* says, "This is, beyond all comparison, the most important case that has ever been in this court since the formation of the government. The fate of many most important public improvements hangs on our decision. If all municipal subscriptions are void, railroads, which are necessary to give the State those advantages to which every thing else entitles her, must stand unfinished for years to come, and large sums expended on them must be lost. Not less than fourteen millions of these stocks have been taken by boroughs, cities, and counties within this commonwealth. It may be well supposed that a large amount of the bonds are in the hands of innocent holders. The reverse of the picture is no less appalling. It is even more so, as some view it. If the power exists, it will continue to be exerted, and generally it will be used under the influence of those who are personally interested, and who do not see or care for the ultimate injury it may bring to the people at large. . . . This plan, if unchecked by this court, will probably go on until it results in some startling calamity to rouse the masses of the people." The long and able opinion of the learned judge in this case may fairly be said to exhaust the law on the subject, as well as its economic bearings; and he decides the case as one of first impressions.

4. Dubuque Co. *v.* Railroad Co., 4 G. Greene (Iowa), 1.

5. State *v.* Wapello Co., 13 Iowa, 388.

6. Hanson *v.* Vernon, 27 Iowa, 28. Note the virtual but not acknowledged overthrow of the line of authorities denying the powers in Stewart *v.* Polk Co., 30 Iowa, 1. The legislative and judicial history of the subject is fully stated in King *v.* Wilson, 1 Dillon (U. S. C. C.), 555.

7. Railroad Company *v.* Napa Co., 30 Cal. 435.

8. It may limit county subscriptions by conditions precedent. Thompson *v.* Kelly,

4. Liabilities of Counties. — (*a*) *Generally.* — Counties being merely parts of the State government, they partake of the State's immunity from liability. The State is not liable, except by its own consent; and so the county is exempt from liability, unless the State has consented. Counties are not liable to implied common-law liabilities as municipal corporations are.[1]

Their liabilities, whether grounding in tort or contract, are the mere creatures of statutes; and they possess no power, and can incur no obligations, except such as are specially provided for by statute.[2] In the absence of statute, there is no county liability.[3]

(*b*) *Liability for Contracts.* — The statute authorizing a contract must be strictly pursued, or the contract will not bind the county;[4] and the requirements of the statute must be fulfilled;[5] and a contract, unless made pursuant to statutory authority, will not be binding;[6] and a contract *ultra vires* may always be defended.[7]

may refuse to provide funds to pay any portion of the old indebtedness unless the creditors will accept new evidences in place of the old ones, and for a less sum. People v. Morse, 43 Cal. 534.

No creditor of a county acquires any vested right to its revenue until the money is actually in the treasury; and if a law is passed before the money comes into the treasury, which makes other disposition of a part of a certain fund, the holders of the certificates on that fund acquire no vested right to such money until the provisions of the last law have been complied with. Kner v. Spaulding, 17 Nev. 289.

An act will not be construed so as to impair the rights of creditors, unless express words are employed. People v. Williams, 8 Cal. 97. See note, 68 Am. Dec. 300.

1. Browning v. City of Springfield, 63 Am. Dec. 345 (see note); s. c., 17 Ill. 143; Perry v. Worcester, 66 Am. Dec. 431.

There may be no remedy against a debt contracted by authority of law. Hunsacker v. Borden, 63 Am. Dec. 130, see note 132.

2. Granger v. Pulaski Co., 26 Ark. 37.

3. Russell v. Men of Devon, 2 T. R. 671; Crawford Co. v. Le Clerc, 4 Chand. (Wis.) 56; Shawnee Co. v. Carter, 2 Kan. 115; Heller v. Shawnee Co., 23 Kan. 128; Askew v. Hale, 54 Ala. 639; Simpson v. Lauderdale Co., 56 Ala. 64; Wilson v. Commissioners, 7 W. & S. (Pa.) 197.

Their powers must be strictly construed. English v. Chicot Co., 26 Ark. 454; Murphy v. Napa Co., 20 Cal. 497.

Thus, the power to construct buildings does not authorize the issue of commercial paper. Claiborne Co. v. Brooks, 111 U. S. 400. See note, 68 Am. Dec. 343.

The subject of the liability of *quasi* corporations, whose corporate powers are conferred for the benefit of the public at large, discussed in Savage v. Banger, 63 Am. Dec. 658; s. c., 40 Me. 176; Browning v. City of Springfield, 63 Am. Dec. 345; s. c., 17 Ill. 143; Commissioners v. Martin, 69 Am. Dec. 333, 4 Mich. 557; Lorillard v. Town, 62 Am. Dec. 120; s. c., 11 N. Y. 392; Eastman v. Meredith, 72 Am. Dec. 302; s. c., 36 N. H. 284.

4. Murphy v. Napa Co., 20 Cal. 497; Hight v. Monroe Co., 68 Ind. 575; Turnpike Co. v. Bartholomew Co., 72 Ind. 226; Steines v. Franklin Co., 48 Mo. 167; Shawnee Co. v. Carter, 2 Kan. 115; Treadwell v. Commissioners, 11 Ohio St. 190; Richardson v. Grant Co., 27 Fed. Rep. 495.

5. Hall v. Marshall Co., 12 Iowa, 142. As a regular meeting of the county board is necessary before entering upon the contract. Archer v. Commissioners, 3 Blackf. (Ind.) 501; Commissioners v. Ross, 46 Ind. 404; Rice v. Plymouth Co., 43 Iowa, 136; Crump v. Supervisors, 52 Miss. 107. A county may become liable on a promise, informally undertaken, if ratified by subsequent acts. Kawk v. Marion Co., 48 Iowa, 23. Thus it may be ratified at a subsequent meeting of the board in legal session. Mitchell v. The Commissioners, 18 Kan. 188; Clark v. Lion Co., 7 Nev. 75; Talbott v. Iberville Parish, 24 La. Ann. 135.

6. Rayburn v. Davis, 2 Ill. App. 548; Stamp v. Cass Co., 47 Mich. 330; Robertson v. Breedlove, 61 Texas, 316.

7. Turnpike Company v. Bartholomew Co., 72 Ind. 226; Henderson v. Sibley Co., 28 Minn. 515; Fowle v. Alexandria, 3 Pet. (U. S.) 409.

Acceptance and occupancy of a public building by a county will not enable the contractor to recover of the county, on a *quantum meruit*, an amount in excess of that authorized by the vote, caused by changes and extensions of the original

some States that counties have not the power to make bonds or negotiable paper of any kind, the consideration or validity of

county unless they are in the form prescribed, even though possibly valid. Merced Co. v. University, 66 Cal. 25.

In railroad aid bonds, technical advantages will not be allowed to involve a breach of the public good. Street Comrs. v. Craven, 70 N. C. 644.

Illegal Rates. — State v. Sanderson, 54 Mo. 203; Rubey v. Schain, 54 Mo. 207; Smith v. Green Co., 54 Mo. 58.

Where a rate of interest is not prescribed, any legal rate may be fixed. Beattie v. Andrew Co., 56 Mo. 42.

Where counties are restricted by statute from issuing bonds to an amount greater than a certain percentage of the assessed valuation of the county, the term bonds must include all bonds: it cannot be restricted to funding bonds. State v. Babcock, 18 Neb. 141.

Where county bonds are issued in excess of legal limits by the county court, a simple certificate of a judge of that court, not a recital in the bond, does not estop the county, neither statute, note, nor order authorizing such certificate. Daviess Co. v. Dickinson, 117 U. S. 657.

The legislature has the power to direct by what agency claims against a county shall be ascertained and adjusted, and by what officials county bonds, authorized to be issued in payment therefor, shall be attested and pledged. But the bonds when issued are the bonds of the county. People v. Ingersoll, 58 N. Y. 1.

County bonds issued for purpose of erecting a public bridge over the Platte River, conformable in all respects to the laws of the State authorizing the issuance of bonds in aid of works of internal improvement, are valid. Union Pacific R. R. v. Commissioners, 4 Neb. 450.

Where the legislature has authorized a special board to contract for certain improvements, and the county to issue bonds for one hundred thousand dollars, and a contract is made for that sum, a subsequent act reducing the bonds to two hundred thousand dollars will not relieve the county of liability. Slaughter v. Mobile Co., 73 Ala. 134.

Where a statute says the commissioners "may" submit any proposed expenditure to the approval of the voters, "may" is construed shall. Steines v. Franklin Co., 48 Mo. 167; State v. Saline Co., 48 Mo. 390.

The validity of a submission as to a proposition to borrow money determined, there being a substantial compliance with the requirements of the statute. Lynde v. County, 16 Wall. (U. S.) 6.

Not liable for bonds issued *ultra vires*. Dent v. Cook, 45 Ga. 323; Whitwell v. Pulaski Co., 2 Dill. (C. C.) 249.

Bonds issued under the *Missouri* act, in regard to the reclamation of swamp lands, are not "orders" or warrants within the meaning of the act, and are payable at maturity regardless of their order of presentation. Shelley v. St. Charles County, 21 Fed. Rep. 699.

The Supreme Court of *Tennessee* having decided the Board of Commissioners of Shelby County to have been an unorganized and illegal body, without lawful existence, *held*, in an action on certain bonds issued by said board, that the principle of *de facto* officers could not be invoked in the plaintiff's aid, as there cannot be officers *de facto* where there is no office *de jure*, and the facts failed to show any ratification by the county. Norton v. Shelby Co., 118 U. S. 425.

County bonds issued in 1862 to raise money for the support of indigent families of soldiers of the Confederate Army were not in aid of the rebellion, and are valid. Bartow Co. v. Newell, 64 Ga. 699.

As to municipal debt in excess of constitutional limit, for which county bonds were issued in *Indiana*, see Kimball v. Board of Commissioners, 21 Fed. Rep. 145.

Bonds of a county were authorized to be issued by a vote of the people; and the law authorizing the vote provides that the bonds should be executed by certain officers, and countersigned by the treasurer of the county. *Held*, that the omission of the treasurer to countersign the bonds was a mere defect in the execution of them, which a court of equity would, in the absence of a remedy at law, ordinarily supply; and that an injunction restraining the collection of taxes for the payment of such bonds should not be allowed. Melvin v. Lisenby, 72 Ill. 63.

Where the county court was empowered by law to issue the bonds of the county, upon a vote to be taken upon the subject, in the manner prescribed by the law, authorizing such vote and the issue of bonds, and such bonds were issued, the fact that the evidence of the compliance with the law in calling and conducting the election, giving notice thereof, etc., may be lost or destroyed, does not affect the validity of the bonds, if, in fact, the law was complied with. Maxey v. Williamson County, 72 Ill. 207.

In an action by a *bona fide* purchaser for value against a county, upon a bond issued by the former county court of such county, under an act of the legislature, the records of such court are conclusive upon the

another or the general fund.[1] It is not lawful for any county board to issue warrants for a greater sum than is actually due, and warrants must be issued at par.[2] The statute of limitations runs against a county, liable to be sued on its warrants, and compelled by *mandamus* to levy a tax to pay them from the date of the issue of the warrants.[3] County warrants payable to bearer are not negotiable. All holders take them subject to any defence against the original payee.[4]

(*e*) *Liability of County for Beneficial Use of Money, Labor, or Property, though not formally obligated therefor.* — Counties have sometimes been held liable when they have enjoyed the beneficial use of any thing, although the formalities ordinarily necessary to bind them have not been complied with;[5] and money made use of

1. Campbell *v.* Polk Co., 49 Mo. 214; Moody *v.* Cass Co., 85 Mo. 477.

But unless a claim against a county is by law required to be paid out of a particular fund, the validity of a warrant therefor will not be affected, because it is drawn upon a fund not appropriate to the character of the allowance. Supervisors *v.* Klein, 51 Miss. 807.

A county which diverts the money of a special fund from the payment of the warrant drawn against it, and uses it for other purposes, becomes liable upon such warrant, though it is not ordinarily liable upon it as for a general debt. Valleau *v.* Newton Co., 72 Mo. 593.

A county warrant for building a jail, drawn on a special fund, which the county has used for other purposes, can be enforced against the general fund. Valleau *v.* Newton Co., 81 Mo. 591.

Under the tax laws of *Georgia*, each county order is entitled to be paid out of the proper fund appropriated for expenditures of that class in the order of date; but orders belonging to one fund cannot be paid out of another. Mitchell *v.* Speer, 39 Ga. 56.

2. *Mississippi* Code, 1871, § 1382, which declares that "it shall not be lawful for any Board of Supervisors to allow any greater sum for any account, claim, or demand against the county than the amount actually due thereon, dollar for dollar, according to the legal or ordinary compensation for such services rendered, or for salaries or fees of officers or materials furnished, or to issue county warrants or orders upon such accounts, claims, or demands, when allowed, for more than the actual amount as allowed dollar for dollar," operates as a limitation on the power of the Board of Supervisors in the allowance of accounts, claims, and demands against the county, and makes void any allowance or warrant prohibited by it; and under section 1520 of the code, by which the action of *mandamus* is assimilated in "the pleadings and other proceedings, as nearly as may be, to an ordinary action for the recovery of damages," the Board of Supervisors may, when the payment of county warrants is sought to be enforced by *mandamus*, go behind the allowance of the claim by the board, and question its validity as having been allowed in violation of section.

The language of section 1382, "dollar for dollar, according to the legal or ordinary compensation" prescribed to the board as the standard for their allowances, is not a restriction to the standard of cash prices. It is competent for the board to make allowances upon the basis of credit prices, if the issuance of the warrants is in anticipation of taxes to be collected. Hence, evidence that the allowances made were at a rate equal to double the cash prices, is insufficient to establish the illegality of the warrants. Board of Supervisors *v.* Kline, 57 Miss. 807.

The fact that a demand on the county will be payable in county warrants, which are at a discount, does not authorize the county court to allow a larger sum than the actual debt, for the purpose of covering the discount. So *held*, under Gantt. Dig. § 601, prohibiting allowance of more than the amount actually due, dollar for dollar. Gayne *v.* Ashley Co., 31 Ark. 552.

In *Mississippi*, the holder of a county warrant issued during the Rebellion can only require in payment the equivalent in lawful currency of the amount of the bond in Confederate money at the date of the warrant. Clayton *v.* McWilliams, 49 Miss. 311.

3. Coquard *v.* Chariton Co., 14 Fed. Rep. 203.

4. Jerome *v.* Rio Grande Co., 18 Fed. Rep. 873; County of Ouachita *v.* Wolcott, 103 U. S. 559; Wall *v.* Monroe Co., 103 U. S. 74. But see Mercer Co. *v.* Hackett, 1 Wall. (U. S.) 83; and Coms. *v.* Aspinwall, 21 How. 539.

5. See County *v.* Bredenhart, 16 Pa. St.

to perform an act when no duty to perform such act is imposed on them by statute.[1]

There is a minority of authority that holds that where this duty is imposed by statute, the county will be liable for its neglect.[2] And, in some States, liability is provided for by statute.[3]

There is some apparent difference of authority upon the liability of counties in the erection, maintenance, and repair of highways, bridges, etc.; but this difference is rather apparent than real. An examination of the cases tends to show, that, where this liability is held to attach, it is founded either upon express statute, from necessary implication therefrom, or because the duty of skilful erection and repair has been considered to be imposed directly or by implication by the legislature.[4]

man v. Supervisors, 54 Miss. 363; Reardon v. St. Louis Co., 36 Mo. 555; Woods v. Colfax Co., 10 Neb. 552; Cooley v. Freeholders of Essex, 27 N. J. L. 415; State v. Hudson Co., 30 N J. L. 137; Freeholders v. Strader, 18 N. J. L. 108; Livermore v. Freeholders, 29 N. J. L. 245; Pray v. Jersey City, 32 N. J. L. 394; Kinsey v. Magistrates of Jones, 8 Jones L. (N. Car.) 186; White v. Chowan Co., 90 N. Car. 437; s. c., 47 Am. Rep. 534; Whitehead v. Phila., 2 Phila. (Pa.) 99; Young v. Commissioners, 2 Nott & M. (S. Car.) 537; Wood v. Tipton Co., 7 Baxt. (Tenn.) 112; Nevasota v. Pearce, 46 Tex. 525.

1. Covington Co. v. Kinney, 45 Ala. 176; Swineford v. Franklin Co., 73 Mo. 279.

2. Ferguson v. Davis Co., 57 Iowa, 601; Huft v. Poweshiek, 60 Iowa, 529; Eyler v. Allegheny Co., 49 Md. 257; Commissioners v. Gibson, 36 Md. 229; Shelby Co. v. Deprez, 87 Ind. 509; Morgan Co. v. Pritchett, 85 Ind. 68; House v. County Coms., 60 Ind. 580; Rigony v. Schuylkill Co., 103 Pa. St. 382.

Counties are liable for infringement of patents. May v. County of Logan (Ohio), 30 Fed. Rep. 250; May v. Mercer Co. (Ky.), 30 Fed. Rep. 246; May v. County Fond du Lac, 27 Fed. Rep. 695.

Judge Dillon, upon a consideration of the authorities respecting the liability for defects in bridges and highways, makes the following deductions: "On examination, it will be found that the cases may be grouped into the following classes: —

"I. Where neither chartered cities nor counties are held to an implied civil liability. Only a few States have adopted this extreme view.

"II. Where the reverse is held, and both chartered cities and counties are alike considered to be impliedly liable for their neglect of duty in question. This doctrine prevails in a small number of States.

"III. Where municipal corporations proper, such as chartered cities, are held to an implied civil liability for damages caused to travellers for defective and unsafe streets under their control, but denying that such liability attaches to counties or other *quasi* corporations, as respects highways and bridges under their charge. This distinction has received judicial sanction in a large majority of the States, where the legislature is silent in respect of corporate liability." Dillon on Mun. Corp. § 999.

3. Ripley v. Essex Co., 40 N. J. L. 45.

But in the absence of statute the county will not be liable for a nuisance caused by the erection of a jail, and its filthy and disorderly condition. Wehn v. Gage Co., 5 Neb. 494; Crowell v. Somona Co., 25 Cal. 313.

4. As the consideration of this particular phase of responsibility is of general and practical importance, it has been thought well to cite the important cases.

In *Alabama* the liability imposed on counties for injuries resulting from defective or unsafe public bridges is special and defined by statute. Barbour Co. v. Horn, 48 Ala. 649; Covington Co. v. Kinney, 45 Ala. 176.

Where the duty of keeping a bridge in repair devolves by law on the county, the county is bound to close it if it becomes dangerous (Humphreys v. Armstrong, 3 Brews. (Pa.) 49), and is liable for injuries resulting from its ordinary use. See also Rigony v. Schuylkill Co., 103 Pa. 382. See 68 Am. Dec. 294, note.

Repairs, Liability for. — One of two counties jointly bound to keep a bridge in repair was compelled to pay damages sustained by its breaking down. *Held*, the other county was bound to contribute. Armstrong Co. v. Clarion Co., 66 Pa. St. 218.

A county and town being jointly, by statute, liable for the erection and maintenance of a bridge, *held*, that one injured by a defect in the bridge could maintain an action against the county. Lyman v. Hampshire Co., 140 Mass. 311.

2. *For Attorney's Fees.* — A member of the bar appointed by the court to defend a prisoner indicted on a criminal charge, the prisoner having expressed a desire for counsel, cannot charge the county for his services.[1] The rule seems to be otherwise in Indiana.[2]

3. *For Physician's Services.* — A county has been held liable for services properly rendered to paupers.[3]

(h) *Liability for Acts and Negligence of Officers and Agents.* — It may be laid down as a general rule that counties are not liable for the acts or negligence of officers; and an action will not lie for injury resulting from the non-performance by its officers of a corporate or official duty, unless a remedy is given by statute:[4] nor does liability attach for the acts or negligence of its servants which cause injury to others; in this it differs from a municipal corporation.[5]

A county, being a political division of the State, has no more

Not liable for interest on an unpaid salary. 49 Ga. 115.

Not liable to a clerk *de jure* for salary wrongly paid to a clerk *de facto*, although it was known that the office was in litigation. Saline *v.* Anderson, 20 Kan. 298.

1. Posey *v.* Mobile Co., 50 Ala. 6; Lamont *v.* Solano Co., 49 Cal. 158; Vise *v.* Hamilton Co., 19 Ill. 78; Johnson *v.* Whiteside, 110 Ill. 22; Davis *v.* Linn Co., 24 Iowa, 508; Case *v.* Shawnee Co., 4 Kan. 511; Bacon *v.* Wayne Co., 1 Mich. 461; Kelley *v.* Andrew Co., 43 Mo. 338; People *v.* Albany, 28 How. (N. Y.) Pr. 22; Weisbrod *v.* Winnebago Co., 20 Wis. 418.

2. Montgomery Co. *v.* Courtney, 105 Ind. 311; Gordon *v.* Commissioners, 52 Ind. 322; Webb *v.* Baird, 6 Ind. 13.

The earlier authorities in *Wisconsin* and *Iowa* looked the same way. Hall *v.* Washington Co., 2 Greene (Iowa), 473; Carpenter *v.* Dane, 9 Wis. 274. See also State *v.* Comrs., 26 Ohio, 599.

3. Comrs. *v.* Wilson, 1 Ind. 478; Bartholomew Co. *v.* Ford, 27 Ind. 17; Johnson *v.* Santa Clara Co., 28 Cal. 545. See also Roberts *v.* Comrs., 10 Kan. 29; Conner *v.* Franklin Co., 57 Ind. 15; Mitchell *v.* Leavenworth, 18 Kan. 188.

County A. is not liable for medical services to its prisoners confined in County B. Smith *v.* Osborne, 29 Kan. 72.

As to power of coroner to employ a physician, Farrell *v.* Commissioners, 57 Ga. 107; Gaston *v.* Marion Co., 3 Ind. 497. Employed by the district attorney, see People *v.* St. Laurence, 30 How. (N. Y.) Pr. 173.

As to costs and fees when a proper charge, Dover *v.* State, 45 Ala. 244.

Counties are liable for costs in all cases of acquittals on indictment. County *v.* Bond, 37 Ark. 226. But see York Co. *v.* Jacobs, 3 Pa. 365; Comr. *v.* Phila. Co., 4 S. & R. (Pa.) 541; Comr. *v.* Huntingdon, 3 Rawle (Pa.), 487; Hutt *v.* Winnebago Co., 19 Wis. 116.

A county is not liable for the board of a jury in a capital case during the pendency of the trial. Young *v.* Commissioners, 76 N. Car. 316.

4. Commissioners *v.* Mighels, 7 Ohio, 109; Wehn *v.* Gage Co., 5 Neb. 494; McConnell *v.* Dewey, 5 Neb. 385; Woods *v.* Colfax Co., 10 Neb. 552; Clark *v.* Adair Co., 79 Mo. 536; Sutton *v.* Board, 41 Miss. 236; Dosdall *v.* Olmstead Co., 30 Minn. 96; Soper *v.* Henry Co., 26 Iowa, 264; Pike Co. *v.* Norrington, 82 Ind. 190; White *v.* County, 58 Ill. 297; Waltham *v.* Kemper, 55 Ill. 346; Hedges *v.* Madison Co., 1 Gilm. (Ill.) 567; R. R. Co. *v.* Santa Clara Co., 62 Cal. 180; Granger *v.* Pulaski, 26 Ark. 37.

A county is only liable to an officer for rent of an office, when the office is one required to be kept open daily for use of the public. Owen *v.* Nye Co., 10 Nev. 338.

A county is not liable for the acts of her Board of Commissioners wholly *ultra vires*. Browning *v.* Owen Co., 44 Ind. 11.

Nor is it liable for loss of a horse bailed to a sheriff, to be used in his duties: such officer engaged in legal duties is the agent of the State, and not of the county. County *v.* Kemp, 55 Ga. 252.

One of the latest and most instructive cases of the general subject, liability of corporations for the wrongful acts of their agents, resulting in benefit to the corporation, is that of Salt Lake City *v.* Hollister, 118 U. S. 259. *Contra*, see House *v.* County, 60 Ind. 580; Pritchett *v.* Morgan Co., 62 Ind. 210.

5. See note to Perry *v.* Worcester, 66 Am. Dec. 431; s. c., 6 Gray (Mass.), 544.

have arisen wherein the statutes which have been passed in several States, and which are very similar, have been construed.[1] The property owner, when there is time, knowledge, and opportunity, should give notice to the authorities of any threatened attack.[2] Acts of the legislature imposing liability on counties for damages resulting from mobs and riots, are constitutional.[3]

5. Remedies for Enforcement of County Liability. — As has been already stated, the county is a creation of the legislature and a part of the sovereign government, and as such it cannot be sued, except by the consent of the State.[4] Therefore persons dealing with a county, for whose liabilities the legislature has provided no means of enforcement, must rely wholly upon its good faith,[5] or they must seek a remedy by application to the legislature.[6]

Where acts have been passed prescribing where and how actions may be commenced, it has been held that such legislation authorizes the bringing of actions generally against counties.[7] As the right of action against counties is dependent on statute, the mode pointed out must be strictly followed.[8] Where no action has been

Abb. (N. Y.) Pr. 270; Sarles v. Mayor of New York, 47 Barb. 447; Atcheson v. Twine, 9 Kans. 350; Underhill v. Manchester, 45 N. H. 214; Richmond City v. Smith, 15 Wall. (U. S.) 429.

1. Statutes have been passed imposing such liability in *Alabama, California, Kansas, Kentucky, Louisiana, Maryland, New Hampshire, New York, Pennsylvania*. See also in *England*, stat. 7 & 8, Geo. IV. c. 31, § 2. See note to Pruether v. City of Lexington, 56 Am. Dec. 589; s. c., 13 B. Mon. (Ky.) 599; Fouvia v. New Orleans, 20 La. Ann. 410; Williams v. N. O., 23 La. Ann. 507; Ely v. Supervisors, 36 N. Y. 297; Dale Co. v. Gunter, 46 Ala. 118; Moody v. Supervisors, 46 Barb. (N. Y.) 659; Wing Chung v. Los Angeles, 47 Cal. 531; Atcheson v. Twine, 9 Kan. 350; Loomis v. Board of Supervisors, 6 Lans. (N. Y.) 269; Chadbourne v. New Castle, 48 N. H. 196; Hagerstown v. Dechert, 32 Md. 369; Bank v. Shaber, 52 Cal. 322.

The fact that a person murdered, and his widow, were aliens, is no defence against a claim against the county. Luke v. Calhoun, 52 Ala. 115.

Liability to widow of a man murdered by an outlaw, *held* not to mean outlaw in the common-law sense, but the lawless persons prevalent at the time the act was passed. Dale Co. v. Gunter, 46 Ala. 118.

A claim on a county for damages for property destroyed by a mob need not be presented to the commissioners. Company v. Lake Co., 45 Cal. 90.

2. The property owner is excused from giving notice to the officers required of assembling of mob, etc., when he has not sufficient time, or is prevented by the mob, or the officers have such knowledge from other sources. Alleghany Co. v. Gibson, 90 Pa. St. 397; Ely v. Niagara Co., 36 N. Y. 297; Moody v. Supervisors, 46 Barb. (N. Y.) 659.

3. Acts subjecting counties and cities to liability for damages to property by mobs and riots within them are not unconstitutional, under the provision that no one shall be deprived of his property without due process of law. Darlington v. City of New York, 31 N. Y. 164. See s. c., 88 Am. Dec. 248, and a carefully edited note collating the authorities on this subject, p. 269; Allegheny Co. v. Gibson, 90 Pa. 397.

4. Russell v. Men of Devon, 2 T. R. 671; Lyell v. St. Clair Co., 3 McLean (U. S. C. C.), 580; Hunsacker v. Borden, 5 Cal. 288; s. c., 63 Am. Dec. 130; Price v. Sacramento, 6 Cal. 254; Sharp v. Contra Costa, 34 Cal. 284; Word v. Hartford Co., 12 Conn. 404; Schuyler Co. v. Mercer, 4 Gilm. (Ill.) 20; Rock Island v. Steele, 31 Ill. 543; Anderson v. State, 23 Miss. 459; Carroll v. Board of Police, 28 Miss. 38; Taylor v. Salt Lake County Court, 2 Utah, 405.

5. Hunsacker v. Borden, 5 Cal. 288; s. c., 63 Am. Dec. 130; Sharp v. Contra Costa Co., 34 Cal. 284.

6. Rose v. Estudillo, 39 Cal. 270.

7. Waitz v. Ormsby Co., 1 Nev. 376.

A county is suable by virtue of statute extending the word "person" to bodies politic and corporate. Donaldson v. San Miguel Co., 1 N. M. 263.

8. Rock Island v. Steele, 31 Ill. 543; Schuyler Co. v. Mercer, 4 Gilm. (Ill.) 20.

8. Audit of Claims. — In the matter of the audit of claims against any county, in any particular State, as is the case in regard to the application of every question of law affecting the powers, rights, or liabilities of counties, recourse must be first had to the statute law of the State. Counties are so utterly the creatures of the State, that their fundamental organization, powers, and duties must ever be found in the will of the creator. The audit of claims against counties forms no exception to this rule.[1]

appeal from the decision of the county board. Wapello Co. *v.* Sinnamon, 1 G. Greene (Iowa), 413; Curtis *v.* Cass Co., 49 Iowa, 421; Murphy *v.* Steele Co., 14 Minn. 67; Taylor *v.* Marion Co., 51 Miss. 731; Washington Co. Ct. *v.* Thompson, 13 Bush (Ky.), 239.

Under the *Alabama* statute, an action does not lie against a county on a claim that has been allowed by the commissioners' court. Marshall Co. *v.* Jackson Co., 36 Ala. 613.

And as a general rule, an act providing an appeal from the action of the Board of Commissioners, upon a claim against the county, does not take away the claimant's right of action against the county which he possessed before. Waitz *v.* Ormsby Co., 1 Nev. 370; Boswell *v.* County Commissioners, 1 Wy. T. 235; Endriss *v.* Chippewa Co., 43 Mich. 317. But see Stamp *v.* Cass Co., 47 Mich. 330.

And in Wood *v.* Bangs, 1 Dak. Ter. 179, it was *held* that where one has an appeal from the decision of the commissioners, this legal remedy must be followed, and equitable relief will not be rendered.

And in general it may be asserted, that suit may be brought against a county upon any complete cause of action, for which no other specific remedy is provided. Adams *v.* Tyler, 121 Mass. 380; Lowndes Co. *v.* Hunter, 49 Ala. 507; Randolph Co. *v.* Hutchings, 46 Ala. 397; Covington Co. *v.* Ramsey, 45 Ala. 176; Comrs. *v.* Hurd, 49 Ga. 462; Taylor *v.* Mayor, 82 N. Y. 10; Brady *v.* Supervisors, 2 Sandf. (N. Y.) 460.

The holder of county warrants drawn on a ditch fund, may sue the county if it fails to levy taxes for that fund without first making a request that taxes be levied. Wills Co. Bank *v.* County, 67 Iowa, 697.

This rule is founded upon the propriety of giving the county notice of the claim and an opportunity to pay without suit. McLendon *v.* Comrs., 71 N. Car. 38.

But in *Iowa* it has been held that counties may be sued originally, both upon liquidated and unliquidated claims. See Clapp *v.* County of Cedar, 5 Iowa, 15; s. c., 68 Am. Dec. 678; and State *v.* County Judge, 2 Iowa, 280.

The provisions of the *Iowa* Code, requiring the presentation of unliquidated demands to the Board of Commissioners, before suit can be brought, applies to actions for infringement of patents. May *v.* Buchanan, 29 Fed. Rep. 469; May *v.* County of Cass, 30 Fed. Rep. 762.

Claims under acts providing remedies for injuries to person and property from outlaws and mobs do not have to be presented to county boards, but suit can be commenced on them directly. Dale Co. *v.* Gunter, 46 Ala. 118; Clear Lake Co. *v.* Lake Co., 45 Cal. 90; Bank *v.* Shaber, 55 Cal. 322.

A man whose claim has been allowed in part may receive county orders without prejudice to his right to appeal: this applies to allowance of items or percentage of claims. Bell *v.* Waupaca Co., 62 Wis. 214.

In some States, claims for damages for torts, as well as claims arising out of contracts, must be presented to the county board before suit. Barbour Co. *v.* Horn, 41 Ala. 114; McCann *v.* Sierra Co., 7 Cal. 121; Hohman *v.* Comal Co., 34 Tex. 36; Jackson *v.* Dinkins, 46 Ala. 69.

A complaint upon a claim against a county must aver a demand and refusal. Love *v.* Chatham Co., 64 N. Car. 706; Maddox *v.* Randolph Co., 65 Ga. 216; Chapman *v.* Wayne Co., 27 W. Va. 496.

This requirement, when demanded at all, cannot be dispensed with. Fenton *v.* Salt Lake City, 3 Utah, 423.

But no formal complaint is necessary. All that is necessary is a detailed statement of items and dates of charge. Howard Co. *v.* Jennings, 104 Ind. 108.

Though in others this is not so. Brady *v.* Supervisors, 2 Sandf. (N. Y.) 460.

And it has been held that where the commissioners refuse to allow or pay an account duly presented, the county may be sued, and the presentment need not be alleged. Gillett *v.* Lyon Co., 18 Kan. 410; Washington Co. *v.* Thompson, 13 Bush (Ky.), 239.

1. No county court or board can audit a claim against a county, or order the same to be paid by the county treasurer, except by authority of some statute. *Re* Tinsley, 90 N. Y. 231.

In *Arkansas* a county court has power to audit, settle, and direct payment of all

The more common method of enforcement of such judgments is by *mandamus* to the county boards to compel the levy of a tax to pay the claim.[1] A county or its officers cannot be garnisheed.[2]

10. County Officers. — See CORONERS, COUNTY COMMISSIONERS, OFFICERS OF MUNICIPALITIES, SHERIFF.

COUNTY COMMISSIONERS, SUPERVISORS, CHOSEN FREEHOLDERS, and POLICE JURY.[3]

has not been delegated to them, the legislature must be invoked for additional authority.

1. Gooch v. Gregory, 65 N. Car. 142; Lutterloh v. Cumberland Co., 65 N. Car. 403; Covington Co. v. Dunklin, 52 Ala. 28; Elmore Co. v. Zeigler, 52 Ala. 277; Commissioners v. Moore, 53 Ala. 25; Lyle v. St. Clair Co., 3 McLean (C. C.), 580; People v. Supervisors, 28 Cal. 431; Emeric v. Gilman, 10 Cal. 404.

In some States the method of payment of an audited claim is by warrants or orders; and, if the proper officers refuse to issue them, *mandamus* will lie. Cuthbert v. Lewis, 6 Ala. 262.

In other States, executions are allowed by statute, and then mandamus will not lie to compel the levy of a tax unless there is no property subject to execution. "But in general, when a claim is reduced to judgment, the duty to provide for its payment becomes perfect; and if it can be paid in no other way, it must be done by the levy and collection of a tax for that purpose; and this duty will be enforced by *mandamus*." Dillon on Mun. Corp. §§ 576, 850, 861.

A bill in equity does not lie against counties to subject equities to the payment of the judgment. Boalt v. Williams Co., 18 Ohio, 13. But see Lyell v. St. Clair Co., 3 McLean (U. S. C. C.), 580.

2. **Garnishment.** — The same considerations that exempt officers of the State and National Government from the process of garnishment and the like, as far as the public funds intrusted to them are concerned, apply with equal force to counties. Gilman v. Contra Costa Co., 8 Cal. 52; Garnishees of Brashears v. Root, 8 Md. 90; Bulkley v. Eckert, 3 Pa. 368; State v. Eberly, 12 Neb. 616; Freeman on Executions, sect. 133; Drake on Attachments, sect. 516; Williams v. Boardman, 9 Allen (Mass.), 570; Boone Co. v. Keck, 31 Ark. 387; Randolph v. Ralls, 18 Ill. 29; but see Adams v. Tyler, 121 Mass. 380.

In McDougal v. Hennepin Co., 4 Minn. 189, the learned judge, in delivering the opinion of the court deciding that counties being public corporations, and their officers public officers, cannot be proceeded against as garnishees, says, "The varied relations which such bodies through their officers hold toward individuals as their debtors, would render them liable to be constantly attacked with such process, and would very seriously embarrass them in the performance of their official duty. Public policy cannot tolerate such an obstacle to the exercise of official duties."

Authorities for Counties. — This subject cannot be found treated, except very incidentally, in any other work or law articles than in the notes to the American Decisions, to the following of which especial reference may be had and credit given. 37 Am. Dec. 413; 56 Am. Dec. 589; 68 Am. Dec. 291; 85 Am. Dec. 100.

3. County commissioners exist in most of the States.

Boards of supervisors are known in several important commonwealths, notably *New York*, *Michigan*, *Illinois*, *Wisconsin*, *Iowa*, *California*, and *Mississippi*.

Corresponding bodies are known as chosen freeholders in *New Jersey*, and police juries in *Louisiana*.

the body or political entity remains the same, notwithstanding any change in the individuals who compose it; and boards composed of new members are bound by the acts of their predecessors within the scope of their authority.[1] Being creatures of statute, endowed only with special powers and created for special purposes, they can exercise only such powers as are expressly conferred by statute, or which are necessarily implied.[2]

have a supervisory power and control over their proceedings, to the exercise of which appellate power is not necessary. This may be done by *mandamus* prohibition, or injunction, but not by *certiorari*. People *v.* Hester, 6 Cal. 679.

Police juries are political corporations, whose powers are specially defined by the legislature, and they can legally exercise no other powers than those delegated to them. Stering *v.* Parish of West Feliciana, 26 La. Ann. 59.

For all purposes for which they are authorized to create debts, they are authorized to levy and collect a tax, but without special authority they cannot issue negotiable paper. Stering *v.* Parish, 26 La. Ann. 59.

They are public agents for the county with respect to all money concerns, and are a *quasi* corporation for the purpose of suing and being sued. Irwin *v.* Commissioners of Northumberland, 1 S. & R. (Pa.) 505; Lyon *v.* Adams, 4 S. & R. (Pa.) 443; Vankirk *v.* Clark, 16 S. & R. (Pa.) 289.

The board of supervisors of a county is a constitutional body, and not dependent for its lawful existence upon the existence of a county clerk, constitutionally elected, but, in default of such, may appoint one who becomes such *de facto*. Carelton *v.* People, 10 Mich. 250.

The board of supervisors, acting under the constitution and laws of *West Virginia*, is a tribunal having no common-law powers, with a special and limited jurisdiction, and, therefore, within the spirit and letter of the constitution giving the supervision and control of inferior tribunals to the circuit courts. Cunningham *v.* Squires, 2 W. Va. 422.

In *Massachusetts* the powers now possessed by the county commissioners were at different times vested in the general sessions of the peace, the court of sessions, the common pleas, and the commissioners of highways. Strong, Petitioner, 20 Pick. (Mass.) 484.

In a county which has adopted township organization, the board of county commissioners continue to act until the board of supervisors have met and organized. State *v.* Musselman (Neb.), 29 N. W. R. 307.

1. A board of county commissioners has perpetual existence, and the body remains the same notwithstanding a change in the individuals who compose it. Pegram *v.* Cleveland Co., 65 N. C. 114.

The powers of a county are vested in the board of commissioners as a corporate entity, and not in commissioners as individuals. Therefore, before a county board can act, it must convene in legal session, either regular, adjourned, or special; and a casual meeting of a majority of the commissioners does not create a legal session. A special session may be convened upon call of the chairman upon request of two members; but personal notice of such case must be served, if practicable, upon every member of the board. Paola, etc., R. R. Co. *v.* Anderson Co., 16 Kan. 302.

New county commissioners are bound by the acts of the old ones within the scope of their authority. Comrs. *v.* Gherky, Wright (Ohio), 494.

Boards of supervisors are bound by the acts of their predecessors. Supervisors *v.* Birdsall, 4 Wend (N.Y.) 453.

2. A board of county commissioners can act only according to the statute. Boise Co. Commissioners, 1 Idaho, 553.

Counties and county boards can only exercise such powers as are expressly conferred by statute, and such grants must be strictly construed. State *v.* Commissioners of Lincoln (Neb.), 25 N. W. Rep. 91.

The creation of the office of county commissioner, the manner of the selection of such officers, whether by election or appointment, the term of period during which they shall act, the character of duties which are to be performed, and the compensation to be paid, are entirely the subject of legislative enactment. Territory *v.* Van Gaskin (Mont.), 6 Pac. Rep. 30.

The above case goes very fully into the power of the legislature as to the principle cited.

The supervisors of a county in *New York* are a corporation with special powers, and for special purposes, and it is questionable whether they were competent, without expressly conferred powers, to take a grant of land. Jackson *v.* Hartwell, 1 Johns. (N. Y.) 422.

The board of county commissioners act under limited statutory authority, and, in order to bind the county for any contract,

The legislature, of course, may, and sometimes does, confer upon the county boards powers of a local, legislative, and administrative character; and when this is done by general words, they acquire the right to pass all such necessary ordinances as may be covered by a fair intendment, and the presumption is in favor of the validity of their action, and as such deliberative body they cannot be bound by acts *in pais*.[1]

The legislature may also authorize them to perform various discretionary and administrative acts.[2]

(*b*) *Election, Appointment, etc.*—In the discussion of the autonomy of bodies, like those under consideration, whose existence and tenure of office are so absolutely dependent upon the changing phases of the statute law, it is not only difficult, but impossible, to lay down, with any degree of accuracy, any general rules

official acts. Webster *v.* Washington Co., 26 Minn. 220.

If county commissioners had jurisdiction of proceedings instituted to annex territory to a town, the regularity of such proceedings cannot be attacked collaterally. Cicero *v.* Williamson, 91 Ind. 541.

The proceedings, orders, and judgments of a board of county commissioners cannot be assailed in a collateral way, as a suit for an injunction, on account of errors and irregularities which might have been made the ground of an appeal. Argo *v.* Barthand, 80 Ind. 63.

An order of annexation made by commissioners in the exercise of their proper jurisdiction, though liable to be reviewed and set aside by the court of common pleas, is not void, and cannot be impeached collaterally. Blanchard *v.* Bissell, 11 Ohio St. 96.

1. Under the *Wisconsin* constitution, which empowers the legislature to confer upon boards of county supervisors "powers of a local legislative and administrative character," when any subject of legislation is intrusted to county boards, by general words they acquire a right to pass any ordinance necessary or convenient for the purpose of disposing of the whole subject, and for that purpose have all the powers of the State legislature over that subject. La Pointe Supervisors *v.* O'Malley, 47 Wis. 332.

In auditing claims against a county, the board of supervisors acts in a legislative, not in a judicial, capacity, and may repeal or reconsider its action when found erroneous. It has power, therefore, to rescind a resolution auditing and allowing such a claim upon discovery of a mistake or error. People *v.* Supervisors, 65 N. Y. 222.

The action of a board of supervisors in setting off a new town, is legislative; the presumptions are in favor of its validity, and the *onus* of proving irregularity or insufficiency are upon the party impeaching the act. People *v.* Carpenter, 24 N. Y. 86.

A deliberative body, like the board of supervisors, cannot be bound by acts *in pais*; the best and only evidence of its intentions is to be drawn from the record of its proceedings. Phelan *v.* San Francisco, 6 Cal. 531.

The relations existing between a State and its several counties, and their respective rights and powers, examined at length, and numerous authorities collated and reviewed with especial reference to the question of the power of the legislature to confirm deeds made by the county commissioners under authority, but void on account of irregularity in the sales. Barton Co. *v.* Wosler, 47 Mo. 189.

2. The legislature may authorize county commissioners to provide funds for paying a valid indebtedness of the county by issuing and selling county bonds. Comrs. of Jefferson *v.* People, 5 Neb. 127.

Where certain members of the board of freeholders were empowered by statute to deal with certain matters of minor importance, the board itself can ratify action taken in good faith by persons other than those designated by which expense is incurred. Cory *v.* Somerset Co. Freeholders, 44 N. J. L. 445.

Where there are not sufficient funds in the treasury to repair all the county bridges, the commissioners have discretion which to repair, which courts will not control save upon clear abuse of the trust. State *v.* Kearney & Buffalo County Comrs., 12 Neb. 6.

The commissioners of Philadelphia County have power to inquire into the irregularities of a ward election. The constables' return is not conclusive on them. Com. *v.* Leslie, 5 Rawle (Pa.), 75.

for by law, and the members enter upon their office, they are officers *de facto*.[1]

3. Powers. — (*a*) *Generally.* — It has been said that these county boards have power to do whatever the political entity the county might do if capable of rational action, except in respect to matters the cognizance of which is exclusively vested in some other officer or person, and that in an enlarged sense they are the guardians of the county, having the management and control of its financial interests.[2] The judicial interpretation as to the powers vested in the county boards will, therefore, be found to be a construction of the powers of the county in so far as they may be vested in the commissioners or supervisors, and they will, of course, vary in different States, according to the distribution of county functions by acts of the legislature among them and the other county officers. They exercise judicial functions in the matter of the approval of the bonds of county officers.[3] They have power to change an appropriation of money raised for a legitimate object, and devote the money to another object equally within the scope of their powers.[4]

They have authority under their general power to compromise a judgment;[5] to sell shares of stock belonging to the county;[6] may

1. If the office of county commissioners is provided for by law, and they enter upon the duties thereof, they are officers *de facto*, and their acts not void for irregularity in the manner of their election. Waller *v.* Perkins, 52 Ga. 233.

County officials *de facto* can perform all acts lawfully appertaining to their office. State *v.* Jacobs, 17 Ohio, 143.

2. Shanklin *v.* Madison Co., 21 Ohio St. 575.

The *Pennsylvania* act of 1836 as to power of the county commissioners, construed and defined. Com. *v.* Corren (6 Phila.), 623.

The California statute, 1855, transfers from the courts of sessions to the supervisors all general and special powers and duties of a civil nature. People *v.* Berchon, 12 Cal. 90. See also Gaines *v.* Robb, 8 Iowa, 193.

The act of a board of freeholders not properly organized, but acting in good faith, will be sustained as to the tenure of office of a collector by them so elected. Sate *v.* Farrier (N. J.), 1 Cent. Rep. 694.

A resolution of a board of county commissioners authorising two of its members to take such action as in their judgment is necessary to utilise the labor of county prisoners on public works, is not an illegal delegation by the board of powers authorizing county commissioners to employ at hard labor all county prisoners. Holland *v.* State (Fla.), 1 Southern Rep. 521.

3. Miller *v.* Supervisors, 25 Cal. 93. And in assessing taxes. People *v.* Schenectady, 35 Barb. (N. Y.) 408; Phœnix *v.* Clark, 2 Mich. 327.

The board of supervisors has jurisdiction to increase or diminish the valuation of personal property in any town or township in the county, and may add or deduct a given percentage to or from the assessed valuation. Harney *v.* Supervisors, 44 Iowa, 203.

The duty of passing upon the question of a corrected assessment-roll, and certifying to its accuracy and completeness, is a judicial one, and cannot be delegated. People *v.* Hagadorn, 104 N. Y. 516.

The levy and collection of a special tax to the amount of the estimate, by the highway commissioners, of the cost of a public improvement, is entirely discretionary with the board of supervisors. People *v.* Vermillion Co., 47 Ill. 256.

4. People *v.* Baker, 29 Barb. (N. Y.) 81.

5. The supervisors have authority to compromise a judgment against the county under their general authority to represent their respective counties, and to have the care and management of the property and business of the county in all cases where no other provision is made. Collins *v.* Welch, 58 Iowa, 72.

The board of supervisors have power to compromise and settle a judgment recovered by the county pending an appeal by the defendant, and a succeeding board cannot rescind and reverse the former acts. Orleans Co. *v.* Bowen, 4 Lans. (N. Y.) 24.

6. County commissioners have power to sell shares of stock belonging to the

They have authority to erect or rent suitable county buildings, and to provide money therefor, and for repairing the same either by appropriation of county funds by taxation, or by borrowing money, according to the limitations of the statute law.[1]

In them is sometimes vested the power to contract for the public printing,[2] and frequently, also, the power to purchase land for county purposes, or take it by devise for like ends, or to buy it in on a tax or other judicial sale to protect a county debt.[3] And

by a public officer in the arrest and prosecution of offenders, where the exigencies of the case and the ends of justice require the expenditure, though they may not be taxable as costs, nor recoverable by action. State v. Freeholders of Hudson, 37 N. J. L. 254.

1. In *Mississippi* the board of police in each county has power to build and repair court-houses, and to levy taxes for that purpose. The legislature locates the seat of justice, but it is in the discretion of the board of police as to what part of the seat of justice shall be the site of the court-house. Odeneal v. Barry, 24 Miss. 9.

The board of county commissioners has power to make a contract for the erection of a court-house, and provide in such contract that the contractor shall not be paid until all claims for material and work against him have been satisfied. Knapp v. Swaney (Mich.), 23 N. W. R. 162.

Under the *Virginia* act of 1870, the board of supervisors may provide land for building of a court-house. Culpepper v. Gorrell, 20 Gratt. (Va.) 484.

The commissioners of a county are empowered, in case the county does not own buildings reasonably suited or adequate therefor, to rent any requisite number of rooms for county offices. And under all ordinary circumstances the judgment of the commissioners is conclusive as to the unfitness or insufficiency of the buildings owned by the county. Comrs. v. Barnett, 14 Kan. 627.

A county board, with power to make a building contract, may provide for payment in county orders bearing interest. Kendleman v. Jackson Co., 8 Ill. Ap. 287.

A board of county commissioners has authority to issue bonds, which shall be valid and binding upon the county, to pay for the building of a court-house, jail, or other necessary county buildings, for the use of the county. Chaska Co. v. Carver, 6 Minn. 204.

County commissioners can appropriate money, without first submitting the question to the voters of the county, to make repairs or alterations to a court-house already existing. State v. Harrison, 24 Kan. 268.

2. County supervisors in *California*, and no other county or township officials, have the power to contract for the county printing. Times Publishing Co. v. Alameda Co., 64 Cal. 469.

The ten days' notice required by California Code is essential to the validity of the supervisors' contract for the county printing. Maxwell v. Stanislaus Co. Supervisors, 53 Cal. 389.

Prior to the enactment of California Pol. Code, § 4047, there was no limitation upon the general powers of the board of supervisors to contract for printing or publication. Maxwell v. Stanislaus Co. Supervisors, 56 Cal. 114.

The powers and duties of the boards of supervisors, county clerks, etc., in the State of *New York*, as to making contracts, and fixing compensation for official printing, and the right of the contractor to compel auditing and payment of his claim, explained and defined. People v. Cortland Co. 58 Barb. (N. Y.) 139.

The board of supervisors have power to determine whether legal notices should be published in one or more newspapers. People v. Hamilton Co. Supervisors, 73 N. Y. 604.

3. Commissioners have a *prima facie* right to purchase a tract of land to be used as a home for the poor of their county, and such right cannot be questioned in a collateral proceeding. Holton v. Comrs. of Lake Co., 55 Ind. 194.

The provisions of *Ohio* Rev. Stat. § 877, requiring county commissioners to publish notice of their intention to purchase any land or to erect any building, do not apply to proceedings under §§ 929 *et seq.*, relating to the purchase of lands for a children's home; these latter sections providing a complete scheme in themselves, which embraces the whole subject. State v. Darke County Auditor, 43 Ohio St. 311.

The rejection by the board of freeholders of a motion to take certain land for public use, was held to be a finality, and to exhaust the power given by a special statute therefor. (Affirming Mabon v. Halsted, 39 N. J. L. 640.) O'Neill v. Hudson Co. Freeholders, 41 N. J. L. 161.

Under a rule of a board of county commissioners, allowing motions to be reconsidered within two business days, an acceptance of a proposal for sale of land for a

3. *To employ Counsel.* — It may be laid down as a general rule, that commissioners or supervisors have power to employ counsel on behalf of the county, or in litigation arising out of their official duty.[1] But in *Nebraska* the rule seems to be otherwise.[2]

4. *Miscellaneous Powers.* — County commissioners and supervisors are sometimes endowed by the legislature, with the power to appoint certain subordinate officers,[3] and to remove such offi-

to railroad companies, although such bonds have not been registered with the auditor of state, as provided in the act of March 6, 1871. 1876, Commissioners of St. Louis County v. Nettleton, 22 Minn. 356.

1. The county commissioners or supervisors have power to employ an attorney on behalf of the county, and the county is liable for his services. State *v.* Franklin Co., 21 Ohio St. 648; Ellis *v.* Washoe Co., 7 Nev. 291; Hopkins *v.* Clayton, 32 Iowa, 13.

County commissioners may employ counsel to defend a *mandamus* against them. Thurber *v.* Commissioners, 13 Kan. 182.

In employing counsel, the board of county commissioners acts as a corporation, and, like other corporations, may employ agents and attorneys without making such employment a matter of record; but this must be done by the concurrent act of a majority of the board at a legal session. McCabe *v.* Comrs., 46 Ind. 380. See also Board of Comrs. *v.* Ross, 46 Ind. 404.

County commissioners have power to employ a special attorney to represent the county in a particular cause instead of the official attorney. 1877, Taylor *v.* Umatilla County, 6 Oreg. 394.

The board of chosen freeholders must pay associate counsel employed by the prosecutor of the pleas in a homicide case on certificate of the presiding judge; *mandamus* will lie to enforce payment. State *v.* Freeholders (1886) (N. J.), 1 Cent. Rep. 484. See same case as to rights, powers, duties, and liabilities of chosen freeholders under acts of 1880 and 1883.

A board of county commissioners has authority to contract with an attorney to defend the board in the supreme court. Dexter *v.* Howe, 28 Kan. 353; Hornblower *v.* Duden, 35 Cal. 664.

County commissioners, when collecting claims due the county, have a right to employ counsel, and to agree with them for a reasonable compensation; but they have no power to agree to pay counsel an unreasonably large contingent fee. Chester Co. *v.* Barber, 97 Pa. St. 455.

Commissioners may employ counsel in litigation arising out of their official duty. Jack *v.* Moore, 66 Ala. 184.

Where a board of county commissioners requested the county attorney to go into another county and render services there for his county, *held,* that the said board was liable to pay him a reasonable compensation in addition to his salary. Huffman *v.* Greenwood Co. Comrs., 23 Kan. 281.

The provision of *Mississippi* Code authorizing county boards to employ counsel to conduct civil cases instead of the district attorney, refers to cases pending or about to be instituted. Marion Co. *v.* Taylor, 55 Miss. 187.

Under *Nevada* Statutes, 1864, 257, § 8, authorizing commissioners to control the prosecution and defence of all suits to which the county is a party, *held,* that an allowance by them of fees of extra counsel, in a suit against the county, was the ratification of the unauthorized employment of such counsel by the district attorney. Clarke *v.* Lyon Co., 8 Nev. 181.

A board of county commissioners has no power to employ an attorney to prosecute one indicted for embezzling county funds. Ripley Co. Comrs. *v.* Ward, 69 Ind. 441.

County commissioners cannot authorize the treasurer to employ an attorney to assist in the collection of delinquent taxes. Miller *v.* Embree, 88 Ind. 133.

While counties have power to contract for collection of county property, the board of supervisors in the exercise of that power is not authorized to delegate it to others to determine whether to commence a suit, select attorneys, and prosecute the same, nor to make a compromise or settlement dependent upon the written consent of strangers; and contracts so attempting to delegate such powers are *ultra vires.* Scollay *v.* Butte Co. (Cal.), 7 Pacific Rep. 661.

2. In *Nebraska,* independently of statute, commissioners have no authority to employ an attorney. Platte Co. *v.* Gerard, 12 Neb. 244.

County commissioners are not liable for the services of assistant district attorneys, or of persons appointed by the court to perform the duties of the district attorney in his absence. Cuming Co. Comrs. *v.* Tate, 10 Neb. 193.

They cannot, at the expense of the county, employ an attorney to aid the district attorney in a criminal prosecution. Montgomery *v.* Jackson Co., 22 Wis. 69.

3. County commissioners in *Maryland* have power to appoint a collector of taxes

3. *To employ Counsel.*— It may be laid down as a general rule, that commissioners or supervisors have power to employ counsel in behalf of the county, in litigation arising out of their official duty.[1] But in Nebraska the rule seems to be otherwise.[2]

4. *Miscellaneous Powers.*— County commissioners and supervisors are sometimes endowed by the legislature with the power to appoint certain subordinate officers,[3] and to remove such offi-

They have been authorized to pay bounties for hedges,[1] to build and regulate highways and ditches,[2] to pass orders as to animals running at large,[3] and under certain conditions to divide the county;[4] under their general power to provide for prisoners they may without express authority transfer insane prisoners from jail to the asylum.[5] The power to issue a county warrant is vested only in the board, and must be drawn and signed after action by the board.[6] They may adjourn from time to time;[7] they have power to regulate the sale of spirituous liquors.[8]

(c) *Powers as a Tribunal.* — The county boards are often authorized to act as courts, with judicial or *quasi* judicial powers.[9] Such

regular meeting to amend their records in accordance with facts. Dresden *v.* Comrs., 62 Me. 365. See also Water Power Co. *v.* Comrs., 112 Mass. 206; Gloucester *v.* Comrs. of Essex, 116 Mass. 579.

1. A board of county commissioners has the power, under *Kansas* Comp. Laws, 1879, to pay a bounty out of the general county fund to one who has grown an Osage-orange hedge, in accordance with the provisions of said laws. Marion County Comrs. *v.* Hech, 24 Kan. 778.

2. The chosen freeholders of a county have power to determine that a highway bridge shall be built over an artificial water course, and — McKinley *v.* Freeholders, 29 N. J. Eq. 164 — their action in such matters within the limits of their authority is not open to review by the courts.

As to power of county commissioners, under *Ohio* act, April 5, 1886, to construct roads, the necessary preliminaries thereto and the assessments therefor, Burgett *v.* Norris, 25 Ohio St. 308.

Where an act is passed authorizing the building of a tall bridge across a river, and the collection of such tolls as the supervisors may fix, the power of the board in the premises is not exhausted when they once fix the tolls; but it may change the same from time to time, subject to the supervising control of the legislature. Bridge Co. *v.* Goodrich, 47 Cal. 488.

The commissioners in *Maine* have power to establish a highway from one point to another within the same town. New Vineyard *v.* Somerset, 24 Me. 151.

Under the statutes of *Massachusetts*, county commissioners have authority to authorize the owner of marshy and wet land to dig a ditch across his neighbor's land to some outlet, where the water may be discharged without injury to him. Sherman *v.* Tobey, 3 Allen (Mass.), 7.

The *Ohio* statutes conferring power on the county commissioners to locate and establish ditches, construed. Cupp *v.* Seneca Co., 19 Ohio St. 173.

3. Under *Indiana* act of May 31, 1852, authorizing county commissioners to pass orders as to the regulation of animals running at large, *held*, that the commissioners might make, modify, and repeal orders as often as the public interest demanded. Welch *v.* Bowen, 103 Ind. 252.

4. Under act of March, 1857, the county commissioners of a county which contains the requisite area may be divided, the county acting through a single committee of freeholders. Commissioners *v.* Spitler, 13 Ind. 235.

5. Although the commissioners of a county may have no express statutory authority to transfer insane prisoners from a county jail to the insane-asylum, there to be supported at the expense of the county, yet, having no place to secure such persons properly, they may, under their general duty of providing for persons, exercise this power. Allegheny *v.* Western Hospital, 48 Pa. St. 123.

6. The power to issue a county warrant is vested only in the board of commissioners, and can be exercised only at a meeting of the board. If drawn and signed without action by the board, it is a nullity in the hands of one chargeable with notice of its defect. Stoddard *v.* Benton, 6 Col. 508.

7. A board of supervisors of a county has power to adjourn from time to time, until its business is completed. *Ex parte* Mirande, 14 Pacific Rep. 888.

8. A board of supervisors has power to regulate the sale of spirituous liquors within the county. *Ex parte* Walter (Cal. 1884), 3 Pacific Rep. 894.

9. The board of county commissioners is a court of record in *Indiana*, and its acts, consequently, can only be proved by the record. State *v.* Conner, 5 Blackf. (Ind.) 325; Board *v.* La Grange Co., 7 Ind. 6.

The authority of commissioners acting judicially to determine whether the requisite number of qualified electors have petitioned for an election, affirmed. Hetzel *v.* Comrs., 8 Nev. 309.

The board of county commissioners, in acting upon claims against the county, acts in a judicial capacity; and its decisions are conclusive and binding alike upon the

must make a specific decree, and not one in the alternative.[1] Where they issue a warrant to the sheriff to summon a jury to assess damages, it should be made returnable to them.[2]

They are not concluded by the finding of a road jury in auditing its assessments.[3] Two commissioners cannot sit to try a third.[4] In the absence of fraud, equity will not interfere with the action of a county board in settling a claim; but a tax-payer can obtain an injunction against an appropriation not authorized by law.[5] Their action in disallowing cost and fees is not reviewable.[6] In proceedings before them, the strict rules of evidence in courts cannot always be insisted upon.[7]

In some States they are not endowed with judicial powers, and are not considered a court.[8] Where they act as agents for the State, in making settlements with collectors, their orders entered on their records are but memoranda.[9] In *Connecticut*, commissioners are not judges within the meaning of the constitution as to the age limit.[10]

4. Rights, Duties, Limitations. — (*a*) *Generally.* — Where county commissioners received a ***per diem*** compensation, it was held that they could base no right to additional compensation upon a custom

tribunal of limited jurisdiction. It has no power to require a sheriff to execute a new bond when a prior bond becomes insufficient, and to declare the office vacant in case of a failure to file such bond. Ruckles v. State, 1 Oreg. 347; Wren *v.* Fargo, 2 Oreg. 19.

1. County commissioners, in the exercise of jurisdiction conferred, must make a specific decree, and not one in the alternative. Roxbury *v.* Boston R. R., 6 Cush. (Mass.) 424.

2. Where county commissioners were authorized to issue a warrant to the sheriff to empanel a jury to assess damages for the location of a canal, the warrant should be made returnable to them, and not to the common pleas; and the latter court could not cure the error, the return of the warrant being of the substance of the proceedings. Hampshire Canal Co. *v.* Ashley, 15 Pick. (Mass.) 496.

3. The supervisors are not concluded by the finding of a road jury when called on to audit its assessments of damages, but have authority to reduce the amount. People *v.* Supervisors, 7 Wend. (N. Y.) 530.

4. Two members of a board of commissioners cannot sit to try a third for misdemeanor, and remove him from office therefor. Hutchinson *v.* Ashburn, 5 Neb. [illegible].

5. Fitzgerald *v.* Harms, 92 Ill. 372.

6. Arapahoe Co. Comrs. *v.* Graham, 4 Col. [illegible].

7. In proceedings before boards of supervisors for organizing new townships, the strict rules governing the introduction of evidence in courts cannot be insisted upon. Matthews *v.* Otsego Co. Comrs., 48 Mich. 587.

8. The board of supervisors, under the laws and constitution of *Virginia*, is not a court, and a petition by a creditor to the board praying the allowance of his claim is not a suit. Gurnee *v.* County, 1 Hugh (Va.), 270.

County commissioners having no judicial powers cannot review the certificate of probable cause, in event of which costs may be paid by the county. The statute giving them power to disallow any bill of costs must be construed conformably with law. Hedges *v.* County Commissioners, 4 Mont. 280. See also Davis *v.* County Commissioners, 4 Mont. 292.

The *Georgia* law, 1872, as to commissioners for Whitfield County, did not confer upon them judicial powers, except as to roads. Cox *v.* Whitfield Co. Comrs., 65 Ga. 741.

9. Where county commissioners act as agents of the State in making settlements with the collectors of revenue, their orders entered on their records are but memoranda of transactions, and may be inquired into. Mistakes made in such settlements may be corrected, as well as those of an individual acting on his own behalf. La Salle *v.* Simmons, 10 Ill. 232.

10. County commissioners are not judges within the meaning of the constitution of *Connecticut*, which provides that no judge shall be capable of holding his office after he arrives at the age of seventy. Betts *v.* New Hartford, 25 Conn. 180.

against county officers;[1] providing fuel and furniture, etc., for county offices;[2] fixing compensation for services of county officers not otherwise defined and provided for;[3] and on them is generally imposed the examination and allowance of claims against the county.[4]

Where an order has been improvidently granted by the county commissioners, it is not only competent for them to rescind it, but it is their duty so to do.[5]

(*c*) *Limitations in Powers of County Boards.* — The instances where the courts have defined certain acts, or attempted acts, of commissioners, supervisors, etc., as *ultra vires*, are numerous, and the examples almost as various as the cases. It would be impossible, therefore, to group all of the rulings under distinct headings or classifications. The underlying principle on this point is not difficult to discover from a study of these cases. As has been shown, the county boards, as representing the counties, have only such implied powers as the county, if a sentient being, would have to carry out the necessary objects of its creation, to the extent that such duties and powers have not been conferred upon other county officers. It follows, therefore, that, being corporations, they have no powers, except such as are given them by statute.[6]

The limits of all powers, therefore, except those necessarily implied from the county entity, must be found within the four corners of the statutory provisions made by the legislature in each State, whether they have to do with the general or special powers and duties of commissioners and supervisors. The cases cited will serve to show how this principle of almost universal application has been applied in a variety of particular cases.[7]

The board of supervisors in such counties of *Illinois* as have adopted township organization are required to provide for the support of the poor; nor is there any distinction as to town and county paupers. Supervisors v. South Ottawa, 12 Ill. 480.

Under the statute, the superintendents of the poor were empowered to draw on the county treasurer for necessary expenses. *Held*, that the board of supervisors cannot regulate the manner of drawing. People v. Demorest, 16 Hun (N. Y.), 123.

1. A county board of supervisors in *Nebraska* is bound to hear complaints duly preferred against county officers. Such complaints may be heard by a quorum. Costs may be imposed and arguments confined within reasonable limits. State v. Saline County, 18 Neb. 422.

2. Under *Indiana* Revised Statutes, 1852, it is the duty of the commissioners to furnish fuel for the recorder's office. Board of Jackson Co. v. King, 7 Ind. 721.

3. Supervisors fix the amount of compensation of the judges of the county courts who attend at the clerk's office on notice from the clerk to witness the drawing of jurors. People v. Supervisors, 12 Wend. (N. Y.) 257.

4. Boards of supervisors have no general authority to establish claims in favor of the county against townships. People v. Wright, 19 Mich. 351.

5. Lemly v. Forsyth Co. Commissioners, 85 N. C. 379.

6. County commissioners have no power to release a sheriff from his liability to pay the county taxes. Being a corporation, they have no powers except such as are given them by statute. State v. Clarke, 73 N. C. 255.

7. **Limitations on Commissioners' Powers: Generally.** — As to the limitation on the powers of commissioners, supervisors, etc., generally, see the following cases:

Boards of supervisors have no authority to make bills of exchange, — Chemung Canal Bank v. Supervisors of Chemung, 5 Den. (N. Y.) 517, — nor to set aside a portion of the revenue of the county for cur-

fication of the change in contract. Mallory v. Montgomery Co., 48 Iowa, 681.

The chairman of a board of county commissioners has no authority to lease premises on behalf of the county, except so far as he is authorized to do so by the board. Gardner v. Comrs. of Dakota Co., 21 Minn. 33.

A board of commissioners cannot let the building of a court-house at any other time than that specified in the advertisement for such letting, and an injunction would lie at the suit of a tax-payer of the county to prevent the building of such court-house. Commissioners v. Templeton, 51 Ind. 266.

A board of county commissioners has no power to enter into contracts for boring wells for oil, or sinking shafts for coal, either alone or in partnership with others. Bennett v. Abbott, 51 Ind. 254.

The provision of Illinois constitution, that the county board shall not increase or diminish the compensation of any county officer during his term of office, is merely a limitation as to compensation for the personal discharge of official duty by him, and does not refer to the fixing of the amount of necessary clerk hire, stationery, fuel, and other expenses. The allowances for these are to be determined from time to time by the necessity which the business of the office may develop. Briscoe v. Clark Co., 95 Ill. 309.

The board of commissioners of a county have no power to consolidate two or more towns without first submitting the question to a vote of the people of the towns. People v. Brayton, 94 Ill. 341.

A board of commissioners, convened in special session, cannot make a valid order for annexation of contiguous territory to an incorporated city. Vincennes v. Windman, 72 Ind. 218.

Limitations on Commissioners' Power to Contract, Lease and Sell County Property.—The board of supervisors is the official agent of the county to scrutinize the reports of the county treasurer to discover if his statement of receipts is correct, and if his charges for disbursements are supported by proper vouchers, and to count the money on hand to see if it is the true amount. But they cannot fix liability on the treasurer by deciding any question against him, or discharge him by any judgment in his favor. In examining and approving his reports, the duties of the board of supervisors of the county are ministerial, and not judicial, and they have no power to decide what commissions the county treasurer should have. Howe v. State, 53 Miss. 57.

If the board of supervisors consolidate the offices of record and auditor of the county, the ordinance making the consolidation must not only be passed and published, but must be published by order of the board. People v. Bailhache, 52 Cal. 310.

Being the inhabitant of a town through which a proposed road is to pass, does not disqualify a commissioner from acting on account of interest. Wilbraham v. Comrs., 11 Pick. (Mass.) 322; Monterey v. Berkshire, 7 Cush. (Mass.) 394.

The board of supervisors has no power to change the method of rendering deeds and mortgages prescribed by statute. People v. Nash, 62 N. Y. 484.

The board of chosen freeholders of Union County has not the custody of the jails and prisoners. State v. Union Co., 9 Cent. Rep. 506.

Under Indiana Revised Statutes, giving county commissioners power to punish contempt by fines, etc., they cannot suspend an attorney from practice before them. Garrigus v. State, 93 Ind. 239.

Where the office of city jailer has been abolished by law, it follows that the board of county commissioners has no authority to create the office. State v. Canavan, 17 Nev. 422.

There being no statute provision on the subject, the director at large, of the board of chosen freeholders of Hudson County, has no power to appoint standing committees unless empowered by a rule adopted by the board of the then present year. State v. Hudson County Freeholders, 44 N. J. L. 392.

Highways and roads are, by the constitution of *Michigan*, put under the control of the boards of supervisors, not absolutely, but under legal restrictions; and those restrictions have confined them to State and territorial roads; and they can have no occasion to raise money for other roads, and they must exercise their own judgment in expending such moneys as they may lawfully raise. Attorney-General v. Supervisors of Bay County, 34 Mich. 47.

County commissioners have no authority to extend the time prescribed by law for the payment of revenue by the collector of the county revenue. Goman v. State, 4 Blackf. (Ind.) 241.

It is not competent for the county commissioners, on taking security for a fine, to discharge from prison a person convicted of a misdemeanor, and sentenced to pay a fine to the State; and the person so discharged may be re-taken, and re-committed by the sheriff. Schwable v. Sheriff, 22 Pa. St. 18.

County commissioners are authorised by statute to establish roads of a certain width; and an order by them establishing a road of an undefined width is void. White v. Conover, 5 Blackf. (Ind.) 462.

If a resolution by the board of freeholders

(*d*) *Liability for Misconduct or Neglect of Duty.* — They are liable to the sheriff for not providing a sufficient jail where it is their duty to furnish one.[1] A member who has been prevented from attending a meeting by the wrongful neglect of his colleagues, may proceed directly against the offending members.[2] The duty to take a sufficient bond as security for a tax-collector is judicial, and not ministerial; and in the absence of corruption charged action will not lie, because of the insufficiency of the security taken,[3] and a refusal to accept non-residents as sureties.[4] Irregular and improper conduct cannot be made out by inference.[5] The

There is no statute in *Indiana* which expressly or by implication authorizes a board of commissioners to appropriate money of the county in the working, improvement, or repair of the ordinary highways of the county; still less, if possible, is any authority conferred upon the board to furnish aid to a gravel road or turnpike company in building or repairing its road at the expense of the county. Turnpike Co. *v.* Bartholomew Co., 72 Ind. 226.

Under *Maryland* act of 1865, ch. 85, amending Maryland Code, art. 28, and empowering the county commissioners of Baltimore County to appoint officers necessary to keep the bridges, etc., in repair, the commissioners are liable to one injured by a defect occasioned by their omission to appoint the same. Commissioners of Baltimore County *v.* Baker, 44 Md. 1.

They have no power to appropriate county funds to aid in the construction of toll-bridges, or to aid a private person in the construction of a free bridge. Colton *v.* Hanchett, 13 Ill. 615.

Nor can they appropriate county funds to the compensation of a circuit judge. Perry *v.* Kinnior, 42 Ill. 160; Beauchamp *v.* Supervisors, 45 Ill. 274.

They cannot delegate their powers and duties in the matter of the approval of guarantees by a majority vote. People *v.* County Officers, 15 Mich. 85.

They have no power to hold land for any other purpose than county purposes. Jackson *v.* Cory, 8 Johns. (N. Y.) 385; Jackson *v.* Hartwell, 8 Johns. (N. Y.) 422.

In *New York* neither the board nor a committee has any power to draw on the treasurer: they can only audit the claim for services, and give a certificate therefor. Supervisors *v.* Weed, 35 Barb. (N. Y.) 136.

A board of supervisors is not authorized by law to appropriate money in the county treasury to pay for the surveying and grading of public roads. But when an appropriation has been made under an honest mistake that the facts justified it, the members of the board are not personally liable. Paxton *v.* Arthur, 60 Miss. 832.

The county commissioners of Alabama have no authority to determine out of which fund a claim against a county is to be paid, and any such judgment is a nullity. Cuthbert *v.* Lewis, 6 Ala. 262.

Where, under the statute, two-thirds of the revenue arising from certain taxes must be set aside by the commissioners for the general county fund, there can be no restraint upon the treasurer as to the manner of paying out such fund except that imposed by law. People *v.* Board of Commissioners of Washoe Co., 1 Nev. 460.

1. When made their duty to furnish a sufficient jail, they are liable to the sheriff for not providing one, when he has been subjected to damages for the escape of prisoners, by reason of the want of a jail. Comrs. *v.* Butt, 2 Ohio, 348.

2. A supervisor who is prevented from being present at a meeting of the board by the wrongful neglect of other members to give him proper notice, cannot on that ground sustain an application for an injunction to restrain other officers from proceeding with the payment of appropriations directed by such meeting. His remedy is by proceeding directly against the offending supervisors. Ely *v.* Connolly, 7 Abb. (N. Y.) Pr. N. S. 8.

3. A duty imposed on county commissioners, by an act of legislature, to take a sufficient bond from the person appointed to collect taxes, is judicial, and not ministerial, and an action will not lie for not taking a bond with sufficient security, unless fraud or corruption is alleged. State *v.* Dunnington, 12 Md. 340.

4. To refuse to accept non-residents as sureties is no abuse of the discretionary power vested in the county commissioners in taking bonds for the faithful performance of a contract to erect county buildings. Guckes *v.* Darke Co., 21 Ohio St. 311.

5. Irregular and improper conduct on the part of county commissioners cannot be made out by inference; but if such exists, the same must be directly alleged and

elect has been held good.[1] They may be sued before a justice of the peace,[2] but cannot be called out of their county.[3] The proper form of action is against "the board of supervisors," without naming the individual members.[4] A tax-payer cannot intervene in an action to enforce a claim against a county agreed to by the supervisors, but he may intervene to restrain an illegal exercise of powers.[5]

County commissioners are not liable, as a general rule, for acts or damages occurring in the honest discharge of their official duty.[6] The election of a clerk by them, at the organization of the

for the prices of a press for the seal of the court of common pleas, it being a county charge; but they are not liable for the price of the seal itself, it being a State charge. Commissioners *v.* Hutchins, 11 Ohio, 368.

A board of county commissioners is not liable for services rendered by a district prosecutor. Bradford *v.* Commissioners, 1 Morr. (Iowa) 219.

A board of supervisors which has provided suitable accommodations for the surrogate cannot be compelled to pay for other accommodations. People *v.* Montgomery Co., 34 Hun (N. Y.), 599.

County commissioners are not bound to furnish the county superintendent with an office,—Greene Co. *v.* Artice, 96 Ind. 384,—nor the county surveyor with fuel or stationery, or to reimburse him for money expended therefor. Towsley *v.* Ozaukee Co., 60 Wis. 251.

The sheriff cannot call upon the commissioners to refund the daily sums he has paid the crier of the court. Commissioners of Mercer *v.* Patterson, 2 R. (Pa.) 106.

No action by an individual lies against the board of chosen freeholders for injuries in consequence of their not completing or repairing a county bridge. Cooley *v.* Essex, 27 N. J. L. 415; Livermore *v.* Freeholders, 29 N. J. L. 245.

The county supervisors, after levying the maximum rate for ordinary expenses and bridge purposes, cannot be compelled to levy an additional tax to pay a judgment rendered upon a warrant issued for such purpose. Polk *v.* Winett, 37 Iowa, 34.

1. Service of a writ of summons against a county upon two commissioners who have been elected, although they have not taken the oath of office, is good. Kleckner *v.* Lehigh Co., 6 Whart. (Pa.) 66.

2. They may be sued before a justice of the peace; and, although individually named, yet if the description of their office is added, and the subject of the suit is public, the suit is against the corporation. Pelts *v.* Comrs., Wright (Ohio), 417.

3. County commissioners cannot be called out of their county to answer for a petition for a *mandamus* complaining of their acts and doings, as such within the county. Woodman *v.* Somerset, 24 Me. 151.

4. The proper form of an action is against "the board of supervisors," without naming the individual supervisors. Hill *v.* Supervisors, 12 N. Y. 52; Magee *v.* Cutler, 43 Barb. (N. Y.) 239.

5. A tax-payer has not such an interest as entitles him to intervene in an action against a county to enforce a claim against it agreed to by the supervisors, unless it appear from the facts stated that the board, in their action respecting the claim, assumed the exercise of powers not conferred by law, or that they acted in bad faith. Cornell College *v.* Iowa Co., 32 Iowa, 520.

Tax-payers may maintain an action for themselves and all other tax-payers of the county, to restrain the county commissioners from an illegal exercise of their powers to the injury of such tax-payers. Normand *v.* Otoe County Comrs., 8 Neb. 18.

6. County commissioners are not personally liable for damages occurring in the honest discharge of their official duty. Thomas *v.* Wilton, 40 Ohio St. 516; Bosseker *v.* Wabash Co. Comrs., 88 Ind. 267.

When commissioners act within their authority in making contracts for county purposes, they are not personally liable. M'Donald *v.* Franklin Co., 2 Mo. 217.

County commissioners are personally liable for costs paid by their direction before the county has become legally fixed for the payment. Commissioners *v.* County of Lycoming, 46 Pa. St. 496.

A board of county commissioners appointed a committee to contract with A. for a county building on county land. The committee did so, and the work was accepted by them. *Held*, that A. could not maintain an action of assumpsit against the committee for the value of the work, his remedy being against the county. McClure *v.* Secrist, 5 Ind. 31.

Where the supervisors of a county are enjoined from building a county jail at the

of statutes, and audit claims only at regular meetings, otherwise their acts are a nullity.[1] Their contracts should be made at regular meetings,[2] though they need not always be entered on their minutes.[3] In some States it has been held that their judgments are as conclusive as those of a court of record, and only reviewable on appeal or some other direct proceeding;[4] an allowance for work done admits that it was done according to contract;[5] an action for work stipulated to be done to acceptance of the commissioners will not lie against the county without proof of their acceptance of

vide him a residence, the lessor, if he has no knowledge of the character of the act, may recover rent from the county. County v. Bredenburt, 16 Pa. St. 458.

The decision of county commissioners of Alabama, that a claim against a county is valid, is conclusive against the county. Cuthbert v. Lewis, 6 Ala. 262. And under the code, an action cannot be maintained against a county to recover a claim which has been allowed by the court of county commissioners. Marshall Co. v. Jackson Co., 36 Ala. 613.

The declarations of county commissioners are not evidence against the county unless made while officially representing the county, and engaged in transactions concerning which the declarations are made. County of La Salle v. Simmons, 10 Ill. 513.

A duty imposed on the road supervisor to carry into effect all orders of the township trustee does not relieve the county commissioners from their liability for failure to keep the bridges in repair. Gibson Co. Commissioners v. Emmerson, 95 Ind. 579.

Where commissioners were authorized to make certain improvements in a bridge, the time and the manner of so doing to be left wholly to their judgment and discretion, a failure to exercise the discretion cannot be made a cause of action for damages against the county. Lehigh Co. v. Hoffart (Pa.), 9 At. Rep. 177.

1. The acts of supervisors in auditing accounts, except at the regular meetings provided by law, or at a special meeting notified in accordance with the statute, are a nullity. El Dorado v. Reed, 11 Cal. 130; Campbell v. Brackenridge, 8 Blackf. (Ind.) 47.

2. A contract made by county commissioners to be binding upon the county must be made by the board at a regular session of their court. Potts v. Henderson, 2 Ind. 327; Campbell v. Brackenridge, 8 Blackf. (Ind.) 47.

Under statute law in *Nebraska*, contracts made by the commissioners at any other place than the county-seat are void. Merrick Co. Comrs. v. Batty, 10 Neb. 176.

3. A contract with county supervisors need not be entered on their records, but may be proved by parol. Jordan v. Osceola Co., 59 Iowa, 388. See, however, Bridges v. Clay Co., 58 Miss. 817.

A county can be bound by its board of supervisors upon a contract only by an affirmative act within the scope of its authority evidenced by an entry on its minutes.

The supervisors can only contract on behalf of the county by an official act of the board, as such, entered on its minutes, and not by oral orders; though the county may be liable, upon a use of property pursuant to oral orders, for the value. Crump v. Supervisors of Colfax, 52 Miss. 107.

Where an ordinance has been properly passed by the county board of supervisors, the omission of the clerk to add the seal of the board to the record of it in the ordinance book, does not render it invalid. Santa Clara County v. Southern Pacific R. R. Co., 66 Cal. 642.

It is not necessary to the validity of the proceedings of a board of supervisors, that the minutes be signed before adjournment: an approval and signing at the next meeting is sufficient. Beck v. Allen, 58 Miss. 143.

4. When the board of commissioners has jurisdiction, the fact that its decision was erroneous does not render it void, but it is binding unless appealed from or avoided in some legitimate mode. Snelson v. State, 16 Ind. 29; Waugh v. Chauncey, 13 Cal. 11.

After a claim against a county has been presented to the board of supervisors for allowance, and has been passed upon by that body, the amount determined to be due declared, and its payment provided for in the mode prescribed by law, no action will lie against the county upon the ground that the decision was erroneous in respect to the amount due to the plaintiff. Martin v. Green, 29 N. Y. 645.

5. An allowance made by the board for work done, admits that it was done according to contract, and cannot be rescinded by the board, and the auditor will be compelled to issue the warrant. Lyons v. Miller, 17 Ind. 250.

rule, however, only applies when the board acts judicially:[1] but where the board does not so act, there is no appeal, and the remedy, if any, is by a civil action.[2] The county cannot be made

prosecuting an action on such claims is by appeal from its decision. Dixon Co. v. Barnes, 13 Neb. 294.

An appeal lies from the decision of the commissioners. Coms. v. Wheeldon, 15 Ind. 147; Coms. v. State, 15 Ind. 250; Inhabitants of Windham, 32 Me. 452; Graham v. Coms., 25 Ind. 333; Connover v. Supervisors, 5 Wis. 478.

An appeal will lie in *Montana* to district court from the decision of the county commissioners, where accounts against the county are disallowed. The discretion of a commissioner in allowing claims against a county is not arbitrary, but is controlled by legal considerations, is subject to review. Davis v. Comrs. of Lewis and Clarke Co. (1882), 1 Pacific Rep. 750.

The *Indiana* act of 1879 providing that "any person, etc., feeling aggrieved by any decision of the board of commissioners, may appeal to the circuit court of such county; and that no court shall have original jurisdiction of any claim against any county except as in this act," *held* to repeal the act of 1852 providing that, if a claim were disallowed by the board, the claimant might, at his option, appeal, or sue the county. Fulton Co. v. Maxwell, 101 Ind. 268.

An appeal from the order of a county board levying a tax in aid of a railroad goes to the circuit court, not for correction of errors, but for a trial as an original cause. Garin v. Decatur Co. Comrs., 81 Ind. 480.

After the court of county commissioners orders the change of a road, appoints viewers, and accepts their report, the right of a person aggrieved to a *certiorari* is complete; and the court in its return should certify its records as they existed when the writ was issued, and not a record subsequently made, whose validity has not been questioned. County Comrs. v. Hearne, 59 Ala. 371.

On an appeal from the decision of a board of county commissioners refusing to allow a claim, the decision was reversed, and it was *held* that the provision of the statute designating the method of allowing claims by county commissioners, is only permissive, and not mandatory, as to requiring further evidence, and an omission to require it is not error at law. Green v. Co. of Richland (S. C.), 2 S. E. Rep. 618.

Boards of supervisors being no longer in existence, either as courts or corporations, having been extinguished by the constitution of this State, and this fact having been judicially known, the appeals were directed to abate. Board of Supervisors v. Livesay, 6 W. Va. 44.

The decision of the circuit court or common pleas in *Indiana* upon an appeal from the action of a board of county commissioners in granting or refusing license to sell intoxicating liquors, is final. Brown v. Porter, 37 Ind. 206.

When the records of the county board, kept by the clerk, show the proper presentation of the claim, and that they refuse to grant it, this is enough to authorize an appeal by the claimant to the district court. Black v. Saunders Co. Comrs., 8 Neb. 440.

1. When a board of county commissioners acts judicially, an appeal lies from its decision. White Co. Comrs. v. Karp, 90 Ind. 236.

A right of appeal lies from the decision of county commissioners under *Indiana* act of 1879, concerning the draining and reclaiming of wet lands, the duties of the commissioners being judicial, and not discretionary. Bryan v. Moore, 81 Ind. 480.

2. There is no statute in *Indiana* which authorizes an appeal from the action of a board of commissioners upon a matter involving no question of legal right, but simply a matter for the exercise of the discretion of the board. Sims v. Comrs., 39 Ind. 40; Board of Comrs. v. Elliott, 39 Ind. 191.

The board of county commissioners is not such a judicial body that its decisions in passing upon claims against the county can be reviewed on appeal. The proper remedy to test the validity of a rejected claim is by civil action. Jones v. Franklin Co. Comrs., 88 N. C. 56.

Where a board of county commissioners refuses to grant a petition to set off and organize a new township, one of the petitioners has no right to appeal from such refusal to the district court. Fulkerson v. Harper Co. Comrs., 31 Kan. 125.

In North Carolina there can be no appeal from the refusal of the county commissioners to allow credits claimed by a sheriff in his settlement with the county: his remedy is by action. McMillan v. Robeson Co. Comrs., 90 N. C. 28.

There is no right of appeal from the joint decision of the county commissioners of two or more counties to locate an inter-county road. Freeman v. Franklin Co. Comrs., 74 Me. 326.

An order of the county commissioners for the sale of railroad stock owned by the county, is not such a decision within the meaning of the act which authorizes appeals rule, however, only applies when the board acts judicially;[1] but where the board does not so act, there is no appeal, and the remedy, if any, is by a civil action.[2] The county cannot be made other clearly enjoined duty.[1] But the courts will not assume to control the exercise of discretion of county commissioners so long as they act within their powers;[2] nor will they be compelled to act upon claims where there are no funds in the county treasury for their payment,[3] nor to pay an unliquidated demand.[4] *Mandamus* does not lie to compel the county clerk to issue a warrant on a rescinded order,[5] nor to correct the record which is under his control;[6] and *mandamus* will not lie to compel an appropriation for claims before they have been audited and allowed,[7] or to compel payment of interest on their order.[8]

6. Resignation and Removal. — As a county officer, a commissioner ordinarily would, in the absence of other statutory regulations, resign to the governor, who would have the power to fill any vacancy in the board.[9] In *Nebraska* a county commissioner

ject to *mandamus* to compel collection. *Ex parte* Rowland, 104 U. S. 604.

Where a statute absolutely requires county commissioners to set apart certain funds in the treasury for a particular purpose, and they refuse to do so, *mandamus* is the proper remedy to compel them to do so. Humboldt Co. *v.* Churchill Co., 6 Nev. 30.

Where the fund raised by taxation is required to meet the necessary expenses of a county government, and no part thereof can be legally applied to the satisfaction of a debt, the commissioners acting in good faith, in the execution of their powers, cannot be put in contempt for failure to pay such debt. But in such case, an *alias* writ of *mandamus* should be awarded, to the end that any excess of revenue raised under the law may be applied to the debt. Cromartie *v.* Bladen County Comrs., 87 N. C. 134.

1. Where county commissioners are empowered to build a new county bridge, the duty to do so may be enforced by *mandamus*. Howe *v.* Crawford Co., 47 Pa. St. 361.

If the county commissioners refuse to pay the sheriff, when there are county funds in the county treasury liable to his claims, his remedy is by *mandamus*, and not by an action of damages against them personally. Hunter *v.* Moblery (S. C.), 1 S. E. Rep. 690.

2. Long *v.* Commissioners, 76 N. C. 273.

County commissioners refused to order an election to determine whether the township should subscribe to railroad stock, until a pending question of a division of the township should be first settled. *Held*, that a *mandamus* would not issue to compel their action. State *v.* Anderson Co. Comrs., 26 Kan. 67.

As the *Michigan* constitution confers upon boards of supervisors exclusive power to adjust all claims against their respective counties, the supreme court cannot by *mandamus* compel the allowance by the board of a claim by a sheriff for hire of a watchman for the jail, or for rent of an office hired for himself. Peck *v.* Kent Co. Comrs., 47 Mich. 477.

3. County commissioners will not be compelled by *mandamus* to act upon claims against the county, where no estimates have been made for taxes to be levied to pay the same, unless there are funds in the treasury for the payment of such claims. Lancaster Co. Comrs. *v.* State, 13 Neb. 523.

4. *Mandamus* is not the proper remedy to compel a county board to pay an unliquidated demand. Cox *v.* Comrs., 65 Ga. 741.

5. *Mandamus* does not lie to compel the county clerk to issue a warrant upon the treasurer under a rescinded order of the county board, whether rightfully or wrongfully rescinded. People *v.* Klokke, 92 Ill. 134.

6. *Mandamus* will not lie to compel the clerk of the board of supervisors to correct the record; it is under his control. Wiggington *v.* Markley, 52 Cal. 411.

7. In *Alabama* the commissioners' court cannot be compelled, by *mandamus* from the circuit court, to make an appropriation for the payment of claims against the county before they have been audited and allowed. Falkner *v.* Comrs. of Randolph Co., 19 Ala. 177; Commonwealth *v.* Coms. of Allegheny, 16 S. & R. (Pa.) 317.

8. Nor will *mandamus* be granted to commissioners to compel payment of interest on their order. Commonwealth *v.* Comrs. of Lancaster, 6 Bin. (Pa.) 5.

9. When one who has been elected commissioner for three years, and resigns during the first year, it is provided by law that the governor, with the advice of the council, shall appoint a person who shall hold the office until the 1st of January after another election has been held to fill the vacancy.

it may select a certain place to be the seat of justice, according to the fundamental law of the State.[1]

The question of the location of a county-seat can only be inquired into in a direct proceeding for that purpose; it cannot be determined collaterally;[2] and an order made in a suit in equity directing the removal of county offices and records to a place designated therein as the county-site, is not a bar to a proceeding by *mandamus* to determine the legal location of such county-site.[3]

3. Removal. — (*a*) *Generally.* — The removal of county-seats is a subject over which the law-making power has plenary jurisdiction and control. In the absence of constitutional restrictions, a removal could be authorized upon any vote, great or small, which that body deemed advisable. And when the lowest limit only is fixed in the fundamental law, the legislature may act without restraint in the ascending scale; and, having fixed in the statute the vote which shall be required, it becomes the paramount law, and nothing is left for implication.[4]

(*b*) *Power to remove.* — No one has a vested right in the continuance of a county-seat at a particular place, and in the absence of constitutional restrictions the legislature has the power of removing it.[5] Nor does the location at a given town, provided the citizens will make specified donations towards the expense of erecting buildings, constitute a contract between the State and the citizens, restricting the right of the State to remove the county-seat.[6] Neither is it an objection to a statute, authorizing the

places, but contiguous to each other, — the commissioners are not authorized to select the place situated at the centre. Smith *v.* [illegible], 44 Ga. 163.

The Territorial Statute of Wisconsin of [illegible] referred the location of the seat of justice of Scott County to the people, and directed the returns of votes to be made to the sheriff of D. County, "who, with the commissioners, should examine the returns, and on being satisfied," etc., the town having the greatest number of votes should be the seat of justice. *Held*, that they were not authorized to examine into the legality of the votes. United States *v.* Commissioners of Dubuque County, 1 Morr. (Iowa) 31.

1. In [illegible] the legislature of Mississippi passed a statute, the first section of which provided "that the seat of justice for Hancock County be, and the same is, hereby located in the town of Gainesville." A subsequent section provides that the town of Gainesville shall erect, at their own expense, suitable buildings for that purpose, one-third of which should be repaid by the State. The seventh section provided that, at a certain time, the officers affected by the removal should remove their books and papers to Gainesville. *Held*, that the seat of justice was located absolutely by the statute at Gainesville, and not subject to the condition that that town should erect suitable buildings. Monet *v.* Jones, 18 Miss. 237.

2. Robinson *v.* Moore, 25 Ill. 135.

Irregularities in an election fixing a county-seat will not be inquired into collaterally fourteen years thereafter, and when the place selected has been in fact the county-seat for nine years. State *v.* Piper, 17 Neb. 614.

3. State *v.* Padgett, 19 Fla. 518.

4. Alexander *v.* People, 7 Col. 155.

A county was organized by the legislature, and a temporary county-seat named until the next general election, when it provided for the selection of a permanent one. *Held*, that such election of a permanent county-seat could not be regarded as the removal of a county-seat once established, and the law was not unconstitutional for not conforming to the requirements of the constitution regarding removals. Attorney-General *v.* Board of Canvassers (Mich.), 31 N. W. Rep. 539.

5. Alley *v.* Denson, 8 Tex. 297; Walker *v.* Tarrant, 20 Tex. 16; Elwell *v.* Tucker, 1 Blackf. (Ind.) 285; Blood *v.* Marcelliott, 53 Pa. St. 391.

6. Gilmore *v.* Hayworth, 26 Tex. 89; Newton *v.* Commissioners of Mahoning, 26 Ohio St. 618.

This case came before the United States

removal of a seat of justice of a county, that a former st
vided that the town in which it was already located shoul
continue to be the permanent seat of justice.[1]

The legislature has a constitutional right to pass an
ging the location of the seat of justice of a county, al
contract for the purchase of a particular site had alre
made by the commissioners appointed by law for that

Supreme Court in Newton v. Commissioners of Mahoning, 100 U. S. 548. The following case was shown:—

In the year 1846 the legislature of Ohio passed an act whereby it was provided that the county-seat of Mahoning County should be permanently established at Canfield, upon the fulfilment of certain prescribed terms and conditions, which were fully complied with. The county-seat was established accordingly, and remained at Canfield for about thirty years. In 1874 the legislature passed another act, providing for its removal to Youngstown. A bill was filed, setting forth that the act of 1846, and what was done under it, constituted an executed contract within the meaning and protection of the contract clause of the Constitution of the United States, and praying for a perpetual injunction against the removal contemplated by the latter act. The court, per *Swayne, J., held,*—

1. That the contract clause of the Constitution had no application.

2. That the act of 1846 was a *public law*, relating to a *public subject*, with respect to which a prior had no right to bind a subsequent legislature.

3. Conceding that there was a contract as claimed, it was satisfied on the part of the State, by establishing the county-seat at Canfield, *with the intent* that it should remain there.

4. There was no stipulation that the county-seat should be *kept* or remain there in perpetuity.

5. The rule of interpretation in cases like this, as against the State, is, that nothing is to be taken as conceded but what is given in express and explicit terms, or by an implication equally clear. Silence is negation, and doubt is fatal to the claim.

After reviewing certain authorities, the court say, "In all these cases, there can be no contract and no irrepealable law, because they are 'governmental subjects,' and hence within the category before stated. They involve *public interests*, and legislative acts concerning them are necessarily *public laws*. Every succeeding legislature possesses the same jurisdiction and power with respect to them as its predecessors. The latter have the same power of repeal and modification which the former had of enactment, neither more nor less. All occupy in this respect a footing of perfect eq
must necessarily be so in th
things. It is vital to the pu
that each one should be able
to do whatever the varying c
and present exigencies touchin
involved may require. A d
would be fraught with evil.
considerations apply with full
times and places of holding c
are both purely public things,
concerning them must necessa
same character. If one may l
about, so may the other. In
there is no difference in princ
them. The same reasoning, p
farther in the same direction, w
the same result with respect to
government of a State. If a S
were sought to be removed u
cumstances of this case with r
county-seat, whatever the publ
or the force of the public sent
demanded it, those interested
plaintiffs in error, might, accor
argument, effectually forbid an
and this result could be broug
a bill in equity and a perpetual

The county-seat of a county
ordinary legislation, permanent
Canfield; the county commissi
agreed that Canfield should be
nent county-seat, if the plain
prietor of the town, would
county certain lands, which de
tiff had duly executed and deli
that the plaintiff could not clai
right that the county-seat sh
remain at Canfield, and that
could not be deprived of th
change the location by vote.
Allamakee, 4 Greene (Iowa), (

1. Armstrong v. Commi
Blackf. (Ind.) 208.

The provisions of a statute
the manner in which the count
county may be re-located by a
people at a general election,
the counties in the State, incl
whose county-seats were decl
nent in the special act of th
creating such counties. Wel
Court of Wetzel County (W.
Rep. 337.

2. State v. Jones, 1 Ired. (N.

But where a constitution provides that no local law shall be enacted where a general law can be made applicable, it is held that the removal of county-seats can be made the subject of a general law; and an act authorizing the re-location of a certain county-seat is unconstitutional.[1] And a county site, though temporarily located at the adoption of a State constitution, is free from all contingencies to which its removal might have been subject by statutory provision before; and a different location cannot be fixed otherwise than by resorting to the mode prescribed by the constitution.[2]

A provision of an act for the removal of county-seats, that whenever an election has been held *in pursuance of this act*, and the county-seat changed in compliance therewith, it shall not be lawful to change the county-seat again under ten years, does not apply to a removal had under the provisions of a prior act;[3] and a statute providing that when an election to vote on a change of county-seat has been held, "and the county-seat changed in compliance therewith, it shall not be lawful to change the county-seat again under ten years," does not bar a petition for such a change, and an election in pursuance thereof, before the ten years had expired, where the vote at the former election was against any change.[4]

An act of the legislature providing for the transfer of certain records and suits from the county-seat of one county to the county-seat of a newly created county, does not effect such a change of the venue in the cases mentioned in the act as to be in conflict with that clause of a State constitution which declares that the legislature shall not pass local or special laws "providing for changing the venue in civil or criminal cases."[5]

And while the constitution of a State may forbid a change of the county-seat without the consent of a majority of the electors of the county, yet there is no constitutional restriction upon the power of the legislature, after such consent has been given, to either make the selection of a new county-seat itself, or provide for the manner of its selection by the electors.[6]

The power to remove or change a county-seat to a specified place is not temporarily exhausted or suspended by the pendency of a proposal to remove it to another place.[7]

(c) *Imposition of Conditions.*—In addition to the conditions precedent to the removal of a county-seat, imposed by a State constitution, the legislature may impose a condition: as, that after the vote is taken in favor of removal to a certain city, the city

The seat of justice in a county is the place originally selected in pursuance of law; and the county court has not, under the laws of Missouri, any authority to remove it to another site. State v. Smith, 46 Mo. 60.

1. Thomas v. Board of Comm'rs, 5 Ind. 4.

2. Matter of La Fayette Co., 2 Chand. (Wis.) 212.

3. Varner v. Simmons, 53 Ark. 212.

4. Cochran v. Edwards, 38 Ark. 136.

5. State v. McKinney, 5 Nev. 194.

6. County-seat of Osage Co., 16 Kan. 296.

7. People v. Wands, 23 Mich. 385.

public use under the condition that the location shall be permanent, it should be re-conveyed to the grantor in case of removal.[1] And a donation of land to a county for a county-seat, "or for what other use the county may see proper to convert the same," vests in the county an absolute title thereto; and on the removal of the county-seat, there is no reversion thereof to the donor or to his heirs.[2]

But the legislature may, in their discretion, in providing for the removal of a county-seat, direct a reconveyance of property donated to the county, to the parties who originally donated said property to the county, or their legal representatives, and the county authorities cannot lawfully refuse to make the conveyance to them accordingly.[3]

(*e*) *Does not give Rise to an Action against the County.* — The establishment of the seat of justice in the different counties of a State is an act of sovereignty, at all times under the control of the sovereign, and the change of that place cannot give rise to an action of damages.[4]

(*f*) *Petitions for Removal.* — Petitions merely asking that an election be held to locate the county-site, or to locate the court-house and county offices, and not asking for a change of location of the county-site, do not show that they desire a change; and an election ordered upon such petitions is of no effect to locate or change the county-site.[5] But where two petitions are at the same time presented to the county board, the language of one of which is for "permanently *re-locating* the county-seat," and that of the other for "permanently *locating* the county-

would raise a sufficient consideration for a promise; and that, therefore, the court ought not to interfere by injunction, to save the county from the payment of a demand having the sanctions of moral obligation.

1. Twiford *v.* Alamakee County, 4 G. Gr. (Iowa) 60.

2. Gilmore *v.* Hayworth, 26 Tex. 89.

Where property was given to a county in consideration that the county-seat should be located thereon, and no reservation was expressed in the deed, or could be implied therefrom, whereby the property was to revert to the donors, in case such location was not made or continued, and the county-seat was afterwards moved therefrom by an act of the legislature, *held*, that the donors could not maintain an action for damages, in consequence of such removal, and that, even if there had been an express agreement that the land should revert in case of the removal, in order to protect the donors, it should have appeared in the deed, or otherwise in a separate instrument, and not in a parol agreement. Adams *v.* County of Logan, 11 Ill. 337.

In Harris *v.* Shaw, 13 Ill. 463, land was conveyed on condition that the county-seat should be "permanently located" upon it. The location was made accordingly with that intent, but some years later the county-seat was removed. The grantor sued to recover the land. The court said it was no part of the contract that the county-seat should *remain forever* on the premises; that the grantor must be presumed to have known that the legislature had the power to remove it at pleasure, and that he must be held to have had in view at least the probability of such a change when he made the deed.

3. Harris *v.* Whiteside Co., 105 Ill. 445.

4. Megret *v.* Vermillion, 10 La. Ann. 670; Alley *v.* Denson, 8 Tex. 297. See "Effect on Property donated to County," *supra*.

"The removal of a county or State capital will often reduce very largely the value of all the real estate of the place from whence it was removed; but in neither case can the parties whose interests would be injuriously affected enjoin the act or claim compensation from the public." Cooley's Const. Lim. 4th ed. 481.

5. Lanier *v.* Padgett, 18 Fla. 842.

seat," the mere verbal difference between the two does nc either.[1]

The names of persons appearing upon a petition for mission of the question of the re-location of a county-sea appear also upon a remonstrance against the submissio question, are not to be counted on the petition;[2] and petition is presented to the board of county commissi a county for the removal and re-location of a county-seat, missioners should strike therefrom the names of all per make application to have their names stricken off, bef action is taken upon the petition. If this is not done, th

1. Benton *v.* Nason, 26 Kan. 658.

Sufficiency of Petitions. — Iowa. — To entitle the applicants for a change of county-seat to a submission of the question to the people, the number of signers to the petition should not only be at least one-half the legal voters of the county, but should also be greater than the number of remonstrants thereto. Loomis *v.* Bailey, 45 Iowa, 400.

Kansas. — Where a petition is presented to the board of county commissioners for the removal and re-location of a county-seat, and, after disregarding all of the ineligible petitioners and the signers who asked their names to be stricken off before final action was taken thereon, the petition contains less than three-fifths of the legal electors of the county whose names appear upon the last assessment-rolls of the county, such petition is wholly insufficient upon which to order an election for the re-location of the county-seat; and the county attorney of the county in which the petition is presented may, in the name of the State, maintain an action to enjoin the board of county commissioners from canvassing the votes cast at and returned from the several precincts of the county at an election ordered upon such a petition. State *v.* Eggleston, 34 Kan. 714.

Where a petition is presented to the board of county commissioners, asking it to order an election for the re-location of the county-seat in a county where, under § 2 of the County-Seat Act, it is necessary that the petition should contain three-fifths of all the legal electors of the county, and the petition does contain three-fifths of the legal electors as shown by the last assessment-rolls, but does not contain three-fifths of all the legal electors, as may be ascertained from the papers from which such assessment-rolls are or should be made, to wit, the personal-property statements made out for the assessors by the various persons, companies, corporations, and designated listing agents, *held*, that while the county board might be permitted to order an election for the re-location of the county-seat upon such petition and rolls without any examination sonal-property statements, yet be compelled to do so by State *v.* Phillips Co. Comrs. 410.

Where a petition for the re a county-seat has been presen county commissioners, and on them, an election ordered, two-al the votes canvassed, and the p ing the majority of the votes a election declared the county-sea under the amendment of 1875 t sas Contest Act, will not inqu sufficiency of the petition, and mony to show that some of thereon were improperly the therefore it did not contain t number of petitioners. Co Linn County, 15 Kan. 500.

Florida. — Several copies o form for a petition for a chan tion in the county-site were c the county, and signed by dif ors. After they had been sig natures to all the petitions b cut off, and attached to the c having its original and atta tures, was presented to the boa ty commissioners, who, at a meeting, ordered an election f tion of the county-site. The as to the petition was underta before making the order. No shown. *Held*, that the irregula invalidate the election. Dougla of Baker (Fla.), 2 So. Rep. 77

2. Duffees *v.* Sherman, 4 Jamison *v.* Supervisors, 47 Iowa in Loomis *v.* Bailey, 45 Iowa, 4 that names appearing both on strance and the re-petition are on the remonstrance. This is the board can only consider remonstrances; and as the stat provide for such a paper as a signed by parties who have signed the remonstrance, no can be considered.

of the petition who asked their names to be stricken off, should not be counted by the board of commissioners, in determining the number of petitioners for the removal and re-location of the county-seat.[1] It is sufficient to show, as to the citizenship of the signers of the petition, that they were legal voters at the time of signing.[2]

In *Iowa* it is held that a petition for the submission of the question of the re-location of a county-seat, must be presented at a regular session of the board of supervisors. The board is not authorized to receive it at an adjourned session.[3] Also that the county court may, in its discretion, require that the evidence introduced in opposition to the petition shall be in writing.[4]

(*g*) *Offer of Building or Property.* — The offer of a public building, if the county-seat is changed, is in no sense bribery. A proposition of this kind looking to the public welfare, and for the benefit of all the people alike, contains no element of criminality or immorality. The thing offered is of a public nature, pertaining to the public, and not to individuals; and the party to be influenced is a whole county, and in a manner to benefit every inhabitant thereof.[5]

(*h*) *The Election.* — In a proceeding to contest an election held for the purpose of locating a county-seat, it is competent for the contestee, or any other party to the action, to plead by way of answer any facts which would show a want of jurisdiction on the part of the county commissioners to call said election;[6] and where an election on the question of re-location of a county-seat results favorably to the proposition, an action will not lie to enjoin

1. State *v.* Eggleston, 34 Kan. 714; State *v.* Nemaha County Comrs., 10 Neb. 32. But in Loomis *v.* Bailey, 45 Iowa, 400, it is held that after a petition and remonstrance have been presented to the board of supervisors, the board cannot entertain an application by signers of the remonstrance that their names be stricken off.

2. Stone *v.* Miller, 60 Iowa, 243.

3. Ellis *v.* Harrison County, 40 Iowa, 301.

4. Mather *v.* Converse, 12 Iowa, 350.

5. Wells *v.* Taylor (Mont.), 3 Pac. Rep. 255. In Dishon *v.* Smith, 10 Iowa, 212, *Woodward, J.*, said, "We do not think the giving facilities for public convenience to the whole county, such as furnishing a building for the courts and offices, and thus relieving the county from a burden of expense, amounts to bribery. Nor would the giving property, though not of that specific character, but yet adapted to reducing the expense of a change. If the people of a town desire a county-seat located at such place, there is no wrong and no corruption in their offering and giving facilities to produce that result. Either in buildings and offices direct, for the use of the public, or in property or money to procure the facilities, they may offer to take away or to lessen the pecuniary burden which would come upon that public, the county, by the location, or by a change of location. And this cannot be bribery. And it may be doubted whether such an act can become bribery when the offer is to the whole county, and upon a matter of county interest only. In a case like the present there is no duty upon the county from which it or its citizens may be induced to swerve. They may adopt which place they see fit, and it is offering additional inducements only to offer as above mentioned." See also State *v.* Purdy, 36 Wis. 225.

The county board has power to accept a contract of subscription from individuals, payable on condition of the removal of the county-seat. Thompson *v.* Mercer Co., 40 Ill. 379.

And an offer by a private party to build a court-house at a particular place in the county without expense to the county, if the electors should vote to locate the county-site there, and the subsequent performance of such offer, do not invalidate the election of such place as the county-site of the county. Douglass *v.* County of Baker (Fla.), 2 So. Rep. 775.

6. Laws *v.* Vincent, 16 Neb. 208.

electors of the county."[1] So where a statute authorizes a special election for a change of county-seat, but provides no method of holding, the election is good if conducted according to the general law on the subject, whether the general law referred to in the special statute or not; and it cannot be attacked on the ground of the incompleteness of such statute, there being no charge of fraud, or of illegal voting.[2]

(*l*) *Powers and Duties of County Officers and Special Commissioners.* — Proceedings for the re-location of a county-seat are special in their character. The board of supervisors is clothed with no other powers with reference thereto than those conferred by statute.[3] It is not improper for them, while considering the question of removing the county-seat, to take into the account any local provision that may be made to relieve the county from the expenses incident to the removal; and where they have passed an unconditional resolution for removal, and the people have voted upon and approved it, no inquiry into motives, either of the supervisors or the people, can be gone into to invalidate the proceedings.[4] An order of election by the board of supervisors, assuming the validity of preliminary proceedings, is also conclusive, until set aside by *certiorari*;[5] and the decision of the board that a petition for a submission of the question has been sufficiently signed, and the notice is sufficient and has been duly published, is conclusive until reversed and set aside in some of the ways provided by the statute.[6] But fraud may be a ground for enjoining the carrying

1. County-Seat of Linn County, 15 Kan. 500.

A constitutional provision, that no county-seat shall be changed "without the consent of the majority of the qualified voters of the county," means a majority of the qualified voters voting at the election, but does not prohibit the legislature from prescribing a larger vote; and a statute fixing the number assessed for poll-taxes on the last assessment as the number of voters in the county, is consistent with the constitutional provision. Vance *v.* Austell, 45 Ark. 400.

An act providing for the removal of a county-seat, to take effect after submission to the electors of the county at the next general election, and its adoption by a majority of such electors *voting thereon*, is contrary to sec. 1, Art. II., of the Minnesota constitution, which provides that "all laws for removing county-seats shall, before taking effect, be submitted to the electors of the county to be affected thereby, at the next general election after the passage thereof, and be adopted by a majority of such electors." Bayard *v.* Klinge, 16 Minn. [illegible].

Under a constitutional provision declaring that the seat of justice of a county shall not be removed without the concurrence of two-thirds of the qualified voters of the county, there must be an active concurrence, and not a passive acquiescence; and therefore two-thirds of the qualified voters must actually vote in favor of the removal. Braden *v.* Stumph, 16 Lea (Tenn.), 581.

A statute requiring a two-thirds vote of the "legally registered voters" to warrant the transfer of a county-seat, construed to prohibit a transfer without a vote of "two-thirds of the qualified voters." State *v.* Sutterfield, 54 Mo. 391. And under a provision requiring the removal of a county-seat in case "a majority of the voters of the county" shall vote in favor of the removal, *held*, that it must appear that a majority of all the votes cast at the election were for the removal; and the vote at another election held at the same time, as for circuit judge, must be considered. People *v.* Wiant, 48 Ill. 263.

2. Wells *v.* Taylor (Mont.), 3 Pac. Rep. 255.

3. Loomis *v.* Bailey, 45 Iowa, 400.

4. Attorney-General *v.* Supervisors of Lake County, 33 Mich. 289.

5. Bennett *v.* Hetherington, 41 Iowa, 142.

6. Baker *v.* Supervisors of Louisa Co., 40 Iowa, 226; Bennett *v.* Hetherington, 41 Iowa, 142.

out of an order of commissioners for re-locating a com if it enters into the order itself, but not so of fraud p upon the commissioners in procuring petitions, or an matter which might be contested during the proceedings.[1]

In determining the sufficiency of a petition for the remo county-seat, and the genuineness of the signatures ther board of supervisors acts in a judicial capacity, but their tion is limited to a determination of the matters prescribed statute, upon the evidence therein specified; they have no to consider evidence other than the affidavits which acc the petition and remonstrance.[2] And special commis appointed by the governor have no authority in canvass votes cast at an election called by them to throw out vo for a certain place, and thereby give another place a maj all the votes cast; and mandamus will lie to compel them vass all the votes cast.[3] The board of supervisors, howe special meeting called to canvass the votes cast upon the q of re-locating the county-seat, may declare the result; but at the same time order the removal thither of the records fixed time, etc., this order may be treated as nugatory, no ing the proceedings, nor restraining the removal, which sh made by the proper officers without such order.[4] And, th of the board in canvassing and declaring the result of a vote being final, any subsequent action by them, recon and reversing their previous canvass and declaration, is force.[5]

1. Markle v. County Comm'rs of Clay, 55 Ind. 185.

2. Herrick v. Carpenter, 54 Iowa, 340.

3. State v. Stearns *et al.*, 11 Neb. 104.

They have no power to inquire into the circumstances under which the signers have fixed their names to a petition or remonstrance, or whether, after having done so, their views or wishes have been changed. Loomis v. Bailey, 45 Iowa, 400.

4. Cole v. Supervisors, 11 Iowa, 552.

Where the county-seat was changed by election, the failure of the county commissioners to order the removal of the books of the offices to the newly designated town cannot defeat the result of the election; and if the officers effect the removal on their own motion, they cannot be compelled by *mandamus* to return and await the order which the statute required the commissioners to give. Wells v. Taylor (Mont.), 3 Pac. Rep. 255.

5. People v. Benzie, 34 Mich. 211. See also People v. Benzie, 41 Mich. 6.

The county board, however, must act in a proper and regular manner, or their canvass will not be upheld. Thus, under the provisions of the act relating to the organization of new counties, an election was held for township and county of also for the permanent locati county-seat of the county, and returns from each precinct were the board of county commissio Saturday following the election t commissioners examined the ret to them, and canvassed and de result for township and county thereupon, one of the commissio a motion that the board proceed the votes to determine the perma tion of the county-seat. Anoth moved that the motion so mad upon the table: this was carrie announcement of the vote on th seat was then made. The board journed to Monday, but no hour for the adjourned meeting, as the of the board did not want the frie place they intended to declare th the contest for county-seat, to b On Monday at three o'clock in the by moonlight, and without the a books, ballots, or tally-sheets, members of the board of coun sioners and the county clerk town site of the temporary county without notice to or the presen

The action of the board in canvassing the vote is ministerial; but its action in ordering a removal in accordance with the count is judicial, and may be reviewed on *certiorari.*[1]

Pending a suit in equity to revise an election the apparent result of which was to approve a change of a county-seat, it was held to be the duty of the county judge to hold his court at the new county-seat.[2] And the fact that there is a controversy pending, as to which of two places is duly selected as the county-seat, is a proper ground for enjoining a county official from ordering the erection of a county building at one of such places.[3]

(*j*) ***When Proceedings to remove may be instituted.*** — The fact that proceedings for removal are instituted while a movement is in progress for a removal to another place, and are pushed to a popular vote after the electors had decided in favor of the removal to another place, but before the change thereto was in fact carried out, does not render them invalid.[4]

(*k*) ***Particular Statutes and Local Decisions.*** — Decisions construing particular statutes which have no general application, and such as are altogether local in their nature, are collected in the note.[5]

third member of the board, pretended to make a canvass of the votes cast for the county-seat, and declared one of the places voted for as the permanent county-seat of that county. *Held*, that the alleged canvass of the returns of the election for the county-seat, and the declaration of the result, were not only irregular, but wholly invalid. State *v.* Harwood *et al.*, 36 Kan. 136.

1 Herrick *v.* Carpenter, 54 Iowa, 349.

Decided also, that where the board has decided the petition for submission to be legal, and such action has been reversed upon *certiorari*, the board will be guilty of an error, which may be corrected, if they canvass the votes at an election upon such question, and make an order for removal thereon.

2. Massey *v.* Mack, 30 Ark. 472.

Where the county-seat of a county has been permanently located by a vote of the electors of the county, at a place not incorporated, but mentioned and described in a town plat duly executed, acknowledged, and filed, which plat embraced fifty-six and ten-elevenths acres of land, the board of county commissioners of the county has no authority, in the absence of any vote therefor, to arbitrarily remove the county-seat, or the county offices, or the books, records, etc., belonging to the county, to an addition subsequently laid out and platted, adjoining the original town site where the county-seat was located, although such addition is subsequently incorporated with the original town site, as a city of the third class. State *v.* Harwi, 36 Kan. 588.

3. Rice *v.* Smith, 9 Iowa, 570.

4. People *v.* Wands, 23 Mich. 385.

In this case it was *held* that the validity of the proceedings to remove was not affected by any decision for or against the location at another place, or by any omission to state from what place it would be removed, or by any uncertainty as to the place where it was then legally established.

5. **Arkansas.**—The removal of the county-seat is a matter of local concern, over which the county court has exclusive original jurisdiction. The circuit court has no authority to determine the result of an election for removal in the first instance, and before the county court has acted in the premises; and where it assumes to do so, a writ of prohibition will lie from this court. Russell *v.* Jacoway, 33 Ark. 191.

Under the Arkansas act of April 25, 1873, appointing commissioners to locate the county-seat of Pope County, Russellville became the temporary county-seat, and judgments rendered by courts at that place were valid. McNair *v.* Williams, 28 Ark. 200.

The removal of a county-seat being a matter of local concern, equity cannot interfere in the matter. The county court, and on appeal the circuit court, have exclusive jurisdiction in the matter of determining the votes. Willeford *v.* State, 43 Ark. 62.

California. — Where an election is held for the removal of a county-seat, under Cal. Pol. Code, part iv. tit. 1, ch. 2, and a majority of the electors vote in favor of retaining the county-seat where it is, the

site. Such legislative determination is final, except in the cases specially enumerated in section 17. State *v.* Padgett, 19 Fla. 518.

Indiana. — The act of Feb. 24, 1869 (3 Ind. Stat. 371), in reference to the location of county-seats, does not require that it shall be stated in the petition that the requisite number of voters had signed it; but it must contain the requisite number, and the deed must be executed, conveying a good title to two sites for a court-house and jail, and the $290 must be paid, before the order for re-location can be made, or the new county buildings erected. Board of Commissioners *v.* Markle, 46 Ind. 96.

A proceeding before a board of county commissioners to re-locate a county-seat, is a special proceeding, for a special purpose, based upon a special statute, which gives no right of appeal; and such proceeding, being special, cannot be governed by the general statute granting appeals (1 Gav. & H. 353, § 31); and therefore no appeal lies from the decision of the board of county commissioners therein. Bosley *v.* Ackelmire, 39 Ind. 536; Commissioners of Scott County *v.* Smith, 40 Ind. 61; Moffit *v.* Flemming, 40 Ind. 217.

Iowa. — An election upon the question of removal of the county-seat is not invalidated, in a case where the people are actually notified of such election, for the reason that notice of the presentation of a petition for such removal is not given in the manner prescribed in ch. 46 of the Laws of 1855, or because the record does not show that notice of the election was posted in the townships. Dishon *v.* Smith, 10 Iowa, 212.

An election for the removal of a county-seat cannot be legally held on the first Monday of April; the act of Jan. 22, 1885, having been repealed by the act of March 23, [illegible]. Mather *v.* Converse, 12 Iowa, 352.

The notice of the presentation of a petition respecting removal of a county-seat, required by § 284 of the Iowa Code, is sufficient, if one of the three publications is made sixty days before the petition is presented. Bennett *v.* Hetherington, 41 Iowa, 142.

Michigan. — Proceedings for the removal of a county-seat are not rendered invalid by reason of the board of supervisors leaving the giving of the requisite notice to the clerk, without prescribing its form or contents, where no mischief is shown to have resulted, and the notice given was in due form, and the supervisors have sanctioned and ratified what was done by canvassing the votes, and declaring the result. Attorney-General *v.* Supervisors of Lake Co., 33 Mich. 289.

Under the constitution and laws of Michigan, the proposition for the removal of a county-seat may originate with the board of supervisors. No previous action of the legislature is necessary to give the board authority to act. It is immaterial that in the particular case the county-seat was permanently located by the legislature when the county was organized. The permanent location is only until a removal takes place in accordance with law. Bagot *v.* Board of Supervisors, 43 Mich. 577.

It is not necessary to the validity of an election for a permanent county-seat to be held at the general election, that notice of it should be given, the statute not requiring it. Separate ballot-boxes may be used at such election for county-seat ballots; and a vote for "Crystal Falls" will be held to mean the settlement of that name, and will not be considered too indefinite because there is a large township of the same name. Attorney-General *v.* Board of Canvassers (Mich.), 31 N. W. Rep. 539.

Minnesota. — Laws of Minnesota, 1885, c. 272, providing a mode for removing county-seats, is unconstitutional and void, as in the nature of special legislation, and not uniform in its operation throughout the State, and so in violation of the constitution of Minnesota, amend. 1881, art. 4, sec. 33, subd. 5, and sec. 34. Nichols *v.* Walter (Minn.), 33 N. W. Rep. 800.

Missouri. — A writ of error will not lie to a county court in Missouri, appointing commissioners to locate a permanent seat of justice. Tetherow *v.* Grundy County Court, 9 Mo. 118.

Nebraska. — In 1871 an election was held in H. County, under the provisions of an act of the legislature, for the location of a county-seat and the election of county officers. A majority of the votes cast were in favor of A. as the county-seat. The returns of the election were duly certified to and filed by the secretary of state, but the county officers elected failed to qualify. In 1872 the acting governor of the State issued his proclamation, calling an election for the election of county officers and the location of a county-seat. At this election county officers were elected who subsequently qualified. There being no choice as to the location of the county-seat, two other successive elections were held, resulting in an apparent majority for M.; but the final vote was not canvassed by the county clerk, and the result of said election was not officially declared. The county offices were not held, nor were the records kept at any one place until the year 1875. From that time to the present the county offices and records have all been kept, and the district courts have all been held at A. In 1881 the board of county commissioners, without the presentation of a petition therefor, called an election for the location of a county-seat. *Held*, they had no au-

COUNTY WARRANTS. — See COUNTIES.

COUPLED *with an interest.* — See POWER.

thority or jurisdiction to call said election. Laws *v.* Vincent, 16 Neb. 208.

North Carolina. — The justices of a county are presumed to know the statute in relation to their county site, and the acts done in pursuance of the same. McCoy *v.* Justices, etc., 6 Jones (N. Car.), L. 488.

Tennessee. — The Tennessee Act of Dec. 14, 1871, providing for the removal of a county-seat from one place to another, is unconstitutional. Tenn. Const. art 10, § 4, provides that a county-seat cannot be removed without the concurrence of two-thirds of the voters of the county. Stuart *v.* Blair, 8 Baxt. (Tenn.) 141.

Texas. — By sect. 2 of the Act of Texas of May 9, 1838, providing for the removal of county-seats of justice, the chief justice of the county is made the judge of what shall be a sufficient number of petitioners to authorize the ordering of an election; that section does not require the petition to be signed by a majority or any specified number of persons. Alley *v.* Denson, 8 Tex. 297.

In order to remove a county-seat from a place not within five miles from the centre of the county, to a place within five miles from the centre, only a majority of all the votes cast is required, not a majority of all the votes which might possibly have been cast if all the qualified electors had voted. Alley *v.* Denson, 9 Tex. 297.

The judges of the State courts appointed by the provisional governor of Texas were clothed with political as well as judicial powers; and the chief justices of the counties had authority to order an election to determine upon the removal of a county-seat. McClelland *v.* Shelby County, 32 Tex. 17.

Where the statute requires an application to remove a county-seat to be made to the county court, which is to determine whether it has been made by a majority of the registered voters of the county, and to order the election and give notice thereof, it may be inferred that the legislature intended to confide to the county court the investigation and determination of all the other facts necessary to a fair and legal election Worsham *v.* Richards, 46 Tex. 441. See *ex parte* Towles, 48 Tex. 413.

The district courts of Texas have no jurisdiction to try cases of contested elections for county-seats; and it is settled there, as well as elsewhere, that a court of equity, on application for injunct[ion], not try and determine such ques[tions in] cases involving the title to office. [Caru]thers *v.* Harnett (Tex.) 2 S. W. R[ep.]; Caruthers *v.* Slaughter (Tex.), 2 [S. W.] Rep. 526.

Wisconsin. — Where, before the [adoption] of the constitution of Wisconsin, t[he terri]torial legislature had adopted a [county-]seat, but afterwards passed an act p[roviding] for the selection, by commission[ers, of] another place for the establishment [of pub]lic offices and the holding of the [courts] until suitable buildings should be [erected] at the site adopted, *held*, that t[he site] became the permanent seat until a [change] should be made by positive legisl[ation, or] the happening of the contingency [referred] to in the act providing for lo[cation]. Matter of La Fayette Co., 2 Cham[d.] 212.

West Virginia. — Under sect. 1 [of ch.] 39 of the Code as amended by ch. [of] Acts of 1881, the petition should [ ] with a prayer that the county cou[rt] make an order that a vote be take[n at the] next general election to be held in th[e county] upon the question of the re-locatio[n of the] county-seat at the place named [in the] petition; and this place is designa[ted with] sufficient certainty when it is calle[d a cer]tain city or town, and there shoul[d be no] designation of the particular lo[cation in] such city or town as the place w[here the] county-seat is to be located, no ma[tter how] much extent of land is covered [by the] boundaries of such city or town, [or how] sparse in portions of these bounda[ries may] be the population. Doolittle *v.* [County] Court, 28 W. Va. 159.

The questions whether such [petition] should be allowed to be filed, and [whether] the order asked for in the petition [should] be granted by the county court, [are not] judicial questions; but it is an [official] duty imposed upon the county cou[rt, when] such a petition as is prescribed [by] law is presented and duly verified [by affi]davit, and signed by the requisite [number] of legal voters of the county to p[ermit it] to be filed, and to make the orde[r asked] for in the petition; and the cour[t has] no discretion to refuse to permit su[ch peti]tion to be filed, or to make such [order; if] it refuses so to do, such ministe[rial duty] can be enforced by *mandamus.* [Doolittle] *v.* County Court, 38 W. Va. 199.

COUPLING CARS, INJURIES BY. — See also CONTRIBUTORY NEGLIGENCE, FELLOW-SERVANTS, MASTER AND SERVANT.

1. Obligation of the Company as to Cars and Apparatus. — A railroad company is under obligation to its employees to exercise reasonable care and diligence in furnishing them cars with safe and suitable coupling apparatus.[1]

1. **Height of Bumpers.** — It is the duty of a railroad company to further the safety of its employees by furnishing as far as possible bumpers of nearly equal height. Muldowney v. Illinois Central R. Co., 36 Iowa, 462. But the mere fact that one car is higher than another, so as to render it difficult to effect a coupling, does not constitute negligence of such a kind as to render the company liable. Ft. Wayne, I. & S. R. Co. v. Gildersleeve, 33 Mich. 133; St. Louis, etc., R. Co. v. Higgins, 44 Ark. 293; s. c., 21 Am. & Eng. R. R. Cas. 629; Kelly v. Wisconsin Cent. R. Co. (Wis.), 21 Am. & Eng. R. R. Cas. 633. And where a servant, in coupling cars of unequal height, neglected to use the crooked link ordinarily employed, and was injured in consequence, he was *held* guilty of such contributory negligence as precluded recovery. Hulett v. St. Louis, etc., R. Co., 67 Mo. 239.

In Railway Co. v. Black, 88 Ill. 112, the complaint was, that the coupling bars of a flat car, loaded with iron, of one company, and of a caboose of another company, were of different heights; and the plaintiff, in stooping down between the cars to do the coupling, had his hand crushed between the bars. It is said, in the opinion by *Mr. Justice Sheldon*, that it was the plaintiff's own fault "in not ascertaining the condition of the cross-bars before attempting the coupling;" and that, "from his experience as a switch-man in the yard, and the frequent coming-in of cars thus constructed from other roads, he had reason to suppose that the case in question was liable to have a draw-bar in the situation it was here; and it was his plain duty to examine and ascertain, as he safely might have done, what was the condition of the car in this respect before venturing upon the coupling."

Where the allegations in a petition were that the draw-head of a certain car was out of repair, and the evidence simply showed that it was of unequal height with those of the cars commonly in use, *held*, that the court could not be required to give instructions as to the rights and duties of the respective parties where draw-heads were of unequal height. Kline v. Kansas City, etc., R. Co., 90 Iowa, 656.

Double Deadwoods. — In order to obviate the difficulties occasioned in coupling cars of unequal heights of the platforms, a device has recently been introduced known as "double deadwoods." This device consists of two blocks or bumpers placed one under the other, so that the car may be coupled by either of them according as it may be found most convenient. Much greater care is required in using "double deadwoods" than with the ordinary coupling apparatus. But the mere use of them by a company on its cars does not constitute negligence. Indianapolis, etc., R. Co. v. Flanigan, 77 Ill. 365.

And where cars are received from another company having such a device, it is not negligence on the part of the railroad company to fail to inform its servants of that fact. Mich. Cent. R. Co. v. Smithson, 45 Mich. 212; s. c., 1 Am. & Eng. R. R. Cas. 101.

Where a servant has been in the habit of coupling cars with double deadwoods to others without this appliance, it was *held* that this was a risk of his employment. Toledo, etc., R. Co. v. Black, 88 Ill. 112.

Draw-Bars. — Where a servant was injured in coupling two cars one of which had the Miller draw-bar, and the other the ordinary draw-bar, so that the ends of the coupling apparatus did not strike squarely against each other, but overlapped, the company was not held liable, the risk being held incident to the servant's employment. T. W. & W. R. Co. v. Asbury, 84 Ill. 429. And in Pennsylvania Co. v. Long (Ind.), 15 Am. & Eng. R. R. Cas. 345, a similar case, it was *held* that the company was not guilty of culpable negligence *per se*, but that the question of negligence was for the jury. If, however, the draw-bar and bumper be defective, and on that account injury ensues, the company is liable, provided it has had time to correct the defect, and had notice thereof, either actual or constructive. Lake Erie & W. R. Co. v. Everett, 11 Am. & Eng. R. R. Cas. 221; Belair v. Chicago & N. W. R. Co., 43 Iowa, 662; and see Skellinger v. Chicago, etc., R. Co. (Iowa), 12 Am. & Eng. R. R. Cas. 206.

It is a common defect, in coupling appa-

The company is not, however, obliged to observe the measure of duty in regard to the adoption of improved pate couplings upon their lines to their servants as to passenge

ratus, for the draw-bar to be too short. The company is liable for accidents occasioned by this cause. Toledo, W. & W. R. Co. *v.* Fredericks, 71 Ill. 294.

But it is not negligence *per se* on the part of a railroad company to use upon its road an engine the draw-bar of which is too short to permit one of its cars to be safely coupled to or detached from such engine. Whitman *v.* Wisconsin & M. R. Co. (Wis.), 12 Am. & Eng. R. R. Cas. 214.

And at the trial of an action against a railroad corporation for personal injuries occasioned to the plaintiff while in its employ as a brakeman, by reason of the draw-bar on a locomotive engine being too low for the work for which it was used, if the facts are in dispute, the defendant is not entitled to a ruling that, upon all the evidence in the case, the plaintiff cannot recover; and that, if the jury find that the only defect in the engine was the height of the draw-bar, the plaintiff cannot recover. Lawless *v.* Connecticut River R. Co., 136 Mass. 1; s. c., 18 Am. & Eng. R. R. Cas. 96.

A brakeman upon a railroad train was crushed while coupling cars. The accident was caused by reason of the fact that the draw-bar of one car was lower than that of the other car. Ordinarily there was no difference in the height of draw-bars on defendant's cars, but the draw-bar of the car in question was five or six inches lower than the usual height. This fact had been observed by defendant's inspector, and the car reported for repairs. On the trial the court directed a verdict for defendant. *Held*, that the court below did not err in so instructing the jury. The court say, "It is very evident that the defendant was not in the exercise of the highest care when making use of this car in its business. But the car is hardly to be considered dangerous machinery in the sense that a defective engine is, or a car with a weakness in some part, which, in its ordinary use, may result in a breaking down, and put property and persons being transported in peril. This car, for any thing that appears, was in perfect running order, and might safely have been run for an indefinite period. The objection to its being run was, that in coupling it to other cars more care was required than if one end were not so low; but with care it could be coupled safely, and had been so coupled regularly from day to day, and sometimes by the plaintiff himself. The danger, such as there was, would arise mainly from thoughtlessness; but attention would be kept alive, and in a measure compelled, by

the fact that defendant was receiv
from other roads not correspon
height with its own, so that it w
necessary for brakemen at all t
take notice of the relative heig
about to make a coupling." B
Flint & P. M. R. Co., 56 Mich.
Open and Solid Draw-Heads.—
company had its cars furnished
draw-heads instead of open
latter being the safer and most
invention, but just coming into
company was not held liable for t
draw-heads of the older pattern.
etc., R. Co. *v.* Wheeler, 4 Am. & E
Cas. 633.

Miscellaneous Defects.—If the
of a particular car should be too
company is liable,—Toledo, etc.,
v. Fredericks, 71 Ill. 294; Cra
Richmond, etc., R. Co., 78 N. Ca
or defective. Le Clair *v.* First
etc., R. Co., 20 Minn. 9.

And where the company per
long bolt to project out from
the brake-beam, and a servant, in
tripped thereon, and was injured,
pany was held liable. Wedge
Chicago & N. W. R. Co., 41 Wis
Wis. 417.

But the mere failure of the co
provide couplings which will
readily is not such negligence as wi
it liable. Williams *v.* Central R
Iowa, 396.

In Houston, etc., R. Co. *v.*
(Tex.), 21 Am. & Eng. R. R. C
plaintiff, a brakeman on the tr
ordered to couple certain cars on
track, to be attached to and carrie
the train. The injury occurred
attempt to use the links which he
the draw-heads of said cars. U
question of negligence of the defe
contributory negligence of plain
court correctly charged as follow
law imposes on the defendant th
furnishing to its employees machi
appliances of all kinds, includi
and pins, reasonably suitable an
to enable such employees to per
duties required of them, and als
reasonable diligence to keep s
chinery and appliances in such re
proper condition after they are fu
and if plaintiff was injured by rea
failure of defendant in this respect,
be entitled to recover, unless yo
from the evidence that it was a
plaintiff's duty as brakeman to exa
link before undertaking to use it."

is, nevertheless, bound to something like reasonable care.[1] But it is bound to exercise reasonable care and caution to keep its coupling apparatus in sound repair.[2]

These obligations of a railroad company toward its employees extend to cars which it receives from another company under a general agreement for transporting them over its road. It is bound to inspect cars brought to its road under such an agree-

1. Toledo, W. & W. R. Co. v. Asbury, 84 Ill. 429; Nashville, etc., R. Co. v. Wheeler (Tenn.), 4 Am. & Eng. R. R. Cas. 633; Gibson v. Pacific, etc., R. Co., 46 Mo. 163. In Missouri Pac. R. Co. v. Lyde (Tex.), 11 Am. & Eng. R. R. Cas. 188, a charge was held erroneous which instructed the jury that "defendant is bound to protect his servant from injury by reason of latent or unseen defects, so far as human care and foresight can accomplish the result," for the reason that this measure of duty is greater and more stringent than that required by law. It is not bound to discard cars of an old style because the coupling of them with cars of a new pattern is attended with increased danger. Ft. Wayne, etc., R. Co. v. Gildersleeve, 33 Mich. 133; Indianapolis, etc., R. Co. v. Flanigan, 77 Ill. 365; Toledo, etc., R. Co. v. Asbury, 84 Ill. 429; Toledo, etc., R. Co. v. Black, 88 Ill. 112.

It is not bound at its peril to make use only of the best implements, the best machinery, and the best methods. Mich. Cent. R. Co. v. Smithson, 45 Mich. 212; s. c., 1 Am. & Eng. R. R. Cas. 101. In this case, Judge Cooley said, "Any form of cars a railroad company may select for use must be one that with care can be coupled safely, or the company could not afford to operate its road by means of them. With the needless exposure of its men to danger by the use of unsuitable cars, the company would inevitably subject itself to public odium and disfavor; casualties to property would be increased; and if it could succeed in manning its road with laborers, it must pay them wages increased by the risks of danger. These are potent facts, and they justify an inference, when a particular form of car is deliberately chosen and adhered to, that it is believed by those who make use of it to be as safe as any other. It is no doubt true that a company may make serious mistakes in such a case. It is quite possible for a company to adhere unreasonably to something which has been thoroughly demonstrated to be dangerous, and the mere fact that it does so cannot be conclusive in its favor of the want of negligence. But on the other hand, no railroad company, and no manufacturing or business establishment of any kind, is bound at its peril to make use only of the best implements, and the best machinery, and the safest methods. The State does not require it, and could not require it, without keeping such minute and constant supervision of private affairs, and interfering with such frequency, as in all cases would be irritating and damaging, and in many cases would become intolerable. In the main the State must leave every man to manage his own business in his own way. If his way is not the best, but nevertheless others, with a full knowledge of what his way is, see fit to co-operate with him in it, the State cannot interfere to prevent, nor punish him in damages when the risks his servants voluntarily assume are followed by injuries." Hulett, etc., v. St. Louis, etc., R. Co., 67 Mo. 240; Lovejoy v. Boston, etc., R. Co., 125 Mass. 79.

2. Indianapolis, etc., R. Co. v. Flanigan, 77 Ill. 365.

Thus, in an action by a servant against a railroad company for injuries sustained by reason of the breaking of certain car-couplings, and the consequent falling of the cars upon the plaintiff's foot, it appeared that the defect in the couplings was known to the superintendent, and that it was not known to plaintiff, nor was it any part of plaintiff's duty to have such knowledge. *Held*, that the evidence was sufficient to entitle plaintiff to recover. Bowers v. Union Pac. R. Co. (Utah), 7 Pac. Rep. 251.

But if the coupling of a freight car suddenly becomes out of repair, the railway company using the same will not be liable for an injury to an employee received in consequence thereof, unless its attention had been called to the defect, or the company, by the exercise of a reasonable degree of care, could have discovered the defect, and had an opportunity to make the needed repairs. Indianapolis, etc., R. Co. v. Flanigan, 77 Ill. 365.

In an action brought by a brakeman of a railroad for injuries alleged to have been received in consequence of a defect in a car which he was coupling, the fact that said car had been safely coupled before and after the accident does not necessarily show that it was not broken; and, in spite of the proof of that fact, the jury would be warranted in finding that the car was broken. Reed v. Burlington, etc., R. Co. (Iowa), 33 N. W. Rep. 451.

Cent. R. Co. (Wis.), 21 Am. & Eng. R. R. Cas. 633. And the fact that the draw-heads of two cars which plaintiff was attempting to couple were not perfectly matched, and that, in attempting to make the coupling, he moved along with the cars and caught his foot in a frog, and was injured, *held* insufficient to show negligence in the company, rendering it liable for the injury. Williams *v.* Central R. Co., 43 Iowa, 396.

In Atchison, T., & S. F. R. Co. *v.* Wagner, 33 Kan. 660, a brakeman upon a railroad train was attempting to couple a car and engine. Owing to a defect in the coupling-pin, he was unable to withdraw it in time. The draw-bar, which had a defective spring, in consequence slipped past the draw-head, struck and injured him. He knew of the defect in the coupling-pin, but it was not shown that any of the officers of the railroad company knew of such defect. Neither party was shown to have any knowledge of the defect in the draw-bar. *Held*, that the party had assumed all the risk of his employment, and was not entitled to damages.

In Redman *v.* Michigan Cent. R. Co., 55 Mich. 57, s. c., 17 Am. & Eng. R. R. Cas. 321, the engineer and fireman in charge of the locomotive of a railroad train, having temporarily left their respective posts, the conductor, who it was alleged was incompetent for the purpose, undertook to take the place of the engineer, and ordered a brakeman to make a coupling; and while he was obeying this order, and in consequence of the unskilfulness of the conductor, the brakeman was injured. *Held*, that in an action against the railroad for such injury, he had assumed the risk of his employment, and was not entitled to recover.

In Watson *v.* Houston, etc., R. Co. (Tex.), 11 Am. & Eng. R. R. Cas. 213, it was *held*, that, where it is, by the custom and usage of a railroad company, part of the duty of a brakeman to couple defective or broken cars, so that they may be taken to the shops for repair, he will be held to have assumed the risks incident to that particular employment, and cannot recover in case of an injury sustained therein.

In Philadelphia, etc., R. Co. *v.* Schertle (Pa.), 2 Am. & Eng. R. R. Cas. 158, A., a brakeman on a railroad train, was engaged in coupling and uncoupling cars. It became his duty, in order to couple a car to an engine, to take his stand on the back of the tank as the engine approached the car. Just before the engine began backing towards the car, A. jumped from the step where he had been standing on the back of the tank, and which was his customary and appropriate place to effect the coupling at the proper moment, and crossed the track. A moment after the engine began backing, A. was heard to cry out, and seen to spring back from the tank, the wheels passed over him, and he was killed. No one saw the accident, or could tell whether A. was endeavoring to climb on the tank, or not, when he fell. There was evidence that the steps were imperfect in number and construction, although A., who had been employed on the engine a long time, had never complained of them, or desired to have them altered, as it was the company's habit to have done on the request of employees; also, that that part of the road-bed where the accident occurred was rough from recent repairs. In an action by A.'s widow and children against the railroad company to recover damages for A.'s death, alleged to have been caused while he was stepping on the tank, by reason of his missing his footing in consequence of the negligence of defendant in providing insufficient steps and a rough road-bed, *held*, that there was no evidence of negligence to go to a jury, and that the court should have given binding instructions to find for defendant.

In Chicago, etc., R. R. Co. *v.* Ward, 61 Ill. 130, a brake was out of repair, and, while coupling, a brakeman was thrown by it, and injured. The company was in the habit of sending damaged cars for repair to the place where the accident occurred. The man ran every day to this place, and his duties required him to assist in handling these damaged cars. This car had been damaged, and was going to be repaired, but there was nothing to show that it was badly constructed originally. As the man was constantly and of necessity exposed to such risks, *held*, that the company was not liable.

In Indianapolis, etc., R. R. Co. *v.* Flanigan, 77 Ill. 365, the danger of double deadwoods was passed upon. A freight conductor attempted to couple a car which was moving to one which was stationary. One of the cars was equipped with a double deadwood. The pin in the draw-bar of the standing car stuck. In the attempt his arm was crushed. It did not appear that the draw-bar was ill-constructed, or that it had been so long out of order as to charge the company with negligence. It appeared that more care was needed in handling cars with double buffers than others, but such cars were in use on this and other roads, and that they could safely be used if care was observed. *Held*, that the use of such cars by a company was not negligent; that the man ought to have known his danger; that, by remaining in the service, he assumed the risk, and could not recover for his injury.

In Chicago, etc., R. R. Co. *v.* Munroe, 85 Ill. 25, it appeared that the injured man knew that the coupling apparatus, which he was using when hurt, was defective, had complained of it, but had continued to work in the service. *Held*, that he thus assumed the risk, and could not recover for his injury.

In Toledo, etc., Co. *v.* Black, 88 Ill. 112, man injured while coupling cars whose draw-bars were of different heights. One had double deadwoods, and one was loaded with iron, which projected over the front of the car. It appeared that he frequently had to couple cars similarly loaded, and with similar coupling apparatus, and that it was more than usually dangerous to couple cars whose draw-bars were of different heights. *Held*, that this was an ordinary peril of the employment, and one which he assumed.

In Fort Wayne, etc., *v.* Gildersleeve, 33 Mich. 133, an employee was injured in coupling cars, one of which had a platform lower than was usual. The car was not in itself unsafe or unfit for use. The servant knew the car was more dangerous than ordinary cars, and it did not appear that complaint had been made to the company, or that any assurances had been given that its use should be discontinued. *Held*, that employee could not recover for his injury, because, while the employer must use reasonable care in selecting machinery and appliances, he need not use the safest known.

In Hulett *v.* St. Louis, etc., 67 Mo. 239, an experienced brakeman tried to couple cars of unequal height. The inequality was apparent, but, instead of using a crooked link as usual in such cases, he tried to couple with a straight one. The whole matter was under his control. He failed to make the coupling, and was injured. *Held*, that the company was not negligent nor liable.

In Wolsey *v.* L. S. R. R. Co., 33 Ohio St., servant injured while coupling by hand. A rule of the company provided for use of a stick in all cases, but there was evidence the rule was impracticable and not observed. *Held*, that the reasonableness of such rules cannot depend on the judgment of the employees; that the company was not liable.

Plaintiff's intestate was injured in attempting to couple cars at a side track, adjacent to a platform used for loading stone. In making the coupling, he got between the platform and cars, and his lantern, from some cause, got between him and the cars, and was so pressed against him as to inflict injuries from which he died. It was claimed that the defendant was negligent in constructing the platform so near the track. The court instructed the jury that if the track and platform were dangerous, and the company by reasonable care could have learned the fact, and deceased was

without knowledge, and co
sonable care, have learned t
gerous, and by reason there
injuries complained of, they
defendant guilty. *Held*, that
was erroneous; that reason
exercised by the company,
expected to reach the sa
would follow from the san
part of the deceased; that i
diligence could not learn th
was dangerous, it was unrea
pute notice or negligence i
to the defendant. Chicago
Clark (Ill.), 15 Am. & Eng.

Plaintiff, a brakeman in t
railroad company, who, alth
was allowed by his father
ment for himself, had his h
being caught between the de
coupling cars. According t
timony, he thought the car
too fast, and signalled to s
although they did not sto
thought that they were mov
stepped in between, and att
the coupling. He understo
tion of draw-heads and d
knew that it was danger
hand between the dead-
that the plaintiff, in accepti
ment, assumed the risks inc
that his injury resulted fron
his own negligence, and the
was not responsible. Norf
v. Cotterell (Va.), 3 S. East.

Where the conductor of
who was not bound to coup
cars except in case of em
took to perform this duty
emergency existed, and w
doing, it was *held* that he
run a risk outside the scope
ment, and that the compa
ble. Sears *v.* Central R. &
Ga. 630. So where a ma
ployed as a switchman, c
orders of his superiors,
dangerous work of couplin
ner *v.* Mich. Cent. R. Co. (
& Eng. R. R. Cas. 435. Se
& A. R. Co. *v.* Bishop, 5
ledo, etc., R. Co. *v.* Asbury,

Where a servant know
pling apparatus employed
tive, and yet makes no com
tinues to use the same, he
run all the risks inciden
cago, etc., R. Co. *v.* Ward,
go, etc., R. Co. *v.* Munroe,
field *v.* Richmond & D. R.
300; Le Clair *v.* St. Paul,
Minn. 9. Particularly doe
apply where the cars a
marked, and set aside as d
this is the case, the servant

But the severity of this principle is relaxed in favor of the employee, in case the defect or danger is not such as is open to

has the strongest possible reason to exercise caution, and will be *held* to have assumed much more than ordinary risks. Watson v. Houston & T. C. R. Co. (Tex.), 11 Am. & Eng. R. R. Cas. 213; Chicago, etc., R. Co. v. Ward, *supra*.

Coupling Cars with Loads projecting.— Where a railroad company is in the habit of receiving from other railroads cars loaded with timbers which project over the ends of the cars so far as to make it dangerous for any one, except a careful, skilful, and prudent person, to attempt to couple the cars together, it is not negligence for the railroad company to order and permit such a person, who has been in the employ of the railroad company doing that kind of business for about five months, to attempt to make such a coupling, where the attempt is to be made in broad daylight, although it may be raining at the time. Atchison, etc., R. Co. v. Plunkett, 25 Kan. 188; s. c., 2 Am. & Eng. R. R. Cas 127.

And where an experienced brakeman was ordered by the conductor to attach a car loaded with lumber which projected forward, and compelled him to stoop in making the coupling, and in so doing he delayed a little and his fingers were caught in the coupling-link and hurt, it was *held* that he could not maintain an action against the railway company, as he fully understood the difficulty to be guarded against, and the conductor was not shown to have been in fault in any way. Day v. Toledo, etc., R. Co., 42 Mich. 523; s. c., 2 Am. & Eng. R. R. Cas 126.

A., an employee of a railroad company, while engaged in coupling cars from the top of which certain bridge-irons projected, was caught by the head between the ends of said bridge-irons and crushed to death. It was customary upon said railroad to load cars in said manner; and A. had knowledge both of this fact, and also that they were so loaded in this particular instance. The regulations of the company required its employees to stoop in coupling below the body of the cars. A. knew of this regulation, but had failed to comply with it. Had he done so, he could have effected the coupling with safety. In an action by A.'s widow and minor children against the railroad company to recover damages for his death, *held*, that there was no evidence that the risk run by decedent was extraordinary in its nature, and that therefore it was error to submit that question to the jury. *Held*, further, that the risk was ordinarily incident to the decedent's employment, and that he had failed to take ordinary care in the premises, and that therefore the company defendant was entitled to judgment. Northern Cent. R. Co. v. Husson, 101 Pa. St. 1; s. c., 12 Am. & Eng. R. R. Cas. 241; and see Chicago, etc., R. Co. v. Munroe, 85 Ill. 25.

So, the acceptance by a railroad company of a flat car loaded with lumber which projects eighteen inches from the end of the car, does not entitle a brakeman who is injured thereby in coupling such car to a box-car, to an instruction that the company is, as a matter of law, guilty of negligence. Louisville, etc., R. Co. v. Gower (Tenn.), 4 S. W. Rep. 820.

In Louisville & N. R. Co. v. Brice (Ky.), 28 Am. & Eng. R. R. Cas. 542, it was *held* that where a brakeman on a railroad train was killed while engaged in coupling cars, the mere fact that one of the cars was improperly loaded, by reason of the fact that lumber projected over the end of it so as to interfere with the space necessary for coupling it, or even the fact that the conductor knew that the car was thus improperly loaded, does not of itself show wilful neglect. To constitute wilful neglect in such a case, it must also appear that the conductor, or other person in charge of the train, knew, or by the use of ordinary care could have known, that the car was so improperly loaded as to imperil the life of the servant or employee. As the jury did not, by its special verdict in this case, find that the conductor knew, or should have known, that the car was so improperly loaded as to imperil the life of the brakeman, and the question was not submitted to the jury by the instructions under which the general verdict was found, a new trial should have been awarded the defendant.

But where the evidence introduced on the trial tended to show that the plaintiff's intestate, who was a yard switchman in the employ of the defendant railroad company, and whose duty it was to couple cars, and who was a new man in the yard, and had but little knowledge of the same, while attempting to couple a flat car loaded with projecting bridge-timbers, and a box-car, properly went in between them to couple them, and stepped into a ditch made by the railroad company, of which ditch he did not have previous knowledge, and slipped, and in recovering himself so raised his head that it came between the projecting timbers and the box-car, and was so crushed that he immediately died, *held*, that such evidence tended to show negligence on the part of the railroad company, and did not necessarily show negligence on the part of the plaintiff's intestate. Brown v. Atchi-

of sufficient capacity or experience to apprehend the danger, or to know how to perform the required service, and yet avoid the obvious hazard.[1]

& Railroads, and the leased lines of the latter; and probably that one car in a thousand on appellant's road was of this character. There was no evidence that cars of this unusual construction were used upon any railroad except those named in the testimony of the general manager. *Held*, that the company should have instructed plaintiff as to this kind of coupler; that the injury was not one of the risks assumed by plaintiff, and company was liable. Mo. Pac. R. Co. v. Callbreath, 6 Tex. Law Review, [illegible].

In T. W. & W. R. R. Co. *v.* Fredericks, 71 Ill. 294, a switchman was injured while coupling an engine and a certain caboose. The draw-bar of the caboose was too short. Had it been of the usual length, the accident would not have occurred. This caboose was faulty in original construction, and was generally known by the employees to be dangerous. The injured man had not been long in the service, and did not know the defect, which was not readily perceived. *Held*, that under the circumstances the man used due care; that the dangerous character of the car could with reasonable diligence have been known to the company; that the continued use of the car made the company liable.

In Gibson *v.* Pacific, etc., R. R. Co., 46 Mo. 163, a careful and prudent brakeman, acting under orders, was injured while coupling. Jury found that he was using due care, and was ignorant of the defect in the apparatus. The coupling was dangerous originally, and the company was changing others of the same kind for a safer sort. *Held*, that the company was negligent and liable.

In Belair *v.* Chicago, etc., Co., 43 Ia. 662, the evidence showed that the draft-iron was too short, was out of repair; that the company had actual knowledge of the fact, the servant having previously notified the company of the defect; that sufficient time elapsed after the notification and before servant again handled the car to afford him ground to suppose the defect remedied. The jury found he did so suppose. *Held*, that the company was liable.

It is the duty of a railway company to cover culverts on the line of its road in its yards, and within a reasonable distance of switches, wherever it would naturally be anticipated that brakemen in the proper discharge of their duties would be apt to go in making couplings. Franklin *v.* Winona, etc., R. Co. (Minn.), 34 N. W. Rep. 898.

1. In Louisville, etc., R. Co. *v.* Frawley (Ind.), 28 Am. & Eng. R. R. Cas. 308, these rules were applied to the case of an inexperienced minor who was injured while coupling cars with "double deadwoods," and the company held liable. But in Veits *v.* Toledo, etc., R. Co., 55 Mich. 120; s. c., 18 Am. & Eng. R. R. Cas. 11, the evidence failing to establish negligence on the part of the defendant railroad company or its employees, and showing that deceased, who was killed while coupling cars, was a youth of ordinary intelligence, and that he was fully aware of the dangerous business in which he was employed, and not entirely inexperienced, a judgment in favor of the defendant was affirmed.

In Russell *v.* Minneapolis & St. L. R. Co., 32 Minn. 230, the plaintiff, who was brakeman upon a railroad train, was injured while attempting to couple a baggage car equipped with a "Miller coupler," to the tender of an engine equipped with an ordinary coupler. The latter was not provided with wooden buffers to prevent the car and tender from colliding, as they sometimes do in such case. In the present instance they did so collide. Plaintiff had been for some time employed in the service of the company. *Held*, that whether or not plaintiff had notice of the danger involved in making the coupling was a question for the jury. The court said, "Now, in this case, plaintiff undoubtedly knew the character of these two couplers. He knew that one was a Miller and the other a common one. He also knew that the former had a certain amount of lateral motion; also that there was no goose-neck or wooden buffers on the tender. But conceding this, and assuming that he must be held to the ordinary skill and experience of brakemen, it does not appear, certainly not conclusively, that he, by the exercise of ordinary observation, ought to have understood the risks to which he was exposed by using such couplers. He was not bound to be an experienced machinist or car-builder. It does not appear that he knew, or by the exercise of ordinary observation ought to have known, that the lateral motion of the Miller coupler was sufficient to permit it to slip past the end of the draw-head on the tender. It does not appear that the use of these two kinds of couplers together in this way was usual or common, so that brakemen generally would or should understand fully the dangers incident to such a practice. Indeed, from the evidence, it is to be presumed that prudent railroad companies do not ordinarily adopt any such practice. Plaintiff had been using them

3. Contributory Negligence. — Negligence on the part of the employee which contributes proximately to the injury will defeat a recovery.[1]

on this train for some time, and it does not appear that he had ever seen the two couplers slip past each other before, — a fact which distinguishes this case from Toledo, etc., R. R. Co. *v.* Asbury, 84 Ill. 429, cited by defendant. Neither does it appear that such a thing would be likely to occur except under peculiar circumstances; as, for example, where, as in this case, the coupling was being made on a curve. As remarked by the court below, the convexity of the draw-head on the tender being so slight, and the lateral motion of the Miller coupler being resisted by a spring, we cannot say that it was obvious or apparent that they would be likely to slip past each other if they came together as they ordinarily would on a straight track. The matter was properly for the jury."

1. When the Employee is guilty of Contributory Negligence. — In the following instances the conduct of the employee was *held* to amount to contributory negligence, and the company was not held liable: —

Where the cars did not couple readily, and the brakeman failed to step out, as was his duty, but remained between the cars, endeavoring to effect the coupling while they were in motion. Williams *v.* Central R. Co. of Iowa, 43 Iowa, 396. And see, to effect that coupling or uncoupling cars while in motion is contributory negligence, Burlington, etc., R. Co. *v.* Coates (Iowa), 15 Am & Eng. R. R. Cas. 265. And in Furguson *v.* Central Iowa R. Co. (Iowa), 5 Am. & Eng. R. R. Cas. 614, it was *held* that if a particular manner of uncoupling cars while in motion was a customary way of doing the work, and was negligent and wrong, the plaintiff himself for the time being in command of the movements of the train, he is himself in part responsible for the injury, and should not be heard to complain. But see Plank *v.* New York, etc., R. Co., 60 N. Y. 607. In an action against a railroad company, for injuries sustained by a brakeman while endeavoring to uncouple cars in motion, the written contract with the company, signed by the brakeman, which advises him that the uncoupling of moving cars is dangerous, and is forbidden, is admissible in evidence, not only for the purpose of showing notice of the danger, but also to show the existence of the rule, and notice of it to the brakeman; and the offer of plaintiff to consent to its admission for the purpose of showing notice of the danger, does not cure its erroneous exclusion. Sedgwick *v.* Illinois Cent. R. Co. (Iowa), 34 N. W. Rep. 790.

A brakeman of some experience, in the employ of a railroad comp[any] between two box-cars which [were] in order to couple them. W[hile] his foot slipped into a cert[ain] frog. He fell, was run over, [and] In an action to recover dam[ages for his] death, his administrator call[ed] to the stand, and asked th[e] danger was, in running alon[g] coupling and uncoupling car[s]. He also asked whether a pe[rson] between two slowly moving [cars to] couple them, could see a frog. *Held*, that when the railroad [company] showed that deceased had actu[al notice] of the alleged danger to whi[ch he ex]posed, the burden of proof [was on the] representatives of the deceas[ed to show] some excuse for his conduct [in exposing] himself to danger. In the ab[sence of] excuse, there could be no rec[overy, as] deceased had clearly been g[uilty of con]tributory negligence. Burling[ton, etc., R.] Co. *v.* Coates (Iowa), 15 Am. [& Eng. R. R.] Cas. 265.

Contributory negligence an[d] from the fact that the emp[loyee was on the] inside instead of the outside of a switch upon which the c[ars were] placed, by which he was th[rown] the projecting ends of the tw[o cars] came nearer together on the i[nside than on] the outside of the curve. Mc[...] *v.* Lyde (Tex.), 11 Am. & Eng[...] 188. Thus, plaintiff's intest[ate, em]ployed in coupling cars in [a] depot yard, in Detroit, Mich[...] coupling certain cars standin[g on a] curve, the draw-heads of the [...] meet, and passed each other[, causing the] cars to come so close together [that he was] crushed to death. The evid[ence showed] that deceased was standing [...] of the draw-bar while coupli[ng, ...] the outside was free from d[anger. Held] that the plaintiff was not [entitled to] recover, the deceased having [as]sumed the risk of remaining [...] of the draw-bar when he [...] to the other side; and that, ha[ving assumed] the risks of the employment, [...] to look out for and avoid the d[anger arising] from the sharpness of the cu[rve ...] as an experienced brakem[an ...] must have known he was exp[osed ...] *v.* Detroit, etc., R. Co., 122 [...]

A servant who undertakes t[o ...] by using the end of a switch-ch[ain ...] a coupling-link, is guilty of con[tributory neg]ligence. Houston, etc., R. Co[...] Tex. 110; s. c., 8 Am. & Eng. [...]

Where a railway company has in use on its road freight cars without end ladders, steps, and handles, which are necessary in coupling or uncoupling while the cars are in motion, and a freight conductor is cognizant of this fact, it is clearly his duty, before attempting to pass from the side to the end of the car for the purpose of uncoupling it, to ascertain whether it is one of that kind, and, if he finds it is, it is negligence on his part to attempt to make the uncoupling while the train is in motion. Chicago, etc., R. Co. v. Warner, 108 Ill. 538; s. c., 18 Am. & Eng. R. R. Cas. 100.

And where an employee, engaged in coupling cars, was injured by reason of the alleged defective condition of the bumper or draw-head, and the evidence showed that, shortly before the accident, he had uncoupled the same car, and that it was his duty to have known of the defect, if it existed, and to have reported it, and that it was his duty to observe the cars and the couplings so as to determine, before attempting to couple them, what kind of a link to use, and, by failing to observe the disparity in the height of the draw-heads, he had used a straight link, *held*, that he was guilty of such contributory negligence as precluded recovery. Norfolk & W. R. Co. v. Emmert (Va.), 3 S. E. Rep. 145.

Plaintiff, a brakeman, sought, in his action against the railroad company by which he was employed, to recover for an injury to his hand, received while trying to couple two freight cars, one of which was stationary, and behind which plaintiff stood while the other was moving towards plaintiff, who had ample opportunity to observe the fact that the coupling on the latter car was the "three-link coupling." There was evidence tending to show that plaintiff was warned of this, and to be particular, and not to go between the cars. Plaintiff, however, denied having received these warnings. A rule of the company, of which plaintiff had knowledge, forbade employees entering cars, when in motion, to uncouple them, "and all such imprudences;" while another rule, designed to lessen the danger of coupling, required that, when possible, a stick should be used. Both these rules plaintiff disregarded. *Held*, that his contributory negligence precluded his recovery. Darracotts v. Chesapeake, etc., R. Co. (Va.), 28 East. Rep. 511.

Rules. — Where a servant was injured while coupling by hand, and a rule of the company provided that in such cases a stick should always be used, evidence was not admissible that the rule was impracticable and not observed, inasmuch as the employees have no right to judge of the reasonableness of the rules, but are bound in any event to obey them. Wolsey v. Lake Shore R. Co., 33 Ohio St. 227. And see Hulett v. St. Louis, etc., R. Co., 67 Mo. 239. But the fact that plaintiff was injured while disobeying a rule of defendant, that a stick must be used in coupling cars, does not prevent him from recovering in such action when it appears that the injury actually suffered would have been received even if the stick had been used in making the coupling. Reed v. Burlington, etc., R. Co. (Iowa), 33 N. W. Rep. 451.

An employee is not bound by a rule of the company which has not been properly published or brought to his attention, and which it has habitually neglected to enforce. This principle applied to a rule forbidding coupling by hand. Fay v. Minneapolis & St. L. R. Co., 30 Minn. 231; s. c., 11 Am. & Eng. R. R. Cas. 193.

A complaint seeking to hold a railroad company liable for an injury to an employee, resulting from an alleged breach of duty in failing to provide cars that could be coupled by hand without injury to the brakeman, is met by an answer which alleges a contract between the company and the employee, embraced in a notice as follows: "Coupling cars by hand is dangerous and unnecessary. This work can be effectually done by the use of a coupling-stick, which will be supplied to employees by yardmasters at —— From this date the company will not assume any liability or pay any expense incurred by employees on account of injuries received in coupling cars." The receipt of this notice, and the employee's continuance in the service of the company, made its terms part of the contract of employment, and a breach of duty by the employee to undertake to couple cars by hand; and the only obligation resting on the railroad company was that of providing cars that might safely be coupled by the use of a coupling-stick. Pennsylvania Co. v. Whitcomb (Ind.), 9 West. Rep 823.

Employee not guilty of Contributory Negligence — Where a brakeman cannot easily uncouple cars when the train is standing still, and, in endeavoring to uncouple them when the train is in motion, steps between the cars, and there meets with an injury which is caused by want of repair in the road-bed, it cannot be ruled that he is careless as a matter of law; but the question is one for the jury. Gardner v. Mich. Cent. R. Co. (Mich.), 24 Am. & Eng. R. R. Cas. 435.

A brakeman was engaged in switching cars. He was on a car which was being pushed by an engine. At the proper moment he uncoupled the car, and signalled to the engine to stop, sufficient momentum having been communicated. When the engine was left some twelve or fifteen feet behind, thinking it had stopped, he jumped down on the track in pursuance of his duty, was struck by the engine, which was still

4. **Fellow-Servants.** — Where the injury happens to the employee through the negligence of a fellow-servant, he is, of course, precluded from recovering wherever the "fellow-servant rule" prevails. As to who is and who is not a fellow-servant with a train-man engaged in coupling cars, the decisions are many and often conflicting.[1]

with the deceased; and that the evidence of defendant's negligence was sufficient to require the submission of the question to the jury; also, that the fact of the knowledge of the deceased of the existence of the trench was not sufficient to charge him, under the circumstances, with contributory negligence, as the act in which he was engaged necessarily required his whole attention and thought; and that the act itself of coupling cars while in motion was the usual, and almost the only, method of doing it.

1. **Who are Fellow-Servants with Car-Coupler.** — Where there is a defect in the coupling apparatus of cars received from another road, and the same has escaped the attention of the car inspector, whose business it was to observe the same, the company cannot be held liable for an injury to a brakeman in consequence, as this is considered to be attributable to the negligence of a fellow-servant. Smith *v.* Potter, 46 Mich. 258; s. c., 2 Am. & Eng. R. R. Cas. 140. See, however, King *v.* Ohio, etc., R. Co., 8 Am. & Eng. R. R. Cas. 119; and Fay *v.* Minneapolis, etc., R. Co., 3 Minn. 231; s. c., 11 Am. & Eng. R. R. Cas. 193, where it is held differently, the car-inspector not being viewed as a fellow-servant, but rather as a vice-principal.

The engineer in charge of the engine and the car-coupler have been held to be fellow-servants, and the company has been held to be not liable for an injury to one occasioned by the negligence of the other. Fowler *v.* Chicago & N. W. R. Co. (Wis.), 19 Am. & Eng. R. R. Cas. 536; Farwell *v.* Boston & W. R. Co., 4 Metc. (Mass.) 29; Hayes *v.* Western R. Corp., 3 Cush. 270; Dow *v.* Kansas Pac. R. Co., 8 Kans. 642; St. Louis, etc., R. Co. *v.* Britz, 72 Ill. 256; Summerhays *v.* Kansas Pac. R. Co., 2 Col. 484; Henry *v.* Staten Island R. Co., 2 Am. & Eng. R. R. Cas. 60; Smith *v.* Potter, 2 Am. & Eng. R. R. Cas. 140; Nashville, C. & St. L. R. Co. *v.* Wheeler, 4 Am. & Eng. R. R. Cas. 633; Pittsburgh, etc., R. Co. *v.* Ranney, 5 Am. & Eng. R. R. Cas. 533; Jeffery *v.* Keokuk, etc., R. Co., 5 Am & Eng. R. R. Cas 568; Gormley *v.* Ohio, etc., R. Co., 5 Am. & Eng. R. R. Cas. 581; Harvey *v.* New York Central & H. R. R. Co., 8 Am. & Eng. R. R. Cas 518; Randall *v.* Baltimore & Ohio R. R. Co., 15 Am. & Eng. R. R. Cas. 243; Nashville & St. L. R. Co. *v.* Wheeler, 15 Am. & Eng. R. R. Cas. 315; Wilson *v.* Madison, etc., R. Co., 18 Ind. 226.

The fact that a yardmaster of a railroad company has authority to discharge a car-coupler does not make him any the less a fellow-servant of the car-coupler. Webb *v.* Richmond, etc., R. Co. (N. Car.), 2 S. East. Rep. 440.

Who are not. — As to car inspectors, see note, *supra*, "Who are Fellow-Servants with Car-Coupler."

In Louisville, etc., R. Co. *v.* Moore (Ky.), 24 Am. & Eng. R. R. Cas. 443, a freight train was uncoupled at a highway crossing to allow travellers to pass, both the engineer and the conductor going to the telegraph, leaving the fireman, an inexperienced boy of twenty years, in charge of the engine, and directing Moore, the head brakeman, to make the coupling. The fireman backed the engine and the cars together with unusual force, and Moore was injured. *Held*, that the company was liable, the engineer and conductor occupying toward Moore the position of vice-principals of the company.

At the trial of an action against a railroad corporation for personal injuries occasioned to the plaintiff while in its employ as brakeman, by reason of the draw-bar on a locomotive engine being too low for the work for which it was used, the defendant has no ground of exception to a refusal to rule that "if the jury find that the conductor, or any person in charge of the cars at the time, directed the coupling of an engine to a car the draw-bars of which were of unequal height, whereby the injury was caused, the plaintiff cannot recover, the injury being the result of the carelessness of a fellow-servant." Lawless *v.* Connecticut River R. Co., 136 Mass. 1, 18 Am. & Eng. R. R. Cas. 96.

In a Wisconsin case, Brabbits *v.* Chicago, etc., R. Co., 38 Wis. 289, a railroad brakeman was injured, in the course of his employment, while coupling two sections of a railroad train; and there was evidence tending to show that the injury was caused by the use of a defective switch-engine. The engineer, whose duty it was, had several times previously notified the foreman of one of the company's repair shops of the defective condition of said engine. Such foreman had charge of all the men in said repair shop, and was the person to whom, by the rules of the company, such

5. Evidence. — Brakemen, baggage-masters, and the like a[re not]
competent to testify as experts in regard to what they co[nsider]
the danger to a brakeman to be in coupling under certain c[ircum-]
stances.[1] This is not a proper question for expert testimon[y; it]
is a matter of common experience, upon which a jury is com[petent]
to pass. In a like manner, it is not a question for an exper[t]
whether a brakeman is negligent in standing a certain wa[y in]
coupling cars.[2]

COUPONS. — See also BILLS AND NOTES, BONDS, INT[EREST,]
MORTGAGE, MUNICIPAL CORPORATIONS, MANDAMUS, RAI[LROAD]
COMPANIES, TAXATION.

1. Definition. — The term "coupon" is derived from the F[rench]
"*couper*, to cut," and is defined by Worcester, in his diction[ary, to]
signify "one of the interest certificates attached to transf[erable]
bonds, and of which there are usually as many as there ar[e]

defect should have been reported; and it was his duty to see it repaired. Another person, known as the master mechanic, had general supervision of all repairs of the motive power, tools, and machinery of the company, and general charge of all the men employed in the locomotive department, including the power to employ men in or discharge them from service in that department; while said foreman had no power to employ or discharge men without the master mechanic's consent. *Held*, that an instruction to the effect that notice to such foreman of the defect was notice to the company, was correct. The court *held* that the company owed a duty to its employee to keep in proper repair the engine used to propel the train [ ] the latter was employed; and [ ] man being the person designated [to] whom notice of any defect in th[e engine] was to be given, and whose du[ty it was] to repair it on receiving such [notice,] negligence in that behalf was th[e negli-]*gence of the company*, and not th[at of a] fellow-servant, and the company w[as liable] for the injury caused thereby. A[ ] similar case in which same resul[t was] reached, Chicago, etc., R. Co. v. [ ] Ill. 641.

1 Muldowney v. Illinois Cent. [ ] 36 Iowa, 462.

2. Belair v. Chicago, etc., R. [ ] Iowa, 662.

ments to be made;—so called because it is *cut off* when presented for payment."[1]

2. Parts of Coupon.—(*a*) *Wording and Form.*—It is entirely immaterial in what words the coupons are expressed, provided they indicate by whom they are due, and the amount and time of payment.[2] They have been issued in the form of promissory notes,[3] bill of exchange, or draft, upon the treasury of the corporation issuing them,[4] ticket or "interest warrant,"[5] check upon a banking-house,[6] and draft or bill with no drawee named.[7]

(*b*) *Signature.*—Coupons of bonds may be signed by a printed *facsimile* of the maker's autograph, adopted by the maker for that purpose, though not expressly authorized by statute;[8] and where commissioners have power to issue coupons accompanying bonds, a statement in the bonds that they have caused one of their number to sign the coupons is equivalent to a signing of the coupons by all of them.[9]

(*c*) *Seal.*—Municipal bonds and coupons must be executed in the manner provided by statute. Thus, where the statute provided that the bonds should be under the hands and seals of the commissioners, and neither the bonds nor coupons were sealed, although the wording of the bonds showed that a sealing was contemplated, it was held, in a suit on the coupons, that the bonds and coupons were void.[10]

1. 2 Daniel's Neg. Inst. (3d ed.) 488.

"Coupons are written contracts for the payment of a definite sum of money on a given day." City of Aurora *v.* West, 7 Wall. (U. S.) 82.

2. 2 Daniel's Neg. Inst. (3d ed.) 494.

3. "Promise to pay the bearer, at the Continental Bank, in the city of New York, forty dollars, interest on bond No. ——." Thompson *v.* Lee County, 3 Wall. (U. S.) 327.

4. "The treasurer of said county will pay the legal holder hereof, one hundred dollars, on the first day of September, 1857, on presentation thereof, being for interest due on the obligation of said county, No. 16, given to the Peru and Indianapolis R. Company." Moran *v.* Comrs. of Miami Co., 2 Black. (U. S.) 722.

5. "County of Lawrence —— Warran, No. ——, for thirty dollars, being for six months' interest on bond No. ——, payable on the —— day of ——, at the office of the Pennsylvania R. Company, in the city of Philadelphia." Woods *v.* Lawrence Co., 1 Black. (U. S.) 360.

6. "Duncan, Sherman, & Co. of New York will pay the bearer thirty dollars, the half-yearly interest on the Wheeling bond, due 1st January, 1867." Arents *v.* Commonwealth, 18 Gratt. (Va.) 753.

7. "Six per cent stock, Mercer County, State of Illinois, railroad bond No. 20. Pay the bearer sixty dollars on the first day of July, 1863, interest to that date. John Cowden, Chairman Board of Supervisors, Mercer County." Mercer County *v.* Hubbard, 45 Ill. 140.

8. Pennington *v.* Baehr, 48 Cal. 565; *s. c.*, 2 Cent. L. J. 92.

Bonds were issued by order of the county court, and were signed by the presiding justice, and sealed with the seal of the county. The deputy clerk also signed the clerk's name, with the knowledge of the presiding justice. These bonds not meeting with favor, they were taken up and destroyed, and new bonds issued, corresponding in style and date with the old ones. The old clerk being then out of office, his name was signed by the deputy, who had become the clerk, the signatures on the coupons being lithographed. The statute made no provision as to the mode of executing the bonds. The county paid interest on the new bonds, and received and retained a certificate of stock. The agent of the county participated in all the proceedings. *Held*, that the bonds were valid in the hands of a *bona fide* holder. McKee *v.* Vernon Co., 3 Dill. (C. C.) 210.

9. Phelps *v.* Lewiston, 15 Blatchf. (C. C.) 131.

County bonds signed only by the chairman of the county board are valid. Thayer *v.* Montgomery County, 3 Dill. (C. C.) 389.

10. Avery *v.* Town of Springport, 14 Blatchf. (C. C.) 272.

(*d*) *Payee.* — The validity of the coupon is not affected by the fact that no payee is mentioned, for it is sufficiently evident from the general character of the instrument that it was issued as the binding obligation of the payor to the purchaser of the bond, and was designed to be paid to him or to the bearer.[1]

(*e*) *Place of Payment.* — The power of a municipal corporation to make any contract does not depend upon the place of performance, but upon its scope and object. It is therefore held to be perfectly legal for such a corporation to specify in its bonds and coupons some particular banking-house, in New York or elsewhere, as the place of payment.[2]

3. Coupons not Bills of Credit. — Bonds or coupons issued by States or counties for money lawfully borrowed by them are not necessarily within the prohibition of the constitution upon bills of credit.[3]

4. Coupons as Negotiable Instruments. — (*a*) *Generally.* — Coupons which promise payment to bearer are in legal effect promissory notes by the law merchant, and possess all the attributes of negotiable paper.[4] It does not deprive them of their negotiable

But in the absence of statutory provisions "it is now pretty well settled by authority, as indeed it is clear in reason, that it is not necessary to constitute a corporate obligation a bond that it should bear its seal." 2 Daniel's Neg. Inst. 496 (3d ed.).

1. Woods *v.* Lawrence Co., 1 Black. (U. S.) 386. See COUPONS AS NEGOTIABLE INSTRUMENTS, *infra*.

2. Connecticut Mut. Life Ins. Co. *v.* Cleveland, etc., R. Co., 41 Barb. (N. Y.) 9; Thompson *v.* Lee County, 3 Wall. (U. S.) 327; City of Kenosha *v.* Lamson, 9 Wall. (U. S.) 478; Lynde *v.* Winnebago Co., 16 Wall. (U. S.) 13; City of Lexington *v.* Butler, 14 Wall. (U. S.) 289; Evansville, etc., R. Co. *v.* City of Evansville, 15 Ind. 413.

The supreme court of Illinois, however, has held that when the legislature, in authorizing a payment abroad, expressly mentions the interest alone, the inference is strong that they intended to exclude the principal from that provision. Prettyman *v.* Supervisors of Tazewell Co., 19 Ill. 406; s. c., 71 Am. Dec. 230; People, etc., *v.* County of Tazewell, 22 Ill. 147.

But when the corporation exceeds its authority by making its securities payable outside the State, although that particular provision is invalid, nevertheless the security is binding, and payable at its treasury in like manner as if it had been so expressed upon its face. The unauthorized portion of the coupon may be rejected as surplusage. Johnson *v.* County of Stark, 24 Ill. 91.

3. McCoy *v.* Washington County, 3 Wall. Jr. (C. C.) 281.

4. Jones on Ry. Sec. § 320, citing Mercer Co. *v.* Hacket, 1 Wall. (U. S.) [illegible]; Thompson *v.* Lee County, 3 Wall. (U. S.) 227; Aurora City *v.* West, 7 Wall. (U. S.) 105; Clark *v.* Iowa City, 20 Wall. (U. S.) 583; Kennard *v.* Cass County, 3 Dill. (C. C.) 147; Chesapeake & Ohio Canal Co. *v.* Blair, 45 Md. 102; Town of [illegible] *v.* Clifford, 53 Ind. 191; [illegible] *v.* Norfolk, etc., R. Co., 1 Hughes (C. C.) [illegible]; Arents *v.* Commonwealth, 18 Gratt. (Va.) 750; Miller *v.* Town of Berlin, 13 Blatchf. (C. C.) 245; Cooper *v.* Town of Thompson, Ib. 434; Haven *v.* Grand Junc. R. & D. Co., 109 Mass. 88; Spooner *v.* Holmes, 102 Mass. 503; s. c., 3 Am. R. [illegible]. See also Town of Eagle *v.* Kohn, 84 Ill. [illegible]; Roberts *v.* Bolles, 101 U. S. [illegible]; Town *v.* Culver, 19 Wall. (U. S.) 84; Commissioners *v.* Aspinwall, 21 How. (U. S.) [illegible]; Ketchum *v.* Duncan, 96 U. S. 659; [illegible] *v.* City of Bridgeport, 17 Conn. [illegible]; Maddox *v.* Graham, 2 Metc. (Ky.) 56; Commonwealth *v.* Emigrant Ind. Ass'n, 98 Mass. 12; Brainard *v.* New York, etc., R. Co., 25 N. Y. 496; Beaver County *v.* Armstrong, 44 Pa. St. 63; Nat. Ex. Bank *v.* [illegible], etc., R. Co., 8 R. I. 375; Langston *v.* South Car. R. Co., 2 S. Car. 249; [illegible] *v.* [illegible] County, Wolw. 69; City of Lexington *v.* Butler, 14 Wall. (U. S.) 282.

Contra, but not authorities, Clarke *v.* City of Janesville, 1 Biss. (C. C.) [illegible]; Myers *v.* New York & Cumberland R. Co., 43 Me. 252; Evertson *v.* National Bank, 66 N. Y. 14.

Coupons are more closely assimilated to promissory notes than to bank notes, bills of exchange, or checks, although in their

…ter that it may be necessary to resort to the bonds to prove …execution,[1] and they retain their negotiability after being …ed from bonds not yet due.[2]

…Negotiable Words in Coupons. — Where interest coupons or …ts are not made payable to bearer or order, they are not …able when separated from the bonds, although the latter …emselves negotiable, and a purchaser of these detached … takes them subject to all defects in the title of his …rrer.[3]

… resemble them. 2 Dan.

… are promissory notes within the …tates statutes concerning national …nd therefore such banks may take, … sue upon coupons. First National … Bennington, 10 Blatch. (C. C.) 53. … drawn in the form of checks upon …hey are regarded as due upon the … for payment, and not as payable …nd, like bank notes. Arents *v.* …nwealth, 18 Gratt. (Va.) 750. …ertson *v.* National Bank, 66 N. Y. …ourt say, "If these warrants are …missory notes, they are not nego- …hey are neither checks nor bills of …e."

…e the coupon is in the form of a … the interest in favor of the bearer, … strictly a bill of exchange, as it is …ded for acceptance. It is usually …gainst funds deposited to meet it, …erefore more like a check. Jones …ec. § 317.

… also differ from bills of exchange …hey are not entitled to graces upon …nt, however, there is some conflict …rity. See *Days of Grace, infra.*

… negotiability of coupons is not … by the fact that they are, by their …leclared to be for interest upon …pecified by their numbers. Evert- …ational Bank, 66 N. Y. 14.

…per *v.* Town of Thompson, 13 … C. C.) 434.

…ompson *v.* Perrine, 16 Otto (U. S.),

…ertson *v.* National Bank of New- … N. Y. 14.

… is case there were two classes of … involved. One class read as fol-

"… The Indianapolis, Bloomington …tern R. Co., will pay the bearer, at …y in the city of New York, thirty- …ars in gold coin, on the first day of …871, for semi-annual interest on … —.

"A. T. Lewis, *Secretary.*"

…hers were in the following terms: — …est warrant for thirty-five dollars, …pon bond No. — of the Danville, Urbana, Bloomington, and Pekin Railroad Company. Payable in gold coin at the office of the Farmers' Loan and Trust Co. in the city of New York, April 1st, 1871.

"W. J. Ermentrout, *Secretary.*"

Both of these coupons were decided to be negotiable instruments by the Supreme Court of New York. Evertson *v.* First Nat. Bank, 4 Hun (N. Y.), 692.

But the court of appeals reversed this decision, and *held* that coupons of Indiana, B. & W. only, were negotiable, concerning which the court say, "The coupons of the Indiana, Bloomington, and Western Railway Company, being promissory notes, they necessarily had all the characteristics of such instruments, and were entitled to the benefit of the days of grace allowable on bills and notes, payable at a given day or on time."

In regard to the other coupons the opinion says, "The coupons of the Danville, Urbana, Bloomington, and Pekin Railroad Company, termed on their face 'Interest Warrants,' are in somewhat different form. Whether they are within that description of property to which a title may be acquired by a *bona fide* transferee for value, notwithstanding a defect of title in the transferrer, depends upon their negotiability," and then the court holds that as they are not payable to any person by name, or his order, or to the bearer, or to the order of a fictitious person, they are not negotiable.

In Partridge *v.* Bank of England, 9 Q. B. 396, dividend warrants of the Bank of England, payable to a particular person, were held to be not negotiable, although they had been so treated by custom for sixty years.

In Jackson *v.* York, etc., R. R. Co., 48 Me. 147, the coupons read, "Coupon No. 1. Bond No. 60. On the first day of May, 1852, the Y. and C. R. R. Co. will pay nine dollars on this coupon in Portland," signed by the treasurer of the company. *Held,* that, without some statutory provision, no action can be maintained in the name of an assignee, upon interest coupons which contain no negotiable words, nor language from which it can be inferred that it was the design of the corporation issuing them to (*c*) *Days of Grace.* — The most recent authority [illegible] that such instruments are entitled to days of grace; [illegible] chasing after the expiration of the time of payment [illegible] before the expiration of the days of grace, is a purchaser [illegible] maturity.[1]

(*d*) *Overdue Coupons.* — Aside from the question of day[s of] grace, a coupon becomes due and payable upon the day [illegible]

treat them as negotiable paper, or as creating an obligation, distinct from and independent of the bonds to which they were severally attached when the bonds were issued. The negotiability of such coupons is a question of law, to be determined from the papers themselves, by fixed and well-settled rules.

To be negotiable, a coupon must be so upon its face, without reference to any other paper: if it is not payable to bearer or order, and does not contain other equivalent words, it is not negotiable. Augusta Bank *v.* Augusta, 49 Me. 507. See also Cranch *v.* Credit Foncier L. R., 8 Q. B. 374; Myers *v.* York, etc., R. Co., 43 Me. 232; Crosby *v.* New London, etc., R. Co., 26 Conn. 121.

It is conceded, however, by the New York court, Evertson *v.* National Bank, *supra*, that the object of the interest warrants may be fully accomplished by regarding them as authority to the financial agent of the company to pay the amount named therein upon presentation, although detached from the bonds. "It is possible," says the court, "that as between such agent and the debtor corporation, the possession and presentment of the interest warrants at maturity would be evidence of an authority to receive the money by the person presenting it, even as against the true owner. But if this be conceded, it does not make them negotiable as between third persons."

Upon this point, however, the authorities are conflicting. In *Missouri* it has been held that a coupon may be negotiable though it name no particular person as payee, and is not made payable to bearer or holder. Smith *v.* County of Clarke, 54 Mo. 58. The coupons read as follows: "State of Missouri. Bond No. 51. $35.00. The County of Clarke will pay thirty-five dollars on this coupon on the first day of January, 1867, at the treasury of the county."

In McCoy *v.* Washington County, 3 Wall. Jr. (C. C.) 281, the coupons were in form as follows: "W. County bonds —— warrant for thirty dollars' interest on bond No. 108, payable in W., on the fifteenth day of May, 1857. For the commissioners, S. Clark." *Held*, that such coupons are not in words an instrument in writing of a commercial nature, and having their negotiability by virtue of the law merchant. [illegible] they are not made payable to any [illegible] person, or his order, or even to [illegible] They partake of the nature of the [illegible] instrument to which they are [illegible] They are intended by the parties to [illegible] dence of debt in the hands of the [illegible] and proof of payment when in the [illegible] of the debtor. They pass by deliv[ery] [illegible] by the contract of the parties [illegible] usage of the country are sufficient [illegible] of a debt to the holder as again[st] [illegible] obligors of the bond. They are of [illegible] invention, and should have the [illegible] tended by the parties, and be [illegible] the usage of the country, and not [illegible] sharp rules of law applicable to [illegible] ments of different nature.

In *Virginia* it is made [illegible] to the negotiability of notes, [illegible] payable at a bank. This statute, ho[wever,] has been held not to apply to bon[ds and] coupons issued by corporations whic[h con]tain negotiable words. Arents *v.* [Com]monwealth, 18 Gratt. (Va.) 750.

1. Evertson *v.* First National B[ank], [illegible] N. Y. 14, *Allen, J.*, says, "It does no[t seem] to have been decided, that, being a p[romis]sory note, although something more, [it is] within the rule allowing days of gr[ace to] commercial instruments of that cha[racter.] . . . It is probably true that they [are re]garded and treated, as well by promi[sor as] promisee, as payable at the day, an[d not] as if, in terms, payable without grac[e. But] this cannot destroy the character, or [change] the legal effect, of the instruments, [the in]terpretation of which is for the cour[t. It] is only as negotiable commercial [paper] that the plaintiff, as a *bona fide* pur[chaser] could acquire a good title to the c[oupons] from one having no title thereto; [he] can only acquire such title by a pu[rchase] under the same circumstances that [would] give him a title to other commercial [paper,] and if there were no days of gr[ace for] the payment of these coupons, they [could] not be transferred so as to give goo[d title.]" Mr. Jones, in his work on Railroad [Securi]ties, adopts the view of the Ne[w York] Court. Jones, Ry. Sec. § 326. Mr. D[aniel,] however, follows a Virginia d[ecision] (Arents *v.* Commonwealth, 18 Gratt. 773), and holds to the contrary. [Daniel,] Neg. Inst. (3d ed.) § 1496 a.

ms of the bond and coupon for the payment of the interest nted by the coupon.[1] Such a coupon, as to the time of its y, is different from a note payable on demand. It becomes hout any demand or presentation.[2]

r the expiration of the days of grace, when they are , the coupons become overdue, and are dishonored; and, if by any person after they are due, they are taken subject to equities which properly attach to them in the hands of the s holder.[3]

coupons detached from bonds, and payable to bearer, though e, are still negotiable instruments.[4]

tolen Coupons. — Negotiable coupons being transferable by , although detached from the bonds, a purchaser, in good efore maturity, from one who has stolen them, acquires a tle.[5] But if the coupons are not negotiable, or if they have urchased after maturity, the purchaser acquires no better an the thief could give.[6]

Presumption that Coupons were purchased in Good Faith, rior to Maturity. — Where a person purchases coupons ket overt, the presumption is that he acquired them before ere due; that he paid a valuable consideration for the and that he took them without notice of any defect which render them invalid;[7] and the burden of proof lies on

nts v. Commonwealth, 18 Gratt.

es on Railway Securities, § 325; tional Bank v. Scott County, 14

nts v. Commonwealth, 18 Gratt.); Union Bank of Louisiana v. New Orleans, 5 Am. Law Reg. ; Gilbough v. Norfolk, etc., R. Co., s (C. C.), 410. See "Stolen Coupons."

st Nat. Bank v. Scott County, 14 , county bonds, with interest couached, were lost, and bought by at their market value, with all the attached thereto. *Held*, that the it thus appeared from the face of , that the interest for several years due and unpaid, was a sufficient nce, sufficient to put the plaintiff uard. The bonds were thus dison their face. The interest equally principal was a part of the debt ey were intended to secure, and it aterial whether the whole or only the debt was overdue. The fact oupons were payable on presentald not relieve the plaintiff. An nt payable at a certain time is as soon as that time has passed. payable generally or at a specified d he who takes it by indorsement ry when overdue, has no better title than the one from whom he received it. See also National Bank v. Texas, 20 Wall. (U. S.) 72; Murray v. Lardner, 2 Wall. (U. S.) 110; Hotchkiss v. National Banks, 21 Wall. (U. S.) 354; Evertson v. National Bank, 66 N. Y. 14.

4. Grand Rapids & Indiana R. Co. v. Sanders, 54 How. (N. Y.) Pr. 214; Thompson v. Perrine, 16 Otto (U. S.), 589.

5. Evertson v. Nat. Bank, 66 N. Y. 14; Arents v. Commonwealth, 18 Gratt. (Va.) 773; Spooner v. Holmes, 102 Mass. 503; s. c., 3 Am. Rep. 491; Murray v. Lardner, 2 Wall. (U. S.) 110.

The bonds of a railroad company, payable to bearer, with interest coupons attached, were stolen from the State of Virginia, which held them in exchange for bonds of the State delivered to the railroad company. They were sold for value to certain bankers, who had no knowledge of the theft; nor was there any circumstances attending their purchase tending to put the bankers on inquiry, except that they purchased of a stranger, and eight coupons were overdue. The bankers were held entitled to recover against the company, except as to the overdue coupons. Gilbough v. Norfolk & P. R. Co., 1 Hughes (C. C.), 410.

6. Evertson v. National Bank, 66 N. Y. 14.

7. City of Lexington v. Butler, 1 Wall. (U. S.) 282.

the person who assails the right claimed by the party in possession.[1]

(*g*) *Presentment for Payment.* — Where coupons do not provide for presentment for payment, the party issuing the bonds may be put in default without presentment, unless it be shown that funds were provided for the payment of the coupons as they became due;[2] and though they be in the form of orders, demand and protest is not necessary in order to maintain a suit upon the coupons.[3] But if there be an indorser or guarantor upon the coupon, it must be presented at the time usual to charge such parties.[4]

(*h*) *Lis Pendens.* — The rule that all persons are bound to take notice of pending suit, does not apply to the purchaser of negotiable securities; and although a suit be pending at the time of the issuance of bonds, to prevent that issuance, the subsequent purchaser in open market is not affected by notice arising from *lis pendens* of which he has no actual notice, and may recover the amount of the coupons attached to said bonds.[5]

1. Murray *v.* Lardner, 2 Wall. (U.S.) 110.

But in Bailey *v.* Town of Lansing, 13 Blatchf. (C. C.) 424, it was *held* that the holder of a municipal bond must show himself to be a *bona fide* holder. The town of Lansing had authority to issue bonds in aid of a railroad company, upon the judgment rendered by the county judge, that the petition of the tax-payers for the issue of bonds represented a majority of the tax-payers and of the taxable property. Pending a *certiorari* to review the judgment of the county judge, upon which such judgment was afterwards reversed and annulled, the commissioners appointed by the judge for that purpose issued the bonds, and delivered them to the company, the latter having due notice of the *certiorari* proceedings, and giving a bond of indemnity. The holder of a part of these bonds, having shown himself to be a *bona fide* holder, was held entitled to recover; but the holder of other of the bonds, failing to establish his *bona fides*, was defeated.

2. Warner *v.* Rising Fawn Iron Co., 3 Woods (U. S.), 514; Smith *v.* Tallapoosa Co., 2 Woods (U. S.), 574; Walnut *v.* Wade, 103 U. S. 683; s. c., 3 Am. & Eng. R. R. Cas. 36; City of Jeffersonville *v.* Patterson, 26 Ind. 16; First Nat. Bank *v.* Scott Co., 14 Minn. 77; Arents *v.* Commonwealth, 18 Gratt. (Va.) 773; Langston *v.* South Car. R. Co., 2 S. Car. (N. S.) 248. But see Gorman *v.* Sinking Fund Comrs., 25 Fed. Rep. 647, *holding* that, where the holder of State coupons has the right to have them funded, he must offer them, and demand that they be funded in order that his right may be fixed. It is no excuse that his demand would have been fruitless.

In an action upon coupons, of bonds of a county in Alabama, where it is provided by statute that county commissioners must audit all claims, and that no suit can be brought upon a claim against a county until presentment of the claim and the statutory provisions have been complied with, the complaint need not aver that the coupons sued upon were presented to the court of county commissioners for allowance before the suit was brought. County of Greene *v.* Daniel, 12 Otto (U. S.) 187.

3. Mayor, etc., of Nashville *v.* First Nat. Bank, 57 Tenn. 402; Mayor, etc., *v.* Potomac Ins. Co., 58 Tenn. 296.

4. Bonner *v.* City of New Orleans, 2 Woods (U. S.), 135; Arents *v.* Commonwealth, 18 Gratt. (Va.) 773.

The liability of an indorser of a negotiable bond issued by the State, when fixed as to the principal sum by due demand and notice, is also fixed as to the interest represented by coupons not detached from the bond, without additional demand and notice. Lane *v.* E. Tenn., Va., etc., R. Co., 13 Lea (Tenn.), 547.

5. County of Warren *v.* Marcy, 97 U. S. 96; Phelps *v.* Lewiston, 15 Blatch. (U. S.) 131; County of Cass *v.* Gillett, 10 Otto (U. S.), 585.

Not a Bar to Recovery. — The pendency of an action for the foreclosure of a mortgage given to trustees by a railroad company upon its road and franchises, as security for an issue of negotiable coupon bonds, and containing the usual powers found in such instruments, authorizing them, upon default in the payment of any instalment of interest coupons, to declare the bonds due, and thereupon to proceed to realise upon the security by foreclosure *ligence of Purchaser does not affect his Title.* — Suspicion of title, or the knowledge of circumstances which would ch suspicion in the mind of a prudent man, or gross neg- n the part of the taker of negotiable bonds or coupons, ne of the transfer, will not defeat his title.[1]

upons of Municipal Bonds. — The principle is well settled suit by a *bona fide* holder against a municipal corporation er the amount of coupons due or bonds issued under conferred by law, no questions of form merely, or irregu- fraud or misconduct on the part of the agents of the on, can be considered. The only matters left open in for inquiry are, (1) the authority to issue the bonds by of the State, and (2) the *bona fides* of the holder.[2] But

, as prescribed in the mortgage, y the proceeds, but with no fur- r power or interest in respect ations or their collection, is no ction in favor of any holder or ly such overdue coupons to re- nount due thereon by judgment ion. Welsh *v.* First Div. St. R. Co., 25 Minn. 314.

as a Bar. — In an action against Iowa upon certain interest cou- lly attached to bonds issued by or the erection of a court-house, l and determined that the bonds against the county in the hands ho did not acquire them before value; and, inasmuch as the hat action had not proved that n such value, it was adjudged not entitled to recover. *Held*, lgment did not estop the plain- other bonds of the same series, coupons attached to the same coupons in the original action, ng, in a second action against that he acquired such other coupons for value before ma- omwell *v.* County of Sac, 94

y *v.* Lardner, 2 Wall. (U. S.) 110. se, *Swayne, J.*, after stating the as above, says, "Such is the of this court, and we feel no to depart from it. The rule s be said to resolve itself into of honesty and dishonesty, for ledge and wilful ignorance alike result of bad faith. They are n effect. Where there is no can be no question. The cir- mentioned, and others of a aracter, while inconclusive in are admissible in evidence; stablished, whether by direct or ial evidence, is fatal to the title er. The rule laid down in the ses of which Gill *v.* Cubitt is the antetype, is hard to comprehend and difficult to apply. One innocent holder may be more or less suspicious under similar circumstances at one time than at another, and the same remark applies to prudent men. One prudent man may also suspect where another would not, and the standard of the jury may be higher or lower than that of other men equally prudent in the management of their affairs. The rule established by the other line of decisions had the advantage of greater clearness and directness. A careful judge may readily so submit a case under it to the jury that they can hardly fail to reach the right conclusion." See also Cromwell *v.* County of Sac, 96 U. S. 351.

2. Roueder *v.* Mayor, etc., of Jersey City, 18 Fed. Rep. 719; East Lincoln *v.* Davenport, 94 U. S. 801; Pompton *v.* Cooper Union, 101 U. S. 196; Miller *v.* Town of Berlin, 13 Blatch. (U. S.) 245; Phelps *v.* Town of Yates, 16 Blatch. (U. S.) 192; Irwin *v.* Town of Ontario, 18 Blatch. (U. S.) 259; Stewart *v.* Lansing, 14 Otto (U. S.), 505.

When by legislative enactment a town is empowered to raise money by a loan for a specified purpose, and the act is silent as to the officers who shall make the loan and issue the bonds, the municipal officers would be authorized to perform those duties; and before issuing the bonds, such officers must determine whether the town had executed the power conferred upon it in accordance with the provisions of the act; and their recital upon the face of the bond of the facts in regard to that matter, as they had determined them to be, would be conclusive upon the town in an action by a bondholder for value to recover the amount of an interest coupon. Lane *v.* Inhabitants of Embden, 72 Me. 354.

In an action thereon by a *bona fide* holder for value of interest coupons, it is no defence that the amount of the bonds issued was in excess of the amount allowed by

there can be no *bona fide* holders without notice when there is no power to issue the bonds.[1]

(*k*) *Effect of Overdue Coupons attached to Bond.* — Overdue and unpaid coupons for interest attached to a negotiable bond which has several years to run, does not render the bond, and subsequently maturing coupons, dishonored paper, so as to subject them in the hands of a purchaser for value to defences good against the original holder.[2]

the act of the legislature authorizing such issue, which limited the amount of the issue to a certain proportion of the amount of the taxable property of the township. Wilson *v.* Salamanaca, 9 Otto (U. S.), 499; Humbolt Township *v.* Long, 2 Otto (U. S.), 642.

In Stewart *v.* Lansing, 104 U. S. 505, coupon bonds of a town in New York were executed by commissioners to a railroad company pursuant to an order of a county judge, which was reversed by the supreme court in a proceeding whereof, before they were issued, the commissioners and the company had due notice. *Held*, that, as between the company and the town, the bonds were invalid; and hence that, in an action upon coupons detached therefrom, the plaintiff must, to make out his right to recover against the town, establish his *bona fide* ownership of them.

In First National Bank of Oxford *v.* Wheeler, 72 N. Y. 201, it was *held* that railroad commissioners of a town who have received from the collector of the town moneys raised by tax to pay interest coupons on bonds of the town, issued in payment of a subscription to the capital stock of a railroad, cannot draw in question the validity of the bonds, to justify them in refusing to pay over the moneys to the owners of the coupons; and the fact that the commissioners resist payment, and defend an action against them by the holder of such coupons, pursuant to a resolution of a town-meeting, and under a promise of indemnity from the town, does not make the invalidity of the bonds a defence to the action.

Where a town has paid interest on its bonds for a number of years, and has accepted and retained the stock of the railroad company to which the bonds were issued, and the bonds have passed from hand to hand in the market, the town is estopped to deny the validity of the bonds. First Nat. Bank *v.* Town of Walcott, 7 Fed. Rep. 892; Whiting to Town *v.* Potter, 18 Blatch. (U. S.) 165.

Where certain county bonds and a number of detached coupons were placed in the hands of an agent of the county to be issued by him conditionally, and the agent issued them fraudulently, and transferred the detached coupons to A., his brother-in-law; and where B., who, while said county was disputing the validity of said bonds and coupons, and negotiating for a compromise with the holders thereof, had, with a full knowledge of the facts, entered into a contract with said county to procure said bonds and coupons for surrender, purchased the coupons transferred to A., in the name of C.; and C. brought suit thereon against the county, — *held*, that C. was not a *bona fide* holder for value, and could not recover. Whitford *v.* Clark County, 13 Fed. Rep. 837.

1. Smith *v.* Town of [illegible] (U. S.) 267; Lewis *v.* City of Shreveport, 3 Woods (U. S.), 205; Township of East Oakland *v.* Skinner, 4 Otto (U. S.), [illegible]; County of Dallas *v.* [illegible], 4 Otto (U. S.), 663.

2. Cromwell *v.* County of Sac, 96 U. S. 58; Morton & Bliss *v.* N. O. & S. R. Co., 79 Ala. 590; Indiana, etc., R. Co. *v.* Sprague, 2 Am. & Eng. R. R. Cas. [illegible]; [illegible] *v.* Jersey City, 18 Fed. Rep. 7[illegible]; s. c. 6 Am. & Eng. Corp. Cas. 316.

In the latter case the court says, "In Parsons *v.* Jackson, 99 U. S. 434, the payment of the bonds of a railway company in Louisiana was in controversy. The bonds had never been issued by the company, but had been seized and carried away during the late Rebellion. They were drawn payable to bearer either in London, New York or New Orleans, and the president of the company was authorised to fix the place of payment by his indorsement. When taken they contained no such indorsement. They were offered for sale, and were sold for a very small consideration in the market of New York, with due and unpaid coupons for several years attached to them. The court *held* that the absence of the required indorsement was a defect which deprived the bonds of the character of negotiability, and that the purchaser was affected with notice of their invalidity. Mr. Justice [illegible], speaking for the court, remarked that the presence of the past due and unpaid coupons was itself an evidence of [illegible] sufficient to put the purchaser on inquiry. But in the subsequent case of Indiana, etc., R. Co. *v.* Sprague, 103 U. S. 756, this expression of the learned justice is commented on [illegible] erest on Overdue Coupons. — *(a) Generally.* — Coupons being contracts for the payment of money, and negotiable payable to bearer, and passing from hand to hand, as gotiable instruments, it is quite apparent, on general prinhat they should draw interest after payment of the principal tly neglected or refused.[1] Interest is accordingly allowed ons from the time they were due until the date of the t,[2] and exchange at the place where, by their terms, they payable.[3]

there is a right of interest upon interest coupons from turity till paid, such a right cannot be impaired by an act after the issue of the bonds, construing past legislation.[4]

rior Demand of Payment. — The failure to present coupons nent does not prevent the running of interest.[5] But if a

ind matriculated; and it was again nay now be accepted as the law, lue and unpaid interest coupons to municipal bonds are not in sufficient to put the purchaser ." See also Indiana B. & W. R. ague, 103 U. S. 760; Gilbaugh v. P. R. Co., 1 Hughes (U. S.), 410. First Nat. Bank v. Scott County, 77, the court held that the fact the plaintiff purchased the bonds d from their face that the interal years was overdue and una suspicious circumstance suffit the plaintiff on his guard. The c thus dishonored on their face. st, equally with the principal, was he debt which they were intended and it is not material whether or a part of the debt was overs. decision, however, is not reauthority.

of Aurora v. West, 7 Wall.

of Genoa v. Woodruff, 92 U. S. well v. Sac County, 96 U. S. 51; . Chesapeake, etc., Canal Co., 32 Amy v. Dubuque, 98 U. S. 471; v. Lee County, 3 Wall. (U. S.) eke v. City of Dubuque, 1 Wall. 5; Walnut v. Wade, 103 U. S. 3 Am. & Eng. R. R. Cas. 36; Commonwealth, 18 Gratt. (Va.) to Bowler, 107 U. S. 529; Koshlburton, 104 U. S. 668; Phelps 15 Blatch. (U. S.) 131; Gibert d Co., 33 Gratt. (Va.) 599; Hol v. City of Detroit, 3 McLean 2; City of Jeffersonville v. Pat-Ind. 18; North Pa. R. R. Co. v. Pa. St. 94; Welsh v. First Div., 25 Minn. 320; Forstall v. Lounters' Ass'n, 34 La. Ann. 770; R. Co. v. Elliott, 57 N. Y. 397; o. v. Armstrong, 6 Wright (Pa.), ton v. South Car. R. Co., 2 S. Car. 248; San Antonio v. Lane, 32 Tex. 405; Mills v. Town of Jefferson, 20 Wis. 54; Mayor, etc., of Nashville v. First Nat. Bank, 57 Tenn. 402; Connecticut, etc., Ins. Co. v. Cleveland, etc., R. Co., 41 Barb. (N. Y.) 9; Burrough v. Richmond Co., 65 N. Car. 234; McLendon v. Commissioners, 71 N. Car. 38; North Penn. R. R. Co. v. Adams, 54 Pa. St. 94; National Ex. Bank v. Hartford, etc., R. Co., 8 R. I. 375.

Where coupons have been lost, the owner, upon tendering indemnity, is entitled to recover the amount of them with interest from the date of demand and tender of indemnity. Fitchett v. North Pa. R. Co., 5 Phila. (Pa.) 132.

Interest upon the coupons of the Chesapeake & Ohio Canal Company was not allowed as against the State of Maryland, which, having a prior lien upon the property, waived it in favor of the bonds, "so as to make the said bonds, and the interest to accrue thereon, preferred and absolute liens," until the bonds and interest should be fully paid. This waiver was construed to extend only to the principal and interest of the bonds, so that interest on the overdue coupons could not be paid until the lien of the State had been satisfied. Corcoran v. Chesapeake & Ohio Canal Co., 1 McArthur (D. C.), 358.

Under an act providing that in all actions founded on contracts, whenever, in the prosecution thereof, any amount of money shall be liquidated or ascertained in favor of either party, it shall be lawful to receive and allow interest until payment thereof: interest may be recovered on interest-coupons of bonds from the day when they were due. Hollingsworth v. Detroit, 3 McL. (U. S.) 472.

3. Gelpeke v. City of Dubuque, 1 Wall. (U. S.) 175.

4. Koshkonong v. Burton, 14 Otto (U. S.), 668; s. c., 7 Am. & Eng. R. R. Cas. 203.

5. Town of Walnut v. Wade, 103 U. S.

bond be made payable on demand at a particular place, on default of payment could be averred without a compliance with the condition precedent of making demand; and consequently there can be no recovery of interest, except from the time of a demand.[1]

(*c*) *Rule as to Foreign Bondholders.*—A corporation is not bound to seek its creditors in a foreign country, and therefore it is not obliged to pay interest on overdue coupons to bondholders resident or absent in a foreign country, when payment has not been demanded, nor the inability or want of readiness to pay them, at the time and place they were made payable, proven.[2]

(*d*) *Abatement of Interest.*—If the corporation shows that it had money ready to pay the coupons at the time and place they were payable, this will be a defence to the claim for interest.[3] To make available a defence of readiness to pay the coupons at the time and place they were payable, it must be alleged; and inasmuch as such a plea is affirmative, it casts the burden of proof upon the defendant.[4]

(*e*) *Rate of Interest.*—The interest on bonds, after maturity, continues at the rate stipulated for in the bond;[5] but the interest on coupons, after their maturity, is allowed only at the legal rate.[6]

6. Coupons are secured by the Mortgage.—Coupons are a part of the mortgage debt, and the holder, upon a foreclosure of the mortgage, is entitled to share in the distribution *pro rata* with the holders of the remainder of the debt.[7] And if, by some condition

683; Gelpeke *v.* City of Dubuque, 1 Wall. (U. S.) 175; City of Aurora *v.* West, 7 Wall. (U. S.) 82; Town of Genoa *v.* Woodruff, 92 U. S. 502; Ohio *v.* Frank, 103 U. S. 697; North Penna. R. Co. *v.* Adams, 54 Pa. St. 97; Langston *v.* South Car. R. Co., 2 S. Car. N. S. 248; City of Jeffersonville *v.* Patterson, 26 Ind. 16; Mills *v.* Jefferson, 20 Wis. 54; Pennsylvania R. R. Co. *v.* Adams, 54 Pa. St. 97; Burroughs *v.* Richmond County, 65 N. Car. 234. *Compare* Whitaker *v.* Hartford, etc., R. Co., 8 R. I. 47; City of Pekin *v.* Reynolds, 31 Ill. 531; Chicago *v.* People, 56 Ill. 327; Johnson *v.* Stark Co., 24 Ill. 75; Alexander *v.* Commissioners, 67 N. Car. 198; McLendon *v.* Comm'rs, 71 N. Car. 38; Corcoran *v.* Chesapeake, etc., Canal Co., 1 McArthur (D. C.), 538.

1. Jones on Ry. Securities, § 332; Aurora City *v.* West, 7 Wall. (U. S.) 82; Gelpeke *v.* City of Dubuque, 1 Wall. (U. S.) 175; Corcoran *v.* Chesapeake & Ohio Canal Co., 1 McArthur (D. C.), 358; Whitaker *v.* Hartford, etc., R. Co., 8 R. I. 47.

2. Emlen *v.* Lehigh, etc., Coal Co., 47 Pa. St. 76.

3. Walnut *v.* Wade, 103 U. S. 683; s. c., 3 Am. & Eng. R. R. Cas. 36; North Pennsylvania R. Co. *v.* Adams, 54 Pa. St. 94; Mayor, etc., of Nashville *v.* First National Bank, 57 Tenn. 402.

It is not necessary to escape, after tendering interest, that the amount of the loan, with accumulated interest at the time of the payment, should be kept separate from the other funds of the company, if it can be shown that funds sufficient for the payment were at all times on hand. Emlen *v.* Lehigh Coal Co., 47 Pa. St. 76.

4. North Pennsylvania R. Co. *v.* Adams, 54 Pa. St. 94; Jones on Railroad Sec. § [illegible].

5. Ohio *v.* Frank, 103 U. S. 697.

6. Cromwell *v.* County of Sac, 96 U. S. 51; Langston *v.* South Car. R. Co., 2 S. Car. (N. S.) 248; Spencer *v.* Pierce, 5 R. I. 63.

7. Miller *v.* Rutland & Washington R. Co., 40 Vt. 399; Haven *v.* Grand Junc. R. & D. Co., 109 Mass. 88; County of Beaver *v.* Armstrong, 44 Pa. St. 63; Union Trust Co. *v.* Monticello, etc., R. Co., [illegible].

Where a railroad company, not having been able to pay the interest on its bonds, gave to the holders of the interest coupons the coupon bonds of the company for the amount of said interest, *held*, that this was not a novation of the debt for the interest; that the coupons bore interest from the time they were payable, and the bonds for which they were exchanged are secured by the mortgage. Gilbert *v.* Washington City, etc., R. Co., 33 Gratt. (Va.) 586; s. c., 1 Am. & Eng. R. R. Cas. 473.

in the mortgage, the bonds become prematurely due, the holder is entitled to recover the amount of subsequently maturing coupons.[1]

As against bondholders who have presented their coupons for payment, and not for sale, and who had the right to assume that they were paid and extinguished, a person who advances the money to take them up under an undisclosed agreement with the company, that the coupons should be delivered to him uncancelled as security for his advances, is not entitled to an equal priority in the lien, or the proceeds of the mortgage by which the coupons are secured.[2]

But as against the corporation who issued the bonds, the coupons so delivered up are valid securities in the hands of the

1. A railroad company issued bonds for the payment to bearer, of money with interest, coupon in the usual form being attached. Before the time fixed for the payment of the principal in the bonds, they became due at once, under a condition contained in the mortgage securing the bonds. In an action upon interest coupons for a time subsequent to the bonds thus becoming due, *held*, that the holder of such coupons is entitled to recover the amount of them, the damages allowed by law for default in payment of the principal being at the same rate as the stipulated interest. Welsh v. First Div., etc., R. Co., 25 Minn. 314.

2. Cameron v. Tome, 24 Am. & Eng. R. R. Cas. 203; Union Trust Co. of New York v. Monticello, etc., R. Co., 63 N. Y. 311; Virginia v. Chesapeake & Ohio Canal Co., 32 Md. 501; Harbeck v. Vanderbilt, 20 N. Y. 398; Robinson v. Leavitt, 7 N. H. 100; James v. Johnson, 6 Johns. Ch. (N.Y.) 423.

There is, however, no presumption that the coupons have been paid and cancelled, when the transaction on its face is a transfer rather than a payment. In Ketchem v. Duncan, 96 U. S. 659, it was *held* that where a corporation which had previously paid its coupons at its own office directed the holders to take the coupons to a bank where they would receive payment, and the holders there received the amounts due on the coupons, and left them in possession of the bank, they might properly presume that the company was not paying the coupons; that inasmuch as the holders of the coupons received from the corporation no checks upon the bank, they must have known that the bank had no vouchers for its payments unless the coupons continued in force after the bank received them; and hence it is regarded as a fair presumption, that, when they delivered the possession, they assented to a transfer of ownership. Mr. *Justice Strong*, in delivering the opinion of the court, said, "It is within common knowledge that interest coupons, alike those that are not due and those that are due, are passed from hand to hand, the receiver paying the amount they call for without any intention on his part to extinguish them, and without any belief in the other party, that they are extinguished by the transaction. In such a case the holder intends to transfer his title, not to extinguish the debt. In multitudes of cases, coupons are transferred by persons who are not the owners of the bonds from which they have been detached. To hold that in all these cases the coupons are paid and extinguished, and not transferred or assigned, unless there was something more to show an assent of the person parting with the possession that they should remain alive and be available in the hands of the person to whom they were delivered, would, we think, be inconsistent with the common understanding of business men."

In Haven v. Grand Junction R. Co., 109 Mass. 88, such a course was adopted; and the belief thereby created, that the company was able to pay, and did pay, the coupons at maturity, was held and acted on by another corporation in subsequent purchases of the bonds from individual holders of them; but these purchases were made at or below the par value of the bonds and accrued interest, and were not made till between eight and nine years afterwards, and then with a view to acquire title to lands which constituted the mortgaged security, and which this corporation had voted to buy. *Held*, that after a judicial sale of the lands, upon foreclosure of the mortgage the person who advanced the money was not estopped to maintain a claim for the amount of the coupons paid by him, with interest from the date of payment, against a surplus of the proceeds of the sale remaining after full satisfaction of the claims of all the other creditors.

holder; and a mortgage upon the corporate property given to pay the bonds, may be enforced for his benefit.[1]

While the coupons are entitled to be paid out of the proceeds of the mortgage, they have no equity superior to that of the bonds from which they were taken, and the coupon holder is entitled to no priority over the holder of the bond, in a final distribution of the proceeds of the whole mortgaged property.[2]

7. Order of Payment of Coupons. — All coupon holders are on the same level, and the mortgage secures no priority to the coupons past due, nor to those first due.[3]

8. Action upon Coupons. — (*a*) *Form of Action.* — Where coupons containing a promise to pay are not under seal, assumpsit is a proper remedy, though not the only one; debt will lie.[4]

(*b*) *By Whom to be brought.* — Coupons payable to holder or bearer, and therefore being negotiable instruments, may be sued upon by the holder in his own name;[5] but, without some statu-

1. Union Trust Co. *v.* Monticello, etc., R. Co., 63 N. Y. 311.

2. Sewall *v.* Brainard, 38 Vt. 364; Miller *v.* Rutland, etc., R. Co., 40 Vt. 399.

In Ketchum *v.* Duncan, 96 U. S. 659, *Strong, J.*, says, "The mortgage was given as a security for the principal of the bonds as well as the interest, with no priority to either. The coupons are mere representatives of the claim for interest. The obligation of the debtor evidenced by them cannot be higher, or entitled to greater privileges, than it would be, had the bonds in their body undertaken the payment of the interest. Cutting them from the several bonds of which they were a part, and transferring them to other holders, can give them no increased equities, so far as we can perceive. Had they been assigned with a guaranty of payment, it may well be they would be entitled to payment before the assignors could claim the fund. Then they might have an equity to prior payment, growing out of the guaranty. But there was no such undertaking of the assignors in this case."

Where a railroad company issued bonds, with coupons for interest attached, which were guaranteed by the State, and, to secure the payment thereof, gave to the State a statutory lien on all the franchises, rights, and property of the company; and the company afterwards failed to pay the coupons, and became insolvent; and before the bonds became due the statutory lien or mortgage was foreclosed in an action by the State, and all the rights, franchises, and property of the company were sold, — *held*, that the holders of the coupons past due at the time of the sale were not entitled to priority of payment over the owners of the principal debt, which was not then due, but that such proceeds were distributable, *pari passu*, between the holders of the coupons past due and the owners of the bonds. State *v.* [illegible] R. Co., 8 S. Car. 129.

In Dunham *v.* Cincinnati, P. & C. R. Co., 1 Wall. (U. S.) 254, it was *held* that a decree of the circuit court which gives precedence to the past due coupons over the principal of the bonds is erroneous, where the terms of the mortgage are that in case of default in the payment of interest or principal, and a sale to [illegible] the same, all bonds and the interest accrued thereon shall be equally due and payable, and entitled to a *pro rata* dividend of the proceeds of said sale or other proceedings.

3. Ketchum *v.* Duncan, 96 U. S. 659; Sewall *v.* Brainard, 38 Vt. 364.

4. First Nat. Bank *v.* Town of Bennington, 16 Blatchf. (U. S.) 53. Compare New London, etc., Bank *v.* Ware River R. Co., 41 Conn. 542.

Coupons attached to county bonds are admissible in evidence under the appropriate money counts. Mercer Co. *v.* Hubbard, 45 Ill. 139; Johnson *v.* Stark, 24 Ill. 75.

Where a declaration set out in a single count eight interest coupons of thirty dollars each, distinguished from each other by a reference to the numbers of the bonds to which they severally belonged, *held*, that the count was not bad for duplicity; that the coupons, though severally below the jurisdiction of the court, could be thus aggregated, and the case brought within the jurisdiction; and that no profert of the bonds was necessary. New London, etc., Bank *v.* Ware River R. Co., 41 Conn. 542. See ACTION ON MUNICIPAL BONDS, *infra*.

5. Johnson *v.* County of Stark, 24 Ill. 75; Carr *v.* Le Fevre, 27 Pa. St. 413.

[illegible], no action can be maintained in the name of an assignee upon coupons which contain no negotiable words, nor language from which it can be inferred that it was the design of the corporation issuing them to treat them as negotiable paper. Such coupons can be enforced only in the name of the bondholder.[1]

([illegible]) *Enforcement of Coupon as an Independent Security.*—An interest warrant which does not import a promise, but is a mere acknowledgment of indebtedness for interest on the bond itself, cannot be made the ground of an action. The holder's right to interest is founded on the bond alone, which must be specially declared upon.[2]

([illegible]) *Connection between Bond and Coupon.*—The holder of coupons which refer to the bonds to which they belong, is chargeable with notice of all the bonds contain.[3] In contemplation of law a detached coupon is still a part of the bond, and the holder is bound by all the covenants contained therein.[4]

([illegible]) *Production of Bond.*—As coupons or warrants for interest are drawn and executed in a form and mode for the very purpose of separating them from the bond, and thereby dispensing with the necessity of its production at the time of the accruing of each instalment of interest, a suit may be maintained upon the coupons without the production of the bonds to which they had been attached.[5]

([illegible]) *Effect of Mortgage Conditions.*—When, by the terms of the mortgage, the coupons are payable from the net revenues of the company, in a suit upon them, it is necessary to allege and prove the existence of such revenues before there can be any recovery. Unless revenue comes into the treasury of the company, the bondholders cannot claim its appropriation to the payment of the coupons. A demand for payment when, without the company's fault, there are no revenues on hand to meet the coupons, is premature, and properly refused; therefore, in such case, interest

1. [illegible] v. York, etc., R. Co., 48 Me. [illegible]; [illegible] v. Brainard, 38 Vt. 364; Wright v. [illegible], etc., R. Co., 1 Dis. (Ohio) 465.

2. [illegible] v. New London, etc., R. Co., 26 Conn. [illegible]; Jackson v. York, etc., R. Co., [illegible] Me. [illegible]; s. c., 2 Am. Law Reg. N. S. [illegible].

Mr. [illegible], in his work on negotiable instruments, criticises these decisions, quoting from a note to the latter case by Judge Redfield in the Amer. Law Register, and citing the case of Virg. & Tenn. R. Co. v. Clay. (Va. Special Court of Appeals, unreported.)

In Mayor, etc., of Nashville v. Potomac Ins. Co., 58 Tenn. 296, the coupons were held to be valid obligations against the city that issued them, although they contained no promise of payment, and that profert of the bonds was not necessary when the stipulations of the bonds were set forth in the declaration.

3. McClure v. Township of Oxford, 4 Otto (U. S.), 429.

4. State v. Spartansburg, etc., R. Co., 8 S. Car. 129.

5. Commissioners of Knox Co. v. Aspinwall, 21 How. (U. S.) 539; Thompson v. County of Lee, 3 Wall. (U. S.) 327; National Exchange Bank v. Hartford, etc., R. Co., 8 R. I. 375; County of Beaver v. Armstrong, 44 Pa. St. 63; Mayor, etc., v. Potomac Ins. Co., 58 Tenn. 296; Walnut v. Wade, 103 U. S. 695; s. c., 3 Am. & Eng. R. R. Cas. 36; Welsh v. First Div., etc., R. Co., 25 Minn. 320; Cicero v. Clifford, 53 Ind. 191; Kennard v. Cass Co., 3 Dill. (U. S.) 147; First Nat. Bank v. Mount Tabor, 52 Vt. 87; Beaver v. Armstrong, 44 Pa. St. 63; Arents v. Commonwealth, 18 Gratt. (Va.) 767.

is not recoverable upon the coupons from the time of such demand, but only from a demand when there are such revenues and an unjust refusal.[1]

(*g*) *Jurisdiction of United States Courts.*—The holder of a coupon payable to bearer is not an assignee, and he may sue in the federal courts without reference to the citizenship of antecedent holders.[2] But interest coupons cannot be sued upon in a federal court, where the municipal bonds to which they are attached, under the seal of the corporation, are made payable to a railroad company in the same State; and the coupons contain no obligation in themselves, but refer to the bonds for their vitality, the plaintiff being an assignee of the railroad company, and his assignor being unable, on account of its citizenship, to sue in a federal court.[3] The amount of the interest determines the jurisdiction without regard to the face value of the bonds.[4] The sum of the amounts of the coupons sued upon also determines the jurisdiction.[5]

(*h*) *Statute of Limitations.*—It is well-settled law that a suit upon a coupon is not barred by the statute of limitations, unless the lapse of time is sufficient to bar also a suit upon the bond.[6] The statute begins to run against detached coupons from their respective maturities, though it does not begin to run against the bond until its own maturity;[7] and where the bonds are not barred by the statute of limitations, the coupons are not.[8]

(*i*) *Holder's Negligence in collecting.*—Where the holders of municipal bond coupons could, with reasonable diligence, have collected their amount, one who transferred the coupons to him

1 Jones on Railroad Securities, citing Corcoran v. Chesapeake & O. Canal Co., 1 McArthur (D. C.), 358.

2 Cooper v. Town of Thompson, 13 Blatch. (U. S.) 434; Pettit v. Town of Hope, 18 Blatch. (U. S.) 180, McCoy v. Washington County, 3 Wall Jr (U S) 381; Rich v. Seneca Falls, 19 Blatch (U. S) 558; Thompson v. Perrine, 16 Otto (U. S.), 589.

3 Clarke v. Janesville, 1 Biss. (U S.) 98.

4 Bruch v. Manchester & R. R. Co. (U S. S. Ct) 25 Am & Eng R. R. Cas -6

5. Smith v. Clarke Co., 54 Mo. 58.

6 City of Lexington v. Butler, 14 Wall (U. S.) 282.

Clifford, J., said, "The coupon, if in the usual form, is but a repetition of the contract in respect to the interest for the period of time therein mentioned, which the bond makes upon the same subject, being given for interest thereafter to become due upon the bond, which interest is a parcel of the bond, and partakes of its nature, and is not barred by lapse of time, except for the same period as would bar a suit upon the bond to which it was attached." City of Kenosha v. Lamson, 9 Wall. (U. S.) 477.

7 Clark v. Iowa City, 20 Wall. (U. S.) 583.

It was attempted in this case to [illegible] the above two decisions as [illegible] the effect that the coupons [illegible] and existing cause of action, not only for the period prescribed for actions on the bond after its maturity, but for the additional period intervening between the maturity of the coupon and the maturity of the bond, however great this might be. But the court *held* that the whole purport of the decisions in those cases was to the effect that the coupons, being given for interest on the bonds, partook of their nature, and were equally high as security, and, therefore, the statute could only run against them when it would run against instruments of the dignity of bonds. See also Amy v. Dubuque, 98 U. S. 470; Town of Koshkonong v. Burton, 104 U. S. 668; s. c. 7 Am. & Eng. R. R. Cas. [illegible]. *Compare* Meyer v. Porter, 1 W. C. Rep. (Cal.) 874.

8. Meyer v. Porter, 2 Pac. Rep. (Cal.) 884. Roeding v. Porter, 2 Pac. Rep. (Cal.) 888.

held liable after the bonds have been declared invalid
eding *in quo warranto* by the State.[1]
ion on Municipal Coupons. — In an action on interest
which had been attached to negotiable bonds issued by
a declaration which does not allege either the tenor
of the bonds, or the authority for their issue, and with
copy of a bond is filed, and none set out therein, is
le. The plaintiff must allege the general authority to
bonds, and show that the bonds sued on were issued for
oses authorized, since a municipal corporation has no
ssue bonds except it is given by the legislature, and then
uch purposes as the legislature authorizes.[2]

E. (See BOUNDARIES.) — Direction of motion;[3] stated
rly method of proceeding; usual manner.[4]

. Hill, 16 N. W. Rep. (Iowa)

v. Town of Covington, 8 Fed.
on v. New Providence, 47 N.
Thayer v. Montgomery Co., 3
389. *Compare* Ring v. John-
wa, 265.
In Kennard v. Cass County,
S.) 147, it was *held* that the
nay aver the authority of the
ue the bonds, either by a dis-
t of the special act conferring
, or by stating the recital of
that respect. But a declara-
oes not show the authority is

n action on coupons to county
ing that the plaintiff was not
etc., of the bonds and coupons
l in the declaration," was held
ral demurrer, though faulty in
like ruling was made as to a
action averring that the cou-
were the property of a third
not the property of the plain-
on Co. v. Amy, 13 Wall. (U.S.)

n action on coupons of county
he "county did not sign, seal,
e bonds as in the declaration
authorize any one to do so,
efendant says the alleged acts
are not its acts and deeds,"
d on general demurrer. Pen-
Amy, 13 Wall. (U. S.) 297.
be no objection to the admis-
ence of bonds and coupons in
n, when the execution of the
in issue, this fact being in sub-
d on the part of the plaintiff,
ied on oath by the defendant
required by local law. Cham-
Clews, 21 Wall. (U. S.) 317.
uments in the suit should be
the face of the declaration by the number of the bond, date, sum, and time of payment. Kennard v. Cass Co., 3 Dill. (U. S.) 147.

3. Webster.

The "course of a river" is a line parallel with its banks, and may vary in direction from the current. Atty.-Genl. v. Railroad Co., 1 Stock. Ch. (N. J.) 550.

4. Webster.

Course of Business or Trade. — See BILLS AND NOTES.

Under a provision in a bankrupt act that any creditor, by and in respect of any bill or bills of exchange really and *bona fide* drawn, negotiated or accepted by the bankrupt in the usual and ordinary course of trade or dealing, or who received money in the usual and ordinary course of trade before the suing out of the commission, should not be liable to repay the same to the assignees, it was *held* that the payment of a bill of exchange upon which time had been given on the allowance of interest, was not in the ordinary course of trade; the transaction was a loan of money at interest. Vernon v. Hall, 2 T. R. 648. So a note reserving interest half-yearly might, for aught that appears, be to secure a loan of money, and cannot be said by the court to be drawn in the usual and ordinary course of business. Harwood v. Lomas, 11 East, 127.

For a retail merchant in a small country town to sell his entire stock to one or more persons, is out of his usual and ordinary course of business, within the meaning of that portion of sect. 35 of the Bankrupt Act of 1867, by which it is enacted, that if one insolvent or in contemplation of insolvency makes a sale not in the usual and ordinary course of his business, that fact shall be *prima facie* evidence of fraud. Walbron v. Babbitt, 16 Wall. (U. S.) 577.

A statute exempting from distress prop-

COURTESY — COURT-HOUSE — COURT-MARTIAL.

COURTESY. — See CURTESY.

COURT-HOUSE. — A building occupied and appropriated for the holding of courts.[1]

COURT-MARTIAL. — See MILITARY LAW.

erty deposited with a tavern-keeper "in the usual course of business," only includes property deposited by a guest for safe keeping. Harris v. Boggs, 5 Blackf. (Ind.) 489.

Carriages belonging to a circus, and used for carrying the band and performers in a street parade, are not carriages "used solely for the conveyance of any goods or burden in the course of trade" so as to exempt them from a duty on carriages under an act making such an exception. Speak v. Powell, L. R. 9 Ex. 25.

Due Course of Law. — See CONSTITUTIONAL LAW, COLLECT and its compounds.

A discharge from the prison rules fraudulently obtained by one imprisoned under an insolvent act, is a discharge by due course of law within the terms of a bond given by him not to depart from the prison rules or bounds till he should be discharged in due course of law, or should pay the debt for which he was imprisoned. Simms v. Slacum, 3 Cranch (U. S.), 300.

In an action of covenant on a warranty to recover back purchase-money, an allegation that the plaintiff was "ousted and dispossessed of the premises by due course of law" was *held* not to be sustained by proof of a constructive eviction by the purchase by the plaintiff of a paramount title hostilely asserted by the party holding it. "The words 'by due course of law' are synonymous with 'due process of law' or 'law of the land,' and the general definition thereof is 'law in its regular course of administration through the courts of justice;' and, while not always necessarily confined to judicial proceedings (as, for instance, the collection of taxes is held to be within the phrase 'by due process of law'), yet these words have such a signification when used to designate the kind of eviction or ouster from real estate by which a party is dispossessed as to preclude thereunder proof of a constructive eviction." Kansas P. R. Co. v. Dunmeyer, 19 Kan. 539.

Course of an Action. — In a statute providing that when, "in the course of any civil action or proceeding whatever," it is made to appear to the court that the defendant is in the military service of the United States or of the State, the action or proceeding shall be stricken from the calendar, "course" signifies "progressive action — in a suit or proceeding not yet determined," and the act is not applicable where the rights of the defendant have been fixed by final judgment before the enlistment. Williams v. [illegible]

Course of the Trial. — After an issue of fact joined in a criminal case, every step thereafter taken for the purpose of a determination of that issue in the court where the cause is pending, up to and including the verdict upon such issue, must be regarded as a step or proceeding 'arising during the course of the trial' within an act regulating motions for new trials. The misconduct of a juror between the time when sworn and examined on his voir dire, and the rendering of the verdict, is within the above expression, and is ground for a motion for a new trial. People v. Turner, 39 Cal. 371.

1. Where the "door of the court-house" is named in a deed of trust as the place at which the sale of the property, when sold, must be held, the provision is sufficiently complied with by a sale at the door of a building temporarily occupied and appropriated for the holding of the courts, while the court-house proper was undergoing repairs. "The object of such deeds . . . is to secure a sale at a public place; and when a court-house is mentioned, it is obviously designed to designate the building where courts are held, and where the people attending such courts are supposed to congregate." Hambright v. Brockman, 59 Mo. 52. And where the provision was that the sale should be "at the north door of the court-house," the sale might properly be held at the north door of a building occupied as a court-house, the court-house proper having been burned down. Alden v. Goldie, 82 Ill. 581. Or where the destruction of the court-house by fire was partial only, the sale might take place at the ruins of the north door, or at the place where the north door had stood. Waller v. Arnold, 71 Ill. 350. In this case it was also said that if the old court-house were entirely demolished, and a new one erected, a sale at the north door of the new edifice would be valid.

Similar are the decisions in reference to judicial sales required by statute in some of the States to be held at the court-house door. Such sales made at the door of a church, at the time occupied by the courts, because the court-house was occupied by troops of the United States, are not invalid. "The obvious meaning of the execution law is to require sales at the door of the building occupied and used as a court-house." Hane v. McCown, 55 Mo. 181.

Where the court-house had been burned

[illegible] — See also Appeal; Attorney and Client; [illegible] Jurisdiction; Jury; Practice; Sheriffs; Writ of

[illegible] — A court is a body in the government, organized [for the] public administration of justice at the time and place pre[scribed] by law.[1]

[Composition]. — A court is composed of a judge,[2] or judges,

[illegible] the courts were held in a school-[house on] private property, and the clerk's [office in] a rented room in another build[ing. The sher]iff, on sale-day, went to the [illegible] burned court-house, and, the sun [being hot,] adjourned the sale to a grove a [hundred and] fifty yards distant, on county [land, and th]ere conducted it. The sales [were held] to be valid, the statute having [been subst]antially complied with. Long[illegible] Featherston, 65 Ga. 165.

[illegible] v. Hobart, 45 Iowa, 501.

[A court] is a place where justice is judi[cially adm]inistered. Co. Litt. 58 a.; 3 [Black]st. Com. 23.

[It has] been defined as the presence [of a suffic]ient number of the members of a [body in] government, to which the pub[lic admin]istration of justice is delegated, [regularly] convened in an authorized place [at an app]ointed time, engaged in the full [and regul]ar performance of its functions. [Bouvier's] Law Dict.; Wightman v. Karsner, [illegible]; Brumley v. The State, 20 Ark.

[The ter]m court is also used for the judge, [or judges] themselves, when duly convened. "[A sessi]on of the judges so sitting for [the admi]nistration of justice." Finch's [illegible] ch. 1; Burrill's Law Dict.; [illegible] Central R. R. Co. v. North In[diana] R. R. Co., 5 Ind. 239; McClure v. [illegible], 33 Mo. 273.

[The ter]m court, in a statute, may be con[strued to] mean the judges of the court, or [to mean] the judges and jury, according [to the] connection and object of its use. [Regard m]ust be had, for the purpose of de[termining] the form of trial where there is [no] legislative provision, other than the use of the general term, to the nature of the question submitted to the court, and the mode previously in use, of determining similar questions. Gold v. Vt. Cent. R. R. Co., 19 Vt. 478.

A statute passed in pursuance of a treaty stipulation to receive and adjust claims, authorizing certain judges to do so on *ex parte* applications, and to transmit the evidence and the decision to the executive department, does not create a court or judicial tribunal; but the judges act as commissioners, and their decisions are not appealable. United States v. Ferreira, 13 How. (U. S.) 40. See also Jecker v. Montgomery, 13 How. (U. S.) 498, and Porte v. United States, Dev. 59 (Court of Claims); *In re* Petition of Pacific Railway Commission, Am. Law Reg. Oct. 1887, 681.

In Glass v. The Betsy, 3 Dallas (U. S.), 6, it was *held* that no foreign power could, of right, institute or erect any court of judicature within the jurisdiction of the United States, except such as were warranted by treaties, and that consequently the admiralty jurisdiction exercised in the United States by French consuls was not of right.

2. In *England* the judges are appointed by the crown. In the United States the federal judges are appointed by the President, by and with the advice and consent of the Senate. In most of the States the judges of the State courts are elected, but in some they are appointed by the governor. A judge having any pecuniary interest in a case on trial is thereby incapacitated for sitting in the cause. This is the case, both by common law and the statutes of most of the States. Ochus v. Sheldon, 12 Fla. 138; Buckingham v. Davis, 9 Md. 324; Pearce

and subordinate officers. Courts of law usually have juries to decide questions of fact.

v. Atwood, 13 Mass. 340; Commonwealth v. Ryan, 5 Mass. 90; Hill v. Wells, 6 Pick. (Mass.) 109; Knight v. Hardeman, 17 Ga. 253; Gregory v. C. C. & C. R. R., 4 Ohio St. 675; Trustees' Fund v. Bailey, 10 Fla. 213; Bank of North America v. Fitzsimmons, 2 Binn. (Pa.) 454.

When the lord chancellor, who was a shareholder in a company in whose favor the vice-chancellor had made a decree, affirmed this decree, the House of Lords reversed the decree on the ground of interest. Dimes v. Grand Junction Canal, 3 H. L. C. 759.

In the above case Lord Campbell said, "It is of the last importance that the maxim that 'no man is to be a judge in his own case,' should be held sacred. And that it is not to be confined to a cause in which he is a party, but applies to a cause in which he has an interest. . . . We have again and again set aside proceedings in inferior tribunals because an individual who had an interest in a cause took a part in the decision. And it will have a most salutary effect on these tribunals, when it is known that this high court of last resort, in a case in which the Lord Chancellor of England had an interest, considered that this decree was on that account a decree not according to law, and was set aside. This will be a lesson to all inferior tribunals to take care, not only that in their decrees they are not influenced by their personal interest, but to avoid the appearance of laboring under such an influence."

It is a question whether the legislatures of the American States can by express enactment permit one to act judicially when interested in the controversy. The maxim of the common law, it is said, in some cases, does not apply where, from necessity, the judge must proceed in the case, there being no other tribunal authorized to act. Ranger v. Great Western R., 5 House of Lords Cases, 72; Stuart v. Mechanics and Farmers' Bank, 19 Johns. (N. Y.) 496.

In *New York*, however, it was *held* that in such a case it belongs to the power which created such a court to provide another in which an interested judge may be a party; and whether another tribunal is established or not, he at least is not intrusted with authority to determine his own rights, or his own wrongs. Washington Ins. Co. v. Price, Hopk. ch. 1.

The rule laid down in the above case meets the approval of Judge Cooley, who says (Const. Lim. 510), "We do not see how the legislature can have any power to abolish a maxim which is among the fundamentals of judicial authority. The people of the State, when [illegible], may possibly [illegible] anomaly, if they see fit; but, if the legislature is intrusted with [illegible] providing for the [illegible] power, we cannot [illegible] authorized, in the [illegible] to do that which has [illegible] as being within the [illegible] authority. To [illegible] controversy to decide it [illegible] within the [illegible] not the [illegible] or decision, but is a [illegible] party, so far as that [illegible] is concerned, out of the [illegible] the law, and submitting him to the control of one whose interest it will be to decide arbitrarily and unjustly." Ames v. Port Huron Log Driving and Booming Co., 11 Mich. 139; Hall v. Thayer, 105 Mass. 219; State v. Crane, 36 N. J. L. 394; Cypress Pond Draining Co. v. Hooper, 2 Met. (Ky.) 350; Scuffletown Fence Co. v. McAllister, 12 Bush (Ky.), 312; Reams v. Kearns, 5 Cold. (Tenn.) 217; Lanfear v. Mayor, 4 La. 97; s. c., 23 Am. Dec. 477.

An objection of interest will avail in an appellate court. Richardson v. Welcome, 6 Cush. (Mass.) 331; Sigourney v. Sibley, 21 Pick. (Mass.) 101; Oakley v. Aspinwall, 3 N. Y. 547.

If one of the judges constituting a court is disqualified on this ground, the judgment will be void, even though the proper number may have concurred in the result, not reckoning the interested party. Queen v. Justices of Hertfordshire, 6 Q. B. 753; Queen v. Justices of Suffolk, 18 Q. B. 416; Queen v. Justices of London, 18 Q. B. 421; Peninsula R. R. Co. v. Howard, 20 Mich. 18.

Mere formal acts necessary to enable the case to be brought before a proper tribunal, for adjudication, an interested judge may do; but that is the extent of his power. Cooley, Const. Lim. 511; Richardson v. Boston, 1 Curtis (C. C.), 250; Washington Ins. Co. v. Price, Hopk. Ch. 1; Buckingham v. Davis, 9 Md. 324; Heydenfeldt v. Towns, 27 Ala. 423.

For the general subject of interest, see also Pearce v. Atwood, 13 Mass. 324; Peck v. Freeholders of Essex, 20 N. J. L. 457; Commonwealth v. McLane, 4 Gray (Mass.), 427; Dively v. Cedar Falls, 21 Iowa, 565; Clark v. Lamb, 2 Allen (Mass.), 396; Stockwell v. White Lake, 22 Mich. 341; Petition of New Boston, 49 N. H. 328; Re Ryers, 72 N. Y. 1; Bedell v. Bailey, 58 N. H. 62.

It has been *held* that where the interest

at of a corporator in a municipal ation, the legislature might provide should constitute no disqualification the corporation was a party. But ound of this ruling appears to be, e interest is so remote, trifling, and ficant, that it may fairly be supposed ncapable of affecting the judgment, influencing the conduct, of an indi- Commonwealth v. Reed, 1 Gray), 472; Justices v. Fennimore, 1 N. 90; Commissioners v. Little, 3 Ohio, ooley's Const. Lim. 509.

re penalties are imposed, to be re- l only in a municipal court, the or jurors in which would be in- d as corporators in the recovery, providing such recovery must be ed as precluding the objection of . Commonwealth v. Ryan, 5 Mass. ill v. Wells, 6 Pick. (Mass.) 104; onwealth v. Emery, 11 Cush. (Mass.)

decision of a judge holding himself lified by interest from sitting in a ill not be reversed unless there is st error. Childress v. Grim, 57 .

a judge is related to the parties, squalified to sit in the case. De La v. Burton, 23 Cal. 592; People v. Guerra, 24 Cal. 73; Kelly v. Hockett, 299; Sanborn v. Fellows, 22 N. H. ayard v. McLane, 3 Harr. (Del.) 139; ork & New Haven R. R. Co. v. er, 28 How. (N. Y.) Pr. 187; Gill v. 61 Ala. 169.

no objection to the qualification of esiding judge to enter up a decree court above that his wife is a daugh- the sister of the whole blood of the wife of one of the defendants below, the defendant is but a trustee, and interest in the controversy. Fowler , 16 Ark. 296.

re the judge of probate was uncle to sband of one of the devisees and -law of the estate in settlement, he t disqualified to act as judge in the ent of the estate. Nettleton v. on, 17 Conn. 542; Fort v. West, 53 .

sband of a judge's wife's sister is ated by consanguinity or affinity to ge so as to render the latter incom- to hear the case. Hume v. Com- Bank, 10 Lea (Tenn.), 1; s. c., 43 p. 290.

dgment is not void because the judge lated in equal degree to both the , especially when neither objected, re has been five years' acquiescence. . Senquefield, 73 Ga. 48; Russell v. r, 76 Me. 501; Re Dodge & Steven- anufacturing Co., 77 N. Y. 101; Gill , 61 Ala. 169.

Unless the attention of a judge is called to the fact that he is disqualified to sit by reason of relationship to one of the parties, an objection on this account is waived. Pettigrew v. Washington Co., 43 Ark. 33.

It is said in Bacon's abridgment, that it is discretionary with a judge whether he will sit in a cause in which he has been counsel. It is customary to refuse to sit in such a case. Commonwealth v. Child, 10 Pick. (Mass.) 252; Owings v. Gibson, 2 Marsh. (Ky.) 516; Jewitt v. Miller, 12 Iowa, 85; Moon v. Stevens, 53 Mich. 144; Joyce v. Whitney, 57 Ind. 550.

It was *held* in *Tennessee*, that, where the judge who rendered the judgment in the case had been counsel in it, the judgment was a nullity. Reams v. Kearns, 5 Cold. (Tenn.) 217.

In *California* it was *held* that a judge is not disqualified from sitting at the trial of a cause, because, before his election to the bench, he had been attorney for one of the parties in another action involving one of the issues in the case on trial. Cleghorn v. Cleghorn, 66 Cal. 309. See also McMillan v. Nichols, 62 Ga. 36; Kean v. Lathrop, 58 Ga. 355.

In *England* it was *held* that a counsel in a cause, being afterwards raised to the bench, is not thereby precluded from taking part in the hearing and discussion of that case; but he may properly (unless his doing so would entail great inconvenience and expense on the parties, or perhaps from his being, as in chancery, the sole judge of the court, amount to a denial of justice) decline to take part in such hearing and decision. Thellusson v. Rendlesham, 7 H. L. Cases, 429.

Legal disqualification of a judge may result from sickness, as well as from interest and relationship. State v. Blair, 53 Vt. 24.

No action lies against a judge or magistrate for an erroneous judicial opinion or act in a case of which he has jurisdiction. Mostyn v. Fabrigas, Cowp. 172; Fray v. Blackburn, 3 B. & S. 576; Ward v. Freeman, 2 Ir. C. L. R. 460; Taafe v. Downes, 3 Moore, P. C. C. 36; Kemp v. Neville, 10 C. B. N. S. 523; Holden v. Smith, 14 Q. B. 841; Brodie v. Rutledge, 2 Bay (S. C.), 69; Ambler v. Church, 1 Root (Conn.), 211; Phelps v. Sill, 1 Day (Conn.), 315; Moor v. Ames, 3 Cai. (N. Y.) 170; Young v. Herbert, 2 Nott & M. (S. Car.) 172; Yates v. Lansing, 5 Johns. (N. Y.) 282, 9 Johns. (N. Y.) 395; Vanderheyden v. Young, 11 Johns. (N. Y.) 150; Ely v. Thompson, 3 A. K. Marsh. (Ky.) 70; Little v. Moore, 4 N. J. Law, 74; Tracy v. Williams, 4 Conn. 113; Tompkins v. Sands, 8 Wend. (N. Y.) 462; Evans v. Foster, 1 N. H. 374; Lining v. Bentham, 2 Bay (S. Car.), 1; Burnham v. Stevens, 33 N. H. 247; Ross v. Ritten-

The officers[1] of a court subordinate to the judge are a ing officer, variously known as clerk,[2] prothonotary, or re attorneys,[3] counsellors, solicitors, or barristers; and mir officers, as sheriffs,[4] constables, bailiffs, criers,[5] and tipstav

2. Rules of Court. — Every court of record has an inherent irrespective of statute, to make rules for the transaction an lation of its business.[7] Such rules, however, must not

house, 2 Dall. (U. S.) 160; Reid v. Hood, 2 Nott & M. (S. Car.) 168; Hamilton v. Williams, 26 Ala. 527; Bailey v. Wiggins, 5 Harr. (Del.) 462; Carter v. Dow, 16 Wis. 317; Maguire v. Hughes, 13 La. Ann. 281; Way v. Townsend, 4 Allen (Mass.), 114; Wood v. Ruland, 10 Mo. 143; Stone v. Graves, 8 Mo. 148; Lenox v. Grant, 8 Mo. 254; Upshaw v. Oliver, Dudley (Ga.), 241; Morrison v. McDonald, 21 Me. 550; Gault v. Wallis, 53 Ga. 675. See 15 Am. L. Rev. 442.

If, however, a ministerial duty is annexed to a judicial office, and the officer execute that duty wrongfully, whether by mistake or fraud, he is answerable to the party injured in a suit at law. Taylor v. Doremus, 16 N. J. Law, 473. See also Stewart v. Cooley, 23 Minn. 347; Beaurain v. Scott, 3 Campb. 388; Holden v. Smith, 14 Q. B. 841, 14 Jur. 598, 19 L. J. Q. B. 170.

1. It is a power which essentially belongs to every court to superintend the conduct of its officers, and to see by what authority they act. King of Spain v. Oliver, 2 Wash. (C. C.) 429.

2. Clerk of Court. — The *Clerk of the Court* is an officer who keeps its minutes, or records its proceedings, and has the custody of its records and seal. Burrill's Law Dict. The clerk is sometimes called the prothonotary. He takes charge of the moneys deposited in court, and certifies to the correctness of transcripts from the court records. The clerk is a ministerial officer who acts under the direction of the court: he is therefore not liable for executing an order of the court, though the order may be bad. He is liable for taking insufficient security if he acts negligently. Brock v. Hopkins, 5 Neb. 231.

In *Michigan* it was decided that a simple order from the Supreme Court is enough to compel a county-court clerk to return files which have been remitted to him by mistake. *Mandamus* was not necessary. Wright v. Huron Co. Clerk, 48 Mich. 642. See also Moore v. Muse, 47 Tex. 210.

In *North Carolina* it was decided that the terms of a bond executed by a clerk of the Superior Court obliged him to account for and pay over all money received by virtue of his office: and he is liable as an insurer at all events, or debtor in respect to

such money, and can only be re
payment. Havens v. Lathene, 7
505; State v. Blair, 76 N. Car.
mington v. Nutt, 78 N. Car. 177
Wood, 58 Tenn. 408; Swift v.
Ind. 81.

Where a person was appointe
the Superior Court by a *de facto* j
siding in the judicial district, in
against him to oust him from the
one who had been declared judg
it was *held* that the appointee of
de jure was not entitled to the offi
ple v. Stanton, 73 N. Car. 546.

Where a statute declared tha
should hold office for six years,
clerks for the same period as the
and a clerk was appointed by
when the latter had been two
office, it was *held* that the clerk's
six years and not four. People
6 Daly (N. Y.), 547.

3. Attorney. — For attorneys,
ATTORNEY AND CLIENT.

4. See SHERIFF.

5. Criers. — A crier is an offi
duty it is to make the various
tions in court, under the directi
judges. Bouvier's Law Dict.

6. Tipstaff. — A tipstaff is a
whose duty it is to wait on the c
serve its process. Bouvier's Law

7. "Every court of record has
ent power to make rules for the tr
of its business, provided they ar
tradictory to the laws of the lan
out this power it would be impo
courts of justice to despatch t
business. Delays would be inte
and delay not unfrequently is t
of one of the parties. Every co
fore, must have stated rules to g
they are the properest judges of t
of practice." Snyder v. Bauch
& R. (Pa.) 336; Robinson v. Bl
Black. 264; Fullerton v. Bank c
States, 1 Peters (U. S.), 604; Bar
dolph, 3 Binney (Pa.), 277; Dub
ner, 4 Yeates (Pa.), 361; Kenne
ningham, 2 Metc. (Ky.) 538;
Boswell, 34 Mo. 474; Resber v. T
Mo. 98; Vail v. McKernan, 21
Redman v. State, 28 Ind. 205;
Carpenter, 27 Mo. 497; Vanatta
son, 3 Binney (Pa.), 493; Harris

c constitution or the law of the land.[1] They should be of record within a reasonable time,[2] and should not be ·ctive in their terms.[3] Courts may rescind their rules, or establishing them, reserve the exercise of discretion for ar cases; but a rule made without such qualification must ied to all cases that fall within it, until it is rescinded.[4] In , the construction of its own rules by a court of original tion is conclusive; and it is only where wrong is manifest, is discretion will be interfered with or invaded by an e court.[5]

neral Divisions. — Courts may be arranged under certain classes, which are determined by the character and extent

', 35 Pa. St. 426; Walker v. La. Ann. 703; Hill v. Harney, 607; Ogden v. Robertson, 15 24; Ferguson v. Kays, 21 N. J. state of Boyd, 25 Cal. 511; Shoe-ain, 23 Ind. 169; Coffin v. Mc-nd. 356; Ottum v. Shaw, 27 Ind. v. Conway Fire Ins. Co., 53 Me. in v. Brooke, 22 Md. 288; Bell v. N. H. 43; Towamencin Road, 195; Gannon v. Fritz, 79 Pa. St. er v. Herts, 13 Lea (Tenn.), 315; v. Travellers' Ins. Co., 79 Ind. iour v. Phillips Construction Co., . C.) 460; Texas Land Co. v. 48 Texas, 602; Haley v. David-exas, 615; Fisher v. National Commerce, 73 Ill. 34; Angell v. Manufacturing Co., 73 Ill. 412; Rolling-Mills Co. v. Robinson, 28; People v. Chew, 6 Cal. 636; tate, 9 Ind. 541; De Lorme v. Ga. 280.

le v. McClellan, 31 Cal. 101; . Rotchford, 12 Gratt. (Va.) 60; fifth Circuit Judges, 37 La. Ann. pbell v. Shivers, 1 Ariz. 161; v. McGlynn, 84 N. Y. 284.

a law is imperfect in its details, such an extent as to render it to execute it, the imperfections ils may be supplied by rules of chran v. Loring, 17 Ohio, 409.

need not be spread in full upon , but should be filed within a time in the clerk's office. State 18 Iowa, 149; Owens v. Ran-Ill. 281; Mix v. Chandler, 44 Ill.

y v. Humphrey, 5 Pick. (Mass.)

l court retrospective in its terms, ting as an act of limitation, is ist v. Hellbrenner, 11 S. & R. ; Burlington, etc., R. R. Co. v. 5 Iowa, 466.

Massachusetts a rule of the court n pleas provided that a plea in "may be filed at any time during the first four days of the return term, and not afterwards." A plea in abatement, in consequence of misinformation from a judge of the court of common pleas, was not offered until the fifth day of the term, and was then, by leave of the judge, filed as of the fourth day. The supreme court, in reversing this action of the lower court, said, "But a rule of court thus authorized and made has the force of law, and is binding upon the court as well as upon parties to an action, and cannot be dispensed with to suit the circumstances of any particular case. In the case before us the plea was allowed to be filed on the fifth day of the term, although the rule allows but four days for that purpose. The circumstances were such as would justify that order of the court, if it had power to pass it; but we are satisfied that no one judge of the court of common pleas or of this court has authority to dispense with rules deliberately made and promulgated, on account of the hardship of any particular case, any more than he would have authority to dispense with any requisition of the legislature itself. The courts may rescind or repeal their rules, without doubt, or, in establishing them, may reserve the exercise of discretion for particular cases; but the rule, once made without any such qualification, must be applied to all cases which come within it, until it is repealed by the authority which made it." Thompson v. Hatch, 3 Pick. (Mass.) 512. See also Wall v. Wall, 2 Har. & G. (Md.) 79; Hughes v. Jackson, 12 Md. 450; Tripp v. Brownell, 2 Gray (Mass.), 402; Coyote Gold and Silver Mining Co. v. Ruble, 9 Or. 121.

In *New Hampshire* it was *held* that a court may make special rules in any particular case, although the effect may be to exempt such case from the ordinary rules of court. Deming v. Foster, 42 N. H. 165. See also Pickett v. Wallace, 54 Cal. 147; United States v. Breitling, 20 How. (U. S.) 522.

5. Gannon v. Fritz, 79 Pa. St. 303; Dailey v. Green, 3 Harris (Pa.), 118.

of their jurisdiction, the principles upon which they adminis justice, or by their forms of procedure. Among these classes the following: (*a*) courts of record, and courts not of reco (*b*) civil and criminal courts; (*c*) inferior, superior, supreme, appellate courts; (*d*) courts of law, and courts of equity; (*e*) cou of general jurisdiction, and courts of limited or special juris tion.[1]

(*a*) *Courts of Record, and Courts not of Record.* — A court record is a judicial, organized tribunal, having attributes exercising functions independently of the person of the magistr designated generally to hold it, and proceeding according to course of the common law.[1] Its acts or proceedings are enrol or recorded; and what is contained in the record cannot be cal in question, except by a writ of error from a higher court. Cou not of record are courts of inferior dignity and limited pow whose proceedings, if disputed, may be tried and determined b jury.

(*b*) *Civil and Criminal Courts.* — Civil courts are those est lished to redress private wrongs. Criminal courts are those wh redress public wrongs.[2]

1. **Courts of Record.** — Bouvier, Law Dict.; *Ex parte* Gladhill, 8 Met. (Mass.) 171. "A court of record is one whereof the acts and judicial proceedings are enrolled for a perpetual memorial and testimony, which rolls are called the records of the court, and are of such high and supereminent authority that their truth is not to be called in question; for it is a settled rule and maxim, that nothing shall be averred against a record, nor shall any plea, or even proof, be admitted to the contrary. And if the existence of a record be denied, it shall be tried by nothing but itself; that is, upon bare inspection whether there be any such record or no, else there would be no end of disputes. Every court of record has authority to fine and imprison for contempt of its authority; while, on the other hand, the very erection of a new jurisdiction, with power of fine or imprisonment, makes it instantly a court of record. But the common-law courts, not of record, are of inferior dignity, and in a less proper sense the king's courts; and these are not, as a general rule, intrusted by the law with any power to fine or imprison the subjects of the realm. And in these the proceedings not being enrolled or recorded, as well their existence, as the truth of the matters therein contained shall, if disputed, be tried and determined by a jury." 3 Stephen's Commentaries, 269; 3 Black. Com. 24; Co. Litt. 117 b., 260 a.

A court of record is one which has jurisdiction to fine or imprison, or one having jurisdiction of civil cases above forty shillings, and proceeding according to the course of the common law. Woodma Somerset, 37 Me. 29; Groenvelt v. Bur 1 Salk. 144; Groenvelt v. College of I sicians, 12 Mod. 388.

In Woodman v. Somerset, 37 Me. : was decided that the courts of county c missioners in *Maine* were not court record. In Lester v. Redmond, 6 (N. Y.), 591, the marine court of the of New York was held not to be a cou record for certain purposes. The justi court of the city of Albany is not a c of record. Wheaton v. Fellows, 23 W (N. Y.) 375. In *Alabama* the court justice of the peace was held to be n court of record. Ellis v. White, 25 540. See also Mills v. Martin, 19 J (N. Y.) 33; Warren v. Flagg, 2 Pick. (Ma 448; Snyder v. Wise, 10 Pa. St. 157, the cases there collected.

The mere fact that a permanent re is kept, does not, in modern law, st the character of the court: since m courts, as probate courts, and other limited and special jurisdiction, are obl to keep records, and yet are held t courts not of record. Bouvier, I Dict.; Smith v. Morrison, 22 Pick. (M 430.

A writ of error lies to correct an erro the proceedings of a court of record Blackstone, Com. 407.

A court has power to replace its records when lost or destroyed, to su pleadings, or other papers before or judgment. Railroad Co. v. Stuve, 32 I 95.

2. See Criminal Law.

Inferior Courts are those which are subordinate to other ; also those of a very limited jurisdiction.

erior Courts are those of intermediate jurisdiction between iferior and supreme courts ; also those of controlling as disished from those of subordinate jurisdiction.

reme Courts are those which possess the highest and conig jurisdiction ; also in some States a court of higher jurisdichan the superior courts, though not the court of final resort.

ellate Courts are those which take cognizance of causes ed from another court by appeal or writ of error.[1]

Courts of Law are those which administer justice according course of the common law.

rts of Equity are those which administer justice according principles of equity.

Courts of General Jurisdiction are those which have a jurisn over causes various in their nature.

rts of Limited Jurisdiction are those which have jurisdiction a few specified matters only.[2]

e distinction between courts of original and general jurisn over any particular subject, and courts of special and d jurisdiction, is this: the former are competent by their itution to decide upon their own jurisdiction, and to exercise final judgment, without setting forth in their proceedings icts and evidence upon which it is rendered. Their records t absolute verity, and cannot be impugned by averment or to the contrary: there can be no judicial inspection behind idgment, save by appellate power. The latter are so constithat their judgments may be looked through for the facts vidence necessary to sustain them: their decisions do not h evidence of themselves to show jurisdiction, and its lawful ise. Every requisite for either must appear upon the face of proceedings, or they are nullities.[3]

English Courts.[4] — In the note is given an approximately comlist of the courts which exist, or have existed, in England.

ouvier, Law Dict. title "Courts."

uvier, Law Dict. If a court of jurisdiction does not proceed according the mode prescribed by the statute h it is created, its acts are nullities. . Ev. 987. Such courts must not t within the scope of their jurisdict it must appear on the face of their lings that they so acted, or their pros are *coram non judice*, and void. v. Kennedy, 5 Cranch (U. S.), 173; v. Ward, 8 Mass. 86; Walbridge v. Vt. 114; Smith v. Rice, 11 Mass. lliams v. Blunt, 2 Mass. 213; Turner of North America, 4 Dallas (U. S.). t v. Hapgood, 4 Mass. 117; Clapp rdsley, 1 Aik. (Vt.) 168; Martin inney, Sneed (Ky.), 321; Hall v. Howd, 10 Conn. 514; Hendrick v. Cleveland, 2 Vt. 329; Powers v. People, 4 Johns. (N. Y.) 292; Hamilton v. Burum, 3 Yerg. (Tenn.) 355; Latham v. Edgerton, 9 Cow. (N. Y.) 227; Stockett v. Nicholson, 1 Miss. 75; Wooster v. Parsons, Kirby (Conn.), 27; Wickes v. Caulk, 5 Har. & J. (Md.) 36; McKenzie v. Ramsay, 1 Bailey (S. Car.), 459; Harvey v. Huggins, 2 Bailey (S C.), 267; Den v. Turner, 9 Wheat. (U. S.) 541; Hill v. Pride, 4 Call. (Va.) 107; Owen v. Jordan, 27 Ala. 608; Procter v. State, 5 Harr. (Del.) 387; City of Chicago v. Rock Island R. R. Co., 20 Ill. 286; State v. Metzger, 26 Mo. 65.

3. Grignon v. Astor, 2 How. (U. S.) 319, 341.

4. A definition and short description of

It is not within the scope of this work to treat of them in **and reference may be had** for information concerning them **sources mentioned in the note.**

most of the courts given in the list below may be found in Bouvier's Law Dictionary and in Rapalje & Lawrence's Law Dictionary.

Admiralty.—Abbott, Shipping, 230; 1 Kent, sec. xvii.; 12 Wheaton (U. S.), 611; 2 Pars. Maritime Law, 479 n.

Ancient Demesne.—2 Black. Com. 99; 1 Steph. Com. 224.

Appeal, Her Majesty's Court of.—Established by the *Supreme Court of Judicature*, acts of 1873 and 1875. 3 Steph. Com. 319. See article in 8 American Law Rev. 296.

Archdeacon, Court of.—3 Black. Com. 64; 3 Steph. Com. 305.

Arches.—3 Black. Com. 64; 3 Steph. Com. 306; 2 Chitty, Gen. Pr. 496; 2 Add. Eccl. 406.

Assise and Nisi Prius.—3 Black. Com. 57; 3 Steph. Com. 352.

Attachments.—3 Black. Com. 171; Wharton's Law Dict. Attachment of the Forest.

Augmentation.—Bouvier's Law Dict.

Bankruptcy.—3 Black. Com. 428; 2 Steph. Com. 199.

Bail, Court.—Wharton's Law Dict.; Holthouse's Law Dict.

Baron, Court.—3 Black. Com. 33; 3 Steph. Com. 279.

Chancery.—3 Black. Com. 46; Story, Eq. Jur.; Dan. Chan. Pr.

Christian Courts.—3 Black. Com. 67.

Cinque Ports, Courts of.—2 Steph. Com. 499 n.; 3 Steph. Com. 347; 3 Black. Com. 79.

Clerk of the Market, Court of.—4 Steph. Com. 323.

Conscience, Court of.—Wharton, Law Dict.

Commissioners of Sewers, Court of.—3 Black. Com. 73.

Common Pleas.—3 Steph. Com. 353.

Crown Cases reserved.—4 Steph. Com. 442.

Consistory Court.—2 Steph. Com. 230; 3 Steph. Com. 430; 3 Black. Com. 64.

Convocation.—2 Burn. Eccl. Law, 18; 1 Black. Com. 279; 2 Steph. Com. 525, 668.

Coroner, Court of the.—4 Steph. Com. 323; 4 Black. Com. 274.

County Courts.—Poll. County Court Pr. 1; Rapalje & Lawrence's Law Dict.

Counties Palatine, Courts of the.—1 Steph. Com. 129; 3 Steph. Com. 348.

Delegates.—3 Black. Com. 66; 3 Steph. Com. 307.

Divorce and Matrimonial Cases.—3 Steph. Com. 319.

Duchy of Lancaster, Court of the.—3 Black. Com. 78.

Exchequer.—3 Steph. Com. 338; Com. 44.

Exchequer Chamber.—3 Black. C 3 Steph. Com. 333.

Franchises, Court of.—2 Chitty, 907.

Great Sessions in Wales, Court Black. Com. 77; 3 Steph. Com. 31

High Commission, Court of.—Law Dict.

High Court of Justice.—3 Step 353.

Hundred Court.—1 Steph. Com.

Hustings, Court of.—3 Black. n.; 3 Steph. Com. 493.

House of Lords.—4 Black. Co May, Parliamentary Pr. c. 23; 4 Com. 299. See also Bagehot's Constitution, Ewald's Crown and visers, Stubbs's Constitutional Hi England, 1 Black. Com.

Insolvent Debtors.—3 Steph. C 426.

Inquiry, Court of.—1 Coleridge, Com. 418 n.; 2 Steph. Com. 590.

Judicial Committee of the Privy —1 Black. Com.

Justice Seat.—3 Steph. Com. Black. Com. 71.

Justiciary, Court of.—Bouvier Dict.

King's Bench.—Wharton's La 3 Steph. Com. 319.

Leet, Court.—4 Black. Com. 273 in's Courts-Leet.

Lord High Steward, Court of.— Com. 261.

Lord High Steward of the Univer 3 Black. Com. 83; 4 Black. Com. Steph. Com. 67; 3 Steph. Com. Steph. Com. 325.

Steward of the King's Househ Black. Com. 276.

Marshalsea.—3 Steph. Com. 31

Orphans, Court of.—3 Steph. Co

Oyer and Terminer, and Gener Delivery.—3 Steph. 352.

Passage, Court of.—Rapalje an rence's Law Dict.

Palace at Westminster, Court of.— Com. 317 n.

Peculiars.—3 Black. Com. 65; Com. 306.

Prepoudre.—3 Black. Com. 32; Com. 317.

Policies of Insurance, Court of.— Com. 74; 3 Steph. Com. 317 n.

Prerogative Court.—3 Black. C 2 Steph. Com. 237.

Probate, Court of.—3 Steph. Co

Queen's Bench.—See King's B

4. American Courts.—American courts fall under two general divisions: *first*, State courts, organized under the constitution and laws of the several States; and *second*, United States courts, organized under the constitution and laws of the United States government.

(a) ***State Courts.***—All the States have complete judicial systems.[1]

(b) ***United States Courts.***—The Constitution of the United States provides that "the judicial power of the United States shall be vested in one supreme court and in such inferior courts as the Congress may from time to time establish.[2] The judges, both of the supreme and inferior courts, shall hold their offices during good behavior, and shall, at stated intervals, receive for their services a compensation which shall not be diminished during their continuance in office." The several courts embraced in the federal judicial system are as follows:—

The Supreme Court.
The Circuit Court.
The District Court.
The Territorial Courts.
The Supreme Court of the District of Columbia.
The Court of Claims.

Request, Court of.—3 Black. Com. 71; 3 Steph. Com. 449.

[illegible], Court of.—3 Steph. Com. 449.

Session, Court of.—Bouvier's Law Dict.

Sheriff's Tourn.—4 Black. Com. 273.

Sheriffs' Court in London.—3 Steph. Com. 449.

Stannaries, Court of.—3 Black. Com. 80.

Steward and Marshal, Court of.—See Court of Marshalsea.

[illegible].—3 Black. Com. 71; 3 Steph. Com. 317 n.

Survey, Court of.—Rapalje & Lawrence's Law Dict.

Wards and Liveries.—1 Steph. Com. [illegible]; 2 Black. Com. 68; 3 id. 258; 4 Reeve's Hist. Eng. Law, 259.

1. The court of last resort is called the *Supreme Court* in New Hampshire, Maine, Vermont, Rhode Island, Pennsylvania, Ohio, Indiana, Michigan, Wisconsin, Iowa, Minnesota, Kansas, Nebraska, North Carolina, Tennessee, Missouri, Arkansas, California, Oregon, Nevada, Colorado, South Carolina, Georgia, Alabama, Mississippi, Florida, Washington, Dakota, Idaho, Montana, Wyoming, Utah, New Mexico, Arizona, District of Columbia, Illinois, Louisiana; *Supreme Judicial* in Massachusetts; *Supreme Court of Errors* in Connecticut; *Court of Appeals* in New York, Kentucky, Maryland, Virginia, West Virginia; *Court of Errors and Appeals* in Delaware and New Jersey; *Supreme* (civil) and *Court of Appeals* (criminal) in Texas.

An elaborate table showing all the courts of the various States may be found in Stimson's American Statute Law, p. 114.

2. Congress can vest the judicial power of the United States only in courts ordained and established by itself. Martin *v.* Hunter, 1 Wheaton (U. S.), 304; Stearns *v.* United States, 2 Paine, 300.

The power of Congress to establish courts inferior to the Supreme Court is considered in Stuart *v.* Laird, 1 Cranch (U. S.), 299; Livingston *v.* Story, 9 Peters (U. S.), 632; Hubbard *v.* Northern R. R. Co., 3 Blatch. (C. C.) 84; United States *v.* Taylor, 3 McLean (C. C.), 539.

Neither the president nor any military officer can establish a court in a conquered country, and authorize it to decide upon the rights of the United States or of individuals. Jecker *v.* Montgomery, 13 How. (U. S.) 498.

But it is within the constitutional powers of Congress to create a special tribunal or board of commissioners to determine the amounts to be paid to parties who are entitled to receive compensation by the provisions of a treaty with a foreign nation. United States *v.* Ferreira, 13 How. (U. S.) 40; United States *v.* Ritchie, 17 How. (U. S.) 525.

Congress, however, has no power to confer judicial power upon the courts of a State. *Ex parte* Knowles, 5 Cal. 300; Ferris *v.* Coover, 11 Cal. 175.

Nor can a State legislature confer judi-

In addition to these, the Senate of the United States is a court for the trial of impeachments.

1. *Supreme Court of the United States.* — The Supreme Court consists of a chief justice and eight associate justices,[1] any six of whom constitute a quorum.[2] It holds one term annually, with such adjourned terms as may be necessary for the despatch of business.[3] It has the power to appoint a clerk, a marshal, and a reporter of its decisions.[4]

2. *Circuit Courts of the United States.* — The circuit courts are the principal inferior tribunals established by Congress under the authority of the Constitution. They are held[5] by the justice of the Supreme Court allotted to the circuit,[6] or by the circuit judge

cial power upon a federal court. Greeley v. Townsend, 25 Cal. 604.

1. Rev. Stat. § 673. The associate justices shall have precedence according to the dates of their commissions, or, when the commissions of two or more of them bear the same date, according to their ages. Rev. Stat. § 674.

In case of a vacancy in the office of chief justice, or of his inability to perform the duties and powers of his office, they shall devolve upon the associate justice who is first in precedence, until such disability is removed, or another chief justice is appointed and duly qualified. This provision shall apply to every associate justice who succeeds to the office of chief justice. Rev. Stat. § 675.

The chief justice of the Supreme Court of the United States shall receive the sum of ten thousand five hundred dollars a year, and the justices thereof shall receive the sum of ten thousand dollars a year each, to be paid monthly. Rev. Stat. § 676.

2. If at any session of the Supreme Court a quorum does not attend on the day appointed for holding it, the justices who do attend may adjourn the court from day to day for twenty days after said appointed time, unless there be sooner a quorum. If a quorum does not attend within said twenty days, the business of the court shall be continued over till the next appointed session; and if during a term, after a quorum has assembled, less than that number attend on any day, the justices attending may adjourn the court from day to day until there is a quorum, or may adjourn without day. Rev. Stat. § 685.

The justices attending at any term when less than a quorum is present, may, within the twenty days mentioned in the preceding section, make all necessary orders touching any suit, proceeding, or process depending in or returned to the court, preparatory to the hearing, trial, or decision thereof. Rev. Stat § 686.

3. The Supreme Court shall hold at the seat of government one term annually, commencing on the second Monday in October, and such adjourned or special terms as it may find necessary for the despatch of business; and suits, proceedings, recognizances, and processes pending in or returnable to said court shall be tried, heard, and proceeded with as if the time of holding said sessions had not been hereby altered. Rev. Stat. § 684.

4. Rev. Stat. § 677. One or more deputies of the clerk of the Supreme Court may be appointed by the court on the application of the clerk, and may be removed at the pleasure of the court. Rev. Stat. § 678.

The marshal is entitled to receive a salary of thirty-five hundred dollars a year. He shall attend the court, and serve its processes. Rev. Stat. § 680.

The reporter shall cause the decisions of the Supreme Court made during his office to be printed and published within eight months after they are made. Rev. Stat. § 681.

Women as Attorneys in United States Supreme Court. — By act Feb. 15, 1879, women may be admitted to practice in the Supreme Court.

5. Rev. Stat. § 609.

6. The chief justice and associate justices of the Supreme Court shall be allotted among the circuits by an order of the court, and a new allotment shall be made whenever it becomes necessary or convenient by reason of the alteration of any circuit, or of the new appointment of a chief justice or associate justice, or otherwise. Rev. Stat. 606.

It shall be the duty of the chief justice and of each associate justice of the Supreme Court to attend at least one term of the circuit court in each district of the circuit to which he is allotted, during every period of two years. Rev. Stat. § 610.

After the establishment of the government in 1789 it became customary for the justices of the Supreme Court to sit in the circuit courts, though not expressly authorized by circuit,[1] or by the district judge of the district sitting alone,[2] any two of the said judges sitting together. Cases may be and tried by each of the judges holding a circuit court sitting by direction of the presiding justice or judge, who shall the business to be done by each.[3] And circuit courts held at the same time in the different districts of the same .[4] There are nine circuits, as follows:[5] —

First Circuit consists of the districts of Maine, New Hamp- Massachusetts, and Rhode Island.

Second Circuit. — Vermont, Connecticut, and New York.

Third Circuit. — Pennsylvania, New Jersey, and Delaware.

Fourth Circuit. — Maryland, Virginia, West Virginia, North na, and South Carolina.

Fifth Circuit. — Georgia, Alabama, Mississippi, Florida, na, and Texas (act of June 11, 1879).

Sixth Circuit. — Ohio, Michigan, Kentucky, and Tennessee.

Seventh Circuit. — Indiana, Illinois, and Wisconsin.

Eighth Circuit. — Nebraska, Minnesota, Iowa, Missouri, s and Arkansas, Colorado (act of June 26, 1876).

Ninth Circuit. — California, Oregon, and Nevada.

re all the judges are disqualified by interest from hearing se, the papers are certified to the most convenient circuit n the next adjoining State or in the next adjoining circuit.[6]

ble. In Stuart v. Laird, 1 Cranch 299, decided in 1803, objection was this practice; but the court *held* construction of the constitution hich the practice became estab- as a contemporary interpretation t forcible nature, and that acqui- and practice under it for a period al years, commencing with the or- on of the judicial system, afforded stible answer to the objection.

each circuit there shall be ap- a circuit judge, who shall have power and jurisdiction therein as ce of the Supreme Court allotted rcuit, and shall be entitled to re- salary of six thousand dollars a Every circuit judge shall reside s circuit. Rev. Stat. § 607.

district judge sitting in a circuit ll not give a vote in any case of r error from his own decision, but gn the reasons for such decision; . that such a cause may, by con- parties, be heard and disposed of hen holding a circuit court sitting When he holds a circuit court with the other judges, the judgment in such cases shall be rendered mity with the opinion of the pre- stice or judge. Rev. Stat. § 614. States v. Lancaster, 5 Wheat. (U. S.)

A district judge may alone hold a circuit court, though no justice of the Supreme Court may be allotted to that circuit. Pollard v. Dwight, 4 Cranch (C. C.), 421; Hussey v. Whitely, 1 Bond (C. C.), 407; Appleton v. Smith, 1 Dill. (C. C.) 202; Robinson v. Satterlee, 3 Sawyer (C. C.), 134.

3. Rev. Stat. § 611.

4. Rev. Stat. 612.

5. Rev. Stat. 604.

6. When it appears, in any civil suit in any circuit court, that all of the judges thereof who are competent by law to try said case are in any way interested therein, or have been of counsel for either party, or are so related or connected with either party as to render it, in the opinion of the court, improper for them to sit in such trial, it shall be the duty of the court, on the application of either party, to cause the fact to be entered on the records, and to make an order that an authenticated copy thereof, with all the proceedings in the case, shall be forthwith certified to the most convenient circuit court in the next adjoining State or in the next adjoining circuit; and said court shall, upon the filing of such record and order with its clerk, take cognizance of, and proceed to hear and determine, the case in the same manner as if it had been rightfully and originally commenced therein; and the proper process for the due execution of the judgment or decree rendered

When a circuit judge deems it advisable, on account of [illegible] absence, or accumulation of business, the judge of any other circuit court may be requested to hold the court.[1] The circuit judge of the circuit has power to appoint a clerk for each circuit court.[2] Each circuit court may also appoint "commissioners of the circuit courts."[3]

The terms of the circuit courts are prescribed by law.[4] If neither of the judges be present to open the sessions, the marshal may adjourn the court from day to day; or if neither of them attend before the close of the fourth day, the marshal may adjourn the court to the next regular term;[5] or the court may be adjourned by the marshal or clerk, on a written order directed to them alternately by either of the judges, to a day before the next regular term.[6] The court may at its discretion, or at the discretion of the Supreme Court, hold special sessions for the trial of criminal cases;[7] and such special sessions may be directed to be holden at any convenient place within the district nearest to the place where the offences are said to have been committed.[8]

The Marshal of the District is the ministerial officer of the circuit court. In case of a vacancy in the office of marshal or district attorney, the justice of the Supreme Court allotted to such circuit has power to fill the position until an appointment shall have been made by the president, and the appointee is duly qualified.[9]

3. *District Courts of the United States.* — The United States is divided into judicial districts, in each of which a district court

in the cause shall run into, and may be executed in, the district where such judgment or decree was rendered, and also into the district from which the cause was removed. Rev. Stat. § 615.

1. Whenever any circuit justice deems it advisable, on account of his disability or absence, or of his having been counsel or being interested in any case pending in the circuit court for any district in his circuit, or for the accumulation of business therein, or for any other cause, that said court shall be held by the justice of any other circuit, he may, in writing, request the justice of any other circuit to hold the same during a time to be named in the request; and such request shall be entered upon the journal of the circuit court so to be holden. Thereupon it shall be lawful for the justice so requested, to hold such court, and to exercise within and for said district, during the time named in said request, all the powers of the justice of such circuit. Rev. Stat. § 617.

It is discretionary with the judge requested to hold the court. The condition of his own circuit may render it inexpedient or his refusal unavoidable. Supervisors *v.* Rogers, 7 Wall. (U. S.) 175.

2. Rev. Stat. § 619. There are special provisions as to the appointment of clerks in *Kentucky* (Rev. Stat. § [illegible]), Western District of *North Carolina* (Rev. Stat. § [illegible]), Western District of *Virginia* (Rev. Stat. § 622), Western District of *Wisconsin* (Rev. Stat. § 622).

One or more deputies of any clerk of a circuit court may be appointed by such court on the application of the clerk, and may be removed at the pleasure of judges authorised to make the appointments. For any default or misfeasance in office of such deputies, the clerk and the sureties on his official bond shall be liable. Rev. Stat. § 624.

3. Rev. Stat. § 627. The duties of commissioners of circuit courts are defined in Rev. Stat. §§ 945, 1014, 2025, 2026. Such commissioners are not officers of the court. 3 Blatchf. (C. C.) 166.

4. See Rev. Stat. § 658.

5. Rev. Stat. § 671.

6. Rev. Stat. § 672.

7. Rev. Stat. § 661; U. S. *v.* Pennsylvania Insurgents, 3 Dall. (U. S.) 513.

8. Rev. Stat. § 662.

9. Rev. Stat. § 793.

[illegible][1] A district judge is appointed to each district[2] except in a few States where one judge is appointed for all the districts within the State.[3] A district judge is required to reside in the district for which he is appointed, or in one of the districts if he is a judge for several. A violation of this provision is declared a high misdemeanor.[4] The regular terms of the district courts are held at times and places regulated by law.[5] The duration of the term is not fixed, but the courts are required to hold monthly adjournments of their regular terms, for the trial of criminal causes, when their business requires it to be done.[6]

If the judge of any district court is unable to attend at the commencement of a term, the court may be adjourned by the marshal on a written order from the judge, to the next regular term or any earlier day.[7] When a district judge is disabled to hold a district court, on the application of the district attorney or marshal of the district, the circuit judge or justice may order the clerk of the district court to certify into the next circuit court to be held in the district the business of the district court, and all cases will then be heard and determined by the circuit court.[8] If the judge or justice of the circuit court deem it proper when a district judge is disqualified, they may designate and appoint the judge of any other district in the same circuit to hold a district court, and to discharge the duties of the judge disqualified.[9] If the judge of a district court is disqualified by interest or relationship with the parties, it shall be his duty, on application by either party, to cause the fact to be entered on the records of the court, and certify all the proceedings in the case to the next circuit court for the district or State.[10]

A clerk is appointed for each district court by the judge thereof.[11] He is required to give bond for the faithful performance of his

1. Rev. Stat. § 530–550.
2. Rev. Stat. § 551.
3. Rev. Stat. § 552.
4. Rev. Stat. § 551.
5. Rev. Stat. § 572.
6. Rev. Stat. § 578.

A special term of any district court may be held at the same place where any regular term is held, or at such other place in the district as the nature of the business may require, and at such time and upon such notice as may be ordered by the district judge. And any business may be transacted at such special term which might be transacted at a regular term. Rev. Stat. § 581.

7. Rev. Stat. § 583.
8. Rev. Stat. § 587.

When such an order has been made, the clerk of the district court shall continue, during the disability of the district judge, to certify all cases thereafter begun, to the circuit court next to be held in the district. When the disability of the district judge is removed, the circuit court shall order all suits and proceedings in which the district court has an exclusive jurisdiction, to be removed to the district court. Rev. Stat. § 588; Wallace *v.* Loomis, 97 U. S. 146.

9. Rev. Stat. § 591.

When there is a great accumulation of business in one district, the circuit judge or justice, or, in their absence or disqualification, the Chief Justice of the United States, may designate and appoint the judge of any other district in the same circuit to have and exercise within the first named district the same powers that are vested in the judge thereof; and each of the said district judges may, in case of such appointment, hold separately, at the same time, a district court in such district, and discharge all the judicial duties of a district judge therein. Rev. Stat. § 592.

10. Rev. Stat. § 603.
11. Rev. Stat. § 555

duties, in a sum not less than five thousand dollars, nor more than twenty thousand dollars, to be fixed by the attorney-general, and with sureties to be approved by the court.[1] One or more deputies may be appointed by the court, on the application of the clerk, removable at the pleasure of the judge. In case of the death of the clerk, his deputy or deputies shall, unless removed, continue in office and perform the duties of the clerk, in his name, until a clerk is appointed and qualified; and for the default or misfeasance of such deputy, the clerk and his estate, and the sureties in his official bond, shall be liable; but his personal representatives shall have such remedy for any default committed after his death as the clerk would have been entitled to, if the same had occurred in his lifetime.[2] The clerk is required by law to reside permanently in his district, and to give personal attention to his duties on pain of removal.[3]

The marshal is the ministerial officer of the court. His duties are similar to those of a sheriff.[4] He is appointed by the President, by and with the advice and consent of the Senate, for a term of four years.[5] The marshal is required to reside within his district, and to give personal attention to his official duties.[6] The records of a district court are kept at the place where the court is held. When it is held at more than one place, and the place of keeping the records is not specially provided by law, they are kept at either of the places of holding the court, which may be designated by the district judge.[7]

1. Act of February 22, 1875, § 3.

2. Rev. Stat. § 558.

Such deputy clerks may be required to give bond, without affecting the legal responsibility of the clerk for the acts of such deputy. Rev. Stat. § 796.

In case of the absence or disability of the judges, the clerks are empowered to take recognizances of bail *de bene esse*, where such bail is demandable. Rev. Stat. § 947.

3. Act of June 20, 1874.

4. Rev. Stat. § 788.

5. Rev. Stat. § 779, 1767, 1768.

Before the marshal enters upon his duties, he is required to give bond for the faithful performance of his duties, with two sureties to be approved by the district judge. Rev. Stat. § 783; Act of Feb. 22, 1875, § 2; 18 Stat. 333.

He may appoint one or more deputies, who are removable from office by the judge of the district court, or by the circuit court for the district, at the pleasure of either. Rev. Stat. § 780.

The deputy is an officer of the court, and, as such, liable to attachment for not paying over moneys collected on an execution in his hands. Bagley *v.* Yates, 3 McLean (C. C.), 465; U. S. *v.* Mann, 2 Brock. (C. C.) 9.

In case of the marshal's death, his deputies shall continue in office, unless specially removed, and shall execute the same in the name of the deceased, until another marshal is appointed and duly qualified; and their defaults shall render the marshal's sureties liable, as in the case of a deputy clerk. Rev. Stat. § 789.

Any person injured by the breach of the condition of a marshal's bond, may bring suit thereon in his own name, and recover his damages. Rev. Stat. § [illegible]; [illegible] *v.* Newcomb, 2 Dill. (C. C.) 45.

The judgment shall remain as a security for future breaches, until the whole penalty has been recovered. Rev. Stat. § 785.

Suit upon a marshal's bond must be brought within six years after the right of action accrues, unless the party be under disability; and then, within three years after the removal thereof. Rev. Stat. § 786.

6. Act of June 20, 1874, [illegible] 18 Stat. 109.

7. Rev. Stat. § 562. The proceedings to restore records in the United States courts must conform to the act of Congress, and not to the State statute. Turner *v.* Newman, 3 Biss. (C. C.) 307.

erritorial Courts of the United States. — In the Territories *w Mexico, Utah, Washington, Dakota, Idaho, Montana,* and *ing*, the judicial power is vested in a supreme court, district , probate courts, and in justices of the peace.[1] In *Arizona* dicial power is vested in a supreme court and such inferior as the legislative council may by law prescribe.[2]

upreme Court of the District of Columbia. — The Supreme of the District of Columbia was established by act of 3, 1863. It now consists of six justices. R. S. Supp., . With the exception of one justice, who is designated chief justice, the justices are appointed by the President of nited States, and hold their office during good behavior.

Court of Claims. — The Court of Claims[3] consists of a chief and four judges, appointed by the President, by and with vice of the Senate.[4] It is authorized to have a seal with device as it may order.[5] It holds one annual session at ngton, beginning on the first Monday of December, and uing as long as may be necessary for the prompt disposition business of the court. Any two of the judges may con- a quorum, and hold a court for the transaction of business;[6] e concurrence of three judges is necessary to any judgment.[7] ers of either House of Congress are forbidden to practise in ourt.[8] The court is authorized to appoint a chief clerk, an nt clerk, a bailiff, and a messenger.[9]

. Stat. § 1907. upreme Court consists of a chief nd two associate justices, any two constitute a quorum. Their term is four years. They are required term of court annually at the seat nment of the Territory. Rev. Stat.

Territory is divided into three districts. A district court is re- o be held in each district of the y by one of the justices of the Su- ourt, at such time and place as prescribed by law; and each judge ignment shall reside in the district he is assigned. Rev. Stat. § 1865. upreme courts and district courts owered to appoint clerks who shall ce at the pleasure of the court for ey are respectively appointed. The ial officer is a marshal appointed by

. Stat. § 1908.

United States v. Klein, 13 Wall. 144, *Chief Justice Chase* stated the f the court of claims as follows: the establishment of the court of claimants could only be heard by . That court was established in r the triple purpose of relieving , and of protecting the govern- regular investigation, and of bene- fiting the claimants by affording them a certain mode of examining and adjudicating upon their claims. It was required to hear and determine upon claims founded upon any law of Congress, or upon any regulation of an executive department, or upon any contract, express or implied, with the Government of the United States. Originally it was a court merely in name, for its power extended only to the preparation of bills to be submitted to Congress. In 1863 the number of judges was increased from three to five, its jurisdiction was enlarged, and, instead of being required to prepare bills for Congress, it was authorized to render final judgment, subject to appeal to this court, and to an estimate by the secretary of the treasury of the amount required to pay each claimant. This court being of opinion that the provision for an estimate was inconsistent with the finality essential to judicial decisions, Congress repealed that provision. Since then the court of claims has exercised all the functions of a court, and this court has taken full jurisdiction on appeal."

4. Rev. Stat. § 1049.
5. Rev. Stat. § 1050.
6. Rev. Stat. § 1052.
7. Act of June 23, 1874.
8. Rev. Stat. § 1058.
9. Rev. Stat. § 1053.

7. *Senate of the United States for the Trial of Impeachments.*—The Constitution of the United States provides that the Senate shall have the sole power to try all impeachments. When sitting for that purpose, they shall be on oath or affirmation. When the President of the United States is tried, the chief justice shall preside; and no person shall be convicted without the concurrence of two-thirds of the members present.[1]

COUSIN.—Any collateral relative, except brothers and sisters and their descendants, and the brothers and sisters of any ancestor.[2] Anciently it was a term for any collateral relative.[3] When used alone "cousin" means cousin-german, or first cousin; that is, one who has the same grandfather or grandmother.[4] The children and grandchildren of a first cousin are first cousins once and twice removed, and so on. Second cousins are [illegible] related, who have the same great-grandfather or great-grandmother, and so on; and the children and grandchildren of [illegible] the same relation to the other, once and twice removed.[5]

1. Constitution of the United States, art. I. § 3.

2. Whart. Law Lex.

A testatrix gave a share of her residuary estate to her "cousin Harriet Cloak." She had no cousin of that name; but she had a married cousin Harriet Crane, whose maiden name was Cloak, and also a cousin T. Cloak, whose wife's name was Harriet. Extrinsic evidence was admitted to show which was meant; and it was held that "cousin" might be understood in a popular sense as the wife of a cousin. The share was accordingly awarded to Harriet, wife of T. Cloak. (*Bowen, L. J.*, dissented.) *Fry, L. J.*, admitted that "cousin" was a term of which the dominant idea was consanguinity, but said, "I think that, in popular language, the word does apply to persons who are not related by consanguinity. In the present case we must either reject the name of the legatee, or else give a secondary or tertiary signification to the word 'cousin.' I think the latter the more correct course." *In re* Taylor, L. R. 34 Ch. Div. 255; s. c., 56 L. J. R. N. S. Ch. Div. 173.

3. Litt. §§ 389, 660, Adams's Gloss.

4. *In re* Parker, L. R. 15 Ch. Div. 528.

Where a bequest is to "cousins" simply, in the absence of any thing to explain the testator's meaning, first cousins only are entitled. Stoddart *v.* Nelson, 6 D. M. & G. 68; Stevenson *v.* Abingdon, 31 Beav. 305.

A gift to "all my first cousins, or cousins-german," does not extend to a first cousin once removed, who is, in fact, a cousin in the second degree, though not called a second cousin, as being of the second class of persons to whom the appellation is given. Sanderson *v.* Bayley, 4 M. & C. 56.

A testator gave legacies to several persons by name, describing each of them as a cousin, and then gave the residue to all such of his cousins as should be living at his death, and to all the children of such of his said cousins as might have theretofore died, or might die in his lifetime. The persons described by name were all first cousins; and it was held that "cousins" in the residuary clause meant first cousins. Caldecott *v.* Harrison, 9 Sim. [illegible].

5. A bequest to second cousins includes only those properly second cousins as defined in the text, and not all those who are in the degree of second cousins, viz., the sixth degree of consanguinity. It has been contended that it was a principle that the term was inclusive of all who were of this degree; but the contention was distinctly repudiated in *In re* Parker, L. R. 15 Ch. Div. 528; 28 W. R. [illegible].

In this case the testator gave one-third of his property to his first cousins, and two-thirds to his second cousins. It was decided that "first cousins" meant cousins-german and that first cousins once removed were not included in the term "second cousins." *Sir George Jessel, M. R.*, who delivered the opinion of the court, said, "The term 'second cousins' has a well-known, definite meaning: it means persons having the same great-grandfathers and great-grandmothers. The relationship is a perfectly well-known and perfectly well-settled relationship. There never was any doubt about its meaning suggested by anybody that I am aware of. Why should the meaning of it here be altered without a context? It is one of the first principles of construction that there should be no alteration in the proper sense of words

n. — The action of covenant is the name of one of the
s of action *ex contractu*, which lies for the recovery

2. Here there is no con-
y be an exception, how-
time of making his will
o second cousins, in which
ve meant something else;
the court must determine.
d are explained some of

the residue of his estate to
first and second cousins.
aking his will, and at his
second cousins, his only
es being a first cousin,

three first cousins once removed, and a great-niece. The court *held* the intention of the testator to be, to give to relatives not more remote than second cousins, and accordingly divided the estate equally among the seven mentioned. Mayott *v.* Mayott, 2 Br. C. C. 125.

In Silcox *v.* Bell, 1 Sim. & Stu. 301, it was decided that the great-grandchildren of uncles and aunts were not second cousins, but first cousins twice removed; but that they were, however, of the degree of relationship of second cousins, and entitled as of damages for the breach of a covenant, or [illegible] in writing under seal.[1]

It is one of the *brevia formata* of the register, and is said sometimes to be a concurrent remedy with debt, though never with assumpsit, and is the only proper remedy where the contract is under seal, and the damages are unliquidated in nature, the contract being under seal.[2]

II. Nature of the Action. — 1. *Generally.* — Covenant can be maintained only upon a writing under seal; and, if a contract is unattested by a seal, or is underwritten, redress for non-performance is by debt or assumpsit, according to the subject-matter.[3]

In covenant there must be a breach of some covenant contained in the instrument in suit, before an action can be maintained;[4] and if there has been a breach of any of the covenants in a deed, the plaintiff may maintain an action in covenant, although the instrument is so defectively executed on his part that only assumpsit can be maintained against him.[5]

such under a bequest. The latter part of this decision was disapproved of by *Jessel, M. R.*, in *In re* Parker, L. R. 15 Ch. Div. 528; 28 W. R. 823.

Where the bequest was to testatrix's second cousins of the name of S., and she had no second cousins, but had three first cousins once removed, two of whom survived, and the third had died leaving children, it was held that the two survivors and the children of the third took, to the exclusion of the children of the survivors, who were of the degree of second cousins, on the ground that it was very common for people to call children of first cousins, second cousins. Slade *v.* Fook, 9 Sim. 386.

But, as a rule, a first cousin once removed is not entitled to share in a fund bequeathed to second cousins. "Those only who have either the same great-grandfather or the same great-grandmother, are second cousins to each other." Corp. of Bridgenorth *v.* Collins, 15 Sim. 541.

Under a bequest to testator's first and second cousins and the children of his kinsman G. C., which children were his first cousins twice removed, all persons related in the degree of second cousins were admitted to take, in Charge *v.* Goodyer, 3 Russ. 140. See this case remarked on in *In re* Parker, L. R. 15 Ch. Div. 528; 28 W. R. 823.

1. Burrill's L. Dict. 397. See 1 Archb. *Nisi Prius*, 250; 1 Chitty, Pl. 115; Brown on Actions, 352; 2 Bouvier's Inst. 355, § 3443; McVoy *v.* Wheeler, 6 Port. (Ala.) 201; Tribble *v.* Oldham, 5 J. J. Marsh. (Ky.) 137; Ludlum *v.* Wood, 2 N. J. L. (1 Penn.) 55; Bilderback *v.* Pouner, 7 N. J. L. (2 Halst.) 64; Gale *v.* Nixon, 6 Cow. (N. Y.) 55; Vicary *v.* Moore, 2 Watts (Pa.), 451; s. c., 27 Am. Dec. 323; Moore *v.* Jones, 2 Ld. Raym. 1536; Lee *v.* [illegible], Cro. Jac. 560.

2. 2 Bouv. L. Dict. (14th ed.) 405, tit. *Covenant*; 1 Chitty, Pl. 116, 113; Fitzherbert, Nat. Brev. 340; 2 Stephens' *Nisi Prius*, 1058.

3. McVoy *v.* Wheeler, 6 Port. (Ala.) 201.

When Covenant lies. — By the common law, an action of covenant cannot be maintained except on an instrument sealed by the party, or by his attorney duly authorized. Tribble *v.* Oldham, 5 J. J. Marsh. (Ky.) 137; Ludlum *v.* Wood, 2 N. J. L. (1 Penn.) 55; Bilderback *v.* Pouner, 7 N. J. L. (2 Halst.) 64; Gale *v.* Nixon, 6 Cow. (N. Y.) 445; Davis *v.* Judd, 6 Wis. 85.

Covenant lies, generally, where the covenantor has done an act contrary to his agreement, or fails to do or perform that which he has undertaken. 4 Dana Ab. 115. Covenant also lies where the covenantor does that which disables him from performing his contract. Heard *v.* Bowers, 23 Pick. (Mass.) 455; Hopkins *v.* Young, 11 Mass. 302; Grebert-Borgnis *v.* Nugent, L. R. 15 Q. B. Div. 85; Scot *v.* Mayn, Cro. Eliz. 449.

Kentucky Statute. — By a statute of Kentucky, passed in 1812, it is provided that all writings thereafter executed without seal, stipulating for a payment of money, or property, or for a performance of any other act, duty, or duties, shall be placed upon the same footing with sealed instruments containing like stipulations, and shall have the same force and effect; and the same species of action may be founded upon them as on the sealed instruments. Hughes *v.* Parks, 4 Bibb (Ky.), 60.

4. Merriman *v.* Bush (Pa.), 8 Cent. Rep. 87.

5. See Poor Directors *v.* McFadden, 1

Though an equitable defence is admissible in an action of covenant, yet, as to the plaintiff, it is strictly a legal action.[1]

2. *Form of Action.* — An action in the nature of waste will lie against a lessee of a mine for an injury to the reversion, by the removal of a barrier or boundary between it and an adjoining mine, although the act complained of might also be the subject of an action for the breach of an express covenant.[2]

A parol agreement by one party to a covenant to waive the performance of a certain part of the covenant by the other party, is not such an alteration of the contract as will render necessary a change in the form of action.[3]

Where, in an agreement under seal for constructing a building, it is stipulated that no extra charges shall be made for alterations unless agreed on in writing, and the price fixed, the owner reserving the right to make them, compensating the builder therefor, the remedy for the recovery of the additional expenses incurred thereby is held to be in covenant on the contract, and not in assumpsit.[4]

When A., by a deed under seal, gave and granted unto B., to take effect at his death, "the sum of five hundred dollars, to have, hold, and enjoy all and singular the said sum of five hundred dollars, to the said B., his executors, etc.," and then warranted the said

Grant Cas. (Pa.) 230; School Directors v. McBride, 22 Pa. St. (10 Harr.) 215.

1. Lehigh Coal & Nav. Co. v. Harlan, 27 Pa. St. 429.

Agreement for Sale of Land. — An action of covenant upon articles of agreement for the sale of land, to recover the purchase-money, is in effect an equitable proceeding to compel specific performance of the contract, and is governed by the same equitable principles. Nicol v. Carr, 35 Pa. St. 381.

2. Marker v. Kenrick, 13 C. B. 188; s. c., 17 Jur. 44; 22 L. J., C. P. 129.

3. McCombs v. McKennan, 2 Watts & S. (Pa.) 216; s. c., 37 Am. Dec. 505.

Modifying Agreement by Parol. — Where there is an oral agreement modifying the original covenant in an essential point, to take advantage of such oral agreement, the covenant must be abandoned, and an action brought in assumpsit. Lehigh Coal & Nav. Co. v. Harlan, 27 Pa. St. 429; Sherwin v. Rutland & B. R. R. Co., 24 Vt. 347.

4. Shaeffer v. Geisenberg, 47 Pa. St. 500.

Contract to do Work. — Where A. covenanted with B. to build and complete a certain house, according to specifications, for a specified price, within a specified time, and the parties further covenanted, that in case B. directed any more work to be done than was mentioned, he should pay A. what it should be worth on a reasonable valuation, it was *held*, that time was not of the essence of the contract; that A. could recover for the work when finished, notwithstanding it was not finished within the time specified; that it was not necessary that he should procure an estimate to be made of the value of the extra work before bringing the action; and that covenant, and not assumpsit, was the proper form of action in order to recover for the extra work. Ramsburg v. McCahan, 3 Gill. (Md.) 341. *Compare* Ellmaker v. Franklin Fire Ins. Co., 6 Watts & S. (Pa.) 439.

Where an agreement under seal stipulated for the construction, by the plaintiff, of a steam-engine for the defendants within a certain time, "unavoidable accidents only excepted," and the defendants' covenant to pay for the same by instalments at certain periods after the commencement and completion of the work, and an unavoidable accident happened by which the completion of the work was delayed, and the time for performance was enlarged by parol, it was *held* that the plaintiff must proceed by covenant, and that he cannot maintain an action of assumpsit, although the cause of action should happen after the time for performance has expired. Green v. Roberts, 5 Whart. (Pa.) 84.

An agreement to perform certain work within a limited time, under a certain penalty, has been held not a liquidation of the damages which the party is to pay for the breach of his covenant. Tayloe v. Sandiford, 20 U. S. (7 Wheat.) 13; bk. 5, L. ed. 384.

sum of five hundred dollars, to take effect at his death, to B., his executors, etc., the court held that an action of lay, on this instrument, against the administratrix of A. debt would also have lain.[1]

3. *Election.* — Covenant is the only remedy where the is created by an agreement under seal; but where the lav the liability independently of the covenant, an action on may also be maintained.[2] And where the obligation und not direct, collateral merely, and where the damages are dated, covenant is the peculiar remedy, and debt will not

When money is secured by an instrument under seal, t in instalments, and they are not all due, no action but will lie, unless there be a penalty which becomes due on payment of any one instalment, in which case debt will li penalty.[4]

Covenant lies only between parties privy to the contrac

Where the covenant creates the liability, no action can be maintained; but where the law creates a liabili pendent of the covenant, an action on the case may maintained.[6]

1. Taylor *v.* Wilson, 5 Ired. (N. C.) L. 214.

2. Luckey *v.* Rowzee, 1 A. K. Marsh. (Ky.) 295.

3. **Several Covenantors.** — Where several covenantors bind themselves, or some one of them, to pay a certain sum of money, an action of debt cannot be maintained against one of them only. Harrison *v.* Matthews, 2 Dowl. N. S. Bail, 318. See also Montague *v.* Smith, 13 Mass. 405; Tileston *v.* Newell, 13 Mass. 406.

And when a lease was made by several owners of a house, reserving rent to each in proportion to his interest, and there was a covenant on part of the lessee that he would keep the premises in good repair, and surrender them in like repair, this covenant was held to be joint as respects the lessors, and that one of them (or two representing) cannot maintain an action in covenant for the breach of such covenant by the lessee. Calvert *v.* Bradley, 57 U. S. (16 How.) 580; bk. 14, L. ed. 1066.

4. Windsor *v.* Gover, 2 Saund. 303, note b.

Where Debt is payable in Instalments. — But it is said that where the sums payable at different times are independent sums, and not instalments of a larger sum, debt lies as well as covenant. See Comyn, Dig. tit. *Action*, F.

Where part of an entire sum due on a sealed instrument is payable by instalments at fixed periods, and the residue in specific articles on demand, covenant will lie for the instalments, although there has been no legal demand of the speci Stevens *v.* Chamberlain, 1 Vt. ·

5. **Action on Covenant by** Thus, a personal covenant in a suit by the assignee of the or covenantee. Lyon *v.* Parker.

But where the covenant ru land, the action may be bro assignee. 2 Hosp. Inst. 356, § *infra*, KINDS OF COVENANTS.

6. Luckey *v.* Rowzee, 1 A. (Ky.) 295.

When Covenant the Only Where tenants in common c course, dam, and several mills, tion, and mutually covenanted repair certain portions of the tively, it was held that an act against the other for failure should be covenant, and not ca *v.* Brown, 3 Denio (N. Y.), 356.

A person who has been co pay money, in consequence of covenant by another, may recov action of covenant, or assumpsit *v.* Waer, Anth. (N. Y.) 130.

The evidence of a contract, t slave sound, consisted of a writing, executed since 1812, i It was *held* in a suit brought in that the writing, though made, ing to its face, to be performed, came within the Kentucky A relating to written instrument covenant, not assumpsit, was priate remedy upon it. Steel 4 Dana (Ky.), 381.

An action of debt will not lie upon articles of agreement to pay certain sum in bank notes, for they are not money. The action ould be covenant, in which the plaintiff can recover his real mages, according to the value of the bank notes.[1]

Covenant, and not assumpsit, should be brought to enforce the bility of one who assigns a specialty by an indorsement under al.[2]

III. When Maintainable. — 1. *In General.* — Covenant can be intained only upon a writing under seal,[3] and against a person o, by himself or some other person duly authorized, acting in behalf, has executed a deed under seal.[4] But the covenant ist impose an affirmative obligation.[5]

In the case of covenant under seal, the action of covenant may maintained, whether such covenant be contained in a deed-poll an indenture,[6] or be expressed on the face of the instrument, implied by law from the terms thereof.[7]

1. Scott v. Conover, 6 N. J. L. (1 Halst.) 1.

2. Somerville v. Stephenson, 3 Stew. (Ala.) 271.

3. McVoy v. Wheeler, 6 Port. (Ala.) 201.

When Covenant lies. — Covenant lies on instrument under seal, generally, when covenantor has done some act contrary his general agreement, or failed to perform that which he has undertaken, or does t which disables him from performing contract, which he has undertaken. In case of reciprocal covenants, the same applies to the covenantee. See Heard Towers, 23 Pick. (Mass.) 455; Hopkins Young, 11 Mass. 302; Grebert-Borgnis Nugent, L. R. 12 Q. B. Div. 85; Scot v. wn, Cro. Eliz. 449; 4 Dana Abr. 115.

Written Obligation. — Debt or covenant the appropriate remedy on a writing obligatory. French v. Tunstall, Hempst. C. 204.

Covenant is the only remedy where the bility is created by an agreement under l; but when the law creates the liability ependently of the covenant, an action the case may also be maintained. Luckey Rowzee, 1 A. K. Marsh. (Ky.) 295.

An action for a breach of covenant must prosecuted in the name of the real party interest, — the person entitled to the mages. Sisker v. Floyd, 104 Ind. 291; , 2 West. Rep. 218.

4. See Bassett v. Jordan, 1 Stew. (Ala.) ; Somerville v. Stephenson, 3 Stew. (Ala.) 271; Powers v. Ware, 2 Pick. (Mass.) ; Bell v. Curtis, 1 N. J. L. (1 Penn.) ; Powell v. Clark, 3 N. J. L. (2 Penn.) ; Rees v. Overbaugh, 6 Cow. (N. Y.) ; Vicary v. Moore, 2 Watts (Pa.), 451; 27 Am. Dec. 323; United States v. wn, 1 Paine, C. C. 422.

5. **Negative Restriction.** — A covenant creating a purely negative restriction is not enforceable; covenants must "touch and concern" or "support," and be for the "benefit of the estate;" unusual incidents cannot attach to land. Norcross v. James, 140 Mass. 188; s. c., 1 New. Eng. Rep. 327.

6. See 1 Rol. Abr. 517, pl. 40.

Deed-Poll. — It has been said that the technical action of covenant cannot be maintained against a grantee in a deed-poll, because he did not seal the deed. Hinsdale v. Humphrey, 15 Conn. 432; Nugent v. Riley, 1 Metc. (Mass.) 167; s. c., 35 Am. Dec. 355; Newell v. Hill, 2 Metc. (Mass.) 180; Goodwin v. Gilbert, 9 Mass. 510; Atlantic Dock Co. v. Leavitt, 54 N. Y. 35, 38; Maule v. Weaver, 7 Pa. St. 329; Johnson v. Muzzy, 45 Vt. 419; Burnett v. Lynch, 5 Barn. & C. 589. But a contrary doctrine has been held in New Jersey in a well-considered case. See Finely v. Simpson, 22 N. J. L. (2 Zab.) 331; s. c., 53 Am. Dec. 252.

A statute in Pennsylvania, passed April 22, 1850, gives to the owner of a ground-rent the remedy by action of covenant, whether the premises out of which the rent issues be held by deed-poll or otherwise.

In those of the States of the Union where the common law still prevails, it is held that the action on the grantor's covenant in a deed-poll must be assumpsit, since the agreement or covenant is not one under his seal, — Hinsdale v. Humphrey, 15 Conn. 432; Nugent v. Riley, 1 Metc. (Mass.) 117; s. c., 35 Am. Dec. 355; Newell v. Hill, 9 Metc. (Mass.) 180; Goodwin v. Gilbert, 2 Mass. 510; Maule v. Weaver, 7 Pa. St. 329; — but in all those States that have adopted codes, the common-law distinction has passed away with the abolition of all forms of actions. Atlantic Dock Co. v. Leavitt, 54 N. Y. 38.

7. See Frost v. Raymond, 2 Cai. (N. Y.)

Covenant will lie upon a sealed instrument, notwithstanding a parol enlargement of the time of performance, if the breaches assigned go only to the manner in which the work was done.[1]

Covenant will lie for the performance of something *in futuro*, or when that something has been done;[2] but as a rule, the action of covenant will not lie on a contract *in presenti*.[3]

It is not essential that the word "covenant" occur in the instrument, in order to render the party executing it liable in covenant;[4] for covenants, like conditions, do not depend upon precise or technical words.[5] Whatever shows the intent of the parties to

188; s. c., 2 Am. Dec. 228; Kent *v.* Welsch, 7 Johns. (N. Y.) 258; s. c., 5 Am. Dec. 266; Dorsey *v.* Jackman, 1 Serg. & R. (Pa.) 42; s. c., 7 Am. Dec. 611; Andrews *v.* Ellison, 6 J. B. Moore, 199, 202, note a.; Saltoun *v.* Houstoun, 1 Bing. 433; Sampson *v.* Easterby, 9 B. & C. 505; s. c., 1 C. & J. 105.

Pleading Implied Covenants. — It has been held that implied covenants may be set forth in the declaration in the same manner as if they were expressed in the instrument. Grannis *v.* Clark, 8 Cow. (N. Y.) 36; Barney *v.* Keith, 6 Wend. N. Y. 555.

1. Crane *v.* Maynard, 12 Wend. (N. Y.) 408.

2. Sharington *v.* Strotton, Plowd. 308; Adams *v.* Gibney, 6 Bing. 666.

3. Sharington *v.* Strotton, Plowd. 308; Powel *v.* Morgan, Finch 49.

Matters in Presenti. — The action of covenant is said to be maintainable in some cases, although the covenant relates to matters *in presenti*, as where one covenants that he is seised and has a good title. Browning *v.* Wright, 2 B. & P. 13; Wotton *v.* Hele, 2 Saund. 181 *b.*; Kingdon *v.* Nottle, 4 M. & S. 53; Adams *v.* Gibney, 6 Bing. 656. See *infra*, COVENANT OF SEISIN, and BREACH OF COVENANT OF SEISIN.

4. Randel *v.* Chesapeake & Del. Canal Co., 1 Har. (Del.) 151; Kendal *v.* Talbot, 2 Bibb (Ky.), 614; Bull *v.* Follett, 5 Cow. (N. Y.) 170; Andrews *v.* Ellison, 6 Moore, 203.

5. Davis *v.* Lyman, 6 Conn. 252; Newcomb *v.* Presbrey, 8 Metc. (Mass.) 406; Myers *v.* Burns, 33 Barb. (N. Y.) 401.

Words implying a Covenant. — Among the words and forms of expression from the use of which covenants have been held to be implied, are "grant," — Grannis *v.* Clark, 8 Cow. (N. Y.) 36; Baber *v.* Harris, 9 Ad. & E. 532, — "give," — Kent *v.* Welch, 7 Johns. (N. Y.) 258; s. c., 5 Am. Dec. 266; Vanderkarr *v.* Vanderkarr, 11 Johns. (N. Y.) 122. *Compare* Allen *v.* Sayward, 5 Me. 227; s. c., 17 Am. Dec. 221; Dow *v.* Lewis, 4 Gray (Mass.), 468, — "lease," — Maule *v.* Ashmead, 20 Pa. St. 482; [illegible] *v.* Cartwright, 22 L. J. Rep. (N. S.) Exch. 285; s. c., 20 Eng. L. & Eq. [illegible], — "demise," — Sumner *v.* Williams, 8 Mass. [illegible]; s. c., 6 Am. Dec. 83; Bruce *v.* Fulton Nat. Bank, 79 N. Y. 162; Williams *v.* Burrell, 1 C. B. 402, 429, — "yielding and paying," — Kimpton *v.* Walker, 9 Vt. [illegible], — "grant, bargain, and sell," — Hawk *v.* McCullough, 21 Ill. 220; Bush *v.* Cooper, 26 Miss. [illegible]; s. c., 59 Am. Dec. 270; [illegible], 23 Mo. 151; Blossom *v.* Van Court, 34 Mo. 390; Gratz *v.* Ewalt, 2 Binn. (Pa.) 95. *Compare* Frost *v.* Raymond, 2 Cai. (N. Y.) 188; Huntly *v.* Waddell, 12 Ired. (N. C.) L. 32, — and other words of like character and import. See Crouch *v.* [illegible], 222; Frost *v.* Raymond, 2 Cai. (N. Y.) 188; Mack *v.* Patchin, 42 N. Y. [illegible]; Adams *v.* Gibney, 6 Bing. 656.

That the word "lease" is equivalent to "demise" in creating an implied covenant, has been held in some cases, — see Hamilton *v.* Wright, 28 Mo. 199; Maule *v.* Ashmead, 2 Pa. St. 482; Ross *v.* Dysart, 33 Pa. St. 452, — and denied in others. Lovering *v.* Lovering, 13 N. H. 513; [illegible] *v.* Brace, 8 Paige, Ch. (N. Y.) [illegible]; Kinney *v.* Watts, 14 Wend. (N. Y.) 38; [illegible] *v.* Mabie, 13 N. Y. 160; Sheets *v.* Selden, [illegible] U. S. (7 Wall.) 416, 423; bk. 19 L. ed. 166, 169; Williams *v.* Burrell, 1 C. B. [illegible]; Hart *v.* Windsor, 12 Mees. & W. 85.

Although a deed contains an express covenant, other covenants may still be implied. Roebuck *v.* Duprey, 2 Ala. 535; Morris *v.* Harris, 9 Gill. (Md.) [illegible]; Sumner *v.* Williams, 8 Mass. [illegible]; Funk *v.* Voneida, 11 Serg. & R. (Pa.) [illegible]; s. c., 14 Am. Dec. 617. *Compare* Vanderkarr *v.* Vanderkarr, 11 Johns. (N. Y.) 122; [illegible] *v.* Stenton, 43 N. Y. 462; Merritt *v.* Closson, 36 Vt. 172. But a covenant will not be implied in the absence of language tending to a conclusion that the covenant sought to be set up was intended by the parties. Booth *v.* Cleveland Rolling Mill Co., 74 N. Y. 15; Hudson Canal Co. *v.* Pennsylvania Coal Co., 75 U. S. (8 Wall.) 276; bk. 19, L. ed. 349. An express covenant in a deed will qualify the generality of

iselves to the performance of a stipulation, may be covenant, without regard to the form of expression;[1] construction is to be preferred which renders the whole
[2]

venant, and restrain it so that
held broader than the express
rouch v. Fowle, 9 N. H. 219;
. Dec. 350; Lynch v. Onon-
., 64 Barb. (N. Y.) 558; Line
n, 5 Bing. N. C. 183.
Statute. — But by statute in
o covenant shall be implied in
ice of real estate in that State.
. Watts, 14 Wend. (N. Y.) 38.
venants are still implied in
rs in that State. Mayor, etc.,
. Y. 168; Lynch v. Onondaga
Barb. (N. Y.) 558.
ll v. Craig, 1 Bibb (Ky.), 379;
Dec. 647; Gardner v. Cosson,
4; Lovering v. Lovering, 13
Jull v. Follett, 5 Cow. (N. Y.)
v. Wylie, 3 Johns. (N. Y.) 85;
wart, 20 Johns. (N. Y.) 85;
ston, 79 Pa. St. 436; Trutt v.
a. St. 339; Rigby v. Great
Co., 14 Mees. & W. 811; Samp-
by, 9 Barn. & C. 505.
y Recital. — A covenant ex-
ay of recital may be as binding
s as though expressed in the
of the deed, — De Forest v.
t. (N. Y.) 43; Horry v. Frost,
C.) Eq. 109. *Compare* Anon.
— and will be binding upon all
o the instrument, their privies
state, and in law — Robbins v.
Miss. 434; McBurney v. Cut-
(N. Y.) 203; Jackson v. Park-
d. (N. Y.) 209; Scott v. Doug-
287; Kaine v. Denniston, 22
, Rankin v. Warner, 2 Lea
; Carver v. Jackson, 29 U. S.
86, 7 L. ed. 761, 790; — but
l not be bound by such recitals.
Garnett, 3 Bush (Ky.), 402.
a deed will not be bound by
the deeds through which he
itle. Wilkins v. Dingley, 29
ggs v. Smith, 12 N. J. L. (7
Doe v. Shelton, 3 Ad. & E.
ter v. Buller, 8 Mees. & W.

ll not be affected by the reci-
executed under judicial com-
cDougald v. Dougherty, 11 Ga.
misrecitals — Lewen v. Mody,
7; s. c., 3 Leon. 135, — espe-
they are impertinent and irrel-
en v. Mudy, Cro. Eliz. 127;
135.
ecitals in a deed will not be
control the operation of the

instrument, if the plain intent would be thereby defeated. Schermerhorn v. Negus, 2 Hill (N. Y.), 335; Cole v. Patterson, 25 Wend. (N. Y.) 456; Boutell v. Summers, 2 Young & J. 407.

The recital of an agreement in a deed only operates as a covenant when it is apparent from the whole scope of the instrument that it was intended to so operate. Douglass v. Hennessy (R. I.), 3 New Eng. Rep. 525. Courts are bound in each case to ascertain the intention of an instrument, and give it effect accordingly. Douglass v. Hennessy (R. I.), 3 New Eng. Rep. 525.

Where a bond was given to secure a conveyance of real estate, in which an agreement was set forth by way of recital, and the court *held* that an action in covenant would not lie on the agreement. Huddle v. Worthington, 1 Ohio, 423. In Tomlinson v. Ousatonic Water Co., 44 Conn. 99, the words of recital in the condition of a bond given by the company were, "Whereas, the Ousatonic Water Company has, made, taken, and does hereby undertake and agree;" and the court *held* that covenant would lie on the recital. However, the court said if the words "and does hereby undertake and agree" were stricken from the clause, the remainder is manifestly nothing more nor less than the condition of the bond, and that in that case the plaintiff's remedy would be on the bond.

Condition. — A covenant or condition may be created by the same words. Chapin v. Harris, 8 Allen (Mass.), 594; Parmlee v. Oswego & S. R. Co., 6 N. Y. 80; Harting v. Witte, 59 Wis. 285; s. c., 18 N. W. Rep. 175.

When a covenant in form is followed by a clause of forfeiture, it will be construed a condition. Ayer v. Emery, 14 Allen (Mass.), 69; Gray v. Blanchard, 8 Pick. (Mass.) 284; Moore v. Pitts, 53 N. Y. 85.

In the construction of deeds, courts will always incline to interpret the language as a covenant rather than a condition. Gallaher v. Herbert, 117 Ill. 160; s. c., 4 West. Rep. 166; Board of Education v. Trustees, 63 Ill. 204.

2. Hulloway v. Lacy, 4 Humph. (Tenn.) 468.

Construction. — In construing written instruments, that construction is to be preferred which renders the whole covenant operative, — Randel v. Chesapeake & Del. Canal Co., 1 Har. (Del.) 154, — and generally the interpretation should be in accord-

It has been held that it is not necessary that the covenantee

ance with the reasonable sense of the words employed. Pavey v. Burch, 3 Mo. 447; s. c., 26 Am. Dec. 682; Killian v. Harshaw, 7 Ired. (N. C.) L. 497; Rogers v. Danforth, 9 N. J. Eq. (1 Stockt.) 289; Thorns v. Wilson, 4 Best & S. 442.

The intention of the parties, as ascertained from the instrument itself, will be enforced when this can be done consistently with the rules of law. Mulford v. Le Franc, 26 Cal. 88; Kenworthy v. Tullis, 3 Ind. 96; Allen v. Holton, 20 Pick. (Mass.) 463; Rutherford v. Tracy, 48 Mo. 325; s. c., 8 Am. Rep. 104; Jackson v. Myers, 3 Johns. (N. Y.) 388; s. c., 3 Am. Dec. 504; Mills v. Catlin, 22 Vt. 98; Collins v. Lavelle, 44 Vt. 230; Roberts v. Robertson, 53 Vt. 690; s. c., 38 Am. Rep. 710; Parkhurst v. Smith, Willes, 332. And in arriving at the intention of the parties, regard should always be had of their situation and the circumstances attending the transaction,—Abbott v. Abbott, 53 Me. 356; Derby v. Hall, 2 Gray (Mass.), 243; Dunn v. English, 23 N. J. L. (3 Zab.) 126; Wolfe v. Scarborough, 2 Ohio St. 361; Shore v. Wilson, 9 Clark & F. 569; Mumford v. Gething, 7 C. B., N. S. 305,—and the practical interpretation which they by their conduct have given the provisions in controversy. Lowber v. Bangs, 69 U. S. (2 Wall.) 728; bk. 17, L. ed. 768. But the court will not assume to make a contract for the parties which they did not choose to make for themselves. Morgan Co. v. Allen, 103 U. S. (13 Otto) 515; bk. 26, L. ed. 583.

In construing covenants, the grammatical sense is not to be adhered to where a contrary intention is apparent,—Hancock v. Watson, 18 Cal. 137; Jackson v. Topping, 1 Wend. (N. Y.) 388; s. c., 19 Am. Dec. 515. *Compare* Deering v. Long Wharf, 25 Me. 51; Waugh v. Middleton, 8 Ex 357; Gray v. Pearson, 6 H. L. Cas. 61;—and punctuation should be wholly disregarded, unless all other means fail. Bruensmann v. Carroll, 52 Mo. 313; Ewing v. Burnet, 36 U. S. (11 Pet.) 41; bk. 9, L. ed. 624. *Compare* English v. McNair, 34 Ala. 40; Churchill v. Ramer, 8 Bush (Ky.), 260; White v. Smith, 33 Pa. St. 186; s. c., 75 Am. Dec. 589. The Supreme Court of the United States say, in the case of Ewing v. Burnet, *supra*, that "punctuation is a most fallible standard by which to interpret a writing. It may be resorted to when all other means fail; but the court will first take the instrument by its four corners, in order to ascertain its true meaning. If that is apparent on judicially inspecting the whole, the punctuation will not be suffered to change it."

Courts, in construing written instruments, have held "and" to mean "or," and [illegible] *versa*, in order to effect the [illegible] intention of the parties. White v. [illegible], 10 Mass. 183; Jackson v. Topping, 1 Wend. (N. Y.) 388; s. c., 19 Am. Dec. 515. And they have omitted [illegible] which were repugnant to the other parts of the instrument and to the manifest general intent of the parties. [illegible], 4 Mass. 196; White v. Gay, [illegible]; s. c., 31 Am. Dec. [illegible]; Jackson v. [illegible], 7 Johns. (N. Y.) 217; [illegible], 355; s. c., 27 Am. Dec. 564; [illegible] v. Harwood, 11 U. S. (7 Cr.) [illegible]; bk. 3, L. ed. 386, 388.

It has been *held*, that where a covenant cannot operate in the manner intended by the parties, it will be so construed, if possible, that it may operate in some other way,—Bryan v. Bradley, 16 Conn. [illegible]; Thomas v. Hatch, 3 Sumn. C. C. [illegible]; Doe v. Woodroffe, 10 Mees. & W. [illegible];—and that where the words are so [illegible] or so unmeaning as to render the intention of the parties absolutely [illegible], the instrument and covenant will be void for uncertainty. Musick v. [illegible], [illegible] 297; Shackelford v. Bailey, [illegible]; Bean v. Thompson, 19 N. H. [illegible] Am. Dec. 154; Mason v. White, 11 Barb. (N. Y.) 173; United States v. King, 41 U. S. (3 How.) 773; bk. 11, L. ed. 824.

It is a well-settled rule in the construction of covenants and other written instruments, that where there is doubt or ambiguity, the construction should be most favorable to the party in whose favor the covenant is made, and most strongly against the party imposing such covenant upon himself. Randel v. Chesapeake & Del. Canal Co., 1 Har. (Del.) 151; Coffing v. Taylor, 16 Ill. 457; Watson v. Boylston, 5 Mass. 411; Gifford v. First Presbyterian Society, 56 Barb. (N. Y.) 114; Rung v. Shoneberger, 2 Watts (Pa.), 23; s. c., 26 Am. Dec. 95; Hogg's Appeal, 22 Pa. St. 479; Johnson v. Webster, 4 De G. M. & G. 474; s. c., 31 Eng. L. & Eq. 98, 1 Jur. (N. S.) 145, 24 L. J. Ch. 300; Warde v. Warde, 16 Beav. 103; Hookes v. Swain, 1 Lev. 102. *Compare* Falley v. Giles, 29 Ind. 114; Palmer v. Warren Ins. Co., 1 Story, C. C. 360.

And the same rule applies to exceptions and restrictions. Duryea v. Mayor, etc., 62 N. Y. 592.

Where a covenant will inure in several ways, the covenantee may elect which way it shall be taken. Sharpe v. Thompson, 100 Ill. 447; s. c., 39 Am. Rep. 61; Esty v. Baker, 50 Me. 325; Jackson v. Hudson, 3 Johns. (N. Y.) 375; s. c., 3 Am. Dec. 500.

A covenant, being a part of a deed, is

should have executed the deed;[1] and a covenant purporting to bind the grantee will be sufficient to sustain an action against him, although he did not sign, if there be evidence of his acceptance of the deed.[2]

A stranger to a deed-poll may sometimes sue on a covenant therein to pay him money; although it is otherwise in the case of a deed *inter partes*.[3] But it has been said that where a deed-poll,

subject to the same rules of construction as the deed itself, and should be so expounded as to give effect to the actual intention of the parties. Watchman *v.* Crook, 5 Gill & J. (Md.) 239; Wadlington *v.* Hill, 10 Miss. 560; Marvin *v.* Stone, 2 Cow. (N. Y.) 781; Ludlow *v.* McCrea, 1 Wend. (N. Y.) 228; Schoenberger *v.* Hay, 40 Pa. St. 132.

In construing a deed where the grantors covenant generally against incumbrances made by them, it will be held to extend to several, as well as joint, incumbrances. Duvall *v.* Craig, 15 U. S. (2 Wheat.) 45, 58; bk. 4, L. ed. 180.

Where the words of plaintiff's covenant are "that he will make a deed" to his vendee on receipt of the first instalment, these words require that the deed shall convey the land,—Washington *v.* Ogden, 66 U. S. (1 Black.) 450; bk. 17, L. ed. 203,—the legal effect of a covenant to sell being, that the land shall be conveyed by a deed from one who has a good title. Washington *v.* Ogden, 66 U. S. (1 Black.) 450; bk. 17, L. ed. 203.

A covenant that if the grantors obtain the "fee-simple" to the property conveyed "from the Government of the United States, they will convey the same" to the grantee, his heirs or assigns, "by a deed of general warranty," only takes effect in case the grantors acquire the title directly from the United States, and does not cover the acquisition of the title of the United States from any intermediate party. Davenport *v.* Lamb, 80 U. S. (13 Wall.) 418; bk. 20, L. ed. 655.

But if the grantor is guilty of fraud, or can convey, but will not, either from perverseness, or to secure a better bargain; or if he has covenanted to convey when he knew he had no authority to contract to convey, or where it is in his power to remedy a defect in his title, and he refuses or neglects to do so; or where he refuses to incur such reasonable expenses as would enable him to fulfil his contract,—in all such cases the vendor is liable to the vendee for the loss of the bargain, under rules analogous to those applied in the sale of personal property. Margraf *v.* Muir, 57 N. Y. 155.

An agreement to perform certain works within a limited time, under a certain penalty, is not to be construed as liquidating the damages which the party is to pay for the breach of his covenant. Tayloe *v.* Sandiford, 20 U. S. (7 Wheat.) 13; bk. 5, L. ed. 384.

It is held that express covenants are to be construed more strictly than implied ones. Shubrick *v.* Salmond, 3 Burr. 1639.

1. Smith *v.* Ransom, 21 Wend. (N. Y.) 202; Olcott *v.* Dunklee, 16 Vt. 478; 2 Rol. Abr. 22; Fait (F.), pl. 2, 22; Hunt *v.* Bourne, Lutw. 305; Petrie *v.* Bury, 3 Barn. & C. 353; Laythoarp *v.* Bryant, 2 Bing. N. C. 735; s. c., 3 Scott, 238; Liverpool Borough Bank *v.* Eccles, 4 H. & N. 139; Seton *v.* Slade, 7 Ves. 275; Egerton *v.* Mathews, 6 East, 307; Allen *v.* Bennet, 3 Taunt. 169.

When Covenantee may sue. — As to when a covenantee may sue for a breach of covenant, although he has not executed the deed, see Wetherell *v.* Langston, 1 Ex. 634; Pitman *v.* Woodbury, 3 Ex 4; British Emp. Ass. Co *v.* Browne, 12 C. B. 723; Morgan *v.* Pike, 14 C. B. 473; Swatman *v.* Ambler, 8 Ex. 72.

It cannot be said that unless the plaintiff also executes the deed, there is a want of mutuality, because the defendant had it in his power to require the plaintiff's signature, and if he does not do so it is his own fault. See Laythoarp *v.* Bryant, 2 Bing. N. C. 743.

2. Atlantic Dock Co. *v.* Leavitt, 54 N. Y. 35.

3. Hinkley *v.* Fowler, 15 Me. 285; Robbins *v.* Ayres, 10 Mo. 538; s. c., 47 Am. Dec. 125; Smith *v.* Emery, 12 N. J. L. (7 Halst.) 53; Hornbeck *v.* Westbrook, 9 Johns. (N. Y.) 73; Hornbeck *v.* Sleight, 12 Johns. (N. Y.) 199; Strohecker *v.* Grant, 16 Serg. & R. (Pa.) 237; Berkley *v.* Hardy, 8 Dowl. & Ryl. 102; Bushell *v.* Beavan, 1 Bing. N. C. 120; Storer *v.* Gordon, 3 M. & S. 308, 322; Barford *v.* Stuckey, 5 Moore, 23; s. c., 2 B. & B. 333.

Promise to pay the Debt of Another. — A promise on a valid consideration, as distinguished from a bond conditioned for such payment, — Turke *v.* Ridge, 41 N. Y. 201, — to pay a third person, will sustain an action by the latter in his own name, although he was not privy to the consideration. Hall *v.* Robbins, 61 Barb. (N. Y.) 338; s. c., 4 Lans. (N. Y.) 463; Lawrence *v.* Fox, 20 N. Y. 268;

not being a deed *inter partes*, contains a covenant with A. to pay B. a sum of money, it is doubtful whether B. could sue in his own name; because the covenant being with A., although for the benefit of B., and the contract being under seal, it would seem that A. should be the plaintiff,[1] for the terms of the express covenant invest him with legal interest.[2]

Where a person covenants with two other persons jointly to pay a sum of money to one of them, they take a joint legal interest, and must jointly sue upon the covenant.[3]

In covenant for non-payment of rent, payable at different times, a new action lies as often as the respective sums become due and payable, and there is a breach of the covenant to pay.[4]

If a party, by his covenant, charge himself with an obligation possible to be performed, he must make it good unless its per-

Hutchings *v.* Miner, 46 N. Y. 456; Barlow *v.* Myers, 64 N. Y. 41; reversing s. c., 3 Hun (N. Y.), 720; Hendrick *v.* Lindsay, 93 U. S. (3 Otto) 143; bk. 23, L. ed. 855.

A contrary doctrine prevails in Massachusetts, except in cases of trust, agency, and the like. See Exchange Bank of St. Louis *v.* Rice, 107 Mass. 37; s. c., 9 Am. Rep. 1.

A promise to pay may be implied from the acceptance of a conveyance stipulating to be subject to the payment of a specified incumbrance, — Collins *v.* Rowe, 1 Abb. Pr. N. C. (N. Y.) 97; Binsse *v.* Paige, 1 Abb. Ct App. Dec. (N. Y.) 138, note, — or a specified sum. Dingeldein *v.* Third Ave. R. R. Co., 37 N. Y. 575; reversing s. c., 9 Bosw. (N. Y.) 79.

If the precise obligation incurred is identified by the promise, as in a covenant to assume and pay a designated mortgage upon land purchased, the defendant cannot deny the existence or validity of the obligation, but he may show that it has been paid. Hartley *v.* Tatham, 2 Abb. Ct. App. Dec. (N. Y.) 339; Ritter *v.* Phillips, 53 N. Y. 586; affirming 34 N. Y. Super. Ct. (J. & S.) 289; 35 id. 388.

1. Millard *v.* Baldwin, 3 Gray (Mass.), 484; Bird *v.* Washburn, 10 Pick. (Mass.) 223; Sanders *v.* Filley, 12 Pick. (Mass.) 551; Montague *v.* Smith, 13 Mass. 396, 404; Watson *v.* Cambridge, 15 Mass. 286.

Covenant for Benefit of Third Person. Suit on. — A. is a trustee for B., and the obligatory part of the instrument, and the acknowledgment of legal responsibility, are to him. See Offy *v.* Warde, 1 Lev. 235; Gilby *v.* Copley, 3 Lev. 139; Lowther *v.* Kelley, 8 Mod. 115; Pigott *v.* Thompson, 3 B. & P. 149, note a; Anderson *v.* Martindale, 1 East, 501.

Upon suit brought by A., he need not set out in his complaint, or show in the evidence, that he has paid the debt. Stout *v.* Folger, 34 Iowa, 71; s. c., 11 Am. Rep. 138; Furnas *v.* Durgin, 119 Mass. 500; s. c., 20 Am. Rep. 341; 15 Alb. L. J. [illegible]. But it will be otherwise where the promise was simply to indemnify.

2. See Chaplin *v.* Canada, 8 Conn. [illegible]; Fellows *v.* Gilman, 4 Wend. (N. Y.) [illegible]; Anderson *v.* Martindale, 1 East, [illegible].

Where A. and B. gave a bond to C., conditioned to pay C.'s debts, and the holder of a promissory note, executed by C. before the date of the bond, brought, an action of assumpsit, on the money covenant, against A. and B., to recover the amount of the note, the court of Massachusetts *held* the action could not be maintained. See Johnson *v.* Foster, 12 Metc. (Mass.) 167; Sanders *v.* Filley, 12 Pick. (Mass.) 551.

Action under the Codes. — Under the codes, an action for the breach of a covenant must be prosecuted in the name of the real party in interest; that is, the party who is entitled to the damages. Sinker *v.* Floyd, 104 Ind. 291; s. c., 2 West. Rep. 218. See Pence *v.* Aughe, 101 Ind. 317.

3. Anderson *v.* Martindale, 1 East, 497; Withers *v.* Bircham, 3 B. & C. 256.

Where there are Several Covenantees. — Where a person covenanted with the rector, wardens, and vestry of a church to pay to the rector or wardens a specified sum of money, it was held that neither separately, nor the rector and wardens jointly, could maintain an action on the covenant, but that the vestry should be joined with the rector and wardens; that is, that the action should be sued in the name of the parties with whom it was made. Montague *v.* Smith, 13 Mass 405. See also Harrison *v.* Matthews, 2 Dowl. N. S. Bail, 318.

Where all the members of a corporation enter into a covenant for themselves and heirs, that the corporation do certain things, they will all be bound in their individual capacities, and be parties to the covenant. See Tileston *v.* Newell, 13 Mass. 406.

4. Cross *v.* United States, [illegible] U. S. (14 Wall.) 479; bk. 20, L. ed. [illegible].

be rendered impossible by the act of God, the law, or party.[1] And a plaintiff cannot recover for a part per- unless prevented by the act of the defendant, from com- s contract.[2]

it is the proper action to be brought on a sealed guaranty; of no consequence to the maintenance of such action he contract is conditional, so that it is a covenant, and ition merely.[3]

it may be brought on a sealed agreement that, in consid- certain services rendered, and materials furnished on aintiff should receive one-half the crops.[4] Covenant lies d instrument between tenants in common of land,[5] for ful dissolution of a partnership, by articles under seal;[6] yment of a stipulated sum of money, either by way of otherwise;[7] for a breach of an indenture of appren-

v. Jones, 69 U. S. (2 Wall.) ed. 762.

v. Debloise, 1 Cr. C. C. 156.

v. Read, 7 R. I. 576.

. Heustis, 26 N. J. L. (2 Dutch.) v. Horner, 3 N. J. L. (2

to Share Profits. — A cove- share of the crops for ser- aterials does not, *per se*, con- tership or tenancy in common, covenant may be maintained. ustis, 26 N. J. L. (2 Dutch.)

men enter into a contract to kind of business, one to fur- ital and the other to do the profits or proceeds are to be ly, such agreement does not artnership. Moore v. Smith, Randle v. State, 49 Ala. 14; Crocker, 25 Ark. 327; Parker Conn. 250; s. c., 9 Am. Rep. ay v. Brinkley, 42 Ga. 226; merlind, 48 Ga. 425; Blue v. Ill. 31; Holbrook v. Oberne, ; s. c., 9 N. W. Rep. 291; one, 30 Me. 384; Holmes v. R. Co., 5 Gray (Mass.), 58; ot, 6 Metc. (Mass.) 82; Brad- 10 Metc. (Mass.) 303; Beecher ich. 188; Donnell v. Harshe, Musser v. Brink, 68 Mo. 242; Clark, 53 N. H. 276; s. c., 16 ; Lamb v. Grover, 47 Barb. Harrower v. Heath, 79 Barb. ; Putnam v. Wise, 1 Hill s. c., 37 Am. Dec. 309; Cas- ich, 15 Wend. (N. Y.) 379; cherson, 54 N. Y. 1; s. c., 13 ; Leggett v. Hyde, 58 N. Y. Am. Rep. 244; Smith v. Bo- . 301 Richardson v. Hughett, s. c., 32 Am. Rep. 267; Ea- ger v. Crawford, 76 N. Y. 97; Burnett v. Snyder, 76 N. Y. 344; s. c., 81 N. Y. 550; Lewis v. Wilkins, Phil. (N. C.) Eq. 303; Holt v. Kernodle, 1 Ired. (N. C.) L. 199; Reynolds v. Pool, 84 N. C. 37; s. c., 37 Am Rep. 607; Ambler v. Bradley, 6 Vt. 119; Vinson v. Beveridge, 3 McA. D. C. 597; Dry v. Boswell, 1 Camp. 329. *Compare* Autrey v. Freize, 59 Ala. 587; Parker v. Canfield, 37 Conn. 250; s. c., 9 Am. Rep. 317; Manhattan Brass and Manuf. Co. v. Sears, 45 N. Y. 797; s. c., 6 Am. Rep. 177.

But where the expenses are shared, one party contributing the capital or land or the like, and the other the experience and labor or personal attention, it is a partnership, at least as to third persons. Emanuel v. Draughn, 14 Ala. 306; McCrary v. Slaughter, 58 Ala. 230; Parker v. Canfield, 37 Conn. 250; s. c., 9 Am. Rep. 317; Holifield v. White, 52 Ga. 567; Adams v. Carter, 53 Ga. 160; Pettee v. Appleton, 114 Mass. 114; Patten v. Heustis, 26 N. J. L. (2 Dutch.) 293; Champion v. Bostwick, 18 Wend. (N. Y.) 183.

5. Hall v. Stewart, 12 Pa. St. 211.

Partnership in Realty. — Where A. & B., by an agreement under seal, were to hold land as equal partners, A. to remain in possession, and to hold for the use of both, and to pay B. one-half of what should be adjudged a reasonable rent, it was *held*, that a covenant would lie upon this agreement, although B. might have expended money in improving the land. Hall v. Stewart, 12 Pa. St. 211.

6. Addams v. Tutton, 39 Pa. St. 447.

7. Bassett v. Jardan, 1 Stew. (Ala.) 352.

A covenant that a note shall be paid first out of a sale, does not bind covenantor that such note shall be paid at all events. Richards v. Holmes, 59 U. S. (18 How.) 143; bk. 15, L. ed. 304.

ticeship;[1] on a penal bond;[2] for a breach of covenant[3] in a deed

1. Sayre *v.* Rose, 3 N. J. L. (2 Penn.) 743.

Apprenticeship. — Covenant is the usual remedy upon an indenture of apprenticeship against the master for not instructing his apprentice or the party who covenanted for the due service of such apprentice, but it will not lie against an infant apprentice. Gylbert *v.* Fletcher, Cro. Cas. 179.

But it would seem to be otherwise where the remedy is given by statute, and where an infant cannot be bound apprentice unless by an instrument under seal. See Commonwealth *v.* Wiltbanks, 10 Serg. & R. (Pa.) 416.

2. But the breach assigned must be the non-payment of the penalty, — United States *v.* Brown, Paine, C. C. 422, — and not of the condition of the bond, or of the condition or obligatory part of the bond separated from the penalty. Huddle *v.* Worthington, 1 Ohio, 423.

3. **Definition of Covenant.** — A covenant is defined to be "an agreement between two or more persons, entered into in writing under seal, by which either party stipulates for the truth of certain facts, or promises to perform or give something to the other, or to abstain from the performance of certain things." Bouv. L. Dict. tit. *Covenant.*

A guaranty, if expressed to be in consideration of one dollar paid by the other party thereto, the receipt whereof is acknowledged, or contains other consideration, is not an unaccepted proposal, but is, without notice of acceptance, binding on delivery. Davis *v.* Wells, Fargo, & Co., 104 U. S. (14 Otto) 159; bk. 26, L. ed. 686.

Kinds of Covenant. — Covenants are either express or implied, personal or real, dependent or independent. Covenants real are sometimes farther divided into those which run with the estate in land, and those which run with the land itself. Norcross *v.* James, 140 Mass. 188; s. c., 1 New Eng. Rep. 327. It was observed in an early English case, that there is "a diversity between a use or warranty, and the like things annexed to the estate of the land in privity, and commons, advowsons, and other hereditaments annexed to the possession of the land. Dillon *v.* Fraine, Poph. 70, 71; s. c., *Sub nom.* Candleigh's Case, 1 Co. Rep. 122 b. See Wilder *v.* Davenport's Estate, 58 Vt. 642; s. c., 2 New Eng. Rep. 810.

Express and Implied Covenants. — All covenants are either created by the express words of the parties to the deed declaration of their intention, or created by implication of law from the use of certain words, — Emerson *v.* Wiley, 10 Pick (Mass.) 310; Parker *v.* Smith, 17 Mass. 413; s. c., 9 Am. Dec. 757; Frey *v.* Johnson, 22 How. Pr. (N. Y.) 323; Taylor *v.* Hopper, 62 N. Y. 649; Williams *v.* Burrell, 1 C. B. 429, — such as "give," "grant," "demise," and the like. See Hawk *v.* McCullough, 21 Ill. 220; Webster *v.* Conley, 46 Ill. 14; Gratz *v.* Ewalt, 2 Binn. (Pa.) 95; Allen *v.* Sayward, 5 Me. 227; Dow *v.* Lewis, 4 Gray (Mass.), 468; Sumner *v.* Williams, 8 Mass. 201; s. c., 5 Am. Dec. 83; Bush *v.* Cooper, 26 Miss. 599; s. c., 59 Am. Dec. 270; Dickson *v.* Desire, 23 Mo. 151; Blossom *v.* Van Court, 34 Mo. 390; Crouch *v.* Fowle, 9 N. H. 222; s. c., 32 Am. Dec. 351; Frost *v.* Raymond, 2 Cai. (N. Y.) 188; s. c., 2 Am. Dec. 228; Grannis *v.* Clark, 8 Cow. (N. Y.) 36; Kent *v.* Welch, 7 Johns. (N. Y.) 258; s. c., 5 Am. Dec. 266; Vanderkarr *v.* Vanderkarr, 11 Johns. (N. Y.) 122; Mack *v.* Patchin, 42 N. Y. 167; Rence *v.* Fulton Nat. Bank, 79 N. Y. 162; Maule *v.* Ashmead, 20 Pa. St. 482; Kimpson *v.* Walker, 9 Vt. 191; Baker *v.* Harris, 9 Ad. & E. 532; Adams *v.* Gibney, 6 Bing. 656; Williams *v.* Burrell, 1 C. B. 402, 429; Bandy *v.* Cartwright, 8 Ex. 913; s. c., 22 L. J. (N. S.) Ex. 285.

A covenant by lessee to occupy premises as a dwelling-house, implies a covenant by lessor of fitness for occupancy; and the amount expended for necessary repairs is a set-off against a claim for rent. Wolfe *v.* Arrott, 109 Pa. St. 473; s. c., 1 Cent. Rep. 128.

But a covenant cannot be implied in the absence of language tending to a conclusion that the covenant sought to be set up was intended. Booth *v.* Cleveland Rolling Mill Co., 74 N. Y. 15; Hudson Canal Co. *v.* Pennsylvania Coal Co., 75 U. S. (8 Wall.) 276; bk. 19, L. ed. 349. And in New York the statute prevails that no covenant shall be implied in the conveyance of real estate, — see Kinney *v.* Watts, 14 Wend. (N. Y.) 38, — but the statute does not affect leases for years, and in these covenants are still implied. See Lynch *v.* Onondaga Salt Co., 64 Barb (N. Y.) 558; Mayor, etc., *v.* Mabie, 13 N. Y. 158; s. c., 64 Am. Dec. 538.

Express covenants are regarded with greater strictness than those which are simply implied. Shubrick *v.* Salmond, 3 Burr. 1639.

Personal Covenants are those which bind only the covenantor and his estate, does not run with the land, — Mason *v.* Rogers, 109 Pa. St. 319; s. c., 1 Cent. Rep. 97, — and can be taken advantage of only by the covenantee. Fitzherbert, Nat. Brev. 340.

Personal covenants are broken, if at all, as soon as they are made; and an action in covenant may at once be brought by the covenantee to recover his damages. See 4 Kent, Comm. 471, 472; Rawle on Cov. (4th [illegible] L. Cas. (5th Am. ed.)

. [illegible] consideration of the re- [illegible], by a lessee, of its [illegible]le, and interest in oil-producing [illegible]ler [illegible] leases, the owner of co[illegible] and agreed for him- the lessee to pay and deliver to [illegible]cessors and assigns, upon leased a certain part of all the oil, etc., therefrom daily during the re- [illegible]f the terms granted in the leases, [illegible]yance and agreement were duly ; and on the same day the owner his interest to different parties, each grantee into possession. [illegible]ntees produced large quantities of refused to account to the lessee. brought, the court *held* that such t was personal, and did not run land, so as to bind the grantee to perform the same. Newburgh [illegible] Co. v. Weare, 44 Ohio, 604; [illegible]est. Rep. 783.

[illegible]venants. — A covenant real is one [illegible] related to the realty that its owner [illegible] to the benefit of such covenant, [illegible]ring an action in covenant thereon broken, whether a party to the [illegible]not. To constitute such a cove- [illegible]s necessary, *first*, that it should [illegible]and concern the land; *second*, that [illegible]uld be some privity of estate be- co[illegible]nator and covenantee. See [illegible] v. Carver, 16 Pick. (Mass.) 183; [illegible] v. Schad, 7 Nev. 204.

[illegible]enants for title are real covenants, [illegible] v. Starr, 1 Conn. 244; s. c., 6 Am. [illegible]; Claycomb v. Munger, 51 Ill. [illegible]ter v. Rawson, 1 Metc. (Mass.) [illegible]ite v. Whitney, 3 Metc. (Mass.) [illegible] v. Weston, 12 N. H. 413; Moore [illegible], 17 N. H. 80; s. c., 43 Am. Dec. [illegible]hy v. Mumford, 5 Cow. (N. Y.) [illegible]kinson v. Hoomes, 8 Gratt. (Va.) [illegible]d in England run with the land; [illegible]st of the States of the Union, only [illegible]enants real as are future, as dis- [illegible]d from those that are *in presenti*, the land.

[illegible]venant of warranty is said to run land, and passes by assignment. [illegible]oken, it becomes a *chose in action*. [illegible]quent grantee may sue the war- the name of the holder. There [illegible]t one satisfaction. A sheriff's or [illegible]im deed will carry the covenant, breach, to the grantee. Peters [illegible]n, 98 U. S. (8 Otto) 56; bk. 25, L.

[illegible]ect to real covenants, or those [illegible] which run with the land, it has [illegible] in New York and Massachu- [illegible], if the grantor be not seised at [illegible] of conveyance, the covenant of [illegible]mmediately broken, and no action can be brought by the assignee of the grantee against the grantor; for, after the covenant is broken, it is a *chose in action*, and incapable of assignment. Bickford v. Page, 2 Mass. 455; Greenby v. Wilcocks, 2 Johns. (N. Y.) 1; s. c., 3 Am. Dec. 379.

But in England a different doctrine is held. It has been there adjudged that a covenant running with the land, though broken in the lifetime of a testator, is a continuing breach in the time of his devisee; and it is sufficient for such devisee to allege, in an action of covenant for damage, that thereby the lands are of less value to the devisee, and that he is prevented from selling them so advantageously. Kingdon v. Nottle, 4 Maule & S. 53. See also Kingdon v. Nottle, 1 Maule & S. 355; Chamberlain v. Williamson, 2 Maule & S. 408; King v. Jones, 5 Taunt. 418; s. c., 1 Marshall's Rep. 107.

Dependent Covenants. — Where the performance of one covenant depends upon the performance of another, they are dependent covenants, and the precedent condition must be performed before an action can be maintained on the other. So that where two acts are to be done by the parties at the same time, neither can maintain an action without showing performance, or offer to perform on his part; as, where the vendor covenants to convey an estate, and the vendee covenants to pay the purchase-money on the same day. Williams v. Healey, 3 Denio (N. Y.), 363; Gazley v. Price, 16 Johns. (N. Y.) 267; Dunham v. Pettee, 8 N. Y. 508; Lester v. Jewett, 11 N. Y. 453; Campbell v. Gittings, 19 Ohio, 347; Tilghman v. Tilghman, 1 Bald. C. C. 464; Bank of Columbia v. Hagner, 26 U. S. (1 Pet.) 455; bk. 7, L. ed. 219; Hyde v. Booraem, 41 U. S. (16 Pet.) 169; bk. 10, L. ed. 925; Slater v. Emerson, 60 U. S. (19 How.) 224; bk. 15, L. ed. 626; Washington v. Ogden, 66 U. S. (1 Black.) 450; bk. 17, L. ed. 203. See also Leonard v. Bates, 1 Blackf. (Ind.) 172, note; Kane v. Hood, 13 Pick. (Mass.) 281; Champion v. White, 5 Cow. (N. Y.) 509; Northrup v. Northrup, 6 Cow. (N. Y.) 296; Robb v. Montgomery, 20 Johns. (N. Y.) 15; Slocum v. Despard, 8 Wend. (N. Y.) 615; Halloway v. Davis, Wright (O.), 129; Adams v. Williams, 2 Watts & S. (Pa.) 227; Buckingham v. Jackson, 4 Biss. C. C. 295; Boody v. Rutland & B. R. R. Co., 3 Blatchf. C. C. 25; s. c., 24 Vt. 660; Buckingham v. Jackson, 4 Biss. C. C. 295; McNamera v. Gaylord, 1 Bond, C. C. 302; Thompson v. Cincinnati W. & Z. R. Co., 1 Bond C. C. 152; Langdon v. Purdy, 1 McA. C. C. 23; Hitchcock v. Galveston, 2 Wood. C. C. 272; Philadelphia W. & B. R. R. Co. 54 U. S. (13 How) 307, 339; bk. 14, L. ed. 157; The Florida Railway Co. v. Smith, 88 U. S. (21 Wall.) 255; bk. 22, L. ed. 513; Woodruff v. Hough, 91 U. S. (1 Otto) 596; bk. 23, L. ed. 332.

There are many adjudicated cases where it has been held that an agreement to pay by instalments, or at different times, would make the covenants mutual and independent, as by doing so the party had manifested a willingness to rely on the covenant or promise of the other contracting party for title or performance, by parting with at least a part of his money before he could with propriety call for performance on the other side. This rule of construction is adhered to both in England and the United States. Some of the authorities hold that the payment of part is still more conclusive as to the character of the agreement. Robb v. Montgomery, 20 Johns. (N. Y.) 151 Champion v. White, 5 Cow. (N. Y.) 509; Mason v. Chambers, 4 Litt. (Ky.) 253; Saunders v. Beal, 4 Bibb (Ky.), 342; Gardiner v. Corson, 15 Mass. 471, 500; Pordage v. Cole, 1 Saund. 319, note 4; Terry v. Duntze, 2 H. Bl. 389.

Where a plaintiff sues on one part of a contract, consisting of mutual stipulations made at the same time, and relating to the same subject-matter, the defendant may recoup his damages arising from the breach of that part which is in his favor; and this, whether the different parts are contained in one instrument, or several; and though one part be in writing, and the other in parol. *Aliter*, where the contract for the breach of which damages are claimed by the defendant, is entirely distinct and independent of the one on which the plaintiff sues. McAllister v. Reab, 4 Wend. (N. Y.) 483, 493; Ives v. Van Epps, 22 Wend. (N. Y.) 155; Withers v. Greene, 50 U. S. (9 How.) 213; bk. 13, L. ed. 109; Van Buren v. Digges, 52 U. S. (11 How.) 461; bk. 13, L. ed. 771; Batterman v. Pierce, 3 Hill (N. Y.), 171, 175.

Covenants are said to be dependent "according to the intentions of the parties and the good sense of the case," and that "technical words will always give way to such intention." Bean v. Atwater, 4 Conn. 3; s. c., 10 Am. Dec. 91; Howland v. Leach, 11 Pick. (Mass.) 154; Johnson v. Reed, 9 Mass. 78; s. c., 4 Am. Dec. 36; Tileston v. Newell, 13 Mass. 410; Gardner v. Corson, 15 Mass. 500; Barruso v. Madan, 2 Johns. (N. Y.) 145; Tompkins v. Elliott, 5 Wend. (N. Y.) 496; Durggins v. Shaw, 6 Ired. (N. C.) L. 46; McCrelish v. Churchman, 4 Rawle (Pa.), 26; Adams v. Williams, 2 Watts & S. (Pa.) 227; Wright v. Smith, 4 Watts & S. (Pa.) 527; Todd v. Summers, 2 Gratt. (Va.) 167; s. c., 44 Am. Dec. 379; Brockenbrough v. Ward, 4 Rand. (Va.) 352.

For cases of dependent contracts, see Gazley v. Price, 16 Johns. (N. Y.) 267; Heard v. Wadham, 1 East, 619; Glaze-

brook v. Woodrow, 8 T. R.
Emmons, 5 Johns. (N. Y.) 1,
Stanley, 11 Johns. (N. Y.)
v. Vanderlip, 12 Johns. (N.
v. Rose, 12 Johns. (N. Y.)
White, 13 Johns. (N. Y.) 5
Camp, 13 Johns. (N. Y.)
Duckingfield, 13 Johns. (N.
v. Stipp, 3 Munf. (Va.) 1
Adm'rix v. Miller's Exrs.,
170; Appleton v. Crownins
443; Johnson v. Reed, 9 Ma

Independent Covenants.
acts are stipulated to be do
times, the covenants are to b
independent of each other.
v. Orr, 21 U. S. (8 Wheat.)
ed. 600.

Covenants may be wholl
although relating to the san
made by the same parties, a
the same instrument. In t
are two separate contracts.
must then perform what l
without reference to the di
obligation by the other pa
party may have his action ag
for the non-performance of
whether he has performed l
Goldsborough v. Orr, 21 U.
217; bk. 5, L. ed. 600, note.

The dependence or indep
covenant will be determine
the fair intention of the part
certained from the languag
them. An intention to mak
stipulation a condition prec
clearly and unambiguously e
Robinson v. Harbour, 42 Mis
v. Lowber, 2 Cliff. C. C. 15

Covenants will not be he
pendent, so that one party n
yet enforce performance, u
be construed in no other w
Peoria & O. R. R. Co., 21 Il
v. Mosley, 15 Miss. (7 Sm. &
dell v. Sims, 17 Miss. (9 Sm
Clopton v. Bolton, 23 Miss.

But where the acts stipulat
are to be done at different ti
nants are to be construed a
of each other. Mullins v. C
(Ala.), 21; Craddock v. Al
(Ky.), 15; Couch v. Inge
(Mass.) 300; Tilleston v. N
406; McKaven v. Crisler,
Cunningham v. Morrell, 10
203; s. c., 6 Am. Dec. 332
Holbrook, 4 Wend. (N. Y
borough v. Orr, 21 U. S. (8
bk. 5, L. ed. 600.

As to when covenants ar
see Bean v. Atwater, 4 Con
Am. Dec. 91; Leonard v. B
(Ind.) 172; McClure v. Rush
64; Payne v. Bettisworth, 2

l estate;[1] for the breach of a contract under seal for the

...1 Allen v. Sanders, 7 B. Mon. ...3; Harrison v. Galloway, 2 Har. & ...) 461; Lord v. Belknap, 1 Cush. ...279; Kane v. Hood, 13 Pick (Mass.) ...illdam Foundry v. Hovey, 21 Pick. 417; Tillotson v. Newell, 13 Mass. ...rant v. Johnson, 5 Barb. (N. Y.) 161; ...Barb. (N. Y.) 339, 5 N. Y. 247; ...ough v. Cox, 6 Barb. (N. Y.) 386; ...Pond, 18 Barb. (N. Y.) 179; Pepper ...ht, 20 Barb. (N. Y.) 429; Underhill ...toga & W. R. Co., 20 Barb. (N. Y.) ...orris v. Miller, 1 Denio (N. Y.), 59; ...v. Finley, 7 Johns. (N. Y.) 219; ...gham v. Morrell, 10 Johns. (N. Y.) ...c., 6 Am. Dec. 333; Robb v. Mont..., 20 Johns. (N. Y.) 15; Tompkins v. 5 Wend. (N. Y.) 496; Dey v. Dox, ...(N. Y.) 129; s. c., 24 Am. Dec. ...bermyer v. Nichols, 6 Binn. (Pa.) ...c., 6 Am. Dec. 439; Edgar v. Boies, ...& R. (Pa.) 445; Stevenson v. Klep... 5 Watts (Pa.), 420; Lowry v. Me... 10 Watts (Pa.), 387; Keenan v. 21 Vt. 86; Kittle v. Harvey, 21 Vt. ...odd v. Summers, 2 Gratt. (Va.) 167; ...Am. Dec. 379; Franklin v. Miller, ...E. ...; Seavers v. Curling, 3 Bing. ...; Boone v. Eyre, 1 H. Bl 273. ...Eastern Counties Ry. Co. v. Philip... C. B. ...; Northampton G. L. Co. v. ..., 15 C. B. 630; s. c., 29 Eng. L. & ...; Ritchie v. Atkinson, 10 East, 295; ...ck v. Geddes, 10 East, 555; Mayor of ...h v. Norfolk R. Co., 4 El. & B. 397; ...v. Webb, 4 El. & B. 933; s. c., 30 ...& Eq. 331; Jonassohn v. Great ...n R. Co., 10 Ex. 439; s. c., 28 Eng. ...; Fishmongers' Co. v. Robert... ...Man. & G. 131; Storer v. Gordon, 3 ...; Wilks v. Smith, 10 Mees. & ...; Thorp v. Thorp, 12 Mod. 460; ...Salk. 171; Fothergill v. Walton, 2 ...oore, 630; Pordage v. Cole, 1 Saund. ...Peters v. Opie, 2 Saund. 350.

...re the covenants are mutual and in...ent, either may recover damages in ...on of covenant from the other for ...ary which he may have sustained by ...formance.—Cook v. Johnson, 3 Mo. ...without showing a compliance with ...pulation on his part. Bean v. At... 4 Conn. 3; s. c., 10 Am. Dec. 91; ...v. Bettisworth, 2 A. K. Marsh. (Ky.) ...anning v. Brown, 10 Me. 49; Morri... Galloway, 2 Har. & J. (Md.) 467; ...v. Hobbs, 4 Har. & J. (Md.) 285; ...v. Gibson, 15 Mass. 112; s. c., 8 ...Dec. 94; Obermeyer v. Nichols, 6 ...Pa.) 164; s. c., 6 Am. Dec. 439.

...tiality of.—In the conveyance of ...ate, there is no warranty of title, as ...in the transfer of chattels, unless there are covenants in the deed. Scott v. Scott, 70 Pa. St. 246; Co. Litt. 386 a. And where a purchaser of land accepts a conveyance, without covenants respecting the title, etc., he has no remedy on failure of title, either in law or in equity, if there was no fraud on the part of the vendor. Murray v. Ballow, 1 Johns. Ch. (N. Y.) 566; Maney v. Porter, 3 Humph. (Tenn.) 347; Commonwealth v. McClanachan, 4 Rand. (Va.) 482.

Covenants in Deeds.—There are six principal covenants usually found in modern conveyances. These are, (1) covenant of seisin, (2) covenant of right to convey, (3) covenant against incumbrances, (4) covenant for quiet enjoyment, (5) covenant of warranty, and (6) covenant for further assurance. It has been said that covenant of warranty is generally the only one employed in the Western and Southern States, but that all the other covenants are recognized in all the States, and that in all the Northern and Middle States, with the possible exception of Pennsylvania, it is customary to employ most, if not all, of the covenants enumerated. See Caldwell v. Kirkpatrick, 6 Ala. 60; s. c., 41 Am. Dec. 36; Funk v. Creswell, 5 Iowa, 62; Van Wagner v. Van Nostrand, 19 Iowa, 426; Colby v. Osgood, 29 Barb. (N. Y.) 339; Foote v. Burnet, 10 Ohio, 317; s. c., 36 Am. Dec. 90.

The covenants of seisin and of the right to convey are practically synonymous. Brandt v. Foster, 5 Iowa, 294; Griffin v. Fairbrother, 10 Me. 91; Raymond v. Raymond, 10 Cush. (Mass.) 134; Slater v. Rawson, 1 Metc. (Mass.) 455; Marston v. Hobbs, 2 Mass. 437; Prescott v. Trueman, 4 Mass. 627; s. c., 3 Am. Dec. 246; Rickert v. Snyder, 9 Wend. (N. Y.) 421. *Contra*, Richardson v. Dorr, 5 Vt. 9.

1. Autcalt v. Huffman, 3 N. J. L. (2 Penn.) 818.

Covenants of Seisin and Right to convey.—The covenants of seisin and the right to convey are general covenants that the grantor is lawfully seised, and had a right to convey at the time of the execution of the conveyance; and in a case where the grantor is not at the time possessed of the legal title, and is not in possession of the premises, the covenant is broken as soon as made, and the covenantee may at once bring an action of covenant for damages for such breach. Mitchell v. Warner, 5 Conn. 497; Griffin v. Fairbrother, 10 Me. 91; Raymond v. Raymond, 10 Cush. (Mass.) 134; Slater v. Rawson, 1 Met. (Mass.) 450; Bartholomew v. Candee, 14 Pick. (Mass.) 170; Prescott v. Trueman, 4 Mass 627; s. c., 3 Am. Dec. 246; Pecare v. Chauteau, 13 Mo. 527; Greenby v. Wilcocks, 2 Johns. (N. Y.) 1; s. c., 3 Am. Dec. 379; Backus

v. McCoy, 3 Ohio, 218; s. c., 17 Am. Dec. 585; Devore v. Sunderland, 17 Ohio, 60; s. c., 49 Am. Dec. 442; Garfield v. Williams, 2 Vt. 327; Dickinson v. Hoomes, 8 Gratt. (Va.) 397; Pollard v. Dwight, 8 U. S. (4 Cr.) 421, 430; bk. 2, L. ed. 666, 669; Howell v. Richards, 11 East, 642.

It is *held* by many courts that if the grantor is in actual possession at the time of the conveyance, even though his possession be tortious and adverse to a paramount outstanding title, and the grantee is subsequently evicted, that this does not constitute a breach of the covenant of seisin, and that an action of covenant will not lie. Salmon v. Vallejo, 41 Cal. 481; Mitchell v. Warner, 5 Conn. 497; Redwine v. Brown, 10 Ga. 314; Brady v. Shurck, 27 Ill. 478; King v. Gilson, 32 Ill. 348; Baker v. Hunt, 40 Ill. 265; Richard v. Bent, 59 Ill 43, 45; s. c., 14 Am. Rep. 1; Schofield v. Iowa Homestead Co., 32 Iowa, 317; Dale v. Shively, 8 Kan. 276; Birney v. Hann, 3 A. K. Marsh. (Ky.) 324; s. c., 13 Am. Dec. 167; Fitzhugh v. Croghan, 2 J. J. Marsh (Ky.) 429, 438; s. c, 19 Am. Dec. 140; Griffin v. Fairbrother, 10 Me. 95; Donnell v. Thompson, 10 Me. 170; Wilson v. Widenham, 51 Me. 567; Raymond v. Raymond, 10 Cush. (Mass.) 134; Slater v. Rawson, 1 Metc. (Mass.) 450; Clark v. Swift, 3 Metc. (Mass.) 390; Bartholomew v. Candee, 11 Pick. (Mass.) 167; Thayer v. Clemence, 22 Pick. (Mass.) 490; Marston v. Hobbs, 2 Mass. 433, s. c., 3 Am. Dec. 61; Moore v. Merrill, 17 N. H. 79; s. c., 43 Am. Dec. 593; Morrisson v. Underwood, 20 N. H. 369; Withy v. Mumford, 5 Cow. (N. Y.) 137; McCarthy v. Leggett, 3 Hill (N. Y.), 135; Greenby v. Wilcocks, 2 Johns. (N. Y.) 1; s. c., 3 Am. Dec. 379; Hamilton v. Wilson, 4 Johns. (N. Y.) 72; s. c., 4 Am. Dec. 253; Beddoe v. Wadsworth, 21 Wend. (N. Y.) 124; Mott v. Palmer, 1 N. Y. 573; Wilson v. Forbes, 2 Dev. (N. C.) L. 30; Wilson v. Cochran, 46 Pa. St. 229; Kincaid v. Brittain, 5 Sneed (Tenn.), 119; Wheaton v. East, 5 Yerg. (Tenn.) 41; s. c., 36 Am. Dec. 251; Catlin v. Hulburt, 3 Vt. 403; Swasey v. Brooks, 30 Vt. 692.

Other States *hold* that a covenant of lawful seisin is both present and future in its operation, and that, if the grantor has actual possession at the time of the conveyance, the covenant is broken on eviction of the grantee by a permanent title, and on action of covenant will lie. See Martin v. Baker, 5 Blackf. (Ind.) 232; Coleman v. Lyman, 42 Ind. 289; Brandt v. Foster, 5 Iowa, 294; Schofield v. Iowa Homestead Co., 32 Iowa, 317; s. c., 7 Am. Rep. 197; Parker v. Brown, 15 N. H. 176; Partridge v. Hatch, 18 N. H. 498; Backus v. McCoy, 3 Ohio, 218; s. c., 17 Am. Dec. 585; Great Western Stock Co. v. Saas, 24 Ohio St. 542; [illegible] Kingdon v. Nottle, 5 [illegible].

[illegible]—[illegible] soul that the covenant [illegible] defeasible estate" is [illegible] in the present tense. [illegible] nant of indemnity, and [illegible] held that it runs with the land [illegible] that if the covenantee [illegible] however defeasible, or [illegible] panies the deed, though [illegible] in either event this covenant [illegible] land, and enures to the [illegible] tee upon whom the loss [illegible]." [illegible] Kennedy, 91 Mo. 324; s. c., [illegible] 845. See Dixon v. [illegible] Chambers v. Smith, 23 Mo. [illegible] v. Riggin, 44 Mo. 512; [illegible] 79 Mo. 188.

Cause of Conflict.—It is [illegible] that a failure to distinguish between a *lawful* seisin and an *indefeasible* estate in the earlier cases is what gave rise to the variance of judicial opinion. The better doctrine, and that which is [illegible] to be the American doctrine, is that the covenant of *lawful* seisin does not covenant for the conveyance of an *indefeasible* estate, and consequently is not broken by a subsequent eviction. But everywhere in the United States, if the grantor expressly or impliedly covenants that he is seised of an *indefeasible* estate, it is a future covenant which runs with the land, and any one who holds under the covenantee may sue on the covenant, whenever he has been evicted by the person holding the paramount title. See Lockwood v. Sturdevant, 6 Conn. 373; Raymond v. Raymond, 10 Cush. (Mass.) 134; Smith v. Strong, 14 Pick. (Mass.) 128; Prescott v. Trueman, 4 Mass. 627; s. c., 3 Am. Dec. 246; Collier v. Gamble, 10 Mo. 467; Dickson v. Desire, 23 Mo. 151; Maguire v. Riggin, 44 Mo. 512; Abbott v. Allen, 14 Johns. (N. Y.) 248; Stanard v. Eldridge, 16 Johns. (N. Y.) 254; Wilson v. Forbes, 2 Dev. (N. C.) L. 30; Kincaid v. Brittain, 5 Sneed (Tenn.), 123; Garfield v. Williams, 2 Vt. 328.

Action for Breach of Covenant of Seisin.—For a breach of the covenant of seisin, the covenantee may recover his actual damages, though in undisturbed possession. Akerly v. Vilas, 21 Wis. 88; Hall v. Sall, 14 Wis. 54; Walker v. Wilson, 13 Wis. 522.

Whether a remote grantee can maintain an action in covenant for the breach of a covenant of seisin, quære, see Coleman v. Layman, 42 Ind. 289; [illegible] v. Peele, 78 Ind. 384; Wright v. [illegible], 92 Ind. 310; Dehority v. Wright, [illegible] Ind. 389; Sinker v. Floyd, 104 Ind. [illegible]; s. c., 2 West. Rep. 218.

Breach of Covenant of Seisin, What amounts to a.—The covenant of good convey is synonymous with the t of seisin. The covenants, if at all, are broken when they are They are personal, and do not run e land. Bacon v. Bowman, 98 Otto), 56; bk. 25, L. ed. 91.

ovenant of seisin is broken at the the execution of the deed, where ntor has not possession either by or another, and covenant will lie. . Burnet, 10 Ohio, 317, 332; s. c., Dec. 90. Some courts, however, t where possession has been given e deed, a covenant of seisin is not until eviction. See Scott v. Twiss, 133; Great Western Stock Co. v. Ohio St. 548.

venant of seisin is broken, and an f covenant will lie, if there is any ding right or title which diminishes lity or quantity of the technical The covenant will be broken if ate is less in duration or quantity at described. Comstock v. Com- 3 Conn. 352; Lindley v. Dakin, 13 ; Brandt v. Foster, 5 Iowa, 294; agner v. Van Nustrand, 19 Iowa, heeler v. Hatch, 12 Me. 389; Phipps ey, 24 Minn. 507; Kellogg v. Malin, 496; Sedgwick v. Hollinback, 7 (N. Y.) 376; Mott v. Palmer, 1 ; Wilson v. Forbes, 2 Dev. (N. C.) Vilder v. Ireland, 8 Jones (N. C.), Downer v. Smith, 38 Vt. 468. And nant of seisin will be broken when ate described is not the property rantor. Morrison v. McArthur, 43 7; Basford v. Pearson, 9 Allen , 389; Bacon v. Lincoln, 4 Cush. 210; s. c., 50 Am. Dec. 765; Wheel- Thayer, 16 Pick. (Mass.) 68.

ovenant is also broken when the y conveyed has upon it buildings er improvements and erections be- to third persons, if there is no ing clause in the deed. Van Wag- an Nostrand, 19 Iowa, 427; Mott er, 1 N. Y. 564; Tifft v. Horton, . 377; West v. Stewart, 7 Pa. St. wers v. Dennison, 30 Vt. 752.

enant of seisin is not affected by tence of easements, which do not he technical seisin of the grantee. soner v. Edmundson, 5 Ind. 394; v. Stumber, 16 Ind. 340; Stock- ouillard, 129 Mass. 231; Lewis v. Pa. St. 350; s. c., 44 Am. Dec.

a public highway, a right of way, lroad, will not constitute a breach covenant. Vaughn v. Stuzaker, 16 ; Fitzhugh v. Croghan, 2 J. J. (Ky.) 429; s. c., 19 Am. Dec. 140; v. Malin, 50 Mo. 496; s. c., 11 Am. 6; Whitbeck v. Cook, 15 Johns. 483; s. c., 8 Am. Dec. 270; Tuite v. Miller, 10 Ohio, 383; Mills v. Catlin, 22 Vt. 98.

And it has been held that a right of dower or an outstanding judgment or mortgage does not constitute a breach of covenant of seisin. Reasoner v. Edmundson, 5 Ind. 394; Fitzhugh v. Croghan, 2 J. J. Marsh. (Ky.) 429; s. c., 19 Am. Dec. 139; Sedgwick v. Hollenback, 7 Johns. (N. Y.) 376, 380; Stanard v. Eldridge, 16 Johns. (N. Y.) 254; Tuite v. Miller, 10 Ohio, 383; Massey v. Craine, 1 McCord (S. C.), 489; Lewis v. Lewis, 5 Rich. (S. C.) L. 12.

But the covenant has been *held* to be broken by an outstanding right to use the water of a spring. — Lamb v. Danforth, 59 Me. 324; Clark v. Conroe, 38 Vt. 469, — and by a right to restrain the damming of water. Traster v. Snelson, 29 Ind. 96; Walker v. Wilson, 13 Wis. 522; Hall v. Gale, 14 Wis. 55.

If a vendor sells land with a special warranty of title, and at the time it was rented for a year by his agent without his knowledge or express directions, and he believes at the time the deed is made that the farm is unoccupied, and the vendee cannot get possession for nearly a year, the tenant refusing to vacate until his term has expired, this constitutes a breach of the warranty. Moreland v. Metz, 24 W. Va. 119; s. c., 49 Am. Rep. 246; 19 Cent. L. J. 376.

It has been *held* that on the trial of an action in Connecticut for breach of a covenant of seisin of lands in Virginia, the question whether a patent from the State of Virginia for the lands be voidable is not examinable. Pollard v. Dwight, 8 U. S. (4 Cr.) 421; bk. 2, L. ed. 666.

Instances of Breach of Covenant of Seisin. — Covenant of seisin has been said to be broken by the existence of an outstanding estate, — Comstock v. Comstock, 23 Conn. 352; Mills v. Catlin, 22 Vt. 98, — as an estate for life, — Woolley v. Newcomb, 87 N. Y. 605; Wilder v. Ireland, 8 Jones (N. C.), L. 90; Mills v. Catlin, 22 Vt. 106. *Compare* Van Wagner v. Van Nostrand, 19 Iowa, 422, — if there is an adverse possession of part of the land by a stranger, — Brandt v. Foster, 5 Iowa, 295; Wheeler v. Hatch, 12 Me. 389; Sedgwick v. Hollenback, 7 Johns. (N. Y.) 376; Mott v. Palmer, 1 N. Y. 564; Wilson v. Forbes, 2 Dev. (N. C.) L. 35, — or a concurrent seisin in another as a tenant in common, — Wheeler v. Hatch, 12 Me. 389; Downer v. Smith, 38 Vt. 464; — if there is no such land as that purporting to be conveyed, — Basford v. Pearson, 9 Allen (Mass.), 389; Bacon v. Lincoln, 4 Cush. (Mass.) 210; s. c., 50 Am. Dec. 765; Wheelock v. Thayer, 16 Pick. (Mass.) 68, 70. *Compare* Morrison v. McArthur, 43 Me. 567, — or there is a material deficiency in the amount of the land conveyed, — see Mann v. Pierson, 2 Johns.

(N. Y.) 37; Pringle v. Witten, 1 Bay (S. C.), 256; s. c., 1 Am. Dec. 612; Kincaid v. Brittain, 5 Sneed (Tenn.), 123; — if the grantor at the time of conveyance did not own such things affixed to the freehold as would pass with it to the grantee, — Van Wagner v. Van Nostrand, 19 Iowa, 427; Burke v. Nichols, 1 Abb. App. Dec. (N. Y.) 260; Ritchmyer v. Morris, 3 Keyes (N. Y.), 349; s. c., 37 How. Pr. (N. Y.) 388; Mott v. Palmer, 1 N. Y. 572; Loughran v. Ross, 45 N. Y. 792; s. c., 6 Am. Rep. 173; Tift v. Horton, 53 N. Y. 381; West v. Stewart, 7 Pa. St. 122; Powers v. Dennison, 30 Vt. 752; — or if there is a judgment for taxes, sale, and a tax-deed, — Vorhis v. Forsythe, 4 Biss. C. C. 409, — and if the grantor has only an estate tail, — Comstock v. Comstock, 23 Conn. 352, — and an action will lie in covenant for damages.

Yet it has been *held* that one who purchases under a warranty deed, containing the usual covenants of seisin and quiet possession, cannot rescind the bargain on the ground of mistake as to the vendor's title, if the mistake does not go to the entire consideration, as where he supposed the vendor had title in fee-simple, instead of a mere life estate. Leal v. Terbush, 52 Mich. 100; s. c., 17 N. W. Rep. 713; 18 Cent. L. J. 97.

Nominal Damages for Breach. — On a breach of the covenant of *seisin*, an action in covenant to recover any thing more than nominal damages for the breach will not lie until after eviction by the party holding the paramount title, or other actual injury. King v. Gilson, 32 Ill. 356; Richard v. Bent, 59 Ill. 38; s. c., 14 Am. Rep. 1; Funk v. Creswell, 5 Iowa, 62; Runnells v. Webber, 59 Me. 488; Whitney v. Dinsmore, 6 Cush. (Mass.) 127; Clarke v. Swift, 3 Metc. (Mass.) 39; Tufts v. Adams, 8 Pick. (Mass.) 547; Thayer v. Clemence, 22 Pick. (Mass.) 493; Prescott v. Trueman, 4 Mass. 629; s. c., 3 Am. Dec. 246; Wyman v. Ballard, 12 Mass. 304; Cockrell v. Proctor, 65 Mo. 41; Wyatt v. Dunn (Mo.), 6 West. Rep. 863; Andrews v. Davison, 17 N. H. 416; s. c., 43 Am. Dec. 606; Russ v. Perry, 49 N. H. 547; Churchill v. Hunt, 3 Denio (N. Y.), 321; Funk v. Voneida, 11 Serg. & R. (Pa.) 112; s. c., 14 Am. Dec. 617; Ardesco Oil Co. v. N. A. Mining Co., 66 Pa. St. 375; Smith v. Hughes, 20 Wis. 630; s. c., 12 Cent. L. J. 17; Noonan v. Ilsley, 22 Wis. 27; Mecklem v. Blake, 22 Wis. 495; Eaton v. Lyman, 30 Wis. 41.

The reason for this rule is the fact that the devisee may never be disturbed in his possession; and, until actual loss or eviction, the damages recoverable for the breach of the covenant against incumbrances are merely nominal; and when possession is had by the grantee, the covenant runs with the land. Wyatt v. Dunn (Mo.), 6 West. Rep. 863.

New York Doctrine. — It is held in New York that the rule is well settled that when the vendor enters into a contract to sell and convey real estate under a belief that he has a good title, and that the same is free from incumbrances, and he fails to perform for the reason that the title is defective, or an incumbrance unknown to him previously is discovered, which prevents a fulfilment of the contract, in an action by the vendee against him for a breach of the contract, the latter is only liable for nominal damages, aside from the purchase-money paid, and the expense of examining the title. Cockcroft v. New York & H. R. Co., 69 N. Y. 201.

Covenant against Incumbrances. — There is considerable conflict of opinion among the courts, as to whether a covenant against incumbrances is one *in praesenti*, and broken, if at all, as soon as made, and consequently one that does not pass to the grantee's assigns; or whether it is a future covenant enforceable by an action in covenant by whoever is injured by the incumbrance. The prevailing doctrine in this country is that it is a covenant *in praesenti*, and does not run with the land. Logan v. Moulder, 1 Ark. 313; s. c., 33 Am. Dec. 338; Richard v. Bent, 59 Ill. 38; s. c., 14 Am. Rep. 1; Frink v. Bellis, 33 Ind. 135; Funk v. Creswell, 5 Clarke (Ia.), 62; Runnells v. Webber, 59 Me. 488; Whitney v. Dinsmore, 6 Cush. (Mass.) 127; Clark v. Swift, 3 Metc. (Mass.) 392; Thayer v. Clemence, 22 Pick. (Mass.) 490; Russ v. Perry, 49 N. H. 547; Stewart v. Drake, 9 N. J. L. 130; Garrison v. Sanford, 12 N. J. L. 261; Funk v. Voneida, 11 Serg. & R. (Pa.) 109; s. c., 14 Am. Dec. 617; Cathcart v. Bowman, 5 Pa. St. 317; Potter v. Taylor, 6 Vt. 676; Pillsbury v. Mitchell, 5 Wis. 17.

However, some of the States of the Union hold that a covenant against incumbrances is *in futuro*, runs with the land, and is broken when the outstanding right is enforced, and that an action in covenant may be maintained by the party in possession. Sprague v. Baker, 17 Mass. 586; Foote v. Burnet, 10 Ohio, 317; s. c., 36 Am. Dec. 90; McCrady v. Brisbane, 1 Nott & M. (S. C.) 104; s. c., 9 Am. Dec. 676.

Indiana and Iowa Doctrine. — In Indiana and Iowa, while covenants against incumbrances are regarded as *in praesenti*, the courts *held* that they run with the land, and will support an action on the covenant by the second and third grantee under the covenantee. Richard v. Bent, 59 Ill. 38; s. c., 14 Am. Rep. 1; Martin v. Baker, 5 Blackf. (Ind.) 232; Nadler v. Sharpe, 1 Iowa, 236.

Massachusetts Doctrine. — In Massachusetts it was originally held that a covenant

ıst incumbrances was not assignable,
lid not run with the land. Whitney v.
more, 6 Cush. (Mass.) 124; Clark v.
, 3 Metc. (Mass.) 302; Tufts v. Adams,
k. (Mass.) 547; Thayer v. Clemence,
Pick. (Mass.) 490. But this is now
ged by a statute giving a right of ac-
for a breach of the covenant "in the
ee, his heirs, executor, successors, or
ns."

braska Doctrine. — The supreme court
ebraska have *held* that a covenant
ıst incumbrances is a present engage-
, that the grantor has an unincumbered
and is not in the nature of a covenant
demnity. Chapman v. Kimball, 7 Neb.

t it is said that if the covenant merely
nds to quiet enjoyment against incum-
es, that it is broken only by an entry
pulsion from the premises, or other
rbance in the possession. Anderson
ox, 20 Ala. 156.
here the grantors covenant generally
st incumbrances made by them, it may
nstrued as extending to several as
as joint incumbrances. Duvall v.
, 15 U. S. (2 Wheat.) 45, 58; bk. 4, L.
ls

en Covenant against Incumbrances is
a. — In general terms, it is *held* that
right to and interest in the land
ed, to the diminution of the value
of, consistent with the passing of the
y conveyance, must be deemed in law
cumbrance. Mitchell v. Warner, 5
, 527; Cary v. Daniels, 8 Metc. (Mass.)
s. c., 41 Am. Dec. 532; Prescott v.
man, 4 Mass. 630; s. c., 3 Am. Dec.
Bronson v. Coffin, 108 Mass. 175.
covenant against incumbrances has
held to be broken, — Bean v. Mayo, 5
4; Cary v. Daniels, 8 Metc. (Mass.)
s. c., 41 Am. Dec. 532; Carter v.
ıan, 33 N. J. L. 273; McMullin v.
ley, 2 Lans. (N. Y.) 394; Hutchins v.
ly, 34 Vt. 433, — and entitles the party
session to maintain an action in cove-
by the existence of a right of dower,
rter v. Noyes, 2 Me. 22; s. c., 11 Am.
30; Runnells v. Webber, 59 Me. 488;
ow v. Hubbard, 97 Mass. 195; Jones
rdner, 10 Johns. (N. Y.) 276; Heim-
r Losey, 35 N. Y. Super. Ct. Rep. (3
& S.) 35; McAlpine v. Woodruff, 11
St. 120. *Compare* Bostwick v. Wil-
, 36 Ill. 65; Powell v. Munson, 3 Mason,
355, — though inchoate only, — Porter
yes, 2 Me. 22; s. c., 11 Am. Dec. 30;
v. Ward, 4 Metc. (Mass.) 412; Shearer
nger, 22 Pick. (Mass.) 447; Hender-
Henderson, 13 Mo. 152; Fletcher v.
Bank, 37 N. H. 397; Russ v. Perry,
H. 590; McAlpine v. Woodruff, 11
St. 120, — by a judgment lien, — see
v. McCampbell, 1 Blackf. (Ind.) 100; Holman v. Creagmiles, 14 Ind. 177; Jenkins v. Hopkins, 8 Pick. (Mass.) 346; Hall v. Dean, 13 Johns. (N. Y.) 105, — by an outstanding mortgage or deed of trust in the nature of a mortgage, — Brooks v. Moody, 25 Ark. 452; Bean v. Mayo, 5 Me. 94; Freeman v. Foster, 55 Me. 508; Prescott v. Trueman, 4 Mass. 630; s. c., 3 Am. Dec. 246, — other than that which the covenantee has assumed and is bound to pay, — Kinnier v. Lowell, 34 Me. 299; Freeman v. Foster, 55 Me. 508; Estabrook v. Smith, 6 Gray (Mass.), 572; s. c., 66 Am. Dec. 445, — by taxes, when ascertained, — Almy v. Hunt, 48 Ill. 45; Richards v. Bent, 59 Ill. 38; Cheney v. City Nat. Bank, 77 Ill. 562; Ingalls v. Cooke, 21 Iowa, 560; Cochran v. Guild, 106 Mass. 29; Hill v. Bacon, 110 Mass. 388; Rundell v. Lakey, 40 N. Y. 514; Barlow v. St. Nicholas Bank, 63 N. Y. 399; Long v. Moler, 5 Ohio St. 271; Pierce v. Brew, 43 Vt. 292; Mitchell v. Pillsbury, 5 Wis. 407; Peters v. Myers, 22 Wis. 602, — by existence of a collateral inheritance tax, — Large v. McClain (Pa. St.), 5 Cent. Rep. 761, — by an outstanding lease in possession, — Edwards v. Gale, 52 Me. 360; Batchelder v. Sturgiss, 3 Cush. (Mass.) 201; Weld v. Traip, 14 Gray (Mass.), 330; Pease v. Christ, 31 N. Y. 141; Cross v. Noble, 67 Pa. St. 77; Porter v. Bradley, 7 R. I. 538; Grice v. Scarborough, 2 Speer (S. C.), L. 649; s. c., 43 Am. Dec. 391; James v. Litchfield, L. R. 9 Eq. 51, — by outstanding conditions and covenants restricting the use of the premises, — Parish v. Whitney, 3 Gray (Mass.), 516; Plymouth v. Carver, 16 Pick. (Mass.) 183; Bronson v. Coffin, 108 Mass. 175; Burbank v. Pillsbury, 48 N. H. 475; Kellogg v. Robinson, 6 Vt. 276, — by outstanding life estate or term of years, — Van Wagner v. Van Nostrand, 19 Iowa, 422; Grice v. Scarborough, 2 Speer (S. C.), 649; s. c., 42 Am. Dec. 391, — by outstanding paramount title, — Cornell v. Jackson, 3 Cush. (Mass.) 506; Prescott v. Trueman, 4 Mass. 627, 630; s. c., 3 Am. Dec. 246, — and by any charge constituting a lien upon the estate, and enforcible against it, — Kelsey v. Remer, 43 Conn. 129; Holman v. Creagmiles, 14 Ind. 177.

But where a land-owner, having assumed a mortgage, conveyed the land with covenants against all incumbrances, his subsequent mortgage to secure his note made to satisfy the mortgage assumed by him is not a breach of his covenant of warranty before eviction. Foster v. Woodward, 141 Mass. 160; s. c., 2 New Eng. Rep. 365.

Easements and Servitudes. — A right to an easement or servitude of any kind in the land outstanding at the time of conveyance, is a breach of the covenant against incumbrances, — see Desvergers v. Willis, 56 Ga. 515; Burk v. Hill, 48 Ind. 52; overruling Scribner v. Holmes, 16 Ind. 142;

Lamb v. Danforth, 59 Me. 322; s. c., 8 Am. Rep. 426; McMullin v. Wooley, 2 Lans. (N. Y.) 394; Brooks v. Curtis, 4 Lans. (N. Y.) 283; s. c., 50 N. Y. 639; 10 Am. Rep. 545; Giles v. Dugro, 1 Duer (N. Y.), 331; Kutz v. McCune, 22 Wis 628,—such as an existing right in a third person to cut and maintain a drain,—Smith v. Sprague, 40 Vt. 43,—or other artificial water-course, —Prescott v. White, 21 Pick. (Mass.) 341; s. c., 32 Am. Dec. 266;—to erect and maintain dams,—Ginn v. Hancock, 31 Me. 42. *Compare* Wetherby v. Bennett, 2 Allen (Mass.), 428,—aqueducts, and the like,—Mitchell v. Warner, 5 Conn. 497; Burk v. Hill, 48 Ind. 52; s. c., 17 Am. Rep. 731; Beach v. Miller, 51 Ill. 206; s. c., 2 Am. Rep. 290; Barlow v. McKinley, 24 Iowa, 70; Lamb v. Danforth, 59 Me. 322; s. c., 8 Am. Rep. 426; Spurr v. Andrews, 6 Allen (Mass.), 420; Prescott v. White, 21 Pick. (Mass.) 341; s. c., 32 Am. Dec. 266; Kellogg v. Malin, 50 Mo. 496; s. c., 11 Am. Rep. 426; Brooks v. Curtis, 50 N. Y. 639; s. c., 10 Am. Rep. 545; Cathcart v. Bowman, 5 Pa. St. 319; Wilson v. Cochran, 46 Pa. St. 233; Smith v. Sprague, 40 Vt. 43; Russ v. Steele, 40 Vt. 310; Kutz v. McCune, 22 Wis. 628;—a right to cut and remove standing trees,—Spurr v. Andrews, 6 Allen (Mass.), 420;—and a right to pass over the land, and take water from a spring. Mitchell v. Warner, 5 Conn. 497; Harlow v. Thomas, 15 Pick. (Mass.) 68. *Compare* Russ v. Steele, 40 Vt. 310.

Party Wall.—A decree compensating the owner of land for damages for the encroachment thereon of a party wall, built by the adjoining owner, legalises the encroachment; and the owner having subsequently deeded the land, with a covenant against incumbrances and special warranty, to one ignorant of the encroachment, it was *held* that such encroachment was a breach of the covenant, and the grantee could recover of the grantor damages therefor. Edmunds' Appeal (Pa.), 6 Cent. Rep. 423.

It is *held* by some courts, that where a purchaser takes land subject to an easement, it will be presumed that he was willing to take the property with the burden as it was at the time of the purchase, where the easement upon it is visible and of a continuous character, and that such an easement is not embraced in a covenant of special warranty. Desvergers v. Willis, 56 Ga. 515; Scribner v. Holmes, 16 Ind. 142; James v. Jenkins, 1 Md. 1. *Compare* Burk v. Hill, 48 Ind. 52; s. c., 17 Am. Rep. 731; overruling Scribner v. Holmes, *supra.*

Knowledge of Incumbrances.—The rights of the parties claiming under a covenant against incumbrances in a conveyance will not be affected by the fact that the covenantee knew of the incumbrance at the time of the conveyance. Beach v. Miller, 51 Ill. 206; s. c., 2 Am. Rep. 290; Snyder v. Lane, 10 Ind. 424; Harvey v. [illegible], 2 Pick. (Mass.) 29; Funk v. Voneida, 11 Serg. & R. (Pa.) 110; s. c., 14 Am. Dec. [illegible]. But it has been *held* in North Carolina that the fact that both parties to a conveyance of a tract of land, with a covenant against incumbrances, have full knowledge of the existence of a valid outstanding incumbrance, in the absence of fraud or mistake in procuring the covenant, that such knowledge furnishes no reason why the purchaser and covenantee is not entitled to recover on the covenant. Gragg v. Wagner, [illegible] N. C. 316.

Taxes.—In Connecticut, taxes are not a lien upon the land of a party taxed where he has other property sufficient to pay the tax,—Briggs v. Morse, 42 Conn. [illegible],—and an action of covenant will not lie.

It has been questioned whether taxes assessed after a conveyance, but on a lien existing at the time of such conveyance, constitute a breach of the covenant against incumbrances. See Blossom v. [illegible], 34 Mo. 394; Rundell v. [illegible], 513; Harlow v. St. Nicholas [illegible], N. Y. 399; Pierce v. Brew, [illegible] Vt. [illegible]; Hutchins v. Moody, 30 Vt. [illegible].

But it is said that the right of the government to hold land for non-payment of taxes which have been assessed upon the premises, is an incumbrance within a covenant against incumbrances, notwithstanding the fact that the grantor is personally liable for the taxes,—Cochran v. Guild, 106 Mass. 29,—and that an action in covenant will lie.

Assessment for Street, etc.—Where, at the time of the sale of the premises to the plaintiffs, the premises were charged with a valid assessment, it was an incumbrance on the premises, and plaintiffs are entitled to recover for a breach of the covenant against incumbrances. Bemis v. Caldwell, 143 Mass. 299; s. c., 3 New Eng. Rep. 430.

In an action for breach of covenant against incumbrances, contained in a warranty deed in the usual form, where an original assessment for opening a street was in existence at the time of the execution of the deed, and afterwards a re-assessment was made, it was held that the lien of the re-assessment related back to the lien of the original assessment, and attached when the assessment was affirmed, and not when the work was completed, and that the covenant was broken as soon as made. Cadmus v. Fagan, 47 N. J. L. (17 Vr.) 549; s. c., 4 Cent. Rep. 800.

When Right of Action arises.—Right of action upon covenants of warranty against incumbrances arises upon covenantee's payment of money to protect his interests.

[illegible], [illegible] Mo. App. 276; s. c., 4 [illegible]; Taylor v. Priest, 21 Mo. [illegible]; s. c., 4 West. Rep. 329.

Covenant for Quiet Enjoyment: Definition. — The covenant for quiet enjoyment is an assurance against a defective title, and of any disturbance thereunder by the grantor or others. Fowler v. Poling, 6 Barb. (N. Y.) 170; Connor v. Bernheimer, 6 Daly (N. Y.) 295; Rea v. Minkler, 5 Lans. (N. Y.) 199; Howell v. Richards, 11 East, 633, 641; Newman v. Foster, 1 Mod. 101.

In this covenant the guaranty extends to the possession merely, and not to the title of the land. Fowler v. Poling, 6 Barb. (N. Y.) 170; Whitbeck v. Cook, 15 Johns. (N. Y.) 482; s. c., 8 Am. Dec. 272.

This covenant for quiet enjoyment is not an absolute covenant for the protection of the grantee's possession against acts of the whole world, but only extends to the acts of the grantor, and of strangers asserting a paramount title, and not to the acts of strangers who do not claim a superior title. Schilling v. Holmes, 23 Cal. 230; Branger v. Manciet, 30 Cal. 626; Wade v. Halligan, 16 Ill. 507; Dexter v. Manley, 4 Cush. (Mass.) 24; Morse v. Goddard, 13 Metc. (Mass.) 177; Sherman v. Williams, 113 Mass. 481; s. c., 18 Am. Rep. 522; Hamilton v. Wright, 28 Mo. 199; Lovering v. Lovering, 13 N. H. 518; Edgarton v. Page, 1 Hilt. (N. Y.) 320, 333; Mack v. Patchin, 42 N. Y. 167; s. c., 1 Am. Rep. 506; Ross v. Dysart, 33 Pa. St. 452; Schuylkill & D. R. R. Co. v. Schmoele, 57 Pa. St. 273; Moore v. Weber, 71 Pa. St. 429; s. c., 10 Am. Rep. 708.

It is said that there is an implied covenant for quiet enjoyment in the grant of an incorporeal, as well as a corporeal, hereditament, — Mayor, etc., v. Mabie, 13 N. Y., 157, — and an action in covenant for the breach will lie on either; but to support this implied covenant, the lease must be a valid one. Webster v. Cooley, 46 Ill. 17.

What a Breach of the Covenant of Quiet Enjoyment. — Nothing but an actual or constructive eviction, by the assertion of a paramount title, will constitute a breach of the covenant for quiet enjoyment. McGary v. Hastings, 39 Cal. 360; s. c., 2 Am. Rep. 456; Sterling v. Peet, 14 Conn. 254; Hand v. Armstrong, 34 Ga. 232; Moore v. Vail, 17 Ill. 190; Clark v. Lineberger, 44 Ind. 223; Thomas v. Stickle, 32 Iowa, 76; Pence v. Duvall, 9 B. Mon. (Ky.) 49; Smith v. Shepard, 15 Pick. (Mass.) 147; s. c., 25 Am. Dec. 432; Moore v. Frankenfield, 25 Minn. 540; Murphy v. Price, 48 Mo. 250; Drew v. Towle, 30 N. H. 537; Greenvault v. Davis, 4 Hill (N. Y.), 645; Whitbeck v. Cook, 15 Johns. (N. Y.) 483; s. c., 8 Am. Dec. 272; Rea v. Minkler, 5 Lans (N. Y.) 199; Cowdrey v. Coit, 44 N. Y. 382; s. c., 4 Am. Rep. 690; Johnson v. Nyce, 17 Ohio, 66; s. c., 49 Am. Dec. 444; Ross v. Dysart, 33 Pa. St. 452; Mayor, etc., v. Whitt, 15 Mees. & W. 577. Thus this covenant is broken whenever there is an involuntary loss of possession by reason of the hostile assertion of an irresistible paramount title, whether that title be established by judgment or not, — McGary v. Hastings, 39 Cal. 360; s. c., 2 Am. Rep. 456; Clark v. Lineberger, 44 Ind. 223; Smith v. Shepard, 15 Pick. (Mass.) 147; s. c., 25 Am. Dec. 432; Stewart v. Drake, 9 N. J. L. (4 Halst.) 141; Adams v. Conover, 22 Hun (N. Y.), 424; Cowdrey v. Coit, 44 N. Y. 382; s. c., 4 Am. Rep. 690; Home Life Ins. Co. v. Sherman, 46 N. Y. 370; Upton v. Townend, 17 C. B. 30; — when the land is in possession of a stranger under a paramount title, who keeps the grantee out of possession, — Playter v. Cunningham, 71 Cal. 229; Witty v. Hightower, 12 Smed. & M. (Miss.) 478; Shattuck v. Lamb, 65 N. Y. 499; s. c., 22 Am. Rep. 656; Noonan v. Lee, 67 U. S. (2 Black) 499, 507; bk. 17, L. ed. 278; — and when the title and possession of the land is disturbed by reason of a suit in equity, — Martin v. Martin, 1 Dev. (N. C.) L. 413; Calthrop v. Heyton, 2 Mod. 54, — but it is otherwise where such disturbance extends only to a particular mode of enjoyment of the land, without otherwise affecting the title or possession. Dennett v. Atherton, L. R. 7 Q. B. 326.

This covenant will not be broken by wrongful and unlawful evictions of third persons, — Jones v. Worley, 21 La. An. 404; Ellis v. Welch, 6 Mass. 250; Rautin v. Robertson, 2 Strobh. (S. C.) L. 366; Dudley v. Folliott, 3 T. R. 584, — or by evictions under rights acquired subsequently to the conveyance, — Ellis v. Welch, 6 Mass. 250; Frost v. Earnest, 4 Whart. (Pa.) 85, — but it will be broken by an entry by the grantor tortiously and without title. Sedgwick v. Hollenback, 7 Johns. (N. Y.) 376. Yet an entry by the grantor upon the demised premises for the purpose of making repairs is not a breach of the covenant for quiet enjoyment, and no action will lie therefor. Bostwick v. Williams, 36 Ill. 69; Dospe v. Genin, 37 How. Pr. (N. Y.) 5; s. c., 1 Sweeney (N. Y.), 25; Mayor, etc., v. Mabie, 13 N. Y. 156.

Terre-Tenant. — Serving a notice on the terre-tenant, forbidding him to use the land, and threatening suit for disobedience, or filing a bill for an injunction, which is refused, to restrain him from using the land, is not a breach of the covenant for quiet enjoyment in a ground-rent deed. Jarden v. Lafferty (Pa.), 6 Cent. Rep. 593.

Lease for Years. — And the implied covenant for quiet enjoyment contained in a lease for years is not broken where an adjoining owner, under statute, condemns and tears down a party wall, which is also a wall to the house leased, for the purpose of erecting one suitable for a larger building. Barns *v.* Wilson (Pa.), 8 Cent. Rep. 454; s. c., 25 Cent. L. J. 14; 9 Atl. Rep. 437.

Although it is true that every lease contains an implied covenant for quiet enjoyment, yet that covenant extends only to acts of the lessor himself, and to injuries inflicted under a paramount title: it is not designed as an indemnity against every disturbance of the lessee's enjoyment of the land under the law. Barns *v.* Wilson (Pa.), 8 Cent. Rep. 454; s. c., 25 Cent. L. J. 14; 9 Atl. Rep. 437. See Frost *v.* Earnest, 4 Whart. (Pa.) 86; Dobbins *v.* Brown, 12 Pa. St. 75; Moore *v.* Weber, 71 Pa. St. 429. The mere fact that a house leased becomes uninhabitable, is not enough to sustain an action on the covenant. Carson *v.* Godley, 26 Pa. St. 117; Hazlett *v.* Powell, 30 Pa. St. 293. This condition of the property must arise from the act of the lessor, or from those holding a title paramount. Barns *v.* Wilson (Pa.), 8 Cent. Rep. 454; s. c., 25 Cent. L. J. 14; 9 Atl. Rep. 437.

Flooding Lands. — It has been held that flooding lands conveyed by deed, with full warranty, by the owner of a mill-privilege situated below, in the exercise of a paramount right, is a breach of the covenant for quiet enjoyment entitling the grantee to recover damages in an action in covenant. Scriver *v.* Smith, 100 N. Y. 471; s. c., 1 Cent. Rep. 763. See Story *v.* N. Y. Elev. R. R. Co., 9 N. Y. 185; Eaton *v.* Boston, C. & M. R. R. Co., 51 N. H. 504; Pumpelly *v.* Green Bay Co., 80 U. S. (13 Wall.) 166; bk. 20, L. ed. 557.

What constitutes an Eviction: Actual Evictions. — Actual eviction is where the grantee is actually ousted of his possession of the premises by a stranger under paramount title, or by acts of dispossession by the grantor, — Robinson *v.* Deering, 56 Me. 358; Bordman *v.* Osborn, 23 Pick. (Mass.) 295; Fitchburg Co. *v.* Melven, 15 Mass. 268; Russell *v.* Fabyan, 27 N. H. 529; Home Life Ins. Co. *v.* Sherman, 46 N. Y. 372; — but a disturbance by a stranger without claim to a paramount title will not constitute an eviction, and an action in covenant on the covenant in the deed. Welles *v.* Castles, 3 Gray (Mass.), 323; Royce *v.* Guggenheim, 106 Mass. 205; s. c., 8 Am. Rep. 322; Palmer *v.* Wetmore, 2 Sandf. (N. Y.) 316; Hazlett *v.* Powell, 30 Pa. St. 293; Schuylkill & D. R. R. Co. *v.* Schmoele, 57 Pa. St. 273; Moore *v.* Weber, 71 Pa. St. 429; s. c., 10 Am. Rep. 708.

Dispossession by an exercise of the right of eminent domain, or other acts of the State, — Ellis *v.* Welch, 6 Mass. 246; s. c., 4 Am. Dec. 353; Frost *v.* Earnest, 4 Whart. (Pa.) 86, — or the Federal Government, — Osborn *v.* Nicholson, 80 U. S. (13 Wall.) 655; bk. 20, L. ed. [illegible]. [illegible] Fitzpatrick *v.* Hearne, 44 Ala. [illegible]; [illegible] *v.* Gatlin, 12 Fla. 9; [illegible] *v.* [illegible], 6 Bush (Ky.), 665; [illegible] *v.* [illegible], 41 Miss. 61, — or by the public enemy, — [illegible]ling *v.* Holmes, 23 Cal. [illegible]; [illegible] *v.* White, 4 Har. & J. (Md.) [illegible]; [illegible] *v.* Watts, L. R. 5 C. P. [illegible]. *Compare* [illegible] *v.* Lawrence, 1 Bay (S. C.), [illegible], — does not amount to an act of eviction for which an action of covenant will lie, but does give a right of action for damages against the public for the lands so confiscated. McLarren *v.* Spalding, 2 Cal. [illegible]; [illegible] *v.* Boston, 15 Pick. (Mass.) [illegible]; [illegible] *v.* Boston, 20 Pick. (Mass.) [illegible]; [illegible] *v.* Huntley, 7 Wend. (N. Y.) [illegible]; [illegible] *v.* Cincinnati, 11 Ohio, [illegible]; s. c., [illegible] Am. Dec. 737; Workman *v.* [illegible], [illegible] Pa. St. 362; Peck *v.* Jones, 70 Pa. St. [illegible].

Missouri Rule. — A different rule [illegible] in Missouri, according to which, if a part of the premises be appropriated to public use, in case of lease the rent will be abated *pro tanto*. Biddle *v.* [illegible], [illegible] Mo. 597; Kingsland *v.* Clark, 24 Mo. 24.

New York Doctrine. — It is *held* in New York, that where premises are held for a term of years, and a portion thereof is taken in the opening and widening of a street, the tenant is entitled to an abatement of the rent reserved in the lease, although by the improvement the part of the premises left is rendered more valuable than the whole premises were previous thereto. Gillespie *v.* Thomas, 15 Wend. (N. Y.) 464, 468. See, on this subject, Vin. Abr. tit. Apportionment, B.; 2 Inst. 503, 504; Bac. Abr. tit. Rent, L., N.; 10 Co. 128 a; 3 Kent, Comm. 469; Collins *v.* Harding, Cro. Eliz. 622, a.; Anonymous, Cro. Eliz. 771.

Constructive Evictions. — Where the grantor, by his own acts or by his own procurement, diminishes the enjoyment of the demised premises in a material degree, or renders such enjoyment impossible, there will be a constructive eviction, such as renting a part of a house for immoral purposes. — Dyett *v.* Pendleton, 8 Cow. (N. Y.) 727. See also Morris *v.* Tillotson, 81 Ill. 607; Rogers *v.* Ostrom, 35 Barb. (N. Y.) 523; Denison *v.* Ford, 7 Daly (N. Y.), 384; Truesdell *v.* Booth, 4 Hun (N. Y.), 100; Cohen *v.* Dupont, 1 Sandf. (N. Y.) 260; Gilhooley *v.* Washington, 4 N. Y. 217; West Side, etc., Bank *v.* Newton, 76 N. Y. 616; *contra* Dewett *v.* Pierson, 112 Mass. 8; s. c., 17 Am. Rep. [illegible]; Bartlett *v.* Farrington, 120 Mass. 284, — erections constructed by the lessor, or with his consent, so near the premises as to materially lessen their enjoyment, — Wright *v.* Lattin, 38 Ill. 293; Royce *v.* Guggenheim, 106 Mass.

, 8 Am. Rep. 322; Sherman v. , 103 Mass. 481; s. c., 18 Am. , — or any acts which render the useless or destroy them, — Halliade, 21 Ill. 479; s. c., 74 Am. Dec. tley v. Hill, 35 Ill. 414; Hayner v. Ill. 430; s. c., 14 Am. Rep. 124; Martin, 7 Md. 375; s. c., 61 Am. ; Fuller v. Ruby, 10 Gray (Mass.), kson v. Eddy, 12 Mo. 209; St. Palmer, 5 Hill (N. Y.), 599; Law- French, 25 Wend. (N. Y.) 443; v. Page, 20 N. Y. 281; Bennet v. Rawle (Pa.), 339; Pier v. Carr, . 326; Wilson v. Smith, 5 Yerg. 379; Alger v. Kennedy, 49 Vt. 109; Am. Rep. 117.

slight acts of trespass which do rially interfere with the enjoyment emises, and compel the grantee to the possession, do not amount to active eviction, yet the grantor is them, like any other trespasser. ner v. Smith, 63 Ill. 430; s. c., 14 . 124; Day v. Watson, 8 Mich. ott v. Aiken, 45 N. H. 35; Gardner as, 3 Hill (N. Y.), 330; Edgerton 20 N. Y. 281; Bennet v. Bittle, Pa.), 339; Wilson v. Smith, 5 Yerg. 99; Briggs v. Hall, 4 Leigh (Va.), , 26 Am. Dec. 526.

the enjoyment of demised premken away altogether, if the grantee ssession, there will be no eviction, grantee, if a lessee, will be liable on in covenant on his covenants. Guggenheim, 106 Mass. 201; s. c., ep. 322; Jackson v. Eddy, 12 Mo. ribut v. Post, 1 Bosw. (N. Y.) 28; Pendleton, 8 Cow. (N. Y.) 727; v. Page, 20 N. Y. 281; Lounsbery , 31 N. Y. 514; Alger v. Kennedy, 9; s. c., 24 Am. Rep. 117.

Eviction. — A tenant will be reom payment of rent, in an action venant in the lease, to the extent viction, where a partial eviction om the acts of strangers, in violahe lessor's covenant for quiet en- Martin v. Martin, 7 Md. 375; Pendleton, 8 Cow. (N. Y.) 727; v. McArthur, 1 E. D. Smith 147; Lawrence v. French, 25 N. Y.) 443; Blair v. Claxton, 18 ; Morrison v. Chadwick, 7 C. B.

ere the partial eviction of the by the procurement of the lessor, e rent is suspended during the ce of such eviction, and the lessee to abandon the premises, and his liability for rent altogether. v. Holmes, 23 Cal. 230; Reed v. . 37 Conn. 469; Smith v. Stigel- Ill. 141; Leishman v. White, 1 Mass.), 489; Shumway v. Collins, 6 Gray (Mass.), 227; Royce v. Guggenheim, 106 Mass. 201; s. c., 8 Am. Rep. 322; Colburn v. Morrill, 117 Mass. 262; s. c., 19 Am. Rep. 415; Lewis v. Payn, 4 Wend. (N. Y.) 423; Christopher v. Austin, 11 N. Y. 216; Edgerton v. Page, 20 N. Y. 281; Pier v. Carr, 69 Pa. St 326; Wilson v. Smith, 5 Yerg. (Tenn.) 379.

But neither total nor partial eviction will prevent the lessor from collecting rent already due when the eviction took place. Giles v. Comstock, 4 N. Y. 270; s. c., 53 Am. Dec. 374; Kessler v. McConachy, 1 Rawle (Pa.), 435.

Covenant of Warranty. — The covenant of warranty is an assurance by the grantor of the estate that the grantee shall enjoy the same without interruption, by virtue of a paramount title. Rindskopf v. Farmers' Loan & Trust Co., 58 Barb. (N. Y.) 36; Moore v. Lanham, 3 Hill (S. C.), 304.

On breach of his covenant, an action of covenant for damages for such breach will lie.

This is the most effective covenant in American deeds, — Leary v. Durham, 4 Ga. 601; Foote v. Burnet, 10 Ohio, 329; s. c., 36 Am. Dec. 90; note Dickinson v. Hoomes, 8 Gratt. (Va.) 399, — goes to the title as well as to the possession, — Patton v. Kennedy, 1 A. K. Marsh. (Ky.) 389; s. c., 10 Am. Dec. 744; Blanchard v. Brooks, 12 Pick. (Mass.) 57; Fowler v. Poling, 6 Barb. (N. Y.) 170; Rowe v. Heath, 23 Tex. 614; Williams v. Wetherbee, 1 Aik. (Vt.) 233; Brown v. Jackson, 16 U. S. (3 Wheat.) 449; bk. 4, L. ed. 432, — is a personal covenant, — Cole v. Raymond, 9 Gray (Mass.), 217; Townsend v. Morris, 6 Cow. (N. Y.) 126; Tabb v. Binford, 4 Leigh (Va.), 132; s. c., 26 Am. Dec 317, — and runs with the land. Wead v. Larkin, 54 Ill. 489; s. c., 5 Am. Rep. 149; Moore v. Merrill, 17 N. H. 81; s. c., 43 Am. Dec. 593; Rindskopf v. Farmers' Loan Co., 58 Barb. (N. Y.) 36; Suydam v. Jones, 10 Wend. (N. Y.) 180; s. c., 25 Am. Dec. 552; King v. Kerr, 5 Ohio, 154; s. c., 22 Am. Dec. 777; Wilson v. Taylor, 9 Ohio St. 595; s. c., 15 Am. Dec. 488.

A special warranty in a deed has not the effect of controlling a precedent general covenant. Bender v. Fromberger, 4 U. S. (4 Dall.) 436; bk. 1, L. ed. 899.

The covenant "to warrant and defend" property for which a quit-claim deed is executed "against all claims, United States excepted," does not cover the interest of the United States, nor preclude its acquisition by the covenantors or their heirs for themselves. Davenport v. Lamb, 80 U. S. (13 Wall.) 418; bk. 20, L. ed. 655.

Breach of Warranty, what constitutes. — To constitute a breach of the warranty, and entitle the grantee to an action on the covenant, the eviction must be by paramount title, — Fowler v. Poling, 6 Barb. (N. Y.) 165, — and there must be an actual or constructive eviction of the whole or a part of the premises. Beebe v. Swartwout, 8 Ill. 179; Bostwick v. Williams, 36 Ill. 69; Funk v. Creswell, 5 Iowa, 88; Mott v. Palmer, 1 N. Y. 564; West v. Stewart, 7 Pa. St. 122.

But it is *held* in South Carolina that the covenant is broken by the existence of a paramount title in a third person, without either actual or constructive eviction. Biggus v. Bradley, 1 McC. (S. C.) 500; Macke v. Collins, 2 Nott & M. (S. C.) 186; s. c., 10 Am. Dec. 586.

In order to sustain an action for a breach of covenant of warranty, an eviction by process of law is not necessary. Patton v. Kennedy, 1 A. K. Marsh. (Ky.) 389; s. c., 10 Am. Dec. 744; Greenvault v. Davis, 4 Hill (N. Y.), 643. *Compare* Stewart v. Drake, 9 N. J. L. (4 Halst.) 139; Stipe v. Stipe, 2 Head (Tenn.), 169. A grantee may voluntarily yield the possession upon demand of the owner of the paramount title, — McGary v. Hastings, 39 Cal. 360; s. c., 2 Am. Rep. 456; Claycomb v. Munger, 51 Ill. 376; Funk v. Creswell, 5 Iowa, 65; Brandt v. Foster, 5 Iowa, 297; Hooker v. Bell, 3 Bibb (Ky.), 173; s. c., 6 Am. Dec. 641; Donnell v. Thompson, 10 Me. 170; s. c., 25 Am. Dec. 216; Gilman v. Haven, 11 Cush. (Mass.) 330; Estabrook v. Smith, 6 Gray (Mass.), 572; s. c., 66 Am. Dec. 445; Hamilton v. Cutts, 4 Mass. 349; s. c., 3 Am. Dec. 222; Sprague v. Baker, 17 Mass. 586; Loomis v. Bedel, 11 N. H. 73; Kellogg v. Platt, 33 N. J. L. (4 Vr.) 328; Greenvault v. Davis, 4 Hill (N. Y.), 643; Clarke v. McAnulty, 3 Serg. & R. (Pa.) 364; Knepper v. Kurtz, 58 Pa. St. 484; Peck v. Hensley, 20 Tex. 673; *contra*, Ferris v. Harshea, 1 Mart. & Y. (Tenn.) 52; s. c., 17 Am. Dec. 782; — but he does so at his peril, and in a subsequent action on the covenant the burden of proof is on him to show that the title to which he yielded was really the paramount title. Claycomb v. Munger, 51 Ill. 377; Crance v. Collenbaugh, 47 Ind. 256; Ryerson v. Chapman, 66 Me. 557; Smith v. Shepard, 15 Pick. (Mass.) 147; s. c., 25 Am. Dec. 432; Hamilton v. Cutts, 4 Mass. 352; s. c., 3 Am. Dec. 222; Merritt v. Morse, 108 Mass. 276; Hall v. Bray, 51 Mo. 288; Stone v. Hooker, 9 Cow. (N. Y.) 154; Clarke v. McAnulty, 3 Serg. & R. (Pa.) 364; Smith v. Sprague, 40 Vt. 43; Somers v. Schmidt, 24 Wis. 417. A judgment in ejectment is a breach of the covenant without an actual eviction, — Norton v. Jackson, 5 Cal. 263; Hannah v. Henderson, 4 Ind. 174; Cummings v. Kennedy, 3 Litt. (Ky.) 118; s. c., 14 Am. Dec. 45; Hale v. New Orleans, 13 La. An. 499; Cowdrey v. Coit, 44 N. Y. 382; s. c., 4 Am. Rep. 690; Loughran v. Ross, 45 N. H. 792; King v. Kerr, 5 Ohio, 158; s. c., 22 Am. Dec. [illegible]; [illegible] v. Britain, 5 Sneed (Tenn.) [illegible]; [illegible] v. Wetherbee, 1 Aik. (Vt.) [illegible]; [illegible] v. Shumway, 1 D. Chip. (Vt.) [illegible]; s. c., 1 Am. Dec. 704; Gleason v. Smith, 41 Vt. 293; Noonan v. Lee, 67 U. S. (2 Black) 499; bk. 17, L. ed. 278. *Compare* Ferris v. Harshea, 1 Mart. & Y. (Tenn.) 52; s. c., 17 Am. Dec. 782, — for an eviction is complete when a constructive dispossession [illegible] place. McGary v. Hastings, 39 Cal. 360; s. c., 2 Am. Rep. 456; Jones v. Warner, 81 Ill. 346; Kansas & Pac. R. R. Co. v. Dunmeyer, 19 Kan. 539; Whitney v. Dinsmore, 6 Cush. (Mass.) 124. *Compare* [illegible] v. Croghan, 2 J. J. Marsh. (Ky.) [illegible]; s. c., 19 Am. Dec. 139; Burrus v. Wilkinson, 31 Miss. 537; Dyer v. Britton, 53 Miss. [illegible].

But a covenant of warranty is not broken by eviction, unless under a lawful and paramount title. Gleason v. Smith, 41 Vt. 296. Thus, where land is condemned in the exercise of the right of eminent domain, this will not constitute a breach of the covenant of warranty. Gee v. Moore, 14 Cal. 474; Kimball v. Thompson, [illegible] Cal. 452; Doe v. Dowdall, 3 Houst. (Del.) [illegible]; Raymond v. Raymond, 10 Cush. (Mass.) 134; Sweet v. Brown, 12 Metc. (Mass.) 175; s. c., 45 Am. Dec. 243; [illegible] v. Brooks, 12 Pick. (Mass.) 47; [illegible] fee, 14 N. H. 215; Adams v. [illegible], 30 N. J. L. (1 Vr.) 505; White v. [illegible], 14 Ohio St. 344; Peck v. Jones, 70 Pa. St. [illegible]; Brown v. Jackson, 16 U. S. (3 Wheat.) 449; bk. 4, L. ed. 432.

Instances of Breach of Covenant of Warranty. — Instances of a breach of the covenant of warranty, for which an action of covenant will lie, are eviction by legal process under a prior mortgage, — [illegible] v. Whitney, 3 Metc. (Mass.) [illegible]; [illegible] v. Adams, 8 Pick. (Mass.) 547; Sprague v. Baker, 17 Mass. 586; Furnas v. Durgin, 119 Mass. 500; Smith v. Dixon, 27 Ohio St. 471. *Compare* Curtis v. Deering, 12 Me. 499; Cowdry v. Coit, 44 N. Y. 382; s. c., 4 Am. Rep. 690, — or under an unexpired term for years, — Rickert v. Snyder, 9 Wend. (N. Y.) 416; — the existence of an easement of right of way over a whole or a part of the premises, — Haynes v. Young, 36 Me. 561; Lamb v. Danforth, 59 Me. 324; Harlow v. Thomas, 15 Pick. (Mass.) 66; Russ v. Steele, 40 Vt. 310, — but the opening of a highway over the land conveyed in the exercise of the right of eminent domain is not, — Alabama R. R. Co. v. Kennedy, 39 Ala. 307; Spader v. N. Y. Elevated R. R. Co., 3 Abb. (N. Y.) Pr. N. C. 467; Frost v. Earnest, 4 Whart. (Pa.) 86; Dobbin v. Brown, 12 Pa. St. 75; Bailey v. Miltenberger, 31 Pa. St. 37; Peck v. Jones, 70 Pa. St. 83; — and by an existing right in another to draw water from the premises by an aqueduct. Lamb v.

payment of a certain sum of money to be discharged in good cur-

Danforth, 59 Me. 324; Clark v. Conroe, 38 Vt. 469; Day v. Adams, 42 Vt. 510.

A covenant of warranty is not broken by the existence of an incumbrance which the grantee agreed to pay as part of the consideration. Pitman v. Connor, 27 Ind. 337.

An illegal or tortious eviction is not a breach of a general covenant of warranty. Patton v. Kennedy, 1 A. K. Marsh. (Ky.) 389; s. c., 10 Am. Dec. 744. But where a special covenant is given against the claims or acts of certain persons therein named, it will be broken by an eviction by the persons, or under the claims specified. Kimball v. Temple, 25 Cal. 452; Patton v. Kennedy, 1 A. K. Marsh. (Ky.) 389; s. c., 10 Am. Dec 744; Ballard v. Child, 46 Me. 152; Comstock v. Smith, 13 Pick. (Mass.) 116; s. c., 23 Am. Dec. 670; Davenport v. Lamb, 80 U. S. (13 Wall.) 418; bk. 20, L. ed 655.

Exercise of Right of Eminent Domain. — It is a well-established principle of law that the legislature may not destroy or impair the rights of individuals secured to them by virtue of their contracts. U. S. Const. Art. I. § 10. See also Jones v. Walker, 2 Paine, C C. 688.

The clause of the federal constitution, which guarantees to individuals their rights in and to the property contained in their contracts of transfer, by declaring that all contracts shall remain inviolate, does not interfere with the power of the State to condemn the property affected, on giving due compensation therefor. All property and contracts must yield to the good of the people and the demands of the sovereign. Brown v. Corey, 43 Pa. St. 495.

But the contract rights of the individuals are not thereby impaired, because full compensation is given. While a State or government may not annul or modify a grant of land or a lease, or a mortgage upon it, yet it may take the whole or a part of the land, on making due compensation therefor; and such an appropriation by the public is held not to impair the obligations of the contract contained in the grant — Young v. McKenzie, 3 Ga. 31; Fletcher v. Peck, 10 U. S. (6 Cr.) 87; bk. 3, L. ed. 162; West River Bridge Co. v. Dix, 47 U S. (6 How.) 507; bk. 12, L. ed. 535; Johnson v. United States, 8 Ct. of Cl. 243 — or lease, — Alabama & F. R. R. Co. v. Kenney, 39 Ala. 307; Frost v. Earnest, 4 Whart. (Pa.) 86, — or of covenants of warranty. — Dobbins v. Brown, 12 Pa. St. 75; Bailey v. Miltenberger, 31 Pa. St 37; — for quiet enjoyment, — Frost v. Earnest, 4 Whart. (Pa.) 86; — or against incumbrances. Alabama & F. R. R. Co. v. Kenney, 39 Ala. 307.

An exercise of the right of eminent domain, in condemning the estate of a lessee, is held not to impair the obligation of the covenant to surrender or any other covenant in the lease. Kip v. New York & Har. R. R. Co., 67 N. Y. 227.

And it has been said that the contract of a railroad company with one telegraph company, to allow the exclusive use of its right of way, will not prevent a condemnation of a use of way by another telegraph company. New Orleans, M. & T. R. R. Co. v. Southern Tel. Co., 53 Ala. 211.

All persons hold their property subject to requisitions for the public service. Donaher v. Mississippi, 8 Smed. & M. (Miss.) 649; Bonaparte v. Camden R. R., Bald. C. C. 205.

Thus it has been held that land just granted by the State may be taken for the purposes of a public highway. Enfield Bridge Co. v. Hartford R. R. Co., 17 Conn. 40; s. c., 42 Am. Dec. 716

Public Highway: An Incumbrance. — Any right of a third person, in the land conveyed, to the diminution of the value of the land, is an incumbrance, though that interest be consistent with the passing of the fee by the deed of conveyance. The effect is the same, whether that third person is an individual, a company, or a corporation, either private or public. The diminution is as great, whether the property is incumbered by a public highway, as by a private passage, obtained by contract; because the public has such a right in its highways that it cannot be divested of them by a private individual. The fact that the incumbrance is of a public nature, and the records of the State furnish a constructive notice to the vendee of the rights of the public, or that he had actual personal notice of its existence, is no bar to a right of action. It has been *held* from an early date in many of the States, — notably Massachusetts, Maine, New Hampshire, and Connecticut, — that a public highway over and upon property sold, with a warranty against incumbrances, comes within the warranty, and that an action in covenant will lie. See Hubbard v. Norton, 10 Conn. 431; Burk v. Hill, 48 Ind. 52; s. c., 17 Am. Rep. 731; Haynes v. Young, 36 Me. 557; Parish v. Whitney, 3 Gray (Mass.), 516; Kellogg v. Ingersoll, 2 Mass. 97, 101; Ellis v. Welsh, 6 Mass. 246; s. c., 4 Am. Dec. 122; Pritchard v. Atkinson, 3 N. H. 335; Wilson v. Cochran, 46 Pa. St. 232; Butler v. Gale, 27 Vt. 739.

And this is true, even though the grantee was aware of its existence when he took the deed and paid the consideration. Dunn v. White, 1 Ala. 645; Hubbard v. Norton, rent bank notes;[1] for breach of a covenant to save [illegible] from a judgment; for the breach of the covenant in a lease,[2] to [illegible]

10 Conn. 431; Beach v. Miller, 51 Ill. 206; s. c., 2 Am. Rep. 290; Medler v. Hyatt, 8 Ind. 171; Snyder v. Lane, 10 Ind. 424; Hoovey v. Newton, 7 Pick. (Mass.) 29; Harlow v. Thomas, 15 Pick. (Mass.) 68; Long v. Moler, 5 Ohio St. 271; Funk v. Voneida, 11 Serg. & R. (Pa.) 112; s. c., 16 Am. Dec. 617; Kincaid v. Brittain, 5 Sneed (Tenn.), 119. *Compare* Kutz v. McCune, 22 Wis. 628.

It was formerly *held* in Indiana (Scribner v. Holmes, 16 Ind. 142) that a public road was not an incumbrance within a warranty against incumbrances; but the doctrine of Scribner v. Holmes was reversed in Burk v. Hill, 48 Ind. 52; s. c., 17 Am. Rep. 713, and has never since obtained in that State. But in New York, Pennsylvania, and Wisconsin, the courts *hold* that the purchase is made subject to the public highway; that there is no breach of the warranty, and that an action in covenant will not lie. See Whitbeck v. Cook, 15 Johns. (N. Y.) 483; s. c., 8 Am. Dec. 272; Patterson v. Arthurs, 9 Watts (Pa.), 152; Wilson v. Cochran, 46 Pa. St. 232; Kutz v. McCune, 22 Wis. 628.

In Georgia, if the highway is known to the purchaser to exist at the time of the purchase, the covenant is not broken. Desvergers v. Willis, 56 Ga. 515; s. c., 21 Am. Rep. 289.

Railway's Right of Way.—There are numerous cases holding that a right of way in a railroad is an incumbrance for which the covenantee may recover in an action in covenant. See Hubbard v. Norton, 10 Conn. 431; Beach v. Miller, 51 Ill. 206; s. c., 2 Am. Rep. 290; Burk v. Hill, 48 Ind. 52; s. c., 17 Am. Rep. 731; Van Wagner v. Van Nostrand, 19 Iowa, 422; Barlow v. McKinley, 24 Iowa, 69; Haynes v. Young, 36 Me. 557; Lamb v. Danforth, 59 Me. 522; Kellogg v. Ingersoll, 2 Mass. 97; Prescott v. Trueman, 4 Mass. 627; s. c., 12 Am. Dec. 752; Harlow v. Thomas, 15 Pick. (Mass.) 66; Kellogg v. Malin, 50 Mo. 496, 500; s. c., 11 Am. Rep. 426; Williams v. Hall, 62 Mo. 405; Giles v. Durgo, 1 Duer (N. Y.), 331.

And this is true, although he had full knowledge of the incumbrance at the time he accepted the conveyance. Beach v. Miller, 51 Ill. 207; s. c., 2 Am. Rep. 290; Barlow v. McKinley, 24 Iowa, 69.

Illegal Tax Sale.—A tax deed of land is no incumbrance within the meaning of a covenant against incumbrances, where the sale was illegal for want of compliance with statutory requirements, and the tax purchaser having paid the taxes, extinguished them, and therefore not even the tax was an incumbrance. [illegible] v. Holt, 56 Vt. 384; s. c., [illegible] Cent. L. J. [illegible].

Covenant for Further Assurance.—The covenant for further assurance, [illegible] extensively in England, is but [illegible] in American deed. See Gwynn v. Thomas, 2 Gill & J. (Md.) 420; Colby v. Osgood, [illegible] Barb. (N. Y.) 339; Nelson v. [illegible], [illegible] Call (Va.) 394.

By this covenant the grantor [illegible] to do such additional reasonable acts as may be necessary for the completion of the transfer, at the requirement of the covenantee. See Armstrong v. Darby, [illegible] 517; Miller v. Parsons, 9 Johns. (N. Y.) 336; Fields v. Squires, Deady, [illegible] 388; King v. Jones, 5 Taunt. 418; [illegible]well's Case, 5 Co. Rep. 19 b. It is a covenant which runs with the land. Colby v. Osgood, 29 Barb. (N. Y.) 339.

In the execution of the covenant [illegible] anty for further assurance, the grantee is not required to do unnecessary—[illegible] v. Bickford, 7 Price, 550; s. c., [illegible] or impossible acts. Pet and Colly's Case, 1 Leon. 304. And the request for the performance of this covenant must be made within a reasonable time, or an action [illegible] covenant for its breach will not lie. [illegible] Miller v. Parsons, 9 Johns. (N. Y.) [illegible]; Heron v. Treyne, 2 Ld. Raym. 750.

A covenant for further assurance contained in a void conveyance is [illegible] the nullity of the original [illegible]. Union Trust Co. of N. Y. v. [illegible], [illegible] N. Y. 729; s. c., *sub nom.* Union Trust Co. of N. Y. v. Rochester & P. R. R. Co., [illegible] Cent. Rep. 840; Nash v. [illegible], [illegible] Jones, 195.

1. Jackson v. Waddill, 1 Stew (Ala.) 579; Scott v. Conover, 6 N. J. L. (1 Halst.) 222.

Indemnity against Judgment.—An action for damages on a covenant of indemnity against a judgment may be maintained immediately upon the recovery of the judgment; and this, although the judgment has not been paid by covenantee, and although covenantee was not a party, and had no notice of the former action. Conner v. Reeves, 103 N. Y. 527; s. c., 5 Cent. Rep. 415.

A covenant to indemnify against a future judgment, charge, or liability, is broken by the recovery of a judgment, or the fixing of a charge or liability, and an action in covenant will lie. Conner v. Reeves, 103 N. Y. 527; s. c., 5 Cent. Rep. 415.

2. An agreement in a lease to "pay all taxes assessed," includes special assessments for local improvements. Cassady v. Hammer, 62 Iowa, [illegible]; s. c., 17 N. W. Rep. 588; 18 Cent. L. J. [illegible].

repairs,[1] to pay rent,[2] to reside on the premises,[3] to cultivate them in a particular manner,[4] not to carry on a particular trade,[5] and to allow the lessor certain privileges.[6]

Covenant lies on a covenant to deliver boards;[7] on a bond or other sealed contract for the delivery of goods.[8] And it is held that a plaintiff may maintain several different actions in covenant for different instalments of a debt as they become due.[9]

1. Harris v. Goslin, 3 Har. (Del.) 338; Stretch v. Forsyth, 3 N. J. L. (2 Penn.) 713; Dean and Chapter of Windsor's Case, 5 Coke, 1049. 24.

2. Van Rensselaer v. Smith, 27 Barb. (N. Y.) 104; Van Rensselaer v. Dennison, 35 N. Y. 393; Worthington v. Hewes, 19 Ohio St. 66; Hurst v. Rodney, 1 Wash. (Va.) 375.

The covenant to pay rent is constantly binding upon the lessee, during the whole continuance of the term, notwithstanding any assignment he may make. Williams on Real Prop., 396.

An action of covenant will lie against a lessee, on an express covenant for payment of rent, although after an assignment by him of the term, and although the lessor has accepted rent from the assignee. Kunckle v. Wynick, 1 U. S. (1 Dall.) 305; bk. 1, L. ed. 149.

A lessor may maintain an action for rent against his lessee, on an expressed covenant to pay rent during the term continued in a lease for nine years, and renewable forever, though the rent accrued after the lessee had assigned all his interest in the leasehold estate, and after the lessor had accepted rent from the assignee of the term. Taylor v. De Bus, 31 Ohio St. 468; s. c., 6 Cent. L. J. 356; limiting and explaining, Worthington v. Hewes, 19 Ohio St. 66; Kunckle v. Wynick, 1 U. S. (1 Dall.) 305; bk. 1, L. ed. 149.

Rent-Service.—A rent-service is apportionable; that is, a release of a part of the land from the rent does not release the whole; but a rent-charge is not apportionable. See Ingersoll v. Sergeant, 1 Whart. (Pa.) 337.

Where a lessor covenanted to keep the main walls and timbers of a warehouse in repair, there being a proviso in the lease for abatement of rent in case the premises became untenantable through "flood, fire, storm, tempest, or other inevitable accident," and the warehouse was seriously damaged during the user of the defendant, the lessee, but such user was not shown to be improper, and the lessor had entered and spent some money in doing extensive repairs, in an action it was *held* that the lessor's covenant to keep in repair amounted to a covenant to put and keep in repair, with regard to the class of tenement demised, and that, therefore, having regard to the user, proved he had no right of action against the lessee for waste. It seems that, in the absence of such covenant, no user of a tenement which is reasonable and proper, having regard to the kind of tenement, is waste. On a counter-claim for abatement of rent for the period during which the premises were partly unfit for use and occupation, the court *held* that "inevitable accident" must be *ejusdem generis* with the accidents specified, and that the term did not apply to any thing arising from the acts or defaults of either of the contesting parties. Saner v. Bilton, 26 W. R. 394.

3. Tatim v. Chaplin, 2 H. Bl. 133.

4. Cockson v. Cock, Cro. Jac. 125.

5. Barron v. Richard, 3 Edw. Ch. (N. Y.) 96; s. c., affirmed, 8 Paige Ch. (N. Y.) 351; Mayor v. Pattison, 10 East, 316. *Compare* St. Andrew's Church Appeals, 67 Pa. St. 512.

Covenants against Sale of Liquor.—Where a lease contained a covenant by the lessee not to allow any house on the lands demised "to be used as a beer-shop," and the lessee carried on the trade of a grocer in a house on the demised premises in partnership with his brother, and the brother took out an excise license to sell beer at the house by retail, to be consumed off the premises, and did so sell beer there, it was *held* to be a breach of the covenant. Bishop of St. Albans v. Battersby, L. R. 3 Q. B. Div. 259; s. c., 26 W. R. 679.

6. Such as to allow him access to a certain room, and the like. See Norfleet v. Cromwell, 64 N. C. 1; Brew v. Van Deman, 6 Heisk. (Tenn.) 433; Bush v. Cales, 1 Show. 389.

7. Bell v. Curtis, 2 N. J. L. (1 Penn.) 142.

8. Bell v. Curtis, 2 N. J. L. (1 Penn.) 142; Powell v. Clark, 3 N. J. L. (2 Penn.) 517.

9. Hepburn v. Mans (Pa.), 31 Leg. Int. 356; s. c., 1 Cent. L. J. 575. See Cross v. United States, 81 U. S. (20 Wall.) 479; bk. 20, L. ed. 721.

Judgment charging an Annuity.—On the breach of a covenant against incumbrances in a deed where the incumbrance is a judgment charging an annuity on the land, a new right of action in covenant accrues to the covenantee upon the pay-

The waiver of parts of a covenant by the defendant does not render it a new contract; the remedy is by action of the covenant.[1]

a. Particular Cases. — Where a covenant was broken by defendant's failure to deliver a deed at the time therein specified, it was held that the plaintiff had a right, in strict law, to his action of covenant to recover back his money paid and damages.[2] But equity may allow performance or compensation.[3]

An instrument purporting to be an assignment of a judgment, which does not exist, and by which instrument the party covenants that the judgment is due and unpaid, will subject him to an action for a breach of covenant.[4]

When a deed is executed, or a contract made, on behalf of a State by a public officer duly authorized, and this fact appears upon the face of the instrument, it is the deed or contract of the State, and the officer is not personally liable.[5]

But where the agent contracts for an individual, a different rule prevails; and if the agent covenants personally, he will be personally bound. The fact that he describes himself as "agent," or the like, will not relieve him from responsibility. Thus, on a covenant by the defendants describing themselves as a committee on the part of a company (naming it), reciting that they had sold to the plaintiffs certain property, and binding themselves to deliver such property to the plaintiffs, on demurrer it was held that it was a personal covenant, on which an action would lie against the covenantors.[6]

ment of each instalment of the annuity; and recovery in an action for the first instalment will be no bar to a recovery on the second and subsequent instalments. Priest *v.* Deaver, 22 Mo. App. 276; s. c., 4 West. Rep. 308. See Taylor *v.* Priest, 21 Mo. App. 685; s. c., 4 West. Rep. 329.

1. Monocacy Bridge Co. *v.* American Iron Bridge Manuf. Co., 83 Pa. St. 517.

Where no time is fixed for performance of a covenant, the party desirous of a performance must hasten it by request. Tilghman *v.* Tilghman, 1 Bald. C. C. 465.

2. Haverstick *v.* Erie Gas Co., 29 Pa. St. 254.

3. Haverstick *v.* Erie Gas Co., 29 Pa. St. 254.

4. Jansen *v.* Ball, 6 Cow. (N. Y.) 628.

5. Sheets *v.* Selden, 69 U. S. (2 Wall.) 177; bk. 17, L. ed. 822.

Covenants of Public Officers: Succession in Office. — Where public officers, such as selectmen acting as overseers of the poor, but designating themselves as selectmen, enter into indentures of apprenticeship or the like, an action may be brought by their successors in office, — subsequent overseers of the poor. Sanford *v.* Sanford, 2 Day (Conn.), 559; Powers *v.* Ware, 2 Pick. (Mass.) 451; Warner *v.* Racey, 20 Johns. (N. Y.) 74; Lawton *v.* Erwin, 9 Wend. (N. Y.) 233.

Where an agent of the government contracts for its benefit and on its behalf, and describes himself as such in the contract, he is held not to be personally responsible, although the terms of the contract might, in cases of a mere private nature, involve him in a personal responsibility. Brown *v.* Austin, 1 Mass. 208; Freeman *v.* Otis, 9 Mass. 272; Sheffield *v.* Watson, 3 Cai. (N. Y.) 69; Hodgson *v.* Dexter, 5 U. S. (1 Cr.) 363; bk. 2, L. ed. 130; Jones *v.* Le Tombe, 7 U. S. (3 Dall.) 384; bk. 1, L. ed. 647; Myrtle *v.* Beaver, 1 East, 135; Rice *v.* Chute, 1 East, 579; Macbeath *v.* Haldimand, 1 Term. Rep. 172; Unwin *v.* Wolseley, 1 Term. Rep. 674.

6. Henderson *v.* Martin, 19 Ark. 477; s. c., 70 Am. Dec. 606.

Covenants by Agents: Personal Responsibility. — Where a person acts as agent for another, if he executes a deed for his principal, and does not mean to bind himself personally, he should execute the deed in the name of his principal only, in the body of the deed. White *v.* Cuyler, 6 Term. Rep. 176; Wilks *v.* Back, 2 East, 142. If, instead of pursuing this course, the agent names himself in the deed, and covenants in his own name, he will be personally

The act of Pennsylvania of April 25, 1850, was designed to give the action of covenant for rent reserved by a deed-poll; and where both parties seal a ground-rent deed, a covenant running with the land is created, and it is the same as a deed-poll.[1]

If one covenant with another to do a certain act, in consideration of a reward, and the other prevent the stipulated thing from being literally performed, and accept of an equivalent, he may be sued for the reward; and the reason of the non-compliance with the literal terms may be averred.[2]

When something is covenanted to be performed by each of two parties at the same time, the one who was ready and offered to perform his part, but was discharged by the other, may maintain an action in covenant against the other for not performing his part.[3]

liable on the covenants, notwithstanding he describes himself as agent.

In the case of Duvall *v.* Craig, 15 U. S. (2 Wheat.) 56; bk. 4 L. ed. 180, *Judge Story* says that "a trustee, merely as such, is in general only suable in equity. But if he chooses to bind himself by personal covenant, he is liable at law for a breach thereof in the same manner as any other person, although he describe himself as covenanting as trustee; for, in such case, the covenant binds him personally; and the addition of the words 'as trustee' is but matter of description, to show the character in which he acts for his own protection, and in no degree affects the rights or remedies of the other party. The authorities are very distinct on the subject. An agent or executor who covenants in his own name, and yet describes himself as agent or executor, is personally liable, for the obvious reason that the one has no principal to bind, and the other substitutes himself for his principal." There are numerous cases to be found in the books illustrative of this doctrine. Thus, in Appleton *v.* Binks (5 East, 148), where the defendant entered into an agreement, under seal, with the plaintiff, by the name of T. B., of, etc., "for, and on the part, and on behalf of the Right Honorable Lord Viscount Rokeby," and covenanted for himself, his heirs, executors, etc., "on the part and behalf of the said Lord Rokeby," and executed the agreement in his own name, it was *held* that he was personally liable on the covenant. And where a committee for a turnpike corporation contracted under their own hands and seals, describing themselves as a committee, they were held personally responsible. Tippetts *v.* Walker, 4 Mass. 595.

Where a person signed a promissory note in his own name, describing himself as guardian, he was held bound to the payment of the note in his personal capacity. Thatcher *v.* Dinsmore, 5 Mass. 299; Forster *v.* Fuller, 6 Mass. 58. And where administrators of an estate, by proper authority from a court, sold the lands of their intestate, and covenanted in the deed, "in their capacity as administrators," that they were seised of the premises, and had good title to convey the same; that the same were free of all incumbrances, and that they would warrant and defend the same against the lawful claims of all persons, it was *held* that they were personally responsible. Sumner *v.* Williams, 8 Mass. 162; Thayer *v.* Wendell, 1 Gall. C. C. 37.

1. Louer *v.* Hummel, 21 Pa. St. 450.

2. Hotham *v.* East Ind. Co., Doug. 272.

3. Jones *v.* Barkley, Doug. 684.

When Right of Action arises. — Thus an action for damages on a covenant of indemnity against a judgment may be maintained immediately upon the recovery of the judgment, and this although the judgment has not been paid by the covenantee, and although the covenantor was not a party, and had no notice of the former action. See Conner *v.* Reeves, 103 N. Y. 527; s. c., 5 Cent. Rep. 415.

And a right of action upon covenants of warranty against incumbrances arises upon the covenantee's payment of money to protect his interest. The statute of limitations does not begin to run until the covenantee has made such payment. Taylor *v.* Priest, 21 Mo. App. 685; s. c., 4 West. Rep. 329; Priest *v.* Deaver, 22 Mo. App. 276; s. c., 4 West. Rep. 308.

Where a breach of the guaranty against incumbrances is a judgment charging an annuity on the land, a new right of action accrues to covenantee upon payment of each instalment; and a recovery of one instalment is not a bar to a recovery of the second. Priest *v.* Deaver, 22 Mo. App. 276; s. c., 4 West. Rep. 308.

2. *Obligation to pay Money: Bonds.*—Covenant lies on an obligation under seal to pay money,[1] and on a writing obligatory for the payment of a certain sum in land-office money,[2] or for the payment of a certain sum of money to be discharged in good, current bank notes.[3]

Several actions of covenant will lie for a debt, payable by instalments.[4]

Covenant will lie upon a bond with a penalty; and in such case there may be a recovery beyond the amount of the penalty.[5] It will lie upon the bond itself, but the breach assigned must be the non-payment of the penalty.[6] And on a penal bond the breach assigned must be the non-payment of the penalty.[7]

Covenant lies upon an attachment bond; and, if the damages alleged to have been sustained exceed the penalty, non-payment of the penalty may be assigned; if not, the damages actually sustained.[8]

3. *Cases of Defective Execution, Alterations, etc.*—Covenant lies upon a sealed instrument, duly executed by the defendant, notwithstanding a defective execution by the plaintiff.[9] And a plaintiff may sustain covenant on a sealed instrument, although it be so defectively executed on his part that only assumpsit can be maintained against him.[10]

Covenant lies on an instrument under seal, notwithstanding a parol agreement by the covenantee to cancel the specialty, on the performance of certain conditions.[11]

Where there has been an entry and possession, according to the terms of a contract, covenant may be maintained upon it, although

1. Basset v. Jordan, 1 Stew. (Ala.) 352; January v. Henry, 2 T. B. Mon. (Ky.) 58.

2. Hedges v. Gray, 1 Blackf. (Ind.) 216.

3. Jackson v. Waddill, 1 Stew. (Ala.) 579; Scott v. Conover, 6 N. J. L. (1 Halst.) 222.

4. Hepburn v. Mans (Pa.), 31 Leg. Int. 356; s. c., 1 Cent. L. J. 575.

Payment in Instalments.—When part of an entire sum due on a sealed instrument, is payable by instalments at fixed periods, and the residue in specific articles on demand, covenant will lie for the instalments, though there has been no legal demand of the specific articles. Stevens v. Chamberlin, 1 Vt. 25.

In an agreement under seal for the payment of $324, in monthly instalments of $27, covenant will lie for any of the instalments as they fall due; but a declaration which counts for a part of a month not due, and also for the residue of the unexpired term, is bad on demurrer. North v. Eslava, 12 Ala. 240.

5. New Holland Turnpike Co. v. Lancaster County, 71 Pa. St. 442.

6. Sumner v. Watson, 1 Cr. C. C. 254; United States v. Brown, 1 Paine, C. C. 422.

7. United States v. Brown, 1 Paine, C. C. 422.

8. Hill v. Rushing, 4 Ala. 212.

9. Directors of the Poor v. McFadden, 1 Grant (Pa.), Cas. 230.

Personal Contracts.—The exceptions to the general rule that an action of covenant can only be sustained where the instrument upon which the action is founded is actually signed and sealed by the party or his authorized agent, do not embrace those personal contracts, by which no estate in land passes. Harrison v. Vreeland, 38 N. J. L. (9 Vr.) 366.

10. Directors of the Poor v. McFadden, 1 Grant (Pa.), Cas. 230.

11. Elmaker v. Franklin Fire Ins. Co., 6 Watts & S. (Pa.) 439.

Alteration by Parol.—A parol agreement by one party to waive the performance of a particular stipulation by the other, is not such an alteration of the contract as will preclude the former from maintaining covenant. McCombs v. McKennan, 2 Watts & S. (Pa.) 216; s. c., 37 Am. Dec. 505.

not valid as a lease, by reason of not being recorded as required by statute;[1] and such entry and possession may be shown by parol.[2]

In *Kentucky*, a party who had had a negro on hire, wrote to his master, proposing to hire the negro for another year at a hundred dollars, and he was sent accordingly, and remained the year out. The master brought covenant upon the letter, setting out those facts, and averring non-payment of the hire. The court held that by virtue of the act of 1831, the offer being accepted, the writing, though not under seal, became a covenant, and that the action was maintainable.[3]

4. *Upon what Words.* — No particular technical words are required to make a covenant. Any words which import an agreement between the parties to a deed, will be sufficient for that purpose.[4]

Covenant lies on an agreement, the words of which create an obligation,[5] and upon words which create an implied covenant or covenants in law.[6]

Covenant will lie where the vendor covenanted that he was "lawfully seised in fee," etc, without an eviction, for a defect of title,[7] and also for a deficiency in the quantity of land sold.[8]

1. Bridgman v. Wells, 13 Ohio, 43.
2. Bridgman v. Wells, 13 Ohio, 43.
3. Graves v. Smedes, 7 Dana (Ky.), 344.
4. Hallett v. Wylie, 3 Johns. (N. Y.) 44; s. c., 3 Am. Dec. 457; Harris v. Nicholas, 5 Munf. (Va.) 483; Stevens v. Carrington, [illegible] 27; Chancellor v. Poole, Doug. [illegible].
5. Hill v. Carr, 1 Cas. Ch. 294.

Thus, if it be said in a deed that an obligation is in the hands of B., and that C. will deliver it, covenant will lie for not delivering it. 1 Rol. Abr. 519, l. 10.

If a man gives a release for money received by him, and at the end of the deed mentions that he will not sue execution, if he afterwards sues it, covenant lies against him upon this deed. 1 Rol. Ab., 517, l. 45.

If a deed be, "I oblige myself to pay," at such a day covenant lies. Pordage v. Cole, 1 Saund. 320; s. c., Sir T. Raym. 183; 1 Sid. 423; 1 Lev. 274.

6. Thus, covenant lies on the word "demise," which amounts in general, in the absence of an express covenant, to a stipulation for quiet enjoyment. Grannis v. Clark, 8 Cow. (N. Y.) 86. And the words, "I have purchased of K. a tract of land supposed to be five hundred acres at four dollars per acre," have been construed to be a covenant to pay four dollars an acre for land. Kendal v. Talbot, 2 Bibb (Ky.), [illegible]; Beall v. Bodley, 6 J. J. Marsh. (Ky.) [illegible].

7. Pringle v. Witten's Exrs., 1 Bay (S. C.) [illegible]; s. c., 1 Am. Dec. 612.

Rule of Damages. — Under the Roman law, and by the codes which have been derived from it, where the vendee is evicted, he has a right to demand of the vendor (1) the restitution of the price; (2) the value of the fruits, or *mesne* profits, in case the vendee has been obliged to account for them to the owner; (3) the costs and expenses incurred both in the suit on the warranty and the prior suit of the owner, by whom the vendee has been evicted; and (4) damages and interest with the expenses legally incurred. Pothier, De la Vente, Nos. 118, 123, 128, 130; Code Napoleon, liv. 3, tit. 6, Art. 1630; De la Vente Dig. of La. And the vendee is also entitled to recover from the vendor, not only the value of all improvements made, but also the increased value, if any, which the property may have acquired independently of the acts of the purchaser. 1 Domat. 77, §§ 15, 16; Pothier, De la Vente, Nos. 132, 133; Code Napoleon, liv. 3, tit. 6, Arts. 1633, 1634; De la Vente Dig. of the Civ. L. of La. 355.

8. **Deficiency in Quantity of Land Sold.** — But it is held by the Supreme Court of Vermont, in the recent case of Church v. Stiles, 5 New. Eng. Rep. 104, that where a grantee has all the land described in his deed, but not all that the grantor agreed to convey, that his remedy is not an action upon the covenants.

Assertions as to Boundaries. — A person is not at liberty to make positive assertions about the boundaries of land he is selling, unless he knows them to be true; and if such statements are false, the assertor cannot relieve himself from the imputation of fraud by pleading ignorance, but must respond, in an action in covenant, in damages to the vendee who has sustained loss by acting in reasonable reliance upon such assertions. Lynch *v.* Mercantile Trust Co. (U. S. C. C. D. Minn.), 5 McCrary, C. C. 623; s. c., 18 Fed. Rep. 486; 18 Cent. L. J. 156; 8 Va. L. J. 68.

An action of covenant sounding in damages depends on matters outside of the record, and cannot be determined from the instrument itself; and an admission of a cause of action does not dispense with proof of the damages. Simonton *v.* Winter, 30 U. S. (5 Pet.) 141; bk. 8, L. ed. 75.

Where it is shown that the vendor did not own the land sold and conveyed, he becomes liable for damages on his covenant of warranty; and the measure of damages is the consideration of the land thus lost to the vendee. Hood's Appeal (Pa.), 5 Cent. Rep. 851.

In Covenant for Quiet Enjoyment. — The rule of damages for breach of the covenant for quiet enjoyment is *held* by some courts to be the value of the land at the time of the eviction, — Horsford *v.* Wright, Kirby (Conn.), 3; s. c., 1 Am. Dec. 8; Coleman *v.* Ballard, 13 La. An. 512; Hardy *v.* Nelson, 27 Me. 525; Smith *v.* Strong, 14 Pick. (Mass.) 128; Wyman *v.* Ballard, 12 Mass. 304; Liber *v.* Parson's Exrs., 1 Bay (S. C.), 19; Guerard's Exrs. *v.* Rivers, 1 Bay (S. C.), 265; Smith *v.* Sprague, 40 Vt. 43; — others hold that it is the consideration money, together with interest and costs. McGarry *v.* Hastings, 39 Cal. 360; s. c., 2 Am. Rep. 456; Crisfield *v.* Storr, 36 Md. 150; Nichols *v.* Walter, 8 Mass. 243; Phipps *v.* Tarpley, 31 Miss. 433; Martin *v.* Long, 3 Mo. 391; Dickson *v.* Desire, 23 Mo. 166; Nutting *v.* Herbert, 35 N. H. 126; Foster *v.* Thompson, 41 N. H. 379; Staats *v.* Ten Eyck, 3 Cai. (N. Y.) 111; s. c., 2 Am. Dec. 254; Adams *v.* Conover, 22 Hun (N. Y.), 424; Mack *v.* Patchin, 42 N. Y. 167; s. c., 1 Am. Rep. 506; Wade *v.* Comstock, 11 Ohio St. 82; Blake *v.* Burnham, 29 Vt. 437.

Price paid. — In applying the latter rule, the amount actually paid for the property may be ascertained by evidence, and may be shown to be more or less than the sum mentioned in the deeds. Lacey *v.* Marnan, 37 Ind. 168; Lawton *v.* Buckingham, 15 Iowa, 22; Dale *v.* Shiveley, 8 Kan. 276; Cox *v.* Strode, 2 Bibb (Ky.), 277; s. c., 5 Am. Dec. 603; Cornell *v.* Jackson, 3 Cush. (Mass.) 506; Smith *v.* Strong, 14 Pick. (Mass.) 128; Harlow *v.* Thomas, 15 Pick. (Mass.) 70; Hodges *v.* Thayer, 110 Mass. 286; Guinotte *v.* Chouteau, 34 Mo. 154; Partridge *v.* Hatch, 18 N. H. 498; Morris *v.* Phelps, 5 Johns (N. Y.) 49; s. c., 4 Am. Dec. 323; [illegible] Sandf. Ch. (N. Y.) 90; [illegible] derwas, 1 N. Y. 516; [illegible] Glenn, 68 N. C. 35; [illegible] (Pa.) 331; [illegible] St. 124; Kincaid *v.* [illegible] (Tenn.), 123; [illegible] 463; Rich *v.* Johnson, [illegible] s. c., 52 Am. Dec. 164.

Purchase by Barter. — Where the purchase was by barter, the value of the things given in exchange for the land may be proven. Lacey *v.* Marnan, 37 Ind. 168; Dale *v.* Shiveley, 8 Kan. 276; [illegible] *v.* Rich, 5 Gray (Mass.) [illegible]; Hodges *v.* Thayer, 110 Mass. 286; [illegible] idge, 15 Minn. 205; Farmers' Bank *v.* Glenn, 68 N. C. 35.

Where the actual consideration or the value of the articles given in exchange cannot be shown, the rule of damages will be the value of the land at the time of the intended conveyance, with interest from the date of the deed. Smith *v.* Strong, 14 Pick. (Mass.) 128. The *mesne* profits received by the grantee should be deducted from the interest on the purchase money, — see Burton *v.* Reeds, 20 Ind. 91; Combs *v.* Tarlton, 2 Dana (Ky.), 467; Whiting *v.* Dewey, 15 Pick. (Mass.) 428; Foster *v.* Thompson, 41 N. H. 373; Winslow *v.* McCall, 32 Barb. (N. Y.) 241; Young *v.* Divine (N. Y.), 12 Week. Dig. 18. Costs incurred in defending the title will include reasonable counsel fees. Harding *v.* Larkin, 41 Ill. 413; Robertson *v.* Lemon, 2 Bush (Ky.), 301; Taylor *v.* Holter, 1 Mon. Ter. 688; Dalton *v.* Bowker, 8 Nev. 190; Smith *v.* Sprague, 4 Vt. 43. *Contra*, Turner *v.* Miller, 42 Tex. 418, — unless there is a special agreement to pay such fees.

In Partial Failure of Title. — Where there is a failure of title as to part only of the land granted, it has been *held* that the grantee cannot recover back the whole consideration money, but the damages will be allowed *pro rata*. Hubbard *v.* Norton, 10 Conn. 122; Boyle *v.* Edwards, 114 Mass. 373; Morrison *v.* McArthur, 43 Me. 567; Hatch *v.* Partridge, 35 N. H. 145; Guthrie *v.* Pugsley, 12 Johns. (N. Y.) 126; Dummick *v.* Lockwood, 10 Wend. (N. Y.) 142.

If the title has failed as to an undivided part of an entire tract, the grantee is entitled to a like proportion of the consideration: but if it be of a specific proportion of the tract, the damages are to be apportioned according to the measure of value between the land lost and the land preserved: that is, the portion of the consideration money to be recovered is to be in the same ratio to the entire consideration that the value of the part, as to which the title has failed, is to the value of the tract.

is v. Phelps, 3 Johns. (N. Y.) 49; 3 Am. Dec. 434.

Breach of Seisin. — The measure of ...ges for a breach of the covenant of ..., or of right to convey, is the considera... paid with interest. Mitchell v. Hazen, ...n. 495; s. c., 10 Am. Dec. 169; Lacey ...man, 37 Ind. 168; Dale v. Shiveley, ...n. 276; Cox v. Strode, 2 Bibb (Ky.), s. c., 6 Am. Dec. 603; Stubbs v. Page, 378; Leland v. Stone, 10 Mass. 459; ...n v. Tarpley, 31 Miss. 433; Nutting ...rbert, 35 N. H. 120; Park v. Cheek, ...d. (Tenn.) 20; Blake v. Burnham, 29 ...7.

...York and Pennsylvania Doctrine. — ...ourts of New York and Pennsylvania that in the covenants of seisin, and of right and title to convey, that the ...e is entitled to the value of the land ...time of the purchase. Staats v. Ten ...'s Exrs., 3 Cai. (N. Y.) 111; s. c., 2 ...Dec. 254; Pitcher v. Livingston, 4 ... (N. Y.) 1; s. c., 4 Am. Dec. 229; ...r v. Fleckberger, 4 U. S. (4 Dall.) ...bk. 1, L. ed. 900.

...same rule has been adopted in Mas...etts. Bickford v. Page, 2 Mass. 455; ...on v. Hobbs, 2 Mass. 433; s. c., 48 ...Dec. 611; Caswell v. Wendell, 4 Mass.

If the grantee has actually enjoyed ...ands for a long time, the purchase... and interest for a term not exceed... years prior to the time of the evic... given; for the grantee, upon a ...ry against him, is liable to account ...e *mesne* profits for that period only. ...v. Ten Eyck's Exrs., 3 Cai. (N. Y.) s. c., 2 Am. Dec. 254; Caulkins v. ..., 9 Johns. (N. Y.) 324; Bennet v. ..., 13 Johns. (N. Y.) 50.

Breach of Warranty. — The measure ...mages for breach of covenant of war... is the loss actually sustained, not ...ing the consideration paid, with in... and expenses of suit. Griffin v. Rey... 58 U. S. (17 How.) 609; bk. 15, L. ...9.

...y nominal damages can be recovered ...breach of the covenant of warranty, ...it is shown that the grantee has suf... actual loss, been evicted, or compelled ... money to remove the incumbrance ...er to prevent eviction, — King v. Gil... 2 Ill. 356; Richard v. Bent, 59 Ill. 38; 14 Am. Rep. 1; Mason v. Cooksey, ...l. 519. See Cockrell v. Proctor, 65 ...1; Myers v. Brodbeck (Pa.), 1 Cent. 407, — in either of which cases he ...tled to recover, in an action on the ...ant, a just compensation for such in... Bronson v. Coffin, 108 Mass. 175; 11 Am. Rep. 335, — or what money ...ght reasonably to have paid to extin... the incumbrance, — Schofield v. Iowa Homestead Co., 32 Iowa, 317; s. c., 7 Am. Rep. 197; Guthrie v. Russell, 46 Iowa, 269; s. c., 26 Am. Rep. 135; Reed v. Pierce, 36 Me. 455; Eastbrook v. Smith, 6 Gray (Mass.), 572; Comings v. Little, 24 Pick. (Mass.) 266; Johnson v. Collins, 116 Mass. 392; Hall v. Bray, 51 Mo. 288; Morrison v. Underwood, 20 N. H. 369; Willson v. Willson, 25 N. H. 229; Delavergne v. Mortis, 7 Johns. (N. Y.) 358; s. c., 5 Am. Dec. 281; Barlow v. St. Nicholas Nat. Bank, 63 N. Y. 402; Eaton v. Lyman, 30 Wis. 41; — but in no case will the covenantee be allowed a sum greater than the value of the land. Kelsey v. Remer, 43 Conn. 129; s. c., 21 Am. Rep. 638.

Some of the cases hold that in no instance should the amount of the recovery exceed the value of the land, — Hennings v. Withers, 3 Brev. (S. C.) 458; s. c., 6 Am. Dec. 589; Ware v. Weathnall, 2 McC. (S. C.) 413, — together with interest and costs, if any. Logan v. Moulder, 1 Ark. 313; s. c., 33 Am. Dec. 338; McGary v. Hastings, 39 Cal. 360; Davis v. Smith, 5 Ga. 274; s. c., 40 Am. Dec. 279; Brady v. Spurck, 27 Ill. 482; Phillips v. Reichert, 17 Ind. 120; s. c., 79 Am. Dec. 463; Burton v. Reeds, 20 Ind. 93; Swafford v. Whipple, 3 Greene (Iowa), 261; s. c., 54 Am. Dec. 498; Brandt v. Foster, 5 Iowa, 298; Wilhelm v. Fimple, 31 Iowa, 137; Durbin v. Garrard, 5 T. B. Mon. (Ky.) 317; Pence v. Duvall, 9 B. Mon. (Ky.) 48; Crisfield v. Storr, 36 Md. 129; Phipps v. Tarpley, 31 Miss. 433; Coffman v. Huck, 19 Mo. 435; Dickson v. Desire, 23 Mo. 166; Taylor v. Holter, 1 Mon. Ter. 688; Dalton v. Bowker, 8 Nev. 198; Foster v. Thompson, 41 N. H. 373; Stewart v. Drake, 9 N. J. L. (4 Halst.) 139; Andrews v. Appel, 22 Hun (N. Y.), 429; Bennet v. Jenkins, 13 Johns. (N. Y.) 50; Demmick v. Lockwood, 10 Wend. (N. Y.) 142; Grant v. Tallman, 20 N. Y. 191; s. c., 75 Am. Dec. 384; Mack v. Patchin, 42 N. Y. 167; s. c., 1 Am. Rep. 506; Williams v. Beeman, 2 Dev. (N. C.) L. 483; Grist v. Hodges, 3 Dev. (N. C.) L. 198; Foote v. Burnet, 10 Ohio, 334; s. c., 36 Am. Dec. 90; Wade v. Comstock, 11 Ohio St. 82; McClure v. Gamble, 27 Pa. St. 288; Cox v. Henry, 32 Pa. St. 21; Terry v. Diabenstatt, 68 Pa. St. 400; Wallace v. Talbot, 1 McC. (S. C.) 466; Stout v. Jackson, 2 Rand. (Va.) 132. But see Porter v. Bradley, 7 R. I. 542; Mills v. Catlin, 22 Vt. 106; Hopkins v. Lee, 19 U. S. (6 Wheat.) 109; bk. 5, L. ed. 218; Lewis v. Campbell, 8 Taunt. 715.

Some States hold that the measure of the damages is the value of the land at the time of eviction. Sterling v. Peet, 14 Conn. 245; Swett v. Patrick, 12 Me. 1; Hardy v. Nelson, 27 Me. 525; Norton v. Babcock, 2 Metc. (Mass.) 518; Gore v. Brazier, 3 Mass. 523; s. c., 3 Am. Dec. 182; Caswell v.

Wendell, 4 Mass. 108; Park *v.* Bates, 12 Vt. 381; s. c., 36 Am. Dec. 347.

In Covenant against Incumbrances. — As to the covenant against incumbrances, it seems generally held that the grantee is entitled to nominal damages only, unless he extinguishes the incumbrance; and if he extinguishes it for a reasonable and fair price, he is entitled to recover that sum with interest from the time of payment, — Prescott *v.* Trueman, 4 Mass. 627; s. c., 3 Am. Dec. 246; Delavergne *v.* Norris, 7 Johns. (N. Y.) 358; s. c., 5 Am. Dec. 281; Hall *v.* Dean, 13 Johns. (N. Y.) 105, — and the costs, if any, to which he has been put by an action against him on account of the incumbrance. Waldo *v.* Long, 7 Johns. (N. Y.) 173.

Extinguishment of Incumbrance. — The question of the reasonableness of the amount paid to extinguish the lien of an incumbrance is a question for the jury. St. Louis *v.* Bissell, 46 Mo. 157.

Where the incumbrance is of a permanent character, such as a right of way, or other easement, and cannot be removed, the damages will be measured by the diminished value of the estate, occasioned by the existence of such permanent incumbrance. Haynes *v.* Young, 36 Me. 557; Lamb *v.* Danforth, 59 Me. 322; s. c., 8 Am. Rep. 426; Jacobs *v.* Davis, 34 Md. 204; Batchelder *v.* Sturgis, 3 Cush. (Mass.) 201; Sturtevant *v.* Phelps, 16 Gray (Mass.), 50; Harlow *v.* Thomas, 15 Pick. (Mass.) 66; Williamson *v.* Hall, 62 Mo. 405.

Where the permanent incumbrances is an easement granted to a railroad, evidence of the enhanced value of the land by reason of the railroad is not admissible. Kellogg *v.* Malin, 62 Mo. 429.

Upon a breach of covenant in an exchange of lands, the measure of damages is the value of the land conveyed, and not of the land received. Cummins *v.* Kennedy, 3 Litt. (Ky.) 118; s. c., 14 Am. Dec. 45. *Compare* Farmers' Bank *v.* Glenn, 68 N. C. 635.

In Quiet Enjoyment. — The measure of damages for a breach of the covenant for quiet enjoyment, implied in a lease, is the value of the unexpired term at the time of the eviction, over and above the rent reserved by the terms of the lease. Myers *v.* Burns, 35 N. Y. 272; Mack *v.* Patchin, 42 N. Y. 167; s. c., 1 Am. Rep. 506; 29 How. Pr. (N. Y.) 20; Myers *v.* Burns, 35 N. Y. 272; Williams *v.* Burrell, 1 Man. G. & S. 402; s. c., 50 Eng. C. L. 401; Lock *v.* Furze, L. R. 1 C. P. 441; s. c., 115 Eng. C. L. 94; Rolph *v.* Crouch, L. R. 3 Ex. 44.

The measure of damages for the breach of a covenant for quiet enjoyment depends largely upon the nature of the estate or title granted, and the character of the landlord's default. The covenant always relates to,

and never extends beyond, the
estate, and privileges granted.
strained and limited to the estate
Hoagland *v.* New York, C. & St.
(Ind.), 9 West. Rep. 492.

Thus, where the subject-matte
lease was so much of the surplus
required for navigation, to be tak
lessees from the Wabash & Erie
should be adequate to propel a de
amount of machinery in their
lessors not having assumed any o
to maintain the canal in repair, or
it in such a condition that there wo
surplus of water above that needed
gation, nor bound themselves to fu
supply the lessees with water, and
ing no provision restricting the les
using all the water for purposes o
tion, or from entirely abandoning
at pleasure; the canal being aban
an action by the lessees for dam
breach of covenant, the court *hel*
no event "did the lessors become
any other consequence than the in.
collect rent from the lessees." I
v. New York, C. & St. L. R. C
9 West Rep. 252. See also Hu
Toledo, 21 Ohio St. 379; Fox *v.* Ci
104 U. S. (14 Otto) 783; bk. 26, L.
Sheets *v.* Selden, 74 U. S. (7 W
bk. 19, L. ed. 166.

Every lessee of the surplus w
canal takes his lease of the power.
up his improvements subject to f
of the reserved right of the State
tinue its canal and stop the supply
at any time. See Trustees of
Canal *v.* Brett, 25 Ind. 409; Fis
Woodruff, 51 Ind. 102; Hubbard *v.*
21 Ohio St. 379; Elevator Co. *v.* Ci
30 Ohio St. 629; Commonwealth
sylvania R. R. Co., 51 Pa. St. 351.

Improvements and Increase of
In an action for a breach of the
of title, the plaintiff cannot rec
value of the improvements made
after purchase from the covenanto
der *v.* Fromberger, 4 U. S. (4 Da
bk. 1, L. ed. 901.

And in covenant for breach of
nant after eviction by paramount
is error to allow damages for inc
value prior to the eviction, in the
of evidence of such increase.
Shay (Ia.), 25 Cent. L. J. 157;
N. W. Rep. 690.

In New York and Pennsylvania
of damages adopted in respect to
nant for quiet enjoyment and of
warranty, is to give the purchas
with interest and the costs of
suit; but no allowance is made
value of any improvements. Staat
Eyck's Exrs., 3 Cal. (N. Y.) 111;
Am. Dec. 254; Pitcher *v.* Livin

(N. Y.) 1; s. c., 4 Am. Dec. 229; ... v. Jenkins, 13 Johns. (N. Y.) 90; ... v. Fromberger, 4 U. S. (4 Dall.) ... bk. 1, L. ed. 920.

... same rule has been adopted in Ten... 5 Hall's Am. Law Jour. 330.

... in other States, in relation to cove... of warranty, the rule of damages has ... said to be the value of the property ... time of eviction. Gore v. Brazier, ... 523; s. c., 3 Am. Dec. 182.

... same rule appears to be adopted in ... Carolina — Liber v. Parsons, 1 Bay ... 19; Guerard's Exrs. v. Rivers, 1 ... C.), 265; Virginia Mills v. Bell, 3 ... (Va.) 326; Humphrey's Admr. v. ... nachan Admr., 1 Munf. (Va.) 493 — ... Connecticut. Horsford v. Wright, ... (Conn.), 3; s. c., 1 Am. Dec. 8.

... and Contracts. — In an action by a ... ser of land to recover damages for ... ire to convey, the value of the land ... time the conveyance is to be made ... true measure of damages. Pinkston ... ie, 9 Ala. 252; Gibbs v. Jemison, 12 ... 20; Wells v. Abernethy, 5 Conn. 222; ... aster v. Grundy, 1 Scam. (Ill.) 310; ... e v. Brandon, 2 Scam. (Ill.) 339; Gale ... n, 20 Ill. 320; Plummer v. Rigdon, ... 222; Hill v. Hobart, 16 Me. 164; ... n v. Wheeler, 21 Me. 484; Lawrence ... se, 54 Me. 196; Dyer v. Dorsey, 1 ... J. (Md.) 520; Cannell v. McAhean, ... & J. (Md.) 297; Kirkpatrick v. ... ing, ... Mo. 32; Drake v. Baker, 34 ... (5 Vr.) 358; Barbour v. Nichols, 3 ... 87; Boardman v. Keeler, 21 Vt. 84; ... ns v. Lee, 19 U. S. (6 Wheat.) 109; ... L. ed. 218.

... a contract for the purchase of real ... if the title prove bad, and the vendor ... out fraud, unable to make a good ... the purchaser is not entitled to dam... the loss of his bargain. Hammond ... nin, 21 Mich. 374; Flurean v. Thorn... W. Black. 1078; Bain v. Fothergill, ... Eng. & Ir. App. 158.

... where the vendor knew at the time ... tracting that he had not title or the ... of conveyance, although he acted in ... aith, and believed that he should be ... procure a good title, it was held ... the vendee was entitled to recover of ... dor the difference between the con... rice and the value of the land at the ... f the breach. Pumpelly v. Phelps, ... Y. 59. See Brinckerhoff v. Phelps, ... h. (N. Y.) 100; s. c., 43 Barb. (N. Y.) ... ornell v. Granger, 8 N. Y. 155.

... Virginia the same general rule has ... aid down. — Thompson's Exrs. v. ... e, 4 Leigh (Va.), 101; Wilson v. ... r, 11 Leigh (Va.), 261, — also in ... ky. Patrick v. Marshall, 2 Bibb ... 40; 4 Am. Dec. 670; Allen v. Ander... Bibb (Ky.), 415; Fisher v. Kay, 2 Bibb (Ky.), 434; McConnell v. Dunlap, Hardin (Ky.), 41; s. c., 3 Am. Dec. 723; Handley v. Chambers, 1 Litt. (Ky.) 358.

New York Rule. — The general rule in New York in the case of executory contracts for the sale of land, is that, in case of breach by the vendor, the vendee can, in an action of covenant, recover only nominal damages, unless he has paid part of the purchase-money, in which case he can also recover such purchase-money and interest. Peters v. McKeon, 4 Denio (N. Y.), 546; Stanton v. Miller, 14 Hun (N. Y.), 383; Baldwin v. Munn, 2 Wend. (N. Y.) 399; s. c., 20 Am. Dec. 627; Conger v. Weaver, 20 N. Y. 145; Mack v. Patchin, 42 N. Y. 167; Margraf v. Muir, 57 N. Y. 155.

In a later case in New York, the court say that the rule is well settled, that, where the vendor enters into a contract to sell and convey real estate under a belief that he has a good title, and that the same is free from incumbrances, and he fails to perform for the reason that the title is defective, or an incumbrance unknown to him previously is discovered, which prevents a fulfilment of the contract, in an action by the vendee against him for a breach of the contract, the latter is only liable for nominal damages aside from the purchase-money paid and the expense of examining the title. Cockroft v. New York & H. R. Co., 69 N. Y. 201.

In an action against vendee for damages for breach of contract to purchase land, the measure of damages is the difference between the contract price and the price for which the land could be sold at the time of the breach. Old Colony R. R. v. Evans, 72 Mass. (6 Gray) 25; s. c., 66 Am. Dec. 394; Griswold v. Sabin, 51 N. H. 167.

An agreement to perform certain work within a limited time, under a certain penalty, does not liquidate the damages which the party is to pay for the breach of his covenant. Tayloe v. Sandiford, 20 U. S. (7 Wheat.) 13; bk. 5, L. ed. 384.

Public Contractors. — One who contracts to deliver wood to the government is entitled to extra compensation for being required to cut it farther from the place of delivery than that named in his contract, and for the expense of keeping his teams during the delay caused thereby. United States v. Peck, 102 U. S. (12 Otto) 64; bk. 26, L. ed. 46.

Covenant running with the Land. — All covenants which relate to land, and are for its benefit, run with the land, and may be enforced by an action in covenant by each successive assignee. See Sterling Hydraulic Co. v. Williams, 66 Ill. 393; 1 Smith Lead. Cas. (Hare & W. notes) pt. 1, p. 179. And while a parol agreement to maintain fences does not run with the land, but affects the parties to the agreement only, yet a written agreement showing an intention to charge the land runs with it, and is enforceable against subsequent grantees. Kentucky Cent. R. Co. *v.* Kearney, 6 Ky. L. Rep. 17; s. c., 19 Cent. L. J. 96.

Where grantees of different lots at several times covenanted not to build beyond a specified line, such covenant, being and continuing for the benefit of future purchasers, may be enforced against an earlier purchaser by a later purchaser. Lattimer *v.* Livermore, 72 N. Y. 174.

Charge upon Land. — Where the performance of a covenant is expressly or impliedly made a charge upon the land, it runs with the land. See Thomas *v.* Von Kapff, 6 Gill & J. (Md.) 372; Astor *v.* Miller, 2 Paige, Ch. (N. Y.) 68; Van Rensselaer *v.* Dennison, 35 N. Y. 393; Goudy *v.* Goudy, Wright (Ohio), 410; Worthington *v.* Hewes, 19 Ohio St. 66; Sandwith *v.* De Silver, 1 Browne (Pa.), 221; Hurst *v.* Rodney, 1 Wash. C. C. 375; Wooliscroft *v.* Norton, 15 Wis. 198.

But if the thing to be done is merely collateral to the land, the assignee will not be charged, and covenant will not lie against him. Dolph *v.* White, 12 N. Y. 296; Webb *v.* Russell, 3 T. R. 393-402.

Thus, a covenant that the grantee shall remain in the quiet and peaceable possession of the land, runs with the land, and is binding upon those to whom the land may be subsequently conveyed by such grantee. Schwalback *v.* Chicago, M. & St. P. R. Co. (Wis.) 33 N. W. Rep.

There must be a privity of estate between the covenantor and covenantee, in order to to create a covenant that will run with the land, and enable an assignee to maintain an action of covenant. Taylor *v.* Owen, 2 Blackf. (Ind.) 301; Morse *v.* Aldrich, 19 Pick. (Mass.) 449; Bronson *v.* Coffin, 108 Mass. 175; s. c., 11 Am. Rep. 335; Wheeler *v.* Schad, 7 Nev. 204; Brewer *v.* Marshall, 19 N. J. Eq. (4 C. E. Gr.) 537; Kirkpatrick *v.* Peshine, 24 N. J. Eq. (9 C. E. Gr.) 206; Cole *v.* Hughes, 54 N. Y. 444; s. c., 13 Am. Rep. 611.

Such a covenant can only be assigned with the land. Martin *v.* Gordon, 24 Ga. 533; Wilson *v.* Widenham, 51 Me. 566; Nesbit *v.* Brown, 1 Dev. (N. C.) Eq. 30; Randolph *v.* Kinney, 3 Rand. (Va.) 394.

Division of Covenants. — Where land conveyed with full covenants consists of several distinct pieces, or is divided up into parcels, and conveyed to different grantees, the covenant is divided up among them, and each may sue in covenant, or be sued on his portion of the covenant. Astor *v.* Miller, 2 Paige, Ch. (N. Y.) 68; Johnson *v.* Blydenburg, 31 N. Y. 427.

English Doctrine. — In England all covenants for title are termed real covenants, and *held* to run with the land. [illegible] Nottle, 1 [illegible] 756.

In America, the [illegible] that covenants of [illegible] convey are covenants in [illegible] broken, if at all, [illegible] *v.* Bent, 39 Ill. [illegible] Bethell *v.* Bethell, [illegible]; s. c., 23 Am. Rep. [illegible]; [illegible] *v.* Callaghan, 8 Hun (N. Y.), [illegible]; [illegible] *v.* Burnet, 10 Ohio, 317, [illegible]; s. c., [illegible] Am. Dec. 90, — and do not [illegible] with the land, and the right of action for a breach does not pass to the assignee of the covenantee. Salmon *v.* Vallejo, 41 Cal. 481; Wilson *v.* Cochran, 46 Pa. St. 229. However, it is *held* in some of the States, that the covenant of seisin runs with the land. See Coleman *v.* Lyman, [illegible] Ind. 289; Schofield *v.* Iowa Homestead Co., 32 Iowa, 317; s. c., 7 Am. Rep. [illegible]; Knadler *v.* Sharp, 36 Iowa, 232; [illegible] *v.* Riggin, 44 Mo. 512; Roberts *v.* Levy, 3 Abb. (N. Y.) Pr. N. S. 311; Hall *v.* Plaine, 14 Ohio St. 417. And the covenant of indefeasible seisin is everywhere *held* to run with the land. Dickson *v.* Desire, [illegible] Mo. 151; Abbott *v.* Allen, 14 Johns. (N. Y.) 248; Garfield *v.* Williams, 2 Vt. [illegible].

Covenants for quiet enjoyment, for further assurance, and of warranty, are prospective in their nature, — McGary *v.* Hastings, 39 Cal. 360; s. c., 2 Am. Rep. 456; Shelton *v.* Codman, 3 Cush. (Mass.) 318; Hurd *v.* Curtis, 19 Pick. (Mass.) 459; Hunt *v.* Amidon, 4 Hill (N. Y.), 345; Abbott *v.* Allen, 14 Johns. (N. Y.) 248, — run with the land, — Logan *v.* Moulder, 1 Ark. 313; s. c., 33 Am. Dec. 338; Hunt *v.* Amidon, 4 Hill (N. Y.), 345; Markland *v.* Crump, 1 Dev. & B. (N. C.) L. 94; Campbell *v.* Lewis, 3 Barn. & Ald. 392; s. c., 5 Eng. C. L. 322, — and an action in covenant for damages for a breach may be maintained by the covenantee and his representatives, heirs, devisees, and alienees. Claycomb *v.* Munger, 51 Ill. 373; Crisfield *v.* Storr, 36 Md. 129; Rindskopf *v.* Farmers' Trust Co., 58 Barb. (N. Y.) 36; Withy *v.* Mumford, 5 Cow. (N. Y.) 137; Burtners *v.* Keran, 24 Gratt. (Va.) 42.

Party Wall. — It is held by some courts that an agreement to build or pay for a party wall is merely a personal covenant, — Bloch *v.* Isham, 28 Ind. 37; Curtiss *v.* White, 1 Clarke, Ch. (N. Y.) 389; Coffin *v.* Talman, 8 N. Y. 465; Cole *v.* Hughes, 54 N. Y. 444, — and does not pass to a grantee; other courts hold that such covenants are real covenants, and run with the land. Savage *v.* Mason, 3 Cush. (Mass.) 500; Maine *v.* Cumston, 98 Mass. 317; Standish *v.* Lawrence, 111 Mass. 113; Richardson *v.* Tobey, 121 Mass. 457; Burlock *v.* Peck, 2 Duer (N. Y.), 90; Hart *v.* Kucher, 5 Serg.

action of covenant will not lie upon a clause in a deed ded solely to prevent the conveyance being treated as an icement.[5]

has been held that an action of covenant will lie upon the s of a deed, "will warrant and defend the premises to A. B., his heirs forever,"[1] as well as the words "grant, bargain, and "[2] and to be maintainable upon a covenant by grantors "for , —— heirs," etc., the clause being construed to mean "them-

Pa.) 3; Todd v. Stokes, 10 Pa. St. rr) 155; Gilbert v. Drew, 10 Pa. St. r) 219; Jaques v. Bringhurst, 1 U. Dall.) 311; bk. 1, L. ed. 167.

ssachusetts Doctrine. — The Massa- ts courts *held* that such a covenant direct and immediate reference to the that it relates to the mode of occu- and enjoying the land; that it is ial to the owner merely as owner; is inherent in and attached to the nd necessarily passes into the hands heir or grantee, who may maintain on in covenant for its breach. See Boston Penny Savings Bank, 115

r States. — Opposed to this doctrine, irts of New York, Pennsylvania, and States, *held* that where the owner of uilds a party wall under an agree- with the adjoining owner, and that the latter shall use it he will pay penses of building his portion of the he right to compensation is personal builder, and does not pass by a grant land and bind subsequent grantees, it the burden of liability is confined original covenantor. Cole v. Hughes, Y. 444; Davids v. Harris, 9 Pa. St. odd v. Stokes, 10 Pa. St. 155; Gil- Drew, 10 Pa. St. 219.

ute of Frauds. — A parol agreement d a party wall is within the statute ds; but if the party builds such a ion the faith of the defendant's agree- o pay one-half the cost when he uses it building is a part performance suffi- o take the agreement out of the stat- d an action in covenant will lie. n v. Ball, 46 Ga. 19. See also Bindge er, 57 N. Y. 207.

ere an adjoining owner, in a city, a statute condemns and removes a wall which forms one side of a build- ased for years, for the purpose of g a suitable wall for a larger build- ich condemning and tearing down of ll will not constitute a breach of the l covenant for quiet enjoyment con- in the lease. Barns v. Wilson (Pa.), . Rep. 454; s. c., 25 Cent. L. J. 14; Rep. 437.

nant for Quiet Enjoyment. — Al- . every lease contains an implied covenant for quiet enjoyment, yet that covenant extends only to the acts of the lessor himself, and to injuries inflicted under paramount title: it is not designed as an indemnity against any and all disturbances of the lessee's enjoyment of the land under the law. Barns v. Wilson (Pa.), 8 Cent. Rep. 454; s. c., 25 Cent. L. J. 14; 9 Atl. Rep. 437. See Frost v. Earnest, 4 Whart. (Pa.) 86; Dobbins v. Brown, 12 Pa. St. 75; Moore v. Weber, 71 Pa. St. 429.

Uninhabitable House. — The mere fact that a house leased becomes uninhabitable is not enough to sustain an action in covenant. Carson v. Godley, 26 Pa. St. 117; Hazlett v. Powell, 30 Pa. St. 293. This condition of the property must result from the act of the lessor, or from those holding a paramount title. Barns v. Wilson (Pa.), 8 Cent. Rep. 454; s. c., 25 Cent. L. J. 14; 9 Atl. Rep. 437. Yet it has been held that a covenant by a lessee to occupy premises as a dwelling-house, implies a covenant by the lessor of fitness for a dwelling-house, and that, in case of unfitness, the amount expended by the lessee for necessary repairs is a set-off against a claim for rent. Wolfe v. Arrott, 109 Pa. St. 473; s. c., 1 Cent. Rep. 128.

See on this subject Phipps v. Tarpley, 24 Miss. 597; Mann v. Pierson, 2 Johns. (N. Y.) 37; Pringle v. Witten, 1 Bay (S. C.), 256; s. c., 1 Am. Dec. 612; Kincaid v. Brittain, 5 Sneed (Tenn.), 123.

1. Hummel v. Hummel, 80 Pa. St. 420.

2. Rickets v. Dickens, 1 Murph. (N. C.) 343; s. c., 4 Am. Dec. 555.

3. "Grant, Bargain, and Sell." — Under a deed of general warranty containing the words "grant, bargain, and sell," the grantee has a right to recover of his grantor's administrator the money paid by him as a collateral inheritance tax, which was a lien upon the property when conveyed by said deed. Large v. McClain (Pa.), 5 Cent. Rep. 761.

In Pennsylvania. — The words "grant, bargain, and sell," in a deed under act of May 28, 1715, created a covenant against incumbrances, which was broken as soon as made by an existing lien; and plaintiff, being compelled to pay it to save his property, has a right to recover in covenant. Large v. McClain (Pa.), 5 Cent. Rep. 761.

selves, their heirs," etc.;[1] but an action is not maintainabl "and the said ——, for ——, heirs, etc., does covenant," etc.; cause the effect of the blanks is to render the entire clause [illegible] tory, and the inference naturally arises that no such covenant [illegible] intended to be made; nor can the context, by construction [illegible] ply the omission.[3]

A court of chancery will decree the performance of a [illegible] covenant to indemnify "against all claims or suits at law, or [illegible]

No action but covenant will lie on an instrument, under se the words "Due A. B. $10.43, value received, payable in cotton [illegible] but will lie on the words "to which payment, well and truly [illegible] made, I bind myself;"[5] on the words "I am content to g[illegible] etc.;[6] on the words "I oblige myself to pay so much mon[illegible] such a day, and so much at another time."[7]

A receipt in these words, "Received fourteen barrels of whi[illegible] of J. S., for sale," does not create a covenant to pay over the ceeds, so as to authorize an action of covenant.[8]

IV. When not Maintainable. — In general, covenant cannot maintained upon a contract not under seal, by the party or [illegible] attorney;[9] because a mere recognition of the contract, [illegible] under seal, will not sustain the action.[10]

1. Baker v. Hunt, 40 Ill. 264.

Illinois Rule. — But in the Illinois case above given the intention is clearly manifest, and the error of the clerk very palpable. The question of construction in such a case is comparatively simple, the imperfect words show the intention of the grantor. The neglect in this instance to insert the word "their" was immaterial, as would have been the word "heirs," for the legal effect of the covenant would have been the same if all reference to the heirs, executors, and administrators had been omitted. See Hall v. Bumstead, 20 Pick. (Mass.) 2; Bell v. Boston, 101 Mass. 506.

2. Day v. Brown, 2 Ohio, 345.

3. Wilson v. Davidson County, 3 Tenn. Ch. 536.

4. Fortenbury v. Tunstall, 5 Ark. 263.

5. Douglass v. Hennessy (R. I.), 5 New Eng Rep. 94.

No demand need be made before action is brought on such a covenant. Douglass v. Hennessy (R. I.), 4 New Eng. Rep. 94.

Burden of Proof. — Defendant has the burden of proving his plea of performance, although a breach of the condition of the bond is alleged in the declaration. Douglass v. Hennessy (R. I.), 5 New Eng Rep. 94.

6. The court *held* the words to mean "did amount to as much as I promise to pay." Anonymous, 3 Leon. 119.

7. Norrice's Case, Hardres, 178.

8. Wilcoxen v. Rix, 1 A. K. Marsh. (Ky.) 421.

9. Tribble v. Oldham, 5 J. J. Marsh. (Ky.) 137; Ludlum v. Wood, 2 [illegible] (1 Penn.) 55; Hilderbach v. [illegible] N. J. L. (2 Halst.) 64; Gale v. [illegible] Cow. (N. Y.) 445; Davis v. [illegible] 85; 2 Bouv. Inst. 356, § [illegible] 118.

Omission to do Act. — If the [illegible] the covenant sued upon is [illegible] sion to do the act, by the perform[illegible] which the bond might [illegible] action of contract will not lie; [illegible] case there is no promise [illegible] Powell v. Clark, 3 N. J. L. (2 [illegible]

English Rule. — But it is [illegible] land that covenant lies against a [illegible] a patentee, although he did [illegible] lease, or any counterpart of the [illegible] cause it is a matter of record, and [illegible] see's acceptance of the [illegible] be[illegible] such a case as obligatory as on e[illegible] covenant. Ewre v. Strickland, Cro [illegible] 240; Bret v. Cumberland, Cro. Ja[illegible] 521; Comyn's Dig. tit. *Covenant*, [illegible] Viner, Abr. tit. *Covenant*, B. Pl. 1.

Where covenant was brought upo[illegible] following words in a letter from one br[illegible] to another, "Dear brother, Preston' [illegible] ting the money that he did from yo[illegible] caused me many painful hours. If [illegible] health I would soon get out of debt. [illegible] amount is sure to you or your heirs [illegible] court *held* that covenant would no[illegible] and that the words imported no prom[illegible] obligation. Bright v. Bright, 8 P[illegible] (Ky.) 104.

10. Gale v. Nixon, 6 Cow. (N. Y.) [illegible]

Covenant will not lie upon a contract where, by the law of the lace in which the remedy is sought, it is not a sealed instru-ient, although it would be considered as under seal in the place here it was made.[1] The reason for this is, that, where a contract is made in one State, and intended to have effect in another, it ust conform to the laws of such other State.[2]

Covenant cannot be maintained by parties not privy to the con-ract, and a personal covenant cannot be set up in a suit by or ainst the assignee of the covenantor or covenantee;[3] neither y it be maintained where the party claiming the benefit of the venant is not named therein as the covenantee.[4]

It has been held that covenant cannot be maintained by one artner against another on the articles of partnership, although nder seal, to compel the pa ment of a balance due the partner-hip from such partner;[5] on a lease executed by a lessor only, though the lessee enters and enjoys the possession;[6] or by the xecutors of the lessor against the executors of the lessee, for rent accrued after the death of the testator;[7] on a contract under seal,

1. Broadhead v. Noyes, 9 Mo. 56; Dorsey Hardesty, 9 Mo. 157.

Scroll Seals. — An instrument in the form a promissory note made in Pennsylvania, a scroll "L. S." being at the end of the aker's name (which by the law of that ate constitutes a seal), and payable in ew York, is governed by the laws of New ork and is but a simple contract. Andrews Herriot, 4 Cow. (N. Y.) 508; Warren v. ynch, 5 Johns. (N. Y.) 239; Ayer's Case, 6 . H. Rec. 30. See Trasher v. Everhart, 3 ill & J. (Md.) 234; Watson v. Brewster, 1 a. St. 381; Bank of United States v. Don-lly, 33 U. S. (8 Pet.) 361; bk. 8, L. ed. 974. It has been *held* that covenant cannot be aintained on a contract made in New ork to be performed in Pennsylvania, ith a scrawl and the word "seal" in the *cus sigilli*; though, by the law of that ate, that constitutes a seal. See Mere-th v. Hinsdale, 2 Cai. (N. Y.) 362; An-rews v. Herriot, 4 Cow. (N. Y.) 508; Warren v. Lynch, 5 Johns. (N. Y.) 239; ank of United States v. Donnally, 33 U. S. Pet.) 361; bk. 8, L. ed. 974; Le Roy v. eard, 49 U. S. (8 How.) 451; bk. 12, L. . 1151; Adam v. Kerr, 1 Bos. & Pull. 360.

2. Stricker v. Tinkham, 35 Ga. 176; ewis v. Headley, 36 Ill. 433; Wooten v. iller, 15 Miss. (7 Smed. & M.) 380.

3. Lyon v. Parker, 45 Me. 474.

Privity of Contract. — Where the defend-t became bound by his bond, jointly and verally to A. C., and others, owners of rtain mills, dam, and water-power, and so unto the grantees of either and all of em (naming the obligees in the bond), to mplete, and keep in repairs for twenty ars, the dam, in an action of covenant broken, brought by a grantee of some of the owners, for damages for defendant's non-performance of his covenant, it was *held*, that, as the defendant was a stranger to the title, his covenant was personal, and that, as the plaintiff was no party to the bond when it was executed, there was no privity of contract between him and the defendant; and, there being neither privity of contract nor of estate, the action was not maintainable. Lyon v. Parker, 45 Me. 474.

4. De Bolle v. The Pennsylvania Ins. Co., 4 Whart. (Pa.) 68; Green v. Horne, 1 Salk. 197; s. c., Comb. 219; Nourse v. Frampton, 1 Ld. Raym. 28; s. c., 1 Salk. 214. *Ex parte* Richardson, 14 Ves. 184, 187; Collins v. Plumb, 16 Ves. 454.

On Deed-Poll. — But it has been *held*, that, in the case to a deed-poll, a stranger to it may sue on the covenant therein to pay him a sum of money; but it is otherwise in the case of a deed *inter partes*. Smith v. Emery, 12 N. J. L. (7 Halst.) 53; Berk-ley v. Hardy, 8 Dow. & Ryl. 102.

5. In such a case the proper remedy under the common-law practice, is an action of account or a bill in chancery. See Niven v. Spickerman, 12 Johns. (N. Y.) 401.

6. Hinsdale v. Humphrey, 15 Conn. 431; Trustees v. Spencer, 7 Ohio (pt. 2), 151. See Burnett v. Lynch, 5 B. & C. 589, 602; s. c., 8 Dow. & R. 368; Hawkins v. Sher-man, 3 Car. & P. 59; East India Co. v. Lewis, 3 Car. & P. 358.

But it will lie, although the covenantee did not sign the indenture in which he is named as a party. Lucke v. Lucke, Lutw. 305; Comyn's Dig. tit. *Covenant*, A. 1.

7. Van Rensselaer v. Platner, 2 Johns. Cas. (N. Y.) 24.

the material part of which is subsequently varied by a parol agreement;[1] on a policy of insurance, renewed by indorsement, not under seal;[2] on a deed, the seal to which has been torn off by one to whom such deed was intrusted by both parties for safe keeping;[3] on a condition in a title-bond to convey land;[4] against the grantee in a deed-poll for non-performance of any condition of any thing therein stipulated to be done by him;[5] on the condition of a bond;[6] on a special agreement under seal to do work,

1. McVoy v. Wheeler, 6 Port. (Ala.) 201; Raymond v. Fisher, 6 Mo. 29; Vicary v. Moore, 2 Watts (Pa.), 451; s. c., 27 Am. Dec. 323; Ellmaker v. Franklin Fire Ins. Co., 6 Watts & S. (Pa.) 443; Heard v. Wadham, 1 East, 630; Littler v. Holland, 3 T. R. 590.

The remedy is on the substituted agreement. McVoy v. Wheeler, 6 Port. (Ala.) 201; Raymond v. Fisher, 6 Mo. 29.

Written Assent. — Where defendants covenanted to pay for work that should be done with their written assent, if such written assent be dispensed with by parol, covenant will not lie. To bring down a covenant to parol in the declaration, is to defeat the action. Lehigh Coal & Nav. Co. v. Harlan, 27 Pa. St. 429.

Parol Alteration. — A parol agreement by one party to a covenant to waive the performance of a part of the agreement by the other party, is held not to be such an alteration of the contract as will defeat an action of covenant. McCombs v. McKennan, 2 Watts & S. (Pa.) 216; s. c., 37 Am. Dec. 505.

It has been *held* that if a person enters into a bond for the performance of certain matters, and afterwards a parol agreement is made between the parties, varying the time of performance, an action cannot be maintained upon the bond for the penalty, but that the plaintiff must seek his remedy upon the agreement enlarging the time of performance. Ford v. Campfield, 11 N. J. L. (6 Halst.) 327.

And it has been *held* that where a plaintiff sues on a covenant which has been modified by parol, in a point essential to the defendant's liability, the action should be *assumpsit*, the written contract being treated as abandoned, or used no further than to mark the terms and extent of the new stipulation. Lehigh Coal & Nav. Co. v. Harlan, 27 Pa. St. 429.

2. Luciana v. American Fire Ins. Co., 2 Whart. (Pa.) 167.

3. Rees v. Overbaugh, 6 Cow. (N. Y.) 746. See Powers v. Ware, 2 Pick. (Mass.) 451; s. c., 4 Pick. (Mass.) 106.

Covenant will not lie against a grantor where the grantee has all the land described in the deed, but not all the grantor agreed to convey. Church v. Stiles (Vt.), 5 New Eng. Rep. 104.

4. Western v. Mayor of Brooklyn, 23 Wend. (N. Y.) 334; Huddle v. Worthington, 1 Ohio, 423; Abrams v. Kounts, 4 Ohio, 214.

Title-Bond to convey. — Where A. sells B. four hundred acres of land, and binds himself to procure a patent for the same, on the payment of the last instalment; and B. sells to C. a part of the said land, and covenants to procure the patent on the reasonable request of C., and by the same instrument empowers C. to procure the patent from A., for which he is to be allowed a valuable consideration, B. cannot support an action of covenant against C. for not procuring a patent. [illegible] v. Tate, 1 Serg. & R. (Pa.) [illegible].

Conditional Covenant. — It has been held that a covenant providing that if the grantors "obtain the fee-simple" to property conveyed "from the government of the United States they will convey the same" to the grantee, his heirs or assigns, "by deed of general warranty" — Davenport v. Lamb, 80 U. S. (13 Wall.) 418; bk. 20, L. ed. 655, — is a covenant of further assurance, and entitles the grantee, his heirs or assigns, to a conveyance of the title on the happening of the contingency specified. Davis v. Tarwater, 15 Ark. 286; Dussaume v. Burnett, 5 Iowa, [illegible]. Such covenant is a special and limited covenant, and takes effect only in case the grantees acquire title directly from the United States, and does not cover the acquisition of title from any other source or intermediate party. Davenport v. Lamb, 80 U. S. (13 Wall.) 418; bk. 20, L. ed. 655.

5. Maule v. Weaver, 7 Pa. St. 329.

Rent reserved. — So where a deed of land purported to be an indenture, and contained a covenant by the grantee to pay a rent reserved to the grantor, but the deed was signed and sealed only by the grantor, and accepted by the grantee, who afterwards conveyed, subject to the rent reserved, it was *held* that covenant would not lie against the grantee to recover the rent reserved in the deed. Maule v. Weaver, 7 Pa. St. 329.

6. Summers v. Watson, 1 Cr. C. C. 234; United States v. Brown, 1 Paine, C. C. 422.

Penal Bond. — Thus covenant will not lie on a penal bond, conditioned to be defeated if the work is not done strictly within the time,[1] nor if it be not done in the manner prescribed, unless the party for whom the work was done has accepted the performance as full and perfect.[2]

Upon an agreement, signed by several, to pay each an equal share of certain expenses, under which agreement some have paid more and some less, an action of covenant against one of the parties to the agreement by the others cannot be maintained.[3]

Covenant will not lie against one who has not signed the deed.[4]

An action of covenant cannot be maintained upon agreement under seal modified or altered by parol.[5]

An action in covenant for a breach of the implied covenant of quiet enjoyment, contained in a lease for years, will not lie where a house in a city has been leased to a tenant for years, and the owner of the adjoining lot, under a statute, condemns and removes a party wall which forms one side of the house leased, for the purpose of erecting a suitable wall for a larger building.[6]

by the performance of collateral conditions, — State v. Woodward, 8 Mo. 353; — on the condition of an injunction bond, — Summers v. Watson, 1 Cr. C. C. 254; United States v. Brown, 1 Paine, C. C. 422; — on a bond with a penalty, conditioned for the performance of a marriage contract between the obligee and one of the obligors, — Abrams v. Kounts, 4 Ohio, 214; — on the condition of a bond, separated in the declaration from the penal and obligatory parts, — Huddle v. Worthington, 1 Ohio, 423; United States v. Brown, 1 Paine, C. C. 422; — on an assignment under seal of a bond for tobacco, the breach assigned being, that the obligor did not pay. Brickell v. Batchelor, Cam. & N. (N. C.) 109.

But it was remarked by *Lord Nottingham*, in the case of Hill v. Carr, 1 Ch. Cas. 294, that "covenant will lie on a bond, for it proves an agreement." Commenting on this case, the learned author of a recent work says that "a bond undoubtedly proves an agreement, but is the agreement proved the one stated in the penalty?" 2 Sedgwick on Dam. (7th ed.) 263. It would seem that, if there be no agreement in the condition, the only agreement possible is an agreement to pay penalty.

Bond of Defeasance. — Where a bond is strictly a bond of defeasance, and not a covenant to perform the act recited in the condition, covenant will not lie, debt being the appropriate remedy. See Hathaway v. Crosby, 17 Me. 448.

Where action of covenant was brought upon an attachment bond, alleging as breaches that the defendants had not paid the penalty, nor prosecuted the action, it was *held* that the action could be maintained. Hill v. Rushing, 4 Ala. 212.

Suit on Officer's Bond. — Where covenant was brought on a sheriff's bond, alleging two breaches of the condition, followed by an averment that the defendant had not paid the penalty, the court say, "It is clear that, by the common law, an action of covenant was a concurrent remedy with debt on a single bill obligatory, or a penal bond subject to be defeated by the performance of the conditions. In such an action the breach of covenant would be the non-payment of the debt in the one case, in the other the non-payment of the penalty." But as the breaches assigned were breaches of the condition, it was *held* covenant would not lie. See State v. Woodward, 8 Mo. 353; Taylor v. Wilson, 5 Ired. (N. C.) L. 214.

In a case — United States v. Brown, 1 Paine, C. C. 422 — where covenant was brought on a bond, conditioned for the faithful performance of the duties of an officer, the court remarked that covenant might probably be maintained upon the penalty of the bond, if the breach was properly assigned, because it contained an acknowledgment of indebtedness, and promise to pay, and the breach would be the non-payment of the money; but that, as the breach alleged was misfeasance in office, an action of covenant would not lie.

1. Jewell v. Schroeppel, 4 Cow. (N. Y.) 564.

2. Stagg v. Munro, 8 Wend. (N. Y.) 399.

3. Belknap v. Paddock, 52 Vt. 1.

4. Maule v. Weaver, 7 Pa. St. 329.

5. Vicary v. Moore, 2 Watts (Pa.), 451; s. c., 27 Am. Dec. 323; Carrier v. Dilworth, 59 Pa. St. 406.

Covenant modified by Parol. — Where a covenant has been modified by parol, the old contract will be treated as abandoned. Appeal of Hall, 112 Pa. St. 42; s. c., 3 Cent. Rep. 132.

6. Barns v. Wilson (Pa.), 8 Cent. Rep.

The mere fact that a house leased becomes uninhabitable, is not enough to sustain an action in covenant;[1] this condition of the property must result from the act of the lessor or from those holding a title paramount.[2] Yet, where a lease contained a covenant by the lessee to occupy premises as a dwelling-house, it was held that there was an implied covenant on the part of the lessor that the premises were fit for the purposes of a dwelling-house; and that, in case of unfitness, the amount expended by the lessee for necessary repairs is a set-off against a claim for rent.[3]

An action for breach of covenant in a lease against sub-letting will not lie for an agreement to let the sign of a third person remain on the outer wall of the building, because such privilege is a license, not a lease, and does not infringe the covenant. A lease of the first floor of a building includes the front wall thereof.[4]

An action of covenant does not lie upon the statute of 3 William and Mary, ch. 14, against the devisee of land, to recover damages for a breach of covenant made by the devisor; the remedy thereby given is confined to cases where an action of debt lies.[5]

Where two persons for valuable consideration, as between themselves, covenant to do some act for the benefit of a mere stranger, that stranger cannot enforce the covenant against the two, though either of the two might do so against the other.[6]

Where an instrument of writing is what is technically called an instrument *inter partes*, that is, expressed to be made between the parties who are named in it, as executing it, in such case it is a settled rule, that, although a covenant be expressed in the instrument for the benefit of a third person named in it, an action can be brought in the name of one of the parties only, and not in the name of such third person.[7]

An attorney who covenants in that capacity to convey, and sets his own hand and seal to the covenants, is competent to bring an action for the purchase-money covenanted to be paid him in his own name.[8]

A. by an indenture, executed by himself and B., assigned to B. premises, subject to the payment of the rent and to the perform-

454; s. c., 25 Cent. L. J. 14, 9 Atl. Rep. 437.

Quiet Enjoyment, Implied Covenant for. — While it is true that every lease contains an implied covenant for quiet enjoyment, yet that covenant extends only to acts of the lessor himself, and to injuries inflicted under title paramount; it is not designed as an indemnity against any and every disturbance of the lessee's enjoyment of the land under the law. Barns v. Wilson (Pa.), 8 Cent. Rep. 454; 25 Cent. L. J. 14, 9 Atl. Rep. 454. See Frost v. Earnest, 4 Whart. (Pa.) 86; Dobbins v. Brown, 12 Pa. St. 75; Moore v. Weber, 71 Pa. St. 429.

1. Carson v. Godley, 26 Pa. St. 117; Hazlett v. Powell, 30 Pa. St. 293.

2. Barns v. Wilson (Pa.), 8 Cent. Rep. 454; 25 Cent. L. J. 14, 9 Atl. Rep. 437.

3. Wolfe v. Arrott, 109 Pa. St. [illegible]; 1 Cent. Rep. 128.

4. Lowell v. Strahan (Mass.), [illegible] New Eng. Rep. 650; 25 Cent. L. J. [illegible] N. E. Rep. 401.

5. Wilson v. Knubley, 7 East, [illegible]; 3 Smith, 128.

6. Colyear v. Mulgrave (Countess), 2 Keen, 81.

7. Smith v. Emery, 12 N. J. L. (7 Halst.) 53.

8. Johnson v. Applegate, 1 N. J. L. (Coxe) 7, 233; Sheldon v. [illegible] Harr. (Del.) 245.

such of the covenants and agreements reserved and contained in the original lease. B. entered under this assignment, and afterwards assigned over to a third person; it was held that B. was not liable to A. for rent which the latter had been called upon to pay, in consequence of the default of B.'s assignee; the words "subject to the payment of the rent," etc., being words of qualification, and not of contract.[1]

V. By Whom Maintainable. — 1. *Generally.* — The right to sue upon a covenant depends upon privity of estate with the original covenantee, and not with the original covenantor.[2]

Under the codes an action for the breach of a covenant must be brought in the name of the real party in interest — the party who is entitled to the damages.[3]

A person who has obtained a discharge in bankruptcy may maintain a bill in equity, based upon his liability upon a covenant of warranty in a deed. The privilege of the bar of a bankrupt discharge, like the statute of limitation, is purely personal to the bankrupt: if he does not choose to avail himself of it, no one else can for him. He may treat the covenant in the deed as binding upon him, notwithstanding the discharge.[4]

2. *Contracting Parties.* — It has been held in this country that action in covenant must be brought by one of the parties between whom the covenant is made, and that a third person cannot maintain an action on a covenant, though made for his benefit;[5] but the English courts hold to a different rule.[6] Where there are

1. Wolveridge v. Steward, 3 Moore & S., 561; s. c., 1 Cromp. & M. 644.

2. Norcross v. James, 140 Mass. 188; s. c., 2 New Eng. Rep. 327.

3. Slater v. Floyd, 104 Ind. 291; s. c., 3 West. Rep. 218. See Pence v. Aughe, 101 Ind. 317.

4. Bush v. Stanley (Ill.), 11 West. Rep. 382.

Discharge in Bankruptcy. — The original cause of action is not destroyed by the discharge in bankruptcy. It is well settled that the bar which the discharge interposes may be removed by an unconditional new promise and debt revived upon the original consideration. See Marshall v. Tracy, 74 Ill. 379; Classen v. Schoenemann, 80 Ill. 304; Bush v. Stanley (Ill.), 11 West. Rep. 382.

The discharge in bankruptcy is analogous in effect to the statute of limitations, in so far as it does not annul the original debt, but merely suspends the right of action for its recovery. Farmers & Merchants' Bank v. Flint, 17 Vt. 508; s. c., 44 Am. Dec. [illegible].

5. Montague v. Smith, 13 Mass. 404, 405; Howe v. How, 1 N. H. 49; Smith v. Emery, 2 N. J. L. (1 Halst.) 53; Hornbeck v. Westbrook, 9 Johns. (N. Y.) 73; Gardner v. Gardner, 10 Johns. (N. Y.) 47.

Thus, where rent was reserved by a lease to a person who was not a party to the instrument, and the lessees covenanted with him and the lessors to pay rent, it was *held* that an action of covenant would not lie for a breach of the covenant at the suit of such person and the lessors. Southampton v. Brown, 6 Barn. & C. 718.

6. See Wetherell v. Langston, 1 Ex. 634; Pitman v. Woodbury, 3 Ex. 4; British Emp. Ass. Co. v. Browne, 12 C. B. 723; Morgan v. Pike, 14 C. B. 473; Swatman v. Ambler, 8 Ex. 72.

Action on Indentures. — Thus, they *hold* that a covenantee in an ordinary indenture who is a party to it, may sue the covenantor who executed it, although he himself has not executed it, notwithstanding there may be cross-covenants on the part of the covenantee, which are stated in the deed to be the consideration for the covenants on the part of the covenantor. Morgan v. Pike, 14 C. B. 473; s. c., 23 L. J. C. P. 64. *In re* Mathew, 7 Taunt. 696; 2 C. L. R. 696.

Mutuality. — It is *held* by the English courts that it cannot be said that, unless the plaintiff also executes the deed, there is want of mutuality, because the defendant had it in his power to require the plaintiff's signature, and if he did not do so it several covenantees, as, for instance, to pay to A. [illegible] dollars, and B. two hundred dollars, each may sue alone on his several covenants.[1]

Where the covenant purported to be made between two persons by name of the first part, and a corporate company of the second part, and only one of the persons of the first part signed the instrument, and the covenant ran "between the party of the first part and the party of the second part," it was held proper for the person who had signed on the first part to sue alone; because the covenant inured to the benefit of those who were parties.[2]

In a case where A. contracted with B. to sell him land, to be paid for by the assignment of a mortgage on other land worth four thousand dollars, and the assignment when made, however, contained no covenant as to the value of the land, it was held that its acceptance was not in satisfaction or extinguishment of the covenant of value in the agreement, and that B. could maintain an action.[3] A covenant in a deed *inter partes* is only available between those who are parties to it.[4] Where, in a lease, the lessor reserves a right to enter and cut timber, making reasonable satisfaction to the lessee for any damage occasioned thereby, an action of covenant does not lie by such lessee for any wrongful act of cutting down by a third person, if without the consent or authority of the lessor, however he may countenance the act afterwards.[5]

Where a lease is executed by a corporation under the corporate seal, individuals composing the corporation cannot maintain an action in covenant thereon.[6]

was his own fault, and he will not be permitted to take advantage of his own *laches*. See Laythoarp *v.* Bryant, 2 Bing. N. C. 743.

1. Farni *v.* Tesson, 66 U. S. (1 Black) 309; bk. 17, L. ed. 67.

2. Philadelphia W. & B. R. R. Co. *v.* Howard, 54 U. S. (13 How.) 307; bk. 14, L. ed. 157.

3. Smith *v.* Holbrook, 82 N. Y. 562.

4. Barford *v.* Stuckey, 8 Moore, 88; s. c., 1 Bing. 225.

Deed Inter Partes. — When a deed is made *inter partes*, no one who is not expressed to be a party can sue on a covenant contained in it. This is not a mere rule of construction, but a rule of positive law. Chesterfield & Midland Silkstone Colliery Company *v.* Hawkins, 3 Hurls. & C. 677; s. c., 11 Jur. N. S. 468.

5. Griffiths *v.* Brome, 6 T. R. 66.

Where it only appeared that the lessor had promised to make compensation afterwards for such wrongful act, if the wrongdoer himself did not, this was not considered as an adoption of the act, nor as evidence of a prior consent to it whereon to found an action on the covenant. Griffiths *v.* Brome, 6 T. R. 66.

6. **Corporation Deed: Suit by Individuals.** — Thus, where a declaration by A., B., and C. stated that, by deed, they demised premises to the defendant for a term; that he covenanted to yield up the premises in good repair at the end of the term, and that, at the end of the term, he yielded up the premises out of repair; and the defendant set out the deed, which appeared to be made between A., the master, and B. and C., the governors of an hospital, of the one part, and the defendant of the other part, and stated that the master and governors demised the premises to the defendant, and that the covenant was made with the master and governors, and their successors; and it also contained covenants by the master and governors, for themselves and their successors, and concluded thus: "In witness whereof, the master and governors have hereunto affixed their common seal;" and a seal purporting to be a common seal was affixed on the part of the lessors; and the deed purported to have been signed, sealed, and delivered by the defendant, — the defendant then pleaded that the deed was not signed by the plaintiffs or their agent, lawfully authorized by writing; and that there was no demise of

Where a conveyance of land is executed, the purchaser can have no remedy for a failure of title except such as may be provided for by covenants contained in the conveyance.[1]

The cause of action for breach of the covenant of seisin in a deed is assignable; and if, before enforcing his remedy for the breach, the covenantee executes a conveyance of the land, it is, unless there be something to show a contrary intention, presumed that he intends to pass his grantee the benefit of the covenant; that is, all his right to sue for the breach, so far as the grantee sustains injury by reason of it.[2]

A right of action for a breach of a covenant of warranty does not arise to the grantee, where the holder of the superior title is not in possession of the land, nor positively asserting title as against the grantee.[3]

A judgment against the covenantee does not conclude the covenantor, unless he has distinct and unequivocal notice from the covenantee that he is looked to for aid in the defence. Mere knowledge of the pendency of the suit is insufficient.[4]

A grantor may maintain a suit in covenant against a grantee for breach of stipulation by the grantee that the latter will pay off an existing mortgage.[5]

3. *Parties: Joint and Several.* — Though a covenant is joint

the premises signed by them or their agent, lawfully authorised by writing. The court *held* that it appeared by the record that the lease was made by a corporation, and that no action could be maintained upon it in the names of the plaintiffs. Couch *v.* Goodman, 2 Gale & D. 159; s. c., 2 Q. B. 580; 6 Jur. 779.

1. Phillips *v.* City of Hudson, 31 N. J. L. (2 Vr.) 143.

Covenant to deliver in Good Condition. — Thus, where a vendor covenanted to deliver premises at a future day to the vendee in as good condition as they then were, the vendee, by accepting a deed, and taking possession of the premises, does not waive his right to recover damages for a breach of the covenants to deliver the premises in the condition stipulated. Green *v.* Kelley, 18 N. J. L. (3 Harr.) 246.

2. Kimball *v.* Bryant, 25 Minn. 496.

Assignment of Covenant of Seisin: Suit on Breach. — Where a grantee in possession under covenants of seisin conveyed to A., with similar covenants, while a judgment of ejectment was still in force against him, under which he was evicted after his conveyance to A., it was *held* that the covenants passed to A., who alone could maintain action thereon. Betz *v.* Bryan, 39 Ohio St. 320.

3. Jones *v.* Paul, 59 Tex. 41.

Covenant of Warranty: Annuity charged on land. — Where there is a breach of a covenant of warranty against incumbrances, and the incumbrance is a judgment charging an annuity on the land, a new right of action accrues to the covenantee upon the payment by him of each instalment; and a recovery of one instalment is not a bar to a recovery for a second instalment afterwards paid. Priest *v.* Deaver, 22 Mo. App. 276.

Taxes and Assessments. — Where A. conveyed by warranty to B., and B. to C., it was *held* that C., on paying money to redeem the land from sales for taxes and assessments, which were liens upon it at the time of the conveyance from A. to B., may maintain an action against A. on the covenant against incumbrances, thus avoiding circuity. Andrews *v.* Appel, 22 Hun (N. Y.), 429.

A grantee under a warranty deed, who has purchased an existing mortgage, is not bound to foreclose that, and so protect himself, but may recover on his covenants of warranty. Royer *v.* Foster, 62 Iowa, 321.

4. Collins *v.* Baker, 6 Mo. App. 588.

Action for Benefit of Holder of Notes. — A grantee who has successfully defended an action on notes given for purchase-money, partly on the ground of an eviction, may maintain an action upon his covenant of warranty, for the benefit of the holders of the notes. Reeside's Appeal (Pa), 10 Pitts. L. J. 296.

5. Golden *v.* Knapp, 41 N. J. L. (12 Vr.) 215.

in its terms, yet, if the interests of the covenantees are several, each may sue separately for a breach.[1]

Joint covenantees who may sue must sue jointly, unless they have expressly disclaimed the covenant, which it lies upon the party suing to show.[2]

The rule as to joint and several covenants is one merely of construction; and parties may, by apt words, covenant severally, although there is a joint interest. If the words are capable of two constructions, then the legal construction will depend upon the nature of the interest.[3] Where the words of a covenant are expressly joint, it will be so construed, although the interest may be several, and *vice versâ;*[4] but where the words are ambiguous

1. Withers *v.* Bircham, 5 Dowl. & R. 106; s. c., 3 Barn. & Cress. 254; Palmer *v.* Sparshott, 4 Scott, N. R. 743; s. c., 4 Man. & G. 137.

If two persons be named in a deed as "the party of the first part," and only one of them executes it, he may sue alone on the covenants therein. Philadelphia, W. & B. R. R. Co. *v.* Howard, 54 U. S. (13 How.) 307, 318; bk. 14, L. ed. 157.

If an obligee of a bond covenants not to sue one of two joint and several obligors, and, if he does, that the deed of covenant may be pleaded in bar, he may still sue the other obligor. Dean *v.* Newhall, 8 T. R. 168.

A covenant with the part-owners of a ship, and their several and respective executors, to pay money — to accrue for the hire of the ship, for freight of goods, and for compensation for the use of the ship's tackle — to the covenantees, their and every of their several and respective executors, at a certain banking-house, in such parts and proportions as were set against their several and respective names, is a several covenant, and cannot be sued upon by the covenantees jointly. Servante *v.* James, 5 Man. & R. 299; s. c., 10 Barn. & Cress. 410.

Where rent was reserved by a lease to a person who was not a party to the lease, and the lessees covenanted with him and the lessors to pay rent, it was *held* that an action of covenant would not lie at the suit of him and the lessors. Southampton *v.* Brown, 6 Barn. & Cress. 718.

Where, in an action against A. and B. on a covenant supposed to be implied as incident to a demise by lease, on production of the lease it appears that, in a point of law, A. only demised, and that B., who had an equitable interest, merely confirmed the action, is not maintainable against A. and B. jointly. Smith *v.* Pocklington, 1 Cromp. & Jerv. 445; s. c., 1 Tyr. 309.

2. Petrie *v.* Bury, 5 Dow. & R. 152; s. c., 3 Barn. & Cress. 353.

3. Keightley *v.* Watson, 18 L. J. Exch. 339; s. c., 3 Exch. 716.

4. **Construction of Joint Covenants.** — Where by articles of agreement, under seal, between L. and the defendant, of the one part, and the plaintiff and H. of the other part, after reciting that L. and the defendant, as solicitors of D., had applied to the plaintiff to lend D. £2,000 out of moneys of H., in the plaintiff's hands, and belonging to him in trust for her, upon the security of a policy of insurance and other securities, but that the plaintiff had declined to do so without further security, and that, thereupon, L. and the defendant proposed to enter into the covenant thereinafter contained, L. and the defendant, in pursuance of the agreement, and in consideration of the premises, and of the plaintiff having so advanced £2,900 to D. at the request of L. and the defendant, did covenant with and to the plaintiff, and also as a separate and distinct covenant to H., that L. and the defendant, or one of them, would pay to the plaintiff the interest on the £2,000, or such part thereof as should remain unpaid, the court *held* that the plaintiff could not maintain an action upon this covenant without joining H. Hopkinson *v.* Lee, 6 Q. B. 964; s. c., 9 Jur. 616, 14 L. J. Q. B. 101.

Lease: Covenants with Tenants in Common. — By an indenture of lease, reciting that L. had agreed to take premises of C., and that R. should enter into the covenant after mentioned for securing payment of the rent, it was witnessed, that, in consideration of the covenants after mentioned on the part of L. to be performed, and particularly after the covenant thereinafter entered into by R., C., at the request of R., demised to L., etc., and L. and R. covenanted to C. that they would pay him the rent on the appointed days, and that L., his executors, etc., should and would keep the premises in repair. There were other covenants similarly framed to this last for matters to be performed by L., and a proviso for re-entry if the rent should be in arrear, or if L., his executors, etc., should pect, they may be construed to be joint or several, to the interest.[1]

erion by which the propriety of the joinder or the non-parties to a covenant in an action for breaches is to be , is the nature of the interest of the covenantees. If it is several, the action must be several; if joint, it must and the terms of language of the covenant do not con-rinciple.[2]

he covenants in the indenture his and their part to be per-there was a covenant by C. enjoyment, L., his executors, he rent and performing the the indenture before con-action in covenant for breach, the court that R. was jointly by the covenant to repair, covenant to pay rent. Cop-e, 3 Adol. & E. 517.

t Lease. — A covenant with mmon, and each and every of nd each and every of their ors, administrators, and as-ir, is a joint and not a several that an action on it must be ll the tenants in common or of them. Bradburne v. Bot-s. & W. 559; s. c., 14 L. J.

to pay Annuity. — In consid-co, T. D. and R. D. severally ely, and for their several and irs, executors, and adminis-ed, covenanted, and agreed, L. and B., their heirs, execu-rators, and assigns, to pay to ir executors, etc., an annuity ly sum of £30 in the shares ons following; viz., of £15, iety of the annuity, unto L., etc., and £15, the remaining B., his executors, etc., to be paid quarterly. The powers uring the payment of the an-ed in the deed were all given ointly, and the deed also con-t power of attorney to them joint judgment; and a joint anted to them to dispose of of a close of land, with a of attorney to sell certain e annuity was redeemable, on otice in writing being given, nt to L. and B. of £307 10s., rs of the annuity. In an ac-ainst T. and D., to recover annuity, it was held that the a joint covenant, and that m the annuity was joint, and not sue alone. Lane v. Drink-ap. M. & R. 599; s. c., 5 Tyrw. P. C. 223.

A covenant to and with A., his executors, administrators, and assigns, to and with B. and her assigns, to pay an annuity to A., his executors, etc., during B.'s life, is a joint covenant to A. and B., in which they have a joint legal interest, although the benefit is for A. only; and therefore, on the death of A., the right of action survives to B., and A.'s administrator cannot sue on the covenant. Anderson v. Martindale, 1 East, 497.

1. Sorsbie v. Park, 12 Mees. & W. 146; s. c., 13 L. J. Exch. 9.

Joint Covenants, Separate Interests, Action in. — Where a demise is joint, and the covenants upon which an action is brought are made jointly with both lessors, the cause of action is joint, and both covenantees must sue, although as between themselves their interest may be separate. Foley v. Addenbrooke, 3 Gale & D 64; s. c., 4 Q. B. 197; 7 Jur. 234; 12 L. J. Q. B. 163.

Where the interest of the covenantees is joint, although the covenant is in terms joint and several, the action follows the nature of the contract, and must be brought in the names of all the covenantees. Pugh v. Stringfield, 3 C. B. N. S. 2; s. c., 27 L. J. C. P. 34.

2. James v. Emery, 5 Price, 529; s. c., 2 J. B. Moore, 195; s. c., 8 Taunt. 245.

Covenant to repair in Joint Demise. — Thus, a covenant to repair in a joint demise by tenants in common, runs with the entire reversion, and all the tenants in common of the reversion at the time of the breach, or their representatives, must join in an action on such covenant. Thompson v. Hakewill, 19 C. B. N. S. 713; s. c., 11 Jur. N. S. 732; 35 L. J. C. P. 18; 14 W. R. 11; 13 L. T. N. S. 289.

Lease by Several Owners. — Where a lease was made by several owners of a house, reserving rent to each one in proportion to his interest, and there was a covenant on the part of the lessee that he would keep the premises in good repair, and surrender them in like repair, this covenant was joint as respects the lessors, and one of them (or two representing) cannot maintain an action for the breach of it by the lessee. Calvert v. Bradley, 57 U. S. (16 How.) 580; bk. 14, L. ed. 1066.

A joint and several covenant by A., and other parties that "they, or some one of them," will pay a certain sum, may be declared upon as covenant by A. to pay.[1]

The heirs or devisees of the grantee may maintain a joint action upon a covenant of warranty.[2]

4. *Personal Representatives, Executors, etc.* — The right of action for the breach of a covenant of seisin passes to the personal representative of the covenantee.[3]

When Interest Several. — Where, by articles of agreement for the sale of premises, the defendant covenanted with the plaintiff, and with the several other parties beneficially interested in the premises, it was *held* that their interest was several, and that the plaintiff might sue alone. Poole v. Hill, 9 Dowl. P. C. 300; s. c., 6 Mees. & W. 835.

In a case where A. covenanted with B., and, as a separate covenant, with C., it was *held* that B. could sue alone, although the deed showed that the consideration moved partly from C., and that C. would, under some circumstances, be interested in the amount recovered. Keightly v. Watson, 18 L. J. Exch. 339; s. c., 3 Exch. 716.

In a lease of colliery, the two lessees covenanted jointly and severally, with the lessor, in manner following, viz., etc.; then followed several other covenants, after which was a covenant that moneys due should be accounted for and paid by the lessees, their executors, etc., not saying, "and each of them." In an action on the covenants, it was held that this and the former covenants were several as well as joint. Northumberland v. Errington, 5 T. R. 522.

Where a party covenanted by deed, for himself, his heirs, executors, and administrators, with each of certain parties thereto (proposed shareholders, the plaintiff being one, in the term and coal mines thereafter mentioned), his executors, administrators, and assigns, that he would produce and show a good marketable title to a term of forty-two years in the seams of coal, by the deed demised and granted; and that he would effectually assign, assure, and vest the same according to the true intent and meaning of the deed; and that he would, with all practicable speed, proceed with, and within four years complete, the harbor and works, — upon an action brought by the plaintiff alone, for a breach of these covenants, the court held that they were in their nature several, and, therefore, that the action was rightly brought. Mills v. Ladbroke, 7 Scott, N. R. 1005; s. c., 7 Man. & G. 218; 8 Jur. 247; 13 L. J. C. P. 122.

1. Caldwell v. Becke, 2 Exch. 318.

A covenant, whereby "A., B., and C., and any two of them jointly, and each of them severally," covenanted with D., that A., B., and C., "or some or one of them," shall pay D. a sum of [illegible], declared upon in an action [illegible] against A. alone, as a covenant that A would pay that sum to D. [illegible] son, 10 Q. B. [illegible]; s. c., 41 Jur. [illegible] L. J. Q. B. 165.

A covenant "with two and each of them" is joint, though the "two" are several parties to the deed. [illegible] Hoare, 3 Taunt. 87.

2. Paul v. Witman, 3 [illegible].

3. Lowry v. Tilleny, [illegible] 500.

Lease for Years; [illegible] Covenant Action. — Declaration on a covenant for rent by the representative of a mortgagor for a term of five thousand years, [illegible] indenture of lease for [illegible] mortgagee S., to which the [illegible] Y. was a confirming party, [illegible] of the lessee, L.; the [illegible] to the making of the lease. The *reddendum* was in the following words: "Yielding and paying yearly, [illegible] year during the term, unto S., [illegible] etc., during the [illegible] of the mortgage, and after payment thereof, unto Y., his executors, etc., the yearly rent of £18 18*s*." The covenant was by L., "to and with S., his executors, etc., and also to and with Y., his executors," etc., that L., his executors, administrators, and assigns, would pay the yearly rent "on the several days and times, and in manner, as the same was reserved and made payable." The plaintiff traced title from S., by deeds, to all of which Y.'s name appeared as a party; but the declaration did not aver that any one of them was executed by Y. Averment, that the plaintiff became possessed of the demised premises for all the residue and remainder of the term of five thousand years, and that, after the making of the indenture of lease, and during the term granted, and after the defendant became assignee, and while he continued assignee, two years' rent became in arrear. The court *held* that the covenant was several, and the action was properly brought by the representative of the mortgagor alone. Harrold v. Whitaker, 10 Q. B. 147; s. c., 10 Jur. 1004; 15 L. J. Q. B. 345. Affirmed in error, 11 Q. B. [illegible] s. c., 12 Jur. 303; 17 L. J. Q. B. 343.

Where a covenant is broken in the lifetime of the covenantee, and possession is surrendered by him to the holder of the paramount title, the action should be brought by his administrator or executor.[1]

An executor, though not named, may sue upon a covenant made with the testator in reference to a chattel.[2]

Where an executrix declared that the defendant, by deed, conveying to her testator lands in fee subject to redemption on payment of a sum certain, covenanted with the testator that he was, at the time of the execution of the deed, seised in fee, and had a right to convey, and assigned for breach that the defendant was not seised in fee, and had not a right to convey, it was held that the executrix could not maintain an action for such breaches of covenant, without showing some special damage to the testator in his lifetime, or that she claimed some interest in the premises.[3]

5. *Heirs and Devisees.* — Although it is true where a covenant of warranty is broken during the lifetime of the covenantee, his executor or administrator must bring suit;[4] yet, on a breach of a covenant for further assurance, where the breach happened in the lifetime of the covenantee, but the damage accrued to the heir, the heir has a preferable title to the executor to bring the action of covenant.[5]

An action lies by the heir, upon a covenant made to the ancestor and his heirs, to whom lands are conveyed in fee by husband and wife, that he and his wife will make further assurance upon request of the ancestor and his heirs; and the heir may well assign,

By an indenture *tripartite* between A. 1, B. 2, and C. 3, A., tenant for life, demised to C., and C. covenanted with B. (a receiver) and another, the receiver or receivers for the time being, and to and with such other person, who, for the time being, should be entitled to the freehold, and to and with every of them. A. died. An action was brought by his executrix, and the court held that she could not maintain an action for a breach in her testator's lifetime, but that the action was joint, and survived to B. Southcote v. Hoare, 3 Taunt. 87.

1. Wilson v. Peele, 78 Ind. 384.

Covenant broken in Lifetime of Testator, Action upon. — If a covenant of warranty is broken in the lifetime of the covenantee, or one holding the covenant, his executor must sue upon it, and not his heirs. Frink v. Bellis, 33 Ind. 135. See also Tufts v. Adams, 8 Pick. (Mass.) 547; Prescott v. Trueman, 4 Mass. 629; s. c., 3 Am. Dec. 246; Wyman v. Ballard, 12 Mass. 304; Chapel v. Bull, 17 Mass. 220; Stewart v. Drake, 9 N. J. L. (4 Halst.) 139; Garrison v. Sandford, 12 N. J. L. (7 Halst.) 261; Funk v. Voneida, 11 Serg. & R. (Pa.) 109; s. c., 14 Am. Dec. 617; Richardson v. Dorr, 5 Vt. 9; Potter v. Taylor, 6 Vt. 676.

Covenant broken after Testator's Death, Action on. — An executor of a lessor, tenant from year to year, may sue for a breach of covenant in a lease, for twenty-one years, granted by the lessor, though the breach was committed after the lessor's death. Mackay v. Mackreth, 2 Chitt. 461; s. c., 4 Doug. 213.

But such declaration should state the termor's interest and title in the premises. Mackay v. Mackreth, 2 Chitt. 461; s. c., 4 Doug. 213.

2. Doe *ex d.* Rogers v. Rogers, 2 Nev. & M. 550.

3. Kingdon v. Nottle, 1 Maule & S. 355.

4. See Frink v. Bellis, 33 Ind. 135; Tufts v. Adams, 8 Pick. (Mass.) 547; Prescott v. Trueman, 4 Mass. 629; s. c., 3 Am. Dec. 246; Wyman v. Ballard, 12 Mass. 304; Chapel v. Bull, 17 Mass. 220; Stewart v. Drake, 9 N. J. L. (4 Halst.) 139; Garrison v. Sandford, 12 N. J. L. (7 Halst.) 261; Funk v. Voneida, 11 Serg. & R. (Pa.) 109; s. c., 14 Am. Dec. 617; Richardson v. Dorr, 5 Vt. 9; Potter v. Taylor, 6 Vt. 676.

5. King v. Jones, 1 Marsh. 107; s. c., 5 Taunt. 418. And see Kingdon v. Nottle, 1 Maule & S. 355.

for breach, that his ancestor requested the husband should
fine to pass the estate of the wife legally to him and hi
which they refused to do before their decease, *per quod* a
death of the ancestor, the devisee of the wife ejected the h

An action lies by a devisee of lands in fee, upon a co
made by the defendant, to whom the defendant conveyed th
in fee, that he was lawfully seised, and had a good right to c
for such covenant runs with the land, and, though broken
lifetime of testator, it is a continuing breach in the time
devisee, and it is sufficient to allege for damage, that t
the lands are of less value to the devisee, and that he is pre
from selling them so advantageously.[2]

6. *Assignee; Strangers; Beneficiaries.* — On a coven
warranty an assignee of the vendee may sue the executors
vendor.[3]

1. Jones v. King, 4 Maule & S. 188.

2. Kingdon v. Nottle, 4 Maule & S. 53.

Devise in Trust: Damages. — Where there was a devise to trustees and their heirs during the life of A., in trust for A., and after his decease to B. in fee, and the trustees recovered in A's. lifetime damages for breach of covenant in a lease granted by the testatrix, and still subsisting, upon A's. death it was *held* that the damages belonged to her estate. Noble v. Cass, 2 Sim. 343.

3. Chapman v. Holmes, 11 N. J. L. (6 Halst) 20.

Right of Assignee to sue. — As to right of assignee of covenantee to sue on a covenant to which he is not a party, see Norcross v. James, 140 Mass. 188; s. c., 1 New Eng. Rep. 328.

In the case of Norcross v. James, *Justice Holmes* says that "from a very early date down to comparatively modern times lawyers have been perplexed with the question how an assignee could sue upon a contract to which he was not a party. West. Symb. I. § 35; Wing. Max. 44, pl. 20; 55, pl. 10; Co. Litt. 117 a; Sir Moyle Finch's Case, 4 Inst. 85. But an heir could sue upon a warranty of his ancestor, because for that purpose he was *eadem persona cum antecessor*. See Year-Book, 20, 21, ed. I. 232, Rolls' Ed.; Oates v. Ferth, Hob. 130; Bain v. Cooper, 1 Dowl. Pr. Cas. N. S. 11, 14. And the conception was gradually extended in a qualified way to assigns, where they were mentioned in the deed. Broct. fol. 17 b, 67 a, 380 b, 381; Fleta. III. ch. 14, § 6; 1 Britton, Nich. 255, 256; Year-Book, 20, ed I. 232-234, Rolls' Ed.; Fitz Abr. tit. *Covenant*, pl. 28; Viner, Abr. tit. *Voucher*, N. 59; Year-Book, 14 H. 4. 56; 20 H. 6, 34 b; Old Nat. Brev. tit. *Covenant*. 67, B. C., in Rastell's Law Tract (ed. 1534); Dr. & Stud. I. ch. 8;
F. N. B. 145, 5; Co. Litt. 384 b;
Dig. tit. *Covenant*, B, 3; Middl
Goodale, Cro. Car. 503, 505;
Jones, 406; Philpot v. Hoare, 2

Covenants running with the
respect to those covenants run
the land, it has been held in New
Massachusetts, that if the grantc
seised at the time of conveyance,
nant of seisin is immediately br
that no action can be brought by th
of the grantee against the gra
after the covenant is broken, it is
action, and incapable of assignmen
ford v. Page, 2 Mass. 455; Gr
Wilcocks, 2 Johns. (N. Y.) 1; s.
Dec. 379.

But in England a different d
held. It has there been adjudge
covenant running with the land
broken in the lifetime of a test
continuing breach in the time of
visee; and it is sufficient to alle
action of covenant for damages,
lands are of less value to the dev
that he is prevented from selling
advantageously. Kingdon v. N
Maule & S. 53. See also Kingdo
tle, 1 Maule & S. 355; Chamb
Williams, 2 Maule & S 408; King
5 Taunt. 418; s. c., 1 Marshall's

L., being seised in fee, demised
twenty-one years, from June, 1814
mised to M. for twenty-one yea
June, 1814, wanting twenty-one d
then by deed-poll granted to L. tl
ture of lease to M., the premises
granted, and the rent reserved, to
his executors, etc., for the term m
in the demise to M. L., by lease
lease, conveyed the premises, the
and reversions, rents, issues, and
and all his interest, in fee to the
by way of mortgage. M. assi

[illegible] of land by estoppel cannot maintain an action [illegible].[1] So also an action for the breach of the covenants [illegible]mbrances and of warranty in a deed to plaintiff's [illegible] be maintained, when the breach occurred before [illegible] became the owner of the land. The right of action [illegible] covenantee.[2] Neither can the assignee of the ground-[illegible] breach, sue in his own name.[3]

[illegible] ground-rent and the land out of which it issues are [illegible] breach of a building covenant, the assignee of [illegible] maintain covenant against the alienee of the land, [illegible] same at the time of the breach.[4]

[illegible]ction of covenant in the name of the original covenantee, [illegible]dant averred that the plaintiff had, before the suit was [illegible]ed, assigned to a third person; but, it appearing that the [illegible] had again become the real owner, it was held that he [illegible] an action in his own name, though the assignment [illegible] cancelled.[5]

[illegible]t of the plaintiff being assignee only of a part of the [illegible] by the lease will not preclude him from suing [illegible], and recovering damages for, the breach of the [illegible]

[illegible]es arising from the breach of the covenants in a deed

[illegible] by way of mortgage, [illegible] never entered. The [illegible] plaintiff might sue the de-[illegible] the covenants in M.'s lease. [illegible], 7 Bing. 745; s. c., 5 [illegible].

[illegible] to the use of L. for life, [illegible] of waste, remainder [illegible] the plaintiff for life, it was [illegible] plaintiff, after the death of L., [illegible] within the statute of 32 [illegible] might maintain an action [illegible] lessee for rent in arrear [illegible] L., and during the continu-[illegible]. Isherwood v. Oldknow, [illegible].

[illegible] Estate. — A., having [illegible] interest, made a lease of [illegible] in 1762, subject to cer-[illegible], to be performed by the [illegible] assigns. In 1775 he obtained [illegible]. In an action brought, it [illegible] the assignee of the reversion [illegible] an action against the [illegible] lessee for breach of the cove-[illegible]. After the lessor had ob-[illegible] estate, he granted another [illegible] the former lease of 1762 was [illegible] was agreed that it should [illegible], and the same rent remain [illegible] was *held* that the assignee of [illegible] could not sue for breach [illegible] contained in the lease of [illegible] v. Peacock, 1 Hodges, 376.

[illegible] of Covenantee. — The rule that, upon a simple contract between A. and B., B. shall pay money to C., an action may be maintained by C. in his own name, does not extend to specialties. Thus, where the purchaser of land executed to the vendor a mortgage to secure the purchase-money, which contains a covenant on the part of the mortgagor to pay the mortgagee the sum of six hundred dollars in one year after its date, and also a covenant to pay a mortgage given by the mortgagee to a third party of five hundred and fifty dollars on the same land, it was *held* that such third party could maintain an action of covenant on the mortgage, but that the suit should have been brought in the name of the mortgagee. Gautzert v. Hoge, 73 Ill. 30.

1. Nesbit v. Montgomery, 1 Tayl. (N. C.) 82.

2. Ladd v. Noyes, 137 Mass. 151.

Where A. conveyed by warranty to B., and B. to C., it was *held* that C., on paying money to redeem the land from sales for taxes and assessments which were liens upon it at the time of the conveyance from A. to B., might maintain an action against A., on the covenant against incumbrances, thus avoiding circuity. Andrews v. Appel, 22 Hun (N. Y.), 429.

3. Fisher v. Lewis, 1 Clark (Pa.), 431.

4. Fisher v. Lewis, 1 Clark (Pa.), 422.

5. Dodd v. Noble, 5 Blackf. (Ind.) 30.

6. Simpson v. Clayton, 4 Bing. N. C. 758; s. c., 1 Arn. 299, 6 Scott, 469.

may be assigned; in which case the assignee, and he alone, can sue.[1]

The grantee becomes the assignee of the covenant; and such assignee has a right of action for damages for the breach of the covenant after his eviction under a judgment against the grantor, equally as if he had been evicted under a mortgage foreclosure.[2]

But it has been said that where a railroad company took from A. a deed to a strip of land for a right of way, the deed containing a covenant that the company should maintain a good farm-crossing, one who subsequently enters into possession, under an executory contract to purchase, is not the proper party plaintiff in an action to enforce the covenant.[3]

An assignee of the reversion may sue on an express covenant for payment of rent; but not for rent which accrued prior assignment, unless it were executed in pursuance of the act of 1715.[4]

An action of covenant will lie by the assignees of the rever-

1. Allen *v.* Kennedy, 91 Mo. 324; s. c., 6 West. Rep. 845.

Action by Assignee. — Where a grantee in possession under covenants of seisin conveyed to A., with similar covenants, while a judgment of ejectment was still in force against him, and under which he was evicted subsequent to his conveyance to A., it was *held* that the covenants passed to A., who alone could maintain an action thereon. Betz *v.* Bryan, 39 Ohio St. 320.

And where A. leased certain premises to B., who afterwards assigned the lease to C., and A. sold and conveyed the land to D., and D. conveyed the same to E. without mentioning the lease, the court *held* that E. could not maintain an action of covenant in his own name against B. upon an express covenant for the payment of rent contained in the lease. Crawford *v.* Chapman, 17 Ohio, 449.

2. Wyatt *v.* Dunn (Mo.), 6 West. Rep. 863.

3. Haynes *v.* Buffalo, N. Y. & P. R. R. Co., 38 Hun (N. Y.), 17.

4. Newbold *v.* Comfort, 2 Clark (Pa.), 331.

Assignee of Ground-rent Lease. — In a case where a ground-rent was reserved to P., his assigns to pay to P., his heirs and assigns, the principal after ten years, the court *held* that an alienee of P., after the ten years, might maintain covenant against the alienee of the grantee; that the right to demand the principal did not lapse, nor the rent become irredeemable after the ten years by owner's continuing to receive it. Springer *v.* Phillips, 71 Pa. St. 60.

Demise under Power. — Where by a deed to lead the uses of a recovery, lands were limited to the use of such a person as A. should by deed or will appoint, to the use of B. in trust for A., his heirs and assigns, reserving to A. a leasing power, A. (reciting the power) demised for a term to C., "yielding and paying unto A., his heirs and assigns, during the term," a certain rent, with covenants to pay rent, to repair, etc., and a proviso for re-entry by A., his heirs and assigns, in case of breach, it was held that the covenants enured in favor of the assignees of the reversion. Greenway *v.* Hart, 14 C. B. 340; s. c., 2 C. L. R. 370.

By a will, power was given to a tenant for life to lease for twenty-one years, and to executors to mortgage in fee, or for years. In 1812, after the testator's death, the tenant for life made a grant for ninety-nine years, if he should so long live. In 1814 he demised under his power for twenty-one years. In 1828 the executors mortgaged for a thousand years under their power. The court *held* that the leasing power under the will was not suspended by the lease of 1812, so far as regarded the grantee of the term under the power to demise by way of mortgage given to the executors, and, consequently, that such grantee had the immediate reversion in him, and might sue on the covenant in the lease of 1814. Bringloe *v.* Goodson, 6 Scott, 502; s. c., 4 Bing. N. C. 726; 1 Arn. 322.

Assignee of Reversion. — Where the assignee of the reversion, who sued the defendant, alleging that the lessor was seised (without stating of what estate), and, being so seised, devised to the plaintiff in fee, is a sufficient allegation of title after verdict. Hardy *v.* Beavan, 4 Bing. 646; s. c., 1 Moore & P. 633.

sion or part of the demised premises against the lessee for not repairing.[1]

The owner of one undivided moiety, jointly with the mortgagor and mortgagee of the other, joining in demise, the covenants being with all three (though the *reddendum* was general and indefinite), is entitled to sué the assignees in bankruptcy of the lessee for the rent.[2]

A county treasurer received a fund under direction to invest for the benefit of G., an infant; and invested it, received theinterest for several years, disposed of the securities, deposited the proceeds in a bank, commingled them with his own and the county's funds, misappropriated them, at the end of his term paid over to his successor the balance of county moneys in his hands, and untruly reported that G.'s money was invested in bonds and mortgages. It was held that G. could not maintain an action against the county to recover the money thus misappropriated.[3]

VI. Against Whom Maintainable. — 1. *Contracting Parties, Joint and Several.* — An action of covenant lies only against the person who has leased and delivered the instrument.[4] Thus, where, in a covenant supposed to be implied as incident to a demise by lease, A. demises, and B., who has but an equitable interest in the premises, merely confirms the action, a suit on the covenant is not maintainable against B.[5]

An action of covenant for rent cannot be sustained against a person, without evidence of some privity of contract.[6] And an

1. Twynam v. Pickard, 2 Barn. & Ald. [illegible]

2. Magnay v. Edwards, 13 C. B. 479; s. c., 1 C. L. R. 141; 17 Jur. 839; 22 L. J. C. P. 171.

3. Gray v. Tompkins Co. Supervisors, [illegible] (N. Y.), 265.

4. Wilson v. Brechemin, Bright (Pa.), [illegible]

Action on Deed inter Partes: By Whom to be Brought. — An action of covenant only lies upon a deed *inter partes* between parties thereto; therefore, where, in an action upon an indenture of lease, it appeared that the landlord by writing, not under seal, authorised his attorney to execute a lease for and on his (landlord's) behalf, and the attorney signed and sealed the lease in his own name, it was *held*, that the landlord could not maintain an action against the tenant upon the indenture, although the covenants were expressly stated to have been made by the tenant to and with the landlord. Berkeley v. Hardy, 8 Dowl. & R. 102; s. c., 5 Barn. & C. 355.

Where a deed is *inter partes*, the party who has the legal interest in a covenant must always sue, although the beneficial interest may be in another. Barford v. Stuckey, 2 Bro. & Bing. 333; Storer v. Gordon, 3 Maule & S. 308.

5. Smith v. Pocklington, 1 Cromp. & Jerv. 445; s. c., 1 Tyrw. 309.

6. Howard v. Ramsay, 7 Har. & J. (Md.) 113. Adams v. French, 2 N. H. 387; Port v. Jackson, 17 Johns. (N. Y.) 239; Williams v. Bosanquet, 1 Brod. & Bing. 238; Shep. Touch. 179.

Presumptive Evidence of Assignment. — The evidence to charge one as an assignee may be presumptive. Adams v. French, 2 N. H. 387. Thus, the possession of the defendant soon after the departure of the lessee, and his exercise of such acts, in subletting, as would be natural in an assignee, furnish presumptive evidence of actual assignment. Adams v. French, 2 N. H. 387; Doe *ex d.* v. Rickarby, 5 Esp. 4.

Where the interest of the assignee of a term was set off to the defendant, on execution, and he entered into possession, and executed sub-leases, the court held that he was chargeable as assignee of the term in covenant for the rent. Adams v. French, 2 N. H. 387.

And where judgment was recovered against one as the assignee of a term of years, in an action of covenant for rent, and the defendant afterwards caused an execution to be extended upon the premises as the estate in fee-simple of the assignee, the court held that the judgment action in a covenant for rent will not lie against a lessee where the lease is a deed-poll, signed by the lessor only, although the lessee may have accepted the lease, and occupied and held under it during the full term, without paying the rent reserved.[1]

against the assignee was an admission by him that he was the assignee of the term, and that it was binding upon a defendant who entered under him. Adams v. French, 2 N. H. 387, 389.

Assignee of Lease by Deed-Poll: Action against for Rent. — It has been *held* that where a lessee, by deed-poll, assigned his interest in the demised premises, subject to the payment of rent and the performance of the covenants in the lease, and the grantee of the lessee took and held possession of the premises and occupied them, and before the end of the term assigned to a third person, and the lessor having sued the lessee and recovered for a breach of the covenants, that the lessee may maintain an action against this grantee who held under the deed-poll. Burnett v. Lynch, 5 Barn. & C. 589.

It was held in Burnett v. Lynch, *supra*, that the action of covenant could not be maintained except against a person who, by himself or some other person acting in his behalf, has executed a deed, under seal, or who, under very peculiar circumstances, has agreed, by deed, to do a certain thing; and also that where the defendant has not engaged, by deed, to perform the covenants covenant will not lie. See Rockford, R. I. & St. L. R. R. Co. v. Beckemeier, 72 Ill. 267, 269.

1. Johnson v. Muzzy, 45 Vt. 419; following Hinsdale v. Humphrey, 15 Conn. 433; Finley v. Simpson, 22 N. J. L. (2 Zab.) 311; s. c., 53 Am. Dec. 252; Trustees v. Spencer, 7 Ohio, pt. 2, 149.

Assignment of a Term: Liability for Rent. — Where B. being in possession of a term of years, of which 1690 years remained unexpired, sold and assigned the same to P. for 1600 years, for a specified yearly rent; P. sold and assigned the same to the defendant, who covenanted to perform all the covenants contained in the indenture of demise from B. to P., and on the part of P. to be performed. In an action of covenant by P. against the defendant, to recover the amount alleged to be due and unpaid to B. for above 24 years, the defendant pleaded that, before any rent accrued or became payable to the lessor, he assigned all his interest to G., who entered into possession of the premises, and was accepted by B. as his tenant: the court held the plea bad; also that the covenant on the part of the defendant was a positive and express covenant to pay rent, as it should become due, to the lessor, and for which the plaintiff remained liable on his covenant to B., by privity of contract, [illegible] assignment by the defendant [illegible] acceptance of him by B. as his tenant; and that it is not necessary that the plaintiff should allege in his declaration, [illegible] that he had been obliged to pay the rent to B., or had been damnified, [illegible] defendant's covenant was broken by the non-payment of the rent, [illegible] no answer to the plaintiff's declaration, and that the plaintiff was, therefore, [illegible] recover the whole rent in arrear [illegible] for which he was liable on his covenant with the lessee. Port v. Jackson, 17 Johns. (N. Y.) 239.

When Action Several. — [illegible] that although a covenant be joint and several in the terms in which it is expressed, yet that if the interest and cause of action be joint, the action must be brought by all the covenantees; and that if, on the other hand, the interest and cause of action be several, the action may be brought by each only. Eccleston v. Clipsham, 1 Saund. 153. See also James v. Emery, 8 Taunt. 245; s. c. 2 J. B. Moore, 195; 5 Price, 529; Slingsby v. Beckwith, 5 Co. 18; Saunders v. Johnson, 1 Saund. 154, note; Spencer v. Durant, 1 Show. 8; Bull. N. P. Prius, 157, 158.

Where the plaintiff, the defendant, and twelve others, tenants in common of certain lands, entered into a deed, and each one for himself only, and not for the others, covenanted to abide by the award of A., it was objected that all of the parties, except the defendant, should have been made plaintiffs, for that each man's covenant was made with all the rest; but the court *held* that the action was maintainable, and that the parties had each a separate interest. Johnson v. Wilson, Willes, 248.

Where the part-owners of a ship agreed "each and every of them with the others and each and every of them," that the ship should be under the management of one of them as husband, and that on her return an account should be taken and the net profits divided ratably, it was *held* that one part-owner might sue the ship's husband without joining the other part-owners as plaintiffs. Owston v. Ogle, 13 East, 538.

When Action Joint. — But where one of the two covenantees has no beneficial interest, the action must be joint. Thus if a man covenant with A., and also with B., to pay an annuity to A., his executors and administrators, during the life of B., this will be a joint covenant, and upon A.'s death his re execution of a contract by one party, in which he does not nant to do any thing, but merely assents, under the provis- of a statute, to the performance of certain acts to be done nother, does not render himself liable in covenant on the iment.[1]

here interests are joint, all the parties must be joined in an n on the covenant;[2] and in covenants between several part- if the interest be several, an action may be brought against of the partners only.[3]

action of covenant will not lie against the grantee in a deed ited by the plaintiff, for a failure by the grantee, after accept- he deed and taking possession under it, to perform the condi- upon which the deed, as therein expressed, was executed.[4]

here land has been conveyed by successive warranty deeds, he last grantor has been compelled to indemnify his grantee, ay look to his grantor, and so on.[5] But where a grantee has ndered possession to one claiming adversely, such grantee ot sue his grantor on the covenants of warranty, without ing that such person's title was paramount to the grantor's.[6]

nants in common may sue a lessee of a house for negligence pair, who after the demise, but before the breach alleged, ne a co-tenant of the plaintiff's in the same house.[7]

ors cannot maintain an action, but ht of action survives to B., because gal interest is joint, although the uts are separate. Anderson v. Mar- , 1 East, 497; Southcote v. Hoare, nt. 87; Scott v. Goodwin, 1 Bos. & 7.

ackett v. Johnson, 3 Blackf. (Ind.) 61.

Several Covenantors. — Thus, where l covenantors bind themselves, or one of them, to pay a certain sum of , an action cannot be maintained t one of them only. See Montague th, 13 Mass. 405; Tileston v. Newell, 13 Mass. 406; Harrison v. Matthews, 2 N. S. Wall, 318.

ral Covenantees. — And where A. nted with B. and C., their executors, istrators, and assigns, to pay a sum ney, to be held by them on certain C. did not assent to or execute the and subsequently, by another deed ch neither A. nor B. was a party, dis- d all the trusts of the first deed, the held that B. could not alone sue A. the covenant during the lifetime of 'etherell v. Langston, 1 Exch. 634; 7 L. J. Exch. 338.

Thomas v. Pyke, 4 Bibb (Ky.), 418.

t and Several Interests, What are. — where an agreement contains a claim ich it is provided that "it is under- that the machines, etc., are to be paid the parties," it creates a covenant on an action will lie in favor of a part- ner who furnishes the machines, etc. In construing the contract, the court say that "it is plain, as well from the matter of the instrument as from its whole tenor and im- port, that the obligation to pay was several, and that neither of the parties intended to bind himself for his co-partners. In such a case the action ought to be several; for it is well settled that although a man may covenant with two or more jointly, yet if the interest and cause of action be several, the covenant should be taken to be several, though the words of the covenant be joint." Thomas v. Pyke, 4 Bibb (Ky.), 418, 420.

4. Rockford, R. I. & St. L. R. R. Co. v. Beckemeier, 72 Ill. 267.

5. Jones v. Whitsett, 79 Mo. 188.

"Grant, bargain, and sell." — In the case of Jones v. Whitsett, supra, the Supreme Court of Missouri say, "It has been held in this court that the covenant of warranty implied in the words 'grant, bargain, and sell,' runs with the land to each subsequent grantee, and that the course of action enures to the person who is owner of the title at the time the eviction is suffered and the covenants are broken." See Dickson v. Desire, 23 Mo. 151; Chambers v. Smith, 23 Mo. 174; Cockrell v. Proctor, 65 Mo. 41; Conklin v. Hannibal & St. J. R. R. Co., 65 Mo. 533.

6. Snyder v. Jennings, 15 Neb. 372.

7. Yates v. Cole, 2 Brod. & B. 660; s. c., sub nom. Gates v. Cole, 5 J. B. Moore, 554.

Where a tenant for life and a remainder-man are parties to an indenture, whereby they (so far as they legally can and may, according only to their respective interests) demise their estate for a term of years, and the lessee enters into possession, the tenant for life may sue him for breach of covenant, although the indenture has not been executed by the remainder-man.[1]

A married woman is not liable to an action of covenant, though she join her husband in warranting the land, as to which she releases her right of dower.[2]

An action does not lie against the chairman of the board of directors of a company, not incorporated by act of parliament, upon a deed under the seal of a former chairman, though sealed by him for and on behalf of the company.[3]

2. *Personal Representatives, Executors, etc.* — A grantee may maintain an action in covenant against the administrator of his grantor;[4] and an action on a covenant of warranty may be maintained against the executors of the vendor by an assignee.[5] And a covenant by two joint lessees, if it is joint and several, will bind the executors of the deceased lessee.[6] But the personal representatives of a covenantor cannot be sued for the breach of a real covenant, running with the land, whereby the covenantor bound himself and his heirs, and which breach occurred after his decease.[7]

Covenant lies against executors and administrators of a grantee in fee, to recover rent, where the grantee covenants for himself, his executors, etc., to pay a rent in fee, although the land goes to the heirs.[8] And an action of covenant for arrears of ground-rent, which accrued after the death of the covenantee, is properly

1. How v. Greek, 3 Hurls. & C. 391.

2. Griffin v. Reynolds, 58 U. S. (17 How.) 609; bk. 15, L. ed. 229.

3. Hall v. Bainbridge, 1 Scott, N. R. 151; s. c., 1 Man. & G. 42.

4. Large v. McClain (Pa.), 5 Cent. Rep. 761.

Under a deed of general warranty containing the words "grant, bargain, and sell," the grantee has a right of action against the administrator of his grantor for money paid by him as a collateral inheritance tax, which was a lien upon the property when conveyed. Large v. McClain (Pa.), 5 Cent. Rep 761.

Pennsylvania Act of May 28, 1715. — The words "grant, bargain, and sell," in a deed under the Pennsylvania act of May 28, 1715, create a covenant against incumbrances, which is broken as soon as made by the existence of a lien. Large v. McClain (Pa.), 5 Cent. Rep. 761.

5. Chapman v. Holmes, 10 N. J. L. (5 Halst.) 20; Townsend v. Morris, 6 Cow. (N. Y.) 123; Hamilton v. Wilson, 4 Johns. (N. Y.) 72; s. c., 4 Am. Dec. 253; Lewis v. Ridge, Cro. Eliz. 863.

Deed of Bargain and Sale. — Thus where in a deed of bargain and sale of lands, the grantor covenanted as follows: "And the said A. doth hereby covenant, for himself and his heirs, to and with the said B., that he the said A. will warrant and forever defend to the said B., his heirs and assigns, the title of the said parcels of land against all persons whatever," it was held that the covenant was not a mere warranty real, but was a personal covenant upon which an action of covenant lay for the grantee on being evicted, against the administrator of the grantor. Tabb v. Binford, [illegible] (Va.), 132; s. c., 26 Am. Dec. [illegible].

6. Enys v. Donnithorne, 2 Burr. 1190.

Action on, against Executors. — In an action against executors, in their own right on a covenant for good title and quiet enjoyment against any person or persons whatever, contained in an assignment of a lease of the testator (by way of mortgage), the declaration must show a breach by some act of the covenantors. Noble v. 1 H. Bl. 34.

7. Kershaw v. Supplee, 1 Rawle 131.

8. Van Rensselaer v. Platner, 2 Johns. (N. Y.) Cas. 17.

brought against his personal representatives; but the judgment must be *de terris*.[1]

If a tenant in tail male demises for a term of ninety-nine years, and his lessee assigns over to another, but, before such assignment, the tenant in tail male dies without issue male, no action upon the lease can be maintained against the representatives of the grantor by such assignee, the lease being void at the time of the assignment, and no interest passing under it.[2]

3. *Heirs and Devisees.* — On a breach of covenant occurring after the death of the covenantor, and the complete settlement of his estate, the covenantee may sue the heirs directly, and they will be liable to the extent of the assets descended.[3] And in an action upon a covenant of warranty in a deed, an heir of an heir is a necessary party.[4]

4. *Assignee.* — Covenant does not lie against a party occupying demised premises as assignee, unless he has actually received an assignment of the lease.[5] But an action of covenant for non-

1. Gardiner *v.* Painter (Pa.), 3 Phila. 365; Quain's Appeal, 22 Pa. St. (10 Harris) 510; William's Appeal, 47 Pa. St. 283; Scott *v.* Lunt's Admr., 32 U. S. (7 Pet.) 596; bk. 8, L. ed. 797.

Liability on Covenant to pay Rent. — It was settled as early as Spencer's Case, 5 Co. 16, that in a covenant in relation to the payment of rent, in which the executors and administrators are expressly named, speaking generally, they are bound to the performance of the covenant. Gardiner *v.* Painter (Pa.), 3 Phila. 365, 367.

It has been said, that, so long as the executor has assets, he must perform the covenants contained in a lease granted to the testator; nor will an assignment over, with an acceptance of the rent by the lessor from the assignee, relieve the executor from the charge. See Kunckle *v.* Wynick, 1 U. S. (1 Dall.) 305; bk. 1, L. ed. 149; Bachelour *v.* Gage, Cro. Cas. 188; Britt *v.* Cumberland, Cro. Jac. 522. And the fact that there may be a good remedy against the assignee will not relieve the personal representative. See Scott *v.* Lunt's Admr., 32 U. S. (7 Pet.) 596, 604; bk. 8, L. ed. 797; Orgill *v.* Kemshead, 4 Taunt. 642; Barnard *v.* Godscall, Cro. Jac. 309; Bacon's Abr. tit. *Covenant*, E. 1, 4; Comyn's Dig. tit. *Covenant*, C. 1.

2. Andrew *v.* Pearce, 1 Bos. & P. N. R. 158.

3. Walker *v.* Deaver, 79 Mo. 664.

Liability of Heir or Devisee. — The heirs and devisees, to the extent of the estate taken by them, are liable in a direct action on the covenant of their ancestor or devisor. Metcalf *v.* Smith, 40 Mo. 572; Walker *v.* Deaver, 79 Mo. 664, 673.

Where the heir or devisee has received and appropriated assets which were bound to make good the covenant of the ancestor or devisor, the case differs from that of an ordinary claim against the estate. In the latter case it is held in Missouri that the doctrine of equitable assets, the marshalling of assets, and bills of discovery, is suspended by the statutory administration law. See Titterington *v.* Hooker, 58 Mo. 593; Walker *v.* Deaver, 79 Mo. 664, 673.

Where the heirs or devisees are proceeded against on account of the debt of their ancestor or devisor, they are not liable *in solido*, but only *pro rata* on account of assets received. An estate by descent renders the heir liable for the debts of the ancestor to the value of the property descended, and he holds the land subject to the payment of the ancestor's debts. Metcalf *v.* Smith's Heirs, 40 Mo. 572.

Missouri Statute. — But the failure of personal assets of the estate will not, under the administration laws of Missouri, after final settlement of the administration, authorize a bill in equity on behalf of the creditors against the heirs, to have lands descended to them sold to satisfy their claims. Titterington *v.* Hooker, 58 Mo. 593.

4. Crocker *v.* Smith, 10 Ill. App. 376.

New Jersey Statute. — An action of covenant will, by force of the statute of New Jersey, lie against heirs and devisees for the breach of a covenant against incumbrances contained in a conveyance of the ancestor. New Jersey Ins. Co. *v.* Meeker, 37 N. J. L. (8 Vr.) 282; Morris *v.* Rowan, 17 N. J. L. (2 Harr.) 304.

5. Armstrong *v.* Wheeler, 9 Cow. (N. Y.) 88; Williams *v.* Woodard, 2 Wend. (N. Y.) 487; Quackenboss *v.* Clarke, 12 Wend. (N. Y.) 555. And see Van Alstyne *v.* Van Slyck, 10 Barb. (N. Y.) 383.

payment of rent lies against an assignee of a lease, though the assignment is by way of mortgage security, although he has not entered, or taken actual possession.[1]

The devisee of the equity of redemption (the legal fee being in a mortgagee) is not liable as assignee of all the estate, right, title and interest of the original covenantor.[2] But, under an absolute assignment of a term, the assignee may be sued on the covenants before he had taken actual possession.[3]

The assignee of a term declared against as such is not liable for rent accruing after he has assigned over, though it is stated that the lessor was a party executing the assignment, and agreed thereby that the term, which was determinable at his option, should be absolute.[4] But it has been held that a trustee to whom two leases were assigned in trust for securing an annuity, saying to the occupier of one of the demised houses, "You must pay the rent to me; I am become landlord for my client, who has the annuity, so you must pay the ground-rents for me," is liable to the lessor, as assignee of both leases, for non-payment of rent and not repairing.[5]

VII. When to be brought.—On a sale of land, with covenant of warranty when any thing passes to the vendee, there can be no action on the covenant until eviction;[6] but where a grantor [illegible]

Assignee of a Covenant, Evidence to charge.—But it is *held* that the execution of a lease, and the possession by the defendant, is evidence sufficient to charge a defendant in an action of covenant as assignee for the non-payment of rent, because the fact of assignment is sufficient evidence of an assignment in the first instance.—Quackenboss v. Clarke, 12 Wend. (N. Y.) 555; Williams v. Woodard, 2 Wend. (N. Y.) 482,—but the defendant is at liberty to prove that he is not assignee, as by showing that the estate created by the lease declared or ceased before his entry. Williams v. Woodard, 2 Wend. (N. Y.) 487.

Pennsylvania Act.—Under the act of April 25, 1850 (Platt, Leases, 571), covenant for ground rent lies against the assignee of the covenantor, for arrears which accrued prior to the assignment. McQuesney v. Hiester, 33 Pa. St. 435.

Theatre Boxes: Personal Covenant.—The lessees of a theatre, by a deed, agreed to pay certain money lent to them by the plaintiff, on a certain day, and that until payment the plaintiff, and such persons as he might appoint, should have the free use of two boxes in the theatre, one in the dress circle, and one in the circle above, no specific boxes being mentioned. The lessees afterwards assigned their interest in the theatre to the defendant. In an action for breach of covenant it was *held* that this was a mere personal contract, and that no action could be maintained against the assignee for refusing to permit the plaintiff to use the boxes in the theatre. Flight v. Glossop, 2 Scott, 220; 2 Bing. N. C. 125; 1 Hodges, 263.

1. Williams v. Bosanquet, [illegible] Moore, 500; s. c., 1 Bro. & Bing. 238.

2. Carlisle Mayor, etc., v. Blamire, 8 East, 487.

3. Walker v. Reeves, 2 Doug. 461, n.

Mortgagee of a Lease: Liability of the Mortgagee.—It was said in McMurphy v. Minot, 4 N. H. 251, that he who takes an assignment of the whole estate of a lessee, by way of mortgage, is liable, on a covenant for the payment of rent, for rent which becomes due after he takes the mortgage, although he never actually entered under the mortgage. See also Williams v. Bosanquet, 1 Bro. & Bing. 238. But this doctrine was questioned in the later case of Lord v. Ferguson, 9 N. H. 380.

4. Chancellor v. Poole, 2 Doug. 764.

5. Gretton v. Diggles, 4 Taunt. 766.

6. Abbott v. Rowan, 33 Ark. 593.

Eviction from Part of Premises: Constructive Eviction, what does not amount to.—An ouster or eviction from a part of the premises is enough to maintain the action. Carter v. Denman, 23 N. J. L. (3 Zab.) 260.

The existence of a paramount title, and the acquisition of it by the covenantee by purchase, on his mere volition, will not amount to a constructive eviction sufficient veyed with covenants of seisin, land belonging to the government, or to a stranger in possession, the covenant is broken as soon as made, and the grantee may sue for damages.[1]

In a conveyance to a city for a street and market-house, a covenant that the grantee shall re-convey when the land ceases to be used for a market, relieves the grantors from the rule which requires them or their reversioners to enter, before they can maintain a claim of forfeiture for breach of the covenant.[2]

Where, in a conveyance, the description of the property is so defective that it can carry no title, an action for breach of a covenant of seisin cannot be maintained before a reformation of the deed.[3]

VIII. Pleadings in Covenant. — 1. *Venue: Before Whom Action to be brought.* — Under the English statute,[4] actions upon express covenants in a lease running with the estate in the law, by an assignee of the reversion against the lessee, or by the lessee against the assignee of the reversion, are transitory actions.[5]

Where there are several facts material to the plaintiff's action arising in different counties, an action of covenant may be brought in either.[6]

In an action on a covenant by the assignee of the lessee of a term, the action is local, and the venue must be laid in the county where the lands are situate.[7]

to support an action in the covenant of [illegible]. Kellog *v.* Platt, 33 N. J. L. (4 Vr.) 328.

2. Abbott *v.* Rowan, 33 Ark. 593.

When Action lies: Eviction. — To sustain an action on the covenant of warranty, or for quiet enjoyment, there must be either an actual eviction, or a disturbance of title, or possession by paramount title, equivalent to an eviction. Carter *v.* Denman, 23 N. J. L. (3 Zab.) 260. But in order to maintain an action on a covenant against incumbrances, it is not necessary that the grantee should wait until eviction or disturbance, or until he has paid the debt or interest secured by the mortgage, or has been impleaded, prosecuted, or put to costs, trouble, or expense. Garrison *v.* Sandford, 12 N. J. L. (7 Halst.) 261. See Washer *v.* Brown, 5 N. J. Eq. (1 Halst.) 81.

By the weight of authority, or upon principle, it cannot be *held* that an eviction by ejecting the covenantee from the actual possession of the premises, whether by process of law or otherwise, is necessary to complete his remedy upon his covenant of warranty. Kellog *v.* Platt, 33 N. J. L. (4 Vr.) 328.

An actual eviction is not necessary to equitable relief, provided there has been a trial and judgment in ejectment, although the court will not act upon a mere suggestion that the title is defective. Coster *v.* Monroe Co., 2 N. J. Eq. (1 H. W. Gr.) 467.

As to what shall be deemed a sufficient ouster or disturbance to sustain an action on the covenant of warranty, notwithstanding there was no actual dispossession, see Kellog *v.* Platt, 33 N. J. L. (4 Vr.) 328.

3. Baker *v.* St. Louis, 7 Mo. App. 429.

3. Gordan *v.* Goodman, 98 Ind. 269.

And an action in covenant upon an insurance policy should not be brought after a judgment in assumpsit upon the same policy. Marine Ins. Co. of Alexandria *v.* Young, 5 U. S. (1 Cr.) 332; bk. 2, L. ed. 126.

4. **32 Hen. 8, c. 34.** — This statute transfers the privity of contract with respect to the covenants in a lease, to and against the assignee of the lessor, in the same plight as the lessor had then against the lessee, or the lessee against the lessor. See Thursby *v.* Plant, 1 Saund. 237, 241 c., n. 6; Webb *v.* Russell, 3 T. R. 394, 395, 401, 402; Thrale *v.* Cornwall, 1 Wils. 165.

5. Thursby *v.* Plant, 1 Saund. 237, 241 c., n. 6; Thrale *v.* Cornwall, 1 Wils. 165; Webb *v.* Russell, 3 T. R. 394, 395.

English Statute in Pennsylvania. — The English statute of 32 Hen. 8, c. 34, is in force in Pennsylvania, excepting those parts that relate to the King of England and his grantees. See Rob. Dig. 227. Henwood *v.* Cheesman, 3 Serg. & R. (Pa.) 502.

6. London (Mayor of) *v.* Cole, 7 T. R. 583.

7. Berwick (Mayor of) *v.* Shanks, 11 Moore, 372; s. c., 3 Bing. 459.

In Delaware, an action of covenant may

2. *Declaration.* — *a. Form.* — The uniformity of process act,[1] imperatively required that the form of action should be concisely stated in each of the writs therein prescribed, whether serviceable or bailable; and if the form was omitted, or substantially varied from the one enjoined by that act, even in serviceable process, the writ would, on summons or motion, be set aside.[2] This act related to and regulated the action of covenant, as well as the other forms of action.[3]

In a declaration in covenant it should be set out without any intermediate inducements or statement of the consideration; but where averments are made, which may be treated as mere surplusage, they will not violate the declaration.[4] It is a well-established rule of pleading, that only so much of the covenant as is essential to the cause should be set out in the declaration.[5]

b. General Rules. — In an action of covenant the declaration must state that the contract was under seal; and it should not only state such a contract, but should also allege its delivery.[6]

be brought before a justice of the peace, in some cases. Walker *v.* Byrd, 15 Ark. 33; Colesbury *v.* Stoops, 1 Harr. (Del.) 448.

1. 2 W. 4, c. 39.

2. "**Promises.**" — But "promises" omitting "on" or "upon," have been held a mere clerical mistake. Cooper *v.* Wheale, 4 Dowl. P. C. 281; s. c., 1 Harr. & W. 525. See also Keen *v.* Skiffington, 3 Tyr. 318; s. c., 1 Dowl. P. C. 686; 1 C. & M. 363.

The omission of the words "on promise" in a writ of summons, is only a ground for setting aside the copy served, and not the writ itself. Chalkley *v.* Carter, 4 Dowl. P. C. 481.

3. 1 Chitt. Pl 253.

4. Jones *v.* Thomas, 21 Gratt. (Va) 96.

Where A. executed his bond as follows, — "March 12, 1863. I hereby bind myself, my heirs, etc., to pay —— the amount of principal and interest due from B, on the tract of land purchased by him of C. and wife. Witness my hand and seal the day and date above," — and delivered it to B., the court held that B. could recover upon it, although the declaration did not, in its commencement, aver that A. covenanted with the plaintiff to pay the debt, but did so aver in a subsequent part of it; such subsequent averment being substantially sufficient. Jones *v.* Thomas, 21 Gratt. (Va.) 96.

5. Wilcox *v.* Cohn, 5 Blatchf. C. C. 346.

Rules for pleading Breach of Covenant. — In the case of Wilcox *v.* Cohn, *Justice Shipman* laid down the rules of pleading applicable to a declaration for the breach of a covenant. He says that "in order to avoid prolixity, so much of the covenant as is essential to the cause of action should be set forth, and no more. Distinct breaches of separate covenants in the deed may be assigned in the same count. It is sufficient if the breach be assigned in words which contain the sense and substance of the covenant. The breach may be assigned according to the legal effect, or in the words of the deed. When the right of action depends upon a condition precedent, its performance must be averred; but it is never necessary to anticipate and negative matters of defence, such as payment, waiver, discharge," etc.

See, regarding the form of a declaration on a bond given for part of the purchase-money of land, Barrow *v.* Bispham, 11 N. J. L. (6 Halst.) 121; on a bond assigned and guaranteed to plaintiff, see Sibley *v.* Stull, 15 N. J. L. (3 J. S. Gr.) 332; on a breach of covenant in a mortgage deed, for not paying the money secured, see Finley *v.* Simpson, 22 N. J. L. (2 Zab.) 311; s. c., 53 Am. Dec. 252; on a breach of covenant of warranty in a deed, see Carter *v.* Denman, 23 N. J. L. (3 Zab.) 261; on covenant in a license by a patentee, see Wilcox *v.* Cohn, 5 Blatchf. C. C. 346.

6. Perkins *v.* Reeds, 8 Mo. 33.

Pleading Seal. — The declaration in an action of covenant should show that the agreement on which it is founded was originally sealed by the defendant, and remained under seal at the time of declaring, or accounting for the omission of such averment. It is not sufficient to say, "and for the faithful performance of the said covenant and agreement, and the said parties did thereunto set their hands and affix their seals." Smith *v.* Emory, 12 N. J. L. (7 Halst.) 53.

and make a profert of the instrument, or show some excuse for the omission.[1] The declaration must always aver, and the evidence show, the delivery of the deed.[2] But the defendant may aver and show that the deed was delivered, and still remains as an escrow,[3] or that it was void from the beginning,[4] that it became void by subsequent acts,[5] or that the deed was delivered to a stranger for the use of the plaintiff, and that he refused to accept it.[6]

It is not in general necessary that the declaration should set out the consideration of the defendant's covenant, because the seal of itself imports and is evidence of a consideration; but when the performance of the covenant is constituted a condition precedent, then such performance must be averred,[7] or the declaration must show that performance was prevented by the defendant.[8]

The declaration should set forth so much of the deed declared on as is essential to the cause of action.[9] The instrument may

1. [illegible] v. Brookman, 3 T. R. 151.

2. **Proving Delivery of Deed.** — The delivery of the deed by the defendant may be proved by showing that the grantor or obligor parted with the dominion over it with an intent that it should pass to the grantee or obligee. The delivery of a deed may be proved, like most facts *in pais*, either by direct evidence or by circumstances. Long v. Ramsay, 1 Serg. & R. (Pa.) 72; Brown v. Bank of Chambersburg, 3 Pa. St. 187. See 2 Greenl. Ev. [illegible].

In general, where a deed is found in the hands of the grantee therein, it is presumed to have been delivered, — Green v. [illegible], 6 Mo. 326; Dunn v. Games, 1 [illegible] C. C. 321, — and where a deed is found in the hands of the grantor or obligor, the presumption is that it has not been delivered. Hatch v. Haskins, 17 [illegible].

Where a deed is registered at the request of the grantor for the use of the grantee, and the latter assents thereto, such registry is evidence of delivery. [illegible] v. Drew, 12 Pick. (Mass.) 141; s. c., 22 Am. Dec. 416. But the simple act of recording a deed is not conclusive evidence of delivery, — Maynard v. Maynard, 10 Mass. 456; s. c., 6 Am. Dec. 146; Harrison v. Phillips' Academy, 12 Mass. 456, — but only *prima facie*, — Gilbert v. North American Fire Ins. Co., 23 Wend. (N. Y.) 43; s. c., 35 Am. Dec. 543. See Union Mutual Insurance Co. v. Campbell, 95 Ill. 231; 35 Am. Rep. 168; Van Valen v. Schermerhorn, 22 How. (N. Y.) Pr. 419; Fryer v. Rockefeller, 63 N. Y. 272, — and the presumption of delivery may be rebutted. Gilbert v. North American Fire Insurance Co., 23 Wend. (N. Y.) 43. See Stephens v. Buffalo & New York City R. R. Co., 20 Barb. (N. Y.) 338; Dietz v. Farish, 44 N. Y. Super. Ct. (11 J. & S.) 205. Parol evidence is always admissible to show that a deed was not delivered. Black v. Lamb, 12 N. J. Eq. (1 Beas.) 116; Black v. Shreve, 13 N. J. Eq. (2 Beas.) 457; Stephens v. Buffalo Ins. Co., 20 Barb. (N. Y.) 332; Roberts v. Jackson, 1 Wend. (N. Y.) 478; Jackson v. Perkins, 2 Wend. (N. Y.) 308; Deitz v. Farish, 79 N. Y. 520; Paris v. Gere, 14 Week. Dig. 387; Johnson v. Baker, 4 Barn. & Ald. 440.

3. See Union Bank v. Ridgely, 1 Harr. & G. (Md.) 324; Wheelwright v. Wheelwright, 2 Mass. 447; Blight v. Schenck, 10 Pa. St. 285.

4. **Defences to a Deed.** — As, for example, that it is a forgery, or was obtained by fraud, or was executed by the defendant while he was insane or intoxicated or an infant. Marine Ins. Co. of Alexandria v. Hodgson, 10 U. S. (6 Cr.) 206; bk. 3, L. ed. 200.

5. **Alteration of Deed.** — As by being materially altered or cancelled by tearing of the seal.

6. Read v. Robinson, 6 Watts & S. (Pa.) 329.

7. Harrison v. Taylor, 3 A. K. Marsh. (Ky.) 168; Gardiner v. Corson, 15 Mass. 503; Keatly v. McLaugherty, 4 Mo. 221; West v. Emmons, 5 Johns. (N. Y.) 179; Knox v. Rinehart, 9 Serg. & R. (Pa.) 45; Wilcox v. Cohn, 5 Blatchf. C. C. 346; Goodwin v. Lynn, 4 Wash. C. C. 714.

8. Clandennen v. Paulsel, 3 Mo. 232; Faunen v. Beauford, 1 Bay (S. C.), 237.

9. **Allegation of Breach: Sufficiency.** — When, in an action for breach of a covenant, the plaintiff stated that the defendant, by deed, etc., sold to him a certain slave, and covenanted to warrant and for-

be stated according to its legal effect,[1] but ... is to declare in the words of the deed.[2]

In an action of covenant, implied covenants ... the same as though they were expressed in ...

A declaration in covenant must clearly show ... is broken,[4] the allegation of the breach must ... the plaintiff must show by sufficient averments ... able certainty, that he has been actually damnified ...

If the breach of contract for which an action ... brought was accompanied with fraud, the fraud ... of inquiry, and may be specially averred in the ...

In covenant on an agreement to indemnify ...

ever defend the sale of the said slave to the plaintiff, against all persons lawfully claiming any estate, right, or title to the slave, etc., and averred that the person so sold as a slave was not a slave, but free at the time of sale, on demurrer to the declaration the court *held* that there was sufficient assignment of a breach of the covenant of warranty. Quackenboss *v.* Lansing, 6 Johns (N. Y.) 49.

1. In an action upon an indenture of lease against the surviving executrix of the lessee, the declaration stated that, upon the death of the lessee, all his estate and interest in the premises came to and vested in the defendant and P., who were executrixes of the last will and testament of the lessee, by reason whereof the defendant and P., as executrixes, became and were possessed. It was *held* a sufficient averment that the term vested in the defendant and P. as executrixes. Ackland *v.* Prinz, 3 Scott, N. R. 297; s. c., 2 Man. & G. 937. *Held* also that it was unnecessary to state that the term had vested in the defendant and P. as executrixes, as the vesting of a term in the lessee's personal representatives, together with the liability of such personal representatives to be sued upon the covenants of the lease, is in effect a conclusion of law. Southcote *v.* Hoare, 3 Taunt 87.

2. **Setting out Deed.** — But the practice of merely setting out the deed as a part of the pleading, has been said to be bad. McCampbell *v.* Vastine, 10 Iowa, 538.

It is sufficient to state so much of the instrument as contains the contract, the breach of which is complained of. Clarke *v.* Gray, 6 East, 567. If the declaration states more of the covenant than composes the foundation of the action, it will be faulty, — Grannis *v.* Clark, 8 Cow. (N. Y.) 36, 42, — but all unnecessary matters stated, which is foreign to the cause of action, may be rejected as surplus. Grannis *v.* Clark, 8 Cow. (N. Y.) 36, 42, 1 Chitt. Pl. 232–234.

3. Grannis *v.* Clark, 8 Cow. (N. Y.) 36, 42; Barney *v.* ... s. c., 6 Wend. (N. Y.) ...

4. Ridgell *v.* ...

5. English *v.* ... Penn.) 816.

Alleging ... covenant, one ... Gaster *v.* Ashley, 1 ...

An assignment of ... same covenant, is ... on special demurrer ... Wend. (N. Y.) ... Comyn, Dig. ... tinct breaches of ... be assigned in the ... *v.* Cole, 5 ... eral breaches may be ... declaration; and if ... assigned, the declaration ... bad on general demurrer ... 1 Dana (Ky.) ... (Ky.) 374; Comyn, ... 2, 3.

6. Gould *v.* Allen, ...

Damnification. — ... ant purchased an ... annuity to S., and, ... covenanted to pay the ... demnify the vendor ... spect to it. In a declaration ... assigning non-payment ... out adding that the ... by damnified, the ... Saward *v.* Anstey, ... J. B. Moore, 55.

7. Cutler *v.* Cox, ... s. c., 18 Am. Dec. ...

Alleging ... seeking to recover ... found in the covenant ... is brought, the ... be part of the contract ... through fraud, ... that one or both parties ... tion. So *held*, as to ... by the seller of a ... good will, that he ... printing-press in the ... man, 65 Ga. 11.

id, an allegation in the complaint, as a breach, that the has been forced and compelled to pay the bond, without how he was compelled to pay, is bad, on special demurrer.[1] a covenant for quiet enjoyment, without lawful disturb- allegation of breach merely stating that the plaintiff was d, is insufficient; it should be, that he was *legitimo modo* d, or the plaintiff should otherwise show by what he was d and how.[2]

action for the breach of a covenant of seisin in a lease, ment that the grantor neither at the date of the lease nor is seised of the premises, is insufficient in not stating that of the person keeping the plaintiff out of possession at the date of the lease; for otherwise the averment of aration may be true, without showing a cause of action, the plaintiff may have been kept out of possession by the ner; but that owner may have derived title under the plain- self.[3] And in an action by an assignee of the reversion, ation that the lessor was seised, without stating of what nd being so seised, devised to the plaintiff in fee, this will icient allegation of title after verdict.[4]

action against executors, in their own right, for covenant title and quiet enjoyment against any person or persons r, contained in an assignment of a lease of the testator of mortgage), the declaration must show a breach by t of the covenantors.[5]

action against an heir for the breach of warranty in a m the deceased grantor, the declaration must allege that te has been settled, and that the defendant has received ng therefrom. If the declaration fails to so state, objec- uld be taken thereto by demurrer; it comes too late at

Words of Covenant: Negativing. — It is not necessary reach of covenant be assigned in the very words of the t; it is enough that a substantial breach be shown.[7]

ard v. Hill, 7 Cow. (N. Y.) 442; Foote, 1 Wend. (N. Y.) 207.
n v. Foote, 1 Wend. (N.Y.) 207; Hale, 2 Saund. , 181 b; g. tit. Plead. C. 47, 48.
Assessment. — The complaint n covenant for the breach of a gainst incumbrances, by reason of ent for the construction of a free d upon the land conveyed, must t there was at least a proceed- pending at the time of the con- hich resulted in the assessment he committee. Kirkpatrick v. Ind. 220; s. c., 5 West. Rep. 798. in v. Clark, 8 Cow. (N. Y.) 36.
House becoming Uninhabit- action in covenant on the lease of a house for the purpose of a dwelling-house cannot be founded upon the mere fact that the house has become uninhabitable. — Carson v. Godley, 26 Pa. St. 117; Hazlett v. Powell, 30 Pa. St. 293; Harns v. Wilson (Pa.), 8 Cent. Rep. 454, 25 Cent. L. J. 14, 9 Atl. Rep. 437. — unless it appears from the complaint that such condition of the property resulted from the acts of the lessor, or from those of persons holding paramount title. Harns v. Wilson (Pa.), 8 Cent. Rep. 454, 25 Cent. L. J. 14, 9 Atl. Rep. 437.
4. Harris v. Beavan, 4 Bing. 646; s. c., 1 Moore & P. 633.
5. Noble v. King, 1 H. Bl. 34.
6. Eddy v. Chace, 140 Mass. 471; s. c., 1 New Eng. Rep. 573.
7. Fletcher v. Peck, 10 U. S. (6 Cr.) 87;

In an action for the breach of covenant of seisin, quiet enjoyment, and against incumbrances, the brea assigned in the words of the covenants,[1] and it is assign the breach in the words of the deed.[2]

In covenant for purchase-money, an averment o plaintiff is indispensable.[3]

When the covenant is to do, or forbear to do, a it is sufficient to assign the breach in the words of But on a covenant of warranty the declaration mu and show an eviction by title paramount.[4]

The breach may be assigned by negativing the covenant,[5] where such general assignment amounts

bk. 3, L. ed. 162; Harmony v. Bingham, 1 Duer (N. Y.), 209; s. c., 12 N. Y. 99; 62 Am. Dec. 142; Bender v. Fromberger, 4 U. S. (4 Dall.) 436; bk. 1, L. ed. 898.

Alleging Breach. — Where the covenant was that a legislature had a right to convey, it was *held* that an allegation that the legislature had no authority to convey was a good assignment of a breach. Fletcher v. Peck, 10 U. S. (6 Cr.) 87; bk. 3, L. ed. 163.

The breach may be assigned according to the legal effect, or in the words of the deed. Wilcox v. Cohn, 5 Blatchf. C. C. 346.

It is sufficient if the breach be assigned in words which contain the sense and substance of the covenant. Wilcox v. Cohn, 5 Blatchf. C. C. 346.

In order to avoid prolixity, only so much of the covenant as is essential to the cause of action should be set forth in the declaration. Wilcox v. Cohn, 5 Blatchf. C. C. 346.

In covenant a breach may be assigned according to the substance, though not according to the letter, of the covenant. Potter v. Bacon, 2 Wend. (N. Y.) 583.

Where an action upon a deed, in which it was recited in effect that the defendant had accepted securities from B., which were to be valid upon the advance of money by the defendant to B., and void upon the repayment of the same by B. to the defendant; and that the defendant had, after taking the securities, but before making the deed, advanced £269 to B., and that the money had not been repaid at the time of making the deed; and that, in order to induce the plaintiff, in his turn, to advance money to the defendant, the defendant, by the deed, assigned to the plaintiff the securities which he held from B., and in which the defendant covenanted that he had neither done nor omitted, at any time, any act by which the securities, or any estate or interest therein, should or might be in any manner affected, and that £269 remained at the time of making the deed due upon the securities to the defendant, — the breach alleged was, that the defendant never made any advance securities, nor was the any part of it, owing to the time of the making court *held* that the breach and that the plaintiff was denying that the defend advance; for, as this fac the validity to the plainti on which he advanced defendant, and as he to the defendant to secure of that fact, the true con denture was, that the reci intended by the parties of the covenantor only. 14 Q. B. 781; s. c., 14 Ju

1. Sedgwick v. Hollen Y.) 376.

2. Bender v. Fromb Dall.) 436; bk. 1, L. ed.

Setting out Title. — I breach of covenant of s complaint need not set o tail, but simply negative covenant. Wooley v. Ne 605; s. c., 9 Daly (N. Y.

Where, in the declar in covenant, for a brea warranty, it was averred "had not a good and su said tract of land, and by said plaintiffs were ouste of the said premises, by it was *held* to be a subst an eviction by a param Chism, 23 U. S. (10 Wh ed. 363.

As to the sufficiency o a covenant of warranty murrer, see Sweack v. St 470.

3. Burk v. Bear, 3 Cla

4. Carter v. Denman, 260.

5. **Negativing Words o** assigning breaches it is eral, to follow and nega

[illegible], though must be placed upon the record to show the breach of [the] covenant, and the plaintiff's right of action.[1] And a breach [m]ay be assigned according to the substance, though not according [to] the letter, of the covenant.[2]

Although it is sufficient, as a general rule, to follow and negative [th]e words of the covenant, yet if the pleader undertake to assign [a] breach coming within the substance, effect, or intent of the cov[en]ant, he is held to a more strict rule of pleading.[3]

d. Setting out Copy; Seals; Profert. — In an action of covenant, [it] is not necessary to set out the whole deed; it is sufficient to set [ou]t those covenants only which contain the mutual stipulations [an]d conditions which are essential to the plaintiff's cause of action.[4] [A]nd it is sufficient to assign the breach in terms as general as [th]ose in which the covenant is expressed.[5] But it is not sufficient [to] set out in the declaration simply the writing obligatory: a [de]livery must also be alleged.[6]

In declaring upon a covenant, any exception in the body thereof [m]ust be set out, and the subject-matter thereof excluded from the [br]eaches assigned.[7]

[illegible] instrument declared upon. McGeehan [v.] McLaughlin, 1 Hall (N. Y.), 33; Hur[ls]gh v. Jones, 5 N. Y. Leg. Obs. 19.

[2.] Breach need not be assigned in the [ve]ry words of the covenant, if perform[anc]e according to its true meaning and [i]nt be negatived by a necessary impli[cati]on. Harmony v. Bingham, 1 Duer (N. [Y.]) 209; s. c., 12 N. Y. 99; 62 Am. Dec. [1]8.

[C]ovenants of Seisin and Title to convey. [I]n the case of the covenants of seisin, [an]d of good right and title to convey, it is [suf]ficient to allege the breach by negativ[ing] the words of the covenant, — Marston [v.] Hobbs, 2 Mass. 433; s. c., 3 Am. Dec. [6]1; Greenby v. Wilcocks, 2 Johns. (N. Y.) [1]; s. c., 3 Am. Dec. 379; Sedgwick v. Hol[lenb]ack, 7 Johns. (N. Y.) 376; Rickert v. [Sny]der, 9 Wend. (N. Y.) 415; Bender v. [Fro]mberger, 4 U. S. (4 Dall.) 436; bk. 1, [L.] ed. 898; Pollard v. Dwight, 8 U. S. (4 [Cr.]) 421; bk. 2, L. ed. 666; Salmond v. [Sk]idmore, 9 Co. 60 b.; s. c., Cro. Jac. 304; [Be]nshire v. Glover, 2 Show. 460; Wot[to]n v. Hele, 2 Saund. 181, note (a) by Mr. [Ser]geant Williams, — and the same rule [ap]plies to the covenant that the grantor [ha]s good right to convey; but the cove[nan]ts for quiet enjoyment, and of general [wa]rranty, require the assignment of a [brea]ch by a specific ouster, or eviction by [titl]e paramount. Rickert v. Snyder, 9 [We]nd. (N. Y.) 415.

[3.] Randel v. Chesapeake Co., 1 Harr. [(Del.)] 151; Camp v. Douglass, 10 Iowa, [58].

[B]reach to be specifically set forth. — In [cove]nant broken, the breach of each of the covenants against incumbrances, of warranty, and for quiet enjoyment, must be specifically set forth; but it is not sufficient merely to negative the language of the covenants of seisin, and a right to sell. Blanchard v. Hoxie, 34 Me. 376.

2. Potter v. Bacon, 2 Wend. (N. Y.) 583.

3. Brown v. Stebbins, 4 Hill (N. Y.), 154.

4. Killian v. Herndon, 4 Rich (S. C.), 196.

Craving Oyer. — It is only necessary to set forth in the declaration such parts of the agreement as relate to the breaches assigned: if a material part be omitted, the defendant must crave oyer and demurrer. Henry v. Cleland, 14 Johns. (N. Y.) 400; Williams v. Healey, 3 Den. (N. Y.) 363.

5. Bender v. Fromberger, 4 U. S. (4 Dall.) 436; bk. 1, L. ed. 898.

Substantial Breach. — It is not necessary that the breach of the covenant should be assigned in the very words of the covenant. It is sufficient if it show a substantial breach. Fletcher v. Peck, 10 U. S. (6 Cr.) 87; bk. 3, L. ed. 162.

6. Perkins v. Reeds, 8 Mo. 33.

Delivery need not be set out. — But it has been *held* that, although the delivery of the deed is essential to the covenant, yet that such delivery need not be set out in the declaration. See Farrall v. Shaen, 1 Saund. 292, and n. 1; 1 Chitt. P. 364.

7. So *held*, as to a covenant in a deed to warrant and defend, etc., against all persons, etc., "except as against the United States." Dunn v. Dunn, 3 Colo. 510.

The declaration in an action of covenant should show that the agreement upon which it is founded was originally sealed by the defendant,[1] and remained under seal at the time of declaring or accounting for the omission of such averment.[2] Because covenant only lies against one who has sealed the deed.[3]

In an action of covenant the agreement is the foundation of the action, and not merely matter of inducement; the declaration should contain a *profert in curia* of the agreement set forth, or an excuse for the omission of it,[4] or that it is lost,[5] or destroyed, or misplaced by accident, and for that reason the plaintiff cannot bring it into court.[6]

c. Statement of Deed. — (1) *Generally.* — In an action on a lease, it is sufficient if the declaration sets out the legal operation and effect of the demise.[7] But the contract must be stated correctly:

1. **Seals.** — In an action of covenant, it must appear than the instrument upon which the action is founded is a sealed instrument. Commonwealth v. Griffith, 2 Pick. (Mass.) 17; Pierson v. Pierson, 6 N. J. L. (1 Halst.) 168; Bilderback v. Pouner, 7 N. J. L. (2 Halst.) 64. See Van Santwood v. Sandford, 12 Johns. (N. Y.) 197; Warren v. Lynch, 5 Johns. (N. Y.) 239.

The plaintiffs must allege that the parties in the covenant sealed it, although it is set out in *hæc verba*, and contains the words, "witness our hands and seals." Hays v. Lasater, 3 Ark. 565.

Words importing a Seal. — There are some technical words, such as "indenture," "deed," or "writing obligatory," and the like, which of themselves import that the instrument is sealed, and are of themselves sufficient. See Van Santwood v. Sandford, 12 Johns. (N. Y.) 198; Lee v. Adkins, Minor (Ala.), 187; Cabell v. Vaughan, 1 Saund. 291, note 1, 320, note 3; Comyn, Dig. tit. Fait.; Platt on Cov. 6.

Admitting Seal. — If the plaintiff in his declaration neglects to aver that the instrument is under seal, but the defendant in his plea admits that the writing was sealed, the plea will be aided, and the objection waived. Cabell v. Vaughan, 1 Saund. 291, note 1, 320, note 3; Moore v. Jones, Ld. Ray. 1536, 1541; Courtney v. Greenville, Cro. Car. 209.

2. **Insufficient Allegation of Seal.** — It is not sufficient to say, "And on agreement, the said parties did thereunto set their hands, and affix their seals." Smith v. Emery, 12 N. J. L. (7 Hal.) 53.

In a declaration in covenant, there must be an express averment that the writing or contract was sealed by the defendant. Van Santwood v. Sandford, 12 Johns. (N. Y.) 197.

A declaration in covenant, setting forth the instrument in *hæc verba*, and concluding with "sealed and delivered," etc., but not otherwise alleging that it was sealed by the defendant, is bad on general demurrer. Hacomb v. Thompson, 14 Johns. (N. Y.) 207.

3. Wilson v. Brechemin, Bright (Pa.), 445; Maule v. Weaver, 7 Pa. St. 329. See Act, Apr. 25, 1850, § 8; Platt Leas. 571.

"Covenant" does not import a Seal. — It is not sufficient to allege that the parties made their covenant, the word "covenant" not importing a sealed instrument. Hays v. Lasater, 3 Ark. 565.

4. **Profert of a deed** need not be made where it appears from the declaration that the deed is in the possession of the adverse party. Barbour v. Archer, 3 Bibb (Ky.), 8; Francis v. Hazlerig, 1 A. K. Marsh. (Ky.) 93.

5. Paddock v. Higgins, 2 Root (Conn.), 482; Kelley v. Riggs, 2 Root (Conn.), 126; Republica v. Coates, 1 Yeates (Pa.), 2.

6. See Scott v. Curd, Hard. (Ky.) 61; Powers v. Ware, 2 Pick. (Mass.) 451; Bender v. Sampson, 11 Mass. 42; Smith v. Emery, 12 N. J. L. (7 Halst.) 53; Rees v. Overbaugh, 6 Cow. (N. Y.) 748; Cutts v. United States, 1 Gall. C. C. 69; Read v. Brookman, 3 T. R. 151; Bensil v. Leigh, 8 T. R. 571; Carlisle v. Lonsdale, 2 H. Bl. 259; Hawley v. Peacock, 2 Campb. 557; Hardy v. Stephenson, 10 East, 57. See also Phillips' Ev. 348; Tidd's Pr. (9th ed.) 487, 587; Comyn's Dig. tit. Plead. O. 1.

The words of reference, "As by the said covenant and agreement, reference being thereunto had, may more fully appear," inserted in the declaration, after the statement of the contents of the instrument, are no profert, nor sufficient to supply the want. Smith v. Emery, 12 N. J. L. (7 Halst.) 53.

In a declaration of covenant, contained in a recorded conveyance of land, the plaintiff may make profert of the certified copy, without the original. Clark v. Nixon, 5 Hill (N. Y.), 36.

7. Wilson v. Bramhall, 1 Younge & J. a

ıc [illegible] differs from the statement in the declaration.

Allegation.—It is a general [illegible]ding, that it is sufficient if the [illegible] is stated according to the legal [illegible]ams v. Davis, 16 Ala. 748; An-[illegible]illiams, 11 Conn. 326; Fish v. [illegible] Conn. 341; Keyes v. Dearborn, [illegible]2; Close v. Miller, 10 Johns. [illegible] Morris v. Fort, 2 McC. (N. C.) [illegible]shell v. Bowen, 1 Bing. (N. C.) [illegible]er v. Wilson, 2 Saund. 97 and [illegible]yn, Dig. tit. Pleader, C. 37; [illegible]r. tit. Pleas f, 7. [illegible]ntiff is not required to follow [illegible] form of words in which the [illegible]is made. Walsh v. Gilmor, 3 ([illegible]) 407; Ridgely v. Riggs, ([illegible]) 213; Hopkins v. Young, [illegible] 3 Hastings v. Lovering, 2 Pick. [illegible]; s. c., 13 Am. Dec. 420; Dorr [illegible]12 Pick. (Mass.) 521; Churchill [illegible]ts' Bank, 19 Pick. (Mass.) 532; [illegible]endrick, 2 N. H. 160; Lent v. [illegible]10 Mass. 230; s. c., 6 Am. Dec. [illegible]er v. Whitney, 10 Mass. 320; [illegible]lark, 8 Cow. (N. Y.) 36; Thomas [illegible], 4 Wend. (N. Y.) 549; Osborne [illegible], 9 Wend. (N. Y.) 135.

[illegible]claring on a special contract, it [illegible] be set out in its very terms or [illegible]o its legal effect. Dickerson v. [illegible] 5 Pike (Ark.), 316; White v. [illegible]ackf. (Ind.) 228; Pye v. Rutter, [illegible] Moore v. Platt County, 8 Mo. [illegible] v. Dearborn, 12 N. H. 52; [illegible] Scott, 17 Vt. 634.

[illegible]n instrument is set out as a part [illegible]dings, it is not necessary that [illegible]e described by its right name. [illegible] Helms, 4 Tex. 228; Salinas v. [illegible] Tex. 572.

[illegible]ation alleging that, by indenture [illegible] to be made between the plaintiff [illegible]lant, it was witnessed that the [illegible]ovenanted, is sufficiently certain. [illegible] Batley, 8 Bing. 256; s. c., 1 M. [illegible]9.

[illegible]ion against a surety on an an-[illegible] who had become bound to pay [illegible]ight days from the time specified [illegible]t by the grantor, in case of fail-[illegible]atter, the declaration by mistake [illegible] the payment had become due [illegible]rety on the day on which it had [illegible]e only from the principal. The [illegible]that, as the bond and covenant [illegible] the whole, set forth with suffi-[illegible]nty to prevent any reasonable [illegible] to the ground of action, the [illegible]t allegation might be rejected [illegible]ge. Hearn v. Cole, 1 Dow.

[illegible] declaration in covenant set out for several lots of ground and rent reserved, and contained a count for rent due on particular lots, and a general assignment of breach, it was *held* good. Associates, etc., v. Halsey, 5 N. J. L. (2 South.) 750.

In covenant broken, breaches of the covenants of seisin and good right to convey having been sufficiently alleged, but breaches of the other covenants insufficiently, though the declaration go on to allege the seisin of third persons of a certain part of granted premises, yet the declaration is not bad on general demurrer, and the plaintiff may recover for the breach of the covenants of seisin and right to convey as damages the consideration paid by him for that part of the granted premises of which defendant was not seised, with interest to the time of judgment. Blanchard v. Hoxie, 34 Me. 376.

Where A. covenanted to pay to B. a certain sum of money, viz., part to the United States and the residue to the covenantee, in the covenantor's promissory notes,—breach, that the covenantor had not paid the plaintiff in the manner mentioned in said agreement, was *held* to be a good assignment. Dale v. Roosevelt, 9 Cow. (N. Y.) 307.

A defendant covenanted that he would pay over the first-fruits and proceeds which should be first realized, and be at his disposition under a sequestration, forthwith upon the receipt thereof, to the plaintiff. In an action upon the covenant, the declaration stated, that, although divers first-fruits and proceeds were realized, and at the defendant's disposition, yet that he had not paid them over. The court *held* this to be sufficient, and also that it was necessary to aver a receipt of them by the defendant. Smith v. Nesbitt, 2 C. B. 286; 15 L. J. C. P. 9.

Lease of a Coal Mine.—It has been *held*, that, in an action on a covenant to do no act whereby an annuity charged upon the profits of a coal mine shall be impeached, it is no ground of demurrer that the declaration does not allege that any profits have been made. Pitt v. Williams, 4 Nev. & M. 412; s. c., 2 Adol. & E. 419, 5 Adol. & E. 885.

But where A. and B., lessees of a coal mine, A. being also lessee in trust for himself and B. of land adjoining, necessary for the working of the mine, covenanted with C. that they would do nothing whereby an annuity, charged (with power of entry upon the mine, and sale, in case the annuity should be in arrear) upon the profits which, after the payment charged thereon, might be made under the leases of the mine and land by the sale of the coal or otherwise, the whole foundation of the action fails, because the contract may be impeached; and in an action on the covenant C. assigned as breaches, (1) that A. surrendered the land, and took a new lease to himself and B. jointly, in trust for other persons, whereby the annuity became and was impeached, and the plaintiff lost his remedies to enforce it; (2) that A. and B. accepted a new lease of the land at an increased rent, and in other respects upon less advantageous terms, for the fraudulent purpose of obtaining from the lessor a demise of mines under the land upon terms advantageous to A. and B., whereby the annuity became and was impeached; and (3) that A. and B. assigned such neighboring mine and the land to D., whereby the annuity became and was impeached, — it was *held* by the court that the declaration was insufficient, for not showing in what manner the acts complained of operated to impeach the annuity. Pitt *v.* Williams, 4 Nev. & M. 412; s. c., 2 Adol. & E. 419; 5 Adol. & E. 885.

Insufficient Assignment of Breach. — A declaration for breach of a covenant for quiet enjoyment is defective if it does not allege that one who recovered against the plaintiff in trespass had lawful title. Webb *v.* Alexander, 7 Wend. (N. Y.) 281; Rickert *v.* Snyder, 9 Wend. (N. Y.) 416.

Lease of Brewery. — In an action upon an indenture whereby the defendant demised to the plaintiffs, for ten years, a brewery at S., and also "the exclusive or such other privilege as the defendant then enjoyed of supplying ale" to certain public houses, "then the property of the defendant or then under his control, that is to say, the Punch Bowl," the declaration averred, that, at the time of making the indenture, the defendant was the landlord and owner of the Punch Bowl, and in the occupation thereof, and that afterwards he demised it to G., who covenanted with the defendant to purchase all the ale consumed on the premises from the plaintiff. The breach assigned was that G., during his tenancy of the Punch Bowl, did not purchase all the ale from the plaintiff, but purchased it from the defendant and others. The court *held* that this breach was not well assigned, and also that the declaration should have shown what privilege the defendant possessed. Hinde *v.* Gray, 1 Man. & G. 195; s. c., 1 Scott N. R. 123, 4 Jur. 392.

Covenant to manufacture Clocks. — Where the plaintiff, in an action of covenant commenced in 1835, averred that the defendants, in 1818, covenanted with him to manufacture certain materials into clocks, and make and finish them as fast as they could be made, by faithfully employing, constantly, ten workmen, until two thousand were completed; and that, as fast as such clocks should be made and completed, one-half of the first three hundred should be delivered to the plaintiff at the shop where they were made, in E., and that three-fourths of the remainder should be delivered to the plaintiff, as aforesaid, until the clocks delivered to him should amount to a certain sum, — the breach assigned was, that the defendants neglected and refused to perform said covenant on their part, and never delivered said clocks, or any part thereof, although they were often demanded; that the defendants manufactured the materials in clocks and privily and clandestinely conveyed them away out of the State, to places unknown, deceitfully substituting in their place boxes filled with stones and rubbish; and that the defendants conveyed away all their property, and secreted said materials, and defrauded the plaintiff of said clocks; without averring that a reasonable time had elapsed for the making of the three hundred clocks, or that the defendants, having made them, refused or neglected to deliver the one-half, or that the defendants neglected to employ the stipulated number of workmen. It was *held* by the court that no breach was well assigned, and that the declaration was ill on demurrer. Newell *v.* Roberts, 13 Conn. 427.

Covenant to save Harmless. — In a declaration on a covenant to "save harmless and keep indemnified W., his heirs and assigns, and also certain closes, etc., from and against all actions, suits, claims, and demands whatsoever, both in law and equity, which should or might be had, made, commenced, or prosecuted by any person or persons claiming any right, title, or demand in, to, or upon the closes, as heir-at-law of H. P. and others, of and from all costs, charges, and expenses which W. should sustain or be put to, for or by reason or means of such actions, suits, claims, or demands, or otherwise howsoever:" to which the breaches assigned were, (1) that P. made claim and demand, and claimed to have right and title of, in, to, and upon the closes, and entered into and upon the same, and cut down grass, and felled trees there growing, and converted them to his own use; and (2) that he caused and procured, and suffered and permitted, one B., who then held and enjoyed the closes, to attorn to him, and withhold the payment of the rents, issues, and profits; and (3) that certain title deeds relating to closes were kept, detained, and withholden by one A., at the instance and through the means and by and through the claim and demand of T. R., W. P., etc., — it was *held*, entire in its nature, must be proved as laid.[1] Where the ict is in the alternative, it must be stated in the declaration, ling to its terms, or there will be a fatal variance.[2] And

e defendant had pleaded over, that reaches were well assigned on the it declared upon. Fowle v. Welsh, . & R. 133; s. c., 1 Barn. & Cress. d see Nash v. Palmer, 5 Moule &

claration stated, that, by deed, the nt covenanted that he would appear fice for the insurance of lives within , and answer such questions as might l respecting his age, etc., in order to the plaintiff to insure his life, and not afterwards do, or permit to be y act whereby such insurance should ded or prejudiced. It alleged that ndant, in part performance of his it, did, at the plaintiff's request, at the office of the Rock Life In- Company, and did answer certain ns asked of him; and that the l insured the defendant's life with mpany, by a policy containing a , that, if the defendant went beyond its of Europe, the policy should be d void. The breach assigned was, defendant went beyond the limits pe, to wit, to the province of Canada, th America. The declaration was be bad, for not averring that the nt had notice that the policy was . Vyse v. Wakefield, 6 Mees. & ; s. c., 8 Dow. P. C. 377; 4 Jur. ffirmed in error, 7 Mees. & W. 126; Dow. P. C. 912; 4 Jur. 611. Obert v. Whitehead, 11 N. J. L. L.) 294; Wheelwright v. Moore, 1 . Y.) 201; Snell v. Moses, 1 Johns.) 105; Perry v. Aaron, 1 Johns. 133; Allaire v. Ouland, 2 Johns. . Y.) 55; Pool v. Court, 4 Taunt. ristow v. Wright, Doug. 640; Gwin- Phillips, 3 T. R. 646; 1 Chitt. Pl. d n. 19; Phillips, Ev. (Dunl. ed.) t, and n. a.

ntracts in the Alternative. — Thus, a contract to transport fifteen or tons of marble from one place to , was stated as an absolute contract, iance was held to be fatal. See . Knowlton, 3 Wend. (N. Y.) 374; Wellings, 3 T. R. 531.

where the contract for the delivery hundred bags of wheat, forty or fifty elivered at a particular time, at the of the defendant, and the defendant to deliver forty, was declared on as ract for the absolute delivery of ags, the variance was held to be Penny v. Porter, 2 East, 2.

re the declaration alleges a consid- for the contract in addition to the true considerations moving thereto, not supported by the proof, it will be a fatal variance. See New Hampshire Fire Ins. Co. v. Hunt, 10 Fost. (N. H.) 219; Stone v. Knowlton, 3 Wend. (N. Y.) 374.

Variance. — A declaration in an action on a covenant for the assignment of a share in stock professed to set out the covenant, and described it as a covenant to assign a certain sum of £2,000. The defendant set out the deed, and demurred, as for a variance, that the covenant was to assign stock, not money; but the court held that it was no variance. Ross v. Parker, 2 Dowl. & R. 662; s. c., 1 Barn. & Cress. 358.

Where a declaration alleged that the defendant covenanted that he, and all persons claiming under him, would, upon request, and at the expense of the defendant, execute such further assurance as might be required, it appeared by the deed, when produced, that the covenant was, that the defendant "would, upon the request, and at the expense, of the defendant, execute," etc. This was held a variance. Whyte v. Burnby, 16 L. J. Q. B. 156.

A declaration on a lease which stated that the plaintiffs derived their titles from two lessors only, and that two other lessors, who were also parties to the demise, had no interest therein, was supported by the production of the lease, which appeared to be a demise by the four. Wood v. Day, 1 J. B. Moore, 389; s. c., 7 Taunt. 646.

In an action against a mortgagor, a statement that the defendant bound himself, his heirs, executors, etc., is no variance, though the word "heirs" was not mentioned in the covenants. Swallow v. Beaumont, 1 Chit. 518 and n.; Hamborough v. Wilkie, 4 Maule & S. 474, n.

In an action on a lease for not repairing, the instrument was described in the declaration to be made by the plaintiff of the one part and the defendant of the other. On the production of the lease, it appeared to have been made by plaintiff and his wife of the one part and the defendant of the other. The court *held* that this was no variance, although the premises demised were the property of the wife before marriage. Arnould v. Revoult, 4 J. B. Moore, 66; s. c., 1 Brod. & B. 443.

Clerical Misprison. — In an action of covenant, the plaintiff set out a covenant by the defendant to deliver among other things "seventy-five head of stock hogs, also twenty-five head of cattle," and, in assigning a breach, averred the failure to deliver "the said seventy-five head of cat-

where the covenant is general, with an exception, the declaration must set out the exception.[1]

In an action of covenant, each assignment of breach may be regarded as a separate declaration, and may be severally traversed.[2]

In a declaration upon a covenant for general performance of duty, if no breach be assigned, or a breach which is bad, as not being, in point of law, within the scope of the covenant, the defect is fatal even after verdict.[3]

It is held in England that a covenant running with the land, though broken in the lifetime of a testator, is a continuing breach in the time of his devisee, and that it is sufficient for such devisee to allege, in an action of covenant for damages for the breach, that the lands are thereby rendered of less value to the devisee, and that he is prevented from selling them so advantageously.[4] But in New York and Massachusetts, in respect to those covenants that run with the land, it has been held that if the grantor be not seised at the time of conveyance, the covenant of seisin is immedi-

tle," it was *held* that the breach referred to the last clause of the covenant, and that the variance was a mere clerical misprison, and not a material error. Sorell v. Sorell, 5 Ala. 576.

Covenant to Repair. — By deed it was covenanted that the defendant should obtain a license from the lord of the manor, and should grant a license to the plaintiff, and that such lease should contain a covenant that the defendant would, during the term, repair the premises demised, and that, till such license was obtained and such lease granted, the plaintiff should hold the premises as tenant from year to year, subject to the terms and conditions specified. In an action upon the deed, the plaintiff, in his declaration, set out the covenant that the defendant should obtain the license and grant the lease, and the proposed covenant to repair, and alleged that the parties further covenanted that, till the license should be obtained and the lease granted, the plaintiff should be considered as tenant from year to year, and that, whilst the plaintiff should be possessed of the premises as tenant from year to year, under the provisions of the deed, the defendant should repair the premises. This was *held* no variance. Price v. Birch, 4 Man. & G. 1; s. c., 1 Dowl. N. S. 720.

1. **Exceptions in Covenants.** — In an action for not repairing, if the covenant to repair contains an exception of "casualties by fire," it is fatal on *non est factum* to state it in the declaration as a general covenant to repair, omitting the exception. Brown v. Knill, 5 Moore, 164; s. c., 2 B. & B. 395.

But where there was a provision in the contract that any disagreement as to its construction, and also the sufficiency of the certificates of title, should be submitted to and determined by, D. & E., it was held that such provision need not be named in the declaration. Williams v. Healey, 3 Den. (N. Y.) 362.

2. **Separate Declarations.** where non-payment of rent, keep in repair, were assigned as breaches of the covenants of a lease. Burroughs v. Clancey, 53 Ill. 30.

3. Minor v. Mechanics' Bank, 26 U. S. (1 Pet.) 46, 67; bk. 7, L. ed. 47.

Contract to divide Money pending Suit. — The complainant and respondent in a suit in chancery entered into a mutual covenant, that, pending the suit, they would divide the money in controversy between them, in certain proportions, and that if in the suit it should be decreed that these were not the correct proportions, they would respectively pay the difference so as to conform to the decree. The result of the suit, however, was the dismissal of the complainant's bill with costs. The respondent then brought an action on the covenant, reciting it, and averring that, by virtue of the decree of dismissal, he was entitled to receive a certain sum of money; but he did not aver that the rights of the parties had been judicially determined by the decree. The court *held* that the declaration was defective, and that the defect was not cured by a verdict for the plaintiff. McDonald v. Hobson, 48 U. S. (7 How.) 745; bk. 12, L. ed. 897.

4. Kingdon v. Nottle, 4 Maule & S. 53. See also Kingdon v. Nottle, 1 Maule & S. 355; Chamberlain v. Williamson, 2 Maule & S. 408; King v. Jones, 5 Taunt. 418; s. c., 1 Marshall's Rep. 107.

broken; and no action can be brought by the assignee of ntee against the grantor, because, after the covenant is it becomes a *chose in action*, and is incapable of assign-

viction, etc.: Notice. — In an action on a covenant of gen- ranty, the grantee must assign as a breach an ouster or by a paramount legal title.[3]

ord v. Page, 2 Mass. 455; Green- ocks, 2 Johns. (N. Y.) 1; s. c., 3 379.
owell v. Hunter, Dudley (Ga.). n v. Wiset, 1 Mass 464; s. c., 2 34; Marston v. Hobbs, 2 Mass. 3 Am. Dec. 61; Bearce v. Jack- s. 408; Kellog v. Platt, 33 N. J.) 328; Greenby v. Wilcocks, 2 . Y.) 1; s. c., 3 Am. Dec. 379; Velch, 7 Johns. (N. Y.) 258; s. Dec. 286; Sedgwick v. Hollen- bins. (N. Y.) 376; Vanderkarr v. r, 11 Johns. (N. Y.) 122; Rick- ler, 9 Wend. (N. Y.) 416; Day v. U. S. (10 Wheat.) 449; bk. 6, L.

on of Eviction. — Where it was a declaration upon a covenant, said O. had not a good and suffi- to the said tract of land, and by reof the said plaintiffs were d dispossessed of the said prem- e course of law," it was held s a substantial averment of an title paramount. Day v. Chism, (10 Wheat.) 449; bk. 6, L. ed.

n, in a suit for breach of a war- le, the premises are in the actual of a third person under para- c, it is not necessary to allege ctual eviction. Sheffey v. Gardi- . 313.

ion on Covenant of Warranty. — ration of warranty, while it is to allege substantially an eviction ramount, no formal terms are in which the averment is to be y v. Chism, 23 U. S. (10 Wheat.) . L. ed. 363; Kellog v. Platt, 33 Vr.) 328.

ases where an eviction must be is *held* to be necessary to aver viction was had under a lawful ng before or at the date of the he plaintiff; and an averment of e without this qualification is after verdict. Grannis v. Clark, N. Y.) 36; Wotton v. Hele, 2 1 a, note 10; Nokes' Case, 4 Co. esolution.

necessary to state all the facts g an eviction. Rickert v. Sny- end. (N. Y.) 416. It is sufficient to allege substantially on eviction by title paramount, — Day v. Chism, 23 U. S. (10 Wheat.) 449; bk. 6, L. ed. 363, — or to aver generally that the grantee was evicted by lawful right and title of a third person, — Townsend v. Murris, 6 Cow. (N. Y.) 123, — and an averment of "ouster by due course of law" is sufficient. Day v. Chism, 23 U. S. (10 Wheat.) 449; bk. 6, L. ed. 363. It is not necessary to allege the eviction to be by legal process. Wotton v. Hole, 2 Saund. 181 a, note; Foster v. Pierson, 4 T. R. 617, 620.

Declaration on Covenant for Quiet Enjoy- ment. — Where the covenant is that the grantee shall enjoy, without the interrup- tion of the grantor himself, his heirs, or executors, it is *held* to be a sufficient breach to allege that he or his heirs or executors entered, without showing it to be a lawful entry, or setting forth his title to enter. Lloyd v. Tomkies, 1 T. R. 671, and cases cited; Sedgwick v. Hollenback, 7 Johns. (N. Y.) 376; Wotton v. Hele, 2 Saund. 181, note.

An averment that an assignment and patent was a prior conveyance, which was still in full force and virtue, "by reason of which said patent and incumbrance the said plaintiff had been prevented from having and enjoying all or any part of the prem- ises," is, upon general demurrer, a sufficient averment that possession was legally with- held from the plaintiff under such prior title by the parties in possession. Duvall v. Craig, 15 U. S. (2 Wheat.) 45; bk. 4, L. ed. 180.

Averring Abandonment. — In an action of covenant upon a warranty, it is neces- nary for the plaintiff to aver, if not an eviction, that he had abandoned the pos- session of the land after it had been found subject to the execution, or that the land had been sold by virtue of the execution, and that he had been deprived of his pos- session thereof, or he will be non-suited. McDowell v. Hunter, Dudley (Ga.), 4.

Averring Title in Third Person at Time of Conveyance. — In an action of covenant upon a general warranty, the averment that the lawful freehold and possession in the land was, when the deed was exe- cuted, and still continued to be, in a third person, by reason whereof the grantee is and always has been unable to recover the

If the declaration be defective in this respect, the defect is not fatal on general demurrer if the matter of fact averred in substance show an eviction tantamount to a breach of the covenant relied on.[1] But where the covenant is broken immediately, no eviction need be averred in the declaration or proven on the trial.[2]

Where a grantee has been evicted under a judgment in ejectment between strangers to the grantor, the plaintiff must set out in his declaration that the grantor had notice of such action, or the breach will not be sufficiently assigned.[3]

Where the grantor is not a party to an ejectment suit, and not notified, he can set up against the grantee a valid defence, which the grantee could have had against the eviction.[4]

The covenant for quiet enjoyment is not broken unless some particular act is shown by which the plaintiff is interrupted; and therefore it is necessary to set forth in the declaration the breach assigned and an actual eviction or disturbance of the possession of the grantee.[5] Where the eviction or disturbance is by a

possession, shows a sufficient breach of the covenant, and is equivalent to the assertion of the legal ouster. Banks v. Whitehead, 7 Ala. 83

In an action for breach of a covenant of warranty, the complaint must show that the title to which possession was surrendered was paramount. Wilson v. Peelle, 78 Ind. 384.

Averring ˚ale and Judgment. — In covenant on general warranty, the declaration averred that, at the time of the grant, there existed a judgment against the grantor, by virtue of which the premises were sold on execution, subsequently to the grant, and purchased by the grantor and others, as partners, in the name of a trustee, and that afterwards, by an action of ejectment, in the name of trustee, the covenantee was evicted, was *held*, on demurrer, to contain a good assignment of a breach. Smith v. McCampbell, 1 Blackf. (Ind.) 100.

Averring Partition under Paramount Title. — Where, in an action for breach of covenant of title, the declaration alleged in it that parties claiming one undivided third part of the land by a superior title had recovered judgment in partition against the plaintiffs, it was *held* to aver an eviction. Wright v. Nipple, 92 Ind. 310.

Averring Eviction on Mortgage Foreclosure. — On a foreclosure the defendant set up the arrest of some of his servants on a part of the premises, their bail, and transfer of the suit to the county circuit. The court *held* no proper allegation of eviction or proper proof of a suit pending. Price v. Lawton, 27 N. J. Eq. (12 C. E. Gr.) 325.

Independent Covenants. — Where the parties to a deed covenanted severally against their own acts and incumbrances, but also to warrant and defend against their own acts and those of all other persons, with an indemnity in lands of an equivalent value in case of eviction, it was *held* that these covenants were independent, and that it was unnecessary to allege in the declaration any eviction, or any demand or refusal to indemnify with other lands, but that it was sufficient to allege a prior incumbrance by the acts of the grantors, etc., and that the action might be sustained on the first covenant, in order to recover pecuniary damages. Duvall v. Craig, 5 U. S. (2 Wheat.) 45; bk. 4, L. ed. [illegible]

1. Kellog v. Platt, 33 N. J. L. [illegible]

2. Grannis v. Clark, 8 Cow. (N. Y.) [illegible]; Quackenboss v. Lansing, 6 Johns. (N. Y.) 50.

3. **Notice to Covenantor.** — In an action for breach of covenant of warranty in a deed, plaintiff cannot rest upon proof of his eviction, under judgment in ejectment between strangers to the covenantor, of which action the covenantor had no notice. Hines v. Estate of Jenkins (Mich.), 7 West. Rep. 795.

The notice to be given to a covenantor of warranty to appear and defend in any action involving the validity of the title he has conveyed, must be in writing, though notice may perhaps be waived by attendance and action without objection. [illegible] v. Kellogg, 38 Mich. 132.

4. Walton v. Cox, 67 Ind. [illegible]

5. Waldron v. McCarty, 3 Johns. (N. Y.) 471; Kortz v. Carpenter, 5 Johns. (N. Y.) 120; Francis' Case, 8 Co. 91 a; Wotton v. Hele, 2 Saund. 181 a, note. [illegible] Comyn's R. 228.

stranger, it is further necessary to allege that the eviction was by a lawful title.[1]

An action may be supported upon a covenant of seisin, although the plaintiff has never been evicted, and the declaration need not aver an eviction.[2]

In an action for the breach of a covenant of seisin, an averment, that a stranger was seised of three undivided seventh parts of the premises, is a good assignment of a breach.[3]

It is not necessary to allege an ouster or eviction, on the breach of a covenant against incumbrances, but only necessary to allege the special incumbrance as a good and subsisting one.[4]

And an averment of an eviction under an elder title is not always necessary to sustain an action on a covenant against incumbrances: if the grantee be unable to obtain possession or seisin by a person claiming and holding under an elder title, it is equivalent to an eviction, and is a breach of the covenant.[5]

f. Requisites and Sufficiency of Declaration: Instances. — Where, by the terms of a contract, there was to be delivered between specified places, the recipients need not to specify a particular point, nor to aver notice of such point, before the time fixed for delivery, in an action of covenant.[6]

Where the circumstances showed that a contract to accept a deed, pay money, etc., was to be performed on a certain day and in a certain place and State, a count alleging that the plaintiff was then and there ready and willing to perform his part, after setting forth what was required of him, but that the defendant was not

1. Marston v. Hobbs, 2 Mass. 433; s. c., 3 Am. Dec. 61; Greenby v. Wilcocks, 2 Johns. (N. Y.) 1; s. c., 3 Am. Dec 379; Pollard v. Wallace, 2 Johns. (N. Y.) 395; Kent v. Welch, 7 Johns. (N. Y.) 258; s. c., 5 Am. Dec. 266; Vanderkarr v. Vanderkarr, 11 Johns. (N. Y.) 122; s. c., 3 Am. Dec. 61; Hodgson v. The East Ind. Co., 8 T. R. 281; Holden v. Taylor, Hob. 12; Foster v. Pierson, 4 T. R. 617.

2. Pollard v. Dwight, 8 U. S. (4 Cr.) 421; bk. 2, L. ed. 665.

Breach without Eviction. — A covenant that one is seised of an indefeasible estate in fee, may be broken without an eviction. Bender v. Fromberger, 4 U. S. (4 Dall.) 436; bk. 1, L. ed. 898.

In New York. — But in New York, where the action is brought for breach of a covenant of seisin or against incumbrances, the cause of action is deemed to have accrued upon an eviction, and not before. N. Y. Code Civ. Proc. § 381.

3. Sedgwick v. Hollenback, 7 Johns. (N. Y.) 376.

Subsisting Mortgage. — But an averment of an outstanding mortgage and judgment, without stating a foreclosure or possession under the mortgage, is not a sufficient averment of a breach of the covenant of seisin. Sedgwick v. Hollenback, 7 Johns. (N. Y.) 376.

A deed conveyed land by the words "grant, bargain, and sell," without limiting their force by other words. The grantor, when he executed the deed, was not the owner in fee-simple. On action brought, it was *held* that the statutory covenant of seisin, expressed by the words, was instantly broken, and that the grantee need not show an eviction in suing for the breach. Benton Co. v. Rutherford, 33 Ark. 610.

4. Prescott v. Trueman, 4 Mass. 629; s. c., 3 Am. Dec. 246.

Averring Incumbrances. — An averment, that, by reason of an existing incumbrance, the covenantee has been prevented from enjoying the premises, is a sufficient allegation of breach of a covenant against incumbrances. Duvall v. Craig, 15 U. S. (2 Wheat.) 45, bk. 4, L. ed. 180.

5. Duvall v. Craig, 15 U. S. (2 Wheat.) 45, 58, bk. 4, L. ed 180.

6. Hartfield v. Patton, 1 Hempst. C. C. 268.

at the place on that day, but was absent from the State, th held the plea to be good.[1]

In covenant upon an obligation to pay to the plaintiff [illegible] upon a particular day, it is not necessary to aver a special d[illegible] The debtor is bound to pay at the day, or to be ready to [illegible] such place as the law would designate as the place of paym[illegible]

In covenant for rent against the assignee of the [illegible] plaintiff need not aver in his declaration that the lessee [illegible] paid the rent: it is sufficient if he states that the rent [illegible] after the assignment to the defendant, and that the same and owing.[2]

In an action on a covenant to allow a business to be car[illegible] in a certain shop, a breach that the defendant improperly [illegible] the shop is sufficient, without alleging that the shop w[illegible] up at unreasonable or improper times.[4]

A. covenanted to work for B. for thirteen months for a sti[illegible] compensation. He served a portion of the time, and t[illegible] parol agreement, C. was substituted in the place of A., who [illegible] B, the balance of the time. In an action of covenant [illegible] against B. for his wages, the court held that he could not [illegible] and prove by parol, that C.'s services were substituted in [illegible] his own.[5]

Where a certain amount of work is to be completed by a [illegible] time, and to be paid for in instalments as the work progre[illegible] action in covenant to recover the whole consideration mon[illegible] not be maintained without averring and proving a perform[illegible] the whole work; and where an action is brought for a ratal[illegible] of the money, the complaint must aver, and the proof [illegible] ratable performance.[6]

g. Time; Consideration; Performance; Tender. — [illegible] declare, in an action for the breach of a covenant, that [illegible] was indented, made, and concluded on a day subsequent to [illegible] on which the deed itself is stated on the face of it to ha[illegible] indented, made, and concluded.[7] And where the covenan[illegible]

1. Kern v. Zeigler, 13 W. Va. 707.

2. Hughes v. Sloan, 8 Ark. (3 Eng.) 146.

Defective Writ. — But a writ "to answer unto J. H. that he render to him $2,000, which to him he owes upon covenant," is defective; it is neither in debt nor covenant, and has no style of action. Brown, Adm'r, v. Hoy, 16 N. J. L. (1 Harr.) 157.

3. Dubois v. Van Orden, 6 Johns. (N. Y.) 105.

Averment for Non-payment of Rent. — In an action against the assignee, it is not necessary to aver non-payment by the lessee. Van Rensselaer v. Bradley, 3 Den. N. Y. 135; s. c., 45 Am. Dec. 451.

An averment that a certain amount of rent, for a particular time, [illegible] of the premises of which [illegible] was assignee, had accrued and [illegible] and was in arrear, was held [illegible] otherwise of a count [illegible] tain sum was due for the [illegible] premises. Van Rensselaer [illegible] 3 Den. (N. Y.) 135; s. c., 45 [illegible] 451.

4. Hodges v. Gray, [illegible]

5. McClanahan v. [illegible] (Tenn.) 120.

6. Cunningham v. [illegible] (N. Y.) 203; s. c., 6 Am. Dec. [illegible]

7. Hall v. Cazenove, [illegible] 1 Smith, 272. And see [illegible] Palmerston, 1 Mood. & [illegible] & P. 474.

it a particular time and place, a declaration averring a coveto pay at the particular time is good.[1]

eat accuracy is required in the allegation of the consideraof the deed, because, if there be error in describing it, the contract will be misdescribed.[2] Where the consideration is red to be set out, the whole consideration must be stated; if part of an entire consideration, or of a consideration consist- f several things, be omitted, there will be a fatal variance.[3] where no consideration is stated in the declarations, or where onsideration stated is clearly insufficient or illegal, it will be y defective on demurrer.[4]

e consideration set out in the declaration must be proved to xtent alleged.[5]

ovenant to pay at Particular Time ace. — A declaration stated that the ant covenanted to pay a certain sum ey at a certain time. Upon oyer, venant appeared to be to pay the at that time, and also at a particular The defendant demurred, and assthe variance as a cause of demurrer. urt held that there was no material . Paine v. Emery, 4 Dowl. P. C. c., 1 Gale, 266; 5 Tyr. 1097; 2 C. & 304.

ee Cooley v. Dean, 4 Conn. 178; ick v. Seeley, 6 Conn. 178. Russell ith Britain Society, 9 Conn. 508; r. Collins, 2 Bibb (Ky.), 429; Ben- Manning, 2 N. H 289; Lansing v. lip, 3 Cai. (N. Y.) 286; De Forest ry, 6 Cow. (N. Y.) 151; Stone v. ton, 3 Wend. (N. Y.) 374; Brooks ric, 1 Nott and McC. (S. C.) 342.

utory and Executed Consideration. , where the consideration alleged utory, and that which is proved is d, the mis-description is fatal, d and executory considerations in their nature materially distinct. v. Landon, 3 Conn. 76; Robertson h, 18 Johns. (N. Y.) 451.

ance, What is. — And where a decla- alleged a deed to have been made for rations therein mentioned, and the self contained only one (a pecuniary ration), it was held no variance. Gully er, 12 Moore, 591; s. c., 4 Bing. 290. eclaration stated that by an inden- was witnessed that, as well in con- ion of certain furnaces to be erected plaintiff, B. did demise. The de- t pleaded non est factum. On pro- the deed, it appeared to be that, in consideration of the erection of naces, "as also for building certain , and payment of rent, B. did de- and this was held to be a variance. w v. Beaumont, 2 Barn. & A. 765; Chitt. 518.

3. Pennsylvania, Delaware and Maryland Nav. Co. v. Dandridge, 8 Gill & J. (Md.) 248; Woods v. Rice, 46 Mass. (4 Metc.) 481; Badger v. Burleigh, 13 N. H. 507; Brooks v. Lowrie, 1 Nott & McC (S. C.) 342. See Morrison v. Ives, 13 Miss. (4 Smed. & M.) 652; Livingstone v. Rogers, 1 Cai. (N. Y.) 583; Briggs v. Tillotson, 8 Johns. (N. Y.) 235; Tucker v. Woods, 11 Johns. (N. Y.) 190; Porter v. Rose, 12 Johns. (N. Y.) 209; Clarke v. Gray, 6 East, 568; Miles v. Sheward, 8 East, 7; Leeds v. Burrows, 12 East, 1; Andrews v. Whitehead, 13 East, 102; King v. Robinson, Cro. Eliz. 79; Bull. N. P. 147.

Warranty of Horse. — Thus, where the declaration on a warranty of a horse stated the transaction as upon a single horse, and upon evidence it appeared that two horses had been sold at an entire price and with a joint warranty, the variance was held fatal, the purchase of the two horses constituting the consideration for the warranty. Symonds v. Carr, 1 Campb. 361.

4. Dalmer v. Barnard, 7 T. R. 248; Dartnall v. Howard, 4 Barn. & Cres. 345; s. c., 6 Dow. & R. 438.

Defective Declaration. — And when the mode in which the consideration is stated is defective or informal, the declaration will be bad on special demurrer. Jones v. Ashburnham, 4 East, 455; Andrews v. Whitehead, 13 East, 102.

But after verdict a defective statement will be aided, — Shaw v. Redmond, 11 Serg. & R. (Pa.) 27, — provided it sufficiently appears, from a reasonable construction of the whole instrument, that there was a consideration capable of supporting the promise. Ward v. Harris, 2 Bos. & P. 265; Marshall v. Birkenshaw, 1 New. Rep. (4 Bos. & P.) 172; Jones v. Ashburnham, 4 East, 464; Whitehead v. Greetham, 2 Bing. 464; s. c., McClel. & Y. 205.

5. Proof of Declaration. — In general, when the consideration proved falls short of that which is stated in the declaration

In alleging a breach of covenant against incumbrances, the complaint is sufficient on demurrer, if the facts alleged show an actual incumbrance on the property at the date of the deed.[1]

In covenant upon a bond for the conveyance of land, it is not necessary to aver or prove a consideration.[2] But a state of demand for not doing repairs should show how the defendant is liable.[3]

Where two acts are to be done by the parties at the same time, the complaint must show performance, or offer to perform, on part of the plaintiff, or it will be bad.[4]

Where the mutual covenants go to the whole consideration on both sides, they are mutual conditions, and performance must be averred.[5]

If the defendant has given notice of his abandonment of the contract, the plaintiff may set forth such notice, without any averment of a readiness to perform on his part.[6]

Where it is necessary, on the part of the plaintiff, to aver performance, it must be set forth with such certainty as to enable the court to judge whether the intent of the covenant has been fulfilled.[7]

as the foundation for the promise, the variance will be fatal: the same is true when the proof exceeds the statement. Stone *v.* Knowlton, 3 Wend. (N. Y.) 374.

1. Sheets *v.* Longlois, 69 Ind. 491.

2. Buckmaster *v.* Grundy, 2 Ill. (1 Scam.) 310.

3. Stretch *v.* Forsyth, 3 N. J. L. (2 Penn.) 713.

4. Williams *v.* Healey, 3 Den. (N. Y.) 363; Gazley *v.* Price, 16 Johns. (N. Y.) 267; Dunham *v.* Pettee, 8 N. Y. 508; Lester *v.* Jewett, 11 N. Y. 453; Campbell *v.* Gittings, 19 Ohio, 347; Tilghman *v.* Tilghman, 1 Bald. C. C. 464; Bank of Columbia *v.* Hagner, 26 U. S. (1 Pet.) 455; bk. 7, L. ed. 219; Hyde *v.* Booraem, 41 U. S. (16 Pet.) 169; bk. 10, L. ed. 925; Slater *v.* Emerson, 60 U. S. (19 How.) 224; bk. 15, L. ed. 626; Washington *v.* Ogden, 66 U. S. (1 Black) 450; bk. 17, L. ed. 203. See also Leonard *v.* Bates, 1 Blackf. (Ind.) 172, note; Kane *v.* Hood, 13 Pick. (Mass.) 281; Champion *v.* White, 5 Cow. (N. Y.) 509; Northrup *v.* Northrup, 6 Cow. (N. Y.) 296; Robb *v.* Montgomery, 20 Johns. (N. Y.) 15; Slocum *v.* Despard, 8 Wend. (N. Y.) 615; Halloway *v.* Davis, Wright (Ohio), 129; Adams *v.* Williams, 2 Watts & S. (Pa.) 227; Buckingham *v.* Jackson, 4 Biss. C. C. 295; Boody *v.* Rutland & B. R. R. Co., 3 Blatchf. C. C. 25; s. c., 24 Vt. 660; Thompson *v.* Cincinnati, W. & Z. Ry. Co., 1 Bond, C. C. 152; McNamara *v.* Gaylord, 1 Bond, C. C. 302; Langdon *v.* Purdy, 1 McA. C. C. 23; Hitchcock *v.* Galveston, 2 Wood, C. C. 272; Philadelphia, W. & B. R. R. Co. *v.* Howard, 54 U. S. (13 How.) 307; bk. 14, L. ed. [illegible]; The Florida Ry. Co. *v.* Smith, [illegible] U. S. ([illegible] Wall.) 255; bk. 22, L. ed. [illegible]; [illegible] *v.* Hough, 91 U. S. (1 Otto) [illegible]; bk. [illegible], L. ed. 332.

5. Dakin *v.* Williams, 11 Wend. (N. Y.) 67; St. Albans *v.* Shore, 1 H. [illegible]; Graves *v.* Legg, 9 Exch. 709; s. c., [illegible] Eng. L. & Eq. 552; Grey *v.* Friar, 4 H. L. Cas. 565; s. c., 26 Eng. L. & Eq. 27.

Performance: How averred. — The performance must always be averred [illegible] to the interest of the parties. Washington *v.* Ogden, 66 U. S. (1 Black) 450; bk. 17, L. ed. 203.

It is not sufficient to pursue the words, if performance according to the intent be not alleged. Washington *v.* Ogden, 66 U. S. (1 Black) 450; bk. 17, L. ed. 203.

6. North *v.* Pepper, 21 Wend. (N. Y.) [illegible].

7. Thomas *v.* Van Ness, 4 Wend. (N. Y.) 549.

What should be averred: [illegible]. — The plaintiff must allege the performance on his part, or readiness to perform, or excuse for non-performance [illegible] condition precedent (if any there be) [illegible] place within the time required. [illegible] McLaugherty, 4 Mo. 221. Thus, [illegible] tion for the breach of a covenant [illegible] land on the payment of a [illegible] certain time, the plaintiff must [illegible] prove payment of such sum at [illegible] if at some subsequent day, he must [illegible] and prove also the payment of [illegible] such sum from the day of [illegible]; Hunter *v.* Miller, 6 B. Mon. (Ky.) [illegible].

Where the covenants in an agreement are dependent or concurrent, the plaintiff must aver and prove performance, or an offer to perform, on his part.[1]

It is not always sufficient to aver performance in the words of the contract; the terms of the contract must be shown to have been performed; and where the words do not clearly and unequivocally import, in terms that which they might import in judgment of law, their legal import constitutes the contract that must be averred to have been done. Thomas *v.* Van Horn, 4 Wend. (N. Y.) 549.

In covenant for not conveying a lot of ground, which the covenantor had agreed to convey when the covenantee paid a certain note, the plaintiff must aver an offer of payment and demand of a deed. Sage *v.* Ranney, 2 Wend. (N. Y.) 532; William *v.* Healey, 3 Den. (N. Y.) 363.

In covenant on an agreement to sell lands, the vendor, in averring performance, must set forth the nature of the conveyance executed by him. Thomas *v.* Van Horn, 4 Wend. (N. Y.) 549.

To sustain an action against a vendee for not accepting the property sold, the plaintiff must aver his readiness and offer to perform, on the day fixed by the contract. Bank of Columbia *v.* Hagner, 26 U. S. (1 Pet.) 455; bk. 7, L. ed. 219.

In covenant on an executory contract, the plaintiff must aver performance on his part of any covenant necessary to be performed, in order to entitle him to performance by the defendant. Hunter *v.* Miller, 6 B. Mon. (Ky.) 612.

A declaration in covenant against an administrator, which barely avers a non-performance by the intestate, is insufficient, as he may have died before the time for performance: it must aver facts showing a breach of covenant by the testator. Warfield *v.* Hudson, 4 Dana (Ky.), 73.

A declaration against the assignee of the reversion, founded on a covenant of the lessor to repair during the term, must aver that such repairs were not done before the conveyance to the defendant: the allegation of such fact by way of *protestando* is not sufficient. Gerselbek *v.* Lord, 33 N. J. L. (4 Vr.) 240.

Where, by an article of agreement, part of the price of the erection of certain houses was "to be paid out of the rents of said houses quarterly, the whole amount to be applied to that purpose," and the houses were burned down soon after they were completed and rented, in covenant to recover that part of the price, the plaintiff should allege and prove that the defendant had received rents from the houses, or should, on account of default or negligence, be charged as if he had received the same. Chambers *v.* Jaynes, 4 Pa. St. 39.

In an action of covenant by A. against B., the declaration set forth a covenant whereby A., a carpenter, undertook the carpenter's work of a wooden house for B. at certain specified prices per piece, the whole to be done in a workmanlike manner, and defendant contracted to furnish the materials as they should be wanted. It was alleged that the plaintiff entered upon and executed a great part of the work, and then the breaches were alleged that B. did not furnish materials, and that, in consequence of B.'s own negligence, after A. had erected the house, and executed a large portion of the work, the house was blown down by a tempest, and the defendant refused to pay the plaintiff for the work he had done. On general demurrer it was *held* that the declaration was good. Clark *v.* Franklin, 7 Leigh (Va.), 1.

It is necessary that the plaintiff should allege that he had title to the premises agreed to be conveyed; if such defence exists, it must be shown by plea. North *v.* Pepper, 21 Wend. (N. Y.) 636.

What need not be alleged. — Where, on the dissolution of a firm, one of the parties covenanted to pay all the firm debts, in an action against him by the other partner, who had been compelled to pay a debt of the firm, it is not necessary to aver notice to the defendant of the debt, nor of the suit, recovery, and payment. Clough *v.* Hoffman, 5 Wend. (N. Y.) 499.

In an action of covenant on an express contract contained in the condition of a penal bond, the declaration need not aver the non-payment of the penalty. Hughes *v.* Houlton, 5 Blackf. (Ind.) 180.

The declaration in such case, not professing to describe the contract in *hæc verba*, may set it out according to its legal effect. Hughes *v.* Houlton, 5 Blackf. (Ind.) 180.

1 Goodwin *v.* Lynn, 4 Wash. C. C. 714.

Condition Precedent. — The plaintiff must set forth precisely the performance of a condition precedent, and such circumstances as are material to raise the corresponding obligation. Glover *v.* Tuck, 24 Wend. (N. Y.) 153; s. c., 1 Hill (N. Y.), 66.

It is not sufficient to allege that the plaintiff was ready and willing to perform acts which, by the covenant itself, in a definite form, constituted a condition precedent. It is sufficient, however, to allege generally that he has performed them according to

In an action upon a dependent covenant, an averment of a readiness to perform on the part of the plaintiff is not sufficient; he must show a tender of performance.[1]

An averment of the execution of a deed, and of the plaintiff's readiness to perform, is sufficient, without alleging a tender of the deed.[2] And a plaintiff who sues upon a contract for the sale of land, whereby he covenanted to "make a deed" for the property, must aver and prove that he had a good title, and was ready and willing to convey.[3]

Where there is a covenant for the sale and purchase of a farm, the conveyance to be made, and the consideration to be paid at a future day, if previous to the day the purchaser notifies the vendor that he has concluded to abandon the contract, and not accept the deed, it is enough to support an action of covenant by the vendor to allege such notice; and it is not necessary to aver a tender of the deed or a readiness to perform.[4]

h. Parties. — An action of covenant must be brought in the name of the covenantee, not of the person for whose benefit it was made.[5] And it must appear in the declaration with whom

the true intent and meaning of the covenant. Kern *v.* Zeigler, 13 W. Va. 707.

1. Frey *v.* Johnson, 22 How. (N. Y.) Pr. 316.

What Declaration must show. — Where the declaration avers that the plaintiff has been ever ready to deliver defendants a deed, but there is no averment that the plaintiff had a good and sufficient title, free from incumbrance, it is insufficient. Washington *v.* Ogden, 66 U. S. (1 Black.) 450; bk. 17, L. ed. 203.

Dependent Covenants. — Where the covenants in a contract for the sale and purchase of land are dependent, the averment in the declaration that "the plaintiff has always been ready and willing to perform his part of the contract, at the time and in the manner set forth in such contract, as soon as the defendant performed his covenants as set forth in the contract," is not sufficient. The plaintiff must aver tender of the deed. Sanford *v.* Cloud, 17 Fla. 532, 550; Green *v.* Reynolds, 2 Johns. (N. Y.) 207, 209; Jones *v.* Gardner, 10 Johns. (N. Y.) 266; Parker *v.* Parmele, 20 Johns. (N. Y.) 130, 135; Barbee *v.* Willard, 4 McL. C. C. 356; Bank of Columbia *v.* Hagner, 26 U. S. (1 Pet.) 455; bk. 7, L. ed. 219.

By an agreement between A. and B., A. covenanted to sell to B. a certain lot of land at a certain price per acre, to have the same surveyed by C., and on a certain day to exhibit to C. a certificate of a clear title, and execute a deed. B. covenanted, at the same time, to give his bond for the purchase-money secured by a mortgage of the same and other lands, of which latter he was to exhibit a certificate of clear title. In an action of covenant by B. against A. for non-performance, it was *held* that the covenants were dependent; that the declaration must allege a tender of performance on B.'s part, and must aver that he had exhibited a certificate of title of his lands, which were to be included in the mortgage. Williams *v.* Healey, 3 Den. (N. Y.) 363.

2. North *v.* Pepper, 21 Wend. (N. Y.) 636.

3. Washington *v.* Ogden, 66 U. S. (1 Black.) 450; bk. 17, L. ed. 203.

4. North *v.* Pepper, 21 Wend. (N. Y.) 636.

5. Strohecker *v.* Grant, 16 Serg. & R. (Pa.) 237. See Seitzinger *v.* Weaver, 1 Rawle (Pa.), 377.

Who may be Parties. — In an action to recover the purchase-money of real estate, the right of the vendee, under 67 Ohio L. 116, to make any person claiming an adverse interest a party, exists only where there has been a breach of the covenants in his deed. Cincinnati *v.* Brachman, 35 Ohio St. 289.

Action in Name of Covenantee. — The party beneficially interested may use the name of the covenantee without his consent. Riley *v.* Vandyke, 1 Phila. (Pa.) 180.

But where one covenants to pay an existing debt due by another (the creditor being no party to the agreement, and the sole consideration being between the covenantor and covenantee), the action for a breach must be brought by the covenantee. The creditor cannot sue in the name of the covenantee without his authority. Mississippi Cent. R. R. Co. *v.* Southern R. R. Assoc., 4 Brewst. (Pa.) 79.

nt was made.[1] An action for the breach of a covenant
with the land can only be brought in the name of him,
ic owner at the time of the breach, not by a subsequent

er the interest of the covenantees is joint, although
nt be in terms joint and several, the action follows the
the interest, and must be brought in the name of all
ntees; and where the legal interest and cause of action
enantees is several, they may maintain separate actions
of the subject-matter, though the language be joint.[3]
here are several covenantees, or where one covenants
A. a hundred dollars, and to B. a hundred dollars, each
one on his several covenants.[4] But when several cove-
nd themselves, or some one of them, to pay a certain
oney, an action cannot be maintained against one of
5

ses. — In an action on a covenant running with the land
tion must designate the land conveyed with convenient

eirs. — Where the plaintiffs
ovenant both as heirs and
ut showing in particular how
s, and without setting out the
eld not to be fatal on general
ey v. Chism, 23 U. S. (10
bk. 46, L. ed. 363.
Where the act to be per-
gle and indivisible, non-per-
oses the offending party to
of an entire breach, and suit
t be brought by the parties
l in the performance of the
venant. Atwood v. Norton,
.) 618.
es Joint. — If there be a cove-
ersons jointly, and a breach,
he survivor may sue alone.
il, 1 Low. U. S. D. C. 416.
n on a covenant purporting
tween two persons by name,
, and a corporate company of
rt, and only one of the per-
s of the first part signed the
d the covenant ran, "between
he first part and the party
part," the person who signed
art may bring an action in
ut joining with him the other
s of the party of the first
the covenant inures to the
e who are in reality parties.
W. & B. R. R. Co. v. Howard,
low.) 307; bk. 14, L. ed. 157.
n upon a covenant contained
nt between the covenantor
uch other parties as he may
him under the name of S. &
ned and sealed by the cove-
ned "S. & Co." by the hand

of S., acting in behalf and by authority of the partnership, covenanting to pay to "the said S. & Co., parties of the second part," for work to be done by them, etc., all those who are partners at the time of the agreement may join. Seymour v. Western R. R. Co., 106 U. S. (16 Otto) 320; bk. 27, L. ed. 103; 1 Supr. Ct. Rep. 123.

1. Keatly v. McLaugherty, 4 Mo. 221.

When the action is by an assignee of the covenant, it is not necessary that he should be described as "assignee." Carter v. Denman, 23 N. J. L. (3 Zab.) 260.

2. Dailey v. Beck, Bright (Pa.), 107; s. c., 4 Clark (Pa.), 58.

3. Bardill v. School Trustees, 4 Ill. App. 94.

Who must Join. — Where the title to land, warranted by a remote grantor, becomes vested in one for life, with remainder to his children, all those entitled to the remedy must join in an action for a breach of the covenant. McClure v. Gamble, 27 Pa. St. 288.

Where the reversion of lands demised to the defendant for years is conveyed to A. and B., and the heirs of B., in trust for A. and his heirs; and A. declares singly on a covenant contained in the lease, and after setting out the above title, without averring the death of B., states himself to be "thereby seised of the reversion in his demesne as of fee," this was held bad on general demurrer. Scott v. Godwin, 1 Bos. & P. 67.

4. Farni v. Tesson, 66 U. S. (1 Black) 309; bk. 17, L. ed. 677.

5. See Montague v. Smith, 13 Mass. 405; Tileston v. Newell, 13 Mass. 406; Harrison v. Matthews, 2 Dowl. N. S. Bail. 318.

certainty.[1] In covenant for rent reserved by deed, it is sufficient to refer to the premises as "particularly described in said indenture."[2]

IX. Pleas. — 1. *Forms.* — The forms of pleas in covenant are governed by the same rules that regulate the formal parts of pleas generally.[3]

2. *General Rules.* — It is a well-established rule,[4] of ancient standing,[5] that a defendant shall, in terms, deny particular parts of the plaintiff's declaration,[6] and plead specifically every matter of defence not merely consisting of a denial of the allegations contained in the declaration.[7] It has been said that there never

1. Carter *v.* Denman, 23 N. J. L. (3 Zab). 200.

Allegations in the Alternative. — A count stating that the demised premises "or some part thereof" had come to the defendant by assignment, is bad for being in the alternative. Van Rensselaer *v.* Bradley, 3 Den. (N. Y.) 135; s. c., 45 Am. Dec. 451.

Where the declaration sets out that the defendant is assignee of "all the estate," etc., in certain premises, and the evidence shows that he is assignee of part, it is a variance. Hare *v.* Cator, Cowp. 766.

Variance. — Where a declaration in an action by the reversioner against A., the assignee of a lease for years (granting license to B., to continue a channel open through the bank of a navigable river upon conditions), imported that the grantors had the entire right and absolute possession of the channel, and full power to grant the use of it to B., and it appeared from the indenture that they were described merely as the persons who had the greatest proportion or share in the profits of the navigation, and that they, by virtue of all or any powers and authorities vesting or enabling them, granted the license to B., his executors, administrators, and assigns, it was *held* that this was a variance, as the grantor had not the privilege which the deed, as set out in the declaration, purported to grant. Portmore *v.* Burn, 3 Dowl. & R. 145; s. c., 1 Barn. & C. 694.

Where a declaration stated the consideration to be that the plaintiff would assign to the defendant a bill of exchange, and that he did assign it to the defendant, and set out a promise by the latter accordingly, and it was proved that the parties had agreed that the plaintiff should give up the bill to the defendant, the latter, however, paying over the proceeds to the plaintiff; and, in pursuance of the agreement, the plaintiff by deed assigned to the defendant the bill, and all sums of money due thereon, for the defendant's own use; and the defendant covenanted to pay the plaintiff a sum equal to any money that he should receive on account of the bill, — the court [illegible] as the declaration imported that the plaintiff had made an absolute assignment of the bill, and as the assignment [illegible] conditional only, it was a variance. [illegible] sandan *v.* Burt, 5 Barn. & Ald. 42.

Repugnance. — In covenant by B. against A., the assignment of a breach that A. did not "give" B. the ground, is bad, as being broader than the contract, which is to give the use only. And, if such breach further avers that the plaintiff was disseised and dispossessed by A., this is inconsistent with the former averment of non-compliance by A., and is bad for repugnance. [illegible] case, to support the action, the plaintiff must allege a special request [illegible] possession. Humphries *v.* [illegible] Ark. 581.

2. Van Rensselaer *v.* Bradley, 3 Den. (N. Y.) 135; s. c., 45 Am. Dec. 451.

3. 1 Chitt. Pl. 542.

Forms of Pleas. — For form of plea setting up that a bond given for the purchase money of land was procured by [illegible] also a defect in title, see [illegible] ham, 11 N. J. Eq. (6 Halst.) [illegible].

For form of plea of fraud in a sealed certificate signed by defendant as conditions of sale of land sold by the orphans' court, see Stryker *v.* Vanderbilt, 25 N. J. L. (1 Dutch.) 483. For form of demurrer to the last-mentioned plea, see Stryker *v.* Vanderbilt, 25 N. J. L. (1 Dutch.) 483.

4. 1 Chitt. Pl. 512, 513.

5. See 2 & 3 W. 4, c. 72, § 5, and Reg. Gen. Hil. T. 4 W. 4.

6. In covenant, that part of the declaration not answered by the plea is admitted. Freeman *v.* Henry, 48 Vt. 553.

7. Marine Ins. Co. of Alexandria *v.* Hodgson, 10 U. S. (6 Cr.) 206; bk. 3, L. ed. 200.

The defendant may plead any matters specially, as infancy, coverture, release, duress, gaming, and the like, which cannot be given in evidence unless pleaded. The defendant must answer all the breaches laid in the declaration; and if he plead to the whole action a plea which is good as

, strictly speaking, any plea of general issue,[1] for the plea of *est factum* only puts the deed in issue, not the breach of the ·nant, or any matters of defence,[2] and, when pleaded, simply its the breach of the covenant and every other material avert contained in the allegation, except the execution of the deed f.[3]

/here several breaches are assigned in an action of covenant, defendant may plead to a part, and demur to a part.[4]

e only, such plea is bad on demurrer. kenbridge v. Lee, 3 Bibb (Ky.), 330; hrow v. McClelland, 1 Litt. (Ky.) 1.

s to the Whole. — Where several ches are assigned, a plea to the whole ration is bad unless it contains matter h is a legal answer to all breaches. h v. Barons, 13 Barb. (N. Y.) 305.

gative Restriction. — A covenant ing a purely negative restriction is nforceable, and the objection may be d either by answer or demurrer. Norv. James, 140 Mass. 188; s. c., 1 New Rep. 327.

3 Rules Reg. Gen. Hil. T. 4 W. 4 prothat, "in debt on specialty or covethe plea of *non est factum* shall opers a denial of the execution of the deed oint of fact only; and all other des shall be specially pleaded, including ts which make the deed absolutely as well as those which make it void-But where a public body is incorted by statute, with a special power to ute a deed in a certain form, then *non ctum* simply puts in issue whether the was executed in legal form. See 1 L. Pl. 518.

an action on the covenants of a deed, nswer alleging that the deed, by the ake of the scrivener, was made to ain other land than that intended to be eyed, etc., without alleging how the ener fell into the mistake, or whether mistake was mutual, was *held* insuffi-Howell v. Caffron, 68 Ind. 196.

General Issue. — In covenant, it is no sion to a special plea that it amounts he general issue, although there is, tly speaking, no general issue in cove-Smith v. Justice, 6 Phila. (Pa.)

See McNeish v. Stewart, 7 Cow. Y.) 474; Dale v. Roosevelt, 9 Cow. Y.) 307; Goulding v. Hewitt, 2 Hill Y.) 644; Hebbard v. Deplain, 3 Hill Y.) 189; Gardner v. Gardner, 10 Johns. Y.) 47; Kane v. Sanger, 14 Johns. Y.) 89; Barney v. Keith, 6 Wend. Y.) 555; Cooper v. Watson, 10 Wend. Y.) 205.

Ohio. — But it has been held in Ohio a plea of *non est factum* is a plea to general issue in covenant, to which a notice of set-off may be appended. Granger v. Granger, 6 Ohio (Ham.), 41.

3. Thomas v. Woods, 4 Cow. (N. Y.) 173; McNeish v. Stewart, 7 Cow. (N. Y.) 474; Dale v. Roosevelt, 9 Cow. (N. Y.) 308; Gardner v. Gardner, 10 Johns. (N. Y.) 47; Kane v. Sanger, 14 Johns. (N. Y.) 89; Legg v. Robinson, 7 Wend. (N. Y.) 94; Cooper v. Watson, 10 Wend. (N. Y.) 202; Norman v. Wells, 17 Wend. (N. Y.) 136; Marine Ins. Co v. Hodgson, 10 U. S. (6 Cr.) 206; bk. 3, L. ed. 200; 1 Chitt. Pl. 428; Tidd, Pr. 593; Peake, Ev. 264, 265, 266.

4. Angell v. Kelsey, 1 Barb. (N. Y.) 16.

Mistake of Attorney. — Where a defendant, by mistake of his attorney, pleads a plea which does not cover his defence, and on trial a verdict is therefore rendered against him, the Supreme Court will not, for that reason, grant a new trial, but *semble* equity will give relief. McNeish v. Stewart, 7 Cow. (N. Y.) 474.

Demurrer. — If some of the breaches be well, and some ill, assigned, the defendant should plead to the former, and demur to the latter. Brown v. Stebbins, 4 Hill (N. Y.), 154.

When several breaches are assigned, some of which are sufficient and others not, the defendant should demur to such as are bad; and if he demur to the whole declaration, judgment must be given against him. Gill v. Stebbins, 2 Paine, C. C. 417.

The objection, in an action against heirs for a breach of their ancestor's covenant in a deed, that the declaration did not formally set out the settlement of his estate, etc., cannot first be taken at the trial, if not taken by demurrer. Eddy v. Chace, 140 Mass. 471; s. c., 1 New-Eng. Rep. 573. And where, in an action against an heir on the breach of a covenant of warranty by a deceased grantor, the declaration fails to set forth that the estate has been settled, and that the defendant has received something, a demurrer will lie. Eddy v. Chace, 140 Mass. 471; s. c., 1 New Eng. Rep. 573.

Where the plaintiffs declared in covenant both as heirs and devisees, without showing in particular how they were heirs, and without setting out the will, it was *held* not to be fatal on general demurrer. Das

3. ***Of Performance and Tender thereof.*** — ***a.*** *Omnia Perform* ***vit.*** — ***Omnia performavit*** **is a good** plea where all the covenan **are in the affirmative.**[1] **Under this plea** the burden of proof on the defendant, for it is **a well-established** rule, that, whenev the plea is in avoidance of the deed, the defendant **has the** *probandi* cast upon him.[2]

Where a specialty is assigned in the declaration, a general pl of performance is bad.[3]

v. Chism, 23 U. S. (10 Wheat.) 449; bk. 6, L. ed 363

A covenant creating a purely negative restriction is not enforceable; and the objection may be raised by demurrer, or taken by answer. Norcross *v* James, 140 Mass. 188; s. c., 1 New Eng. Rep. 327.

1. Bailey *v.* Rogers, 1 Me. 189.

Covenants performed. — In Alabama a plea of covenants performed does not admit the deed: the plaintiff is required to prove his cause of action as if no such plea had been filed. Batre *v.* Simpson, 4 Ala. 309.

In Illinois the plea of covenants performed, if not sustained, admits the plaintiff's right to recover only nominal damages. Reed *v.* Hobbs, 3 Ill. (2 Scam.) 297.

But in Pennsylvania it admits the execution of the instrument, and supersedes the necessity of other proof; however, it does not admit that the opposite party has performed his covenant. Roth *v.* Miller, 15 Serg. & R. (Pa.) 105; Neave *v.* Jenkins, 2 Yeates (Pa.), 107. But it seems that a different doctrine is held in later cases. See Zents *v.* Legnard, 70 Pa. St. 192.

In Tennessee it has been held that evidence in avoidance of a deed cannot be admitted under a plea of covenants performed. Kincaid *v.* Brittain, 5 Sneed (Tenn.), 119.

Under the plea of covenants performed, as a defence to an action of covenant on a policy under seal, the defendant cannot give evidence which goes to vacate the policy. Marine Ins. Co. *v.* Hodgson, 10 U. S. (6 Cr.) 206; bk. 3, L. ed. 200.

2. **Right to begin and reply.** — And in such cases the defendant has the right to open and close. Sott *v.* Hull, 8 Conn. 296; Norris *v.* Insurance Co. of North America, 3 Yeates (Pa.), 84; s. c., 2 Am. Dec. 360.

Evidence on Plea of Omnia Performavit. — Under the plea of "covenants performed, with leave to give any special matter he might have in evidence," the defendant may, in Pennsylvania, give evidence of any matter he might have pleaded, and which in law can protect him, and is not required to give notice of special matter unless called for. Kangler *v.* Morton, 4 Watts (Pa.), 265; Webster *v.* Warren, 2 Wash. C. C. 456; Bender *v.* Fromberger, 4 U. S. Dall.) 439; bk. 1, L. ed. 899.

Under the plea of covenants perform the defendant will not be able to avail hi self of the defence of the difficulty of p forming his covenants in excuse of n performance. Stone *v.* Dennis, 3 P (Ala.) 231.

But in no instance will a defendant allowed to excuse performance where, fore the time of performance, he disabl himself from so doing. Heard *v.* Bowe 23 Pick. (Mass.) 455; Hopkins *v.* You 11 Mass. 302. Thus, where a brewer co nanted to deliver grains from his bre house, and before the time fixed for t delivery rendered them unfit for use mixing hops with them, he was held lial on his covenant. Griffith *v.* Goodhand, Raym. 464. The same doctrine was he where a man covenanted to deliver a hor and then poisoned him. Anonymous, Ski 42. See Bacon, Abr. tit. "Covenant," I

3. Simonton *v.* Winter, 30 U. S. (5 Pe 141; bk. 8, L. ed. 35; s. c., 3 Cr. C. C.

General Issue: Allegation of Speci Breach. — If, in an action of covenant, t plaintiff assigns particular breaches, t defendant should not plead general pe formance; he should plead separately each breach. Marshall *v.* Haney, 9 G (Md.), 251.

A general plea of performance is ba on general demurrer, to a declaration covenant, assigning a particular breac the defendant must answer the breach a signed. Beach *v.* Barons, 13 Barb. (N. Y 305; Bradley *v.* Osterhoudt, 13 Johns. (Y.) 404.

Double and Inconsistent Pleas. — A pl in covenant alleging performance on t part of the defendant, and non-performan by the plaintiff, of any part of his covenan although his covenants were conditio precedent, is both double and inconsiste Witter *v.* McNeel, 4 Ill. (3 Scam.) 433.

In Pennsylvania the defendant in action of covenant may plead performan with leave to give in evidence any thi which amounts to a legal defence, and th may give in evidence any thing which might plead, or which might be a legal d fence, without giving notice to the plaint of the real defence which he intends to

Performance pleaded otherwise than in the terms of the covenant itself, is bad, even on general demurrer.[1]

Under the plea of "covenants performed," the defendant may give evidence of a tender before suit brought,[2] but not of the breach of an independent covenant.[3]

The plea of "covenants performed, *absque hoc*," puts in issue the averments in the declaration.[4]

The plea of "covenants performed" admits the execution of the instrument, but not the plaintiff's performance of his part of the agreement.[5] And a plea of covenants performed with

op. Webster v. Warren, 2 Wash. C. C. 456.

1. Scuddamore v. Stratton, 1 Bos. & P. 455.

In covenant for rent, against an assignee of the term, to entitle the defendant to an apportionment on account of an eviction from part of the demised premises, he must plead the fact specially, and not in bar of the whole action. Lansing v. Van Alstyne, 2 Wend. (N. Y.) 561.

The plaintiff, in an action of covenant, set forth, in the first count of his declaration, a covenant of the defendant to pay him, for his services, a certain sum per year, alleged a general performance, and assigned, as a breach, that there was due to him, at the end of the term, a specific sum, which the defendant refused to pay. In a second count he set forth the same covenant, averring performance to a given time, readiness to complete performance, and a dismissal by the defendant. The defendant, in one plea, pleaded that he did pay the plaintiff so long as he served. Another plea was the same, except that the plaintiff was paid so long as he faithfully served. Both these pleas concluded to the country. Two other pleas were transcripts of these, except that they concluded with a verification. The court *held* that in any event two of these pleas were bad, because the same plea could not conclude indifferently to the country or with a verification, and that all were bad, because neither answered the whole declaration. Norris v. Wolfe, 2 Spears (S. C.) 322.

Charter Party. — Thus, in covenant on a charter party, by which the owners of a brig let her to the defendant for a certain time, the hire to be paid at certain periods, under certain circumstances; and after the brig had earned a certain sum of money, she was lost by perils of the sea, and the declaration set out the covenants, and averred performance by the plaintiff, and that $2234.17 was due and unpaid; and the defendant pleaded that he had paid the plaintiff all that was due, according to the charter party; and the court instructed the jury, upon trial of the issue joined on this plea, that the plaintiff was not bound to prove his declaration, but that the burden of proof was on the defendant to maintain his plea, — the court *held* that such instruction was erroneous, the plea not meeting the allegations in the declaration, nor amounting to an admission that the brig had earned the sum demanded. Simonton v. Winter, 30 U. S. (5 Pet.) 141; bk. 8, L. ed. 75.

2. McCormick v. Crall, 6 Watts (Pa.) 207.

3. Kates v. Dougherty, 1 Phila. (Pa.) 264.

4. Wilkinson v. Turnpike Co, 6 Pa. St. 398; Martin v. Hammon, 8 Pa. St. 270.

"Covenants performed, absque hoc." — But it has been held in Pennsylvania that the plea of "covenants performed," with no *absque hoc*, to a declaration averring performance, admits the plaintiff's performance. Zents v. Legnard, 70 Pa. St. 192.

The plea of "covenants performed, *absque hoc*," admits the execution of the instrument, and only puts in issue performance on the part of the plaintiff. Farmers' and Mechanics' Turnpike Co. v. McCullough, 25 Pa. St. 303.

In covenant for purchase-money, the plea of "covenant performed, *absque hoc*," does not put the plaintiff's title in issue. Hite v. Kier, 38 Pa. St. 72.

5. Roth v. Miller, 15 Serg. & R. (Pa.) 105; Neave v. Jenkins, 2 Yeates (Pa.), 107. *Compare* Zents v. Legnard, 70 Pa. St. 192.

Admission of Title. — In covenant by vendor against vendee, where the declaration contains a general averment of performance, the plea of "covenants performed" admits that the title to the land for which a deed was tendered was good. Martin v. Hammon, 8 Pa. St. 270.

Negative Pregnant. — Where the defendant covenants, in case of the breach of another covenant, to pay a certain sum as liquidated damages, under the plea of "covenants performed," the plaintiff must prove a breach of the prior covenant; in such case the affirmative plea is pregnant with a negative. Stewart v. Bedell, 79 Pa. St. 336.

leave, etc., does not admit liability of *narr*, where [illegible] t distinct and inconsistent kinds of liability.[1]

Under the plea of performance, with notice of special ma an equitable defence may be given in evidence.[2]

When, in a declaration in a covenant, a material breach of agreement declared on is averred, a plea denying the charge, alleging that the defendants had well and truly kept all o covenants, must conclude to the country.[3]

On the plea of covenants performed, the defendant has the to open and close.[4]

b. Of Tender thereof. — Upon a bare covenant for the pay of money the defendant may plead a tender.[5]

4. *Special Pleas.* — *a. Generally.* — All special matters of fence must be pleaded.[6]

1. Middleton *v.* Stone, 111 Pa. St. 589; s. c., 2 Cent. Rep. 547.

2. Beadle *v.* Hopkins, Col. & Cai. 486; s. c., 3 Caines, 150.

Special Matters. — Under the plea of "performance with leave," etc., and notice, the defendant may give any thing in evidence which he might have pleaded. Bender *v.* Fromberger, 4 U. S. (4 Dall.) 436; bk. 1, L. ed. 898.

Under the plea of "covenants performed," without notice of special matter, the defendant cannot give evidence of failure of consideration, or non-performance of other collateral covenants on the part of the plaintiff. Evans *v.* Negley, 13 Serg. R. (Pa.) 218.

3. Star Brick Co. *v.* Ridsdale, 34 N. J. L. (5 Vr.) 428; Overton *v.* Crabb, 4 Hayw. (Tenn.) 109.

4. Norris *v.* Ins. Co. of North America, 3 Yeates (Pa.), 84; s. c., 2 Am. Dec. 360.

5. Johnson *v.* Clay, 7 Taunt. 486; s. c., 1 Moore, 200.

Frivolous Pleas. — In an action on a covenant for the delivery of goods levied on by the sheriff as the property of A., where the breach assigned is the not delivering of the property according to agreement, it is not a good plea that the goods were the property of B., and that the defendants were ready to deliver them subject to the legal rights of B. Hogencamp *v.* Ackerman, 24 N. J. L. (4 Zab.) 133.

In an action upon a covenant "not to remove certain goods off the premises where they were levied upon," it is a frivolous plea to a breach assigning that they were removed off the premises, and were not delivered on the day of the sale, to plead that the defendants had the goods there on the day of the sale, ready to deliver, because it does not answer the whole breach; and because, on a covenant to deliver goods at a certain day and place, it is not sufficient for the defendant to allege that he was there ready to deliver them. Hogencamp *v.* Ackerman, 24 N. J. L. (4 Zab.) 133.

6. **What must be pleaded.** — The defendant must plead special performance of the covenants. Stone *v.* Dennis, 3 (Ala.) 231; Champ *v.* Ardery, 2 A. Marsh. (Ky.) 246; Rangler *v.* Morton, Watts (Pa.), 265; Norris *v.* Ins. Co. of North America, 3 Yeates (Pa.), 84; 2 Am. Dec. 360; Overton *v.* Crabb, 4 H. (Tenn.) 109; Shum *v.* Farrington, 1 B. & P. 640; Comyn, Dig. tit. Pleader, 2 v. Bull. N. P. 165.

In action of covenant against the assi of a term, the defendant, under a ge plea that he does not hold as assi cannot ask for an apportionment of the because he has been evicted from a pa the premises. In order to entitle hi an apportionment on this account, he plead the facts specially, and not in b the whole action. Lansing *v.* Van Als 2 Wend. (N. Y.) 561.

The plea of tender admits all the that are well alleged, covenants perfor and assumes the burden of the pro performance. Bryant *v.* Simpson, 3 S (Ala.) 339; Pollard *v.* Taylor, 2 Bibb (K 234; Barnett *v.* Crutcher, 3 Bibb (Ky.), Harrison *v.* Park, 1 J. J. Marsh. (172; Marston *v.* Hobbs, 2 Mass. 438; 3 Am. Dec. 61; Roth *v.* Miller, 15 Ser R. (Pa.) 105; Neave *v.* Jenkins, 2 Ye (Pa.) 414.

Excusing Performance. — The defen may excuse for non-performance, b showing eviction. Salmon *v.* Smit Saund. 204, n. 2; Wotton *v.* Hele, 2 Sa 176; Stevenson *v.* Lambard, 2 East, 5 Eviction of the whole or any part of demised premises is a good plea in b an action of covenant for rent. Smi Shepard, 15 Pick. (Mass.) 147; s. c., 25 Dec. 432; Pendleton *v.* Dyett, 4 (N. Y.) 581.

A plea of "not guilty" is wholly inapplicable to an action in ovenant for damages for the breach of a covenant in a contract

And where a master brought an action n the covenants of an indenture of ap- renticeship, alleging, as a breach, that he apprentice had left his service within the tipulated time, it was *held* to be a good efence that the plaintiff had neglected to nstruct the apprentice in his trade, and ad, unnecessarily, obliged him to work on unday. Warner v. Smith, 8 Conn. 14.

Non-Performance by Plaintiff. — The efendant may plead non-performance — arker v. Parmelee, 20 Johns. (N. Y.) 130; . c., 11 Am. Dec. 253 — by the plaintiff of condition precedent, — Glazebrook v. Woodrow, 8 T. R. 366, — or the surrender f the lease, and the like, — Thursby v. lant, 1 Saund. 235; — but the defendant annot plead that the plaintiff intended to iolate a covenant as an excuse for his wn violation of it. Coffin v. Basset, 2 ick. (Mass.) 357.

Pleading Discharge. — The defendant ay admit the breach alleged to have been ommitted, and plead specially that he is ischarged, — Comyn, Dig. tit. Pleader, 2 . 8, — by discharge in bankruptcy, — harlston v. King, 4 T. R. 156; Thursby v. lant, 1 Saund. 241, n. 6, — by accord and atisfaction after breach, — Kaye v. Wag- orne, 1 Taunt. 428; Holmes v. Blogg, 8 aunt. 37; Thompson v. Brown, 1 J. B. loore, 358, — by arbitrament, — Peytoe's ase, 9 Co. 79; Comyn, Dig. tit. Pleader, v. 8, 9, — former recovery, — Vooght v. Vinch, 2 B. & Ald. 668, — foreign attach- ent, set-off, release, and the like. John- on v. Kerr, 1 Serg. & R. (Pa.) 25; Comyn, Dig. tit. Pleader, 2 v. 8; 1 Chitt. Pl. 478.

But a said accord and satisfaction made efore a breach cannot be pleaded in bar f an action of covenant, — Kaye v. Wag- orne, 1 Taunt. 428, — neither can a parol greement for a substituted contract be leaded. Heard v. Wadham, 1 East, 630; ordy v. Armand, 3 T. R. 596.

Pleading Tender. — A tender may be leaded in an action on a covenant for the ayment of money. Johnson v. Clay, 7 aunt. 486; s. c., 1 J. B. Moore, 200; nonymous, 5 Mod. 18; Paramore v. John- on, 1 Ld. Raym. 566; s. c., 12 Mod. 376. *compare* Gilb. C. P. 63.

Instances. — A plea of eviction by title aramount must aver it to have been by tle existing before the demise, and that here was an entry under the recovery. agleе v. Ingersoll, 7 Pa. St. 185.

In action of covenant upon an executory ontract for the sale of the land, for a part f the consideration, the declaration averred hat the plaintiff had conveyed the land, nd delivered possession according to the agreement. The defendant pleaded that the plaintiff, knowing that he had not a perfect title, fraudulently deceived the defendant in that respect, representing that he had such a title. The plea, containing no averment of an offer to rescind the contract, was held bad. Tinsley v. Ogg, 7 Dana (Ky.), 385.

In an action of covenant by which the vendee bound himself to pay for certain land conveyed to him, so soon as it could be ascertained whether the same could be held under and by virtue of the vendor's conveyance, the vendee pleaded (1) that he did not hold said land mentioned in said deed, under said deed of conveyance; (2) that he did not, on the —— day of ——, nor at any time before or since, ascertain that said deed of conveyance, mentioned in the covenant, held the land; (3) that the vendor was entitled to but one-fourth of the land conveyed, and that there were three other persons who were entitled to, and did actually hold, said lands by virtue of their right as co-heirs, with the vendor, or have disposed of three-fourths to their own use, in exclusion of the vendee claiming under the deed aforesaid; (4) that there was no assignment of the covenant of the plaintiff. On demurrer to these pleas, the court *held* that the first and second were bad, but that the third and fourth were substantially good. Whitesides v. Caldwell, 9 Yerg. (Tenn.) 421.

By deed, after reciting a grant to A. in fee, and that the defendant's wife was the heiress of deceased, who died intestate, and reciting an appointment in fee by the defendant and his wife, in favor of the plaintiff, the defendant covenanted, that, notwithstanding any act by him or his wife or A. committed, he and his wife were lawfully seised, and that, notwithstanding any act as aforesaid, he and his wife had a good right to convey; and that it should be lawful for the plaintiff to quietly occupy, without interruption by the defendant and his wife, or any person lawfully claiming under them or A.; and that the defendant and his wife, and all persons claiming under them or A., would execute to the plaintiff all further assurances. In an action for breach of this covenant for quiet enjoyment, the declaration averred that P. claimed, as heir-at-law of A., deceased, lawful right and title to the premises; and then set out a recovery in ejectment by P., by which the plaintiff was evicted. The defendant set out the deed, and pleaded that A. died intestate, leaving the defendant's wife her only child and heiress-at-law; and that the plaintiff instigated P. to claim -

for the purchase of land, and may be withdrawn at [illegible] the defendant.[1]

b. Fraud and Deceit. — Fraud and deceit in procurin[illegible] tion may be set up as a defence to an action on a c[illegible] the facts constituting the alleged fraud must be set up [illegible]

right and title to the premises; and that P., in consequence, made the claim and prosecuted the ejectment. At the trial, the jury found that the defendant's wife was not the heiress-at-law of A.; it was *held*, first, that the jury was not estopped, by the recital in the deed of the heirship of the defendant's wife, from finding that she was not, in fact, such heiress, — Young v. Raincock, 7 C. B. 310; s. c., 13 Jur. 539; 18 L. J. C. P. 193; — second, that the plea, without such allegation of the heirship of the defendant's wife, was no answer to the action, — Young v. Raincock, 7 C. B. 310; s. c., 13 Jur. 539; 18 L. J. C. P. 193; — third, that the allegation in the declaration, that P claimed, as heir-at-law of A., lawful title, sufficiently showed, after being pleaded over to, that he had a lawful title, — Young v. Raincock, 7 C. B. 310; s. c., 13 Jur. 539; 18 L. J. C. P. 193; — and, fourth, that the generality of terms of the covenant for quiet enjoyment was not restricted by the introductory words of the covenant for the title and power to convey, to any act done by the defendant and his wife, or A. Young v. Raincock, 7 C. B. 310; s. c., 13 Jur. 539, 18 L. J. C. P. 193.

In an action of covenant on a policy of insurance under seal, all special matters of defence must be pleaded. Under the plea of covenants performed, the defendant cannot give evidence which goes to vacate the policy. Marine Ins. Co. v. Hodgson, 10 U. S. (6 Cr.) 206; bk 3, L. ed 200.

In covenant to recover the price of labor covenanted to be performed, the plaintiff alleged an extension of the time of performance. Issue was taken on the plea that the defendant did not extend the time, and that the contract was not performed within the time of extension. The court *held* that the pleas admitted performance, except as to the extension. McKee v. Brandon, 3 Ill. (2 Scam.) 339.

By a deed expressed to be made between G. of the first part, the defendant and two others, as sureties of G., of the second part, and the plaintiff of the third part, G., the defendant, and the other two sureties, jointly and severally covenanted to repay the plaintiff moneys advanced by him to G. The defendant having been sued for a breach of this covenant, a plea that he executed the deed in the faith that P. (one of the sureties) should join therein and execute the same, and that P. never did join therein or execute the same, is a bad plea. Cumberledge v. Lawson, [illegible] C. [illegible] s. c., 26 L. J. C. P. 120.

A declaration in covenan[illegible] to P. of a certain steam-e[illegible] the plaintiff gave P. an o[illegible] that the defendant became[illegible] payment. The defendant [illegible] plaintiff made false and fr[illegible] sentations as to the eng[illegible] whereof the contract of sal[illegible] P. refused to perform the s[illegible] fore the contract to be s[illegible] It was *held*, that, after ver[illegible] ficiently averred that P. ha[illegible] contract. Hazard v. Irwin, [illegible] 95.

The defendant covenante[illegible] tiff to use his best endeav[illegible] diligence, to forward certai[illegible] the same works should be [illegible] short a time as practicable. [illegible] tion alleging as a breach tha[illegible] did not nor would use his [illegible] or due or any diligence, [illegible] works, so that the same [illegible] pleted in as short a time as [illegible] defendant pleaded that he [illegible] endeavors, and all due di[illegible] ward the works, so that th[illegible] completed in as short a tim[illegible] but by causes wholly beyo[illegible] and without any default [illegible] was hindered and prevente[illegible] ing the works. On demurr[illegible] *held* good, as a traverse [illegible] Vickers v. Overend, 20 L. [illegible]

1. Sanford v. Cloud, [illegible]

2. Misrepresentation. — [illegible] a complaint in covenant [illegible] covenant of purchase of la[illegible] that the plaintiff "obtained [illegible] misrepresentation, deceptio[illegible] this that the plaintiff [illegible] defendant at and before [illegible] ing, and delivering of the [illegible] that he, the plaintiff, had [illegible] cumbered title, in fee [illegible] said tract of land described [illegible] in said contract, while [illegible] the plaintiff, at the time [illegible] contract, had not, and [illegible] had not, a good and [illegible] and to said tract of land, [illegible] which fact was not known [illegible] ant," and alleging that [illegible] the defendant was "induced [illegible] by the plaintiff by fraud, [illegible] execute said contract," [illegible]

Statute of Limitations. — In an action for the breach of :nant to warrant and defend, the statute of limitations is not fence, because such covenant runs with the land.[1]

nd it has been held that the statute of limitations does not n to run against an action for breach of covenant of warranty nst incumbrances until the covenantee has paid money to ect his interest.[2]

Non est Factum. — The plea of *non est factum* only puts execution of the deed in issue.[3] It admits a breach, and

se it does not specially set up the committing the alleged fraud, and not set up a defence or other action. rd v. Cloud, 17 Fla. 532, 548, 549.

cumbered Title. — It does not, in of fact, necessarily amount to a fraud he plaintiff had not, at the time of good, indefeasible, and unincumbered It is not a part of the contract that le shall pass on the day of the sale, t is therefore immaterial whether a iff had at that time an unincumbered r not. If he was prepared to make a title as he contracted for at the time dertook to convey, that is all the de- nt has a right to require. Gibson v. nan, 1 How. (Miss.) 346; Champion rrs, 5 Cow. (N. Y.) 510; Greenby v. vers, 9 Johns. (N. Y.) 126.

ere, in a suit in covenant for breach ntract for the purchase of land, a laint setting out an execution and ry of the deed, and a delivery of ssion under it, and the defendant ed that the plaintiff had not, at the of filing the plea, such title as he sold, epresented that he had; and that the dant, in a reasonable time after dis- ing the fraud, offered to rescind the act, and tendered a deed of reconvey- —the court *held* that his plea was in- ient, (1) because it did not aver that efendant had not discovered the fraud he received the deed, and, if he had, aived it by receiving the deed; (2) se it did not aver that the plaintiff not a good title when he made the for, if he had, it was insufficient, h he was without title when he made ntract; and, though he had no good hen the plea was filed, he might have one either when the deed was made contract was made; and (3) because, eed of reconveyance not being in the l, the court could not judge of its iency. Tinsley v. Ogg, 7 Dana (Ky.).

se of Hotel: Defective Drainage. — ea alleging that the premises were d for hotel purposes upon the false entations of the lessor that the drain- as adequate, on the discovery of the falsity of which the possession was returned to, and accepted by, the lessor, was *held* to be bad for not alleging at what time the defendant rescinded; *non constat;* but he occupied nearly to the end of the term without any relinquishment of rent by the lessor. Burroughs v. Clancey, 53 Ill. 30.

In such case a plea alleging a compromise and settlement of the subject-matter in controversy, under which the lease had been surrendered and cancelled, and possession given to the plaintiff, was *held* to be bad for not averring that he had accepted the possession. Burroughs v. Clancey, 53 Ill. 30.

1. Wilder v. Davenport's Estate, 58 Vt. 642; s. c., 2 New Eng. Rep. 810.

2. Priest v. Deaver, 22 Mo. App. 276; s. c., 4 West. Rep. 308; Taylor v. Priest, 21 Mo. App. 685; s. c., 4 West. Rep. 329; Dickson v. Desire, 23 Mo. 151-163; Chambers v. Smith, 23 Mo. 174; Maguire v. Riggin, 44 Mo. 512; Walker v. Deavey, 79 Mo. 664.

3. Denton v. Bours, Anth. (N. Y.) 177; Thomas v. Woods, 4 Cow. (N. Y.) 173; McNeish v. Stewart, 7 Cow. (N. Y.) 474; Dale v. Rosevelt, 9 Cow. (N. Y.) 307; Goulding v. Hewitt, 2 Hill (N. Y.), 644; Hebbards v. Delaplaine, 3 Hill (N. Y.), 187; Gardner v. Gardner, 10 Johns. (N. Y.) 47; Kane v. Sanger, 14 Johns. (N. Y.) 89; Barney v. Keith, 6 Wend. (N. Y.) 555; Legg v. Robinson, 7 Wend. (N. Y.) 194; Cooper v. Watson, 10 Wend. (N. Y.) 202; Norman v. Wells, 17 Wend (N. Y.) 136.

What admitted by: Evidence. — In an action of covenant on a deed, all the material allegations, except the execution of the deed, are admitted by the plea of *non est factum*. Norman v. Wells, 17 Wend. (N. Y.) 136.

Under *non est factum*, neither an abandonment of the contract nor the non-performance of conditions precedent on the part of the plaintiff can be given in evidence. Laraway v. Perkins, 10 N. Y 371.

In covenant, by a lessee against his lessor, no question of title can arise on a plea of *non est factum*. Barney v. Keith, 6 Wend. (N. Y.) 555

Election. — Where a declaration in cove-

requires the defendant to take the *onus* of showing the contrary.[1]

nant contained several counts, each of which set out the instrument, but only one breach was assigned, the defendant craved oyer, then pleaded *non est factum*, and demurred to each count; and the court *held* that he must elect to rely upon his pleas or demurrers, both pleas and demurrers covering the whole declaration. Angell *v.* Kelsey, 1 Barb. (N. Y.) 16.

A declaration stated that, by a deed of July 20, 1825, between the plaintiff E., the defendant's testator, and W., E. for himself, his executors, etc., covenanted with the plaintiff to pay to W. £1,200. The breach assigned was non-payment by E. in his lifetime or by the defendant, as his executor, to the plaintiff or W. The defendant pleaded first *non est factum*, and in the second plea set out the deed. In this deed it was stated that, by a mortgage dated April 12, 1825, W. had become mortgagee of the premises to the plaintiff for £1,200, with a proviso that if the plaintiff should, within six months after the demand of payment of the £1,200 (such demand to be in writing, but not to be good or valid unless made after April 12, 1828), pay to W. £1,200 and interest, W would assign the premises to the plaintiff. The deed declared on, then stated that, for the considerations therein mentioned, the plaintiff sold to E., his executors, etc, the premises for the residue of the term, subject to the mortgage to W. of April 12, 1825, and to the payment of £1,200 thereby secured, and interest. The plea then alleged that, after the breaches in the declaration on Oct. 24, 1825, the plaintiff became bankrupt; that the plaintiff obtained his certificate, and that the £1,200 became payable by the plaintiff to W. before the bankruptcy of the plaintiff. The third plea stated that the deed declared on was the same as that set forth in the second plea; it then set out the proviso and covenant contained in the mortgage of April 12, 1825, and alleged that no demand in writing of payment of the £1,200 had been given to the plaintiff. These pleas having been demurred to, it was *held*, first, that the declaration was good; second, that the £1,200 was not due until after six months' demand in writing subsequent to April 12, 1828, and that the second plea was a sufficient answer to the principal of £1,200; third, that the interest on the £1,200, being payable absolutely, and not on demand, the plea which was pleaded to the interest, as well as to the principal, being bad in part was bad altogether, and that the same objection applied to the first special plea; fourth, that the first plea was bad, as it negatived on the face of it any possibility of interest in the covenant on the part of the plaintiff's assignees, and therefore that it was not necessary for the plaintiff to reply to that fact. Trott *v.* Smith, 12 Mees. & W. 688; s. c., 13 L. J. Exch. 178.

Statutory Provisions. — *Non est factum* was, under a former statute of Ohio, a plea of the general issue in covenant, to which a notice of set-off may be appended. Granger *v.* Granger, 6 Ohio, 41.

The statutory provision in Illinois, that a defendant shall not be permitted to deny the execution of an instrument declared on, if he is a party to the same, unless he support his plea by affidavit, does not apply to the plea of *non est factum* in covenant. Gale's Stat. 531, 532; Longley *v.* Norvall, 2 Ill. (1 Scam.) 389.

Evidence in Plea of Non est Factum. — When the deed is not put in issue by the plea of *non est factum*, the defendant at common law admits that portion of the deed which is spread upon the record: if other parts of the deed are required to support his case, the plaintiff must prove them in the usual way. Williams *v.* Sills, 2 Campb. 519.

When the plaintiff has pleaded *non est factum*, he must, of course, prove the allegations contained in his declarations, as well as the formal execution of the instrument on which he has declared. This is done by producing the instrument, and proving by the attesting witnesses, when they can be had, that the deed was signed, sealed, and delivered by the grantor or obligor. Where there are any alterations or erasures, from which suspicions may arise of alteration, these must be removed before the deed can be read in evidence Whether erasures and interlineations were made before delivery, is a question for the jury. When the alteration is against the interest of the party claiming under it, the presumption is, that such alteration was made before or at the time the instrument was executed. Heffelfinger *v.* Shutz, 16 Serg. & R. (Pa.) 44; Van Amringe *v.* Morton, 4 Whart. (Pa.) 382; Withers *v.* Atkinson, 1 Watts (Pa.), 236; Arrison *v.* Harmstead, 2 Pa. St. 191; Bacon's Abr tit. "Evidence," F.

A mistake in drawing a deed, by which the covenants were inverted, may be shown under the plea of *non est factum*. Gove *v.* Wooster, Hill & Den. (N. Y.) 30.

1. Goulding *v.* Hewitt, 2 Hill (N. Y.), 644.

In an action on specialties, the plea *non est factum* shall operate as a denial of the

Where a deed is pleaded according to its supposed legal effect, *non est factum* (the deed not being set out on oyer) not only puts in issue the facts of its execution, but the construction of it, as alleged in the previous pleading.[1]

Where a defendant sets out the deed, and pleads *non est factum*, the deed so set out becomes part of the declaration; and the only question at the trial upon that issue is, whether the deed set out was executed by the defendant.[2]

If, in an action for breach of covenant for quiet enjoyment, the defendant plead *non est factum*, with notice denying an eviction, he must prove that there was no eviction.[3]

To an action against the heir, on a covenant by his ancestor, for himself, his heirs, executors, administrators, and assigns, a plea that he has not any lands by hereditary descent in fee-simple from his ancestor, is bad for omitting to negative that he had estates *pur autre vie* by descent from the covenantor.[4]

Where the defendant is a party to the deed, he cannot traverse its operation by pleading that "he did not grant," etc., but must plead *non est factum*; but the rule is otherwise in case of a stranger.[5]

a. Non Infregit Conventionem. — The plea of *non infregit conventionem* merely denies that the defendant has broken the covenants as set forth in the declaration; it does not deny the deed, and is not, therefore, the general issue; yet it may be pleaded in bar.[6] But where the breach assigned is in the negative, then the plea of *non infregit conventionem* is bad, because, both the breach and the plea being negative, there can be no issue.[7]

The plea of *non infregit conventionem* is bad on demurrer, but the defect is cured by verdict.[8] But if, in a covenant of warranty

execution of the deed in point of fact only; and all other defences shall be specially pleaded, including matters which make the deed absolutely void, as well as those which make it voidable. Reg. Gen Q. B., C. P. and Exch. T. T. 16 Vict. 10; 1 El. & B. App. L XXX.

1. Smith v. Wakefield, 13 Q. B. 536; s. c., 18 L. J. Q. B. 214.

2. Snell v. Snell, 7 Dowl. & R. 249; s. c., 4 Barn. & C. 741.

3. Kane v. Sanger, 14 Johns. (N. Y.) 89.

4. Fitzgerald v. Fitzgerald, 1 Ir. C. L. R. 1[illegible].

5. Taylor v. Needham, 2 Taunt. 278; s. c., 3 Rev. & Man. 90 in note Doct. Plac. 1[illegible]; Stephen's Pl. (2d ed.) 237, 238, 239.

As to what the general traverse puts in issue, see Cowlenshaw v. Cheslyn, 1 Cramp. & Jerv. 48; Taylor v. Needham, 2 Taunt. 2[illegible].

6. Roosevelt v. Fulton, 7 Cow. (N. Y.) 71; Phelps v. Sawyer, 1 Aik. (Vt.) 150; Kinsler v. Fromberger, 4 U. S. (4 Dall.) 4[illegible]; bk. 1, L. ed. 898.

Such plea admits the deed, but denies the breaches, and puts in issue all such matters as show that the covenant is not broken, or that the defendant never was under an obligation to fulfil it. Roosevelt v. Fulton, 7 Cow. (N. Y.) 71; Davis v. Clayton, 5 N. Y. Leg. Obs. 100.

7. Bacon, Abr. tit. "Covenant," L.

Non Infregit Conventionem is not an issuable plea to a breach of covenant assigned in the negative. Boone v. Eyre, 2 W. Bl. 1312; s. c., 1 H. Bl. 273, n.

Non infregit conventionem cannot be pleaded where a plaintiff assigns a breach without setting forth the particulars of the title of a third person, adding, "and so the defendant did not keep his covenant." Hodgson v. East India Co., 8 T. R 278.

8. Roosevelt v. Fulton, 7 Cow. (N. Y.) 71; Davis v. Clayton, 5 N. Y. Leg. Obs. 100.

If a plaintiff assigns as a breach that the defendant did not repair, a plea that the defendant did not break his covenant is bad, on special demurrer, although the declaration concluded by averring that "so of seisin, the defendant plead *non infregit conventionem*, the issue, though informal, will support a judgment.[1]

f. Nil Habuit in Tenementis. — In covenant for ground-rent, *nil habuit in tenementis* is bad on general demurrer.[2] And in covenant for rent, the plea of an eviction by title paramount must allege that it was by a title existing before the demise, and that there was an actual entry by the evictor.[3]

g. Non Damnificatus. — *Non damnificatus* is not a good plea to a breach of covenant.[4]

h. Oyer. — Where a deed is set out in the schedule annexed to a declaration, it is not necessary to crave oyer; but the declaration may be pleaded to as if it had set out the deed.[5]

5. *Defences and Pleas in Bar.* — *a. Defence.* — In an action of covenant, the defendant must plead specially every matter of defence of which, under the circumstances of the case, he is at liberty to avail himself; and the evidence must be confined to the issue made by such plea.[6]

In covenant against one who sealed the instrument declared on, it is no defence that it was not also sealed by the plaintiff.[7] And matters which show how the defendant paid for the premises when he purchased, form no bar to an action brought against him for breach of covenant with the plaintiff, who is another person.[8]

the defendant has broken his covenant;" but it will be good after verdict. Taylor *v.* Needham, 2 Taunt. 278.

1. Bender *v.* Fromberger, 4 U. S. (4 Dall.) 436; bk. 1, L. ed 898.

In covenant upon a warranty, in which one of the breaches assigned is, that the defendant was not seised of a good estate in fee, etc., the plea of *non infregit conventionem*, etc., though it presents an informal issue, is still sufficient for the court to enter judgment on. Bender *v.* Fromberger, 4 U. S. (4 Dall.) 436; bk. 1, L. ed. 898.

2. Naglee *v.* Ingersol, 7 Pa. St. 185.

In Covenant for Rent reserved by deed indenture, *nil habuit in tenementis* is bad on general demurrer. Naglee *v.* Ingersol, 7 Pa. St. 185.

3. Naglee *v.* Ingersol, 7 Pa. St. 185.

4. Hogencamp *v.* Ackerman, 24 N. J. L. (4 Zab.) 133.

Non-Performance. — In covenant for non-performance of an act agreed to be done by the defendant, a plea, that, if the plaintiff was damnified, it was by his own wrong, is bad on demurrer; such plea is only applicable to a bond of indemnity. Harmony *v.* Bingham, 12 N. Y. 99; s. c., 1 Duer (N. Y.), 209.

5. Hogencamp *v.* Ackerman, 24 N. J. L. (4 Zab.) 133.

But where, in a declaration in covenant, profert is made of the deed, and the covenant is misrecited, the defendant cannot demur specially, alleging the misrecital as the cause of demurrer, without first craving oyer of the deed, and setting it out *in hæc verba*, so as to make it part of the record. Killian *v.* Herndon, 4 Rich. (S. C.) 195.

A declaration in covenant contained several counts, each of which set out the instrument, but one breach only was assigned. The defendant craved oyer, then pleaded *non est factum*, and demurred to each count generally. The court *held* that he must elect to rely upon his pleas or demurrers, both pleas and demurrers covering the whole declaration. Angell *v.* Kelsey, 1 Barb. (N. Y.) 16.

6. Jones *v.* Johnson, 10 Humph. (Tenn.) 184.

Defences. — As to what defences are admissible in actions of covenants, see United States *v.* Clarke, Hempst. U. S. D. C. 315; Gill *v.* Patton, 1 Cr. C. C. 143; Wise *v.* Resler, 2 Cr. C. C. 182; Scott *v.* Lunt, 3 Cr. C. C. 285; Kurtz *v.* Becker, 5 Cr. C. C. 671; Wilder *v.* Adams, 2 Woodb. & M. C. C. 329.

Insurance Policy. — In covenant on a policy under seal, all special matters of defence must be pleaded. Marine Ins. Co. of Alexandria *v.* Hodgson, 10 U. S. (6 Cr.) 206; bk. 3, L. ed. 200.

7. Directors of the Poor *v.* McFadden, 13 N. J. L. (1 Gr.) 230; Gilhousen *v.* Wilink (Pa.), 3 Pitts. L. J. 214.

8. Miller *v.* Halsey, 14 N. J. L. (2 Gr.) 48.

A covenant not to sue one of several obligors is not pleadable in bar; it is a covenant only, and the covenantee is put to his cross-action to recover the damages which a breach may occasion him.[1]

A covenant not to sue one joint contractor is no bar to a suit against another. To allow it so to operate would defeat the very object of resorting to a covenant not to sue, instead of giving a release, which is to preserve the remedy against the other parties.[2] And if there be a joint decree against the executors of two persons, and a creditor receive a moiety of the debt from the representatives of one of them, and covenants not to levy the residue of the decree on the estate of that one, it does not discharge the representative of the other.[3]

Where an action of covenant on a sealed instrument sounds entirely in damages, it is a good plea and sufficient defence to show an accord and satisfaction by parol, though the general rule is, that a sealed instrument should be avoided by one of as high a nature.[4]

An answer that the defendants conveyed one-third to plaintiffs by mistake, was held no defence.[5]

Where a covenant is assigned, notice of the breach from the assigned is sufficient to support the action.[6]

Where the conduct of one party to a contract prevents the other from performing his part, this is an excuse for such non-performance.[7]

Where a building contract contained the following stipulation, "The said houses to be completely finished on or before the 24th of December next, under a penalty of $1,000 in case of failure," it was held that this was not intended as liquidated damages for the breach of that single covenant only, but applied to all the covenants made by the same party in that agreement; that it was in the nature of a penalty, and could not be a set-off in an action brought by the party to recover the price of the work.[8]

In an action by a grantee, ejected under a paramount title, against his grantor, it is no defence that defendant in ejectment was not in possession, if the grantor himself defended the ejectment.[9]

1. But, as an exception to this rule, a sole obligor may plead such covenant in bar to avoid circuity of action. See Line v. Nelson, 38 N. J. L. (9 Vr.) 358.

2. Tuthill v. Babcock, 2 Woodb. & M. C. C. 138. And see Ferson v. Sanger, 1 Woodb. & M. C. C. 138.

3. Garnett v. Macon, 2 Brock. (Marsh. Dec.) 185.

4. Cabe v. Jameson, 10 Ired. (N. C.) L. [illegible].

5. Wright v. Nipple, 92 Ind. 310.

6. Van Vechten v. Graves, 4 Johns. (N. Y.) 403.

7. United States v. Peck, 102 U. S. (12 Otto) 64; bk. 26, L. ed. 46.

8. Tayloe v. Sandiford, 20 U. S. (7 Wheat.) 13; bk. 5, L. ed. 384.

9. Jones v. Whitsett, 79 Mo. 188.

Notice to Grantor: Defence.—A grantee sued his grantor for breach of covenant, alleging the eviction of the grantee by the holder of a paramount title in an action to which the grantor was a party. The court *held*, first, that the grantor in his answer could set up that he was not a party, and had no notice, and could place on the grantee the burden of proving that the

In an action for breach of covenant of warranty, the defence that the covenant sued upon was a joint one, and that it was sued upon as several, can be made under an answer denying that there is any thing due.[1]

In covenant for breach of warranty of title, the defendant may show that the deed, though absolute on its face, was in reality a collateral security for a debt due to a third person, and that the plaintiff had no real interest in the title.[2] And where, by the terms of a contract for the sale of the land, A. agreed to deliver to B. a good deed to the land upon the performance of certain covenants by B., and A. sued B. for breach thereof, it was held that it was no defence that A., at the time of the making of the contract, had not a good title to the land.[3]

Where a purchaser had obtained a decree for conveyance upon his securing the balance of the purchase-money, but, upon the vendor's filing the deed, failed to take it and comply with the decree, it was held that he could not contest an action of covenant brought by the vendor for a subsequent instalment.[4]

In an action of covenant for the breach of a covenant of warranty, the defendant is estopped to say that his prior deed to the said land, by virtue of a judgment in a special proceeding, is not valid and paramount to his deed to the plaintiff. The existence of a better title, with actual possession under it, is a breach of the covenant of warranty.[5]

Notice of incumbrance does not affect the right of a grantee to recover for the breach of an express covenant against incumbrances.[6]

In an action in covenant for the breach of a contract for the purchase of land, a plea of want of title in the vendor should show specifically the defects in his title;[7] and the defendant must show by allegation and proof who claims title to the land, and that the title thus claimed is good.[8]

A verbal agreement between the parties to a deed made at the time of the delivery, or previous thereto, that one of them should be released from the covenants contained in the deed, cannot defeat an action for an alleged breach of those covenants.[9]

eviction was right; second, that the grantor if not a party, and not notified, could set up against the grantee a valid defence which the grantee could have had against the eviction. Walton *v.* Cox, 67 Ind 164.

1. Patrick *v.* Leach, 1 McCr. C. C. 250.

2. Parke *v.* Chadwick, 8 Watts & S. (Pa.) 96.

3. Sanford *v.* Cloud, 17 Fla. 532.

4. Herdic *v.* Woodward, 75 Pa. St. 479.

5. Hodges *v.* Latham (N. C.), 25 Cent. L. J. 497; s. c., 3 S. E. Rep. 495.

6. Watts *v.* Fletcher, 107 Ind. 391; s. c., 5 West. Rep. 795.

Notice of Defective Title. — And the fact that the vendee of land, at the time of his purchase, knew of the insufficiency or invalidity of the vendor's title, is not an available defence to an action on the covenants of the deed received by him from the vendor, either at law or in equity. Sparrow *v.* Smith (Mich.), 5 West. Rep. 763.

7. Capeland *v.* Loan, 10 Mo. 266.

8. Walker *v.* Towns, 23 Ark. 147.

The "bare naked" allegations of a want of title, even when it is a good plea, is not sufficient. Sanford *v.* Cloud, 17 Fla. 532, 549; Gibson *v.* Newman, 1 How. (Miss.) 346.

9. Wadsworth *v.* Warren, 79 U. S. (12 Wall.) 307; bk. 20, L. ed. 402.

That the estate has been fully settled, and land apportioned, is no defence in action against the administrator by decedent's [illegible].[1]

A covenant by a lessee, to occupy the premises as a dwelling-house, implies a covenant by the lessor of fitness for occupancy; and the amount expended by the lessee for necessary repairs is a set-off against a claim for rent.[2] Yet it has been held that the mere fact that a house leased for a residence becomes uninhabitable, will not sustain an action in covenant,[3] unless this condition of the property resulted from the act of the lessor, or from those holding a paramount title.[4]

5. Pleas in Bar. — Where there are mutual covenants, one cannot be pleaded in bar of the other.[5]

An obligation under seal can be discharged before a breach only by a sealed instrument. After a breach, any agreement or transaction that would operate as an accord and satisfaction in ordinary cases may be pleaded in discharge.[6]

In covenant on a policy of insurance, the defendant may plead in bar that one of the plaintiffs has assigned all his interest in the policy to the other, with the assent of the company.[7]

In an action on an instrument under seal, if the contract is still executory, or has been rescinded before suit brought, or the consideration has entirely failed, the defence of fraud in the consideration should be pleaded in bar: but where the contract, having been executed, has not been rescinded, and the consideration has entirely failed, such defence cannot be pleaded in bar; it can only be used at the trial to reduce the amount of the plaintiff's recovery.[8]

Eviction of the whole or any part of the demised premises is a good plea in bar to an action in covenant for rent.[9]

In an action for breach of covenant of warranty in a deed, the title having failed to one-third of the property, an answer which alleged that the defendant was the owner of the land described, subject to the rights of a married woman to one-third thereof, and

1. Taylor *v.* Priest, 21 Mo. App. 685; s. c., 4 West. Rep. 329.

2. Wolfe *v.* Arrott, 109 Pa. St. 473; s. c., 1 Cent. Rep. 128.

3. Carson *v.* Goodley, 26 Pa. St. 117; Hazlett *v.* Powell, 30 Pa. St. 293.

4. Barns *v.* Wilson (Pa.), 8 Cent. Rep. 454; 25 Cent. L. J. 14; 9 Atl. Rep. 437.

5. Boone *v.* Eyre, 2 Wm. Bl. 1312; s. c., 1 H. Bl. 273, n.

6. Herzog *v.* Sawyer, 61 Md. 344.

7. Perrins *v.* North America Fire Insurance Co., 1 Hill (N. Y.), 71.

8. Lord *v.* Brookfield, 37 N. J. L. (8 Vr.) [illegible].

Instances. — A plea to an action of covenant, that since it was made, so much thereof as required the defendant to deliver [illegible] bushels of corn, 20,000 pounds of [illegible], 6 horses, 65 head of hogs, and 25 head of cattle, was waived by a subsequent contract between said defendant and said testator, in his lifetime, so that said defendant was not bound to deliver said horses, cattle, oxen, and hogs, as may happen to die or be lost without any neglect of defendant, before the day appointed for their delivery, — and defendant avers that a large number of said horses, cattle, and oxen did die, or were lost, without his default, before the time appointed for their delivery, etc., — is bad because an executory parol contract cannot be pleaded in bar of an action on a sealed instrument, and also because of uncertainty in not alleging how many of the horses, etc., had died or were lost. Sorrell *v.* Craig, 8 Ala. 566.

9. Smith *v.* Shepard, 15 Pick. (Mass.) 147; s. c., 25 Am. Dec. 432; Pendleton *v.* Dyett, 4 Cow. (N. Y.) 581.

country, and for that reason replications do not occur in this action so often as in the other forms of action;[1] but when proper, they are governed by the same general rules relating to replications in other actions.[2]

7. *Matters of Practice.* — In an action of covenant to recover the price stipulated for building a mill-dam, which the plaintiff covenanted to fill with rocks and gravel in a proper manner, so as to keep the dam safe and tight, the plaintiff, in his declaration, alleged that the defendant directed what rocks and gravel should be used, and that the same were used, and the dam made as close and tight as it could be with such materials. The defendant pleaded that he did not designate the materials, and direct them to be put in the dam. Upon this plea, issue was taken; and on the trial, the defendant moved the court to instruct the jury that the issue was immaterial, and to be disregarded by them, which was refused. It was held that this refusal was correct.[3]

1. See Morris *v.* Wadsworth, 11 Wend. (N. Y.) 100.

2. In an action for the breach of a covenant of seisin, where the declaration assigns a breach by negativing the words of the covenant, and the defendants plead that they were seised, in the words of the covenant, the replication may simply reiterate the breach assigned; for the burden of proving a seisin is on the defendants, and the facts are not supposed to be within the plaintiff's knowledge. Abbott *v.* Allen, 14 Johns. (N. Y.) 248.

De Injuria. — To a plea of lease and license to a count for breach of covenant, *de injuria* is a good replication. Douglass *v.* Hoppaugh, 46 N. J. L. (17 Vr.) 114.

Departure from Declaration. — A declaration by A., the surviving lessor in a lease for years, granted by A., B., and C., to the defendant, on a covenant to repair and leave in repair, assigning breaches in not repairing, and in not leaving in repair at the end of the term, to which the defendant pleaded that A., B., and C., from the time of making the demise until the death of B., and A. and C. afterwards, had a reversion for a longer term of years expectant on the lease; and that after B.'s death, and before any breach of covenant, A. and C. assigned such reversion to D., and thenceforward ceased to have any reversion in the premises. Replication, that A., B., and C. were not, until the death of B., nor were A. and C. afterwards, possessed of the reversion in the premises, is bad, as being a departure from the declaration. Green *v.* James, 6 Mees. & W. 656.

Where, in an action against the assignee of the lease for the non-payment of rent, a plea was interposed, that, before the rent became due, he assigned all his estate and interest in the premises to A. and B., to which plaintiff alleged, by way of replication, that in and by the indenture the lessee, for himself, his executors, administrators, and assigns, covenanted that he, his executors and administrators, should not assign the premises without the consent of the lessor, and that no consent was given, the court *held*, first, that the replication was bad, inasmuch as the covenant of the lessee not to assign did not stop the assignee from setting up the assignment; and secondly, that the action being founded on privity of the estate, the liability of the assignee ceased as soon as the privity of estate was destroyed. Paul *v.* Nurse, 8 Barn. & C. 486.

Where the plaintiff owned a steamboat which was about to be sold on certain chattel mortgages, and the defendant agreed with him, under seal, that he would become the purchaser, if the boat could be bought for $30,000, and would allow the plaintiff an interest therein, in covenant on the agreement, the plaintiff declared that the defendant neglected to make the purchase, though he might have done so for the sum mentioned. The defendant pleaded that he attended the sale, and bid $30,000; but that the boat was sold to a higher bidder, to wit, for $30,300. The plaintiff replied, that the purchase by a higher bidder, and the higher bids, were made by fraud and collusion with the defendant, for the purpose of evading his agreement. To this replication the defendant demurred specially. The court *held*, that the replication was good, and was not a departure. Barne *v.* Drew, 4 Den. (N. Y.) 287.

3. McKee *v.* Brandon, 3 Ill. (2 Scam.) 339.

An action on a covenant in a lease to pay rent, brought before the rent is due, is premature, and should be dismissed.[1]

X. Evidence. — 1. *Onus Probandi.* — In an action in covenant, the burden of proof is usually on the plaintiff to establish the allegations in his complaint;[2] but the defendant has the burden of establishing his plea, although a breach of the condition of the covenant is alleged in the declaration.[3]

But where the defendant is defaulted, in an action of covenant, the plaintiff is not bound to prove the averments in his declaration.[4]

1. Duryee *v.* Turner, 20 Mo. App. 34; s. c., 2 West. Rep. 442.

2. **Prima Facie Proof.** — It is *prima facie* sufficient if the plaintiff proves the execution of the covenant by the defendant: he is not required to produce or prove the counterpart. Patten *v.* Heustis, 26 N. J. L. (2 Dutch.) 293.

If a lease describes the demised land as meadow land, no other evidence is necessary to prove that it was meadow land at the commencement of the term. Birch *v.* Stevenson, 3 Taunt. 469.

In covenant, the obligation on which it is brought is *prima facie* evidence of a consideration; and the defendant cannot, by pleading negatively that it "was given without consideration," throw the burden of proof on the obligee. Boone *v.* Shackleford, 4 Bibb (Ky.), 67.

Damages. — Thus, in an action on covenant sounding in damages, the damages, depending on matters outside of the record, and not being capable of determination from the instrument itself, must be proved, although the cause of action is admitted. Simonton *v.* Winter, 30 U. S. (5 Pet.) 141; bk. 8, L. ed. 75.

Failure to deliver Property. — In covenant for not delivering property according to the covenant, if issue be joined upon the plea that the defendant has not broken his covenant, the burden is upon the plaintiff to show that the property was not delivered. Sawtelle *v.* Sawtelle, 34 Me. 228.

Action against Assignee. — On an issue tendered by the defendant, denying his holding as assignee, the plaintiff holds the affirmative, and has the burden of proof. Lansing *v.* Van Alstyne, 2 Wend. (N. Y.) 561.

It is obviously a question of fact whether the possession of the covenantee has been transferred from his elder title to the newer and better title, which he has acquired by purchase, under such circumstances as that he may be said to have suffered an involuntary loss of possession tantamount to an eviction therefrom. Kellog *v.* Platt, 33 N. J. L. (4 Vr.) 328.

Impotent Pleas. — Matter that is not well pleaded, and is not an answer to the breach assigned in the declaration, cannot be considered as an admission of the cause of action set forth in the declaration, so as to excuse the plaintiff from proving the allegations in his declaration. Simonton *v.* Winter, 30 U. S. (5 Pet.) 141; bk. 8, L. ed. 75.

3. Douglass *v.* Hennessy (R. I.), 5 New Eng. Rep. 94. See also s. c., 3 New Eng. Rep. 525; Index Z, 31.

Breach by Lessee of Public House. — Thus, in an action by a lessee of a house, that he would use his best endeavors to continue it open as a public licensed victualling house, and to increase its trade, and that he would not remove the trade or the license to any other public house, the breach assigned was that he did not use his best endeavors to continue the house open as a public licensed victualling house, but allowed it to be discontinued, and the license to be removed. The plea was only that the defendant did use his best endeavors to continue the house open and increase the trade according to the covenant. After the lease was granted, in consequence of complaints of irregularities in the conduct of it by the tenant, the license was taken away by the magistrates; and from that time till the lease expired, the house had not been licensed. The court *held* that it lay on the defendant to show that he did some act after the license was taken away, such as applying for a re-hearing of the case, or some other act, endeavoring to obtain the continuance of the license, and to get the house open again. Linder *v.* Pryor, 8 Car. & P. 518.

4. Courcier *v.* Graham, 1 Ohio, 347.

Default: Deductions. — The defendant, after judgment by default, cannot give in evidence an agreement signed by the plaintiff, engaging to make deduction on the happening of certain events. Templeton *v.* Pearse, 2 Hayw. (N. C.) 339.

But where, in an action for a breach of the covenant of *seisin*, the defendant has been defaulted because he failed to file an answer, he may offer evidence upon the question of damages, when the averment is bad. Bartelt *v* Braunsdarf, 57 Wis. 1.

Proof of an absolute refusal before the expiration of the time fixed for performance of a covenant, is not enough,[1] unless the defendant has put it out of his power to perform,[2] or unless refusal was communicated for the purpose of influencing, and did influence, the conduct of the other party to his damage.[3] But the defendant's omission to deny a due allegation of a request and refusal dispenses with the necessity of proving a demand.[4]

A prima facie case is made by the plaintiff in an action for breach of covenant of warranty, when the deed is introduced, and evidence is given to show that the grantor had no title to the land which he assumed to convey.[5]

In an action on a covenant for breach of warranty in a deed, plaintiff need not prove an eviction by judgment of law, but the burden is upon him clearly to establish the paramount title.[6]

Where the plaintiff's title is in issue in an action on his executory contract to convey, the burden of proof is on him to show

1. Daniels v. Newton, 114 Mass. 530; s. c., 19 Am. Rep. 384.

2. Sears v. Conover, 4 Abb. (N. Y.) Ct. App. Dec. [illegible].

When this fact is relied on as an excuse for not performing or tendering performance, it must be pleaded. Van Rensselaer v. Miller, Hill & D. Supp. (N. Y.) [illegible].

3. See Skinner v. Tinker, 34 Barb. (N Y.) [illegible]; Thomas v. Wickmann, 1 Daly (N.Y.), [illegible].

[illegible] v. Davison, 2 Duer (N. Y.), [illegible].

[illegible] v. Woods, 109 Ind. 291; s. c., 7 West. Rep. 534.

Conveyance under Statute.—To prove a covenant broken, it is not enough to prove that the conveyance was ostensibly made under the provisions of the statute: it must also be proved that the land was embraced within the provisions of the law. Wine v. Woods, 109 Ind. 291; s. c., 7 West. Rep. [illegible].

[illegible] Callis v. Cogbill, 9 Lea (Tenn.), 137.

Eviction: Yielding Possession.—Where, by the agreement for quiet possession, the title of him who brought ejectment is admitted to be paramount to that of the party under whom the possessor holds, it is both the right and duty of the possessor to yield possession to the party having paramount title, without engaging in further litigation. Wilson v. Holly, 57 Miss. 335.

While the covenantee may yield to a paramount title in his suit against the covenantor, the burden of showing that the title to which he yielded was, in fact, a paramount title, is on the covenantee. Clark v. Mumford, 62 Tex. 531.

In a suit on the covenants in a deed by the grantee, if he sets up that he had been evicted from the premises because he had yielded possession thereof to a paramount title, he must show, by sufficient evidence, not only that he had yielded possession to what he supposed, or was claimed, to be a paramount title, but that the title to which he had then yielded was, in fact, paramount to the title of any one else to such property. Sheets v. Lonlois, 69 Ind. 491.

Incumbrances: Taxes.—The foundation of an action for the recovery of taxes paid by the grantee, under a deed containing covenants of warranty, is proof of such a deed, and the existence of the taxes as an incumbrance, and their payment by the grantee. Hillhouse v. Houts (Mo.), 6 West. Rep. 833.

The defence of breach of warranty, whereby a grantee had been compelled to pay taxes, cannot be maintained by the evidence of the tax-receipt alone without further evidence that the taxes were properly assessed. Hanna v. Fisher, 95 Ind. 383.

Where A. conveyed to B. by warranty deed a lot of land, and B. conveyed one-half to C., and there were taxes unpaid on the land, to pay which the land was sold after the conveyance to C., in an action on the covenant in his deed, A. was held liable to C. only for that portion of the consideration paid to A. which the value of his portion of the lot bore to the whole lot, and that the burden was on C. to establish this value. Mischke v. Baughn, 52 Iowa, 528.

As to evidence of incumbrance, see Anonymous, 2 Abb. (N. Y.) Pr. N. S. 56; Reeder v. Schneider, 1 Hun (N. Y.), 121; Riggs v. Pursell, 66 N. Y. 193.

Respecting offer to discharge, see Rinaldo v. Housmann, 1 Abb. (N. Y.) Pr. N. S. 312.

either that he has a good title,[1] or that the purchaser agreed to accept such title as he had.[2]

In covenant upon a general warranty contained in a deed of conveyance, an eviction by paramount title is *prima facie* evidence of the plaintiff's right to recover; and if the warrantor was notified of the eviction, and required to defend, the eviction will be conclusive.[3]

2. *Under Special Pleas.* — The plea of conditions performed[4] does not admit evidence of a waiver, or other excuse for non-performance.[5] But an allegation of tender, where such tender is not a party of the contract, but is an act *in pais*, does admit evidence of a waiver.[6]

a. In General: Instances. — In order to enable a party suing in covenant upon a contract under seal to prove a parol contemporaneous agreement as a part of the contract,[7] he must aver in his declaration either fraud or mistake in omitting such agreement from the terms of contract.[8]

1. Wilson *v.* Holden, 16 Abb. (N. Y.) Pr. 133, 136.

2. Wilson *v.* Holden, 16 Abb. (N. Y.) Pr. 130, 133, 136; Negley *v.* Lindsay, 67 Pa. St. 217; s. c., 5 Am. Rep. 427.

3. Paul *v.* Witman, 3 Watts & S. (Pa). 407.

Paramount Title. — In an action of covenant, a grantee, ousted under a legal proceeding of which his grantor had no notice, and to which he was not a party, cannot recover on the warranty of title without showing that the title of the party by whom he was ousted was valid, and grew out of no act of the plaintiff. Dugger *v.* Oglesby, 3 Ill. App. 94.

A., in possession of land, was sued for the possession by one having a paramount title. A.'s grantor made himself a defendant to the suit, and undertook the control of the defence, but died pending the suit, whereupon it abated. A. was defaulted, and judgment of ouster rendered. A. sued his grantor's executor for a breach of the covenants of seisin and warranty. It was *held* that, in consideration of the action of his grantor, it was immaterial whether A. had served written notice on him or not; that his executor was concluded by the judgment, and could not show that the title of the plaintiff in suit against A. was not paramount to that of A.'s grantor. Margan *v* Muldoon, 82 Ind. 347.

4. Respecting the cases in which performance or tender of performance must be proved, see Burling *v.* King, 66 Barb. (N. Y.) 633, 642; s. c., 2 N. Y. Supr. Ct. (2 T. & C.) 545; McCotter *v.* Lawrence, 4 Hun (N. Y.), 107; s. c., 6 N. Y. Supr. Ct. (6 T. & C.) 392; Hoag *v.* Parr, 13 Hun (N. Y.), 95, 100; Delavan *v.* Duncan, 49 N. Y. 485; Hartley *v.* James, 50 N. Y. 38, 42; Doyle *v.* Harris, 11 R. I. 539.

5. Baldwin *v.* Munn, 2 Wend. (N. Y.) 399; s. c., 20 Am. Dec. 627; Oakley *v.* Morton, 11 N. Y. 25.

But if the covenant be independent, evidence cannot be given, under such plea, which amounts to a bar of the plaintiff's claim, or to a set-off of damages sustained by a breach of other independent covenants. Webster *v.* Warren, 2 Wash. C. C. 456.

Insurance Policy. — In an action on the covenant of a policy of insurance under seal, under the plea of covenants performed, the defendant cannot give evidence which goes to vacate the policy. Marine Ins Co. *v.* Hodgson, 10 U. S. (6 Cr.) 206; bk. 3, L. ed. 200.

Covenant of Seisin. — To prove a breach of covenant of seisin, evidence cannot be given to show irregularities which would render the defendant's protest merely void. Pollard *v.* Dwight, 8 U. S. (4 Cr.) 421; bk. 2, L. ed 666.

6. Holmes *v* Holmes, 9 N. Y. 525, affirming 12 Barb. (N. Y.) 137; Carman *v* Pultz, 21 N. Y. 547.

7. **Promissory Note: Agreement to sue the Maker.** — In an action of covenant on a guaranty of a note under seal, evidence of a parol agreement that the payee should bring his action against the maker is inadmissible. Nixon *v.* Long, 11 Ired. (N. C.) L. 428.

8. Hunter *v.* McHose, 100 Pa. St. 38.

Varying Contract by Parol. — In covenant upon an indenture, the plaintiff may show, by parol evidence, that a partial and formal performance of a stipulation on his part to deliver certain articles, with an agreement of a third person to deliver the residue, has been accepted by the other party as full performance of the covenant

On a writ of inquiry in covenant, the plaintiff cannot give evidence of any breach not set forth in his declaration.[1] And where in the complaint in an action of covenant it is assigned as breach, "that the defendant has not used a farm in a husband-like manner, but on the contrary has committed waste," the plaintiff cannot give evidence of the defendant's using the farm in an unhusband-like manner, if it does not amount to waste.[2]

b. Of Title, Damages, Plea of Non est Factum. — (1) *Evidence as to Title.* — The general rules of evidence relative to title are applicable in actions for the breach of a covenant in which questions of title arise.[3]

A lessee, by executing a lease, is estopped from disputing the title of either of his lessors.[4] And where a plaintiff produces an

and such evidence will support a general averment of performance by him. Morrill v. Chadwick, 9 N. H. 84.

In covenant on an agreement to convey land, payment for which was to be made in lawful currency of New Jersey, the vendee may prove that, before the day for payment, the vendor agreed to receive bank bills, which were tendered and refused. McWhorter v. Rose, 5 N. J. L. (2 South.) 582.

1. Matthews v. Sims, 2 Mill (S. C.), Const. 103.

In Pennsylvania. — In Pennsylvania the plea of "covenants performed, with leave, etc.," enables the defendant to give in evidence any thing which, in point of law, can protect him from the plaintiff's claim. Webster v. Warren, 2 Wash. C. C. 456.

Agreement to raise Dam. — In covenant for breach of an agreement to raise a dam and keep it in order, it was *held* that the plaintiff could not show the state of the dam before the agreement. McCready v. Schuylkill Co., 3 Whart. (Pa.) 424.

Merchandise Estimated: Fraud. — In covenant, when merchandise is estimated at a specific price in the agreement, the value of the merchandise cannot afterwards be controverted, unless fraud be alleged. Depreier v. Graham, 1 Ohio, 351.

Special Cases. — For admissibility and competency of evidence determined in cases depending upon particular facts, see Davis v. Kingsley, 13 Conn. 285; Armstrong v. Munday, 5 Den. (N. Y.) 166.

Instances. — In an action on a covenant which runs with the land, evidence that the defendant is an heir will support a declaration charging him as assignee. Derisley v. Custance, 4 T. R. 75.

By a written agreement under seal, C. agreed to convey to E. a parcel of land. E., on this agreement, brought an action of covenant against C. for failure to convey and deliver possession of five and one-half acres, on which there was a mill-site, being part of the land agreed to be conveyed. Evidence was offered to show that C., some time after the date of the agreement, purchased the five and one-half acres, and offered to convey them to E., under the term of the contract, and that E. refused to accept the offer. It was *held*, first, that evidence of the yearly rental value of a mill suitable for such site was inadmissible, as there could be no recovery of the rents and profits of a mill which never had an existence; second, that evidence that C. knew that E. was purchasing the land as a mill-site, and intended to erect a mill on it, was admissible; third, that the measure of damages was the fair rental value of the five and one-half acres in the condition they were in at the time of the agreement, from the date of the agreement to the time when C. offered to convey the five and one-half acres, if the jury should find that he made such offer; fourth, that in order to determine the rental value of the five and one-half acres, evidence was admissible to show that there was a mill-site on it; and fifth, that it was not necessary for E. to rescind the contract in order to enable him to recover for the time during which any part of the land was withheld from him. Clagett v. Easterday, 42 Md. 617.

2. Harris v. Mantle, 3 T. R. 307.

3. **Declarations affecting Title.** — Thus, a grantor's declarations before making a deed are admissible to show that certain liens, or defects in title, known to the grantee, were intended to be covered by the warranty. Skinner v. Moye, 69 Ga. 476.

4. Wood v. Day, 1 J. B. Moore, 389; s. c., 7 Taunt. 646.

Power under Will: Execution of. — In an action on an indenture of lease which purported to be granted to S. in exercise of a power given him by will, the lessee, by holding under the lease, and executing a part, admits the due execution of the will. Bringloe v. Goodson, 5 Bing. N. C. 738.

Presumption of Underletting. — If a person is found on the premises, appearing as original lease for a long term, and proves possession for seventy years, the mesne assignments will be presumed.[1]

(2) *Evidence in Action for Damages.* — In an action for damages for the breach of a covenant, the evidence must support the plea.[2] In an action to recover damages for the breach of a covenant against incumbrances, evidence tending to establish or controvert the execution and breach of the covenant only is admissible under the general pleas;[3] and where there are special defences they may be set up in the answer, and established on the trial.[4]

In an action for breach of covenant of seisin, if the complaint states the conveyance was upon a valuable consideration, without stating its amount, this is sufficient to make evidence of damages admissible. If the allegation in the complaint was defective for indefiniteness, the defect could be reached only by motion to make more certain, not by objections to the admission of evidence.[5]

the tenant, it is *prima facie* evidence of an underletting sufficient to maintain an action for a breach of covenant not to assign or underlet. Doe *ex d.* Hindly *v.* Rickarby, 5 Esp. 4.

1. Earl *ex d.* Goodwin *v.* Baxter, 2 W. Bl. 1228.

On Action for Rent: Assignment of Lease. — Where, in an action of covenant for rent, brought against the assignee of the lessee, the plaintiff alleged that all the estate, right interest, etc., of the lessee in the demised premises, came to and vested in the defendant by assignment thereof, and that the defendant entered into possession of said premises after said assignment, and retained the possession thereof until the rent sued for became due, and the defendant pleaded that the estate, right, etc., of the lessee did not come to and vest in him, as alleged in the declaration, and that he was not possessed of and in the said demised premises in manner and form as the plaintiff had alleged, it was *held* that the fact of the assignment was the only material part of the issue, and the only part which the plaintiff was required to prove, and that the defendant could not be allowed to prove that he did not, in fact, take the possession of the premises after the assignment. Pingry *v.* Watkins, 17 Vt. 379.

2. **Plea of Eviction.** — Thus a declaration in covenant for breach of warranty alleging that by due process of law the plaintiff had been ejected by a person lawfully entitled to the premises, is not supported by evidence that he had recovered a verdict in ejectment fixing the value of the premises and improvements, and had elected to abandon them, and taken judgment for their value, and is insufficient. Long *v.* Sinclair, 38 Mich. 90.

Covenant to deliver Hogs. — Where the pleadings in an action of covenant required the plaintiff to prove a tender of a particular description of hogs to the defendant, and the proof failed as to the description, — proof that the plaintiff had other hogs in the neighborhood that did answer the description was *held* inadmissible, especially when it did not appear that the defendant knew it. Hawley *v.* Mason, 9 Dana (Ky.), 32; s. c., 33 Am. Dec. 522.

3. **Knowledge of Incumbrances.** — Where real estate is conveyed with warranty against incumbrances, knowledge on the part of the grantee that incumbrances exist cannot be shown to defeat his action for damages occasioned by the incumbrances. McGowen *v.* Myers, 60 Iowa, 256.

In an action for breach of covenant of seisin, the defendant, although he has made default by failing to answer, may offer evidence upon the question of damages when the assessment is had. Bartelt *v.* Braunsdorf, 57 Wis. 1.

4. **Indemnity against Incumbrances.** — In an action on a covenant against incumbrances, defendant may show that he left property in plaintiff's hands to cover the incumbrances. Wachendorf *v.* Lancaster, 66 Iowa, 458.

Where, in an action for breach of a covenant of warranty, there was evidence that at the time of the delivery of the deed there were unpaid taxes and penalties on the premises to the amount of $130, that the grantee received from a debtor of the grantor $150, which he agreed to use in discharge thereof, and that he failed to do so until the tax liens greatly exceeded $150, the court *held* that he was not entitled to recover. Perley *v.* Taylor, 21 Kan. 712.

5. Bartelt *v.* Braunsdorf, 57 Wis. 1.

Action by Lessee. — Where a lessee, who had been evicted by a paramount title, sued his lessor for breach of the covenant of

(b) *Under Plea of Non est Factum.* — Under the plea of *non est factum* the lessee in possession cannot controvert the title of his lessor to a demise,[1] or give in evidence what amounts to license.[2]

A fraudulent misrepresentation of the legal effect of a deed, by which a party is induced to execute it, cannot be given in evidence under *non est factum*;[3] but proof that the deed was delivered as an escrow is admissible in evidence under *non est factum*.[4] And under the general issue in covenant, the defendant may show the deed is not his, by proving a lack of power in the agent who executed it on his behalf.[5]

In an action of covenant for rent, before a justice, where the defendant pleaded the general issue, and "gave notice of special matters," and on trial, at a subsequent day, the justice allowed him to give evidence of an eviction, the court held that the justice was right, it being clear that there was no surprise.[6]

c. *Documentary Evidence.* — The admission of documentary evidence in actions for the breach of covenants is controlled by the general rules relating to the admission of such instruments in evidence.[7]

quiet enjoyment, it was *held* that the defendant could not show that plaintiff took a new lease from the paramount owner at a higher rate, and sold it at a profit. Fitzgibbons v. Freisem, 12 Daly (N. Y.), 419.

But where the covenantee, in a suit for the breach of a covenant for quiet use and enjoyment for a term of years, introduces the records of an ejectment suit wherein there was a recovery by one having a paramount title, and a judgment for damages for use and occupation, not disclosing affirmatively the period of occupation, — the covenantor, not being a party or privy to the suit, may show by parol that there was no recovery for a portion of the time. Watson v. Moffy, 57 Miss. 335.

1. Friend v. Estabrook, 2 W. Bl. 1152.

2. [illegible] v. Pemberton, 1 Esp. 35.

3. Edwards v. Brown, 1 Tyr. 182, 281; s. c., 1 C. & J. 307, 3 Y. & J. 423.

4. [illegible] v. Pearson, 4 Esp. 255. And see Bull. N. P. 172.

5. Agent of State Prison v. Lathrop, 1 [illegible] 4[illegible].

6. [illegible] v. Dupont, 1 Sandf. (N. Y.) [illegible].

7. *Judgments as Evidence.* — In an action for breach of a covenant against incumbrances, a judgment for the breach of a similar covenant in another later deed of the same property is no evidence on the question of damages. Myers v. Munson, 65 Iowa, 423.

In order that a grantor may be held liable on his covenants of warranty by virtue of an adjudication in a suit against the covenantee, it must appear that the grantor was notified in the manner prescribed by law. Even without such notice, however, the record of the former suit may be put in evidence on the issue of whether there was an eviction. Clark v. Mumford, 62 Tex. 531.

In an action of covenant for a breach of warranty of the title to real estate, it was *held* that a verdict and judgment against the covenantee in an action of ejectment by him instituted against a third person in possession, with notice to appear and prosecute the action, were no evidence of a better outstanding title. Ferrell v. Alder, 8 Humph. (Tenn.) 44.

Instances. — In an action of covenant for part of the price of land, upon an agreement to convey and deliver possession, the plaintiff averred that he had done so. The defendant traversed the allegation of delivery of possession, and issue was joined to the plea. The court *held*, that, in permitting the plaintiff to read the deed he had made, there was no error injurious to the defendant, who had admitted the fact thus proved. The court *held* also that there was no error in rejecting a reconveyance of the land, which the defendant had tendered to the plaintiff, it being irrelevant to the issue. Tinsley v. Ogg, 7 Dana (Ky.), 385.

Where A., by deed, covenanted to pay B. a sum of money on a certain day, and such deed also contained an assignment by A. to B. of certain goods, as per schedule, in an action brought for a breach of the covenant for the non-payment of the money, and *non est factum* pleaded, it was *held* that it was not necessary for the plaintiff to produce the schedule referred to in proof of *d. Parol Evidence.* — Under the common law rules of pleading an action of covenant on a specialty, in the absence of fraud, the plaintiff is confined to the written covenants, and is not permitted to prove by parol evidence an agreement different from that on which he declares.[1] But where fraud is specially averred in the declaration, and the instrument is sought to be reformed, parol evidence is admissible.[2]

3. *Variance.* — In an action of covenant, the special breach proven must be the breach alleged.[3]

his case. Daines *v.* Heath, 3 C. B. 938; s. c., 11 Jur. 185, 16 L. J. C. P. 117.

1. See Barndollar *v.* Tate, 1 Serg. & R. (Pa.) 160; Vicary *v.* Moore, 2 Watts (Pa.), 451; s. c., 27 Am. Dec. 323; Lyon *v.* Miller, 24 Pa. St. 392, 395; Carrier *v.* Dilworth, 59 Pa. St. 406; Phillips & Colby Construction Co. *v.* Seymour, 91 U. S. (1 Otto) 646; bk. 23, L. ed. 341.

Prior Claims. — Parol testimony is not admissible, in an action on the covenant of seisin, to prove prior claims to the land. Pollard *v.* Dwight, 8 U. S. (4 Cr.) 421; bk. 2, L. ed. 666.

In an action in covenant to recover damages for the breach of a covenant in a deed against incumbrances, proof of a contemporaneous oral undertaking of a larger scope, upon the same consideration, and to add a further obligation to those assumed by the covenantor, is inadmissible; but it is otherwise where the attempt is to cut the latter down. Flynn *v.* Bourneuf, 143 Mass. 277; s. c., 3 New Eng. Rep. 343.

Memorandum on Lease. — A memorandum, indorsed on a lease, signed by the parties, but not dated or under seal, that "it is agreed that the said second parties are not to drill any wells in the barnyard, orchard, or garden without consent of first parties, but nobody else to have the right" was held inadmissible in an action of covenant on an oil lease. Bradford Oil Co. *v.* Blair, 113 Pa. St. 83; s. c., 4 Cent. Rep. 101.

Pointing out Boundary to Land sold. — Where B. sold M. standing timber upon twelve tracts of land, and covenanted that he was the legal and equitable owner of the tracts, M. brought covenant on the deed, and alleged that B., before the deed was delivered, went upon the ground and pointed out to M. the lines, etc., of two of the tracts, upon the faith of which M. began cutting timber therefrom, but was dispossessed by paramount title. It was *held* that parol testimony was not admissible to prove that the covenant for title referred to the tracts as pointed out. Merriman *v.* Bush (Pa.), 8 Cent. Rep. 87.

Assessment for Construction of Road. — In a suit for a breach of covenant against incumbrances by reason of an assessment for construction of a free gravel road upon the land conveyed, it must appear at least that there was a proceeding resulting in the assessment made by the committee. A certificate of the county auditor of the amount assessed for a free gravel road against certain land, not accompanied with proof of such fact, is inadmissible. Kirkpatrick *v.* Pearce, 107 Ind. 520; s. c., 5 West. Rep. 798.

The court say that Robinson *v.* Murphy, 33 Ind. 483, and Barker *v.* Hobbs, 6 Ind. 385, would not, under present laws, be enforced to the rule there stated.

2. Hunter *v.* McHose, 100 Pa. St. 38; Thorne *v.* Warfflein, 100 Pa. St. 519.

3. **What a Variance.** — Accordingly, an allegation by O., the grantee, that the paramount title was not in D., the grantor, but in P., it was *held* not to be supported by proof that P. had purchased the premises at a foreclosure sale in chancery, without proof also of a deed, etc. Dugger *v.* Oglesby, 3 Ill. App. 94.

A declaration in covenant for breach of warranty, alleging that by due process of law the plaintiff had been ejected by a person holding a paramount title, is not supported by evidence that he had recovered a verdict in ejectment, fixing the value of the premises and improvements, and had elected to abandon them, and take judgment for their value. Long *v.* Sinclair, 38 Mich. 90.

A plaintiff covenanted to build two houses for five hundred pounds by a certain day, and averred, in an action, that the houses were built within the time. It was *held* that evidence that the time had been enlarged by parol agreement, and the houses finished within the enlarged time, did not support the declaration. Littler *v.* Holland, 3 T. R. 590. See Bailey *v.* Homan, 3 Bing. N. C. 915; s. c., 5 Scott, 94, 3 Hodges, 184.

In covenant for not employing the plaintiff as clerk, the declaration averred that on the day stipulated in the covenant the plaintiff was ready, and tendered his services to the defendant. The court *held* that this averment was not supported by evidence that on the day stipulated the plaintiff was sick, and that the defendant agreed to dispense with his services until he

XI. Damages. — 1. *In General.* — In an action of covenant, the plaintiff is entitled to recover damages, only on the breaches alleged. This is the rule, either where there is an issue on the plea of performance, or where there is a judgment by default, and a writ of inquiry.[1]

An action of covenant sounds in damages, and such damages depend upon matter *dehors* the instrument declared on, and which must be ascertained by proof *aliunde*. If, therefore, judgment is given for the plaintiff on demurrer, the damages must be assessed by a jury.[2]

The time at which the breach of the covenant is made to sell and convey land is the time when the value of the land should be estimated in assessing damages;[3] and in an action of covenant

should recover; and that on a subsequent day he tendered his services, and that the defendant refused to employ him. Marks v. Robinson, 1 Bailey (S. C.), 89.

In covenant, the defendant took oyer of the covenant, and afterwards pleaded covenants performed. The court *held* that the defendant by oyer made the covenant itself a part of the record, and could not, at the trial of the issue, object to the covenant as evidence, on the ground of variance between it and the covenant set forth in the declaration. Armstrong *v.* Armstrong, 1 Leigh (Va.), 491.

In a declaration, on a covenant in a lease by the defendant, that the plaintiff shall have and enjoy the demised premises from a day named, during a certain term, the breach alleged being that the plaintiff on the day entered upon and became possessed of the premises for the term, but was not able to enjoy the premises in this, viz., that the plaintiff being so possessed, the defendant entered into the premises and upon the plaintiff's possession, and expelled and kept him out, the defendant pleaded that he did not keep plaintiff out; and it was *held* that such breach was not proved by evidence that the plaintiff came to take possession, but was refused entrance by the defendant, who continued occupying the premises, and never admitted him. Hawkes *v.* Orton, 5 A. & E. 367; s. c., 6 Nev. & M. 842.

What not Variance. — In covenant by the assignee of the lessor against the assignee of the lessee, the declaration charged "that all the estate, right, title, and interest of the lessee of, in, and to the demised premises, with appurtenances thereof, legally came to and vested in the defendant," and the defendant, besides the plea of *non est factum*, took issue on the assignments. The court *held* that it was not a variance entitling the defendant to non-suit, and that the defendant was shown by the evidence to be assignee of only a part of the demised premises. Van Rensselaer *v.* Jones, 2 Barb. (N. Y.) 643.

In covenant against the assignee of the lessee for non-payment of rent, the declaration alleged that all the estate of the lessee in the premises leased had come to, and vested in, the defendant by assignment. Issue being joined upon this averment, it was *held* that the point of such issue was whether the defendant was assignee of the whole estate of the lessee in any part of the land, and it being proved that he was lessee of the whole estate in a part only of the land, and, further, that there was no variance, and that the plaintiffs could recover such part of the rent reserved as the defendant was liable to pay in respect to the part of the premises held by him. Van Rensselaer *v.* Gallup, 5 Den. (N. Y.) 454.

1. Eastham *v.* Crowder, 10 Humph. (Tenn.) 194.

Abatement of Writ. — Where, in an action of covenant broken, the summons left with the defendant in the service of the writ, does not set forth what sum in damages is demanded, and for what, it is a good cause to abate the writ. Putney *v.* Cram, 5 N. H. 174.

2. Simonton *v.* Winter, 30 U. S. (5 Pet.) 141; bk. 8, L. ed. 75.

In Pennsylvania. — In Pennsylvania a jury may, in an action of covenant, certify a balance due to the defendant. Vicary *v.* Moore, 2 Watts (Pa.), 451; s. c., 27 Am. Dec. 323.

3. Marshall *v.* Haney, 9 Gill (Md.), 251.

In Negotiable Paper. — The note accompanying a mortgage, having been assigned with it, its value at the time of trial — not at the time of the assignment — was properly considered in diminution of damages, and an offer to return the note before suit was not necessary. Smith *v.* Holbrook, 82 N. Y. 562.

In an action of covenant on a sealed contract to pay $12,000 in Confederate money, by a certain date, and, on failure to pay by for the non-payment of a certain amount borrowed in bank bills, the measure of damages is the value of such bills when obtained in coin.[1]

In an action for damages for breach of covenants in a deed, the court, under the "prayer for general relief," will give such relief as the justice of the case demands.[2]

2. *Measure of: Nominal Damages, etc.* — *a. Measure of Damages.*[3] — The measure of damages for vendee or lessee, evicted by paramount title, is the consideration paid,[4] with interest and costs of the ejectment suit.[5]

that time, to pay $12,000 in 6 per cent bonds of the $500,000,000 loan within twelve months from that date, it was *held* that the measure of damages was the value of the bonds at the time the contract was made. Fleming *v.* Robertson, 3 S. C. (N. S.) 118.

1. **Value of Property purchased.** — Evidence as to the value of the property which the covenantor has afterwards purchased with the money thus borrowed, is incompetent. Harris *v.* Davis, 64 N. C. 574.

2. Price *v.* Deal, 90 N. C. 290.

Conveyance to Third Person. — It is of no legal concern to a grantor bound to pay off incumbrances, that the conveyance was not in fact made to the other party to the land contracts, but to the latter's wife, at his request: the grantor's obligations are not increased or diminished. Norton *v.* Colgrove, 41 Mich. 544.

3. As to measure of damages for breach of the various covenants, see *ante*, COVENANTS IN DEEDS.

4. **Rent.** — If the consideration is rent, paid for the term of possession, damages are nominal. Lanigan *v.* Kille, 13 Phila. (Pa.) 60; s. c., 97 Pa. St. 120; 39 Am. Rep. 797.

Breaches of Covenant in Deeds. — The damages for breach of a covenant of seisin is *prima facie* the amount of consideration paid, where the plaintiff was assignee of the cause of action arising upon the breach. Kimball *v.* Bryant, 25 Minn. 496.

Where improved land was sold with warranty, and a recovery was afterward had in ejectment for the value of the naked lot at the time of such recovery, it was *held* that, in an action on the covenant, the damages could not exceed the value of the lot alone at the date of the covenant. Mason *v.* Kellogg, 38 Mich. 132.

In an action for a breach of a covenant of seisin, the measure of plaintiff's damages is the consideration paid for the land, and interest thereon from the date of payment, in lieu of *mesne* profits; the grantee being left to his remedy against the evictor who has established a paramount title, to obtain pay for improvements. Conrad *v.* Druids' Grand Grove, 64 Wis. 258.

Where the breach of a covenant against incumbrances or for quiet enjoyment consists simply of the existence of an unexpired term or lease, the measure of damages is the value of the use of the premises for the time the grantee has been deprived of the use of them. Fritz *v.* Pusey, 31 Minn. 368.

In an action for breach of a covenant against incumbrances, the recovery cannot exceed the amount paid to relieve the premises therefrom; nor, in any case, exceed the actually received consideration of the deed. Andrews *v.* Appel, 22 Hun (N. Y.), 429.

In case of a recovery by an assignee of the covenantee against the covenantor, for a breach of the covenant, the measure of damages is the amount paid by such assignee for the premises, not exceeding the consideration paid to the covenantor, with interest from the time of the eviction. Moore *v.* Frankenfield, 25 Minn. 540.

If, pending an action for a breach of the covenant of seisin, the grantee's title becomes perfect by reason of the enurement, to his benefit, of an after-acquired title by the grantor, the consideration paid for the land is not the measure of damages, but only the amount necessary to indemnify the grantee for acts done by the holder of the adverse title. McInnis *v.* Lyman, 62 Wis. 191.

Rental Value. — If a vendor sells land with warranty of title, and at the time the land has been rented by his agent, without his direction or knowledge, and the vendee is thereby delayed in getting possession, the measure of damages is the fair rental value for the lost time; and, *prima facie*, the rent agreed to be paid by the tenant is the fair rental value. Moreland *v.* Metz, 24 W. Va. 119; s. c., 49 Am. Rep. 246.

5. Kingsbury *v.* Milner, 69 Ala. 502.

Consideration with Interest and Costs. — The measure of damages for a breach of a covenant against incumbrances is the amount paid, if reasonable, to extinguish the incumbrance, whether it exceeds the purchase-money or not: whether the amount paid was reasonable, is a question for the

The rule is the same, though the lessor has set off the value of [illegible]'s improvements, in an action for mesne profits against the lessor by the paramount owner.[1]

In action for breach of warranty of title, plaintiff cannot recover more than the paramount title cost.[2]

[illegible]. On such question the record of a recovery against the covenantee, of which the covenantor had no notice, is not conclusive; but is the fact of payment any evidence of what the incumbrance was worth. Dickson *v.* Desire, 23 Mo. 151; Walker *v.* Deaver, 5 Mo. App. 139.

In an action for breach of covenant of warranty brought by a purchaser from the covenantee, the measure of damages is the consideration money paid by the covenantee, with interest from the time of the sale, and the costs of the action to eject the plaintiff, and not the price paid by the plaintiff for the land. The rule is the same where the land was sold to the purchaser at a sale by an officer of court, under an order of the court. Lawrence *v.* Robertson, 10 S. C. 8.

The amount of damages in such a case cannot be offset by a voluntary payment by the covenantor of the bond given by the plaintiff to the officer of the court for the purchase-money, nor by payments made by the covenantor to the true owner of the land, in satisfaction of his claim for *mesne* profits. Lawrence *v.* Robertson, 10 S. C. 8.

[illegible]. — In an action for the breach of the covenant of seisin, the measure of damage is the purchase-money and interest. [illegible] *v.* Millner, 69 Ala. 502; Wilson *v.* [illegible], 78 Ind. 384; Williamson *v.* Williamson, 71 Me. 442; Conrad *v.* Druids' Grand Grove, 64 Wis. 258; Price *v.* Deal, 90 N. C. 290.

Where a lot of land is conveyed to two grantees, either grantor may recover from the grantee a moiety of the purchase-price, with interest from the date of the eviction. [illegible] *v.* Dow, 9 Lea (Tenn.), 93.

No interest on the consideration money is recoverable for the time during which the grantee occupies the premises, without liability to the holder of the paramount title. Stebbins *v.* Wolf, 33 Kan. 765.

Rate of Interest. — Where a note given for the purchase-money of a tract of land [illegible] unpaid, the measure of damages for a breach of the covenant in the deed was *held* to be the amount of the purchase-money, and interest at the same rate as that borne by the note. Zent *v.* Picken, [illegible] Iowa, 535.

[illegible]. — The rule of damages is, not only the value of the land, but the legal costs and necessary expenses of such action of ejectment. Pitkin *v.* Leavitt, 13 Vt. 379.

In an action for breach of warranty in a deed, the measure of damages is the value of the land as agreed on at the time of the conveyance, with reasonable costs and expenses incurred in resisting eviction. Stebbins *v.* Wolf, 33 Kan. 765.

The expense of defending the title may be recovered by the covenantee in an action on the covenant. Allis *v.* Nininger, 25 Minn. 525. And the measure of damages is the cost of extinguishing the incumbrance without regard to the purchase-price or value of the land. Walker *v.* Deaver, 79 Mo. 664.

Where defendant, in an action of covenant broken, had notice of the pendency of the real action against plaintiff, and was cited to defend under his covenant, but refused to defend, and judgment was for the plaintiff in such real action, the costs of that suit, the expense to which plaintiff was subjected in defending it, with interest from the time of payment, and the value of the premises at the time of eviction, with interest therefrom, are the legal elements of damage. Williamson *v.* Williamson, 71 Me. 442.

In A.'s action against B. for breach of covenant of warranty as to land recovered from A. by paramount title, it was *held* that B. was liable for the taxed costs in the ejectment against A., having received due notice to defend the same. Not so for counsel fees incurred by A. in defending the suit. Williams *v.* Burg, 9 Lea (Tenn.), 455.

Attorney Fees. — In an action for breach of a warranty, the grantee can recover attorney's fees only to the extent of proof of actual liability therefor. Swartz *v.* Ballou, 47 Iowa, 188. See also Williams *v.* Burg, 9 Lea (Tenn.), 455.

1. Lanigan *v.* Kille, 13 Phila. (Pa.) 60; s. c., 97 Pa. St. 120; 39 Am. Rep. 797.

Mesne Profits. — Upon the assessment of plaintiff's damages in a suit for breach of covenant of seisin and warranty, if plaintiff has had the use of the premises, he can recover no interest for the period prior to his eviction, unless he has been compelled to pay mesne profits to the holder of the paramount title, which, under the Missouri statute of ejectment, cannot have been for more than five years. Hutchins *v.* Roundtree, 77 Mo. 500.

2. Snell *v.* Iowa Homestead Co., 59 Iowa, 701; Andrews *v.* Appel, 22 Hun (N. Y.), 429; Moore *v.* Frankenfield, 25 Minn. 540.

The measure of damages, where a third person has recovered judgment in partition for an undivided third part of the land, is one-third of the purchase-money with interest.[1]

Where parts of a covenant are waived by a defendant, the waiver does not render it a new contract, and the remedy is by action of covenant. If there has been substantial performance, the plaintiff is entitled to recover, but not necessarily the whole contract price. There may be defects, in the fulfilment, of such a nature as to preclude the plaintiff from recovery, for which the jury would have a right to make a deduction as compensation to defendant.[2]

Extinguishment of Incumbrances to protect Title. — Where land is conveyed with a covenant against incumbrances, in case of breach, the covenantee may recover the amount which he is required to pay in extinguishment of incumbrances. Morehouse *v.* Heath, 99 Ind. 509.

Where the vendor held under a tax deed, and the vendee recovered, in the action for eviction by the holder of the paramount title, all taxes paid, it was *held* that the amount so received should be allowed in reduction of damages. Stebbins *v.* Wolf, 33 Kan. 765.

L. purchased one-fourth of a quarter-section of land for $350, but took possession of the whole quarter-section, for all of which he afterwards suffered judgment in ejectment, and elected to pay its value, which was adjudged to be $800; it was *held* that in an action on the covenant of seisin in the deed to him he could recover only $200, in the absence of any showing that the forty-acre lot which he bought was worth any more than either of the other forties in the quarter-section. Long *v.* Sinclair, 40 Mich. 569.

For breach of a covenant to secure a certain release, the damages will be what it costs to obtain such release, although more is paid therefor than it is worth. Robbins *v.* Arnold, 11 Ill. App. 434.

Where a vendee, to protect his title, buys an outstanding title, the measure of damages, in his suit for breach of covenant, is the amount so paid, if it does not exceed the original price paid the defendant. Price *v.* Deal, 90 N. C. 290.

1. Wright *v.* Nipple, 92 Ind. 310.

Joint Vendees: Damages for Breach. — Where A. conveyed to B., by warranty deed, a lot of land, and B. one-half of it to C., and there were unpaid taxes on the land, to pay which the land was sold after the conveyance to C., in an action on the covenant, A. was held liable to C. only for that proportion of the consideration paid to A. which the value of his portion of the lot bore to the whole lot, and that the burden was on C. to establish this value. Mischke *v.* Baughn, 52 Iowa, 528.

A., by deed containing a covenant of general warranty of title, conveyed to B., his co-tenant, an undivided half of a lot of land. B. subsequently conveyed the entire lot to C., who was afterward evicted, and sued A. on his covenant. The court *held* that he could recover one-half the amount paid by him to B., with interest from the date of eviction. Mette *v.* Dow, 9 Lea (Tenn.), 93.

A. and B. owned portions of the same building, B. having a right of way over a staircase in A.'s portion. A. conveyed to C. with a warranty against incumbrances, and B. conveyed to D. C. and D. moved the building back twelve feet, and repaired the staircase at their joint expense. Later C. tore out the staircase, and therefore had to pay damages to D. C. sued A. for breach of his covenant. The court *held* that he could not recover for damages brought upon him by his own misconduct, and that he could only recover the value of the incumbrance from the date of his deed to that of the removal of the building, when the easement ceased, and for the expense of the removal of the incumbrance. Wilcox *v.* Danforth, 5 Ill. App. 378.

An action for breach of a covenant of title, in which the plaintiff claimed to be entitled to recover for two undivided thirds of the value of the land, was restrained by a bill in equity, and it was decided that the plaintiff in the action at law was estopped to claim damages for more than one-sixth of the value of the land. It was *held*, that, although the *ad damnum* named in the writ was less than two-thirds of the value of the land, he was entitled to one-sixth of the entire value, if this did not exceed the *ad damnum*. Lucas *v.* Wilcox, 135 Mass. 77.

2. Monocacy Bridge Co. *v.* American Iron Bridge Manuf. Co., 83 Pa. St. 517.

Note Payable in Bank-Bills. — Where, in covenant, there was a plea of covenants performed, and no proof was introduced except a note for —— dollars, payable in current bank-notes, it was *held* that the jury were warranted in giving a verdict for

Where a deed purporting to convey a fee, with covenants of seisin and warranty, conveyed only a life estate, it was held that the grantee, who sued on the covenants without an offer to rescind the conveyance, could recover only the difference between the value of the fee and the life estate.[1]

In the absence of any showing of fraud a partial failure of title cannot be shown, in reduction of damages, in an action for the price of land conveyed by a deed, with the usual covenants of title. The defendant's remedy is by an action on the covenants.[2]

If a plaintiff bring covenant upon a penal bond, he cannot have judgment for the penalty; he can only recover his actual damages.[3]

b. Nominal Damages. — In an action on a covenant, the grantee can recover only nominal damages, unless he has been actually evicted, or has paid the whole or a part of the incumbrance.[4] And where the plaintiff makes no proof of consideration, and shows no threatened disturbance of possession, the damages recoverable will be nominal.[5]

XII. Judgment. — Defects in the declaration cannot be cured by the verdict, where no proof was offered to aid the insufficient averments of the declaration.[6]

A grantor against whom, in an action on his warranty, a judgment has been rendered, is entitled to a re-conveyance free from any incumbrances created by the grantee.[7]

In an action of covenant on a warranty of title, a verdict rendered against the purchaser in a suit against him, in which suit the vendor was vouched to defend his title, is conclusive against the vendor, unless it can be shown that the verdict was procured by collusion or negligence on the part of the purchaser.[8]

Where two out of three joint covenantors suffer judgment by default on counts in several deeds, and the third defends and

the number of dollars called for in the note. Baker v. Jordan, 5 Humph. (Tenn.) 485.

1. Recohs v. Younglove, 8 Baxt. (Tenn.) 385.

2. Bowley v. Holway, 124 Mass. 395.

3. Vaughn v. Van Storch (Pa.), 1 Luz. L. Obs. 3.

4. Hundy v. Ridenour, 63 Ind. 406.

Where Grantee has not discharged Incumbrance. — A grantor is liable for only nominal damages on a covenant against incumbrances, unless the grantee has to pay them. Norton v. Colgrove, 41 Mich. 544.

One who, before his suit for breach of the covenant against incumbrances, has discharged none, can recover only nominal damages. Kirkendall v. Keogh, 2 Ill. App. 493.

A grantee of land whose possession has never been disturbed, can recover only nominal damages for a merely technical breach of the covenant of seisin in his deed. Boon v. McHenry, 55 Iowa, 202.

A. sold to B. a portion of certain premises subject to a mortgage, and covenanted to pay the mortgage when due. He failed to do this, and, the rest of the land being worth more than the mortgage debt, it was *held* that B. could only recover nominal damages. Wilcox v. Musche, 39 Mich. 101.

Conveyance by Widow. — A grantee in a warrantee deed of land by a widow, in which she had but an undivided third interest, who has never been disturbed in his possession by either the widow or her heirs, can recover only nominal damages for breach of warranty. Hencke v. Johnson, 62 Iowa, 555.

5. Norman v. Winch, 65 Iowa, 263.

6. Washington v. Ogden, 66 U. S. (1 Black) 450; bk. 17, L. ed. 203.

7. Shorthill v. Ferguson, 47 Iowa, 284.

8. Wilson v. McElwee, 1 Strobh. (S. C.) L. 65.

succeeds on some counts, the plaintiff cannot hold his judgment on those counts against the other two.[1]

In an action in covenant against the administrator, widow, and heirs of the covenantor, the judgment should be against them *in solido*, with an order, as to the administrator, *quando acciderint*. The widow and heirs should be subjected to no greater liability than the value of the estate descended to them, exclusive of the widow's award, and the court should ascertain this value.[2]

COVERTURE. — See HUSBAND AND WIFE.

COVER.[3]

COVIN. (See FRAUD; COLLUSION.) — "Covin is a secret assent determined in the minds of two or more to the prejudice of another."[4]

COW. — See ANIMALS.[5]

1. Morgan *v.* Edwards, 6 Taunt. 398; s. c., 2 Marsh. 201.

2. Dugger *v.* Ogglesby, 3 Ill. App. 94.

3. "There can be no doubt that the policy which they obtained purported to *cover* not only goods which belonged to them, but also such as they held in trust or on commission."

. . . "Will be *covered* by insurance as soon as received in store." Johnson *v.* Campbell, 120 Mass. 449.

Held, that the canal and the filter-beds were land *covered* with water within the meaning of § 17, etc. East London Water Works Co. *v.* The Leyton Sewer Authority, L. R. 6 Q. B. 669.

"If the dock with the surrounding buildings were taken as a whole, it would become something more than 'land *covered* with water;' but that part which is the basin or reservoir is within that description." Dock Co. *v.* Board of Health, 2 Best & Smith, 716.

4. . . . "As if tenant for life or tenant in tail secretly conspire with another that the other shall recover against the tenant for life lands which he holds, etc., to the prejudice of the one in reversion; or if an executor or administrator permit judgments to be entered against him by fraud, and plead them to a bond, or any fraudulent assignment or conveyance be made, the injured party may plead *covin*, and obtain relief." Termes de la Ley (ed. 1708). Co. Litt. 357 b.; Comyn's Dig. "Covin," A.; 1 Viner's Abr. 473. "Now it can hardly be questioned that it was by collusion that the judgment was obtained against the defendants by the defendants in the name of Rolfe, for whatever purpose it was obtained, and as to its being covinous, the definition of *covin* was given in the argument from Coke upon Littleton, and we have it very clearly given in the 'Termes de la Ley' (ed. 1708), 'Covin is a secret assent determined in the minds of two or more to the prejudice of another.' In the present case the secret assent was the assent of Rolfe to the defendants' borrowing his name to bring the action against themselves; and the prejudice of another was the judgment being used, as in the present case, to defeat the rights of others. It matters not whether Rolfe was kept in ignorance of the purpose to which the action was to be applied or not: it was not the less covinous in the defendants." Girdlestone *v.* Brighton Aquarium, L. R. 3 Ex. D. 142.

"The plea of *covin* and collusion is not proved in its legal effect, unless the jury find there was something wrong in the mind of the parties who had agreed to the judgment. I think the jury would have to find that there was something wrong in the minds of both the parties." Brett, L. J. L. R. 4 Ex. D. 109.

. . . "Such a transaction would be a fraud upon the other partner, or, more properly, it would be what is called *covin*, which is by Lord Ellenborough defined to be 'a contrivance between two to defraud or cheat a third.' It would be a contrivance between Muzzy and the Merrimans to appropriate the property of Huntly to pay a debt of Muzzy's, which, of course, Huntly was under no obligation to pay, and it would therefore operate as a fraud or cheat upon him; and this, too, would be done with a full knowledge of all the facts by Muzzy and the Merrimans, who also knew that Huntly was ignorant of the whole proceeding." Mix *v.* Muzzy, 28 Conn. 191.

5. If the indictment charge the malicious and unlawful killing of a *cow*, it is good without the use of the word "beast," as a *cow* is a beast within the meaning of the statute. Taylor *v.* State, 6 Humph. (Tenn.) 285.

CRAFT. (See ADMIRALTY; SHIPPING.)—1. Art, skill, cunning.[1] 2. Vessels of any kind.[2]

CRANK.—Some strange action caused by a twist of judgment; a caprice; a whim; a crotchet; a vagary; violent of temper.[3]

CREATE.[4]

An indictment for stealing *a cow* cannot be supported by evidence of stealing *a heifer*. The King *v.* Cook, 1 Leach's Crown Law, 105 (1774).

A steer is an "animal of the *cow kind*" within the meaning of the statute, etc. Watson *v.* State, 55 Ala. 150.

"One certain calf of the neat-cattle kind" is sufficient description of the animal stolen. Grant *v.* State, 3 Tex. App. 1.

"The statute in terms exempts one *cow* from attachment and execution. Possibly, if it were a penal statute, it might be considered that the term only applies to the animal after she has brought forth a calf. This is, undoubtedly, not only the common but the correct meaning of the term. In the case of Dow *v.* Smith, 7 Vermont, 465, it was considered that the term made use of had, in this statute, a more extensive meaning, and included a heifer, adopting the definition which, in some dictionaries and by some writers, is given to that term, to wit, a *young cow*. Freeman *v.* Carpenter, 10 Vt. 434.

A heifer, twenty months old, and which has not begun to give milk, is exempt from execution as a *cow* under the statute, if its owner intends to keep it as a *cow*, and has no other *cow*. Carruth *v.* Grassie, 11 Gray (Mass.), 211.

"A *heifer*, between two and three years old, that has never had a calf," may be described in an indictment for larceny as a cow. Parker *v.* State, 39 Ala. 365.

It is no ground for dismissing a writ of replevin that an animal described in the writ as a heifer is described in the certificate of appraisement as a *cow*. Pomeroy *v.* Trimper, 8 Allen (Mass.), 398.

"Good custom *cow-hide* boots." Wait *v.* Fairbanks, Brayton's (Vt.) 77.

Cow-keeper. *Held*, that A. was not a cow-keeper within the bankrupt act. Bell *v.* Young, 15 Com. B. 524.

1. Web. Dict.

2. The expression "bay or river *craft*, or other boat," in the code of *Virginia*, includes steamboats of five hundred tons burden. And the word craft includes all kinds of sailing vessels. The Wenonah *v.* Bragdon, 21 Gratt. (Va.) 685.

A small pleasure boat, without deck, propelled by a small steam engine, and run occasionally by its owners for pleasure only, was *held* not within the provisions of the United States steam inspection laws, which require every ferry-boat, canal-boat, yacht, "or other small craft of light character propelled by steam," to be inspected. United States *v.* The Mollie, 2 Woods (C. C.), 318.

The words of a statute were "wherry, lighter, or *other craft*," and the term "craft" was *held* not to include a steam-tug, because, though a steam-tug is a *craft*, it is not one of the same character as a wherry or a lighter. Reg. *v.* Reed, 23 L. T. Rep. 156; 26 Eng. L. & Eq. 133; Reed *v.* Ingham, 3 El. & Bl. 888.

3. The word "crank" has no necessary defamatory meaning; and for a newspaper to publish an item that a certain pamphlet, written by a lawyer who was also the author of a text-book on the law of patents, was "the effusion of a crank," is not actionable without a charge in the declaration of the alleged defamatory meaning of the word by an appropriate innuendo, and an averment and proof of special damage.

"It is urged, in a brief filed by plaintiff, that, since the assassination of President Garfield by Guiteau, the word 'crank' has obtained a definite meaning in this country, and is understood to mean a crack-brained and murderously inclined person, and is so used by the public press. I do not think so short a term of use would give to such a word a libellous sense or meaning without an allegation or innuendo as to the sense in which it was used by the defendant. In Ogilvie's Imperial Dictionary, published in England in 1883, and republished in this country in 1885, the word is found in the Supplement with the following definition: 'Crank. Some strange action caused by a twist of judgment; a caprice; a whim; a crotchet; a vagary; violent of temper; subject to sudden cranks. Carlyle.' So that by this authority, which, I think, must be deemed the latest, and probably the best, the word would seem to have no necessarily defamatory sense. It would not necessarily imply that a man had been guilty of a crime, nor tend to subject him to ridicule or contempt, to say of him that he is capricious, or subject to vagaries or whims; as such implication or intent could only be shown by an apt averment, and proof in support of such averment." Blodgett J. Walker *v.* Tribune Co., 29 Fed. Rep. 827 (Feb. 14, 1887), and The Reporter (Mass.), vol. 23, p. 520.

4. To *create* a charter or a corporation, is to make one which never existed before; while to renew one, is to give vitality to

CREATURE. — See ANIMALS.[1]

CREDIBLE, CREDIBILITY. — See WITNESSES.

CREDIT. (See CONSTITUTIONAL LAW; EXECUTION; GUARANTY; LOANS; LETTER OF CREDIT; MONEY; TAXATION.) — A transfer of goods, money, or other valuable thing, in confidence of future payment. That which is due to any person, as distinguished from that which he owes.[2] As a verb the word means to trust, to sell, or loan, in confidence of future payment; to set to the credit of; to enter upon the credit side of an account.[3]

one which has been forfeited or has expired; and to extend one, is to give an existing charter more time than originally limited. Moers *v.* City of Reading, 21 Pa. St. 188.

The continuance of an old charter is not the *creation* of a new corporation, and does not infringe a constitutional provision restricting the creation of new corporations, but recognizing and continuing existing ones. People *v.* Marshall, 1 Gilm. (Ill.) 672.

An act remedying a technical defect in the organization of a corporation, e.g., insufficiency in the proof or acknowledgment of a certificate of organization of a banking association formed under a general statute, is not an act to *create* a corporation. Syracuse City Bank *v.* Davis, 16 Barb. (N. Y.) 188.

A sub-lessee is within the provisions of the fifth section of the Representation of the People Act, 1867, which gives the right of voting to the lessee or assignee of lands or tenements for the unexpired residue of any term originally *created* for a period of not less than sixty years, etc.

The words "originally created" refer to the creation of the term in respect of which the claim is made. Chorlton *v.* Stretford, L. R. 7 C. P. 198.

To change of phraseology in the revision of the statutes from "created and manifested" to "created or declared," wrought a change of the law, so that under R. S. c. 73, § 11, an express trust need not be created by a writing: it is sufficient that it be subsequently declared by a writing signed by the party charged with the trust. McClellan *v.* McClellan, 65 Me. 500.

"A debt *created* by fraud." See Palmer *v.* Preston, 45 Vt. 154.

1. "From an examination of the various general statutes providing for the establishment of pounds, and the manner in which they shall be maintained and kept, the impounding of *creatures* in them, their care and sustenance while in the pound, etc., . . . we are also of the opinion that they were intended to apply as well to *creatures* which should be liable to be impounded under the provisions of statute, as those which should be impounded for other causes. . . . It has also been justly remarked that the use of the word *creatures* in the third clause favors the construction of defendants." Whitlock *v.* West, 26 Conn. 406; State *v.* Bogardus, 4 Mo. App. 215.

2. See Webster's Dict. and Bouv. Law Dict.

Credits, in an act making them the subject of taxation, are defined to be "the excess of the sum of all legal claims and demands, whether for money, or other valuable thing, or for labor, or for services, due, or to become due, to the person liable to pay taxes thereon, . . . when added together (estimating every such claim or demand at its true value in money), over and above the sum of all legal *bona fide* debts owing by such person." Payne *v.* Watterson, 37 Ohio St. 123; and see also Life Ins. Co. *v.* Lott, 54 Ala. 499.

Shares of stock are not "credits" within the meaning of a tax act, stock being "in no sense a debt owing to the stockholder." Bridgeman *v.* Keokuk (Iowa), 33 N. West. Rep. 355.

But a loan of money secured by a mortgage on real estate is a credit within such an act. Myers *v.* Seaberger (Ohio), 12 N. East. Rep. 796.

Credits, including promissory notes within that term, are not "property," so as to be subject to taxation as such. People *v.* Hibernia Bank, 51 Cal. 243; s. c., 3 Cent. L. J. 260.

Choses in action, and the notes of a bank as being choses in action, are not "goods, effects, and credits" within an act making such subject to trustee process. Perry *v.* Coates, 9 Mass. 537. Nor are legacies. Barnes *v.* Treat, 7 Mass. 271.

The contrary is held in Maine, legacies there having been made the subject of execution. Cumming *v.* Garvin, 65 Me. 301.

3. Webster's Dict.

"Credit in cash" means "pay;" and a request to credit in cash, is a sufficient order to pay to make the instrument which contains it a bill of exchange. Ellison *v.* Collingridge, 9 C. B. 571.

"Credit my account" indorsed on a bill

CREDITOR. (See ASSIGNMENT FOR BENEFIT OF CREDITORS; BANKRUPTCY; DEBTOR AND CREDITOR; INSOLVENCY.) — One to whom a debt or obligation is due.[1]

CREDITORS' BILLS, OR CREDITORS' SUITS.

1. Definition and Kinds. — Creditors' bills are bills in equity filed by creditors for the purpose of collecting their debts out of the real or personal property of the debtor, under circumstances in which the process of execution at common law could not afford relief.[2] They may be classified according to the character or condition of the debtor, as, *first*, against a debtor in his lifetime; *second*, against corporations or their stockholders; and *third*, against decedents' estates. In this article the subject will be treated generally, as relating to the first class: the others will be considered specially, under paragraphs 8 and 9, *post*.

2. Jurisdiction. — The jurisdiction of a court of equity to reach the property of a debtor justly applicable to the payment of his debts, even where there is no specific lien on the property, is undoubted. It is a very ancient jurisdiction; but for its exercise, the debt must be clear and undisputed, and there must exist some special circumstances requiring the interposition of the court to obtain possession of and apply the property. Unless the suit relate to the estate of a deceased person, the debt must be established by some judicial proceeding; and it must generally be shown that legal means for its collection have been exhausted.[3]

of exchange is restrictive, and puts an end to its negotiability. It is an appropriation of the proceeds of the bill which renders any other illegal. Lee *v.* Bank, 1 Biss. (C. C.) 325.

1. "The term creditor does not mean singly a person to whom a debt is due, — that is but its usual meaning; but it further denotes a person to whom any obligation is due, — and this is its unusual meaning. A creditor, according to the definition of Bouvier, 'is he who has a right to require the fulfilment of an obligation or contract.' In this large sense it means more than the person to whom money is owing. Webster's definition of the word is, 'A person to whom a sum of money, or other thing, is due by obligation, promise, or in law.'" *Beasley, C. J.*, in N. J. Ins. Co. *v.* Meeker, 37 N. J. L. 300.

"In a strict legal sense a creditor is he who voluntarily trusts and gives credit to another for a sum of money, or other property, upon bond, bill, note, book, or simple contract. In a more liberal sense he is a creditor who has a legal demand upon another for money, or other property, which has got into the hands of another without his consent by mistake or accident, which he is entitled to have, or to a compensation in damages for, upon the ground of an implied promise.

"In the more general or extensive sense of the term, he is a creditor who has a right by law to demand and recover of another a sum of money on any account whatever." Stanley *v.* Ogden, 2 Root (Conn.), 261.

2. Bisp. Eq. sec. 525.

Bills of this description had their origin in the limited scope of the ordinary writs of execution. These writs, being common-law writs, were confined in their operation to legal interests. Equitable interests could be reached, if reached at all, in equity alone. The narrowness of the common-law remedy naturally led to a jurisdiction in equity to afford the necessary relief. Ibid. sec. 526; Pomeroy, Eq. Jur. sec. 1415.

3. *Field, J.*, in Public Works *v.* Columbia College, 17 Wall. 521, 530.

"It is within the general jurisdiction of a

In this country, there have been enacted in several States various statutory provisions, intended to accomplish more speedily or effectively the object of the creditor's bill in the court of chancery.[1] In other States the creditor's bill, as a branch of the equitable jurisdiction, is still the appropriate remedy.[2] The employment of special statutory writs and processes, especially those for the attachment of debts due to the defendant, has greatly restricted the use of the creditor's bill in this country.

3. Exhausting Remedy at Law. — The jurisdiction in equity attaches only when the creditor's legal remedies have proved inadequate. For this reason the creditor must usually allege that he has obtained a judgment, and issued execution, and that there has been a return thereto of *nulla bona.*[3] There are,

court of chancery to assist a judgment creditor to reach and apply to the payment of his debt any property of the judgment debtor, which, by reason of its nature only, and not by reason of any positive rule exempting it from liability for debt, cannot be taken on execution at law, as in the case of most property, in which the debtor has the entire beneficial interest, of shares in a corporation, or of choses in action. *Gray, J.*, in Ager *v.* Murray, 105 U. S. 126; Bayard *v.* Hoffman, 4 John. Ch. (N. Y.) 450; Hadden *v.* Spader, 20 John. (N. Y.) 554.

1. The statutes and decisions on this subject will generally be found under the name "Supplementary Proceedings;" i.e., proceedings by the creditor supplementary to the usual means of execution, in compelling discovery by the defendant himself of his assets, or by joining others in whose hands the defendant's assets are supposed to be. Statutes of this kind are in force in *Arkansas, California, Colorado, Indiana, Iowa, Kentucky, Maine, Minnesota, Missouri, Nebraska, Nevada, New Jersey, New York, Ohio, Oregon, South Carolina,* and *Wisconsin.*

The procedure in supplementary proceedings is usually by order made upon proof of return of an execution unsatisfied, requiring the debtor to appear in person in court, to be examined concerning his property: a receiver is then appointed to collect the assets, and, upon qualifying, he becomes vested with the assets without conveyance or assignment by the debtor. The receiver also represents the creditors in bringing any suits which may be necessary to establish title to the property. Wait, Fraud Conveyances, sec. 62; High on Receivers (2d ed.), § 401, *et seq*

2. This is the case in those States in which there is either the general chancery jurisdiction, or a special jurisdiction conferred by statute for assisting creditors in enforcing their rights against the debtor's property. It follows, that, where there is no such equitable jurisdiction, the creditor's bill, as known in chancery, cannot be used. For the jurisdiction in equity in the several States, see EQUITY; also Bisp. Eq. (4th ed.) sec. 15; Pomeroy, Eq. Jur. sec. 41.

In *Pennsylvania* a judgment creditor desiring to avoid a fraudulent alienation of land by his debtor, must levy on the land, buy it in, and bring ejectment: he is not entitled to relief in equity. Girard National Bank's Appeal, 13 Weekly Notes Cas. (Pa.) 101.

3. "Courts of equity are not tribunals for the collection of debts, and yet they afford their aid to enable creditors to obtain payment, when their legal remedies have proved to be inadequate. It is only by the exhibition of such facts as show that these have been exhausted, that their jurisdiction attaches. Hence it is, that, when an attempt is made by a process in equity to reach equitable interests, choses in action, or the avails of property fraudulently conveyed, the bill should state that judgment has been obtained, and that execution has been issued, and that it has been returned by an officer without satisfaction." Webster *v.* Clark, 25 Me. 313. Quoted and approved as the established rule of equity in Taylor *v.* Bowker, 111 U. S. 110; s. c., 6 Am. & Eng. Corp. Cas. 609; Baxter *v.* Moses, 10 Am. & Eng. Corp. Cas. 307.

A creditor's bill should be dismissed when it is apparent that no *bona fide* attempt has been made by the officer to find property to satisfy the judgment. As the basis for a creditor's bill, an execution upon the judgment should be in good faith issued, and should be returned unsatisfied by the officer upon a reasonable and actual, but ineffectual, effort to find property. If the return shows on its face a failure in this respect, there is no foundation for equity jurisdiction. Bassett *v.* Orr, 7 Biss. (C. C.) 296.

"The court, when its aid is invoked, looks only to the execution, and the return er, a few exceptions to this rule, which are stated in the.

ficer to whom the execution was
The execution shows that the
afforded at law has been pursued,
course is the highest evidence of
The return shows whether the
has proved effectual or not; and
e embarrassments which would
ny other rule, the return is held
re. The court will not entertain
as to the diligence of the officer
voring to find property upon which
If the return be false, the law
s to the injured party ample
' *Field, J.*, in Jones *v.* Green, 1
', S.) 330.
re allegation of insolvency is not
o sustain the averment of a want
ly at law. Hall *v.* Joiner, 1 S. Car.
186.
is proved that there is sufficient
other than that described in the
tisfy the judgment, the bill cannot
ined. Vacrhees *v.* Howard, 4 Abb.
. (N. Y.) 503; High on Receivers
§ 402. See also Birely's Executors
, 5 Gill & J. (Md.) 432; s. c., 25 Am.
; Newman *v.* Willett, 52 Ill. 101;
Burdett, 1 Paige (N. Y.), 305;
. Long, 1 Ired. Eq. (N. C.) 190;
' *v.* Eastland, 10 Yerg. (Tenn.)
ese *v.* Bradford, 13 Ala. 837; Tap-
vans, 11 N. Hamp. 312; Bassett *v.*
ns Co., 47 Vt. 313; Allen *v.* Mont-
48 Miss. 106; Preston *v.* Colby
West. Rep. 33.
th regard to the extent to which a
ditor must proceed at law, before
laim the aid of a court of chancery,
a difference, depending on the
f the property which he seeks to
where lands or chattels, of which
title was in the debtor, have been
ntly conveyed, it is enough to have
nt in the former case, and to issue
tion to the sheriff in the latter, be-
: application to chancery is to re-
obstruction which prevents a legal
operating upon the property; but
is desired to reach equitable assets,
ssary to have the execution levied
rned unsatisfied, or something
nt to that, because chancery does
creditor in upon that fund until
l assets appear to be exhausted;
re legal assets have been fraudu-
nveyed, a creditor is entitled to set
reyance aside in equity without
that there is no property retained
btor from which satisfaction might
Note to Sexton *v.* Wheaton, 1 Am.
s. *54; Beck *v.* Burdett, 1 Paige
308.

Whether an equitable suit analogous to the creditor's suit will be allowed in aid of the lien created by an attachment, before the recovery of judgment, is a question to which the American courts have given directly conflicting answers. Pom. Eq. Jur. § 1415, and note.

It is unnecessary, in order to maintain a creditor's suit to cancel judgments alleged to be paid, that the creditor should have issued execution in the county in which the debtor's lands lie: it is sufficient that an execution has been returned unsatisfied in the county where the debtor resides, and that his judgment is a lien on the land. Shaw *v.* Dwight, 27 N. Y. 244.

Where the property of the judgment debtor sought to be reached is land only, and the debtor has no other property out of which the judgment can be satisfied, and that has been conveyed to another in fraud of the judgment, it is not essential to relief for the judgment creditor to show that he has issued execution. Payne *v.* Sheldon, 63 Barb. (N. Y.) 169.

A return of an unsatisfied execution against one of two joint judgment debtors, is sufficient to support a creditor's suit against the other. Hill *v.* Hetrick, 5 Daly (N. Y.), 33.

It is unsettled whether the debtor's insolvency precludes the necessity of proceeding at law as if he were solvent. It has been *held* that where the debtor is insolvent, and the issue of an execution would be of no practical utility, its issue may be dispensed with, and the judgment creditor may resort directly to chancery. Turner *v.* Adams, 46 Mo. 95; Postlewait *v.* Howes, 3 Iowa, 365; Botsford *v.* Beers, 11 Conn. 369; Payne *v.* Sheldon, 63 Barb. (N. Y.) 169.

Where it was alleged that the debtor was insolvent, and that executions on other judgments had been returned *nulla bona*, on demurrer it was *held* that it was not necessary to allege that execution on the present judgment had issued. Tabb *v.* Williams, 4 Jones, Eq. (N. C.) 352. But see *contra*, Mixon *v.* Dunklin, 48 Ala. 455; Parish *v.* Lewis, Freem. (Miss.) Ch. 299.

Whenever the creditor has a trust in his favor or a lien upon property for a debt due him, he need not exhaust his remedy at law. Case *v.* Beauregard, 101 U. S. 688.

If the debtor has absconded, so that no judgment can be obtained against him, and he has no property in the State subject to attachment, but has money in a city treasury belonging to him, it may be reached by bill in equity without even a previous judgment, and without showing fraud. Pendleton *v.*

4. Effect of the Bill. — The filing of the creditor's bill, and the service of process, creates a lien upon the effects of the judgment debtor.[1] It has been aptly termed an "equitable levy."[2]

5. Nature of Remedy. — The objects sought by the creditor in chancery are generally, (1) to remove some obstruction, fraudulently or inequitably imposed to prevent a sale of the debtor's property on execution at law; or (2) to obtain satisfaction of his debt out of property of the defendant, which cannot be reached by execution at law.[3] In the first class of cases, the court acts in the methods usually adopted for the enforcement of decrees in equity: the remedy by *injunction* against any transfers of the debtor's property, made with intent to defraud and delay his judgment creditors, is the immediate relief afforded,[4] which is followed by the various forms of relief *in rem* or *in personam* given by equity in cases of fraud.[5] In the second class of cases, the relief sought is best obtained by the appointment of a receiver, who shall take possession of the property, and hold and dispose of it under the order of the court.[6] The necessity of obtaining both

Perkins, 49 Mo. 565. See also Scott *v.* McMillan, 1 Litt. (Ky.) 302; Peay *v.* Morrison's Executors, 10 Gratt. (Va.) 149; Farrar *v.* Haselden, 9 Rich. Eq. (S. C.) 331; Pope *v.* Solomon, 36 Ga. 541.

The return of an execution unsatisfied before its return-day, and in the lifetime of the writ, does not lay the foundation for a receiver upon a bill in behalf of the judgment creditor. High on Rec. (2d ed.) § 404; Thayer *v.* Swift, Harring. (Mich.) 430.

1. *Swayne, J.*, in Miller *v.* Sherry, 2 Wall. (U. S.) 237, 249.

Where the property is not liable to an execution at law, the plaintiff obtains no lien upon the property or fund by the issuing or return of the execution. But it is the filing of the bill in equity, after the return of the execution at law, which gives to the plaintiff a specific lien. *Lord Hardwicke* in Edgell *v.* Haywood, 3 Atk. Rep. 357; Beck *v.* Burdett, 1 Paige (N. Y.), 309.

The judgment creditor who first files his bill in chancery obtains a priority in relation to the property and effects of the defendant which cannot be reached by execution at law. Coming *v.* White, 2 Paige (N. Y.), 567.

2. The *lis pendens* is an equitable levy, and secures a priority of lien to the complainant. Tilford *v.* Burnham, 7 Dana (Ky.), 109.

3. *Walworth, Chancellor*, in Beck *v.* Burdett, 1 Paige (N. Y.), 308.

"It is a familiar and unquestioned doctrine of equity that the court has power to aid a judgment creditor to reach the property of his debtor, either by removing fraudulent judgments or conveyances which obstruct or defeat the plaintiff's remedy under the judgment, or by appropriating, in satisfaction of the judgment, rights or equitable interests of the defendant which are not the subject of legal execution." *Green, Chancellor*, in Robert *v.* Hodges, 16 N. J. Eq. 302.

4. Where the main purpose of the bill is to set aside a fraudulent transfer of a debtor's goods and effects, made to delay and hinder his creditors, an injunction is considered as a necessary adjunct, and is granted as auxiliary to the general relief sought. Hyde *v.* Ellery, 18 Md. 496; Witmer's Appeal, 45 Pa. St. 455; High on Inj. (2d ed.) § 1402.

5. *Paxson, J.*, speaking of the applicability of the equitable jurisdiction to this class of cases, says, "Its process is plastic, and may be readily moulded to suit the exigencies of the particular case. A court of equity proceeds with but little regard to mere form. It moves with celerity, and seizes the fruits of a fraud in the hands of the wrong-doer." Fowler's Appeal, 87 Pa. St. 454.

The creditor's bill or a suit to clear the fraudulent transfer is preferable to seizure under execution. If the creditor attempts to sell the disputed property arbitrarily under execution, the market value is injured, and the debtor's transfer of title must be proved to be fraudulent. But by filing the creditor's bill, the only risk incurred is as to the costs and expense of the suit, and generally no seizure is effected unless the suit is successful, in which event the covinous transfer and cloud on the title is cleared away. Wait, Fraud. Con. § 60

6. No branch of the law of receivers is more frequently invoked than this. Under

Remedies is frequently met in the same case. Discovery is an important incident to either remedy.

2. What Property may be reached. — From the nature of the jurisdiction, it is obvious that all property of the debtor which ought in equity to be applied to the payment of his debts, may be reached by this process. It is not essential that the property sought should have been fraudulently withdrawn from the creditor's reach at law.[1] Property held in trust for the debtor may in general be reached in equity.[2] A patent or copyright is property which may be subjected by this means to the payment of the owner's debts.[3] A right of action for injury to debtor's property

the practice of the *New York* court of chancery, the appointment of receivers on creditors' bills, after return of execution unsatisfied, was almost a matter of course for the preservation of the debtor's property pending the litigation. Bloodgood *v.* Clark, 4 Paige (N. Y.) 574; High, Rec. (2d ed.) §§ 399, 400.

The creditor must have used due diligence in the assertion of his rights. Gould *v.* Tryon, Walk. (Mich.) 353.

The power of appointing a receiver on the debtor's property is exercised with caution when the contest is as to the title to real estate which is in possession of, and claimed by, third parties. Vause *v.* Woods, 46 Miss. 120; High, Rec. (2d ed.) § 416.

When a receiver has been appointed, his possession is that of the court; and any attempt to disturb it, without leave of the court first obtained, will be a contempt on the part of the person making it. Wiswall *v.* Sampson, 14 How. (U. S.) 52.

The receivership may extend to property of any nature, real or personal, in which the debtor has such an interest as may avail his creditor. High, Rec. (2d ed.) § 43[illegible].

Form of Decree. — "In an equitable proceeding of this kind, a decree in the nature of a judgment for damages cannot be rendered against the defendant, who is alleged to have taken a fraudulent assignment of the property. The decree against him must be a decree for an account. He must be called to account for just what property has come into his hands, and no more; and he will be entitled, under ordinary circumstances, to a rebate for the amount that was justly and honestly his due. The mode of taking such an account is well known in equity proceedings. The defendant is to exhibit an account either in his answer or in the master's office, and, if it is not satisfactory to the complainant, it may be surcharged or falsified; and as the account is finally found to stand, so will the responsibility of the defendant be. But if the complainant wishes to make him answerable in damages, either for the waste of the property or for its disposal by the original proprietor by aid of the wrongful complicity of the defendant, he must sue for damages in an action at law." *Bradley, J.*, in Dunphy *v.* Kleinsmith, 11 Wall. (U. S.) 610.

1. Pendleton *v.* Perkins, 49 Mo. 565. See, however, Donovan *v.* Finn, 1 Hopk. Ch. (N. Y.) 59; s. c., 14 Am. Dec. 531 and note.

A debt due by a municipal corporation to its creditor may be reached by a creditor's bill against the latter. Furlong *v.* Thomssen, 1 West. Rep. 729.

2. Groff *v.* Bonnett, 31 N. Y. 9; s. c., 88 Am. Dec. 236; Halstead *v.* Davison, 10 N. J. Eq. 290; Smith *v.* Moore, 37 Ala. 327.

Under the *New York* legislation, property held in trust for the debtor, or arising from a fund proceeding from a third person, and intended to secure the debtor a support, cannot be reached, except as to a surplus after providing for such support. Groff *v.* Bonnett, 88 Am. Dec. 236 and note.

In other jurisdictions this exception has not been made. Frazier *v.* Barsium, 19 N. J. Eq. 316; Starr *v.* Keefer, 1 MacArthur (D. C.), 166; Pickrell *v.* Zell, 2 MacArthur (D. C.), 65.

3. Stephens *v.* Cady, 14 How. (U. S.) 528; Ager *v.* Murray, 105 U. S. 126; Gillette *v.* Bate, 86 N. Y. 87; Pacific Bank *v.* Robinson, 57 Cal. 520.

A part-owner of the right with the debtor should be joined as co-defendant in the bill. A proper form of decree is that, in default of the debtor's paying the judgment by a certain day, with interest and costs, the patent rights be sold, and an assignment thereof be executed by him, and that, in default of his executing such assignment, some suitable person be appointed trustee to execute the same. Ager *v.* Murray, 105 U. S. 126.

But this jurisdiction cannot be maintained on the ground of fraud. There is no jurisdiction in *Pennsylvania* for such a bill. Bakewell *v.* Keller, 11 Weekly Notes Cas. (Pa.) 300; Rutter's Appeals, 6 Cent. Rep. 619.

may be reached.[1] But exempt property cannot be reached,[2] nor the possibility of inheriting property,[3] nor unearned salary.[4]

7. Parties to the Bill. — In a creditor's suit, the rule of equity which requires all parties having interests in the subject-matter in controversy, to be joined as parties, is relaxed so far as to allow one or more creditors to file a bill on behalf of themselves and others: this is done as a matter of convenience, as it tends to prevent a multiplicity of suits.[5] It has been said that the judgment debtor is an indispensable party defendant to the creditor's suit;[6] but it seems that, in suits brought against fraudulent alienees to avoid specific conveyances, the action is a proceeding *in rem*, and as the debtor cannot be prejudiced by a decree, he need not be a party defendant.[7] But the fraudulent grantee or assignee must be joined.[8]

8. Against Corporations and Stockholders. — This remedy is frequently applied in modern times for the relief of creditors of insolvent corporations. The jurisdiction is both on account of the advantages of the form of action,[9] and the nature of the corporate property, and the liabilities of the stockholders thereto.[10] It is now well established that the capital stock of a corporation, especially its unpaid subscriptions, is a trust fund for the benefit of the general creditors of the corporation.[11] The suit to enforce payment of

There is no jurisdiction in the federal courts for granting this relief under the patent laws. Ryan *v.* Lee, 10 Fed. Rep. 917.

1. Hudson *v.* Plets, 11 Paige (N. Y.), 180.

2. Tillotson *v.* Wolcott, 48 N. Y. 188.

3. Smith *v.* Kearny, 2 Barb. Ch. 533.

4. Browning *v.* Bettis, 8 Paige (N. Y.) 568.

5. Dan. Chan. Pr. 236, 237; Barbour on Parties, 438.

Parties who are creditors by several judgments, may, as a general rule, join as complainants in an action to reach property fraudulently alienated by a debtor. Wait, Fraud. Conv. § 108; Conro *v.* Port Henry Iron Co., 12 Barb. (N. Y.) 27.

"The practice of permitting judgment creditors to come in and make themselves parties to the bill, and thereby obtain the benefit, assuming at the same time their portion of the costs and expenses of the litigation, is well settled." *Nelson, J.*, in Myers *v.* Fenn, 5 Wall. (U. S.) 207; Pomeroy, Remedies (2d ed.), § 394.

The complainant may properly make every one a party who is a participator in the fraud alleged: he has a right to do this for purpose of discovery. Bank *v.* Littell (N. J.), 4 Cent. Rep. 868.

6. Pomeroy, Remedies (2d ed.), § 347.

It has been *held* that the defendant is a necessary party in a creditor's bill to reach a chose in action, — Miller *v.* Hall, 70 N. Y. 252; — and, in a receiver's suit, to set aside a fraudulent conveyance, and apply the proceeds on the plaintiff's judgment. Sharer *v.* Brainard, 29 Barb. (N. Y.) 25. He is the principal party in a suit to set aside a prior assignment made by him for the benefit of creditors. Lawrence *v.* Bank, 35 N. Y. 324. See also Gaylords *v.* Kelshaw, 1 Wall. (U. S.) 81.

7. Fox *v.* Moyer, 54 N. Y. 130; Buffington *v.* Harvey, 95 U. S. 103; Campbell *v.* Jones, 25 Minn. 155; Potter *v.* Phillips, 44 Iowa, 357; Wait, Fraud. Conv. § 129.

8. Wait, Fraud. Conv. § 131. See, generally, as to assignees for benefit of creditors, receivers, lien claimants, etc. Ibid. §§ 133–138.

9. Tanesma *v.* Schuttler, 114 Ill. 156.

10. "In equity the capital stock of a corporation is regarded as a trust fund for the payment of debts. The creditors have a lien upon it, which is prior in point of right to any claim which the stockholders as such can have upon it; and courts will be astute to detect and defeat any scheme or device which is calculated to withdraw this fund, or in any way to place it beyond the reach of creditors." Crandall *v.* Lincoln, 52 Conn. 73, 95. In this case it was *held* that receivers of an insolvent corporation could recover back the money paid by the corporation for its own stock. See Wood *v.* Dummer, 3 Mason (C. C.), 308.

11. *Miller, J.*, in Sawyer *v.* Hoag, 17 Wall. (U. S.) 610, in which it was *held*

subscriptions may be brought by an assignee of the corporation, or by any creditor. The remedy at law must be pursued and exhausted as against the corporation.[1] The creditor is not required to join all the stockholders, or to settle the affairs of the corporation, and adjust the equities between its various stockholders and debtors.[2] It is essential that there be a call upon the stockholders for the amount or share of their unpaid assessments, in order to entitle the creditor to be benefited by it; but if this call has not been made, or, by reason of a contract with the stockholders, cannot be made, by the corporation, the assessment must be made by the court upon proper proceedings. An assessment so made can be recovered in an action at law, or can be enforced by a decree against the stockholder; and the fund so raised will be administered for the benefit of all creditors.[3] A creditor's bill may be main-

that the assignee of an insolvent corporation could recover back from a stockholder the amount of a pretended payment to the capital stock which the corporation had at once loaned back to the stockholder: this was held to be a mere simulated payment, by which the trust could not be defeated. "The capital stock of an incorporated company is a fund set apart for the payment of its debts. It is a substitute for the personal liability which subsists in private copartnerships. When debts are incurred, a contract arises with the creditors that it shall not be withdrawn or applied otherwise than upon their demands, until such demands are satisfied. The creditors have a lien upon it in equity. If diverted, they may follow it as far as it can be traced, and subject it to the payment of their claims, except as against holders who have taken it *bona fide* for a valuable consideration and without notice. It is publicly pledged to those who deal with the corporation for their security. Unpaid stock is as much a part of this pledge and as much a part of the assets of the company as the cash which has been paid upon it. Creditors have the same right to look to it as to any thing else, and the same right to insist upon its payment as upon the payment of any other debt due to the company. As regards creditors, there is no distinction between such a demand and any other asset which may form a part of the property and effects of the corporation." *Swayne, J.*, in Sanger *v.* Upton, 91 U. S. 56; Hatch *v.* Dana, 101 U. S. 205. These principles apply as well to enforcing the subscription of a county as of an individual. County of Morgan *v.* Allen, 103 U. S. 498. For practice under *New York* statutes, see Morgan *v.* N. Y. & R. R. Co., 10 Paige (N. Y.), 290; s. c., 40 Am. Dec. 244.

1. Ogilvie *v.* Ins. Co., 22 How. (U. S.) 380; Hatch *v.* Dana, 161 U. S. 205; Taylor *v.* Bowker, 111 U. S. 110; 6 Am. & Eng. Corp. Cas. 609.

2. Ogilvie *v.* Ins. Co., 22 How. (U. S.) 380; Bartlett *v.* Drew, 57 N. Y. 587; Pierce *v.* Construction Co., 38 Wis. 253. "A judgment creditor who has exhausted his legal remedy may pursue in a court of equity any equitable interest, trust, or demand of his debtor, in whosesoever hands it may be. And if the party thus reached has a remedy over against other parties for contribution or indemnity, it will be no defence to the primary suit against him that they are not parties. If a creditor were to be stayed until all such parties could be made to contribute their proportionate share of the liability, he might never get his money." *Bradley, J.*, in Marsh *v.* Burroughs, 1 Woods (U. S. C. C.), 468; Hatch *v.* Dana, 101 U. S. 205. But where it is sought to impose on stockholders a statutory liability "in proportion to their stock," the obligations of all the stockholders must be considered, and the proper mode of proceeding is by bill in equity for an account. Pollard *v.* Bailey, 20 Wall. 520; Terry *v.* Tubman, 92 U. S. 156; Terry *v.* Little, 101 U. S. 216. See Hatch *v.* Dana, 101 U. S. 213.

A creditor is entitled to a decree against such of the stockholders as he has sued for the full amount of the assets wrongfully received by them: each stockholder must restore his part *in toto* without regard to the non-joinder of other stockholders. Stang's Appeal, 10 Weekly Notes Cas. (Pa.) 409.

3. Lane's Appeal, 105 Pa. St. 49. An attachment execution will not lie to recover the unpaid portion of the stock against the stockholders. Lane's Appeal, 3 Am. & Eng. Corp. Cas. 1. But *compare In re* Glen (U. S. Dist. Ct.), 13 Weekly Notes Cases Iron Works (Pa.), 387; s. c., 20 Fed. Rep. 764; Peterson *v.* Sinclair, 83 Pa. St. 250.

An agreement between the corporation

tained against the directors of an insolvent corporation for mismanagement of its affairs.[1]

9. Against Decedents' Estates. — Creditors' bills filed after the death of the debtor, generally result in an administration of the estate, unless the executor or administrator admits assets in his hands applicable to the payment of the demand.[2] The jurisdiction of special courts for the administration of decedents' estates in this country renders the creditor's bill as practised in chancery a somewhat exceptional remedy.[3] Creditors' bills of this kind are usually filed by one or more on behalf of all; the bill enures to the benefit of all who may come in and prove their debts under it, so as to prevent the running of the statute of limitations; but, up to the time of the decree for an account, the suit is under the control of the creditor who has filed the bill; after the decree the fund is in court, and the creditor who has filed the bill ceases to have absolute control of the suit.[4] The

and its stockholders that the latter shall not be subject to calls for assessments, and that the stock should be considered full paid, is binding as against the corporation; but such a contract is a fraud in law upon the creditors, and they can set it aside, and require the stockholders to pay in full. Sawyer *v.* Hoag, 17 Wall. (U. S.) 610; Scovill *v.* Thayer, 105 U. S. 143.

But in *England* it has been *held* that such a contract is binding upon creditors as well as upon the corporation. Waterhouse *v.* Jamieson, L. R. 2 H. L. (Sc.) 29; Currie's Case, 3 De G. J. & S. 367; Carling's Case, L. R. 1 Ch. D. 115.

"It is well settled, that when stock is subscribed to be paid upon call of the company, and the company refuses or neglects to make the call, a court of equity may itself make the call if the interests of the creditor require it. The court will do what it is the duty of the company to do. . . . But under such circumstances, before there is any obligation upon the stockholder to pay without an assessment and call by the company, there must be some order of a court of competent jurisdiction, or, at the very least, some authorized demand on him for payment." *Woods, J.*, in Scovill *v.* Thayer, 105 U. S. 155.

An action will not lie by a judgment creditor against one stockholder for payment of an uncalled subscription in satisfaction of the judgment. Patterson *v.* Lynde, 106 U. S. 519; s. c., 1 Am. & Eng. Corp. Cas. 76; Ladd *v.* Cartwright, 7 Oreg. 329. See Glenn *v.* Williams, 1 Am. & Eng. Corp. Cas. 58, and note. *Cf.* Patterson *v.* Lynde (Illinois), 10 Am. & Eng. Corp. Cas. 195.

1. The pending of such a suit is a good plea in abatement to an action at law subsequently brought for the same cause by the assignee for benefit of creditors in the name of the corporation against the directors. Penn Bank *v.* Hopkins, 111 Pa. St. 328.

2. Bisp. Eq. (4th ed.) § 528; Pom. Eq. Jur. § 1152, *et seq.*

3. "In England, courts of chancery took jurisdiction of bills against executors and administrators for discovery and account of assets, and to reach property applicable to the payment of the debts of deceased persons, not merely from their general authority over trustees and trusts, but from the imperfect and defective power of the ecclesiastical courts. It was sufficient that a debt existed against the estate of a decedent, and that there was property which should be applied to its payment to justify the interposition of the court; but, where a distribution of the fund had been made, another creditor could not ask for a return of the moneys or for a proportional part if he had received notice of the original proceeding, and had been guilty of laches or unreasonable neglect. In this country, there are special courts established in all the States, having jurisdiction over estates of deceased persons, called probate courts, orphans' courts, or surrogate courts, possessing, with respect to personal assets, nearly all the the powers formerly exercised by the court of chancery and the ecclesiastical courts in England. They are authorized to collect the assets of the deceased, to allow claims, to direct their payment and the distribution of the property to legatees or other parties entitled, and generally to do every thing essential to the final settlement of the affairs of the deceased and the claims of creditors against his estate." *Field, J.*, in Public Works *v.* Columbia College, 17 Wall. (U. S.) 531.

4. Bisp. Eq. (4th ed.) § 530.

validity of the creditor's claim need not be established by judgment.[1] The court has jurisdiction of a bill against the administrator and the decedent's fraudulent alienee; and in such a bill it is proper to make a prior incumbrance a party, in order to make a clear title, though a sale may be made subject to the incumbrance.[2]

CREEK. — This term has no definite legal meaning. According to Webster it sometimes signifies a small bay, inlet, or cove, and generally in this country a small river.[3]

CREMATION. — See Dead Body.

CREW. (See Maritime Law; Prize, etc.) — The ship's company, including officers as well as seamen. The term is occa-

1. Hogan v. Walker, 14 How. (U. S.) 29. "The authorities are abundant and well settled that a creditor of a deceased person has a right to go into a court of equity for a discovery of assets and the payment of his debt. When there, he will not be turned back to a court of law to establish the validity of his claim. The court, being in rightful possession of the cause for a discovery and account, will proceed to a final decree upon all the merits." Bradley, J., in Kennedy v. Creswell, 101 U. S. [illegible], citing Thompson v. Brown, 4 Johns. (N. Y.) Ch. 619; 1 Story, Eq. Jur. [illegible]; 2 Wms. Exrs. 1718, 1719.

2. Hogan v. Walker, 14 How (U. S.) 29.

Jurisdiction of Federal Courts. — The jurisdiction in equity in the circuit courts does not receive any modification from the legislation of the States or the practice of their courts having similar powers. The fact of the pending of proceedings in insolvency in a State probate court, will not oust the jurisdiction of the circuit court; and a foreign creditor may establish his debt in the federal court against the representative of the decedent, notwithstanding the local laws relative to the administration and settlement of insolvent estates, and the court will interpose to arrest the distribution of any surplus among the heirs. Kendall v. Creighton, 23 How. (U. S.) [illegible].

A federal court may entertain jurisdiction of a creditor's bill, although the parties to the suit may be compelled to testify under an act of Congress, and although the code of the State gives special proceedings having the same end in view, — to reach any property of the judgment debtor, and subject it to execution under the judgment. Frazer v. Colorado Dressing Co., 5 Fed. Rep. 163.

Where the demands of the several creditors joining in the bill exceed the amount necessary to give jurisdiction to the Supreme Court on appeal, but the claim of no individual creditor equals that amount, neither party can appeal. Seaver v. Bigelows, 5 Wall. (U. S.) 208; Schwed v. Smith, 106 U. S. 188.

A creditor's suit to reach the defendant's interest in a patent right is not a suit arising under the patent laws within Rev. Stat. § 629. Ryan v. Lee, 10 Fed. Rep. 917.

Authorities. — The subject is discussed in the treatises on equity. See especially Bispham on Equity (4th ed.), §§ 525–530; Pomeroy on Equity Jurisprudence, § 1415; High on Receivers (2d ed.), §§ 399–471; High on Injunctions (2d ed.); Wait on Fraudulent Conveyances and Creditors' Bills; Pomeroy on Remedies and Remedial Rights (2d ed.); Bump on Fraudulent Conveyances (3d ed.); Thompson on Liability of Stockholders.

3. French v. Carhart, 1 N. Y. 107. It has, however, been said, that "the term 'creek' itself properly imports a recess, cove, bay, or inlet in the shore of a river, and not a separate or independent stream, though sometimes used in the latter meaning." Schermerhorn v. Hudson R. R. Co., 38 N. Y. 103. In this case, it was applied to that part of a river flowing between an island and the shore. The word is used in its ordinary acceptation in Wilson v. B. B. Creek Marsh Co., 2 Pet. (U. S.) 245; Surgett v. Lapice, 8 How. (U. S.) 48; and see Oyster Co. v. Baldwin, 42 Conn. 255.

A creek does not cease to be such, merely because its course may be opposed by some natural or artificial obstruction. French v. Carhart, 1 N. Y. 107.

Third Creek. — Where an entry of land is designated as beginning 640 poles north from the mouth of the third creek running into the Ohio above the mouth of the Little Miami, the creek which is third numerically must be taken to be meant, unless some other stream can be shown by reputation or notoriety to have been considered the third creek. Watts v. Lindsey's Heirs, 7 Wheat. (U. S.) 158.

sionally used as exclusive of the officers; and sometimes, but rarely, as including the master as well as the officers and seamen.[1]

CRIB.[2]

CRIMINAL CONSPIRACY.

1. U. S. *v.* Winn, 3 Sumn. (C. C.) 209. In deciding this case, *Story, J.*, said, "Now, the word 'crew' has several well-known significations. In its general and popular sense, it is equivalent to 'company.' Thus, for example, we find the most general definition of it, laid down in Johnson's Dictionary, to be, 'a company of people associated for any purpose.' And the same learned lexicographer adds, that, when spoken with reference to a ship, the crew of a ship, or ship's crew, means 'the company of a ship.' . . . Falconer, in his 'Marine Dictionary,' says, 'The crew of a ship (*equipage*, French) comprehends the officers, sailors, seamen, marines, ordinary men, servants, and boys.' . . .

"The general sense of the word 'crew' being, then, as I think, equivalent to ship's company, which, it can scarcely be doubted, embraces all the officers, as well as the common seamen, that sense ought not to be displaced, unless it is manifest that the legislature have used the word 'crew' in a more restrictive sense; and this must be ascertained, either from the context, or from the object to be accomplished by the enactment. Now, in examining our laws upon maritime subjects, it will be found that the word 'crew' is used sometimes in the general sense above stated, and sometimes in other senses, more limited and restrained. It is sometimes used to comprehend all persons composing the ship's company, including the master; sometimes to comprehend the officers and common seamen, excluding the master; and sometimes to comprehend the common seamen only, excluding the master and officers. But in the last two classes, I think, upon close examination, it will be found that the context always contains language which explains and limits the general to the particular sense." It was accordingly *held* that in an act providing "that, if any master or other officer, etc., shall, without justifiable cause, beat, wound, or imprison any one or more of the crew, he shall be punished," etc., "crew" included the officers.

The master is included in the expression, "officers, sailors, and others of the crew," in an act by which actions for wages by those enumerated, are subjected to a limitation of one year. Millandon *v.* Martin, 6 Rob. (La.) 534.

A passenger is not one of the crew or ship's company. U. S. *v.* Libby, 1 W. & M. (C. C.) 231.

A provision in articles of service, signed by a seaman, that the crew were, if required, to be transferred to any other ship in the same employ, was *held* to be several as to each of the crew, and not merely joint as to all. Frazer *v.* Hatton, 2 C. B. N. S. 525.

"Any of the crew" means any one or more of the crew. U. S. *v.* Harriman, 1 Hughes (C. C.), 525.

2. A "crib of corn" is an indefinite quantity, not only because the capacity of a crib is not fixed, but because the expression does not necessarily indicate that the crib is full. A contract to redeliver a crib of corn does not require the delivery of a full crib, but only of the amount of corn originally delivered; and evidence may be given to show that amount. Masterson *v.* Goodlett, 46 Tex. 402.

I. Conspiracy at Common Law. — 1. *Definition.* — A criminal conspiracy is (1) a corrupt combination (2) of two or more persons, (3) by concerted action, to commit (4) a criminal or an unlawful act, (*a*) or an act not in itself criminal or unlawful, by criminal or unlawful means; (*b*) or an act which would tend to prejudice the public in general, to subvert justice, disturb the peace, injure public trade, affect public health, or violate public policy; (5) or any act, however innocent, by means neither criminal nor unlawful, where the tendency of the object sought would be to wrongfully coerce or oppress either the public or an individual.[1]

1. By criminal law, a conspiracy is an agreement between two or more persons, by concerted action, to do some unlawful act, or a lawful act in an unlawful manner. The agreement constitutes the offence, whether the act is done or not. United States *v.* Warner, 17 Fed. Rep. 145; Owens *v.* State, 16 Lea (Tenn.), 1; Spies *v.* People, 122 Ill. 1; s. c., 10 West. Rep. 701, and note.

Historical. — The earliest definition of the crime of conspiracy is that contained in the "Ordinatio de Conspiratoribus," in the statutes 33 Edw. I., which was simply declaratory of the common law. 2 Coke, Inst. 561.

Lord Denman's Antithesis. — A conspiracy may be described in general terms as a combination of two or more persons, by some concerted action, to accomplish some criminal or unlawful purpose, or to accomplish some purpose, not in itself criminal or unlawful, by criminal or unlawful means. Spies *v.* People (The Anarchists' Case), 122 Ill. 1; s. c., 10 West. Rep. 769; Heaps *v.*

It is the corrupt agreeing together of two or more persons to do, by concerted action, something unlawful, either as a means or an end, that constitutes a criminal conspiracy. The unlawful thing must either be such as would be indictable if performed by one alone, or of a nature particularly adapted to injure the public or some individual by reason of the combination.[1]

It is not necessary, in order to constitute a conspiracy, that the acts agreed to be done should be acts which, if done, would be criminal: it is enough if they are wrongful, — that is, amount to a civil wrong.[2]

And a confederation of two or more persons wrongfully to prejudice another in his property, person, or character, or to injure public traffic, or to affect public health, or to violate public policy, or to obstruct public justice, or to do any act in itself illegal, is a criminal conspiracy.[3]

Every conspiracy to do an unlawful act, or to do a lawful act for an illegal, fraudulent, malicious, or corrupt purpose, or for a purpose which has a tendency to prejudice the public in general, is an indictable offence regardless of the means whereby it is to be accomplished.[4]

A consultation or agreement between two or more persons, either falsely to accuse another with a crime punishable by law, or wrongfully to injure or prejudice a third person, or any body of

Dunham, 95 Ill. 583; State *v.* Rowley, 12 Conn. 101; State *v.* Hewett, 31 Me. 396; State *v.* Ripley, 31 Me. 386; State *v.* Mayberry, 48 Me. 218; Commonwealth *v.* Hunt, 45 Mass. (4 Metc) 111; s. c., 38 Am. Dec. 346; Alderman *v.* People, 4 Mich. 414; s. c., 69 Am. Dec. 321; State *v.* Burnham, 15 N. H. 394, 396; Rex *v.* Jones, 4 Barn. & Ad. 345; Rex *v.* Richardson, 1 Moo. & R. 402; Rex *v.* Seward, 1 Adol. & E. 706; 2 Greenl. Ev. sec. 89; Commonwealth *v.* Manson, 2 Ashm. (Pa.) 31; Lambert *v.* People, 9 Cow. (N. Y.) 601; Smith *v.* People, 25 Ill. 17; s. c., 76 Am. Dec. 780; State *v.* Bartlett, 30 Me. 132; United States *v.* Cole, 5 McL. C. C. 513; Commonwealth *v.* Judd, 2 Mass. 329; s. c., 3 Am. Dec. 54; Rex *v.* Hilbers, 2 Chit. 163; Reg. *v.* Roy, 11 L. C. Jur. 89; Reg. *v.* Vincent, 9 Car. & P. 91. See 2 Bish. Cr. L. (6th ed.) sec. 171; 2 Arch. Cr. Pr. 1044; 4 Blackst. Com. 136; 2 Whart. Cr. L. (8th ed.) secs. 1337, 1340; 3 Russ. on Cr. (9th ed.) 116, 144.

This antithesis was invented by Lord Denman in Rex *v.* Jones, 4 Barn. & Ad. 345, and was by him reviewed, and its correctness doubted, in Regina *v.* Peck, 9 Adol. & E. 686, and explained in Reg. *v.* King, 7 Q. B. 782; and is now understood to contain a limitation, and not a definition of what combinations are criminal. Reg. *v.* Peck, 9 Ad. & E. 686; Reg. *v.* King, 7 Q. B. 782; Wright, Conspiracy, sec. 14; State *v.* Glidden, 55 Conn. 46; s. c., 3 New Eng. Rep. 849.

1. Bish. Cr. L. § 171. See also 3 Greenl. Ev. § 89. State *v.* Mayberry, 48 Me. 218; State *v.* Rowley, 12 Conn. 101; Smith *v.* People, 25 Ill. 17; s. c., 76 Am. Dec. 780; Commonwealth *v.* Hunt, 45 Mass. (4 Metc.) 111; s. c., 38 Am. Dec. 346; Alderman *v.* People, 4 Mich. 414; s. c., 79 Am. Dec. 321, State *v.* Burnham, 15 N. H. 394, 396; Hinchman *v.* Richie, Bright (Pa.), 143; Commonwealth *v.* Bliss, 12 Phil. (Pa.) 580; United States *v.* Watson, 17 Fed. Rep. 145; s. c., 4 Cr. L. Mag. 391; State *v.* Murphy, 6 Ala. 765; s. c., 41 Am. Dec. 79; Heaps *v.* Dunham, 95 Ill. 583, State *v.* Potter, 28 Iowa, 556; State *v.* Bartlett, 30 Me. 132, 134; State *v.* Hewett, 31 Me. 396; Commonwealth *v.* Ridgeway, 2 Ashm. (Pa.) 247; Mifflin *v.* Commonwealth, 5 Watts & S. (Pa.) 461; s. c., 40 Am. Dec. 527; Reg. *v.* Vincent, 9 Car. & P. 109; Reg. *v.* Bunn, 12 Cox, Cr. Cas. 316. The common-law offence is not abolished by statute. State *v.* Norton, 23 N. J. L. (3 Zab.) 33.

2. Reg. *v.* Warburton, L. R. 1 C. C. 274; 2 Bish. Cr. L. (7th ed.) sec. 172; Wright, Cr. Consp. 50.

3. Johnson *v.* State, 26 N. J. L. (2 Dutch.) 313.

4. State *v.* Buchanan, 5 Har. & J. (Md.) 317, 362.

tion, in any manner; or to commit any offence punishable by law; or to do any act with intent to prevent the course of justice, or to effect a legal purpose with a corrupt intent, or by improper means, — is a conspiracy;[1] but where it is to accomplish an unlawful purpose not criminal, it depends on the circumstances of each case.[2] It is not necessary that the subject should be unlawful,[3] or that a civil wrong only be inflicted.[4] Neither is it essential that the parties should have conspired for their own benefit.[5] And it is held that a conspiracy to commit an indictable offence is a crime.[6]

Many acts which, if done by an individual, are not indictable criminally, when done in pursuance of a conspiracy between two or more persons are indictable.[7]

2. *Previous Concert and Agreement.* — A criminal conspiracy consists not merely in the intention of two or more, but on the agreement of two or more to do an unlawful act, or to do a lawful act by unlawful means.[8]

The agreement must be to do some act embraced in the definition of the offence.[9]

There must have been a previous concert between the conspirators to do the unlawful act.[10]

The agreement may be express or implied; and it is not essential that any but the leading conspirator know the exact part which each is to perform.[11]

But a conspiracy cannot exist without the consent of two or more persons: their agreement is an act in advancement of the intent of each.[12]

1. Reg. v. Tailor's Co., 8 Mod. 11; Reg. v. Best, 6 Mod. 185; 1 Russ. Cr. (9th ed.) 117.

2. Smith v. People, 25 Ill. 17, 24; s. c., 76 Am. Dec. 780; Reg. v. Warburton, L. R. 1 C. C. 274.

It is generally a matter of inference deduced from acts of the parties, done in pursuance of a common criminal purpose. Rex v. Brisac, 4 East, 164; Mulcahy v. Reg., L. R. 3 Eng. & Ir. App. 317; United States v. Babcock, 3 Dill. C. C. 566, 581; United States v. Graff, 14 Blatchf. C. C. 381; United States v. Cole, 5 McL. C. C. 513; Commonwealth v. Warren, 6 Mass. 74; [illegible] v. State, 48 Md. 521; Kelley v. People, 55 N. Y. 565, 566; Commonwealth v. Crowninshield, 27 Mass. (10 Pick.) 497; Rex v. Cope, 1 Strange, 144; Rex v. Parsons, 1 W. Black. 392; Reg. v. Whitehouse, 6 Cox, C. C. 38.

3. Rex v. Mawbey, 6 T. R. 619; 3 Russ. Cr. (9th ed.) 141.

4. Reg. v. Warburton, L. R. 1 C. C. 276.

5. Commonwealth v. Harley, 48 Mass. (7 Metc.) 462. See Webster v. Commonwealth, 59 Mass. (5 Cush.) 402.

Thus, it is an indictable offence to conspire to induce a party to forego a just claim. Reg. v. Carlisle, 6 Cox, C. C. 366.

6. Commonwealth v. Putnam, 29 Pa. St. 296.

And is an indictable offence at common law. Commonwealth v. Hunt, 45 Mass. (4 Metc.) 111; Reg. v. Roy, 11 L. C. Jur. 89.

7. State v. Rowley, 12 Conn. 101; Whart. Cr. L. (9th ed.) sec. 1338.

In the States of the Union. — In the States generally, a conspiracy is indictable as a common-law offence. State v. Pulle, 12 Minn. 164; State v. Norton, 23 N. J. L. (3 Zab.) 33. However, in some of the States, there is no common-law jurisdiction of conspiracy. Key v. Vattier, 1 Ohio, 132; Beal v. State, 15 Ind. 378; State v. Ohio, etc., R. R., 23 Ind. 362; Estes v. Carter, 10 Iowa, 400.

8. Mulcahy v. Reg., L. R. 3 Eng. & Ir. App. 317; Rex v. Jones, 4 Barn. & Ad. 345; Reg. v. Vincent, 9 Car. & P. 91; Rex v. Seward, 1 Adol. & E. 706; Reg. v. Peck, 9 Adol. & E. 686; R. v. Parnell, 14 Cox, C. C. 508.

9. See 1 Russ. Cr. (9th ed.) 116; 1 Whart. Cr. L. (8th ed.) sec. 1342 *et seq.*; 2 Bish. C. L. (6th ed.) sec. 186.

10. Reg. v. Absolon, 1 Fost. & F. 498.

11. United States v. Rindskopf, 6 Biss. C. C. 259.

12. Mulcahy v. Reg., L. R. 3 H. L. Eng. &

But the least degree of consent or collusion between parties to an illegal transaction makes the act of one the act of the others.[1]

As soon as the union of two wills for the unlawful purpose is perfected, the offence of conspiracy is complete. This joint assent of minds, like all other parts of a criminal case, may be established as an inference of the jury from the other facts proved; in other words, by circumstantial evidence.[2]

An agreement to commit an act, unless it amounts to a conspiracy, is not indictable:[3] so a mere intention or solicitation is not sufficient.[4]

3. *The Combination.* — Any confederation to do any act which amounts to a civil wrong, is a criminal conspiracy.[5] There must be a combination of two or more persons to commit some act known as an offence at common law, or that has been declared such by statute.[6]

It is not necessary, however, that the accused should have been an original contriver of the mischief; for he may become a partaker in it by joining the others at any time while it is being executed.[7]

The conspirators might not even be acquainted with each other.[8]

And it would not be a defence to say that the whole scheme was concocted before the accused become an associate,[9] nor need the means be settled and resolved on at the time of the conspiracy,[10] much less need the conspirators succeed in their object.[11]

Ir. App. 306; s. c., 1 Ir. R. C. L. 13; State v. Glidden, 55 Conn. 46; s. c., 3 New Eng. Rep. 349; Alderman v. People, 4 Mich. 414; s. c., 69 Am. Dec. 321; United States v. Johnson, 26 Fed. Rep. 682.

1. State v. Anderson, 82 N. C. 782.

2. Spies v. People (The Anarchists' Case), 122 Ill. 1; s. c., 10 West. Rep. 701.

3. Torrey v. Field, 10 Vt. 353. See 2 Whart. Cr. L.

4. United States v. Goldberg, 7 Biss. C. C. 175; United States v. Nunnenmacher, 7 Biss. C. C. 111; Mulcahy v. Rex, L. R. 3 Eng. & Ir. App. 306.

5. **Agreement to commit Adultery.** — An agreement to commit adultery or fornication is not a conspiracy. Miles v. State, 58 Ala. 390; denying Shannon v. Commonwealth, 14 Pa. St. 226.

Crimes which necessarily require the concurrence of two persons, as adultery, bigamy, duelling, etc., are not the subjects of conspiracy. Miles v. State, 58 Ala. 390; Shannon v. Commonwealth, 14 Pa. St. 226.

6. Alderman v. People, 4 Mich. 414; s. c., 69 Am. Dec. 321; State v. Glidden, 55 Conn. 46; s. c., 3 New Eng. Rep. 849; United States v. Johnson, 26 Fed. Rep. 682.

7. Spies v. People (The Anarchists' Case), 122 Ill. 1; s. c., 10 West. Rep. 701.

8. People v. Mather, 4 Wend. (N. Y.) 229; s. c., 21 Am. Dec. 122.

Time not an Element. — It is immaterial at what time one charged as a member of a conspiracy to commit crime is shown to have entered the conspiracy. Smith v. State, 21 Tex. App. 96.

It is competent to show a conspiracy to murder among others than the defendant, although its existence be unknown to him, if he be afterward connected with it by competent evidence. Lamar v. State, 63 Miss. 265.

9. Stewart v. Johnson, 3 Har. & J. (Md.) 87.

When a new party, with a full knowledge of the facts, concurs in the plans of the conspirators as originally formed, and comes in and aids in the execution of them, he is from that moment a fellow-conspirator: his concurrence, without particular proof of any agreement, is conclusive against him. He commits the offence whenever he agrees to become a party to the transaction, or does any act in furtherance of the original design. People v. Mather, 4 Wend. (N. Y.) 229; s. c., 21 Am. Dec. 122.

10. Rex v. Gill, 2 Barn. & Ald. 204.

11. State v. Norton, 23 N. J. L. (3 Zab.) 33.

A conspiracy must be a joint, wilful, and malicious common purpose.[1]

The gist of the offence is the fraudulent and corrupt combination, with intent that injury shall result.[2]

It is sufficient if two or more, in any manner, through any contrivance, positively or tacitly, come to a mutual understanding to accomplish a criminal or unlawful design.[3]

The bare combination with the joint design is sufficient;[4] but a mere passive cognizance of fraud, or the illegal action of others, is not sufficient to show a conspiracy: an active participation is necessary.[5]

a. Must be Corrupt. — The confederation must be corrupt.[6]

A criminal conspiracy is the corrupt agreeing. The object of the conspiracy, or the means to be employed, must be criminal;[7] and the object and motive appear from the conduct of the parties.[8]

A corrupt intent and design is necessary to constitute the offence.[9]

The law encourages combinations for good; and combinations of workmen to better their condition by legitimate and fair means are commendable, and should be encouraged. But combinations for evil purposes, whether by one class of men or another, are detrimental to the public weal, and cannot be regarded with favor by the courts.[10] So associations to bring criminals to punishment for the public good are not illegal.[11] But under the English system, an association, the members of which are bound by oath not to disclose its secrets, is an unlawful combination and conspiracy, unless declared by statute to be legal.[12]

When an association is formed for innocent purposes, and its

1. People *v.* Petheram (Mich.), 7 West. Rep. 592.

2. Commonwealth *v.* Ridgeway, 2 Ashm. (Pa.) 217; March *v.* People, 7 Barb. (N. Y.) 391; State *v.* Rickey, 8 N. J. L. (4 Halst.) 293; State *v.* Buchanan, 5 Har. & J. (Md.) 317; Horseman *v.* Reg., 16 Up. Can. Q. B. 543; Rex *v.* Seward, 1 Ad. & E. 706; Rex *v.* Richardson, 1 Moody & R. 402; Reg. *v.* Kenrick, 5 Q. B. 49. See 3 Russ. Cr. (9th ed.) 116, and Hazen *v.* Commonwealth, 23 Pa. St. 355.

Any act done in pursuance of it is no constituent part of the offence, but merely an aggravation of it. Commonwealth *v.* Judd, 2 Mass. 329; s. c., 3 Am. Dec. 54; State *v.* Rickey, 9 N. J. L. (4 Halst.) 293; State *v.* Buchanan, 5 Har. & J. (Md.) 317.

3. United States *v.* Babcock (U. S. D. C. Mo.), 3 Cent. L. J. 144; United States *v.* Nunnemacher, 7 Biss. C. C. 123; United States *v.* Goldberg, 7 Biss. C. C. 180.

4. Commonwealth *v.* Judd, 2 Mass. 329; s. c., 3 Am. Dec. 54; State *v.* Buchanan, 5 Har. & J. (Md.) 317; Hazen *v.* Commonwealth, 11 Harris (Pa.), 355; United States *v.* Cole, 5 McL. C. C. 513; Poulterer's Case, 9 Coke, 55; Rex *v.* Best, Salk. 174.

5. Evans *v.* People, 90 Ill. 384; Miles *v.* State, 58 Ala. 390; Reg. *v.* Barry, 4 Fost. & F. 389.

A concurrence in the common design. Reg. *v.* Boulton, 12 Cox, C. C. 87.

6. People *v.* Powell, 63 N. Y. 92; Wood *v.* State, 47 N. J. L. (18 Vr.) 461; s. c., 1 Cent. Rep. 441; State *v.* Young, 37 N. J. L. (8 Vroom) 184; Rex *v.* Gill, 2 Barn. & Ald. 204.

7. State *v.* Jones, 13 Iowa, 269.

8. State *v.* Ripley, 31 Me. 386.

9. Hudson *v.* State, 34 Ala. 254.

10. State *v.* Glidden, 55 Conn. 46; s. c., 3 New Eng. Rep. 849.

11. This has been the recognised doctrine since the time of Lord Coke. Floyd *v.* Barker, 12 Coke, 23; 2 Bish. Cr. L. sec 220; Russ. Cr. *667.

12. Rex *v.* Lovelass, 6 Car. & P. 596; s. c., 1 Mood. & R. 349.

power and authority are afterwards abused, only those so abusing them are liable.[1]

By "corrupt" is meant an evil purpose, but not necessarily an intent to do what, if accomplished by a single individual, would be indictable.[2]

4. *Two or More must unite.* — Two at least must conspire. One cannot be convicted, unless he has been indicted with persons unknown;[3] for it is in its nature a joint offence, and cannot be committed by one alone; but the proof must show that two or more persons were engaged in its promotion.[4]

Where one of the parties was legally capable of doing the act, it is sufficient,[5] and all who join at any time are conspirators.[6]

5. *Intent and Act.* — Evil intent is necessary to constitute the crime.[7] It is an act done with the intent to commit, but without accomplishing, a felony or a misdemeanor.[8] The offence is committed when to the intention to conspire is added the actual agreement.[9]

1. Carew *v.* Rutherford, 106 Mass. 10. See Snow *v.* Wheeler, 113 Mass. 186; Bowen *v.* Matheson, 96 Mass. (14 Allen) 503.

2. 2 Bish. Cr. L. (7th ed.) sec. 172.

3. State *v.* Adams, 1 Houst. Cr. C. (Del.) 361; Turpin *v.* State, 4 Blackf. (Ind.) 72; People *v.* Howell, 4 Johns. (N. Y.) 296; Commonwealth *v.* Manson, 2 Ashm. (Pa.) 31; Commonwealth *v.* Irwin, 8 Phila. (Pa.) 380; State *v.* Jackson, 7 S. C. 283; State *v.* Allison, 3 Yerg. (Tenn.) 428; Johnson *v.* State, 3 Tex. App. 590.

4. Evans *v.* People, 90 Ill. 384; State *v.* Christianbury, Busb. L. (N. C.) 48; Commonwealth *v.* Manson, 2 Ashm. (Pa.) 31; Commonwealth *v.* Irwin, 8 Phila. (Pa.) 380; Pollard *v.* Evans, 2 Show. 50; Reg. *v.* Manning, L. R. 12 Q. B. Div. 241; 1 Hawk. P. C. 72, sec. 8; 1 Russ. Cr. (9th ed.) 39.

Conspiracy by Man and Wife. — A husband and wife, being deemed but one person in law, cannot commit this offence, unless it be entered into before marriage, or unless another person joins with them in its promotion. State *v.* Covington, 4 Ala. 603; Kirtley *v.* Deck, 2 Munf. (Va.) 15; s. c., 5 Am. Dec. 445; Rex *v.* Locker, 5 Esp. 107; Rex *v.* Robinson, 1 Leach, 37; 2 Bish. Cr. L. sec. 162; 1 Hawks, P. C 448.

But if a man marry a woman in the name of another for the purpose of raising a specious title to the estate of the person whose name is assumed, it is a conspiracy. Rex *v.* Robinson, 1 Leach, Cr. Cas. 37; 2 East, P. C. 1010; 2 Bish. Cr. L. sec. 162; 1 Hawks, P. C. 448.

Or they may be guilty of a conspiracy where there is another conspirator joined with them. State *v.* Covington, 4 Ala. 603; Rex *v.* Hodson, 7 Law Rep. 58; Rex *v.* Locker, 5 Esp. 107.

Thus, a husband and wife and their servants have been held guilty of a conspiracy to ruin a card-maker. Rex *v.* Cope, 1 Strange, 144; 2 Stark, Ev. (2d ed.) 232; 3 Russ. Cr. (5th ed.) 149.

And it has been said that a man and wife may be charged with conspiracy with persons unknown, although the names of the unknown must necessarily have transpired to the grand jury. People *v.* Mather, 4 Wend. (N. Y.) 231: s. c., 21 Am. Dec. 122; State *v.* Covington, 4 Ala. 603; Commonwealth *v.* Wood, 7 Law Rep. 58.

5. United States *v.* Bayer, 4 Dill. C. C. 407; State *v.* Sprague, 4 R. I. 257; Boggus *v.* State, 34 Ga. 275; Rex *v.* Potts, Russ. & R. C. C. 353. See 1 East, P. C. 96.

6. State *v.* Trexler, 2 N. C. 90; Den. *v.* Johnson, 18 N. J. L. (3 Harr.) 87; People *v.* Mather, 4 Wend. (N. Y.) 229; s. c., 21 Am. Dec. 122; Reg. *v.* McMahon, 26 Up. Can. Q. B. 195.

7. People *v.* Powell, 63 N. Y. 88.

8. State *v.* Jordan, 75 N. C. 27.

9. United States *v.* Donau, 11 Blatchf. C. C. 168; State *v.* Glidden, 55 Conn. 46; s. c., 3 New Eng. Rep. 847.

The general doctrine as to specific intent is illustrated in Reg. *v.* Sanderson, 1 Fost. & F. 37, and notes; Rex *v.* Price, 5 Car. & P. 510; People *v.* Getchell, 6 Mich. 496; Shannon *v.* People, 5 Mich. 71; Durant *v.* People, 13 Mich. 351; Wilson *v.* People, 24 Mich. 410; People *v.* Chappell, 27 Mich. 486; People *v.* Petharam (Mich.), 7 West. Rep. 592; Bish. Cr. L. secs. 427, 429.

Conspiracy to murder Unborn Infant. — In case of conspiracy to murder an unborn

It has been held that A. cannot be convicted of conspiracy with B. to commit a crime where B. only feigned a purpose to draw A. on.[1]

5. *Overt Act not Necessary.* — The previous concert and agreement constitute the intent and act which constitute the crime, and no overt act is necessary unless required by statute.[2]

It is, in general, complete without an overt act,[3] for it is itself an overt act.[4]

The offence consists in the commission of certain acts, or in conspiring to commit the same; and the manner of committing them may furnish, if unexplained, a sufficient proof of the malice necessary under the statute, to be proved in the same way as malice is established in other cases.[5]

6. *Gist of the Offence.* — The gist of the offence of conspiracy is the unlawful confederacy to do an unlawful act, or to do a lawful act by unlawful means.[6]

And the offence has been held to consist in the conspiracy, and not in the acts committed for carrying it into effect; and the charge has been held to be sufficiently made in general terms describing an unlawful conspiracy to effect a bad purpose; and

infant, the agreement and intention must commence subsequent to the birth. Reg. *v.* Banks, 12 Cox, C. C. 393.

1. Woodworth *v.* State, 20 Tex. App. 375.

2. State *v.* Wilson, 30 Conn. 507; Alderman *v.* People, 4 Mich. 414; s. c., 38 Am. Dec. 346; Commonwealth *v.* Gillespie, 7 Serg. & R. (Pa.) 469; s. c., 10 Am. Dec. 475.

3. Landringham *v.* State, 49 Ind. 186; 1 Am. Cr. R. 104; State *v.* Straw, 42 N. H. 393; State *v.* Pulle, 12 Minn. 164; Commonwealth *v.* Eastman, 55 Mass. (1 Cush.) 189; s. c., 48 Am. Dec. 596; State *v.* Noyes, 25 Vt. 415; Commonwealth *v.* Davis, 9 Mass. 415; State *v.* Rickey, 9 N. J. L. (4 Halst.) 239; People *v.* Mather, 4 Wend. (N. Y.) 229; s. c., 21 Am. Dec. 122; Alderman *v.* People, 4 Mich. 414; s. c., 69 Am. Dec. 321; State *v.* Ripley, 31 Me. 386; Hazen *v.* Commonwealth, 23 Pa. St. 355; Isaacs *v.* State, 48 Miss. 234. *Compare* State *v.* Norton, 23 N. J. L. (3 Zab.) 33; Rex *v.* Gill, 2 Barn. & Ald. 204; Mulcahy *v.* Reg., L. R. 3 Eng. & Ir. App. 306; Heymann *v.* Reg., 12 Cox, C. C. 303; s. c., L. R. 8 Q. B. 102; Poulterer's Case, 9 Coke, 55 b; Reg. *v.* Best, 2 Ld. Raym. 1167.

4. Commonwealth *v.* Eastman, 55 Mass. (1 Cush.) 189; s. c., 48 Am. Dec. 596; Rex *v.* Kinnersly, 1 Strange, 193.

It is an act done with intent to commit, but without accomplishing, a felony or a misdemeanor. State *v.* Jordan, 75 N. C. 27.

Making a false oath is a sufficient overt act on a charge of conspiracy to extort by false charges of fraudulently obtaining goods. Raleigh *v.* Cook, 60 Tex. 438.

5. People *v.* Petheram (Mich.), 7 West. Rep. 592.

6. State *v.* Rowley, 12 Conn. 101, 112; State *v.* Bradley, 48 Conn. 549; State *v.* Adams, 1 Houst. Cr. Cas. (Del.) 361; State *v.* Potter, 28 Iowa, 554; State *v.* Sterling, 34 Iowa, 444; State *v.* Buchanan, 5 Har. & J. (Md.) 317; Commonwealth *v.* Judd, 2 Mass. 329, 337; s. c., 3 Am. Dec. 54; Commonwealth *v.* Tibbets, 2 Mass. 536; Commonwealth *v.* Warren, 6 Mass. 74; Morgan *v.* Bliss, 2 Mass. 112; Commonwealth *v.* Davis, 9 Mass. 415; Commonwealth *v.* Wallace, 82 Mass. (16 Gray) 223; Commonwealth *v.* Hunt, Thach. Cr. Cas. (Mass.) 609; People *v.* Richards, 1 Mich. 216; s. c., 51 Am. Dec. 75; People *v.* Saunders, 25 Mich. 124; State *v.* Pulle, 12 Minn. 164; State *v.* Burnham, 15 N. H. 396; State *v* Cawood, 2 Stew. (Ala.) 360; State *v.* Rickey, 8 N. J. L. (3 Halst.) 50; People *v.* Mather, 4 Wend. (N. Y.) 229; s. c., 21 Am. Dec. 122; State *v.* Christianbury, Busb. (N. C.) L. 48; Collins *v.* Commonwealth, 3 Serg. & R. (Pa.) 220; Respublica *v.* Ross, 2 Yeates (Pa.), 8; Commonwealth *v.* McKisson, 8 Serg. & R. (Pa.) 420; s. c., 11 Am. Dec. 630; Commonwealth *v.* Corlies, 8 Phila. (Pa.) 450; Twitchell *v.* Commonwealth, 9 Pa. St. 211; United States *v.* Miller, 3 Hughes, C. C. 553; United States *v.* Donau, 11 Blatchf. C. C. 168; Reg. *v.* Button, 11 Q. B. 929; Rex *v.* Gill, 2 Barn. & Ald. 204; Reg. *v.* Best, 1 Salk. 174.

numerous authorities[1] have all added their indorsement of the doctrine advanced as early as the work of Hawkins, and it is manifest that we are compelled to forsake the literature of doubt and to cleave unto that of authority.[2]

The unlawful thing agreed to be done must either be such as would be indictable if performed by one alone, or of a nature particularly adapted to injure the public, or some individual, by reason of the combination.[3]

It is not necessary that the "unlawful" act done should be such as to lay the foundation of an action for damages when done.[4]

7. *A Substantive Offence.*—A conspiracy is a substantive offence, and is punishable at common law, though nothing be done in execution of its purpose.[5] The offence is complete when the confederacy is made; and an act done in pursuance of it is no part of the offence, which is in fact punished to prevent the execution of the act proposed to be done.[6] The original corrupt agreement is itself the offence; and overt acts charged to have been done in pursuance thereof are mere matters of aggravation, and not necessary to the consummation of the crime.[7] To complete the crime, it is not necessary that any act should be done by the conspirators, or that any one should be aggrieved or defrauded in pursuance of, or in consequence of, the unlawful agreement.[8]

1. Reg. *v.* Selsby, 5 Cox, Cr. Cas. 495, note; Reg. *v.* Harris, 1 Car. & Marsh. 661; Hilton *v.* Eckersley, 6 E. & B. 47; Rex *v.* Mawbey, 6 T. R. 619; Rex *v.* Eccles, 1 Leach, C. C. 274; Walsby *v.* Anley, 3 Ell. & E. 516; Reg. *v.* Rowlands, 17 Ad. & E. N. S. 670; Reg. *v.* Bunn, 12 Cox, Cr. Cas. 316; Springhead Spinning Co. *v.* Riley, L. R. 6 Eq. 551; Mogul S. S. Co. *v.* McGregor, L. R. 15 Q. B. Div. 476; Commonwealth *v.* Hunt, 45 Mass (4 Metc.) 111, 128; s. c., 38 Am. Dec. 346; Smith *v.* People, 25 Ill. 71; Commonwealth *v.* Carlisle, Bright (Pa.), 36; Carew *v.* Rutherford, 106 Mass. 1.

2. See also Rex *v.* Ferguson, 2 Stark. N. P. 489; Rex *v.* Bykerdike, 1 Moo. & R. 179; People *v.* Fisher, 14 Wend. (N. Y.) 9; s. c., 28 Am. Dec. 501; State *v.* Donaldson, 32 N. J. L. (3 Vr.) 151; Snow *v.* Wheeler, 113 Mass. 186; State *v.* Noyes, 25 Vt. 415; State *v.* Burnham, 15 N. H. 396; Morris Run Coal Co. *v.* Barclay Coal Co., 68 Pa. St. 173; State *v.* Stewart, 59 Vt. 273; s. c., 4 New Eng. Rep. 378.

3. State *v.* Murphy, 6 Ala. 765; s. c., 41 Am. Dec. 71; State *v.* Rowley, 12 Conn. 101; State *v.* Glidden, 55 Conn. 46; s. c., 3 New Eng. Rep. 849; Smith *v.* People, 25 Ill. 17; s. c., 76 Am. Dec. 780; Heaps *v.* Dunham, 95 Ill. 583; State *v.* Potter, 28 Iowa, 556; State *v.* Mayberry, 48 Me. 213, 218; State *v.* Bartlett, 30 Me. 132, 134; State *v.* Hewett, 31 Me. 388, 396; Commonwealth *v.* Hunt, 45 Mass. (4 Metc.) 111; s. c., 38 Am. Dec. 346; Alderman *v.* People, 4 Mich. 414; s. c., 69 Am. Dec. 321; State *v.* Burnham, 15 N. H. 394, 396; Commonwealth *v.* Bliss, 12 Phila. (Pa.) 580; Commonwealth *v.* Ridgway, 2 Ashm. (Pa) 247; Mifflin *v.* Commonwealth, 5 Watts & S (Pa.) 461; s. c., 40 Am. Dec. 527; United States *v.* Watson, 17 Fed. Rep. 145; Reg. *v.* Vincent, 9 Car. & P. 109; Reg. *v.* Bunn, 12 Cox, C. C. 316.

4. State *v.* Donaldson, 32 N. J. L. (3 Vr.) 151.

5. People *v.* Fisher, 14 Wend. (N. Y.) 9; s. c., 28 Am. Dec. 501; Poulterer's Case, 9 Coke, 55; Rex *v.* Eccles, 1 Leach, C. C. 274; Rex *v.* Edwards, 1 Strange, 707; Rex *v.* Gill, 2 Barn. & Ald. 204; Respublica *v.* Ross, 2 Yeates (Pa.), 1; s. c., 2 U. S. (2 Dall.) 239; bk. 1, L. ed. 364; Leach, Crown Cas. 38.

6. Commonwealth *v.* Judd, 2 Mass. 329; s. c., 3 Am. Dec. 54; State *v.* Rickey, 9 N. J. L. (4 Halst.) 293; O'Connell *v.* Reg., 11 Clark & F. 155; s. c., 9 Jur. 25; United States *v.* Watson, 17 Fed. Rep. 145.

7. Commonwealth *v.* Judd, 2 Mass. 329; s. c., 3 Am. Dec. 54; Commonwealth *v.* Hunt, 45 Mass. (4 Metc.) 111; s. c., 38 Am. Dec. 346; State *v.* Rickey, 9 N. J. L. (4 Halst.) 293.

8. People *v.* Geiger, 49 Cal. 643; State *v.* Sterling, 34 Iowa, 443; Alderman *v.*

The offence is complete when the conspirators enter into the agreement, notwithstanding they do not proceed to its consummation;[1] for the conspiracy and consummation are separate and distinct offences,[2] in the sense, at least, that the fact that the offence has been completed is no legal bar to the prosecution for the conspiracy.[3] So, if the means employed were sufficient to possibly effect the purpose, the offence is complete.[4]

A bare engagement and association of two or more to break the law, without an overt act, is sufficient.[5] And it is not necessary to allege that the purpose was carried into effect.[6] The agreement itself constitutes the offence whether an act is done in furtherance of the object or not.[7]

8. *Doctrine of Merger.*—A conspiracy is a misdemeanor; and when its object is only a misdemeanor, it cannot be merged.[8] But where the conspiracy is to commit a higher crime, as a felony, it is merged in the higher crime.[9] Yet in New Jersey it has been held that a charge of conspiring to procure an indictment by perjury, does not charge a felony which merges the conspiracy.[10]

People, 4 Mich. 414; s. c., 69 Am. Dec. 321; Isaacs v. State, 48 Miss. 234; Heine v. Commonwealth, 91 Pa. St. 148.

1. Johnson v. State, 3 Tex. App. 590, distinguishing Speiden v. State, 3 Tex. App. 156, and Pegg v. State, 43 Tex. 108; Reg. v. Roy, 11 L. C. Jur. 89; Isaacs v. State, 48 Miss. 234; 1 Am. Cr. R. 103; Mulcahy v. Reg., L. R. 3 Eng. & Ir. App. 306.

2. State v. Straw, 42 N. H. 393.

3. United States v. Bayer, 13 Bankr. Reg. 400; United States v. Boyden, 1 Low. C. C. 266; United States v. Rindskopf, 6 Biss. C. C. 259; s. c., 21 Int. Rev. Rec. 326; People v. Fisher, 14 Wend. (N. Y.) 9; s. c., 28 Am. Dec. 501; People v. Chase, 16 Barb. (N. Y.) 495; Reg. v. Boulton, 12 Cox, C. C. 87; Reg. v. Rowlands, 5 Cox, C. C. 436.

4. March v. People, 7 Barb. (N. Y.) 391.

5. Bloomer v. State, 48 Md. 521; State v. Buchanan, 5 Har. & J. (Md.) 362; Landringham v. State, 49 Ind. 186; Alderman v. People, 4 Mich. 414; s. c., 69 Am. Dec. 321; State v. Pulle, 12 Minn. 164; Collins v. Commonwealth, 3 Serg. & R. (Pa.) 220; Commonwealth v. McKisson, 8 Serg. & R. (Pa.) 420; s. c., 11 Am. Dec. 630; State v. Young, 37 N. J. L. (8 Vr.) 184; Respublica v. Ross, 2 Yeates (Pa.), 1.

6. Commonwealth v. Wallace, 82 Mass. (16 Gray) 221; Bowen v. Matheson, 96 Mass. (14 Allen) 503.

7. United States v. Watson, 17 Fed. Rep. 145; Commonwealth v. Eastman, 55 Mass. (1 Cush.) 189; s. c., 48 Am. Dec. 596; Hazen v. Commonwealth, 23 Pa. St. (11 Harris) 362.

8. State v. Murray, 15 Me. 100; State v. Mayberry, 48 Me. 218; People v. Richards, 1 Mich. 216; s. c., 51 Am. Dec. 75; Commonwealth v. Drum, 35 Mass. (18 Pick.) 479; Commonwealth v. Walker, 108 Mass. 309; Commonwealth v. Goodhue, 43 Mass. (2 Metc.) 193; Commonwealth v. Bakeman, 105 Mass. 53; Commonwealth v. Dean, 109 Mass. 349; People v. Mather, 4 Wend. (N. Y.) 265; s. c., 21 Am. Dec. 122; Hartman v. Commonwealth, 5 Pa. St. 60; Commonwealth v. McGowan, 2 Pars. Cas. (Pa.) 341.

9. State v. Murphy, 6 Ala. 765; s. c., 41 Am. Dec. 79; Commonwealth v. Blackburn, 1 Duval (Ky.), 4; State v. Mayberry, 48 Me. 218; State v. Murray, 15 Me. 100; Commonwealth v. Kingsbury, 5 Mass. 106; Commonwealth v. Goodhue, 43 Mass. (2 Metc.) 193; Commonwealth v. Walker, 108 Mass. 309; Commonwealth v. Dean, 109 Mass. 349; People v. Richards, 1 Mich. 216; s. c., 51 Am. Dec. 75; People v. Mather, 4 Wend. (N. Y.) 215; s. c., 21 Am. Dec. 122; Commonwealth v. McGowan, 2 Pars. Cas. (Pa.) 341; Hartman v. Commonwealth, 5 Pa. St. 60; Commonwealth v. Parr, 5 Watts & S. (Pa.) 345; State v. Noyes, 25 Vt. 415; Reg. v. Button, 3 Cox, Cr. Cas. 229; 1 Bish. Cr. L. (6th ed.) sec. 814.

A Conspiracy to commit a felony is merged in the felony when actually consummated; and so an indictment for a conspiracy to commit a felony must allege that the felony was not committed. After the felony is consummated, the conspiracy is not indictable. Elsey v. State, 47 Ark. 572.

10. Johnson v. State, 26 N. J. L. (2 Dutch.) 313.

A conspiracy to commit a felony is merged in the consummated act; but a conspiracy to commit a misdemeanor, being only a misdemeanor, is not merged in the consummated act;[1] for on a simple charge of conspiracy, carrying the conspiracy into effect does not merge the offence charged into the greater offence; but if the conspiracy is proven, the conviction follows, although the defendant might have been found guilty of the greater crime had he been charged with it.[2]

9. *The Civil Remedy.—a. Action for Damages.*—Conspiracy being a misdemeanor, the parties affected may waive criminal prosecution, and bring an action for damages, where a personal injury has been sustained.[3] And an action may be maintained against a corporation for damages caused by, or resulting from, a conspiracy, as well as against an individual.[4]

A complaint alleging that the defendant company, in conspiracy with others, requested plaintiff's customers not to purchase its oil, and threatened suits for infringement of patents which it falsely professed to own, is sufficient; and charging the acts as being the acts of the company is sufficient, without averring that such acts were done by and through its agents.[5]

1. State *v.* Murray, 15 Me. 100; State *v.* Mayberry, 48 Me. 218; Commonwealth *v.* O'Brien, 66 Mass. (12 Cush.) 84; Commonwealth *v.* Kingsbury, 5 Mass. 106; People *v.* Mather, 4 Wend. (N. Y.) 229; s. c., 21 Am. Dec. 122; White *v.* Fort, 3 Hawks (N. C.), 251; 1 Leach, Cr. Cas. 34; Commonwealth *v.* Walker, 108 Mass. 309; Commonwealth *v.* Bakeman, 105 Mass. 53; Commonwealth *v.* Dean, 109 Mass. 349; Commonwealth *v.* Goodhue, 43 Mass. (2 Metc.) 193; People *v.* Richards, 1 Mich. 216; s. c., 51 Am. Dec. 75; Commonwealth *v.* McGowan, 2 Pars. Cas. (Pa.) 341; Commonwealth *v.* Drum, 36 Mass. (19 Pick.) 479; People *v.* Mather, 4 Wend. (N. Y.) 265; s. c., 21 Am. Dec. 122; State *v.* Noyes, 25 Vt. 415; Commonwealth *v.* Hartman, 5 Pa. St. 60.

2. People *v.* Petheram (Mich.), 7 West Rep. 592.

3. See *infra*, "Compromising offence."

4. Buffalo Lubricating Oil Co. *v.* Standard Oil Co., 42 Hun (N. Y.), 153; s. c., affirmed, 106 N. Y. 669; 8 Cent. Rep. 667; Morton *v.* Metropolitan Life Ins. Co., 34 Hun (N. Y.), 366; s. c., affirmed, 103 N. Y. 645; Western News Co. *v.* Wilmarth, 33 Kan. 510; Krulevitz *v.* Eastern R. R. Co., 140 Mass. 573; s. c., 2 New Eng. Rep. 37; Reed *v.* Home Savings Bank, 130 Mass. 443.

Malice and Wicked Intent in Corporations.—In affirming the case of Buffalo Lubricating Oil Co. *v.* Standard Oil Co., *supra*, the court say, "If actions can be maintained against corporations for malicious prosecution, libel, assault and battery, and other torts, we can perceive no reason for holding that actions may not be maintained against them for conspiracy. It is well settled that the malice and wicked intent needful to sustain such actions may be imputed to corporations."

By the great weight of modern authority, a corporation may be liable even when a fraudulent or malicious intent in fact is necessary to be proved, the fraud or malice of its authorized agents being imputable to the corporation, as in actions for fraudulent representations,—Reed *v.* Home Savings Bank, 130 Mass. 443; National Exchange Co. *v.* Drew, 2 Macq. 103; New Brunswick & C. R. *v.* Conybeare, 9 H. L. Cas. 711, 738, 740; Barwick *v.* English Joint Stock Co., L. R. 2 Ex. 259,—for libel,—Philadelphia, W. & B. R. R. *v.* Quigley, 62 U. S. (21 How.) 202; bk. 16, L. ed. 73; Whitfield *v.* Southeastern R., 1 E. B. & E. 115,—or for malicious prosecution,—Goodspeed *v.* East Hamden Bank, 22 Conn. 530; Stove *v.* Crocker, 41 Mass. (24 Pick.) 81; Ripley *v.* McBarrow, 125 Mass. 272; Carter *v.* Howe Machine Co., 51 Md. 290; Wheless *v.* Second Nat. Bank, 1 Baxt. (Tenn.) 469; Williams *v.* Planters' Ins. Co., 57 Miss. 759; Iron Mountain Bank *v.* Mercantile Bank, 4 Mo. App. 505; Vance *v.* Erie R. Co., 32 N. J. L. (3 Vr.) 334; Stewart *v.* Sonnebarn, 98 U. S. (8 Otto) 187; bk. 25, L. ed. 116; Copely *v.* Grover & Baker Co., 2 Woods, C. C. 494; Mitchell *v.* Jenkins, 5 Barn. & Ad. 588; s. c., 2 Nev. & Man. 301; Walker *v.* Southeastern Ry., L. R. 5 C. P. 640; Edwards *v.* Midland Ry., L. R. 6 Q. B Dev. 287.

5. Lubricator Oil Co. *v.* Standard Oil

The charge of the conspiracy must show that damage resulted to the plaintiff from acts done in furtherance of it.[1] No action lies for simply conspiring to do an unlawful act: the act itself, and the resulting damages to the plaintiff, are the only ground of action.[2] Where defendants do nothing unlawful, it is immaterial whether they conspire or not.[3]

Where the conspiracy charged is one, though embracing within its scope many transactions, one suit is sufficient.[4]

Where a judgment has been procured by a conspiracy, the judgment must be reversed or set aside before an action for damages lies.[5] Where a several judgment is rendered against one of defendants, it is unnecessary to determine whether complaint states a good cause against other defendants. Trespass on the case for conspiracy to defame and thereby injure another in his particular vocation or business, may be maintained whenever, in pursuance of such unlawful combination, means have been employed which tended to effectuate, or to a greater or less extent accomplished, the object of the conspiracy.[6] And a cause of action for a conspiracy to cheat or defraud the intestate is for an injury to property right, and does not die with its owner.[7]

Pendency of an action for conspiracy to defraud is not notice to one not a party thereto, of infirmity in the subject of the conspiracy.[8]

Fraudulently effecting an insurance on a fictitious cargo is a good defence to an action on the policy.[9]

Where certain inhabitants of a county combined and conspired to prevent the collection of a tax, or to pay a judgment, and by threats to prevent such collection, an action lies against them.[10]

On the trial of a question whether there has been a combination between the debtor and one creditor to defraud the others, the judge charged, "A slight degree of collusion is sufficient to establish fraud;" and the appellate court held that the use of the word "fraud," as meaning a combination to defraud, was not error.[11]

6. *Acts and Declarations as Evidence.* — All acts and declarations performed or made for the purpose of carrying the unlawful design into effect, are accomplished after the existence of such design

Co., 42 Hun (N. Y.), 153; s. c., affirmed, 106 N. Y. 669; 8 Cent. Rep. 667.

1. Douglass v. Winslow, 52 N. Y. Super. Ct. 410.

2. Kimball v. Harman, 34 Md. 407.

3. McHenry v. Sneer, 56 Iowa, 649.

4. Northern Pac. R. Co. v. Kindred, 14 Fed. Rep. 77.

5. **Unreversed Judgment.** — Thus, where B. procured a judgment against A by inducing C. to testify falsely, so long as the judgment remains A. cannot maintain an action for damages against them for conspiracy. Stevens v. Rowe, 59 N. H. 578; s. c., 47 Am. Rep. 231; Lubricating Oil Co. v. Standard Oil Co., 42 Hun (N. Y.), 153; s. c., affirmed, 106 N. Y. 699; 8 Cent. Rep. 667.

6. Wildee v. McKee, 111 Pa. St. 335; s. c., 56 Am. Rep. 271.

7. Brackett v. Griswold, 103 N. Y. 425; s. c., 5 Cent. Rep. 35; 2 Rev. Stat. 1, p. 448.

8. Zoller v. Riley, 100 N. Y. 102; s. c., 1 Cent. Rep. 8.

9. Phoenix Ins. Co. v. Moog, 78 Ala. 284.

10. Findlay v. McAllister, 113 U. S. 104; bk. 28, L. ed. 930.

11. Nusbaum v. Loucheim (Pa.), 1 Cent. Rep. 327.

has been presumptively established.[1] Yet, before such evide can be admitted, the court must decide for itself that there is s cient evidence *primâ facie* to prove such combination, which jury may nevertheless negative.[2]

In an action for trespass, the declarations of one conspir. are admissible to prove the conspiracy.[3] But to authorize admission of acts and declarations as evidence against the o conspirators, a proper predicate must be first laid by the in duction of evidence *aliunde, primâ facie* sufficient, to the opini of the presiding judge, to establish the existence of such spiracy; as in the analogous case of agency, where the act. declarations of the agent are offered in evidence against the p cipal, and are only received when the fact of agency has been *primâ facie* established.[4]

Where a combination is shown between assignor and assig to defraud, the declarations of each, while acting in furtheranc the wrongful scheme, are competent against the other, even w made without the knowledge of the other;[5] and in an action enticing away plaintiff's wife, declarations and conversation defendant, during his absence, with her, are admissible as evid against him.[6] Declarations of the father, in his son's absence, a bond was given to keep off creditors, are admissible.[7]

At the hearing of the suit in equity against A. and B., for spiring to defraud the plaintiff, no exception lies to the admis in evidence, in behalf of the plaintiff, of declarations of B. r ing to the conspiracy, if there is then evidence of the existenc the conspiracy, and the plaintiff offers to produce further evide although B. was not served with process, and has not appeare a party defendant.[8]

c. Compromising Offence.—The law will permit a compro of all offences, though made subject of a criminal prosecution, which offences the injured party might recover damages,[9] provi the rights of the public are preserved inviolate.[10] But no mi meanor can be compromised if it tends to the injury of the munity at large.[11]

1. Amer. Fur. Co. *v.* United States, 27 U. S. (2 Pet.) 358, 364; bk. 7, L. ed. 450; Page *v.* Parker, 40 N. H. 47; Lee *v.* Lamprey, 43 N. H. 13; Lincoln *v.* Claflin, 74 U. S. (7 Wall.) 132; bk. 19, L. ed. 106.

2. Clayton *v.* Anshaving, 6 Rand. (Va.) 285; United States *v.* Cole, 5 McL. C. C. 513; Preston *v.* Bowers, 13 Ohio St. 1; Kimmerle *v.* Geeting, 2 Grant (Pa.), 125; Price *v.* Jones, 4 Watts (Pa.), 85.

3. Solomon *v.* Kirkwood, 55 Mich. 256; Amer. Fur. Co. *v.* United States, 27 U. S. (2 Pet.) 358; bk. 7, L. ed. 450; Preston *v.* Bowers, 13 Ohio St. 13; Cowles *v.* Coe, 21 Conn. 229; 2 Stark. Ev. 403; 1 Phill. Ev. 103.

4. Phoenix Ins. Co *v.* Moog, 78 Ala. 284

5. Cuyler *v.* McCartney, 40 N. Y Lee *v.* Huntoon, Hoff. Ch. (N. Y.) Adams *v.* Davidson, 10 N. Y. 309; *v.* Burrows, 91 U. S. (1 Otto) 438; b L. ed. 280.

6. Bosler *v.* Webb, 113 Ill. 436.

7. Reitenbach *v.* Reitenbach, 1 I (Pa.), 62.

8. Bole *v.* Wooldrege, 142 Mass. See TRESPASS.

9. Keir *v.* Leeman, 6 Q. B. 308; 2 L C. C. 316.

10. Rex *v.* Hardey, 14 Q. B 529; I *v.* Wingfield, 11 East, 46; Baker *v.* send, 7 Taunt. 422.

11. Dwight *v.* Ellsworth, Up. Q. B. 540.

Where an offence is a personal tort, and there is no attempt to suppress the prosecution, it may be compromised.[1]

II. Under Statute. — 1. *Under the Revised Statutes of the United States.* — As defined by the United States statute, criminal conspiracy is an unlawful agreement to do some act which by some law of the United States has been made a crime.[2] The conspiracy exists when two or more persons agree together to do an unlawful act, or to do some lawful act in an unlawful manner; and the crime is complete when such combination is formed, and an act is done to further it.[3] An indictment under the federal statute which fails to state with certainty the acts relied on effecting the conspiracy, is defective.[4]

1. Stancel v. State, 50 Ga. 155.

2. *Re* Wolf, 27 Fed. Rep. 606.

The sections of the Revised Statutes and Acts of Congress define offences which are forbidden whether an act be a conspiracy or not. United States v. Watson, 17 Fed. Rep. 145.

3. United States *v.* Wootten, 29 Fed. Rep. 702.

4. United States v. Watson, 17 Fed. Rep. 145.

Revised Statutes, § 440. — In an indictment for a conspiracy to commit an offence against the United States under Revised Statutes, sec. 440, the conspiracy must be sufficiently charged: it cannot be aided by averments of acts done by one or more of the conspirators. United States v. Britton, 108 U. S. 199; bk. 27, L. ed. 703.

Under Section 3169 United States Revised Statutes, every officer or agent, appointed and acting under the authority of any revenue law of the United States, conspiring or colluding with any other person to defraud the United States, is guilty of a misdemeanor. United States v. McDonald, 3 Dill. C. C. 543; United States v. McKee, 3 Dill. C. C. 546; United States v. Babcock, 3 Dill. C. C. 566..

Revised Statutes, § 5336. — A conspiracy to drive the Chinese out of the country, or to maltreat or to intimidate them, is *primâ facie* a conspiracy to prevent or hinder the operation of a law of the United States. Revised Statutes, § 5336; *In re* Grand Jury, 26 Fed. Rep. 749; *In re* Baldwin, 27 Fed. Rep. 187; Baldwin v. Franks, 120 U. S. 678; bk. 30, L. ed. 766.

Revised Statutes, § 5364. — Under section 5364 United States Revised Statutes, a conspiracy to cast away a vessel is made an indictable offence. United States v. Cole, 5 McL. C. C. 513; United States v. Hand, 6 McL. C. C. 274.

Revised Statutes, § 5440. — All parties to a conspiracy to defraud the United States under section 5440 are liable to a penalty, if any one does any act in furtherance of the design of the conspirators. United States v. Boyden, 1 Low. C. C. 266; United States v. Fehrenback, 2 Woods, C. C. 175; United States v. Dennee, 3 Woods, C. C. 47; United States v. Sacia, 2 Fed. Rep. 754; The Mussel Slough Case, 5 Fed. Rep. 680; United States v. Sanches, 6 Fed. Rep. 715; United States v. Watson, 17 Fed. Rep. 145; United States v. Gordon, 22 Fed Rep 250; *In re* Wolf, 27 Fed. Rep. 606; United States v. Frisbie, 28 Fed. Rep. 808; United States v. Donau, 11 Blatchf. C. C. 168; United States v. Hirsch, 100 U. S. (10 Otto) 33; bk. 25, L. ed. 539; United States v. Britton, 108 U. S. (1 Davis) 199; bk. 27, L. ed. 703; United States v. Hammond, 2 Woods, C. C. 197.

Post-Office; Using Mail to defraud; Revised Statutes, § 5480. — The elements in the offence of using the mail for the purpose of defrauding, created by Revised Statutes of the United States, § 5480, are (1) the devising, or intending to devise, a scheme or artifice to defraud; (2) the opening, or intending to open, correspondence or communication with some other person, or inciting such person to open correspondence, by means of the post-office department, with the one devising the scheme; and (3) in pursuance of the scheme, putting a letter or packet in the mail, or taking one out. United States v. Wootten, 29 Fed. Rep. 702.

It is not fraudulent, within the meaning of the statute, if one, not in solvent circumstances, should seek credit, or order goods without the present means of paying for them: nor would it come within the meaning of the statute if one had ordered goods, and afterwards devised a purpose of escaping from paying for them. United States v. Wootten, 29 Fed. Rep. 702.

Revised Statutes, § 5508. — Section 5506 of the Revised Statutes of the United States punishes by fine and imprisonment a conspiracy to prevent citizens from voting. United States v. Reese, 92 U. S.

2. ***Under State Statutes.*** — The common-law offence is n[illegible] abolished by statute.[1]

(2 Otto) 214; bk. 23, L. ed. 563; United States *v.* Cruikshank, 92 U. S. (2 Otto) 542; bk. 23, L. ed. 588; Seeley *v.* Knox, 2 Wood-, C. C. 368.

Revised Statutes, §§ 5506, 5508, 5520. — An indictment charging a conspiracy to intimidate a citizen of African blood in the exercise of his right to vote; and in the exercise of his rights, and beating and wounding him, is good under Revised Statutes, §§ 5506, 5508, 5520. *Ex parte* Yarborough, 110 U. S. 651; bk. 28, L. ed. 274.

Aliens. — In section 5508, Revised Statutes, to punish conspiracies against the free exercise or enjoyment by any citizen of any right or privilege under the Constitution or laws of the United States, the word citizen does not include aliens or mere residents or inhabitants. Baldwin *v.* Franks, 120 U. S. 678; bk. 30, L. ed. 766.

Infamous Crimes. — As defined by United States Revised Statutes, § 5508, conspiracy is an infamous crime, and must be prosecuted by indictment. United States *v.* Butler, 4 Hughes, C. C. 512.

But a conspiracy to make counterfeit coin has been held not to be an infamous crime within the meaning of the statute. United States *v.* Burgess, 3 McCrary, C. C. 278

Revised Statutes, § 5519. — To punish a conspiracy to deprive persons of the equal protection of the laws, or of equal privileges or immunities, is unconstitutional as to its operation within a State, even though the conspiracy be to deprive one of his rights under the Constitution, laws, or treaties of the United States. Baldwin *v.* Franks, 120 U. S. 678; bk. 30, L. ed. 766.

And so it has been held that a conspiracy directly or indirectly to deprive any person of the equal protection of the laws, or equal privileges or immunities under the laws, is punishable by a fine. Revised Statutes, § 5519; *Re* Baldwin, 27 Fed. Rep. 187; United States *v.* Harris, 106 U. S. (16 Otto) 629; bk. 27, L. ed. 290.

Indians: Revised Statutes, § 5440. — Two Indians may be indicted in the Indian country for conspiracy to commit offences against the United States under Revised Statutes, § 5440. *In re* Wolf, 27 Fed. Rep. 606.

Settlers on Public Lands. — A conspiracy to deprive a settler upon public lands of his right to make a settlement, is a crime under the Revised Statutes. United States *v.* Waddell, 16 Fed. Rep. 221. But a conspiracy to make a settlement on Indian lands, and to return to the Indian country, after being removed therefrom, is not indictable. United States *v.* [illegible] 22 Fed. Rep. 426.

1. State *v.* Norton, 23 N J. L. (3 Z[illegible]) 33.

In Alabama. — Under the Alabama [illegible] utes any two or more persons conspi[illegible] together to commit a [illegible] doing some act to carry [illegible] purposes, are each guilty of the offence[illegible] a conspiracy to forge, or utter a forged [illegible]strument. Scully *v.* State, 39 Ala. [illegible] Cleveland *v.* State, 34 Ala. [illegible]; State [illegible] Murphy, 6 Ala. 765; s. c., 41 Am. Dec. [illegible]

In Connecticut. — The offence is co[illegible]mitted when to the intention to conspi[illegible] added the actual agreement. State *v.* G[illegible]den, 55 Conn. 46; s. c., 3 New Eng. R[illegible] 849. See United States *v.* [illegible], Blatchf. C. C. 168.

In Indiana. — For discussions of the p[illegible]visions of the statutes of Indiana [illegible] to indictment for conspiracy, [illegible] *v.* State, 49 Ind. 186; State *v.* [illegible] 90 Ind 465.

The provisions of the Federal Consti[illegible]tion respecting the presentment of [illegible] for felony, and the mode of trial, [illegible] apply to prosecutions under the laws of [illegible] States. State *v.* Barwell, 104 Ind. [illegible] s. c., 2 West. Rep. 726.

In Iowa. — Under the Iowa statut[illegible] criminal conspiracy is made [illegible] State *v.* Flynn, 28 Iowa, 26; State *v.* [illegible]ter, 28 Iowa, 554; State *v.* [illegible], Iowa, 391; State *v.* Savoye, 48 Iowa, [illegible]

In Maine. — In Maine, conspiracy [illegible] fined by statute. State *v.* [illegible] 102; State *v.* Ripley, 31 Me. [illegible] Mayberry, 48 Me. 236; State *v.* [illegible] 30 Me. 135; State *v.* [illegible], 31 Me. [illegible] State *v.* Clary, 64 Me. 370.

In Michigan. — The Michigan statute [illegible]lating to conspiracies was [illegible] tect the business interests of the [illegible] from such combinations. It [illegible] quire malice to be shown against [illegible] of the business disturbed, or its [illegible] in the same sense as does the [illegible] in cases of malicious mischief. People [illegible] Petheram (Mich.), 7 West. Rep. [illegible]

An information charging a [illegible]acy to obstruct and impede the [illegible] a manufacturing company, has [illegible] unlawfully to do so by [illegible] means (describing them), but [illegible] where alleges that any of [illegible] actually committed by the defendants[illegible] simply that they conspired to [illegible] charges only the offence of [illegible] Rev. Stat. § 9275; People *v.* [illegible] (Mich.), 7 West. Rep. [illegible]

In Missouri. — In Missouri, a [illegible]

III. Subjects of Conspiracy. — *A. Where the Object to be attained is Criminal.* — *1. To commit a Criminal Act.* — A conspiracy to commit a felony is indictable: as to commit an abortion,[1] or bigamy or incest,[2] or arson,[3] or burglary,[4] or forgery,[5] or larceny,[6] or murder,[7] or rape,[8] or robbery,[9] or treason.[10]

A conspiracy to commit an offence made a felony by statute is indictable.[11]

A conspiracy to commit any crime is an indictable offence:[12]

held guilty of a misdemeanor for a criminal conspiracy. State v. Ross, 29 Mo. 32; State v. Daubert, 42 Mo. 239.

In New Jersey. — In New Jersey the agreement must be followed by some act done to effect the object by one or more of the parties to the agreement. State v. Rickey, 9 N. J. L. (4 Halst.), 293; State v. Norton, 23 N. J. L. (3 Zab.) 33; Johnson v. State, 26 N. J. L. (2 Dutch.) 313; State v. Donaldson, 32 N. J. L. (3 Vroom) 151; State v. Young, 37 N. J. L. (8 Vroom) 184; Stewart v. Johnson, 18 N. J. L. (3 Harr.) 90.

In New York. — By the Revised Statutes of New York, conspiracies are specifically defined. March v. People, 7 Barb. (N. Y.) 391; People v. Chase, 16 Barb. (N. Y.) 495; Pepper v. Haight, 20 Barb. (N. Y.) 438; Adams v. People, 9 Hun (N. Y.), 89; Hooker v. Vandewater, 4 Denio (N. Y.), 352; People v. Seaman, 5 Denio (N. Y.), 371; People v. Fisher, 14 Wend. (N. Y.) 9; Priest v. Cummings, 20 Wend. (N. Y.) 352; Hamilton v. Wright, 37 N. Y. 508; People v. Brady, 56 N. Y. 190; People v. Powell, 63 N. Y. 88.

In North Carolina. — A conspiracy to abduct children is made indictable by statute. State v. Sullivan, 85 N. C. 506.

Or a conspiracy to destroy State government by any means. State v. Jackson, 82 N. C. 565.

In Pennsylvania. — An indictment lies under the Pennsylvania statute for a conspiracy to lay out townships under powers usurped from the State. Act Apr. 11, 1795. Commonwealth v. Franklin, 4 U. S. (4 Dall.) 255; bk. 1, L. ed. 823.

1. R. v. Banks, 12 Cox, C. C. 393; Solander v. People, 2 Colo. 48; Commonwealth v. Demain, Bright (Pa.), 441.

2. Shannon v. Commonwealth, 14 Pa. St. 226; Miles v. State, 58 Ala. 390.

3. State v. Chapin, 17 Ark. 561.

4. Brown v. State, 2 Tex. App. 115; Wilson v. State, 32 Ark. 238; State v. Ridley, 48 Iowa, 370; Scudder v. State, 62 Ind. 13; Rex v. Pullman, 2 Camp. 229.

5. Gard v. State, 109 Ind. 415; s. c., 7 West. Rep. 81.

6. Lawson v. State, 32 Ark. 220; State v. Grady, 34 Conn. 118; Neville v. State, 60 Ind. 308; Miller v. Commonwealth, 78 Ky. 15; Clinton v. Estes, 20 Ark. 216; State v. Wilson, 30 Conn. 500; Reid v. State, 20 Ga. 681; State v. Sterling, 34 Iowa, 443; State v. Dean, 13 Ired. (N. C.) L. 63.

7. Spies v. People (The Anarchists' Case), 122 Ill. 1; s. c., 10 West. Rep. 701; Frank v. State, 27 Ala. 37; Glory v. State, 13 Ark. 236; People v. Woody, 45 Cal. 289; People v. Geiger, 49 Cal. 643; People v. Leith, 52 Cal. 251; State v. Allen, 47 Conn. 121; Brennan v. People, 15 Ill. 511; Lamb v. People, 96 Ill. 73; Williams v. State, 47 Ind. 568; Jones v. State, 64 Ind. 475; Walton v. State, 88 Ind. 9; Archer v. State, 106 Ind. 426; State v. Nash, 7 Iowa, 347; State v. Winner, 17 Kans. 305; Cummins v. Commonwealth, 81 Ky. 465; State v. Ford, 37 La. An. 443; Commonwealth v. Crowninshield, 27 Mass. (10 Pick.) 497; Carrington v. People, 6 Park. Cr. Rep. (N. Y.) 336; State v. Tom, 2 Dev. (N. C.) L. 569; State v. George, 7 Ired. (N. C.) L. 321; Rufer v. State, 25 Ohio St. 465.

If A. and B. have a quarrel with C., and C. approaches them, and A. commands C. to halt or he will shoot him, and B. then shoots C., the circumstances do not necessarily import a common criminal intent between A. and B. to kill C. so as to make A. guilty. People v. Leith, 52 Cal. 251.

8. State v. Shields, 45 Conn. 256; State v. Trice, 88 N. C. 627.

9. Landringham v. State, 49 Ind. 186; People v. Poole, 27 Cal. 572; State v. Sterling, 34 Iowa, 443; Lisle v. Commonwealth, 82 Ky. 250; State v. Heyward, 2 Nott & McC. (S. C.) 312.

Even though it was the intention of one of the conspirators to convict the robber. Rex v. McDonald, 1 Leach, 45.

To compel a person to sign a check, and then take it from him by force, is robbery. People v. Richards, 67 Cal. 412.

10. Commonwealth v. Blackburn, 1 Duval (Ky.), 4.

11. State v. McKinstry, 50 Ind. 465; State v. Murray, 15 Me. 100; Commonwealth v. O'Brien, 66 Mass. (12 Cush.) 84.

12. R. v. Bunn, 12 Cox, C. C. 316; Rex v. Pollman, 2 Camp. 229.

so is a conspiracy to commit a misdemeanor,[1] as bigamy or incest,[2] or to kidnap.[3]

B. Where the Object to be attained is Illegal or Unlawful.— 1. To commit an Illegal or Unlawful Act.—It is not necessary, in order to constitute a conspiracy, that the acts agreed to be done be acts which, if done, would be criminal. It is enough if the acts agreed to be done, although not criminal, are wrongful; that is, that they amount to a civil wrong.[4]

Immoral acts and indictable cheats are subjects of conspiracy, and may be punished as crimes.[5]

Many acts are said to be unlawful which would not be the subject of criminal conspiracy. Other acts are unlawful because they are in violation of the criminal law, or some penal statute. If the ends or the means are criminal in themselves, or contrary to some penal statute, the conspiracy is clearly an offence.[6]

Whatever may be the doctrine of the early cases, the later and better-considered American cases hold that an agreement and combination is not criminal unless it be for acts or omissions, either as ends or means, and which would be criminal as apart from the agreement.[7]

In conspiracy the unlawful thing proposed, whether as a means or an end, need not be such as would be indictable if proposed, or even done, by a single individual.[8]

1. State *v.* Murray, 15 Me. 100; State *v.* Mayberry, 48 Me 218; Commonwealth *v.* Kingsbury, 5 Mass. 106; People *v.* Mather, 4 Wend. (N. Y.) 229; s. c., 21 Am Dec. 122; White *v.* Fort, 3 Hawks (N. C), 251; 1 Lead. Cr. Cas. 34.

2. Shannon *v.* Commonwealth, 14 Pa. St. 226; Miles *v* State, 58 Ala. 390.

3. *Ex parte* Blossom, 10 Low. Can. L. Jur 30

4. Reg. *v.* Warburton, L. R. 1 C. C. 273.

To constitute an indictable conspiracy, it is not necessary that the act to be done should be of itself an indictable offence,—State *v* Buchanan, 5 Har. & J (Md) 317, 362, a leading case,—nor that it should be such as to lay the foundation of an action for damages when done. State *v.* Donaldson, 32 N. J L. (3 Vr.) 151.

5. State *v.* Rowley, 12 Conn. 101; Reg. *v.* Rowlands, 2 Denison, 364; s c, 17 Q. B. 671; Reg. *v* Carlisle, Dears. 337.

Quasi-Criminal Acts.—In cases of quasi-criminal acts, it is not essential that the means employed should be *per se* the ground of the indictment. State *v.* Burnham, 15 N H. 396

6. State *v.* Glidden, 55 Conn. 46; s. c, 3 New Eng Rep. 849

Many acts which, if done by an individual, are not indictable criminally, when done in pursuance of a conspiracy between two or more persons are indictable. State *v* Rowley, 12 Conn. 101; Whart. C. L. (9th ed) § 1338.

7. Commonwealth *v.* Hunt, 45 Mass (4 Metc.) 111, 324; s. c., 38 Am. Dec. 346; Commonwealth *v.* Eastman, 55 Mass. (1 Cush.) 189; s c, 48 Am. Dec 596; Commonwealth *v.* Shedd, 61 Mass. (7 Cush.) 514; State *v.* Rickey, 9 N. J. L. (4 Halst.) 293; State *v.* Straw, 42 N. H. 393; State *v.* Stevens, 30 Iowa, 392; State *v* Jones, 13 Iowa, 269; State *v* Potter, 28 Iowa, 554; Alderman *v.* People, 4 Mich. 414; s. c., 69 Am. Dec. 321; 3 Greenlf. Ev (Redf. ed.) 79, § 90 a.

8. State *v.* Simpson, 1 Dev. (N C.) L. 504; 2 Bish. Cr. L. (7th ed.) 3181.

Thus, a conspiracy to commit an act may be indictable, although the act committed by a single person is not indictable Commonwealth *v* Manley, 29 Mass. (12 Pick.) 173; State *v.* Straw, 42 N. H. 393; Rex *v.* Turner, 13 East, 228; Reg. *v.* Warburton, L. R. 1 C. C 274; s. c, 12 Cox, C. C. 584; State *v* Rowley, 12 Conn. 101.

The unlawful thing agreed to be done must either be such as would be indictable if performed by one alone, or of a nature particularly adapted to injure the public, or some individual, by reason of the combination. State *v.* Murphy, 6 Ala 765. s. c., 41 Am. Dec. 79; State *v* Rowley, 12 Conn. 101; State *v.* Glidden, 55 Conn 46; s. c., 3 New Eng. Rep. 849; Smith *v.* People.

2. *Acts against Law and Social Order.* — The intention of any number of men acting separately, so long as they do nothing, is not a crime of which the law will take cognizance: but when several men form the intent and come together, and agree to carry it into execution, the case is changed. The combination becomes dangerous, and subversive of the rights of others; and the law wisely says it is a crime.[1] And all conspiracies to "excite disaffection" are indictable at common law.[2]

a. Anarchy. — Anarchy is the absence of government: it is a state of society where there is no law or supreme power. If the conspiracy had for its object the destruction of the law and the government, and of the police and militia as the representatives of the law and the government, it had for its object the bringing about of practical anarchy.[3]

25 Ill. 17; s. c., 6 Am. Dec. 780; Heaps v. Dunham, 95 Ill. 583; State v. Potter, 28 Iowa, 556; State v. Mayberry, 48 Me. 218; State v. Bartlett, 30 Me. 132, 134; State v. Bowen, 31 Me. 396; Commonwealth v. Hunt, 45 Mass. (4 Metc.) 111; s. c., 38 Am. Dec. 346; Alderman v. People, 4 Mich. 414; s. c., 79 Am. Dec 321; State v. Burnham, 15 N. H. 394, 396; Commonwealth v. Ellis, 12 Phila (Pa.) 580; Commonwealth v. Ridgway, 2 Ashm. (Pa.) 247; Mifflin v. Commonwealth, 5 Watts & S. (Pa.) 461; s. c., 40 Am. Dec. 527; United States v. Watson, 17 Fed. Rep. 145; s. c., 4 Cr. L. Mag. 391; Reg. v. Vincent, 9 Car. & P. 109; Reg. v. Bunn, 12 Cox, C. C. 316.

1. State v. Glidden, 55 Conn. 46; s. c., 3 New Eng. Rep. 849.

2. Spies v. People (The Anarchists' Case), 122 Ill. 1; s. c., 10 West. Rep 701; Reg. v. Vincent, 9 Car. & P. 91; Reg. v. Shellard, 9 Car. & P. 277; Rex v. Hunt, 3 Barn. & Ald. 566; Russ. Cr. 681.

To stir up Strife. — A conspiracy to stir up jealousies, hatred, and ill will between different classes of citizens is unlawful, — O'Connell v. Rex, 11 Clark & F. 155, — or to induce others to violate the laws. Hagan v. Commonwealth, 23 Pa. St 355; Commonwealth v. Kostenbander (Pa), 3 Cent. Rep. 632.

Test of Criminality. — The influence of an act upon society determines whether it is a criminal conspiracy to combine to accomplish it, and not whether the act itself is criminally punishable. Smith v. People, 25 Ill. 17, 24; s. c., 76 Am. Dec. 780.

The acts of all the public meetings throughout the land looking to, and providing for, coercive means, no matter in what form, or through what channels applied, are criminal; and all those participating in them must be subject to the very severe penalties denounced by the statute. *In re* [illegible], 27 Fed. Rep. 193.

3. Spies v. People (The Anarchists' Case), 122 Ill. 1; s. c., 10 West Rep. 701.

"International Arbeiter Association." — An organization known as the "International Workingmen's Association," or the "International Arbeiter Association," generally called the "Internationals," and designated for brevity as the "I. A. A.," which urges that the present system of property ownership should be destroyed by force, through the crimes of robbery, theft, and murder, and the destruction of the existing system of social order, and of all the laws and institutions upon which the system is based, and organized into "sections" or groups, armed with Springfield rifles, and publishing newspapers in the German and English languages, inciting the workingmen to revolution against the present system of social order, and advising them to arm, and provide themselves with dynamite bombs, for the purpose of murdering the police and militia, is an unlawful conspiracy. Spies v. People (The Anarchists' Case), 122 Ill. 1; s. c., 10 West. Rep. 701.

Armed Groups. — The arming and drilling of groups is in violation of the militia-law of the State, which prohibits such organizations without compliance with the provisions of the statute. And whether or not the defendants were Anarchists, may be a proper circumstance to be considered to show what connection they had with the conspiracy, and their purposes in joining it. Spies v. People (The Anarchists' Case), 122 Ill. 1; s. c., 10 West. Rep. 701.

The design of the organization to bring about a "social revolution," meaning the bringing about a state of society in which all property should be held in common, and to this end to make war upon the police and militia as representatives of law and order, was unlawful. Spies v. People (The Anarchists' Case), 122 Ill. 1; s. c., 10 West. Rep. 701.

Denouncing Police. — Where the purpose

3. *Acts against Public Justice.* — Any confederation tending to interfere with, or obstruct or pervert, the course of public justice, is criminal conspiracy;[1] as by abuse of legal process, so as to enforce the payment of money known not to be due.[2] And to pervert public justice by the suppression or fabrication of evidence, is indictable,[3] as where several persons hire one to go to another State to testify falsely;[4] or to make false charges and accusations;[5] or to procure an acquittance by bribery;[6] or to charge one with crime, though no process be obtained;[7] or to procure criminal process for improper purposes,[8] and in such case the officer, prosecutor, and all others concerned, are liable;[9] or to hinder an officer in the discharge of his duties;[10] or to decoy one into the jurisdiction;[11] or to suppress competition at public sales;[12] or to commit a prison breach.[13]

4. *Acts against the Public Peace.* — Combinations against law, or against individuals, are always dangerous to public peace and public security.[14]

of the meeting called by the association was to denounce the acts of the police while in performance of their duty on the day previous, such purpose was unlawful; and the plan adopted at the meeting of the night previous was an unlawful conspiracy. Spies *v.* People (The Anarchists' Case), 122 Ill. 1; s. c., 10 West Rep. 701.

"**Social Revolution.**" — Where the time was definitely fixed for the inauguration of the "social revolution," and practical measures in the work of preparation were taken by the association, and books and publications were freely circulated among the groups of the association, instructing them in the mode of preparing and using dynamite, the jury were warranted in finding that the bomb which exploded at the meeting was made by one of the defendants in furtherance of the conspiracy. Spies *v.* People (The Anarchists' Case), 122 Ill. 1; s. c., 10 West. Rep 701.

1. State *v.* McKinstry, 50 Ind. 465; State *v.* De Witt, 2 Hill (S. C.), 282; s. c., 27 Am. Dec. 371; Commonwealth *v.* Douglas, 46 Mass. (5 Metc.) 241; State *v.* Norton, 23 N. J. L. (3 Zab.) 33; People *v.* Washburn, 10 Johns. (N. Y.) 160; Commonwealth *v.* McLean, 2 Pars. Cas. (Pa.) 367; State *v.* Noyes, 25 Vt. 415; State *v.* Keyes, 8 Vt. 57; s. c., 30 Am. Dec. 450; State *v.* Carpenter, 20 Vt. 9; United States *v.* Staats, 8 Howe (U. S.), 41; bk. 12, L. ed. 976; R. *v.* Mawbey, 6 T. R. 619; R. *v.* Jolliffe, 4 T. R. 285; R. *v.* Thompson, 16 Q. B. 832; 20 L. J. M. C. 183; R *v.* MacDaniel, 1 Leach, C. C. 145 Claridge *v.* Hare, 14 Ves. 65; Bushell *v.* Barrett, Ry. & M. 434; s. c., 1 Saund. 300; 1 Hawk. P. C. 21, § 15; Fost. 130.

2. R. *v.* Taylor, 15 Cox, C. C. 265.

3. State *v.* De Witt, 2 Hill (S. C.), 282; Rex *v.* Steventon, 2 East, 362; Rex *v.* Mawbey, 6 T. R. 619; Rex *v.* Johnson, 2 Show. 1; 3 Russ. Cr. (9th ed.) 117; 1 Whart. C. L. (8th ed.) § 1342; 2 Bish. C. L. (6th ed) § 186.

4. See 3 Russ Cr. (9th ed.) 117. But see State *v.* McKinstry, 50 Ind. 465.

5. Slomer *v.* People, 25 Ill. 70; s. c., 76 Am. Dec. 786; State *v.* Buchanan, 5 Har. & J. (Md.) 317; Commonwealth *v.* Tibbetts, 2 Mass. 536; Johnson *v.* State, 26 N. J. L. (2 Dutch.) 313; Elkin *v.* People, 28 N. Y. 177; Lambert *v.* People, 9 Cow. (N. Y.) 599; Commonwealth *v* McLean, 2 Pars. Cas. (Pa.) 367; Hood *v.* Palm, 8 Pa. St. 237; Rex *v* Sprague, 2 Burr. 993; Rex *v.* Best, 1 Salk. 174; Reg. *v.* Best, 2 Ld. Raym. 1167; Child *v.* North, 1 Keble, 203; Rex *v.* Timberly, 1 Keble, 254, 264; Rex *v.* McDaniel, 1 Leach, C. C. 45. See also Fost 130; 1 Hawk. P. C. 72; 2 Russ. Cr. 683; 2 Bish. Cr. L. (6th ed.) §§ 169, 240.

6. State *v.* McKinstry, 50 Ind. 465; State *v.* De Witt, 2 Hill (S. C.), 282; s. c., 27 Am. Dec. 371; Rex *v.* Mawbey, 6 Term Rep. 619.

7. Commonwealth *v.* Tibbetts, 2 Mass. 536

8. Slomer *v.* People, 25 Ill. 70; s. c., 76 Am. Dec. 786.

9. Slomer *v.* People, 25 Ill. 70; s. c., 76 Am Dec. 786.

10. State *v.* Noyes, 25 Vt. 415.

11. Phelps *v.* Goddard, 1 Tyler (2 Vt.), 60; s. c., 4 Am. Dec. 720; Cook *v.* Brown, 125 Mass 503.

12. Levi *v.* Levi, 6 Car. & P. 239.

13. State *v.* Murray, 15 Me. 100.

14. State *v.* Burnham, 15 N. H. 396.

An agreement to commit a trespass is a conspiracy;[1] or an agreement to condemn a play, and hiss an actor;[2] or to commit riots;[3] or to induce others to violate laws forbidding the circulation of notes;[4] or to induce a man to violate the Sunday law;[5] or to defeat the enforcement of the prohibitory liquor laws;[6] or to excite disaffection.[7] And an agreement of officials to violate a statute constitutes a conspiracy.[8]

5. *To cheat and defraud.* — A conspiracy to cheat and defraud is an indictable offence,[9] and a division of the profits of a fraudulent transaction is sufficient as evidence of a combination to defraud.[10]

As the words "cheating" and "defrauding" do not necessarily import a thing forbidden by law, it is necessary for the indictment to state the means proposed to be used, in order that the court may see whether the means are in fact illegal.[11]

All combinations to effect an evil purpose are dangerous; and when their object is to cheat, by whatever means, they are criminal.[12]

And an indictment lies for a conspiracy to cheat or defraud,

1. State *v.* Straw, 42 N. H. 393; King *v.* Mawbey, 6 T. R. 628.

Civil Trespass. — That a mere agreement to commit a civil trespass would not be the subject of indictment, — R. *v.* Turner, 13 East, 228, — was overruled in Reg. *v.* Rowlands, 17 Q B. 686.

2. Clifford *v.* Brandon, 2 Camp. 358; King *v.* Mawbey, 6 T. R. 628; 4 Bl. Comm. 136.

3. Reg. *v.* Vincent, 9 Car. & P. 91.

4. Hazen *v.* Commonwealth, 23 Pa. St. 355.

5. Commonwealth *v.* Leeds, 9 Phila. (Pa.) 569. But see Commonwealth *v.* Kostenbader (Pa.), 3 Cent. Rep. 632; People *v.* Saunders, 25 Mich. 119.

6. State *v.* Potter, 28 Iowa, 554.

7. Reg. *v.* Vincent, 9 Car. & P. 91. See Reg. *v.* Shellard, 9 Car. & P. 277; Rex *v.* Hunt, 3 Barn. & Ald. 566.

8. Woods *v.* State, 47 N. J. L. (18 Vr.) 461; s. c., 1 Cent. Rep. 441. See People *v.* Powell, 63 N. Y. 88.

9. State *v.* Murphy, 6 Ala. 765; s. c., 41 Am. Dec. 79; Johnson *v.* People, 22 Ill. 314; s. c., 76 Am. Dec. 780; Commonwealth *v.* Davis, 9 Mass. 415; Commonwealth *v.* Boynton, 84 Mass. 160; Commonwealth *v.* Walker, 108 Mass. 309; Commonwealth *v.* Eastman, 55 Mass. (1 Cush.) 189; s. c., 48 Am. Dec. 596; State *v.* Norton, 23 N. J. L. (3 Zab.) 33; State *v.* Clary, 64 Me. 369; State *v.* Simons, 4 Strob. (S. C.) L. 266; People *v.* Underwood, 16 Wend. (N. Y.) 546; Clary *v.* Commonwealth, 4 Pa. St. 210; United States *v.* Cruikshank, 92 U. S. (2 Otto) 542; bk. 23, L. ed. 588.

Meaning of "Cheat." — In the forms of indictment for a conspiracy to cheat, the word "cheat" implies a corrupt act. Wood *v.* State, 47 N. J. L. (18 Vr.) 461; s. c., 1 Cent. Rep. 441.

10. Kimmell *v.* Geeting, 2 Grant (Pa.), 125.

11. United States *v.* Cruikshank, 92 U. S. (2 Otto) 542; bk. 23, L. ed. 588; State *v.* Parker, 43 N. H. 88; Alderman *v.* People, 4 Mich. 414; s. c., 79 Am. Dec. 321; Commonwealth *v.* Eastman, 55 Mass. (1 Cush.) 189; s. c., 48 Am. Dec. 596; approved, Commonwealth *v.* Shedd, 61 Mass. (7 Cush.) 515; Commonwealth *v.* Wallace, 82 Mass. (16 Gray) 223; Commonwealth *v.* Hunt, 45 Mass. (4 Metc.) 111; s. c., 38 Am. Dec. 346.

The gist of the offence of conspiracy to cheat and defraud is the conspiracy, and the specific pretences need not be set out. State *v.* Adams, Houst. Cr. R. (Del.) 361; Rex *v.* Gill, 2 Barn. & Ad. 204.

12. Twitchell *v.* Commonwealth, 9 Pa. St. 211.

A conspiracy to defraud individuals or a corporation of their property may in itself constitute an indictable offence, though the act done in pursuance of the conspiracy is not in itself indictable. State *v.* Norton, 23 N. J. L. (3 Zab.) 33; State *v.* Donaldson, 32 N. J. L. (3 Vr.) 151; State *v.* Young, 37 N. J. L. (8 Vr.) 184; State *v.* Cole, 39 N. J. L. (10 Vr.) 324; State *v.* Hickling, 41 N. J. L. (12 Vr.) 208; Noyes *v.* State, 41 N. J. L. (12 Vr.) 418; Johnson *v.* State, 26 N. J. L. (2 Dutch.) 313; s. c., 29 N. J. L. (5 Dutch.) 453.

though the means of affecting it have not been determin[illegible] A conspiracy to defraud need not be by means of any [illegible] written or similar device, and it may be by acts, without [illegible] words.[2]

6. *To extort.* — A conspiracy to extort money is [illegible] offence at common law;[3] as to charge one falsely for the [illegible] of extortion,[4] whether the offence charged is criminal or not,[5] whether the party charged be guilty or not.[6]

A conspiracy to charge an innocent person with an offence [illegible] indictable.[7] It is immaterial whether the charge be true or fal[illegible] successful or unsuccessful, if any of the means resorted to [illegible] unlawful.[8] A conspiracy to cause one person to accuse anoth[illegible]

1. Rex *v.* Gill, 2 Barn. & Ald. 204.

2. People *v.* Clark, 10 Mich. 310.

Cheating. — So an agreement to cheat is a conspiracy, the cheating being but an aggravation. State *v.* Murphy, 6 Ala. 765; s. c., 41 Am. Dec. 79; Commonwealth *v.* Davis, 9 Mass. 415.

Agreement to defraud. — An agreement to defraud any person, class, company, or corporation, constitutes a conspiracy, — Reg. *v.* Orbell, 6 Mod. 42. See 3 Russ. Cr. (9th ed.) 126; — or an agreement by a bank clerk and another to cheat the bank, — Commonwealth *v.* Foering, Brightly (Pa.), 315, — or to defraud a bank, and thereby impair the circulation of its securities, — State *v.* Norton, 23 N. J. L. (3 Zab.) 33; State *v.* Buchanan, 5 Har. & J. (Md.) 317; *contra*, State *v.* Rickey, 9 N. J. L. (4 Halst.) 293, — or to defraud creditors, — State *v.* Simons, 4 Strob. (S. C.) L. 266; Johnson *v.* Davis, 7 Tex. 173; Whitman *v.* Spencer, 2 R. I. 124; Hall *v.* Eaton, 25 Vt. 458; Reg. *v.* Peck, 9 Ad. & E. 686; People *v.* Underwood, 16 Wend. (N. Y.) 546, — or to dispose of goods in contemplation of bankruptcy, — Reg. *v.* Hall, 1 Fost. & F. 33, — even if no adjudication of bankruptcy has taken place. Heymann *v.* Reg., L. R. 8 Q. B. 102; ——— *v.* ———, 12 Cox, 383. See United States *v.* Bayer, 4 Dill. C. C. 407.

An indictment lies for a conspiracy to defraud an individual out of goods and merchandise, — Commonwealth *v.* Ward, 1 Mass. 473; — or to obtain goods by purchase, with no expectation of paying for them. — Commonwealth *v.* Eastman, 55 Mass. (1 Cush.) 189; s. c., 48 Am. Dec. 596, — or by representations of solvency of a bank or merchant. Reg. *v.* Esdaile, 1 Fost. & F. 213.

To cheat by Bank Notes. — An indictment lies for a conspiracy to cheat by bank notes, — Twitchell *v.* Commonwealth, 9 Pa. St. 211; Clary *v.* Commonwealth, 4 Pa. St. 210; State *v.* Van Hart, 17 N. J. L. (2 Harr.) 327, — for to make false or illegal notes is indictable at common law, — [illegible] *v.* Commonwealth, 4 Pa. St. [illegible]; Commonwealth *v.* McGowan, 2 Pars. Cas. (Pa.) [illegible] — so also is a conspiracy to obtain [illegible] *in action* by fraud, — Lambert *v.* People, [illegible] Cow. (N. Y.) 578, — or to obtain money [illegible] filing a fraudulent bond, — Commonwealth *v.* Gallagher, 2 Clark (Pa.), [illegible], — or to [illegible] tort money by charging a person [illegible] offence or a scandal, — Commonwealth [illegible] Wood, 7 Bost. L. R. 58; Rex *v.* Holl[illegible] berry, 4 Barn. & C. 329, — or to fraudulently induce a broker to advance money. Commonwealth *v.* Wrigley, 6 Phila. (Pa.) [illegible]

Spurious Goods. — To make spurious goods with intent to sell them as genuine, although no sale be made, — Commonwealth *v.* Hunt, 45 Mass. (4 Metc.) [illegible]; 38 Am. Dec. 346, — or to manufacture base and spurious article of merchandise with a fraudulent intent to sell the same as genuine, — Commonwealth *v.* Judd, 2 Mass. 329; s. c., 3 Am. Dec. 54; — or by manufacturing spurious indigo, intending [illegible] it as good, — Commonwealth *v.* Judd, [illegible] Mass. 329; s. c., 3 Am. Dec. 54, — [illegible] destroy a will to defraud devisees. [illegible] *v.* De Witt, 2 Hill (S. C.), 282.

Cheating at Cards. — A conspiracy [illegible] cheat at cards is indictable. [illegible] Younger, 1 Dev. (N. C.) L. 357; [illegible] P. C. 446, § 2.

3. State *v.* Shooter, 8 Rich. (S. C.) L. [illegible] Rex *v.* Hollingberry, 6 Dow. & R. [illegible] s. c., 4 B. & C. 329. See State *v.* [illegible] 59 Vt. 273; s. c., 7 West. Rep. [illegible] note.

4. Rex *v.* Rispal, 1 W. Bl. 386; s. c. [illegible] Burr 1320.

5. Rex *v.* Rispal, 3 Burr. 1320; s. c. [illegible] W. Bl. 386.

6. Rex *v.* Hollingberry, 4 Barn. & [illegible] 329; s. c., 2 Lead. C. C. [illegible]

7. Reg *v.* Best, 2 Ld. Raym. [illegible] Salk. 174; 3 Russ. Cr. (9th ed.) 118.

8. Rex *v.* Hollingberry, 4 Barn. & C. 329; 1 Hawk. P. C. 72, § 2; [illegible] 112.

person falsely of the theft of a bank note, as a means to extort money, is indictable.[1]

Making a false oath is a sufficient overt act on a charge of conspiracy to extort by false charges of fraudulently obtaining goods.[2]

It is an indictable conspiracy to extort a deed,[3] or to obtain money as a reward for an appointment to an office.[4]

C. Where the Object is not Criminal or Unlawful, but the Means employed are Illegal or Unlawful. — 1. *Where the Means are Unlawful.* — If the conspiracy is to do an act not in itself unlawful, the means used must be unlawful.[5]

It is not necessary that the illegal or unlawful means should be an indictable offence: it is sufficient if they are fraudulent or immoral.[6]

When the combination is to effect by lawful means an object in itself not unlawful, the means must be particularly set out, and they must be such as to constitute a statutory or common-law offence.[7]

In such cases it is necessary to show that some unlawful device was used, to show the intent of the combination.[8] Thus, a conspiracy to procure the marriage of a pauper could amount to a crime only by the practice of some undue means.[9]

2. *Acts affecting the Public Injuriously.* — An indictment will lie at common law for a conspiracy to do an act neither illegal nor immoral, which is intended to effect a purpose tending to the prejudice of the public at large.[10] And a conspiracy to do an act which, if done by an individual singly, may not be indictable, if calculated to affect the community injuriously, is an indictable conspiracy:[11] as, to defraud the public generally, though no specific persons were made its object;[12] or to defraud the government of revenue,[13] or taxes;[14] or to fraudulently tamper with elections

1. State *v.* Cawood, 2 Stew. (Ala.) 360.

2. Raleigh *v.* Cook, 60 Tex. 438.

3. State *v.* Shooter, 8 Rich. (S. C.) L. 72.

4. Rex *v* Pollman, 2 Camp. 229.

5. Alderman *v.* People, 4 Mich 414; s. c., 69 Am. Dec. 321; State *v.* Mayberry, 48 Me. 218; Cole *v.* People, 84 Ill. 216; State *v.* Potter, 28 Iowa, 554; Rex *v.* Tanner, 1 Esp. 304; Reg. *v.* Edwards, 8 Mod. 320; Rex *v.* Tarrant, 4 Burr. 2106; Reg. *v.* Seward, 1 Ad. & E. 706.

6. State *v.* Burnham, 15 N. H. 396; State *v.* Parker, 43 N. H. 83.

7. Cole *v.* People, 84 Ill. 216; State *v.* Potter, 28 Iowa, 554; State *v.* Mayberry, 48 Me. 218; Alderman *v.* People, 4 Mich. 414, s. c., 69 Am. Dec. 321; Rex *v.* Fowler, 1 East, P C. 461; Rex *v.* Seward, 3 Nev. & M. 557.

8. Rex *v.* Tanner, 1 Esp. 304; Rex *v.* Edwards, 8 Mod. 320.

9. Rex *v.* Fowler, 1 East, P. C. 461; Reg. *v.* Seward, 1 Adol. & E. 706; s. c., 3 Nev. & M. 557.

10. King *v.* Journeymen Tailors, 8 Mod. 10; King *v.* Edwards, Strange, 707.

11. State *v.* Straw, 42 N. H. 393; State *v.* Burnham, 15 N. H. 396; Commonwealth *v.* Manley, 29 Mass. (12 Pick.) 173; State *v.* Rowley, 12 Conn. 101; Rex *v.* Turner, 13 East, 228; Reg. *v.* Warburton, 11 Cox, C. C. 584.

12. Gardner *v.* Preston, 2 Day (Conn.), 205; Rex *v.* Roberts, 1 Camp. 399; Rex *v.* De Berenger, 3 Maule & S. 67.

13. United States *v.* Rindskopf, 6 Biss. C. C. 259; United States *v.* Smith, 2 Bond, C. C. 323; United States *v.* Boyden, 1 Low. C. C. 266; United States *v.* Babcock, 3 Dill. C. C. 581; United States *v.* Graff, 14 Blatchf. C. C. 381. See United States *v.* Hirsch, 20 Alb. L. J. 454.

14. United States *v.* Dustin, 2 Bond, C. C. 332; United States *v.* Smith, 2 Bond. C. C. 323; United States *v.* Boyden, 1 Low C. C. 266.

appointed by the State;[1] or to corruptly procure an [illegible] obtain money by selling a public office;[2] or to fraudulently [illegible] tolls on public works;[4] or to procure one to be appointed inspector of elections;[5] or to lay out townships under [illegible] powers.[6] And the members of a public body are crimi[nally] liable for illegal combination in their official conduct.[7]

a. To endanger Public Health.—An agreement to do an act injurious to public health is indictable; as, to barter unwh[ole]some wine.[8]

b. To commit Acts against Morality and Virtue.—An indictm[ent] will lie at common law for conspiracy to do an act not illegal [or] punishable, if done by an individual, but which is merely immor[al]. A combination to seduce a female is criminal conspiracy,[10] [illegible] a false marriage.[11] A combination to assist in the elopement [of a] female is indictable;[12] or to entice and carry off a female, [although] the seduction and abduction be not indictable;[13] or to effect [the] escape of a female infant with the view to her marriage [against] her father's will;[14] or to procure the defilement of a girl;[15] [or to] entice a girl under age to leave her father's house, and live [in] fornication with one of the conspirators;[16] or for the purpose [of] prostitution;[17] or to procure a minor female to have illicit [con]nection with a man;[18] or to obtain a fraudulent divorce.[19]

1. United States v. Crosby, 1 Hughes, C. C. 448; Reg. v. Haslam, 1 Denison, 73.

2. Commonwealth v. Callaghan, 2 Va. Cas. 460; Rex v. Pollman, 2 Camp. 229.

3. Rex v. Vaughan, 4 Burr. 2494; Rex v. Pollman, 2 Camp. 229.

4. See Whart. Prec. 658.

5. United States v. Watson, 17 Fed. Rep. 145.

6. Commonwealth v. Franklin, 4 U. S. (4 Dall.) 255; bk. 1, L. ed. 823.

7. Wood v. State, 47 N. J. L. (18 Vr.) 461; s. c., 1 Cent. Rep. 441.

Intent as an Element.—Where, on a trial for conspiracy among public officers to violate a statute, the court charged the jury that, without regard to the defendants' ignorance of the existence of the statute, the agreement between them to violate the act, followed by conduct in furtherance of the general agreement, constituted a conspiracy, this was held to be error, the court remarking that "the general rule is, that, to constitute a crime, there must not only be the act, but also a criminal intention; and these must concur, the latter being equally essential with the former." Stokes v. People, 53 N. Y. 179; People v. Powell, 63 N. Y. 88, 91.

8. Rex v. Mackarty, 2 Ld. Raym. 1179. See State v. Rowley, 12 Conn. 101.

9. King v. Grey, 9 How. St. Tri. 127; Rex v. Delaval, 3 Burr. 1434; 1 East, P. C. 460.

10. Smith v. People, 25 Ill. 17; s. c., 76 Am. Dec. 780; King v. Grey, 9 How. St. Tr. 127; State v. Savoye, [illegible]; State v. Murphy, 6 Ala. 765; s. c., 41 Am. Dec. 79; Reg. v. Mears, 2 Den. C. C. [illegible]; s. c., 4 Cox, C. C. 423; Anderson v. Commonwealth, 5 Rand. (Va.) 627; s. c., 16 Am. Dec. 776.

11. State v. Murphy, 6 Ala. 765; s. c., 41 Am. Dec. 79.

12. Anderson v. Commonwealth, 5 Rand. (Va.) 627; s. c., 16 Am. Dec. 776; Smith v. People, 25 Ill. 17, 23; s. c., 76 Am. Dec. 780; Mifflin v. Commonwealth, 5 Watts & S. (Pa.) 461; s. c., 40 Am. Dec. [illegible].

13. Anderson v. Commonwealth, 5 Rand. (Va.) 627; s. c., 16 Am. Dec. 776; Smith v. People, 25 Ill. 23; s. c., 76 Am. Dec. 780; Mifflin v. Commonwealth, 5 Watts & S. (Pa.) 461; s. c., 40 Am. Dec. [illegible].

14. Mifflin v. Commonwealth, 5 Watts & Serg. (Pa.) 461; s. c., 40 Am. Dec. [illegible]; Commonwealth v. Hunt, 4 Metc. (Mass.) 111; s. c., 38 Am. Dec. 346.

15. Rex v. Mears, 2 Den. C. C. [illegible].

16. Anderson v. Commonwealth, 5 Rand. (Va.) 627; s. c., 16 Am. Dec. 776; King v. Grey, 9 How. St. Tri. 127.

17. Reg. v. Powell, 4 F. & F. [illegible]; Reg. v. Mears, 2 Den. C. C. 79; s. c., [illegible] M. 414; 15 Jur. 66; 20 L. J. M. C. [illegible]; 4 Cox, C. C. 423; Rex v. Grey, 9 How. St. Tr. 127; Rex v. Delaval, 3 Burr. [illegible]; s. c., 1 W. Bl. 439.

18. Reg. v. Mears, 2 Den. C. C. [illegible]; L. J. M. C. 59.

19. Cole v. People, 84 Ill. 216.

An indictment lies at common law for a conspiracy to inveigle a young girl into matrimony,[1] or to take away an heiress from the custody of her friends for the purpose of marrying her to one of the conspirators.[2]

c. Interference with Business. — The doctrine of criminal conspiracy rests upon the proposition, that the power of many for mischief against one person is so great that the State should protect him.[3] No one is authorized to unlawfully destroy or hinder the lawful business of another for the purpose of helping himself.[4] It does not require malice to be shown against the owner of the business disturbed, or his property, in the same sense as does the common law in cases of malicious mischief.[5]

A conspiracy to injure trade is indictable.[6] And an information charging a mere conspiracy to obstruct and impede the business of a manufacturing company, by combining unlawfully to do so by certain acts and means, describing them, but which nowhere alleges that any of these acts were actually committed by the defendants, but simply that they conspired to commit them, charges only the offence of conspiracy under the Michigan revised statutes.[7]

3. *To obtain Property by Fraudulent Means.* — An indictment lies at common law for a conspiracy to defraud by means of an act not in itself unlawful, and even though no person be injured thereby.[8]

Many acts which, if done by an individual, are not indictable, are punishable criminally when done in pursuance of a conspiracy among a number of individuals.[9]

1. Respublica v. Hevice, 2 Yeates (Pa.), 114.

2. Wakefield's Case, 2 Lewin, Cr. Cas. 279.

3. State v. Rowley, 12 Conn. 112; Reg. v. Duffield, 5 Cox, Cr. Cas. 432; 2 Bish. Cr. L. sec. 181.

4. People v. Petheram (Mich.), 7 West. Rep. 592.

To Injure a Man in his Trade. — A conspiracy to injure a man in his trade or profession is indictable ever since Eccles's Case. People v. Petheram (Mich.), 7 West. Rep. 592; Rex v. Eccles, 1 Leach, 274; s. c., 3 Doug. 337; affd. in 1885, Mogul Steamship Co. v. McGregor, L. R. 15 Q. B. Div. 476, 482. See also Reg. v. Hewitt, 5 Cox, Cr. Cas. 163; Carew v. Rutherford, 106 Mass. 10-15; Walker v. Cronin, 107 Mass. 564; Master Stevedores' Association v. Walsh, 2 Daly (N. Y.), 1; Rex v. Byerdike, 1 Moody & R. 179; State v. Donaldson, 32 N. J. L. (3 Vr.) 151; Walsby v. Anley, 3 L. T. N. S. 666.

5. People v. Petheram (Mich.), 7 West. Rep. 592.

6. Rex v. Cope, 1 Str. 144.

7. Mich. Rev. Stat., § 9275. See People v. Petheram (Mich.), 7 West. Rep. 592.

8. Rex v. Robinson, 1 Leach, 37; Rex v. Edwards, 2 Strange, 707; Rex v. Berenger, 3 Maule & S. 67.

Cheating. — An indictment lies at common law for a conspiracy to cheat and defraud by means of an act which would not in law amount to an indictable cheat if perpetrated by a single individual. Rex v. Lara, 2 Leach, 647; Rex v. Wheatly, 2 Burr. 1127; Rex v. Skirret, 1 Sid. 312; Reg. v. Orbell, 6 Mod. 42; Reg. v. Mackarty, 2 Ld. Raym. 1179.

9. State v. Rowley, 12 Conn. 101.

Instances. — As cheating by false pretences without false tokens, even when such cheating by one person is not punishable, — Commonwealth v. Boynton, 84 Mass. 160; Commonwealth v. Hunt, Thach. Cr. Cas. (Mass.) 609, 610, — or where developed to show a fraudulent scheme. See 2 Whart. C. L. (8th ed.) sec. 1370.

Getting Money by False Pretences. — Thus, it is an indictable conspiracy to obtain money by false pretences mediately, or by a contract, — *In re* Wolf, 27 Fed. Rep. 606; Bloomer v. State, 48 Md. 521; State v. Norton, 23

N. J. L. (3 Zab.) 33; State v. De Witt, 2 Hill (S. C.), 282; s. c., 27 Am. Dec. 371; Cole v. People, 84 Ill. 216; Commonwealth v. Wrigley, 6 Phila. (Pa.) 169; Clary v. Commonwealth, 4 Pa. St. 210; Commonwealth v. McGowan, 2 Pars. Cas. (Pa.) 341; Commonwealth v. Fuering, Brightly (Pa.), 315; Commonwealth v. Judd, 2 Mass. 329; s. c., 3 Am. Dec. 54; Commonwealth v. Gallagher, 2 Clark (Pa.) 58; State v. Spouten, 8 Rich. (S. C.) 72. See 2 Whart. Cr. L. (8th ed.) sec. 1370; Rex v. Robinson, 1 Leach (Eng.), 37; Reg. v. Bailey, 4 Cox, C. C. 390; Reg. v. Hudson, 8 Cox, C. C. 305; s. c., Bell, C. C. 263; 6 Jur. (N. S.) 566; Reg. v. Esdaile, 1 Fost. & F. 213; Reg. v. Brown, 7 Cox, C. C. 442; Reg. v. Carlisle, 6 Cox, C. C. 366; Reg. v. Stenson, 12 Cox, C. C. 111; Reg. v. Kenrick, Dav. & M. 208; Rex v. Hollingberry, 4 Barn. & C. 329; s. c., 2 Lead. Crim. Cas. 34; Reg. v. Kenrick, 5 Q. B. 49, — or by false pretences or fraudulent devices to cheat one out of his money, — Reg. v. Hudson, Bell, C. C. 263; s. c., 8 Cox, C. C. 305; 6 Jur. N. S. 566; 29 L. J. M. C. 145; 8 Week. R 421; 2 L. T. N. S. 263, — or by means of a mock auction, with sham bidders, — Reg. v. Lewis, 11 Cox, C. C. 404, — or by offering to sell forged bank notes of a denomination prohibited by statute, — Twichell v. Commonwealth, 9 Pa. St. 211, — or to obtain money under a feigned name. Rex v. Robinson, 1 Leach, 37.

Obtaining Property by Fraud. — A conspiracy to obtain property by false and fraudulent representations of insolvency is indictable, — Bush v. Sprague, 51 Mich. 41; Reg. v. Timothy, 1 Fost. & F. 39; — so also is a conspiracy to obtain goods under false pretences indictable, — Johnson v. People, 22 Ill. 314; Reg. v. Gompertz, 9 Q. B. 824; Sydserff v. Reg., 11 Q. B. 245; People v. Richards, 1 Mich. 216; s. c., 51 Am. Dec. 75; Commonwealth v. Walker, 108 Mass. 309; Clary v. Commonwealth, 4 Pa. St. 210; State v. Norton, 23 N. J. L. (3 Zab.) 33; Reg. v. Parker, 3 Q. B. 292; Reg. v. Whitehouse, 6 Cox, C. C. 38; Heymann v. Reg., 12 Cox, C. C. 338; Reg. v. Bunn, 12 Cox, C. C. 316; Commonwealth v. Eastman, 55 Mass. (1 Cush.) 190; s. c., 48 Am. Dec. 596, — or on credit with intent not to pay for them, — Commonwealth v. Eastman, 55 Mass. (1 Cush.) 189; s. c., 48 Am. Dec. 596; Reg. v. King, Dav. & M. 741, — as by causing themselves to be reputed men of property, — Rex v. Roberts, 1 Camp. 399; Gardner v. Preston, 2 Day (Conn.), 205; State v. Clary, 64 Me. 369. See 3 Russ. Cr. (9th ed.) 126, — or wrongfully to obtain possession of real estate. People v. Richards, 1 Mich. 216; s. c., 51 Am. Dec. 75; State v. Shooter, 8 Rich. (S. C.) 72.

Where two are charged with obtaining property by fraud, and the fraud of one is not denied, [illegible] fraud and [illegible] the other. Lincoln v. [illegible] Wall.) 132; [illegible]

But a charge cannot [illegible] against several persons [illegible] money from a bank [illegible] when they had no funds [illegible] v. Rickey, 9 N. J. L. [illegible]

Conspiracy to Issue Fictitious [illegible] or Bills, etc. — A combination [illegible] member of a partnership and [illegible] to issue and circulate the notes [illegible] drawn by such parties for the [illegible] paying his individual debts, [illegible] being fraudulent, is indictable, — [illegible] Cole, 39 N. J. L. (10 Vr.) [illegible] Warburton, L. R. 1 Cr. Cas. [illegible] or by issuing fictitious bills in the [illegible] a fictitious firm, — Reg. v. [illegible] P. C. 858. See State v. Norton [illegible] L. (3 Zab.) 33, — or by [illegible] of an indorsement on a [illegible] — State v. Norton, 23 N. J. L. [illegible] — or to fraudulently [illegible] tickets, — Bloomer v. State, [illegible] or to publish false [illegible] a corporation, — Reg. v. Esdaile [illegible] F. 213; Reg. v. Brown, 7 Cox, [illegible] See Reg. v. Gurney, 11 Cox, C. [illegible] v. Aspinwall, 13 Cox, C. C. [illegible] — [illegible] spire to induce persons to [illegible] new company, to which was [illegible] business of the old company, [illegible] of defrauding and cheating, — [illegible] ney, 11 Cox, C. C. [illegible] — or [illegible] prices of public funds by false [illegible] Rex v. De Berenger, 3 [illegible] to procure by false means [illegible] stock on the stock exchange, [illegible] Aspinall, L. R. 1 Q. B. Div. [illegible] defraud a broker by a [illegible] — Commonwealth v. Supt. [illegible] Prison, 6 Phila. (Pa.) [illegible] — or [illegible] of goods fraudulently, at a [illegible] — Reg. v. Lewis, 11 Cox, C. C. [illegible] dispose of goods by false [illegible] of their quality, — Reg. v. Kenrick [illegible] 49, — or as to their soundness [illegible] Carlisle, 23 L. J. M. C. 109.

False Representations in the [illegible] Horse. — A conspiracy to [illegible] lently misrepresent the value of [illegible] induce the acceptance of [illegible] the agreed price, is an indictable [illegible] Reg. v. Carlisle, Dears. C. C. [illegible] L. J. M. C. 109.

That an agreement between [illegible] to give a false warranty [illegible] a horse is not indictable, [illegible] v. Pywell, 1 Stark. N. P. C. [illegible] overruled in Reg. v. Kenrick [illegible] R. v. Orman, 14 Cox, C. C. [illegible]

Overvaluing a Commodity [illegible] spiracy is indictable where [illegible] cheat by fraudulently [illegible]

D. Where neither the Object to be attained, nor the Means to be employed, are Illegal or Unlawful. — 1. *What Indictable.* — It is said [1] that a combination is a conspiracy in law whenever the act to be done has a necessary tendency to prejudice the public, or oppress individuals, by unjustly subjecting them to the power of the confederates, and giving effect to the purposes of the latter, whether of extortion or mischief; and the same proposition, in one form of expression and another, is laid down in all the leading works on criminal law.[2]

2. *What not Indictable.* — But an indictment will not lie for conspiracy to commit a mere civil trespass,[3] or against township officers for a conspiracy to get public money into their hands, there being no overt act.[4] An agreement to prosecute a person who is guilty, or against whom there is reasonable ground of suspicion, is not an indictable conspiracy.[5]

A mere preparation for crime is not indictable;[6] nor is a con-

modity, — Reg. v. Levine, 10 Cox, C. C. 374; Reg. v. Stenson, 12 Cox, C. C. 111; Reg. v. Kenrick, Dav. & M. 208, — or against a body of men, where the object of the conspiracy is to procure fraudulently the election of certain persons as directors of an incorporated company, by an issuance of false policies, — State v. Burnham, 15 N. H. 396, — or by fabricating shares in a joint-stock company, — Rex v. Mott, 2 Car. & P. 521; Reg. v. Gurney, 11 Cox, C. C. 414, — or to cheat by betting, — Reg. v. Bailey, 4 Cox, C. C. 390; Reg. v. Hudson, 8 Cox, C. C. 305 — or to induce making an absurd bet, — Reg. v. Hudson, 8 Cox, C. C 305, — or by false representations to induce a purchase, — Reg. v. Kenrick, 5 Q. B. N. S. 49; s. c., Dav. & M. Jur. 848; Reg. v. Timothy, 1 Fost & F. 39, — or by false representations to induce a person to forego a claim, — Reg. v. Carlisle, Dears. C. C. 337; s. c., 18 Jur. 386; 23 Law J. M. C. 109; 6 Cox, C. C. 366, — or to marry by false personation, with the purpose to defraud relations out of the estate, — Rex v. Robinson, 1 Leach, 37, — or to gain the consent of a father and mother to a marriage through a forged license, and falsely stating one of their number was a justice of the peace, — State v. Murphy, 6 Ala. 765; s. c., 41 Am. Dec. 79, — or to cause a marriage falsely to appear upon record, and to obtain a false certificate of the same, — Commonwealth v. Waterman, 122 Mass. 43, — or to solemnize a marriage to defraud, — Rex v. Robinson, 1 Leach, 37.

Inducing Pauper or Fraudulent Marriages. — It is an indictable offence by fraudulent means to bring about a marriage between paupers of different parishes, — Rex v. Seward, 3 Nev. & M. (K. B.) 557; s. c., 1 A. & E. 706, — or to procure a forced and fraudulent marriage. Respublica v. Hevice, 2 Yeates (Pa.), 114; Rex v. Wakefield, Towns. St. Tr. 112; 3 Russ. Cr. (9th ed.) 130.

1. 2 Whart. Cr. L. § 2322.

2. Bish. Cr. L. § 172; Desty, Cr. L. § 11; 3 Chitty, Cr. L. 1138; Archb. Cr. Pr. Pl. 1830. See also Queen v. Kenrick, 5 Q. B. 49; State v. Stewart, 59 Vt. 273; s. c., 4 New Eng. Rep. 378; Commonwealth v. Carlisle, Bright. (Pa.) 36; Morris Run Coal Co. v. Barclay Coal Co., 68 Pa. St. 173.

Where the act is lawful for an individual, it can be subject of a conspiracy when done in concert only where there is a direct intention that injury shall result from it, or where the object is to benefit the conspirators to the prejudice of the public, or to the oppression of individuals, and where such prejudice or oppression is the natural or necessary consequence. Commonwealth v. Carlisle, Bright. (Pa.) 36.

Conspiracies which involve mischief to the public are indictable, although neither the object sought to be accomplished, nor the means used for its accomplishment, is criminal. Commonwealth v. Ward, 1 Mass. 473; Commonwealth v. Judd, 2 Mass. 329; s. c., 3 Am. Dec. 54; State v. Burnham, 15 N. H. 396.

3. State v. Straw, 42 N. H. 393. See Rex v. Turner, 13 East, 228.

A mere sympathy not exhibited in overt acts is not sufficient. People v. Leith, 52 Cal. 251; State v. Cox, 65 Mo. 29; Connaughty v. State, 1 Wis. 169.

4. Horseman v. Reg., 16 Up. Can. Q. B. 543.

5. Commonwealth v. Tibbetts, 2 Mass. 536; Commonwealth v. Dupuy, Bright. (Pa.) 44; Rex v. Best, 1 Salk. 174.

6. United States v. Nunnemacher, 7 Biss. C. C. 111; United States v. Goldberg, 7 Biss. C. C. 175.

spiracy to procure an over-insurance indictable;[1] nor to sell man an unsound horse, if there be no fraudulent devices.[2]

3. *To commit Acts against Public Polity.* — A combination restrain trade so as to impoverish a man in his business, is indic able.[3]

Conspiracies to injure trade were indictable at common law And a "corner," when accomplished by confederation, to rai or depress prices and operate on the market, is a conspiracy, the means be unlawful.[5] And so is a conspiracy to monopoliz by fraudulent means, any particular business staple, so as to for its purchase at exorbitant prices,[6] such as coal.[7]

a. Contests between Capital and Labor. — The labor and skill the workman, the plant of the manufacturer, and the equipme of the farmer, are, in an equal sense, property.[8] Every man h the right to employ his talents, industry, and capital as he please free from the dictation of others; and, if two or more perso combine to coerce his choice in this behalf, it is a criminal co spiracy, whether the means employed are actual violence, or species of intimidation that works upon the mind.[9] While tl law accords this liberty to one, it accords a like liberty to anothe and all are bound to use and enjoy their own liberties and pri leges with regard to those of their neighbors.[10]

It is a criminal offence for two or more persons corruptly

1. Commonwealth *v.* Prius, 75 Mass. (9 Gray) 127.

2. Rex *v.* Pywell, 1 Stark. 402.

3. Commonwealth *v.* Hunt, 45 Mass. (4 Metc.) 111; s. c., 38 Am. Dec. 346; Commonwealth *v.* Wallace, 82 Mass. (16 Gray) 221; Commonwealth *v.* Prins, 75 Mass. (9 Gray) 127; Rex *v.* Turner, 13 East, 228. But see Commonwealth *v.* Eastman, 55 Mass. (1 Cush.) 189; s. c., 48 Am. Dec. 596.

4. Rex *v.* Cope, 1 Strange, 144; Rex *v.* De Berenger, 3 Maule & S. 68; Rex *v.* Norris, 2 Ld. Ken. 300; Reg. *v.* Gurney, 11 Cox, Cr. Cas. 414; Levi *v.* Levi, 6 Car. & P. 239.

5. Morris Run Coal Co. *v.* Barclay Coal Co., 68 Pa. St. 173; People *v.* Melvin, 2 Wheel. Cr. Cas. 262.

An agreement by the proprietors of five lines of canal boats on the Erie and Oswego canals to charge a uniform rate, and divide the earnings, being injurious to trade and commerce, has been held to be a conspiracy. Hooker *v.* Vandewater, 4 Denio (N. Y.), 349; s. c., 47 Am. Dec. 258. A contract arising out of such agreement is illegal and void. Stanton *v.* Allen, 5 Denio (N. Y.), 434; s. c., 49 Am. Dec. 282; Hooker *v.* Vandewater, 4 Denio (N. Y.), 349; s. c., 47 Am. Dec. 258.

6. Rex *v.* Norris, 2 Keny. 300.

7. Morris Run Coal Co. *v.* Barclay Co Co., 68 Pa. St. 173.

8. State *v.* Stewart, 59 Vt. 273; s. c. New Eng. Rep. 378.

9. State *v.* Stewart, 59 Vt. 273; s. c. New Eng. Rep. 378.

It is said in the case of State *v.* Stew *supra*, that, from a careful examination the English and American authorities, it clear to a demonstration that a combi tion of persons to prevent and hinder violence, threats, and intimidation a co pany corporation, or individual from e ploying or retaining the services of certa workmen, or by threats to terrify, inti date, and drive away the workmen, i conspiracy at common law; and, furth that the subject-matter of the offence bei the same in this country as in Englai namely, an interference with the proper rights of third persons, and a restrai upon the lawful prosecution of their dustries, as well as an unlawful cont over the free use and employment by wor men of their own personal skill and lab at such times, for such prices, and for su persons, as they please, — the common l of England is "applicable to our lo situation and circumstances" in this half, and is therefore the common law Vermont.

10. State *v.* Stewart, 59 Vt. 273; s. 4 New Eng. Rep. 378.

maliciously to confederate together, and agree among themselves to deprive another of his liberty or property.[1]

All confederacies whatsoever, which wrongfully prejudice a third person, are highly criminal at common law.[2]

(1) *To compel Discharge of Employees.* — Conspiring to compel an employer to discharge certain workmen, and threatening to quit the employment if he does not, is an indictable conspiracy.[3]

1. State v. Glidden, 55 Conn. 46; s. c., 3 New Eng. Rep. 849; State v. Ripley, 31 Me. 386; Wood v. State, 47 N. J. L. (18 Vr.) 180; Reg. v. Timothy, 1 Fost. & F. 39; Reg. v. Peck, 9 Adol. & E. 686; s. c., *sub nom.* Peck v. Queen, 1 Perry & D. 508.

2. State v. Stewart, 59 Vt. 273; s. c., 4 New Eng. Rep. 378, 2 Russ Cr. 674.

Confederation to injure or prejudice a Third Person. — It is laid down in 1 Hawkins's P. C. ch. 72, sect. 2, that "all confederacies whatsoever, wrongfully to prejudice a third person, are highly criminal at common law." The same proposition in one form of expression and another is laid down in 2 Bish. Cr. L. § 172; and in Desty, Cr. L. § 11; and in 3 Chitty, Cr. L. 1138; and in Archb. Cr. Pr. Pl. 1830. And by *Baron Rolfe*, in Reg. v. Selsby, 5 Cox, Cr. Cas. 495, note; and *Tindal, Ch. J.*, in Reg. v. Harris, 1 Car. & Marsh. 661; and *Crompton, J.*, in Hilton v. Eckersley, 6 E. & B. 47; and *Grose, J.*, in Rex v. Mawbey, 6 T. R. 619; and *Lord Mansfield*, in Rex v. Eccles. 1 Leach, Cr. Cas. 274; and *Hill, J.*, in Walsby v. Anley, 3 E. & E. 516; and *Campbell, Ch. J.*, in Reg. v. Rowlands, 17 A. & E. N. S. 670; and *Baron Bramwell*, in Reg. v. Druitt, 10 Cox, Cr. Cas. 592; and *Brett, J.*, in Reg. v. Bunn, 12 Cox, Cr. Cas. 316; and *Malins, V. C.*, in Springhead Co. v. Riley, L. R. 6 Eq. 551; and *Coleridge, Ch. J.*, in Mogul S. S. Co. v. McGregor, L. R. 15 Q. B. Div. 476; and *Shaw, Ch. J.*, in Commonwealth v. Hunt, 45 Mass. (4 Metc.) 111, 128; s. c., 38 Am. Dec. 346; and *Caton, J.*, in Smith v. People, 25 Ill. 17; and *Gibson, Ch. J.*, in Commonwealth v. Carlisle, Journal Jurisp. 225; and *Chapman, Ch. J.*, in Carew v. Rutherford, 106 Mass. 1, — have all added their indorsement of the doctrine advanced as early as the work of Hawkins, *supra*; and it is manifest that we are compelled to forsake the literature of doubt, and to cleave unto that of authority. See also Rex v. Ferguson, 2 Stark. N. P. 489; Rex v. Hverdike, 1 Moo. & Rob. 179; People v. Fisher, 14 Wend. (N. Y.) 9; State v. Donaldson, 32 N. J. L. (3 Vr.) 151; Snow v. Wheeler, 113 Mass. 186; State v. Noyes, 25 Vt. 415; State v. Burnham, 15 N. H. 396; Morris Run Coal Co. v. Barclay Coal Co., 68 Pa. 173.

Vice-Chancellor Malins, in Springhead Co. v. Riley, L. R. 6 Eq. 551, states the law of the subject in brief but intelligible words: "Every man is at liberty to enter into a combination to keep up the price of wages; but, if he enters into a combination for the object of interfering with the perfect freedom of the action of another man, it is an offence, not only at common law, but under Act 6, Geo. IV. chap. 129."

Foundation of the Doctrine. — The principle upon which the cases, English and American, proceed, is, that every man has the right to employ his talents, industry, and capital as he pleases, free from the dictation of others; and if two or more persons combine to coerce his choice in this behalf, it is a criminal conspiracy. The labor and skill of the workman, be it of high or low degree, the plant of the manufacturer, the equipment of the farmer, the investments of commerce, are all, in equal sense, property. If men by overt acts of violence destroy either, they are guilty of crime. The anathemas of a secret organization of men combined for the purpose of controlling the industry of others by a species of intimidation that works upon the mind, rather than the body, are quite as dangerous as, and generally altogether more effective than, acts of actual violence. And, while such conspiracies may give to the individual directly affected by them a private right of action for damages, they at the same time lay a basis for an indictment, on the ground that the State itself is directly concerned in the promotion of all legitimate industries and the development of all its resources, and owes the duty of protection to its citizens engaged in the exercise of their callings. The good order, peace, and general prosperity of the State is directly involved in the question. State v. Stewart, 59 Vt. 273; s. c., 4 New Eng. Rep. 378.

3. State v. Donaldson, 32 N. J. L. (3 Vr.) 151; People v. Trequier, 1 Wheel. Cr. Cas. 142; Commonwealth v. Hunt, 45 Mass. (4 Metc.) 111; s. c., 38 Am. Dec. 346; Collins v. Hayte, 50 Ill. 355; Hooker v. Vandewater, 4 Denio (N. Y.) 349; s. c., 47 Am. Dec. 258; Rex v. Journeymen Tailors, 8 Mod. 11, citing Tubwomen v. Brewers of London; Reg. v. Rowlands, 17 Q. B. 671; Reg. v. Bunn, 12 Cox, Cr. Cas. 316; Reg. v. Banks, 12 Cox, Cr. Cas. 393.

b. To coerce and oppress Workmen. — (1) *Combinations of* [illegible] *ployers.* — A combination of employers to [illegible] journeymen, having a necessary tendency to [illegible] or to oppress individuals, is an indictable conspiracy.[1]

(2) *Combinations of Employees.* — Associations of [illegible] endeavor peaceably, and in a reasonable manner, [illegible] others to cease or abstain from work; but if by force or [illegible] tion they endeavor to control the free agency, or overcom[illegible] free will, of their fellow-workmen, they become guilty of a [illegible] offence.[2] And the fact that the threat is designed as a [illegible] an end, and that end in itself considered a lawful one, does [illegible] divest the transaction of its criminality.[3]

A count in an indictment for a conspiracy is sufficient [illegible] charges that the respondents, with a malicious intent, [illegible] and injure a person, or a company, or the business of [illegible] unlawfully conspired to terrify, intimidate, and drive [illegible] threats, its workmen;[4] or to prevent and hinder by [illegible]

An indictment lies where journeymen shoemakers enter into an agreement not to make coarse boots for less than $1 a pair, and not to work for any master who paid any shoemaker less than $1 a pair; pursuant to which agreement, defendants forced a master to discharge from his employ one who had worked for less than that sum. People *v.* Fisher, 14 Wend. (N. Y.) 9; s. c., 28 Am. Dec. 501.

Several employees notified their master, that, if he did not discharge two fellow-workmen, they would leave; and they did refuse to work until their demand was complied with. They were then indicted for conspiracy, and convicted; and the language of Chief Justice Beasley embodies about all that can be said for that side of the question in State *v.* Donaldson, 32 N. J. L. (3 Vr.) 151. *Dicta* to the same effect may be found in Morris Run Coal Co. *v.* Barclay Coal Co., 63 Pa. St. 173; Master Stevedores' Asso. *v.* Walsh, 2 Daly (N. Y.), 1, a very elaborately considered case, embracing a review of, and criticism upon, many, if not all, the early decisions in this country and England. People *v.* Petheram (Mich.), 7 West. Rep. 592.

1. Commonwealth *v.* Carlisle, Bright (Pa.), 36; Philadelphia Boot and Shoe Makers, Phila. 1807; Twenty-four Journeymen Shoemakers, Phila. 1827.

2. Reg. *v.* Shepherd, 11 Cox, Cr. Cas. 325.

Threats: Indictment. — It is not necessary to set out specifically the kind of threats or intimidation made use of. State *v.* Stewart, 59 Vt. 273; s. c., 4 New Eng. Rep. 849.

3. State *v.* Glidden, 55 Conn. 46; s. c., 3 New Eng. Rep. 849.

Molesting Workmen. — Thus, it is indictable to molest or obstruct workmen to induce them to leave their [illegible] Reg. *v.* Hibbert, 13 Cox, Cr. Cas. [illegible] *v.* Rowlands, 5 Cox, C. C. [illegible]

Shouting and hooting [illegible] considered intimidation. [illegible] 11 Cox, Cr. Cas. [illegible] 5 Cox, Cr. Cas. 437; Reg. *v.* [illegible] Cr. Cas. 432.

Expelling Chinese. — [illegible] public meetings throughout the [illegible] ing to, and providing for, [illegible] subjects of the rights, [illegible] ties, and exemptions [illegible] our treaties with China, [illegible] ularly known as "boycotting," [illegible] coercive means, [illegible] through what [illegible] nal. *Re* Baldwin, 27 Fed. [illegible]

Intimidating Miners. — [illegible] of men collect about the [illegible] the intention of intimidating the m[illegible] working, such combination would b[illegible] lawful; and all persons engaged th[illegible] would be guilty of conspiracy, wh[illegible] actually present at the commission o[illegible] act of violence or riot. Newman *v.* [illegible] monwealth (Pa.), 5 Cent. Rep. 497.

Coercing a Newspaper. — An inform[illegible] which alleges that the defendants cons[illegible] to threaten and use means (the boyco[illegible] intimidate a publishing company, to [illegible] pel it, against its will, to abstain from [illegible] an act (to keep in its employ workm[illegible] its own choice) which it had a legal [illegible] to do, and to do an act (employ th[illegible] fendants and such persons as they sh[illegible] name) which it had a legal right to ab[illegible] from doing, charges acts clearly cri[illegible] by the statute. State *v.* Glidden, 55 C[illegible] 46; s. c., 3 New Eng. Rep. 849.

4. State *v.* Stewart, 59 Vt. 273; s. [illegible] New Eng. Rep. 378.

threats, and intimidations, the company from retaining and taking into its employ certain workmen.[1]

c. To coerce and oppress Employers. — The exposure of a legitimate business to the control of an association that can order away its employees, and frighten away others that it may seek to employ, and thus be compelled to cease the further prosecution of its work, is a condition of things utterly at war with every principle of justice, and with every safeguard of protection that a citizen under our system of government is entitled to enjoy.[2] An

The workmen sought to be injured, and deprived of their employment, have just as good a right to work for their employers as the conspirators have, and their right is entitled to the same consideration and protection. In such cases, it has been said, "The combination is not against capital, or against their employers, to better their condition, but against fellow-workmen, — men whose earnings are comparatively small, and who, presumably, need all their earnings for the support of themselves and their families. They are ordinarily poor men, and men whose entire capital consists in their trade and time. The combination is to wantonly deprive them of a livelihood, and practically of all means of support, by securing their discharge. If a capitalist is driven from his business, he has other resources; but the poor mechanic, driven from his employment, — and, as is often the case, deprived of employment elsewhere, — is compelled to see his loved ones suffer or depend upon charity. It is a combination of the many to impoverish and oppress a few. The weak party needs, and must receive, the protection of the law. If in any case it is criminal for the many to combine to do what any one may lawfully do singly, it would seem that this would be such a case." State *v.* Glidden, 55 Conn. 46; s. c., 3 New Eng. Rep. 849.

1. **Indictment for intimidating Workmen** for unlawfully molesting by using threats, or intimidating workingmen; by unlawfully molesting their employer, and obstructing him in his business, where a charge of the means by which the conspiracy was to be carried on are stated in the words of the statute, it is sufficient. Reg. *v.* Rowlands, 17 Q. B. 671; 21 L. J. M. C. 81; 4 Cox, Cr. Cas. 436; Hilton *v.* Eckersley, 1 Jur. N. S. 875; 24 L. J. Q. B. 353; 6 El. & B. 47.

A count is sufficient which merely charges a conspiracy to do an unlawful act; and, *a fortiori*, one that charges a conspiracy to do an unlawful act by unlawful means. State *v.* Stewart, 59 Vt. 273; s. c., 4 New Eng. Rep. 378.

Combining of Journeymen. — It is an indictable conspiracy for journeymen to combine to compel by force of numbers and discipline, and by fines and penalties, other journeymen to join their societies, and masters to employ none but members. Commonwealth *v.* Hunt, 45 Mass. (4 Metc.) 111; s. c., 38 Am. Dec. 346; Thach. C. C. 609; People *v.* Fisher, 14 Wend. (N. Y.) 9; s. c., 28 Am. Dec. 501; Collins *v.* Hayte, 50 Ill. 355; Hooker *v.* Vandewater, 4 Den. (N. Y.) 349; s. c., 47 Am. Dec. 258; Stanton *v.* Allen, 5 Den. (N. Y.) 434; s. c., 49 Am. Dec. 282; Rex *v.* Byerdike, 1 Moody & R. 179; Rex *v.* Tailors' Co., 8 Mod. 11; Rex *v.* Eccles, 1 Leach, 274; Reg. *v.* Hewitt, 5 Cox, C. C. 162; Reg. *v.* Duffield, 5 Cox, C. C. 286. See Reg. *v.* Rowlands, 17 Q. B. 671; 2 Den. C. C. 364; Walsby *v.* Anley, 30 L. J. M. C. 121; O'Neil *v.* Longman, 4 Best & S. 376; O'Neil *v.* Kruger, 4 Best & S. 389; Reg. *v.* Druitt, 10 Cox, C. C. 592; Reg. *v.* Shepherd, 11 Cox, C. C. 325; Reg. *v.* Selsby, 5 Cox, C. C. 495; Hornby *v.* Close, L. R. 2 Q. B. 153; Reg. *v* Hunt, 8 Car. & P. 642.

2. State *v.* Stewart, 59 Vt. 273; s. c., 4 New Eng. Rep. 378.

Effect of Intimidation. — The direct tendency of such intimidation is to establish over labor, and over all industries, a control that is unknown to the law, and is exerted by a secret association of conspirators, who are actuated solely by personal considerations, and whose plans, carried into execution, usually result in violence and the destruction of property. State *v.* Stewart, 59 Vt. 273; s. c., 4 New Eng. Rep. 378.

Combination to compel Discharge of Workmen. — In State *v.* Stewart, 59 Vt. 273; s. c., 4 New Eng. Rep. 378, where an indictment for conspiracy was found against workmen for combining to compel their employer, the Ryegate Granite Co., to discharge certain workmen in its employ, the court say, —

"By the law of the land, these respondents have the most unqualified right to work for whom they please, and for such prices as they please. By the law of the land, O'Rourke and Goodfellow have the same right. By the same law, the Ryegate Granite Company has the right to employ the respondents or O'Rourke on such terms as may be mutually agreed upon, without

engagement and combination between the defendants, or so
them, and others, to interfere with the master by molesting
so as to control their will, if the molestation was such as
be likely to deter them from carrying on their business acco
to their own will, is an illegal conspiracy, for which the defen
are liable.[1]

(1) *To prevent hiring Employees.* — It is unlawful for wor
wrongfully to coerce, intimidate, or hinder employers in the
tion of such workmen as they choose to employ,[2] or to pr
and hinder by violence, threats, and intimidation the cor
from taking into its employ certain workmen.[3] An indict
lies where journeymen seek to prevent their employers
taking apprentices.[4] An agreement between employees to
the service if the master does not comply with some demand
conspiracy to molest and obstruct the employer.[5]

let, hinderance, or dictation from any man or body of men whatever.

"Suppose the members of a bar association in Caledonia County should combine and declare that the respondents should employ no attorney not a member of such association to assist them in their defence in this case, under the penalty of being dubbed a 'scab,' and having his name paraded in the public press as unworthy of recognition among his brethren, and himself brought into hatred, envy, and contempt, would the respondents look upon this as an innocent intermeddling with their rights under the law? The proposition has only to be stated to discern its utter inconsistency with every principle of justice that permeates the law under which we live.

"If such conspiracies are to be tolerated as innocent, then every farmer in Vermont, now resting in the confidence that he may employ such assistance in carrying on his farm as he thinks he can afford to hire, is exposed to the operation of some such code of law, in the framing of which he had no voice, and upon the terms of which he has no veto; and every manufacturer is handicapped by a system that portends certain destruction to his industry. If our agricultural and manufacturing industries are sleeping upon the fires of a volcano, liable to eruption at any moment, it is high time our people knew it. But happily such is not the law, and among English-speaking people never has been the law. The reports, English and American, are full of illustrations of the doctrine that a combination of two or more persons to effect an illegal purpose, either by legal or illegal means, whether such purpose be illegal at common law or by statute; or to effect a legal purpose by illegal means, whether such means be illegal at common law or
by statute, — is a common-law co
Such combinations are equally
whether they promote objects or
means that are *per se* indictable.
mote objects or adopt means that ar
oppressive, immoral, or wrongfully
dicial to the rights of others. If th
to restrain trade, or tend to the dest
of the material prosperity of the c
they work injury to the whole

"A conspiracy to hinder, preve
deter a man from retaining, and tak
his employ, an attorney to defend hi
is a clear violation of his as well
attorney's personal rights; and equ
is a combination to terrify, alar
drive away his attorney already em
The natural tendency and inevitabl
sequence of such combinations is
strain the prosecution of legitimate
and industries, and thereby injure tl
lic as well as individuals. The c
intent, emphasized and expanded
aggregation of members and amou
a show of force, gives to such comb
its character of illegality. If, in f
respondents had prevented, hinder
deterred the Granite Works from
ing O'Rourke, the act would conf
have been criminal. It logically
that a conspiracy to do this thing w
equally so."

1. Reg. v. Bunn, 12 Cox, Cr. Ca
People v. Petheram (Mich.), 7 Wes
592.

2. State v. Stewart, 59 Vt. 273;
New Eng. Rep. 378.

3. State v. Stewart, 59 Vt. 273;
New Eng. Rep. 378.

4. Rex v. Ferguson, 2 Starkie, 48
ple v. Fisher, 14 Wend. (N. Y.) 9;
Am. Dec. 501.

5. Reg. v. Hewitt, 5 Cox, Cr. Ca
Walsby v. Anley, 3 L. T. (N. S.) 66

d. Boycotting. — The "boycott" is not the remedy to adjust the difference between capital and labor.[1] To incite persons to prevent others from taking or occupying farms from which others have been evicted for non-payment of rents, is an offence at common law.[2] A combination to prevent persons buying goods taken in execution is an offence at common law, and is a crime, if the means to carry out this object were those commonly known as boycotting.[3]

The acts of all the public meetings through the land looking to, and providing for, depriving Chinese subjects of the rights, privileges, immunities, and exemptions secured to them by our treaties with China, by means popularly known as "boycotting,"

1. State *v.* Stewart, 59 Vt. 273; s. c., 4 New Eng. Rep. 378.

That evils exist in the relations of capital and labor, and that workmen have grievances that oftentimes call for relief, are facts that observing men cannot deny. With such questions the court have no function to discharge, further than to say that the remedy cannot be found in the boycott. State *v.* Stewart, 59 Vt. 273; s. c., 4 New Eng. Rep. 378.

Origin of the Term. — Conspiracy contemplates boycotting as a means to the end sought. The word "boycotting" is not easily defined. It is frequently spoken of as passive, merely: a let-alone policy, a withdrawal of all business relations, intercourse, and fellowship. If that is its only meaning, it will be difficult to find any thing in it criminal. We may gather some idea of its real meaning, however, by a reference to the circumstances in which the word originated. Those circumstances are thus narrated by Mr. Justin H. McCarthy, an Irish gentleman of learning and ability, who will be recognized as good authority. In his work, entitled, "England under Gladstone," he says, "The strike was supported by a form of action — or rather inaction — which soon became historical. Captain Boycott was an Englishman, an agent of Lord Earne, and a farmer of Lough Mask, in the wild and beautiful district of Connemara. In his capacity as agent he had served notices upon Lord Earne's tenants, and the tenantry suddenly retaliated in a most unexpected way, by, in the language of schools and society, sending Captain Boycott to Coventry in a very thorough manner. The population of the region for miles round resolved not to have any thing to do with him, and, as far as they could prevent it, not to allow any one else to have any thing to do with him. His life appeared to be in danger: he had to claim police protection. His servants fled from him as servants flee from their masters in some plague-stricken Italian city. The awful sentence of excommunication could hardly have rendered him more helplessly alone for a time. No one would work for him: no one would supply him with food. He and his wife had to work in their own fields themselves, in most unpleasant imitation of Theocritan shepherds and the shepherdesses, and play out their grim eclogue in their deserted fields, with the shadows of the armed constabulary ever at their heels. The Orangemen of the North heard of Captain Boycott and his sufferings, and the way in which he was holding his ground, and they organized assistance, and sent down armed laborers from Ulster. To prevent civil war, the authorities had to send a force of soldiers and police to Lough Mask; and Captain Boycott's harvests were brought in, and his potatoes dug, by the armed Ulster laborers, guarded always by the little army." State *v.* Glidden, 55 Conn. 46; s. c., 3 New Eng. Rep. 849. Whenever courts of law have made use of the term "boycotting," they have applied it to some phase of conspiracy.

It has been *held* that a combination and agreement among defendants, owners of steamers, with intent to injure plaintiffs, and prevent them from obtaining cargoes for their steamers between ports, agreeing to refuse, and refusing, to accept cargoes from shippers, except upon terms that shippers should not ship by plaintiffs' steamers, and threatening to stop shipment of homeward cargoes altogether, which threats they carried into effect, was boycotting. Mogul S. S. Co. *v.* McGregor, L. R. 15 Q. B. Div. 476.

2. Reg. *v.* Parnell, 14 Cox, Cr. Cas. 508.

3. Reg. *v.* Parnell, 14 Cox, Cr. Cas. 508.

Agreement not to ship Sailors. — To conspire with the keepers of sailors' boarding-houses not to ship seamen at the offices of certain notaries, is an indictable offence, — is boycotting. Emanuel's Case, 6 City Hall Rec. 33.

or any other coercive means, no matter in what form, or throu what channels applied, are criminal.[1]

An information which alleges that the defendants conspired threaten and use means (the boycott) to intimidate a company individual, to compel it, against its will, to abstain from doing act (to keep in its employ workmen of its own choice) which had a legal right to do, and to do an act (employ the defendan and such persons as they should name) which it had a le right to abstain from doing, charges acts clearly prohibited the statute.[2]

e. Picketing. — "Picketing," which means watching, and spea ing to the workmen as they go to or return from their empl ment, to induce them to leave the service, is not necessari unlawful; nor is it unlawful to use terms of persuasion towar them to accomplish that object; but if the besetting and watchi is carried to such an extent that it occasions dread of loss, it unlawful.[3]

There is nothing unlawful either in a strike to compel a mast to comply with certain regulations, or informing him of the obj of the strike, or in picketing his premises, so long as there is violence or molestation.[4]

f. Associations of Workmen. — Where the object of the ganization of workingmen is to better their own condition, th designs are not unlawful; and while they are free from engag ment, and have the option of entering into employment or n they have a right to agree among themselves not to go into a employment unless they can get a certain rate of wages.[5] A

1. *Re* Baldwin, 27 Fed. Rep. 193.

2. State *v.* Glidden, 55 Conn. 46; s. c., 3 New Eng. Rep. 849.

Boycotting a Newspaper. — An information charging the object of a conspiracy to have been to compel a newspaper company, against its will, by means of the boycott, to discharge workmen of its own choice, and employ defendants and such persons as they should name, charges acts prohibited by the Connecticut statute, 1887. State *v.* Glidden, 55 Conn. 46; s. c., 3 New Eng. Rep. 849.

And the charge that this conspiracy contemplated the wholesale boycotting of the patrons of the newspaper, states an offence within the statute. State *v.* Glidden, 55 Conn. 46; s. c., 3 New Eng. Rep. 849.

3. Reg. *v.* Hibbert, 13 Cox, Cr. Cas. 82; Reg. *v.* Bauld, 13 Cox, Cr. Cas. 282.

4. Sheridan's Case, Wright, Comp. 50; Reg. *v.* Shepherd, 11 Cox, Cr. Cas. 325.

5. Reg. *v.* Duffield, 5 Cox, Cr. Cas. 404, 431; and also Reg. *v.* Hibbert, 13 Cox, Cr. Cas. 82; Commonwealth *v.* Hunt, 45 Mass. (4 Metc.) 111, 130; State *v.* Donaldson, 32 N. J. L. (3 Vr.) 151; Carew *v.* Rutherford, 106 Mass. 1; Master Stevedores' Asso Walsh, 2 Daly (N. Y.), 1.

Combination to better Condition. — England and here it is lawful — and, may be added, commendable — for a body of men to associate themselves gether for the purpose of bettering th condition in any respect, financial or cial. The very genius of free institutio invites them to higher levels and bet fortunes. They may dictate their o wages, fraternise with their own associat choose their own employment, and serve m and mammon according to the dictates their own conscience. But while the l accords this liberty to the one, it accord like liberty to every other one; and all bound to so use and enjoy their own lil ties and privileges as not to interfere w those of their neighbors. State *v.* Stewa 59 Vt. 273; s. c., 4 New Eng. Rep. 378.

Labor Legislation. — All the legislat in England and America has been p gressively in the direction of according laborers the enjoyment of equal rig with others. The early English statut beginning with the middle of the fourtee century, are to be read in the light of t workmen have a right to combine for their own protection to obtain such wages as they choose to agree to demand; and while they have the option of entering the employment or not, they have a right to agree, that, unless they get a certain remuneration, they will not go into employment.[1] They are not indictable for exercising their option, but for the conspiracy among themselves to refuse.[2]

g. Labor Strikes. — Every association is criminal, the object of which is to raise or depress wages beyond or under what they would be if they were left without artificial aid or stimulus.[3] Strikes are criminal if they are part of a combination for the purpose of injuring or molesting either the master or his employees.[4]

There is nothing unlawful either in a strike to compel a master to comply with certain regulations, or informing him of the object of the strike, or in picketing his premises, so long as there is no violence or molestation.[5]

4. *Acts against Personal and Property Rights.* — Any combination of two or more persons, to injure either the character or property of an individual, is indictable.[6] Conspiracies are indictable where injury results to an individual.[7]

civilization of that day: and their provisions — to us, of the nineteenth century, harsh, illiberal, and tyrannical — were but the reflex of the prevalent notions of class distinctions that shaped and guided the social and political policy of those days. From time to time, however, down to 1875, this legislation has been called liberalized and Christianized; and to-day, in England or in America, workmen stand on the same broad level of equality before the law with all other vocations, professions, or callings, whatsoever, respecting the disposition of their labor and the advancement of their associated interests. Here, as there, it is unlawful for employers wrongfully to coerce, intimidate, or hinder the free choice of workmen in the disposal of their time and talents. There, as here, it is unlawful for workmen wrongfully to coerce, intimidate, or hinder employers in the selection of such workmen as they choose to employ. There, as here, no employer can say to a workman he must not work for another employer; nor can a workman say to an employer he cannot employ the service of another workman. State *v.* Stewart, 59 Vt. 273; s. c. 4 New Eng. Rep. 378.

1. Reg. *v.* Rowlands, 5 Cox, Cr. Cas. 436; Reg. *v.* Duffield, 5 Cox, Cr. Cas. 404; R. *v.* Hibbert, 13 Cox, Cr. Cas. 82; Commonwealth *v.* Hunt, 45 Mass. (4 Metc.) 111; State *v.* Donaldson, 32 N. J. L. (3 Vr.) 151; Carew *v.* Rutherford, 106 Mass. 1; Master Stevedores' Asso. *v.* Walsh, 2 Daly (N. Y.), 1.

2. Rex *v.* Journeymen Tailors, 8 Mod. 11.

3. State *v.* Glidden, 55 Conn. 46; s. c., 3 New Eng. Rep. 849; Smith *v.* People, 25 Ill. 24; Carew *v.* Rutherford, 106 Mass. 10; Snow *v.* Wheeler, 113 Mass. 186; Bowen *v.* Matheson, 96 Mass. (14 Allen) 503; People *v.* Petheram (Mich.), 7 West. Rep. 592; State *v.* Donaldson, 32 N. J. L. (3 Vr.) 151; Master Stevedores' Asso. *v.* Walsh, 2 Daly (N. Y.), 1; Rex *v.* Ferguson, 2 Starke, 489; Reg. *v.* Rowland, 17 Q. B. 671; s. c., 5 Cox, Cr. Cas. 436; Reg. *v.* Duffield, 5 Cox, Cr. Cas 404; Reg. *v.* Hewitt, 5 Cox, Cr. Cas. 162; Reg. *v.* Shepherd, 11 Cox, Cr. Cas. 325; Reg. *v.* Bunn, 12 Cox, Cr. Cas. 316; Reg. *v.* Hibbert, 13 Cox, Cr. Cas. 82; *Re* Perham, 5 Hurl. & N. 30; 2 L. & E. 383; Reg. *v.* Byerdyke, 1 Moody & R. 179; Hilton *v.* Eckersley, 6 El. & Bl. 47; 3 Russ. Cr. (9th ed.) 134.

4. Farrar *v.* Close, L. R. 4 Q. B. 603; Hilton *v.* Eckersley, 6 Ellis & B. 47; 3 Russ. Cr. (9th ed.) 134; Reg. *v.* Hibbert, 13 Cox, Cr. Cas. 82; Reg *v.* Shepherd, 11 Cox, Cr. Cas. 325; Reg. *v.* Rowlands, 5 Cox, Cr. Cas. 437; Reg. *v.* Duffield, 5 Cox, Cr. Cas. 432; Newman *v.* Commonwealth (Pa.), 5 Cent. Rep. 497.

5. Sheridan's Case, Wright, Consp. 50; Reg. *v.* Shepherd, 11 Cox, C. C. 325.

6. That an indictment will lie for a conspiracy to commit a civil injury, was denied in State *v.* Rickey, 9 N. J. L. (4 Halst.) 293; but this case was overruled in State *v.* Norton, 23 N. J. L. (3 Zab.) 33.

7. As to commit a trespass, — State *v.* Straw, 42 N. H. 393. But see Rex *v.* Turner, 13 East, 228, — to obtain a horse; a

a. To cause Private Injury.—All confederacies wron[illegible] injure another in any manner are misdemeanors:[1] as t[illegible] his reputation, whether by charging him with an indictabl[illegible] or not.[2]

IV. Responsibility of Parties.—1. *Instigators to a Crim*[illegible] —The instigator to a crime is guilty of the offence co[illegible] through his instigation.[3] The advice, procurements, en[illegible]

mere trespass,—State *v.* Clary, 64 Me. 369,—or to injure the property of another,—State *v.* Ripley, 31 Me. 386,—as to chase and kill cattle,—Lowery *v.* State, 30 Tex. 402.

Injury to Profession or Business.—An indictment lies at common law for a conspiracy to impoverish a person by ruining his profession or trade,—Rex *v.* Eccles, 1 Leach, 274; Rex *v.* Leigh, 1 Car & K 28, Rex *v.* Cope, 1 Strange, 144; Reg. *v.* Rowlands, 5 Cox, Cr. Cas. 436; s. c., 17 Q. B. 671,—also to impoverish a tailor, and prevent him from carrying on his trade. Rex *v.* Eccles, 1 Leach, 274; s. c., 3 Doug. 337.

Maliciously speaking of and publishing a person in his profession, imputing to him want of integrity, and capacity, mental and moral, to the special damage of the relation, is an indictable offence. Wildee *v.* McKee, 111 Pa. St. 335.

Personal Injury.—A conspiracy to slander a person by charging him with a criminal offence is indictable, although a civil remedy is available,—State *v.* Hickling, 41 N. J. L. (12 Vr) 208,—or to charge one with crime, though no process is obtained,—Commonwealth *v.* Tibbetts, 2 Mass. 536,—or injure his character,—State *v.* Hickling, 41 N. J. L. (12 Vr.) 208,—as to charge one with being the father of a bastard,—Lambert *v.* People, 9 Cow. (N. Y.) 599; Reg. *v.* Best, 2 Ld. Raym. 1167; Child *v.* North, 1 Keble, 203; Rex *v.* Tymberly, 1 Keble, 254. 264. See 2 Russ. Cr, 683,—or to charge him with fornication,—Child *v.* North, 1 Keble, 203. See 2 Bish. C. L. (6th ed) secs. 169, 240,—or other disgraceful offence,—Hood *v.* Palm, 8 Pa. St. 237,—or to make false charges and accusations. Johnson *v.* State, 26 N. J. L. (2 Dutch.) 313; State *v.* Buchanan, 5 Har. & J. (Md.) 317; Slomer *v.* People, 25 Ill. 70; Commonwealth *v.* Tibbetts, 2 Mass. 536; Elkin *v.* People, 28 N. Y. 177; Rex *v.* MacDaniel, 1 Leach, 45; Rex *v* Spragg, 2 Burr. 993; Reg. *v.* Best, 1 Salk. 174. See Fost. 130; 1 Hawk. P. C. 72, sec. 2. And even the legal conviction of an innocent man is no bar. Commonwealth *v.* McClean, 2 Pars. Cas. (Pa.) 367.

1. 3 Chit. Cr. L. 1163.

Private Injury.—This was the law until the decision of Lambert *v.* People, 9 Cow. (N. Y.) 578, where the question whether an indictment lies for a conspiracy [illegible] a mere private injury by mean[illegible] not in themselves criminal, [illegible] would not affect the public n[illegible] justice, was left in doubt until [illegible] by the Revised Statutes of that [illegible]

2. Rex *v.* Armstrong, 1 Ven[illegible] *v.* Kinnersley, 1 Strange, 193; Re[illegible] 2 Strange, 866; Rex *v.* Rispal[illegible] 368; s. c., 3 Burr. [illegible]; Rex [illegible] W. Bl. 392; Reg. *v.* Best, 2 Ld. [illegible] Child *v.* North, 1 Keb. 203.

3. People *v.* Hodges, 27 Cal. [illegible] ly *v.* State, 15 Ga. 346; Comm[illegible] Hurley, 99 Mass. 433; Reg. [illegible] Ders. & B. 288.

Advising or encouraging Co[illegible] a Crime.—It is a mistake to a[illegible] a defendant cannot be charged [illegible] ing, encouraging, aiding, and [illegible] unknown principal in the perp[illegible] a crime. Suppose that A. inst[illegible] hire some person to kill C. B. [illegible] son whose name is unknown [illegible] never becomes known to the [illegible] that person kills C. in pursua[illegible] employment. Will it be said [illegible] not guilty as an accessory befo[illegible] because the instrument emplo[illegible] unknown by name or personal d[illegible] Archbold says, that, if the prin[illegible] be unknown, the indictment of [illegible] sory may state it accordingly. [illegible] Cr. Pr. p. 67. It is also *held*, [illegible] principal is declared to be u[illegible] the indictment, and the proof o[illegible] shows that he is known, there [illegible] variance. Rex *v.* Walker, 3 C[illegible] Rex *v.* Blick, 4 C. & P. 377.

But where there are two sepa[illegible] one charging the principal to [illegible] and the other charging him to b[illegible] it is sufficient if either is proven. [illegible] Cr. L. §§ 207, 225, 226, 231; 1 [illegible] §§ 651, 677; Reg. *v.* Tyler, 8 C. [illegible] State *v.* Green, 26 S. C. 105, [illegible] *v.* Commonwealth, 112 Pa. St. [illegible] nan *v.* People, 15 Ill. 516; Bax[illegible] ple, 4 Ill. (3 Gilm.) 368; Kitzma[illegible] 110 Ill. 362.

Inciting to an Offence.—"I[illegible] posely excites another to com[illegible] fence,—as, if he harangues peo[illegible] ing them to a riot,—and the[illegible] accordingly committed, he is gu[illegible] ments, etc., may be direct or indirect; by words, signs, or motions; personally, or through the intervention of an agent.[1] No matter how long a time elapses, or how great a space intervenes, between the instigation and the consummation of the deed, if there is immediate causal connection between the instigator and the act, the instigator is liable.[2]

he personally takes no part in it." 1 Bish. Cr. L. 640.

In Reg. v. Sharpe, 3 Cox, C. C. 228, *Chief Justice Wilde*, in charging the jury, said, "If persons are assembled together to the number of three or more, and speeches are made to those persons to excite and inflame them, with a view to incite them to acts of violence, and if that same meeting is so connected in point of circumstances with a subsequent riot that you cannot reasonably sever the latter from the incitement that was used, it appears to me that those who incited are guilty of the riot, although they are not actually present when it occurs. I think it is not the hand that strikes the blow or that throws the stone (bomb), that is alone guilty under such circumstances, but that he who inflames people's minds, and induces them by violent means to accomplish an illegal object, is himself a rioter, though he take no part in the riot. It will be a question for the jury whether the riot that took place was so connected with the inflammatory language used by the defendants that they cannot reasonably be separated by time or other circumstances."

Illinois Statute. — The Illinois statute upon this subject provides, ch. 38, div. 2, §§ 2, 3, that, —

"§ 2. An accessory is he who stands by, and aids, abets, or assists, or who, not being present aiding, abetting, or assisting, hath advised, encouraged, aided, or abetted the perpetration of the crime. He who thus aids, abets, assists, advises, or encourages, shall be considered as principal, and punished accordingly.

"§ 3. Every such accessory, when a crime is committed within or without this State, by his aid or procurement in this State, may be indicted and convicted at the same time as the principal, or before or after his conviction, and whether the principal is convicted or amenable to justice or not, and punished as principal."

This statute abolishes the distinction between accessories before the fact and principals; by it all accessories before the fact are made principals. As the acts of the principal are thus made the acts of the accessory, the latter may be charged as having done the acts himself, and may be indicted and punished accordingly. Baxter v. People, 3 Ill. (3 Gilm.) 368; Dempsey v. People, 47 Ill. 326. If, therefore, the defendants advised, encouraged, aided, or abetted the killing, they are as guilty as though they took his life with their own hands. If any of them stood by and aided, abetted, or assisted in the throwing of the bomb, those of them who did so are as guilty as though they threw it themselves. See Spies v. People (The Anarchists' Case), 122 Ill. 1; s. c., 10 West. Rep. 701.

1. Kennedy v. People, 40 Ill. 488; Reg. v. Blackburn, 6 Cox, Cr. Cas. 333; Somersetts Cases, 19 St. Tri. 804; Rex v. Cooper, 5 Car. & P. 535; Reg. v. Williams, Den. Cr. Cas. 39; Rex v. Giles, 1 Moody, Cr. Cas. 166.

Inflaming Public Mind. — He who inflames people's minds, and induces them by violent means to accomplish an illegal object, is himself a rioter, though he takes no part in the riot. Reg. v. Sharpe, 3 Cox, C. C. 228. See Spies v. People, 122 Ill. 1; s. c., to West. Rep. 701.

"One is responsible for what wrong flows directly from his corrupt intentions. . . . If he set in motion the physical power of another, he is liable for its result. If he contemplated the result, he is answerable, though it is produced in a manner he did not contemplate. . . . If he awoke into action an indiscriminate power, he is responsible. If he gave directions vaguely and incautiously, and the person receiving them acted according to what he might have foreseen would be the understanding, he is responsible." 1 Bish. Cr. L. § 641.

It can make no difference whether the mind is affected by inflammatory words addressed to the reader through the newspaper organ of a society to which he belongs, or to the hearer through the spoken words of an orator whom he looks up to as a representative of his own peculiar class. Spies v. People, 122 Ill. 1; s. c., 7 West. Rep. 701; Queen v. Most, L. R. 7 Q. B. Div. 244.

2. Commonwealth v. Glover, 111 Mass. 395; Reg. v. Sharpe, 3 Cox, Cr. Cas. 288; Reg. v. Blackburn, 6 Cox, Cr. Cas. 333.

In an Indictment for a Conspiracy to murder. — If the defendants advised, encouraged, aided, or abetted the killing, they are as guilty as though they took the life with their own hands. Spies v. People (The Anarchists' Case), 122 Ill. 1; s. c., 10 West. Rep. 701.

One who inflames the people's minds, and induces the lent means to accomplish an illegal object, is himself liabl he takes no part in the act; and it can make no differenc the mind is affected by inflammatory words addresse reader through the newspaper organ of a society, or to th through the spoken words of an orator whom he looks u representative of his class. It will be a question for whether the riot that took place was so connected with flammatory language by the defendant that they cannot re be separated by time or other circumstances.[1]

2. *Accessory before the Fact.* — An accessory before th one who, being absent at the time the crime is commi procures, counsels, encourages, incites, or commends an commit the crime; but it is necessary that he have t intent as the principal.[2] And he who procures a felo done, is a felon: so, if a murder be committed with the kn or consent or connivance of a person, he is accessory.[3] tinction between principals and accessories, as at common been abolished by statute in some of the States; and ac before the act are all principals.[4] In such States there a cessories in murder, all being principals.[5] As the act principal are thus made the acts of the accessory, the la be charged as having done the acts himself, and may be and punished accordingly.[6]

At common law all offences admit of accessories, except unpremeditated offences, and misdemeanors.[7]

The statute of Illinois abolishes the distinction betwe sories before the fact and principals.[8]

1. Spies v. People (The Anarchists' Case), 122 Ill. 1; s. c., 10 West. Rep. 701, 764; Reg. v. Sharpe, 3 Cox, C. C. 288; 1 Bish. Cr. L. § 640.

2. Rex v. Gordon, 1 Leach, 515. See 4 Bl. Com. 37; 1 Hale, P. C. 617; State v. Lymburn, 1 Brev. (S. C.) L. 397; s. c., 2 Am. Dec. 669; People v. Davidson, 5 Cal. 133; People v. Hodges, 27 Cal. 340; Norton v. People, 8 Cow. (N. J.) 137; United States v. Lyles, 4 Cranch, C. C. 469; State v. Mann, 1 Hayw. (N. C.) 4; Commonwealth v. Hurley, 99 Mass. 433; People v. Knapp, 26 Mich. 112; Baker v. State, 12 Ohio St. 214; People v. McMurray, 4 Parker, Cr. R. (N. Y.) 234; Keithler v. State, 10 Smedes & M. (Miss.) 192; 4 Bl. Com. 36; 1 Hale, P. C. 615, 617; 1 Russ. Cr. (9th ed.) 49, 57; 1 Bish. C. L. (6th ed.) 662, 666.

3. United States v. Harries, 2 Bond, C. C. 311; Commonwealth v. McAtee, 8 Dana (Ky.), 28; State v. Cheek, 13 Ired. (N. C.) L. 114; Commonwealth v. Macomber, 3 Mass. 254; Commonwealth v. Barlow, 4 Mass. 439; Williams v. State, 12 Smedes & M. (Miss.) 58; Un v. Gooding, 25 U. S. (12 Whea 6, L. ed. 693; Carlin v. Sta (Tenn.) 143; Stratton v. Sta 468; Clem v. State, 33 Ind. v. State, 13 Tex. 174.

4. Spies v. People (The Case), 122 Ill. 1; s. c., 10 West Raiford v. State, 59 Ala. 10 v. Bearss, 10 Cal. 68; State 12 Kan. 550; s. c., 1 Am. Cr. v. State, 11 Ind. 62; People son, 5 Cal. 133; 1 Whart. Cr 205.

5. State v. Westfield, 1 Bail. Lowenstein v. People, 54 Ba 299.

6. Spies v. People (Anarch 122 Ill. 1; s. c., 10 West. Rep.

7. English v. State, 35 Ala. 4 States v. White, 5 Cranch, Bieber v. State, 45 Ga. 570; State, 43 Ga. 197; 4 Bl. Comm. Cr. (9th ed.) 57.

8. Spies v. People, 122 Ill. West. Rep. 701.

3. *Responsibility for Consummated Act.* — Where several persons take part in the execution of a criminal purpose, all are equally liable for the acts of each, and for the incidental and probable consequences of the joint purpose.[1] But a man is not to be proved to be a conspirator having a joint illegal intent with others in a particular assault which he does not personally commit, by showing the misconduct of others on previous occasions.[2] Yet when men form the intent, and come together, and agree to carry it into execution, this agreement is a step in the direction of accomplishing the purpose, and it is a crime.[3] If a number of men combine to attack another with deadly weapons, and one kills the person attacked, all are guilty of the murder.[4]

Where the defendants, as a means of bringing about a social revolution, also conspired to excite classes of workingmen into sedition, tumult, and riot, and to murder the authorities of the city, and a murder of a policeman resulted from such advice and encouragement, the defendants are responsible therefor.[5]

Where persons agree to stand by each other in a breach of the peace, with a general resolution to resist all opposers, and in the execution of their design a murder is committed, all of the company are equally principals in the murder, if the murder be in furtherance of the common design.[6]

4. *Aiders and Abettors in Common Design.* — One who is present aiding or abetting others in a common purpose, is responsible for

1. Frank v. State, 27 Ala. 37; Thompson v. State, 25 Ala. 41; People v. Woody, 45 Cal. 289; Griffin v. State, 26 Ga. 493; Hanna v. People, 86 Ill. 243; Brennan v. People, 15 Ill. 511; Williams v. People, 54 Ill. 478; Williams v. State, 47 Ind. 568; Commonwealth v. Campbell, 89 Mass. (7 Allen) 541; Commonwealth v. Knapp, 26 Mass. (9 Pick.) 496; s. c., 20 Am. Dec. 491, 496; People v. Knapp, 26 Mich. 112; Green v. State, 13 Mo. 382; Norton v. People, 8 Cow. (N. Y.) 137; Ruloff v. People, 18 N. Y. 179; Carrington v. People, 6 Park. Cr. R. (N. Y.) 336; Commonwealth v. Neills, 2 Brewst. (Pa.) 553; Commonwealth v. Daley, 2 Clark (Pa.), 196; Breese v. State, 12 Ohio St. 146; s. c., 80 Am. Dec. 340; Commonwealth v. Hare, 2 Clark (Pa.), 457; Moody v. State, 6 Cold. (Tenn.) 299; Berry v. State, 4 Tex. App. 492; United States v. Ross, 1 Gall. C. C. 624; Miller v. State, 25 Wis. 384; Reg. v. Hilton, 5 Up. Can. L. J. 70; Reg. v. Slavin, 17 Up. Can. C. P. 205; Rex v. Lockett, 7 Car. & P. 300; Rex v. Passey, 7 Car. & P. 282; Reg. v. Cruse, 8 Car. & P. 541; Reg. v. Howell, 9 Car. & P. 437; Rex v. Higgins, 2 East, 5; Rex v. Duffevs, 1 Lewin, 194; Rex v. Hodgson, 1 Leach, C. C. 6; s. c., *sub nom.* Rex v. Hobson, 1 East, P. C. 258; Reg. v. Taylor, L. R. 2 C. C. 147; Rex v. Standley, Russ. & R. 305; 1 Hale, P. C. 439, 462; 2 Hawk. P. C. ch. 29, § 8.

2. Strout v. Packard, 76 Me. 148; s. c., 49 Am. Rep. 604; Rex v. Nicholls, 13 East, 412.

3. State v. Glidden, 55 Conn. 46; s. c., 3 New Eng. Rep. 849.

4. Williams v. State, 81 Ala. 1.

Thus, where defendant was engaged in a conspiracy to forcibly compel new men to leave an employer, and in carrying out the conspiracy a homicide was committed, such homicide is binding on him. State v. McCahill (Iowa), 33 N. W. Rep. 599.

5. Spies v. People (The Anarchists' Case), 122 Ill. 1; s. c., 10 West. Rep. 701.

Where A. and B. by pre-arrangement attack C. and kill him, and D., not being privy to their common design, joins in the fight, D. is not guilty of murder, — Frank v. State, 27 Ala. 37; — the same is true in a conspiracy to rob, — State v. Heyward, 2 Nott & McC. (S. C.) 312; s. c., 10 Am. Dec. 604; — but if some of the parties, combined to escape, commit a crime, the one who did not consent, and was not engaged in its commission, will not be liable. People v. Knapp, 26 Mich. 112. And see State v. Phillips, 24 Mo. 475.

6. Spies v. People (The Anarchists' Case), 122 Ill. 1; s. c., 10 West. Rep. 758; Williams v. People, 54 Ill 422; Whart. Hom. (2d ed.) 338.

the act of one of the party, providing the act was in pur of, or incidental to, such purpose;[1] but if the act committ no connection with the common object, the party committir alone responsible for its consequences.[2] Where parties co to commit an offence, the one who did not consent, and w privy to the fact, is not responsible.[3] After the common p is at an end, the act or dictation of one cannot affect the o

All conspirators are liable for the act of each if done prosecution of the common design.[5] It is a that every one who enters into a common purpose or de generally, in law, a party to every act which has before bee by the others, and a party to every act which may afterwa done by any of the others, in furtherance of such common d

A conspiracy is not destroyed by connection, at a subs time, of new parties therewith;[7] as a new party, agreeing plans of the conspirators, and coming in and assisting becomes one of them.[8] And individuals who, though not cally parties to the killing, are present, and consenting assemblage by whom it is perpetrated, are principals, wh killing is in pursuance of the common design.[9]

Confederates in a common design, of which the offence c spiracy is a part, are all principals.[10] Any participatio

1. Weston v. Commonwealth, 111 Pa. St. 251; s. c., 2 Cent. Rep. 35; Wicks v. State, 44 Ala. 398; United States v. Wilson, Bald. C. C. 104; United States v. Gooding, 25 U. S. (12 Wheat.) 460; bk. 6, L. ed. 693; Sharp v. State, 6 Tex. App. 650; Rex v. Royce, 4 Burr. 2073; Reg. v. Jackson, 7 Cox, Cr. Cas. 357.

Under the Illinois Statute and the construction given to it by the decisions of the Supreme Court of that State (Baxter v. People, 3 Gilm. 368, and other cases), the man, who, "not being present aiding, abetting, or assisting, hath advised, encouraged, aided, or abetted the perpetration of the crime," may be considered as the principal in the commission of the crime, may be indicted as principal, and may be punished as principal. The indictment need not say any thing about his having aided and abetted either a known principal or an unknown principal. It may simply charge him with having committed the murder as principal. Then, if, upon the trial, the proof shows that he aided, abetted, assisted, advised, or encouraged the perpetration of the crime, the charge that he committed it as principal is established against him. It would make no difference whether the proof s that he so aided and abetted, etc., a known principal or an unknown principal.

2. Frank v. State, 27 Ala. 37; People v. Leith, 52 Cal. 251; Heine v. Commonwealth, 91 Pa. St. 148.

Association for Innocent Power Abused.—Thus, where an tion is formed for innocent purp its power and authority are a abused, only those so abusing liable. Carew v. Rutherford, 10. See Snow v. Wheeler, 113 M Bowen v. Matheson, 96 Mass. (503.

3. People v. Knapp, 26 Mich. 1 Car. Law Rep. 282.

4. Snowden v. State, 7 482.

5. State v. Wilson, 30 Conn. 500 kins v. State, 17 Ga. 356; State v. Iowa, 347; State v. Arnold, 48 Io State v. Larkin, 49 N. H. 39; State, 13 Mo. 382; People v. Sau Mich. 119; Cuyler v. McCartney, 224; Heine v. Commonwealth, 9 148; Hardin v. State, 4 Tex. Ap

6. McKee v. State (Ind.), 9 W 838; Card v. State, 109 Ind. 415 West. Rep. 81, 82.

7. United States v. Nunnemach C. C. 111.

8. People v. Mather, 4 Wend. 229; s. c., 21 Am. Dec. 122.

9. Spies v. People (The An Case), 122 Ill. 1; s. c., 10 West. R Commonwealth v. Daley, 2 Cla 150; Reg. v. Jackson, 7 Cox, C. C Whart. Hom. § 202.

10. Williams v. State, 47 Ind. 56 v. State, 13 Mo. 382.

concerted felonious plan renders a party liable as principal.[1] All concerned in the execution of the common purpose are equally guilt .[2]

Though the common design is the essence of the charge of conspiracy, it is not necessary to prove that the defendants came together, and actually agreed in terms to that design, and to pursue it by common means. If they pursued by their acts the same object often by the same means, one performing one part, and another another part of the same, so as to complete it with a view to the attainment of that same object, the jury will be justified in the conclusion that they were engaged in a conspiracy to effect that object.[3]

Where the means are not specifically agreed upon or understood, each conspirator becomes responsible for the means used by any co-conspirator in the accomplishment of the purpose in which they are all at the time engaged, although there was no specific intent, and no special malice against the party slain.[4]

5. *The Act of One the Act of All.* — Where men combine with intent to do an unlawful thing, and in the prosecution of their intent one goes a step beyond the rest of the party, and does acts which they do not perform, all are responsible for what he does; but there should be concert of action, — an agreement to do some unlawful thing.[5] The least degree of concert or collusion between

1. Commonwealth *v.* Knapp, 26 Mass. (9 Pick.) 496; s. c., 20 Am Dec. 491; Norton *v.* People, 8 Cow (N. Y.) 137; Breese *v.* State, 12 Ohio St. 146; Rex *v.* Manners, 7 Car. & P. 801; Sissinghurst's Case, 1 Hale, P. C. 462.

2. United States *v.* Goldberg, 7 Biss. C. C. 175; United States *v.* Nunnemacher, 7 Biss. C. C. 111; Commonwealth *v.* Harley, 48 Mass. (7 Metc.) 462; Reg. *v.* Fellowes, 19 Up. Can. Q. B. 48; Rex *v.* Parsons, 1 W. Bl. 392; Reg. *v.* Murphy, 8 Car. & P. 297; Reg. *v.* Slavin, 17 Up. Can. C. P. 205; Reg. *v.* Shellard, 9 Car. & P. 277; Reg. *v.* Blake, 6 Q. B. 126; United States *v.* Donau, 11 Blatchf. C. C. 168; Smith *v.* State, 52 Ala. 407; Jackson *v.* State, 54 Ala. 234; Glory *v.* State, 13 Ark. 236; Lawson *v.* State, 32 Ark. 220; State *v.* Jackson, 29 La. An. 354; Brown *v.* Smith, 83 Ill. 294; Collins *v.* Commonwealth, 3 Serg. & R. (Pa.) 220. See 3 Arch C. Pr 622.

Where there was a conspiracy to commit an offence, and both conspirators were present, aiding and abetting the common design, both are equally liable for all the consequences. People *v.* Woody, 45 Cal. 289; Brister *v.* State, 26 Ala. 107; Commonwealth *v.* O'Brien, 66 Mass. (12 Cush.) 84.

If five or six persons conspire to invade a man's household, and go there armed for the purpose of attacking and beating him, and, in furtherance of this common design, one of them gets into a difficulty with him, and kills him, the others, being present, or near at hand, are guilty of murder, although they did not intend to kill. Williams *v.* State, 81 Ala. 1. And it is immaterial who fired the fatal shot, as all are guilty. People *v.* Woody, 45 Cal. 289; Spies *v.* People (The Anarchists' Case), 122 Ill. 1; s. c., 10 West. Rep. 701.

3. Spies *v.* People (The Anarchists' Case), 122 Ill. 1; s. c., 10 West. Rep. 701; The Mussel-slough Case, 5 Fed. Rep. 680; Frank *v.* State, 27 Ala. 37; Thompson *v.* State, 25 Ala. 41; Hanna *v.* People, 86 Ill. 243; Carrington *v.* People, 6 Park. C. R. (N. Y.) 336; Reg. *v.* Hilton, 5 Up. Can. L. J. 70; Reg. *v.* Lee, 2 McNally, Ev. 634; Reg. *v.* Slavin, 17 Up. Can. C. P. 205.

4. Spies *v.* People (The Anarchists' Case), 122 Ill. 1; s. c., 10 West. Rep. 701.

5. United States *v.* Kinne, 23 Fed. Rep. 748; People *v.* Powell, 63 N. Y. 88.

It is well settled, that, when the fact of a conspiracy is once established, any act of one of the conspirators in the prosecution of the enterprise is considered the act of all. Nudd *v.* Burrows, 91 U. S. (1 Otto) 426; bk. 23, L. ed. 286; 1 Whart. Cr. L. (6th ed.) § 702; 3 Greenl. Ev. § 94.

the parties to an illegal transaction, makes the act of on
of all.[1]

Where a party is shown to have acted [illegible] wi
he cannot complain if he is charged with [illegible] consp
them in producing the results, even though [illegible] name
conspirators were not known to the grand jury, [illegible] the i
so states.[2] It might be otherwise if all the co-conspira
known to the grand jury;[3] for he who enters into a co
or conspiracy to do such an unlawful act as will probably
the unlawful taking of human life, must be presumed
understood the consequences which might reasonably be
to follow from carrying it into effect.[4] Individuals wh
not specifically parties to the killing, are present, and
to the assemblage by whom it is perpetrated, are princi
the killing is in pursuance of the common design.[5] Ye
presence on the occasion of the conspiracy is not su
make one guilty. One must incite, procure, or encourag
but, if a person joins the conspiracy after it is formed, he
a co conspirator, and the acts of others become his acts
tion.[6]

Where several conspire to do an unlawful act, all are
the acts of each, if done in the prosecution of their pur

V. The Indictment. — 1. *Venue.* — The venue may be la
county in which an act was done by either of the consp
furtherance of their common design,[8] and may charge a
with parties unknown.[9] In the States generally, a co
indictable as a common-law offence.[10] But it must app

1. Jackson *v.* State, 54 Ala. 234; Smith *v.* State, 52 Ala. 407; State *v.* Wilson, 30 Conn. 500; Tompkins *v.* State, 17 Ga. 356; Ferguson *v.* State, 32 Ga. 658; Reid *v.* State, 20 Ga. 681; Smith *v.* People, 25 Ill. 17; s. c., 76 Am. Dec. 180; Brown *v.* People, 83 Ill. 291; State *v.* Nash, 7 Iowa, 347; State *v.* Shelledy, 8 Iowa, 477; State *v.* Myers, 19 Iowa, 517; State *v.* Jackson, 29 La. An. 354; State *v.* Buchanan, 5 Harr. & J. (Md.) 317; Commonwealth *v.* Harley, 47 Mass. (7 Metc.) 462; Green *v.* State, 13 Mo. 382; Carrington *v.* People, 6 Park. Cr. R. (N. Y.) 336; Collins *v.* Commonwealth, 3 Serg. & R. (Pa.) 220; Hannon *v.* State, 5 Tex. App. 549; Phillips *v.* State, 6 Tex. App. 364; United States *v.* Goldberg, 7 Biss. C. C. 175; United States *v.* Donau, 11 Blatchf. C. C. 168; Reg. *v.* Fellows, 19 Up. Can. Q. B. 48; Reg. *v.* Slavin, 17 Up. Can. C. P. 205; 3 Arch. Cr. Pr. 622; 2 Whart. on Ev. § 1206.

2. People *v.* Mather, 4 Wend. (N. Y.) 229; . ., 21 Am. Dec. 122; Rex *v.* Steele, 1 Moody, Cr. Cas. 246.

3. Whart. Cr. Pl. & Pr. §§ 104, 111.

4. Spies *v.* People (The Anarchists' Case), 122 Ill. 1.; s. c., 10 West. Rep. 701.

5. Spies *v.* People (The
Case), 122 Ill. 1.; s. c., 10
701.

6. United States *v.* J[illegible]
Rep. 682; Johnson *v.* [illegible]
529.

7. State *v.* Wilson, 30 [illegible]
kins *v.* State, 17 Ga. [illegible]
Ga. 681; State *v.* Nash, 7 [illegible]
v. Shelledy, 8 Iowa, [illegible]
19 Iowa, 517; Green *v.* [illegible]
Ferguson *v.* State, 32 Ga. [illegible]
People, 25 Ill. 17; s. c., 76 [illegible]
State *v.* Buchanan, 5 Har. [illegible]
As where a homicide [illegible]
some person with whom [illegible]
in concert. Carrington *v.* [illegible]
Cr. R. 336; 4 Am. [illegible]
ACCOMPLICES.

8. Commonwealth *v.* [illegible]
(Pa.) 575; Rex *v.* [illegible]
489.

9. People *v.* Mather, 4 [illegible]
229; s. c., 21 Am. Dec. [illegible]

10. Commonwealth [illegible]
Metc.) 111; s. c., 38 Am. [illegible]
Pulle, 12 Minn. 164; [illegible]
N. J. L. (3 Zab.) 33.

face of the indictment that the object of the conspiracy, or the means to be employed, are criminal.[1] Active participation in, not simply passive cognizance of, the illegal action, must be shown.[2]

Where the offence is in the conspiracy, and not in the acts committed for carrying it into effect, the charge is sufficiently made in general terms describing an unlawful conspiracy to effect a had purpose.[3]

In a conspiracy to commit a felony or a misdemeanor, a general allegation describing it in general terms is sufficient;[4] but a general allegation is not sufficient where the object is not criminal.[5]

1. State *v.* Jones, 13 Iowa, 269; Commonwealth *v.* Eastman, 55 Mass. (1 Cush.) 189; s. c., 48 Am. Dec. 596; Commonwealth *v.* Shedd, 61 Mass. (7 Cush.) 514. *Compare* State *v.* Parker, 43 N. H. 83.

Such facts must be stated upon the record as in the judgment of law constitute an offence, whether in the object or means. State *v.* Stevens, 30 Iowa, 392; State *v.* Ormiston, 66 Iowa, 143; State *v.* Potter, 28 Iowa, 554; State *v.* Hewett, 31 Me. 396.

2. Evans *v.* People, 90 Ill. 384.

Thus, an allegation that A. and B. conspired to do an act so that C. should commit a felony, is not a sufficient allegation that the purpose of the act was to induce him to commit it, or abet in its perpetration. Commonwealth *v.* Barnes, 132 Mass. 242.

3. Reg. *v.* Selsby, 5 Cox, Cr. Cas. 495, note; Reg. *v.* Harris, 1 Car. & Marsh. 661; Hilton *v.* Eckersley, 6 El. & Bl. 47; s. c., Jur. N. S. 587; 25 L. J. Q. B. 199; Rex *v.* Mawbey, 6 T. R. 619; Rex *v.* Eccles, 1 Leach, C. C. 274; Walsby *v.* Anley, 3 El. & E. 516; s. c., 7 Jur. N. S. 465; 30 L. J. M. C. 121; 9 W. R. 271; 3 L. T. N. S. 666; Reg. *v.* Rowlands, 17 Ad. & E. (N. S.) 670; 17 Q. B. 671; 21 L. J. M. C. 81; 5 Cox, C. C. 436; Reg. *v.* Druitt, 10 Cox, Cr. Cas. 592; Reg. *v.* Bunn, 12 Cox, Cr. Cas. 316; Springhead Co. *v.* Riley, L. R. 6 Eq. 551; Mogul Steamship Co. *v.* McGregor, L. R. 15 Q. B. Div. 476; Commonwealth *v.* Hunt, 45 Mass. (4 Metc.) 111, 128; s. c., 38 Am. Dec. 346; Smith *v.* People, 25 Ill. 17; s. c., 76 Am. Dec. 780; Commonwealth *v.* Carlisle, Bright. (Pa.) 36; Carew *v.* Rutherford, 106 Mass. 1.

Knowledge of Character of Act. — It was unnecessary to aver knowledge in the respondents of the wrongful character of the matters and things charged against them. If an act in its natural characteristics and quality is unlawful, knowledge of its wrongful character is presumed. It is otherwise when it becomes wrongful by the presence of accidental or fortuitous features not ordinarily attendant upon it. Thus in State *v.* Carpenter, 54 Vt. 551, the respondent was presumed to know that it was unlawful to assault Larose as an individual. So, for such assault, no averment was necessary to bring home to him knowledge of the wrongful quality of his act. But when the same act was enlarged to the grade of an offence for impeding Larose as a public officer, it took on a character so abnormal that knowledge of this artificial quality of his act in the respondent must be alleged in order to lay a basis for a guilty intent. State *v.* Stewart, 59 Vt. 273; s. c., 4 New Eng. Rep. 378.

4. Commonwealth *v.* Eastman, 55 Mass. (1 Cush.) 189; s. c., 48 Am. Dec. 596; Wood *v.* State, 47 N. J. L. (18 Vr.) 461; s. c., 1 Cent. Rep. 442.

5. Commonwealth *v.* Shedd, 61 Mass. (7 Cush.) 514; Commonwealth *v.* Wallace, 82 Mass. (16 Gray) 221.

If the means to be used are not necessarily unlawful, either by statute or the common law, and are laid as the *corpus delicti*, then a particular statement of the means to be used must be set out, so that the court can see on the face of the indictment that a crime has been committed. In State *v.* Keach, 40 Vt. 113, the court laid down the rule as follows: "The adjudged cases uniformly recognize the rule that a general allegation that two or more persons conspired to effect an object criminal in itself, — as, to commit a misdemeanor or felony, — is sufficient, even though the indictment omits all charges of the particular means to be used; and the cases are now equally uniform in holding that if the agreement or combination be to do an act or to effect an object not criminal, by the use of unlawful means, a general charge of a conspiracy to effect the object is not sufficient; and the charge of such a conspiracy must be accompanied with a particular statement of the means by which the object of the conspiracy was to be effected, so that those means may appear to be criminal, or the indictment will be bad." State *v.* Stewart, 59 Vt. 273; s. c., 4 New Eng. Rep. 378.

If the indictment be too general, the court will order ticulars, though not a statement of specific acts, place of their occurrence.[1] Where the object of is the commission of a misdemeanor, or any unla means to be used need not be set forth.[2] And w spiracy to do an act is to do an act *per se* indictabl means nor the overt acts need be stated: merely stati is sufficient.[3]

2. *No Overt Act need be alleged.* — It is not necess overt acts when the conspiracy to do the acts is its

1. Reg. *v.* Kenric, 5 Q. B. 49; Reg. *v.* Hamilton, 7 Car. & P. 443; State *v.* Bartlett, 30 Me. 132; State *v.* Buchanan, 5 Har. & J. (Md.) 317; Commonwealth *v.* Ward, 1 Mass. 473; Commonwealth *v.* Tibbetts, 2 Mass. 536; Commonwealth *v.* Warren, 6 Mass. 72; People *v.* Richards, 1 Mich. 216; s. c., 51 Am. Dec. 75; Commonwealth *v.* McKisson, 8 Serg. & R. (Pa.) 420; s. c., 11 Am. Dec. 354; Reg. *v.* Esdaile, 1 Fost. & F. 213; Reg. *v.* Roycroft, 6 Cox, C. C. 76; Reg. *v.* Brown, 8 Cox, C. C. 69; Reg. *v.* Hamilton, 7 Car. & P. 443.

2. State *v.* Ormiston, 66 Iowa, 143; People *v.* Petheram (Mich.), 7 West. Rep. 592; People *v.* Clark, 10 Mich. 310; Ros. Cr. Ev. 387.

Unlawful Act by Unlawful Means. — Where the counts in an indictment charge a conspiracy to commit an act, unlawful at common law, by means unlawful under the statute, it is not necessary to set out specifically the kind of threats, or methods of intimidation, made use of. The words of the statute may be used without setting forth their meaning. Thus, in Reg. *v.* Rowlands, 17 A. & E. N. S. 671, the indictment, among other things, charged a conspiracy to force workmen to quit the employment of the Messrs. Perry, by using threats and intimidation. The statute (6 Geo. IV. chap. 129, § 3) forbids the use of such means. The court said, "It is objected that some counts do not disclose the nature of the molestation or intimidation by which the conspiracy was to take effect; but this is quite unnecessary. The words of the legislature are used; the terms in question have a meaning stamped upon them by the Act (6 Geo. IV. chap. 159, § 3), and we must take it that they are used here in that sense. And they are not employed as describing the substantive offence for which the indictment is preferred: that offence consists in the conspiracy, which is a conspiracy at common law."

In Commonwealth *v.* Dyer, 128 Mass. 70, under a statute similar to that of Vermont, a like decision was made; and such is the general rule in even where the statutory offence. 1 Whart. Cr. Cook, 38 Vt. 437; State 273; s. c., 4 New Eng.

3. O'Connell *v.* Reg., 155; Reg. *v.* Carlisle, s. c., 6 Cox, C. C. 366.

Means need not be set dictment for conspiracy dictable offence, the mean set out. It is enough for out the offence to be such as will describe it law. Thomas *v.* People State *v.* Ormiston, 66 Io Dent, 3 Gill & J. (Md.) lett, 30 Me. 132; State 386; People *v.* Bush, 4 Hazen *v.* Commonwealth Commonwealth *v.* Rogers (Pa.) 463; State *v.* Noyes *v.* Higgins, 2 East, 5 Am. ed.) 263.

Sufficiency of. — A which merely charges a an unlawful act; and, charges a conspiracy to act by unlawful means. 59 Vt. 273; s. c., 4 New

Charging Offence in W Where the language of adopted, all the element enumerated, and the have been with the inte sufficient. Commonweal Mass. 70; Reg. *v.* Rowla 5 Cox, C. C. 436; State 443; State *v.* Cook, 38 Stewart, 59 Vt. 273; s. c. 378; 1 Whart. Cr. L. §

4. State *v.* Bartlett, *v.* Ripley, 31 Me. 386; Eastman, 55 Mass. (1 Cu Am. Dec. 596; Commonw 61 Mass. (7 Cush.) 514; State, 49 Ind. 136; Alde 4 Mich. 414; s. c., 58 Am *v.* State, 48 Miss. 234; 7 Barb. (N. Y.) 398; Mich. 268; State *v.* Me

it is an offence complete in itself.[1] Where the conspiracy is elf unlawful, pleading the offence is sufficient; and charging overt acts may be considered as surplusage, or as mere gravation.[2] An indictment is not bad for duplicity because it rges the overt act by way of aggravation, where the conspiracy s complete without the overt act.[3] If overt acts were charged the indictment, and sustained by proof, such acts would be rely matter of aggravation,[4] or evidence of crime;[5] for the ert act, wherever committed, is a renewal of the original conracy by all the conspirators.[6]

}. *Where the Means are Unlawful.* — Where the gist of the ence consists in the unlawful means used, these means should set forth by direct averments of facts sufficient to continue the ence.[7] But when the object to accomplish which the alleged spiracy is formed, is not unlawful, but the offence consists in use of unlawful means, the means must be particularly set th in the indictment.[8] When the object or purpose of the

ted States v. Dustin, 2 Bond, C. C. ; Rex v. Kinnersley, 1 Strange, 195; Reg. 'ompertz, 9 Q. B. 824; Reg. v. Heyn, 12 Cox, C. C. 383; Reg. v. Seward, dol. & El. 706.

The Poulterer's Case, 9 Coke, 55; v. Kinnersley, 1 Strange, 193; Reg. v. , 2 Ld. Raym. 1167; State v. Cawood, ew. (Ala.) 360; Landringham v. State, nd. 189; Isaacs v. State, 48 Miss. 234; e v. Straw, 42 N. H. 392; State v. ley, 9 N. J. L. (4 Halst.) 293; People lather, 4 Wend. (N. Y.) 229; s. c., 21 . Dec. 122; State v. Younger, 1 Dev. C.) L. 357; Respublica v. Ross, 2 tes (Pa.), 1; s. c., 2 U. S. (2 Dall.) 239; 1. L. ed. 364; Commonwealth v. Bliss, Phila. (Pa.) 580; Heine v. Commonlth, 91 Pa. St. 145; Johnson v. State, 3 . App. 590; State v. Noyes, 25 Vt. 415.

New Jersey Doctrines. — But in New sey, although it is acknowledged that were the common-law doctrines, still, *held* that, under the statute, some act t be done in execution of the design ed upon to complete the offence. State ortou, 23 N. J. L. (3 Zab.) 33.

State v. Cawood, 2 Stew. & P. (Ala.) ; State v. Bartlett, 30 Me. 132; State ipley, 31 Me. 386; Commonwealth v. setts, 8 Mass. 536; Commonwealth v. is, 9 Mass. 415; State v. Buchanan, 5 . & J. (Md.) 317; State v. Straw, 42 H. 393; Collins v. Commonwealth, 3 . & R. (Pa.) 220; State v. Noyes, 25 415.

State v. Ormiston, 66 Iowa, 143.

Averring Means. — Where the conspiritself is the crime, it is wholly unnecesto aver the means by which the conspirwas to be carried out. State v. Noyes, Vt. 415, 422. Herein lies the distinction between the case of State v. Stewart, 59 Vt. 273; s. c., 4 New Eng. Rep. 378, and Commonwealth v. Hunt, 45 Mass. (4 Metc.) 111; s. c., 38 Am. Dec. 346. In the latter case the substantive offence was a conspiracy, but not to do an unlawful act; and the means laid for its accomplishment were laid as mere matters of aggravation, and for that reason no crime whatever was charged in the indictment. But it was otherwise in State v. Stewart.

4. State v. Noyes, 25 Vt. 415; Collins v. Commonwealth, 3 Serg. & R. (Pa.) 220.

5. Commonwealth v. Corlies, 8 Phila. (Pa.) 450; s. c., 3 Brewst. (Pa.) 575.

6. State v. Chapin, 17 Ark. 561; Johns. v. State, 19 Ind. 421; Bloomer v. State, 43 Md. 321; Commonwealth v. White, 123 Mass 430; State v. Hamilton, 13 Nev. 386; Commonwealth v. Corlies, 3 Brewst. (Pa.) 575.

7. Commonwealth v. Hunt, 45 Mass. (4 Metc.) 111; s. c., 38 Am. Dec. 346.

8. Cole v. People, 84 Ill. 216; Smith v. People, 25 Ill. 17; Commonwealth v. Eastman, 55 Mass. (1 Cush.) 189; s. c., 48 Am. Dec. 596; Alderman v. People, 4 Mich. 414; s. c., 69 Am. Dec. 321; People v. Petheram (Mich.), 7 West. Rep. 592; People v. Barkelow, 37 Mich. 455; State v. Burnham, 15 N. H. 396; Commonwealth v. Shedd, 61 Mass. (7 Cush.) 515.

Allegation of Means to show Purpose. — The allegation of means then becomes important to show the criminal or unlawful purpose. People v. Petheram (Mich.), 7 West. Rep. 592; People v. Richards, 1 Mich 216; s. c., 51 Am. Dec. 75; State v. Crowley, 41 Wis. 271; People v. Barkelow, 37 Mich. 455; Commonwealth v. Eastman, 55 Mass. (1 Cush.) 190; s. c., 48 Am Dec. 596.

conspiracy is to commit a criminal act, the off
without reference to the means by which it is to be
and the criminal purpose should be distinctly alleg
offence consists in unlawful means to be emplo
should be distinctly stated.[1] If the end be unl
need be alleged; but if the end be not lawfu
means must appear. The criminality must appear
the indictment.[2]

The means must be particularly set out, and the
as to constitute a statutory or common-law offence

4. *Joinder of Counts.* — Felonies and misdeme
ent felonies, may be joined in the same indictmen
cover the same transactions.[4] The conspiracy n
as the substantive offence, or counts for the con
joined with counts for the substantive offence.[5]
the counts in an information are manifestly b
and the same transaction, it will be assumed that i
tion to charge but one offence.[6]

If more than one unlawful act was to be accomp
relating to each may be set up in separate coun
count must set out the offence in full: referen
sufficient.[8]

The charge is sufficient where the object of
could be sufficiently inferred from the prior av
indictment: its insufficiency would be cured by th

5. *Charging Consummated Act.* — When the co
cuted, the fact should be alleged. The better prac
the consummated act.[10] Where the proof intended
to the jury is proof of the actual commission of
the proper course to charge the parties with con
mit it.[11]

An indictment jointly charging several defenda
der, implies a conspiracy; and proof may be ad
formal allegation of conspiracy.[12]

1. State *v.* Ripley, 31 Me. 384, 386; State *v.* Roberts, 34 Me. 320, 322.
When Means to be set out. — In the former case it is not necessary to set out the means, while in the latter it is. Smith *v.* People, 25 Ill. 17.

2. People *v.* Clark, 10 Mich. 310.

3. Cole *v.* People, 84 Ill. 216; State *v.* Potter, 28 Iowa, 554; State *v.* Mayberry, 48 Me. 218; Alderman *v.* People, 4 Mich. 414; s. c., 69 Am. Dec. 321; Rex *v.* Fowler, 1 East, P. C. 461; Rex *v.* Seward, 3 Norm. & M. 557.

4. State *v.* Stewart, 59 Vt. 273; s. c., 4 New Eng. Rep. 378.

5. State *v.* Coleman, 5 Port. (Ala.) 32; Burk *v.* State, 2 Har. & J. (Md.) 426; Harman *v.* Commonwealth, 12 Serg. & R. (Pa.) 69; State *v.* Bolen, 1 State *v.* Montague, 2 State *v.* Gaffney, 1 Ri

6. State *v.* Glidden, 3 New Eng. Rep. 849

7. State *v.* Kennedy

8. State *v.* Norton,

9. R. *v.* Aspinwall, 730; s. c., 45 L. J. M. Cas. 48; 46 L. J. M.

10. State *v.* Clary, Kinstry, 50 Ind. 465; N. Y. 177; United S 62 U. S. (2 Otto) 51 Reg. *v.* Boulton, 12 C

11. R. *v.* Boulton, 1 *v.* Selsby, 5 Cox, C. C

12. State *v.* Ford, 3

The relation between the conspiracy and the act need not be [illegible]ecifically declared.[1]

6. *Offences under the Statute.* — In an indictment for conspiracy [illegible] do acts prohibited by statute, it is sufficient to charge the [of]fence in the words of the statute.[2] And the words of the statute [m]ay be used without setting forth their meaning.[3]

As to statutory offences, all are principals where no mention is [m]ade of principal in the second degree.[4]

An indictment under the federal statute which fails to state [w]ith certainty the acts relied on effecting the conspiracy, has been [h]eld to be defective.[5]

7. *Indictment for Specific Offences.* — In an indictment for a [co]nspiracy to accuse one of crime, the procurement, or intended [pr]ocurement, of an indictment or other legal process need not be [se]t out.[6] But an indictment for a conspiracy to commit a burglary [w]ith intent to steal, must charge the intent to "feloniously steal."[7]

The substantive felony must be described accurately: so, in an [in]dictment for a conspiracy to rob, the charge should aver, "by [vi]olence, or by putting in fear."[8] And an indictment for a con[sp]iracy to cheat and defraud must set forth such allegations as [w]ill show the object to be criminal either by statute or at common [la]w.[9]

No particular description of the goods is necessary,[10] nor need [th]e scienter be alleged.[11] The superfluous words "divers other [go]ods" and "divers other persons" do not render the indictment [vo]id.[12]

The allegation in the information that one object of the defend-

1. United States v. Donau, 11 Blatchf. C. C. 168.

2. State v. Hewett, 31 Me. 396; State v. [Ke]yes, 25 Vt. 415.

3. State v. Stewart, 59 Vt. 273; s. c., 4 [Ne]w Eng. Rep. 378; Reg. v. Rowlands, 2 [De]n. Cr. Cas. 304; s. c., 16 Jur. 265; 21 L. [J.] M. C. 81.

4. United States v. Bayer, 13 Bankr. Reg. [400]; United States v. Harbison, 13 Int. [Re]v. Rec. 118; Thornton v. State, 25 Ga. [30]; Commonwealth v. Gannett, 83 Mass. [2 B]ishop, Stat. Cr. 136; 1 Arch. Cr. Pr. 13.

5. United States v. Watson, 17 Fed. [Re]p. 221.

[Co]nspiracy must be sufficiently charged. — In an indictment for a conspiracy to [comm]it an offence against the United [Sta]tes under Rev. Stat. § 5440, the con[spir]acy must be sufficiently charged: it [m]ust be aided by averment of acts done [by] one or more of the conspirators. United [Sta]tes v. Britton, 108 U. S. 199; bk. 27, L. [ed.] 698.

[R]evised Statute, § 5440. — Under sect. [544]0 of the United States Revised Statutes, [to] constitute good information or indict[me]nt it must state with sufficient certainty the offence intended to be committed, and must then state some act done by one of the conspirators toward effecting the object. United States v. Watson, 17 Fed. Rep 221.

6. Commonwealth v. Tibbetts, 2 Mass. 536.

7. Smith v. State, 93 Ind. 67.

8. Landringham v. State, 49 Ind. 186.

Conspiracy to rob. — An indictment charging that defendants conspired to rob, and did rob, another of a silver dollar, and a warrant of arrest in his hands against them, does not allege two distinct offences. Lisle v. Commonwealth, 82 Ky. 250.

9. Commonwealth v. Eastman, 55 Mass. (1 Cush.) 190; s. c., 48 Am. Dec. 596; Rhoads v. Commonwealth, 5 Pa. St. 272; Twitchell v. Commonwealth, 9 Pa. St. 211; Haxen v. Commonwealth, 23 Pa. St. 355; Williams v. Commonwealth, 34 Pa. St. 178.

10. Commonwealth v. Goldsmith, 12 Phila. (Pa.) 632.

11. Commonwealth v. Goldsmith, 12 Phila. (Pa.) 632.

12. Commonwealth v. Goldsmith, 12 Phila. (Pa.) 632.

ant was to extort money from a particular person means which are unlawful, charges a crime.[1] And ment charges a conspiracy to extort through false crime, if there is evidence to sustain the former verdict will not be set aside.[2]

An information under a statute making "crimina to unlawfully and maliciously obstruct and impede of corporations," etc., need not set forth that the act committed by the defendants, but merely that the commit them.[3]

An indictment for a conspiracy to obstruct justi false pretences, subtle means, and devices," and alle defendants have prevented and defeated the trial of sufficient.[4]

In an indictment for a conspiracy to procure the pauper, it is not necessary to aver that the mar against the consent of the parties, though that proved.[5]

An indictment for conspiracy to do a wrongful a of another's rights, which is a statutory but not offence, must set out the facts showing it to be illegal means are charged.[6]

An indictment for conspiring to hinder persons to assemble, must allege the object of the defenda vent a meeting for the purpose of petitioning Co something connected with the powers and duties of

An indictment against a board of freeholders for vote away county money, but not charging that the was corrupt, or that the payee was, to the knowle ants, disentitled to the money, is bad.[8]

8. *To cheat.* — The indictment must charge the overt act,[9] but there need be no allegation that obtained.[10] In such a case, it is necessary to sh unlawful device was used, and also to show the combination.[11] And it must appear from the in

1. State v. Glidden, 55 Conn. 46; s. c., 3 New Eng. Rep. 849.
2. Commonwealth v. Nichols, 134 Mass. 531.
Conspiracy to extort Money. — The indictment for conspiracy to extort money must allege from whom. Commonwealth v. Andrews, 132 Mass. 263.
3. People v. Petheram (Mich.), 7 West. Rep. 592.
4. Schwab v. Mahley, 47 Mich. 572.
Obstructing Justice. — That defendants "did knowingly and willingly oppose and obstruct the said sheriff in attempting to execute said writ," is a sufficient charge. Schwab v. Mahley, 47 Mich. 572.
5. Re Parkhouse, 1 East, P. C. 462.
6. Commonwealth v. (1 Cush.) 189; s. c., 48
7. United States v. S. (2 Otto) 542; bk. 23,
8. Wood v. State, 47 s. c., 1 Cent. Rep. 446.
9. Wood v. State, 47 461; s. c., 1 Cent. Rep.
10. Miller v. State,
Rule in Montana. — der sec. 187, div. 3, Territory, for a conspi defraud, must allege the conspiracy was to be a ritory v. Carland, 6 Mon
11. Rex v. Tanner, 1 Edwards, 8 Mod. 320.

property sought to be obtained was not the property of ndant.[1]

i an indictment to cheat by false pretences, it is sufficient to ge "divers false pretences."[2] Where the object was to de- d many persons, the indictment may charge the purpose to aud the public: if the names of persons defrauded, or intended e defrauded, are ascertainable, they should be stated.[3] And re the conspiracy was to defraud a class of persons, or the lic generally, the parties injured need not be specifically ied.[4]

t is not necessary to set out any overt act, or any actual injury the person to be defrauded.[5] But an indictment for a con- acy to obtain goods by false pretences must charge the doing n overt act, or it will be void.[6]

I. Evidence. — 1. *Proof of Conspiracy.* — The conspiracy may proved by facts and circumstances,[7] and slight evidence of nion is all that is required.[8] But active participation in, not ply passive cognizance of, the illegal action must be shown.[9] dence that the same persons were, shortly prior to the time of alleged crime, engaged in a conspiracy to commit similar crimes, ompetent.[10]

he evidence of the conspiracy is either direct of a meeting consultation for the illegal purpose, or it is circumstantial.[11]

[illegible] Allegation. — That defendants [illegible], fraudulently, and deceitfully [illegible], combine, confederate, and together to cheat and defraud," has held sufficient. Sydserff v. Reg., 11 Q [illegible] Reg v. Whitehouse, 6 Cox, Cr. Cas. Reg. v. Heymann, L. R. 8 Q. B. 102; 12 Cox, Cr. Cas. 383; White v. Reg., [illegible], Cr. Cas. 318.

[illegible] divers false pretences against the [illegible] made and provided, did defraud [illegible] the form of the statute," was held [illegible] in Latham v. Reg., 9 Cox, Cr. [illegible].

Reg. v. Parker, 3 Q. B. 292; s. c., 11 [illegible]) 234.

[illegible] v. Gill, 2 Barn. & A. 204; Reg. [illegible]ker, 3 Q. B. 555; Reg. v. Heymann, 8 Q. B. 102; s. c., 12 Cox, Cr. Cas.

McKee v. State (Ind.), 9 West. Rep.

Commonwealth v. Judd, 2 Mass. 329; 3 Am. Dec. 54; Reg. v. Peck, 9 Adol. [illegible]; Rex v. De Berenger, 3 Maule &

Commonwealth v. Fuller, 132 Mass. United States v. Waddell, 16 Fed. [illegible].

Wood v. State, 47 N. J. L. (18 Vr.) s. c., 1 Cent. Rep. 441.

The Mussel-slough Case, 5 Fed. Rep. State v. Wolcott, 21 Conn. 281; Riehl v. Evansville Found. Asso., 104 Ind. 70; s. c., 1 West. Rep. 885; United States v. Sacia, 2 Fed. Rep. 754; Kelley v. People, 55 N. Y. 566; Bloomer v. State, 48 Md. 521; United States v. Cole, 5 McL. C. C. 513; United States v. Graff, 14 Blatchf. C. C. 381; United States v. Babcock, 3 Dill. C. C. 581; Reg. v. Whitehouse, 6 Cox, Cr. Cas. 38; 3 Whart. C. L. § 2351.

8. McDowell v. Rissel, 37 Pa. St. 164; Peterson v. Speer, 29 Pa. St. 479; Clinton v. Estes, 20 Ark. 216; Johnson v. State, 29 Ala. 62, Evans v. Watson, 56 Pa. St. 54; Benham v. Cary, 11 Wend. (N. Y.) 83; Crary v. Sprague, 12 Wend. (N. Y.) 41.

9. Evans v. People, 90 Ill. 384.

10. Tarbox v. State, 38 Ohio St. 581.

11. R. v. Cope, 1 Strange, 144; 2 Stark. (2d ed.) 232; R. v. Parsons, 1 W. Bl. 392; Spies v. People (Anarchists' Case), 122 Ill. 1; s. c., 10 West. Rep. 701.

Resolutions passed at a Meeting. — Resolutions passed at one meeting, the object of which meeting was to fix the meeting mentioned in the indictment, are admissible to show the intention of the defendants in assembling and attending the latter meeting. Spies v. People (Anarchists' Case), 122 Ill. 1; s. c., 10 West. Rep. 701; Rex v. Hunt, 3 Barn. & A. 566.

Handbills. — A handbill circulated where it is probable the conspirators would see it, and it indicates what they should do, is

Directions given by one of the party on the day of t
as to where they were to go, and for what purpose, are

Where the prosecution is not for the conspiracy,
tive crime, proof of conspiracy is only proper so f
tend to show a common design. It may be introd
purpose of establishing the position of the members
bination as accessories to the crime.[2]

The mere fact that defendant stood outside a store
was offering stolen property for sale, is insufficien
conspiracy.[3] But proof of illegal purpose alone i
sustain a criminal prosecution for conspiracy.[4] Evide
misdemeanors on different days may be given under a
for several misdemeanors on the same day.[5]

2. *Proof of Previous Plan.* — When a number of
together for different purposes, and afterwards join t
common purpose to the injury of the property of
a conspiracy, and it is not necessary to prove any
amongst them against the person injured.[6] If the

admissible in evidence against the conspirators. Reg. v. Duffield, 5 Cox, C. C. 404; Spies v. People (Anarchists' Case), 122 Ill. 1; s. c., 10 West. Rep. 701.

After proof that a particular defendant had been active in attempting to induce the public not to patronize the company, evidence tending to show that he had distributed circulars is admissible. State v. Glidden, 55 Conn. 46; s. c., 3 New Eng. Rep. 849.

If defendants in their circular, reading, "A word to the wise is sufficient. Boycott the company," used the word boycott in its original sense, in its application to the company, there can be no doubt of their criminal intent. State v. Glidden, 55 Conn. 46; s. c., 3 New Eng. Rep. 849.

A Notice to Newspaper that it would be charged a certain sum per week as its share of the expenses of the boycott, was admissible for the same reasons. State v. Glidden, 55 Conn. 46; s. c., 3 New Eng. Rep. 849.

Letters. — Letters from one conspirator to another are, under certain circumstances, admissible in his favor, to show that he was a dupe of the other. Rex v. Whitehead, 1 C. & P. 67; Spies v. People (Anarchists' Case), 122 Ill. 1; s. c., 10 West. Rep. 701.

Drilling of Armed Sections. — Evidence of drilling a short time before, and hissing an obnoxious person, are admissible. R. v. Frost, 9 Car. & P. 126; 3 Russ. Cr. (5th ed.) 190; Spies v. People (Anarchists' Case), 122 Ill. 1; s. c., 10 West. Rep. 701.

1. R. v. Hunt, 3 Barn. & Ald. 566; Spies v. People (Anarchists' Case), 122 Ill. 1; s. c., 10 West. Rep. 701.

2. Spies v. People (The Anarchists' Case), 122 Ill. 1; s. c.,
701.

Bombs. — As specimens
weapons which the consp
paring, and as showing t
the intended use of suc
cated, the bombs prepar
properly introduced, to c
compare their structure w
did the killing. Spies
Anarchists' Case), 122
West. Rep. 701.

Evidence offered by d
a conspiracy was properl
nothing was offered to c
it. Waugh v. Bridgeford

3. People v. Stevens, G
4. Schwab v. Mabley,
5. Rex v. Levy, 2 Star
6. Myers v. State, 1 Co
v. State, 24 Ind. 77; Rin
Ind. 80; Ulrich v. Comm
(Ky.), 400; Commonwea
Mass. (2 Cush.) 577; C
Rogers, 48 Mass. (7 Met
Am. Dec. 458; Commonw
84 Mass. (2 Allen) 160; C
Farren, 91 Mass. (9 Alle
wealth v. Waite, 93 Mas
Commonwealth v. Emm
Commonwealth v. Went
441; Heckman v. Nac
Miller v. State, 3 Ohio
Smith, 10 R. I. 258; Lo
Tex. 402 State v. Hart
State v. Cain, 9 W. Va.
State, 7 Humph. (Ten
States v. Pearce, 2 McL
win v. Clark, L. R. 1 Q
Robbins, 1 Carr. & P. 45

spiracy to kill policemen at a police station, but the agents of the conspiracy kill them at a distance from the station, it is no such departure from the original plan as to relieve the conspirators from the responsibility.[1]

Where a series of notes are forged in pursuance of a system of conspiracies, they are all admissible in evidence to show and explain the system.[2] And where there are two separate counts, — one charging the principal to be known, and the other charging him to be unknown, — it is sufficient if either is proved.[3]

3. *Acts and Declarations of Co-Conspirators.* — When two or more persons combine or associate together, for the prosecution of some fraudulent or illegal purpose, the acts and declarations of any one of them, made in furtherance of the common purpose, and forming a part of the *res gestæ*, are admissible as evidence against the others; otherwise, however, as to subsequent acts, admissions, or declarations.[4] After the fact of the conspiracy is proved, the declarations of any of the conspirators during the pendency of the criminal project are admissible against all.[5]

It is a rule of ancient standing, that the conspiracy should be first established *prima facie*, before the acts and declarations of a co-conspirator can be received in evidence against another.[6]

10 Cox, C. C. 402; Reg. v. Mycock, 12 Cox, C. C. 28; Reg. v. Booth, 12 Cox, C. C. 231; Reg. v. Prince, Law Rep. 2 C. C. 154. See also Desty, Am. Crim. Law, p. 101.

1. Spies v. People (The Anarchists' Case), 122 Ill. 1; s. c., 10 West. Rep. 701.

Variance from Previous Plan. — The circumstance that the man who threw the bomb, and his confederates who fired the shots, waited before doing their work until the policemen had left the station, contrary to the plan adopted at the previous meeting, would make no difference as to the guilt of the parties to the conspiracy. Spies v. People (The Anarchists' Case), 122 Ill. 1; s. c., 10 West. Rep. 701.

2. Card v. State, 109 Ind. 415; s. c., 7 West. Rep. 81.

3. Reg. v. Tyler, 8 Car. & P. 616; State v. Green, 26 S. C. 128; Pilger v. Commonwealth, 112 Pa. St. 220; Brennan v. People, 15 Ill. 516; Baxter v. People, 4 Ill. (3 Gilm.) 368; Kitzman v. People, 110 Ill. 362.

4. Phœnix Ins. Co. v. Moog, 78 Ala. 284; Sundry Goods v. United States, 27 U. S. (2 Pet.) 358; bk. 7, L. ed. 450; Nudd v. Burrows, 91 U. S. (23 Wall.) 438; bk. 23, L. ed. 286.

5. Jones v. State, 1 Ga. (1 Kelly) 610; Malone v. State, 8 Ga. 408; Walker v. Hunter, 17 Ga. 408; Taylor v. Johnson, 17 Ga. 536; Armistead v. State, 18 Ga. 704; Reid v. State, 20 Ga. 681; Boggus v. State, 34 Ga. 275.

6. But before such acts and declarations can be admitted in any event, a *prima facie* case of conspiracy must appear to the trial court, and then the declarations and acts during the performance of the conspiracy can be submitted to the jury to be used by them if they find such conspiracy existed; but to be discarded in case it is not established. Such acts and declarations cannot be used to show the conspiracy, without other independent evidence. People v. Parker (Mich.), 11 West. Rep. 182.

Exception to the Rule. — But the general rule cannot well be enforced "where the proof of the conspiracy depends upon a vast amount of circumstantial evidence, a vast number of isolated and independent facts; and, in any case, where such acts and declarations are introduced in evidence, and the whole of the evidence introduced on the trial, taken together, shows that such a conspiracy actually exists, it will be considered immaterial whether the conspiracy was established before or after the introduction of such acts and declarations." State v. Winnid, 17 Kan. 298; Spies v. People, 122 Ill. 1; s. c., 10 West. Rep. 701.

It has been said that the prosecutor may either prove the conspiracy which renders the acts of the conspirators admissible in evidence, or he may prove the acts of the different persons, and thus prove the conspiracy. Roscoe, Cr. Ev. (7th ed.) 415. In many important cases, evidence has been given of a general conspiracy, before any proof of the particular part which the ac-

Where evidence has been adduced *prima facie*, est
spiracy among the several defendants, the acts and d
each in furtherance of the common design, are the a
rations of all.[1] But only those declarations are adn
were made during the process of the conspiracy, and i
of its objects.[2] When the common design has been c
nothing said or done by one can affect the others.[3]
the admission of acts and declarations of one conspi
nal evidence against each member of the conspiracy,
the same rule applies in criminal as in civil cases.[4]
on which the acts and declarations of other conspira
done at different times are admitted in evidence agair
prosecuted, is, that, by the act of conspiring togethe
ators have jointly assumed to themselves, as a body,
of individuality so far as regards the prosecution of
design, thus rendering whatever is said or done b
furtherance of that design a part of the *res gestæ*,
the acts of all.[5] And where a conspiracy has been
sayings, and movements of other conspirators, before
tion of the crime, are admissible against the defe
occurring in his absence.[6] But such acts and declar
be used to show the conspiracy without other
evidence.[7]

When the fact of conspiracy is once established,
of the conspirators in the prosecution of the enterp

cused parties have taken. In some peculiar instances, in which it would be difficult to establish the defendant's privity without first proving the existence of a conspiracy, a deviation has been made from the general rule, and evidence of the acts and conduct of others has been admitted to prove the existence of a conspiracy previous to the proof of the defendant's privity. Roscoe, Cr. Ev. 414.

The term "acts," as here used, includes written correspondence and other papers relative to the main design. 1 Greenl. Ev. § 111; Spies *v.* People, 122 Ill. 1; s. c., 10 West. Rep. 701.

1. Williams *v.* State, 81 Ala. 1; Brown *v.* Herr, 21 Neb. 113; State *v.* Glidden, 55 Conn. 46; s. c., 3 New Eng. Rep. 489; Tucker *v.* Finch, 66 Wis. 17; Owen *v.* State, 16 Lea (Tenn.), 1; Spies *v.* People (The Anarchists' Case), 122 Ill. 1; s. c., 10 West. Rep. 701; Rhiel *v.* Evansville Found. Asso., 104 Ind. 70; s. c., 1 West. Rep. 81; Miller *v.* Commonwealth, 8 Ky 15; McKee *v.* State (Ind.), 9 West. Rep. 838; Card *v.* State, 109 Ind. 415; s. c., 7 West. Rep. 81; Nudd *v.* Burrows, 91 U. S. (1 Otto) 426; bk. 23, L. ed. 286; Ford *v.* State (Ind.), 11 West. Rep. 858; 1 Whart. Cr. L. (6th ed.) 702; 3 Green. Ev. 394.

Speeches and Publicati
perpetration of the act
the common design, are
tions of the conspirators
ble. Spies *v.* People
Case), 122 Ill. 1; s. c
701; Campbell *v.* Com
St. 187; State *v.* Cahill
Rep. 599; Card *v.* State,
7 West. Rep. 81; Peo
Wend. (N. Y.) 229; s. c.
United States *v.* Cole, 5
Queen *v.* West, L. R. 1
Rex *v.* Hammond, 2 Esp

2. United States *v.* G
Cent. Rep. 764.

3. Owens *v.* State,
1.

4. Card *v.* State, 109
West. Rep. 81; Walk
293; Daniels *v.* McGin
Hogue *v.* McClintock, 7
v. Freeman, 71 Ind. 85

5. Ford *v.* State (Ind
858.

6. Williams *v.* State
5 S. W. Rep. 655; s.
38.

7. People *v.* Parker
Rep. 182.

all.[1] **But acts and declarations of co-conspirators not in pur-ance of the common design are not admissible.**[2]

After **a conspiracy is established, only those declarations which** in **furtherance** of the common design can be introduced in idence **against the other members.**[3] To make declarations missible, they must accompany acts done in pursuance of the nspiracy.[4] While all the acts and declarations of one con-irator may be given in evidence against himself, they cannot be ceived against his co-conspirators, unless made during the ogress of the conspiracy, and in furtherance of its objects.[5]

On the trial of an indictment for arson, where the *gravamen* of e offence charged is not a conspiracy, declarations made months fore the time at which it is claimed that the defendant had y thing to do with any scheme to commit the offence, and, at e time the declarations were made, there was no conspiracy, d the declarations were but mere threats, it was held that ch declarations were not so connected with the commission of e offence in time and character as properly to be said to be a part the *res gestæ*. If it be said that such evidence is competent r the purpose of proving a conspiracy, it may be answered that atever weight it might have in that regard, it would also have connecting defendant with the conspiracy, where there is no im that there was any conspiracy, except as between defendant d the person making the declarations; and it is well settled at one person cannot be connected with a conspiracy by the clarations of another, and declarations are incompetent for that rpose.[6]

After the accomplishment or abandonment of the common terprise, no declaration of one conspirator will affect another, d should be excluded as to the latter.[7]

. Card v. State, 109 Ind. 415; s. c., 7 st. Rep. 81; Spies v. People (The An-hists' Case), 122 Ill. 1; s. c., 10 West. p. 701; Nudd v. Burrows, 91 U. S. (1 o) 426; bk. 23, L. ed. 286.

They are admissible on a *prima facie* ablishment of the fact. Phœnix Ins. . v. Moog, 78 Ala. 284; Miller v. Day-, 57 Iowa, 423; Spies v. People (The archists' Case), 122 Ill. 1; s. c., 10 West. p. 701; Johnson v. Miller, 69 Iowa, 562.

. Long v. State, 13 Tex. App. 211.

. Spies v. People (The Anarchists' Case). Ill. 1; s. c., 10 West. Rep. 701; Card State, 109 Ind. 415; s. c., 7 West. Rep. . Horton v. State, 66 Ga. 690.

They are part of the *res gestæ*, and are acts and declarations of all. State v. rkin, 49 N. H. 39; Phœnix Ins. Co. v. og, 78 Ala. 284; Rex v. Salter, 5 Esp. ; Rex v. Hammond, 2 Esp. 719.

. 2 Stark. Ev. 405; 3 Russ. Cr. 160; 1 eenl. Ev. 126, §§ 110, 111; 1 Phill. Ev. 95; 2 Whart. Ev. 1206.

5. United States v. Gunnell (D. C.), 3 Cent. Rep. 764.

Joint Illegal Intent. — A conspiracy being proved among a certain number of men, an act in pursuance of the common plan may be the act of all; but a man is not to be presumed to be a conspirator having a joint illegal intent with others in a particular assault which he does not personally commit, by showing the misconduct of others on previous occasions. Strout v. Packard, 76 Me. 148; s. c., 49 Am. Rep. 604; State v. Fredericks, 85 Mo. 145; Rex v. Nicholls, 13 East. 412.

6. Ford v. State (Ind.), 11 West. Rep. 858.

7. State v. Fredericks, 85 Mo. 145; State v. McGraw, 87 Mo. 161; s. c., 8 West. Rep 448. See State v. Duncan, 64 Mo. 263; Laytham v. Agnew, 70 Mo. 48; State v. Reed, 85 Mo. 194.

Distraining for Church Rates. — On a charge of conspiracy to annoy a broker who distrained for church rates, evidence

It is competent to show a conspiracy to murder persons than the defendant, though its existence was him, if he be afterward connected with it by compet If murder was the result of the conspiracy, the acts spirators are admissible, although defendant was not such acts were done;[2] and although he was not in indictment.[3] And they are admissible on the sep one, even though made in his absence.[4] But decla in the absence of the defendant, and after the con the conspiracy, are not admissible against him.[5] Th sible only when made pending the criminal enterpris

While it is a general rule of evidence, that the act tions of a person, in the absence of the prisoner, ar ble in evidence against him, yet there are exceptions, is in a case of a conspiracy to do an unlawful act, and declarations of conspirators, in furtherance of the pose, are competent, although made in the absence c

The rule admitting evidence of declarations of on the hearing of the other, before the common purpose mated, is not varied by the fact that after one's arres into a new conspiracy, upon the purpose whereof th were made.[8] Such declarations are admissible with tion.[9]

4. *Statements and Confessions.* — It is competent, conspiracy, to connect the several parties charged not only of their statements, but of separate acts.[10] two unite in a common undertaking to defraud, th of one are competent against both, although there is conspiracy.[11] Upon a separate trial of one jointly another, evidence of what was said by the latter in th the defendant is competent to prove the purpose of th

of what a person, who was at the meeting, said some days after, when he was distrained for church rates, is not admissible. Reg. v. Murphy, 8 Car. & P. 297; Reg. v. Blake, 6 Q. B. 126; 13 L. J. M. C. 131.

1. Lamar v. State, 63 Miss. 265.
2. State v. McCahill (Iowa), 33 N. W. Rep. 599; State v. Anderson, 82 N. C. 732.
3. State v. Glidden, 55 Conn. 46; s. c., 3 New Eng. Rep. 849.
4. O'Neal v. State, 14 Tex. App. 582.
5. Ricks v. State, 19 Tex. App. 308; Willey v. State (Tex.), 8 S. W. Rep. 570.
6. Armistead v. State (Tex.), 2 S. W. Rep. 627.
7. State v. Anderson, 82 N. C. 732.
8. State v. Buchanan, 35 La. An. 89.
9. Cohea v. State, 11 Tex. App. 153.
10. People v. Saunders, 25 Mich 119.

Printing Circular. — Thus, a conspirator, not a defendant, having declined to testify for the State on tl crimination, evidence to made on another trial by he had printed the circu evidence, was admissible 55 Conn. 46; s. c., 3 New

11. Riehl v. Evansvill 104 Ind. 70; s. c., 1 Wes

Conversation of Membe evidence is admissible c between five or six meml which inaugurated and l cott, among whom was c defendant, and others which it was stated, but could not say, that they cents a week for the su cott, and that it would b company. State v. Glid s. c., 3 New Eng. Rep. 8

12. People v. Davy Rep. 897.

On a conspiracy to liberate a prisoner, the acts of the prisoner thin the prison, and articles found on him, are admissible against rsons charged with the conspiracy.[1] But the admissions and clarations of a co-conspirator are admissible against the defendt, although made after the consummation of the enterprise, if fendant was present and acquiesced.[2] Declarations which are erely narrative are incompetent, and should not be admitted cept against the one making them.[3]

Letters and statements of a co-conspirator written or spoken in rtherance of the common design, are admissible against all the nspirators.[4]

What was done or said by one of the conspirators before the nspiracy was formed, or after its object had been attained, or work fully completed, not in the presence or hearing of the hers, and not brought to their knowledge, and ratified by them, not admissible against them, or either of them.[5] And statents of one of them as to part of the transactions, accompanying act done in furtherance of, or in connection with, such enterise, are not competent against the others.[6] But they are missible to prove his own participation under instructions to e jury.[7]

Confession of one joint offender, made after the enterprise is ded, is admissible only against himself.[8] But confession of one t on trial is not evidence against a co-defendant.[9]

Subsequent evidence of the conspiracy cures any defect in the mission of statements of a confederate.[10]

5. *Order of Proof.* — Before acts and declarations can be admitted any event, a *prima facie* case of conspiracy must appear to the al court, and then the declarations and acts during the perrmance of the conspiracy can be submitted to the jury to be ed by them, if they find such conspiracy existed, but to be dis-

1. Reg. v. Desmond, 11 Cox, C. C. 146. **Acts and Declarations in Absence of Co-conspirator.** — A. and G., having united in common intention of robbing I., knocked from a moving train. The train was pped, and, while I. was being carried off, in a short time re-appeared alone, and in attempted to rob I. It was *held* that acts and words of A., whether G. was sent or not, in this second attempt, ght be proven on the trial of G., such atapt being in furtherance of the common rpose from which the defendant had not hdrawn. Grogan v. State, 63 Miss. 147.

2. Holder v. State, 18 Tex. App. 91.

3. Spies v. People (The Anarchists' se), 122 Ill. 1; s. c., 10 West. Rep. 701; wles v. Coe, 21 Conn. 230; State v. rkin, 49 N. H. 39; 2 Phill. Ev. 179; 2 rr. Tri. 578.

4. Card v. State, 109 Ind. 415; s. c., 7 st. Rep. 81; Spies v. People (The Anarchists' Case), 122 Ill. 1; s. c., 10 West. Rep. 701.

5. People v. Parker (Mich.), 11 West. Rep. 182; Legg v. Olney, 1 Den. (N. Y.) 202. **Evidence of Interview.** — It has been *held* proper, on the cross-examination of a State witness, to exclude evidence of an interview to which one defendant was a party, and of declarations then made by him, to which no allusion had been made by the State on the direct examination. State v. Glidden, 55 Conn. 46; s. c., 3 New Eng. Rep. 849.

6. N. Y. Guaranty & Ins. Co. v. Gleason, 78 N. Y. 504.

7. People v. Arnold, 46 Mich. 268.

8. Studstill v. State, 7 Ga. 2; Parsons v. State, 43 Ga. 197; Johnson v. State, 48 Ga. 116.

9. Lyons v. State, 22 Ga. 399.

10. State v. Ward, Nev. 1887; Dole v. Wooldredge, 135 Mass. 140.

carded in case it is not established.[1] And where th
separate counts, — one charging the principal to be
the other charging him to be unknown, — it is suffici
is proven.[2]

The conspiracy must be established by proof, bef
dence can be given of the acts of any person not in t
of the prisoner; and, generally speaking, by evid
party's own act. It cannot be collected from the act
as, by express evidence of the fact of a previous cons
a concurrent knowledge and approbation of each othe

A conspiracy must be shown; and evidence that ea
illegally or maliciously will not support an action for
without proof that the defendants conspired together.

But a deviation has been made from the general r
dence of the acts and conduct of others has been
prove the existence of the conspiracy previous to
defendants' privity.[5]

In an ordinary conspiracy, it is not necessary to pro
design between defendants before proving the ac
Proof of the fact of the conspiracy need not always b
fore evidence is admissible of the acts and declara
conspirators when the proof of the conspiracy consist
ous and independent circumstances.[7]

The fact that some of the acts and declarations
spirators were allowed to come in before proof was
conspiracy, or of the connection of the defendants v
ground of objection. This matter is largely discre
evidence of a general conspiracy may be given before
part taken by the conspirators.[8]

The prosecutor may either prove the conspiracy, wh
the acts of the conspirators admissible in evidence
prove the acts of the different persons, and thus pro

1. People *v.* Parker (Mich.), 11 West. Rep. 182.

The Joint Assent of Mind, like all other parts of a criminal case, may be established as an inference of the jury from the other facts proved. Spies *v.* People (The Anarchists' Case), 122 Ill. 1; s. c., 10 West. Rep. 701; 2 Bish. Cr. L. 190, n. 7.

Any joint action on a material point, or a collection of independent but co-operating acts, by persons closely associated with each other, is held sufficient to enable the jury to infer concurrence of sentiment. Archer *v.* State, 106 Ind. 426; s. c., 4 West. Rep. 726, 729.

It has been *held* that it is competent to prove that other property, stolen about the same time, was found in possession of one of the defendants, for the purpose of developing the *res gestæ*, and showing common intent. Smith *v.* Sta
96.

2. Spies *v.* People (T
Case), 122 Ill. 1; s. c.,
701.

3. 1 East, P. C. 96.

4. Newell *v.* Jenkins,
Compare Rex *v.* Cope, 1 S

5. 2 Stark. Ev. (2d ed.)

6. Reg. *v.* Brittain, 3 Co

7. Loggins *v.* State, 12
Spies *v.* People (The A
122 Ill. 1; s. c., 10 West.

8. Spies *v.* People (T
Case), 122 Ill. 1; s. c., 10

9. R. *v.* Stafford, 7 St.
Russell, 9 St. Tri. 578; R.
Tri. 530; R. *v.* Hardy, 24
v. Horne Tooke, 25 St. Tri
Case, 2 Brod. & B. 310;
Cox, C. C. 332; 2 Stark.

racy.[4] Where a member of a society was permitted to prove printed regulations and rules, and that he and others acted der them in execution of the conspiracy, as introductory to oof that they were members and equally concerned, such evince could not affect the defendants until they were made parties the conspiracy.[2] Before the evidence of the conspiracy can ect the prisoner materially, it is necessary to make out that he nsented to the extent that the others did.[3]

The sufficiency of the evidence of the combination to form a indation is held to be a question for the jury.[4]

6. *Testimony of Co-Conspirator.* — On a joint indictment, one her convicted or acquitted may be a witness for the other defendts.[5] But a defendant who suffers judgment by default, cannot called as a witness on behalf of a co-conspirator.[6] And where o conspire to rob, and one withdraws and the other proceeds, d a murder is committed, his co-conspirator may testify to the reement to rob.[7]

Where a defendant offers himself as a witness to prove the iminal charge, he cannot excuse himself from answering on e ground that by so doing, he may criminate himself. By mak- g himself a witness, he waives his privilege to all matters concted with the defence.[8]

And where one of several defendants is acquitted, the record his acquittal is admissible in favor of another subsequently ed.[9]

VII. The Trial and its Incidents. — One of several persons may be ed separately,[10] and judgment be passed upon him, although e others who have appeared and pleaded have not been tried.[11] ne alone may be convicted upon proof that there was a criminal nspiracy of which he was a member.[12] But if two persons

. Spies v. People (The Anarchists' se), 122 Ill. 1; s. c., 10 West. Rep. .

. R. v. Hammond, 2 Esp. N. P. 720.

. 2 Stark. Ev. (2d ed.) 234.

. State v. Ross, 29 Mo. 32; Burkee v. ller, 61 Mass. (7 Cush.) 547; Jones v. rilliam, 29 Barb. (N. Y.) 403; State v. sh, 7 Iowa, 347; Oldham v. Bentley, 6 B. Mon. (Ky.) 428; Heiser v. McGrath, Pa. St. 458.

. State v. Hunt, 91 Mo. 490; s. c., 8 est. Rep. 627.

. Rex v. Lafone, 5 Esp. 155.

Wife of Co-Conspirator: English Practice. — Under the English practice, the wife a co-conspirator cannot be a witness for other defendants. Rex v. Locker, 5 p. 107.

. People v. Collins, 64 Cal. 293.

. Spies v. People (The Anarchists' se), 122 Ill. 1; s. c., 10 West. Rep. .

. Paul v. State, 12 Tex. App. 346.

10. Rex v. Kinnersley, 1 Str. 193.

Death of Co-Conspirators: Trial of Survivor. — As where the rest have died. Rex v. Nicholls, 2 Str. 1227; s. c., 13 East, 412 n.

11. Reg. v. Ahearne, 6 Cox, C. C. 6.

12. 2 Bish. Cr. Proc. § 186; 3 Whart. Cr. L. (6th ed.) §§ 2340, 2344, 2346; State v. Adams, 1 Houst. Cr. C. (Del.) 361; Commonwealth v. Irwin, 8 Phila. (Pa.) 380.

If three persons were engaged in a conspiracy, and one of them died before trial, and another was acquitted, the survivor may be tried and convicted. People v. Olcott, 2 Johns. (N. Y.) Cas. 301; Rex v. Nicholls, 13 East, 412 n.; Reg. v. Kenrick, 5 Q. B. 49; s. c., D. & M. 208; 7 Jur. 848; 12 L. J. M. C. 135.

On an indictment of three persons tried separately, if one of them is convicted before the others are tried, the possibilities of the others being not found guilty is not a sufficient reason for holding the judgment irregular. Reg. v. Ahearne, 6 Cox, C. C. 6.

alone are indicted, they must both be convicted: a[illegible]
one would be an acquittal of the other.[1]

Upon a count charging one conspiracy, the jury n[illegible]
some guilty of conspiring to effect one or more c[illegible]
specified.[2] The fact that the object of the conspira[illegible]
plished, and that the unlawful thing conspired to
performed and completed, does not prevent a convic[illegible]
charge simply that the defendants conspired to com[illegible]

On an indictment containing several counts, if a sin[illegible]
is proved, the verdict may nevertheless be taken o[illegible]
the counts as describe the conspiracy consistently wi[illegible]

1. *Procedure and Practice.* — Separate trials may
an indictment for conspiracy,[5] and all conspirators
with full knowledge of a common design may be
indictment.[6]

2. *Continuance.* — A continuance will not be give[illegible]
conspirator, who is evading arrest, to testify for ano[illegible]

3. *Motion to Quash.* — A motion to quash is add[illegible]
discretion of the court, and its refusal is not rever[illegible]
the indictment does not state any thing done to effe[illegible]
the object and purpose, it must be quashed.[9] A m[illegible]
of the clerk is not a good ground for quashing the i[illegible]

4. *Formation of Jury.* — Unless objection is sho[illegible]
more of the jury who tried the case, the antecedent
court upon the competency or incompetency of jur[illegible]
been challenged and stood aside, will not be inquire[illegible]
appellate court.[11] The mere fact that a juror h[illegible]
against a crime does not disqualify him as a juror.[12]

1. State *v.* Tom, a Slave, 2 Dev. (N. C.) L. 569; Jones *v.* Baker, 7 Cow. (N. Y.) 445.

2. O'Connell *v.* Reg., 11 Clark & F. 155; s. c., 9 Jur. 25.

3. People *v.* Petheram (Mich.), 7 West. Rep. 592.

Carrying the conspiracy into effect does not merge the offence charged into the greater offence; but, if the conspiracy is proved, the conviction follows, although the defendant might have been found guilty of the greater crime had he been charged with it. People *v.* Petheram (Mich.), 7 West. Rep. 529.

4. Reg. *v.* Gomperts, 9 Q. B. 824; s. c., 11 Jur. 204; 16 L. J. Q. B. 121.

5. Casper *v.* State, 47 Wis. 535. *Compare* Commonwealth *v.* Manson, 2 Ashm. (Pa.) 31.

It is within the discretion of the trial court to allow separate trials of defendants jointly indicted; and where there has been no abuse of discretion, the appellate court will not interfere. Spies *v.* People (The Anarchists' Case), 122 Ill. 1; s. c., 10 West. Rep. 701.

One conspirator may [illegible] formed against, tried a[illegible] naming his co-conspirat[illegible] the information bad. [illegible] 67 Cal. 412.

6. Reg. *v.* Hudson, 8 [illegible] Reg. *v.* Pollman, 2 Cam[illegible]

7. Lisle *v.* Commonw[illegible]

Testimony of Co-Consp[illegible] spirator cannot testify [illegible] *v.* Commonwealth, 82 K[illegible]

8. State *v.* Stewart, [illegible] New Eng. Rep. 378.

9. United States *v.* [illegible] Rep. 145.

10. State *v.* Norton, [illegible] 33.

11. Spies *v.* People [illegible] Case), 122 Ill. 1; s. c[illegible] 701.

12. Robinson *v.* Ran[illegible] Winnesheik Insurance [illegible] 60 Ill. 465; Spies *v.* [illegible] archists' Case), 122 Ill. [illegible] Rep. 701.

Prejudice against [illegible] archy. — Any prejudice [illegible]

The prosecuting attorney is entitled to the same number of **remptory challenges as** the defendants, — equal to the sum of the **allenges** of all the defendants.[1]

§ *Argument of Counsel.* — Mere statements of the prosecuting **orney derogatory** to the character of the defendant are not **ound for reversal.**[2]

5. *Instructions to Jury.* — The court is at liberty to instruct in discretion, if it reduces its instructions to writing.[3] The charge the court must be taken together; and when so taken, if it rly presents the law, a cause should not be reversed merely cause one of the instructions may lay down the law without fficient qualification.[4]

Although an instruction, considered by itself, is too general, t, if it is properly limited, by others given on the other side, so it it is not probable it could have misled the jury, judgment ll not be reversed on account of such instruction.[5]

. or anarchism would not render a or incapable of trying fairly and imparly the issue of whether the defendants, mmunists or anarchists, were guilty or guilty of murder. Spies *v.* People e Anarchists' Case), 122 Ill. 1; s. c., 10 st. Rep. 701.

. Spies *v.* People (The Anarchists' se), 122 Ill. 1; s. c., 10 West. Rep. .

. Heyl *v.* State, 109 Ind. 589; s. c., 8 st. Rep. 393.

xceeding Limits of Debate. — The gment will not necessarily be reversed rely because the prosecuting attorney eeds the limit of legitimate debate in statement to the jury. Epps *v.* State, Ind. 539; s. c., 3 West. Rep. 380.

Exhibiting Caricature to Jury. — Under indictment charging defendants with spiracy against the employees of cer- coal operators, to compel them to t working by force, threats, and men- s of harm, the exhibition by the coun- for the prosecution, as part of his ument to the jury, of a caricature from uck," entitled "Suckers of the Work- men's Sustenance," under permission the court, will not be ground for revers- a judgment of conviction. The use of h matter in argument is within the dis- tion of the court, unless it appears that reby serious wrong has been done. wman *v.* Commonwealth (Pa.), 5 Cent. p. 497.

. Brown *v.* People, 5 Ill. (4 Gilm.) 439; een *v.* Lewis, 13 Ill. 642.

Discretion of Trial Judge. — Under the nois statute, a judge of the circuit court at liberty to instruct at his discretion, if reduces his instructions to writing, so t the jury can take them with them in nsidering their verdict. Brown *v.* People, 5 Ill. (4 Gilm.) 439; Green *v.* Lewis, 13 Ill. 642. In this case, the judge who presided at the trial in the court below, himself wrote an instruction, and read it to the jury, which contained the following words: "What are the facts, and what is the truth, the jury must determine from the evidence, and from that alone. If there are any unguarded expressions in any of the instructions, which seem to assume the existence of any facts, or to be any intimation as to what is proved, all such expressions must be disregarded, and the evidence only looked to, to determine the facts." It is difficult to see how, after such a clear and explicit injunction as this, the jury could have made any finding that was not based on the evidence.

4. Rice *v.* Des Moines, 40 Iowa, 638.

While some instructions may be subject to criticisms, yet if, when taken as a whole, they are substantially correct, they are sufficient. Spies *v.* People (The Anarchists' Case), 122 Ill. 1; s. c., 10 West. Rep. 701; People *v.* Cleveland, 49 Cal. 577; Toledo W. & W. Ry. Co. *v.* Ingraham, 77 Ill. 309.

5. Spies *v.* People (The Anarchists' Case), 122 Ill. 1; s. c., 10 West. Rep. 701.

Requesting Instruction. — If counsel desired to have the jury differently instructed as to the form of the verdict, they should have prepared an instruction indicating such form as they deemed to be correct, and should have asked the trial court to give it. Where this is not done, the parties are in no position to claim it in the appellate court. Spies *v.* People (The Anarchists' Case), 122 Ill. 1; s. c., 10 West. Rep. 701; Dunn *v.* People, 109 Ill. 646; Dacey *v.* People, 116 Ill. 555.

It is error to charge the jury to the effect that evidence of good character is available only in a doubtful case.[1]

It is the duty of the jury to consider all the instructions together; and when the court can see that an instruction in the series, although not stating the law correctly, is qualified by others, so that the jury were not likely to be misled, the error will be obviated.[2]

7. *Verdict.*—The conspiracy being a joint offence, all must be convicted, or none, unless the indictment is for conspiring with persons unknown to the grand jury.[3]

If a reasonable doubt of the guilt of the prisoner is entertained by them, the jury have no discretion, but must acquit.[4]

8. *New Trial.*—In a prosecution for conspiracy against several co-conspirators, a new trial of one involves a new trial of all.[5]

It is dangerous practice to allow verdicts to be set aside upon *ex parte* affidavits as to what jurors are claimed to have said before they were summoned to act as jurymen.[6]

1. United States *v.* Gunnell, 5 Mackey (D. C.), —; s. c., 3 Cent. Rep. 764.

2. Spies *v.* People (The Anarchists' Case), 122 Ill. 1; s. c., 10 West. Rep. 701.

Instructions considered together: Duty of Jury.—It is the duty of the jury to consider all the instructions together; and when the court can see that an instruction in the series, although not stating the law correctly, is qualified by others, so that the jury were not likely to be misled, the error will be obviated. Toledo, W. & W. Ry. Co *v* Ingraham, 77 Ill. 309.

Although an instruction, considered by itself, is too general, yet, if it is properly limited by others given on the other side, so that it is not probable it could have misled the jury, judgment will not be reversed on account of such instruction. Kendall *v.* Brown, 86 Ill. 387; Skiles *v.* Caruthers, 88 Ill. 458.

The Supreme Court of Iowa has said, "It is usually not practicable, in any one instruction, to present all the limitations and restrictions of which it is susceptible. These very frequently must be presented in other and distinct portions of the charge. The charge must be taken together; and if, when so considered, it fairly presents the law, and is not liable to misapprehension, nor calculated to mislead, a cause should not be reversed simply because some one of the instructions may lay down the law without sufficient qualification." Rice *v.* Des Moines, 40 Iowa, 638.

The same court *held*, in a criminal case, where the indictment was for murder, that "instructions are all to be considered and construed together;" and that an omission to state the law fully in one instruction, where the omission is fully supplied in another, does not constitute error. State *v.* Maloy, 44 Iowa, 104.

The Supreme Court of California said, in a criminal case, "While some of the instructions are subject, perhaps, to criticism, and may not state the law with precise accuracy, yet, taken as a whole, they were substantially correct, and could not have misled the jury to the prejudice of the defendant." People *v.* Cleveland, 49 Cal. 577.

The principle that an instruction which is general in its character may be limited or qualified by other instructions in the series, does not contravene the rule that, in a criminal case, "material error in one instruction calculated to mislead is not cured by a subsequent contradictory instruction." Whart. Cr. Pl. (8th ed.) § 793.

3. Commonwealth *v.* Irwin, 8 Phila. (Pa.) 380; United States *v.* Cole, 5 McL. C. C. 513; Reg. *v.* Thompson, 16 Q. B. 832.

But the defendants may be convicted of the conspiracy, and acquitted on the other counts. Wilson *v.* Commonwealth, 96 Pa St. 56; State *v.* Noyes, 25 Vt. 415.

Where two are indicted, the acquittal of one is the acquittal of both,—State *v.* Tom, 2 Dev. (N. C.) L. 569;—but where more than two are indicted, the acquittal of one will not necessarily relieve the others. People *v.* Olcott, 2 Johns. (N. Y.) Cas. 301.

4. Spies *v.* People (The Anarchists' Case), 122 Ill. 1; s. c., 10 West. Rep. 701.

5. Commonwealth *v.* McGowan, 2 Pars. Sel. Cas. (Pa.) 314.

6. Because the parties making such affidavits submitted to no cross-examination, and the correctness of their statement is subject to no test whatever. Spies *v.* Peo-

Judgment. — On indictment for conspiracy, judgment should gainst each defendant severally, and not jointly against all.[1] ere the indictment charges a conspiracy to extort through false sation of crime, and another count charges a conspiracy dy to accuse one of the crime of adultery, if there is evidence stain the former count, a general verdict will not be set aside.[2]

IMINAL CONVERSATION. See ADULTERY.

IMINAL LAW.[3]

he Anarchists' Case), 122 Ill. 1; s. c., st. Rep. 701; Hughes v. People, 116).

arch v. People, 7 Barb. (N. Y.) 391. Commonwealth v. Nichols, 134 Mass.

use the general verdict includes a upon the second count, and could not have been found without proof of the purpose therein alleged. Commonwealth v. Nichols, 134 Mass. 531. See Crowley v. Commonwealth, 52 Mass. (11 Metc.) 575; Commonwealth v. Nickerson, 87 Mass. (5 Allen) 518; Commonwealth v. Andrews, 132 Mass. 263.

3. For the various specific offences, as

I. Definition. — Criminal law has been properly defined as "that branch of jurisprudence which treats of crimes and offences." [1]

1. *Crime defined.* — A crime or public offence is an act committed or omitted in violation of a law forbidding or commanding

Arson, Homicide, etc., see the various titles of this work.

1. 1 Bouv. L. Dict. (15th ed.) 457.

Salus Populi Suprema Lex. — All municipal law is founded upon the social compact in which every man, upon entering or joining the society or community, gives up a portion of his natural liberty to the laws enacted for the benefit and protection of all, which, in certain cases, authorize the infliction of certain penalties for the doing of specified prohibited acts, or the failure to perform duties enjoined, including the privation of liberty, and even the destruction of life, for the purpose of preventing and suppressing crime, and to thereby insure the safety and welfare of society, and the public generally, on the principle that the welfare of the people is the paramount law.

The Leading Principles of American and English criminal law have been summarized as follows: "(1) Every man is presumed to be innocent till the contrary is shown; and if there is any reasonable doubt of his guilt, he is entitled to the benefit of the doubt. (2) In general, no person can be brought to trial until a grand jury, on examination of the charge, has found reason to hold him for trial. (3) The prisoner is entitled to trial by a jury of his peers, who are chosen from the body of the people with a view to impartiality, and whose decision on questions of fact is final. (4) The question of his guilt is to be determined without reference to his general character. By the systems of Continental Europe, on the contrary, the tribunal not only examines the evidence relating to the offence, but looks at the probabilities arising from the prisoner's previous history and habits of life. (5) The prisoner cannot be required to criminate himself, nor permitted to exculpate himself by giving his own testimony on his trial. The justice and expediency of this latter restriction are now much questioned [and repudiated in some of the States]. (6) He cannot be twice put in jeopardy for the same offence. (7) He cannot be punished for an act which was not an offence by the law existing at the time of its commission, nor can a severer punishment be inflicted than was declared by law at that time." 1 Bouv. L. Dict. (15th ed.) 457, 458.

it, and to which is annexed, upon conviction, the punishment of death, imprisonment, fine, removal from office, or disqualification to hold and enjoy any office of honor, trust, or profit in the State.[1]

A crime is a wrong directly or indirectly affecting the public, to the commission of which the State has annexed certain pains and penalties, and which it prosecutes and punishes in its own name in what is called a criminal proceeding.[2]

But a private injury is not an indictable offence,[3] as pulling off the thatch of a dwelling-house,[4] or selling as two chaldrons of coal a less quantity,[5] or delivering less beer than contracted for.[6]

The word "crime" is properly applicable to both a felony and a misdemeanor.[7]

2. *Statutory Offences.* — The violation of a statute of a public nature is a crime.[8]

Under a statute declaring that if one voluntarily, before prosecution within a reasonable time, returns property which he has stolen, the offence is reduced to a misdemeanor; the return may be voluntary if induced by repentance, although fear of punishment may also constitute a motive; the return must be actual, not constructive, and all the property unchanged in form must be returned.[9]

a. Construction of Statutes. — Criminal statutes are to be construed strictly in those parts which are against defendants, but liberally in those which are in their favor. No person can be made subject to such statutes by implication; and, when doubts arise concerning their interposition, such doubts are to weigh only in favor of the accused.[10]

1. **In General.** — Slattery *v.* People, 76 Ill. 218. See 4 Bl. Com. 5; 1 Whart. Cr. L. (8th ed.) 314; 1 Bish. Cr. L. (6th ed.) 332.

In Indiana. — It was enacted in 1852, as a part of the Indiana revised system of laws passed during that year, that thereafter "crimes and misdemeanors shall be defined, and punishment therefor fixed, by statutes of this State, and not otherwise," and that provision of law still continues in force. Rev. Stat. 1881, § 237.

In giving a construction to that enactment, it has been uniformly *held* that they have no longer any common-law offences in that State, and that however immoral, reprehensible, or revolting an act may be, it cannot be punished either as a crime or misdemeanor, unless it has been defined and declared to be either the one or the other by some statute. Rosenbaum *v.* State, 4 Ind. 599; Hackney *v.* State, 8 Ind. 494; [illegible] *v.* State, 9 Ind. 408; Beal *v.* State, [illegible] Ind. 398; State *v.* Ohio & M. R. R. Co., [illegible] Ind. 362; Jones *v.* State, 59 Ind. 229; [illegible] *v.* State (Ind.), 5 West. Rep. [illegible].

2. Amer. Jur. 318; 1 Whart. Cr. L. (8th ed.) 315; 4 Bl. Com. 5; Rob. El. Law, 78; 1 Bish. Cr. L. (6th ed.) 332.

3. Rex *v.* Storr, 3 Burr. 1698.

4. Rex *v.* Atkins, 3 Burr. 1706.

5. Rex *v.* Osborn, 3 Burr. 1697.

6. Rex *v.* Wheatley, 1 W. Black. 273; s. c., 2 Burr. 1125; Rex *v.* Dunnage, 2 Burr. 1130.

7. Lehigh Co. *v.* Schock, 113 Pa. St. 373; s. c., 4 Cent. Rep. 744.

8. 1 Whart. Cr. L. (8th ed.) 324; *Re* Lucas, 23 Up. Can Q. B. 92.

"**Conviction of Crime.**" — Under the statute, the terms "offence" and "crime" are synonymous; and one convicted of an "offence" has "been convicted of a crime," disqualifying him from being a member of the police force. People *v.* N. Y. Police Comrs., 39 Hun (N. Y.), 507; People *v.* French, 102 N. Y. 583.

9. Bird *v.* State, 16 Tex. App. 525.

10. State *v.* Bryant, 90 Mo. 534; s. c., 7 West. Rep. 748; Howell *v.* Stewart, 54 Mo. 400; Kritzer *v.* Woodson, 19 Mo. 327; [illegible] *v.* Spaunhorst, 67 Mo. 256; United States *v.* Wiltberger, 18 U. S. (5 Wheat.) 76; bk. 5, L. ed. 37.

That construction of a statute defining an offence is not to be preferred which would make one guilty regardless of his intent.[1]

When a statute makes an act indictable which is merely *malum prohibitum*, when done "wilfully and maliciously," the existence of an evil mind, as a general rule, is a constituent part of the offence.[2]

To constitute a statutory offence, neither knowledge nor intent need be shown.[3]

Under a statute making it a crime to obstruct a railroad track, the obstruction need not be such as would endanger the passage of trains, or throw the engine or cars from the track.[4]

And it has been held that where, under the provisions of a statute, it is sufficient that an act be "maliciously" and "wantonly" done, an instruction that it must be done "wilfully" is erroneous.[5]

When the commission of certain acts is declared to be a misdemeanor, it is in effect declared unlawful.[6]

A statute making an act a criminal offence prohibits its performance.[7]

And where acts are prohibited by statute, it is unnecessary for the jury to find that defendant was actuated by express malice.[8]

When a statute creates a new offence by prohibiting and making unlawful any thing which was lawful before, and appoints a specific remedy by a particular method of proceeding, that particular method must be pursued.[9]

3. *Infamous Crimes.* — A crime punishable by imprisonment in the State prison is an infamous crime,[10] and it may be committed

1. Bradley *v.* People, 8 Colo. 599.

2. Falwell *v.* State (N. J. Nov. 1886), 6 Atl. Rep. 619.

3. People *v.* Schaeffer, 41 Hun (N. Y.), 23. See *infra*, "Ignorance of Law."

Minor in Saloon. — Thus, a saloon-keeper may be convicted without proof that he knew of the presence of a minor in his billiard saloon, or the fact of his minority, where the law declares it unlawful "to permit any minor . . . to remain in such hall." State *v.* Probasco, 62 Iowa, 400.

4. Riley *v.* State, 95 Ind. 446.

5. Garrett *v.* Greenwell (Mo.), 10 West. Rep. 351.

6. State *v.* Mulhisen, 69 Ind. 145.

Pointing Gun at Person. — Thus, pointing a gun for fifteen minutes at the door of a house, and calling upon the occupant to come out, as defendant wanted to "shoot him dead," is within a statute making it unlawful "to point or aim any . . . fire-arm . . . toward any other person." Lange *v.* State, 95 Ind. 114.

Deadly Weapon. — A "deadly weapon" is not exclusively one designed to take life or inflict bodily injury; and when not of this character, the question is one of fact. Blige *v.* State, 20 Fla. 742; s. c., 51 Am. Rep. 628.

7. Wilson *v.* Joseph, 107 Ind. 681; s. c., 5 West. Rep. 681.

8. People *v.* Richards, 44 How. (N. Y.) 278.

9. Reg. *v.* Lovibond, 24 L. T. N. S. 357; s. c., 19 W. R. 753; Rex *v.* Wright, 1 Burr. 543.

The "Offence of Intoxication" created by statute is a crime within the New York Consolidation Act. People *v.* French, 102 N. Y. 583.

10. Mackin *v.* United States, 117 U. S. 348; bk. 29, L. ed. 909.

At Common Law. — The punishment for misdemeanors at common law was fine or imprisonment, or both, unlimited, but in the most aggravated cases seldom exceeding two years. See note to Inwood *v.* State, 1 Am. L. J. 77; United States *v.* Williams, 1 Cr. C. C. 178; Adams *v.* Barrett, 5 Ga. 404; State *v.* Dewer, 65 N. C. 572; United States *v.* Smith, 18 U. S. (5 in three ways: (1) by forgery, (2) by perjury, (3) by acts, as dealing with false weights, altering coin, making false keys, etc.[1]

Any crime which may be punished by imprisonment at hard labor is an infamous crime within the meaning of the fifth amendment to the United States Constitution, and therefore must be prosecuted by presentment, not by information.[2]

In early times the character of the crime was determined by the punishment inflicted; but in modern times the act itself, its nature and purpose, determine that question.[3]

But a crime is not infamous, within the meaning of the Fifth Amendment to the Constitution of the United States, unless it not only involves the charge of falsehood, but may also affect the public administration of justice by the introduction therein of falsehood and fraud.[4]

It has been said that, "at common law, a crime involving a charge of falsehood must, to be infamous, not only involve a falsehood of such a nature and purpose as to make it probable that the party committing it is devoid of, and insensible to, the obligation of an oath, but the falsehood must be calculated to injuriously affect the public administration of justice."[5]

No crime is infamous, within the meaning of the Constitution, unless expressly made infamous, or declared to be a felony, by act of Congress.[6] And in the absence of some positive provision in a statute, the presumption is against an intention to make an offence an infamous crime.[7]

In most of the States, the disqualification of infamy has been

Wheat.) 153; bk. 5, L. ed. 57; United States v. Staats, 49 U. S. (8 How.) 41; bk. 12, L. ed. 979; 1 Bish. Cr. L. §§ 580–590; 1 Russ. on Cr. 42; 1 Hale's P.C. 411, 574; 4 Bacon's Abridg. titles, "Felony" and "Forfeiture;" Viner's Abridg. title, "Forfeiture;" 4 Bl. Com. 94; 3 Inst. 43; Tomlin's Dict. title, "Felony."

1. 1 Bouvier's L. Dict.

2. *Ex parte* Wilson, 114 U. S. 417; bk. 29, L. ed. 89.

Confinement in Penitentiary. — In the case of *Ex parte* Karstendick, 93 U. S. (3 Otto) 396; bk. 23, L. ed. 889, it is *held* that it is not the intention of our statutes to limit confinement in the penitentiary to those cases where hard labor is imposed. And the fact that an offence may or must be punishable by imprisonment in a penitentiary, does not make it in law infamous. United States v. Reid, 53 U. S. (12 How.) 361; bk. 13, L. ed. 1023; United States v. Maxwell, 3 Dill. C. C. 275; United States v. Coppersmith, 4 Fed. Rep. 198; United States v. Wynn, 9 Fed. Rep. 886; United States v. Block, 4 Saw. C. C. 211.

"Infamous" Punishment. — Offences punishable by imprisonment for more than one year may upon conviction subject the criminal to an "infamous" punishment. United States v. Tod, 25 Fed. Rep. 815.

3. United States v. Yates, 6 Fed. Rep. 861; People v. Whipple, 9 Cow. (N. Y.) 708; 2 Starkie's Ev. pt. 4, 715.

4. United States v. Block, 4 Saw. C. C. 211, 214; United States v. Yates, 6 Fed. Rep. 861.

5. United States v. Yates, 6 Fed. Rep. 861. This position is criticised by Dr. Wharton in his note to United States v. Field, 16 Fed. Rep. 778. He says that "the common-law test of infamy, heretofore generally accepted, is disqualification as a witness; in other words, an offence, a conviction of which disqualifies a person at common law as a witness, is infamous; an offence, not working such disqualifications at common law, is not infamous." See United States v. Mann, 1 Gall. C. C. 3; United States v. Isham, 84 U. S. (17 Wall.) 728; bk. 21, L. ed. 496; United States v. Buzzo, 85 U. S. (18 Wall.) 125; bk. 21, L. ed. 812; United States v. Ebert, 1 Cent. L. J. 205.

6. United States v. Wynn, 9 Fed. Rep. 886.

7. United States v. Cross, 1 McAr. C. C. 149.

removed by constitutional provision, or by statute; but the conviction may be proved as affecting the credibility of the witness.[1]

a. What are Infamous Crimes.—It has been said[2] that the following crimes have been held to be infamous; to wit, larceny,[3] knowingly receiving stolen goods,[4] forgery,[5] suppressing testimony by bribery or conspiracy,[6] perjury,[7] subornation of perjury,[8] and all crimes which create a strong presumption against the truthfulness of the party under oath.[9]

b. What not Infamous Crimes.—It has been held that uttering and passing counterfeit money is not an infamous crime,[10] and may be prosecuted by information.[11]

Embezzlement is not an infamous crime within the intention of the Fifth Amendment to the Constitution,[12] and stealing from the mails is not an infamous crime,[13] and may be prosecuted by

1. Reynold's Ev. 116; 1 Wharton's Ev. sec. 397.

2. Desty's Am. Cr. L. § 490.

3. State *v* Gardner, 1 Root (Conn.), 485.

Exceptions to the Rule.—But it has been held otherwise in Tennessee as to horse-stealing,—Wilcox *v.* State, 3 Heisk. (Tenn.) 110,—and in most of the States petit larceny has been reduced to the grade of a misdemeanor,—Shay *v.* People, 22 N. Y. 317; People *v.* Alde, 3 Parker, C. C. (N. Y.) 249; People *v.* Rawson, 61 Barb. (N. Y.) 619; State *v.* Gray, 14 Rich. (S. C.) 174; State *v.* Hurt, 7 Mo. 321; Carpenter *v.* Nixon, 5 Hill (N. Y.), 260; Pruitt *v.* Miller, 3 Ind. 16; Commonwealth *v.* Keith, 49 Mass. (8 Met.) 531; Uhl *v.* Commonwealth, 6 Gratt. (Va.) 706. See Rex *v.* Davis, 5 Mod. 75, notes; Pondock *v.* Mackin, Willes, 665,—which renders it no longer infamous. In New Hampshire, however, a person convicted of petit larceny cannot be a witness. See Lyford *v.* Farrar, 11 Fost (N. H.) 314.

4. Commonwealth *v.* Rogers, 48 Mass. (7 Metc) 500.

Receiving Stolen Goods.—Otherwise, however, where receiving stolen goods is only a misdemeanor. Commonwealth *v.* Murphy, 3 Pa. L. J. 290.

5. Poage *v.* State, 3 Ohio St. 229; State *v.* Chandler, 3 Hawks (N. C) 393; Rex *v.* Davis, 5 Mod. 74 See 2 East, P. C. 1003.

6. Rex *v.* Priddle, 1 Leach, 442; Bushel *v.* Barrett, 1 Ryan & M 434.

Spiriting away Witness.—But it has been *held*, that, where the conspiracy to get a witness away fails, it is not infamous, although it is an indictable offence. State *v.* Keyes, 8 Vt. 57.

7. Howard *v.* Shipley, 4 East, 180; Anonymous, 3 Salk. 15; Rex *v.* Peal, 11 East, 307. See 1 Greenl. Ev. sec. 373.

8. *In re* Sawyer, 2 Gale & D. 141; *Ex parte* Hannan, 6 Jur. 669.

9. Utley *v.* Merrick, 52 Mass. (11 Met.) 302.

10. United States *v.* Coppersmith, 4 Fed. Rep. 198; United States *v.* Yates, 6 Fed. Rep. 861; *In re* Wilson, 18 Fed. Rep. 33, United States *v.* Field, 16 Fed. Rep. 778.

Counterfeiting.—Making counterfeit coin was, by the ancient common law, treason, and subsequently a felony, while uttering or passing it was only a misdemeanor. Fox *v.* Ohio, 46 U. S. (5 How.) 410; bk. 12, L. ed. 213; United States *v.* McCarthy, 4 Cr. C. C. 304; United States *v.* Shepherd, 1 Hughes, C. C. 521; 1 Hale's P. C. 210; Tomlin's Dict. tit. "Coin;" United States *v.* Field, 16 Fed. Rep. 778; United States *v.* Wynn, 9 Fed. Rep 886; *contra*, United States *v.* Cultus Joe, 15 Int. Rev. Rec. 57.

11. United States *v.* Field, 16 Fed. Rep. 778.

12. United States *v.* Reilley, 20 Fed Rep. 46.

The court cited United States *v.* Shepard, 1 Abb. C. C. 437; United States *v.* Waller, 1 Saw. C. C. 701; United States *v.* Block, 4 Saw. C. C. 211; Spear's Law of the Federal Judiciary, 406; Thatch. Pr 650–652.

13. United States *v.* Wynn, 9 Fed. Rep. 886.

The court cited and examined Wheaton *v.* Donaldson, 33 U. S. (8 Pet.) 591; bk. 8, L. ed. 1055; United States *v.* Reid, 53 U S. (12 How.) 361; bk. 13, L. ed. 1023; People *v.* Whipple, 9 Cow. (N. Y.) 707; Clark's Lessees *v.* Hall, 2 Har. & McH. (Md.) 378; People *v.* Herrick, 13 Johns. (N. Y.) 82; Cushman *v.* Loker, 2 Mass. 106; Pendock *v.* Mackender, 2 Wilson, 18; Rex *v.* Priddle, Leach, 462; Rex *v.* Davis, 5 Mod. 75; State *v.* Gardner, 1 Root (Conn.), 485; Commonwealth *v.* Keith, 49 Mass. (8 Met.) 531; Lyford *v.* Farrar, 11 Fost. (N. H.) 314; United States *v.* Maxwell, 3 Dill. C. C. 275; *In re* Truman, 44 Mo. 181;

information.[1] *c. Conviction and Punishment for Infamous Crimes.* —A conviction of an infamous crime or offence disqualifies the party convicted from being a witness, unless pardoned[2] in the State where convicted,[3] if the court rendering the judgment had jurisdiction;[4] but whether it disqualifies him in other States or jurisdictions, depends upon the local statutes of such other States.[5] However, the disqualifications do not arise until after conviction.[6]

It is not easy to determine in all cases what are felonies and what are *crimen falsi*.[7]

There is no uniformity in the state legislation and that of

Fox v. State, 46 U. S. (5 How.) 410; bk. 12, L. ed. 213; Moore v. State, 55 U. S. (14 How.) 13; bk. 14, L. ed. 306; United States v. Shepard, 1 Abb. C. C. 431; United States v. Magill, 1 Wash. C. C. 464; United States v. Hawthorne, 1 Dill. C. C. 422; State v. Keyes, 8 Vt. 63, 66; 5 Watts & S. (Pa.) 348; United States v. Hudson, 7 Cr. C. C. 32, 34; United States v. Lancaster, 2 McL. C. C. 431; United States v. Wiltberger, 18 U. S. (5 Wheat.) 76; bk. 5, L. ed. 37; United States v. New Bedford Bridge, 1 Woodb. & M. C. C. 401; State v. Stephenson, 2 Bail. (S. C.) 334; United States v. Wilson, 3 Blatchf. C. C. 435; United States v. Coolidge, 14 U. S. (1 Wheat.) 415; bk. 4, L. ed. 124; United States v. Beavans, 16 U. S. (3 Wheat.) 336; bk. 4, L. ed. 404; United States v. Burr, 4 Cr. C. C. 500; Marhney v. Madison, 1 Cr. C. C. 176; United States v. Cross, 1 McAr. C. C. 149; United States v. Coppersmith, 4 Fed. Rep. 198; s. c., 2 Flippin, 546; 1 Crim. L. Mag. 741; 26 Int. Rev. Rec. 308; 10 Reper. 517; 22 Alb. L. J. 250; United States v. Shepherd, 1 Hughes, C. C. 520; United States v. Block, 4 Sawy. C. C. 212; United States v. Yates, 6 Fed. Rep. 861; United States v. Baugh, 1 Fed. Rep. 784; United States v. Waller, 1 Sawy. C. C. 701; United States v. Okie, 5 Blatchf. C. C. 516; United States v. Clark, Crabe, U. S. D. C. 584; United States v. Golding, 2 Cr. C. C. 212; United States v. Patterson, 6 McL. C. C. 477; United States v. Mills, 32 U. S. (7 Pet.) 138; bk. 8, L. ed. 636; United States v. Clayton, 2 Dill. C. C. 219, 226; Wilson v. State, 1 Wis. 184, 189; Commonwealth v. Barlow, 4 Mass. 439; Commonwealth v. Macomber, 3 Mass. 257; and [illegible] Cases (unreported); 1 Kent, Comm. 336, 337; Coke's Litt. 6, a, b; [illegible] a, 6 b, note 1; 1 Bl. Comm. 370; 4 Bl. Comm. 94, 95, 230; 1 Phil. Ev. 22, note, 45; 1 Chit. Cr. L. 600, 601; 1 Starkie's Ev. 94, 95; 1 Hale, 43; 2 Hale, 227; 1 Bish. Cr. L. secs. 580, 581, 621, 743, 974; 1 Greenl. Ev. secs. 372, 373; 1 Rus. Cr. ([illegible] ed.) 44, 46, 47; 3 Wilson's Works, 370; Willis, 665; Seargeant's Coast Law, 345; 4 Tucker's Bl. No. 10 of Ap.; Conkling's Treaties, 83; Whart. Crim. L. (3d ed.) 354 *et seq.*

1. United States v. Baugh, 4 Hughes, C. C. 501; United States v. Wynn, 3 McCrary, C. C. 206.

Nor is a libel an infamous crime. People v. Parr, 42 Hun (N. Y.), 313.

2. Desty's Am. Cr. L., sec. 49.

Erroneous Judgment: Disqualification under. — Where the judgment is erroneous, the disqualification attaches and subsists until vacated. Commonwealth v. Keith, 49 Mass. (8 Met.) 531.

3. People v. Whipple, 9 Cow. (N. Y.) 707; Commonwealth v. Green, 17 Mass. 515; United States v. Brockins, 3 Wash. C. C. 99; Schuylkill v. Copley, 17 Smith (Pa.), 386. See State v. Harston, 63 N. C. 294; Regna v. Alternun, 1 Gale & D. 261. Regna v. Webb, 11 Cox, C. C. 133; 1 Greenl. Ev. sec. 372.

4. Cooke v. Maxwell, 2 Stark. 183.

5. Kirschner v. State, 9 Wis. 140.

6. Skinner v. Perot, 1 Ashm. (Pa.) 57; United States v. Dickerson, 2 McL. C. C. 325; People v. Whipple, 9 Cow. (N. Y.) 707; Gibbs v. Osborn, 2 Wend. (N. Y.) 555; State v. Valentine, 7 Ired. (N. Y.) L. 225; Dawley v. State, 4 Ind. 128; Barber v. Ginzell, 3 Esp. 60; Fitch v. Smalbrook, T. Raym. 32; Lee v. Gausel, 1 Cowp. 1; s. c., Lofft. 374; Rex v. Castell, 8 East, 77.

7. Harrison v. State, 55 Ala. 239.

Crimen Falsi is a fraudulent alteration or forgery to conceal the truth to the prejudice of another. 1 Bouvier's L. Dict. (15th ed.) 456. It not only involves the charge of falsehood, but also is one which may injuriously affect the administration of justice by the introduction of falsehood and fraud. 1 Greenl. Ev. sec. 373.

In Ohio. — The Supreme Court of Ohio say that to "a predicate of an act that it is felonious, is simply to assert a legal conclusion as to the quality of the act; and unless the act charged, of itself, imports a felony, it is not made so by the application of the epithet." Mathews v. State, 4 Ohio St. 539.

Congress as to the punishment of criminal offences, and we often find statutory misdemeanors punished more severely than statutory felonies; and while some of the statutes prescribe hard labor as a part of the punishment, when necessarily the confinement must be in some prisons where it can be so enforced, on the other hand the simple imprisonment prescribed may become confinement with hard labor, by selecting a prison where it is part of the discipline; so that we often find prisoners convicted of the same offence, and sentenced to the same punishment, undergoing, in fact, different punishment.[1]

Where Congress uses a common term in defining a crime, or in any statute, we must look to the common law for a definition of the term used.[2]

The State statutes are not by any means harmonious on the subject of infamous crimes; and, if they were, that fact would avail nothing, for the federal courts take no cognizance of State statutes in criminal proceedings.[3]

The Revised Statutes of the United States,[4] adopting the laws of the several States, applies only to civil cases.[5]

4. *Doctrine of Merger.*—The higher crime necessarily merges the inferior offence, and dispenses with a finding of *non culpabilis* as to that count,[6] because the lesser offence is included in the greater,[7] as larceny in burglary.[8]

In Pennsylvania, where the statute raises the offence from a lower to a higher grade of crime, the misdemeanor becomes merged, the offence becomes felony, and it must be prosecuted as such.[9] But in Michigan a misdemeanor is not merged in a felony.[10]

An assault and battery, when committed in an attempt to murder, is merged in the felony.[11]

1. United States *v.* Coppersmith, 4 Fed. Rep. 198; *Ex parte* Karstendick, 93 U. S. (3 Otto) 396; bk. 23, L. ed. 889.

2. United States *v.* Coppersmith, 4 Fed. Rep. 198; United States *v.* Palmer, 16 U. S. (3 Wheat.) 610; bk. 4, L. ed. 471; United States *v.* Wilson, Baldw. C. C. 78; United States *v.* Barney, 5 Blatchf. C. C. 294; United States *v.* Magill, 1 Wash. C. C. 463; 2 Abb. (N. Y.) Pr. 171; Conk. Treat. (5th ed.) 178.

3. United States *v.* Reid, 53 U. S. (12 How.) 361; bk. 13, L. ed. 1023; United States *v.* Lancaster, 2 McL. C. C. 431; United States *v.* Paterson, 1 Woodb. & M. C. C. 306; United States *v.* Shepherd, 1 Hughes, C. C. 520; United States *v* Taylor, 1 Hughes, C. C 514; United States *v.* Maxwell, 3 Dill. C. C. 275; United States *v.* Shepard, 1 Abb. C. C. 431; United States *v.* Cross, 1 McAr. C. C. 149; United States *v.* Block, 1 Saw. C. C. 211; United States *v.* Ebert (U. S. D. C. Mo.), 1 Cent. L. J. 205; United States *v.* Williams, 1 Cliff. C. C. 5; United States *v.* Barney, 5 Blatchf. C. C. 294; United States *v.* Watkins, 3 Cr. C. C. 441; United States *v.* Hammonds, 2 Woods, C. C. 197; United States *v.* Magill, 1 Wash. C. C. 463; s. c., 1 Abb. (N. Y.) Pr. 197; 2 Abb. (N. Y.) Pr. 171.

4. U. S. Rev. Stat. § 721.

5. *In re* Wilson, 18 Fed. Rep. 33.

6. Manly *v.* State, 7 Md. 151; Stevens *v.* State (Md.), 5 Cent. Rep. 586.

7. Reynolds *v.* People, 83 Ill. 479; Carpenter *v.* People, 5 Ill. (4 Scam.) 197, Beckwith *v.* People, 26 Ill. 500.

8. Commonwealth *v.* Tuck, 37 Mass. (20 Pick.) 356; West *v.* State, 35 Tex. 89, Wilcox *v.* State, 31 Tex. 587; Shepherd *v.* State, 42 Tex. 503.

9. Whart. Cr. Law (old ed.), pp. 34, 133; Commonwealth *v.* Gable, 7 Serg. & R. (Pa.) 423; Commonwealth *v.* Weiderhold, 112 Pa. St. 504; s. c., 3 Cent Rep. 401.

10. People *v.* Arnold, 46 Mich. 268.

11. Wright *v.* State, 5 Ind. 527; 1 Russ. Cr (9th ed.) 88; 2 id. 1026.

The same is true of an attempt to commit rape;[1] so that a person charged with rape may be convicted of a felonious assault,[2] but not of a common assault.[3]

Thus, it has been held that a person charged with rape may be acquitted of that charge, and convicted of an assault and battery, because the charge necessarily includes an assault and battery.[4]

One indicted for murder may be convicted of a lower degree of criminal homicide.[5] But he cannot be convicted of the crime of being accessory after the fact.[6] And upon an indictment for murder in the first or second degree, the defendant may be convicted of voluntary or involuntary manslaughter.[7]

So, too, it has been held, that, upon an indictment for an assault and battery with intent to commit murder, there may be a conviction of an assault and battery with intent to commit murder in the second degree, or voluntary manslaughter, or there may be a conviction for an assault and battery only.[8]

But one indicted for riot cannot be convicted of an assault.[9]

It is held that where a statute provides that upon an indictment for an offence, consisting of different degrees, the jury may find the defendant not guilty of the degree charged, but guilty of any degree inferior thereto, or of an attempt to commit the offence; and that, in all cases, the defendant may be found guilty of any offence, the commission of which is necessarily included in that with which he is charged.[10]

Thus, a person indicted for malicious mayhem may, if the evidence warrants it, be convicted of simple mayhem, or of an assault and battery.[11]

The doctrine of merger did not obtain at common law except in treason and common-law felonies.[12] Mayhem was not within the rule,[13] nor piracy,[14] nor manslaughter by negligence,[15] nor impeding an officer in the performance of his duties.[16]

And where a misdemeanor at common law is made a felony by statute, the misdemeanor is merged in the felony.[17]

1. People v. Saunders, 4 Park. C. R. (N. Y.) 196.
2. Hall v. People, 47 Mich. 636.
3. State v. Pennell, 56 Iowa, 20; State v. Peters, 56 Iowa, 263; State v. Jay, 57 Iowa, 164. Compare State v. Porter, 57 Iowa, 691.
4. See Mills v. State, 52 Ind. 187; State v. Fisher, 103 Ind. 530; s. c., 1 West. Rep. 560; Ritchie v. State, 58 Ind. 355.
5. United States v. Leonard, 18 Blatchf. C. C. 187; Allen v. State, 37 Ark. 433.
6. Wade v. State, 71 Ind. 535.
7. See Powers v. State, 87 Ind. 144; State v. Fisher, 103 Ind. 530; s. c., 1 West. Rep. 560.
8. See Gillespie v. State, 9 Ind. 380; State v. Throckmorton, 53 Ind. 354; Behymer v. State, 95 Ind. 140; Barnett v. State, 100 Ind. 171; State v. Fisher, 103 Ind. 530; s. c., 1 West. Rep. 560.
9. Price v. People, 9 Ill. App. 36.
10. State v. Fisher, 103 Ind. 530; s. c., 1 West. Rep. 560.
11. State v. Fisher, 103 Ind. 530; s. c., 1 West. Rep. 560.
12. See Neal v. Farmer, 9 Ga. 555; White v. Fort, 3 Hawks (N. C.), 251; Dacy v. Gay, 16 Ga. 203.
13. Commonwealth v. Newell, 7 Mass. 245. See Adams v. Barrett, 5 Ga. 404.
14. Manro v. Almeida, 23 U. S. (10 Wheat.) 473; bk. 6, L. ed. 369; Rex v. Morphes, 1 Salk. 85.
15. Commonwealth v. Gable, 7 Serg. & R. (Pa.) 423; Shields v. Yonge, 15 Ga. 349; s. c., 60 Am. Dec. 698.
16. State v. Noyes, 25 Vt. 415.
17. People v. Fish, 4 Park. Crim. Rep. (N. Y.) 206.

II. Classification of Crimes. — 1. *General Divisions.* — Crimes may be divided into two general classes, which will include all conceivable crimes, whether common law or statutory; to wit, (1) acts which are in themselves wrong,[1] and (2) acts that are wrong because they are prohibited by statute.[2]

2. *According to Nature of the Offence.* — While crimes are sometimes arranged according to the degree of punishment inflicted for the commission of them,[3] yet they are more generally classified according to the nature of the offence committed. As thus classified, crimes may be subdivided into, —

a. Acts affecting the Sovereignty of the State. — Under this division fall (1) treason, (2) misprision of treason, and (3) high crimes and misdemeanors.[4]

b. Acts affecting the Persons and Lives of Individuals. — The acts affecting the persons and lives of the individuals composing the State are (1) abduction, (2) assault and battery, (3) false imprisonment, (4) kidnapping, (5) rape, (6) robbery, (7) murder, (8) attempts to murder and kill, and (9) manslaughter.

c. Acts affecting Property. — (1) *Acts affecting Public Property.* — Under this head fall (1) burning public property, (2) destroying public property, and (3) injuries to public property.

(2.) *Acts affecting Private Property.* — Those acts which affect private property are divided into (1) arson, (2) burglary, (3) embezzlement, (4) larceny, (5) malicious mischief, and (6) obtaining goods by false pretences.

d. Acts affecting the Public, or Individuals, or their Property. — Under acts affecting the public at large, or individuals or their property, may be classed all those combinations known as conspiracies.[5]

e. Acts affecting Public Polity. — Those acts which affect public polity are (1) gambling, (2) exhibiting immoral shows, (3) lotteries, (4) nuisance, (5) violating or obstructing the right of suffrage, (6) destroying game, fish, etc.

f. Acts affecting the Currency and Public and Private Securi-

1. **Malum in se.** — Any act which shocks the moral sense of the community, and is denounced as grossly immoral and injurious, is in itself wrong, and accounted a crime. Of this class are the specific offences of arson, burglary, larceny, murder, rape, etc., and are universally condemned by men everywhere. See 1 Bouv. L. Dict. (15th ed.) 456; 1 Russ. on Cr. (9th ed.); . . . Bl. Comm. . . .

2. **Malum Prohibitum.** — Some acts are prohibited because it is regarded as for the best interests of society that they should not be done. Such acts are wrong or crimes because, and only because, they are prohibited. Of this general class is adultery, drunkenness, polygamy, and the like. See Bl. Comm.; 1 Russ. on Cr. (9th ed.).

It has been said that "an offence is regarded as strictly a *malum prohibitum* only when, without the prohibition of statute, the commission or omission of it would in a moral point of view be regarded as indifferent. The criminality of the act or omission consists not in the simple perpetration of the act, or the neglect to perform it, but in its being a violation of a positive law." 1 Bouv. L. Dict. (15th ed.) 456.

3. As formerly in Ohio. See Ohio Rev. Stat. (Swan's ed.) 266.

4. The "high crimes" under the federal statutes correspond with felonies under the State statutes, and are punished as felonies by confinement in some one of the various State penitentiaries.

5. See *ante*, title "Criminal Conspiracies."

— The acts which fall under this subdivision are (1) counter-
ng, (2) passing counterfeit money, and (3) circulating a false
ency.

. *Acts affecting the Public Peace and Security.* — The acts
cting the public peace and security are (1) breach of the peace,
challenging to fight a duel, (3) accepting a challenge to fight a
l, (4) libel, (5) riot, (6) rout, (7) unlawful assembly.

. *Acts affecting Public Justice.* — Those acts which affect
lic justice are (1) barratry, (2) bribery, (3) champerty, (4) com-
nding felony, (5) contempt of court, (6) counterfeiting public
s, (7) destroying public records, (8) escape, (9) extortion,
jail-breach, (11) maintenance, (12) misprision of felony, (13) ob-
cting legal process, (14) oppression, (15) perjury, (16) resist-
e of officer, and (17) suppression of evidence.

Acts affecting Chastity. — Acts affecting chastity are purely
ters of statutory regulation, and generally consist of (1) adul-
, (2) bestiality, (3) bigamy, (4) fornication, (5) frequenting house
ll-fame, (6) incest, (7) keeping house of ill-fame, (8) lascivious
iage, (9) seduction, and (10) sodomy.

Acts affecting Religion, Morality, and Decency. — Those acts
ch affect religion, morality, and decency, like those affecting
stity, are purely matters of statutory regulation, and are gen-
ly (1) blasphemy, (2) cruelty to animals, (3) drunkenness,
obscenity, (5) profanity, (6) promoting intemperance, (7) sab-
h-breaking.[1]

. *Felonies.* — Crimes are distinguished as felonies and mis-
ieanors.[2]

he distinction between felonies and misdemeanors is rather
the consequences which follow the commission of the offence,
conviction, than by any particular element or ingredient of
offence itself.[3]

nd a discretion to assess a lesser punishment does not reduce
grade of the crime.[4]

. *Felony defined.* — A felony is a crime punishable, on convic-
, with death, or imprisonment in the State prison, or for the
mission of which the perpetrator may be so punished.[5]

See 2 Sharsw. Bl. Comm. 42 *et seq.*; ouv. L. Dict. (15th ed.) 456
he various acts above enumerated as inal will be found treated as specific ces in their appropriate places in this under the letters where they naturally ify. Only so much will be said of in this article as is necessary to ob- a distinct idea of the general subject iminal law.

Bl. Com. 74; 1 Arch. Cr. Pr. 1; Broom, . 892; 1 Russ. Cr. 78; 1 Whart. Cr. L. ed.) 321; *In re* Lucas, 29 Up. Can. Q. ; 3 Wels. 16.

New York. — The common-law distinction between felonies and misdemeanors is not wholly abolished in New York. People *v.* Lyon, 32 Hun (N. Y.), 623.

3. Lewis *v.* State, 33 Ga. 137.

4. Chandler *v.* Johnson, 39 Ga. 85; State *v.* Murdock, 9 Mo. 730; State *v.* Joiner, 19 Mo. 224; State *v.* Thompson, 30 Mo. 470.

5. People *v.* War, 20 Cal. 117; Miller *v.* State, 58 Ga. 200; State *v.* Smith, 8 Blackf. (Ind.) 489; Weinzorpflin *v.* State, 7 Blackf. (Ind.) 186; Johnston *v.* State, 7 Mo. 183; Ingram *v* State, 7 Mo. 293; A. *v.* B., R. M. Charlt. (Ga.) 228.

b. Statutory Felonies.—Offences may be designated as felonies by statute, and felonies at common law.[1]

Statute felonies are such crimes as are made felonies by the statute, or misdemeanors, where prosecution is by statute made to follow the procedure in felonies.[2]

And where a statute defines felony as an offence punishable by death, or by confinement in the penitentiary, a statute which makes slander thus punishable, or punishable by fine at the discretion of the court, in effect declares slander a felony.[3]

Under a statute making it a felony to assault and beat another with a cowhide whip or stick, "having at the time in his possession a pistol or other deadly weapon, with intent to intimidate the person assaulted, and prevent him from defending himself," defendant may be guilty, though the pistol was not exposed, and the person assaulted did not know that his assailant had one.[4]

A second offence of petit larceny may be made a felony by statute punishable by imprisonment in the State prison.[5] And an act respecting conviction upon second and third offences is not unconstitutional.[6] The second conviction need not be for the same offence.[6]

An act incorporating a certain bank, and providing that, if any of the officers, agents, or servants of that bank should embezzle the funds thereof, or make false entries, they should be guilty of felony, was held unconstitutional, because it did not apply generally to officers, agents, or servants of banks committing like offences.[7]

An enactment that an offence shall be a felony, which was a felony at common law, does not create a new offence.[8]

Where prohibition and penalty are contained in the same section, the remedy must be by proceeding for the penalty; but where the prohibition is in one section, and the penalties are in another section, an indictment will lie.[9]

And an act of the legislature providing for a fine to be paid for disturbing public ditches, with the alternative of fifteen days' labor on public works, does not create a crime.[10]

No penalty can be inflicted under a statute which has been repealed, unless a provision be made for that purpose.[11]

1. Reg. *v.* Horne, 4 Cox, C. C. 263. And the word "feloniously," used in the statute, makes the crime defined therein a felony. Rex *v.* Johnston, 3 Maule & S. 539; Rex *v.* Solomon, Ryan & M. 252.

2. State *v.* Darrah (Del.), Houst. Cr. Rep. 112; 1 Bish. C. L. (6th ed.) 3616.

Obtaining Money under False Pretences. The statute may make the obtaining of money under false pretences a felony, although but eight dollars is involved. Jackson *v.* Commonwealth (Ky. June, 1887), 4 S. W. Rep. 685.

3. State *v.* Waller, 43 Ark. 381.

4. Lawson *v.* State, 62 Miss. 556.

5. State *v.* Lehr, 16 Mo. App. 491.

6. Kelley *v.* People, 115 Ill. 583; s. c., 3 West. Rep. 46.

7. Millett *v.* People, 117 Ill. 294; s. c., 5 West. Rep. 155, 157. See Budd *v.* State, 3 Hump. (Tenn.) 483; Wally *v.* Kennedy, 2 Yerg. (Tenn.) 554; *In re* Jacobs, 98 N. Y. 109; People *v.* Marx, 99 N. Y. 377; Austin *v.* Murray, 33 Mass. (16 Pick.) 121; Watertown *v.* Mayo, 109 Mass. 315.

8. Williams *v.* Reg., 7 Q. B. N. S. 250.

9. Reg. *v.* Buchanan, 8 Q. B. N. S. 883; s. c., 10 Jur. 736; 15 L. J. Q. B. 227.

10. Territory *v.* Baca, 2 New Mex. 183; Territory *v.* Tafoya, 2 New Mex. 191.

11. Wheeler *v.* State (Miss. March, 1887), 1 South. Rep. 632.

A person charged with an offence under a statute which is ealed before time of trial, must not be put upon his trial.[1]

A statute covering the entire ground of a previous statute, estab-ing an entirely different system, repeals the previous statute.[2]

. *What Acts are Felonies.* — Forgery of an indorsement on a k check is a felony.[3]

Stealing cotton not severed from the soil is in South Carolina lony.[4] But it has been held that it was not a felony where a ty bought cotton of a firm which stored it in a certain house, and, emoving it, carried off cotton belonging to the firm from another se, openly and under claim of right, as a part of the trade.[5]

n the absence of statutory definition, offences are felonies which e such at common law.[6] Under the common law, felony com-ed every species of crime which resulted in forfeiture of either ds or goods, or both, and to which capital or other punishment ht be added.[7] At common law, a felony was an atrocious ne, while faults and omissions less than atrocious were termed demeanors.[8]

One present aiding and abetting in the commission of a felony, y be convicted on an indictment charging him directly with nmitting the felony.[9]

The court has no jurisdiction over a prosecution for felony begun affidavit and information filed during its vacation.[10]

. *Misdemeanors.* — *a. Generally.* — The word "crime" is prop-y applicable both to a felony and to a misdemeanor.[11]

That which is declared by statute to be a misdemeanor, cannot a felony.[12]

And where an act is prohibited by law, but no penalty is pro-ed, the doing of the act cannot be punished as a misdemeanor.[13]

. *Misdemeanors defined.* — Misdemeanors are such public of-ces as are penal at common law, or are made penal by statute.[14]

A misdemeanor is a crime, either of commission or omission, which punishment other than death or imprisonment in the te prison is awarded: it is an offence less than felony.[15]

Anonymous, 2 Lewin, C. C. 22.
Stebbins v. State (Tex. App. Octo-1886), 2 S. W. Rep. 617.
Hawthorn v. State, 56 Md. 530.
State v. Washington (S. C. June,), 2 S. E. Rep. 623.
Newton Mfg. Co. v. White, 63 Ga.

State v. Dineen, 10 Minn. 407; Ward eople, 3 Hill (N. Y.), 395.
1 Arch. Cr. Pr. 1; 4 Bl. Com. 94, 95; h. C. L. (6th ed.) 614; 1 Whart. Cr. L. ed.) § 22; 1 Russ. Cr. (9th ed.) 78.
4 Bl. Com. 6; 2 East, P. C. 5, 21; 1 . Cr. L. (6th ed.) 608.
State v. Kirk, 10 Or. 505. See "Aid-and Abettors," 1 Am. & Eng. Ency. of 53.

10. Hoover v. State, 110 Ind. 349; s. c., 9 West. Rep. 86; 11 N. E. Rep. 434.
11. Lehigh Co. v. Schock, 113 Pa. St. 373; s. c., 4 Cent. Rep. 744.
12. Rex v. Walford, 5 Esp. 62.
13. State v. Gaunt, 13 Or. 115.
14. 4 Bl. Com. 65; 1 Russ. Cr. (9th ed.) 78; 1 Whart. Cr. L. (8th ed.) § 24.
15. People v. War, 20 Cal. 117; Pillsbury v. Brown, 47 Cal. 477; Hall v. State, 3 Ga. 21; State v. Rohfrischt, 12 La. An. 382; State v. Dewer, 65 N. C. 572; Welsh v. State, 3 Tex. App. 114; State v. Rowe, 8 Rich. (S. C.) L. 17; Barker v. Commonwealth, 2 Va. Cas. 122. See 4 Bl. Com. 65; 1 Arch. Cr. Pr. 2; 1 Whart. Cr. L. (8th ed.) § 24; 1 Russ. Cr. (9th ed.) 78; 1 Bish. Cr. L. (6th ed.) § 623.

Misdemeanors are either *mala in se*, or penal at common law, and such as are *mala prohibita*, or penal by statute. Those *mala in se* are such as mischievously affect the person or property of another, or outrage decency, disturb the peace, injure public morals, or are breaches of public duty.[1] Thus, it is no crime to make use of false pretences, unless, by means of such pretences, the party making them obtains money or property from another to which he has no right. The crime is consummated only where money or property is received.[2]

c. Statutory Misdemeanors.—The federal and State statutes declare what shall be accounted and punished as misdemeanors.[3]

1. State *v.* Appling, 25 Mo. 315; State *v.* Craighead, 32 Mo. 561; State *v.* Boll, 59 Mo. 321. See 1 Russ. Cr. (9th ed.) 73; 1 Whart. Cr. L. (8th ed.) § 24.

Trespass. — Misdemeanors include trespass. United States *v.* Flanakin, Hempst. C. C. 30.

Offences against the Post-Office Laws are misdemeanors, not felonies. United States *v.* Lancaster, 2 McL. C. C. 431.

2. State *v.* Shaeffer, 89 Mo. 271; s. c., 5 West. Rep. 465; People *v.* Sutty, 5 Park. Cr. Rep. (N. Y.) 142.

False Pretences.—It is no crime to make use of false pretences, unless, by means of such pretences, the party making them obtains money or property from another to which he had no right. And the crime is consummated where the money or property is received. Commonwealth *v.* Van Tuyl, 1 Met. (Ky.) 1; State *v.* House, 55 Iowa, 466; Stewart *v.* Jessup, 51 Ind. 415.

In Stewart *v.* Jessup, *supra*, the substantial fact was, that one Kerr, relying upon false representations of Stewart, sold the latter twelve horses which Kerr had shipped to New York, where Stewart got possession of them. Stewart was arrested in Indiana on the charge of obtaining the horses by false pretences, and, on a preliminary examination before a justice of the peace, was adjudged guilty, and required to give security in the sum of three thousand dollars for his appearance in the circuit court to answer the charge. Stewart, not having given the security, was committed to jail, and, upon a writ of *habeas corpus*, was brought before the circuit court of Hamilton County, was remanded, and appealed to the Supreme Court of the State, from the judgment of the circuit court against him. The Supreme Court reversed the judgment, holding that the crime was not committed in Indiana, where the false representations were made, but in the State of New York, where the property was received.

In Norris *v.* State, 25 Ohio St. 217, the defendant was a resident of Clark County; and by fraudulent representations as to his solvency, contained in a letter, he induced the Akron Sewer Pipe Company, located in Summit County, to ship him by rail, to Clark County, a lot of sewer pipe. He was indicted in Clark County, but the Supreme Court held that the crime was committed in Summit County, and remarked that "the weight of authority is clear that the railroad company was the agent of defendant for receiving the goods at Akron, and carrying them to Springfield; and the delivery to it by the sewer-pipe company was in legal contemplation a delivery of the goods to the defendant at Akron."

When the defendant was indicted for obtaining by false pretences a lot of mules, and the question was whether he had received the mules in Randolph County or in the city of St. Louis, in delivering the opinion of the court, *Judge Norton* said, "It is, however, earnestly insisted by counsel, that, if any offence was committed, the evidence shows that it was committed in the city of St. Louis, and not in Randolph County; and that the demurrer to the evidence should have been sustained, on the ground that the Moberly Court of Common Pleas of Randolph County had no jurisdiction. If the premises assumed be well founded, the legal conclusion drawn from them is undoubtedly correct." The judgment was affirmed, the majority of the court holding that the mules were received by defendant in Randolph County. State *v.* Dennis, 80 Mo. 594.

3. **Federal Statutes.** — By § 3954. United States Rev. Stat., it is made a misdemeanor for the bidder for a mail contract to refuse to enter into the contract and perform the contract service. Oregon Steamship Co. *v.* Otis, 100 N. Y. 446; s. c., 1 Cent. Rep. 734, note.

Missouri Statute. — Any person who shall cruelly mistreat a domestic animal, is deemed guilty of misdemeanor under Missouri Revised Statutes § 1609. Evidence that defendant struck an animal in a cruel manner, and killed it, will support a conviction, although he did not intend to kill

Under a statute declaring that if one voluntarily, before prose... ...tion, within a reasonable time, returns property which he has ...olen, the offence is reduced to a misdemeanor; the return may ... voluntary if induced by repentance, although fear of punish... ...ent may also constitute a motive; the return must be actual, not ...nstructive, and all the property unchanged in form must be ...turned.[1]

Upon an indictment for a misdemeanor, it is no ground for ...quittal that the evidence necessary to prove the misdemeanor ...so shews it is part of a felony, and that the felony has been ...mpleted.[2]

(1) *City Ordinances.* — Misdemeanors and offence under ordi... ...nce of city is not the same as offence under statute.[3]

(a) *An Ordinance making it a Misdemeanor* to carry on business ... real-estate agent without license, will not prevent enforcement ... contract between unlicensed agent and vendor.[4]

(b) *Suppressing Bawdy Houses.* — A city has power under its ...arter to pass an ordinance to suppress and prohibit bawdy houses, ...d prescribes a punishment for its violation. It is no objection ... such an ordinance that the act prohibited is criminal in its ...ture, or that it is a crime under the general laws of the State.[5]

5. *Misprision of Felony.*[6] — Misprision of felony is having ...owledge that a felony has been committed, or is about to be ...mmitted, and concealing such knowledge, or procuring the con... ...alment thereof.[7] Mere silence or approval of an act after its ...mmission, cannot be held to "countenance" it.[8] Mere knowl... ...ge that a murder is to be committed, but not being present, or ...couraging its perpetration, does not render one an accomplice.[9]

... State v. Hackfath, 20 Mo. App. 614; ..., 2 West. Rep. 588.

New York Statute. — An owner of a ...ating-rink refusing to sell tickets to a ...ored person, is guilty of a misdemeanor ...der the New York Penal Code, § 383. ...ople v. King, 42 Hun (N. Y.), 186.

Ohio Statute. — Under the Ohio statute ... April 5, 1866, supplying liquor to a ...nor, to be drank by him, is a misde... ...meanor; and so also is furnishing liquor ... a minor, although it may have been pur... ...chased by another, and supplied by the ...ler to the minor, in pursuance of such ...rchase. State v. Munson, 25 Ohio St. ...

2. Bird v. State, 16 Tex. App. 525.
3. Reg. v. Button, 3 Cox, C. C. 229.
4. Ex parte Schmidt, 24 S. C. 363.
5. Prince v. Eighth-street Baptist Church, ... Mo. App. 332; s. c., 2 West. Rep. ...
6. Wong v. Astoria, 13 Or. 538.
7. Misprision. — A misprision is the con... ...ment of a crime, and is used to signify ...y considerable misdemeanor which has not a specific name given to it by law. See 3 Coke, Inst. 36.

It is said to be the duty of every good citizen, who has knowledge that treason or a felony has been committed, to make known such fact to the proper officers of the law; and that silently to observe the commission of a felony, without using any endeavors to apprehend the offender, is a misprision. See 1 Bish. Cr. L. § 720; 4 Bl. Comm. 119; Hawk. P. C. ch. 59, § 6; 1 Russ. Cr. 43.

Kinds of Misprision. — Misprision may consist in the mere concealment of something which should be made known to the officers of the law, and is called negative misprision; or it may consist in the doing of an act which should not be done, and is then positive misprision. 4 Bl. Comm. ch. 9.

7. Connaughty v. State, 1 Wis. 159, 165; s. c., 60 Am. Dec. 370; Reg. v. Daly, 9 Car. & P. 342; 1 Bish. Cr. L. (6th ed.) sec. 604; 1 Russ. Cr. (9th ed.) 194; 1 Hale, P. C. 374, 618, 708; 4 Bl. Com. 121.

8. Cooper v. Johnson, 81 Mo. 483.

9. Melton v. State, 43 Ark. 367.

But one, knowing that a crime has been determined on, who keeps away from the spot to facilitate the same, is a principal, though not near enough to aid manually, as where the foreman of a railway was held guilty of larceny of cotton from a freight depot.[1]

Where knowledge of the commission of an offence, and intent to shield from the law, is declared criminal, an indictment must charge knowledge, or it will be bad.[2]

6. *Compounding Offences.* — *a. Generally.* — Entering into a agreement with a person charged with a crime for a valuable consideration, or where any peculiar advantage is thereby gained, not to prosecute, or to put an end to the prosecution of an action already brought, is compounding the offence.[3]

To constitute the crime of compounding a criminal prosecution, the State need not show that a crime had actually been committed by the person prosecuted.[4]

And it is not necessary that the principal offender should be convicted to sustain an indictment for compounding.[5]

The bare taking of one's goods back, or receiving reparation, is not compounding the offence[6] in the absence of any agreement that the offender is not to be prosecuted.[7]

Neither is a simple failure to prosecute for an assault with intent to kill.[8]

And it seems that the loaning of money to a forger, by the person whose name has been forged, for the purpose of paying and taking up the forged paper, is not a compounding of the felony.[9]

After compounding, the compounder having prosecuted the felon to conviction, he is entitled to an acquittal for the compounding.[10]

An officer being privy to a crime, and accepting any thing as a consideration for his official conduct, is guilty: any attempt to thwart justice by suppressing evidence is unlawful.[11]

In case of a prosecution for compounding a crime, and agreeing to withhold evidence, the acquittal of the principal offender is not competent evidence for the defence.[12]

The record of conviction of a felony is *prima facie*, but not conclusive as against the compounder.[13]

1. State *v.* Poynier, 36 La. An. 572.
2. State *v.* Davis, 14 R. I. 281.
3. State *v.* Duhammel, 2 Harr. (Del.) 532. See also 1 Bish. Cr. L. (6th ed.) sec. 604; 2 Arch. Cr. Pr. 1065; 2 Whart. Cr. L. (8th ed.) sec. 1559; 4 Bl. Com. 133; 1 Russ. Cr. (9th ed.) 194; 1 Hawk. chap. 59, sec. 5.
4. Fribly *v.* State, 42 Ohio St. 205. See Adam *v.* State, 31 Ohio St. 462.
5. People *v.* Buckland, 13 Wend. (N. Y.) 593; State *v.* Dandy, 1 Brev (S. C.) L. 395.
6. Plumer *v.* Smith, 5 N. H. 553; s. c., 22 Am. Dec. 478; Reg. *v.* Stone, 4 Car. & P. 379. See 1 Hawk. ch. 59, § 7.
7. 1 Chitt. Cr. L. 4; Hale, P. C. 546.
8. Phillips *v.* Kelly, 29 Ala. 628.
9. *In re* Mapleback, L. R. 4 Ch. Div. 150; s. c., 19 Moak's Eng. Rep. 735.
10. Reg. *v.* Stone, 4 Car. & P. 379. People *v.* Buckland, 13 Wend. (N. Y.) 592; State *v.* Dandy, 1 Brev. (S. C.) L. 395.
11. Plumer *v.* Smith, 5 N. H. 553; s. c., 22 Am. Dec. 478; Collins *v.* Blantern, 2 Wils. 341; State *v.* Henning, 33 Ind. 189. See also Desty, Am. Cr. L. p. 18.
12. People *v.* Buckland, 13 Wend. (N. Y.) 592.
13. State *v.* Duhammel, 2 Harr. (Del.) 532; State *v.* Williams, 2 Harr. (Del.) 532.

2. Compounding a Felony. — Compounding a felony is an offence unishable by fine and imprisonment,[1] and at common law the erson committing it was regarded as an accessory.[2] In the nited States, the offence of compounding a felony is indictable;[3] nd no action can be maintained on any contract into which uch offence enters as the consideration in whole or in part.[4] A

1. 1 Bouv. L. Dict. (15th ed.) 353; 18 lis. ch. 5.

2. Hawk. P. C. 125.

3. Commonwealth v. Pease, 16 Mass. 1; People v. Buckland, 13 Wend. (N. Y.) 1.

"Theft bote." — "Theft bote" is where e robbed not only knows the felon, but so agrees to take his goods again, or to ccept other amends upon the condition at he will not prosecute. 1 Hale, P. C. 9.

Accepting a promissory note, by a party ilty of a larceny, as a consideration for t prosecuting, is sufficient to constitute e compounding of a felony. Commonealth v. Pease, 16 Mass. 91.

4. Jones v. Rice, 35 Mass. (18 Pick.) 0; Swood v. Commonwealth, 6 Dana Ky.) 318; Plumer v. Smith, 5 N. H. 3; Vose v. Summers, 5 N. J. L. (2 outh.) 578; Mattocks v. Owen, 5 Vt. 42; inesburgh v. Sumner, 9 Vt. 23.

Receipt in Full. — Thus, a receipt in full f all demands given in consideration of an greement not to prosecute a criminal acon, is void. Bailey v. Buck, 11 Vt. 252.

Agreement to pay Money. — Where a erson was indicted for maintaining a pubc nuisance on his premises, and entered to an agreement with the prosecutor to y him a certain sum of money, in connsideration of which the prosecutor was to op the prosecution on the indictment, and ch the plaintiff's land, the court *held* at the agreement to stop the prosecution as illegal, and rendered the entire conact void. Lindsay v. Smith, 78 N. C. 328; c., 24 Am. Rep. 463. See also Garner Qualls, 4 Jones (N. C.), L. 223.

Giving Note to stifle Prosecution. — here a promissory note is given to stifle criminal prosecution, it is void. Thus, here a note was given to one who had en robbed, in consideration that he would tition the court to mitigate the punishent of the felon, it was held to be void. uch v. First Nat. Bank, 27 Mich. 293; c., 15 Am. Rep. 189.

But where a clerk in a post-office emzzled funds, for which the postmaster as liable to the government, and to secure imself the postmaster induced the clerk give him a note with security, at the me time agreeing not to prosecute him iminally for the embezzlement, upon a suit ereon the court *held* that the note was valid and the surety liable. Bibb v. Hitchcock, 49 Ala. 468; s. c., 20 Am. Rep. 288. The court said, that, if the postmaster was bound to make good the amount of the clerk's embezzlement, then he stood in the attitude of surety for such clerk, and that the clerk would be bound to refund to him the amount he would be forced to pay on account of the embezzlement; that the giving of the note by the clerk showed that he accepted the payment which the postmaster had made for him, and that this would establish the relation of debtor and creditor between them, citing Ross v. Pearson, 21 Ala. 473. The court also *held*, that, inasmuch as the note was valid and binding upon the clerk as principal, it would also be binding upon his surety. 2 Kent. Comm. 468; Howe v. Synge, 15 East, 440.

The decision of Bibb v. Hitchcock, *supra*, is open to serious doubt. It is evident that the agreement not to prosecute criminally, was in fact, at least, a part of the consideration for which the note was given; and a note, part of the consideration for which is an agreement not to prosecute criminally, being against public policy, is void, — Brown v. Padgett, 36 Ga. 609; Murphy v. Bottomer, 40 Mo. 67, — even in the hands of an innocent holder for value. Smith v. Richards, 29 Conn. 232; Brown v. Padgett, 36 Ga. 609; Swan v. Chandler, 8 B. Mon. (Ky.) 97; Commonwealth v. Johnson, 57 Mass. (3 Cush.) 454; Clark v. Pomeroy, 86 Mass. (4 Allen) 534; Murphy v. Bottomer, 40 Mo. 67; Plumer v. Smith, 5 N. H. 553; Hinds v. Chamberlain, 6 N. H. 225; Porter v. Havens, 37 Barb. (N. Y.) 343; Oakford v. Johnson, 2 Miles (Pa.), 203; Jackson v. Polack, 2 Miles (Pa.), 362; Dickson v. Primrose, 2 Miles (Pa.), 366; Bell v. State, 1 Bay (S. C.), 249; Corley v. Williams, 1 Bailey (S. C.), 588; Hinesburgh v. Sumner, 9 Vt. 23; Bowen v. Buck, 28 Vt. 308.

Note after Conviction on Suggestion by Court. — But it seems that where a promissory note is given after trial and conviction for a misdemeanor, and before sentence, in pursuance of a recommendation by the court to compromise the matter, it is valid. Kirk v. Strickwond, 1 Nev. & M. 275; Beeley v. Wingfield, 11 East, 46; Edgecombe v. Rodd, 5 East, 294; s. c., reported in 1 Smith, 515.

Note and Mortgage. — And the same is true of notes secured by mortgage; the original contract being void, the mortgage person cannot take care of his private interest by depriving the State of a witness or an active prosecutor, which is the means relied on for the conviction of offenders: much less can he pollute the very fountain of criminal justice by suppressing an indictment already instituted against him.[1]

c. Compounding a Misdemeanor. — Compounding a misdemeanor, being also a perversion or defeating of public justice, is in like manner an indictable offence at common law.[2]

securing it is also void. See Henderson *v.* Palmer, 71 Ill. 579; s. c., 22 Am. Rep. 117; Peed *v.* McKee, 42 Iowa, 689; s. c., 20 Am. Rep. 631; Catlin *v.* Henton, 9 Wis. 476; Reg. *v.* Daly, 9 Carr. & P. 342.

Agreement to use "Influence." — Where a person was indicted and convicted of robbery, and in consideration that a person would use his influence with, or petition, the court to mitigate the sentence, executed to such person his promissory note it was held that the contract was void. Buck *v.* First Nat. Bank, 27 Mich. 293; s. c., 15 Am. Rep. 189.

The court say, "It may be proper to remark, that, even as to such petitions, any promise to pay money in consideration of signing the same, or of the employment of solicitations, to influence or secure official action in any form whatever, other than by the use of open and legitimate evidence or argument, would be entirely without consideration, because opposed to public policy. This has been so often decided, and under such a variety of circumstances, that we content ourselves with a reference to a few of the reported cases," citing Pingry *v.* Washburn, 1 Aik. (Vt.) 264; Clippenger *v.* Hepbaugh, 1 Watts & S. (Pa.) 315; Hatzfield *v.* Gulden, 7 Watts (Pa.) 152; Fuller *v.* Dame, 35 Mass. (18 Pick.) 472; Wood *v.* McCann, 6 Dana (Ky.), 366; Marshall *v.* Baltimore & O. R. R. Co., 57 U. S. (16 How.) 314; bk. 14, L. ed. 953; Harris *v.* Roof, 10 Barb. (N. Y.) 489; Frost *v.* Belmont, 88 Mass. (6 Allen) 152; Sedgwick *v.* Stanton, 14 N. Y. 289; Frankfort *v.* Winterport, 54 Me. 250; Martin *v.* Wade, 37 Cal. 168.

1. Lindlay *v.* Smith, 78 N. C. 328; s. c., 24 Am Rep. 463; Thompson *v.* Whitman, 4 Jones (N. C.) L. 47; Ingram *v.* Ingram, 4 Jones (N. C.) L. 188; Blythe *v.* Lovinggood, 2 Ired. (N. C.) L 20.

Power of Individuals to compromise Offences. — The Supreme Court of Massachusetts in Jones *v.* Rice, 35 Mass. (18 Pick.) 440, say, "We do not think that such a power is vested in individuals. It would enable them to use the claim of the government for their own emolument, and greatly to the oppression of the people. It has a direct tendency to obstruct the course of the administration of justice, and the mischief extends, we think, as well to misdemeanors as to felonies." 1 Russ. on Cr. 210; Edgecombe *v.* Rodd, 5 East, 301; s. c., 1 Smith, 515.

2. Jones *v.* Rice, 35 Mass. (18 Pick.) 440; Edgecombe *v.* Rodd, 5 East, 301; Elworthy *v.* Bird, 2 Bing. 258; 1 Russ. Cr. 258. See Westmeath *v.* Westmeath, 1 Jac. Rep. 126; 4 Bl. Com 134, note by Christian.

Permitting Reference. — But in some cases of public offences which have more immediately injured a private individual or individuals, such as assaults and batteries, libels, and the like, if the public remedy by prosecution be adopted, the court will sometimes permit a reference. Baker *v.* Townshend, 1 J. B. Moore, 120; s. c., 7 Taunt. 442; Blanchard *v.* Lilly, 9 East, 497; Rex *v.* Moate, 3 Barn. & Adol. 237.

"Speaking" to Prosecutor. — And the court will sometimes allow the defendant, even after conviction, to "speak" (as it is termed) with the prosecutor before any judgment is pronounced; and a trivial punishment will be inflicted, if, as a result of such "speaking," the prosecutor declare himself satisfied; that is, if an adequate apology or compensation has been made. Baker *v.* Townshend, 1 J. B. Moore, 120; Elworthy *v.* Bird, 2 Sim. & Stu. 372; Gurford *v.* Daley, 1 Dow. N. S. 519; 4 Bl. Comm. 363, 364.

Compromising Bastardy Suit. — A contract or note to compound a private misdemeanor, such as a suit for slander or bastardy proceedings, is good. Wallridge *v.* Arnold, 21 Conn. 434; Merrill *v.* Fleming, 42 Ala. 234; Clark *v.* Riker, 14 N. H. 44; Beeley *v.* Wingfield, 11 East, 46; Kirk *v.* Strickwood, 4 B. & Ad. 421; Baker *v.* Townshend, 1 J. B. Moore, 120; Bell *v.* Wood, 1 Bay (S. C.) L. 249; Cameron *v.* McFarland, 2 Car. Law Repos. 415; Corley *v.* Williams, 1 Bail. (S. C.) L. 588; Ford *v.* Cratty, 52 Ill. 313; Keir *v.* Leeman, 6 Q. B. 308; Burgen *v.* Straughan, 7 J. J. Marsh. (Ky.) 583; Hays *v.* McFarlan, 32 Ga. 699; Weaver *v.* Waterman, 18 La. An. 241; Howe *v.* Litchfield, 85 Mass. (3 Allen) 443; Rice *v.* Maxwell, 21 Miss. (3 Smed. & M.) 289; Stephens *v.* Spiers, 25 Mo. 386; Sharp *v.* Teese, 9 N. J. L. (4 Halst.) 352; Payne *v.* Eden, 3 Cai. (N. Y.) 212; Maxwell *v.* Campbell, 8 Ohio St. 265; Knight *v.* Priest, *l. When Offences may be compounded.* — The law will permit : compromise of any offence, although made the subject of minal prosecution. Where the party injured might recover dam- :s in an action for the offence,[1] and there is no attempt to sup- ss the prosecution, it may be compromised.[2]

. When Offences may not be compounded. — Where the offence of a public nature, no agreement can be valid that is founded the consideration of stifling a prosecution for it.[3]

Thus, where, by a misdemeanor, injury is done to the commu- y at large, it cannot be compromised.[4] And an offence which the discretion of the court may be punished by imprisonment in : penitentiary, cannot be compromised.[5]

No person can compromise a felony or criminal charge, where : offender is under arrest, or otherwise held to answer.[6]

III. Attempts.[7] — 1. *Definition.* — An attempt is an endeavor to :omplish an object or purpose. In criminal law, an attempt is endeavor to accomplish a crime carried beyond the mere eparation, but falling short of the execution of the ultimate sign, or any part of it.[8]

An attempt to commit an offence is an intent to do a wrongful :, coupled with an overt act, toward its commission. The so- itation of another to commit an offence is an attempt to commit : crime. And an attempt may be made to commit more than e offence at the same time.[9]

To constitute an attempt, there must be an intent to commit ne act which would be indictable, if done, because of its nature, the probable consequences.[10] And the act must be apparently

. 507; Robinson v. Crenshaw, 2 Stew. . (Ala.) 276.

ut in Massachusetts an action will not on an agreement entered into for the pose of compounding any misdemeanor, ss it appears that satisfaction has been nowledged in and approved by the court which the prosecution was pending, ording to General Statutes 1875. Par- ge v. Hood, 120 Mass. 403; s. c., 21 Am. . 524.

Keir v. Leeman, 6 Q. B. 308.

Stancel v. State, 50 Ga. 155.

Keir v. Leeman, 6 Q. B. 308; s. c., 9 B. 371; 1 Benn. & H. Lead. Cr. Cas. .

Dwight v. Ellsworth, 9 Up. Can. Q. B. Rex v. Hardy, 14 Q. B. 529; Beeley Wingfield, 11 East, 46; Baker v. Town- , 7 Taunt. 422.

Chandler v. Johnson, 39 Ga. 85; Peo- v. Lyon, 99 N. Y. 210; reversing s. c., Hun (N. Y.), 623.

Saxon v. Conger, 6 Oreg. 388; Ivin- v. Pease, 1 Wyom. Tr. 277; Keir v. man, 6 Q. B. N. S. 308. See also 2 Cr. Cas. 216.

See ante, CRIMINAL CONSPIRACY.

8. Commonwealth v. McDonald, 59 Mass. (5 Cush.) 365.

To attempt to make an effort to effect some object, to make a trial or experiment, to endeavor, to use exertion for some purpose. A man may make an attempt, an effort, a trial, to steal, by breaking open a trunk, and be disappointed in not finding the object of his pursuit, and so not steal in fact. So a man may make an attempt, an experiment, to pick a pocket, by thrusting his hand into it, and not succeed because there happens to be nothing in the pocket. Still, he has clearly made an attempt, and done the act towards the commission of the offence. Commonwealth v. McDonald, 59 Mass. (5 Cush.) 365; Josslyn v. Commonwealth, 47 Mass. (6 Metc.) 236; People v. Bush, 4 Hill (N. Y.), 133; Rogers v. Commonwealth, 5 Serg. & R. (Pa.) 463; King v. Higgins, 2 East, 5.

9. Rex v. Fuller, 1 Bos. & P. 180.

10. Moore v. State, 18 Ala. 532; State v. Jefferson, 3 Harr. (Del.) 571; People v. Shaw, 1 Park. Cr. Cas. (N. Y.) 327; Davidson v. State, 9 Humph. (Tenn.) 455; Regina v. Cruse, 8 Car. & P. 541;

adapted to produce the result intended.[1] Some authorities say a "complete adaption."[2]

Any act done by the prisoner immediately and directly tending to the execution of the principal crime, where the act is done under such circumstances that he has the power of carrying his intention into execution, is an attempt.[3]

To assault, with intent to commit a higher crime, is a crime.[4] And whatever is punishable in its consummation, is punishable in its attempt;[5] as, to commit larceny,[6] or to bribe,[7] and, at common law, to commit suicide;[8] but with the latter it is otherwise under the statute.[9]

An attempt to commit a felony is punishable at common law as a misdemeanor.[10] And, although an attempt to commit a crime is unsuccessful, it is a misdemeanor;[11] as, to bribe,[12] to commit larceny,[13] or to steal cattle.[14]

s. c., 1 Crawf. & D. 156; 1 Bish. Cr. L. § 731.

1. Kunkle *v.* State, 52 Ind. 220; Commonwealth *v.* McDonald, 59 Mass. (5 Cush.) 365; Henry *v.* State, 18 Ohio, 32; State *v.* Rawles, 65 N. C. 334; United States *v.* Morrow, 4 Wash. C. C. 733; Rex *v.* Coe, 6 Car. & P. 403; Regina *v.* Leddington, 9 Car. & P. 79; Regina *v.* St. George, 9 Car. & P. 483; King *v.* Parfait, 1 Leach, 19.

2. 1 Bish. Cr. L. 749.

3. Regina *v.* Taylor, 1 Fost. & F. 511.

This includes solicitations of another. State *v.* Shepard, 7 Conn. 54, 266; People *v.* Bush, 4 Hill (N. Y.), 133; Commonwealth *v.* Harrington, 20 Mass. (3 Pick.) 26; United States *v.* Mitchell, 2 U. S. (2 Dall.) 384; bk. 1, L. ed. 410.

4. Hayes *v.* State, 15 Lea (Tenn.), 64.

5. Berdeaux *v.* Davis, 58 Ala. 611; State *v.* Danforth, 3 Conn. 112, Demarest *v.* Haring, 6 Cow. (N. Y.) 76; Griffin *v.* State, 26 Ga. 493, State *v.* Maner, 2 Hill (S. C.), 453; State *v.* Boyden, 13 Ired. (N. C.) L. 505; People *v.* Washburn, 10 Johns. (N. Y.) 160; State *v.* Murray, 15 Me. 100; Commonwealth *v.* Barlow, 4 Mass. 439; Commonwealth *v* Kingsbury, 5 Mass. 106; Commonwealth *v.* Harrington, 20 Mass. (3 Pick.) 26; Hackett *v.* Commonwealth, 15 Pa. 95; Randolph *v.* Commonwealth, 6 Serg. & R. (Pa.) 398; State *v.* Keyes, 8 Vt. 57; Reg. *v.* Goff, 9 Up. Can. C. P. 438; Rex *v.* Higgins, 2 East, 5; Rex *v.* Phillips, 6 East, 464; Rex *v.* Kinnersley, 1 Strange, 193; Reg. *v.* Chapman, 2 Carr. & K. 846.

6. Simpson *v.* State, 59 Ala. 1; Berdeaux *v.* Davis, 58 Ala. 611; Commonwealth *v.* Barlow, 4 Mass. 439; Nicholson *v.* State, 9 Baxt. (Tenn.) 258; Miller *v.* State, 58 Ga. 200.

7. United States *v.* Worrall, 2 U. S. (2 Dall.) 384; bk. 1, L. ed. 426; People *v.* Bush, 4 Hill (N. Y.), 133; State *v.* Keyes, 8 Vt. 57; State *v.* Carpenter, 20 Vt. 9; State *v.* Biebusch, 32 Mo. 276.

8. Reg. *v.* Doody, 6 Cox, C. C. 463; Reg. *v.* Burgess, 9 Cox, C. C. 247.

9. Commonwealth *v.* Dennis, 105 Mass. 162.

10. Nicholson *v.* State (Tenn.), 6 Cent. L. J. 478.

One may be properly convicted of a misdemeanor for attempting to commit a felony. Reg. *v.* Bain, L. & C. 129; 9 Cox, C. C. 198; 31 L. J. M. C. 88; 8 Jur. N. S. 418; 10 W. R. 236.

11. State *v.* Danforth, 3 Conn. 112; Berdeaux *v.* Davis, 58 Ala. 611; Ross *v.* Commonwealth, 2 B. Mon. (Ky.) 417; Demarest *v.* Haring, 6 Cow. (N. Y.) 76; Griffin *v.* State, 26 Ga. 493; State *v.* Maner, 2 Hill (S. C.), 453; State *v.* Boyden, 13 Ired. (N. C.) L. 505; People *v.* Washburn, 10 Johns. (N. Y.) 160; State *v.* Murray, 15 Me. 100; Commonwealth *v.* Barlow, 4 Mass. 439; Commonwealth *v.* Kingsbury, 5 Mass. 106; State *v.* Jordan, 75 N. C. 27; Commonwealth *v.* Smith, 54 Pa. St. 209; Commonwealth *v.* Harrington, 20 Mass. (3 Pick.) 26; Hackett *v.* Commonwealth, 15 Pa. St. 95; State *v.* Keyes, 8 Vt. 57; Rex *v* Kinnersley, 1 Str. 196; Rex *v.* Higgins, 2 East, 5; Rex *v.* Phillips, 6 East, 464; Reg. *v.* Chapman, 2 Car. & K. 846; Reg. *v.* Goff, 9 Up. Can. C. P 438.

12. United States *v.* Worrall, 2 U. S. (2 Dall.) 384; bk. 1, L. ed. 426; People *v.* Bush, 4 Hill (N. Y.), 133; State *v.* Keyes, 8 Vt. 57; State *v.* Carpenter, 8 Vt. 9; State *v.* Biebusch, 32 Mo. 276.

13. Simpson *v.* State, 59 Ala. 1; Berdeaux *v.* Davis, 58 Ala. 611; Commonwealth *v.* Barlow, 4 Mass. 439. See 1 Whart. Cr. L. § 173.

14. Miller *v.* State, 58 Ga. 200.

he attempt to commit a felony can only be made out where, if interruption had taken place, the felony itself could have been ited;[1] as where one goes to a stack with the intention of set- fire to it, and lights a lucifer-match for that purpose, but ndons the attempt because he finds that he is watched.[2]

lerely delivering poison to a person, asking him to put it in spring of another person, is not "an attempt to administer ion"[3] under a statute providing a punishment for such an :mpt.

Vhen the attempt is to commit a felony, the responsibility fol- s the law of principal and accessory.[4]

f an attempt, when in process of its execution, is abandoned any cause, as from surprise, or the interruption or force of ers, such abandonment is no defence.[5]

Vhere two convicts determined to break out of prison together, deliberately supplied themselves with deadly weapons to kill one who resisted them, and the watchman was wilfully killed one while they were acting in concert, both were guilty of rder in the first degree; and one would be guilty of murder the first degree, although in fact he abandoned the attempt scape just before the fatal shot was fired by his companion, 1out informing his companion by word or act that he had aban- ed the attempt.[6]

Vhere one made a hole in the roof of a building with intent to er and steal, but was disturbed, he was properly convicted of a demeanor in attempting to commit a felony.[7]

Reg. v. Collins, Leigh & C. 471; s. c., , C. C. 497; 10 Jur. N. S. 686; L. J. . 177; 12 W. R. 886; 10 L. T. N. S.

proximate Act. — An act approximate commission of the intended crime is ly essential; as, renting a house for ses of prostitution, — Commonwealth rrington, 20 Mass. (3 Pick.) 26, — or ring indecent prints with intent to sh them, — Dugdale v. Reg., Dears. er procuring a die for coining, — v. Roberts, 7 Cox, C. C. 39; s. c., . 553, — or taking the impression of a with intent to commit larceny from ses. Griffin v. State, 26 Ga. 503. a subsequent attempt to accomplish same purpose by different means is ible to show intent. Lamb v. State ; 3 Cent. Rep. 774.

Reg. v. Taylor, 1 F. & F. 511; Reg. v. , 3 Cox, C. C. 186.

Thus, S., having a grievance against solicited N. to put poison in W.'s , so that the latter would be poi- , and offered him a reward for so . N. refused, and handed the pack- of poison back to S., but afterwards wed it in his pocket. *Held*, that S. could not be convicted of an attempt to commit murder by poisoning. Stabler v. Commonwealth, 95 Pa. St. 318; s. c., 40 Am. Rep. 653; 11 Cent. L. J. 404.

4. Collins v. State, 3 Heisk. (Tenn.) 14; Reg. v. Hapgood, L. R. 1 C. C. 221.

5. Goff v. Prime, 26 Ind. 196; Reg. v. McCann, 28 Up. Can. Q. B. 517; Stephens v. Myers, 4 Car. & P. 349; State v. McDaniel, 1 Winst. (N. C.) 249; Lewis v. State, 35 Ala. 380; State v. Elick, 7 Jones (N. C.) L. 68. See State v. Blair, 13 Rich. (S. C.) L. 93; Kelly v. Commonwealth, 1 Grant (Pa.) 484; Reg. v. Taylor, 1 Fost. & F. Cr. L. (8th ed.) sec. 187.

English Doctrine. — It is *held* in Reg. v. Taylor, 1 Fost. & F. 511, that an attempt is not the less an offence because the offender voluntarily desists — a proposition to which Sir James Stephens seems to allude with some dubiety, when observing, "This, however, rests upon the decision of a single judge." 3 Hist. Cr L. 44. And the case of R. v. Howarth, Moody, C. C. 207, seems to hold that the offender may at all events be arrested, though he give over his attempt and run away.

6. State v. Allen, 42 Conn. 121.

7. Reg. v. Bain, Leigh & C. 129; s. c.,

But there is no law in the United States for the punishment of the crime of an attempt to commit murder upon land in places within the exclusive jurisdiction of the Federal Government, unless committed by some means other than an assault with a dangerous weapon, as by poisoning, drowning, and the like.[1]

An attempt to commit a misdemeanor is itself a misdemeanor.[2]

Every step towards a misdemeanor, by an act done, is punishable as a misdemeanor;[3] but not every intention to commit a misdemeanor is a misdemeanor.[4] And this is so, whether the offence was created by statute, or was an offence at common law.[5]

When the attempt is to commit a misdemeanor, all participants are principals.[6]

An attempt to do a wrongful act, coupled with overt acts towards its commission, constitutes an attempt which is itself a crime. It may consist of words only, as in soliciting another to commit a crime.[7] But a mere effort, without any step taken towards its commission, is not an attempt.[8] Although an unlawful coincident intent to commit the offence is necessary, yet this may logically be deduced from the facts.[9] There must be a physical ability to complete the immediate offences,[10] but an apparent capacity is sufficient.[11]

9 Cox, C. C. 98; 8 Jur. N. S. 418; 31 L. J. M. C. 88; 10 W. R. 236.

1 United States v. Williams, 6 Sawy. C. C. 244; 2 Fed. Rep. 61; 9 Rep. 369.

The United States Revised Statutes, § 5346, is confined to attempts not made with a dangerous weapon.

2. Wolf v. State, 41 Ala. 412; Commonwealth v. Kingsbury, 5 Mass. 106; Smith v. Commonwealth, 54 Pa. St. 209; United States v Lyles, 4 Cr. C. C. 469; Rex v. Butler, 6 Car. & P. 368; Rex v. Martin, 9 Car. & P. 213, 215; s. c., 2 Moody, C. C. 123.

It is a misdemeanor the moment a man takes one necessary step towards the completion of a misdemeanor. Reg. v. Chapman, 2 C. & K. 846; s. c., 1 Den. C. C. 432; T. & M. 90; 18 L. J. M. C. 152; 15 Jur. 885.

A False Oath taken before a surrogate, and to obtain from him a license for a marriage, is punishable as a misdemeanor, although it is not alleged in the indictment, nor proved in evidence, that the marriage was in fact celebrated, and although the party found guilty was not the person about to be married. Reg. v. Chapman, 2 C. & K. 846; s c., 1 Den. C. C. 432; T. & M. 90; 18 L. J. M. C. 152; 13 Jur. 885.

3. Reg. v. Chapman, 2 C. & K. 846; s. c., 1 Den. C. C. 432; T. & M. 90; 18 L. J. M. C. 152; 13 Jur. 885.

4. Reg v. Martin, 9 Car. & P. 215; s. c., 2 Moody, C. C. 123.

5. Rex v. Roderick, 7 Car. & P. 795; Rex v. Cartwright, Russ. & R. C. C. 107; Rex v. Butler, 6 Car. & P. 368.

6. Commonwealth v. Fortune, 105 Mass. 592; Uhl v. Commonwealth, 6 Gratt. (Va.) 706; Reg. v. Wyatt, 39 L. J. M. C. 82; s. c., 18 W. R. 356; Reg. v. Hapgood, L. R. 1 C. C. 221.

7. McKay v. State, 44 Tex. 43; s. c., 1 Am. Cr. Rep. 51; People v. Lawton, 56 Barb. (N. Y.) 126; McDermott v. People, 5 Park. Cr. R. (N. Y.) 102. See 1 Russ Cr. (9th ed.) 83; 1 Whart. Cr. L. (8th ed.) § 173.

8. Cox v. People, 82 Ill. 191.

9. Reg. v Roberts, 7 Cox, C. C. 39; s c., Dears. 539; Reg. v. Ryan, 2 Moody & R 213; Reg. v. Lallement, 6 Cox, C. C 204; Reg. v. Donovan, 4 Cox, C. C. 399; Reg. v. Cheeseman, Leigh & C. 140; Griffin v. State, 26 Ga. 503; Commonwealth v. Harney, 51 Mass. (10 Met.) 422.

10. Reg. v. Phillips, 8 Car. & P. 736; Rex v. Eldershaw, 3 Car. & P. 396; Reg. v. Collins, Leigh & C. 471; s. c., 2 Lead. C C. 478; 9 Cox, C. C 49. See 1 Whart. Cr. L. (8th ed.) § 184.

Attempt to commit Rape. — So, a boy incapable of committing rape cannot be guilty of an attempt. Williams v. State, 14 Ohio, 222; State v. Handy, 4 Harr. (Del.) 566; People v. Randolph, 2 Parker, Cr. R. (N. Y.) 203; State v. Sam, Winst. (N. C.) L. 300; Rex v. Phillips, 8 Car. & P. 736; Rex v. Eldershaw, 8 Car. & P. 396. *Compare* Commonwealth v. Green, 19 Mass. (2 Pick.) 380; Smith v. State, 12 Ohio St. 466.

11. Lewis v. State, 35 Ala. 380; State v. Elick, 7 Jones (N. C.), L. 68.

2. *Attempts to commit Specific Offences.*—An attempt to bribe is an indictable offence, although not consummated.[1]

An attempt to commit a burglary may be established on proof of a breaking with intent to rob the house, without proof of an actual entry.[2]

It is a misdemeanor for a prisoner to attempt escape, and he may be indicted and punished therefor.[3]

And an unsuccessful rescue may be indicted as an attempt.[4]

Attempts to commit homicide are indictable.[5]

The overt act necessary to constitute an attempt to commit larceny must be such as would apparently naturally result in the commission of the crime.[6]

An attempt to produce a miscarriage[7] is indictable, though the woman was not pregnant at the time.[8] The fact that he used a substance which would not produce a miscarriage, is no defence, if he employed it with a criminal intent.[9]

In order to commit an assault with intent to commit a rape, the jury must be satisfied not only that the prisoner intended to gratify his passions on the person of the prosecutrix, but that he intended to do so at all events, and notwithstanding any resistance on her part.[10]

A person attempting to carnally know and abuse a girl of tender years, with her consent, is indictable for the attempt;[11] the same is true of an attempt to corrupt or intimidate a witness;[12] or to blackmail; or to extort money by threats of criminal prosecution;[13] or to obtain money from a county on a false bill.[14]

1. Walsh *v.* People, 65 Ill. 58; Hutchinson *v.* State, 36 Tex. 294. See Barefield *v.* State, 14 Ala. 603.

2. Reg. *v.* Spanner, 12 Cox, C. C. 155.

To maliciously enter a Storehouse, and attempt to steal any thing of the value of thirty five dollars or more, is an "attempt to commit a felony," within the meaning of sec. 6, tit. 1, chap. 4, of the Crimes Act. 74 Ohio L. 249; Griffin *v.* State, 34 Ohio St. 299.

An attempt to commit a burglary may be established on proof of a breaking with intent to rob the house, although there is no proof of an actual entry. Reg. *v.* Spanner, 12 Cox, C. C. 155.

3. People *v.* Rose, 12 Johns. (N. Y.) 339. See Luke *v.* State, 49 Ala. 30.

Attempt to escape.—However, an attempt to escape may at times be justifiable on the ground of necessity to save lives, as in case of a conflagration,—Shattuck *v.* State, 51 Miss. 575,—because an act done from necessity raises no presumption of intent,—Oliver *v.* State, 17 Ala. 587. See 4 Bl. Com. 28; 1 Hale, P. C. 43, 52; 1 Whart. Cr. L. (8th ed.) § 95; 1 Bish. Cr. L. (6th ed.) § 346;—but the necessity must in all cases be actual, imminent, and apparent.—Runyan *v.* State, 57 Ind. 80; s. c., 2 Am. Cr. R. 318; Erwin *v.* State, 29 Ohio St. 186; s. c., 2 Am. Cr. 251; Long *v.* State, 52 Miss. 23,—with no probability or possible means of escape.

4. See 2 Whart. Cr. L. (8th ed.) § 1680.

5. Desty's Am. Cr. L. § 123 a.

6. Sipple *v.* State, 46 N. J. L. (17 Vr.) 197.

7. Lamb *v.* State (Md.), 5 Cent. Rep. 774.

8. Commonwealth *v.* Wood, 77 Mass. (11 Gray) 86; Reg. *v.* Goodall, 2 Cox, C. C. 40. *Compare* State *v.* Howard, 32 Vt. 380.

9. State *v.* Owens, 22 Minn. 238.

10. Rex *v.* Lloyd, 7 C. & P. 318.

If Offence committed, Jury cannot find guilty of Attempt only.—On an indictment for an assault with intent to commit rape, if penetration is proved, the prisoner cannot be convicted of the attempt. Reg. *v.* Nicholls, 2 Cox, C. C. 182.

11. Reg. *v.* Martin, 9 Car. & P. 213; s. c., 2 M. C. C. 123; Reg. *v.* Johnson, Leigh & C. 632; s. c., 10 Cox, C. C. 114; Reg. *v.* Beale, 35 L. J. M. C. 60.

12. Cover *v.* Commonwealth (Pa.), 6 Cent. Rep. 585.

13. People *v.* Wightman, 104 N. Y. 598; s. c., 6 Cent. Rep. 657.

14. People *v.* Brage, 10 Abb. (N. Y.) New Cas. 300.

An attempt to commit the offence of sodomy is indictable at common law, as well as assaults with intent to commit it.[1]

To attempt to obtain property by false pretences is criminal, although defendant failed in his effort.[2]

3. *Preparations.* — Mere preparations are not indictable as attempts.[3] So, where one purchased spirituous liquors with intent to introduce it into prohibited territory, it is not sufficient to constitute an attempt to introduce it in violation of law.[4] So, buying a gun is not an attempt to commit murder,[5] nor is buying a box of matches an attempt to set fire to a stack of corn;[6] nor

1. Rex *v* Rowed, 3 Q. B. 180; Reg. *v.* Lock, L. R. 2 C. C. 12; Reg. *v.* Eaton, 8 Car. & P. 417.

Attempts to commit Sodomy. — In Iowa it is held to be a common-law offence, — Estes *v.* Carter, 10 Iowa, 100, — but the Texas Code makes no provision for punishing and attempting to commit it. Commonwealth *v.* Goodhue, 43 Mass. (2 Metc.) 193.

2. State *v.* Decker, 36 Kan. 717; 14 Pac. Rep. 283.

One going into a Pawnbroker's for a loan, representing his pledge as silver when in fact it was base metal, is guilty of an attempt to commit the statutory misdemeanor of obtaining money under false pretences. Reg. *v.* Ball, 1 Carr. & M. 249.

Where a man went to a pawnbroker's shop, and laid down eleven thimbles on the counter, saying, "I want 5 s. for them," and the pawnbroker's assistant asked the man if they were silver, and he said they were, and the assistant tested them, and found them not to be silver, and he gave the man no money, but sent for a policeman and gave him in custody, it was *held* that the conduct of the man who presented the thimbles amounted to an attempt to commit the offence of obtaining money by false pretences. Reg. *v.* Ball, 1 Carr. & M. 249.

An Employee in a Tannery clandestinely removed certain skins of leather from the warehouse to another part of the tannery, for the purpose of delivering them to the foreman and getting paid for them as if they had been his own work: it was *held* that this amounted to an attempt to commit the misdemeanor of obtaining money by false pretences. Reg. *v.* Holloway, 1 Den. C. C. 370; s. c., T. & M. 48; 3 New Sess. Cas. 410; 2 C. & K. 942; 18 L. J. Moody, C. C. 60; 13 Jur. 86.

When Prosecutor knows Pretences are False. — The prisoner wrote a begging letter to the prosecutor, in which, by certain false statements, he attempted to obtain money. The prosecutor sent the prisoner five shillings, but stated at the trial that he knew the pretences were false. It was *held* that the prisoner might be convicted of an attempt to obtain money by false pretences. Reg. *v.* Hensler, 11 Cox, C. C. 570; s. c., 22 L. T. 691; 19 W. R. 108.

3. Brockway *v.* People, 2 Hill (N. Y.), 558; People *v.* Lawton, 56 Barb. (N. Y.) 126; Commonwealth *v.* Morse, 2 Mass. 138; Cunningham *v.* State, 49 Miss. 685; Randolph *v.* Commonwealth, 6 Serg. & R. (Pa.) 398; Commonwealth *v.* Clark, 6 Gratt. (Va.) 675; Commonwealth *v.* Newell, 7 Mass. 245; Cassels *v.* State, 4 Yerg. (Tenn.) 149; Reg. *v.* Woodrow, 15 Mees. & W. 404; Rex *v.* Meredith, Russ. & R. C. C. 46; Rex *v.* Heath, Russ. & R. 184; Reg. *v.* Eagleton, Dears. C. C. 515; Reg. *v.* Cheeseman, 9 Cox, C. C. 103.

Mere Preparations. — Herr Geyser, an eminent German jurist, has devoted a great deal of consideration to the subject of attempts to commit crime in a recent work, in which he maintains that preparations are indictable when they are made for the purpose of committing specific crimes. This must, according to most European codes, appear, in order to sustain a conviction; and to this it may be added, that, to make an attempt penal, it must be such a movement, directed towards such consummation of a crime, as would apparently end, if not extraneously interrupted, in such consummation. Otherwise, the area of crimes would be dangerously increased. Few "preparations" can be conceived of, which could not be made use of as instruments of crime; and to say that an intent to commit a crime is sufficient to convict one who has made any such preparations, is virtually to say that there may be convictions for the bare intent. It is better to say that there is to be no conviction unless the preparations were such as to be likely to end, unless there were an extraneous interruption, in a consummated crime which the parties intended to effect. Geyser, Holz. Enc. See 17 Cent. L. J. 26.

4. United States *v.* Stephens, 8 Sawy. C. C. 116.

5. Reg. *v.* Cheeseman, 9 Cox, C. C. 103.

6. Reg. *v.* Taylor, 1 Fost. & F. 511.

is sending for a magistrate to solemnize a marriage an attempt to contract an incestuous marriage;[1] nor is procuring false weights an attempt to cheat by using them.[2] But preparations where means appropriate are used, and by reason of an unforeseen impediment, or from extraneous circumstances, the purpose is frustrated, or fails of its accomplishment, constitute a criminal attempt;[3] as purchasing poison, and putting it in the way of others.[4]

4. *Suitable Means.* — If the means used are apparently adapted to the end sought to be accomplished, it constitutes an attempt.[5]

5. *Unsuitable Means.* — Where the means are absolutely unsuitable, there should be no conviction.[6] This view obtains in this country in cases where the means are not absolutely, but apparently, unsuitable. But it is thought that to require the test of absolute unsuitability would be unduly to limit the indictability of attempts:[7] the best test is that of apparent adaptability.[8] If the instrument used is one apparently fitted to injure, the effect on the public peace and on the party assaulted is the same as if the instrument was absolutely fitted to injure. And this has been held to be the law in this country with regard to assaults.[9]

1. People v. Murray, 14 Cal. 159.

2. Reg. v. Cheeseman, Leigh & C. 140.

3. Mullen v. State, 45 Ala. 43; Kunkle v. State, 32 Ind. 220; Reg. v. Meredith, 8 Car. & P. 589; Reg. v. St. George, 9 Car. & P. 483; Reg. v. Dale, 6 Cox, C. C. 14; Weaver v. State, 24 Tex. 387; United States v. Pryor, 3 Wash. C. C. 234.

4. Mullen v. State, 45 Ala. 43.

5. Commonwealth v. Jacobs, 91 Mass. (9 Allen) 274; Mullen v. State, 45 Ala. 43; Tarver v. State, 43 Ala. 354; United States v. Dorr, 11 Blatchf. C. C. 346; People v. Lawton, 56 Barb. (N. Y.) 126; People v. Yslas, 27 Cal. 630; Commonwealth v. McDonald, 59 Mass. (5 Cush.) 365; Allen v. State, 28 Ga. 395; State v. Shepard, 10 Iowa, 126; Tyra v. Commonwealth, 2 Metc. (Ky.) 1; State v. Davis, 1 Ired. (N. C.) L. 125; Slatterly v. People, 58 N. Y. 354; State v. Hampton, 63 N. C. 13; State v. Rawles, 65 N. C. 334; O'Leary v. People, 4 Park. Cr. R. (N. Y.) 187; Long v. State, 34 Tex. 566. See also 1 Whart. Cr. L. (9th ed.) sec. 182.

6. Geyser, Holz Enc.; 17 Cent. L. J. 26.

7. "Of what means can we say that they are absolutely capable of producing a particular effect? What poison can we be sure will not, in the person for whom it is prepared, find a system so tempered by antidotes as to resist the effects? How can we tell that a particular wound will be deadly, or that it may not be warded off by armor worn by the party assailed?" Dr. Wharton, 17 Cent. L. J. 26.

8. This would exclude the case, put by Geyser, — Holz. Enc.; 17 Cent. L. J. 26, — of an attempt to kill by sorcery. But it would not exclude cases in which a gun is fired, in which, at the moment of firing, the powder turns out to be wet; or in which the poison has been given, whose strength has been so weakened (this being unknown to the accused party) that it can have no fatal effect.

9. An Assault. — It has been repeatedly ruled that an assault, when apparently fitted to do harm if pressed to a battery, does not cease to be indictable because it turns out that no battery could have been effected. See "Assault," 1 Am. & Eng. Encyc. of L. 778. And a similar distinction should be taken as to attempts.

"Unsuitable" and "Inadequate" Means. — A distinction has been made between means which are "absolutely unsuitable" — that is, means which under no circumstances could produce the intended effect — and means "relatively unsuitable;" that is, means which are in themselves suitable, but which are applied in insufficient quantity or in an ineffective way. Regarding this distinction, it has been observed that there is no agency of which it can be absolutely said that it will necessarily produce the intended result; that there is no cup between which and the lip there may not be a slip; and that there can be no certainty that the means will operate until there has been a trial of the means. The attempt which is made with "unsuitable"

6. *Unsuitable Object.* — An attempt may be made to commit a crime which it is impossible to commit.[1]

means, and that which is made with "inadequate" means, are, objectively considered, of the same character. Neither is adapted to effect the desired end. Neither is actually "dangerous." Thus, an insufficient dose of poison may be not only innocent, but beneficial, and hence not a poison at all. An insufficient dose of arsenic may be as ineffective as a sprinkling of sugar, and hence, not merely "inadequate," but "unsuitable." Consequently, if an attempt with "inadequate" means is indictable, so must be an attempt with "unsuitable" means; and, if an attempt with "unsuitable" means is not indictable, neither should an attempt with "inadequate" means be indictable. The same observation is extended to means whose failure is imputable to the defective action of the offender himself, — thus, "where the ball, which fails because the gun is badly aimed, is as ineffective as the ball aimed from too great a distance. A false belief that the powder with which a gun is loaded is sufficient to make the ball effective, is as potent in defeating the offender's purpose as is the false belief that an unloaded gun is loaded. And an error as to the length of a ladder to be used in entering a house, or as to the fitness of a skeleton key, operates to defeat the criminal purpose as effectively as does an error as to the explosive capacity of a powder to be used, to burst open a gate." 17 Cent L. J. 26.

Unfit Instrument. — However, it is maintained that "the use of an instrument in itself unfit, leaves us no means of determining what was the intention of the party charged. Thus, what right have we to assume that a person aiming a broomstick at another is attempting to shoot? To prove the criminal intention, it is necessary to put in evidence acts consistent with such intention, not acts as to which the hypothesis of such an intention is repugnant. And a mere confession of the party cannot convict when it is a confession that plainly shows there is no offence. Thus, if A. says, 'I meant to shoot B. with the broomstick,' this is a confession of something, that, whatever it is, is not an attempt to shoot with a gun. And so a person confessing that he gave another sugar, believing it to be such, or not knowing it to be poison, cannot, on his confession, be convicted of attempt to poison." 17 Cent. L. J. 26.

Criminal Will. — Yet it is *held* that the existence of a criminal will, and of an act performed with the intention to effectuate this will, is as much present when unsuitable means are used as when inadequate means are used; the first being an error as to quality, the second an error with regard to quantity: and want of accuracy of perception in the one case is no more a defence than defective appreciation of the quantity required is a defence in the other case. However, from the use of absolutely unsuitable means, we may infer that the intention charged did not exist; and this exception does not apply to cases in which the means used, though really unsuitable, did not appear so to the party employing them. Thus, where a person goes to the apothecary to buy arsenic in order to poison another, and the apothecary, suspecting the object, gives the purchaser a harmless drug, instead of the arsenic, the purchaser, where an intent to kill is established, will be indictable for the attempt.

It has been said that it is absurd to assume that there can be a "beginning" of an undertaking of which there cannot possibly be a "completion." But it is of the very essence of an attempt, that the initiatory act has not worked the intended result. The reason of the non-concurrence of the result is indifferent: the only requisite is, that the result should not have occurred. A different doctrine would establish the immunity of all attempts, since the interruption of the offender's purpose in all cases of attempt shows the inadequacy of the means. Thus, a shot which fails because the intended victim is cased in armor, is, on this reasoning, as little of an attempt as is a shot which fails because the gun is unloaded. In such cases, the intent to kill is that which makes up the offence. To say that the attempt is only indictable when the object is attainable, and yet that whether the object is attainable depends upon what was the intent, is to argue in a vicious circle. Dr. Wharton in 17 Cent. L. J. 26.

The True Theory is the subjective; that is to say, the test is, did the offender intend to hurt, and did he take means in his view calculated to effect his end? If so, the unsuitableness of the means makes no defence. To this rule, an exception is advanced by those who maintain its general validity, excluding cases when unsuitable superstitious agencies are employed. And the validity of this exception is conceded in cases in which the agency of supernatural beings is invoked, it being left discretionary with such beings to intervene or not. Hence, it is not an indictable attempt for a person, intending thereby to kill another, to resort to incantations or invocations of supposed magicians or malevolent spirits. Dr. Wharton in 17 Cent. L. J. 26.

1. Kunkle *v.* State, 32 Ind. 220.

A man may make an attempt, an experiment, to pick a pocket by thrusting his hand into it, and not succeed because there happens to be nothing in the pocket. It is not presumable that the person had in view any particular article, or had any knowledge whether there was any thing in the pocket; but he attempted to pick the pocket of whatever he might find in it, if, happily, he should find any thing; and the attempt, with the act done of thrusting his hand into the pocket, made the offence complete.[1] So a man may make an effort to steal by breaking open a trunk, and be disappointed in not finding the object of his pursuit, and so not steal in fact.[2]

If the object sought to be obtained is probably in existence, or probably attainable, as attempting to steal from a pocket in which there is nothing to take;[3] or to forge, though the paper could not defraud;[4] or to alter a counterfeit note, though the intended receiver had no property of which to be defrauded;[5] or to personate a person who at the time is dead;[6] or to shoot at a person

1. Commonwealth *v.* McDonald, 59 Mass. (5 Cush.) 365.

Attempt to Steal: Nothing to be Stolen.—But it seems that a different rule prevails in England. It has there been *held*, that if a man puts his hands into the pockets of another, with intent to steal what he can find there, and the pocket is empty, he cannot be convicted of an attempt to steal. Reg. *v.* Collins, L. & C. 471; s. c., 9 Cox, C. C. 497; 33 L. J. M. C. 177; 10 Jur. N. S. 686; 10 L. T. 581; 12 W. R. 886.

2. Commonwealth *v.* McDonald, 59 Mass. (5 Cush.) 365.

Attempts on Unsuitable Objects.—"Must an attempt, in order to be indictable, be on an object on which the complete crime could be consummated? An attempt is made to steal an article from a room which is either empty, or has in it other articles than that which is sought. Or a wound is inflicted on a corpse whom the assailant believes to be a living man. In such cases we have on the subjective side the conditions of an attempt. The punishability of the act, however, is denied, because the offender assumed a non-existent quality in the object, which defect excluded the possibility of the completion of the offence. But the same contradictions result from this view, as result from the theory that an attempt with unsuitable means is not indictable. How do we know that any object actually exists as conceived? And if it does not exist as conceived, how can there be in this view an indictment for an attempt? If entire correspondence between intention and object be required, the person who attempts to pick a pocket can in no case be convicted, since in no case could he find exactly what he seeks. An assassin, in this view, who sees a carriage belonging to his intended victim approach, and shoots into the carriage, is not punishable if the owner had a moment or two before stepped out, though it would be otherwise if the owner had shifted his seat from the back seat, which he usually occupied, to the front. But is not the peril and the disturbance of public order in each case the same? Can we hold that it is not an indictable offence to attempt to produce a miscarriage on a non-pregnant woman, or attempt to murder a person by setting a spring-gun on his chamber-door on a night in which it so happened that he would be necessarily absent?

"In these cases it is said there is an existent object, though not an object in the condition that was supposed. But is this distinction tenable? Is there an existent object in cases where a pocket is searched unavailingly by a thief, and yet is not this an attempt? So far as concerns liability to hurt, a man covered all over with impenetrable armor is as non-existent as is a dead person; yet no one holds that to shoot a man incased in armor is not an attempt." Dr. Wharton in 9 Cent. L. J. 42.

3. People *v.* Jones, 46 Mich. 441; Commonwealth *v.* McDonald, 59 Mass. (5 Cush.) 365; State *v.* Wilson, 30 Conn. 500; Hamilton *v.* State, 36 Ind. 280; Spears *v.* State, 2 Ohio St. 584; Rogers *v.* Commonwealth, 5 Serg. & R. (Pa.) 463; Reg. *v.* Collins, 33 L. J. M. C. 177.

4. Reg. *v.* Nash, 2 Den. C. C. 493; Reg. *v.* Dodd, 18 L. T. N. S. 89.

5. Commonwealth *v.* Starr, 86 Mass. (4 Allen) 301.

6. Rex *v.* Martin, Russ. & R. C. C. 324; Rex *v.* Cramp, Russ. & R. C. C. 327.

with fire-arms not capable of doing the harm intended;[1] or to poison another with a non-poisonous substance, believing at the time that it was poisonous;[2] or to destroy a vessel to recover the insurance, though it is not in fact insured;[3] or to produce a miscarriage, when in fact the woman was not pregnant,[4] — the attempt is indictable. But where the subject of the intention has no existence, the attempt is not considered as made;[5] as to personate one who never had an existence.[6] For when the object is unsuitable, — that is, when it is an object on which the intended wrong could not have been perpetrated, — then the act complained of is not an attempt to effect the object in question.[7]

7. *Minor Offences.* — In respect to minor offences which are not *mala in se*, but are made indictable by statute on police grounds, the doctrine of attempts does not apply, and hence it is not in itself an offence to attempt such minor offences.[8]

1. Vaughan *v.* State, 3 Smedes & M. (Miss.) 553.

2. State *v.* Clarissa, 11 Ala. 57; Reg. *v.* Childeray, 1 Den. C. C. 514; s. c., 3 Camp. 76.

3. United States *v.* Cole, 5 McL. C. C. 513.

4. Reg. *v.* Goodchild, 2 Carr. & K. 293; s. c., 2 Cox, C. C. 4041; s. c., 1 Den. C. C. 187; Wilson *v.* State, 20 Ohio St. 319; State *v.* Howard, 32 Vt. 380. See Commonwealth *v.* Wood, 77 Mass. (11 Gray) 85.

5. Rex *v.* Lovel, 2 Moody & R 39; Reg. *v.* McPherson, Dears. & B. C. C. 197.

6. Rex *v.* Tannet, Russ & R. C. C. 351.

7. Thus, when A. intends to kill B., but, in the execution of this intent, shoots at a dead body, which he mistakes for B. Geyser, Holz. Enc.; 17 Cent. L. J. 26.

Dr. Wharton's Criticism. — Dr. Wharton criticises this doctrine. He says, "Now, supposing this was a case in which, apparently as well as actually, the object was one on which the attempt could not have been consummated, we may agree in holding with Geyser that the offence could not be called an attempt to kill A. But suppose that the attempt was apparently likely to succeed, is the same conclusion to be reached? Ought we not, in such case, to take the same distinction as is made in respect to means, and to hold that where the object is apparently one on which the offence could be consummated, then an attempt to perpetrate the offence on such an object is indictable? A., for instance, intends to assassinate B., and lurks in a street through which B.'s carriage is to pass, and then shoots at the carriage at a time when he thinks B. is in it. B., however, is not in it, but, it may be, in his place a bundle of clothes. But this A. does not know at the time the gun is discharged, nor is it apparent to other people that B. is not in the carriage. And if the distinction above taken with regard to unsuitable means be good, it is an indictable offence to attempt to commit a crime on an object which, though not actually, is apparently, the object the perpetrator intended to injure. This distinction is applied in an English case, in which it was *held* that the fact that a woman was not with child is no defence to an indictment for an attempt to commit an abortion on her person. The truth is, if we reject the test of apparent susceptibility, and introduce in its place that of absolute susceptibility, we will encounter interminable difficulties. It is impossible to say of any one that a shot would inevitably take effect on him, or that he would certainly yield to a particular poison. If so, it is better in respect to attempts, as is the case with assaults, to take the test of apparent as distinguished from actual adaptability or susceptibility." See 17 Cent. L. J. 26.

8. **German View.** — This seems to be the view generally held in Germany, and there is a good deal to commend it. Dr. Wharton summarizes what can be said as follows: First, an offence must be of a certain magnitude to make it the object of attempts and accessoryships. A thing must be of a certain degree or size to make it cognizable at a distance; and if, in addition to its smallness, it is as easy to execute a particular wrong as to attempt it, the attempt would be an absurdity for which it would be irrational to indict. Secondly, the wheels of police prosecutions would be clogged if attempts to commit offences of this class were indictable. The selling of whiskey by retail is made in many States indictable. If in such States it was ruled to be indictable to attempt such sales, not only would a new and enormous mass of offences be created, which would choke the courts, but, when

8. *Solicitations to commit Crime.* — Solicitations to commit a crime are indictable and punishable as distinct offences.[1] Some

the vendee in such cases was called as a witness, he could refuse to answer, on the ground that to agree to buy was to take part in, if not attempt, a sale. Our courts, however, have negatived this claim, and have held that the vendee of illicit drinks is not privileged because he is not indictable. The reason given for this, that the law which makes an accessory indictable does not apply to minor offences not *mala in se*, applies as logically to attempts as it does to accessoryships; and the public convenience of making such application is manifest. Not only do we thus keep out of the courts many cases which ought not to be tried, but, in cases which ought to be tried, we obtain evidence we would otherwise lose. If we make all persons in any way encouraging such offences indictable, we would subject whole sections of the community to indictment. And, as all parties in any way promoting or encouraging such sales would be indictable, no such parties could be compelled to answer. The consequence of thus extending indictments to everybody would be to relieve everybody from prosecution.

Great Offences. — It is not so with great offences. Great offences cannot ordinarily be committed without drawing within the range of their observers numerous parties who have no part or lot in them. As to such offences, there is, therefore, no processual reason why we should not maintain the old and salutary rules which make attempts indictable. It is otherwise, however, as to minor offences not *mala in se*, the application of the law of attempts to which is as irrational as it is inconvenient. 17 Cent. L. J. 26.

1. **English Authorities: Leading Cases.** — The leading case upon the subject is that of Rex *v.* Higgins, 2 East, 5. In that case the traverser was indicted for soliciting and inciting a servant to steal his master's goods: it was *held*, upon full consideration, that it was a punishable misdemeanor for any one to solicit another to steal, and this, although it be not charged in the indictment that the party solicited stole the goods, or that any other act was done more than the simple acts of soliciting and inciting by the traverser. There, in answer to the argument that a mere intent to commit evil was not indictable, without an act done, *Lord Chief Justice Kenyon* replied, "But is there not an act done, when it is charged that the defendant solicited another to commit a felony? The solicitation is an act; and the answer given at the bar is decisive, that it would be sufficient to constitute an overt act of high treason." *Mr. Justice Grose*, after referring to the cases upon the subject, said, "All these cases prove that inciting another to commit a misdemeanor is itself a misdemeanor; *a fortiori*, therefore, it must be such to incite another to commit felony." And *Mr. Justice Lawrence* said, "The whole argument for the defendant turns upon a fallacy in assuming that no act is charged to have been done by him; for a solicitation is an act. The offence does not rest in mere intention; for, in soliciting Dixon to commit the felony, the defendant did an act towards carrying his intention into execution. It is an endeavor or attempt to commit a crime."

Distinction between Felony and Misdemeanor. — And the principle of that case was fully adopted and applied in the recent case of Reg. *v.* Ransford, 13 Cox, C. C. 9, by the court of criminal appeal in England; and the attempted distinction made here between the cases of felony and misdemeanor was in that case utterly ignored, as being without foundation. See Lamb *v.* State (Md.), 8 Cent. Rep. 881.

Attempt to corrupt by Solicitations. — In the case of Rex *v.* Vaughan, 4 Burr. 2494, the charge was for an attempt to corrupt the Duke of Grafton, a member of the Privy Council, by solicitation to induce him for a bribe to procure an office for the applicant. *Lord Mansfield*, with the concurrence of the other judges, said that he was clear that the offence charged was a misdemeanor, and punishable as such. And in the course of his judgment his lordship said, "If a party offers a bribe to a judge, meaning to corrupt him in a case depending before him, and the judge taketh it not, yet this is an offence punishable by law, in the party that offers it. 3 Inst. 147. So, also, a promise of money to a corporator to vote for a mayor of a corporation, as in Rex *v.* Plympton, 2 Ld. Raym. 1377. And so also must be an offer to bribe a privy councillor to advise the King."

Challenge to fight a Duel. — In the case of Rex *v.* Philipps, 6 East, 464, it was *held* upon full argument and examination of authorities, that an endeavor to provoke or incite another to commit the misdemeanor of sending a challenge to fight a duel is itself a misdemeanor, and therefore indictable at common law. And so, to attempt to suborn one to commit perjury, or to solicit and persuade a witness to absent himself from a public prosecution when summoned as a witness, or to solicit a party to commit adultery or any other misdemeanor of an evil and vicious nature, are indictable offences, and punish-have classed them with attempts to commit a crime.[1] This, however, is hardly permissible.[2] But a mere solicitation, not directed to the procurement of some specific offence or crime, is not an attempt, and is not punishable as such.[3]

Thus, it is an indictable offence to solicit a servant to steal his master's goods,[4] or to commit murder,[5] or arson,[6] or sodomy,[7] or adultery, where adultery is punishable criminally;[8] or to incite to larceny,[9] or to request one to post up a threatening notice,[10] or to offer a bribe.[11] Yet merely soliciting one to do an act, is not an attempt to do that act.[12]

able at the common law. Rex *v.* Lady Lawly, Fitzg. 263; State *v.* Keyes, 8 Vt. 57; State *v.* Carpenter, 20 Vt. 9; State *v.* Avery, 7 Conn. 267; Commonwealth *v.* Harrington, 20 Mass. (3 Pick.) 26.

1. 1 Whart. Cr. L. (8th ed.) 179.

2. Solicitations as Attempts. — There is a dispute whether a mere solicitation is an attempt. Bishop says, "The law as adjudged holds, and has held from th ebeginning, in all this class of cases, an indictment sufficient which simply charges that the defendant, at a time and place mentioned, 'falsely, wickedly, and unlawfully did solicit and incite' a person named to commit the substantive offence without any further specification of overt acts. It is in vain, then, to say that mere solicitation, the mere entire thing which need be averred against a defendant as the ground for his conviction; is no offence." Bishop, Cr. L. § 768 c.

Wharton says, that, "To make bare solicitations or allurements indictable as attempts, not only unduly and perilously extends the scope of penal adjudication, but forces on the court psychological questions which they are incompetent to decide, and a branch of business which would make them despots of every intellect in the land. What human judge can determine that there is such a necessary connection between one man's advice and another man's action, as to make the former the cause of the latter? An attempt, as has been stated, is such an intentional guilty act as will apparently result, in the usual course of natural events, if not hindered by extraneous causes, in the commission of a deliberate crime. But this cannot be affirmed of advice given to another, which advice such other person is at full liberty to accept or reject. Following such reasoning, several eminent European jurists have declined to regard any solicitations as indictable, when there is interposed between the bare solicitation on the one hand, and the proposed illegal act on the other, the resisting will of another, which other person refuses assent and co-operation.

"We must, however, remember, that such solicitations, when in any way attacking the body politic, either by way of treason, scandal, or nuisance, are, under any view of the case, indictable as independent offences." 1 Whart. Cr. L. § 179.

The True Doctrine seems to be, as Irving Browne has pointed out in his note to Stabler *v.* Commonwealth, 95 Pa. St. 318; s. c., 40 Am. Rep. 653, 657, that any direct mere solicitation to commit a specific criminal offence against a particular individual or the community, although not consummated, is indictable as a solicitation, but not as an attempt. See also Respublica *v.* Roberts, 1 U. S. (1 Dall.) 39; bk. 1, L. ed. 27; Reg. *v.* Harris, Crawf. & D. 149; s. c., 1 C. & M. 661 n.

3. See Respublica *v.* Roberts, 1 U. S. (1 Dall.) 39; bk. 1, L. ed. 27; Reg. *v.* Harris, 1 Crawf. & D. 149; s. c., 1 C. & M. 661 n.

4. State *v.* Avery, 7 Conn. 266; Commonwealth *v.* Harrington, 20 Mass. (3 Pick.) 26; Hately *v.* State, 15 Ga. 346; Demarest *v.* Haring, 6 Cow. (N. Y.) 76; State *v.* Carpenter, 20 Vt. 9; State *v.* Keyes, 8 Vt. 57; Reg *v.* Quail, 4 Fost. & F. 1076; Rex *v.* Higgins, 2 East, 5.

5. Demarest *v.* Haring, 6 Cow. (N. Y.) 76; 1 Russ. Cr. (9th ed.) 970.

6. People *v.* Bush, 4 Hill (N. Y.), 133; 1 Bish. Cr. L. (6th ed.) 767.

7. Reg. *v.* Ransford, 13 Cox, C. C. 9; s. c., 31 L. T. N. S. 488; Rex *v.* Hickman, 1 Moody, 34.

8. State *v.* Avery, 7 Conn. 266; s. c., 18 Am. Dec. 105.

Solicitations to commit Adultery. — But it is otherwise where there is no statutory punishment for adultery, because solicitations to commit adultery are not indictable at common law, — Smith *v.* Commonwealth, 54 Pa. St. 209; Kelly *v.* Commonwealth, 1 Grant, Cas. (Pa.) 484; — and the same is true of an endeavor to persuade to commit incest, — Cox *v.* People, 82 Ill. 191; s. c., 2 Am. Cr. R. 329, — or to sell liquor. Commonwealth *v.* Willard, 39 Mass. (22 Pick.) 476.

9. Rex *v.* Higgins, 2 East, 5.

10. Reg. *v.* Darcy, 1 Crawf. & D. 33.

11. United States *v.* Worrell, 2 U. S. (2 Dall.) 384; bk. 1, L. ed. 426.

12. Smith *v.* Commonwealth, 55 Pa. St.

A solicitation to commit a misdemeanor is not an attempt to commit the misdemeanor, although a solicitation to commit a felony does constitute an attempt to commit the felony.[1] And it is indictable at common law to solicit another to commit a felony, or other aggravated offence, although the solicitation is of no effect, and the crime counselled is not committed.[2]

Solicitations are indictable where they involve the employment of means to effect illegal ends.[3] Thus, sending a letter which solicits and entices the commission of a crime, will, if such letter is intercepted, and never reaches the person for whom it was intended, and to whom it was addressed, render the sender liable for an attempt to solicit and incite.[4]

Counselling, advising, or inciting another to commit a breach of the peace, or other offence, constitutes the crime.[5] Thus, at common law, solicitations to commit adultery or incest, or statutory offences, are not indictable unless they incite to a breach of the peace;[6] but solicitations to commit crime are always indictable when their object is to provoke a breach of the public peace,[7] or an interference with public justice.[8] Yet attempts or solicitations have been regarded as not indictable when there is interposed between the attempt or solicitation on the one hand, and the proposed illegal act on the other, the resisting will of another person, and that person refuses assent or co-operation.[9]

A mere solicitation inciting to the corruption of an officer, if not consummated, is not indictable, nor is it when invited by the officer himself.[10]

Procuring, counselling, or inciting another to commit an offence, renders the instigator liable.[11] Thus, a person inciting another in

(4 P. F. Smith) 209; Stabler *v.* Commonwealth, 95 Pa. St. 318; s. c., 40 Am. Rep. 653; Rex *v.* Butler, 6 Car. & P. 368.

In a High Moral Sense it is said it may be true that solicitation is an attempt, but in a legal sense it is not. Smith *v.* Commonwealth, 55 Pa. St. (4 P. F. Smith) 209.

1. Smith *v.* Commonwealth, 55 Pa. St. (4 P. F. Smith) 209; Stabler *v.* Commonwealth, 95 Pa. St. 318; s. c., 40 Am. Rep. 653.

2. State *v.* Avery, 7 Conn. 265; s. c., 18 Am. Dec. 105; Commonwealth *v.* Flagg, 135 Mass. 545; Commonwealth *v.* Willard, 39 Mass. (22 Pick.) 476; Rex *v.* Higgins, 2 East, 5; Rex *v.* Phillips, 6 East, 464; Reg. *v.* Ransford, 13 Cox, C. C. 9.

3. Collins *v.* State, 3 Heisk. (Tenn.) 14; State *v.* McGill, Addis. (Pa.) 21.

4. Regina *v.* Banks, 12 Cox, C. C. 393; s. c., 5 Moak's Eng. Rep. 471.

5. Commonwealth *v.* Willard, 39 Mass. (22 Pick.) 476; Commonwealth *v.* Harrington, 20 Mass. (3 Pick.) 26; Walsh *v.* People, 65 Ill. 58; People *v.* Hoag, 2 Park. Cr. Rep. (N. Y.) 36; Penn *v.* McGill, Addis. (Pa.) 21.

6. United States *v.* Ravara, 2 U. S. (2 Dall.) 297; bk. 1, L. ed. 388; Cox *v.* People, 82 Ill. 191; s. c., 2 Am. C. R. 329; Commonwealth *v.* Willard, 39 Mass. (22 Pick.) 476; Commonwealth *v.* Tibbs, 1 Dana (Ky.), 524; State *v.* Farrier, 1 Hawk. (N. C.) 487; State *v.* Taylor, 3 Brev. (S. C.) L. 243.

7. United States *v.* Ravara, 2 U. S. (2 Dall.) 297; bk. 1, L. ed. 388; Commonwealth *v.* Whitehead, 2 Rep. 148; State *v.* Farrier, 1 Hawks (N. C.), 487; State *v.* Taylor, 3 Brev. (S. C.) L. 243; Commonwealth *v.* Tibbs, 1 Dana (Ky.), 524.

8. State *v.* Calwell, 2 Tyler (Vt.), 212.

9. 2 Whart. Cr. L. sec. 2691; Smith *v.* Commonwealth, 54 Pa. St. 209; Commonwealth *v.* Willard, 39 Mass. (22 Pick.) 476. *Compare* State *v.* Avery, 7 Conn. 267; s. c., 18 Am. Dec. 105.

10. Miller *v.* State, 58 Ga. 200; Walsh *v.* People, 65 Ill. 58; Cox *v.* People, 82 Ill. 191; 2 Am. Cr. R. 329; Commonwealth *v.* Willard, 39 Mass. (22 Pick.) 476; Smith *v.* Commonwealth, 54 Pa. St. 209; 2 Whart. Cr. L. sec. 2691. *Compare* Hutchinson *v.* State, 36 Tex. 293.

11. Hately *v.* State, 15 Ga. 346; People

a tumultuous crowd to strike another, is guilty of the assault;[1] and at common law the instigator and the perpetrator may be guilty in different degrees.[2] The instigator of manslaughter may be convicted of murder.[3]

The advice, procurement, or encouragement may be direct or indirect, by words, signs, or motions, personally, or through the intervention of a third party.[4] And the instigator need not be the originator of the criminal design: if he encourage the perpetrator, he is guilty as accessory.[5]

If the procurement is through an intervening agent, it is not necessary that the instigator should know the name of the perpetrator.[6]

No matter how long a time, or how great a space, intervenes between the advice or instigation and the consummation of the deed, if there is immediate causal connection between the instigation and the act, it is sufficient.[7] The instigator is responsible for the incidental consequences of the crime he counsels, but not for collateral crimes.[8]

Where the person instigated commits a crime different from the crime instigated, the instigator is not responsible.[9] Thus, if A. instigates B. to murder C., and B. murders D., A. is not liable, although he would be responsible for all the probable consequences upon an unlawful act which he has encouraged or advised; as where the perpetrator by mistake commits a different crime.[10] But he is liable where the perpetrator commits the crime instigated in a different way from that proposed.[11]

Where the instigator countermands the execution of the crime before it is executed, he ceases to be liable only if the perpetrator has timely notice of the countermand.[12]

IV. Elements of Crime. — To constitute crime, there must be (1) an act, and (2) a criminal intent, or (3) criminal negligence, (4) which must concur in point of time.[13] Thus, an assault is complete if

v. Hodges, 26 Cal. 340; Commonwealth *v.* Hurley, 99 Mass. 433; Reg. *v.* Gaylor, Dears. & B. 288.

1. Commonwealth *v.* Tryon, 99 Mass. 443; People *v.* Hodges, 27 Cal. 340.

2. Klein *v.* People, 31 N. Y. 229; Mask *v.* People, 32 Miss. 405.

3. Reg. *v.* Gaylor, Dears. & B. C. C. 288.

4. Kennedy *v.* People, 40 Ill. 488; Reg. *v.* Blackburn, 6 Cox, C. C. 333; Rex *v.* Lee, 6 Car. & P. 536; Somersett's Case, 19 How. State Tri. 804; Rex *v* Giles, 1 Moody, 166; Rex *v.* Cooper, 5 Car. & P. 535; 1 Hale, P. C. 616.

5. Keithler *v.* State, 10 Smedes & M. (Miss.) 192; Reg. *v.* Tuckwell, Car. & M. 215.

6. Reg. *v.* Williams, 1 Den. C. C. 39; Rex *v.* Giles, 1 Moody, C. C. 166.

7. Commonwealth *v.* Glover, 111 Mass. 395; Reg. *v.* Sharpe, 3 Cox, C. C. 288; Reg. *v.* Blackburn, 6 Cox, C. C. 333.

8. People *v.* Knapp, 26 Mich. 112; Watts *v.* State, 5 W. Va 532; 1 Hale, P. C. 687.

9. Desty, Am. Cr. L. § 42*a*.

10. Brennan *v.* People, 15 Ill. 511; Rex *v.* Saunders, 2 Plowd. 475; 4 Bl. Com. 371; 1 Hale, P. C. 617; Fost Cr L. 369, sec. 1; 1 Whart. Cr. L (8th ed.) sec. 229; 1 Russ. Cr. (9th ed.) 62.

11. Desty, Am. Cr. L.

12. Saunders's Case, Plowd. 474; 1 Hale, P. C. 618; 1 Whart Crim L. (8th ed.) sec. 228; 1 Russ. Cr. (9th ed) 63.

13. Allen *v* State, 52 Ala. 393; Miles *v.* State, 58 Ala. 300; People *v.* Harris, 29 Cal. 679; People *v.* White, 34 Cal. 183; Yoes *v.* State, 9 Ark. 42; Ross *v.* Commonwealth, 2 B. Mon. (Ky) 419; State *v.* Will, 1 Dev. & B. (N. C.) L. 121; Long *v.* State,

a dangerous weapon, or the semblance of one, is used in a threatening manner with intent to alarm; and the ability to commit a battery need not be shown.[1] And setting fire to a storehouse, with the intent that the fire should be communicated to a barn and dwelling-house, constitutes the crime of arson.[2] But setting fire to a jail by a prisoner merely for the purpose of making his escape, is not arson,[3] although the jail is to be deemed as an inhabited dwelling-house within the meaning of the statute declaring the punishment of crimes.[4]

1. *Overt Act Essential.* — Although the essence of every criminal offence is the wrongful intent, yet an overt act is necessary to constitute crime, as mere intention is not punishable.[5]

2. *Criminal Intent.* — The intent to do an act forbidden by law is the criminal intent, which imparts to the act the character of an offence.[6]

38 Ga. 507; Slattery *v.* People, 76 Ill. 218; Walker *v.* State, 8 Ind. 290; Gates *v.* Lounsbury, 20 Johns. (N. Y.) 427; Commonwealth *v.* Morse, 2 Mass. 138; Torrey *v.* Field, 10 Vt. 353; Hopkins *v.* Commonwealth, 50 Pa. St. 10; Morse *v.* State, 6 Conn. 9; State *v.* Weston, 9 Conn. 526; State *v.* Roper, 3 Dev. (N C.) L. 473; Long *v.* State, 12 Ga. 293; Kelly *v.* Commonwealth, 1 Grant (Pa.), 484, People *v.* Cogdell, 1 Hill (N. Y.), 94; People *v.* Anderson, 14 Johns. (N. Y.) 204; State *v.* Ferguson, 2 McMull (S C.), L. 502; People *v.* Reynolds, 2 Mich. 422; State *v.* Braden, 2 Tenn. 68; State *v* Smith, 2 Tyler (Vt), 272. And see Norton *v.* State, 4 Mo. 461; Ransom *v.* State, 22 Conn. 153; State *v* Conway, 18 Mo. 321.

Sale of Property by Bailee. — Thus, if, at the time a bailee sells the property, he has the intent to appropriate the proceeds, it is immaterial that he had authority to sell. Epperson *v.* State (Tex. App. Jan. 1887).

1 Kief *v.* State, 10 Tex. App. 286.

2 Grimes *v.* State, 63 Ala. 166.

3. People *v.* Cotterel, 18 Johns. (N. Y.) 115; s. c., 5 City H Rec. 71; State *v.* Mitchell, 5 Ired. (N. C.) L. 350; Delaney *v.* State, 41 Tex. 601; s. c., 6 Cent. L. J. 99. *Compare* Lockett *v.* State, 63 Ala. 5; Smith *v* State (Tex. Ct. App.), 5 S. W. Rep 219; s. c., 25 Cent. L. J. 256

Burning Hole in Jail. — Defendants burning a hole in a jail in order to escape, may be indicted for arson, if they intended to burn the jail; and if they set fire to it in such a way as in reasonable probability would burn it up, the jury is justified in finding the intent. State *v.* Nevel, 2 W. L. M. 494.

If a prisoner burns a hole in the door, or attempts to burn one through the floor, of a guard-house, situate in an incorporate town, merely for the purpose of effecting his escape, and not with the intent to "consume or to generally injure the building," and neither of such results occurs, he is not guilty of the offence of attempting to burn a house, as defined in sects. 4376 and 4381 of the Georgia Code. Jenkins *v.* State, 53 Ga. 33.

4. People *v.* Cotterel, 18 Johns. (N. Y.) 115. See N. Y. Sess. L. 36, c. 20.

5. State *v.* Hawkins, 8 Port. (Ala.) 461; s. c., 33 Am. Dec. 294; Stein *v.* State, 37 Ala. 123; Roseberry *v.* State, 50 Ala. 160; Miles *v.* State, 58 Ala. 390; Allen *v.* State, 58 Ala. 393; Yoes *v.* State, 4 Eng. (Ark.) 42; Riley *v.* State, 16 Conn. 47; State *v.* Wilson, 30 Conn. 500; Cummins *v.* Spruance, 4 Harr. (Del.) 315; Slattery *v.* People, 76 Ill. 218; Walker *v.* State, 8 Ind. 290; Stephens *v.* State (Ind.), 5 West. Rep. 258; Ross *v.* Commonwealth, 2 B. Mon. (Ky.) 417; Commonwealth *v.* Morse, 2 Mass. 138; State *v.* Rider, 90 Mo. 54; s. c., 6 West. Rep. 458; State *v.* Gardner, 5 Nev. 377; Sturges *v.* Maitland, Anth. N. P. (N. Y.) 153; People *v.* Lohman, 2 Barb. (N. Y.) 218; State *v.* Garland, 3 Dev. (N. C.) L. 114; Commonwealth *v.* Sheriff, 1 Leg. Gaz. (Pa.) 340; Commonwealth *v.* Ridgway, 2 Ashm. (Pa.) 247; Randolph *v.* Commonwealth, 6 Serg. & R. (Pa.) 398; State *v.* Nicholas, 2 Strob. (S. C.) 278; Lovett *v.* State, 19 Tex. 174; Torrey *v.* Field, 10 Vt 353; Commonwealth *v.* Clark, 6 Gratt. (Va.) 675; United States *v.* Pearce, 2 McL. C. C. 14; The William Gray, 1 Paine, C. C. 16; United States *v.* Bazzo, 85 U. S. (18 Wall.) 128; bk. 21, L. ed. 813; Case of Le Tigre, 3 Wash. C. C. 567; United States *v.* Riddle, 9 U. S. (5 Cr.) 311; bk. 3, L. ed. 110, Fowler *v.* Padgett, 7 Term Rep. 509. See also 1 Bish. Cr. L. § 287 (6th ed.); 1 Greenl. Ev. § 18; 3 Greenl. Ev. § 13; 1 Russ. Cr. 184.

6. State *v.* King, 86 N. C. 603; State *v.* Voight, 90 N. C. 741.

The intent determines the criminality of the act; and when a specific design is required by statute to constitute the crime, such specific design enters into the nature of the act itself, and must be alleged and proved beyond a reasonable doubt.[1]

And even an act, lawful in itself, may be punished as criminal, because of a criminal intent connected therewith.[2]

a. Establishing Intent. — Where the act becomes criminal only by reason of the intent, then, unless that intent is proved, the offence is not proved.[3]

Ordinarily we are compelled to infer the intent from the nature and surroundings of the act.[4]

Felonious purpose or intent is seldom established by direct evidence, but, in the very great majority of cases, is inferred from circumstances.[5]

Testimony in reference to similar transactions is admissible to show the criminal intent: hence, a confession which relates to the general course of conduct of defendant in reference to such transactions is admissible.[6]

The evidence must show that the intent was directed to the commission of the offence charged: so, an intent to commit a malicious mischief will not sustain a conviction for a larceny.[7]

(1) *Motive.* — If, among all the motives leading to a particular act, one is illegal, it is sufficient to add to the act the essential evil intent.[8]

1. Roseberry *v.* State, 50 Ala. 160; Simpson *v.* State, 59 Ala. 1; United States *v.* Learned, 1 Abb. U. S. 483; State *v.* Dowd, 19 Conn. 388; State *v.* Stanton, 37 Conn. 421; People *v.* Sanchez, 24 Cal. 17; Hill *v.* People, 1 Colo. 451; Rex *v.* Woodfall, 5 Burr. 2661; Bivens *v.* State, 4 Eng. (Ark.) 455; White *v.* State, 53 Ind. 595; State *v.* Gillick, 7 Iowa, 287; Roberts *v.* People, 19 Mich. 401; People *v.* Potter, 5 Mich. 1; s. c., 71 Am. Dec. 763; Barcus *v.* State, 49 Miss. 17; s. c., 1 Am. Cr. R. 249; Whiteford *v.* Commonwealth, 6 Rand. (Va.) 722; Reg. *v.* Prince, L. R. 2 C. C. 154; s. c., 1 Am. Cr. R. 15; Brown, Cr. L. 871; McKay *v.* State, 44 Tex. 43; s. c., 1 Am. Cr. R. 46; Mullins *v.* State, 37 Tex. 337. See also 1 Bish. Cr. L. (6th ed.) §§ 288, 735.

2. Morse *v.* State, 6 Conn. 9; State *v.* Weston, 9 Conn. 527; Ransom *v.* State, 22 Conn. 153; Rex *v.* Horner, Caldc. 295; State *v.* Will, 1 Dev. & B. (N. C.) L. 121; State *v.* Roper, 3 Dev. (N. C.) L. 473; Long *v.* State, 12 Ga. 293; Kelly *v.* Commonwealth, 1 Grant (Pa.), 484; People *v.* Cogdell, 1 Hill (N. Y.), 94; s. c., 27 Am. Dec. 297; Fairlee *v.* People, 11 Ill. 1; People *v.* Anderson, 14 Johns. (N. Y.) 294; s. c., 7 Am. Dec. 462; People *v.* Reynolds, 2 Mich. 422; Norton *v.* State, 4 Mo. 461; State *v.* Connay, 18 Mo. 321; State *v.* Braden, 2 Tenn. 68; State *v.* Smith, 2 Tyler (Vt.), 272; State *v.* Ferguson, 2 McMull. (S C.) 502.

3. State *v.* King, 86 N. C. 603.

In New York. — Under the New York Laws, unless the intent appears, a conviction cannot be maintained for making imitations of butter with intent to sell the same. People *v.* Kerin, 39 Hun (N. Y.), 631.

4. People *v.* Beckwith, 103 N. Y. 360; s. c., 4 Cent. Rep 539.

5. Padgett *v.* State, 103 Ind. 550; s. c., 1 West. Rep. 584; Archer *v.* State, 106 Ind. 426; s. c., 4 West. Rep. 726.

6. Commonwealth *v.* Sawtelle, 141 Mass. 140; s. c., 1 New Eng. Rep. 590; Commonwealth *v.* Shepard, 83 Mass. (1 Allen) 575; Commonwealth *v.* Tuckerman, 76 Mass. (10 Gray) 173; Commonwealth *v.* Eastman, 55 Mass. (1 Cush) 189, 216.

7. Pence *v.* State, 110 Ind. 95; s. c., 8 West. Rep. 511.

8. **Gravamen of the Offence.** — Thus, the *gravamen* of the offence of obstructing a public road, is that such obstruction is wilful. Murphy *v.* State (Tex. App. May, 1887).

"**Getting Even.**" — Where the evidence showed that the intent of the defendant in removing and burning a buggy was to "get even" with the owner for a real or imagi-

(2) *Deliberation.*[1] — Deliberation shows intent. The time need not be long, and may be short. If it furnishes room and opportunity for reflection, and the facts show that such reflection existed, and the mind was busy with its design, and made the choice with full chance to choose otherwise, the condition of the statute is fulfilled.[2]

b. Felonious Assault. — If, with a felonious intent, A. shoots at B., with intent to kill him, and misses B., but wounds C., the law transfers the felonious intent from B. to C.[3]

And if a party brings on a quarrel with no felonious intent, or malice, or premeditated purpose, of doing bodily harm or killing, it is not murder, let the result of the quarrel be what it will; but if one provokes a combat, or produces the occasion to kill, and kills his adversary, it is murder, no matter to what extremity he may have been reduced in the combat.[4] Thus, it has been said, that where, without provocation, a man draws his sword upon another, who draws in defence, whereupon they fight, and the first slays his adversary, he is guilty of murder; because he who seeks and brings on a quarrel cannot, in general, avail himself of his own wrong in defence. But that, where an assault, which is neither intended nor calculated to kill, is returned by violence beyond what is proportionate to the aggression, the character of the combat is changed; and if, without time for his passion to cool, the assailant kills the other, it is only manslaughter.[5]

nary wrong, by the malicious injury or destruction of the buggy, a verdict of the jury finding the defendant guilty of grand larceny cannot be sustained. Pence *v.* State, 110 Ind. 95; s. c., 8 West. Rep. 511.

The court say that the evidence absolutely precluded the jury from finding that the buggy was taken and carried away with the felonious intent, the *animus furandi*, which is an essential and inseparable ingredient in every larceny, and in the absence of which there can be no larceny. Umphrey *v.* State, 63 Ind. 223; Starck *v.* State, id. 285; Lamphier *v.* State, 70 Ind. 317; State *v.* Wingo, 89 Ind. 204.

1. See "Deliberation," *post.*

2. People *v.* Beckwith, 103 N. Y. 360; s. c., 4 Cent. Rep. 539.

Murder in First Degree. — For the existence of the deliberation required to constitute the statutory crime of murder in the first degree, the time need not be long, and may be short. If it furnishes room and opportunity for reflection, and the facts show that such reflection existed, and the mind was busy with its design, and made the choice with full chance to choose otherwise, the condition of the statute is fulfilled. People *v.* Beckwith, 103 N. Y. 360; s. c, 4 Cent. Rep. 539.

3. State *v.* Montgomery, 91 Mo. 52; s. c., 8 West. Rep. 220; State *v.* Payton, 90 Mo. 220; s. c., 7 West. Rep. 129; State *v.* Henson, 81 Mo. 384. *Compare* Lacefield *v.* State, 34 Ark. 275; s. c., 36 Am. Rep. 8.

Evidence introducedon the part of the State tending to show that defendant sought, provoked, and brought on a fight in a public street, in which he fired three shots with intent to kill the party he assaulted, and that one of the shots missed and struck another person, inflicting a severe wound, was properly admitted upon the question of intent. State *v.* Henson, 81 Mo. 384; State *v.* Payton, 90 Mo. 220; s. c., 7 West. Rep. 129; State *v.* Montgomery, 91 Mo. 52; s. c., 8 West. Rep. 220.

4. State *v.* Partlow, 90 Mo. 608; s. c., 8 West. Rep. 274.

5. 2 Bish. Cr. L. (8th ed.) § 702. See State *v.* Partlow, 90 Mo. 608; s. c., 8 West. Rep. 274; State *v.* Lane, 4 Ired. (N. C.) L. 113; Reg. *v.* Smith, 8 Carr. & P. 160; Slaughter *v.* Commonwealth, 11 Leigh (Va.), 681; Murphy *v.* State, 37 Ala. 142; Adams *v.* People, 47 Ill. 376; State *v.* Hildreth, 9 Ired. (N. C.) L. 111, 440; State *v* Hogue, 6 Jones (N. C.) L. 381; State *v.* Martin, 2 Ired. (N. C.) L. 101; Atkins *v.* State, 16 Ark. 568; Cotton *v.* State, 31 Miss. 504; Stewart *v.* State, 1 Ohio St. 66; State *v.* Hill, 4 Dev. & B. (N. C.) L. 491.

Provoking Combat — It has been said, that if the defendant provoked the combat, or produced the occasion, in order to have a pretext for killing his adversary or doing him great bodily harm, the killing will be murder, no matter to what extremity he may have been reduced in the combat; but that if he provoked the combat or produced the occasion without any felonious intent, intending, for instance, an ordinary battery merely, the final killing in self-defence will be manslaughter only. Harrigan & Thompson on Self-Defence, 227. See also Stoffer *v.* State, 15 Ohio St. 47; Reed *v.* State, 11 Tex. App. 509.

Judge Sherwood says in State *v.* Partlow, 90 Mo. 608; s. c., 8 West. Rep. 274, that the assertion of the doctrine that one who begins a quarrel, or brings on a difficulty, with the felonious purpose to kill the person assaulted, and, accomplishing such purpose, is guilty of murder, and cannot avail himself of the doctrine of self-defence, carries with it in its very bosom the inevitable corollary, that, if the quarrel be begun without a felonious purpose, the homicidal act will not be murder. To deny this obvious deduction is equivalent to the anomalous assertion that there can be a felony without a felonious intent; that the act done characterizes the intent, and not the intent the act. See State *v.* McDonnell, 38 Vt. 491; 2 Bishop, Cr. L. § 701; 1 Hale, P. C. 456; 6 How. St. Tr. 769; Foster, 276.

Thus, where the defendant, with a spade in his hand, took a position near the deceased, and gradually approached him, for the purpose of inducing an altercation, and getting a chance to kill him, and commenced raising his spade at the same time the deceased commenced drawing his pistol, and then struck him, and killed him, he is guilty of murder in the first degree; and in such case, it would be no defence, even if the evidence showed that the deceased drew his pistol before the defendant commenced raising his spade; for the law will not permit a man thus to induce a provocation, and so take advantage of it. The court say, "Although the jury may believe from the evidence that the deceased was attempting to draw his pistol, or had it drawn at the time the defendant struck, and that the defendant's life or person was in imminent danger, yet, if they further believe that the defendant intentionally brought on the difficulty for the purpose of killing the deceased, he is still guilty of murder in the first degree." State *v.* Hays, 23 Mo. 287; State *v.* Partlow, 90 Mo. 608; s. c, 8 West. Rep. 274.

Pleading Provocation. — The principle thus announced in State *v.* Hays was followed in that of State *v.* Starr, 38 Mo. 270; for there a qualifying instruction, given by the court of its own motion, was expressly approved, which told the jury that the right of self-defence, which justifies homicide, does not imply the right of attack; and the plea of justification in self-defence cannot avail in any case where it appears that the difficulty was sought for and induced by the act of the party in order to afford him a pretence for wreaking his malice; *Wagner, J.*, remarking, "The qualification was necessary in view of the evidence in the case. The testimony tended to show that the accused sought the altercation, and was instrumental in bringing it on; and if the jury found such to be the fact, the law would not permit him to shield himself behind the doctrine of self-defence. Besides, the qualification is couched in the very language of Wharton, and commends itself for its justice, and is well supported by authority." Whart. Hom. 197.

Dr. Wharton, when speaking of a case "where the attack is sought by the party killing," says, "The plea of provocation will not avail in any case, where it appears that the provocation was sought for and induced by the act of the party in order to afford him a pretence for wreaking his malice; and it will presently be seen, that, even where there may have been previous struggling or blows, such plea cannot be admitted, where there is evidence of express malice, and it must appear, therefore, that, when he did the act, he acted upon such provocation, and not upon any old grudge." Whart. Hom. § 197. And the same learned author uses similar language in another work. 1 Whart. Cr. L. (8th ed.) §§ 474, 476.

Seeking a Quarrel. — Treating of the subject of seeking a quarrel, Bishop says, "If a man determines to kill another, or to do him great bodily harm, and seeks a quarrel, he cannot avail himself of the passion it excites; because he acts from an impulse which his mind receives in its cool moments." 2 Bish. Cr. L. § 715. See State *v.* Partlow, 90 Mo. 608; s. c., 8 West. Rep. 274.

Judge Thurman says in Stewart *v.* State, 1 Ohio St. 66, that "the combat must not have been of his own seeking, and he must not have put himself in the way of being assaulted, in order that, when assaulted and hard pressed, he might take the life of his assailant. . . . Now, it does seem to us clear that defendant sought to bring on the affray; that he desired and intended, if assaulted, to make good his previous threats of using his knife. True, he had a right to dun deceased for his money, but he had no right to do so for the purpose of bringing on an affray in order to afford him a pretext to stab his enemy."

Provoking an Assault. — In a case which arose in Tennessee, *Deadrick, Ch. J.*, observed, "The charge in this case la[illegible]

(1) *Locus Penitentia.* — Although a man should be in the wrong in the first instance, yet a space for repentance is always open; and where a combatant in good faith withdraws as far as he can, really intending to abandon the conflict, and his adversary pursues him, then, if the taking of life becomes necessary to save his own, he will be justified.[1]

c. Abandonment of Intent. — A mere unexecuted intention does not bind or commit the person who conceives or indulges it.[2]

If a party abandoned his evil intention at any time before so much of an act is done as constitutes a crime, such abandonment takes from what has been done its indictable quality.[3]

Where an act is done with intent to commit an assault, but the intent is voluntarily abandoned, or is prevented while the distance between the parties is too great for an actual assault, there can be no conviction as for an assault.[4] And to maintain a prosecution for an evil intention, some concurring act must have followed the unlawful thought.[5]

3. *Criminal Negligence.* — Every person who does an unlawful act carelessly or negligently, or a lawful act in a grossly careless and negligent manner, or who through wanton or reckless conduct, or wilful misconduct or neglect, or gross want of skill and attention, or through wilful omission or neglect of duty, endangers, or causes to be endangered, the life or safety of another, is guilty of a crime.[6]

The failure to do an act of duty is as criminal as to commit a criminal act; as where an officer or other person employed to tend a steam-engine is guilty of negligence, or leaves it in the care of an incompetent person, and thereby an accident happens causing death, he is guilty of manslaughter.[7] And a man may be indicted for either murder or manslaughter if death ensues from the negligent omission of a legal duty.[8]

in effect, that a person who may, by improper conduct, provoke an assault, cannot be allowed to rely on the plea of self-defence; nor can he rely upon such defence if he willingly engage in a fight, even if first assaulted and stricken. . . . Provoking words and gestures might be used from heat of blood, in a sudden quarrel, and a fight might, under such circumstances, be engaged in, during which a party might have the right to defend himself from impending danger of death or great bodily harm." Daniel *v.* State, 10 Lea (Tenn.), 261.

1. State *v.* Partlow, 90 Mo. 608; s. c., 8 West. Rep. 274.

2. Stephens *v.* State, 107 Ind. 185; s. c., 5 West. Rep. 258; Clements *v.* State, 50 Ala. 117.

3. Stephens *v* State, 107 Ind. 185; s. c., 5 West. Rep. 258.

4. People *v* Lilley, 43 Mich. 521.

5. Stephens *v.* State, 107 Ind. 185; s. c., 5 West. Rep. 258; Parmlee *v.* Sloan, 37 Ind. 482; Clements *v.* State, 50 Ala. 117; 1 Bish. Cr. L. § 204.

6. Studstill *v.* State, 7 Ga. 13; Commonwealth *v.* Rodes, 6 B. Mon. (Ky.) 174; Sturges *v.* Maitland, Anth. (N. Y.) 153; Ann *v.* State, 11 Humph. (Tenn.) 159; United States *v.* Freeman, 4 Mason, C. C. 505. See also 1 Bish. Cr. L. (6th ed.) sec. 313; 1 Whart. Cr. L. (8th ed.) sec. 125.

7. United States *v.* Taylor, 5 McL. C C. 242; United States *v.* Farnham, 2 Blatchf. C. C. 528; Reg *v.* Lowe, 4 Cox, C. C. 449; Reg. *v.* Spence, 1 Cox, C C. 352; Reg. *v.* Haines, 2 Carr. & K. 368; Reg. *v.* Hughes, 26 L. J. M. C. 202; Reg. *v.* Benge, 4 Fost. & F. 504.

8. Oliver *v.* State, 17 Ala. 587; Culbreath *v.* Culbreath, 7 Ga. 71; s. c., 50 Am. Dec. 375; State *v.* Goodenow, 65 Me. 30; s. c.,

The law attributes malice to reckless acts of homicide, where no particular motive can be traced.[1] But malice, as distinguished from negligence, is the intent from which flows any unlawful and injurious act committed without legal justification, as shooting into a crowd, in an attempt to shoot a particular individual.[2] And the same is true where a person by mistake shoots another person than the one intended.[3]

Where the gist of the offence is criminal negligence or carelessness, intent will be presumed, as discharging a fire-arm intentionally and carelessly into a crowd of people.[4] Thus, where a defendant standing in a car discharged a pistol downward by his side, intending the ball to go into the floor, and it passed through the foot of a passenger standing behind him, it was held to be a malicious assault.[5]

Where a person deliberately shoots into a crowd with intent to kill A., and wounds B., it is held that he can be convicted of an assault with intent to murder B.[6] And where one who, intending to kill A., assails B. in the dark, he may be indicted for assault with intent to kill B.[7]

But malice is not an element of the offence created by statute for "unlawfully or wantonly" killing, etc., certain animals.[8]

In a prosecution for maliciously shooting with intent to kill, malice must be shown.[9] And the malice required to constitute malicious stabbing is malice in its common-law signification.[10] At common law, a mere police offence is not indictable, where it involves no malice.[11]

Express malice is never to be inferred from the act, or the weapon used, or from a cruel and unnecessary act done, but may be proved by matters *aliunde*; by external circumstances, as well as by verbal declarations.[12] Implied malice is not a fact, but an

1 Am. Cr. Rep. 42, State *v.* O'Brien, 32 N. J. L. (3 Dutch.) 169; Etchberry *v.* Levrelle, 2 Hilt. (N. Y.) 40; People *v.* Enoch, 13 Wend (N. Y.) 159; s. c., 27 Am. Dec. 197; State *v.* Williams, 12 Ired. (N. C.) L. 172; State *v.* Hoover, 4 Dev. & B. (N. C.) L. 365; Commonwealth *v.* Keeper of Prison, 2 Ashm. (Pa.) 227; Wilson *v.* Commonwealth, 10 Serg. & R. (Pa) 373; Ann *v.* State, 11 Humph. (Tenn) 159; United States *v.* Warner, 4 McL. C. C. 463; United States *v.* Freeman, 4 Mason, C. C. 505.

1. Conn *v.* People, 116 Ill. 458; s. c., 3 West. Rep. 481.

2. Reg. *v.* Fretwell, 9 Cox, C. C. 471; s. c., Leigh & C. 443.

3. Rex *v.* Holt, 7 Car. & P. 518.

4. Vandermark *v.* People, 47 Ill. 122; Golliher *v.* Commonwealth, 2 Duvall (Ky.), 116.

5. Commonwealth *v.* Lister, 15 Phila. (Pa.) 405.

6. Dunaway *v.* People, 110 Ill. 333; s. c., 51 Am. Rep. 686.

7. McGehee *v.* State, 62 Miss. 772; s. c., 52 Am. Rep. 209.

8. Tatum *v.* State, 66 Ala. 465.

9. Cline *v.* State, 43 Ohio St. 332.

10. Taylor *v.* State, 6 Lea (Tenn.), 234.

11. Ross *v.* Commonwealth, 2 B. Mon. (Ky.) 417; Commonwealth *v.* Willard, 39 Mass. (22 Pick.) 476; Dobkins *v.* State, 2 Humph. (Tenn.) 424; Pulse *v.* State, 5 Humph. (Tenn.) 108; Rex *v.* Upton, 2 Str 816; Rex *v.* Bryan, 2 Str. 866.

12. Dill *v.* State, 25 Ala. 15; Martin *v.* State, 47 Ala. 564; Miller *v.* State, 37 Ind. 432; *Ex parte* Moore, 30 Ind. 197; People *v.* Barry, 31 Cal. 357; Farris *v.* Commonwealth, 14 Bush (Ky.), 362; State *v.* Hays, 23 Mo. 287; People *v.* Lamb, 3 Keyes (N. Y.), 360; s. c., Harr. & T. Self-Def. 646; Richarte *v.* State, 5 Tex. App. 359; Summers *v.* State, 5 Tex. App. 365; Murray *v.* State, 1 Tex. App. 417; Singleton *v.* State, 1 Tex. App. 501.

A "**Malicious Act**" is where a person wilfully does an act which is illegal, or wil-

inference to be deduced from facts and circumstances; but the distinction between implied and express malice does not affect the criminality of the act.[1]

A man, by mere carelessness, may be guilty of manslaughter; as, permitting an animal of vicious propensities to go at large;[2] or recklessly discharging fire-arms at night, causing the death of a human being.[3] And a physician is criminally liable for causing death by gross ignorance in the selection or application of remedies, but not for a mistake of judgment.[4] If he cause death through lack of skill or inattention, he is guilty of manslaughter, unless he acts in good faith, and with a reasonable degree of skill.[5]

Negligence of a servant, resulting in injury to person or property, cannot be imputed to the master unless it is the natural consequence of such relation, or the master has neglected his duty in the supervision of such employment.[6] But the government, under an indictment against a railroad company for criminal negligence in colliding with a team at a public crossing, must show affirmatively the company's negligence, and the injured person's want of contributory negligence.[7] However, contributory negligence of the person injured is no defence if the injury is the result of recklessness or misconduct of defendant, if the injury inflicted could have been avoided by the defendant.[8]

4. *Act and Intent must unite.* — In every crime, there must be a joint operation of act and intent, or criminal negligence.[9] Intent

fully departs from a known duty, and which in its necessary consequence must result in injury to another. Holland *v.* State, 12 Fla. 117; The Yankee *v.* Gallagher, McAll. C. C. 477; United States *v.* Cutler, 1 Curt. C. C. 501; Reg. *v.* Ward, L. R. 1 C. C. 360; 1 Whart. Cr. L. (8th ed.) sec. 107.

1. Toonev *v.* State, 5 Tex. App. 165; Buckner *v.* Commonwealth, 14 Bush (Ky.), 601; Farris *v.* Commonwealth, 14 Bush (Ky.), 362; Ewing *v.* State, 4 Tex. App. 417; Johnson *v.* State, 4 Tex. App. 598. Wilson *v.* State, 4 Tex. App. 637.

2. Stumps *v.* Kelley, 22 Ill. 140; People *v.* Fuller, 2 Parker, Cr. Rep. (N. Y.) 16.

3. People *v.* Keefer, 18 Cal. 636; Rigmaidon's Case, 1 Lew. C. C. 180.

4. State *v.* Hardister, 38 Ark. 605; s. c., 42 Am. Rep. 5.

5. Fairlee *v.* People, 11 Ill. 1; Commonwealth *v.* Thompson, 6 Mass. 134; Rice *v.* State, 8 Mo. 561; Rex *v.* Long, 4 Carr. & P. 398; Knight's Case, 1 Lew. C. C. 168. See also 1 Hale, P. C. 429; 4 Bl. Com. 14; 1 Bish. Cr. L. (6th ed.) sec. 314.

6. Commonwealth *v.* Boston & L. R. R. Corp., 126 Mass. 61; Commonwealth *v.* Nichols, 51 Mass. (10 Met.) 259; Commonwealth *v.* Morgan, 107 Mass. 199; Commonwealth *v.* Mason, 94 Mass. (12 Allen) 185; State *v.* Smith, 65 Me. 257; Barnes *v.* State, 19 Conn. 398; Anderson *v.* State, 39 Ind. 553; Hipp *v.* State, 5 Blackf. (Ind.) 149; s. c., 33 Am. Dec. 463; State *v.* Berkshire, 2 Ind. 207; State *v.* Bailey, 1 Fost. (N. H.) 185; State *v.* Privett, 4 Jones (N. C.), L. 100; State *v.* Dawson, 2 Bay (S. C.), L. 360; United States *v.* Knowles, 4 Sawy. C. C. 517; Reg. *v.* Lowe, 4 Cox, C. C. 449; Reg. *v.* Vann, 5 Cox, C. C. 379; Reg. *v.* Gray, 4 Fost. & F. 1098; Reg. *v.* Hughes, 7 Cox, C. C. 301; Reg. *v.* Willmett, 3 Cox, C. C. 281; Reg. *v.* Michael, 9 Carr. & P. 356.

7. State *v.* Maine Central R. R. Co., 77 Me. 538.

8. Bowles *v.* State, 58 Ala. 335; State *v.* Hardie, 47 Iowa, 647; Harvey *v.* State, 40 Ind. 516; United States *v.* Jones, 3 Wash. C. C. 209; Blackburn *v.* State, 23 Ohio St. 146; Reg. *v.* Kew, 12 Cox, C. C. 355; Reg. *v.* Haines, 2 Carr. & K. 368; Reg. *v.* Murton, 3 Fost. & F. 492; Reg. *v.* Longbottom, 3 Cox, C. C. 439; Rex *v.* Hickman, 5 Carr. & P. 151; Reg. *v.* Pitts, Carr. & M. 284; Reg. *v.* Swindall, 2 Carr. & K. 230; Reg. *v.* Chamberlain, 10 Cox, C. C. 486; Reg. *v.* Bennett, 8 Cox, C. C. 74.

9. Allen *v.* State, 52 Ala. 393; Miles *v.* State, 58 Ala. 390; Voes *v.* State, 9 Eng. (Ark.) 42; People *v.* Harris, 29 Cal. 679; People *v.* White, 34 Cal. 183; Long *v.* State, 38 Ga. 507; Slattery *v.* People, 76 Ill. 218; Walker *v.* State, 8 Ind. 290; Ross *v.* Com-

may be simultaneous with the act: it need not have existed for any appreciable time before the commission of the act.[1]

Where one enters a house with the intent to commit any crime, it justifies a conviction of the crime of burglary.[2] And it has been said that if, at the time the bailee sells the property, he has the intent to appropriate the proceeds, it is immaterial that he had authority to sell;[3] but the evidence must establish the intent as of the time of the act.[4]

5. *Intent inferred from Act.*—The intent which characterizes the act is generally inferred from the act itself;[5] and it is inferred from the circumstances of the case, and the conduct of the accused, at the time of the act, and subsequent to its commission.[6] However, guilt cannot be inferred from the mere fact that the accused had the ability to commit the act.[7]

Intent draws to itself the consequences of acts done in carrying them into execution.[8] And where the act is done by one of sound mind, and capable to commit crime, the law presumes that the natural, necessary, and even probable consequences were intended by the actor; and where the act was in itself unlawful, even the possible consequences will be presumed to have been intended.[9]

monwealth, 2 B. Mon. (Ky.) 419; Commonwealth *v.* Moise, 2 Mass. 138; State *v.* Will, 1 Dev. & B. (N. C.) L. 121; Gates *v.* Lounsbury, 20 Johns. (N. Y.) 427; Hopkins *v.* Commonwealth, 50 Pa. St. 10; Torrey *v.* Field, 10 Vt. 353. See also 1 Bish. Cr. L. (6th ed.) §§ 204, 206; 3 Greenl. Ev. § 12; 4 Bl. Com. 20; Broom, Com. 874; 1 Hale, P. C. 15.

1. People *v.* Bealoba, 17 Cal. 389.

2. People *v.* Richards, 44 Hun (N. Y.), 278.

3. Epperson *v.* State (Tex. Ct. App. Jan. 1887), 3 S. W. Rep. 789.

4. Cain *v* State (Tex. Ct. App. June 1886), 2 S. W. Rep. 888.

5. Commonwealth *v.* McLaughlin, 87 Mass. (5 Allen) 507; United States *v.* Learned, 1 Abb. C. C. 483; Bain *v.* State, 61 Ala. 76; Hadley *v.* State, 55 Ala. 31; Commander *v.* State, 60 Ala. 1; Stein *v.* State, 37 Ala. 123; Rex *v.* Woodfall, 5 Burr. 2661; Rex *v.* Hunt, 3 Barn. & Ald. 566; Reg. *v.* Regan, 4 Cox, C. C. 335; People *v.* Trim, 39 Cal. 75; Woodward *v.* State, 54 Ga. 186; s. c., 1 Am. Cr. R. 366; Holley *v.* State, 10 Humph. (Tenn.) 141; Ann *v.* State, 11 Humph. (Tenn) 159; Hood *v.* State, 56 Ind. 263; Cluck *v.* State, 40 Ind. 263; Walker *v.* State, 8 Ind. 290; Undermark *v.* People, 47 Ill. 122; Rex *v.* Robinson, 2 Leach, C. L. 149; State *v.* Underwood, 57 Mo. 40; s. c., 1 Am. Cr. R. 251; Commonwealth *v.* Stout, 7 B. Mon. (Ky) 247; State *v.* Goodenow, 65 Me. 30; s. c., 1 Am. Cr. R. 42; Commonwealth *v.* Drew, 4 Mass. 391; State *v.* Smith, 32 Me. 369; Commonwealth *v.* York, 50 Mass. (9 Met.) 103; s. c., 43 Am. Dec. 373; State *v.* Welch, 21 Minn. 22; Stokes *v.* People, 53 N. Y. 164; State *v.* Smith, 2 Strobh. (S. C.) 77; Felton *v.* United States, 96 U. S. (6 Otto) 699; bk. 24, L. ed. 875; State *v.* Patterson, 45 Vt. 308; People *v.* Herrick, 13 Wend. (N. Y.) 87. See also Broom, Com. 876; 1 Bish. Cr. L. (6th ed.) § 288; 1 Russ. Cr. (9th ed.) 82; 3 Green. Ev. § 130.

6. Griggs *v.* State, 58 Ala. 425; People *v.* Bealoba, 17 Cal. 389; People *v.* Soto, 53 Cal. 415; Hill *v.* People, 1 Colo. 436; Slattery *v.* People, 76 Ill. 218.

7. State *v.* Hopkins, 50 Vt. 316.

8. Weston *v.* Commonwealth (Pa.), 2 Cent. Rep. 35.

9. Meredith *v.* State, 60 Ala. 441; Hadley *v.* State, 55 Ala. 31; Commander *v.* State, 60 Ala. 1; Miller *v.* People, 5 Barb. (N. Y.) 203; State *v.* Stanton, 37 Conn. 421; People *v.* Honshell, 10 Cal. 83; Rex *v.* Jones, 2 Carr. & P. 629; State *v.* Merrill, 2 Dev. (N. C.) L. 269; Mitchum *v.* State, 11 Ga. 615; Hill *v.* Commonwealth, 2 Gratt. (Va.) 594; State *v.* Cooper, 13 N. J. L. (1 J. S. Green) 361; s. c., 25 Am. Dec. 490; Jones *v.* State, 29 Ga. 608; Clarke *v.* State, 35 Ga. 383; Studstill *v.* State, 7 Ga. 2; State *v.* Zellers, 7 N. J. L. (2 Halst.) 220; Woodsides *v.* State, 2 How. (Miss.) 656; Rex *v.* Woodburne, 16 How. St. Tr. 54; Walker *v.* State, 8 Ind. 290; Cluck *v.* State, 40 Ind. 263; Hood *v.* State, 56 Ind.

In case of a statutory offence, proof of knowledge that the act was prohibited by law is essential, and a knowledge of the distinction between right and wrong is not sufficient.[1]

Where the statute contains nothing requiring acts to be done knowingly, and the acts done are not *malum in se*, nor infamous, but are merely prohibited, the offender is bound to know the law, and a criminal intent need not be proved.[2]

The intent, if an element of the crime as defined by statute, is implied in the allegation "falsely" making the instrument in an indictment for counterfeiting.[3] And the *gravamen* of the statutory offence of obstructing a public road is that such obstruction is wilful[4] And the intent is immaterial where the statute declares it a misdemeanor to obstruct a public road.[5]

When the statute does not make intent an element of the crime, intent need not be alleged, although, under general principles, it must be proved.[6] And it is held that one who does that which the law forbids, is presumed to have had the criminal intent.[7]

An act is "wilfully" done when done without reasonable ground to believe it to be lawful.[8] And where, in the statute defining the offence, it is declared that the intent may be presumed from the act, the words are to be taken in their literal sense.[9]

Although there must be a former design to take life to constitute murder, yet such design is not necessary where the party killing seeks the quarrel, and uses a deadly weapon.[10]

6. *Malice.* — Malice in the legal sense denotes a wrongful act done intentionally without just cause or excuse; and the intention is an inference of law resulting from the doing of the act, except where the circumstances rebut the presumption of its existence.[11]

263; State *v.* Mitchell, 5 Ired. (N. C.) L. 250; State *v.* Jarrott, 1 Ired. (N. C.) L. 76; Hanrahan *v.* People, 91 Ill. 143; People *v.* Cotteral, 18 Johns. (N. Y.) 115; State *v.* Goodenow, 65 Me. 30; s. c., 1 Am. Cr. R. 42; Commonwealth *v.* Drew, 4 Mass. 391; Commonwealth *v.* York, 50 Mass. (9 Metc.) 93; s. c., 43 Am. Dec. 373; Commonwealth *v.* Bonner, 50 Mass. (9 Met.) 410; Commonwealth *v.* Snelling, 32 Mass. (15 Pick.) 337; State *v.* Gilman, 69 Me. 163; People *v.* Clark, 7 N. Y. 385; Copperman *v.* People, 56 N. Y. 591; Weed *v.* People, 56 N. Y. 628; Coleman *v.* People, 58 N. Y. 555; People *v.* Kirby, 2 Parker, Cr. Rep. (N. Y.) 28; People *v.* Herrick, 13 Wend. (N. Y.) 87; Cathcart *v.* Commonwealth, 1 Wright (Pa.), 108; Hill *v.* State, 5 Tex. App. 2; Weyman *v.* People, 6 Thomp. & C. (N. Y.) 696. See also 1 Greenl. Ev. § 18; 2 Greenl Ev. § 13; Stark. Ev. 738.

1. Parker *v.* State, 20 Tex. App. 451.

2. United States *v.* Leathers, 8 Sawy. C. C. 17.

3. United States *v.* Otey (Or. Cir. Ct.), 31 Fed. Rep. 68.

4. Murphy *v.* State (Tex. Ct. App. May, 1887), 4 S. W. Rep. 906.

5. McKibbin *v.* State, 40 Ark. 480; Clifton *v.* State, 73 Ala. 473; United States *v.* Adams, 2 Dak. 305.

6. State *v.* Hurds, 19 Neb. 316.

7. State *v.* Smith, 93 N. C. 516.

8. Owens *v.* State, 19 Tex. App. 242; Loyd *v.* State, 19 Tex. App. 321.

9. Lane *v.* State, 16 Tex. App. 172.

10. State *v.* Partlow, 90 Mo. 608; s. c., 8 West. Rep. 274.

11. Maynard *v.* F. F. Ins. Co., 34 Cal. 48; People *v.* Taylor, 36 Cal. 255; Hayes *v.* State, 58 Ga. 35; Beauchamp *v.* State, 6 Blackf. (Ind.) 299; Lossen *v.* State, 62 Ind. 437; State *v.* Hays, 23 Mo. 287; Commonwealth *v.* Goodwin, 122 Mass. 19; State *v.* Town, Wright (Ohio), 75; Commonwealth *v.* Green, 1 Ashm. (Pa.) 289; Lander *v.* State, 12 Tex. 462; McCoy *v.* State, 25 Tex. 33; Plasters *v.* State, 1 Tex. App. 673; Farrer *v.* State, 42 Tex. 265; Williams *v.* State, 3 Tex. App. 316; Worley *v.* State, 11 Humph. (Tenn.) 172; Wiggin *v.* Coffin, 3 Story, C. C. 7; United States *v.* Coffin, 1 Sumn. C. C. 394; United

Malice is always presumed where one person deliberately injures another. It is the deliberation with which the act is performed that gives it character. It is the opposite of an act performed under uncontrollable passion, which prevents all deliberation or cool reflection in forming a purpose.[1]

Where, in a homicide, there was no provocation for the shooting, and it was accompanied by threats, the law will infer the existence of malice.[2]

V. Capacity to commit Crime. — All persons capable of exercising their will, or of entertaining a motive, are capable of committing crime.[3] But no act is a crime, if the person, who, at the time the act is done, is prevented by idiocy, defective mental power, or by a diseased mind, from knowing the nature of his act, or that his act is wrong, or from controlling his own conduct, unless the want of power of control has been superinduced by his own fault.

1. *Corporations.* — Corporations are persons within the purview of the criminal law, and are liable for a breach of duty imposed by law, and for any neglect which would be indictable in a natural person, and for misfeasance as well as nonfeasance; but not for felonies or public wrongs, nor for any act which is not in their power to prevent.[4] At common law an indictment will lie against

States *v.* Taylor, 2 Sumn. C. C. 586; Blunt *v.* Little, 3 Mason, C. C. 102; Dexter *v.* Spear, 4 Mason, C. C. 192; United States *v.* Outerbridge, 5 Sawy. C. C. 620; Wason *v.* Walter, L. R. 4 Q. B. 73; Bromage *v.* Prosser, 4 Barn. & C. 247; Duncan *v.* Thwaites, 3 Barn. & C. 556; Rex *v.* Philip, 1 Moody, C. C. 264; Rex *v.* Selten, 11 Cox, C. C. 674; McIntyre *v.* McBean, 13 Up. Can. Q. B. 542. See also 1 Russ. Cr. (9th ed.)667; 1 Whart. Cr. L. (8th ed.) §§ 106, 122; 1 Bish. Cr. L. (6th ed.) 429; 4 Bl. Com. 199; 1 Arch. Cr. Pr. 368.

1. Spies *v.* People (The Anarchists' Case), 122 Ill. 1; s. c., 10 West. Rep. 701.

2. Boyler *v.* State, 105 Ind. 469; s. c., 2 West. Rep. 788.

3. **A Governor as a Criminal.** — It would seem that the governor of a State may be amenable to a criminal process. See State *ex rel.* Herron *v.* Smith, 44 Ohio St. 349; s. c., 4 West. Rep. 110.

It is said in Dalton *v.* State, *ex rel.* Richardson, 43 Ohio St. 682; s. c., 1 West. Rep. 773, that "it is a fundamental principle that every citizen and every public officer, however high his grade, is amenable to judicial control. It was but a few years since that the governor of this State was arrested by the sheriff of an adjoining county, and compelled to stand at the bar of the court and plead as a common criminal. He did not claim, nor could he claim, exemption from obedience to the mandates of the court."

The opinions in which the above doctrine is enunciated are dissenting opinions, but the opinions of such judges as William W. Johnson and Selwyn N. Owen are well worthy of careful consideration on all subjects.

4. Barnett *v.* State, 54 Ala. 579; State *v.* Ohio & M. R. R., 23 Ind. 362; State *v.* Great Wks., etc., Co., 20 Me. 41; s. c., 38 Am. Dec. 38; Commonwealth *v.* Boston & L. R. R. Co., 126 Mass. 61; Commonwealth *v.* Worcester T. Co., 20 Mass. (3 Pick.) 327; Commonwealth *v.* New Bedford Bridge, 68 Mass. (2 Gray) 339; State *v.* Morris & E. R. R. Co, 23 N. J. L. (3 Zab.) 360; People *v.* N. Y. Cent., etc., R. R. Co., 74 N. Y. 302; People *v.* Corp. of Albany, 11 Wend. (N. Y.) 539; s. c., 27 Am. Dec. 95; People *v.* Long Island R. R. Co., 4 Park Cr Rep. (N. Y.) 602; State *v.* Cin. Fert. Co., 24 Ohio St. 611; Louisville, etc., R. R. Co. *v.* State, 3 Head (Tenn.), 523; s. c., 75 Am. Dec. 778; State *v.* Vermont Cent. R. R. Co., 30 Vt. 108; Copley *v.* G. & B. S. M. Co., 2 Wood, C. C. 494; Reg. *v.* Birmingham & G. R. Co., 9 Car. & P. 469; Reg. *v.* Grt. North of Eng. R. Co., 9 Q. B. N. S. 315; s. c., 2 Cox, C. C. 70. See 2 Russ. Cr. (9th ed.) 327; 1 Bish. Cr. L. (6th ed.) sec. 417; Kyd, Corp. 225; 3 Chitt. Cr. L. 566.

A Corporation Aggregate may be guilty of a misdemeanor, as in the non-repair of bridges, which it is their duty to repair. Reg. *v.* Birmingham & G. R. Co., 3 Eng. Ry. & C. Cas. 148; s. c., 2 Gale & D. 236; 9 Carr. & P. 469; 6 Jur. 804.

a corporation for misfeasance.[1] And a railway may be indicted, if it so construct its railway across any established road or way, as to be a serious inconvenience, or dangerous obstruction, along the road or way.[2]

A street-car company is responsible for the criminal acts of its driver, while acting within the scope of his employment.[3] And a railroad company owning connecting lines under the federal statutes[4] is liable only for a default occurring on its own line.[5]

Corporations may be indicted for libel,[6] or for nuisances,[7] or for neglect to repair highways and bridges when it is their duty to do so; or for failure to open roads, or for not maintaining them.[8]

2. *Infancy.* — An infant under seven years of age is conclusively presumed incapable of committing crime; for the legal presumption is, he cannot have discretion.[9] He cannot be capitally punished, nor be indicted for an offence in its nature capital, nor for a felony.[10]

1. Reg. *v.* Great N. of Eng. R. Co., 9 Q. B. N. S. 315; s. c., 10 Jur. 755; 16 L. J. M. C. 16.

2. Northern Central Railway Co. *v.* Commonwealth, 90 Pa. St. 300.

3. Commonwealth *v.* Brockton Street Ry., 143 Mass. 501; s. c., 3 New Eng. Rep. 707

4. United States Rev. Stat. sec. 4386, *et seq.*

5. United States *v.* Louisville & Nashville R. R. Co., 18 Fed. Rep. 480.

6. Maynard *v.* F. F. Ins. Co., 34 Cal. 48; Whileman *v.* Wilmington R. R. Co., 2 Harr. (Del.) 514; Dater *v.* Troy T. Co., 2 Hill (N. Y.), 629; Bloodgood *v.* Mohawk & H. R. R. Co., 18 Wend. (N. Y) 9; s. c., 31 Am. Dec. 313; Orr *v.* Bank of U. S., 1 Ohio, 36; s. c., 13 Am. Dec. 588; Lyman *v.* White Riv. B. Co., 2 Aik. (Vt.) 255; s. c., 16 Am. Dec. 705; Eastern Co.'s R. R. *v.* Broom, 6 Exch. 314; Whitfield *v.* S. E. R. Co., Ellis, B. & E. 113.

7. Prim *v.* State, 36 Ala. 244; State *v.* Great Wks. Co., 20 Me. 41; s. c., 38 Am. Dec. 38; Commonwealth *v.* New Bedford Bridge, 68 Mass. (2 Gray) 339; Benson *v.* Monson & B. M. Co., 50 Mass. 562; State *v.* Morris & Essex R. R. Co., 23 N. J. L. (3 Zab) 360; State *v.* Cincinnati Fert. Co., 24 Ohio St. 611; Chestnut Hill T. Co. *v.* Rutter, 4 Serg. & R. (Pa.) 6; Delaware Div. C. Co. *v.* Commonwealth, 60 Pa. St. 367; Wartman *v.* Philadelphia, 33 Pa. St. (9 Casey) 102; Commonwealth *v.* Ohio, etc., R. R., 1 Grant (Pa.), 329; Simpson *v.* State, 10 Yerg. (Tenn.) 525; Hill *v.* State, 4 Sneed (Tenn.), 443; State *v.* Shelbyville, 4 Sneed (Tenn.), 176; Louisville, etc., R. R. Co. *v.* State, 3 Head (Tenn.), 523; s. c., 75 Am. Dec. 778; State *v.* Vermont R. R. Co., 30 Vt. 103; Commonwealth *v.* Turnpike Co., 2 Va. Cas. 362; Wilkes *v.* Hungerford Market Co., 2 Bing. (N. C.) 281; Mayor of Lyme Regis *v.* Henley, 1 Bing. (N. C.) 222; Chichester *v.* Lethbridge, Willes, 74; Reg. *v.* Medley, 6 Car. & P. 299.

8. Malone *v.* State, 51 Ala. 55; Smoot *v.* Wetumpka, 24 Ala. 112; State *v.* Kittery, 5 Me. 254; Mower *v.* Leicester, 9 Mass 247; s. c., 6 Am. Dec. 63; Biddle *v.* Proprietors, 7 Mass. 169; Commonwealth *v.* Inhab. of Deerfield. 88 Mass. (6 Allen) 449; Commonwealth *v.* Wilmington, 105 Mass. 199; State *v.* Dover, 10 N. H. 394; Waterford, etc., T. Co. *v.* People, 9 Barb. (N. Y.) 161; State *v.* N. J T. Co., 16 N. J. L. (1 Harr.) 222; Stoors *v.* Utica, 17 N. Y. 104; s. c., 72 Am. Dec. 431; Susquehanna Road *v.* People, 15 Wend. (N. Y.) 267; State *v.* Barksdale, 5 Humph. (Tenn.) 154; State *v.* Murfreesboro, 11 Humph. (Tenn.) 217; State *v.* Patten, 4 Ired. (N. C.) L. 16; State *v.* Whittingham, 7 Vt. 391; State *v.* Town of Fletcher, 13 Vt. 124; Commonwealth *v.* Turnpike Co., 2 Va. Cas. 362; Henly *v.* Mayor of Stratford, 14 East, 348; Reg. *v.* Birmingham & G. R. Co., 3 Q. B. 223; Rex *v.* Severn R. R. Co., 2 Barn. & Ald. 646; Matthews *v.* West London W. W. Co., 3 Camp. 403; Lancaster C. Co. *v.* Parnaby, 11 Adol. & E. 223; Church *v.* Imperial G. L. & C. Co., 6 Adol. & E. 246.

9. Willet *v.* Commonwealth, 13 Bush (Ky.), 230; People *v.* Townsend, 3 Hill (N. Y.), 479; Reniger *v.* Fogossa, 1 Plowd. 19; Marsh *v.* Loader, 14 C. B. N. S. 535. See 4 Bl. Com. 22; 1 Hale, P. C. 27; 1 Hawk. P. C. Ch. 2; Dalt. Just. 334; 1 Bish Cr. L. (6th ed.) sec. 68; 1 Whart. Cr. L. (8th ed.) sec. 67; 2 Greenl. Ev. sec. 4.

Infant under Seven. — Hence it follows that an infant under the age of seven years cannot incur the guilt of felony. Marsh *v.* Leader, 14 C. B. (N. S.) 535; s. c., 11 W. R. 784. See AGE, vol. 1, p 326.

10. People *v.* Townsend, 3 Hill (N. Y.),

At seven years of age criminal responsibility begins, subject to the presumption in favor of infancy; but malice supplies age; and where the infant understands the nature and consequence of his acts, and where his acts indicate design and malice, he may be convicted.[1] The presumption of law is, that a child between seven and fourteen years of age had not guilty knowledge that he or she was doing wrong under an indictment for felony. It is a question for the jury.[2]

Where an infant is arraigned for a felony, the disputable presumption of the law, that, in the interval between seven and fourteen years of age, he is incapable of committing crime, is to be rebutted, and the evidence of malice, which is to supply age, should be strong and clear beyond all doubt and contradiction.[3]

At common law, an infant under fourteen was presumed incapable of committing rape, but the presumption gave way on proof that he had reached the age of puberty.[4] But the presumption is only *prima facie*, and may be rebutted by clear evidence of a mischievous discretion, or by proof of knowledge of good and evil, which knowledge must be distinctly made to appear from the circumstances.[5]

A boy under fourteen is not liable for ordinary assault and battery, unless it be aggravated, or be prompted by lust.[6] And infants under fourteen years of age may be convicted or acquitted of high crimes, as the degree of intelligence and the circumstances

479; Reniger *v.* Fogossa, 1 Plowd. 19. See 4 Bl. Com. 23.

1. Godfrey *v.* State, 31 Ala. 323; Willet *v.* Commonwealth, 13 Bush (Ky.), 230; Commonwealth *v.* Mead, 92 Mass. (10 Allen) 396, 398; State *v.* Learnard, 41 Vt. 585; State *v.* Goin, 9 Humph. (Tenn.) 175; People *v.* Randolph, 2 Park. Cr. Rep. (N. Y.) 174; State *v.* Aaron, 4 N. J. L. (1 South.) 231; 4 Bl. Com. 22.

2. State *v.* Adams, 76 Mo. 355; Rex *v.* Owen, 4 Car. & P. 236.

3. State *v.* Tice, 90 Mo. 112; s. c., 6 West. Rep. 677.

Doli Incapax. — Under seven years of age an infant cannot be guilty of felony. In the interval between that age and that of fourteen years, he is *prima facie* adjudged to be *doli incapax*. And when an infant is arraigned for a felony, this disputable presumption of the law — for the *onus* in such cases is on the State — is to be rebutted, and the "evidence of that malice which is to supply age, ought to be strong and clear beyond all doubt and contradiction." 4 Bl. Com. 24. In this way only can the legal maxim be applied that "*malitia supplet ætatem*." State *v.* Tice, 90 Mo. 412; s. c., 6 West. Rep. 677.

4. People *v.* Randolph, 2 Park. Cr. Rep. 174; State *v.* Handy, 4 Harr. (Del.) 566; State *v.* Pugh, 7 Jones (N. C.) L. 61; State *v.* Sam, Winst. (N. C.) 300; Williams *v.* State, 14 Ohio, 222; s. c., 45 Am. Dec. 536; Moore *v.* State, 17 Ohio St. 521; O'Meara *v.* State, 17 Ohio St. 515; Commonwealth *v.* Green, 19 Mass. (2 Pick.) 380; Rex *v.* Eldershaw, 3 Car. & P. 396; Reg. *v.* Phillips, 8 Car. & P. 736; Reg. *v.* Jordan, 9 Car & P. 118; Reg. *v.* Brindlow, 9 Car. & P. 366.

5. Godfrey *v.* State, 31 Ala. 323; Willet *v.* Commonwealth, 13 Bush (Ky.), 230; Commonwealth *v.* Mead, 92 Mass. (10 Allen) 396, 398; State *v.* Guild, 10 N. J. L. (5 Halst.) 163; s. c., 18 Am. Dec. 404; People *v.* Davis, 1 Wheel. Cr. Cas. (Mass.) 230; People *v.* Teller, 1 Wheel. Cr. Cas. (Mass.) 231; State *v.* Doherty, 2 Tenn. 80; Miller *v.* People, 5 Barb. (N. Y.) 203; Walker's Case, 5 City Hall Rec. (N. Y.) 137; State *v.* Goin, 9 Humph. (Tenn.) 175; State *v.* Pugh, 7 Jones (N. C.) L. 61; State *v.* Learnard, 41 Vt. 585; State *v.* Arnold, 13 Ired. (N. C.) L. 184; Rex *v.* York, 1 Fost. C. L. 70; Reg. *v.* Smith, 1 Cox, C. C. 260; Rex *v.* Owen, 4 Car. & P. 236; Reg. *v.* Groombridge, 7 Car. & P. 582; Reg *v.* Vamplew, 3 Fost. & F. 520; Staundeforde, P. C. ch. 19; 1 Hale, P. C. 27.

6. State *v.* Pugh, 7 Jones (N. C.) L. 61; Reg. *v.* Allen, 1 Den. C. C. 264; Rex *v.* Eldershaw, 3 Car. & P. 396; Rosc. Cr. Ev. 973; 1 Hale, P. C. 630.

of the case may warrant.[1] The capacity of an infant under fourteen years of age is determined from the facts of the case: independent evidence is not necessary.[2]

At the age of fourteen all presumption in favor of infancy ceases; and above that age an infant is presumed to be capable of committing any offence, except such as consist in nonfeasance merely.[3] A school-boy of such years and discretion as to be responsible for crime, was held guilty of a criminal assault and battery, though he acted without malice, when he threw a stone at a comrade and hit him.[4]

The ordinary opinions of medical experts are admissible to prove age; and when it cannot be ascertained by inspection, the court and jury must decide.[5] And the confessions of an infant otherwise competent are admissible against him in the same manner as confessions of adults, if the *corpus delicti* be otherwise proved.[6]

3. *Idiocy.*—The understanding may be immature from idiocy, or it may be affected by lunacy, or some derangement arising from disease of the brain subsequently to its full development.[7] Idiocy consists in a deficiency of the mental faculties, either congenital or the result of arrested development during infancy: it is sterility of mind, and not a perversion of the understanding.[8] An idiot is a person without understanding, and who is legally presumed

1. Godfrey *v.* State, 31 Ala. 323; State *v.* Guild, 10 N. J. L. (5 Halst.) 163; s. c., 18 Am. Dec. 404; State *v.* Bostick, 4 Harr. (Del.) 563; State *v.* Aaron, 4 N. J. L. (1 South.) 231; s. c., 7 Am. Dec. 5; Commonwealth *v.* McKeagy, 1 Ashm. (Pa.) 246, 248; Rex *v.* York, 1 Fost. C. L. 70; Case of Dean, 1 Hale, P. C. 25; Spigurnel's Case, 1 Hale, P. C. 26; Case of Alice de Waldeborough, Fitzh. Abr. 118, 170; Rosc. Cr. Ev. 972; 4 Bl. Com. 23.

Convicting Infant of Felony.—Felony can be established against an infant of eleven years, only by the strongest and clearest proof of his capacity to entertain a criminal intent. Angelo *v.* People, 96 Ill. 209; s. c., 36 Am. Rep. 132.

Rape by Infant.—A male infant about twelve years old assisting his elder brother to commit rape cannot be convicted as principal in the second degree. Law *v.* Commonwealth, 75 Va. 885; s. c., 40 Am. Rep. 780.

2. State *v.* Toney, 45 S. C. 409.

Presumption as to Discretion.—Where an infant is arraigned for a felony, the disputable presumption, that between seven and fourteen years of age he is incapable to commit crime, must be rebutted by evidence of malice, which is to supply age, and such evidence should be clear and strong, and beyond all doubt. State *v.* Tice, 90 Mo. 112; s. c., 6 West. Rep. 677.

3. Irby *v.* State, 32 Ga. 496; State *v.* Bostick, 4 Harr. (Del.) 536; State *v.* Handy, 4 Harr. (Del.) 566; McDaniel *v.* State, 5 Tex. App. 475; People *v.* Kendall, 25 Wend. (N. Y.) 399; s. c., 37 Am. Dec. 240; State *v.* Goin, 9 Humph. (Tenn.) 175; Rex *v.* Sutton, 3 Adol. & E. 597. See 1 Hale, P. C. 20; 1 Bish. Cr. L. sec. 368.

4. Hill *v.* State, 63 Ga. 578; s. c., 36 Am. Rep. 120.

5. People *v.* Townsend, 3 Hill (N. Y.), 479; State *v.* Smith, Phill. (N. C.) 302; State *v.* Arnold, 13 Ired. (N. C.) L. 184.

6. State *v.* Guild, 10 N. J. L. (5 Halst.) 163; State *v.* Bostick, 4 Harr. (Del.) 563. See 1 Arch. Cr. Pr. 13; Mather *v.* Clark, 2 Ark. 209; Rex *v.* Wild, 1 Moody, 452; Rex *v.* Upchurch, 1 Moody, 465; Reg. *v.* Reeve, 12 Cox, C. C. 179; 1 Green. Cr. Rep. 398; Rosc. Cr. Ev. (7th ed.) 38; 1 Bish. Cr. L. (6th ed.) sec. 370; 1 Hale, P. C. 27; 4 Bl. Com. 24.

7. 4 Bl. Com. 21; 1 Russ. Cr. (9th ed.) 6; 1 Whart. Cr. L. (8th ed.) sec. 32; 1 Beck, Med. Jur. 721; Reg. *v.* Shaw, L. R. 1 C. C. 145.

8. Somers *v.* Pumphrey, 24 Ind. 231; 1 Beck, Med. Jur 722; Chitt. Med. Jur. sec. 345; 1 Bl. Com. 302; 1 Bouv. Law Dic. (15th ed.) 764; 1 Whart. Cr. L. (8th ed.) sec. 34; 1 Russ. Cr. (9th ed.) 11; 1 Bish. Cr. L. (6th ed.), sec. 379.

never to be likely to have any; as where a person cannot count twenty, nor tell the names of his parents, or his own age.[1]

An idiot is considered at law incapable of committing crime; and when idiocy exists in reference to the particular act, the court will direct an acquittal;[2] for one mentally imbecile is incapable of committing crime.[3]

4. *Deaf and Dumb Persons.* — A man deaf and dumb from his infancy is, in presumption of law, an idiot.[4] But a person born deaf and dumb, but not blind, is not an idiot.[5]

The want of hearing may exist in connection with responsibility for crime, and if such a person is shown to be able to comprehend the nature of his act, he may be convicted; but persons born deaf, dumb, and blind, are presumed to be idiots, and not capable of committing crime, yet the presumption may be rebutted.[6]

In the case of deaf-mutes, malice cannot be implied.[7]

VI. Consent. — Consent to the perpetration of an act affecting the consenting party, and not leading to a breach of the peace, deprives such act of its criminal character,[8] as where one whips another with his consent;[9] but not if done in public, or likely to disturb the public peace.[10] (See CONSENT, vol. 3, p. 662.)

VII. Accident or Mistake. — 1. *Accident.* — Where accidental mischief results from the proper performance of a lawful act, the party committing it is excused from all guilt;[11] but if in the performance of an act which is morally wrong, it is otherwise.[12]

If a physician or surgeon, in the exercise of his profession,

1. Ball *v.* Mannen, 3 Bligh, N. S. 1; Co. Lit. 247; Fitzh. Natura Brevium, 233; 1 Arch. Cr. Pr. 16; 2 Kent Com. 573; Shelford, Lun. 2.

2. McAllister *v.* State, 17 Ala. 434; s. c., 52 Am. Dec. 180; United States *v.* Shultz, 6 McL. C. C. 121; People *v.* Sprague, 2 Park. Cr. Rep. (N. Y.) 43; Vance *v.* Commonwealth, 2 Va. Cas. 132; 4 Bl. Com. 24; 1 Russ. Cr. (9th ed.) 11; Reg. *v.* Southey, 4 Fost. & F. 864.

3. Pettigrew *v.* State, 12 Tex. App. 225.

4. Hale, P. C. 34. See DEAF AND DUMB, vol. 4, p. .

5. Coll. Lun. 4, sec. 5.

6. Commonwealth *v.* Hill, 14 Mass. 207; State *v.* Harris, 8 Jones (N. C.) L. 136; s c., 78 Am. Dec, 272; Rex *v.* Steel, 1 Leach, 451; Reg. *v.* Whitfield, 3 Car. & K. 121; Rex *v.* Pritchard, 7 Car. & P. 303; Shelford, Lun.; 3 Co. Lit. 42; 1 Bish. Cr. L. (6th ed) sec. 396; 1 Russ. Cr. (9th ed.) 11, 12

7. State *v.* Draper, Houst. Cr. Rep. (Del.) 291.

8. Richie *v.* State, 58 Ind. 355; Commonwealth *v.* Stratton, 114 Mass. 303; Don Moran *v.* People, 25 Mich. 356; Pillow *v.* Bushnell, 3 Barb. (N. Y.) 156; Reg. *v.* Bennett, 4 Fost. & F. 1105; Reg. *v.* Case, 4 Cox, C. C. 220; Reg. *v.* Flattery, 13 Cox, C. C. 388; Reg. *v.* Read, 2 Carr. & K. 957; Rex *v.* Martin, 2 Moody, 123; Reg. *v.* Meredith, 8 Car. & P. 589; 1 Bish. Cr. L. (6th ed.) sec. 257; 1 Whart. Cr. L (8th ed.) sec. 142.

9. Duncan *v.* Commonwealth, 6 Dana (Ky.), 295; Commonwealth *v.* Parker, 50 Mass. (9 Metc.) 263; State *v.* Beck, 1 Hill (S. C.), 363; State *v.* Cooper, 22 N. J. L. (2 Zab.) 52; Champer *v.* State, 14 Ohio, 437; Commonwealth *v.* Welch, 73 Mass. (7 Gray) 324; Commonwealth *v.* Barrett, 108 Mass. 302.

10. Commonwealth *v.* Wood, 77 Mass. (11 Gray) 85; Reg. *v.* Billingham, 2 Car. & P. 234; Reg. *v.* Perkins, 4 Car. & P. 537; 1 East, P. C. 270; Fost. Cr. L. 260.

11. McPherson *v.* State, 22 Ga. 479; Aaron *v.* State, 31 Ga. 167; State *v.* Benham, 23 Iowa, 154; Commonwealth *v.* Campbell, 89 Mass (7 Allen) 541; Duncan *v.* State, 7 Humph. (Tenn.) 148; Plummer *v.* State, 4 Tex. App. 310; Hinchcliffe's Case, 1 Lewin, 161; Rex *v.* Hall, Kelyng, C. C. 40; 4 Bl. Com. 26; 1 Hale, P. C. 42.

12. Epps *v.* State, 19 Ga. 103; Webster *v.* Commonwealth, 59 Mass. (5 Cush.) 295; Commonwealth *v.* Dana, 43 Mass. 329; 1 Hale, P. C. 39; 1 Hawk. P. C. chap. 1, sec. 3; 1 Bish. Cr. L. (6th ed.) sec. 346.

using his best skill and judgment, accidentally causes the death of his patient, he is not criminally liable, even though he acts with gross ignorance as to the means of cure.[1]

2. *Mistake.* — If an act is unlawful, but mistakenly believed to be innocent, its commission is not a criminal offence.[2] A man will be excused where he acts under a mistake, provided he acts honestly and in good faith, — where the act, but for the mistake, would not have been unlawful.[3]

Ignorance or mistake of fact sometimes renders that innocent which would otherwise be criminal, and will or will not excuse acts according to the original intention; but ignorance of facts which might have been known by reasonable diligence will not excuse.[4] Thus, an honest misapprehension of the ownership of property will excuse larceny.[5] And one cannot be convicted of obstructing a highway, when he was ignorant of the fact that it was a highway.[6] But ignorance of fact is no defence where the statute makes the crime indictable irrespective of guilty knowledge.[7]

1. Commonwealth *v.* Thompson, 6 Mass. 134; Rice *v.* State, 8 Mo. 561. *Compare* McCandless *v.* McWha, 10 Harris (Pa.), 261; Reg. *v.* Whitehead, 2 Car. & K. 202; Reg. *v.* Crook, 1 Fost. & F. 521; Rex *v.* Long, 4 Car. & P. 440; Rex *v.* Williamson, 3 Car. & P. 635; Rex *v.* Simpson, 4 Car. & P. 407; Reg. *v.* Senior, 1 Moody. 346; Rex *v.* Spilling, 2 Moody & R. 107.

2. Dickens *v.* State, 30 Ga. 383; Hull *v.* State, 34 Ga. 208.

3. The Marianna Flora, 24 U. S. (11 Wheat.) 1; bk. 6, L. ed. 405; United States *v.* The Malek Adhel, 43 U. S. (2 How.) 210; bk. 11, L. ed. 239; United States *v.* Liddle, 2 Wash. C. C. 205; United States *v.* Ortega, 2 Wash. C. C. 531; United States *v.* Benner, Baldw. C. C. 234; People *v.* Torres, 38 Cal. 141; State *v.* Matthews, 20 Mo. 55; State *v.* Graham, 46 Mo. 490; Cutter *v.* State, 36 N. J. L. (7 Vr.) 125; Logue *v* State, 38 Pa. St. 265; State *v.* Belk, 76 N. C. 10; People *v.* Muldoon, 2 Parker, Cr. R. (N. Y.) 13; Johnson *v.* State, 26 Tex. 117; Commonwealth *v.* Kirby, 56 Mass. (2 Cush.) 577; Rex *v.* Ricketts, 3 Camp. 68; Yates *v.* People, 32 N. Y. 500.

In Maryland. — But under the Maryland statute an honest mistake of fact, leading to the publication of libellous matter, is no defence. Richardson *v.* State (Md.), 5 Cent. Rep. 565.

4. Commonwealth *v.* Kirby, 56 Mass. (2 Cush.) 577; United States *v.* Pearce, 2 McL. C. C. 14; State *v.* Cain, 9 W. Va. 559; Myers *v.* State, 1 Conn. 502; Unwin *v.* Clark, L. R. 1 Q. B. 417. See 1 Hale, P. C. 6; 1 Russ. Cr. (9th ed.) 46; 4 Bl. Com. 27; Broom, Leg. Max. 190; 1 Whart. Cr. L. (9th ed.) § 87; Duncan *v.* State, 7 Humph. (Tenn.) 148; Farbach *v.* State, 24 Ind. 77; Rineman *v.* State, 24 Ind. 80; Commonwealth *v.* Rogers, 48 Mass. (7 Metc.) 500; Commonwealth *v.* Boynton, 84 Mass. (2 Allen) 160; Commonwealth *v.* Farren, 91 Mass. (9 Allen) 489; Commonwealth *v.* Waite, 93 Mass. (11 Allen) 54; Commonwealth *v.* Emmons, 98 Mass. 6; State *v.* Smith, 10 R. I. 258; Ulrich *v.* Commonwealth, 6 Bush (Ky.), 400; Commonwealth *v.* Wentworth, 118 Mass. 441; State *v.* Hartfiel, 24 Wis. 60; Beckham *v.* Nacke, 56 Mo. 546; Reg. *v.* Robbins, 1 Car. & K. 452; Reg. *v.* Olifier, 10 Cox, C. C. 402; Reg. *v.* Mycock, 12 Cox, C. C. 28; Reg. *v.* Booth, 12 Cox, C. C. 231; Reg. *v.* Prince, L. R. 2 C. C. 154. *Compare* Miller *v.* State, 3 Ohio St. 475; 1 Bish. Cr. L. (6th ed.) § 301.

5. Commonwealth *v.* Doane, 55 Mass. (1 Cush.) 5; State *v.* Homes, 17 Mo. 379; State *v.* Bond, 8 Iowa, 540.

6. Guthrie *v.* State (Tex. Ct. App.), May, 1887.

7. Smith *v.* State, 55 Ala. 1; Schuster *v.* State, 48 Ala. 199; State *v.* Hallett, 8 Ala. 159; Barnes *v.* State, 19 Conn. 398; Farmer *v.* People, 77 Ill. 322; McCutcheon *v.* People, 69 Ill. 601; Hood *v.* State, 56 Ind. 263; Brown *v.* State, 24 Ind. 113; Farbach *v.* State, 24 Ind. 77; Goetz *v.* State, 41 Ind. 162; Stern *v.* State, 53 Ga. 229; State *v.* Ruhl, 8 Iowa, 447; State *v.* Newton, 44 Iowa, 45; Davis *v.* Commonwealth, 13 Bush (Ky.), 318; Ulrich *v.* Commonwealth, 6 Bush (Ky.), 400; Commonwealth *v.* Mash, 48 Mass. (7 Met.) 472; Commonwealth *v.* Elwell, 43 Mass. (2 Met.) 190; Commonwealth *v.* Thompson, 88 Mass. (6 Allen)

Ignorance of fact is admissible to negative a particular intent.[1] Thus, it is not extortion to receive money believed to be due; nor is it an offence to resist an officer, honestly supposing him to be a private person; nor to capture a vessel, when the captured vessel was honestly supposed to be piratical.[2]

3. *Mistake of Legal Rights.* — Where a man acts in good faith upon a mistaken view of his legal rights, and not from wantonness or evil intent, or in the honest execution of a supposed duty, his acts will be excused;[3] as there can be no conviction for a criminal offence without proof of guilty knowledge and guilty intent.

591; s. c., 93 Mass. (11 Allen) 23; Thompson *v* Thompson, 114 Mass. 566; Commonwealth *v.* Emmons, 98 Mass. 6; Commonwealth *v.* Goodman, 97 Mass. 117; Commonwealth *v.* Lattinville, 120 Mass. 385; Commonwealth *v.* Finnegan, 124 Mass. 324; Commonwealth *v.* Boynton, 84 Mass. (2 Allen) 160; Commonwealth *v.* Farren, 91 Mass. (9 Allen) 489; Commonwealth *v.* Nichols, 92 Mass. (10 Allen) 199; Commonwealth *v.* Waite, 93 Mass. (11 Allen) 264; Commonwealth *v.* Smith, 103 Mass. 444; Commonwealth *v.* Raymond, 97 Mass. 567; Commonwealth *v.* Bradford, 50 Mass. (9 Met.) 268; State *v.* Heck, 23 Minn. 549; Beckham *v.* Nacke, 56 Mo. 546; State *v.* Griffith, 67 Mo. 287; State *v.* Balt. St. Nav. Co., 13 Md. 187; Minor *v.* Happersett, 53 Mo. 58; State *v.* Stimson, 24 N. J. L. (4 Zab.) 478; State *v.* Hause, 71 N. C. 518; State *v.* Hart, 6 Jones (N. C.), L. 389; Crabtree *v.* State, 30 Ohio St. 382; Farrell *v.* State, 32 Ohio St. 456; State *v.* Goodenow, 65 Me. 30; State *v.* Smith, 10 R. I. 258; State *v.* Melville, 11 R. I. 417; Duncan *v.* State, 7 Humph. (Tenn.) 148; McGuire *v.* State, 7 Humph. (Tenn.) 54; Lawrence *v.* Commonwealth, 30 Gratt. (Va.) 845; State *v.* Cain, 9 W. Va. 559; United States *v.* Dodge, Deady, U. S. D. C. 186; United States *v.* Anthony, 11 Blatchf. C. C. 200; People *v.* Zeiger, 6 Parker, Cr. R. (N. Y.) 355; Rex *v.* Myddleton, 6 T. R. 739; Reg. *v.* Robins, 1 Carr. & K. 456; Reg. *v.* Olifier, 10 Cox, C. C. 402; Reg. *v.* Booth, 12 Cox, C. C. 231; Reg. *v.* Green, 3 Fost. & F. 274; Reg. *v* Hibbert, L. R. 1 C. C. 184. See also 1 Whart. Cr. L. (8th ed.) sec. 88.

1. People *v.* Reed, 47 Barb. (N. Y.) 235; United States *v.* Carr, 1 Woods, C. C. 480; Reg. *v.* Reed, Carr. & M. 306; Merry *v.* Green, 7 Mees. & W. 623; Rex *v.* Levett, Cro. Car. 538; Hudson *v.* MacRae, 4 Best & S. 585; Reg. *v.* Macleod, 12 Cox, C. C. 534; Reg. *v.* Hicklin, L. R. 3 Q. B. 360; Hearne *v.* Garton, 2 El. & E. 66. See also 1 Whart. Cr. L. (8th ed.) sec. 87; 4 Bl. Com. 179, 1 Hale, P. C. 42, 501; 2 Hale, P. C. 411; 3 Inst. 52, 211; Oliver *v.* State, 17 Ala. 587; Isham *v.* State, 38 Ala. 213; Farbach *v.* State, 24 Ind. 77; Rineman *v.* State. 24 Ind. 80, Squire *v.* State, 46 Ind. 459; People *v.* Wilson, 64 Ill. 195; Commonwealth *v.* Smaltz, 3 Bush (Ky.), 32; Commonwealth *v.* Kirby, 56 Mass. (2 Cush.) 577; Commonwealth *v.* Rogers, 48 Mass. (7 Met.) 500; Commonwealth *v.* Power, 48 Mass. (7 Met. 596; Curtis *v.* Mussey, 72 Mass. (6 Gray) 261; Commonwealth *v.* Wentworth, 118 Mass. 441; Hourigan *v.* Nowell, 110 Mass. 470; Commonwealth *v.* Presby, 80 Mass. (14 Gray) 65; State *v.* Shippey, 10 Minn. 223; State *v.* O'Connor, 31 Mo. 389; Commonwealth *v.* Viall, 84 Mass. (2 Allen) 512; State *v.* Rutherford, 1 Hawks (N. C.), 457; State *v.* Roane, 2 Dev. (N. C.) L. 58; State *v.* Scott, 4 Ired. (N. C.) L. 409; Grainger *v.* State, 5 Yerg. (Tenn.) 459; Tom *v.* State, 8 Humph. (Tenn.) 86; Duncan *v.* State, 7 Humph. (Tenn.) 148; United States *v.* Taylor, 5 McL. C. C. 242; United States *v.* Pearce, 2 McL. C. C. 14; Yates *v.* People, 32 N. Y. 509.

2. Yates *v.* People, 32 N. Y. 509; State *v.* Cutter, 36 N. J. L. (7 Vr.) 125; Logue *v.* Commonwealth, 38 Pa. St. 265; State *v.* Belk, 76 N. C. 10; People *v.* Muldoon, 2 Parker, Crim. Rep. (N. Y.) 13; Johnson *v.* State, 26 Tex. 117; Commonwealth *v.* Kirby, 56 Mass. (2 Cush.) 577; Rex *v.* Ricketts, 3 Camp. 68; United States *v.* Liddle, 2 Wash. C. C. 205; United States *v.* Ortega, 4 Wash. C. C. 531; United States *v.* Benner, Baldw. C. C. 234; People *v.* Torres, 38 Cal. 141; The Marianna Flora, 24 U. S. (11 Wheat.) 1; bk. 6, L. ed. 405; Clow *v.* Wright, Brayt. (Vt.) 118. *Compare* United States *v.* The Malek Adhel, 43 U. S. (2 How.) 210; bk. 11, L. ed. 239.

3. Witt *v.* State, 9 Mo. 663; State *v.* Homes, 17 Mo. 379; State *v.* Newkirk, 49 Mo. 84; Stern *v.* State, 53 Ga 229; Brown *v.* State, 24 Ind. 77; Goetz *v.* State, 41 Ind. 162; Crabtree *v.* State, 30 Ohio St. 382; Farrell *v.* State, 32 Ohio St. 456; People *v.* Anderson, 44 Cal. 65; People *v.* Lamb, 54 Barb. (N. Y.) 342; Patterson *v.* People, 46 Barb (N. Y.) 625; Yates *v.* People, 32 N. Y. 509; United States *v.* Railroad Cars, 1 Abb. C. C. 196; State *v.* Gardner, 5 Nev. 377.

And the guilt or innocence of the person accused depends on the circumstances as they appear to him.

A man will be excused who acts in good faith upon a mistaken view of his rights, and not from wantonness or evil intent; as there can be no conviction for a criminal offence without proof of guilty knowledge and guilty intent, and his guilt or innocence depends on the circumstances as they appear to him; so where one unlawfully removed a certain seal in ignorance of its character, but in the honest execution of a supposed duty; or where an officer, supposing he had authority to issue a license, there being no fraudulent intent, the issuance is not criminal; or where a person by mistake kills the hogs of the wrong person, he is not liable.[1]

And an honest misapprehension of the law, unless induced by gross carelessness, or gross ignorance of the law, may be set up by executive or *quasi* judicial officers.[2]

VIII. Ignorance of Fact.—It is a well-established principle of law, that ignorance of fact is no defence where the statute makes the offence indictable irrespective of guilty knowledge.[3] But

1. People *v.* Anderson, 44 Cal. 65; Stern *v.* State, 53 Ga. 229; Brown *v.* State, 24 Ind. 113; Farbach *v.* State, 24 Ind. 77; Goetz *v.* State, 41 Ind. 162; Witt *v.* State, 9 Mo. 663; State *v.* Homes, 17 Mo. 379; State *v.* Newkirk, 49 Mo. 84; State *v.* Matthews, 20 Mo. 55; State *v.* Graham, 46 Mo. 490; State *v.* Gardner, 5 Nev. 377; Crabtree *v.* State, 30 Ohio St. 382; Farrell *v.* State, 32 Ohio St. 456; People *v.* Lamb, 54 Barb. (N. Y.) 342; Patterson *v.* People, 46 Barb. (N. Y.) 625; Yates *v.* People, 32 N. Y. 509; United States *v.* Railroad Cars, 1 Abb. C. C. 196.

2. Lining *v.* Bentham, 2 Bay (S. C.) 1; State *v.* Johnson, 2 Bay (S. C.), 385; State *v.* Johnson, 1 Brev. (S. C.) 155; State *v.* Porter, 3 Brev. (S. C.) 176; State *v.* McDonald, 3 Dev. (N. C.) L. 468; Cutter *v.* State, 36 N. J. L. (7 Vr.) 125; State *v.* Gardner, 2 Mo. 28; Commonwealth *v.* Shed, 1 Mass. 227; State *v.* McDonald, 4 Harr. (Del.) 555; State *v.* Porter, 4 Harr. (Del.) 556; Hoggatt *v.* Bigley, 6 Humph. (Tenn.) 236; Jacobs *v.* Commonwealth, 2 Leigh (Va.), 709; People *v.* Calhoun, 3 Wend. (N. Y.) 420, People *v.* Coon, 15 Wend. (N. Y.) 277; Rex *v.* Jackson, 1 T. R. 653; Rex *v.* Fielding, 2 Burr. 719; Rex *v.* Barrat, 2 Doug. 465; Rex *v.* Stukely, 12 Mod. 493.

3. Smith *v.* State, 55 Ala. 1; Schuster *v.* State, 48 Ala. 199; State *v.* Hallett, 8 Ala. 159; Barnes *v.* State, 19 Conn. 398; Farmer *v.* People, 77 Ill. 322; McCutcheon *v.* People, 69 Ill. 601; Hood *v.* State, 56 Ind. 263; Brown *v.* State, 24 Ind. 113; Farbach *v.* State, 24 Ind 77; Goetz *v.* State, 41 Ind. 162; Stern *v.* State, 53 Ga. 229; State *v.* Ruhl, 8 Iowa, 447; State *v.* Newton, 44 Iowa, 45; Davis *v.* Commonwealth, 13 Bush (Ky.), 318; Ulrich *v.* Commonwealth, 6 Bush (Ky.), 400; Commonwealth *v.* Mash, 48 Mass. (7 Met.) 472; Commonwealth *v.* Elwell, 48 Mass. (2 Met) 190; Commonwealth *v.* Thompson, 88 Mass. (6 Allen) 591; s. c., 93 Mass. (11 Allen) 23; Thompson *v.* Thompson, 114 Mass. 566; Commonwealth *v.* Emmons, 98 Mass. 6; Commonwealth *v.* Goodman, 97 Mass. 117; Commonwealth *v.* Lattinville, 120 Mass. 385; Commonwealth *v.* Finnegan, 124 Mass. 324; Commonwealth *v.* Boynton, 84 Mass. (2 Allen) 160; Commonwealth *v.* Farren, 91 Mass. (9 Allen) 489; Commonwealth *v.* Nichols, 92 Mass. (10 Allen) 199; Commonwealth *v.* Waite, 93 Mass. (11 Allen) 264; Commonwealth *v.* Smith, 103 Mass. 444; Commonwealth *v.* Raymond, 97 Mass. 567; Commonwealth *v.* Bradford, 50 Mass. (9 Met.) 268; State *v.* Heck, 23 Minn 549; Beckham *v.* Nacke, 56 Mo. 546; State *v.* Griffith, 67 Mo. 287; State *v.* Balt. St. Nav. Co., 13 Md. 187; Minor *v.* Happersett, 53 Mo. 58; State *v.* Stimson, 24 N. J. L. (4 Zab.) 478; State *v* Hause, 71 N. . 518; State *v.* Hart, 6 Jones (N C.), L 389 [Crabtree *v.* State, 30 Ohio St. 382; Farrell *v.* State, 32 Ohio St. 456; State *v.* Goodenow, 65 Me. 30; State *v.* Smith, 10 R. I. 258. Duncan *v* State, 7 Humph. (Tenn) 148; McGuire *v.* State, 7 Humph. (Tenn) 54, State *v.* Melville, 11 R. I. 417; Lawrence *v.* Commonwealth, 30 Gratt. (Va) 845; State *v* Cain, 9 W. Va. 559; United States *v.* Dodge, Deady, U. S. D. C. 186; United States *v.* Anthony, 11 Blatchf. C. C 200; People *v* Zeiger, 6 Parker, Cr. R. (N. Y.) 355; Rex *v.* Myddleton, 6 T. R. 739; Reg. *v.* Robins, 1 Carr. & K. 456; Reg. *v.* Olifier,

ignorance of fact is admissible to negative a particular intent.[1] And an honest misapprehension of the ownership of property, it has been held, will excuse larceny.[2]

IX. Ignorance of Law.—Ignorance of law is no excuse for the commission of crime, nor does it justify an unlawful act, nor constitute a defence in a prosecution for the violation of the law,[3] because every one is presumed to know the laws of the country in which he dwells, or in which he transacts business.[4] And this is true, even though the statute rendering the act illegal is so recently passed that it was impossible to know of its existence.[5]

Ignorance of the law after promulgation of a statute by publica-

10 Cox, C. C. 402; Reg. *v.* Booth, 12 Cox, C. C. 231; Reg. *v* Green, 3 Fost. & F. 274; Reg. *v.* Hibbert, L. R. 1 C. C. 184. See also 1 Whart. Cr. L. (8th ed.) § 88.

Obstructing Highway.—Thus, an indictment lies, though it is in dispute whether the land is a highway. State *v.* Eiscle (Minn.), 33 N. W. Rep 785.

1. Oliver *v* State, 17 Ala. 587; Isham *v.* State, 38 Ala. 213; Farbach *v.* State, 24 Ind. 77; Rineman *v.* State, 24 Ind. 80; Squire *v.* State, 46 Ind. 459; People *v.* Wilson, 64 Ill 195; Commonwealth *v.* Smaltz, 3 Bush (Ky.), 32; Commonwealth *v.* Kirby, 56 Mass. (2 Cush.) 577; Commonwealth *v.* Rogers, 48 Mass. (7 Met.) 500; Commonwealth *v.* Power, 48 Mass. (7 Met.) 596; Curtis *v.* Mussey, 72 Mass. (6 Gray) 261; Commonwealth *v.* Wentworth, 118 Mass. 441; Hourigan *v.* Nowell, 110 Mass. 470; Commonwealth *v.* Presby, 80 Mass. (14 Gray) 65; State *v.* Shippey, 10 Minn. 223; State *v.* O'Connor, 31 Mo. 389; Commonwealth *v.* Viall, 84 Mass. (2 Allen) 512; State *v.* Rutherford, 1 Hawks (N. C.), 457; State *v.* Roane, 2 Dev. (N. C.) L. 58; State *v.* Scott, 4 Ired. (N. C.) L. 409; Grainger *v.* State, 5 Yerg. (Tenn.) 459; Tom *v.* State, 8 Humph. (Tenn.) 86; Duncan *v.* State, 7 Humph. (Tenn.) 148; U. S. *v.* Taylor, 5 McL. C. C. 242; U. S. *v.* Pearce, 2 McL. C. C. 14; Yates *v.* People, 32 N. Y. 509; People *v.* Reed, 47 Barb. (N. Y.) 235; U. S. *v.* Carr, 1 Woods, C. C. 480; Reg. *v.* Reed, Carr. & M. 306; Merry *v.* Green, 7 Mees. & W. 623; Rex *v.* Levett, Cro. Car. 538; Hudson *v.* MacRae, 4 Best & S. 585; Reg. *v.* Macleod, 12 Cox, C. C. 534; Reg. *v.* Hicklin, L. R. 3 Q. B. 360; Hearne *v.* Garton, 2 El & E. 66. See also 1 Whart. Cr. L. (8th ed.) § 87; 4 Bl. Com. 179; 1 Hale, P. C. 42, 501; 2 Hale, P. C. 411; 3 Inst. 52, 211.

2. Commonwealth *v.* Doane, 55 Mass. (1 Cush.) 5; State *v.* Homes, 17 Mo. 379; State *v.* Bond, 8 Iowa, 540.

3. United States *v.* Learned, 1 Abb. U. S. 483; s. c, 11 Inter. Rev. Rec. 149; The Shark, Blatchf. Prize Cas. 215; The Ann, 1 Gall. 62; United States *v.* Anthony, 11 Blatchf. C. C. 200; United States *v.* Taintor, 11 Blatchf. C. C. 374; United States *v.* Conner, 3 McL. C. C. 573; Schuster *v.* State, 48 Ala. 199; Hoover *v.* State, 59 Ala. 57; Brent *v.* State, 43 Ala. 297; Dickens *v.* State, 30 Ga. 383; Sumner *v.* Beeler, 50 Ind. 341; Winehart *v.* State, 6 Ind. 30; Wayman *v.* Commonwealth, 14 Bush (Ky.), 467; State *v.* Goodenow, 65 Me. 30; s. c., 1 Am. Cr. Rep. 42; Commonwealth *v.* Bagley, 24 Mass. (7 Pick.) 279; Commonwealth *v.* Elwell, 43 Mass (2 Met.) 190; Commonwealth *v.* Goodman, 97 Mass. 117; Commonwealth *v.* Emmons, 98 Mass 6; Black *v.* Ward, 27 Mich. 191; Whitton *v.* State, 37 Miss. 379; Cutter *v.* State, 36 N. J. L. (7 Vr.) 125; State *v.* Halsted, 39 N. J. L. (10 Vr.) 402; State *v.* Boyett, 10 Ired. (N. C.) 336; People *v.* Powell, 63 N. Y. 88; McGuire *v.* State, 7 Humph. (Tenn.) 54; Walker *v.* State, 2 Swan (Tenn.), 287; Chaplin *v.* State, 7 Tex. App. 87; Reg. *v.* Moodie, 20 Up. Can. Q. B. 389; Unwin *v.* Clarke, L. R. 1 Q. B. 417; Reg. *v.* Mailloux, 3 Pugs. 493; Rex *v.* Bailey, Russ. & R. C. C. 1; Rex *v.* Esop, 7 Carr. & P. 456; Reg. *v.* Good, 1 Carr. & K. 185; Reg. *v.* Hoatson, 2 Carr. & K. 777; Reg. *v.* Price, 11 Ad. & E. 727. See also 4 Bl. Com. 27; 1 Hale, P. C. 42; Broom, Leg. Max. 190; 3 Greenl. Ev. sec. 20; 1 Whart. C. L. (8th ed.) 84; 1 Russ. Cr. (9th ed.) 46; 1 Bish. C. L. (6th ed.) sec. 294.

4. McConico *v.* State, 49 Ala. 6; The Joseph, 21 U. S. (8 Cr.) 451; bk. 3, L. ed. 621; Wilson *v.* The Brig Mary, Gilp. C. C 31, Webster *v.* Sanborn, 47 Me. 471; Lincoln *v.* Shaw, 17 Mass. 410; Commonwealth *v.* Bagley, 24 Mass. (7 Pick.) 279; Shattuck *v.* Woods, 18 Mass. (1 Pick.) 171; Whitton *v.* State, 37 Miss. 379; Walker *v.* State, 2 Swan (Tenn.), 287; Lyon *v.* Richmond, 2 Johns. Ch. (N. Y.) 51; Cambioso *v.* Maffett, 2 Wash. C. C. 98; Reg. *v.* Moodie, 20 Up Can. Q. B. 389.

5. Bank of Mobile *v.* Murphy, 8 Ala. 119; Heard *v.* Heard, 8 Ga. 380; The Ann, 1 Gall. C. C. 62.

tion is criminal negligence.[1] Even resident foreigners are not excused by ignorance of the law, and this rule applies to ministerial officers resident abroad.[2]

Ignorance of the law of a foreign country is merely ignorance of a fact which no one can be conclusively presumed to know.[3] And a custom of a country to do an act cannot be used as a defence in an action for violating the positive law.[4] While ignorance of the law is no excuse for crime, yet it is a matter to be considered in mitigation of punishment.[5] It is only in cases where a special mental condition is involved, or where intent is of the essence of the crime, that the existence of knowledge of the law is open to inquiry.[6]

Where parties riotously destroy a house, believing at the time that it belonged to one of their number, ignorant of the law, the question of knowledge of the law may be raised.[7] Or, where one converts the money of another to his own use, under the erroneous impression that it became his by finding it.[8]

But where an act is unlawful, an intent to do the act, with full knowledge of the facts, is a criminal intent, irrespective of the knowledge of the law, or that the act was unlawful.[9]

X. Self-Defence. — If defendant was assaulted by deceased in such manner as to induce in his mind a well-grounded belief that he was actually in danger of death or great bodily harm, he was justified in defending himself, whether the danger was real or only apparent.[10] And when an unlawful and violent attack is made on one, which reasonably indicates that serious bodily injury is about to be inflicted, the assailed may kill his assailant at once.[11]

1. Culbreath *v.* Culbreath, 7 Ga. 64; Dickens *v.* State, 30 Ga. 383; State *v.* Goodenow, 65 Me. 30; s. c., 1 Am. Cr. R. 42; United States *v.* Fourteen Packages, Gilp. C. C. 235; The Ship Cotton Planter, 1 Paine, C. C. 23.

2. Cambioso *v.* Maffett, 2 Wash. C. C. 98; Sumner *v.* Beeler, 50 Ind. 341.

3. Haven *v.* Foster, 26 Mass. (9 Pick.) 112.

4. Bankus *v.* State, 4 Ind. 114.

5. Rex *v.* Esop, 7 Carr. & P. 456.

6. Cutter *v.* State, 36 N. J. L. (7 Vr.) 125; State *v.* Gates, 17 N. H. 373; State *v.* Knox, Phil. (N. C.) 312; Lossen *v.* State, 62 Ind. 437; Commonwealth *v.* Cornish, 6 Binn. (Pa.) 249; Dye *v.* Commonwealth, 7 Gratt. (Va.) 662; Commonwealth *v.* Cook, 1 Rob. (Va.) 729; United States *v.* Conner, 3 McL. C. C. 573; Reg. *v.* Langford, Carr. & M. 602; Rex *v.* Pedley, 1 Leach, C. C. 325; Reg. *v.* Schlesinger, 10 Q. B. N. S. 670; Reg. *v.* Muscot, 10 Mod. 192.

7. Reg. *v.* Reed, Car. & M. 303.

8. Reg. *v.* Langford, Car. & M. 602.

9. Hoover *v.* State, 50 Ala. 57; Culbreath *v.* Culbreath, 7 Ga. 64; Dickens *v.* State, 30 Ga. 383; State *v.* Goodenow, 65 Me. 30; s. c., 1 Am. Cr. R. 42; United States *v.* Anthony, 11 Blatchf. C. C. 200.

10. Crews *v.* People, 120 Ill. 317; s. c., 8 West. Rep. 691; Panton *v.* People (Ill.), 1 West. Rep. 357; Brennan *v.* People, 15 Ill. 512; Chicago *v.* Smith, 48 Ill. 107; Pollard *v.* People, 69 Ill. 148.

The Common-Law Right of Self-Defence is not impaired by statute, making it an indictable offence to fight in a public place with deadly weapons. Hunter *v.* State, 62 Miss 540.

In Illinois. — If a person is assaulted in such a manner as to produce in a reasonable person a belief that he is in danger of losing his life, or of suffering great bodily harm, he will be justified in defending himself, though the danger be not real, but only apparent. Crews *v.* People, 120 Ill. 317; s. c., 8 West. Rep. 691.

In Michigan. — Where one strikes another in a quarrel provoked by the latter and his friends, the former should not be confined to the right to repel the actual assault. People *v.* Ross (Mich.), 9 West. Rep. 555.

11. Williams *v.* State (Tex. App. Dec. 1886).

To justify homicide as having been done in self-defence, accused must have apparently been, and must have believed, he was in imminent danger at the time of the act.[1] But a person is not justified in killing his assailant who is unarmed, and is not his superior in physical power.[2] Nor is a person justified in killing another merely because the latter carried a pistol, whether he had a right to carry it or not, where no attempt was made to use it.[3]

The right of self-defence depends upon defendant's belief, with reasonable grounds therefor, that he was then in danger of death, or of great bodily harm.[4] And the fact that deceased was intoxicated, and that defendant sold him liquor, did not deprive defendant of the right to protect himself against the assault of deceased.[5] Where a person has reasonable cause to apprehend a design on the part of another to do him great bodily harm, and there is reasonable cause to apprehend immediate danger, he may act upon appearances, and may kill his assailant, if necessary, to avoid the danger.[6]

1. *Duty to retreat.* — It is the duty of the assailed to retreat, unless he thereby incurs greater danger; and the fact that he will not be safer by such retreat does not excuse from this duty.[7]

Although a man should be in the wrong in the first instance, yet a space for repentance is always open; and where a combatant withdraws as far as he can, and his adversary pursues him, if the taking of life becomes necessary to save his own, he will be justified.[8]

2. *Insulting Words and Menacing Gestures.* — Insulting epithets or opprobrious words will not justify an assault.[9] Words of reproach, or gestures, however irritating or provoking, do not constitute justification or excuse in law for killing.[10]

3. *Threats.* — Threats made by deceased are not admissible in evidence except under the defence of self-defence.[11] The threats must have been directed to the accused, and not to his son who was the party attacked.[12]

Threats alone unaccompanied by any overt act or outward demonstration will not justify hostile acts toward those making the threats.[13]

One against whom threats have been made by another is not justified in assaulting him unless the threatener makes some attempt to execute his threats.[14]

1. People v. Gonzales (Cal. Jan. 1887).
2. Wall v. State (Miss. Feb. 1887).
3. State v. Griffin (Mo.), 3 West. Rep. 820.
4. Short v. Commonwealth (Ky.), 4 S. W. Rep. 810
5. Nichols v. Winfrey, 90 Mo. 403; s. c., 7 West. Rep. 150.
6. Nichols v. Winfrey, 90 Mo. 403; s. c., 7 West. Rep. 150.
7. Carter v. State (Ala.), 2 Southern Rep. 766.
8. State v. Partlow, 90 Mo. 608; s. c., 8 West. Rep. 274.
9. State v. Griffin (Mo.), 3 West. Rep. 820.
10. State v Elliott, 90 Mo. 350; 7 West. Rep. 285.
11. State v. Clum, 90 Mo. 482; s. c., 8 West. Rep. 209.
12. State v. Downs, 91 Mo. 19; s. c., 8 West. Rep. 24
13. State v. Clum, 90 Mo. 482; s. c., 8 West. Rep. 209; Anderson v. Territory (N Mex.), 90 Mo. 482; s. c., 8 West. Rep 209.
14. State v. Rider (Mo.), 6 West. Rep 458.

Where defendant provoked the difficulty, threats made by the deceased, or what his character may have been for violence, will not excuse the homicide.[1]

XI. Acting under Legal Advice. — Acting under legal advice is no protection against responsibility for acts done resulting in the killing of a person.[2] But, where A., honestly following the advice of counsel, withholds property from his schedule in bankruptcy proceedings, his affidavit thereto is not perjury, although false in law.[3]

An official opinion, or the advice of a justice, under which a person acts, affords no excuse for the violation of law, and constitutes no defence.[4]

An illegal act cannot be justified by an order from a superior authority, whether parent, master, or military superior, in the absence of actual duress. But the illegality of the act must appear on the face of the order.[5] But a soldier acting under the orders of his superior officers will be protected, where he is bound by law to obedience.[6]

XII. Excuse and Justification. — Uncontrollable passion or excitement is no excuse for acts of violence, whatever may be the provocation.[7] And an officer has no right to kill one attempting to rescue another unless there is a necessity.[8]

In a case of homicide, the burden of proof of circumstances excusing the crime, or in mitigation, is on the accused.[9]

An instruction that "Mere weakness of mind does not excuse the commission of crime. If one is of sound mind he is responsible for his criminal act, even though his mental capacity be weak, or his intellect of an inferior order," is a correct statement of the law. The law recognizes no standard of exemption from crime, less than some degree of insanity or mental unsoundness.[10]

XIII. Responsibility for Criminal Acts. — All persons capable of exercising their will are responsible for their criminal acts, and no person shall be excused from punishment unless he be expressly

1. Jackson *v.* State (Ala. Jan. 1887).
2. Weston *v.* Commonwealth, 111 Pa. St. 251; s. c., 2 Cent. Rep. 35.
3. United States *v.* Conner, 3 McL., C. C. 573.
4. Dodd *v.* State, 18 Ind. 56; State *v.* Goodenow, 65 Me. 30; s. c., 1 Am. Cr. R. 42.
5. State *v.* Bell, 5 Port. (Ala.) 365; Hately *v.* State, 15 Ga. 346; Skeen *v.* Monkeimer, 21 Ind. 1; Commonwealth *v.* Hadley, 52 Mass. 66; Commonwealth *v.* Drew, 57 Mass. (3 Cush.) 279; Commonwealth *v.* Hadley, 52 Mass. (11 Met) 66; Commonwealth *v.* Blodgett, 59 Mass. (12 Met.) 56; Kliffield *v.* State, 4 How. (Miss.) 304; Hays *v.* State, 13 Mo. 246; State *v.* Bryant, 14 Mo. 340; Schmidt *v.* State, 14 Mo. 137; Curtis *v.* Knox, 2 Denio (N. Y.), 341; Brown *v.* Howard, 14 Johns. (N. Y) 119; Weatherspoon *v.* Woody, 5 Cold. (Tenn) 149; State *v.* Sparks, 27 Tex. 627; State *v.* Bugbee, 22 Vt. 32; State *v.* Mann, 1 Hayw. (N. C.) 4; Mitchell *v.* Harmony, 54 U. S. (13 How.) 115; bk. 14. L. ed. 75; 1 Blatchf. C. C. 549; Kendall *v.* United States, 37 U. S. (12 Pet.) 524; bk. 9, L. ed. 1181; Mitchell *v.* Harmony, 1 Blatchf. C. C. 549; United States *v.* Jones, 3 Wash. C. C. 209; United States *v.* Carr, 1 Woods. C. C. 480; Mostyn *v.* Fabrigas, Cowp. 161; 1 Bish. Cr. L. (6th ed.) § 355.
6. Clark *v.* State, 37 Ga. 195; State *v.* Rogers, 37 Mo. 367; State *v.* Sutton, 10 R. I. 159; Weatherspoon *v.* Woody, 5 Cold. (Tenn.) 149; Simmons' Ct. Mar. 1 De Hart's Mil. Law, 166; United States *v.* Carr, 1 Woods. C. C. 480.
7. People *v.* Mortimer, 48 Mich. 37.
8. State *v.* Bland (N. C. May, 1887).
9. People *v.* Bush (Cal. Jan. 1887).
10. Wartena *v.* State, 105 Ind. 445; s. c., 2 West. Rep. 757.

defined and exempted by the law itself. A person is responsible for all the consequences of his act, whether the harm inflicted was intended or not; as, if one shoots with intent to kill a certain person, but through mistaken identity he wounds another, he may be convicted of wounding with intent to kill, and, if he kills, he is guilty of murder.[1] And if a person wilfully does any unlawful and criminal act, he takes upon himself all the legal and penal consequences of such act, regardless of his knowledge, unless knowledge is made an essential ingredient of the crime.[2]

1. *Idiots, Imbeciles, and Deaf-Mutes.* — But the understanding may be immature from idiocy, or it may be affected by lunacy, or some derangement arising from disease of the brain subsequent to its full development, in which case there is generally no criminal responsibility.[3]

Idiocy consists in a deficiency of the mental faculties, either congenital, or the result of arrested development during infancy: it is sterility of mind, and not a perversion of the understanding.[4] An idiot is a person without understanding, and who is legally presumed never likely to have any; as where a person cannot count twenty, nor tell the names of his parents, or his own age.[5] An idiot is considered at law incapable of committing crime; and where idiocy exists in reference to the particular act, the court will direct an acquittal.[6]

One mentally imbecile is incapable of committing crime;[7] and a man deaf and dumb from his infancy is, in presumption of law, an idiot.[8] A person born deaf and dumb, but not blind, is not an idiot.[9] Yet the want of hearing may exist in connection with responsibility for crime, and if such a person is shown to be able to comprehend the nature of his act, he may be convicted; but persons born deaf, dumb, and blind, are presumed to be idiots, and not capable of committing crime; yet the presumption may be rebutted.[10] But, in the case of deaf-mutes, malice cannot be implied.[11]

1. Meredith *v.* State, 60 Ala. 441; People *v.* Honshell, 10 Cal. 83; People *v.* Keefer, 18 Cal. 636; State *v.* Staunton, 37 Conn. 421; Studstill *v.* State, 7 Ga. 2; Commonwealth *v.* Webster, 59 Mass. 306; State *v.* Turner, Wright (Ohio), 20; State *v.* Smith, 2 Strob. (S. C.) 77; Ann *v.* State, 11 Humph. (Tenn.) 159.

2. State *v.* Wyman (Vt.), 4 New Eng. Rep. 126; State *v.* Dana (Vt.), 5 New Eng. Rep. 108.

3. 4 Bl. Com. 21; 1 Russ. Cr. (9th ed.) 6; 1 Whart. C. L. (8th ed.) § 332; 1 Beck, Med. Jur. 721; Reg. *v.* Shaw, Law Rep. 1 C. C. 145.

4. Somers *v.* Pumphrey, 24 Ind. 231; 1 Beck, Med. Jur. 722; Chitt. Med. Jur. § 345; 1 Bl. Com. 302; Bouv. Law Dict.; 1 Whart. Cr. L. (8th ed.) § 34; 1 Russ. Cr. (9th ed.) 11; 1 Bish. Cr. L. (6th ed.) § 379.

5. Ball *v.* Mannen, 3 Bligh, N. S. 1; Co. Lit. 247; Fitzh. *Natura Brevium*, 233; 1 Arch. Cr. Pr. 16; 2 Kent, Com. 573; Shelford, Lun. 2.

6. McAllister *v.* State, 17 Ala. 434; United States *v.* Shultz, 6 McL. C. C. 121; People *v.* Sprague, 2 Park. Cr. Rep. (N. Y.) 43; Vance *v.* Commonwealth, 2 Va. Cas. 132; 4 Bl. Com. 24; 1 Russ. Cr. (9th ed.) 11; Reg. *v.* Southey, 4 Fost. & F. 864.

7. Pettigrew *v.* State, 12 Tex. App. 225.

8. Hale, P. C. 34.

9. Coll. Lun. 4, § 5.

10. Commonwealth *v.* Hill, 14 Mass. 207; State *v.* Harris, 8 Jones, (N. C.) L. 136; Rex *v.* Steel, 1 Leach, 451; Reg. *v.* Whitfield, 3 Car. & K. 121; Rex *v.* Prichard, 7 Car. & P. 303; Shelford, Lun. 3; Co. Litt. 42; 1 Bish. Cr. L. (6th ed.) § 396; 1 Russ. Cr. (9th ed.) 11, 12.

11. State *v.* Draper (Del.), Houst. Cr. Rep. 291.

To be responsible for crime, the party committing the act must be of sane mind, as the act does not constitute guilt unless the mind is guilty; hence, sanity is an essential ingredient in crime.[1] The mere fact that a person is insane does not relieve him from criminal responsibility.[2] If one is of sound mind he is responsible for his criminal act, even though his mental capacity be weak, or his intellect of an inferior order: the law recognizes no exemption from rime less than some degree of insanity or mental unsoundness.[3]

The law requires something more than occasional oddity or hypochondria to exempt the perpetrator of an offence from its punishment.[4] Permanent insanity, when clearly proved, excuses from all crimes, except such as are committed in lucid intervals.[5] Permanent insanity produced by habitual intoxication excuses a criminal act.[6] But temporary insanity, or unconsciousness of what one is doing, occasioned by intoxication, is no excuse for crime.[7] So, partial insanity is not sufficient to exempt a person from responsibility for crime.[8]

The delusions which indicate a defect of sanity such as will relieve a person from criminal responsibility, are delusions of the senses, or such as relate to facts or objects, — not mere wrong notions or impressions, or of a moral nature; and the aberration must be mental, not moral, to affect the intellect of the individual.[9] A party acting under the influence of an insane delusion, with a view of redressing or avenging some supposed grievance, or of producing some public benefit, is nevertheless punishable, if he knew, at the time, he was acting contrary to law.[10] To constitute insanity, there must be a disease which impairs, or totally destroys, either the understanding or the will, or both.[11] If the accused was under such defect of reason from disease of mind as not to know the quality of the act he was doing, or was under such delusion as not to understand its nature, or not sufficient consciousness to discern that his act was criminal, or was led by an uncontrollable impulse, he is not responsible.[12] It must be

1. 1 Russ. Cr. (9th ed.) 6; 1 Hale, P. C. 434; 1 Bish. C. L. (6th ed.) § 375; Co. Lit. 247 *b*; Long *v.* State, 38 Ga. 507; Chase *v.* People, 40 Ill. 358.

2. People *v.* O'Connell, 62 How. Pr. (N. Y.) 436.

3. Wartena *v.* State, 105 Ind. 445; s. c., 2 West. Rep. 757; Somers *v.* Pumphrey, 24 Ind. 231; Studstill *v.* State, 7 Ga. 3; People *v.* Hurley, 8 Cal. 390; Lowder *v.* Lowder, 58 Ind. 538.

4. Hawe *v.* State, 11 Neb. 537; s. c., 38 Am. Rep. 375; Anderson *v.* State, 43 Conn. 514; s. c., 21 Am. Rep. 669.

5. 1 Russ. Cr. (9th ed.) 11, 12; 1 Bish. C. L. (6th ed.) § 375.

6. State *v.* Robinson, 20 W. Va. 713; s. c., 43 Am. Rep. 799.

7. Upstone *v.* People, 109 Ill. 169; State *v.* Thomas (Del.), Houst. Cr. Rep. 511.

8. Dejarnette *v.* Commonwealth, 75 Va. 867; State *v.* Danby (Del.), Houst. Cr. Rep. 166.

9. Reg. *v.* Burton, 3 Fost. & F. 772.

10. McNaghten's Case, 10 Clark & F. 200; s. c., 8 Scott, N. R. 595; Reg. *v.* Higginson, 1 C. & K. 130.

11. Bradley *v.* State, 31 Ind 492.

12. Stevens *v* State, 31 Ind. 485; State *v.* Felter, 25 Iowa, 67; Smith *v.* Commonwealth, 1 Duvall (Ky.), 224; Kriel *v.* Commonwealth, 5 Bush (Ky.), 362; Scott *v.* Commonwealth, 4 Met. (Ky.) 227; Shannahan *v.* Commonwealth, 8 Bush (Ky.), 464, People *v.* McDonell, 47 Cal. 134; State *v.* Huting, 21 Mo. 464; Commonwealth *v.*

such as to render the accused incapable of governing his actions at the time, and so controlling as not to be resisted, creating an overpowering impulse to do the act.[1]

The circumstance of a person having acted under an irresistible influence to the commission of the crime, is no defence, if at the time he committed the act he knew he was doing wrong.[2] It must appear, that, at the commission of the offence, accused was affected by an uncontrollable impulse to do the act, overriding his reason and judgment.[3] A mere uncontrollable impulse of the mind co-existing with the full possession of the reasoning powers, will not warrant an acquittal;[4] for an irresistible impulse does not absolve the actor if at the time, and in respect to the act, he could distinguish between right and wrong.[5]

The test of responsibility for crime lies in the capacity or power of the person to commit the act; and the inquiry is, whether the accused was capable of having, and did have, a criminal intent, and the capacity to distinguish between right and wrong in reference to the particular act charged.[6] The test of

Rogers, 48 Mass. (7 Met.) 500; s. c., 1 Lead. C.C. 94; Commonwealth v. Mosler, 4 Pa. St. 264; United States v. Holmes, 1 Cliff. C. C. 119; Freeman v. People, 4 Denio (N. Y.), 9; Reg. v. Law, 2 Fost. & F. 836; Reg. v. Davies, 1 Fost. & F. 69; McNaghten's Case, 10 Clark & F. 200; Reg. v. Oxford, 9 Carr & P. 527; Rex v. Offord, 5 Carr. & P. 168; Reg. v. Higginson, 1 Carr. & K. 129; People v. Sprague, 2 Park. Cr. R. (N. Y.) 43. See also 1 Russ. Cr. (9th ed.) 19; Rosc. Cr. Ev. 953.

1. State v. Johnson, 40 Conn. 136; Roberts v. State, 3 Ga. 329; Spann v. State, 47 Ga 553; s. c., 1 Green, C. L. Rep. 391; United States v. Hewson, 7 Bost. L. R. 361; Bradley v. State, 31 Ind. 492; Stevens v. State, 31 Ind. 485; Hopps v. People, 31 Ill. 385; State v. Felter, 25 Iowa, 67; Smith v. Commonwealth, 1 Duvall (Ky.), 224; Scott v. Commonwealth, 4 Met. (Ky.) 227; Kriel v. Commonwealth, 5 Bush (Ky.), 365; Shannahan v Commonwealth, 8 Bush (Ky.), 464; Commonwealth v Rogers, 48 Mass. (7 Met.) 500; s. c., 1 Lead. C. C. 94; *In re* Forman, 54 Barb. (N. Y) 274; People v. Sprague, 2 Parker, Cr. Rep. (N. Y.) 43; Commonwealth v. Schneider, 59 Pa. St. 328; Bitner v. Bitner, 65 Pa. St. 347; Commonwealth v. Mosler, 4 Pa. St. 267.

2. Reg. v. Haynes, 1 F. & F. 666.

3. Dacy v. People (Ill.), 4 West. Rep. 180; State v. Pratt, Houst. Cr. Rep. (Del.) 249.

4. Reg. v. Barton, 3 Cox, C. C. 275.

5. People v. Hoin, 62 Cal. 120; s. c., 45 Am. Rep. 651. See Reg. v. Stokes, 3 C. & K. 185; Reg. v. Haynes, 1 Fost. & F. 666; Reg. v. Barton, 3 Cox, C. C. 275.

6. Life Ins. Co. v. Terry, 82 U. S. (15 Wall.) 590; bk. 21, L. ed. 236; U. S. v. McGlue, 1 Curt. C. C. 1, 8; U. S. v. Clarke, 2 Cr. C. C. 158; U. S. v. Shults, 6 McL. C. C. 121; McAllister v. State, 17 Ala. 434; People v. McDonell, 47 Cal. 134; People v. Coffman, 24 Cal. 230; State v. Richards, 39 Conn. 591; State v. Johnson, 40 Conn. 136; Roberts v. State, 3 Ga. 310; Choice v. State, 31 Ga. 424; Anderson v. State, 42 Ga. 9; Humphreys v. State, 45 Ga. 190; Loyd v. State, 45 Ga. 57; Westmoreland v. State, 45 Ga. 225; Hopps v. People, 31 Ill. 385; Fouts v. State, 4 Greene (Iowa), 500; Sawyer v. State, 35 Ind. 80; Smith v. Commonwealth, 1 Duvall (Ky.), 224; Kriel v. Commonwealth, 5 Bush (Ky.), 362; Bovard v. State, 30 Miss. 600; State v. Huting, 21 Mo. 464, 476; Commonwealth v. Rogers, 48 Mass. (7 Met.) 500; Commonwealth v. Heath, 77 Mass. (11 Gray) 303; State v. Lawrence, 57 Me. 574; Walker v. People, 88 N. Y. 81; Reg. v. Higginson, 1 Car. & K. 129; Freeman v. People, 4 Denio (N. Y.), 9; Willis v. People, 32 N. Y. 715, 719; Am. Seam. Soc. v. Hopper, 33 N. Y. 619; People v. Kleim, 1 Edm. Sel. Cas. (N. Y.) 13; Flanagan v. People, 52 N. Y. 467; s. c., 1 Green, C. L. Rep. 377; People v. Pine, 2 Barb (N. Y.) 566; State v. Pike, 49 N. H. 399; Boardman v. Woodman, 47 N. H. 120; State v. Jones, 50 N. H. 369; Jones v. State, 11 N. H. 269; State v. Porter, 34 Iowa, 131; s. c., 1 Green, C. L. Rep. 241; Loeffner v. State, 10 Ohio St. 598; Blackburn v. State, 23 Ohio St. 146; Ortwein v. Commonwealth, 76 Pa. St. 414; s. c., 1 Am. Cr. Rep. 283; Commonwealth v. Mosler, 4 Pa. St. 264; Brown v. Commonwealth, 78 Pa. St. 122; Commonwealth v. Farkin, 2 Pa. L. J. 480; State v. Spencer, 21 N. J. L. (1 Zab.) 196; State v. Gardiner, Wright

responsibility where insanity is asserted, is the capacity to distinguish between right and wrong with respect to the act, and the absence of insane delusions respecting the same.[1] If the accused knew what he was doing, and that the act was forbidden by law, and had power of mind enough to be conscious of what he was doing, he is responsible.[2]

2. *Husband and Wife.*—An offence committed by the wife in the immediate presence of her husband is *prima facie* done by his coercion.[3] The presumption of coercion of the wife acting in the presence of her husband is not conclusive, but may be rebutted by evidence.[4] But the husband must be actually present

(Ohio), 392; Dove *v.* State, 3 Heisk. (Tenn.) 348; s. c., 1 Green, C. L. Rep. 760; Stuart *v.* State, 1 Baxter (Tenn.), 178; Williams *v.* State, 7 Tex. App. 163; Webb *v.* State, 7 Tex. App. 607; s. c., 5 Tex. App. 596; Vance *v.* Commonwealth, 2 Va. Cas. 132; People *v.* Sprague, 2 Parker, Cr. R. (N. Y.) 43; Winchester's Case, 6 Coke, 23; Combes' Case, F. Moore, 759; Haskell's Case, cited in, on Insan. 83; Reg. *v.* Goode, 7 Ad. & E. 536; Rex *v.* Offord, 5 Carr. & P. 168; Reg. *v.* Oxford, 9 Carr. & P. 525; Reg. *v.* Vaughan, 1 Cox, C. C. 80; Reg. *v.* Barton, 3 Cox, C. C. 275; Reg. *v.* Layton, 4 Cox, C. C. 149; Reg. *v.* Higginson, 1 Carr. & K. 129; Reg. *v.* Stokes, 3 Carr. & K. 185; Burrows' Case, 1 Lewin, C. C. 238; Hadfield's Case, 27 How. St. Tr. 1282; Reg. *v.* Vyse, 3 Fost. & F. 247. See also 1 Hawk. ch. 1, § 3; 4 Bl. Com. 24; Collinson, Lun. 573; 1 Inst. 247; 1 Russ. Cr. (9th ed.) 19; 1 Whart. C. L. (8th ed.) 34.

1. Casey *v.* People, 31 Hun (N. Y.), 158; People *v.* O'Connell, 62 How. (N. Y.) Pr. 436; Hart *v.* State, 14 Neb 572; United States *v.* Young, 25 Fed. Rep 710.

2. State *v.* Nixon, 32 Kans. 205. See Grissom *v.* State, 62 Miss. 167; State *v.* Marler, 2 Ala. 43; State *v.* Brinyea, 5 Ala. 241; McAllister *v.* State, 17 Ala. 434; People *v.* McDonell, 47 Cal. 134; People *v.* Hobson, 17 Cal. 424; Roberts *v.* State, 3 Ga. 310; State *v.* Jones, 50 N. H. 369; Clark *v.* State, 12 Ohio, 483; State *v.* Thompson, Wright (Ohio), 617; Brown *v.* Commonwealth, 78 Pa. St. 122; United States *v.* Holmes, 1 Cliff. C. C. 120; Flanagan *v.* People, 52 N. Y. 467; s. c., 1 Green, Cr Rep. 377; State *v.* West (Del.), Houst. Cr. Rep. 371; State *v.* Pagels (Mo.), 10 West. Rep. 288; Reg. *v.* Barton, 3 Cox, C. C. 275; Reg. *v.* Stokes, 3 Carr. & K. 185; Rex *v.* Offord, 5 Carr. & P. 168; Lord Ferrer's Case, 19 How. St. Tr. 947; Reg. *v.* Vamplew, 3 Fost. & F. 520.

3. **Acts in Presence of Husband.**—The presumption that acts done by the wife in the immediate presence of the husband were done by his command or authority, may be contradicted by evidence. Commonwealth *v.* Hill (Mass.), 5 New Eng. Rep. 277.

House of Prostitution: Rightful Power of Husband.—A husband has the rightful power to prevent his wife from using, as a resort for prostitution, a house owned by her as her separate property, and occupied by both as the home of the family. If she kept such tenement for such purpose of her own free will, and without her husband's consent, and against his will, he cannot be convicted of thereby maintaining a nuisance in such tenement, although he did not use all practicable means to control her conduct. His whole conduct, including what he did and said as well as what he could reasonably have done, and did not do, may be shown for the purpose of proving or disproving his consent in fact to the acts done by his wife. Evidence that, prior to the time covered by the indictment, he had ordered, directed, persuaded, and used all means in his power to prevent his wife from doing any of the acts charged, and that his wife told him the property was hers, and she would do as she pleased, is admissible, on his behalf, on the trial of such indictment. Commonwealth *v.* Hill (Mass.), 5 New Eng. Rep. 277; Commonwealth *v.* Kennedy, 119 Mass. 211; Commonwealth *v.* Carroll, 124 Mass. 30; Commonwealth *v.* Pratt, 126 Mass. 462; Commonwealth *v.* Barry, 115 Mass. 148; Commonwealth *v.* Wood, 97 Mass. 225; Commonwealth *v.* Tryon, 99 Mass. 442; Commonwealth *v.* Cheney, 114 Mass. 281; Commonwealth *v.* Welch, 97 Mass. 593; Commonwealth *v.* Putnam, 70 Mass. (4 Gray) 16.

4. Edwards *v.* State, 27 Ark. 493; s. c., 1 Green, Cr. Rep. 741; State *v.* Nelson, 29 Me. 329; Ferguson *v.* Brooks, 67 Me. 251; Commonwealth *v.* Burk, 77 Mass. (11 Gray) 437; Commonwealth *v.* Welch, 97 Mass. 593; Commonwealth *v.* Eagan, 103 Mass. 71; Commonwealth *v.* Trimmer, 1 Mass. 476; Martin *v.* Commonwealth, 1 Mass. 347; Commonwealth *v.* Neal, 10 Mass. 152; s. c., 1 Lead. Cr. Cas. 91; Commonwealth *v.* Murphy, 68 Mass. (2 Gray)

when the act is done; and a moment's absence from the room might still leave her under his influence.

The wife is not liable for her act, even when her husband is absent, if it can be proved that she acted under his coercion; and actual restraint, except in cases of treason and capital crimes, will relieve her from legal guilt of a crime committed in his presence; but his mere presence without coercion will not excuse.[1] At common law, if the husband was present when the wife committed the act, except it be treason, murder, manslaughter, or robbery, the law presumed that she acted under his coercion, and the husband only was punishable.[2]

Coercion by the husband is a presumption of law, both in favor of the wife and against the husband.[3] The doctrine of coercion of the wife raises only a disputable presumption of law in her favor.[4] The disputable presumption of law exists in misdemeanors, as well as in felonies, the question for the jury being the same in both.[4] It does not apply to murder.[5] A wife cannot be convicted of comforting, harboring, and assisting her husband, who is charged with murder.[6]

The *prima facie* presumption is, that a felony committed by a wife, in the presence of her husband, was done through his coercion.[7] So, a wife uttering base coin is deemed in the presence of her husband who accompanies her, although he stands outside the house she enters.[8] If the wife acts in the absence of her husband, there is no presumption that she acts under his coercion.[9] While it is true, that, if the wife acts in the absence of her husband, there is no presumption that she acts under his coercion; yet if the husband is near enough for the wife to act under his immediate influence and control, although not in the same room, he is not absent, within the meaning of the law.[10] But the mere

513; Quinlan *v.* People, 6 Park. Cr. R (N. Y.) 1; State *v.* Williams, 65 N. C. 398; Davis *v.* State, 15 Ohio, 72; Tabier *v.* State, 34 Ohio St. 127; State *v.* Parkerson, 1 Strob (S. C.) L. 169; City Council *v.* Van Roven, 2 McCord (S. C.), 465; Miller *v.* State, 25 Wis. 384.

1. Freel *v.* State, 21 Ark. 212; Edwards *v.* State, 27 Ark. 493; Commonwealth *v.* Murphy, 68 Mass. (2 Gray) 510; Commonwealth *v.* Welch, 97 Mass. 593; Commonwealth *v.* Neal, 10 Mass. 152; Commonwealth *v.* Feeney, 95 Mass. (13 Allen) 560; Davis *v.* State, 15 Ohio St. 72; State *v.* Parkerson, 1 Strob. (S C.) L. 169; State *v.* Potter, 42 Vt. 495; Rex *v.* Knight, 1 Car. & P. 116; Reg. *v.* Wardroper, 8 Cox, C. C 284; Reg. *v.* Smith, 8 Cox. C. C. 27; 1 Hale, P. C. 45; 1 Russ Cr. (9th ed.) 39; 1 Bish. Cr. L. (6th ed.) § 358

2. State *v.* Banks, 48 Ind. 197; State *v.* Nelson, 29 Me. 329; Commonwealth *v.* Gannon, 97 Mass. 547; Commonwealth *v.* Lewis, 42 Mass. (1 Met.) 151; 48 Ind. 197; Haines *v.* State, 35 N. H. 207; Davis *v.* State, 15 Ohio St. 72; Uhl *v.* Commonwealth, 6 Gratt. (Va.) 706; Miller *v.* State, 25 Wis. 384; Rex *v.* Sargeant, 1 Ryan & M. 352; Case of Morris, Russ. & R. 270; Dr. Foster's Case, 11 Coke, 61; Rex *v.* Crofts, 2 Strange, 1120; Reg. *v.* Smith, Dears. & B. 553; The King *v.* Stapleton, Jebb, C. C. 93; Case of Matthews, 1 Denison, 596.

3. State *v.* Boyle, 13 R. I. 537.

4. Reg. *v.* Torpey, 12 Cox, C. C. 45.

5. Reg. *v.* Manning, 2 C. & K. 903.

6. Reg. *v.* Good, 1 C. & K. 185.

7. Rex *v.* Hughes, 2 Lewin, C. C. 229.

8. Connolly's Case, 2 Lewin, C. C. 229.

9. Commonwealth *v.* Flaherty, 140 Mass. 454; s. c., 1 New Eng. Rep. 530.

10. Commonwealth *v.* Flaherty, 140 Mass. 454; s. c., 1 New Eng. Rep. 530; Commonwealth *v.* Burk, 77 Mass. (11 Gray) 437.

Proximity of Husband.—This principle was restated and applied in a case where, if it appeared at all where the husband proximity of the husband, not actually present, will not raise in her favor the presumption that she acted under his coercion.[1] But if the husband is near enough for the wife to act under his immediate influence, although not in the same room, he is not absent within the meaning of the law.[2]

A wife cannot commit larceny in the presence of her husband: it is deemed done through his coercion.[3] But an act done in his absence, though done at his command, is deemed her voluntary act, and she is responsible.[3] And a wife may be guilty of false swearing, although her husband be present when she takes the oath.[4] The wife must rely upon coercion as a defence; and it must be shown to have been exercised at the time of the act, and it must be made to appear that she was not acting of her own volition, in order to an acquittal.[5]

If a married woman commits a crime of her own volition, or not under the immediate control of her husband, or if she lives apart from her husband, she may be indicted alone.[6]

The wife who takes an independent part in the commission of a crime, when her husband is not present, is not protected by her coverture.[7]

Where the husband is absent, the wife may be convicted of uttering, and the husband who commanded the act may be convicted of procuring.[8]

A married woman may be convicted of maintaining a common

was, he was in the barn while the sales were made in the house. Commonwealth *v.* Munsey, 112 Mass. 287; Commonwealth *v.* Patterson, 138 Mass. 498; Commonwealth *v.* Flaherty, 140 Mass. 454; s. c., 1 New Eng. Rep. 530.

1. State *v.* Shee, 13 R. I. 535; Commonwealth *v* Gormley, 133 Mass. 580.

When Husband's Influence not presumed. —Where the husband "was a cripple, generally at home, except that he could hop out," it is conceivable that his wife might be so far free from his influence as to be answerable for the sale, and yet not so independent as to be deemed to have acquired control of the place. See Commonwealth *v.* Churchill, 136 Mass. 148, 151.

The ruling sustained in Commonwealth *v.* Roberts, 132 Mass. 267; Commonwealth *v.* Flaherty, 140 Mass. 454; s. c., 1 New Eng. Rep. 530.

2. Commonwealth *v.* Flaherty, 140 Mass. 454; s. c., 1 New Eng. Rep. 530.

3. Anon. 2 East, P. C. 559.

4. Reg. *v.* Dick, Rosc. Cr. Ev. 986.

5. Edwards *v.* State, 27 Ark. 493; s. c., 1 Green, Cr. Rep. 741; Freel *v.* State, 21 Ark. 212; Commonwealth *v.* Neal, 10 Mass. 152; Commonwealth *v.* Eagan, 103 Mass. 71; Commonwealth *v.* Tryon, 99 Mass. 442; Commonwealth *v.* Burk, 77 Mass. (11 Gray) 437; Commonwealth *v.* Murphy, 68 Mass. (2 Gray) 516; Commonwealth *v.* Munsey, 112 Mass. 287; State *v.* Bentz, 11 Mo. 27; Quinlan *v.* People, 6 Park, Cr. R. (N. Y.) 1; State *v.* Parkerson, 1 Strob. (S. C.) L. 169; State *v.* Potter, 42 Vt. 495; Reg. *v.* Manning, 2 Car. & K. 903, note; 1 Hale, P. C. 45; 1 Russ. Cr. (9th ed.) 39.

6. Martin *v.* Commonwealth, 1 Mass. 347; Commonwealth *v.* Trimmer, 1 Mass. 476; Commonwealth *v* Neal, 10 Mass 152; s. c., 1 Lead. Cr. Cas. 81; Commonwealth *v.* Murphy, 68 Mass. (2 Gray) 510; Commonwealth *v.* Welch, 97 Mass. 593; Commonwealth *v* Butler, 83 Mass. (1 Allen) 4; Commonwealth *v.* Burk, 77 Mass. (11 Gray) 437; Commonwealth *v.* Whalen, 82 Mass. (16 Gray) 25; Commonwealth *v.* Cheney, 114 Mass. 281; Commonwealth *v.* Lewis, 42 Mass. (1 Metc.) 151; Pennybaker *v.* State, 2 Blackf. (Ind.) 484; State *v.* Bentz, 11 Mo. 27; State *v.* Haines, 35 N H. 207; Geuing *v.* State, 1 McCord (S. C.) 573; Reg. *v.* Buncombe, 1 Cox, C. C. 183; Reg. *v.* Hughes, 1 Russ. Cr. 40; Reg. *v.* Crofts, 7 Mod. 397; Reg. *v.* Dixon, 10 Mod. 335; 1 Whart. Cr. L. (8th ed.) § 81; 1 Russ. Cr. (9th ed.) 39; 1 Bish. Cr. L. (6th ed.) § 361.

7. Reg. *v.* John, 13 Cox, C. C. 100.

8. Rex *v.* Morris, Russ. & R. C. C. 270.

nuisance [1] or a disorderly house.[2] And coverture is no protection against the consequence of a criminal act, when the part taken by the wife is shown to have been active and willing.[3]

If the offence is of such a character that she could commit it alone, and without the concurrence of her husband, although he was living with her at the time, she may be convicted.[4]

Where a wife procured a check, and suggested to her husband the idea of raising the check, and he in her presence erased the payee's name and the amount, and when she was not present filled the space with a larger amount, she receiving nearly one-half the proceeds of the crime, it was held that she was not properly convicted as a principal.[5] Under a joint indictment for feloniously wounding with intent to disfigure, where the wife acted under coercion of her husband, she could not be convicted.[6]

A wife jointly indicted with her husband is entitled to an acquittal where she uttered the false coin in the presence of her husband.[7] And if larceny is committed jointly by husband and wife, the latter is entitled to be acquitted, as having acted under coercion.[8] But if the husband is absent, the wife may be convicted of uttering; and the husband who commanded the act may be convicted of procuring.[9]

A husband may be punished for an indictable offence, not *malum in se*, committed by the wife in his presence, and with his knowledge, or by his command, or with his concurrence.[10] But the husband must be actually present when the act is done, for, if absent, coercion will not be presumed; but a moment's absence from the room might still leave her under his influence; and she will not be liable, even in his absence, if she can satisfactorily establish that she acted under his coercion. In all cases of actual constraint imposed on a wife, except in cases of treason and capital offences, the coercion will relieve her from the legal guilt of a crime committed in the presence of or under the control of her husband.[11]

1. Commonwealth *v.* Roberts, 132 Mass. 266.
2. Commonwealth *v.* Hopkins, 133 Mass. 381.
3. People *v.* Ryland, 28 Hun (N. Y.), 568.
4. Pennybaker *v.* State, 2 Blackf. (Ind.) 484; Commonwealth *v.* Cheney, 114 Mass. 281; Commonwealth *v.* Lewis, 42 Mass. (1 Metc.) 151; State *v.* Bentz, 11 Mo. 27; State *v.* Collins, 1 McCord (S. C.), 355; State *v.* Potter, 42 Vt. 495; 4 Bl. Com. 29; 1 Russ. Cr. (9th ed.) § 39; Reg. *v.* Williams, 10 Mod. 63; Rex *v.* Fenner, 2 Keble, 468; Rex *v.* Jordan, 2 Keble, 634; Rex *v.* Crofts, 2 Strange, 1120; Somersett's Case, 2 State Trials, 951; Reg. *v.* Foxby, 6 Mod. 178.
5. People *v.* Ryland, 97 N. Y. 126.
6. Reg. *v.* Smith, Dears. & B. C. C. 553; s. c., 4 Jur. N. S. 395; 27 L. J. M. C. 204; 8 Cox, C. C. 27.
7. Rex *v.* Price, 8 Carr. & P. 19.
8. Rex *v.* Knight, 1 Carr. & P. 116.
9. Rex *v.* Morris, Russ. & R. C. C. 270.
10. Hensly *v.* State, 52 Ala. 16; s. c., 1 Amer. Cr. Rep. 465; Williamson *v.* State, 16 Ala. 431; Mulvey *v.* State, 43 Ala. 316; Commonwealth *v.* Barry, 115 Mass. 146; Commonwealth *v.* Carroll, 124 Mass. 30; Commonwealth *v.* Pratt, 126 Mass. 462; Commonwealth *v.* Kennedy, 119 Mass. 211; Commonwealth *v.* Wood, 97 Mass. 225; Reg. *v.* Manning, 2 Carr. & K. 903; Rex *v.* Hill, 3 New Sess. Cas. 648; Reg. *v.* Dring, 7 Cox, C. C. 382; Reg. *v.* Woodward, 9 Cox, C. C. 95; Reg. *v.* McAthey, 9 Cox, C. C. 251; Reg. *v.* Clayton, 1 Car. & K. 128; State *v.* Brown, 31 Me. 520; State *v.* Dow, 21 Vt. 484; State *v.* Potter, 42 Vt. 495; Commonwealth *v.* Nichols, 51 Mass. (10 Metc.) 259; Schmidt *v.* State, 14 Mo. 137.
11. King *v.* Stapleton, Jebb, C. C. 93.

a. Separate Liability of Wife. — Where a wife commits a crime of her own voluntary act, or by the simple command of her husband, she is punishable, as much as if she were unmarried; and the same is true when the act is done in his absence, and not under his immediate command; but not if he is near enough to exercise control, or if, as agent of her husband, she delivers liquor, under her husband's contract with his buyer, in violation of law. Where the wife lives apart from her husband, she may be indicted alone for any crime she may have committed, the same as though she were unmarried. And, where she lives with her husband, the wife is liable, if the offence is of such a nature that she could commit it alone, and without the concurrence of her husband. Thus, a married woman may be indicted and punished for keeping a house of ill-fame, although her husband lives in the house, and furnishes and supplies it, or was actually living with her at the time, and a participant.[1]

Commonwealth *v.* Butler, 83 Mass. (1 Allen) 4; Commonwealth *v.* Murphy, 68 Mass. (2 Gray) 510, 513; State *v.* Nelson, 29 Me. 329; Commonwealth *v.* Martin, 1 Mass. 348; Commonwealth *v.* Trimmer, 1 Mass. 476; Commonwealth *v.* Neal, 10 Mass. 152; s. c., 1 Lead. C. C. 81; Commonwealth *v.* Lewis, 42 Mass. (1 Metc) 151; Eagan *v.* Commonwealth, 103 Mass. 71; State *v.* Collins, 1 McCord (S. C.), 355; State *v.* Bentz, 11 Mo. 27; State *v.* Harvey, 3 N. H. 65; Uhl *v.* Commonwealth, 6 Gratt. (Va.) 706; Davis *v.* State, 15 Ohio, 72; State *v.* Williams, 65 N. C. 399; State *v.* Parkerson, 1 Strob (S. C.) L. 169; State *v.* Potter, 42 Vt. 495; Rex *v.* Morris, Russ. & R. C. C. 270; Rex *v.* Fenner, 1 Sid. 410; Rex *v.* Jordan, 2 Keb. 634; Rex *v.* Crofts, 2 Strange, 1120; Rex *v.* Taylor, 3 Burr. 1679; Rex *v.* Sergeant, 1 Ryan & M. 352; Reg *v.* Price, 8 Carr. & P. 19; Reg. *v.* Braddy, 3 Cox, C. C. 425; Reg. *v.* Hill, 1 Denison, 453; Reg. *v.* Cohen, 11 Cox, C C. 99; Rex *v.* Hughes, 2 Lew. C. C. 229; 1 Hawk. P. C. ch. 1, § 9; 1 Hale, P. C. 45, 47; 4 Bl. Com. 29, 444; Commonwealth *v.* Welch, 97 Mass. 593; Rex *v.* Connolly, 2 Lew. C. C. 29; Commonwealth *v.* Munsey, 112 Mass. 287; Quinlan *v.* People, 6 Park. Cr. R. (N. Y.) 1; Commonwealth *v.* Burk, 77 Mass. (11 Gray) 437; Commonwealth *v.* Tryon, 99 Mass. 442; Commonwealth *v.* Whalen, 82 Mass. (16 Gray) 23; Rosc. Cr. Ev. 986.

1. Martin *v.* Commonwealth, 1 Mass. 347; Commonwealth *v.* Trimmer, 1 Mass. 476; Commonwealth *v.* Neal, 10 Mass. 152; s. c, 1 Lead. C. C. 81; Reg *v.* Buncombe, 1 Cox, C. C. 183; Reg. *v.* Hughes, 1 Russ. Cr. 40; 1 Russ. Cr. (9th ed.) 39; 1 Bish. Cr. L (6th ed.) § 361; Commonwealth *v.* Murphy, 68 Mass. (2 Gray) 510; State *v.* Haines, 35 N. H. 207; Commonwealth *v.* Welch, 97 Mass. 593; Geuing *v.* State, 1 McCord (S. C.), 573; Reg. *v.* Crofts, 7 Mod. 397; Commonwealth *v.* Butler, 83 Mass. (1 Allen) 4; Commonwealth *v.* Burk, 77 Mass. (11 Gray) 437; Commonwealth *v.* Whalen, 82 Mass. (16 Gray) 25; Reg. *v* Dixon, 10 Mod. 335; Commonwealth *v.* Cheney, 114 Mass. 281; Commonwealth *v.* Lewis, 42 Mass. (1 Metc.) 151; State *v.* Collins, 1 McCord (S. C.), 355; State *v.* Bentz, 11 Mo. 27; Pennybaker *v.* State, 2 Blackf. (Ind.) 484; 1 Wharton C. L. (8th ed.) § 81; 4 Bl. Com 29; Reg. *v.* Williams, 10 Mod. 63; s. c., 1 Salk. 384; Rex *v.* Fenner, 2 Keble, 468; Rex *v.* Jordan, 2 Keble, 634; People *v.* Townsend, 3 Hill (N. Y.), 479; Reg. *v.* Squires, 1 Russ. Cr. 38, 678, Reg. *v.* Foxby, 6 Mod. 178; Somersett's Case, 2 St. Tr. 951; Rex *v.* Crofts, 2 Strange, 1120; State *v.* Potter, 42 Vt. 495; Commonwealth *v.* Hartnett, 69 Mass. (3 Gray) 450; Reg. *v.* Cohen, 11 Cox, C. C. 99; Reg. *v.* Tollett, 1 Carr. & M. 112; Rex *v.* Willis, 1 Moody, 375; 1 Hawk. P. C. ch. 72, § 8; Reg. *v.* Robinson, L. R. 1 C. C. 80; 1 Hale, P. C. 514; Rosc. Cr. Ev. 654, 987; Reg. *v.* Brooks, Dears. C. C. 184; Reg. *v.* Archer, 1 Moody, 143; Matthews' Case, 1 Denison, 596; Reg. *v.* McClarens, 3 Cox, C. C 425; Rex *v.* March, 1 Moody, 182; People *v.* Mather, 4 Wend. (N. Y) 229; Commonwealth *v.* Manson, 2 Ashm. (Pa.) 31; Commonwealth *v.* Wood, 7 Boston L. R. 58; Rex *v.* Locker, 5 Esp. 107; Reg. *v.* Goode, 1 Carr. & K. 185; Reg. *v.* Manning, 2 Carr. & K 903; 1 Russ. (9th ed) 35; 1 Hale, P. C. 48, 516; 1 Hawk P. C. ch. 1, § 7; 2 Hawk P. C. ch. 29, § 34; 4 Bl. Com. 39; Commonwealth *v.* Feeney, 95 Mass. (13 Allen) 560; 2 East, P. C 537; Freel *v.* State, 21 Ark. 212; Edwards *v.* State, 27 Ark. 493; s. c., 1 Green, C. C. Rep. 741; 1 Bish. Cr. L. (6th ed.) § 358; Rex *v.* Knight, 1 Carr. & P.

But a wife cannot commit larceny by stealing her husband's goods, neither can she embezzle them; neither can a stranger acting under her direction, except when done in adulterous intercourse. Neither can a wife be convicted of receiving stolen goods from her husband, where they were stolen by him, and delivered to her.[1] And while it is ordinarily true that the wife cannot steal the goods of her husband, nor can an indifferent person steal his goods by delivery of the wife,[2] yet, if the person to whom she delivers the goods is her adulterer, he may be properly convicted.[3] So, if the goods are delivered to her intended adulterer, it is larceny.[4]

b. When jointly liable. — It is well established, that, where the offence is joint, the wife cannot be convicted without her husband; and, when the offence appertains chiefly to the husband, she cannot be convicted unless her husband is also.[5] Where the wife voluntarily accompanies her husband, and both engage in an attempt to commit a felony, and the husband commits it in her presence, she is guilty, although she gave no intentional assistance in the commission of the act, as in a case of breaking and entering.[6]

116; Reg. *v.* Manning, 2 Carr. & K. 903; Reg. *v.* Cruse, 8 Carr. & P. 541; 1 Russ. Cr. (9th ed.) 39; Reg. *v.* Smith, 8 Cox, C. C. 27; Reg. *v.* Wardroper, 8 Cox, C. C. 284; Commonwealth *v.* Gannon, 97 Mass. 547; State *v.* Nelson, 29 Me. 329; Miller *v.* State, 25 Wis. 384; State *v* Banks, 48 Ind. 197; Haines *v.* State, 35 N. H. 207; Matthews' Case, 1 Denison, 596; Foster's Case, 11 Coke, 61; Reg. *v.* Buncombe, 1 Cox, C. C. 183.

1. State *v.* Potter, 42 Vt. 495; Commonwealth *v.* Hartnett, 69 Mass. (3 Gray) 450; Reg. *v.* Cohen, 11 Cox, C. C. 99; Reg. *v.* Tollett, 1 Car. & M. 112; Rex *v.* Willis, 1 Moody, 375; Hawk. P. C. ch. 72, § 8; Reg. *v.* Robinson, L. R. 1 C. C. 80; Reg. *v.* Tollett, Harr. & M. 112; Reg. *v.* Brooks, Dears. C. C. 184; Reg. *v.* Archer, 1 Moody, 143; Case of Matthews, 1 Den. C. C. 184; Reg. *v.* McClarens, 3 Cox, C. C. 425. See Rosc. Cr. Ev. 654, 987; 1 Hale, P. C. 514; 1 Russ. Cr. (9th ed.) 42.

2. Reg. *v.* Tollett, Car. & M. 112.

3. Commonwealth *v.* Hartnett, 69 Mass. (3 Gray) 450; Rex *v.* Willis, 1 Moody, 375; Reg. *v.* Cohen, 11 Cox, C. C. 99; Reg. *v.* Tollett, 1 Carr. & M. 112; Reg. *v.* Robinson, L. R. 1 C. C. 80; 1 Hawk. P. C. ch. 72, § 8; 1 Hale, P. C. 514; 1 Russ. Cr. (9th ed.) 42; Rosc. Cr. Ev. 654.

Elopement with Adulterer. — If a wife elopes with an adulterer who takes her clothes with them, it is larceny. Reg. *v.* Tollett, Car. & M. 112.

4. Reg. *v.* Tollett, Carr. & M. 112.

5. Rather *v.* State, 1 Port. (Ala.) 132; Commonwealth *v.* Trimmer, 1 Mass. 476; State *v.* Parkerson, 1 Strob. (S. C.) L. 169. See 4 Bl. Com. 29; 1 Russ. Cr. (9th ed.) 37.

6. Rather *v.* State, 1 Port. (Ala.) 132; State *v.* Parkerson, 1 Strob. (S. C) L. 169; Commonwealth *v.* Trimmer, 1 Mass. 476; 4 Bl. Com. 29; 1 Russ. Cr. (9th ed.) 37; Reg. *v.* Cruse, 8 Carr. & P. 541; Reg. *v.* Manning, 2 Carr. & K. 887; 1 Russ. Cr. (9th ed.) 35; 1 Hale, P. C. 47, 516; Commonwealth *v.* Murphy, 68 Mass. (2 Gray) 510; Phillips *v.* Phillips, 7 B. Mon. (Ky.) 268; Commonwealth *v.* Tryon, 99 Mass. 442; State *v.* Bentz, 11 Mo. 27; Curd *v.* Dodds, 6 Bush (Ky.), 681; State *v.* Nelson, 29 Me. 329; Reg. *v.* Dixon, 10 Mod. 335; 1 Whart. Cr. L. (8th ed.) § 76; 1 Bish. Cr. L. (6th ed.) § 363; Somerville's Case, 1 And. 104; Reg. *v.* Ingram, 1 Salk. 384; Reg. *v.* Price, 8 Carr. & P. 19; Park *v.* Hopkins, 2 Bailey (S. C), 411; Commonwealth *v.* Lovel, Addis. (Pa.) 18; Rex *v.* Hammond, 1 Leach, 499; Rex *v.* Cross, 1 Ld. Raym. 711; State *v.* Harvey, 3 N. H. 65; Commonwealth *v.* Neal, 10 Mass. 152; Commonwealth *v.* Kennedy, 119 Mass. 211; Commonwealth *v.* Hamor, 8 Gratt (Va.) 698; Commonwealth *v.* Barry, 115 Mass. 146; Commonwealth *v.* Van Stone 97 Mass. 548; Commonwealth *v.* Gannon 97 Mass. 547; Commonwealth *v.* Welch 97 Mass. 593; Reg. *v.* Williams, 10 Mod. 63; Baldwin *v.* Blackmore, 1 Burr. 601; Miller *v.* State, 25 Wis. 384; Reg. *v.* McAthey, 9 Cox, C. C. 251; Reg. *v.* Matthews, 1 Dennison, 596; State *v.* Potter, 42 Vt. 495; Commonwealth *v.* Wood, 7 Boston L. R. 58; Commonwealth *v.* Manson, 2 Ashm. (Pa.) 31; Rex *v.* Locker, 5 Esp. 107; **Rex *v.* Robinson, 1 Leach, 37.**

If larceny is committed jointly by husband and wife, the latter is entitled to be acquitted, as having acted under coercion.[1] A wife and her husband may be jointly convicted for receiving stolen goods.[2] And merely indicting her as "the wife of A." is sufficient, without further proof of that fact.[3] But where the charge against them was joint, and it had not been left to the jury to say whether she received the goods in his absence, her conviction was wrong.[4]

A wife, jointly indicted with her husband, is entitled to an acquittal where she uttered the false coin in the presence of her husband.[5] Under a joint indictment for feloniously wounding, with intent to disfigure, where the wife acted under coercion of her husband, she could not be convicted.[6]

A married woman is liable jointly with her husband for her torts, as for murder or treason; and also for her misdemeanor, as for assault and battery, forcible entry and detainer, keeping a liquor nuisance, or a bawdy house, or a gambling-house. And, if jointly indicted, one may be convicted, and the other acquitted.[7]

3. *Principal and Agent.* — The principal is *prima facie* liable for acts done by his agent in the general course of business authorized by him, but not for illegal acts done without his knowledge, consent, or direction; and the agent cannot excuse himself from liability for acts done in the course and duty of his agency.[8]

The principal is not responsible for the criminal acts of his agent, unless they were done by his express authority, or by his command, or under his orders; and when the agent acts under the orders of his principal, the latter cannot evade responsibility by the mere fact that he was absent at the time.[9] The presump-

1. Rex *v.* Knight, 1 Carr. & P. 116.
2. Rex *v.* Archer, 1 Moody, C. C. 143.
3. Rex *v.* Knight, 1 Carr. & P. 116.
4. Rex *v.* Archer, 1 Moody, C. C. 143.
5. Rex *v.* Price, 8 C. & P. 19.
6. Reg. *v.* Smith, Dears. & B. C. C. 553; s. c., 4 Jur. N. S. 395; 27 L. J. M. C. 204; 8 Cox, C. C. 27.
7. Curd *v.* Dodds, 6 Bush (Ky.), 681; Commonwealth *v.* Tryon, 99 Mass. 442; Commonwealth *v.* Barry, 115 Mass. 146. See Commonwealth *v.* Trimmer, 1 Mass. 476; Commonwealth *v.* Neal, 10 Mass. 152; Commonwealth *v.* Kennedy, 119 Mass. 211; Commonwealth *v.* Van Stone, 97 Mass. 548; Commonwealth *v.* Gannon, 97 Mass. 547; Commonwealth *v.* Murphy, 68 Mass. (2 Gray) 510; Commonwealth *v.* Welch, 97 Mass. 593; State *v.* Nelson, 29 Me. 329; State *v.* Bentz, 11 Mo. 27; State *v.* Harvey, 3 N. H. 65; Penna. *v.* Lovel, Addis. (Pa.) 18; State *v.* Parkerson, 1 Strob. (S. C.) 169; Park. *v.* Hopkins, 2 Bail. (S. C.) 411; Commonwealth *v.* Hamor, 8 Gratt. (Va.) 698; Miller *v.* State, 25 Wis. 384; 1 Whart. Cr. L. (8th ed.) sec. 76; 1 Bish. Cr. L. (6th ed.) sec. 363; 1 Lead. C. C. 81; Somerville's Case, 1 And. 104; Reg. *v.* Cruse, 8 Car. & P. 541; Reg. *v.* Price, 8 Car. & P. 19; Reg. *v.* Dixon, 10 Mod. 335; Reg. *v.* Williams, 10 Mod. 63; Reg. *v.* Ingram, 1 Salk. 384; Reg. *v.* Cohen, 11 Cox, C. C. 99; Reg. *v.* McAthey, 9 Cox, C. C. 251; Rex *v.* Hammond, 1 Leach, 499; Rex *v.* Cross, 1 Ld. Raym. 711; Reg. *v.* Matthews, 1 Denison, 596.
8. Nall *v.* State, 34 Ala. 262; Patterson *v.* State, 21 Ala. 571; Seibert *v.* State, 40 Ala. 60; State *v.* Bell, 5 Port. (Ala.) 365; Winter *v.* State, 30 Ala. 22; Barnes *v.* State, 19 Conn. 398; State *v.* Hull, 34 Conn. 132; Jordan *v.* State, 22 Ga. 545; Hately *v.* State, 15 Ga. 347; Hipp *v.* State, 5 Blackf. (Ind.) 149; Lathrope *v.* State, 51 Ind. 192; Commonwealth *v.* Nichols, 51 Mass. (10 Metc.) 259; State *v.* Dawson, 2 Bay (S. C.), 360; Watts *v.* State, 5 W. Va. 352; Lathrope *v.* State, 1 Am Cr. R. 468; O'Leary *v.* State, 44 Am. Cr. R. 91; Wreidt *v.* State, 48 Am. Cr. R. 579; Rex *v.* Dixon, 3 Maule & S. 11; Roberts *v.* Reston, 9 C. B. N. S. 208; *In re* Stephens, L. R. 1 Q. B. 702.
9. Nall *v.* State, 34 Ala. 262; Patterson *v.* State, 21 Ala. 571; Seibert *v.* State, 40 Ala. 60; Commonwealth *v.* Lewis, 4 Leigh

tion is, that the agent was authorized by his principal, but the servant's want of authority will excuse the master; and if a servant executes a lawful direction in an unlawful manner, he is himself responsible.[1]

a. Master and Servant. — A master may be liable for an injury caused by the negligent acts of his servants; and, where he assists his servant in the perpetration of the criminal act, both are liable.[2] Thus, the owner of works is liable for a nuisance, although committed by his agents or servants without his knowledge, and even against his express orders.[3]

If a servant, in the absence of his employer, and with his authorization, performs an illegal act in the pursuit of his employ-

(Va.), 664; 1 Whart. Cr. L. (8th ed.) § 246; 1 Russ. Cr. (9th ed) 53; Commonwealth *v.* Gillespie, 7 Serg. & R. (Pa.) 469; Reg. *v.* Williams, 1 Carr. & K. 589; Rex *v.* Hench, Russ. & R. C. C. 163; 1 Russ. Cr. (9th ed.) 57; 1 Arch. Cr. Pr. 58; Sloan *v.* State, 8 Ind. 312; Rex *v.* Spiller, 5 Carr. & P. 333; Reg. *v.* Michael, 9 Carr. & P. 356; U. S. *v.* Davis, 2 Sumn. C. C. 482; People *v.* Adams, 3 Denio (N. Y.), 190; s. c., 1 N. Y. 173; Commonwealth *v.* Pettes, 114 Mass. 307; Reg *v.* Garrett, 6 Cox, C. C. 260; Norton *v.* People, 8 Cow. (N. Y.) 137; Welsh *v.* State, 3 Tex. App. 413; U. S. *v.* Nunnemacher, 7 Biss. C. C. 111; Commonwealth *v.* Park, 67 Mass. (1 Gray) 553; Commonwealth *v.* Nichols, 51 Mass. (10 Metc.) 259; Commonwealth *v.* Morgan, 107 Mass. 199; Commonwealth *v.* Boston, etc., R. R., 126 Mass. 61; State *v.* Mathis, 1 Hill (S. C.), 37; Britain *v.* State, 3 Humph. (Tenn.) 203; Commonwealth *v.* Major, 6 Dana (Ky.), 293; State *v.* Abrahams, 6 Iowa, 117; State *v.* Stewart, 31 Me. 515; State *v.* Wentworth, 65 Me. 234; State *v.* Dow, 21 Vt. 484; Molihan *v.* State, 30 Ind. 266; Schmidt *v.* State, 14 Mo. 137; Rex *v.* Medley, 6 Carr. & P. 292; Tuberville *v.* Stampe, 1 Ld. Raym. 264; Rex *v.* Almon, 5 Burr. 2686; s. c., 1 Lead. C. C. 145; Rex *v.* Dodd, 2 Sess. Cas 33; Rex *v.* Cutch, Moody & M. 433; Rex *v.* Dixon, 3 Maule & S. 11; Wixon *v.* People, 5 Park. Cr. R. (N. Y) 120; People *v.* Hall, 57 How. Pr. (N. Y.) 342; 1 Hale, P. C. 615, 617; 4 Bl. Com. 37; Fost. 369, 370; Roberts *v.* Reston, 9 C. B. N. S. 208; *In re* Stephens, L. R. 1 Q. B. 702; Barnes *v.* State, 19 Conn. 398; State *v.* Dawson, 2 Bay (S. C.), 360; Hipp *v.* State, 5 Blackf. (Ind) 140; Thompson *v* State, 45 Ind. 495; Hanson *v.* State, 43 Ind. 550; Anderson *v.* State, 39 Ind. 553; U. S. *v.* Halberstadt, Gilp U. S. D. C. 262; State *v.* Privitt, 4 Jones (N C.), L. 100; Anderson *v.* State, 22 Ohio St. 305; Miller *v.* Lockwood, 17 Pa. St. 248; Louisville, etc., R. R. Co. *v.* Blair, 1 Tenn. Ch. 351; Ewing *v* Thompson, 13 Mo. 132; Naish *v.* East India Co., 2 Comyns, 462; Watts *v.* State, 5 W. Va. 352; Lathrope *v.* State, 51 Ind. 192; O'Leary *v.* State, 44 Ind. 91; Wreidt *v.* State, 48 Ind. 579; State *v.* Bell, 5 Port. (Ala) 365; Winter *v.* State, 30 Ala. 22; State *v.* Hull 34 Conn. 132; Jordan *v.* State, 22 Ga. 545; Hately *v.* State, 15 Ga. 347; McCutcheon *v.* People, 69 Ill 601; s. c., 1 Am. Cr. R. 471; Verona Cent. C. Co. *v* Murtaugh, 50 N. Y. 314; Commonwealth *v.* Mason, 94 Mass. 185; State *v.* Berkshire, 2 Ind. 207, Overholtzer *v.* McMichael, 10 Pa. St. 139; *In re* Stephens, 1 Ga. 584; The Emulous, 1 Gall. U. S. D. C. 563

1. Barnes *v.* State, 19 Conn. 398; McCutcheon *v.* People, 69 Ill. 601; s. c., 1 Am. Cr. R. 471; Hipp *v.* State, 5 Blackf. (Ind.) 149; Thompson *v.* State, 45 Ind. 495; Hanson *v.* State, 43 Ind. 550; Anderson *v.* State, 39 Ind. 553; Hipp *v.* State, 5 Blackf. (Ind.) 140; Commonwealth *v.* Mason, 94 Mass. 185; State *v.* Dawson, 2 Bay (S. C.), 360; Ewing *v.* Thompson, 13 Mo. 132; Verona Cent. C. Co. *v.* Murtaugh, 50 N. Y. 314; State *v.* Privitt, 4 Jones (N. C.) L. 100; Anderson *v.* State, 22 Ohio St. 305; United States *v.* Halberstadt, Gilp. U. S. D. C. 262; Miller *v.* Lockwood, 17 Pa. St. 248; Louisville, etc., R. R. Co. *v.* Blair, 1 Tenn. Ch. 351; Naish *v.* East India Co., 2 Comyns, 462; 1 Whart. Cr. L. (8th ed.) sec. 135; 1 Russ. Cr. (9th ed.) 32.

2. *In re* Stephens, 1 Ga. 584; State *v.* Berkshire, 2 Ind. 207; Commonwealth *v.* Nichols, 51 Mass. (10 Metc.) 259; Commonwealth *v.* Morgan, 107 Mass. 199; Commonwealth *v.* Boston & Lowell R. R., 126 Mass. 61; Norton *v.* People, 8 Cow (N. Y.), 137; Overholtzer *v.* McMichael, 10 Pa. St. 139; Miller *v.* Lockwood, 17 Pa. St. 248; Commonwealth *v.* Lewis, 4 Leigh (Va), 664; Rex *v.* Medley, 6 Carr. & P. 292; Reg. *v.* Michael, 9 Carr & P. 356; The Emulous, 1 Gall. C. C. 563.

3. Reg. *v.* Stephens, L. R. 1 Q. B. 702; 12 Jur. N. S. 961; 14 W. R. 859; L. J. Q. B. 251; 14 L. T. N. S. 593.

ment, both may be found guilty.[1] But where the servant acts in the presence or under the control of his employer, he cannot be convicted for maintaining a liquor nuisance.[2]

b. Agency in Crime. — To constitute one a principal in a felony, he must be present at its commission ; but such presence may be constructive, as where it is shown that he acted with another in pursuance of a given design, and was so situated as to be able to give aid to his associates to insure the success of a common purpose.[3]

Where one watches while his confederate robs a house, both are equally guilty.[4] But to constitute one a principal in a felony, he must be present at its commission ; but such presence may be constructive, as where it is shown that he acted with another in pursuance of a given design, and was so situated as to be able to give aid to his associates, to insure the success of a common purpose.[5] Where three men went together to rob a store, and one was posted some distance therefrom to watch, the others entering the storehouse, killing the owner, and robbing the store, the first sharing the booty, he was held to be a principal in the crime of murder in the first degree.[6]

To constitute one a principal rather than an accomplice, he must do some act during the time when the offence is committed to connect him with its commission.[7] An accessory before the fact to a felony may be convicted as though he were the principal felon.[8] To hold one liable with others as a principal, there must be a combination of act and intent.[9]

One cannot be convicted as principal in the second degree where there is no evidence of the guilt of the principal in the first degree.[10] Thus, two boys, without V.'s presence or co-operation, stole certain hogs, and delivered them at his pen, he having promised them a certain price if they would so steal and deliver them : V. was held as an accomplice, but not as a principal offender.[11]

The rule that one agreeing to the offence is a principal offender, although not aiding in the act, applied on trial of T. for the murder of B., shot by either T. or by a brother of T., who had fled and escaped ; T. being proved to have been present with his brother at an appointed interview with B., in a field, and, owing to a feud, all three being armed with loaded pistols.[12]

Where a person employs another to do an unlawful act, the act becomes his own, and he is liable ; but both will, in general, be guilty, as the contract is illegal.[13] And the fact that the defendant

1. Commonwealth *v.* Galligan, 144 Mass. 171 ; s. c., 3 New Eng. Rep. 801.
2. Commonwealth *v.* Galligan, 144 Mass. 171 ; s. c., 3 New Eng. Rep. 801.
3. McCarney *v.* People, 83 N. Y. 408.
4. Thomas *v.* State, 43 Ark. 149.
5. McCarney *v.* People, 83 N. Y. 408.
6. Mitchell *v* Commonwealth, 33 Gratt. (Va.) 845.
7. Bean *v.* State, 17 Tex. App. 60.
8. Commonwealth *v.* Hughes, 11 Phila. (Pa.) 43.
9. Rountree *v.* State, 10 Tex. App. 110.
10. Jones *v.* State, 64 Ga. 697.
11. Vincent *v.* State, 9 Tex. App. 46.
12. Taylor *v.* State, 9 Tex. App. 100.
13. Hays *v.* State, 13 Mo. 246 ; State *v.*

was acting as the agent of another in the commission of an offence, will afford no excuse or justification.[1]

One who, by the intervention of an innocent agent, commits a felony, he, and not the agent, is responsible, where the person employed is ignorant of the intention of his employer, unless the act was wholly illegal, and out of the usual course of the employment.[2]

One who procures the commission of a crime by a person who, from idiocy, insanity, or infancy, is deemed incapable of committing crime, is himself liable, as though he had himself committed the act.[3] And for an act done by an innocent agent, the principal or employer is responsible.[4]

So, where A., by letter, asks B. to sign the name of S. to a post-office order, A. is a principal in the forgery, even if the letter merely says that B. is at liberty to sign the name.[5]

4. *Instigation to commit Crime.* — The instigator need not be the originator of the criminal design: if he encourage the perpetrator by falsehood or otherwise, he is guilty as an accessory.[6] At common law the instigator and perpetrator of a crime may be guilty in different degrees.[7] The advice, procurement, encouragement, etc., may be direct or indirect,[8] by words, signs, or motions,[9] personally, or through the intervention of another;[10] and it is not necessary that the instigator should know the name of the perpetrator.[11] While the instigator is responsible for incidental consequences, it is otherwise as to collateral offences.[12]

5. *Compulsion and Duress.* — *a. Compulsion.* — No person can be held liable criminally for an act which it is not in his power to prevent.[13] And acts committed under the compulsion of law, where the will is not freely exercised, are excusable; as, killing to prevent an escape after a felony has been committed.[14]

Whatever is necessary to save life, is, in general, considered as

Schmidt, 14 Mo. 137; State *v.* Bryant, 14 Mo. 340; United States *v.* Nunnemacher, 7 Biss. C. C. 111; 1 Whart. Cr. L. (8th ed.) sec. 161; Reg. *v.* King, 20 Up. Can. C. P. 246. See also Attorney-General *v.* Siddon, 1 Tyrw. 47; Attorney-General *v.* Riddle, 2 Cromp. & J. 493.

1. Allyn *v.* State, 21 Neb. 593.

2. Commonwealth *v.* Nickerson, 87 Mass. (5 Allen) 518; State *v.* Matthews, 20 Mo. 55; Blackburn *v* State, 23 Ohio St. 146; Wixon *v.* People, 5 Parker, Cr. R. (N. Y.) 119; People *v.* McMurray, 4 Parker, Cr. R. (N. Y.) 234; Reg. *v.* Clifford, 2 Carr. & K. 202; Reg. *v.* Bleasdale, 2 Carr. & K. 765; *Ex parte* Parks, 85 Mass. (3 Allen) 237; Rex *v.* Gutch, Moody & M. 433. See Rex *v.* Almon, 5 Burr. 2686; s. c., 1 Lead. C. C. 150; Reg. *v.* Donaghue, 5 L. C. Jur. 104; Reg. *v.* Stephens, L. R. 1 Q. B. 702; Reg. *v.* King, 20 Up. Can. C. P. 246; Reg. *v.* Brewster, 8 Up. Can. C. P. 208.

3. Berry *v.* State, 10 Ga. 518; Commonwealth *v.* Hill, 11 Mass. 136; State *v.* Learnard, 41 Vt. 585; Reg. *v.* Tyler, 8 Car. & P. 618.

4. Reg. *v.* Bleasdale, 2 Carr. & K. 765.

5. Reg. *v.* Clifford, 2 Carr. & K. 202.

6. Keithler *v.* State, 10 Smedes & M. (Miss.) 192; Reg. *v.* Tuckwell, Car. & M. 215.

7. Klein *v.* People, 31 N. Y. 229; Mask *v.* State, 32 Miss. 405.

8. Reg. *v.* Blackburn, 6 Cox, C. C. 333.

9. Kennedy *v.* People, 40 Ill. 488.

10. Rex *v.* Cooper, 19 How. State Tr. 804.

11. Rex *v.* Lee, 6 Carr. & P. 536; Rex *v.* Giles, 1 Moody, 166.

12. People *v.* Knapp, 26 Mich. 112; Watts *v.* State, 5 W. Va. 532.

13. State *v.* Vermont Cent. R. Co., 30 Vt. 108.

14. State *v.* Rutherford, 1 Hawks (N. C.) 457; State *v.* Roane, 2 Dev. (N. C.) L. 58. See also 4 Bl. Com. 28, 179; 1 Hale, P. C. 43; 1 Bish. Cr. L. (6th ed.) sec. 347; 1 Whart. Cr. L. (8th ed.) sec. 94.

done under compulsion; as, joining with rebels for fear of present death,[1] or where one is attacked by a ruffian.[2] And in cases of extreme peril from shipwreck, where there is a necessity that a part should be sacrificed to save the remainder, a decision by lot should be resorted to, unless the peril is so sudden and overwhelming as to leave no choice of means, and no moment for deliberation; but seamen, being common carriers, have no right, even in extreme peril, to sacrifice the lives of passengers for the sole purpose of saving their own.[3]

b. Duress. — Direct physical force exempts from punishment.[4] Actual force upon the person, and present fear of death, are a legal excuse, provided they continue all the time the party remains with rebels.[5] Threats of future injury, or commands from any other than a husband, do not excuse; so, a mere threat to take one's life is not sufficient to excuse homicide, felony, or treason; so, a threat to burn one's house, or destroy his property, is not sufficient duress to excuse the commission of an offence.[6]

An apprehension, though never so well grounded, of suffering mischief not endangering the person, affords no excuse for joining or continuing with rebels,[7] but otherwise when one joins from fear of death.[8] The apprehension of personal danger does not furnish an excuse for assisting an illegal act.[9]

Actual force upon the person, or personal restraint, or fear of personal injury or imprisonment, excuses acts committed during the continuance of such duress.[10] Compulsion to excuse must be such as deprives a person of his free agency.[11]

6. *Effect of Intoxication on Responsibility for Crime.* — *a. Voluntary Intoxication.* — An act is none the less a crime because the

1. **Joining Rebels.** — An apprehension, though never so well grounded, of suffering mischief not endangering the person, affords no excuse for joining or continuing with rebels. McGrowther's Case, 1 East, P. C. 71; but otherwise, when one joins from fear of death. Rex *v.* Gordon, 1 East, P. C. 71.

2. Oliver *v.* State, 17 Ala. 587; People *v.* Doe, 1 Mich. 451; Respublica *v.* McCarty, 2 U. S. (2 Dall.) 86; bk. 1, L. ed. 300; United States *v.* Thomas, 82 U. S. (15 Wall.) 337; bk. 21, L. ed. 89; United States *v.* Vigol, 2 U. S. (2 Dall.) 346; bk. 1, L. ed. 409; United States *v.* Haskell, 4 Wash. C. C. 402; Rex *v.* Gordon, 1 East, P. C. 71. See also 1 Bish. Cr. L. (6th ed.) sec. 347; 1 Allison, Cr. L. 673; 4 Bl. Com. 183.

3. United States *v.* Holmes, 1 Wall. Jr. C. C. 1.

4. United States *v.* Vigol, 2 U. S. (2 Dall.) 346; bk. 1, L. ed. 409; United States *v.* Haskell, 4 Wash. C. C. 402. See also 1 Bish. Cr. L. (6th ed.) sec. 346; 1 Whart. Cr. L. (8th ed.) sec. 97.

5. United States *v.* Vigol, 2 U. S. (2 Dall.) 346; bk 1, L. ed. 409; United States *v.* Haskell, 4 Wash. C. C. 402; Reg. *v.* Tyler, 8 Carr. & P. 616. See also 1 East, P. C. 294.

6. People *v.* Butler, 8 Cal. 435; United States *v.* Holmes, 1 Wall. Jr. C. C. 1; Reg. *v.* Grimwade, 1 Den. C. C. 30; Rex *v.* McGrowther, 18 St. Tr. 391; Rex *v.* Crutchley, 5 Carr. & P. 133.

7. McGrowther's Case, 1 East, P. C. 71.

8. Rex *v.* Gordon, 1 East, P. C. 71.

9. Reg. *v.* Tyler, 8 Carr. & P. 616.

10. United States *v.* Vigol, 2 U. S. (2 Dall.) 346; United States *v.* Haskell, 4 Wash. C. C. 402; Brown *v.* Pierce, 74 U. S. (7 Wall.) 205; bk. 19, L. ed. 134; Strong *v.* Grannis, 26 Barb (N. Y.) 122; State *v.* Learnard, 41 Vt. 585; Simmons *v.* Trumbo, 9 W. Va. 358; Skeate *v.* Beale, 11 Adol. & E. 983; Reg. *v.* Tyler, 8 Car. & P. 616; 1 Bish. Cr. L. (6th ed.) sec. 346; 1 Whart. Cr. L. sec. 97; 1 Bouvier, L. Dict. tit. "Duress."

11. Commonwealth *v.* Hadley, 52 Mass. (11 Met.) 66; Commonwealth *v.* Drew, 57 Mass. (3 Cush.) 279; State *v* Bryant, 14 Mo. 340; State *v.* Mathis, 1 Hill (S. C.), 37; Commonwealth *v.* Gillespie, 7 Serg. & R. (Pa.) 469.

person perpetrating it happened to be in a state of intoxication at the time,[1] because voluntary intoxication is no excuse for crime, even when the intoxication is so extreme that the person is insensible to his surroundings, and unconscious of his acts.[2]

Drunkenness affords no excuse for crime, even though it causes temporary insanity, or renders one unconscious of what he is doing,[3] unless such drunkenness was occasioned by the fraud,

1. Hanvey *v.* State, 68 Ga. 612; State *v.* Hurley, Houst. Cr. Rep. (Del.) 28; Pearson's Case, 2 Lewin, C. C. 144; Rex *v.* Thomas, 7 Carr. & P. 817; Reg. *v.* Gamlen, 1 Fo-t. & F. 90.

It neither excuses nor justifies crime,— Scott *v.* State, 12 Tex. App. 31,—although the result of an irresistible appetite overcoming the will, and amounting to a disease, — Flanigan *v.* People, 86 N. Y. 554; s. c., 40 Am. Rep. 556,—unless the act was committed from insanity produced thereby. State *v.* Paulk, 18 S. C. 514.

2. State *v.* Bullock, 13 Ala. 413; People *v.* King, 27 Cal. 507; People *v.* Lewis, 36 Cal. 531; People *v.* Bell, 49 Cal. 485; United States *v.* Clarke, 2 Cr. C. C. 158; State *v.* Johnson, 40 Conn. 136; State *v.* McGonigal, 5 Har. (Del.) 510; State *v.* Jones, 20 Ga. 534; Wise *v.* State, 34 Ga. 354; Choice *v.* State, 31 Ga. 424; Estes *v.* State, 55 Ga. 31; Golden *v.* State, 25 Ga. 527; Westmoreland *v.* State, 45 Ga. 225; Mercer *v.* State, 17 Ga. 146; Rafferty *v.* People, 66 Ill. 118; McIntyre *v.* People, 38 Ill. 514. See Co Litt. 247 a; Bailey *v.* State, 26 Ind. 422; Bradley *v.* State, 31 Ind. 492; Cluck *v.* State, 40 Ind. 263; Dawson *v.* State, 16 Ind. 428; O'Herrin *v.* State, 14 Ind. 420; Patterson *v.* State, 66 Ind. 185; Gillooley *v.* State, 58 Ind. 182; Reedy *v.* Harper, 25 Iowa, 87; State *v.* Hart, 29 Iowa, 268; State *v.* White, 14 Kan. 538; Shannahan *v.* Commonwealth, 8 Bush (Ky.), 464; Smith *v.* Commonwealth, 1 Duv. (Ky.) 224; Golliher *v.* Commonwealth, 2 Duv. (Ky.) 163; Tyra *v.* Commonwealth, 2 Met. (Ky) 1; State *v.* Millen, 14 La. An. 570; State *v.* Graviotte, 22 La. An. 587; State *v.* Coleman, 27 La. An. 691; Lawton *v.* Sun Mu. Ins. Co., 56 Mass. (2 Cush.) 500; Commonwealth *v.* Hawkins, 69 Mass. (3 Gray) 463; Commonwealth *v.* Malone, 114 Mass 295; People *v.* Garbutt, 17 Mich. 9; Roberts *v.* People, 19 Mich. 401; State *v.* Welch, 21 Minn. 22; State *v.* Gut, 13 Minn. 341; Kelly *v.* State, 3 Sme. M. (Miss.) 518; Schaller *v.* State, 14 Mo. 502; Whitney *v.* State, 8 Mo. 165; State *v.* Hundley, 46 Mo. 414; State *v.* Cross, 27 Mo. 332; State *v.* Pitts, 58 Mo. 556; State *v.* Harlow, 21 Mo. 446; State *v.* Dearing, 65 Mo. 530 State *v.* John, 8 Ired. (N. C.) L. 330; State *v.* Thompson, 12 Nev. 140; State *v.* Avery, 44 N. H. 392; Shannahan *v.* Commonwealth, 1 Green, C. L. (N. J.) 373; Cole's Ca. 7 Abb. Pr. N. S. (N. Y.) 321; People *v.* Pine, 2 Barb. (N. Y.) 566; Lanergan *v.* People, 50 Barb. (N. Y.) 266; Friery *v.* People, 14 Barb. (N. Y.) 319; People *v.* Rogers, 18 N. Y. 9; Kenney *v.* People, 31 N. Y. 330; People *v.* Porter, 2 Parker, Cr. R. (N. Y.) 14; People *v.* Robinson, 1 Parker, Cr. R. (N. Y.) 649; Willis *v.* People, 5 Parker, Cr. R. (N. Y.) 621; People *v.* Hammill, 2 Parker, Cr. R. (N. Y.) 223; People *v.* Willey, 2 Parker, Cr. R. (N. Y.) 19; Real *v.* People, 42 N. Y. 279; State *v.* Turner, Wright (Ohio), 120; Commonwealth *v.* Hart, 2 Brewst. (Pa.) 546; United States *v.* Forbes, Crabbe, U. S. D. C. 558; Respublica *v.* Weidle, 2 U. S. (2 Dall.) 88; bk. 1, L. ed. 301; State *v.* Stark, 1 Strob. (S. C.) 479; Pirtle *v.* State, 9 Humph. (Tenn.) 663; Haile *v.* State, 11 Humph. (Tenn.) 154; Swan *v.* State, 4 Humph. (Tenn.) 136; Cornwell *v.* State, Mart. & Y. (Tenn.) 147; Bennett *v.* State, Mart. & Y (Tenn.) 133; Henslie *v.* State, 3 Heisk. (Tenn.) 202; Carter *v.* State, 12 Tex. 500; Colbath *v.* State, 2 Tex. App. 391; s. c., 4 Tex. App. 76; Outlaw *v.* State, 35 Tex. 481; McCarty *v.* State, 4 Tex. App. 461; Boswell *v.* Commonwealth, 20 Gratt. (Va.) 860; State *v.* Tatro, 50 Vt. 483; Schmidt *v.* Pfeil, 24 Wis. 452; United States *v.* McGlue, 1 Curt. C. C. 1; United States *v.* Willey, 2 Curt. C. C. 19; United States *v.* Cornell, 2 Mason, C. C. 91; United States *v.* Drew, 5 Mason, C. C 28; s. c., 1 Lead. Cr. Cas. 131; 1 Whart. Cr. L (8th ed.) 49; 1 Russ. Cr. (9th ed.) 12; 1 Bish. Cr. L. (6th ed.) sec. 400; 1 Hale, P. C. 32; Pearson's Case, 2 Lewin, 144; Burrows' Case, 1 Lewin, 75; Rennie's Case, 1 Lewin, 76; Reg. *v* Carroll, 7 Car. & P. 145; Reg *v.* Thomas, 7 Car. & P. 817; Reg. *v.* Meakin, 7 Car. & P. 297; Reg. *v.* Grindley, 1 Russ. 8.

3. Upstone *v.* People, 109 Ill. 169; People *v.* Garbutt, 17 Mich. 9.

When Drunkenness considered.—But it may, in cases where the law makes the condition of the criminal's mind an essential element in the crime, be taken into consideration as showing that no crime was committed. People *v.* Robinson, 1 Park. (N. Y) Cr. 235.

Drunkenness is no Excuse for Crime, although the result of an irresistible appetite artifice, or contrivance of another. Nor does it make any difference that a man by constitutional infirmity, or by accidental injury to the head or brain, is more liable to be maddened by liquor than another man. If he has legal memory and discretion when sober, and voluntarily deprives himself of reason, he is responsible for his acts in that condition.[1]

As voluntary drunkenness neither excuses nor justifies crime,[2] therefore intoxication at the time of committing an offence cannot be set up as a defence.[3]

But the accused may show, that, about the time the crime was committed, he was in such a physical condition as to render it improbable that he committed it; and the fact that such condition was caused by intoxication makes no difference in the rule, the intoxication not being set up as a defence.[4]

Drunkenness is no excuse for crime, neither is any state of mind resulting from drunkenness, unless it be a permanent and

overcoming the will, and amounting to a disease. Flanigan *v.* People, 86 N. Y. 554; s. c., 40 Am. Rep. 555.

Temporary Insanity produced by Intoxication does not destroy responsibility for crime, if the accused, being sane and responsible, voluntarily made himself intoxicated. State *v.* Thompson, 12 Nev. 140.

1. Choice *v.* State, 31 Ga. 424.

2. Estes *v.* State, 55 Ga. 31; Hanvey *v.* State, 68 Ga. 612; State *v.* Hurley, Houst. Cr. Rep. (Del.) 28; Scott *v.* State, 12 Tex. App. 31; Pearson's Case, 2 Lewin, C. C. 144; Rex *v.* Thomas, 7 Carr. & P. 817; Reg. *v.* Gamlen, 1 Fost. & F. 90.

3. United States *v.* Drew, 5 Mass. 28; United States *v.* McGlue, 1 Curt. C. C. 1; United States *v.* Roudenbush, Baldw. C. C. 514; United States *v.* Forbes, Crabbe, U. S. D. C. 558.

Drunkenness is no Excuse for Homicide, although the result of an irresistible appetite, overcoming the will, and amounting to a disease, and it is immaterial on the question of premeditation. Flannigan *v.* People, 86 N. Y. 554; s. c., 40 Am. Rep. 556. Drunkenness is no excuse for homicide by shooting, if the act is voluntary. To be too drunk to form an intent to kill, one must be too drunk to form an intent to shoot the victim. Marshall *v.* State, 59 Ga. 154.

Voluntary drunkenness that merely excites the passions, and stimulates men to the commission of crime, in a case of homicide by one in such a condition, without any provocation, neither excuses the offence nor mitigates the punishment. Shannahan *v.* Commonwealth, 8 Bush (Ky.), 464.

Use of Deadly Weapon. — Where defendant used a deadly weapon while in a drunken condition, the fact that he was drunk does not alter the nature of the case; but if he had intemperately used an instrument, not in its nature deadly, the jury might less strongly infer a malicious intent on his part. Rex *v.* Meakin, 7 Carr. & P. 297.

Where a Drunken Man retains Mind enough to plan and execute a crime, it is enough to subject him to legal responsibility. People *v.* Robinson, 1 Park. (N. Y.) Cr. R. 235.

If the defendant, who was drunk at the time of the act, was conscious, and understood what was done and said, so as to give an intelligent and true account of it at the trial, he is responsible. Territory *v.* Franklin, 2 New Mex. 307.

Illegal Voting. — To an indictment for voting more than once at the same election, it is no defence that the prisoner was so drunk when he cast his second vote that he did not know what he was doing, and did not remember that he had already voted at the same election. State *v.* Welch, 21 Minn. 22.

An Instruction in a murder trial, that if defendant (who was drunk at the time of killing) was conscious of and understood what was done and said by himself and others, so as to give an intelligent and true account of it at the trial, he was responsible, *held* correct. Territory *v.* Franklin, 2 New Mex. 307.

Voluntary drunkenness affords no excuse for crime; and a charge to this effect, but with the addition that the drunkenness might be considered by the jury, like any fact, to shed light on the transaction, being quite as favorable to a defendant charged with murder as he could claim, could not be complained of by him. Hanvey *v.* State, 68 Ga. 612.

4. Ingalls *v.* State, 48 Wis. 647.

continuous result.[1] But while drunkenness is no excuse for crime, it cannot in law be held to aggravate an offence.[2]

(1) *Intent and Degrees of the Offence.* — Whenever the actual existence of any particular purpose, motive, or intent is a necessary element to constitute any particular species or degree of crime, the jury may take into consideration the fact that the accused was intoxicated at the time of committing the act, in determining the purpose, motive, or intent with which the offence was committed. Therefore intoxication may be admitted in evidence as to the degree of the crime, and in mitigation of the offence. When the degree of guilt depends on premeditation, the intoxication of the accused may be taken into consideration in determining what specific offence has been committed, or the grade of the offence, or to test the capacity of the accused to form a purpose, or to decide between right and wrong, as tending to show that the accused was not capable of deliberation, or incapable of attack or defence, or unable to form a wilful, deliberate, and premeditated design, or incapable of judging of his acts or their legitimate consequences.[3]

1. State *v.* Coleman, 27 La. An. 691.

2. McIntyre *v.* People, 38 Ill. 514.

Intoxication as an Aggravation. — But it has been *held* in Pennsylvania that intoxication is an aggravation of, rather than an excuse for, crime: short of destruction of reason, it is in no case a full defence. Where it is so great as to render it impossible for a man to form any complete design, the law allows it to reduce the grade of homicide from murder in the first to murder in the second degree. The burden of proof is on the defendant. Commonwealth *v.* Hart, 2 Brewst. (Pa.) 546.

3. State *v.* Bullock, 13 Ala. 413; Mooney *v.* State, 33 Ala. 419; People *v.* Belencia, 21 Cal. 544; People *v.* King, 27 Cal. 507; People *v.* Williams, 43 Cal. 344; People *v.* Lewis, 36 Cal. 531; State *v.* Johnson, 41 Conn. 584; s. c., 40 Conn. 136; People *v.* Odell, 1 Dak. Ter. 197, 203; Golden *v.* State, 25 Ga. 527; Jones *v.* State, 29 Ga. 594; Henry *v.* State, 33 Ga. 441; Rafferty *v.* People, 66 Ill. 118; People *v.* Dawson, 16 Ind. 428; State *v.* Horne, 9 Kan. 119; Curry *v.* Commonwealth, 2 Bush (Ky.), 67; Kriel *v.* Commonwealth, 5 Bush (Ky.), 362; Blimm *v.* Commonwealth, 7 Bush (Ky.), 320; Shannahan *v.* Commonwealth, 8 Bush (Ky.), 463; Smith *v.* Commonwealth, 1 Duv. (Ky.), 224; Golliher *v.* Commonwealth, 2 Duv. (Ky.), 163; Roberts *v.* People, 19 Mich. 401; Kelly *v.* State, 3 Smedes & M. (Miss.) 518; Smith *v.* State, 4 Neb. 277; Rogers *v.* People, 18 N. Y. 9; s. c., 3 Parker, Cr. R. (N. Y.) 632; Kenny *v.* People, 31 N. Y. 330; Commonwealth *v.* Hart, 2 Brewst. (Pa.) 546; Penna. *v.* McFall, Addis. (Pa.) 255; Kelly *v.* Commonwealth, 1 Grant. Cas. (Pa.) 484; Jones *v.* Commonwealth, 75 Pa. St. 403; Keenan *v.* Commonwealth, 44 Pa. St. 55; State *v.* McCants, 1 Spear (S. C.), 384; Pirtle *v.* State, 9 Humph. (Tenn.) 663; Swan *v.* State, 4 Humph. (Tenn.) 136; Haile *v.* State, Swan (Tenn.), 248; Lancaster *v.* State, 2 Lea (Tenn.), 575; 11 Humph (Tenn.) 154; Cornwell *v.* State, Mart. & Y. (Tenn.) 147; Clark *v.* State, 8 Humph (Tenn.) 671; Colbath *v.* State, 2 Tex. App. 391; Ferrell *v.* State, 43 Tex. 503; Brown *v.* State, 4 Tex. App. 275; McCarty *v.* State, 4 Tex. App 461; Wenz *v.* State, 1 Tex. App. 36; Boswell *v.* Commonwealth, 20 Gratt. (Va.) 860; Commonwealth *v.* Jones, 1 Leigh (Va.), 598; 1 Green, C. L. Rep. 373, 412; Commonwealth *v.* Haggerty, Lewis, C. R. L. 402; State *v.* Horne, 1 Green, C. L. Rep. 718; 1 Russ. Cr. (9th ed.) 12; 1 Whart. Cr. L. (8th ed.) sec. 51; 1 Bish. Cr. L. (6th ed.) sec. 414; Rex *v.* Moore, 3 Car. & K. 319; Rex *v.* Meakin, 7 Car. & P. 297; Rex *v.* Thomas, 7 Car. & P. 817; Reg. *v.* Doody, 6 Cox, C. C. 463; Reg. *v.* Monkhouse, 4 Cox, C. C. 55.

Intent. — Though drunkenness cannot of itself constitute an excuse for crime, yet, in cases which involve intention as well as acts, it may be proper to hear proof of the condition of the accused as to sobriety at the time of the offence, in order to test his capacity to decide between right and wrong. Wenz *v.* State, 1 Tex. App 36.

Although drunkenness neither aggravates nor excuses an act done by a party while under its influence, yet it is a fact which may affect both physical ability

As a general rule, intoxication cannot be proven to reduce the grade of the crime, or to show that the act was not a crime, or to prove no crime was committed;[1] but in some cases it is admissible to show that no crime has been committed, or to show the degree or grade of the crime. Thus, in a prosecution for maliciously shooting, evidence that defendant was so intoxicated that he could not form an intent to wound, is admissible.[2]

(2) *Rebuttal of Malice.* — Although intoxication will not excuse crime, yet it may be considered in rebuttal of malice in connection with other facts, and it may be admitted in evidence to show the impulse of sudden passion under provocation; but where the accused determined upon the act when sober, and fortified himself with liquor to commit the act, it furnishes no extenuation of the offence.[3]

and mental condition, and may be essential in determining the nature and character of the acts of the accused as well as the purpose and intent with which they were done. Ferrell *v.* State, 43 Tex. 503.

Showing Mental State. — Voluntary intoxication is no excuse for crime, and can only be considered in cases involving the condition of the defendant's mind when the act was done. On a charge of murder, the drunkenness of the defendant may be considered with a view of determining whether there was that deliberation, premeditation, and intent to kill, necessary to constitute the offence. State *v.* Mowry, (Kan.); s. c., 15 Pac. Rep. 286.

Voluntary intoxication is no defence; but evidence thereof is admissible to prove the mental status of the accused, and thereby the degree of the crime. Colbath *v.* State, 4 Tex. App. 76; Brown *v.* State, 4 Tex. App. 275; McCarty *v.* State, 4 Tex. App. 461; Payne *v.* State, 5 Tex. App. 35; Pocket *v.* State, 5 Tex. App. 552.

An instruction "that drunkenness can never be received as a ground to excuse or palliate a crime," is erroneous, as it may depend on its motive, its degree, and its effect on the mind. Golliher *v.* Commonwealth, 2 Duv (Ky.) 163.

As affecting Degree of Offence. — Where an offence is divisible into degrees, evidence of the intoxicated condition of the accused is admissible to determine how the act was affected by volition. People *v.* Odell, 1 Dak. Ter. 197.

If drunkenness exists to such a degree as to render one incapable of forming a premeditated design to kill, it cannot be murder in the first degree. Cartwright *v.* State, 8 Lea (Tenn.), 376.

In Order to reduce the Offence of Murder to Manslaughter, when committed by a drunken man, it is not essential that he should be intoxicated at the time of killing to such a degree as to be unconscious of his acts, or incapable of forming a deliberate purpose of taking life. McIntyre *v.* People, 38 Ill. 514.

Attempt to Suicide. — Where the prisoner, at the time of the act, was so drunk that he did not know what he did, the fact negatived the attempt to commit suicide. Reg. *v.* Moore, 3 Carr. & K. 319; s. c., 16 Jur. 750.

Shooting into Train. — One may be guilty of the offence of shooting at a railroad train with intent to injure, although he was very drunk at the time. State *v.* Barbee, 92 N. C. 820.

1. State *v.* Sneed, 88 Mo. 138; s. c., 3 West. Rep. 797.

Intoxication cannot reduce an Assault with intent to murder to an aggravated assault. Jeffries *v.* State, 9 Tex. App. 598.

2. Cline *v.* State, 43 Ohio St. 332; s. c., 1 West. Rep. 81; Barber *v.* State, 39 Ohio St. 660.

3. State *v.* Bullock, 13 Ala. 413; Mooney *v.* State, 33 Ala. 419; People *v.* Williams, 43 Cal. 344; People *v.* Belencia, 21 Cal. 544; People *v.* King, 27 Cal. 507; People *v.* Harris, 29 Cal. 678; Malone *v.* State, 49 Ga. 210; Hudgins *v.* State, 2 Ga. 173; Golden *v.* State, 25 Ga. 527; Henry *v.* State, 33 Ga. 441. See Guilford *v.* State, 24 Ga. 323; Long *v.* State, 38 Ga. 491; Jones *v.* State, 29 Ga. 594; Wise *v.* State, 34 Ga. 348; Estes *v.* State, 55 Ga. 30; Dawson *v.* State, 16 Ind. 428, State *v.* Bell, 29 Iowa, 316; State *v.* White, 14 Kan. 538; Shannahan *v.* Commonwealth, 8 Bush (Ky.), 463; Smith *v.* Commonwealth, 1 Duv. (Ky) 224; Blimm *v.* Commonwealth, 7 Bush (Ky.), 320; Commonwealth *v.* Hawkins, 69 Mass. (3 Gray) 463; Kelly *v.* State, 3 Smedes & M. (Miss.) 518; State *v.* Harlow, 21 Mo. 446; Shannahan *v.* State, 1 Green, Cr. R. 273, 379; People *v.*

Drunkenness may be considered by the jury like any other fact to shed light on the transaction.[1] Where provocation by a blow has been given to one who kills another with a weapon which he happens to have in his hands, his drunkenness may be considered on the question of malice, and whether his expressions manifested a deliberate purpose, or were merely idle expressions of a drunken man.[2]

Drunkenness may be admitted to show that the accused was, at the time, in hot blood, and peculiarly susceptible to a supposed insult; but if he determined upon the act when he was sober, and fortified himself with liquor for its perpetration, or did the act deliberately, his intoxication furnishes no extenuation.[3]

(3) *Disproving Criminal Intent.* — Drunkenness at the time of committing the act is not admissible to disprove criminal intent

Rogers, 18 N. Y. 9; Lanergan *v.* People, 6 Park. Cr. R. (N. Y.) 200; People *v.* Hammill, 2 Park. Cr. R. (N. Y.) 223; People *v.* Robinson, 2 Park, Cr. R. (N. Y.) 649; Kenny *v* People, 27 How. Pr. (N. Y.) 202; Penna. *v.* McFall, Addis. (Pa.) 255; Keenan *v.* Commonwealth, 44 Pa. St. 55; Pirtle *v.* State, 9 Humph. (Tenn.) 663; Swan *v.* State, 4 Humph. (Tenn.) 154; Haile *v.* State, 11 Humph. (Tenn.) 154; Cornwell *v.* State, Mart. & Y. (Tenn.) 147; Johnson *v.* State, 1 Tex. App. 146; Loza *v.* State, 1 Tex App. 488; Gwatkin's Case, 9 Leigh (Va.), 678; State *v.* Tatro, 50 Vt. 483; State *v.* Johnson, 41 Com. 584; People *v.* Williams, 1 Green, C. L. Rep. 412; U. S. *v.* Rondenbush, Bald. C. C. 514; State *v.* McCants, 1 Speers (S. C.), 384. See 4 Bl. Com. 26; Rosc. Cr. Ev. 985; 1 Bish. Cr. L. (6th ed.) sec. 414; Rex *v.* Carrol, 7 Car. & P. 145; Rex *v.* Thomas, 7 Car. & P. 817.

1. Hanvey *v.* State, 68 Ga. 612.

Homicide while Drunk: Instruction. — In a trial of one indicted for homicide committed while drunk, the fact of drunkenness, while it may be a circumstance showing the absence of malice, should not be singled out from the other proof, and the jury told that it mitigates the offence. The proper rule is, that one in a voluntary state of intoxication is subject to the same rule of conduct, and the same rules and principles of law, that a sober man is; and that, where a provocation is offered, and the one offering it is killed, if it mitigates the offence of the man drunk, it should also mitigate the offence of the man sober. Shannahan *v.* Commonwealth, 8 Bush (Ky.), 464.

2. Rex *v.* Thomas, 7 Carr. & P. 817.

3. People *v.* Williams, 43 Cal. 344; State *v.* Johnson, 41 Conn. 584; Jones *v.* State, 29 Ga. 594; Malone *v.* State, 49 Ga. 210; McIntyre *v.* People, 38 Ill. 514; Dawson *v.* State, 16 Ind. 428; Cluck *v.* State, 40 Ind. 263, Smith *v.* Commonwealth, 1 Duv. (Ky.) 224; Shannahan *v.* Commonwealth, 8 Bush (Ky.), 463; Kriel *v.* Commonwealth, 5 Bush (Ky.), 362; Curry *v.* Commonwealth, 2 Bush (Ky.), 67; State *v.* Mullen, 14 La. An. 570; Commonwealth *v.* Hawkins, 69 Mass. (3 Gray), 463; Commonwealth *v.* Malone, 114 Mass. 295; State *v.* Garvey, 11 Minn. 154; State *v.* Gut, 13 Minn. 341; State *v.* Harlow, 21 Mo. 446; State *v.* Cross, 27 Mo. 332; State *v.* Hundley, 46 Mo. 414; State *v.* John, 8 Ired. (N.C.) L. 330; People *v.* Rogers, 18 N. Y. 9; Friery *v.* People, 54 Barb. (N. Y.) 319; People *v.* Fuller, 2 Park. Cr. R. (N. Y.) 16; Jones *v.* Commonwealth, 75 Pa. St. 403; Keenan *v.* Commonwealth, 44 Pa. St. 55; Haile *v.* State, 11 Humph. (Tenn.) 154; Ferrell *v.* State, 43 Tex. 503; Wenz *v.* State, 1 Tex. App. 36; People *v.* Williams, 1 Green, C. L. Rep. 412; Shannahan *v.* Commonwealth, 1 Green, C. L. Rep. 373; State *v.* McCants, 1 Speers (S. C.), 384; U. S. *v.* Cornell, 2 Mason, C. C. 91; Rex *v.* Carrol, 7 Car. & P. 145.

Homicide in "Hot Blood:" Effect of Drunkenness. — If drunkenness exists to such an extent as to render one incapable of forming a premeditated and deliberate design to kill, there cannot be murder in the first degree. If drunkenness exists to a less extent, it may be considered in connection with all the facts, to ascertain whether the purpose to kill was formed in passion produced by a cause operating upon a mind excited with liquor, — not such adequate provocation as would reduce the grade of the homicide to manslaughter, but such as to produce passion, and so reduce the killing to murder in the second degree; or whether, notwithstanding the drunkenness, the purpose to kill was formed deliberately and with premeditation, which may exist if the drunkenness is not too great to render the mind incapable of such operations. Cartwright *v.* State, 8 Lea (Tenn.), 376.

in the case of a wanton killing without provocation; but if a man was so drunk that he did not know what he was doing, that fact may be proved to show the absence of a specific intent; and the same is true when, from the facts, the intent is uncertain or doubtful.[1]

Intoxication is always available to disprove a specific intent,[2] such as passing counterfeit money with intent to cheat, or an assault with intent to murder or to do bodily harm, and the like.[3]

(4) *Insanity resulting from Intoxication.* — Although drunkenness in itself is no palliation or excuse for crime, yet mental unsoundness, superinduced by excessive intoxication, and continuing after the intoxication has subsided, may excuse; or when the mind is destroyed by long-continued habit of drunkenness, or where the habit of intoxication caused an habitual madness; and where a person is insane at the time he commits the crime, he is

1. People *v.* Nichol, 34 Cal. 211; People *v.* Williams, 43 Cal. 344; Choice *v.* State, 31 Ga. 424; Humphreys *v.* State, 45 Ga. 190; Estes *v.* State, 55 Ga. 30; Guilford *v.* State, 24 Ga. 315; Rafferty *v.* People, 66 Ill. 118; O'Herrin *v.* State, 14 Ind. 420; Gates *v.* Meredith, 7 Ind. 440; State *v.* Bell, 29 Iowa, 316; People *v.* Garbutt, 17 Mich. 9; State *v.* Garvey, 11 Minn. 154; State *v.* Gut, 13 Minn. 341; People *v.* Rogers, 18 N. Y. 9; Nichols *v.* State, 8 Ohio St. 435; Ferrel *v.* State, 43 Tex. 503; Wenz *v.* State, 1 Tex. App. 36; Boswell *v.* Commonwealth, 20 Gratt. (Va.) 860; State *v.* Schingen, 20 Wis. 74; s. c., 5 Chic. Leg. News, 100; Rex *v.* Meakin, 7 Car. & P. 297. See Reg. *v.* Gamlen, 1 Fost. & F. 90; Reg. *v.* Monkhouse, 4 Cox, C. C. 55; Reg. *v.* Stopford, 11 Cox, C. C. 645; Reg. *v.* Cruse, 8 Car. & P. 541.

2. **Where Statute requires Intent.** — Where a statute makes an offence to consist of an act committed with a particular intent, the rule that voluntary intoxication does not excuse acts which constitute an offence, includes only the consequences which do actually ensue, — the crime actually committed, and not the intent charged, if the defendant was at the time incapable of entertaining it, and did not, in fact, entertain it. Roberts *v.* People, 19 Mich. 401.

Specific Intent. — Although drunkenness is not an excuse for crime, the condition of the accused, caused by drunkenness, may be taken into consideration by the jury, with the other facts of the case, to enable them to decide in respect to the question of intent. People *v.* Harris, 29 Cal. 678; People *v.* Eastman, 14 N. Y. 562.

In Larceny. — Larceny involves a felonious intent; and if one who takes property is too drunk to have any intent, he is not guilty thereof. People *v.* Walker, 38 Mich. 156. And if, at the time the defendant appropriated another's property, he was under the influence of liquor, so as to be unable to form a felonious intent, he is not guilty of larceny. Wood *v.* State, 34 Ark. 341; s. c., 36 Am. Rep. 13.

Assault with Intent to Murder. — On a trial for an assault with intent to murder, the drunkenness of the accused at the time charged may be considered by the jury: it may have produced a state of mind unfavorable to premeditation, although not so excessive as to render him utterly incapable of forming a deliberate purpose. Lancaster *v.* State, 2 Lea (Tenn.), 575.

3. Mooney *v.* State, 33 Ala. 410; Golliher *v.* Commonwealth, 2 Duv. (Ky.) 163; Roberts *v.* People, 19 Mich. 401; State *v.* Garvey, 11 Minn. 154; State *v.* Avery, 44 N. H. 392; Real *v.* People, 42 N. Y. 270; Pigman *v* State, 15 Ohio, 555; Nichols *v.* State, 8 Ohio St. 435; Lytle *v.* State, 31 Ohio St. 196; United States *v.* Roudenbush, Bald. C. C. 514; State *v.* McCants, 1 Speers (S. C.), 384; Reg. *v.* Cruse. 8 Car. & P. 541; Reg. *v.* Moore, 3 Car. & K. 310.

Drunkenness affecting Motive. — Drunkenness may be taken into account by the jury when considering motive or intent of the one acting under its influence. Reg. *v.* Gamlen, 1 Fost. & F. 90.

Where the offence charged embraces deliberation, premeditation, some specific intent or the like, evidence of intoxication may be important. People *v.* Harris, 29 Cal. 678; State *v.* Johnson, 40 Conn. 136; Roberts *v* People, 19 Mich. 401; State *v.* Welch, 21 Minn. 22; People *v.* Robinson, 2 Park. Cr. R. (N. Y.) 235; Pigman *v.* State, 14 Ohio, 555; Nichols *v.* State, 8 Ohio St. 435; Davis *v.* State, 25 Ohio St. 369; Lytle *v.* State, 31 Ohio St. 196; Hopt *v.* People, 104 U. S. 631; bk. 26, L. ed. 873.

not punishable, although such insanity be remotely occasioned by undue indulgence in spirituous liquors, or from what, in a moral sense, is a criminal neglect of duty. For if the reason be perverted or destroyed by a fixed disease, though brought on by his own vices, the law holds him not accountable.[1] But temporary insanity, resulting immediately from voluntary intoxication, does not destroy legal responsibility, or constitute a defence for crime; but when the question is, whether a murder is of the first or of the second degree, the fact of drunkenness may be proved to show the mental *status* of the accused at the time of the act, and thereby enable the jury to determine whether or not the killing resulted from a deliberate and premeditated purpose.[2]

A fixed frenzy or insanity, as delirium tremens, or *mania a potu*, destroys all legal responsibility, and, although induced by voluntary intoxication, is a good defence. It annuls responsibility, provided the mental condition can stand the tests applied in other forms of insanity. The insane person is no more punishable for his acts

1. Beasley *v.* State, 50 Ala. 149; United States *v.* Clarke, 2 Cr. C. C. 158; People *v.* Odell, 1 Dak. Ter. 197; State *v.* McGonigal, 5 Harr. (Del.) 510; State *v.* Dillahunt, 3 Harr. (Del.) 551; Estes *v.* State, 55 Ga. 30; Bailey *v.* State, 26 Ind. 422; Cluck *v.* State, 40 Ind. 263; Gates *v.* Meredith, 7 Ind. 440; Smith *v.* Commonwealth, 1 Duv. (Ky.) 224; Roberts *v.* People, 10 Mich. 401; s.c., 19 Mich. 402; State *v.* Hundley, 46 Mo. 414; State *v.* Thompson, 12 Nev. 140; O'Brien *v.* People, 48 Barb. (N. Y.) 275; People *v.* Eastwood, 14 N. Y. 562; Lanergan *v.* People, 50 Barb. (N. Y.) 266; People *v.* Rogers, 18 N. Y. 9; Maconnehey *v.* State, 5 Ohio, 77; Commonwealth *v.* Green, 1 Ashm. (Pa.) 289; United States *v.* Forbes, Crabbe, U. S. D. C. 558; Bennett *v.* State, Mart. & Y. (Tenn.) 133; Cornwell *v.* State, Mart. & Y. (Tenn.) 147; Stuart *v.* State, 57 Tenn. 178; Haile *v.* State, 11 Humph. (Tenn.) 154; Pirtle *v.* State, 9 Humph. (Tenn.) 663; Carter *v.* State, 12 Tex. 500; Boswell *v.* Commonwealth, 20 Gratt. (Va.) 860; United States *v.* McGlue, 1 Curt. C. C. 1; United States *v.* Cornell, 2 Mason, C. C. 91; United States *v.* Drew, 5 Mason, C. C. 28; 1 Russ. Cr. (9th ed.) 12; 1 Bish. Cr. L. (6th ed.) 406; 1 Whart. Cr L (8th ed.) sec. 48; McDonald's C. L. of Scot. 16; 1 Hale, P. C. 23; 4 Blackst. Com. 26; Reniger *v.* Fogossa, Plow. 1; Rex *v.* Meakin, 7 Car. & P. 297; Rennie's Case, 1 Lewin, 76.

Voluntary intoxication affords no excuse for crime, unless insanity was produced thereby, and the defendant was insane when the act was committed. State *v.* Paulk, 18 S. C. 514.

Predisposition to Insanity from Intoxication. — If a person be subject to a tendency to insanity which is liable to be excited by intoxication, of which he is ignorant, having no reason from his past experience, or from information derived from others, to believe that such extraordinary effects are likely to result from intoxication, he ought not to be held responsible for such extraordinary effects; and so far as the jury believe that his actions resulted from these, and not from the natural effects of drunkenness, or from previously formed intentions, the same degree of competency should be required to render him capable of entertaining or responsible for the intent, as when the question is one of insanity alone. Roberts *v.* People, 19 Mich. 401.

Where the defence of temporary insanity proceeds upon the theory that it was induced by the operation of strong drink upon a mind rendered unsound by an injury to the brain, it is error to leave the question of criminal responsibility to be determined upon the facts of injury and mental unsoundness alone, or upon the effects of intoxication apart from the other facts. People *v.* Cummins, 47 Mich. 334.

Mental Unsoundness superinduced by Drink. — Although "drunkenness in itself is no excuse or palliation for crime" committed while under its influence, yet mental unsoundness superinduced by excessive drunkenness, and continuing after the intoxication has subsided, may be an excuse. Beasley *v.* State, 50 Ala. 149.

Permanent Insanity. — If permanent insanity is produced by habitual drunkenness, then, like insanity produced by any other cause, it excuses an act which otherwise would be criminal. State *v.* Robinson, 20 W. Va. 713; s. c., 43 Am. Rep. 799.

2. Colbath *v.* State, 2 Tex. App. 391.

than if the delirium had proceeded from causes not under his control.[1]

b. Involuntary Intoxication as an Excuse for Crime. — If a person be made drunk by fraud or stratagem of another, or by the unskilfulness of his physician, he is not responsible for his acts; and a man, owing to temporary debility or disease, maddened by the quantity of wine which he usually takes in his normal condition, is not voluntarily insane.[2]

7. *Insanity.* — To be responsible for crime, the party committing the act must be of sane mind, as the act does not constitute guilt unless the mind is guilty; hence sanity is an essential ingredient in crime.[3] And while soundness of mind is presumed, yet if the jury entertain a reasonable doubt as to the sanity of accused, they should acquit.[4]

Sanity is presumed;[5] but where insanity is once established, it is presumed to continue.[6]

The mere fact that a person is insane does not relieve him from criminal responsibility.[7] The insanity must have been such as to prevent the accused from distinguishing between right and wrong in the particular act.[8]

1. People *v.* Williams, 43 Cal. 344; U. S. *v.* Clarke, 2 Cr. C. C. 158; State *v.* Dillahunt, 3 Harr. (Del.) 551; State *v.* McGonigal, 5 Harr. (Del.) 510; Cluck *v.* State, 40 Ind. 563; Bradley *v.* State, 31 Ind. 492; Gates *v.* Meredith, 7 Ind. 440; Bailey *v.* State, 26 Ind. 423; O'Herrin *v.* State, 14 Ind. 420; Dawson *v.* State, 16 Ind. 428; Fisher *v.* State, 64 Ind. 435; Smith *v.* Commonwealth, 1 Duv. (Ky.) 224; Roberts *v.* People, 10 Mich. 401; State *v.* Hundley, 46 Mo. 414; State *v.* Sewell, 3 Jones (N. C.), L. 245; Lanergan *v.* People, 50 Barb. (N. Y.) 266; s. c., 6 Parker, Cr. R. (N. Y.) 209; O'Brien *v.* People, 48 Barb. (N. Y.) 274; People *v.* Rogers, 18 N. Y. 9; Maconnehey *v.* State, 5 Ohio St. 77; Commonwealth *v.* Green, 1 Ashm. (Pa.) 280; U. S. *v.* Forbes, Crabbe, U. S. D. C. 558; Cornwell *v.* State, Mart. & Y. (Tenn.) 147; Carter *v.* State, 12 Tex. 500; Boswell *v.* Commonwealth, 20 Gratt. (Va.) 860; U. S. *v.* McGlue, 1 Curt. C. C. 1; U. S. *v.* Drew, 5 Mason, C. C. 28; 1 Whart. Cr. L. (8th ed.) sec. 48; Watson's Case, Tayl. Med. Jur. 650; Simpson's Case, Tayl. Med. Jur. 650.

Mania a Potu is a species of insanity. State *v.* Hurley, Houst. Cr. Rep. (Del.) 28.

"Fixed Frenzy." — While it is true that the voluntarily contracted and temporary madness produced by drunkenness is rather an aggravation of, than an apology for, a crime committed during that state, yet, when an habitual and fixed frenzy is produced by drunkenness, the man is in the same condition as if it was contracted involuntarily. United States *v.* Forbes, Crabbe, U. S. D. C. 558; United States *v.* Drew, 5 Mason, C. C. 28; United States *v.* McGlue, 1 Curt. C. C. 1; United States *v.* Clarke, 2 Cr. C. C. 158; State *v.* McGonigal, 5 Harr. (Del.) 510; Mercer *v.* State, 17 Ga. 146; Tyra *v.* Commonwealth, 2 Met. (Ky.) 1; Schaller *v.* State, 14 Mo. 502; Kenny *v.* People, 31 N. Y. 330; Carter *v.* State, 12 Tex. 500.

But if a man is insane when sober, the fact that he increased the insanity by the superadded excitement of liquor does not thereby make him responsible for his acts when in that condition. Choice *v.* State, 31 Ga. 424.

2. State *v.* Johnson, 40 Conn. 136; Choice *v.* State, 31 Ga. 424; Rogers *v.* State, 33 Ind. 543; Roberts *v.* People 19 Mich. 401; People *v.* Robinson, 2 Parker, Cr. R. (N. Y.) 649.

3. Long *v.* State, 38 Ga. 507; Chase *v.* People, 40 Ill. 358; 1 Russ. Cr. (9th ed.) 6; 1 Hale, P. C. 434; 1 Bish. Cr. L. (6th ed.) sec. 375; Co. Lit. 247 b.

Actual Insanity is a Defence to a Crime, not a mitigating circumstance. Sage *v.* State, 91 Ind. 141.

4. Dacy *v.* People, 116 Ill. 555; s. c., 4 West. Rep. 180.

5. State *v.* Brown (Del.), Houst. Cr. Rep. 539.

6. **In Texas,** however, this is not the rule. Leacher *v.* State, Tex. Ct. App. Nov. 1886.

7. People *v.* O'Connell, 62 How. Pr. (N. Y.) 436.

8. State *v.* Erb, 74 Mo. 199; State *v.*

If one is of sane mind, he is responsible for his criminal act, even though his mental capacity be weak, or his intellect of an inferior order: the law recognizes no exemption from crime less than some degree of insanity or mental unsoundness.[1] And mere weakness of mind is not insanity, as the memory may be impaired, and still the mind be sound.[2] Neither can immunity from crime be predicated upon a merely weak or low order of intellect, coupled with a sound mind.[3] One conscious that his act is wrong, and with sufficient power of mind to refrain from committing the offence, cannot claim exemption from punishment on the plea of insanity.[4]

The law requires something more than occasional oddity or hypochondria to exempt the perpetrator of an offence from its punishment.[5] But permanent insanity, when clearly proved, excuses from all crimes, except such as are committed in lucid intervals.[6] So, permanent insanity produced by habitual intoxication excuses criminal acts.[7] But it has been said that temporary insanity, or unconsciousness of what one is doing, occasioned by intoxication, is no excuse for crime.[8]

To constitute insanity, there must be a disease which impairs or totally destroys either the understanding or the will, or both.[9] And if the accused was under such defect of reason from disease of mind as not to know the quality of the act he was doing, or was under such delusions as not to understand its nature, or not sufficiently conscious to discern that his act was criminal, or was led by an uncontrollable impulse, he is not responsible.[10] But the defect must be such as to render the accused incapable of governing his actions at the time, and so controlling as not to be resisted, creating an overpowering impulse to do the act.[11]

Kotovsky, 74 Mo. 247; Rex *v.* Offord, 5 Car. & P. 168.

1. Wartena *v.* State, 105 Ind. 445; s. c., 2 West. Rep. 757.

2. People *v.* Hurley, 8 Cal. 390; Studstill *v.* State, 7 Ga. 3; Somers *v.* Pumphrey, 24 Ind. 231; Lowden *v.* Lowden, 58 Ind. 538.

3. Somers *v.* Pumphrey, 24 Ind. 231; Patterson *v.* People, 46 Barb. (N. Y.) 625; Wartena *v.* State, 105 Ind. 445; s. c., 2 West. Rep. 757; Buswell, Insanity, ¶ 8.

4. Dunn *v.* People, 109 Ill. 635.

5. Hawe *v.* State, 11 Neb. 537; s. c., 38 Am. Rep. 375.

6. 1 Russ. Cr. (9th ed.) 11, 12; 1 Bish. Cr. L. (6th ed.) sec. 375.

7. State *v.* Robinson, 20 W. Va. 713; s. c., 43 Am. Rep. 799.

8. State *v.* Thomas, Houst. Cr. Rep. (Del.) 511; Upstone *v.* People, 109 Ill. 169.

9. Bradley *v.* State, 31 Ind. 492

10. People *v.* McDonell, 47 Cal. 134; Stevens *v.* State, 31 Ind. 485; State *v.* Felter, 25 Iowa, 67; Smith *v.* Commonwealth, 1 Duv. (Ky.) 224; Kriel *v.* Commonwealth, 5 Bush (Ky.), 362; Scott *v.* Commonwealth, 4 Met. (Ky.) 227; Shanahan *v.* Commonwealth, 8 Bush (Ky.), 464; Commonwealth *v.* Rogers, 48 Mass. (7 Metc.) 500; s. c., 1 Lead. C. C. 94; State *v.* Huting, 21 Mo. 464; People *v.* Sprague, 2 Parker, Cr. R. (N. Y.) 43; Freeman *v.* People, 4 Denio (N. Y.), 9; Commonwealth *v.* Mosler, 4 Pa. St. 264; United States *v.* Holmes, 1 Cliff. C. C. 119; Reg. *v.* Law, 2 Fost. & F. 836; Reg. *v.* Davies, 1 Fost. & F. 69; McNaghten's Case, 10 Clark & F. 200; Reg. *v.* Oxford, 9 Carr. & P. 527; Rex *v.* Offord, 5 Carr. & P. 168; Reg. *v.* Higginson, 1 Carr. & K. 129. See also 1 Russ. Cr. (9th ed.) 19; Rosc. Cr. Ev. 953.

11. State *v.* Johnson, 40 Conn. 136; Roberts *v.* State, 3 Ga. 329; Spann *v.* State, 47 Ga. 553; s. c., 1 Green, C. L. Rep. 391; Hopps *v.* People, 31 Ill. 385; Bradley *v.* State, 31 Ind. 492; Stevens *v.* State, 31 Ind. 485; State *v.* Felter, 25 Iowa, 67; Smith *v.* Commonwealth, 1 Duv. (Ky.) 224;

a. Test of Responsibility. — The test of responsibility for crime lies in the capacity or power of the person to commit the act; and the inquiry is, whether the accused was capable of having, and did have, a criminal intent, and the capacity to distinguish between right and wrong in reference to the particular act charged.[1]

The test of responsibility where insanity is asserted, is the capacity to distinguish between right and wrong with respect to the act, and the absence of insane delusions respecting the same.[2]

(1) *Knowledge of Right and Wrong.* — If the accused knew what he was doing, and that the act was forbidden by law, and had power of mind enough to be conscious of what he was doing, he is responsible.[3]

Scott *v.* Commonwealth, 4 Met. (Ky.) 227; Kriel *v.* Commonwealth, 5 Bush (Ky.), 365; Shannahan *v.* Commonwealth, 8 Bush (Ky.), 464; United States *v.* Hewson, 7 Rep. 361; Commonwealth *v.* Rogers, 48 Mass. (7 Metc.) 500; s. c., 1 Lead. C. C. 94; *In re* Forman, 54 Barb. (N. Y.) 274; People *v.* Sprague, 2 Park. Cr. Rep. (N. Y.) 43; Commonwealth *v.* Schneider, 59 Pa. St. 328; Bitner *v.* Bitner, 65 Pa. St. 347; Commonwealth *v.* Mosler, 4 Pa. St. 267.

1. Life Ins. Co. *v.* Terry, 82 U. S. (15 Wall.) 590; bk. 21, L. ed. 236; United States *v.* McGlue, 1 Curt. C. C. 1, 8; United States *v.* Clarke, 2 Cr. C. C. 158; United States *v.* Shults, 6 McL. C. C. 121; McAllister *v.* State, 17 Ala. 434; People *v.* McDonell, 47 Cal. 134; People *v.* Coffman, 24 Cal. 230; State *v.* Richards, 39 Conn. 591; State *v.* Johnson, 40 Conn. 136; Roberts *v.* State, 3 Ga. 310; Choice *v.* State, 31 Ga. 424; Anderson *v.* State, 42 Ga. 9; Humphreys *v.* State, 45 Ga. 190; Loyd *v.* State, 45 Ga. 57; Westmoreland *v.* State, 45 Ga. 225; Hopps *v.* People, 31 Ill. 385; Fouts *v.* State, 4 Greene (Iowa), 500; State *v.* Porter, 34 Iowa, 131; s. c., 1 Green, C. L. Rep. 241; Sawyer *v.* State, 35 Ind. 80; Smith *v.* Commonwealth, 1 Duv. (Ky.) 224; Kriel *v.* Commonwealth, 5 Bush (Ky.), 362; Bovard *v.* State, 30 Miss. 600; State *v.* Huting, 21 Mo. 464, 476; Commonwealth *v.* Rogers, 48 Mass. (7 Metc.) 500; Commonwealth *v.* Heath, 77 Mass. (11 Grav) 303; State *v.* Lawrence, 57 Me. 574; Walker *v.* People, 88 N. Y. 81; Reg. *v.* Higginson, 1 Car. & K. 129; Freeman *v.* People, 4 Denio (N. Y.), 9; Willis *v.* People, 32 N. Y. 715, 719; Am. Seam. Soc. *v.* Hopper, 33 N. Y. 619; People *v.* Kleim, 1 Edm. Sel. Cas. (N. Y.) 13; Flanagan *v.* People, 52 N. Y. 467; s. c., 1 Green, C. L. Rep. 377; People *v.* Pine, 2 Barb. (N. Y.) 566; People *v.* Sprague, 2 Park. Cr. R. (N. Y.) 43; State *v.* Pike, 49 N. H. 399; Boardman *v.* Woodman, 47 N. H. 120; State *v.* Jones, 50 N. H. 369; Jones *v.* State, 11 N. H. 269; Loeffner *v.* State, 10 Ohio St. 598; State *v.* Gardiner, Wright (Ohio), 392; Blackburn *v.* State, 23 Ohio St. 146; Ortwein *v.* Commonwealth, 76 Pa. St. 414; s. c., 1 Am. Cr. Rep. 283; Commonwealth *v.* Mosler, 4 Pa. St. 264; Brown *v.* Commonwealth, 78 Pa. St. 122; Commonwealth *v.* Farkin, 2 Pa. L. J. 480; State *v.* Spencer, 21 N. J. L. (1 Zab.) 196; Dove *v.* State, 3 Heisk. (Tenn.) 348; s. c., 1 Green, C. L. Rep. 760; Stuart *v.* State, 1 Baxter (Tenn.), 178; Williams *v.* State, 7 Tex. App. 163; Webb *v.* State, 7 Tex. App. 607; s. c., 5 Tex. App. 596; Vance *v.* Commonwealth, 2 Va. Cas. 132; Reg. *v.* Goode, 7 Ad. & E. 536; Rex *v.* Offord, 5 Carr. & P. 168; Reg. *v.* Oxford, 9 Carr. & P. 525; Reg. *v.* Vaughan, 1 Cox, C. C. 80; Reg. *v.* Barton, 3 Cox, C. C. 275; Reg. *v.* Layton, 4 Cox, C. C. 149; Reg. *v.* Higginson, 1 Carr. & K. 129; Reg. *v.* Stokes, 3 Carr. & K. 185; Burrows' Case, 1 Lewin, C. C. 238; Hadfield's Case, 27 How. St. Tr. 1282; Reg. *v.* Vyse, 3 Fost & F. 247. See also 1 Hawk. ch. 1, sec. 3; 4 Bl. Com. 24; Collinson, Lun. 573; 1 Inst. 247; 1 Russ. Cr. (9th ed) 19; 1 Whart. Cr. L. (8th ed.) 34.

2. Casey *v.* People, 31 Hun (N. Y.), 158; People *v.* O'Connell, 62 How. Pr. (N. Y.) 436; Hart *v.* State, 14 Neb. 572; United States *v.* Young, 25 Fed Rep. 710.

3. State *v.* Nixon, 32 Kans. 205. See also Grissom *v.* State, 62 Mass. 167; State *v.* Marter, 2 Ala. 43; State *v.* Brinyear, 5 Ala. 241; McAllister *v.* State, 17 Ala. 434; People *v.* McDonell, 47 Cal. 134; People *v.* Hobson, 17 Cal 424; State *v.* West, Houst. Cr. Rep. (Del.) 371; Roberts *v.* State, 3 Ga. 310; State *v.* Pagels, 92 Mo. 300; s. c., 10 West. Rep. 288; State *v.* Jones, 50 N. H. 369; Flanagan *v.* People, 52 N. Y. 467; s. c., 1 Green, C. L. Rep. 377; Clark *v.* State, 12 Ohio, 483; State *v.* Thompson, Wright (Ohio), 617; Brown *v.* Commonwealth, 78 Pa. St. 122; United States *v* Holmes, 1 Cliff. C. C. 120; Reg. *v.* Barton, 3 Cox, C. C. 275; Reg. *v.* Stokes, 3 Carr. & K. 185; Rex *v.* Offord, 5 Carr. &

Insanity must have been such as to prevent the accused to distinguish between the right and wrong of the particular act,[1] although he suffers from mental aberration as to other matters.[2]

One conscious that his act is wrong, and with sufficient power of mind to refrain from committing it, cannot claim exemption from punishment on the plea of insanity.[3] And the question of capacity to know good from evil is one of fact for the jury.[4]

b. Irresistible Impulse. — The circumstance of a person having acted under an irresistible influence in the commission of a crime

P. 168; Lord Ferrer's Case, 19 How. St. Tr. 947; Reg. *v.* Vamplew, 3 Fost. & F. 520.

In Georgia. — If defendant could distinguish between right and wrong, in the act charged, he is responsible, though he suffers from mental aberration as to other matters. United States *v.* Ridgway, 31 Fed. Rep. 144.

In Kansas. — In State *v.* Mowry, 37 Kan.; s. c., 15 Pac. Rep. 282, the defendant interposed the defence of insanity to the charge of murder in the first degree; and on the trial the court charged substantially that the test of the defendant's responsibility was whether, at the time of the homicide, he had capacity and reason sufficient to enable him to distinguish between right and wrong as to the particular act he was doing, and had power to know that the act was wrong and criminal, and would subject him to punishment. This was *held* to be a proper instruction.

In the course of the opinion in this case, the court say, "There is an objection made to an instruction wherein the court states the *test of responsibility* in a prosecution where insanity is asserted as a defence. The court directed the jury that 'if he was laboring under such a defect of reason from disease of the mind as not to know the nature and quality of the act he was doing; or, if he did know it, that he did not know that he was doing wrong, — then the law does not hold him responsible for his act. On the other hand, if he was capable of understanding what he was doing, and had the power to know that his act was wrong, then the law will hold him criminally responsible for it. . . . If this power of discrimination exists, he will not be exempted from punishment because he may be a person of weak intellect, or one whose moral perceptions are blunted or illy developed, or because his mind may be depressed or distracted from brooding over misfortunes or disappointments, or because he may be wrought up to the most intense mental excitement from sentiments of jealousy, anger, or revenge. . . . The law recognizes no form of insanity, although the mental faculties may be disordered or deranged, which will furnish one immunity from punishment for an act declared by law to be criminal, so long as the person committing the act had the capacity to know what he was doing, and the power to know that his act was wrong.' We think the court stated the correct rule of responsibility where insanity is asserted as a defence. The 'right and wrong test' was approved by this court in State *v.* Nixon, 32 Kan. 205. It is there said that 'where a person, at the time of the commission of an alleged crime, has sufficient mental capacity to understand the nature and quality of the particular act or acts constituting the crime, and the mental capacity to know whether they are right or wrong, he is generally responsible if he commits such act or acts, whatever may be his capacity in other particulars; but, if he does not possess this degree of capacity, then he is not so responsible.' This test has received the almost universal sanction of the courts of this country. Lawson, Insan. 231–270."

In Missouri. — The criterion of insanity is whether the accused knew at the time he committed the act that it was wrong, and a violation of law. State *v.* Pagels, 92 Mo. 300; s. c., 10 West. Rep. 288.

1. State *v.* Erb, 74 Mo. 199; State *v.* Kotovsky, 74 Mo. 247; Rex *v.* Offord, 5 Car. & P. 168.

2. State *v.* Murray, 11 Or. 413; United States *v.* Ridgway, 31 Fed. Rep. 144.

3. Dunn *v.* People, 109 Ill. 635.

4. People *v.* Davis, 1 Wheel. Cr. Cas. (N. Y.) 230; State *v.* Doherty, 2 Tenn. 79; People *v.* Walker, 5 City Hall Rec. (N. Y.) 137; People *v.* State, 5 City Hall Rec. (N. Y.) 177; Reg. *v.* Smith, 1 Cox, C. C. 260.

In New Hampshire all tests of insanity as matters of law are rejected, and neither delusion, hallucination, nor knowledge of right and wrong, affords an inflexible test of criminal responsibility; but all symptoms of disease, and its effect upon the faculties, are submitted to the jury, and the testimony of non-expert witnesses is excluded. State *v.* Pike, 49 N. H. 399; State *v.* Jones, 50 N. H. 369; Boardman *v.* Woodman, 47 N. H. 120. See Sawyer *v.* State, 35 Ind. 80.

is no defence, if at the time he committed the act he knew he was doing wrong.[1] A mere uncontrollable impulse of the mind co-existing with the full possession of the reasoning powers, will not warrant an acquittal.[2] And an irresistible impulse does not absolve the actor if, at the time, and in respect to the act, he could distinguish between right and wrong.[3] Thus, where the defence of insanity was interposed by a defendant indicted for murder in the first degree, it was held that the omission to charge that, if the defendant knew the act to be wrong, but was driven to it by an irresistible impulse arising from an insane delusion, he would not be responsible, was not error.[4]

c. Delusion. — A delusion which indicates a defect of sanity such as will relieve a person from criminal responsibility, is a delusion of the senses, or such as relates to facts or objects, — not mere wrong notions or impressions, or of a moral nature. The aberration must be mental, not moral, such as to affect the intellect of the individual.[5]

A party acting under the influence of an insane delusion, with a view of redressing or avenging some supposed grievance, or of producing some public benefit, is, nevertheless, punishable, if he knew, at the time, that he was acting contrary to law.[6]

d. Temporary Insanity. — Where the intellectual power of a

1. Reg. *v.* Haynes, 1 Fost. & F. 666.
2. Reg. *v.* Barton, 3 Cox, C. C. 275.
3. People *v.* Hoin, 62 Cal. 120; s. c., 45 Am. Rep. 641; Reg. *v.* Haynes, 1 Fost. & F. 666.
4. State *v.* Mowry, 37 Kan.; s. c., 15 Pac. Rep. 282.

Irresistible Impulse: Moral Insanity. — In the above case the court say, "The defendant urges that the instruction is erroneous, because it excluded the theory of an *irresistible impulse* or moral insanity. This question received the attention of the court, and was practically decided, in State *v.* Nixon, 32 Kan. 205, although the question was not fairly presented in that case. It is there recognized as a dangerous doctrine, to sustain which would jeopardize the interests of society and the security of life. *Mr. Justice Valentine* says that 'it is possible that an insane, uncontrollable impulse is sometimes sufficient to destroy criminal capacity; but this is possible only where it destroys the power of the accused to comprehend rationally the nature, character, and consequences of the particular act or acts charged against him, and not where the accused still has the power of knowing the character of the particular act or acts, and that they are wrong.' Farther along he says that 'the law will hardly recognize the theory that any uncontrollable impulse may so take possession of a man's faculties and powers as to compel him to do what he knows to be wrong and a crime, and thereby relieve him from all criminal responsibility. Whenever a man understands the nature and character of an act, and knows that it is wrong, it would seem that he ought to be held legally responsible for the commission of it, if, in fact, he does commit it.' In a very recent case the Supreme Court of Missouri considered the refusal of the trial court to charge that, if the defendant obeyed an uncontrollable impulse springing from an insane delusion, he should be acquitted. The court repudiated that doctrine, and *Judge Sherwood* remarked, in deciding the case, that 'it will be a sad day for this State when uncontrollable impulse shall dictate a rule of action to our courts.' State *v.* Pagels, 92 Mo. 300; s. c., 10 West. Rep. 288; 4 S. W. Rep. 931. It is true that a few of the courts have adopted this principle, but by far the greater number have disapproved of it, and have adopted the test which was given in the present case. Lawson, Insan. 270, 308."

Illinois and Delaware Doctrine. — It is *held* in Illinois and Delaware that to excuse crime it must appear that at the time of the commission of the offence the accused was affected by an uncontrollable impulse, overruling his reason and judgment. Dacy *v.* People, 116 Ill. 555; s. c., 4 West. Rep. 180; State *v.* Pratt, Houst. Cr. Rep. (Del.) 249.

5. Reg. *v.* Burton, 3 Fost. & F. 772.
6. McNaghten's Case, 10 Clark & F. 200; s. c., 8 Scott, N. R. 595; Reg. *v.* Higginson, 1 Car. & K. 130.

person to resist is for a time obliterated through an overwhelming violence of mental disease, he is not a responsible moral agent; but if he had power of mind enough to be conscious of what he was doing at the time, or if he could distinguish between right and wrong, he is responsible.[1]

A crime committed under the impulse of passion, anger, or jealousy, which may temporarily dethrone reason, cannot be excused on the ground of insanity; but adventitious insanity during the frenzy is entitled to the same indulgence as fixed insanity.[2]

e. Partial Insanity. — Where the mind is clouded or weakened, but without incapacitating the remembrance, the reasoning faculties, or the judgment, it can excuse crime only where it deprives the party of his reason in regard to the act charged, and will not excuse where there was reason sufficient to distinguish between right and wrong as to the particular act.[3]

One may be sane and insane at different times, and sane and responsible as to one subject, and insane and irresponsible as to another subject; and such insanity will not save him from the consequences of his acts.[4]

(1) *Dementia.* — Dementia is a derangement accompanied by a general enfeeblement of the faculties; and either mania or dementia may be limited to particular subjects, and is an excuse only when it deprives of reason in regard to the act charged.[5]

(2) *Melancholia.* — Melancholia is excessive and unwarranted fears and griefs. It does not excuse crime, unless it deprives the party of reason in regard to the act charged.[6]

(3) *Mania.* — Mania is a mental derangement, which may be limited to particular objects. It is characterized by intellectual disturbance and emotional disorder of more or less intensity.[7]

(4) *Monomania.* — Monomania exists where the mind has imbibed a single notion or delusion contrary to common experience,

1. People *v.* Best, 39 Cal. 690; Hopps *v.* People, 31 Ill. 285; State *v.* Lawrence, 57 Me. 574; Commonwealth *v.* Rogers, 48 Mass. (7 Metc.) 500; State *v.* Shippey, 10 Minn. 223; State *v.* Jones, 50 N. H. 369; People *v.* Klein, 1 Edm. Sel. Cas. (N. Y.) 13; People *v.* Griffin, 1 Edm. Sel. Cas. (N. Y.) 123; Commonwealth *v.* Mosler, 4 Pa. St. 264; Brown *v.* Commonwealth, 78 Pa. St. 122; Bovard *v.* State, 30 Miss. 600; Commonwealth *v.* Stark, 1 Strob. (S. C.) 479; Thomas *v.* State, 40 Tex. 60; 1 Whart. Cr. L. (8th ed.) § 43.

2. Guetig *v.* State, 63 Ind. 94; State *v.* Strickley, 41 Iowa, 232; Bovard *v.* State, 30 Miss. 600; Willis *v.* People, 32 N. Y. 715; Freeman *v.* People, 4 Denio (N. Y.), 9; Beverley's Case, 4 Coke, 125.

3. State *v.* Lawrence, 57 Me. 74; Commonwealth *v.* Rogers, 48 Mass. (7 Metc.) 500; State *v.* Gut, 13 Minn. 341; Bovard *v.* State, 30 Miss. 600; State *v.* Huting, 21 Mo. 464; Commonwealth *v.* Mosler, 4 Pa. St. 264; 1 Beck, Med. Jur. 729; 1 Hale, P. C. 412.

4. State *v.* Geddis, 42 Iowa, 264; State *v.* Mewherter, 46 Iowa, 88; Bovard *v.* State, 30 Miss. 600; State *v.* Huting, 21 Mo. 464; Freeman *v.* People, 4 Denio (N. Y.), 9; Hall *v.* Unger, 2 Abb. C. C. 512; State *v.* Gut, 13 Minn. 341; Commonwealth *v.* Mosler, 4 Pa. St. 264.

5. State *v.* Lawrence, 57 Me. 74; Bovard *v.* State, 30 Miss. 600; State *v.* Huting, 21 Mo. 464; Commonwealth *v.* Mosler, 4 Pa. St. 264.

6. Bovard *v.* State, 20 Miss. 600; State *v.* Huting, 21 Mo. 464.

7. Hall *v.* Unger, 2 Abb. C. C. 512; Dew *v.* Clark, 3 Add. Ec. Rep. 79; Beck, Med. Jur. 725; 1 Russ. Cr. (9th ed.) 12; 1 Bish. Cr. L. (6th ed.) § 388; 1 Whart. Cr. L. (8th ed.) §§ 41, 47.

the mind retaining its other intellectual powers; and it may be confined to a single subject, which leads by an insane impulse to the commission of the act, which impulse controls the will and judgment, obliterates the understanding of right and wrong, and renders it impossible to do otherwise than yield to its influence.[1]

Monomania excuses only when it deprives the party of reason in regard to the act committed; and the delusion must be mental, not moral, nor one which ordinary reason might have produced.[2]

f. Moral or Emotional Insanity. — Moral or emotional insanity has no foundation in law; but if a person is not conscious of the moral turpitude of the act, or is deprived of his understanding, and ignorant that he is committing an offence, the law will not infer a criminal intent; but in such case the moral power must be so deranged as to overcome any resistance made by the intellect.[3]

XIV. Punishment. — Punishment is inflicted as a precaution against future offences. The object sought is effected in three ways: (1) by the amendment of the offender himself; (2) by de-

1. Stevens *v.* State, 31 Ind. 485; State *v.* Johnson, 40 Conn. 136; Commonwealth *v.* Rogers, 48 Mass. (7 Metc.) 500; s. c., 1 Lead. C. C. 94; Bradly *v.* State, 31 Ind. 492; Commonwealth *v.* Haskell, 2 Brewst. (Pa.) 491; Commonwealth *v.* Freth, 5 Clark (Pa. L. J.), 455; Life Ins. Co. *v.* Terry, 21 U. S (15 Wall.) 580; bk. 21, L. ed. 236; United States *v.* Hewson, 7 Bost. L. R. 361; Spann *v.* State, 47 Ga. 553; Roberts *v.* State, 3 Ga. 310; Hopps *v.* People, 31 Ill. 385; State *v.* Felter, 25 Iowa, 67; Wesley *v.* State, 37 Miss. 327; Scott *v.* Commonwealth, 4 Met. (Ky.) 227; Smith *v.* Commonwealth, 1 Duv. (Ky.) 224. *Compare* State *v.* Brandon, 8 Jones (N. C.), L. 463; State *v.* Pike, 49 N. H. 399; Commonwealth *v.* Mosler, 4 Pa. St. 264; 1 Bish. Cr. L. (6th ed.) § 392.

2. Commonwealth *v.* Mosler, 4 Pa. St. 264; State *v.* Huting, 21 Mo. 464; Boyce *v.* Smith, 9 Gratt. (Va.) 704; Rex *v.* Offord, 5 Car. & P. 168; Willis *v.* People, 5 Park. Cr R. (N. Y.) 621; Reg. *v.* Burton, 3 Fost. & F. 772; Rex *v.* Townley, 3 Fost. & F. 839.

3. United States *v.* Schultz, 6 McL. C. C. 121; United States *v.* Holmes, 1 Cliff. C. C. 98; State *v.* Richards, 39 Conn. 591; s. c., 1 Green, C. L. Rep. 377, 395; People *v.* Coffman, 24 Cal. 230; People *v.* McDonell, 47 Cal. 134; Martin *v.* State, 25 Ga. 494; State *v.* Lawrence, 57 Me. 574; Freeman *v.* People, 4 Den. (N. Y) 9; Snorter *v.* People, 2 N. Y. 193; Flanagan *v.* People, 52 N. Y. 467; Farrer *v.* State, 2 Ohio St. 54; State *v.* Gardiner, Wright (Ohio), 392; Commonwealth *v.* Rogers, 48 Mass. (7 Metc.) 500; s. c., 1 Lead. C. C. 94; Commonwealth *v.* Heath, 77 Mass. (11 Gray) 303; McFarland's Case, 8 Abb. (N. Y.) Pr. N. S. 57; State *v.* Spencer, 21 N. J. L. (1 Zab.) 196; State *v.* Brandon, 8 Jones (N. C.), L. 463; Vance *v.* Commonwealth, 2 Va. Cas. 132; State *v.* Windsor, 5 Harr. (Del.) 512; Loyd *v.* State, 45 Ga. 57; Humphreys *v.* State, 45 Ga. 190; affirming Choice *v.* State, 31 Ga. 424; Spann *v.* State, 47 Ga. 553; Reg. *v.* Haynes, 1 Fost. & F. 666; Rex *v.* Townley, 3 Fost. & F. 839; Reg. *v.* Barton, 3 Cr. C. 275; Reg. *v.* Layton, 4 Cr. C. 149; Reg. *v.* Oxford, 9 Car. & P. 525; Rex *v.* Goode, 7 Ad. & E. 536; Reg. *v.* Higginson, 1 Car. & K. 129; 1 Whart. Cr. L. (8th ed.) 43; 1 Russ. Cr. (9th ed.) 11; 1 Bish. Cr. L. (6th ed.) §§ 381, 387; Anderson *v.* State, 43 Conn. 514; Smith *v.* Commonwealth, 1 Duv. (Ky.) 224; St. Louis Mut. Ins. Co. *v.* Graves, 6 Bush (Ky.), 268; *In re* Forman, 54 Barb. (N. Y.) 274; State *v.* Kring, 64 Mo. 244; s. c., 2 Am. Cr. R. 313; United States *v.* McGlue, 1 Curt. C. C. 9; United States *v.* Clark, 2 Cr. C. C. 158; McAllister *v.* State, 17 Ala. 434; People *v.* Pine, 2 Barb. (N. Y.) 571; State *v.* Felter, 25 Iowa, 67; State *v.* Shippey, 10 Minn. 223; Baldwin *v.* State, 12 Mo. 223; State *v.* McCoy, 35 Mo. 531; State *v* Klinger, 48 Mo. 127; State *v.* Huting, 21 Ind. 464; Commonwealth *v.* Mosler, 4 Pa. St. 266; People *v.* Sprague, 2 Park. Cr. R. (N. Y.) 43; Willis *v.* People, 5 Park. Cr. R. (N. Y.) 621; Rex *v.* Offord, 5 Car. & P. 168. People *v.* Kleim, 1 Edm. Sel. Cas. 13; Commonwealth *v.* Euchenberg, 59 Pa. St. 328; Bitner *v.* Bitner, 65 Pa. St. 347; 1 Whart. Cr. L. (8th ed.) § 34; 1 Arch. Pr. 12.

The Law rejects the theory of emotional insanity, which begins on the eve of the criminal act, and ends on its commission. People *v.* Kernaghan (Cal.), 14 Pac. Rep. 566.

terring others through his example; and (3) by depriving the guilty party of the power to do future mischief.[1] The right to punish, in a state of society, depends on the right of society to protect and preserve itself, even to the taking of life.[2]

Among crimes of different natures, those should be most severely punished which are most destructive to public safety and happiness.[3] And the quantity of punishment must be such as is warranted by the laws of nature and society, and such as appears to be best calculated to answer the ends of precaution against future offences;[4] but excessive fines shall not be imposed, nor cruel and unusual punishments inflicted;[5] and a sentence inflicting such punishments may be reversed on that ground,[6] or one which attempts to validate a punishment which would otherwise be illegal, because it is an *ex post facto* law;[7] but fine and imprisonment are not cruel and unusual punishment,[8] nor are disfranchisement and forfeiture of citizenship,[9] neither are stripes inflicted in the discretion of the court.[10]

Retrospective statutes awarding punishment are inoperative;[11] and every law which makes an act, innocent before the law, a crime, or aggravates a crime, and punishes, or enhances the punishment, or that provides for less evidence for conviction, is retrospective and retroactive, and therefore void.[12]

1. *Jurisdiction.* — Jurisdiction to punish offences exists at common law.[13]

1. See 4 Bl. Com. 11; Becc. Cr. & Pun. ch. 12.

2. See 4 Bl. Com. 11; Becc. Cr. & Pun. ch. 12.

3. See Becc. Cr. & Pun. ch. 6.

4. See 4 Bl. Com. 12, 13.

5. See Const. U. S. Amdt. art. 8.

This amendment is a restriction on the National Government, and not on the power of the States. Barker *v.* People, 3 Cow. (N. Y.), 686; s. c., 20 Johns. (N. Y.) 457; Barron *v.* Mayor of Baltimore, 32 U. S. (7 Pet.) 243; bk. 7, L. ed. 672; Pervear *v.* Commonwealth, 72 U. S. (5 Wall) 475; bk. 17, L. ed. 608; James *v.* Commonwealth, 12 Serg. & R. (Pa.) 220; United States *v.* Cruikshank, 92 U. S. (2 Otto) 542; bk. 23, L. ed. 588; s. c., 1 Woods, C. C. 308.

Michigan Doctrine. — Where, at the worst, the offence was merely an assault, how the larger crime should be qualified need not be considered; and where, under the conviction and imprisonment, defendant had already suffered punishment greater than for a common assault, he should not be subjected to further punishment. People *v.* Ross (Mich.), 9 West. Rep. 555.

6. State *v.* Driver, 78 N. C. 423.

7. *In re* Murphy, 1 Woolw. C. C. 141.

8. Ligan *v.* State, 3 Heisk. (Tenn.) 159. And see Turnipseed *v.* State, 6 Ala. 664; State *v.* Adams, 1 Brev. (S. C.) L. 279.

Three years has been held not excessive for arson, — Hester *v.* State, 17 Ga. 132, — and a fine of forty dollars, or ten days' imprisonment, not unusual for gaming, — Williams *v.* State, 6 Tex. App. 147; — but a forfeiture of the weapon as part of the penalty is unconstitutional. Leatherwood *v.* State, 6 Tex. App. 244.

9. Huber *v.* Reily, 3 Smith (Pa.), 112. See Wilson *v.* State, 28 Ind. 393.

10. Commonwealth *v.* Wyatt, 6 Rand. (Va.) 694. See Aldridge *v.* Commonwealth, 2 Va. Cas. 447; Gotchens *v.* Matheson, 40 How. (N. Y.) Pr. 97.

11. See 1 Whart. Cr. L. (8th ed.) sec. 29.

12. Calder *v.* Bull, 3 U. S. (3 Dall.) 386; bk. 1, L. ed. 648; Fletcher *v.* Peck, 6 Cr. C. C. 87; Cummings *v.* State of Missouri, 71 U. S. (4 Wall.) 277; bk. 17, L. ed. 356; Shepherd *v.* People, 25 N. Y. 406; Lapeyre *v.* United States, 84 U. S. (17 Wall.) 191; bk. 21, L. ed. 606; Carpenter *v.* Pennsylvania, 58 U. S. (17 How.) 456; bk. 15, L. ed. 127; Matter of Dorsey, 7 Port. (Ala.) 293; Gut *v.* State, 76 U. S. (9 Wall.) 35; bk. 19, L. ed. 576; U. S. *v.* Gilbert, 2 Sumn. C. C. 101; Dickinson *v.* Dickinson, 3 Murph. (N. C.) L. 327; Wilson *v.* Ohio, etc., R. R. Co., 64 Ill. 542; Falconer *v.* Campbell, 2 McL. C. C. 195; State *v.* McDonald, 20 Minn. 136.

13. State *v.* Ellis, 3 Conn. 186; Ferrill *v.* Commonwealth, 1 Duv. (Ky.) 153; Meyers

2. *Punishment in either of Two Counties.* — Where a crime is composed of several elements, and a material one exists in either of two counties, the courts of either county may, under statutory regulation to that effect, rightfully take jurisdiction of the entire crime.[1]

3. *Discretion of the Court.* — Punishment for crime is, and ought to be, largely in the discretion of the court;[2] but the discretion given to the court in some cases to assess a lighter punishment, does not reduce the grade of the offence.[3]

Where the law gives the court a discretion in awarding punishment, they will look at any evidence proper to influence a judicious mind.[4]

When a party is convicted, and sentenced to pay a fine, it is within the discretion of the court to order his imprisonment till

v. People, 26 Ill. 173; State *v.* Bennett, 14 Iowa, 479; State *v.* Underwood, 49 Me. 181; Cummings *v.* State, 1 Harr. & J. (Md.) 340; Commonwealth *v.* Andrews, 2 Mass. 14; Commonwealth *v.* Holder, 75 Mass. (9 Gray) 7; Watson *v.* State, 36 Miss. 593; State *v.* Williams, 35 Mo. 229; People *v.* Williams, 24 Mich. 156; State *v.* Newman, 9 Nev. 48; Hamilton *v.* State, 11 Ohio, 435; Stanley *v.* State, 24 Ohio St. 166; State *v.* Johnson, 2 Oreg. 115; State *v.* Brown, 1 Hayw. (N. C.) 100. That it does not exist without a statutory provision, see Simmons *v.* Commonwealth, 5 Binn. (Ky.) 619; State *v.* Rennels, 14 La. An. 278; People *v.* Gardner, 2 Johns. (N. Y.) 477; People *v.* Schenck, 2 Johns. (N. Y.) 479; State *v.* LaBlanche, 2 Brown (Pa.), 8. If an offence be created by law, and before prosecution the law is repealed, it cannot be punished, unless a reservation of jurisdiction is provided for in the repealing act. Anonymous, 1 Wash. C. C. 84.

1. Archer *v.* State, 106 Ind. 426; s. c., 4 West. Rep. 726.

There is, perhaps, some diversity of opinion as to whether a statute is constitutional which provides for the punishment of a crime in a county where no material part of the crime was committed; but even upon this question the very decided weight of authority is that the legislature may provide for the punishment of the crime in either of the two counties where any part of the crime is committed. Tippins *v.* State, 14 Ga. 422; Steerman *v.* State, 10 Mo. 503; State *v.* Pauley, 12 Wis. 537; Commonwealth *v.* Parker, 19 Mass. (2 Pick.) 258; Tyler *v.* People, 8 Mich. 320; Commonwealth *v.* Macloon, 101 Mass. 1; State *v.* Johnson, 38 Ark. 568; Hanks *v.* State, 13 Texas App. 289; Ham *v.* State, 4 Texas App. 645; *Ex parte* Rogers, 10 Texas App. 655; Adams *v.* People, 1 N. Y. 173; Archer *v.* State, 106 Ind. 426; s. c., 4 West. Rep. 726.

This power is often necessary in order to prevent an absolute failure of justice; nor is its existence doubtful, for it has ever been the law, illustrated and declared by a great number of cases, that a crime committed partly in one jurisdiction, and partly in another, may be punished in either jurisdiction. 1 Hale, P. C. 430, 431, 615, 617; Regina *v.* Michael, 9 Car. & P. 356; People *v.* Adams, 3 Den. (N. Y.) 207; Bulwer's Case, 7 Coke, 28 *b*; Rex *v.* Burdett, 4 B. & Ald. 175; Commonwealth *v.* Andrews, 2 Mass. 14; Commonwealth *v.* Holder, 75 Mass. (9 Gray) 7; Simmons *v.* Commonwealth, 5 Binn. (Pa.) 619; Simpson *v.* State, 4 Humph. (Tenn.) 461; Beal *v.* State, 15 Ind. 378; Archer *v.* State, 106 Ind. 426; s. c., 4 West. Rep. 726.

2. Malory *v.* State, 56 Ga. 545; Miller *v.* State, 58 Ga. 200.

Sentencing an Infant. — As in sentencing an infant to be executed or imprisoned for a felony. Creed *v.* People, 81 Ill. 565; Monoughan *v.* People, 24 Ill. 341.

3. See Nettles *v.* State, 58 Ala. 268; People *v.* Haun, 44 Cal. 96; Johnston *v.* State, 7 Mo. 183; Ingram *v.* State, 7 Mo. 293; State *v.* Joiner, 19 Mo. 224; State *v.* Murdock, 9 Mo. 730.

4. Morton *v.* Princeton, 18 Ill. 383; State *v.* Townsend, 2 Harr. (Del.) 543; Wilson *v.* The Mary, Gilp. U. S. D. C. 31; State *v.* Smith, 2 Bay (S. C.), L. 62; Robbins *v.* State, 20 Ala. 36; Sarah *v.* State, 18 Ark. 114; People *v.* Cochran, 2 Johns. (N. Y.) Cas. 73; Rex *v.* Mahon, 4 Ad. & E. 575; Rex *v.* Lynn, 2 T. R. 733; Rex *v.* Grey, 2 Keny. 307; Rex *v.* Turner, 1 Strange, 139; Rex *v.* Burdette, 4 Barn. & Ald. 314; Rex *v.* Sharpness, 1 T. R. 228; Rex *v.* Withers, 3 T. R. 428; Rex *v.* Williams, Lofft. 760; Rex *v.* Pinkerton, 2 East, 357; Rex *v.* Mawbey, 6 T. R. 619; Rex *v.* Cox, 4 Car. & P. 538; Rex *v.* Esop, 7 Car. & P. 456.

the fine is paid.[1] The prisoner is entitled to a credit for each day he may remain in prison, and may at any time pay the sum remaining due, and claim his discharge.[1]

The question as to what punishment is generally within the limits of the law, is for the judicial discretion.[2] Accessories after the fact of the crime of murder may be punished by fine and imprisonment at discretion;[3] and though an agent cannot excuse himself from liability because the act was done in the course of his agency, yet that fact may be considered in fixing the punishment.[4]

In some States the statute directs that the jury shall assess the punishment,[5] and in others a division of the responsibility between the court and the jury is provided for.[6] In States where it is competent for the jury to fix the punishment, the statute must be followed.[7]

In construing penal statutes, the reasonable sense designed by the legislature must be applied.[8] Restrictive and punitive clauses are to be construed favorably to the accused,[9] and matters of doubt are to be resolved in favor of life and liberty.[10]

If an attempt, with a felonious intent, is a matter of aggravation, the punishment is not other or additional, but only severer

1. *Ex parte* Jackson, 96 U. S. (6 Otto) 727; bk. 24, L. ed. 877; People *v.* Markham, 7 Cal. 208; *Ex parte* Kelley, 28 Cal. 414.

2. United States *v.* Mundel, 6 Call. (Va.) 245.

3. Tully *v.* Commonwealth, 13 Bush (Ky.), 142.

4. State *v.* Bell, 5 Port. (Ala.) 365.

5. McWhirt's Case, 3 Gratt. (Va.) 594; Cook *v.* United States, 1 Greene (Iowa), 56; State *v.* Douglass, 1 Greene (Iowa), 550; Commonwealth *v.* Frye, 1 Va. Cas. 19; Doty *v.* State, 6 Blackf. (Ind.) 529; Dias *v.* State, 7 Blackf. (Ind.) 20; Leech *v.* Waugh, 24 Ill. 228; Morton *v.* Princeton, 18 Ill. 383; O'Herrin *v.* State, 14 Ind. 420; Ervine *v.* Commonwealth, 5 Dana (Ky.), 216; Nemo *v.* Commonwealth, 2 Gratt. (Va.) 558; Chesley *v.* Brown, 2 Fairf. (Me) 143; Blevings *v.* People, 2 Ill. 172; State *v.* Bean, 21 Mo. 269; Fooxe *v.* State, 7 Mo. 502; Hawkins *v*, State, 3 Stewart & Porter (Ala.), 63; Rice *v.* State, 7 Ind. 332.

In Cases of Homicide, in several of the States it is incumbent on the jury to designate the punishment. Walston *v.* State, 54 Ga. 242. See Buster *v* State, 42 Tex. 315; People *v.* Welch, 49 Cal. 174.

6. Cook *v.* United States, 1 Greene (Iowa), 56; State *v.* McQuaig, 22 Mo. 319; Behler *v.* State, 22 Ind. 345; Moss *v.* State, 42 Ala. 546; Melton *v.* State, 45 Ala. 56.

7. Walston *v.* State, 54 Ga. 242.

8. United States *v.* Staats, 49 U. S. (8 How.) 41; bk. 12, L. ed. 979; United States *v.* Brewster, 32 U. S. (7 Pet.) 164; bk. 8, L. ed. 645; United States *v.* Jones, 3 Wash. C. C. 200; Hodgman *v.* Peoples, 4 Denio (N. Y.), 235; State *v.* Gerkin, 1 Ired. (N. C.) L. 121; Thomas *v.* Commonwealth, 2 Leigh (Va.), 741; State *v.* Fearson, 2 Md. 310; State *v.* Smith, 32 Me. 360; State *v.* Taylor, 2 McC. (S. C.) L. 483; Commonwealth *v.* Houghton, 8 Mass. 107; Commonwealth *v.* Whitmarsh, 21 Mass. (4 Pick.) 233; Stone *v.* State, 20 N. J. L. (1 Spenc.) 401; People *v.* Mather, 4 Wend. (N. Y.) 229; s. c., 21 Am. Dec. 122; People *v.* Hennessey, 15 Wend. (N. Y.) 147; Commonwealth *v.* King, 1 Whart. (Pa) 448; Ream *v.* Commonwealth, 3 Serg. & R. (Pa.) 207; Angel *v.* Commonwealth, 2 Va. Cas. 228.

9. United States *v.* Ragsdale, Hempst. C. C. 497; Andrews *v.* United States, 2 Story, C. C. 202; Carpenter *v.* People, 8 Barb. (N. Y.) 603; State *v.* Stephenson, 2 Bail. (S. C.) L. 334; State *v.* Jaeger, 63 Mo. 403; Commonwealth *v.* Martin, 17 Mass. 359; Warner *v.* Commonwealth, 1 Pa. St. 154; Randolph *v.* State, 9 Tex. 521. See People *v.* Soto, 49 Cal. 67; Commonwealth *v.* Davis, 12 Bush (Ky.), 240.

10. United States *v.* Wiltberger, 18 U. S. (5 Wheat.) 76; bk. 5, L. ed. 37; United States *v.* Sheldon, 15 U. S. (2 Wheat.) 119; bk. 4, L. ed. 199; United States *v.* Clayton, 2 Dill. C. C. 219; United States *v.* Morris, 39 U. S. (14 Pet.) 464; bk. 10, L. ed. 543.

in degree;[1] but punishment for attempts should be less than for the consummated offence.[2]

Changes in the punishment prescribed by a statute, subsequent to the commission of an offence, have no application to such offence.[3]

4. *Consequences of Conviction.* — Persons convicted of felony are thereafter incompetent as witnesses in court proceedings,[4] even though the judgment against them be erroneous, until it is vacated,[5] if the prosecution was by a tribunal having jurisdiction;[6] but whether a foreign judgment operates to disqualify a person as a witness, depends on the statute of the State where the convicted party offers himself as a witness.[7] The following crimes have been held infamous, and conviction thereof sufficient to disqualify a person as a witness: larceny,[8] or knowingly receiving stolen goods,[9] forgery,[10] perjury,[11] subornation of perjury,[12] suppressing testimony by bribery or conspiracy,[13] and all the crimes which create a violent presumption against the truthfulness of a party under oath;[14] but the disqualification does not arise till judgment has been rendered against the convicted party.[15] So, a party attainted of an infamous crime is disqualified to act as a juror.[16]

a. Disfranchisement. — Disfranchisement and forfeiture of citizenship is not a cruel or unusual punishment.[17] A conviction for felony in some States works a forfeiture of office, and of the

1. Simpson *v.* State, 59 Ala. 1; Beasley *v.* State, 18 Ala. 535; Meredith *v.* State, 60 Ala. 441; Norman *v.* State, 24 Miss. 54. See 2 Arch. C. Pr. 285.

2. See 1 Whart. Cr. L. (8th ed.) sec. 200.

3. Hartung *v.* People, 22 N. Y. 95. See Shepherd *v.* People, 25 N. Y. 406; Ratzky *v.* People, 29 N. Y. 124; Kuckler *v.* People, 5 Park. Cr. R. (N. Y.) 212; Miles *v.* State, 40 Ala. 39; Moore *v.* State, 40 Ala. 49; Stephens *v.* State, 40 Ala. 67; Miller *v.* State, 40 Ala. 54.

In South Carolina, it has been undecided whether the substitution of a less penalty than death, without the repeal of so much of an act as declares the offence to be a felony, reduces the crime to a misdemeanor. State *v.* Rowe, 8 Rich. (S. C.) L. 17. And see State *v.* Williams, 2 Rich. (S. C.) L. 418; State *v.* Rohfrisch, 12 La. An. 382; Barker *v.* Commonwealth, 2 Va. Cas. 122; State *v.* Dewer, 65 N. C. 578; Herber *v.* State, 7 Tex. 69; Strong *v.* State, 1 Blackf. (Ind.) 193; State *v.* Willis, 66 Mo. 131.

4. People *v.* Whipple, 9 Cow. (N. Y.) 707; Commonwealth *v.* Green, 17 Mass. 515; U. S. *v.* Brockius, 3 Wash. C. C. 99; Schuylkill *v.* Copley, 17 Smith (Pa.), 386. See State *v.* Hartson, 63 N. C. 294; Reg. *v.* Alternum, 1 Gale & D. 261; Reg. *v.* Webb, 11 Cox, C. C. 133; 1 Greenl. Ev. sec. 372.

5. Commonwealth *v.* Keith, 49 Mass. (8 Met.) 531.

6. Cooke *v.* Maxwell, 2 Stark. 183.

7. Kirschner *v.* State, 9 Wis. 140.

8. State *v.* Gardner, 1 Root (Conn.), 485.

9. Commonwealth *v.* Rogers, 48 Mass. (7 Met.) 500. But see Commonwealth *v.* Murphy, 3 Pa. L. J. 290.

10. Poage *v.* State, 3 Ohio St. 229; State *v.* Candler, 3 Hawks (N. C.), L. 393; Rex *v.* Davis, 5 Mod. 74. See 2 East, P. C. 1003.

11. Howard *v.* Shipley, 4 East, 180; Anonymous, 3 Salk. 155; Rex *v.* Teal, 11 East, 307. See 1 Greenl. Ev. sec. 373.

12. *In re* Sawyer, 2 Gale & D. 141; *Ex parte* Hannan, 6 Jur. 669.

13. Rex *v.* Priddle, 1 Leach, 442; Bushel *v.* Barrett, 1 Ryan & M. 434.

14. Utley *v.* Merrick, 52 Mass. (11 Metc.) 302.

15. Skinner *v.* Perot, 1 Ashm. (Pa.) 57; U. S. *v.* Dickenson, 2 McL. C. C. 325; People *v.* Whipple, 9 Cow. (N. Y.) 707; Gibbs *v.* Osborn, 2 Wend. (N. Y.) 555; State *v.* Valentine, 7 Ired. (N. C.) L. 225; Dawley *v.* State, 4 Ind. 128; Barber *v.* Gingell, 3 Esp. 60; Fitch *v.* Smalbrook, T. Raym. 32; Lee *v.* Gansel, 1 Cowp. 1; s. c., Lofft. 374; Rex *v.* Castell, 8 East, 77.

16. Desty's Am. Cr. Law, p 127.

17. Huber *v.* Reily, 3 Smith (Pa.), 112. See Wilson *v.* State, 28 Ind. 393.

capacity to hold office;[1] but the usual punishment for felony is imprisonment in the State prison.[2]

5. *Adjustment of Punishment.*—When an offence is committed against two sovereignties, the first prosecuting the offence absorbs it, and its punishment is a bar to a prosecution by the other;[3] but when the offence is partly against one, and partly against the other, the sentence of one is to be taken into account in adjusting the sentence of the other.[4] In adjusting the sentence, the grade of the offence will be taken into consideration, and an adequate punishment imposed, allowing for what has been inflicted by the other jurisdiction.[5]

6. *Increased Punishment.*—Increased punishment may be imposed for a subsequent offence.[6] This will not be putting the party twice in jeopardy, nor is it punishment for the first offence.[7] But laws imposing several penalties cannot be applied retrospectively; and doubtful questions as to the severity of the penalty are to be determined in favor of the accused;[8] and where the severer penalty has been abolished by statute, it cannot be imposed.[9]

7. *Discipline.*—A convict can be punished only according to law; and for any excessive or violent punishment, those in charge are liable.[10]

1. Commonwealth *v.* Fugate, 2 Leigh (Va.), 724; State *v.* Carson, 27 Ark. 469; Doty *v.* State, 6 Blackf. (Ind.) 529; Barker *v.* People, 3 Cow. (N. Y.) 686; s. c., 20 Johns. (N. Y.) 457.

2. See 1 Bish. Cr. L. (6th ed.) sec. 939.

3. Coleman *v.* State of Tennessee, 97 U. S. (7 Otto) 309; bk. 24, L. ed. 1118.

4. See Whart. Cr. Pl. & Pr. secs. 441, 453.

5. See Whart. Cr. Pl. & Pr. sec. 441; Whart. Confl. of L. sec. 920.

6. Calder *v.* Bull, 3 U. S. (3 Dall.) 386; bk. 1, L. ed. 648; 5 Rawle (Pa.), 383; Commonwealth *v.* Ross, 19 Mass. (2 Pick.) 165; Plumbly *v.* Commonwealth, 43 Mass. (2 Metc.) 413; Rand *v.* Commonwealth, 9 Gratt. (Va.) 743; People *v.* Stanley, 47 Cal. 113; Maguire *v.* State, 47 Md. 485; People *v.* Butler, 3 Cow. (N. Y.) 347; Phillips *v.* Commonwealth, 44 Mass. (3 Metc.) 588; Evans *v.* Commonwealth, 44 Mass. (3 Metc.) 453; Newton *v.* Commonwealth, 49 Mass. (8 Metc.) 535; Bump *v.* Commonwealth, 49 Mass. (8 Metc.) 533; Kite *v.* Commonwealth, 52 Mass. (11 Metc.) 581; Commonwealth *v.* Phillips, 28 Mass. (11 Pick.) 28; Commonwealth *v.* Getchell, 33 Mass. (16 Pick.) 452; Commonwealth *v.* Mott, 38 Mass. (21 Pick.) 492; *Ex parte* Seymour, 30 Mass. (14 Pick.) 40; Russel *v.* Commonwealth, 7 Serg. & R. (Pa.) 489; Smith *v.* Commonwealth, 14 Serg. & R. (Pa.) 69; Scot *v.* Turner, 1 Root (Conn.), 163; Commonwealth *v.* Morrow, 9 Phila. (Pa.) 583; Long *v.* State, 36 Tex. 6; *Ex parte* Gutierrez, 45 Cal. 429; Ross *v.* Riley, 19 Mass. (2 Pick.) 165. And see People *v.* Butler, 3 Cowen (N. Y.), 347; 1 Bish. Cr. L. secs 959–965.

Subsequent Offence.—A mere conviction of the prior offence is sufficient without sentence. Stevens *v.* People, 1 Hill (N. Y.), 261. *Contra*, Smith *v.* Commonwealth, 14 Serg. & R. (Pa.) 69. And see Wood *v.* People, 53 N. Y. 511; Johnson *v.* People, 55 N. Y. 512; Gibson *v.* People, 5 Hun (N. Y.), 542; State *v.* Volmer, 6 Kan. 379. If he plead guilty, conviction need not be proved. People *v.* Delany, 49 Cal. 394.

Former Conviction in Another State.—But provisions in statutes for increased punishment for a subsequent offence, are not to be considered to include a former conviction in another State or county. People *v.* Ceasar, 1 Park. Cr. R. (N. Y.) 645.

7. People *v.* Stanley, 47 Cal. 114.

8. See 1 Whart. Cr. L. (8th ed.) sec. 30. United States *v.* Harper (U. S. D. C. Southern District of Ohio), 26 Cent. L. J. 2.

9. Commonwealth *v.* Wyman, 66 Mass. (12 Cush.) 237.

10. State *v.* Roberts, 52 N. H. 492; State *v.* Hull, 34 Conn. 132; Harrison *v.* Hodgson, 10 Barn. & C. 445; Rex *v.* Friend, Russ. & R. 20; Reg. *v.* Porter, 9 Cox, C. C. 449; Rex *v.* Miles, 6 Jur. 243. See 1 East, P. C. 297; 1 Hale, P. C. 481.

8. *Bonds to keep the Peace.* — In all cases of misdemeanor, the court in its discretion may require, as a part of the sentence, that the defendant give bonds to keep the peace and be of good behavior.[1]

9. *Fine and Imprisonment.* — Fine and imprisonment is the ordinary common-law punishment for misdemeanors,[2] or cases where the statute is silent as to the punishment.[3] If the statute provides for both fine *and* imprisonment, both must be awarded;[4] but if fine *or* imprisonment, only one can be imposed:[5] yet, where a party is subject to two distinct punishments, he cannot object that only one was inflicted.[6]

If a statute imposes a specific fine, a judgment for a less amount than that specified in the statute will be reversed.[7]

Till judgment is entered, the sentence may be modified.[8]

10. *For Distinct Offences.* — Where a party is convicted of two crimes carved out of one transaction, that fact ought to be considered in fixing the measure of his punishment.[9] One person may be liable for two distinct offences committed in the same act, as selling liquor, and keeping open on Sunday;[10] so, one and the same act may be punishable as a crime under the general law of the State, and also as a violation of a city ordinance:[11] but where a person has been indicted for distinct offences, and sentenced on some of the counts, he cannot, at a subsequent term, be sentenced anew upon another count.[12]

11. *Joint Conviction.* — When two persons are jointly indicted and convicted of an offence, the sentence against them is several, each to suffer the whole of the penalty provided by law.[13] Each one who contributes to the crime is guilty, as though it was done by his own hands.[14] If the offence is punishable by imprison-

1. Terr *v.* Nugent, 1 Mart. (La.) 103; Estes *v.* State, 2 Humph. (Tenn.) 496; Rex *v.* Hart, 30 How. St. Tri. 1131; LeRoy *v.* Rainer, 1 Sid. 214; Dunn *v.* Reg., 12 Q. B. 1031; O'Connell *v.* Reg, 11 Clark & F. 155.

2. State *v.* Roberts, 1 Hayw. (Tenn.) 176; Northampton's Case, 12 Coke, 733.

3. United States *v.* Coolidge, 1 Gall. C. C. 488. See Beecher's Case, 8 Coke, 59; Cro. Jac. 211; Noy, 38; 2 Inst. 131.

4. United States *v.* Vickery, 1 Harr. & J. (Md.) 427.

5. State *v.* Kearney, 1 Hawks (S. C.), 53; Wilde *v.* Commonwealth, 43 Mass. (2 Metc.) 408.

6. Kane *v.* People, 8 Wend. (N. Y.) 203; McQuoid *v.* People, 3 Gilm. (Ill.) 76; Dodge *v.* State, 24 N. J. L. (4 Zab.) 455. See Barth *v.* State, 18 Conn. 431.

7. Taff *v.* State, 39 Conn. 82; *In re* Sweatman, 1 Cow. (N. Y.) 144; State *v.* James, 37 Conn. 355.

8. Jobe *v.* State, 28 Ga. 235.

9. United States *v.* Harmison, 3 Sawy. C. C. 556.

10. Commonwealth *v.* Trickey, 95 Mass. (13 Allen) 559.

11. State *v.* Bergman, 6 Oreg. 341.

12. Commonwealth *v.* Foster, 122 Mass. 317.

13. McLeod *v.* State, 35 Ala. 395; Jones *v.* Commonwealth, 1 Gall. C. C. 555; Caldwell *v.* Commonwealth, 7 Dana (Ky.), 229; Commonwealth *v.* Harris, 7 Gratt. (Va.) 600; State *v.* Hunter, 33 Iowa, 361; State *v.* Gay, 10 Mo. 440; State *v.* Smith, 1 Nott. & McC. (S. C.) 13; Waltzer *v.* State, 3 Wis. 785; Curd *v.* Commonwealth, 14 B. Mon. (Ky.) 386; Calico *v.* State, 4 Pike (Ark.), 430; Rex *v.* Morris, 2 Leach, 1096; Rex *v.* Manning, 2 Comyn, 619.

Husband and Wife. — Even in the case of husband and wife. Commonwealth *v.* Ray, 1 Va. Cas. 262.

14. Commonwealth *v.* McAtee, 8 Dana (Ky.), 28; United States *v.* Babson, 1 Ware, U. S. D. C. 450; State *v.* Hopkins, 7 Blackf. (Ind) 494; State *v.* Berry, 21 Mo. 504; Godfrey's Case, 11 Coke, 42 a; Reg. *v.* King, 1 Salk. 182. See 2 East,

ment for an additional term, such as will pay costs,[1] the sentence of each should be for such a term as will pay half the costs.

12. *Separate Punishment.* — Punishment for crime does not begin until after the criminal has been convicted and sentenced.[2] When a prisoner is convicted of a second offence, the judgment may direct that each succeeding period of imprisonment shall commence on the termination of the period next preceding,[3] as in case of pardon, or reversal of the sentence on writ of error.[4]

13. *Punishment of Accessories.* — If a statute says nothing of accessories when it makes an act a felony, the punishment extends to an accessory as much as to the principal, unless there is an express provision to the contrary.[5] So far as punishment is concerned, there is no difference between accessories before the fact and aiders and abettors at the fact.[6]

14. *Capital Punishment.* — Following the common law, death is the award of the law for any statute felony, unless the statute specially directs otherwise.[7]

The day for the execution of the sentence need not be inserted in the judgment.[8] It may be in the warrant;[9] but if in the judgment, and the sheriff dies, or the prisoner temporarily escapes, the court may direct the execution of the sentence on a day subsequent to that named in the judgment.[10]

P. C. 740; 1 Bish. Cr. L. (6th ed.) sec. 955.

1. Coleman *v.* State, 55 Ala. 173.

2. People *v.* Wardens, 66 N. Y. 343; State *v.* Frazier, 6 Baxt. (Tenn.) 539.

3. People *v.* Forbes, 22 Cal. 136; *Ex parte* Dalton, 49 Cal. 463; State *v.* Smith, 5 Day (Conn.), 175; Kite *v.* Commonwealth, 52 Mass. (11 Metc.) 581; Cole *v.* State, 10 Ark. (5 Eng.) 318; *Ex parte* Mayers, 4 Mo. 279; Williams *v.* State, 18 Ohio St. 46; *Ex parte* Turner, 45 Mo. 331; Mills *v.* Commonwealth, 13 Pa. St. (1 Harr.) 631; Commonwealth *v.* Leath, 1 Va. Cas. 151; Wilkes *v.* Rex, 4 Brown, Parl. C. 360; Rex *v.* Bath, 1 Leach, 441; Reg. *v.* Cutbush, L. R. 2 Q. B. 379. *Compare* Miller *v.* Allen, 11 Ind. 389.

4. Kite *v.* Commonwealth, 52 Mass. (11 Metc.) 581; *Ex parte* Roberts, 9 Nev. 44; Brown *v.* Commonwealth, 4 Rawle (Pa.), 259; Opin. of Justices, 79 Mass. (13 Gray) 618.

5. Hughes *v.* State, 12 Ala. 458. See 1 Hale, P. C. 613, 632.

6. Thornton *v.* State, 25 Ga. 304. See 3 Bl. Com. 39.

In Tennessee, accessories in murder may be sentenced to imprisonment for life. Nuthill *v.* State, 11 Humph. (Tenn.) 247.

7. State *v.* Scott, 1 Hawk. (N. C.) L. 24. See Adams *v.* Barrett, 5 Ga. 404; United States *v.* Jacoby, 12 Blatchf. C. C. 491; United States *v.* Cross, 1 McAr. (C. C.) 149. See 1 Bish. Cr. L. (6th ed.) sec. 615.

Under the Laws of the United States, the manner of inflicting the death penalty is by hanging. See Rev. Stat. U. S. sec. 5325.

In Texas the death penalty cannot be inflicted on one under seventeen years of age. Ake *v.* State, 6 Tex. App. 398.

In Utah capital punishment is inflicted by shooting, hanging, or beheading, at the option of the criminal. Wilkerson *v.* Utah, 99 U. S. (9 Otto) 130; bk. 25, L. ed. 345.

8. People *v.* Murphy, 45 Cal. 137; Webster *v.* Commonwealth, 59 Mass. (5 Cush.) 386; Rex *v.* Doyle, 1 Leach, 67; Rex *v.* Wyatt, Russ. & R. 230; Atkinson *v.* Rex, 3 Brown, Parl. C. 517; Rex *v.* Hartnett, Jebb, 302.

9. Rex *v.* Doyle, 1 Leach, 67.

10. State *v.* Kitchen, 2 Hill (S. C.), 612; Bland *v.* State, 2 Ind. 608.

CRIMINAL PROCEDURE.

I. Definition. — Criminal procedure may be properly defined as the method pointed out by law for the apprehension, trial, or "prosecution," and fixing the punishment, of those persons who have broken or violated, or are supposed to have broken or violated, the laws prescribed for the regulation of the conduct of the people of the community, and who have thereby laid themselves liable to fine or imprisonment, or both.

II. Modes of originating Process. — There are two modes of originating process, or instituting a prosecution, against a person known or suspected to be guilty of the commission of a criminal act, (1) by a complaint made before a magistrate who is authorized to arrest the person charged with, or suspected of, having committed any crime, for the purpose of examining into the truth of the charge, and inflicting upon him the punishment prescribed by law, if the case be within the jurisdiction of such examining magistrate, and of holding him to bail, or sending him to prison, to answer to a higher tribunal where the offence is not within his cognizance; (2) by a complaint made directly to the grand jury, or to the officer charged with the duty of prosecuting all offences, and the finding of an indictment or the filing of an information, upon either of which process issues, and the arrest and trial of the person accused follow.

1. *Preliminary Examination.* — *a. Arrest.* — When an arrest[1] has been made, the accused should be taken before a magistrate or magistrates[2] with all reasonable speed. But when arrested on sus-

1. As to warrant, see that title, 1 Am. & Eng. Encyc. of L. 730.

An Omission of a Magistrate to secure an order from the prosecuting attorney before issuing process in criminal cases, as provided by How. Stat. § 7135 a, does not deprive him of jurisdiction: the appearance of the prosecuting attorney and his prosecution of the case are sufficient approval. People *v.* Griswold (Mich.), 7 West. Rep. 899.

2. The magistrates here referred to are those officers of the law who answer to those who in England are known as justices of the peace. Washb. Man. Cr. L. 104. This office was created as early as the statute of I. Edw. III. c. 16. See Com. Dig. tit. "Justice of the Peace;" Beache, Man. of a Just. of Peace; Burn, Just.; 15 Viner, Abr. 3; Bacon, Abr. tit. "Justice;" 2 Phill. Ev. 239.

In the American States. — In most, if not

picion, he should be detained before he is so taken before the magistrate, in order that evidence against him may first be collected.[1]

b. Examination. — The magistrate is bound to forthwith examine into the circumstances of the charge.[2] In order to secure the attendance of witnesses to the fact, they may be served with a summons or warrant, in a manner similar to that in which the presence of the accused is secured. If a witness refuses to be examined, he is liable to imprisonment. The room in which the examination is held is not to be deemed an open court, and the magistrate may exclude any person if he thinks fit.[3] When the witnesses are in attendance, the magistrates takes,[4] in the presence of the accused (who is at liberty by himself or his counsel to put questions to any witness produced against him), the statement on oath or affirmation of those who know the facts of the case, and puts the same in writing.[5]

all, of the States of the American Union, a justice of the peace is a public officer, invested with judicial powers, for the purpose of preventing and punishing misdemeanors, and breaches of the peace, and violations of the law. In many of the States they possess civil as well as criminal jurisdiction. See 2 Bouv. L. Dict. (15th ed.) 31.

The Massachusetts. — But under the colony of Massachusetts the office of justice of the peace was not known for many years. However, under the Providence Charter, and ever since, it has been a well-defined and important office in the preservation of peace and public order, as well as the punishment of petty offences, notwithstanding the fact that other officers have been clothed with similar powers, to whom the principal part of the jurisdiction in criminal matters has been transferred. See 6 Dane, Abr. 412; Mass. Gen. Stat. c. 120, §§ 32, 36; id. c. 116, § 12; id. c. 169, § 1; and also Acts of 1869, c. 415.

1. **For Forms and Modes of Procedure,** reference may be made to those in use in Massachusetts, which correspond in most respects to the requirements of the common law. See Commonwealth *v.* Leach, 1 Mass. 59; Commonwealth *v.* Foster, 1 Mass. 488.

2. **Preliminary Examination.** — Where respondent charged with a criminal offence had never had a preliminary examination, or waived the same, and the witness claimed to have been examined did not sign his evidence given on such examination in the police court, as required by the positive terms of the statute, it was error to overrule his motion to quash the information, and compel him to plead and go to trial thereon. People *v.* Smith, 25 Mich. 497; People *v.* Chapman, 28 N. W. Rep. 900; People *v.* Gleason (Mich.), 6 West. Rep. 393; People *v.* Brock (Mich.), 7 West. Rep. 885.

When the examination, before a magistrate, of one arrested for crime, is in other respects legal, and in conformity with the other express terms of the statute, a deposition taken and filed without being read by or to the witnesses before signing, cannot affect the status of the defendant in the trial court, to which he is bound over at such examination. He has an undoubted right to require at the examination that the testimony shall be so read before it is signed; but if he makes no objection then, he cannot be heard afterward to complain of it. People *v.* Gleason (Mich.), 6 West. Rep. 393.

3. **In England** this is regulated by statute. See 11 & 12 Vict. c. 42, § 19. And the same is true in most of the States of the Union.

4. The omission of the district attorney and magistrate, on preliminary examination, to ask a witness for the prosecution his profession or business, is not prejudicial to the defendant. People *v.* Rodrigo, 69 Cal. 601.

5. **Reducing Evidence to Writing.** — The statutes of the States are not uniform in their requirements regarding the reducing of the evidence of the witnesses on the preliminary hearing to writing. The statute of Massachusetts, following the common law closely, so requires, and so also does the statute of Illinois. See Rev. Stat. 1874, p. 401, § 348. On the other hand, the statutes of Michigan — see Laws, 1871, § 7844 — and New York — see Rev. Stat. pt. 4, c. 2, tit 2, § 2 — do not require the evidence of the witnesses to be taken down in writing, and signed by the witnesses deposing. See People *v.* Lynch, 29 Mich. 278.

Signing Depositions. — Where depositions of witnesses, on an examination before a magistrate of one charged with robbery, were taken and filed without being read by or to the witnesses before signing, and the examination in all other respects was regular, under How. Stat. § 9469, *held*, the action of the court was proper in refus-

The magistrate then asks the accused whether he desires to call any witnesses. If he does, the magistrate, in the presence of the accused, takes their statement, on oath or affirmation, whether such statement is given on examination, for they may be submitted to both. These statements, in the same way as those of the prosecution, are read to, and signed by, the witnesses and by the magistrate. And the same rules apply to witnesses, both for the prosecution and for the defence (other than those merely to character), as to being bound over by recognizance to appear and give evidence at the trial. If a witness refuses to enter into such recognizance, he may be committed to prison until the trial. The recognizances, depositions, etc., are transmitted to the court in which the trial is to take place.

(1) *Adjournment of Examination.* — If the investigation before the magistrate cannot be completed at a single hearing, he may from time to time remand the accused to jail for any period not exceeding eight days; or may allow him his liberty in the interval upon his entering into recognizances, with or without sureties, for re-appearance.[1]

After the defendant has been examined for the offence, there is nothing in the statutes to prevent filing an information as soon as it is found convenient.[2]

c. Commitment and Discharge. — (1) *Discharge.* — If, when all the evidence against the accused has been heard, the magistrate does not think that it is sufficient to put the accused on his trial for an indictable offence, he is forthwith discharged. But if he thinks otherwise, or the evidence raises a strong or probable presumption against the accused, he commits him for trial, either at once sending him to jail so as to be forthcoming for trial, or admitting him to bail. Under certain circumstances a third course is open to the magistrate: he may dispose of the case and punish the offender himself.

(2) *Commitment for Trial.* — It will be noticed that there are two forms of commitment to prison:[3] *(a) For safe keeping; (b) In execution* either as an original punishment, or as a means of

ing to allow defendant to withdraw a plea of not guilty, and to discharge the defendant for the reason of non-reading of the depositions, it appearing that defendant did not at the examination object to the omission. People *v.* Gleason (Mich.), 6 West. Rep. 393.

1. After the person charged with the commission of an offence has been arrested and brought before a magistrate, for examination or trial, the magistrate is allowed a reasonable time for this purpose before making his final decision. In most of the States this matter is regulated by statute. Thus, in Illinois — Rev. Stat. 1874, 402, § 356 — and in Massachusetts, — Gen. Stat. Mass. c. 170, § 17, — the magistrate may adjourn an examination for a period not exceeding ten days, and in the mean time require the accused to give recognizance for his appearance, if the offence is a bailable one, and, if not, to commit him to prison. In Iowa, — Code 1873, § 4230, — no examination can be adjourned for a longer period than thirty days. Under the Michigan statute, — See Laws, 1871, § 7852, — an adjournment may be made from time to time. See Hamilton *v.* People, 29 Mich. 176; Pardee *v.* Smith, 27 Mich. 43.

2. People *v.* Mason (Mich.), 6 West. Rep. 183.

3. For form of warrant of commitment under N. Y. Rev. Stat. § 31, Code Crim. Proc. 721, 725, see People *v.* Holmes, 41 Hun (N. Y.), 55.

enforcing payment of a pecuniary fine, or of enforcing obedience to the sentence or order of a magistrate under the hand and seal of the officer committing, directed to the jailer, containing a concise statement of the cause of commitment.[1]

(3.) *Imprisonment pending Trial.* — The imprisonment pending trial is merely for safe custody, and not for punishment: therefore, those imprisoned are treated with much less rigor than those who have been convicted.[2]

(4.) *Bail.*[3] — Admitting to bail consists in the delivery (or bailment) of a person to his sureties, on their giving security (he also entering into his own recognizance) for his appearance at the time and place of trial, there to surrender and take his trial. In the mean time, he is allowed to be at large, being supposed to remain in their friendly custody. The bailability of offences is regulated by statute.[4]

Under acts of Congress, bail must be taken upon all arrests in criminal cases, where the offence is not punishable by death; and in capital cases, the person charged may be admitted by the Supreme Court, the circuit court, a justice of the Supreme Court, a circuit judge, or a judge of a district court.[5]

III. Indictment. — An indictment is a plain, brief narrative of an offence committed by any person, and the necessary circumstances that concur to ascertain its fact and nature.[6]

1. **The Statutory Requirements** in the recitals of a commitment to the house of correction, on conviction of several offences at the same time, as to fines and costs, must be strictly followed; and where the offence is not defined in the commitment, in the language of the statute, the defendant will be discharged on *habeas corpus*. *Re* McLaughlin, 58 Vt. 136; s. c., 2 New Eng. Rep. 481.

A Commitment indorsed upon the depositions, and signed by the justice in the following form, viz., "It appearing to me that the offence in the written depositions mentioned has been committed, and that there is sufficient cause to believe the within named (giving name) guilty thereof, I order that he be held to answer to the same," etc., is in the language of sect. 872 of the Penal Code, and sufficient. People *v.* McCurdy, 68 Cal. 576.

Mere Irregularities or informalities before the committing magistrate, which do not deprive the defendant of any substantial right, will not warrant the quashing of an information. People *v.* Rodrigo, 69 Cal. 601.

A Magistrate's Certificate that the complainant in a criminal prosecution was made on affirmation, implies that it was in the form prescribed, and that the witness had conscientious scruples against taking an oath. State *v.* Adams, 78 Maine, 486; s. c., 3 New Eng. Rep. 243.

2. Thus, they may have sent to them food, clothing, etc., subject to examination, and the rules made by the visiting magistrates. In some places they have the option of employment, but are not compelled to perform any hard labor; and if they choose to be employed, and are acquitted, or no bill is found against them, an allowance is paid for the work. See Harris's Cr. L. (Force's ed.), c. iv. p. 253.

3. For a general discussion of the question of bail, see that title, 2 Am. & Eng. Encyc. of L. 1.

4. When an officer has the custody of a prisoner charged with a bailable offence, it is his duty to keep him until he has given a good and sufficient bond for his appearance; and if he accepts a bond which the sureties sign on the express agreement and condition that the officer himself shall also sign it as a surety, but fails to do so, he is guilty of reprehensible conduct. King *v.* State, 81 Ala. 92.

5. United States Rev. Stat. 189.

6. Richardson *v.* State (Md.), 5 Cent. Rep. 765; Hale, P. C. 168.

Harris says that an indictment is a written accusation of one or more persons of a crime preferred to, and presented on oath by, a grand jury. It lies for all treasons and felonies, for misprisions of either, and for all misdemeanors of a public nature at common law. See 2 Hawk. c. 25, § 4.

If a statute prohibits a matter of a public

1. *What Crimes prosecuted by Indictment.* — Any crime punishable by death or imprisonment in the penitentiary can be prosecuted by indictment only.[1] And the legislature cannot authorize the institution of a criminal prosecution in any other mode.[2] But an indictment does not lie upon a statute which creates a new offence and prescribes a particular remedy.[3]

Under the statutes in some States a prosecution for offences not capital are authorized to be by indictment, or information, in the discretion of the district attorney.[4]

grievance, or commands a matter of public convenience (such as the repairing of highways, or the like), all acts or omissions contrary to the prohibition or command of the statute, being misdemeanors at common law, are punishable by indictment if the statute specifies no other mode of proceeding. If the statute specifies a mode of proceeding different from that by indictment, then, if the matter was already an indictable offence at common law, and the statute introduces merely a different mode of prosecution and punishment, the remedy is cumulative, and the prosecutor has still the option of proceeding by indictment at common law, or by the mode pointed out by the statute. Rex *v.* Robinson, 2 Burr. 799. See Harris, Cr. L. (Force's Ed.) 261.

1. **Any Crime Punishable by Imprisonment in the Penitentiary** for more than one year is infamous within the meaning of the Fifth Amendment, and the prosecution must be by indictment. Parkinson *v.* United States, 121 U. S. 281; bk. 30, L. ed. 959.

Form of Prosecution. — The declaration of the Fifth Amendment, that "no person shall be held to answer for a capital or otherwise infamous crime, unless on a presentment or indictment of a grand jury," is jurisdictional; and no court of the United States has authority to try a prisoner without indictment or presentment in such cases. *Ex parte* Bain, 121 U. S. 1; bk. 30, L. ed. 849.

In Military Court. — By the 66th and 97th Articles of War, courts martial have jurisdiction to punish larceny when committed by persons in the military service to the prejudice of good order and military discipline; and it was not intended that proceedings should be in technical forms of criminal proceedings founded on indictments. *Re* Esmond (D.C.), 3 Cent. Rep. 520.

2. State *v.* Kelm, 79 Mo. 515; State *v.* Briscoe, 80 Mo. 643; State *v.* Russell, 88 Mo. 648; s. c., 5 West. Rep. 368.

3. Rex *v.* Wright, 1 Burr. 543.

Asportation of Goods. — Every asportation constitutes a new offence. Thus, when goods are stolen in one county, and are taken by the thief into another county, he may be indicted and tried in such county. Such indictments are upheld, on the distinct ground that each asportation of stolen property from one county to another is a new or fresh theft. State *v.* Smith, 66 Mo. 61; State *v.* McGraw, 87 Mo. 161; s. c., 2 West. Rep. 448.

4. State *v.* Cole, 38 La. An. 843.

An Information cannot be prosecuted where defendant was arrested but was not indicted. State *v.* Boswell, 140 Ind. 541; s. c., 2 West. Rep. 726. Cited in Shular *v.* State, 105 Ind. 289; s. c., 2 West. Rep. 805.

Provisions in Illinois. — Under the Illinois statute, all offences cognizable in the county court must be prosecuted by information of the State's attorney, the attorney-general, or some other person; and when presented by such other person, the county judge shall indorse thereon that there is probable cause for filing the same. Where the information was presented by the State's attorney, and an affidavit accompanies the same, such affidavit does not make it the information of the affiant. Gallagher *v.* People, 120 Ill. 179; s. c., 8 West. Rep. 687. Ill. Rev. Stat. 343, § 182.

Under the Indiana Practice the only instance in which a person may be tried on a criminal charge in a criminal or circuit court, upon an affidavit alone, is upon an appeal from a justice of the peace under Rev. Stat. 1881, § 1643. When complaint is made, and the person charged is taken before a justice of the peace. Rev. Stat. 1881, § 1836, requires that "such justice or jury, if they find the prisoner guilty of a misdemeanor, shall assess his punishment; or, if in their opinion the punishment they are authorized to assess is not adequate to the offence, they may so find; and in such case the justice shall hold such prisoner to bail for his appearance before the proper court, or commit him to jail in default of such bail." When a justice of the peace reaches the conclusion that he is not authorized to inflict adequate punishment, and accepts a recognizance from the prisoner for his appearance before the proper court, the affidavit filed with him as a complaint has performed its office, and has no longer any force or effect as a pleading in the cause. While it is proper for him to file a transcript of his proceed-

It has been held that a State is not forbidden by the United States Constitution from prosecuting felonies by information;[1] but prosecution by information is in derogation of the common law, and a departure from the general policy of law. Statutes providing therefor, being in opposition to a long-settled policy, must be strictly construed.[2]

2. *What should contain.* — An indictment, like every other document, should contain time, place, person, and circumstance, and must in all cases be sufficiently explicit to inform the person accused of the offence charged against him; but it is not necessary that an indictment should state that it was presented by the grand jury, in the name and by the authority of the State.[3] The essential parts of every indictment are the caption, the commencement, the statement, and the conclusion.

a. Caption. — Where the caption of the indictment sets forth the State, parish and district, and contains an averment that the crime was committed in the State, parish and district aforesaid, it is sufficient.[4] Where the county is omitted in the caption

ings, together with the original papers in the cause, with the clerk, he is not required to do so; and his failure does not affect the proceedings which may thereafter be taken against the prisoner in the criminal or circuit court, which have no dependence upon those had before the justice, who has discharged his duty when he files the recognizance with the clerk of the court in which the prisoner is required to appear. Under the recognizance, the prisoner charged is simply required to appear in the court named in his recognizance, to answer such charge as may be preferred against him, whether by indictment or affidavit and information, as an original proceeding in that court; and a further trial on the complaint filed with the justice is erroneous, and a motion in arrest of judgment for such error should be sustained. The fact that the recognizance was entered into at the request of the party charged before the justice, and by agreement of the parties, is immaterial. State *v.* Butler (Ind.), 11 West. Rep. 836; Hoover *v.* State, 110 Ind. 350; s. c., 9 West. Rep. 86; Lindsey *v.* State, 72 Ind. 40.

Affidavit as Basis of Criminal Proceeding. — It was said, in the case of Byrne *v.* State, 47 Ind. 120, that an information is a well-recognized pleading in criminal prosecution in courts of superior jurisdiction, but that an affidavit is not.

In Texas. — An affidavit is an indispensable prerequisite to the sufficiency of an information to charge a misdemeanor, and must appear as a part of the record on appeal. Wadgymar *v.* State, 21 Tex. App. 495.

1. State *v.* Boswell, 104 Ind. 541; s. c., 2 West. Rep. 726. Cited in Shular *v.* State, 105 Ind. 289; s. c., 2 West. Rep. 801, 805.

2. State *v.* Boswell, 104 Ind. 541; s. c., 2 West. Rep. 728; Brady's Case, 3 Cr. L. Mag. 77.

Mr. Wharton, in speaking of this subject in a note appended to Brady's Case, *supra*, says, "The ordeal of a grand jury is a proper one in all cases of serious crime. It is a terrible thing for a man to be put on trial for an offence involving ignominy and contingent heavy punishment. The expense is heavy; the mere fact of being put on trial is a great discredit; there is always a risk of an unjust conviction. Under these circumstances, the protection afforded by a grand jury is just, as well as politic."

3. Holt *v.* State, 47 Ark. 196.

4. **Sale of Liquors without License.** — State *v.* Crittenden, 38 La. An. 448.

In an indictment for being interested in the sale of liquor without license, it is not necessary that the offence be stated in the caption. It is sufficient to charge it in the body of the indictment. Williams *v.* State, 47 Ark. 230.

In Indiana the Criminal Code makes the caption and upper marginal title for many purposes a preliminary part of the indictment; and when the name of the State there appears, it sufficiently indicates that the county is within the State. Anderson *v.* State, 104 Ind. 467; s. c., 2 West. Rep. 341.

Dakota Doctrine. — A caption, "In the District Court . . . having and exercising the same jurisdiction in all such cases as is vested in the circuit and district courts of of an indictment, it may be amended, and the defect is not fatal.[1]

b. Venue. — The venue must be properly laid; that is, the county or other division of the country from which the grand jury by whom the indictment was found came, must be set out. This is an index to the place where, in regular course, the trial is to be had.[2]

(1) *Where laid.* — The nature of the crime in some cases requires the place to be stated; otherwise, the venue in the margin, that is, the county or other division, is taken as the venue for all facts in the indictment.[3]

It is a general rule that a crime is to be tried in the place in which the criminal act is committed. It is not sufficient that part of such acts shall have been done in such place: it is the completed act alone which gives jurisdiction.[4]

Where the names of the State and county are stated in the caption of the indictment, and the county only is stated in the body of the indictment, the venue is sufficiently laid.[5]

Where a crime is composed of several elements, and a material one exists in either one of two counties, the courts of either county may[6] rightfully take jurisdiction of the entire crime.[7]

If a material act, part of the crime, as an assault and battery, is performed in one county, and death results in another county, the place of the crime, according to the weight of authority, was held by the common law to be the county where the first material act

the United States," *held* sufficient. United States *v.* Spaulding, 3 Dak. 85.

Texas Practice. — Transcript showing, in the caption of the case, that the judge who tried the case presided by exchange with the regular judge of the district, sufficiently shows the lawful authority of the judge who presided. Wyers *v.* State, 21 Tex. App. 448.

1. State *v.* Moore, 24 S. C. 150.

2. See Harris' Cr. L. (Force's ed.) 262; State *v.* Quaite, 20 Mo. App. 485; s. c., 3 West. Rep. 275; State *v.* Dawson, 90 Mo. 149; s. c., 6 West. Rep. 461.

Venue as laid in the indictment must be shown in the record. Wells *v.* State (Tex.), October, 1886.

But the defendant cannot deny the jurisdiction of a court to which he has caused the case to be removed. McBain *v.* Enloe, 13 Ill. 76; Logston *v.* State, 3 Heisk. (Penn.) 414; Hitt *v.* Allen, 13 Ill. 592; People *v.* Zane, 105 Ill. 667; Goodhue *v.* People, 94 Ill. 37.

3. The following are the most common cases in which a local description is required: (1) burglary, (2) housebreaking, (3) stealing in a dwelling-house, (4) sacrilege, (5) nuisances to highways, etc. Harris' Cr. L. 339.

False Pretence. — In a prosecution for obtaining money or property by false pretences, the place where goods or money is obtained, without regard to where the representations were made, is the place where the party should be prosecuted. Hoge *v.* People, 117 Ill. 35; s. c., 4 West. Rep. 197; State *v.* Wycoff, 31 N. J. L. (2 Vr.) 68.

4. State *v.* Shaeffer, 80 Mo. 271; s. c., 5 West. Rep. 465, 468. See also State *v.* Dennis, 80 Mo. 594; Norris *v.* State, 25 Ohio St. 217; People *v.* Sully, 5 Park. Cr. R. (N. Y.) 142; State *v.* Wycoff, 31 N. J. L. (2 Vr.) 68.

5. State *v.* Dawson, 90 Mo. 149; s. c., 6 West. Rep. 461.

An Information good upon its face, and regularly filed by the district attorney after an examination and commitment by a magistrate, cannot be set aside on the ground that the offence was not committed in the county alleged in the information. Such an objection may be taken advantage of under a plea of not guilty, and is then a question for the jury to determine. People *v.* Moore, 68 Cal. 500.

6. Under Section 1580, Ind. Rev. Stat. 1881.

7. Archer *v.* State, 106 Ind. 426; s. c., 4 West. Rep. 726, 728.

was committed. There is a conflict of authorities as to whether the jurisdiction is in the courts of the place where death occurred, or where the fatal blow was given; and, in order to remove doubt, the body was sometimes taken to the county where the blow was struck.[1]

Thus, where deceased was shot in A County, kept there for a few days, and then taken just across the river into another county, to be more convenient to his attending physician, and died there, proof that death occurred in A County is not necessary;[2] or, if A hires a horse in Alabama and sells it in Tennessee, a conviction is properly had in Tennessee for fraudulent appropriation;[3] or, where goods embezzled were received in a certain county, the venue could be properly laid there under a statute authorizing prosecution in any county in which defendant may have taken or received the property, or through or into which he may have undertaken to transport it.[4] A statute is valid declaring that one committing burglary and larceny in one county may be indicted, tried, and convicted, in the county to which he has carried the stolen property.[5] And a statute allowing a prosecution for larceny in any county, where the thief may be found with the property stolen in another State, was not abrogated by the Constitution.[6] But a person cannot be indicted and tried for burglary in the county into which he brings the stolen property.[7] And it is held that theft, and theft from the person, are distinct offences; the latter can occur only at one place, the former is committed in any county into which the thief takes the property.[8]

1. Archer v. State, 106 Ind. 426; s. c., 4 West. Rep. 726, 727.

Blow struck in one County, Death in another.—There is some conflict in the old common-law authorities as to whether the jurisdiction is in the courts of the place where death occurred, or in those of the place where the fatal blow was given; and in order to remove all doubt, the body was sometimes taken to the county where the blow was struck. Riley v. State, 9 Humph. (Tenn.) 657; People v. Gill, 6 Cal. 637; State v. Gessert, 21 Minn. 369; Commonwealth v. Macloon, 101 Mass. 1; Commonwealth v. Parker, 19 Mass. (2 Pick.) 550; Tyler v. People, 8 Mich. 320; Green v. State, 66 Ala. 40; s. c., 41 Am. Rep. 744; Steerman v. State, 10 Mo. 503; Hunter v. State, 40 N. J. L. (12 Vr.) 495. If, however, the crime was committed in part in one county and consummated in another, jurisdiction, at common law, would seem to be in the county where the first material step in the crime was taken. Archer v. State, 106 Ind. 426; s. c., 4 West. Rep. 726.

However, it was recently held that there is no real conflict of opinion as to the power of the Legislature to provide for the punishment of a crime, committed partly in one jurisdiction and partly in another, in either jurisdiction; but there is a sharp conflict as to whether death can be said to be a part of the crime of murder, many of the authorities maintaining that death is merely by the consequence of the crime, many of the authorities, on the other hand, maintaining, with much reason, that death is a part of the crime, for, unless it results within a year and a day, the offence cannot be murder. Archer v. State, 106 Ind. 426; s. c., 4 West. Rep. 726, 728. Dynamiting and Extra-territorial Crime, 16 Crim. Law Mag. 155.

2. Binfield v. State, 15 Neb. 484.

3. Lovelace v. State, 12 Lea (Tenn.) 721.

4. Cole v. State, 16 Tex. App. 461; Reed v. State, 16 Tex. App. 586.

5. Mack v. People, 82 N. Y. 235.

6. State v. Johnson, 38 Ark, 568.

And an accused may be tried for wilfully driving stock, under the provisions of Article 749 of the Texas Penal Code, in any county into or through which the stock is driven. McElmurray v. State, 21 Tex. App. 691.

7. State v. McGraw, 87 Mo. 161; s. c., 2 West. Rep. 448.

8. Gage v. State (Tex. App.), Oct. 1886.

(2) *Proof of.* — Proof of the venue is indispensable to a conviction.[1] Venue is an issue which must be affirmatively proved;[2] and a failure to prove that the offence was committed in the county where the indictment was found, is a fatal defect.[3]

Where the record fails to show that the offence charged was committed in the county where the venue is laid, judgment must be reversed.[4] To support a conviction, it is as important to prove that the offence was committed in the county where it is charged to have been committed, as to prove that the defendant committed it.[5] The court will not take judicial notice of the location of a town;[6] and proof that the offence was committed in a certain town, in the absence of evidence tending to show that such town was in the county laid in the venue, is not proof of the venue.[7]

The venue must be proved as alleged.[8] A judgment will be reversed where the bill of exceptions fails to show that the venue, as laid in the indictment, was directly or indirectly proved.[9] The venue may be established by circumstantial evidence;[10] but it must be proved absolutely: it cannot be inferred from the evidence,[11] for inference alone cannot establish the venue of an

1. West *v.* State (Tex. App.), June, 1886.

2. Ryan *v.* State, 22 Tex. App. 699.

3. State *v.* Kindrick, 21 Mo. App. 507; s. c., 3 West. Rep. 928; State *v.* Hogan, 31 Mo. 340; Wheat *v.* State, 6 Mo. 455; State *v.* Wacker, 16 Mo. App. 417, 421.

Where the Venue laid was not directly proved, and there was no evidence from which to infer that the offence was committed in the county, judgment against defendant must be reversed. State *v.* Apperger, 80 Mo. 174; State *v.* Wheeler, 79 Mo. 366; State *v.* Hartnett, 75 Mo. 251; State *v.* Burgess, 75 Mo. 541; State *v.* McGrath, 73 Mo. 186; State *v.* Hughes, 71 Mo. 634; State *v.* McGinniss, 74 Mo. 245; s. c., 2 West. Rep. 140; State *v.* McKay, 19 Mo. App. 149; s. c., 2 West. Rep. 543; State *v.* Buckner, 20 Mo. App. 420; s. c., 2 West. Rep. 544; State *v.* Hopper, 21 Mo. App. 510; s. c., 4 W. Rep. 276; State *v.* Roach, (Mo.) 4 West. Rep. 340.

A Conviction will be reversed where the record does not contain proof of the venue of the offence. State *v.* Buckner, 20 Mo. App. 420; s. c., 2 West. Rep. 544.

4. State *v.* Roach, (Mo.), 4 West. Rep. 340.

The Record on Appeal must show that the offence charged was committed in the county where the venue was laid. State *v.* Roach (Mo.), 4 West. Rep. 340; Williams *v.* State, 21 Tex. App. 256; West *v.* State, 21 Tex. App. 427; Wells *v.* State, and Perry *v.* State, 22 Tex. App. 182; State *v.* Hopper, 21 Mo. App. 510; s. c, 4 West. Rep. 276.

Where the record brought to the supreme court on writ of error in a criminal case purports to contain all the evidence given on the trial, it must appear affirmatively from the evidence that the homicide charged was committed in the county alleged in the indictment, otherwise a judgment of conviction will be reversed. Dougherty *v.* People, 118 Ill. 160; s. c., 6 West. Rep. 96.

5. State *v.* Hughes, 71 Mo. 633; State *v.* McGinniss, 74 Mo. 245; State *v.* Hartnett, 75 Mo. 251; State *v.* Burgess, 75 Mo. 541; State *v.* Babb, 76 Mo. 503; State *v.* Hooper, 21 Mo. App. 510; s. c., 4 West. Rep. 276.

6. State *v.* Quaite, 20 Mo. App. 405; s. c., 3 West. Rep. 275.

7. State *v.* Quaite, 20 Mo. App. 405; s. c., 3 West. Rep. 275.

8. Crawford *v.* State (Tex. App.), 5 S. W. Rep. 130.

9. State *v.* Quaite, 20 Mo. App. 405; s. c, 3 West. Rep. 275.

10. **Proof of Venue.** — Although there is no direct evidence that the crime was committed in the county, yet where there is sufficient circumstantial evidence to enable the jury to arrive at the same result the conviction will be sustained. State *v.* Burns, 48 Mo. 438; State *v.* West, 69 Mo. 404; State *v.* McGinniss, 76 Mo. 326.

11. Ryan *v.* State (Tex. App.), Jan. 1887; State *v.* Hopper, 21 Mo. App. 510; s. c., 4 West. Rep. 276; Hughs *v.* State, 71 Mo. 633; State *v.* McGinniss, 74 Mo. 245; State *v.* Hartnett, 75 Mo. 251; State *v.* Burgess, 75 Mo. 541; State *v.* Babb, 76 Mo. 503.

Proof of the venue, by direct or indirect

offence: it must be established by the evidence.[1] But the testimony of the prosecutor is sufficient to establish the venue.[2]

Where, by the statute,[3] the jurisdiction of a crime lies in either of two counties, the court which first obtains jurisdiction of the person of the accused retains it to the end, to the exclusion of the court of the other county, even though he may have been indicted first in such other county.[4] But a provision that, when an offence shall[5] be committed within five hundred yards of the boundary of two counties, it may be examined, and a trial thereof had in either county, is unconstitutional as far as it provides for the examination or trial of an offense in a county other than that in which it is alleged in the indictment to have been committed.[6]

c. Description of Offence. — The facts, circumstances, and intent, which are the ingredients of the offence, must be given with certainty, so that the defendant may be able to perceive what charge he has to meet, the court may know what sentence should be given, and that on future reference to the conviction or acquittal, it may be known exactly what was the alleged offence.[7]

evidence, is essential to a conviction of an offence under the statute. State *v.* Hopper, 21 Mo. App. 510; s. c., 4 West. Rep. 276.

1. Sedberry *v.* State, 14 Tex. App. 233.

2. Pike *v.* State, 8 Lea (Tenn.), 577.

3. As by Iowa Code, § 4159.

4. *Ex parte* Baldwin, 69 Iowa, 502.

5. As by the provision of sec. 1697, Mo. Rev. Stat.

6. *Re* McDonald, 19 Mo. App. 370; s. c., 1 West. Rep. 691.

7. **Technical Words, when to be used.** — In indictments for certain crimes, particular technical words must be used, namely, in murder, *murdravit;* in rape, *rapuit;* in larceny, *felonicè cepit et asportavit.* Again, as to the intent, treason must be laid to have been done "traitorously;" a felony, "feloniously;" burglary, "feloniously and burglariously;" murder, "feloniously and of his malice aforethought." Harris, Cr. L. 339.

When indictments were drawn in Latin, it was fatal error to write "collis" for "colli," or "murderavit" instead of "murdravit." Harris, Cr. L. (Force's Ed.) 266. And an indictment was fatally defective at common law which averred the offence was committed "on the third day of August, eighteen hundred and forty-three," instead of "the year eighteen hundred and forty-three." State *v.* Lane, 4 Ired. (N. C.) L. 113. And it has been held that an allegation in an indictment is not sufficient if the words "the year" were added, unless other words were also added, showing that it was a year in the Christian era. Com. *v.* Loon, 1 Mass. (5 Gray) 91. An indictment which alleges that "the defendant stole the goods of the aforesaid A. B.," no A. B. having been previously named therein, is equally fatally defective. See 1 Stark, Cr. Pl. 182; 2 Hawk. P. C. c. 25, § 72.

Middle Name. — An averment, in an indictment for bigamy, that defendant was lawfully married to Mary I. Bennett, is proved by showing a marriage to Mary Bennett, as the letter "I" was no part of the name of the person mentioned in the indictment. Tucker *v.* People (Ill.), 11 West. Rep. 765.

However, it seems that while it is not necessary, in giving the name of the person on whose premises a burglary was committed, to insert a middle letter which may form part of his name; but when it is inserted, it becomes an important part of the name, and must be proved as laid. Davis *v.* People, 19 Ill. 77; State *v.* Homer, 40 Me. 438; Commonwealth *v.* Perkins, 18 Mass. (1 Pick.) 389; Commonwealth *v.* Hall, 20 Mass. (3 Pick.) 262; State *v.* Hughes, 1 Swan (Tenn.) 261; Rex *v.* Deeley, 4 Car. & P. 579.

Misspelled Words. — Where an indictment charged that a wound was inflicted on the "brest," it was held defective; anonymous, 2 Hayw. (N. C.) 140; also where the indictment concluded "against the peace of the State," instead of "against the peace and dignity of the State." Cain *v.* State, 4 Blackf. (Ind.) 512; also where it concluded "against the peace and dignity of W. Virginia" instead of "against the State of West Virginia." Lemons *v.* State, 4 W. Va. 755.

And it was recently held in Texas that an indictment omitting the words "on their oaths present," or their equivalent, is insufficient to show an accusation of the

An indictment under the statute must contain all the substantial requirements of an indictment at common law.[1]

Where there are any formal defects in the indictment objection thereto must be taken before the jury is sworn; and such defects may then be amended by the court.[2]

When an indictment contains two counts charging the same crime, one ending with and the other without the words, "contrary to the form, force, etc., and against the peace" and dignity of the State, the defective count can be amended by adding those words, although the Constitution provides that indictments shall conclude with the words, "against the peace and dignity of the State;" as it is a matter of form, and not of substance.[3]

defendant by the grand jury. Vanvickle *v.* State, 22 Tex. App. 625.

1. State *v.* Miles, 4 Ind. 577; Mount *v.* State, 7 Ind. 654; Surber *v.* State, 99 Ind. 71; Doles *v.* State, 97 Ind. 555; Wood *v.* State, 92 Ind. 269; Hays *v.* State, 77 Ind. 450; Bryant *v.* State, 72 Ind. 400; Howard *v.* State, 67 Ind. 401; Adams *v.* State, 65 Ind. 565; Shepherd *v.* State, 64 Ind. 43; Agee *v.* State, 64 Ind. 340; Greenley *v.* State, 60 Ind. 141; Jones *v.* State, 60 Ind. 241; Bruner *v.* State, 58 Ind. 159; Jarell *v.* State, 58 Ind. 293; Veatch *v.* State, 56 Ind. 584; Shepherd *v.* State, 54 Ind. 25; State *v.* Blan, 69 Mo. 317; Lester *v.* State, 9 Mo. 658.

Information. — It is not necessary that an information charging the defendant with receiving stolen property of the value of twenty-five dollars should contain any allegation that this was other than a first conviction for a like offence; that the act of stealing the property received by defendant was not a simple larceny; that defendant made no restitution; nor, where the conviction is upon a plea of guilty, is any inquiry, finding, or determination by the court or jury, of record or otherwise, showing any of these matters, necessary; nor need such matter appear in the judgment following upon the plea of guilty. People *v.* Caulkins (Mich.), 11 West. Rep. 560.

Violating Local Option Law: Indictment. — Chapter 462 of Maryland, Act of 1878 (a local option law for certain districts in Dorchester County), though local, is a public and not a private law, and any question affecting the legal existence of such a law belongs to the court. Hence it is not necessary for an indictment charging a violation thereof to contain a statement of all the formalities necessary to precede the law's becoming operative.

Where said local option law of 1878 had been adopted by an election district, and thereafter by chapter 456 of Act of 1880, a portion of said district was cut off and formed into another district without changing the name of the old district, *held*, that this did not change the operation of the local option law in the old district as it was left. Jones *v.* State (Md.), 8 Cent. Rep. 897.

It was not necessary, therefore, for the indictment to contain a statement of all the formalities necessary to precede the law's becoming operative. They were not facts for the jury to pass upon, and had no proper place in the indictment. Slymer's Case, 62 Md. 238; Mackin's Case, 62 Md. 244; Jones *v.* State (Md.), 8 Cent. Rep. 898.

The passage of the Acts of 1880, taking a part of District No. 7 from it, and with it and portions of other districts forming a new district, could not possibly change the law operating on District No. 7 as it was left. It was still District No. 7, if it was not as large. Higgins *v.* State, 64 Md. 419; s. c., 1 Cent. Rep. 703; Jones *v.* State (Md.), 8 Cent. Rep. 898.

2. **The Law as to the Amendment of Defects in the Indictment** is now on a much more reasonable footing than it was at one time. Instead of requiring the evidence rigorously and servilely to correspond with the indictment as it stands when drawn up, extensive powers of amendment are given to the court. Whenever there is a variance in certain points between the indictment and the evidence, it is lawful for the court before which the trial is had, if it considers that the variance is not material to the merits of the case, and that the defendant cannot be prejudiced thereby in his defence on such merits, to order the indictment to be amended on such terms as to postponing the trial, as the court thinks reasonable. Harris' Cr. L. 340.

3. State *v.* Amadon, 58 Vt. 524; s. c. 1 New Eng. Rep. 355.

Amendment of Indictment. — The respondent excepted to the allowance, by the county court, of an amendment to the first count in the indictment, by adding at its close, the words "contrary to the form

The power of the legislature to prescribe the form of the indictment, and to dispense with certain matters of description, provided the nature and substance of the charge is preserved, is not questioned.[1] And where a statute makes it an offence to do this or that or another thing, mentioning several things disjunctively, either one of which would constitute one and the same offence, subject to one and the same punishment, it is the general rule that all the things mentioned in the statute may be charged conjunctively in a single count, as constituting but a single offence.[2]

(1) *Certainty.* — An indictment must be so specific as to state the exact offence charged.[3]

force and effect of the statute in such case made and provided, and against the peace and dignity of the State." The indictment is for an assault with a dangerous weapon, and contains two counts. The second count closes with the words allowed to be added to the first count. The counsel for the respondent contended that the amendment was one of substance, and, for that reason, beyond the jurisdiction of the county court to allow; and he based his contention upon § 32 of the Constitution of the State, which declares: "All indictments shall conclude with these words, 'against the peace and dignity of the State.'" The court say "He insists that what the Constitution declares that an indictment shall contain is a matter of substance. Suppose this contention is conceded. Does not this indictment close with the very words prescribed? The indictment does not close at the end of the first count thereof. That count ends in the middle of the indictment. The two counts taken together form the indictment. As the indictment closes with the very words prescribed by the Constitution, the contention upon that basis is without support or foundation. In indictments, matters of form may be amended; matters of substance may not be. It may be difficult to express in exact language, that will be applicable to every case, what constitutes the substance of an indictment, and what is merely formal. In general, I think, it may be laid down, that the statement of every fact necessary to be proven, to make the act complained of a crime, is matter of substance in an indictment; and that all beyond — the order of arrangement, the precise words, unless particular words alone will convey the proper meaning — is formal." State *v.* Amadon, 58 Vt. 524; s. c., 1 New Eng. Rep. 355.

Says *Judge Barrett*, in State *v.* Arnold, 50 Vt. 735, "It is obvious, without illustration, that a defect that does not effect the merits of the case, or the evidence necessary to be given to maintain the indictment, can be regarded as only formal."

Says *Lord Chief-Justice De Grey*, in Rex *v.* Horne, 2 Cowp. 682, and adopted by Mr. Chitty, in vol. 1, p. 215, of his work on Pleadings, "The charge must contain such a description of the crime that the defendant may know what crime it is which he is called upon to answer; that the jury may appear to be warranted in their conclusion of 'guilty, or not guilty,' upon the premises delivered to them, and that the court may see such a definite crime that they may apply the punishment which the law prescribes."

Again, says *Lord Chief-Justice De Grey*, "As to the matter to be charged, whatever circumstances are necessary to constitute the crime imputed must be set out; and all beyond is surplusage."

Mr. Chitty says, "Hence the science of special pleading may be considered under two heads: 1, the facts necessary to be stated; and 2, the form of the statement." Chitt. Cr. L. 214.

1. Commenting on the provision in the Bill of Rights, guaranteeing to an accused party the right "to demand the nature and cause of the accusation against him," *Whit, J.*, said, in Turpin *v.* State, 19 Ohio St. 544, "We do not understand that it was intended by this provision to place the rules of the common law prescribing the particularity with which offences were required to be charged, beyond all legislative control. And where, as in this case, the indictment clearly informs the accused of the transaction for which he is called upon to answer, it is, we think, in this respect free from constitutional objection." State *v.* Granville, 45 Ohio St.; s. c., 10 West. Rep. 656.

2. Davis *v.* State, 100 Ind. 154; Fahnestock *v.* State, 102 Ind. 156; State *v.* Stout (Ind.), 11 West. Rep. 358.

3. State *v.* Clevenger, 20 Mo. App. 626; s. c., 2 West. Rep. 589.

Information. — The same certainty and particularity are required in proceedings by information as in proceedings by indictment. State *v.* Beebe, 83 Ind. 171.

But the jurisdictional facts, giving the right to so prosecute, need not be stated in

Thus, an indictment for an attempt to poison must allege that the drug or other substance administered was a deadly poison, or such as was calculated to destroy human life; and the better practice is, to specify the name of the drug or other substance, or that it was unknown.[1] And where an act only becomes a crime when done in a particular place, the complaint should charge the act done in that particular place.[2] But when place is not essential to the description of a crime, omission of place not fatal.[3]

As a rule, more than one offence cannot be charged in the same count. This is commonly expressed by saying that a count must not be double, or is bad for duplicity. Thus, one count cannot charge the prisoner with having committed a murder and a robbery.[4]

the information. Hodge *v.* State, 85 Ind. 561.

An affidavit and information for erecting and maintaining a public nuisance need not point out and specifically describe the particular location of the alleged nuisance. Dronberger *v.* State (Ind.), 11 West. Rep. 106; Wertz *v.* State, 42 Ind. 161; Howard *v.* State, 6 Ind. 444.

1. Shackleford *v.* State, 79 Ala. 26.

Whatever is included in, or is necessarily implied from, an express allegation, need not be otherwise averred. Baysinger *v.* People, 115 Ill. 419; s. c., 2 West. Rep. 839.

Following Language of the Statute. — In an indictment under Ind. R. S. 1881, § 2079, substantially in the words of the statute, for unlawfully and knowingly permitting a room and building to be used for gaming purposes, it is sufficient to state the county and State in which the building is situated, without specially describing the room and its location in the house; and in a count for renting the building for such use, it is not necessary to state the name of the tenant. Kleespies *v.* State, 106 Ind. 383; s. c., 4 West. Rep. 717.

2. State *v.* Turnbull, 78 Me. 392; s. c., 3 New Eng. Rep. 45, 46.

Thus, under Me. R. S. chap. 28, § 8, providing that it shall be an offence to deposit any of certain poisons "within two hundred rods of a highway, pasture, field, or other improved land, for the purpose of killing wolves, foxes, dogs, or other animals," an indictment alleging a deposit made in a certain field, without naming its distance from any other field or improved land, or from a highway, is good on demurrer. State *v.* Bucknam (Me.), 2 New Eng. Rep. 697.

3. State *v.* Moore, 24 S. C. 150.

4. **Exceptions to the Rule.** — There are two exceptions to the rule: (1) an indictment for burglary usually charges the defendant with having broken and entered the house with intent to commit a felony, and also with having committed the felony intended. And (2) in indictments for embezzlement by clerks, or servants, or persons employed in the public service or in the police, the prosecution may charge any number of distinct acts of embezzlement, not exceeding three, which may have been committed against the same master within six months inclusive. But even here it is usual to charge the different acts in different counts. Harris' Cr. L. 342.

An Indictment is not Duplex which charges one or more acts contemporaneously, making one offence, each act constituting a minor offence. State *v.* Hendricks, 38 La. An. 682.

But a count is bad for duplicity that charges a sheriff with refusing to execute process, and with making a false return. State *v.* Walworth, 58 Vt. 502; s. c., 2 New Eng. Rep. 118.

The indictment charged in effect that the defendant was the tax collector of Del Norte County from the first Monday in January, 1883, at 12 o'clock, M., to the like day and time on the fifth day of January, 1885; that as tax collector he had on the fifth day of January, 1885, received and collected certain public money, and on that day, and for five days thereafter, and ever since then, had wholly and wilfully refused and omitted to pay it over to the county treasurer. *Held*, the indictment charged but one offence, and was sufficient under section 424 of the California Penal Code. People *v.* Otto, 70 Cal. 523.

Joinder of Felony and Misdemeanor. — If a count for a felony is joined with a count for a misdemeanor, the indictment will be held bad if demurred to, or judgment may be arrested if the verdict has been general (i.e., guilty or not guilty on the whole indictment), but not if the prisoner is convicted of the felony alone. Rex *v.* Ferguson, 24 L. J. M. C. 61.

An indictment for misdemeanor may con-

The indictment must be so framed as to enable the accused to defend himself against a second prosecution.[1] But the law does not require that an indictment shall contain any allegations of fact which are useless or unnecessary to be proven;[2] yet if an indictment contains a necessary allegation which cannot be rejected, and the pleader makes it unnecessarily minute in the way of description, the proof must satisfy the description as well as the main part.[3]

Every travesable fact in an indictment must be directly alleged.[4] Thus, if a thing is claimed to be "lawful or unlawful,"

tain several counts for different offences, even though the judgments upon each be different, so that the legal character of the substantive offences charged be the same. Young *v.* R., 3 T. R. 105. Thus, evidence of several assaults or several libels will be received on the several counts of the same indictment. But there are limits, not precisely defined, to this rule; when convenience and justice demand it, the judge compelling the prosecution to elect upon which charge they will proceed. In all cases of this character, the important consideration is, whether all the acts were substantially one transaction.

In Illinois embezzlement is declared by statute (Rev. Stat. 1871, 360) to be larceny; hence a single count for larceny would be supported by proof of either embezzlement or strict larceny.

The Statute of Indiana (Rev. Stat. 1876, vol. 2, p. 389) provides that the counts for murder in the first and second degree, and for manslaughter, may be joined in the same indictment. But in a case where a count for embezzlement was joined in the same indictment with a count for larceny, the court refused to require the State to elect on which count the defendant should be tried. Griffith *v.* State, 36 Ind. 406.

The Iowa Code (§ 4300) provides, "The indictment must charge but one offence; but it may be charged in different forms, to meet the testimony; and if it may have been committed in different modes and by different means, the indictment may allege the modes and means in the alternative, provided, that in case of compound offences, where, in the same transaction, more than one offence has been committed, the indictment may charge the several offences, and the defendant may be convicted of any offence included therein." See Rev. Stat. 1873, p. 668. This provision is a concise statement of the common-law rule.

The Criminal Code of Kentucky provides (sect. 126), "An indictment, except in the cases mentioned in the next section, must charge but one offence; but if it may have been committed in different modes and by different means, the indictment may allege the modes and means in the alternative. Sect. 127. The offences named in each of the subdivisions of this section may be charged in one indictment: 1. Larceny and knowingly receiving stolen property. 2. Larceny and obtaining money or property on false pretences. 3. Larceny and embezzlement. 4. Robbery and burglary. 5. Robbery and an assault with intent to rob. 6. Passing, or attempting to pass, counterfeit money or United States currency or bank-notes, knowing them to be such, and having in possession counterfeit money or United States currency or bank-notes, knowing them to be such, with the intention to circulate the same."

The Michigan Statute (Rev. Stat. 1871, p. 2174) provides that "an indictment for larceny may contain also a count for obtaining property by false pretences, or for embezzlement, or for receiving or concealing stolen property; and the jury may find all or any of these persons indicted, guilty on either count."

The Ohio Code provides that "an indictment for larceny may contain a count for obtaining the same property by false pretence, a count for embezzlement thereof, and a count for receiving or concealing the same property, knowing it to have been stolen; and the jury may find any or all the persons indicted guilty of either of the offences charged in the indictment." 74 Ohio L. 366.

1. Mincher *v.* State (Md.), 5 Cent. Rep 769.

2. Hutchins *v.* Kimmell, 31 Mich. 128; Fleming *v.* People, 27 N. Y. 329; Whart. Conf. L. §§ 170–173.

3. The State was bound to prove the allegation as laid. Withers *v.* State, 21 Tex. App. 210.

Where the indictment alleged the brand, age, and color of the horse involved, it was *held* that such allegations became material because of the identity of the animal, and it devolves upon the State to establish the allegations by proof. Coleman *v.* State, 21 Tex. App. 520.

4. State *v.* La Bore, 26 Vt. 765.

the facts which make it so must be set out; and the mere allegation "lawful or unlawful" is a conclusion of law and insufficient, and particularly is this so where the unlawfulness of the act is so only by virtue of a statute.[1] But an indictment need not negative facts which are matters of defence.[2]

The indictment must charge the crime with certainty and precision. A statement of a legal result is bad;[3] and it has been frequently held that it is insufficient to allege a material part of the charge by way of recital.[4]

An indictment is sufficient if the offence is clearly set forth, and charged with such certainty that the court can pronounce judgment according to the right of the case;[5] but it must contain an allegation of every fact which is legally essential to the punishment to be inflicted. All that is to be proved must be alleged.[6] Thus, where two persons are charged as principals, one as the immediate perpetrator of the injury, and the other as aiding and abetting, it is immaterial which of them is charged as having inflicted the wound, inasmuch as the law imputes the injury given by one as the act of the other. So that an indictment that A. gave the blow and B. was present and abetting, is sustained by evidence that B. gave the blow and A. was present and abetting.[7]

In certain cases if the prisoner has been *previously convicted*, a count is inserted in the indictment charging him with such previous conviction. He will have to plead to this, and proof may be given, if he denies it, as on any other count. The object of putting in this count is, that the prisoner may have his identity with

1. People *v.* Crotty, 93 Ill. 181–190; Collins *v.* People, 39 Ill. 233; Williams *v.* State, 2 Ind. 439.

2. People *v.* West, 44 Hun (N. Y.), 162.

3. 1 Chitty, Cr. L. (4th Am. ed.) 227.

Thus to sustain a prosecution for obtaining goods under false pretences, it must be, in legal effect, charged in the indictment as well as proved at the trial, that the goods were obtained by means of the alleged false pretences. State *v.* Orvis, 13 Ind. 569; Todd *v.* State, 31 Ind. 514; State *v.* Williams, 103 Ind. 235; s. c., 1 West. Rep. 188; State *v.* Connor, 110 Ind. 469; s. c., 9 West. Rep. 226. Whart. Cr. L. § 1175; 2 Bish. Cr. L. § 461; Moore, Cr. L. § 739.

A general charge of conspiracy in an indictment is sufficient. Wood *v.* State, 47 N. J. L. (18 Vr.) 461; s. c., 1 Cent. Rep. 441.

4. Moore, Cr. L. § 788.

It is a general rule that the charge should be expressed positively, and not with a whereas, or by way of recital. 1 Bish. Cr. Proc. § 555; Stark. Cr. Pl. (1st ed.) 270.

5. Thomas *v.* State, 103 Ind. 419; s. c., 1 West. Rep. 309; State *v.* Anderson, 102 Ind. 170; s. c., 1 West. Rep. 175; Ind. Rev. Stat. 1881, § 1755.

6. State *v.* Buster, 90 Mo. 514; s. c., 7 West. Rep. 723, 724.

7. State *v.* Payton, 90 Mo. 220; s. c., 7 West. Rep. 129; State *v.* Dalton, 27 Mo. 14. It was *held* in State *v.* Blan, 69 Mo. 318, that an indictment for murder in the first degree was not faulty in failing to state separately the individual acts of each defendant. The indictment may either allege the matter according to the fact, or charge them both as principals in the first degree. State *v.* Anderson, 89 Mo. 312; s. c., 5 West. Rep. 420.

And in State *v.* Dalton, 27 Mo. 14, the indictment was *held* to be sufficient to support a conviction, though it alleged that both defendants held the same knife, club, or pistol in the right hand. In the present case it cannot be said which of the defendants fired the particular shot which killed the child, but in the eye of the law both are equally responsible. Bishop in his Criminal Practice (3d ed.), § 471, says, "The common method is simply to name them (defendants), and add that they did so and so. Offences jointly committed being in law several, such an allegation is equivalent to saying that each defendant did the criminal act. The indictment is therefore well enough."

the person so previously convicted proved before the severer punishment consequent on a previous conviction is awarded.[1]

Where the indictment purports to set out the crime specifically and circumstantially in the common-law method, it must be construed by common-law rules.[2]

(2) *Time and Place.* — The indictment must allege the specific day on which the offence was committed.[3] And an indictment failing to set forth the time, although it is not essential that the offence charged be proved to have been committed on the day alleged, cannot be sustained.[4] The day upon which the State claims that the offence was committed should be stated in the indictment with certainty and precision.[5]

Except where time is of the essence of an offence, a crime alleged to have been committed on a certain day may be shown to have been committed on a subsequent day, if the latter is prior to the filing of the indictment or information.[6] But it must appear

1. Harris' Cr. L. (Force's ed.) 275.

Previous Conviction. — An indictment based on Mo. Rev. Stat. § 1664, prescribing punishment upon a second conviction for petit larceny, is sufficient which alleges, in substance, that defendant on a particular date, previous to the finding of the indictment, was convicted in St. Louis Court of Criminal Correction of petit larceny, and fined one dollar and costs; that he complied with the sentence and was discharged; and that thereafter, he did in the city of St. Louis feloniously steal, take, and carry away fifty pounds of iron of the value of ten cents per pound, the property of the Missouri Pacific Railroad Company, a corporation duly organized. State *v.* Loehr, (Mo.) 11 West. Rep. 473.

The court say in the above case, "It is also insisted that the court erred in allowing the State, over defendant's objection, to put in evidence the record of the St. Louis Court of Criminal Correction, showing the conviction of defendant, in 1881, of petit larceny. Inasmuch as defendant had been examined as a witness on his own behalf, the evidence received was properly admitted for the purpose of affecting his credibility." State *v.* Rider, 90 Mo. 54; s. c., 6 West. Rep. 458; State *v.* Bulla, 89 Mo. 595; s. c., 6 West. Rep. 440; State *v.* Palmer, 88 Mo. 568; s. c., 5 West. Rep. 387.

2. People *v.* Carr (Mich.), 7 West. Rep. 890.

Rule of Construction. — An indictment charging that defendant did, with intent to feloniously cheat and defraud, attempt to obtain by trick and deception, and by false and fraudulent representations, a certain sum of money, tested by the rules of the common law, would be insufficient; and where it fails to give the name or names of the persons, firms, or corporations, or the names of the persons forming the voluntary association alleged to be defrauded, it is sufficient under Mo. R. S. § 1561. State *v.* McChesney, 90 Mo. 120; s. c., 6 West. Rep. 643.

There is no rule of construction which requires the pronoun shall relate to the last noun mentioned for its antecedent; but the construction will be governed by the sense and meaning intended to be conveyed. Miller *v.* State, 107 Ind. 152; s. c., 4 West. Rep. 501. Steeple *v.* Downing, 6 Ind. 478; State *v.* Hedge, 6 Ind. 330.

3. State *v.* Brown, 24 S. C. 224.

4. State *v.* Fenlason, 78 Me. 495; s. c., 3 New. Eng. Rep. 834. State *v.* Hanson, 39 Me. 340; State *v.* Baker, 34 Me. 52; State *v.* Thurstin, 35 Me. 206; Commonwealth *v.* Adams, 67 Mass. (1 Gray) 483; 1 Bish. Cr. Proc. §§ 237, 251.

Indictments for Cruelty to Animals may allege a period of time instead of a single date, the offences involving continuous action. State *v.* Bosworth, 54 Conn. 1; s. c., 1 New Eng. Rep. 928.

5. State *v.* Fenlason, 78 Me. 495; s. c., 3 New Eng. Rep. 834

In an Indictment for frequenting an Opium Den for the purpose of smoking opium, where the offence is in its nature continuing from day to day, or constituted out of a series of minor acts, it is sufficient to charge the act as having been committed upon a particular day. State *v.* Ah Sam, 14 Oreg. 347.

Selling Liquor. — An indictment charging keeping and selling liquors at a time and place stated, is not bad for omission, to repeat the time in further allegation that defendant thereby maintained a nuisance. State *v.* Buck, 78 Me. 193; s. c., 1 New Eng. Rep. 903.

6. People *v.* Sheldon, 68 Cal. 434.

from the proof that the offence was committed anterior to the presentment of the indictment.[1]

The allegation of an impossible date vitiates an indictment.[2]

d. The Intent. — When, by common law or statute, a particular intention is essential to an offence, it is necessary to allege the intent with distinctness and precision, and support the allegation by proof.[3] The intent may be inferred from the facts in the case.[4] But where the intent with which an act is done forms no part of the offence, it is unnecessary to aver it in the indictment.[5]

When an act contains several provisions, an indictment must state the peculiar provision which the person charged intended to violate.[6]

e. Of Statutory Offences. — Statutory crimes, as distinguished from common-law crimes, are such crimes as are ***malum prohibitum.***[7]

In an Indictment for Bribery, or promise of benefit to influence official action, an omission of the year is not fatal, time not being of the essence of the offence. State *v.* McDonald, 106 Ind. 233; s. c., 3 West. Rep. 752.

Amendment. — Where the blank for the year in an indictment is unfilled, it may be amended, even after the evidence has closed. State *v.* Fontenette, 38 La. An. 61.

1. Clement *v.* State, 22 Tex. App. 23.

An Indispensable Prerequisite to the sufficiency of an information is, that it charges the offence to have been committed anterior to the filing of the same. The complaint cannot be resorted to in order to supply such an omission. Kennedy *v.* State, 22 Tex. App. 693.

Indictment which charges the offence to have been committed upon a date subsequent to its presentment is fatally defective. Lee *v.* State, 22 Tex. App. 547.

Illegal Voting. — Where an indictment charges illegal voting on Nov. 4, 1886, which was three days after the return of the indictment; but immediately following that statement, it was alleged that, "the same being the day upon which the general election was being held in said State for the election of governor, as was then and there required by law," the latter statement shows the offence to have been committed in the past, fixes the date thereof, and is sufficient, under Ind. R. S. 1881, § 1756. State *v.* Patterson (Ind.), 7 West. Rep. 410.

2. State *v.* Noland, 29 Ind. 212; Moore, Cr. L. § 162.

An indictment which charges the offence to have been committed "on the 16th day of August, 18184," should have been quashed on motion. Murphy *v.* State, 106 Ind. 96; s. c., 3 West. Rep. 741.

And an indictment alleging an illegal sale of intoxicating liquors on an impossible date — as June 11, 18184 — should be quashed on motion. Murphy *v.* State, 106 Ind. 94, 96; s. c., 3 West. Rep. 741; 107 Ind. 598, 600; 5 West. Rep. 549, 815; State *v.* Patterson (Ind.), 7 West. Rep 410, 411.

3. Commonwealth *v.* Smith, 143 Mass, 169; s. c., 3 New Eng. Rep. 305.

All that need be done is to characterize by appropriate words the intent essential to the existence of the crime charged. Garmire *v.* State, 104 Ind. 444; s. c., 2 West. Rep. 284, 285; Harding *v.* State, 54 Ind. 359; Powers *v.* State, 87 Ind. 97; Myers *v.* State, 101 Ind. 379.

An allegation in a complaint for the violation of a city ordinance, that the defendant "wilfully and unlawfully" did the act complained of, is equivalent to alleging that it was "knowingly" done. Wong *v.* Astoria, 13 Oreg. 538.

It is as essential to charge the specific intent, as it is to prove it, in cases of assault with intent to murder. Bartlett *v.* State, 21 Tex. App. 500.

4. Brown *v.* State, 52 Ala. 345; People *v.* Shainwold, 51 Cal. 468; Brooks *v.* State, 51 Ga. 612; McDonald *v.* People, 47 Ill. 533; State *v.* Rolifrischt, 12 La. An. 382; State *v.* Watson, 63 Me. 128; Commonwealth *v.* Harney, 51 Mass. (10 Metc.) 422; Commonwealth *v.* McCarthy, 119 Mass. 354; Tullis *v.* State, 41 Tex. 598; Reg. *v.* Dossett, 2 Car. & K. 306; Reg. *v.* Taylor, 5 Cox, C. C. 138; Rex *v.* Farrington, Russ & R. C. C. 207.

5. State *v.* Hackfath, 20 Mo. App. 614, s. c., 2 West. Rep. 588, 589.

6. People *v.* Martin, 52 Cal. 201.

7. **Malum prohibitum and Malum in se.** — Crimes are generally divided into two general classes, *mala in se* and *mala prohibita;* a distinction which is of little practical importance in a system which must

When a statute makes indictable an act which is merely ***malum prohibitum***, when done "wilfully and maliciously," the existence of an evil mind in doing the forbidden act is, as a general rule, a constituent part of the offence.[1]

necessarily vary with the standard of good and bad. Austin Jur. 590. There will always be some crimes which naturally take their place in the one class or the other; for example, no one will hesitate to say that murder is ***malum in se***, or that the secret importation of articles liable to custom is merely ***malum quia prohibitum***; but between these offences there are many acts which it is difficult to assign to their proper class. Harris' Cr. L. 5.

Common Law and Statutory Crimes. — Some acts have been recognized as crimes in the English law from time immemorial, though their punishment and incidents may have been affected by legislation. Thus murder and rape are crimes at common law. In other cases acts have been pronounced crimes by particular statutes, which have also provided for their punishment; e.g., offences under the bankruptcy laws. Harris' Cr. L. 5.

There are no common-law crimes in some of the States. This was declared by the Supreme Court of the State in Key *v.* Vattier, 1 Ohio, 132, and in many subsequent cases; consequently there is no crime, or punishment, or criminal procedure in Ohio other than what has been defined or prescribed by statute. Misprisions, attempts, conspiracy, and all accessorial offences are substantive crimes, so far as they have been declared by statute; and, in the absence of statute, are not punishable. The common law is used, however, to define words used in the statutes. The same rule prevails in Indiana (Beals *v.* The State, 15 Ind. 378; State *v.* O. & M. R. R. Co., 23 Ind. 362), and in Iowa (Estes *v.* Carter, 10 Iowa, 400). In Indiana and Iowa the rule is prescribed by statute. But the States generally hold that common-law crimes are indictable, and common-law punishments can be imposed by courts having general criminal jurisdiction, except so far as the common law has been repealed or modified by statute. Hence, an indictment for conspiracy is good in Minnesota, though there is no mention of conspiracy in the statutes. State *v.* Pulle, 12 Minn. 164.

In Scotland, the common-law power of courts extends to declaring and punishing as crimes, acts not made criminal by statute, and which have never before been indicted. Greenhuff's Case, 2 Swiss. 236; 1 Bish. Cr. L. (ed. 1868) 18.

1. Folwell *v.* State, 49 N. J. L. (20 Vr.) 31; s. c., 5 Cent. Rep. 353.

The word "maliciously" when used in the definition of a statutory crime, the act forbidden being merely ***malum prohibitum***, has almost always the effect of making a bad intent or evil mind a constituent of the offence. The whole doctrine of that large class of offences falling under the general denomination of malicious mischief is founded on this theory. For example, it was declared by the Supreme Court of Massachusetts, in the case of Commonwealth *v.* Walden, 57 Mass. (3 Cush.) 558, that the word "maliciously" as used in the statute relating to malicious mischief, was not sufficiently defined as "the wilfully doing of any act prohibited by law, and for which the defendant has no lawful excuse," but that on the contrary, in order to justify a conviction under the Act referred to, the jury must be satisfied that the injury was done, either out of a spirit of wanton cruelty or of wicked revenge. And even the word "wilfully," in the ordinary sense in which it is used in statutes, was said by *Chief Justice Shaw* to mean not merely "voluntarily," but to imply the doing of the act with a bad purpose. Commonwealth *v.* Kneeland, 37 Mass. (20 Pick.) 220.

This same signification of the term "wilful" was adopted in the case of State *v.* Clark, 29 N. J. L. (5 Dutch) 96, the charge being that the defendant, in the language of the statute, wilfully destroyed a fence on land in the possession of another; the defendant was permitted to show that he did the act under claim of title to the premises. Folwell *v.* State, 49 N. J. L. (20 Vr.) 31; s. c., 5 Cent. Rep. 353.

Evil Design. — A person was indicted under the Act prohibiting the wilfully and maliciously tearing down of a sheriff's advertisement. *Held*, that the defendant had the right to show that he tore down such paper without any evil design. Folwell *v.* State, 49 N. J. L. (20 Vr.) 353; s. c., 5 Cent. Rep. 353.

When a statute prohibits an act if done intentionally, without any words being added to such inhibition indicating that, to render the forbidden act criminal, it must be the product of an evil mind, it becomes a pure question of statutory construction whether or not the ***animus*** of the person inculpated was an element of the crime.

This was the rule adopted in New Jersey in the case of Halsted *v.* State, 41 N. J. L. (12 Vr.) 552, and exemplified in the case of State *v.* Cutter, 36 N. J. L. (7 Vr.) 125, — in the latter case the court deciding that the *mens rea* was an ingredient of the

Indictments for attempts, whether brought under statutes or under common law, should set forth in direct terms that the defendant attempted to commit the crime.[1] The acts constituting the alleged attempt should be set forth in the indictment.[2]

An indictment under a statute may state the act in the language of the statute, or it may state the offence by setting out the substance of the statute.[3]

statutory offence although the legislative language was simply prohibitive of the act described. Folwell *v.* State, 49 N. J. L. (20 Vr.) 31; s. c., 5 Cent. Rep. 353

Violating Insurance Laws. — An information under Vermont statute, No. 463, Acts of 1884 (Rev. L. 3615), charging an agent with receiving risks for insurance in behalf of a foreign insurance company which has not complied with the statute, must allege assured's name. State *v.* Hover, 58 Vt. 496; s. c., 2 New Eng. Rep. 201.

1. Commonwealth *v.* Roosnell, 143 Mass. 32; s. c., 3 New Eng. Rep. 109; Commonwealth *v.* Shedd, 140 Mass. 451; s. c., 1 New Eng. Rep. 389; Commonwealth *v.* Dennis, 105 Mass. 162; Commonwealth *v.* Sherman, 105 Mass. 169; Commonwealth *v.* McLaughlin, 105 Mass. 460; Christian *v.* Commonwealth, 23 Gratt. (Va.) 954 See also Commonwealth *v.* Thompson, 116 Mass. 346.

Where an indictment alleged that the defendant "in the night-time feloniously did attempt to break and enter, with intent the goods and chattels in said building then and there being found, then and there feloniously to steal, take and carry away; and in such attempt did certain acts, but "was then and there intercepted and prevented in the execution of said offence," it was held to be sufficient. Commonwealth *v.* Flynn, 57 Mass. (3 Cush.) 529; Commonwealth *v.* McLaughlin, 105 Mass. 460; Commonwealth *v.* Shedd, 140 Mass. 451; s. c., 1 New Eng. Rep. 389.

2. State *v.* Brown, 95 N. C. 685.

In an indictment under 2 N. Y. Rev. Stat. 698, § 3, for attempting to commit an offence, the particular manner in which the attempt was made is immaterial, and need not be alleged. People *v.* Bush, 4 Hill (N. Y.) 131.

3. **Criminal Negligence.** — Thus an indictment under the statute charging manslaughter in causing the death of a human being, by culpable negligence in the construction of a building, is good. People *v.* Buddensiek, 103 N. Y. 487; s. c., 4 Cent. Rep. 787.

Evidence. — A piece of brick and mortar from the fallen wall of the alleged defective building was properly admitted in evidence, as confirming the opinion of a competent witness as to the quality of the mortar, and to enable the jurors to understand the difference in effect between the mortar used by the defendant and that properly prepared. People *v.* Buddensiek, 103 N. Y. 487; s. c., 4 Cent. Rep. 787.

Violating Election Laws. — In an indictment under Ohio Rev. Stat. § 7061, as amended Feb. 17, 1881 (78 Ohio L. 30), it is not necessary to set out a copy of the poll-book or tally-sheet on which the offence was committed, nor is the purport thereof required. It is sufficient to describe it by the designation "poll-book," or "tally-sheet," and to aver that the defendant wrongfully and fraudulently changed, altered, erased, or tampered with a "name," "word," or "figure" contained in such poll-book or tally-sheet, as the facts may require, setting forth the nature and character of the alteration made, and that it was done with intent to defeat, hinder, or prevent a fair expression of the will of the people at an election. State *v.* Granville, 45 Ohio St.; s. c., 10 West. Rep. 656.

Blackmailing. — Where one was indicted under the New York Penal Code, § 558, for blackmail, in sending a letter to the prosecutor, stating that the writer had been informed that complainant had gotten a certain unmarried female with child, and intimating that legal proceedings would be taken to enforce prosecutor's liability unless he made voluntary provision for the mother and child, and asking whether he was willing to do this to avoid publicity, *held*, that an averment in the indictment that the defendant, for the purpose of extorting money from the prosecutor, threatened to expose him, to disgrace him with the criminal acts stated, implies that defendant knew the charge contained in the letter was false; that an admission in the record that evidence was given tending to prove the acts charged covered an averment that it was a scheme to extort money by making a false charge; that the indictment was good in substance, and the conviction should stand. People *v.* Wightman, 104 N. Y. 598; s. c., 6 Cent. Rep. 657.

Lottery. — A criminal information which charges the "wrongful and unlawful sale of a certain share or shares in a certain lottery and device in the nature of a lottery,

In an indictment for obtaining goods by false pretences from a partnership, it is proper to charge the false pretences to have been made to the partnership by its firm name, and the ownership in the same form.[1]

known as the Louisiana State Lottery," is sufficient. State *v.* Kaub, 19 Mo. App. 149; s. c., 1 West. Rep. 411. See State *v.* McWilliams, 7 Mo. App. 99.

Upon an information which charges defendant with the "wrongful and unlawful sale of a certain share or shares, in certain lottery-tickets, in a certain lottery and device in the nature of a lottery, known as the Louisiana State Lottery," etc, he was tried, found guilty, and sentenced to pay a fine of $1,000. He thereupon moved in arrest of judgment, on the ground that the information states no cause of action against him, because it fails to state where the Louisiana State Lottery is located, or that said lottery has a veritable and *bona fide* existence, or that defendant conducted the business of selling as a vocation. The court *held* that the information was sufficient. State *v.* Kaub, 19 Mo. App. 149; s. c., 1 West. Rep. 411; State *v.* McWilliams, 7 Mo. App 99.

Verification.—Such an information is sufficiently verified "upon information and belief" of the affiant. State *v.* Kaub, 19 Mo. App. 149; s c., 1 West. Rep. 411.

That the information is not verified by an affidavit stating affiant's knowledge of the facts sworn to, but only by an affidavit stating that the facts are true according to affiant's knowledge and belief, is an objection without merit. This objection was fully examined in State *v.* Fitzporter, 16 Mo. App. 282, and was found untenable. See State *v.* Kaub, 19 Mo. App. 149; 1 West Rep. 411.

Perjury.—Averments, in an indictment for perjury in the verification of a quarterly report required of a State bank, that the defendant had full and certain knowledge as to the real and true condition of the bank in respect to the matters in question, and well knew that the facts were other than as stated in the report, and well knew that the statements in the report were false, —amount to an allegation that the statements were false. The objection that such indictment is argumentative goes only to its form, and is not fatal. People *v.* Clements (N Y.), 9 Cent. Rep. 698; N. Y. Code Crim Proc. § 285.

In an indictment for perjury under sect. 2006 of the Revised Statutes of 1881, it must appear by a specific averment, or by the statement of facts, that the false swearing was touching matters material to the point in question; and this rule applies to an affidavit to secure a continuance, in a cause, in which the facts stated do not themselves show their materiality, and there is no allegation of the materiality of the facts stated in the affidavit, as to the point in question. State *v.* Anderson, 103 Ind. 170; s. c., 1 West. Rep. 175; Weathers *v.* State, 2 Blackf. (Ind.) 278; State *v* Hall, 7 Blackf. (Ind.) 25; State *v.* Johnson, 7 Blackf. (Ind) 49. In this last case it was *held*, also, that it is perjury to swear falsely to a material point in an affidavit for the continuance of a cause. Gallaway *v.* State, 29 Ind. 442; Hendricks *v.* State, 26 Ind. 493; State *v* McCormick, 52 Ind. 169. See also State *v.* Flagg, 25 Ind. 244; Bishop's Crim. Pro. § 921.

In the case of State *v.* Flagg, 27 Ind. 24, an affidavit was filed with interrogatories for the purpose of procuring a continuance It was said: "The indictment in this case alleges that the interrogatories and affidavit were filed for the purpose of procuring a continuance. It was, therefore, an affidavit required by law, and if false, and wilfully and corruptly made, as the indictment charges, was clearly within the statute defining perjury. It was *held* that the materiality of the facts stated in the affidavit must be shown. Under these decisions, the affidavit for a continuance upon which, in the case before us, perjury is predicated, is an affidavit required by law; and hence the materiality must appear from the facts stated, or by an express allegation in the indictment, if such an allegation is the proper mode of showing it, under our criminal practice." See Burk *v.* State, 81 Ind. 128.

1. State *v.* Williams, 103 Ind. 235; s. c., 1 West. Rep. 188.

In the case of Commonwealth *v.* Harley, 48 Mass (7 Metc.) 462, the charge was, that the defendants "did designedly and falsely pretend and represent to said George B. Blake & Co. that," etc., it was *held* that the indictment was sustained by proof that the representation was made to a clerk of the firm. See Stoughton *v.* State, 2 Ohio St. 562; Commonwealth *v.* Call, 38 Mass. (21 Pick.) 515; 2 Whart. Cr. L. §§ 1171-1212.

False Pretences.—An averment in the indictment that "relying on said false representations," etc, is a sufficient averment that the representations were believed to be true. State *v.* Williams, 103 Ind. 235; s. c., 1 West. Rep. 188; Clifford *v.* State, 56 Ind. 245.

Averments that, for the purpose of ob-

Under a statute providing that whoever maliciously or mischievously injures the property of another shall be fined not more than twofold value of the damage done, — in order that the court may determine the amount of the fine to be imposed, the amount of damages done must be alleged and proved; and it must be made to appear by the affidavit, information, or indictment, that the property was injured.[1]

(1) *Setting out Statutes.* — An indictment which follows substantially the language of the statute, and apprises the defendant of the offences charged, sufficiently describes the statutory offence.[2] And when a statute in defining a crime refers by name

taining "credit," certain false representations were made, and that by means of the representations thus made defendant did, then and there, obtain "on credit" certain goods, etc., where it does not appear from the allegations whether the goods were obtained as a result of negotiations for a purchase, loan, or exchange, but simply that they were obtained "on credit," are too uncertain, no connection appearing between the false pretences and obtaining of the goods. State *v.* Williams, 103 Ind. 235; s. c., 1 West. Rep. 188.

In Commonwealth *v.* Strain, 51 Mass. (10 Metc.) 521, it was said "that the sale or exchange ought to be set forth in the indictment, and that the false pretences should be alleged to have been made with a view to effect such sale or exchange, and that by reason thereof the party was induced to buy or exchange, as the case may be." See also State *v.* Philbrick, 31 Me. 401.

In the case last cited, the indictment averred that, by means of certain false pretences, the accused did then and there knowingly and designedly obtain one horse of the value of fifty dollars from one Goff. It was *held* bad because it contained no allegation that by reason of such false pretences Goff was induced to sell or exchange his horse. See Todd *v.* State, 31 Ind. 514; State *v.* Orvis, 13 Ind. 569; Johnson *v.* State, 11 Ind. 481; Jones *v.* State, 50 Ind. 473; Wagoner *v.* State, 90 Ind. 504.

1. State *v.* McKee, 109 Ind. 497; s. c., 7 West. Rep. 920.

Malicious Mischief. — In order that the court may determine the amount of fine to be imposed, the amount of damages done must be alleged and proved. The damages, too, must result from an injury to the property; and hence it must be made to appear by the affidavit, information, or indictment, that the property was injured. If no injury is shown, no crime, as defined by the statute, is shown; and if injury to the property be shown, and no amount of damage resulting from that injury, the affidavit, information, or indictment is insufficient, because the court cannot measure the fine to be imposed, and hence cannot pronounce the judgment provided by the statute. These things must be so shown by the affidavit, information, or indictment, that the defendant may be apprised of what he is to meet. Brown *v.* State, 76 Ind. 85; State *v.* Cole, 90 Ind. 112; Sample *v.* State, 104 Ind. 289; s. c., 2 West. Rep. 258.

Malicious Trespass. — An affidavit that the defendant on, etc., at, etc., "did then and there unlawfully and maliciously throw down the fence, and pass over the enclosed lands of this affiant, situated in said county and State, to this affiant's damage in the sum of five dollars, contrary," etc., is too vague and indefinite. Wherever, in a prosecution for malicious trespass, it may be sufficient to allege damage to the owner instead of injury to the property, it must appear that the property was injured, that it was the property of the person damaged, and that the damages to the owner resulted directly from such injury. State *v.* McKee, 109 Ind. 497; s. c., 7 West. Rep. 290.

2. Baysinger *v.* People, 115 Ill. 419; s. c., 2 West. Rep. 839; Commonwealth *v.* Bearse, 108 Mass. 487; Commonwealth *v.* Galavan, 91 Mass. (9 Allen), 271; Commonwealth *v.* Hobbs, 140 Mass. 443; s. c., 1 New Eng. Rep. 541; State *v.* West, 21 Mo. App. 309; s. c., 4 West. Rep. 747; State *v.* Bayne, 88 Mo. 604; s. c., 4 West. Rep. 649; State *v.* Fulton, 19 Mo. 680; State *v.* Batson, 31 Mo. 343; State *v.* Stubblefield, 32 Mo. 563; State *v.* Roehm, 61 Mo. 82; State *v.* Hedrick, 20 Mo. App. 629; s. c., 2 West. Rep. 591; 1 Bish. Crim. Proc. §§ 611, 612; State *v.* West, 21 Mo. App. 309; s. c., 4 West. Rep. 747; Mincher *v.* State (Md.), 5 Cent. Rep. 768.

The court say, in State *v.* West, *supra*, that, "conceding to appellant that the indictment is technically defective in this respect, his objection comes too late. It was not raised in the court below. After verdict such defects are cured by the Statute of Jeofails," § 1821, Mo. R. S.

An indictment for a statutory offence

to another well-known crime, and makes such named crime a constituent of the defined crime, — in an indictment for the latter it is not sufficient to use the mere statutory language, but the particulars constituting the named crime must be shown.[1]

need not be in the exact words of the statute, but other words, if conveying the same meaning, may be used; hence an indictment under the statute for perjury, where the word "falsely" is omitted, and in its stead the word "feloniously" is used, taken in connection with the charge, that the affidavit sworn to by defendant was false, and that defendant well knew that the affidavit and all matters stated therein were wholly false, and that he wilfully, knowingly, and voluntarily committed wilful and corrupt perjury, render the word "feloniously" equivalent to the word "falsely," as used in the statute. State *v.* Anderson, 103 Ind. 170; s. c., 1 West. Rep. 175; Shinn *v.* State, 68 Ind. 423; State *v.* Walls, 54 Ind. 561; State *v.* Gilbert, 21 Ind. 474; Malone *v.* State, 14 Ind. 219.

It is sufficient where the indictment charges the offence in the language of the statute, changing the disjunctive to the conjunctive form. Seacord *v.* People (Ill.), 10 West. Rep. 915; McCutcheon *v.* People, 69 Ill. 601; Warringer *v.* People, 74 Ill. 346; Cole *v.* People, 84 Ill. 216; Fuller *v.* People, 92 Ill. 184.

Cruelty to Animals. — An affidavit which charges that the defendant "did then and there unlawfully and cruelly torture, torment, and needlessly mutilate a certain animal, to wit, a goose, the property of some person or persons to the affiant unknown, by then and there unlawfully turpentining and burning, in a cruel and wanton manner, the said goose," is a sufficient charge of an offence under Ind. Rev. Stat. 1881, § 2101. State *v.* Bruner, 111 Ind. 98; s. c., 9 West. Rep. 602.

Forgery. — An indictment for forgery is sufficient where it charges the offence in the language of the statute, and sets forth the instrument according to its tenor; and it is not necessary to its validity, under Mo. Rev. Stat. 1879, § 1386, that it should charge an intent on the part of defendant to defraud any particular person. State *v.* Rucker (Mo.), 11 West. Rep. 457.

A Complaint for a Penalty for a statutory offence may be in the words of the statute, without a particular detail of facts and circumstances, when, by using those words, the act in which the offence consists is fully and expressly alleged. Commonwealth *v.* Richardson, 142 Mass. 71; s. c., 2 New Eng. Rep. 153.

It is a well-settled rule that an indictment may be made in the words of a statute, without a particular detail of facts and circumstances, when by using those words the act in which an offence consists is fully, directly, and expressly alleged, without any uncertainty or ambiguity. Commonwealth *v.* Welsh, 73 Mass. (7 Gray) 324; Commonwealth *v.* Barrett, 108 Mass. 302; Commonwealth *v.* Tiffany, 119 Mass. 302; Mass. Pub. Stat. chap. 91, § 27.

Violation of Game and Fish Laws. — In an indictment under the Act of March 22, 1886, relating to game-fish, it is sufficient to describe the interdicted material alleged to have been unlawfully put in the lake as "acid" in the language of the statute, without specifying what particular acid it was. The first two counts of the indictment are defective in this case, because there is no averment that the acid was discharged into the water in such quantity as would prove fatal to the fish therein, nor that any of said fish had perished in consequence of the defendant's act. It is not necessary, in legislation amending statutes, to set forth the amended statute, and also the statute as it was before amendment. The mischief to be remedied by the constitutional amendment does not require it, nor does the language of the Constitution. It is sufficient to set forth the amended Act in full. State *v.* Amer. Forcite P. M. Co. (N. J.), 9 Cent. Rep. 495.

In Indictments for Misdemeanors created by statute, it is sufficient to charge the offence in the words of the statute, subject to the qualification that the crime must be set forth with such certainty as will apprise the accused of the offence imputed to him. State *v.* Stimson, 24 N. J. L. (4 Zab.) 9; State *v.* Thatcher, 35 N. J. L. (6 Vr.) 445; State *v.* Halsted, 39 N. J. L. (10 Vr.) 402; State *v.* Startup, 39 N. J. L. (10 Vr.) 423; State *v.* Amer. Forcite P. M. Co. (N. J.) 9 Cent. Rep. 495.

Indictment for Murder. — In an indictment for murder, when the fact that the killing was in the commission of a rape is relied on to make such killing murder in the first degree, a count in the general form authorized by section 45 of the Criminal Procedure Act is sufficient. Titus *v.* State, 49 N. J. L. (20 Vr.) 36; s. c., 5 Cent. Rep. 816.

1. Titus *v.* State, 49 N. J. L. (20 Vr.) 36; s. c., 5 Cent. Rep. 816.

"Generally where a statute merely designates an offence by the use of some word, technical or otherwise, yet does not describe

Offences prescribed and defined by a statute must be charged in the language of the statute, or in language equivalent thereto;[1] and an indictment which sets forth the offence created by the statute neither in the words of the statute nor in equivalent words, is insufficient.[2]

Where a statute denounces an offence bearing close relation to a common-law offence, such offence may be charged in the language of a statute,[3] and must set forth all the constituent facts and circumstances necessary to bring the accused within the statutory provisions.[4]

Acts forbidden disjunctively by statute may generally be charged conjunctively in one count of the indictment.[5]

An indictment based on a statute must contain forms of expression and descriptive words contained therein to bring the offence

the constituents of the offence, the indictment must state it according to its legal, and sometimes its actual, particulars." 1 Bish. Cr. Proc. § 373; Titus *v.* State, 49 N. J. L. (20 Vr.) 36; s. c., 5 Cent. Rep. 816.

An Indictment for Manslaughter by Culpable Negligence in the construction of a building, under N. Y. Penal Code, secs. 193-195, which substantially complies with the provisions of the sections, and with sec. 284 of the Code Criminal Procedure, is sufficient. People *v.* Buddensiek, 103 N. Y. 487; s. c., 4 Cent. Rep. 787.

1. Tilly *v.* State, 21 Fla. 242; Baysinger *v.* People, 115 Ill. 419; s. c., 2 West. Rep. 839; Commonwealth *v.* Dyer, 128 Mass. 70; State *v.* Jones, 33 Vt. 443; State *v.* Cook, 38 Vt. 439; Reg. *v.* Rowlands, 5 Cox C. C. 437; 1 Whart. Cr. L. § 364.

Other Words of Equivalent Meaning to these employed by the statute may be used. Franklin *v.* State, 108 Ind. 47; s. c., 6 West. Rep. 270, 271; State *v.* Anderson, 103 Ind. 170; s. c., 1 West. Rep. 175; State *v.* Ah Sam, 14 Oreg. 348; State *v.* McGaffin, 36 Kan. 315.

The Supreme Court of Indiana say that it is well settled that an indictment or information will be upheld if it uses words of equivalent meaning to those employed by the statute in defining the offence. Henning *v.* State, 106 Ind. 386; Riggs *v.* State, 104 Ind. 261; State *v.* Anderson, 103 Ind. 170; s. c, 1 West. Rep. 175.

The word "feloniously" is used instead of the word "unlawful," and it is a word of much more force and more comprehensive meaning than the word "unlawful." Shinn *v.* State, 68 Ind. 423; Hays *v.* State, 77 Ind. 450; Franklin *v.* State, 47 Ind. 47; s. c., 6 West. Rep. 270; Whart. Cr. Pl. & Pr. § 269.

2. Plum *v.* Studebaker Bros., 89 Mo. 162; s. c., 4 West. Rep. 646.

An Indictment for Obstruction of Highway, good at common law, will be upheld, although it is not within the express terms of the statute. State *v.* Turner, 21 Mo. App. 324; s. c., 4 West. Rep. 259.

"**Burglariously.**" — In an indictment under chapter 3463, Florida Laws 1883, it is not necessary to charge that the entry was "burglariously," nor is it necessary to allege the ownership of the building in any particular individual. The crime is a statutory one. Tilly *v.* State, 21 Fla. 242.

The Illustrated Police News and The Police Gazette are publications specially enumerated in the Texas statute (Art. 4675, Gen. Laws, 17 Leg. Special Sess. p. 18) as among those the sale of which cannot be pursued as an occupation, without the payment of the tax levied therefor; and it was not necessary that the indictment should further describe them than by name. Baldwin *v.* State, 21 Tex. App. 591.

The Texas Penal Code, Art. 756, requiring dealers in cattle to make report of all animals slaughtered, those raised, and those purchased, an indictment charging that defendant failed to make report of all animals purchased and slaughtered, is sufficient. Kinney *v.* State. 21 Tex. App. 348.

3. State *v.* Philbin, 38 La. An. 964.

4. State *v.* Gabriel, 88 Mo. 631; s. c., 5 West. Rep. 340.

The rule is, that, where the indictment is based upon a statute creating the offence, an offence unknown to the common law, the indictment must set forth all the constituent facts and circumstances necessary to bring the accused perfectly within the statutory provisions. People *v.* Allen, 5 Denio (N. Y.), 76; Hall *v.* State, 3 Coldw. (Tenn.) 125; State *v.* Gabriel, 88 Mo. 631; s. c., 5 West. Rep. 340; Bish. Stat. Cr. §§ 418, 421, 422; 1 Arch. Cr. Pr. p. 68, note 1.

5. State *v.* Wood, 14 R. I. 151. See State *v.* Colwell, 3 R. I. 284.

precisely within the definition. A less degree of precision is required where descriptive words are not used. When words of equivalent import may make the charge certain, it will be sufficient.[1]

(2) *Negativing Provisions and Exceptions.* — An indictment need not negative an exception contained in the statute, unless such exception be necessary to a complete definition of the offence,[2] because negative averments are not required unless an exception is made in the enactment clause.[3]

Exceptions not so incorporated with the clause defining a statutory offence as to become a material part of the definition of the offence, is matter of defence, and need not be negatived in the indictment.[4] If the statute forbids the doing of an act without the

1. State *v.* Emerich, 87 Mo. 110; s. c., 1 West. Rep. 760.

2. Territory *v.* Burns, 6 Mont. Ter. 72.

According to Chitty, when a statute contains provisions and exceptions in distinct clauses, it is not necessary to state in the indictment that the defendant does not come within the exceptions, or to negative the provisions it contains. 1 Chit. Cr. L. 283 b, 284. See also Whitwicke *v.* Osbaston, 1 Lev. 26; Wade *v.* Ripton, 1 Sid. 303; Southwell's Case, Poph. 93, 94; Rex *v.* Jarvis, 1 Bur. 148; Rex *v.* Pemberton, 2 Burr. 1037; s. c., 1 W. Bl. 230; 3 Barn. & Cres. 135; Rex *v.* Bryan, 2 Str. 1101; Rex *v.* Stone, 1 East, 646, and notes; Rex *v.* Baxter, 5 T. R. 83; 1 Hale, P. C. 171; 2 Hawk. P. C. 25, § 112; Bac. Abr. tit. "Indictment," H 2; Burn. Jur. tit. "Indictment," IX.; 1 Chit. Pl. (4th ed.) 322.

Neither is it necessary to allege that he is not within the benefit of its provisos, though the purview should expressly notice them, as by saying that none shall do the act prohibited, except in the cases therein enumerated. Wells *v.* Iggulden, 3 Barn. & Cres. 186; Steel *v.* Smith, 1 Barn. & Ald. 94; Southwell's Case, Poph. 93, 94; 2 Hawk. P C. chap. 25, § 113.

The reason is, all these are matters of defence, which the prosecutor need not anticipate, because they are more properly to come from the prisoner. Rex *v.* Baxter, 5 T. R. 83; Rex *v.* Pemberton, 1 W. Bl. 230; s. c., 2 Bur. 1037; 2 Hawk. P. C. chap. 25, § 113.

3. State *v.* Duggan (R. I.), Index Z, 17; s. c., 3 New Eng. Rep. 137; State *v.* Rush, 13 R. I. 198; State *v.* O'Donnell, 10 R. I. 472.

The Rule of pleading a Statute containing an exception or a proviso is usually expressed in the text-books as follows: namely, "If there is an exception in the enacting clause, the party pleading must show that his adversary is not within the exception; but if there be an exception in a subsequent clause or a subsequent statute, that is matter of defence, and is to be shown by the other party." See 1 Ben. & H. Lead. Cas. 255, 256; 8 Am. Jur. 234.

Bishop says, that "while this rule is a correct one as applied in most circumstances, it is not of universal application; or, at least, it is not full enough to furnish a universal guide." 1 Bish. Cr. Proc. 384, § 635.

It is laid down as a general rule, that "when an indictment is drawn upon a statute, the pleader must keep reasonably near to the words of the statute, or there will be a variance," and the indictment therefore defective. See State *v.* Keen, 34 Me. 500; State *v.* Wade, 34 N. H. 495; State *v.* Abbey, 29 Vt. 60, 66.

The Indiana Rev. Stat. 1881, sec. 2066, declares the doing of any one of a number of distinct and separate acts a crime, to which precisely the same punishment is affixed. The doing of any one or more of the prohibited acts by the same person, at the same time, constitutes but a single offence, which may be charged in the same count of an indictment, without subjecting it to the imputation of duplicity. Thus the indictment need not negative the exception contained in the proviso, authorizing towns and cities to enact ordinances to protect the public health. Mergentheim *v.* State, 107 Ind. 567; s c., 5 West. Rep. 851.

4. State *v.* Elam, 21 Mo. App. 290; s. c., 3 West. Rep. 787; 1 Ben. & H. Lead. Cas. 255, 256; 8 Am. Jur. 234.

Negativing Exceptions. — Thus, where a statute providing that a person "shall not, except" under circumstances named, do a certain thing, as to work on the Lord's Day, — State *v* Barker, 18 Vt. 195, — or selling liquor on such day, — Commonwealth *v.* Maxwell, 19 Mass. (2 Pick.) 139, — or selling liquors without a license, — see Elkins *v.* State, 13 Ga 435; Brutton *v.* State, 4 Ind. 601; Kinser *v* State, 9 Ind. 543; Howe *v.* State, 10 Ind. 423; Rex *v.* Palmer, 1 Leach authority of one of two things, the indictment must negative the existence of both. Exceptions in the enactment clause must be negatived in the indictment, but an exception in a subsequent clause, or subsequent statute, is matter of defence.[1] When a proviso to a statute attaches a qualification or limitation by which particular cases are excepted from the operation of the enactment, it is not necessary that an indictment under the statute shall negative the proviso; but, when the proviso makes the existence of any fact an essential element of the offence, or necessary to a conviction under it, the indictment must allege the existence of the fact.[2]

It is a general rule recognized by all courts, that no indictment is sufficient which alleges an act or omission in itself innocent, unless it proceed to disclose circumstances which render such act or omission illegal.[3]

f. Counts. — An indictment very frequently contains more than one count or charge. The object of the insertion of more than one count is either to charge the defendant with different offences, or with a previous conviction; or to describe the single offence in other terms, so that, proof of one description failing, he may be convicted under another.[4]

It is a general rule, that more than one offence cannot be charged in the same count; that is, a count must not be double, or is bad for duplicity. Thus, one count cannot charge the prisoner with having committed a murder and a robbery.[5]

(4th ed.), 102; 1 East, P. C. 166, 167, — when the indictment omits to negative the exception, it will be bad. See 1 Bishop's Cr. Proc. § 636.

1. Jefferson *v.* People, 101 N. Y. 19; s. c., 1 Cent. Rep. 719. See also 1 Ben. & H. Lead. Cas. 234.

2. Smith *v.* State, 81 Ala. 74.

3. 1 Stark. Cr. Pl. (2d ed.) 171; 1 Bishop, Cr. Proc. (2d ed.) 637.

But it is sometimes necessary to allege a negative in order to show affirmatively a *prima facie* case of an offence committed. See Crandall *v.* State, 10 Conn. 339; Mills *v.* Kennedy, 1 Bailey (S. C.), L. 17; 1 Bishop, Cr. Proc. (2d ed.) § 637. But see Steel *v.* Smith, 1 Barn. & Ald. 94.

4. Thus, an indictment for wounding generally contains a count for doing grievous bodily harm. Again, an indictment for obtaining goods by false pretences must state the false pretence correctly. Therefore, in order to prevent a failure of justice in consequence of the false pretence not being properly stated, it is often necessary to insert different counts laying the pretence in different ways. The different counts are tacked on by the insertion of "and the jurors aforesaid, upon their oath aforesaid, do say that," etc. Harris, Cr. L. 342-3.

5. **Exceptions to the Rule.** — There are two exceptions to the rule: an indictment for burglary usually charges the defendant with having broken and entered the house with intent to commit a felony, and also with having committed the felony intended. And in indictments for embezzlement by clerks, or servants, or persons employed in the public service, or in the police, the prosecution may charge any number of distinct acts of embezzlement, not exceeding three, which may have been committed against the same master within six months inclusive; but even here it is usual to charge the different acts in different counts. Harris, Cr. L. 343. But this matter is subject of statutory regulation in most of the States.

Rules as to charging Offences. — The rules as to charging a defendant with different offences in different counts of the same indictment are as follows: —

In Treason. — In an indictment for *treason*, there may be different counts, each charging the defendant with different species of treason; for example, compassing the queen's death, levying war, etc.

In an Indictment for Felony, there is no objection in point of *law* to charging several different felonies in different counts, whether such felonies be of a different *g. Duplicity.* — Charging two or more distinct offences in the same count of an indictment is denominated "duplicity," which is defined as "multiplicity of distinct matter to one and the same thing, whereunto several answers are required;" [1] also as "alleging for one single purpose or object two or more distinct grounds of complaint or defence, when one of them would be as effectual in law, or both, or all." [2]

Duplicity in criminal pleading is bad. Two or more distinct offences should in no instances be joined in one count of an indictment.[3]

character, or distinct cases of the same sort of felony; for example, whether they be a burglary and a murder, or two cases of murder. But in *practice*, as this course would embarrass the prisoner in his defence, it is not adopted; and it will be ground for quashing the indictment, though not for demurrer or arrest of judgment. If it is discovered, before the jury are charged, that it has been done, the judge may quash the indictment; if after, he may put the prosecutor to his election on which charge he will proceed. The same felony may, however, be charged in different ways in different counts; as, if there is a doubt whether the goods stolen are the property of A. or of B., they may be stated in one count as the goods of A., in another as the goods of B. There are certain exceptions to the rule forbidding the charging of distinct felonies in different counts. In an indictment for feloniously stealing any property, it is expressly declared lawful to add a count or several counts for feloniously receiving the same property, knowing it to have been stolen, and *vice versa;* and the prosecutor is not put to any election, but the jury may find a verdict of guilty on either count, against all or any of the persons charged. Also, in an indictment for larceny, it is lawful to insert several counts against the same person for any number of distinct acts of stealing, not exceeding three, which may have been committed by him against the same person within the space of six calendar months from the first to the last of such acts, and to proceed thereon for all or any of them. We have already noticed a similar rule with regard to embezzlement. Harris, Cr. L. 272, 273.

Joinder of a Felony and Misdemeanor. — If a count for a felony is joined with a count for a misdemeanor, the indictment will be held bad if demurred to, or judgment may be arrested if the verdict has been general (i.e., guilty, or not guilty on the whole indictment), but not if the prisoner is convicted of the felony alone. R. *v.* Ferguson, 24 L. J. (M. C.) 61.

Charging Different Misdemeanors in Different Counts. — An indictment for misdemeanor may contain several counts for different offences, even though the judgments upon each be different, so that the legal character of the substantive offences charged be the same. Young *v.* R., 3 T. R. 105. Thus, evidence of several assaults or several libels will be received on the several counts of the same indictment. But there are limits, not precisely defined, to this rule; when convenience and justice demand it, the judge compelling the prosecution to elect upon which charge they will proceed. In all cases of this character, the important consideration is, whether all the acts were substantially one transaction.

Previous Conviction, when a Count for. — In certain cases if the prisoner has been previously convicted, a count is inserted in the indictment charging him with such previous conviction. He will have to plead to this, and proof may be given, if he denies it, as on any other count. The object of putting in this count is, that the prisoner may have his identity with the person so previously convicted proved before the severer punishment consequent on a previous conviction is awarded. The cases in which such a count may be inserted are indictments for (1) felonies (not misdemeanors) mentioned in the Larceny Act, or (2) for offences under the Coinage Act, provided that the previous conviction be for some offence against that or some other Coinage Act. Harris, Cr. L. 343, 344.

1. 1 Bouv. L. Dict. (15th ed.) tit. "Duplicity."

2. See 1 Bish. Cr. L. (3d ed.) § 432; Gould, Pl. c 8, § 1.

3. Gahagin *v.* State, 17 Fla. 665; State *v.* Shields, 8 Blackf. (Ind.) 151; Knopf *v.* State, 84 Ind. 316; s. c., 17 West. Jur. 33; State *v.* Weil, 89 Ind. 286; State *v.* McPherson, 9 Iowa, 53; State *v.* Stauderman, 6 La. An. 286; State *v.* Taylor (La.), 17 Rep. 788; State *v.* Palmer, 35 Me. 9; Commonwealth *v.* Symonds, 2 Mass. 163; State *v.* Nelson, 8 N. H. 163; Morse *v.* Eaton, 23 N. H. 415; State *v.* Fowler, 28 N. H. 184; People *v.* Wright, 9 Wend. (N. Y.) 193; Reed *v.* People, 1 Park. Cr. R. (N. Y.) 481; Hutchinson *v.* Commonwealth, 82 Pa. St.

h. Joinder of Offences. — There is no objection, in point of law, to the joinder in one count of several distinct felonies of the same degree, though committed at different times; and such joinder will not be ground either for demurrer or arrest of judgment.[1] However, two or more misdemeanors may be joined in the same indictment, although they arise out of separate and distinct transactions.[2]

472; Commonwealth *v.* Bartilson, 85 Pa. St. 487; Fulmer *v.* Commonwealth, 97 Pa. St. 503; s. c., 10 W. N. C. 437; Commonwealth *v.* Schaub (Pa.), 16 Chic. L. News, 204; Greenlow *v.* State, 4 Humph. (Tenn.) 25; Davis *v.* State, 3 Coldw. (Tenn.) 77; Womack *v.* State, 7 Coldw. (Tenn.) 508; Weathersby *v.* State, 1 Tex. App. 643; United States *v.* Sharp, 1 Pet. C. C. 131.

Joinder of Offences. — But there may be a joinder of several offences of the same class or kind, growing out of the same transaction, though committed at different times, if set out in several distinct counts; and such joinder is not ground for demurrer or arrest of judgment. United States *v.* Wentworth, 11 Fed. Rep. 52; United States *v.* O'Callahan, 6 McL. C. C. 596.

It has been held that an indictment is not objectionable for duplicity, because it charges the accused with having sent a "false writing and affidavit," if the context clearly shows the meaning to be that the accused sent a single false instrument, described as "a writing and affidavit," not that he sent a false writing and a false affidavit. United States *v.* Corbin, 11 Fed. Rep. 238.

Each Count of an indictment, it has been said, charges a distinct and separate offence in judgment of law, and is, in fact and theory, a separate indictment. Consequently, where a prisoner is charged in two separate counts with having two different stills at different times on the same day, and at the same place, he may be acquitted on one count, and convicted on the other. United States *v* Malone, 2 Blatchf. C. C. 137; s. c., 9 Fed. Rep. 879; 13 Rep. 67.

But Counts of Different Classes cannot be joined in the same count. Thus, it has been *held* that counts for conspiracy cannot be joined with counts to murder. United States *v.* Scott, 4 Biss. C. C. 29 See Spies *v.* People, 122 Ill. 1; s. c., 10 West. Rep. 701.

And where an indictment charged in the same count a capital offence and a misdemeanor, it was quashed. United States *v.* Sharp, 1 Pet. C. C. 131. So also where, in an indictment for forgery, two distinct offences, requiring different punishment, are joined in the same count; as where the forging of a mortgage, and of a receipt indorsed thereon, are both charged in the same count, and the defendant is convicted, the judgment will be arrested. People *v.* Wright, 9 Wend. (N. Y.) 193. But see People *v.* Stearns, 21 Wend. (N. Y.) 409.

Joinder of Misdemeanors. — But the joinder of several distinct misdemeanors in the same indictment is not a cause for a reversal of judgment thereon, on writ of error, when the sentence is single, and is appropriate to either of the counts upon which the conviction is had. Polinsky *v.* People, 73 N. Y. 72.

Exceptions. — However, there are exceptions to this general rule. Thus, where the indictment charges the defendant with an offence which in its nature includes several smaller ones, it is not multifarious; as a murder for murder which includes manslaughter, a battery and an assault; or in an indictment for manslaughter which includes a full and technical charge of an assault and battery. Commonwealth *v.* Harney, 51 Mass. (10 Metc.) 422-425; 1 Bish. Cr. Proc. 190.

1. 1 Chit. Cr. L. 253; 2 Colby, Cr. L. 121.

However, not more than one distinct offence or criminal transaction should regularly be charged upon the prisoner in one indictment, because, if that should be shown to the court before plea, they would quash the indictment, lest it confound the prisoner in his defence. Should the fact not be discovered until after plea, the court may, in its discretion, require the prosecutor to elect upon which he will proceed. This, however, is merely a matter of prudence and discretion resting entirely with the trial judge. 1 Chit. Cr. L. 253; 1 Colb. Cr. L. 362.

The Practice is, in indictments for felonies, to include but one transaction in a single indictment, and, if two or more distinct offences are contained in the same indictment, either to quash it, or compel the prosecutor to elect on which charge he will proceed. Whart. Cr L. (5th ed.) 416-422; 1 Bish. Cr. Proc. 201.

However, where it appears, on the opening of the case, and on the trial of the prisoner, that there is no more than one criminal transaction involved, and that the joinder of the different counts is only meant to meet the various aspects in which the evidence may present itself, the court will not restrict the prosecutor to particular counts, and will suffer a general verdict to be taken on the whole. People *v.* Austen, 1 Park. Cr. R. (N. Y.) 154.

2. 1 Chit. Cr. L. 254; Rex *v.* Jones, 2 Camp. 133.

i. The Conclusion. — Each count of an indictment must conclude, "against the peace and dignity of the State," or it will be defective.[1] But an error in the form of the conclusion is not now material, inasmuch as it has been enacted that no indictment shall be held insufficient for the omission of the words "against the peace," nor for the insertion of the words, "against the form of the statute," instead of "against the form of the statutes," or *vice versa;* nor for want of a proper or formal conclusion.[2]

j. The Signature. — To render an indictment valid, it must be signed by the prosecuting attorney.[3] If the name of the prosecuting attorney be legibly attached, it is a sufficient signing of the indictment; and when appended to an indictment, the presumption is that it was by his authority.[4] If the name of the prosecutor is written on the indictment with his knowledge or consent, it is sufficient.[5] And the deputy appointed by a prosecuting attorney may sign the indictment.[6]

An information, though filed by the prosecuting attorney, if not verified as required by statute, cannot be prosecuted.[7]

k. The Indorsement. — Every indictment should be indorsed by the foreman of the grand jury which found it; and an indictment

1. Williams *v.* State, 47 Ark. 230.

Allegations in the Conclusion of an indictment beyond the words "against the peace, government, and dignity of the State," are immaterial, and may be rejected as surplusage. Richardson *v.* State (Md.), 5 Cent. Rep. 765; Rex *v.* Horne, Cowp. 672; Rawlings *v.* State, 2 Md. 251.

2. Harris, Cr. L. 341.

Yet it has been held that where two counts charge the same crime, one ending with, and the other without, the words "contrary to the form, force, etc., and against the peace," the defective count may be amended by adding the words prescribed by the Constitution. State *v.* Amadon, 58 Vt. 524; s. c., 1 New Eng. Rep. 355.

3. **Substantial Rights of Defendant.** — Whether failure of the prosecuting attorney to sign the indictment tends to prejudice substantial rights of the defendant, under the Indiana Rev. Stat. 1881, § 1756, is an open question. Hamilton *v.* State, 102 Ind. 96; 1 West. Rep. 146, 147; Heacock *v.* State, 42 Ind. 393; Dukes *v.* State, 11 Ind 557.

4. Hamilton *v.* State, 102 Ind. 96; s. c., 1 West. Rep. 146.

A complaint charging an unlawful sale of intoxicating liquors is not sufficient for the reason that the person making the same is described therein by his full Christian name, while it is signed with an initial. Commonwealth *v.* Intoxicating Liquors, 142 Mass. 470; s. c, 3 New Eng. Rep. 36.

The defendant in a criminal case produced written complaints, and, being a witness, testified that such complaints were signed by the prosecutor in his presence: the court refused to receive the same thus proved, and required the prosecutor in such complaints to be called to prove his own signature; such prosecutor was produced, and was a witness hostile to the defence. *Held,* error entitling the defendant to a reversal of the judgment. Lefferts *v.* State, 49 N. J. L. (20 Vr.) 26; s. c., 4 Cent. Rep. 883.

5. Parr *v.* State, 74 Ga. 406.

6. Hamilton *v.* State, 102 Ind. 96; s. c., 1 West. Rep. 147; Stout *v.* State, 93 Ind. 150; Ind Rev. Stat. 1881, §§ 5568, 5570.

In Missouri. — It is *held* in Missouri that an indictment signed by the assistant circuit attorney is a sufficient compliance with R. S. § 1798, requiring it should be signed by the circuit attorney. State *v.* Hayes, 88 Mo. 344; s. c., 2 West. Rep. 110.

7. State *v.* Calfee (Mo), 10 West. Rep. 272; State *v.* Haywood, 83 Mo. 303.

An Affidavit taken before the clerk of a court, who is *ex officio* clerk of the criminal court of the county, is sufficient. State *v.* Downing, 22 Mo. App. 504; s. c., 5 West. Rep. 64.

The Competency of a Witness, whose name is appended to the affidavit to the truth of the information, is a matter of judicial inquiry, and it is not necessary that he should state his competency, or that he had knowledge that an offence had been committed, where the affidavit is in positive terms, and not upon information and belief. State *v.* Downing, 22 Mo. App. 504; s. c., 5 West. Rep. 64.

not indorsed by the foreman of the grand jury, as required by the statute, is bad for want of such indorsement, on a motion to quash.[1] And where the indictment upon which appellant was tried and convicted was not indorsed by the foreman of the grand jury, the judgment must be reversed.[2]

The fact that the number of the indictment and the number of the case are different, is immaterial, where it affirmatively appears that the indictment set out in the transcript was returned into court, and defendant pleaded thereto.[3] And where, by inadvertence, the county attorney indorsed on a substituted information a different number than that by which the case was originally entered upon the docket, and the defence therefore objected to the substitute, *held*, that the mistake should have been corrected upon the motion of the county attorney, or by the trial court upon its own motion.[4] And an indictment indorsed on the back in printing with the words "A true bill," which indorsement is signed by the foreman of the grand jury as such foreman, it is a compliance with the statute in that respect.[5]

It is immaterial on what part of the bill the foreman's signature appears.[6] Error in the form of the indorsement of the indictment by the foreman of the grand jury, which could not have prejudiced the rights of the defendant, will be disregarded.[7]

A statute requiring a noting on the indictment of the names of the witnesses, is mandatory, and, if disregarded, it is sufficient to quash indictment; but the names of all witnesses need not be noted.[8] Thus, where an indictment had indorsed upon it the

1. Cooper *v.* State, 79 Ind. 206; State *v.* Bowman, 103 Ind. 69; s. c., 1 West. Rep. 138; Johnson *v.* State, 23 Ind. 32; Heacock *v.* State, 42 Ind. 393; Beard *v.* State, 57 Ind 8; Strange *v.* State, 110 Ind. 354; s. c., 8 West. Rep. 928; Ind. Rev. Stat., 1881, § 1669.

Omission of Clerk. — No exception to the omission of the clerk of the circuit court to put the usual file mark on an indictment which has been pleaded to, and of which the record shows due presentation by a grand jury in open court, can be raised primarily in the appellate court. Willingham *v.* State, 21 Fla. 761.

The Minutes of the Evidence upon which an indictment is found are sufficiently filed with the clerk, under Iowa Code, § 4293, when they are handed to him, and he receives them to be kept on file in his office. The indorsement of the filing by the clerk, although proper, is not necessary. State *v.* Briggs, 68 Iowa, 416.

It is not necessary to indorse a verdict upon an indictment at all; and if indorsed upon a wrong indictment, judgment may nevertheless be entered upon the one on which the trial was had. O'Bryan *v.* State, 48 Ark. 42.

2. Strange *v.* State, 110 Ind. 354; s. c., 8 West. Rep. 928.

Iowa Code; Private Prosecution; Duty of Grand Jury. — Section 4292 of the Iowa Code, requiring the grand jury, when an indictment is found at the instance of a private prosecutor, to indorse that fact on the indictment, is directory merely, and such indorsement is not essential to the validity of the indictment. State *v.* Briggs, 68 Iowa, 416.

3. Mergentheim *v.* State, 101 Ind. 567; s. c., 5 West. Rep. 851.

4. Stiff *v.* State, 21 Tex. App. 255.

5. Tilly *v.* State, 21 Fla. 242.

6. State *v.* Bowman, 103 Ind. 69; s. c., 1 West. Rep. 138; 1 Bish. Cr. Proc. (3d ed.) § 698.

7. Thus, where the foreman signed above the words, "A true bill," and not the bill with the words "Foreman," the indorsement is sufficient on a motion to quash the indictment. State *v.* Bowman, 103 Ind. 69; s. c., 1 West. Rep. 138; Johnson *v.* State, 23 Ind. 32; Heacock *v.* State, 42 Ind. 363; Cooper *v.* State, 79 Ind. 272.

8. Andrews *v.* People, 117 Ill. 195; s. c., 4 West. Rep. 139. *Vide infra*, III. 2, i.; and IV., 1.

names of three witnesses, the presumption must be indulged, that it was found upon their evidence, and that the grand jury, in making the indorsement, complied with the mandate of the statute.[1]

l. Return of the Grand Jury.—Indictments found by a grand jury should be presented to the court by their foreman, in their presence, and are filed, and remain as public records.[2]

A return by the grand jury, "at true bill," is sufficient.[3]

The record showing that the grand jury came into open court, and, through their foreman, returned an indictment, etc., it is a full compliance with the statute.[4]

Under Mo. R. S. § 1802, if the grand jury fail to indorse on the indictment the names of the witnesses on whose evidence the same was found, it will be a good ground for a motion to quash. State *v.* O'Day, 89 Mo. 559; s c., 6 West. Rep. 449.

Determining Identity.—Where the name of "Mrs. H." was indorsed on the indictment as one of the witnesses, and the State on the trial offered "Mrs. Mary E. H." as a witness, and it was objected that her name was not indorsed on the indictment, *held*, that it was the duty of the court to determine whether "Mrs. H." and "Mrs. Mary E. H." were the same person, and that, in so doing, it was competent to consult, not the indorsement upon the indictment, but the minutes of the evidence; and, further, that, since the court overruled the objection, it must be presumed that it did consult such minutes, and therein found sufficient evidence. State *v.* Briggs, 68 Iowa, 416. Code, § 4293.

1. State *v.* O'Day, 89 Mo. 559; s. c., 6 West. Rep. 449.

2. Barb. Cr. L. 317.

But where an indictment is found against a person for a felony where he is not in actual confinement, it is not open to the inspection of any one except the district or prosecuting attorney, until the defendant therein has been arrested. 2 N. Y. Rev. Stat. §§ 39, 40.

3. Epps *v.* State, 102 Ind. 539; s. c., 3 West. Rep. 380.

Indictment not returned by Grand Jury.—A special plea which alleged that the indictment was never returned in the court by the grand jury, but was brought in by their bailiff and handed to the clerk, who thereupon entered it on the minutes of the court, at which time none of the grand jurors were present, but which did not allege that the bailiff making the return was not the duly qualified officer of the grand jury, sworn in accordance with law or that the indictment was tampered with or altered in any respect, or that, in consequence thereof, the accused suffered injury or detriment, was *held* demurrable, and properly stricken out by the court. The history and reason of the manner of returning indictments is discussed in Danforth *v.* State, 75 Ga. 614.

A special plea to the effect that the indictment was improperly delivered to the court, being brought into the court by the bailiff of the grand jury, but not alleging that it had been tampered with, or was out of the bailiff's hands from the time he left the grand jury room until he delivered it to the court, or that there was any improper conduct on his part, has been properly stricken out on demurrer. Davis *v.* State, 74 Ga. 869.

Where the indictment itself states that the grand jury was duly impanelled, sworn and charged, the record sufficiently discloses that it was lawfully impanelled. Walter *v.* State, 105 Ind. 589; s. c., 2 West. Rep. 759, 760; Alley *v.* State, 32 Ind. 476; Powers *v.* State, 87 Ind. 144; Stout *v.* State, 93 Ind. 150; Epps *v.* State, 102 Ind. 539; Padgett *v.* State, 103 Ind. 550; s. c., 1 West. Rep. 584.

An indictment is good which purports to be found by the grand jurors "upon their oath or affirmation," some of whom affirmed. State *v.* Adams, 78 Me. 486; s. c, 3 New Eng. Rep. 243, 244; Lincoln *v.* Taunt. Cop. Mfg. Co., 65 Mass. (11 Cush.) 440; Horne *v.* Haverhill, 113 Mass. 344.

Information for a Felony cannot be lodged against a defendant at a term of court to which he has been recognized to appear after discharge of the grand jury without finding an indictment. State *v.* Boswell, 104 Ind. 541; s. c., 2 West. Rep. 726.

He may be again arrested, a preliminary examination may be again had, and he be placed under recognizance. State *v.* Boswell, 104 Ind. 541; s. c., 2 West. Rep. 726.

4. Rev. Stat. 1879, sec. 1797. State *v.* Payton, 90 Mo. 220; s. c., 7 West. Rep. 129.

A failure of the record to show the return is not ground for motion in arrest of judgment where the cause assigned is that the facts do not constitute the offence.[1]

IV. Process and Appearance. — The grand jury having found a true bill, process is issued to compel the attendance of the accused to answer the charge. This is not required if he is already in custody, or surrenders to his bail: in such case he may be tried as soon as is convenient. If he is in custody of another court for some other offence, the course is to remove him by a writ of *habeas corpus*, and bring him up to plead.[2]

If, however, an indictment has been found in the absence of the accused, he having fled or secreted himself so as to avoid the warrant of arrest, or has not been bound over to appear at the session of the court in which the indictment is found, then process must issue to bring him into court. This process in ordinary cases is regulated by statute in the various States of the Union. In most, if not all, of the States, when an indictment or information is filed, a warrant issues from the court in which it is filed, unless the defendant is already in arrest on bail.[3] From and after the return day of a served writ,[4] such defendant is held to be continuously present in court, till final disposition of the prosecution.

Another mode of proceeding is, for the court before whom the indictment is found to issue a bench warrant for the arrest of the accused, and to bring him immediately before such court.

Process on informations is similar to that on indictments.

The appearance of the accused having been enforced in this way, or voluntarily made, the next step is to arraign him. After arraignment, and before plea, the defendant makes any objections which he may have to the form of the indictment, the constitution or conduct of the jury finding the indictment, and the like.

V. Arraignment[5] and Plea. — The arraignment, or requiring the prisoner to answer to the charge of an indictable offence, consists of three parts: (1) calling the prisoner to the bar by name; (2) reading the indictment to him; (3) asking him whether he is guilty or not of the offence charged.[6] If several defendants are charged in the same indictment, they ought all to be arraigned at

1. Padgett *v.* People, 103 Ind. 550; s. c., 1 West. Rep. 584; followed in Walter *v.* State, 105 Ind. 589; s. c., 2 West. Rep. 760.

2. Harris, Cr. L. 361.

3. In Kentucky, in cases of misdemeanor, a summons issues, unless the court orders a warrant. (Criminal Code, sect. 148.)

Process on Corporation. — In Ohio (74 Ohio L. 337) and Iowa (Rev. Stat. 1877, p. 672) a corporation is brought into court by summons.

4. In Iowa, from and after two days after service.

5. *Ad rationem; ad reson; a resu.*

6. The former practice of requiring him to hold up his hand for the purpose of identification is now generally disused, unless it be adopted in order to distinguish between two or more prisoners who are being arraigned at the same time. Nor is the prisoner now asked how he will be tried, it being taken for granted that he will be tried by a jury. He is to be brought to the bar without irons, or any manner of shackles or bonds, unless there is evident danger of escape, or other good cause. In felonies he must be placed at the bar of the court, though in misdemeanors this does not seem necessary. See R. *v.* Lovett, 9 Carr. & P. 462; Harris, Cr. L. 370, 371.

the same time. It is usual, for convenience' sake, to arraign several prisoners immediately in succession, and then to proceed to the trial of one, the rest being put down for the time.[1]

The indictment having been read to the prisoner, the clerk, or other proper officer of the court, demands of him whether he is "guilty or not guilty?" Thereupon the prisoner will either (1) move to quash the indictment, (2) demur to the indictment, (3) stand mute, (4) confess by saying that he is guilty, or (5) he will plead to the indictment.

An arraignment and plea are essential and necessary preliminaries to a legal trial upon an indictment;[2] and the record must show that the defendant was arraigned,[3] or that he waived it, and that a plea was entered for him.[4]

The record failing to show arraignment or waiver or plea, or that a plea was entered by or for him,[5] the judgment will be reversed.[6]

1. Harris, Cr. L. 371.

2. People *v.* Bradner, 107 N. Y.; s. c., 9 Cent. Rep. 172; 4 Bl. Com. 322; Bishop, Cr. Proc. § 684; 3 Wharton, Cr. L. § 3154.

A Verdict in a case where there has been neither arraignment nor plea is a nullity (Schoeffler *v.* State, 3 Wis. 823; People *v.* Corbett, 28 Cal. 328; People *v.* Gaines, 52 Cal. 479; Graeter *v.* State, 54 Ind. 159; Grigg *v.* People, 31 Mich. 471; Anderson *v.* State, 3 Pin. (Wis.) 367; State *v.* Saunders, 53 Mo. 234; 1 Tex. App. 408. *Contra*, State *v.* Cassady, 12 Kan. 550, and the **Judgment** rendered thereon is invalid. State *v.* West, 84 Mo. 440.

Separate Arraignment; Joint Trial; Judgment. — Where defendants were separately arraigned, although tried together, the verdict is a separate finding as to each; and judgment may be affirmed as to one, and reversed as to the other. State *v.* Stair, 87 Mo. 268; s. c., 1 West. Rep. 765.

Indiana Practice. — Although no statute of the State requires either an arraignment or a plea in a criminal case, before a justice of the peace, yet the proper practice requires defendant to enter a plea to the charge. Johns *v.* State, 104 Ind. 257; s. c., 2 West. Rep. 276.

Texas Practice. — The record entry of the arraignment of the defendant, conforming substantially to No. 685 of Willson's Criminal Forms, is sufficient that the indictment was read to the defendant before he was required to plead to it, and this constitutes an arraignment. Smith *v.* State, 21 Tex. App. 277.

3. Hanson *v.* State, 43 Ohio St. 376; s. c., 1 West. Rep. 331; Steagard *v.* State (Tex. App.), Dec. 1886.

4. Hicks *v.* State, 111 Ind. 402; s. c., 10 West. Rep. 261; Steagard *v.* State (Tex. App.), Dec. 1886.

5. Hicks *v.* State, and Steagard *v.* State, *supra*.

6. Hicks *v.* State, 111 Ind. 402; s. c., 10 West. Rep. 261; Bowen *v.* State, 108 Ind. 411; s. c., 6 West. Rep. 897; Shoffner *v.* State, 93 Ind. 519; Tindall *v.* State, 71 Ind. 314.

Where the record in a criminal cause fails to disclose affirmatively that a plea to the indictment was entered, either by or for the defendant, such record, on its face, shows a mis-trial, and that the proceedings were consequently erroneous. Hicks *v.* State, 111 Ind. 402; s. c., 10 West. Rep. 261; Bowen *v.* State, 108 Ind. 411; s. c., 6 West. Rep. 897; Johns *v.* State, 104 Ind. 557; s. c., 2 West. Rep. 276; Shoffner *v.* State, 93 Ind. 519; Tindall *v.* State, 71 Ind. 314; Fletcher *v.* State, 54 Ind. 462; Graeter *v.* State, 54 Ind. 159.

Arraignment in Misdemeanor. — In an action for a misdemeanor, where the record fails to show that defendant was arraigned for trial, judgment will be reversed. State *v.* Vanhook, 88 Mo. 105; s. c., 4 West. Rep. 423; State *v.* Jacques, 68 Mo. 260; State *v.* Saunders, 53 Mo. 234.

Arraignment in Felony. — A trial for forgery, had without arraignment or plea, is irregular; and a conviction and sentence must be set aside. Ray *v.* People, 6 Cal. 231.

Arson. — In a case where the defendants were prosecuted for the crime of arson by an information which alleged that the offence was committed on a day subsequent to the date of its filing, under which information they were arraigned, and pleaded not guilty; and, on the trial, the information was amended by charging the offence to have been committed prior to the filing of the information; and the trial thereupon proceeded without an arraignment or plea

If arraignment had been made in the place where the indictment was found, it need not be made at the place to which the trial is removed,[1] though a double arraignment would not be error.[2] When a defendant has been once arraigned, and has pleaded to an indictment on a former trial, re-arraignment is unnecessary.[3]

The arraignment in cases of felony must be by the defendant in person.[4] If the defendant, when arraigned, asks for and obtains time to plead, he waives any defect in the statutory details of the arraignment.[5] And where, after reading the indictment, the counsel for the accused causes it to be entered by the court, the plea of not guilty, it is a sufficient arraignment.[6]

Where the indictment was not read to the defendant, nor a copy of it, with the indorsements, delivered or tendered to him, nor was he then or thereafter asked to plead, there was no arraignment.[7] The defendant does not waive arraignment and plea by submitting to a trial introducing witnesses, and allowing the case to be argued on his behalf.[8] But an arraignment is not void because of the omission to inform defendant of his right to have counsel, if the court so informed him during the arraignment.[9]

1. *Motion to quash.* — At common law, a motion to quash was addressed to the discretion of the court;[10] and courts differed in their practice as to the cases in which the motion should be granted, and as to the stage of the procceding at which it could be presented.

It has been remarked that, "(1) in general, this motion could be properly presented as a speedy means of disposing of the indictment, where the indictment for defect in substance was bad on general demurrer; but where the indictment was for a grave offence, a motion made on this ground would be overruled, unless the defect were obviously clear; (2) where the indictment was defective in form, in which case the motion was a substitute for a

to the amended information, — the court *held* that the original information stated no offence, and that the trial under the amended information, without an arraignment and plea, was error, as no issue was joined. People *v.* Moody, 69 Cal. 184.

1. Davis *v.* State, 39 Md. 355; Vance *v.* Commonwealth, 2 Va. Cas. 162; Hayes *v.* State, 58 Ga. 35; Paris *v.* State, 36 Ala. 232.

2. Gardner *v.* People, 4 Ill. (3 Scam.) 83.

3. State *v.* Boyd, 36 La. An. 374.

Mis-trial. — After a mis-trial a re-arraignment is not necessary. Hayes *v.* State, 58 Ga. 35.

4. People *v.* Redinger, 55 Cal. 298.

5. People *v.* Lightner, 49 Cal. 226.

6. Bateman *v.* State, Miss. Jan. 1887.

7. People *v.* Corbett, 28 Cal. 328.

8. Schoeffler *v.* State, 3 Wis. 823; People *v.* Corbett, 28 Cal. 328; McQuillen *v.* State, 8 Smed. & M. (Miss.) 587.

9. People *v.* Villarins, 66 Cal. 228.

10. And to-day the question whether or not an indictment will be quashed, for the reason that different felonies are charged in different counts, is much in the discretion of the court. In no case should an indictment be quashed because of misjoinder, unless it clearly appears upon the face of the indictment that different and distinct crimes are charged. Different counts cannot be joined in the same indictment; and unless the prosecutor declines to elect, but manifests a purpose to insist upon a conviction upon each count, the indictment will not be quashed. Glover *v.* State, 109 Ind. 391; s. c., 7 West Rep. 565; Hamilton *v.* People, 29 Mich. 173; Rex *v.* Kingston, 8 East, 41; 1 Bish. Cr. Proc. 447.

special demurrer; (3) for fatal irregularity in the record other than the face of the indictment. (4) It was also allowed by some courts for irregularity in the proceedings not appearing on the record, in which case the motion filled the place of a plea in abatement. It must ordinarily be presented before issue joined, but was in a proper case allowed after issue joined.[1] In such case, it has been held by some courts, the plea should be withdrawn before the motion to quash can be received;"[2] but the practice in this country has been reduced to certainty in most States by statute.[3]

1. Commonwealth *v.* Chapman, 65 Mass. (11 Cush.) 422; Reg. *v.* Heane, 9 Cox, C.C. 433.

2. Nicholls *v.* State, 5 N. J. L. (2 South) 539.

3. Thus, by statutory provision,—

In Illinois, all exceptions which go merely to the form of an indictment, shall be made before trial; and no motion in arrest of judgment or writ of error shall be sustained, for any matter not affecting the real merits of the offence charged in the indictment. No indictment shall be quashed for the want of the words "with force of arms," or of the occupation or place of residence of the accused, nor by reason of the disqualification of any grand juror. Ill. Rev. Stat. 1877, p. 403.

In Indiana, the court may quash an indictment on motion when it appears upon its face either: (1) that the grand jury had no legal authority to inquire into the offence charged; (2) that the facts stated do not constitute a public offence; (3) that the indictment contains any matter which, if true, would constitute a legal justification of the offence charged, or (4) other legal bar to the prosecution. Ind. Rev. Stat. 1876, 399.

In Iowa, a "motion to set aside an indictment" made by the defendant must be sustained: 1. When the indictment is not indorsed "a true bill" by the foreman of the grand jury. 2. When the names of all the witnesses examined before the grand jury are not indorsed on the instrument; also, where the minutes of the evidence of the witnesses examined before the grand jury are not returned with it. 3. When it has not been presented and marked "filed" as prescribed by the code. 4. When any person other than the grand jurors was present before the grand jury when the question was taken upon the finding of the indictment, or when any person other than the grand jurors was present before the grand jury during the investigation of the charge, except as required or permitted by law. 5. That the grand jury were not selected, drawn, or summoned, impanelled, or sworn as prescribed by law. A motion made on the ground of error in the indorsement of the names of witnesses upon the indictment, will be overruled where the error or omission is corrected. Since all persons "bound over" by an examining magistrate after a preliminary hearing, have under the code the right to challenge the array of the grand jury, or any member of it, no such person is allowed to base his motion on the fifth ground above enumerated. Iowa Rev. Stat. 1873, p. 674.

In Kentucky, a "motion to set aside the indictment" can be made only on the following grounds: 1. A substantial error in the summoning or the formation of the grand jury. 2. That some person other than the grand jurors was present before the grand jury when they acted upon the indictment. 3. That the indictment was not found and presented as required by the code. Ky. Cr. Code, § 158.

In Michigan it is provided that no indictment shall be quashed (1) for the omission or misstatement of the occupation, estate, or degree of the defendant, or of the name of the city, township, or county of his residence; (2) for the omission of the word "feloniously," or of the words "with force and arms," or any words of similar import; (3) for omitting to charge any offence to have been committed contrary to the form of the statute or statutes; (4) for any other defect or imperfection in matters of form, which shall not tend to the prejudice of the defendant. See Mich. Rev. Stat. 1871, pp. 2169, 2170. The statute also provides that every objection to any indictment for any formal defect apparent on the face thereof shall be taken by motion to quash or demurrer before the jury shall be sworn; and the court may, if it be thought necessary, cause the indictment to be forthwith amended in any particular, and thereupon the trial shall proceed as if no defect had appeared. Ibid. p. 2172.

In Ohio, a motion to quash may be made in all cases when there is a defect apparent upon the face of the record, including defects in the form of the indictment, or in the manner in which the offence is charged.

But it may be laid down as a general rule, applicable alike in all the States, that a motion to quash and a demurrer precede the arraignment:[1] and a motion to quash must be made before plea;[2] it cannot be entertained after verdict.[3] And a motion to quash, if taken too late, is properly overruled.[4]

Where a motion to quash is made after plea, and too late to frame a new indictment, the motion must fail, unless the defects in the indictment would be clearly fatal after verdict.[5] Merely making out and filing a written application to set aside the indictment is not sufficient to constitute a motion: the attention of the court must be called to it, and the court be moved to grant it.[6]

A motion to quash does not have the effect of withdrawing the plea of not guilty at the special term, and a second arraignment is not necessary.[7]

An order setting aside an indictment is a final order, and appealable,[8] and it must be assigned for error;[9] but the general rule is, that the refusal of the lower court to quash an indictment on motion is not reviewable on error; and if such motion may be sustained, when it was shown that there was no evidence before the grand jury, the court may properly refuse to enter into an inquiry into the sufficiency of the evidence to sustain the finding.[10]

a. When granted. — Where the essential part of the offence is omitted, a motion to quash should be sustained.[11]

A plea in abatement may be made when there is a defect in the record which is shown by facts extrinsic thereto. The accused shall be taken to have waived all defects which may be excepted to by a motion to quash, or a plea in abatement, by demurring to the indictment, or pleading in bar or the general issue. 74 Ohio L. 341.

1. Epps *v.* State, 102 Ind. 539; s. c., 3 West. Rep. 380.

2. **Waiver of Error.** — A motion to set aside the indictment must be made before plea, or it will be deemed waived. Stacey *v.* People, 34 Cal. 308; People *v* Turner, 39 Cal. 377; People *v.* Johnston, 48 Cal. 550.

A failure to move to set aside the indictment is a waiver of any error which might have been reached by such motion. Haggard *v.* Commonwealth, 79 Ky. 366.

Objection to Grand Jury. — The objection to a grand juror, if made before plea, is made in time. State *v.* Haywood, 94 N. C. 847.

The Nolle Prosequi of a count destroys all basis for quashing the indictment for defects in that count. State *v.* Lockwood, 58 Vt. 378; s. c., 2 New Eng. Rep. 196.

3. State *v.* Barbee, 93 N. C. 498.

4. Commonwealth *v.* Hallahan, 143 Mass. 167; s. c., 3 New Eng. Rep. 308.

A merely formal objection cannot be taken for the first time in the superior court. Commonwealth *v.* Hersey, 144 Mass. 297; 3 New Eng. Rep. 515, 910; Commonwealth *v.* Keefe, 143 Mass. 467; s. c., 3 New Eng. Rep. 515.

They should be taken in the trial court. Commonwealth *v.* Hallahan, 143 Mass. 167; s. c., 3 New Eng. Rep. 300.

5. United States *v.* Bartow, 20 Blatchf. C. C. 349.

6. People *v.* Ah Sam, 41 Cal. 650.

7. State *v.* Bishop, 22 Mo. App. 435; s. c., 4 West. Rep. 793.

8. People *v.* Young, 31 Cal. 564.

9. Bowen *v.* State, 108 Ind. 411; s. c., 6 West. Rep. 897.

10. Bryant *v.* State, 79 Ala. 282.

11. State *v.* Jackson, 89 Mo. 561; s. c., 6 West. Rep 445.

Texas Code. — The Texas Code Crim. Proc. art. 523, enumerates but two grounds upon which an indictment can be set aside, the first being "that if it appears from the record of the court that the indictment was not found by at least nine of the grand jurors," and the second being "that some person not authorized by law was present when the grand jury were deliberating upon the accusation against the defendant, or were voting upon the same." Neither of those grounds covers the conditions of a case wherein the grand jury, voting originally to indict the defendant only for murder of the second or other degree, upon

A prosecution cannot be maintained on an affidavit alone. If no information is filed, the proceedings should be quashed.[1] And where the affidavit does not support the information, a motion to quash must be sustained.[2] A motion to quash an indictment which avers an impossible time of commission of the act, should be sustained.[3]

An indictment should be quashed where the defendant never had a preliminary examination, nor had he ever waived it, and the being advised by the district attorney and the regular district judge (not then presiding) that the offence of murder could be charged only in the first degree, voted to indict in the first degree. Johnson *v.* State, 22 Tex. App. 206.

An Indictment for obtaining Property under False Pretences was properly quashed, although both counts averred the falsity of the representations alleged to have been made by the defendant, and that the owner of the goods relied on such representations, believing them to be true, and was thereby deceived, where it was not even inferentially charged that it was by means of such false representations that the owner was induced to part with the possession of the goods some eighteen days after the false representations were so made and relied on. State *v.* Connor, 110 Ind. 469; s. c., 9 West. Rep. 226.

1. State *v.* First, 82 Ind. 81.

2. Dyer *v.* State, 85 Ind. 525.

The Affidavit and Information take the place of an indictment, and, in a certain generic sense, constitute the indictment. Their sufficiency may consequently be tested by either a motion to quash or a motion in arrest, under the same general rules which apply to indictments. Lindsey *v.* State, 72 Ind. 39; Hoover *v.* State, 110 Ind. 349; s. c., 9 West. Rep. 88.

3. Murphy *v.* State, 107 Ind. 598; s. c., 5 West. Rep 549, 741.

On a motion to quash where the indictment charges the offence to have been on a particular day, which date is anterior to the finding of the indictment, it is sufficient. People *v.* Littlefield, 5 Cal. 355; People *v.* Lafuente, 6 Cal. 202; U. S. *v.* Bowman, 2 Wash. C. C. 328; Commonwealth *v.* Dillane, 67 Mass. (1 Gray) 483; State *v.* Magrath, 19 Mo. 678; McBryde *v.* State, 34 Ga. 202; Cook *v.* State, 11 Ga. 53; Wingard *v.* State, 13 Ga. 396; McDade *v.* State, 20 Ala. 81; Shelton *v.* State, 1 Stew. & P. (Ala.) 208; Turner *v.* People, 33 Mich. 363; People *v.* Van Santvoord, 9 Cow. (N. Y.) 660; Wells *v.* Commonwealth, 78 Mass. (12 Gray) 326; State *v.* Woodman, 3 Hawks (N. C.), 384.

An indictment alleging an impossible date, as 18184, of an unlawful sale of liquors, should be quashed on motion. Murphy *v.* State, 107 Ind. 598; s. c., 3 West Rep. 741.

A motion to quash an indictment for selling less than a quart of intoxicating liquor without a license, averring impossible time as date of sale, should have been sustained, upon authority of Murphy *v.* State, 106 Ind. 96; s. c., 3 New Eng. Rep. 300, 3 West. Rep. 741; Murphy *v* State, 107 Ind. 598; s. c., 5 West. Rep. 549.

But if the day assigned be subsequent to the finding, the indictment is bad. State *v.* Noland, 29 Ind. 212; Commonwealth *v.* Doyle, 110 Mass. 103; Jacobs *v.* Commonwealth, 5 Serg. & R. (Pa.) 316; Joel *v.* State, 28 Texas, 642; State *v.* Fox, 15 Vt. 22; State *v.* Litch, 33 Vt. 67.

When time is important, courts will inquire into a day or fractional portion of a day. People *v.* Beatty, 14 Cal. 571.

The allegation of a day within a limitation is material when the offence is subject to limitation. People *v.* Miller, 12 Cal. 294.

In bigamy the date of the unlawful marriage is immaterial. State *v.* Hughes, 58 Iowa, 165.

An indictment charging keeping and selling liquors at a time and place stated, is not bad for omission to repeat the time in further allegation that defendant thereby maintained a nuisance. State *v.* Buck, 78 Me. 193; s. c., 1 New Eng. Rep. 903.

Indictment for cruelty to animals may allege a period of time instead of a single date, the offences involving continuous action. State *v.* Bosworth, 54 Conn. 1; s. c., 1 New Eng. Rep. 928.

Where an indictment charged defendant with having opened his saloon after nine o'clock in the "afternoon" instead of "evening," *held* immaterial. People *v.* Husted, 52 Mich. 624.

In an indictment for bribery, or for promise of benefit to influence official action, omission of the year is not fatal, time not being of the essence of the offence. State *v.* McDonald, 106 Ind. 233; s. c., 3 West. Rep. 752.

Where there are several counts, in the first of which the time and place are specially stated, it is sufficient to allege in the subsequent counts that the offence therein described was then and there committed. Fisk *v.* State, 9 Neb. 62.

witness had never signed his evidence given;[1] or, where the wife appeared before the grand jury against the husband;[2] or, where the grand jury received testimony of a person not under oath;[3] or, where a grand juror was falsely personated by another of the same surname.[4] And it is not error to quash an indictment for murder, where death resulted from an attempt to produce an abortion.[5]

Objection that names of all material witnesses for the State were not indorsed on indictment, should be made on motion to quash indictment.[6]

A motion to quash on the ground of the pendency of another information, is merely a plea in abatement, and must be supported by evidence.[7]

A complaint must allege facts, not belief, or it will be quashed on motion.[8] And where a bill of rights provides "that no warrant shall issue but on probable cause, supported by oath or affirmation," a complaint or information charging a misdemeanor on hearsay and belief will not authorize a warrant where no preliminary examination has been had or waived.[9]

Where, under the facts of the case, in a criminal prosecution for a statutory offence, respondent should have been charged under a section of the statute other than that under which the charge was laid, as there can be no conviction under the information as framed, the prisoner must be discharged.[10]

A motion by a defendant to be discharged from custody need not be in writing; and it is not required to state the reasons upon which the discharge is asked.[11] And the motion may be based upon matter lying entirely outside of the record. It may be supported by affidavits or records or other evidence *aliunde*, in which

1. People *v.* Brock (Mich.), 7 West. Rep. 885.

2. People *v.* Moore, 65 How. (N. Y.) Pr. 177.

3. Mackin *v.* People, 115 Ill. 312; s. c., 2 West. Rep. 912, 915.

4. Nixon *v.* State, 68 Ala. 535.

5. Commonwealth *v.* Railing, 113 Pa. St. 37; s. c., 3 Cent. Rep. 531; Commonwealth *v.* Jackson, 81 Mass. (15 Gray) 188; Robbins *v.* State, 8 Ohio St. 131.

6. State *v.* Griffin, 87 Mo. 608; s. c., 8 West. Rep. 820, 89 Mo. 49; 4 West. Rep. 630.

The Names of the Witnesses need not be stated in the affidavit,—State *v.* Bunnell, 81 Ind. 315,—and they cannot be added to the information without showing that they were not known in time to give notice to the defendant before trial. People *v.* Hall, 48 Mich. 482.

7. State *v.* Bishop, 22 Mo. App. 435; s. c., 4 West. Rep. 793.

8. People *v.* Heffron, 53 Mich. 527.

In a Justice's Court, however, a complaint in a criminal proceeding upon information and belief is sufficient. State *v.* Davie, 62 Wis. 305.

9. State *v.* Gleason, 32 Kan. 245. *Compare* State *v* Babbitt, 32 Kan. 253.

A complaint charging the commission of a crime is not invalidated by the addition of the words, "the affiant verily believes the defendant is guilty of the facts." Brown *v.* State, 16 Neb. 658.

10. People *v.* Calderwood (Mich.), 9 West. Rep. 554.

11. State *v.* Cooper, 103 Ind. 75; s. c., 1 West. Rep. 135.

This Rule can only be applied to cases where the error, if error occurred, is apparent upon looking at what properly belonged to the record. In speaking of matters which appear on the record, only such things are meant as pertain to the legal record. Scotten *v.* Divilbiss, 60 Ind. 37; Lippman *v.* City of South Bend, 84 Ind. 276; Hancock *v.* Fleming, 85 Ind. 571; State *v.* Cooper, 103 Ind. 75; s. c., 1 West. Rep. 135.

case neither the motion, affidavits, records or other evidence, nor the ruling thereon, are legally a part of the record unless made so by order of the court, or by bill of exceptions.[1]

b. When not granted. — Where the indictment is sufficient, it is error in the court to quash it;[2] and a motion to quash an indictment consisting of several counts is properly overruled, if either count is sufficient.[3]

Where the evidence is conflicting, the court may refuse to set aside the indictment.[4] And a motion to quash an indictment, or to strike it from the files, on the ground that it was not found on legal evidence, or that the evidence was insufficient, is properly overruled, when it appears that a competent witness was sworn and examined before the grand jury.[5]

In no case should an indictment be quashed because of mis-

1. State *v.* Cooper, 103 Ind. 75; s. c., 1 West. Rep. 135.

Motion to discharge from Custody. — In the case of Beard *v.* State, 57 Ind. 8, the defendant moved to dismiss the proceedings and to be discharged from custody. The motion was overruled; and in delivering the judgment of the court on the defendant's appeal, *Howk, J.*, said, "Appellant's motion to dismiss the proceedings in this case, and for his discharge from the custody of the sheriff, the decision of the court below thereon, and appellant's exception to such decision, were not made part of the record by a proper bill of exceptions. The second alleged error complained of by appellant is not apparent, therefore, in the record of this cause, and no question is thereby presented for our consideration." State *v.* Cooper, 103 Ind. 75; s. c., 1 West. Rep. 135.

2. State *v.* Cave, 81 Mo. 450; State *v.* Huckeby, 87 Mo. 414; s. c., 4 West. Rep. 337.

An indictment should not be quashed for any defect or imperfection which does not tend to the prejudice of the substantial rights of the defendant upon the merits. Stout *v.* State, 96 Ind. 407; Galvin *v.* State, 93 Ind. 550; Wood *v.* State, 92 Ind. 269, see p. 272; State *v.* Bowman, 103 Ind. 69; s. c., 1 West. Rep. 138; Ind. Rev. Stat. § 1756.

Thus, it is no ground to quash that the indictment was found by a second grand jury. State *v.* Hughes, 58 Iowa, 165.

And error in the general charge to the grand jury is not ground for quashing the indictment. State *v.* White, 37 La. An. 172.

The fact that the first grand jury was illegally drawn, is not a ground for quashing an indictment found by the second grand jury. State *v.* Hart, 67 Iowa, 142.

Illegal Arrest of Accused. — A motion to quash an indictment on the ground that, previous to the finding of the indictment, defendant had been illegally arrested, and was in custody under such arrest when it was found, presents no error. State *v.* Brooks, 92 Mo. 542; s. c., 10 West. Rep. 679.

The court say, "Conceding (without deciding) that, previous to the finding of the indictment, the forms of law had not been pursued in arresting the defendant, and that such arrest was illegal, it affords no ground for quashing the indictment, and it has been so ruled in the following cases, and we have not been able to find a contrary ruling by any court of last resort. People *v.* Rowe, 4 Park. Cr. R. (N. Y.) 253; State *v.* Brewster, 7 Vt. 118; United States *v.* Lawrence, 13 Blatchf. C. C. 295; Dow's Case, 18 Pa. St. 37."

The Supreme Court of Missouri *held* that the wrongfulness of the arrest of the defendant, or the wrongfulness of his detention after arrest, cannot affect, or in any wise impair, the validity of the indictment afterwards found against him; and a motion to quash for either reason should be overruled. State *v.* Chyo Chaigk, 92 Mo. 395; s. c., 10 West. Rep. 308.

3. Bryant *v.* State, 106 Ind. 549; s. c., 4 West. Rep. 524.

Arson. — On an information for the crime of setting fire to a dwelling-house in the night-time, with intent to burn the same, in the main expressed in the language of the statute (How. Stat. § 9128), if the word "did" had been used in the place of "was" after the word "situate" and before "willfully," it would have charged the offence positively; but where the complaint correctly stated the offence, the error must be regarded as merely clerical and formal, and the defect should have been taken advantage of by demurrer or motion to quash. People *v.* Duford (Mich.), 9 West. Rep. 561.

4. People *v.* Ah Chung, 54 Cal. 399.

5. Jones *v.* State, 81 Ala. 79.

joinder, unless it clearly appears upon the face of the indictment that different and distinct crimes are charged, in different counts, which cannot be joined in the same indictment, and unless the prosecutor declines to elect, and manifests a purpose to insist upon a conviction upon each count.[1]

Charging burglary with intent to commit larceny, does not make an indictment bad for duplicity.[2] And an allegation that defendant "caused to be issued a false certificate of the ownership of certain stock signed in blank, and of the following tenor," is bad for duplicity.[3]

Where the record shows that the grand jury came into open court, and through the hand of their foreman returned into open court one indictment, etc., the objection that it does not show that the indictment in this prosecution was so returned, cannot be sustained.[4]

Where the complaint substantially follows the language of the revised standing regulations of the board of aldermen of a city under which it was brought, the obvious meaning of which is, that no vehicle shall make a continuous stop for more than twenty minutes, it is sufficient, on motion, to quash.[5]

Error in the form of indorsement of the indictment by the foreman of the grand jury, which could not have prejudiced the rights of the defendant, will be disregarded on appeal. Hence, where the foreman signs above the words "a true bill," and not on a line with the word "foreman," the indorsement is sufficient, on a motion, to quash the indictment.[6]

1. Glover *v.* State, 109 Ind. 391; s. c., 7 West. Rep. 562. In the case of McGregg *v.* State, 4 Blackf. (Ind.) 101, the court quoted with approval the following, taken from an opinion by Justice Buller: "On the face of an indictment every count imports to be for a different offence, and is charged as at different times. And it does not appear in the record whether the offences are or are not distinct. But if it appears before the defendant has pleaded, or the jury are charged, that he is to be tried for separate offences, it has been the practice of the judges to quash the indictment, lest it should confound the prisoner in his defence, or prejudice him in his challenge of the jury. . . . But these are only matters of prudence and discretion. If the judge who tries the prisoner does not discover it in time, I think he may put the prosecutor to make his election on which charge he will proceed." See McGregor *v.* State, 16 Ind. 9; Engleman *v* State, 2 Ind. 91; Maynard *v.* State, 14 Ind. 427.

The Supreme Court of Indiana say, in Glover *v.* State, 109 Ind. 391; s. c., 7 West. Rep 562, that the appellate courts should not be swift to reverse judgments in criminal cases on account of a refusal by the trial court to put the prosecutor to an election, because the court may, when justice requires it, compel an election after it may be developed by the evidence that the different counts in the indictment charge different and distinct offences which cannot be joined in the same prosecution. Long *v.* State, 56 Ind. 182.

Objection that Defendant cannot be tried First Day of Next Term. — Where defendant had been examined for the offence before the police court, during the then present term of the recorder's court, and he was bound over for his appearance for trial at the next term of the recorder's court, the objection that defendant could not be tried till the first day of the next term is not tenable. There is nothing in the statute to prevent filing an information as soon as it is found convenient. People *v.* Mason (Mich.), 6 West. Rep. 183.

2. Becker *v.* Commonwealth (Pa.); s. c., 8 Cent. Rep. 388.

3. State *v.* Haven, 59 Vt. 399; s. c., 4 New Eng. Rep. 617.

4. State *v.* Payton, 90 Mo. 220; s. c., 7 West. Rep. 129.

5. Commonwealth *v.* Rowe, 141 Mass. 79; s. c., 1 New Eng. Rep. 911; Commonwealth *v.* Barrett, 108 Mass. 302; Commonwealth *v.* Fenton, 139 Mass. 197.

6. State *v* Bowman, 103 Ind. 69; s. c., 1 West. Rep. 138; Johnson *v.* State, 23

c. Misnomer. — The defendant's *name* must be given correctly; or, if it is not known, he must be described as a person unknown.[1] So also with regard to the name of the person against whom the crime has been committed.[2] But a plea of not guilty waives a misnomer.[3]

Where two names are derived from the same source, both taken by common use to be the same, the use of one for the other is not a misnomer.[4] And where two names, though spelled differently, necessarily sound alike, the court may, as matter of law, pronounce them to be *idem sonans;* but, if they do not necessarily sound alike, the question is for the jury.[5]

A literal variance in the spelling of a word is not alone fatal,

Ind. 32; Heacock *v.* State, 42 Ind. 353; Cooper *v.* State, 79 Ind. 272.

1. However, a mistake in the name of the defendant does not occasion a variance, because it is not necessary to prove the name of the accused. If the defendant desires to take advantage of such mistake, he does so by a plea in abatement Where this plea is sustained, the indictment is amended, and the case proceeds. Harris, Cr. L. (Force's ed.) 367.

In New York. — The provisions of the New York Code Criminal Procedure, §§ 203-295, authorizing the amendment of indictments in respect to the name of any person, are not in violation of the Constitution. People *v.* Johnson, 104 N. Y. 213; s. c, 6 Cent. Rep. 792.

2. Harris, Cr. L. (Force's ed.) 263.

The name of the alleged injured party, as it is designated in the indictment, must be sufficiently proved to identify the party; and unless this is done the proof will not only be held insufficient, but the variance between the proof and the allegata will be held fatal. Humbard *v.* State, 21 Tex. App. 200.

Variance in Name of Party injured. — Where the indictment alleges the name of the injured party as E. S. Woods, and the proof establishes the name to be E. S. Wood, it is *held,* that "Wood" and "Woods" are neither the same nor *idem sonans,* and that the variance is fatal. Neiderluck *v.* State, 21 Tex. App. 320.

3. State *v.* Drury, 13 R. I. 540.

4. Walter *v.* State, 105 Ind 589; s. c., 2 West. Rep. 759, 761; 1 Bish. Cr. Proc. 689.

"Jack" for "John," in an indictment, is not a misnomer. Walter *v.* State, 105 Ind. 589; s. c, 2 West. Rep. 759.

5. Commonwealth *v.* Warren, 143 Mass. 568; s. c., 3 New Eng. Rep. 887.

Massachusetts Doctrine. — The Supreme Judicial Court of Massachusetts said in a recent case, that the trial court properly submitted to the jury to determine from their general knowledge, in the absence of evidence showing how they were usually pronounced, the question whether the names "Celestia" and "Celeste" were usually and ordinarily pronounced alike. Commonwealth *v.* Warren, 143 Mass. 568; s. c., 3 New Eng. Rep. 887.

The court say, that, "If two names spelled differently, necessarily sound alike, the court may, as matter of law, pronounce them to be *idem sonans;* but, if they do not necessarily sound alike, the question whether they are *idem sonans* is a question of fact for the jury. Queen *v.* Davis, 4 New Sess. Cas. 411; s. c, 5 Cox, C. C. 237, 2 Den. C. C. 233. In that case the court *held* as a matter of law that 'Darius' and 'Trius' were *idem sonans.* The conviction was quashed; *Coleridge, J.,* saying that if the question had been left to the jury, there can be no doubt that a Dorsetshire jury would have found that 'Darius' and 'Trius' were not the same name.

"The case at bar is similar to that of Commonwealth *v.* Donovan, 95 Mass. (13 Allen) 57, which was an indictment for larceny from John Mealey. The witness testified that his name was spelled Malay or Maley, and that he was called Maley, but never Mealey. The court left it to the jury to say whether the name proved was *idem sonans* with the one in the indictment. After verdict of guilty, this court *held* that the instructions were correct.

"The court submitted to the jury in the case at bar the question whether the names 'Celestia' and 'Celeste' were usually and ordinarily pronounced alike. The jury were to determine this from their general knowledge, in the absence of evidence showing how they were usually pronounced, as in the cases above cited.

"In Commonwealth *v.* Jennings, 121 Mass. 47, evidence was before the jury as to the way the name was ordinarily pronounced. The ruling of the Superior Court was correct." Commonwealth *v.* Warren, 143 Mass. 568; s. c., 3 New Eng. Rep. 887

when the omission or addition of a letter does not make it a different word; and the diversity in the spelling of a name is not material where it is *idem sonans.*[1]

A merely clerical error in writing a name in an indictment cannot be invoked as vitiating the proceeding.[2] And the addition of the word "junior" to the name of a person referred to in an indictment is a mere matter of description, constituting no part of the name, and need not be proved where proof of the name is necessary.[3]

d. Formal and Immaterial Defects. — A defect that does not affect the merits of the case, or the evidence necessary to be given to maintain the indictment, can be regarded as only formal.[4]

1. State *v.* Fitzgerald, 20 Mo. App. 408; s. c., 2 West. Rep. 557, 558; 1 Greenl. Ev. § 167.

Variance. — There is a material variance between the names Tarpley and Tapley, which would support a plea in abatement on the ground of misnomer; consequently a pending prosecution against the defendant, by the latter name, cannot be pleaded in abatement of a prosecution by the former. Tarpley *v.* State, 79 Ala. 271.

And where the complaint and information impleaded "Clements Turner," but the evidence names, and the verdict and judgment condemn, "Turner Clements," if the record fails to identify the party prosecuted as Clements Turner as the person who was convicted as Turner Clements, the variance is fatal. Clements *v.* State, 21 Tex. App. 258

An indictment was *held* defective by the Texas court of appeals because in one place it denominated the defendant one "Kiney," and in another place as one "McKiney." Kinney *v.* State, 21 Tex. App. 348.

But where the defendant was indicted for perjury, charged to have been committed upon the trial of one Willis Fain for larceny, and the record introduced as evidence of the indictment described the person charged with the larceny as Willie Fanes, the court *held* that it was within the rule of *idem sonans*, and that there was no variance. State *v.* Hare, 95 N. C. 682.

In a prosecution under an indictment for forgery, where the writing was offered in evidence, the mere fact that another name was written upon the note by the company, after it was delivered to it, to indicate the agent in whose hands it was placed for collection, creates no variance, inasmuch as, in describing the note in the indictment, it was not necessary to set forth that fact. State *v.* Jackson, 89 Mo. 561; s. c., 6 West. Rep. 445.

2. State *v.* Ford, 38 La An. 797.

Clerical Error in writing Name. — An indictment for an assault with intent to kill and murder George J. Farley, whose name thus appeared four times in the indictment, ended thus: "With a felonious intent . . to kill and murder said Frank I. Farley," *held*, that the court properly instructed the jury that if it was apparent that the writing of Frank I. Farley was a clerical error in draughting the indictment, and that George J. Farley was meant, and that defendant was not misled by the mistake, the variance was not fatal, and the defendant should not be acquitted on the ground thereof. State *v.* McCunniff, 70 Iowa, 217.

3. Geraghty *v.* State, 110 Ind. 103; s. c., 8 West. Rep. 868.

4. State *v.* Amadon, 58 Vt. 524; s. c., 1 New Eng. Rep. 355; State *v.* Arnold, 50 Vt. 735; Rex *v.* Horne, 2 Cowp. 682.

Omission of Material Word. — But if an indictment omits a material word, although it be but a preposition or a helping verb, the court will not, from a knowledge of the language, supply the missing word so as to supply the probable intention of the grand jury, where the charging part of the indictment read as follows: ". . . Adam Carpenter and R. Jones, on the tenth day of May, 1884, did then and there, unlawfully and with malice aforethought, make an assault in and upon the person of John Long, with intent him the said Long, then and there kill and murder," etc., *held* that the omission of the preposition "to" before the words "kill and murder" was fatal to the sufficiency of the indictment. Jones *v.* State, 21 Tex. App. 349.

Omission to serve Names of Witnesses. — Where a justice of the peace was indicted for malpractice in office in wilfully and knowingly demanding and receiving more costs than he was entitled to under the law, a service on him of a copy of the indictment, except that it did not contain the names of the grand jurors, was a substantial compliance with the law; and a special plea alleging that this service was insufficient, was properly stricken on demurrer. Ridenhour *v.* State, 75 Ga. 382.

Neither verbal nor grammatical inaccuracies, nor the misspelling of words in an indictment,[1] are fatal to it where they do not affect the sense, and where, from the whole context, the words, as well as the meaning, can be determined with certainty by a person of ordinary intelligence.[2] A conviction will not be reversed for a mere formal defect in the indictment which might have been amended in the court below, or might be amended in the appellate court.[3] And an indictment shall not be deemed invalid for any defect which does not tend to prejudice the substantial rights of the defendant.[4]

Objections to a complaint for formal defects should be taken in the trial court; and a motion to quash on this ground, made for

Where an instrument is set forth, a mistake of the pleader in designating its character does not vitiate the indictment. Garmire *v.* State, 104 Ind. 444; s. c., 2 West. Rep. 284.

Reversal for "Imperfection, Formal Defect." — By § 87 of the Criminal Procedure Act it is provided that no judgment given upon any indictment shall be reversed for any imperfection, omission, defect in or lack of form, or for any error except such as shall have prejudiced or may prejudice the defendant in maintaining his defence upon the merits. *Re* Esmond (D. C.), 3 Cent. Rep. 520.

1. **Misspelling Words in Indictment.** — A transposition of the letters "e" and "a" in the word "steal," so as to make "stael," does not render a count defective. State *v.* Lockwood, 58 Vt. 378; s. c., 2 New Eng. Rep. 196. In State *v.* Carville (Me.), 5 New Eng. Rep. 354, it is *held* that an indictment for incest is not bad because the word "incestuous" is spelled "incestous." The court say, —

"In this indictment for incest between father and daughter, the word 'incestuous' is spelled 'incestous,' a letter 'u' being omitted by chance. It is, however, not a fatal omission. It is not only nearly enough *idem sonans*, but the spelling is not grammatically incorrect. The essential part of the meaning of the term is in the noun 'incest,' a word borrowed from the Latin language, into which it was imported from the Greek. The adjective may not incorrectly be incestous, although it is, for merely the sake of euphony, spelled 'incestuous.' No one could mistake its meaning in its connection in this indictment."

A defect in an information for forgery by using the word "affiant" for words "prosecuting attorney," if the charge was preferred by the proper officer, will not be available to reverse the judgment. Billings *v.* State, 107 Ind. 54; s. c., 4 West. Rep. 519.

In an indictment under Mo. R. S. § 1307, for stealing cattle, the use of the word "steer" is sufficient, without employing the term "cattle," or "neat cattle." State *v.* Bowers (Mo.), 4 West Rep. 588.

An indictment for larceny which substitutes the word "haul" for the word "carry," used in the statutory definition of the offence, is sufficient. Spittorff *v.* State, 108 Ind. 171; s. c., 6 West. Rep. 307.

2. State *v.* Halida, 28 W. Va. 499.

Where the indictment charged the offence to have been committed at and near the dwelling of one Henry F. Miller, and the proof was that it was near the residence "of a man by the name of Miller," and a Mrs. Miller lived there with her son Henry, who was sickened by the odors complained of, the jury was authorized to infer that the son was the person whose dwelling-house was affected by the acts complained of. The failure to prove the initial letter of the middle name was not a variance. If a variance, it had reference only to a matter of unnecessary description, the failure to prove which with technical exactness would not authorize the reversal of a judgment in a criminal case. Mergentheim *v.* State, 107 Ind. 567; s. c., 5 West. Rep. 851.

3. Davis *v.* Commonwealth (Pa.), 4 Cent. Rep. 711.

4. Ind. Rev. Stat. 1881, § 1756. State *v.* Bowman, 103 Ind. 69; s. c., 1 West. Rep. 138; State *v.* Anderson, 103 Ind. 170; s. c., 1 West. Rep. 175, 176; Thomas *v.* State, 103 Ind. 309; s. c., 1 West Rep. 309, 316; Sample *v.* State. 104 Ind 289; s c., 2 West. Rep. 258, 259; State *v.* McDonald, 106 Ind. 233; s. c., 3 West. Rep. 752, 754.

Repugnant Indictment: Validity. — An indictment, though lamentably repugnant, must be held valid under the saving provisions of the statute, § 1821, where it does not tend to the prejudice of the substantial rights of the defendant on the merits. State *v* Chamberlain, 89 Mo. 129; s. c., 5 West. Rep. 386.

the first time in the superior court, comes too late, and is properly overruled.[1]

But no indictment should be quashed for any surplusage or repugnant allegations, when there is sufficient matter alleged to indicate the crime and person charged.[2]

On arraignment, where the defendant neither stands mute nor confesses, he pleads;[3] that is, he alleges some defensive matter.[4]

The pleas are divided into (1) dilatory pleas, consisting of (*a*) plea of guilty or not guilty, (*b*) pleas to the jurisdiction, and (*c*) pleas in abatement; (2) special pleas in bar, consisting of (*a*) former

1. Commonwealth *v.* Hallahan, 143 Mass. 167; s. c., 3 New Eng. Rep. 300; Commonwealth *v.* Legassy, 113 Mass. 10; Commonwealth *v.* Doherty, 116 Mass. 13.

2. State *v.* Patterson (Ind.), 7 West. Rep. 410, 412; Myers *v.* State, 101 Ind. 379; State *v.* McDonald, 106 Ind. 233; s. c., 3 West. Rep. 752.

Whatever Circumstances are Necessary to constitute the crime imputed must be set out, and all beyond is surplusage. State *v.* Amadon, 58 Vt. 524; s. c., 1 New Eng. Rep. 355.

It is a well-settled principle of criminal pleading, that if, eliminating surplusage, an indictment so avers the constituents of the offence as to apprise the defendant of the charge against him, and enables him to plead the judgment in bar of another prosecution, it is good in substance under the Texas Code. McConnel *v.* State, 22 Tex. App. 354.

An indictment for shooting with intent to murder, need not charge an assault: such charge is surplusage. State *v.* Crittenden, 38 La. An. 448.

3. Every plea must be put in orally. People *v.* Redinger, 55 Cal. 298; People *v.* Johnson, 47 Cal. 124.

And two pleas, when not repugnant with each other, may be pleaded at the same time. Commonwealth *v.* Long, 2 Va. Cas. 318.

A mistake in a plea may be corrected after entry on the minutes. Davis *v.* State, 20 Ga. 674.

Plea Essential. — It is essential to the sufficiency of a conviction, that the defendant pleaded to the indictment, or that the plea of not guilty was entered for him, which fact, on appeal, must appear in the final judgment brought up with the record. Pate *v.* State, 21 Tex. App. 191; State *v.* Cunningham, 94 N. C. 824; People *v.* Heller, 2 Utah, 133; Dale *v.* Copple, 53 Mo. 321; State *v.* Montgomery, 63 Mo 296; People *v.* Gaines, 52 Cal 481; Douglass *v.* State, 3 Wis. 820.

And where the record in a criminal case fails to disclose affirmatively that a plea to the indictment was entered either by or for the defendant, such record on its face shows a mis-trial, and that the proceeding was erroneous, at least; and a recital in a bill of exceptions, that the defendant pleaded not guilty, will not supply the omission. Bowen *v.* State, 108 Ind. 411; s. c., 6 West. Rep. 897.

Exception to the Failure of the Court to arraign a defendant, or require him to plead to an indictment for forgery, can only be saved by presenting the omission as a ground for a new trial. Billings *v.* State, 107 Ind 54; s. c, 4 West. Rep. 519.

Arraignment before Justice of the Peace. — An arraignment or plea in a criminal case, before a justice of the peace, is nowhere affirmatively required by the Indiana statute; but it is *held* that the proper practice requires that a defendant should enter a plea in order to present an issue for trial. Johns *v.* State, 104 Ind. 557; s. c., 2 West. Rep. 276.

Arraignment in Misdemeanors. — It has been *held* that where a defendant is put on trial for a misdemeanor without a plea to the indictment having been entered, it is a mere technical error or irregularity which does not affect any of his substantial rights, and affords no ground for reversal of a judgment of conviction. See State *v.* Hayes, 67 Iowa, 27; s. c., 24 N. W. Rep. 575; Allyn *v.* State, 21 Neb. 593.

Special Pleas must always be tried before the general issue. Commonwealth *v.* Merrill, 90 Mass. (8 Allen) 545; Salliday *v.* Commonwealth, 28 Pa. St.; Foster *v.* State, 39 Ala. 229; Henry *v.* State, 33 Ala. 389; Nonemaker *v.* State, 34 Ala. 211; Mountain *v.* State, 40 Ala. 344; Faulkner *v.* State, 3 Heisk. (Tenn.) 33; Clem *v.* State, 42 Ind. 420.

4. The learning on the subject of the different pleas has become, to a great extent, a matter of history rather than of practice, on account of the comprehensive character of the plea of the general issue of not guilty, and also on account of the right to move in arrest of judgment. Harris Cr. L. 375.

conviction, (*b*) former acquittal, and (*c*) pardon; and (3) pleading the general issue.[1]

The first steps to be taken after the prisoner is brought into court, is to call upon him by name to answer the matter charged against him.[2] If, when arraigned, he fails to give his true name on request, he cannot afterwards complain if he is tried by the name specified in the indictment.[3] But if he gives his true name, it must be substituted, and the subsequent proceedings be had in that name.[4]

2. *Plea of Guilty or Not Guilty.* — By pleading guilty, defendant confesses his guilt as charged in the indictment; but if none is charged therein, none is confessed.[5] After the plea of guilty, there is nothing for the court to do other than to pronounce sentence.[6] If defendant be of age, the court must sentence

1. The defendant is not permitted to go through the whole of these pleas in succession, resorting to the subsequent plea as a previous one fails. The rule is, that not more than one plea can be pleaded to an indictment for misdemeanor, or a criminal information. In felonies, if the accused pleads in abatement, he may afterwards, if the plea is adjudged against him, plead over to the felony; that is, plead the general issue of not guilty. Harris, Cr. L. 375, 376.

2. Rex *v.* Hensey, 1 Burr. 643; 2 Hale, P. C. 119.

3. State *v.* Burns, 8 Nev. 251.

4. People *v.* Jim Ti, 32 Cal. 60; People *v.* Kelly, 6 Cal. 210.

5. Fletcher *v.* State, 7 Eng. (Ark.) 169; 1 Bish. Cr. Proc. 464.

Effect of Plea of Guilty. — The plea of guilty is a confession of the offence which subjects the defendant to precisely the same punishment as though he had been tried and found guilty by the verdict of a jury. The fact that defendants often imagine that by pleading guilty they are likely to receive some favor from the court in the sentence that will be passed upon them, makes it not an uncommon practice for the judge to undeceive them in this respect, by apprising them that their pleading guilty will make no alteration in their punishment. 1 Arch. Cr. Pr. § 110; 1 Colby, Cr. L. 286; Rice *v.* State (Tex. Ct. App.), 9 Crim. L. Mag. 577; s. c., 3 S. W. Rep. 791.

But where defendant pleaded guilty under a belief, induced by something said by the judge, that by so doing he would escape the maximum penalty of the law, it was *held* he should not be sentenced to the maximum, but rather be allowed to plead not guilty. State *v.* Stephens, 71 Mo. 535.

It has been said that a plea of guilty is the highest kind of conviction of which the case admits, — 2 Hale, P. C. 225, — and may be received after a plea of "not guilty" has been entered on the record, whenever the accused chooses to withdraw such plea, and confess the accusation. Ward *v.* People, 3 Hill (N. Y.), 395; 1 Colb. Cr. L. 287; 2 Hawk. P. C. c. 31, § 1.

In Michigan, under the provisions of the statute (How. Stat. § 9558), the judge is to satisfy himself, by private examination, whether the defendant voluntarily pleads guilty, and, if satisfied that he does so plead, must proceed to judgment. See People *v.* Brown, 53 Mich. 531; s. c., 5 Crim. L. Mag. 868, 877; People *v.* Stickney, 50 Mich. 99; People *v.* Ferguson, 48 Mich. 41; Clark *v.* People, 44 Mich. 308; Henning *v.* People, 40 Mich. 733; Edwards *v.* People, 39 Mich. 760.

6. People *v.* McEwen, 67 How. (N. Y.) Pr. 105; Gray *v.* State, 107 Ind. 177; s. c., 5 West. Rep. 264; Boswell *v.* State, 111 Ind. 47; s. c, 9 West. Rep. 262, 264; Rev. Stat. 1881, § 1767

If the accused makes a simple, unqualified confession that he is guilty of the offence charged in the indictment, if he adheres to this confession, the court has nothing to do but to award judgment, generally hearing the facts of the case from the prosecuting counsel. But the court usually shows reluctance to accept and record such confession in cases involving capital or other great punishment; often they advise the prisoner to retract the confession and plead to the indictment. The reason of this is obvious: the defendant may not fully understand the nature of the charge, he may be actuated by a morbid desire for punishment, etc. Harris, Cr. L. 373.

Stay of Sentence. — The Supreme Court of Michigan say in People *v.* Brown, 53 Mich. 531; s. c., 5 Crim. L. Mag. 868, 878, that it is no doubt competent for a criminal court, after conviction or confession, to stay for a time its sentence; and that many good reasons may be suggested for doing so, him, or place him in the custody of the sheriff until such sentence.[1]

A plea of guilty can be put in only by defendant personally in open court.[2] And if the plea of guilty be drawn out by the court's admonishing the prisoner that, if he does not plead, he will be heavily punished, it is a nullity.[3] A plea of guilty cures formal defects.[4]

A plea of guilty includes a plea of former conviction, if charged in the indictment, and renders the defendant liable accordingly.[5] But if the plea of *nolo contendere* is accepted, it is not necessary or proper that the court should adjudge the party to be guilty, for that follows as a legal inference from the implied confession; but the court proceeds thereupon to pass the sentence of the law.[6]

The plea of not guilty puts in issue all the material averments[7]

such as to give opportunity for motion in arrest, or to enable the judge to better satisfy his own mind what the punishment should be. Commonwealth *v.* Dowdican's Bail, 115 Mass. 133.

1. Gray *v.* State 107 Ind. 177; s. c., 5 West. Rep. 264.

2. People *v.* McCrary, 41 Cal. 461.

In Misdemeanors, however, a plea of guilty may be put in by an attorney, but in felonies it must be put in by defendant in person. Gordon *v.* Gibbs, 3 Smedes & M. (Miss.) 587; United States *v.* Mayo, 1 Curt. C. C. 433; People *v.* Ebner, 23 Cal. 158; People *v.* Corbett, 28 Cal. 328.

3. O'Hara *v.* People, 41 Mich. 623.

4. Casper *v.* State, 27 Ohio St. 572.

Defects on a complaint in not following the precedents are cured by a plea of guilty. State *v.* Knowles, 34 Kans. 393.

5. People *v.* Delany, 49 Cal. 395.

6. Commonwealth *v.* Horton, 26 Mass. (9 Pick.) 206; Commonwealth *v.* Ingersoll, (Mass.), 5 New Eng. Rep. 383.

The Plea of Nolo Contendere is not common, but is sometimes allowed in misdemeanors, as a sort of compromise between the prosecuting officer and the defendant, and differs but slightly in its effect from the plea of not guilty. 1 Colby, Cr. L. 287; 1 Bish. Cr. Proc. 469. Hawkens says that "it is an implied confession, when the defendant in a case not capital doth not directly own himself guilty, but in a manner admits it by yielding to the king's mercy, and desiring to submit to a small fine." 2 Hawk. P. C. c. 31, § 3.

A plea of *nolo contendere*, when accepted by the court, is, in its effect upon the case, equivalent to a plea of guilty. It is an implied confession of guilt only, and cannot be used against the defendant as an admission in any civil suit for the same act. But there is a difference between the two pleas, in that defendant cannot plead *nolo contendere* without the leave of the court. If such plea is tendered, the court may accept or decline it at its discretion.

If the plea is accepted, it is not necessary or proper that the court should adjudge the party to be guilty, but the court proceeds thereupon to pass the sentence of the law.

If the record does not certainly show that the plea *nolo contendere* was accepted, and sentence passed thereupon, in the police court, the defendant has the right to plead anew in the superior court, and to have a trial by jury. Commonwealth *v.* Ingersoll (Mass.), 5 New Eng. Rep. 382.

It seems that the chief or only difference between this plea where it is received, and the plea of guilty, is, that, while the latter is a solemn confession which may bind the defendant in other proceedings, the former is held to be a confession only for the purposes of the particular case. See Commonwealth *v.* Fulton, 49 Mass. (8 Metc.) 232; Commonwealth *v.* Tilton, 26 Mass. (9 Pick.) 206; 1 Bish. Cr. Proc. 469, 1 Colby, Cr. L. 287.

7. People *v* Aleck, 61 Cal. 137.

Pleading the General Issue. — When the prisoner, on being charged with the offence, answers *vivâ voce* at the bar, "Not guilty," he is said to plead the general issue. The consequence is, that he is to be tried by a jury, or, as it is frequently stated, he puts himself upon the country for trial Harris, Cr. L. 380.

Advantages of pleading "Not Guilty." — This is much the most common and advantageous course for the prisoner to take; unless, indeed, he pleads guilty, and thereby the court is induced to take a more lenient view of his case. Pleading the general issue does not necessarily imply of the indictment, including that of the *locus delicti*.[1] The plea of not guilty should be made by the defendant in person in open court, and a plea of not guilty by an attorney in a prosecution for felony is a nullity. The personal plea should appear by the record.[2]

Where a plea of not guilty is interposed, the jury must acquit if, on the whole evidence, they have a reasonable doubt as to any material fact covered by the essential averments, including the actual participation in the crime.[3]

a. Standing Mute. — By "standing mute" is meant, not answering when called upon to plead to the indictment, or, if answering at all, answering irrelevantly.[4] Where a party refuses to plead, a plea of not guilty may be entered for him.[5]

that the prisoner contends that he did not do the actual deed in question, inasmuch as it does not prevent him from urging matter in excuse or justification. More, this is practically the only way in which he can urge matter in excuse or justification. Thus, on an indictment for murder, a man cannot plead that the killing was done in his own defence against a burglar; he must plead the general issue, — not guilty, — and give the special matter in evidence. The pleading of the general issue lays upon the prosecutor the task of proving every material fact alleged in the indictment or information; while the accused may give in evidence any thing of a defensive character. Harris, Cr. L. 380.

Thus, under the plea of not guilty, insanity may be shown. People *v.* Olwell, 28 Cal. 461.

If, in a capital case, the record on appeal shows that the defendant pleaded "not guilty," but is silent respecting his arraignment, the court presuming that an arraignment was waived, will not reverse the judgment of conviction for want of an arraignment; but if the record shows neither an arraignment nor a plea, the judgment will be set aside. Steagald *v.* State, 22 Tex. App. 464.

1. People *v.* Bevans, 52 Cal. 470; People *v.* Roach, 48 Cal. 382.

Thus, if an offence is committed in another State, that is matter of defence under the plea of not guilty. State *v.* Mitchell, 83 N. C. 674.

But the question of jurisdiction will not be considered on a plea of not guilty. State *v.* Day, 58 Iowa, 678.

2. State *v.* Conkle, 16 W. Va. 736.

Joint Plea of "Not Guilty." — A general plea of not guilty by several defendants is a several plea. State *v.* Smith, 2 Ired. (N. C.) L. 402.

3. People *v.* Fairchild, 48 Mich. 31; s. c., 11 N. W. Rep. 773.

4. Harris, Cr. L. (Force's ed.) 300.

Historical. — In former times, if, in cases of felony, this standing mute was obstinate, the sentence of *peine forte et dure* followed. See 2 Reeves, Hist. Eng. Law, 134; 3 id. 133, 250, 418. In treason and misdemeanor the standing mute was equal to a conviction. Later, in every case it had the force of a conviction. 12 Geo. III. c. 20. If the prisoner was dumb *ex visitatione Dei*, the trial proceeded as if he had pleaded not guilty. But now, if the prisoner stands mute of malice, or will not answer directly to the indictment or information, the court may order the proper officer to enter a plea of not guilty on behalf of such person; and the plea so entered has the same force and effect as if the person had actually so pleaded. 7 & 8 Geo. IV. c. 28, § 2. If it is doubtful whether the muteness be of malice or *ex visitatione Dei*, a jury of any twelve persons present may be sworn to discover this. If they find him mute of malice, 7 & 8 Geo. IV. c. 28 will apply; if mute *ex visitatione Dei*, the court will use such means as may be sufficient to enable him to understand the charge, and make his answer; or, if this be found impracticable, a plea of not guilty will be entered, and the trial proceed. Harris, Cr. L. (Force's ed.) 300.

5. United States *v.* Berger, 19 Blatchf. C. C. 249; Weaver *v.* State, 83 Ind. 289.

Indiana Doctrine. — Section 1762 of Indiana R. S. provides for arraignment of defendant. Section 1763 provides, except in certain cases, that defendant may plead the general issue; section 1766 provides that if he stands mute, a plea of not guilty may be entered. These sections are in substance the same as 2 R. S. 1876, 398, §§ 96–98. Under these sections a trial without an arraignment, unless waived, erroneous; the record must show the plea entered by the court. Johns *v.* State, 104 Ind. 557; s. c., 2 West. Rep. 277.

Trial without Plea. — It is error to put the prisoner on trial without entering his

3. *Withdrawal of Plea.* — It has long been held that where a defendant has pleaded guilty, and sentence has been passed upon him, he cannot retract his plea, and plead not guilty;[1] but, on the other hand, a person who has been indicted, and has plead not guilty, may, by leave of the court, on the advice of his counsel, or of his own motion or otherwise, withdraw that plea, and enter a plea of guilty.[2]

plea, but announcing himself ready for trial is in effect an entry of a plea. Spicer *v.* People, 11 Ill. App. 294; Avery *v.* People, 11 Ill. App. 332.

1. Reg. *v.* Tell, 9 Car. & P. 346, 348; State *v.* Buck, 59 Iowa, 382; s. c., 13 N. W. Rep. 342; Mastromada *v.* State, 60 Miss. 86.

And this is true, even in a capital case where his punishment has been assessed at death. People *v.* Lennox, 67 Cal. 13; s. c., 6 West. Coast Rep. 691.

In United States *v.* Rayaud, 15 Reporter, 200, defendants were indicted for violations of internal revenue laws, and pleaded guilty; but the district attorney delayed moving for sentence until a subsequent term, in order to allow defendants an opportunity to endeavor to effect a compromise at Washington. The commissioner of internal revenue having rejected the offer of compromise, the district attorney moved the court for sentence, and the prisoners then made a motion for leave to withdraw their pleas of guilty, and substitute not guilty. The motion was denied.

Massachusetts Doctrine. — In Massachusetts it has been *held* that after plea of not guilty and a trial thereon in the police court, the defendant cannot file another plea in the superior court on his appeal without leave of court. Commonwealth *v.* Lannan, 95 Mass. (13 Allen) 563; Commonwealth *v.* Hagarman, 92 Mass. (10 Allen) 401.

And in the late case of Commonwealth *v.* Ingersoll (Mass.), 5 New Eng. Rep. 382, it was *held* that, when defendant pleads guilty in a municipal or police court, and appeals from the sentence to the superior court, he cannot of right claim a trial by jury, but is liable to be sentenced upon his original plea in the court below, unless the court gives him leave to plead anew.

On Reversal of Conviction. — In a proper case, where a judgment on a plea of guilty has been reversed, the prisoner is entitled to plead not guilty. Commonwealth *v.* Ervine, 8 Dana (Ky.), 30. See Whart. Crim. Pl. & Pr. (8th ed.) p. 285, sec. 414.

2. See Reg. *v.* Brown, 17 L. J. (M. C.) 145; Harris, Cr. L. 373.

Discretion of Court. — It is discretionary with the trial court in most cases, whether a plea will be allowable to be withdrawn and another substituted. It is held to be addressed to the sound discretion of the court, — Pattee *v.* State, 109 Ind. 545; s. c., 8 West. Rep. 41; Epps *v.* State, 102 Ind. 536; s. c., 3 West. Rep. 380; Hubbard *v.* State, 72 Ala. 164; State *v.* Delahenssaye, 37 La. An. 551; Commonwealth *v.* Ingersoll (Mass.), 5 New Eng. Rep 382; Commonwealth *v.* Mahoney, 115 Mass. 151; United States *v.* Bayaud, 21 Blatchf. C. C. 217; s. c., 15 Rep. 200, — and nothing short of a clear abuse of it can be assigned as error. Phillips *v.* People, 55 Ill 429. See also People *v.* Lee, 17 Cal. 76, 80, and Reg. *v.* Brown, 17 L. J. (M. C.) 145 The prisoner is not entitled to withdraw a plea of not guilty as a right. People *v.* Lewis, 64 Cal. 401, 403; s. c, 1 West. Coast Rep 131, 132; 17 Rep. 361; 5 Crim. L. Mag. 627; Norton *v.* People, 47 Ill. 468; Kinlock's Case, Foster's Crown Law, 16; Page *v.* Commonwealth, 27 Gratt. (Va.) 954; Conover *v.* State, 86 Ind. 99; Hensehe *v.* People, 16 Mich. 46; Sanders *v.* State, 97 Ind. 147; s. c., 4 Crim. L. Mag. 359; Wickwise *v.* State, 16 Conn. 477; Pattee *v.* State, 109 Ind. 545, s. c., 8 West. Rep. 41; Sunday *v.* State, 14 Mo. 417; Rex *v.* Fitzharris, 8 Howell, St. Tr. 243, 385; People *v.* Lee, 17 Cal. 76; Norwood *v.* State, 45 Md. 68, 76; State *v.* Kring, 71 Mo. 551; Watson *v.* Walker, 33 N. H. 132, 143; State *v.* Salge, 2 Nev. 321; 1 Bishop, Crim. Proc. sects. 747, 798; 2 Archb Crim. L. 334; Reg. *v.* Brown, 17 L. J. (M. C.) 145; 2 Hawk. P. C. 469; 2 Hale, P. C. 225; 1 Chitty, Cr. L. 436.

In the recent case of Mostronda *v.* State, 60 Miss. 87, the defendant pleaded guilty to the charge of unlawfully retailing liquors; but before sentence had been passed upon him, he moved the court for leave to withdraw his plea of guilty. In support of his motion he filed an affidavit to the effect that, upon a previous occasion, he had pleaded guilty to a similar offence, and had been sentenced with the mildest penalty allowed by the law, and that he filed his plea of guilty in the belief that the court would be as lenient with him in this case as the former; but that, since entering his plea, he had heard a rumor that he would be more severely dealt with than before, and therefore he wished to withdraw his plea. The affidavit did not aver

The statutes in some of the States provide for the withdrawal of pleas of guilty, and permitting the plea of "not guilty," or other pleas, to be substituted; but this must be done previous to judgment.[1] But a plea of guilty cannot be withdrawn after sentence under statute.[2]

But if the proposed plea to be substituted is not sufficient, in law, as a defence, the court may refuse the withdrawal, as in pleading a prior judgment which has been reversed by the Supreme Court.[3]

VI. Demurrer. — A demurrer is an objection on the part of the defendant, who admits the facts alleged in the indictment to be true,[4] but insists that they do not, in point of law, amount to the crime with which he is charged.[5] A demurrer should always be in writing.[6]

that he was innocent of the offence with which he was charged. The court refused to grant the motion. On appeal, this was held to be a proper exercise of discretion. But see State *v.* Stephens, 71 Mo. 535; s. c., 10 Cent. L. J. 497, where it is *held* that if a defendant enters a plea of guilty under the belief induced by something said or done by the judge, that, by so doing, he will receive a punishment less severe than the maximum allowed by law, he should not afterwards be sentenced to the maximum, but should rather be permitted to withdraw his plea, and file a plea of not guilty. See State *v.* Kring, 71 Mo. 551, where this case is followed.

Exception to the Rule. — However, there is this qualification to the rule: If the defendant desires to plead something that would be a good defence, and which has taken place since the last continuance, then he has an absolute right to do so. State *v.* Salge, 2 Nev. 321, 324. Thus, the court could not deny a prisoner the right to plead a pardon which had been granted since the last continuance of the cause. 2 Nev. 321, 324. And where there is evidence sufficient to raise a doubt of the sanity of defendant at the time the plea of guilty was interposed, he should, as a right, be permitted to withdraw his plea of guilty, and substitute "not guilty." People *v.* Scott, 59 Cal. 341. So where a youth, a foreigner, ignorant of the language and institutions of this country, upon being charged with a capital offence, says that he is guilty, but says so under circumstances which show that he is ignorant of his rights, it is error for the court, without appointing counsel or submitting the case to the jury, to accept his statement as a plea of guilty, and to enter judgment and pass sentence of death. Gardner *v.* People, 106 Ill. 76; s. c., 4 Crim. L. Mag. 881. And even where the defendant, after pleading guilty, has moved in arrest of judgment, and the motion been overruled, should justice require, the court should permit, before judgment rendered, a withdrawal of the plea of guilty, and the substitution of the plea of not guilty. 1 Bish. Crim. Proc. sect. 747. Thus, in State *v.* Cotton, 24 N. H. 143, the defendant pleaded guilty, and moved in arrest of judgment. He also moved, that, if judgment should not be arrested, he be permitted to withdraw his plea of guilty. *Eastman, J.*, thought the motion to withdraw rather novel, but said it is "one to be addressed to the discretion of the common pleas, and is proper for their consideration, and the consideration of the prosecuting officers." So, where a defendant inadvertently pleaded guilty to one indictment when intending to plead guilty to another, the plea being entered through misapprehension, the mistake should be corrected. Davis *v.* State, 20 Ga. 674. In any case where justice requires it, the plea of guilty should be permitted to be withdrawn. 1 Bish. Crim. Proc. sect. 747.

1. For instance, in Iowa, it is enacted that, "at any time before judgment, the court may permit the plea of guilty to be withdrawn, and other plea, or pleas, substituted." Miller's Code of Iowa, 1880, p. 1022, sec. 4362. This practice has been recognized in two cases by the Supreme Court of that State. State *v.* Kraft, 10 Iowa, 330, 331; State *v.* Oehlslager, 38 Iowa, 297.

2. State *v.* Buck, 59 Iowa, 382; s. c., 13 N. W. Rep. 342.

3. State *v.* Salge, 2 Nev. 321, 324.

4. Demurrer admits the offence, but not the legal effect of the facts therein pleaded, and puts in issue the legality of the whole proceeding. Quigley *v.* Commonwealth, 84 Pa. St. 18.

5. Thus, if a person is indicted for *feloniously* stealing goods which are not the subject of larceny at common law or by statute, he may demur to the indictment, denying it to be a felony. It is for the court, on hearing the arguments, to decide whether the objection be good. Harris, Cr. L. 382.

6. McGarr *v.* State, 75 Ga. 155.

If, on the demurrer, judgment is given *for* the defendant, it is to the effect that he be discharged, provided that the objection be a substantial one; that the indictment be quashed if it is a merely formal one. If judgment is given *against* the defendant, in felonies the judgment is final: in misdemeanors it is final, unless the court should afterward permit the defendant to plead over.[1] When a demurrer is overruled, it is now generally provided by statute that the defendant shall have leave to plead. It is also provided in some States, as in Iowa, that, if he then fails to plead, final judgment may be rendered against him on the demurrer.[2] And where the indictment is adjudged good on demurrer, the prisoner may except; and if the exception is sustained, judgment may be rendered in his favor: if overruled, judgment may be rendered for the State, unless the prisoner has reserved his right to plead anew.[3]

Demurrers in criminal cases seldom occur in practice. Not only is there the risk of having final judgment against the defendant, but the same objections may be brought forward in other and safer ways. In cases of defects in substance apparent on the face of the indictment, generally the defendant may, instead of demurring, plead not guilty, and then, if convicted, move in arrest of judgment. Thus he has a double chance of getting off: first, on the facts of the case, then on the point of law. But this course cannot be taken when the defect in the indictment is cured by verdict.[4]

Formerly there was another kind of demurrer besides the general demurrer to which we have been referring; namely, a special demurrer, usually termed a "demurrer in abatement." This was founded on some formal defect in the indictment, whereas a general demurrer is founded on some substantial defect.[5]

1. This seems to be the state of the law as settled in R. *v.* Faderman, 1 Den. 569; s. c., 3 C. & K. 353; though some still contend that in felonies, after judgment against the defendant, he may still plead not guilty; and a defendant has been allowed to demur and plead not guilty at the same time. See Harris, Cr. L. 383.

2. Iowa Rev. Stat. 1873, p. 676.

3. State *v.* Dresser, 54 Me. 569.

4. 7 Geo. IV. c. 64, s. 21. Heymann *v.* R., L. R. 8 Q. B. 105; R. *v.* Goldsmith, L. R., 2 C. C. R. 74; s. c., 42 L. J. (M. C.) 94.

5. Harris, Cr. L. 383.

English Doctrine.—But now no demurrer lies in respect of the defects specified in the 24th section of 14 & 15 Vict. c. 100; and demurrers for other formal defects are practically rendered useless by sect. 25 of the same statute, which provides that every objection to an indictment for any formal defect apparent on the face thereof shall be taken by demurrer or motion to quash the indictment before the jury are sworn, and not afterwards; and the court before which such objection is taken for any formal defect may, if it be thought necessary, cause the indictment to be forthwith amended in such particulars, and thereupon the trial will proceed as if no such defect had appeared.

In Alabama, in a *quasi* criminal prosecution for the violation of a municipal ordinance, removed by appeal into the circuit court, if a demurrer is interposed to the statement (or complaint), and the plea of not guilty is afterwards filed, before any action of the court is had or invoked on the demurrer, the appellate court will hold the demurrer to have been waived, and will not consider the sufficiency of the complaint as assailed by it. Pitts *v.* Dist Opelika, 79 Ala. 527.

In Kentucky, where all pleadings in criminal cases are required to be oral, when the defendant says he demurs, an entry is made by the clerk on the record as

An indictment defective in substance and form may be demurred to;[1] but demurrer will not lie for a defect in indorsing and filing the indictment.[2] If it appears from the caption that the court had no jurisdiction, the indictment will be adjudged invalid.[3] Where there are two counts, and one of them is good, a general demurrer will be overruled;[4] nor will demurrer lie to a part of a count.[5]

follows: "The defendant demurs to the indictment." In Kentucky a demurrer is proper, (1) if it appear from the indictment that the offence was not committed within the local jurisdiction of the court; (2) if the indictment do not substantially conform to the requirements of the code as to its form and structure; (3) if more than one offence be charged in the indictment, except as permitted by the code; (4) if the facts stated do not constitute a public offence; (5) if the indictment contain matter which is a legal defence or bar to the prosecution. If it appear that the offence is a felony, and was committed in some other county in the State, the defendant, together with the indictment and all original papers, is transferred to the county having jurisdiction. If there is an improper joinder of offences, the demurrer will be overruled upon the prosecuting attorney's dismissing one of the charges. If the demurrer is sustained on the fifth ground, the defendant must be discharged, and judgment entered in his favor. If sustained on any other ground, the indictment may be submitted to another grand jury, and the defendant held meanwhile on bail. Ky. Crim. Code, §§ 164-170.

In Iowa, an indictment is not demurrable on the ground that the minutes of the evidence on which it was found have not been filed with the clerk, as required by Code, § 4293. State *v.* Briggs, 68 Iowa, 416. But the defendant may demur when it appears upon the face of the indictment either, (1) that it does not conform substantially to the requirements of the Criminal Code; (2) that the indictment contains any matter which, if true, would constitute a legal defence or bar to the prosecution. If the demurrer is sustained on the ground that the offence charged was within the exclusive jurisdiction of another county in the State, the same proceedings are taken as in Kentucky. If sustained on the second ground, the judgment is final, and the defendant is discharged. If sustained on any other ground, the defendant is discharged, unless the court is of opinion the objection can be remedied or avoided in another indictment; in which case the court may order it to be submitted to another or the same grand jury, the defendant being held meanwhile on bail. Iowa Rev. Stat. 1873, p. 676.

In Michigan, objection for a formal defect appearing on the face of the indictment may be taken by demurrer as well as by motion to quash; and, if sustained, the court may order the indictment to be forthwith amended and the case proceed. Rev. Stat. (1871) p. 2172.

In Ohio, the only ground of demurrer allowed by the code, is that the facts stated in the indictment do not constitute a punishable offence, or that the intent is not alleged, when proof of it is necessary to make out the offence charged. 74 Ohio L. 341.

1. Lazier *v.* Commonwealth, 10 Gratt. (Va.) 708.

Material Defects. — An indictment which fails to show the offence committed within the jurisdiction is demurrable. People *v.* Craig, 59 Cal. 370.

That the indictment did not contain the particular circumstances of the offence, is a ground for demurrer. People *v.* Swenson, 49 Cal. 390; People *v.* Cox, 40 Cal. 277; People *v.* Bogart, 36 Cal. 247.

The objection to a pleading, that its allegations are argumentative, is not one of substance, but of form, and can only be taken advantage of by special demurrer. Spencer *v.* Southwick, 9 Johns. (N. Y.) 314; Marie *v.* Garrison, 83 N. Y. 14.

But a demurrer "because the indictment is an absurdity on its face," was properly overruled as frivolous. State *v.* Belew, 79 Mo. 584.

Objection to an Indictment for a Formal Defect, apparent on its face, should be taken by demurrer, before the jury is sworn, and not afterwards. Commonwealth *v.* Hughes, 11 Phila. (Pa.) 430.

Objection to the insufficiency of the indictment must be taken at the trial; and a failure to demur at the proper time is a waiver of the objections. People *v.* Burgess, 35 Cal. 115; People *v.* Johnston, 48 Cal. 550; Amesti *v.* Castro, 49 Cal. 330.

Duplicity in a Plea in Abatement is reached by general demurrer. State *v.* Emery, 59 Vt. 84; s. c., 3 New Eng. Rep. 377.

2. State *v.* Brandon, 28 Ark. 410.

3. King *v.* Fearnley, 1 Term Rep. 316; s. c., 1 Leach, 425.

4. Turner *v.* State, 40 Ala. 21; Ingram *v.* State, 39 Ala. 247; Commonwealth *v.* Webster, 59 Mass. (5 Cush.) 295.

5. Wheeler *v.* State, 42 Md. 563; Mulcahy *v.* Queen, L. R. 3 H. L. 306.

1. *Amendments.* — It has been said that an information may be amended,[1] but that an indictment, which is a finding upon the oaths of the grand jury, can only be amended with their consent before they are discharged.[2]

VII. Plea in Abatement. — This is a dilatory plea, formerly principally used in the case of the defendant being misnamed in the indictment.[3] It is sufficient for the purposes of the plea as to misnomer, to state that the defendant's name is so and so, giving

1. Rex *v.* Holland, 4 T. R. 457.

2. Barb. Cr. L. (2d ed.) 347; 2 Hawk. P. C. c. 25, §§ 97, 98.

When an Indictment is quashed on Demurrer, and its defects, real or supposed, can be easily amended by resubmission of the matter to the grand jury, it should be done instead of appealing the judgment on the demurrer to a higher court. State *v.* Withrow, 47 Ark. 551.

In New York. — Power of court to allow erroneous allegations in an indictment in respect to any thing or person, to be corrected under sects. 281, 293, 294, Code Crim. Proc.; People *v.* Richards, 44 Hun (N. Y.), 278.

Power of Court to amend. — It is questionable whether the court can authorize any amendment to an affidavit on which a criminal proceeding before a justice is based; but, if permissible, it can only be made by interlineation, and swearing anew to the original affidavit, or by substitution of a new one. Strong *v* State, 105 Ind. 289; s. c, 2 West. Rep. 289.

A Nolle Prosequi may be directed to be entered on an indictment demurred to in order to permit a new indictment, conforming to the facts, to be brought, instead of allowing an amendment to the original indictment. State *v.* Baron (N. H.), 2 New Eng. Rep. 851.

3. Harris, Cr. L. 377; 2 Hale, P. C. 238; Arch. Cr. Pl. 30. See Commonwealth *v.* Lewis, 42 Mass. (1 Metc.) 151. As, for example, if a wrong Christian name or addition were given. But, even if the defendant was successful on this plea, a new bill of indictment with the correction might at once be framed. Harris, Cr. L. 377.

Descriptio Personæ. — Where words are added which are mere *descriptio personæ*, and which need not be proved on a plea of not guilty, as where a woman is indicted as "the wife of A. B.," such addition, if wrong, must be excepted to by a plea in abatement. Commonwealth *v.* Lewis, 42 Mass. (1 Metc.) 151.

But the want of an addition to the name, such as title, occupation, estate, or degree, or pleading a wrong one, cannot be pleaded in abatement in New York and other States. See 2 N. Y. Rev. Stat. 728, § 54; Barb. Cr. L. 343; 1 Colby, Cr. L. 285.

In the Absence of any Defect to a plea of misnomer, the prosecution can raise either of two questions by replication: (1) that the defendant was as well known by the name in the complaint as by that in the plea; (2) that the two names were pronounced alike. Neither of these questions is presented by a demurrer to the plea. State *v.* Malia (Me.), 5 New Eng. Rep. 355.

In State *v.* Malia, *supra*, the county attorney filed a demurrer to the defendant's plea of misnomer. The court say, "No question is raised as to the form of the plea, and we perceive no defect therein." State *v.* Flemming, 66 Me. 142.

"The demurrer having been sustained by the judge, the defendant was found guilty on his plea of not guilty. By going to trial he waived no right to his exceptions on the pleading. State *v.* Pike, 65 Me. 111.

"In the absence of any defect in the plea of misnomer, the State could have raised either of two questions by replication: (1) that the defendant was known as well by the name in the complaint as by that in the plea, — State *v.* Corkrey, 64 Me. 521, — or (2) that the two names were pronounced alike. The county attorney filed no replication, but demurred, and now contends in substance that the two names are *idem sonans*, which is not a question of law, but of fact, which the defendant has the right to submit to a jury. Rex *v.* Shakespeare, 10 East, 87, and cases in note *a*; Commonwealth *v.* Mehan, 77 Mass. (11 Gray) 323."

In England. — The plea is now, however, virtually obsolete. It has been enacted that no indictment or information shall be abated by reason of any dilatory plea of misnomer, or of want of addition, or of wrong addition, if the court be satisfied of the truth of the plea. The court will cause the indictment or information to be amended, and will call upon the party to plead thereto, and will proceed as if no such dilatory plea had been pleaded. 7 Geo. IV. c. 64, § 19. And no indictment is to be held insufficient for want of, or imperfection in, the addition to the name of any defendant. Harris, Cr. L. 377.

his true name, and add that by that name he has always been called and known, without stating that he was baptized by it.[1]

Pleas in abatement are always founded upon some defect apparent on the face of the record, or some fact extrinsic to the record which renders the indictment insufficient.[2] The incompetency of the grand jury, or of any of the jurors, which find the indictment, is a matter which may properly be pleaded in abatement.[3]

1. Walden *v.* Holman, 6 Mod. 116; s. c., 1 Salk. 6; Hardw. 286.

2. 1 Bish. Cr. Proc. 416; 1 Colby, Cr. L. 284.

Any Defect which at any stage of the proceedings will vitiate the indictment, may be taken advantage of by a plea in abatement. 1 Colby. Cr L. 284; 2 Hale, P. C. 236.

By Statutory Provision, in some States, a pending prosecution is not abated by the repeal of the statute on which it is founded, unless otherwise provided by the repealing statute (Ala. Code, § 4459); but this statute does not apply to municipal ordinances, and pending prosecutions under such ordinances are abated by their repeal, unless expressly excepted from the operation of the repealing ordinance. Barton *v.* Gadsden, 79 Ala 495.

3. **Objections to Grand Jurors: not Freeholder.** — Thus, under a statute requiring that grand jurors be freeholders, a plea in abatement setting forth that some of the grand jury were not freeholders, is good. Colby, Cr. L. 285; 1 Arch. Cr. Pl. (ed. 1860) § 111, and cases cited.

New York Doctrine. — However, it has been *held* in New York, and such would seem to be the rule there still, that it is not a ground for a plea in abatement, that one of the grand jurors who found the indictment is not a freeholder. People *v.* Jewett, 6 Wend. (N. Y.) 386. The court say that "the prevailing opinion among the professional men of this State, previous to the Act of April 16, 1827, was, that a freehold qualification was not dispensable to a grand juror. From the earliest period of our government, the legislature has expressly enacted that petit jurors should be freeholders; but in acts passed contemporaneously in relation to grand jurors, they have merely provided that they should be good and lawful men 1 N. Y. Rev. L. 327, 339; 2 id. 150. These Acts have repeatedly come under the consideration of the legislature, in the various revisions, through which our laws have passed; and it appears to me that an express provision upon this subject would have been introduced, if it had been supposed that a property qualification was necessary for a grand juror."

When Objection to Grand Juror to be made. — It has been *held* that an objection to the qualifications of a grand juror comes too late when made after the jury have been sworn. See Commonwealth *v* Smith, 9 Mass. 107, 110; Commonwealth *v.* G.e, 60 Mass. (6 Cush.) 174; People *v.* Jewett, 3 Wend. (N. Y.) 314, 321. Particularly where the accused has been previously held to answer. People *v.* Beatty, 14 Cal. 566.

However, a contrary doctrine prevails in many States, where it is *held* that the objection may be taken by plea in abatement. See State *v.* Middleton, 5 Port. (Ala.) 484; State *v.* Rockfellow, 6 N. J. L. (1 Halst.) 332; Kitrol *v.* State, 9 Fla. 9; Doyle *v.* State, 17 Ohio, 222; Huling *v.* State, 17 Ohio St. 583; State *v.* Duncan, 6 Yerg. (Tenn.) 271; Stanley *v.* State, 16 Tex. 557; Commonwealth *v.* Cherry, 2 Va. Cas. 20; Barney *v.* State, 12 Smed. & M. (Miss.) 68.

Rhode Island Doctrine. — The court say in State *v.* Davis, 12 R. I. 492; s. c., 34 Am. Rep. 704, that these cases "rest on the stronger reasons. It is certainly not reasonable to require a person, who has not been held to answer, to object to the jury before it is impanelled for he may be on the other side of the globe, or he may have no reason to suppose that he is going to be indicted, being guiltless. And even if a person has been held to answer, he may be in prison, sick at home, or, if in court, he may be ignorant, without fault, of the disqualification of the juror until after he has been sworn. Indeed, a person may be indicted for an offence committed pending the inquest Moreover, the act of the grand jury is *ex parte* and preliminary, and it is contrary to principle to hold that a person shall forfeit his rights by not intervening in a proceeding to which he is not a party. No English case has been cited, but English treaties recognize the plea 2 Hale, P. C. 155; Bacon, Abr tit. 'Juries, A;' 1 Chitt. Cr. L. 309. The statute of Henry IV. ch. 9 is declaratory of the common law. State *v.* Foster, 9 Tex. 65; Commonwealth *v.* Cherry, 2 Va. Cas 20. And on this question, whether it may not be considered a part of the law of this State by adoption, see Dig. of 1767, p. 56; R. I Col. Rec. vol. 5, p. 289; and Gen Stat. R. I. ch. 260, § 3."

But it is *held* by the same court, in the recent case of State *v.* Duggan, Index, Z. 17; s. c., 3 New Eng. Rep. 135, 136, that upon a

The objection that the drawing, summoning, and impanelling of the grand jury was not done according to law, must be made by plea in abatement;[1] but the plea must point out specifically wherein the grand jury were not legally chosen and impanelled.[2]

plea in abatement that the grand jury were not "reputable freeholders or house-holders of county, and taxable therein," that the plea was bad (1) because whether they were reputable was only a question for the persons selecting them, and (2) because, disregarding that, the plea was too uncertain as to the particular disqualification intended to be relied upon.

Ohio Doctrine. — But it is *held* in a recent Ohio case that an objection to the personal qualifications of a grand juror cannot be raised by plea in abatement. See State *v.* Easter, 30 Ohio St. 542; s. c., 27 Am. Rep. 478.

In Illinois it seems that the common law governs as to the time of making the objection to the grand juror, as well as to the manner and cause. It is there *held* that the right to challenge exists, and may be exercised by any person charged with crime, whose case is likely to be made the subject of investigation. Musick *v.* People, 40 Ill. 268.

In Indiana it was formerly permitted to the accused to challenge the grand jury before they are sworn. Jones *v.* State, 2 Blackf. (Ind.) 476; Hudson *v.* State, 1 Blackf. (Ind.) 318; Ross *v.* State, 1 Blackf. (Ind.) 390. But this limit of the right to challenge was confined to those under prosecution for crime. But it is now *held* that where one under indictment has had no opportunity of challenging the grand jury, he may plead in abatement any matter which would have been sufficient cause of challenge to that tribunal or any member thereof; and having failed to plead in abatement, he waives his right by a plea in bar. Pointer *v.* State, 89 Ind. 255.

In Massachusetts it has been *held* that the objection to the qualification of a grand juror must be made before the indictment is found, and that such objection may be received from any person who is under presentment for crime, or from one as *amicus curiæ*. Commonwealth *v.* Smith, 9 Mass. 107. But in Commonwealth *v.* Parker, 19 Mass. (2 Pick.) 550, this decision is commented on, and doubts expressed as to the proposition that objections to the qualifications of a grand juror must always be made before the indictment is found. See State *v.* Hendon, 5 Blackf. (Ind.) 75; Thayer *v.* People, Doug. (Mich.) 417; State *v.* Ostrand, 18 Iowa, 438; State *v.* Ried, 20 Iowa, 414; Brading *v.* State, 11 Tex. 257; Glassinger *v.* State, 24 Ohio St. 206; Meeks *v.* State, 57 Ga. 329; United States *v.* Williams, 1 Dill. C. C. 486. See also 1 Bish. Crim. Proc. §§ 853, 875, and 881; 1 Whart. Cr. L. § 489; 1 Chitt. Cr. L. 307.

1. State *v.* Greenwood, 5 Port. (Ala.) 474; State *v.* Seaborn, 4 Dev. (N. C.) L. 305; State *v.* Freeman, 6 Blackf. (Ind.) 248; Rawls *v.* State, 8 Smed. & M. (Miss.) 599; Bass *v.* State, 37 Ala. 469; Floyd *v.* State, 30 Ala. 511. But see Bellair *v.* State, 6 Blackf. (Ind.) 104; McCann *v.* People, 3 Park Cr. R. (N. Y.) 272; Noakes *v.* People, 25 N. Y. 380; People *v.* Allen, 43 N. Y. 28; Horton *v.* State, 47 Ala. 58; Commonwealth *v.* Chauncey, 2 Ashm. (Pa.) 90.

Unsealed Venire. — An objection that the venire summoning the jury was not sealed, should be taken by plea in abatement. State *v.* Flemming, 66 Me. 142; s. c., 22 Am. Rep. 552.

Defects in Constitution of Grand Jury. — Pleas in abatement for mere defects in the constitution of grand juries are not favored. Such pleas, if they do not allege in what regard the persons named as grand jurors are not qualified to serve, are not good. State *v.* Duggan (R. I.), Index, Z. 26; s. c., 3 New Eng. Rep. 135.

An averment in a plea that grand jurors were not legally elected, impanelled, and sworn, is only one of conclusion, not of facts from which the court may draw its own conclusion. State *v.* Duggan, R. I. Index, Z. 26; s. c., 3 New Eng. Rep. 136.

In Indiana it was recently *held* that for errors and irregularities in the selection or impanelling of the grand jury, a plea in abatement is properly taken. Henning *v.* State, 106 Ind. 386; s. c., 4 West. Rep. 470.

Errors in the Impanelling of the Grand Jury must be taken advantage of by plea in abatement, not in arrest of judgment. Henning *v.* State, 106 Ind. 386; s. c., 4 West. Rep. 470.

A plea in abatement, that one of the grand jurors was not qualified because he usurped the place of one drawn on a day too long before the term, is insufficient. State *v.* Mead, R. I. Index, Z. 30; s. c., 3 New Eng. Rep. 142.

2. Priest *v.* State, 10 Neb. 393; Baldwin *v.* State, 12 Neb. 61; Brennan *v.* People, 15 Ill. 511; State *v.* Duggan, R. I. Index, Z. 26; s. c., 3 New Eng. Rep. 135. 136.

The Tennessee Supreme Court say, in the case of Dyer *v.* State, 11 Lea (Tenn.), 509, that "the plea does aver broadly that the grand jurors were not legally elected, impanelled, and sworn, which is only an averment of a conclusion, not of facts from

An objection to a portion of the panel may be pleaded in abatement.[1]

A plea in abatement must be certain,[2] and should set forth the grounds of objection specifically.[3] It is always essential that the facts should be stated out of which the defence arises, and it should negative that state of facts which is to be presumed from the existence of a record.[4]

A plea in abatement, or a special plea not involving a statement of fact, is exclusively for the court,[5] and the defendant may file two or more pleas in abatement;[6] but the plea must always be filed at the proper time, for a failure to file will be considered as a waiver of rights. Thus, a plea in abatement alleging prior proceedings comes too late after defence made and recognizance given;[7] and a plea in abatement filed after a general continuance,[8] or after the defendant has gone to trial on the merits,[9] will be stricken out.[10]

which the court may draw its own conclusion," and for this reason *held* it to be insufficient.

1. United States *v.* Richardson, 28 Fed. Rep. 61. But a plea in abatement to an indictment that one of the grand jurors was not qualified to vote upon any proposition to impose the tax, or for the expenditure of money, is too general. State *v.* Duggan, R. I. Index, Z. 26; s. c., 3 New Eng. Rep. 135.

Alien Grand Juror. — Thus, where one of the grand jurors is an alien, the objection may be taken by plea in abatement. Reich *v.* State, 53 Ga. 73; s. c., 21 Am. Rep. 265.

Objection to Grand Juror who has expressed an Opinion cannot be taken by a plea in abatement. State *v.* Hamlin, 47 Conn. 95; s. c., 36 Am. Rep. 54; United States *v.* Williams, 1 Dill. C. C. 492; United States *v.* Burr, Burr's Trial, 38. See Tuck's Case, 8 Mass. 286; Commonwealth *v.* Smith, 9 Mass. 107; Musick *v.* People, 40 Ill. 268.

2. **In Vermont** it was recently said that a plea in abatement must be certain to every intent, and must stand or fall on its own allegations, unless there be express reference to the indictment. State *v.* Emery, 59 Vt. 84; s. c., 3 New Eng. Rep. 377.

3. Brennan *v.* People, 15 Ill. 511.

Thus, a plea in abatement to impeach the verity of the record must negative every reasonable intendment in favor of the record. Dyer *v.* State, 11 Lea (Tenn.), 509.

Pleas in abatement must leave, on the one hand, nothing to be supplied by intendment of construction, and, on the other, no supposable or special answer unobviated. State *v.* Duggan, R. I. Index, Z. 26; s. c., 3 New Eng. Rep. 136; Billings *v.* State, 107 Ind. 54; s. c., 4 West. Rep. 519.

Vermont Doctrine. — A plea in abatement must be certain to every intent; thus it was *held*, on general demurrer to a plea purporting to raise the disqualification of one of the grand jurors and the illegality of the grand jury, that the plea was bad, in that it was not properly alleged that the objectionable grand juror acted with the panel in finding the indictment; that the allegation that he was not a "legal voter of the county" was lacking in certainty as to what county; that the allegations that he was not one of the "judicious men of the county," and that the panel did not constitute a legal grand juror, present conclusions of law; that the mere reference in the plea to "said indictment" did not show, except by inference, what indictment had been pleaded to; and because duplicity could be reached by general demurrer. State *v.* Emery, 59 Vt. 84; s. c., 3 New Eng. Rep. 377.

4. State *v.* Brooks, 9 Ala. 10; State *v.* Newer, 7 Blackf. (Ind.) 307.

5. Chase *v* State. 46 Miss. 683.

The Court cannot go behind an Indictment properly returned, and inquire into the evidence on which it was found upon a plea in abatement. Terry *v.* State, 15 Tex. App. 66.

6. United States *v.* Richardson, 28 Fed. Rep. 61.

7. Smith *v.* People (Mich.), 1 West. Rep. 615.

8. State *v.* Myers, 10 Lea (Tenn.), 717.

9. Dyer *v.* State, 11 Lea (Tenn.), 509.

10. **Striking out Plea in Abatement.** — In order for the striking out of a plea in abatement to furnish a ground for reversal, it must affirmatively appear that such plea was filed before arraignment; otherwise it will be presumed that the judgment of the court was right, and that the plea was filed

An agreement by defendant to aid State officers in detecting criminals cannot be pleaded in abatement.[1]

When the plea in abatement is found on hearing in favor of the defendant, the judgment, in case of a misdemeanor, is, that he be not compelled to answer to the indictment, and is dismissed from the court without day;[2] but in cases of felony the judgment is, that the defendant do answer over.[3] Where the plea is overruled, the jury, or the court where the case is submitted to the court, without the intervention of a jury, proceed to fix the penalty.[4]

1. *Limitation of Action.* — As a rule, there is no time limited after the commission of a crime within which the indictment must be preferred. The offender is continually liable to be apprehended and visited with the penalties of the criminal law. By particular statutes, however, there are exceptions to this rule, a stated time being fixed after which criminal proceedings cannot be commenced. When a time is thus fixed within which the prosecution shall be commenced, if an indictment is found after the expiration of such time, the "plea of limitation" will be valid.[5] But the Statute of Limitations must be specially pleaded.[6]

The time while a prosecution for a crime is pending, the period of limitation does not run.[7] And the Statute of Limitations does

after arraignment. Moseley *v.* State, 74 Ga. 404.

A Motion to quash, on the ground of the pendency of another information, is in effect a plea in abatement, and subject to Mo. R. S. sec. 1846, requiring an affidavit or other evidence of the truth of a plea in abatement or other dilatory plea. State *v.* Bishop, 22 Mo. App. 435; s. c., 4 West. Rep. 793.

1. Holmes *v.* State, 20 Tex. App. 509.

2. Rex *v.* Cowhoneyborne, 10 East, 88; 2 Hale, P. C. 238; Barber, Cr. L. 343.

3. Id. 1 Arch. Cr. Pl. ch. "Plea in Abatement."

4. Guess *v.* State, 1 Eng. (Ark.) 147.

On an Accusation for a Capital Crime, after the indictment has been abated for a misnomer, the court does not dismiss the prisoner, but causes him to be indicted *de novo* by the proper name as disclosed in his plea. Ferrer's Case, Cro. Car. 371; 2 Hale, 176-238; Hawk. B. 2, ch. 34, § 2; 1 Arch. Cr. Pr. III. note.

5. Harris, Cr. L. 345.

Thus, where the indictment must be found within one year from the date of the offence, proof showing that it was committed more than a year prior to finding of indictment will not support conviction. State *v.* Hopper, 21 Mo. App. 510; s. c., 4 West. Rep. 276.

Previous Prosecution. — Where a *nol. pros.* is entered, and defendant's discharge ordered, it amounts to setting aside the proceedings, and is within the saving clause of the section limiting a second indictment for the same offence. Swalley *v.* People, 116 Ill. 247; s. c., 2 West. Rep. 391.

Proof of the previous prosecution of another "person" accused of some "offence" is not proof of knowledge of the prosecuting officer that the accused had committed the offence, and will not sustain his plea for prescription. State *v.* Hanks, 38 La. An. 468.

In Texas prosecutions for larceny are barred after five years from the commission of the offence. Wimberley *v.* State (Tex. App.), Dec. 1886.

6. State *v.* Thrasher (Me.), 3 New Eng. Rep. 61.

7. The statute, section 318 of the Ill. Criminal Code, R. S. 1874, p. 348, specifies three modes of disposing of an indictment, information, or suit, in which the time of the pendency shall not be recond within the time limited to bring a new proceeding for the same offence: they are, when the indictment is quashed, or the proceedings are set aside, or reversed on error or appeal. Swalley *v.* People, 116 Ill. 247; s. c., 2 West. Rep. 391.

When a prosecution is dismissed because the indictment is not signed and indorsed as required by the statute (Ala. Code, § 4777), an entry of record may be made stating the facts, and ordering another indictment to be found (Code, § 4819); and a new indictment being found, the time not run against the State in favor of one charged with a felony, who shall "flee from justice." Within the meaning of the statute, it is not necessary to constitute a fugitive from justice that the accused should leave the State. One who conceals himself to avoid arrest is a fugitive from justice, although such concealment be upon his own premises.[1]

A plea in writing of not guilty, and the Statute of Limitations, is bad for duplicity.[2]

2. *Alibi.* — Regarding the plea of alibi, see that title in this work.[3]

VIII. Pleas in Bar. — These pleas are termed "special" to distinguish them from the general issue, and "in bar" because they show reason why the defendant ought not to answer at all, nor put himself upon his trial for the crime alleged; and thus they are distinguished from dilatory pleas, which merely postpone the result. All matters of excuse and justification may be given in evidence under the general issue; therefore it is hardly ever necessary to resort to a special plea in bar, except in the four cases to be examined more in detail below.[4]

1. *Plea to the Jurisdiction.* — When an indictment is taken before a court which has no cognizance of the offence, the defendant may plead to the jurisdiction without answering at all to the crime alleged. This want of jurisdiction may arise either from the fact that the offence was not committed within the district of the jurisdiction, or because the tribunal in question has not cognizance of that class of crimes.[5]

which elapsed between the finding of the two indictments must be deducted (Code, § 4820) in computing the bar of the Statute of Limitations. Smith *v.* State, 79 Ala. 21.

1. State *v.* Hawell, 89 Mo. 588; s. c., 6 West. Rep. 432.

The Statute of Limitations applying to crimes deducts from the limitations such time "during which the party charged was not usually and publicly a resident within the State." Hence, it is not mere absence from the State which the statute refers to, but such absence as destroys residence.

Criminal cases do not stand on the same necessity as civil cases, for absence does not prevent an indictment, while it does prevent the beginning of a civil action; and the fact of a temporary absence during the running of the statute on a criminal charge would not, in case of a long delay in complaining, take the case out of the statute. People *v.* McCausey (Mich.), 8 West. Rep. 132.

2. State *v.* Ward, 49 Conn. 429.

3. 1 Am. & Eng. Encyc. of L. 454.

4. Harris, Cr. L. 276.

In England. — It is said that in England the only instance in which a special plea in bar seems requisite in criminal cases, is where a parish or county is indicted for not repairing a road or bridge, etc., and wishes to throw the *onus* of repairing upon some person or persons not bound of common right to repair it. Arch. Cr. Pl. 140.

Where Defendant pleads in Bar and the General Issue, and both are submitted at the same time, there must be a verdict in each, and it is error to take a verdict on the plea of not guilty alone. People *v.* Kinsey, 51 Cal. 278; Solliday *v.* Commonwealth, 28 Pa. St. 14.

5. But this plea is very seldom resorted to, inasmuch as relief can be obtained in other ways. Thus, the objection that the offence was committed out of the jurisdiction, may generally be urged under the general issue, or, in certain cases, by demurrer, or by moving in arrest of judgment, or by writ of error. If the objection is that the crime is not cognizable in a court of that grade, though committed within the jurisdiction, the defendant may demur, or have advantage of it under the general issue, or by removing the indictment to a higher court, and there quashing it. Harris, Cr. L. 376.

Irregularities and Errors. — Irregularities in the course of judicial proceedings do not render them void. Kelley *v.* People, 115 Ill. 583; s. c., 56 Am. Rep. 184; 3 West. Rep. 46.

Error in changing the *venue* is not available by plea to the jurisdiction it was subject of exception in the court which ordered the change. Bowden *v.* State, 12 Tex. App. 246.

In Alabama the accused may be prosecuted for murder in the county in which deceased was shot, although death occurred in another State. Green *v.* State, 66 Ala. 40; s. c., 41 Am. Rep. 744. The court say, "The principal question involved in this case is that of sovereign jurisdiction in the matter of homicide where the fatal shot or blow occurs in one State, and death ensues in another. The appellant Green, being under indictment, was convicted of the murder of Ephraim Thompson, and sentenced to the penitentiary for life. The evidence showed that the act of shooting, which caused the death, occurred in Colby County, Alabama, where the indictment was found and the trial occurred, and that Thompson died within a year and a day, in the State of Georgia.

"It was formerly doubted at common law, where a blow was inflicted in one county, and death by reason of the injury ensued in another, whether the offence could be prosecuted in either county. 1 East, P. C. 361; 1 Hale, P. C. 426. The better opinion seems to have been, however, that the jurisdiction attached to the *venue* where the blow was inflicted. Id. This difficulty, as noted by Mr. Starkie, was sought to be avoided by the legal device of 'carrying the dead body back into the county where the blow was struck; and the jury might there,' he adds, 'inquire both of the stroke and death.' 1 Stark. Cr. Pl. (2d ed.) 3, 4, note. It was to quiet doubts and obviate this difficulty that the Statute of 2d and 3d Edward VI., ch. 24, and the later one of 2 Geo. II., ch. 21, were enacted by the British Parliament. The example has been followed in some fourteen or fifteen of the States of the American Union, and by our own State among the others. These statutes, though different in phraseology, are similar in substance and purpose. Their manifest design seems to be to prevent a defeat of justice in administering the law of felonious homicide and other crimes, by rendering the jurisdiction certain. . . .

"The validity of this statute is assailed as being beyond the scope of legitimate legislative power. It may be conceded that the laws of no nation can operate beyond its own territorial domain or jurisdiction, being local in their nature, and co-extensive only with the limits of the State by which they are enacted. As said by *Story, J.*, in the case of The Apollon, 22 U. S. (9 Wheat.) 362; bk. 6, L. ed., 'They must always be restricted, in construction, to places and persons upon whom the legislature had authority and jurisdiction.' It is a safe principle, perhaps, to be asserted, that a crime committed in a foreign country, and in violation of the laws thereof, cannot, by mere legislative fiction or construction, be constituted an offence of another country. This reasoning, however, does not apply to a case where a crime is perpetrated partly in one State or country, and partly in another; 'provided,' as suggested by Mr. Bishop, 'that what is done in the country which takes jurisdiction, is a substantial act of wrong, and not merely some incidental thing, innocent in itself alone.' . .

"The sovereign right of States to enact jurisdictional laws of this kind, though often questioned, has been uniformly sustained, and notably in the recent case of Hunter *v.* State, 40 N. J. L. (11 Vr.) 495. There the mortal blow was given within the jurisdiction of New Jersey, and the death occurred in Pennsylvania. It is said that the courts of the former State had cognizance of the crime by force of a statute not unlike our own. So in the State of Michigan and Missouri. Tyler *v.* People, 8 Mich. 321; Steerman *v.* State, 10 Mo. 503."

In California it is *held* that although the superior court has no jurisdiction over a simple assault, yet, if one is indicted for a felonious assault, he may be convicted of the lesser crime. People *v.* Holland, 59 Cal. 364; State *v.* Griffin, 34 La. An. 37.

In the District of Columbia.—It is *held* that murder is committed within the District of Columbia when the felonious blow is struck there, although the death occurs without the District. United States *v.* Guiteau, 1 Mackey (D. C.), 498.

In Georgia it has been *held* that where a party is illegally arrested in A. County, and forcibly taken into B. County, and there detained, the court of B. County has jurisdiction to try the offence of false imprisonment. Lavina *v.* State, 63 Ga. 513.

In Indiana it is *held* that the court has no jurisdiction over a prosecution for felony begun by affidavit and information filed during its vacation. Hoover *v.* State, 110 Ind. 349; s. c., 9 West. Rep. 86.

But where a crime is composed of several elements, and a material element exists in each of two counties, jurisdiction of the entire crime attaches in either county. Archer *v.* State, 106 Ind. 426; s. c., 4 West. Rep. 726.

In Iowa an indictment may properly be found for false pretences made in another county where the property was delivered in the county where the indictment was found. State *v.* House, 55 Iowa, 466.

2. *Former Acquittal.* — Where a person has been indicted for an offence, and regularly acquitted, he cannot afterwards be indicted for the same offence, provided the indictment was such that he could have been lawfully convicted on it.[1] It is against the policy of the law that a person should be put in peril more than once for the same offence;[2] and therefore if he is indicted a second time,

In Michigan, a conspiracy to obtain property by false pretences may be tried wherever an overt act in pursuance of the conspiracy has been committed. People *v.* Arnold, 46 Mich. 260.

How. Stat. § 7135 *a* was not intended to limit or curtail the jurisdiction of justices of the peace in criminal cases. While an omission to secure an order from the prosecuting attorney before issuing process in criminal cases might subject the magistrate to censure, and possibly in some cases to pecuniary injury or official embarrassment, it was not intended by the statute to deprive the magistrate of his jurisdiction for such omission. The appearance of the prosecuting attorney, and his prosecution of the case, are sufficient approval. People *v.* Griswold (Mich.), 7 West. Rep. 899.

In Missouri it is *held* that the purpose of the clause in the Bill of Rights was individual protection and limitation upon power, and any construction which would leave with the legislature this unbridled authority would render the restriction nugatory. State *v.* Berkley, 92 Mo. 67; s. c., 10 West. Rep. 67.

In Nebraska it is *held* that the courts have jurisdiction over crimes committed on Indian reservations in the same State. Marion *v.* State, 20 Neb. 233.

In New York, there is nothing in the statutes which confers on the court of special sessions jurisdiction over offences committed without the county. People *v.* Bates, 38 Hun (N. Y.), 180.

In Ohio. — Where a forged deed was made in another State, and uttered and published in Ohio by an innocent agent, the latter is indictable for the uttering and publishing. Lindsey *v.* State, 38 Ohio St. 507. But see Exp. Carr, 28 Kans. 1, a case of a forged check upon a railroad company.

In South Carolina an assault and battery upon peace officers, while in discharge of their duties, gives the court of general sessions jurisdiction. State *v.* Sims, 16 S. C. 486.

In Pennsylvania, the court of quarter sessions has jurisdiction over the first offence of receiving stolen goods. Commonwealth *v.* Kelly, 13 Phila. (Pa.) 422.

In Tennessee it is *held* that one in charge of the sheriff journeying to S. County is indictable in S. County for a theft committed on the journey. State *v.* Margerum, 9 Baxt. (Tenn.) 362.

In Texas. — A forgery in another State is punishable within the State under the criminal code of Texas. Hawks *v.* State, 13 Tex. App. 289; Rogers *v.* State, 11 Tex. App. 608.

By the Texas code the trial should be had in the county where the offence was committed, although the county has been since divided. Hernandez *v.* State, 19 Tex. App. 408.

And a plea that the place of trial, though the *de facto* county-seat, is not the *de jure* county-seat, should be overruled. Watts *v.* State (Tex. App.), Dec. 1886.

In Wisconsin. — Where one enters a moving car with intent to commit larceny therein, he is indictable in any county in which the act is committed. Powell *v.* State, 52 Wis. 217.

In Federal Courts. — Where the circuit court to which a cause was removed, quashed the indictment found in the State court, it had no jurisdiction to proceed against the accused for a crime against the State. Bush *v.* Kentucky, 107 U. S. (17 Otto) 110, bk. 27, L. ed. 354.

Where there has been no cession of the territory by the State, the United States court has no jurisdiction. United States *v.* Penn, 4 Hughes, C. C. 491.

The United States Circuit Court has jurisdiction of a murder committed on an Indian reservation, by an Indian upon a white man. United States *v.* Martin (Or.), 8 Sawy. C. C. 473; s. c., 14 Fed. Rep. 817.

After conviction the indictment cannot be remitted to the circuit court. United States *v.* Haynes, 26 Fed. Rep. 857.

Offences against United States Laws. — An indictment for depositing obscene matter in the mail must be found in the district where the matter was deposited. United States *v.* Comerford, 25 Fed. Rep. 902.

1. On a plea of former acquittal, if the court holds the defendant could have been lawfully convicted on the former proceeding, the plea is good. State *v.* Norvell, 2 Yerg. (Tenn.) 24; State *v.* Parish, 43 Wis. 395.

2. One put on trial for the statutory offence of burning an untenanted house, is not in second jeopardy from having been acquitted, by direction of the judge, of arson. State *v.* Jenkins, 20 S. C. 351.

he may plead *autrefois acquit*, and thus bar the indictment.[1] Where there is any difficulty in determining whether the second indictment bears such a relation to the first that the latter is a bar to the former, the true test seems to be this: whether the facts charged in the second indictment would, if true, have sustained the first.[2]

An acquittal for murder may be pleaded in bar to an indictment for manslaughter, and *vice versa*. The same is true with larceny and embezzlement; robbery, and assault with intent to rob;

1. **When Plea Good.** — An acquittal under indictment for larceny, alleging ownership in one person, is a bar to a subsequent indictment for the same larceny, alleging ownership in another, and that the crime was committed on a different day. Good *v.* State, 70 Ga. 752.

When the evidence necessary to support the second indictment would have been sufficient to procure a legal conviction upon the first, the plea of *autrefois acquit* is generally good, but not otherwise. Hilands *v.* Commonwealth, 111 Pa. St. 1; s. c., 5 Cent. Rep. 267.

A verdict of guilty on one count in a criminal complaint, saying nothing as to other counts, is equivalent to a verdict of not guilty as to such other counts. And where such a verdict has been rendered, and the defendant procures a new trial, he can be tried at the new trial only for the offences charged in the count upon which he was found guilty at the former trial. State *v.* McNaught, 36 Kan. 624.

When a court of its own motion discharged the jury impanelled and sworn in a capital case, before any evidence had been given, a plea of former jeopardy will be good, and the accused cannot be again tried for the same offence. Hilands *v.* Commonwealth, 111 Pa. St. 1; s. c., 1 Cent. Rep. 899.

Discharge of a jury in a capital case, because the court had permitted them to separate, is not such an extreme necessity as will warrant bringing the accused to trial anew. Hilands *v.* Commonwealth, 111 Pa. St. 1; s. c., 5 Cent. Rep. 899.

Acquittal, even without a judgment of the court, is a bar, — State *v.* Elden, 41 Me. 165; West *v.* State, 22 N. J. L. (2 Zab.) 212, — but convictions do not follow this rule. United States *v.* Negro Herbert, 5 Cr. C. C. 87; Commonwealth *v.* Frasher, 126 Mass. 265; West *v.* State, 22 N. J. L. (2 Zab.) 212; Pennsylvania *v.* Huffman, Addis. (Pa.) 140; Mount *v.* State, 14 Ohio, 295; Brennan *v.* People, 15 Ill. 511; State *v.* Norvell, 2 Yerg. (Tenn.) 24; State *v.* Spear, 6 Mo. 644; 1 Tex. Ct. App. 323. But see Preston *v.* State, 25 Miss. 383; Ratzky *v.* People, 29 N. Y. 124, where the prosecuting officer, after conviction, concedes the badness of the indictment, and proceeds on a second indictment, — Pennsylvania *v.* Huffman, Addis. (Pa.) 140, — or where the case is pending in error, — Commonwealth *v.* People, 126 Mass. 265; Coleman *v.* Tennessee, 97 U. S. 530; bk. 24, L. ed. 1127; Jackson *v.* Moyer, 13 Johns. (N. Y.) 531, — or where the indictment was stolen after verdict and before judgment, — Mount *v.* State, 14 Ohio, 295; — but, ordinarily, a verdict of guilty will sustain the plea. State *v.* Parish, 43 Wis 395. See State *v.* Elden, 41 Me. 165.

When Plea Bad. — A former acquittal of a co-defendant is not a bar to a subsequent prosecution of defendant, though they were partners. Goforth *v.* State (Tex. App.), Nov. 1886. A judgment quashing an indictment will not bar a subsequent prosecution on the same charge. State *v.* Taylor, 34 La. An. 978. Where the jury was discharged and the indictment quashed for a clerical error in the allegation of time, in charging a future time, a plea of *autrefois acquit* on the trial under a new indictment, is properly overruled. State *v.* Jenkins, 20 S. C. 351. A man indicted for adultery cannot plead in bar the former acquittal of his paramour and co-defendant. Alonzo *v.* State, 15 Tex. App. 378; s. c., 49 Am. Rep. 207. A trial on an indictment held bad on motion in arrest is no ground for a plea of *autrefois acquit*. State *v.* Owen, 78 Mo. 367. A plea of *autrefois acquit*, showing upon its face that there was no identity of the former case, on trial, it was properly held bad on demurrer. Brothers *v.* State, 22 Tex. App. 447. A plea of former acquittal, which is bad upon its face, is properly stricken out. Shubert *v.* State, 21 Tex. App. 551.

Plea Demurrable. — On an indictment for involuntary manslaughter, a plea of a discharge or former acquittal, under an indictment for murder, is demurrable. Hilands *v.* Commonwealth, 111 Pa. St. 1; s. c., 5 Cent. Rep. 264.

2. R. *v.* Vandercomb, 2 Leach, 708.

Autrefois Acquit applies where the transaction is the same, and must be established by the same proof; while *autrefois convict* only requires the facts to be the same. Schubert *v.* State (Tex. App.), June, 1886.

felony, and an attempt to commit a felony.[1] It is a general rule that a former conviction of a lower degree of the offence charged operates on an acquittal of the higher degree.[2]

After a prisoner indicted for a crime in the first degree has been convicted of that crime in the third degree, which was reversed on appeal, he cannot thereafter be tried for the same crime in any degree.[3] And the defendant will be discharged without day, where the original proceedings are reversed for insufficiency of a special verdict.[4]

The prisoner must satisfy the court (1) that the former indictment, on which an acquittal took place, was sufficient in point of law, so that he was in jeopardy upon it; (2) that, in the indictment, the same offence was charged, for the indictment is in such a form as to apply equally to several different offences;[5] (3) of his identity with the defendant in the former prosecution. To prove his acquittal, he may obtain a certificate thereof from the officer or deputy having custody of the records of the court where the acquittal took place.

Former conviction or acquittal, to be available as a defence, must be pleaded: it cannot be considered on a motion to arrest the judgment.[6] And the plea of former acquittal is not admissible under the general issue.[7]

A plea of former acquittal or conviction need not be traversed by the Commonwealth.[8] And the burden is on the accused pleading former acquittal or conviction to show that he has been acquitted or convicted of the identical offence for which he is being tried.[8]

1. Harris, Cr. L. 309.

False Pretences. — But an acquittal for larceny is no bar to an indictment for false pretences; nor will an acquittal as accessory bar an indictment as principal, and *vice versa.* Nor, again, is an acquittal on a charge of stealing "certain goods" on the ground that such goods are a fixture in a building, a bar to an indictment for stealing the fixture. R. *v.* O'Brien, 46 L. T. N. S. 177.

2. Smith *v.* State (Tex. App.), Nov. 1886; Parker *v.* State, 22 Tex. App. 105. *Compare* Curtis *v.* State (Tex. App.), Nov. 1886.

In Texas. — It is a well-settled principle of law in this State, that, if a defendant upon trial for the higher grade of an offence consisting of degrees is convicted of an inferior grade of such offence, such conviction operates as an acquittal of all the grades higher than that for which the conviction was had, and will bar subsequent prosecution for any of such higher grades. Parker *v.* State, 22 Tex. App. 105.

If the offence charged be one consisting of different degrees, the statute (Code Crim. Proc. art. 713) which declares that "the jury may find the defendant not guilty of the higher (naming it) but guilty of any degree inferior to that charged in the information or indictment," is not mandatory so far as acquittal of the higher degree is concerned, but the finding of the lesser degree is *per se* an acquittal of the higher. Robinson *v.* State, 21 Tex. App. 160.

In New York, after a prisoner, indicted for a crime in the first degree, has been convicted of that crime in the third degree, and such conviction has been reversed on appeal, the prisoner, having been acquitted of the crime in the higher degree, cannot, under sec. 36 of the Penal Code, "be thereafter indicted or tried for the same crime in any other degree." People *v.* Palmer, 43 Hun (N. Y.), 397.

3. People *v.* Palmer, 43 Hun (N.Y.), 397.

4. Rhoads *v.* Commonwealth (Pa.), 4 Cent. Rep. 725.

5. Parke, B., in R. *v.* Bird, 2 Den. 94, 98; Bainbridge *v.* State, 30 Ohio St. 264; State *v.* Small, 51 Mo. 197.

6. State *v.* Morgan, 95 N. C. 641.

7. Rickles *v.* State, 68 Ala. 538.

8. Vowells *v.* Commonwealth, 83 Ky. 193.

3. *Former Conviction.* — A former conviction may be pleaded in bar of a subsequent indictment for the same offence,[1] and that whether judgment has been given or not;[2] for the law will not suffer a man to be twice put in jeopardy for the same offence.[3]

1. **In Indiana** it is said that it is too well settled to be open to doubt, that if a defendant has been put upon trial for a criminal offence; or, as is sometimes said, if a competent jury has been "charged" with the offence, and a *nolle prosequi*, or any thing equivalent thereto, is afterwards entered without his consent, — he cannot be again put upon trial for the same offence. Hensley *v.* State, 107 Ind. 587; s. c., 5 West. Rep. 473; Kingan *v.* State, 46 Ind. 132; Hines *v* Ohio, 24 Ohio St. 134; Bish. Cr. L. § 1016; Whart. Cr. Pl. §§ 517, 447; Moore, Cr. L. § 400; Boswell *v.* State, 111 Ind. 47; s. c., 9 West. Rep. 262, 264.

In Pennsylvania the Supreme Court recently held that where defendant is in jeopardy under the indictment and evidence, he cannot be again tried under the same indictment. Rhoads *v.* Commonwealth (Pa.), 4 Cent. Rep. 725.

2. People *v.* Goldstein, 32 Cal. 432; 2 Hale, 241, 242; 2 Hawk. P. C. ch. 3, sec. 1.

3. 2 Hale, 241, 242; 2 Hawk. P. C. ch. 35, sec 1.

Judgment on Conviction: Necessity for, on Plea. — To sustain the plea of *autrefois convict*, no judgment sentencing the prisoner need have been pronounced on the verdict. State *v.* Elden, 41 Me. 165.

But to sustain the plea of *autrefois acquit*, it is necessary that the defendant should produce a record of acquittal. Bailey *v.* State, 26 Ga. 579.

And the plea should set out the record of the former conviction or acquittal, and allege that the two offences are the same, and that the defendant in the former suit is the same person who is the defendant in the latter suit. Rex *v.* Wildey, 1 M. & S. 183; Wortham *v.* Commonwealth, 5 Rand. (Va.) 669; 2 East, P. C. 519; 2 Leach (4th ed), 708; Rex *v.* Taylor, 3 Barn. & Cress. 502.

When a Bar. — The plea of former jeopardy will protect a defendant from a second trial, only upon such charges as he might have been convicted of upon the first indictment. Hilands *v.* Commonwealth, 111 Pa. St. 1; s. c., 56 Am. Rep. 235, 5 Cent Rep. 264.

But the fact that another indictment had been previously found against the defendant for the same offence, is not a valid objection. Rev. Stat. sec. 1808; State *v.* Arnold (Mo.), 7 West. Rep. 283.

It has been *held* in Arkansas, that under the statute a conviction or acquittal by a judgment or verdict will bar any other prosecution for the same offence, notwithstanding a defect in form or substance of the indictment; but by any proceeding short of conviction or acquittal, the defendant is not in jeopardy if the indictment is so defective that a conviction under it would be reversed for error. State *v.* Ward, 48 Ark. 36.

However, if the former indictment was so defective that judgment might have been reversed, yet, if the judgment has been executed and performed, the plea of former conviction will prevail. Commonwealth *v.* Loud, 44 Mass. (3 Metc.) 328.

When one act constitutes two distinct offences, a conviction of one offence is not a bar to a subsequent indictment for the other offence. As, where the same acts constitute the offence of keeping a tippling-shop, and the distinct offence of being a common seller of intoxicating liquors. State *v.* Inness, 53 Me. 536; Commonwealth *v.* McShane, 110 Mass. 502. So, it has been *held* that a conviction of being a common seller of intoxicating liquors, is not a bar to an indictment for a single illegal sale during the time embraced in the first indictment. State *v.* Maher, 35 Maine, 225. But the contrary has been *held*. State *v.* Nutt, 23 Vt. 698.

It has been said in Texas that inasmuch as a conviction for wilfully driving stock from its accustomed range, etc., can be had under an indictment charging the theft of the stock, it is no objection to the sufficiency of a plea of former jeopardy interposed upon trial for the wilful driving of the stock, etc., that the indictment under which the former trial was had, charged the theft of the stock. McElmurray *v.* State, 21 Tex. App. 691.

A conviction of murder in the second degree is a bar to trial of the higher offence. Smith *v.* State, 68 Ala. 424.

And it is said that where defendant has been acquitted upon an information before a justice of the peace, charging him with selling whiskey and stomach bitters, *held*, that, on a second information charging the sale of an intoxicating mixture called "dandelion bitters," it was error to allow evidence of any sales of such mixture during the time covered by the first information. State *v.* Sterrenburg, 69 Iowa, 544.

After acquittal on an indictment for rape, the prisoners were indicted for assault and battery with intent to commit a rape, and for assault and battery; it was *held* that the former acquittal was a bar to the first charge in the indictment, but not to the second. Sargeant's Case, 2 City H. Rec. 44. And where, to an indictment for rape, the prisoner pleaded that he had been convicted before a justice of the peace, on the oath of the prosecutrix, of an assault and battery upon her, and fined twenty dollars, which fine was paid by him, and that the assault and battery of which he was so convicted, was the same assaulting, beating, ravishing, and carnally knowing of the said prosecutrix charged in the indictment for rape, on demurrer to such plea, it was adjudged bad on the ground that the facts set forth constituted no defence to the indictment for rape, and that an acquittal upon an indictment for felony constitutes no bar to an indictment for a misdemeanor; and that an acquittal for a misdemeanor is no bar to an indictment for a felony; that to make the plea of *autrefois convict* or *autrefois acquit* a bar, it is necessary that the crime charged in both cases be precisely the same. The above case does not come within the provision of the Revised Statutes which makes an acquittal or conviction on a former trial for an offence a bar to an indictment for such offence in any other degree or for an attempt to commit such offence. People *v.* Saunders, 4 Park. Cr. Cas. (N. Y.) 196.

Where a defendant, by a subsequent deposition, expressly contradicts a former one made by him, and makes apparent his corrupt motive, and negatives the probability of a mistake in the first, a conviction upon an indictment for perjury in either deposition would bar an indictment for perjury in the other. People *v.* Burden, 9 Barb. (N. Y.) 467.

And a conviction for misdemeanor, consisting in the commission of certain acts, e.g., administering drugs to procure an abortion, will bar a prosecution for felony based on a charge that such act was performed with an intent which would render it felonious, e.g., with intent to destroy the life of the child. Lohman *v.* People, 1 N. Y. 379; s. c., 2 Barb. (N. Y.) 216.

Ruling on Demurrer. — Sustaining a demurrer to an information, no direction for a new information being given, is a bar to another prosecution, notwithstanding the fact that a new information was filed before the judgment on the demurrer (People *v.* Jordan, 63 Cal. 219), for the hearing of a demurrer to an indictment does not constitute putting the defendant in jeopardy. A man has only been in jeopardy when he has had a trial. United States *v.* Phillips (D. C.), 4 Cent. Rep. 617, 620. A decision on a demurrer only bars a prosecution for same offence. People *v.* Richards, 44 Hun (N. Y.), 278, N. Y. Code Crim. Proc. sec. 327.

Discharging Jury. — Where the jury was discharged for an irregularity in separating over night, and another jury was impanelled, a plea of former jeopardy should be sustained. Hilands *v.* Commonwealth, 111 Pa. St. 1; s. c., 56 Am. Rep. 235; 5 Cent. Rep. 264.

The consent of a defendant that the jury may separate during the recess of the court, is not a consent that one of them may absent himself and necessitate the discharge of the jury; and such discharge, without his consent, will not deprive him of the defence of former jeopardy against a subsequent prosecution for the same offence. State *v.* Ward, 48 Ark. 36.

Where a juror, pending trial, and after the evidence was nearly in, was taken sick and the panel discharged, the prisoner has not been in jeopardy. State *v.* Emery, 59 Vt. 84; s. c., 3 New Eng. Rep. 377.

The record disclosing that the jury on the former trial were not discharged until they had been considering the verdict for two days, and that they were discharged because they had been kept together until it became altogether improbable that they could agree, the defendant's plea of former jeopardy was properly overruled and stricken out. Smith *v.* State, 22 Tex. App. 196.

When no Bar. — The discharge of a jury who have disagreed constitutes no bar to further prosecution. Kelly *v.* United States, 27 Fed. Rep. 616. And plea of once in jeopardy not sustained by proof of former trial with verdict of guilty set aside on motion of the defendant for mistake of a date under same indictment. State *v.* Blaisdell, 59 N. H. 328.

The fact that the offence charged in an information was committed before the filing of another complaint on which an acquittal was had, constitutes no bar. State *v.* Kuhuke, 30 Kan. 462.

The pendency of one indictment is no bar to a second one for the same offence. United States *v.* Neverson, 1 Mackey (D. C.), 152. And one charged with being a disorderly person, and discharged on objection to the jurisdiction, may be re-arrested on a warrant on like complaint. State *v.* Britton, 47 N. J. L. (13 Vr.) 251.

In pleading a former jeopardy to an indictment for a felony, it is not sufficient to show that a jeopardy had once attached to the defendant, but it must be shown that such jeopardy had not been discharged by operation of law, or waived by some act of the defendant. Hensley *v.* State, 107 Ind. 587; s. c., 5 West. Rep. 827. And if a juror so acts that no verdict can be rendered, as if he escapes before the verdict is rendered, this does not, like a wrongful discharge of the jury by the judge, entitle the defendant to go free, or protect him from a second jeopardy. Henning *v.* State,

106 Ind. 386; s. c., 4 West. Rep. 470, 475.

Accessory. — It is said to be clear, however, that if a man be indicted as accessory after the fact, and acquitted, he may be afterwards tried as a principal, for proof of one will not at all support the other. Knightley's Case, 1 Hale, 625; 2 Hale, 244; Hawk. bk. 1, ch. 34. sec. 11.

The Arresting of Judgment after conviction of a felony is no bar to a second indictment for the same offence, though the second indictment be similar to the first. People *v.* Casboras, 13 Johns. (N. Y.) 351.

Assault. — Proceedings for a contempt is no bar to a prosecution for the assault. Rex *v.* Offulfton, 2 Strange, 1107; State *v.* Woodfin, 5 Ired. (N. C.) L. 199; State *v.* Williams, 2 Spears (S. C.) L. 26. A trial and conviction before a court of special sessions for an assault and battery are no bar to a subsequent indictment for manslaughter, where the person assaulted dies subsequently of the wounds caused by the blows for the inflicting which the complaint for assault and battery was made; a former trial is no bar unless the first indictment was such as the accused might have been convicted upon by proof of the facts set forth in the second indictment. To constitute a bar, the offence charged in both indictments must be identically the same in law as well as in fact. Burns *v.* People, 1 Park. Cr. R. (N. Y.) 182. *Vide* 1 Park. Cr. R. 338, 445.

And where a conviction of assault and battery with a stick is a bar to a subsequent indictment for the same act, for assault with intent to murder. Moore *v.* State, 71 Ala. 307.

A Conviction for Aggravated Assault and battery, under an indictment for assault with intent to murder, will not operate to bar a prosecution for murder after the death of the assaulted party, the death resulting from the same transaction. Curtice *v.* State, 22 Tex. App. 227.

Burglary. — An acquittal of burglariously entering, and committing a larceny of A.'s clothes, is no bar to a trial for larceny of B.'s clothes. Philips *v.* State (Tenn.), March, 1887.

Larceny. — An acquittal upon an indictment for stealing the goods of Jenkins, the acquittal being had upon the ground that the goods belonged to Jenkinson, is no bar to a subsequent indictment for stealing the same goods as belonging to Jenkinson. Hughes' Case, 4 City H. Rec. 132.

Nuisance. — An acquittal of the defendant, on an indictment for a nuisance caused by a dam erected by him, is no bar to a subsequent indictment for a nuisance arising from the same cause years after. People *v.* Townsend, 3 Hill, 479.

Passing Counterfeit Money. — An acquittal by a jury, on a charge of having a single counterfeit bill in possession with an intention of passing the same, was held no bar to a prosecution against the prisoner so acquitted; and another, for having a large quantity of counterfeit money in possession. Van Houton's Case, 2 City H. Rec. 73.

Murder. — A failure to convict of felonious manslaughter on an indictment for murder will not preclude conviction on an indictment for involuntary manslaughter. Hilands *v.* Commonwealth, 111 Pa. St. 1; s. c., 56 Am. Rep. 235; 5 Cent. Rep. 264.

And a former conviction for concealing the birth of a bastard child is no defence to an indictment for the murder of such child. State *v.* Morgan, 95 N. C. 641. The Code, sec. 1004.

Rape. — Upon an indictment for rape, a plea that the charge was brought before a magistrate who decided that there was probable cause for a charge of assault and battery only, and convicted the prisoner of that offence, constitutes no defence. People *v.* Saunders, 4 Park. Cr. R. (N. Y.) 196.

Robbery. — A previous trial on the charge of robbery is not a bar to a subsequent indictment for assault with a dangerous weapon at the same time on the same person. State *v.* Helveston, 38 La. An. 314.

Forgery. — An acquittal on an indictment for forging indorsements on a note was held a bar to a subsequent indictment for uttering the note, knowing the indorsement to be forged; the evidence of the guilt in the latter case being such as would necessarily have established the guilt in the former case. People *v.* Allen, 1 Park. Cr. R. (N. Y.) 445. But a previous acquittal, on an indictment for forging a certificate of deposit, is no bar to an indictment for attempting to obtain money by means of a forged letter enclosing the certificate to the bank. People *v.* Ward, 15 Wend. (N. Y.) 231. *Contra*, People *v.* Krummer, 4 Park. Cr. R. (N. Y.) 445.

Nolle Prosequi. — After a new trial is granted, the State's attorney, the court consenting, may enter a *nolle prosequi*, without prejudice to a fresh prosecution, — State *v.* Rust, 31 Kan. 509, — for the entry of a *nolle prosequi* is not an acquittal, and cannot be pleaded in bar to a subsequent indictment for the same offence, — Commonwealth *v.* Wheeler, 2 Mass. 172; Wortham *v.* Commonwealth, 5 Rand. (Va.) 669; — therefore entry of a *nolle prosequi*, unless made without the prisoner's consent, and after the cause has been submitted to the jury, will not bar a subsequent indictment. Doyal *v.* State, 70 Ga. 134.

A plea to an indictment alleged that the defendant had been arraigned and pleaded not guilty to an indictment containing three

A former acquittal or conviction must be availed of by this plea; it cannot be availed of on motion in arrest of judgment;[1] but technical accuracy is not required in setting out a former conviction.[2]

counts, and that a *nolle prosequi* was thereupon entered to the second count, and a jury was impanelled and sworn, and evidence introduced; and before argument, and over the exception of the defendant, the prosecuting attorney was permitted to withdraw the third count of the indictment. A demurrer having been sustained to this plea, on appeal it was *held* that, there being no averments of a conviction or an acquittal on the first count, the inference was that there was no final judgment on that count, because either the jury failed to return a verdict, or a new trial was granted, or the judgment was arrested, and therefore another trial might be had on that count. The cause having thus stood over, the prosecuting attorney might have abandoned the cause on that count, and have had a new indictment returned, based upon and covering the same facts, either in one or more counts. Hensley *v.* State, 107 Ind. 587; s. c., 5 West. Rep. 827.

Habeas Corpus. — The question whether a former trial and conviction for abduction are a bar to a subsequent indictment found for murder alleged to have been previously committed, cannot be raised and made a ground for discharge on *habeas corpus*. Such defence can only be made available, if at all, on the trial of the indictment for murder. People *v.* Rulloff, 3 Park. Cr. R. (N. Y.) 126.

Reversal, etc. — Where a judgment of conviction is reversed on appeal, the accused may be tried again. Territory *v.* Dorman, 1 Ariz. 56.

A discharge on formal objections will not sustain the plea of former jeopardy. State *v.* Britton, 47 N. J. L. (18 Vr.) 251.

And where a verdict of guilty has been set aside on the defendant's motion, a plea of once in jeopardy cannot avail him on a second trial. State *v.* Patterson, 88 Mo. 88; s. c., 3 West. Rep. 226.

As to the Identity of the offence, if the crimes charged in the former and present prosecution are so distinct that evidence of the one will not support the other, it is inconsistent with reason, as it is repugnant to the rules of law, to say that the offences are so far the same that an acquittal of the one will be a bar to the prosecution of the other. King *v.* Vandercomb, 2 Leach, 717; Commonwealth *v.* Roby, 29 Mass. (12 Pick.) 505.

A judgment of conviction of an offence on a specified day, rendered upon a plea of guilty, will not sustain a plea of former conviction in bar of another indictment for a like offence at a different time, without proof that both indictments were for the same offence. State *v.* Blahut, 48 Ark. 34.

Whether the accused has been previously tried for same offence is a question of fact to be determined by the record and parol evidence in connection therewith, for the purpose of identification. Walter *v.* State, 105 Ind. 589; s. c., 2 West. Rep. 759.

A Verdict of Guilty upon a Former Indictment, where there was no judgment on the verdict, but where the court virtually set the verdict aside by sustaining a motion in arrest of judgment, and also set the indictment aside, was not such a former conviction as to bar a prosecution upon a new indictment for the same offence, under sect. 4364 of the Code. State *v.* Clark, 69 Iowa, 196.

Continuance. — Where, on the trial of a criminal case, the State introduced evidence and rested, and the defendant introduced his evidence, and the district attorney then moved for leave to introduce a witness who had not been before the grand jury, and of whose examination notice had not been given, and the motion was sustained, and the defendant then elected to have the cause continued (Code, sect. 4421), which was done accordingly, *held*, that defendant could not object to another trial on the ground that, by the proceedings above referred to, he had already been put in jeopardy. State *v.* Falconer, 70 Iowa, 416.

Trial on Change of Venue. — The court to which a change of venue in a criminal cause is taken, acquires no jurisdiction of the cause until there is filed in it a transcript of the record of the proceedings in the cause from the original court, duly certified by the clerk under the seal of the court; and therefore a trial of the defendant upon a transcript without a seal would be no jeopardy, and no defence against a trial upon the same record after it is perfected by the seal. Bald. *v.* State, 48 Ark. 94.

1. State *v.* Barnes, 32 Maine, 530.
2. State *v.* Welch (Maine), 3 New Eng. Rep. 627.

Indictment for Gaming. — A plea of former conviction to an indictment for gaming, which does not aver the identity of the offence charged in the indictment with that for which the former conviction was had, is fatally defective. Pope *v.* State, 63 Miss. 53.

The issue joined upon a special plea of a former trial can only be tried by a jury: the consent of a defendant cannot confer jurisdiction upon the court to try the issue without a jury.[1] On a plea of *autrefois acquit*, a jury are sworn instantly to try the cause.[2] The proof of the issue lies upon the defendant;[3] and to prove it, he has first merely to prove the record, and secondly to prove the averment of identity contained in his plea.[4]

In cases where a plea of *autrefois acquit* is interposed, if the indictment be for a felony the defendant should also plead over to the felony.[5] But if the defendant plead *autrefois acquit* without pleading over to the felony, after his special plea is found against him, he may still plead over to the felony.[6] And in cases of felony, where he pleads over at the same time with the plea of *autrefois acquit*, the jury are charged again to inquire of the second issue.[7]

Where the plea of not guilty is tendered at the same time with that of a previous acquittal, the defendant cannot have both issues submitted to the jury at once, but the court will order the special plea to be passed on first.[8]

It seems to be doubted, whether, in cases of misdemeanor, the defendant may plead over by leave of the court.[9]

The same rules as in the plea of *autrefois acquit* generally apply; thus, there is the same test as to the identity of the crime.[10] And the plea of former conviction need not aver that judgment was rendered on the verdict,[11] for a verdict of acquittal is a finality: it operates as a discharge of the accused, and judgment thereon is a matter of course.[12]

1. Grant *v.* People, 4 Park. Cr. R. (N. Y.) 527.
2. 2 Leach, 541.
3. Arch. 90.
4. 2 Russ. 721, n.
5. Arch. Cr. Pl. & Ev., note.
6. 2 Hawk. P. C. ch. 23, sec. 128; Rex *v.* Sheen, 2 Car & P. 634; 13 Mass. 455.
7. 2 Leach, 448, 708.
8. Rex *v.* Roche, 1 Leach, 134; 90 Mass. (8 Allen) 545.
9. R. *v.* Strahan, 7 Cox, C. C. 85, 86.
10. Harris, Cr. L. 379.

Form and Requisites of Plea. — The form, requisites, and consequences of this plea are very nearly the same as in a plea of former acquittal. Like that plea, it must set forth the former record, and plead over to the felony. 2 Hale, 255–392. And as in that the identity must be shown by averments, both of the offence and of the person, so the same forms are here requisite. 2 Hale, 255–392. Also, like that plea, in order to constitute it an available defence in bar of another prosecution, the former conviction must have been had before a tribunal having competent jurisdiction. The State *v.* Spencer, 10 Humph. (Tenn.) 431; Commonwealth *v.* Goddard, 13 Mass. 455; Rector *v.* State, 1 Eng. (Ark.) 187; Dunn *v.* State, 2 Ark. 229; R. *v.* Welsh, Ry. & M. 175; Commonwealth *v.* Peters, 53 Mass. (12 Metc.) 387; State *v.* Odell, 4 Blackf. (Ind.) 156.

In a Complaint of Search and Seizure, an averment of prior conviction that "defendant has been before convicted of unlawfully keeping and depositing in this State intoxicating liquors, with intent that the same should be sold in this State in violation of law," and stating the time, place, and court in which the conviction was had, *held* sufficient. State *v.* Longley (Me.). s. c., 3 New Eng. Rep. 617.

11. If judgment were so rendered, the appropriate plea was formerly, when the forms were established, *autrefois attaint*: and if the verdict of guilty had been set aside, that was matter for replication by the prosecution.

12. **The English Rule,** however, is, that the plea of former acquittal should aver judgment on the verdict. 2 Hale, P. C. 243; Rex *v.* Sheen, 2 C. & P. 634, where the form of the plea is commended by the court.

The Constitution of the United States provides that no person shall be subject, for the same offence, to be twice put in jeopardy of life or limb.[1] The equivalent provision in the State Constitutions is more commonly in the form that no person shall be put in jeopardy twice for the same offence.[2]

Jeopardy begins when the trial jury is sworn. If, after that, without assent of the defendant, the prosecuting attorney enters a *nolle prosequi*, or the court, without sufficient cause, discharges the jury, the effect is the same as an acquittal, — the defendant is finally discharged, and cannot be tried again. The defence of "once in jeopardy" is therefore broader than the strict plea of "former acquittal."[3] Legal jeopardy does not arise if the court has no jurisdiction of the offence.[4] Therefore, in order to make

In the United States, however, it is generally held that judgment need not be averred in a plea of former acquittal. *Dictum* in State *v.* Elden, 41 Maine, 185; State *v.* Benham, 7 Conn. 414; West *v.* State, 22 N. J. L. (2 Zabr.) 212; State *v.* Novell, 2 Yerg. (Tenn.) 24; Mount *v.* State, 14 Ohio, 295.

1. **Article V. of the Amendments to the Constitution** of the United States, *inter alia*, declares, "Nor shall any person be subject, for the same offence, to be twice put in jeopardy of life or limb." Article 1, sec. 10, of Declaration of Rights of the Constitution of Pennsylvania declares, "No person shall, for the same offence, be twice put in jeopardy of life or limb." This identical language was in the Constitution of 1790, and retained in the amended one of 1838. The declaration is not that a person shall not be twice tried for the same offence, but that he shall not be twice put in jeopardy. Hilands *v.* Commonwealth, 111 Pa. St. 1; s. c., 56 Am. Rep. 235; 5 Cent. Rep. 899.

This Restriction is limited, and applies only to the General Government, and does not apply to State government. State *v.* Flynn (R. I.), 5 New Eng. Rep. 329; Barron *v.* Baltimore, 32 U. S. (7 Pet.) 243; bk. 8, L. ed. 672.

Withdrawing Juror. — Where, on a trial for a felony, after the public prosecutor has entered upon his case and given evidence to the jury, he finds himself unprepared with the proper evidence to convict, and obtains leave of the court to withdraw a juror, and thus arrest the trial, such withdrawal not being the result of improper practice on the part of the defendant, or any one acting with or for him, or of any overruling, inevitable necessity, the defendant cannot again be put on trial for the same offence; but the objection to a second trial in such a case does not rest upon the constitutional provision that no person shall be subject to be put twice in jeopardy for the same offence. That provision is a protection only where there has been a conviction or acquittal by the verdict of a jury, and judgment has passed thereon, and does not apply to a case where the jury have been discharged without giving any verdict, or where judgment has been arrested. The objection lies back of the constitution, and rests upon the principles of the common law, which are essential to the protection of the accused, by securing him a speedy and impartial trial and the best means of vindicating his own innocence. Klock *v.* People, 2 Park. Cr. R. (N. Y.) 676.

Former Jeopardy: How Pleaded. — The prisoner, in taking advantage of a former jeopardy, brings the fact to the attention of the court by two pleas in bar known to the common law: the one of which is produced when the jeopardy has resulted in a conviction, and is called the plea of *autrefois convict*; the other of which is brought forward when the jeopardy has resulted in an acquittal, and is called the plea of *autrefois acquit*. Bish. Cr. Pro. 572.

Second Offence. — An act providing for conviction for second and third offences is not unconstitutional; second conviction need not be for same crime as former. Kelley *v.* People, 115 Ill. 583; s. c., 3 West. Rep. 45.

2. **The Maxim that a Man ought not to be brought twice into Danger,** *Justice Story* remarks, is embodied in the very element of the common law, and has been uniformly construed to present an insurmountable barrier to a second prosecution where there has once been a verdict of acquittal or conviction regularly had upon a sufficient indictment. United States *v.* Gilbert, 2 Sumn. C. C. 42.

3. Such defence and forms, however, are undoubtedly included in the general designation, "plea of former acquittal."

4. Commonwealth *v.* Peters, 53 Mass. (12 Metc.) 387; Commonwealth *v.* Goddard,

a plea of former acquittal or former conviction available, the

13 Mass. 455; People *v.* Tyler, 7 Mich. 161.

Former Jeopardy. — Where accused has entered a plea of guilty, and nothing remains but to pass judgment, he has been in jeopardy. Boswell *v.* State, 111 Ind. 447; s. c., 9 West. Rep. 262.

And where a jury is impanelled and sworn, in a court of competent jurisdiction, to try a prisoner under an indictment sufficient in form and substance to sustain a conviction, he is in jeopardy. State *v.* Ward (Ark.), Dec. 1886; Hilands *v.* Commonwealth, 111 Pa. St. 1; s. c., 56 Am. Rep. 235; 5 Cent. Rep. 899. *Compare* United States *v.* Bigelow, 3 Mackey (D. C.), 393; United States *v.* Phillips (D. C.), 4 Cent. Rep. 617.

But the plea of former jeopardy will protect from a second trial only upon such charges as might have convicted upon the first indictment. Hilands *v.* Commonwealth, 111 Pa. St. 1; s. c., 56 Am. Rep. 235; 5 Cent. Rep. 264; 2 Hawk. ch. 35, sec. 8; E. *v.* Vandercombe, 2 Leach, 708; Vaux's Case, 3 Co. 45; Wigg's Case, 4 Co. 46, b.

Thus, an acquittal upon an invalid and insufficient indictment was no bar to another indictment for the same offence, as if the offence was alleged to have been committed in another district than the one in which the bill was found, or if an impossible date was assigned to the commission of the offence, as a day posterior to the finding of the indictment. State *v.* Ray, 1 Rice (S. C.) 1; Commonwealth *v.* Cunningham, 13 Mass. 245; Hite *v.* State, 9 Yerg. (Tenn.) 357; Commonwealth *v.* Curtis, Thach. C. C. (Mass) 202; Gerard *v.* People, 3 Scamm. (Ill.) 363; Le Prince *v.* Guillemot, 1 Rich. (S. C) 219; Commonwealth *v.* Cook, 6 Serg. & R. (Pa.) 577; Commonwealth *v.* Clue, 3 Rawle (Pa.), 498; Commonwealth *v.* Purchase, 19 Mass. (2 Pick.) 521; People *v.* Barrett, 1 John. (N.Y.) 66; Commonwealth *v.* Roby, 29 Mass. (12 Pick) 496.

A plea of former jeopardy cannot be sustained on proceedings before a justice of the peace, on their face void. Johnson *v.* State (Ala.), June, 1887. And no jeopardy arises from trial and conviction in a court having no jurisdiction. Montross *v.* State, 61 Miss. 429. But if a party is once placed upon trial before a competent court and jury upon a valid indictment, the jeopardy attaches, to which he cannot be again subjected, unless the jury be discharged from rendering a verdict by a legal necessity, or by his consent; or in case a verdict is rendered, if it be set aside at his instance. People *v.* Horn, 70 Cal. 17.

If a man be acquitted on an indictment for murder, he cannot afterwards be indicted for manslaughter of the same person, for he might have been convicted of manslaughter on the former indictment. 2 Hale, 246. A trial for robbery involves the question of larceny, and an acquittal is a perfect bar to a prosecution for larceny in respect to the same property. People *v.* McGowan, 17 Wend. (N. Y.) 386. An acquittal of arson for burning a mill is a bar to a subsequent prosecution for arson of books of account at the same time. State *v.* Colgate, 31 Kan. 511; s. c., 47 Am. Rep. 507. And if one person was indicted singly, he may plead that he was before indicted jointly with other persons, and, on such indictment, convicted or acquitted. Rex *v.* Dann, 1 Moody, 424.

A mis-trial and consequent discharge of the jury does not put the accused in legal jeopardy, — State *v.* Blackman, 35 La. An. 483, — but former jeopardy may be pleaded where the judge discharged the jury in a murder trial, after deliberating three and a half hours, for failure to agree. Whitten *v.* State, 61 Miss. 717. Where the trial had commenced, and the evidence was nearly in when a juror was taken sick and the panel discharged, it was *held* that the prisoner had not been in jeopardy. State *v.* Emery, 59 Vt. 84; s. c., 3 New Eng. Rep. 377. It is not sufficient to show that the jeopardy had once attached, but that it had not been discharged by operation of law, or waived. Hensley *v.* State, 107 Ind. 587; s. c., 5 West. Rep. 827.

An information for murder charged the commission of the offence on a day subsequent to the date of its filing. The mistake being discovered on the trial, the jury were discharged, on motion of the prosecution, before verdict. A new information was then filed, to which the defendant pleaded that he had been once in jeopardy for the same offence. *Held*, that a conviction upon this information would have been a nullity, and that it was not admissible to sustain the plea. People *v.* Larson, 68 Cal. 18.

If a juror fraudulently procured himself to be put on the jury to acquit the prisoner of murder, the judge may direct the withdrawal of a juror, even if the prisoner was innocent of the fraud; and this constitutes no jeopardy. State *v.* Washington, 89 N. C. 585; s. c., 45 Am. Rep. 700. And there was no jeopardy where, in a murder case, the jury having been out ten days, the judge withdrew a juror, and ordered a mis-trial. State *v.* Washington, 90 N. C. 664; State *v.* Carland, 90 N. C. 668. Also where the trial had commenced, and the court must have been competent having jurisdiction,[1] and the proceedings must have been regular;[2] but where the court has final jurisdiction, an acquittal or conviction is a bar, although the proceedings were defective.[3] Nor is such party put in legal jeopardy if it appears that the first indictment was clearly insufficient and invalid,[4] nor if, by any overruling necessity, the jury are discharged without a verdict.[5] Nor is such party put in legal jeopardy if the term of court, as fixed by law, comes to an end before the trial is finished;[6] nor if the verdict is set aside on motion of the accused, or writ of error based on his behalf;[7] nor in case the judgment is arrested on his motion;[8] nor if the jury is discharged after considering the cause for such a length of time as to leave no reasonable expectation that they will be able to agree upon a verdict.[9]

But an acquittal, even though erroneous, is conclusive until the judgment is reversed;[10] so that if a judge direct the jury to acquit the prisoner on any ground, however fallacious, he is entitled to the benefit of the verdict.[11] However, a former acquittal

evidence was nearly in, when one of the jurors was taken sick, and the panel was thereupon discharged, *held*, that the prisoner had not been in jeopardy. State *v.* Emery, 59 Vt. 84; s. c., 3 New Eng. Rep. 377.

1. Marston *v.* Jenness, 11 N. H. 156; Commonwealth *v.* Myers, 1 Va. Cas. 188; State *v.* Hodgkins, 42 N. H. 475; Commonwealth *v.* Goddard, 13 Mass. 456; Commonwealth *v.* Peters, 53 Mass. (12 Metc.) 387; Canter *v.* People, 38 How. (N. Y.) Pr. 91; Dunn *v.* State, 2 Ark. 229; State *v.* Odell, 4 Blackf. (Ind.) 156; O'Brian *v.* State, 12 Ind. 369; Weaver *v.* State, 14 Tex. 387; State *v.* Payne, 4 Mo. 376; Thompson *v.* State, 6 Neb. 102; Rector *v.* State, 1 Eng. (Ark.) 187; Mikels *v.* State, 3 Heisk. (Tenn.) 321; Commonwealth *v.* Alderman, 4 Mass. 477; State *v.* Morgan, 62 Ind. 35.

2. Commonwealth *v.* Bosworth, 113 Mass. 200.

3. Stevens *v.* Fassett, 27 Me. 266. See State *v.* Thornton, 37 Mo. 360; Commonwealth *v.* Miller, 5 Dana (Ky.), 320.

4. Commonwealth *v.* Bakeman, 105 Mass. 53; Gerard *v.* People, 3 Ill. 362; People *v.* Cook, 10 Mich. 164: Mount *v.* Commonwealth, 2 Duv. (Ky.) 93.

5. United States *v.* Perez, 22 U. S. (9 Wheat.) 579; bk 6, L. ed. 579; People *v.* Goodwin, 18 Johns. N. Y. 187; Commonwealth *v.* Bowden, 9 Mass 494; Commonwealth *v.* Purchase, 19 Mass. (2 Pick.) 521.

6. State *v.* Brooks, 3 Humph. (Tenn.) 70; State *v.* Mahala, 10 Yerg (Tenn.) 532; State *v.* Battle, 7 Ala. 259. *In re* Spier, 1 Dev. (N. C.) 491; Wright *v.* State, 5 Ind. 290.

Nor if the jury are discharged before verdict, with the consent of the accused, expressed or implied. State *v.* Slack, 6 Ala. 676.

7. State *v.* Redman, 17 Iowa, 329.

8. People *v.* Casborns, 13 Johns. (N. Y.) 351. See Coleman *v.* Tennessee, 97 U. S. (7 Otto) 509-521; bk. 24, L. ed. 1118.

9. Dobbins *v.* State, 14 Ohio St. 493.

10. **Trial on Reversal of Conviction.** — To subject a prisoner to a second trial, where a former conviction has been reversed, and a new trial ordered by a court of review on the application of the prisoner, is not a violation of the constitutional provision which declares that no person shall be subject to be twice put in jeopardy for the same offence. People *v.* Ruloff, 5 Park. Cr. R. (N. Y.) 77.

11. State *v.* Norvell, 2 Yerg. (Tenn.) 24.

After the submission of a criminal case to a jury, their retirement to their room for deliberation, and their failure to agree upon a verdict, they were discharged by the court. The following entry was thereupon made by the court upon the trial docket: "Jury impanelled and sworn. Trial had. Jury discharged for the reason that there was no probability of jurors agreeing. Recognizance fixed at one thousand dollars. Recognizance with sureties entered into. Continued." At the second term of the court thereafter, the defendant was again put upon his trial to a jury upon the same indictment. He moved the court to discharge him from further prosecution, offering in evidence in support of his motion the journal entry of the proceedings at the former trial, from which had been omitted the recital from the court docket of the or conviction will not be a defence, if it was procured by the fraud of the defendant.[1]

If judgment be given in favor of the defendant, it is that "he go thereof without day;" and if the issue be found against the defendant, it is that he answer over to the felony, if such be the nature of the indictment, or, in the case of a misdemeanor, that he receive judgment for the offence.[2]

4. *Pardon.* — A pardon may be pleaded not only in bar to the indictment, but also after verdict in arrest of judgment, and after judgment in bar of execution; but it must be pleaded as soon as the defendant has an opportunity of doing so, or he will be considered as having waived the benefit of it.[3]

a. Pardon must be produced. — Where a pardon has been granted, and this release is set up on the trial in arrest of judgment, or in bar of execution, the pardon must be proved by the production of the warrant itself, or its loss must be accounted for.[4]

IX. Plea of General Issue. — Under the plea of the general issue, or not guilty, the defendant may set up (1) infancy, (2) insanity, (3) intoxication, (4) justification, and (5) compulsion and duress.

1. *Infancy.* — Infancy may be set up as an excuse for crime, but will be available only in the absence of evidence of criminal intention; though there are certain presumptions of the law on the subject, some of which may, some of which may not, be rebutted.[5]

reason of the discharge of the jury. Thereupon the State moved the court to supply such omission by an order *nunc pro tunc*, which was done, the motion to discharge the defendant overruled, and the trial allowed to proceed. *Held*, there was no error in such action of the court. Benedict *v.* State, 44 Ohio St. 679; s. c., 9 West. Rep. 425.

1. State *v.* Reed, 26 Conn. 202; State *v.* Green, 16 Iowa, 239; Commonwealth *v.* Alderman, 4 Mass. 477; State *v.* Cole, 48 Mo. 70; State *v.* Little, 1 N. H. 257; State *v.* Colvin, 11 Humph. (Tenn.) 599; State *v.* Epps, 4 Sneed (Tenn.), 552; Commonwealth *v.* Jackson, 2 Va. Cas. 501.

2. 2 Colby, Cr. L. 336; People *v.* Saunders, 4 Park. Cr. R. (N. Y.) 196; 1 Arch. Cr. Pr. 113; 2 Hale, 253-257; 2 Hawk. ch. 36; R. *v.* Scott, 1 Leach, 401; R. *v.* Bowman, 6 Car. & P. 337; R. *v.* Goddard, 2 Ld. Raym. 920. But see Commonwealth *v.* Goddard, 13 Mass. 455; Foster *v.* Commonwealth, 8 Watts & S. (Pa.) 77.

3. Harris, Cr. L. 379. For a full discussion of pardon, see that title, this series.

Conditional Pardon. — Where a pardon is granted on condition, and there is a breach of the condition, the pardon becomes void, and the convict may be remanded to undergo sentence. People *v.* Potter, 1 Park. Cr. R. (N. Y.) 47; State *v.* Smith, 1 Bailey (S. C.), 123; State *v.* Fuller, 1 McCord (S. C.), L. 178; Commonwealth *v.* Haggerty, 4 Brewst. (Pa.) 326.

4. Spalding *v.* Saxton, 6 Watts (Pa.), 338; Commonwealth *ex rel.* Lawson *v.* Ohio & Pa. R. R. Co., 1 Grant Cas. (Pa.) 329.

5. Harris, Cr. L. 26. As to effect of infancy on ability to commit crime, *vide ante*, 683.

Age of Discretion. — The age of discretion, and, therefore, of responsibility, varies according to the nature of the crime. What the law technically terms "infancy" does not terminate till the age of twenty-one is reached; but this is not the "infancy" which is the criterion in the criminal law. Two other ages have been fixed as points with reference to which the criminality of an act is to be considered.

First Period. — Under the age of seven an infant cannot be convicted of a felony; for, until he reaches that age, he is presumed to be *doli incapax*; and this presumption cannot be rebutted by the clearest evidence of a mischievous discretion.

Presumptio Juris et de Jure. — Presumptions of this character are absolute, conclusive, and irrebuttable. No evidence is allowed to be given to the contrary. For example, an infant under the age of seven is incapable of committing a felony. Harris, Cr. L. 435.

But infants who have arrived at years of discretion are not to be allowed to commit crimes with impunity. In certain cases, the law deals with juvenile offenders in an exceptional way, in order, if possible, to prevent their becoming confirmed criminals.[1]

2. *Insanity.* — Insanity may be set up in defence to an indictment for crime, and, if the plea is established, it will excuse for the offence; but if, at the time of the homicide, the accused had capacity and reason sufficient to enable him to distinguish between right and wrong[2] as to the particular act he was doing, and had power to know that the act was wrong and criminal, he will be held responsible for his act.[3]

Second Period. — Between seven and fourteen he is still, *prima facie*, deemed by law to be *doli incapax;* but this presumption may be rebutted by clear and strong evidence of such mischievous discretion, the principle of the law being *malitia supplet ætatem.* Thus, a boy of the age of ten years was hanged for killing his companion, he having manifested a consciousness of guilt, and a discretion to discern between good and evil by hiding the body. See York's Case, Fost. 70; 1 Hale, P. C. 26, 27.

Exception to the Rule. — There is one exception to this rule, grounded on presumed physical reasons. A boy under the age of fourteen cannot be convicted of rape or similar offences, even though he has arrived at the full state of puberty. He may, however, be convicted as principal in the second degree. Harris, Cr. L. 26.

Third Period. — Between fourteen and twenty-one an infant is presumed to be *doli capax*, and, accordingly, as a rule, may be convicted of any crime, felony, or misdemeanor. But this rule is subject to exceptions, notably in the case of offences consisting of mere non-feasance; as, for example, negligently permitting felons to escape, not repairing highways, etc. It is given as a reason for the exemption in cases of the latter character, that, not having the command of his fortune till twenty-one, the person wants the capacity to do those things which the law requires. 4 Bl. Com. 22; Harris, Cr. L. 26.

1. Harris, Cr. L. 27.

2. To warrant the jury in acquitting under the defence of insanity, it must be proved affirmatively that the prisoner was at the time insane, — so insane that he did not know right from wrong. Walker *v.* State, 102 Ind. 502; s. c., 3 West. Rep. 354; Reg. *v.* Higginson, 1 C. & K. 129. If the fact be left in doubt, and if the crime charged is proved, it is the duty of the jury to convict. Reg. *v.* Stokes, 3 C. & K. 185.

3. State *v.* Mowry (Kan.), 10 Cr. L. Mag. 23; s. c., 15 Pac. Rep. 282. Lawson on Insanity, 1-326; Wharton & Stille's Medical Jurisprudence, Browne's Medical Jurisprudence of Insanity, Reese's American edition of Taylor's Medical Jurisprudence, and the note to Commonwealth *v.* Rogers, 1 Leading Crim. Cas. 100; see also tit. "Insanity," this series.

Definition and Kinds of Insanity. — In Commonwealth *v.* Rogers, 48 Mass. (7 Metc.) 500, the court define insanity as recognized by the law as (1) a want of capacity and reason to enable a person to distinguish between right and wrong, and understand the nature, character, and consequences of his act, and mental powers sufficient to apply that knowledge to his own case; (2) a delusion, or real and firm belief of the existence of a fact which is wholly imaginary, and under which he does an act which would be justifiable if such fact existed; (3) an uncontrollable impulse, which is the result of mental disease. The Supreme Court of Pennsylvania adopt substantially the same doctrine. Commonwealth *v.* Mosler, 4 Barr, Pa 267.

The Insanity of Uncontrollable Impulse occurs in criminal prosecutions mainly under the forms of homicidal mania and kleptomania, though several other forms are recognized by medical writers. A voluntary vicious indulgence, which grows into an inveterate habit, beyond control, is not insanity. It must be an irresistible impulse, "which is the result of mental disease." In The People *v.* Sprague, 2 Parker's Cr. R. (N. Y.) 43, where the defence of kleptomania was successfully pleaded, it was proved that insanity had been hereditary for several generations in the family of the defendant, and had been developed in him by an injury to his head, though it was manifested only in an uncontrollable propensity to a singular species of theft.

The insanity of uncontrollable impulse produced by mental disease is recognized in Commonwealth *v.* Rogers, 48 Mass. (7 Metc.) 500; State *v.* Johnson, 40 Conn. 136; Commonwealth *v.* Mosler, 4 Barr, 267; People *v.* Sprague, 2 Parker's Cr. R. (N. Y.) 43; Scott *v.* Commonwealth, 4

The law recognizes no standard of exemption from crime less than some degree of insanity or mental unsoundness. Mere

Met. (Ky.) 227; Smith *v.* Commonwealth, 1 Duv. (Ky.) 225; Kriel *v.* Commonwealth, 5 Bush (Ky.), 365; Shannahan *v.* Commonwealth, 8 Bush (Ky.), 464; Stevens *v.* State, 31 Ind. 485; State *v.* Felter, 25 Iowa, 67.

The Insanity of Delusion is recognized in Commonwealth *v.* Rogers, 48 Mass. (7 Metc.) 500.

Inability to distinguish between Right and Wrong, as to the act charged as a crime, is the generally accepted, and, in some States, the exclusively accepted, test of such insanity as exempts from criminal responsibility. Commonwealth *v.* Rogers, 48 Mass. (7 Metc.) 500; State *v.* Johnson, 40 Conn. 136; Willis *v.* People, 32 N. Y. 717; Flannigan *v.* People, 52 N. Y. 467; State *v.* Spencer, 21 N. J. L. (1 Zab.) 196; Commonwealth *v.* Mosler, 4 Barr (Pa.), 267; Ortwein *v.* Commonwealth, 76 Pa. St. 414; McAllister *v.* State, 17 Ala. 434; Bovard *v.* State, 30 Miss. 600; Dove *v.* State, 3 Heisk. (Tenn) 348; Loeffner *v.* State, 10 Ohio St. 598; Blackburn *v.* State, 23 Ohio St. 146; Hopps *v.* People, 31 Ill. 385; State *v.* Huting, 21 Mo. 476; People *v.* McDonnell, 47 Cal. 134; United States *v.* McGlue, 1 Curt. C. C. 8.

New Hampshire Doctrine. — The Supreme Court of New Hampshire, in State *v.* Pike, 49 N. H. 399, and State *v.* Jones, 50 N. H. 369, discarded all tests of insanity as rules of law. It is there *held* that insanity is a mental disease; neither delusion, nor knowledge of right and wrong, etc., is, as a matter of law, a test of mental disease; but all symptoms and tests of mental disease are purely matters of fact, to be determined by the jury; whether the defendant had a mental disease, and whether the act charged as a crime was the product of such disease, are the decisive questions, and they are questions of fact for the jury. In harmony with this, the same court has adopted, as a rule of evidence, that it is not competent for a witness who is not an expert to give his opinion as to the sanity of the defendant, though such opinion is based upon the witness's observation of the appearance and conduct, and the facts so observed are in evidence. Boardman *v.* Woodman, 47 N. H. 120; State *v.* Pike, 49 N. H. 399.

What constitutes Insanity: Difficulty of the Subject. — Mr. Harris says that with regard to no subject in criminal law is there so much obscurity and uncertainty as on the question of the responsibility or irresponsibility of a prisoner when the state of his mind at the time of the commission of the act is the point at issue. It has often been asserted, and not without a considerable degree of truth, that the acquittal or conviction of a prisoner, when insanity is alleged, is more or less a matter of chance. The subject is one on which the views taken by medical men differ most widely from those taken by lawyers; and, as the former are generally the most important witnesses in cases of alleged insanity, the confusion is by no means diminished. "There is great difference of opinion as to the cause of the uncertainty; the lawyers asserting that it is owing to the fanciful theories of medical men, who never fail to find insanity when they earnestly look for it, the latter protesting that it is owing to the unjust and absurd criterion of responsibility which is sanctioned by the law." Maudsley's Responsibility in Mental Disease (1874), 101.

There are two classes of mental alienation usually recognized: —

1. *Dementia naturalis*, or *a nativitate* — in other words idiocy, or continuous weakness of mind from birth, without lucid intervals: a person deaf and dumb from birth is by presumption of law an idiot, but it may be shown that he has the use of his understanding.

2. *Dementia accidentalis*, or *adventitia* — usually termed insanity, in the narrower signification. The mind is not naturally wanting or weak, but is deranged from some cause or other. It is either partial (insanity upon one or more subjects, the party being sane upon all others) or total. It is also either permanent (usually termed madness) or temporary (the object of it being afflicted with his disorder at certain periods only, with lucid intervals), which is usually denominated lunacy. Harris, Cr. L. 21. See Bacon, Abr. tit. "Idiots."

There are Three Stages in the History of the Law of Insanity. — The first, outrageous as it was, may be illustrated by the following dictum of an English judge: A man who is to be exempted from punishment "must be a man that is totally deprived of his understanding and memory, and doth not know what he is doing, no more than an infant, than a brute, or a wild beast." R. *v.* Arnold, 16 St. Tr. 764. The second stage regarded as the test of responsibility the power of distinguishing right from wrong in the abstract. R. *v.* Bellingham, Coll. 636. The third stage, unhappily, is that in which we live; though common sense may soon inaugurate a fourth. The existing state of doctrines dates from the trial of M'Naughten in the year 1843. 10 Cl. & Fin. 200; 1 C. & K. 130.

M'Naughten's Case. — Certain questions were propounded by the House of Lords weakness of mind does not excuse the commission of crime.[1] It must be shown that the act was done under mental delusion, and that the defendant did not know the act was wrong or criminal.[2]

The plea of insanity is itself, and of necessity, a plea in the nature of a plea of confession and avoidance; and where the fact of the killing was abundantly established by the evidence, as well as by the admissions of the defendant, and such a plea is interposed, it becomes immaterial whether testimony as to the dying

to the judges. The substance of their answers was to the following effect: "To establish a defence on the ground of insanity, it must be clearly proved, that, at the time of the committing of the act, the party accused was laboring under such a defect of reason, from disease of the mind, as not to know the nature and quality of the act he was doing, or, if he did know it, that he did not know he was doing what was wrong" *Cf.* Alison's Principles of Criminal Law of Scotland, pp. 645, 654. "The insanity must have been of such a kind as entirely to deprive the prisoner of the use of reason, *as applied to the act in question*, and of the knowledge that he was doing wrong in committing it." Thus, the question of knowledge of right or wrong, instead of being put generally and indefinitely, is put in reference to the *particular act* at the *particular time* of committing it. Harris, Cr. L. 22.

Partial Insanity. — As to partial insanity, that is, when a person is sane on all matters except one or more, the judges declared that "he must be considered in the same situation as to responsibility as if the facts with respect to which the delusion exists were real. For example, if, under the influence of his delusion, he supposes another man to be in the act of attempting to take away his life, and he kills that man, as he supposes, in self-defence, he would be exempt from punishment. If his delusion was, that the deceased had inflicted a serious injury to his character and fortune, and he killed him in revenge for such supposed injury, he would be liable to punishment. Maudsley says that "here is an unhesitating assumption that a man, having an insane delusion, has the power to think and act in regard to it *reasonably*; that, at the time of the offence, he ought to have and exercise the knowledge and self-control which a sane man would have and exercise, were the facts with respect to which the delusion exists real; that he is, in fact, bound to be reasonable in his unreason, sane in his insanity." Maudsley, 97.

After laying down, as above, what may be called the "particular right and wrong theory," they abandon it here, and also in another answer, where, still dealing with partial delusions, they express their opinion that "notwithstanding the party accused did the act complained of with a view, under the influence of insane delusion, of redressing or revenging some supposed grievance or injury, or of producing some public benefit, he is nevertheless punishable if he knew at the time of committing such crime that he was acting contrary to the law of the land." For strictures on these principles of "exquisite inhumanity," see remarks of Judge Ladd in State *v.* Jones, 50 N. H. 369.

1. Wartena *v.* State, 105 Ind. 445; s. c., 2 West. Rep. 757.

Temporary Insanity. — Where the defence of temporary insanity proceeds upon the theory that it was induced by strong drink upon a mind rendered unsound by an injury to the brain, responsibility must be determined by all the facts, not by the intoxication alone. People *v.* Cummins, 47 Mich. 334.

The Burden of proving Insanity rests upon defendant; and he is not entitled to the benefit of a reasonable doubt whether he was, or was not, insane. State *v.* Johnson, 90 Mo. 439; s. c., 8 West. Rep. 711, 712; Leach *v.* State, 22 Tex. App. 279; Parsons *v.* State, 81 Ala. 577; State *v.* Hanley, 34 Minn. 430; State *v.* Bundy, 24 S C. 439. And to establish the defence of insanity, it must be clearly proved. Walker *v.* People, 88 N Y. 81.

Under the Pennsylvania Act of May 14, 1874, providing for the removal to a hospital of a person acquitted of crime on the ground of insanity, application must be made to a judge of a court in which the accused could be legally tried. If the person convicted becomes insane in confinement, application for his removal must be made to a court or judge in the county where the conviction was had. Clarion Co. *v.* Western Pa. Hospital, 111 Pa. 339; s. c., 1 Cent. Rep. 909.

2. State *v.* Bundy, 24 S. C. 439.

Act without Apparent Motive. — Evidence that the act was sudden without apparent motive, and that the prisoner had been addicted to drink, and had been suffering under depression, was not enough to raise the defence of insanity. Reg. *v.* Dixon, 11 Cox, C. C. 341.

declarations of the deceased was properly introduced in evidence or not.[1]

3. *Intoxication.* — Voluntary intoxication is no excuse for crime;[2]

1. State *v.* Pagels, 92 Mo. 300; s. c., 10 West. Rep. 288; 1 Whart. Cr. L. (9th ed.) § 61.

2. State *v.* Bundy, 24 S.C. 439; Mix *v.* McCoy, 22 Mo. App. 488; s. c., 4 West. Rep. 895; McKenzie *v.* State, 26 Ark. 335; s. c., Lawson's Insanity as a Defence, 533; Kenny *v.* People, 31 N. Y. 330; s. c., Lawson's Insanity as a Defence, 562; Carson's Case, 2 Lew. C. C. 144. See Lawson's Insanity as a Defence, 533–768. See also *ante*, this vol., tit. "Criminal Law," XIII. 6; "Effect of Intoxication on Responsibility for Crime," pp. 707–715.

View of Early Text Writers. — Blackstone says that "the law of England, considering how easy it is to counterfeit this excuse, and how weak an excuse it is (though real), will not suffer any man thus to privilege one crime by another." 4 Bl. Com. 25, 26.

Coke says, that, "As for a drunkard, who is *voluntarius dæmon*, he hath no privilege thereby, but what hurt or ill soever he doeth, his drunkenness doth aggravate it." 1 Inst. 247.

Hale says, "By the laws of England such a person shall have no privilege by his voluntary contracted madness, but shall have the same judgment as if he were in his right sense." 1 Hale, P. C. 30.

Lord Bacon says that, "If a madman commit a felony, he shall not lose his life for it, because his infirmity came by act of God; but if a drunken man commit a felony, he shall not be excused, because the imperfection came by his own fault." "Maxims of the Law," rule 5.

An Early English Case declares "that if a person that is drunk kills another, this shall be felony, and he shall be hanged for it; and yet he did it through ignorance, for when he was drunk he had no understanding or memory; but inasmuch as that ignorance was occasioned by his own act and folly, and he might have avoided it, he shall not be privileged thereby." Reniger *v.* Zogossa, Plowd. 19. See Beverly's Case, 4 Co. 123 b, 125 a.

Recent English Cases. — In a case where the accused was indicted for rape, and he urged in his defence that he was intoxicated, the court said, "It is a maxim in the law if a man gets himself intoxicated, he is answerable to the consequences, and is not excusable on account of any crime he may commit when infuriated by liquor, provided he was previously in a fit state of reason to know right from wrong. If, indeed, the infuriated state at which he arrived should continue and become a lasting malady, then he is not answerable." R. *v.* Burrow, 1 Lew. C. C. 75.

The American Doctrine: In Georgia. — In the case of Choice *v.* State, 31 Ga 424, the court said, "Whether any one is born with an irresistible desire to drink, or whether such thirst may be the result of accidental injury to the brain, is a theory not yet satisfactorily established. For myself, I doubt whether it ever can be; and if it were, how far this crazy desire for liquor would excuse from crime is not for me to say. That this controlling thirst for liquor may be acquired by force of habit until it becomes sort of second nature, in common language, I entertain no doubt. Whether even a long course of indulgence will produce a pathological or organic change in the brain, I venture no opinion. Upon this proposition, however, I plant myself immutably, and from it nothing can dislodge me but an act of the legislature; namely, that neither moral nor legal responsibility can be avoided in that way. This is a new principle sought to be ingrafted upon criminal jurisprudence. It is neither more nor less than this: that a want of will and conscience to do right will constitute an excuse for the commission of crime, and that, too, where this deficiency in will and conscience is the result of a long and persevering course of wrong-doing. If this doctrine be true, — I speak it with all seriousness, — the Devil is the most irresponsible being in the universe. For, from his inveterate hostility to the Author of all good, no other creature has less power than Satan to do right. The burglar and the pirate may indulge in robbing and murder until it is as hard for an Ethiopian to change his skin as for them to cease to do evil; but the inability of Satan to control his will to do right is far beyond that; and yet our faith assures us that the fate of Satan is unalterably and eternally fixed in the prison-house of God's enemies. The fact is, responsibility depends upon the possession of will, not the power over it. Nor does the most desperate drunkard lose the power to control his will, but he loses the desire to control it. No matter how deep his degradation, the drunkard uses his will when he takes his cup. It is for the pleasure of the relief of the draught that he takes it. His intellect, his appetite, and his will, all work rationally, if not wisely, in his guilty indulgence; and, were you to exonerate the inebriate from responsibility, you would do violence, both to his consciousness and to his conscience, for he not only feels the self-prompted use of every rational power involved in accountability, but he feels, also, precisely what this new philosophy denies,—his solemn and actual wrong-doing in the very act of indulgence. Converse seriously with the greatest drunkard this side of actual insanity, just compose him so as to reach his clear, constant experience, and he will confess that he realizes his guilt, and therefore the responsibility of his conduct. A creature made by God never loses his responsibility, save by some sort of insanity. There have always existed amongst men a variety of cases wherein the will of the transgressor is universally admitted to have little or no power to dictate a return to virtue. But mankind have never, in any age of the world, exonerated the party from responsibility, except when they were considered to have lost rectitude of intellect by direct mental aberration." This case was quoted with approval in Goodwin *v.* State, 69 Ind. 550, 579.

In Indiana.—In the case of Goodwin *v.* State, 69 Ind. 550; s. c., 4 Cr. L. Mag. 565, the court say, "It was not error to refuse permission to ask a non-expert witness whether the accused could control his appetite for intoxicating liquor. Men who are not insane must control their appetites and passions. With quite as much propriety might a witness ask in a case of rape whether the accused could control his lustful desire, and with just as much reason might a witness be asked whether a prisoner could control his anger or master his desire for revenge; and to permit such things to excuse crime would be to break down all law, and set a premium on masterful evil passions. While the law shields from punishment one who does an act when insane from the continued use of intoxicating liquor, it does not permit him to set up his voluntary drunkenness as an excuse for taking human life. If the rule for which counsel contends should prevail, then the common drunkard, whose appetite controls his mind and will, may with impunity commit the gravest crimes, but, happily, the law is subject to no such reproach. People *v.* Ferris, 55 Cal. 589; s. c., 2 Cr. L. Mag. 18; Gillooley *v.* State, 58 Ind. 182; Cluck *v.* State, 40 Ind. 263; Bradley *v.* State, 30 Ind 492; Hudley *v.* State, 46 Mo. 44; Carter *v.* State, 12 Tex. 500; United States *v.* McGlue, 1 Curt. C. C. 44. The question in this case was not whether the appellant could refrain from strong drink, but whether he was insane when he slew his brother. If, however, the question had been the power of the accused to refrain from the use of liquor, the interrogatory would have been improper, for the reason that it is not competent to ask a witness whether a man has capacity to do, or refrain from doing, a particular thing. It is proper to inquire generally as to mental capacity; but it is not proper to inquire whether there is, or is not, capacity to do a specific act, as, for instance, to execute a will, make a contract, or commit a designated crime."

In Michigan, the Supreme Court said in People *v.* Garbutt, 17 Mich. 9; s. c., 7 Am. L. Reg. (N. S.) 554, that "A man who voluntarily puts himself in a condition to have no control of his actions must be held to intend the consequence. The safety of the community requires this rule. Intoxication is so easily counterfeited, and when real it is so often resorted to as a means of nerving the person up to the commission of some desperate act, and is withal so inexcusable in itself, that the law has never recognized it as an excuse for crime."

In New York, where the defendant was indicted for killing a man with a knife, on the trial evidence was introduced tending to show that the defendant was drunk at the time of the murder. The court say, "It will . . . occur to every mind that such a principle is absolutely essential to the protection of life and property. In the forum of conscience, there is, no doubt, considerable difference between a murder deliberately planned and executed by a person of unclouded intellect, and the reckless taking of life by one infuriated by intoxication; but human laws are based upon considerations of policy, and look rather to the maintenance of personal security and social order than to an accurate discrimination as to the moral qualities of individual conduct. But there is, in truth, no injustice in holding a person responsible for his acts committed in a state of voluntary intoxication. It is a duty which every one owes to his fellow-men and to society, to say nothing of more solemn obligations, to preserve, so far as lies in his own power, the inestimable gift of reason. If it is perverted or destroyed by fixed disease, though brought on by his own vices, the law holds him not accountable. But if, by a voluntary act, he temporarily casts off the restraints of reason and conscience, no wrong is done him if he is considered answerable for any injury which in that state he may do to others or to society." People *v.* Rogers, 18 N. Y. 9. The court, after referring to the English authorities cited *supra*, in this note, proceed, "Assuming the foregoing positions to be established, I proceed to an examination of the exceptions to the charge of the judge. It is difficult to know precisely what was meant by the request to charge, but I think its sense may be expressed thus: that drunkenness might exist to such a degree that neither an intention to commit murder, nor a motive for such an act, could be imputed to the prisoner. It was, therefore, asked that it should be left to the jury to determine whether such a degree of intoxication had been shown, and that they should be instructed that, if it had, the prisoner should be found guilty of manslaughter only. We must lay out of view, as inapplicable, the case of a person who had become insensible from intoxication, and who was performing an act unaccompanied by volition. There was nothing in the evidence to show that the prisoner's conduct was not entirely under the control of his will, or which would render it possible for the jury to find that he did not intend to stab the deceased with his knife. The mind and will were, no doubt, more or less perverted by intoxication, but there was no evidence tending to show that they were annihilated or suspended. Assuming, therefore, that the request did not refer to such a hypothesis, the only other possible meaning is, that it supposes that the jury might legally find that the prisoner was so much intoxicated that he could not be guilty of murder, for the want of the requisite intention and motive; and the request was, that they might be so instructed. This would be precisely the same thing as advising them that they might acquit of murder on account of the prisoner's intoxication, if they thought it sufficient in degree. It has been shown that this would be opposed to a well-established principle of law. The judge was not at liberty so to charge, and the exceptions to his refusal cannot be sustained. What he did charge on the subject of intoxication was more favorable to the prisoner than he had a right to claim. It implies, that, if he was so far intoxicated as to be deprived of his reasoning faculties, it was an excuse for the crime of murder, or, as perhaps it was intended to state, that he could not be guilty of murder. The rule which I have endeavored to explain, assumes that one may be convicted of murder or any other crime, though his mind be reduced by drunkenness to a condition which would have called for an acquittal if the obliquity of mind had arisen from any other cause. The judge ought to have charged, that, if a man makes himself voluntarily drunk, that is no excuse for any crime he may commit while he is so, and that he must take the consequences of his own voluntary act. Rex *v* Thomas, *supra*. The charge, therefore, gave the prisoner the chance of an acquittal to which he was not entitled, but this was not an error of which he can take advantage."

In Tennessee, in a case where the prisoner was convicted of murder, and urged his intoxication as an excuse, the court say, "Three cases of conviction for murder have been brought before this court at the present term, in two of which the prisoner was defended in the court below on the ground of madness occasioned by drunkenness; and yet in neither does it seem to us was there a colorable foundation for such a defence. This court would be remiss in the performance of their duty if they did not, under these circumstances, declare the law explicitly on this most important subject. In the argument of these causes, very untenable positions have been assumed, and very dangerous doctrines have been advanced, by counsel. And, from what was stated by some of those counsel, these doctrines have been repeatedly urged, and sometimes sanctioned in the courts below. It has become fashionable of late to discourse and philosophize much on mental sanity and insanity. New theories have been broached, and various grades and species of mania have been indicated. Some reasoners have gone so far as to maintain that we are all partial maniacs. Whatever difference of opinion there may be as to the construction and operations of the mind of man, whatever difficulty in discovering the various degrees of unsoundness, it is only necessary for us to ascertain the kind of prostration which is requisite to free a man from punishment for crimes by the law of the land. It is with this alone we have to do. What the law has said, we say. In all things else we are silent. We put our feet in the tracks of our forefathers. 'Non mens hic sermo, sed quæ præcepit affectus' Let us, then, for a moment resort to the sages of the law of different ages, and learn from them whether that species of frenzy which is produced by inebriety constitutes an excuse for crime, and what sort of insanity it is which will serve this purpose." Cornwell *v.* State, Mart. & Y. (Tenn.) 147.

Evidence of Drunkenness: When Inadmissible. — Accused's drunken condition at time of killing is inadmissible to show that no crime was committed, or to reduce the grade from murder in the first to second degree. State *v.* Sneed, 88 Mo. 138; s. c., 3 West. Rep. 797.

If defendant, who was drunk at the time of the act, was conscious, and understood what was done and said so as to give an intelligent and true account of it at the trial, he is responsible. Territory *v.* Franklin, 2 New Mex. 307. Although it is true intoxication cannot reduce an assault with intent to murder, to an aggravated assault, — Jeffries *v.* State, 9 Tex. App. 598, — yet in some cases it is admissible to show that no crime has been committed, or to show the degree or grade of the crime; so, in a prosecution for maliciously shooting, evidence that defendant was so intoxicated that he could not form an intent to wound, is admissible. Cline *v.* State, 43 Ohio St. 332; s. c.

intoxication is neither an aggravation of, nor an excuse for, crime,[1] and can only be considered in cases involving the condition of the defendant's mind when the offence was committed;[2]

1 West. Rep. 81; Barber v. State, 39 Ohio St. 660.

Drunkenness is sometimes termed *dementia affectata*,—acquired madness. But the sanctions of the law cannot be supposed to exert an equal influence on the mind and conduct of a person in this state, but the initiation of the crime may be said to date back to the time when the offender took steps to deprive himself of his reason. It is evident, that, if drunkenness were allowed to excuse, the gravest crimes might be committed with impunity by those who either counterfeited the state, or actually assumed it. Harris, Cr. L. 25.

1. **Aggravation.**—In early cases it was said that drunkenness "only aggravates the offence." People v. Porter, 2 Park. Cr. R. (N. Y.) 14. Such, however, is not now the law.

The Illinois Supreme Court say, "We are aware that text-writers frequently say that drunkenness is no excuse for crime, but rather an aggravation of the offence. That it is no excuse, is certainly true; but that it should be held in law to aggravate crime, is not, we conceive, a correct proposition. In ethics, it is, no doubt, true; but how can it aggravate a wilful deliberate murder, perpetrated with malice preconceived and deliberately perpetrated, we are unable to comprehend. Or that it will aggravate what in law is only manslaughter, if perpetrated by a sober man, into murder if committed by a drunken man, is not, we conceive, true. Or that it increases a minor offence to one of the higher grade, is not true. Whilst it is not ground for reversing a judgment, it is, perhaps, calculated to prejudice the defendant's case; and a court might well omit to give it, or at least to modify it before it should be given." McIntyre v. People, 38 Ill 515

In a Texas case it was said, "The court told the jury that the condition of the defendant, at the time of the homicide, the result of intoxication, was an aggravation of the offence, and should be so regarded by the jury, thus, in effect, telling them if the defendant was intoxicated he might be properly convicted of a higher grade of offence than the facts otherwise required; for, it will be observed, it is the offence, and not its penalty, which the court tells the jury is aggravated by appellant's intoxication. It is needless for us to say that the law of this State gives no warrant for such doctrine. While intoxication is no excuse, much less justification, for crime, it is certainly a startling idea that the bare fact of one being in this condition when the homicide is committed converts murder in the second into murder in the first degree, or will authorize, if not require, the jury to impose the penalty of death or confinement for life instead of a term of years. This would be directly the reverse of the rule laid down by the code, and would make that the homicide was committed when the perpetrator was incapable of a deliberate intention and formed design to take life or do other serious bodily injury for want of a sedate mind, an aggravation instead of a mitigation of the heinousness of murder." Farrell v. State, 43 Tex. 503. See also United States v. Claypool, 14 Fed. Rep. 127; United States v. Forbes, Crabbe, C. C. 559; Commonwealth v. Hart, 2 Brewst. (Pa.) 546; State v. Donovan, 61 Iowa, 369.

When resorted to, to blunt the Moral Responsibility, drunkenness heightens the culpability of the offender. United States v. Claypool, 14 Fed. Rep. 127.

And where the act is done wilfully, the intoxication is no extenuation of the offence. People v Jones, 2 Edm. (N. Y.) Sel. Cas. 86; Pugh v. State, 2 Tex. App 539.

2. State v. Mowry (Kan.), 10 Cr. L. Mag. 23; s. c., 15 Pac. Rep. 282.

It would be incorrect to say that the consideration of drunkenness is never entertained in the criminal law. Though it is no excuse for crime, yet it is sometimes an index of the quality of an act. Thus, it may be taken into account by the jury when considering the motive or intent of a person acting under its influence; for example, on the question whether a person who struck a blow was excited by passion, or acted from ill will; whether expressions used by the prisoner were uttered with a deliberate purpose, or were merely the idle expressions of a drunken man. Rex v. Thomas, 7 Car. & P. 817; Harris, Cr. L. 25

Intent.—Where the offence charged embraces deliberation, premeditation, some specific intent, or the like, evidence of intoxication may be important. People v. Harris, 29 Cal. 678; State v. Johnson. 40 Conn. 136; Roberts v. People, 19 Mich. 401; State v. Welch, 21 Minn. 22; People v. Robinson, 2 Park. Cr. R. (N. Y.) 235; Pigman v. State, 14 Ohio, 555; Nichols v. State, 8 Ohio St. 435; Davis v. State. 25 Ohio St. 369; Lytle v. State, 31 Ohio St. 196; Hopt v. People, 104 U. S. (14 Otto) 631; bk. 26, L. ed. 873.

Evidence that the accused was intoxicated at the time of the killing, is admissible to show whether he was in such a state of mind as to be capable of premeditation. Hopt *v.* People, 104 U. S. (14 Otto) 631; bk. 26, L. ed. 873.

In a prosecution for maliciously shooting with intent to wound, evidence that the defendant was so much intoxicated that he could not form any such intent, is admissible. Cline *v.* State, 43 Ohio St. 332; s. c., 1 West. Rep. 81.

Drunkenness may be taken into account by the jury when considering motive or intent of the one acting under its influence. Reg. *v.* Gamlen, 1 F. & F. 90.

Drunkenness may be considered by the jury like any other fact to shed light on the transaction. Hanvey *v.* State, 68 Ga. 612.

If drunkenness exists to such a degree as to render one incapable of forming a premeditated design to kill, it cannot be murder in the first degree. Cartwright *v.* State, 8 Lea (Tenn.), 376.

The accused may show, that, about the time the crime was committed, he was in such a physical condition as to render it improbable that he committed it; and the fact that such condition was caused by intoxication makes no difference in the rule, the intoxication not being set up as a defence. Ingalls *v.* State, 48 Wis. 647.

One may be guilty of the offence of shooting at a railroad train with intent to injure, although he was very drunk at the time. State *v.* Barbee, 92 N. C. 820.

If, at the time the defendant appropriated another's property, he was under the influence of liquor so as to be unable to form a felonious intent, he is not guilty of larceny. Wood *v.* State, 34 Ark. 341; s. c., 36 Am. Rep. 13.

Whether defendant was so intoxicated as to be unable to form intent to commit assault, is question for jury. Commonwealth *v.* Hogenlock, 140 Mass. 125; s. c., 1 N. E. Rep. 105, note.

Where the prisoner, at the time of the act, was so drunk that he did not know what he did, the fact negatived the attempt to commit suicide. Regina *v.* Moore, 3 Car. & K. 319; 16 Jur. 750; 1 Am. L. Reg. O. S. 37. But in such a case it is also held that the mere fact of drunkenness is no excuse; yet it is a material fact for the jury to consider, before coming to the conclusion that the prisoner really intended to destroy his life. Regina *v.* Doody, 6 Cox, C. C. 463.

Where provocation by a blow has been given to one who kills another, with a weapon which he happens to have in his hands, his drunkenness may be considered on the question of malice, and whether his expressions manifested a deliberate purpose, or were merely idle expressions of a drunken man Rex *v.* Thomas, 7 Car. & P. 817.

In Rex *v.* Thomas, *supra*, it is said that "drunkenness may be taken into consideration in cases where what the law deems sufficient provocation has been given, because the question is, in such cases, whether the fatal act is to be attributed to the passion of anger excited by the previous provocation, and that passion is more easily excited in a person when in a state of intoxication than when sober."

Effect on Specific Crimes: Assault and Battery. — It is no excuse for an assault and battery, for there no specific intent is necessary to constitute the offence. Commonwealth *v.* Malone, 114 Mass. 295.

Assault with Intent. — In Roberts *v.* People, 19 Mich. 401, the charge was shooting with intent to kill; and it was *held* that if the prisoner was so intoxicated as to be unable to entertain the intent to kill, he was not guilty. On a charge of an assault with intent to rob, evidence of drunkenness was *held* admissible, in Scott *v.* State, 12 Tex. App. 31; but where evidence is admissible to show drunkenness in order to reduce murder in the first to murder in the second degree, but not to manslaughter, it is *held* that evidence on a charge of assault with intent to murder is not admissible to reduce the crime to an aggravated assault. Jeffries *v.* State, 9 Tex. App. 598. See Gaitan *v.* State, 11 Tex. App. 544.

So, drunkenness may excuse one charged with an assault with intent to commit a rape. State *v.* Donovan, 61 Iowa, 369; s. c, 16 Rep. 488. However, if a rape was actually committed, the rule would be different Marshall *v.* State, 59 Ga. 154.

Generally, on this subject, see State *v.* Garvey, 11 Minn. 154; State *v.* Gut, 13 Minn. 341.

Blasphemy. — Drunkenness, in a case of blasphemy, has been held to aggravate the offence. People *v.* Porter, 2 Park. Cr. R (N. Y.) 14. See also Lanergan *v.* People, 50 Barb. (N. Y.) 266; s. c., 6 Park. Cr. R. (N. Y.) 209; Friery *v.* People, 54 Barb. (N. Y.) 319; Kenny *v.* People, 31 N. Y. 330; O'Brien *v.* People, 48 Barb. (N. Y) 274; s. c., 36 N. Y. 276. However, if the prisoner was so drunk as not to know what he was doing, it would probably be now held to be an excuse. People *v.* Porter, 2 Park. Cr. R. (N. Y.) 14.

Forgery. — On a charge of forgery, the accused may show that he was, at the time of the forgery, afflicted with dipsomania; that, from protracted habits of intemperance, his mind had been impaired; that, when he was under the influence of liquor, he was insane, did not know what he was doing, could not distinguish right from wrong, and that he was in such a state when he committed the act of which he is accused. People *v.* Blake, 5 Crim. L. Mag

722. *Contra*, People *v.* Willey, 2 Park. Cr. R. (N. Y.) 19.

Illegal Voting. — Where a statute made it an offence to "knowingly" vote twice at the same election, it was *held* that the accused might show that he was too drunk at the time of the voting, and immediately preceding it, to know what he was doing. People *v.* Harris, 29 Cal. 678. But where a statute made it a penal offence to cast an illegal vote regardless of knowledge of its illegality, drunkenness was held to be no excuse. State *v.* Welsh, 21 Minn. 22.

Incest. — Of drunkenness, as an excuse for the crime of incest, it was said in an Indiana case, "In the eighth instruction the jury were told, in substance, that voluntary drunkenness neither excused nor palliated an offence such as that with which the accused was charged. This was right. Voluntary drunkenness cannot be used as a shield to ward off punishment for a crime of such a character as that charged against the appellant. The instruction under immediate mention also told the jury that a man with ordinary capacity and will-power, unimpaired by disease, was bound to restrain his lustful passions. The counsel for appellant contend that this is not the statement of a rule of law, and that it prejudiced appellant's cause. The statement of the court was correct, although probably so plain a rule of common sense, as well as of law, as to have been unnecessarily embodied in an instruction; but, however this may be, it was not error to state it to the jury." Colee *v.* State, 75 Ind. 511.

Larceny. — What is true of an assault with intent to commit a felony, is true of a larceny. In such an instance, there must be not only the trespass committed that is necessary in every larceny, but there must be the specific larcenous intent entertained at the moment the trespass is committed. If, therefore, the prisoner was too drunk to know what he was about, or to entertain the specific intent to deprive the owner of his property, no crime is committed. Ingalls *v.* State, 48 Wis. 647; Wood *v.* State, 34 Ark. 341; s. c., 36 Am. Rep. 13; People *v.* Walker, 38 Mich. 156; Wentz *v.* State, 1 Tex. App. 488; State *v.* Schingen, 20 Wis. 74.

In Indiana, the courts, it is said, have fallen into error on this subject; that the earliest case is ill considered. In that case it was held that drunkenness could be no excuse for the crime of larceny. O'Harrin *v.* State, 14 Ind. 420. Respecting this case Mr. Bishop says, "Plainly, to sustain this Indiana doctrine would be to overturn the whole law of larceny, which rests on the idea of a specific intent in distinction from general malice. If a man too drunk to know what he was about, should carry off the goods of another, and then, on becoming sober, should appropriate them to himself instead of returning them, there would be a larceny committed after he became sober. But if he should return them on learning what he had done, it would be a monstrosity in the criminal law to hold him guilty of this offence." 1 Bish. Cr. L. (3d ed.) sec. 490. But the doctrine of this case has been followed, and is still the law of that State. Dawson *v.* State, 16 Ind. 423; Bailey *v.* State, 26 Ind. 422; Rogers *v.* State, 33 Ind. 543.

Murder. — Drunkenness is no excuse for homicide, although the result of an irresistible appetite, overcoming the will and amounting to a disease, and is immaterial on the question of premeditation. Flannigan *v.* People, 86 N. Y. 554; s. c., 40 Am. Rep. 556.

In a case of stabbing, where the prisoner has used a deadly weapon, the fact that he was drunk does not at all alter the nature of the case; but if he had intemperately used an instrument, not in its nature a deadly weapon, at a time when he was drunk, the fact of his being drunk might induce the jury to less strongly infer a malicious intent in him at the time. Rex *v.* Meakin, 7 Car. & P. 297.

So, it was held that drunkenness may be taken into account by the jury, when considering the motive or intent of the person acting under its influence. Rex *v.* Gamlen, 1 Fost. & F. 90. "Such a state of drunkenness may, no doubt, exist, or would take away the power of forming any specific intention." Regina *v.* Monkhouse, 4 Cox, C. C. 55.

Passing Counterfeit Money. — On a charge of passing counterfeit money, the defendant may show his intoxication, and that his condition prevented him from distinguishing between good and spurious money. This evidence is not conclusive. The prosecution may, in reply, show that the accused procured the money for the purpose of passing it. Pigman *v.* State, 14 Ohio, 555. See United States *v.* Roudenbush, 1 Baldw. C. C. 518; Nichols *v.* State, 8 Ohio St. 438.

Perjury. — So, on a charge of perjury, if the accused was so drunk as not to know what he was saying, it would manifestly be abhorrent to hold him guilty of violating his oath. The specific intent is absent which constitutes the crime; for it is to be remembered that a witness may swear falsely under a mistaken view of the facts, and yet not be guilty of this offence. Lytle *v.* State, 31 Ohio St. 196. In New York the court has held the same doctrine. People *v.* Willey, 2 Park. Cr. R. (N. Y.) 19.

Provocation. — It has been said, "if a man makes himself voluntarily drunk, that

and this is true, although the intoxication amounts to a frenzy.[1]

it is no excuse for any crime he may commit whilst he is so; he must take the consequences of his own voluntary act, or most crimes would otherwise be unpunished But drunkenness may be taken into consideration in cases where what the law deems sufficient provocation has been given, because the question is, in such cases, whether the fatal act is to be attributed to the passion of anger excited by the previous provocation, and that passion is more easily excitable in a person when in a state of intoxication than when he is sober." R. v. Thomas, 7 Car. & P. 817. See also Jones v. State, 29 Ga. 607; State v. McCanto, 1 Spears (S. C.), 384; State v Hurley, 1 Houst (Del.) Cr. Cas. 28; Haile v. State, 11 Humph. (Tenn) 154; Swan v. State, 4 Humph. (Tenn.) 136.

But inadequate provocation for a sober man, insufficient to mitigate his act, will not, *in and of itself*, have such an effect in case of an intoxicated person. There are not two rules of sufficient provocation, one for the sober man, and one for the drunken man. Keenan v. Commonwealth, 44 Pa. St. 55.

Self-Defence. — On an indictment for stabbing, the judge told the jury that they might take into consideration the fact of the person being drunk at the time, in order to determine whether he acted under a *bona fide* apprehension that his person or property was about to be attacked. Marshall's Case, Lew. C C. 76. So, where a charge arose out of an affray, and there was ground to believe that the accused acted under an apprehension of an attack on himself, the judge charged as follows: "Drunkenness is no excuse for crime; but, in considering whether the prisoner apprehended an assault on himself, you may take into account the state in which he was." Regina v. Gamlen, 1 Fost. & F. 90. See *contra*, Golden v. State, 25 Ga. 527.

1. This doctrine is supported by the following cases: —

In *Alabama:* Mooney v. State, 33 Ala. 419; Beasley v. State, 50 Ala. 149; s. c., 20 Am Rep. 292; Ross v. State, 62 Ala. 225; Ford v. State, 71 Ala. 385; s. c., 5 Crim. L. Mag 32; Tedwell v. State, 70 Ala. 33; State v. Bullock, 13 Ala. 413.

In *Arkansas:* McKenzie v. State, 26 Ark. 335.

In *California:* People v. Belencia, 21 Cal. 544; People v. Williams, 43 Cal 344; People v. Ferris, 55 Cal. 588; s. c., 2 Crim. L Mag. 18; 2 Ky. L. Rep. 190; 10 Rep. 588.

In *Connecticut:* State v. Johnson, 41 Conn. 584; State v. Smith, 49 Conn. 376.

In *Dakota:* People v. Odell, 1 Dak. T. 197.

In *Delaware:* State v. Hurley, 1 Houst. (Del.) Cr. Cas. 28; State v. Till, 1 Houst. (Del.) Cr. Cas. 233; State v. Thomas, 1 Houst. (Del.) Cr. Cas. 511; State v. McGonigal, 5 Harr. (Del.) 510

In *Georgia:* Choice v. State, 31 Ga 424; Estes v. State, 55 Ga. 31; Marshall v. State, 59 Ga. 154; Harvey v. State, 63 Ga. 612; Moon v. State, 68 Ga. 687; Mercer v. State, 17 Ga. 146; Golden v. State, 25 Ga. 527; Pierce v State, 53 Ga. 365.

In *Illinois:* Rafferty v. People, 66 Ill. 118; Uptone v. People, 18 Rep. 208.

In *Indiana:* Goodwin v. State, 96 Ind. 550; Gillooley v State, 58 Ind. 182; Bradley v. State, 31 Ind. 492; Cluck v. State, 40 Ind. 263; Smurr v. State, 88 Ind. 504; Sanders v. State, 94 Ind. 147; Surber v. State, 99 Ind. 71.

In *Iowa:* State v. Maxwell, 42 Iowa, 208.

In *Kansas:* State v. Mowry, 5 Cr. L. Mag 23; s. c., 15 Pac. Rep. 282; State v. White, 14 Kan. 538

In *Kentucky:* Blimm v. Commonwealth, 7 Bush (Ky.), 320; s. c., 10 Am. L. Reg. 577; Nichols v. Commonwealth, 11 Bush (Ky.), 576; Shannahan v. Commonwealth, 8 Bush (Ky.), 463; s. c, 8 Am. Rep. 465; Smith v. Commonwealth, 1 Duv. (Ky.) 227.

In *Louisiana:* State v. Mullen, 14 La. An. 570.

In *Maine:* State v. Verrill, 54 Me. 408.

In *Massachusetts:* Commonwealth v. Malone, 114 Mass 295; Commonwealth v. Hawkins, 69 Mass. (3 Gray) 463; Commonwealth v. Dorsey, 103 Mass. 412.

In *Michigan:* People v. Finley, 38 Mich. 482; People v. Cummins, 47 Mich. 334; People v. Garbutt, 17 Mich. 9; s. c., 7 Am. L. Reg. 554.

In *Minnesota:* State v. Welch, 21 Minn. 22; State v. Herdina, 25 Minn. 161; State v. Grear, 28 Minn 426

In *Mississippi:* Kelly v. State, 3 Sm. & M. (Miss.) 518.

In *Missouri:* Schaller v State, 14 Mo. 502; State v. Hundley. 46 Mo. 414. State v. Pitts, 58 Mo. 556; State v. Edwards, 71 Mo 312; State v. Harlow, 21 Mo. 446.

In *Nebraska:* Schleneker v. State, 9 Neb. 242.

In *Nevada:* State v. Thompson, 12 Nev. 140.

In *New Hampshire:* State v. Avery, 44 N. H. 392; State v. Pike, 49 N. H. 399.

In *New York:* People v. Rogers, 18 N. Y. 9; People v. Cavanagh, 62 How. (N. Y.) Pr 187; People v. O'Connell, 62 How. (N. Y) Pr. 436; People v. Jones, 2 Edm. (N. Y.) Sel. Cas. 86.

In *North Carolina:* State v. Keath, 83 N. C. 626.

But a person accused of crime has a right to show that at the time of its commission he was physically incapable of committing it by reason of his intoxication.[1]

Although drunkenness is no excuse for crime, yet if it is held that delirium tremens caused by excessive drinking produces such a degree of madness as to render the person incapable of distinguishing right from wrong at the time the offence is committed, he is relieved from responsibility.[2] And where a man has voluntarily drank to such an extent as to permanently destroy his reason and render him insane, while he is thus insane he will be excused from a crime committed while in this condition, the same as if his mental faculties had been destroyed by disease.[3] But temporary

In *Ohio:* Nichols *v.* State, 8 Ohio St. 435; Davis *v.* State, 25 Ohio St. 369.

In *Pennsylvania:* Commonwealth *v.* Crozier, 1 Brewst. (Pa.) 349; Commonwealth *v.* Fletcher, 33 Leg. Int. (Pa.) 13; Jones *v.* Commonwealth, 75 Pa. St. 403; Commonwealth *v.* Platt, 11 Phil. (Pa.) 421; Commonwealth *v.* Hart, 2 Brewst. (Pa.) 546; Commonwealth *v.* Dougherty, 1 Browne (Pa.), 20.

In *South Carolina:* State *v.* Paulk, 18 S. C. 514; State *v.* McCants, 1 Spears (S. C.), 393.

In *Tennessee:* Cornwell *v.* State, Mart. & Y. (Tenn.) 147, 157; Pirtle *v.* State, 9 Humph. (Tenn.) 663; Stuart *v.* State, 1 Baxt. (Tenn.) 178; Cartwright *v.* State, 8 Lea (Tenn.), 376; Lancaster *v.* State, 2 Lea (Tenn.), 575.

In *Texas:* Payne *v.* State, 5 Tex. App. 35; Colbath *v.* State, 2 Tex. App. 391; s. c., 4 Tex. App. 76; Brown *v.* State, 4 Tex. App. 275; Jeffries *v.* State, 9 Tex. App. 598; Gaitan *v.* State, 11 Tex. App. 544; Farrell *v.* State, 43 Tex. 503; Carter *v.* State, 12 Tex. 500.

In *Vermont:* State *v.* Tatro, 50 Vt. 483; s. c., 18 Am. L. Reg. 153.

In *Virginia:* Willis *v.* Commonwealth, 32 Gratt. (Va.) 929; s. c., 3 Va. L. J. 741; Boswell *v.* Commonwealth, 20 Gratt. (Va.) 860.

In *West Virginia:* State *v.* Robinson, 20 W. Va. 713; s. c., 43 Am. Rep. 799.

In *Wisconsin:* Cross *v.* State, 55 Wis. 261; s. c., 14 Rep. 479.

In *United States* courts: United States *v.* McGlue, 1 Curt. C. C. 1; United States *v.* Forbes, Crabbe, C. C. 558; United States *v.* Cornell, 2 Mason, C. C. 111; United States *v.* Drew, Baldw. C. C. 28; United States *v.* Claypool, 14 Fed. Rep. 127; Hopt *v.* Utah, 104 U. S. (14 Otto) 631; bk. 26, L. ed. 873; United States *v.* Clarke, 2 Cr. C. C. 158.

1. "If a man, by voluntary drunkenness, render himself incapable of walking for a limited time, it is just as competent evidence tending to show that he did not walk during the time he was so incapable, as though he had been so rendered incapable by paralysis of his limbs from some cause over which he had no control. The cause of the incapacity, in such case, is immaterial: the material question is, was he, in fact, incapable of doing the acts charged?" Ingalls *v.* State, 48 Wis. 647; s. c., 1 Crim. L. Mag. 476; 4 N. W. Rep. 785; 2 Wis. L. N. 208; State *v.* Horne, 9 Kan. 119.

2. Regina *v.* Davis, 14 Cox, C. C. 563; s. c., 28 Moak, Eng. Rep. 657.

3. See Willis *v.* Commonwealth, 32 Gratt. (Va.) 929; s. c., in note 40 Am. Rep. 560; Schlenker *v.* State, 9 Neb. 241; People *v.* Rogers, 18 N. Y. 9; State *v.* Thompson, 12 Nev. 144; Hopt *v.* People, 104 U. S. (14 Otto) 631; bk. 26, L. ed. 873; Commonwealth *v.* Dorsey, 103 Mass. 412; Pirtle *v.* State, 9 Humph. (Tenn.) 663; Haile *v.* State, 11 Humph. (Tenn.) 156; Kelly *v.* Commonwealth, 1 Grant (Pa.), 484; Keenan *v.* Commonwealth, 44 Pa. St. 55; Jones *v.* Commonwealth, 75 Pa. St. 403; People *v.* Belencia, 21 Cal. 544; People *v.* Williams, 43 Cal. 344; State *v.* Johnson, 40 Conn. 136; s. c., 41 Conn. 584; State *v.* Robinson, 20 W. Va. 713; s. c., 43 Am. Rep. 799; State *v.* Trivas, 32 La. An. 1086; s. c., 36 Am. Rep. 293; Blynn *v.* Commonwealth, 7 Bush (Ky.), 320; s. c., 10 Am. L. Reg. 577; Holmes *v.* State, 11 Tex. App. 223; Ford *v.* State, 71 Ala. 385; s. c., 5 Crim. L. Mag. 32; Tedwell *v.* State, 70 Ala. 33; People *v.* Cassiano, 30 Hun (N. Y.), 388; State *v.* Martin (N. J.), 3 Crim. L. Mag. 44; Cartwright *v.* State 8 Lea (Tenn.), 376; People *v.* Ferris, 55 Cal. 589; s. c., 2 Crim. L. Mag. 18; Commonwealth *v.* Platt, 11 Phil. (Pa.) 421; State *v.* Gut, 13 Minn. 341; Golden *v.* State, 25 Ga. 527; Jones *v.* State, 29 Ga. 594; Dawson *v.* State, 16 Ind. 428.

These views have not always met with favor, and by some courts they are expressly held to be unsound. In Vermont the fact insanity produced immediately by intoxication is no excuse for homicide.[1]

Of course, if the drunkenness be involuntary, — as, for example, if it be by the contrivance of the prisoner's enemies, — he will not be accountable for his action while under that influence.[2]

4. *Justification.* — If there are any facts or circumstances which justify or mitigate the offence charged, the accused may plead

of actual drunkenness was held not to be of any weight in determining the degree of murder. State *v.* Tatro, 50 Vt. 483; s. c., 18 Am L Reg. 153, 40 Am. Rep. 567, note; Shannahan *v.* Commonwealth, 8 Bush (Ky.), 463; s. c., 8 Am. Rep. 465; Ball *v.* Commonwealth, 18 Rep. 49; State *v.* Edwards, 71 Mo. 324; State *v.* Dearing, 65 Mo. 530; State *v.* Cross, 27 Mo. 332; Harvey *v.* State, 68 Ga. 612; Moon *v.* State, 68 Ga. 687; State *v.* Bullock, 13 Ala. 413.

Texas Doctrine. — The Supreme Court of Texas have said, that, "while intoxication *per se* is no defence to the fact of guilt, yet, when the question of intent and premeditation is concerned, evidence of it is material for the purpose of determining the precise degree. In all cases where the question is between murder in the first or murder in the second degree, the fact of drunkenness may be proved to shed light upon the mental *status* of the offender, and thereby to enable the jury to determine whether or not the killing resulted from a deliberate and premeditated purpose." Colbath *v.* State, 9 Tex. App. 391.

In another case it was said, "The mere fact of drunkenness alone will not reduce to manslaughter a homicide which would otherwise be murder, much less extract from it its indictable quality. The fact of being drunk, or mere mental excitement, or ungovernable rage, which may be engendered by drinking intoxicating liquors, will not reduce the crime of a voluntary killing below the grade of murder." Pugh *v.* State, 2 Tex. App. 539.

Doctrine of the United States Courts. — Judge Story has said, "We are of the opinion that the indictment upon these admitted facts cannot be maintained. The prisoner was unquestionably insane at the time of committing the offence. And the question made at the bar is, whether insanity, whose remote cause is habitual drunkenness, is or is not an excuse in a court of law for a homicide committed by the party while so insane, but not at the time intoxicated or under the influence of liquor. We are clearly of opinion that insanity is a competent excuse in such a case. In general, insanity is an excuse for the commission of any crime, because the party has not the possession of that reason which includes responsibility. An exception is, when the crime is committed by a party while in a fit of intoxication, the law not permitting a man to avail himself of the excuse of his own gross vice and misconduct to shelter himself from the legal consequences of such crime. But the crime must take place and be the immediate result of the fit of intoxication while it lasts, and not, as in this case, a remote consequence superinduced by the antecedent exhaustion of the party, arising from gross and habitual drunkenness. However criminal, in a moral point of view, such an indulgence is, and however justly a party may be responsible for his acts, there is no law for punishing them, since they are not the acts of a reasonable being. Had the crime been committed while Drew was in a fit of intoxication, he would have been liable to have been convicted of murder. As he was not then intoxicated, but merely insane from an abstinence from liquor, he cannot be pronounced guilty of the offence. The law looks to the immediate, and not to the remote, cause; to the actual state of the party, and not to the cause which remotely produced it. Many species of insanity arise remotely from what, in a moral view, is a criminal neglect or fault of the party, or from religious melancholy, undue exposure, extravagant pride, ambition, etc. Yet such insanity has always been deemed a sufficient excuse for any crime done under its influence." United States *v.* Drew, 5 Mas. C. C. 28. See Bradley *v.* State, 31 Ind. 492; Fisher *v.* State, 64 Ind. 435; Gillooley *v.* State, 58 Ind. 182; Cluck *v.* State, 40 Ind. 263; Jones *v.* Commonwealth, 13 Pitts. L. J. 423; State *v.* Grear, 29 Minn. 221; People *v.* Cummins, 47 Mich. 334; s. c., 11 N. W. Rep. 134; People *v.* O'Connell, 62 How. (N. Y.) Pr. 436; Cross *v.* State, 55 Wis. 261; s. c., 12 N. W Rep. 425; People *v.* Ferris, 55 Cal. 589; s. c., 2 Crim. L. Mag. 18; Colbath *v.* State, 4 Tex. App. 76; State *v.* Robinson, 20 W. Va. 713; s. c., 43 Am. Rep. 799; Maconnehey *v.* State, 5 Ohio St. 77; United States *v.* McGlue, 1 Curt. C. C. 1; Erwin *v.* State, 10 Tex. App. 700; Rennie's Case, Lew. C. C. 76; R. *v.* Dixon, 11 Cox, C. C. 41; R. *v.* Leigh, 4 Fost. & F. 915.

1. Upstone *v.* People, 18 Rep. 203.

2. Bartholomew *v.* People, 114 Ill. 605; Harris, Cr. L. 25.

them. Thus, a necessity for defence, which is the result of an attack on the part of the defendant, cannot be made available in excuse.[1] And contributory negligence of the party aggrieved may sometimes be pleaded as a defence, — as in larceny, confiding property to a bailee; in forgery, allowing defendant to sign for him; permitting one's self to be robbed in order to subject the robber to prosecution, — but not if the scheme is laid with the view of apprehending the thief, unless legal rights are waived.[2]

A person negligently inflicting a wound is responsible for the result of his act, even though the wounded person would have recovered with better nursing and proper care.[3]

The concurrent negligence of a third person is no defence.[4] Insulting epithets or opprobrious words will not justify an assault.[5] In a case of homicide, it is immaterial whether or not the deceased had a right to carry a pistol; so long as he did not attempt to use it, defendant was not justified in killing him for that reason.[5]

In an action for perjury, defendant cannot plead that he believed what he swore to, to be true, if there was no probable cause for such belief.[6]

1. State *v.* Hicks, 92 Mo. 431; s. c., 10 West. Rep. 415. *Vide* tit. "Self-Defence," *ante*, 691.

Self-Defence. — "It may be divided into two general classes, to wit, perfect and imperfect right of self-defence. A perfect right of self-defence can only obtain and avail where the party pleading it acted from necessity, and was wholly free from wrong or blame in occasioning or producing the necessity which required his action. If, however, he was in the wrong — if he was himself violating, or in the act of violating, the law — and on account of his own wrong was placed in a situation wherein it became necessary for him to defend himself against an attack made upon himself which was superinduced or created by his own wrong, then the law justly limits his right of self-defence, and regulates it according to the magnitude of his own wrong. Such a state of case may be said to illustrate and determine what in law would be denominated the imperfect right of self-defence. Whenever a party by his own wrongful act produces a condition of things wherein it becomes necessary for his own safety that he should take life or do serious bodily harm, then indeed the law wisely imputes to him his own wrong and its consequences to the extent that they may and should be considered in determining the grade of offence which, but for such act, would never have been occasioned. . . . How far and to what extent he will be excused or excusable in law must depend on the nature and character of the act he was committing, and which produced the necessity that he should defend himself. When his own original act was in violation of law, then the law takes the fact into consideration in limiting his right to defence and resistance whilst in the perpetration of such unlawful act. If he was engaged in the commission of a felony, and, to prevent its commission, the party seeing it, or about to be injured thereby, makes a violent assault upon him, calculated to produce death or serious bodily harm, and, in resisting such attack, he slay his assailant, the law would impute an original wrong to the homicide and make it murder; but if the original wrong was, or would have been, a misdemeanor, then the homicide growing out of, or occasioned by, it, though self-defence from any assault made upon him, would be manslaughter under the law." Reed *v.* State, 11 Tex. App. 509; King *v.* State, 13 Tex. App. 277.

2. Parsons *v.* State, 21 Ala. 301; Thompson *v.* State, 18 Ind. 386; State *v.* Weaver, Busbee (N. C.), 9; State *v.* Preslar, 3 Jones (N. C.) L. 421; State *v.* Covington, 2 Bailey (S. C.), L. 569; Dodge *v.* Brittain, Meigs (Tenn.), 84; Alexander *v.* State, 12 Tex. 540; Pigg *v.* State, 43 Tex. 108; United States *v.* Foye, 1 Curt. C. C. 364; Reg. *v.* Ady, 7 Carr. & P. 140. See also Desty, Am. Crim. Law, p. 15, and cases cited.

3. Bowles *v.* State, 58 Ala. 335; Commonwealth *v.* State (Miss.), Nov. 1886.

4. State *v.* Bantley, 44 Conn. 537; Commonwealth *v* McPike, 57 Mass. (3 Cush.) 181; Reg. *v.* Pym, 1 Cox, C. C. 339.

5. State *v.* Griffin, 87 Mo. 608; s. c., 3 West. Rep. 820.

6. Commonwealth *v.* Cornish, 6 Binn. (Pa.) 249.

5. *Compulsion and Duress.* — For offences committed under compulsion and duress, the party is not liable.[1]

X. Personal Rights. — 1. *Constitutional Rights.* — All persons in this country possess certain constitutional rights which it is declared by the organic law "shall remainin violate." Thus, it is a constitutional right of every person accused of a crime to be tried by a jury of his peers;[2] he is also entitled to a speedy, fair, and public trial,[3] and, as a rule, has a right to appear in person, free from shackles or bonds.[4]

a. Right to Trial by Jury. — The right to a trial by jury is a sacred right, and one secured by the guarantees of the constitution.[5] The fact that the party is not able to obtain it in the inferior court, is not a deprivation of the right of trial by jury, if

1. See, for a full treatment of this question, *ante*, "Criminal Law," XIII. 5, "Compulsion and Duress," p. 706.

2. Har. Cr. L. 384

Jury for Trial of Alien. — Aliens are not entitled to a jury of one-half aliens. People *v* Chin Mook Sow, 51 Cal. 597.

3. **The Right to a Public Trial** does not abridge the power of the trial court in certain emergencies, as when necessary to support public morals, to expel a boisterous and insubordinate audience, and protect an intimidated or embarrassed witness, and to clear the court-room temporarily of all but a reasonable and respectable number of the public. Grimmet *v.* State, 22 Tex. App. 36.

In Missouri it is *held* that the requirement that there shall be a public trial is fairly met if, without partiality or favoritism, a reasonable portion of the public is suffered to attend, notwithstanding those whose presence would be of no service to the accused are excluded altogether. Where, for a short time during the impanelling of the jury, without authority from the court, two men excluded persons not having business in court from the room, and no request was made for the re-examination of jurors accepted during this period, no error can be assigned. State *v.* Brooks, 92 Mo. 542; s. c., 10 West. Rep. 697.

4. People *v.* Harrington, 42 Cal. 168.

5. People *v.* Fair, 43 Cal. 146.

The right to a trial in all cases of felony, by a common-law jury of twelve men, cannot be taken away by the legislature, nor even waived by the accused. Cooley, Const. 319.

It is *held* in Indiana, in a recent case, that it is not within the power of the legislature to deprive one accused of crime of the right to demand information of the nature of the crime with which he is charged. Riggs *v.* State, 104 Ind. 261; s. c., 2 West. Rep. 205.

In Rhode Island one charged under § 6 of the statute is entitled to a trial by jury on any question of fact arising under the complaint; and under the former conviction with which he may be charged, the right of trial by jury has been secured to him, and the statute does not therefore violate provisions of the State constitution which secure the right of trial by jury. State *v.* Flynn (R. I.), 5 N. Eng. Rep. 329.

The Missouri Revised Statutes, sect. 1903, giving the State the right, in certain localities, of peremptorily challenging a larger number of persons than it possesses in other localities, does not deprive defendant of any right, and is constitutional; and the fact that the statute applied to all cities having a population of over a hundred thousand inhabitants does not make it a special law, and unconstitutional. State *v.* Hayes, 88 Mo. 344; s. c., 4 West. Rep. 666.

Provisions of United States Constitution respecting accusations and trials do not apply to prosecutions under State laws, or prohibit States proceeding by information. State *v.* Boswell, 104 Ind. 541; s. c., 2 West. Rep. 726; Shular *v.* State, 105 Ind. 289; s. c., 2 West. Rep. 805.

Entering Noll. Pros. — After the jury is impanelled in a criminal action, the State cannot enter a *noll. pros.* without the consent of the accused. State *v.* Thompson, 95 N. C. 596.

The constitutional rule which prohibits non-jury trial in felony cases, even upon the plea of guilty, does not extend to misdemeanors, or trials for violating city ordinances. Wong *v.* Astoria, 13 Oreg. 538; Moore *v.* State, 22 Tex. App. 117.

The Action of a Police Magistrate in committing a minor child to the industrial school does not amount to a criminal prosecution, nor to procedure according to the course of the common law; and the minor, therefore, is not entitled to a trial by jury. *Ex parte* Ah Peen, 51 Cal. 280.

provision is made whereby it can be secured upon an appeal by a reasonable, simple procedure.[1] But the trial must be by a jury of twelve and not a less number, although defendant consent thereto.[2]

(1) *Right to a Speedy Trial.* — In prosecutions, the accused has a right to a speedy trial by a jury of the vicinage.[3]

(2) *Right to a Fair Trial.* — All persons accused of crime are entitled to a fair trial.

The constitutional right of a person accused of crime to have process to compel the attendance of witnesses in his behalf[4] is excepted out of the general powers of government, and all laws interfering with that right are void. Hence a statute which permits the prosecuting attorney to admit that the absent witness would testify to the facts as set forth in the affidavit on motion by defendant for a continuance, were he personally present, and thereby compel defendant to go to trial without the benefit of his testimony, is void.[5]

1. Wong *v.* Astoria, 13 Oreg. 538; Moore *v.* State, 22 Tex. App. 538.

2. People *v.* Guidici, 100 N. Y. 503; s. c., 1 Cent. Rep. 721, 722.

3. Const. 1820, art. XIII. sec. 9; Consts. 1865, 1875. *Re* McDonald, 19 Mo. App. 370; s. c., 1 West. Rep. 691, 693.

4. See *Ex parte* Marmaduke (Mo.), 8 West. Rep. 575.

5. State *v.* Berkley, 92 Mo. 41; s. c., 10 West. Rep. 67.

In the above case the court say, "From whence does the legislature derive the power to deny the simple right conferred by the organic law, and, in lieu thereof, compel the accused to accept such a beggarly substitute as § 1886 offers? If such legislation is valid, then there is no boundary and no limit imposed by the constitution which may not be overridden and destroyed in the same way whenever the legislature so wills it. I have already suggested the inestimable value to the accused of having the testimony of his witnesses delivered *ore tenus* at the time and place of his trial. All the sages of the law have so regarded it. Speaking on this subject Blackstone observes, 'This open examination of witnesses, *viva voce*, in the presence of all mankind, is much more conducive to the clearing-up of truth than the private and secret examination taken down in writing before an officer or his clerk, . . . where a witness may frequently depose that in private which he will be ashamed to testify in a public and solemn tribunal. . . . Besides, the occasional questions of the judge, the jury, and the counsel, propounded to the witness on a sudden, will sift out the truth much better than a formal set of interrogatories previously penned and settled; and the confronting of adverse witnesses is also another opportunity of obtaining a clear discovery, which can never be had upon any other method of trial. . . . In short, by this method of examination, and this only, the persons who are to decide upon the evidence have an opportunity of observing the quality, age, education, understanding, behavior, and inclinations of the witness; in which points all persons must appear alike, when their depositions are reduced to writing, and read to the judge in the absence of those who made them; and yet as much may be frequently collected from the manner in which the evidence is delivered as from the matter of it.' 3 Cooley's Bl. 373.

"Touching the same matter Starkie says, 'In these, as in so many other cases, it is for the jury to estimate the degree of influence by which the testimony of a witness is likely to be corrupted, and to determine whether, under all the circumstances, he may be the witness of truth. In arriving at this conclusion, a consideration of the demeanor of the witness upon the trial, and of the manner of giving his evidence, both in chief and upon cross examination, is oftentimes not less material than the testimony itself. An over-forward and hasty zeal on the part of the witness in giving testimony which will benefit the party whose witness he is; his exaggeration of circumstances; his reluctance in giving adverse evidence; his slowness in answering; his evasive replies; his affectation of not hearing or not understanding the question, for the purpose of gaining time to consider the effect of his answer; precipitancy in answering, without waiting to hear *b. Right to Day in Court.*—Another of the constitutional rights of every person is the right to a day in court, for no man can be condemned without an opportunity to be heard in his own defence.[1]

c. Right to be confronted by Witnesses. — The right to be confronted by the witnesses against him is also a right accorded to all persons; but the constitutional provision, that accused shall be confronted with witnesses against him, does not apply to the proof of facts in their nature purely documentary, and which can only be proved by the original or an officially certified copy.[2]

2. *Other Rights.* — Among the rights of the accused which are not regarded as constitutional rights, are (1) a right to a copy of the indictment and a list of the grand jurors, (2) to be present at the trial, (3) to a severance, and (4) to compel election between counts.

or to understand the nature of the question; his inability to detail any circumstances wherein, if his testimony were untrue, he would be open to contradiction, or his forwardness in minutely detailing those where he knows contradiction to be impossible; an affectation of indifference, —are all to a greater or less extent obvious marks of insincerity. On the other hand, his promptness and frankness in answering questions without regard to consequences, and especially his unhesitating readiness in stating all the circumstances attending the transaction, by which he opens a wide field for contradiction if his testimony be false, are, as well as numerous others of a similar nature, strong internal indications of his sincerity. The means thus afforded by a *viva voce* examination, of judging of the credit due to witnesses, especially where their statements conflict, are of incalculable advantage in the investigation of truth; they not unfrequently supply the only true test by which the real characters of the witnesses can be appreciated.' Starkie, Ev. (9th ed.) 727, 728.

"Elsewhere the same learned author observes, 'As the depositions of dead or absent witnesses are, in point of law, of a secondary nature to the *viva voce* testimony of witnesses subjected to the ordeal of cross-examination, so are they inferior and weaker in point of force and effect: so true is it that a witness will frequently depose that in private which he would be ashamed to certify before a public tribunal. It is by the test of a public examination, and by that alone, that the credit of a witness, both as to honesty and ability, can be thoroughly tried and appreciated. *Nam minus obstitisse videtur pudor inter paucos signatores* is an ancient and a powerful observation in favor of oral testimony.' Starkie, 766."

Chief Justice Marshall says, "The right of an accused person to the process of the court to compel the attendance of witnesses, seems to follow, necessarily, from the right to examine those witnesses; and whenever the right exists, it would be reasonable that it should be accompanied by means of rendering it effectual. . . . The genius and character of our laws and usages are friendly, — not to condemnation, at all events, but to a fair and impartial trial; and they consequently allow to the accused the right of preparing the means to secure such a trial. . . . The Constitution and laws of the United States will now be considered for the purpose of ascertaining how they bear upon the question. The sixth amendment to the Constitution gives to the accused in all criminal prosecutions a right to a speedy and public trial, and to compulsory process for obtaining witnesses in his favor. The right given by this article must be deemed sacred by the courts; and the article should be so construed as to be something more than a dead letter." 1 Burr, Tr. 158, 159.

Section 1886 is equally obnoxious to § 1 of the fourteenth amendment to the Constitution of the United States, which forbids any State to deny to any person the equal protection of the laws. State *v.* Berkley, 92 Mo. 41; s. c., 10 West. Rep. 67.

1. See Baltimore & O. R. R. *v.* Wagner, 43 Ohio St. 75; s. c., 1 West. Rep. 87.

2. People *v.* Dow (Mich.), 7 West. Rep. 897, 898.

Amendment to tne United States Constitution, requiring the accused to be confronted with the witnesses against him, is not applicable to trials in State courts for State offences. The similar provision in the bill of rights of the State of New York is satisfied if the accused has been once confronted with, and had opportunity to cross-examine, the witness. People *v.* Penhollow, 42 Hun (N. Y.), 103.

a. To Copy of Indictment and List of Jurors. — A copy of the indictment, together with the names of the grand jurors who composed the jury returning such bill, must be served upon the accused before he can be required to proceed to trial.[1] But if the defendant proceed to trial without objection that a copy of the indictment and list of jurors was not served on him, the presumption is conclusive that they were served.[2] But an accused whose case is fixed for the second week of the term, has not the right to require service of the list of jurors drawn for the third week of the term;[3] and objection that the indictment and list of jurors was not served on defendant should be taken before trial.[4]

b. Right to be present at Trial. — The defendant has a right to be present at the trial,[5] unless he forfeits such right by misconduct, and his removal from the court-room is a necessity;[6] although a plea of not guilty may, in some States, be properly entered by defendant's counsel in his absence.[7]

The defendant must be present when evidence is given against him.[8] Thus, it is held that, examining the jurors when the accused was not personally present, is not a mere irregularity, not reviewable unless some actual prejudice to defendant is made to appear,

1. **It is unnecessary for the Record** to show that a copy of the indictment and list of jurors was served as required by the statute. Compliance with the statute will be presumed. Patterson *v.* State, 48 N. J. L. (19 Vr.) 381; s. c., 3 Cent. Rep. 486; *Re* Esmond (D. C.), 3 Cent. Rep. 520.

Texas Practice. — Article 617 of the Code of Criminal Procedure requires no more than that the names of all the jurors summoned under the special venire shall be served upon the defendant more than one day before the case is called for trial. The provisions of the said article are not subverted by the mere fact that the certified copy served on the defendant contained other names which were erased. Murray *v.* State, 21 Tex. App. 466.

2. Patterson *v.* State, 48 N. J. L. (19 Vr.) 381; s. c., 3 Cent. Rep. 486.

Missouri Practice. — The names of persons summoned under a special venire for a case tried in the criminal court of the city of St. Louis need not be furnished by the jury commissioned. State *v.* Hayes, 88 Mo. 344; s. c., 2 West. Rep. 110.

3. State *v.* Pierre, 38 La. An. 91.

4. *Re* Esmond (D. C.), 3 Cent. Rep. 520.

5. **It is not essential** that accused should be present at the filing and trial of motions and pleas not involving the question of guilt or innocence on the merits. State *v.* Gonsoulin, 38 La. An. 459.

Missouri Practice. — In all cases of felony, Missouri Revised Statutes, sec. 1891, makes it necessary that the defendant should be personally present in court at each and every material step taken during the trial, up to the time when the verdict is to be received, when the particular steps mentioned in the statute, of receiving and entering the verdict, may be taken in his absence, if the same is wilful and voluntary. Impanelling and examining the jury is a material, substantive, and important step "during the trial," within the meaning of this section. For every purpose involved in the requirement of defendant's presence, where the indictment is for a felony, the trial commences at least when the work of impanelling a jury begins. State *v.* Crocket (Mo.), 6 West. Rep. 651.

Viewing Premises without Defendant. — Power of the court in a criminal action to allow a jury to view the premises, — Code Crim. Proc. secs. 411, 412. It cannot be done in the absence of the defendant and his counsel. People *v.* Palmer, 43 Hun (N. Y.), 397; People *v.* Lowrey, 70 Cal 193.

6. But see *infra*, "Waiver of Rights."

The Right of the Accused to be heard in Person, however, applies only to the *nisi prisi* court. Tooke *v.* State (Tex. App.), Jan. 1887.

7. State *v.* Jones, 70 Iowa, 505.

8. Shular *v.* State, 105 Ind. 289: s. c., 5 West. Rep. 801.

Objection not made on Trial is waived. — In Boggs *v.* State, 8 Ind. 463, it was *held* that an objection that a deposition was taken without the consent of the accused was waived by a failure to make it in the trial court. Shular *v.* State, 105 Ind. 289, s. c., 5 West Rep. 801.

but, on the contrary, is a breach and infringement of the statute requiring the accused to be personally present at this step during the trial, and prejudice under such circumstances is presumed.[1]

c. Right to a Severance. — Severance upon the request of any one of several defendants jointly indicted is a matter of right when the application therefor has been made in conformity with the statutes.[2] And when a defendant has been denied the benefit of certain testimony by reason of a refusal of the trial judge to grant a severance, and it can be seen that probable injustice has been done the defendant by depriving him of the said testimony, a new trial will be granted.[3]

The court may expressly suggest separate trials, and defendants may demand a separate trial;[4] but after having elected to be tried jointly, and after evidence has been heard on the trial, it is then too late for either of the defendants to demand a severance, and to insist upon the right to be tried severally.[5]

A prisoner may be ordered by the court to be tried separately from others indicted with him.[6]

d. Right to compel Election between Counts. — Separate offences of the same nature, charged in separate counts, may be included in the same indictment;[7] and several indictments preferred at different times, but alleging the same facts in different forms, will be treated as separate counts of one indictment.[8] But a felony and a misdemeanor, growing out of the same transaction, cannot be charged in separate counts in the same indictment.[9]

Where all the counts in an information are manifestly based upon one and the same transaction, it will be assumed that it was the intention to charge but one offence.[10]

1. State *v.* Crocket (Mo.), 6 West. 651.

Right of Accused to argue by Counsel before the Jury both upon the law and the fact, see this title, *infra*, XVII. "Argument of Counsel"

2. Willey *v.* State, 22 Tex. App. 408.

3. Watson *v.* State, 16 Lea (Tenn.), 604.

4. Shular *v* State, 105 Ind. 289; s. c., 2 West. Rep. 801.

5. Trowbridge *v.* State, 74 Ga. 431.

New York Practice. — Under New York Code Crim Proc sec. 462, a prisoner may be ordered by the court to be tried separately from others indicted with him. People *v.* Clark, 102 N. Y. 735; s. c., 3 Cent Rep. 801.

6. People *v* Clark, 103 N. Y. 735; s. c, 3 Cent Rep. 801.

7. State *v.* Frazier (Me.), 3 New Eng. Rep 629.

Where the defendant has been acquitted under a certain count in an indictment, it cannot be urged as error that the trial court refused to compel the prosecution to elect as to which of the several transactions set out in that count the State would rely upon for a conviction. Clark *v.* State, 47 N. J. L (18 Vr.) 556; s. c., 4 Cent. Rep. 806.

8. State *v.* Brown, 95 N. C. 685.

9. Burk *v.* State, 2 Harr. & J. (Md.) 426; Hays *v.* People, 1 Hill (N. Y), 352; Commonwealth *v.* Thompson, 116 Mass. 348; Stevens *v.* State (Md), 5 Cent. Rep. 586.

10. State *v.* Glidden, 55 Conn. 46; s. c., 3 New Eng. Rep. 849.

Thus, where defendant was arraigned upon an information containing three counts, the first charging murder of a female, and the second alleging female quick with child, and no objection was taken to the form of the information, upon the trial of the information the people cannot be compelled to elect upon which of the counts they would rely. People *v.* McDowell (Mich.), 5 West. Rep. 777.

In this case the court said, "Before impanelling the jury for the trial, respondent's counsel asked that the people be compelled to elect upon which of the counts they should rely. The court declined to grant the request, and respondent excepted. We

Where an indictment contains two counts, one for larceny, and one for receiving stolen goods, which relate to the same transaction, the prosecution will not be required to elect on which count a conviction will be asked.[1] But where an indictment consists of two counts, each of which is sufficient as an indictment for simple larceny, the defendant cannot require the State to elect and try him on one count only, unless it appears that the counts charge separate and distinct offences.[2]

Where counts are for different felonies connected with one transaction, or where one felony is set out in various ways in the different counts to meet the varying forms of proof, no election of counts will, in ordinary circumstances, be required.[3] And where a party is indicted for a given offence, he is bound by law to take notice of whatever offence he may be convicted of thereunder, as the law governing the subject-matter and practice then stands.[4]

e. Waiver of Rights. — A defendant cannot, without express statutory authority, waive his right to a trial by jury on a plea of not guilty.[5] However, if a defendant elects to take depositions

think the ruling was right under the decisions of this court." Stuart *v.* People, 42 Mich. 257; People *v.* Sweeney, 55 Mich. 586; People *v.* Sessions, 58 Mich. 594; People *v.* Annis, 13 Mich. 511; Turner *v.* People, 33 Mich. 363; People *v.* McKinney, 10 Mich. 54. See also Jennings *v.* Commonwealth, 34 Mass. (17 Pick.) 80; United States *v.* Furlong, 18 U. S. (5 Wheat.) 184; bk. 5, L. ed 64; 1 Arch. Cr. Pr. 292, 295; Commonwealth *v.* Hawkins, 69 Mass. (3 Gray) 464; People *v.* McDowell (Mich.), 5 West. Rep. 777.

Cohabiting with more than one Woman within the meaning of the Act of March 22, 1882, is a single continuous offence subject to but one indictment or prosecution for all the time prior to such indictment or prosecution. *Ex parte* Snow, 120 U. S. 274; bk. 30, L. ed. 658.

1. Andrews *v.* People, 117 Ill. 195; s. c., 4 West. Rep. 139.

2. State *v.* Halida, 28 W. Va. 499.

3. Andrews *v.* People, 117 Ill. 195; s. c., 4 West. Rep. 139, 141.

Texas Doctrine. — When several counts in the same indictment are substantially for the same offence, and are introduced for the purpose of meeting the evidence as it may transpire, the State will not be required to elect on which it will rely. Green *v.* State, 21 Tex. App. 64.

4. State *v.* Burk, 89 Mo. 669; s. c., 6 West. Rep. 669.

5. State *v.* Maine, 27 Conn. 281; Hill *v.* People, 16 Mich. 351; Neales *v* State, 10 Mo. 498; Wilson *v* State, 16 Ark. 601; Dillingham *v.* State, 5 Ohio St. 283; Williams *v.* State, 12 Ohio St. 622; State *v.* Lockwood, 43 Wis. 403; Bond *v.* State, 17 Ark. 290; People *v.* Smith, 9 Mich. 193; League *v.* State, 36 Md. 259. See State *v.* Mansfield, 41 Mo. 470; Cooper *v.* State, 21 Ark. 228; State *v.* Kaufman, 20 Alb. L. J. 291. See also Cooley, Const. 319.

In California. — The point that the defendant could not, by pleading guilty, waive a trial by jury, is answered adversely to him by the decision in People *v* Noll, 20 Cal 164.

In Indiana. — A party in a criminal action may waive his constitutional rights. Shular *v.* State, 105 Ind. 289; s. c., 2 West. Rep. 805

In Texas. — Under Code Crim. Proc. art. 535, defendant has a right to waive a jury, and enter a plea of guilty. Moore *v.* State, 22 Tex. App. 117.

Waiver of Trial by Jury. — Where one accused in a criminal case of felony waives a trial by jury, and is tried by consent by the court, and, upon a finding of guilty on such trial, is sentenced, and undergoes the punishment, such conviction, even if erroneous, is not a nullity, and cannot be collaterally questioned. Kelley *v.* People, 115 Ill. 583; s. c., 3 West Rep. 45

Waiver of Right to be present at Trial. It has been *held* in Ohio and Indiana, that the presence of the accused at his trial for a felony is a personal right which he may waive; and, if he voluntarily absents himself, the trial may proceed, and verdict be rendered in his absence. Fight *v.* State, 7 Ohio (pt. 1), 180; McCorkle *v.* State, 14 Ind 39; s. c, 16 Ind. 537.

But the contrary is the prevalent **rule.**

under the statute, he concedes to the State a like privilege, thus waiving his constitutional privilege.[1]

XI. Change of Venue. — When a fair and impartial trial cannot be had in the county where the venue is laid, the court will, upon an affidavit stating that fact, permit a suggestion to be entered on the record, so that the trial may be had in an adjacent county.[2] The application for a change of venue is addressed to the sound discretion of the court,[3] the exercise of which must be reason-

State *v.* Hurlburt, 1 Root (Conn.), 90; People *v.* Perkins, 1 Wend. (N. Y.) 91; Prine *v.* Commonwealth, 6 Harris (Pa.), 103; State *v.* Hughes, 2 Ala 102; Cole *v.* State, 5 Eng. (Ark.) 318; Clark *v.* State, 4 Humph (Tenn.) 254; Nomaque *v.* People, Breese (Ill.), 109; People *v.* Kohler, 5 Cal 72.

It is now provided by statute, in Ohio, that if the defendant escapes or forfeits his recognizance after the jury are sworn, the trial shall proceed and the verdict be received and recorded. If the trial is for misdemeanor, the sentence shall also be pronounced in his absence; but if for felony, the case shall be continued until the convict appears in court or is retaken. 74 Ohio L. 350 The Kentucky Criminal Code, § 183, has the same provision as to the trial of felonies, except that in such case it is at the option of the prosecuting attorney whether the trial shall proceed or not. The statute of Indiana provides that no person, prosecuted for an offence punishable by death or imprisonment, shall be tried unless personally present during the trial. Act of 1852, in Rev. Stat. (1876), pp. 397, 398. The Illinois statute leaves the rule as at common law. In Iowa and Michigan, the statute provides that no person indicted for felony shall be tried unless personally present. Harris, Cr. L. (Force's ed.) 301.

1. Shular *v.* State, 105 Ind. 289; s. c., 5 West. Rep. 801.

This doctrine is firmly supported by the authorities. In addition to those cited in that case may be cited the following: Williams *v.* State, 61 Wis. 281; Wills *v* State, 73 Ala. 362; State *v.* Wagner, 78 Mo. 644; Hancock *v.* State, 14 Tex. App. 392.

A striking illustration of the doctrine that a defendant in a criminal case may waive a constitutional right, is supplied by those cases which hold that, where an accused takes a new trial under a statute, he waives his right to insist upon the constitutional provision prohibiting a citizen from being put in jeopardy twice for the same offence. It would seem that if a party takes a new trial in a criminal case, he takes it on the terms prescribed by the statute, and consents to be placed in the same position as if no trial had been had. Veatch *v.* State, 6 Ind. 291; Morris *v.* State, 1 Blackf. (Ind) 37; United States *v.* Perez, 22 U. S. (9 Wheat.) 579; bk. 6, L. ed. 165; State *v.* Davis, 80 N. C. 384; Conn *v.* Arnold, 6 Cr. L. Mag 61; Lesslie *v.* State, 18 Ohio St. 390; Livingston *v.* Commonwealth, 14 Gratt. (Va.) 593; United States *v.* Harding, 1 Wall. Jr. C. C. 127; State *v.* McCord, 3 Kan. 232; s. c., 12 Am. Rep. 469.

2. See Roscoe's Cr. Ev. 260.

3. People *v.* Perdue, 49 Cal. 425, 427; People *v.* Mahoney, 18 Cal. 186; People *v.* Fisher, 6 Cal. 155; Dronberger *v.* State (Ind.), 11 West. Rep. 106; People *v.* Congleton, 44 Cal. 95; Sloan *v.* Smith, 3 Cal. 410; Spittorff *v.* State, 108 Ind. 171; s. c., 6 West. Rep. 307; Martin *v.* State, 21 Tex. App. 1; People *v.* Yoakum, 53 Cal 567; Williams *v.* State, 48 Ala. 85; Taylor *v.* State, 48 Ala. 180; McPherson *v.* State, 29 Ark. 225; Brinkley *v.* State, 54 Ga. 371; People *v.* Harris, 4 Denio (N. Y.), 150; People *v.* Webb, 1 Hill (N Y.), 179; Manly *v.* State, 52 Ind. 215; Bissot *v.* State, 53 Ind. 408; State *v.* Spurbeck, 44 Iowa, 667; State *v.* O'Rourke, 55 Mo. 440; State *v.* Lawther, 65 Mo. 454; State *v.* Bohan, 15 Kan. 407, State *v.* Adams, 20 Kan. 311; State *v.* Coleman, 8 S. C. 237; Auschicks *v* State, 45 Tex. 148; Martin *v.* State, 35 Wis. 294; State *v.* Rowan, 35 Wis. 303.

In Alabama. — An application for a change of venue, in a criminal case, is required to be made "as early as practicable before the trial." Code, sec. 4911. And it comes too late when made after several postponements of the case, after an application for a continuance has been overruled, after the witnesses have been sworn and put under the rule, and after the solicitor has expressed himself satisfied with the jury. Shackleford *v.* State, 79 Ala. 26.

In California. — The only provisions of law for the removal of the place of trial of a criminal action are contained in the Penal Code, commencing with sec. 1033; and the only ground is, that a fair and impartial jury cannot be obtained in the county. Where the court transferred the case to another county on the ground of disqualification of the judge, it exceeded its jurisdiction. Bias or prejudice of the presiding judge is no legal ground. People *v.* Shuler, able,[1] to be disposed of in furtherance of justice;[2] and the order of removal will not be disturbed except in case of gross abuse of discretion.[3]

28 Cal. 495; People *v.* Williams, 24 Cal. 31; People *v.* Mahoney, 18 Cal. 185; McCauley *v.* Weller, 12 Cal. 523.

That the judge previously in the same case made an erroneous ruling, is no evidence of the existence of bias and prejudice. People *v.* Williams, 24 Cal. 31.

In Indiana. — The granting or refusing an application for a change of venue from the county, under an indictment for larceny, is within the discretion of the court. Spittorff *v.* State, 108 Ind. 171; s. c., 6 West. Rep. 307.

In a prosecution for maintaining a public nuisance, a motion for a change of venue from the county, on account of the bias and prejudice of the citizens, is addressed to the discretion of the court. Dronberger *v.* State (Ind.), 11 West. Rep. 106.

On change of venue, the county from which the change is made is liable for the payment of the attorney appointed to defend the poor prisoner. Montgomery Co. *v.* Courtney (Ind.), 2 West. Rep. 657.

In Iowa. — An application for a change of venue on the ground of prejudice in the county is addressed to the sound discretion of the court. State *v.* Perigo, 70 Iowa, 657.

In Kentucky. — When the evidence shows that there are reasonable grounds to believe that the defendant cannot have a fair trial in the county where the offence was committed, it is the duty of the court to grant such change. Johnson *v.* Commonwealth, 82 Ky. 116.

The adoption of the amendment of April 1, 1880, makes it no less the duty of the court now as before its adoption, to grant the order. Johnson *v.* Commonwealth, 82 Ky. 116.

In Missouri. — A presiding judge duly elected and qualified under Rev. Stat. 1879, §§ 1106, 1107, in the absence of the regular judge, is a judge within the meaning of § 1878 of the statute, and equally incompetent as the regular judge of said court to proceed to hear and try a criminal cause, when the affidavit as to prejudice of the judge has been made in compliance with the requirements of said section. State *v.* Shipman (Mo.), 12 West. Rep. 110.

The statute confers no authority to award a change of venue to another circuit, where the ground of the application is the prejudice of the inhabitants of the county in which the cause is pending. State *v.* Gabriel, 88 Mo. 631; s. c., 5 West. Rep. 340.

Where an application for change of venue, under Rev. Stat. 1879, sec. 1881, has been granted, the defendant has no power to divest the court of jurisdiction by withdrawal of his application. State *v.* Hayes, 88 Mo. 344; s. c., 4 West. Rep. 666.

In New York. — By sec. 344 of the Code of Criminal Procedure, and those which follow, a prisoner may apply for a removal of his case; but, if denied, a second application is punishable as a contempt and also a misdemeanor. People *ex rel.* Munsell *v.* Court of Oyer & Terminer, 101 N. Y. 245; s. c., 1 Cent. Rep. 812.

In Pennsylvania. — The Supreme Court has power to remove by writ of *certiorari* into that court, a criminal cause pending in a county court of quarter sessions, before trial, and to order a trial in another county. Commonwealth *v.* Ralph, 111 Pa. St. 365; s. c., 1 Cent. Rep. 663.

In Texas. — The granting or refusing an application for a change of venue from the county is within the discretion of the court. Martin *v.* State, 21 Tex. App. 1.

Article 583 of the Code of Crim. Proc. provides two modes in which the application of an accused for a change of venue may be contested. The first is by filing the affidavit of a credible person attacking the credibility of the compurgators. The second is by filing the affidavit of a credible person attacking the means of knowledge possessed by the compurgators. Smith *v.* State, 21 Tex. App. 277.

Whether or not the controverting affiant is himself a credible person, is an issue to be tried and determined by the trial judge. His credibility cannot be impugned merely upon the ground that he was the physician who attended the deceased in his last illness, and was a witness for the State in the prosecution of the accused for the murder of the deceased. Smith *v.* State, 21 Tex. App. 277.

The filing by the State of a sufficient controverting affidavit raises, upon the application for the change of venue, an issue of fact as to the truth of the grounds set up in the application; and evidence *pro* and *con* the application, in addition to the testimony of the compurgators and the controverting affiants, is admissible upon the issue thus raised, the burden of proof resting upon the applicant. That the trial court imposed that burden upon the State, was an error of which the defendant cannot be heard to complain. Pierson *v.* State, 21 Tex. App. 14.

1. People *v.* Yoakum, 53 Cal. 567; People *v.* Mahoney, 18 Cal. 186.

2. People *v.* Congleton, 44 Cal. 95; People *v.* Fisher, 6 Cal. 155.

3. People *v.* Fisher, 6 Cal. 155; People *v.* Mahoney, 18 Cal. 180.

The finding of the court on an issue under an application for a change of venue is conclusive, unless it appears that palpable injustice has been done, or there has been an abuse of judicial discretion [1] in refusing the application.[2]

The venue may be changed as to one of several defendants.[3] And the application for a change of venue may be made by one of two jointly indicted without the presence of the other.[4]

The circuit court may certify an indictment to the county court, but not after arraignment and plea.[5] And when a change of venue in a criminal case is awarded, a failure of the court to make an order that the body of the defendant be removed does not deprive the court of the power thereafter to make it. It can be made at a subsequent term.[6]

1. State *v.* Hunt, 91 Mo. 490; s. c., 7 West. Rep. 625.

2. State *v.* Guy, 69 Mo. 431; State *v.* Whitton, 68 Mo. 91; State *v.* Wilson, 85 Mo. 134; State *v.* Hunt, 91 Mo. 490; s. c., 7 West. Rep. 625.

3. State *v.* Wetherford, 25 Mo. 439; State *v.* Martin, 2 Ired. (N. C.) 101; State *v.* Carothers, 1 Greene (Ia.), 464.

One of two defendants jointly indicted has a right to apply for a change of venue; and the effect of granting the order is to sever the d fences, leaving the defendant who does not apply for a change to be tried in the court where the indictment was found, and carrying the trial of the other defendant to the court to which the cause was ordered upon his application. State *v.* Carothers, 1 Greene (Ia.), 464; State *v.* Martin, 2 Ired. (N. C.) L. 101; State *v.* Wetherford, 25 Mo. 439; Hunter *v.* People, 1 Scam (Ill.) 453; John *v.* State, 2 Ala. 290; 1 Bish. Cr. L. § 75; Whart. Cr. Pl. & Pr. (8th ed.) 602; Shular *v.* State, 105 Ind. 289; s. c., 2 West. Rep. 801.

In Brown *v.* State, 18 Ohio St. 496, it was *held* that a change of venue upon the application of one of several defendants was proper, and that it operated as a severance. The court there said, "It seems quite clear to us that a motion by one of two persons jointly indicted for a change of venue necessarily involves and includes a motion for a separate trial, and that the granting of such motion necessarily involves and includes the granting of a separate trial also." See Shular *v.* State, 105 Ind. 289; s. c, 2 West. Rep. 801.

The defendant need not be present when an application for a change of venue is made in his own behalf. State *v.* Elkins, 63 Mo. 159; Hopkins *v.* State, 10 Lea (Tenn.), 204; Rothschild *v.* State, 7 Tex. App. 519

This rule is in harmony with the decision in Epps *v.* State, 102 Ind. 539, that a defendant need not be present at the hearing of motions, although he must be present on the trial. There are authorities supporting this doctrine, among them, State *v.* Jefcoat, 20 S. C. 383; State *v.* Fahey, 35 La. An. 9; State *v.* Clark, 32 La. An. 560; State *v.* Harris, 34 La. An. 121; Shular *v.* State, 105 Ind. 289; s. c., 2 West. Rep. 801.

4. Shular *v.* State, 105 Ind. 289; s. c., 2 West. Rep. 801.

5. Fanning *v.* People, 10 Ill. App. 70.

6. State *v.* Gleason, 88 Mo. 582; s. c., 5 West Rep. 407.

Where the venue in a criminal case was changed at the request and upon the application of the defendant, and the record and papers transmitted at his request, it was the duty of the defendant, before the trial began, to point out any defects in the records or certificates of the clerk. Such an objection made for the first time upon appeal is too late under Rev. Stat. chap. 146, § 35. Tucker *v.* People (Ill.), 11 West. Rep. 765.

The court say, "Under such circumstances can he now be heard to complain that the Circuit Court of Livingston County had no right to proceed with the trial of the cause? We think § 35 of chapter 146, *supra*, furnishes the answer. That section is as follows: 'All questions concerning the regularity of proceedings in obtaining changes of venue, and the right of the court to which the change is made, to try the cause and execute the judgment, shall be considered as waived after trial and verdict.'"

"In Gardner *v.* People, 4 Ill. 83, where a change of venue had been taken from the Circuit Court of Scott to the Circuit Court of Morgan County, after a conviction on writ of error, it was objected, as here, that the Circuit Court of Morgan County had no right to try the prisoner, because the record of the proceedings in Scott County was not properly certified by the clerk, as required by the statute. In deciding the point raised, it is there said, 'No objection

The application must be made by a party to the record verified by his affidavit,[1] and cannot be made after twelve competent jurors are obtained;[2] and the burden is on the petitioner to make out a case.[3]

Good ground must be stated in the affidavit, for the belief that a fair trial cannot be had.[4] The affidavit must state facts and circumstances from which the conclusion is deduced that a fair and impartial trial cannot be had in the county where the indictment is found.[5] A mere opinion or belief set forth in the affidavit that a fair trial cannot be had, is not sufficient.[6]

The affidavit that he cannot have a fair and impartial trial in the county, is not alone sufficient;[7] nor is the mere fact that thirty or forty persons in the county had subscribed money to procure a lawyer to aid the prosecuting attorney.[8]

If the affidavit is in conformity with the statute, it is the duty of the court to remove the cause.[9]

was made in the court below, before or after verdict, to the regularity of the proceedings in Scott County, or to the authentication of the same when changed to Morgan County. If the authentication of the record was defective, the prisoner should have availed himself of it in the circuit court before trial. Not having done so, the irregularity, if in fact any existed, is cured by the statute [citing it] as above."

"The same rule was laid down in Perteet *v.* People, 70 Ill. 172, and the doctrine has been approved in other cases, but it will not be necessary to cite them. If the transcript from Kankakee County, or the certificate thereto, was defective or irregular, it was the duty of the defendant to interpose the objection before the trial. As he failed to speak when duty required, the objection now made for the first time comes too late. Tucker *v.* People (Ill.) 11 West. Rep. 765.

1. State *v.* Shaw, 43 Ohio St. 324; s. c., 1 West. Rep. 221.

2. People *v.* Cotta, 49 Cal. 170.

3. People *v.* Sammis, 3 Hun (N. Y.), 560.

4. R. *v.* Clendon, 2 Str. 911; R. *v.* Harris, 3 Burr. 1330; 1 W. Bl. 378; Rosc. Cr. Ev. 260, 261.

English Doctrine. — This suggestion need not state the facts from which the inference is drawn, that a fair trial cannot be had. R. *v.* Hunt, 3 B. & A. 444. And when entered is not traversable. 1 Chitty, Crim. Law, 201. And the venue in the indictment remains the same, the place of trial alone being changed. Ib. In R. *v.* Casey, 13 Cox, C. C. R. (Irish) 614, which was a case of libel, the court of crown cases reserved, appear to have been of opinion that the venue in a criminal case will not be changed, but in two subsequent cases of murder the Court of Queen's Bench in Ireland changed the venue on the ground that an impartial trial could not be had, and no reference seems to have been made to the previous case. R. *v.* McEneany, 14 Cox, C. C. 87; R. *v.* Walter, 14 Cox, C. C. 79. It is only, however, in case of misdemeanor that the Court of King's Bench will, in general, award a *venire* to try in a foreign country, though cases may occur in which the court would change the venue in felony. R *v.* Holden, 5 B & Ad. 347; 2 Nev. & M. 167. And even in cases of misdemeanor, the court has not exercised its discretionary power, unless there has been some peculiar reason which made the case almost one of necessity. Ib. Upon an indictment for a misdemeanor, the application to change the venue ought to be made before issue joined. R. *v.* Forbes, 2 Dowl. P. C. 440; Roscoe's Cr. Ev. 260, 261.

5. People *v.* McCauley, 1 Cal. 379; Sloan *v.* Smith, 3 Cal. 412.

6. People *v.* Congleton, 44 Cal. 95; People *v.* Shuler, 28 Cal. 495.

7. People *v.* Graham, 21 Cal. 265; State *v* Williams, 2 McCord (S. C.), 302; Wormeley *v.* Commonwealth, 10 Gratt. (Va.) 658; People *v.* Bodine, 7 Hill (N. Y.), 47; Rex *v.* Holden, 5 Barn. & Adol. 347; People *v.* Mahoney, 18 Cal. 186.

8. People *v.* Graham, 21 Cal. 265; People *v.* Lee, 5 Cal. 353.

9. State *v.* Shaw, 43 Ohio St. 324; s. c., 1 West Rep. 221.

In Ohio. — Where, under sec. 550 of the Revised Statutes, the required statute affidavit for a change of venue is filed with the clerk of the court of common pleas, the duties of the clerk in regard to such change of venue are ministerial, and not judicial. State *v.* Shaw, 43 Ohio St. 324; s. c., 1 West. Rep. 219, note.

The granting of time to file counter-affidavits is in the discretion of the court.[1]

XII. Trial Jury. — Every person accused of the commission of a crime, and indicted therefor, is entitled to a fair trial[2] by an impartial[3]

1. Pierson *v.* McCahill, 22 Cal. 131.

2. **Right of Trial by Jury.** — When a person is charged with any offence (except assault) for which he is liable on summary conviction to imprisonment for more than three months, he may, before the charge is gone into, claim to be tried by a jury; and thereupon the case will be treated as an indictable offence. Before the charge is gone into, he should be informed of his right of trial by jury, and asked if he desires such a trial. And in the case of a child, similar information must be given to the child's parent or guardian, if present; and such parent or guardian has the right of claiming trial by jury. Harris, Cr. L. 481.

3. As to the necessary qualifications of a juror, see Byrd *v.* State, 1 How. (Miss.) 163; Quinn *v.* State, 35 Ind. 489; Bish. Cr. § 243; Curtis *v.* State, 6 Cold. (Tenn.) 9; Lindley *v.* State, 11 Tex. App. 285; 20 Am. L. Reg. 436, 497.

Impressions as to Guilt or Innocence: Effect on Qualification. — Although a juror had an impression as to the guilt or innocence of the prisoner, yet if he testified that he would be governed by the evidence, and his previous impression would not influence his verdict, and that he believed he could render an impartial verdict according to the evidence, and that he would give the prisoner the benefit of every reasonable doubt, and acquit him if such doubt existed, he is a competent juror. People *v.* Clark, 103 N. Y. 735; s. c., 3 Cent. Rep. 801.

Opinion formed or expressed: Effect on Qualification. — A person who has formed and expressed an opinion as to the guilt or innocence of the accused, which it would require evidence to remove, is a competent juror if he testifies that he can nevertheless render an impartial verdict on the evidence. People *v.* Buddensiek, 103 N. Y. 487; s. c., 4 Cent. Rep. 787.

The court say, "The challenge was upon the ground of actual bias existing in the minds of those proposed jurors; but each also testified in substance that he could, nevertheless, go into the jury-box, and render an impartial verdict upon the evidence submitted from the witness-stand, without being influenced by the opinion or impression derived or formed from what he had read. There remained, therefore, no sufficient ground of challenge or reason why the trial court could not, in the exercise of a sound discretion, determine that these several persons could try the issue impartially and without prejudice to the substantial rights of the party challenging. They were, therefore, competent within the letter of the Code of Criminal Procedure relating to such questions, and the defendant's objections were properly overruled." People *v.* Otto, 101 N. Y. 690; s. c., 2 Cent Rep. 899; People *v.* Crowley, 102 N. Y. 234; s. c., 2 Cent. Rep. 896; People *v.* Carpenter, 102 N. Y. 238; s. c., 3 Cent. Rep. 179.

An expressed opinion, founded on reports in newspapers of evidence given at a preliminary examination of a respondent, does not disqualify a juror, when his opinion was dependent upon the correctness of the reports. To disqualify, there must be an abiding bias in the mind, based upon the substantial facts in the case, in the existence of which the juror believes. State *v.* Meyer, 58 Vt. 457; s. c., 2 New Eng. Rep. 209.

The question of the competency of a juror, under his statements, is left, in a measure, to the sound discretion of the trial judge, which will not be reviewed unless facts show that it was abused. Moore, Cr. L § 308; Bradford *v.* State, 15 Ind. 347; Fahnestock *v.* State, 23 Ind 231–237; Elliott *v.* State, 73 Ind. 10; Stout *v.* State, 90 Ind. 1; Stephenson *v.* State, 110 Ind 358; s. c., 9 West. Rep. 228. Thus, where a juror answered upon his *voir dire* that, notwithstanding his conscientious scruples upon the subject of capital punishment, and his conviction that the law providing for the infliction of such punishment is unjust and wrong, he could yet render a verdict enforcing the law, the exclusion of the juror by the court will not furnish ground for the reversal of the judgment: the record showing nothing to the contrary, the appellate court should presume that the juror called in the place of the excluded juror was impartial and in every way competent. Stephenson *v.* State, 110 Ind. 358; s. c., 9 West. Rep. 228. In People *v.* Otto, 101 N. Y. 690; s. c., 2 Cent. Rep. 899, the court say, "It was apparent that he (the juror challenged) had no prejudice against the prisoner, and his mind was free to receive the evidence, and decide upon it fairly and impartially. He was, therefore, qualified to sit." People *v.* Otto, 101 N. Y. 690; s. c., 2 Cent. Rep. 899.

Bias: When disqualifies. — In State *v.* Meaker, 54 Vt. 112, *Ross, J.*, in delivering the opinion of the court, says that the opinion, in order to disqualify the juror, jury[1] of his countrymen. This jury, where not otherwise

"must be an abiding bias of the mind, based upon the substantial facts in the case in the existence of which he believes." State *v.* Meyer, 58 Vt. 457; s. c., 2 New Eng. Rep. 209.

Opinion as to the Defence of Insanity. — A juror is not disqualified because of his aversion to a "bogus plea of insanity." State *v.* Burns, 85 Mo. 47; State *v.* Baber, 74 Mo. 292; State *v.* Pagels, 92 Mo. 300; s. c., 10 West. Rep. 288.

1. As to juries generally, competency, methods of selection, formation, etc., see this work, title "Juries."

Freehold Qualification of Jurors. — It has been said that, "The doctrine that the jurors must be freeholders is found in, and running through, the common law of England from the very earliest times, and has in that country been aided by a series of statutes on the subject from the time of Henry V. down to that of George II. It was a doctrine sacredly maintained likewise in the Bill of Rights of 1688, under which William and Mary ascended the English throne. It was a doctrine brought by our ancestors to the American colonies, where it uniformly prevailed; and when the Declaration of Independence of 1776 'was submitted to a candid world' by the thirteen original States, charging that the 'king of Great Britain had given his assent to acts of pretended legislation (among others) for depriving us, in many cases, of the benefits of trial by jury, the freehold qualification was a distinguished feature of that system, then justly held in such esteem by the American people."

It was the early law of Virginia, from whence were derived the early laws of many States; it was the law of the Northwest Territory, whose inhabitants were guaranteed forever "the benefits of the trial by jury, and of judicial proceedings according to the course of the common law." See ordinance of 1787.

It was the law of most of the Territories at the time of the adoption of nearly all our different State constitutions, which declare that "the right of trial by jury shall remain inviolate;" and this has been generally construed as meaning a preservation of that mode of trial, as it was understood to exist at the time of the adoption of the Constitution. See Ross *v.* Irving, 14 Ill. 171; Norval *v.* Rice, 2 Wis. 22; Proffatt on Jury Trial, sect. 84.

It is admitted, on all hands, that this ought to be the law, because of the fact that it is a rule tending to the elevation and preservation of trial by jury; and also because it is one which forever eliminates the "professional juror" from the system, as well as that class of persons, who, having no stake in the community, are most easily liable to be bribed or suborned. 20 Am. L. Rep. 436.

The Common-Law Doctrine. — In the very earliest history of trial by jury, it appears that juries were composed of freeholders: an instance of this is found in the ancient treaty between Alfred the Great and Guthram, where the practice on trial by compurgators (the trial by jury of that period) is brought out, and where it appears that the accused, together with eleven freeholders, was required to make oath of not guilty. Anglo-Saxon Laws, p. 155; Proffat on Jury Trial, sect. 12.

In speaking of the court of the hundred, in the time of Alfred, Hume says, "Their method of decision deserves to be noted, as being the origin of juries, an institution admirable in itself, etc. Twelve freeholders were chosen, who, having sworn, together with the hundreder, or presiding magistrate of that division, to administer impartial justice, proceeded to the examination of that cause, which was substituted to their jurisdiction." "The next superior court to that of the hundred was the county court, and consisted of the freeholders of the county, who possessed an equal vote in the decision of causes." 1 Hume's Hist. Eng. (ed. 1854) ch. 2, p. 72.

In the Year Book of 3 Hen. IV. p. 4, is found the following report: That a juror was challenged because he did not have sufficiency of freehold, and then at the prayers of the triers, he was sworn to say what his freehold was worth per annum, and he said five shillings, and then the triers were charged (to answer) if he spoke truly, which then was sufficient, and he (the juror) was sworn in chief thereupon. Another juror was challenged by defendant because he was not of sufficient freehold, and Read asked that this challenge should be tried by those who were sworn, who were of the same county as the juror who was challenged, and not by those of a different county, because these could not have knowledge of his freehold; and yet the challenge was tried by those who were (already) sworn *quod nota*. Year Book, 4 Hen. IV. p. 1.

In a case where one W. De K. brought a writ of formedon, and in the formedon aforesaid a juror was challenged for non-sufficiency of freehold, and the triers say that a certain one was seised of certain land for the term of his life, reversion to the wife of him challenged; and this one (the life tenant) leased his estate to the man and wife, they paying certain rent; and there was an entry for default of payment; the challenge was allowed. Year Book, 7 Hen. IV. p. 1.

In Keilwey's Cases, temp. Henry VII. p. 46, we read, "Yaxley showed that at the last term the defendant in trespass justified damage done, etc, where he had feoffees to his use, and the demurrer was sustained; and it seems that the plea is good, for notwithstanding his feoffment, yet the land is his own land, and he would be impanelled (as juror) the same as he who had the land in possession, as it was at the common law. If a juror had but a fraction of land he would be sworn; and then comes the statute of 2 Hen. V. c. 3, and advanced the common law, and commanded that a juror who should pass upon the death of a man, in an action real or action personal, where the damages amount to forty marks, ought to expend forty shillings per year, and they construe (it to) the tenant at sufferance by equity, for that is in the intention of the framers of the statute; it being the common law at this day in a personal action under forty marks, that it is enough if he (the juror) can expend one penny."

Where one of the panel was challenged because he had nothing in the hundred, and upon that the triers pray that he upon that may be examined; and being done, he said he had half an acre of land in the hundred, and the triers report that much, and then he was sworn, *quod nota*. Year Book, 16 Edw. IV. p. 8. And in the case of Filpott *v.* Fielder, 2 Rolle, 395; s. c., Palmer, 386, it was urged that the statutes regulating the qualifications of jurors only governed the law courts, and did not apply to that case because it was (although a law case) tried in the court of chancery; that the *venire facias* specifying at least forty-one [shillings], as the quantum of freehold of the jurors summoned, was erroneous, and the plaintiff moved to arrest judgment on that ground. The court *held* "that at common law, *venire facias* was general, that jurors should have sufficient freehold, but in special cases the judges, in their discretion, could add a caution to the *venire* that the sheriff should not return any but such as had lands of the value of fifty-one [shillings], or more or less" (2 Rolle, 395); "and the values were inserted in the writ by the statutes, 2 Henry V., 25 Henry VIII., and 27 Elizabeth, by which the plaintiff took judgment accordingly, and the same day another case was decided accordingly between Horwood and Sabyn." Palmer, 386.

Rule as to Property Qualification did not extend to Suits by the Sovereign. — In Sir Christopher Blunt's Case, 1 Cro. Eliz. 413, which was an information upon an intrusion by the Queen against Sir C. Blunt, we read, "A juror was challenged for non-sufficiency of freehold, and by examination of the juror it appeared that he had freehold of the value only of fifteen shillings per annum, yet it was ruled by the court that he had sufficient to pass on that jury: for at the common law if a juror had any freehold it was sufficient But by the 2 Henry V. c. 3, he ought to have forty shillings per annum, and by 27 Eliz. 6, he ought to have forty-one per annum, where the damages exceeded forty marks. But the statutes speak only between party and party, which extends not to the Queen, wherefore the juror was sworn. But it was ruled that he ought to have some freehold, and, therefore, one who had not any freehold was there challenged and withdrawn."

In "De Laudibus Legum Angliæ," by Sir John Fortescue, Lord Chief Justice and Lord Chancellor in the reign of Henry VI., a work which fills the same authoritative place in English law of the fifteenth century which the Institutes of Coke and the Commentaries of Blackstone occupy in subsequent periods, is found the common-law rule as to freehold qualifications of jurors: he says, "Every one of the jury shall have lands or revenues (redditus, i.e., revenues arising out of lands) for the term of his life, of the yearly value, at least, of twelve scutes (i e., forty shillings). This method is observed in all actions and causes criminal, real or personal, except where, in personal actions, the damages, or thing in demand, shall not exceed forty marks, English money, because, in such like actions of small value, it is not necessary nor required that the jurors should be able to expend so much; but they are required to have lands or revenues to a competent value, at the discretion of the justices, otherwise they shall not be accepted, lest by reason of the meanness and poverty they may be liable to be easily bribed or suborned." Gregor's Translation, c. 25, p. 88.

The Statute 2 Hen. V. c. 3 is as follows: "The king, considering the great mischief and disinherisons which daily happen through all the realm of England, as well in case of the death of a man, as in cases of freehold, and in other cases, by them which pass in inquests in said cases, which be common jurors, and others that have but little to live upon but by such inquests, and which have nothing to lose because of their false oaths, and willing thereof to have correction and amendment, hath ordained and established, by assent of the lords and commons, that no person shall be admitted to pass in any inquest upon such trial of the death of a man, nor in any inquest between party and party in plea real, nor in plea personal, where the debt or the damage declared amount to forty marks, if the same person have not lands or tenements of the yearly value of forty shillings above all charges of the same." 3 Statutes at Large of England, 34.

In Coke's Commentary it is said that the statute 2 Hen. V. c. 3 "was made to remedy a mischief that the sheriff used to return simple men of small or no understanding, and therefore the statute provided that he should return sufficient men." 2 Co. Lit. sect. 464, p. 272 a.

In the Bill of Rights of 1688, which was the charter under which William and Mary ascended the British throne (1 W. & M. 2d sess. cap. 2, v. 9, Statutes at Large of England), is found a solemn declaration of the grievances suffered by the people under the Stuarts. It is recited, 'That King James did endeavor to subvert the laws and liberties of this kingdom. . . . Sect. 9. . . . 'And whereas of late years, partial, corrupt, and unqualified persons have been returned and served on juries in trials, and particularly divers jurors in trials for high treason, which were not freeholders, all which are utterly and directly contrary to the known laws, statutes, and freedom of this realm,' therefore the Parliament, 'for the vindication and asserting the ancient rights and liberties of the people, declare,' — sect. 11, — that jurors ought to be duly impanelled and returned; and jurors which pass upon men in trials for high treason ought to be freeholders."

In the Age when the Commentaries of Blackstone were written, the doctrine that jurors should be freeholders had already been settled and crystallized in the statutes of England for centuries. Hence we find in Blackstone (3 Bl. Com. 361), under the head of challenges to the polls for cause, simply a reference to the various statutes passed, from that of 2 Henry V. down to that of Geo. II.' "But," says Blackstone, in reviewing the various causes of challenge *propter defectum*, "the principal deficiency is defect of estate sufficient to qualify him to be a juror," thus clearly indicating the importance attached to this element of the trial by jury in the common law.

The American Doctrine. — The freehold qualification required by the common law was protected and perpetuated by the early State constitutions, which preserved inviolate, and without essential change, the right of trial by jury; and the more recent statutes, in many of the States, retain the freehold qualifications. See Bradford *v.* State, 15 Ind. 354; State *v.* Babcock, 1 Conn. 401; Work *v.* State, 2 Ohio St. 269; Norval *v.* Rice, 2 Wis. 22; Byrd *v.* State, 1 How. (Miss.) 163; Murick *v.* People, 40 Ill. 268. See also Rev. Stat. Ill. (1874) ch. 78; 3 Rev. Stat. N. Y. ch. 7, tit. 4; 2 Davis, Rev. Stat. Ind. (1876) 31; Gen. Stat. (1873) 571.

It is a notable fact, that, at the time the people of Virginia and of the United Colonies published their celebrated declarations against the King of England, among other things, "for depriving them, in many cases, of the trial by jury," the people of the Far North-West were equally dissatisfied with the courts organized by the English military commander in the Illinois country, and "insisted," says the historian, "upon trials by jury." Brown's Hist. Illinois. The laws of Illinois, Kentucky, Indiana, and other Western States, were originally founded upon, and derived from, those of Virginia.

Virginia Statutes. — Among the early statutes of Virginia are the following: "An act concerning juries, in force June 10, 1751. Henning's Stat. at Large, Va., vol. 5, p. 525. Sect. 3 provides for a grand jury of twenty-four freeholders. Sect. 6 provides "that no person shall be capable to be of a jury in any cause whatsoever depending in the general court, unless such person be a freeholder, and possessed of a visible estate, real and personal, of the value of one hundred pounds current money at the least." Sect. 59 of "an act for establishing a general court in this Commonwealth," passed in 1777, found in 9 Hen. Stat. at Large of Virginia, p. 416, provides "that when any person is removed (to the general court) to be tried for treason or felony, the clerk of the county from whence the prisoner is removed shall issue a venire to the sheriff of that county commanding him to summon twelve good and lawful men, being freeholders of the county, to come before the general court, which freeholders, or so many of them as shall appear not being challenged, together with so many other good and lawful freeholders of the bystanders as will make up the number twelve, shall be a lawful jury for the trial of such prisoner."

The Constitution of Virginia (Bill of Rights) of 1776 provides (sect. 11), "In controversies respecting property, and in suits between man and man, the ancient trial by jury is preferable to any other, and ought to be held sacred."

The Ordinance of 1787, which became a fundamental law, to remain "forever unalterable, unless by common consent," guarantees to the people of the North-west Territory "the benefits of the trial by jury, and . . . of judicial proceedings, according to the course of the common law." Ord. 1787, art. 2.

In the Laws of Illinois of 1819, p. 201, is found an act passed March 23, 1819, providing that the sheriff of each county where a circuit court is to be holden, shall, before the sitting of every such court, "summon twenty-four discreet freeholders, part of them from each township in their respective counties," "and the said twenty-four free-

regulated by statute, is the common-law jury.[1] A jury at com-

holders, or any sixteen of them, shall be a grand jury." "And if a sufficient number of freeholders do not attend, the sheriff shall summon from among the b.standing freeholders qualified according to law, a sufficient number to form, together with such of the first mentioned freeholders as do attend, a grand jury."

In the "Territorial Laws of Indiana," approved Sept. 17, 1807, p. 144, is found an act regulating the practice in forcible entry and detainer, and providing that the sheriff shall "summon twelve good and lawful men of the same county, each of whom having freehold lands and tenements, and they shall be impanelled to inquire into the entry or forcible detainer complained of." The form of venire is thus prescribed: "You are commanded, on behalf of the United States, to cause to come before us upon the day of , at the , in said county, twelve good and lawful men of your county, each of whom being a freeholder, to be impanelled and sworn," etc.

In same "Territorial Laws of Indiana," chap. 70, p. 450, is an act regulating the duties of sheriffs, where the right of property taken in execution is called in question, where (sect. 6) it is declared to be the duty of the sheriff to impanel twelve freeholders as a jury to try the right of property.

Delaware. — Const. of 1792, art. 1, sect. 4: "Trial by jury shall be as heretofore."

Georgia. — Const. of 1777, art. 61: "Trial by jury to remain inviolate forever."

Kentucky. — Const. of 1792, art. 12, provides that "Trial by jury shall be as heretofore, and the right thereof remain inviolate"

The Constitution of Illinois of 1818 (art. 8, sec. 6) declares, "That the right of the trial by jury shall remain inviolate." The words are clear and definite, for it is not any kind of trial that is preserved inviolate, but "the trial by jury," a particular kind and system of trial, without essential change. Ross v. Irving, 14 Ills. 171.

Maryland. — Const. of 1776, art. 3: "The inhabitants of Maryland are entitled to the common law of England and the trial by jury, according to the course of that law."

The New Jersey Constitution of 1776, sect. 22, provides, "The inestimable right of trial by jury shall remain as a part of the law of this colony without repeal forever."

New York. — The Constitution of 1777 of New York, sect. 41, provides, "Trial by jury in all cases, in which it hath heretofore been used in the colony of New York, shall be established and remain inviolate."

North Carolina. — Const. of 1776, art. 14, provides, "That in all controversies at law respecting property, the ancient mode of trial by jury is one of the best securities of the rights of the people, and ought to remain sacred and inviolable." See "United States Charters and Constitutions," compiled by Ben: Perley Poore.

"Wherever," says Judge Cooley, in his Constitutional Limitations, p. 319, "the right to this trial is guaranteed by the Constitution, without qualification or restriction, it must be understood as retained in all those cases which were triable by jury at the common law, and with all the common-law incidents to a jury trial, so far, at least, as they can be regarded as tending to the protection of the accused" And in commenting upon this constitutional clause, and others like it, Proffat, in his work on "Trial by Jury," says (sect. 84), "No matter how expressed, whether 'shall be inviolate' or 'shall remain inviolate,' there is a reference to the mode and nature of the trial, as known and used at the time of the constitutional provision, and in judicial instruction there has been a remarkable unanimity in the interpretation of these clauses. Courts have held that it was not the intent of the people either to create, enlarge, or restrict the right, but to secure and establish it as it was previously known and practised in civil and criminal cases."

1. Naturalized Citizen Competent Juror. — One who, in compliance with the terms of the State Constitution, has acquired the right to vote, is competent to serve as a juror. State v. Pagels, 92 Mo. 300; s. c., 10 West. Rep. 288. The court say in this case, "Was Lang competent to serve as a juror? He had lived in this country about eighteen years, resided in the city of St. Louis some three years, was over twenty-one years of age, had declared his intention of becoming a citizen according to law, not less than one year, nor more than five years. prior to the defendant's trial. He was therefore a citizen under the terms of § 2 of art. VIII. of our State Constitution, so far as being a voter is concerned; and that privilege is one of the highest marks and attributes of citizenship. Taken in its 'plain, ordinary, and usual sense,' as words are required to be taken by Rev. Stat. § 3126, — and this is the general rule (Smith. Com. § 481), — the word 'citizen' may well mean one entitled to vote. If so, Lang was competent to serve as a juror under the provisions of Rev. Stat. § 2777."

Jury de Medietate Linguæ. — The statute 28 Edw. III. c. 13, § 2, which provides for the trial of aliens by a jury *de medietate linguæ*, was repealed as to England by statute 26 & 27 Vict. c. 125; and the statute of mon law was a jury of twelve men; and this is the interpretation given to the word "jury" as used in our State Constitutions, for a trial by less than twelve is void.[1] It is now well settled that there can be no waiver and trial by a less number.[2]

1. *Formation of Jury.* — In the formation of a jury, the statute with respect to selecting jurors is directory. The trial court may order its officers to bring in additional jurors, or an entire new panel, as the despatch of business may demand.[3] It has been held proper, in the formation of a jury, to ask jurors on examination on their *voir dire*, who had admitted the formation of an opinion upon newspaper reports, whether, if sworn as jurors, they could give the accused a fair and impartial trial.[4]

Where, upon the calling of the names of persons summoned for a special jury, one of them answered, when his name was called, that his name varied from the list, an objection to further

6 Geo. IV. c. 50, § 47, which contained further provisions as to such trials, is repealed by the 33 Vict. c. 14, which enacts that "from and after the passing of this act an alien shall not be entitled to be tried by a jury *de medietate linguæ*, but shall be triable in the same manner as if he were a natural-born subject."

1. See Brown *v.* State, 16 Ind. 496; Jackson *v.* State, 6 Blackf. (Ind.) 461; Brown *v.* State, 8 Blackf. (Ind.) 561; Allen *v.* State, 54 Ind. 461; Moore *v.* State, 72 Ind. 358; Allen *v.* Anderson, 57 Ind. 388; Reynolds *v.* State, 61 Ind. 392, 406; Cooley, Const. Lim. *319.

2. Cancemi *v.* People, 18 N. Y. 128; Norval *v.* Rice, 2 Wis. 22; Cooley, Const. Lim. *319.

3. State *v.* Gleason, 88 Mo. 582; s. c., 5 West. Rep. 407; State *v.* Pitts, 58 Mo. 556; State *v.* Knight, 61 Mo. 373; State *v.* Ward, 74 Mo. 256.

In Indiana. — Under Code, art. 50, §§ 9, 13, providing that in all civil cases tried before a jury, and in all criminal cases where the right of peremptory challenge is not allowed, lists of names of the twenty petit jurors drawn by the clerk shall be delivered "to the respective parties or their counsel, and the said parties or their counsel may each strike out four persons from said lists, and the remaining twelve persons shall be immediately impanelled and sworn as the petit jury in such cause;" all who are joined as plaintiffs constitute one party, and all who are joined as defendants the other, and the privilege of striking out jurors is confined to four on a side, and does not extend to each individual in the case. State *v.* Reed, 46 N. H. 466; Snodgrass *v.* Hunt, 15 Ind. 274; Stone *v.* Segur, 95 Mass. (11 Allen) 568.

In Maryland The parties have, however, the right to interpose challenges to the array or polls for favor or cause, and to have such challenges passed upon before the list of twenty names is drawn or made out. Hamlin *v.* State (Md.), 9 Cent. Rep. 59.

The latter right is expressly reserved to "any person" by statute. Code, art. 50, § 10. To secure the full enjoyment of this privilege, the list, before it is stricken from, should present twenty names beyond the reach of challenge either as a principal cause or to the favor; and the parties have the right to have their cause of challenge heard and determined upon before the list is drawn from the box. Lee *v* Peter. 6 Gill & J (Md.) 447; Hamlin *v.* State (Md), 9 Cent. Rep. 59.

In Michigan. — Under How. Stat. § 7578, the court could order the jury drawn from the county at large, or from specified townships near the county-seat. In this case the order was that the jurors be drawn and summoned according to law, which would be from the county at large as specified and directed by the statute. The objection to the jury drawn in the case of People *v.* Hall, 48 Mich. 487, was, that they were neither a jury of the vicinage, nor a jury of the county at large, nor one desired by the judge himself for the general purposes of the term. "It was therefore not sanctioned by law." See People *v.* Hall, 48 Mich. 487.

It was *held* in People *v* Coffman, 59 Mich. 1, that the omission of the supervisor to return a list of names from one township would not destroy the legality of a jury drawn from the body of the county, and from the lists returned from the other townships, according to law. People *v.* Coughlin (Mich.), 11 West. Rep. 556.

4. State *v.* Brooks, 92 Mo. 542; s. c., 10 West. Rep. 679.

proceedings until a corrected list be furnished the defendant, entered in his behalf, will be properly overruled.[1]

It has also been held that exemption, not being a disqualification, is a personal privilege of the person exempted, which he may waive; and, if he does so, parties have no ground of complaint.[2] Thus, a postmaster of the United States, though exempt, is not disqualified to serve as a juror.[3]

a. Challenge. — Challenges are either (1) to the array, or (2) to the polls; and challenges to the polls are either (1) peremptory, or (2) for cause.[4]

Parties may waive their right to challenge. If either party, knowing the existence of ground for challenge, omits to challenge before the juror is sworn, he waives his right to except to the juror on such ground. It is held by some courts that if the party

1. State *v.* Brooks, 92 Mo. 542; s. c., 10 West. Rep. 697.

Miscalling Juror. — In case of Reg *v.* Mellor, J. L. 27, Mag. Cas. 121, where a juror was addressed by and answered to the wrong name, and was afterwards sworn, upon a case reserved, the court said, "The mistake is not a mistake of the man, but only of his name. At the bottom of the objection is but this, that the officer of the court, the juryman being present, called and addressed him by a wrong name. Now, it is an old and familiar maxim of law that when a party to a transaction, or the subject of a transaction, are either of them present, the calling of either by a wrong name is immaterial. *Præsentia corporis tollit errorem nominis.*"

English Doctrine. — On a trial for murder the panel returned by the sheriff contained the names of J. H. T. and W. T. The name of J. H. T. was called from the panel as one of the jury; and J. H. T., as was supposed, went into the box, and was duly sworn by the name of J. H. T. The prisoner was convicted. The following day it was discovered that W. T. had by mistake answered to the name of J. H. T., and that W. T. was really the person who had served on the jury. It was held in the court of criminal appeal, by Lord Campbell, C J., Cockburn, C. J, Coleridge, J., Martin and Watson, BB. (five), that there had been a mis-trial; by Erle, Crompton, Crowder, Willes, and Byles, JJ., and Channell, B. (six), that there had been no mis-trial. It was doubted in this case whether the objection was matter of error; and Pollock, C. B., Erle, Williams, Crompton, Crowder, and Willes, JJ, and Channell, B, thought that this was not a question of law arising at the trial over which the court of criminal appeal had jurisdiction. R. *v.* Mellor, Dears & B. C. C. 468. And see R. *v.* Martin, L. R. 1 C. C. R. 378; 41 L. J. M. C. 113.

2. State *v.* Wright, 53 Me. 344; State *v.* Forshner, 43 N. H. 89; State *v.* May (Me.), 3 New Eng. Rep. 846.

3. State *v* Quimby, 51 Me. 395; State *v.* May (Me.), 3 New Eng Rep. 846.

4. **Statutory Regulation.** — In this country the whole subject of challenging is provided for and determined in great detail by the statutes in some of the States, while in others the matter is left substantially as at common law. One of the grounds of challenge is "previously formed or expressed opinion," a fruitful source of decision. 1 Bish Cr. Proc. § 771.

Conscientious Scruples. — If the proposed juror, in a capital case, has such conscientious scruples against capital punishment that he would not find a verdict of guilty, he must, if challenged, be excluded. When he admits he has a fixed opinion against capital punishment, but does not say he would not find a verdict of guilty, it has been held he should be excluded. O'Brien *v.* People, 36 N. Y. 276; Walker *v.* State, 40 Ala. 325.

Other cases hold the contrary doctrine. Atkins *v.* State, 16 Ark. 568; People *v.* Stewart, 7 Cal. 140; Commonwealth *v.* Webster, 5 Cush. 295.

Opinions of Juror as Grounds of Challenge. — It has likewise been held good ground for challenge, that the juror would not render a verdict of guilty on circumstantial evidence, — Gales *v.* People, 14 Ill. 433. — that he does not think the matter charged against the defendant is a crime, — Choteau *v.* Pierre, 9 Mo. 3, — that he holds the statute under which the defendant is indicted unconstitutional, and, therefore, would not bring in a verdict of guilty. Commonwealth *v.* Austen, 73 Mass. (7 Gray) 51.

When Talesmen are required to fill the jury, the court directs the sheriff to call the required number. The sheriff is not restricted to persons in the court-house. State *v.* Damon, 3 Hawks (N. C.), 175.

omits to use the means given to him by the law, of ascertaining the juror's competency, — if he omits to inquire of the juror, or challenge him before he is sworn, — it is too late to except to him.[1] In other courts, this is denied or qualified.[2]

If a challenge is erroneously overruled, and the juror is then peremptorily challenged, this is not cause for new trial or reversal, if the challenging party goes to trial without exhausting his peremptory challenges.[3]

1. State *v.* Howard, 27 N. H. 171; Stalls *v.* State, 28 Ala. 25; Gillespie *v.* State, 8 Yerg. (Tenn.) 507; Beck *v.* State, 20 Ohio St. 228, the principle stated in a civil case, Kenrick *v.* Reppard, 23 Ohio St. 333.

2. Commonwealth *v.* Wade, 24 Mass. (17 Pick.) 395; Commonwealth *v.* Flannagan, 7 Watts & S. (Pa.) 515; Thompson *v.* Commonwealth, 8 Gratt. (Va.) 637; State *v.* Underwood, 6 Ired. (N. C.) 96; Ogle *v.* State, 33 Miss. 383; State *v.* Bunger, 14 La. An. 461; Stoner *v.* State, 4 Mo. 368; State *v.* Groome, 10 Iowa, 316.

3. Nimms *v.* State, 16 Ohio St. 221; Erwin *v.* State, 29 Ohio St. 186; Carroll *v.* State, 3 Humph. (Tenn.) 315; State *v.* Elliott, 45 Iowa, 486. *Compare* Dowdy *v.* Commonwealth, 9 Gratt. 727.

Challenges improperly allowed or disallowed. — It is said that, if a challenge be overruled without demurrer, the ruling may be made the subject of a bill of exceptions. R. *v.* City of Worcester, Skin. 101. If there is a demurrer and judgment thereon, there would be matter of error on the record. See R. *v.* Edmonds, 4 B. & Ald. 471. If a challenge be improperly allowed, it is doubtful whether there is any matter for error. See Mansell *v.* Reg., Dears. & B. C. C. 375.

Time and Mode of taking them. English Doctrine. — When one or more defendants have pleaded the general issue, they are informed by the officer of the court that the persons whose names he is about to call will form the jury which is to try them, and that they are at liberty to challenge any who may be called, as they come to be sworn. The practice as to the mode of getting a jury together is not very clearly defined, and probably differs considerably in different parts of the country. It is difficult to understand whether the rule laid down in Vicars *v.* Langham, Hob. 235, that there can be no challenge either to the array or to the polls until a full jury appear, is of perfectly general application. It is repeated, and no limits indicated, in R. *v.* Edmonds, 4 B. & Ald. 471; 3 Burn, Just. ed. 30, p. 90; and Joy on Confessions and Challenges, § 10. It is probably stated somewhat too broadly, and what is meant is, that before the prisoner is put to his challenges, he has a right to have the whole panel called over to see who does and who does not appear. Fost. Cr. Cas. fol. ed. p. 7; R. *v.* Frost, 9 C. & P. 135. However this may be, it is the constant practice in some counties to swear the first juryman who answers as soon as he enters the box, without any further inquiry. In other places it is the practice to get a full jury into the box, and then to commence swearing them; then, if any one is rejected, to call another in his place, and so on, *toties quoties*. If there is a defect of jurors, and either party pray a tales, he does not thereby lose his right to challenge. Vicars *v.* Langham, Bull. N. P. 307. But Hawkins doubts whether a tales can be prayed by the prosecutor, upon an indictment or criminal information, without a warrant from the attorney-general. Hawk. P. C. c. 41, § 18. On the other hand, it is said by Blackstone, J., that "if by reason of challenges, or defaults of jurors, a sufficient number cannot be had of the original panel, a *tales* may be awarded as in civil causes, till the number of twelve is sworn." 4 Bl. Com. 355. See 14 Eliz. c. 9 (repealed 6 Geo. IV. c. 50, § 62); P. *v.* Dolby, 2 B. & C. 104; Arch. Cr. L. 18th ed. p. 157. But, inasmuch as if the panel is exhausted, and no *tales* prayed, the court may, of its own accord, order the sheriff or other officer to return a fresh panel *instanter*. 1 Hale, P. C. 28, 260.

There is no doubt that the time for the prisoner to challenge the polls is, as each juryman comes to the book to be sworn; that is, after the juryman has been called for the purpose of being sworn, and before the oath has commenced. It seems that the formal delivery of the book into the hands of a juryman is the commencement of the oath. R. *v.* Frost, 9 C. & P. 126; R. *v.* Brandreth, 32 How. St. Tr. 770. See also R. *v.* Giorgetti, 4 F. & F. 546. But if the juryman, of his own accord, takes the book into his hands, his doing so not being directed by the court, or sanctioned by the court, that does not take away the right of challenge. R. *v.* Frost, *supra*. It is not absolutely necessary that the names should be called in the order in which they stand on the panel, but that order may be departed from if convenience requires it. Mansell *v.* Reg., Dears. & B. C. C. 375.

The challenge to the array is an objection to the whole body of jurors returned by the sheriff, not on account of their individual defects, but for some partiality or default in the sheriff, or his under-officer, who arrayed the panel. It may be either (1) a *principal* challenge, which is founded on some manifest partiality, as if the sheriff be the prosecutor or person injured, or be closely connected with such person, or if he has any pecuniary interest in the trial, or be influenced in his return of jurors by the prosecutor or defendant, or if he be counsel, attorney, etc., in the case; or it may be founded on some error on the part of the sheriff. If the cause of challenge is substantiated, the court will quash the array. (2) Challenge for *favor*, in cases where the ground of partiality is less apparent and direct, as when one of the parties is tenant to the sheriff. The challenge to the array ought to be in writing, and must state specifically the ground of objection.[1]

The challenge to the array must, of course, be before any juryman is sworn.

Where the indictment charged a subsequent felony in one count, and a previous conviction in another, and the prisoner, at the request of his counsel, was arraigned separately on the subsequent felony, and afterwards on the previous conviction, it was doubted if it was necessary to re-swear the jury, and give the prisoner his challenges. R. *v.* Key, 3 C. & K. 371. But an express provision for separate arraignment without re-swearing the jury is now made in most cases.

Persons unfit to serve not challenged.—A juror who is not qualified may object to serve, though not challenged; and if, upon examin tion on oath, he be found not to be so, he will be ordered to retire. 4 Harg. St. Tr. 740. A juryman, on being called to serve on a trial for murder, stated that he had conscientious scruples to capital punishment. Upon this the judge ordered him to withdraw, although the counsel for the prisoner demanded that he should serve. The Court of Queen's Bench, on a writ of error, without stating whether they considered that this was the right course, said that they wished it to be understood that they by no means acquiesced in the doctrine contended for on the authority of an anonymous case in Brownlow & Gold Rep. 41, that a judge, on the trial of a criminal case, has no authority, if there be no challenge on either side, to excuse a juryman on the panel when he is called, or to order him to withdraw, if he be palpably unfit, by physical or mental infirmity, to do his duty in the jury-box. Mansell *v.* Reg., *ubi supra.*

1. **In Michigan.**—Under How. Stat. § 7567, the list and box containing the names from which the jurors are to be drawn are placed in the charge of the clerk, and the clerk is required to draw from the box in the presence of the officer or officers attending. His oath of office applies to the duty of drawing, and the oaths of the others apply to the duties assigned to them; and where the sheriff drew from the box the names, and the defendant in a criminal action challenged the array of jurors called, the challenge should have been sustained. People *v.* Labadie, (Mich.) 10 West. Rep. 643.

The court say, "It appears from the record that when the cause was reached at the circuit a jury was called, and, before being sworn, counsel for the respondent challenged the array of jurors called, alleging a large number of reasons, and among which it is alleged that when the panel of jurors was obtained, the names were drawn from the box by the sheriff, and not by the clerk.

"The record shows that this allegation is true; and if so, the challenge to the array was well taken. The statute was not complied with. It was the duty of the clerk to take the names from the box. How Stat. § 7567; Atkinson *v.* Morse (Mich.), 5 West. Rep. 917. The statutes which establish the rule for the drawing of jurors leave no discretion in the officers designated to conduct such drawing, but plainly indicate how the proceeding shall be conducted. People *v.* Hall, 48 Mich. 486.

"Mr. Justice Graves, speaking for this court in the case of Gott *v.* Brigham, 45 Mich. 429, while considering this section of the statute, and speaking of the duties of the clerk on these occasions, said, 'The legislature has seen fit to provide expressly that the clerk, and no one else, shall handle the box, and draw therefrom in the presence of the officer or officers attending, and that one of the attending officers shall keep a minute of such drawing. The law has

If the challenge to the array be determined against the prisoner, he may challenge to the polls. This challenge is either (1) principal, or (2) for favor. Challenges for cause may properly be divided into three classes: to wit, (1) *propter defectum*, that is, on account of some personal objection, as alienage, infancy, old age, or a want of the requisite qualification;[1] (2) *propter affectum*, where there is supposed to be a bias or prospect of partiality, as on account of the relationship of a juror, or where an actual partiality is manifested, or where a juror has expressed an opinion as to the result of the trial; and (3) *propter delictum*, if a person has

apportioned the duties with extreme care. The list and box are under the sworn custody of the clerk. His oath of office applies to the duty of drawing, and the oaths of the others apply to the duties assigned to them; and, if they exchange duties, their respective oaths do not accompany the exchange.'" People *v.* Labadie (Mich.), 10 West Rep. 643.

In Pennsylvania. — To constitute a court of oyer and terminer, it is necessary that forty-eight jurors be drawn and returned; but it is not cause of challenge to the array that only forty-eight jurors were summoned, one of whom was not qualified. Foast *v.* Commonwealth, 33 Pa. St. 338; Buchanan Commonwealth, (Pa.) 5 Cent. Rep. 783.

English Doctrine. — The learning on this subject has to be sought out of old books, and there is great difficulty in deriving from them any precise rules. It is, however, quite clear that any partiality in the sheriff, under-sheriff, or other officer who is concerned in the return of the jury, is a good cause of challenge to the array. And that this partiality will be assumed to exist, if the sheriff or other officer be of kindred or affinity to either party; or if any dispute be pending between the sheriff and either party which would be likely to influence the sheriff; or if the sheriff or other officer have been concerned for either party in the same matter, either as counsel, attorney, or the like. Co. Litt. 156 a; Bac. Abr. tit. "Juries" (E).

There can be no challenge to the array on the ground of the partiality of the master of the crown office, in a case where he is the officer by whom the jury is to be nominated under a rule of court, according to the statute 3 Geo. II. c. 25, § 15 (repealed 6 Geo. IV. c. 50, § 64); R *v.* Edmonds, 4 B. & Ald. 471. The only remedy in such a case is to apply to the court to appoint another officer to nominate the jury.

By the 6 Geo. IV. c. 50, § 13, the want of four hundreders in the panel is declared to be no cause of challenge; and by § 28, the same is declared with respect to the want of a knight.

Whether there is the same right in a subject as in the crown to challenge for favor, has been doubted. See 2 Hawk. P. C. c. 44, § 32. But that doubt is obsolete.

A challenge to the array should be in writing, so that it may be put upon the record, and the other party may plead or demur to it; and the cause of challenge must be stated specifically. R. *v.* Hughes, 1 C. & K. 235.

When the opposite party pleads to the challenge, two triers are appointed by the court; either two coroners, two attorneys, or two of the jury, or indeed any two indifferent persons. If the array be quashed against the sheriff, a *venire facias* is then directed *instanter* to the coroner; if it be further quashed against the coroner, it is then awarded to two persons, called *elisors*, chosen at the discretion of the court, and it cannot be afterwards quashed. Co Litt. 158 a.

It has been said that there is some distinction between trying challenges; those that are manifest or principal challenges, as they are called, being tried by the court without the appointment of any triers. See Co. Litt. 156 a; Bac. Abr. tit. "Juries," E. 12.

The truth of the matter alleged as cause of challenge must be made out by witnesses to the satisfaction of the triers. The challenging party first addresses the triers, and calls his witnesses; then the opposite party addresses them, and calls witnesses if he thinks fit; in which case the challenger has a reply. The judge then sums up to the triers, who give their decision. See R. *v.* Dolby, 2 B. & C. 104. If a challenge to the array be found against the party, he may afterwards, notwithstanding, challenge to the polls.

1. Not a Citizen. — The objection that one of the jurors was not a citizen of the county would have been a good ground of challenge, but it comes too late after his acceptance and qualification as a juror. State *v.* Waller, 88 Mo. 402; s. c., 4 West. Rep 433, Mo R. S. § 2778.

Age is not a disqualification as a juror. State *v.* May (Me.), 3 New Eng. Rep. 846.

been convicted of an infamous crime (e.g., treason, felony, perjury, etc.), and has not been pardoned.[1]

Other Disqualifications. — The court always sustains a challenge to a juror where he is not a voter, householder, or freeholder. Block *v.* State, 100 Ind. 357. See *ante*, p. 823, "Freehold Qualifications."

1. Harris, Cr. L. 390.

Where the defendant, on his trial for murder, claimed and was allowed forty-eight hours, after a panel of forty-seven jurors had been qualified, within which to make his challenges, the jury being first duly cautioned, it was not error in the court to refuse to permit him thereafter to interrogate the jury as to whether they had read a newspaper report of the crime charged, the counsel stating that he had no knowledge that the jury had seen the report State *v.* Rose, 90 Mo. 201; s. c., 10 West. Rep. 279.

The English Doctrine is admirably set forth by Roscoe in his "Criminal Evidence," p. 214, *et seq.* He says respecting challenges for cause or principal challenges that, by the common law, the king, or the prosecutor who represented him, might challenge peremptorily any number of jurors, simply alleging *quod non boni sunt pro rege;* but by the 33 Edw. I. st. 4 this right is taken away, and the king is bound to assign the cause of his challenge; and this enactment is repeated in the same words in the 6 Geo. IV. c. 50, § 29.

A practice, however, which has continued uniformly from the time of Edw. I. to the present enables the prosecutor to exercise practically the right of peremptory challenge; because, when a man is called, the juror will, on his request, be ordered to stand by; and it is only when the panel has been exhausted, that is, when it appears that, if the jurors ordered to stand by are excluded, there will be a defect of jurors, that the prosecutor is compelled to show his cause of objection. Mansell *v.* Reg., Dears & B. C. C. 375. When it appears that, in consequence of the peremptory challenges by the defendant, and the juryman ordered to stand by at the request of the prosecutor, a full jury cannot be obtained, then the proper course is to call over the whole panel again, only omitting those that have been peremptorily challenged by the defendant. R. *v.* Geach, 9 Car & P. 499. And even on the second reading over of the panel a juryman may be ordered to stand by at the request of the prosecutor, if it reasonably appears that sufficient jurymen may yet appear. Mansell *v.* Reg., *supra.*

The prisoner has, in cases of felony, twenty peremptory challenges and no more, — 6 Geo. IV c. 50, § 29, — and the right exists whether the felony be capital or not. Gray *v.* Reg., 11 Cl. & Fin. 427. The number in cases of high treason is thirty-five but this is reduced to twenty in such cases of treason as are, by the 39 & 40 Geo. III c. 93, and the 5 & 6 Vict. c. 51, directed to be tried in the same manner as charges of murder. In cases of misdemeanor, there is no right of peremptory challenge. Co Litt. 166. But the defendant is generally allowed to object to jurors as they are called, without showing any cause, till the panel is exhausted; and that practice was approved of by *Williams*, *J*, in R. *v.* Blakeman, 3 C. & K. 97. If the panel be thus exhausted, the list must be gone through again, and then no challenge allowed except for cause.

The trial proceeds in the same manner as a challenge to the array. The juror challenged may be himself examined as to any cause of unfitness. Bac. Abr. *ubi supra.*

A juror may be challenged on the ground that he is not *liber et legalis homo;* and this would hold good against outlaws, aliens, minors, villains, and females. He may also be challenged on the ground of infamy, which ground is said not to be removed by pardon, — Bac. Abr. tit. "Juries," E. 2, — or that he is not fit to serve from age, — but see Mulcahy *v.* Reg., L. R. 3 H. of L. 306, — or some other personal defect; or that he is not qualified. The qualification of jurors is fixed by the 6 Geo. IV. c. 50, § 1, which provides that "all persons between the ages of twenty-one and sixty years, residing in any county in England, who shall have in his own name or in trust for him, within the same county, ten pounds by the year above reprizes, in lands or tenements, whether of freehold, copyhold, or customary tenure, or of ancient demesne, or of rents issuing out of any such lands or tenements, or in any such lands, tenements, and rents taken together, in fee-simple, fee-tail, or for the life of himself or some other person; or who shall have within the same county twenty pounds by the year above reprizes in lands or tenements, held by lease or leases for the absolute term of twenty-one years, or some longer term, or for any term of years determinable on any life or lives, or who, being a householder, shall be rated or assessed to the poor-rate, or to the inhabited house duty in the county of Middlesex, on a value of not less than thirty pounds, or in any other county on a value of not less than twenty pounds, or who shall occupy a house containing not less than fifteen windows, shall be qualified to serve on juries on all issues in all the

Challenges *for favor* are made when there is reasonable ground for suspicion (as if a fellow-servant be one party), but there is not sufficient ground for a principal challenge *propter affectum*.

The challenge to the polls is generally made orally, and must be made before the juror has been sworn.[1] In felonies the prisoner is allowed to arbitrarily challenge, and so exclude a certain number of jurors without showing any cause at all. He cannot claim this right in misdemeanors.[2]

In the absence of statutory regulation, the court may require both parties to make their peremptory challenges, after having exhausted their challenges for cause, to each juror as called, and, upon default, may require the juror to be sworn as such at once, before calling another.[3]

superior courts, both civil and criminal, and in all courts of assizes, *nisi prius*, oyer and terminer, and gaol delivery, and in all issues joined in courts of sessions of the peace, such issues being respectively in the county in which every man so qualified respectively shall reside." And every man, being between the aforesaid ages, "residing in any county in Wales, and being there qualified to the extent of three-fifths of any of the foregoing qualifications," shall be qualified to serve on juries in all issues joined in the courts of great sessions, and in courts of sessions of the peace, in every county in Wales in which every man so qualified shall reside. By the 45 & 46 Vict. c. 50, § 186, every burgess of a borough having a separate court of quarter-sessions is qualified and liable to serve on juries in that court, unless exempted by law; but by the schedule of 33 & 34 Vict. c. 77, they are exempt from serving on county sessions. By 33 & 34 Vict. c. 77, schedule, members of the council, justices of the peace, the town clerk, and treasurer within the borough, are disqualified from serving on any jury in the county where the borough is situate. Justices are also exempt from serving on any sessions for the jurisdiction of which they are justices.

Challenge of Juror not Indifferent. — A juror may also be challenged on the ground that he is not indifferent. The same circumstances which would support a challenge to the array for unindifferency in the sheriff would support a challenge to the poll for the same defect in a juryman. It is no cause of challenge of a juror by the prosecutor that the juror is a client of the prisoner, who is an attorney, — R. *v.* Geach, 9 C. & P. 499, — nor that the juror has visited the prisoner as a friend since be has been in custody. Id. It is not allowable to ask a juryman if he has not previously to the trial expressed himself hostilely to the prisoner, in order to found a challenge; but such expressions must be proved by some other evidence. R. *v.* Edmonds, 4 B. & Ald. 471; R. *v.* Cooke, 13 How. St. Tr. 333. And they must amount to something more than an expression of opinion in order to constitute a good cause of challenge; they must lead directly to the conclusion that the juryman is not likely to act impartially after he has heard the evidence. "Joy on Confessions and Challenges," p. 189. On the trial of an indictment for a riot, it is ground for challenge by the prosecution that the juror challenged is an inhabitant of the town where the riot took place, and that he took an active part in the matter which led to it. *Per Coleridge, J.*, R. *v.* Swain, 2 Moo. & R. 112.

After the prisoner has challenged twenty jurors peremptorily, he may still challenge others for cause. R. *v.* Geach, 9 Car. & P. 499.

As in a challenge to the array, the ground of challenge should be specifically stated in writing, in order that it may be placed on the record with the judgment thereon. R. *v.* Hughes, 1 C. & K. 235.

1. Harris, Cr. L. 388.

2. "It is equally absurd that in the case of a trifling theft the prisoner should have the right of peremptorily challenging twenty jurors, whilst a man accused of perjury might see his bitterest enemy in the jury-box, and be unable to get rid of him as a juror, unless he could give judicial proof of his enmity." Fitz. St. 106.

Number of Peremptory Challenges allowed: English Rule — The defendant may peremptorily challenge to the number of thirty-five in treason, except in that treason which consists of compassing the queen's death by a direct attempt against her life or person. In such excepted case, in murder, and all other felonies, the number is limited to twenty. If challenges are made beyond the number allowed, those above the number are entirely void, and the trial proceeds as if no such extra challenge had been made.

3. Schufflin *v.* State, 20 Ohio St. 233.

2. *Misconduct of Jury.* — Regarding the misconduct of a juror, which will be ground for a new trial, see the title "Jury and Juryman" in this series.

XIII. Continuance and Adjournment. — If the trial is not concluded on the same day on which it is commenced, the judge may adjourn from day to day; and where the trial cannot be finished during the term, it may properly be continued at six o'clock, P.M., of the last day of the term.[1]

When a case is postponed, either until a later day in the same term or until the next term, it is in legal contemplation continued.[2]

The failure of a party to object until after trial, excludes him from questioning the regularity of the proceedings at an adjourned term.[3]

A judge[4] may adjourn a case, and proceed with another if the

In Iowa and Kentucky all the defendants constitute one party, and a challenge by any one of them is a challenge by all. See Iowa Rev. Stat. (1873) 681; Kentucky Cr. Code, § 198.

In Ohio, where there are several defendants, and there has been no severance, each defendant is entitled to as many peremptory challenges as if he were tried alone. See 74 Ohio L. 346.

In Missouri. — On the trial of an indictment charging defendant with putting out the eye of a designated person, on purpose and with malice aforethought, by shooting him with a gun, based on Rev. Stat. 1879, § 1261, the defendant is entitled only to eight challenges, as provided in the third subdivision of Rev. Stat. § 1900. State *v.* Stevenson (Mo.), 11 West. Rep 449.

Nature of Peremptory Challenge. — The right of peremptory challenge is a right, not to select, but simply to reject, jurors, without cause assigned. Turpin *v.* State, 55 Md. 462; U. S. *v.* Marchant, 25 U. S. (12 Wheat.) 480; bk. 6, L. ed. 700; Hayes *v.* Mo., 120 U. S. 71; bk. 30, L. ed. 578.

And where the accused has exercised the right of peremptory challenge in respect to any member of the panel, and the juror thus challenged has retired from the box, the court will not allow the challenge to be recalled or withdrawn. Rex. *v.* Parry, 7 Carr. & P. 836; 3 Wharton, Crim. Law, § 3061. Biddle *v.* State (Md.), 9 Cent. Rep. 207.

The defendant is entitled to a full panel of qualified jurors before he is required to make his peremptory challenges. State *v.* McCarron, 51 Mo. 27; State *v.* Waters, 62 Mo. 196; State *v.* Davis, 66 Mo. 684. It therefore becomes important to learn whether there was a full general panel from which to make selection. State *v.* Bryant (Mo.), 12 West. Rep. 335.

When disallowed. — The trial court correctly refused to sustain defendant's peremptory challenge to a juror who, on the *voir dire* examination as to his qualifications as a juror, stated that he had formed an opinion from rumor and newspaper accounts purporting to give the evidence on the former trial; that it would take evidence to remove the opinion, but that, notwithstanding such opinion, he could hear the case impartially and decide it according to the evidence and instructions of the court; and that he could try the case as impartially as if he had never heard of it. The legislature has expressly provided that opinions formed from newspaper reports and rumors should not disqualify a person from being a juror unless it should further appear that such opinion would bias his judgment, and prevent him from treating the case impartially and according to the evidence adduced on the trial. State *v.* Bryant (Mo.), 12 West. Rep. 324; Baldwin *v.* State, 12 Mo. 223; State *v.* Brooks (Mo.), 10 West. Rep. 679; State *v.* Davis, 29 Mo. 392; State *v.* Rose, 32 Mo. 346; State *v.* Core, 70 Mo. 491; State *v.* Brown, 71 Mo. 454; State *v.* Walton, 74 Mo. 270; State *v.* Hoprick, 84 Mo. 283; State *v.* Cutler, 82 Mo. 623.

1. Walker *v.* State, 102 Ind. 502; s. c., 3 West. Rep. 354.

2. Morris *v.* State, 104 Ind. 457; s. c., 2 West. Rep. 259.

3. Snurr *v.* State, 105 Ind. 125; s. c., 2 West. Rep. 722.

4. Where, after due opening of a term, an order is made that if no judge shall be in attendance at a specified later hour, the sheriff shall then continue court until next morning, no notice of such adjournment is required to be posted. Bressler *v.* People (Ill.), 5 West. Rep. 185.

The continuance of a criminal cause by a clerk of court beyond the period authorized by statute operates as a discontinuance, and a new warrant of arrest cannot be issued on the old complaint. State *v.* Meagher, 57 Vt. 398.

emergency requires it; as, for example, to give time for the production of something essential to the proof, or for the witnesses to arrive.[1]

Right of Prosecuting Attorney to pass upon Application for Continuance. — The legislature has no more authority to authorize the prosecuting attorney to pass upon the defendant's application for a continuance, than it has to pass upon defendant's application for a change of venue, or his motion for a new trial. State *v.* Berkley, 92 Mo. 41; s. c., 10 West. Rep. 67.

There is a limit to the power of the legislature; there is a boundary over which it may not pass. It cannot make the impossible possible, nor, in defiance of the Bill of Rights, compel the accused to accept a piece of paper instead of a man.

"The question presents itself whether any thing may be made the law of the land, or may become due process of law, which the legislature, under the proper forms, has seen fit to enact? To solve this question, we have only to consider for a moment the purpose of the clause under examination. That purpose, as is apparent, was individual protection and limitation upon power; and any construction which would leave with the legislature this unbridled authority, as has been well said by an eminent jurist, 'would render the restriction absolutely nugatory, and turn this part of the Constitution into mere nonsense.' The people would be made to say to the two houses, 'You shall be vested with the legislative power of the State, but no one shall be disfranchised or deprived affidavit, in so far as it states what the defendant expects to prove as the evidence of the absent witness.' The defendant may show that he has used all reasonable efforts to have his witnesses summoned; that they are within the jurisdiction of the court, and can be served; or he may show that they have been served, but do not appear, and can and ought to be attached; yet, in all these cases, he must go to trial without them. The statute makes no exception. Its evident purpose is to substitute the affidavit for the witnesses, and thus avoid the necessity of bringing the witnesses before the court. The plain sense of the law is to deprive the accused of the right 'to have process to compel the attendance of witnesses in his own behalf,' as is secured to him by the State Constitution; but I do not agree that the statute violates any other provision of the State or Federal Constitution." State *v.* Berkley, 92 Mo. 41; s. c., 10 West. Rep. 67.

1. Where Witnesses Resident out of State. — An application on account of witness out of the State, must show materiality of the evidence, due diligence, and that they can and will be produced at the future term. State *v.* Duffy (La. An.), April, 1887.

But it was recently *held* in Mississippi that a continuance will not be granted on account of the absence of a witness who does not reside in the State. Skates *v.* State (Miss.), April, 1887.

Cumulative Evidence. — Continuances will not be allowed to enable the party to produce evidence that is merely cumulative, unless there is some necessity shown therefor, — such as that there will be a conflict in the evidence in reference to the particular matter in regard to which the absent witness is expected to testify. Shook *v.* Thomas, 21 Ill. 87; Dacy *v.* People, 116 Ill. 555; s. c., 4 West Rep. 180.

Evidence of a merely cumulative character is not sufficient on which to ground the application. Sutherlin *v.* State (Ind.), 7 West. Rep. 60.

Continuance for Sentence. — When the term of the district court was begun two weeks before the session of the circuit court, and the accused had been tried and convicted before the beginning of the latter term, and the circuit court does not meet, the district court may continue its term for the purpose of passing sentence. State *v.* Boyd, 38 La. An. 374.

Validity of Proceedings at Adjourned Term. — Where a judge makes an order in term time for an adjourned term, appears at the time appointed and opens court, proceedings at such adjourned term are not void, although another court of the same circuit was in session at the time, presided over by a special judge. Snurr *v.* State, 105 Ind. 125, s. c., 2 West. Rep. 722.

Validity of a trial held at an adjourned term depends on the steps taken to appoint and convene the adjourned term. Snurr *v.* State, 105 Ind. 125; s. c., 2 West. Rep. 722.

Illness of Judge. — The failure to bring a person charged with crime to trial within sixty days after the filing of the information will not warrant a dismissal of the prosecution, if the delay was caused by the illness of the trial judge, or his engagements in the trial of other causes. People *v.* Camilo, 69 Cal. 540.

Indiana Practice. — Ind. R. S. 1881, sec. 1784, contemplates that one accused of crime is not to be discharged from arrest as a matter of course, after the expiration of two terms of continuous confinement, or at any other time, under the provisions of sec. 1782, except upon application to the court in which the indictment is pending. If, upon such application, the court shall be

If the prisoner is taken so ill as to render him incapable of remaining at the bar, the jury is discharged, and the prisoner is afterwards tried by another jury.[1]

The statutory provisions concerning continuance have reference as well to temporary postponements; and motions are addressed to the sound discretion of the court, and are not matter of right except upon cause shown.[2] Neither a continuance nor a postponement can be demanded as matter of right, except upon cause shown.[3] But where nothing in the record casts suspicion on the good faith of the application, the witnesses named in the application are all real, and the testimony at the trial shows that they

satisfied that the delay was the result of one of the causes within the exception contained in sec. 1783, it would be its duty to continue its cause until the next term, and remand the prisoner unconditionally to await his trial. As long and as often as the State is able to make it appear that the occasion of the delay is one of the excepted causes, the application must fail. McGuire *v.* Wallace, 109 Ind. 284; s. c., 7 West. Rep. 415.

1. Harris, Cr. L. 450.

Time to prepare Defense. — Defendant in a criminal case is entitled to a reasonable time to prepare for trial, and to have the aid of counsel; but a mere statement of counsel that the respondent is not prepared for trial, is not a sufficient basis for a continuance of the cause. The practice and rules of court require such applications to be supported by affidavit showing the necessity for delay; and in the absence of such showing, it is not error to overrule the motion. People *v.* Mason (Mich.), 6 West. Rep. 183.

The motion, where the offence was committed but nine days before the application, should be granted, where counsel was procured only the day before the application. State *v.* Brooks (La. An.), Feb. 1887.

Art. 54, Texas Code Crim. Proc., provides that, if a "motion to set aside an indictment or information, or an exception to the same, is sustained, the defendant, in a case of misdemeanor, shall be discharged, but may be again prosecuted within the time allowed by law. The defendant in such case cannot be held, as in a felony case, but must be discharged; and this rule applies whether the indictment is set aside on the motion of the State, or on the motion of the defendant In this case, after the defence announced that they were ready, the county attorney quashed the information because of a fatal defect, and filed another *instanter*. The defendant asked leave to withdraw his announcement, because not ready to answer to the new information, which application was refused, and the trial on the new information was proceeded with. *Held*, error, and that the defendant was entitled to his discharge, and was not triable until arrested under the new information. Turner *v.* State, 21 Tex App. 198.

Requiring defendant to answer whether he is ready for trial or not, after the State has asked for a continuance, and before the application has been disposed of, is not the proper practice: it is for that State to answer first whether ready or not. State *v.* Emerson, 90 Mo. 236; s. c., 6 West. Rep. 666.

Illness of Counsel. — It will be presumed that the court properly overruled a motion for a continuance at a second term, on the ground of sickness of counsel. State *v.* Stegner (Iowa), June, 1887.

Infant Witness. — Where a case depends upon the testimony of an infant, it is usual for the court to examine him as to his competency to take an oath previously to his going before the grand jury; and if found incompetent, for want of proper instruction, the court will, in its discretion, put off the trial, in order that the party may, in the mean time, receive such instruction as may qualify him to take an oath. 1 Stark. Ev. 2d ed 94. This was done by Rooke, J., in the case of an indictment for a rape, and approved of by all the judges. 1 Leach, 430 n.; 2 Bac. Abr. by Gwill, 577 n. An application to postpone the trial upon this ground ought properly to be made before the child is examined by the grand jury; at all events, before the trial has commenced, for if the jury are sworn, and the prisoner is put upon his trial, before the incompetency of the witness is discovered, the judge ought not to discharge the jury upon this ground. 1 Phill. Ev. 10th ed. 19, citing R. *v.* Wade.

2. Morris *v.* State, 104 Ind. 457; s. c., 2 West. Rep. 259; State *v.* Bradley, 90 Mo. 160; s. c., 7 West. Rep. 97; Brown *v.* State (Tenn.), Feb. 1887; Tucker *v.* State (Tex. App.), June, 1886.

3. Morris *v.* State, 104 Ind. 457; s. c., 2 West. Rep. 259.

were present at the act, the motion for a continuance should be granted.[1]

Where the discretion of the court has been arbitrarily or unsoundly exercised, it is ground for reversal.[2] But this is the case only where error is shown.[3]

1. Sutton *v.* People (Ill.), 7 West. Rep. 702.

2. State *v.* Bradley, 90 Mo. 160; s. c., 7 West. Rep. 97.

3. Morris *v.* State, 104 Ind. 457; s. c, 2 West Rep. 259.

Where the Trial is before the Court, the admission in evidence of the defendant's affidavit for a continuance, which has been previously filed before the same judge, is not ground for reversal. Phillips *v.* State (Ind.), 6 West. Rep. 893.

Refusal: Ground for Reversal when. — Where the affidavit for defendant for continuance, under Missouri R. S. sec. 1884, set forth the absence of a witness, and the testimony he would give as to the facts relating to an alleged assault, which materially confirmed the testimony of defendant, and contradicted that of the prosecuting witness, *held*, ground for reversal. State *v.* Bradley, 90 Mo. 160; s. c., 7 West. Rep. 97.

Where, upon application for a continuance on the ground of absence of a witness, the prosecuting attorney admitted that, if present, the witness would testify to the facts stated in the affidavit filed in support of the motion; where the application was seasonably made, and nothing in the application or in the record indicated that the subpœna had not been issued in good faith, or that the same could not be served, — it was error to deny the application. State *v.* Dawson, 90 Mo. 149; s. c., 6 West. Rep. 461.

When Continuance refused. — Diligence to procure the attendance of a witness is essential to a postponement of a criminal case May *v.* State (Tex. App.), Dec. 1886.

Where the application for a continuance failed to show proper diligence, and all the evidence of the witness, had he been present, would have been inadmissible, the refusal of the application was not error. State *v.* Sneed, 91 Mo. 552; s. c., 10 West. Rep. 84.

And the application may be refused where the evidence on the trial shows that the testimony sought to be obtained is probably untrue, — Doss *v.* State (Tex. App.), June, 1886, — or is simply cumulative. Dacy *v.* People, 116 Ill. 555; s. c., 4 West. Rep. 180.

After a special plea to an indictment had been stricken on demurrer, there was no reason for continuing the case, and it was proper to proceed to a trial on the merits. Carter *v.* State, 75 Ga 747.

English Practice. — Roscoe says in his "Criminal Evidence" (pp. 199 to 203) that where the courts deem it necessary for the purposes of justice, they will postpone the trial until the next assizes or sessions; and that misdemeanors are put on the same footing in this respect as felonies; the 14 & 15 Vict. c. 100, § 27, enacting that "no person prosecuted shall be entitled to traverse or postpone the trial of *any* indictment found against him at any session of the peace, session of oyer and terminer, and general gaol delivery: provided always, that if the court, upon the application of the person so indicted or otherwise, shall be of opinion that he ought to be allowed a further term, either to prepare for his defence or otherwise, such court may adjourn the trial of such person to the next subsequent session, upon such terms as to bail or otherwise as to such court shall seem meet, and may respite the recognizances of the prosecutor and witnesses accordingly, in which case the prosecutor and witnesses shall be bound to attend to prosecute and give evidence at such subseqnent session without entering into any fresh recognizance for that purpose."

Instances have occurred in which a principal witness has been of such tender years and so ignorant as not to understand the nature and obligation of an oath, that the judge has ordered the trial to be put off until the next assizes, and directed the child in the mean time to be instructed in religion. *Vide ante*, "Infant Witness," p. 836. Also where it appears by affidavit that a necessary witness for the prisoner is ill, — R. *v.* Hunter, 3 C. & P. 591, — or that a witness for the prosecution is ill, or unavoidably absent, or is kept out of the way by the contrivance or at the instigation of the prisoner, the court will postpone the trial, unless it appear that the requirements of justice can be satisfied by reading the witness's depositions before a magistrate.

If it is moved on the part of the prosecution in a case of felony, to put off the trial on the ground of the absence of a material witness, the judge will require an affidavit stating the points which the witness is expected to prove, in order to form a judgment whether the witness is a material one or not. R. *v.* Savage, 1 C. & K. 75. An affidavit of a surgeon, that the witness is the mother of an unweaned child afflicted with an inflammation of the lungs, who could neither be brought to the assize

On application for a continuance where the State admits that

town nor separated from the mother without danger to life, is a sufficient ground on which to found a motion to postpone the trial. Ib. Where a prisoner's counsel moved to postpone a trial for murder, on an affidavit which stated that one of the witnesses for the prosecution, who had been bound over to appear at the assizes, was absent, and that on cross-examination this witness could give material evidence for the prisoner, *Cresswell, J.*, after consulting *Patteson, J.*, held that this was a sufficient ground for postponing the trial, without showing that the prisoner had at all endeavored to procure the witness's attendance, as the prisoner might reasonably expect, from the witness having been bound over, that he would appear. R *v.* Macarthy, Carr. & M. 625. In R. *v.* Palmer, 6 C. & P. 652, the judges of the Central Criminal Court postponed until the next session the presentment of a bill for a capital offence to the grand jury, upon the affidavit of the attorney for the prosecution, that a witness, whose evidence was sworn to be material, was too ill to attend, and they refused to refer to the deposition of the witness to ascertain whether he deposed to material facts. Where in a case of murder committed in Newcastle-upon-Tyne, which had created great excitement, a newspaper published in the town had spoken of the prisoner as the murderer, and several journals down to the time of the assizes had published paragraphs, implying or tending to show his guilt, and it appeared that the jurors at such assizes were chosen from within a circle of fifteen miles round Newcastle, where such papers were chiefly circulated, but that at the summer assizes they would be taken from the more distant parts of the county of Northumberland (into which the indictment had been removed), Alderson and Parke, BB., postponed the trial until the following assizes. *Alderson, B.*, however, said, "I yield to the peculiar circumstances of the case, wishing it to be understood that I am by no means disposed to encourage a precedent of this sort." R. *v.* Bolam, Newcastle Spring Ass. 1839, MS.; 2 Moo. & R. 192. See also R. *v.* Joliffe, 4 T. R. 285. And in R. *v.* Johnson, 2 C. & K. 354, the same learned judge refused to postpone the trial of a prisoner charged with murder, on the ground that an opportunity might be thereby afforded of investigating the evidence and characters of certain witnesses who had not been examined before the committing magistrate, but who were to be called for the prosecution to prove previous attempts by the prisoner on the life of the deceased. A trial for murder was postponed till the next assizes by *Channell, B.*, upon an affidavit of a medical man as to a witness being unable to travel, although such witness was not examined before the magistrate, and although the trial had been fixed for a particular day. R. *v.* Lawrence, 4 F. & F. 901.

In general a trial will not be postponed to the next assizes before a bill is found. R. *v.* Heesom, 14 Cox, C. C. 40. But where it was shown that the attendance of witnesses, inmates of a workhouse in which small-pox had broken out, was necessary, *Bagallay, L. J.*, did not require any bill to be sent up before the grand jury, but postponed the trial to the next assizes, admitting the prisoner to bail in the mean time. R. *v.* Taylor, 15 Cox, C. C. 8. No objection appears to have been taken on the part of the prisoner to the postponement.

In no instance will a trial be put off on account of the absence of witnesses to character. R. *v.* Jones, 8 East, 34.

Where the prisoner applies to postpone the trial, he will be remanded and detained in custody till the next assizes or sessions, or will be admitted to bail, but he is never required to pay the costs of the prosecutor. R. *v.* Hunter, 3 C. & P. 591. Where the application is by the prosecutor, the court in its discretion will either detain the prisoner in custody, or admit him to bail, or discharge him on his own recognizances. R. *v.* Beardmore, 7 C. & P. 497; R. *v.* Parish, id 782; R. *v* Osborne, id. 799. See also R. *v.* Crowe, 4 C. & P. 251. A motion to put off a trial on an indictment for felony made on behalf of the prisoner, cannot be entertained until after plea pleaded. R. *v.* Bolam, 2 Moo & R. 192. Previous to the spring assizes A. was committed to take his trial for shooting B. The trial was postponed till the summer assizes, on the ground that B. (who shortly afterwards died) was too ill from his wounds to attend to give evidence. At the summer assizes a true bill was found against A. for the murder of B., and an application was made to put off the trial until the following spring assizes, on account of the illness of a material witness. *Williams, J.*, granted the application, and held that A. was not entitled to his discharge under the seventh section of the Habeas Corpus Act. R. *v.* Bowen, 9 C. & P. 509. See R. *v* Chapman, 8 C. & P. 558.

The application should be made before the prisoner is given in charge to the jury, as it is very doubtful whether, if the adjournment of the trial involved a discharge of the jury, it would be granted. See *post*, p. 222. It seems that, after the prisoner is given in charge, a judge has no authority the testimony of the desired witness would be such as stated in the affidavit, the application may be refused.[1]

A mere statement of counsel that defendant is not prepared for trial, is not sufficient basis for a continuance.[2] The applications must be supported by affidavits showing necessity for the delay,[3] or the presumption is that the court rightfully refused to postpone the trial.[4] The affidavit must set out and verify all the

to adjourn the trial till another day on account of the absence of witnesses. See R. *v.* Parr, 2 F. & F. 861.

1. State *v.* Jewell, 90 Mo. 467; s. c., 8 West. Rep. 211.

An Application for a Continuance, made at a previous term of the court, if the accused was in actual custody at the time, and was not merely upon bond, partakes so far of the nature of a confession or admission that the same cannot be used against him on his subsequent trial, unless he was warned previously that it might be so used. This doctrine is not affected by the fact that since the application was made the indictment was quashed for invalidity, and a new one charging the same offence was found But the defendant in this case being upon bail, no error in this respect is apparent. Wimberly *v.* State, 22 Tex. App. 506.

Where, on an affidavit under the provisions of Rev. Stat. 1879, § 1886, which has been held unconstitutional, but, while in vogue, was only regarded as a temporary admission, — one *pro hac vice*, and not intended to extend beyond the term at which it was made, — the prosecuting attorney had admitted that Barber, a non-resident, would, if present, swear as stated in the affidavit for continuance, and this affidavit was used in the former trial, it was properly rejected when again offered in evidence. State *v.* Bryant (Mo.), 12 West. Rep. 324.

Charge of Court regarding. — Where, on an application for continuance in a criminal case, the prosecuting attorney admitted that what appellant alleged he could prove by the absent witness was true, there was no error in an instruction given to the jury that, "as a matter of law, I will say to you, that the facts stated in the affidavit for a continuance, (in) which the defendant alleged (what) he expected to prove by his mother, . . . must, for the purpose of the trial, be taken as true. The weight and effect of such facts, upon the merits, is a matter exclusively for your determination." Mayfield *v.* State, 110 Ind. 591; s. c., 9 West. Rep. 386.

Where Evidence Immaterial. — Where the facts to which the absent witnesses would swear were wholly immaterial and irrelevant, the motion was properly denied. State *v.* Dale (Mo.), 6 West. Rep. 434.

In Murder Trial. — In a criminal prosecution for the crime of murder, an application for a continuance, where the State admits that the witness desired to be produced, would, if present, testify as stated in the affidavit filed with the application, may be properly refused. State *v.* Jewell, 90 Mo. 467; s. c., 8 West. Rep. 211.

2. People *v.* Mason (Mich.), 6 West. Rep. 183.

Unsupported Allegations on motion cannot be reviewed on appeal. State *v.* Jewell, 90 Mo. 467; s. c., 8 West. Rep. 211.

3. People *v.* Mason (Mich.), 6 West. Rep. 183.

4. Morris *v.* State, 104 Ind. 457; s. c., 2 West. Rep. 259.

Affidavits for a Continuance will not necessarily be taken as true, if contradictory or equivocal, — Dacy *v.* People, 116 Ill. 555; s. c., 4 West. Rep. 180, — for it is presumed, that, in making the showing for a continuance, the defendant will make the strongest possible statement in his own favor that the facts will warrant. And, so far as the showing made is equivocal or uncertain, the intendments must be taken against it. Steele *v.* People, 45 Ill. 155; State *v.* Eisenmeyer, 94 Ill. 96; Dacy *v.* People, 116 Ill. 555; s. c., 4 West. Rep. 180.

Counsel not ready. — Where the counsel are not ready, the affidavit should state that, for want of time, counsel could not prepare for trial, and that absent witnesses could be procured if time was given, and that affiant had no opportunity for preparation. Dacy *v.* People, 116 Ill. 555; s. c., 4 West. Rep. 180.

An affidavit that, since notification of his appointment as counsel for defendant, there had not been sufficient time to prepare for trial, must state special facts or reasons to support the statement. State *v.* Jewell, 90 Mo. 467; s. c., 8 West. Rep. 211.

Affidavits are fatally defective if they do not state that, for want of time, such counsel could not prepare for trial, nor that absent witnesses could be procured if more time was given, nor any want of opportunity for preparation. Eubanks *v.* People, 41 Ill 487; Pertect *v.* People, 70 Ill. 171; Wilhelm *v.* People, 72 Ill. 468; Dacy *v.* People, 116 Ill. 555; s. c., 4 West. Rep. 180

facts, as they then exist, which are essential to support the application.[1]

XIV. Trial. — 1. *Modes of.* — All criminal prosecutions are now[2] by (*a*) *Complaint*, (*b*) *Indictment*, and (*c*) *Information.*[3]

2. *Conduct of Trial.* — It is the undoubted province of the *nisi prius* courts, in the exercise of a sound discretion, to regulate the course of business during the progress of trials. Included in this is the right during the term, in a proper way, to control its own sittings; and unless the action taken affects any right of the parties in pending proceedings, it cannot be considered on appeal,

An Affidavit by the Attorney appointed by the court to defend the party accused, that, since he was notified of his appointment, there had not been sufficient time for him to prepare the case for trial on the set day, is sufficient where there was no statement of special facts or reasons showing why a longer period was asked or required. State *v.* Jewell, 90 Mo. 467; s. c., 8 West. Rep. 211.

1. Sutherlin *v.* State (Ind.), 7 West. Rep. 60.

It cannot be aided by attaching an affidavit made at a previous term. Sutherlin *v.* State (Ind.), 7 West. Rep. 60.

Where accused, on being interrogated, contradicted his affidavit, it was improper practice of the attorney of accused to prove such contradictions. Hubbard *v.* State (Miss.), Feb. 1887.

Evidentiary Facts. — Affidavits for continuance are required to state material evidentiary facts affirmed by the affiant to be true; and this admission may be used against the defendant in a criminal prosecution. In affidavits for change of venue, no evidentiary facts are stated, and they cannot, therefore, supply evidence to be used on the trial. An accused may show that he was mistaken as to some or all of the statements contained in his affidavit for a continuance, and he has a right to explain the statements, if he can, by competent evidence; but they are nevertheless admissions, and, as such, entitled to go to the jury. There is nothing privileged in the statement in an affidavit for a continuance, nor is there any thing which imposes upon them any compulsory or confidential features. The paper belongs to the files, being public in its character, and freely executed. Behler *v* State (Ind), 11 West. Rep. 105.

An affidavit upon which is founded a motion for a continuance to procure the evidence of certain witnesses, must negative the fact that they were absent by the procurement of the party who asks the continuance. Crews *v.* People, 120 Ill. 317; s. c., 8 West. Rep. 691.

Where the Desired Witness is a Non-Resident, it should state the grounds of expectation that his testimony could be procured. Dacy *v.* People, 116 Ill. 555; s. c., 4 West. Rep. 180.

Witness to prove Insanity. — In an affidavit for continuance based upon evidence proposed to be introduced as to the insanity of the defendant, where there is no averment that the defence of insanity will be interposed, the materiality of the evidence is not shown. Where it is not alleged in the affidavits that the affiants believe the testimony desired will be true; that the witnesses are not absent by the connivance, procurement, or consent of the defendant; that the subpœnas could not have been issued on the day of the receipt of the information in time to have secured the attendance of witnesses living within reach of the subpœnas, — the affidavits were properly overruled. State *v.* Bryant (Mo.), 12 West. Rep. 324.

2. Harris says in his Criminal Law, p. 384, "It will not be necessary to describe the various modes of trial which have been long abolished; namely, the ordeal, the corsned, trial by battle, a full account of which will be found in the various editions of Blackstone, Hallam's 'Middle Ages,' Reeves's 'History of English Law,' and the other works dealing with the history of the law. The last of these was suppressed by 59 George III. c. 46, in consequence of the case of Ashford *v.* Thornton, 1 Barn. & Ald. 405, in which the person accused demanded the settlement of the question by a fight."

On the subject of trials by ordeals, see 1 Stephens's Hist Cr. L. in Eng. 250, 252, 253, 299; 3 id. 241.

3. **Indictment for Misdemeanor.** — Upon an indictment for a misdemeanor, it is no ground for acquittal that the evidence necessary to prove the misdemeanor also shows it is part of a felony, and that the felony has been completed. Reg *v.* Button, 3 Cox, C. C. 229.

Assaults. — An assault is a misdemeanor, of which circuit courts have original jurisdiction, and is prosecuted in those courts by indictment. Kennedy *v.* People (Ill.), 11 West. Rep. 48.

although it imposes personal discomfort upon counsel, and exacts labor where rest is needed.[1]

In the order of trial, special pleas must always be tried before the general issue.[2]

1. Wartena *v.* State, 105 Ind. 445; s. c., 2 West. Rep. 757.

Time to prepare for Trial. — When the case was called for trial, the defence asked for time in which to prepare and file a plea of former conviction. The trial court awarded fifteen minutes, to which the defence objected as insufficient time, whereupon the court ordered the trial to proceed. After a part of the State's evidence was introduced, the trial court refused to entertain the plea, and the defendant excepted. *Held*, error. Coon *v.* State, 21 Tex. App. 332.

In a Theft Case, wherein the "Rule" was invoked, one N. advised the defendant's counsel, during the examination of a defence witness, that he knew important facts in connection with the said witness's testimony. N. was then offered by the defence as a witness, but was excluded upon the State's objection that the "rule" had not been applied to him, and that he had heard all of the testimony of the preceding witness. After the examination of other witnesses, N. was again offered as a witness, and was again excluded upon the same objection, and the further one that the defence had failed to place him under the rule after his former rejection, and that he had since heard the testimony of several witnesses *Held*, correct. Rummel *v.* State, 22 Tex. App. 558.

Before the commencement of the trial, counsel for the accused moved the court for an order that all articles in the possession of the State, intended to be used in evidence, be placed in the hands of the clerk or other officer of the court for their inspection. The State attorney filed a statement by which it appears that all such articles had been seen and examined by counsel for defence and the experts in their behalf, and that they were fully acquainted with such articles, and further agreeing that such articles should be submitted to counsel for defence before they were so offered in evidence. No denial of this statement was made by defence. *Held*, that, in overruling the motion, there was no error. Newton *v.* State, 21 Fla. 53.

Interrogation of Witness by Judge. — It is proper for the judge presiding at a criminal trial to interrogate a witness, to supply some omitted and legitimate question, or to fully develop the facts bearing on the case. State *v.* Pagels, 92 Mo. 300; s. c., 10 West. Rep. 288

There can be no doubt of the right of a trial judge to interrogate a witness if he deems it necessary to supply some omitted and legitimate question, or to fully develop the facts bearing on the case. Whart. Cr. Ev. § 452, and cases cited.

Failure to file Complaint in County Court. — The defence moved the trial court to strike out the complaint, because the same had not been filed in the county court. The court overruled the motion, and the prosecutor ordered the complaint filed. *Held*, correct. Day *v.* State, 21 Tex. App. 213.

Where an Offence is set out with Aggravating Circumstances which enlarge the offence, the prosecutor may *nol. pros.* the aggravation, and obtain a conviction for the lesser offence, which is well charged. Commonwealth *v.* McMonagle, 1 Mass. 517; Commonwealth *v.* Briggs, 24 Mass. (7 Pick.) 177; Commonwealth *v.* Tuck, 37 Mass. (20 Pick) 356; Commonwealth *v.* Jenks, 67 Mass. (1 Gray) 490; Commonwealth *v.* Cain, 102 Mass. 487; Jennings *v.* Commonwealth, 105 Mass. 586; Commonwealth *v.* Holmes, 119 Mass. 195; Commonwealth *v.* Mead, 92 Mass. (10 Allen) 396, Commonwealth *v.* Dunster, 5 New Eng. Rep. 115.

2. Commonwealth *v.* Merrill, 90 Mass. (8 Allen) 545; Salliday *v.* Commonwealth, 28 Pa. St. 13; Foster *v.* State, 39 Ala. 229; Henry *v.* State, 33 Ala. 389; Nonemaker *v.* State, 34 Ala. 211; Mountain *v.* State, 40 Ala. 344; Faulkner *v.* State, 3 Heisk. (Tenn.) 33; Clem *v.* State, 42 Ind. 420.

The Admission of Further Evidence after a criminal case had been closed, and before the jury had retired, was a matter resting in the sound discretion of the court; and the omission of the attorney for the people to read in evidence the statute of Minnesota being a mere oversight, it was proper that he should be allowed to introduce it, the court having offered the defendant the right to rebut the evidence, and to argue its force and effect to the jury. Tucker *v.* State (Ill.), 11 West Rep. 765.

After the Evidence had been closed by both people and defendant, the attorney for the people made an argument to the jury, and he was followed by an argument in favor of the defendant. At the conclusion of the argument on behalf of defendant, the court took a recess for dinner. When the court met after recess, the counsel for the people entered a motion for leave to introduce in evidence certain portions of the statute of Minnesota: this

3. *Regulation by Court.* — The right of the court to regulate the course of the trial and control its sittings cannot be considered on appeal, unless the rights of parties are affected.[1]

4. *Appointment of Counsel.* — The court may appoint an attorney to defend where the accused is without means.[2] And it is within the discretion of the trial court to direct the employment of counsel to assist the prosecuting attorney in conducting a trial against a person accused of felony.[3]

a. Limiting Number of Counsel. — The court may limit the number of counsel which may prosecute; and the appointment of more than one counsel to prosecute, in case of disability of the prosecuting attorney, is a practice not to be approved, but it is not a reversible error.[4]

XV. Evidence.[5] — 1. *Rules in Criminal Cases.* — The general

motion was allowed, and the statute was read in evidence, and the ruling of the court is relied upon as error. It appears from the bill of exceptions that the court, upon allowing the evidence to be introduced, offered to allow the defendant the right to introduce further evidence on his behalf if he desired, and to further argue his case to the jury.

"The admission of further evidence after the case had been closed, and before the jury had retired, was a matter resting in the sound discretion of the court; and, as it does not appear that the discretion was abused, we do not think the court erred.

"The failure on the part of the attorney for the people to read in evidence the statute of Minnesota was a mere oversight, and it was but just that he should be allowed to introduce the evidence, as the defendant was in no manner injured, the court having allowed him the right to rebut the evidence if he wished, and to argue its force and effect to the jury." Whart. Cr. L. (8th ed.) § 1696.

Confessions are only authoritative where there is clear proof of the *corpus delicti*; and here (in bigamy) the *corpus delicti* is the alleged first marriage, which must be clearly proved independently of the defendant's confessions; and secondary evidence cannot be received. Whart. Cr. L. (8th ed.) § 1696.

1. Wartena *v.* State, 105 Ind. 445; s. c., 2 West. Rep. 757.

Admission of Evidence on the part of the prosecution in rebuttal, after the defence has closed, is in the discretion of the trial court. McMeen *v.* Commonwealth (Pa.), 5 Cent. Rep. 887.

The Kentucky Civil Code, section 601, puts the matter of excluding witnesses from the court-room in the discretion of the court. Johnson *v.* Clem, 82 Ky. 84.

Separation of the Witnesses is within the discretion of the court, — State *v.* Cole, 38 La. An. 843; State *v.* Harrison, 38 La. An. 501; People *v.* Sam Lung, 70 Cal. 515, — or permitting a witness to correct his testimony. State *v.* Gonsoulin, 38 La. An. 459.

Limiting Time of Argument of Counsel. — There must be some restraint of the volubility of counsel, since there must be a limit to a criminal trial. State *v.* Boasso, 38 La. An. 202.

It is discretionary with the Court to recall the Jury after they have retired to consider their verdict, for the purpose of explaining instructions already given, giving additional instructions, or admitting evidence of some fact overlooked during the trial; and the defendant being at the time present in person, with his attorney, and being allowed an opportunity to cross-examine the witness, there is nothing of which he can complain. Cooper *v.* State, 79 Ala. 54.

Request to discharge Juror. — The discharge of a juror, after he has been accepted and sworn, is, under the New York Code, within the discretion of the trial judge. Code Crim. Proc. § 371. People *v.* Beckwith, 103 N. Y. 360; s. c., 4 Cent. Rep. 539.

2. Dukes *v.* State, 11 Ind. 557; Tull *v.* State, 99 Ind. 238. See Siebert *v* State, 95 Ind. 471.

3. Wood *v.* State, 92 Ind. 269; Siebert *v.* State, 95 Ind. 471; Tull *v.* State, 99 Ind. 238; Bradshaw *v.* State, 22 N. W. Rep. 361; State *v.* Montgomery, 22 N. W. Rep. 639; Shular *v.* State, 105 Ind. 289; s. c., 2 West. Rep. 801.

4. **Counsel so appointed** should not be under private retainer. State *v.* Griffin, 87 Mo. 608; s. c., 3 West. Rep. 820.

5. It is not the purpose here to fully discuss the question of evidence, — which question will be taken up later on in the series under that title, — but simply to set forth those principles of evidence peculiar

rules of evidence are the same in criminal as in civil cases.[1] Thus, in each it is the first and most signal rule that the best evidence of which the case is capable shall be given; for, if the best evidence be not produced, it affords a presumption that it would make against the party neglecting to produce it.[2]

All facts and circumstances stated in the indictment which cannot be rejected as surplusage, must be proved, and all descriptive averments must be strictly proved;[3] and the testimony in crimi-

to a criminal prosecution, and which do not properly, or so properly, fall anywhere else.

1. Thomas *v.* State, 103 Ind. 419; s. c., 1 West. Rep. 309, 316.

In criminal cases the State must resort to the ordinary course of proof to establish every material fact charged in the indictment. Bird *v.* State, 104 Ind. 384; s. c., 2 West. Rep. 227.

"There is no difference as to the rules of evidence," says *Abbott, J.*, "between criminal and civil cases: what may be received in the one may be received in the other, and what is rejected in the one ought to be rejected in the other." R. *v.* Watson, 2 Stark. N. P. C. 155; R. *v.* Murphy, 8 C. & P. 306.

2. Gilb. Ev. 3 Bull, N. P. 293, *per* Jervis, C. J., in Twyman *v.* Knowles, 13 C. B. 224. Best on Ev. Pt. 1, ch. 1, §§ 87, 89.

Upon a Trial for Murder in the First Degree, there is no warrant in the statute for reading against the accused, as the testimony of an absent witness, that which the prosecuting attorney states, in his affidavit filed with a motion for a continuance, to be what the absent witness would testify if present, unless defendant agrees that it may be so read. State *v.* Emerson, 90 Mo 236; s. c., 6 West. Rep. 666.

Insanity cannot be proved by reputation. Walker *v.* State, 102 Ind. 502; s. c., 3 West. Rep. 354.

A physician cannot be asked whether, having heard the whole evidence, he was of opinion that the prisoner, at the time he committed the alleged act, was of unsound mind. Reg. *v.* Frances, 4 Cox, C. C. 57.

3. **Descriptive Averments.** — Thus, where the statute provided against stealing "any horse, mare, or gelding," and the indictment charges the stealing of a horse, but the evidence shows the theft of a gelding, the defendant must be acquitted. Hooker *v.* State, 4 Ohio, 350; Truley *v.* State, 3 Humph. (Tenn.) 323. The court say, in Hooker *v.* State, *supra*, that "the term horse, being a generic name, ought to include every variety of the animal, as diversified by age, sex, occupation, and modification. The English authorities, however, and which have been recognized in several States of the Union as sound law, are too strong to be resisted, and too pointed to be evaded. It is the duty of the court not to make, but to declare, the law. *Ita lex scripta est* precludes all inquiry into the reasonableness or propriety of the objection." But see Reg. *v.* Aldridge, 4 Cox, C. C. 143.

So, if the charge is stealing two turkeys, and the evidence shows the stealing of two dead turkeys, — Rex *v.* Halloway, 1 C. & P. 128, — because the allegation of an animal means a live animal, unless it is described as dead. Rex *v.* Edwards, R. & R. 497; Commonwealth *v.* Beaman, 7 Mass. (8 Gray) 497; State *v.* Jenkins, 6 Jones (N. C.), 19. A variance as to a person named in the indictment is fatal, unless it is a variance in spelling merely, which does not affect the sound. Thus, where the name in the indictment was Dougal McInnis, and the name proved was Dougal McGinnis, the variance was *held* fatal, — Barnes *v.* People, 18 Ill. 52, — while proof of Winyard in place of Whyneard, as averred, has been *held* not. Rex *v.* Foster, R. & R. 412.

When a Paper is set out in the Indictment by its tenor, where the omission or addition of a letter does not change the word so as to make it another word, the variance is not material. Reg. *v.* Drake, 11 Modern, 78. Where the allegation was "not," and the proof was "nor," although the sense was not affected thereby, the variance was *held* fatal, — Rex *v* Beech, Camp. 229, — but where the allegation was "undertood," and the proof was "understood," the variance was *held* not fatal. Reg. *v.* Drake, 11 Mod. 78.

Though the Descriptive Averment be unnecessary, still it must be strictly proved. Thus where, in an indictment for the theft of a horse, the failure to prove that the stolen horse was black, was fatal. 1 Stark. Ev. 374. And where, in an indictment for bigamy, the woman was needlessly described as a widow, the failure to prove her widowhood was fatal. Rex *v.* Deeley, 4 C. & P. 579.

The Effect of Variance in Particulars not Material to the merits of the case is overcome in Michigan by a statute authorizing the indictment to be amended to correspond with the evidence, when such a vari-nal cases is always to be given in open court and in the presence of the accused.[1]

a. Burden of Proof. — In criminal cases the burden of proof is on the prosecutor to show that the accused is guilty of the offence charged.[2] But when an accused relies upon any substantive, dis-

ance occurs, — Mich. Rev. Stat. (1871) 2172, — and in Ohio by the statutes declaring that no such variance shall be ground for acquittal. 74 Ohio L. 334. Under the Ohio statute, it was *held* that the defendant was correctly convicted where the indictment charged him with stealing certain articles of silverware, and the evidence showed the articles were of plated ware, consisting of only one twenty-fifth part silver. Goodall *v.* State, 22 Ohio St. 203.

Exception to the Rule. — The rule that a descriptive averment must be strictly proved, has one qualification in cases of homicide and felonious assault. If the averment is that the homicide was caused, or the assault made, in a designated manner, it is not necessary to prove strictly the details of the means averred to have been used in so committing the offence. If the indictment is for murder by poisoning, and, it is averred, by poisoning with a certain drug, the indictment is supported by proof of poisoning with a different drug. East, P. C. c 5, § 107 A charge of felonious assault with a staff will be sustained by proof of such assault with another bruising implement, as a stone, — Sherwin's Case, cited East, P. C. c. 5, § 107, — and a charge of strangling by clasping both hands about the throat, is sustained by proof of strangling by placing one hand over the mouth. Rex *v.* Culkins, 5 Car. & P. 121.

1. People *v.* Dowdigan (Mich.), 10 West. Rep 865. See Chadwick *v.* Chadwick, 52 Mich. 545; *Re* Foster's Will, 34 Mich. 21.

Sending Evidence to Jury-Room. — Thus, on the trial of respondents under an indictment for a criminal assault, it was error for the court, in the absence of their counsel, who had previously refused their consent, and after the retirement of the jury, to allow, at the request of the jury, to be given to them the evidence of the witness upon whom the assault was made, taken on her examination before the magistrate, to which was attached the evidence of another witness, reduced to writing at the preliminary examination before the justice, and the original written complaint upon which the warrant for the arrest of the accused was based, together with such warrant. The court was not justified in sending the papers to the jury-room. It is a dangerous practice, even in civil cases, and one not often to be indulged in, and in criminal cases never. People *v.* Dowdigan (Mich), 10 West. Rep. 865

2. People *v.* Coughlin (Mich.), 9 West. Rep. 129; Day *v.* State, 21 Tex. App. 213.

The State must prove, beyond a Reasonable Doubt, every essential element of the crime charged. Criminal intent, unless otherwise provided by statute, is an essential element. If the defendant was insane, the law holds he was incapable of criminal intent. Hence, the defence of insanity is merely a denial of criminal intent, and is, therefore, provable under the general issue. Hence, if the evidence raises a reasonable doubt of the sanity of the defendant, it raises a doubt as to his criminal intent, and, logically, he is entitled to an acquittal. See State *v.* Bartlett, 43 N. H. 224; State *v.* Jones, 50 N. H. 369; State *v.* Johnson, 40 Conn. 136; People *v.* McCann, 16 N. Y. 58; Wagner *v.* People, 4 Abb (N. Y.) App. Dec. 509; McFarland's Case, 8 Abb. (N. Y.) App. Dec. 57; Dove *v.* State, 3 Heisk. (Tenn.) 348; People *v.* Garbutt, 17 Mich. 1; Polk *v.* State, 19 Ind. 170; Bradley *v.* State, 31 Ind. 492; Hopps *v.* People, 31 Ill. 385; Chase *v.* People, 40 Ill. 352; State *v.* Crawford, 11 Kan. 32; Wright *v.* People, 4 Neb. 407.

Burden of Proof in Presumptions of Insanity. — In some cases, it is held that the presumption of sanity throws the burden of proof on the defendant; that the defence of insanity is in the nature of a plea of confession and avoidance; and that the defendant must establish the fact of his insanity by a preponderance of proof. Commonwealth *v.* Eddy, 73 Mass. (7 Gray) 583; Ortwein *v.* Commonwealth, 76 Pa. St. 414; Lynch *v.* Commonwealth, 77 Pa. St. 205; Myers *v.* Commonwealth, 83 Pa. St. 131; Boswell *v.* Commonwealth, 20 Gratt. (Va.) 860; State *v.* Coleman, 27 La. An. 691; McKenzie *v.* State, 26 Ark. 334; Graham *v.* Commonwealth, 16 B. Mon. (Ky.) 589; Kriel *v.* Commonwealth, 5 Bush (Ky.), 362; Loeffner *v.* State, 10 Ohio St. 598; Bergin *v.* State, 31 Ohio St. 111; State *v.* Felter, 32 Iowa, 49; State *v.* Stickley, 41 Iowa, 232; State *v.* Klinger, 43 Mo. 127; State *v.* Smith, 53 Mo. 267. But, in this last case, though the court says it is necessary for the defendant to make out insanity by a preponderance of testimony, it also says it is irregular to tell the jury so. Bonfanti *v.* State, 2 Minn. 123; People *v.* McDonnell, 47 Cal. 134; People *v.* Wilson, 49 Cal. 13. The court say, in tinct, separate, and independent matter as a defence which is outside of, and does not necessarily constitute a part of, the act or transaction with which he is charged (such as the defence of insanity, etc.), then it devolves upon him to establish such special and foreign matter by a preponderance of evidence. It is not error to instruct in such cases that the burden of proving such defences devolves upon the accused.[1]

Ortwein *v.* Commonwealth, 76 Pa. St. 414, that, "And if this reasoning were less conclusive, the safety of society would turn the scale. Merely doubtful insanity would fill the land with acquitted criminals." The influence of this consideration may be estimated by comparing the ruling of this court in cases of homicide with the ruling made in the case of a contested will. Egbert *v.* Egbert, 78 Pa. St. 326.

The Claim of Self-Defence is merely a denial of the malice which the prosecution is bound to establish beyond a reasonable doubt. Accordingly, some cases hold that the defendant is entitled to an acquittal, if, upon the evidence, it is doubtful whether the homicide or assault was malicious or was in self-defence. State *v.* People, 53 N. Y. 164; State *v.* Porter, 34 Iowa, 131; State *v.* Wingo, 66 Mo. 181. And, in Massachusetts, in cases of assault. Commonwealth *v.* McKie, 67 Mass. (1 Gray) 61. While others hold the defendant must make out a case of self-defence by a preponderance of proof. People *v.* Shroyer, 42 N. Y. 1; Silvus *v.* State, 22 Ohio St. 99; Weaver *v.* State, 24 Ohio St. 584.

Where the Possession of Stolen Goods by the defendant is established, he is not required to prove by preponderance of proof that he is innocent. State *v.* Merrick, 19 Me. 401. In a case of forgery, where it was proved that the paper came into the hands of the defendant unaltered, and left his hands altered, it was held error to charge that thereby the burden was cast on the defendant to prove that he did not alter it. The court said, "If the result of the case depends upon the establishment of the proposition of the one on whom the burden was first cast, the burden remains with him throughout, though the weight of evidence may have shifted from one side to the other, according as each may have adduced fresh proof. There is a wide difference between a requirement, in a criminal prosecution, that the accused shall prove his innocence, when a presumption is raised against him, and the necessity of explaining, in some degree, the fact on which that presumption rests." State *v.* Flye, 26 Me. 312.

Shifting of Burden of Proof. — If the defendant relies upon no separate, distinct, or independent facts, but confines his defence to the original transaction on which the charge is founded, with its accompanying circumstances, the burden of proof never shifts, but remains upon the government throughout the case to prove the act a criminal one beyond a reasonable doubt. People *v.* Rodrigo, 69 Cal. 601.

1. Leache *v.* State, 22 Tex. App. 279; State *v.* Johnson, 91 Mo. 439; s. c., 8 West. Rep. 711, 712.

Innocence to be established.—The phrase in an instruction to the jury, "You may consider this as a circumstance in determining the guilt or innocence of the defendant," does not imply that innocence is a fact to be established. State *v.* O'Neil, 13 Oreg. 183.

Insanity. — Where insanity is relied on as a defence to a criminal prosecution, the burden of proof is on the defendant, the same as upon an affirmative issue. Leache *v.* State, 22 Tex. App. 279; People *v.* Walter, 1 Idaho (N. S.), 386; Reg. *v.* Layton, 4 Cox, C. C. 149.

Reasonable Doubt. — And he is not entitled to the benefit of a reasonable doubt, whether he was, or was not, insane. State *v.* Huting, 21 Mo. 464; State *v.* McCoy, 34 Mo. 531; State *v.* Klinger, 43 Mo. 127; State *v.* Johnson, 91 Mo. 439; s. c., 8 West. Rep. 711.

To establish the Defence of Insanity, it must be clearly proved. Walker *v.* People, 88 N. Y. 81.

And to warrant the jury in acquitting under the defence of insanity, it must be proved affirmatively that the prisoner was at the time insane, — so insane that he did not know right from wrong. Reg. *v.* Higginson, 1 C. & K. 129.

Presumption as to Insanity. — The general rule is, that, where insanity once exists, it is presumed to continue. But this is not the rule in Texas. Leache *v.* State, 22 Tex. App. 279.

In Manslaughter. — It is incumbent on the people to show, in a case of manslaughter, such facts and circumstances as convince the jury that the killing was not done in self-defence. People *v.* Coughlin (Mich.), 9 West. Rep. 129.

Self-Defence. — Where the defence of self-defence is interposed, the burden of proof is on the State to negative it. People *v.* Coughlin (Mich April, 1887), 9

2. *Admissibility*. — Any facts tending to prove the main fact, and contemporaneous and connected with it, are admissible as a general rule.[1]

a. Relevancy. — All relevant and material evidence must be received, and evidence is not to be rejected because it fails to be conclusive: it is sufficient if it fairly tends to prove a point sought to be established.[2]

Testimony in reference to similar transactions is admissible to show the criminal intent of a party, when other transactions of the same general character and connected therewith are investigated.[3]

West. Rep. 129. Where one strikes another in a quarrel provoked by the latter and his friends, the former should not be confined to the right to repel the actual assault. People *v.* Ross (Mich. May, 1887), 9 West, Rep. 555.

1. People *v.* Foley (Mich.), 7 West. Rep. 347. See tit. "Evidence," this series.

It is Error to refuse Testimony in Defence, and then permit State to testify to such matter in reply. State *v.* Mays, 24 S. C. 190. It was not error to allow a witness to state "whom he understood was referred to" by the respondent, when he said that he had "found the tin can of old Johnnie," and that he "supposed it was Johnson." State *v.* Lockwood, 58 Vt. 378; s. c, 2 New Eng. Rep. 196.

Failure to Object. — Counsel cannot, after omission to object to testimony offered, take the chances of the testimony making in his favor, and, if it happens to be adverse, then interpose an objection to it Clark *v.* State, 102 N. Y. 735; s. c., 3 Cent Rep 801.

It is a Statutory Rule of Evidence, that when a detailed act, declaration, conversation, or writing is given in evidence, any other act, declaration, or writing which is necessary to make it fully understood, or to explain the same, may also be given in evidence. Gaither *v.* State, 21 Tex. App. 527.

Documentary Evidence. — A copy of the record of the collector of internal revenue, when sworn to in court by a competent witness, is admissible in evidence. State *v.* Hall (Me.), 5 New Eng. Rep. 235.

Where a witness on his cross-examination admitted that he had signed and sworn to a complaint, and identified a copy thereof presented to him as a true copy, the contents of the complaint are admissible to contradict him. Commonwealth *v.* Luce (Mass.), 5 New Eng. Rep. 249.

Where a Receipt is admissible as evidence of the guilt of the defendant, and is shown to have been taken into the possession of the defendant and his counsel, and they have refused to produce it, a copy of it is admissible. Commonwealth *v.* Goldstein, 114 Mass. 272; Commonwealth *v.* Spurn (Mass.), 5 New Eng. Rep. 170.

In Larceny. — In the prosecution of an indictment for larceny, where the people have not yet concluded their testimony, and the testimony offered — that the stolen oxen were afterwards seen in another county — was competent to go to the jury; and the testimony given not being stated in the record, but only what it tended to show in the opinion of the circuit judge, — this court cannot say that it was error to allow the case to proceed. Error, to avail, must be made to appear upon the record, and not be left in doubt. People *v.* La Munion (Mich.), 7 West. Rep. 893.

In Homicide. — On a trial for homicide, it is proper to admit in evidence, and to permit the jury to inspect, clothing worn by the accused on, and soon after, the day of the commission of the crime, and bearing blood-stains. The fact that such garments cannot be filed with the bill of exceptions, is no reason for excluding them; the descriptive evidence being sufficient to enable the court to pass upon the competency of the evidence. State *v.* Stair, 87 Mo. 268; s. c., 1 West. Rep. 765.

2. Commonwealth *v.* Shepard, 83 Mass. (1 Allen) 573; Commonwealth *v.* Eastman, 55 Mass. (1 Cush.) 189; Commonwealth *v.* Tuckerman, 76 Mass. (10 Gray) 173.

3. **A Confession,** which relates to a course of conduct pursued by defendant during his whole employment in the service of the person whose property he is alleged to have embezzled, and necessarily has reference to, and characterizes all, his acts charged to have been done within that time, is admissible to show criminal intent, although it does not, in terms, refer to the specific matters charged in the indictment. Commonwealth *v.* Shepard, 83 Mass. (1 Allen) 573; Commonwealth *v.* Eastman, 55 Mass. (1 Cush.) 189; Commonwealth *v.* Tuckerman, 76 Mass. (10 Gray) 173.

In a Prosecution for compounding a Crime and agreeing to withhold evidence, the acquittal of the principal offender is not

It is competent to prove that the matters of defence set up on the preliminary examination were contradictory of those relied upon at the trial.[1] And trial courts are authorized to admit apparently immaterial testimony, upon the assurance of the party offering it that its materiality will be shown by other evidence, to be introduced at a subsequent stage of the trial. The failure of such party, however, to produce such qualifying evidence, imposes upon the trial court the duty of withdrawing the immaterial evidence from the jury, and instructing them to disregard the same.[2]

Improper and inadmissible evidence must be objected to in season. Counsel cannot listen to a witness's answer evidently irresponsive to the question, and, when he finds it to be unfavorable, move to strike it out.[3] He should object to the answer as soon as its objectionable character is perceived.[4]

b. Materiality. — Evidence which fairly tends to prove the point sought to be established is material, and should be admitted.[5] All evidence not material is properly excluded.[6]

Where the intoxication of the accused at the time of committing the offence charged is in question, it is competent for the State to prove that, a short time previous to the commission of the offence, the accused was intoxicated; provided such testimony makes it

competent evidence for the defence. People *v.* Buckland, 13 Wend. (N. Y.) 592.

In Murder. — The question upon a trial for murder, is, did the prisoner do the act under a delusion, believing it to be other than it was? Reg. *v.* Townley, 3 Fost. & F. 839.

1. State *v.* Conrad, 95 N. C. 666.

2. Phillips *v.* State, 22 Tex. App. 139.

Failure to introduce Qualifying Evidence: Withdrawal: Effect. — Upon the understanding that the State would introduce other qualifying evidence, a State's witness was permitted to testify. The trial judge certified that, the State having failed to introduce the qualifying evidence, the evidence complained of was withdrawn from the jury. *Held*, that the evidence having been withdrawn without prejudice to the defendant, he cannot now be heard to complain. Further, that, being a part of the *res gestæ* of the transaction and the declaration of one of the co-conspirators pertinent to the transaction, the evidence was, in any event, competent. Smith *v.* State, 21 Tex. App. 133.

3. Quin *v.* Lloyd, 41 N. Y. 349.

4. **Hearsay Evidence: When Harmless.** — When the case on an appeal from a conviction for murder discloses undisputed and ample evidence of premeditation and deliberation, error in receiving hearsay evidence tending merely to corroborate the fact of premeditation may be disregarded as harmless. People *v.* Chacon, 102 N. Y. 669; s. c., 2 Cent. Rep. 910.

5. Commonwealth *v.* Sawtelle, 141 Mass. 140; s. c., 1 New Eng Rep. 590.

Defendant a Witness: Record of Prior Conviction. — Where defendant had been examined as a witness on his own behalf, it was proper to permit the State to put in evidence the record showing the prior conviction of the defendant; and the evidence of a witness that he had warned defendant from taking the iron, and informed him as to the ownership of the railroad company, was admissible as tending to show knowledge in defendant of such ownership. State *v.* Loehr (Mo.), 11 West. Rep. 473.

6. **Exclusion of Evidence.** — Thus, it has been *held* that an accused is not prejudiced by the exclusion of evidence which would not have impaired the circumstantial evidence against him, — State *v.* Beaudet, 53 Conn. 536; s. c., 1 New Eng. Rep. 833, — and the improper exclusion of a question is cured by the admission thereafter of the evidence sought by the question. Anderson *v.* State, 104 Ind. 467; s. c., 2 West. Rep. 341.

On burning Wife's House. — On the trial of a defendant for burning a house belonging to his wife, in which he resided with her, there is no available error in the exclusion of evidence offered by the defendant, which tended to prove that he had furnished certain money to pay for the building of the house. Garrett *v.* State, 109 Ind. 527; s. c., 8 West. Rep. 391.

probable that the intoxication continued, and existed at the time the alleged criminal act was done.[1]

Where the defendant was indicted for arson, in burning his house, to defraud an insurance company which had issued a policy of insurance thereon, it was proper for the prosecution to introduce in evidence a claim made by the defendant for property destroyed by the fire, and also to prove that he had put a value upon the property beyond its real worth, for the purpose of showing a motive for the commission of the crime charged.[2]

The defendant was entitled to an instruction, that if the over-valuation of the property was the result of an erroneous judgment,

1. Peirce *v.* State, 53 Ga. 365.

2. Stitz *v.* State, 104 Ind. 359; s. c., 2 West. Rep. 296.

The law recognizes the principle that men are impelled to commit crime from some motive. There are, indeed, few motiveless crimes; and among the motives impelling men to crime is that of gain. In a thoughtful and philosophical treatise it is said, "As there must pre-exist a motive to every voluntary action of a rational being, it is proper to comprise in the class of moral indications such particulars of external relation as are usually observed to operate as inducements to crime;" and among the motives that influence human conduct, this author classes that of gain. Wills, Cir. Ev. 39. Another author says, "In looking at the motives which instigate human conduct, we ascend to the very origin of crime." Burr. Cir. Ev. 281. At another place this author says, "The motive of gain, in the stricter sense of the term, may be excited by two different classes of objects: first, by something visible and tangible, which the party meditating the crime desires to possess; and, secondly, by some substantial benefit which is expected to accrue as the result of the contemplated act." Burr. Cir. Ev.

The case of State *v.* Cohn, 9 Nev. 179, supplies an illustration of the practical application of these principles. In that case the appellant was charged with arson, and it was *held* that evidence of over-large insurance upon his goods was competent to show a possible or probable motive, such motive being a material link in the chain of circumstances. In the course of the opinion in that case it was said, "Now, it is not a natural thing for a man to fire his own premises: presumptively, appellant was innocent. What, then, is the logical and natural course of human thought at such a juncture? Is it not to inquire what motive, if any, existed which could have influenced a sane person to do such an act? Such was the course pursued by the prosecution: the motive was sought, and by it claimed to be found in the fact of an undue insurance; not only a perfectly proper proceeding, but, indeed, the only one open." The same principle is declared in Commonwealth *v* Hudson, 97 Mass. 565, and in Shepherd *v.* People, 19 N. Y. 537.

In this last case, *Denio, J.*, speaking for the court, said, "The prisoner's house had been burned, and he was charged, upon circumstantial evidence, with having set it on fire. *Prima facie* he had no motive for the act, but a strong pecuniary one against it. But if he had a contract of indemnity, and especially if, under it, he might probably obtain more than the value of the property, the case would be quite different."

Mr. Bishop says, "Evidence that the insurance was for more than the worth of the building, is pertinent; also that the defendant attempted to procure payment of what was thus excessive." 1 Bish. Cr. Pro. § 50.

These cases are in harmony with the general rule which that author thus states: "Hence, proof of motive is never essential to a conviction, but it is always competent against the defendant." 1 Bish. Cr. Pro. § 1107; Wills, Cir. Ev. 41; Goodwin *v.* State, 96 Ind. 550. See p. 560.

While it is competent to prove facts tending to show an evil motive, yet such facts are always susceptible of explanation. Motive is but a circumstance, and it is always proper to explain the act which is adduced as evidence of a wicked motive. This is true of the present case. If the valuation of the property was made by mistake, or was a mere honest error of opinion, the probatory force of the fact that there was a claim made for a value greater than the actual one, would be materially weakened if not entirely destroyed. It is not uncommon for men to place too great a value on their own property, and an error in doing so is not necessarily a criminating circumstance. Citizens' Ins. Co. *v.* Short, 62 Ind. 316.

or was a mistake in fact, it was not necessarily evidence of a wicked motive or criminal intent.[1]

(1) *On Former Trials.* — Evidence taken on a former trial, as a rule, cannot be used except in impeachment.[2] Thus, where the defendant offered in evidence a transcript containing the evidence of a witness on a former trial, without showing that such witness was either dead or beyond the jurisdiction of the court, the transcript was properly rejected.[3]

On the trial of an indictment, a member of the grand jury which found it may testify as to evidence given before the grand jury.[4]

While it is competent to prove by members of the grand jury that witnesses testified differently before them, yet this cannot be done without first calling the attention of the witnesses to their testimony before the grand jury, and asking them as to it.[5]

1. Stitz *v.* State, 104 Ind. 359; s. c., 2 West. Rep. 296.

2. **Evidence before Coroner.** — On a trial under an information charging the defendant with murder, the proceedings before the coroner's jury, including the evidence and verdict of the jury, offered by defendant's counsel to show that the defendant testified before such jury substantially as upon the trial, and that such jury found the shooting was done in self-defence, was properly excluded. People *v.* Coughlin (Mich.), 11 West. Rep. 556.

3. State *v.* Houser, 26 Mo. 431; State *v.* Rose, 90 Mo. 208; s. c., 10 West. Rep. 279.

Reading Defendant's Evidence on Former Trial. — Where the defendant did not except to the State's reading in evidence, in rebuttal, the transcript of defendant's evidence given on a former trial, no question is presented; but the court would have been justified in overruling such an objection had it been presented. State *v.* Rose, 90 Mo. 208; s. c., 10 West. Rep. 279.

But if an objection had been made when it was offered, the court would have been justified in overruling it and receiving the evidence, under the ruling made in the case of State *v.* Eddings, 71 Mo. 545, and subsequently followed in the case of State *v.* Jefferson, 77 Mo. 136.

On Trial for Bribery. — On the trial of an indictment charging the defendant with having given a bribe to a certain member of the common council of the city of New York to influence his official action upon the application of the Broadway Surface Railway Company for the consent of the common council to the construction of a street railway, admission of evidence on the part of the prosecution as part of its affirmative case, to the effect that the defendant had, previously to the commission of the alleged offence charged in the indictment, proposed to pay a third party, who was at the time engrossing clerk of the Assembly, a certain sum for the alteration of a bill then pending before that body, so that it might authorize the construction of a railway on Broadway in said city, was erroneous. The thing in dispute on the trial being whether the defendant gave the money alleged to the member of the common council, evidence that upon a former and different occasion he had offered money with a guilty purpose to another person cannot fairly be held relevant to the question on trial, nor admissible as tending to show the intent or motive of the defendant in the commission of the crime charged. People *v.* Sharp (N. Y.), 8 Cent. Rep. 699.

4. Allen *v.* State, 79 Ala. 34; Bressler *v.* People, 117 Ill. 422; s. c., 5 West. Rep. 185.

5. Hoge *v.* People, 117 Ill. 35; s. c., 4 West. Rep. 197; State *v.* Leeper, 70 Iowa, 748.

Impeaching Witness by Grand Juror. — It is competent to prove by members of the grand jury that witnesses testified differently before them from what they did at the trial; but this cannot be done without first calling the attention of the witnesses to their testimony before the grand jury, and asking them as to it. Hoge *v.* People, 117 Ill. 35; s. c., 4 West. Rep. 197; Granger *v.* Warrington, 3 Gilm. 299; Bressler *v.* People, Sept. Term, A. D. 1885.

But the attention of the witnesses should have been first called to the testimony they gave before the grand jury, and they should then have been allowed to state whether they did testify as claimed. If they had admitted that they did, they would have been then entitled to give any explanation they could why their present testimony was different.

There is no error shown in allowing the prosecutor to testify to the fact that he was examined before the grand jury, since such evidence may sometimes be material, or it may have been introduced as merely preliminary to something else.[1]

(2) *Of Other Crimes.* — It is not generally competent to prove a man guilty of one felony by proving him guilty of another unconnected felony; but where several felonies are connected together, and form part of one entire transaction, then the one is evidence of the character of the other.[2]

And the State, for the purpose of showing that defendant would be likely to commit the crime charged, cannot prove that he committed other crimes, although of a like nature.[3]

Admission of another crime of defendant may be considered in determining his credibility.[4]

To show a former conviction, as common seller of intoxicating liquors, a record is admissible, which says, "Indictment for being common seller of intoxicating liquors," instead of copying the indictment itself. It is for the jury to say whether the defendant is the same person named in the record.[5]

3. *Written and Parol Evidence.* — The ***best evidence*** must always

If they had denied that they had so testified, the defendant would have been entitled to contradict them. Regnie *v.* Cabot, 2 Gilm. 34; N. W. R. R. Co. *v.* Hack, 66 Ill. 238.

1. Allen *v.* State, 79 Ala. 34.

Indictment for Perjury. — The indictment alleging that the false statements were made upon the trial of one P., the trial court properly permitted the State to prove the proceedings had and the evidence delivered by the defendant upon that trial. Such evidence was admissible to show that the alleged false statements were made in a judicial proceeding, and that they were material to an issue in the said proceeding. Partain *v.* State, 22 Tex. App. 100.

2. Lamb *v.* State (Md.), 5 Cent. Rep. 775.

Texas Doctrine. — It is not well settled that an indictment against a defendant for an offence different from that for which he is on trial, may be introduced in evidence against him, if such indictment, in any degree, tends to show a motive on the part of the defendant to commit the offence for which he is on trial. Kunde *v.* State, 22 Tex. App. 65.

3. Clark *v.* State, 47 N. J. L. 556; s. c., 4 Cent. Rep. 806.

Gaming. — Evidence that rooms in which gaming implements were found were resorted to for gaming prior to seizure, tends to prove implements were kept for gaming at time of seizure, and is competent. Commonwealth *v.* Certain Gaming Implements, 114 Mass. 576; s. c., 1 New Eng. Rep. 576.

Letters tending to prove the offence charged (false pretences) are not incompetent evidence because they disclose the fact that other crimes or attempts had been committed, as a general swindling business. Commonwealth *v.* Blood (Mass.), 2 New Eng. Rep. 393.

Under R. S. § 1561, providing that any one, who, with intent to cheat or defraud or obtain money "by use of any trick or deception, or false or fraudulent representation, shall be guilty of a felony," *held,* that evidence that defendant obtained money on the representation that he was an agent for another person, and gave the prosecuting witness instruction in the making of pictures, and a promise to furnish him with a job, and it appeared that he had no authority as such agent, and failed to procure the job, although the instruction in making pictures was of some value, was sufficient to sustain conviction. In such case, evidence of other similar transactions was competent to show intent. State *v.* Bayne, 88 Mo. 604; s. c., 4 West. Rep. 649.

4. Boyle *v.* State, 105 Ind. 469; s. c., 2 West. Rep. 788.

5. State *v.* Lashus (Me.), 5 New Eng. Rep. 237.

Identity of a Party at the Bar is a matter of fact for the trial court. State *v.* Whitney, 38 La. An. 579.

But the record of conviction for a felony is *prima facie* as against the compounder. State *v.* Duhammel, 2 Harr. (Del.) 532; State *v.* Williams, 2 Harr. (Del.) 532.

be given; that is, if it is possible to be had; if not, then inferior evidence will be admitted. But before this inferior (or *secondary*) evidence is let in, the absence of the better evidence must be accounted for. By this is meant, that merely substitutionary evidence — that is, such as indicates more original sources of information — must not be received so long as the original evidence is attainable. It does not imply that weaker proofs (which are not substitutionary) may not be selected instead of stronger ones. Thus, an act may be equally proved by a written instrument, and also by some one who saw it. Both these modes of proof are primary.[1]

1. Harris, Cr. L. 429.

Admissions as to Recorded Facts. — It is settled that an admission, whether under oath or on examination or otherwise, is not admissible to prove record facts. Whart. Cr. Ev. §§ 153, 687; 2 Greenl. Ev. (13th ed.) §§ 49, 461, 462; People *v.* Humphrey, 7 Johns. (N. Y.) 314; State *v.* Roswell, 6 Conn. 446; Miner *v.* People, 58 Ill. 59; South *v.* People, 98 Ill. 261; Miller *v.* White, 80 Ill. 580.

The Most Common Application of this Rule is in the case of written instruments. It is plain that the best evidence of the contents of a written document is the writing itself; and therefore before a copy, or parol evidence, of its contents can be received, the absence of the original instrument must be accounted for by proving that it is lost or destroyed, or that it is in the possession of the opposite party, and that he has had reasonable notice to produce it. If once secondary evidence is admitted, any proof may be given, as there are no degrees of secondary evidence: thus, if an original deed cannot be produced, parol evidence of its contents may be given, although there is an attested copy in existence. But for the sake of convenience, copies may be given, in evidence of all records, other than those of the court requiring proof of them, generally of the official documents of other courts, and parish registers, entries in corporation books, and books of public companies relating to things public and general. Harris, Cr. L. 429.

Oral Testimony is admissible to prove the contents of a lost indictment. State *v.* Whitney, 38 La. An. 579.

The indictment, after charging the forgery, alleged that the instrument "is in the possession of the defendant, or is lost or destroyed, and that access to the same cannot be had." *Held,* that the trial court erred in permitting the State to prove the contents of the instrument by parol, without having served notice upon the defendant to produce it. Rollins *v.* State, 21 Tex. App. 148.

Parol to show Election to Office. — The parol evidence that he held the office, etc., was admitted at the trial without objection on the part of defendant. The objection cannot be made for the first time on appeal. Had it been made timely, the State, doubtless, would have obviated the objection by introducing the better proof. Walker *v.* Owen, 79 Mo. 563-568; State *v.* West, 21 Mo. App. 309; s. c., 4 West. Rep. 747.

For the purpose of showing title in the person whose name is alleged to be forged to a deed, the testimony of the register of deeds — that a careful examination of the records fails to show any transfer of the land, since the title was acquired, save the alleged forged instrument — is admissible. People *v.* Parker (Mich.), 11 West. Rep. 182.

Public Records: Certificate of Examiner. — Where a witness has examined a public record, and swears that he has made a true copy, such copy may be admitted to show the contents of the record. State *v.* Lynde, 77 Me. 561; s. c., 1 New Eng. Rep. 290.

Examined Copies are, in England, resorted to as the most usual mode of proving records. Whart. Ev. § 94. The mode is explained and commended in Best's work on Evidence, § 486. It seems to have prevailed in many of the States, including Pennsylvania and New York. It was at an early date adopted in some of the federal circuit courts. U. S. *v.* Johns, 4 U. S. (4 Dall.) 412; bk. 1, L. ed. 888. It is not an unknown mode of proof in New England. It is spoken of as a well-settled doctrine in New Hampshire. Whitehouse *v.* Bickford, 29 N. H. 471. In Spaulding *v.* Vincent, 24 Vt. 501, it is said, "The more usual method" (of proving a discharge in a foreign court of bankruptcy) "is a sworn copy." Mr. Greenleaf says, — 1 Ev. § 485,— "Where the proof is by copy, an examined copy, duly made and sworn to by any competent witness, is always admissible." In Atwood *v.* Winterport, 60 Me. 250, the rule is casually approved; *Appleton, Ch. J.,* there saying, whilst speaking of the mode of proving an army record, "A sworn copy is admissible, or a copy certified by the proper certifying officer." State *v.* Goshun, 65 Me. 270.

Public Records: Certificate of Officer. — A certificate from a public officer, that certain facts exist or appear by the records of his office, is not competent evidence of such facts. Robbins *v.* Townsend, 37 Mass. (20 Pick.) 345; Wayland *v.* Ware, 109 Mass. 248; Hanson *v.* South Scituate, 115 Mass. 336; Commonwealth *v.* Richardson, 142 Mass. 71; s. c., 2 New Eng. Rep. 153.

A certificate of a public officer, as to matters which he is not authorized by law to attest, is extra-official, and insufficient to prove such matters. Commonwealth *v.* Richardson, 142 Mass. 71; s. c., 2 New Eng. Rep. 153.

The certificate of the secretary of the Commonwealth does not prove the signatures to a lease made by the commissioners of inland fisheries, recorded in the records of a town. Commonwealth *v.* Richardson, 142 Mass. 71; s. c., 2 New Eng. Rep. 153.

He is not authorized by law to attest them. As to matters which he is not authorized by law to attest, his certificate is extra-official, can have no higher weight than that of a private citizen, and is therefore inadequate to make the proof required. Oakes *v.* Hill, 31 Mass. (14 Pick.) 442–448.

Records of Hospitals. — Under Mo. Rev. Stat. § 2285, to render records of the hospitals for the insane in Illinois admissible, it is necessary to show that such institutions were public offices "of a sister State;" and under § 2272, the printed statute-book of such State was competent evidence of such fact. A private letter from the superintendent of the poorhouse of the city of St. Louis could not be introduced in evidence, under Rev. Stat. § 2285. State *v.* Pagels, 92 Mo. 300; s. c., 10 West. Rep. 283.

Under the provisions of § 1802, it was competent for Officer Emmett to testify on behalf of the State, though his name was not indorsed on the indictment. State *v.* Roy, 83 Mo. 268; State *v.* Griffin, 87 Mo. 608; s. c., 3 West. Rep. 820; State *v.* O'Day, 89 Mo. 561; s. c., 6 West. Rep. 449; State *v.* Pagels, 92 Mo. 300; 10 West. Rep. 288.

In Prosecution for Bigamy: Marriage License. — A copy of the marriage license and certificate of the officer or person solemnizing the marriage, indorsed on the license and properly authenticated by the officer in whose office the license and certificate were filed, is admissible proof of marriage in a prosecution for bigamy. Jackson *v.* People, 3 Ill. 231.

The Supreme Court of Illinois has *held*, that on a trial for criminal conversation, where strict proof is required, a marriage license issued in Tennessee, with a certificate indorsed thereon by a justice of the peace, that he solemnized the marriage, was properly admitted in evidence. King *v.* Dale, 2 Ill. 513; Miller *v.* White, 80 Ill. 580; Conant *v.* Griffin, 48 Ill. 410.

The people's attorney is not obliged to prove either of the marriages by the register or certificate thereof, or other record evidence; but the same may be proved by such other evidence as is admissible to prove a marriage in other cases. Jackson *v.* People, 3 Ill. 232; Miner *v.* People, 58 Ill. 60; Bergen *v.* People, 17 Ill. 426; Hays *v.* People, 25 N. Y. 396; Rev. Stat. chap. 38, § 29.

In Jackson *v.* People, 3 Ill. 231, which was a prosecution for bigamy, the record evidence of marriage was held admissible. In that case, however, the constitutional question does not seem to have been raised; but, if it had been raised and relied upon, we do not think the result would have been different. Under the constitutional guaranty, the deposition of witnesses could not be taken and read in evidence in a criminal prosecution, as is done in a civil case, because this would be a direct denial of the right to meet the witnesses face to face. But the provision, "In all criminal prosecutions the accused shall have the right to meet the witnesses face to face," in our judgment, has no reference to record evidence which may, during the progress of a criminal trial, become necessary to establish some material fact to secure a conviction.

The offered transcript consisted of a public record which is declared by the law to be evidence. The record imports verity; and a cross-examination is foreign to, and has no application to, this character of evidence. Tucker *v.* People, 122 Ill. . s. c, 11 West. Rep. 765.

The constitutional guaranty, to the defendant, of the right to meet the witnesses face to face, has no reference to record evidence which may, during the progress of a criminal trial, become necessary to establish some material facts to secure conviction. A certified copy, from the records of the county clerk, of the certificate of the person who performed the marriage ceremony, entered on the back of the license, was properly admitted, under Rev. Stat. 1874, chap. 89, §§ 9, 12. Tucker *v.* People, 122 Ill. ; s. c., 11 West. Rep. 765.

On the Trial of an Indictment for Violations of the Election Laws, a material question was whether the persons named in the indictment as those whose names had been falsely entered in the poll-books as having voted, did in fact vote. The State introduced as a witness one Crawford, who testified that he was a challenger at the polls, and had there a duly certified copy of the registration poll-book, in which he checked off the names of all those who voted while he was present; that he was at the polls the whole day except for about an hour, when he left said book with Foxwell and Hamilton; and that he could identify nearly all the checks made by him in the book. Foxwell testified that during Crawford's absence Hamilton held the book, and he, Foxwell, was present all the time and saw Hamilton check off the name of every one who voted. Due efforts were made to obtain the attendance of Hamilton as a witness, but the summons for him was returned "*non est.*" Thereupon the book was offered in evidence, and admitted over the objection of defendants. *Held*, that, while the book would not have been admissible as independent evidence, it was properly admitted with the check-marks therein, in connection with the testimony of the witnesses, as showing original entries or memoranda made in accordance with the facts at the time they were made. Owings *v.* Low, 5 Gill & J. (Md.) 134; Ins. Co. *v.* Weide, 76 U. S. (6 Wall.) 677; bk. 19, L. ed. 810.

If a witness swears that he made an entry or memorandum in accordance with the truth of the matter, as he knew it to exist at the time of the occurrence, such entry or memorandum is admissible in evidence in confirmation of what the witness states from memory, whether he retains a present recollection of the facts or not. The admissibility of such memoranda does not depend upon the distinction made in the law between primary and secondary proof. Owens *v.* State (Md.), 8 Cent. Rep. 871.

Letters. — Unanswered letters found on person of accused, and not shown to be acted on, are not evidence against him. State *v.* Stair, 87 Mo. 268; s. c., 1 West. Rep. 766.

But when letters supposed to have been written by defendant were offered against him, and there was evidence tending to prove that he wrote them, *held* that the letters were properly admitted, along with the evidence as to their genuineness. State *v.* Briggs, 68 Iowa, 416.

Where one of two joint defendants was arrested for homicide, there was found in a pocketbook in his possession a paper with the following words in his handwriting: "Do you think it safe to kill them and wrap them up in the clothes, and tell that they went off in a buggy?" *held*, that this writing was competent evidence against said defendant, the proof tending to show that he acted on the suggestion. State *v.* Stair, 87 Mo. 268; s. c., 1 West. Rep. 765.

Proving Handwriting. — Comparison of signatures for the purpose of showing that one of them is forged, can only be made with such writings as are legally in evidence for some other purpose than that of being compared. It is error, on the trial of an indictment for forgery, to introduce the probate files for the express purpose of putting a will in evidence, that the signature to it may be used in comparison with the one alleged to have been forged. People *v.* Parker (Mich.), 11 West. Rep. 182.

It is proper to allow the bonds of the respondent and his co-defendant, recognizing for their appearance to answer the information, and the affidavit of his co-defendant for a continuance in the case, to be admitted in evidence, and to be used in making comparisons of the handwriting.

They were part of the files in the cause, and, as such, belong to the case, to be used for any material and relevant purpose therein. People *v.* Parker (Mich.), 11 West. Rep. 182.

A paper alleged to be in the handwriting of defendant is sufficiently proved to go to the jury, where a witness called to identify it, testifies that he had seen defendant write two or three notes and sign his name to another; that he thought he could tell defendant's handwriting; that he judged the paper handed him was in his handwriting; that he was not positive, but judged so from a comparison with his memory of what defendant wrote. State *v.* Stair, 87 Mo. 268; s. c., 1 West. Rep. 765.

All evidence of handwriting, except when the witness saw the document written, is, in its nature, comparison. If the witness has the proper knowledge, he may declare his belief. One of the modes of acquiring that knowledge is from having seen the person write. It is held sufficient for this purpose that the witness has seen the party write but once, and then only his name. Greenl. Ev. §§ 576, 577; State *v.* Scott, 45 Mo. 303.

Such writing, however, was not competent as against the other defendant, wife of the one in whose possession it was found, it not being shown when it was written or that she had any knowledge of it, and it not being proved to be part of the *res gestæ*. State *v.* Stair, 87 Mo. 268; s. c., 1 West. Rep. 765. State *v.* Talbott, 73 Mo. 347.

In People *v.* Thoms, 3 Park. Cr. R. (N. Y.) 256, the defendant was indicted for having in his possession an altered bank bill; and, while under arrest, his wife was searched, and the State showed that she had in her possession engraved figures cut from genuine bills, suited to that species of forgery, and this evidence, it was held, was improperly admitted.

A paper in handwriting of defendant is sufficiently proved to go to the jury where a witness identifies it, having seen the writer make two or three notes and sign another. State *v.* Stair, 87 Mo. 268; s. c., 1 West. Rep. 765.

The Testimony of a Person in Regard to his own Signature is not evidence of a grade superior to the testimony of a witness acquainted with the handwriting. Lefferts *v.* State, 49 N. J. L. (20 Vr.) 26; s. c., 4 Cent. Rep. 883.

Proof of Contents of Written Instrument. — If a witness admits a certain writing, produced but not put in evidence, to be his, he cannot be asked, on cross-examination, as to statements such as counsel may suggest are contained in it. The writing itself must be read as the only competent evidence of its contents. State *v.* Mathews, 88 Mo. 121; s. c., 4 West. Rep. 429.

The general rule is, that if the witness admits the writing to be his, as was done here, he cannot be thus asked as to statements such as counsel may suggest are contained in it; but the writing itself must be read as the only competent evidence of the contents. Romertze *v.* E. Riv. Nat. Bank, 49 N. Y. 577; Prewitt *v.* Martin, 59 Mo. 325; State *v.* Mathews, 88 Mo. 121; s. c., 4 West. Rep. 429; 1 Greenl. Ev. § 463; 1 Phill. Ev. *576.

Documentary Evidence: Exceptions. — In a case where any documentary evidence is excluded by the trial court, or a portion is admitted, and the claim is that the whole should have been introduced, such evidence not introduced or excluded should be made a part of the bill of exceptions, so that the court can judge of its admissibility. If the whole document was not presented, through the refusal of the circuit judge and the protest of the prosecuting attorney, so that the court can determine its tenor and effect, the conviction would be reversed; but where, on an examination, it is apparent that the part of the article excluded could have had no other effect than to injure instead of benefiting the respondent, he cannot complain. People *v.* Coughlin (Mich.), 11 West. Rep. 556.

Marriage License. — An objection that a marriage license introduced in evidence was signed by the "clerk of the county court," is not well taken, as Rev. Stat. 1874, chap. 131, § 1, declares that the words "county clerk" shall be held to include "clerk of the county court," and the words "clerk of the county court" to include "county clerk." Tucker *v.* People, 122 Ill. ; s. c, 11 West. Rep. 765.

English Doctrine. — Roscoe says in his work on Cr. Ev. pp. 2-4, that the most important application of this principle is that which rejects secondary and requires primary evidence of the contents of written documents of every description, by the production of the written documents themselves. The rule was so stated by the judges in answer to certain questions put to them by the House of Lords on the occasion of the trial of Queen Caroline (2 B. & B. 286), and is perfectly general in its application; the only exceptions to it being founded on special grounds. These may be divided into the following classes: (1) Where the written document is lost or destroyed; (2) Where it is in the possession of an adverse party who refuses or neglects to produce it; (3) Where it is in the possession of a party who is privileged to withhold it, and who insists on his privilege; (4) Where the production of the document would be, on physical grounds, impossible, or highly inconvenient; (5) Where the document is of a public nature, and some other mode of proof has been specially substituted for reasons of convenience. It is apparent, therefore, that, in order to let in the secondary evidence in these cases, certain preliminary conditions must be fulfilled: what these conditions are, we shall explain more particularly when we come to treat of "Secondary Evidence"

It is not necessary, in every case where the fact that is to be proved has been committed to writing, that the writing should be produced, but (unless the contents of the written document is itself a fact in issue) only in those cases where the documents contain statements of facts, which by law, are directed or required to be put in writing, or where they have been drawn up by the consent of the parties for the express purpose of being evidence of the facts contained in them. Indeed, in many cases the writing is not evidence, as in the case of R. *v.* Layer, 16 How. St. Tr. 93. 285

The following cases are cited as instances of the general rule. Upon an indictment for setting fire to a house with intent to defraud an insurance company, in order to prove that the house was insured, the policy must be produced as being the best evidence, and the insurance office cannot give any evidence from their books unless the absence of the policy is accounted for. R. *v.* Doran, 1 Esp. 126; R. *v.* Kitson, 1 Dears. C. C. 187; 22 L. J. M. C. 118. Upon the same principle, the records and proceedings of courts of justice, existing in writing, are the best evidence of the facts there recorded. As, for instance, where it was necessary to prove the day on which a cause came on to be tried, Lord Ellenborough said that he could not receive parol evidence of the day on which the court sat at *nisi prius*, as that was capable of other proof by matter of record. Thomas *v.* Ansley, 6 Esp. 80. So, on an indictment for disturbing a Protestant congregation, Lord Kenyon ruled that the taking of the oaths under the Toleration Act, being matter of record, could not be proved by parol evidence. R. *v.* Hube, Peake, N. P. 180; 5

a. Depositions and Commissions. — To avoid the necessity of the issuing of a commission to examine a witness, it is not sufficient for the prosecutor to admit that the witness would testify to the facts stated in the affidavit: the admission must be of the absolute truth of the facts so stated.[1] Testimony of witnesses since deceased, taken before the justice of the peace on the preliminary examination, are admissible in evidence.[2]

T. R. 542. In R. *v.* Rowland, 1 F. & F. 72, Bramwell, B., *held* that on an indictment for perjury, in order to prove the proceedings of the county court, it was necessary to produce either the clerk's minutes, or a copy thereof bearing the seal of the court; the county court act (9 & 10 Vict. c. 95, § 111) directing that such minutes should be kept, and that such minutes should be admissible as evidence. And it has been said generally, that where the transactions of courts which are not, technically speaking, of record are to be proved, if such courts preserve written memorials of their proceedings, those memorials are the only authentic modes of proof which the law recognizes. 3 Stark. Ev. 1st ed. 1043. On indictments for perjury, where it appears that there was an information in writing, such writing is the best evidence of the information, and must be produced. R. *v.* Dillon, 14 Cox, C. C. 4. On an indictment under the repealed statute 8 & 9 Will. 3, c. 26, § 81, for having coining instruments in possession, it was necessary to show that the prosecution was commenced within three months after the offence committed. It was proved, by parol, that the prisoners were apprehended within three months, but the warrant was not produced or proved, nor were the warrant of commitment or the depositions before the magistrate given in evidence to show on what transactions, or for what offence, or at what time, the prisoners were committed. The prisoners being convicted, a question was reserved for the opinion of the judges, who held that there was not sufficient evidence that the prisoners were apprehended upon transactions for high treason respecting the coin within three months after the offence committed. R. *v.* Phillip, Russ. & Ry. 369.

But, on the other hand, where a memorandum of agreement was drawn up, and read over to the defendant, which he assented to, but did not sign, it was *held* that the terms of the agreement might be proved by parol. Doe *v.* Cartwright, 3 B. & Ald. 326; Trewhitt *v.* Lambert, 10 A. & E. 470. So facts may be proved by parol, though a narrative of them may exist in writing. Thus, a person who pays money may prove the fact of payment, without producing the receipt which he took. Rambert *v.* Cohen, 4 Esp. 213. So where, in trover to prove the demand, the witness stated that he had verbally required the defendant to deliver up the property, and at the same time served upon him a notice in writing to the same effect, Lord Ellenborough ruled that it was unnecessary to produce the writing. Smith *v.* Young, 1 Campb. 439. So a person who takes notes of a conversation need not produce them in proving the conversation, as they would not be evidence if produced. Thus, in R. *v.* Layer, 16 How. St. Tr. 93, 285, a prosecution for high treason, Mr. Slaney, an under-secretary of state, gave evidence of the prisoner's confession before the council, though it had been taken down in writing. 12 Vin. Ab. 96. So, on an indictment for perjury committed upon a trial in the county court, any witness, present at the time, is competent to prove what evidence was given, inasmuch as a county court judge is not bound to take any notes. R. *v.* Morgan, 6 Cox, Cr. C. 107 per Martin, B.; Harmer *v.* Bean, 3 C. & K. 307, per Parke, B. So the fact of a marriage may be proved by a person who was present, and it is not necessary to produce the parish register as the primary evidence. Morris *v.* Miller, 1 W. Bl. 632. So the fact that a certain person occupied land as tenant, may be proved by parol, although there is a written contract. R. *v.* Inhab. of Holy Trinity, 7 B. & C. 611; 1 M. & R. 444. But the parties to the contract, the amount of rent and the terms of the tenancy, can only be shown by the writing. S. C. and Strother *v.* Burr, 5 Bing. 136; Doe *v.* Harvey, 8 Bing. 239; R. *v.* Merthyr Tydvil, 1 B. & Ad. 29.

1. Newton *v.* State, 21 Fla. 53.

Florida Laws. — Sect. 1, chap. 3125, 1879, gives to the court no discretion in the matter of issuing a commission to take testimony. Newton *v.* State, 21 Fla. 53.

2. State *v.* McO'Blenis, 24 Mo. 402, which was subsequently followed in the cases of State *v.* Houser, 26 Mo. 431; State *v.* Harman, 27 Mo. 120; State *v.* Carlisle, 57 Mo. 105; State *v.* Able, 65 Mo. 357; State *v.* Elliott, 90 Mo. 350; s. c., 7 West. Rep. 285. See also "Bill to Perpetuate Testimony," 2 Am. & Eng. Ency. of L. 277; and "Bill to take Testimony De Bene Esse," 2 Am. & Eng. Ency. of L. 285.

4. *Admissions and Confessions.*[1]

5. *Presumptions.* — In a criminal prosecution, the presumption of innocence of defendant continues until his guilt has been established by evidence to the satisfaction of the jury, and beyond a reasonable doubt, which means, convinced to a moral certainty.[2] The presumption of innocence continues until guilt is established by evidence.[3]

The principle is recognized in criminal jurisprudence, that proof of certain facts may lead irresistibly to the presumption that another act, of which there is no direct proof, was committed or done.[4]

Soundness of mind is presumed; but, if the jury entertain a reasonable doubt as to the sanity of the accused, they should acquit.[5]

6. *Judicial Notice.* — The *corpus delicti* must be proven. The court will not take judicial notice that certain places are within the county or jurisdiction of the court.[6]

7. *Weight of the Evidence.* — It is the province of the jury in a criminal case to pass upon the weight of evidence and credibility of witnesses, and to render such a verdict as their own judgment and consciences affirm.[7]

Where it is not claimed that there is an absolute failure of evidence, on any material point, to sustain a verdict, and it has been approved by the trial court, the supreme court cannot disturb the verdict, even in a criminal case, upon the weight or sufficiency of the evidence.[8]

1. See "Confessions," 3 Am. & Eng. Ency. of L. 349.

2. State *v.* Johnson, 91 Mo. 439; s. c., 8 West. Rep. 711.

The court should instruct the jury that innocence is presumed until overcome by evidence convincing beyond a reasonable doubt that accused is guilty. People *v.* De Fore (Mich.), 7 West. Rep. 886.

3. State *v.* Johnson, 91 Mo. 439; s. c., 8 West. Rep. 711.

The Presumption is first in Favor of Innocence, and then of the lesser crimes in their order, of which the respondent may be convicted under the indictment; and the prisoner is entitled to the benefit of any reasonable doubt which the jury may have as to the degree of murder. State *v.* Meyer, 58 Vt. 457; s. c., 2 New Eng. Rep. 209.

4. Roberts *v.* People, 9 Colo. 458.

5. Dacy *v.* People, 116 Ill. 555; s. c., 4 West. Rep. 180.

Soundness of mind is presumed to continue. State *v.* Brown (Del.), Houst. Cr. Rep. 539.

But where insanity once exists, it is presumed to continue. However, this is not the rule in Texas. Leache *v.* State, 22 Tex. App. 279.

6. **Judicial Notice.** — Thus, the court will not, in a criminal case, take judicial notice that certain streets referred to by the witnesses are in the city of Chicago or elsewhere in Cook County, although there are streets of the same names in that city. Dougherty *v.* People, 118 Ill. 160; s. c, 6 West. Rep. 96. However, in a later case the same court say that, Where it is proved that the offence was committed "on Emerson Avenue," and that such avenue is a street in Chicago, the proof that the crime was committed in Cook County is sufficient. Sullivan *v.* People, 123 Ill. ; s. c., 11 West. Rep. 566.

7. Baysinger *v.* People, 115 Ill. 419, s. c., 2 West. Rep. 839; State *v.* Anderson, 89 Mo. 312; s. c., 5 West. Rep. 420; State *v.* Falconer, 76 Iowa, 416; State *v.* McDevitt, 69 Iowa, 549; State *v.* Hicks, 92 Mo. 431; s. c., 10 West. Rep. 415; State *v.* Gee, 85 Mo. 647; State *v.* Wisdom, 84 Mo. 190; State *v.* McGinnis, 76 Mo. 328; State *v.* Jones, 86 Mo. 623; s. c., 1 West. Rep. 747.

The Issuance by a Trial Judge of a Bench Warrant to detain a witness that has just testified, is not a violation of the statute forbidding the judge to express any opinion as to what facts have been proved. State *v.* Strade, 38 La. An. 562.

8. Garrett *v.* State, 109 Ind. 527; s. c.,

Although the evidence is weak and unsatisfactory, yet where there was not a failure of evidence, judgment will not be reversed.[1] And if there is evidence in some degree tending to sustain the material averments in the indictment, the court should not reverse, although apprehensive that the jury may have been mistaken in their conclusion.[2]

8. *Credibility of Witnesses.* — It is the peculiar province of a jury to pass upon the credibility of witnesses; and, where there is a conflict in the evidence, the fact that the testimony of a witness interested in the result may be rejected or disbelieved by the jury, forms no ground to disturb the judgment.[3]

9. *Sufficiency of the Evidence.* — Where evidence has been given which directly tends to support the allegations of the indictment, the jury are authorized to convict.[4]

8 West. Rep. 391; Hudson *v.* State, 107 Ind. 372; s. c., 5 West. Rep. 628; Clayton *v.* State, 100 Ind. 201; Padgett *v.* State, 103 Ind. 550; s. c., 1 West. Rep. 584; Kleespies *v.* State, 106 Ind. 383; s. c., 4 West. Rep. 717; Skaggs *v.* State, 108 Ind. 53; s. c., 6 West. Rep. 261; State *v.* Williams, 38 La. An. 371; Ledbetter *v.* State, 21 Tex. App. 344; and Dos *v.* State, 21 Tex. App. 505.

The Weight of the Evidence and the Credit to be given to the Testimony of the complaining witness are questions exclusively for the jury; and it was error for the court to charge the jury that they should consider the facts testified to by the complaining witness as established, simply because she had testified to them, and had not been contradicted. People *v.* De Fore (Mich.), 7 West. Rep. 886.

The Accuracy of the Interpretation of the sworn interpreter may be impeached, and is ultimately to be determined by the jury. Skaggs *v.* State, 108 Ind. 53; s. c., 6 West. Rep. 261.

1. Padgett *v.* State, 103 Ind. 550; s. c., 1 West. Rep. 584.

2. Anderson *v.* State, 104 Ind. 467; s. c., 2 West. Rep. 341.

3. Aholtz *v.* People (Ill.), 11 West. Rep. 391; McMahon *v.* People, 120 Ill. 581; s. c., 9 West. Rep. 520; Commonwealth *v.* Moore (Mass.), 5 New Eng. Rep. 301.

The Court has no Authority to say to the jury that certain allegations are uncontradicted, and therefore may be considered as proved. The credibility of the witnesses must be submitted to the jury. Heldt *v.* State, 20 Neb. 493.

And it is not error to refuse, in an action for illegal sale of intoxicating liquors, to charge that testimony of "spotters" or informers, employed to procure sales and bring prosecutions, is to be received with great caution and distrust. State *v.* Hoxsie (R. I.), 1 New Eng. Rep. 29.

Credibility of Accomplices. — It is not for the court to determine the credibility of the accomplice; and the court cannot, as matter of law, advise the jury that they must acquit the respondent by reason of lack of credibility of the accomplice when his testimony is not corroborated by other evidence. State *v.* Potter, 42 Vt. 495; Lindsay *v.* People, 63 N. Y. 143; Roscoe, Cr. Ev. 143; Rex *v.* Jones, 2 Camp. 131; Rex *v.* Hastings, 7 Carr. & P. 152; Jordaine *v.* Lashbrooke, 7 T. R. 601; Rex *v.* Atwood, 1 Leach, C. C. 464; State *v.* Dana (Vt.), 5 New Eng. Rep. 108; 1 Greenl. Ev. § 380.

Fits of Madness. — Where a person is in a state of mind in which he is liable to fits of madness, it is for the jury to consider whether the act was done during such a fit. Reg. *v.* Richards, 1 Fost. & F. 87.

4. Commonwealth *v.* Wood (Mass.), 3 New Eng. Rep. 94.

In Forgery. — Where it is shown, by the one whose name was signed to the check, that he never signed it; and by another witness that on the day of its date the defendant uttered the check in his store in the city, by passing it to him in payment for goods; and by another witness that he saw the defendant go into the bank upon which it was drawn with the check, — a demurrer to the evidence was properly overruled. State *v.* Rucker (Mo.), 11 West. Rep. 457. The possession of a forged instrument, or the uttering of it by one in the county where the indictment is found, is strong evidence that the forgery of the instrument was committed by him in the same county. State *v.* Yerger, 86 Mo. 33; State *v.* Rucker (Mo.), 11 West. Rep. 457.

"Winning Money." — Evidence in a prosecution by indictment brought against defendant for winning money at a game of pool, that defendant and another played at the game, and that the party with whom defendant played lost the game and paid for it, is insufficient to sustain a verdict find-

In order to convict upon circumstantial evidence, the circumstances should be strong, and the result of the whole leave no doubt that the offence has been committed, and that accused, and no other, could have committed it.[1]

10. *Of Intent.* — Evidence of intent is essential[2] in all prosecutions for crime.[3]

ing defendant guilty of winning money. Clark *v.* Middaugh, 103 Ind. 78; s. c., 1 West. Rep. 137.

Delirium Tremens. — Evidence which rather tends to show wilful excesses, causing fits of delirium tremens, but not showing that the prisoner was laboring under such a fit at the time of the act, is insufficient to establish the defence. Reg. *v.* Leigh, 4 Fost. & F. 915.

In Insanity. — Evidence that the act was sudden without apparent motive, and that the prisoner had been addicted to drink, and had been suffering under depression, was not enough to raise the defence of insanity. Reg. *v.* Dixon, 11 Cox, C. C. 341.

It was no Error for the Court to refuse to rule upon the Government's Evidence if the defendant intended to introduce other evidence; and no exception lies to the refusal to rule that the evidence of the government was insufficient, if other evidence was afterwards introduced by the defendant. Commonwealth *v.* Chadwick, 142 Mass. 595; s. c., 3 New Eng. Rep. 126.

1. People *v.* Foley (Mich.), 7 West. Rep. 344.

2. **When Intent not Essential.** — Where an act in general terms is made indictable, a criminal intent need not be shown, unless, from the language or effect of the law, a purpose to require the existence of such an intent can be discovered. Halstead *v.* State, 41 N. J. L. ( ) 552; s. c., 10 Cent. L. J. 290.

3. *Vide* tit. "Intent," this series.

Where it does not appear that the injury was wanton or excessive punishment, or if it was done under the belief that the defendant had a right to commit it, and not from malice against the owner, it has been *held* that the offence was not committed. Rex *v.* Pierce, 2 East, P. C. 1072; State *v.* Robinson, 3 Dev. & Bat. (S. C.) 130; State *v.* Newby, 64 N. C. 23; Hill *v.* State, 43 Ala. 335; Hobson *v.* State, 44 Ala. 381; State *v.* Wilcox, 3 Yerg. (Tenn.) 278; Goforth *v.* State, 8 Humph. (Tenn.) 37; State *v.* Enslow, 10 Iowa, 115.

It is a general law governing the law of malice, that, when a man commits an act unaccompanied by any circumstances justifying its commission, the law presumes that he has acted advisedly and with an intent to produce the consequences which have ensued. People *v.* Petheram (Mich.), 7 West. Rep. 596.

To maintain a presumption of an evil intent, some concurring act must have followed the unlawful thought. If a party abandoned his evil intent any time before so much of an act is done as constitutes a crime, such abandonment takes from what has been done its indictable quality. Stephens *v.* State (Ind.), 5 West. Rep. 260.

Acts Malum Prohibitum. — When a statute makes indictable an act which is merely *malum prohibitum*, when done "wilfully and maliciously," the existence of an evil mind in doing the forbidden act is, as a general rule, a constituent part of the offence. Folwell *v.* State, 29 N. J. L. (20 Vr.) 31; s. c., 5 Cent. Rep. 353.

Where the defendant was indicted under the act (N. J. Rev. Stat. 229, 15) prohibiting the wilfully and maliciously tearing down of a sheriff's advertisement, it was *held* that he had the right to show that he tore down such paper without any evil design. Folwell *v.* State, 49 N. J. L. (20 Vr.) 31; s. c., 5 Cent. Rep. 353.

Assault and Battery. — Under an indictment for assault and battery, with intent to commit felony, the State need not prove the intent by positive testimony: it is sufficient that evidence will satisfy triers beyond a reasonable doubt. Padgett *v.* State, 103 Ind. 550; s. c., 1 West. Rep. 584.

In a Charge of Assault and Battery with Intent to murder, evidence that deceased attacked the defendant being first introduced, proof of previous threats by him is admissible upon the ground that such threats may tend to illustrate the character of the attack made, although never communicated to the defendant; and the discovery of evidence of such threats after conviction of the defendant is a ground for granting a new trial. Leverich *v.* State, 105 Ind. 277; s. c., 3 West. Rep. 314.

Attempts. — Upon the trial of an indictment for attempting to procure a miscarriage and abortion by furnishing a pregnant woman with medicines for that purpose, any declarations or acts of the defendant, either before or after the particular act mentioned in the indictment, tending to show his intention and purpose to procure such abortion, are admissible. Lamb *v.* State (Md.), 5 Cent. Rep. 747.

That the defendant made a subsequent attempt to accomplish the same purpose by different means, is admissible, to show with what purpose and intent he made the

Felonious purpose or intent is seldom established by direct evidence, but circumstantial evidence is mainly relied upon; yet where the evidence is of such a character, it is never deemed to

attempt charged in the indictment, as well as to corroborate the evidence of the first attempt. Lamb *v.* State (Md.), 5 Cent. Rep. 747. *Vide ante*, 650; tit. "Criminal Law," III. "Attempts."

False Pretences: Intent to defraud. — As in other cases, the intent is generally to be gathered from the facts of the case. It is sufficient to allege in the indictment, and to prove at the trial, an intent to defraud generally, without alleging or proving an intent to defraud any particular person.

Evidence of other Pretences. — It has been *held* that to support the evidence of intent to defraud, proof that the defendant has *subsequently* obtained other property from some other person by the same pretence is not admissible, — R. *v.* Holt, 30 L. J. M. C. 11, — but that evidence of similar false pretence on a *prior* occasion is admissible. R. *v.* Francis, L. R. 2 C. C. R. 128; 43 L. J. M. C. 97.

Forgery: Intent to defraud. — It is not necessary to prove an intent to defraud any particular person: it will suffice to prove generally an intent to defraud. So it need not appear that the prisoner had any intention ultimately to defraud the person whose signature he had forged, he having defrauded the person to whom he uttered the instrument. R. *v.* Trenfield, 1 Fost. & H. 43. And it is not necessary that any person should be actually defrauded, or that any person should be in a situation to be defrauded by the act. R. *v.* Nash, 21 L. J. M. C. 147.

In a prosecution for forgery of a promissory note, where intent is an element of the offence, evidence may be introduced to show that the defendant was affected with dipsomania; that from protracted habits of intemperance his mind had become impaired; that when he was under the influence of liquor he was insane, did not know what he was doing, could not distinguish right from wrong, and that he was in such a state when he committed the act complained of. People *v.* Blake (Col.), May 27, '84; 3 W. C. Rep. 38; 1 Am. L. J. 162, 4 Pac. Rep. 1.

Intent to injure or defraud. — When it is necessary to allege this, there is no need to allege an intent to injure or defraud any particular person.

When a person wilfully sets fire to the house of another, the intent to injure that person is inferred from the act. But if the setting fire is the result of accident, though the accused be engaged in the commission of some other felony, there can be no intent to defraud. Harris, Cr. L. 277.

The exposing of oleomargarine unmarked, with other pure butter, or groceries, upon the shelves or counter of a salesroom, is an act from which an intent to sell may be inferred in the absence of rebutting evidence. State *v.* Dunbar, 13 Oreg. 591.

Intoxication. — Evidence of intoxication may be admitted where offence charged embraces deliberation, premeditation, or specific intent. Cline *v.* State, 43 Ohio St. 332; s. c., 1 West. Rep. 81. *Vide ante*, "Criminal Law," "Intoxication as a Defence to Crime."

Larceny: Intent permanently to deprive the Owner of his Property: The Animus Furandi. — The felonious intent is an essential constituent of larceny, and therefore are excepted from criminal liability those who are merely trespassers. Thus, if I take my neighbor's horse out of his stables, and ride it in open day for a few miles, where I am well known, there would be a mere trespass, and no ground for a charge of larceny, however much I may be at enmity with my neighbor. So, also, are exempted those who take goods under a *bona fide* claim of right, however unfounded that claim may be; as if under color of arrears of rent, although none is actually due, I distrain or seize my tenant's cattle: this may be a trespass, but is no felony. Harris, Cr. L. 216.

In Homicide. — On an indictment for murder where the death was caused by a pistol-shot which pierced the *medulla oblongata*, and where it became important to determine the effect of the shot in order to ascertain whether a pistol had been placed near the body of the deceased to suggest that the killing was committed in self-defence, the evidence of a physician, that, after the *medulla oblongata* was struck by the bullet, the deceased would have neither volition nor consciousness, was competent. King *v.* Commonwealth (Pa.), 6 Cent. Rep. 806.

It was *held* in Fouts *v.* State, 8 Ohio St. 98, and affirmed in subsequent cases, that the intent to kill is essential, and that an indictment for murder is bad on demurrer, which omits to charge such intent.

Permitting the appellant to state that his intention in firing a gun, which was the assault charged, was to frighten the trespasser from his premises, and that he did not intend to kill when he shot at him, sufficiently explained the motive of the shooting, and was inconsistent with any theory of self-defence. Rauck *v.* State, 110 Ind. 384; s. c., 9 West. Rep. 197.

impair or impeach the validity of the proof.[1] Evidence in reference to similar transactions of the same general character is admissible to show criminal intent.[2]

11. *Of Alibi.* — Alibi, like every other defence not arising out of the *res gestæ*, must be proved by a preponderance of evidence.[3]

12. *Of Attempts to escape.* — An attempt to escape from custody is a circumstance to be considered in connection with other evidence to determine the question of intent.[4]

Evidence of the flight of the accused after the return of indictment against him, and of his effort to obtain false testimony to be used on his trial, is always admissible for the State, and especially when the inculpatory evidence is circumstantial.[5]

13. *Of Attempts to procure False Testimony.* — Fabrication of false and contradictory accounts by a criminal for the purpose of diverting inquiry, or casting off suspicion, is always a circumstance indicatory of guilt.[6] And testimony is admissible on behalf of the prosecution to show that the accused, after the commission of the crime charged against him, attempted to manufacture testimony in his own defence, or to destroy testimony tending to prove his guilt.[7]

1. Archer *v.* State, 106 Ind. 426; s. c., 4 West Rep. 726, 728.

2. Commonwealth *v.* Sawtelle, 141 Mass. 590; s. c., 1 New Eng. Rep. 590; Thomas *v.* State, 103 Ind. 419; s. c., 1 West. Rep. 309, 314.

3. *Vide* tit. "Alibi," 1 Am. & Eng. Encyc. of L. 454. In California, — People *v.* Lee Sare, June, 1887, — Georgia, — Ledford *v* State, 75 Ga. 856; Bryan *v.* State, 74 Ga. 393, — Iowa, — State *v.* Sutton, 7 Iowa, 268; State *v.* Rivers, 68 Iowa, 611, — Maine, — State *v.* Fenlason, 78 Me. 495; s. c., 3 New Eng. Rep. 273, — and Missouri, — State *v.* Johnson, 91 Mo. 439; s. c., 8 West. Rep. 711; State *v.* Rockett, 87 Mo. 666; s. c., 3 West. Rep. 249, — it is *held* that the burden of proof rests on the defendant to establish an alibi by a preponderance of evidence. But in Illinois — Hoge *v.* People, 117 Ill. 35; s. c., 4 West. Rep. 197 — and in Texas, — Ayres *v.* State, 21 Tex. App. 399. — it is *held* that the burden of proof does not rest upon the defendant to establish an alibi by a preponderance of evidence. An alibi merely traverses the issue tendered by the indictment, and is sufficient to raise a reasonable doubt of guilt. Ledford *v.* State, 75 Ga. 856; State *v.* Rockett, 87 Mo. 666; s. c., 3 West. Rep. 249.

In Texas, wherever alibi is the only ground of defence, upon request the court is bound to give a special instruction. Ayres *v.* State, 21 Tex. App. 399. It seems that in Georgia and Maine the evidence of alibi should show that the defendant was so far from the scene of action as to render it impossible that he should have participated. Bryan *v.* State, 74 Ga. 393; State *v.* Fenlason, 78 Me. 495; s. c., 3 New Eng. Rep. 273. See Stewart *v.* People, 42 Mich. 255.

4. Anderson *v.* State, 104 Ind. 467; s. c., 2 West. Rep. 341; State *v.* Griffin, 87 Mo. 608; s. c., 3 West. Rep. 820; Hart *v.* State, 22 Tex. App. 563.

5. Williams *v.* State, 22 Tex. App. 497.

Threats of Lynching. — Where evidence has been given tending to show that defendant, after his arrest, fled, and forfeited his bail, *held*, that the court properly excluded evidence of threats to lynch defendant, where there was nothing to show that the flight was soon enough after his knowledge of the threats, to indicate that he fled on that account. State *v.* McDevitt, 69 Iowa, 549.

Until the State introduces evidence showing that defendant had gone away under circumstances indicating a purpose to avoid arrest, evidence of his purpose in leaving is immaterial. Welch *v.* State, 104 Ind. 347; s. c., 2 West. Rep. 228.

6. McKeen *v.* Commonwealth (Pa.), 5 Cent. Rep. 890.

7. Cover *v.* Commonwealth (Pa.), 6 Cent. Rep. 585.

Evidence of the Flight of the Accused after the return of indictment against him, and of his effort to obtain false testimony to be used on his trial, is always admissible for the State, and especially when the in-

It is immaterial that the theory of defence was manufactured by another, if adopted by the defendant, and his evidence failed to establish it.[1]

14. *Of Character and Reputation.* — Evidence of good character must be considered by the jury in all cases.[2] A defendant in a criminal case may prove not only his general good reputation in the community, but also his good character as a fact within the knowledge of the witness.[3]

culpatory evidence is circumstantial. Williams *v.* State, 22 Tex. App. 497.

If a Party attempts to practise a Fraud on the Court, by procuring, or assisting to procure, testimony which he knows to be false, this is a circumstance which the jury may properly consider to his disadvantage; but, to justify a charge invoking this principle, there must be evidence tending to show such procurement of false testimony, and mere conflict of testimony as to some of the facts of the case is insufficient. State *v.* Vance, 80 Ala. 356; Beck *v.* State, 80 Ala. 1.

Attempt to manufacture Evidence. — Upon the trial of one indicted for a crime, testimony is admissible on behalf of the Commonwealth to show that the accused, after the commission of the crime charged against him, attempted to manufacture testimony in his own defence, or to destroy testimony tending to prove his guilt. Cover *v.* Commonwealth (Pa. St.); s. c., 6 Cent. Rep. 585.

Attempt to corrupt Witnesses. — Especially is it admissible to prove an attempt by the defendant to corrupt or intimidate the prosecution's witnesses. Cover *v.* Commonwealth (Pa. St.); s. c., 6 Cent. Rep. 585.

Attempt to destroy Evidence. — Upon the trial of one indicted for a crime, testimony may be introduced to show that the accused attempted to destroy testimony tending to prove his guilt. Cover *v.* Commonwealth (Pa. St.); s. c., 6 Cent. Rep. 585.

The Court charged the Jury, "If any testimony has been introduced by the defendant, upon which he relies, that is false, and you believe it is sworn to with his knowledge and consent, that is, of itself, an incriminating circumstance, and would be an admission of the truth of all that had been stated by the witnesses who say to the contrary, and whom you believe to be credible in themselves." *Held*, that the proposition above stated is sustained by no principle of law, and takes away the right of the jury to weigh the testimony. Boyd *v.* State, 16 Lea (Tenn.), 149.

1. Pilger *v.* Commonwealth, 112 Pa. St. 220; s. c., 2 Cent. Rep. 835.

2. People *v.* Clements, 42 Hun (N. Y.), 353; People *v.* Wileman, 44 Hun (N. Y.), 187.

Proof of Good Character, by the rules of evidence, is limited to general reputation for honesty, and more is matter of favor, and not of right. State *v.* Emery, 59 Vt. 84; s. c., 3 New Eng. Rep. 377.

3. State *v.* Sterrett, 68 Iowa, 76; State *v.* Cross, 68 Iowa, 180.

Good character is to be considered, but the judge could not charge that it is strong presumption of innocence. State *v.* Tarrant, 24 S. C. 593.

It frequently occurs that witnesses, after speaking of the general opinion of the prisoner's character, state their personal experience and opinion of his honesty; and when this statement is admitted, it is rather from favor to the prisoner than strictly as evidence of his general character. State *v.* Emery, 59 Vt. 84; s. c., 3 New Eng. Rep. 377, 379.

Weight of Evidence of Good Character is for the jury to determine: the old rule, that only in cases of doubt, such evidence is considered, is now the law. Commonwealth *v.* Leonard, 140 Mass. 473; s. c., 1 New Eng. Rep. 370.

In an Action for Damages for Assault and Battery, the reputation of a defendant as a peaceable citizen is not in issue, and testimony as to his good reputation is not admissible. It is only where the proceedings are such as to put the character of parties in issue, that a different rule prevails. Fahey *v.* Crotty (Mich.), 6 West. Rep. 135.

In Missouri. — Under the rulings in this State, a witness may be impeached, not only by a general reputation as to veracity, but the inquiry may extend to the general moral character or reputation of the witness. State *v.* Grant, 79 Mo. 113; State *v.* Miller (Mo.), 12 West. Rep. 97.

General Reputation. — It was error to admit testimony offered by the State respecting the general reputation of one of defendant's witnesses, without the State having first laid the proper foundation. State *v.* Brady, 87 Mo. 142; s. c., 2 West. Rep 131.

While a statute making a reputation evidence of guilt is unconstitutional, a statute (R. I. Pub. Stat. chap. 80, § 3) making the reputation of premises admissible in evidence to prove sale of liquors, but leaving

Upon the trial of an indictment, evidence of the defendant's good character is a substantive fact, and must be treated as such. It is not a mere make-weight to be thrown in to determine the balance in a doubtful case.[1] And in a case of homicide, the defendant may show the character and reputation of the deceased.[2]

15. *Of Declarations as of Res Gestæ.* — Those declarations which are a part of the *res gestæ* will be competent evidence in a prosecution for the crime.[3] But statements by a defendant to a crimi-

the jury free to find the accused guilty or not, is not unconstitutional. State *v.* Wilson (R. I.), 1 New Eng. Rep. 888.

A statement in the charge to the jury, that evidence of good character is admitted in criminal cases for the purpose of leading the jury to believe that the accused is not likely to have committed the crime, but where the facts constituting the crime are clearly proved, such evidence can have little or no effect, is *held* not to have been error where, taking the whole charge together, the jury were, in effect, told that the case was not one where the facts constituting the crime were clearly proved so as to render evidence of good character of little or no effect, but one where the testimony was contradictory, and hence such evidence should be considered in connection with all the other evidence, and that if they had any reasonable doubt of the defendant's guilt, upon all the facts of the case, including his good character, then he should be acquitted. State *v.* Leppere, 66 Wis. 355.

1. Heine *v.* Commonwealth, 91 Pa. St. 145; Hanney *v.* Commonwealth (Pa.), 8 Cent. Rep. 184.

On the trial, a witness was asked to state the general reputation of the defendant for peace and quietness in the county, so far as he knew. The witness had not stated that he lived in the county, or knew the general reputation of the defendant therein. The court excluded the evidence. *Held*, that the ruling of the court was proper. People *v.* Rodrigo, 69 Cal. 601.

It is error to charge the jury in a prosecution for a conspiracy to the effect that evidence of good character is available only in a doubtful case. The law gives to such evidence a positive defensive force, and it is for the jury to assign its value upon a comparison of all the facts and circumstances which envelop the transaction. United States *v.* Grunnell (D. C.), 3 Cent. Rep. 764.

2. **In Homicide.** — After evidence has been given by a defendant, tending to show that the homicide was committed in self-defence, he may follow it by proof of the general reputation of the deceased for quarrelsomeness and violence; but evidence of specific acts of violence towards third persons is inadmissible.

When the voluntary confession of a defendant is otherwise admissible against him on trial for the crime, it is immaterial that he was under arrest when the confession was made. People *v.* Druse, 103 N. Y. 655; s. c., 4 Cent. Rep. 770.

3. **Nature of Act.** — When it is necessary, on the trial of a cause, to inquire into the nature of a particular act, or the intention of the person who did the act, proof of what the person said at the time of doing the act is admissible in evidence as part of the *res gestæ* for the purpose of showing its true character: but, to render such declarations competent, the act with which it is connected should be pertinent to the issue; for, when the act is *per se* incompetent, the union of the two will not render the declaration admissible. Brumley *v.* State, 21 Tex. App. 222.

Declarations regarding the Act. — If the defendants in a prosecution under an indictment for murder have said any thing in relation thereto, the jury should consider it all together; what they said against themselves, the law presumes to be true; but what they said for themselves, the jury are not bound to believe, but may believe or disbelieve as it may be shown to be true or false; and statements and admissions are only binding upon the party making the same. State *v.* Anderson, 89 Mo. 312; s. c., 5 West. Rep. 420.

What a Defendant has said against himself after the act of killing, the law presumes to be true; but his statements favorable to himself, in any different conversation, not proved by the State, are to be disregarded. State *v.* Hicks, 92 Mo. 431; s. c., 10 West. Rep. 415; State *v.* Bryant, 55 Mo. 77; State *v.* Evans, 65 Mo. 579; State *v.* Christian, 66 Mo. 138.

Such Evidence should be limited to the identification of the prisoner and the deceased, and to the act of killing and circumstances forming part of the *res gestæ*. State *v.* Chambers, 87 Mo. 406; s. c., 2 West. Rep. 453.

The Quo Animo and all actions and words whereby that is demonstrated, form part of the *res gestæ*, and thus become admissible.

nal prosecution, which are no part of the *res gestæ*, but which are

Garber *v.* State, 4 Coldw. (Tenn.) 161, and cases cited; State *v.* Gabriel, 88 Mo. 631; s. c., 5 West. Rep. 340.

Surrounding Circumstances. — "Human affairs consist of a complication of circumstances so intimately interwoven as to be hardly separable from each other. Each owes its birth to some preceding circumstances, and in its turn becomes the prolific parent of others, and each during its existence has its inseparable attributes and its kindred facts materially affecting its character, and essential to be known, in order to a right understanding of its nature. These surrounding circumstances, constituting parts of the *res gestæ*, may always be shown to the jury along with the principal fact, and their admissibility is determined by the judge in the exercise of a sound judicial discretion." 1 Greenl. Ev. 138.

Declarations of a Third Party are the natural and inartificial concomitants of an act done by him, and are explanatory of such act, and such act is part of the *res gestæ*: such declarations are not hearsay, and are therefore admissible. Hunter *v.* State, 40 N. J. L. (11 Vr.) 495; State *v.* Hayden, 9 Rep. 237; State *v.* Gabriel, 88 Mo. 631; s. c., 5 West. Rep. 340.

Declarations of a third person are not admissible as tending to prove the commission of the crime by him, in defence of the accused on trial therefor, when not part of the *res gestæ*, nor definite and specific in relation to the crime. State *v.* Beaudet, 53 Conn. 536; s. c., 1 New Eng. Rep. 833.

The only Plausible Ground for the Admission is, that, as the accused might exculpate himself by showing that another was the guilty party, so any item of evidence which would have been admissible had such other person been on trial should be received in his favor. We concede the premises, but not the conclusion; for, under the rules of evidence, it makes a vast difference whether declarations offered in evidence come from the party on trial or not. In the one case they are universally admitted, unless irrelevant or self-serving. In the other, they are by general rule excluded, subject to a few well-marked exceptions. In 2 Best on Evidence, § 506, under the head of "*Res inter alios acta*," it is said, "No person is to be affected by the words or acts of others, unless he is connected with them, either personally, or by those whom he represents, or by whom he is represented."

In Texas. — Article 751 of the Texas Code of Crim. Proc. reads as follows: "When part of an act, declaration, conversation, or writing is given in evidence by one party, the whole on the same subject may be inquired into by the other; as when a letter is read, all other letters on the same subject between the same parties may be given. And when a detailed act, declaration, conversation, or writing is given in evidence, any other act, declaration, or writing which is necessary to make it fully understood, or to explain the same, may also be given in evidence." That portion of the written testimony of the deceased witness, M., read by the State in this case, related solely to the prosecution of the defendant and his co-defendants. That part proposed to be read by the defence related solely to a prosecution against the deceased. *Held*, that the portion of the testimony offered to be read by the defence had no relation whatever to that portion read by the State, was not necessary to explain the portion read, was clearly inadmissible under the provisions of said article. Kunde *v.* State, 22 Tex. App. 65.

Declarations of the Defendant's Father in Relation to the Stolen Article, made in the presence of the defendant, and acquiesced in by him, are admissible in evidence against him. Clement *v.* State, 22 Tex. App. 23. Confessions made by one of the defendants, both while drunk and while sober, being in evidence before the jury, and being inconsistent with each other, a charge asked, instructing the jury to believe the latter in preference to the former, is properly refused. Finch *v.* State, 81 Ala. 41.

Confessions or Declarations of One Conspirator, made after the consummation of the conspiracy, and not in the presence of his co-conspirator, cannot be used in evidence against the latter. Willey *v.* State, 22 Tex. App. 408. *Vide ante*, "Criminal Conspiracy," VI. 3, p. 582.

Declarations by Co-Defendant. — Statements made to a witness by a co-defendant, at a time when the defendant was under arrest for the crime, are evidence against such co-defendant, and are properly admitted on the trial of the two defendants together. Smith *v.* People, 115 Ill. 615; s. c., 1 West. Rep. 615.

In Rape. — On the trial of an indictment for rape, it is competent to prove, on the examination in chief, that the party alleged to have been injured made complaint while the injury was recent; but the details and circumstances of the transaction cannot be proved on such examination by her declarations. Parker *v.* State (Md.), 9 Cent. Rep. 87.

Such declarations are not admissible as evidence in chief to prove the commission of the offence, but only to corroborate the testimony of the injured person given in in the nature of self-serving declarations, open to the suspicion of court. Dunn *v.* State, 45 Ohio, St. ; s. c., 10 West. Rep. 493.

Thus, D., over seventeen years of age, was indicted for carnally knowing and abusing C., a female child under ten years of age, with her consent, on the 20th day of December, 1886. On the evening of that day, and on the next succeeding day, C. made complaint to her mother of the alleged injury. After a delay until the 30th day of December, 1886, C., in response to inquiries by her mother, made a statement to her in detail of the particulars of the offence. The statement was admitted in evidence on the trial of the accused, but the delay in making it to the mother was not explained and excused by proof of sufficient cause therefor. *Held*, that it was error to permit such statement to be given in evidence to the jury. Dunn *v.* State, 45 Ohio St. ; s. c., 10 West. Rep. 493.

Carnally knowing a Female Child. — On the trial of one indicted under Rev. Stat. § 6816, for carnally knowing and abusing a female child under ten years of age, with her consent, the declarations made by the injured person, in reference to the offence, several days after its perpetration, are not admissible in evidence to the jury, unless the delay in making such declarations is first explained and excused by proof of sufficient cause therefor. Dunn *v.* State, 45 Ohio St. ; s. c., 10 West. Rep. 493.

In a case of rape, when the person upon whom the offence is charged to have been committed has not been examined as a witness, no evidence of her assertions or declarations descriptive of the offence or offender should be received except when made *in extremis*. They are merely hearsay, and are not competent as evidence in chief to prove the commission of the offence. If, however, the injured person has been sworn and has testified, her declarations in relation to the injury, made immediately after it was inflicted, would be competent in corroboration of her statements made in court. Her credibility would be strengthened or weakened as it would be found to be in accordance with, or contradictory to, the statements and disclosures which she would naturally make immediately after an outrage upon her person, — disclosures which she would instinctively shrink from if not true. Dunn *v.* State, 45 Ohio St. ; s. c., 10 West. Rep. 493.

Evidence of Declarations. — In England, and in several American jurisdictions, evidence of the declarations of the injured person has been limited to the mere fact that a complaint was made, and the bare nature of it Thus, the rule is laid down in New York, that, on the trial of an indictment for rape, although proof of the fact that the prosecutrix made complaint recently after the commission of the offence is competent, yet evidence of the particulars of such complaint is inadmissible on behalf of the prosecution. Roscoe, Cr. Ev. 26; 1 Russ. Cr. 923; Baccio *v.* People, 41 N. Y. 265. But in Ohio the prosecution is permitted to give the substance of what the prosecutrix stated immediately after the event. In McCombs *v.* State, 8 Ohio St. 643, the court says, "Whatever may be the rule elsewhere, it is settled in Ohio, that in a prosecution for rape, the substance of what the prosecutrix said immediately after the offence was committed may be given in evidence in the first instance to corroborate her testimony." And in Burt *v.* State, 23 Ohio St. 394, — in which it was *held*, that, in giving in evidence the declarations of the prosecutrix made immediately after the alleged transaction in corroboration of her testimony, it is competent to show that in and by such declarations she charged the crime upon the defendant, — *Welsh, J.*, says, "How far the prosecution shall be permitted to go into details in giving the declarations of the female, must, to a great extent at least, be left to the discretion of the court." See also Johnson *v.* State, 17 Ohio, 593; Laughlin *v.* State, 18 Ohio, 99; Hornbeck *v.* State, 35 Ohio St. 277; Brown *v.* People, 36 Mich. 204, in which Burt *v.* State, 23 Ohio St. 394, is followed.

Time of making Declarations. — A controlling question, however, is, How soon after the offence is committed must the female who has suffered the injury make the declarations, in order to render evidence of such declarations admissible? It is well settled in Ohio that the declarations must be made immediately. Immediateness is essential to their admissibility. Such is the language substantially of our decisions on the subject. Whether or not the declarations constitute a part of the *res gestæ*, when made immediately after the injury, they largely preclude the idea of the injured party having been practised upon to fabricate a story. They are presumed to be the natural outburst of outraged feelings, and, if made at all, would naturally be made at the first opportunity, while the injury is yet fresh and aggravating. Silence and delay in making known the wrong would be likely to awaken suspicion and doubt as to the truth of the complainant's statement If, says Blackstone, she conceals the injury for any considerable time after she has had an opportunity to complain, such a circumstance would carry a strong presumption — though not conclusive — that her testimony is false or feigned. 4 Bl. Com. 213. But being part of a hastily formed plan of defence, are not competent evidence.[1]

Declarations of a party to the offence committed, made after the crime was complete, are not part of the *res gestæ;* such as to declarations of a woman on whom an abortion had been committed.[2]

when delay by the prosecutrix in making complaint or declaring the circumstances of the wrong has occurred, such delay may be explained and excused by proof of sufficient cause therefor; as, for instance, want of suitable opportunity, or duress or threats by the perpetrator of the wrong. Higgins *v.* People, 58 N. Y. 377; State *v.* Shettleworth, 18 Minn. 208; State *v.* Knapp, 45 N. H. 148; State *v.* De Wolf, 8 Conn. 93. Yet, if there has been a want of promptness in making complaint or declaration as to the particulars of the injury after its perpetration, the court should not admit evidence of the complaint or declaration until the delay has been excused or justified. People *v.* Gage (Mich), 8 Cr. L. Mag. & Rep. 195, was a case of prosecution for rape, and the silence of the outraged party in making complaint was the direct consequence of fears of chastisement induced by threats of the defendant. "It is contended," said *Champlin, J.*, "that the testimony ought not to have been received because of the lapse of time after the outrage and the statement to the mother. The lapse of time occurring after the injury and before complaint made is not the test of admissibility of the evidence, but it may be considered as affecting its weight; and when complaint is not made promptly, the delay calls for explanation before the court will admit it."

1. Spittorff *v.* State, 108 Ind. 307; s. c., 6 West. Rep. 307.

2. People *v.* Murphy (N. Y.), 2 Cent. Rep. 107. Applied to the case of a co-conspirator. State *v.* McGraw, 87 Mo. 161; s. c., 2 West. Rep. 448; State *v.* Duncan, 64 Mo. 263.

Declarations, to be Admissible, must be concomitant with the principal act, and so connected with it as to be regarded as the mere result and consequence of co-existing motives. 2 Poth. Obl. 248; Ambrose *v.* Clendon, Hardw. 267; Doe *v.* Webber, 1 Ad. & El. 733; Boyden *v.* Moore, 28 Mass. (11 Pick.) 362; Walton *v.* Green, 1 Car. & P. 521; Reed *v.* Dick, 8 Watts (Pa.), 479; O'Kelly *v.* O'Kelly, 47 Mass. (8 Met.) 436; Stiles *v.* Western R. R. Corp., 47 Mass. (8 Pick.) 44.

Declarations of Co-Conspirators. — The same principles apply to acts and declarations of a co-conspirator, but the foundation must first be laid by proof sufficient to establish *prima facie* the fact of conspiracy between the parties. Rex *v.* Watson, 32 How. St. Tri. 7; Rex *v.* Brandreth, 32 How. St. Tr. 857; Rex *v.* Hardy, 24 How. St. Tr. 451; American Fur Co. *v.* U. S., 27 U. S. (2 Pet.) 358, 365, bk. 7, L. ed. 450, 453; Commonwealth *v.* Crowninshield, 27 Mass. (10 Pick.) 497; Nichols *v.* Dowding, 1 Stark. 81.

The points to be considered are whether the circumstances and declarations were contemporaneous with the main fact, and whether they were so connected with it as to illustrate its character. *In re* Taylor, 9 Paige, Ch. (N. Y.) 611; Carter *v.* Buchanan, 3 Ga. (3 Kelley) 513; Blood *v.* Rideout, 54 Mass. (13 Met.) 237; Boyden *v.* Burke, 55 U. S. (14 How.) 575, bk. 14, L. ed. 548.

Extra-Judicial Statements. — In Wharton's Criminal Evidence, § 225, it is said, "Extra-judicial statements of third persons cannot be proved by hearsay, unless such statements were part of the *res gestæ*, or made by deceased persons in the course of business, or as admissions against their own interest, or are material for the purpose of determining the state of mind of a party who cannot be examined in court. . . . Hence, on an indictment for murder, the admissions of other persons that they killed the deceased, or committed the crime in controversy, are not evidence; and evidence of threats by other persons are inadmissible. . . . On an indictment for larceny also, declarations of third parties that they committed the theft are inadmissible."

It was shown that the witness, by whom the defendant proposed to prove his declarations, was two hundred yards distant when the difficulty occurred; that he went to the place of the difficulty after it was over, and asked the defendant what was the matter; that the defendant told him to catch his horse first, and he would tell him; that he accordingly caught the defendant's horse, occupying about three minutes of time in doing so, when the defendant made the statement proposed to be introduced in evidence. *Held*, that the statements so made by the defendant were no part of the *res gestæ*. Bradberry *v.* State, 22 Tex. App. 273.

A Declaration accompanying and explanatory of an Act indefinite in itself is always admissible as part of the *res gestæ*. Thus, on a trial for murder, where the

How far back the prosecution shall be permitted to go, is in the discretion of the trial judge. The general rule is, that the evidence should be admitted if, under the facts, there can be a reasonable inference that the same state of mind continued to exist up to and during the particular time which is the subject of inquiry.[1]

16. *Of Threats.* — Evidence of threats, general or special, or verbal indications of a similar nature of the intended commission of a wrongful or criminal act, are admissible in both civil and criminal cases.[2] Evidence of threats, to be admissible, must be of threats directed against the person of the defendant, not against his property, or the person of another.[3]

Threats by the defendant are always admissible; and it is properly held that there is equal reason, supposing a collision between the deceased and the defendant to be first proved, for the admission of such threats by the deceased.[4]

Threats alone, unaccompanied by any overt act or outward demonstration, will not justify hostile acts towards those making the threats: the danger must be immediate.[5]

proof showed that the deceased when last seen alone was asked "whither he was going," and answered "to look for N." (the accused), *held*, that this statement was not within the rule against hearsay. U. S. *v.* Nardello, 4 Mackey (D. C.), 503; s. c., 2 Cent. Rep. 666.

Where, after the shooting, deceased went about two hundred yards and called to his wife, who went to him travelling one hundred yards, and she testified that he said either "O Hun, he has killed me!" or, "O Hun, he has shot me! Pray for me! O my children!" *held*, the testimony was not admissible as part of the *res gestæ*, or as a dying declaration. If the exclamation was, "O Hun, he has killed me!" it would, in connection with the nature of the wound and the short time which elapsed before his death, show that he was under a sense of impending death; but if the exclamation was, "He has shot me!" there is nothing to show that the statement was made under a sense of impending death. State *v.* Rider, 90 Mo. 54; s. c., 6 West. Rep. 458.

1. Commonwealth *v.* Hill (Mass.), 5 New Eng. Rep. 277.

2. Culbertson *v.* Hill, 87 Mo. 553; s. c., 2 West. Rep. 477.

Declarations of Intentions to commit a crime are no less susceptible of being false than the declarations of the opposite cast; namely, declarations of intention to abstain from the commission of that or a similar crime. State *v.* Beaudet, 53 Conn. 536; s. c., 1 New Eng. Rep. 835.

3. State *v.* Downs, 91 Mo. 19; 8 West. Rep. 241.

It is not necessary that the accused should be previously shown to be connected with the crime, to render his threats in relation thereto admissible. State *v.* May (Me.), 3 New Eng. Rep. 846.

The Exclusion of a Letter, without signature or date, conveying threats to the defendant, and offered in evidence where no injury was shown, is not ground for a new trial. Linneus City *v.* Dusky, 19 Mo. App. 20; s. c., 1 West. Rep. 321, 322, Mo. R. S. 3775.

4. As to the same subject, see also Holler *v.* State, 37 Ind. 57; Wood *v.* State, 92 Ind. 269; Boyle *v.* State, 97 Ind. 322; Campbell *v.* People, 16 Ill. 17.

Threats made by Deceased are not admissible in evidence, except under the defence of self-defence. State *v.* Clum, 90 Mo. 482; s. c., 8 West. Rep. 209. Defendant cannot introduce proof of previous threats, unless it is first shown that he was attacked or was threatened with immediate danger by the deceased. State *v.* Brooks (La. An.), June, 1887.

Where Self-Defence is sought to be established, evidence of mere threats made by the deceased is not admissible. State *v.* Clum, 90 Mo. 482; s. c., 8 West. Rep. 209.

Evidence of threats, to be admissible, must be of threats directed against the person of the defendant, not against his property or the person of another. State *v.* Downs, 91 Mo. 19; 8 West. Rep. 241.

5. State *v.* Clum, 90 Mo. 482; s. c., 8 West. Rep. 209.

Threats of Third Person. — It is, therefore, going far enough in favor of the accused, to allow him to exculpate himself by showing the fact of another's guilt, by some appropriate evidence directly connecting that person with the *corpus delicti*. The *animus* of a third person is no defence, and by itself it cannot prove the ultimate fact which is a defence. Even as to the threats of the person on trial, Wharton, in his "Criminal Evidence," 8th ed. § 756, says, They "are admissible in evidence, not because they give rise to a presumption of law as to guilt, which they do not; but because from them, in connection with other circumstances and on proof of the *corpus delicti*, guilt may be logically inferred." In 3 Bentham's Jud. Ev. 75, it is said that "Declarations of an intention to commit a crime are no less susceptible of being false than declarations of the opposite cast; namely, declarations of an intention to abstain from the commission of that or a similar crime."

In State *v.* Johnson, 30 La. An. 921, the State, in a prosecution for murder based entirely on circumstantial evidence, found it necessary to trace to the accused a motive for the homicide in a previous quarrel with the deceased, when the accused while in liquor uttered threats against the deceased; and upon cross-examination the witness for the State, who had in chief testified to the quarrelsome character of the deceased and to the threats of the accused, was asked what other quarrels the deceased had besides that with the accused, a few days prior to the murder; and the trial court excluded it. The court of review cites no authorities and enters into no discussion of the question upon principle, but simply says in effect that, although it was of doubtful admissibility, yet on the whole they will give the accused the benefit of a new trial. State *v.* Beaudet, 53 Conn. 536; s. c., 1 New Eng. Rep. 833.

The case of State *v.* Davis, 77 N. C. 483, was an indictment for murder. On the trial the prisoner proposed to prove by one Peck that George Nicks had malice towards the deceased, and had a motive to take his life, and opportunity to do so, and had threatened to do so before the court. He further offered to prove by one Rice, "that one Peck took a gun, and went in the direction of the house of the deceased some time before the deceased was killed." The court says, "Both exceptions are untenable, and have been repeatedly so held by this court; the first, because they are declarations of a third party, and are *res inter alios acta*, and have no legal tendency to establish the innocence of the prisoner; and the second for the same and additional reason that the time is too vaguely and indefinitely set forth. . . . Such evidence is inadmissible because it does not tend to establish the *corpus delicti*. Unquestionably it would have been competent to prove that a third party killed the deceased, and not the prisoner. But this could only have been done by proof connecting Peck with the fact, that is, with the perpetration of some deed entering into the crime itself. Direct evidence connecting Peck with the *corpus delicti* would have been admissible. After proof of the *res gesta* constituting Peck's alleged guilt had been given, it might be that the evidence which was offered and excluded in this case would have been competent in confirmation of the direct testimony connecting him with the fact of killing. No such direct testimony was offered here. It is unnecessary to elaborate, as the questions of evidence here made have been fully discussed and decided by this court in many cases. It is only necessary to refer to the principal ones. State *v.* Bishop, 73 N. C. 44; State *v.* May, 4 Dev. (N. C.) 328; State *v.* Duncan, 6 Ired. (N. C.) L. 236; State *v.* White, 68 N. C. 158."

These cases are all pertinent, and supported by similar and some additional reasons. We will not take the time and space necessary for a particular statement of the evidence offered, and the reasoning of the court sustaining its exclusion. To the above list we will add the case of State *v.* Haynes, 71 N. C. 79.

In Crookham *v.* State, 5 W. Va. 510, it was *held* that it was no error to exclude testimony offered by the prisoner, to the effect that another and a different person from himself had made threats to kill the deceased, just before the commission of the offence with which he was charged, and that immediately after the offence such other person left the country, and has not since been heard from.

In Boothe *v.* State, 4 Tex. App. 202, and in Walker *v.* State, 6 Tex. App. 576, both being indictments for murder, it was *held* not competent for the accused to prove that a very short time before the homicide a person other than the accused made threats to take the life of the deceased. In the last case the court supported the ruling by saying, "The issue of the trial was the guilt or innocence of the defendant on trial. Evidence is admissible if it tends to prove the issue, or constitutes a link, in the chain of proof; and this seems to be the limit, and excludes all evidence of collateral facts, or those which are incapable of affording any reasonable presumption or inference as to the principal fact or matter in dispute; and for the good reason stated for the rule by Mr. Greenleaf, that such evidence tends to draw away the minds of the jury from the point in issue, and to excite prejudice and mislead them. 1 Greenl. Ev. §§ 51, 52."

We may add that the doctrine of these cases has received the recent approval of jurists and text-writers of high authority. Wharton, in his treatise on Criminal Evidence, § 225, says, "Evidence of threats by other persons are inadmissible." The same doctrine is found in Wharton on Homicide, § 693. In 2 Bishop on Criminal Procedure, § 623, it is said, "The declarations of the deceased, as of any third person, when not of the *res gestæ*, or dying declarations, or communicated to the defendant so as possibly to influence his conduct, are excluded by rules which have been supposed to promote justice on the whole; at all events, which have become parts of the common law, not within the discretion of the courts to set aside. Hence they are not admissible." And again, in the first volume of the same treatise, § 1248, it is said, "In general what one says, as, for example, that he committed the crime in question, will not be admitted for or against another."

In the early case of Commonwealth *v.* Chabbock, 1 Mass. 143, the prisoner was tried on an indictment for breaking into a house, and also for stealing goods therein. The defendant offered to prove by a witness present that another person had acknowledged to the witness that he had stolen some of the articles mentioned in the indictment. The court held that the evidence could not be admitted, saying, "It was no more than hearsay. If a person other than the defendant had stolen the goods, it was undoubtedly competent for the defendant to prove the fact in exculpation of himself, but not by the mode of proof now offered."

In Smith *v.* State, 9 Ala. 990, the prisoner (a slave) was indicted for the murder of one Edmund (also a slave). All the evidence was circumstantial. Sam, another slave, had been tried and acquitted for the same murder previously. On the trial, it seems there was a strong array of circumstantial evidence against him; but Sam stated, that, a few days after the murder, Smith told him that he killed Edmund. The particulars of the statement we omit. But on the trial of Smith, evidence was offered in his behalf that Sam, during his own trial, had become alarmed, and had told the witness that he had wrongfully accused Smith of the murder of Edmund, and he did not wish to die with a lie in his mouth, etc. The counsel for the accused claimed that it was competent for the prisoner under the circumstances to show that another committed the murder; and that in this view the declarations of Sam should have been received, as they tended to inculpate him as well as to show that the prisoner was not the offender.

Ormond, J., in delivering the opinion of the court, said, "Conceding the true meaning of these declarations of Sam in jail to be an admission of his own guilt, and that he had killed Edmund himself, it does not vary the case in the slightest degree. . . . The declaration of Sam was not an act within the meaning of the doctrine I have been discussing. . . . To give effect to the mere declarations of third persons, would be a most alarming innovation upon the criminal law. Such a declaration would not be obligatory on the person making it. He might afterwards demonstrate its falsity when attempted to be used against him. Such testimony may be a mere contrivance to procure the acquittal of the accused."

In West *v.* State, 76 Ala. 98, the question was again before the highest court of the same State, and it was held "that the admission of a third person that he committed the offence with which the accused was charged, not made under oath, though on his death-bed, is mere hearsay, and is not admissible as evidence for the accused."

In Sharp *v.* State, 6 Tex. App. 650, it was held no error to refuse to allow a witness for the defence to testify that certain other men confessed that they committed the crime.

A similar ruling was also sustained in Rhea *v.* State, 10 Yerg. (Tenn.) 258.

Greenfield *v.* People, 85 N. Y. 75, was an indictment for murder. Upon the trial the accused offered the letter of one Royal Kellogg to his brother, in which, after alluding to the murder, he said among other things, "If they want me, they can come and get me;" and in connection with the above, and certain anonymous letters containing confessions, they offered the declarations of Kellogg and his brother and another person, made within an hour after the murder, and at a place three-fourths of a mile distant. The witness being awakened at the barking of a dog at about four o'clock in the morning, on looking out of the window recognized the two Kelloggs and one Taplin, and they had a gun and a bag, etc. The witness, after giving in detail their suspicious actions at this place, was offered to prove that Taplin said to the Kelloggs on that occasion before they left, "You were damned fools to do it," and that one of the Kelloggs replied, "If we had not done it, we should all have been hung."

Miller, J., in delivering the opinion of the court, said, "Even if this letter could be regarded as a confession of Kellogg that he committed the murder, it was only the declaration of a third party, merely hearsay testimony, and upon no rule of evidence admissible. If such declarations were competent upon any trial for homicide, they would tend to confuse the jury, and to divert their attention from the real issue. The letter did not tend to establish that Kellogg committed the offence; was not a part of the *res gestæ;* and in no sense relieved the prisoner from the charge for

XVI. Witnesses.[1] — 1. *Competency.* — The same general rules governing the competency of witnesses and the admissibility of evidence is applicable alike in civil and criminal cases.[2] Other

which he was upon trial, or raised any presumption that Kellogg was the guilty party. Confessions of this character are sometimes made to screen offenders, and no rule is better established than that extra-judicial statements of third persons are inadmissible. Whart. Ev. § 644; Whart. Cr. L. §§ 662, 684; 2 Best, Ev. §§ 559, 560, 563, 565, 578. . . . While evidence tending to show that another party might have committed the crime, would be admissible, before such testimony could be received there must be such proof of connection with it, such a train of facts or circumstances, as tend clearly to point out some one besides the prisoner as the guilty party. Remote acts disconnected, and outside the crime itself, cannot be separately proved for such a purpose. In considering the question we have carefully examined the numerous authorities cited to sustain the position that the evidence was competent, and none of them hold that under such circumstances it could lawfully be received; and it was neither admissible alone nor in connection with the letters referred to"

Threats by a Mob that they would hang a person who had killed another, made within a few minutes after the occurrence, are mere declarations of the opinions of those who composed the mob that the person was guilty of murder, and are inadmissible in evidence on the trial of an indictment for the offence. State *v.* Sneed, 88 Mo. 138; s. c., 3 West. Rep. 797.

Assault to Murder: Evidence: Threats. — On a trial for assault with intent to murder, a question to a witness by the accused, as to whether he had, shortly before the assault, heard a third person make any threats against the person assaulted, was properly excluded, there being no evidence that such third person had committed the crime. State *v.* Beaudet, 53 Conn. 536; s.c., 1 New Eng. Rep. 833.

The court say, "The offer was simply to prove the threats of Dougherty against Dr. Zink. Any threats of any kind would have filled the offer. What act Dougherty threatened to do, or when or how he was to do it, was not indicated; nor was the offered evidence accompanied with any claim, or even a hint, that it could or would be supplemented by further testimony. Indeed, it nowhere appears in the record that it was even claimed in behalf of the prisoner that Dougherty committed the offence, or that any evidence admitted or to be offered would show it. The threats, whatever they were, so far as appears, were entirely isolated from the transaction in question, and tended in no way to elucidate, or give character to, any material act or fact in the case. They could not, therefore, have been received as parts of the *res gestæ*. As to the threats in the saloon, the only thing, it would seem, which they characterized was the drunken condition of the one who uttered them."

1. For a full discussion of the subject of witnesses, see that title in this series.

2. **Infant Witness.** — Where it appears to the presiding judge that a child, offered as a witness, does not sufficiently understand the nature and obligations of an oath, he may permit the child to be properly instructed, if of sufficient age and intellect to receive instructions. If the judge find the witness competent, it is no objection that she has been instructed by a Christian minister since the last adjournment of the court. Commonwealth *v.* Lynes, 142 Mass. 577; s. c., 3 New Eng. Rep. 89.

Interpreter as Witness. — A person appointed to act as an interpreter on the trial of a criminal action, is not disqualified by reason of the fact that he was a witness for the prosecution. People *v.* Fong Ah Sing, 70 Cal. 8.

Testimony of Deceased Witness. — Testimony of witnesses, since deceased, taken before the justice of the peace on the preliminary examination, is admissible in evidence. State *v.* Elliott, 90 Mo. 350; s. c., 7 West. Rep. 285.

An Ex-Convict who has not been restored to citizenship, cannot be admitted as a witness to testify for the State. State *v.* Sutherland (Mo.), 6 West. Rep. 214.

Where an objection was made to the competency of a witness on the ground that he had been convicted of grand larceny, and, to sustain the objection, the defendant offered the record of the conviction of one "Reuben Bradshaw," and the witness testified that he had never been known by the name of Bradshaw; and the evidence of another person was to the effect that he was not certain that the witness ever went by the name of Bradshaw, but had heard him called Bradshaw several times, — on this evidence the court was justified in overruling the objection. State *v.* Rose, 90 Mo. 208; s. c., 10 West. Rep. 279.

Husband and Wife. — The provision of a statute that "neither husband nor wife shall be allowed to testify as to private conversations with each other," is not confined to conversations upon subjects which are confidential in their nature, but includes conversations between them relating to witnesses than those whose names are indorsed upon the indictment may be examined by the State.[1]

a. Defendant as a Witness. — If a person accused of crime testifies in his own behalf, he is to be treated as any other witness; and if he fails to deny a material fact which has been testified against him, the district attorney may comment upon such omission in his argument.[2] In such case the jury should weigh the testimony of the defendant as that of any other witness, and consider his interest in the result of the case.[3]

(1) *Rules Applicable when he elects to testify.* — Where a defendant takes the witness-stand, he assumes the character of a witness, and is entitled to the same privileges, and subject to the same tests, and to be contradicted, discredited, or impeached the same as

business done by one as agent of the other. Commonwealth *v.* Hayes (Mass.), 5 New Eng. Rep. 268; Dexter *v.* Booth, 84 Mass. (2 Allen) 559; Jacobs *v.* Hesler, 113 Mass. 157; Drew *v.* Tarbell, 117 Mass. 90; Brown *v.* Wood, 121 Mass. 137.

Evidence on Former Trial. — The testimony of a witness, in the presence of the defendant on the hearing of his application for bail, may be read on the final trial, if the witness is out of the jurisdiction of the court, or cannot be found. Sneed *v.* State, 47 Ark. 180. However, it has been *held* in Mississippi that evidence of the testimony delivered in a previous trial of the same case by a witness not dead, but beyond the jurisdiction of the court or the limits of the State, is not admissible. Owens *v.* State, 63 Miss. 450.

In Texas it devolves upon the party proposing to use as evidence the written testimony of an absent witness, taken upon the examining trial of the accused, to first establish that the witness resided out of the State, or had removed beyond the limits of the State, or that he was dead, or that he had been prevented from attending court through the act or agency of the opposing party. Menges *v.* State, 21 Tex. App. 413.

A Signal-Service Station Official Record, without the presence of the party making the observation and record, as a witness, is not admissible in a criminal case, to show the condition of the weather. People *v.* Dow (Mich.), 7 West. Rep. 897.

1. State *v.* O'Day, 89 Mo. 559; s. c., 6 West. Rep. 449; State *v.* Phelps, 91 Mo. 478; s. c., 8 West. Rep. 724.

2. Heldt *v.* State, 20 Neb. 493.

Failure of Defendant to explain Prominent Facts. — When a defendant in a criminal case takes the stand as a witness, and fails to explain prominent and damaging facts peculiarly within his own knowledge, the inferences from such failure are as adverse as though he were a witness as a party to the record in a civil cause, or, being thus a party, failed to produce evidences confessedly under his control and peculiarly within his own knowledge. State *v.* Anderson, 89 Mo. 312; s. c., 5 West. Rep. 420.

3. Anderson *v.* State, 104 Ind. 467; s. c., 2 West. Rep. 341.

Where the defendant in a criminal case testifies in his own behalf, and the jury know him to be the defendant, there need be no further showing that he is a party to the suit; and the jury are authorized to consider to what extent that circumstance should affect his credibility. Bressler *v.* People, 117 Ill. 422; s. c., 5 West. Rep. 185.

A Charge that, if the jury believe defendant, as a witness, has testified falsely, then they have the right to disregard his evidence, is erroneous, as omitting the essential element "wilfully and knowingly." Panton *v.* People, 114 Ill. 505; s. c., 1 West. Rep. 357.

An instruction which, in the language used, is equivalent to telling the jury that it was their duty to keep in mind that the witness was the defendant, and that his testimony, for that reason, could not be taken as of controlling weight, unless consistent with all the facts and circumstances in evidence, is erroneous, as discrediting the witness. The defendant has a right to put his evidence before the jury unprejudiced by any adverse criticisms of the court. Bird *v.* State, 107 Ind. 54; s. c., 5 West. Rep. 279.

In a criminal trial it is error for a court to instruct the jury that it may at pleasure, and without regard to other considerations, reject the evidence wholly or in part of any witness interested in the case or having any motive to swear falsely, unless such witness be corroborated by other evidence; and such instruction is erroneous as much when aimed at a defendant who testifies as at any other witness. Owens *v.* State, 63 Miss. 450.

any other witness.[1] And a defendant who elects to testify as a witness, must be treated the same as any other witness upon cross-examination.[2] He may be impeached or contradicted in the same manner as any other witness, and he is not entitled to notice of the intention of the State to introduce evidence for that purpose,[3] the only exception being certain statutory restrictions as to the extent of cross-examinations.[4]

(2) *Not compelled to testify.* — The defendant cannot be compelled to be a witness against himself,[5] and no inference can be drawn from failure of defendant to testify.[6]

2. *In Case of Joint and Several Defendants.* — In a criminal prosecution against two jointly indicted, where the cause as to

1. State *v.* Pfefferle, 36 Kan. 90.

Discrediting Defendant. — In a criminal trial, where defendant offers himself as a witness in his own behalf, it is not error to allow the State, over defendant's objections, to introduce and examine witnesses touching his general moral character. He may be impeached as any other witness, except that on his cross-examination he can only be examined as to matters he has testified to on his examination in chief. State *v.* Bulla, 89 Mo. 595; s. c., 6 West. Rep. 440.

Where, on a Trial for Murder, defendant becomes a witness for himself, his conduct, demeanor, and appearance on the stand become a subject of fair observation, as much as those of any other witness. State *v.* Grayor, 89 Mo. 600; s. c., 6 West. Rep. 207.

2. Boyle *v.* State, 105 Ind. 469; s. c., 2 West. Rep. 788; Thomas *v.* State, 103 Ind. 419; s. c., 1 West. Rep. 309, 316.

Cross-Examination of Defendant. — The section of the statute providing that defendant may testify in his own behalf, provides also that he shall be liable to cross-examination as to any matter referred to in his examination in chief. State *v.* Chamberlain, 89 Mo. 129; s. c., 5 West. Rep. 386; State *v.* McGraw, 74 Mo. 573; State *v.* Turner, 76 Mo. 350; State *v.* McLaughlin, 76 Mo. 320; State *v.* Porter, 75 Mo. 171; State *v.* Douglass, 81 Mo. 231; State *v.* Patterson, 88 Mo. 88; s. c., 3 West. Rep. 226.

Where a party voluntarily takes the witness-stand, and denies the offence charged, much latitude should be allowed in his cross-examination. Thomas *v.* State, 103 Ind. 419; s. c., 1 West. Rep. 309. Followed in Boyle *v.* State, 105 Ind. 469; s. c., 2 West. Rep. 790, 792.

Where defendant, in his direct examination, had given an account of his movements on a day named, it is proper, on cross-examination, to go fully into the subject; and the State is not confined, on cross-examination, to some designated indirect examination of defendant. Boyle *v.* State, 105 Ind. 469; s. c., 2 West. Rep. 788.

Discretion of the Court. — When a defendant in a criminal trial becomes a witness in his own behalf, it is in the discretion of the court to allow him to be cross-examined on the whole case; and the exercise of such authority is not reviewable on error. Disque *v.* State, 49 N. J. L. (20 Vr.) 249; s. c., 6 Cent. Rep. 331.

But where defendant offered himself as a witness on his own behalf, it is not permissible to cross-examine him as to matters not testified to in his examination in chief. State *v.* Mills, 88 Mo. 417; s. c., 4 West. Rep. 316; State *v.* Patterson, 88 Mo. 88; s. c., 3 West. Rep. 226.

And upon the admission of the attorney-general that error was committed in extending the cross-examination of the defendant beyond the matter of his examination in chief, the judgment was reversed. State *v.* Beeman (Mo.), 7 West. Rep. 117.

3. State *v.* Teeter, 69 Iowa, 717.

In a Trial for Burglary and Larceny, the defendant, having been a witness in his own behalf, may be impeached by the record of a former conviction for grand larceny; and the record in which the name is identical with the name of defendant, is *prima facie* evidence of identity. State *v.* McGuire, 87 Mo. 642; s. c., 4 West. Rep. 417.

4. Mo. R. S sec. 1918; State *v.* Palmer, 88 Mo. 568; s. c., 5 West. Rep. 387.

5. People *v.* Guidici, 100 N. Y. 503; s. c., 1 Cent. Rep. 721, 722.

6. Commonwealth *v.* Hanley, 140 Mass. 457; s. c., 1 New Eng Rep. 743.

The prosecuting attorney is not authorized by Maine R. S. chap. 134, sec. 19, to call the attention of the jury to the fact that defendant did not testify in his own behalf. State *v.* Banks, 78 Me. 490; s. c., 3 New Eng. Rep. 240.

But a reference properly checked by the

one defendant is disposed of by a plea of guilty, or a verdict of conviction or acquittal, he may be a witness for the other.[1]

court is not ground for reversal. Norton *v.* State, 106 Ind. 163; s. c., 3 West. Rep. 730.

1. State *v.* Hunt, 90 Mo. 490; s. c., 8 West. Rep. 627; State *v.* Glotts, 26 Mo. 307.

Under Illinois Rev. Stat. 1874, sec. 6, relating to qualifications of parties as witnesses, a joint defendant in an indictment is a competent witness against his co-defendant. Smith *v.* People, 115 Ill. 17; s. c., 1 West. Rep. 615.

Missouri Statute: Co-Defendant as Witness for Defence. — Under Missouri Rev. Stat. § 1918, co-defendants jointly indicted with the defendant, but not put on trial, are competent witnesses to testify in his behalf. State *v.* Chyo Chiagk, 92 Mo. 395; s. c., 10 West. Rep. 308; State *v.* Goom (Mo.), 10 West. Rep. 112.

At the Common Law, the central idea was to prohibit a party to the record from testifying. People *v.* Bill, 10 Johns. (N. Y.) 95. That prohibition no longer prevails. On the contrary, the controlling principle of the section under discussion is to remove the ancient landmarks of evidence, and to make it entirely optional whether a defendant, in any given criminal case, shall bear witness for himself or for his fellows. Bearing this in mind, it is altogether inconceivable that the legislature intended that a defendant might testify in his own behalf and on behalf of those tried with him, and yet be denied the privilege of testifying for his co-defendant, or of having the latter testify for him when their trials are separate. Such a construction would be an absurdity contrary to reason, and which should not be attributed to a man in his right senses. State *v.* Hayes, 81 Mo. 585. On the other hand, if a different construction be given that section, such a construction accords well with its evident fundamental purpose, — that of being a remedial section, giving a testifying capacity where none existed before, therefore to be construed liberally, — to receive an equitable interpretation which will enlarge the letter of the act so as more effectually to meet the beneficial end in view, and prevent a failure of the remedy. 1 Kent, Com. 465; Smith, Com. §§ 520, 547. In such cases the reason of the law prevails over its letter, and general terms are so limited in their application as not to lead to injustice, oppression, or an absurd consequence; the presumption being indulged that the legislature intended no such anomalous results. United States *v.* Kirby, 74 U. S. (7 Wall.) 482; bk. 7, L. ed. 278; People *v.* McRoberts, 62 Ill. 38; St. Louis & S. F. R. Co. *v.* Evans, 85 Mo. 329.

Missouri Practice: Co-Defendant as Witness for Prosecution. — But under Missouri Rev. Stat. § 1917, a defendant jointly indicted with others, but not put upon his trial, cannot testify on behalf of the State against his co-defendants. State *v.* Chyo Chiagk, 92 Mo. 395; s. c., 10 West. Rep. 308.

History of the Doctrine. — In the endeavor to ascertain the present status of the law in this State, as involved in this question, it is necessary to give a summary of what has been heretofore decided by this court, as well as to quote from the text-writers, and to set forth certain statutory provisions bearing on the point in hand.

Bishop says, "One of two or more joint defendants cannot be a witness for or against another, even on a separate trial, until the case as to himself is disposed of by a plea of guilty, or a verdict of conviction or acquittal, or a discharge on a plea in abatement; then he may be. Sentence need not be rendered. Of course, if the indictments are separate, he may be a witness, though the offence is supposed to be joint. . . . According to Lord Hale, it was the usage in his time not to indict one who was to be a witness, because this would disparage his testimony. But, in our day, no good reason appears for attempting to veil from a jury the real facts, with a gauze so transparent. Hence, with us, one of the methods is for the prosecuting officer to require the accomplice to submit to be indicted with the rest. Whereupon the law is that a joint defendant cannot be a witness for or against the others, even on a separate trial, till the case is disposed of as to him by a conviction or acquittal, or by a *nolle prosequi*. But judgment on the conviction need not be rendered; therefore the defendant who is to testify pleads guilty, and then testifies. If his testimony entitles him to be discharged, there is a *nolle prosequi*, or other appropriate proceeding; or, if not, the court has only to render sentence on the plea of guilty" 1 Bish. Cr. Proc. §§ 1020, 1166, and cases cited.

In Best's "Principles of Evidence," by Chamberlayne, 180, it is said, "Except as above stated, the incompetency of accused parties to give formal evidence in criminal proceedings still subsists; nor even can parties jointly indicted be called as witnesses for or against themselves or against each other."

Another author says, "But as in civil actions against several defendants, a co-defendant may sometimes be so circumstanced as to be a competent witness; so, in criminal prosecutions, one of several

On trial against two jointly indicted for false pretences, evidence may be admitted against one which does not tend to prove

persons jointly indicted may be rendered competent to give evidence, either for the prosecution or for his co-defendants. Thus, upon an information by the crown against two or more, if a *nolle prosequi* be entered by the attorney-general, either before or at the trial, as to one of the defendants, such defendant may be called as a witness for the crown against his co-defendant. So, where, upon a joint indictment against two, one had pleaded in abatement, and for want of replication judgment had been entered that he should be dismissed and discharged, he was admitted, without objection, as a competent witness for the other defendant, being himself no longer interested in the event of the prosecution. . . . It has been *held* in a recent case that a prisoner who has pleaded guilty to an indictment is a competent witness against other defendants joined in the same indictment. It was contended in this case that the defendant was not admissible as a witness against two other prisoners included in the same indictment, because he was a party to the record; but *Alderson, B.*, observed that he was not a party to the issues, the only issues being whether the two other prisoners were guilty or not." 1 Phill. Ev. 64, 65

Greenleaf says, "In regard to defendants in criminal cases, if the State would call one of them as a witness against others in the same indictment, this can be done only by discharging him from the record, — as by the entry of a *nolle prosequi;* or by an order for his dismissal and discharge, where he has pleaded in abatement as to his own person, and the plea is not answered; or by a verdict of acquittal, where no evidence, or not sufficient evidence, has been adduced against him. In the former case, where there is no proof, he is entitled to the verdict; and it may also be rendered at the request of the other defendants, who may then call him as a witness for themselves, as in civil cases. In the latter, where there is some evidence against him, but it is deemed insufficient, a separate verdict of acquittal may be entered, at the instance of the prosecuting officer, who may then call him as a witness against the others. On the same principle, where two were indicted for assault, and one submitted, and was fined, and paid the fine, and the other pleaded 'not guilty,' the former was admitted as a competent witness for the latter, because as to the witness the matter was at an end. But the matter is not considered as at an end, so as to render one defendant a competent witness for another, by any thing short of a final judgment, or a plea of guilty. Therefore, where two were jointly indicted for uttering a forged note, and the trial of one of them was postponed, it was *held* that he could not be called as a witness for the other. So, where two, being jointly indicted for an assault, pleaded separately 'not guilty,' and elected to be tried separately, it was *held* that the one tried first could not call the other as a witness for him." 1 Greenl. Ev. § 363.

Elsewhere the same author states, "The usual course is to leave out of the indictment those who are to be called as witnesses; but it makes no difference as to the admissibility of an accomplice, whether he is indicted or not, if he has not been put on his trial at the same time with his companions in crime. He is also a competent witness in their favor; and if he is put on his trial at the same time with them, and there is only very slight evidence, if any at all, against him, the court may, as we have already seen, and generally will, forthwith direct a separate verdict as to him, and, upon his acquittal, will admit him as a witness for the others. If he is convicted, and the punishment is by fine only, he will be admitted for the others, if he has paid the fine." 1 Greenl. Ev. § 379.

Wharton says, "An accomplice is a competent witness for the prosecution, although his expectation of pardon depends upon the defendant's conviction, and although he is a co-defendant, provided in the latter case his trial is severed from that of the defendant against whom he is offered." Whart. Cr. Ev 9th ed. § 439. In another place he says, "At common law an accomplice, not a co-defendant, is always a competent witness for the defendant on trial; but when indicted jointly with the defendant on trial, although he has pleaded and defended separately, he is not, at common law, a competent witness for his co-defendants, unless immediately acquitted by a jury, or a *nolle prosequi* be entered; and the same rule applies to accessories. Whether the trial be joint or several, the rule is said to be the same."

History of the Missouri Adjudications. — In Garret *v.* State, 6 Mo. 1, it was ruled that an accomplice jointly indicted with others, who is not put on his trial with them, may be a witness for them. In McMillan *v.* State, 13 Mo. 30, this view of the admissibility of a witness in such circumstances was disapproved, though no ruling was made.

In Fitzgerald *v.* State, 14 Mo. 413, where several were jointly indicted, it was ruled that it was discretionary with the trial judge the offence against the other.[1] In the separate trial of one of two persons jointly charged in an information with burglary, evidence as to what one said in the presence of the other as to the purchase of railroad tickets for the purpose of leaving the city shortly after the crime was committed, is competent.[2] Where evidence is offered against several defendants, on trial jointly, which is admissible against one of them only, it cannot be excluded from the jury on motion, but a charge should be asked limiting its effect.[3] Where two defendants, jointly indicted, elect to be tried jointly, and make no reservation of the right to testify for each other, as though they had severed, and were tried separately, there is no error in refusing to permit the wife of one of the defendants to testify in favor of the other defendant then on trial.[4]

3. *Accomplices.*[5]

4. *Experts.*[6]

5. *Limiting Number of Witnesses.* — It is within the discretion of court to limit number of witnesses.[7]

6. *Examination of Witnesses.*[8]

7. *Corroboration of Witnesses.*[8]

whether a severance should be allowed the defendants.

All were then put upon their trial, and it was then asked that the jury be permitted to pass on the case of Ward, so that he might be used as a witness for his co-defendants This request was also refused, and the result was that Ward was acquitted, and the other defendants convicted. And the second ruling was also approved by this court.

This case was followed in 1851 by that of State *v.* Roberts, 15 Mo. 24, where quite an extensive discussion of the point decided in Garret *v.* State, 6 Mo. 1, was had; and the conclusion reached after an examination of the authorities was that, where two defendants are jointly indicted, neither is admissible as a witness for his co-defendant, no matter whether they be jointly or separately tried.

In 1852 it was ruled to be the proper practice for the State to enter a *nolle prosequi* in order to render one defendant a competent witness against his co-defendant. State *v.* Clump, 16 Mo. 385.

In 1854 the ruling made, that jointly indicted parties cannot be witnesses for each other, whether jointly or severally tried, was again announced. State *v.* Edwards, 19 Mo. 674.

In 1855 the legislature enacted the following section: "When two or more persons shall be jointly indicted, the court may, at any time before the defendants have gone into their defence, direct any defendant to be discharged, that he may be a witness for the State. A defendant shall also, when there is not sufficient evidence to put him on his defence, at any time before the evidence is closed, be discharged by the court, for the purpose of giving testimony for a co-defendant. The order of discharge shall be a bar to another prosecution for the same offence." 2 Rev. Stat. 1855, p. 1193, § 25. The section just quoted is now § 1917, Rev. Stat. 1879.

1. Commonwealth *v.* Blood, 141 Mass. 571; s. c., 2 New Eng. Rep. 393.

2. People *v.* Dow (Mich.), 7 West. Rep. 897.

3. Williams *v.* State, 81 Ala. 1.

4. Trowbridge *v.* State, 74 Ga. 431.

5. For a full discussion of this topic, see tit. "Accessories," 1 Am. & Eng. Ency. of L. 61, and particularly division "18 Evidence," pp. 74 to 82.

6. See tits. "Experts" and "Witness," this series.

7. *Ex parte* Marmaduke, 91 Mo. 228; s. c., 8 West. Rep. 575.

Limiting Number of Witnesses.—Where the defendant moved the court to establish the State's limit at three witnesses to a fact, and the court fixed the limit at seven, the defendants were bound to infer that a like limit would be applied to them. Mergentheim *v.* State, 107 Ind. 567; s. c., 5 West. Rep. 851.

The State in Rebuttal is not limited to the witnesses who were examined before the grand jury, or of whose introduction the prescribed notice has been given. State *v.* Rivers, 68 Iowa, 611.

8. See this series, tit. "Witness," where these divisions are fully treated.

XVII. Argument of Counsel. — The conduct and management of the argument upon the trial of either a civil or criminal prosecution is largely within the discretion of the trial court; and it is only when some abuse of this discretion, to the probable injury of a party, is shown, that an appellate court will interfere.[1]

As a general rule, counsel, in argument, must confine themselves to the facts brought out in evidence.[2] But, when counsel grossly abuses his privilege to the manifest prejudice of the opposite party, it is the duty of the judge to stop him; and if he fails to do so, and the impropriety is gross, it is good ground for a new trial.[3]

1. Epps *v.* State, 102 Ind. 539; s. c., 3 West. Rep. 380; 1 N. E. Rep. 492; Scripps *v.* Reilly, 35 Mich. 371; Kaime *v.* Omro, Trustees, 49 Wis. 371; s. c., 5 N. W. Rep. 838; Rehberg *v.* Mayor, 99 N. Y. 652; s. c., 2 N. E. Rep. 11; State *v.* Hamilton, 55 Mo. 520; Lafayette *v.* Weaver, 92 Ind. 477; Morgan *v.* Hugg, 5 Cal. 409; Duffin *v.* People, 107 Ill. 113; Shular *v.* State, 105 Ind. 289; s. c., 2 West. Rep. 801; 4 N. E. Rep. 870.

The Routine Matters of the Trial, such as what shall be admitted in argument to the jury outside of the evidence, the degree of invective allowed, and the time during which the argument shall continue, are largely in the discretion of the court at *nisi prius.* Proffat, Jury Trial, sec. 249; State *v.* Hamilton, 55 Mo. 520; State *v.* Waltham, 46 Mo. 55; Scripps *v.* Reilly, 35 Mich. 371; s. c., 24 Am. Rep. 575; St. Louis, etc., R. Co. *v.* Mathias, 50 Ind. 65; Larkins *v* Tartar, 3 Sneed (Tenn.), 681, Lloyd *v.* Hannibal & St. J. R. Co., 53 Mo. 509; Kaime *v.* Trustees, 49 Wis 371; Barden *v.* Briscoe, 36 Mich. 254; Hilliard, New Trial, 225.

As to what is an Abuse of Discretion, as to just how far courts may permit counsel to go in argument, the authorities are not agreed. The line separating what is proper or allowable from what it is improper and erroneous to permit counsel to comment upon, is dim and ill defined; and cases may be found close to the line on either side. 14 Cent. L. J. 406.

2. Dickerson *v.* Burke, 25 Ga. 225; Doster *v.* Brown, 25 Ga. 24; Cook *v.* Ritter, 4 E. D. Smith (N. Y.), 253; Lloyd *v.* Hannibal & St J. R. Co., 53 Mo. 509; Read *v.* State, 2 Ind. 438; Walker *v.* State, 6 Blackf (Ind.) 1; State *v.* Lee, 66 Mo. 165.

It is Error and sufficient cause for a new trial to permit counsel, over objection and exception, to comment upon facts pertinent to the issues but not in evidence, — Brown *v.* Swineford, 44 Wis. 282; s. c., 28 Am. Rep. 582; 7 Cent L. J. 208; Yoe *v.* People, 49 Ill. 410; Kennedy *v.* People, 40 Ill 489; Bill *v.* People, 14 Ill 432, — or to appeal to prejudices foreign to the case made by the evidence, and calculated to have an injurious effect. Ferguson *v.* State, 49 Ind. 33; Hennier *v.* Vogel, 66 Ill. 401; Kinnaman *v.* Kinnaman, 71 Ind 417; Tucker *v.* Henniker, 41 N. H. 317; State *v.* Smith, 75 N. C. 306.

The Allowance of an Improper and Irrelevant Course of Argument is no ground of exception, without showing that the jury were erroneously instructed as to the weight to be given to it. Commonwealth *v.* Byce, 74 Mass. (8 Gray) 461.

3. State *v.* Underwood, 77 N. C. 50; Cable *v.* Cable, 79 N. C. 589; State *v.* Hamilton, 55 Mo. 520; State *v.* Guy, 69 Mo. 430; Proctor *v.* DeCamp, 83 Ind. 559; Dickenson *v.* Burke, 25 Ga. 225; Furgeson *v.* State, 49 Ind. 33; Hilliard on New Trials, 225; State *v.* Williams, 65 N. C. 505; Deories *v.* Haywood, 63 N. C. 53; Junkins *v.* N. C. Ore Dressing Co. (N. C. 1887).

Exhibition of Pictures from "Puck." — In the case of Newman *v.* Commonwealth (Pa.), 5 Cent. Rep. 497, it was *held,* that under an indictment charging defendants with conspiracy against the employees of certain coal-operators, to compel them to quit working by force, threats or menaces of harm, the exhibition by the counsel for the prosecution, as part of his argument to the jury, of a caricature from "Puck" entitled "Suckers of the Workingmen's Sustenance," under permission of the court, will not be ground for revising a judgment of conviction. The court say that "With reference to the exhibition of the picture, exhibited by the counsel for the prosecution as part of his argument to the jury, we cannot say that the court was wrong in permitting it. Things of this kind are very much a matter of discretion, and we are not disposed to review them unless we are satisfied that some serious wrong has been done."

Use of Engravings to Illustrate Propositions of Counsel. — The case of Newman *v.* Commonwealth, *supra,* was perhaps based upon the civil case of Ordway *v.* Haynes, 50 N. H. 159, in which it was *held* that an engraving may be used before the jury, to illustrate the positions of coun-

Within the limits of the testimony, the argument of counsel should be free; but that freedom does not extend either to the statement or assumption of facts, or to commenting on facts not in evidence, to the prejudice of the adverse party. When counsel are permitted to state facts not in evidence, and to comment upon them, the usage of courts regulating trials is departed from, the laws relating to evidence are violated, and the full benefit of trial by jury is denied.[1]

sel, or the statements of a witness, as well as a sketch made by pen or pencil, or in any other way, unless the court can see that there is something about it that is calculated to mislead the jury.

Transgressing Privileges of Debate. — In Heil *v.* State (Ind.), 8 West. Rep. 393, which was a prosecution for larceny, the prosecuting attorney was held not to have transgressed the privileges of fair debate because he referred to recent riots in Cincinnati and the burning of the court-house by a mob, assigning as a cause the lax administration of criminal law in that city; the court saying, "The remarks alluded to above had reference to an historical event, concerning which the jury was supposed to be familiar, both in respect to its occurrence and the causes to which it was attributed. As there was no allusion made to the defendant in that connection, or to his being in any manner concerned in the riots, we cannot say that the privileges of fair debate were transgressed."

In Ferguson *v.* State, 49 Ind. 33, it was *held*, that on the trial of an indictment for murder, it was error for counsel for the State, in argument to the jury, to comment on the frequent occurrence of murder in the community and the formation of vigilance committees and mobs, and to state that the same are caused by laxity in the administration of the law, and that they should make an example of the defendant, and for the court, upon objection by the defendant to such language, to remark to the jury that such matters are proper to be commented upon. But it was *held* in another trial for murder, that, where counsel was allowed to say in his address to the jury, "Three or four men have been recently executed at Indianapolis, most of whom set up the plea of insanity," the error was not of sufficient materiality to justify a reversal. Combs *v.* State, 75 Ind. 215.

So, in an action against a railroad company, the appellate court refused to interfere where counsel had told the jury that the question for them to determine was, "whether this country shall be governed by railroad companies or by the people." St. Louis, etc., R. Co. *v.* Mathias, 50 Ind. 65.

A statement by the county attorney, that "the defendant has been guilty of one offence, and would commit a greater offence to cover the other up," which was not objected to, *held* not ground for new trial, it not appearing whether reference was intended to the offence on trial, or some other offence. State *v.* McCool (Kan.), 9 Pac. Rep. 618.

In a trial for murder, the district attorney referred to another man convicted of murder, then in jail, who should be released, if no conviction should be found in the case: *held*, ground for reversal. Newton *v.* State, 21 Fla. 53.

Where, at the close of the opening address, persons in the court-room applauded, and in his closing argument the prosecuting attorney alluded to and approved it, and the court neither checked the audience nor cautioned the jury, *held* ground for new trial. Cartwright *v.* State, 16 Tex. App 473.

Instruction not to consider. — Where the court, over objection, has erroneously permitted counsel to persist in such misconduct, an instruction to the jury that they should disregard or not consider such matters, will not cure the error. Scripps *v.* Reilly, 35 Mich. 371; s. c., 24 Am. Rep. 575; Forsyth *v.* Cothran, 61 Ga. 278; Tucker *v.* Henniker, 41 N. H. 317; Martin *v.* Orndorff, 22 Iowa, 505. *Contra*, Kennedy *v.* People, 40 Ill. 489.

1. Proctor *v.* DeCamp, 83 Ind. 539; Combs *v.* State, 75 Ind. 215; Morrison *v.* State, 76 Ind. 335; Epps *v.* State, 102 Ind. 539; Anderson *v.* State, 103 Ind. 170; s. c., 1 West. Rep. 175; Deicker *v.* Henniker, 41 N. H. 317; Perkins *v.* Guy, 55 Miss. 153; Cavanah *v.* State, 56 Miss. 299; Cross *v.* State, 68 Ala. 476; Wolffe *v.* Minis, 79 Ala. 386; State *v.* Smith, 75 N. C. 306; Proffat on Jury Trials, sec. 250; McNabb *v.* Lockhart, 18 Ga. 495; Ferguson *v.* State, 49 Ind. 33; Hennies *v.* Vogel, 66 Ill. 401; Bohanan *v.* State, 18 Neb. 57; s. c., 53 Am. Rep. 791; 24 N. W. Rep. 390; Brown *v.* State, 105 Ind. 385; s. c., 2 N. E. Rep. 296; State *v.* Lee, 66 Mo. 165; Dickerson *v.* Burke, 25 Ga. 225; Cartwright *v.* State, 16 Tex. App. 473; Union Ins. Co. *v.* Cheever, 36 Ohio St. 201; Brown *v.* Swineford, 44 Wis. 282; Yoe *v.* People, 49 Ill. 410; Bill *v.* People, 14

Ill. 432; Kennedy *v.* People, 40 Ill. 489; Beassette *v.* State, 101 Ind. 85; People *v.* Dane (Mich.), 26 N. W. Rep. 781; Read *v.* State, 2 Ind. 438.

Abusive Language. — In order to make vituperation and abuse grounds for reversing a judgment, it must appear that the remarks were grossly unwarranted and improper, that they were of a material character, and calculated injuriously to affect the defendant's rights. Pierson *v.* State, 18 Tex. App. 524.

Where the county attorney, in his closing address, said, "The defendant, in this case, has stooped so low as to drag before you the infidelity of his dead wife, and publish her before the court-house as a prostitute," the court *held* this language not cause for new trial, remarking, "We cannot deny that this remark was unfair. A defendant has a right unquestionably to introduce all such matters of defence as are advisable and calculated to mitigate, excuse, or justify his actions; and while the prosecuting officer has a right to comment upon the nature and character of such defences, still in doing so it is most improper to denounce and vilify him on account of his defences." Pierson *v.* State, 18 Tex. App. 524.

Where the prosecutor declared in argument, that he had personal knowledge that the defendant was reputed to be a hotel-thief, and that he had been published and portrayed in "The Police Gazette" as such, the court *held* that the speech of the prosecutor went beyond the bounds of propriety, but the evidence in the record, fully sustaining the verdict, refused to grant a reversal. Heil *v.* State, 109 Ind. 589; s. c., 8 West. Rep. 393.

Where, in the opening address, the prosecuting attorney called the defendant a "dirty dog," and that, in separating the prosecuting witness from her companions, he acted "like a dirty dog as he was," the court refused to grant a new trial, saying, "It was, strictly speaking, a breach of professional decorum to apply opprobrious epithets to the appellant in advance of the introduction of any evidence from which disparaging inferences might have been drawn, and the circuit court would have been justified in restraining the prosecuting attorney from the use of such epithets in a merely opening statement; but the breach of professional decorum thus involved ought not to be regarded as of sufficient importance to cause a reversal of the judgment." Anderson *v.* State, 104 Ind. 467; s. c., 2 West. Rep. 341; 4 N. E. Rep. 63.

Where defendant's character had not been impeached, but a witness for plaintiff had been contradicted by a witness for defendant, counsel said, "that no man who lived in defendant's neighborhood could have any thing but a bad character; that defendant polluted every thing near him, or that he touched; that he was like the Upas tree, shedding pestilence and corruption all around him." It was *held* ground for new trial. Coble *v.* Coble, 79 N. C. 589.

The prosecuting attorney said, "that saloon-keepers always had a gang organized to swear them through, and that the jury should not believe a saloon-keeper under oath; that only a short time ago a saloon-keeper had sold liquor to a man and made him drunk, and he froze to death; that he knew personally the saloon-keeper in this case, and that he was guilty of this, and, he was sure, of other crimes." This language the court *held* ground for a new trial, remarking, "The constitution guarantees to every person accused of crime a right to meet the witnesses against him face to face; but the guaranty stands for nothing if, after the evidence is closed, the State may avail itself of the personal knowledge of the prosecutor concerning the defendant's guilt, not only of that, but of other crimes, conveyed to the jury, accompanied with other statements ingeniously contrived to excite their prejudice against him. If a conviction is had, in any case, it is essential that it should have been secured according to the facts in the case legally produced to the jury, agreeably to established rules in judicial proceedings, and not by methods which afford the accused no opportunity of meeting the assertions made by any one claiming to have personal knowledge of his character or guilt." Brow *v.* State, 103 Ind. 133; s. c., 1 West. Rep. 180.

On the second trial of the case, the public prosecutor denounced the defendant as a "fellow" and a "land-thief," and "as guilty as hell," and asserted that the new trial had been obtained "by a dodge and technicality," boasting of his ability to convict him as many times as he could get a new trial. A new trial was granted, although the trial judge admonished the jury to disregard the language. Hatch *v.* State, 8 Tex. App. 416.

In a murder trial, the prosecutor said, "Defendant is a man of bad, dangerous, and desperate character; but I am not afraid to denounce the butcher-boy, although I may, on returning to my home, find it in ashes over the heads of my defenceless wife and children." *Held*, ground for reversal. Martin *v.* State, 63 Miss. 505.

The county attorney used the following language: "This defendant is a contemptible and pusillanimous puppy. He comes into this court with the swaggering insolence of a grocery bully, and pleads not

It has been held that the misconduct may be so flagrant that the court should interfere without objection.[1]

guilty to this charge. During the dead hours of the night, while his family were at their humble home shedding tears of regret over the sad downfall of the husband and father, this man — this biped — is bedding up with these prostitutes. Had I the command of language to stand here and express my contempt of this thing, I could stand until the dawn of the resurrection-day, and then say less than he merits. If I were going to establish a hell on earth, and invade the realms of darkness for one to supervise it, I would leave there and come back here and take defendant, for he is a fair representative of the Devil." *Held*, ground for new trial. Stone *v.* State, 22 Tex. App. 185.

Where the prosecuting attorney said, "Will you believe this man, this person, who has told so many lies, and who has just seen the shadow of the gallows?" it was *held* not so distinct a reference to a verdict upon a former trial as would require a reversal. Boyle *v.* State, 105 Ind. 469; s. c., 2 West. Rep. 788.

1. Berry *v.* State, 10 Ga. 511; Saunders *v.* Baxter, 6 Heisk. (Tenn.) 369.

It is the Duty of the Presiding Judge to interfere of his own motion to prevent a breach of the privilege of counsel; and if he fail to do so, and the abuse produce the conviction, so that injustice resulted therefrom, it is the duty of the appellate court to award a new trial. Perkins *v.* Guy, 55 Miss. 153; Cavanah *v.* State, 56 Miss. 299; Martin *v.* State, 63 Miss. 505. But the great weight of authority is the other way, and failure to so interfere is not ground for a new trial, — St. Louis, etc., R. Co. *v.* Myrtle, 51 Ind. 566; Gilhooly *v.* State, 58 Ind. 182; Tucker *v.* Henniker, 41 N. H. 317; Davis *v.* State, 33 Ga. 98, — though the court may interfere of its own accord, and stop counsel, or even grant a new trial, because of misconduct; and such action will be sustained by the appellate court unless there has been a gross abuse of discretion. Kinnaman *v.* Kinnaman, 71 Ind. 417; St. Louis, etc., R. Co. *v.* Myrtle, 51 Ind. 566; Farman *v.* Lauman, 73 Ind. 568; Forsyth *v.* Cothran, 61 Ga. 278.

Commenting on Evidence at Former Trial. — Under the rule restricting the argument to the evidence, it is improper for counsel to comment on minutes of evidence taken at a former trial, — Martin *v.* Orndorff, 22 Iowa, 505; Walker *v.* State, 6 Blackf. (Ind.) 1; State *v.* Whit, 5 Jones (N. C.) L. 224, — or to state and assume as a fact any thing that has not been proved or put in evidence Bill *v.* People, 14 Ill. 432; Wightman *v.* Providence, 1 Cliff. C. C. 524; Rolfe *v.* Rumford, 66 Me. 564; s. c., 4 Am. L. T. R. 461. One court has gone so far in enforcing this rule, as to hold that where there is no evidence legally sufficient, no argument should be allowed. Bankard *v.* Baltimore R. Co., 34 Md. 197. However, this cannot be so in criminal cases in those States where counsel are allowed to argue the law as well as the facts to the jury. Lynch *v.* State, 8 Ind. 541.

As not pertinent to the Issue, but calculated to prejudice the Case, it has been held improper for counsel to refer to the fact that a change of venue was taken, — Farman *v.* Lauman, 73 Ind. 568, — or, in a criminal case, that defendant failed to testify, — Long *v.* State, 56 Ind. 182, — or that he had not called as witness two accessories, — State *v.* Degonia, 69 Mo 485, — or that he failed to produce evidence of good moral character, — Fletcher *v.* State, 49 Ind. 124; State *v.* Lee, 66 Mo. 165; — but acts showing bad faith or dishonesty, appearing in the record, may be commented upon. Cross *v.* Garrett, 35 Iowa, 480.

Attack of Character. — It is improper to attack the opposite party's character when he has not been impeached, and to use language tending to degrade and humiliate him, — Coble *v.* Coble, 79 N. C. 589; s. c., 28 Am. Rep. 338, — but it is proper to allude to the manner and change in countenance of a party while testifying. Huber *v.* State, 57 Ind. 341.

Indiana Doctrine. — The Supreme Court of Indiana say in a recent case, that "to rigidly require counsel to confine themselves directly to the evidence would be a delicate task, both for the trial and appellate courts, and it is far better to commit something to the discretion of the trial court, than to attempt to lay down or enforce a general rule defining the precise limits of the argument. If counsel make material statements outside of the evidence, which are likely to do the accused injury, it should be deemed an abuse of discretion and a cause for reversal; but where the statement is a general one, and of a character not likely to prejudice the cause of the accused in the minds of honest men of fair intelligence, the failure of the court to check counsel should not be deemed such an abuse of discretion as to require a reversal." Combs *v.* State, 75 Ind. 215. See also McNabb *v.* Lockhart, 18 Ga. 495; Haderlein *v.* St. Louis R. Co., 3 Mo. App. 601; Winter *v.* Sass, 19 Kan. 557; Hilliard, New Tr. 225. If the counsel, in summing up, misstate the evidence to the jury, the court below may grant a new trial;

The prosecutor may comment upon the appearance of defendant in giving his testimony where the defendant has elected to testify.[1] But where the prosecuting attorney refers to the fact that the defendant has not testified in his own behalf, the defendant is entitled to a new trial.[2]

XVIII. Charge of the Court.[3] — 1. *Questions of Law and Fact.*[3] *a. Reasonable Doubt.*[3] 2. *Instructions.*[3]

XIX. Retirement and Deliberation. — The questions governing the retirement and deliberation of the jury in a criminal case are substantially the same as in a civil action.[4]

1. *Viewing the Premises.* — The statute authorizing the jury to inspect the place in which any material fact occurred, is constitutional, and does not intend that the view of the premises shall be deemed part of the evidence, but that the view may be had for the purpose of enabling the jury to understand and apply the evidence placed before them in the presence of the accused in open court; and it is not contemplated that the judge or the accused shall accompany the jury. It is proper to send the jury at the defendant's request to make such inspection.[5]

however, their refusal to do so is not the subject of review upon a writ of error. Thompson *v.* Barkley, 27 Pa. St. 263.

The Rule, as stated in Shular *v.* State, 105 Ind. 289; s. c., 2 West. Rep. 801, 806, is, that "If counsel go beyond the evidence, and bring in foreign and improved matters, courts should interfere; and if the trial court does not interfere, and the matter improperly brought before the jury is of a material character, the court may revise the judgment. But it is not every violation of the rules governing the discussion of causes before the jury that will entitle the complaining party to have the verdict set aside; for if the statement be an unimportant one, or one not likely to wrongfully influence the jury, the verdict will be upheld."

1. Huber *v.* State, 57 Ind. 341.

In a Prosecution for Murder, to refer to the defendant as "a murderer" is not ground for reversal. State *v.* Griffin, 87 Mo. 608; s. c., 3 West. Rep. 820.

2. Commonwealth *v.* Scott, 123 Mass. 239; Long *v.* State, 56 Ind. 12; State *v.* Ryan, 70 Iowa, 154.

Comment on Failure of Defendant to testify. — Reference to the fact that the defendant did not testify, while matter for objection at the time, is not a cause for taking the case from the jury. Commonwealth *v.* Worcester, 140 Mass. 58; s. c., 2 New Eng. Rep. 38.

Commenting upon Absence of Defendant's Witness. — As to the right of district attorney to commit upon the absence of one of defendant's former witnesses, see Commonwealth *v.* Harlow, 110 Mass. 411; Learned *v.* Hall, 133 Mass. 417; Woodward *v.* Leavette, 107 Mass. 453.

Reference to a Former Trial is improper; but if the court checks the reference, and the speaker immediately desists, it is not ground for new trial. Petite *v.* People, 8 Colo. 518; s. c., 9 Pac. Rep. 622.

3. The various matters naturally falling under the head of charge of the court in criminal trials, — the doctrine relating to questions of fact and law; to reasonable doubt, and the instructions which may be given upon request of either party, which it was originally intended to treat in this place, — will be found treated under "Charge to Jury," 3 Am. & Eng. Encyc. of L. 121, "Instructions," and "Jury Trials," to be hereafter treated in this series.

4. See, for a full discussion of this subject, tit. "Jury Trials," this series.

5. Shular *v.* State, 105 Ind. 281, 289; s. c, 2 West. Rep. 801.

The Jury viewing the Premises. — In the recent case of Shular *v.* State, *supra*, the Supreme Court of Indiana say, "Our statute provides that, 'whenever, in the opinion of the court and with the consent of all the parties, it is proper for the jury to have a view of the place in which any material fact occurred, it may order them to be conducted in a body, under the charge of an officer, to the place, which shall be shown to them by some person appointed by the court for that purpose. While the jury are thus absent, no person, other than the officer and the person appointed to show them the place, shall speak to them on any subject connected with the trial.' This statute does not intend that

Photographs, proved to be accurate representations of an actual scene, are admissible in evidence as appropriate aids to the jury in applying the evidence, whether it relates to persons, things, or places.[1]

the view of the premises where a crime was committed shall be deemed part of the evidence, but intends that the view may be had for the purpose of enabling the jury to understand and apply the evidence placed before them in the presence of the accused in open court. Evidence can only be delivered to a jury in a criminal case in open court; and unless there is a judge or judges present, there can be no court. The statute does not intend that the judge shall accompany the jury on a tour of inspection. The statute expressly provides who shall accompany the jury, and this express provision implies that all others shall be excluded from that right or privilege. It is quite clear from these considerations that the statute does not intend that the defendant or the judge shall accompany the jury; and it is equally clear that the view obtained by the jury is not to be deemed evidence. Turning to the authorities, we shall find our conclusion well supported. The statute of Kansas is substantially the same as ours, except that it does not, as ours does, require the consent of all of the parties; and in a strongly reasoned case, it was *held* that it was not error to send the jury, unaccompanied by the defendant, to view the premises where a burglary had been committed. *Brewer, J.*, by whom the opinion of the court was prepared, said, in speaking of the statute, 'Nothing is said in it about the presence of the defendant, the attorneys, the officers of the court, or the judge. On the contrary, the language seems clearly to imply that only the jury and the officer in charge are to be present. The trial is not temporarily transferred from the court-house to the place of view. They are to be conducted in a body while thus absent. This means that the place of trial is unchanged, and that the jury, and the jury only, are temporarily removed therefrom. Just as when the case is finally submitted to the jury, and they retire for deliberation, there is simply a temporary removal of the jury. The place of trial is unchanged; and whether the jury retire to the next room, or are taken to a building many blocks away, the effect is the same. In contemplation of law, the place of trial is not changed. The judge, the clerk, the officers, the records, the parties, and all that go to make up the organization of a court, remain in the court-room.'" State *v.* Adams, 20 Kan. 311; Shular *v.* State, 105 Ind. 289; s. c., 2 West. Rep. 801.

"It seems to us that it was to enable the jury, by a view of the premises or place, better to understand the evidence and comprehend the testimony of the witnesses respecting the same, and thereby the more intelligently to apply the testimony, and not to make them silent witnesses in the case, burdened with testimony unknown to both parties, and in respect to which no opportunity for cross-examination or correction of error, if any, could be afforded either party." Clare *v.* Samm, 27 Iowa, 503; Jeffersonville M. & I. R. R. Co. *v.* Bowen, 40 Ind. 545; Heady *v.* Vevay, etc., Tpke. Co., 52 Ind. 117; Gagg *v.* Vetter, 41 Ind. 228; Indianapolis *v.* Scott, 72 Ind. 196; Shular *v.* State, 105 Ind. 289; s. c., 2 West. Rep. 801. *Compare* Carroll *v.* State, 5 Neb. 31; State *v.* Bertin, 24 La. An. 46; Benton *v.* State, 30 Ark. 348.

"The court had discretion to permit the jury to view these physical facts; and this was neither in contemplation of the act nor otherwise any part of the trial. It was rather a suspension of the trial to enable the jury to view the ground, etc., that they might better understand the testimony. We do not see what good the presence of the prisoner would do, as he could neither ask nor answer any questions, nor in any way interfere with the acts, observations, or conclusions of the jury. If he had desired to see the ground, that he might be assisted in his defence by the knowledge thus obtained, possibly the court would have granted him the privilege; but the fact that the jury went upon the ground without being accompanied by him, is no good reason for setting aside the verdict, especially as he neither made objection nor asked permission to accompany at the time." People *v.* Bonney, 19 Cal. 426.

1. People *v.* Buddensiek, 103 N. Y. 735; s. c., 4 Cent. Rep. 787.

Photographs as Evidence.—The court say in People *v.* Buddensiek, *supra*, that "the next exception brought to our attention is the use in evidence of a photograph of the premises. It was taken during the trial; but it appeared that the part represented was in the same condition as when first seen by the witness on the 25th of April, or soon after the structure fell. No objection was made that the person taking the picture was not competent or skilled in his art, nor that the then condition of the ruins was unimportant as throwing light upon the manner of the construction of the buildings. It exhibited the surface, condition, and state of

XX. Verdict. — 1. *Return.* — The verdict of the jury in criminal cases is to be considered and delivered with the same form as in civil cases.[1]

2. *Polling Jury.* — It has been long established, that, when the jury say they are agreed, the court may examine them by poll.[2] And the defendant has the right to require that the jury be polled.[3]

3. *Recording Verdict.* — The delivery and recording of the verdict are essential to its validity, because it is not perfected until recorded.[4]

4. *Impeachment.* — A verdict may be impeached for (5) *Misconduct*, or (6) *Separation* of jury during the trial; (7) *Setting aside* for that reason.[5]

XXI. Motion for New Trial. — Where a defendant is convicted upon the trial of an indictment, and his counsel is of opinion that the proceedings upon the trial were, in some respects, irregular, or that the conviction is illegal, or there has been newly discovered evidence, he may make a motion for a new trial upon the merits, because of the irregularities, or on the ground of the newly discovered evidence.[6]

1. *Grounds for.* — The grounds for a new trial are (1) newly discovered evidence, (2) surprise, (3) irregularity in summoning and returning jurors, (4) bias or hostility of jurors, (5) tampering with jury, (6) misconduct of the jury, (7) that the verdict is against the evidence, (8) that the verdict is against the law.[7]

2. *Proceedings on Second Trial.* — Where a verdict has been rendered, and the defendant procures a new trial, he can be tried at the new trial only for the offence charged in the count upon which he was found guilty at the former trial.[8]

the wall; and it, no doubt, carried to the minds of the jurors a better image of the subject-matter concerning which negligence was charged, than any oral description by eye-witnesses could have done. Its accuracy as a faithful representation of the actual scene was proven; and in such a case it must be deemed established that photographic scenes are admissible in evidence as appropriate aids to a jury in applying the evidence, whether it relates to persons, things, or places. Cozzens *v.* Higgins, 1 Abb. Ct. App. Dec. 451; Cowley *v.* People, 83 N. Y. 464; Durst *v.* Masters, L. R. 1 Prob. Div. 373, 378.

1. 1 Arch. Cr. Pr. § 173, note. For a full discussion of this subject, see the titles, "Jury Trials" and "Verdict," to be hereafter treated in this series.

2. See Watts *v.* Brains, Cro. Eliz. 778.

The Object of polling the Jury is to ascertain whether the verdict returned by the foreman, in behalf of himself and the rest, is really concurred in by the others. State *v.* Bogain, 12 La. An. 264; State *v.* John, 8 Ired. (N. C.) L. 330.

Although a juror has consented to a verdict, and even where it is in writing, and he has signed it, yet he has the right to deny it at any time before it is recorded. See Burk *v.* Commonwealth, 5 J. J. Marsh. (Ky.) 675; Rex *v.* Parkin, 1 Moody, 45; Hale's P. C. 299.

3. People *v.* Perkins, 1 Wend. (N. Y.) 91.

4. 3 Robinson's Cr. Pr. 268; 2 Arch. Cr. Pr. ; See tit. "Verdict," this series.

5. *Vide* "Verdict," *loc. cit.*

6. See a full discussion of this question in tit. "New Trials," in this series.

7. See "New Trials," *loc. cit.*

8. State *v.* McNaught, 36 Kan. 624.

The Texas Criminal Code. — Article 783, which declares that "the effect of a new trial is to place the cause in the same position in which it was before any trial had taken place," does not apply in cases admitting of degrees where a party, having been convicted of a lesser degree, is accorded a new trial. In such cases the rule is, that the case stands for trial upon the degree for which the conviction was had,

A second trial is a re-examination of the issue in the same court; and the former verdict shall not be referred to on the subsequent trial, either in the evidence or the argument. This rule is applicable to new trials granted by the court in which the accused was tried, and trials had on the reversal of a judgment by this court, and remanded for another trial to the court which rendered the judgment.[1]

XXII. Judgment. — 1. *Arrest of Judgment.* — After the jury have rendered their verdict, and before the sentence of the court is pronounced, the defendant may move in arrest of judgment for all defects or matters of objection which are not cured by verdict.[2]

2. *Sentence.* — After the verdict of the jury has been duly returned and recorded by the clerk, if no motion in arrest of judgment has been granted, the court proceeds to sentence the prisoners.[3]

a. Suspension of Sentence. — In those cases where a motion in arrest of judgment has been allowed, the passing of sentence by the court will be suspended.[4]

b. Fines and Costs.[5] —

XXIII. Error and Appeal. — As a rule, the only way in which judgment can be reversed is by writ of error,[6] though such writ is not necessary if the objection is to some matter *dehors*, or foreign to the record, as if judgment be given by persons who have no authority.[7]

and the degrees inferior thereto, and that, with respect to such degrees, the case stands as if no previous trial had been had. Robinson *v.* State, 21 Tex. App. 160.

1. State *v.* Leabo, 89 Mo. 247; s. c., 5 West. Rep. 401.

The prosecuting attorney in a criminal case is equally bound by the rule that prohibits attorneys, in their arguments before the jury, from commenting on the evidence of defendant as a witness, or making objectionable allusions to the verdict in a former trial; but this alone is not a sufficient ground for reversal. State *v.* Leabo, 89 Mo. 247; s. c., 5 West. Rep. 401.

2. 1 Arch. Cr. Pr. § 178. See a full discussion of the various questions relating to judgments and arrest of judgment under the title "Judgment" in this series.

3. The formalities and other matters pertaining to the passing of sentence upon the prisoner will be found fully treated under the title "Sentence," this series.

4. See title "Sentence," *loc. cit.*

5. See that title.

6. As a rule, an appeal does not lie in a criminal case. Harris, Cr. L. 467.

7. Harris, Cr. L. 468.

A Writ of Error is a writ directed to an inferior court which has given judgment against the defendant, requiring it to send up the record and proceedings of the indictment in question to the Queen's Bench division, for that court to examine whether the errors alleged took place, and to affirm or reverse the judgment of the inferior court. It must be grounded on some substantial defect, apparent on the face of the record, as if the indictment be bad in substance, or the sentence be illegal. It will never be allowed for a formal defect.

If judgment is affirmed, the defendant may be at once committed to prison; and if he does not surrender within four days, a judge may issue a warrant for his apprehension.

If judgment is reversed, all the former proceedings are null and void, and the defendant is in the same position as if he had never been charged with the offence: therefore, he may be indicted again on the same ground.

In the interval before the result of the proceedings in error is known, in cases of misdemeanor, the defendant is discharged from custody on entering into the recognizances with sureties required by the acts mentioned below: in felonies he remains in custody. Harris, Cr. L. 469.

The American Doctrine has been summarized by Judge Force in his edition of Harris's Criminal Law (pp. 411-416) as follows: —

"The judgment upon a verdict of conviction can be reviewed by the proper appellate court. The proceeding, varying in form, and called by different names in the different States, is everywhere substantially the same. In Illinois and Michigan, the proceeding is called writ of error; in Ohio, petition in error; in Kentucky, Indiana, and Illinois, it is called appeal. In all, the object of the proceeding is to transmit the record of the trial court to the appellate court, in order that the appellate court may determine if there is error in the record, to the prejudice of the plaintiff in error or appellant, and thereupon render appropriate judgment.

"In Ohio, in any criminal case, a judgment of a court or officer inferior to the court of common pleas may be reviewed in the court of common pleas; judgment of any court inferior to the district court may be reviewed in the district court; and the judgment of any court inferior to the Supreme Court may be reviewed in the Supreme Court.

"The plaintiff in error files his petition in error with a transcript of the record in the appellate court. Petition in error cannot be filed in the Supreme Court, without an allowance by the Supreme Court or a judge thereof; in capital cases, the allowance must be by the court or by two judges thereof. Upon hearing, the court may affirm the judgment, or reverse it, in whole or in part, and order the accused to be discharged, or grant a new trial. 74 Ohio L. 359–361.

"In Kentucky, the court of appeals has appellate jurisdiction in all cases of felony, and also in penal actions and prosecutions for misdemeanors, where the judgment is for a fine exceeding fifty dollars or imprisonment exceeding thirty days. The circuit court has appellate jurisdiction from the judgments of inferior tribunals, where the sentence is a fine of twenty dollars or more, or is imprisonment. Where an appeal is taken to the circuit court, the defendant files in the circuit court a copy of the summons or warrant, and of the judgment, together with a statement of the costs; and the case is tried in the circuit court as if no judgment had been rendered.

"Where, after judgment in the circuit court, the defendant, at the same term, prays an appeal, the appeal is granted as a matter of right. The appeal is perfected by lodging in the clerk's office of the court of appeals, within sixty days after the judgment, a certified transcript of the record. The clerk issues a certificate that the appeal has been taken, but no summons or notice is necessary. A judgment of conviction must be reversed for any error of law, to the defendant's prejudice, appearing on the record. But it shall not be reversed for error in instructing or refusing to instruct the jury, unless the bill of exceptions contains all the instructions given to the jury. Crim. Code, title 9.

"It is provided in the chapter on Bills of Exceptions, that decisions of a court upon challenges to the panel, and for cause, upon motions to set aside an indictment, and upon motions for new trial, shall not be subject to exception. Crim. Code, tit. 9, § 281.

"In Indiana, an appeal to the Supreme Court can be taken as a matter of right, by the defendant, from any judgment against him. It must be taken within one year after the rendering of the judgment. It is taken by serving on the clerk of the trial court notice that the defendant appears, and a similar notice upon the prosecuting attorney. The appellate court must give judgment without regard to technical errors or to exceptions which do not affect the substantial rights of the parties, and may reverse, affirm, or modify the judgment appealed from, and may, if necessary, order a new trial. Rev. Stat. (1876) vol. 2, pp. 410–412.

"In Illinois, in capital cases, the party aggrieved by manifest and material error appearing on the record may be relieved by writ of error, if the writ be allowed to issue by the Supreme Court in session, or by a judge thereof in vacation. In all other cases, a writ of error is a writ of right, and is issued of course. Rev. Stat. (1877) p. 409. The jury, in criminal cases, is judge of law and fact. Ibid. p. 405. But the defendant may except to any ruling or decision of the judge, as in civil cases, — Ibid. p. 406, — and, hence, may except to the court's overruling a motion for new trial. Ibid. p. 742.

"The provisions for appeal in Iowa are substantially the same as in Indiana. Rev. Stat. (1873) pp. 696–699. In Iowa, if the judge to whom a bill of exceptions is tendered does not sign it within a day, it may be signed and sworn to by two or more attorneys or officers of the court, or disinterested by-standers, and filed with the clerk, and thereupon becomes part of the record. Ibid. p. 692.

"In Michigan, no writ of error, upon a judgment of conviction for treason or for murder in the first degree, issues, unless allowed by one of the justices of the Supreme Court, after notice to the attorney-general. In all other cases, the writ issues as a matter of course. All proceedings upon writs of error are to be according to the course of the common law, as modified by practice and usage in the State, and by such general rules as may be made by the Supreme Court. Rev. Stat. (1871) pp. 1969, 1970.

"In Ohio, Kentucky, Indiana, and Iowa, the State, as well as the defendant, can take a case by petition in error or by appeal

1. *Rights of State.* — In a criminal prosecution, under the statute, the State is only allowed an appeal from the judgment of the trial court, sustaining a motion to quash an indictment, or from its judgment sustaining a demurrer thereto.[1]

2. *Time to Appeal.*[2] — Where a statute furnishes an adequate remedy for the review of decisions in criminal cases, it alone must be looked to for guidance on that subject.[3]

A statute which requires an appeal to be taken immediately after conviction will not be so literally construed as to have the effect of denying to defendant the right of appeal.[4]

to the appellate court. In Indiana, the State can appeal only upon a judgment for the defendant, on quashing or setting aside an information or indictment; upon an order of court arresting the judgment; or upon a question reserved by the State. Upon such appeal in Indiana, the Supreme Court can reverse a judgment quashing or setting aside an indictment or information, or an order arresting judgment; but in all other cases of appeal by the State, the decision of the Supreme Court only settles the question of law reserved, but does not affect the judgment rendered in the case. Rev. Stat. (1876) vol. 2, p. 411. In Kentucky, a judgment in favor of the defendant which operates as a bar to a future prosecution for the offence cannot be reversed by the court of appeals. Crim. Code, § 339. In such cases in Kentucky, and in all cases in Ohio and Iowa, the judgment of the appellate court has no effect upon the judgment rendered below, but only settles for future cases the law upon the questions considered.

"Judgments in criminal cases in the federal courts are final, and are not subject to review by proceeding in error or an appeal. The district court must remit every indictment found therein for a capital offence, and may remit any indictment involving difficult and important questions of law to the circuit court; whereupon the circuit court proceeds as if the indictment had originally been found therein. Rev. Stat. p. 192. When the judges of a circuit court are divided in opinion upon any question in a criminal proceeding, the point shall, on request of either party, be certified to the Supreme Court. But this shall not prevent the cause from proceeding, if, in the opinion of the court, further proceedings can be had without prejudice to the merits. Rev. Stat. p. 117. If the circuit or district court render judgment without having jurisdiction, the defendant can be discharged by the Supreme Court on *habeas corpus*. *Ex parte* Lange, 85 U. S. (18 Wall.) 163; bk. 21, L. ed. 872."

1. State *v.* Stegman, 90 Mo. 486; s. c., 8 West. Rep. 210.

The defendants pleaded in abatement, that no such person as Harry Blue, by whom the affidavit purported to be signed and sworn to, existed at the time it was made, but that the person who signed and swore to it was one Henry, alias Harry Little. A demurrer was overruled to the plea; and the State refusing to reply, or plead further, it was ordered by the court, that the defendants be discharged from custody, and that "they go hence without delay." Thereupon the State appealed to this court, and the order of the circuit court was reversed. State *v.* Cooper, 96 Ind. 331; State *v.* Cooper, 103 Ind. 75; s. c., 1 West. Rep. 135.

2. For a full discussion of time of appeal in both civil and criminal cases, see tit. "Appeal," 1 Am. & Eng. Encyc. of L. 616, *et seq.*

3. Well's Case, 2 Me. 322; People *v.* Carnal, 6 N. Y. 463; People *v.* Clark, 7 N. Y. 385; Bish. Cr. Proc. § 1401; Frazier *v.* State, 106 Ind. 564; s. c., 4 West. Rep. 711.

4. State *v.* Herman, 20 Mo. App. 548; s. c., 3 West. Rep. 786; State *v.* Andrews, 76 Mo. 101.

Thus, where defendant was convicted late at night for illegally selling intoxicating liquors, and was immediately placed under arrest on another charge of the same nature, his demand for an appeal made next day immediately after his trial on the last charge was in time. State *v.* Herman, 20 Mo. App. 348; s. c., 3 West. Rep. 786.

In Caldwell *v.* Hawkins, 46 Mo. 263, it is *held* that the duty of filing the transcript in proper time is a personal duty devolving on the appellant, and he cannot transfer it to the clerk; nor will it avail the appellant that he had several times asked the circuit clerk to make it out and send it up, and that the latter had promised to do so. The Supreme Court adds that the statutory duty of the appellate court in such a case is "plain and imperative, and cannot be dispensed with." The present case is, if possible, stronger against the appellants, since it appears that only one request was made of the clerk. State *v.* Caldwell, 21 Mo.

3. *When Appeal lies.* — The right of appeal in a capital case is necessarily coincident with that of a stay of execution, until that appeal can be heard.[1]

No appeal lies for merely formal errors.[2]

One who pleads guilty, and voluntarily pays the fine, cannot appeal.[3]

Where an appeal upon a constitutional question was taken to the appellate court, it was properly dismissed.[4]

The finding of the court on the issue raised on motion for change of venue was conclusive, unless it appears that palpable injustice has been done, or there has been an abuse of judicial discretion in refusing the application, which does not appear in this case.[5]

Where, upon a former writ of error, the indictment was held to be sufficient, that decision is conclusive in all future proceedings.[6]

On a judgment of the criminal court sustaining a demurrer to an indictment, the United States has no right of appeal to the general term.[7]

App. 645; s. c., 4 West. Rep. 301; State *v.* Chapman, 48 Mo. 218.

Bill of Exceptions: Power of Prosecuting Attorney. — Under Indiana Rev. Stat. § 1847, a prosecuting attorney has no power to fix the time in the first instance, or to extend the time after, within which a bill of exceptions in a criminal prosecution must be prepared, signed, and filed. Bartley *v.* State, 111 Ind. 358; s. c., 9 West. Rep. 814

Indiana Rev. Stat. 1881, § 1847, which constitutes a part of our present Criminal Code, is as follows: "All bills of exceptions in a criminal prosecution must be made out and presented to the judge at the time of the trial, or within such time thereafter as the judge may allow, not exceeding sixty days from the time judgment is rendered; and they must be signed by the judge, and filed by the clerk." The power of the court, therefore, to extend the time within which the bill of exceptions may be filed, after the close of the term, is, in a criminal cause, limited to sixty days after judgment is rendered. A prosecuting attorney may, when further appearing in a criminal cause, withhold any objection to a bill of exceptions on account of its not having been filed in time; but he has no power to fix the time in the first instance, or to extend the time after, and, consequently, cannot enter into any agreement concerning such extension of time which would be binding upon any other person or tribunal. If he has the power to extend the time beyond the statutory limit of sixty days, he has, in that respect, an authority greater than is conferred upon the court, and no such claim of authority on his part either has been or will be asserted.

1. State *v.* Pagels, 92 Mo. 300; s. c., 10 West. Rep. 288.

Insanity: Continuance. — The fact that a defendant on the trial relied on the defence of insanity, would not render sufficient an affidavit for continuance filed before the trial commenced, which stated facts to be proved by absent witnesses, tending to show that he was insane. The relevancy of the statement in the application to the issue joined must always appear. State *v.* Pagels, 92 Mo. 300; s. c., 10 West. Rep. 288.

2. Harris, Cr. L. 467.

Formal Defects. — A conviction will not be reversed for a mere formal defect in the indictment which might have been amended in the court below, or might be amended in this court. Davis *v.* Commonwealth (Pa.), 4 Cent. Rep. 711.

3. State *v.* Barthe (La. An.), March, 1887.

4. Williams *v.* People, 118 Ill. 444; s. c., 6 West. Rep. 335.

5. State *v.* Guy, 69 Mo. 431; State *v.* Whitton, 68 Mo. 91; State *v.* Wilson, 85 Mo. 134; State *v.* Hunt, 91 Mo. 490, 491; s. c., 8 West. Rep 625, 627.

6. Tucker *v.* People, 122 Ill. ; 11 West. Rep. 765.

7. United States *v.* Phillips (D. C.), 4 Cent. Rep. 617.

The court say, "This question is to be determined solely by an interpretation of the statute, for it is a settled doctrine that the right of appeal rests with the legislature alone. If the statute is silent on the subject, it leaves the complaining party

The court cannot review the action of trial courts upon unsupported allegations in motions for new trial.[1]

Where no objections were made or saved at the trial, or in the motion for a new trial, it is too late to raise that objection for the first time on appeal.[2]

4. *Bill of Exceptions.* — Regarding bills of exceptions, (*a*) *Assignment of Errors*, and (*b*) *Technical Errors*, see title "Bills of Exceptions," 2 Am. & Eng. Encyclopædia of Law, 218.

5. *Record and Transcript.*[3]

6. *Review on Appeal.* — *a. What considered.* — The subject of review on appeal, and what is open to the consideration of the court, has heretofore been treated in this series.[4]

unrelieved, since the grant of appeal in terms to one party necessarily by the expression of that grant confers no such right upon the other."

1. State *v.* Jewell, 90 Mo. 467; s. c., 8 West. Rep. 691.

2. State *v.* Marshal, 36 Mo. 400; State *v.* Pints, 64 Mo. 317; State *v.* Preston, 77 Mo. 294; State *v.* Williams, 77 Mo. 310; State *v.* Burnett, 81 Mo. 119; State *v.* McDonald, 85 Mo. 539; State *v.* Burk, 89 Mo. 635; s. c., 6 West. Rep. 669.

Discretion of Court. — The action of the judge of the criminal court, in determining whether the official stenographer "shall attend upon the said court" in given cases, is not a subject of review on appeal, and furnishes no ground for reversal of the judgment. State *v.* Pagels, 92 Mo. 300; s. c., 10 West. Rep. 288.

Reversal for Failure to instruct. — It is only where a proper and material instruction covering some omitted matter of law has been requested and refused, that the judgment will be reversed for a failure to instruct as to such omitted matter. Rollins *v.* State, 62 Ind. 46; Adams *v.* State, 65 Ind. 565; Powers *v.* State, 87 Ind. 144; Ireland *v* Emerson, 93 Ind. 1; Fitzgerald *v.* Goff, 99 Ind. 28; Louisville, N. A. & C. R. Co. *v.* Grantham, 104 Ind. 353; s. c., 2 West. Rep. 280; Louisville, N. A. & C. R. Co. *v.* Jones, 108 Ind. 551; s. c., 7 West. Rep. 33; Cline *v.* Lindsey, 110 Ind. 337; s. c., 9 West. Rep. 218; Rauck *v.* State, 110 Ind. 384; s. c., 9 West. Rep. 197.

Nuisance: Recognizance. — Where a party has been convicted of maintaining a common nuisance in an inferior court, and appeals to the Superior Court, and enters into a recognizance to appear on the first term of the Superior Court, the fact that a statute was passed after the appeal taken, changing the term of the Superior Court from the second Monday in the month to the first Monday in the month, in no way prejudices defendant, nor is it a ground for dismissing the complaints. Commonwealth *v.* Parker, 140 Mass. 439; s. c., 1 New Eng Rep. 722. See Jones *v.* Robbins, 74 Mass. (8 Gray) 329, 349; Lewis *v.* Robbins, 95 Mass. (13 Allen) 552.

Exclusion of Evidence: When cured. — Where an excluded fact is afterwards fully proved on the same trial, this cures any error in the exclusion. People *v.* Clark, 102 N. Y. 735; s. c., 3 Cent. Rep. 801; Graham *v.* People, 115 Ill. 566; s. c., 2 West. Rep. 897.

Although evidence given on a criminal trial was incompetent, unless objection was made and exception taken to its introduction, this court is precluded from examining the question.

Unless this court can see that the finding of the jury in a criminal case is so contrary to the evidence as to impress the court with the belief that the verdict is the result of passion or prejudice, this court will not disturb it.

Although the verdict is not supported by the evidence, this court cannot reverse the judgment for that reason, unless the bill of exceptions shows that a motion was made in the court below for a new trial on that account: a mere entry of the same by the clerk in the record is insufficient. Graham *v.* People, 115 Ill. 566; s. c., 2 West. Rep. 897.

3. Regarding the record and transcript on error or appeal, how made, when made, and what must contain, see titles, "Appeal," 1 Am. & Eng. Encyc. of L. 617, 623, 628; "Error," "Record," "Transcript," hereafter treated in this series.

The failure of the clerk, upon request, to make out and transmit to the clerk of the appellate court a transcript of the record within the proper time, is not good cause for refusing to affirm the judgment. State *v.* Caldwell, 21 Mo. App. 645; s. c., 4 West. Rep. 301.

4. See 1 Am. & Eng. Encyc. of L. 616.

CROPPER. (See CROPS.) — One who is hired to work land, receiving for his compensation a part of the land. He is not a tenant: he has no estate in the land, but receives his share of its fruits as the price of his labor. The possession is still in the owner of the land, who alone can maintain trespass. Nor has the owner the remedy of distress, for the property and possession of the crop also are in him; the possession of the cropper being that of a servant, who gains no property in his share of the crop until the division, which is made by the landlord.[1]

CROPS. — See also LANLORD AND TENANT.

1. Definition. — A crop is the harvested products of grain and other cultivated plants; and also those plants while growing.[2]

2. Growing Crops. — (*a*) *Real or Personal Property.* — Growing crops, before maturity and unsevered from the soil, are part and parcel of the land on which they grow, and pass with a conveyance of the land.[3]

1. Fry *v.* Jones, 2 Rawle (Pa.), 12; Adams *v.* McKesson, 53 Pa. St. 81; Steel *v.* Frick, 56 Pa. St. 175; Harrison *v.* Ricks, 71 N. Car. 7.

2. **Fair Average Crop.** — A contract by an overseer to make "a fair average crop," calls for an average crop, making due allowance for the season and for unforeseen events beyond the control of a prudent and faithful overseer: it is not an agreement that the crop shall be an average one at all events. Wright *v.* Morris, 15 Ark. 444.

His Crop. — While "his crop of flax, 200,000 pounds," in a bill of sale would ordinarily mean the crop raised by the seller, yet it does not necessarily do so; and parol evidence is admissible to show the usage and custom of the flax trade in relation to the meaning of "his crop," and to show that it meant what he owned of the present year's growth. Goodrich *v.* Stevens, 5 Lans. (N. Y.) 230.

Outstanding Crop. — An allegation in an indictment for the larceny of fifteen ears of corn, that they were a portion of an outstanding crop, precludes the idea of their severance from the freehold. Holly *v.* State, 54 Ala. 238.

Crop-Time. — The portion of the year occupied in making and gathering the crop. The period of time intervening between the time when the crop no longer requires working — in popular phrase, "when the crop is laid by" — and the time when the crop has matured, and it is necessary to begin gathering it, is that portion of the year not considered "crop-time." Martin *v.* Chapman, 6 Port. (Ala.) 344.

3. Heavilon *v* Heavilon, 29 Ind. 509; Turner *v.* Cool, 23 Ind. 56; Chapman *v.* Long, 10 Ind. 465; Tripp *v.* Hasceig, 20 Mich. 254; Coman *v.* Thompson, 47 Mich. 22; s. c., 41 Am. Rep. 706; Pitts *v.* Hendrix, 6 Ga. 452; Coombs *v.* Jordan, 3 Bland's Ch. (Md) 284; s. c., 22 Am. Dec. 236; Bittinger *v.* Baker, 29 Pa. St. 66; Backenstoss *v.* Stahler, 33 Pa. St. 251; s. c., 75 Am. Dec. 592; Wilkins *v* Vashbinder, 7 Watts (Pa.), 378; Bank of Pennsylvania *v* Wise, 3 Watts (Pa.), 394; Bear *v.* Bitzer, 16 Pa. St. 175; s. c., 55 Am. Dec. 490; Sallade *v.* James, 6 Barr (Pa.), 144; Crews *v.* Pendleton, 1 Leigh (Va.), 305; s. c., 19 Am. Dec. 750; Foot *v.* Calvin, 3 Johns. (N. Y.) 222; Foster *v.* Fletcher, 7 T. B. Monr. (Ky.) 534; s. c., 18 Am. Dec. 208; Kinsman *v.* Kinsman, 1 Root (Conn.) 180; s. c., 1 Am. Dec. 37; McIlvaine *v.* Harris, 20 Mo. 457; s. c., 64 Am. Dec. 196; Pratte *v.* Coffman, 27 Mo. 426; State *v.* Faber, 37 Mo. 80; Porche *v.*

Bodin, 28 La. Ann. 761; Bloom *v.* Welsh, 27 N. J. L. 183.

A transfer of the legal title of land without reservation passes the title to crops growing thereon at the time of such transfer; and a subsequent chattel mortgage of such crops by such grantor, though still remaining in possession, will pass no rights as against one claiming under the grantee in the conveyance of the land. Coman *v.* Thompson, 47 Mich. 22, Gibbons *v.* Dillingham, 10 Ark. 9; s. c., 50 Am. Dec. 233.

There may be an interest in growing crops in one man, whilst the title to the land is in another. The one does not necessarily follow the other: but when the right to any portion of the crop exists in the owner of the soil, there, unless in certain excepted cases, the ownership of the land draws after it that of the crops; and it cannot admit of a doubt that a sale of the land simply, by the owner of both the land and the crop, carries the property of the crop to the purchaser. Foote *v.* Calvin, 3 Johns. (N. Y.) 216, 222; Willis *v.* Moore, 59 Tex. 628; s. c., 46 Am. Rep. 284.

A landlord cannot, during a subsisting lease, support trespass against one entering and carrying away the crop, nor can his grantee support any such action; in such a case the right of action is in the tenant. Gibbons *v.* Dillingham, 10 Ark. 9; s. c., 50 Am. Dec. 233.

Crops on leased land belong to the lessee, and a subsequent sale of the land does not divest him from his title. Porch *v.* Bodin, 28 La. Ann. 761; Pickens *v.* Webster, 31 La. Ann. 870. See Dayton *v.* Vandoozer, 39 Mich. 749. *Compare* Edwards *v.* Perkins, 7 Oreg. 149.

A conveyance of the reversion carries the crop growing upon it. Burnside *v.* Weightman, 9 Watts (Pa.), 46.

Where rent is payable out of the grain raised, if the landlord sells the land, the vendee becomes entitled to that proportion of the grain growing at the time of the conveyance which the landlord would have been entitled to, had he not conveyed. Johnson *v.* Smith, 3 P. & W. (Pa.) 496.

In Ohio, where lands are valued for judicial sale, and the value of the crop is not included in the estimate, the sale of lands, under a decree of foreclosure, does not pass to a purchaser under the decree. Cassilly *v.* Rhodes, 12 Ohio, 88.

And the sale of real estate by a sheriff, under proceedings in partition, does not pass growing crops of grain to the purchaser. Honts *v.* Schowalter, 10 Ohio St. 124.

Although in Indiana the statutory regulations in respect to the sale of real estate upon execution are nearly identical with those of Ohio, it has been *held* there that growing crops do pass to the purchaser at such sale. Jones *v.* Thomas, 8 Blackf. (Ind.) 428.

The lessee of a farm is entitled to a crop of wheat growing upon it at the time of executing the lease, and which matured during the term of the lease. Emery *v.* Fugina, 32 N. West. Rep. (Wis.) 236.

Ripe crops, although no longer drawing nourishment from the ground, will, if still unsevered, pass by a conveyance of the land so held where the land was sold on the 13th of December, while corn was still standing unsevered where it grew. Tripp *v.* Hasceig, 20 Mich. 254.

In this case the court said that the authorities, in alluding to this subject, generally use the words "growing crops" as those embraced by a conveyance of the land; but this expression appears to have been commonly employed to distinguish crops still attached to the ground rather than to mark any distinction between "ripe and unripe" crops. *Compare* Powell *v.* Rich, 41 Ill. 466. And see Kittredge *v.* Woods, 3 N. H. 503; Bear *v.* Bitzer, 4 Harris (Pa.), 175.

The purchaser of land at sheriff's sale is entitled to the growing grain thereon which had not been severed before a sale. If there has been a severance, it does not pass to him who purchases the land subsequent to the severance. The plaintiffs conveyed a farm to defendant, and took a judgment for part of the purchase-money. They issued a *fi. fa.* thereon, and levied on the real and personal estate. Defendant claimed his exemption, and elected to take the growing grain, which was duly appraised in the presence of one of plaintiffs. The land was subsequently purchased by the plaintiffs, who claimed that the growing grain passed to them. *Held*, that the appraisement under these circumstances was a severance of the grain, and that plaintiffs were not entitled thereto. Hershey *v.* Metzgar, 90 Pa. St. 217. See also Stambaugh *v.* Yeates, 2 Rawle (Pa.), 161; Ulrich's Appeal, 12 Wright (Pa.), 489.

A mortgagor assigned all his property for the benefit of his creditors; it was *held* that the growing grain passed to the assignees, and not to the purchaser at sheriff's sale of the land by virtue of the *levari facias*, because the assignment amounted to a severance. Myers *v.* White, 1 Rawle (Pa.), 353. *Compare* Bittinger *v.* Baker, 29 Pa. St. 66.

Where one sells his growing crop, however, and afterward sells the land, the conveyance of the latter will pass no title to the crops. Austin *v.* Sawyer, 9 Cow. (N. Y.) 39; Stambaugh *v.* Yeates, 2 Rawle (Pa.), 161. But in Westcott *v.* Delano, 20

Wis. 514, it was held that the grantee of land takes the growing grass, notwithstanding a prior sale thereof by the grantor, of which he had no notice.

Crops growing on Lands held adversely. —An action cannot be maintained to recover grain sown and harvested by defendant upon lands to which he claimed title, and of which he had the actual adverse and exclusive possession. Martin *v* Thompson, 62 Cal. 618; s. c., 45 Am. Rep. 663. See Reilly *v.* Ringland, 39 Iowa, 106. *Compare* Lampton *v.* Preston, 1 J. J. Marsh. (Ky.) 454.

Crops sowed on land by a stranger to the title, and without authority or consent of the owner, belong to the owner of the soil. Freeman *v.* McLennan, 26 Kan. 151; Simpkins *v.* Rogers, 15 Ill. 397; Crotty *v.* Collins, 13 Ill. 567; Thomes *v.* Moody, 11 Me. 139. *Compare* Lindsay *v.* Winona, etc., R. Co., 29 Minn. 411; s. c., 43 Am. Rep. 228; Brothers *v.* Hurdle, 10 Ired. (N. Car.) 490; De Mott *v.* Hagerman, 8 Cow. (N. Y.) 220.

Where a person entered upon the land of another without license, and cut grass therefrom and made the same into hay, *held*, that he acquired no property in such hay, and could not maintain an action for its destruction, caused by the negligence of another, while it was stacked upon such land. Murphy *v.* Sioux City, etc., R. Co., 55 Iowa, 473; Lindsay *v.* Winona, etc., R. Co., 29 Minn. 411; s. c., 43 Am. Rep. 228.

The owner of timber trees cut from his land by a trespasser cannot be divested of his title thereto, although the trespasser has converted them into railroad ties, and sold them to a *bona fide* purchaser. Strubbee *v.* Trustees, 78 Ky. 481; s. c., 39 Am. Rep. 251.

Where, during the pendency of an action of ejectment, brought by a lessor against a lessee, under a condition of the lease giving a right to re-enter in case of nonpayment of rent, the lessee sublets to another, who, with full knowledge of the facts, puts in a crop upon the land, which is harvested but not removed therefrom at the time the lessor is put into possession under and by virtue of the judgment in the ejectment suit, the crop belongs to the lessor. Samson *v.* Rose, 65 N. Y. 411; McLean *v.* Bovee, 24 Wis. 295. See also Gardner *v.* Kersey, 30 Ga. 664.

By purchasing land from the United States, the purchaser acquires title to all improvements and crops growing thereon, whether severed or unsevered. Consequently, a mere possessor of public land, who has planted a crop thereon, cannot maintain trespass against a purchaser who enters and removes such crops. Floyd *v.* Ricks, 14 Ark. 286; s. c., 58 Am. Dec. 374; Boyer *v.* Williams, 5 Mo. 335; s. c., 32 Am. Dec. 324.

A pre-emptor planting a crop, which matures after his pre-emption right expires, because of his failure to purchase during the time allowed him by law, may be dispossessed of it by one who, after the expiration of the right, purchases from the government. Rasor *v.* Qualls, 4 Blackf. (Ind.) 286; s. c., 30 Am. Dec. 658.

A promise to pay for improvements erected on public lands, to which the promisor has acquired title from the government, is without consideration and void. Carson *v.* Clark, 1 Scam. (Ill.) 113; s. c., 25 Am. Dec. 79; Hutson *v.* Overturf, 1 Scam. (Ill.) 170; Merrell *v.* Legrand, 1 How. (Miss.) 150; McFarland *v.* Mathis, 10 Ark. 560; Blair *v.* Worley, 1 Scam. (Ill.) 179; Roberts *v.* Garen, 1 Scam. (Ill.) 396; Townsend *v.* Briggs, 1 Scam. (Ill.) 472; Turney *v.* Saunders, 4 Scam. (Ill.) 535; Blackenship *v.* Cutrill, 16 Ill. 62. See also Boston *v.* Dodge, 1 Blackf. (Ind.) 19; s. c., 12 Am. Dec. 203, where the same principle was held in regard to improvements.

Where, at the time of the purchase, the growing crops are reserved by the vendor as a part of the consideration of the sale, the agreement, though by parol, is valid. Or, where the purchaser has permitted the vendor, under such a parol reservation, to harvest and remove the crops, the contract is executed, and the purchaser cannot set off the value of the crop against a suit by the vendor. Heavilon *v.* Heavilon, 29 Ind. 509; Baker *v.* Jordan, 3 Ohio St. 438.

But, in general, a reservation of interest in growing crops cannot be shown by parol evidence where the deed of the land makes no reservation of it. Gibbons *v.* Dillingham, 10 Ark. 9; s. c., 50 Am. Dec. 233; Turner *v.* Cool, 23 Ind. 56; McIlvaine *v.* Harris, 20 Mo. 457; s. c., 64 Am. Dec. 196; Brown *v.* Thurston, 56 Me. 126. *Compare* Backenstoss *v.* Stahler, 33 Pa. St. 251; s. c., 75 Am. Dec. 592, where it was *held* that parol reservation of growing crops is severance thereof, and prevents them from passing as realty under an orphan's court sale of the land; although it is otherwise as to the natural products of the earth which grow spontaneously, such as trees, etc., a reservation of which must be in writing. Green *v.* Armstrong, 1 Den. (N. Y.) 550.

Where, under a parol contract for the sale of land, the vendee, with the consent of the vendor, in pursuance of the terms of the contract, enters into possession, and puts in crops, the invalidity of the contract to sell and convey does not affect the vendee's title to the crops; and if the vendor refuses to perform, and ejects the vendee, the title of the latter to the crops is not thereby divested. In such cases, the crops, as between the parties, are not a part of the realty, but chattels. Harris *v.* Frink, 49 N. Y. 24.

A reservation of growing crops gives right to enter and cut and carry them away and if they are wrongfully taken by the vendee, trover will lie for them. Backenstoss *v.* Stahler, 33 Pa. St. 251; s. c., 75 Am. Dec. 592.

The purchaser of mortgaged premises under a foreclosure sale is entitled to the crops sown by the mortgagor, and growing on the land at the time of the sale. So *held* where such crops had been sold under an execution against the mortgagor before the foreclosure sale, and were harvested by the purchaser under the foreclosure. Shepard *v.* Philbrick, 2 Den. (N. Y.) 174. See Sherman *v.* Willett, 42 N. Y. 146; Simers *v.* Saltus, 3 Den. (N. Y.) 214; Jewett *v.* Keenhaltz, 16 Barb. (N. Y.) 193: Aldrich *v.* Reynolds, 1 Barb. Ch. (N. Y.) 613; Gillett *v.* Balcom, 6 Barb. (N. Y.) 370; Crews *v.* Pendleton, 1 Leigh (Va.), 297; s. c., 19 Am. Dec. 750; Howell *v.* Schenck, 24 N. J. L. 89; Hamblet *v.* Bliss, 55 Vt. 535; Jones *v.* Thomas, 8 Blackf. (Ind.) 428.

A mortgage of land without reservation passes the title to crops growing thereon at the time of such transfer; and a subsequent chattel mortgage of such crops by such grantor, though still remaining in possession, will pass no rights as against one claiming under the grantee in the conveyance of the land. Coman *v.* Thompson, 47 Mich. 22; s. c., 41 Am. Rep. 706.

Until they are severed, the crops growing on mortgaged land are covered by the mortgage, whether planted before or after its execution. The record is notice to all subsequent purchasers of the crops. Rankin *v.* Kinsev, 7 Ill. App. 215. See Chelton *v.* Green, 65 Md. 272.

Where one mortgages his land, and afterward leases it, the lessee is not entitled to crops growing on the premises as against a purchaser under a foreclosure sale. Lane *v.* King, 8 Wend. (N. Y.) 584; s. c., 24 Am. Dec. 105. See also Sallade *v.* James, 6 Pa. St. 144. *Compare* Porche *v.* Bodin, 28 La Ann. 761; Willis *v.* Moore, 59 Tex. 628; s. c., 46 Am. Rep. 284.

Where, at the foreclosure sale, the crops are specially reserved, they do not pass under the sale. Sherman *v.* Willett, 42 N. Y. 146.

Plants and shrubs, the growth of cuttings from plants and shrubs mortgaged, pass to the mortgagee by accession. Bryant *v.* Pennell, 61 Me. 108; s. c, 14 Am. Rep. 550.

Pending foreclosure proceedings under a mortgage of certain land, together with the rents, issues, and profits thereof, the court is authorized to appoint a receiver to take possession of the mortgaged premises, and harvest and market the crop growing thereon which had been planted by defendant: the crops in such case would be part of the mortgaged property. Montgomery *v.* Merrill, 65 Cal. 432.

Where a mortgagor brought trover for the conversion of a crop of growing corn, *held*, that he was entitled to recover the value of the corn in the crib in which it had been put by the defendant after husking, and that, if the defendant had commingled it with his own corn, the duty of separating it lay on him; also, that the cost of husking and gathering could not be deducted. Stuart *v.* Phelps, 39 Iowa, 14. See Lewis *v.* Whittenmore, 5 N. H. 364; Benjamin *v.* Benjamin, 15 Conn. 347; Backenstoss *v* Stahler, 33 Pa. St. 251; Cook *v.* Steel, 42 Tex. 53. *Compare* Lake Shore, etc., R. Co. *v.* Hutchins, 32 Ohio St. 571, 237 id. 82.

Where mortgaged lands were sold under foreclosure while a crop of wheat was growing on the land, and redeemed after the crops had been harvested by the purchaser, the crop or its value was held to belong to the mortgagor, and not to the purchaser. Cartwright *v.* Savage, 5 Oreg. 397.

A mortgage of land does not affect the growing crops until entry under the mortgage, and then all crops not severed pass with the land. A mortgage of the crops made by the mortgagor of the realty, in possession, is a sale of the crops, and in law operates such a severance that they do not pass at a subsequent sale under the mortgage of the realty. White *v.* Pulley, 27 Fed. Rep. 436.

A mortgagor is entitled to sever, in law or in fact, the crops which stand upon his land at any time prior to the destruction of his title by sale or entry under the mortgage. This results from his ownership, and consequent right to the use and profit of this land. Willis *v.* Moore, 59 Tex. 628. See Bittinger *v.* Baker, 29 Pa. St. 70; Buckout *v.* Swift, 27 Cal. 433.

In Myers *v.* White, 1 Rawle (Pa.), 353. it was decided, that, even after the commencement of a suit on a mortgage, the mortgagor may dispose of his growing crop, and then it will not pass to the sheriff's vendee, though it be still growing on the land. See also Hershey *v.* Metzgar, 90 Pa. St. 217.

A mortgagor, and those claiming under him, having the right to the possession and use of the mortgaged property after foreclosure sale until his title is divested by due course of law, may cut and remove all crops growing upon the mortgaged premises, in the usual course of good farming, until the confirmation of the mortgage sale. Allen *v.* Elderkin, 62 Wis. 627.

(*b*) *Ripe Crops.* — Crops ripe for harvest are personal property: they pass to the executor, and not to the heir. They are liable to be seized on execution; and the officer may enter, cut down, seize, and sell the same as other personal estate.[1]

A party in possession of land sold under a foreclosure sale is not divested of his title to the standing crop until the period of redemption has expired, and until the execution of the sheriff's deed. Everingham *v.* Braden, 58 Iowa, 133.

After the foreclosure of a mortgage upon a tract of real estate, the mortgagor planted a crop of corn thereon, which was immature and growing when the land was sold pursuant to the decree of foreclosure. One day before the sale of the land, the mortgagor sold the corn to another, who claimed the same as against the purchaser of the land. *Held*, that the lien of the mortgage and decree of foreclosure attached to the growing crop as well as to the land, and that the purchaser of the land under the decree will be entitled to the growing and unsevered crop in preference to the vendee of the mortgagor, unless there was a reservation of the crop, or unless the purchaser had waived his right to claim the same. Beckman *v.* Sikes, 35 Kan. 120, citing Smith *v.* Hague, 25 Kan. 246; Chapman *v.* Veach, 32 Kan. 167; s. c., 4 Pac. Rep. 100; Caranflo *v.* Cooley, 33 Kan. 137; s. c., 5 Pac. Rep. 766; Jones, Mortg. §§ 676, 780, 1658; 1 Washb. Real Prop. (3d ed.) 124; Jones *v.* Thomas, 8 Blackf. (Ind.) 428; Downard *v.* Groff, 40 Iowa, 597; Shepard *v.* Philbrick, 2 Denio (N. Y.), 174; Lane *v.* King, 8 Wend. (N. Y.) 584; Gillett *v* Balcom, 6 Barb. (N. Y.) 370; Scriven *v.* Moote, 36 Mich. 64; Howell *v.* Schenck, 24 N. J. Law, 89; Pitts *v.* Hendrix, 6 Ga. 452; Rankin *v.* Kinsey, 7 Bradw. 215; Sherman *v.* Willett, 42 N. Y. 146; 1 Schouler, Pers. Prop. 133.

Timber growing upon land mortgaged is a portion of the realty, and is embraced in the mortgage as security. Mortgagors have no right to cut it after default made in any of the payments of the mortgage; and the sale of it by them after it was cut, does not divest the lien of the mortgage; the purchaser takes the timber subject to its paramount rights. Hutchins *v.* King, 1 Wall. (U. S.) 53.

At common law, larceny cannot be committed of things which are a part of the freehold at the time they are taken; but by statute in this State, any vegetable or other product, cultivated for food or market, growing, standing, or remaining ungathered in any field, is the subject of larceny. State *v.* Thompson, 93 N. Car. 538; State *v.* Ballard, 1 South Eastern Rep'r (N. Car.) 685; State *v.* Hills, 78 N. Car. 496; State *v.* Bragg, 86 N. Car. 690; State *v.* Foy, 82 N. Car. 679.

1. Penhallow *v.* Dwight, 7 Mass. 34; s. c., 5 Am. Dec. 21; Heard *v.* Fairbanks, 5 Metc. (Mass.) 111; s. c., 38 Am. Dec. 394; Mulligan *v.* Newton, 16 Gray (Mass.), 212; Cheshire Nat. Bank *v.* Jewett, 119 Mass. 241, 244; Sherman *v.* Willett, 42 N. Y. 146; Stewart *v.* Doughty, 9 Johns. (N. Y.) 108; Shepard *v.* Philbrick, 2 Den. (N. Y.) 174; Bradner *v.* Faulkner, 34 N. Y. 347; Shannon *v.* Jones, 12 Ired. L. (N. Car.) 208; Brittain *v.* McKay, 1 Ired. L. (N. Car.) 268.

Courts will take judicial notice that in the general course of agriculture and the seasons of the year, a crop will not be ready to harvest by the 10th of August. Floyd *v.* Ricks, 14 Ark. 286; s. c., 58 Am. Dec. 374.

A deed of land will not pass grain raised thereon, which has been set apart as the landlord's portion, in the absence of a contract to that effect. Moffett *v.* Armstrong, 40 Iowa, 484.

Vegetable productions growing on land are parcel of it, but, on severance, become mere chattels belonging to the owner of the inheritance unless severed and removed at the same time when they are regarded as part of the land. Coombs *v.* Jordan, 3 Bland's Ch. (Md.) 284; s. c, 22 Am. Dec. 236.

The statutory exemption from attachment and execution of provisions necessary, procured and intended for the use of the family of the debtor, extends to corn, potatoes, and cabbages, planted and raised by the debtor for the use of his family, and ripe for harvest, though not severed from the soil. Mulligan *v.* Newton, 16 Gray (Mass.), 211.

Under the general rule that chattels sold under execution must be present at the place of sale, a sale of growing crops, made two miles from the place where they stand, was held to be invalid. Smith *v.* Tritt, 1 Dev. & B. (N. Car.) L. 241; s. c., 28 Am. Dec. 565.

To constitute attachment of standing corn and potatoes in the ground, ripe for harvesting, actual possession must be taken by gathering them, and putting them in a place of safety. Heard *v.* Fairbanks, 5 Metc. (Mass.) 111; s c., 38 Am. Dec. 394.

Tobacco stored in barns, hanging on poles in process of curing, and in such condition that it cannot be moved without great damage to it, is subject to attachment.

(*c*) *Personalty so as to be Subject to Execution.* — Although growing crops are part of the realty, unless severed from the soil, yet, for the purpose of levy and sale on execution, they are suffered to be treated as personalty.[1]

Cheshire Nat. Bank *v.* Jewett, 119 Mass. 241.

As between a purchaser of land on a foreclosure sale, and the mortgagor's tenant, crops planted by the latter, and mature when the sheriff's deed is executed, although not severed, do not pass by the sale. Hecht *v.* Dettman, 56 Iowa, 679; s. c., 41 Am. Rep. 131. See Johnson *v.* Camp, 51 Ill. 220; Curtis *v.* Millard, 14 Iowa, 128; Everingham *v.* Braden, 58 Iowa, 133. *Compare* McLean *v.* Bovee, 24 Wis. 295; Rankin *v.* Kinsey, 7 Bradw. 215.

1. Preston *v.* Ryan, 45 Mich. 174; Stewart *v.* Doughty, 9 Johns. (N. Y.) 108, 112; Whipple *v.* Foot, 2 Johns. (N. Y.) 422; s. c., 3 Am. Dec. 442; Long *v.* Seavers, 103 Pa. St. 519; Thompson *v.* Craigmyle, 4 B. Monr. (Ky.) 391; s. c., 41 Am. Dec. 240; Parham *v.* Thompson, 2 J. J. Marsh. (Ky.) 159; Craddock *v.* Riddlesbarger, 2 Dana (Ky.), 206; Coombs *v.* Jordan, 3 Bland's Ch. (Md.) 284; s. c., 22 Am. Dec. 236; Smith *v.* Tritt, 1 Dev. & B. (N. Car.) L. 241; s. c., 28 Am. Dec. 565; McKenzie *v.* Lampley, 31 Ala. 526; Stambaugh *v.* Yeates, 2 Rawle (Pa.), 161; Crine *v.* Tifts, 65 Ga. 644; Northern *v.* Lathrop, 1 Ind. 113; Pickens *v.* Webster, 31 La. Ann. 870. *Compare* Shannon *v.* Jones, 12 Ired. (N. Car.) 206.

Crops growing on land at the time of the testator's death go to the executors as against the heir; but, as between the executor and the devisee of the land, the latter is entitled to them. Smith *v.* Barham, 2 Dev. Eq. (N. Car.) 420; s. c., 25 Am. Dec. 721. And see Blair *v.* Murphree, 81 Ala. 454, and cases cited; Creel *v.* Kirkham, 47 Ill. 344.

"When a product of the soil is claimed not to be subject to seizure and sale under a *fieri facias*, the claim must be determined by ascertaining whether such product is real or personal estate; and this last question is in turn to be settled by inquiring whether the product is chiefly the result of roots permanently attached to the soil, or of the labor and skill of the defendant in sowing and cultivating the soil. The decisions holding certain crops to be personal estate, and therefore subject to execution, have generally embraced nothing beyond those crops which, being sown or planted, are capable of reaching perfection within one year. But we think a crop which could not reach perfection in less than two or three years would also be personal property, if its growth can be regarded as chiefly attributable to the skill and labor of the owner. We think, too, that the purpose for which the product is cultivated may be taken into consideration in determining its character as real or personal estate. Thus, fruit-trees planted in an orchard to permanently enhance the value of the real estate ought to be regarded in a very different light from trees growing in a nursery for the purposes of sale, and which the owner treats as merchandise to be sold to whomsoever may apply. But the general rule undoubtedly is, that 'growing trees, fruit, or grass, the natural produce of the earth, and not annual productions raised by the manurance and industry of man, are parcel of the land itself, and not chattels.' 'Annual productions or fruits of the earth, as clover, timothy, spontaneous grapes, apples, pears, peaches, cherries, etc., are considered as incidents to the land in which they are nourished, and are therefore not personal.' Of course, the rule is otherwise where fruit, grass, or any other natural product of the earth has been severed therefrom, and therefore converted into personalty. The fact that a crop is produced by perennial roots is by no means conclusive that it is to be ranked as real estate. The true test is, whether the crop is produced chiefly by the manurance and industry of the owner." Freeman on Executions, § 113.

Growing grain may be levied on at any period of its growth, whether the growth is going on below or above the surface of the soil. Gillitt *v.* Truax, 29 Minn. 528.

Fruit-trees growing upon land become part of the freehold. Adams *v.* Smith, 1 Ill. 221. See Griffin *v.* Bixby, 12 N. H. 454.

A. and B. were partners in the business of fruit-growing; A. furnishing the land and money, and B. the labor. By the terms of a submission to arbitration between them to wind up the partnership, A. was to be charged with the value of all permanent improvements made by the firm. *Held*, that he was not chargeable with the increase, by reason of growth, during the continuance of the partnership, in the value of vines which were growing on the land when the partnership was formed. Squires *v.* Anderson, 54 Mo. 193.

Grass already grown, and ready to be cut, may be sold by parol. Cutler *v.* Pope, 13 Me. 377. *Compare* Crosby *v.* Wadsworth, 6 East, 622.

Though grass, growing, is, in general, parcel of the realty, yet, where it is owned

3. Statute of Frauds. — (a) *Fructus Industriales.* — As growing crops are, for the sake of a sale, personal property, it follows that such sale does not come within the statute of frauds. A parol contract for the sale of growing crops is valid.[1]

by one who does not also own the land, it is personal property, and may be mortgaged and sold as such. Smith v. Jenks, 1 Denio (N. Y.), 579. See Norris v. Watson, 22 N. H. 364; s. c., 55 Am. Dec. 160.

Growing fruit-trees are part and parcel of the land on which they grow, and cannot be considered as goods and chattels, and sold on execution. Adams v. Smith, 1 Ill. 221.

Peaches on trees cannot be taken in execution on a writ of *fi. fa.*, but they may be after they are gathered. State v. Gemmill, 1 Houst. (Del.) 9.

A purchaser of a growing crop at an execution sale shall have free entry, egress and regress to cut and carry it away. Brittain v. McKay, 1 Ired. L. (N. Car.) 265; s. c., 35 Am. Dec. 738; Lewis v. McNatt, 65 N. Car. 65.

Where corn sold under a *fi. fa.* is not ripe at the time of the sale, the vendee has a reasonable time after it is ripe to cut it, and carry it away; and whilst remaining on the land it is not liable to a distress for rent, or to a sale for taxes; for, during all that time, it is considered in *custodia legis.* Smith v. Tritt, 1 Dev. & B. (N. Car.) L. 241; s. c., 28 Am. Dec. 565; Coombs v. Jordan, 3 Bland's Ch. (Md.) 284; s. c., 22 Am. Dec. 236; Whipple v. Foot, 2 Johns. (N. Y.) 418; s. c., 3 Am. Dec. 442; Hartwell v. Bissell, 17 Johns. (N. Y.) 128; Craddock v. Riddlesbarger, 2 Dana (Ky.), 205; Raventas v. Green, 57 Cal. 254.

The lien of an execution issued upon the judgment or decree of a court of record relates to its *teste*, and attaches to all personalty owned by the debtor between the *teste* and the levy of the execution, so as to defeat all intermediate transfers; but a growing corn-crop, being exempt from levy until the 15th of November, is not subject to this lien of the execution until that date, so as to overreach or defeat a prior *bona fide* sale thereof by the owner. Edwards v. Thompson, 85 Tenn. 720.

See also Personal Property, Real Property.

1. Austin v. Sawyer, 9 Cow. (N. Y.) 39; Whipple v. Foot, 2 Johns. (N. Y.) 422; Stewart v. Doughty, 9 Johns. (N. Y.) 112; Bryant v. Crosby, 40 Me. 9; Bricker v. Hughes, 4 Ind. 146; Northern v. State, 1 Ind 113; Matlock v. Fry, 15 Ind. 483; Davis v. McFarlane, 37 Cal. 634.

Growing crops, if *fructus industriales*, are chattels; and an agreement for the sale of them, whether mature or immature, whether the property in them is transferred before or after severance, is not an agreement for the sale of any interest in land, and is not governed by the fourth section of the statute of frauds. Benjamin on Sales, 4th Am. ed. § 126; Marshall v. Ferguson, 23 Cal. 65; Bernal v. Hovions, 17 Cal. 541; Bull v. Griswold, 19 Ill. 631. *Compare* Powell v. Rich, 41 Ill. 469; Graff v. Fitch, 58 Ill. 377. And see Parker v. Staniland, 11 East, 362; Warwick v. Bruce, 2 M. & S. 205; Evans v. Roberts, 5 B. & C. 836; Jones v. Flint, 10 Ad. & El. 753; Emmerson v. Heelis, 2 Taunt. 38.

Growing crops are not "goods and chattels" within the meaning of the section of the statute of frauds which requires immediate delivery, and actual and continued change of possession, of goods and chattels to render a sale valid as against creditors, as they are not susceptible of manual delivery until harvested and reduced to actual possession, and hence they pass by deed or conveyance. The fact, therefore, that after a sale the vendor continues to live on the premises, will not render the sale void as against creditors. Bernal v. Hovions, 17 Cal. 541; s. c., 79 Am. Dec. 147; Bours v. Webster, 6 Cal. 661; Vischer v. Webster, 13 Cal. 58; Davis v. McFarlane, 37 Cal. 638.

A contract for the sale, at a certain price, of growing cabbages not yet ready to be gathered, but which afterwards, when ready for gathering, are counted by the parties and left on the land with an agreement that the purchaser may take them away at any time, makes a sufficient sale and delivery of the whole number, notwithstanding the statute of frauds. Ross v. Welch, 11 Gray (Mass.), 235.

In the case of the sale of standing crops, the possession is in the vendee until it is time to harvest them; and until then he is not required to take manual possession of them. Ticknor v. McClelland, 84 Ill. 471; Thompson v. Wilhite, 81 Ill. 356; Graff v. Fitch, 58 Ill. 373; Bull v. Griswold, 19 Ill. 631; Raventas v. Green, 57 Cal. 254; Williamson v. Steele, 3 Lea (Tenn.), 527; Davis v. McFarlane, 37 Cal. 634. *Compare* Smith v. Champney, 50 Iowa, 174; Stone v. Peacock, 35 Me 385; Lamson v. Patch, 5 Allen (Mass), 586; Stearns v. Washburn, 7 Gray (Mass.), 188.

A license to enter the land of another to cut and carry off corn may be by parol, and cannot be revoked when given for a valuable consideration. Miller v. State, 39 Ind. 267.

(*b*) *Fructus Naturales.* — Growing crops, if *fructus naturales*, are part of the soil before severance; and an agreement therefor, vesting an interest in them in the purchaser before severance, is governed by the fourth section; but if the interest is not to be vested till they are converted into chattels by severance, then the agreement is an executory agreement for the sale of goods, wares, and merchandise, governed by the seventeenth, and not by the fourth, section of the statute.[1]

Where a field of corn is sold, the purchaser has a reasonable time to harvest and remove it, even after notice by the vendor. Ogden *v.* Lucas, 48 Ill. 492.

See also PERSONAL PROPERTY.

1. Benjamin on Sales, 4th Am. ed. § 126; Owens *v.* Lewis, 46 Ind. 488; Kingsley *v.* Holbrook, 45 N. H. 313; Olmstead *v.* Niles, 7 N. H. 523; Putney *v.* Day, 6 N. H. 430; S. C., 25 Am. Dec. 470; Buck *v.* Pickwell, 27 Vt. 401; Ellison *v.* Brigham, 38 Vt. 64; Sterling *v.* Baldwin, 42 Vt. 306; Yeakle *v.* Jacob, 33 Pa. St. 376; Huff *v.* McCauley, 53 Pa. St. 208; Mizell *v.* Burnett, 4 Jones L. (N. Car.) 249; S. C., 69 Am. Dec. 744; Lawrence *v.* Smith, 27 How. Pr. (N. Y.) 327; Green *v.* Armstrong, 1 Denio (N. Y.), 551; McGregor *v.* Brown, 10 N. Y. 114; Harrell *v.* Miller, 35 Miss. 700; S. C., 72 Am. Dec. 154; Anderson *v.* Simpson, 21 Iowa, 399; Slocum *v.* Seymour, 36 N. J. L. 138; Craddock *v.* Riddlesbarger, 2 Dana (Ky.), 205; Jones *v.* Flint, 10 Ad. & El. 753; Teal *v.* Anty, 2 Brod. & B. 99. *Compare* Bostwick *v.* Leach, 3 Day (Conn.), 476, 484.

A sale of standing trees by the owner of the freehold is a sale of an interest in land. Such trees are part of the inheritance, and can only become personalty by actual severance, or by severance in contemplation of law as the effect of a proper instrument in writing. Slocum *v.* Seymour, 36 N. J. L. 139; S. C., 13 Am. Rep. 432; Owens *v.* Lewis, 46 Ind. 488.

Trees annexed to the land are not, in contemplation of the law, severed therefrom: they cannot be sold by verbal contract, although a sale of growing crops of annual culture is not a contract or sale of an interest in land. Buck *v.* Pickwell, 27 Vt. 164. *Compare* Sterling *v.* Baldwin, 42 Vt. 306.

A sale of growing trees, if not made with a view of immediate severance from the soil, is a sale of an interest in real estate, and must be in writing. Huff *v.* McCauley, 53 Pa. St. 210; Bowers *v.* Bowers, 95 Pa. St. 477; Miller *v.* Zufall, 113 Pa. St. 317; Pattison's Appeal, 61 Pa. St. 294.

The sale of trees growing upon land made in prospect of immediate separation from it, is not a sale of the land, or any interest in it, and is not within the statute of frauds. Cain *v.* McGuire, 13 B. Monr. (Ky.) 340; Byassee *v.* Reese, 4 Metc. (Ky.) 372; McClintock's Appeal, 71 Pa. St. 365; Sterling *v.* Baldwin, 42 Vt. 306.

A contract for the sale of standing wood or timber, to be cut and severed from the freehold by the vendee, does not convey to him any interest in the land within the meaning of the statute of frauds. Such a contract is to be construed as passing an interest in the trees when they are severed from the freehold, and not any interest in the land. Claflin *v.* Carpenter, 4 Metc. (Mass.) 580, 583; Whitmarsh *v.* Walker, 1 Metc. (Mass.) 313; Parsons *v.* Smith, 5 Allen (Mass.), 578, 580; Nettleton *v.* Sikes, 8 Metc. (Mass.) 34; Woodbury *v.* Parshley, 7 N. H. 237; Erskine *v.* Plummer, 7 Greenl. (Me.) 447.

Such contracts are held to be at least executory contracts for the sale of chattels, as they shall be thereafterwards severed from the real estate, with a license to enter on the land for the purpose of removal. White *v.* Foster, 102 Mass. 375, 378; Giles *v.* Simonds, 15 Gray (Mass.), 441, 442.

The license to enter upon the land to cut and remove the trees, is, however, revocable so long as the contract remains executory; and if revoked, the purchaser has his remedy by an action against the seller for a breach of the contract. It becomes irrevocable as soon as the contract is executed, or for so far as it has been executed; viz., so far as the trees have been severed from the freehold, and so converted into personal property vested in the vendee. Giles *v.* Simonds, 15 Gray (Mass.), 441, 444, citing Cook *v.* Stearns, 11 Mass. 533; Cheever *v.* Pearson, 16 Pick. (Mass.) 273; Ruggles *v.* Lesure, 24 Pick. (Mass.) 190; Claflin *v.* Carpenter, 4 Metc. (Mass.) 580; Nettleton *v.* Sikes, 8 Metc. (Mass.) 34; Buck *v.* Pickwell, 27 Vt. 157; Barnes *v.* Barnes, 6 Vt. 388; Riddle *v.* Brown, 20 Ala. 412; Russell *v.* Richards, 1 Fairf. (Me.) 429; Erskine *v.* Plummer, 7 Greenl. (Me.) 447; Cutter *v.* Pope, 13 Me. 377. See also Drake *v.* Wells, 11 Allen (Mass.), 141, 143; Nelson *v.* Nelson, 6 Gray (Mass.), 385; Douglas *v.* Shumway, 13 Gray (Mass.), 498; Delaney *v.* Root, 99 Mass. 546, 548; McNeall *v.* Emerson, 15 Gray (Mass.), 384; Heath *v.* Randall, 4 Cush. (Mass.) 195; Owens *v.*

4. Letting on Shares. — Where a farm is let out on shares, it depends upon the stipulations of the contract, and the intention of the parties, whether they are tenants in common, or partners, or whether the relation of landlord and tenant, or of master and servant, exists; and the rights of the parties to the crops raised are determined accordingly.[1]

Lewis, 46 Ind. 488, 519; Selch *v.* Jones, 28 Ind. 255; Pierrepont *v.* Barnard, 2 Seld. (N. Y.) 284; Mumford *v.* Whitney, 15 Wend. (N. Y.) 380; Smith *v.* Benson, 1 Hill (N. Y.), 176. *Compare* Marshall *v.* Green, 33 L. T. R. (N. S.) 404; s. c., 13 Alb. L. J. 9.

A tree growing upon land constitutes a part thereof, and a parol contract for the sale of such a tree passes no title thereto which can be enforced by legal proceedings. Such a contract may amount to a license to enter upon the land, cut down and remove the tree, but the license is one which may be revoked at any time before the tree is cut down; therefore, the reservation by *parol* of a growing tree by the grantor in a conveyance of real estate, by consent of the grantee, with the right to enter thereon and remove such tree after the conveyance is made, constitutes a mere license on the part of the grantee to the grantor to enter upon the land to remove the tree, for the revocation of which no action will lie. Armstrong *v.* Lawson, 73 Ind. 498.

If the owner of land, for a valuable consideration, orally licenses another to cut off within a certain time the trees standing upon it, and afterwards executes an absolute deed of the land to a third person, such deed, when made known to the licensee, will operate as a revocation of the license, although the grantee had knowledge of it. Drake *v.* Wells, 11 Allen (Mass.), 141; Cook *v.* Stearns, 11 Mass. 533, 538; Byassee *v.* Reese, 4 Metc. (Ky.) 372.

Where timber or other produce of land, or any other thing annexed to the freehold, is specifically sold, whether it is to be severed from the soil by the vendor, or taken by the vendee under a special license to enter for that purpose, it is still a sale of goods only. Smith *v.* Bryan, 5 Md. 141; s. c., 59 Am. Dec. 104. This case criticised in Owen *v.* Lewis, 46 Ind. 488, 501.

A., by a written contract of sale, sold certain trees standing upon his land to B., who, having cut and removed some of them, resold the residue to A. by a parol contract. *Held*, that both the original and the resale were sales of goods within the seventeenth section of the statute of frauds; but A. being owner and in possession of the land on which the trees were growing, the resale gave instantly, by force of law, possession of them to him, and the delivery was perfect. Smith *v.* Bryan, 5 Md. 141.

A sale of a crop of peaches then growing in the seller's orchard, the buyer to gather and remove the peaches as they mature, *held* not within the statute of frauds as a sale of an interest in land. Purner *v.* Piercy, 40 Md. 212; s. c., 17 Am. Rep. 591. *Compare* Rodwell *v.* Phillips, 9 M. & W. 502.

A contract to cut trees standing upon the contractor's land into cord-wood, and to deliver the wood at so much per cord, is not a contract for the sale of an interest in lands, and a writing is not necessary to give it validity. Killmore *v.* Howlett, 48 N. Y. 569.

See also Real Property.

1. "In construing contracts for the cultivation of land at halves, it is impossible to lay down a general rule applicable to all cases, because the precise nature of the interest or title between the contracting parties must depend upon the contract itself, and very slight provisions in the contract may very materially affect the legal relations of the parties, and their consequent remedies for injuries as between themselves. In some cases, the owner of the land gives up the entire possession, in which event it is a contract in the nature of a lease, with rent payable in kind; in other cases, he continues to occupy the premises in common with the other party, or reserves to himself that right, and so a tenancy in common to that extent is created, and each is entitled to the joint possession of the crops, or the possession of the one is the possession of the other, until division; or he may retain the sole possession of the land, and the other party may have the right to perform the labor and receive half the crops as compensation; or the two parties may become tenants in common of the growing crops, while no tenancy in common as such exists in the land." Warner *v.* Abbey, 112 Mass. 355, 359, citing Chandler *v.* Thurston, 10 Pick. (Mass.) 205; Walker *v.* Fitts, 24 Pick. (Mass.) 191; Merriam *v.* Willis, 10 Allen (Mass.), 118; Delaney *v.* Root, 99 Mass. 546; Cornell *v.* Dean, 105 Mass. 435. See also Alwood *v.* Ruckman, 21 Ill. 200; Dixon *v.* Nicholls, 39 Ind. 372; Walls *v.* Preston, 25 Cal. 59; Johnson *v.* Hoffman, 53 Mo. 504.

There is no doubt, that where one man farms land of another, under an agreement by which he is to give the owner a part of the crop raised for its use, he and the owner, in the absence of a stipulation pro-

(*a*) *Tenancy in Common in Crops.* — Every form of agreement by which land is let to one who is to cultivate the same, and give the owner as compensation therefor a share of the produce, creates a tenancy in common in the crops. The true test seems to lie in the question whether there be any provision, in whatever form, for dividing the specific products of the premises. If there be, a tenancy in common arises at least in such products as are to be divided.[1]

viding otherwise, become tenants in common of the crops raised. But it is just as clear that the agreement between the parties may be so framed as to secure to the owner of the land the ownership of the product until the performance of a certain stated condition. Howell *v.* Foster, 65 Cal. 169; Wentworth *v.* Miller, 53 Cal. 9; Andrew *v.* Newcomb, 32 N. Y. 419; Lewis *v.* Lyman, 22 Pick. 437; Ponder *v.* Rhea, 32 Ark. 435; Smith *v.* Atkins, 18 Vt. 461.

1. Freeman on Cotenancy and Partition, § 100; Walker *v.* Fitts, 24 Pick. (Mass.) 191; Delaney *v.* Root, 99 Mass. 546; Cornell *v.* Dean, 105 Mass. 435; Putnam *v.* Wise, 1 Hill (N. Y.), 234, 247; s. c., 37 Am. Dec 309, 316; Otis *v.* Thompson, Hill & Denio (N. Y.), 131; Jackson *v.* Brownell, 1 Johns. (N. Y.) 267; De Mott *v.* Hagerman, 8 Cow. (N. Y.) 220; s. c. 18 Am. Dec. 443; Caswell *v.* Districh, 15 Wend. (N. Y.) 379; Burdick *v.* Washburn, 36 How. Pr. (N. Y.) 468, 475; Bertrand *v.* Taylor, 32 Ark. 470; Ponder *v.* Rhea, 32 Ark. 436; Brown *v.* Lincoln, 47 N. H. 468; Wentworth *v.* Portsmouth, etc., R. Co., 55 N. H. 540; Moulton *v.* Robinson, 27 N. H. 550; s. c., 69 Am. Dec. 505; Daniels *v.* Brown, 34 N. H. 454; Hatch *v.* Hart, 40 N. H. 93; State *v.* Jewell, 34 N. J. L. 259; Cooper *v.* McGrew, 8 Or. 327; Currey *v.* Davis, 1 Houst. (Del.) 598; Herskell *v.* Bushnell, 37 Conn. 43; Henderson *v.* Allen, 23 Cal. 521; Smith *v.* Rice, 56 Ala. 417; Brown *v.* Coats, 56 Ala. 439; Swanner *v.* Swanner, 50 Ala. 66; Strother *v.* Butler, 17 Ala. 733; Williams *v.* Nolan, 34 Ala. 167; Ellerson *v.* State, 69 Ala. 1; Ferrall *v.* Kent, 4 Gill (Md.), 209; Lowe *v.* Miller, 3 Gratt. (Va.) 205; Maverick *v.* Lewis, 3 McCord (S. Car.), 212; Scott *v.* Ramsey, 82 Ind. 334; Fiquet *v.* Allison, 12 Mich. 328; Aiken *v.* Smith, 21 Vt. 172; Esdon *v.* Colburn, 28 Vt. 631.

If land is occupied on the shares, and the occupiers covenant to yield and pay to the owners one-half of all the grain raised on the farm, to be delivered at a place designated, and one of the occupiers afterwards enters into an agreement with other persons to do certain work, and to receive therefor one-third of such occupier's share, all the parties are, until the grain is delivered and divided, tenants in common thereof, and not partners. Putnam *v.* Wise, 1 Hill (N. Y.), 234; s. c., 37 Am. Dec. 309.

Where the reservation is of an undivided share, the property of that share is always in the lessor by virtue of his reservation; while the property of the residue is always in the tenant by the implied grant of profits, and they are, therefore, tenants in common of the crop until division. Hatch *v.* Hart, 40 N. H. 98; Car *v.* Dodge, 40 N. H. 407; Taylor *v.* Bradley, 39 N. Y. 140; Foote *v.* Calvin, 3 Johns. (N. Y.) 215; Guest *v.* Opdyke, 31 N. J. L. 554.

Letting on shares for a single crop makes the parties tenants in common thereof. Putnam *v.* Wise, 1 Hill, 234; s. c., 34 Am. Dec. 309; Bradish *v.* Schenck, 8 Johns. (N. Y.) 151.

But after division the property of either party becomes at once absolute in his share. Scott *v.* Ramsey, 82 Ind. 330.

After a lease was cancelled, the landlord told the tenant to put in and harvest fall wheat, and promised that he should have his part and lawful share of it, but afterwards harvested and kept it himself. *Held*, that they were tenants in common of the wheat under a valid agreement, and that the tenant could maintain *assumpsit* on the common counts for the value of his share. McLaughlin *v.* Salley, 46 Mich. 219.

The agreement need not provide for the division of the produce itself. It may contain a particular provision for disposing of the crop in a convenient time and manner, in order to close the transaction by paying the expenses out of the proceeds, and dividing the residue in proportions agreed on. The point is, that there is to be a division, and that the occupier or cultivator is not to pay a certain number of bushels of grain or a certain number of tons of hay as rent of the premises so as to make him a tenant. A provision for disposing of the crop before division, is but a mode of ascertaining the value. and dividing the proceeds. Tanner *v.* Hills, 44 Barb. (N. Y.) 430; Wilber *v.* Sisson, 53 Barb. (N. Y.) 262; Moore *v.* Spruill, 13 Ired. (N. C.) 56.

Where, by the contract, a tenancy in common is created, both parties are entitled to be in possession of the crops before division made, and the possession of one is the (*b*) *Lessor and Lessee.* — Where the owner parts with his entire possession of the land to his lessee or tenant, and is to receive his half by way of rent in kind, the relation of tenants in common does not exist, but it is that of lessor and lessee. The lessor has no right to disturb the lessee in his possession, or to interfere with or take his half; for, the possession of the land being in the lessee, the property in the crop must necessarily follow the interest in the land until the time for division.[1]

possession of the other. Thompson *v.* Mawhinney, 17 Ala. 368; Putnam *v.* Wise, 1 Hill (N. Y.), 234; s c., 37 Am. Dec. 309; Daniels *v.* Brown, 34 N. H. 454; s. c., 69 Am. Dec. 505; Miller *v.* Darling, 22 Minn. 303; Melin *v.* Reynolds, 32 Minn. 52.

And, although the possession of the land remains undisturbed in the owner, who alone may bring trespass for breaking the close, the tenants in common with him may join in an action of trespass for spoiling the crops, because they were tenants in common of the crop. Delaney *v.* Root, 99 Mass. 546; Cornell *v.* Dean, 105 Mass. 435; Foote *v.* Calvin, 3 Johns. (N. Y.) 216; Bradish *v.* Schenck, 8 Johns. (N. Y.) 151; Stewart *v.* Doughty, 9 Johns. (N. Y.) 108; De Mott *v.* Hagerman, 8 Cow. (N. Y.) 220; Caswell *v.* Districh, 15 Wend. (N. Y.) 379.

But neither one may sue the other for damage to the crop, as they are tenants in common. Wells *v.* Hollenbeck, 37 Mich. 504.

If the relation of tenants in common in the land or crop exists between the parties by virtue of their contract, on familiar principles trespass *quare clausum* or *de bonis asportatis* would not lie, and trover for conversion of the share of one party in the crops by the other can be maintained only where there is such destruction, sale, or other disposition of the crops by the one, that the other party is precluded by that act from any further enjoyment of it. Warner *v.* Abbey, 112 Mass. 355, 360; Daniels *v.* Daniels, 7 Mass. 135; Weld *v.* Oliver, 21 Pick. (Mass.) 559; Burbank *v.* Crooker, 7 Gray (Mass.), 158; Delaney *v.* Root, 99 Mass. 546; Daniels *v.* Brown, 34 N. H. 454, s. c, 69 Am. Dec. 505. See Kennon *v.* Wright, 70 Ala. 434.

1. Warner *v.* Abbey, 112 Mass. 355, 360; Darling *v.* Kelly, 113 Mass. 29; Chandler *v.* Thurston, 10 Pick. (Mass.) 205; Cornell *v.* Dean, 105 Mass. 435; Taylor *v.* Bradley, 39 N. Y. 129; Jackson *v.* Brownell, 1 Johns. (N. Y.) 267; Stewart *v.* Doughty, 9 Johns. (N. Y.) 107; Overseers *v.* Overseers, 14 Johns. (N. Y.) 365; Alexander *v.* Pardue, 30 Ark. 359; Birmingham *v.* Rogers, 46 Ark. 254; Person *v.* Wright, 35 Ark. 169; Anderson *v.* Bowles, 44 Ark. 108; Dixon *v.* Niccolls, 39 Ill. 372; Alwood *v.* Buckman, 21 Ill. 200; Rees *v.* Baker, 4 G. Greene (Iowa), 461; Blake *v.* Coats, 3 G. Greene (Iowa), 548; Johnson *v.* Shank, 67 Iowa, 115; Harrison *v.* Ricks, 71 N. Car. 7; Lacy *v.* Weaver, 49 Ind. 373; Doremus *v.* Howard, 23 N. J. L. 390; Rinehardt *v.* Olwine, 5 W. & S. (Pa.) 486; Burns *v.* Cooper, 31 Pa. St. 426; Ream *v.* Harnish, 45 Pa. St. 376; Hoskins *v.* Rhodes, 1 Gill & J. (Md.) 266; Turner *v.* Bachelder, 17 Me. 257; Aikin *v.* Smith, 21 Vt. 180; Moulton *v.* Robinson, 7 Fost. (N. H.) 550; Hatch *v.* Hart, 40 N. H. 98; Garland *v.* Hilborn, 23 Me. 442. *Compare* Jordan *v.* Staples, 57 Me. 352.

A written instrument duly executed by G. and S., whereby G. "does lease unto S. her farm for the term of one year, date to commence Dec. 1, 1882 [describing the land], . . . S. to give one-third of all grain or roots raised, to be delivered in the half-bushel, and one-third of all the hay cut in the stack; to furnish all seed and tools, and pay all threshing expenses; and to keep the buildings and fences in as good repair as they now are, damage by the elements excepted. And it is mutually agreed between the parties that they bind their heirs, executors, and assigns, as well as themselves, to the faithful performance of these covenants," — creates the relation of landlord and tenant between G. and S. Strain *v.* Gardner, 61 Wis. 174; Walls *v.* Preston, 25 Cal. 59.

The exclusive possession of a farm in a tenant for a series of years, a rent agreed upon, though payable in a share of the crop, and non-residence of the owner, all conspire to show the relation of landlord and tenant, and not a tenancy in common of the crop. Dixon *v.* Niccolls, 39 Ill. 372.

A lessor of land on the shares for a single crop, whose share is to be delivered to him off the premises, is to be regarded as entitled to such share as rent, and as not having a right to any part prior to its severance. Before such severance, the lessee is the only person who can maintain an action of trespass for an entry upon the land. It will be different if the landlord is to receive his share on the premises. Woodruff *v.* Adams, 5 Blatchf. (Ind.) 317; s. c., 35 Am. Dec. 122. See Sargent *v.* Courrier, 66 Ill. 245; Darling *v.* Kelly, 113 Mass. 29.

Where "letting on shares" amounts to a lease, the tenant is the owner of the soil during the term of the lease, and he who owns the soil during the year owns the crop raised on it. Waltson v. Bryan, 64 N. Car. 764.

A lease with rent reserved in kind confers upon the lessee an estate in possession in severalty, and the entire property in the whole crop raised and growing upon the land during the term is in the lessee. The landlord has no lien on the crop in preference to other creditors, even where the lessee agreed that he should take all the corn standing in a particular field, except when given by statute. Deaver v. Rice, 4 Dev. & B. L. (N. Car.) 431; s. c., 34 Am. Dec. 388; Rose v. Swaringer, 9 Ired. (N. Car.) 481; Gordon v. Armstrong, 5 Ired. (N. Car.) 409; Harrison v. Ricks, 71 N. Car. 7; Haywood v. Rogers, 73 N. Car. 320.

Under Code N. C. § 1754, which vests the title to crops grown in the landlord until the rent is paid, and the other stipulations of the lease fulfilled, and until the lessor "shall be paid for all advancements made, and expenses incurred, in making and saving said crops," advances by the landlord to a sub-lessee, made without the knowledge and privity of the lessee, are not entitled to priority over advances procured by the lessee for the sub-lessee from a third person. Moore v Faison, 2 S. Eastern Rep. (N Car.) 169.

Under a lease with rent reserved in kind, the tenant may maintain trespass against a stranger for injury to the crop, without joining the landlord. Larkin v Taylor, 5 Kans. 433; Darling v. Kelly, 113 Mass. 29.

Or he may sue a third person whose cattle he has agreed to pasture on the land, without joining his lessors. Cornell v. Dean, 105 Mass. 435.

Where a person has rented a place to another to make a crop, in which they were to go halves, the owner furnishing a horse, it was held to be a tenancy, and that the tenant might bring trespass against his landlord for forcibly entering and breaking the close. Hatchell v. Kimbrough, 4 Jones L. (N. Car.) 163. See also Front v. Hardin, 56 Ind. 165.

Where the rent of a farm is payable in a share of the grain raised on it, division and delivery are essential to vest the title to the grain in the landlord. Burns v. Cooper, 31 Pa. St. 31; Ream v. Harnish, 45 Pa. St. 376; Dockham v. Parker, 9 Greenl. (Me.) 137; Geer v Flemming, 110 Mass. 39; Darling v. Kelly, 113 Mass. 29; Warner v. Abbey, 112 Mass. 355.

Where a tenant holds under a verbal lease giving him half the crop grown upon the land, and allowing him and the landlord the equal right to dig and use the potato crop for family use during the season, the landlord may, without violating the rights of the tenant, go upon the leased premises and request a division of the crop, to the end that each might not encroach upon the other's rights. State v. Forsythe, 89 Mo. 667.

Where the owner of a farm orally leases it to be "carried on at the halves" for a year, the tenant to leave as much hay as he found at the beginning, and having exclusive possession, it cannot be *held* as a matter of law that the owner has such an interest as enables him to mortgage the crops during the year. Orcutt v. Moore, 134 Mass. 48; s. c., 45 Am. Rep. 278.

The interest of a lessor in the crop is not liable to levy under execution against him before division. Howard Co. v. Kyte, 28 N. Western Rep'r. (Iowa) 609; Waltson v. Buyan, 64 N. Car. 764; Gordon v. Armstrong, 5 Ired. L. (N. Car) 409; Deaver v. Rice, 4 Dev. & B. L. (N. Car.) 431; Williams v. Smith, 7 Ind. 559; Long v. Seavers, 103 Pa. St. 517.

Unless the landlord and tenant are tenants in common of a crop, the share of the former cannot, until the crop has been divided, be levied upon. Hansen v. Denison, 7 Ill. App. 73.

The landlord's interest in the crops can in such a case only be attached by garnishment of the tenant. Howard Co. v. Kyte, 28 N. Western Rep'r. (Iowa) 609.

A purchaser at a judicial sale of real estate is entitled to the crops growing thereon, in preference to a landlord to whom part of such crops are reserved for rent, but before it is set apart to him. Townsend v. Isenbarger, 45 Iowa, 670.

The growing crops on leased property is subject to be seized and sold by a judgment creditor of the lessee. Pickens v. Webster, 31 La Ann. 870.

While as between landlord and tenant, in the case of farming on shares, until a division of the crop, the ownership and right to the possession may be said to be in the tenant, still he is not the owner in such a sense that the crop, regardless of the interests of the landlord, can be appropriated to the payment of the debts of the tenant. Atkins v. Womeldorf, 53 Iowa, 150. See Sunol v. Molloy, 63 Cal. 369.

Where a farm is leased for a share of the crops, the hay to be spent on the farm, a mortgage by the tenant on his share of the hay creates no lien which will entitle the mortgagee to remove the hay from the farm. Jewell v. Woodman, 59 N. H. 520.

Execution for the debt of a tenant at will of a farm, may be levied on hay in the barn, which has not been actually delivered to the lessor, notwithstanding an agreement by such tenant that the lessor may hold all (*c*) *Croppers: Master and Servant.*—Where the property of the crop does not at any time vest in the tenant, neither in whole nor in part, but remains in the owner of the soil who controls it at all times, and divides to the occupier his share, neither the relation of tenants in common, nor of landlord and tenant, is created. The occupier is the servant of the land-owner, and is frequently

the hay cut on the farm at security for the rent. Bailey *v* Fillebrown, 9 Greenl (Me.) 12; s. c., 23 Am. Dec. 529; Butterfield *v.* Baker, 5 Pick. (Mass.) 522.

But where the landlord agreed to let a tenant, who was in arrears, remain on the farm upon consideration that he should have all the hops raised thereon, and that the tenant would harvest, cure, and bag them for him, delivery of the hops was not necessary to pass the title, as it never was in the tenant. Kelley *v.* Weston, 20 Me. 233.

Where a lessee of a farm agrees to pay the lessor a part of the crop in lieu of rent, and to give him possession of the whole crop until such part is paid, a sale of the crop by the lessee conveys no title as against the owner of the land. Wentworth *v.* Miller, 53 Cal 9.

Where a tenant dies before the landlord's part of the crop of hay was cut and set off to him, and there is no new agreement between the widow and administratrix and the landlord, the hay cut afterwards is the property of the estate; and where the widow remains on the land, with the landlord's consent, as his tenant at will, after her husband's death, she is the legal owner of all the produce gathered by her on the farm, and is not bound by any contract of her husband as to paying the rent in produce. Dockham *v.* Parker, 9 Greenl. (Me.) 137; s. c., 23 Am. Dec. 547.

Where the lease of a farm provides that half of the hay raised on it shall be consumed thereon by cattle kept by the lessee, and the other half be divided between the lessor and the lessee, the property in the whole of the hay remains in the lessee until the division is made. The lessor has no claim *in rem* upon it before division. But when the division is made under the contract, the portions divided vest separately in the lessor and lessee; but the undivided half to be consumed on the farm still remains the property of the lessee. Symonds *v.* Hall, 37 Me. 354; s. c., 59 Am. Dec. 53.

Where, under a lease, rent is payable out of the grain raised, if the landlord sells the land, the vendee becomes entitled to that portion of the grain growing at the time of the conveyance which the landlord would have been entitled to had he not conveyed. Johnson *v.* Smith, 3 P. & W. (Pa.) 496; s. c., 24 Am. Dec. 339.

Where the relation of landlord and tenant exists, the tenant may mortgage his interest in the crop raised without the consent of the lessor, and the mortgagee will hold the title of the lessee to the mortgaged property, but subject to all the rights of the lessor; and such mortgage will be no violation of his rights. Yates *v.* Kinney, 19 Nebr. 275; Dworak *v.* Graves, 16 Nebr. 706.

A lease upon shares is a personal contract, and not assignable where the amount of rent received must depend on the character and skill of the lessee, or where it gives the lessee the use of lessor's tools on condition that they may be properly kept. A personal lease is forfeited by an assignment and attempt to give the assignee possession, and the lessor may take immediate steps to recover the premises. Randall *v.* Chubb, 46 Mich. 311; s. c., 41 Am. Rep. 165.

Under a statute which provides that every lessor of land shall have a lien on all agricultural products of the leased premises, for the payment of rent, which shall be paramount to all other liens; and that any person shall be fined who, without the consent of the lessor, and with notice of the lien, and with intent to defeat it, shall remove or conceal, or aid in removing and concealing, any thing subject to such lien,—one who purchases cotton from a lessee, with notice of the tenancy of his vendor, is liable to the landlord, in an action on the case, whether the vendee had or had not joined with the tenant in removing the property from the leased premises. But the right to bring an action on the case under such statute is waived where the landlord consents to the sale of cotton by his lessee, although the purchaser may have known nothing of such consent, and it was without consideration. Cohn *v.* Smith, 2 Southern Repr. (Miss.) 244. See also Westmoreland *v.* Wooten, 51 Miss. 825; Wooten *v.* Gwin, 56 Miss. 423; Dunn *v.* Kelly, 57 Miss. 825; Thornton *v.* Strauss, 79 Ala. 164; Knowles *v.* Steed, 79 Ala. 427; Hardin *v.* Pulley, 79 Ala. 381.

Such lien will be paramount to the claim of a mortgagee of the crop. Roberts *v.* Sims, 2 Southern Repr. (Miss.) 72.

See also LANDLORD AND TENANT, LEASES.

called a "cropper." The cropper has no interest in the land, and receives his share as the price of his labor.[1]

(*d*) *Partnership.* — Where an agreement is made to farm on shares, the form of the agreement may be made so as to constitute a partnership between the parties; the ordinary test of a person being a partner, being his participation in the profits of the business.[2]

1. Harrison *v.* Ricks, 71 N. Car. 7; Denton *v.* Strickland, 3 Jones (N. Car.), 61; Haywood *v.* Rogers, 73 N. Car. 320; Parrish *v.* Commonwealth, 81 Va. 1; Walls *v.* Preston, 25 Cal. 59; Romero *v.* Dalton, 11 Pac. Rep. (Ariz.) 863; Fry *v.* Jones, 2 Rawle (Pa.), 11; Adams *v.* McKesson, 53 Pa. 81; Wallace *v.* Maples, 14 Pac. Rep. (Cal.) 19; Jeter *v.* Penn, 28 La Ann. 230; s. c, 26 Am. Rep. 98; Leland *v.* Sprague, 28 Vt. 746; Ponder *v.* Rhea, 32 Ark. 436; Christian *v.* Crocker, 25 Ark. 327; Burgie *v.* Davis, 34 Ark. 179; Sentell *v.* Moore, 34 Ark. 687; Gardenhire *v.* Smith, 39 Ark. 280; Hammock *v.* Creekmoore, 3 S. Western Rep. (Ark.) 180; Porter *v.* Chandler, 27 Minn. 301; s. c., 38 Am. Rep. 293.

Where A. was to pay B. a certain rent for the use of his land, and it was stipulated that no part of the crop was to belong to A. before the rent was paid, A. was *held* to be a cropper. Haywood *v.* Rogers, 73 N. Car. 320; Neal *v.* Bellamy, 73 N. Car. 384; see Pender *v.* Rhea, 32 Ark. 435; Wentworth *v.* Miller, 53 Cal. 9; Esdon *v.* Colburn, 28 Vt. 631. *Compare* Ross *v.* Swaringer, 9 Ired (N. Car.) 481.

A cropper has no assignable title to his share of the crop before division. McNeeley *v.* Hart, 10 Ired. L. (N. Car.) 63; s. c., 51 Am. Dec. 377; Parkes *v.* Webb, 3 S. Western Rep. (Ark.) 521; Hammock *v.* Creekmoore, 3 S. Western Rep. (Ark.) 180. See Beard *v.* State, 43 Ark. 284.

A cropper has no such interest in the crop as can be subjected to the payment of his debts while it remains *en masse;* until a division, the whole is the property of the landlord. Brazier *v.* Ansley, 11 Ired. L. (N. Car.) 12; s. c, 51 Am. Dec. 408; State *v.* Jones, 2 Dev. & B. L. (N. Car.) 544; Hare *v.* Pearson, 4 Ired. L. (N. Car.) 76; Smith *v.* Meech, 26 Vt. 233; Hasbrouck *v.* Bouton, 41 How. Pr. (N. Y.) 208; Provis *v.* Cheves, 9 R. I. 53.

Where, in a lease of a farm, it was stipulated that "all the hay and fodder raised should be fed out on the farm," and that "the calves should be half raised if suitable and promising for that purpose, and be kept on the farm until the expiration of the lease, and then divided," it was *held* that the property in the hay never passed to the tenant, and in the calves not before division at the end of the term, and that, consequently, neither hay nor calves could be attached by his creditors. In regard to these he was the mere servant of the land-owner. Lewis *v.* Lyman, 22 Pick. (Mass.) 437. See Jordan *v.* Staples, 57 Me. 352; Heald *v.* Builders' Ins. Co., 111 Mass. 38. *Compare* Moulton *v.* Robinson, 27 N. H. 550.

By a parol contract between B. and the plaintiff, B. was to cultivate the plaintiff's land, find part of the seed, harvest the crop, and then take one-half of it as a compensation for his labor, and deposit the other half in such place as the plaintiff should direct. Before the crop was harvested, B. absconded, being insolvent. It was *held* that B., whether lessee or cropper, had not such interest in the crop as rendered it liable to attachment for his debts. Chandler *v.* Thurston, 10 Pick. (Mass.) 205.

A contract for working a farm on shares does not amount to a lease; it vests no title to the property in the laborer, nor gives him more than the right to enter for the purpose of cultivation: after the crop is severed, and the owner's share is deposited in a portion of the land, he has no further right to enter that portion, and any subsequent entry will be trespass. Warner *v.* Hoisington, 42 Vt. 94.

One who hires laborers to be paid with a share of the crops raised by them, has no lien on such share for advances made during the year. Shields *v.* Kimbrough, 64 Ala. 504.

Where a land-owner contracts with one to crop his land, and to give him part of the crop after paying all advances, and the crop has not been divided, such cropper is not a tenant, but a mere employee, and the ownership of the entire crop is in the land-owner; and if the cropper forcibly, or against the consent of the land-owner, takes the crop from the possession of the latter, such taking is larceny, robbery, or other offence according to the circumstances of the case. Parrish *v.* Commonwealth, 81 Va. 1.

See also Master and Servant.

2. McCrary *v.* Slaughter, 58 Ala. 230.

An agricultural agreement between two persons, one to furnish the outfit and the land, and the other to hire the laborers and superintend the farm during the year, the (*e*) *Husband and Wife.* — Crops raised on land owned by husband and wife are not subject to the individual debts of the husband;[1] neither are crops raised by the husband on lands owned by the wife;[2] but where land is owned by the husband, and worked by him, the crops may be sold for his debts.[3]

5. Statutory Lien on Crops. — (*a*) *By Landlord.* — In several States the landlord has a statutory lien for his rent on the crops grown during the term of the lease, unless an agreement waiving the lien has been made; and this lien extends in some States for supplies, money, utensils, and other articles advanced by him to enable a farmer to raise his crops.[4]

former to provide money to carry on the business, half of which to be repaid him, and the profits to be divided between them, creates the relation of partners. Reynolds *v.* Pool, 84 N. Car. 37; s. c., 37 Am. Rep. 607, citing Holt *v.* Kernodle, 1 Ired. (N. Car.) 199; Lewis *v.* Wilkins, Phil. Eq. (N. Car.) 303.

Where one furnishes land, team, and its feed, and another gives the time and attention, and meets the expenses, requisite to the making of a crop upon such land, under an agreement that the gross products are to be evenly divided between the parties, the relation of copartners is thereby constituted between them. Curtis *v.* Cash, 84 N. Car 41.

The parties may be partners, even where the agreement is to share the "crops," and not the "profits." Where parties have a joint interest in, and share, the profits and losses arising from the use of property or skill, either separately or combined, they are partners. Autrey *v.* Frieze, 60 Ala. 587; Emanuel *v.* Draugh, 14 Ala. 306; Adams *v.* Carter, 53 Ga. 160; Holifield *v.* White, 52 Ga. 567; Taylor *v.* Bradley, 4 Abb. App. Dec. (N. Y.) 363

It is, however, essential to a partnership, that there be a community of interest in the subject of it, and this community of interest must not be that of mere joint tenants, or tenants in common. When the effect of the agreement is, that one should occupy and cultivate the farm, and the crops should be divided equally between the occupant and the owner, no partnership is necessarily intended or created. Donnell *v.* Harshe, 67 Mo. 170, 172; Musser *v.* Brink, 68 Mo. 242; Johnson *v.* Hoffman, 53 Mo. 504; Dwinel *v* Stone, 30 Me. 384; Putnam *v.* Wise, 1 Hill (N. Y.), 234; s. c., 37 Am. Dec. 309; Christian *v.* Crocker, 25 Ark. 327.

See also PARTNERSHIP.

1. Patton *v.* Rankin, 68 Ind. 245.

2. Dayton *v.* Walsh, 47 Wis. 113; s. c, 32 Am. Rep. 757; Feller *v.* Alden 23 Wis. 301; Rush *v.* Vaught, 55 Pa. St. 437. *Compare* Moreland *v.* Myall, 14 Bush (Ky.), 474; Cunningham *v.* Mitchell, 30 Ind. 362.

But if the husband, who has received the crops or the income of his wife's land during a certain period, can hold the same against her, he, and not she, must bring an action for injuries done to the crops during that period. Lyon *v.* Green Bay, etc., R. Co., 42 Wis. 548.

3. Although a wife is by statute entitled to the fruits of her own labor, yet if she expends money, and furnishes mules in the cultivation of crops on land leased by her husband, and mainly worked by himself and his two minor sons, the crops belong to him, and are subject to his debts. Hamilton *v.* Booth, 55 Miss. 60; s. c., 30 Am. Rep. 500.

See also HUSBAND AND WIFE.

4. Stimson's Am. Stat. Law, § 2034, and statutes of Indiana, Illinois, Iowa, Kansas, Maryland, North Carolina, Kentucky, Tennessee, Missouri, Arkansas, Texas, South Carolina, Georgia, Alabama, Mississippi, Florida, Louisiana, and Arizona. Thigpen *v* Leigh, 93 N. Car 47; Montague *v.* Mial, 89 N. Car. 137; Ledbetter *v.* Quick, 90 N. Car. 276; Belcher *v.* Grimsley, 88 N. Car. 88; Slaughter *v.* Winfrey, 85 N Car. 159; Evans *v.* Howell, 84 N Car. 460; Durham *v.* Speeke, 82 N. Car. 87; Henry *v.* Davis, 60 Miss. 212; Fitzgerald *v.* Fowlkes, 60 Miss. 270: Okolona Sav. Inst. *v.* Trice, 60 Miss. 262; Bacon *v* Howell, 60 Miss. 362; Strauss *v.* Baley, 58 Miss. 131; Burrow *v.* Sanders, 57 Miss. 211; Dunn *v.* Kelly, 57 Miss. 825; Meyer *v.* Bloom, 37 Ark. 43; Roth *v.* Williams, 45 Ark. 447; Bloom *v.* McGehee, 38 Ark. 329; Knox *v.* Hellums, 38 Ark. 413; Lemay *v.* Johnson, 35 Ark. 225; Volmer *v.* Wharton, 34 Ark. 691; Patton *v.* Garrett, 37 Ark. 605; Reavis *v.* Barnes, 36 Ark. 575; Bell *v.* Matheny, 36 Ark. 572; Hammond *v.* Harper, 39 Ark. 248; Sarner *v.* Rice, 39 Ark. 344; Roberts *v.* Jacks, 31 Ark. 597; Bernays *v.* Field, 29 Ark. 218; Nolen *v.* Royston, 36 Ark. 561; Franklin *v.* Meyer, 36 Ark. 96; Buck *v.* Lee, 36 Ark. 525; Kurtz *v.* Dunn, 36 Ark. 648; Herron *v.* Gill, 112 Ill. 247; Cunnea

(*b*) *For Advances.* — So may, under some statutes, any one who advances money or materials to a farmer to enable him to raise a crop, have a lien on the crop, provided an agreement to that effect be made in writing, and, in some instances, recorded. Such a lien has in general a preference over all other previous or subsequent liens, although there are exceptions in some States. A laborer may also have a lien on the crops for the value of labor performed.[1]

6. Mortgage of Growing Crops. — A growing crop, however immature its state, and whatever of labor may be required for its cultivation to maturity, and its severance from the soil, may also be the subject of mortgage.[2]

v. Williams, 11 Ill. App. 72; Gittings *v.* Nelson, 86 Ill. 591; Gooding *v.* Outhouse, 95 Ill. 346; Hunter *v.* Whitfield, 89 Ill. 229; Martin *v.* Blanchett, 77 Ala. 288; Folmar *v.* Copeland, 57 Ala. 588; Thompson *v.* Powell, 77 Ala. 391; Hudson *v.* Vaughan, 57 Ala. 609; Bell *v.* Hurst, 75 Ala. 44; Abraham *v.* Hall, 59 Ala. 386; Lake *v.* Gaines, 75 Ala. 143; Lavender *v.* Hall, 60 Ala. 214; Agee *v.* Mayer, 71 Ala. 88; Kennon *v* Wright, 70 Ala. 434; Lomax *v* Le Grand, 60 Ala. 537; Robinson *v.* Lehman, 72 Ala. 401; Tucker *v.* Adams, 59 Ala. 254; Hussey *v.* Peebles, 53 Ala. 432; Scaife *v.* Stovall, 67 Ala. 237; Tuttle *v.* Walker, 69 Ala. 172; Busbin *v.* Ware, 69 Ala. 279; Wilson *v.* Stewart, 69 Ala. 302; Wilkinson *v.* Ketler, 69 Ala. 435; Fitzsimmons *v.* Howard, 69 Ala. 590; Lehman *v.* Howze, 73 Ala. 302; Ware *v.* Blalock, 72 Ga. 804; Zachry *v.* Stewart, 67 Ga. 218; Scott *v.* Pound, 61 Ga. 579; Lathrop *v.* Clewis, 63 Ga. 282; Hempstead Real Est., etc., Assoc. *v.* Cochran, 60 Tex. 620; Wise *v.* Old, 57 Tex. 514; Rosenberg *v.* Shaper, 51 Tex. 134; Stone *v.* Bohm, 79 Ky. 141; English *v.* Duncan, 14 Bush (Ky.), 377; Haseltine *v.* Ansherman, 87 Mo. 410; Meier *v* Thomas, 5 Mo. App. 584; Carter *v.* Du Pre, 18 S. Car. 179; Kennedy *v.* Reames, 15 S. Car. 548; Richardson *v.* Blakemore, 11 Lea (Tenn), 290; Lewis *v.* Mahon, 9 Baxt. (Tenn.) 374; Armstrong *v.* Walker, 9 Lea (Tenn.), 156; Dougherty *v.* Kellum, 3 Lea (Tenn), 643; Tarpy *v.* Persing, 27 Kans. 745; Fejavary *v.* Broesch, 52 Iowa, 88; Holden *v* Cox, 60 Iowa, 449; Atkins *v.* Womeldorf, 53 Iowa, 150; Cathcart *v.* Turner, 18 Fla. 837; Kennard *v.* Harvey, 80 Ind. 37; Ellis *v.* Martin, 60 Ind. 394. See Shields *v.* Atkinson, 67 Ala. 244. *Compare* Thomas *v.* Bacon, 34 Hun (N. Y.), 88. See also Buswell *v.* Marshall, 51 Vt. 87.

See also Liens.

1. See statutes of Virginia, North Carolina, Alabama, Florida, Tennessee, South Carolina, Georgia, Mississippi, Louisiana, Kansas. Stimson's Am. Statute Law, § 1954; Reese *v.* Cole, 93 N. Car. 87; Rawlings *v.* Hunt, 90 N. Car. 270; Cottingham *v.* McKay, 86 N. Car. 241; Gay *v.* Nash, 84 N. Car. 333; Whitaker *v.* Smith, 81 N. Car. 340; Emerson *v* Hedrick, 42 Ark. 263; Franklin *v.* Meyer, 36 Ark. 96; Purgie *v.* Davis, 34 Ark. 179; Brown *v.* Thomas, 14 Ill. App. 428; Carter *v.* Wilson, 61 Ala. 434; Stern *v.* Simpson, 62 Ala. 194; Hamilton *v.* Maas, 77 Ala. 283; Peard *v.* Woodard, 78 Ala. 317; Foster *v.* Napier, 74 Ala 393; Watson *v.* Auerbach, 57 Ala. 353; Grady *v.* Hall, 59 Ala. 341; Griel *v.* Lehman, 59 Ala. 419; Connor *v.* Jackson, 74 Ala. 464; Comer *v.* Daniel, 69 Ala 434; Flexner *v.* Dickerson, 65 Ala. 129; Johnston *v.* Hannah, 66 Ala. 127; Brown *v.* Hamil, 76 Ala. 506; Marens *v.* Robinson, 76 Ala. 550; Sheussler *v.* Gairs, 68 Ala. 556; Lalouire *v.* Wiltz, 31 La. Ann. 436; Chaffe *v.* Heyner, 31 La. Ann. 594; Gay *v.* Daigre, 30 La. Ann. Pt. II 1007; Lenton *v.* Mahan, 30 La. Ann. Pt. II. 1401; Saloy *v.* Dragon, 37 La. Ann. 71; Citizens' Bank *v.* Wiltz, 31 La. Ann 244; Hogue *v.* Lewis Co. Sheriff, 1 Wash. Ter. 172; Carpenter *v.* Strickland, 20 S Car. 1; Richey *v.* Du Pré, 20 S. Car. 6; Jones *v.* Clarkson, 16 S. Car. 628; Isbell *v* Dunlap, 17 S. Car. 581; Sternberger *v.* McSween, 14 S. Car 35; Warren *v.* Lawton, 14 S. Car. 476; Mabry *v.* Judkins, 66 Ga. 732; Stallings *v.* Harrold, 60 Ga. 478; Hardwick *v* Burtz, 59 Ga. 773; Eve *v.* Crowder, 59 Ga. 799; Ware *v.* Macon City Bank, 59 Ga. 840; Wooten *v.* Gwin, 56 Miss. 422; Polk *v.* Foster, 7 Baxt. (Tenn.) 98; Whitmore *v.* Poindexter, 7 Baxt. (Tenn.) 248. See also Commission Merchants or Factors, vol. 3, p. 317.

2. Booker *v.* Jones, 55 Ala. 266; Adams *v.* Tanner, 5 Ala 740; Evans *v.* Lamar, 21 Ala. 333; Ellis *v.* Martin, 60 Ala. 394; McKenzie *v.* Lampley, 31 Ala. 528; Sealy *v.* McCormick, 68 Ala. 649; Robinson *v.* Mauldin, 11 Ala. 977; Melin *v.* Reynolds, 32 Minn. 52; Cotten *v.* Willoughby, 83

N. Car. 75; s. c., 35 Am. Rep. 564; Clay *v.* Currier, 17 Rep. (Iowa) 683; Hansen *v.* Dennison, 7 Ill. App. 73; Parker *v.* Webb, 3 S. Western Rep. (Ark.) 521; Hammock *v.* Creekmoore, 3 S. Western Repr. (Ark.) 180; Beard *v* State, 43 Ark. 284; Jarratt *v.* McDaniel, 32 Ark. 598; Meadow *v.* Wise, 41 Ark. 285; Greer *v.* Turner, 47 Ark. 17; Kimball *v.* Sattley, 55 Vt. 285; s. c., 45 Am. Dec. 614; Fitch *v.* Burk, 38 Vt. 683; Sterling *v.* Baldwin, 42 Vt. 306; Cudworth *v.* Scott, 41 N H. 456.

A crop is a "growing" crop, so that it can be mortgaged, giving a legal title to the mortgagee from the time the seed is deposited in the ground. Wilkinson *v.* Ketler, 69 Ala. 435; Hansen *v.* Dennison, 7 Ill. App. 73. *Compare* Comstocks *v.* Scales, 7 Wis 159.

Unplanted Crops. — It is even *held* that a crop to be planted on one's own land or on land to be let to him, as well as a crop planted and in process of cultivation, is the subject of a valid mortgage. Rawlings *v.* Hunt, 90 N. Car 270; Cotten *v.* Willoughby, 83 N. Car. 75; Harris *v.* Jones, 83 N. Car. 317; Robinson *v.* Ezzell, 72 N. Car. 231; Senter *v.* Mitchell, 16 Fed. Rep. 206; Thrash *v.* Bennett, 57 Ala. 156; Hurst *v.* Bell, 72 Ala. 336; Watkins *v.* Wyatt, 9 Baxt. (Tenn.) 250; s. c, 30 Am. Rep. 63. *Compare* Hutchinson *v.* Ford, 9 Bush (Ky.), 318; Comstocks *v.* Scales, 7 Wis. 159; Milliman *v.* Neher, 20 Barb. (N. Y.) 37.

The lessee of land in possession executed a mortgage of the crops to be raised by him the coming season, and which were not yet planted. *Held*, that the mortgage was valid. Arques *v.* Wasson, 51 Cal. 620; s. c., 21 Am. Rep. 718; Conderman *v.* Smith, 41 Barb. (N. Y.) 404; Harris *v.* Jones, 83 N. Car. 317; Robinson *v.* Ezzell, 72 N. Car. 231; Sanborn *v.* Benedict, 78 Ill 309; Minnesota Linseed Oil Co. *v.* Maginnis, 32 Minn. 193; McCarty *v.* Blevins, 5 Yerg. (Tenn.) 195.

A mortgage on crops yet to be planted is a good and enforceable lien where the mortgagee takes the property in his possession after it is acquired, and before the rights of others as creditors or purchasers have attached thereon. Moore *v.* Byrum, 10 S Car. 452; s. c, 30 Am. Rep. 58; Wyatt *v.* Watkins, 16 Alb. L J. (Tenn.) 205; Cook *v.* Corthell, 11 R. I. 482; s. c., 23 Am Rep. 518; Williams *v* Briggs, 11 R. I. 176; s. c., 23 Am. Rep. 518; 22 Am. Rep. 653, note; Rees *v.* Coats, 65 Ala. 258; Columbus Iron Works *v.* Renfro, 71 Ala. 577; Collier *v.* Faulk, 69 Ala. 58; Hurst *v.* Bell, 72 Ala. 336; Thompson *v.* Powell, 77 Ala. 391; Mayer *v.* Taylor, 69 Ala. 403; Cole *v.* Kerr, 19 Neb. 553; Lamson *v.* Moffatt, 61 Wis. 153.

A cotton planter, cultivating land, for the purchase-price of which he had mortgaged his crop for the ensuing year, made two mortgages on the same crop, one before and one after it was sown, to other parties, to cover past and future advances from them. Advances were made thereafter, and the mortgagor continued in their debt. He sold part of his crop through a broker, and received the proceeds. In a suit against the broker by the second mortgagees for conversion, *held*, that the first mortgage of the plaintiffs, though not notice to third parties under the Alabama registration law, being made before the crop was planted, was a valid executory contract, conveying to the mortgagees an equity which, on their taking possession of the crop, would become a legal title. In such a case the mortgagor in possession, having a legal title against all but the prior mortgagee, could convey to the second mortgagees such a title as would enable them to maintain trover against any one but the prior mortgagee, or those claiming under him. Marks *v.* Robinson, 2 Southern Rep. (Ala.) 292.

Where a mortgage is executed on an unplanted crop, a lien attaches in equity as soon as the subject of the mortgage comes into existence, and in a proceeding to foreclose will be enforced against the mortgagor and those holding under him with record notice. Apperson *v.* Moore, 30 Ark. 56; s. c., 21 Am. Rep. 170; Butt *v.* Ellett, 19 Wall. (U. S.) 544; McCaffrey *v.* Woodin, 65 N. Y. 459; s. c., 22 Am. Rep. 644; Smith *v.* Atkins, 18 Vt. 465; Everman *v.* Robb, 52 Miss. 653; s. c., 25 Am. Rep. 682; White *v.* Thomas, 52 Miss. 49; Sillers *v.* Lester, 48 Miss. 513; Booker *v.* Jones, 55 Ala. 266; Stewart *v.* Fry, 3 Ala. 573; Kirksey *v.* Means, 42 Ala. 426; Smith *v.* Fields, 79 Ala. 335.

In case of crops to be grown, a mortgage vests potentially from the time of the executory bargain, and actually as soon as the subject arises. Andrew *v.* Newcomb, 32 N. Y. 417; Senter *v.* Mitchell, 16 Fed. Rep. 206.

A mortgage executed by the owner or lessee of land on a crop which is not planted, but is to be planted *in futuro*, conveys to the mortgagee a mere equitable interest or title, which will not support an action of detinue, trover, or trespass; but this title attaches instantly on the planting, and is superior to a second mortgage executed prior to the planting, the second mortgagee having notice of the former mortgage. Mayer *v.* Taylor, 69 Ala. 403; s. c., 44 Am. Rep. 522, citing Grant *v.* Steiner, 65 Ala. 499; Rees *v.* Coats, 65 Ala. 256; Booker *v.* Jones, 55 Ala. 266; Abraham *v.* Carter, 53 Ala. 8; Moore *v.* Byrum, 10 S. Car. 452; s. c., 30 Am. Rep. 58; Sillers *v.* Lester, 48

Miss. 513; Fonville *v.* Casey, Murph. (N. Car.) 389; s. c., 4 Am. Dec. 559. See also Collins *v.* Faulk, 69 Ala. 58; Seay *v.* McCormick, 68 Ala. 549; Wilkinson *v* Keller, 69 Ala. 435. *Compare* Hutchinson *v.* Ford, 9 Bush (Ky.), 318; s. c., 15 Am. Rep. 711, where it was held that a mortgage of a crop to be raised on a farm during a certain term, but which is not yet sown, passes no title, and the mortgagee has no claim against a purchaser of the crop for it or its value. See also Cudworth *v.* Scott, 41 N. H. 456; Redd *v.* Burrus, 58 Ga. 574.

A chattel mortgage can have no valid operation upon a crop of grain given at or about the time of planting the same, and before it is up, or has any appearance of a growing crop. Comstock *v.* Scales, 7 Wis. 159.

A mortgage may embrace a crop of which the seed is planted, and which is growing. Stephens *v.* Tucker, 55 Ga. 543.

A mortgage of a crop thereafter to be raised is void as against a subsequent purchaser from the mortgagor, unless before such purchase the mortgagee took actual possession of the property. Lamson *v.* Moffat, 61 Wis. 153, citing Comstock *v.* Scales, 7 Wis. 159; Chynometh *v.* Tenney, 10 Wis. 397, 407; Farmers' L. & T. Co. *v.* Comm. Bank, 11 Wis. 207; Single *v.* Phelps, 20 Wis. 398; Mowry *v.* White, 21 Wis. 417; Hunter *v.* Bosworth, 43 Wis. 583; Farmers' L. & T. Co. *v.* Fisher, 17 Wis. 114; Farmers' L. & T. Co. *v.* Cary, 13 Wis. 110.

A mortgage of crops to be sown is too indefinite and uncertain to be valid against third persons, unless at least designating the year or term in which they are to be grown. Pennington *v.* Jones, 57 Iowa, 37.

A mortgage may be of part of a growing crop, if the part mortgaged is so described as to be identified by parol evidence; and whether so identified or not, is a question for the jury upon the proof. Stephens *v.* Tucker, 55 Ga. 543.

The sale or mortgage of *a crop to be planted*, as well as one planted and in process of cultivation, is valid, provided the *place* where the crop is to be produced is designated with certainty sufficient to identify it. *It seems* parol testimony is competent to fit the description to the property, and show the agreement of the parties. A mortgage conveying "my entire crop of every description" is too vague to pass any title to the property mentioned. Rountree *v.* Britt, 94 N. Car 104; Atkinson *v.* Graves, 91 N. Car. 99.

A mortgage which conveys "all of the crops of corn, cotton, and cotton-seed, and crops of every other name and description, to be grown this year in said county," is not void for uncertainty, but is valid and operative to convey all the crops grown in said county by the grantor or mortgagor. Hamilton *v.* Maas, 77 Ala. 283.

A chattel mortgage upon a growing crop, as against an attaching creditor, continues to be a lien upon the crop, in the possession of the mortgagor, after severance and removal from the land, — Rider *v.* Edgar, 54 Cal. 127, — and upon the proceeds of the crop after sale. Muse *v.* Lehman, 30 Kan. 514.

Section 2972 of Civil Code keeps alive the lien of a mortgage upon a growing crop only so long as the same remains on the land of the mortgagor. Waterman *v.* Green, 59 Cal. 142; Goodyear *v.* Williston, 42 Cal. 11.

A mortgagee of a cotton crop, who, in order to gather and secure the crop, makes further advances to the mortgagor, does not thereby obtain a lien on the proceeds of the sale of the crop that takes precedence of a lien created by a second mortgage or deed of trust executed to a trustee to secure an indebtedness due from the mortgagor to his wife for moneys advanced to him. Weathersbee *v.* Farrar, 1 S. Eastern Repr. (N. Car.) 616.

In 1879, N. conveyed to B. a farm for $5,610, payable in six equal annual instalments. B. then conveyed the land and ten bales of each annual crop of cotton to be produced on it for the six years, to a trustee to secure the payments, with power to take possession, and sell on default of payment. In 1881, N. took possession of ten bales, including three made by a tenant of B., to pay the instalment for that year. The tenant had mortgaged his whole crop of that year to D. for supplies. *Held*, that the first mortgage was void for uncertainty as against D., the second mortgagee, and he could maintain replevin against N. for the three bales. Dodds *v.* Neel, 41 Ark. 70.

A mortgage describing the property as "all the cut and growing, and having grown," on the premises. *Held* insufficient to give third persons notice of a lien on the crops grown on the land. Cray *v.* Currier, 62 Iowa, 535.

A mortgage which describes the crops intended to be conveyed as "my entire crop of corn, cotton, [cotton] seed, fodder, pease, potatoes, and cane that I may raise the present year on my place," is not void for uncertainty. While the description of the crops is very general and indefinite, it is capable of being rendered certain by showing the lands cultivated by the mortgagor during that year, and the quantity of the respective crops raised by him. Seay *v.* McCormick, 68 Ala. 549; Ellis *v.* Martin, 60 Ala. 394.

The description of the property in a mortgage was as follows: "All and the entire crop of flax and wheat, and other grain or produce, *raised* on the east half,"

CROSS.[1]

CROSS-BILL. — A cross-bill is brought by a defendant in a suit against the plaintiff in the same suit, or against other defendants in the same suit, or against both, touching the matters in question in the original bill. It is brought either to obtain a discovery of facts in aid of the defence to the original bill, or to obtain full and complete relief to all parties, as to the matters charged in the original bill.[2]

etc.; and the year when the same were to be "raised" was not stated. *Held* insufficient to put defendants on inquiry as to crops, — none of which were "raised," and only five acres of which were sown at the time of the execution of the mortgage, — and that the description could not be aided by parol testimony. Eggert *v.* White, 59 Iowa, 464; Pennington *v.* Jones, 57 Iowa, 37. *Compare* Muir *v.* Blake, 57 Iowa, 662.

A mortgage of "all of a crop of ten acres of cotton to be grown" by the mortgagor upon a field containing forty acres in cotton, is, as to strangers to the mortgage, void for uncertainty, and parol evidence to designate the particular ten acres intended is not admissible. Krone *v.* Phelps, 43 Ark. 350.

"One-half of all the crop growing" on certain described lands, means one undivided half of such crop; and, as a description (in a chattel mortgage) of the property mortgaged, is sufficiently definite. Melin *v.* Reynolds, 32 Minn. 52.

A mortgage of land including "the rents, issues, and profits thereof," was *held* to be a lien on the crops growing on the premises. Montgomery *v.* Merrill, 165 Cal. 432.

A mortgage which described the property mortgaged as "thirty bales of good lint cotton, the first picking of our crop of 1882, to average four hundred and fifty pounds each," describes the cotton with sufficient certainty. Senter *v.* Mitchell, 16 Fed. Rep. 206.

A chattel mortgage on a growing crop executed after a transfer of the legal title to the land on which it grows, will pass no rights as against one claiming under the grantee in the convevance of the land. Coman *v.* Thompson, 47 Mich. 22; Gibbons *v.* Dillingham, 10 Ark. 9; s. c., 50 Am. Dec. 233.

One who takes a mortgage of growing crops during the pendency of an action of ejectment, is bound by the judgment against the mortgagor, and may be evicted under the writ issued on such judgment. As between him and the successful plaintiff such growing crops are part of the realty, and pass to the plaintiff, and the mortgagee is not entitled to possession of the premises for the purpose of harvesting such crops. Huerstal *v.* Muir, 64 Cal. 450.

See also Mortgages, Chattel Mortgages.

1. **Cross, Intersect.** — "The word 'intersect' ordinarily means the same as to cross; literally, to cut into or between. The two words seem to be used in the same sense, as is apparent from the fact that the word *intersected* is only used in the latter part of the quotation, whereas, if they were used in different senses, we should expect to find the words 'or crossed' also used." State *v.* New Haven & Northampton Co., 45 Conn. 344.

A railroad *held* to "cross a public highway," though they did not cross upon the same level. People *v.* N. Y. Cent. R. R. Co., 13 N. Y. 78.

Cross Street. — Where a proviso is made as to the assessment of real estate fronting upon a "cross-street, or street fronting upon" another, its language does not contemplate the assessment of *any* street upon *one side* alone of that other. Schumacker *v.* Toberman, 56 Cal. 510.

"Cross the Lake." — Where an act provides that it shall not be law for a person to cross the lake within three miles of a certain bridge without paying toll, it applies also to a person crossing on *ice*, but not to one who does not enter the lake within three miles of the bridge. Cayuga Bridge Co. *v.* Stout, 7 Cow. (N. Y.) 33.

"Cross the Bar." — Where a boundary is described as "crossing the bar" between two islands, "crossing the bar" means passing clear across the entire width of the bar on the line of low water, and drawing the subsequent boundary-line from the farther edge or limit of the bar on that line of low water. Bremen *v.* Bristol, 66 Me. 357.

"Cross a Road." — The exemption from payment of toll of a passenger "crossing a road and not going one hundred yards thereon," applies only to persons actually *crossing* the road. Phillips *v.* Harper, 2 Chit 412.

But it was *held* to apply to a person going along the road and continuing thereon till he reached a lane turning off on the same side on which he entered. Major *v.* Oxenham, 5 Taunt. 340.

2. Ayres *v.* Carver, 17 How. (U. S.) 595.

"It should not introduce new and distinct matters not embraced in the original

CROSS-COMPLAINT.[1]

CROSS-EXAMINATION. — See TRIAL; WITNESSES.

CROSSINGS. — See also CARRIERS OF PASSENGERS; COMPARATIVE NEGLIGENCE; CONTRIBUTORY NEGLIGENCE; MUNICIPAL CORPORATIONS; NEGLIGENCE; RAILROADS.

bill, as they cannot be properly examined in that suit, but constitute the subject-matter of an original, independent suit. The cross-bill is auxiliary to the proceeding in the original suit, and a dependency upon it. It is said by *Lord Hardwicke*, that both the original and cross bill constitute but one suit, so intimately are they connected together."

"A cross-bill is a mere auxiliary suit, and a dependency of the original. It may be brought by a defendant against the plaintiff in the same suit, or against other defendants, or against both; but it must be touching the matters in question in the bill, as where a discovery is necessary, or as where the original bill is brought for a specific performance of a contract, which the defendant at the same time insists ought to be delivered up and cancelled; or where the matter of defence arises after the cause is at issue, where in cases at law the defence is by plea *puis darrein continuance*." Cross *v.* De Valle, 1 Wall (U. S.) 14.

"A cross-bill, *ex vi terminorum*, implies a bill brought by a defendant in a suit against the plaintiff in the same suit or against other defendants in the same suit, or against both, touching the matters in question in the original bill." Kemp *v.* Mitchell, 36 Ind. 256, quoting Story's Eq. Pl sec. 389.

"A cross-bill is a bill brought by a defendant against a plaintiff, or other parties in a former bill depending, touching the matter in question in that bill. . . . It is treated as a mere auxiliary suit, or as a dependency upon the original suit. . . . A bill of this kind is usually brought either to obtain a necessary discovery of facts in aid of the defence to the original bill, or to obtain full relief to all parties in reference to the matters of the original bill." Kidder *v.* Barr, 35 N. H. Rep. 251.

"In the very elementary nature of the thing, a cross-bill is a bill filed by a *party defendant* to a suit." McDougald *v.* Dougherty, 14 Ga 679.

"A cross-bill is nothing more than an addition to the answer. It makes a part of the pleading which states the defence, the answer being the other part. . . . If a cross-bill is added to an answer, the answer is amended." Canant *v.* Mappin, 20 Ga. 731

1. "A cross-complaint is allowed 'when a defendant has a cause of action against a co-defendant, or a person not a party to the action, and affecting the subject-matter of the action.' . . . 'The only real difference between a complaint and a cross-complaint,' says the author we have quoted, 'is, that the first is filed by the plaintiff, and the second by the defendant. Both contain a statement of the facts, and each demands affirmative relief upon the facts stated' . . . And we may add, the difference between a counter-claim and a cross-complaint is this. in the former, the defendant's cause of action is against the plaintiff; and in the latter, against a co-defendant, or one not a party to the action." White *v.* Reagan, [illegible] Ark. 289, 290

1. Preliminary. — The term "crossing," as used in this article, cannot well be defined. It is rather a term of description. We here deal principally with the duties and rights of railroads, and of travellers at "crossings" created by the intersection at grade of public highways and railroad tracks; and consequently the greater part of this discussion relates to rights and liabilities arising from the injury of property and persons by accidents at such crossings.

2. Kinds of Crossings. — A crossing, in the sense of the term as used in this article, is the intersection at grade of a railroad track (*a*) by a public highway, or (*b*) by a private road, or (*c*) by another railroad. So, also, the intersection at grade of either a public or private street or way by another of either class, may be said to be "a crossing," within the scope of this discussion; but the litigation that has arisen from accidents at such crossings is so limited that they will only be treated of incidentally. Rights and liabilities of railroad companies for accidents at places where their tracks cross highways either above or below grade, may also properly be considered as incident to the general discussion.

3. What a Part of Crossing. — The crossing itself is the portion of the highway and the railway that are used in common. But the embankment, which is constructed as a necessary approach to the railway tracks, is, in legal contemplation, a part of the crossing.[1]

4. Duty of Railroad to construct and maintain. — It is generally the duty of a railroad company to construct, maintain, and repair the crossing where it intersects a public highway at grade.[2] It

1. Beatty v. Cent., etc., R. Co., 58 Ia. 242; s. c., 8 Am. & Eng. R. R. Cas. 210; Farley v. Chicago, etc., R. Co., 42 Ia. 234.

2. Farley v. Chicago, etc., R. Co., 42 Ia. 234; Ferguson v. V. & T. R. Co., 13 Nev. 184; Pittsburg, etc., R. Co. v. Dunn, 56 Pa. St. 280; Paducah, etc., R. Co. v. Commonwealth, 80 Ky. 147; s. c., 10 Am. & Eng.

is bound to keep the approaches in a safe condition.[1] And this seems to be true, even though the highway was laid out after the construction of the railroad;[2] but, perhaps, only when a fair construction of statutory provisions seems to require it to be so held.[3] And the company must so construct, repair, and improve the crossing as to meet the increasing wants of the public.[4] The obligation to maintain the crossing begins when the railroad is located over it,[5] and is a continuing duty.[6] Having crossed a highway, the railroad company must restore it to such a condition that its usefulness will not be unnecessarily impaired.[7] The railroad company is not bound, in restoring or maintaining a crossing, to actually improve the highway,[8] but it is liable for a failure to construct and maintain suitable crossings at all points where it intersects a public highway at grade.[9] The crossing is generally sufficient if it does not unnecessarily impair the usefulness of the highway, and its enjoyment by the public.[10] The duty to construct and maintain crossings usually applies only to lawful public highways or streets.[11] But if a railroad company has made a crossing public by license, it will be required to maintain it in repair.[12] It must keep in repair bridges which constitute a highway crossing,[13] but is not obliged to build that part of the highway crossing its right of way, except at the crossing.[14] It is not relieved from the duty to repair because a street railway using the crossing is under a like obligation.[15] And for a failure to comply with its duty to construct, maintain, or repair, a railroad company may be indicted.[16]

R. R. Cas. 318; People *v.* Chicago, etc., R. Co., 67 Ill. 118; State *v.* Dayton, etc., R. Co., 36 Ohio St. 436; s. c., 5 Am. & Eng. R. R. Cas. 312; Buchner *v.* Chicago, etc., R. Co., 60 Wis. 264; s. c., 14 Am. & Eng. R. R. Cas. 447.

1. Maltby *v.* Chicago, etc., R. Co., 52 Mich. 108; s c., 13 Am. & Eng. R. R. Cas. 606.

2. Louisville, etc., R. Co. *v.* Smith, 91 Ind. 119; s. c., 13 Am. & Eng. R. R. Cas. 608.

3. Northern Cent. R. Co. *v.* Baltimore, 46 Md. 425.

4. Cooke *v.* Boston, etc., R. Co., 133 Mass. 185; s. c., 10 Am. & Eng. R. R. Cas. 328; Manley *v.* St. Helen's Can. & R. Co., 2 H. & N. 840; English *v.* New Haven, etc., R. Co., 32 Conn. 241.

5. Pittsburg, etc., R. Co. *v.* Commonwealth, 101 Pa. St. 192; s. c., 10 Am. & Eng. R. R. Cas. 321; Buchner *v.* Chicago, etc., R. Co., 60 Wis. 264; s. c., 14 Am. & Eng. R. R. Cas. 447.

6. Pittsburg, etc., R. Co. *v.* Dunn, 56 Pa. St. 280; People *v.* Chicago, etc., R. Co., 67 Ill. 118; Ergler *v.* County Comr's, 49 Md. 257; Willcome *v.* Leeds, 51 Me. 313; Chicago, etc., R. Co. *v.* Moffit, 75 Ill. 524. But see Missouri, etc., R. Co. *v.* Long, 27 Kan. 684; s. c., 6 Am. & Eng. R. R. Cas. 254.

7. People *v.* New York, etc., R. Co., 89 N. Y. 266; s. c., 10 Am. & Eng. R. R. Cas. 230.

8. Beatty *v.* Chicago, etc., R. Co., 58 Ia. 242; s. c., 8 Am. & Eng. R. R. Cas. 210.

9. Farley *v.* Chicago, etc., R. Co., 42 Ia. 234.

10. Patterson's Ry. Ac. Law, 155; People *v.* New York Cent., etc., R. Co., 89 N. Y. 266; s. c., 10 Am. & Eng. R. R. Cas. 230.

11. International, etc., R. Co. *v.* Jordan (Texas, 1883), 10 Am. & Eng. R. R. Cas. 301; Missouri, etc., R. Co. *v.* Long, 27 Kan. 684; s. c., 6 Am. & Eng. R. R. Cas. 254; Flint, etc., R. Co. *v.* Willey, 47 Mich. 88; s. c., 5 Am. & Eng. R. R. Cas. 305.

12. Kelly *v.* Southern, etc., R. Co., 28 Minn. 98; s. c., 6 Am. & Eng. R. R. Cas. 264.

13. South. & N. Ala. R. Co. *v.* McLendon, 63 Ala. 266.

14. People *v.* Lake Shore, etc., R. Co., 52 Mich. 108; s. c., 13 Am. & Eng. R. R. Cas. 611.

15. Masterson *v.* N. Y. Cent. R. Co., 84 N. Y. 247; s. c., 3 Am. & Eng. R. R. Cas. 408.

16. Paducah, etc., R. Co. *v.* Commonwealth, 80 Ky. 147; s. c., 10 Am. & Eng. R. R. Cas. 318; Pittsburg, etc., R. Co. *v.*

And the duty to re-form and re-lay the highway applies to footways.[1] But whether the railroad company has properly constructed the crossing so as to render it as convenient and little dangerous as possible, is for the jury.[2] All of the foregoing doctrines of this section would seem to be sustainable on common-law principles; but most of them, and many analogous rules, are based upon decisions construing particular statutes, so that in every case, in order to determine the exact rule in a particular State, the special statutes and decisions must be examined, and all general statements of doctrine as to the duty of railroad companies to construct, maintain, and repair crossings, must be taken with caution.[3]

5. Duties at Established Crossings. — A railway-highway crossing once established, certain general duties, rights, and obligations arise upon the part of and toward (*a*) the railway company in the use of its track over the crossing, and (*b*) travellers upon the highway. The consideration of these relative rights and duties, first in their general principles, and then in their special applications, is the main subject of this article.

6. The Mutuality of Rights and Duties. — At places other than crossings, a railroad track is the private property of the company; and strangers who go upon or cross the track at such places are naked trespassers, to whom the railway company owes no duty.[4] But a traveller on a highway at a railway crossing is not a trespasser, and toward him at such a crossing the railway company must use that reasonable degree of care due toward a person having equal rights with itself.[5] In such cases, the rights and obligations of the railway company and the traveller are mutual and reciprocal.[6] Both must exercise ordinary care, in view of the

Commonwealth, 101 Pa. St. 192; s. c., 10 Am. & Eng. R. R. Cas. 321.

1. Queen *v.* Manchester, etc., R. Co., 2 Eng. R. R & Canal Cas. 711.

2. Roberts *v.* Chicago, etc., R. Co., 35 Wis. 679.

3. See, for full collection of authorities upon the doctrines of this section, 3 Am. & Eng. R. R. Cas. 415, note; 10 Am. & Eng. R. R. Cas. 330, note; 13 Am. & Eng. R. R. Cas. 610, 614, notes; 20 Am. & Eng. R. R. Cas. 16, 58, notes; 24 Am. & Eng. R. R. Cas. 481, note; 29 Am. & Eng. R. R. Cas. 439, note.

4. Tit. "Contributory Neg." 4 Am. & Eng. Ency. § 25.

It is time it should be understood . . . that the use of a railroad track, cutting or embankment, is exclusive of the public everywhere, except where a way crosses it. Philadelphia, etc., R. Co. *v.* Hummell, 44 Pa. St. 375; s. c., 84 Am. Dec. 457; Jackson *v.* Rutland, etc, R. Co, 25 Vt. 150; s. c., 60 Am. Dec. 246; Edgerton *v.* Huff, 26 Ind. 46; Isabel *v.* Hannibal, etc., R. Co., 60 Mo. 475; Kansas Pac. R. Co. *v.* Ward, 4 Col. 30; Finlayson *v.* Chicago, etc., R. Co., 1 Dill. (U. S. C. C.) 579; Sweeney *v.* Boston, etc, R. Co, 128 Mass. 5; s. c., 1 Am. & Eng. R. R. Cas. 138 and note; Illinois, etc., R. Co. *v.* Hetherington, 83 Ill. 510; Cauley *v.* Pittsburg, etc., R. Co., 95 Pa. St. 398; s. c., 2 Am. & Eng R. R. Cas. 4.

5. Kay *v.* Penna. R. Co., 65 Pa. St. 269; Pierce on Railroads, 340–342, 346, 347.

6. Continental, etc., Co. *v.* Stead, 95 U. S. 161; Indianapolis, etc., R. Co. *v.* McLin, 82 Ind. 435; Toledo, etc., R. Co. *v.* Goddard, 25 Ind. 185; Penna. R. Co. *v.* Krick, 47 Ind. 368; Beisiegel *v.* N. Y. Cent. R. Co., 40 N. Y. 9; Black *v.* Burlington, etc., R. Co., 38 Ia. 515; Rockford, etc., R. Co. *v.* Hillmer, 72 Ill. 235; Penna. R. Co. *v.* Goodman, 62 Pa. St 329; Baltimore, etc, R. Co. *v.* Owings (Md. 1880), 28 Am. & Eng. R. R. Cas 639; Louisville, etc., R. Co. *v.* Goetz, 79 Ky. 442; s. c., 14 Am. & Eng. R. R. Cas. 627.

circumstances and their respective situations;[1] and each, within certain limitations, may rely upon the other so to do.[2] But, by reason of the momentum of its trains, their fixed place of movement, and the necessities of railway traffic, it is the privilege of the railway to have precedence for its trains at highway crossings.[3]

7. General View of the Duty of the Company. — In approaching a highway crossing with its train, it is the duty of a railway company to exercise such care to avoid and prevent collisions with travellers on the highway, as a reasonable and prudent person engaged in its business would use, under the circumstances, at the particular crossing.[4] In other words, the duty required of it is ordinary care;[5] and extraordinary care, or unusual precautions and foresight, are not required of it.[6] Trains should approach and pass crossings with care, and should not pass each other at speed on the crossings.[7] It is the common-law duty of the railroad company to provide suitable warnings of danger at highway crossings,[8] and to so regulate the speed of its trains, and give such signals of their approach to the crossing, that travellers using the crossing with reasonable care will be apprised of the approach of trains in time to avoid injury.[9] Where, owing to surrounding cir-

1. Louisville, etc., R. Co. *v.* Goetz, 79 Ky. 442; s. c., 14 Am. & Eng. R. R. Cas. 627; Penna. R. Co. *v.* Krick, 47 Ind. 368; Cohen *v.* Eureka, etc., R. Co., 14 Nev. 376; Baltimore, etc., R. Co. *v.* Owings (Md. 1886), 28 Am. & Eng. R. R. Cas. 639; Tit. "Contributory Neg." 3 Am. & Eng. Ency. of Law, § 32. Neither is bound to use extraordinary care. Willoughby *v.* Chicago, etc., R. Co., 37 Ia. 432.

2. This doctrine is correct, both in theory and practice, as will appear in the concrete farther on; but it is often misapprehended and misapplied. For its real meaning, see 3 Am. & Eng. Ency. of Law, tit. "Contributory Negligence," § 16 and note 4. In this connection it may be stated thus: Either party may rely upon the other to perform a required duty, provided that such reliance does not, under the circumstances, amount to a want of ordinary care. See Beach on Con. Neg. § 13; 2 Thompson on Neg. 1172, § 18; Shearman & Redf. on Neg. § 31; Deering on Neg. § 16; Beisiegel *v.* N. Y. Cent. R. Co, 34 N. Y. 622; s. c., 90 Am. Dec. 741; Fox *v.* Sackett, 10 Allen (Mass.), 535. And see cases collected in note 4 to § 16, tit. "Con. Neg."

3. Warner *v.* New York, etc., R. Co., 44 N. Y. 465; Black *v.* Burlington, etc., R. Co., 38 Ia. 515; Continental Imp. Co. *v.* Stead, 95 U. S. 161; Galena, etc., R. Co. *v.* Dill, 22 Ill. 264; Toledo, etc., R. Co. *v.* Goddard, 25 Ind. 185; Penna. R. Co. *v.* Goodman, 62 Pa. St. 329.

A railway train is entitled to precedence at highway crossings, on condition that it shall give reasonable and timely warning of the approach of its trains; and a failure to give such warnings is negligence. Indianapolis, etc., R. Co. *v.* McLin, 82 Ind. 435; s. c., 8 Am. & Eng. R. R. Cas. 237.

4. Patterson, Ry. Ac. Law, 158, § 157.

5. Weber *v.* New York Cent. R. Co., 58 N. Y. 451; Western, etc., R Co. *v.* King, 70 Ga. 261; s. c, 19 Am. & Eng. R. R. Cas. 255; Baltimore, etc., R. Co. *v.* Breinig, 25 Md. 378; s. c., 90 Am. Dec. 49 and note.

6. Weber *v.* New York Cent., etc., R. Co., 58 N. Y. 451; Western, etc., R. Co. *v.* King, 70 Ga. 261; s. c., 19 Am. & Eng. R. R. Cas. 255; Shaw *v.* Boston, etc., R. Co., 8 Gray (Mass.), 45; Gruppen *v.* N. Y., etc., R. Co., 40 N. Y. 34.

The railroad company is not required to use all the means and measures to avoid injury which the highest prudence could suggest, and which it was in its power to employ. Weber *v.* New York Cent., etc, R. Co., 58 N. Y. 451.

7. Patterson, Ry. Ac. Law, 166; West *v.* New Jersey, etc., R. Co., 3 Vroom (N. J.), 91.

8. Chicago, etc., R. Co. *v.* Still, 19 Ill. 499; s. c., 71 Am. Dec. 236.

9. Linfield *v.* Old Colony R. Co., 10 Cushing (Mass.), 562; s. c, 57 Am. Dec. 124, notes; Chicago, etc., R. Co. *v.* Cauffman, 38 Ill. 428; Rockford, etc., R. Co. *v.* Hillmer, 77 Ill. 240; Chicago, etc., R. Co. *v.* Gretzner, 46 Ill. 84; Philadelphia, etc., R. Co. *v.* Troutman (Pa. 1882), 6 Am. &

cumstances, a crossing is known to be peculiarly dangerous to travellers, the railroad company must exercise care commensurate with the danger when it approaches such crossing with its trains.[1] And where the railroad company has created an extra danger at a crossing, it must use extra precautions to avoid inflicting injury.[2] Such are the general principles governing the duty of a railroad company, in approaching a highway crossing with its trains and locomotives. Where, however, the crossing is that of a public street in a city or village, the duty of the railroad company is increased, and the precautions necessary to constitute ordinary care are greater than would be required in the open country.[3] But

Eng. R. R. Cas. 117 and note; Philadelphia, etc., R. Co. *v.* Hogan, 47 Pa. St. 244; s. c., 86 Am. Dec. 541; Murray *v* S. Car. R. Co., 10 Richardson's Law, So. Car. 227; s. c., 70 Am. Dec. 219; Reeves *v.* Delaware, etc., R. Co., 30 Pa. St. 454; s. c., 72 Am. Dec. 713.

1. James *v.* Gt. West. Ry. Co., L. R. 2 C. P. 634, note; Bilbie *v.* Railroad Co., 18 C. B. N. S 584; Cliff *v.* Midland R. Co., L. R. 5 Q. B. 258; Continental Imp. Co *v.* Stead, 95 U. S. 161; Mackey *v.* New York Cent. R. Co., 35 N. Y. 75; Richardson *v.* New York Cent. R. Co., 45 N. Y. 846; Funston *v.* Chicago, etc., R. Co., 61 Ia. 452; s c, 14 Am. & Eng. R. R. Cas. 640; Nehrbas *v* Cent. Pac. R. Co., 62 Cal. 320, s. c., 14 Am. & Eng. R. R. Cas. 370; Thomas *v.* Delaware, etc., R. Co., 19 Blatchf. (U. S. C. C.) 533; Pennsylvania R. Co. *v.* Matthews, 36 New J. L. 531; Roberts *v.* Chicago, etc., R. Co., 35 Wis. 679; Eilert *v.* Railroad Co, 48 Wis. 606; Dimick *v.* Chicago, etc., R. Co., 80 Ill. 338; C. R. R. Co *v.* Feller, 84 Pa St. 226.

2. Thus, where the construction of the track is such that trains cannot be seen when they are close to a highway crossing, an extraordinary danger is created which it is the duty of the railroad company to reduce to a minimum by taking more than ordinary precautions at such crossing, and giving such warnings of danger or signals as will suffice to warn travellers, using ordinary care, of the approach of trains. New York, etc., R. Co. *v.* Randel, 47 New J. L. 144; s. c., 23 Am. & Eng. R. R. Cas. 308.

3. For a test of "ordinary care," see 4 Am. & Eng. Ency. of Law, tit. "Contributory Neg." § 9 and note.

A higher degree of care is required of a railroad company when running its trains through a village or city than when running them in the open country. Beisiegel *v.* New York Cent. R. Co., 34 N. Y. 622; s. c., 90 Am. Dec. 741; Pierce on Railroads, 354, 355.

A railway company operating its cars through a populous street on which many children live, must omit nothing which can be done to prevent injury to the children on the street. Norfolk, etc., R. Co. *v.* Ormsby, 27 Gratt. (Va.) 455.

It is the duty of a railroad company, in the operation of its trains, to approach the crossing of a public street in a city at a moderate rate of speed, and to give timely warning to those passing along the street. Philadelphia, etc., R Co. *v.* Hagan, 47 Pa. St. 244; s. c., 86 Am. Dec. 541.

A railroad company is to be held to the exercise of a very high degree of care in operating its road through the public streets of a city, and will not be permitted to omit with impunity any reasonable precaution that may tend to the safety of the public while using the thoroughfare. Chicago, etc., R. Co. *v.* Stumps, 69 Ill. 409. And it is said that the railway company must so control and regulate the speed of its trains while running through and over the streets of a city, that the sound of a whistle or bell will be an effectual warning to persons on the highway and themselves in the exercise of due care. Patterson's Ry. Ac. Law, 158, § 157, citing C. I. Co. *v.* Stead, 95 U. S. 161; the State *v.* B. & O Co., 24 Md. 84; Quimby *v.* Vt. Cent. R. Co., 23 Vt. 387; Wilson *v.* Cunningham, 3 Cal. 241; P. R. Co. *v.* Long, 75 Pa. St. 257; Schultz *v.* P. R. Co. (Pa.), 6 Weekly Notes of Cases, 69; P. R. Co. *v.* Ackerman, 74 Pa. St. 265; P. R. Co. *v.* Lewis, 79 Pa. St. 33; Penna. Co. *v.* James, 81½ Pa. St. 194; P. R. Co. *v.* Coon (Pa), 17 Weekly Notes of Cases, 137.

Where there is a dangerous crossing in a city, a railroad company must exercise care to avoid the infliction of injury commensurate with the danger of accident; and on the other hand, those using the crossing must exercise care to avoid injury commensurate with the danger to which they are exposed. Harlan *v* St. Louis, etc., R. Co., 65 Mo. 22. And see, generally, upon the subject of the operation of trains over city streets, Frick *v.* St. Louis, etc., R. Co., 75 Mo. 595; 5 Mo. App. 435; s. c., 8 Am. & Eng. R. R. Cas. 280; Zimmer *v.* New while such precautions as have been stated are required of the railroad company in approaching crossings with its trains, yet it does not have to yield the right of way, and check its train for a traveller approaching the crossing, and to whom it has given due warning of the proximity of the train.[1] A railroad company is not liable for exercising its rights in a usual and ordinary manner at or near crossings,[2] but will be liable for doing a thing rightful in itself at an improper place or time, and regardless of the rights of others.[3]

A railroad company cannot escape liability by a mere compliance with statutory requirements, if by its conduct it renders them unavailing as warnings of danger.[4]

The railroad company must have good and sufficient machinery and appliances for the control and operation of its trains, and must keep its employees, whose duty it is to operate such trains, free from distracting influences, such as strangers in the cab of the locomotive.[5]

York Cent., etc., R. Co., 7 Hun (N. Y.), 554; Fero *v.* Buffalo, etc., R. Co, 22 N. Y. 209; s. c., 78 Am. Dec. 178; Longabaugh *v.* Virginia, etc., R. Co., 9 Nev. 295; Kinney *v.* Crocker, 18 Wis. 81; Gregg *v.* Vetter, 41 Ind. 242.

1. Chicago, etc., R. Co. *v.* Lee, 68 Ill. 576; Purl *v.* St. Louis, etc., R. Co., 73 Mo. 168; s. c., 6 Am. & Eng. R. R. Cas. 27.

2. Hahn *v.* Southern, etc., R. Co., 51 Cal. 605; Flint *v.* Norwich, etc., R. Co., 110 Mass. 222; Beatty *v.* Cent., etc., R. Co., 58 Ia. 242; s. c., 8 Am. & Eng. R. R. Cas. 210; Burton *v.* Philadelphia, etc, R. Co., 4 Harr. (Del.) 252; Whitney *v.* Maine Cent. R. Co., 69 Me. 208; Favor *v.* Boston, etc., R. Co., 114 Mass. 350.

3. In Manchester, etc., R. Co. *v.* Fullarton, 14 C. B. N. S. 54; s. c., 108 E. C. L. 54, it was said, "It appears that the plaintiff's horses were using the road as of right, and that the company were also as of right exercising the power given them by their act of crossing the highway; and, if there had been nothing to show that they were not exercising their rights in the ordinary way and with due and reasonable care, the company undoubtedly would not be liable for the misfortune which has happened. But I am of the opinion that the evidence abundantly shows that the company, by their servants, exercised their right of crossing the highway in an inconvenient and improper manner. Whilst near the gate which separates the railway from the road, the driver blew off the steam from the mud-cocks in front of the engine, so that the plaintiff's horses became enveloped therein and frightened, and so became unmanageable. It is clear that the company have not used their railway with that attention to the rights and safety of the Queen's subjects which, under the circumstances, they were bound to exercise." Louisville, etc., R. Co. *v.* Schmidt, 81 Ind. 264; s. c., 8 Am. & Eng. R. R. Cas. 248; Billman *v.* Indianapolis, etc., R. Co., 76 Ind. 166; s. c., 6 Am. & Eng. R. R. Cas. 41; Gibson *v.* St. Louis, etc., R. Co., 8 Mo. App. 488; Stott *v.* Gd. Trunk R. Co., 24 W. C. C. P. 347; Borst *v.* Lake Shore, etc., R. Co., 66 N. Y. 639; Toledo, etc., R. Co. *v.* Harmon, 47 Ill. 298; Geveke *v.* Grand Rapids, etc., R. Co. (Mich. 1885), 22 Am. & Eng. R. R. Cas. 551; Pennsylvania R. Co. *v.* Barnett, 59 Pa. St. 259; Philadelphia, etc., R. Co. *v.* Stinger, 78 Pa. St. 219; Kase *v.* Greenough, 88 Pa. St 405; Chicago, etc., R. Co. *v.* Dunn, 52 Ill. 451; Chicago, etc., R. Co. *v.* Dickson, 88 Ill. 431; Culp *v.* Atchison, etc., R. Co., 17 Kan. 475; Georgia R. Co. *v.* Newsome, 60 Ga. 492; Georgia R. Co. *v.* Thomas, 68 Ga. 744.

4. Thus, the giving of the statutory signals by a train run so close behind another at a crossing that the signals could not be heard, and at a time when one in the exercise of ordinary care would not have anticipated the coming of such train, is not sufficient to excuse the company from a charge of negligence in so running such trains. Chicago, etc., R. Co. *v.* Boggs, 101 Ind 522; s. c., 23 Am. & Eng. R. R. Cas. 282.

5. Marcott *v.* Marquette, etc., R. Co., 47 Mich. 1; s. c., 4 Am. & Eng. R. R. Cas. 548; Smith *v.* New York, etc, R. Co., 19 N. Y. 127; Costello *v.* Syracuse, etc., R. Co., 65 Barb. (N. Y.) 92; Smedis *v.* Brooklyn, etc, R. Co., 88 N. Y. 13; s. c., 8 Am. & Eng. R. R. Cas. 445; Gregg *v.* Vetter,

All of these general duties at crossings must be observed continuously at places where a railroad is operated along and in a public street or highway, as travellers have a right to cross such street or highway at any point, and are not restricted to its points of intersection with other highways.[1] And a railroad company is not relieved of its general duty to travellers upon highways because it is operating its trains over the track of another company, but is chargeable with injuries caused by its trains through the negligence of flagmen or others engaged in the signal service of the other company.[2]

8. General View of Traveller's Duty. — Farther on, special applications of the doctrines relating to the rights and duties of travellers at crossings will be shown. Here only general principles will be stated.

The track of a railroad intersecting a highway at grade is itself a warning and a proclamation of danger which the traveller should heed.[3] He must exercise care commensurate with the impending danger at a crossing;[4] and if familiar with the crossing, and aware that it is usually dangerous, he must the more vigilantly exercise his faculties, in order to escape injury from the known danger.[5] But he is not precluded from using a crossing because it is environed with special dangers, if, in doing so, he acts as a careful and prudent man would under the circumstances.[6] Yet, if he fails to so act, the unusual dangers of the place will not excuse him from the charge of negligence.[7] And he should "approach the crossing under the apprehension that a train is liable to come at any moment.[8] He has no right to shut his eyes, and close his ears, to the danger he is liable to incur at such a place,"[9] and cannot escape the charge of contributory negligence if he drives upon the crossing at a trot[10] or at a rate of speed too great for him to readily check his team,[11] without having taken ordinary precautions for his own safety.[12] It is the duty of a traveller near a

41 Ind. 228; Nashville, etc., R. Co., 6 Heisk. (Tenn.) 174.

1. Louisville, etc., R. Co. *v.* Head, 80 Ind. 117; s. c., 4 Am. & Eng. R. R. Cas. 619; Frick *v.* St. Louis, etc., R. Co., 75 Mo. 595; s. c., 8 Am. & Eng. R. R. Cas. 280; Smedis *v.* Brooklyn, etc., R. Co., 88 N. Y. 13; s. c., Am & Eng. R. R. Cas. 445.

2. Leonard *v.* New York Cent. R. Co., 42 N. Y. Supr. Ct. Rep. 225.

3. Stubley *v.* London, etc., R. Co., L. R. 1 Ex. 13; Gillespie *v.* Newburgh, 54 N. Y. 471.

4. Toledo, etc., R. Co. *v.* Shuckman, 50 Ind. 42.

5. Cincinnati, etc., R. Co. *v.* Butler, 103 Ind. 31; s. c., 23 Am. & Eng. R. R. Cas. 262.

6. Shearman & Redf. on Neg. § 31; Turner *v.* Buchanan, 82 Ind 147; s. c., 42 Am. Rep. 485; Mahoney *v.* Metropolitan R. Co., 104 Mass. 73; Dewire *v.* Bailey, 131 Mass. 169; s. c., 41 Am. Rep. 219.

7. Cincinnati, etc., R. Co. *v.* Butler, 103 Ind. 31, 34; s. c., 23 Am. & Eng. R. R. Cas. 262.

8. Cincinnati, etc., R. Co. *v.* Butler, 103 Ind. 31, 35; s. c., 23 Am. & Eng. R. R. Cas. 262.

9. Chicago, etc., R. Co. *v.* Still, 19 Ill. 499; s. c., 71 Am. Dec. 236; Railroad Co. *v.* Houston, 95 U. S. 697, 702.

10. Mantel *v.* Chicago, etc., R. Co., 33 Minn. 62; s. c., 19 Am. & Eng. R. R. Cas. 362.

11. Salter *v.* Utica, etc., R. Co., 13 Hun, 187; Haring *v.* New York, etc., R. Co., 13 Barb. 9; Grippen *v.* New York, etc., R. Co., 40 N. Y. 34; Snows *v.* Maine, etc., R. Co., 67 Me. 100.

12. See 4 Am & Eng. Essay of Law, tit. "Contributory Neg." §§ 9, 33.

crossing to look out for trains.[1] And the fact that a train is behind time does not relieve a traveller of this duty. A railroad company has the right to run trains at all times, and those crossing the tracks are entitled to no exemption from care and vigilance because trains are irregular or extra.[2] Neither does a failure to give statutory signals exempt a traveller on a highway from the duty to use ordinary care in approaching a crossing.[3] And it is erroneous to charge a jury that a traveller need only exercise such care as would avoid injury if the railroad company be free from fault.[4] While a traveller has a right to expect the railroad company to do its duty, yet this will not excuse him for failing to take ordinary care to guard against a possible breach of duty on its part.[5] Neither physical infirmities nor voluntary intoxication will excuse a traveller for failing to exercise ordinary care at a crossing.[6] But when a traveller has exercised such ordinary care, no matter what his condition, age, or capacity, he has done all that the law requires of him. What the standard of ordinary care is in general, has already been shown, and it is illustrated by a multitude of cases.[7]

9. Private Crossings. — At private crossings, the rules, both as to the rights and obligations of railroad and traveller, are somewhat different from those that govern at public highway crossings. A railroad company is not ordinarily bound to maintain or repair a private way over its track; but it may become obligatory upon it to do so, either by charter or contract.[8]

1. Pennsylvania R. Co. *v.* Ogier, 35 Pa. St. 60; s. c., 78 Am. Dec. 322.

2. Salter *v.* Utica, etc., R. Co., 75 N. Y. 273.

3. Wabash, etc., R. Co. *v.* Wallace, 110 Ill. 114; s. c., 19 Am. & Eng. R. R. Cas. 359.

4. Toledo, etc., R. Co. *v.* Shuckman, 50 Ind. 42.

5. Railroad Co. *v.* Houston, 95 U. S. 397; Schofield *v.* Chicago, etc., R. Co., 2 McCrary, U. S. C. C. 268; s. c., on appeal, 14 U. S. 618; Chicago, etc., R. Co. *v.* Natzki, 66 Ill. 455; Bellefontaine R. Co. *v.* Hunter, 33 Ind. 335; Hinckley *v.* Cape Cod R. Co., 120 Mass. 257; Ormsbee *v.* Boston, etc., R. Co., 14 R. I. 102; Gorton *v.* Erie R. Co., 45 N. Y. 664. But see Ernst *v* Hudson River R. Co., 35 N. Y. 9; s. c., 90 Am. Dec. 761; Klanawski *v.* Grand Trunk R. Co. (Wis.), 24 N. W. Rep. 802.

6. See 4 Am. & Eng. Ency. of Law, tit. "Contributory Neg." §§ 34 and 35; as to deafness, see New Jersey, etc., R. Co. *v.* West, 32 N. J. L. 91; Morris, etc., R. Co. *v.* Haslan, 38 N. J. L. 147; Cleveland, etc., R. Co. *v.* Terry, 8 Ohio St. 570; Central, etc., R. Co. *v.* Fellar, 84 Pa. St. 226; Zimmerman *v.* Hannibal, etc., R. Co., 71 Mo. 476; s. c., 2 Am & Eng R R. Cas. 191; Purl & St. Louis, etc., R. Co. 73 Mo. 168; s. c., 6 Am. & Eng. R. R. Cas. 27; Chicago, etc., R. Co. *v.* Miller, 46 Mich. 532; s. c., 6 Am. & Eng. R. R. Cas. 89. As to intoxication; see Toledo, etc., R. Co. *v.* Riley, 47 Ill. 514; Chicago, etc., R. Co. *v.* Bell, 70 Ill. 102; Houston, etc., R. Co. *v.* Reosor, 61 Tex. 613; Kern *v.* Baltimore, etc., R. Co., 61 Md. 154; s. c., 19 Am. & Eng. R. R. Cas. 321.

7. "A traveller upon a highway, when approaching a railroad-crossing, ought to make a vigilant use of his senses of sight and hearing, in order to avoid a collision This precaution is dictated by common prudence. He should listen for signals. and look in the directions from which a train may come. If, by neglect of this duty, he suffers injury from a passing train, he cannot recover of the company, although it may itself be chargeable with negligence, or have failed to give the signals required by statute, or be running at the time at a speed exceeding the legal rate." And for a collection of cases, see 3 Am. & Eng Ency. of Law, tit. "Contributory Neg." § 33, p. 70, note 2.

8. Keefe *v.* Sullivan County R. Co., 62 N. H. 271; s. c., 23 Am. & Eng. R. R Cas. 301; Ferguson *v.* Virginia, etc., R Co., 13 Nev. 185.

In crossing a railroad track at a private crossing, the person using the crossing is required to assume a greater burden of care than would be necessary were the crossing public, and the duties and responsibilities of the railroad are correspondingly lessened.[1] The railroad is not required to guard against accidents at old abandoned ways which were never legally laid out.[2] And in approaching a private crossing, it is not obliged to give statutory signals, as for a public highway.[3] Yet it may be a question for the jury whether, in a particular case, ordinary care would not have required the giving of warning signals.[4] And even where a railroad company, by permitting people to cross its track repeatedly at a place where there is no public right of passage, has given an implied license to do so, it is not liable for injuries received at such place by collision with its trains, except when its conduct was of such a character that it might reasonably have foreseen it was likely to result in injury to some one.[5]

10. Crossings by Custom and License. — This brings us to the consideration of the mutual duties and rights of a railroad company and a traveller at crossings, not legally public highways, but made public crossings by license, custom, or use. While a merely passive permissive use of a crossing not a public highway will not warrant a recovery, because of a failure on the part of a railroad company to provide safeguards, and give signals at and for such way,[6] yet when a crossing has been commonly and notoriously used by the public for many years as a public crossing, and without let or hinderance from the railroad company, those who use it are not trespassing.[7] And when a railroad company knowingly permits a place not a highway crossing to be used as a crossing by the general public for years, it is bound to use reasonable care at such crossing, and to give notice and warning of the approach of its trains.[8]

And at such a crossing, the railroad company must exercise care similar to that required at a legally established public highway crossing.[9] And a person injured thereat by the negligence of the company is not a trespasser, and can recover against the

1. O'Connor *v.* Boston, etc., R. Co., 135 Mass. 352; s. c., 15 Am. & Eng. R. R. Cas 362.

2. Omaha, etc., R. Co. *v.* Martin, 14 Neb. 295; s. c., 19 Am. & Eng. R. R. Cas. 236.

3. Johnson's Admr. *v.* Louisville, etc., R. Co. (Ky. 1883), 13 Am. & Eng. R. R Cas. 623; Thomas *v* Delaware, etc., R. Co., 8 Fed. Rep. 728; Bennett *v.* Grand Trunk, etc., R. Co., 3 Ontario, Rep. C. P. Div. 446; s. c., 13 Am. & Eng. R. R. Cas. 627.

4. Thomas *v.* Delaware, etc., R. Co., 8 Fed. Rep. 728.

5. Sutton *v.* New York Cent., etc., R. Co., 66 N. Y. 243.

6. Illinois Cent. R Co., *v.* Godfrey, 71 Ill. 500; s. c., 22 Am. Rep. 112; Morrissey *v.* Eastern R. Co., 126 Mass. 377; s. c., 30 Am. Rep. 686, and note; Nicholson *v.* Erie R. Co., 41 N. Y. 525.

7. Philadelphia, etc., R. Co. *v.* Troutman, 6 Am. & Eng. R. R. Cas. 117.

8. Byrne *v.* New York Cent. R. Co., 104 N. Y. 362; s. c., 58 Am. Rep. 512; Barry *v.* New York Cent. R. Co., 92 N. Y. 289.

9. Harriman *v.* Pittsburg, etc., R. Co. (Ohio, 1887), 12 N. E. Rep. 451; Taylor *v.* Delaware, etc., R. Co., 113 Pa. St. 162; s. c., 28 Am. & Eng. R. R. Cas. 656; s. c., 57 Am. Rep. 446; Kelly *v.* So. Minn. R. Co., 28 Minn. 98; s. c., 6 Am. & Eng. R. R. Cas. 264.

company, if free from contributory negligence.[1] It seems, however, that the conduct of the company must be such as to amount to an invitation, express or implied, to the public to use the crossing, in order to make its liabilities as great as at a legal highway crossing.[2] And a mere permission or license to a person to cross the track is not necessarily an invitation.[3] But the construction of the crossing, and its character, may constitute an invitation.[4] And whether there is an invitation, express or implied, is generally for the jury.[5]

11. Liability for Defects in Crossings. — A railroad company is liable for injuries caused by defects in crossings, or structures thereat, which it is bound to maintain.[6] And where injury flows from defects in a crossing at a street, the municipality, as well as the railroad company, will be liable, in the first instance, to the person injured.[7] But in case the city is held liable, it may recover over against the railroad company if, as between the city and the company, it was the duty of the latter to maintain and repair the crossing.[8]

12. Sign-Boards at Crossings. — Whether, in the exercise of ordinary care, a railroad company, in the absence of any statutory requirement, should erect a sign-board at any particular crossing,

1. Murphy *v.* Boston, etc., R. Co., 133 Mass. 121; s. c., 14 Am. & Eng. R. R. Cas. 675; Weil *v.* Portland, etc., R. Co., 57 Me. 117; Sweeney *v.* Old Colony, etc., R. Co., 10 Allen (Mass.), 368; Delaney *v.* Milwaukee, etc., R. Co., 33 Wis. 67.

2. Stewart *v.* Pennsylvania R. Co., 14 Am. & Eng. R. R. Cas. 679, and note.

3. Wright *v.* Boston, etc., R. Co., 142 Mass. 296; s. c., 28 Am. & Eng. R. R. Cas. 652.

4. Wright *v.* Boston, etc., R. Co., 142 Mass. 296; s. c., 28 Am. & Eng. R. R. Cas. 652; Stewart *v.* Pennsylvania R. Co., 14 Am. & Eng. R. R. Cas. 679; Taylor *v.* Delaware, etc., R. Co., 113 Pa. St. 162; s. c., 28 Am. & Eng. R. R. Cas. 656; s.c., 57 Am. Rep. 446; Kelly *v.* So. Minn. R. Co., 28 Minn. 98; s. c., 6 Am. & Eng. R. R. Cas. 264.

5. Taylor *v.* Delaware, etc., R. Co., 113 Pa. St. 162; s. c., 28 Am. & Eng. R. R. Cas. 656; s. c., 57 Am. Rep. 446. And see as analogous in principle, Fitchburg R Co. *v.* Page, 131 Mass. 391; s. c., 7 Am. & Eng. R. R. Cas. 86.

6. Wasmer *v.* Delaware, etc., R. Co., 80 N. Y. 212; s. c., 36 Am. Rep. 608; Payne *v.* Troy, etc., R. Co., 83 N. Y. 572; s. c., 6 Am. & Eng. R. R. Cas. 54; Farley *v.* Chicago, etc., R. Co., 42 Ia. 234; State *v.* Dayton, etc., R. Co., 36 Ohio St. 436; s. c., 5 Am. & Eng. R. R. Cas. 312; People *v.* Chicago, etc., R. Co., 67 Ill. 118; Pittsburg, etc., R. Co *v.* Dunn, 56 Pa. St. 280; Baughman *v.* Shenango, etc., R. Co., 92 Pa. St. 335; Roberts *v.* Chicago, etc., R. Co., 35 Wis. 679; Indianapolis, etc., R. Co. *v.* Stout, 53 Ind. 143; Louisville, etc., R. Co. *v.* Smith, 91 Ind. 119; s. c., 13 Am. & Eng. R. R. Cas. 608 and note; O'Connor *v.* Boston, etc., R. Co., 135 Mass 352; s. c., 15 Am. & Eng. R. R. Cas. 362; Oliver *v.* North E. R. Co., L. R. 9 Q. B. 409; Johnson *v.* St. Paul, etc., R. Co., 31 Minn. 283; s. c., 15 Am & Eng. R. R. Cas. 467; Beatty *v.* Cent., etc., R. Co., 58 Ia. 242; s. c., 8 Am. & Eng. R. R. Cas. 210; Sweeney *v.* Old Colony, etc., R. Co., 10 Allen (Mass.), 368; s. c., 87 Am. Dec. 644; Kearney *v.* London, etc., R. Co., L. R. 5 Q. B. 411; s. c., 6 Q. B. 759; Byrne *v.* Boadle, 2 Hurl. & C. 722; Pennsylvania, etc., Co. *v.* Graham, 63 Pa. St. 290; Hays *v.* Gallagher, 72 Pa. St. 136; Masterson *v.* New York Cent., etc., R. Co., 84 N. Y. 247; s. c., 38 Am. Rep. 510; Mann *v.* Cent. Vt., etc., R. Co., 55 Vt. 484; s. c., 45 Am. Rep. 628; Milwaukee, etc., R. Co. *v.* Hunter, 11 Wis. 160; Brownell *v.* Troy, etc., R. Co., 55 Vt. 218; s. c., 15 Am. & Eng. R. R. Cas. 498; Brown *v.* R. Co., 113 Mass. 52; Dickie *v.* Boston, etc., R. Co., 131 Mass. 516; s. c., 8 Am. & Eng. R. R. Cas. 203; Pierce on Railroads, 248.

7. 2 Dillon's Munc. Corp. (3d ed.) §§ 1027 and 1037; Pierce on Railroads, 249; Schmidt *v.* Chicago, etc., R. Co., 83 Ill. 405; Gillett *v.* Western, etc., R. Co., 8 Allen (Mass.), 560.

8. 2 Dillon's Munc. Corp. (3d ed.) § 1037, and cases cited.

is a question of fact for a jury.[1] But where signs are required by statute, the failure to erect them may be conclusive evidence of carelessness upon the part of the railroad company;[2] yet such careless breach of duty will not be such actionable negligence as renders the company liable unless it proximately causes the injury.[3] Hence the failure to erect sign-boards as required by statute, is not, in itself, sufficient to sustain a recovery by one injured at a crossing of whose existence he knew, and with which he was familiar;[4] nor does the failure to have such statutory sign-board confer any right of action on persons not intending to use the crossing, but only approaching it;[5] nor will its absence warrant a recovery where, by ordinary care, the person injured might have known of the crossing without a sign-board.[6]

13. Warnings required at Common Law. — At common law it is the duty of a railroad company to give reasonable and proper warnings for the protection of travellers on the highway when its trains are approaching a highway crossing.[7] And the right of the company's trains to precedence at the crossing does not relieve it of this duty.[8] These are merely the requirements of ordinary care;[9] and the warning must be of such a character, and made at such time, that it will serve to protect a traveller from injury at the crossing, if he be in the exercise of ordinary care.[10]

1. Shaber *v.* St. Paul, etc., R. Co., 28 Minn. 103; s. c., 2 Am. & Eng. R. R. Cas. 185; Baltimore, etc., R. Co. *v.* Whitacre, 35 Ohio St. 627; Elkins *v.* Boston, etc., R. Co., 115 Mass. 190.

2. Field *v.* Chicago, etc., R. Co., 14 Fed. Rep. 332; s. c., 8 Am. & Eng. R. R. Cas. 425; Shaber *v.* St. Paul, etc., R. Co., 28 Minn. 103; s. c., 2 Am. & Eng. R. R. Cas. 185.

3. Field *v.* Chicago, etc., R. Co., 14 Fed. Rep. 332; s. c., 8 Am. & Eng. R. R. Cas. 425.

4. Haas *v.* Grand Rapids, etc., R. Co., 47 Mich. 401; s. c., 8 Am. & Eng. R. R. Cas. 268.

5. East Tenn., etc., R. Co. *v.* Feathers, 10 Lea (Tenn.), 103; s. c., 15 Am. & Eng. R. R. Cas. 446; Rosenberger *v.* Grand Trunk R. Co., 8 Ont. App. (Can.) 482; s. c., 15 Am. & Eng. R. R. Cas. 448 and note.

6. Gulf, etc., R. Co. *v.* Greenlee, 62 Tex. 344; s. c., 23 Am. & Eng. R. R. Cas. 322; Lang *v.* Holiday Creek R. Co., 49 Ia. 469; Payne *v.* Chicago, etc., R. Co., 39 Ia. 523; s. c., 44 Ia. 236.

7. "Railroad companies, in operating their cars, must be held, in crossing public highways and thoroughfares, to so regulate the speed of their trains, and to give such signals to persons passing, that all may be apprised of the danger of crossing the railroad track." Chicago, etc., R. Co. *v.* Still, 19 Ill. 499; s. c., 71 Am. Dec. 236; Rockford, etc., R. Co. *v.* Hillmer, 72 Ill. 240.

"At common law it would be the duty of the corporation to exercise all reasonable care in the running of engines and the general use of the railroad, and to adopt all proper precautions against accidents likely to happen by reason of the road." Wakefield *v.* Connecticut, etc., R. Co., 37 Vt. 330; s. c., 86 Am. Dec. 711; Philadelphia, etc., R. Co. *v.* Hagan, 47 Pa. St. 244; s. c., 86 Am. Dec. 541. And even though no statute requires signals, yet, when care and prudence dictate that they would serve to prevent the infliction of injury, they should be given. Loucks *v.* Chicago, etc., R. Co., 31 Minn. 526; s. c., 19 Am. & Eng. R. R. Cas. 305; Peoria, etc., R. Co. *v.* Clayberg, 107 Ill. 644; s. c., 15 Am. & Eng. R. R. Cas. 356.

8. Indianapolis, etc., R. Co. *v.* McLin, 82 Ind. 435. See also Rockford, etc., R. Co. *v.* Hillmer, 72 Ill. 235.

9. Tolman *v.* Syracuse, etc., R. Co., 98 N. Y. 198; Guggenheim *v.* Lake Shore, etc., R. Co., 57 Mich. 488; s. c., 22 Am. & Eng. R. R. Cas. 546; Kelly *v.* St. Paul, etc., R. Co., 29 Minn. 1; s. c., 6 Am. & Eng. R. R. Cas. 93; Shaber *v.* St. Paul, etc., R. Co, 28 Minn. 103; s. c., 2 Am. & Eng. R. R. Cas. 185; Peoria, etc., R. Co. *v.* Clayberg, 107 Ill. 644; s. c., 15 Am. & Eng. R. R. Cas. 356.

10. Louisville, etc., R. Co. *v.* Goetz, 79 Ky. 442; s. c, 14 Am. & Eng. R. R. Cas.

But what notice of approach is sufficient, is ordinarily for the jury,[1] although it may sometimes present a question of law for the court.[2] So well settled is the rule requiring a railroad company to give warning before moving its trains over a crossing, that a traveller has the right to presume it will do so.[3] But this doctrine will not excuse a want of ordinary care on his part to guard against injury.[4] He has no right to omit proper precautions on the assumption that the railroad company will comply with statutory requirements.[5]

14. Duty of Traveller when View obstructed. — When the view of and from a crossing is obstructed, this fact imposes additional obligations as to care upon both traveller and railroad company; and while the standard is still that of ordinary care,[6] yet, by reason of the circumstance, it may require greater care and precaution on the part of one party than of the other to constitute such care.[7] Considering, first, the duty of the traveller where the view is obstructed, the general rule is, that the question of his care in view of the condition of things at the crossing is for the jury.[8] And in Pennsylvania it has been held that when a traveller cannot see along the track, he should get out and lead his horse, or go forward, and look up and down the track;[9] and that a failure to do so, if he could not otherwise see, would be negligence *per se*.[10] But this doctrine has been somewhat limited by later decisions in Pennsylvania,[11] and is not the rule in other jurisdictions.[12] The

427; Chicago, etc., R. Co. *v.* Still, 19 Ill. 699; s. c., 71 Am. Dec. 236.

1. Shaber *v.* St. Paul, etc., R. Co., 28 Minn. 103; s. c., 2 Am. & Eng. R. R. Cas. 185; Loucks *v.* Chicago, etc., R. Co., 31 Minn. 526; s. c., 19 Am. & Eng. R. R. Cas. 305, 309.

2. Loucks *v.* Chicago, etc., R. Co., 31 Minn. 526; s. c., 19 Am. & Eng. R. R. Cas. 305, 309. See Philadelphia R. Co. *v.* Stinger, 78 Pa. St. 219, 225, 227; Louisville, etc., R. Co. *v.* Commonwealth, 13 Bush (Ky.), 388; Roberts *v.* Chicago, etc., R. Co, 35 Wis. 679.

3. Robinson *v.* West Pac. R. Co., 48 Cal. 409; Loucks *v.* Chicago, etc., R. Co., 31 Minn. 526; s. c., 19 Am. & Eng. R. R. Cas. 305; 2 Dillon's Munc. Corp. (3d ed.) § 713, note 2; Beisiegel *v.* N. Y. Cent. R. Co., 34 N. Y. 622; s. c., 90 Am. Dec. 741; Klanowski *v.* Grank Trunk R. Co., 24 N. W. Rep. 802; Ernst *v.* Hudson River R. Co., 35 N. Y. 9; s. c., 90 Am. Dec. 761, and note.

4. Railroad Co. *v.* Houston, 95 U. S. 397; Schofield *v.* Chicago, etc., R. Co., 2 McCrary (U. S. C. C.), 268; s. c. on appeal, 114 U. S. 618; Bellefontaine, etc., R. Co. *v.* Hunter, 33 Ind. 335; Hinckly *v.* Cape Cod R. Co., 120 Mass. 257; Bowers *v.* Chicago, etc., R. Co., 61 Wis. 457; s. c., 19 Am. & Eng. R. R. Cas. 301.

5. Colligan *v.* N. Y. Cent., etc., R. Co., 59 N. Y. 651. See Cordell *v.* N. Y. Cent., etc., R. Co., 75 N. Y. 330.

6. 4 Am. & Eng. Ency. of Law, tit. "Contributory Neg." § 9.

7. 4 Am. & Eng. Ency. of Law, tit. "Contributory Negligence," §§ 16, 19.

8. Artz *v.* Chicago, etc., R. Co., 34 Ia. 153; Bunting *v.* Cent. Pac. R. Co., 14 Nev. 351; Beisiegel *v.* N. Y. Cent. R. Co., 34 N. Y. 622; s. c., 90 Am. Dec. 741.

9. Pennsylvania R. Co. *v.* Beale, 73 Pa. St. 504; s. c., 13 Am. Rep. 753; North Pennsylvania R. Co. *v.* Heileman, 49 Pa. St. 60; s. c., 1 Thomps. on Neg. 401; Lehigh Valley, etc., R. Co. *v.* Brandtmaier, 113 Pa. St. 610; Cent., etc., R. Co. *v.* Feller, 84 Pa. St. 226.

10. Pennsylvania R. Co. *v.* Weber, 76 Pa. St. 157; s. c., 18 Am. Rep. 407; Reading etc., R. Co. *v.* Ritchie, 102 Pa. St. 425; s. c., 19 Am. & Eng. R. R. Cas. 267; Penna. R. Co. *v.* Bentley, 66 Pa. St. 30.

11. Penna. R. Co. *v.* Ackermann, 74 Pa. St. 265; Philadelphia, etc., R. Co. *v.* Carr (Pa. 1882), 6 Am. & Eng. R. R. Cas. 185; Baughman *v.* Shenango, etc., R. Co., 92 Pa. St. 335; s. c., 6 Am. & Eng. R. R. Cas. 51.

12. In Wisconsin it is expressly repudiated, the court saying that "this would be exercising extraordinary care and diligence,

test of the traveller's care is found in the general principles of the law relating to negligence;[1] and he is only required to take into consideration the surrounding circumstances and conditions, and make such use of his senses as a careful and prudent man would when so situated.[2] If such care and prudence require him to stop, or even to get out of his vehicle, and lead his horse, or go ahead and view the track from the crossing, or beyond the obstructions, then he must do so.[3] But these are questions of fact for a jury, not of law for the court.[4] The general duty of a traveller at crossings where the view is obstructed, can best be shown by a consideration of cases dealing with it in the concrete. It is scarcely a subject for any generalizations of a specific character. Each case rests upon its own particular facts, when viewed in the light of the general doctrines of the law of negligence.[5]

15. Duty of Railroad Company when View obstructed.—When there are obstructions at a crossing that interfere with the field of vision from the crossing and its approaches, or make it more than usually difficult to see or hear, a railroad company must take special care to give timely warning of the approach of its trains to such crossing.[6] It is negligent not to give ordinary signals on approaching

greater than the law imposes upon him." Duffy *v.* Chicago, etc., R. Co., 32 Wis. 274; Mackay *v.* N. Y. Cent. R. Co., 35 N. Y. 75; Dolan *v.* Delaware, etc., Co., 71 N. Y. 285; Richardson *v.* N. Y. Cent. R. Co., 45 N. Y. 846; Pittsburg, etc., R. Co. *v.* Wright, 80 Ind. 182; s. c., 5 Am. & Eng. R. R. Cas. 628; Continental Imp. Co. *v.* Stead, 95 U. S. 161; Huckshold *v.* St. Louis, etc., R. Co. (Mo. 1887), 28 Am. & Eng. R. R. Cas. 659.

1. Patterson's Ry. Ac. Law, p. 170, § 175.

2. Tucker *v.* Duncan (U. S. C. C.), 6 Am. & Eng. R. R. Cas. 268; Kansas Pac. R. Co. *v.* Richardson, 25 Kan. 391; s. c., 6 Am. & Eng. R. R. Cas. 96.

3. Nicholson *v.* Erie R. Co., 41 N. Y. 525; Hanover R. Co. *v.* Coyle, 55 Pa. St. 396; Rothe *v.* Milwaukee R. Co., 21 Wis. 256; Butterfield *v.* Western R. Co., 10 Allen (Mass.), 532; Elkins *v.* Boston, etc., R. Co., 115 Mass. 190; Chicago, etc., R. Co. *v.* Still, 19 Ill. 499; Steves *v.* Oswego, etc., R. Co., 18 N. Y. 422; Ill., etc., R. Co. *v.* Ebert, 74 Ill. 399; Penna. R. Co. *v.* Werner, 89 Pa. St. 59; Penna. R. Co. *v.* Maryland, 61 Md. 108; s. c., 19 Am. & Eng. R. R. Cas. 326; Dolan *v.* Delaware, etc., Co., 71 N. Y. 285.

4. Kelly *v.* St. Paul, etc., R. Co., 29 Minn. 1; s. c., 6 Am. & Eng. R. R. Cas. 93; Kansas Pac R. Co. *v.* Richardson, 25 Kan. 391; s. c., 6 Am. & Eng. R. R. Cas. 96; Cleveland, etc., R. Co. *v.* Crawford, 24 Ohio St. 631; s. c., 15 Am. Rep. 633. And see, generally, the cases heretofore cited in this section as bearing on questions of law and fact.

5. A more specific treatment of this subject will be given farther on, when we come to deal with contributory negligence of travellers at crossings, *post.* See also tit. "Contributory Negligence," § 33, *ante.* See Funston *v.* Chicago, etc., R. Co., 61 Ia. 452; s. c., 14 Am. & Eng. R. R. Cas. 640; Thomas *v.* Delaware, etc., R. Co., 8 Fed. Rep. 728; Kansas Pac. R. Co. *v.* Richardson, 25 Kan. 391; s. c., 6 Am. & Eng. R. R. Cas. 96; Tucker *v.* Delaware, etc., R. Co., 6 Am. & Eng. R. R. Cas. 268; Haas *v.* Grand Rapids, etc., R. Co., 47 Mich. 401; s. c., 8 Am. & Eng. R. R. Cas. 268; Lehigh Valley R. Co. *v.* Brandtmaier, 5 Cent. Rep. 144; Lehnertz *v.* Minneapolis, etc., R. Co (Minn. 1883); s. c., 15 Am. & Eng. R. R. Cas. 370; Dimick *v.* Chicago, etc., R. Co., 80 Ill. 338; Kelly *v.* St. Paul, etc., R. Co., 29 Minn. 1; Philadelphia, etc., R. Co. *v.* Carr, 99 Pa. St. 505; s. c., 6 Am. & Eng. R. R. Cas. 185; Ingersoll *v.* N. Y. Cent. R. Co., 66 N. Y. 612; Garland *v.* Chicago, etc., R. Co., 8 Bradw. (Ill. App.) 571; Cordell *v.* N. Y. Cent. R. Co., 70 N. Y. 119; Chicago, etc., R. Co. *v.* Miller, 46 Mich. 532; s. c., 6 Am. & Eng. R. R. Cas. 89; Cent. R. Co. *v.* Fellar, 84 Pa. St. 226; Hixson *v.* St. Louis, etc., R. Co., 80 Mo. 335.

6. Cordell *v.* New York, etc., R. Co., 75 N. Y. 330; s. c., 70 N. Y. 119; s. c., 64 N. Y. 535; s. c., 26 Am. Rep. 550; Louisville, etc, R. Co. *v.* Commonwealth, 13 Bush (Ky.), 388; s. c., 26 Am. Rep. 207 and note.

a crossing, the view of which is obstructed;[1] and this is true whether signals are required by statute or not.[2] So the company is chargeable with negligence when it carries its track across a highway in such a manner and at such a place that those travelling the highway, when using ordinary care, can neither see nor distinctly hear approaching trains until too late to avoid injury, when trains are run over such crossing without travellers being warned of their approach.[3] And where the railroad company is at fault in creating an obstruction, or obscuring the view, at a crossing, evidence of this is admissible as bearing upon the question of negligence.[4] And, in order to avoid the charge of negligence, the company must show an exercise of care commensurate with the increase its conduct made in the hazards of the crossing.[5]

16. Temporary Obstructions of View. — It frequently happens that the view from a crossing is temporarily obstructed. If such obstructions are the result of causes beyond the control of either railroad company or traveller, the relative degree of care required of each is not altered by the existence of the obstructions; but if either party causes them, when they might have been avoided, the degree of care required of such party becomes greater.[6] In other words, the party at fault must see to it that the other has as good an opportunity to avoid inflicting or receiving injury as he would have had in the absence of the obstructions. The one at fault in creating the obstructions must use so much care that, notwithstanding the obstructions, the other party, by the use of ordinary care, would avoid either sustaining or inflicting injury.[7] Thus, where a railroad company obstructs a private crossing, it must use more care than would otherwise be necessary to avoid inflicting an injury at such crossing.[8] And it may be negligence to leave empty cars on a side track in such a position that they obscure the view of a crossing;[9] or to obstruct a public crossing with a train, and then fail to exercise greater care toward those

1. Funston *v.* Chicago, etc., R. Co., 61 Ia. 452; s. c., 14 Am. & Eng. R. R. Cas. 640. But it seems this question may be for the jury. Nehrbas *v.* Cent. Pac. R. Co., 62 Cal. 320; s. c., 14 Am. & Eng. R. R. Cas. 670.

2. Eilert *v.* Green Bay, etc., R. Co., 48 Wis. 606; Roberts *v.* Chicago, etc., R. Co., 35 Wis 679

3. Richardson *v.* N. Y. Cent. R. Co., 45 N. Y. 846.

4. Cordell *v.* N. Y. Cent., etc., R. Co., 70 N. Y. 119; s. c., 26 Am. Rep. 550.

5. Dimick *v.* Chicago, etc., R. Co., 80 Ill. 338; Rockford, etc., R. Co. *v.* Hillmer, 72 Ill. 235; Indianapolis, etc., R. Co. *v.* Smith, 75 Ill. 112; Chicago, etc., R. Co. *v.* Lee, 87 Ill. 454; Mackay *v.* N. Y., etc., R. Co., 35 N. Y. 75; Klein *v.* Jewett, 26 N. J. Eq. 474; s. c., 27 N. J. Eq. 550; Indianapolis, etc., R. Co. *v.* Stable, 62 Ill. 313; Penna. R. Co. *v.* Matthews, 36 N. J. L. 531; Duffy *v.* Chicago, etc., R. Co., 32 Wis. 269; Continental Imp. Co. *v.* Stead, 95 U. S. 161.

6. This is but a general statement of a rule that governs throughout the law of negligence. Numbers of the authorities already cited support it. See Thomas *v.* Delaware, etc., R. Co., 19 Blatchf. (U. S. C. C.) 533; s. c., 8 Fed. Rep. 729.

7. See, for analogous doctrines, tit. "Contributory Negligence," §§ 16, 19, 23, *ante;* Mackey *v.* N. Y., etc., R. Co., 35 N. Y. 75.

8. Thomas *v.* Delaware, etc., R. Co., 19 Blatchf. (U. S. C. C.) 533; s. c., 8 Fed. Rep. 729.

9. Kissenger *v.* N. Y. Cent., etc., R. Co., 56 N. Y. 538.

forced to use a private crossing in passing around the train.[1] So, where obstructions, either temporary or permanent, exist at a crossing, the railroad company should not so use its locomotives, cars, or machinery in the vicinity as to drown the noise of trains approaching such crossing, thereby increasing its hazards.[2]

17. Warning-Signals at Crossings. — The common law does not absolutely require warning-signals at all highway crossings approached by railway trains;[3] but if the giving of warning-signals at any particular crossing would be necessary in order to constitute ordinary care on the part of the railroad company when its trains were approaching such crossing, then the omission to give such signals would be negligence at common law.[4] And the necessity for such signals would be a question of fact for the jury.[5]

18. Signals required by Statute. — Warning-signals to notify travellers that a train is approaching a highway crossing are now considered so necessary that in most, if not all, of the United States they are required by statute;[6] and in some States it is provided that a failure to give the statutory signals shall, *prima facie*, be negligence *per se*,[7] although the company may show, by way of defence, that such failure was not the *proximate* cause of a subsequent injury.[8] In general, however, the rule is, that it must not only be shown that the statutory signals were omitted, but also that the omission was the proximate cause of injury before any liability to respond in damages for the injury arises.[9] And

1. Brown *v.* Hannibal, etc., R. Co., 50 Mo. 461; s. c., 11 Am. Rep. 420.

2. Ritchie *v.* Caledonian R. Co., 7 Scotch Sess Cas. (4th series, 1879) 148.

3. 2 Wood's Ry. Law, 1309; Spencer *v.* Ill., etc., R. Co., 29 Ia. 55; Brown *v.* Milwaukee, etc., R. Co., 22 Minn. 165.

4. *Ante*, § 13; Chicago, etc., R. Co. *v.* Still, 19 Ill. 499; s. c., 71 Am. Dec. 236; Rockford, etc., R. Co. *v.* Hillmer, 72 Ill. 240; Loucks *v.* Chicago, etc., R. Co., 31 Minn. 526; s. c., 19 Am. & Eng. R. R. Cas. 305. Peoria, etc., R. Co. *v.* Clayberg, 107 Ill. 644; s. c., 15 Am. & Eng. R. R. Cas. 356; Penna. Co. *v.* Krick, 47 Ind. 368; Dyer *v* Erie R. Co., 71 N. Y. 288.

5. Linfield *v.* Old Colony R. Co., 10 Cush. (Mass.) 562; s. c., 57 Am. Dec. 124 and note; Norton *v.* Eastern R. Co., 113 Mass. 369; Favor *v.* Boston, etc., R. Co., 114 Mass. 352; Cordell *v.* N. Y. Cent. R. Co., 64 N. Y. 535.

6. It would be useless to collect here all the statutory provisions in regard to warning-signals. In general, they require the bell or whistle, sometimes both, to be sounded a given distance from the crossing. For the rule in each State, the statutes and decisions of such State should be looked to. Many references, both to the statutes and the cases, will be found in the annotations to the American and English Railroad Cases. See 29 Am. & Eng. R. R. Cas. 433–440; 26 Am. & Eng. R. R. Cas. 162; 23 Am. & Eng. R. R. Cas. 249, 268, 307; 19 Am. & Eng. R. R. Cas. 260, 361, and many other volumes of the series.

7. Missouri Acts of 1881, p. 79, amending § 806 R. S. of Mo. 1879, so that the last sentence in said section as amended reads, "And said corporation shall also be liable for all damages which any person may hereafter sustain at such crossing when such bell shall not be rung, or such whistle sounded, as required by this section, provided, however, that nothing herein contained shall preclude the corporation sued from showing that the failure to ring such bell, or sound such whistle, was not the cause of such injury."

8. Huckshold *v.* St. Louis, etc., R. Co. (Mo. 1887), 28 Am. & Eng. R. R. Cas. 659.

9. When a traveller nearing a railway crossing on a highway has notice of the approach of a train, a failure to give statutory signals, or to have a flagman at the crossing, is not negligence as to him. Pakalinsky *v.* N. Y. Cent., etc., R. Co., 82 N. Y. 424; s. c., 2 Am. & Eng. R. R. Cas. 251. The omission to ring a bell, or sound a whistle, at a highway crossing does not render a railroad company liable for per-

except where an absolute liability is created by statute for a failure to give signals, and their omission is declared to be conclusive on the question of negligence, the failure to signal is not proximate negligence in itself, but the causal connection between the omission and the injury must be shown.[1] Negligence *per se* can only exist when something is carelessly done or omitted by one person which directly causes the injury of another, when, in the exercise of ordinary care, the person inflicting the injury would not have done, or omitted to do, the thing, the doing or failure to do which caused the injury.[2] As the entire doctrine of responsibility for injuries caused by negligence rests upon the maxim *causa proxima et non remota spectatur*, there can be no negligence *per se*, for which liability arises, when such negligence is not the proximate cause of a subsequent injury.[3] But, as we have seen, the doctrine of causation may be affected by statutes which raise a presumption that the omission of signals required by statute caused a subsequent injury, or a statutory liability to the injured party, penal in its character, may be created. So, invoking familiar principles on

sonal injuries, unless it is made to appear that the warning might have prevented the injury. Toledo, etc., R. Co. *v.* Jones, 76 Ill. 311; Chicago, etc., R. Co. *v.* Harwood, 90 Ill. 425; Parker *v.* Wilmington, etc., R. Co., 86 N. C. 221; s. c., 8 Am. & Eng. R. R. Cas. 420. The negligence of defendant must have been the proximate cause of injury to render it liable. Its negligence, followed by an accident, will not render it liable, if such negligence did not cause the accident. Harlan *v.* St. Louis, etc., R. Co., 65 Mo. 22; Karle *v.* Kansas City, etc., R. Co., 55 Mo. 476; Stepp *v.* Chicago, etc., R. Co., 85 Mo. 225; Atchison, etc., R. Co. *v.* Morgan (Kan. 1883); s. c., 13 Am. & Eng. R. R. Cas. 499 and note.

1. For a statute that places an absolute liability upon a railroad company for a failure to observe statutory precautions, see Code of Tenn. 1884, §§ 1298–1300. Under these sections of the Tennessee Code the company is said to be liable, even though the observance of the precautions would not have prevented the injury. Railroad Co. *v.* Walker, 11 Heisk. (Tenn.) 383–385; Nashville, etc., R. Co. *v.* Thomas, 5 Heisk. (Tenn.) 262; Collins *v.* East Tenn., etc., R. Co., 9 Heisk. (Tenn.) 841; Hill *v.* Louisville, etc, R. Co., 9 Heisk. (Tenn.) 823; Louisville, etc., R. Co. *v.* Connor, 9 Heisk. (Tenn.) 20. And under these statutory provisions, contributory negligence does not bar the action, but may be considered in mitigation of damages. The company will also be excused when there was not time for its employees to conform to the statutory requirements. For a fuller discussion of these statutory provisions, and the authorities sustaining the construction of them, just given, see *ante*, tit. "Contributory Negligence." In support of the doctrine of the text, that proof of the omission of the signals and a subsequent accident is not sufficient, as a general rule, to establish liability, but that the causal connection between the omission and the injury must be shown, see the cases cited in the last note, and also the following: Sellick *v.* Lake Shore, etc., R. Co. (Mich. 1885); s. c., 23 Am. & Eng. R. R. Cas. 338, and note; Karle *v.* Kansas City, etc., R. Co., 55 Mo. 476; Stepp *v.* Chicago, etc., R. Co., 85 Mo. 225; Pakalinsky *v.* N. Y. Cent, etc., R. Co., 82 N. Y. 424; s. c., 2 Am. & Eng. R. R. Cas. 251; Holman *v.* Chicago, etc., R. Co., 62 Mo. 562; Moore *v.* Chicago, etc., R. Co., 62 Mo. 584; Jackson *v.* Chicago, etc., R. Co, 36 Ia. 451; Flattes *v.* Chicago, etc., R. Co., 35 Ia. 191.

2. This is but equivalent to saying that a want of ordinary care proximately causing an injury is the only negligence *per se*. If to so state it, works a *reductio ad absurdum*, the fault is with those who mistake negligence which is so held as a matter of law for negligence *per se*, and who consequently say that some act or omission was negligent *per se*, when, in fact, it was only negligent, upon a given state of facts, as a matter of law. We have fully presented this distinction elsewhere. *Ante*, tit. "Con. Negligence," § 33, pp. 72, 73, and notes.

3. Broom's Maxims (7th ed.), 228; Lewis *v.* Flint, etc., R. Co. (Mich. 1884); s. c., 18 Am. & Eng. R. R. Cas. 263, opinion by Cooley, J.; Pittsburg, etc., R. Co. *v.* Staley, 41 Ohio St. 118; s. c., 19 Am. & Eng. R. R. Cas. 381.

the border line between the civil and the criminal branches of our law, the failure to comply with a positive statutory requirement may be treated as wilful, and consequences that would be remote if the omission had been merely negligent be held proximate because of the intent which the law imputes to the actor or non-actor.[1] It is not usual, however, to apply these *quasi* criminal-law doctrines to cases involving the omission of statutory signals by railroad companies, and they are generally determined by the rules that govern in cases of negligence.[2] When so determined, the term "negligence *per se*" is really a misnomer; what is meant being, that, on a given state of facts, negligence is held established as a matter of law.[3] Such distinctions are subtle, but, when observed, greatly facilitate the application of legal principles to given states of facts.[4]

(*a*) *Illustrative Doctrines.* — How the principles have been applied may be seen by a consideration of some illustrative cases. Thus, where a traveller nearing a crossing has notice of the approach of a train, a failure to give the statutory signals is not negligence as to him;[5] yet the duty to give statutory signals on approaching a highway crossing is a positive duty, and to disregard it is negligence;[6] but it is not such negligence as will war-

1. In other words, the lawfulness or unlawfulness of the act done or omitted may, in the eye of the law, make certain consequences proximate or remote in the legal chain of causation. Thus, where the act or omission is wrong in itself, the law may conclusively presume that *all* the consequences flowing from it were foreseen and intended, no matter how improbable or unlikely to have been foreseen. 1 Bish. Cr. Law (7th ed.), §§ 328, 334, 335, 343; 2 Bish. Cr. Law (7th ed.), § 693; Reg. *v.* Hicklin, L. R. 3 Q. B. D. 360; Bigelow on Torts, 313; Bloom *v.* Franklin Ins. Co., 97 Ind. 478; Billman *v.* Railway Co, 76 Ind. 178; Binford *v.* Johnson, 82 Ind. 427, 429; Weick *v.* Lander, 75 Ill. 93; Forney *v.* Geldmacher, 75 Mo. 113; Carter *v.* Louisville, etc., R. Co., 98 Ind. 555; Reynolds *v.* Clarke, Lord Raym. 1401 Stra. 635; Scott *v.* Shepherd (Squibb Case), 2 W. Black. 892, opinions of Nares and De Gray, JJ.

2. This sufficiently appears from the numerous cases cited throughout this article wherein omissions to comply with statutory requirements are treated as merely negligent. It is proper to so treat them, because the statutory requirements are generally only intended to raise the standard of care, and make precautions necessary that would not have been required at common law.

3. In other words, the courts sometimes hold, that, when certain facts appear as proven and undisputed, it should be said, as a matter of law, that the things done or omitted were negligent, and proximately caused a subsequent injury. Chicago, etc., R. Co. *v.* Boggs, 101 Ind. 522; s. c., 23 Am. & Eng. R. R. Cas. 282; s. c., 51 Am. Rep. 761.

Thus, contributory negligence is often held established as a matter of law. Chicago, etc., R. Co. *v.* Houston, 95 U. S. 697; Schofield *v.* Chicago, etc., R. Co., 114 U. S. 615; s. c., 19 Am. & Eng. R. R. Cas. 353; Hixson *v.* St. Louis, etc., R. Co., 80 Mo. 335; Tully *v.* Fitchburg, etc., R. Co., 134 Mass. 499; s. c., 14 Am. & Eng. R. R Cas. 682; Tolman *v.* Syracuse, etc., R. Co., 98 N. Y. 198; s. c., 23 Am. & Eng. R. R Cas. 313.

4. All these distinctions are plain when the doctrines of causation are borne in mind. They are too often overlooked or misapplied in cases of negligence. See tit. "Contributory Negligence," *ante*, dealing with "Proximate and Remote Causes."

5. Pakalinsky *v.* N. Y. Cent., etc., R. Co., 82 N. Y. 424; s. c., 2 Am. & Eng. R. R. Cas. 251; Houston & Texas Cent. R. Co. *v.* Nixon, 52 Tex. 19.

6. Chicago, etc., R. Co. *v.* Boggs, 101 Ind. 522; s. c., 23 Am. & Eng. R. R. Cas. 282; Cincinnati, etc., R. Co. *v.* Butler, 103 Ind. 31; s. c., 23 Am. & Eng. R. R. Cas. 262; Pittsburgh, etc., R. Co. *v.* Martin, 82 Ind. 476; s. c., 8 Am. & Eng. R. R. Cas. 253; Zimmerman *v.* Hannibal, etc., R. Co., 71 Mo. 476; s. c., 2 Am. & Eng. R. R. Cas. 191; Atlanta, etc., R. Co. *v.* Wyly, 65 Ga. 120; s. c., 8 Am. & Eng. R. R. Cas. 262;

rant a recovery, unless it appears that the signals might have prevented the injury.[1] It is not a compliance with the statute, or the exercise of ordinary care, to give the signals, and at the same time, by careless acts or omissions, render them unavailing as warnings of danger.[2] But a failure to give the statutory signals will not excuse contributory negligence on the part of a traveller.[3] A railroad company is not bound to give statutory signals for highways when approaching a switch-crossing on its own ground, but it may be negligence in fact for it not to give some warning.[4] Statutory signals are, in some jurisdictions, only necessary at lawfully established public highways.[5] Statutes requiring signals by bell *or* whistle do not require the use of both.[6] And where statutory signals are given at the proper place before the crossing is reached, and kept up until the crossing is passed, the statutory duty is fully performed.[7] A traveller has a right to assume that a railroad company will thus perform its statutory duty;[8] but in doing so he must, nevertheless, vigilantly use his senses of sight and hearing.[9] Statutory provisions requiring signals are in the

Leavenworth, etc., R. Co. *v.* Rice, 10 Kan. 426; Missouri Pac. R. Co. *v.* Wilson, 28 Kan. 639; Faber *v.* St. Paul, etc., R. Co., 29 Minn 465; s. c., 8 Am. & Eng. R. R. Cas. 277; Bitner *v.* Utah Cent. R. Co., 11 Pac Rep. 620.

1. Toledo, etc., R. Co. *v.* Jones, 76 Ill. 311; Chicago, etc., R. Co. *v.* Harwood, 90 Ill. 425; Parker *v.* Wilmington, etc., R Co., 86 N. C. 221; s. c., 8 Am. & Eng. R. R. Cas. 420.

2. Chicago, etc., R. Co. *v.* Boggs, 101 Ind. 522; s. c., 23 Am. & Eng. R. R. Cas. 282.

3. "The doctrine has been declared by this court, and re-affirmed, that a traveller approaching a railroad track is bound to use his eyes and ears, so far as there is an opportunity, and when, by the use of those senses, danger may be avoided, notwithstanding the neglect of the railroad servants to give signals, the omission of the plaintiff to use his senses and avoid the danger is concurring negligence, entitling the defendant to a non-suit." Gorton *v.* Erie R. Co., 45 N. Y. 664; Briggs *v.* N. Y. Cent., etc., R. Co, 72 N. Y. 26; Shaw *v.* Jewett, 86 N. Y. 616; s. c., 6 Am. & Eng. R. R. Cas. 111; Artz *v.* Chicago, etc., R. Co., 34 Ia. 153; 38 Ia. 293; 44 Ia. 284; Baltimore, etc., R. Co. *v.* State, 29 Md. 252; Stoneman *v.* Atlantic, etc., R. Co., 58 Mo. 503; Zimmerman *v.* Hannibal, etc., R. Co., 71 Mo. 476; s. c., 2 Am. & Eng. R. R. Cas. 191; Cleveland, etc., R. Co. *v.* Elliott, 28 Ohio St. 340; Dodge *v.* Burlington, etc., R. Co., 34 Ia. 276; Meeks *v.* Southern Pac. R. Co., 52 Cal. 602; 56 Cal. 513; s. c., 8 Am & Eng. R. R. Cas. 314.

4. Hodges *v.* St. Louis, etc., R. Co., 17 Mo. 50; s. c., 2 Am. & Eng. R. R. Cas. 190.

5. Cordell *v.* N. Y. Cent. R. Co., 64 N. Y. 535.

6. Terry *v.* St. Louis, etc., R. Co. (Mo. 1887), 2 S. W. Rep. 746; Chicago, etc., R. Co. *v.* Damerell, 81 Ill. 450.

7. Chicago, etc., R. Co. *v.* Dougherty, 110 Ill. 521; s. c., 19 Am. & Eng. R. R. Cas. 292; Zimmerman *v.* Hannibal, etc., R. Co., 71 Mo. 476; s. c., 2 Am. & Eng. R. R. Cas. 191.

8. "The citizen who on a public highway approaches a railway track, and can neither see nor hear any indications of a moving train, is not chargeable with negligence for assuming that there is no car sufficiently near to make the crossing dangerous. He has a right to assume that in handling their cars the railroad company will act with appropriate care, that the usual signals of approach will be reasonably given, and that the managers of the train will be attentive and vigilant." Kenayde *v.* Pac. R. Co., 45 Mo. 255; Donohue *v.* St. Louis, etc., R. Co. (Mo. 1886), 28 Am. & Eng. R. R. Cas. 673; Petty *v.* Hannibal, etc., R. Co. (Mo. 1886), 28 Am. & Eng. R. R. 618; Newson *v.* N. Y. Cent. R. Co, 29 N. Y. 390; Ernst *v.* Hudson River R. Co., 35 N. Y. 9; s. c., 90 Am. Dec. 761, and note; Wabash, etc, R. Co. *v.* Cent. Trust Co., 23 Fed. Rep. 738; Pittsburgh, etc, R. Co. *v.* Martin, 82 Ind. 476, 482; Philadelphia, etc, R. Co. *v.* Hagan, 47 Pa. St. 244; s. c., 86 Am. Dec. 541; Patterson's Ry. Ac. Law, 173, § 180. "Contributory Negligence," *ante*, § 16, pp. 34, 35, notes.

9. "The court told the jury that the

nature of police regulations,[1] and in some instances are of such character that the only liability for a failure to observe them is in the nature of a penalty.[2] The requirements of such statutes are mandatory, and the court should not leave it to the jury to say what signals were necessary.[3] For a failure to give the signals, a railroad company may be indicted;[4] but their omission is excusable when the ordinances of a particular municipality forbid them in its limits.[5] It is not for the legislature to prescribe the standard of ordinary care. Consequently, when signals or warnings required by statute are insufficient to give notice of danger, other and additional signals or warnings will be necessary.[6] The statutory requirements represent the mimimum of care exacted of the company,[7] but there are cases that apparently support contrary doctrines.[8]

(*b*) ***Duty to signal for Animals.*** — Statutory signals are usually for the protection of cattle as well as men; and when their careless omission is the cause of an injury to an animal upon a crossing, the actionable negligence of the railway company is established.[9] And this is true in cases where, had the signals been given, they might probably have frightened the animal from the crossing.[10] But there is no liability where the giving of the

plaintiff had a right to assume that the defendant would do his duty and ring a bell. It is claimed that this was erroneous. When that portion of the charge was excepted to, the court supplemented it by saying to the jury that the plaintiff, though he might make that assumption, was not relieved thereby from the duty on his part to vigilantly use his senses to avoid danger. The charge as thus restricted is sustainable upon the authority of this court." Folger, J., in Shaw *v.* Jewett, 86 N. Y. 616; s. c., 6 Am. & Eng. R. R. Cas. 111, citing Voak *v.* N. Y. Cent. R. Co., 75 N. Y. 320; Weber *v.* N. Y. Cent. R. Co., 58 N. Y. 451; Terry *v.* Jewett, 78 N. Y. 338. See this doctrine and that of the preceding paragraph fully treated: tit. "Contributory Neg.," *ante*, § 16, pp. 34, 35.

1. West. Union R. Co. *v.* Fulton, 64 Ill. 271; Tiedeman Lim. Police Power, 599.

2. Chicago, etc., R. Co. *v.* McDaniels, 63 Ill. 122.

3. Havens *v.* Erie R. Co., 53 Barb. (N. Y.) 328; Semel *v.* N. Y., etc., R. Co., 9 Daly (N. Y.), 321.

4. Commonwealth *v.* Boston, etc., R. Co., 133 Mass. 383; s. c., 8 Am. & Eng. R. R. Cas. 297, and note collecting many authorities.

5. Penna. Co. *v.* Hensil, 70 Ind. 569; s. c., 6 Am. & Eng. R. R. Cas. 79; s. c., 36 Am. Rep. 188.

6. A railroad company neglecting reasonable precautions besides ringing bell, as required by statute, to avoid collision with a vehicle at a highway crossing, is liable for an injury resulting from such neglect, and it is for the jury to judge as to whether or not such additional precautions have been neglected. Linfield *v.* Old Colony R. Co., 10 Cush. (Mass.) 562; s. c., 57 Am. Dec. 124, and note; Zimmerman *v.* N. Y. Cent., etc., R. Co., 67 N. Y. 601; s. c., 7 Hun (N. Y.), 552; Weber *v.* N. Y., etc., R. Co., 58 N. Y. 451; Indianapolis, etc., R. Co. *v.* Stables, 62 Ill. 313.

7. Richardson *v.* N. Y. Cent. R. Co., 45 N. Y. 846; Bradley *v.* Boston, etc., R. Co., 2 Cush. (Mass.) 539; Barry *v.* N. Y. Cent. R. Co., 92 N. Y. 289; s. c., 13 Am. & Eng. R. R. Cas. 615; Eaton *v.* Fitchburg, etc., R. Co., 129 Mass. 364; s. c., 2 Am. & Eng. R. R. Cas. 183.

8. Chicago, etc., R. Co. *v.* Dougherty, 110 Ill. 521; s c., 19 Am. & Eng. R. R. Cas. 292; Chicago, etc., R. Co. *v.* Robinson, 106 Ill. 142; s. c., 19 Am. & Eng. R. R. Cas. 396; Beisiegel *v.* N. Y. Cent. R. Co., 40 N. Y. 9; Grippen *v.* N. Y. Cent. R. Co., 40 N. Y. 34.

9. Kansas City, etc., R. Co. *v.* Turner, 78 Mo. 578; s. c., 19 Am. & Eng. R. R. Cas. 506, and note; East Tenn., Va. & Ga. R. Co. *v.* Scales, 2 Lea (Tenn.), 688; Chicago, etc., R. Co. *v.* Reid, 24 Ill. 144; Springfield, etc., R. Co. *v.* Andrews, 68 Ill. 56; Gt. Western R. Co. *v.* Geddis, 33 Ill. 304; Mobile, etc., R. Co. *v.* Malone, 46 Ala. 391.

10. Kansas City, etc., R. Co. *v.* Turner,

statutory signals at the proper place results in frightening animals on to the crossing;[1] although the unnecessary sounding of bell or whistle, when not required by statute, and at such time and place that it will probably cause animals to go upon the track at the crossing, is negligent when injury to an animal is caused thereby.[2] In a common-law action for killing cattle at a crossing, evidence of the omission of statutory signals is admissible against the company;[3] and the railroad company is always bound to use ordinary care and diligence as to cattle rightfully on the highway.[4] Whether the carelessness of an owner in permitting his animals to run at large is contributory negligence *proximate* to their injury upon a crossing by the negligent failure of a railroad company to give statutory signals when its trains approach the crossings, is differently decided in different jurisdictions.[5] From the giving of statutory signals at a place where the law requires them, no liability arises; but when not absolutely required by

78 Mo. 578; s. c., 19 Am. & Eng. R. R. Cas. 506; Tabor *v.* Missouri, etc., R. Co., 46 Mo. 354; Owens *v.* Hannibal, etc., R. Co., 58 Mo. 387; Gates *v.* Burlington, etc., R. Co, 39 Ia. 45; Pennsylvania Co. *v.* Krick, 47 Ind. 369; Illinois, etc., R. Co. *v.* Peyton, 76 Ill. 340; Bemis *v.* Connecticut, etc., R. Co., 42 Vt. 375; Lapine *v.* New Orleans, etc., R. Co., 20 La. Ann. 128; Washington *v.* Baltimore, etc., R. Co., 17 W. Va. 190; s. c., 10 Am. & Eng. R. R. Cas. 749.

1. Manhattan, etc., R. Co. *v.* Stewart (Kan. 1883) 13 Am. & Eng. R. R. Cas. 503.

2. Philadelphia, etc., R. Co. *v.* Stinger, 78 Pa. St. 219; Pennsylvania R. Co. *v.* Barnett, 59 Pa. St. 259. See Billman *v.* Indianapolis, etc., R. Co., 76 Ind. 166, as illustrating the principle that governs in such cases.

3. Braxton *v.* Hannibal, etc., R. Co., 77 Mo. 455; s. c., 13 Am. & Eng. R. R. Cas. 494.

4. Lane *v.* Kansas City, etc., R. Co. (Kan. 1884), 15 Am. & Eng. R. R. Cas. 526; Chicago, etc., R. Co. *v.* Keridig, 79 Mo. 207; s. c., 19 Am. & Eng. R. R. Cas. 493.

5. It would be outside the scope of this article, to enter at length into the discussion of the principles that should govern in the determination of this question. It would seem that there should be no arbitrary holding as a matter of law either way. In some cases, allowing the animals to run at large might be proximate to a subsequent injury, and in others not. It would be a question of fact, not of law, at least in all cases where the animal was injured on a crossing, and the element of trespass was absent. The conflict of authority may be seen by an examination of the following: Tonawanda R. Co. *v.* Munger, 5 Denio (N. Y.), 255; s. c., 49 Am. Dec. and note collecting many cases *pro* and *con;* Alabama, etc., R. Co. *v.* McAlpine, 71 Ala. 545; s. c., 15 Am. & Eng. R. R. Cas. 544; Alabama, etc., R. Co. *v.* Jones, 71 Ala. 487; s. c., 15 Am. & Eng. R. R. Cas. 549, and note; Savannah, etc., R. Co. *v.* Geiger, 21 Fla. 669; s. c., 29 Am. & Eng. R. R. Cas. 274; Price *v.* New Jersey, etc., R. Co., 32 N. J. L. 19; Eames *v.* Salem, etc., R. Co., 98 Mass. 561; Maynard *v.* Boston, etc., R. Co., 115 Mass. 458; McDonald *v.* Pittsfield R. Co., 115 Mass. 564; Baltimore, etc., R. Co. *v.* Lamborn, 12 Md. 257; Keech *v.* Baltimore, etc., R. Co., 17 Md. 33; Locke *v.* St. Paul, etc., R. Co., 15 Minn. 351; Indianapolis, etc., R. Co. *v.* McClure, 26 Ind. 370; Indianapolis, etc., R. Co. *v.* Harter, 38 Ind. 557; Jeffersonville, etc., R. Co. *v* Underhill, 48 Ind. 389; Cincinnati, etc., R. Co. *v.* Street, 50 Ind. 225; Railroad Co. *v.* Skinner, 19 Pa. St. 298; North. Pa. R. Co. *v.* Rehman, 49 Pa. St. 101; Drake *v.* Philadelphia, etc., R. Co., 51 Pa. St. 240; Toledo, etc., R. Co. *v.* Johnston, 74 Ill. 83; Ohio, etc., R. Co. *v.* Fowler, 85 Ill. 21; Cairo, etc, R. Co. *v.* Woolsey, 85 Ill. 370; Stucke *v.* Milwaukee, etc., R. Co., 9 Wis. 203; McCandless *v.* Chicago, etc., R. Co., 45 Wis. 365; Estes *v.* Atlantic, etc., R. Co., 63 Me. 308; Towne *v.* Nashua, etc., R. Co., 124 Mass. 101; Isbell *v.* N. Y., etc., R. Co, 27 Conn. 393; s. c., 71 Am. Dec. 78; Buckley *v.* N. Y., etc., R. Co., 27 Conn. 479; Pacific R. Co *v.* Brown, 14 Kan. 469; Pittsburgh, etc., R. Co. *v.* Howard, 40 Ohio St. 6; s. c., 11 Am. & Eng. R. R. Cas. 488; Washington *v.* Baltimore, etc., R. Co., 17 W. Va. 190; s. c., 10 Am. & Eng. R. R. Cas. 749.

statute, it may be negligence to sound whistle or bell in the vicinity of a crossing so that it frightens horses on the highway, even though it is the custom to give such signal at such place.[1] But "the railway owes to persons on the highway, whose horses may be frightened by the sudden appearance of a train, the duty of giving notice of the approach of its trains."[2] And the same rule applies where a railway passes over or under a highway by bridge or cut;[3] yet it would be contributory negligence upon the traveller's part to drive upon a bridge knowing a railway train was about to pass under it.[4] When the signals required by statute are not given by an approaching train, and in consequence of such omission the horses of a traveller, upon a highway crossing the railroad track, are frightened by the sudden and unheralded appearance of the train, the railroad company is liable for resulting damage.[5] And in some cases this principle has been applied where the traveller was not intending to use the crossing, or was only driving along a parallel highway.[6] But it will not be extended to cases where a team has been carelessly tied or left standing near the crossing by the driver.[7]

(*c*) *Who entitled to Benefit of Signals.* — Some of the foregoing cases show a conflict of authority upon the question of what persons are entitled to the benefit of statutory signals.[8] In some jurisdictions the doctrine is, that only travellers on the highway who are approaching or using the crossing can complain of the omission of statutory signals;[9] but in others it is held that all persons in the vicinity of a crossing, whether intending to use it or not, are entitled to the benefit of the statutory signals, and

1. Hill *v.* Portland, etc., R. Co., 55 Me. 438; s. c., 92 Am. Dec. 601; Cincinnati, etc., R. Co. *v.* Gaines, 104 Ind. 526; s. c., 54 Am. Rep. 334.

2. Patterson's Ry. Ac. Law, 152–153; Hudson *v.* Louisville, etc., R. Co., 14 Bush (Ky.), 303; Sacramento, etc., R. Co. *v.* Strong, 61 Cal. 326; s. c., 8 Am. & Eng. R. Cas. 273; Cosgrove *v.* N. Y. Cent., etc., R. Co., 87 N. Y. 88; s. c., 41 Am. Rep. 355.

3. Pennsylvania R. Co. *v.* Barnett, 59 Pa. St. 255. But see Cincinnati, etc., R. Co. *v.* Gaines, 104 Ind. 526; s. c., 54 Am. Rep. 334; Favor *v.* Boston, etc., R. Co., 114 Mass. 350; s. c., 19 Am. Rep. 364.

4. Pennsylvania R. Co. *v.* Barnett, 59 Pa. St. 255.

5. Patterson's Ry. Ac. Law, 153; Norton *v.* Eastern R. Co., 113 Mass. 366; Prescott *v.* Eastern R. Co., 113 Mass. 370; Pollock *v.* Eastern R. Co., 124 Mass. 158; Grand Trunk R. Co. *v.* Rosenberger, 9 Sup. Ct. Can. 311; s. c., 19 Am. & Eng. R. R. Cas. 8; Texas, etc., R. Co. *v.* Chapman, 57 Tex. 75.

6. Ransom *v.* Chicago, etc., R. Co., 62 Wis. 178; s. c., 19 Am. & Eng. R. R. Cas. 16, and note; Wakefield *v.* Connecticut, etc., R. Co., 37 Vt. 330; s. c., 86 Am. Dec. 711.

7. St. Louis, etc., R. Co. *v.* Payne, 29 Kan. 166; s. c., 13 Am. & Eng. R. R. Cas. 632, and note.

8. Generally this conflict may be traced to the construction of particular statutory provisions, but sometimes it is due to radical differences of view among the judges as to the purpose of the statutory enactments requiring signals.

9. Randall *v.* Baltimore, etc., R. Co., 109 U. S. 478, 485; Rosenberger *v.* Grand Trunk R. Co., 8 Ont. App. (Can.) 482; s. c., 15 Am. & Eng. R. R. Cas. 448, and note; Clark *v.* Missouri Pac. R. Co., 11 Pac. Rep.; Bell *v.* Hannibal, etc., R. Co., 72 Mo. 50; s. c., 4 Am. & Eng. R. R. Cas. 580; Hodges *v.* St. Louis, etc., R. Co., 71 Mo. 50; s. c., 2 Am. & Eng. R. R. Cas. 190; East Tenn., etc., R. Co. *v.* Feathers, 10 Lea (Tenn.), 103; s. c., 15 Am. & Eng. R. R. Cas. 446; St. Louis, etc., R. Co. *v.* Payne, 29 Kan. 166; s. c., 15 Am. & Eng. R. R. Cas. 632, and note; Harty *v.* Cent. R. Co., etc., 42 N. Y. 468; Cordell *v.* N. Y. Cent. R. Co., 64 N. Y. 535; Byrne *v.* N. Y

have a right to rely upon their being given.[1] The true rule is, to look to the terms of the particular statute, and hold the railroad company liable for injuries caused by a failure to give signals on which the person injured had a right, in the exercise of ordinary care, to rely.[2]

(*d*) *Evidence as to Signals.* — Positive evidence that the statutory signals were given outweighs negative evidence that they were not heard by other witnesses; but where the evidence is, that a witness who did not hear the signals was listening for them, and would have heard them had they been given, the evidence is in its nature positive, and entitled to the same weight as the evidence that the signals were given.[3]

19. Gates at Crossings. — Unless required by statute, a railroad company does not have to maintain gates at all highway or street crossings along its lines;[4] and the laws requiring railroad companies to fence their lines cannot be construed so as to compel them to fence up public crossings, and put gates thereat.[5] But, upon principles analogous to many already stated, it may be a question for the jury upon all the facts, whether it was not negligent for the railroad company not to have a gate at a particular crossing.[6] And where gates are placed at a crossing, either in obedience to a statute, or by the railroad company of its own motion, it is an implied invitation to travellers to cross when they find the gates open;[7] and to leave the gates open when a train is

Cent. R. Co., 94 N. Y. 12; O'Donnell *v.* Providence, etc., R. Co., 6 R. I. 211; Alabama, etc., R. Co. *v.* Hawk, 72 Ala. 112; Patterson's Ry. Ac. Law, 160, § 160.

1. Ransom *v.* Chicago, etc., R. Co., 62 Wis. 178; s. c., 19 Am. & Eng. R. R. Cas. 16, and note; s. c., 51 Am. Rep. 718; Wakefield *v.* Connecticut, etc., R. Co, 37 Vt. 330; s. c., 86 Am. Dec. 711; Cosgrove *v.* N. Y. Cent. R. Co., 87 N. Y. 88; s. c., 6 Am. & Eng. R. R. Cas. 35; Voak *v.* N. Y. Cent. R. Co, 75 N. Y. 320; Western, etc., R. Co. *v.* Jones, 65 Ga. 631; s. c., 8 Am. & Eng. R. R. Cas. 267.

2. Patterson's Ry. Ac. Law, 161, § 162.

3. Positive outweighs negative evidence as to the giving and non-giving of signals, — Bohan *v.* Milwaukee, etc., R. Co., 61 Wis. 391; s. c., 19 Am. & Eng. R. R. Cas. 276; Chicago, etc., R. Co. *v.* Robinson, 106 Ill. 142; s. c., 13 Am. & Eng. R. R. Cas. 620; 19 Am. & Eng. R. R. Cas. 396; Sutherland *v.* N. Y, etc., R. Co., 9 Jones & S. 17; Chapman *v.* N. Y., etc., R. Co., 14 Hun (N. Y.), 484; Culhane *v.* New York, etc., R. Co., 60 N. Y. 133; McGrath *v.* New York, etc., R Co., 63 N Y. 522; Telfer *v.* Northern R. Co., 30 N. J. L 188; Savannah, etc., R. Co. *v.* Shearer, 58 Ala. 672; Chicago, etc., R. Co *v.* Still, 19 Ill. 499; s. c., 71 Am. Dec. 236, and note; Ellis *v.* Gt West. R Co., L. R. 9 C. P. 551, — but where the witnesses, who did not hear the signals, were paying attention to see if the signals were given, and could have heard them if they had been, the doctrine just stated is not applicable, and the question of the relative weight of the evidence is for the jury. Bunting *v.* Cent. Pac. R. Co., 16 Nev. 277; s. c., 6 Am. & Eng. R. R Cas. 282; Louisville, etc., R. Co. *v.* Shires, 108 Ill. 617; s. c., 19 Am. & Eng. R. R. Cas. 387; Urbauck *v.* Chicago, etc., R. Co., 47 Wis. 59; Berg *v.* Chicago, etc., R. Co., 50 Wis. 419; s. c., 2 Am. & Eng. R. R. Cas. 70; Chicago, etc., R. Co. *v.* Dickson, 88 Ill. 431; Dublin, etc., R. Co. *v.* Slattery, L. R. 3 App. Cas. 1155; Voak *v.* Northern Cent. R. Co., 75 N. Y. 320; Renwick *v.* New York Cent. R. Co., 36 N. Y. 132.

4. Stubley *v.* London, etc., R. Co., L. R. 1 Ex. 13.

5. Indiana, etc., R. Co. *v.* Leak, 89 Ind. 596; s. c., 13 Am. & Eng. R. R. Cas. 521; Long *v.* Cent. Ia. R. Co. (Iowa, 1884), 19 Am. & Eng. R. R. Cas. 541, and note.

6. Eaton *v.* Fitchburg R. Co., 129 Mass. 364; s. c., 2 Am. & Eng. R. R. Cas. 183.

7. Stapley *v.* London, etc., R. Co., L. R. 1 Exch 21; Wanless *v.* Northeastern R. Co, L. R. 6 Q. B. 481; Sharp *v.* Glushing, 96 N. Y. 676; s. c., 19 Am. & Eng. R. R. Cas. 372.

nearly approaching the crossing, is evidence of negligence on the part of the company,[1] and in such cases the questions of negligence and contributory negligence are for the jury.[2] But travellers, in approaching crossings where there are gates, must use ordinary care to avoid injury, and should not depend wholly on the gates or gatemen to save them from injury.[3] It is the duty of gatemen to close the gates when signalled to do so, or when a train is approaching; and travellers, who, seeing the gates in motion, then attempt to cross before they can be closed, cannot maintain an action for injuries on the crossing.[4]

20. Flagmen at Crossings. — As a general rule, in the absence of statutory requirements, a railroad company is not bound to keep a flagman at the points where its road intersects public highways.[5] But where special dangers exist, it may be negligence not to do so, even though no statute requires it.[6] And the question whether ordinary care requires the keeping of a flagman at a crossing that is especially hazardous, is one of fact for a jury.[7] Although it has been held, in some cases, that the duty of a railroad company to provide a flagman was one of law for the court rather than of fact for the jury;[8] but these cases are generally self-contradictory in holding, also, that evidence of the omission to keep a flagman is admissible upon the question of due care, as a part of the *res*

1. Northeastern R. Co. *v.* Wanless, L. R. 7 Eng. & I. App. 12; s. c., 9 Moak's Eng. Rep. 1; Sharp *v.* Glushing, 96 N. Y. 676; s. c., 19 Am. & Eng. R. R. Cas. 372.

2. Bilbee *v.* London, etc., R. Co., 18 Com. B. (N. S.) 584; s. c., 114 E. C. L. 583; Sharp *v.* Glushing, 96 N Y. 676; s. c., 19 Am. & Eng. R. R. Cas. 372.

3. Lunt *v.* London, etc., R. Co., L. R. 1 Q. B. 277; Philadelphia, etc., R. Co. *v.* Boyer, 97 Pa. St. 91; s. c., 2 Am. & Eng. R. R. Cas. 172.

4. Peck *v.* New York, etc., R. Co., 50 Conn. 379; s. c., 14 Am. & Eng. R. R. Cas. 633.

5. Heisiegel *v.* N. Y. Cent., etc., R. Co., 40 N. Y. 9; Ernst *v.* Hudson River R. Co., 39 N. Y. 61; Culhane *v.* N. Y Cent., etc., R. Co., 60 N. Y. 133; Weber *v.* N. Y. Cent., etc., R. Co., 58 N. Y. 459; Commonwealth *v.* Boston, etc., R. Co., 101 Mass. 201; Shaw *v.* Boston, etc., R. Co., 8 Gray (Mass.), 45; Bailey *v.* New Haven, etc., R. Co., 107 Mass. 496; Maryland, etc., R. Co *v.* Newbern (Md. 1884), 19 Am. & Eng. R. R. Cas 261; Cliff *v* Midland R Co., L R. 5 Q. B. 258; Welsch *v.* Hannibal, etc., R. Co., 72 Mo. 451; s. c., 6 Am & Eng. R. R. Cas. 75; 37 Am. Rep. 440, and note; Pennsylvania R. Co. *v.* Matthews, 36 N. J. L. 531; Haas *v.* Grand Rapids, etc, R. Co, 47 Mich. 401; s. c., 8 Am. & Eng. R. R. Cas. 268.

6. Eaton *v.* Fitchburg R. Co., 129 Mass. 364; s. c., 2 Am. & Eng. R. R. Cas. 183; Kansas Pacific R. Co. *v.* Richardson, 25 Kan. 391; s. c., 6 Am. & Eng. R. R. Cas. 96; Kinney *v.* Crocker, 18 Wis. 74; Welsch *v.* Hannibal, etc., R. Co., 72 Mo. 451; s. c., 6 Am. & Eng. R. R. Cas. 75; 37 Am. Rep. 440; Cliff *v.* Midland R. Co. L. R. 5 Q. B. 258; Illinois, etc., R. Co. *v.* Ebert, 74 Ill. 399; Haas *v.* Grand Rapids, etc., R. Co., 47 Mich. 401; s. c., 8 Am. & Eng. R. R. Cas. 268.

7. Eaton *v.* Fitchburg R. Co., 129 Mass. 364; s. c., 2 Am. & Eng. R. R. Cas. 183; Bailey *v.* New Haven, etc., R. Co., 107 Mass. 496; Pennsylvania R. Co. *v.* Killips, 88 Pa. St. 405; Pennsylvania R. Co. *v.* Matthews, 36 N. J. L. 531; Kansas Pacific R. Co. *v.* Richardson, 25 Kan. 391; s. c., 6 Am. & Eng. R. R. Cas. 96; Kinsey *v.* Crocker, 18 Wis. 74; Welsch *v.* Hannibal, etc., R. Co., 72 Mo. 451; s. c., 6 Am. & Eng. R. R. Cas. 75; 37 Am. Rep. 440; Hart *v.* Chicago, etc., R Co., 56 Ia. 166; s. c., 41 Am. Rep. 93; Pittsburgh, etc., R. Co. *v.* Yundt, 78 Ind. 373; s. c., 41 Am. Rep. 580; 2 Wood's Ry. Law, 1313, 1314.

8. Houghkirk *v.* Delaware, etc, Co., 92 N. Y. 219; s. c., 44 Am. Rep. 370; Grippen *v.* N Y. Cent., etc., R Co., 40 N. Y. 41; McGrath *v.* N. Y. Cent., etc., R. Co., 63 N. Y. 528; Dyer *v.* Erie R. Co., 71 N. Y. 228; Weber *v.* N. Y. Cent., etc, R. Co., 58 N. Y. 451; State *v.* Philadelphia, etc., R. Co., 47 Md. 76.

gestæ.[1] Where it is the statutory duty of railroad commissioners to determine the necessity for a flagman at any given crossing, it has been held that a failure to have a flagman at a crossing where no order had been made by the commissioners, requiring one, could not be considered as evidence of negligence.[2] But this is seemingly in conflict with fundamental principles already stated.[3]

Where an ordinance or statute requires a flagman at a crossing, it is not conclusive upon the question of the company's negligence, that none was kept;[4] and, before the liability of the company is established, it must appear that the failure to obey the law was the proximate cause of an injury.[5]

Where a railroad company does keep a flagman at a crossing, although not required to do so by law, so long and continuously as to make his presence at the crossing customary, then travellers have a right to count upon his presence and care.[6] And it is evidence of negligence upon the part of the railway company if he be temporarily absent or permanently removed without notice to the public;[7] and in such cases his negligence is the negli-

1. "And those cases which hold that the question as to the necessity of maintaining a flagman, etc., at a particular crossing, is not for the jury, really nullify the rule by holding that, while the jury may not determine whether or not there is such a necessity, yet they may consider the circumstance that such precautions are not taken as a part of the *res gestæ*, and bearing upon the question of the company's care or negligence in the management of its trains, which is a direct repudiation of the rule itself, and involves the court in an absurd position." 2 Wood's Ry. Law, 1314. See, as subject to Mr. Wood's pertinent criticism, the following cases: viz., Houghkirk *v.* Delaware, etc., R. Co., 92 N. Y. 21; s. c., 44 Am. Rep. 370; Dyer *v.* Erie R. Co., 71 N. Y. 228; Casey *v.* N. Y. Cent. R. Co., 78 N. Y. 518; Ernst *v.* Hudson River R. Co., 39 N. Y. 61, and, generally speaking, the cases cited in the last preceding note.

2. Battishill *v.* Humphrey (Mich. 1887), 29 Am. & Eng. R. R. Cas. 411.

The soundness of the doctrine laid down in this case upon this point may well be questioned. The true principle is, that neither legislature nor railroad commissioners can arbitrarily determine what is a failure to use ordinary care. The question is one of fact for a jury; and in the Battishill case, plaintiff should have been allowed to show that there was no flagman, as bearing on the question of defendant's negligence; while defendant would have been fairly entitled to show that no order had been made by the railroad commissioners requiring a flagman, as tending to show that defendant had used ordinary care.

3. For example, as we have seen in several instances, the mere compliance with statutory requirements may not be the performance of the entire duty of the railroad company. It may be the duty of the company, before it will be in the exercise of ordinary care, to do much more than is required by positive enactment. Such questions are for a jury. The railroad commissioners may not have required a flagman at crossings where not to have one would be extremely careless on the part of the railroad company.

4. Pennsylvania Co. *v.* Hensil, 70 Ind. 569; s. c., 6 Am. & Eng. R. R. Cas. 79; 36 Am. Rep. 188.

5. Pennsylvania Co. *v.* Hensil, 70 Ind. 569; s. c., 6 Am. & Eng. R. R. Cas. 79; 36 Am. Rep. 188; Cordell *v.* N. Y. Cent., etc., R. Co., 70 N. Y. 119; Briggs *v.* N. Y. Cent., etc., R. Co., 72 N. Y. 26; Chicago, etc., R Co. *v.* Notzki, 66 Ill. 455; Fletcher *v.* Atlantic, etc., R. Co., 64 Mo. 484; see Johnson *v.* St. Paul, etc., R. Co. (Minn. 1883), 15 Am. & Eng. R. R. Cas. 467.

6. Ernst *v.* Hudson River R. Co., 39 N. Y. 61; Warner *v.* N. Y. Cent., etc., R. Co., 45 Barb. (N. Y.) 299; Dolan *v.* Delaware, etc., Co., 71 N. Y. 285; Pittsburgh, etc., R. Co. *v.* Yundt, 78 Ind. 373; s. c., 3 Am. & Eng. R. R. Cas. 305; 41 Am. Rep. 580; St. Louis, etc., R. Co. *v.* Dunn, 78 Ill. 197. See McGrath *v.* N. Y. Cent., etc, R. Co., 59 N. Y. 468; s. c., 17 Am. Rep. 359, and note, s. c., second appeal, 63 N. Y. 522; Casey *v.* N. Y. Cent., etc., R. Co., 78 N. Y. 518.

7. Pittsburgh, etc., R. Co. *v.* Yundt, 78

gence of the railway company,[1] even though he was not specially employed as a flagman if customarily permitted to act as such;[2] but, in order that the company may be liable, it must be shown that his negligence proximately caused the injury.[3] Where one rides or drives up to a crossing by the invitation or direction of a flagman or gate-keeper, and receives an injury at the crossing from the trains, machinery, or appliances of the railway company, he is entitled to recover, because the invitation or direction was an assurance of safety upon which he had the right to rely.[4] In such case the traveller is not bound to exercise the same degree of care that would otherwise be required.[5] But such invitation or direction will not excuse him from exercising the care of a prudent man under such circumstances.[6] And one who persists in driving on a crossing after being warned not to do so by a flagman, and is then injured, cannot recover.[7] As bearing upon the question of the negligence of a flagman, evidence that he was intoxicated at the time an injury was sustained by a traveller at the crossing where such flagman was stationed, is admissible; but evidence of his former intoxication is not material.[8]

21. Lookout at Crossings. — It is the duty of a railroad company to keep a lookout when approaching highway crossings, even though no statute commands it.[9] The lookout must be as efficient as circumstances require, and special vigilance is necessary when the chances of access to the track are greater than usual.[10] When an engine is backing a train in a city, there should be a lookout to give notice of any person or obstruction on the track,[11]

Ind. 373; s. c., 3 Am. & Eng. R. R. Cas. 305; 41 Am. Rep. 580; St. Louis, etc., R. Co. v. Dunn, 78 Ill. 197; Dolan v. Delaware, etc, Co., 71 N. Y. 285; Philadelphia, etc., R. Co. v. Killips, 88 Pa. St. 405.

1. Dolan v. Delaware, etc., Co, 71 N. Y. 285; Ernst v. Hudson River R. Co., 35 N. Y. 9; s. c, 90 Am. Dec. 761; Kissenger v. N. Y. Cent., etc., R. Co., 56 N. Y. 538; Peck v. Michigan Cent. R. Co. (Mich. 1885), 19 Am. & Eng. R. R. Cas. 257; Sweeney v. Old Colony R. Co., 10 Allen (Mass.), 368; s. c., 87 Am. Dec. 644.

2. Peck v. Michigan Cent. R. Co. (Mich. 1885), 19 Am. & Eng. R. R. Cas. 257.

3. Pakalinsky v. N. Y. Cent., etc., R. Co., 82 N. Y. 424; s. c., 2 Am. & Eng. R. R. Cas. 251; Pennsylvania Co. v. Hensil, 70 Ind. 596; s. c., 6 Am. & Eng. R. R. Cas. 79

4. Borst v. Lake Shore, etc., R. Co., 66 N. Y. 639; Sharp v. Glushing, 96 N. Y. 676; s. c., 19 Am. & Eng. R. R. Cas 372; Sweeney v. Old Colony R. Co, 10 Allen (Mass), 368; s. c., 87 Am. Dec. 644; Bayley v. Eastern R. Co., 125 Mass 62; Lunt v. London, etc., R. Co., L. R. 1 Q. B. 277.

5. Lunt v. London, etc., R. Co., L. R. 1 Q. B. 277.

6. Philadelphia, etc., R. Co. v. Boyer, 97 Pa. St. 91; s. c., 2 Am. & Eng. R. R. Cas. 172; McGrath v. N. Y. Cent., etc., R. Co., 59 N. Y. 468; s. c., 17 Am. Rep. 359, and note; Chicago, etc., R. Co. v. Spring, 13 Bradw. (Ill. App.) 174.

7. Houston, etc., R. Co. v. Carson (Tex.), 1 So. West. Rep. 107.

8. Warner v. N. Y. Cent., etc., R. Co., 44 N. Y. 465.

9. "The necessity of a careful lookout is recognized by the unwritten law of navigation, and it is apparent on railroads." Marcott v. Marquette, etc., R. Co., 47 Mich. 1; s. c., 4 Am. & Eng. R. R. Cas. 548.

"The servants of the company in charge of the train should be at their posts, observant of the track, and ready, at a moment's notice, to avert, if possible, any apprehended danger." Frick v. St. Louis, etc., R. Co., 75 Mo. 595; s. c., 8 Am. & Eng. R. R. Cas. 280, 288; St. Louis, etc., R. Co. v. Mathias, 50 Ind. 65.

10. East Tennessee R. Co. v. White, 5 Lea, Tenn. 540; s. c., 8 Am. & Eng. R. R. Cas. 65; Marcott v. Marquette, etc., R. Co., 47 Mich. 1.; s. c., 4 Am. & Eng. R. R. Cas. 548.

11. Barley v. Chicago, etc., R. Co., 4 Biss. (U. S. C. C.) 430.

and on whose signal the engineer may depend to avert danger to persons on the crossing behind the train.[1] The lookout must exercise ordinary care; and if the employees of a railroad company, whose duty it is to watch the track, fail to discover the peril of persons at a crossing, when reasonable attention would have enabled them to do so in time to have prevented the infliction of injury, the company is liable.[2] So when they pay no attention to the track ahead of them, or their duty to give signals, but leave such duties to a boy, who is riding and ringing the bell for amusement, the company is chargeable with negligence.[3] It is the duty of both engineer and fireman to keep a lookout ahead of their locomotive; and when one can see, and the other cannot, it is the duty of the one who can see to be vigilant in looking ahead.[4] But some of these doctrines have been laid down in cases construing particular statutory provisions which require the keeping of a lookout ahead, and impose an absolute liability upon the company for injuries occurring when the lookout has not been kept, even though the proximate connection between the violation of the statute and the subsequent injury is not shown.[5]

22. Speed of Trains at Crossings. — It is now well settled that no rate of speed in crossing a highway with a railway train is negligence *per se* at common law.[6] Nor is it negligence, as a matter of law, not to slacken the speed of a train when approaching an ordinary highway crossing.[7] Yet the speed at which a train is run over a crossing may be so great as to be negligent under the circumstances, as a matter of fact,[8] and this is a question for the

1. Robinson *v.* Western Pac. R. Co., 48 Cal 409.

2. East Tennessee, etc., R. Co. *v.* White, 5 Lea (Tenn.), 540; s. c., 8 Am. & Eng. R. R. Cas. 65; Morrissey *v.* Wiggan's Ferry Co., 47 Mo. 521; s. c., Thompson's Carriers of Pass. 243; Tuff *v.* Warman, 2 C. B. (N. S.) 740; 5 C. B. (N. S.) 573; Radley *v.* London, etc., R. Co., L. R. 1 App. Cas. 754; s. c., 2 Thompson on Neg. 1108; Isbell *v.* New York, etc., R. Co., 27 Conn. 393; s. c., 71 Am. Dec. 78; Baltimore, etc., R. Co. *v.* Kean (Md.), 28 Am. & Eng. R. R. Cas. 580; *ante*, pp. 27–29, tit. "Contributory Negligence," § 12.

3. Chicago, etc., R. Co. *v.* Ryan, 70 Ill. 211.

4. Nashville, etc., R. Co. *v.* Nowlin, 1 Lea (Tenn.), 523.

5. Code of Tenn. 1884, §§ 1298–1300; Railroad Co. *v.* Walker, 11 Heisk (Tenn.) 383, 385; Nashville, etc., R. Co. *v.* Thomas, 5 Heisk (Tenn.) 262; Collins *v.* East Tenn., etc., R. Co., 9 Heisk. (Tenn. 841; East Tenn., etc., R. Co. *v.* White, 5 Lea (Tenn.), 540; s. c., 8 Am. & Eng. R. R. Cas. 65.

6. Reading, etc., R. Co. *v.* Ritchie, 102 Pa. St. 425; s. c., 19 Am. & Eng. R. R. Cas. 267, and note; Powell *v.* Mo. Pac. R. Co., 76 Mo. 80; s. c., 8 Am. & Eng. R. R. Cas. 467; Goodwin *v.* Chicago, etc., R. Co., 75 Mo. 73; s. c., 11 Am. & Eng. R. R. Cas. 460; Wallace *v.* St. Louis, etc., R. Co, 74 Mo. 594; Artz *v.* Chicago, etc., R. Co., 44 Ia. 284; Burlington, etc., R. Co. *v.* Wendt, 12 Neb. 76; Chicago, etc., R. Co. *v.* Lee, 68 Ill. 576; Chicago, etc., R. Co. *v.* Harwood, 80 Ill. 88; Cohen *v.* Eureka, etc., R. Co., 14 Nev. 376; Grand Rapids, etc., R. Co. *v.* Huntley, 38 Mich. 537; Grows *v.* Maine, etc., R. Co., 67 Me. 100; Bemis *v.* Connecticut, etc., R. Co., 42 Vt. 375; Zeigler *v.* Northeastern R. Co., 5 So. Car. 222; 7 So. Car. 402; Telfer *v.* Northern, etc., R. Co., 30 N. J. L. 188; Terre Haute, etc., R. Co. *v.* Clark, 73 Ind. 168; s. c., 6 Am. & Eng. R. R. Cas. 84; Warner *v.* N. Y. Cent. R. Co. 44 N. Y. 465; Commonwealth *v.* Fitchburg R. Co., 126 Mass. 472.

7. Zeigler *v.* Northeastern R. Co., 5 So. Car. 222; 7 So. Car. 402; Telfer *v.* Northern R. Co., 30 N. J. L. 188; Cohen *v.* Eureka, etc., R. Co., 14 Nev. 376; Chicago, etc., R. Co. *v.* Robinson, 9 Bradw. (Ill. App.) 89.

8. Salter *v.* Utica, etc., R. Co., 88 N. Y. 42; s. c., 8 Am. & Eng. R. R. Cas. 437;

jury on the facts of each case;[1] but there must be facts and circumstances, apart from the rate of speed itself, tending to show that it was careless to run at the rate of speed complained of, or a finding of negligence will not be warranted.[2] Yet it may be the legal duty of a railway company in approaching a crossing to have its train under such control that it can be stopped in time to avoid injuring those who, in the exercise of ordinary care, have gone upon the crossing.[3] Although it cannot be said, as a matter of law, that trains must be run at such speed at night that they can be stopped within the distance in which objects can be seen ahead by the light of the headlight;[4] on the other hand, it may be negligent for a train to approach a dangerous crossing at a rate of speed as great as permitted by statute,[5] and no law or ordinance permitting a given rate of speed will justify such speed if negligent in view of the surrounding circumstances.[6] It is clearly negligent to cross a public highway with a train at any great speed without giving sufficient warnings of the approach of the

Wilds v. Hudson River R. Co., 29 N. Y. 315; Massoth v. Delaware, etc, Co., 64 N. Y. 531; Indianapolis, etc., R. Co., v. McLin, 82 Ind. 435; s. c., 8 Am. & Eng. R. R. Cas. 237; Pittsburgh, etc., R. Co. v. Martin. 82 Ind. 476; s. c., 8 Am. & Eng. R. R. Cas. 253; Frick v. St. Louis, etc., R. Co., 75 Mo 595; s. c., 8 Am. & Eng. R. R. Cas. 280; Artz v. Chicago, etc., R. Co., 44 Ia. 284; Indianapolis, etc., R. Co. v. Stables, 62 Ill. 313; Chicago, etc., R. Co. v. Payne, 59 Ill. 534; Rockford, etc., R. Co. v. Hillmer, 72 Ill. 235; Shaber v. St. Paul, etc., R. Co., 28 Minn. 103; s. c., 2 Am. & Eng. R. R. Cas. 185.

1. Marcott v. Marquette, etc., R. Co., 47 Mich. 1; s. c, 4 Am. & Eng. R. R. Cas. 548; Frick v. St. Louis, etc., R. Co., 75 Mo. 595; s. c, 8 Am. & Eng. R. R. Cas. 280; Meyer v. M P. R. Co., 2 Neb. 319; Langhoff v. Milwaukee, etc., R. Co., 19 Wis. 489; Louisville, etc., R. Co. v. Goetz, 79 Ky. 442; s. c, 14 Am & Eng. R. R. Cas. 627; Klanowski v. Grand Trunk R. Co. (Mich. 1885), 21 Am. & Eng. R. R. Cas. 648; Salter v. Utica, etc., R. Co, 88 N. Y. 42; s. c., 8 Am. & Eng R. R. Cas. 437; Massoth v. Delaware, etc, Co., 64 N. Y. 531; Wilds v. Hudson River R Co., 29 N. Y. 315; Terre Haute, etc., R. Co v. Clark, 73 Ind. 168; s c., 6 Am. & Eng. R R. Cas. 84; Pittsburgh, etc., R. Co. v. Martin, 82 Ind. 476; s. c., 8 Am. & Eng. R R. Cas. 253.

2. This follows from the doctrine that no rate of speed is negligence *per se.* "While there may be circumstances which require a diminished speed, it is only the force of those circumstances which creates such a duty." Reading, etc., R. Co. v. Ritchie, 102 Pa. St. 425; s. c., 19 Am. & Eng. R. R. Cas. 267; Pierce on Railroads, 354.

3. "The speed of a train at a crossing should not be so great as to render unavailing the warning of its whistle or bell; and this caution is especially applicable when their sound is obstructed by winds and other noises, and when intervening objects prevent those who are approaching the railroad from seeing a coming train. In such cases, if an unslackened speed is desirable, watchmen should be stationed at the crossing." Continental Imp. Co. v. Stead, 95 U. S. 161, 164; Pennsylvania R. Co. v. Ackerman, 74 Pa. St. 265; Pennsylvania R. Co. v. Lewis, 79 Pa. St. 33; Philadelphia, etc., R. Co. v Long, 75 Pa. St. 257; Philadelphia, etc., R. Co. v. Hagan, 47 Pa. St. 244; s. c., 86 Am. Dec. 541; Quimby v. Vermont Cent. R. Co., 23 Vt. 387; State v. Baltimore, etc., R. Co., 24 Md. 84; Wilson v. Cunningham, 3 Cal. 241; South & N. Ala. R. Co. v. Thompson, 62 Ala. 494; Wilds v. Hudson River R. Co., 29 N. Y. 315; Warner v. New York, etc., R. Co., 44 N. Y. 465; Black v. Burlington, etc, R. Co., 38 Ia. 515; Nehrbas v. Cent. Pac. R. Co., 62 Cal. 320; s. c., 14 Am. & Eng. R. R. Cas. 670; Pierce on Railroads, 355.

4. Patterson's Ry. Ac. Law, 158, § 157; Louisville, etc., R. Co. v. Milam, 10 Lea (Tenn.), 223; s. c, 13 Am & Eng. R. R. Cas. 507. But see Railroad Co. v. Lyon, 7 Reporter, 556.

5. Shaber v. St. Paul, etc., R. Co., 28 Minn. 103; s. c., 2 Am. & Eng. R. R. Cas. 185.

6. Frick v. St. Louis, etc., R. Co., 75 Mo. 595; s. c., 8 Am. & Eng. R. R. Cas. 280; Shaber v. St. Paul., etc., R. Co, 28 Minn. 103; s. c., 2 Am. & Eng. R. R. Cas. 185.

train;[1] but it is not necessary to slacken the speed of a train, which has given such warning, because the engineer sees a team approaching the crossing in the open country.[2] And even though the speed be negligent under the circumstances, it affords no excuse for contributory negligence.[3] In determining whether the speed of a train at a particular time was dangerous, evidence of the speed of other trains, practised with the tacit acquiescence of the community, is not admissible.[4] But the rule would seem to be different when it is shown that the speed of the particular train was equal in velocity to that usually practised.[5] And it seems that evidence of the speed of a train when at some distance from the place of a subsequent accident may be considered in determining whether the speed at the place of the accident was dangerous.[6] And so the distance run by the train after striking a person, and before it could be stopped, may be shown as bearing upon the question of negligence.[7]

(*a*) *Speed in Violation of Positive Law.* — A railroad company is liable for injuries caused by running its trains at a speed greater than allowed by statute.[8] But it is not liable in such cases if there was contributory negligence as the violation of the statute; being only negligent, contributory negligence is a defence.[9] The fact that a train was running at a greater rate of speed than permitted by law, is evidence of negligence;[10] but it is no proof of proximate negligence,[11] nor is it negligence *per se* as a matter of law.[12] The question is for the jury.[13] Statutory requirements

1. Continental Imp. Co. *v.* Stead, 95 U. S. 161; Louisville, etc., R. Co. *v.* Commonwealth, 14 Am. & Eng. R. R. Cas. 613; Massoth *v.* Delaware, etc., Co., 64 N. Y. 524.

2. Chicago, etc., R. Co. *v.* Robinson, 9 Bradw (Ill. App.) 89; Telfer *v.* Northern R. Co., 30 N. J. L. 188. But of course where a wagon is on the track, and in danger, the rule is otherwise. Chicago, etc., R. Co. *v.* Hogarth, 38 Ill. 370; Bunting *v.* Cent. Pac. R. Co, 16 Nev. 277.

3. Bell *v.* Hannibal, etc., R. Co., 72 Mo. 50; s. c., 4 Am. & Eng. R. R. Cas. 580; Gorton *v.* Erie R. Co., 45 N. Y. 664; Pierce on Railroads, 343.

4. Cleveland, etc., R. Co. *v.* Newell, 75 Ind. 542; s. c., 8 Am. & Eng. R. R. Cas. 377.

5. Shaber *v.* St. Paul, etc., R. Co., 28 Minn. 103; s. c., 2 Am. & Eng. R. R. Cas. 185.

6. Louisville, etc., R. Co. *v.* Jones, 108 Ind. 551; s. c., 28 Am. & Eng. R. R. Cas. 170.

7. Pennsylvania Co. *v.* Conlan, 101 Ill. 93.

8. Pierce on Railroads, 354; Haas *v.* Chicago, etc., R. Co., 41 Wis. 44; Correll *v.* Burlington, etc., R. Co., 38 Ia. 120; St. Louis, etc., R. Co. *v.* Mathias, 50 Ind. 65; Chicago, etc., R. Co. *v.* Becker, 84 Ill. 483; Baltimore, etc., R. Co. *v.* McDonald, 43 Md. 534; Liddy *v.* St. Louis, etc., R. Co, 40 Mo. 506.

9. Illinois, etc., R Co. *v.* Hetherington, 83 Ill. 510; Railroad Co. *v.* Houston, 95 U. S. 397; Schofield *v.* Chicago, etc., R. Co., 114 U. S. 618.

10. Faber *v.* St. Paul, etc., R. Co. 29 Minn. 465; s. c., 8 Am. & Eng. R. R. Cas. 277; Howard *v.* St. Paul, etc., R. Co., 32 Minn. 214; s. c, 19 Am. & Eng. R. R. Cas. 283; Meek *v.* Penna. Co., 38 Ohio St. 632; s. c., 13 Am. & Eng. R. R. Cas. 643; Western, etc, R. Co. *v.* King, 70 Ga. 261; s. c., 19 Am. & Eng. R. R. Cas. 255.

11. Kelley *v.* Hannibal, etc., R. Co., 75 Mo. 138; s. c., 13 Am. & Eng. R. R. Cas. 638

12. Meek *v.* Penna. Co., 38 Ohio St. 632; s. c., 13 Am. & Eng. R. R. Cas. 643; Hanlon *v.* So. Boston H. R. Co., 129 Mass 310; s. c., 2 Am. & Eng. R. R. Cas 18; Western, etc., R. Co. *v.* King, 70 Ga. 261; s. c., 19 Am. & Eng. R. R. Cas. 255; Howard *v.* St. Paul, etc., R. Co., 32 Minn. 214; s. c., 19 Am. & Eng. R. R. Cas. 283.

13. Western, etc., R. Co. *v* King, 70 Ga 261; s. c., 19 Am. & Eng. R. R. Cas. 255;

relating to speed, signals, etc., in cities and other places, are passed to preserve life, and a strict observance of such statutes is required by the courts.[1] See also for principles governing in the case of violation of statutory requirements, the preceding paragraphs of this article treating of statutory signals, sign-boards, etc.

23. Appliances, etc., for Control of Train. — It is the duty of a railroad company to properly and adequately equip its trains and engines with brakes and appliances to control and arrest the progress of a train; also to furnish a sufficient number of competent employees to control and operate the train with care.[2]

(*a*) *Lights on Cars and Engines.* — A railroad company, moving cars and engines after dark at a crossing, is bound to take means to notify the public of the approach of its cars, and must use ordinary care to adopt precautions that will avoid accidents.[3] It is its duty to provide headlights,[4] but it is not liable because they are temporarily obscured by causes beyond its control.[5]

24. Pushing, Backing, and Switching Cars over Crossings. — It is not negligent to push, back, or switch cars over a crossing, even though the cars be "kicked," or a "flying-switch" be made, if precautions to prevent injury to travellers on the highway are taken that are proportioned to the special danger of the mode adopted.[6] The question is, as we have seen in many similar instances, one of fact for the jury.[7] But a railroad company is required to take extraordinary care to prevent accident when it undertakes to back a train or engine at a highway crossing.[8]

Howard *v.* St. Paul, etc., R. Co., 32 Minn. 214; s. c., 19 Am. & Eng. R. R. Cas. 283.

1. Haas *v.* Chicago, etc., R. Co., 41 Wis. 44. See Vicksburg, etc., R. Co. *v.* McGowan, 62 Miss. 682, for a decision bearing on the violation of a municipal ordinance regulating the speed of trains.

2. O'Mara *v.* Hudson River R. Co., 38 N. Y. 445; St. Louis, etc., R. Co. *v.* Mathias, 50 Ind. 65; Frick *v.* St. Louis, etc., R. Co., 75 Mo. 595; s. c., 8 Am. & Eng. R. R. Cas. 280; Toledo, etc, R. Co. *v.* Maginnis, 71 Ill. 346; Kansas Pac. R. Co. *v.* Pointer, 14 Kan. 37, 9 Kan. 620; Kay *v.* Pennsylvania R. Co., 65 Pa. St. 269; Chicago, etc., R. Co. *v.* Garvey, 58 Ill. 83.

3. Peoria, etc., R. Co. *v.* Clayberg, 107 Ill. 644; s. c., 15 Am. & Eng. R. R. Cas. 356.

4. Nashville, etc., R. Co. *v.* Smith, 6 Heisk. (Tenn.) 174; Smedis *v.* Brooklyn, etc., R. Co., 88 N. Y. 13; s. c., 8 Am. & Eng. R. R. Cas. 445; Cheney *v.* N. Y. Cent. R. Co., 16 Hun (N. Y.), 415.

5. Louisville, etc., R. Co. *v.* Melton, 2 Lea (Tenn.), 262.

6. Bohan *v.* Milwaukee, etc., R. Co., 58 Wis. 30; s. c., 15 Am. & Eng. R. R. Cas. 374; s. c., 61 Wis. 391; 19 Am. & Eng R. R. Cas 276; Hogan *v.* Chicago, etc., R. Co., 59 Wis. 139; s. c., 15 Am. & Eng. R. R Cas. 439.

7. Howard *v.* St. Paul, etc., R. Co., 32 Minn. 214; s. c, 19 Am. & Eng. R. R. Cas 283, and note; Ferguson *v.* Wisconsin, etc., R. Co., 63 Wis. 145; s. c., 19 Am & Eng. R. R. Cas. 285

8. Hutchinson *v.* St. Paul, etc., R. Co, 32 Minn. 398; s. c., 19 Am. & Eng. R. R. Cas. 280, and note; Maginnis *v.* New York Cent., etc., R. Co., 52 N. Y. 215; Kissinger *v.* New York, etc., R. Co., 56 N. Y 538; South, etc., R. Co. *v.* Shearer, 58 Ala. 672; Johnson *v.* St. Paul, etc., R. Co., 31 Minn. 283; s. c., 15 Am. & Eng. R. R. Cas. 467; Levoy *v.* Midland R. Co., 3 Ont. Rep. 623; s. c., 15 Am. & Eng. R. R. Cas. 478.

It is negligence to run a train backward

(*a*) "*Flying-Switches*" *and* "*Kicking-Cars.*" — Where cars are "kicked" or sent on a "flying-switch" over a crossing, the greatest care must be exercised to prevent injury to persons on the highway.[1] Where a "flying-switch" is made over a crossing without notice, warning, or flagman to protect the public, it is negligence as a matter of law if injury follows.[2]

over a crossing in a populous city without warning or lookout at the back, and with defective appliances for stopping the train. Kansas Pac. R. Co. *v.* Pointer, 14 Kan. 37; Kan. Pac. R. Co. *v.* Ward, 4 Col. 30.

The company is bound to sound suitable signals and give other warnings of danger when pushing or backing cars over crossings. Bailey *v.* New Haven, etc., R. Co., 107 Mass. 496; Robinson *v.* Western Pac. R. Co., 48 Cal. 409; Kennedy *v.* North Mo R. Co., 36 Mo. 351; McWilliams *v.* Detroit, etc., R. Co, 31 Mich. 247; Hathaway *v.* Toledo, etc., R. Co., 46 Ind. 25.

The mere sounding of a whistle on an engine attached to a long train of freight cars is not sufficient warning of an intention to back the train at the crossing. Eaton *v.* Erie R. Co., 51 N. Y. 544; McGovern *v.* N. Y., etc, R. Co., 67 N. Y. 417; Chicago, etc., R. Co. *v.* Garvey, 58 Ill. 85; Illinois, etc., R. Co. *v.* Ebert, 74 Ill. 399; Linfield *v.* Old Colony R. Co, 10 Cush. (Mass.) 564.

When a train standing adjacent to a crossing was backed suddenly and without warning, injuring a person on the crossing, the negligence of the company is clear. Robinson *v.* Western, etc., R. Co., 48 Cal. 409.

It is sufficient evidence to support a finding of negligence if it appears that cars were backed over a crossing at night without light, signal, lookout, or flagman, and at a high rate of speed. Bolinger *v.* St. Paul, etc, R. Co. (Minn. 1887), 29 Am. & Eng. R. R. Cas. 408.

So it is negligence to back cars over the crossing of a main street in a village without a lookout or flagman. Cooper *v.* Lake Shore, etc., R. Co. (Mich.), 33 N. W. Rep. 306.

Where a train backed over a crossing without signal, and with a brakeman so placed that he could not see the crossing, the question of negligence was for the jury. Barry *v.* New York, etc, R. Co., 92 N. Y. 289; s. c., 13 Am. & Eng. R. R. Cas. 615.

In such a case, sounding the bell does not relieve the company from liability as a matter of law. Barry *v.* New York, etc., R. Co., 92 N. Y. 289; s. c., 13 Am. & Eng. R. R. Cas. 615.

To permit freight cars detached from an engine to cross a public street at speed, and without having control of them, or giving warning of their approach, is negligent. Chicago, etc., R. Co. *v.* Garvey, 58 Ill. 83.

It is not negligent for a person to start across the track behind a train standing still, at or near a crossing; and he has a right to presume that the train will not be started back without signal or lookout. Robinson *v.* Western, etc., R. Co., 48 Cal. 409; McWilliams *v.* D. C. M. Co., 31 Mich. 274; Solen *v.* Virginia, etc., R. Co., 13 Nev. 106.

1. Kay *v.* Pennsylvania R. Co., 65 Pa. St. 269; Troutman *v.* Philadelphia, etc., R. Co., 11 Weekly Notes of Cases (Pa. 455); Ferguson *v.* Wisconsin, etc., R. Co., 63 Wis. 145; s. c., 19 Am. & Eng. R. R. Cas. 285; Butler *v.* Milwaukee, etc., R. Co., 28 Wis. 487; Howard *v.* St. Paul, etc., R. Co., 32 Minn. 214; s. c., 19 Am. & Eng. R. R. Cas. 283; Brown *v.* New York, etc., R. Co., 32 N. Y. 600; s. c., 87 Am. Dec. 353; Sutton *v.* New York, etc., R. Co., 66 N. Y. 243; Pennsylvania R. Co. *v.* State, 61 Md. 108; s. c., 19 Am. & Eng. R. R. Cas. 326; Illinois, etc., R. Co *v.* Baches, 55 Ill. 379; Chicago, etc, R. Co. *v.* Degman, 56 Ill. 487; Chicago, etc., R. Co. *v.* Garvey, 58 Ill. 83.

2. French *v.* Taunton, etc., R. Co., 116 Mass. 537; Hinkley *v.* Cape Cod R. Co., 120 Mass. 257; Brown *v.* New York, etc., R. Co, 32 N Y. 597; Sutton *v.* New York, etc., R. Co., 66 N. Y. 243; Butler *v.* Milwaukee, etc., R. Co., 28 Wis. 487; Illinois, etc. R. Co. *v.* Hammer, 72 Ill. 347; Illinois, etc., R. Co. *v.* Baches, 55 Ill. 397; Chicago, etc., R. Co. *v.* Taylor, 69 Ill. 461; Philadelphia, etc, R. Co. *v.* Troutman, 6 Am. and Eng. R R. Cas. 117; Ferguson *v.* Wisconsin, etc., R. Co, 63 Wis. 145; s. c., 19 Am. & Eng. R. R. Cas. 285.

The making of a "flying-switch" necessarily implies negligence. Illinois, etc., R. Co. *v.* Hammer, 72 Ill 347.

"The mode of making a running or flying switch, and permitting a detached car to pass over a crossing, is a fruitful source of disasters, and in this case it is a fair inference from the evidence that the company was guilty of negligence in so doing." Grethen *v.* Chicago, etc., R. Co. (U. S. C. C.), 19 Am. & Eng. R. R. Cas. 342.

Where an engine passed a crossing, and its steam obscured the track just as a man started across behind it, his contributory

25. Negligence of Railroad Company: What Sufficient Evidence of. — Many illustrations have already been given of what constitutes negligence on the part of a railroad company in crossing a highway with its trains, or using it for railway purposes. Some special doctrines upon the subject remain to be considered. The injury of a person by cars or engines at a railway highway-crossing raises no presumption that the company has been negligent.[1] But where there is some evidence from which a reasonable mind could fairly infer that there had been negligence on the part of the railroad company, the question becomes one of fact for the jury.[2]

negligence in being struck by a car making a flying switch was held for the jury; the evidence of the negligence of the company being sufficient. Ferguson *v.* Wisconsin, etc., R. Co., 63 Wis. 145; s. c., 19 Am. & Eng. R. R. Cas. 285.

Where a person is injured in the street by the unexpected "kicking" of a car, the question of negligence on both sides is for the jury. Mahar *v.* Grand Trunk R. Co., 26 Hun (N. Y.), 32.

Where an injury was caused by a detached and unseen car following a train which had just passed, the question of plaintiff's contributory negligence in not discovering the car switched from the train was left to the jury. French *v.* Taunton, etc., R. Co., 116 Mass. 537.

But where the flagman of another company was injured by a train making a "flying-switch," it was *held* on the facts of the case that his contributory negligence was established. Clark *v.* Boston, etc., R. Co., 128 Mass. 1; s. c., 1 Am. & Eng. R. R. Cas. 134.

So, where persons were struck at a highway crossing by cars making a "flying-switch," it was held that there could be no recovery, because the persons injured were not using the highway, but were, and had been, walking along the track, which they were using as a footpath regardless of company's trains. Grethen *v.* Chicago, etc., R. Co. (U. S. C. C.), 19 Am. & Eng. R. R. Cas. 242.

1. Penna. R. Co. *v.* Goodman, 62 Pa. St. 329; Cleaveland, etc., R. Co. *v.* Crawford, 24 Ohio St. 631; s. c., 15 Am. Rep. 633; *ante*, pp. 76, 77, tit. "Contributory Negligence"

2. Thus, where a train approached a crossing at night without whistle, bell, or headlight, there was sufficient evidence of negligence to go to the jury. Smedis *v.* Brooklyn, etc., R. Co., 88 N. Y. 13; s. c., 8 Am. & Eng. R. R. Cas. 445.

Where there was no flagman at a crossing, and there was evidence that no signals were given, and that persons about to cross looked and listened, but heard no train, it was *held* that there was sufficient evidence of negligence to sustain a verdict. Guggenheim *v.* Lake Shore, etc., R. Co. (Mich.), 22 Am. & Eng. R. R. Cas. 546.

So the company was held liable where a train was opened for a man to drive across the track, when, just as he got on the track, the engine, which was immediately on one side of the crossing, blew off steam, and enveloped the horses in a cloud of steam, causing them to run away and injure the driver Geveke *v.* Grand Rapids, etc., R. Co (Mich. 1885), 22 Am. & Eng. R. R. Cas. 551.

So, where burning coals were allowed to fall from the firebox of an engine of an elevated railway upon the back of a horse being lawfully driven under the track, the evidence of negligence was sufficient. Lowery *v.* Manhattan R. Co., 99 N. Y. 158.

Where steam was allowed to escape from an unusual part of an engine which had been posted near a crossing, whereby a horse was frightened and injured, the company was chargeable with negligence. Louisville, etc., R. Co. *v.* Schmidt, 81 Ind. 264; s. c., 8 Am. & Eng. R. R. Cas. 248.

Where cars obstruct a crossing longer than permitted by statute, and while so standing, in violation of law, serve to frighten a horse, and cause a runaway, the railroad company is liable. Young *v.* Detroit, etc, R. Co. (Mich. 1885), 19 Am. & Eng. R. R. Cas. 417.

Where cars were left adjacent to a railroad crossing with nothing to prevent them from being set in motion by the wind, and they were set in motion, and injured travellers upon the crossing, the company was held liable for negligence. Nicholson *v.* Erie R Co, 41 N. Y. 525; Brown *v.* Pontchartrain R. Co., 8 Robinson (La.), 45.

Where the company placed a hand-car at a crossing, and plaintiff's wagon collided with it, frightening his horse, the company was held liable for a resulting injury. Myers *v.* Richmond, etc., R. Co., 87 N. Car. 345; s. c., 8 Am. & Eng. R. R. Cas. 293.

But if there is no evidence of negligence, the court should take the case from the jury.[1]

26. Negligence of Railroad Company must be Proximate. — But before there can be any liability on the part of the railroad company for injuries alleged to have been caused by its negligence, it must appear that its negligence was the proximate cause of the injury.[2]

And such is the general rule where injuries result from the fright of horses caused by cars carelessly left adjacent to a highway crossing. Pittsburgh, etc., R. Co. *v.* Spanier, 85 Ind. 165; s. c., 8 Am. & Eng. R. R Cas. 453; Bussian *v.* Milwaukee, etc., R. Co., 56 Wis. 325; s. c., 10 Am. & Eng. R. R. Cas. 716; Vars *v.* Grand Trunk R. Co, 23 Up. Can. (C. P.) 143.

But a box-car at rest at a crossing is not *per se* calculated to frighten horses. Gilbert *v.* Flint, etc., R. Co., 51 Mich. 488; s. c., 15 Am. & Eng R. R. Cas. 491.

And before a railroad company is liable for injuries resulting from the fright of horses at cars left standing at highway crossings, it must appear that the fright of the horses was usual and natural, and that the cars as left would naturally frighten horses not unusually nervous. Gilbert *v.* Flint, etc., R. Co, 51 Mich. 488; s. c., 15 Am. & Eng. R. R. Cas. 491. See also Pittsburgh, etc., R. Co. *v.* Taylor, 104 Pa. St. 306.

But a railroad company is not liable for the fright of horses resulting in injury, or for accidents, resulting from the ordinary movement or situation of its cars, engines, or trains at crossings. Hahm *v.* Southern Pac. R. Co., 51 Cal. 605; Beatty *v.* Central, etc., R. Co., 58 Ia. 242; s. c., 8 Am. & Eng. R. R. Cas. 210; Whitney *v.* Maine, etc., R. Co, 69 Me. 208; Flint *v.* Norfolk, etc, R. Co, 110 Mass. 222; Favor *v.* Boston, etc, R. Co., 114 Mass. 350.

When a train suddenly turned off at a side-track in making a "flying-switch," and injured a person using an established foot-path, the negligence of the railroad company was sufficiently established. Philadelphia, etc., R. Co. *v.* Troutman (Pa.), 6 Am & Eng. R. R. Cas. 117.

For a train to approach a crossing at great speed, and without giving warning-signals to herald its approach, is negligence. Pittsburgh, etc, R. Co. *v.* Martin, 82 Ind. 476; s. c., 8 Am & Eng. R. R. Cas. 253; Kelly *v.* St. Paul, etc, R. Co, 29 Minn. 1; s. c, 6 Am & Eng. R. R. Cas. 93.

It has been *held*, but in this and other respects the decision has been the subject of criticism, that the running of an engine across a much frequented thoroughfare, such as a village street, by a fireman alone, there being no other evidence of negligence, would justify a jury in finding a want of proper care on the part of a railroad company. O'Mara *v.* Hudson River R. Co., 38 N. Y. 445.

Whether it is negligence, in a railroad company, to fail to perform a self-imposed duty at a crossing, seems to be a moot question; but the better doctrine is, that such failure is negligence if the public have been led to rely upon the railroad company to do the thing omitted. Patterson's Ry. Ac. Law, 165; Pennsylvania R. Co. *v.* Killips, 88 Pa. St. 413; Pittsburgh, etc., R. Co. *v.* Yundt, 78 Ind. 373; s. c., 3 Am. & Eng. R. R. Cas. 502. But see Skelton *v.* London, etc., R. Co., 2 C. P. 631; Cliff *v.* Midland R. Co., L. R. 5 Q. B. 258; McGrath *v.* N. Y. Cent., etc., R. Co., 59 N. Y. 468; 63 N. Y. 522.

No absolute rule as to what constitutes negligence can be laid down, — Philadelphia, etc., R. Co. *v.* Spearen, 47 Pa. St. 300; s. c., 86 Am. Dec. 544, — and consequently the illustrative cases cited do not serve to establish any hard and fast rule as to what does or does not constitute negligence on the part of railroad companies at highway crossings. They are negligent if they do not exercise ordinary care under the circumstances: they are not negligent if they do. To finally charge the company, there must be a want of ordinary care on its part, proximately causing an injury which could not have been obviated by reasonable care on the part of the person injured. Baltimore, etc., R. Co. *v.* Fitzpatrick, 35 Md. 32.

1. Hestonville, etc., R. Co. *v.* Connell, 88 Pa. St. 520; s. c., 32 Am. Rep. 472; Nagle *v.* Alleghany, etc., R. Co., 88 Pa. St. 35; s. c., 32 Am Rep. 413; Church *v.* Northern Pac. R. Co., 31 Fed. Rep. 529; Wilds *v.* Hudson, etc., R. Co., 29 N. Y 315; 24 N. Y. 430; Sherman *v.* Hannibal, etc., R. Co., 72 Mo. 62; s. c, 4 Am. & Eng. R. R. Cas. 589. And see *ante*, 46, 47, tit. "Contributory Negligence."

2. The negligence of defendant must have been the proximate cause of the injury to render it liable. Its negligence followed by an accident will not render it liable if its negligence did not cause the accident. Harlan *v.* St. Louis, etc., R. Co., 65 Mo. 22; Stepp *v.* Chicago, etc., R. Co., 85 Mo. 225.

27. Precautions after an Accident. — There are some cases holding that evidence of precautions taken to prevent future accidents at a crossing, of a kind similar to one that has occurred when the precautions were not taken, is admissible as tending to prove it negligent not to have taken such precautions before the accident.[1] But on principle such evidence can scarcely be justified, and is generally rejected.[2]

28. Plaintiff's Negligence apparent to Defendant. — It is a settled principle of the law of negligence, although often overlooked and misapplied, that when the defendant's negligence is subsequent to the negligence of the plaintiff, and the defendant knew, or by the exercise of ordinary care might have known, of the negligence of the plaintiff in time to have avoided inflicting injury upon him, then the defendant is liable for inflicting the injury, and plaintiff's negligence is remote in the chain of causation.[3]

The company must be shown at fault in laying its track or running its trains at a public crossing before it can be held liable for an injury thereat. Wilds *v.* Hudson, etc., R. Co., 29 N. Y. 315; 24 N. Y. 430.

A failure to give statutory signals at a crossing does not render the company liable if the failure was not the proximate cause of a subsequent injury. Atchison, etc., R. Co. *v.* Morgan (Kan.), 13 Am. & Eng. R. R. Cas. 499; Karle *v.* Kansas City, etc., R. Co., 55 Mo. 476; Purl *v.* St. Louis, etc., R. Co., 72 Mo. 168; s. c., 6 Am. & Eng. R. R. Cas. 27; Pakalinsky *v.* N. Y. Cent., etc., R. Co., 82 N. Y. 424; s. c., 2 Am. & Eng. R. R. Cas. 251.

And where the violation of a statute against blocking the highway is not the proximate cause of an injury, there can be no recovery. Sellick *v.* Lake Shore, etc., R. Co. (Mich.), 23 Am. & Eng. R. R. Cas. 338; Jackson *v.* Nashville, etc., R. Co., 13 Lea (Tenn.), 491; s. c., 19 Am. & Eng. R. R. Cas. 433; Pittsburgh, etc., R. Co. *v.* Staley (Ohio, 1884); s. c., 19 Am. & Eng. R. R. Cas. 381.

But where a person started across a street-car track without looking, and would have got across safely, but accidentally stumbled and fell upon the crossing, where he was injured by a horse-car which came up, it was *held* that he was not bound to anticipate an accidental fall, and that the negligence of the street-car driver was the proximate cause of his injury. Mentz *v.* Second Ave. R. Co., 3 Abb. Ct. of App. Dec. (N. Y.) 274.

So, if a person falls on a railroad track because of a defect in a city street, and before he can arise is run over by a locomotive, the city is liable for the injury, and its negligence is its proximate cause. Schmidt *v.* Chicago, etc., R. Co., 83 Ill. 405.

1. Shaber *v.* St. Paul, etc., R. Co., 28 Minn. 103; s. c., 2 Am. & Eng. R. R. Cas. 185; Kelly *v.* Southern Minn. R. Co., 28 Minn. 98; s. c., 6 Am. & Eng. R. R. Cas. 264; Pennsylvania R. Co. *v.* Henderson, 51 Pa. St. 315.

2. Such changes may be a mere measure of precaution suggested for the first time by the peculiar character of the accident, and which before the accident human care would not have foreseen as needful to prevent accident. Patterson's Ry. Ac. Law, 421; Pierce on Railroads, 294; Payne *v.* T. & B. R. Co., 9 Hun (N. Y.), 526; Dale *v.* Delaware, etc., R. Co., 73 N. Y. 468; Salter *v.* Delaware, etc., Co., 3 Hun (N. Y.), 338; Morse *v.* Mankato, etc., R. Co., 30 Minn. 465; s. c., 11 Am. & Eng. R. R. Cas. 168; Ely *v.* St. Louis, etc., R. Co., 77 Mo. 34; s. c., 16 Am. & Eng. R. R. Cas. 342; Nalley *v.* Carpet Co., 51 Conn. 524; s. c., 50 Am. Rep. 47.

3. For a full discussion of this and its related questions in so far as the principles that govern are concerned, see the article on "Contributory Negligence," § 12, pp. 12–31, *ante.* See also the following cases: Davies *v.* Mann, 10 Mee. & W. 545; s. c., 2 Thomp. on Neg. 1105; Tuff *v.* Warman, 2 C. B. (N. S.) 740; 5 C. B. (N. S.) 573; 27 L. J. C. P. 322; Radley *v.* London, etc., R. Co., L. R. 1 App. Cas. 754; s. c., 2 Thomp. on Neg. 1108; Isbell *v.* New York, etc., R. Co., 27 Conn. 393; s. c., 71 Am. Dec. 78; Washington *v.* Baltimore, etc., R. Co., 17 W. Va. 190; s. c., 10 Am. & Eng. R. R. Cas. 749, 755, 756; Morrissey *v.* Wiggins Ferry Co., 47 Mo. 521; s. c., Thomp. on Carriers of Pass. 243; Baltimore, etc., R. Co. *v.* Kean (Md. 1886), 28 Am. & Eng. R. R. Cas. 580–584.

"If the negligence of a defendant, which contributed directly to cause the injury, occurred after the danger in which the in-

29. No Presumption of Contributory Negligence. — When an injury occurs to a person in the lawful exercise of independent rights, at a railway highway crossing, there is no presumption that the person injured was guilty of negligence or contributory negligence.[1]

(*a*) *The Presumption of Care prevails.* — In such cases the presumption of fact, in the absence of evidence to the contrary, is

jured party had placed himself by his own negligence was, or by the exercise of reasonable care might have been, discovered by the defendant in time to have averted the injury, then defendant is liable, however gross the negligence of the injured party may have been in placing himself in such position of danger." Donohue *v.* St. Louis, etc., R. Co. (Mo 1886), 28 Am. & Eng. R. R. Cas. 623.

Where an injury could have been avoided by a railroad company after its servants became aware of the danger of the person injured, who was at a crossing, the company is liable. Kean *v.* Baltimore, etc., R. Co, 61 Md. 154; s. c., 19 Am. & Eng. R. R. Cas. 321; Indianapolis, etc., R. Co. *v.* McLin, 83 Ind. 435; s. c., 8 Am. & Eng. R. R. Cas. 237.

Where the negligence of the injured party is known to the railroad employees, they should take ordinary care in view of such knowledge to avoid inflicting injury. Houston, etc., R. Co. *v* Smith, 52 Tex. 178; Cleveland, etc., R. Co. *v.* Crawford, 24 Ohio St. 631.

So, it is sometimes a question for the jury whether, with ordinary care, the employees of a railroad company should not have discovered the person injured on the track in time to have avoided injuring him; and if the jury find that they should have so discovered him, but did not, the company will be held liable. Texas, etc., R. Co. *v.* Chapman, 57 Tex. 75; Frick *v.* St. Louis, etc., R. Co., 5 Mo. App. 435.

1. "However, as ruled in Railroad Co. *v.* Weber, 76 Pa. St 157; s. c., 18 Am. Rep. 407, it is not incumbent on the plaintiffs, in order to recover damages for the death of Phillip Schum, to show affirmatively that, before attempting to cross the track, he did stop and look and listen. The common-law presumption is, that every one does his duty until the contrary is proved; and in the absence of all evidence upon the subject, the presumption is, that the decedent observed the precautions which the law prescribed. In the case at bar, no witness was called who saw the occurrence. There is no evidence whatever whether in fact the decedent did stop and look and listen: the presumption is that he did. Proof of the fact was no part of the plaintiff's case. The presumption is of fact merely, and may be rebutted, but we are without evidence upon the subject: all that we have is, that, as he came upon the railroad, he was struck down by the locomotive." Schum *v.* Pennsylvania R. Co., 107 Pa. St. 8; s. c., 52 Am. Rep. 468; Pennsylvania R. Co. *v.* Weber, 76 Pa. St. 157; Lehigh Valley, etc., R Co. *v.* Hall, 61 Pa St. 361; Reading, etc., R. Co. *v.* Ritchie, 102 Pa. St. 425; s. c., 19 Am. & Eng. R. R Cas. 267; Louisville, etc., R. Co. *v.* Goetz, 79 Ky. 42; s. c., 14 Am. & Eng. R. R. Cas. 627; 42 Am. Rep. 227; Hoye *v.* Chicago, etc., R. Co, 62 Wis. 666; s. c., 19 Am. & Eng. R. R. Cas. 347; Haasenyer *v.* Michigan, etc., R. Co., 48 Mich. 205; 6 Am. & Eng. R. R. Cas. 59; Guggenheim *v.* Lake Shore, etc., R. Co. (Mich. 1887), 33 N. W. Rep. 161; Petty *v.* Hannibal, etc, R. (Mo. 1887), 28 Am. & Eng. R. R. Cas. 618. See also tit. "Contributory Neg." *ante*, pp. 75, 76, and cases there cited.

It is also *held*, in numerous cases, that the exercise of due care upon the part of a person who has been run over and killed at a railroad crossing may be inferred from the ordinary habits of prudent men to avoid danger. Philadelphia, etc, R. Co. *v.* Stebbing, 62 Md. 504; s c., 19 Am. & Eng. R. R Cas. 36; Northern Cent. R. Co. *v.* State, 29 Md. 420; Northern Cent. R. Co. *v.* Geis, 31 Md. 357; Maryland Cent. R. Co. *v.* Newbern, 62 Md. 391; s. c., 19 Am. & Eng. R. R. Cas. 261; Gay *v.* Winter, 34 Cal. 153; Johnson *v.* Hudson, etc, R. Co., 20 N. Y. 65; Cleveland, etc., R. Co. *v.* Rowan, 66 Pa. St. 393; Weiss *v.* Pennsylvania R. Co, 79 Pa. St. 387; Patterson's Ry. Ac. Law, 174; Cassidy *v.* Angell, 12 R. I. 447; s. c., 34 Am. Rep. 690.

But see, as maintaining a doctrine contrary to that just stated to an extent which holds that there is a presumption of contributory negligence, Chase *v.* Main Cent. R. Co., 77 Me. 62; s c., 19 Am. & Eng. R. R. Cas. 356; s. c., 52 Am. Rep. 744; State *v.* Main Cent. R. Co., 76 Me. 357; s. c., 49 Am. Rep. 622; Indianapolis, etc., R. Co. *v.* Green, 106 Ind. 279; s. c., 25 Am. & Eng. R. R. Cas. 322; s. c., 55 Am. Rep. 736; Cincinnati, etc., R. Co. *v.* Butler, 103 Ind. 31; s. c., 23 Am. & Eng. R. R. Cas. 262.

And see, as holding that there must be evidence of the causal connection of the negligence of the railroad company with the death of a person found dead upon the track, even though there be no presump-

that both the railroad company and the person injured were in the exercise of ordinary care.[1]

(*b*) *This Presumption may be rebutted.* — But this presumption, being one of fact merely, may be rebutted by evidence.[2]

30. Burden of Proof of Contributory Negligence. — In some States the burden of proving freedom from contributory negligence is upon the plaintiff as a part of his case in chief.[3] But perhaps the greater weight of authority tends to establish the rule that contributory negligence is an affirmative defence.[4] The true rule seems to be, that plaintiff should first make out a *prima facie* case of negligent injury by defendant without any negligence upon his own part appearing as a proximate cause of his injury. So far the burden of proof is upon him; but this done, it should devolve upon defendant to rebut plaintiff's case; and one way of doing so is to show the negligence of the plaintiff as a proximate contributory cause of his own injury, combining and concurring with the negligence of the defendant in its production.[5] Into these questions it is not necessary to go more fully here. In other connections they have been treated at length.[6]

31. What Contributory Negligence is. — Contributory negligence is a want of ordinary care upon the part of a person injured by the actionable negligence of another combining and concurring with that negligence, and contributing to the injury as a proximate cause thereof without which the injury would not have occurred.[7]

(*a*) *The Want of Ordinary Care.* — It is apparent from this that there must be a want of ordinary care on the part of the person injured.[8]

tion of contributory negligence on his part, Wakelin *v.* London, etc, R. Co., L. R. 12 H. L. Cas. 41; s. c., 29 Am. & Eng. R. R. Cas 425.

1. Cleveland, etc., R. Co. *v.* Crawford, 24 Ohio St. 631; s. c., 15 Am. Rep. 633; Smedis *v.* Brooklyn, etc, R. Co., 88 N. Y. 13; s c., 8 Am. & Eng. R. R. Cas. 445. And see the cases cited in support of the next preceding proposition.

2. Maryland, etc., R. Co. *v.* Newbern, 62 Md 391; s. c., 19 Am. & Eng. R. R Cas. 261; Philadelphia, etc., R. Co *v.* Stebbing, 62 Md. 504; s c., 19 Am. & Eng R. R. Cas 36. See also the cases cited in the two preceding notes, many of which state the doctrine of the text.

3. See, as illustrative of this class of cases, Cincinnati, etc, R *v.* Butler, 103 Ind. 31; s. c., 23 Am. & Eng. R. R. Cas. 262; Indianapolis, etc., R. Co. *v.* Green, 106 Ind. 279; s. c., 25 Am. & Eng. R R. Cas. 322; s. c, 55 Am. Rep. 736; Chase *v.* Main Cent. R. Co., 77 Me. 62; s. c., 19 Am. & Eng. R. R. Cas. 356; s. c, 52 Am. Rep. 744; tit "Contributory Neg." *ante*, p. 91, note 3

4. Hough *v.* Railroad Co., 100 U. S 216; Railroad Co. *v.* Horst, 93 U. S. 291. And see, for a full collection of the cases in States where the burden of proving contributory negligence is held to be upon the defendant, tit. "Contributory Neg." *ante*, pp. 91, 92, note 5

5. Weiss *v.* Pennsylvania R. Co., 79 Pa. St. 387; see Wakelin *v.* London, etc., R. Co., L R. 12 H L. Cas. 41; s. c., 29 Am. & Eng R. R. Cas. 425; Buesching *v.* St. Louis Gas Co, 73 Mo. 219; s. c., 39 Am. Rep. 503; Cleveland, etc., R. Co. *v.* Crawford, 24 Ohio St. 631; s. c., 15 Am. Rep 633; Cassidy *v.* Angell, 12 R. I. 447; s. c., 34 Am. Rep. 690; Tolman *v.* Syracuse, etc., R Co., 98 N Y. 198; s. c., 50 Am Rep. 649; Wharton on Neg. §§ 423-426; Shearman & Redf. on Neg. § 44; Stephen's Dig. of Ev. Article 95; Patterson's Ry. Ac. Law, § 374, p. 435; tit. "Contributory Neg." *ante*, p 93, notes 1 and 2.

6 See tit. "Contributory Neg." *ante*, §§ 33-40, with notes.

7. Tit. "Contributory Neg." *ante*, p. 17, § 4 and note 3.

8. Tit. "Contributory Neg." *ante*, pp. 18, 19, §§ 6, 7. See also § 9, p. 22, of same article for the test of ordinary care.

(*b*) *Its Causal Connection.* — And that such want of ordinary care must proximately contribute to his injury before contributory negligence can exist.[1]

(*c*) *Contributory Negligence defeats Recovery.* — When, however, there is contributory negligence upon the part of a person injured at a highway railway crossing by the negligence of the company, it bars a recovery, and in nearly every case of such character the existence of contributory negligence is a moot question.[2]

1. Tit. "Contributory Neg." *ante*, pp. 18, 25, §§ 6, 12. See, for a case where the negligence of plaintiff was held remote, Union Pac. R. Co. *v.* Henry (Kan.), 14 Pac. Rep. 1.

2. Tit. "Contributory Neg." *ante*, pp. 19–21, § 7. Butterfield *v.* Western, etc., R. Co., 10 Allen (Mass.), 532; s. c., 87 Am. Dec. 678; Warren *v.* Fitchburg, etc., R. Co., 8 Allen (Mass.), 227; s. c., 85 Am. Dec. 700.

Where a traveller started to drive across a railroad track at a crossing at a time when he saw a train approaching, and at a distance of three hundred and fifty yards, and an accident followed from the backing of his horse just after he got over the track, whereby his wagon was backed on to the track, and struck by the train, it was *held* that he was guilty of negligence, barring a recovery. Kigler *v.* Railroad Co (N. Car. 1886). 26 Am. & Eng. R. R. Cas. 386.

The mere omission of statutory signals, even though negligent, will not excuse contributory negligence. International, etc., R. Co. *v.* Jordan (Tex. 1883), 10 Am. & Eng. R. R. Cas. 301.

Where one, without his own fault, is, through the negligence of another, put in such apparent peril as to cause in him terror, loss of self-possession, and bewilderment, and, as a natural result thereof, he, in attempting to escape, puts himself in a more dangerous position, and is injured, the putting himself in such more dangerous position is not, in law, contributory negligence that will prevent him recovering for the injury. Mark *v.* St. Paul, etc., R. Co, 32 Minn. 208; s. c., 12 Am. & Eng. R. R. Cas. 86.

A person crossing a railroad track at a well established footpath is not a trespasser, and if injured upon such a crossing by the negligence of the company will not be non-suited unless contributory negligence clearly appears. Philadelphia, etc., R. Co. *v.* Troutman (Pa. 1882), 6 Am. & Eng. R. R. Cas. 117.

It is not always contributory negligence *per se* for a person to attempt to cross without waiting until a train just passed has gone so far as to leave the view unobstructed. Philadelphia, etc., R. Co. *v.* Carr, 99 Pa. St. 505; s. c., 6 Am. & Eng. R. R. Cas. 185.

Where the view of a crossing is obstructed, the traveller has a right to presume that the usual and proper signals announcing the approach of trains will be given, and it is not contributory negligence in him to rely thereon, using ordinary care at the same time to avoid injury. Bunting *v.* Cent. Pac. R. Co., 14 Nev. 351; Beisiegel *v.* New York, etc., R. Co., 34 N. Y. 622; s. c., 90 Am. Dec. 741; Ernst *v.* Hudson, etc., R. Co., 35 N. Y. 9; s. c., 90 Am. Dec. 761; See Indianapolis, etc., R. Co. *v.* Stables, 62 Ill. 313.

Where a person looks and listens as well as obstructions will permit, and then drives on a crossing, and is struck by a train which has given no warning of its approach, he is not guilty of contributory negligence, and may recover. Dimick *v.* Chicago, etc., R. Co., 80 Ill. 338; Kelly *v.* St. Paul, etc., R. Co, 29 Minn. 1.

The fact that the view of the track may have been obstructed by other cars left standing on the side track does not lessen the caution required of a person attempting to cross, but imposes upon him the duty of exercising a higher degree of diligence. Garland *v.* Chicago, etc., R. Co., 8 Bradwell (Ill.), 571 (1881); Haas *v.* Grand Rapids, etc., R. Co., 47 Mich. 401; s. c., 8 Am. & Eng. R. R. Cas. 268; Cordell *v.* New York Cent., etc., R. Co, 70 N. Y. 119.

Where both parties are negligent, but the negligence of the person injured contributes to his injury, there can be no recovery. Harlan *v.* St. Louis, etc., R. Co., 64 Mo. 480; Fletcher *v.* Atlantic, etc., R. Co., 64 Mo. 484.

If the negligence of a person injured at a highway crossing contributes at all to his injury, it contributes proximately. Hearne *v.* Southern, etc., R. Co., 50 Cal. 482.

Where the negligence of the plaintiff contributes to his own injury, no mere negligence on defendant's part can render it liable. Evansville, etc., R. Co. *v.* Lowdermilk, 15 Ind. 120.

It is only where the injuries are inflicted wilfully that contributory negligence ceases to be a defence. Terre Haute, etc., R. Co. *v.* Graham, 95 Ind. 286, 293; s. c., 12 Am. & Eng. R. R. Cas. 77; Carter *v.* Louisville, etc., R. Co., 98 Ind. 552; s. c., 22

Am. & Eng. R. R. Cas. 360; Louisville, etc., R. Co. *v.* Bryan, 107 Ind. 51; Chicago, etc., R. Co. *v.* Hedges, 105 Ind. 398; s. c., 25 Am. & Eng. R. R. Cas. 558. And see tit. "Contributory Neg." *ante*, pp. 80, 81, § 36.

The negligent violation of a statute will not render a railroad company liable for an injury to which the negligence of the person injured proximately contributed. Vicksburg, etc., R Co. *v.* McGowan, 62 Miss. 682; Cincinnati, etc., R. Co. *v.* Butler, 103 Ind. 31; s. c., 23 Am. & Eng. R. R. Cas. 262.

The mere fact that a train was a special one, or that some precautions which should have been taken were negligently omitted by the railroad company, will not excuse a want of ordinary care on the part of the person injured. Schofield *v.* Chicago, etc., R. Co., 114 U. S. 615; s. c., 19 Am. & Eng. R. R. Cas. 353; Davey *v.* London, etc., R. Co., 11 Q. B. 213; 12 Q. B. 73; Henze *v.* St. Louis, etc., R. Co., 71 Mo. 636; s. c., 2 Am. & Eng. R. R. Cas. 212; Kelly *v.* Hannibal, etc., R. Co., 75 Mo. 138; s. c., 13 Am. & Eng. R. R. Cas. 638; Mahlen *v.* Lake Shore, etc., R. Co., 49 Mich. 585; s. c., 14 Am & Eng. R. R. Cas. 687.

But the neglect of the railroad company may be of such a character as to excuse the traveller from as high a degree of care, as, but for such neglect, would have been required of him. Wabash, etc., R. Co. *v.* Wallace, 110 Ill. 114; s. c., 19 Am. & Eng. R. R. Cas. 359; Gaynor *v.* Old Colony, etc., R. Co., 100 Mass. 208; Chaffee *v.* Boston, etc, R. Co., 104 Mass. 108; Copley *v.* New Haven, etc., R. Co, 136 Mass. 6; s. c., 19 Am. & Eng. R. R. Cas. 373; Ernst *v.* Hudson, etc, R. Co., 39 N. Y. 61; Butler *v.* Milwaukee, etc., R. Co., 28 Wis. 487; Ferguson *v.* Wisconsin, etc., R. Co., 63 Wis. 145; s. c., 19 Am. & Eng. R. R. Cas. 285; Pennsylvania R. Co. *v.* Ogier, 35 Pa. St. 60; s. c, 78 Am Dec. 322; Philadelphia, etc., R. Co. *v.* Hagan, 47 Pa. St. 244; s. c, 86 Am. Dec. 541; Dublin, etc., R. Co. *v.* Slattery, 3 App. Cas. 1155.

Absent-mindedness is no excuse for a failure to use due care. Lake Shore, etc., R. Co. *v.* Miller, 25 Mich. 274.

It is contributory negligence to persist in the effort to drive a frightened horse over a crossing where cars have been derailed and are lying, when there is another crossing near at hand that could be as readily used. Pittsburgh, etc., R. Co. *v.* Taylor, 104 Pa. St. 306; s. c, 49 Am. Rep. 580. But where a street-crossing was obstructed by a train of cars, and a foot-passenger after waiting twenty minutes undertook to cross between them and was injured, he was permitted to recover. The case, however, is of doubtful authority. Spencer *v.* Baltimore, etc., R. Co., 4 Mackey (D. C.); s. c., 54 Am. Rep. 269, and note collecting numerous contrary cases.

A snow-storm has been held to excuse conduct on a traveller's part that would otherwise have been negligent. Solen *v.* Virginia, etc., R. Co., 13 Nev. 106.

A stranger unfamiliar with a crossing, and ignorant of its presence, may be excused, when one who knew it and its dangers would be held guilty of negligence. Cohen *v.* Eureka, etc., R. Co., 14 Nev. 376.

If a railroad track is so constructed that a train cannot be seen by a person on an intersecting highway, until so near that it is difficult or impossible to avoid being struck after reaching such point, it seems that the company is liable. Lehnertz *v.* Minneapolis, etc, R. Co. (Minn), 15 Am. & Eng. R. R. Cas. 370.

When the plaintiff, before going upon the track at a crossing, looked up and down the track, and saw that it was clear, but, just after he stepped on the crossing, a switch-engine came rapidly around a curve, and, without giving any signal, struck and injured plaintiff, it was *held* that he could not be charged with negligence, especially as the whistle of an adjacent workshop was sounding at the time of his injury by the locomotive. Chicago, etc., R. Co. *v.* Ryan, 70 Ill. 211.

Where piles of lumber obscured the view of a crossing which plaintiff was approaching in a slow trot, and the locomotive passed the crossing just in front of him, frightening his team and causing a runaway, without having given statutory signals, it was *held* that the railroad company was liable, and the evidence failed to show contributory negligence. Strong *v.* Sacramento, etc., R. Co., 61 Cal. 326; s. c., 8 Am. & Eng. R. R. Cas. 273.

But where a traveller approached a crossing between piles of lumber without stopping to look or listen, and drove upon the crossing in a trot, where he was struck and injured by a train, it was *held* that he could not recover. Hixson *v.* St. Louis, etc., R. Co., 80 Mo. 335.

Where a freight train had passed, and was out of hearing, and the person injured drove upon the track, at a crossing the view of which was obstructed by cars standing on a switch-track near the crossing, and was there struck by a coming train and killed, it was *held* that deceased was not guilty of contributory negligence. Ingersoll *v* New York Cent., etc., R. Co., 66 N. Y. 612. See also 4 Hun (N. Y.), 277.

Where a person, to avoid an apparently imminent collision at a crossing, jumps from a buggy and is injured, where, in fact, no collision followed, he is not barred of recovery by such conduct, even though no injury would have been sustained had he remained in the buggy, provided the rail-

(*d*) *Usually a Question for the Jury.* — It is usually a question of fact for the determination of a jury.[1]

(*e*) *But it may be a Matter of Law.* — Yet it may be a question of law for the court, and should be so treated when the facts are undisputed, and no inference but that of a want of ordinary care contributing to the injury, as an immediate cause, can be drawn from them. Consequently, there are many cases where it has

road company was at fault in creating the position of danger. Dyer *v.* Erie, etc., R. Co, 71 N. Y. 228.

It is not necessarily negligence to use a defective railway highway crossing. Kelly *v.* Southern, etc., R. Co., 28 Minn. 98; s. c, 6 Am. & Eng. R. R. Cas. 264

The decedent looked and listened as he drew near a crossing, but did not stop. The train that killed him was two hours late, and running from twenty-five to forty miles an hour; no signals were given, and the view was obstructed. Decedent was driving very slowly. He did not seem to understand warnings of the approach of the train, which persons in the vicinity attempted to give him. On these facts a recovery was sustained. Guggenheim *v.* Lake Shore, etc., R. Co. (Mich. 1887), 33 N. W. Rep. 161.

On the facts of the case, a foot-traveller struck at a crossing by one train while trying to avoid another, was *held* not guilty of contributory negligence. West *v.* New Jersey, etc, R. Co., 3 Vroom (N. J), 91.

The fact that a train which inflicts an injury is behind time, may bear on the question of contributory negligence. State *v.* Philadelphia, etc., R. Co., 47 Md 76.

See also for a full discussion of the doctrine relating to contributory negligence at railroad crossings, tit. "Contributory Negligence," *ante*, pp. 68-78, § 33.

1. Tit. "Contributory Negligence," *ante*, pp. 94, 95, § 41. In an action for an injury to a person on a railroad crossing, it is only when the inference of negligence or contributory negligence, or the absence thereof, is necessarily deducible from the undisputed facts and circumstances proved, that a court is justified in taking the case from the jury; and if such facts and circumstances, though undisputed, are ambiguous, and of such a nature that reasonable men, unaffected by bias or prejudice, might disagree as to the inference or conclusion to be drawn from them, the case should be submitted to the jury. Hoye *v.* Chicago, etc., R Co., 62 Wis. 666, s. c., 19 Am. & Eng R. R. Cas. 347.

When the question on the evidence as to whether due care was exercised by the plaintiff is an open one, it is for the jury. Craig *v.* New York, etc., R. Co., 118 Mass. 431.

It is an error to grant a non-suit where, by any allowable deduction from the facts proved, a cause of action may be sustained by the plaintiff; and it cannot be granted because of the contributory negligence of the plaintiff, unless such negligence is conclusively established by evidence, which leaves nothing of inference or fact for the jury. Greany *v.* Long Island R. Co., 101 N. Y. 419; s. c., 24 Am. & Eng. R. R. Cas. 473.

An old deaf man, while driving a span of colts towards a railway track down a narrow road from which the track was concealed on one side by a high embankment, stopped to listen, but, hearing nothing, drove on; and when close by the track, a train appeared within a few rods. He whipped up his horses, fearing he could could not control them, and tried to cross the track. But the rear of his buggy was struck by the locomotive, and injury followed. The question of his negligence was held for the jury. Chicago, etc., R. Co. *v.* Miller, 46 Mich. 532; s. c., 6 Am. & Eng. R. R. Cas. 89.

Where a traveller's view of the track is obscured by a passing train, and he waits until such train has passed, and then, starting over a crossing, is struck by a train on another track coming in an opposite direction, and which could not be seen because of the train that had passed, the question of the contributory negligence of the traveller is for the jury Philadelphia, etc., R. Co. *v.* Carr, 99 Pa. St. 505; s. c., 6 Am. & Eng. R. R. Cas. 185.

Where a person about to cross a railway has his attention distracted by watching out against one train, and is injured by another, the question of his contributory negligence is for the jury. Leonard *v.* New York, etc, R. Co, 42 N. Y. Super. Ct. 225; Casey *v.* N. Y. Cent. R. Co., 78 N. Y. 518; New Jersey R. Co. *v.* West, 32 N. J. L. 91; Pennsylvania, etc., R. Co. *v.* Fortney, 90 Pa. St. 323.

There are multitudes of cases sustaining propositions similar to those already stated in this note. It is generally held that it would be an invasion of the province of the jury for the courts to attempt to prescribe the exact thing which a traveller should do in order to be in the exercise of ordinary care. Texas, etc, R. Co. *v.* Chap-

been held, as a matter of law, that contributory negligence existed, and a *non-suit* should be ordered.[1]

32. Traveller's Duty to "Stop," "Look," and "Listen." — Elsewhere the principles that the law applies in requiring or not requiring a traveller on a public crossing to stop, look, and listen before crossing a railroad track intersecting the highway, have been carefully treated. To that discussion the reader is referred.[2] That it is frequently the duty of a traveller to stop, look, *or* listen before crossing, cannot be disputed, and often he should do all three. Indeed, it has come to be a definite rule of law, that the traveller must look and listen when it would be possible for him to see or hear by so doing, and there are cases that hold him at fault if he does not also stop.[3]

man, 57 Tex. 75; Houston, etc., R. Co. *v.* Waller, 56 Tex. 331; s. c., 8 Am. & Eng. R. R. Cas. 431; Philadelphia, etc., R. Co. *v.* Carr, 99 Pa. St. 505; s. c., 6 Am & Eng. R. R. Cas. 185; Randall *v.* Connecticut, etc., R. Co., 132 Mass. 269; Sweeney *v.* Boston, etc, R. Co., 128 Mass. 5; s. c., 1 Am & Eng. R R. Cas. 138; Tyler *v.* New York, etc., R. Co., 137 Mass. 238; s. c., 19 Am. & Eng. R R. Cas. 296; Bower *v.* Chicago, etc., R. Co, 61 Wis. 457; s. c, 19 Am. & Eng. R. R. Cas. 301; Hutchinson *v.* St. Paul, etc., R. Co., 32 Minn. 398; s. c., 19 Am. & Eng. R, R. Cas. 280; Young *v.* Detroit, etc., R. Co. (Mich.), 19 Am. & Eng. R. R. Cas. 417; Salter *v.* Utica, etc., R. Co., 88 N. Y. 42; s. c., 8 Am. & Eng. R. R. Cas. 437; Indianapolis, etc., R. Co. *v.* McLin, 83 Ind. 435; s. c., 8 Am. & Eng. R. R. Cas. 237; Corey *v.* Northern Pac. R. Co., 32 Minn. 457; s. c., 19 Am. & Eng. R. R. Cas. 352; Loucks *v.* Chicago, etc., R. Co., 31 Minn. 526; s. c, 19 Am. & Eng. R. R Cas. 305; Kansas, etc., R. Co. *v.* Richardson, 25 Kan. 391; s. c, 6 Am. & Eng. R. R. Cas. 96.

1. Tit. "Contributory Neg." *ante*, pp. 94, 95, § 41. Rigler *v.* Railroad Co. (N. Car. 1885), 26 Am. & Eng R. R. Cas. 386; Schofield *v.* Railroad Co., 114 U. S. 615; Pennsylvania R. Co. *v* Beale, 73 Pa. St. 504; s. c., 13 Am. Rep 753; Tolman *v.* Syracuse, etc., R. Co., 98 N. Y. 198; s. c., 50 Am. Rep. 649, and note; Ivens *v.* Cincinnati, etc., R. Co., 103 Ind. 27; s c, 23 Am. & Eng. R. R Cas. 258, and note; Sherry *v.* New York, etc., R. Co. (N. Y), 6 Cent. Rep. 357; Hinckley *v.* Cape Cod R. Co, 120 Mass. 257; Lesan *v.* Maine Cent. R. Co., 77 Me. 88; s. c., 23 Am. & Eng. R. R. Cas. 245; Pence *v.* Chicago, etc., R. Co., 63 Ia. 746; s. c., 19 Am & Eng. R. R. Cas. 365; Grippen *v.* New York, etc, R. Co., 40 N. Y. 34; Grows *v.* Maine, etc, R. Co., 67 Me. 100; Mantel *v.* Chicago, etc., R. Co., 32 Minn. 62; s. c, 19 Am. & Eng. R. R. Cas. 362; Chicago, etc., R. Co. *v.* Lee, 68 Ill. 576; Baltimore, etc., R. Co. *v.* Hobbs (Md. 1884), 19 Am. & Eng. R. R. Cas. 338; Pzolla *v.* Michigan, etc., R. Co., 54 Mich. 273; s. c., 19 Am. & Eng. R. R. Cas. 334; McLaren *v.* Indianapolis, etc., R. Co., 83 Ind. 319; s. c., 8 Am. & Eng. R. R. Cas. 217; Glasscock *v.* Cent. Pac. R. Co. (Cal. 1887), 14 Pac. Rep. 518, and note; Northern Pac. R. Co. *v.* Holmes (W. T), 14 Pac. Rep. 688; Zimmerman *v.* Hannibal, etc, R. Co., 71 Mo. 476; s. c., 2 Am. & Eng. R. R Cas. 191; Hixson *v.* St. Louis, etc., R. Co., 80 Mo. 335; Henze *v.* St. Louis, etc, R. Co., 71 Mo 636; s. c., 2 Am. & Eng. R. R Cas. 212; Turner *v.* Hannibal, etc., R. Co., 74 Mo. 603; s. c., 6 Am. & Eng. R. R. Cas. 38; Reading, etc., R. Co. *v.* Ritchie, 102 Pa. St. 405; s. c., 19 Am. & Eng. R. R. Cas. 267; Connelly *v.* New York, etc., R. Co, 88 N. Y. 346; s. c., 8 Am. & Eng. R. R. Cas. 459; Rogstad *v.* St. Paul, etc., R. Co., 31 Minn. 208; s. c., 14 Am. & Eng. R. R. Cas. 648; Tully *v.* Fitchburg R. Co., 134 Mass. 499; s. c., 14 Am. & Eng. R. R. Cas. 682; Galveston, etc., R. Co. *v.* Bracken, 59 Tex. 71; s. c., 14 Am. & Eng. R. R. Cas. 691; Potter *v.* Flint, etc., R. Co. (Mich. 1886), 28 N. W. Rep. 714; Central, etc., R Co. *v.* Feller, 84 Pa. St. 226; Louisville, etc., R. Co. *v.* Schmidt, 81 Ind. 264; s. c, 8 Am. & Eng. R. R. Cas. 248; Peck *v.* New York, etc., R. Co, 50 Conn. 379; s. c, 14 Am. & Eng. R. R. Cas. 633.

2. Tit. "Contributory Negligence," *ante*, pp. 68–74. § 33.

3. Schofield *v* Chicago, etc, R. Co, 114 U. S. 615; s. c., 19 Am. & Eng. R R. Cas. 353; Schaefert *v.* Chicago, etc., R. Co, 62 Ia 624; s. c., 14 Am. & Eng. R. Cas. 696; Pennsylvania R. Co. *v.* Righter, 42 N. J. L. 180; s. c., 2 Am. & Eng R. R. Cas. 220; Berry *v.* Pennsylvania R. Co. (N. J. 1886), 26 Am & Eng. R R. Cas. 396; Pennsylvania R. Co *v.* Beale, 73 Pa. St. 504; s c., 13 Am. Rep. 753; Reading, etc., R. Co. *v.* Ritchie, 102 Pa. St. 425; s. c., 19 Am. &

The stop, look, and listen rule cannot be correctly treated as an arbitrary standard of care to be inflexibly applied by the courts in all cases, but is rather a useful legal measure of ordinary care in cases where to have stopped, looked, or listened would have been to effectually guard against injury. In such cases the courts properly say, as a matter of law, that the failure to stop, look, and listen was contributory negligence.[1]

Eng. R. R. Cas. 267; Philadelphia, etc., R. Co. *v.* Boyer, 97 Pa. St. 91; s. c., 2 Am. & Eng. R. R. Cas. 172; Pennsylvania R. Co. *v.* Forney, 90 Pa. St. 323; 1 Am. & Eng. R. R. Cas. 128; North Penna. R. Co. *v.* Heileman, 49 Pa. St. 60; s. c., 88 Am. Dec. 482; Union Pac. R. Co. *v.* Adams, 33 Kan. 427; s. c., 19 Am. & Eng. R. R. Cas. 376; Schaefert *v.* Chicago, etc., R. Co., 62 Ia. 624; s. c., 14 Am. & Eng. R. R. Cas. 696; Haas *v.* Grand Rapids, etc., R. Co., 47 Mich. 401; s. c., 8 Am. & Eng. R. R. Cas. 268; Cordell *v.* New York, etc., R. Co., 64 N. Y. 535: s. c., 70 N. Y. 119; Mitchell *v.* New York, etc., R. Co., 2 Hun (N. Y.), 535; s. c., 64 N. Y. 655: Harty *v.* Cent, etc., R. Co, 42 N. Y. 473; Gorton *v.* Erie R. Co., 45 N. Y. 664; Kellogg *v.* New York Cent. R. Co., 79 N. Y. 72; Weber *v.* New York, etc., R. Co., 67 N. Y. 587; Stapley *v.* London, etc., R. Co., L. R. 1 Ex. 21; Skelton *v.* London, etc., R. Co., 2 C. P. 361; Chicago, etc., R. Co. *v.* Jacobs, 63 Ill. 179; Bellefontaine R. Co. *v.* Hunter, 33 Ind. 359; Maryland Cent. R. Co. *v.* Neubuer, 62 Md. 391; s. c., 19 Am. & Eng. R. R. Cas. 261; Wright *v.* Boston, etc., R. Co., 129 Mass. 440; s. c., 2 Am. & Eng. R. R. Cas. 121; Chaffee *v.* Boston, etc., R. Co., 104 Mass. 116; Ormsbee *v.* Boston, etc., R. Co., 14 R. I. 102; s. c., 51 Am. Rep. 354.

In the Ormsbee case just cited, it is laid down as a general rule "that ordinary prudence requires one who enters upon so dangerous a place as a railroad crossing to use his senses, to listen, to look, or to take some precaution for the purpose of ascertaining whether he may cross in safety; and it is said that those cases where the look and listen rule has been dispensed with are exceptions to the general rule falling within one of the three following classes; viz, 1st, Where the view of the track is obstructed, and hence where the injured party, not being able to see, is obliged to act upon his judgment at the time; in other words, where compliance with the rule would be impracticable or unavailing. 2d, Where the injured person was a passenger, going to or alighting from a train, and hence under an implied invitation and assurance by the company to cross the track in safety. 3d, Where the direct act of some agent of the company had put the person off his guard, and induced him to cross the track without precaution. Many cases are referred to by the court in support of these distinctions, and the rule seems to be as stated. South., etc., R. Co. *v.* Thompson, 66 Ala. 494 Baltimore, etc., R. Co. *v.* Whitacre, 35 Ohio St. 627; Pennsylvania R. Co. *v.* Rathgeb, 32 Ohio St. 73; McCrary *v.* Chicago, etc., R. Co., 31 Fed. Rep. 531; Bower *v.* Chicago, etc., R. Co., 61 Wis. 457; s. c., 19 Am. & Eng. R. R. Cas. 301, Mynning *v.* Detroit, etc., R. Co. (Mich. 1887), 28 Am. & Eng. R. R. Cas. 665; Donohue *v.* St. Louis, etc., R. Co. (Mo. 1886), 28 Am. & Eng. R. R. Cas. 673; Drane *v.* St. Louis, etc., R. Co., 10 Mo. App. 531; Connelly *v.* New York, etc., R. Co., 88 N. Y. 346; s. c., 8 Am. & Eng. R. R. Cas. 459; Terre Haute, etc, R. Co. *v.* Clark, 73 Ind. 168; s. c., 6 Am. & Eng. R. R. Cas. 84; Chicago, etc., R. Co *v.* Dimmick, 96 Ill. 42; s. c., 2 Am. & Eng. R. R Cas. 201; Harris *v.* Minneapolis, etc., R. Co. (Minn.), 33 N. W. 112; Patterson's Ry. Ac. Law, p. 168, § 173, and notes.

1. Patterson's Ry. Ac. Law, p. 170, § 175, tit. "Contributory Neg." *ante*, § 33, pp. 68, 70, 71, 72, 73, 74.

Whether the traveller should stop, as well as look and listen, depends on the attendant circumstances. Pittsburgh, etc., R. Co. *v.* Wright, 80 Ind. 236; Shaber *v.* St. Paul, etc., R. Co., 28 Minn. 103; s. c., 2 Am. & Eng. R. R. Cas. 185; Houston, etc., R. Co. *v.* Waller, 56 Tex. 331; s. c., 8 Am. & Eng. R. R. Cas. 431; Pittsburgh, etc, R. Co. *v.* Martin, 82 Ind. 476; s. c., 8 Am & Eng. R. R. Cas. 253; Laverenz *v.* Chicago, etc., R. Co., 56 Ia. 689; s. c., 6 Am. & Eng. R. R. Cas. 274; Kelly *v.* St. Paul, etc., R. Co., 29 Minn. 1; s. c. 6 Am. & Eng. R. R. Cas. 93: Pennsylvania Co. *v.* Rudel, 100 Ill. 603; s. c, 6 Am & Eng. R. R. Cas. 30; Plummer *v.* Eastern R. Co., 73 Me. 591; s. c, 6 Am. & Eng. R. R. Cas. 165; Duffy *v.* Chicago, etc, R. Co., 32 Wis. 275; Kellogg *v.* New York, etc., R. Co., 79 N. Y. 72; Howard *v.* St. Paul, etc., R. Co., 32 Minn. 214; s. c., 19 Am. & Eng. R. R. Cas. 283.

A failure to look and listen when an approaching train could not be seen, is not contributory negligence. Petty *v.* Hannibal, etc, R. Co. (Mo. 1886), 28 Am. & Eng. R. R. Cas. 618.

33. Mufflings, Snow-storms, Physical Infirmities, etc. — As bearing upon the question of the care to be exercised by both travellers and railroad companies, and the duties required of each, the conditions of the weather, the season of the year, the physical surroundings of the traveller, his infirmities of sight, his dress or mufflings, umbrellas, carriage-tops, etc., are all valuable and important evidence. In each particular case such circumstances are generally controlling upon the question of due care, especially when the traveller went upon the track without having stopped to listen for approaching trains. It is well, therefore, to look at some of the cases in which these matters have been dealt with specifically.[1]

The rule requiring persons, before crossing a railroad track, to look and see whether trains are approaching, is not applied inflexibly in all cases without regard to age, or other circumstances. McGovern *v.* New York, etc., R. Co., 67 N. Y. 417.

Where a failure to stop, look, and listen, is not a proximate cause of injury, it is not contributory negligence. Baughman *v.* Shenango, etc., R. Co., 92 Pa. St. 335; s. c., 32 Am. Rep. 690.

1. Where a man walked upon a railroad track without stopping to look or listen, holding an umbrella over his head in such a position as to obscure his view of the track, it was *held* that he was guilty of contributory negligence in being struck by a detached car sent rapidly along the track. Yancey *v.* Wabash, etc., R. Co. (Mo. 1887), 6 S. W. Rep. 272; Pennsylvania R. Co. *v.* State, 61 Md. 108; s. c., 19 Am. & Eng. R. R. Cas. 326.

Where a man in a covered wagon was struck on a railroad crossing of a city street, it was *held* on the facts of the case that his contributory negligence was for the jury. Sharp *v.* Glushing, 96 N. Y. 676; s. c., 19 Am. & Eng. R. R. Cas. 372.

Where a traveller is compelled, by severity of weather, to protect himself in a manner to interfere with his ability to perceive coming danger, he is not freed from a charge of contributory negligence when injured at a railroad crossing, if the measures adopted to protect him from the weather caused him to be injured; yet, unless it is certain that the means used did have that effect, the question is for the jury, not the court. Salters *v.* Utica, etc., R. Co., 59 N. Y. 631.

It is not contributory negligence, as a matter of law, to approach a crossing in a covered buggy or carriage. Stackus *v.* New York, etc., R. Co., 79 N. Y. 464; reversing same case, 7 Hun (N. Y.), 559.

But see Lendening *v.* Sharpe, 22 Hun (N. Y.), 78; Terre Haute, etc., R. Co. *v.* Clark, 73 Ind. 168.

Where a person could have seen a train approaching, but did not look in that direction, and had his ears so bandaged that he could not hear, he is guilty of contributory negligence. Chicago, etc., R Co. *v.* Still, 19 Ill. 499; s. c., 71 Am. Dec. 236.

When a party approaching a crossing wraps or muffles himself up so as to protect himself from cold or rain, he is bound to use extraordinary care, as he has voluntarily diminished his powers of seeing or hearing a train approaching. Butterfield *v.* Western R. Co., 10 Allen (Mass.), 532; Elkins *v.* Boston, etc., R. Co., 115 Mass. 190; Steves *v.* Oswego, etc., R. Co., 18 N. Y. 420; Hanover, etc., R Co. *v.* Coil, 55 Pa. St. 396; Illinois, etc., R. Co. *v.* Ebert, 74 Ill. 399; Chicago, etc., R. Co. *v.* Sweeney, 52 Ill. 325; Pennsylvania R. Co. *v.* Werner, 89 Pa. St. 59; Roth *v.* Milwaukee, etc., R. Co., 21 Wis. 256; Salters *v.* Utica, etc., R. Co., 75 N. Y. 273.

Deafness should increase vigilance at a crossing. Purl *v.* St. Louis, etc., R. Co., 72 Mo. 168; s. c., 6 Am. & Eng. R. R. Cas. 27; Johnson *v.* Louisville, etc., R Co. (Ky. 1883), 13 Am. & Eng. R. R. Cas 623; New Jersey, etc, Co. *v.* West, 32 N. J. L. 91; Morris, etc., R. Co. *v.* Haslon, 38 N. J. L. 147; Cleveland, etc., R. Co. *v.* Terry, 8 Ohio St. 570; Central R. Co. *v.* Feller, 84 Pa. St. 226; Zimmerman *v.* Hannibal, etc, R. Co., 71 Mo. 476; s. c., 2 Am. & Eng. R. R. Cas. 191.

When a snow-storm is prevailing at the time of an injury, it seems that the question of contributory negligence should be submitted to the jury. Hackford *v.* New York, etc., R. Co., 43 Howard's Pr. (N. Y.) 222; Same *v.* Same, 6 Lans. (N. Y.) 381.

The sobriety or intoxication of a person at the time of his injury at a crossing also bears upon the question of his contributory negligence. Houston, etc., R. Co. *v.* Waller, 56 Tex. 331; s. c., 8 Am. & Eng. R. R. Cas. 431; Keane *v.* Baltimore, etc., R. Co., 61 Md. 154; s. c., 19 Am. & Eng.

34. Crossing in Front of Moving Train. — It is usually negligence in a traveller to attempt a crossing in plain view of a near and rapidly approaching train.[1] And the mere fact that the speed of the train was greater than usual, or in violation of law, will not excuse the traveller's negligence.[2] Yet there may be cases in which it is not negligent to cross in front of an approaching train.[3]

35. Children and Feeble Persons. — The doctrines of the law relating to the injury of adults at railway highway crossings are somewhat modified in their application to children, and old and feeble persons. The same care is not required of a child that is exacted of a man.[4] What would be contributory negligence in a man may not be in a child.[5] And the question of the care to be required of a child is ordinarily to be determined by a jury, in accordance with what a child of similar age and experience similarly situated would have done.[6] Yet there are some cases where children have been held guilty of contributory negligence as a matter of law.[7]

36. Imputable Contributory Negligence. — The doctrines of imputable contributory negligence as applicable in cases of injury at highway crossings, both to children of tender years and adults,

R. R. Cas. 321; Toledo, etc., R. Co. *v.* Riley, 47 Ill. 514.

1. Chicago, etc., R. Co. *v.* Bell, 70 Ill. 102; Gothard *v.* Alabama, etc., R. Co., 67 Ala. 114; State *v.* Maine, etc., R. Co., 76 Me. 657; s. c., 19 Am. & Eng. R. R. Cas. 312; Rigler *v.* Railroad Co (N. Car. 1887), 26 Am. & Eng. R R. Cas 386; Baltimore, etc., R Co *v.* Mali (Md. 1887), 28 Am. & Eng. R. R Cas. 628; Bohan *v.* Milwaukee, etc., R Co, 61 Wis. 391; s. c., 19 Am. & Eng. R. R. Cas. 276; Bellefontaine R. Co. *v.* Hunter, 33 Ind. 335; s. c., 5 Am. Rep. 201; Chicago, etc., R. Co. *v.* Fears, 53 Ill. 115; Schwartz *v.* Hudson, etc., R. Co., 4 Robt. (N. Y.) 347; Pierce on R. R. 345, and note 9; tit. "Contributory Negligence," *ante*, p. 75. See, as to crossing in front of street-cars, Pierce on R. R. 347.

2. One who attempts to cross in front of a train that he sees approaching, cannot escape a charge of contributory negligence by saying that, if the locomotive had run at its usual and lawful pace, he would not have been injured. Kelley *v.* Hannibal, etc., R. Co., 75 Mo. 138 (1881).

3. Bonnell *v.* Delaware, etc., R. Co., 39 N J. L. 189; tit. "Contributory Negligence," *ante*, p. 75, note 6.

4. Tit. "Contributory Negligence," *ante*, pp. 42–48, § 22; Sheriden *v* Brooklyn, etc, R Co, 36 N Y. 43; O'Mara *v.* Hudson, etc, R. Co, 38 N. Y. 449; Thurber *v.* Harlem, etc., R Co, 60 N. Y. 326; Dowling *v.* New York, etc., R. Co, 90 N. Y. 670; s. c, 12 Am. & Eng R. R. Cas. 73.

The rule that a person approaching a railroad crossing must stop, look, and listen, and if injured by a failure to do so cannot recover, does not govern in the case of infants of tender years. Chicago, etc, R. Co *v.* Becker, 84 Ill. 483; Haycroft *v.* Lake Shore, etc., R. Co, 2 Hun (N. Y.), 489; s. c., affirmed, 64 N. Y. 636; Elkins *v.* Boston, etc, R. Co., 115 Mass. 190; Schwier *v.* New York, etc, R. Co., 90 N. Y. 558; 14 Am. & Eng. R. R. Cas. 656, and note.

5. Moore *v.* Metropolitan R. Co., 2 Mackey (D. C.), 437; Nehrbas *v.* Cent. Pac. R. Co., 62 Cal. 320; s. c., 14 Am. & Eng. R. R. Cas. 370; Powell *v.* New York, etc., R. Co., 22 Hun (N. Y.), 56; Meeks *v.* Southern, etc., R. Co., 56 Cal. 513; s. c., 38 Am. Rep. 67.

6. O'Connor *v.* Boston, etc., R. Co, 135 Mass. 352; s. c., 15 Am. & Eng. R. R. Cas. 362; Paducah, etc., R Co. *v.* Hoehl, 12 Bush (Ky.), 41; Dowling *v.* New York Cent., etc., R. Co., 90 N. Y. 670; s. c., 12 Am. & Eng. R. R. Cas. 73; Barry *v.* New York, etc., R. Co., 92 N Y. 289; s. c., 13 Am. & Eng. R. R. Cas. 615; Nehrbas *v.* Cent. Pac. R. Co., 62 Cal. 320; s. c, 14 Am. & Eng. R. R. Cas. 370; tit. "Contributory Neg." *ante*, pp. 43-46.

7. Wendell *v.* New York, etc., R. Co., 91 N. Y. 420; Moore *v.* Pennsylvania R. Co., 99 Pa. St. 301; s. c., 4 Am. & Eng R. R. Cas. 569; tit. "Contributory Neg." *ante*, p. 47, and note 2.

have been sufficiently treated elsewhere in this volume. It is not necessary to repeat those doctrines here. They are applicable, if at all, to cases where one person is injured at a crossing while in the conveyance of, and being driven by, another, or where children of tender years have escaped their custodians, and been injured upon a crossing.[1]

37. Injury of Fellow-Servant. — The general rule, that the master is not liable for the injury of one fellow-servant by another, applies in cases of injuries at crossing. Thus, where an engineer failed to give statutory signals at a crossing, and thereby injured a fellow-servant, it was held there could be no recovery against the company.[2]

38. Comparative Negligence at Crossings. — In Illinois the test of comparative negligence is applied to accidents at railway highway crossings; and the slight negligence of the plaintiff will not prevent him from recovering, if the negligence of the railway company was gross.[3]

39. Peculiar Statutory Provisions, etc. — It is not feasible to collect here all the statutory provisions relating to the duties and obligations of railroads and travellers at highway crossings. Indeed, if done, it would scarcely be useful. In the course of this article, references have been made to many statutory provisions, and to decisions construing them. In each State the doctrines heretofore enunciated should be applied in the light of existing statutory rules. There are some statutory provisions, however, so peculiar as to merit special mention.[4]

1. Tit "Contributory Neg." *ante*, pp. 82–89, § 38, "Imputable Contributory Negligence."

2. Randall *v.* Baltimore, etc., R. Co., 109 U. S. 478; s. c., 15 Am. & Eng. R. R. Cas. 243.

3. 3 Am. & Eng. Ency. of L. tit. "Comparative Negligence," pp. 367–376. Chicago, etc., R. Co. *v.* McKean, 40 Ill. 218; Chicago, etc., R. Co. *v.* Fears, 53 Ill. 115; Illinois, etc., R. Co. *v.* Moffitt, 67 Ill 431; Chicago, etc., R. Co. *v.* Lee, 68 Ill. 576; Illinois, etc, R. Co. *v.* Goddard, 72 Ill. 567; Illinois, etc., R. Co. *v.* Benton, 69 Ill. 174; Chicago, etc., R. Co. *v.* Hatch, 79 Ill. 137; Illinois, etc., R. Co. *v.* Hammer, 85 Ill. 526; Chicago, etc., R. Co. *v.* Lee, 87 Ill. 454; Wabash, etc., R. Co. *v.* Henks, 91 Ill. 406; Stratton *v.* Central, etc, R. Co., 95 Ill. 25; s.c., 1 Am. & Eng. R. R. Cas 115; Chicago, etc, R. Co *v.* Dimmick, 96 Ill. 42; s. c., 2 Am. & Eng. R. R. Cas. 201; Chicago, etc., R. Co. *v.* Johnson, 103 Ill. 512; s. c., 8 Am & Eng. R. R. Cas. 225.

4. In Missouri, in 1881, the legislature amended § 806, Rev St. 1879, so as to make the last sentence of said section read, "And said corporation shall also be liable for all damages which any person may hereafter sustain at such crossing when such bell shall not be rung, or such whistle sounded, as required by this section; provided, however, that nothing herein contained shall preclude the corporation sued, from showing that the failure to ring such bell, or sound such whistle, was not the cause of such injury." Acts 1881 (Mo.), p. 79.

Prior to this act, it was held that a failure to give signals did not make a *prima facie* case of negligence, but, under it, the Supreme Court of Missouri has held that it does raise a *prima facie* case. Huckshold *v.* St. Louis, etc., R. Co. (Mo. 1887), 28 Am. & Eng. R. R. Cas. 659.

There is a statute in Georgia that declares the negligence of the company shall be presumed when an injury is inflicted by the running of the locomotives, cars, or other machinery of a railroad company. Code of Ga. 1882, §§ 30, 33. Central, etc., R. Co. *v.* Sanders, 73 Ga. 513; s. c., 27 Am. & Eng. R. R. Cas. 300.

And in Tennessee certain precautions are required, which, if taken, relieve the company from liability; but, if not taken, render the company absolutely liable for injuries

40. Railroad Liable over to Municipality. — Where an injury occurs at a crossing from a defect in a street at its intersection with a railroad, the municipality is liable in the first instance to the person injured.[1] But if it was the duty of the railroad company, as between it and the city, to keep the crossing in repair, then the municipality may recover over from the railroad company the damages and costs in which the city has been mulcted.[2] And if the company had notice of the suit, the judgment against the city is conclusive as to the city's right of recovery.[3]

41. Legislative Control over Crossings. — The legislature has the right and power to regulate grade crossings of railways and highways, declare established crossings a nuisance, and order changes made conducive to the public welfare.[4]

So, a statute imposing penalties for the failure to give statutory signals, and giving part of the penalty to the person who informs, are constitutional, both under State and federal laws.[5] But a city ordinance undertaking to regulate the speed of trains along and over streets is void if unreasonable in its terms. Municipal regulations, to be valid, must be reasonable.[6]

42. Railroad-Railroad Collisions. — This topic belongs more properly, perhaps, to the subject of railroads; yet a doctrine relating

to which the omission of the statutory duties even remotely contributed. Code of Tenn. 1884, §§ 1298–1300. Railroad Co. *v.* Walker, 11 Heisk. (Tenn.) 383.

In some States, there are proceedings by indictment to recover damages in the nature of a penalty for killing persons at railway highway crossings by the railroad trains. State *v.* Maine, etc., R Co., 76 Me. 357; s. c., 19 Am. & Eng. R. R. Cas. 312.

1. A municipal corporation having the care and control of the streets, is bound to see that they are kept safe for the passage of persons and property. If this duty be neglected, and one should be injured on account of such neglect, the corporation will be liable in the first instance for the damage thus sustained, even though the defect causing the injury result from the failure of a railroad company to keep a crossing in repair. Western, etc., R. Co. *v.* Atlanta (Ga. 1885), 19 Am. & Eng. R. R. Cas. 233; Chicago *v.* Robbins, 2 Black (U S.), 418.

2. Western, etc., R. Co. *v.* Atlanta (Ga. 1885), 19 Am. & Eng. R. R. Cas. 233; Chicago *v.* Robbins, 2 Black (U. S.), 418; Robbins *v.* Chicago, 4 Wallace (U.S.), 657; Lowell *v.* Short, 4 Cush. (Mass.) 275; Milford *v.* Holbrook, 9 Allen (Mass.), 17; Boston *v.* Worthington, 10 Gray (Mass), 496; Woburn *v.* Henshaw, 101 Mass. 193; West Boylston *v.* Mason, 102 Mass. 341; Westfield *v.* Mayo, 122 Mass. 100; Norwich *v.* Breed, 30 Conn. 355; Littleton *v.* Richardson, 34 N. H. 179; Rochester *v.* Montgomery, 72 N. Y. 65; First National Bank *v.* Port Jervis, 96 N. Y. 550; s. c., 6 Am. & Eng. Corp. Cas. 233; Brooklyn *v.* Brooklyn, etc., R. Co., 47 N. Y. 475 Lowell *v.* Boston, etc., R. Co., 23 Pickering, 24 Woburn *v.* Boston, etc., R. Co., 109 Mass. 283; Portland *v.* Richardson, 54 Me. 46; Veazie *v.* Penobscot R. Co., 49 Me. 119; Ottumwa *v.* Parks, 43 Ia. 119.

3. Western, etc., R. Co. *v.* Atlanta (Ga 1885), 19 Am. & Eng. R. R. Cas. 233; Chicago *v.* Robbins, 2 Black (U. S.) 418; Portland *v.* Richardson, 54 Me. 46; Boston *v.* Worthington, 10 Gray (Mass), 496; Milford *v.* Holbrook, 9 Allen (Mass.), 17; Rochester *v.* Montgomery, 72 N. Y. 65; First Nat. Bank *v.* Port Jervis, 96 N. Y 550. 6 Am. & Eng Corp. Cas. 233; Westfield *v.* Mayo, 122 Mass. 100.

4. Tiedeman Lim. Police Pow. 593–602; Woodruff *v.* Catlin (Conn.), 6 Atl. Rep. 849; Textor *v.* Baltimore, etc., R. Co., 59 Md. 63; s. c., 13 Am. & Eng. R. R. Cas. 635, and note; Railroad Company *v.* Richmond, 96 U. S. 521; Knobloch *v.* Chicago, etc, R. Co., 31 Minn. 402; s. c., 14 Am. & Eng. R. R. Cas. 625, and note.

5. State *v.* Wabash, etc., R. Co (Mo. 1886), 1 S. W. Rep 130; State *v.* Hannibal, etc., R. Co. (Mo. 1886), 1 S. W. Rep. 133; Revised Stat. Mo. 1879, § 806.

6. Cooke *v.* Boston, etc., R. Co. (Mass. 1883), 10 Am & Eng. R. R. Cas. 328; Meyers *v.* Chicago, etc., R. Co., 57 Ia. 555; s. c., 7 Am. & Eng. R. R. Cas. 406, and note; s. c., 42 Am. Rep. 50.

to collisions at railroad-railroad crossing may be usefully stated here.[1]

43. Highway-Highway Collisions. — Collisions of one team with another, etc., at the intersection of two highways, are infrequent, but they have been before the courts in a few instances. The rights and duties of parties at the intersection of two highways being in all respects mutual, equal, and reciprocal, the rules that govern in such cases are simple and easily applied.[2]

44. Street-Cars, Collisions of. — Street-cars have a superior right of way at the crossings of streets over ordinary vehicles, but only in a limited degree as compared with steam railroads. The subject is of little practical importance, although some cases have arisen that are worthy of note.[3]

CROW.[4]

CRUDE. — The lexicon definition of *crude* is, in its natural state; not cooked or prepared by fire or heat; undressed; not altered, refined, or prepared for use by any artificial process; raw.[5]

CRUEL. (See ANIMALS; DIVORCE; GUARDIAN AND WARD; MASTER AND SERVANT; PARENT AND CHILD; PUNISHMENT.) — Inhumane conduct towards living creatures; wanton or careless infliction of pain upon the body; injury of the person or feelings;

1. Where a railway passenger is injured by a negligent collision of his train with that of another company, he may maintain an action for the wrong against either company. Wabash, etc., R. Co. *v.* Shacklet, 105 Ill. 364; s. c., 12 Am. & Eng. R. R. Cas. 166; 44 Am. Rep. 791; Cuddy *v.* Horn, 46 Mich. 596; s. c., 41 Am. Rep. 178; Transfer Co. *v.* Kelly, 36 Ohio St. 86; s. c., 38 Am. Rep. 558; Pittsburgh, etc., R. Co. *v.* Spencer, 98 Ind. 186.

2. "There being no statute regulating the manner in which persons shall drive when they meet at the junction of two streets, the rule of the common law applies, and each person must use reasonable care to avoid a collision, such care as is adapted to the place and circumstances. Garrigan *v.* Berry, 12 Allen (Mass.), 84.

A person about to cross a street of a city in which there is an ordinance against fast driving, has a right to presume, in the absence of knowledge to the contrary, that others will respect and conform to that ordinance. But where he knows that others are driving along the street, at the place of crossing, at a forbidden rate of speed, and he has full means of seeing the rate at which they are driving, the existence of such ordinance will not authorize a presumption which is negatived by the evidence of his senses. If the attempt to cross the street, under the circumstances, would be negligence on his part, the fact of the existence of such city ordinance is not evidence tending to free him from culpability. Baker *v.* Pendergast, 32 Ohio St. 494; s. c., 30 Am. Rep. 620.

3. See, for a full collection of the authorities upon the relative duties of street-cars, and persons walking or riding in private vehicles along or across street-car tracks, the note to the case of Market St. Ry. Co. *v.* McKeever, 19 Am & Eng. R. R. Cas. 127, also Wood *v.* Detroit, etc., R. Co., 52 Mich. 402; s. c., 19 Am. & Eng. R. R. Cas. 129, and note; Dahl *v.* Milwaukee, etc, R. Co. (Wis 1885), 19 Am. & Eng R. R. Cas. 121; Hanlon *v.* South Boston, etc., R. Co., 129 Mass. 310; s. c., 2 Am. & Eng R. R. Cas. 18; Maschek *v.* St. Louis, etc., R. Co., 71 Mo. 276; s. c., 2 Am. & Eng. R. R. Cas. 38; Cook *v.* Metropolitan R. Co., 98 Mass. 361.

Authorities. — Patterson's Ry. Ac. Law; Pierce on Railroads; 2 Wood's Ry. Law; 90 Am. Dec.; elaborate notes at pp. 54 to 67; 751 to 752; 780 to 787; and particularly the series of Am. & Eng. R. R. Cas. and the numerous valuable notes and cases upon "Crossings" contained in many of the volumes.

4. "The phrase 'as the crow flies' is a popular and picturesque expression to denote a straight line, which I think is clearly the proper mode of measuring the distance from one given point to another." Stokes *v.* Grissell, 78 Eng. Com. L. Rep. 688

5. Recknagel *v.* Murphy, 12 Otto (U. S.), 198.

abuse; ill-treatment.[1] What constitutes cruelty to a person depends upon the relation of the parties concerned.[2]

CRUELTY TO ANIMALS. — See Vol. I. p. 575.

CRUISE (see ADMIRALTY) is nothing but a voyage for a given purpose, and may, therefore, be properly defined to be a cruising-voyage.[3]

CUCKING-STOOL is an engine invented for the punishment of scolding and unquiet women.[4]

CULPABLE (see NEGLIGENCE) means not only criminal but censurable; and, when the term is applied to the omission by a person to preserve the means of enforcing his own rights, censurable is more nearly equivalent.[5]

CULTIVATE. (See ADVERSE POSSESSION, Vol. I. p. 259.) — To till or husband the ground; to improve or forward the product of the earth by labor.[6]

1. Abbott's Law Dict.

2. Cruelty towards weak and helpless persons takes place where a party, bound to provide for and protect them, either abuses them by whipping them unnecessarily, or by neglecting to provide for them those necessaries which their helpless condition requires. Exposing a person of tender years, under a party's care, to the inclemency of the weather. Rex *v.* Ridley, 2 Campb. 650. Keeping a child, unable to provide for himself, without adequate food. Rex *v.* Friend, Russ & Ryan, 20 Or an overseer neglecting to provide food and medical care to a pauper having urgent and immediate occasion for them. Rex *v.* Meredith, Russ & Ryan, 45, are examples of this species of cruelty. Bouvier's L. Dict.

3. The Brutus, 2 Gall. C. C. 539.

A voyage or expedition in quest of vessels or fleets of the enemy, which may be expected to sail in any particular track at a certain season of the year. The region in which the *cruises* are performed is usually termed the rendezvous, or cruising latitude.

When the ships employed for this purpose, which are accordingly called *cruisers*, have arrived at the destined station, they traverse the sea backwards and forwards, under an easy sail, and within a limited space, conjectured to be in the track of their expected adversaries. Weskett Ins. Lex. Merc. Redid. 271, 284; Dougl. 509; Marshall Ins. 196, 199, 520.

Cruise imports a definite place as well as time of commencement and termination, unless such construction is repelled by the context. When not otherwise specially agreed, a cruise begins and ends in the country to which a ship belongs, and from which she derives her commission. The Brutus, 2 Gall. (C. C.) 539.

4. James *v.* Comm., 12 S. & R. (Pa.) 230; Co. 3d Inst. 219, 4 Bl. Com. 168.

5. As he has merely lost a right of action which he might voluntarily relinquish, and has wronged nobody but himself, culpable neglect conveys the idea of neglect which exists where the loss can fairly be ascribed to the party's own carelessness, improvidence, or folly. Waltham Bank *v.* Wright, 8 Allen (Mass.), 121.

Culpable negligence is the omission to do something which a reasonable and prudent man would do, under the circumstances surrounding each particular case, or it is the want of such care as men of ordinary prudence would use under similar circumstances. Woodman *v.* Nottingham, 49 N. H. 387. See Hot Springs R. Co. *v.* Newman, 36 Ark. 610.

Culpable homicide, described as a crime varying from the very lowest culpability up to the very verge of murder. Lord Moncrieff, Arkley's R. 72. In statute, Sykes *v.* Meacham, 103 Mass. 286.

6. State *v.* Allen, 13 Ired. L. (N. Car.) 36; Clark *v.* Phelps, 4 Cow. (N. Y.) 190.

Cultivated Land, Field or Grounds. — It is not necessary that there should be something actually growing upon the land in order to constitute it "cultivated" land. "The word 'cultivated' may refer either to past or present time. A field on which a crop of wheat is growing is a cultivated field, although not a stroke of labor may have been done to it since the seed was put into the ground; and it is a cultivated field after the crop is removed." Accordingly, the defence to an indictment for removing a fence around "cultivated grounds," that there was nothing growing upon them, is not good. It was sufficient to show that the grounds were cultivated, that they had been prepared for tillage

CUMULATIVE SENTENCE. — Where a person is charged with several offences at the same time of the same kind, he may be sentenced to several terms of imprisonment or penal servitude, one after the conclusion of the other.[1]

by being cleared and fenced, and that a crop had been raised upon them the preceding year. State *v.* Allen, 13 Ired. L. (N. C.) 36.

"Where a piece or tract of land has been cleared and fenced and cultivated, or proposed to be cultivated, and is kept and used for cultivation, according to the ordinary course of husbandry, although nothing may be growing within the enclosure at the time of the trespass, is a 'cultivated field,' within the description of the statute" prescribing a penalty for the removal of fences. State *v.* McMinn, 81 N. C. 585.

Enclosed or Cultivated Field. — A field need not necessarily be enclosed by a lawful fence, in order to be an "enclosed or cultivated field," within an act requiring railroad companies to fence their tracks along such fields. Biggerstaff *v.* St. Louis, etc., R. Co., 60 Mo. 567.

Improved or Cultivated Land. — A power given to commissioners to lay out roads through "improved or cultivated land," does not include the right to prostrate buildings in so doing. These, though improvements, are not within the contemplation of the words of the act. "The terms, to 'improve and cultivate,' may be considered as synonymous. . . . When speaking of improved land, it is generally understood to be such as has been reclaimed, is used for the purposes of husbandry, and is cultivated as such, whether the appropriation is for tillage, meadow, or pasture." Clark *v.* Phelps, 4 Cow. (N. Y.) 190.

Under a statute authorizing the location of private roads from improved or cultivated land to a town or highway, a mill lot upon which a mill was erected was *held* to be such. Lyon *v.* Hamor, 73 Me. 56.

State of Cultivation. — In an act limiting a widow's dower to lands "in a state of cultivation," "'a state of cultivation' must be the converse of a state of nature; and whenever lands have been wrought with a view to the production of a crop, they must be considered as becoming and continuing in 'a state of cultivation,' until abandoned for every purpose of agriculture, and designedly permitted to revert to a condition similar to their original one." Lands "in a state of cultivation" are not necessarily such as "produce an income;" they do not, *ipso facto*, cease to be in a state of cultivation because naturally sterile and unprofitable for agriculture. Johnson *v.* Perley, 2 N. H. 56.

Suitable for Cultivation. — Land situated in the mountains, six miles from the sea, difficult of access for want of roads; of uneven, but not steep, surface; of a rich soil, covered with brush and timber, which must be removed before it can be ploughed; valuable as timber land, but more valuable, after the removal of the timber, for agricultural purposes, — such land is "suitable for cultivation," within a constitutional provision that such land belonging to the State shall be granted only to actual settlers. The phrase includes "all lands ready for occupation, or which by ordinary farming processes are fit for agricultural purposes." It is not confined to those which are "presently or immediately fit for tillage, without other preparation than appertains to the ordinary operations of husbandry," and are capable of cultivation without the necessity of clearing the timber. Manley *v.* Cunningham (Cal.), 13 Pac. Rep. 622.

Things Necessary for Cultivation. — An act gave a lien upon a farm for "all advance of money, purchase of supplies, farming utensils, working stock, or other things necessary for the cultivation of the farm or plantation." In construing this, the court said, "What is embraced in the words 'other things necessary for the cultivation of the farm,' must be learned by resort to the usages and customs of the agricultural interest. The statute implies that the farmer has the land. What he needs, and what the statute proposes to secure, is the common and usual outfit provided from time to time, to make the crop." "The only rule that can be adopted with safety, is to take into account the system of agriculture as we actually have it, — the character of the food, clothing, etc., consumed by the laborers; the implements and provender appropriate for the use, — and in that light determine whether an account in whole or in part is in excess of the statute." There is a rebuttable presumption, that, where the farmer in good faith has taken up goods on the faith of the lien, they are necessary. Where the goods were used to pay laborers with, the seller was protected by the lien. Herman *v.* Perkins, 52 Miss. 813.

1. 1 Russell on Crimes (5th ed.) 82; 1 Bishop, Cr. Proc. (3d ed.), §§ 1326, 1327; R. *v.* Williams, 1 Leach, 536; Williams *v.* State, 18 Ohio St. 46; Johnson *v.* People, 83 Ill. 431; Fletcher *v.* People, 81 Ill. 116; Martin *v.* People, 76 Ill. 499; State *v.* Car-

CUMULATIVE VOTING. — 1. In the Election of Public Officers. — By the Constitution of *Illinois* (each district voting for three representatives), each voter may cast as many votes for each candidate as there are State representatives to be elected, or may distribute his votes, or equal parts thereof, among the candidates as he sees fit.[1]

In *Ohio* it has been held that a statute authorizing the election of four members of the police board at the same election, but which denies to an elector the right to vote for more than two members, is in conflict with the constitution of that State.[2]

lyle, 33 Kan. 716; Kite *v.* Commonwealth, 11 Met. (Mass.) 581; Russell *v.* Commonwealth, 7 S. & R. (Pa.) 489; *In re* Bloom, 53 Mich. 597; *Exp.* Roberts, 9 Nev. 44; People *v.* Forbes, 22 Cal. 135; *Exp* Dalton, 49 Cal. 463; *Exp.* Fry, 3 Mackey (D. C.), 135. See Gregory *v.* R., 15 Q. B. 974; Mims *v.* State, 26 Minn. 498; Barnes *v.* State, 19 Conn. 398. *Compare* People *v.* Liscomb (Tweed's Case), 60 N. Y. 559; Miller *v.* Allen, 11 Ind. 389; Kennedy *v.* Howard, 74 Ind. 87; James *v.* Ward, 2 Met. (Ky.) 271; Baker *v* State, 11 Tex. App. 262; *Exp.* Meyers, 44 Mo. 279

Where the sentence, as shown by the record, is to imprisonment "for a further term of ten years, to commence at the expiration of the sentence aforesaid," and there is nothing in the record showing to what the term "aforesaid" relates, such judgment and sentence will be reversed for uncertainty. Williams *v.* State, 18 Ohio St 46. See *In re* Jackson, 3 MacArthur (D. C.), 24.

Where the defendant is convicted of several offences under different counts of the same indictment, it is error to render judgment ordering imprisonment of the defendant a gross number of days in all. It should fix the imprisonment for a specified number of days on each count on which conviction is had, the imprisonment on several counts to commence at the expiration of each preceding term. Martin *v.* People, 76 Ill. 499; Mullinix *v.* People, 76 Ill. 211; Fletcher *v* People, 81 Ill. 116; Bolun *v.* People, 73 Ill. 488.

It is erroneous in the judgment to fix the day and hour when imprisonment shall commence and end under each count. The sentence to imprisonment should be for a specified number of days under each count upon which conviction is had, the imprisonment under each succeeding count to commence when it ends under the preceding one, without fixing the day and hour of any. Johnson *v.* People, 83 Ill. 431. See *In re* Bloom, 53 Mich 597.

S was convicted separately in a district court of the Territory of Utah on three indictments under that section, covering together a continuous period of time, each covering a different part, but the three parts being continuous, the indictments being found at the same time, by the same grand jury, on one oath and one examination, of the same witnesses, covering the whole continuous time. One judgment was entered on the three convictions. It first imposed a term of imprisonment and a fine. It next imposed two further successive terms of imprisonment, each to begin at the expiration of the last preceding sentence and judgment, with two further fines. It set forth the time embraced by each indictment, and specified each of the three punishments as being imposed in respect of a specified one of the indictments. On a petition to a district court of the Territory by the defendant for a writ of *habeas corpus*, setting forth that he had been imprisoned under the judgment for more than the term first imposed, and had paid the fine first imposed, and that the other two punishments were in excess of the authority of the trial court, the writ was refused. On appeal to this court, *held*, (1) there was but one entire offence for the continuous time; (2) the trial court had no jurisdiction to inflict a punishment in respect of more than one of the convictions; (3) as the want of jurisdiction appeared on the face of the proceedings, the defendant could be released from imprisonment on a *habeas corpus*; (4) the order and judgment of the court below must be reversed, and the case be remanded to that court, with a direction to grant the writ of *habeas corpus* prayed for. *In re* Snow, 120 U. S. 274.

Three separate offences — but not more — against the provisions of U. S. Rev. Stat. § 5480, when committed within the same six calendar months, may be joined; and when so joined, there is to be a single sentence for all. But this does not prevent other indictments for other and distinct offences under the same statute committed within the same six calendar months. *In re* Henry, 123 U. S. 372.

1. Illinois Const. art. IV. §§ 7, 8.

2. State *v.* Constantine, 42 Ohio St. 437.

s. c., 9 Am. & Eng. Corp. Cas. 33. It is believed that the opinion of *McIlvaine, J.*, in this case is the first expression of judicial opinion on the constitutionality of statutory provisions for minority representation. The point was raised in two New York cases, — People *v.* Crissey, 91 N. Y. 616; and Agerstein *v.* Kenney, 7 Am. & Eng. Corp Cas. 677, — but in both cases the court declined to pass upon it. In the latter case the court said, speaking of the constitutionality of minority representation, "The constitutional question which the plaintiff sought to raise by the commencement of this action is a very grave and interesting one, and should not be decided in any case unless properly presented and necessarily involved. It need not be decided in this case." In the former case the court, referring to the discussion of the same constitutional point in the course of the argument by council, said, "We ought not to decide it. It has a possible importance beyond the issues involved. It touches the question of minority representation upon which has been founded very much legislation, and about which there is room for difference and debate."

The constitutional provision on which the court bases its decision in this case is contained in § 1 of art. V. of the Ohio Constitution of 1851, entitled "Elective Franchise," and is to the effect that every duly qualified elector "shall be entitled to vote at all elections." The entire section reads as follows: "Every white male citizen of the United States of the age of twenty-one years who shall have been a resident of the State one year next preceding the election, and of the county, township, or ward, in which he resides, such time as may be provided by law, shall have the qualifications of an elector, and be entitled to vote at all elections."

It would seem that all that the section was intended to provide for was for the fixing of the qualification of electors, and if the last clause in the section was intended to guarantee any constitutional right to qualified electors, it was merely that of equality; that is, that all qualified electors should have *equal rights* of voting at all elections, and for all officers to be voted for. It would seem clear that it was not intended to prohibit minority representation and to give the right to each elector to vote for all officers to be elected. As the court remarks, the subject of minority representation was probably not known or thought of as a particular question at the time the Ohio Constitution was framed (1851), and hence it is plain that the framers of that constitution did not intend to make any constitutional guaranty, or provision in the nature of guaranty, against it.

It is probable that the framers of the constitution contemplated that all officers to be voted for should be voted for by each elector, and that a plurality of votes should elect; but is there any thing in the constitution that amounts to a guaranty that the majority or plurality shall in every case have the absolute right to elect every officer to be voted for? It would seem not. In certain cases the constitution contains express provisions as to the modes in which officers shall be elected. Thus, § 3 — of art. III. provides that a plurality shall elect the executive officers of the State (governor, lieutenant-governor, etc.). In the case of representatives, however, the constitution is not at all explicit; § 2, art. II. merely provides that they shall be elected by the electors in their respective districts. Under this provision it would seem that the legislature might by statute require that a majority vote or even a two-thirds vote was necessary to elect, and in case that the requisite number of votes were not attained by any candidate that the election might be thrown open to the house. Yet such legislation would have the effect of defeating the will of the majority in many cases, as where in a given district one party was in the predominance but not sufficiently so to elect their man, and in the house the opposite party was in the majority. The provisions of the constitution in relation to apportionment, art. XI., would seem to prohibit any minority representation in the case of representatives.

As to the validity of minority representation under the New York Constitution of 1881, the case is more difficult. § 1 of art. II., after fixing the qualifications of an elector, goes on to provide that he "shall be entitled to vote . . . for all officers that now are or hereafter may be elected by the people."

At the time this constitution was being framed, the theory of minority representation had been in practical operation in the State of Illinois for several years under the provision of the constitution of 1870 [art. IV. §§ 7, 8], and was well known to legislators as a practical system of representation. Moreover, the language of the constitution seems to be an almost express prohibition of minority representation. Still, even as to this constitutional provision, it would seem that it might be argued with much force that it intended to provide for equal rights of voting, rather than to prohibit minority representation. It is to be noticed that the system of minority representation provided for by §§ 7, 8, art. IV. of the Illinois Constitution of 1870, is different from that adopted by the statute held unconstitutional in the principal case. §§ 7, 8, art. IV. of the Illinois Constitution provide that three representatives

2. In Private Corporations. — It is provided by several State constitutions that in the election of directors, etc., of a private corporation, the voting power of each stockholder shall be the number of shares he owns multiplied by the number of directors to be elected, and that he may divide this power among as many candidates greater than the whole number to be elected, and in such proportions as he shall see fit.[1]

CURATOR. (See CIVIL LAW.) — The committee of the estate of a minor, spendthrift, imbecile or absent person.[2]

CURE. (See VERDICT; PLEADING.) — The care of souls; spiritual charge;[3] the ordinary duties of an officiating clergyman.[4]

shall be elected in each district, and that, "In all elections of representatives aforesaid, each qualified voter may cast as many votes for one candidate as there are representatives to be elected, or may distribute the same, or equal parts thereof, among the candidates, as he shall see fit; and the candidate highest in votes shall be declared elected." In the statute in question in the principal case each voter was entitled to vote for only two of a board of officers, and the statute was held unconstitutional as infringing on the right of voters to vote for *all* officers to be elected. But a provision similar to that of the Illinois Constitution would not come under this objection, as each member would be entitled to vote for all the members of the board if he chose. Yet of course the purpose and result of provisions like that in the statute in question, and of those like that in the Illinois Constitution, are identical; i e., to give representation to the minority.

1. Such a provision is contained in the following State constitutions: Illinois (1870). art. XI. § 3; Pennsylvania, art. XVI. § 4; West Virginia (1872), art. XI. § 4; Nebraska (1875), art. XI.; Miscellaneous Corporations, § 5; Missouri (1875), art. XIII. § 6; California, art XII. § 12.

It is held that such provisions are unconstitutional as impairing the obligation of contract and infringing on vested rights, as far as they concern corporations chartered before the adoption of the Constitution. In the case of Hays *v.* Commonwealth of Pennsylvania, 82 Pa. St. 518, it was *held* that the constitutional provision allowing cumulative voting (Constitution of Pennsylvania, 1874, art. XVI. § 4), if it applied to existing corporations, was void, as within the constitutional inhibition against impairing the obligation of contracts. The court says, "Now, whilst it cannot be said that this would not be an alteration in the terms of the charter, it is nevertheless urged that it is a mere regulation of the right of suffrage in corporations, but affects the vested rights of no one. But if it be not a vested right in those who own a major part of the stock of the corporation to elect, if they see proper, every member of the board of directors, I would like to know what a vested right means?" The case of The State *v.* Green, 78 Mo. 188; s. c., 8 Am. & Eng. Corp. Cas. 322, is a similar decision as to the constitutional provision of the State of Missouri, providing for cumulative voting in private corporations. Constitution of Missouri (1875), art. XII. § 6.

In Wright *v.* Central California Colony Water Co. (Cal.), 13 Am. & Eng. Corp. Cas. 89, it was *held* that under section 12 of article XII. of the Constitution, each qualified stockholder, present at an election for directors of a corporation, has the right, in exercising his power of voting for directors, to vote, at one time, the whole number of shares in his name, for the whole number of directors to be elected, or to cumulate his shares by voting for one candidate for director as many votes as shall equal the number of his shares multiplied by the number of directors to be elected, or by distributing them, upon the same principle, among as many candidates for directors as he shall think fit. And an election at which the stockholders are denied the right to thus cumulate their votes, is illegal, and will be set aside.

In Pierce *v.* Commonwealth, 104 Pa. St. 150; s. c, 13 Am. & Eng. R. R. Cas. 74, it was *held* that article 16, section 4. of the Constitution of Pennsylvania, providing for cumulative voting for directors of corporations, is not merely directory, and does not require legislation to give it effect.

2. Just. Inst. I. 23; 1 Bla. Com. 460; Adams' Glos.

The term has been adopted in Missouri to apply to the guardian of a ward's estate, as distinguished from the guardian of his person. Duncan *v.* Crook, 49 Mo. 116.

3. Webster.

4. Bouv. L. D.

A mere "licensed preacher" of the Methodist Church is not authorized to perform a marriage ceremony by a statute

CURIOSITY. — See notes to CABINET and COLLECTION.

CURRENCY, CURRENT. (See BILLS AND NOTES;[1] COIN; MONEY; TENDER.) — The term currency is commonly used to include whatever passes among the people for money, both coin and bank notes, or other paper money issued by authority, and which continually pass as and for coin.[2] It is sometimes, however, confined to the substitutes for coin, — bank and treasury notes, which circulate in the community as money.[3]

Current money is lawful money. Tender money,[4] current notes, funds, etc., are those which circulate in the community as money.[5]

CURRICLE[6]

giving power to do so to "all regular ministers of the gospel of every denomination having the cure of souls." Whether a "local preacher" is within the act, cannot be said generally. "It is not supposed that the cure of souls, as used in the act, implies a necessity that the minister should be the incumbent of a church living, or the pastor of any congregation or congregations in particular. But those terms import that the person is to be something more than a minister or preacher merely, and that he has a faculty, according to the constitution of his church, to celebrate matrimony, and, to some extent at least, has the power to administer the Christian sacraments, as acknowledged and held by the church." State *v.* Bay, 13 Ired. L. (N. Car.) 289.

1. Vol. ii. p. 326.

2. Whar. L. L.; Bouv. L. D.; C. F. & M. Ins. Co. *v.* Keiron, 27 Ill. 501; Webster *v.* Pierce, 35 Ill. 158; Cockrill *v.* Kirkpatrick, 9 Mo. 701; Dugan *v.* Campbell, 1 Ohio, 115; Lackey *v.* Miller, Phil. L. (N. Car.) 26; Lampton *v.* Haggard, 3 Mon. (Ky.) 149; Pilmer *v.* Bank, 16 Ia. 323; Butler *v.* Paine, 8 Minn. 329. In the last case, currency was said to be money; but in Griswold *v.* Hepburn, 2 Duval (Ky.), 33, it was *held* not to be necessarily so, but that "whatever circulates conventionally on its credit as a medium of exchange, whether it be bank notes, bills of exchange, or government securities, being thus practically current, is properly current."

"The word currency is far from having a settled, fixed, and precise meaning; and, even if it had such a meaning in general, it might acquire in certain localities, or among certain classes, a different signification;" and evidence is admissible to show its peculiar meaning at the time and place of drawing a draft in which the word occurs. Pilmer *v.* Bank, 16 Ia. 323. The contrary of this is, however, *held* in nearly all of the cases cited.

3. M. & F. Ins. Co. *v.* Tincher, 30 Ill. 399; Osgood *v.* McConnell, 32 Ill. 75; Coffin *v.* Hill, 1 Heisk. (Tenn.) 385; Dull's Case, 25 Gratt. (Va.) 965; State *v.* Gasting, 23 La. Ann. 609; Hulbert *v.* Carver, 57 Barb. (N. Y.) 62; s. c., 40 Barb. 245. Both the general and the restricted signification are recognized in Phelps *v.* Town, 14 Mich. 379. "In currency," by general usage among merchants and bankers, means in notes current in the community, and is in *contra* distinction to "in specie," which means in coin. Trebilcock *v.* Wilson, 12 Wall. (U. S.) 657.

The term will not include depreciated bank notes. C. F. & M. Ins. Co. *v.* Keiron, 27 Ill. 501; M. & F. Ins. Co. *v.* Tincher, 30 Ill. 399; Osgood *v.* McConnell, 32 Ill. 75; *contra*, Coffin *v.* Hill, 1 Heisk. (Tenn.) 385.

"United States currency," as the subject of larceny, embraces treasury notes and national bank notes. Dull's Case, 25 Gratt. (Va.) 965; State *v.* Gasting, 23 La. Ann. 609.

"Greenback currency" means United States legal tender notes only, and does not include national bank notes. Burton *v.* Brooks, 25 Ark. 215.

4. Bouv. L. D.; Bainbridge *v.* Owen, 2 J. J. Marsh. (Ky.) 464; Wharton *v.* Morris, 1 Dall. (Pa) 124; Lee *v.* Biddis, 1 Dall. (Pa.) 175. And see articles on MONEY and TENDER.

5. Baker *v.* Jordan, 5 Humph. (Tenn.) 485; Moore *v.* Gooch, 6 Heisk. (Tenn.) 104; Osgood *v.* McConnell, 32 Ill. 75. The test of currency is not convertibility. Stalworth *v.* Blunn, 41 Ala. 321; *contra*, Fleming *v.* Nall, 1 Tex. 246; Williams *v.* Annis, 30 Tex. 37.

6. It appeared in evidence that the plaintiff had made a written application to the defendants for insurance "on merchandise" to be laden on board the "Margaret," on a voyage to New Orleans; that he did not specify the merchandise to be

CURTESY.

1. Definition.—Tenancy by the curtesy is an estate for life, created by the act of the law. When a man marries a woman, seised, at any time during the coverture, of an estate of inheritance, in severalty, in coparcenary or in common, and hath issue by her born alive, and which might by possibility inherit the same estate as heir to the wife, and the wife dies in the lifetime of the husband, he holds the land during his life by curtesy.[1]

2. Requisites at Common Law.—To entitle a husband to a tenancy by the curtesy, four requisites must exist; viz., there must be a legal marriage; there must be seisin by the wife during coverture; there must be issue capable of inheriting the estate; the wife must be dead.[2]

shipped, nor was he required by the company so to do. Upon this application, an insurance was effected at three per cent. Under the policy, the plaintiff claimed the value of a *curricle*, which, by the perils of the seas, had sustained damages beyond fifty per cent, and had been sold, after survey, for the benefit of the concerned. It also appeared in evidence that three per cent was the common sea-risk on goods, wares, and merchandise, and that carriages and household furniture could not, at that time, have been insured under from twelve to twenty per cent, on account of the increased risk from the nature of the subject, and that such insurances always contained an express exemption from partial losses. Duplanty *v.* Insurance Co., Anthon (N. Y.), 157.

1. 4 Kent's Com. 13th ed. 25; Litt. § 35; 1 Bishop M. W. § 473; 2 Blackst. 126; Heath *v.* White, 5 Com. 228; Rawlings *v.* Adams, 7 Md. 26; Carrington *v.* Richardson, 79 Ala. 101, 104.

2. Jackson *v.* Johnson, 5 Cow. (N. Y.) 74, 95, 102; s. c., 15 Am. Dec. 433; Hunter *v.* Whitworth, 9 Ala. 967; Furguson *v.* Tweedy, 43 N. Y. 543; Stewart *v.* Ross, 50 Miss. 776; Monroe *v.* Van Meter, 100 Ill. 347; Wheeler *v.* Hotchkiss, 10 Conn. 225; Withers *v.* Jenkins, 14 S. Car. 597; McDaniel *v.* Grace, 15 Ark. 465; Carpenter *v.* Garrett, 75 Va. 129, 133; Winkler *v.* Winkler, 18 W. Va. 455.

The four requisites need not all exist at the same time. So will the birth of living children, after the conveyance by a married woman of land held by her to her sole and separate use, entitle her husband, after her death, to an estate by the curtesy therein. Comer *v.* Chamberlain, 6 Allen (Mass.), 166; Stewart *v.* Ross, 50 Miss. 776.

"If a man taketh a woman, seised of lands in fee, and is disseised and then have issue, and the wife die, he shall enter and hold by the curtesy. So if he hath issue which dieth before the descent." Ld. Coke, 1 Inst. 30 a.; Jackson *v.* Johnson, 5 Cowen (N. Y.), 74, 95; s. c., 15 Am. Dec. 433; Guion *v.* Anderson, 8 Humph. (Tenn.) 307.

Where an illegitimate child under a statute becomes legitimated by the subsequent marriage of the parents, the father will be entitled to an estate by the curtesy at the death of the mother, although no other issue was born. Hunter *v.* Whitworth, 9 Ala. 965.

Where the wife has no seisin in fact in the land in her lifetime, the husband is not entitled to curtesy in it. Carpenter *v.* Garrett, 75 Va. 129.

Where there is no issue, there can exist no right to curtesy. Winkler *v.* Winkler, 18 W. Va. 455.

An alien is not entitled to take as tenant by the curtesy. Hatfield *v.* Sneden, 54 N. Y. 280; Reese *v.* Waters, 4 W. & S. (Pa.) 145; Copeland *v.* Sands, 1 Jones (N. Car.) 70.

Not even where he has declared his intention to become a citizen. Foss *v.* Crisp, 20 Pick. (Mass.) 121.

(*a*) *Marriage.* — The marriage must be a lawful one; though, if it be a voidable one, it will give curtesy, unless it is actually avoided during the life of the wife. It cannot be declared void afterwards.[1]

(*b*) *Seisin.* — To entitle the husband to an estate by the curtesy in the real property of his wife, she must have been seised of it during coverture; but it is not necessary that she should be seised of it at the time of her death, or at the time of the birth of issue.[2]

1. 1 Washb. on Real Prop. 5th ed. 172; Stewart on Husband and Wife, § 153.

The marriage must exist at the time of the death of the wife. A divorce, *a vinculo*, will destroy the husband's right to curtesy. Wheeler *v.* Hotchkiss, 10 Conn. 225; Mattocks *v.* Stearns, 9 Vt. 326.

But in *Alabama* a decree of divorce, *a mensa et thoro*, against the husband will be no bar to his right to curtesy. Smoot *v.* Lecatt, 1 Stew. (Ala.) 590.

2. Mercer *v.* Seldon, 1 How. (U. S.) 37; McDaniel *v.* Grace, 15 Ark. 465; Withers *v.* Jenkins, 14 S. Car. 597; Upchurch *v.* Anderson, 59 Tenn. 410; Haynes *v.* Bourn, 42 Vt. 686; Jackson *v.* Johnson, 5 Cow. (N. Y.) 74; Comer *v.* Chamberlain, 6 Allen (Mass), 166.

A father, who was tenant by the curtesy, sold his interest in his deceased wife's lands, and at the same time, as guardian of his children, sold their interest under an order of the probate court, and invested the whole proceeds in other lands, and took the deed to himself as guardian of the children, and took possession, made valuable improvements on it, and received the rents and profits for many years, and maintained his children. When his daughter had married, she brought ejectment against him for her interest in the land. He set up the above facts, and asked to hold the land for his life in lieu of the tract sold in which he had curtesy. *Held*, that he could not have curtesy in the last tract, because his wife was never seised of it. Bogy *v.* Roberts, 48 Ark. 17.

A female of full age, owning land, sold it by verbal contract, received the price, put the purchaser in possession, but failed to convey until she became a *feme covert* and had issue born alive, when her husband united with her in a conveyance to the purchaser. *Held*, that the husband was not tenant by the curtesy. Welch *v.* Chandler, 13 B. Monr. (Ky.) 420.

But if, on the eve of her marriage, a woman should convey her real estate without the consent of the contemplated husband, it is a fraud on his rights, and void as to him. Hobbs *v.* Blandford, 7 T. B. Monr. (Ky.) 473; Baker *v.* Jordan, 73 N. Car. 145; Johnson *v.* Peterson, 6 Jones, Eq. (N. Car.) 12; Spencer *v.* Spencer, 3 Jones, Eq. (N. Car.) 404; Poston *v.* Gillespie, 5 Jones, Eq. (N. Car.) 258; Goodson *v.* Whitfield, 5 Ired. Eq. (N. Car.) 163; Strong *v.* Menzies, 6 Ired. Eq. (N. Car.) 544; Tisdale *v.* Bailey, 6 Ired. Eq. (N. Car.) 358; Williams *v.* Carle, 10 N. J. Eq. 543; Robinson *v.* Buck, 71 Pa. St. 386.

The seisin must be actual. Actual seisin, or seisin in fact, means possession of the freehold by the *pedis positio* of one's self or one's tenant or agent; or by construction of law, as in case of a commonwealth's grant, a conveyance under the statute of uses; or of grant or devise where there is no actual adverse occupancy. Carpenter *v.* Garrett, 75 Va. 129; Mercer *v.* Selden, 1 How. (U. S.) 37, 54; Haynes *v.* Bourn, 42 Vt 686; Furguson *v.* Tweedy, 43 N. Y. 543; Gibbs *v.* Esty, 22 Hun (N. Y.), 266; Jackson *v.* Johnson, 5 Cow. (N. Y.) 74, 98; s. c., 15 Am. Dec. 433; Bush *v.* Bradley, 4 Day (Conn.), 298; Orr *v.* Hollidays, 9 B. Monr. (Ky.) 59; Adams *v.* Logan, 6 T. B. Monr. (Ky) 179; Petty *v.* Malier, 15 B. Monr. (Ky.) 591; Stinebaugh *v.* Wisdom, 13 B. Monr. (Ky.) 467; Vanarsdall *v.* Fauntleroy, 7 B. Monr. (Ky.) 401; Stevens *v.* Smith, 4 J. J. Marsh. (Ky.) 64; s. c., 20 Am. Dec. 205.

G. died in 1845 intestate, leaving a widow and eight children, all but one infants. By the law, as it then was, until dower was assigned to the widow, she was entitled to remain in the mansion-house and the messuage and plantation thereto belonging, without being charged with paying the heir any rent for the same. Dower was never assigned to the widow; and she remained in possession of the mansion-house and plantation until her death in 1866, cultivating and renting out the land in her own name, and using and disposing of the profits at her own pleasure, her children being with her and supported by her until their death or marriage. H., one of the daughters, married C.; had issue born alive, and died in the lifetime of her mother. Upon a bill by C. to have curtesy in his wife's share of the land, *held*, the wife did not have seisin in fact in the land in her lifetime, and C. was not entitled to curtesy in it. Carpenter *v.* Garrett, 75 Va. 129.

Seisin in law of the wife is not sufficient to invest the husband with an estate as tenant by the curtesy. Nothing short of seisin in fact, or actual seisin, will affect this. Seisin in law is a right to the possession of the freehold, when there is no adverse occupancy thereof, such as exists in the heir after descent of lands upon him before actual entry by himself or his tenant. Carpenter v. Garrett, 75 Va. 129; Fulton v. Johnson, 24 W. Va. 95.

Although it is undoubtedly the general language of the English authorities that only seisin in fact during coverture entitles the husband to an estate by the curtesy, this rule, in its literal strictness, has not been adhered to, either in England or in this country. Jackson v. Johnson, 5 Cow. (N. Y.) 74, 97; s. c., 15 Am. Dec 433; Ellsworth v. Cook, 8 Paige (N. Y.), 643; Merritt v. Horne, 5 Ohio St. 307, 317; s. c., 67 Am. Dec. 298; Borland v. Marshall, 2 Ohio St. 308; Bush v. Bradley, 4 Day (Conn.), 298; Kline v. Beebe, 6 Conn. 494; Wass v. Bucknam, 38 Me. 356; McCorry v. King, 3 Humph. (Tenn.) 267; s. c., 39 Am. Dec. 165; Day v. Cochran, 24 Miss. 261; Stephens v. Hume, 25 Mo. 340; Harvey v. Wickham, 23 Mo. 112; Reaume v. Chambers, 22 Mo. 36; McKee v. Cottle, 6 Mo. App. 416; Stoolfoos v. Jenkins, 8 S. & R. (Pa.) 175; Buchanan v. Duncan, 40 Pa. St. 82; Chew v. Commissioners, 5 Rawle (Pa.), 160.

A husband may be tenant by the curtesy, though the wife was never seised in deed, either actually or constructively, and though the land was adversely held during the coverture by another person. Mitchell v. Ryan, 3 Ohio St. 377.

The doctrine that there must be seisin in deed in the wife, only applies in cases where her title is not complete before entry, as where she takes as heir or devisee, and not where she takes by a conveyance which passes the legal title and seisin of the land Adair v. Lott, 3 Hill (N. Y.), 182; Jackson v. Johnson, 5 Cow. (N. Y.) 74; Ellsworth v. Cook, 8 Paige (N. Y.), 643; Davis v. Mason, 1 Pet. (U. S.) 503.

In order to give a right by the curtesy in the wife's lands, it is not sufficient that the wife was seised of an estate of inheritance therein during the coverture. She must also have a right to the present possession of the freehold. Watkins v. Thornton, 11 Ohio St. 367.

The rigid rules of the common law have never been applied to a wife's estate in "wild" or "waste" lands to enable her husband to acquire a tenancy by the curtesy. Davis v Mason, 1 Pet. (U. S) 503, 506; Barr v. Galloway, 1 McLean (U. S.), 416; Wells v. Thompson, 13 Ala. 793; s c., 48 Am. Dec. 76; McCorry v. King, 3 Humph. (Tenn.) 267; s. c., 39 Am. Dec. 165; Jackson v. Sellick, 8 Johns. (N. Y.) 262; Jackson v. Johnson, 5 Cow. (N. Y.) 74, 102; Mercer v. Selden, 1 How. (U. S.) 37, 49; Day v. Cochran, 24 Miss. 261; Reaume v. Chambers, 22 Mo. 36.

The contrary doctrine was *held* in *Kentucky*. Neely v. Butler, 10 B. Monr. (Ky.) 48; Stinebaugh v. Wisdom, 13 B. Monr. (Ky.) 467.

If a man have a title of entry to lands, but does not enter for fear of bodily harm, and he approach as near the land as he dare, and claim the land as his own, he hath presently by such claim a possession and seisin in the land as if he had entered indeed. And, under some circumstances, living within view of the land will give the feoffee a seisin in deed as fully as if he had made an entry. Co. Litt. §§ 417-419; Mercer v. Selden, 1 How. (U. S.) 37, 54.

Possession by trustee has been *held* to be a sufficient seisin. A *feme sole*, in contemplation of marriage, grants a term of seventy-five years of her real estate to a trustee in trust for her own use during the contemplated coverture. The marriage takes effect, and she has issue, but dies before her husband. *Held*, that the husband was entitled to a tenancy by the curtesy. Lowry v. Steele, 4 Ohio, 170.

The possession of a lessee for years is so far the possession of the person entitled to the inheritance, even before the receipt of rent, as to entitle the husband to curtesy. Jackson v. Johnson, 5 Cow. (N. Y.) 74, 98; Ellsworth v. Cook, 8 Paige (N. Y.), 643; Powell v. Gossom, 18 B. Monr. (Ky.) 179, 192; Vanarsdall v. Fauntleroy. 7 B. Monr. (Ky.) 401; Lowry v. Steele, 4 Ohio, 170; Carter v. Williams, 8 Ired. Eq. (N. Car.) 177; De Grey v. Richardson, 3 Atk. 469.

The receipt of the rents and profits is deemed a sufficient seisin in the wife to entitle the husband to an estate in the land as tenant by the curtesy. Powell v. Gossom, 18 B. Monr. (Ky.) 179, 192; Pitt v. Jackson, 3 Bro. 51; Morgan v. Morgan, 5 Madd. 248.

The chief reason why the husband is required to take the lands of the wife in actual possession, is to strengthen her title to, and protect them from adversary claims and from a hostile possession, which might, by its continuance, endanger her rights, all of which is as fully accomplished by the possession taken of them by the husband's vendee as it would be by a possession taken and held by the husband himself. Vanarsdall v. Fauntleroy, 7 B. Monr. (Ky.) 401.

Where a father conveys land to his married daughter, he, however, continuing in possession and control of it until her death, but not in hostility to her right, she

1. *Remainder.* — In order to give a right by the curtesy in the wife's lands, it is not sufficient that the wife was seised of an estate of inheritance therein during the coverture. She must also have had a right to the present possession of the freehold. Hence it is the well-settled rule of law that a husband cannot be tenant by the curtesy of a remainder, expectant upon an estate for life, unless the latter be determined during the coverture.[1]

(*c*) *Birth.* — Without birth of issue, no estate by the curtesy can exist.[2]

and her husband living with the father on the land, her husband, after her death, leaving a child born alive, is entitled to curtesy, the father being considered to have held the land for her use. Sweeney *v.* Montgomery, 2 S. Western Rep. (Ky.) 562.

A peaceable possession under claim of title, though for less than twenty years, when there has been no abandonment, is sufficient *prima facie* evidence of an estate of inheritance in the wife to give the husband a right to an estate by the curtesy. Smooth *v.* Lecatt, 1 Stew. (Ala.) 590.

Possession of land by the wife as a coparcener will be sufficient. Land descended to several coparceners, one of whom afterward married, had issue, and died: neither she nor her husband had ever lived upon, or exercised any act of ownership over, the land, but it remained in the possession of the other coparceners. *Held*, that this was a sufficient seisin in fact to sustain the husband's claim as tenant by the curtesy. Carr *v.* Givens, 9 Bush (Ky.), 679; s. c., 15 Am. Rep. 747.

But a seisin as joint tenant is not sufficient. 1 Washb. on Real Prop. (5th ed.) 180.

A seisin as tenant in common is. 1 Washb. on Real Prop. (5th ed.) 182.

Where the wife has only the right of preemption in public lands, this is not such a seisin as will give her husband a right to a tenancy by the curtesy. McDaniel *v.* Grace, 15 Ark 465.

A decree of a court settling the rights of husband and wife to the land of the wife, is, as far as the husband's right to curtesy is concerned, equal to actual possession. Ellsworth *v.* Cook, 8 Paige (N. Y.), 643.

A seisin as trustee by a wife of the legal estate is not sufficient to entitle her husband to a tenancy by the curtesy, even if she should become entitled to a reversion of the equitable estate if she dies before the intermediate estate is determined. Chew *v.* Commissioners of Southwark, 5 Rawle (Pa.), 160.

1. Watkins *v.* Thornton, 11 Ohio St. 367; Stoddard *v.* Gibbs, 1 Sumner (U. S.), 263; McKee *v.* Cottle, 6 Mo. App. 416; Mackey *v.* Proctor, 12 B. Monr. (Ky.) 433; Stewart *v.* Barclay, 2 Bush (Ky.), 550; Shores *v.* Carley, 8 Allen (Mass.), 425; Baker *v.* Flournoy, 58 Ala. 650; Planters' Bank *v.* Davis, 31 Ala. 626; Malone *v.* McLaurin, 40 Miss. 161; Redus *v.* Hayden, 43 Miss. 614; Prater *v.* Hoover, 1 Coldw. (Tenn.) 544; Reed *v.* Reed, 3 Head (Tenn.), 491; s. c., 75 Am. Dec. 777; Orford *v.* Benton, 36 N. H. 395; Ferguson *v.* Tweedy, 43 N. Y. 543; Tayloe *v.* Gould, 10 Barb. (N. Y.) 388; Hitner *v.* Ege, 23 Pa. St. 305; Chew *v.* Commissioners, 5 Rawle (Pa.), 160; Upchurch *v.* Anderson, 59 Tenn. 410.

Where a father devised certain lands to his wife until she could raise money to pay a certain debt, but devised the land in fee to his daughter, it was held that the daughter became seised, upon the death of the testator, so as to make her husband a tenant by the curtesy, though the daughter died before the particular estate of the mother had expired. Robertson *v.* Stevens, 1 Ired. Eq. (N. Car.) 247.

2. Winkler *v.* Winkler, 18 W. Va. 455; Ryan *v.* Freeman, 36 Miss. 175; Day *v.* Cochrane, 24 Miss. 261.

The child must be born alive; but, even where it dies immediately after birth, the right to curtesy attaches. Taliaferro *v.* Burwell, 4 Call. (Va.) 321; Heath *v.* White, 5 Conn. 228; Doe *v.* Killen, 5 Del. 14.

And must have been born during the life of the mother. The birth of a child after the mother's death by the Cæsarean operation, though it be born alive, is not sufficient to confer the right. Co. Litt. 29 b.; Marsellis *v.* Thalhimer, 2 Paige (N. Y.), 42; *In re* Winne, 1 Lans. (N. Y.) 508; Ryan *v.* Freeman, 36 Miss. 175

It must have been such a child as by possibility might have inherited the estate. Co. Litt. 29 b.; 1 Greenl Cruise, 143; Heath *v.* White, 5 Conn. 228; Day *v.* Cochran, 24 Miss. 261; Paine's Case, 8 Rep. 34.

Where a wife died intestate, leaving children by a former husband, *held*, that the surviving husband was entitled to an estate as tenant by the curtesy, in so much of her real estate as would by law descend to her children of the second marriage. Kingsley *v.* Smith, 14 Wis 360.

A father left to his three children each a lot of land in fee, and added, "If either (*d*) *Death of Wife.* — 2. *Curtesy Initiate.* — The right of estate by the curtesy is not complete before the death of the wife, although it exists after marriage, birth of issue, and seisin. It is then "initiate" and contingent on the death of the wife.[1]

of these three — M., J., and L. — should die without lawful heirs of their body, the estate shall fall to the other two; if two should die, their estate shall fall to the one; if the one should die without heirs, the estate shall be equally divided between C.'s and A.'s heirs." Two of the children died unmarried, before the father. The other one died afterward, but left no issue, although she had one child born alive. *Held*, that her husband had an estate by the curtesy in the three lots. Crumley *v.* Deake, 8 Baxt. (Tenn.) 361.

A wife's declarations, made shortly after birth of child, that it had been born alive, are not competent evidence to establish her husband's title to an estate by the curtesy. Gardner *v.* Klutts, 8 Jones, L. (N. Car.) 375; s. c., 80 Am. Dec. 331.

In *Pennsylvania*, by statute, the birth of issue is no more required. Lancaster Bank *v.* Stauffer, 10 Pa. St. 399; Dubs *v.* Dubs, 31 Pa. St. 154. See also statutes of *Ohio* and *Oregon*, and Kingsley *v.* Smith, 14 Wisc. 390.

1. Rice *v.* Hoffman, 35 Md. 344; Foster *v.* Marshall, 22 N. H. 491; Winne *v.* Winne, 2 Lans. (N. Y.) 21; Schermerhorn, *v.* Miller, 2 Cow. (N. Y.) 439; Wilson *v.* Arentz, 70 N. Car. 670; Porter *v.* Porter, 27 Gratt. (Va.) 599; Chambers *v.* Handley, 3 J. J. Marsh. (Ky.) 98. See Denny *v.* McCabe, 35 Ohio St. 576.

A tenancy by the curtesy initiate is both salable and assignable. Briggs *v.* Titus, 13 R. I. 136.

The right to curtesy initiate is assignable by the husband for the benefit of his creditors in insolvency proceedings. So, in land devised in trust to pay the income to the testator's wife for life, and at her decease to convey the remainder to such of his children, or their issue, as shall survive her, the husband of a daughter of the testator, after issue born alive, has an equitable tenancy by the curtesy, which will pass by an assignment of his property under the insolvent law during the life of the testator's widow. Gardner *v.* Hooper, 3 Gray (Mass.), 398; Mechanics' Bank *v.* Williams, 17 Pick. (Mass.) 438; Wickes *v.* Clarke, 8 Paige (N. Y.), 161; Van Duzer *v.* Van Duzer, 6 Paige (N. Y.), 366.

The interest of the husband is a legal estate: it is a freehold during the lives of himself and wife, with a freehold in remainder to himself for life, as a tenant by the curtesy, and a remainder to the wife and his heirs, in fee. It is a certain and determinate interest, whose value may be easily ascertained by reference to well-known rules. It is in every sense his "land," and liable to respond for his debts. It may be barred by the statute of limitations. Canby *v.* Porter, 12 Ohio, 79. See Melvin *v.* Proprietors of Locks and Canals, 16 Pick. (Mass.) 161; Lang *v.* Hitchcock, 99 Ill. 550; Rose *v.* Sanderson, 38 Ill. 247; Shortall *v.* Hinckley, 31 Ill. 219; Jacobs *v.* Rice, 33 Ill. 369; Kibbie *v.* Williams, 58 Ill. 30; Clark *v.* Thompson, 47 Ill. 25; Cole *v.* Van Riper, 44 Ill. 58, 66; Winkler *v.* Winkler, 18 W. Va. 455; Day *v.* Cochran, 24 Miss. 261; Plumb *v.* Sawyer, 21 Conn. 351; Roberts *v.* Whiting, 16 Mass. 185, 189; Mattock *v.* Stearns, 9 Vt. 326.

A mortgage by husband and wife, of the wife's real estate for the husband's debts, though held void as to the wife, passes the husband's interest as tenant by the curtesy. Central Bank *v.* Copeland, 18 Md. 305; Boykin *v.* Rain, 28 Ala. 332. See Lang *v.* Hitchcock, 99 Ill. 550, 553.

A wife mortgaged her private property, her husband joining her. The proceeds were used by the husband for his own purposes exclusively, without accounting to his wife, after which he assigned all his property to his creditors. At the wife's death, her mortgaged property was left by will to her son, and sold under foreclosure proceedings, leaving a balance. *Held*, that even if the husband had an interest by curtesy in this balance, the amount of the mortgage which he had used being greater than such interest, it belonged to the heirs in preference to the husband's creditors. Shippen's Appeal, 80 Pa. St. 391.

Where a husband and wife join in mortgaging her land, and, she dying, her interest descended to her sons, from one of whom the husband bought her interest, *held*, the interest so purchased was liable, along with the husband's estate by curtesy, to the mortgage, especially as it appeared that the mortgage contained a clause of general warranty. Edmunds *v.* Leavell, 3 S. Western Rep. (Ky.) 134.

Under the North Carolina statute, a husband, as tenant by the curtesy initiate, cannot dispose of his interest in the estate of his wife; but as he is entitled to the rents and profits during coverture, or until such time as the wife objects to such claims by him, he can dispose thereof. Jones *v.* Carter, 73 N. Car. 148.

A husband's right of curtesy is not forfeited by a conveyance in fee of his interest *a. Not a Vested Right.* — The right of curtesy initiate is not a vested right; and as curtesy consummate is regarded as an estate by descent, and rules of descent are determined by the law as existing at the time of the ancestor's death, it follows that, during the lifetime of the wife, curtesy initiate may be destroyed by statute. But if the statute does not expressly refer to existing rights, it will be applied only to those which arise after its passage.[1]

3. *Curtesy Consummate.* — After the death of the wife, curtesy "initiate" becomes curtesy "consummate." The estate is then vested. It vests by operation of law, and without assignment.[2]

of the estate. Wells *v.* Thompson, 13 Ala. 793; s. c., 48 Am. Dec. 76; Koltenbrock *v.* Cracraft, 36 Ohio St. 584; McKee *v.* Pfout, 3 Dall. (U. S.) 486.

Although it was formerly so held. Koltenbrock *v.* Cracraft, 36 Ohio St. 584, 589; Carpenter *v.* Denoon, 29 Ohio St. 398; French *v.* Rollins, 21 Me. 372.

In case of a sale by the husband of his tenancy by the curtesy, neither the wife during coverture, nor her heirs after her death, had, as against the vendee, a right of entry, for he held in the right of the husband during the continuance of his estate. Koltenbrock *v.* Cracraft, 36 Ohio St. 584; Canby *v.* Porter, 12 Ohio, 80; Thompson *v.* Green, 4 Ohio St. 217; Clarke *v.* Clark, 20 Ohio St. 128; Denny *v.* McCabe, 35 Ohio St. 578; Carpenter *v.* Denoon, 29 Ohio St. 398; Borland *v.* Marshall, 2 Ohio St. 308; Gillespie *v.* Worford, 2 Coldw. (Tenn.) 641; King *v.* Nutall, 7 Baxt. (Tenn.) 226; Vanarsdall *v.* Fauntleroy, 7 B. Monr. (Ky.) 401.

A husband cannot, to defraud his creditors, transfer his right of tenancy by the curtesy to his wife, and a court of equity will not interfere in her behalf as against his creditors. Van Duzer *v.* Van Duzer, 6 Paige (N. Y.) 366; Wickes *v.* Clarke, 8 Paige (N. Y.), 161.

In the absence of a fraud, a husband who is embarrassed may convey his curtesy in the real estate of his wife to trustees for her benefit, and for the benefit of their children, when a consideration is received for it which a court of equity may fairly take to be a valuable one. This indebtedness to her is such a valuable consideration, although he may at the time be also indebted to others. Hitz *v.* Nat. Metrop. Bank, 111 U. S. 722.

1. Porter *v.* Porter, 27 Gratt. (Va.) 599; Strong *v.* Clem, 12 Ind. 37; s. c., 74 Am. Dec. 200; Withers *v.* Jenkins, 14 S. Car. 597; Hill *v.* Chambers, 30 Mich. 422; Hathon *v.* Lyon, 2 Mich. 93; Brown *v.* Clark, 44 Mich. 309; Winne *v.* Winne, 2 Lans. (N. Y.) 21; Thurber *v.* Townsend, 22 N. Y. 517; Stewart *v.* Ross, 50 Miss. 776; Denny *v.* McCabe, 35 Ohio St. 576; Ind., Bloom. & West R. Co. *v.* McLaughlin, 77 Ill. 275; Mellinger *v.* Bausman, 45 Pa. St. 522; Kingsley *v.* Smith, 14 Wis. 390; Porter *v.* Bowers, 55 Md. 213; Rice *v.* Hoffman, 35 Md. 344; Watson *v.* Watson, 13 Conn. 83.

The *Michigan* revised statutes of 1846, in creating a statutory estate by the curtesy, did not in any manner interfere with the wife's absolute control of the property during her lifetime, or with her right to dispose of it, but only subjected it after her death to the interest of the surviving husband as a limitation upon the inheritance. The legislative power to subject any existing estate to the rights of tenancy by curtesy is the same as the power to modify the rules of descent for the subsequent transmission of property, and do not interfere with any constitutional right of the wife. Brown *v.* Clark, 44 Mich. 309.

If a woman, being seised of real estate, married, and a child was born of the marriage before the Married Woman's Act of 1861 took effect, the husband will have an estate in her lands for his life; but if the child was born after such law took effect, he will have an estate during coverture, and in either case his estate may be sold on execution. Lang *v.* Hitchcock, 99 Ill. 550.

A statute enacting that the property of a married woman shall not be liable for the debts of her husband, exempts his estate in the curtesy in her real estate from being taken for his debts contracted after the passage of the act. Hitz *v.* Metropolitan Bank, 111 U. S. 722.

To the possession of land given to a wife by her father in 1840, the husband, having children by the wife, became entitled *jure uxoris*, and to the pernancy of profits during their joint lives, and as tenant by the curtesy upon her death, if he should survive her; and this title was not divested by the Act of 1841, ch. 161, or by the provisions of the Code of 1860. Porter *v.* Bowers, 55 Md. 213.

2. Wheeler *v.* Hotchkiss, 10 Conn. 225; Watson *v.* Watson, 13 Conn. 83; Oldham *v.* Henderson, 5 Dana (Ky.), 254; Rice *v.*

3. In what Property does Curtesy exist. — The right of tenancy by the curtesy can exist only in real estate. When, however, money is treated in equity as real estate, the husband may have the interest thereof as curtesy.[1]

Hoffman, 35 Md. 344; Denny v. McCabe, 35 Ohio St. 576; Foster v. Marshall, 22 N. H. 491; Winne v. Winne, 2 Lans. (N. Y.) 21; Marsellis v. Thalhimer, 2 Paige (N. Y.), 35; Stewart v. Ross, 50 Miss. 776, 791; Witham v. Perkins, 2 Me. 400.

Before issue born, husband and wife in her right are jointly seised during their joint lives of a freehold in her fee-simple lands. After issue born alive, in such lands he becomes tenant by the curtesy initiate, and holds an estate therein in his own right, which, after her death, *illo vivente*, becomes an estate by the curtesy consummate. Breeding v. Davis, 77 Va. 639; s. c., 46 Am. Rep. 740.

When the estate by the curtesy is once vested by the death of the wife, the husband cannot by disclaimer divest himself of it. Watson v. Watson, 13 Conn. 85.

The estate partaking of the nature of an inheritance, and not of a sale, is subject to all equities subsisting in respect to it as against the wife. Coleman v. Waples, 1 Harr. (Del.) 196; Willis v. Snelling, 6 Rich. (S. Car.) 280; Watson v. Watson, 13 Conn. 83, 86; Forbes v. Sweezey, 8 Neb. 520; Winne v. Winne, 2 Lans. (N. Y.) 21.

Where a right of tenancy by the curtesy attaches, and the land is in the possession of another, the surviving husband has a right of action to recover the possession thereof. Hall v. Hall, 32 Ohio St. 184.

And so can one claiming lands as heir of his mother recover no judgment in ejectment against an occupant who entered under the father, while there is an outstanding estate for life in the latter as tenant by the curtesy. Grout v. Townsend, 2 Hill (N. Y.), 554; Miller v. Bledsoe, 61 Mo. 96.

A tenant by the curtesy may convey his title; but his deed of bargain and sale conveys no greater estate than he held himself. Meraman v. Caldwell, 8 B. Monr. (Ky.) 32; s. c., 46 Am. Dec. 537; Koltenbrock v. Cracraft, 36 Ohio St. 584, 590; Flagg v. Bean, 25 N. H. 49.

A tenant by the curtesy has a right to reasonable estovers, which is confined strictly to timber and wood for the use of the estate; and it must be actually applied, used, and consumed on the estate, or with its proper use and enjoyment. Armstrong v. Wilson, 60 Ill. 226.

But he has no right to commit waste. Weise v. Welsh, 30 N. J. Eq. 431.

The executors of a wife cannot maintain a bill against the executors of her husband, who survived her, for waste in cutting trees on her lands, which he occupied as tenant by the curtesy after her death, on the ground of equitable conversion, nor for an account of the proceeds of such trees. Recovery can only be had at law. Lippincott v. Barton, 42 N. J. Eq. 272.

Tenant by curtesy cannot maintain a writ of right. Lecatt v. Merchants' Ins. Co., 16 Ala. 177; s. c., 50 Am Dec. 169.

1. 2 Black. Com. 126; 1 Greenl. Cruise, 140; Davis v. Mason, 1 Pet. (U. S.) 503, 508; Sweetapple v. Bindon, 2 Vern. 536; Houghton v. Hapgood, 13 Pick. (Mass.) 154.

A tenant by the curtesy is entitled to interest for life on the proceeds of lands devised to his wife, and sold after her death by the executors of the devisor under a direction in the will. Dunscomb v. Dunscomb, 1 Johns. Ch. (N. Y.) 508; s. c., 7 Am. Dec. 504.

The proceeds arising from the sale of real estate belonging to the wife, under a decree for partition, stand in the place of the real estate, and only so much of the proceeds as may be allowed to the husband in lieu of his interest as tenant by the curtesy is liable to his creditors upon the death of the wife. Rice v. Hoffman, 35 Md. 344.

A husband may have an estate by the curtesy in lands which were conveyed by him to his wife as a gift; and such interest may be taken by his creditors. Robie v. Chapman, 59 N. H. 41.

Curtesy can arise only out of estates of inheritance. Sumner v. Partridge, 2 Atk. 47; Boothby v. Vernon, 9 Mod. 147; Simmons v. Gooding, 5 Ired. Eq. (N. Car.) 382.

And arises equally whether the fee is absolute or determinable. Paine's Case, 8 Coke, 67, 68; Thornton v. Krepps, 37 Pa. St. 391; Withers v. Jenkins, 14 S. Car. 597.

The prevailing opinion of the courts is, that curtesy continues after a determinable fee has determined, although the decisions are not uniform. Mason v. Johnson, 47 Md. 347, 357; Hatfield v. Sneden, 54 N. Y. 284; Graves v. Trueblood, 1 S. East. Rep. 918; Northcut v. Whipp, 12 B. Monr. (Ky.) 65, 71; Thornton v. Knapp, 37 Pa. St 391; Evans v. Evans, 9 Pa. St. 391; Taliaferro v. Burwell, 4 Call. (Va.) 321; Withers v. Jenkins, 14 S. Car. 597; Buckworth v. Thirkell, 3 Bos. & P. 652 n.; Moody v (*a*) *Equitable Estates.* — The right to a tenancy by the curtesy is not confined to legal estates. "A husband is entitled to curtesy in equitable estates of inheritance of the wife in possession."[1]

(*b*) *Wife's Separate Estate.* — It has been held that a husband cannot be tenant by the curtesy of the separate real estate of the wife.[2]

But the better opinion seems to be, that, all the requisites concurring, the husband may be tenant by the curtesy of his wife's separate real estate, notwithstanding he is cut off from any participation in the rents and profits during coverture. But if the purpose to cut him off from the curtesy be clearly expressed in the instrument of settlement, then his right is gone, although formerly this could not be done at law.[3]

King, 2 Bing 447; Smith *v.* Spencer, 6 De Gex, M. & G. 632.

1. Rawlings *v.* Adams, 7 Md. 26, citing 1 Bright on Husband and Wife, 120, 135. See also Lowry *v.* Steele, 4 Ohio, 170; Houghton *v.* Hapgood, 13 Pick. (Mass.) 154; Gardner *v.* Hooper, 3 Gray (Mass.) 398, 404; Cushing *v.* Blake, 30 N. J. Eq. 689; Carrington *v* Richardson, 79 Ala. 101, 105; Robison *v.* Codman, 1 Sumn. (U. S.) 128; Withers *v.* Jenkins, 14 S. Car. 597; Phillips *v.* Ditto, 2 Duv. (Ky) 549; Dugan *v.* Gittings, 3 Gill (Md), 138; s. c., 43 Am. Dec. 306; Sentill *v.* Robeson, 2 Jones, Eq. (N. C.) 510; Taylor *v.* Smith, 54 Miss 50; Alexander *v.* Warrance, 17 Mo. 228; Tremmel *v.* Kleiboldt, 6 Mo. App. 549; Dubs *v.* Dubs, 31 Pa. St. 149; Nightingale *v.* Hidden, 7 R. I. 115; Baker *v.* Heiskell, 1 Coldw. (Tenn.) 641.

A testator directed that the income of one-half of his estate should be paid to his widow during her life, and that upon her death such half should be divided equally among her children absolutely, in fee forever, and that the income of the other half should be divided among his children, until the youngest child should be of age, and then that such half should be divided among his children absolutely in fee forever. *Held*, that the children took a vested remainder in fee, subject to the restrictions contained in the will, and that the husband of a daughter who died having issue born alive was entitled to a tenancy by curtesy in it. Young *v.* Langbein, 7 Hun (N. Y.), 151.

An estate by the curtesy is not incident to a life estate. A deed by a husband conveying land in trust for the benefit of his wife and the heirs of her body born in wedlock with the said husband, creates an estate in fee-tail special, which by a statute in *Missouri*, abolishing estates in fee-tail, is converted into a life estate in the wife with remainder in fee to the heirs named in the deed, who, upon the death of the mother, are entitled to the possession of the premises. It is not in the power of the father or mother, or both together, to do more in such case than dispose of her life estate. Phillips *v.* La Forge, 89 Mo. 72.

2. Bottoms *v.* Corley, 5 Heisk. (Tenn.) 6; Grimball *v* Patton, 70 Ala. 626, 635; Randall *v.* Schrader, 20 Ala. 338; Mayfield *v.* Clifton, 3 Stew. (Ala.) 375; Bibb *v.* McKinley, 9 Port. (Ala.) 636; Bradford *v.* Howell, 42 Ala. 422; Stewart *v.* Stewart, 31 Ala. 207; Lockhart *v.* Cameron, 29 Ala. 355, 363; Vanderveer *v.* Alston, 16 Ala. 494; Welch *v.* Welch, 14 Ala. 76, 83; Andrews *v.* Jones, 10 Ala. 400, 422; Machen *v.* Machen, 15 Ala. 373; s. c., 38 Ala. 364; Cheek *v.* Waldrum, 25 Ala. 152; Brevard *v.* Jones, 50 Ala. 221.

3. Carter *v.* Dale, 3 Lea (Tenn.), 710; s. c., 31 Am. Rep. 660; Stovall *v.* Austin, 16 Lea (Tenn.), 700; Baker *v* Heiskell, 1 Cold. (Tenn.) 642; Frazer *v.* Hightower, 12 Heisk. (Tenn.) 94; Beecher *v.* Hicks, 7 Lea (Tenn.), 207; Cooney *v.* Woodburn, 33 Md. 320; Jones *v.* Brown, 1 Md. Ch. 191; Ege *v.* Medlar, 82 Pa. St. 86; Stokes *v.* McKibbin, 13 Pa. St. 267; Cochran *v.* O'Hern, 4 Watts & S. (Pa.) 95; s. c., 39 Am. Dec. 60; Rigler *v.* Cloud, 14 Pa. St. 361; Talbot *v.* Calvert, 24 Pa. St. 327, Wightman's Appeal, 29 Pa. St. 280; Kimball *v.* Kimball, 2 Miss. 532; De Hart *v.* Dean, 2 McArthur (D. C.), 60; Mitchell *v.* Moore, 16 Gratt. (Va.) 275; Sayers *v.* Wall, 26 Gratt. (Va.) 354; Payne *v.* Payne, 11 B. Monr. (Ky.) 138; Hart *v.* Soward, 14 B. Monr. (Ky.) 243; Neelly *v.* Lancaster, 47 Ark. 175; Tremmell *v.* Kleiboldt, 6 Mo. App. 549; Tillinghast *v.* Coggeshall, 7 R. I. 383; Carrington *v.* Richardson, 79 Ala. 106; Smoot *v.* Lecatt, 1 Stew. (Ala.) 590; 4 Kent, Com. 31, 32; 1 Washb. on Real Prop. 151.

Where a testator provided in his will that no part of the property given to his married daughter should ever, in any event, be liable, in whole or in part,

4. How barred. — A husband may by an agreement with his wife, entered into either before or after marriage, relinquish his right to tenancy by the curtesy.[1]

5. Curtesy by Statutes. — In some States the right of curtesy is expressly abolished by statute, in others retained as it was at common law, in others not mentioned in the statutes, while in

towards the payment of any debt of her husband, but that all of it should be held and kept free from such liability, it was *held*, that, by necessary implication, the husband of the devisee was excluded from any estate by the curtesy, even if that had not been abolished by statute. Monroe *v.* Van Meter, 100 Ill. 347.

Where a husband settled real estate upon his wife by conveyance to a trustee, and allowed her, her heirs and assigns, to have the occupation, possession, and enjoyment of the property, it was *held*, that, upon the death of the wife, the husband was entitled to take the property as a tenant by curtesy Frazer *v.* Hightower, 12 Heisk. (Tenn.) 94. See also Cushing *v.* Blake, 29 N. J. Eq. 399; 30 N. J. Eq. 689; Curtis *v.* Fox, 47 N. Y. 299. *Compare* Sayers *v.* Wall, 26 Gratt. (Va.) 354.

A husband cannot be tenant by the curtesy of real estate conveyed to the wife for her sole and separate use and with power of disposal, where she had disposed of it by will duly executed and attested, or by conveyance. Pool *v.* Blakie, 53 Ill. 495; Stokes *v.* McKibbin, 13 Pa. St. 267; Neelly *v.* Lancaster, 47 Ark. 175.

1. Waters *v.* Tazewell, 9 Md. 291; Hutchins *v.* Dixon, 11 Md. 29, 37; Sayers *v.* Wall, 26 Gratt. (Va.) 354; Rochon *v.* Lecott, 2 Stew. (Ala.) 429.

Where, by a decree in equity, a deed of a woman's land to her intended husband is executed before marriage is annulled, the husband's curtesy will not be affected by the conveyance. Gilmore *v.* Burch, 7 Oreg. 374; s c., 33 Am. Rep. 710.

Where a husband joins his wife in conveying her real estate, he releases his right to curtesy: so does a conveyance, under a power of attorney, by husband and wife, of all the right, title, and interest of the husband and wife in land, pass the estate by curtesy of the husband, and the children of the wife cannot sue for the land after the death of the wife and during the life of the husband. Jackson *v.* Hodges, 2 Tenn. Ch. 276. See also Stewart *v.* Ross, 50 Miss. 776.

Where a husband and wife convey the land of the wife, and the husband agrees to invest the proceeds in land for the use of the children of the wife by a former husband, the husband has no curtesy in the land thus purchased; and if, in violation of his agreement, he takes the title to himself, a court of equity will enforce the trust in favor of his step-children, and will require him to account for rents and profits, even during the lifetime of the wife. Carpenter *v.* Davis, 72 Ill. 14.

A sale by the wife without the husband will not defeat his right to curtesy, even where the consideration for the conveyance is a note held by the purchaser against the husband. Houck *v.* Ritter, 76 Pa. St. 280.

But where a married woman has leased her separate property, and she dies before the term of the lease has expired, the lessee will have a right to the possession of the premises until the end of his term, notwithstanding the husband's right to curtesy. Forbes *v.* Sweezey, 8 Nebr. 520

A sale under legal process of the wife's lands for her debts, defeats the husband's right of curtesy. Stewart *v.* Ross, 50 Miss. 776.

But where land was sold under an order of the orphan's court, without making the tenant by the curtesy a party to the sale, the sale was held to be subject to the curtesy. Jacques *v.* Ennis, 25 N. J. Eq. 402.

A divorce *a vinculo* obtained by the wife against her husband, bars his right to curtesy. Wheeler *v.* Hotchkiss, 10 Conn. 225, Starr *v.* Pease, 8 Conn. 541; Schoch *v.* Schoch, 33 Pa. St. 351; Hays *v.* Sanderson, 7 Bush (Ky.), 489; Oldham *v.* Henderson, 5 Dana (Ky.), 256; Emmert *v.* Hays, 89 Ill. 11; Howey *v.* Goings, 13 Ill 95; Clarke *v.* Lott, 11 Ill. 105; Barber *v.* Root, 10 Mass. 260; Porter *v.* Porter, 27 Gratt. (Va.) 599; Boykin *v.* Rain, 28 Ala. 332; Gould *v.* Webster, 1 Tyler (Vt.), 409; Mattock *v.* Stearns, 9 Vt. 326; Doe *v.* Brown, 5 Blackf. (Ind.) 309; Renwick *v.* Renwick, 10 Paige (N. Y.), 420. *Compare* Gillespie *v.* Worford, 2 Cold. (Tenn.) 632

The husband's right of curtesy may be barred by the conditions contained in the deed conveying the property. Hutchins *v.* Dixon, 11 Md. 30; Waters *v.* Tazewell, 9 Md. 291; Townshend *v.* Matthews, 10 Md. 251; Marshall *v.* Beall, 6 How. (U. S.) 70; Stokes *v.* McKibbin, 13 Pa. St. 267.

So may it be barred by the statute of limitations. Thompson *v.* Green, 4 Ohio St. 216; Carter *v.* Cantrell, 16 Ark. 154; Shortall *v.* Hinckley, 31 Ill. 219; Kibbie *v.* Williams, 58 Ill. 30; Weisinger *v.* Murphy, 2 Head (Tenn.), 674.

other States the common-law rights are greatly modified. Where the right of curtesy is expressly abolished, the statute generally makes another provision for the husband, as where the husband has a right of dower in his wife's estate, the same as the wife has in his estate.[1]

(*a*) *Married Women Acts.* — It has been held that the acts relative to the protection of the rights of married women entirely abrogate the existence of prospective tenancy by the curtesy. Every quality and incident that is necessary to constitute such a tenancy is destroyed by the provisions of these acts.[2]

The law seems now, however, to be substantially settled, that, while those acts excluded the husband during life from control of, or interference with, his wife's real and personal estate, and gave to her alone the power of disposition by deed or will; yet they left the husband the right of curtesy in her real property in so much as remained, at her death, undisposed of and unbequeathed.[3]

1. See the statutes of the various States. Stewart on Husband and Wife, § 160; Stimson, Am. Stat. Law, § 3300 *et seq.*

A statute giving the right of curtesy does not do away with any of the common-law requisites except when expressly mentioned. Winkler *v.* Winkler, 18 W. Va. 455.

And where the statutes neither give nor abolish the right of curtesy, the common-law rule prevails. Reaume *v.* Chambers, 22 Mo. 36; Denny *v.* McCabe, 35 Ohio St. 576; Neelly *v.* Lancaster, 47 Ark. 175.

2. Tong *v.* Marvin, 15 Mich. 60; White *v.* Zane, 10 Mich. 333; Hill *v.* Chambers, 30 Mich. 422; Billings *v.* Baker, 28 Barb. (N. Y.) 343; Thurber *v.* Townsend, 22 N. Y. 517; Gaffney *v.* Peeler, 21 S. Car. 55; Frost *v.* Frost, 21 S. Car. 501.

3. Hatfield *v.* Sneden, 54 N. Y. 280, 287; Ransom *v.* Nichols, 22 N. Y. 110; Bertles *v.* Nunan, 92 N. Y. 160; *In re* Winne, 2 Lans. (N. Y.) 21; Barnes *v.* Underwood, 47 N. Y. 351; Burke *v.* Valentine, 52 (Barb.) N. Y. 412; *Re* Leach, 21 Hun (N. Y.), 381; Zimmerman *v.* Schoenfeldt, 6 Th. & C. (N. Y.) 142; Kingsley *v.* Smith, 14 Wis. 390; Robinson *v.* Eagle, 29 Ark. 202; Neelly *v.* Lancaster, 47 Ark. 175; Luntz *v.* Greve, 102 Ind. 173; Martin *v.* Robson, 65 Ill. 129; Cole *v.* Van Riper, 44 Ill 58; Noble *v.* McFarland, 51 Ill. 226; Armstrong *v.* Wilson, 60 Ill. 226; Wolf *v.* Wolf, 67 Ill. 55; Davenport *v.* Karnes, 70 Ill. 465; Anderson *v.* Tydings, 8 Md. 427; Rice *v.* Hoffman, 35 Md. 344; Leggett *v.* McClelland, 39 Ohio St. 624; Winkler *v.* Winkler, 18 W. Va. 455; Houck *v.* Ritter, 76 Pa. St. 280; Stewart *v.* Ross, 50 Miss. 776; Prall *v.* Smith, 31 N. J. L. 244; Johnson *v.* Cummins, 16 N. J. Eq. 97; Porch *v.* Fries, 18 N. J. Eq. 204; Morris *v.* Morris, 94 N. Car. 613; Houston *v.* Brown, 7 Jones, L. (N. Car.) 161.

By the Married Woman's Act, the wife's property is her separate estate, which she may possess, enjoy, and devise as if *sole*; the husband must unite with her in alienating it; and if he refuse, the court will, if of opinion that her interests will be benefited thereby, cause the absolute title thereto to be conveyed. No interest or estate in the wife's lands vests in husband during the coverture. But if, after issue born alive, he survive her, he has an estate by the curtesy in the *fee-simple* lands of which she was seised, but made no alienation during the coverture. The act only protects the estate of the wife during her life, but does not after her death affect the law of succession as to her real or personal property. Breeding *v.* Davis, 77 Va. 639; s. c., 46 Am. Rep. 740.

A statute permitting a married woman to devise her separate estate as if she were a *feme sole* abolishes the common-law curtesy. The proviso, "if she die intestate," etc., only leaves her husband a life estate in such property as she would have had a right to bequeath. Mason *v.* Johnson, 47 Md. 347.

Under a statute providing that, "Any estate or interest, legal or equitable, in real property belonging to any woman at her marriage, or which may have come to her during coverture, by conveyance, gift, devise, or inheritance, or by purchase with her separate means or money, shall, together with all rents and issues thereof, be and remain her separate property, and under her control; and she may, in her own name, during coverture, lease the same for any period not exceeding three years. This act shall not affect the estate by the curtesy of any husband in the real

CURTILAGE. (See ARSON;[1] BURGLARY; HOUSE; LAND; MESSUAGE.) — A court-yard adjoining a house or messuage, or any piece of ground lying near, enclosed and used with the house, and necessary for its convenient occupation.[2]

property of his wife after her decease; but during the life of such wife, or any heir of her body, such estate shall not be taken by any process of law for the payment of his debts, or be conveyed or incumbered by him, unless she shall join therein with him in the manner prescribed by law in regard to her own estate." It was *held*, that the estate could not be incumbered by the husband after the death of the wife, but during the life of her children. Robert *v.* Sliffe, 41 Ohio St. 225.

The consent by a husband that his wife may devise her real estate to her child by a former marriage does not estop him from asserting title, after her death, to one-third of the premises as given to him by statute. Roach *v.* White, 94 Ind. 510, citing O'Hara *v.* Stone, 48 Ind. 417; Adamson *v.* Lamb, 3 Blackf. (Ind.) 446.

Where, by statute, a limitation is made on the right of a surviving husband to curtesy in his deceased wife's real estate in favor of her issue or legal representative of such issue by a *former marriage*, it was *held*, that the right to curtesy secured by said statute cannot be affected or defeated by showing that the deceased wife left *illegitimate issue*, who, under the same statute, inherited her estate. Bruner *v.* Briggs, 39 Ohio St. 478.

Where a woman, having no children by her surviving husband, died, leaving issue by a former marriage and an estate which did not come to her from her surviving husband or his ancestors, *held*, that under a statute providing that "surviving husbands, whether there be issue born during the coverture or not, shall be entitled to the estate of their deceased wives by the curtesy, provided, however, that if any deceased wife shall leave issue or legal representative of such issue by a former marriage, her surviving husband shall not be entitled to an estate by the curtesy in the interest of such issue or the legal representatives of such issue in her estate, unless the estate came to the deceased wife by deed of gift from the surviving husband, or by devise or deed of gift from his ancestors," the surviving husband is not entitled to curtesy in her estate, notwithstanding she had devised the same to her grandchildren. Tilden *v.* Barker, 40 Ohio St. 411. See also Denny *v.* McCabe, 35 Ohio St. 576.

U., having a daughter by a former husband, married K., by whom she also had a child. After her marriage with K., and before the birth of her second child, she acquired by grant, and became seised in fee of certain real estate. Her child by K. died, and afterward she died, leaving K. and her daughter by her first husband surviving her. *Held*, that under the statute K. was not tenant by the curtesy of the land his wife died seised of, which descended on her death to her daughter by her first husband. Hathon *v.* Lyon, 2 Mich. 94.

Where the statute gives a married woman power to alienate her property, she can defeat the right of curtesy by deed or by will, but the statute must give her expressly the right to convey alone. Porch *v.* Fries, 18 N. J. Eq. 204; Silsby *v.* Bullock, 10 Allen (Mass.), 94; Cole *v.* Van Riper, 44 Ill. 58; Stewart *v.* Ross, 50 Miss. 776; Bagley *v.* Fletcher, 44 Ark. 153; Milwee *v.* Milwee, 44 Ark. 112; Roberts *v.* Wilcoxon, 36 Ark. 355.

1. Washington *v.* State, 3 So. Rep. 357.

2. People *v.* Gedney, 10 Hun (N. Y.), 154.

A curtilage is uncertain in extent. It "seems to connect itself with buildings or messuages, and means the grounds which properly appertain to them, whether they be enclosed within one hundred feet square in a city, or whether they are enclosed within the court, grounds, or park attached to and appertaining to a country-seat, whether the contents be two acres, ten acres, or a hundred acres." Accordingly, where it is requisite that a mechanic's lien contain a description of the building and lot or curtilage, against which it is filed, sufficient to identify the same, it is not fatal to the lien that the description covers too large a quantity of land. Edwards *v.* Derrickson, 4 Dutch. (N. J.) 39.

Under an act prohibiting the use of abusive, vulgar, or insulting language in the dwelling-house of another, upon the curtilage thereof, or upon the adjoining highway, enclosure is not requisite to constitute a piece of ground a curtilage "It is the propinquity to the dwelling, and the use in connection with it for family purposes, which the statute regards, and not the fact of enclosure." Ivey *v.* State, 61 Ala. 58.

Curtilage has reference to dry land only: a lot under the water of a river is not such within the meaning of a mechanic's lien law. Coddington *v.* Dock Co., 2 Vr. (N. J.) 477.

CURVE. See note.[1]

CUSPADORE.[2]

CUSTODY.—Of persons, imprisonment;[3] of things, such a relation towards them as would constitute possession, if the person having custody had it on his own account.[4]

CUSTOM. (See REVENUE LAWS; USAGES AND CUSTOMS.)—1. Frequent repetition of the same act; way of acting; ordinary manner; habitual practice; usage.[5] 2. Habitual buying of goods; practice of frequenting; as a shop, manufactory, etc.[6]

CUSTOMARY.[7]

Land which is convenient to the occupation of a house is a curtilage, so as to be a part of the house, under an act which provides that no one shall be compelled to sell or convey a part only of any house or building, if he shall be willing to sell or convey the whole. Marson *v.* L. C. & D. Ry. Co., L. R. 6 Eq. 101.

1. Where the general course of a railroad track is curved, it is "a curved line," although a short piece taken alone is straight; and the laying of such a piece is in compliance with an enactment that four companies should join in the construction of the tract between two points "extending a curved line." Worcester *v.* Railroad Comrs., 113 Mass. 161.

2. The fact that one patent is granted for a cuspadore, and the other for a spittoon, is of no importance, as the difference is merely of form, and the form itself is old. Ingersoll *v.* Turner, 12 Off. Pat. Gaz. 189.

3. Smith *v.* Comm., 59 Pa. St. 320, where a sentence that one be in custody until he paid a fine and costs and other charges, was *held* to be a sentence to imprisonment, so that a discharge rendered the keeper of the prison liable.

4. Stephen's Cr. Dig. art. 281, 311.

Money intrusted to a solicitor for investment is not intrusted for "safe custody" within the meaning of a larceny act. Queen *v.* Newman, 8 Q. B. D. 706.

It is a sufficient compliance with an act requiring the jury wheel to remain in the custody of the county commissioners, and the keys to be in the custody of the sheriff, to deposit the wheel in a vault in the commissioners' office, under the control of their clerk, and for the sheriff to keep the keys in a desk in his office, which was not always locked, and to which his deputy had access. Rolland *v.* Comm., 82 Pa. St. 306.

Custody of the Law.—Property is in the custody of the law when it has been taken and is held by legal process in a lawful manner and for a lawful purpose. Gilman *v.* Williams, 7 Wis. 329.

5. Web. Dict.; Rapalje & Lawrence's Law Dict.

The distinction between *custom* and prescription is, that the former is common to many, the latter is peculiar to an individual. Burrill's Law Dict. The distinction between a usage of trade and a common-law custom has not always been observed. A custom is something which has by its universality and antiquity acquired the force and effect of law in a particular place or country, in respect to the subject-matter to which it relates, and is ordinarily taken notice of without proof. Thus, when a payee indorses his name on the back of a promissory note, the law, by force of a pervading and universal custom, imports a well-recognized contract into the transaction. Smythe *v.* Scott, 106 Ind. 245; 6 N. E. Rep. 145; Walls *v.* Bailey, 49 N. Y. 466; Hursh *v.* North, 40 Pa. St. 241; Munn *v.* Burch, 25 Ill. 41; Morningstar *v.* Cunningham, 11 N. E. Rep. 494.

6. Web. Dict.

"Good *custom* cowhide boots, etc." Wait *v.* Fairbanks, Brayt. (Vt.) 77.

7. Supposing that the words, "as customary at port of loading," refer to the manner of signing, there is nothing to take away from the defendants their liability. But supposing that those words mean that the master is to sign a bill of lading in the customary form, then the words, "without prejudice to the stipulation of this charter party," prevent it having any effect at variance with the effect of the charter party. Rodocanachi Sons & Co. *v.* Milburn Bros., 56 L. T. (N. S.) 597.

A charter party provided that the vessel to be loaded with lumber should have "customary despatch" in discharging her cargo at New York, and fixed the demurrage for each day's detention by the default of the charterers. *Held*, that such "despatch" meant in accordance with, or consistently with, all known and well-established usages of the port, that charterers were bound to find her a berth where the cargo could be discharged with "custom-

CUSTOM DUTIES. See REVENUE LAWS.

CUSTOMER. A buyer; a purchaser; one who frequents any place of sale for the sake of purchasing or ordering goods.[1]

CUT. — The word *cut* imports a wound with an instrument having an edge.[2]

CY PRES. See CHARITIES AND CHARITABLE ASSOCIATIONS.

DAILY.[3]

ary despatch," and without interruption during customary hours, and was liable for the detention at the agreed rate of demurrage, caused by failure so to do. Smith *v.* Yellow Pine Lumber, 2 Fed. Rep. 396.

Customary, a book containing laws and usages, or customs; as the *customary* of the Normans. Cowell.

1. Web. Dict.

"But we must give to the word 'customer' a reasonable interpretation, and one as nearly as possible in accordance with the expressed intention of the parties. The information would be required as much in the case of an intending customer as an actual customer. Indeed, it would be more requisite in the case of an intending than an actual customer. For these reasons we think the word 'customers,' as used in the notice in front of the book furnished to each subscriber, means intending or actual customers." M'Lean *v.* Dun *et al.*, 39 U. C. Q. B. R. 562.

2. State *v.* Patza, 3 La. Ann. 514. Whereas "*stab* imports a wound made with a pointed instrument."

Where a cutting is inflicted by an instrument *capable of cutting*, the case is within the statute, though the instrument is not intended for cutting, nor ordinarily used to cut. Rex *v.* Hayward. 1 Russ. & Ry. 78.

A striking over the face with the sharp or claw part of a hammer *held* to be a sufficient *cutting* within the statute. Rex *v.* Atkinson, 1 Russ. & Ry. 104.

An indictment for "striking and cutting" is not supported by evidence of "stabbing." Rex *v.* M'Dermot, 1 Russ. & Ry. 356.

Cut down. — *Cutting down* a tree, though it is not thereby totally *destroyed*, is sufficient to bring the case within a statute prohibiting "cutting down or otherwise destroying" trees. Rex *v.* Taylor, 1 Russ. & Ry. 373.

Cut off. — Biting off the end of a person's nose or finger-joint does not come within the offence of "stabbing, cutting, or wounding." Rex *v.* Harris, 7 C. & P. 446.

But see State *v.* Mairs, 1 Coxe (N. J.), 457, where it is said, "The substance of the crime charged upon the defendants, is the wilfully and deliberately cutting off the nose; and whether this is effected by one instrument or another is perfectly immaterial. I think I may go farther, and say, if the party deliberately and with the intention of biting off the nose of another, watches his opportunity, and effects his purpose, the nose may be said to be cut off, and the jury would be bound to find so. It is not necessary to prove it to have been done with a knife, as laid in the indictment."

Where a road was constructed across a deep bay upon a river, about nineteen feet distant from, and in front of, a wharf, but with a sufficient draw placed therein, *held*, that the wharf was not "cut off" by the railroad, within the meaning of an act. "The bays were 'crossed,' but not 'cut off' within the meaning of the act; that is to say, they were not cut off from the navigable communication with the river channel. Drawbridges were directed to keep that communication open, and to prevent their being cut off. If the bays were not 'cut off,' the wharves within them were not, for the same communication was open to them. But wharves not within the bays or inlets were 'cut off,' whenever the railroad should pass between them and the channel; because drawbridges were not directed in those cases." Tillotson *v.* Hudson River R. Co., 9 N. Y. 581.

3. A newspaper published every day of the week except Monday is a "daily newspaper" within the meaning of an act requiring an advertisement to be published "in two daily newspapers . . . for ten days, Sundays and non-judicial days excepted." "It was," said the court, "a 'daily' newspaper in the sense of the statute, which employs the term 'daily newspaper' in contra-distinction to the term 'weekly,' 'semi-weekly,' or 'tri-weekly' newspapers. The term was used, and is to be understood, in its usual popular sense; and in this sense it is clear that a paper which, according to its usual custom, is published every day of the week except one, is a daily newspaper; otherwise a paper which is published every day except Sunday would not be a daily paper. The term in its popular sense does not admit of this construction." Richardson *v.* Tobin, 45 Cal. 30.

DAM.

1. Definition.—The word dam is used in two different senses. It properly means the work or structure raised to obstruct the flow of water in a river; but by well-settled usage it is often applied to designate the pond of water created by this obstruction.[1]

2. Flash-boards are Part of Dams.—The flash-boards used at low water form part of a dam, and measure the height of the flowage.[2]

3. Right to Erect.—(a) *On Unnavigable Streams.*—The owner of land on both sides of a stream not navigable may erect a dam swelling the water of a stream or pond in its natural state, up to the line of his neighbor next above.[3]

1. Colwell *v.* May's Landing Water Power Co., 19 N. J. Eq. (5 C. E. Greene), 245. In this case it was held that an act which authorizes the owner of a mill dam "to raise the dam and water works" to the height of the natural surface of the water at the line of his lands, will be construed to authorize the raising of the water in the dam to that height, and not to authorize the raising the structure of the dam, by which the water would be made to flow back upon the lands of an adjoining proprietor

"A dam is an instrument for turning the water of a stream to the use of a mill . . . but it may not in fact have been used for that purpose at all, or, if at all, in such a way as to affect the original rights of riparian owners on either hand." Burnham *v* Kempton, 44 N. H. 78. A plank structure erected in the bank of a river at a place where the bank had been carried away by former freshets, and not erected across the channel of a river, is not a dam within the meaning of the *Michigan* Statute. Annotated Statutes, 1882, § 9168; People *v.* Gaige, 23 Mich. 93.

2. Amoskeag Mfg. Co. *v.* Worcester, 60 N. H. 522; Lammott *v.* Ewers, 106 Ind. 310; s.c., 55 Am Rep. 746; Dingley *v.* Gardiner, 73 Me. 63.

3. Lancy *v.* Clifford, 54 Me. 487. Wood *v.* Edes, 2 Allen (Mass.), 578; Smith *v.* Agawam Canal Co., 2 Allen (Mass.), 790; Dorman *v* Ames, 12 Minn. 451, Stein *v.* Burden, 29 Ala. 127; s.c., 68 Am. Dec. 453; Dil'ing *v.* Murray, 6 Ind. 324. Webster *v.* Fleming, 2 Humph. (Tenn.) 518; McCalmont *v.* Whitaker, 3 Rawle (Penn), 84; s. c., 23 Am. Dec. 102; Monongahela Navigation Co *v.* Coons, 6 Pa. St. 379; s.c. 47 Am. Dec. 474.

"The owner of soil over which a floatable but not navigable stream passes may build a dam across it, provided he furnishes a convenient and suitable sluice or passageway for the public by or through his dam. Lancey *v* Clifford, 54 Me. 487; s.c. 92 Am. Dec. 561; Forster *v.* Searsport Spool and Block Co. (Me Nov. 19, 1887), 11 Atl. Rep. 273.

(*b*) *When Party Owns but One Side of the Stream.*—But an owner of but one bank of such a stream cannot without legal permission erect a dam which extends beyond the thread of the stream.[1]

(*c*) *Given by Statute.*—For the purpose of encouraging the erection of dams several of the States have, on grounds of public policy, made special statutory enactments giving a riparian owner the right to erect a dam on his own land, even though in so doing he flows the land of the owner above him. In some of these permission is given to the riparian owner to erect his dam, although he is the owner of land on one side of the stream only. In all these cases the statute provides a mode of assessing and collecting damages, which generally supersedes the common-law remedy for similar injuries.[2]

1. "When the proprietors of two opposite banks of a stream of water are desirous of enjoying the advantage of the water-power for propelling machinery, a dam for that purpose cannot be built except by mutual consent, unless indeed it may be what is termed a wing-dam, confined to the soil of the person who erects it, or that half of the bed of the stream which belongs to him If erected by either on the land of the other it would clearly be a trespass, and could lawfully be abated by him on whose land it was built without his consent" Per Sharswood, J., in Lindeman *v.* Lindsay, 69 Pa. St 93. See also Wigford *v* Gill 1 Croke (Eng. C. P & K. B. temp Eliz) 269; Adams *v* Barney, 25 Vt. 225; Canal Trustees *v.* Havens, 11 Ill. 554, Trask *v.* Ford, 39 Me. 437.

But the right may be gained by prescription. Bliss *v.* Rice, 17 Pick. (Mass.) 23.

Where there is an island in the stream. See Stoep *v.* Hovt, 44 Ill. 219; Crooker *v.* Bragg, 10 Wend. (N. Y) 260; s. c, 25 Am. Dec 555

2 **Alabama Statute**—Angell on Water Cour §§ 482-484 The provisions of the statute of *Alabama*, Civil Code, 1887, §§ 3184-3206, are as follows:

Dams for water, grist mill, saw mill, gin or factory, to be operated for the public, may be erected across any water-course not navigable, by owner of land on both sides or one side, and of part of the bed thereof at the place where the dam is proposed to be erected, by proceeding under the Code.

Application verified by affidavit, setting forth the right of the applicant, the purpose for which the dam is to be erected, a full description of the location of the land, the name of the water course, side on which mill is to be erected, and proposed height of the dam, must be made to the probate judge of the county in which it is proposed to erect the mill. If the applicant owns but one side and part of the bed of the stream, the application must be made to the judge of probate of the county in which the land on the opposite side of the stream lies, and must state in addition the name and residence of the opposite owner, whether he is a minor or of full age; and if he is of unsound mind, that fact must be stated.

On the filing of this application, the judge of probate must issue to the sheriff a writ commanding him to summon seven disinterested persons to meet at the place where the dam is to be erected, to inquire into the matters contained in the application. Notice must be given to the opposite owner. The sheriff's jury must, after being sworn, examine the land above and below belonging to others, and ascertain the damages likely to result to the owners from flowage or other injury caused by the dam; they must ascertain whether the residence of any of such owners, or the outhouses, enclosures, gardens, or orchards belonging thereto, will be overflowed; they must ascertain whether the health of the neighborhood will probably be endangered, and whether any other mill will be overflowed. If the applicant does not own both sides of the stream, they must ascertain the value of one acre on the opposite side. The inquest must be reduced to writing, signed by a majority, and returned to the office of the judge of probate.

On the return of the inquest, the judge of probate must summon the owners of land found to be liable to damage (giving them ten days' notice), to show cause why the applicant should not have provision to erect his dam

If on the day appointed to show cause it shall appear to the judge of probate that the residence, etc., of any owner will be overflowed, that the health of the neighborhood will probably be endangered, or that any other mill, etc., would probably be overflowed, the judge must refuse the application, but otherwise it must be granted.

If the application be granted, the applicant must within three months pay to the several owners the sums severally assessed, and a failure so to do operates as a revocation of the grant. Upon making these payments, the applicant is vested with a qualified estate in fee to the acre of land located by the jury, to become absolute on the conditions, first, that the dam or mill shall be finished within three years from the date of the grant, and, second, that whenever it is destroyed or materially impaired, it must be restored within three years. On failure to comply with such conditions, the land reverts to former owner.

Where it is necessary to dig a canal through the land of another, or where a proprietor wishes to raise his dam, application must be made to the judge of probate, and similar proceedings be had.

Persons making affidavit that they are interested against any application under this act, and giving security for costs, may contest the application.

Persons building or raising dams except under the statutory provisions, and who thereby flow the land of another, or work him any other injury, are liable to the person injured in double damages, and may also be prosecuted for creating a nuisance.

Land-owners dissatisfied with assessment of damages may appeal to the circuit court

State Statutes on Dams—There are statutes similar to this in the following States, viz.: *Delaware*, Rev. Code (1874), chap. 61, § 4; *Florida*, McClellan's Digest (1881), pp. 760–761, §§ 1–13; *Kentucky*, Gen. Stat. (1881), pp. 672–675, §§ 1–13; *Mississippi*, Rev. Code (1880) §§ 924–932; *Missouri*, Rev. Stat. (1879), §§ 924–932; *Virginia*, Code (1873), pp. 608–611; *Arkansas*, Digest of Stats. (1884), §§ 4667–4692; *Illinois*, Rev. Stat. (1887), p. 976; *Indiana*, Rev. Stat. (1881), §§ 883–887; *Iowa*, Rev. Code (1884), §§ 1188–1206; *Nebraska*, Comp. Stat. (1885), p. 437 *et seq.*; *West Virginia*, Rev. Stat. (1879), chap 91 §§ 29–36.

The following States have similar statutes, which, however, do not apply except to cases where the person proposing to erect a dam owns the land on both sides of the stream: *Tennessee*, Code (1884), § 1442; *Dakota*, Code of Civil Procedure (1884), p 193; *Kansas*, Dassler's Comp. Laws (1885), §§ 3125–3141; *Minnesota*, Stats. (1878), pp. 328–331, §§ 1–22; *Vermont*, Rev. Laws (1880), §§ 3215–3224.

Connecticut.—The *Connecticut* statute resembles that of Alabama, but after the jury have assessed the damages the court are to add fifty per cent to the amount so assessed, which shall be the damages to be paid. Gen. Stat. (Rev. of 1875), tit. 19 chap. 17, §§ 1–10, p 472 *et seq.*

The question whether, under this act, there is or is not a mill-site on which a mill-dam has been lawfully erected and used, is a question of fact for the decision of the committee. Manilla Co *v.* Olcott, 52 Conn. 452. So where the respondent to a petition under this act had eight years before purchased a mill-site on the land sought to be flowed, on which he then intended to build, but toward which he had done nothing, it was held that the question of abandonment was one of fact. McArthur *v.* Morgan, 49 Conn. 349.

Vermont.—The *Vermont* statute regulating mill-dams did not authorize the committee appointed by the county court to make an order in the first instance to lower his dam. The statute gives the committee the right to direct alterations, repairs, and additions only. Glover *v.* McGaffey, 55 Vt. 171.

Under the Alabama law, the jurisdiction of a probate judge to authorize the erection of a dam is special, and attaches when the application is filed. Folmar *v.* Folmar, 68 Ala. 120

Massachusetts.—The statute of *Massachusetts* (Public Statutes (1882), pp. 1087–1094) differs from these in the manner of proceedings under it and the measure of damages to be assessed. It gives the owner of land on both sides of a stream not navigable the right to erect a dam for mill purposes on his complying with the provisions of the statute. After prohibiting the erection of any dams to the injury of existing ones on the same stream, and providing that the height to which the water may be raised and the length of time for which it shall be kept up in each year may be regulated by the verdict of a jury, it provides that any person injured by the erection of a dam may obtain compensation upon complaint made to the superior court of the county where the lands lie, within three years after the injury was received. The writ is to be served on the owner or occupant of the mill by the proper officer. On agreement of parties the cause may be tried as other civil causes but if either demand it a jury must be appointed to view the premises. In estimating the damages the jury shall

4. Navigable Streams.—In general a riparian owner on a navigable stream,[1] whether navigable by nature, or declared a public high-

take into consideration damage to other property of the plaintiff than that overflowed, and set off any benefit that may have been occasioned him in relation to such land. The jury shall assess the damages for three years preceding the complaint, or for so much thereof as the defendant has held title, and also what sum to be paid annually to the complainant would be a full and proper compensation for injuries that might be occasioned by the dam so long as it is used in conformity with the verdict, and also what sum in gross would be a reasonable compensation for all damages thereafter to be occasioned by such use of such dam, and the right of maintaining and using the same forever. The complainant may elect to take the gross sum instead of the annual damages. If he does not so elect the annual damages are to be paid, which become a lien on the mill and property. If the property is sold under any proceedings to enforce the lien, the person entitled to the premises so sold may redeem at any time within one year, by paying the amount of purchase-money and interest at the rate of twelve per cent. If it is alleged in the complaint that the dam is raised to an unreasonable height, or that it ought not to be kept up and closed for the entire year, the jury shall decide how much, if any, the dam shall be lowered, and if so whether it shall be left open any part of the year, and if so during what part, and shall state such decision as part of their verdict. An appeal lies from so much of such verdict as relates to costs.

The following States have statutes closely resembling this, viz.: *Maine*, Rev. Stat. (1883), pp. 776–782; *Rhode Island*, Pub Stat. (1882), p. 280 *et seq.*; *Wisconsin*, Rev. Stat (1878), §§ 3374–3406.

The *Wisconsin* act has been declared constitutional in Pratt *v.* Brown, 3 Wis. 603, Sheen *v.* Voegtlander, 3 Wis. 461. It is not applicable when dams are erected across navigable streams. Cobb *v.* Smith, 16 Wis. 661. See also Geise *v.* Green, 49 Wis. 334.

The *Maine* act (Rev. Stat. 1883, pp 776–782), does not justify the erection of a dam destroying a public easement. Treat *v.* Lord, 42 Me. 552, s. c., 66 Am. Dec. 298; Parks *v.* Morse, 52 Me. 260. And a mill-owner upon a non-tidal, floatable stream must furnish a log-driver with reasonably convenient facilities for running his logs, but is under no legal obligation to furnish locks or sluices through which large and loosely constructed rafts can be run without being broken or the logs displaced. Foster *v.* Searsport Spool and Block Co. (Me., Nov. 19, 1887), 11 Atl. Rep. 273.

Under the *Massachusetts* statute, a mill-owner may raise his dam so as to use all the unappropriated water-power, even if he thereby causes water of his own pond to flow into the raceway of a mill higher up on the stream, provided it do not obstruct the wheel or injure the mill above. Dean *v.* Colt, 99 Mass. 480.

The statutes of *New Hampshire*, Gen. Laws (1878), p. 340, and of *North Carolina*, Code (1883), §§ 1849–1863, are somewhat peculiar. They both resemble the Alabama statute in general, but in the former State either the party proposing to erect the dam, or the person whose land is likely to be injured, may make the petition, and in the latter State, after petition and return of the verdict, "the court in its discretion may allow either plaintiff or defendant to build the dam," the costs to be paid by the party to whom such leave is granted; parties injured may bring suit, and judgment may be for gross or annual damage.

The law of *South Carolina* prohibits the overflowing of land belonging to another without the consent of the owner. Gen. Stat. (1882), § 1169.

These statutes do not, in general, give any title to the land flowed, but merely an easement in the land. Thus the owner of a dam, who does not own the bed of the stream above the dam, has no interest in the ice formed on it, and where he maliciously and unnecessarily draws down the pond and destroys the ice-field, he is liable in damages to the owner of the land under the pond. Stevens *v.* Kelley, 78 Me. 455; s. c., 57 Am. Rep 813. As to the right to take ice, see Dodge *v.* Berry, 26 Hun (N. Y.), 246; Marshall *v.* Peters, 12 How. Pr. (N. Y.) 217; Cummings *v.* Barrett, 10 Cush. (Mass) 186, State *v* Pottmyer, 33 Ind. 402; Bigelow *v.* Shaw (S. Court Mich., Apr. 14, 1887), 32 N. W. Rep. 800. But *compare* Myer *v.* Whitaker, 5 Abb. N. Cas. (N. Y.) 172. Mill River Woollen Mfg. Co. *v.* Smith, 34 Conn. 463.

1. **Navigable Streams** include all those which in their natural state have the capacity of valuable floatage, whether so used or not. Moore *v.* Sanborne, 2 Mich. 519. For other definitions see Little Rock, Mississippi River & Texas R. Co. *v.* Brooks, 39 Ark. 403; s. c., 43

way by the legislature of the State through which it flows, cannot erect a dam on such stream without the permission of such legislature.[1] This may be granted by general laws, as in *Pennsylvania* and *Michigan*, or by special laws, as in *New York*. The legislature, in granting permission to erect such a dam, will always protect ordinary navigation, and provide for the maintenance of fishways.[2]

Am. Rep 277; Shaw *v.* Oswego Iron Co., 10 Oregon, 371; s. c., 45 Am. Rep. 146; Attorney-General *v.* Woods, 108 Mass. 436; s. c., 11 Am. Rep. 380; Carter *v.* Thurston, 58 N. H. 104; s. c., 42 Am. Rep. 574; Lewis *v.* Coffee County, 77 Ala. 190; s. c. 54 Am. Rep. 55; Spooner *v.* McConnell, 1 McLean (U. S. C. C.). 337.

1. Commonwealth *v.* Church, 1 Pa St. 105; s. c., 44 Am. Dec. 112; Gates *v.* Blincoe, 2 Dana (Ky.), 158; Yolo *v.* City of Sacramento, 36 Cal. 193; Newark Plank-road Co. *v.* Elmer, 9 N. J. Eq. 754; South Carolina R. Co. *v.* Moore, 28 Ga. 398; State *v.* Freeport, 43 Me. 198; State *v.* Dibble, 4 Jones (N. Car.), L. 107; Gold *v.* Carter, 9 Humph. (Tenn.) 369; Selman *v.* Wolfe, 27 Tex. 68, Banns *v.* Racine, 4 Wis. 454.

2. The mill-dam acts of several of the States cited in the note to the preceding section apply as well to navigable streams as to those not navigable. *Kentucky*, Gen. Stat. (1881) p. 672, §§ 1-13; *Mississippi*, Rev. Code (1880) §§ 924-932; *Nebraska*, Comp. Stat. (1885) p. 437; *Virginia*, Code (1873), pp. 608-611.

In *Michigan*, the boards of supervisors of the several counties may permit or prohibit the construction of dams over navigable streams in their respective counties. Howell's Annotated Statutes (1882), §§ 493-495.

In *Wisconsin*, dams are not to be erected on navigable streams without the consent of the legislature. Rev. Stat. (1878) § 1596. But while the State may authorize the construction of a dam at a point where the river is not navigable, though it becomes navigable below, they cannot do so to the injury of other riparian proprietors. Morrill *v.* St. Anthony's Falls Water-power Co., 26 Minn. 222; s. c , 37 Am Rep. 399.

In *Indiana*, dams may be erected across rivers more than 65 feet wide, on complying with the provisions of a statute somewhat similar to the mill-dam acts above cited, but such dam must have a lock constructed around it. Rev. Stat. (1881) §§ 3702-3704. In *Tennessee*, no dam can be erected across navigable streams except under the directions of the court, and in such a way as not to obstruct navigation. Code (1884), § 1441. So in *West Virginia*, Rev. Stat. (1879) ch. 91 § 27. The *Georgia* statute. Code (1882), § 464, forbids the overflowing of land of another. See also Pool *v.* Lewis 41 Ga. 162, to the effect that the statutes of Georgia have in no wise changed the common-law rules in that State.

In *New York*, permission to erect dams on navigable streams is given by the legislature only, and by special laws; e.g., Laws N. Y., ch. 149 of 1811, ch. 20 of 1835, ch. 551 of 1864; in all cases of application to the legislature for such acts, notice of the intended application must be given by advertisement specifying the nature and objects of the parties applying for at least six weeks successively in the State paper, and in a paper printed in the county where the dam is to be erected, or if there be none published in the county, then in the county nearest thereto in which a newspaper shall be printed. Rev. Stat. (7th Ed) p. 432. All dams on rivers recognized by law as public highways must have aprons of prescribed width in the middle of the current, for the purpose of running logs. Rev Stat. (7th Ed.) p. 1265 For list of such streams see Rev. Stat. (7th Ed) p. 1265, and ch. 95 Laws 1887.

In *Pennsylvania*, the mill-dam act of 1803, 4 Sm. L. 20 Purdon's Digest, 1883, p. 1173, provides that any person owning land upon a navigable stream declared by law to be a public highway, except the rivers Delaware, Schuylkill, and Lehigh, may erect dams for a mill or mills or other water-works, upon any such stream adjoining his own lands, and may take off water as may be necessary for those purposes, provided that he does not obstruct or impede the navigation of the stream, or prevent the fish from passing up the same, and does not injure nor infringe on the rights and privileges of the owner of any private property on the stream. When complaint is made that any such dam obstructs navigation or the passage of fish, the court of quarter sessions shall appoint three commissioners to report. Upon their report that an offence has been committed against this act, a bill of indictment shall be sent to the grand jury, and upon prosecution to conviction the person convicted shall pay (*a*) *Power of Congress.*—The power of Congress to regulate commerce carries with it power to change the channels of navigable rivers.[1] But where Congress has not deemed it necessary to take action in the matter of improving the navigation of a river which throughout its whole course runs within the territory of a State, that State may rightfully, for purposes of internal improvement, change the channel of that river[2] or erect dams in the same.[3]

(*b*) *Statutory Right to Erect is No Protection against Injuries to a Private Owner.*—While a dam in a navigable stream, if authorized by the act of the legislature, cannot be indicted as a public nuisance for obstructing the stream, still the act is no protection against injuries to a private owner.[4]

5. Miscellaneous Statutes in Regard to Dams.—There are besides the several mill-dam acts various other statutes depending on the peculiar needs and industries of the different States.[5]

damages to the party injured, and the court shall order the supervisors of highways to remove the dam so as to make it comply with the provisions of the act. There is also a summary method of recovering damages caused to any vessel by delays in the passage of vessels caused by such dams. This act is applicable to streams navigable at common law, as well as to those declared so by act of assembly. Ensworth *v.* Commonwealth, 52 Pa. St. 320. It does not authorize the erection of a dam for other purposes than those specified. Dubois *v.* Glaub, 52 Pa St 238, Commonwealth *v.* Church, 1 Pa. St 105. The right under the act is not indefeasible, but may be taken away by the legislature Monongahela Navigation Co. *v* Coons, 6 W & S. (Pa.) 101; Susquehanna Canal Co. *v.* Wright, 9 W. & S (Pa) 9; N Y. & Erie R. Co. *v.* Young, 33 Pa. St. 175

In *Wyoming*, no dams are permitted in streams large enough to float logs without sufficient chutes or other contrivance to permit the logs and timber to pass without unreasonable delay. Comp. L (1876) p. 468 § 2

1. South Carolina *v.* Georgia 93 U S. 4.

2. Withers *v.* Buckley, 20 How. (U S) 84.

3. Willson *v.* The Blackbird Creek Marsh Co., 2 Pet. (U. S) 245 The facts in this, the leading case on this subject, were that Blackbird Creek was a navigable stream wholly within the State of Delaware; the State of Delaware had authorized the company defendant to erect a dam across the creek. The dam had been built, and was broken and injured by a sloop duly licensed and enrolled under the navigation laws of the United States and owned by Willson. Thereupon the company brought an action of trespass *vi et armis* against the owner of the sloop in a court of the State of Delaware, and he raised, by plea, the question of the right of the State to authorize the obstruction of a navigable stream. A verdict having been found for the plaintiff, judgment thereon was affirmed by the supreme court, the ground of decision being, as stated by Marshall C J: "If Congress had passed any act which bore upon the case, any act in execution of the power to regulate commerce, the object of which was to control State legislation over those small navigable creeks into which the tide flows, and which abound throughout the lower country of the Middle and Southern States, we should feel not much difficulty in saying that a State law coming in conflict with such act would be void But Congress has passed no such act The repugnancy of the law of Delaware to the constitution is placed entirely on its repugnancy to the power to regulate commerce with foreign nations, and among the several States,—a power which has not been exercised so as to affect the question" See also Veazie *v.* Moor, 14 How. (U. S.) 568; Pennsylvania *v.* Wheeling Bridge Co., 9 How (U. S) 647; 11 How. (U. S.) 528; 13 How. (U S) 518; 18 How. (U. S.) 421; Transportation Co. *v.* Chicago, 99 U S. 635; Palmer *v.* Cuyahoga Co., 3 McLean (C C), 226.

4. Crittenden *v.* Wilson, 5 Cow. (N. Y) 165; Lee *v.* Pembroke Iron Co., 57 Me. 481; s. c., 2 Am. Rep. 59; Eastman *v.* Amoskeag Mfg. Co., 44 N. H. 160; Trenton Water Power Co. *v.* Raff, 36 N. J L. 335

5 **Fishways.**—Fishways are required in dams by the statutes of several States.

6. Erection of Dams may be Restrained.—The erection of a dam across a natural stream may be restrained,[1] though the person applying for an injunction must show right.[2]

7. Liability of Person Erecting Dam.—A person who erects a dam is responsible for all the injury caused by it[3] at ordinary stages of

Title "Fisheries," Statutes of *New Jersey*, 1877; Comp. L. *New Mexico* (1884), § 927; Rev. Stat. *New York* (7th Ed). pp. 2098 and 2110; Rev. Stat. *Ohio* (1884), § 4219 *et seq.*; Laws of *Utah*, 1882. p. 41; Laws of *Dakota*, 1885, ch. 60, p. 102; *Iowa*, 17 G. A. chap. 188, and 18 G A., chaps. 123 and 411; Dassler's Comp. Laws *Kansas* (1881), §§ 2652 and 2653; Gen. Stat. *Kentucky* (1881). p. 943, § 5; Laws of *Oregon*, 1878, p. 21; Title "Dams," Code of *Virginia* (1873), and also several special laws in the subsequent pamphlet laws of State; Rev. Stat. *Maine* (1883), p. 376; Pub. St. *Massachusetts* (1882) p. 499.

Chutes.—So in others chutes for logs must be provided. Stats. of *Minnesota*, 1878. p. 333, § 2; Code *North Carolina* (1883), § 3712 *et seq.*; Rev. Stat. *Wisconsin* (1878). §§ 1601–1606; *Arkansas*, Act of 6th April, 1885.

Waste-gates.—So waste gates. Laws of *New Jersey*, 1883, p. 155; Gen. Stat. *South Carolina* (1882), § 1174.

Draining Marshes.—So there are statutes authorizing the erection of dams in order to utilize low-lying lands, to drain marshes, etc. Gen Stat. *Connecticut*, p. 263; Rev. Stat. *Maine* (1883), pp. 274–277.

Log Sluices.—So to sluice logs. Stats. of *Minnesota* (1878) p. 350, § 83.

Cultivating Oysters.—In *Connecticut* the owner of land in which there is a salt-water creek may, after permission properly obtained, erect a dam for the purpose of cultivating oysters. Gen Stat. (1875) title 16, chap 4 § 10, p. 215.

Cranberry Culture.—So *Maine* and *Wisconsin* have laws authorizing the erection of dams for cranberry culture. Laws of *Maine*, 1887, p. 71; Rev Stat. *Wisconsin* (1878), §§ 1472–1479. The constitutionality of the latter law, which allows the flowing of lands of another, and provides for an assessment of damages by arbitrators, has been questioned, though not determined. Ramsdale *v.* Footer, 55 Wis. 557.

Cutting Ice.—So in *Maine* for the purpose of cutting ice and harvesting of ice, and lands may be flowed from November to April. Rev. Stat. 1883, p. 124.

Generally.—Some States go so far as to permit a person proposing to erect dams to overflow public highways upon permission granted by the courts of the county, or supervisors of the highways, or other officers specified, upon paying such damages as may be adjudged, or on complying with such other terms as may be ordered; generally the costs are to be paid by the applicant. Gen. Stat *Connecticut* (1875) title 16, ch. 7, § 18, p. 234; Stats. of *Minnesota* (1878), pp. 331, 332, §§ 22–30; Rev. Stat. *Maine* (1883), pp 782, 783, §§ 36–41; Pub. Stat. *Massachusetts*, 1882, p. 1092, etc.

The *Montana* statute, Rev. Stat. 1879, §§ 493–503, provides that dams must be constructed in a substantial manner, and provides a mode for enforcing the law.

Dams that are sources of danger to the neighborhood must be repaired. Rev. Laws *Vermont* (1880), §§ 3248–3250.

Materials necessary for the erection of a dam may, when they lie adjacent to the site selected, be taken for such purposes by proceedings similar to those for flowing lands under the *Alabama* statute. Del. Rev. Code (1874) chap. 61, § 5.

In *Missouri* the privilege of maintaining a dam may cease if the State or county undertake the improvement of the stream whereon it is erected. Rev. Stat. Mo (1879) § 932.

Rice Fields.—In *South Carolina* all dams flooding rice-fields are to be opened and the land drained before the 10th of March in each year, for the protection of the rice-fields. Gen. Stat. (1884) §§ 1170–1173.

1. Ogletree *v.* McQuaggs, 67 Ala. 580; s. c., 42 Am. Rep 112; Norwood *v.* Dickey, 18 Ga. 528. But see State *v.* City of Eau Claire 40 Wis 533.

2. Wattier *v.* Miller, 11 Oreg. 329.

3. The whole question of the liability of the owner of a dam to persons whose lands are injured thereby is fully discussed in Pixley *v.* Clark, 35 N. Y. 520; s. c., 91 Am. Dec. 72. In this case the defendants purchased land on a creek, and erected an embankment higher than the natural bank to prevent the overflow of water caused by their dam. The water percolated through this embankment, and the land of the plaintiff was drowned by this means. Peckham, J., delivering the opinion of the court, said: "The general rule as to flowing or drowning lands is well settled 'If riparian proprietors

water,[1] or in times of ordinary, usual and expected freshets, such as flowing the lands of another, when not authorized by statute;[2] flowing back water on a mill above;[3] creating a stagnant pool which is likely to endanger the health of the neighborhood;[4]

use a watercourse in such a manner as to inundate or overflow the lands of another, an action will lie on the principle *sic utere tuo ut alienum non lædas.* So if he drown the land of another and rot his grass, an action lies.' Angell Wat. Cour. (7th Ed.) § 330." And he adds: "The law on the subject, as thus laid down, is so well settled and so obviously just as never to have been called in question"

1. What is Ordinary Height of Water.—McCoy *v.* Danley, 20 Pa. St. 85; s. c., 57 Am. Dec. 680; Ames *v.* Cannon River Manufacturing Co., 27 Minn. 245; Decorah Woollen Mill Co. *v.* Greer, 58 Iowa, 86

2. Backing Water upon Land.—Stout *v.* McAdams, 2 Scammon (Ill.). 67; s. c., 33 Am. Dec. 441; Bell *v.* McClintock, 9 Watts (Pa.), 119; s. c., 34 Am. Dec. 507. The meaning of the term "high water," as used in this case, is explained in McCoy *v.* Danby, 20 Pa. St. 85; s. c., 57 Am. Dec. 680; Hoy *v.* Sterrett, 2 Watts (Pa.), 327; s. c., 27 Am. Dec. 313; Odiorne *v.* Lyford, 9 N. H. 502; s. c., 32 Am. Dec. 387; Haso *v.* Toussard, 17 Tex. 588; Wright *v.* Howard, 1 Sim. & Stu. (Eng. Vice Chancery) 190; Monroe *v.* Gates, 48 Me. 463; Hutchison *v.* Chase, 39 Me. 508; s. c., 63 Am. Dec. 645; Heath *v.* Williams, 25 Me. 209; s. c., 43 Am. Dec. 265; Hutchinson *v.* Granger, 13 Vt., 386; Johns *v.* Stevens, 3 Vt. 308; Wabash & Erie Canal *v.* Spears, 16 Ind. 441; s. c., 79 Am. Dec. 444; Simmons *v.* Brown, 5 R. I. 299; s. c., 73 Am. Dec. 66; Roundtree *v.* Brantley, 34 Ala. 544; s. c., 73 Am. Dec. 470; Lohmiller *v.* Indian Ford Water-power Co., 51 Wis 683; Trustees, etc., *v.* Spears, 16 Ind. 441; s. c., 79 Am. Dec. 444; Bristol Hydraulic Co. *v.* Boyer, 67 Ind. 236; Cooper *v.* Hall, 5 Ohio, 320; Brisbane *v.* O'Neall, 3 Strobh. (S. Car.) 348; O'Melvany *v.* Jaggers, 2 Hill (S. Car.), 634; s. c., 27 Am. Dec. 417; Himes *v.* Jarrett (S. Car., Apr. 27, 1887), 2 S. E. Rep. 393; Godfrey *v.* Mayberry, 84 N. Car. 255; Ames *v* Cannon River Mfg. Co., 27 Minn. 245; Felker *v.* Calhoun, 64 Ga. 614.

But if a person has a right to keep his dam at a certain height, it is no ground of complaint under the mill acts that, owing to his mills not being used, the water stands higher on the complainant's land than it otherwise would. Daniels *v.* Citizens' Savings Inst., 127 Mass. 534.

One being sole seised of a mill and privileges and dam, cannot by such dam flow lands above him owned by himself and another in common. Hutchinson *v.* Chase, 39 Me. 508; s.c., 63 Am. Dec 645.

In *North Carolina* the overflow of lands by a mill-pond is a tort: the statute merely gives additional remedy, but does not alter its nature. Wilson *v.* Myers, 4 Hawks (N. Car.). 73.

3. Flowing Back Water on a Mill Above.—Mr. Angell says (Angell on Water-courses, 7th Ed., § 340, p. 517). "The consequences of setting back the water on a mill-wheel above are in most cases more injurious than flowing the land in the absence of any mill on it." In Gilman *v.* Tilton, 5 N. H. 232, the court say: "In general, every man has a right to the use of the water flowing in a stream through his land; and if any one divert the water from its channel, or throw it back on him, so as to deprive him of the use of it, the law will give him redress." See also Hodges *v.* Raymond, 9 Mass. 316; Butz *v.* Ihrie, 1 Rawle (Pa.), 218; Monroe *v.* Gates, 48 Me. 463; Ames *v.* Cannon River Mfg. Co., 27 Minn. 245; Lincoln *v.* Chadborne, 56 Me. 197; Dwinel *v.* Veazie, 44 Me. 167; s. c., 69 Am. Dec. 94; Stout *v.* McAdam, 2 Scam. (Ill.) 67; s. c., 33 Am Dec. 441; Barrow *v.* Landry, 15 La. Ann. 681; s. c., 77 Am. Dec. 199; Babb *v.* Mackey, 10 Wis. 371.

Where the defendant was owner of an existing mill-dam, and the plaintiff had rightfully erected a mill-dam above it on the same stream, the defendant had no right to increase the height of his dam to a level with the plaintiff's wheel by means of flash-boards, and thereby obstruct the wheel by back-water. Sumner *v.* Tileston, 7 Pick. (Mass.) 198; Ripka *v.* Sergeant, 7 W. & S. (Pa) 9. But where the injury was such as could not be foreseen at the time of erecting the dam, it was *damnum absque injuria.* Proctor *v.* Jennings, 6 Nev. 83.

4 Creating a Stagnant Pool which is Likely to Injure the Health of Those Living in the Vicinity.—Neal *v.* Henry. Meigs (Tenn.), 17; s. c., 33 Am Dec. 125. In this case Reese, J., uses the following language: "Every individual indeed has a right to make the most profi-

drowning neighboring lands by percolation,[1] interference with natural drainage;[2] and discharging in large quantities and flooding lands below,[3] or for other injuries.[4]

8. Care in Constructing.—The owner of a dam must use reasonable care and skill in so constructing and maintaining it, that it will not be the means of injuring another, either above or below, by throwing the water back, or being incapable of resisting it in times of ordinary, usual, and expected floods; but his liability extends no further, and he is not held responsible for inevitable accidents or for injuries caused by extraordinary freshets which could not be anticipated or guarded against.[5]

table use of that which is his own, so that he does not injure others in the enjoyment of what is theirs. And it is conceded also that if one, in the cautious and prudent use of his property, in a manner appropriated to its nature and character, produce some annoyance to his neighbors, such person, though sustaining some loss, has suffered no legal injury which can be redressed. But to dam up a stream, and create pools of stagnant water upon or near to the premises of another, poisoning the atmosphere, generating disease, and impairing the enjoyment of that most valuable of absolute rights, health, cannot be called the cautious and prudent use of property in an appropriate manner. To do so is to violate the injunction, *sic utere tuo ut alienum non lædas.*" See also Treat *v.* Bates, 27 Mich. 390; White *v.* Forbes, Walker's Chancery Rep. (Mich.) 112; Ogletree *v.* McQuaggs, 67 Ala. 580; Neal *v.* Cogar, 1 A. R. Marsh. (Ky.) 589; Mayo *v.* Turner, 1 Munf. (Va.) 405.

In *Ohio* dams may be removed as a sanitary measure by the county commissioners, on petition being made by the owners of adjacent lands. The proceedings are regulated by statute. Rev. Stats. (1884) § 4567*a et seq.*, vol. iii. p. 230.

1 **Percolation.**—Pixley *v.* Clark, 35 N. Y. 520; Marsh *v.* Trullinger, 6 Oreg. 356; Wilson *v.* New Bedford, 108 Mass. 261.

2 **Interference with Natural Drainage.**—Bassett *v.* Salisbury Mfg. Co., 43 N. H. 569; s. c. 82 Am. Dec. 179; Treat *v.* Bates, 27 Mich. 391.

3. **Flooding Lower Land.**—Discharging in large quantities and flooding lands below. Gerrish *v.* Newmarket Mfg. Co., 30 N. H. 479; Clinton *v.* Myers, 46 N. Y. 511; Clapp *v.* Herrick, 129 Mass. 292; Kelley *v.* Lett, 13 Ired. L. (N. Car.) 50. Though he is not liable where he allows the water to flow in a reasonable manner. Drake *v.* Hamilton Woollen Co., 99 Mass. 574.

But under the *Maine* statute giving damages to one whose lands are damaged by being flowed by a mill-dam, one whose lands below the dam are damaged by water drawn from the dam cannot maintain complaint. Wilson *v.* Campbell, 76 Me. 94.

4. **Other Injuries.**—Injuries to mining claim by washing away pay-dirt, and preventing owners from working claim. Fraler *v.* Sears Union Water Company, 12 Cal. 555; s. c., 73 Am. Dec. 562.

Where either from neglect or accident there is a sudden and unusual flow of water from a mill-dam, it is the duty of the owner or tenant thereof to give notice as soon as possible to the next mill-owner below him. On failure to do so, the higher owner is liable to double damages. Del. Rev Code (1874), chap. 61, § 2 See McIlvaine *v.* Marshall, 3 Harr. (Del.) 1.

Where a road passes over a dam, the owner of the dam is to keep so much of it as is on the dam in repair. Gen. Stat. *Kentucky*, p. 767, § 39; Amended Code, *West Virginia* (1884), chap. 43, § 39.

5. Washb. on Easements, pp., *288, *289; Angell Wat Cour. § 336; Lehigh Bridge Co. *v.* Lehigh Coal & Nav. Co. 4 Rawle (Pa.). 9; s. c., 26 Am. Dec. 111; Bell *v.* McClintock, 9 Watts (Pa.). 119; s. c., 34 Am. Dec. 507; Monongahela Nav. Co. *v.* Coons, 6 Pa. St. 379; s. c., 47 Am. Dec. 474; Knoll *v* Light, 76 Pa St. 268; Lapham *v.* Curtis, 5 Vt. 371, s. c., 26 Am. Dec. 371; Mayor, etc., of New York *v.* Bailey, 2 Denio (N.Y.), 433. Fraler *v.* Sears Union Water Co., 12 Cal. 555; s. c., 73 Am. Dec. 562; Inhabitants of China *v.* Southwick, 12 Me. 238; Gray *v.* Harris, 107 Mass. 492; s. c., 9 Am. Rep. 61; Everett *v.* Hydraulic, etc., Co., 23 Cal. 225; Neal *v.* Henry, Meigs (Tenn.), 17; s. c., 33 Am. Dec. 125; Procter *v.* Jennings, 6 Nev. 83; s. c., 3 Am. Rep. 240; Ames *v.* Cannon River Mfg. Co., 27 Minn. 245; Bristol Hydraulic Co. *v.* Boyer, 67 Ind.

9. Liability of Joint Owners to Repair.—It is the duty of the owners of a dam to keep it in repair. Where there are more than one owner they are bound to defray the costs of repair in proportion to their several interests, and if one or more refuse to pay their proportion towards the cost of repairs, they may in several States be compelled to do so by statute.[1]

10. Right to Use of Water.—An upper proprietor has a right to detain the water of a stream by his dam so far as is reasonable and necessary for mill purposes, but he cannot detain it unreasonably,[2]

236; State *v.* Water Co., 51 Conn. 137.

And when the defendant so negligently constructed his dams that they were unable to resist the pressure of water and were carried out, thus flooding the stream below, causing injury to lower proprietors, it is an injury for which a common-law action lies, and for which the mill-dam act of Wisconsin affords no remedy. Rich *v.* Keshena Improvement Co., 56 Wis. 287.

Where the stream is subject to extraordinary freshets, the owner of a dam is bound to construct it to resist such freshets. Gray *v.* Harris, 107 Mass. 492.

1. Gen. Laws, *New Hampshire* (1881), p. 339, §§ 1-12; Gen. Laws, *Oregon* (1872), p. 682; Howell's Annotated Statutes, *Michigan* (1882), §§ 1664-1616; Rev. Stat. *Wisconsin* (1878), §§ 3403-3406. See Webb *v.* Laird 59 Vt. 108; s. c., 59 Am. Rep. 699.

2. Tyler *v.* Wilkinson, 4 Mason (C. C.), 397; Union Mill & Mining Co *v.* Ferris, 2 Sawyer (C C.), 176; Gould *v.* Boston Duck Co., 13 Gray (Mass), 442; Barrett *v* Parsons, 10 Cushing (Mass.), 367; Thurber *v.* Martin, 2 Gray (Mass.), 394; s. c., 61 Am. Dec. 468; Pitts *v.* Lancaster Mills, 13 Metc. (Mass.). 156; Bardwell *v.* Ames, 22 Pick (Mass.) 333; Drake *v* Hamilton Woollen Co., 99 Mass. 574; Merritt *v.* Brinkerhoff, 17 Johns. (N. Y) 306; Palmer *v.* Mulligan, 3 Caines (N Y), 307; s. c., 2 Am Dec. 270; Crooker *v.* Bragg, 10 Wend. (N.Y.) 260; s. c., 25 Am Dec. 555; Platt *v.* Johnson, 15 Johns. (N. Y.) 213; s. c., 8 Am. Dec. 233; Canfield *v.* Andrew. 54 Vt. 1; s. c., 41 Am. Rep 828; Snow *v.* Parsons 28 Vt 464; Martin *v.* Bigelow, 2 Aik. (Vt.) 184; s. c., 16 Am. Dec. 696; Hoxsie *v.* Hoxsie 38 Mich. 77; Dumont *v* Kellogg 29 Mich 420; Shreve *v.* Voorhees 2 Green Ch. (N J) 25; Acquachanonk Water Co *v.* Watson 29 N. J Eq. 366, Eddy *v.* Simpson, 3 Cal. 249; s. c., 58 Am. Dec. 408; Stein *v* Burden, 29 Ala 127; s. c , 60 Am. Dec. 453; Pool *v.* Lewis, 41 Ga 162; s c , 5 Am. Rep. 526; Gillett *v.* Johnson, 30 Conn. 180; Keeney, etc., Co., *v.* Union Mfg. Co., 39 Conn. 576; Parker *v.* Hotchkiss, 25 Conn. 321; Buddington *v.* Bradley, 10 Conn. 213; s. c., 26 Am. Dec. 386; Wadsworth *v.* Tillotson, 15 Conn. 365; s. c , 39 Am. Dec. 391; Rudd *v* Williams, 43 Ill. 385; Evans *v.* Merriweather, 3 Scam. (Ill.) 492; s. c., 38 Am. Dec. 106, Plumleigh *v.* Dawson, 1 Gilman (Ill.), 544; s. c., 41 Am. Dec. 199; Shamleffer *v.* Mill Co , 18 Kans. 24; Vliet *v.* Sherwood, 35 Wis. 229; McCalmont *v.* Whitaker, 3 Rawle (Pa.), 84; s. c., 23 Am. Dec. 102; Wheatley *v.* Chrisman, 24 Pa. St. 298; Omelvany *v.* Jaggers, 2 Hill (S. Car.), 634; s. c., 27 Am. Dec. 417; Cowles *v.* Kidder, 24 N. H. 364; Holden *v.* Lake Co., 53 N. H. 552; Pilsbury *v.* Moore, 44 Me. 154; Dwinel *v.* Veazie, 44 Me. 167; s. c., 69 Am. Dec. 94; Davis *v.* Getchell, 50 Me 602; s. c , 79 Am. Dec. 636; Davis *v.* Winslow, 51 Me. 264; s. c., 81 Am. Dec. 573; Phillips *v.* Sherman, 64 Me. 171; Mayor, etc., *v.* Apold, 42 Md. 442.

The right of a lower owner to have the water run uninterruptedly through the gate on the premises of an upper mill on the same stream would be, and is, an easement on the latter. Mabie *v.* Matteson, 17 Wis. 1. See extended note to McCoy *v.* Danley, 57 Am. Dec. 680.

What is Reasonable Detention of Water.—In Gould *v.* Boston Duck Co. 13 Gray (Mass.), 442, the defendant had built a substantial dam upon the stream and drew the water to his factory by means of a canal, and after using the same returned it to its natural channel before it reached the plaintiff's land. The stream, at ordinary stages of water, afforded an ample supply for defendant's factory, but in seasons of great drought the defendants were unable to operate their factory during all the usual working hours of each day, but were obliged, in order to create the requisite head and supply of water, to shut their gates earlier than usual on some days, and sometimes for an entire day, and thus arrest the flow or divert it, unless he has acquired the right by prescription.

of the water. This was the injury complained of by the plaintiff, who was the owner of a mill upon the stream directly below the dam, and who was injured to some extent by being deprived of the use of the water while the natural flow was thus arrested. Shaw, C.J., delivered the opinion of the court, saying (p. 452): "Upon the facts agreed the court are of opinion that the defendants did not exceed their just right in the use of this water-power. . . . What is a reasonable use of water-power may often be a difficult question, depending on a variety of circumstances; somewhat upon usage, upon the state of mechanical and manufacturing advancement. Usage is some proof of what is considered a reasonable and proper use of that which is a common right: because it affords evidence of tacit consent of all the parties interested to the general convenience of such use. The circumstances above stated we think are decisive of the present case, and show that the defendants made no more than a reasonable use of the water; and if this did interfere at times with the use which the plaintiff might have made of the water if the defendants had no occasion to use it, it was *damnum absque injuria*. . . . As there was no detention of the water in the ordinary stages of water, and no other detention of the water by the defendants in times of extreme drought than was necessary to the reasonable use of their own mills, we are of opinion that it was not their duty, in point of law, to open their gates, or leave them open without using the amount to such extent as they might, merely because the plaintiff's works were of such a character that his necessities required such flow of the water."

This case is cited as a leading case in Clinton *v.* Myers, 46 N. Y. 511; s. c., 7 Am. Rep. 373. See also Pitts *v.* Lancaster Mills, 13 Metc. (Mass.) 156; Brace *v.* Gale, 10 Allen (Mass.), 441; Springfield *v.* Harris, 4 Allen (Mass.), 494; McKinney *v.* Smith, 21 Cal. 374; Nevada Water Co *v.* Powell, 34 Cal. 109; Mabie *v.* Matteson, 17 Wis. 1.

In *Rhode Island* "no person owning any dam on any river or stream of water shall detain the natural stream thereof, at any one time, more than twelve hours out of the twenty-four hours, except on Sundays, whenever he shall be requested by the owner of any dam within one mile below on the same stream to suffer the said natural run of said river or stream to pass his said dam." Pub Stat. (1882), p. 282, § 21

As to what is unreasonable detention of water, see Clinton *v.* Myers, 46 N. Y. 511; s. c., 7 Am. Rep. 373. This was an action for an injunction to restrain the defendants from opening the gate of the plaintiff's dam and letting off the accumulated water. The plaintiff had erected a dam across a stream flowing through his land, and used it to detain the water in the pond during the autumn and spring when the factory was adequately supplied with water from another source; when that failed the deficiency was made up from the reservoir thus created. Defendant, the owner of land on the stream below, opened the gates and let off the accumulated waters, claiming the right to do so. Grover, J., delivered the opinion of the court, saying (P. 516): "No proprietor has the right to use the water to the prejudice of other proprietors above or below him, unless he has a prior right to divert it or a title to exclusive enjoyment. . . . But the machinery must be adapted to the power of the stream at its usual stage. An owner has no right to erect machinery requiring for its operation more water than the stream furnishes at an ordinary stage, and operate such machinery by ponds full, discharging upon those below in unusual quantities, by means of which the latter are unable to use it. See also Merritt *v.* Brinkerhoff, 17 Johns. (N. Y.) 306; Brace v. Yale, 10 Allen (Mass.), 441; Pitts *v.* Lancaster Mills, 13 Met. (Mass) 156; Clinton *v.* Myers, 46 N. Y. 511; s. c., 7 Am. Rep. 373; Ferrea *v.* Knipe, 28 Cal. 340; s. c., 87 Am. Dec. 128; Hartzell *v.* Sill, 12 Pa. St. 248, Agawam Canal Co. *v.* Edwards, 36 Conn. 476; Davis *v.* Getchell, 50 Me. 602; Snow *v.* Parsons, 28 Vt. 459; Lawson *v.* Menasha Wooden-ware Co, 59 Wis. 393; s. c., 48 Am. Rep. 528; Timm *v.* Bear, 29 Wis. 254; Gerrish *v.* Newmarket Mfg. Co., 30 N. H. 478; Anderson *v.* Cincinnati Southern Ry. (Ky., June 18, 1887) 5 S. W. Rep 49; Dilling *v* Murray, 6 Ind. 324 *Compare* Whalen *v.* Ahl, 29 Pa St. 98.

The question of reasonableness of detention is for the jury. Hetrich *v.* Deachler, 6 Pa. St. 32; Hoy *v.* Sterrett, 2 Watts (Pa.), 327; s. c., 27 Am. Dec. 313; Hartzell *v.* Sill, 12 Pa. St 248; Nevada Water Co. *v.* Powell, 34 Cal. 109; Pool *v.* Lewis, 41 Ga. 162; s. c., 5 Am. Rep 526.

1. Tillotson *v.* Smith, 32 N. H. 90; Harding *v.* Stamford Water Co., 41 Conn. 87; Van Hoesen *v.* Coventry, 10

11. Rights Acquired by Occupancy.—In common with other riparian proprietors, the owners of dams have only such use in the water as will not interfere with the use of it by other riparian owners. Nor, in the United States, will mere prior occupancy or appropriation of a running stream by a riparian owner, unless continued for such a length of time as to raise the presumption of a grant, give an exclusive right thereto as against the owners on the same stream above or below him, except when the common law has been modified by local usage or statutory enactment.[1]

Barb. (N. Y.) 518; Garwood *v.* N. Y. Central & Hudson River R. Co., 83 N. Y. 400; s. c., 38 Am Rep. 452; Cook *v.* Hall, 3 Pick. (Mass) 269; Manville *v.* City of Worcester, 138 Mass. 89; s. c., 52 Am. Rep. 261; Halsey *v.* Lehigh Val. R. Co., 45 N. J. L. 26; City of Emporia *v.* Soden, 25 Kans. 588; s. c., 37 Am. Rep. 265.

When right is given to divert water from a stream it is to be construed strictly. Thus where a right had been given to take water into a canal for purposes of navigation, it was held that under the grant none could be taken for motive power. Druley *v.* Adam, 102 Ill. 177.

The upper of two neighboring mill-owners on the same stream may divert the water on his own land by an artificial channel, provided he restores it to the natural channel with reasonable care and prudence, and without appreciable injury to the lower owner. Canfield v. Andrews, 54 Vt. 1; s. c., 41 Am. Rep. 828.

1 See the law on this subject very fully discussed in Norway Plains Co. *v.* Bradley, 52 N. H. 109 The American rule as there laid down differs from the English rule as laid down in Bickett *v.* Morris, L. R. 1 H. L. Sc. 47 which is "that an encroachment on the *alveus* of a running stream may be complained of by an adjacent or *ex adverso* proprietor, without the necessity of proving either that damage has been sustained or that it is likely to be sustained from that cause." See also a very extended note to McCoy *v.* Danley, 57 Am. Dec. 680; Hendricks *v.* Johnson, 6 Porter (Ala.) 472; Palmer *v.* Mulligan, 3 Caines (N. Y.) 307; s. c., 2 Am. Dec. 270; Platt *v.* Johnson, 15 Johns (N. Y.), 213; s. c., 8 Am. Dec. 233; Hoy *v.* Sterrett, 2 Watts (Pa.), 321; s. c., 27 Am. Dec. 313; Hartzell *v.* Sill, 12 Pa. St. 248; Martin *v* Bigelow, 2 Aik. (Vt) 184; s. c., 16 Am. Dec. 696; Davis *v.* Fuller, 12 Vt. 178; s. c., 36 Am. Dec. 334; Stout *v.* McAdams, 2 Scam. (Ill.) 67; s. c., 33 Am. Dec. 441; Evans *v.* Merriweather, 3 Scam. (Ill.) 492; s. c., 38 Am. Dec. 106; Gilman *v* Tilton, 5 N H. 231; Cowles *v.* Kidder, 24 N. H. 378; Parker *v.* Hotchkiss, 25 Conn. 321; Keeny, etc., Co. *v.* Union Mfg. Co., 39 Conn. 576; Pugh *v.* Wheeler, 2 Dev. & B. (N.C.) 55; Bliss *v.* Kennedy, 43 N. C. 67; Rudd *v.* Williams, 43 N. Car. 385; Dumont *v.* Kellogg, 29 Mich 420; Buchanan *v.* Grand River & Greenville Log Co., 48 Mich. 364; Stillman *v.* White Rock, etc., Co., 3 Woodb. & M. (U. S. C. C.) 550; Tyler *v.* Wilkinson, 4 Mason (U. S. C. C.), 397; Smith *v.* Agawam Canal Co., 2 Allen (Mass.), 357; Bearse *v.* Berry, 117 Mass. 211.

As a riparian proprietor cannot by prior occupation of a stream acquire a right to divert a water-course as against a lower proprietor, so he cannot by such prior occupation acquire the right to use all the water for mechanical purposes by turning it into steam. Bliss *v.* Kennedy, 43 Ill. 67. Though he use all the water for domestic purposes. Stein *v.* Burden, 29 Ala. 127; s. c., 60 Am. Dec. 453. But his rights must be properly exercised. McCalmont *v.* Whitaker, 3 Rawle (Pa), 84; s. c., 23 Am. Dec. 102; Wadsworth *v* Tillotson, 15 Conn. 366; s. c., 39 Am. Dec. 391.

The right to the exclusive use of the water may undoubtedly be acquired, by adverse enjoyment and possession where it is real and actual. Thus the proprietor who first lawfully erects a dam across the stream to create a fall to operate his mill, has a right afterward to maintain it against all other proprietors above and below, and, to this extent, priority of occupation gives priority of title. Thurber *v.* Martin, 2 Gray (Mass.), 394; s. c., 61 Am. Dec. 468; Pratt *v* Lamson, 2 Allen (Mass.), 288; Gardner *v.* Newburg 2 Johns. Ch. (N. Y.) 161; s c., 7 Am. Dec. 526; Olney *v.* Fenner, 2 R. I. 211; s. c., 57 Am. Dec. 711. So a lower proprietor cannot by occupation acquire the right to flow upper land or mill. Stout *v.* McAdams, 2 Scam. (Ill.) 67; s.c., 33 Am. Dec. 441; Cowles *v.* Kidder, 24 N. H. 378;

12. Rights Acquired by Grant.—The right of the owner of a dam to overflow the lands of another above or below, or to set back water on an upper mill-privilege, may be acquired by special grant or reserved in a conveyance of land like any other easement. The construction of all such conveyances will depend upon the stipulations they contain in connection with the right granted. A grant of a mill with its appurtenances passes not only the mill itself, but whatever naturally and necessarily belongs to it, as the dam, race, flood-gates, water-rights in the stream on which it is situated, and in some cases storage dams, even though they may be at a considerable distance from the mill.[1]

(*a*) *Loss of.*—Where there has been a grant of the right to flow lands, there must be not only disuse, but actual adverse user for twenty years to extinguish the right.[2]

Pugh *v.* Wheeler, 2 Dev. & B. (N. Car.) 57; Burnett *v.* Nicholson, 72 N Car. 334.

The right of this second occupant of a stream for mill purposes is subordinate to that of the first. Tye *v.* Catching, 28 Ky. 463.

In *Wyoming* the right is given to take water from streams, but not so as to impair the rights of any dam-owner previously acquired. Comp. L. (1876) p. 378, § 9.

1. In Baker *v.* Bessey, 73 Me. 472; s. c., 40 Am. Rep. 377, it was decided that a deed of a mill with the appurtenances will pass not only the dam at the mill, but also an easement in a reservoir dam owned by the grantor of the mill and lower dam, and for many years used in conjunction with them, and up to which the lower dam had always been flowed, although the grantor did not own all the land between them. See also Watrous *v.* Watrous, 3 Conn. 373; Albee *v.* Hayden, 25 Minn. 267; Oregon Water Co. *v* Twillenger, 3 Oreg. 1; Conwell *v.* Brookhart, 4 B. Mon. (Ky) 580; s. c., 41 Am. Dec. 244; Hathaway *v.* Mitchell, 34 Mich. 164; Butler *v.* Huse, 63 Me. 447; Estey *v.* Baker, 48 Me. 495; Preble *v.* Reed, 17 Me. 169; Rackley *v.* Sprague, 17 Me. 281; McTavish *v.* Carroll, 7 Md. 352; s. c., 61 Am. Dec. 353; Simmons *v.* Cloonan, 81 N. Y. 557; Voorhees *v.* Burchard, 55 N Y. 98; Adams *v.* Conover, 87 N Y. 422; s. c., 41 Am Rep. 381; Parsons *v.* Johnson, 68 N. Y. 62; s. c., 23 Am. Rep. 149; Vandenburgh *v.* Van Bergen, 13 Johns. (N. Y.) 212; Wetmore *v.* White, 2 Caines Cases (N. Y.), 87; s. c., 2 Am. Dec. 323; Nitzell *v.* Paschal, 3 Rawle (Pa.), 76. Swartz *v.* Swartz, 4 Pa. St. 353; Pickering *v.* Stapen, 5 S. & R. (Pa) 107; s. c., 9 Am. Dec. 336; Frailey *v.* Waters, 7 Pa. St. 221; Frey *v.* Witman, 7 Pa. St. 441; Stricken *v.* Todd, 10 S. & R. (Pa.) 63; s. c, 13 Am. Dec. 648; Leonard *v.* White, 7 Mass. 6; s. c., 5 Am Dec. 19; Crittenden *v* Field, 8 Gray (Mass.), 621; Philbrick *v.* Ewing 97 Mass. 134; Peter *v.* Hawes, 13 Pick. (Mass.) 323; Short *v.* Woodward, 13 Gray (Mass.), 87; Mabie *v* Matteson, 17 Wis. 1; Whitney *v.* Olney, 3 Mas. (R. I.) 280; Perrin *v.* Garfield, 37 Vt. 312; Coolidge *v.* Hager, 43 Vt. 9; s. c., 5 Am. Rep. 256; Goodal *v.* Godfrey, 53 Vt. 219; s. c., 38 Am. Rep 671; Tuthill *v.* Scott, 43 Vt. 525; s. c., 5 Am. Rep. 501; Neaderhouser *v.* State, 28 Ind. 257; Lammott *v.* Ewers, 106 Ind 310; s. c., 55 Am. Rep. 746; Decorah Woollen Mill Co. *v.* Greer, 49 Iowa, 490. New Ipswich Factory *v.* Batchelder, 3 N. H. 190; s. c., 14 Am. Dec. 346; Spaulding *v.* Abbott, 55 N. H 423; Salmon Falls Mfg Co. *v.* Portsmouth Co., 46 N. H. 249; Wilcoxon *v.* McGhee, 12 Ill. 381, s. c., 54 Am. Dec. 509; O'Rorke *v.* Smith, 11 R I 259; s. c., 23 Am. Rep. 440; Ang. Wat. Cour. (7th Ed.) § 353 *et seq* *Compare* Brace *v.* Yale, 4 Allen (Mass.), 393, and see extended note to McCoy *v.* Danley, 57 Am. Dec. 687.

As to right to overflow, or back water, given by parol, see Ang. Wat. Cour. (7th Ed.) § 387; Johnson *v.* Lewis, 13 Conn. 303; s c., 33 Am. Dec. 405; Woodbury *v.* Parshley, 7 N. H. 237; s c., 26 Am. Dec. 739; McKillip *v.* McIlhenny, 4 Watts (Pa), 317; s. c., 28 Am Dec. 711; Leidensparger *v.* Spear, 17 Me. 123; s. c., 35 Am. Dec 234; Stevens *v.* Stevens, 11 Met. (Mass.) 251; s. c., 45 Am. Dec. 203; Woodward *v.* Seely, 11 Ill. 157; s. c., 50 Am. Dec. 158; Hazelton *v.* Putnam, 3 Chandler (Wis.), 117; s. c., 3 Pinney (Wis.), 107; s c., 54 Am. Dec. 158; Cook *v* Prigden, 45 Ga. 33 n.; s. c., 12 Am. Rep. 582; Himes *v.* Jarrett (S Car. Apr 20, 1881) 2 S E. Rep. 593; Case *v.* Weber, 2 Ind 108.

2. Mower *v.* Hutchinson, 9 Vt. 242;

13. Rights Acquired by Prescription.—The right to overflow lands or to raise water by means of a dam to the injury of an upper mill-owner, may, like easements in general, be acquired by an uninterrupted and adverse enjoyment for twenty years, or for the period of time, whatever it may be, limited by the statute of limitations for the right of entry on land.[1]

(*a*) *Measure of.*—A mill-owner having a twenty years' prescriptive right to flow land of another is entitled to keep the water as high as it would be raised by a dam of the same height as that maintained during the period of prescription, having regard to the effective height of the same. The right does not depend on

Smith *v.* Modus Water Co., 35 Conn. 392. *Compare* Pilsbury *v.* Moore, 44 Me. 154.

1. Ang. Wat. Cour. (7th Ed.). § 372; note to McCoy *v.* Danley, 57 Am. Dec. 688.

A party acquires the right to the use of water in a particular manner by an uninterrupted adverse enjoyment of such use for twenty years; but an omission by the owner to make use of his right does not impair his title or confer any right thereto upon another. It is not non-user by the owner, but the adverse enjoyment by another, which destroys the right. Pilsbury *v.* Moore, 44 Me. 154; s. c., 69 Am. Dec. 91. See also Voter *v.* Hobbs, 69 Me. 19, Blanchard *v.* Baker, 8 Greenleaf (Me.), 253; s. c., 23 Am. Dec. 504; Leidensparger *v.* Spear, 17 Me. 123; s. c., 35 Am. Dec. 234; Augusta *v.* Moulton, 75 Me. 284; Burnham *v.* Kempton, 44 N. H. 78; Norway Plains Co *v.* Bradley, 52 N H. 86; Perley *v.* Hilton, 55 N. H 444; Odiorne *v.* Lyford, 9 N. H. 502; s. c., 32 Am. Dec. 387; Taylor *v.* Blake (N. H., July 15, 1887), 10 Atlantic Rep. 698; Stein *v.* Burden, 24 Ala. 130; s. c., 60 Am. Dec. 453; Conwell *v.* Thayer, 5 Metc. (Mass) 253; s. c., 38 Am. Dec. 400; Brace *v.* Yale, 10 Allen (Mass.), 441; Johns *v.* Stevens, 3 Vt. 308; Vail *v.* Mix, 74 Ill. 127; Lane *v.* Miller, 27 Ind. 534; Ogle *v.* Dill, 55 Ind. 130; Wilson *v.* Wilson, 4 Dev. (N. Car. L.) 154; Dumont *v* Kellogg, 29 Mich. 420; Alhambra Addition Water Co. *v.* Richardson (Cal. June 27, 1887), 14 Pac. Rep. 379; Townsend *v.* McDonald, 12 N. Y. (2 Kern) 381; Haas *v.* Choussard, 17 Tex. 588.

When a mill-owner has enjoyed the right to the use of all the water of a stream for twenty years, no riparian owner of land above may divert the water of the stream for purposes of irrigation, if by so doing he impedes the operation of such mill. Cook *v.* Hull, 3 Pick (Mass.) 269; Cary *v.* Daniels, 8 Metc (Mass) 479; s. c., 41 Am. Dec. 532.

And under the mill acts, where authority is given to flow land on payment of damages, if a mill-owner has kept up a dam and flowed the land of another for twenty years without such payment, or question made, it is evidence of the right to maintain the dam, and flow the lands, and a bar to a claim for damages. Williams *v.* Nelson, 23 Pick. (Mass.) 141; s. c., 34 Am. Dec. 45.

But where the defendant in action for the obstruction of a water-course, by raising his dam, proved that the party under whom the plaintiff claimed was frequently present during the erection of the dam, and did not object to or forbid its erection, and even expressed an opinion that it would be beneficial to his mill, and that the plaintiff had said that he was satisfied with the manner in which the defendant used the water, it was held that these facts did not amount to a license to erect the dam, but were merely evidence of such license. Johnson *v.* Lewis, 13 Conn, 303; s. c., 33 Am. Dec. 405.

As to prescriptive authority to erect dams across arms of the sea where the tide ebbed and flowed, see Seely *v.* Brush, 35 Conn 419.

So a proprietor of land on a stream may not, for purposes of irrigation, stop the flow of the water by a dam across the stream. Colburn *v.* Richards, 13 Mass. 420; Anthony *v.* Lapham, 5 Pick. (Mass.) 175; Sampson *v.* Hoddinott, 1 C. B. N. S. 590. Unless he has by prescription gained the right, if the existence of the dam and use of the water has been of sufficient duration. Messinger *v.* Uhler, 2 East. Rep. 602.

No owner or occupier of any mill-dam or other water-power shall acquire by prescription any right against the State or the public to impede or injure navigation, the passage of fish, or any other public easement in any of the waters of the State. Gen. Laws N. H. (1878), p. 325.

what the dam may actually flow at a art cu ar time, but what, in good condition, it will ordinarily flow.P i l

(*b*) *Loss of.*—A prescriptive right to overflow lands, or to interfere with an upper mill-owner by setting back water upon him, may be lost by non-user for the length of time required to gain it, but not for a less period.[2]

14. Remedy of Persons Injured by the Erection or Maintenance of a Dam.—(*a*) *Abatement.*—Where the erection and maintenance of a dam interfere with the rights of other proprietors, equity will interfere and order the abatement of the nuisance, to such an extent as will remedy the injury.[3] The grounds of equitable interference are,

1. Angell Wat. Cour. § 379. Note to McCoy *v.* Danley, 57 Am. Dec. 689; Voter *v.* Hobbs, 69 Me. 19; Carlisle *v.* Cooper, 21 N. J. Eq. 576; Mertz *v.* Dorney, 25 Pa. St. 579; Smith *v.* Russ, 17 Wis. 227; Powell *v.* Lash, 64 N. Car. 456; Morris *v.* Commander, 3 Ired. (N. Car.) L. 510; Whittier *v.* Cocheco Mfg. Co., 9 N. H. 454; s. c., 32 Am. Dec. 382; Guilford *v.* Winnepiseogee Lake Co., 52 N. H. 262; Shepherdson *v.* Perkins, 58 N. H. 354; Cowell *v.* Thayer, 5 Met. (Mass.) 253; s. c., 38 Am. Dec. 400; Powers *v.* Osgood, 102 Mass. 454; Thurber *v.* Martin, 2 Gray (Mass.). 394; s. c., 61 Am. Dec. 468; Maguire *v.* Baker, 57 Ga. 109; Ellington *v.* Bennett, 59 Ga. 286; Mardy *v.* Shults, 29 N. Y. 346.

2. French *v.* Braintree Mfg. Co., 23 Pick. (Mass.) 216; Williams *v.* Nelson, 23 Pick. (Mass.) 141; s. c., 34 Am. Dec. 35. Non user for a less time does not impair his rights, nor confer adverse rights on another. Townsend *v.* McDonald, 12 N. Y. 381; Pilsbury *v.* Moore, 44 Me. 154.

3. Hammond *v.* Fuller, 1 Paige (N. Y. Ch.), 197; Rothery *v.* N. Y. Rubber Co., 90 N. Y. 30; McCormick *v.* Horan, 81 N. Y. 86; s. c., 37 Am. Rep. 479; Ames *v.* Cannon River Mfg. Co., 27 Minn. 245; Finch *v.* Green, 16 Minn 355; Bowman *v.* City of New Orleans, 27 La Ann. 501; Potter *v.* Howe, 141 Mass. 357; Cobb *v.* Smith, 23 Wis. 261; Newell *v.* Smith, 26 Wis. 582.

A court of equity will not interfere to protect complainant from an injury that defendants can at any time make lawful if they choose; therefore, a showing of a subsisting right of flowage for saw-mill or grist-mill purposes will prevent the abatement of a mill-dam erected to supply a paper mill, and causing only the like extent of flowage. Hathaway *v.* Mitchell, 34 Mich 164.

Under a decree of abatement of a mill-dam, so as not to interfere with plaintiff's prior enjoyment of a power, it was held that the proper height at which the dam should stand was to be determined by experiment rather than theoretical conclusions drawn from surveys Decorah Woollen Mill Co *v.* Greer, 58 Iowa, 86. And when such abatement is to be made with reference to the ordinary stage of the water, the meaning is the ordinary stage when the water is high. Decorah Woollen Mill Co. *v.* Greer, 58 Iowa. 86.

But when the petition to compel one to lower his dam does not allege its height at any time, or how much raised by the respondent, it is fatally defective. Tye *v.* Catching, 78 Ky. 463.

Where permission has been granted to raise the water of a stream to a certain height, and a dam had been erected for that purpose which had existed for thirty years, an injunction to abate the dam will be denied where evidence does not conclusively show that the height has ever been exceeded. Cobb *v.* Slimmer, 45 Mich. 176.

In *Pennsylvania*, the mill-dam act of 23 March, 1803 (Purdon's Digest, 1885), p. 1173. 4 Sm. Laws, 20, takes away the common-law remedy by abatement as far as navigable streams are concerned, and gives the courts power to direct the supervisors of highways in the adjoining townships to remove such part of the structure as will bring it within the provisions of the act. Criswell *v.* Clugh, 3 Watts (Pa.), 330; Spigelman *v.* Walter, 3 Watts & Sergeant (Pa.). 549; Ensworth *v.* Commonwealth, 52 Pa. St. 320.

The mill-dam acts of the several States have taken away this remedy so far as it applies to dams lawfully erected under the statute. See note to § 3 (*c*).

In some States unlawful dams are declared by law to be nuisances. Gen. Stat. *Conn.* (1875), p. 253; Rev. Stat *Missouri* (1879), §§ 6,438; Rev. Stat. *West Virginia* (1879), chap. 91, § 24. So in *Maine*, when they become injurious to the public health, offensive to the neighborhod, or occasion injuries or annoy-

first, that the remedy at law is inadequate, and second, to prevent multiplicity of actions.[1]

(*b.*) *When Party Injured May Abate.*—A riparian owner may enter on adjoining land to remove obstructions in a stream whereby the water is flowed back upon his land to the injury of his mill, if he cannot otherwise obtain relief.[2]

(*c*) *Damages.*—Any person injured by the erection or maintenance of a dam may have a common law action against the owner, or in some cases the occupant thereof, for damages for the injury done him, unless the right has been taken away by the mill-dam acts of the several States. These latter acts all provide a special mode of recovering damages, which must be strictly followed, and is generally a bar to any other action for the damages incurred.[3]

ances of a kind not authorized by the statutes regulating dams. Rev. Stat. 1883 p. 234 § 310.

Others have declared navigable streams free and common highways, or have forbidden the obstruction of streams by dams Codes and Statutes of *California* (1876). § 13, 611; Gen. Laws *Oregon*, p. 103.

A dam erected under the statutes of *Missouri*, but not completed within the time prescribed by the statute, is an unlawful structure, and one that cannot be legitimated by lapse of time so as to entitle its owners to the protection of the statute as against other mills. Hoffman *v.* Vaughan, 72 Mo. 465. As to when dam is a nuisance Stone *v.* Peckham, 12 R. I. 27.

In *Delaware*, when an ancient mill is injured by other mills erected on the same stream, upon complaint made, the court will appoint a jury of twelve men to inspect the premises, and upon their report the court may award damages, or if it seem necessary may abate the dam. Rev. Code (1874), chap. 61, § 2, p. 349.

In *Virginia*, where dams interfere with the improvement of any water-course, the State may abate them. Code *Virginia* (1873), p. 605, § 5.

If the owner of a dam does not keep it so as not to obstruct navigation, six months after notice given him, the county or party injured may do it and recover the cost from the owner. Code *Virginia* (1873), p. 606 § 7.

1 Corning *v.* Troy Iron and Nail Factory, 40 N Y. 191. Per Grover, J.: "Upon established principles this is a proper case of equity jurisdiction. First upon the ground that the remedy at law is inadequate. The plaintiffs are entitled to the flow of the stream in its natural channel. Legal remedies cannot restore to them, and secure them in the enjoyment of it. Hence the duty of a court of equity to interpose for the accomplishment of that result. A further ground requiring the interposition of equity is to avoid multiplicity of actions. . . . The right to the plaintiffs to the equitable relief sought is established by authority as well as by principle. Webb *v.* Portland Manufacturing Co., 3 Sumner (U. S. C. C.), 190, and cases there cited. Tyler *v.* Wilkison, 4 Mason (U. S. C. C.), 400; Townsend *v.* McDonald, 12 N. Y. 382."

2. Heath *v.* Williams, 25 Me. 209; s.c. 43 Am Dec. 265; Colburn *v.* Richards, 13 Mass. 420; s.c., 7 Am. Dec. 160, Prescott *v.* White, 21 Pick. (Mass) 341, s.c., 32 Am. Dec. 266; Adams *v.* Barney, 25 Vt. 225; Chapman *v.* Thames Mfg Co., 13 Conn. 269; s.c., 33 Am. Dec. 401; Great Falls Co. *v.* Worster, 15 N. H. 412. So a riparian owner can remove a dam built on his land by another. Richardson *v.* Emerson, 3 Wis. 319; s.c. 62 Am. Dec. 694; Ware *v.* Walker, 70 Cal. 591; s.c., 12 Pac. Rep. 475.

3. **Who May Bring Suit.**—Generally the person bringing suit for damages must show some special injury, and title to the property injured. Thus, a mill-owner whose mill is injured by a dam erected and kept up without right may maintain an action against the person who erected it for injuries sustained after the wrong doer has conveyed to a third person. Prentiss *v.* Wood, 132 Mass. 486 So, the owner of a mill may recover damages for injury thereto by a diversion of the water, and a tenant may also recover for the diminution of the value of the mill resulting from abstractions of the water during his term. Halsey *v.* Lehigh

(*d*) *When Owner of Dam Entitled to Nominal Damages.*—An owner of a dam is entitled to nominal damages for any disturbance of his right, without proof of actual damage.[1]

Val. R. Co., 45 N. J. L. 26. So, against one who so negligently constructs and manages his dams that they are carried away, and plaintiff's lands and crops are flooded, a common-law action may be maintained. Rich *v.* Keshena Improvement Co., 56 Wis. 287. See also Seymour *v.* Carpenter, 51 Wis. 413; Lohmiller *v.* Indian Ford Water Power Co., 51 Wis. 683. See also Burnet *v.* Nicholson, 86 N. Car. 99; Godfrey *v.* Mayberry, 84 N. Car. 256; Cooper *v.* Hall, 5 Ohio, 320; Hovey *v.* Perkins, 63 N. H. 516; Newell *v.* Smith, 15 Wis. 101; Fort Plain Bridge Co. *v.* Smith, 30 N. Y. 44; Groat *v.* Moak, 26 Hun (N. Y.), 380; Great Falls Co. *v.* Worster, 15 N. H. 467; Hendricks *v.* Johnson, 6 Port. (Ala.) 472; Crockett *v.* Millett, 65 Me. 191; Adams *v.* Barney, 25 Vt. 225; Isele *v.* Schwamb, 131 Mass. 337; Fitch *v.* Taft, 126 Mass. 534; Walker *v* Oxford Woollen Mfg. Co. 10 Met. (Mass.) 203; Luller *v.* French, 10 Met. (Mass.) 359.

Under the *Maine* statute, see Wilson *v.* Campbell, 76 Me. 94: Goodwin *v.* Gibbs, 70 Me., 243; Worcester *v.* Great Falls Mfg. Co, 41 Me. 159; s.c., 66 Am. Dec. 217.

Where in an action by a riparian mill-owner for damages, resulting from unlawful obstruction and use by the defendant company of the water of a stream used to run such mill, it appears that the defendant erected across the stream a stone dam, which is the obstruction complained of, the fact that the company has leased its road, including the dam, is no defence in such action. Anderson *v.* Cincinnati Southern R. (Ky., June 18, 1887) 5 S. W. Rep. 49.

Where plaintiff's unlawful acts have contributed to the injury, damages cannot be recovered. Davis *v.* Munroe (S.C. of Mich., June 23, 1887), 33 N. W. Rep. 408.

But the fact that one mill-owner partially obstructs the flow of the water in a stream to his mill, does not prevent his recovering for an additional obstruction by another. Clarke *v.* French, 122 Mass. 419. In such a case the doctrine of contributory negligence does not apply. Brown *v*, Dean, 123 Mass. 254.

What Admissible as Evidence—Ellis *v* Harris, 32 Gratt. (Va.) 684; Godfrey *v.* Mayberry, 84 N. Car. 255; Burnet *v.* Nicholson, 86 N. Car. 99; Johnson *v.* Atlantic & St. Lawrence R Co., 35 N. H. 560; s.c., 79 Am. Dec. 560; Polly *v.* McCall, 37 Ala. 20; Mead *v* Hein, 28 Wis. 533; Lewin *v.* Simpson, 38 Md. 468; Rucker *v.* Athens Mfg. Co., 54 Ga. 84; Ellington *v.* Bennett, 59 Ga. 286. Marsh *v.* Trullinger, 6 Oreg. 356, McArthur *v.* Morgan, 49 Conn. 347

Mill-dam Acts as Bar to Actions.—In all of the States which have special statutory enactments authorizing the flowing of lands, by persons erecting dams (see note to § 5), the statutes provide a mode of assessing and collecting damages which generally supersedes the common-law remedy. Ang. Wat. Cour. (7th Ed.) § 484; Stowell *v.* Flagg, 11 Mass. 364; Waddy *v.* Johnson, 5 Ired. (N. Car) 333; Hendricks *v.* Johnson, 6 Port. (Ala.) 472; Veazie *v.* Dwinel, 50 Me. 485; Williams *v.* Camden & Rockland Water Co. (Me. Dec. 17, 1887), 5 New Eng. Rep. 352. But the statute of *Mississippi* provides: "No inquest taken by virtue of this act, and no opinion or judgment of the court thereupon, shall bar any public prosecution or private action which could have been had or maintained, if this act had never been made, other than prosecutions and actions for such injuries as were actually foreseen and estimated upon in such inquest." Rev. Code (1880) § 932. And to the same effect are the laws of *Oregon* (Genl. Laws (1872) p. 681), and of *West Virginia* (Rev Stat. 1879, chap. 91, § 36). And while a dam in a navigable stream, if authorized by the act of the legislature, cannot be indicted as a public nuisance for obstructing the stream, still the act is no protection against injuries to a private owner Crittenden *v.* Wilson, 5 Cow. (N. Y.) 165; Lee *v.* Pembroke Iron Co., 57 Me. 481; s.c., 2 Am. Rep. 59; Eastman *v* Amoskeag Mfg. Co., 44 N. H, 160; Trenton Water power Co. *v.* Raff, 36 N. J. L. 335.

1. Stein *v.* Burden, 24 Ala. 130; s. c., 60 Am. Dec. 453; Eagle Mfg Co. *v.* Gibson, 62 Ala. 369; Adams *v.* Barney, 25 Vt. 225; Pastorius *v.* Fisher, 1 Rawle (Pa.), 27; Casebeer *v.* Mowry, 55 Pa St. 419; Amoskeag Mfg. Co *v.* Goodale, 46 N. H. 53; Dorman *v.* Ames, 12 Minn. 451; Butman *v.* Hussey, 12 Me. 407. Washb. Easements, 289. But *compare* Garrett *v.* McKie, 1 Rich. L (S. Car.) 444; s. c., 44 Am. Dec. 263; Chalk *v* McAlily, 11 Rich. (S. Car.) 153; Dwight Printing Co. *v.* Boston, 122 Mass. 583.

(*e*) *Measure of Damages.*—The amount of damages to be recovered by a party injured by a dam is, in general, commensurate with the injury done, unless the rule is altered by statute.[1]

(*f*) *Where Action to be Maintained.*—Actions for abatement of dams, or for damages for injuries caused thereby, whether brought at common law or under the mill-dam acts, are local actions, and are to be brought in the county where the lands injured lie, or in the courts provided by the statutes.[2]

(*g*) *Remedy of Mill-owner for Injuries Sustained.*—The owner of a dam who sustains injury by means of unreasonable diversion or detention of the water by an upper proprietor, or the flowing of his mill-site by a lower proprietor, or suffers any other

1. In a suit for damages for ponding water it appeared that the plaintiff sustained injury to his mill by reason of the defendants erecting another mill and dam lower down on the same stream. *Held*, that the measure of damages was the value of the injury actually sustained by the plaintiff at the time of the trial, and in estimating the same, the decrease of custom (in the matter of toll) could not be considered; and that evidence to show how much it would have cost the plaintiff to raise his dam and water-wheel to escape the injury complained of was properly excluded. Burnet *v.* Nicholson, 86 N. Car. 99. So Decorah Woollen Mill Co. *v.* Greer, 49 Iowa, 490; Hovey *v.* Perkins, 63 N. H. 516; Town *v.* Faulkner, 56 N H. 255; Phinizy *v.* Augusta, 47 Ga. 260; Robertson *v.* Woodworth, 42 Conn. 163; Halsey *v.* L. V. R. Co., 45 N. J. L. 26; Harding *v.* Funk, 8 Kans. 315; City of Chicago *v.* Huenerbein, 85 Ill. 594; s. c., 38 Am. Rep 626; Janssen *v.* Lammers, 29 Wis. 89; Chalk *v.* McAlily, 11 Rich. (S. Car.) 153; Howe *v.* Ray, 113 Mass 90

In Taylor *v.* Keeler, 50 Conn. 346, it was decided that where a mill-owner alleged that, by reason of the erection of a dam below, the water backed upon his wheel and stopped it, and it was proved that the water flowed his land, but did not reach his wheel, he could receive no damages for flowage, since none were alleged.

Although the act of 1803 in *Pennsylvania* took away the common-law remedy of abatement, it did not take away the right to a common-law action for damages. Gould *v* Langdon, 43 Pa St. 365.

All of the mill-dam acts of the several States provide for the assessment of damages, providing that the jury shall assess the actual damage. Several of them distinctly provide that punitive damages shall not be imposed, while those of *Connecticut* and *New Hampshire* add fifty per cent to the amount assessed. See notes to sec. 3, *supra*.

Under the *Missouri* law persons building dams otherwise than under the statutory provisions of the State, are liable to double damages to the party injured. Rev. Stat. (1879), § 929.

Under the *North Carolina* statute relating to ponding water, damages are to be assessed separately for each year. Goodson *v.* Mullen, 92 N. Car. 207. And an issue involving the amount of annual damages done is a proper one to be submitted to the jury. Hester *v.* Broach, 84 N. Car. 251.

And in an action before a justice under the *Mississippi* statute the judgment of the justice is final, but he cannot award costs. Lagrove *v.* Trice, 57 Miss 227.

2. Geise *v.* Green, 49 Wis. 339; Oliphant *v.* Smith, 3 Penrose & Watts (Pa.), 180; Worster *v* Winipiseogee Lake Co., 25 N. H. 477; Brown *v.* Bowen, 30 N. Y. 519; s. c , 86 Am. Dec. 406.

Under the *Wisconsin* act, where lands lying in one county were overflowed by a dam in another, an action for the injury might be brought in the former county. Lohmiller *v.* Indian Ford Water-power Co., 51 Wis. 683.

So an action may be maintained in *Massachusetts* for diverting a stream in that State, and preventing it from coming to the plaintiff's mill in Rhode Island. Mannville Co. *v.* City of Worcester, 138 Mass. 89; s. c., 52 Am. Rep. 261. See Stillman *v.* White Rock Mfg. Co., 3 Woodb. & M. (U. S. C. C.) 538. But where the complaint is for flowage of several parcels of land in different counties by the same dam, it may be brought and all the damages recovered in either county. Bates *v.* Ray, 102 Mass. 458.

injury, may bring an action against the party injuring for damages, or, if necessary, may have the nuisance abated.[1]

DAMAGE.—To injure.[2]

1. Decorah Woollen Mill Co. *v.* Greer, 49 Iowa, 490; Lawson *v.* Menasha Wooden-ware Co., 59 Wis. 393; s. c., 48 Am. Rep. 528; Adams *v.* Manning, 51 Conn. 5; Prentiss *v.* Wood, 132 Mass. 486; Halsey *v* Lehigh Valley R. Co., 45 N. J. L. 26. As to rights of joint owners, see Townsend *v.* McDonald, 14 Barb. (N. Y.) 460.

So a mill-owner whose mill is benefited by the reserve of a reservoir dam erected upon his land, is subject to the provisions of the *Maine* statute, though there are other mills benefited by the same reservoir. Dingley *v.* Gardiner, 73 Me. 63. But the owner of a mill cannot recover damages from higher owners for making too great and profitable use of their water-power by their expensive machinery and well-constructed works, to his detriment, when he is making too little use of his own power for want of its improvement. Caldwell *v.* Sanderson (S. C. Wis., June 1, 1887), 33 N. W. Rep. 591.

Many of the States have statutes declaring the wilful and malicious destruction of a mill-dam a misdemeanor, or providing special penalties for such acts. Codes and Statutes of *California* (1876), § 13,607; *Connecticut* Laws of 1875, p 6; Code of *Georgia* (1882) § 4611; Rev. Stat. *Idaho* (1887), § 7162; Rev. Stat. *New York*, 7th Ed., p. 2520; Comp. Laws *Utah* (1876), p. 640, § 349; Code *Washington Ty.* (1881), § 842; Comp. Laws *Wyoming* (1876), p. 278, § 151; Rev. Stat. *Illinois* (1887), p. 485, § 197; Rev. Stat. *Indiana* (1881), § 1967; McClain's Annotated Statutes *Iowa*, § 3978; Gen. Stat. *Kentucky* (1881), pp. 327, 328; Stats. of *Minnesota*, p. 309, § 26; Rev. L. *Vermont* (1880), § 4198; Howell's Annotated Statutes *Michigan* (1882), §§ 9127 and 9168; Pub. Stat. *Rhode Island* (1882), p. 678, § 35; Rev. Stat. *Wisconsin*, § 4439. In *Kansas* malicious destruction of a dam, or the erection of a dam on a stream previously occupied, so as to injure the former proprietor, is a misdemeanor. Dassler's Comp. Laws (1881), § 1851. *Massachusetts* has a similar act, but the latter part does not apply when the State has power to abate the dam. Pub. Stat. (1882), p. 1149.

Lumber put into streams and lodged upon lands adjoining or on dams crossing the stream must be moved by the 1st of May. If not, the owner of lands or dam may detain till damage is paid. §§ 3239, 3240.

Persons floating logs, etc., over dams must give security in such sums as will protect the owner of such dams against all loss and damage that may be done by the parties floating logs across said dam. Laws of *Tennessee*, 1883, p. 265.

Authorities on Dams.—Angell on Water Courses (7th Ed.); Washburn on Easements (4th Ed); Washburn on Real Property (5th Ed); Pomeroy on Riparian Rights (Black's Ed., 1887); Note to McCoy *v.* Danley, 57 Am. Dec. 680.

2. Taking away a part of a stocking-frame so that it will not work is damaging it within an act making it felony to break, destroy, or damage such frames. R. *v.* Tracy, Russ. & R. 452.

A non-adjacent property-holder is not entitled to damages under an act providing for compensation "when property is damaged by the vacation or closing of any street," where by the vacation egress and ingress is not affected, and the damages suffered consist of mere inconvenience common to the general public. Nor is such vacation a taking or damaging within a constitutional provision that private property shall not be taken or damaged for public use without just compensation. E. St. Louis *v.* O'Flynn (Ill.), 10 N. E. Rep. 395.

INDEX.